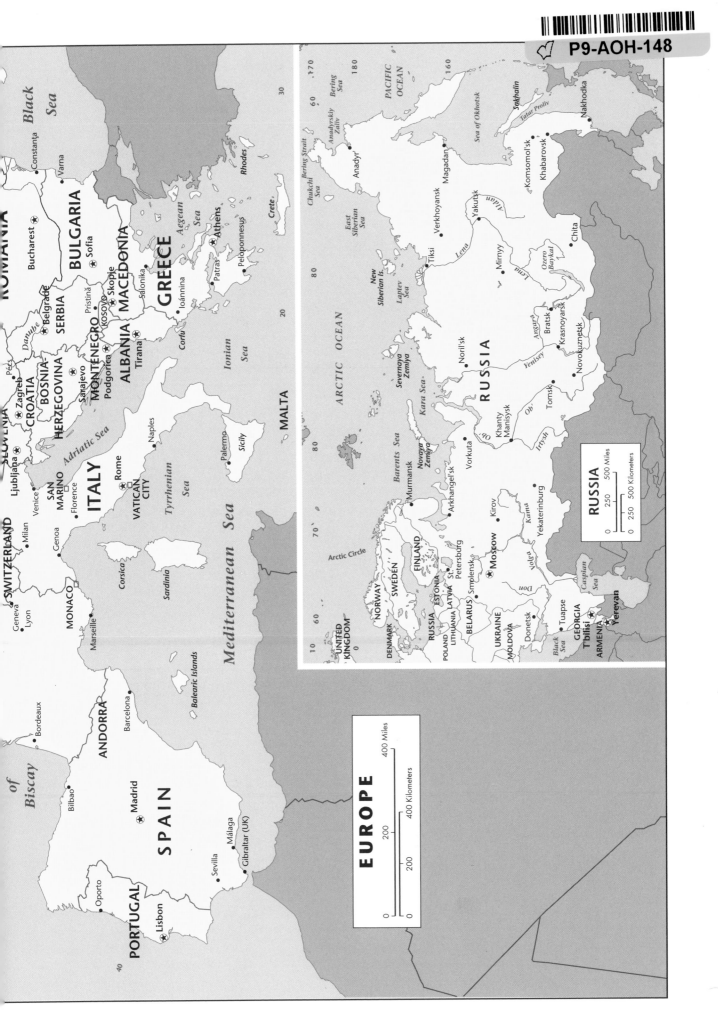

EUROPE

RUSSIA

WORLDMARK
ENCYCLOPEDIA OF THE NATIONS

EUROPE

WORLDMARK
ENCYCLOPEDIA OF THE NATIONS, THIRTEENTH EDITION

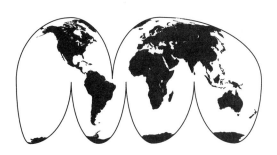

Volume 5
EUROPE

GALE
CENGAGE Learning

Detroit • New York • San Francisco • New Haven, Conn • Waterville, Maine • London

Worldmark Encyclopedia of the Nations, 13th Edition
Timothy L. Gall and Derek M. Gleason, Editors

Project Editors
Jason M. Everett and Kimberley A. McGrath

Contributing Editors
Kathleen J. Edgar and Elizabeth Manar

Managing Editor
Debra Kirby

Rights Acquisition and Management
Christine Myaskovsky

Imaging and Multimedia
John L. Watkins

Composition
Evi Abou-El-Seoud

Manufacturing
Rita Wimberley, Dorothy Maki

Product Manager
Douglas A. Dentino

Product Design
Kristine A. Julien

For product information and technology assistance, contact us at

Gale Customer Support, 1-800-877-4253.

For permission to use material from this text or product, submit all requests online at

www.cengage.com/permissions.

Further permissions questions can be emailed to

permissionrequest@cengage.com

While every effort has been made to ensure the reliability of the information presented in this publication, Gale, a part of Cengage Learning, does not guarantee the accuracy of the data contained herein. Gale accepts no payment for listing; and inclusion in the publication of any organization, agency, institution, publication, service, or individual does not imply endorsement of the editors or publisher. Errors brought to the attention of the publisher and verified to the satisfaction of the publisher will be corrected in future editions.

Library of Congress Cataloging-in-Publication Data

Worldmark encyclopedia of the nations / Timothy L. Gall and Derek M. Gleason, editors. -- 13th ed.
  p. cm.
 Includes bibliographical references and index.
  ISBN 978-1-4144-3390-5 (set) -- ISBN 978-1-4144-3391-2 (vol. 1) -- ISBN 978-1-4144-3392-9 (vol. 2) -- ISBN 978-1-4144-3393-6 (vol. 3) -- ISBN 978-1-4144-3394-3 (vol. 4) -- ISBN 978-1-4144-3395-0 (vol. 5) -- ISBN 978-1-4144-9090-8 (ebook)
 1. Geography--Encyclopedias. 2. History--Encyclopedias. 3. Economics--Encyclopedias. 4. Political science--Encyclopedias. 5. United Nations--Encyclopedias. I. Gall, Timothy L. II. Gleason, Derek M.
 G63.W67 2012
 910.3--dc23

                              2011049990

Gale
27500 Drake Rd.
Farmington Hills, MI 48331-3535

978-1-4144-3390-5 (set)   1-4144-3390-5 (set)
978-1-4144-3391-2 (vol. 1)   1-4144-3391-3 (vol. 1)
978-1-4144-3392-9 (vol. 2)   1-4144-3392-1 (vol. 2)
978-1-4144-3393-6 (vol. 3)   1-4144-3393-X (vol. 3)
978-1-4144-3394-3 (vol. 4)   1-4144-3394-8 (vol. 4)
978-1-4144-3395-0 (vol. 5)   1-4144-3395-6 (vol. 5)

This title is also available as an e-book
ISBN-13: 978-1-4144-9090-8   ISBN-10: 1-4144-9090-9

Contact your Gale, a part of Cengage Learning, sales representative for ordering information.

Printed in the United States
1 2 3 4 5 6 7 16 15 14 13 12

CONTENTS

For Conversion Tables, Abbreviations and Acronyms, Glossaries, World Tables, notes to previous editions, and other supplementary materials, see Volume 1.

READER'S GUIDE

GENERAL NOTE: The Thirteenth Edition of *Worldmark Encyclopedia of the Nations* (WEN) is comprised of five volumes. Volume 1 is dedicated to the United Nations and its related agencies. Volumes 2 through 5, "Africa," "Americas," "Asia and Oceania," and "Europe," contain entries on the countries of the world.

Reflecting the ever-changing status of the world geopolitical situation, the Thirteenth Edition includes entries for 196 countries and the Palestinian Territories, three more entries than the previous edition. This reflects the widely recognized independence of Kosovo and South Sudan that has occurred since the publication of the Twelfth Edition. It also recognizes the unique status of the Palestinian Territories, which, in the months leading up to the publication of this edition, were working to achieve membership in several peripheral United Nations agencies—a push toward formal recognition of statehood. Seven entries describe dependencies of the United Kingdom, United States, and the Netherlands. Previous editions have been cognizant of similar changes, including those in East Timor, Macau, and Hong Kong. Perhaps most dramatically, the Eighth Edition of this encyclopedia (1995) reported on the dissolution of the USSR, Czechoslovakia, and Yugoslavia; the unification of Germany; the unification of Yemen; and the independence of Eritrea. These changes resulted in 25 new country articles. Whereas the First Edition of the *Worldmark Encyclopedia of the Nations,* in one volume, contained 119 articles, the present Thirteenth Edition now contains 204.

Some notable foci for the Thirteenth Edition include coverage of the Arab Spring—the revolutionary fervor that carried across North Africa and the Middle East during 2011 and into 2012, deposing several longstanding dictators—and the global financial crisis, which, despite beginning in 2008, has led to economic recession or stagnation across much of the world that continued through 2011 and into 2012, especially among European countries and in other highly developed economies. Also for the Thirteenth Edition, each entry was submitted for review by subject-matter experts at universities across the United States and around the world, leading to greater continuity within each article and an authorial perspective conscious of region-wide context and historical relevance.

In compiling data for incorporation into the *Worldmark Encyclopedia of the Nations,* substantial efforts were made to utilize national government statistical resources, as well as all pertinent UN agencies, to compile the core information in each entry. Material received from official sources was reviewed and critically assessed by editors as part of the process of incorporation. In some cases, discrepancies between self-reported data and accepted international revisions, occasionally noted in figures such as unemployment and minority ethnic populations, highlight the political influences that weigh on national government statistic reporting. Materials and publications of the UN family and of intergovernmental and nongovernmental organizations throughout the world provided a major fund of geographic, demographic, economic, and social data.

In compiling historical, economic, and political data, primary materials generated by governments and international agencies were supplemented by data gathered from numerous other sources including newspapers (most notably *The European,* the *Financial Times,* the *New York Times,* and the *Wall Street Journal*); periodicals (most notably *Current History, Elections Today, The Economist,* the *Far Eastern Economic Review, Foreign Affairs,* and *World Press Review*); and thousands of World Wide Web sites hosted by government agencies and embassies. The base knowledge and access to a broad range of speciality academic publications enjoyed by subject-matter experts figures heavily in these sections as well.

The reader's attention is directed to the Glossary of Special Terms for explanations of key terms and concepts essential to a fuller understanding of the text.

COUNTRY NAMES: Country names are reported (as appropriate) in three forms: the short-form name (generally conformed to the US Central Intelligence Agency's *World Factbook 2011*), as commonly used in the text; the English version of the official name (generally conformed to the United Nations list of country names); and the official name in the national language(s). When necessary, textual usages of some short-form names have been rectified, usually through the substitution of an acronym for the official name, in order to strike a better balance between official usages and universal terminology. Thus the following short-form names have been adopted throughout (except in historical context to preserve accuracy): DROC (Democratic Republic of the Congo); ROC (Republic of the Congo); DPRK (Democratic People's Republic of Korea/North Korea); and ROK (Republic of Korea/South Korea).

MAPS: Spellings on the individual country maps reflect national usages and recognized transliteration practice. To clarify national boundaries and landforms, dark shading has been applied to waters, and lighter shading to lands not within that nation's jurisdiction. Cross-hatching has been used to designate certain disputed areas. Rivers that run dry during certain times of the year are indicated by dashed instead of solid lines.

FLAGS AND NATIONAL EMBLEMS: All depictions of flags, flag designations, and national emblems have been reviewed and, where necessary, corrected or changed to reflect their official usage as of 2012. In general, the term "national flag" denotes the civil flag of the nation.

CURRENCY: In most cases, currency conversion factors cited in the Thirteenth Edition are derived from figures available during the last quarter of 2011 or the first quarter of 2012. Differences between the official exchange rate and the actual exchange rate are noted as appropriate.

WEIGHTS AND MEASURES: The general world trend toward adoption of the metric system is acknowledged through the use of metric units and their nonmetric (customary or imperial) equivalents throughout the text. The two exceptions to this practice involve territorial sea limits, which are reported in nautical miles, and various production data, for which (unless otherwise stated) units of measure reflect the system in use by the country in question. All tons are metric tons (again, unless otherwise indicated), reflecting the practice of the UN in its statistical reporting.

HOLIDAYS: Except where noted, all holidays listed are official public holidays, on which government offices are closed that would normally be open. Transliterations of names of Muslim holidays have been standardized. For a fuller discussion on these points, and for a description of religious holidays and their origins and meanings, see the Glossary of Religious Holidays in this volume.

GEOGRAPHIC INFORMATION: To update the sections on Location, Size, and Extent; Topography, Climate, Flora and Fauna, and Environment, the World Bank's *World Development Indicators 2011* and CIA *World Factbook 2011* were two primary sources. Additional data was acquired from the Ramsar Convention on Wetlands (http://www.ramsar.org); UNESCO World Heritage Centre (http://www.whc.unesco.org); United Nations Environment Programme (http://www.unep.org); Weather Channel: Averages and Records (http://www.weather.com/common/home/climatology.html); and the International Union for Conservation of Nature (http://www.iucn.org).

POPULATION DATA: Data for the four rubrics describing population (Population, Migration, Ethnic Groups, Languages) were compiled from numerous publications of the US Department of State, the World Bank, the United Nations, and the Organization for Economic Co-Operation and Development (OECD), specifically its publication *Trends in International Migration*. Data on refugee populations generally comes from the United Nations. Population rankings are ordered based on data from the *World Factbook 2011* and include all full country entries in these volumes; this calculation excludes the Palestinian Territories and the seven dependency entries.

RELIGIONS: Data for this section were compiled in large part from the *2010 International Religious Freedom Report* released by the Bureau of Democracy, Human Rights, and Labor, US Department of State. This is an annual report to Congress compiled in compliance with Section 102(b) of the International Religious Freedom Act (IRFA) of 1998. The report includes the work of hundreds of State Department, Foreign Service, and other US government employees. The authors gathered information from a variety of sources, including government and religious officials, nongovernmental organizations, journalists, human rights monitors, religious groups, and academics.

TRANSPORTATION: Sources consulted for updated information on transportation include the *World Factbook 2011* and the World Bank's *World Development Indicators 2011*. Information on recent or ongoing transportation projects most often came from major news organizations such as the *BBC News International* and the *New York Times*.

HISTORY: In writing the History rubric, the entries relied heavily on the expertise of the academics reviewing and revising each country profile. Beyond the contributions of the subject-matter experts, the History rubrics have been maintained in previous editions and in between editions through the use of a variety of news and background information sources. Full country profiles—including information on the history, economy, political institutions, and foreign relations on most nations of the world—are provided by the US Library of Congress and by the US Department of State; similar formats are published by the *BBC News International*. In consulting news sources for up-to-date information on events, only reported facts (not editorials) were used. The *New York Times* and the *Washington Post* are more comprehensive than the *Wall Street Journal*, whose focus is placed on financial and business news. While the Web site of the United Nations was used extensively in compiling Volume 1 "United Nations," of the *Worldmark Encyclopedia of the Nations,* its coverage of such problems as politics in the Middle East and global terrorism pertained to and supported the updating of History rubrics of a number of countries. Other organizations that publish journals or studies on global current events, foreign policy, international relations, and human rights include Amnesty International; Human Rights Watch; *Foreign Affairs*, published by the Council on Foreign Relations; and *Great Decisions*, published by the Foreign Policy Association.

GOVERNMENT: The Government rubric is constructed by outlining the institutions of government as they were formed throughout a nation's modern history, up to those existing under the present constitution.

The US Library of Congress and the US Department of State chronicle constitutional changes and also provide information on the form of government. The online resource ElectionGuide (Electionguide.org) and the *World Factbook 2011* provide information on officeholders in place at the time of publication. The *BBC News International* "Country Profiles" cover current leaders and their political parties, and *The Economist* is comprehensive in its coverage of political structures and political forces in place and at work in the nations it profiles. The official government Web sites of individual nations were also consulted.

POLITICAL PARTIES: The *World Factbook 2011* was consulted for a list of political parties, and often, their leaders. *The Economist* also has sections in its country briefings labeled "political structure" and "political forces," which describe the political climate of each nation the magazine profiles. In addition, *The Economist* provides a brief history of the nation, which often includes the history of political parties. Editors also reviewed profiles of nations prepared by the US Department of State.

LOCAL GOVERNMENT: The *World Factbook 2011* lists the administrative subdivisions in each nation of the world. *The Economist* was consulted for a description of regional legislatures. ElectionGuide provides information on recent and upcoming subnational elections.

JUDICIAL SYSTEM: The US State Department *Background Notes* and the *World Factbook 2011* both provided basic information on each nation's judicial system. *The Economist* was consulted for a description of the legal systems of each nation it profiles. The US State Department's *Human Rights Reports* provide more in-depth details about the independence and fairness of the judiciary.

ARMED FORCES: Statistical data on armed forces was compiled from the *The Military Balance* (The International Institute for Strategic Studies), the *World Factbook 2011*, and other print and online sources including *Current World Nuclear Arsenals* maintained by the Center for Defense Information.

INTERNATIONAL COOPERATION: This section was updated using data provided by news agencies, the *World Factbook 2011,* and US State Department *Background Notes.*

ECONOMY: In addition to numerous official online sources, data on the economies of the world were compiled from the most recent editions of the following publications (and their publishers): *Country Commercial Guides* (US Department of State), *World Development Indicators 2011* (World Bank) and *Doing Business* reports (World Bank). *The Economist* was consulted for detailed information on economic structures and select indicators in its "Country Profiles" archive; it also included economic and political forecasts for the nations it profiled. *The Index of Economic Freedom* (Heritage Foundation) was also consulted for its measurement of independent variables into broad factors of economic freedom.

INCOME: Statistics on national income were obtained from sources published by the United Nations, the World Bank, and the US Central Intelligence Agency. CIA figures are for gross domestic product (GDP), defined as the value of all final goods and services produced within a nation in a given year. In most cases, CIA figures are given in purchasing power parity terms. Actual individual consumption, a statistic maintained by the World Bank, measures the percentage of a nation's GDP spent on various sectors of the consumer economy. Thus, public expenditures in sectors such as education, health, or military are not included in the calculation and account for the remaining percentage of GDP not included in actual individual consumption numbers.

LABOR: Labor statistics were compiled from the World Bank publication *World Development Indicators 2011* and the US State Department's *Human Rights Reports 2010.*

AGRICULTURE, FISHING, AND FORESTRY: In addition to government sources, statistical data for these sections was compiled from the following yearbooks published by the Food and Agriculture Organization of the United Nations: *Fishery Statistics; Production; Agriculture;* and *Forest Products.*

MINING: Data on mining and minerals production came from various online sources and from statistics compiled by the Minerals Information office of the US Geological Survey, US Department of the Interior, including the *Minerals Yearbook.* The *Minerals Yearbook* is published both electronically on the Internet and in various print formats available from the US Government Printing Office Superintendent of Documents. The *Yearbook* provides an annual review of mineral production and trade and of mineral-related government and industry developments in more than 175 countries.

ENERGY AND POWER: Key sources consulted include *Country Analysis Briefs* (US Energy Information Administration, US Department of Energy) and *World Development Indicators* (The World Bank). Special attention was given to renewable energy projects completed or underway in various countries; information for projects typically was found through major news agencies or on official government Web sites.

INDUSTRY: The primary source material for the Industry rubric was the *World Factbook 2011* and the US State Department's *Country Commercial Guides*, which provide a comprehensive look at countries' commercial environments, using economic, political, and market analysis. *Background Notes* were consulted for information on the industrial history and climate of each country profiled. *The Economist* and, to a lesser extent, *BBC News* were useful in providing background material for the Industry rubric.

SCIENCE AND TECHNOLOGY: Information in this section derived primarily from statistics of the UNESCO Institute for Statistics, the World Bank's *World Development Indicators,* and the World Intellectual Property Organization.

DOMESTIC TRADE: Source material for the Domestic Trade rubric came from the US State Department's *Country Commercial Guides* and *Background Notes.* Also used was *The Economist* and, to a lesser extent, the *BBC* for providing background material for the Domestic Trade rubric. The World Bank's *Doing Business* reports were consulted for information on conducting business in a nation, which included business hours and business regulations. Finally, most nations' government Web sites provided information on domestic trade.

FOREIGN TRADE: Sources consulted included the *Direction of Trade Statistics* (IMF Statistics Department, International Monetary Fund). The US State Department's *Country Commercial Guides* and *Background Notes* were also used. *The Economist* and the *World Factbook 2011* were consulted in listing import and export partners and key products traded. Various UN bodies—such as UNCTAD and UNESCO—provided up-to-date trade statistics. The principal trading partners table was constructed with information from the IMF's *Direction of Trade Statistics* publication.

BALANCE OF PAYMENTS: Balance of payments tables were computed from the International Monetary Fund's *Balance of Payments Statistics Yearbook.* In some cases, totals are provided even though not all components of those totals have been reported by the government of the country. Accordingly, in some instances numbers in the columns may not add to the total. Supplementing the IMF's *Balance of Payments Statistics Yearbook* were *The Economist*'s "Country Briefings," the *World Factbook 2011,* and information taken from the US State Department, in particular, the *Country Commercial Guides.*

BANKING AND SECURITIES: Statistical data on securities listings and market activity was compiled from *International Banking Statistics* (www.bis.org/statistics) and the *World Factbook 2011,* which provides both the discount rate and prime lending rate for most nations. Various Web sites specific to the individual countries of the world were also consulted, especially for the most current information on active publicly traded companies and market capitalization for domestic exchanges.

INSURANCE: Primary sources for information on insurance included the online resources of the Insurance Information Institute, Rowbotham and Co. LLP., PricewaterhouseCoopers, the Swiss Reinsurance Company, and J. Zakhour & Co., as well as numerous national Web sites dealing with insurance.

PUBLIC FINANCE: In addition to official government Web sites, analytical reports from the US Department of Commerce, the *World Factbook 2011,* and the *Government Finance Statistics Yearbook* (International Monetary Fund) were consulted.

TAXATION: Information on Taxation was compiled from country data sheets published by international accounting firms (Deloitte and Ernst & Young). Addition informational was obtained from the US Commerce Department, *Doing Business* reports from the World Bank, and government Web sites of the countries of the world.

CUSTOMS AND DUTIES: Information on Customs and Duties was compiled from country data sheets published by the accounting firms of Deloitte and Ernst & Young. Additional information was obtained from the US Commerce Department, the World Trade Organization, and the government Web sites of the countries of the world.

FOREIGN INVESTMENT: Source material for the Foreign Investment rubric included the US State Department's *Country Commercial Guides*, which provided a comprehensive analysis of the foreign direct investment environments of the countries of the world. The International Monetary Fund's publications *International Financial Statistics Yearbook* and *Balance of Payments Statistics Yearbook*, and the US State Department's *Background Notes* were consulted for the information on foreign direct investment. Also used was information contained in the *World Factbook 2011. The Economist* was consulted in providing basic FDI figures and other relevant data.

ECONOMIC DEVELOPMENT: Source material for the Economic Development rubric included the US State Department's *Country Commercial Guides* and *Background Notes. The Economist* was consulted for economic and political forecasts for selected nations. The *Index of Economic Freedom* was also consulted for its broad description of economic freedom and development. Information on foreign aid was taken from the print publications and Web sites of the International Monetary Fund, World Bank, and the United States Agency for International Development (USAID). Information on long-term development plans was found most often on individual government Web sites.

SOCIAL DEVELOPMENT: Publications consulted in the preparation of this rubric include the US State Department's 2010 *Human Rights Reports*, the US Social Security Administration reports for each nation, and the World Bank's *World Development Indicators 2011.* Additional information was obtained from country-specific Web sites and general news publications.

HEALTH: Statistical sources consulted included the World Health Organization health profiles for each country as well as statistical information maintained by UNESCO. Numerous Web sites of individual nations of the world were also utilized. The World Bank's *World Development Indicators 2011* served as an additional resource.

HOUSING: The latest government population and housing census information available was used for each country through access of official government Web sites. Also of use was the World Bank publication *World Development Indicators 2011.* Web sites consulted included Habitat for Humanity (http://www.habitat.org), United Nations Human Settlements Programme (http://unhabitat.org) and the US Agency for International Development (http://www.usaid.gov).

EDUCATION: Data on Education was obtained from various UNESCO publications and statistics from the World Bank. The *World Factbook 2011* and the US State Department's *Background Notes* were also consulted.

LIBRARIES AND MUSEUMS: Some information concerning libraries and museums was accessed through official government Web sites of various countries when links were available to tourism, education, and/or cultural ministries or departments. In addition, the following Web sites were consulted: American Library Association (http://www.ala.org); International Federation of Library Associations and Institutions (http://www.ifla.org); Museums of the World (http://www.museum.com); and UNESCO (http://www.unesco.org).

MEDIA: Primary sources for this section include the annual *Editor & Publisher* publication *International Year Book*—which lists circulation figures for periodicals—online data provided by UNESCO, and media sections of the "Country Profiles" featured on the Web site of *BBC News International.* In addition, government and other Web sites related to the countries of the world were consulted. Additional sources consulted included the *World Development Indicators 2011, World Factbook 2011,* and US State Department's *2010 Human Rights Reports* (particularly with regard to freedom of the press).

ORGANIZATIONS: Lists of member countries were obtained through the official Web sites of a variety of prominent international organizations and associations, such as the International Federation of Red Cross and Red Crescent Societies, Amnesty International, Kiwanis International, the World Alliance of YMCAs, the World Organization of the Scout Movement, etc.

TOURISM, TRAVEL, AND RECREATION: Statistical sources consulted included the *Tourism Factbook,* published by the UN World Tourism Organization in 2011. Tourism Web sites of individual countries were also consulted. US Department of State per diem travel allowances are published online.

FAMOUS PERSONS: Entries are based on information available through March 2012. Where a person noted in one country is known to have been born in another, the country (or, in some cases, city) of birth follows the personal name in parentheses.

DEPENDENCIES: Source material for the Dependencies rubric was taken primarily from statistical Web sites maintained by the sovereign nation overseeing each dependency. Information also came from *Background Notes* and from the Web site of the United Nations. *The Economist* and the Web site of *BBC News* were also consulted.

BIBLIOGRAPHY: Bibliographical listings at the end of country articles are provided as a guide to further reading on the country in question and are not intended as a comprehensive listing of references used in research for the article. Effort was made to provide a broad sampling of works on major subjects and topics as covered by the article; the bibliographies provide, wherever possible, introductory and general works for use by students and general readers, as well as classical studies, recent contributions, and other works regarded as seminal by area specialists. The country article bibliographies were supplemented with information obtained from a search conducted in November 2011. An extensive bibliography listing key references related to the facts in this encyclopedia follows. However, it is not a complete listing since many fact sheets, brochures, World Wide Web sites, and other informational materials were not included due to space limitations.

PRINT PUBLICATIONS CONSULTED

Almanac of Famous People. 10th ed. Farmington Hills, MI: Cengage Gale, 2011.

Balance of Payments Statistics Yearbook. Washington, D.C.: International Monetary Fund, 2011.

Asian Development Bank, ed. *Asian Development Outlook 2011: South-South Economic Links.* Manila, Philippines: Asian Development Bank, 2011.

Central Intelligence Agency. *World Factbook 2011.* Washington, D.C.: US Government Printing Office, 2011.

Commonwealth Yearbook 2011. London: Commonwealth Secretariat, 2011.

Compendium of Tourism Statistics (2005–2009). 2011 ed. Madrid: World Tourism Organization, 2011.

Crystal, David. *The Cambridge Encyclopedia of Language.* 2nd ed. New York: Cambridge University Press, 1997.

Direction of Trade Statistics. Washington, D.C.: International Monetary Fund, quarterly.

Doernberg, Richard L. *Doernberg's International Taxation in a Nutshell.* 9th ed. Eagan, MN: Thomson Reuters Westlaw, 2012.

Dowie, Mark. *Conservation Refugees: The Hundred-Year Conflict between Global Conservation and Native Peoples.* Cambridge, MA: MIT Press, 2011.

Editor and Publisher International Yearbook 2010. New York: The Editor and Publisher Company, 2011.

Ellicott, Karen. *Countries of the World and Their Leaders Yearbook 2012.* Farmington Hills: Cengage Gale, 2011.

Emerging Stock Markets Factbook 2000. Washington, D.C.: International Finance Corporation, 2002.

Entering the 21st Century: World Development Report 1999/2000. New York: Oxford University Press, 2000.

Evandale's Directory of World Underwriters 2010. London: Evandale Publishing, 2011.

Food and Agriculture Organization of the United Nations. *FAO Statistical Yearbook.* New York: United Nations, 2010.

———. *FAO Yearbook: Fishery Statistics.* New York: United Nations, 2009.

———. *FAO Yearbook: Forest Products.* New York: United Nations, 2009.

Future Demographic-Global Population Forecasts to 2030. London: Euromonitor, 2012.

Global Development Finance. Washington, D.C.: The World Bank, 2011.

Global Education Digest. Montreal: UNESCO Publishing, 2011.

Government Finance Statistics Yearbook. Washington, D.C.: International Monetary Fund, 2011.

Health in the Americas. 2007 ed. Washington, D.C.: World Health Organization, 2007.

Health Information for International Travel 2005–2006. Philadelphia, PA: Mosby, 2005.

Historical Statistics 1960-1993. Paris: Organization for Economic Co-Operation and Development, 1995.

Insurance in the Arab World: Facts and Figures. Beirut: J. Zakhour & Co., undated.

International Civil Aviation Organization. *ICAO Statistical Yearbook, Civil Aviation Statistics of the World.* Montreal: International Civil Aviation Organization, annual.

International Committee of the Red Cross. *ICRC Annual Report 2010.* Geneva: ICRC Publications, 2011.

International Finance Corporation. *Doing Business 2012: Doing Business in a More Transparent World.* Washington, D.C.: International Finance Corporation, 2011.

International Financial Statistics Yearbook. Washington, D.C.: International Monetary Fund, 2008.

The International Insurance Fact Book. New York: Insurance Information Institute, 2012.

International Marketing Data and Statistics 2012. London: Euromonitor, 2012.

International Institute for Strategic Studies. *The Military Balance 2011.* London: Routledge, 2011.

International Save the Children Alliance Annual Report 2010, London: Cambridge House, 2011.

International Trade Statistics Yearbook. New York: United Nations, 2011.

Insurance in the Arab World: Facts and Figures. Beirut: J. Zakhour & Co., undated.

The International Insurance Fact Book, New York: Insurance Information Institute, 2011.

Key World Energy Statistics. Paris: International Energy Agency, 2011.

Little Data Book. Washington, D.C.: The World Bank, 2011.

Making Decisions on Public Health: A Review of Eight Countries. Geneva: World Health Organization, 2004.

McCoy, John F., ed. *Geo-Data: The World Geographical Encyclopedia, 3rd ed.* Farmington Hills, MI: Gale Group, 2003.

National Accounts for OECD Countries, Main Aggregates, Volume I, 2003–2010. Paris: Organization for Economic Cooperation and Development, 2011.

National Accounts Statistics: Main Aggregates and Detailed Tables. New York: United Nations, 2011.

Nordic Statistical Yearbook 2010. Stockholm: Nordic Council of Ministers, 2011.

Nuclear Power Reactors in the World. Vienna: International Atomic Energy Agency, 2006.

Organisation for Economic Co-operation and Development (OECD). *OECD Factbook 2011–2012.* Paris: OECD, 2011.

———. *Agricultural Policies in OECD Countries at a Glance 2011.* Paris: OECD, 2011.

———. *Education at a Glance 2011.* Paris: OECD, 2011.

———. *Health at a Glance 2011.* Paris: OECD, 2011.

———. *Government at a Glance 2011.* Paris: OECD, 2011.

Organization for Economic Co-operation and Development (OECD). *Revenue Statistics of OECD Member Countries 1965–1992.* Paris: OECD, 1993.

Population and Vital Statistics Report, January 2011. New York: United Nations, 2011.

Science & Engineering Indicators 2010. Washington, D.C.: National Science Foundation, 2010.

Sivard, Ruth Leger. *World Military and Social Expenditures.* Washington, D.C.: World Priorities, Inc., 1996.

Sources and Methods: Labour Statistics. Geneva: International Labour Office, 1996.

The State of the World's Children 2011. New York: Oxford University Press, 2011.

The State of the World's Refugees: Human Displacement in the New Millenium. New York: Penguin Books, 2006.

The State of the World's Refugees: Fifty Years of Humanitarian Action. New York: Oxford University Press, 2000.

Stockholm International Peace Research Institute. *SIPRI Yearbook 2011: Armaments, Disarmament and International Security.* London: Oxford University Press, 2011.

Tourism Market Trends: Africa, Madrid: World Tourism Organization, 2008.

Tourism Market Trends: Americas, Madrid: World Tourism Organization, 2008.

Tourism Market Trends: East Asia & the Pacific, Madrid: World Tourism Organization, 2008.

Tourism Market Trends: Europe, Madrid: World Tourism Organization, 2008.

Tourism Market Trends: Middle East, Madrid: World Tourism Organization, 2008.

Tourism Market Trends: South Asia, Madrid: World Tourism Organization, 2008.

Trends in International Migration 2004. Paris: Organization for Economic Co-Operation and Development, 2005.

United Nations Department of Economic and Social Affairs. *World Population Policies 2009.* New York: United Nations, 2010.

United Nations Development Program. *Human Development Report 2011.* New York: United Nations, 2011.

US Agency for International Development, Bureau for Management, Office of Budget. *US Overseas Loans and Grants and Assistance from International Organizations (The Greenbook).* Washington, D.C.: US Government Printing Office, 2011.

US Arms Control and Disarmament Agency. *World Military Expenditures and Arms Transfers 2005.* Washington, DC: U.S. Arms Control and Disarmament Agency, 2009.

US Department of the Interior, US Geological Survey. *Mineral Industries of Africa and the Middle East.* Washington, D.C.: US Government Printing Office, 2009.

———. *Mineral Industries of Asia and the Pacific.* Washington, D.C.: US Government Printing Office, 2009.

———. *Mineral Industries of Europe and Central Eurasia.* Washington, D.C.: US Government Printing Office, 2008.

———. *Mineral Industries of Latin America and Canada.* Washington, D.C.: US Government Printing Office, 2009.

Working Time Laws: A Global Perspective. Geneva: International Labour Office, 2005.

World Data on Education. Paris: International Bureau of Education, 2000.

World Development Indicators 2011. Washington D.C.: The World Bank, 2011.

World Development Report 1990: Poverty. New York: Oxford University Press, 1990.

World Development Report 1995: Workers in an Integrating World. New York: Oxford University Press, 1995.

World Development Report 1996: From Plan to Market. New York: Oxford University Press, 1996.

World Development Report 2003: Sustainable Development in a Dynamic World. Washington, D.C.: World Bank, 2003.

World Development Report 2006: Equity and Development. Washington, D.C.: World Bank, 2005.

World Development Report 2011. Washington, D.C.: World Bank, 2011.

The World Health Report: Make Every Mother and Child Count. Geneva: World Health Organization, 2005.

The World Health Report: Working Together for Health. Geneva: World Health Organization, 2006.

The World Health Report: A Safer Future: Global Public Health Security in the 21st Century. Geneva: World Health Organization, 2007.

The World Health Report: Primary Health Care (Now More Than Ever). Geneva: World Health Organization, 2008.

World Health Statistics 2011. Geneva: World Health Organization, 2011.

World Migration Report. New York: United Nations, 2011.

World Population Projections to 2150. New York: United Nations, 1998.

World Population Prospects: 2011. New York: United Nations, 2011.

World Resources Institute; United Nations Environment Programme; United Nations Development Programme; World Bank. *World Resources Report 2010–11.* New York: Oxford University Press, 2011.

World Urbanization Prospects. New York: United Nations, 2011.

Worldwide Corporate Tax Guide. New York: Ernst & Young, 2011.

Yearbook of Labour Statistics 2005. Geneva: International Labour Office, 2011.

WEB SITES CONSULTED

In the course of preparing this edition, hundreds of Web sites were consulted including the official Web site of each country of the world and those of various nongovernmental organizations worldwide. Of special significance are the Web sites listed below. These sites were accessed in 2011 and 2012 for information relevant to the rubrics listed above.

African Development Indicators 2011. http://data.worldbank.org/sites/default/files/adi_2011-web.pdf

American Library Association. http://www.ala.org

Amnesty International. http://www.amnesty.org

Asia Society. http://asiasociety.org/policy

BBC News. *Country Profiles.* http://news.bbc.co.uk/2/hi/country_profiles/default.stm

Central Intelligence Agency. *The World Factbook, 2011.* http://www.cia.gov/cia/publications/factbook/index.html

Council on Foreign Relations. http://www.foreignaffairs.org/

Country Forecasts. http://www.countrywatch.com

Country Overviews. http://www.developmentgateway.org

The Economist. http://www.economist.com/countries/index.cfm

ElectionGuide. http://www.electionguide.org

Energy Information Administration. *Country Analysis Briefs, 2011.* http://www.eia.doe.gov/emeu/cabs/

Foreign Policy Association. http://www.fpa.org/

Growth Competitiveness Index Rankings. http://www.weforum.org

Habitat for Humanity. http://www.habitat.org

Human Rights Watch. http://www.hrw.org/

Index of Economic Freedom. http://www.heritage.org

Insurance Information Institute. http://www.internationalinsurance.org/

International Banking Statistics. http://www.bis.org/statistics/index.htm

International Federation of Library Associations and Institutions. http://www.ifla.org

International Labour Organization, Department of Statistics. http://www.ilo.org/stat/lang--en/index.htm

International Monetary Fund. http://www.imf.org/

International Union for Conservation of Nature. http://www.iucn.org

Jurist World Law. http://jurist.law.pitt.edu/world/

L'Outre-Mer. http://www.outre-mer.gouv.fr/

Latin Business Chronicle. http://www.latinbusinesschronicle.com

Minerals Information Office, US Geological Survey, US Department of the Interior. http://minerals.usgs.gov/minerals/pubs/country/

Museums of the World. http://www.museum.com

National Science Foundation. Science & Engineering Indicators 2012. http://www.nsf.gov/statistics/seind12/

New York Times. http://www.nytimes.com/pages/world/index.html

OPEC Annual Report 2010. http://www.opec.org/opec_web/static_files_project/media/downloads/publications/Annual_Report_2010.pdf

Organization of American States Annual Report of the Inter American Commission on Human Rights. http://www.oas.org/en/iachr/docs/annual/2011/TOC.asp

Patent Applications by Country. http://www.wipo.int/ipstats/en/statistics/patents/

Political Resources on the Net. http://www.politicalresources.net

Population and Vital Statistics Report, January 2011. Series A, Vol. LXIII. http://unstats.un.org/unsd/demographic/products/vitstats/default.htm

Ramsar Convention on Wetlands. http://www.ramsar.org

TradePort. http://www.tradeport.org

United Nations. http://www.un.org/

United Nations Conference on Trade and Development (UNCTAD). http://www.unctad.org

United Nations Educational, Scientific, and Cultural Organization (UNESCO). http://www.unesco.org

———. *Education for All Global Monitoring Report 2011.* http://unesdoc.unesco.org/images/0019/001907/190743e.pdf

———. Statistics on Research and Development. http://www.uis.unesco.org

———. World Heritage Centre. http://www.whc.unesco.org

United Nations Food and Agricultural Organization. http://www.fao.org/

———. Production Statistics. http: http://faostat.fao.org/site/339/default.aspx

———. Trade Statistics. http: http://faostat.fao.org/site/342/default.aspx

———. Resource Statistics. http: http://faostat.fao.org/site/348/default.aspx

———. Forestry Statistics. http: http://faostat.fao.org/site/630/default.aspx

———. Fisheries Statistics. http: http://faostat.fao.org/site/629/default.aspx

United Nations Schedule of Mission Subsistence Allowance (MSA). http://www.un.org/depts/OHRM/salaries_allowances/allowances/msa.htm

United Nations Human Settlements Programme (UN-HABITAT). http://unhabitat.org

United Nations Statistics Division. http://unstats.un.org/unsd/default.htm

US Agency for International Development. http://www.usaid.gov.

US Department of State. *Background Notes.* http://www.state.gov/r/pa/ei/bgn

———. *Country Commercial Guides.* http://www.state.gov/e/eb/rls/rpts/ccg/

———. *International Religious Freedom Report 2010.* http://www.state.gov/g/drl/rls/irf/2010/index.htm

———. *Human Rights Reports, 2010.* http//www.state.gov/j/drl/rls/hrrpt/

US Library of Congress. http://lcweb2.loc.gov/frd/cs/profiles.html

The Wall Street Journal. http://online.wsj.com/public/us

The Washington Post. http://www.washpost.com/index.shtml

The Weather Channel. "Averages and Records." http://www.weather.com

The World Bank. http://worldbank.org

———. *Doing Business* database. http://www.doingbusiness.org

World Development Indicators, Country Overviews. http://www.developmentgateway.org

World Health Organization. Countries. http://www.who.int/countries/en/

World Intellectual Property Organization. http://www.wipo.int/portal/index.html.en

GUIDE TO COUNTRY ARTICLES

All information contained within a country article is uniformly keyed by means of small superior numerals to the left of the subject headings. A heading such as "Population," for example, carries the same key numeral (6) in every article. Thus, to find information about the population of Albania, consult the table of contents for the page number where the Albania article begins and look for section 6 thereunder. Introductory matter for each nation includes coat of arms, capital, flag (descriptions given from hoist to fly or from top to bottom), anthem, monetary unit, weights and measures, holidays, and time zone.

SECTION HEADINGS IN NUMERICAL ORDER

1	Location, size, and extent	27	Energy and power
2	Topography	28	Industry
3	Climate	29	Science and technology
4	Flora and fauna	30	Domestic trade
5	Environment	31	Foreign trade
6	Population	32	Balance of payments
7	Migration	33	Banking and securities
8	Ethnic groups	34	Insurance
9	Languages	35	Public finance
10	Religions	36	Taxation
11	Transportation	37	Customs and duties
12	History	38	Foreign investment
13	Government	39	Economic development
14	Political parties	40	Social development
15	Local government	41	Health
16	Judicial system	42	Housing
17	Armed forces	43	Education
18	International cooperation	44	Libraries and museums
19	Economy	45	Media
20	Income	46	Organizations
21	Labor	47	Tourism, travel, and recreation
22	Agriculture	48	Famous persons
23	Animal husbandry	49	Dependencies
24	Fishing	50	Bibliography
25	Forestry		
26	Mining		

SECTION HEADINGS IN ALPHABETICAL ORDER

Agriculture	22	Income	20
Animal husbandry	23	Industry	28
Armed forces	17	Insurance	34
Balance of payments	32	International cooperation	18
Banking and securities	33	Judical system	16
Bibliography	50	Labor	21
Climate	3	Languages	9
Customs and duties	37	Libraries and museums	44
Dependencies	49	Local government	15
Domestic trade	30	Location, size, and extent	1
Economic development	39	Media	45
Economy	19	Migration	7
Education	43	Mining	26
Energy and power	27	Organizations	46
Environment	5	Political parties	14
Ethnic groups	8	Population	6
Famous persons	48	Public finance	35
Fishing	24	Religions	10
Flora and fauna	4	Science and technology	29
Foreign investment	38	Social development	40
Foreign trade	31	Taxation	36
Forestry	25	Topography	2
Government	13	Tourism, travel, and recreation	47
Health	41	Transportation	11
History	12		
Housing	42		

FREQUENTLY USED ABBREVIATIONS AND ACRONYMS

AD—Anno Domini
a.m.—before noon
b.—born
BC—Before Christ
C—Celsius
c.—circa (about)
cm—centimeter(s)
Co.—company
Corp.—corporation
cu ft—cubic foot, feet
cu m—cubic meter(s)
d.—died
E—east
e.g.—exempli gratia (for example)
ed.—edition, editor
est.—estimated
et al.—et alii (and others)
etc.—et cetera (and so on)
EU—European Union
F—Fahrenheit

fl.—flourished
FRG—Federal Republic of Germany
ft—foot, feet
ft³—cubic foot, feet
GATT—General Agreement on Tariffs and Trade
GDP—gross domestic products
gm—gram
GMT—Greenwich Mean Time
GNP—gross national product
GRT—gross registered tons
ha—hectares
i.e.—id est (that is)
in—inch(es)
kg—kilogram(s)
km—kilometer(s)
kw—kilowatt(s)
kWh—kilowatt-hour(s)
lb—pound(s)
m—meter(s); morning

m³—cubic meter(s)
mi—mile(s)
Mt.—mount
MW—megawatt(s)
N—north
n.d.—no date
NA—not available
oz—ounce(s)
p.m.—after noon
r.—reigned

rev. ed.—revised edition
S—south
sq—square
St.—saint
UK—United Kingdom
UN—United Nations
US—United States
USSR—Union of Soviet Socialist Republics
W—west

A fiscal split year is indicated by a stroke (e.g. 2011/12).
For acronyms of UN agencies and their intergovernmental organizations, as well as other abbreviations used in text, see the United Nations volume.
A dollar sign ($) stands for US$ unless otherwise indicated.
Note that 1 billion = 1,000 million.

ALBANIA

Republic of Albania
Republika é Shqipërisë

CAPITAL: Tiranë

FLAG: The flag consists of a red background at the center of which is a black double-headed eagle.

ANTHEM: *Hymni i Flamúrit (Anthem of the Flag).*

MONETARY UNIT: The lek (ALL) of 100 qindarka is a convertible paper currency. There are coins of 5, 10, 20, 50 qindarka, and 1 lek, and notes of 1, 3, 5, 10, 25, 50, 100, and 500 leks. ALL1 = US$0.01 (or US$1 = ALL105.87) as of 2011.

WEIGHTS AND MEASURES: The metric system is the legal standard.

HOLIDAYS: New Year's Day, 1 January; International Women's Day, 8 March; Independence Day, 28 November; Christmas Day, 25 December. Movable Islamic and Christian religious holidays include Small Bayram, Catholic Easter, Orthodox Easter, and Great Bayram.

TIME: 1 p.m. = noon GMT.

¹LOCATION, SIZE, AND EXTENT

Albania is situated on the west coast of the Balkan Peninsula opposite the "heel" of the Italian "boot," from which it is separated on the SW and W by the Strait of Otranto and the Adriatic Sea. It is bordered on the N and E by Montenegro, Kosovo, and Macedonia and on the SE by Greece, with a total boundary length of 720 km (447 mi). Comparatively, Albania is slightly smaller than Maryland, with a total area of 28,748 sq km (11,100 sq mi) and extends 340 km (211 mi) N–S and 148 km (92 mi) E–W. Albania's capital city, Tiranë, is located in the west central part of the country.

²TOPOGRAPHY

Albania is predominantly mountainous, with 70% of the territory at elevations of more than 300 m (1,000 ft). The rest of the country consists of coastal lowland and the lower reaches of river valleys opening onto the coastal plain. The Albanian mountains, representing a southern continuation of the Dinaric system, rise abruptly from the plains and are especially rugged along the country's borders. The highest peak, Mt. Korabi (2,753 m/9,033 ft) lies in eastern Albania on the Macedonian border. The most important rivers are the Drin, the Buna, the Mat, the Shkumbin, the Seman, and the Vjosa river, all of which empty into the Adriatic. Albania shares Lake Scutari (Liqeni i Shkodrës/Skadarsko Jezero) with Montenegro, Lake Ohrid (Liqeni i Ohrit/Ohridsko Jezero) with Macedonia, and Lake Prespa (Liqeni i Prespës/Prespansko Jezero) with Macedonia and Greece.

³CLIMATE

Albania has a variety of climatic conditions, as it is situated in the transition zone between the typical Mediterranean climate in the west and the moderate continental in the east. The average annual temperature is 15°C (59°F). Rainy winters (with frequent cyclones) and hot, dry summers are typical of the coastal plain. Summer rainfall is more frequent and winters colder in the mountainous interior. Annual precipitation ranges from about 100 cm (40 in) on the coast to more than 250 cm (100 in) in the mountains.

⁴FLORA AND FAUNA

The mountainous topography produces a variety of flora and fauna. The dry lowlands are occupied by a bush-shrub association known as maquis, in which hairy, leathery leaves reduce transpiration to a minimum. There are some woods in the low-lying regions, but larger forests of oak, beech, and other deciduous species begin at 910 m (2,986 ft). Black pines and other conifers are found at higher elevations in the northern part of the country. Wild birds still abound in the lowland forests. The World Resource Institute estimates that there are 3,031 plant species in Albania. In addition, Albania is home to 73 mammal, 303 bird, 37 reptile, and 16 amphibian species. The calculation reflects the total number of distinct species residing in the country, not the number of endemic species. According to a 2011 report issued by the International Union for Conservation of Nature and Natural Resources (IUCN), threatened species included 3 types of mammals, 5 species of birds, 4 types of reptiles, 2 species of amphibians, and 39 species of fish. Endangered species include the Atlantic sturgeon, Mediterranean monk seal, and the hawksbill turtle.

⁵ENVIRONMENT

The World Resources Institute reported that Albania had designated 20,200 hectares (49,915 acres) of land for protection as of 2006. Water resources totaled 41.7 cu km (10 cu mi) while water usage was 1.71 cu km (0.41 cu mi) per year. Domestic water usage accounted for 27% of total usage, industrial for 11%, and agricultural for 62%. Per capita water usage totaled 546 cu m (19,282 cu ft) per year.

Deforestation remains Albania's principal environmental problem, despite government reforestation programs. Forest and woodland account for about 38% of the country's land use. Soil erosion is also a cause for concern, as is pollution of the water by industrial and domestic effluents. About 99% of Albania's urban population and 95% of its rural population have access to pure water.

Albania has three Ramsar Wetlands of International Importance.

The UN reported in 2008 that carbon dioxide emissions in Albania totaled 4,239 kilotons.

⁶POPULATION

The US Central Intelligence Agency (CIA) estimated the population of Albania in 2011 to be approximately 2,994,667, which placed it at number 135 in population among the 196 nations of the world. In 2011, approximately 10.5% of the population was over 65 years of age, with another 21.4% under 15 years of age. The median age in Albania was 30.4 years. There were 1.04 males for every female in the country. The population's annual rate of change was 0.267%. The projected population for the year 2025 was 3,300,000. Population density in Albania was 104 people per sq km (269 people per sq mi).

The UN estimated that 52% of the population lived in urban areas and that urban populations had an annual rate of change of 2.3%. The largest urban area was Tiranë, with a fast-growing population fed especially by Albanian internal migration from agricultural areas.

The population increase in Albania has been exceptionally rapid by European standards. The birthrate, despite a decline from over 40 births per 1,000 of population in the 1950s to 19 by 2000, remains among the highest in Europe. The high birthrate is partially attributed to the ban on birth control during the communist era; as of 2006, the use of birth control remains low, with only 15.3% of married women reportedly using contraceptives. Another contributing factor to the population growth is the increase in life expectancy to an average of 74 years of age.

⁷MIGRATION

Estimates of Albania's net migration rate, carried out by the CIA in 2011, amounted to -3.34 migrants per 1,000 citizens. The total number of emigrants living abroad was 1.44 million, and the total number of immigrants living in Albania was 89,100. In the 19th century, Albanians emigrated to other Balkan countries (Romania, Bulgaria, Turkey, Greece) and to Egypt and Russia. During the first decades of the 20th century, emigration—for economic reasons—was primarily to the United States (largely to Massachusetts), Argentina, Australia, and France. Emigration following World War II occurred on a very limited scale, mainly for political reasons. Between 1945 and 1990, Albania remained virtually isolated from the rest of Europe.

In 1997, rebel fighting and an Italian-led multinational force of 6,000 foreign peacekeeping troops prevented thousands of Albanians from fleeing into Greece or Italy. By 2004, approximately 25% of the total population, or over 35% of the labor force, had emigrated. Of the approximately 900,000 emigrants, most reside in Greece (600,000), Italy (200,000), Western European countries,

the United States, and Canada. Since the 1990s, migration has been five times higher than the average migration flow in developing countries. Included in this flow was a significant "brain drain" of scholars that became a "brain waste" as they became underemployed in their countries of destination.

During the NATO air strikes of 1999, Albania hosted 465,000 refugees from Kosovo. Adoption of the Kosovo Peace Plan on 10 June 1999 prompted the return of an estimated 432,500 refugees to Kosovo from Albania. At the end of 2003, there were around 300 refugees in the country, mainly Albanians from Kosovo and the former Yugoslav Republic of Macedonia, as well as citizens from Iraq and Turkish Kurds. By the end of 2004, Albania's refugee population had declined to just 51.

Between 1992 and 2003, approximately 6,000 foreigners entered Albania as migrant workers employed mainly in construction, trade, service, and education sectors. Around three fourths of them came from Turkey, China, Egypt, other Arab and Muslim countries, and European Union (EU) countries.

⁸ETHNIC GROUPS

Generally regarded as descendants of the ancient Illyrians, the Albanians make up about 95% of the population. Ethnic Greeks comprise as much as 3% of the populace. Other groups, including Roma, Vlachs, Bulgarians, Macedonians, and Serbs, make up the remaining 2%. The Greeks are located primarily in the south. The law grants official minority status to national groups, which include Geeks, Macedonians, and Montenegrins, and ethnolinguistic minority groups, which include Vlachs and Roma. Some Greek communities have continued to file grievances with the government for the right to use Greek in public documents and on public signs in primarily Greek communities. There have been some reports of social discrimination against the Roma and the small number of Balkan Egyptians within the country. In the early 1990s, about two million Albanians lived in Serbia and Montenegro (formerly Yugoslavia).

⁹LANGUAGES

Albanian (Shqip) is an independent member of the Indo-European family of languages. Parallel theories about its origin coexist, with the main being those of Illyrian and Thracian descent. Lexical influences stem from Latin, Slavonic, Greek, and Turkish during centuries of close contacts. The first document of written Albanian is from 1555. It was not until 1908 that a common Latin alphabet was established for Albanian. In addition to letters of the English alphabet, Albanian uses the diacritics ç (representing the sound of ch in church) and ë (the sound of i in dirt). Other unusual letter values are c (the sound of ts in gets), x (the sound of ds in woods), xh (the sound of j in jaw), j (the sound of y in yet), q (the sound of ky in stockyard), and y (the sound of the German ü). There are two distinct dialects—Gheg, spoken in the north, and Tosk, spoken in the south. During the period between World War I and II, a Gheg variety of Central Albania was used in public communication, functioning as standard Albanian, although there was no systematic process of standardization until the 1960s. After World War II, the Tosk dialect was used more extensively in the public communication, and, during an ideologically loaded process of language planning that started in the 1950s and was formally concluded in the 1970s, the Tosk dialect became the base of the new standard that is still used today. Greek is spoken by a minority of the population in the southeast border area and in the southern coast. Vlach, Romani, and other Slavic dialects are also spoken by minority groups.

10 RELIGIONS

In 1990 and 1991, official opposition to religious activities came to an end, and churches and mosques that had been closed under the communist regime were selectively allowed to reopen. Albania is now a self-proclaimed secular state; however, the 1998 constitution calls for freedom of religion. There is no reliable data available concerning membership in religious organizations or participation in religious activities, since the last census that included such information was taken in 1939. During the five centuries of Ottoman domination, Islam has been the most prominent religion of Albania, including Sunni Islam and members of the Bektashi school (Shi'a Sufism). Since 1925, Albania has been considered the world center of the Bektashi school. The Orthodox Autocephalous Church of Albania (Albanian Orthodox) and Roman Catholicism represent the two other traditional faiths in the country. There are several small Protestant groups. The four main groups of Sunnis, Bektashis, Orthodox, and Catholics have maintained a heightened degree of social recognition and status due to their historical presence within the country. Historically, there has been religious harmony among different groups. A large part of the Albanian population, especially in the capital and other big cities, does not demonstrate strong religious feelings. The State Committee on Cults regulates relations between the government and religious organizations and keeps statistics on groups that contact the Committee for assistance. Registration or licensing is not required for religious organizations. In 2010, there were more than 230 religious groups, organizations, foundations, and educational institutions operating in the country. The religious holidays of Catholic and Orthodox Easter and Christmas, Major Bajram, Minor Bajram, and Nevruz are observed as public holidays.

11 TRANSPORTATION

The CIA reports that Albania has a total of 18,000 km (11,185 mi) of roads, of which 7,020 km (4,362 mi) are paved. There are 114 vehicles per 1,000 people in the country. Railroads extend for 423 km (263 mi). There are five airports, which transported 231,263 passengers in 2009 according to the World Bank. Albania has approximately 41 km (25.5 mi) of navigable waterways.

Many side roads are unsuitable for motor transport; bicycles and donkeys are common. There were virtually no private cars in the country before 1990, but they have become more common since the opening of the borders. One of the many recent infrastructural projects was the construction of a 241 km (150 mi) four-lane highway linking Durrës with Greece, via Pogradec and Kapshtica. In the summer of 2011, the government began work on a four-lane, 32-km (20-mi) highway linking the capital city of Tiranë to Elbasan, once the industry hub of Albania. A major new road connects the Albanian coast (Adriatic) with the region of Kosovo.

Railroad construction began in 1947 and continued during the years of the communist state. After 1990, the railroads were completely abandoned. The state of the Albanian railroads today is deplorable, although a few trains still run.

LOCATION: 39°38′ to 42°39′N; 19°16′ to 21°4′ E. BOUNDARY LENGTHS: Montenegro, 172 kilometers (109 miles); Kosovo, 112 kilometers (70); Macedonia, 151 kilometers (94 miles); Greece, 282 kilometers (175 miles); coastline, 362 kilometers (225 miles). TERRITORIAL SEA LIMIT: 15 miles.

Coastwise vessels link the ports of Durrës, Vlorë, Sarandë, and Shëngjin. Durrës is the principal port for foreign trade. The merchant fleet of Albania in 2010 consisted of 25 vessels of 1,000 GRT or over. A freight ferry service between Durrës and Trieste was inaugurated in 1983.

Four airports had paved runways. There was one heliport. Flights from Tiranë's international airport 'Mother Theresa' connect the Albanian capital with Rome, Athens, Belgrade, Switzerland and other European cities.

¹²HISTORY

Origins and the Middle Ages

The Albanians are generally considered descendants of ancient Illyrian or Thracian tribes of Indo-European origin that may have come to the Balkan Peninsula even before the Greeks. Although several Greek colonies were established along the coast, the hinterland remained independent. An Illyrian kingdom was formed in the 3rd century BC, and even after it was conquered by Rome in 167 BC, some mountain tribes were never subdued. Among them were the Albani or Albanoi, whose city Albanopolis was mentioned in the 2nd century BC by Ptolemy in his Geography. Later, while nominally under Byzantine rule, Albania was raided by Slav invaders in the 6th century and annexed to Bulgaria in the 9th century. Temporary inroads were made by Venice, which established coastal colonies, and by the Normans, who seized Durrës in 1082–85. Albanian expansion took place under the Angevin kings of Naples in the 13th century, and again under the Serbs in the 14th century. Short-lived independent principalities flourished during the second half of the 14th century.

From the Ottomans to Independence

Turkish advances began in 1388 and were resisted from 1443 to 1468 by Gjergj Kastrioti, better known as Scanderbeg, the Albanian national hero; however, by 1479, the Turks had attained complete control of the area. Over the succeeding centuries, Islam spread throughout most of the country. Turkish rule continued through the 19th century, which saw an intensification of nationalistic feeling, often erupting into open rebellion. In November 1912, during the First Balkan War, the National Assembly convened in Vlorë under the chairmanship of Ismail Qemali and proclaimed Albania's independence. The proclamation was supported by Austria-Hungary but opposed by Russia, Serbia, Greece, and Turkey. At a conference in London in 1913, Albania's national boundaries were established—they have remained virtually unchanged since that time—and the nation was placed under the tutelage of the great powers. Albania then became a principal battleground during World War I. By the time the war ended, portions of Albania were under Italian, French, and Yugoslav control.

Albania again asserted its independence in 1920, and a provisional government was established as the Italians and French withdrew. Following a period of unstable parliamentary government (1921–24), Ahmet Zogu, the chief of the Mat district, seized power with Yugoslav support. He proclaimed Albania a republic in 1925, with himself as president, and a kingdom in 1928, with himself as King Zog I. A series of concessions to Italy made Albania a virtual Italian protectorate, and after Zog was forced into exile in April 1939, Italy occupied Albania, uniting it with the Italian crown. During World War II, Communist-led guerrillas under Enver Hoxha resisted Italian and German forces. The Congress of Permeti (24 May 1944) formed Albania's provisional government, naming Hoxha as premier; the congress banned the return of former King Zog and called for a constituent assembly to meet after the complete liberation of the country. In November 1944, the communist rule under Hoxha's government was established in Tiranë.

Under Communist Rule

The constitution of 1946 declared Albania a people's republic. Early close relations with Yugoslavia were abruptly severed when the Soviet-Yugoslav break occurred in 1948. Partly because of fundamental differences with Yugoslavia, whose borders included about 1.7 million Albanians, and partly because of ideological divergences, Albanian-Soviet relations worsened at the 22nd Communist Party Congress, and the USSR severed diplomatic relations with Albania in December 1961 and evacuated its naval and submarine bases at Vlorë.

Relations with Communist countries other than China worsened during the 1960s, as Albania ceased to participate in the activities of the Warsaw Treaty Organization by September 1968 following the Soviet invasion of Czechoslovakia. With Yugoslavia, however, there were signs of rapprochement: an Albanian-Yugoslav trade pact was signed in 1970, and trade between the two nations consequently flourished. Gestures were also made to improve relations with Albania's other neighbor, Greece.

Albania's relations with China, its ally and supporter since 1961, seemed to cool somewhat after 1971. China's détente with the United States ran counter to Albania's policy of opposition to the USSR and the United States. China's assistance to Albania ceased when the United States denounced the overthrow of China's "Gang of Four" in October of 1976.

On 28 December 1976, Albania adopted a new constitution that formally established Marxism-Leninism as the dominant ideology and proclaimed the principle of self-reliance. The following year, Albania broke off most of its links with China and accused it of "social imperialist" policies, and, in 1978, trade relations were also suspended. In 1983, however, Albania received a Chinese delegation to discuss the resumption of trade relations. Meanwhile, relations with Yugoslavia worsened following the riots by ethnic Albanians in Yugoslavia's Kosovo province in March 1981; Yugoslavia charged that Albania had instigated the protests, and Albania accused Yugoslavia of ethnic discrimination. (Nevertheless, as of 1987 Yugoslavia was Albania's main trading partner, and Albania's first rail connection with the outside world, the Shkodër-Titograd link, was opened in 1986.)

Internally, Albania seemed to be locked in bitter political conflict as the 1980s began. Prime Minister Mehmet Shehu, relieved of his defense portfolio in April 1980, died in December 1981, an alleged suicide. A year later, Hoxha charged that Shehu had been working for the US, Soviet, and Yugoslav secret services and that Shehu even had orders from Yugoslavia to kill him. Western and Yugoslav press accounts speculated that Shehu had favored an opening to the West and had been executed in the course of a power struggle. Throughout 1981–83, an extensive purge of those even remotely connected with Shehu was conducted. This was in keeping with previous purges in the 1950s of those sympathizing with Yugoslavia, in the 1960s of pro-Soviet officials, and in the late 1970s of pro-West and pro-China policymakers. On 25 September 1982, according to Albanian reports, a group of armed Albanian exiles landed on the coast and was promptly murdered. Hoxha alleged that they had been sent by Yugoslavia.

Hoxha died on 11 April 1985 and was succeeded as first secretary of the Workers Party by Ramiz Alia, who had been chairman of the presidium of the People's Assembly since 1982.

In the mid 1980s, Albania took steps to end its isolation. In 1987, it established diplomatic relations with Canada, Spain, Bolivia, and the Federal Republic of Germany. In August 1987, Albania signed a treaty with Greece formally ending the state of war that had existed between the two countries since World War II.

Democracy and a Free-Market Economy

As unrest spread in the late 1980s through Central and Eastern Europe in opposition to long-lasting Communist dictatorships, economic hardships in Albania grew ever deeper. Albania's political leadership had to open up more diplomatic and trade relationships with Western nations as the only available source of potential assistance. At the same time, internal unrest and a search for alternative democratic political solutions led by 1990 to mass protests and calls for the government's resignation. Thousands of Albanians wanted to emigrate in spite of imposed restrictions and became refugees housed in foreign embassies waiting for ships to take them abroad, particularly to Italy. President Ramiz Alia initiated the process of reestablishing diplomatic relations with the United States, discontinued since the 1939 annexation of Albania by Italy. Restrictions on travel abroad were eased and religious practices allowed again.

The Communist Party government still intended to maintain both its control and its socialist system while allowing for some democracy. But it was not to be, and by December 1990, the opposition Democratic Party was formed. On 7 February 1991, some 8,000 students went on strike in Tiranë demanding economic changes and the government's resignation. In the face of persistent unrest, President Alia scheduled multiparty elections for 31 March 1991. Even with the Communist Party still in control, the Democratic Party managed to win 75 of the 250 People's Assembly seats (mostly in urban areas) with 160 seats won by the Communist Party. Ramiz Alia was reelected president, and a still all-Communist Council of Ministers was appointed under Prime Minister Fatos Nano. By June 1991, continuous unrest forced Alia to agree to a first coalition government between its Communist (renamed Socialist) Party and the new Democratic Party. The latter withdrew from the coalition government in December 1991, claiming that the majority Socialists were preventing any reforms. President Alia then called for new general elections on 22 March 1992, which gave the Democratic Party a majority of seats (92 of 140). Sali Berisha was elected president with Aleksander Meksi his prime minister. Under Berisha, Alia and Nano were arrested and tried for corruption and abuse of power. They were sentenced to long prison terms but were released within a few years of their convictions.

Radical reforms were pushed to create a market economy and democratic institutions internally while bringing Albania back into the international mainstream after half a century of isolation. By the end of 1993, barriers to foreign trade had been removed and the Albanian lek made fully convertible. The privatization of the economy had been successfully initiated, particularly in the agricultural sector, with 90% of land distributed to private farmers. In foreign relations, Albania tried to balance the internal pressure to assist both the repressed Albanian majority in the Kosovo region of Serbia towards its independence and the sizable Albanian minority in Macedonia to obtain human and political rights. Albania's Western trade partners realized its internal economic

and humanitarian needs and have been generous with their assistance, which, between mid 1991 and 1993, amounted to $1 billion, mostly from European Union countries led by Italy. The United States and Albania also developed very close relations. Albania requested membership in NATO and continued its cooperation with NATO. Because of its own border problems with Greece, Albania supported the independence of Macedonia and was one of the first nations to recognize Macedonia in spite of Greece's refusal to do so. Albania, a majority (70%) Muslim country, joined the Organization of the Islamic Conference mainly to gain economic support. Albania also hosted Pope John Paul II's visit in April 1993, having established diplomatic relations with the Vatican in September 1991, and intensified its traditional good relationship with Italy, whose annexation of Albania in 1939 was by then only a faint memory.

In 1994, the border disputes that have occurred since the creation of Albania flared into violence as Greek and Albanian border guards fought against each other in sporadic clashes. Greece expelled over 1,500 Albanians working in Greece without permits.

Albania's borders also became critical in 1994, as smugglers attempted to evade the embargo imposed on Serbia as a consequence of its participation in the war in Bosnia. Fuel was shipped into Albania through the ports of Durrës and Vlorë and then taken by tanker truck inland where it was transported via Lake Shkodër into Montenegro and then into Serbia. Because the oil was legitimately imported into the country, it was subjected to import duties, which provided in excess of $22 million in tax revenue for the Albanian government in 1994.

Domestically, Albania began to see the beginning fruits of its painful transition to a market economy as consumer goods and cafe-filled boulevards began to appear for the first time in post-Communist Albania. While wages remained low in comparison to other European countries, living standards were still higher than they had been under Hoxha's Stalinist economics.

While Albania's parliamentary election in May 1996 returned President Berisha to power, the election was marred by reports of widespread electoral fraud committed by Berisha's Democratic Party and its allies. International observers in Albania to monitor the election confirmed these reports. While the United States and the Organization for Cooperation and Security in Europe expressed private concern over the election tampering, they did not publicly demand that new elections be held. For days after the election, police jailed major opposition leaders and used truncheons and tear gas to disperse crowds protesting the election fraud. In October of 1996, the Democratic Party again won a landslide victory in local elections, but the party was again charged by international observers and opposition parties with massive electoral fraud.

Perhaps the best indicator that the Democratic Party was not as popular as elections indicated came in response to the collapse of several "pyramid schemes" in late 1996 and early 1997, in which at least one third of the population had invested approximately $800 million by late 1996. Not only were these schemes a dubious investment value, but they had retarded the development of the legitimate Albanian economy by draining money away from legitimate investments, as even banks offering 16% annual interest had trouble attracting new deposits.

Rightly or wrongly, most Albanians blamed the government for the pyramid schemes. It was widely believed that the government had used funds provided by the schemes to finance its campaign and that government ministers were involved with starting and running the schemes. The government's own belated actions in reaction to the pyramid schemes—freezing their assets and arresting fund managers—only further infuriated investors because they reduced the already slim chances of seeing a return of any of their capital.

Anger over the collapse of the funds initiated the violence that followed throughout the winter and spring, releasing pent-up frustration that quickly spun out of government control and into anarchy. Protests in Tiranë in January 1997 calling for the resignation of the government were peaceful, but, in provincial areas, Albanians began destroying anything associated with the government and the Democratic Party, including courthouses, police stations, municipal buildings, and property belonging to state-owned industries. Violence was particularly serious in the southern port city of Vlorë, home to many of Albania's smugglers and drug operators who had invested heavily in the schemes. Government officials and soldiers were expelled from most of southern Albania, as citizens (mostly gangsters and smugglers armed with weapons from government stockpiles and even with MIG aircraft from a captured military base) took control of the area.

The government attempted to stop the protests by cracking down on opposition groups and protesters. Curfews were imposed, as well as restrictions on the right of assembly and freedom of the press. Major opposition leaders were secretly arrested and imprisoned, and the offices of the nation's major opposition newspaper were torched by plain-clothes security officers. A military force dispatched to return the south to government control was unable to dislodge the rebel hold on Vlorë.

At the appearance of government impotence in the south, order broke down throughout Albania, and the looting went completely beyond control. Not only were food and goods looted from government and industrial facilities (as well as weapons from government armories), but university libraries and cherished cultural monuments were destroyed by rampaging crowds.

President Berisha eventually accepted the creation of a coalition government with the aim of restoring order and ending the widespread anarchy. At Berisha's request, a "voluntary militia" was created, and Tiranë returned to government control. However, it soon became apparent that the militia was composed mostly of members of the secret police (which Berisha had promised to dissolve) and Berisha loyalists, creating great mistrust among the opposition members of his cabinet.

As the violence came closer to the Albanian capital, there were calls for an international peacekeeping force to restore order. In April, a 6,000-member peacekeeping force led by French and Italian troops was deployed to patrol the countryside and restore order so the country could hold new elections. While the deployment of these troops put an end to the violence that had rocked Albania for over three months and had cost almost 150 lives, the massive looting and destruction left the country in tatters, and the pillaging of government armories meant that nearly every household had an automatic machine gun.

The identification of the Democrats with the corruption of the pyramid schemes hurt them badly in the July 1997 election, and

the Socialist Party and its allies won an overwhelming victory. Nano, who had regained control of the Socialist Party after his release from prison, became prime minister. President Berisha resigned, and the Assembly elected Rexhep Mejdani, of the Democratic Party, as his successor. In November 1998, many of the principles embodied in the country's 1991 interim constitution were given permanent status when a new, Western-style constitution defining Albania as a democratic republic was approved in a nationwide referendum.

Albania was thrust into the international spotlight by the Kosovo crisis in the spring of 1999, as approximately 440,000 Kosovar Albanian refuges fled over the border to escape persecution at the hands of the Serbs after NATO began launching air strikes against Yugoslav military targets in March. Albania served as an outpost for NATO troops. The influx of refugees further strained Albania's weak economy, and millions of dollars' worth of aid was pledged by the World Bank, the European Union, and other sources. By the fall, most of the refugees had returned to their homes, but Albania's struggle with poverty, crime, and corruption continued.

In October 1999, Socialist Prime Minister Pandeli Majko, appointed a year earlier, was ousted after losing favor with senior party leaders; he was replaced by another young, Western-leaning politician, Ilir Meta. Meta immediately moved to modernize the economy, privatize business, fight crime, and reform the judiciary and tax systems. In January 2001, Albania and Yugoslavia re-established diplomatic relations that had been severed during the Kosovo crisis.

Close to Albania's East borders, fighting between ethnic Macedonians and ethnic Albanian rebels in the northwest region of Macedonia around the town of Tetovo intensified in March 2001 (it had begun in 2000). Fears in Macedonia of the creation of a "Greater Albania," including Kosovo and parts of Macedonia, were fueled by the separatist movement. On 13 August, the Ohrid Framework Agreement was signed by the Macedonian government and ethnic Albanian representatives, granting greater recognition of ethnic Albanian rights in exchange for the rebels' pledge to turn over weapons to the NATO peacekeeping force.

General elections were held in June 2001 and were won by the Socialist Party once again, taking over half of the 140 parliamentary seats. In the elections, the Union for Victory, a coalition of five political parties, came in second. By September, a coalition government was in place. Meta listed European integration and an end to energy shortages as his priorities. However, by December, the Socialist Party was plagued by a rift between Meta and party chairman Nano, after Nano accused Meta's government of corruption and incompetence and demanded that the cabinet be restructured. On 29 January 2002, Meta resigned after failing to resolve the split in the party. Pandeli Majko became the country's new prime minister, but feuding in the Socialist Party leadership continued. In June, parliament elected former Defense Minister Alfred Moisiu as president, replacing Mejdani. His election came after days of political infighting, during which Nano and Berisha were barred from running. In the end, both Nano and Berisha backed Moisiu as the sole consensus candidate for the position. Then, in August, Nano became prime minister for the fourth time after the Socialist Party decided to merge the roles of prime minister and party chairman.

In November 2002, the North Atlantic Treaty Organization (NATO) announced that it would accept seven new members in 2004 of the ten countries aspiring to join the organization. This left three—Albania, Macedonia, and Croatia—to wait until a later round of expansion. In January 2003, Albania and Macedonia agreed to intensify bilateral cooperation, especially in the economic sphere, so as to prepare their way to NATO and European Union membership. Also that month, the EU and Albania began Stabilization and Association Agreement talks, seen as the first step toward EU membership.

In the spring of 2004, the failure of Nano's government to bring about economic and social improvements for everyday Albanians led to demonstrations staged by the opposition in Tiranë asking for Nano's resignation. However, general elections were held as scheduled in the summer of 2005. The Democratic Party of Albania (PD) emerged victorious, taking 55 out of 140 seats, while its allies took 18 seats. In spite of having this slim majority in the People's Assembly, the prime minister could not be nominated for another two months due to political wrangling and accusations of rigged elections. Finally, on 3 September 2005, Sali Berisha was nominated prime minister by president Moisiu. Berisha assured the people that he had learned from his past mistakes and pledged to reduce corruption and taxation, improve economic and social conditions, and make progress towards EU and NATO integration. After three years of talks, in June 2006, the Stabilization and Association agreement was signed with the EU. The EU encouraged further reform, particularly regarding doing away with organized crime and corruption, and developing media freedom and property and minority rights. By 2007, although there had been signs of economic progress, with inflation under tighter control and rising levels of GDP growth, the country remained one of the poorest in Europe. Unemployment was high and poverty widespread.

In July 2007, parliament elected the ruling party chairman Bamir Topi president. Albania became a member of NATO in April 2009.

In the legislative elections of June 2009, the PD won enough seats to form a government; however, for the first time since the beginning of the multiparty system, the leading party fell one seat short of a majority in the unicameral assembly. As a result, Berisha remained in office as prime minister, but the center-right governing party had to rule in coalition with the left-wing Socialist Movement for Integration (LSI). Some observers issued reports of widespread irregularities in a vote that was so close that final counts were not confirmed until nearly one month after the poll. The Democratic Party earned about 46% of the vote, while the Socialist Party, led by Edi Rama, won about 45%.

In May 2010, the Socialist opposition took to the streets of Tiranë in protest against the government, claiming to have found new evidence of election fraud and calling for an official recount nearly one year after the election. Rama, who is also the mayor of Tiranë, publicly encouraged those taking part to engage in non-violent resistance against the government until their demands were met. However, Berisha gave no indication that the government would cede to the protesters and dismissed their demands as illegal.

¹³GOVERNMENT

Under the 1976 constitution, Albania was a socialist republic. Legislative authority was vested in the unicameral People's Assembly, elected every four years from a single list of candidates. In elections held 2 February 1987, 250 deputies were elected by 1,830,653 voters, with no votes cast against and one vote invalid. Voter participation was allegedly 100%. Suffrage was extended to men and women from the age of 18 and was compulsory. The 1976 constitution specified that "the rights of citizens are indivisible from the fulfillment of their duties and cannot be exercised in opposition to the socialist order."

Through most of the 1990s, Albania's government was based on the 29 April 1991 Law on Constitutional Provisions that established the principle of separation of powers, the protection of private property and human rights, a multiparty parliament, and a president of the republic with broad powers. After defeating a proposed constitutional measure in 1994, Albanian voters approved a new constitution in November 1998 giving the Albanian government a shape more like those of Western nations. Many provisions of the 1991 interim constitution were made permanent in the new document, which guaranteed a number of basic rights, including religious freedom, property rights, and human rights for ethnic minorities. After being cut to 140 members in 1992, the unicameral People's Assembly was expanded to 155 in 1997; it was subsequently reduced to 140 once again. Of these members, 100 are directly elected, and 40 are elected by proportional representation. The president is elected by the People's Assembly for a five-year term, and the prime minister is appointed by the president. A Council of Ministers is nominated by the prime minister and approved by the president.

¹⁴POLITICAL PARTIES

Before the 1990s, the only political party was the Communist Party, which was founded in 1941 and has been known officially as the Workers Party (Partia e Punes) since 1948. As of November 1986, it had about 147,000 members, as compared to 45,382 in 1948. The Albanian Democratic Front was the party's major subsidiary organization; other subsidiary groups included the Union of Albanian Working Youth and the Women's Union of Albania. Under the 1976 constitution, the first secretary of the Workers Party was commander-in-chief of the armed forces. The constitution described the Workers Party as the "sole directing political power in state and society."

The primary political parties of the first decade after the communist era included the Democrats (led by Sali Berisha), a Western-style conservative party; the Democratic Alliance, a breakaway group of Democrats still largely allied with them; the Socialists, that largely inherited the former Communist Party members but that tried to distance itself ideologically from the former communist party; the Republican Party, a conservative party; and the Social Democrats, a Western-style progressive party largely allied with the socialists. Although in the early years of post-Communist Albania there were genuine ideological differences between the parties, such distinctions have since blurred. Following the election of 4 July 2005, seats in the unicameral National Assembly were distributed as follows: the Democratic Party of Albania (PD), 55; the Socialist Party (PS), 40; the Republican

Party (PR), 11; the Social Democratic Party (PSD), 7; the Socialist Movement for Integration (LSI), 5; and other, 22.

In July 2007, Bamir Topi of PD was elected as president with 85 votes from the assembly after the fourth round of elections.

In the first six elections since independence, allegations of fraud and voting irregularities drew contention among political parties and concern from international observers. The July 2009 parliamentary elections, although markedly improved by international standards, still held some irregularities, such as delayed openings of polling centers. The ruling PD retained its control of the legislature with a narrow 47%, representing 71 of the 140 seats in parliament. PS came in second with 45% of the vote, representing 65 seats. As preliminary results were being tabulated, Prime Minister Sali Berisha invited the third-place splinter group, the Socialist Movement for Integration (LSI), to form a coalition government. The invitation, placed before the final official results of the election were posted, caused tension with PS leaders, who accused Berisha of trying to impose inappropriate influence over the electoral commission. Despite the quarrels over the vote, however, both of the main parties campaigned on similar platforms, including pledges to make the alleviation of poverty a priority and to pursue membership in the European Union. The next legislative elections were scheduled for 2013.

15 LOCAL GOVERNMENT

Albania is divided into 12 regions (qarqe), 36 districts (rrethe), including the city of Tiranë (or Tirana), and 384 municipalities (as of 2007). All subdivisions are governed by people's councils. The councils direct economic, social, cultural, and administrative activity in their jurisdictional areas and appoint executive committees to administer day-to-day activities.

International observers deemed local elections held in 2000 to have achieved a certain level of democracy, but identified irregularities that need to be addressed in reforms in the Albanian electoral code. The third round of local elections held on 12 October 2003 did not address these irregularities. Several international organizations noted that international standards for democratic elections had not been met. Partial run-offs were held in November and December, following a boycott by the Democratic Party commissioners.

Local elections were held on 18 February 2007. The leftist opposition, led by Edi Rama's Socialist Party, won in the majority of the 384 municipalities, including the major cities of Tiranë, Durrës, Fier, Elbasan, Korçë, Berat, Gjirokastër, and Vlorë; the only major city won by the rightist government was Shkodër. International observers criticized the elections, citing a need for improved cross-party cooperation in the preparation and conduct of the elections.

In the local elections held on 8 May 2011, the race for Tiranë was marked by mutual stalls from parties involved, and the active involvement of the intervention of most prominent foreign Ambassadors. The counting lasted six days. After the last ballot box, it revealed that Edi Rama, the socialist candidate of the Coalition for the Future, was ahead by only 10 votes of Lulzim Basha, the candidate of the Coalition for the Citizen. The tally was awaiting final certification by the KQZ. The latter declared that ballots inserted on the wrong ballot boxes should have been counted as well. KQZ overrode local KZAZ's decisions and started to count all invalid

ballots cast on the wrong ballot boxes. The final tally revealed that Lulzim Basha won the Tiranë race by 81 votes over Edi Rama. Thus, the winner for the Tiranë mayoral chair was declared to be Lulzim Basha. Edi Rama filed an appeal at the Electoral College to overthrow the result and re-instate the May 14 tally that pointed to him as the winner of the election. All instances rejected Rama's appeal, and, on July 25 2011, Lulzim Basha was sworn in as the new Mayor of Tiranë. OSCE declared the electoral system in need of immediate reforms.

16 JUDICIAL SYSTEM

The judicial system includes 29 district courts, 6 courts of appeal, and a supreme court, or High Court. The district courts are trial-level courts from which appeal can be taken to a court of appeals and then to the High Court. The High Court is divided into civil, criminal, and administrative/commercial panels. There is also a military court of appeals. Justices of the High Court serve for nine years without the right of reappointment.

There is also a Constitutional Court with jurisdiction to resolve questions of constitutional interpretation that arise during the course of any case on appeal. In a 1993 decision, the Constitutional Court invalidated a law that would have disbarred lawyers who were active during the Communist era and ordered the lawyers reinstated. Justices of the Constitutional Court serve a maximum of nine years.

The members of the High Court and the Constitutional Court are appointed by the president with the consent of parliament. The other judges are appointed by the president upon the proposal of the High Council of Justice.

17 ARMED FORCES

The International Institute for Strategic Studies reports that armed forces in Albania totaled 14,245 members in 2011. The force is comprised of 8,150 members of a Joint Force Command, 4,300 support staff, 1,000 members of the US Army Training and Doctrine Command, and 795 from Ministry of Defense and General Staff. Armed forces represent 1% of the labor force in Albania. Defense spending totaled $355.6 million and accounted for 1.5% of GDP. The Albanian army was reconstructed from 2005–2010.

In July 2010, Albania sent its first combat contingent to Afghanistan to fight alongside British and US troops in the Afghan province of Kandahar. The 44-member commando unit joined 245 Albanian troops already stationed in Afghanistan. Most of the Albanian forces currently in Afghanistan perform protection duties at military bases in Kabul, the capital of Afghanistan. The new batch of troops will actively take part in combat operations, joining more militarily active NATO members, including the United States, Australia, Canada, the UK, and the Netherlands.

18 INTERNATIONAL COOPERATION

Albania, a United Nations member since 14 December 1955, belongs to numerous specialized agencies, such as FAO, IAEA, IFAD, ILO, UNESCO, WHO, WIPO, ICAO, WMO, the World Bank, IFC, IMF, and the WTO (2000). Albania was originally a member of the Council for Mutual Economic Assistance (CEMA) and the Warsaw Pact, but, in 1968, it formally announced its withdrawal from both (it had ended participation in CMEA in 1961). The country is a part of the Central European Initiative and the Agency for the French-Speaking Community (ACCT) and is one of 12 members of the Black Sea Cooperation Zone. Albania is part of the Council of Europe, the Euro-Atlantic Partnership Council, the International Confederation of Free Trade Unions and the World Federation of Trade Unions, the Islamic Development Bank, and the Organization of the Islamic Conference (OIC).

Albania submitted its application for membership to the European Union in April 2009. The nation became a member of NATO on 1 April 2009.

Albania joined the OSCE 19 June 1991. The country also participates in the Organization for the Prohibition of Chemical Weapons, the NATO Partnership for Peace, and the Adriatic Charter (2003). In May 2003, Albania and the United States signed a treaty on the Prevention of Proliferation of Weapons of Mass Destruction and the Promotion of Defense and Military Relations. Albania was one of four nations to contribute troops to the combat phase of Operation Enduring Freedom (2004), a US initiative in Iraq.

In cooperation on environmental issues, Albania participates in the Basel Convention (hazardous waste), the Convention on Biological Diversity, Ramsar, the Montréal Protocol (ozone layer protection), and the UN Conventions of the Law of the Seas, Climate Change, and Desertification.

¹⁹ECONOMY

The gross domestic product (GDP) rate of change in Albania, as of 2010, was 3.5%. Inflation stood at 3.6%, and unemployment was reported at 13.5%.

Albania has always been an underdeveloped country. Before World War II, there were only a few small-scale industrial plants, and only a few of the larger towns had electricity. Subsoil resources were potentially rich, but only coal, bitumen, and oil were extracted—by Italian companies. Transportation was poorly developed. Stockbreeding contributed about half of the agricultural output; by 1938, tilled area represented only 23% of the agricultural land. Forests were exploited and reforestation neglected.

After the war, the Communist regime pursued an industrialization program with a centrally planned economy. Development projects received priority, especially mining, industry, power, and transportation. Consumer goods, agriculture, livestock, and housing were relatively neglected. By 1950, Albania had its first standard-gauge railways, a textile combine, a hydroelectric power plant, a tobacco fermentation plant, and a sugar refinery. Mineral extraction, especially of oil, chrome ore (the main export product), and iron-nickel, was increased. Land cultivated under crops or orchards expanded by over 70% from the 1950s to the 1980s. Although collectivized, farmland was again privatized in 1992 and distributed to peasants. Despite significant progress, living standards in Albania were still among the lowest in Europe. When central planning was abandoned, there was no mechanism to take its place, and GDP fell 45% during 1990–92. It rose by at least 5% in 1995, however. After prices were freed, the inflation rate shot up to 226% in 1992, but dropped to 86% in 1993. Consumer prices and unemployment mounted rapidly in 1994.

More trouble followed in 1997 with the countrywide collapse of financial pyramid schemes. The resulting chaos left the government paralyzed, and over 1,500 Albanians died in the ensuing violence that swept the country before an international peacekeeping force restored order. More economic hardship struck Albania in 1999 as the country received 450,000 Kosovar refugees. Western aid helped the Albanians manage the influx.

As Albania entered the 21st century, its economy had begun to improve. Inflation remained low, the economy was expanding at a rate of approximately 7% a year, and foreign direct investment was growing. Economic growth came largely from the transportation, service, and construction sectors. The state was privatizing industries, and as of 2002, nearly all land in Albania was privately owned. However, the country's transition to a free-market economy did not come without difficulties. Unemployment remained high, and the economy remained based on agriculture (around 50%). Crime and corruption were problems, as were governmental bureaucratic hurdles that hamper business activity. The country's infrastructure was still outmoded, in disrepair, and in dire need of funding. Severe energy shortages caused blackouts and were responsible for small businesses failing; in 2003, the country was increasing its imports of electricity.

In 2001, Albania joined Bosnia and Herzegovina, Bulgaria, Croatia, the former Yugoslav Republic of Macedonia, Romania, and Serbia and Montenegro (Yugoslavia) in creating a Balkan free trade zone. Tariffs on selected goods were to be eliminated under the agreement. In September 2000, Albania joined the World Trade Organization, signaling its commitment to the process of economic reform.

Albania's economic freedom score is 64, making its economy the 70th freest in the 2011 *Index*. Its level of economic freedom declined by 2 points during the past year, due primarily to decreases in trade freedom, investment freedom, freedom from corruption, labor freedom, and its government spending score. Albania is ranked 33rd freest among the 43 countries in the Europe region, and its overall score is above the world average.

The EU remains Albania's main trading partner, with Italy and Greece taking the lion's share. In 2006, Albania entered into an interim free trade agreement with the EU. Albania also consolidated bilateral trade agreements with many of its neighbors into a multiregional agreement based on the CEFTA (Central European Free Trade Agreement) model. Although exports have been growing steadily, they have been outpaced by the increase of imports. Thus, in 2007 exports totaled $1 billion, while imports marked $4.15 billion. Albania's main exports are textiles, footwear, mineral products, and metals; its imports include agricultural products, metals and minerals, and machinery.

Albania enjoyed a relatively stable environment in the early years of the 21st century, and its economic growth was steady and strong, driven mainly by the services and construction sectors and reflecting significant diversification of the economic base. Albania's GDP real growth rate was 3.5% in 2010 (est.), 3.3% in 2009 (est.), and 7.7% in 2008 (est.). However, the country was still one of the poorest in Europe and remained subject to political instability and economic downside risks, such as shortages of the electricity supply and possible delays in the privatization of large enterprises.

Albania was still plagued by energy shortages in 2007, hampering the growth economy. The problems of energy were solved during 2008 and shortages did not occur in the coming years. Albania also had a large underground economy that may be as large as 50% of its official GDP, further obstructing much-needed economic reform.

[20]INCOME

The CIA estimated that, in 2010, the GDP of Albania was $23.86 billion. The CIA defines GDP as the value of all final goods and services produced within a nation in a given year and computed on the basis of purchasing power parity (PPP) rather than value as measured on the basis of the rate of the exchange based on current dollars. The per capita GDP was estimated at $8,000. The annual growth rate of GDP was 3.5%. The average inflation rate was 3.6%. It was estimated that agriculture accounted for 18.9% of GDP, industry 23.5%, and services 57.6%.

According to the World Bank, remittances from citizens living abroad totaled $1.3 billion or about $440 per capita and accounted for approximately 5.5% of GDP.

The World Bank reports that in 2009, household consumption in Albania totaled $10.5 billion or about $3,492 per capita, measured in current US dollars rather than PPP. Household consumption includes expenditures of individuals, households, and nongovernmental organizations on goods and services, excluding the purchases of dwellings. It was estimated that household consumption was growing at an average annual rate of 2.6%.

The World Bank reported that, in 2005, actual individual consumption in Albania was 79.9% of GDP and accounted for 0.04% of world consumption. By comparison, the United States accounted for 25.44% of world individual consumption. The World Bank also estimated that 24.6% of Albania's GDP was spent on food and beverages, 20.5% on housing and household furnishings, 3.8% on clothes, 4.7% on health, 9.9% on transportation, 3.4% on communications, 4.6% on recreation, 4.5% on restaurants and hotels, and 1.3% on miscellaneous goods and services and purchases from abroad.

It was estimated that, in 2008, about 12.5% of the population subsisted on an income below the poverty line.

[21]LABOR

As of 2010, Albania had a total labor force of 1.053 million people. Within that labor force, CIA estimates in 2010 noted that 47.8% were employed in agriculture, 23% in industry, and 29.2% in the service sector.

When communism was abandoned in favor of a free-market economy in 1991, a transitional dislocation of workers and resources took place, resulting in an estimated unemployment rate of 40% in 1992.

In 1991, workers were granted the legal right to create independent trade unions. The Independent Confederation of Trade Unions of Albania (BSPSH) was formed as the umbrella organization for several smaller unions.

As of 2005, all citizens had the right to organize and bargain collectively, except the military and civilian employees of the military. About 20% of the workforce was unionized, but that number is shrinking. Generally, labor unions in Albania operate from a weak position, and those unions that represent employees in the public sector usually negotiate directly with the government. In addition, little privatization has occurred outside the retail and agricultural sectors, and few private employees are unionized.

The minimum work age is 14, with restrictions placed on employment of those under 18 years old. Children between 14 and 16 years old may work part-time. Although the labor code sets the maximum workweek at 40 hours, the actual workweek for many is six days per week. There is no legal minimum wage rate for workers in the private sector, although government workers 18 years of age and older were paid a minimum wage of about $118/month in 2005, which does not provide for a decent living for a family.

The enforcement of occupational health and safety standards and regulations is the responsibility of the Ministry of Labor and Equal Opportunities. However, what regulations and standards that do exist are generally not enforced. In addition, the law provides no remedies for workers who leave the workplace because of hazardous conditions. The enforcement of the labor code is severely limited by the Albanian government's lack of funding.

[22]AGRICULTURE

Roughly 24% of the total land is farmed, and the country's major crops include wheat, corn, potatoes, vegetables, fruits, sugar beets, and grapes. Cereal production in 2009 amounted to 630,900 tons, fruit production 338,579 tons, and vegetable production 738,006 tons in 2009.

About 85% of the economically active population was engaged in agriculture before World War II (1939–45), a number that has been in steady decline since. Albania's mountainous terrain limits the amount of land available for agriculture.

The first collective farm was created in 1946, but collectivization did not move forward on a large scale until 1955. By early 1962, 1,263 collectives included about 2,000 villages and covered almost 80% of the cultivated area. Consolidation reduced the collectives to 1,064 by December 1964. State farms, meanwhile, had expanded, and by 1960, they accounted for about 12% of the cultivated area. By 1964, only 10% of the cultivated area was privately farmed, and, by 1973, 100% of the agricultural land was reported as socialized, either in collective or state farms. Collective farm consolidations and mergers reduced their number to 420 in April 1983, including "advanced type" cooperatives. The cooperatives accounted for 74% of total agricultural production. By the mid 1980s, the number of collective farmers was about 800,000.

After the government abandoned central planning, the economy collapsed from the void. The decline saw the agricultural sector shrink by 21% in 1991, but agricultural production rebounded in 1992 in response to the privatization of cooperative farms and the elimination of fixed pricing. The number of tractors increased from 359 in 1950 to 4,500 in 1960 and to 12,500 in 1991; 7,915 were in service in 2002. In 2002, irrigation systems covered 59% of the cropland. Artificial fertilizers supplied to farms rose from 8,000 tons of active substance in 1960 to 99,900 tons in 1978. However, fertilizer use fell from 145 kg per hectare in 1983 to about 5 kg per hectare in 2002.

Greater emphasis is being placed on the production of cash crops.

[23]ANIMAL HUSBANDRY

The UN Food and Agriculture Organization (FAO) reported that Albania dedicated 484,000 hectares (1.2 million acres) to permanent pasture or meadow in 2009. During that year, the country tended 5.1 million chickens, 494,000 head of cattle, and 160,300 pigs. The production from these animals amounted to 58,137 tons of beef and veal, 37,130 tons of pork, 30,932 tons of poultry, 18,143 tons of eggs, and 880,638 tons of milk. Albania also produced 7,788 tons of cattle hide and 3,200 tons of raw wool.

The major problem of Albanian animal husbandry has been a shortage of fodder. As a result, livestock numbers remained virtually constant or increased very slowly in the postwar decades. When central planning was abandoned, uncertain monetary and credit policies caused inflation to soar, which eroded export earnings. Albania, which had been a net exporter of food products, became heavily dependent on food aid. Sheep, originally the most important livestock, numbered 1.84 million in 1946 and 1.8 million in 2004. Additional estimated numbers of livestock for 2004 included goats, 1,030,000 and horses, 65,000. Estimates of livestock products in 2004 included 70,000 tons of sheep's milk; 65,000 tons of goats' milk, 12,000 tons of mutton and lamb, and 25,800 tons of eggs.

24 FISHING

Fishing is an important occupation along the Adriatic coast. In 1958, a development program for inland fisheries was begun, and the results were improved exploitation and conservation as well as increased fish reserves and catches. Exports of fish products amounted to almost $13.5 million in 2003.

Albania had 146 decked commercial fishing boats in 2008. The annual capture totaled 5,510 tons according to the UN FAO. The export value of seafood totaled $1.7 million.

25 FORESTRY

The UN FAO estimated the 2009 roundwood production at 80,000 cu m (2.83 million cu ft). The value of all forest products, including roundwood, totaled $7.41 million.

Forests cover 1 million hectares (2.5 million acres), or about 36% of the total land area. As a result of exploitation, erosion, and neglect, about 70% of the forested area consists of little more than shoots and wild shrubs, and exploitation of the remaining accessible forests exceeds optimum annual limits. Roundwood production in 2003 totaled 296,000 cu m, with about 56% used for firewood. Between 1971 and 1978, 65,310 hectares (161,380 acres) were forested, compared with a total of 61,900 hectares (153,000 acres) for 1961–70.

26 MINING

After the abandonment of central planning in 1992, Albania's mineral industry was marginal, with technical difficulties contributing to the decline. Nearly half a century of self-imposed isolation during the Communist era crippled the industry with a shortage of capital, aging and inadequate machinery, overstaffing, and environmental damage. In 1995, the government adopted a law to privatize the mineral industry, and administrative preparations for privatization began in 1996.

Mineral deposits traditionally associated with Albania included chromite, copper ore, and nickeliferous iron ore. From the late 1970s through 1990, Albania was the principal chromite-producing country in Europe; the country often ranked second in the world in exports and third in production. In this period, exports of chromite, ferrochromium, and petroleum refinery products constituted the country's chief sources of foreign exchange. For much of the 1990s, the chromite mining and processing industry paralleled the country's moribund economy.

In 2009, chromite production was 256,000 metric tons. The most important chromite mines were at Katjel, Mëmlisht, and Bulqize, in the upper reaches of the Drin River. A chromium-ore enrichment plant was put into operation at Bulqize in 1972. In the 1980s, chromite production amounted to more than one million metric tons per year.

In 2000, the government awarded Hayri Ogelman Madencilik, of Turkey, a long-term concession to upgrade and operate the Kalimash mining and beneficiation complex and to develop mines at the Perollajt and Vllahane deposits in the northeastern part of the country. The Albaninan government reports chromite reserves of 36.9 million metric tons in 2010.

Copper ore concentrate production was 2,000 metric tons in 2009. Copper was mined at Pukë and Rrubig, where the ore was concentrated and smelted. The deposits near Kukës were the richest in Albania.

Albania was one of the few countries producing natural asphalt, mined at Selenicë. Production of bitumen in 2009 totaled 92,000 metric tons.

27 ENERGY AND POWER

The World Bank reported in 2008 that Albania produced 3.8 billion kWh of electricity and consumed 4.31 billion kWh, or 1,441 kWh per capita. Roughly 64% of energy came from fossil fuels, while 16% came from alternative fuels. Per capita oil consumption was 664 kg. Oil production totaled 10,844 barrels of oil a day.

Albania has both thermal and hydroelectric power stations to generate electricity, but the latter are more significant and have the greater potential. Total power production increased from 85 million kWh in 1955 to 578 million kWh in 1967, and to 4.9 billion kWh in 1985. In 2004, electricity generation was 5.68 billion kWh. In 2002, 13% came from fossil fuels, 87% from hydropower, and none from other sources. In the same year, consumption of electricity totaled 5.286 billion kWh, with total capacity at 1.671 million kW. Rural electrification was achieved in 1970.

The 24,000-kW Shkopet plant and the 27,000-kW Bistricë plant became operational in 1962. A 100,000-kW thermal plant at Fier went into operation in 1968, and the Mao Zedong hydroelectric plant was completed in 1971. The "Light of the Party" hydroelectric plant on the Drin River, with a total installed capacity of 500,000 kW, began operations in 1978. The seventh five-year plan (1981–85) provided for construction of a hydropower station at Koman, also on the Drin, with a capacity of 600,000 kW; the first two turbines were installed there by early 1986.

Petroleum production has become significant. Crude oil output rose from 108,000 tons in 1938 to 870,000 tons in 1967, and 3,500,000 tons in 1985. In 2002, production totaled 6,360 barrels per day. Oil refineries are located at Ballsh, Stalin, Fier, and Cërrik. Albania also produced 1.77 billion cu ft of natural gas in 2002. Sizable coal deposits were discovered near Tiranë in 1969.

28 INDUSTRY

Before World War II, industry was confined to a cement plant at Shkodër and to small-scale flour-milling, food-processing, cigarette-making, and fellmongery (processing animal hides). In

Principal Trading Partners – Albania (2010)

(In millions of US dollars)

Country	Total	Exports	Imports	Balance
World	6,150.8	1,550.1	4,600.7	-3,050.6
Italy	2,088.8	789.5	1,299.2	-509.7
Greece	687.0	84.0	603.0	-519.0
Turkey	353.3	92.9	260.4	-167.5
Germany	301.8	43.4	258.4	-215.0
Switzerland	135.7	64.4	71.3	-6.9
Spain	125.3	53.4	71.9	-18.6
France	113.4	13.2	100.2	-87.0
Russia	101.7	0.0	101.7	-101.7
Macedonia, FYR	98.6	26.0	72.6	-46.6
Bulgaria	97.6	15.7	81.9	-66.1

(…) data not available or not significant.

(n.s.) not specified.

SOURCE: *2011 Direction of Trade Statistics Yearbook*, New York: United Nations, 2011.

1937–39, industry's contribution to the GNP was only 10%, by far the lowest in Eastern Europe. There was virtually no export of industrial products. After the war, the government emphasized industrial development, primarily development projects. Gross industrial output increased annually by 20% during 1951–60, by 12% during 1961–70, by 9% during 1971–80, by 5% during 1981–85, and by 3% during 1986–90. The socialized sector accounted for over 95% of gross output by the late 1950s and 100% by the 1970s. The industrial labor force, which virtually tripled between 1946 and 1960, continued to increase rapidly during the 1960s, and, in 1994, 15% of all wage and salary earners were employed in industry (including mining).

Industrial production fell 44% in 1992 and 10% in 1993, but, by 1995, industrial productivity was growing at a rate of 6%. Privatization was proceeding slowly, with joint state-private ventures planned or sale of state enterprises at auction. In 1994, over one half of the non-farm workforce was employed by the state. As of 2002, the industrial sector accounted for 27% of GDP. Major industries include food processing, textiles and clothing, lumber, oil, cement, chemicals, and basic metals. Albania had two oil refineries with a capacity of 26,000 barrels per day in 2002. In 2001, the government privatized a brewery, distillery, dairy, and pharmaceutical company, and planned to sell the Savings Bank of Albania and INSIG, the state-owned insurance company. The construction sector showed potential for growth in 2002–03, as the country had a housing deficit, and existing housing is old and in poor condition.

While the importance of agriculture in Albania's economy has decreased, other sectors (such as services, transport, and construction) have benefited from investment in 2004. The telecommunications industry in particular has grown substantially due to significant inflow of capital from two new mobile companies. Tourism, the only sector to register a net positive trade balance, has the prospective of becoming one of Albania's main growth engines. Another sector that has good future prospects is mining—due in part to increases in the price of raw materials. In addition to these developments, there are plans for a 1600-acre Energy Park at Vlora. This park is supposed to respond to Albania's energy short-ages by means of large foreign direct investments. To date, 80% of Albania's GDP is generated by the private sector.

29 SCIENCE AND TECHNOLOGY

The World Bank reported in 2009 that there were no patent applications in science and technology in Albania. The main scientific organization, the Academy of Sciences (founded in 1972 and located in Tiranë), has a scientific library and numerous attached research institutes dealing with various aspects of agriculture, fisheries, and veterinary science; medicine; natural sciences (biology, computer science and applied mathematics, energetics, nuclear physics, hydrometeorology, seismology, and geology) and technology (oil and gas geology and technology, industrial projects studies and design hydraulics, metallurgy, mining, roads and railways, chemistry mechanics, minerals, building technology); and the food industry.

The University of Tiranë, founded in 1957, has faculties in natural science, medicine, and mechanics and electronics. Its Natural Science Museum has exhibits related to zoology, botany, and geology. Luigj Gurakuqi University of Shkodër, founded in 1991 and based on the former Higher Pedagogical Institute founded in 1957, has a faculty in natural sciences. The Agricultural University of Tiranë, founded in 1971, has faculties in agronomy, veterinary science, and forestry. In 1987–97, science and engineering students accounted for 19% of college and university employment. The Fan S. Noli University in Korçë was founded in 1971 as the Higher Agricultural Institute and renamed in 1992. The Centre for Scientific and Technical Information and Documentation in Tiranë was founded in 1981.

30 DOMESTIC TRADE

Wholesale trade became a state monopoly in 1946. Initially, private retail trade played an important role, but, by 1970, trade was fully socialized. By December 1990, retail units had been privatized again. All price controls were eliminated except for those on a few consumer items and monopoly-controlled products.

Shops in Albania are generally small, but department stores and a few larger supermarkets with limited stocks have been established in Tiranë, Durrës, Korcë, and other larger cities. Consumer cooperatives conduct trade in the rural areas. Albania has a small, but growing, advertising sector.

Albanian business hours are Monday through Friday from 8 a.m. to 5 p.m. However, some are occasionally open on Saturday mornings. Shop hours are Mondays and Tuesdays, 7 a.m. to 2 p.m. and 5 to 8 p.m., and other weekdays, 7 a.m. to 2 p.m. Many shops are open seven days a week since there is no legislation regulating shop hours. Before 1 January 1959, all sales were for cash. Since then, limited consumer credit was sanctioned, but most transactions are still in cash.

31 FOREIGN TRADE

Albania imported $4.59 billion worth of goods and services in 2008 while exporting $1.55 billion worth of goods and services. Major import partners in 2009 were Italy, 28%; Greece, 13%; China, 6.3%; Turkey, 5.6%; and Germany, 5.6%. Its major export partners were Italy, 50.8%; Kosovo, 6.2%; Turkey, 5.9%; Greece, 5.4%; and China, 5.5%.

Before World War II, about 50% of the exports consisted of the entire production of chrome ore and crude oil and some timber; the balance consisted of agricultural goods and fish. Good grains, sugar, and coffee made up about 20% of the imports; textiles, about 24%; and paper, machinery, chemicals, leather, metals, and oil products, about 53%. As the value of imports almost tripled that of exports, the deficit was met largely by Italian loans. Italy received two thirds of Albanian exports and supplied Albania with up to half its imports. Under the Communist government, foreign trade became a state monopoly. The volume of turnover increased substantially and the structure and orientation changed radically.

As of the year 2000, Albania was running a trade deficit of $814 million, a considerable increase since the 1990s. The expansion in imports was largely due to increased domestic demand for foreign goods, as well as increased demand for electronics. Between 1950 and 1967, trade volume increased six fold, to ALL1,043 million in 1967. Total trade volume (imports plus exports) rose 49% between 1966 and 1970. In 1960, trade with the socialist states accounted for about 90% of total trade; the Soviet share of this was half. Political and economic differences between Albania and the United States resulted in suspension of aid to and trade with Albania. In 1961, 54% of total foreign trade was with the United States and 7% with China; by 1964, trade with the former had ceased entirely, while trade with China had risen to 55%. After the Albanian-Chinese split in the late 1970s, economic contacts with China ceased. Talks aimed at renewing trade between the two nations were held in 1983, resulting in trade agreements worth about $5–7 million.

³²BALANCE OF PAYMENTS

In 2010, Albania had a foreign trade deficit of $3 billion.

A decrease in exports has been linked to a decline in industrial production. Recent increases in imports were due to increased domestic demand for imported goods, in addition to large increases in electricity imports. Remittances from abroad have improved Albania's balance of payments.

³³BANKING AND SECURITIES

The Bank of Albania is the country's central bank. It was established on 22 April 1992, after the fall of the communist regime, as the successor to the Bank of the Albanian State that existed under the communist government. The bank is government owned and the nation's sole issuer of bank notes and coins of legal tender. It also controls the money supply, sets interest rates, and is generally responsible for the nation's monetary policy. This is usually accomplished through the buying or selling of treasury bills to the nation's commercial banks, or to the general public. The bank can also set bank reserve requirements. The bank is managed by the Governor, with a Deputy Governor and a nine-member Supervisory Council, of which the Governor and Deputy Governor are the Chairman and Vice Chairman, respectively.

In 2010, the discount rate, the interest rate at which the central bank lends to financial institutions in the short term, was 5%. The commercial bank prime lending rate, the rate at which banks lend to customers, was 12.833%.

The Communist regime nationalized all banking and financial institutions in 1945 and established the Bank of the Albanian

Balance of Payments – Albania (2010)		
(In millions of US dollars)		
Current Account		**-1,403.9**
Balance on goods		-2,757.5
Imports	-4,305.3	
Exports	1,547.9	
Balance on services		232.9
Balance on income		-101.1
Current transfers		1,221.8
Capital Account		**112.3**
Financial Account		**816.4**
Direct investment abroad		-0.2
Direct investment in Albania		1,109.6
Portfolio investment assets		-118.4
Portfolio investment liabilities		421.0
Financial derivatives		...
Other investment assets		-212.6
Other investment liabilities		-383.0
Net Errors and Omissions		**411.0**
Reserves and Related Items		**64.3**

(…) data not available or not significant.

SOURCE: *Balance of Payment Statistics Yearbook 2011,* Washington, DC: International Monetary Fund, 2011.

State (now simply the Bank of Albania), which became the bank of issue. The bank also controlled foreign transactions, helped prepare financial plans for the economy, accepted savings deposits, financed economic activities, and performed other banking functions. An agricultural bank was created in 1970 to provide credit facilities for agricultural cooperatives.

On 10 August 1949, the Directorate of Savings was established to grant loans and to accept savings deposits in branches throughout the country; the system has grown steadily ever since.

When the Soviet Union collapsed in 1991, Albania decided to develop a market economy. However, the government's position was weakened considerably when four of the country's major pyramid investment schemes collapsed, leading to anarchic, nationwide demonstrations by furious investors. In January of 1997, a 20,000-strong crowd marched on Skanderbeg Square, where it demanded that the government guarantee all deposits in the companies. Notable pyramid investment companies included VEFA, Kamberi, Populli, Xhaferri, Gervnasi, Gjallica, and Sudja.

The pyramid investment schemes attracted hundreds of thousands of depositors—local estimates put participation in the companies at about 75% of all households—by guaranteeing to pay high interest rates on cash deposits within a short period of time. Much of the blame for the crisis rested with the government, whose policy towards the companies was not simply cavalier, but actively encouraging. It did not pay attention to requests made by the central bank governor to regulate the pyramid schemes more tightly.

Meanwhile, an informal financial market has absorbed millions of dollars of savings and remittances in recent years (estimates run as high as $1 billion), at the expense of the country's inefficient and uncompetitive banking sector. The privatization of the three state-owned commercial banks has long been advocated by the International Monetary Fund and the World Bank. The government has privatized the Rural Commercial Bank and the National

Public Finance – Albania (2008)		
(In millions of leks, general government figures)		
Revenue and Grants	**291,191**	**100.0%**
Tax revenue	214,576	73.7%
Social contributions	47,253	16.2%
Grants	4,228	1.5%
Other revenue	25,133	8.6%
Expenditures	**351,445**	**100.0%**
General public services	71,615	20.4%
Defense	11,970	3.4%
Public order and safety	16,204	4.6%
Economic affairs	80,210	22.8%
Environmental protection	203	0.1%
Housing and community amenities	16,536	4.7%
Health	26,713	7.6%
Recreational, culture, and religion	3,999	1.1%
Education	37,923	10.8%
Social protection	86,110	24.5%
(…) data not available or not significant.		

SOURCE: *Government Finance Statistics Yearbook 2010,* Washington, DC: International Monetary Fund, 2010.

Commercial Bank and was working towards privatizing the Savings Bank of Albania, which held nearly 80% of all Albanian bank deposits. On 3 May 2004, it was announced that Austrian-based Raiffeisen Zentralbank (RZB) acquired 100% of the Savings Bank of Albania for $126 million.

As of September 2006, the value of all third-party (external) loans made by Albania's banks totaled $114 million, while the value of all third-party (external) deposits held by Albania's banks totaled $830 million.

[34] INSURANCE

Insurance was nationalized by the Communist government after World War II. Under the jurisdiction of the Ministry of Finance, the program is administered by the Institute for Insurance, created in 1950. Half the profits are earmarked for the state budget, the other half for a reserve fund. In 1990, income from social insurance contributions totaled ALL967 million. Total expenditures—for temporary disability, pregnancy, childbirth, rest home stay, and pensions—were ALL1.4 billion. In 2002, Albania's parliament passed a law to privatize the insurance agency, hoping to create a competitive industry.

[35] PUBLIC FINANCE

In 2010, the budget of Albania included $3.205 billion in public revenue and $3.571 billion in public expenditures. The budget deficit amounted to 3% of GDP. Public debt was 59.3% of GDP, with $3.02 billion of the debt held by foreign entities.

Albania began its transition from a centrally planned economy to a market driven economy in 1992, after GDP had collapsed by over 50% in 1989. The government elected in 1992 set in motion a series of aggressive economic reforms to light the path towards a market economy. Among the reforms were price and exchange regime liberalization, fiscal consolidation, monetary restraint, and a rigid income policy. Stalling progress in 1997 was followed by a resumption of growth the next year.

[36] TAXATION

Both personal income and corporate income tax rates were a flat 10% in 2010, with exclusions for low-income households and businesses. There is property tax on agricultural land and buildings. Indirect taxes include a value-added tax (VAT). The VAT rate was 20% in 2010. Exports are exempt from both excise and VAT. Financial transactions are exempt from VAT, and liquefied gas is exempt from excise. Excise duties on tobacco were levied at 60%, on alcohol at 50%, and on fuels at 50%.

[37] CUSTOMS AND DUTIES

Under the jurisdiction of the Ministry of Trade, the general directorate of customs and duties administers customs regulations. With certain exemptions, all goods are subject to duties ranging from 5–10%, depending on product type. Having become a member of the World Trade Organization in September 2000, Albania is working with Bulgaria, Croatia, Macedonia, Romania, and Serbia and Montenegro to create a regional free trade zone.

As of 1 May 2007, Albania is part of CEFTA (The Central European Free Trade Agreement—an organization of non-EU countries), together with Bosnia and Herzegovina, Croatia, Macedonia, Moldova, Montenegro, Serbia and UNMIK on behalf of Kosovo. Most of the members are countries of the Western Balkans.

[38] FOREIGN INVESTMENT

Foreign direct investment (FDI) in Albania was a net inflow of $978 million, according to World Bank figures published in 2009. FDI represented 8.14% of GDP.

Prior to 1990, no foreign capital was invested in postwar Albania, but various communist states aided the Albanian industrialization program, supplying credit, machinery, equipment, and technicians. Prior to 1961, assistance by Soviet-bloc technicians in geologic surveys, construction, and operation of factories was vital to Albanian economic growth. Following the Soviet suspension of credits, withdrawal of technicians, and elimination of trade, China increased its activity in all these areas. In 1978, China terminated all its economic and military cooperation with Albania, and, the following year, Albania was for the first time without any foreign assistance. In the 1980s, some economic assistance was provided by the FRG.

After the fall of communism, foreign investment was encouraged and 149 joint ventures were agreed upon. A $10 million Coca-Cola bottling plant set up in 1994 outside of Tiranë (directly employing about 100 people), the European Bank for Reconstruction and Development, and a local Albanian company were early ventures. In 1995, Albania concluded a bilateral investment treaty with the United States. At the end of 1995, foreign investment was projected to rise to about $600 million, with about one-half of that coming from Italy. However, the prospects for foreign investment dropped sharply in 1997 in the wake of the violence and property destruction that followed the collapse of the pyramid schemes into which many Albanians had sunk their savings. The violent removal of the Prime Minister in 1998 and the influx of Kosovar refugees in 1999 were added deterrents to foreign investment. From 1997 to 1999, FDI in Albania averaged only $44.57 million, but, in 2000, the rate of inflow tripled to $143 million and then in 2001 to

$181 million. The rate of investment decreased slightly in subsequent years but rose again in 2004, reaching $300 million.

In 2003 the UN Development Program assisted the Albanian government in setting up the Investment Promotion Agency (ANIH) that replaces the Economic Development Agency. Previously, the government had put few restrictions on foreign investment but had offered no tax or financial incentives beyond national treatment. There are initiatives aimed at attracting foreign investment, but as of now they remain unimplemented or in the planning stage.

While the climate for investors has definitely improved over the past years, there are still a number of inconsistencies that make the investment process rather cumbersome. Thus, the physical and financial infrastructure still requires considerable development; there are frequent shortages of power and water in certain areas; corruption remains a major concern; and the rule of law (especially in questions regarding property ownership) is not as strong as it should be. During the 2000s, Albania had one of the lowest rates of foreign investment in Europe.

[39]ECONOMIC DEVELOPMENT

Albania formerly had a state-controlled, centrally planned economy with emphasis on industrial development and socialized agriculture. Under Workers Party directives, short-term and long-range plans were formulated by the Economic Planning Commission, a government agency. By the mid 1980s, the economy was virtually under complete state control; enterprises were either directly owned by the state or managed through cooperatives.

From 1951, Albanian economic development was directed by five-year plans, most of which stressed heavy industry. A sweeping economic reform program was announced in 1992. It called for widespread private ownership of farmland, state-owned companies and housing, and the removal of trade restrictions and price controls. Yet after nearly a decade of post-Communist rule, Albania remains by far the poorest country in Europe. For much of the 1990s, economic reforms were stifled by rampant corruption. Only after the collapse of pyramid investment schemes did the situation begin to improve. Nevertheless, Albania relies heavily on foreign aid and seeks to secure more funding for infrastructure improvements.

Economic development in the early 2000s was stimulated by the construction and service industries; the lack of housing under communism led to a demand for new housing construction, and the development of tourism in Albania's seaside resorts has fueled the service sector. The country is undergoing an economic restructuring program with the International Monetary Fund (IMF) and World Bank. A three-year Poverty Reduction and Growth Facility program with the IMF was negotiated in 2002, in the amount of some $38 million. In 2003, Albania entered into negotiations with the European Union for a Stabilization and Association Agreement.

[40]SOCIAL DEVELOPMENT

In 1947, the first law providing benefits for disability, old age, survivors, and retirement was introduced. Current pension law sets retirement age at 60 for males and 55 for females, with 35 years of contributions. Mothers with six or more children are eligible at age 50 with 30 years of contributions. The amount of the pension is up to 75% of average net wages during 3 of the last 10 years of employment. Disability pensions provide as much as twice the basic pension or 80% of the last average wage. Employers' contributions are 26% of payroll. Additional sums are provided by employees and by the state budget.

Unemployment benefits introduced in 1993 require at least one year's contributions and a willingness to undergo training to be eligible. The employer, at 6% of payroll, makes contributions. A flat rate for benefits allows for a minimum standard of living. A program of Family Allowances fully funded by the government was introduced in 1992. Maternity and sickness benefits are also provided. In 1996/7 the pyramid saving scheme scandal wiped out about 60% of private savings. The scandal coupled with the influx and maintenance of Kosovo refugees, undermined public confidence and trust in the government's ability to deliver public services. Corruption remains another major barrier. Social assistance and social welfare systems are in need of fundamental reform.

Albania's constitution prohibits discrimination based on sex. Roughly half of the labor force is comprised of women. The Labor Code incorporates the principle of equal pay for equal work. Women remain underrepresented in higher positions and often are underemployed. Women have equal access to higher education, many obtaining professional positions in the medical and legal fields. However, discrimination in the workplace continues. Abuse, trafficking, and violence against women and children remain significant problems. Albania is a source country for women and children trafficked for the purposes of sexual exploitation. Domestic violence and sexual harassment are prevalent and largely unreported.

Religious tolerance is prevalent, and the constitution provides for coexistence between ethnic groups. The Office of National Minorities was established to monitor Albania's minority issues. Nevertheless, societal discrimination against Roma, the Egyptian community, and homosexuals persists. Blood feuds, or violent rival factions, contribute to an atmosphere of fear in some areas.

In July 2009, Prime Minister Sali Berisha formally announced that his party would support a controversial law to legalize same-sex marriage in the nation. Homosexuality was illegal in Albania until 1995. While there is no open homosexual organization or community within the nation calling for such a reform, Berisha suggested the move was a necessary step in ending discrimination. The predominant religious communities, Muslim and Christian, have offered vehement opposition.

[41]HEALTH

According to the CIA, life expectancy in Albania was 77 years in 2011. The country spent 6.8% of its GDP on healthcare, amounting to $265 per person. There were 12 physicians, 40 nurses and midwives, and 29 hospital beds per 10,000 inhabitants. The fertility rate was 1.9, while the infant mortality rate was 14 per 1,000 live births. In 2008, the maternal mortality rate, according to the World Bank, was 31 per 100,000 births. It was estimated that 97% of children were vaccinated against measles.

Healthcare facilities at the turn of the century remained substandard. There was a medical school in Tiranë and some Albanians received their medical training abroad. Tertiary care, available mostly in Tiranë, included a teaching hospital, an obstetric and gynecological facility, a facility for treating respiratory diseases, and a military hospital.

42 HOUSING

During World II, about 61,000 buildings of all types were destroyed, including 35,400 dwellings. Housing was generally primitive in rural areas and poor elsewhere. After the war, housing continued to be a problem for a variety of reasons: primary emphasis on industrial construction, shortages of materials and skilled labor, and lack of or inadequate assistance for private building. Moreover, the increase of urban population worsened an already desperate situation. Consequently, new housing construction was concentrated in Tiranë, Vlorë, Elbasan, Shkodër, Durrës, and Korçë, as well as in other industrial and mining sites.

According to the results of a 2001 census, there are about 520,936 residential buildings in the country containing about 785,000 dwellings. Most of the existing stock (29%) was built 1961–80. About 27% of all units were built before 1945. Only about 120,000 (15%) units were built 1991–2001. About 30% of all dwelling spaces (over 50% of urban units) are block flats that were constructed and owned by the government during the Communist era; most public housing was privatized during the period from 1992–93. In 2001, there were 253 dwelling units per 1,000 people, and an average of 1 household of about 4.46 people lived in each occupied dwelling. About 13% of all dwellings were vacant in 2001.

43 EDUCATION

In 2009, the World Bank estimated that 85% of age-eligible children in Albania were enrolled in primary school. Secondary enrollment for age-eligible children stood at 74%. Overall, the CIA estimated that Albania had a literacy rate of 98.7%.

Preschool training for children ages three through six is common but not obligatory. The basic educational program lasts for eight years (ages 6 to 14) and is divided into two cycles of five and three years, respectively. Secondary education consists of a four-year program. Vocational programs of three to five years are also open to students who have passed their basic educational requirements. The academic year runs from October to June. The educational system is regulated through the Ministry of Education and Science.

Institutes of higher learning include two agricultural schools, one institute for fine arts, one institute of physical culture, and three teacher-training institutes. In 1957, the Institute of Sciences was elevated to university rank, and Tiranë State University became the first and only institution of university status in Albania. It was later renamed Enver Hoxha University of Tiranë. Between 1990 and 2010, over 20 new public and private universities were founded. Most of them have a very low student enrollment. Approximately 8% of the adult population was enrolled in tertiary education programs in 2005.

44 LIBRARIES AND MUSEUMS

The largest library in Albania is the National Library in Tiranë (1922) with over one million volumes. The University of Tiranë library has 700,000 volumes. Tiranë also has several university libraries with specialized collections, including the Higher Agricultural Institute Library (126,000 volumes) and the Fine Arts Institute Library (40,000 volumes). Albania's Public Assembly maintains a library of 41,000 volumes, also in Tiranë. Public libraries exist in many communities with notable ones in Elbasan (284,000 volumes), Shkodër (250,000 volumes), Durrës (180,000 volumes), and Korçë (139,000 volumes). The Albanian Library Association (ALA), the nation's first and only national association for libraries and librarians, was established in 1993.

The principal museums are the Museum of Archaeology, the Fine Arts Gallery, the Museum of the Struggle for National Liberation, the Natural Science Museum, and the National Historical Museum, all located in Tiranë. There are some 30 provincial museums, among them the Berat Museum, known for its collection of historic documents; the Museum of Architecture in Berat; the Onufri Iconographic Museum, located in Berat's main castle and housing a distinguished collection of medieval icons; the Museum of Education in Elbasan; the Museum of Albanian Medieval Art in Korçë; and the Shkodër Museum in Shkodër, a historical museum tracing Albanian culture to the Neolithic Age. The cities of Berat and Gjirokastër, the first dating from antiquity and the second from the Middle Ages, have been designated "museum-cities" and are both UNESCO World Heritage sites.

45 MEDIA

In 2010, the CIA reported that there were 331,500 telephone landlines in use in Albania. There were 13 FM radio stations, 46 AM radio stations, and 1 shortwave radio station. Internet users numbered 41 per 100 citizens. In 2010, the country had about 15,098 Internet hosts. Internet cafes are popular in Tiranë and have started to spread outside the capital.

In 2009, there were some 4.1 million mobile cellular phones in use. Generally, there were about 7 fixed main telephone lines for every 100 people, the lowest density in Europe. However, cellular phone use is widespread, with service considered to be relatively good. By 2010, multiple companies were providing mobile services, and mobile teledensity exceeded 130 subscriptions per 100 persons.

Radio and TV broadcasting is governed by the National Council of Radio and Television (NCRT), a seven-member bipartisan body elected by the Parliament. The Albanian Radio and Television (RTSh) was the sole public broadcaster in 2004. About 30% of the station's budget comes from the government, and the station tends to devote most of its coverage to government concerns. Television was introduced in 1961, color broadcasts in 1981. About 80% of the population rely on television as a primary source of news and information. In 2003, there were an estimated 260 radios and 318 television sets for every 1,000 people.

CIA factbook reports show that, in 2010, there were 3 public television networks, one of which transmits by satellite to Albanian-language communities in neighboring countries; more than 60 private television stations were operating; many viewers can pick up Italian and Greek TV broadcasts via terrestrial reception; cable TV service is available; 2 public radio networks and roughly 25 private radio stations; several international broadcasters are available.

There are several daily newspapers published in Tiranë. There are about 40 daily newspapers and magazines, and 200 publications overall, including daily and weekly newspapers, magazines, newsletters, and pamphlets. At least 18 papers and magazines were published in Greek, with primary distribution throughout the south. Agjensia Telegrafike Shqiptare (Albanian Telegraphic Agency) is the official news agency.

Though the law protects freedom of speech and press, nearly all news stories are designed to suit the publisher's political and economic interests. The Albanian Telegraphic Agency is the primary news service. The Albanian Media Institute (AMI) was established by the end of 1995. It has been consolidated, constituting at present one of the main actors of civil society in Albania and one of most important journalistic training institutions in Albania and the Balkan region.

46 ORGANIZATIONS

Trade unions in Albania were prohibited until 1991. Before 1991, the official trade unions of the country were responsible for promoting the production goals of the country's Communist government. In 1991, independent trade unions were established to promote the rights of workers. The Union of Independent Trade Unions is the most important umbrella trade organization. Other trade unions operate in the defense, agriculture, food processing, and mining sectors of the economy. The Chamber of Commerce of the republic of Albania promotes the economic and business activities of the country in world markets. Other chambers of commerce are located in Shkodër, Durrës, and Gjirokastër. The Foreign Investors Association promotes foreign investment within the country. The Albanian Consumers Association is based in Tiranë. There are a number of national professional medical organizations, such as the Albanian Medical Association and the Albanian Dental Association. The Organic Agriculture Association was established in 1997, and Tiranë is the site of the Regional Environmental Center for Central and Eastern Europe.

The Open Society Foundation for Albania is a nonprofit organization established in 1992 to encourage the process of the democratization of Albanian society. It is sponsored in part by the SOROS Foundation Network, a fund established by American philanthropist George Soros.

There are a number of youth organizations in the country. The Albanian International Youth Committee (AIYC) serves as the major nongovernmental youth platform that encompasses several different youth and student organizations. It is supported by the Albanian Youth Federation (AYF) and seeks to represent the views of organized Albanian youth. The World Organization of Scouting opened a national chapter in Albania (Beslidhja Skaut Albania) in 2005. There are also organizations of the YMCA/YWCA.

The Red Cross and the Red Cross Youth have active chapters in the country. There are also chapters of the Lions Club and Kiwanis International.

47 TOURISM, TRAVEL, AND RECREATION

The *Tourism Factbook*, published by the UN World Tourism Organization, reported 1.86 million incoming tourists to Albania in 2009, who spent a total of $2.01 billion. Of those incoming tourists, there were 1.5 million from Europe. There were 17,879 hotel beds available in Albania.

Albania was once the most inaccessible country in Eastern Europe, with tight entry regulations keeping most Western visitors out. In the early 1980s, persons explicitly forbidden to visit the country were US citizens, Soviet citizens, and full-bearded men.

However, since the advent of democracy, Albania has slowly become accessible to the outside world. Tourists from the United States, New Zealand, Australia, and members of the European Union and the EFTA no longer have a visa requirement. Upon arrival, a three-month entry-level visa is issued, which can be extended. Citizens of other countries must obtain a visa prior to arrival from the nearest Albanian embassy. In promoting travel to Albania, the official tourist agency cites the Adriatic beaches, especially at Durrës, Vlorë, and Sarandë, and the picturesque lakes. The most popular sports are football (soccer), gymnastics, volleyball, and basketball.

48 FAMOUS PERSONS

Much Albanian popular lore is based on the exploits of the national hero Gjergj Kastrioti (known as Scanderbeg, 1405–68), who led his people against the Turks.

Ahmet Bey Zogu (1895–1961), military commander, minister of the interior, and premier, was elected first president of the new republic in 1925; in 1928, when Albania became a kingdom, he ascended the throne as Zog I. After Italian forces occupied Albania in April 1939, he fled the country, dying in exile in southern France. His son Leka, pretender to the Albanian royal throne, died in Albania on 30 November 2011. Three major political leaders of the communist era were Enver Hoxha (1908–85), postwar Albania's first premier, minister of foreign affairs, and defense minister; Mehmet Shehu (1913–81), who replaced Hoxha as premier in 1954, when Hoxha became first secretary of the Workers Party's Central Committee; and Ramiz Alia, Hoxha's successor after his death in 1985 until 1991.

Albania's written, nationalist literature first developed among emigres, Italo-Albanians in Calabria and Sicily in the mid-19th century, and among the Albanian intellectuals in Constantinople in the second half of the 19th century. Naim Frashëri (1846–1900), Albania's national poet, belonged to the Constantinople group. His most highly regarded works are *Bagëti e Bujqësi* (Cattle and Land), *Histori e Skënderbeut* (History of Scanderbeg), and a collection of short poems, *Lulet e Verës* (Spring Flowers). Kostandin Kristoforidhi (K. Nelko, 1827–95) translated the Old and New Testaments into Albanian and compiled a standard Albanian-Greek dictionary. Faik Konitza (1875–1942), prewar Albanian minister to Washington, edited a literary review, *Albania*, which became the focal publication of Albanian writers living abroad. Gjergj Fishta (1871–1940), a Franciscan friar who was active in the nationalist movement, wrote a long epic poem, *Lahuta e Malcís* (The Lute of the Mountains), which is regarded as a masterpiece of Albanian literature. Bishop Fan Stylian Noli (1882–1965), a political leader in the early 1920s, was Albania's foremost translator of Shakespeare, Ibsen, Cervantes, and other world classics. Lasgush Poradeci (1899–1987) was a highly regarded lyric poet. Ismail Kadare (b. 1926), winner of the Booker International Prize and candidate for the Nobel Prize in Literature, is the most famous Albanian writer of the last 60 years. He takes as his subjects contemporary Albanian society, the communist regime, and Albanian old traditions (*kanun*). He often finds inspiration in Albanian legends and folklore in general. Kadare's works include *City in Stone*, *Gjenerali i Ushtrisë së Vdekur* (The General of the Dead Army) and *Pallati i ëndrrave* (The Palace of Dreams).

⁴⁹DEPENDENCIES

Albania has no territories or colonies.

⁵⁰BIBLIOGRAPHY

Albania Investment and Business Guide: Strategic and Practical Information. Washington, DC: International Business Publications USA, 2012.

Elsie, Robert. *Albanian Literature: A Short History.* London, Eng.: I. B. Tauris, 2005.

———. *Historical Dictionary of Albania.* Lanham, MD: Scarecrow, 2004.

Frucht, Richard, ed. *Eastern Europe: An Introduction to the People, Lands, and Culture.* Santa Barbara, Calif.: ABC-CLIO, 2005.

Green, Sarah F. *Notes from the Balkans: Locating Marginality and Ambiguity on the Greek-Albanian Border.* Princeton, NJ: Princeton University Press, 2005.

Hoshi, Iraj, Ewa Balcerowicz, and Leszek Balcerowicz, eds. *Barriers to Entry and Growth of New Firms in Early Transition: A Comparative Study of Poland, Hungary, Czech Republic, Albania, and Lithuania.* Boston: Kluwer Academic Publishers, 2003.

King, Russell, Nicola Mai, and Stephanie Schwandner-Sievers, eds. *The New Albanian Migration.* Portland, Ore.: Sussex Academic Press, 2005.

Marx, Trish. *One Boy from Kosovo.* New York: HarperCollins, 2002.

Opello, Walter C. *European Politics.* Boulder, CO: Lynne Rienner Publishers, 2009.

Pettifer, James, and Miranda Vickers. *The Albanian Question: Reshaping the Balkans.* London: I. B. Tauris, 2007.

Political Chronology of Europe. London, Eng.: Europa, 2001.

Vickers, Miranda. *The Albanians: A Modern History.* London: I. B. Tauris, 2001.

ANDORRA

Principality of Andorra
Principat d'Andorra

CAPITAL: Andorra la Vella

FLAG: The national flag is a tricolor of blue, yellow, and red vertical stripes. The yellow stripe, which is slightly wider than the others, bears the coat of arms. The coat of arms features a shield, with the emblems of (clockwise from upper left) Urgell, Foix, Bearn, and Catalonia in the quadrants. Printed across the bottom of the shield is the motto VIRTUS UNITA FORTIOR ("Strength united is stronger").

ANTHEM: *El gran Carlemany (The Great Charlemagne).*

MONETARY UNIT: Andorra has no currency of its own; the euro, adopted by both Spain and France, is used. There are coins of 1, 5, 10, 20, and 50 cents and 1 euro and 2 euros. There are notes of 5, 10, 20, 50, 100, 200, and 500 euros. €1 = $1.371 (or $1 = €0.72939) as of September 2011.

WEIGHTS AND MEASURES: The metric system and some historic local standards are used.

HOLIDAYS: New Year's Day, 1 January; Our Lady of Meritxell Day, 8 September; Christmas, 25 December. Movable religious holidays include Good Friday and Easter Monday.

TIME: 1 p.m. = noon GMT.

[1]LOCATION, SIZE, AND EXTENT

Landlocked Andorra lies in southwestern Europe on the southern slopes of the Pyrenees Mountains between the French departments of Ariège and Pyrenees-Orientales to the N and the Spanish provinces of Gerona and Lérida to the S, with a total boundary length of 120.3 km (74.6 mi).

Andorra is about 2.5 times the size of Washington, DC, with a total area of 468 sq km (180 sq mi), extending 30.1 km (18.7 mi) E–W and 25.4 km (15.8 mi) N–S.

Andorra's capital city, Andorra la Vella, is located in the southwestern part of the country.

[2]TOPOGRAPHY

Andorra is situated in a single drainage basin, but its main stream, the Riu Valira, has two distinct branches and six open basins; hence the term Les Valls ("valleys") was traditionally employed as part of the name of the principality. The section of the river flowing through El Serrat by way of Ordino and La Massánan is the Valira del Nord, while that flowing through Canillo, Encamp, and Les Escaldes is the Valira d'Orient. Most of the country is rough and mountainous, and there is little level surface. All the valleys are at least 900 m (3,000 ft) high, and the mean altitude is over 1,800 m (6,000 ft). There are lofty peaks, of which the highest is Coma Pedrosa (2,946 m/9,665 ft).

[3]CLIMATE

Because of its high elevation, Andorra has severe winters. The northern valleys are completely filled with snow for several months. Most rain falls in April and October; annual precipitation averages 808 mm (31.8 in). Humidity is very low. Summers are warm or mild, depending on the altitude. The average high temperature in July, the warmest month, typically reaches 79°F

(26°C); the average low temperature in December, January, and February (the coldest months) is 30°F (-1°C). There are considerable variations between maximum day and night temperatures.

[4]FLORA AND FAUNA

The World Resources Institute estimates that there are 1,350 plant species in Andorra. In addition, Andorra is home to 15 mammal species, 119 bird species, 4 reptile species, and 2 amphibian species. The calculation reflects the total number of distinct species residing in the country, not the number of endemic species.

The plant and animal life is similar to that found in the neighboring areas of France and Spain. Chestnut and walnut trees grow only in the area around Sant Julía de Lòria, the lowest village. Elsewhere, evergreen oaks still are common. Higher regions and many valleys have pines, firs, and various forms of subalpine and alpine plant life. At the highest altitudes there are no trees, but grass is plentiful during the summer. There are carnations, violets, bellflowers, and daisies, as well as blackberries, wild strawberries, and moss. Bears, wolves, foxes, martens, Pyrenean chamois, rabbits, hares, eagles, vultures, wild ducks, and geese may be found in isolated areas. The mountain streams contain trout, brochet, and crayfish.

[5]ENVIRONMENT

The World Resources Institute reported that Andorra had designated 3,300 hectares (8,154 acres) of land for protection as of 2006. The United Nations (UN) reported in 2008 that carbon dioxide emissions in Andorra totaled 539 kilotons.

Andorra was once heavily forested. One explanation for the name of the country is that it came from the Moorish word *aldarra,* meaning "place thick with trees." Andorra's mountainous environment attracts millions of tourists each year. However, forested area has been decreasing steadily. One reason forests are being removed is to make way for development related to tourism. Overgrazing of mountain meadows by sheep, with consequent soil erosion, is another environmental problem. According to a report issued by the International Union for Conservation of Nature and Natural Resources (IUCN), threatened species included one mammal species: the common otter. The Apollo butterfly and the lesser horseshoe bat are vulnerable species.

6 POPULATION

The US Central Intelligence Agency (CIA) estimated the population of Andorra in 2011 to be approximately 84,825, which placed it at number 186 in population among the 196 nations of the world. In 2011, approximately 13% of the population was over 65 years of age, with another 15.6% under 15 years of age. The median age in Andorra was 40.5 years. There were 1.07 males for every female in the country. The population's annual rate of change was 0.274% in 2012. The projected population for the year 2025 was 80,000. Population density in Andorra was calculated at 184 people per sq km (477 people per sq mi).

The UN estimated that 88% of the population lived in urban areas, and that urban populations had an annual rate of change of 1.1%. The largest urban area was Andorra la Vella, with a population of 25,000.

The population is concentrated in the seven urbanized valleys that form Andorra's political districts.

7 MIGRATION

Immigration consists mainly of Spanish, Portuguese, and French nationals who intend to work in Andorra; these groups make up some 70% of the population. There is a small but rapidly growing group of African immigrants, especially from North Africa, who work mostly in agriculture and construction. Immigrant workers are supposed to hold temporary work authorization permits, which are valid only as long as the job exists for which the permit was obtained. The UN estimated that about 60% of the population is foreign-born. The Andorra Department of Statistics reported that 47,300 authorized immigrants (about 56% of the total population) were living in the country as of 2011.

Legal immigrants may obtain citizenship after 20 years of residence in the country.

8 ETHNIC GROUPS

The Andorra Department of Statistics reported that in 2010, native-born Andorrans made up less than 40% of the total population; these reported Catalan ethnicity. That year, about 32% of the population reported that they were of Spanish descent, 15% were Portuguese, about 6% were French, and just over 1% were of British descent. About 6% were from other groups, including Argentine, Italian, Moroccan, and Filipino.

9 LANGUAGES

The official language is Catalan. French, Castilian, and Portuguese are also spoken.

10 RELIGIONS

Traditionally, over 90% of all Andorrans have claimed to be Roman Catholic. Though it is not an official state religion, the constitution acknowledges a special relationship with the Roman Cath-

olic Church, offering some special privileges to that group. Only about half of the nation's Roman Catholics attend church regularly. The Muslim community is primarily made up of North African immigrants and consisted of about 2,000 members in 2010. Other Christian denominations include the Anglican Church, Jehovah's Witnesses, the Reunification Church, the New Apostolic Church, and the Church of Jesus Christ of Latter-day Saints. There are small communities of Hindus and Jews. The Christian holidays of Easter, All Saints' Day, Christmas, and Our Lady of Meritxell Day (Verge de Meritxell or Virgin of Meritxell) on September 8, are celebrated as public holidays.

11 TRANSPORTATION

A north-south highway links Andorra la Vella with the Spanish and French borders. Secondary roads and trails also cross the border but are sometimes closed in winter because of deep snows.

Buses, the principal means of mass transit, provide regular service to Seo de Urgel and Barcelona in Spain, and to Perpignan in France. Among several cable cars, the most important operates between Encamp and Engolasters Lake. Vehicles from neighboring countries transport most merchandise.

Andorra does not have railways or commercial airports, but the airport at Seo de Urgel is only 20 km (12.5 mi) from Andorra la Vella. The nearest international airports are at Barcelona, Spain, located 215 km (134 mi) from Andorra, and at Toulouse, France, 165 km (103 mi) away. There is daily bus service from the Barcelona and Toulouse airports to Andorra.

12 HISTORY

According to one tradition, Charlemagne gave the region the name Andorra for its supposed likeness to the biblical town of Endor. Tradition also asserts that Charlemagne granted the Andorran people a charter in return for their help in fighting the Moors, and that Charlemagne's son Louis I, king of France, confirmed the charter.

It is generally agreed that Charles the Bald, the son of Louis, appointed the count of Urgel (now Seo de Urgel) overlord of Andorra and gave him the right to collect the imperial tribute. The bishop of Urgel, however, also claimed Andorra as part of the endowment of his cathedral. In 1226, the lords of the countship of Foix, in present-day south-central France, by marriage became heirs to the counts of Urgel. The quarrels between the Spanish bishop and the French counts over rights in Andorra led in 1278 to their adoption of a paréage, a feudal institution recognizing equal rights of two lords to a seigniorage.

In 1505, Germaine of Foix married Ferdinand V of Castile, thereby bringing the lordship of Andorra under Spanish rule. On taking over the kingdom in 1519, Emperor Charles V granted the lordship of Les Valls, as it was then known, to Germaine of Foix's line in perpetuity. Henry III of Navarre, who was also count of Foix, in 1589 ascended the French throne as Henry IV, and by an edict of 1607 established the head of the French state, along with the bishop of Urgel, as co-princes of Andorra.

In 1793, the French revolutionary government refused the traditional Andorran tribute as smacking of feudalism and renounced its suzerainty, despite the wish of the Andorrans to enjoy French protection and avoid being under exclusively Spanish influence.

Andorra remained neutral in the Napoleonic wars with Spain. Napoleon restored the co-principality in 1806 after the Andorrans petitioned him to do so. French title to the principality subsequently passed from the kings to the president of France.

Long an impoverished land having little contact with any nations other than adjoining France and Spain, Andorra after World War II (1939–45) achieved considerable prosperity through a developing tourist industry. This development, abetted by improvements in transport and communications, has tended to break down Andorra's isolation and to bring Andorrans into the mainstream of European history. Public demands for democratic reforms led to the extension of the franchise to women in the 1970s and to the creation of new and more fully autonomous organs of government in the early 1980s.

Andorra formally became a parliamentary democracy in May 1993 following approval of a new constitution by a popular referendum in March 1993. The new constitution retained the French and Spanish co-princes although with reduced, and narrowly defined, powers. Civil rights were greatly expanded including the legalization of political parties and trade unions, and provision was made for an independent judiciary.

Andorra entered into a customs union with the European Communities (now the European Union [EU]) in 1991, but is not a member of the EU. It was admitted to the UN on 28 July 1993. The country has been seeking ways to improve its export potential and increase its economic ties with its European neighbors.

13 GOVERNMENT

The governmental system of Andorra is unique. The constitution adopted in 1993 retained the French and Spanish co-princes but reduced their powers. The co-princes are, as of April 2012, the president of France (Nicholas Sarkosy) and the bishop of Urgel, Spain Archbishop Joan-Enric Vives i Sicilia, each of whom has a representative in Andorra. As of 2011, Christian Fremont had been the representative of the French president since September 2008, and Nemesi Marques i Oste had been the representative of the Spanish bishop since 30 July 2003. Both reside in Andorra and acquire Andorran nationality ex officio. The representatives of the co-princes are not typically native Andorrans.

Legislation is enacted by the General Council of the Valley (parliament), consisting of 28 members (14 members chosen from the national constituency and 14 representing the 7 parishes), elected for a four-year term since December 1981. At least one member from each parish must be present for the General Council to hold an official session. Fourteen of the General Council seats were held by women as of 2011, making Andorra second in the world for percentage of women in elected national parliamentary bodies.

As of 12 May 2011, the Executive Council President (*Cap de Govern*) was Antoni Marti Petit. The General Council designates as its head a first syndic (*syndic procureur général*) and a second syndic for the conduct of administration; upon election to their four-year terms, these syndics cease to be members of the General Council.

The right to vote, which at one time was limited to third-generation Andorran males of 25 years of age or over, by 1981 had been extended to include all native Andorrans of Andorran parentage (at age 21) and first-generation Andorrans of foreign parentage (at age 28). In October 1985, the voting age was lowered to 18 years.

LOCATION: 42°25′ to 42°40′N; 1°25′E. BOUNDARY LENGTHS: France, 60 kilometers (37.3 miles); Spain, 65 kilometers (40.4 miles).

14 POLITICAL PARTIES

Prior to 1993, political parties were illegal in Andorra, though the Democratic Party of Andorra (formed in 1979) was tolerated. As of 2011 there were four major political parties in the country: Andorra for Change (ApC); Democrats for Andorra (DA), a coalition that included the Liberal Party of Andorra (PLA) and the Reformist Coalition; Greens of Andorra; and the Social Democratic Party (PS). Among the small parties that influence parish politics is the conservative Lauredian Union.

The general election of December 1993, in which five parties gained representation, was the first under Andorra's new constitution. The PLA dominated politics for 15 years, until the general election held April 2009, when the PS won 45% of the vote and 14 seats. The PLA and the New Center Party formed the Reformist Coalition and garnered 32% of the vote and 11 seats. The ApC party gained 19% of the vote and 3 seats. The Andorran Green party took 4% of the vote, which was not enough to gain a seat. Social Democrat Jaume Bartumeu was appointed as head of government (executive council president) in June 2009.

The next parliamentary elections were scheduled for 2013. However, in February 2011, after the General Council failed to approve a value-added tax plan and a budget for the country, early elections were called to break the deadlock. The election took place in April 2011. The DA, the center-right coalition that includes the PLA and the Reformist Coalition and was led by Antoni Marti Petit, won 55% of the vote and 20 seats in the 28-seat General Council. Petit was elected executive council president. The left-of-center PS, led by former head of government Jaume Bartumeu, won 35% of the vote and 6 seats. The Lauredian Union won 2 seats. While ApC won 7% of the vote and the Green Party about 3%, neither party gained any seats in the General Council.

15 LOCAL GOVERNMENT

Andorra is divided into seven parishes or districts: Andorra la Vella, Canillo, Encamp, La Massána, Escaldes-Engordany, Ordino, and Sant Juliá de Lòria. Eligible voters in each of the districts elect members of its *comú* (parish council).

Parish councils administer local affairs. Each council generally consists of 8 to 14 members elected by universal suffrage for four-year terms at the same time as general councilors. Councils elect a senior consul and a junior consul.

16 JUDICIAL SYSTEM

The 1993 constitution guarantees an independent judiciary and the judiciary has in fact been independent. A Superior Council of Justice oversees and administers the judicial system. The Superior Council of Justice has five members, one of whom was a woman as of 2010. One member each is appointed by the two co-princes, the head of government, the president of the General Council, and members of the lower courts. Members of the judiciary are appointed for six-year terms. The judicial process is fair and efficient.

The constitution also calls for respect for the promotion of liberty, equality, justice, tolerance, defense of human rights, dignity of the person, and privacy, and guarantees against arbitrary arrest and detention.

Under the current system, civil cases in the first instance are heard by four judges. Appeals are heard in the Court of Appeal. Final appeals in civil cases are brought before the Supreme Court of Andorra at Perpignan, France, or the Ecclesiastical Court of the Bishop of Seu d'Urgell, Spain.

Criminal cases are heard in Andorra la Vella by the Tribunal de Cortes (Tribunal of the Courts), consisting of the *veguers*, and the judge of appeal, two judges, and two members of the General Council. Few criminal trials are held, and the principality's jail is used only for persons awaiting sentencing. Sentenced criminals have the choice of French or Spanish jails.

17 ARMED FORCES

Andorra has no defense force, and the police force is small. The sole military expenses are for ammunition used in salutes at official ceremonies, the lone responsibility of Andorra's small army. France and Spain are pledged to defend Andorra.

18 INTERNATIONAL COOPERATION

Andorra was admitted to the United Nations on 28 July 1993. It participates in the Council of Europe, FAO, ICAO, ICRM, IFRCS, Interpol, IOC, IPU, ITU, OIF, OPCW, OSCE, UN, UNCTAD, UNESCO, Union Latina, UNWTO, WCO, WHO, WIPO, and is an observer at the WTO.

Since 1991, Andorra has had a special agreement with the European Union. Andorra is part of the Organization for the Prohibition of Chemical Weapons. In cooperation on environmental issues, Andorra is part of the Basel Convention.

19 ECONOMY

The gross domestic product (GDP) rate of change in Andorra, as of 2011, was -1.8%. Inflation stood at 1.6%, and unemployment was reported at 2.9%.

The Andorran economy is primarily based on trade and tourism, with the traffic between France and Spain providing most of the revenue. Andorra is attractive for shoppers from France and Spain because of low taxes. However, Andorra's comparative advantage has eroded as the economies of France and Spain have been opened up, providing broader availability of goods and lower tariffs. Approximately 10 million tourists visit Andorra each year, although that number began to decline as European economies suffered beginning around 2008. Tourists are drawn by Andorra's summer and winter resorts.

The Andorran banking system, once of significant importance as a tax haven for foreign financial transactions and investments, was dealt a blow in early 2009, when Andorra was one of three nations on the list of uncooperative tax havens compiled by the Organization for Economic Cooperation and Development (OECD). However, an April 2009 report indicated that the government had made a commitment to implement measures towards greater transparency in the banking system.

Prior to the creation of the EU there was an active trade in consumer goods, which were duty-free in Andorra. With the creation of the EU, Andorran-manufactured goods remain tariff free, but Andorran agricultural products are subject to EU tariffs. The production of agricultural goods is limited, though, as only 2% of the land is arable. Most food is imported.

Until 2008, to operate in Andorra, companies were required to be at least two-thirds owned by Andorran citizens. A new law enacted opened selected sectors of the economy to 100% foreign ownership. In 2007 the Grand Council passed by unanimous vote a law requiring all companies with income of €100,000 ($137,000) or more to file accounting reports with the government.

20 INCOME

The CIA estimated that in 2011 the GDP of Andorra was $3.169 billion. The CIA defines GDP as the value of all final goods and services produced within a nation in a given year and computed on the basis of purchasing power parity (PPP) rather than value as measured on the basis of the rate of the exchange based on current dollars. In 2011, the per capita GDP was estimated at $37,200. The annual growth rate of GDP was reported as -1.8% in 2011, when the average inflation rate was 1.6%.

21 LABOR

As of 2010, Andorra's labor force was estimated at 38,220 people. Within that labor force, the CIA estimated that 0.4% were employed in agriculture, 4.7% in industry, and 94.9% in the service sector.

Under the constitution passed in 1993, workers were granted the right to form and maintain trade union associations without prejudice, but implementation has not been provided. In 2009 the government approved a labor relations law to protect the right of unions, but it did not provide for the right to strike; resolution of disputes is through mediation and arbitration.

There are government-mandated health and safety standards, which are regularly enforced with routine inspections. There is a government-set minimum wage, which in 2010 was €5.28 ($7.24) per hour and €915.20 ($1,254.74) per month. The minimum wage was not considered sufficient for a worker and family, due to the high cost of living in the country. The minimum working age is 18, with some exceptions allowing 16- and 17-year-olds to work. The workweek is limited to 40 hours, with an additional 66 hours per month of overtime allowed.

22 AGRICULTURE

Out of 47,000 hectares (116,140 acres) of land in Andorra, 1,000 hectares (2,471 acres) are arable. The country's major crops include small quantities of rye, wheat, barley, oats, and vegetables. Fruit production amounted to 350,000 tons and vegetable production to 1.5 million tons in 2009.

Until the tourism sector in Andorra experienced an upsurge, agriculture had been the mainstay of the economy. Most of the cropped land is devoted to hay production for animal feed. Since there is insufficient sunlight on northward-facing slopes, and the lands in shadow are too cold for most crops, some southward-facing fields high in the mountains must be used even though they are a considerable distance from the farmers' homes.

Tobacco, the most distinctive Andorran crop, is grown on the prime agricultural land. Tobacco was sold and exported, especially to Spain, only in loose form until the late 1800s, and snuff was the main product made from Andorran tobacco. Later, new varieties of tobacco were imported and grown.

Other farm products include cereals, potatoes, and garden vegetables. Grapes are used mainly for raisins and for the making of anisette. The lack of modern methods on Andorra's family farms caused the agricultural sector to decline in importance. Most food is now imported.

23 ANIMAL HUSBANDRY

The UN Food and Agriculture Organization (FAO) reported that Andorra dedicated 17,000 hectares (42,800 acres) to permanent pasture or meadow in 2009. During that year, the country tended 3.7 million chickens and 483 pigs. The production from these animals amounted to 35,617 tons of beef and veal, 11,360 tons of pork, 5,675 tons of poultry, 9,000 tons of eggs, and 387,388 tons of milk. Andorra also produced 3,290 tons of cattle hide and 5,447 tons of raw wool.

For many centuries, until eclipsed by tourism and other service industries, sheep raising was the basis of Andorra's economy. Cattle, sheep, and goats are raised both in the valleys and in some of the higher areas. Cattle are raised mainly for their meat, and there are few dairy cows. When the cattle move up the mountains to begin grazing in the spring, historically, entire families moved to temporary villages in the mountains to herd, mow, and plant; this

practice is less common as of the 2010s, although many families do maintain summer cottages in the mountains.

Large droves of sheep and goats from France and Spain feed in Andorra in the summer, and the Spanish-owned animals in particular are looked after by Andorran shepherds. On their way back to their native land, many of the animals are sold at annual fairs; the Spanish fairs are usually held in Andorra in September and the French in November. Andorra's own animal fairs are also held in the fall.

24 FISHING

The streams are full of trout and other freshwater fish, but Andorra imports most fish for domestic consumption from Spain.

25 FORESTRY

Approximately 36% of Andorra is covered by forest. The value of all forest products, including roundwood, totaled $80,000. Some 16,000 hectares (39,500 acres) are forested.

Fuel wood may be freely gathered by anyone, but it may not be bought or sold. Wood needed for building purposes is cut in rotation from a different district each year. For centuries logs have been shipped to Spain. Most reforestation is in pines.

26 MINING

For hundreds of years, Andorran forges were famous in northern Spain. There are still iron ore deposits in the valley of Ordino and in many of the mountain areas, but access to them is difficult. In 2008 Geo Enviro Group SL, a mining company based in Andorra, acquired an exploration permit for the iron ore mines in Sweden.

Small amounts of lead are still mined, and alum and building stones are extracted. The sulfurous waters of Les Escaldes are used in washing wool.

27 ENERGY AND POWER

A hydroelectric plant, operated since 1934 by FEDA (Andorran Electric Power) at Les Escaldes, has a capacity of 26.5 megawatts. It produces about 15% of the country's electricity. Most of the remainder is imported from France and Spain. In 2009, the country imported 497.7 million kWh of electricity. Domestic production in 2009 totaled 101 million kWh.

28 INDUSTRY

Andorra produces cigars, cigarettes, and furniture, both for local use and for export.

Several firms in Les Escaldes manufacture woolen goods, such as blankets and scarves. There are a number of construction companies, the largest producing building materials from iron.

29 SCIENCE AND TECHNOLOGY

The World Bank reported in 2009 that there were no patent applications in science and technology in Andorra. Students wishing to pursue scientific and technical careers usually receive their training abroad.

The National Motor Car Museum in Encamp, founded in 1988, exhibits achievements in automotive technology, including cars, motorbikes, and bicycles dating from 1898 to 1950. The Electricity Museum, which illustrates the history of hydropower in the country, is housed at the FEDA (Andorran Electric Power) hydroelectric plant in Les Escaldes.

30 DOMESTIC TRADE

Andorra la Vella has an estimated 2,000 shops where commodities of all kinds and origins may be purchased. The larger villages elsewhere also have small general stores. The French, Spanish, and Andorran animal fairs that take place at Andorra la Vella, Encamp, Ordino, and elsewhere are attended by most Andorrans and by many French and Spanish farmers.

There is a high level of competition between the large department stores and the small shops. There are some several thousand retail establishments in the country, of which the department and jewelry stores are the most numerous, followed by food and clothing outlets. Trade in consumer goods, historically very active, particularly with French and Spanish shoppers, declined when the country adopted the euro in 2002, and Andorran merchants lost their ability to set low prices. Handicrafts, cigars, cigarettes, and furniture are major products manufactured for both domestic and export markets.

There are hundreds of hotels and restaurants, and the country was undergoing development in the tourism sector as of 2011.

31 FOREIGN TRADE

Of recorded trade, close to half is with Spain and over one-quarter with France. The majority of imports consist of consumer goods (most of which are sold to tourists), food, and electricity. In 2009, recorded imports amounted to $1.474 billion, while reported exports amounted to just $64 million.

A customs union with the EC (now the EU) took effect in 1991, allowing industrial goods to pass between Andorra and EC members under a uniform customs tariff. The EU's external tariffs are to be applied by Andorra to its trade with non-EU members.

32 BALANCE OF PAYMENTS

Most goods have to be imported, and there is a structural trade deficit.

33 BANKING AND SECURITIES

The banking system attracts foreign financial transactions and investments because there are no direct taxes in Andorra. As the banking sector introduced more transparency (and offered less secrecy as a result) in the first decade of the 21st century, combined assets of Andorra's banks fell by almost 16% during 2009.

There were five private banks in 2011: BancSabadell d'Andorra, Banc Internacional-Banca Mora, Andbanc, Banca Privada d'Andorra, and Credit Andorra.

There is no stock exchange, and therefore, stocks and bonds are not traded in Andorra.

34 INSURANCE

Because Andorra is not a member of the EU, the European Health Insurance Card (EHIC) is not valid in the country. The Oficina Andorrana d'Entitats d'Asseguranca d'Automobil (Bureau Andorra) is the office that oversees car insurance companies operating in the country.

Many insurance companies operate in the country, including Assegurances Bercia, Assegurances Generals, Financera d'Assegurances, Generali, Grupo Catalana Occidente, Patrimoine Assegurances, and Santamaria Cosan Assegurances.

35 PUBLIC FINANCE

In 2010 the budget of Andorra included $872 million in public revenue and $868.4 million in public expenditures.

The US Central Intelligence Agency (CIA) estimated that in 2009 Andorra's central government took in revenues of approximately $872 million and had expenditures of $868.4 million. Revenues minus expenditures totaled approximately $3.6 million.

36 TAXATION

There is no income tax on the individual or corporate level. Employees pay social security taxes at rates of 5–9%; employers pay 13%. As of 2011, a proposed value-added tax of 4.5% was stalled in the parliament.

37 CUSTOMS AND DUTIES

Andorra is a member of the EU Customs Union and generally abides by the EU trade regime. However, its agricultural exports are treated as of non-EU origin and, therefore, are subject to ordinary tariffs.

38 FOREIGN INVESTMENT

Foreign direct investment (FDI) in Andorra was unreported, according to World Bank figures published in 2009. The Foreign Investment Law, which came into effect on November 7, 2008, allowed for foreign entrepreneurs and businesses to enter some 200 sectors of the economy, including industrial production, research and development, e-commerce, audiovisual production, plastic surgery, and education and training. Foreigners can own 100% of a business in the designated sectors; prior to the passage of this bill, foreign business owners were limited to 33% ownership in any Andorra-based business.

Historically Andorran banks attracted foreign depositors and investors, in part due to the lack of taxes but also due to Andorra's bank secrecy laws. In 2001, a Department for the Prevention of Money Laundering was established, which is authorized to carry out unannounced inspections and to provide information to the public prosecutor's office or to the government. In addition, in 2004, Andorra was obliged to accept the EU's Savings Tax Directive, and as of July 2005, imposed a withholding tax of 15% on return of savings paid to citizens of EU member states, of which 75% is remitted onwards to the states concerned.

39 ECONOMIC DEVELOPMENT

Government policy is to encourage local industries and to promote private investment. In addition to handicrafts, manufacturing includes cigars, cigarettes, and furniture. Tourism and finance account for about 75% of gross domestic product (GDP), and the banking sector significantly contributes to the economy.

In 2002, Andorra adopted the EU's common currency, the euro. In 2004, Andorra signed a series of accords with the EU in the fields of economic, social, and cultural cooperation.

40 SOCIAL DEVELOPMENT

There is a social welfare system that was first introduced in 1966. Programs include old-age, disability, and survivors' pensions, health and maternity coverage, and workers' compensation.

There is no legal discrimination against women, although they have only enjoyed full suffrage since 1970. However, since that time, they have begun to play a greater role in the country's government; women held 50% of the seats in the national parliamentary body as of 2011. The law prohibits discrimination against women privately or professionally; however, trade unionists and other observers estimate that women still generally earn 25–35% less than men for comparable work. Women's rights advocates have reported that pregnant women frequently lose their jobs. The country's first women's shelter opened in December 2010.

The constitution prohibits discrimination on the basis of birth, race, sex, origin, religion, or any other personal or social condition. While accorded the same rights and freedoms as citizens, foreigners lack access to some of the social benefits provided by law. Legislation has improved living conditions for immigrant workers, but many still have only temporary work permits and face deportation if they lose their jobs.

The rights of freedom of speech, press, peaceful assembly, religion, and movement are provided by the constitution and are respected in practice.

41 HEALTH

According to the CIA, life expectancy in Andorra was 82.5 years in 2012. The country spent 7.7% of its GDP on healthcare in 2009. There were 20 physicians, 50 nurses and midwives, and 61 hospital beds per 10,000 inhabitants. The fertility rate was 1.36 born per woman, while the infant mortality rate was 3.76 per 1,000 live births in 2012.

42 HOUSING

There is a housing shortage in Andorra, especially in Andorra la Vella, the capital. The mountainous terrain presents challenges for construction.

Most Andorran houses are made of stone. Since the flat land is used for farm crops, the rural houses are frequently backed against the mountainsides. The high villages (*cortals*) are situated on a line between the highest fields and the lowest limits of high-level pastures. Isolated houses (*bordes*) are found at higher elevations. Many families maintain temporary dwellings in the highest pasture areas. All residents have access to safe water and sanitation systems.

43 EDUCATION

In 2009 the World Bank estimated that 82% of age-eligible children in Andorra were enrolled in primary school. Secondary enrollment for age-eligible children stood at 70%. Tertiary enrollment was estimated at 10%. Overall, the CIA estimated that Andorra had a literacy rate of 100%. Public expenditure on education represented 3.2% of GDP.

By law, students must attend school between the ages of 6 and 16. There are essentially three coexisting school systems in the country: French, Spanish, and Andorran. The French government partially subsidizes education in Andorra's French-language schools; schools in the southern section, near Spain, are supported by the Roman Catholic Church. As of 2011, about 32% of Andorran children attend French primary schools, 31% attend Spanish primary schools, and 37% attend Andorran schools. In general, Andorran schools follow the Spanish curriculum, and their diplomas are recognized by Spain.

The University of Andorra was established in July 1997. It has graduate schools of nursing and computer science. As of 2008–09, there were 1,183 Andorrans enrolled in institutions of higher education, 460 of which attended the University of Andorra, 640 attended universities in Spain, 74 attended universities in France, and 9 were enrolled in universities elsewhere in the world.

44 LIBRARIES AND MUSEUMS

The National Library and National Archives founded in 1974 and 1975 respectively are located in Andorra la Vella; the library holds over 45,000 volumes. Small museums reflect a variety of interests. The Museu Nacional de l'Automòbil (National Automobile Museum) is located in Encamp. Museu Postal (Postal Museum) is in Ordino. Also in Ordino is the Nikolaï Siadristy Museum—Museum of Miniatures, the first permanent museum of the artist Siadristy's miniatures. The Sanctuary of Meritxell dedicated to the history of the Andorran people and their patron, the Virgin of Meritxell, is housed in a chapel dedicated to Santa Maria. The chapel was destroyed in a fire after the celebrations on the national holiday, Our Lady of Meritxell Day, September 8, 1972. It was rebuilt in 1994, and is open to the public daily except Tuesdays.

45 MEDIA

In 2010 the CIA reported that there were 38,200 telephone landlines and 65,500 mobile cellular phones in Andorra. In addition to landlines, mobile phone subscriptions averaged 76 per 100 people. Internet users numbered 79 per 100 citizens. Prominent newspapers in 2010, with circulation numbers listed parenthetically, included *Diari D'Andorra* (3,000). French and Spanish newspapers are also widely available.

Automatic telephone service was begun in 1967. Postal and telegraph services are handled by the Spanish and French administrations; a telex system was installed in 1970.

Radio Nacional d'Andorra is the country's public radio; as of 2011, it was operating Radio Andorra and the all-music station Andorra Musica. Radio Valira and Andorra 7 are commercial radio broadcast stations. As of 2010, there were about 10 commercial radio stations. Andorrans also receive broadcasts from Spain, France, and elsewhere over the Internet.

As of 2010 Andorra had one television station. The following year, the country had about 28,131 Internet hosts. As of 2009, there were some 67,100 Internet users. According to International Telecommunication Union statistics for 2011, approximately 79% percent of the population was using the Internet.

The Andorran constitution ensures freedom of speech and press, and the government is said to respect these rights in practice.

46 ORGANIZATIONS

There are about 10 human rights associations in the country, the most active being the Association of Immigrants in Andorra (AIA), which defends the rights of foreign residents. The Andorran International Women's Association (AIWA) and the Andorran Women's Association focus on women's rights.

The Andorra Chamber of Commerce, Industry and Services works to support commercial and economic growth in Andorra by promoting commercial and industrial instruction; collaborating with the educational government in the administration of practical training for companies; coordinating trade fairs, exhibitions, and conventions; and supporting research programs. There are networking and educational associations representing a variety of professions, such as the Andorran Medical Association, the Andorran College of Dentists, the Andorran Bar Association, and the Andorran College of Engineers.

The Youth Council of Andorra (Area de Jovent), founded in 1988, serves as a nongovernmental platform for major youth and student organizations. The General Union of Andorran Students (Agrupacio General dels Estudiants d'Andorra (AGEA), founded in 1990, is a union of university students. Other youth NGOs include: the Andorran Red Cross Youth, Andorran Catholic Student Movement, and youth associations of Andorran Kiwanis, Lions and Rotary clubs. Andorra also sponsors an organization of the Special Olympics and a few national sports organizations, including groups for squash and sailing.

There are national chapters of the Red Cross Society, Caritas, and UNICEF.

[47]TOURISM

The *Tourism Factbook,* published by the UN World Tourism Organization, reported in 2009 that there were 9.11 million incoming tourists to Andorra. There were 33,700 hotel beds available in Andorra. The estimated daily cost to visit Andorra la Vella, the capital, was $332.

Tourism has brought considerable prosperity to Andorra and now constitutes the principal source of income. Visitors, mostly from France and Spain, come to Andorra each summer to attend the fairs and festivals, to buy consumer items at lower prices than are obtainable in the neighboring countries, and to enjoy the pleasant weather and beautiful scenery. There is skiing at Pas de la Casa and Soldeu in winter.

Shrines and festivals are both key attractions to tourists. Romanesque churches and old houses of interest are located in Ordino, Encamp, Sant Julía de Lória, Les Escaldes, Santa Coloma, and other villages. The best known is the shrine of Our Lady of Meritxell, Andorra's patroness, between Canillo and Encamp.

Pilgrims come from France and Spain to pay homage on 8 September, the festival day of Andorra's patroness. Each of the larger villages has its own festival during which the *sardana*, Andorra's national dance, is performed.

There is an International Jazz Festival at Escaldes-Engordany in July and the International Music Festival of Ordino in September.

Andorra's high life expectancy, robust outdoor recreation opportunities, such as hiking and skiing, and peaceful history (Andorra has not been at war for 700 years) helped propel the country to Lonely Planet's 2010 list of the top ten happiest places on earth. Lonely Planet is a well-regarded travel company based in Australia.

[48]FAMOUS PERSONS

There are no internationally famous Andorrans.

[49]DEPENDENCIES

Andorra has no territories or colonies.

[50]BIBLIOGRAPHY

Augustin, Byron. *Andorra.* New York: Marshall Cavendish, 2009.

Cameron, Peter. *Andorra.* New York: Farrar, Straus and Giroux, 1997.

De Cugnac, Pascal. *Pyrenees and Gascony: Including Andorra.* London: Hachette UK, 2000.

Eccardt, Thomas M. *Secrets of the Seven Smallest States of Europe.* New York: Hippocrene, 2005.

Political Chronology of Europe. London: Europa, 2001.

ARMENIA

Republic of Armenia
Hayastani Hanrapetut 'Yu

CAPITAL: Yerevan

FLAG: Three horizontal bands of red (top), blue, and gold.

ANTHEM: *Mer Hayrenik* (*Our Fatherland*).

MONETARY UNIT: The dram (introduced 22 November 1993) is a paper currency in denominations of 1,000, 5,000, 20,000, 50,000, and 100,000 drams. The dram (AMD) replaced the Armenian ruble and the Russian ruble. AMD1 = US$0.00262 (or US$1 = AMD382) as of 2011.

WEIGHTS AND MEASURES: The metric system is in force.

HOLIDAYS: New Year's Day, 1 January; Christmas, 6 January; Army Day, 28 January; International Women's Day, 8 March; Genocide Remembrance Day, 24 April; Victory and Peace Day, 9 May; Anniversary of Declaration of First Armenian Republic (1918), 28 May; Constitution Day, 5 July; Independence Day, 21 September; Spitak Earthquake Remembrance Day, 7 December.

TIME: 4 p.m. = noon GMT.

¹LOCATION, SIZE, AND EXTENT

Armenia is a landlocked nation located in southeastern Europe/southwestern Asia. Comparatively, the area occupied by Armenia is slightly smaller than the state of Maryland with a total area of 29,743 sq km (11,484 sq mi). Armenia shares boundaries with Georgia on the N, Azerbaijan on the E and S, Iran on the S, and Turkey on the W and has a total boundary length of 1,254 km (778 mi). Armenia's capital city, Yerevan, is located in the west-central portion of the country on the Hrazdan River.

²TOPOGRAPHY

The topography of Armenia features the high Armenian Plateau and three primary mountain ranges, the Lesser Caucasus Mountains in the north, the Vardenis Range in central Armenia, and the Zangezur Range in the southeast. There is little forest land and a few fast flowing rivers. The Aras River Valley contains good soil. Mount Aragats, an extinct volcano in the plateau region, is the highest point in Armenia at 4,095 m (13,425 ft).

The nation occasionally suffers from severe earthquakes. In December 1988, a massive earthquake struck near the city of Spitak, killing over 25,000 people and destroying most of Armenia's infrastructure in the region.

³CLIMATE

Armenia's climate ranges from subtropical to alpine-like in the mountains. The mean temperature in midsummer is 25°C (77°F). In midwinter, the mean temperature is 0°C (32°F). Rainfall is infrequent. The capital city receives 33 cm (13 in) of rain annually, though more rainfall occurs in the mountains.

⁴FLORA AND FAUNA

The World Resources Institute estimates that there are 3,553 plant species in Armenia. In addition, Armenia is home to 78 species of mammals, 302 species of birds, 53 species of reptiles, and 7 species of amphibians. The calculation reflects the total number of distinct species residing in the country, not the number of endemic species.

Armenia is located in what geographers call the Aral Caspian Lowland. Much of the country is mountainous, with broad sandy deserts and low grassy plateaus between. It is not naturally highly forested. The region is home to European bison, snow leopards, cheetahs, and porcupines.

⁵ENVIRONMENT

In 2011 Armenia's chief environmental problems resulted from natural disasters, warfare, and pollution as a result of both of industrialization and poor environmental management. A strong earthquake in 1988 resulted in over 25,000 deaths and many more casualties. Radiation from the 1986 meltdown of the nuclear reactor facility at Chernobyl in the former Soviet Union also polluted the environment. The nation's soil has also been polluted by chemicals (including dichlorodiphenyltrichloroethane, DDT), and the Hrazdan and Ares rivers have been polluted by fertilizers and factory run-off.

The 1988–94 war between Armenia and Azerbaijan strained the country's economy, limiting the resources that could be devoted to environmental preservation. It also led to an energy blockade from Azerbaijan and its supporter in the war, Turkey, causing deforestation of Armenia's few forests, as trees were cut for firewood. Yet another environmental hazard was the restarting of the Metsamor nuclear power plant, which was brought online in 1993 without the safety systems recommended by the International Atomic Energy Agency (IAEA). However, in 2007 the Armenian government agreed to close the plant and there are plans to build a replacement up to modern standards.

From 1990–2010 deforestation occurred at an average annual combined rate of 1.22%, a loss of 24.5% of its total forest cover for this period. However, some reforestation projects have been initiated.

Two sites are protected as Ramsar wetlands: Lake Sevan and Lake Arpi. As of 2011, 9 species of mammal were threatened, as were 12 species of bird and 1 higher plant species. Endangered species include the Barbel sturgeon, Dahl's jird, and the field adder. The World Resources Institute reported in 2006 that Armenia had designated 244,000 hectares (602,937 acres) of land for protection.

Armenian water resources totaled 10.5 cu km (2.52 cu mi) while water usage was 2.95 cu km (0.708 cu mi) per year. Domestic water usage accounted for 30% of total usage, industrial for 4%, and agricultural for 66%. Per capita water usage totaled 977 cu m (34,502 cu ft) per year. Poor water management has yet to be addressed robustly. Likewise, carbon dioxide emissions continue to rise as the country's economy grows. The United Nations (UN) reported in 2008 that carbon dioxide emissions in Armenia totaled 5,053 kilotons, up from 3,000 in 2002.

6 POPULATION

The US Central Intelligence Agency (CIA) estimated the population of Armenia in 2012 to be approximately 2,970,495, which placed it at number 138 in population among the 196 nations of the world. In 2011 approximately 10% of the population was over 65 years of age, with another 17.6% under 15 years of age. The median age in Armenia was 32.2 years. There were 0.89 males for every female in the country. The population's annual rate of change was 0.107%. The projected population for the year 2025 was 3,300,000. Population density in Armenia was calculated at 100 people per sq km (259 people per sq mi).

The UN estimated that 64% of the population lived in urban areas in 2010, and that urban populations had an annual rate of change of 0.5%. The largest urban area was Yerevan, with a population of 1.11 million. Other urban centers and their estimated populations in 2009 include Gyumri (168,918) and Vanadzor (116,929). Most of the cities and towns are located along the river valleys in the north and west.

7 MIGRATION

Estimates of Armenia's net migration rate, carried out by the CIA in 2012, amounted to -3.35 migrants per 1,000 citizens. The total number of emigrants living abroad was 870,200, and the total number of immigrants living in Armenia was 324,200. Armenia also hosted 113,295 refugees. Independent Armenia is only a portion of historic Armenia, which at its greatest extent also included lands now in Turkey, Iran, and Azerbaijan. There are Armenian communities in these countries and also in Russia, Georgia, Lebanon, Syria, and the United States. Between 1988 and 1993 around 360,000 ethnic Armenians arrived in Armenia from Azerbaijan as a result of the conflict over the disputed territory of Nagorno-Karabakh. In 1995 a citizenship law, which included special provisions making naturalization much easier for refugees from Azerbaijan, was enacted. By the end of January 2004 the number of refugees from Azerbaijan obtaining Armenian citizenship topped 65,000. One of the largest naturalizations of refugees in recent decades, the UN High Commissioner for Refugees (UNHCR) sup-

ported the process with financial and material assistance. From 1998 to 2003, except for 2000, remittance flows to Armenia grew by 20% per year, although as of 2010 remittances out of the country had increased, while remittances into the country had decreased.

8 ETHNIC GROUPS

In 2010 Armenians comprised an estimated 98% of the population. Minority groups include the Azeri, Russians, Ukrainians, Belarusians, Jews, Assyrians, Georgians, Greeks, and Yezidi Kurds.

9 LANGUAGES

Armenian is spoken by about 97% of the population. Armenian belongs to an independent branch of the Indo-European linguistic family. It is a highly inflective language, with a complicated system of declensions. It is agglutinative, rich in consonants, and has no grammatical gender. The vocabulary includes many Persian loan words. There are two main dialects: East Armenian, the official language of Armenia, and West, or Turkish, Armenian. The alphabet, patterned after Persian and Greek letters, has 38 characters. Armenian literature dates from the early 5th century. Yezidi is spoken by about 1% of the population; Russian and other various languages are spoken by the remaining 2%.

10 RELIGIONS

In 2010 about 90% of the population were nominally members of the Armenian Apostolic Church. The Armenian Apostolic Church is a member of the World Council of Churches. Other Christian congregations include Roman Catholic, Mekhitari (Armenian Uniate Catholic), Pentecostal, Greek Orthodox, Jehovah's Witness, Armenian Evangelical Christian, Molokan, Baptist, Seventh-Day Adventist, and The Church of Jesus Christ of the Latter-day Saints (Mormon).

11 TRANSPORTATION

Armenia has 11 airports, which transported 653,320 passengers in 2009, according to the World Bank. Only one of the airports has an unpaved runway. The Zvartnots airport at Yerevan is fairly well maintained and receives scheduled flights from Moscow, Paris, New York, London, Amsterdam, Athens, Beirut, Dubai, Frankfurt, Istanbul, Prague, Tehrān, Vienna, Zürich, and Sofia.

Cargo shipments to landlocked Armenia are routed through ports in Georgia and Turkey, and then transported by road or by rail. The CIA reports that Armenia has a total of 8,888 km (5,523 mi) of roads, of which 7,079 km (4,399 mi) are paved. As of 2010 there were 869 km (540 mi) of 1.520-m (broad) gauge railroad. An estimated 818 km (508 mi) are electrified. Supplies that arrive from Turkey by rail must be reloaded, due to a difference in rail gauges. Goods that cross Georgia or Azerbaijan are subject to travel delay from strikes and blockages and may be interdicted.

12 HISTORY

Armenian territories were first united into an empire under Tigranes the Great (95–55 BC), whose extensive lands included parts of Syria and Iraq. Defeated by the Roman general Pompey, Armenia became a client state of the Roman Empire. Rome and Sasanian Persia partitioned Armenia, and after them Byzantium and the Ummayed and Abbasid caliphates controlled parts of Armenia. Armenia adopted Christianity at the beginning of the 4th century. The Seljuk Turks invaded Armenia in the 11th century, followed by Genghis Khan and Timur, leading to mass emigrations. Persia and Ottoman Turkey divided Armenia into eastern and western portions in the 16th–18th centuries. Russia took over Persia's holdings in 1828, and during the latter part of the 19th century both Russia and Turkey carried out harsh repression against nationalist activities among Armenians under their sway, leading to many deaths and mass emigrations. During World War I (1914–18) Ottoman Turkey carried out forced resettlement and other harsh policies against Armenians, which Armenians term their national genocide. The historical experience remains a contentious issue in Armenian-Turkish relations.

After the Bolshevik revolution in Russia in 1917, Armenia declared independence in May 1918. Armenia's population of 750,000 included as many as 300,000 who had survived flight from Turkey. The heavy burden of independence among hostile neighbors (it clashed with Turkey, Georgia, and Azerbaijan) and an inhospitable climate may have led to as many as 150,000 deaths from famine and disease. Although the August 1920 Treaty of Sevres accorded international recognition of Armenian independence, the Russian Red Army conquered Armenia in November 1920. In 1922 Armenia was named part of a Transcaucasian Soviet Federated Socialist Republic, which encompassed lands now in Armenia, Azerbaijan, and Georgia, but it became a separate union republic in 1936. During the 1920s Moscow drew internal borders in the Caucasus, which resulted in Nagorno-Karabakh (NK), then a mostly ethnic Armenian region, being incorporated into Azerbaijan, separated from the rest of Soviet Armenia by a few miles of Azerbaijani territory. NK was given the status of an autonomous republic.

Beginning in 1988, conflict engulfed NK. Following a February 1988 call by the Nagorno-Karabakh legislature for unification with Armenia, the Armenian Supreme Soviet in December 1989 declared that NK was part of Armenia. It also proclaimed Armenia's sovereignty over its land and resources. Azerbaijan resisted the secession or independence of its enclave. Casualties were estimated at over 5,000. Emigration of 350,000 Armenians residing in Azerbaijan and over one million Azerbaijanis residing in Armenia or NK followed pogroms in both states and conflict in NK and surrounding areas. In December 1991 a referendum in NK (boycotted by local Azerbaijani) approved NK's independence and a Supreme Soviet was elected, which on 6 January 1992 declared NK's independence and futilely appealed for world recognition. In 1993 Armenian forces gained control over NK and surrounding areas, occupying over 20% of Azerbaijani territory, which they continued to hold despite an Azerbaijani offensive in 1993–94 that reportedly cost 6,000 Azeri casualties. A cease-fire was established in May 1994, but talks on a political settlement remained inconclusive. In the six-year period of conflict from 1988 to 1994 more than 35,000 people were killed and nearly one million have been left homeless.

In November 1989 Levon Ter-Petrosyan became a leader of the Armenian National Movement (ANM), which grew out of the Karabakh Committee to push for Armenia's independence. ANM and other nationalist deputies cooperated to elect him chairman of the Armenian Supreme Soviet in August 1990, inflicting a serious blow on the Armenian Communist Party. A popular referendum on independence was held in Armenia on 21 September

LOCATION: 40°0′ N to 45°0′ E BOUNDARY LENGTHS: Azerbaijan (E), 566 kilometers (352 miles); Azerbaijan (S), 221 kilometers (137 miles); Georgia, 164 kilometers (102 miles); Iran, 35 kilometers (22 miles); Turkey, 268 kilometers (167 miles).

1991, in which 94% of the eligible population reportedly participated; independence was approved by 99% of those who voted. The Armenian legislature declared Armenia's independence two days later. Following Armenia's declaration of independence, presidential elections were held on 16 October 1991. Ter-Petrosyan was supported by the ANM, winning 83% of the vote against six other candidates, including internationally famous dissident Paruir Hairikian of the Association for National Self-Determination and Sos Sarkisyan of the Armenian Revolutionary Federation (ARF). Ter-Petrosyan was sworn into office on 11 November 1991 for a five-year term. Armenia received worldwide diplomatic recognition upon the collapse of the Soviet Union in December 1991. Ter-Petrosyan 's suspension of the activities of ARF in December 1994 and a trial of its leaders raised concerns among some observers about possible setbacks to democratization.

Elections to Armenia's new unicameral 190-member national assembly were held in June 1995, at the same time as a referendum in which Armenian voters adopted the country's first post-Communist constitution. International observers reported many campaign and voting irregularities. Observers from the Organization for Security and Cooperation in Europe (OSCE) judged the elections free but not fair, in part because the main opposition party, the ARF, was banned from participation, the government dominated campaigning, the electoral commission appeared heavily pro-government in its decisions, and security officers constituted a chilling presence in many voting places. Voting irregularities reported on election day by the international observers included the violation of secret voting and pressure in voting places to cast a ballot for certain parties or candidates. In all, the Republic Bloc and other pro-government parties won 166 out of 190 seats, while the opposition won only 18 and independents four (two seats were undecided).

Ter-Petrosyan won reelection as president on 22 September 1996. Ter-Petrosyan's main opponent in the presidential race was Vazgen Manukyan, head of the National Democratic Union (NDU) party. He garnered 41.3% of the presidential vote. Manukyan had worked closely with Ter-Petrosyan in the Karabakh Committee. Following the presidential election, followers of Manukyan's electoral coalition demonstrated against what they and many international observers termed irregular voting procedures. On 25 September 1996, tens of thousands of protesters stormed the legislative building in Yerevan and assaulted the assembly speaker and deputy speaker, both belonging to the ANM. The crowd was dispersed by police with few injuries or deaths.

In March 1997, in an attempt to garner greater public support for his regime, Ter-Petrosyan appointed a highly popular war hero of the NK conflict, Robert Kocharian, to the post of prime minister of Armenia. Ter-Petrosyan and others viewed Kocharian as having the leadership abilities necessary to help revive the slumping economy and to increase tax collection. In accepting the prime ministership, Kocharian resigned as president of NK.

Ter-Petrosyan announced in September 1997 OSCE peace plan as a basis for resolving the NK conflict that would require compromises from Armenia. The two-stage plan called for NK Armenians to withdraw from most territories they had occupied outside of NK and for international peacekeepers to be deployed, followed by discussion of NK's status. The announcement brought open criticism from Kocharian and other Armenian and NK officials. On 1 February 1998 Yerkrapah, a legislative faction and militia group composed of veterans of the NK conflict and headed by the country's defense minister, called for Ter-Petrosyan to resign. Many members of Ter-Petrosyan's ANM legislative faction defected, leading to the resignation of the legislative speaker. Heated debate in the legislature culminated with Ter-Petrosyan's resignation on 3 February 1998. Although the constitution calls for the assembly speaker to assume the duties of acting president pending an election, the resignation of the speaker caused these duties to devolve upon Prime Minister Kocharian. A special presidential election was scheduled for 16 March 1998.

Twelve candidates succeeded in registering for the March presidential election. The main contenders were Kocharian, Vazgen Manukyan, and Karen Demirchyan (head of the Armenian Communist Party from 1974 to 1988). Since none of the candidates won the required 50% plus one of the 1.46 million votes cast (in a 64% turnout), a runoff election was held on 30 March. In the runoff, the acting president and prime minister Kocharian received 59.5% of 1.57 million votes cast (in a 68.5% turnout). The OSCE concluded that the election showed improvement over the 1996 election, but did not meet OSCE standards to which Armenia has committed itself. Observers alleged ballot box stuffing, discrepancies in vote counting, and fraud perpetrated by local authorities that inflated the number of votes for Kocharian. Nevertheless, he was inaugurated on 9 April 1998. The assembly selected Demirchyan as its speaker on 10 June.

On 27 October 1999 gunmen entered the national assembly and opened fire on deputies and officials, killing then prime minister Vazgen Sarkisyan, Demirchyan, two deputy speakers, and four others. The purported leader of the gunmen claimed they were targeting the prime minister and were launching a coup to "restore democracy" and end poverty. They took many hostages. President Robert Kocharian rushed to the assembly and helped negotiate the release of the hostages, promising the gunmen a fair trial. The killings appeared to be the product of personal and clan grievances. Abiding by the constitution, the legislature met on 2 November and appointed Armen Khachatryan (a member of the majority Unity bloc) as speaker. Kocharian named Sarkisyan's brother, Aram, the new prime minister the next day, seeking to preserve political balances. Political infighting intensified. The military prosecutor investigating the assassinations detained a presidential aide, appearing to implicate Kocharian in the assassinations. The Unity and Stability factions in the assembly also threatened to impeach Kocharian in April 2000. Seeking to counter challenges to his power, Kocharian, in May 2000, fired his prime minister and defense minister. In October 2001, on the second anniversary of the shootings in the legislature, thousands of protesters staged demonstrations in Yerevan to demand Kocharian's resignation.

Presidential elections were held on 19 February 2003 with no candidate receiving 50% of the votes; a run-off election was scheduled for 5 March. Kocharian took 48.3% of the first-round vote, with Stepan Demirchyan–son of Karen Demirchyan—taking 27.4% of the vote. The opposition called the election fraudulent and said it would not recognize the vote, and observers from the Organization for Security and Cooperation in Europe (OSCE) declared the election flawed.

In November 2005 a referendum was held on proposed amendments to the constitution that were designed to enhance the role of the legislature while placing some restrictions on the powers of the president. The referendum passed. In 2006, residents of Nagorno-Karabakh again voted for a declaration as a sovereign state, but this was not internationally recognized.

In February 2007, the legislature adopted a measure allowing for dual citizenship. This paved the way for the naturalization of Armenia's huge foreign diaspora, estimated at around 8 million. Unfortunately, it has been estimated that nearly one-quarter of the population has emigrated from Armenia since independence, as citizens and families hope to find greater opportunities in other countries.

In March 2007, Prime Minister Andranik Markaryan died suddenly of a heart attack. Serzh Sargsian replaced him.

In 2008, the presidents of Armenia and Azerbaijan signed an agreement to intensify efforts toward a peaceful resolution of the NK conflict. Though the leaders met again in January 2009, no settlement was determined, and tensions increased after reports surfaced of a troop build-up on Azerbaijan's border with Armenia.

Tension also exists with the government of Turkey over the Nagorno-Karabakh conflict, in which Turkey has allied with Azerbaijan. As a result, Turkey has kept its border closed to Armenia since 1993.

Sargsian went on to win the presidential election of February 2008 with 52.9% of the vote in the first round. Tigran Sargsian (no relation to Serzh Sargsian) was appointed as prime minister. However, protests were staged by thousands of members of the opposition who claimed that the election was rigged. The protests and the crackdown by police turned violent, and ten people were killed. The memory of this event and the government's continued policy of detaining political prisoners were the subject of renewed protests for political and economic reform in January 2011, inspired by the protesters in the Middle East calling for the same types of changes. In April 2011 the assembly agreed to investigate the 2008 violence and passed a bill increasing people's right to peaceful free assembly. In May 2011 the government agreed to begin releasing political prisoners.

13 GOVERNMENT

Armenia adopted its post-Soviet constitution by public referendum on 5 July 1995 with 68% of the voters. It provides for a strong presidential system of government with a weak legislative system, granting the president power to appoint and remove the prime minister, judges, and prosecutors. It also gives him liberal grounds for dissolving the legislature, declaring martial law, and limiting human rights by declaring a state of emergency. The president serves a five-year term and can be elected for one additional term. The prime minister is nominated by the president and is subject to legislative approval. The prime minister with presidential and legislative approval appoints the cabinet of ministers. The unicameral national assembly has 131 members, who serve four-year terms; 90 members are elected by party list and 41 by direct vote. In November 2005 voters approved amendments to the constitution in a national referendum. The amendments were designed to enhance the role of the assembly while placing some restrictions on the powers of the president. The 2011 protests also led to several significant reforms that reduced the government's power of detention and increased citizens' political and civil rights.

14 POLITICAL PARTIES

Armenia held elections to a new single-chamber 131-seat assembly on 30 May 1999, with 75 deputies elected by party list and 56 elected by direct vote. Twenty-one parties and blocs fielded candidates on the party list vote, but only six passed a 5% vote hurdle. The Unity bloc garnered 42% of over two million votes cast, gaining 29 seats, followed by the Communist Party of Armenia with about 12% of the vote. In constituency balloting, the Unity Bloc (which included the country's two largest parties, the People's Party and the Republican Party) garnered the most seats (35), followed by nonparty-affiliated candidates (29). Other major parties that received at least 7% of the party list vote in the 1999 legislative race include the National Democratic Union, Armenian Revolutionary Federation, Law-Governed Country Party, Communist Party of Armenia, the Armenian Pan-National Movement, Law and Unity bloc, and the Mission Party. The other registered parties included both those newly created for the legislative race and more traditional parties. They were the Mighty Motherland,

Homeland bloc, Ramkavar Azatakan Party (Liberal Democratic Party), Freedom Party, Democratic Party of Armenia, Union of Socialist Forces and Intelligentsia bloc, Union of Communist and Socialist Parties, Youth Party of Armenia, Decent Future, National State Party, Free Hayk Mission Party, Shamiram Party, and ONS+ bloc (the National Self-Determination and Homeland-Diaspora).

Legislative elections were held on 25 May 2003. The Republican Party won 23.5% of the vote (23 seats) for deputies elected by party list, followed by Justice Bloc, 13.6% (14 seats); Rule of Law, 12.3% (12 seats); ARF (Dashnak), 11.4% (11 seats); National Unity, 8.8% (9 seats); United Labor Party, 5.7% (6 seats). However, seats by party change frequently as deputies switch parties or declare themselves independent. The next legislative elections were held on 12 May 2007. The Republican Party won 32.82% of the vote and 65 seats; Prosperous Armenia won 14.68% of the vote and 26 seats; the Armenian Revolutionary Federation won 12.72% of the vote and 16 seats; the Rule of Law party won 6.84% of the vote and 10 seats; and the Heritage party won 5.81% of the vote and 7 seats. Voter turnout was 59.35%. The next legislative elections were scheduled for May 2012.

In the 2008 presidential election, Serzh Sargsian of the Republican Party won with 52.9% of the vote. His nearest rival was Levon Ter-Petrosyan of the Armenian National Congress, who won 21.5% of the vote.

15 LOCAL GOVERNMENT

The regional governmental structure is closely modeled after the national structure. The president appoints governors to Armenia's 11 provinces (marzer), including the mayor of the capital of Yerevan, which has the status of a marz. Each province has both executive and legislative bodies that control the provincial budget and businesses within the region. Regional governments do not have authority to pass laws independent of national legislation. Marzer are divided into rural and urban communities (hamainkner), and Yerevan is divided into 12 districts. The communities and Yerevan districts are governed by community chiefs and legislative bodies called councils of elders (avakani). In the cities, community chiefs hold the title of mayor. In 1997 a law on self-government was passed calling for decentralization in some areas and some fiscal independence for local governments.

Elections for mayors, community chiefs, and local councils in 654 constituencies were held 20 October 2002, with a 46% voter turnout rate (an increase of close to 20% from the turnout in 1999). Local elections are held every three years. There were fewer complaints of electoral irregularities than in previous elections. The ruling Republican Party fielded the most candidates, and 18 other parties, in addition to independents, participated. The Law-Governed Country Party came in second, and the Armenian Revolutionary Federation was third. Local elections were held once again in 2005, 2008, and 2011. In these elections, voting went smoothly for the most part, and voters decided not to return many incumbents to office.

16 JUDICIAL SYSTEM

The constitution provides for an independent judiciary, but in practice courts are vulnerable to pressure from the government, though legal reforms are resulting in some changes. The court system consists of district courts of first instance, an appeals court,

and a court of cassation. Judges for the local courts of first instance and the court of appeals began operating under a new judicial system in January 1999. Judges were selected for their posts
based on examinations and interviews by the minister of justice,
approval of a list of nominees by the council of justice, and approval by the president. Unless they are removed for malfeasance,
they serve for life. About one-half of Soviet-era judges have been
replaced. Prosecutors and defense attorneys also began retrain-
ing and recertification. A military bureaucracy continues to follow
Soviet-era practices.

A constitutional court has the power to review the constitutionality of legislation, approve international agreements, and settle
electoral disputes. Its effectiveness is limited. It only accepts cases
referred by the president, two-thirds of the members of the legislature, or election-related cases brought by candidates in legislative or presidential races. The president appoints four of the nine
judges of the constitutional court.

The constitution establishes a council of justice, headed by the
president and including the prosecutor general, the minister of
justice, and 14 other members appointed by the president. The
council appoints and disciplines judges in courts of first instance
and the court of appeals. A council of court chairs has been created to reduce the power of the Ministry of Justice and increase
the independence of the judicial system. It is responsible for financial and budgetary issues involving the courts, and consists of
21 senior judges.

A criminal procedure code entered into force in January 1999
specifies that a suspect may be detained for no more than 12
months pending trial, has the right to an attorney, right to a public
trial and to confront witnesses, and the right to appeal.

[17]ARMED FORCES

The International Institute for Strategic Studies reports that armed
forces in Armenia totaled 48,570 members in 2011. The force is
comprised of 45,343 from the army, 1,146 from joint aviation forces, and 2,031 members of other air defense forces. Armed forces
represent 3.4% of the labor force in Armenia. The army is organized into five corps that include a mix of motorized and standard
rifle regiments, armored, and other support units.

Equipment in 2010 included 200 main battle tanks, 152 armored infantry fighting vehicles, 361 heavy and light armored
personnel carriers, and 229 artillery pieces. The air and defense
aviation forces numbered 3,160 personnel with 16 combat capable
aircraft (one fighter and 15 fighter/ground attack aircraft) and 12
attack helicopters. Paramilitary forces numbered 1,000 and were
made up of border troops and Ministry of Internal Affairs personnel. The military budget in 2011 totaled $386 million, or 2.8% of
gross domestic product (GDP).

[18]INTERNATIONAL COOPERATION

Armenia was admitted to the UN on 2 March 1992. The country
serves as a member of several specialized agencies within the UN,
such as FAO, IAEA, ICAO, IDA, IFC, IFAD, ILO, IMF, UNCTAD,
UNESCO, UNIDO, WIPO, and WHO. Armenia is a member of
the Commonwealth of Independent States (CIS) and the Council
of Europe. The country was admitted to the OSCE on 30 January
1992 and serves as an observer in the OAS. It became a full member of the WTO on 5 February 2003. Armenia is one of 12 mem-

bers of the Black Sea Economic Cooperation Zone, which was established in 1992. It is also a part of the Euro-Atlantic Partnership
Council and the EBRD. Armenia is a member of the Organization
for the Prohibition of Chemical Weapons and the NATO Partnership for Peace. The country ratified the Conventional Armed
Forces in Europe (CFE) Treaty in July 1992. Armenia also joined
the Collective Security Treaty Organization in 1992, a mutual defense alliance that consists of seven member states: Russia, Belarus, Armenia, Kazakhstan, Kyrgyzstan, Tajikistan, and Uzbekistan.

In environmental cooperation, Armenia is part of the Basel
Convention, the Conventions on Biological Diversity, Air Pollution, Ramsar, the Kyoto Protocol, the Montréal Protocol, the Nuclear Test Ban Treaty, and the UN Conventions on the Law of the
Sea, Climate Change, and Desertification.

Armenia has strongly supported the separatist government of
the Nagorno-Karabakh region of Azerbaijan. Nagorno-Karabakh
declared its own independence in 1991, and violence escalated
into civil war. More than 300,000 people were killed, and hundreds of thousands of civilian refugees fled from the region before
a cease-fire was brokered in 1994, under which the region legally became a part of Azerbaijan but de facto controlled by the local ethnic Armenian government. In 2006 residents of Nagorno-
Karabakh again voted for a declaration as a sovereign state, but
this was not internationally recognized. In 2008 the presidents of
Armenia and Azerbaijan signed an agreement to intensify efforts
toward a peaceful resolution of the conflict. Though the leaders
met again in January 2009, no settlement was determined. Relations remained fragile through 2011.

Tensions between Armenia and Turkey stem from the highly
charged issue of the mass killings of Armenians by Ottoman Turks
during 1915–16. The Armenians regard the killings as genocide,
a view that is formally held by several other countries. Turkey denies the allegations of genocide, insisting that the killings were
simply a result of the widespread fighting of World War I. Armenians mark the death toll at about 1.5 million; Turkey claims the
total was about 300,000. The two countries have had no diplomatic ties since 1991. Tension between the governments also exists
over the Nagorno-Karabakh conflict, in which Turkey has allied
with Azerbaijan. As a result, Turkey closed its border to Armenia
in 1993. In April 2009 officials from both countries met and announced an agreement on a process to normalize Turkish-Arme-
nian relations. As of 2011 this agreement has yet to bear significant results, however.

In August 2009 the secretary general of the Collective Security
Treaty Organization (CSTO) reiterated the organization's charter, declaring that CSTO would respond with military support to
any attack against Armenian forces by Azerbaijan over the issue
of Nagorno-Karabakh. Like other security alliances, such as the
North Atlantic Treaty Organization, CSTO members officially regard an attack on any member-state as an attack on all. When the
CSTO secretary-general made the remark, however, no member-
state had ever been attacked, leaving many observers in Armenia
and elsewhere less than confident in the backbone of the alliance.

[19]ECONOMY

As part of the Soviet Union, the Armenian economy featured
large-scale agro-industrial enterprises and a substantial industrial
sector that supplied machine tools, textiles, and other manufac-

tured goods to other parts of the USSR in exchange for raw materials. Trade with its neighbors, on which resource-poor Armenia relies heavily, was jeopardized by the outbreak of conflict over the Nagorno-Karabakh enclave in 1988, and by political instability in Georgia and Azerbaijan. Also, in December 1988 a severe earthquake did considerable damage to Armenia's productive capacity, aggravating its regional trade deficit. The physical damage had not been repaired when the economy suffered the implosion that accompanied the breakup of the Soviet Union in 1991.

With independence, as real GDP fell 60% from 1992–93, small-scale agriculture came to dominate in place of the former agro-industrial complexes, with crops of grain, sugar beets, potatoes, and other vegetables, as well as grapes and other fruit. Growth was not registered until 1994, at 5%, when, in July, a cease-fire was signed by Armenia, Azerbaijan, and Nagorno-Karabakh. In December of that same year, the government embarked on a comprehensive IMF-monitored program of macroeconomic stabilization and structural reform. By 1996 growth was in double digits and inflation in single digits. Still, set-backs, which began in late 1996, reduced real GDP growth to 3% in 1997, while inflation surged to 27%. In 1998 real growth reached 7.3% while inflation fell to a single digit 8.7%, despite the negative impacts of the Russian financial crisis and a continuing Azerbaijan-led economic blockade over the unresolved Nagorno-Karabakh issue.

Growth in the first nine months of 1999 was at an annual rate of 6%, but this was reduced to 3% for the year in the disruptions following the hostage-takings and assassinations of the prime minister and assembly speaker in October, a stated motive for which was the large proportion of Armenians living in poverty (at 55% in 2001 by CIA estimates). Inflation was held to 0.7% in the crisis, due to policy changes that have continued to keep inflation at a low level. Moderate GDP growth of 6% was achieved in 2000 while prices, as measured by the consumer price index, actually declined an estimated 0.8%.

In 2001 targeted real growth under the IMF-guided program was 6% but actual growth was about 10% (CIA estimate) as the effects of economic reforms, the privatization of small and medium-sized enterprises, and increased foreign investment began to impact performance. In February of 2003 Armenia joined the WTO, further solidifying its commitment to the development of international trade.

The IMF-sponsored economic liberalization program encouraged remarkable GDP growth rates: 13.9% in 2003 and 10.1% in 2004. Growth continued at this level in 2007 at a rate of 13.8%. Rising investment levels, exports, and real incomes also contributed to this growth. Inflation, tamed in 2002, was on the rise in 2003 and 2004, at 4.7% and 7.0% respectively. For the most part, the government did a good job of keeping the inflation in check, and stabilizing the local currency. This was reflected when inflation dropped back to 4.4% in 2007. Despite encouraging economic figures, unemployment remained high in 2007 at around 7.1%.

As a result of the global financial crisis of 2008–09, the growth rate that had once averaged about 10% dropped to 6.8% in 2008. After experiencing a difficult 14.4% economic contraction in 2009, Armenia rebounded strongly in the first four months of 2010. In May 2010 Armenia's National Statistical Service reported that the country's economy expanded by 7.2% from January through April 2010, compared to the previous year. The strong economic numbers were linked to Armenia's booming industrial sector, which grew at nearly 13% over the first four months of 2010. As of 2010, the GDP rate of change in Armenia was 2.6%. Inflation stood at 8.2%, and unemployment was reported at 7.1%. By 2011, things had improved even more: GDP growth was 4.6%; inflation was 7.7%; and unemployment was at 5.6%.

20 INCOME

The CIA estimated that in 2011 the GDP of Armenia was $17.95 billion. This includes the value of all final goods and services produced within a nation in a given year, computed on the basis of purchasing power parity (PPP) rather than value as measured on the basis of the rate of the exchange based on current dollars. The per capita GDP was estimated at $5,400. The annual growth rate of GDP was 4.6%. The average inflation rate based on consumer prices was 7.7%. It was estimated that agriculture accounted for 17.8% of GDP, industry 37.7%, and services 44.5%. According to the World Bank, remittances from citizens living abroad totaled $769.5 million or about $259 per capita and accounted for approximately 4.6% of GDP. It was estimated that household consumption was growing at an average annual rate of 6.4%.

As of 2011 the most recent study by the World Bank reported that actual individual consumption in Armenia was 79.6% of GDP and accounted for 0.03% of world consumption. By comparison, the United States accounted for 25.44% of world individual consumption. The World Bank also estimated that 54.2% of Armenia's GDP was spent on food and beverages, 7.1% on housing and household furnishings, 2.4% on clothes, 4.0% on health, 2.6% on transportation, 0.9% on communications, 1.1% on recreation, 0.5% on restaurants and hotels, and 3% on miscellaneous goods and services and purchases from abroad. Despite increases in GDP, employment, and access to goods and services, it was estimated that in 2009 about 34.1% of the population still subsisted on an income below the poverty line established by Armenia's government.

21 LABOR

As of 2011 Armenia had a total labor force of 1.194 million people. Within that labor force, CIA estimates in 2008 noted that 44.2% were employed in agriculture, 16.8% in industry, and 39% in the service sector. Unemployment was reported at 5.6% in 2011.

Legislation passed in 1992 guarantees workers the right to bargain and organize collectively. An independent labor federation was created in 1997. However, organized labor remained weak as of 2010, because of high unemployment and a slow economy. Collective bargaining does not occur because most large employers are still under state control. Labor disputes are generally settled in economic or regular courts of law. According to the Confederation of Labor Unions (CLU) an estimated 250,000 workers belonged to 27 labor unions in 2010.

Armenians are guaranteed a monthly minimum wage which was set at 30,000 drams (about $80) as of 2010. The standard legal workweek is 40 hours, with mandatory overtime and rest periods. Children under the age of 16 are prohibited by law from full-time labor, although children at age 14 can be employed if permission is given by the child's parents and from the labor union. Even though the economic situation has improved in recent years, none of these legal standards are generally followed. Although the government is required to promulgate minimum occupational health and safety standards, such standards have yet to be implemented. In addition, a lack of government resources, corruption, and general worker insecurity prevent any effective enforcement of the nation's labor laws.

22 AGRICULTURE

As of 2011 roughly 19% of the total land was farmed. The country's major crops include fruit (especially grapes) and vegetables. In 2009 cereal production amounted to 377,501 tons, fruit production 540,749 tons, and vegetable production 1 million tons.

23 ANIMAL HUSBANDRY

The UN Food and Agriculture Organization (FAO) reported that Armenia dedicated 1.2 million hectares (3.07 million acres) to permanent pasture or meadow in 2009. During that year, the country tended 4 million chickens, 584,779 head of cattle, and 84,801 pigs. The production from these animals amounted to 49,244 tons of beef and veal, 24,491 tons of pork, 32,566 tons of poultry, 19,162 tons of eggs, and 418,146 tons of milk. Armenia also produced 8,331 tons of cattle hide and 1,307 tons of raw wool. Meat, milk, and butter are the chief agricultural imports.

24 FISHING

Fishing is limited to the Arpa River and Lake Sevan. Commercial fishing is not a significant part of the economy. Trout and carp are the principal species. In 2008 the annual capture totaled 3,700 tons according to the UN FAO.

25 FORESTRY

Armenia officially lists 11% of its territory as forested, yet forests are estimated by external sources to cover 8–9% of Armenia in 2011, down from 25% a century ago. Soviet mismanagement, the 1988 earthquake, hostilities with Azerbaijan, and fuel shortages have impaired development. Available timber is used for firewood during the harsh winters. The UN FAO estimated the 2009 roundwood production at 2,000 cu m (70,629 cu ft). The value of all forest products, including roundwood, totaled $495,000. Imports of forestry products have risen dramatically in the last decade, from a total value of $7.8 million in 2000 to $59.1 million in 2009.

26 MINING

Mineral resources in Armenia are concentrated in the southern region, where several operating copper and molybdenum mines are located. Armenia has been mining one-third of the former Soviet Union's (FSU) output of molybdenum (4,100 metric tons in 2009, up from 3,000 metric tons in 2005). Copper mines are located at Kapan, Kadzharan, Agarak, Shamlugh, and Akhtala; the latter two were not in operation in 2009. Kadzharan and Agarak also have molybdenum mines. Despite relative proximity to rail and port facilities that supply European markets, the mineral sector's ability to compete on the world market has been inhibited by infrastructure problems. Armenia's production of perlite has been estimated at a steady 35,000 metric tons annually, from 2006 through 2010.

In 2009 Armenia produced industrial minerals such as clays, diatomite, dimension stone, limestone (15 million metric tons), salt (35,000 metric tons), and semiprecious stones. It mined cop-

per (19,000 metric tons of copper concentrate), copper-zinc, and native gold deposits. The Zod gold mine annually produced an estimated 1,400 kg during 2005–2009. Significant byproduct constituents in the nonferrous ores in 2009 included barite, gold, lead, rhenium (1,200 kg), selenium, silver (40,000 kg), tellurium, and zinc.

27 ENERGY AND POWER

With only negligible reserves of oil, natural gas, and coal, and with no production, Armenia is heavily reliant on foreign imports. Following the breakup of the Soviet Union, oil consumption has declined. The World Bank reported in 2008 that Armenia produced 5.77 billion kWh of electricity and consumed 4.86 billion kWh, or 1,636 kWh per capita. Roughly 73% of energy came from fossil fuels, while 27% came from alternative fuels. Per capita oil consumption was 974 kg.

Armenia obtains roughly 40% of its power from the country's only nuclear facility. The plant originally featured two nuclear power units, but after a 1988 earthquake caused the facility to go offline for seven years, only one of the two units reopened. In recent years, Armenia has developed plans to construct a new and updated nuclear reactor in the country. In August 2010, these plans appeared to move forward, as a delegation from the International Atomic Energy Agency (IAEA) visited Armenia to examine the country's nuclear infrastructure and the environmental surveys conducted at Armenia's operational nuclear power facility. After the new reactor becomes operational (2017), analysts expect the current reactor to be shut down.

Economic blockades by Turkey and Azerbaijan as part of the continuing dispute over Nagorno-Karabakh have cut Armenia off from an old direct gas pipeline from Azerbaijan, as well as precluded it from participation in any of the east-west pipelines being built in the post-Soviet era. The alternative Armenia has pursued is a gas pipeline from Iran delivering Turkmenistan gas (to avoid sanctions on customers of Iran imposed by the international community). Intergovernmental agreements on the project were signed in 1992 and 1995. In December 1997 the Korpezehe-Kurt-Kwi pipeline feeding Turkmen natural gas directly into the Iranian system was opened. In December 2001 an agreement was reached on a route that bypassed the Azeri exclave of Nakhichevan, running from Kadzharan to the southern border at Megri. Work on the Armenian section of the Iran-Armenian gas pipeline was to have begun in 2002 but was delayed until 2003 by disputes over the price Iran was intending to charge. The pipeline was completed and began operation in late 2006. An oil pipeline between Iran and Armenia has also been discussed, with preliminary estimates made as of 2011 for completion in 2014. If Armenia and Azerbaijan ever resolve their disputes, the transit of oil and gas from the Caspian Sea region abroad will become possible.

28 INDUSTRY

Before the earthquake in 1988 Armenia exported trucks, tires, electronics, and instruments to other republics. A number of these plants were destroyed by the earthquake. Armenia was also a major producer of chemical products, some 59% of which were exported to other republics. Armenia has the highest number of specialists with higher education and second highest number of scientists of all the former Soviet republics. Since the collapse of the Soviet Union, industrial production has been severely disrupted by political instability and shortages of power. Much of Armenia's industry is idle or operating at a fraction of its capacity.

Light industry dominates Armenia's industrial sector and is striking for its diversity. The leading industries include metal-cutting machine tools, forging-pressing machines, electric motors, tires, knitted wear, hosiery, shoes, silk fabric, chemicals, trucks, instruments, microelectronics, gem cutting, jewelry manufacture, software development, food processing, and brandy. Most of the country's small and medium-sized enterprises have been privatized, spurring the recovery of industrial growth.

Progress has been slower with larger industries, often due to the lack of viable bidders. About 70% of the larger operations were privatized by 1998, the year Armenia passed legislation for the sale of the country's electricity transmission and distribution networks, retaining government control over power generation. To support the privatization, the European Bank for Reconstruction and Development (EBRD) bought a 20% share in each of Armenia's four distribution companies in an agreement preserving the government's right to buy back the shares should the agreement be abrogated.

Armenia has the highest number of cooperatives (per capita) in the Commonwealth of Independent States. The country is projecting growth along with partnership opportunities in areas such as power generation, aviation, construction, electronics, apparel, tourism, food processing, industrial property acquisition, banking, and other areas. The industrial production growth rate was estimated at 8% in 2010.

29 SCIENCE AND TECHNOLOGY

The Armenian National Academy of Sciences, founded in 1943 and headquartered in Yerevan, has departments of physical, mathematical, technological, and natural sciences;and 32 research institutes in fields such as agriculture; biological, mathematical, physical, and earth sciences; and technology. Yerevan State University (founded in 1919) has faculties of mechanics, mathematics, physics, radiophysics, chemistry, biology, geology, geography, and mathematical cybernetics and automatic analysis. Also in Yerevan are the State Engineering University of Armenia (founded in 1930), the Yerevan State Medical University (founded in 1922), the Yerevan Zootechnical and Veterinary Institute (founded in 1929), and the Armenian Scientific and Technical Library.

In 2008 high technology exports totaled $11.5 million, 2.5% of the country's manufactured exports. This had fallen to $6.6 million in 2009, but because of the 14.4% contraction in the overall economy the percentage of high technology exports actually increased to 3.7% of GDP. According to the World Bank, patent applications in science and technology in 2009 totaled 116 in Armenia. Public financing of science was 0.21% of GDP.

30 DOMESTIC TRADE

The end of communism led to a rapid increase in private enterprise. By 2001 there were about 4,500 retail shops registered in Armenia. The main retail center is Yerevan. A majority of retail establishments are small food and specialty item shops. Many of these work with wholesalers and sell items on a consignment basis. There are also large open markets in Yerevan and other cities offering a wide variety of food, clothing, housewares, and elec-

Principal Trading Partners – Armenia (2010)

(In millions of US dollars)

Country	Total	Exports	Imports	Balance
World	4,794.3	1,011.4	3,782.9	-2,771.5
Russia	995.8	160.5	835.3	-674.8
China	434.9	30.9	404.0	-373.2
Germany	343.3	132.6	210.7	-78.1
Iran	284.7	84.8	199.9	-115.1
Bulgaria	268.9	156.6	112.4	44.2
Ukraine	242.0	12.1	229.9	-217.9
Turkey	211.7	1.3	210.4	-209.1
United States	194.2	82.9	111.3	-28.4
Belgium	143.9	72.5	71.4	1.1
Italy	127.0	4.8	122.2	-117.4

(…) data not available or not significant.

(n.s.) not specified.

SOURCE: *2011 Direction of Trade Statistics Yearbook*, New York: United Nations, 2011.

tronics. As of 2010 the majority of retail transactions were still made in cash.

Beginning in 1996 the government launched a major privatization drive. By 1999 over 80% of small businesses and over 60% of medium and large corporations were in private hands. As of 2012 the World Bank ranked Armenia 55th (out of 183 economies) in the ease of doing business, up 6 places from 2011. Armenia's rank in the ease of starting a business jumped from 20th to 10th place in the same period. Nearly all farmland is privately owned. Seasonal open-air food markets are also popular. Some of these markets still engage in bartering.

31 FOREIGN TRADE

Due to its delicate geographic placement, Armenia has scored modest foreign trade figures over the past decade. In 2004, exports totaled only $850 million (FOB—Free on Board), while imports climbed to $1.3 billion (FOB). Exports fell to $722 million in 2009 because of the world economic crisis, but had bounced back to $1.1 billion in 2010 and $1.319 billion in 2011. Yet Armenia imports continue to rise, with $3.255 billion worth of goods and services in 2010, a 150% increase from 2004, and $3.538 billion in 2011. Major import partners in 20110 were Russia, 16%; United Arab Emirates, 9.4%; Georgia, 6%; Iran, 5.5%; China, 5.1%; Ukraine, 5.1%; and Turkey, 4.8%. Major export partners were Russia, 16.4%; Germany, 12.1%; Bulgaria, 11.7%; Netherlands, 9%; Iran, 8.3%; the United States, 7.8%; Belgium, 5%; Canada, 5%; and Georgia, 4.6%.

Exports include gold and diamonds, aluminum, transport equipment, electrical equipment, and scrap metal. Main export commodities in the mid-2000s were precious or semiprecious stones and metals (accounting for 42.5% of total exports), base metals (19.5%), mineral products (11.7%), prepared foodstuffs (9.7%). Principal imports included precious or semiprecious stones and metals (22.5%), mineral products (16.2%), machinery and equipment (10.1%), and prepared foodstuffs (7.0%). These last figures indicate that while Armenia has a vibrant industry, it is not exploiting it to its fullest potential. Existing trade barriers with its neighbors, Azerbaijan and Turkey, probably hinder the export

Balance of Payments – Armenia (2010)

(In millions of US dollars)

Current Account		**-1,373.2**
Balance on goods	-2,032.5	
Imports	-3,208.0	
Exports	1,175.4	
Balance on services	-242.3	
Balance on income	338.7	
Current transfers	563.0	
Capital Account		**107.9**
Financial Account		**974.2**
Direct investment abroad	-8.3	
Direct investment in Armenia	570.1	
Portfolio investment assets	-1.5	
Portfolio investment liabilities	12.2	
Financial derivatives	...	
Other investment assets	-245.6	
Other investment liabilities	647.2	
Net Errors and Omissions		**17.6**
Reserves and Related Items		**273.5**

(…) data not available or not significant.

SOURCE: *Balance of Payment Statistics Yearbook 2011*, Washington, DC: International Monetary Fund, 2011.

of manufactured goods, so it has to resort to trading mainly natural resources.

Imports include grain and other foods, tobacco, natural gas, and oil. Inter-republic trade has suffered as a result of border hostilities, particularly the ongoing conflict over the Armenian enclave of Nagorno-Karabakh in Azerbaijan, which may prevent the proposed Caspian Sea oil pipeline from passing through Armenia. There was hope that the 2003 talks between the leaders of Armenia and Azerbaijan represented a positive step toward resolving the dispute, but almost ten years passed, and as of 2012 relations had not appreciably improved.

32 BALANCE OF PAYMENTS

Although the government is working to reduce Armenia's large trade deficits by improving export performance, the conflict over the Armenian enclave of Nagorno-Karabakh in Azerbaijan continues to weaken the economy by disrupting normal trade and supply links. Armenia receives large amounts of humanitarian assistance, especially from the United States and the European Union. Between 2006 and 2011 Armenia received about $175 million from the United States, and will receive over $200 million from the EU between 2011 and 2013.

The CIA reported that in 2001 the purchasing power parity of Armenia's exports was $338.5 million, while imports totaled $868.6 million resulting in a trade deficit of $530.1 million. Exports of goods and services continued to grow in the following years, reaching $696 million in 2003, and $738 million in 2004. Imports followed a similar path, totaling $1.1 billion in 2003, and $1.2 billion in 2004. The resource balance was consequently negative in both years, at around -$400 million. The current account balance was also negative, dropping to -$190 million in 2003, and recuperating to -$161 million in 2004. Reserves of foreign exchange and gold reached $555 million in 2004, covering almost

six months of imports. Reserves had increased to $1.4 billion by 2008, but external debt had also increased over the same period to $3.5 billion. The account balance in 2008 stood at -$1.355 billion, and in 2010 Armenia had a foreign trade deficit of $2.3 billion, amounting to 7.5% of GDP.

33 BANKING AND SECURITIES

The Central Bank of Armenia is charged with regulating the money supply, circulating currency, and regulating the commercial banks of the country. Commercial banks in Armenia include the Ardshinbank, Armagrobank, Armeconombank, Armimplexbank, Arminvestbank, Bank Armcommunication, Central Bank of Armenia, "Gladzor" Joint Stock Commercial Bank, Masis Commercial Bank, and the State Specialized Savings Bank of the Republic of Armenia. Leading foreign banks include Mellat Bank (Iran) and Midland Armenia (UK).

In 2009 the money market rate (i.e. the rate at which financial institutions lend to one another in the short term) was 6.2%. Armenian commercial banks had $2.9 billion extended in the form of economic loan as of 2011, 62% in foreign currency.

As of 2012 there was only one stock exchange operating in Armenia, NASDAQ OMX Armenia, a part of the NASDAQ OMX Group. The value of publicly traded shares was $105 million in 2007, the last accurate estimate taken.

The IMF has been concerned about the direction of policy taken by the National Bank of Armenia and the slow pace of financial reform. Armenia's financial sector is overbanked and beset with nonperforming credits, mainly to large state enterprises. At the same time, Armenia has been a model reforming country among the former Soviet republics, and for this reason multilateral creditors are worried that public pressure may now force the government to loosen monetary and fiscal policies.

34 INSURANCE

Insurance is largely controlled by government organizations inherited from the Soviet system, although private insurance companies are not unknown.

35 PUBLIC FINANCE

In 2010 the CIA estimated that the budget of Armenia included $2.023 billion in public revenue and $2.607 billion in public expenditures. The budget deficit amounted to 4.9% of GDP. In 2010 Armenia had $5.227 billion in debt held by foreign entities. A year later this had risen 25% to $6.965 billion.

In 1994 the government began a three-year effort to privatize the national industries. Loans from the IMF, World Bank, EBRD, and other financial institutions and foreign countries aimed at eliminating the government's budget deficit. However, by 1996, external public debt already exceeded $353 million with annual debt service payments exceeding $55 million. External debt in 2011 was $7.336 billion. Loans to Armenia from 1993 to 2010 total over $800 million.

36 TAXATION

Armenia's complex tax system was revised in 1997 and again in 2001. The top corporate profit tax rate was lowered from 30% to 20%. As of 1 July 2001 a single rate was applied to all taxable profits, defined as the difference between revenues and the sum of

Public Finance – Armenia (2009)

(In millions of dram, central government figures)

Revenue and Grants	722,468	100.0%
Tax revenue	518,557	71.8%
Social contributions	102,903	14.2%
Grants	23,348	3.2%
Other revenue	77,660	10.7%
Expenditures	961,259	100.0%
General public services	...	...
Defense	...	...
Public order and safety	...	...
Economic affairs	...	...
Environmental protection	...	...
Housing and community amenities	...	...
Health	...	...
Recreational, culture, and religion	...	...
Education	...	...
Social protection	...	...

(…) data not available or not significant.

SOURCE: *Government Finance Statistics Yearbook 2010*, Washington, DC: International Monetary Fund, 2010.

wages, amortization payments, raw and intermediate purchases, social security contributions, insurance fees, and interest expenses. Newly formed foreign enterprises are exempt from taxes for the first two years (see below), but there is no provision for carrying forward losses.

Individual income taxes are withheld by enterprises and are paid to the Ministry of Finance monthly. The personal income tax has been reduced from three bands to two: 10% for monthly taxable income up to AMD80,000 ($209) and 20% for incomes above AMD80,000, plus a payment of AMD8,000 ($20.90). Armenians also pay taxes to social security and pension funds. In 1992 Armenia introduced a value-added tax, which stood at 20% in 2011. Excise taxes are applied to diesel fuel, oil, spirits, wine and beer at various rates. There are also land taxes and property taxes. Achieving a higher level of tax collection has been an important part of Armenia's economic reform programs. Taxes and other revenues were computed as 21.5% of GDP in 2010, with a fiscal deficit projected at 4.9% of GDP.

37 CUSTOMS AND DUTIES

All exports are duty-free. Minor customs duties (up to 10%) are imposed on certain imports. Imports of machinery and equipment for use in manufacturing by enterprises with foreign investment are exempt from all customs duties.

38 FOREIGN INVESTMENT

Armenia's investment climate is regulated by the bilateral investment treaty (BIT) signed with the United States on 23 September 1992 and by the law on foreign investment adopted by Armenia on 31 July 1994. Armenia has also concluded BITs on investment and investment protection with 15 other countries: Georgia, Turkmenistan, Kyrgyzstan, Ukraine, Iran, Egypt, Romania, Cyprus, Greece, France, Germany, Canada, Argentina, China, and Vietnam. Its investment policy is geared to attract foreign invest-

ment, with foreign investors accorded national treatment and any sector open to investment. As of 2011 two-year tax holidays are accorded foreign investors whose equity investment in a resident company is at least AMD500 million, or $1.3 million dollars. For the following three years foreign investors enjoy a 50% reduction in tax. There are no limits on the repatriation of profits, or on the import and export of hard currency, so long as the currency is imported or earned in Armenia. Otherwise there is a $10,000 limit on the export of cash.

In late 1997 the government initiated the privatization of 11 of the larger state owned enterprises (SOEs), including the energy sector. It was not until 2002, however, that a suitable and willing foreign investor, Daewoo Engineering, was found to manage privatized electricity distribution. Operations at the Zvartnots International Airport have also been successfully leased. The 2001 debt-for-equity swap with Russia, whereby five unproductive SOEs (Hrazdan Thermal Power Plant, the "Mars" Electronics Factory established in 1986 to build robots, and three research labs) were exchanged for the cancellation of Armenia's debt with Russia (about $100 million of nonconcessional lending that was costing almost $20 million/year to service) promised to increase Russian private investment in Armenia as the Russian government passed the assets on to private investors.

From 1998–2000 annual inflow of foreign direct investment (FDI) ranged from $120 million to $230 million, though it fell to $75.9 million in 2001 in the wake of the global contraction of foreign investment following the 11 September 2001 terrorist attacks on the US World Trade Center. In 2002 FDI increased 12% to about $85 million. The flow of foreign capital into Armenia continued to grow steadily, reaching $155 million in 2003, and $300 million in 2004. At the end of 2003 the accumulated stock of FDI amounted to 32% of the GDP. This investment trend has continued in dramatic fashion, and by 2009 FDI was calculated by the World Bank at a net inflow of $777.5 million, representing 8.92% of GDP. The main FDI sources have been Russia, the United States, Greece, France, and Germany. Unfortunately, only a small part of the capital inflows were geared toward the development of new industrial projects or sectors.

A large share of FDI comes from the Armenian diaspora in the United States, Russia, Iran, France, Greece, the United Kingdom, Germany, and Syria. Since 1998 the Lincy Foundation, begun by Armenian American Kirk Kirkorian, has made available about $165 million to support small and medium enterprise (SME) development (offering concessional loans for businesses that are at least 51% Armenian owned), assistance for tourism development ($20 million in 2000), and infrastructure repair ($60 million in 2002 and $80 million in 2003). Armenia's accession to the World Trade Organization in 2003 helped improve the investment climate as a consequence of meeting the WTO's strictures for membership.

39 ECONOMIC DEVELOPMENT

Development planning in Armenia has been aimed at counteracting the effects of three devastating blows to its economy: the earthquake of 1988; open warfare and economic blockade over Nagorno-Karabakh; and the combination of hyperinflation and industrial collapse following its separation from the Soviet Union. The government has been aggressive in launching economic reform, beginning with its privatization of agricultural land in 1991, which boosted crop output 30% and resulted in a 15% increase in agricultural production. In December 1994 Armenia embarked on a series of ambitious programs of economic reform guided by the International Monetary Fund (IMF), which resulted in 14 years of positive growth rates before losing 14.4% in 2008–09 due to the global economic crisis. A return to positive growth came in 2010. Likewise, from 1999 to 2011 GDP per capita (PPP) grew from $2,900 to $5,400 per year, surpassing pre-independence levels.

By 1997 privatization of most small industry, as well as an estimated 70% of larger enterprises, was complete. Progress has been slower with larger state-owned enterprises (SOEs), not least because the government has had difficulty finding bidders at its cash sales auctions. In 1997 the ministries controlling the SOEs were merged, and their functions changed from direct control to general supervision and special support. The Ministry of Industry and the Ministry of Trade, and certain parts of the Ministry of Economy and the Ministry of Privatization and Foreign Investment were also merged in order to streamline the bureaucracy.

In late 1997, 11 large enterprises were offered for sale, and in 1998 the assembly passed a law allowing for the sale of the state electricity transmission and distribution networks. Viable bidders were not immediately forthcoming, and on 5 December 2000, as a means of supporting the privatization program, the European Bank of Reconstruction and Development (EBRD) agreed to take 20% shares in each of Armenia's four electricity distribution companies, with provision for the Armenian government's right to buy back the shares if the agreements were abrogated. The privatization process of the distribution networks stalled in 2001 and 2002 as twice the government failed to attract any final bids. To make the offer more attractive, the government merged the four distribution companies into one closed-end joint stock company, Electricity Networks of Armenia, and on 31 October 2002, 100% of the shares were acquired by the English company Midland Resources Holding, Ltd. Midland in turn contracted with Daewoo International of South Korea to manage the newly privatized company.

The republic has substantial deposits of gold, copper, zinc, bauxite, and other minerals, which could be developed with Western capital. The government is currently exploring alternative trade routes, and seeking export orders from the West to aid production and earn foreign exchange. Much of Armenia's industry remains idle or operating at low capacity utilization in large part because of the country's political isolation from oil and gas supplies.

Armenia's determination to create a market-oriented economy and democratic society has engaged (in addition to the IMF) the World Bank and EBRD as well as other financial institutions and foreign countries. Nevertheless, Armenia continues to remain economically isolated in comparison with its Caucasian neighbors.

The Armenian economy is expected to continue growing strongly in the coming years, based on increased domestic consumption, which in turn is fueled by higher wages and remittances from abroad. The quick and robust bounce-back following the 2008–2009 global economic crisis is another positive sign. In addition, further investments are expected to come in the country as a result of economic restructuring and trade-oriented policies. Armenia boasts a highly-educated work force, a diverse and dynamic industrial base, and a strategic geographic location. How-

ever, as long as the Nagorno-Karabakh conflict is not resolved (along with the accompanying diplomatic problems between Armenia, Azerbaijan, and Turkey), the economy will find it hard to reach its fullest potential.

40 SOCIAL DEVELOPMENT

Pension and disability benefit systems were first introduced in 1956 and 1964. Additional legislation was passed in 2002 and implemented in 2003. Retirement is set at age 63 for men and age 59.5 for women, although earlier retirement is allowed for those engaged in hazardous work. The cost is covered by employee, employer, and government contributions. Work injury legislation provides 100% of average monthly earnings for temporary disability and a proportion of wages up to a maximum of 100% for permanent disability, depending on the extent of incapacity. Unemployment, sickness, and maternity benefits and family allowances are also provided under Armenian law.

Women in Armenia largely occupy traditional roles despite an employment law that formally prohibits discrimination based on sex. Women do not receive the same professional opportunities as men and often work in low-level jobs, although the World Economic Forum reported in 2011 that this situation was changing positively. Still, in 2011 the ratio of women to men in the workforce was 69:83, and men on average earned twice as much as women. Societal attitudes do not view sexual harassment in the workplace worthy of legal action. Violence against women and domestic violence is widespread and underreported. According to one survey, 45% of women have been subject to psychological abuse, and 25% of women have been physically abused. Most women do not report domestic abuse due to fear of reprisal and embarrassment. Less than 10% of the national legislature is female.

The constitution protects the freedom of assembly and the freedom of religion. The government allows minorities, such as the Russians, Jews, Kurds, Yezidi, Georgians, Greeks, and Assyrians, the right to preserve their cultural practices; the law allows them to study in their native languages. Discrimination is prohibited on the basis of race, sex, religion, language disability, or social status. Human rights abuses appear to be widespread. Prison conditions fail to meet international standards, and accusations of police brutality are not uncommon.

41 HEALTH

According to the CIA, life expectancy in Armenia was 73.49 years in 2012. The country spent 3.8% of its GDP on healthcare, amounting to $129 per person. There were 37 physicians, 49 nurses and midwives, and 41 hospital beds per 10,000 inhabitants. The fertility rate was 1.38 children born per woman, while the infant mortality rate was 18.21 deaths per 1,000 live births. The incidence of tuberculosis was 78 per 100,000 people. In 2007 one-year-old children were immunized against the following diseases: diphtheria, pertussis, and tetanus, 94%; and measles, 90%. By 2011 it was estimated that 96% of children were vaccinated against measles.

The break from the Soviet Union meant a disruption of the system that once provided member states with equipment, supplies, and drugs. Out-of-pocket payments by individual are now required for most health care services. However, the health care delivery itself is still largely organized as it was during the Soviet era, with regional clinics and walk-in centers delivering most primary health care services.

The incidence of heart disease is high compared to other moderately developed countries. The HIV/AIDS adult prevalence rate was 0.1% in 2009. There were an estimated 2,600 people living with HIV/AIDS in the country.

42 HOUSING

Housing throughout Armenia has been somewhat scarce for the past two decades due to a number of factors, including a history of state control, a devastating earthquake in 1988, and civil conflicts. That Armenia is relatively densely populated (the second most densely populated of the former Soviet republics) has also created problems. Since the 1993 passage of a law on privatization for previously state and public-owned housing, about 96% of apartments were privatized and transferred to ownership by the existing tenants.

A large number of buildings are neglected and in serious disrepair, and utilities are limited and expensive. The total number of housing units in 2001 was at about 750,719. Nearly 59% were multiunit dwellings, most of which are in urban areas. About 25% of all multiunit homes were built before 1960; another 52% were built between 1960 and 1980. Only about 96% of the population have access to improved water supplies, and 90% have access to improved sanitation facilities.

Overcrowding and homelessness is a great concern, particularly among the population of refugees and displaced persons. For years following the 1988 earthquake, thousands of families lived in temporary shelters called *domics* within the earthquake zone. In 2001 about 11% of all households lived in one-room homes. In 2011 it was estimated that about 70,000 families had no permanent housing. Another 40,000 families were on waiting lists for new permanent housing because of overcrowding. About 1,200 new housing units were completed in 2001. The same year, there were about 29,000 unfinished housing units (4,487 buildings). Most of these were started in the late 1980s and early 1990s within the earthquake zone, and were simply left incomplete because of lack of funds and materials. As the economy has improved, this situation is beginning to be addressed, but many problems remain.

43 EDUCATION

Education is compulsory between the ages of 7 and 14 years and is free at both the primary and secondary levels. The system is broken into three levels. Primary school lasts for three years, followed by intermediate school, which lasts for five years. This is followed by two years of general secondary education. In 2007 the World Bank estimated that 84% of age-eligible children in Armenia were enrolled in primary school. Secondary enrollment for age-eligible children stood at 87%. Tertiary enrollment was estimated at 50%. Of those enrolled in tertiary education, there were 100 male students for every 133 female students.

Since the early 1990s increasing emphasis has been placed on Armenian history and culture. The school year runs from September to July. Instruction is available in Armenian and Russian. The education system is coordinated through the Ministry of Education and Science and the Council of Rectors of Higher Educational Establishments. Public expenditure on general education represented about 3% of GDP in 2006.

The adult literacy rate was estimated in 2009 to be about 99.5%, with a fairly even rate between men and women. There are two universities in Yerevan: the Yerevan State University (founded in 1919) and the State Engineering University of Armenia. Seven other educational institutions are located in the capital. There are several other institutes of higher education throughout the country. In recent years enrollment in tertiary education has increased dramatically. After falling to a low of 14.7% in 1997, in 2003 the percentage of all age-eligible students enrolled in tertiary education programs had regained the pre-independence high of 25%. By 2009 this figure had more than doubled to 50.1%.

44 LIBRARIES AND MUSEUMS

There are two branches of the National Library, with the main branch in Yerevan comprising 6.6 million volumes as of 2011. The main library of the Armenian Academy of Sciences in Yerevan has 4.4 million volumes. The Armenian Academy of Sciences and the universities each have research libraries. The Armenian Library Association was established in 1995.

Yerevan's museums include the National Gallery of Arts; the Yerevan Children's Picture Gallery, a unique collection of children's art from Armenia and around the world; the Museum of Modern Art; the House Museum of Ovanes Tumanjan, Armenia's most renowned poet; and the Museum of Ancient Manuscripts. There are also museums devoted to the composer Aram Khachaturian (including his piano) and the filmmaker Sergei Paradjanov, two of Armenia's most famous artists. The Genocide Memorial and Museum at Tsitsernakaberd is in Yerevan. The Matenadaran Manuscript Museum, also in Yerevan, was established to preserve the ancient written culture of the region.

45 MEDIA

As of 2011 Armenia's telephone system was privately held and is undergoing expansion and modernization. In 2010 the CIA reported that there were 589,900 telephone landlines in Armenia. However, the system is generally inadequate, with most of the modern equipment and the majority of subscribers located in the nation's capital of Yerevan. In 2010 there were 3.865 million mobile cellular phones in use, an average of more than 100 per 100 people. Yerevan is linked to the Trans-Asia-Europe fiber-optic cable through Iran. Communications links to other former Soviet republics are by land line or microwave, and to other countries by satellite and through Moscow.

A majority of citizens rely on radio and television as a primary source of news and information. Armenian and Russian radio and television stations broadcast throughout the country. In 2009 there were 26 radio stations (9 FM radio stations, 16 AM radio stations, and 1 shortwave radio station) and 48 television broadcasters, most of which were privately owned and operated. In 2011 the country had about 192,541 Internet hosts. As of 2009 there were some 208,200 Internet users in Armenia, an average of 7 per 100 citizens. Prominent newspapers in 2010 included *Aravot* and *Azg*. According to the Yerevan Press Club, the total newspaper circulation in the country in 2004 was 60,000, an increase of 20,000 from 2003. In 2011 this had fallen to an estimated 40,000. There were about 27 newspapers available in the capital.

Armenia's constitution provides for freedom of expression, and it is said to generally uphold freedom of speech and press. However, journalists seem to adhere to an unspoken rule of self-censorship, particularly when reporting on political issues, since they traditionally depend on the government for funding and access to facilities. The government has, it is noted, begun to shed itself of the state publishing apparatus, and it has dissolved the Ministry of Information. The 2008 and 2011 protests led to renewed calls from prominent journalists for civil reforms and anti-corruption efforts.

⁴⁶ORGANIZATIONS

Important political movements in Armenia include the Armenian National Movement and the National Self-Determination Association. Armenian trade unions belong to the umbrella organization Council of Armenia Trade Unions. The Chamber of Commerce and Industry of the Republic of Armenia promotes the economic and business activities of the country in world markets.

The National Academy of Sciences of Armenia encourages the public interest in science and seeks to ensure availability and effectiveness of science education programs. The Armenian Physical Society serves a similar role. The group also works with various research programs. The Independent Media Center promotes the freedom and accuracy of press and other media. The Armenian Medical Association promotes research and education in the field; there are also several professional associations for specialized fields of medicine.

There are a number of national sporting organizations, including the Athletic Federation of the Republic of Armenia, the Armenian National Paralympic Committee, and other groups sponsoring football (soccer), baseball, skiing, and the Special Olympics. The National Youth Council of the Republic of Armenia coordinates youth organizations through the support of the Ministry of Culture, Sports, and Youth. An affiliate of the UN of Youth (UNOY), a foundation based in the Netherlands, was established in Armenia in 1994. Other youth groups include the Aragast Youth Club and the Armenian Euro Club Unipax. There are active chapters of the Girl Guides and Girl Scouts; the World Organization of Scouting is represented by the Armenian National Scout Movement. The Armenian Junior Chamber is a national leadership development organization. The YMCA is also present.

Organizations representing the rights and role of women in society include the League of Armenian Women, the Union of the Protection of Women's, Children and Family Rights, and the Women's Alliance. There are national chapters of the Red Cross Society, World Vision, and Habitat for Humanity. The Armenian Relief Society supports local community health development programming.

⁴⁷TOURISM, TRAVEL, AND RECREATION

The *Tourism Factbook*, published by the UN World Tourism Organization, reported 575,000 incoming tourists to Armenia in 2009, spending a total of $374 million. Of those incoming tourists, there were 311,000 from Europe and 135,000 from the Americas. There were 23,290 hotel beds available in Armenia, which had an occupancy rate of 66%. The estimated daily cost to visit Yerevan, the capital, was $235. The cost of visiting other cities averaged the same.

Although there is a shortage of resources, Armenia has been investing in new hotels to increase tourism. Outdoor activities and scenery seem to be the primary attractions. Lake Sevan, the world's largest mountain lake, is a popular summer tourist spot. The Tsakhador ski resort is open year round for skiing in the winter and hiking and picnicking the rest of the year. Mt. Ararat, the reputed site of the landing of Noah's Ark, is located along the border with Turkey. Yerevan, Armenia's capital, also boasts theaters; the casinos in Argavand are popular with tourists and Albanian citizens.

⁴⁸FAMOUS PERSONS

Gregory Nare Katzi, who lived in the 10th century, was Armenia's first great poet. Nineteenth-century novelists include Hakob Maliq-Hakobian (1835?–1888), whose pen name is "Raffi," and the playwright Gabriel Sundukian (1825–1912). G. I. Gurdjieff (1872?–1949) was a Greek-Armenian mystic and teacher. Soviet aircraft designer Artem Mikuyan (1905–70) served as head of the MiG design bureau. Arshile Gorky (1904–48) was an Armenian-American abstract expressionist painter. Aram Khachaturian (1903–1978) was an Armenian composer. Levon Ter-Petrosyan (b. 1945) was president of Armenia from 1991 until 1998.

⁴⁹DEPENDENCIES

Armenia has no territories or colonies.

⁵⁰BIBLIOGRAPHY

Abrahamian, Levon, and Nancy Sweezy, eds. *Armenian Folk Arts, Culture, and Identity.* Bloomington: Indiana University Press, 2001.

Adalian, Rouben Paul. *Historical Dictionary of Armenia.* Lanham, MD: Scarecrow Press, 2002.

Armenia Investment and Business Guide: Strategic and Practical Information. Washington, DC: International Business Publications USA, 2012.

De Waal, Thomas. Black Garden: *Armenia and Azerbaijan through Peace and War.* New York: New York University Press, 2003.

Karanian, Matthew. *Edge of Time: Traveling in Armenia and Karabagh, 2nd ed.* Washington, DC: Stone Garden Productions, 2002.

Kohut, David R. *Historical Dictionary of the "Dirty Wars."* Lanham, MD: Scarecrow Press, 2003.

Libaridian, Gerard J. *Modern Armenia: People, Nation, State.* New Brunswick, NJ: Transaction Publishers, 2004.

Miller, Donald E, and Lorna T. Miller. *Armenia: Portraits of Survival and Hope.* Berkeley: University of California Press, 2003.

Seddon, David, ed. *A Political and Economic Dictionary of the Middle East.* Philadelphia: Routledge/Taylor and Francis, 2004.

World Bank. *Public Expenditure Review of Armenia.* Washington, D.C.: World Bank, 2003.

AUSTRIA

Republic of Austria
Republik Österreich

CAPITAL: Vienna (Wien)

FLAG: The flag consists of a white horizontal stripe between two red stripes.

ANTHEM: *Land der Berge, Land am Strome (Land of Mountains, Land on the River).*

MONETARY UNIT: The euro (€) replaced the schilling as the national currency in 2002. The euro is divided into 100 cents. There are coins in denominations of 1, 2, 5, 10, 20, and 50 cents and 1 euro and 2 euros. There are notes of 5, 10, 20, 50, 100, 200, and 500 euros. €1 = US$1.407 (or US$1 = €0.7107) as of 2011.

WEIGHTS AND MEASURES: The metric system is in use.

HOLIDAYS: New Year's Day, 1 January; Epiphany, 6 January; May Day, 1 May; Assumption, 15 August; National Day, 26 October; All Saints' Day, 1 November; Immaculate Conception, 8 December; Christmas, 25 December; St. Stephen's Day, 26 December. Movable religious holidays include Easter Monday, Ascension, Whitmonday, and Corpus Christi. In addition, there are provincial holidays.

TIME: 1 p.m. = noon GMT.

¹LOCATION, SIZE, AND EXTENT

Austria, with an area of 83,855 sq km (32,377 sq mi), is a landlocked country in Central Europe, extending 573 km (356 mi) E–W and 294 km (183 mi) N–S. Comparatively, Austria is slightly smaller than the state of Maine. Bounded on the N by Germany and the Czech Republic, on the E by Slovakia and Hungary, on the S by Slovenia and Italy, and on the W by Liechtenstein and Switzerland, Austria has a total boundary length of 2,562 km (1,588 mi).

While not making any territorial claims, Austria oversees the treatment of German speakers in the South Tyrol (now part of the autonomous province of Trentino-Alto Adige), which was ceded to Italy under the Treaty of Saint-Germain-en-Laye in 1919.

Austria's capital city, Vienna, is located in the northeastern part of the country.

²TOPOGRAPHY

Most of the western and southern parts are mountainous with the eastern and northern regions being mostly flat or gently sloping. Valleys and passes permit travel within the country and have made Austria an important bridge between various sections of Europe. The principal topographic regions are the Alps, constituting 62.8% of Austria's land area; the Alpine and Carpathian foothills (11.3%); the Pannonian lowlands of the east (11.3%); the granite and gneiss highlands of the Bohemian Massif (10.1%); and the Vienna Basin (4.5%). The specific landforms have resulted in small yet distinct regions, landscapes, and ecosystems.

The highest point of the Austrian Alps is the Grossglockner, 3,797 m (12,457 ft). The Danube (Donau) River, fully navigable along its 350-km (217-mi) course through northeastern Austria, is the chief waterway, and several important streams—the Inn, Enns, Drava (Drau), and Mur—are tributaries to it. Included

within Austria are many Alpine lakes, most of the Neusiedler See (the lowest point in Austria, 115 m/377 ft above sea level), and part of Lake Constance (Bodensee).

³CLIMATE

Climatic conditions can vary widely over a short range and thus depend on location and altitude. Temperatures often depend on local winds and can range from about -7 to -1°C (20 to 30°F) in winter to about 20 to 30°C (68 to 86°F) in summer. Warm, dry winds from the south, called foehns, can cause quick increases in temperature in mountain valleys in the winter. Rainfall ranges from more than 102 cm (50 in) annually in the western mountains to less than 66 cm (26 in) in the driest region, near Vienna.

⁴FLORA AND FAUNA

The World Resources Institute estimates that Austria is home to 3,100 plant species, 101 species of mammals, 412 species of birds, 16 species of reptiles, and 20 species of amphibians. This calculation reflects the total number of distinct species residing in the country, not the number of endemic species. With regard to native animal and plant species, Austria is one of the most species-rich countries in central Europe. There is a predominantly Central European fauna: deer, stag, rabbit, pheasant, fox, badger, marten, and partridge. Bird populations near the Neusiedler See include heron, spoonbill, scooper, wild goose and many more. Austria is one of Europe's most heavily wooded countries, with many deciduous (oak, beech) and alpine (fir, larch, pine) trees. The alpine climate provides a habitat for edelweiss, gentian, Alpine carnation, arnica, Alpine rose, and heather.

⁵ENVIRONMENT

The federal environmental agency, Umweltbundesamt, is responsible for all environmental issues, media, and statistics. Up until 1990 Austrians battled the problem of acid rain which damaged 25% of the country's forests. Since then the focus has turned to dealing with the health risks related to exposure to particulate matter. According to the Umweltbundesamt, exposure to air pollutants remains a considerable threat to human health, vegetation, and ecosystems. As of 2007, 31.7% of Austrians rated "greenhouse effect/Climate change" as the most pressing environmental problem while 26.2% rated "Increasing volume of traffic" as most pressing, 16.3% rated "Destruction of nature and countryside," 13.2% rated "Increasing consumption of energy and raw materials," 10.5% rated "Increasing volume of waste," and 2% did not know.

The World Resources Institute reported that Austria had placed 2.35 million hectares (5.8 million acres) of land under protection as of 2006. Water resources totaled 84 cu km (20.15 cu mi) while water usage was 3.67 cu km (.88 cu mi) per year. Domestic water usage accounted for 35% of total usage, industrial for 64%, and agricultural for 1%. Per capita water usage totaled 448 cu m (15,821 cu ft) per year. The Umweltbundesamt reported in 2010 that greenhouse gas emissions from traffic rose by 61% between 1990 and 2008. The UN reported in 2008 that carbon dioxide emissions in Austria totaled 68,674 kilotons.

Urban sprawl, transit traffic, and air pollution have had an impact on the Austrian environment. In 2009 critically endangered species included 4 species of mammals, 33 species of birds, 6 species of fish, 3 species of reptiles, 1 species of amphibians, and hundreds of other plants and insects. Endangered species include Freya's damselfly, slender-billed curlew, bald ibis, Danube salmon, and the European mink. The number of non-native species is set to increase, with 17 invasive non-native plant species and 46 non-native animal species already established as of 2004.

6 POPULATION

The US Central Intelligence Agency (CIA) estimated the population of Austria in 2011 to be approximately 8,217,280, which placed it at number 93 in population among the 196 nations of the world. The population's annual rate of change was 0.034%. In 2011 approximately 18.3% of the population was over 65 years of age, with another 14% under 15 years of age. The median age in Austria was 43 years. There were 0.95 males for every female in the country. The projected population for the year 2025 was 8,900,000. Population density in Austria was calculated at 98 people per sq km (254 people per sq mi).

The UN estimated in 2007 that 66.9% of the population lived in urban areas, and that urban populations had an annual rate of change of 0.7%. The largest urban areas was Vienna, with a population of about 1.7 million people.

7 MIGRATION

Estimates of Austria's net migration rate, carried out by the CIA in 2011, amounted to 1.81 migrants per 1,000 citizens. The total number of emigrants living abroad was 598,300, and the total number of immigrants living in Austria was 1.31 million. Every Austrian has the constitutional right to migrate. For several years after the end of World War II (1945), fairly large numbers of Austrians emigrated, mostly to Australia, Canada, and the United States, but as the economy recovered from war damage, emigration became insignificant. Austria retains the principle of the right

of asylum, and the benefits of Austrian social legislation are granted to refugees and displaced persons. Between 1945 and 1983, 1,942,782 refugees from more than 30 countries came to Austria, of whom about 590,000 became Austrian citizens (including some 302,000 German-speaking expatriates from Czechoslovakia, Romania, and Yugoslavia). Following the political upheavals in Hungary in 1956, Czechoslovakia in 1968, and Poland in 1981, Austria received large numbers of refugees from these countries: 180,432 Hungarians, about 100,000 Czechs and Slovaks, and 33,142 Poles. Between 1968 and 1986, 261,857 Jewish emigrants from the Soviet Union passed through Austria, about one-third of them going to Israel and the rest to other countries, primarily the United States. Of Austrians living abroad, some 186,900 were residents of Germany in 1991.

Between 1985 and 2001, over 254,000 foreigners were naturalized. By the end of 2004, the majority of those seeking asylum were from the Russian Federation, Serbia and Montenegro, Moldova, India, Turkey, China, and Pakistan. Approximately 16% of the asylum seekers were from the Russian Federation alone. Citizenship legislation has been changed to allow foreign spouses to become citizens only after five years of marriage to the same Austrian spouse.

8 ETHNIC GROUPS

Austrians are a people of mixed Dinaric, Nordic, Alpine, and East Baltic origin. Austria has a diverse mix of Croatians, Slovenes, Serbs, and Bosniaks (former Yugoslavs) made up about 4% of the population. Turks made up about 1.6% of the population and Germans constitute less than 1%. The Croatians, Slovenes, Slovaks, Roma, Czechs, Serbs, Bosniaks, and Hungarians are legally recognized as national minorities, a designation that allows federal funding for projects such as education and bilingual media in communities where at least 25% of the population belongs to one of these groups.

9 LANGUAGES

The official national language of German is the primary language for about 88.6% of the inhabitants; however, the Austrian Tourist Office states that 98% of the population can speak German although it may not be their first language. People in different parts of the country speak local dialects of German. People in Vorarlberg province speak German with an Alemannic accent, similar to that in Switzerland. In other provinces, Austrians speak various Bavarian dialects. Slovene is the official language in Carinthia and both Croatian (1.6%) and Hungarian are official languages in Burgenland. Turkish is spoken by about 2.3% of the population and Serbian by about 2.2%. There are also small groups of Czech, Slovak, and Polish speakers in Vienna.

10 RELIGIONS

Approximately 73.6% of Austrians are Roman Catholic, 4.7% are Protestant, 4.2% are Muslim, and 5.5 % belonged to other or non-specified faiths. About 12% of respondents claim to be atheists and 2% indicate no religious affiliation at all. The Jewish community stands at about 0.1% of the population. The Church of Scientology reportedly has somewhere between 5,000 and 7,000 members and the Unification Church has about 700 members. Other small groups within the country, which are termed as "sects" by

LOCATION: 46°22′ to 49°1′N; 9°22′ to 17°10′ E BOUNDARY LENGTHS: Germany, 784 kilometers (487 miles); Czech Republic, 362 kilometers (225 miles); Slovakia, 91 kilometers (57 miles); Hungary, 366 kilometers (227 miles); Slovenia, 330 kilometers (205 miles); Italy, 430 kilometers (267 miles); Liechtenstein, 37 kilometers (23 miles); Switzerland, 164 kilometers (102 miles).

the government, include: Hare Krishna, the Divine Light Mission, Eckankar, the Osho movement, Sai Baba, Sahaja Yoga, Fiat Lux, the Holosophic Community, Sri Chinmoy, Transcendental Meditation, and the Center for Experimental Society Formation. In a 2009, of those who stated membership in a specific church or religious groups, only 12% attended services at least once a week. About 24% attended services only on holidays and other special occasions.

Freedom of religion is guaranteed by the constitution and this right is generally respected in practice. The government is secular, but many Roman Catholic holidays are celebrated as public holidays. Religious organizations are divided into three legal categories under the 1874 Law on Recognition of Churches and the 1998 Law on the Status of Religious Confessional Communities, and each division offers a different level of rights. Those divisions are: officially recognized religious societies, religious confessional communities, and associations. Religious societies enjoy some legal benefits, and may receive federal funding to support religious teachers at both public and private schools. In 2010 there were 14 officially recognized religious societies and 10 religious confessional communities. In 2011 the Austrian atheist Niko Alm made international headlines for winning the right to wear a pasta

strainer as religious headgear on his head in his driving license picture.

[11]TRANSPORTATION

Austria has a dense and modern transportation network. The CIA reports that Austria has a total of 107,262 km (66,650 mi) of roads, of which 107,262 km (66,650 mi) are paved. There are 562 vehicles per 1,000 people in the country. Railroads extend for 5,784 km (3,594 mi). There were 55 airports, which transported 8.52 million passengers in 2009, according to the World Bank. There was also one heliport. Austria has approximately 358 km (222 mi) of navigable waterways. Most of Austria's overseas trade passes through the Italian port of Trieste; the rest is shipped from German ports. In 2008 the oceangoing merchant fleet of Austria consisted of four ships of 1,000 gross registered tons (GRT) or over.

[12]HISTORY

Human settlements have existed in what is now Austria since the Paleolithic Age. Around 400 BC, various tribes, including the Celts from Western Europe, settled in the eastern Alps. Noricum, a Celtic state, developed around the region's ironworks in the 2nd century BC. The Romans arrived shortly thereafter and by 15 BC came to dominate the entire area. The Romans founded several towns that survive today including Vindobona (Vienna) and Juvavum (Salzburg). In AD 788 Charlemagne established a territory in the Danube Valley known as Ostmark (Eastern March) and encouraged colonization and Christianity. In AD 996, Ostmark was first referred to as Ostarrichhi, a clear forerunner of the modern German word Österreich (Kingdom of the East).

From the late 13th to the early 20th century, the history of Austria is tied to that of the Habsburg (also Hapsburg) family. In 1282 Rudolf von Habsburg (Rudolf I, newly elected German emperor) gave Austria (Upper and Lower Austria, Carinthia, Styria, and Carniola) to his sons, Albrecht and Rudolf, thus inaugurating the male Habsburg succession that would continue unbroken until 1740. The highest point of Habsburg rule came in the 1500s when Emperor Maximilian I (r. 1493-1519) arranged a marriage between his son and the daughter of King Ferdinand and Queen Isabella of Spain. Maximilian's grandson became King Charles I of Spain in 1516 and, three years later, was elected Holy Roman emperor, as Charles V. Until Charles gave up his throne in 1556, he ruled over Austria, Spain, the Netherlands, and much of Italy, as well as over large possessions in the Americas. Charles gave Austria to his brother Ferdinand, who had already been elected king of Hungary and Bohemia in 1526; the Habsburgs maintained their reign over Austria, Bohemia, and Hungary until 1918.

When the last Habsburg king of Spain died in 1700, France as well as Austria laid claim to the throne. The dispute between the continental powers erupted into the War of the Spanish Succession (1701–14) and drew in other European countries in alliance with the respective claimants. At the end of the war, Austria was given control of the Spanish Netherlands (Belgium), Naples, Milan, and Sardinia. (It later lost Naples, together with Sicily, in the War of the Polish Succession, 1733–35.) In 1740, after the death of Charles VI, several German princes refused to acknowledge his daughter and only child Maria Theresa as the legitimate ruler of Austria, thus provoking the War of the Austrian Succession (1740–48). Maria Theresa lost Silesia to Prussia, but held on to her throne, from which she proceeded to institute a series of major internal reforms as ruler of Austria, Hungary, and Bohemia. After 1765 she ruled jointly with her son, Holy Roman Emperor Joseph II (r. 1765–90). Following his mother's death in 1780, Joseph, an enlightened despot, sought to abolish serfdom and introduce religious freedom, but he succeeded only in creating considerable unrest. Despite the political turmoil, Austria's cultural life flourished during this period, which spanned the careers of the composers Haydn and Mozart.

During the French revolutionary and Napoleonic wars, Austria suffered a further diminution of territory. In 1797 it gave up Belgium and Milan to France, receiving Venice, however, in recompense. In 1805 Austria lost Venice, as well as the Tyrol and part of Dalmatia, to Napoleon. Some restitution was made by the Congress of Vienna (1814–15), convened after Napoleon's defeat; it awarded Lombardy, Venetia, and Istria and restored all of Dalmatia to Austria, but it denied the Habsburgs the return of former possessions in Baden and the Netherlands.

From 1815 to 1848, Austria, under the ministry of Prince Klemens von Metternich, dominated European politics as the leading power of both the German Confederation and the Holy Alliance (Austria, Russia, and Prussia). Unchallenged abroad, the reactionary Metternich achieved peace at home through ruthless suppression of all liberal or nationalist movements among the people in the Habsburg Empire. In 1848, however, revolutions broke out in Hungary and Bohemia and in Vienna itself. Metternich resigned and fled to London. Although the revolutions were crushed, Emperor Ferdinand I abdicated in December. He was succeeded by his 18-year-old nephew Franz Josef I, who was destined to occupy the Austrian throne for 68 years until his death in 1916. During his reign Austria attempted to set up a strong central government that would unify all the Habsburg possessions under its leadership. But nationalist tensions persisted, exacerbated by outside interference. In 1859, in a war over Habsburg-controlled Lombardy, French and Sardinian troops defeated the Austrians, ending Austrian preeminence in Italian politics. In 1866 Prussia forced Austria out of the political affairs of Germany after the Seven Weeks' War. In 1867 Hungarian nationalists, taking advantage of Austria's weakened state, compelled Franz Josef to sign an agreement giving Hungary equal rights with Austria. In the ensuing dual monarchy, the Austrian Empire and the Kingdom of Hungary were united under one ruler. Each country had its own national government, but both shared responsibility for foreign affairs, defense, and finance. Self-government for the empire's Magyar (Hungarian) population was balanced by continued suppression of the Slavs.

On 28 June 1914, at Sarajevo, Serbian patriots, who were members of the Slavic movement, assassinated Archduke Francis Ferdinand, the nephew of the emperor and heir to the Austrian throne. Their act set off World War I, in which Austria-Hungary was joined by Germany (an ally since 1879), Italy (a member, with the first two, of the Triple Alliance of 1882), and Turkey. They became known as the Central Powers. In 1915 Italy defected to the side of the Allies—France, Russia, the United Kingdom, and (from 1917) the United States. After the defeat of the Central Powers and the collapse of their empires in 1918, Austria, now reduced to its German-speaking sections, was proclaimed a republic. The Treaty of Saint-Germain-en-Laye (1919) fixed the borders of the new state and forbade it any kind of political or economic union with Germany without League of Nations approval.

During the next decade, Austria was plagued by inflation, food shortages, unemployment, financial scandals, and, as a consequence, growing political unrest. The country's two major political groupings, the Christian Socialist Party and the Social Democratic Party, were almost equal in strength, with their own private paramilitary movements. A small Austrian Nazi party, advocating union with Germany, constituted a third group. In March 1933 Chancellor Engelbert Dollfuss, leader of the Christian Socialists, dissolved the Austrian parliament, suspended the democratic constitution of 1920, and ruled by decree, hoping to control the unrest. In February 1934 civil strife erupted; government forces broke up the opposition Social Democratic Party, executing or imprisoning many persons. Dollfuss thereupon established an authoritarian corporate state along Fascist lines. On 25 July the Nazis, emboldened by Adolf Hitler's rise in Germany, assassinated Dollfuss in an abortive coup. Kurt von Schuschnigg, who had served under Dollfuss as minister of justice and education, then became chancellor. For the next four years Schuschnigg struggled to keep Austria independent amid growing German pressure for annexation (Anschluss). On 11 March 1938, however, German troops entered the country, and two days later Austria was proclaimed a part of the German Reich. In 1939 Austria, now known as Ostmark, entered World War II as part of the Axis alliance.

Allied troops entered Austria in April 1945, and the country was divided into US, British, French, and Soviet zones of occupation. Declaring the 1920 constitution in force, the occupying powers permitted Austrians to set up a provisional government, but limited Austrian sovereignty under an agreement of 1946. Austria made effective use of foreign economic aid during the early postwar years. The United States and the United Kingdom supplied $379 million worth of goods between 1945 and 1948; another $110 million was provided by private organizations; and Marshall Plan aid amounted to $962 million. Inflation was checked by the early 1950s, and for most of the remainder of that decade the economy sustained one of the world's highest growth rates.

On 15 May 1955, after more than eight years of negotiations, representatives of Austria and the four powers signed, at Vienna, the Austrian State Treaty, reestablishing an independent and democratic Austria, and in October all occupation forces withdrew from the country. Under the treaty, Austria agreed to become permanently neutral. As a neutral nation Austria has remained outside the political and military alliances into which postwar Europe was divided. Economically, however, it began to develop close links with Western Europe, joining the European Free Trade Association (EFTA) in 1960 and concluding free-trade agreements with the European Economic Community (now the European Union) in 1972. Because of its location, Austria served as an entrepôt between the Western trade blocs and the Council for Mutual Economic Assistance (CMEA), with which it also had trade relations. Austria was twice the site of US-USSR summit meetings. In June 1961, President John F. Kennedy and Premier Nikita S. Khrushchev conferred in Vienna, and in June 1979, presidents Jimmy Carter and Leonid I. Brezhnev signed a strategic arms limitation agreement in the Austrian capital. Austria joined the European Union in 1995 and European Economic and Monetary Union in 1999.

On 8 July 1986, following elections in May and June, former UN Secretary-General Kurt Waldheim was sworn in as president of Austria. During the presidential campaign, Waldheim was accused of having belonged to Nazi organizations during World War II and of having taken part in war crimes while stationed in Greece and Yugoslavia with the German army from 1942 to 1945; he denied the charges. After his inauguration, diplomats of many nations made a point of avoiding public contact with the new president, and on 27 April 1987, the US Justice Department barred him from entering the United States. To the dismay of many leaders, Pope John Paul II granted Waldheim an audience at the Vatican on 25 June.

Waldheim declined to run for a second term, and in July 1992 Thomas Klestil was elected federal president. He was reelected on 19 April 1998. Relations with Israel, which had been strained under Waldheim's presidency, returned to normal.

The growing strength of Austria's Freedom Party, headed by Jörg Haider, was evidence of a turn to the right in Austrian politics. Although the party did not capture the votes it wanted to in the 17 December 1995 legislative elections, in the elections for European Parliament on 14 October 1996 the aggressively nationalist, anti-immigrant, anti-European Freedom Party took 28% of the vote, 2% behind the Social Democrats. The People's Party and Social Democrats remained together in a coalition throughout the 1990s and prepared Austria for entry into the European Economic and Monetary Union. Cautious reforms took place. The administration privatized state-owned enterprises, brought down inflation to less than 1% in 1998, and reduced the budget deficit to 2%. Average growth rates between 1997 and 2000 were over 2%. Unemployment fell to 4% in 2000. However, the global economic downturn that began in 2001 caused Austria's economy to suffer; coupled with costs resulting from severe flooding in August 2002, Austria's budget deficit increased sharply. In 2004–05 the economy rebounded: GDP growth was once again at 2%, allowing Austria to retain its position among the top European economies.

The Freedom Party scored a triumph in the general election of October 1999, coming in second behind the Social Democrats with 27% of the vote. After the traditional coalition of Social Democrats and the conservative People's Party failed to reach agreement on the next government in early 2000, the leader of the People's Party, Wolfgang Schüssel, turned to Haider and the Freedom Party to form a new administration. President Klestil had no choice but to accept the new coalition agreement. Its installation on 3 February 2000 provoked widespread protests both within Austria and from other members of the European Union. The EU partners decided to boycott Austria in all official meetings, a decision that caused a severe crisis in the European Union itself. Haider resigned as party chairman in April 2000 although he remained governor of Carinthia. His withdrawal from federal politics did not soften the views of the European Union, which imposed diplomatic sanctions on Austria. (They were lifted in September 2000.)

Following the 11 September 2001 terrorist attacks on the United States, Austria passed a Security and Defense Doctrine, representing a shift in Austria's longstanding policy of neutrality. Although Austria would not agree to participate in military alliances requiring mutual defense commitments, the country expected to gradually move towards closer integration with European security structures, which would allow for participation in the European Union rapid reaction force and NATO's Partnership for Peace program.

A power struggle within the Freedom Party between Haider and Austria's Vice-Chancellor and Freedom Party chair Susanne Riess-Passer in September 2002 resulted in Riess-Passer's resignation, along with that of two Freedom Party ministers. The People's Party/Freedom Party coalition government collapsed and new elections were called for 24 November 2002. In those elections, Schüssel's People's Party made wide gains; the Freedom Party suffered a major defeat. It dropped to 10% of the vote, down from its 2000 showing of 27%. Despite these results, and after failed negotiations with the Social Democrats and Greens, Schüssel formed a coalition government with the Freedom Party, which was sworn in on 1 April 2003. Schüssel subsequently moved closer to the right, notably on asylum and immigration issues (in October 2003, his government introduced a package of asylum legislation which are seen as the most restrictive in Europe). In April 2005 the Freedom Party split when Haider left to form the Alliance for Austria's Future. Members of both groups remain in government.

In April 2004, Heinz Fischer was elected president. In May 2005, the Austrian parliament ratified the EU constitution. However, the rejection of that constitution by the French and Dutch in referenda held later in May and June 2005 doomed the plan for further European integration indefinitely.

Legislative elections were held in October 2006. The Social Democrats led by Alfred Gusenbauer narrowly defeated the ruling conservative People's Party in elections. After weeks of bargaining, the Social Democrats and the People's Party agreed on a coalition government, which went into effect in January 2007 with Gusenbauer taking the post of federal chancellor on 11 January 2007. Wilhelm Molterer took the post as vice chancellor. The agreement for a coalition government turned sour in July 2008. After months of stalemate disputes, the People's Party vice chancellor announced that the party was quitting the government and called for new elections. The Social Democratic Party of Austria (as it became known) won the September 2008 elections. However, large gains were made by the Freedom Party and the Alliance for the Future of Austria. The shift was attributed in part to a larger pool of young voters, as the minimum voting age for the election was dropped to 16. The results also reflected growing anti-immigration sentiments. The far-right was blamed for higher consumer costs on higher numbers of immigrants and foreign competition.

[13] GOVERNMENT

Austria is a federal republic governed under the constitution of 1920, as amended in 1929, with a mixed presidential-parliamentary form of government. The president, who is head of state and commander in chief of the armed forces, is elected by popular vote for a six-year term and may serve any number of terms but no more than two in a row. Generally, the president appoints the federal chancellor (*Bundeskanzler*) from the political party with the most seats in the Nationalrat (National Council). The chancellor, who is head of government, makes cabinet recommendations to the president. The president in turn appoints ministers to make up the Council of Ministers who head government departments and, with the chancellor, formulate and direct national policy. The chancellor and the Council of Ministers are responsible to the Nationalrat which may force the chancellor and ministers to resign with a vote of no confidence.

The federal assembly, known as the Bundesversammlung, consists of the Nationalrat and Bundesrat (Federal Council). The Bundesrat has 62 members, elected by the country's unicameral provincial legislatures (*Landtage*) in proportion to the population of each province. The Nationalrat has 183 members (prior to 1970, 165 members), elected directly in nine election districts for four-year terms by secret ballot on the basis of proportional representation. All citizens 25 years of age or older are eligible to serve in the assembly. As of 2007 all citizens 16 years of age or older may vote. All legislation originates in the Nationalrat; the Bundesrat exercises only a suspensory veto.

[14] POLITICAL PARTIES

The restoration of the republic in 1945 revived political activity in Austria. In general elections that November, the Austrian People's Party (Österreichische Volkspartei–ÖVP), successor to the prewar Christian Socialists, emerged as the strongest party, with the reborn Socialist Party of Austria (Sozialistische Partei Öster-

reichs–SPÖ) trailing slightly. The ÖVP and SPÖ, controlling 161 of the 165 seats in the Nationalrat, formed a coalition government and worked closely with the Allies to construct an independent and democratic Austria. This coalition held until after the elections of 1966, when the ÖVP, with a majority of 11 seats, formed a one-party government headed by Chancellor Josef Klaus. In 1970, the SPÖ won a plurality in the Nationalrat and was able to put together a minority Socialist government under its leader, Bruno Kreisky. Kreisky remained in power until 1983-longer than any other non-Communist European head of government. The Socialist Party was renamed the Social Democratic Party in 1991, and began to advocate free-market oriented policies. It supported Austria's entry into the European Community (now European Union).

The ÖVP, also referred to as Austria's Christian Democratic Party, favors free enterprise, competition, and the reduction of class differences. Organized into three constituencies-businessmen, farmers, and employees-it advocates provincial rights and strongly supports the Catholic Church. The SPÖ, also known as the Social Democratic Party, advocates moderate reforms through democratic processes. It favored continued nationalization of key industries, economic planning, and widespread social welfare benefits. It is closely allied with the Austrian Trade Union Federation and its constituent unions. The economic policy differences between the two parties diminished in the 1990s as both recognized the need to introduce structural reforms and bring down budget deficits. Their main disagreements are on the pace of change, rather than on the need to introduce reforms.

A third political group, the Union of Independents (Verband der Unabhängigen—VdU), appeared in 1949. Strongly antisocialist, with anticlerical, pan-German elements, it challenged the coalition in the elections of that year, winning 16 seats. By the mid-1950s, however, the VdU, consistently denied a voice in government by the two major parties, had begun to disintegrate. In 1955, it was reorganized, under new leadership, as the Freedom Party of Austria (Freiheitliche Partei Österreichs—FPÖ). In 1970, with six seats in the Nationalrat, the FPÖ was accepted as a negotiating partner by the SPÖ. The party favors individual initiative over collective security. By the turn of the 21st century, under the leadership of Jörg Haider, the FPÖ was an extreme nationalist, anti-immigrant, anti-European party. In June 1992 FPÖ dissidents founded the Free Democratic Party. In 2005 Haider split from the FPÖ to form the Alliance for the Future of Austria (BZÖ).

The Communist Party of Austria (Kommunistische Partei Österreichs—KPÖ) has declined steadily in strength since the end of World War II. It has had no parliamentary representation, for example, since 1959, when it lost the three seats won in 1956. The KPÖ was the first party in the Nationalrat to propose, in 1953, that Austria become a neutral nation.

In the elections of 24 April 1983, dominated by economic issues, the SPÖ (with 47.8% of the vote) won 90 seats, down from 95 in 1979; the ÖVP (with 43.21%) 81; and the FPÖ (with 4.97%) 12. The KPÖ polled 0.66% of the vote but won no seats. Two new environmentalist groups, the United Greens of Austria (Vereinten Grünen Österreichs) and the Alternative List-Austria (Alternative Liste Österreichs), likewise failed to gain representation in the Nationalrat. In May, Kreisky, having failed to win a clear majority, resigned. He was succeeded as party leader and chancellor by Fred Sinowatz, who proceeded to form a coalition government with the FPÖ.

Following the election of Kurt Waldheim to the presidency in June 1986, Sinowatz resigned and was succeeded by Franz Vranitzky, a former finance minister. The SPÖ-FPÖ coalition broke down in September 1986. Following parliamentary elections on 23 November 1986, a new government was sworn in on 21 January 1987, with Vranitzky from the SPÖ as chancellor and Alois Mock, FPÖ chairman, as vice-chancellor and prime minister.

In the general election of 7 October 1990, the "grand coalition" continued. The 183 seats in the Nationalrat were distributed as follows: SPÖ (80), ÖVP (60), FPÖ (33), and the Green Alternative (10). It also governed after the 1995 elections.

The 1999 elections finally brought change and was a watershed event. In the legislative election held on 3 October 1999, the 183 seats in the Nationalrat were distributed as follows: SPÖ (65), ÖVP (52), FPÖ (52), Greens (14), and Liberal Forum (0). Compared to the 1995 elections, the SPÖ lost 6 seats, the Liberal Forum lost all of its 10 seats and had no representation in the new assembly, the ÖVP retained more or less its share of the vote, while the Greens went from 9 to 14 seats and the FPÖ went from 40 seats to 52 seats and became, together, with the People's Party, the second-largest bloc in the assembly. The leader of the ÖVP, Wolfgang Schüssel, formed a coalition with the FPÖ, and became chancellor.

Following the 24 November 2002 elections, party strength in the Nationalrat was distributed as follows: ÖVP, 42.3% (79 seats); SPÖ, 36.5% (69 seats); FPÖ, 10% (18 seats); the Greens, 9.5% (17 seats); the Liberal Forum, 1% (no seats); and the KPÖ, 0.6% (no seats). Schüssel remained chancellor, and formed a government with the FPÖ, as he was unable to persuade the SPÖ and the Greens to join in a coalition with the ÖVP.

In the presidential election held on 25 April 2004, Heinz Fischer of the SPÖ was elected president with 52.4% of the vote, defeating Benita Ferrero-Waldner of the ÖVP (47.6% of the vote). Fischer succeeded Thomas Klestil, who had served as president since 1992.

On 1 October 2006 legislative elections were held. The SPÖ bested the ÖVP, winning 68 seats and 35.7% of the vote, to the ÖVP's 66 seats and 34.2% of the vote. The Greens won 21 seats and 11% of the vote, placing them as the third largest political party for the first time. The Freedom Party won 11% of the vote and 21 seats. Haider's Alliance for the Future of Austria (BZÖ) won 4.1% of the vote, and 7 seats in the Nationalrat. Voter turnout was 78.5%.

The coalition government agreement turned sour in July 2008. The OVP vice-chancellor announced that the party was quitting the government and called for new elections. The Social Democratic Party of Austria again won the highest percentage of votes in the September 2008 elections at 29.3%, followed by the OVP with 26%. However, large gains were made by far-right parties, primarily the Freedom Party (17.5%) and the Alliance for the Future of Austria (10.7%).

In the April 2010 presidential election, Heinz Fischer was re-elected with 79.3% of the vote, defeating the Freedom Party candidate, Barbara Rosenkrantz (15.2%) and Christian Party candidate Rudolf Gehring (5.4%).

15 LOCAL GOVERNMENT

Austria is divided into nine provinces (*Bundesländer*): Vienna (Wien), Lower Austria (Niederösterreich), Upper Austria (Oberösterreich), Styria (Steiermark), Carinthia (Kärnten), Tyrol (Tirol), Salzburg, Burgenland, and Vorarlberg. The relationship between the provinces and the central government is defined by the constitution. Most administrative, legislative, and judicial authority-including taxation, welfare, and police-is granted to the central government. The Bundersländer, which enjoy all residual powers, act as executors of federal authority.

Each province has its own unicameral legislature (*Landtag*), elected on the basis of proportional representation. People in each province elect legislative members to either five or six-year terms, depending on the province. Each Landtag chooses the provincial governor (*Landeshauptmann*). All legislation must be submitted through the provincial governor to the competent federal ministry for concurrence. If such concurrence is not obtained, the provincial legislature can reinstate the bill by majority vote. In case of prolonged conflict between the federal authorities and the provincial legislatures, the Constitutional Court may be appealed to for settlement.

The provincial governor is assisted by a cabinet (*Landesrat*) consisting of ministries analogous to those at the federal level. Each province is divided into several administrative districts (*Bezirke*), each of which is under a district commissioner (*Bezirkshauptmann*). Local self-government is vested in popularly elected communal councils which, in turn, elect various local officers, including the mayor (*Bürgermeister*) and his deputies. There are some 2,300 communities in Austria, as well as 15 cities that have independent charters and fall directly under provincial authority rather than that of the districts. Vienna is both a municipality and a province.

16 JUDICIAL SYSTEM

Austria in 2005 had 140 local courts (*Bezirksgerichte*) with civil jurisdiction. There were also 20 provincial and district courts (*Landesgerichte* and *Kreisgerichte*) with civil and criminal jurisdiction and four higher provincial courts (*Oberlandesgerichte*) with criminal jurisdiction, located in Vienna, Graz, Innsbruck, and Linz. The Supreme Court of Justice of Austria (Oberster Gerichtshof und Generalprokuratur Österreich), in Vienna, acts as the final appellate court for criminal and civil cases. The constitutional court (*Verfassungsgerichtshof*) has supreme jurisdiction over constitutional and civil rights issues. The administrative court (*Verwaltungsgerichtshof*) ensures the legal functioning of public administration. A central auditing authority controls financial administration. Judges are appointed by the federal government and cannot be removed or transferred. Trial by jury was reintroduced in 1951. There is no capital punishment.

The judiciary is independent of the other branches. Judges are appointed for life and can only be removed for specific reasons established by law and only after formal court action has been taken.

Prior to the mid 1990s, the law allowed for detention of suspects for 48 hours without judicial review and up to two years of detention during the course of a criminal investigation. Amendments to the law in 1994 required more stringent judicial review of pre-trial and investigative detention. Criminal defendants are afforded a presumption of innocence, public trials, and jury trial for major offenses, as well as a number of other procedural rights.

¹⁷ARMED FORCES

Austrian men must serve at least six months in the army. Women may voluntarily enlist in the army. The International Institute for Strategic Studies reports that armed forces in Austria totaled 25,900 members in 2011. The force is comprised of 12,800 from the army, 2,900 from the air force, and 10,200 members of support staff. Armed forces represent 0.6% of the labor force in Austria. Defense spending totaled $2.7 billion and accounted for 0.8% of gross domestic product (GDP).

In 2011 Austrian armed forces deployed few than 1,500 service members to 13 countries or regions under UN, NATO, or European Union command.

¹⁸INTERNATIONAL COOPERATION

The Federal Constitutional Law on the Neutrality of Austria, adopted on 26 October 1955, bound the nation to neutrality and banned it from joining any military alliances or permitting the establishment of foreign military bases on its territory. However, since 1995, the country has reconsidered this position on neutrality. In December 2001, Austria adopted a Security and Defense Doctrine; although Austria will not participate in military alliances requiring mutual defense commitments, the country is gradually moving toward greater integration with European security arrangements, which would allow for participation in the EU rapid reaction force and NATO's Partnership for Peace program.

Austria became a member of the UN on 14 December 1955. It is a member of ECE and all the non-regional specialized agencies, such as FAO, IFC, ILO, WHO, and the World Bank. The country became a member of the WTO 1 January 1995 and of the OSCE on 30 January 1992. Vienna has served an important role as a meeting place and headquarters site for a variety of international activities. The headquarters of OPEC, IAEA, UNIDO, and the International Institute for Applied Systems Analysis are located in Vienna. Austria belongs to the Council of Europe, the OECD, the Paris Club, the European Space Agency, and the European Union. Austria's interest in the Third World is exemplified by membership in the Asian and Inter-American development banks and by its permanent observer status with the OAS.

Austria is part of the Australia Group, the Zangger Committee, and the Organization for the Prohibition of Chemical Weapons. Austrian troops have been part of UN peacekeeping forces in Kosovo (est. 1999), Western Sahara (est. 1991), Ethiopia and Eritrea (est. 2000), Georgia (est. 1993), and Cyprus (est. 1964).

In environmental cooperation, the country is part of the Antarctic Treaty; the Basel Convention; Conventions on Biological Diversity, Whaling, and Air Pollution; Ramsar; CITES; the International Tropical Timber Agreements; the Kyoto Protocol; the Montréal Protocol; MARPOL; and the Nuclear Test Ban Treaty.

¹⁹ECONOMY

The GDP rate of change in Austria, as of 2010, was 2%. Inflation stood at 1.9%, and unemployment was reported at 4.5%.

Austria is part of the European Union and has benefited from close economic ties with its neighboring countries, especially Germany. The social market economy is well developed and Austrians

enjoy a generally high standard of living. Services account for the largest sector of the economy.

Austria's period of unparalleled prosperity lasted from the 1950s through the early 1970s; the economy was characterized by a high rate of growth, modest price increases, and a favorable climate in industrial relations. By 1975 Austrian industry, the single most important sector of the economy, had more than quadrupled in value over 1945. But the general economic slowdown that followed the oil price hike of late 1973 affected Austria as it did other European countries.

Liberalization inspired by the European Union and greater acceptance of the values of competition have transformed Austria's economy since the 1980s. Previously, the state maintained a strong presence in the Austrian economy, but in the 21st century private enterprise increasingly takes on a primary position. Basic industries, including mineral production, heavy industry, rail and water transport, and utilities, were nationalized during 1946–47 and in 1970 were reorganized under a state-owned holding company, the Austrian Industrial Administration (Österreichische Industrieverwaltungs-Aktiengesellschaft—ÖIAG). In 1986 the ÖIAG was renamed the Österreichische Industrieholding AG, and a process of restructuring and privatization took place that traversed the 1990s and early 2000s. German companies in particular took advantage of the privatization of Austrian firms.

Following the mild recession in 1993, Austria's economy-driven by strong exports, investment, and private consumption-expanded an average of 2% throughout the 1990s. After a period of low growth of only around 1.0% annually during 2001–03, Austria's economy recovered again in 2004 and 2005 and grew 2.5% and 2.9%, respectively, driven by booming exports in response to strong world economic growth. Primarily due to higher growth in Europe, particularly Central and Eastern Europe, and continued export growth, Austrian real GDP grew 3.3% in 2006 and 3.4% in 2007. Public debt in 2007 was estimated at 59.3% of the GDP. The strong economic growth helped reduce Austria's unemployment rate to 4.4% in 2007. Predictions were for the economy to grow 2.2–2.3% in 2008 and 1.4–1.9% in 2009.

Trade with other EU-27 countries accounts for about 73% of Austrian imports and exports. A major element of Austrian economic activity is expanding trade and investment in the new EU members of Central and Eastern Europe that joined the European Union in May 2004 and January 2007. Austrian firms had sizable investments in these countries and continued to move labor-intensive, low-tech production there.

Though the global financial crisis of 2008–09 set the nation in recession, the passage of two major economic stimulus packages and the initiation of tax reforms in the first half of 2009 stabilized the economy somewhat and limited the decline in economic growth to a decrease of 2.1%. A third stimulus package was proposed in August 2009, but was rejected by the government finance minister as unnecessary.

²⁰INCOME

The CIA estimated that in 2010 the GDP of Austria was $332 billion. The CIA defines GDP as the value of all final goods and services produced within a nation in a given year and computed on the basis of purchasing power parity (PPP) rather than value as measured on the basis of the rate of the exchange based on current dollars. The per capita GDP was estimated at $40,400. The annual growth rate of GDP was 2%. The average inflation rate was 1.9%. It was estimated that agriculture accounted for 1.5% of GDP, industry 29.3%, and services 69.2%.

According to the World Bank, remittances from citizens living abroad totaled $3.3 billion or about $400 per capita and accounted for approximately 1% of GDP.

The World Bank reported that in 2009, household consumption in Austria totaled $207 billion or about $25,191 per capita, measured in current US dollars rather than PPP. Household consumption included expenditures of individuals, households, and nongovernmental organizations on goods and services, excluding the purchases of dwellings. It was estimated that household consumption was growing at an average annual rate of 1.3%.

The World Bank estimates that Austria, with 0.13% of the world's population, accounted for 0.51% of the world's GDP. By comparison, the United States, with 4.85% of the world's population, accounted for 22.51% of world GDP.

As of 2011, the most recent study by the World Bank reported that actual individual consumption in Austria was 67.4% of GDP and accounted for 0.52% of world consumption. By comparison, the United States accounted for 25.44% of world individual consumption. The World Bank also estimated that 7.8% of Austria's GDP was spent on food and beverages, 16% on housing and household furnishings, 3.7% on clothes, 6.9% on health, 7.6% on transportation, 1.5% on communications, 7.2% on recreation, 6.9% on restaurants and hotels, and 4.3% on miscellaneous goods and services and purchases from abroad.

It was estimated that in 2008 about 6% of the population subsisted on an income below the poverty line established by Austria's government.

21 LABOR

As of 2010 Austria had a total labor force of 3.648 million people. Within that labor force, the CIA estimates noted that 5.5% were employed in agriculture, 27.5% in industry, and 67% in the service sector in 2009. The unemployment rate was estimated at 4.5%.

As of 2005 workers were organized into 13 trade unions affiliated in the Austrian Trade Union Federation (Österreichische Gewerkschaftsbund—ÖGB), accounting for an estimated 47% of the nation's workforce. This confederation negotiates collective bargaining agreements with the Federal Economic Chamber (Bundeskammer der gewerblichen Wirtschaft), representing employers. Although the right to strike is recognized, strikes are rarely used due to cooperation between labor and management. Collective bargaining is prevalent. Disputes over wages, working hours, working conditions, and vacations are settled by a labor court or an arbitration board.

The workweek is set at a maximum of 40 hours, although most Austrian workers put in 38–38.5 hours per week. A 50% differential is generally paid for overtime on weekdays, 100% on Sundays and holidays. In addition, it is required that an employee be given at least 11 hours off between workdays. There is no national minimum wage. Most employees are covered by collective bargaining agreements, which set wages by industry. However, the unofficial accepted minimum is $14,880 to $17,360 per year, which provides a family with a decent standard of living. The minimum legal age for employment is 15 years, and this is effectively enforced.

22 AGRICULTURE

Although small, the agricultural sector is highly diversified and efficient due to the use of modern machinery and scientific farming methods. Most production is oriented toward local consumption. Roughly 17% of the total land is farmed, and the county's major crops include grains, apples, potatoes, wine, and vegetables.

The best cropland is in the east in the Vienna Basin, which has the most level terrain. Farms are almost exclusively family-owned. Most holdings are small or medium-sized and, in many cases, scattered.

The use of farm machinery has been increasing steadily. Austria today uses less land and manpower and produces more food than it did before World War II (1939–45). Better seeding and more intensive and efficient application of fertilizers have helped raise farm yields and have enhanced self-sufficiency in foodstuffs. Agriculture is highly protected by the government; overproduction, especially evidenced by recurring grain surpluses, requires a hefty subsidy to be paid by the government in order to sell abroad at market prices. Nevertheless, the Austrian government has been able to maintain farm income, although Austria has some of the highest food costs in Europe.

Austria is near self-sufficiency in wheat, oats, rye, fruits, vegetables, sugar, and a number of other items.

23 ANIMAL HUSBANDRY

Dairy and livestock production takes place in geographical areas unfit for raising crops. Milk, butter, cheese, and meat are excellent, and Austria is self-sufficient in dairy products and in most meats. The UN Food and Agriculture Organization (FAO) reported that Austria dedicated 1.7 million hectares (4.28 million acres) to permanent pasture or meadow in 2009. During that year, the country tended 14.5 million chickens, 2 million head of cattle, and 3.1 million pigs. The production from these animals amounted to 14,135 tons of beef and veal, 548,564 tons of pork, 145,241 tons of poultry, 115,699 tons of eggs, and 1.95 million tons of milk. Austria also produced 23,100 tons of cattle hide and 256 tons of raw wool.

By specializing in quality strains of cattle, hogs, and horses, Austrian breeders have gained wide international recognition. Livestock products, primarily milk, account for about 35% of agricultural exports. Dairy and livestock breeding, traditionally the major agricultural activities, account for about three-fifths of gross agricultural income.

24 FISHING

Fishing is not important commercially, and fish do not constitute a large part of the Austrian diet. Commercial catches consist mainly of carp and trout. In 2008 the annual capture totaled 350 tons according to the UN FOA. Aquacultural production in 2003 was 2,233 tons, mostly rainbow trout. A sizable segment of the population engages in sport fishing.

25 FORESTRY

Austria has the second-largest percentage of forest in the European Union. About 47% of Austria's total area is forested, mostly in the foothills and mountains. Styria, in the southeast, is 60% covered with forests, while Burgenland in the east has only 32% forest coverage. About two thirds of the trees are coniferous, primarily spruce; beech is the most important broadleaf type.

Austria's rich, dense forests provide plentiful lumber, paper, and other products. Over-cutting during World War II (1939–45) and in the postwar period resulted in a decline in timber production from 9.5 million cu m (335 million cu ft) in 1936 to a low of about 7.1 million cu m (251 million cu ft). From 1950 to 2003, sawn lumber output rose from 4,000 cu m (141,000 cu ft) to 10.5 million cu m (370.7 million cu ft). Competition reduced the number of sawmills from 5,100 in 1950 to 1,400 in 2003, with about 10,000 employees. Bark beetle infestations adversely affected production in the mid-1990s. The UN FAO estimated the 2009 roundwood production at 12.1 million cu m (428.9 million cu ft).

To prevent overcutting, export restrictions have been introduced, strict conservation laws have been enacted, and reforestation on both public and private land is compulsory. Exports of raw timber and cork are supplemented by exports of such forestry products as paper, cardboard boxes, prefabricated houses, toys, matches, turpentine, and volatile oils. Austria is the world's fourth-largest softwood lumber exporter. The value of all forest products, including roundwood, totaled $6.41 billion in 2009.

26 MINING

After a period of postwar expansion, mineral production has stagnated, and metals mining continues to decline, because of high operating costs, increased foreign competition, low ore grades, and environmental problems. All the metal mines in the country have been closed, except an iron ore operation at Erzberg (producing 1.5 million tons of iron ore and concentrate in 2009) and a tungsten operation at Mittersill, which is the only other metal mine still operating in Austria. Most of the growth in the mineral resources area is in the production of industrial minerals, the area in which future mining activities will most likely be concentrated, mostly for domestic consumption.

Austria is one of the world's largest sources of high-grade graphite. In 2009 estimated output was 250 metric tons. The country produces 1.5% of the world's talc, with a reported output in 2009 of 150,000 tons of crude talc and soapstone. That year, the country's only producer of talc, Luzenac Naintsch AG, operated three mines, in the Styria region, and produced a range of talc, chloritic talc, dolomite talc, and chlorite-mica-quartz ores.

Output of other minerals in 2009 included: limestone and marble, 23 million metric tons; dolomite, 4 million metric tons, for the domestic cement industry, along with calcite and limestone; gypsum and anhydrite, 1,950,000 metric tons; brine salt, 3,500,000 cubic meters (salt mines are owned by the government); tungsten, 1,000 tons; and crude kaolin, 40,000 metric tons. Crude magnesite production was reported at 750,000 metric tons in 2009.

Lignite production has been declining since 1963. In 2009 coke production totaled 1,300,000 metric tons. Production of bituminous coal declined steadily after World War II, and in 1968 ceased altogether.

27 ENERGY AND POWER

Due to Austria's mountains and swift flowing rivers, it is one of the foremost producers of hydroelectric power in Europe. The most important power facilities are publicly owned; 50% of the shares of the large private producers are owned by provincial governments.

The World Bank reported in 2008 that Austria produced 64.4 billion kWh of electricity and consumed 68.5 billion kWh, or 8,338 kWh per capita. Roughly 72% of energy came from fossil fuels, while 11% came from alternative fuels. Per capita oil consumption was 3,988 kg. Oil production totaled 16,745 barrels of oil a day. During the winter, when there is less flowing water for hydroelectric power, domestic electricity demands must be supplemented by imports from neighboring countries.

Oil, first produced in 1863, is found both in Upper Austria, near Wolfsegg am Hausruck, and in Lower Austria, in the vicinity of Vienna. After reaching a peak of about 3,700,000 tons in 1955, oil production gradually declined to 22,000 barrels per day in 2000. Natural gas production was 1.698 billion cu m (60 billion cu ft) in 1998, far short of domestic needs; consumption amounted to 6.862 billion cu m (242 billion cu ft) in that year.

In April 2010 Austria agreed to back the South Stream natural gas pipeline, a joint venture between Russia's Gazprom and Italy's Eni energy corporations. The pipeline was designed to supply natural gas from Russia to several southern and eastern European countries, including Austria, via an undersea pipeline in the Black Sea. Previously, Austrian officials had backed only the rival Nabucco pipeline project, which was supported by the European Union and the United States and completely bypassed Russia.

28 INDUSTRY

Industrial output has increased vastly since the beginning of World War II, and contributed to 29.3% of the GDP in 2010. In 1946 the federal assembly nationalized basic industries. Major parts of the electric and electronics, chemical, iron and steel, and machinery industries remained state controlled until the 1990s, when the Austrian government embarked upon a privatization program. As of 2005 the steel, aluminum, and petroleum industries were majority-owned by private shareholders. Other privatizations in the early 2000s were the Austrian tobacco company, the Vienna airport company, Telekom Austria, Voest-Alpine Steel, and Boehler Uddeholm, an important tool and specialty steel manufacturer.

Iron and steel production greatly expanded its output after 1937. A total of 155,403 automobiles were manufactured in 2001 and 24,988 heavy trucks were produced in 2000. The sale of automotive parts and equipment was a $3 billion industry in 2004, albeit a decline from $3.35 billion in 2003 and $3.87 billion in 2002.

The chemical industry, which was relatively unimportant before World War II, ranks second in value of production, behind the mechanical and steel industry. Other leading industries, in terms of production value and employment, are electrical and electronic machinery and equipment, pulp and paper products, ceramics, furniture, chemical products, cement, textiles, and especially foodstuffs and allied products. Austria, with its focus on high quality products as opposed to high quantity, has always been famous for its skilled craftsmen, such as glassblowers, goldsmiths, jewelers, lacemakers, potters, stonecutters, and wood-carvers. The world famous Swarovski crystal is one of Austria's most well known products.

The country has taken steps to change its image from one in which traditional "rust belt" industries such as steel and heavy engineering dominate. The electronics, biotechnology, and medical and pharmaceutical sectors have been high growth industries throughout the 2000s. In 2011 Austria ranked 19th on INSEAD's Global Innovation Index.

29 SCIENCE AND TECHNOLOGY

Numerous research institutes in Austria play an important role in conducting and coordinating advanced agricultural, medical, scientific, and technical research. The Austrian Research Council supports and coordinates scientific research. The major learned society is the Austrian Academy of Sciences (founded in 1847 and headquartered in Vienna). The Austrian Science Foundation (founded in 1967) and the Austrian Industrial Research Fund together form the Austrian Research Council, which supports and coordinates scientific, applied, and industrial research and development and advises federal and state governments on scientific matters. The Natural History Museum and the Trade and Industrial Museum of Technology, both in Vienna and founded in 1748 and 1907, respectively, each have large libraries.

The World Bank reports that public financing of science was 2.66% of GDP, or nearly $11 billion in 2008. As of 2008 there were 4,123 researchers per million people, and as of 2007 there were 1,960 technicians per million people actively engaged in research and development. According to the World Bank, patent applications in science and technology totaled 2,263 in 2009. High-tech exports were valued at $12.096 billion, a decrease from 2008, and accounted for 11% of all manufactured exports.

30 DOMESTIC TRADE

Vienna is the commercial, banking, and industrial center. Railroad lines passing through it connect Austria with all neighboring countries. Vienna is also the major, but not the only, distribution center; every large provincial city is the hub of marketing and distribution for the surrounding area. Most items are sold in privately owned general or special stores, but consumer cooperatives are also active. Though small specialty shops have accounted for about 90% of retail establishments, larger outlets and shopping malls are becoming popular. For instance, close to the small village of Parndorf, Burgenland, 40 minutes outside of Vienna, there is a designer outlet featuring more than 90 department stores and specialty shops selling over 350 international brands. Although modeled after the American shopping mall, the McArthur Glen Designer Outlet resembles an Austrian baroque village.

Electronic commerce (e-commerce) is growing steadily in Austria, despite high telephone costs and Internet service provider fees, plus a general reluctance by Austrians to use electronic payments over the web. Only 20% of Internet users in Austria engage in online banking. In 2004 Austria's e-commerce market size was estimated at $16.5 billion.

Austria imposes a 20% value added tax on most goods at services. A reduced rate of 10% is levied on food, agriculture, and tourism services.

By law, most Austrian shops may be open no more than 66 hours per week. Stores are generally open from 6 a.m. to 6 p.m. Monday through Friday, and 6 a.m. to 5 p.m. on Saturdays. However, some supermarkets are open later. Food can be bought on Sundays in shops, gas stations, and at railway stations. However, normal business hours are from 8 or 9 a.m. to 6 p.m., Mondays through Fridays. The larger banks usually stay open from 8 a.m.

Principal Trading Partners – Austria (2010)				
(In millions of US dollars)				
Country	Total	Exports	Imports	Balance
World	294,972.0	144,645.0	150,327.0	-5,682.0
Germany	117,009.0	47,814.0	69,195.0	-21,381.0
Italy	22,540.0	11,791.0	10,749.0	1,042.0
Switzerland	16,331.0	7,102.0	9,229.0	-2,127.0
Czech Republic	11,866.0	6,140.0	5,726.0	414.0
France	10,713.0	6,279.0	4,434.0	1,845.0
Hungary	9,175.0	4,892.0	4,283.0	609.0
Netherlands	8,951.0	2,441.0	6,510.0	-4,069.0
Slovak Republic	8,323.0	3,997.0	4,326.0	-329.0
United States	7,725.0	5,208.0	2,517.0	2,691.0
China	7,651.0	3,258.0	4,393.0	-1,135.0

(…) data not available or not significant.

(n.s.) not specified.

SOURCE: *2011 Direction of Trade Statistics Yearbook*, New York: United Nations, 2011.

to 3 p.m. on weekdays, although they usually close at 5:30 p.m. on Thursdays. Smaller banks generally follow the same hours as their larger counterparts, except they tend to close in the afternoon between the hours of 12:30 to 3 p.m. on the weekdays. Retail establishments are governed by stricter rules than in the United States. Sunday hours are generally not permitted.

Advertising is displayed in newspapers, periodicals, and trade journals, and on posters on public conveyances, public stands, and billboards. Considerable advertising is done in cinemas. International fairs are held every spring and autumn in Vienna, and specialized fairs are held regularly in Dornbirn, Graz, Innsbruck, Klagenfurt, Ried im Innkreis, and Wels.

31 FOREIGN TRADE

Austria depends heavily on foreign trade. During the Cold War, the government consistently maintained strong ties with the West while being careful to preserve the country's neutrality. In 1972 Austria achieved association with the EEC without encountering much Soviet opposition. Austria formerly had long-term bilateral trade agreements with CMEA nations, and played an important role as a mediator in East-West trade dealings. Austria became a member of the EU in 1995, and a member of the EMU in 1999; euro notes and coins were introduced in place of the Austrian schilling in 2002.

Austria's commodity trade pattern has changed significantly since the 1930s. Because of its increasing self-sufficiency in agricultural production, expansion in output of certain basic industries, and development of new industries, Austria is no longer as dependent as in pre-World War II years on imports of food and raw materials.

The rise in industrial capacity has resulted in an extensive rise in export volume, with finished and semifinished goods accounting for well over 80% of the total export value. The major industry and export commodity in Austria is the automobile and its components, made up of plates and sheets of iron or steel, internal combustion engines and piston parts, motor vehicle parts and accessories, and complete passenger motor cars. These exports comprise a large portion of Austria's exports, while machinery and paper products continue to be important commodities. Medicinal

Balance of Payments – Austria (2010)

(In millions of US dollars)

Current Account		**11,461.0**
Balance on goods	-4,283.0	
Imports	-151,993.0	
Exports	147,710.0	
Balance on services	17,665.0	
Balance on income	737.0	
Current transfers	-2,658.0	
Capital Account		**517.0**
Financial Account		**-2,467.0**
Direct investment abroad	20,378.0	
Direct investment in Austria	-25,636.0	
Portfolio investment assets	-8,800.0	
Portfolio investment liabilities	-1,099.0	
Financial derivatives	343.0	
Other investment assets	19,455.0	
Other investment liabilities	-7,108.0	
Net Errors and Omissions		**-8,076.0**
Reserves and Related Items		**-1,435.0**

(…) data not available or not significant.

SOURCE: *Balance of Payment Statistics Yearbook 2011,* Washington, DC: International Monetary Fund, 2011.

Public Finance – Austria (2009)

(In millions of euros, central government figures)

Revenue and Grants	**101,081**	**100.0%**
Tax revenue	51,354	50.8%
Social contributions	42,954	42.5%
Grants	560	0.6%
Other revenue	6,213	6.1%
Expenditures	**108,284**	**100.0%**
General public services	12,638	11.7%
Defense	2,229	2.1%
Public order and safety	3,740	3.5%
Economic affairs	7,335	6.8%
Environmental protection	464	0.4%
Housing and community amenities	478	0.4%
Health	17,561	16.2%
Recreational, culture, and religion	912	0.8%
Education	10,182	9.4%
Social protection	52,745	48.7%

(…) data not available or not significant.

SOURCE: *Government Finance Statistics Yearbook 2010,* Washington, DC: International Monetary Fund, 2010.

and pharmaceutical product exports are increasing, but are still low compared to those of the automobile industry.

Austria imported $156 billion worth of goods and service in 2008, while exporting 157.4 billion worth of goods and services. Major import partners in 2009 were Germany 45.1%; Switzerland, 6.8%; Italy, 6.7%; and Netherlands, 4%. Major export partners were Germany, 31%; Italy, 8.2%; and Switzerland, 5%.

32 BALANCE OF PAYMENTS

In 2010 Austria had a foreign trade surplus of $14 billion, amounting to 2.6% of GDP. The UN reports that Austria's account balance in 2008 was at $14.269 billion.

33 BANKING AND SECURITIES

Because Austria is part of the European Monetary Union and uses the euro as its currency, the European Central Bank (ECB) acts as the nation's central bank, a function formally performed by the Austrian National Bank (Österreichische Nationalbank), which originally opened on 2 January 1923. The Austrian National Bank is part of the ECB system and acts as the Austrian banking representative to the ECB.

The Austrian banking system includes joint-stock banks, banking houses, and private banks, as well as postal savings banks, private savings banks, mortgage banks, building societies, and specialized cooperative credit institutions. The most important credit institutions are the joint-stock commercial banks, the two largest of which, the Creditanstalt-Bankverein and the Osterreichische Landerbank, were nationalized in 1946; shares representing 40% of the nominal capital of the two were sold to the public in 1957.

On 12 January 1997 the coalition partners, after long and intensive negotiations, agreed to sell Credit and staff-Bankverein to the indirectly state-owned Bank Austria, which is dominated by the senior coalition party, the Social Democratic Party (SPÖ). The sale created a financial and industrial giant in Austria, which

holds about one-quarter of the assets of all financial institutions. In 2010 Austria's gold reserves were valued at $22.241 billion.

A special decree of Empress Maria Theresa (1 August 1771) provided for the establishment of a stock exchange in Vienna. From the mid-19th century to the beginning of World War I, it was the main capital market of middle and eastern Europe, and from 1918 to 1938, it had continuous international importance as an equity market for the newly founded nations originating from the former monarchy. The exchange also deals in five Austrian and seven foreign investment certificates. Market capitalization as of 2010 stood at $67.682 billion. There were 72 companies listed on the Wiener Borse AG in 2010.

34 INSURANCE

Insurance in Austria is regulated by the Ministry of Finance under legislation effective 1 January 1979. Motor-vehicle third-party liability, aviation accident and third-party liability, workers' compensation, product liability, professional indemnity for certain professions, and nuclear-risk liability coverage are compulsory. Armed sportsmen, accountants, pipeline operators, and notaries are also required to carry liability insurance.

35 PUBLIC FINANCE

The government's proposed annual budget is submitted to the Nationalrat before the beginning of each calendar year (which coincides with the fiscal year). Within certain limits, the finance minister can subsequently permit the maximum expenditure levels to be exceeded, but any other excess spending must receive the approval of the Nationalrat in the form of a supplementary appropriations bill or an amendment to the budgetary legislation. Annual expenditures, which in the early 1960s rose markedly owing to increases in defense expenditures, social services, federal operations, and capital expenditures, were less expansionary in 1965–70. During the 1970s, the annual budget again began to rise, expenditures increasing at a faster rate than revenues, but by the mid-1980s, both expenditures and revenues were increasing at about the same rate. As a result of a mini-recession in 1993, the budget deficit widened to 4.7% of GDP in 1994. The increase in the budget deficit was mainly due to the government's decision to let automatic stabilizers work, when it became apparent that business activity was slowing down. Rising budget deficits present an economic challenge to the government. Despite these problems, Austria managed to meet the criteria necessary to join the European Monetary Union in 1999.

In 2010 the budget of Austria included 172.1 billion in public revenue and $189.4 billion in public expenditures. The budget deficit amounted to 7.2% of GDP. Public debt was 70.4% of GDP.

36 TAXATION

The income tax for individuals in 2005 was progressively set up to 50% on a four-bracket progressive schedule: 21% (on taxable income from €3,640 ($4,898) to €7,270 ($9,784); 31% (€7,270 to €21,800/$9,784 to $29,342); 41% (€21,800 to €50,870/$29,342 to $68,472); and 50% above €51,000 ($68,647). Married people are taxed separately. Payroll withholding tax is in effect.

Taxes are levied on corporations (25% on distributed and undistributed profits), trade income, real estate, inheritance, dividends, gifts, and several miscellaneous services and properties. A value-added tax was introduced 1 January 1973 at a basic rate of 16%. The standard rate in 2005 was 20%. A reduced rate of 10% applied to basic foodstuffs, agricultural products, rents, tourism, and entertainment; banking transactions are exempt and exports are untaxed. There was also an augmented rate of 32% on automobiles, airplanes, and ships.

Capital gains and dividend income are taxed at 25% and are withheld at the source. There is no wealth tax. In accordance with EU guidelines, tax exemptions and reductions are included in incentive packages for investment in economically depressed and underdeveloped areas along Austria's eastern border.

37 CUSTOMS AND DUTIES

Austria is committed to a program of progressive trade liberalization. As a member of the European Union, non-EU imports are covered by the EU's common tariff policy, the TARIC (integrated tariff). For most manufactured goods, this tariff results in the addition of a 3.5% duty. Import quotas affect other imports such as raw materials or parts. In addition, imports are levied an import value-added tax, which is 20% for everything except food products, for which it is 10%.

Import licenses are required for a variety of products, including agricultural produce and products, tobacco and tobacco products, salt, war materials, and poisons. An automatic licensing procedure is applied to certain products. Free trade zones are located at Graz, Linz, Bad Hall, and Vienna.

38 FOREIGN INVESTMENT

Foreign direct investment (FDI) in Austria was a net inflow of $8.71 billion according to World Bank figures published in 2009. FDI represented 2.29% of GDP.

Between 1948 and 1954 an estimated $4 billion was invested in the Austrian economy. Austria raised foreign capital largely through loans rather than as direct investment. Many post-World War II projects were financed by US aid; US grants and loans in the postwar period totaled about $1.3 billion before they began to taper off in 1952. To stimulate domestic and foreign investment, especially in underdeveloped areas of Austria, two specialized investment credit institutions were founded in the late 1950s.

The Austrian government welcomes productive foreign investment, offering a wide range of assistance and incentives at all levels ranging from indirect tax incentives to direct investment grants. Until 2006, 41% of Austria's land area was eligible for support under various EU structural reform programs. In 2005 Austria lowered its corporate tax from 34% to 25%, making the investment climate more agreeable to foreign companies. Of particular interest are investments in industries that are seeking to create new employment in high technology, promoting capital-intensive industries linked with research activities, improving productivity, replacing imports, increasing exports, and are environmentally "friendly." Austria has strict environmental laws, has rejected plans to build nuclear power plants, and has tight restrictions on biotech products. Full foreign ownership is permitted, except in nationalized sectors, and such enterprises have the same rights and obligations as domestic companies.

Austria has sizeable investments in the countries of Central and Eastern Europe, and continues to move low-tech and labor-intensive production to those regions. Austria has the potential to attract EU firms seeking convenient access to developing markets in Central and Eastern Europe and the Balkans.

39 ECONOMIC DEVELOPMENT

The federal government once held a majority share in two of the three largest commercial banks and all or most of the nation's electricity, coal and metal mining, and iron and steel production, as well as part of Austria's chemical, electrical, machine, and vehicle industries. The republic's share in the nationalized industries was handed over on 1 January 1970 to the Austrian Industrial Administration Co. (Österreichische Industrieverwaltungs-Aktiengesellschaft–ÖIAG), of which the government was the sole shareholder. The ÖIAG, in line with the government's industrialization program, regrouped the nationalized industries into six sectors: iron and steel; nonferrous metals; shipbuilding and engineering; electrical engineering; oil and chemicals; and coal. This was later regrouped into five sections: steel; metals; machinery and turnkey operations; electronics, petroleum, petrochemicals and plastics; and chemicals, pharmaceuticals, and fertilizers.

The nationalized establishments operated according to free-enterprise principles and did not receive tax concessions. Private investors were subsequently allowed to buy shares in them. The government, however, maintained voting control in these transactions. The legislation providing for ÖIAG's reorganization of the iron and steel industry included codetermination provisions granting employees the right to fill one-third of the seats on the board of directors. The postal, telephone, and telegraph services and radio and television transmission were state monopolies, as was the trade in tobacco, alcohol, salt, and explosives.

During the 1970s the government placed new emphasis on centralized economic planning. Key elements in the new policy were the planning of public investment, selective promotion of private sector investment, coordinated expansion of the energy sector and state-owned industry, and assistance for the structural improvement of agriculture. Special emphasis was given to the reform of the handicrafts industry.

In 1986 the ÖIAG was renamed the Österreichische Industrieholding AG, and a process of restructuring and privatization took place in 1993. In 1996 the post and telecommunications monopoly was privatized, and other companies were split up and taken over by foreign, and especially German, companies. The agricultural sector has gone through substantial reform through the EU's common agricultural policy. Computer software and services, telecommunications, advertising, and Internet services are growing commercial enterprises.

In the 21st century, Austria has emphasized its knowledge-based sectors of the economy, continued to deregulate the service sector, and encouraged greater participation in the labor market of its aging population. The aging phenomenon, together with already high health and pension costs, poses future problems in tax and welfare policies.

40 SOCIAL DEVELOPMENT

Austria has one of the most advanced and comprehensive systems of social legislation in the world. The General Social Insurance Bill of 1955 unified all social security legislation and greatly increased the scope of benefits and number of insured. All wage and salary earners must carry sickness, disability, accident, old age, and unemployment insurance, with varying contribution levels by employer and employee for each type of insurance. Health insurance is available to industrial and agricultural workers, federal and professional employees, and members of various other occupational groups. For those without insurance or adequate means, treatment is paid for by public welfare funds.

Unemployment benefits mostly range from 40–50% of previous normal earnings. After three years' service, regular benefits are paid up to between 20 and 30 weeks; thereafter, for an indefinite period, a worker, subject to a means test, may receive emergency relief amounting to 92–95% of the regular benefit. Work injury laws were first enacted in 1887. Citizens are eligible for old age pensions after age 65 (men) and age 60 (women) if they have 35 years of contributions paid or credited. In 2004 the age for retirement began increasing by one month per quarter.

Employers must contribute 4.5% of payroll earnings to a family allowance fund. Family allowances are paid monthly, depending on the number of dependent children, with the amount doubled for any child who is severely handicapped. The state provides school lunches for more than 100,000 children annually. In addition, it administers the organization of children's holiday programs and provides for the care of crippled children, for whom there is a state training school. The state also grants a special birth allowance and a payment for newlyweds setting up their first home; unmarried people establishing a common household may apply for tax remission. The government provides maternity benefits, takes care of destitute old people, and provides for war victims and disabled veterans. Administration of social insurance is carried out in the provinces by autonomous bodies in which both employers and employees are represented. Payment is also made to victims of political persecution during the Nazi era and to victims of violent crime.

Women make up an increasing percentage of the work force. While the number of women in government is low in relation to the overall population, there are female members of parliament, cabinet ministers, state secretaries, town councilors, and mayors. The law proscribes sexual harassment in the workplace, and the government generally enforces these laws. It is believed that violence against women is a widespread problem, and cases generally remain unreported. The government provides shelters and hotlines for victims. Children's rights are fully protected by law.

The constitution provides for the freedoms of religion and assembly, and the government respects these rights. A growing problem is right-wing extremism and the emergence of neo-Nazi groups. Racial violence against ethnic minorities in Austria is evident. In 2005, Austria adopted an Equal Treatment Bill to combat racism and discrimination.

In June 2010 the European Court of Human Rights upheld the right of the Austrian government to prohibit same-sex marriages. The ruling addressed a suit brought by two Austrian men who argued that their basic rights were being denied, since Austria does not recognize same-sex marriages. The suit was filed in the European Court based on the fact that six other European Union nations have already legalized same-sex marriages. The ruling stated that, since cultural and social connotations vary from one society to another, individual countries should be permitted to form their own laws on the issue, rather than imposing one rule for all countries. Austria introduced the new legal union of registered partnerships in January 2010. Under this new category, same-sex couples may apply for some of the legal benefits offered to married heterosexual couples. In the first four months of that year, there were 270 registered partnerships. While some hailed the new law, others condemned it as not enough, saying that full equality requires full recognition of marriage under the law. Meanwhile, in May 2010 a heterosexual couple filed a suit in an Austrian court to have their non-marital relationship recognized as a registered partnership, claiming that heterosexual couples should have the same opportunity as homosexual couples in legalizing their union. Supporters of registered partnerships cite easier divorces as a primary reason for favoring such civil unions over traditional marriage.

41 HEALTH

Austria's federal government formulates health policy directive and public hygiene standards are high. According to the CIA, life expectancy in Austria was 80 years in 2011. In the same year, the country spent 10.5% of its GDP on healthcare, amounting to $5,037 per person. There were 48 physicians, 78 nurses and midwives, and 77 hospital beds per 10,000 inhabitants. Virtually every Austrian has benefits of health insurance. In principle, anyone is entitled to use the facilities provided by Austria's health service. The costs are borne by the social insurance plan or, in cases of hardship, by the social welfare program. Vienna's medical school and research institutes are world famous; spas (with thermal springs), health resorts, and sanatoriums are popular among Austrians as well as foreigners.

The total fertility rate in Austria in 2011 was estimated at 1.4 children born per woman, while the infant mortality rate was 3 deaths per 1,000 live births. Maternal mortality was estimated at 5 deaths per 100,000 live births in 2007. An estimated 90% of women (ages 15–49) used contraceptives.

It was estimated that 83% of children were vaccinated against measles. As of 2007 Austria immunized its one-year-old children as follows: diphtheria, pertussis, tetanus, and measles. There were 14 cases of tuberculosis per 100,000 people in 2007. The CIA calculated HIV/AIDS prevalence in Austria to be about 0.3% in 2009.

42 HOUSING

During the First Republic (1919–38), Vienna and several other Austrian municipalities supported a progressive housing policy and built model apartment houses for workers. From the end of World War II until 1967, 157,386 small homes were built under the Federal Accommodation Fund, and 75,663 damaged homes were repaired under the Housing Reconstruction Fund. A system of subsidies for public housing has since been decentralized, and control turned over to local authorities. The Housing Improvement Act of 1969 provided for state support for modernization of outdated housing.

In 2003 there were an estimated 3,863,262 dwellings in the nation. About 74% of all dwellings were privately owned. As of 1990, 25% of Austria's housing stock had been built before 1919; 19% between 1971 and 1980; 18% between 1961 and 1970; 15% between 1945 and 1960; 13% after 1981; and 10% between 1919 and 1944. About 53,000 new dwellings were completed in 2000 and 41,914 were built in 2002.

43 EDUCATION

The Austrian educational system has its roots in the medieval monastic schools that flourished toward the end of the 11th century. The present state education system goes back to the school reforms introduced by Maria Theresa in 1774. In 1869 the Imperial Education Law unified the entire system of compulsory education.

In 1962 Austria's education system was completely reorganized under a comprehensive education law, and compulsory education was extended from eight to nine years. Since 1975 all schools are coeducational and education at state schools is free of charge. Primary education lasts for four years. After primary school, pupils may either attend a general secondary school (*Hauptschule*), which is organized into two four-year courses of study (lower and upper secondary), or an academic secondary school, which also covers an eight-year program. Financial support is provided for postsecondary schooling. Secondary age students may also choose a five-year vocational program. Those who complete their studies at secondary or higher vocational school are qualified to attend the universities. Disabled students either attend special schools or are mainstreamed into regular classrooms. The primary language of instruction is German. The school year runs from October to June.

In 2009 the World Bank estimated that 98% of age-eligible children in Austria were enrolled in primary school. Of those enrolled in tertiary education, there were 100 male students for every 119 female students. In 2009, the pupil to teacher ratio for primary and secondary schools was 11:1. Between 2005 and 2008, public expenditure on education was estimated at 5.4% of GDP.

Austria maintains a vigorous adult education system. Austria has 22 universities throughout the country offering training in humanities, medicine, basic and applied sciences and 13 federal colleges of technology. Austria also has a number of private universities. The adult literacy rate was estimated at 98% in 2009. Almost all adult education bodies owe their existence to private initiative. The Ministry of Education, under the auspices of the Development Planning for a Cooperative System of Adult Education in Austria, has joined private bodies in setting up projects for enhancing the quality of adult education programs.

44 LIBRARIES AND MUSEUMS

Austria is rich in availability of large library collections and is filled with strong, unique collections. The largest and most important of Austria's 2,400 libraries is the Austrian National Library, which contains more than 2.6 million books and over 3 million non-book materials. It includes nine special collections: manuscripts and autographs, incunabula (old and precious prints), maps and globes, music, papyri, portrait and picture archives, Austrian literature archives, pamphlets and posters, and a theater collection. The National Library serves as a center for the training of professional librarians, prepares the Austrian national bibliography, and provides a reference service for Austrian libraries. The largest university libraries are the University of Vienna (5.5 million volumes), Graz University (3 million), and Innsbruck University (1.4 million). There are at least 12 prominent scientific libraries in the country, primarily associated with universities. Austria also has several hundred private libraries, such as the renowned libraries in the monasteries at Melk and Admont. The Austrian Institute of Economic Research in Vienna maintains an internationally renowned research library and electronic databases on international economic trends and forecasts.

The Haus-, Hof-, and Staatsarchiv, founded in Vienna in 1749, was combined in 1945 with the Allgemeine Verwaltungsarchiv to form the Austrian State Archives. The archives' collection ranks as one of the most important in the world, with more than 100,000 manuscripts and documents, some dating as far back as the year 816. Most notable are the state documents of the Holy Roman Empire, including those of the Imperial Court Council (from 1555), the Imperial Court Chancellery (from 1495), and the Mainz Imperial Chancellery (from 1300); documents of the subsequent Austrian State Chancellery; and those of the Austro-Hungarian Foreign Ministry.

There are over 700 museums in Austria, including art museums, archaeology and history museums, science and technology museums, and regional museums. There are eight recognized historical sites in the country. The most important museums had their origins in the private collections of the House of Habsburg. The Museum of Fine Arts (Kunsthistorisches Museum) in Vienna (1871) contains a vast collection of Flemish, Italian, and German paintings by old masters. It also houses distinguished collections of Egyptian and Oriental objects, classical art, sculpture and applied art, tapestries, coins, and old musical instruments. The Albertina Museum houses the world's largest graphic art collection, including the most extensive collection in existence of the works of Albrecht Dürer. The Secular Treasury (Schatzkammer) houses the jewels and insignia of the Holy Roman Empire and of all the Austrian emperors. The numerous collections formerly in the possession of the imperial court have in large part been brought together for display in the Natural History Museum, the Museum of Fine Arts, and the Hofburg (Innsbruck). Vienna's Schönbrunn Palace contains a collection of imperial coaches from the Habsburg court. The Austrian Gallery in Belvedere Castle (Vienna), formerly the summer palace of Prince Eugene of Savoy, houses unique examples of medieval Austrian art as well as works of 19th- and 20th-century Austrian artists. The Museum of Modern Art was opened in Vienna's Palais Liechtenstein in 1979; incorporated into it was the Museum of the 20th Century, founded in 1962. Also of interest is Vienna's Lipizzaner Museum, featuring the city's famous white horses, and a museum of Sigmund Freud's apartment and office.

There are also other castles, manor houses, monasteries, and convents, many of which date from the Middle Ages and which are of interest for their architecture as well as for their contents. Important scientific collections are housed in the Natural History Museum, the Museums of Anthropology and Folklore, and the Technical Museum, all in Vienna; the Joanneum, in Graz; the Ferdinandeum, in Innsbruck; the Carolino Augusteum and the House of Nature, in Salzburg; and the Folk Museum, in Hallstatt, Upper Austria, which contains local prehistoric discoveries dating from the 4th and 3rd centuries BC. Salzburg has two historical museums dedicated to Mozart—the house where he was born and another house in which he lived. In Vienna, there is a museum dedicated to Sigmund Freud.

The Jewish Museum Vienna contains a memorial to Austrian victims of the Holocaust and a 40,000-volume research library on the history of the Jews in Austria and Vienna. There is also a Holocaust memorial at the site of the Maunthausen concentration camp.

45 MEDIA

Austria's telephone system is efficient and highly developed, with some 45 main telephone lines for every 100 persons. In 2009 the CIA reported that there were 3.3 million telephone landlines in Austria. In addition to landlines, mobile phone subscriptions averaged 141 per 100 people.

Oesterreichischer Rundfunk (ORF) is the primary public broadcasting company in Austria. The first national commercial television license was granted to ATV in 2000. Commercial radio stations began in the 1990s. As of 2009 there were 65 FM and 2 AM radio stations. Internet users numbered 74 per 100 citizens. In 2010 the country had about 3.2 million Internet hosts.

Prominent newspapers in 2010, with circulation number listed parenthetically, included *Neue Kronenzeitung* (510,226), *Kleine Zeitung* (300,000), and *Oberösterreichische Rundschau* (259,000), as well as 15 other major newspapers. Vienna accounts for about half of total readership. Other leading dailies include *Der Kurier Salzburger Nachrichten, Tiroler-Tageszeitung, Die Presse,* and *Der Standard.* The leading periodicals include the weeklies *Wochenpresse-Wirtschaftswoche* and *Profil* and the monthly *Trend.*

Freedom of the press is constitutionally guaranteed and there is no state censorship; the Austrian Press Council is largely concerned with self-regulatory controls and the effective application of a code of ethics. The Austrian Press Agency is independent of the government and operates on a nonprofit basis; most major newspapers share in its financing.

46 ORGANIZATIONS

The Federal Economic Chamber, including representatives of commerce, industry, trade, and transport, has official representatives in most counties. Every province has an economic chamber organized in the same way as the federal chamber. District chambers of agriculture are combined into provincial chambers, which are further consolidated in a national confederation. Provincial chambers of labor are combined in a national chamber. Austria has a committee on the International Chamber of Commerce.

The Federation of Austrian Industrialists, with an organizational membership of almost 5,000, is subdivided into departments for trade, industry, finance, social policies, and communications, with sections for press relations and organization. There are associations of bankers, insurance companies, and publishers, as well as other commercial and professional groups.

Austria has a large number of scholarly associations, as well as several groups dedicated to the support and promotion of various arts and sciences. The latter include the Association for Sciences and Politics, the Austrian Academy of Sciences, the Austrian Association of Music, the Austrian Physical Society, the Austrian P.E.N. Center, and the Austrian Science Fund. Filling a specialty niche, Vienna is home to the International Confederation of Accordionists and the International Gustav Mahler Society.

The Austrian Medical Chamber is a notable institution for the promotion of health education, research, and policymaking. There are numerous associations representing a wide variety of specialized medical fields and promoting research for the treatment and prevention of particular diseases and conditions.

The Austrian Sports Federation represents over three million athletes in the country in promoting education and competition in a wide variety of sports. There are numerous associations for particular sports, including Frisbee, football (soccer), baseball, golf, ice hockey, tennis, and badminton. There is an Austrian Paralympic Committee, an Olympic Committee, and a Special Olympics committee.

The Austrian Union of Students (AUS), the national university student coordinating body, is incorporated under Austrian federal public law to serve as a legal representative body for Austrian university students through federal ministries responsible for higher education and through the federal assembly. The secretariat of the National Unions of Students of Europe (ESIB) is housed within the AUS. Other youth organizations, representing a variety of concerns and interests, include the Austrian Socialist Youth Organization, Young Austrian People's Party, Union of Liberal Youth, Communist Youth of Austria, Austrian Catholic Youth Group, Cartel Association of Austrian Catholic Student Unions, Protestant Youth Welfare Organization, Protestant Student Community, Austrian Trade Union Youth Organization, Austrian Friends of Nature Youth Organization, Junior Chamber Austria, and Austrian Alpine Youth Organization. Scouting organizations are also present for both boys and girls.

Organizations of Greenpeace, The Red Cross, and Amnesty International are also present. There are active chapters of Lions Clubs and Kiwanis International.

47 TOURISM, TRAVEL, AND RECREATION

Austria ranks high among European tourist destinations. It has a year-round tourist season: in winter, tourists come to the famous skiing resorts and attend outstanding musical events in Vienna; in summer, visitors are attracted by scenery, sports, and cultural festivals, notably in Vienna and Salzburg. Of the 4,000 communities in Austria, nearly half are considered tourist centers.

The *Tourism Factbook*, published by the UN World Tourism Organization, reported 21.4 million incoming tourists to Austria in 2009, who spent a total of $19.2 billion. Of those incoming tourists, there were 19,613 from Europe. There were 587,899 hotel beds available in Austria, which had an occupancy rate of 37%. The estimated daily cost to visit Vienna was $378. The cost of visiting other cities averaged $344.

Tourist attractions in the capital include 15 state theaters and the Vienna State Opera (which also houses the Vienna Philharmonic); the Vienna Boys' Choir; St. Stephen's Cathedral; the Schönbrunn and Belvedere palaces; and the Spanish Riding Academy, with its famous Lippizaner stallions. Just beyond the city boundary are the Vienna Woods, with their picturesque wine taverns.

About 40 or 50 towns and villages qualify as major resorts for Alpine skiing, and Innsbruck has been the site of two Winter Olympics, in 1964 and 1976. Mountaineering is another Austrian specialty, with Austrian climbers having scaled high peaks all over the world. Austrians have frequently taken titles in world canoeing championships. Football (soccer) is a very popular sport. Austria also puts on a number of prominent annual events for cyclists. Probably the most challenging tour on the amateurs' program is the "Tour d'Autriche," which has been held every year since 1949. This race through Austria's mountains covers a total distance of almost 1,500 kilometers. Motor racing, motorcycle racing and speedway racing are also extremely popular sports in Austria.

Visitors entering Austria for a short stay need only a valid passport if from the United States or the European Union countries, but an Austrian visa is required for visits exceeding three months.

⁴⁸FAMOUS PERSONS

Political Figures

Monarchs who played a leading role in Austrian and world history include Rudolf I of Habsburg (1218–91), founder of the Habsburg dynasty and Holy Roman emperor from 1273; Maria Theresa (1717–80), who succeeded to the Habsburg dominions by means of the Pragmatic Sanction of 1740; her son Joseph II (1741–90), the "benevolent despot" who became Holy Roman emperor in 1765; Franz Josef (1830–1916), emperor of Austria at the outbreak of World War I; and his brother Maximilian (Ferdinand Maximilian Josef, 1832–1867), who became emperor of Mexico in 1864, ruling on behalf of Emperor Napoleon III of France, and was deposed and executed. Prince Klemens Wenzel Nepomuk Lothar von Metternich (1773–1859), Austrian foreign minister from 1809 to 1848, was the architect of the European balance of power established at the Congress of Vienna in 1815. Adolf Hitler (1889–1945), born in Braunau, was dictator of Germany from 1933 until his death. Leading Austrian statesmen since World War II are Bruno Kreisky (1911–90), Socialist Party chairman and chancellor of Austria from 1970 to 1983; and Kurt Waldheim (b. 1918), Austrian diplomat and foreign minister, who was UN secretary-general from 1971 to 1981 and was elected to the presidency in June 1986.

Artists, Writers, and Scientists

Austria has produced many excellent artists, writers, and scientists but is probably most famous for its outstanding composers.

Beginning in the 18th century and for 200 years, Vienna was the center of European musical culture. Among its great masters were Franz Joseph Haydn (1732–1809), Wolfgang Amadeus Mozart (1756–91), Franz Schubert (1797–1828), Anton Bruckner (1824–96), Gustav Mahler (1860–1911), Hugo Wolf (1860–1903), Arnold Schönberg (1874–1951), Anton von Webern (1883–1945), and Alban Berg (1885–1935). Although born in northwestern Germany, Ludwig van Beethoven (1770–1827) and Johannes Brahms (1833–97) settled in Vienna and spent the rest of their lives there. Composers of light music, typical of Austria, are Johann Strauss, Sr. (1804–49), Johann Strauss, Jr. (1825–99), Dalmatian-born Franz von Suppé (Francesco Ezechiele Ermenegildo Cavaliere Suppe-Demelli, 1819–95), Hungarian-born Franz Lehár (1870–1948), and Oskar Straus (1870–1954). Outstanding musicians are the conductors Clemens Krauss (1893–1954), Karl Böhm (1894–1981), and Herbert von Karajan (1908–89); the pianists Artur Schnabel (1882–1951) and Alfred Brendel (b. 1931); and the violinist Fritz Kreisler (1875–1962).

Leading dramatists and poets include Franz Grillparzer (1791–1872), Nikolaus Lenau (1802–50), Ludwig Anzengruber (1839–81), and Hugo von Hofmannsthal (1874–1929). Novelists and short-story writers of interest are Adalbert Stifter (1805–68), Marie von Ebner-Eschenbach (1830–1916), Arthur Schnitzler (1862–1931), Hermann Bahr (1863–1934), Stefan Zweig (1881–1942), Robert Musil (1880–1942), Hermann Broch (1886–1952), Yakov Lind (b. 1927), Peter Handke (b. 1942), and Elfriede Jelinek (b. 1946), who won the 2004 Nobel Prize in Literature. Although born in Czechoslovakia, the satiric polemicist Karl Kraus (1874–1936), the poet Rainer Maria Rilke (1875–1926), the novelist and short-story writer Franz Kafka (1883–1924), and the poet and novelist Franz Werfel (1890–1946) are usually identified with Austrian literary life. Film directors of Austrian birth include Max Reinhardt (Maximilian Goldman, 1873–1943), Erich von Stroheim (Erich Oswald Stroheim, 1885–1957), Fritz Lang (1890–1976), Josef von Sternberg (1894–1969), Otto Preminger (1905–86), and Billy Wilder (1906–2002). Internationally known performers born in Austria include Lotte Lenya (Karoline Blamauer, 1900–81) and Maximilian Schell (b.1930).

Architects and Artists

Two great architects of the Baroque period were Johann Bernhard Fischer von Erlach (1656–1723) and Johann Lucas von Hildebrandt (1668–1745). Four prominent 20th-century painters were Gustav Klimt (1862–1918), Oskar Kokoschka (1886–1980), Egon Schiele (1890–1918), and Friedensreich Regentag Dunkelbunt Hundertwasser (born Friedrich Stowasser, 1928–2000)

Physicians

Psychoanalysis was founded in Vienna by Sigmund Freud (1856–1939) and extended by his Austrian colleagues Alfred Adler (1870–1937), Otto Rank (1884–1939), Theodor Reik (1888–1969), and Wilhelm Reich (1897–1957). Eugen Böhm-Bawerk (1851–1914) and Joseph Alois Schumpeter (1883–1950) were outstanding economists. A renowned geneticist was Gregor Johann Mendel (1822–84). Christian Johann Doppler (1803–53), a physicist and mathematician, described the wave phenomenon known today as the Doppler shift. Lise Meitner (1878–1968) was the physicist who first identified nuclear fission. Austrian Nobel Prize winners in physics are Erwin Schrödinger (1887–1961), in 1933;

Victor Franz Hess (1883–1964), authority on cosmic radiation, in 1936; and atomic theorist Wolfgang Pauli (1900–1958), discoverer of the exclusion principle, in 1945. Winners of the Nobel Prize in chemistry are Fritz Pregl (1869–1930), who developed microanalysis, in 1923; Richard Zsigmondy (1865–1929), inventor of the ultramicroscope, in 1925; biochemist Richard Kuhn (1900–1967), a pioneer in vitamin research, in 1938; and biochemist Max Ferdinand Perutz (1914–2002) for research in blood chemistry, in 1962. Winners of the Nobel Prize in physiology or medicine are otologist Robert Bárány (1876–1936), in 1914; psychiatrist Julius Wagner-Jauregg (1857–1940), for developing a treatment for general paresis, in 1927; Karl Landsteiner (1868–1943), discoverer of blood groups, in 1930; German-born pharmacologist Otto Loewi (1873–1961), for his study of nerve impulse transmission, in 1936; Carl Ferdinand Cori (1896–1984) and his wife, Gerti Theresa Radnitz Cori (1896–1957), whose work with enzymes led to new ways of fighting diabetes, in 1947; and Konrad Lorenz (1903–89), discoverer of the "imprinting" process of learning, in 1973. In 1974, Friedrich August von Hayek (1899–1992), a noted monetary theorist, was awarded the Nobel Prize in economics.

Humanitarians

The Nobel Peace Prize was awarded to Baroness Berta Kinsky von Suttner (b. Prague, 1843–1914), founder of the Austrian Society of Peace Lovers and author of *Lay Down Your Arms!*, in 1905; and to Alfred Hermann Fried (1864–1921), a prolific publicist for the cause of international peace, in 1911. One of the most influential philosophers of the contemporary age was Ludwig Josef Johann Wittgenstein (1889–1951). Rudolf Steiner (1861–1925), the founder of anthroposophy, was an Austrian. Theodor Herzl (b. Budapest, 1860–1904), founder of the Zionist movement, was an early advocate of the establishment of a Jewish state in Palestine. Simon Wiesenthal (b. Poland, 1908–2005), a Nazi concentration camp survivor, searched for Nazi war criminals around the world.

Athletes

Austrians have excelled in international Alpine skiing competition. In 1956, Toni Sailer (b. 1935) won all three Olympic gold medals in men's Alpine skiing events. Annemarie Moser-Pröll (b. 1953) retired in 1980 after winning a record six women's World Cups, a record 62 World Cup races in all, and the 1980 women's downhill skiing Olympic championship. Franz Klammer (b. 1953), who won the 1976 men's downhill Olympic title, excited spectators with his aggressive style. Arnold Schwarzenegger (b. 1947) was once the foremost bodybuilder in the world and became a successful Hollywood actor and governor of California.

⁴⁹DEPENDENCIES

Austria has no territories or colonies.

⁵⁰BIBLIOGRAPHY

Ake, Anne. *Austria*. San Diego: Lucent Books, 2001.

Annesley, Claire, ed. *A Political and Economic Dictionary of Western Europe*. Philadelphia: Routledge/Taylor and Francis, 2005.

Austria. Singapore: APA Publications, 2001.

Austrian Women in the Nineteenth and Twentieth Centuries. Providence, RI: Berghahn Books, 1996.

Bisanz-Prakken, Marian. *Rembrandt and His Time: Masterworks from the Albertina, Vienna*. New York: Hudson Hills Press, 2005.

Brook-Shepherd, Gordon. *The Austrians: A Thousand-Year Odyssey*. New York: Carroll and Graf, 2002.

Fichtner, Paula S. *Historical Dictionary of Austria*. Lanham, MD: Scarecrow Press, 2009.

Healy, Maureen. *Vienna and the Fall of the Habsburg Empire: Total War and Everyday Life in World War I*. New York: Cambridge University Press, 2004.

International Smoking Statistics: A Collection of Historical Data from 30 Economically Developed Countries. New York: Oxford University Press, 2002.

MacHardy, Karin Jutta. *War, Religion and Court Patronage in Habsburg Austria: The Social and Cultural Dimensions of Political Interaction, 1521–1622*. New York: Palgrave, 2002.

Opello, Walter C. *European Politics*. Boulder, CO: Lynne Rienner Publishers, 2009.

Roman, Eric. *Austria-Hungary and the Successor States: A Reference Guide from the Renaissance to the Present*. New York: Facts On File, 2003.

Wessels, Wolfgang, Andreas Maurer, and Jürgan Mittag, eds. *Fifteen into One?: the European Union and Its Member States*. New York: Palgrave, 2003.

BELARUS

Republic of Belarus
Respublika Belarus

CAPITAL: Minsk

FLAG: The national flag consists of a red horizontal band (top) and green horizontal band (bottom) one-half the width of the red band; a white vertical stripe on the hoist side bears Belarusian national ornamentation in red. The red band color recalls past struggles from oppression, and the green band represents hope and the many forests of the country

ANTHEM: *My, Bielarusy (We Belarusians).*

MONETARY UNIT: The Belarus ruble (BYB) circulates along with the Russian ruble. The government has a varying exchange rate for trade between Belarus and Russia. BYB1 = US$0.00047 (or US$1 = BYB4,351.1) as of 2011.

WEIGHTS AND MEASURES: The metric system is the legal standard.

HOLIDAYS: New Year's Day, 1 January; Orthodox Christmas, 7 January; International Women's Day, 8 March; Labor Day, 1 May; Victory Day, 9 May; Independence Day, 3 July; October Revolution Day, 7 November; Day of Commemoration, movable; Christmas, 25 December.

TIME: 2 p.m. = noon GMT.

¹LOCATION, SIZE, AND EXTENT

Belarus is a landlocked nation located in Eastern Europe, between Poland and Russia. Comparatively, the area occupied by Belarus is slightly smaller than the state of Kansas with a total area of 207,600 sq km (80,154 sq mi). Belarus shares boundaries with Latvia on the N, Russia on the N and E, Ukraine on the S, Poland on the SW, and Lithuania on the NW. The boundary length of Belarus totals 3,098 km (1,925 mi).

The capital city of Belarus, Minsk, is located near the center of the country.

²TOPOGRAPHY

The topography of Belarus is generally flat and contains a large amount of marshland. The Belarusian Ridge (Belorusskya Gryda) stretches across the center of the country from the southwest to the northeast. The highest elevation is at Dzerzhinskaya Gora, 346 m (1,135 ft).

³CLIMATE

The country's climate is transitional between continental and maritime. July's mean temperature is 19°C (67°F). January's mean temperature is -5°C (23°F). Rainfall averages between 57 cm (22.5 in) and 61 cm (26.5 in) annually.

⁴FLORA AND FAUNA

The World Resources Institute estimates that there are 2,100 plant species in Belarus. Pine trees are found throughout the north, but spruce, alder, ash, birch, and oak trees are also common. Some of the mammals in the forest include deer, brown bears, rabbits, and squirrels. In addition, Belarus is home to 71 mammal species, 226 bird species, 6 reptile species, and 14 amphibian species. The cal-

culation reflects the total number of distinct species residing in the country, not the number of endemic species. The southern region is a swampy expanse. The marshes are home to ducks, frogs, turtles, archons, and muskrats.

⁵ENVIRONMENT

The World Resources Institute reported that Belarus had designated 1.08 million hectares (2.66 million acres) of land for protection as of 2006. As part of the legacy of the former Soviet Union, Belarus's main environmental problems are chemical and nuclear pollution. Belarus was the republic most affected by the accident at the Chernobyl nuclear power plant in Ukraine in April 1986. Northerly winds prevailed at the time of the accident; therefore, most of the fallout occurred over farmland in the southeastern section of the country (primarily in the Gomel and Mogilev oblasts). Most experts estimate that 25–30% of Belarus's farmland was irradiated and should not be used for agricultural production or to collect wild berries and mushrooms, although it continues to be used for these and other purposes. Belarus has one natural United Nations Educational, Scientific, and Cultural Organization (UNESCO) World Heritage Site, the Bialowieza Forest. There are nine Ramsar Wetland Sites.

Belarus has significant air and water pollution from industrial sources. The most common pollutants are formaldehyde, carbon emissions, and petroleum-related chemicals. In 2008 the United Nations (UN) reported that industrial emissions of carbon dioxide in Belarus totaled 66,747 kilotons. The soils also contain unsafe levels of lead, zinc, copper, and the agricultural chemical dichlorodiphenyltrichloroethane (DDT). All urban and rural dwellers have access to safe drinking water. Water resources totaled 58 cu km (13.91 cu mi) while water usage was 1.01 cu km (.242 cu mi) per year. Domestic water usage accounted for 23% of total usage, industrial for 47%, and agricultural for 30%. Per capita water usage totaled 286 cu m (10,100 cu ft) per year.

According to a 2011 report issued by the International Union for Conservation of Nature and Natural Resources (IUCN), threatened species included 4 types of mammals, 4 species of birds, and 6 species of invertebrates. Endangered species include the European bison and the European mink.

6 POPULATION

The US Central Intelligence Agency (CIA) estimated the population of Belarus in 2011 to be approximately 9,577,552, which placed it at number 88 in population among the 196 nations of the world. In 2011 approximately 14.1% of the population was over 65 years of age, with another 14.2% under 15 years of age. The median age in Belarus was 39 years. There were 0.87 males for every female in the country. The population's annual rate of change was -0.363%. The projected population for the year 2025 is 9,100,000. Population density in Belarus was calculated at 46 people per sq km (119 people per sq mi).

The UN estimated that 75% of the population lived in urban areas, and that urban populations had an annual rate of change of 0.1%. The largest urban area was Minsk, with a population of 1.8 million.

Almost 25% of the population of Belarus was killed during World War II (1939–45) and, combined with the fatalities of the Soviet-era purges, the postwar population was one-third smaller than it had been in 1930. It was not until the 1970s that the population returned to prewar levels.

7 MIGRATION

Estimates of Belarus's net migration rate, carried out by the CIA in 2011, amounted to 0.38 migrants per 1,000 citizens. The total number of emigrants living abroad was 1.78 million, and the total number of immigrants living in Belarus was 1.09 million. With the breakup of the Soviet Union in 1991, some two million Belarusians were among the various nationality groups who found themselves living outside their autonomous regions or native republics. Most of the Belarusians who have returned to Belarus fled other former Soviet republics because of fighting or ethnic tensions. From 1989 to 1995, 3,000 Belarusians returned from Azerbaijan and 3,000 Belarusians returned from Kyrgyzstan. From 1991 to 1995, 16,000 Belarusians returned from Kazakhstan and 10,000 Belarusians returned from Tajikistan. In 1999 Belarus had 131,200 internally displaced people from the ecological effects of the accident at the Chernobyl nuclear power plant and 160,000 "returnees" (ethnic Belarusians who had returned to Belarus from other former republics).

8 ETHNIC GROUPS

As of 2010 an estimated 81.2% of the total population was Belarusian. Russians made up about 11.4% of the populace; Poles, Ukrainians, and other groups combined to make up about 7.4% of the population.

9 LANGUAGES

Belarusian belongs to the eastern group of Slavic languages and is very similar to Russian. It did not become a separate language until the 15th century, when it was the official language of the Grand Duchy of Lithuania. It is written in the Cyrillic alphabet but has two letters not in Russian and a number of distinctive sounds. The vocabulary borrows from Polish, Lithuanian, German, Latin, and Turkic. Belarusian and Russian are both official languages, with Russian being the most widely known. Polish and Ukrainian are also spoken by minority populations.

10 RELIGIONS

As of 2010 approximately 82.5% of all citizens are Belarusian Orthodox, though only about 18% of that group regularly attended church services. Another 12% are Roman Catholics, with about 50% claiming regular church attendance. About 4% of citizens belong to Eastern religious groups, which include Muslims, Hare Krishnas, and Baha'is. Another 2% are Protestants, including Seventh-Day Adventists, Apostolic Christians, Lutherans, Old Believers, and Jehovah's Witnesses. The Jewish community is estimated at between 30,000 and 50,000 people, though most are not religiously active. Other minority religions included the Greek Rite Catholic Church, the Christian Baptist church, Lutheranism, Presbyterian, and Islam. Since the 1994 elections the country's first president, Aleksandr Lukashenko, established a policy of favoring the Belarusian Orthodox Church (BOC—a branch of the Russian Orthodox Church) as the country's chief religion. A 2003 Concordat between the government and the BOC more firmly established the special relationship between the government and the church. The BOC works closely with the government in developing and implementing political policies, including those related to such departments as the ministries of education, defense, health, and labor. The president grants the Orthodox Church special financial aid that is not given to other denominations and has declared the preservation and development of Orthodox Christianity a "moral necessity."

11 TRANSPORTATION

The CIA reports that Belarus has a total of 94,797 km (58,904 mi) of roads, of which 84,028 km (52,213 mi) are paved. There are 67 airports, which transported 333,252 passengers in 2009 according to the World Bank.

The European Bank for Reconstruction and Development (EBRD) initiated a study of railways and roads in 1993 to help determine advantageous locations for future development in Belarus. The focus of the EBRD study also included the development of the trucking industry. Railroads extend for 5,510 km (3,424 mi).

Belarus has approximately 2,500 km (1,553 mi) of navigable waterways. The use of navigable waterways is limited by their location near the country's perimeter and by shallowness. In 1995 Belarus claimed to have retained 5% of the merchant fleet of the former Soviet Union. As of 2009 there were an estimated 35 airports with paved runways. There is also a single heliport.

12 HISTORY

The Belarusians are the descendants of Slavic tribes that migrated into the region in the 9th century. They trace their distinct identity from the 13th century when the Mongols conquered Russia and parts of Ukraine. During this period, Belarus managed to maintain its identity as part of the Grand Duchy of Lithuania. The union of the Grand Duchy with the Polish kingdom in 1569, resulting in the emergence of the Polish-Lithuanian Commonwealth (Rzeczpospolita), put the territory of Belarus under Polish rule. As a result of the partitions of Rzeczpospolita in 1772, 1793, and 1795 by Imperial Russia, Austria, and Prussia, Belarus fell to the Russian Empire.

In March 1918 at the time of the Soviet-German Treaty of Brest-Litovsk in which Moscow agreed to relinquish claim to a substantial amount of territory captured by Germany in exchange for peace, the Belarusian National Republic was formed with German military assistance. However, after the German government collapsed in November 1918 and German forces were withdrawn from the region, Bolshevik troops moved in and set up the Belorussian Soviet Socialist Republic (SSR) in January 1919. In 1922 the Belorussian SSR became one of 15 socialist republics to form the Union of Soviet Socialist Republics (USSR). Two years later, Belarus's borders were enlarged at the expense of Russia and Ukraine. Later, parts of eastern Poland were annexed to Belarus by Stalin under the 1939 Molotov-Ribbentrop pact. However, Belarus was devastated by World War II.

During the decades of Soviet rule, Belarus underwent intense Russification, and its leaders generally complied with Soviet policy. However, after extensive nuclear contamination by the 1986 Chernobyl accident in neighboring Ukraine, Belarusian nationalists, acting from exile in Lithuania, organized the Belarusian People's Front. The nationalist upsurge of the period was intensified by the discovery of mass graves from the Stalinist purges of the 1930s at Kuroplaty and other locations. Although the Belarusian leadership still supported keeping the Soviet Union intact, Belarus's parliament declared Belarus a sovereign state within the USSR in July 1990. Shortly after the abortive August 1991 coup attempt against Soviet leader Mikhail Gorbachev, Belarus declared its independence on 26 August 1991.

Belarus's first president, Aleksandr Lukashenko, was elected in July 1994; the same year the country adopted its first post-Communist constitution. Lukashenko has halted economic and political reform and silenced or even jailed his critics using internal security forces. At the end of 1996 Belarus sent the last of its nuclear missiles back to Russia. Also in November 1996 Lukashenko won a plebiscite to expand his power as president, although most observers agreed that the election was not fair. On 28 November 1996 Lukashenko signed into law a new constitution containing provisions that gave him almost total control of all branches of government and extended his term by two years to 2001. A new bicameral National Assembly replaced the old parliament. During 1996 Lukashenko suspended the registration of new enterprises, stopped privatization, and spurned World Bank assistance. Under the new constitution, the president has the right to hire and fire the heads of the constitutional court and the central bank, and he also has the right to dissolve parliament and veto its decisions. Most members of the international community criticized the plebiscite expanding Lukashenko's power and do not recognize the 1996 constitution or the bicameral legislature that it established.

The constitutional changes implemented by the president sparked strong protests, including public demonstrations and opposition by the constitutional court and members of parliament, some of whom attempted to form their own assembly. However, all dissent was effectively suppressed, and Lukashenko remained in power. After boycotting the April 1999 local elections, his political opponents held an alternative presidential election in July.

LOCATION: 53°53′ N; 28°0′ E; BOUNDARY LENGTHS: Latvia 141 kilometers (88 miles); Lithuania 502 kilometers (312 miles); Poland, 605 kilometers (376 miles); Russia 959 kilometers (596 miles); Ukraine, 891 kilometers (554 miles).

This was followed by a new crackdown that forced opposition leader Semyon Sharetsky into exile. From exile Sharetsky proclaimed himself the nation's legitimate ruler, but his action had little effect on the actual state of political affairs in the country. Another prominent political dissident, Viktar Hanchar, was reported missing in September 1999 and is presumed dead.

In April 1997 Lukashenko and Russia's President Boris Yeltsin signed an initial charter for economic union that included a plan to adopt a common currency. However, over the following two years implementation of the integration plan moved slowly, and in September 1999 Belarus took steps to peg the country's currency to the euro. Nevertheless, at the end of year Belarus and Russia reaffirmed their intentions of forming an economic alliance. The leaders of both countries signed a new treaty in December 1999, and it was approved by both parliaments. In April 2000 Russia's new president, Vladimir Putin, reconfirmed his country's commitment to strengthening ties with Belarus.

Parliamentary elections held in 2001 were criticized by election observers as being neither free nor fair. Lukashenko and his administration manipulated the election process to make sure a minimum of opposition candidates were elected to parliament. Turnout in 13 constituencies was so low that a repeat of the voting was necessary (it was held in March 2001). On 9 September 2001 Lukashenko was reelected president in what Organization for Security and Cooperation in Europe (OSCE) observers described as undemocratic elections. Lukashenko won 75.6% of the vote, with opposition candidate Vladimir Goncharik winning 15.4% and Liberal Democratic Party leader Syargey Gaydukevich winning 2.5%. The government reported 83.9% of eligible voters participated in the election.

In June 2002 Russian president Vladimir Putin refused to follow the path to integration that Belarus had proposed for the two nations, saying it would lead to the recreation of "something along the lines of the Soviet Union." While Lukashenko pledged not to relinquish Belarus's sovereignty in the union with Russia, Putin put forth a proposal for the "ultimate unification" of both countries. Putin envisioned a federation based on the Russian constitution, with the Russian ruble as the state's sole currency and the election of a president in 2004. A constitution for the union was approved in March 2003. In April 2003 the speaker of the Russian Duma indicated Armenia, Ukraine, and Moldova might be probable candidates for joining the Belarus-Russian union. An economic union among Belarus, Russia, and Kazakhstan, agreed to in November 2011, was scheduled for implementation by 2015.

European policy has not been coherent or proactive in facing the human right violations in Belarus. In November 2002, 14 European Union (EU) states imposed a travel ban on Lukashenko and several of his government ministers as a way of protesting Belarus's poor human rights record. However, Lukashenko continued to eliminate political opponents, attack independent press, and expand his powers. In February 2003 Lukashenko pledged support for Iraq in the prelude to war that began on 19 March, led by a US and UK coalition, to project an image of a strong and independent leader. Among European countries, Poland has been playing the most active role in promoting democratic changes and market transformation in Belarus and supporting the country's national revival. However, the Polish government has not developed a strong or consistent policy of dealing with Lukashenko.

In December 2005 presidential elections were declared for March 2006. As the March elections approached, parliament approved a bill spelling out strict penalties for those found guilty of inciting demonstrations or distributing information regarded as harmful to national interests. In February and March 2006 dozens of people were arrested at opposition demonstrations in Minsk as the election date approached. On 19 March Lukashenko was declared the winner with 82.6% of the vote, in an election condemned as neither free nor fair by Western observers. Voter turnout was 92.6%, according to the government. In April the EU imposed a visa ban on Lukashenko and many other Belarusian ministers and officials. Also in April, defeated presidential election candidate Alexander Milinkevich, who received 6% of the vote in March, was jailed for 15 days after attending a rally to mark the anniversary of the Chernobyl disaster in Ukraine. In July 2006 defeated presidential election candidate Alexander Kozulin, who took a mere 2.3% of the vote in March, was convicted of hooliganism and incitement to mass disorder. He was sentenced to five and a half years in prison. That November the youth opposition activist Dmitriy Dashkevich was sentenced to 18 months in prison for

belonging to an unregistered organization. In March 2007 police clashed with protesters in Minsk as thousands of opposition supporters held a rally calling for an end to the Lukashenko regime.

In December 2006 after tense negotiations during which Russia threatened to cut gas supplies to Belarus, a new gas agreement was signed with Belarus more than doubling the price and phasing in further increases over the next four years. In January 2007 Russia cut its supply of oil along an oil export pipeline through Belarus to Europe during a disagreement with Belarus over taxation and allegations of illegal siphoning of oil. The dispute was resolved after Belarus cancelled a transit tax and Russia agreed to cut oil export duties. The EU condemned Russia for cutting off oil supplies without consultation.

In the 19 December 2010 presidential election Lukashenko was declared the winner with 79.7% of the vote. The announcement of the results sparked massive protests, particularly in the capital, when some of the 10,000 anti-Lukashenko demonstrators who were gathered attempted to storm a government building. This led to violent confrontations with police as the crowd was dispersed by force. Within the two days of the completion of the election, about 600 protesters had been arrested and/or detained, including seven of the nine candidates that ran against Lukashenko. Dozens of injuries were reported. Although Lukashenko argued that the election was as democratic as possible, observers from the OSCE called the vote flawed, primarily due to the lack of transparency in the counting process. The OSCE reported that designated observers were restricted from monitoring the counting process in more than 90% of the observed polling stations. Although the government's heavy-handed crackdown on protestors was largely condemned by the international community, Lukashenko accused opposition supporters of banditry and claimed that law enforcement officials acted within the bounds of the law to "defend the country and people from barbarism and ruin."

In August 2011 a bomb explosion in a subway station near Lukashenko's office killed 12 people, wounded 150, and worsened an already tense political situation. Two days later, Lukashenko announced that security services had caught the perpetrators, who had confessed to the crime. No motives or details of the investigation were announced.

13 GOVERNMENT

In May 1993 a draft constitution was presented to the 12th session of parliament, which adopted 88 of the new constitution's 153 articles. Until mid-1994 Belarus was the only former Soviet republic not to have a president. The chairman of the Supreme Soviet was considered the chief of state, but power remained in the hands of the Council of Ministers headed by a prime minister.

On 19 July 1994 elections for president were held in Belarus. Aleksandr Lukashenko received 80.1% of the vote. He was elected on a platform of clearing out the ruling Communist establishment. Lukashenko, however, was considered a Communist populist, with no plans for implementing political or economic reform. By Western standards, he ruled as a dictator.

In November 1996 Lukashenko won a plebiscite to expand his powers. He signed a new constitution into law giving the president power to dissolve parliament and authorized the formation of a new bicameral national assembly with a 64-member upper house, the Council of the Republic, and a 110-member lower house, the House of Representatives. All legislators serve four-year terms. The president's term was also extended until 2001, the year he was reelected. The October 2004 referendum, criticized by observers as fraudulent, revised the constitution to eliminate presidential term limits. Consequently, Lukashenko was eligible to run for a third term in 2006, an election he won. Parliamentary elections held in 2004 resulted in the election of only pro-Lukashenko candidates, with many opposition candidates disqualified on technicalities.

The presidential elections held in 2006 and 2010 failed to meet international standards. They were characterized by a disregard for the basic rights of freedom of assembly, association, and expression and included a highly problematic vote count. The opposition and civic activists were detained by the government during the campaign, and force was used against demonstrators protesting the fraudulent election.

14 POLITICAL PARTIES

The Communist Party was declared illegal after the abortive August 1991 coup attempt against Soviet leader Mikhail Gorbachev, but was re-legalized in February 1993. With two other pro-Communist parties it merged into the People's Movement of Belarus in May 1993. On the whole, political parties have not gathered the momentum evident in other former Soviet republics. None of the parties has had a large public following.

The parties with the greatest representation in the 260-member unicameral Supreme Council elected in 1995 were the Communist Party of Belarus (KPB—42 seats) and the Belarusian Agrarian Party (AP—33 seats). Following the elections in October 2004, which were widely criticized internationally, all the seats were won by pro-Lukashenko candidates. The Supreme Council was disbanded under the terms of the 1996 constitution and replaced with a bicameral legislature, for which the first elections were held in January 1997.

The primary pro-government party is the Belarusian Popular Patriotic Union, which supports President Lukashenko and the proposed union with Russia. Other pro-government parties include the AP, the KPB, the Liberal Democratic Party of Belarus, and the Social-Sports Party. The primary opposition party is the Belarusian Popular Front, whose chairman, Zyanon Paznyak, was in exile in the United States and whose other leaders were jailed at various times. The Popular Front was one of three parties that organized the alternative presidential elections held in 1999 to protest the extension of President Lukashenko's term to 2001. Other opposition parties are the Belarusian Social-Democrat Party Narodnaya Gromada (BSDP NG), the Belarusian Social-Democratic Party Hromada, the United Civic Party (UCP), the Party of Communists Belarusian (PKB), and the Women's Party Nadezhda. The opposition Belarusian Party of Labor was liquidated in August 2004, but remains active.

In presidential elections held on 19 March 2006, Lukashenko won 82.6% of the vote in an election deemed neither free nor fair by Western observers. Contesting Lukashenko's rule were Alexander Milinkevich, who won 6% of the vote; Sergei Gaidukevich, who took 3.5%; and Alexander Kozulin, who won 2.3% of the vote. Kozulin was beaten and arrested during post-election protests. He was sentenced to a five-year jail term but was released in 2008.

In the 2008 legislative elections the KPB took six seats in the 110-seat chamber of representatives. The AP won one seat and the remaining 103 seats were won by candidates with no affiliations.

Lukashenko again won the presidency in the 19 December 2010 election.

15 LOCAL GOVERNMENT

Belarus is divided into six provinces (oblasts) and one municipality. The oblasts are roughly parallel to counties in the United States. Each has a capital city, and the name of the oblast is typically derived from the name of this city. The names of the six oblasts are Brestskaya, Homyel'skaya, Hrodzyenskaya, Mahilyowskaya, Minskaya, and Vitsyebskaya. The municipality is Horad Minsk. Local Councils of Deputies are elected for four-year terms. A 1994 decree gave the president the right to appoint and dismiss senior local officials. The constitutional modifications passed in 1996 gave the president increased powers over local government, including the power of nullifying rulings by local councils.

16 JUDICIAL SYSTEM

The court system consists of district courts, regional courts, and the Supreme Court. Higher courts serve as appellate courts but also serve as courts of first instance. There are also economic courts, and a Supreme Economic Court. Trials are generally public unless closed on grounds of national security. Litigants have a right to counsel and, in cases of need, to appointment of counsel at state expense.

The president appoints all district level and military judges. The 1996 constitution gives the president the power to appoint 6 of the 12 members of the constitutional court, including the chief justice. The Council of the Republic appoints the other remaining 6 members of the constitutional court. The judiciary is not independent and is under the influence of the executive. Legislation concerning independence of the judiciary was passed in 1995, but the laws have not been implemented. The constitutional court was established in 1994 and adjudicates serious constitutional issues, but it has no power to enforce its decisions. Prosecutors are responsible to the procurator general who is appointed by the Council of the Republic according to the 1996 constitution. The offices of prosecutors consist of district offices, regional, and republic level offices.

17 ARMED FORCES

The International Institute for Strategic Studies (IISS) reports that armed forces in Belarus totaled 72,940 members in 2011. The force is comprised of 29,600 from the army, 18,170 from the air force, and 25,170 members of joint forces. Armed forces represent 3.7% of the labor force in Belarus. Defense spending totaled $1.8 billion and accounted for 1.4% of gross domestic product (GDP).

18 INTERNATIONAL COOPERATION

Belarus was admitted to the UN on 22 October 1945 and serves on several specialized agencies, such as IAEA, International Monetary Fund (IMF), UNCTAD, UNESCO, UNIDO, World Health Organization (WHO), and the World Bank. It is an observer in the World Trade Organization (WTO). Belarus joined the OSCE on 30 January 1992. The country is part of the Commonwealth of Independent Nations (CIS) and the Central European Initiative.

In 2000 Belarus, Kazakhstan, Russia, Kyrgyzstan, and Tajikistan established the Eurasian Economic Community.

The country has signed the Nuclear Nonproliferation Treaty and has formal diplomatic ties with many nations. It is a member of the Nuclear Suppliers Group (London Group) and the Non-aligned Movement. The country is also a member of the NATO Partnership for Peace. The United States recognized Belarus's sovereignty 25 December 1991. US diplomatic relations with Belarus were established two days later. Belarus has unresolved boundary disputes with Ukraine and Latvia.

In environmental cooperation, Belarus is part of the Basel Convention, the Conventions on Biological Diversity and Air Pollution, Ramsar, CITES, the London Convention, the Montréal Protocol, MARPOL, and the UN Conventions on Climate Change and Desertification.

In May 2009 Belarus signed an agreement with the European Union (EU) as part of a new Eastern Partnership Initiative (EPI), designed to establish greater economic ties with EU members, without the prospect of EU membership. Through the EPI, the EU promises economic aid and technical and security consultations in return for a commitment to democratic reform. The EU invitation to sign the partnership agreement was extended to five other former Soviet states

[19]ECONOMY

The GDP rate of change in Belarus, as of 2010, was 7.6%. Inflation stood at 7%, and unemployment was reported at 1%. Belarus's economy has been geared toward industrial production, mostly in machinery and metallurgy with a significant military component, although trade and services account for an increasing share of economic activity. Forestry and agriculture, notably potatoes, grain, peat, and cattle, are also important. Belarus's economy was closely integrated with those of Eastern Europe and the other republics of the former Soviet Union, and the breakup of the Soviet Union was highly disruptive to the economy of Belarus. The demand for military products was cut sharply, and supplies of imported energy and raw materials were curtailed.

Even though the economy was suffering, there was a high level of capitalist reform between 1991 and 1994. State enterprises, including banks, were privatized and many institutions of private property were formed.

Even after the break-up, both economic and political ties between Belarus and Russia remained close. In 1994 Aleksandr Lukashenko became president and began reversing many of the capitalist reforms. In 1995 he began to instill a program of "market socialism," and many state enterprises that had been privatized were re-nationalized. The process also allowed government control in all companies with foreign investment. Western analysts also accused the Belarusian government of printing more money to subsidize higher salaries, thereby fueling inflation.

In 1997 Belarus and Russia signed a treaty of union, to provide for close cooperation in foreign affairs and military and economic policies including freedom of movement for citizens, property ownership, and participation in local elections. However, each country retained its sovereignty, independence, territorial integrity, and other aspects of statehood. A constitution for the union was approved in 2003.

As a result of this union, Russia has become Belarus's primary trading partner. The union also preceded an interesting trade situation between Belarus and Russia. Russia exported discounted oil to Belarus, and Belarus would then re-export the oil and gas at world market value and gain the profits.

This situation was remedied with a change in the export duty and an agreement that the profits from the exportation of natural gas and oil must be shared with Russia. This resulted in decreased trade with Russia in 2007.

The business climate remains poor in Belarus. Production has increased, but products are uncompetitive on the world market and many are placed in warehouses for storage. Losses from state-owned businesses are largely written off, which prevents those businesses from going bankrupt and keeps unemployment artificially low. Further borrowing is the main mechanism used to manage the pressures of the economy.

In 2008 about 80% of industry remained state controlled. Belarus has had a hard time attracting foreign investment because of the tight state control on monetary policy and industry.

Despite having an economy that seems to be doing well on paper, most international analysts agree that as long as Lukashenko continues to favor the obsolete industrial base and as long as he continues to pump subsidies into the agricultural sector (the peasants and the blue collar workers are his main constituency), Belarus will not achieve healthy and sustainable economic growth.

[20]INCOME

The CIA estimated that in 2010 the GDP of Belarus was $131.2 billion. The CIA defines GDP as the value of all final goods and services produced within a nation in a given year and computed on the basis of purchasing power parity (PPP) rather than value as measured on the basis of the rate of the exchange based on current dollars. The per capita GDP was estimated at $13,600. The annual growth rate of GDP was 7.6%. The average inflation rate was 7%. It was estimated that agriculture accounted for 9% of GDP, industry 42.9%, and services 48.1%.

According to the World Bank, remittances from citizens living abroad totaled $357.8 million or about $37 per capita and accounted for approximately 0.3% of GDP.

The World Bank reported that in 2009 household consumption in Belarus totaled $27.3 billion or about $2,855 per capita, measured in current US dollars rather than PPP. Household consumption includes expenditures of individuals, households, and nongovernmental organizations on goods and services, excluding the purchases of dwellings. It was estimated that household consumption was growing at an average annual rate of 0.4%.

As of 2011 the most recent study by the World Bank reported that actual individual consumption in Belarus was 64.3% of GDP and accounted for 0.18% of world consumption. By comparison, the United States accounted for 25.44% of world individual consumption. The World Bank also estimated that 24.8% of Belarus's GDP was spent on food and beverages, 9.3% on housing and household furnishings, 3.7% on clothes, 5.7% on health, 3.9% on transportation, 2.3% on communications, 2.7% on recreation, 1.3% on restaurants and hotels, and 4% on miscellaneous goods and services and purchases from abroad.

As of 2011 CIA estimated that about 17% of the population subsisted on an income below the poverty line established by Belarus's government.

21 LABOR

Although the constitution provides for the right of workers to form and join independent unions, these rights are not respected in practice. Union activity is discouraged and almost impossible to conduct in most of the state-owned larger industries. Strikes are legally permitted but tight control by the regime over public demonstrations makes it difficult to strike or hold public rallies. The government has harassed and arrested union leaders and broken up union-sponsored activities. In addition, workers who are fired for union or political activity are not required to be re-hired by their employers.

Forced or compulsory labor by adults or children is prohibited. The statutory minimum employment age is 16, although a child of 14 can be employed if the parent or legal guardian gives written consent. In addition, minors under the age of 18 cannot work at hazardous jobs or those which will adversely affect his or her education. Also they cannot work overtime on government holidays or on the weekend. The workweek is set at 40 hours, with a 24-hour rest period per week. Safety and health standards in the workplace are often ignored. As of 2010 the minimum wage was $132 a month, which does not provide a decent standard of living. However, average real wages were officially reported (as of end 2010) at around $530 per month, although many receive additional income from the underground economy.

As of 2009 Belarus had a total labor force of five million people. Within that labor force, CIA estimates in 2003 noted that 14% were employed in agriculture, 34.7% in industry, and 51.3% in the service sector.

22 AGRICULTURE

Roughly 27% of the total land is currently farmed, and the country's major crops include grain, potatoes, vegetables, sugar beets, and flax. Cereal production in 2009 amounted to 8.2 million tons, fruit production 691,704 tons, and vegetable production 2.3 million tons.

23 ANIMAL HUSBANDRY

The UN Food and Agriculture Organization (FAO) reported that Belarus dedicated 3.3 million hectares (8.11 million acres) to permanent pasture or meadow in 2009. During that year, the country tended 29.2 million chickens, 4.1 million head of cattle, and 3.7 million pigs. The production from these animals amounted to 212,707 tons of beef and veal, 313,211 tons of pork, 173,047 tons of poultry, 147,172 tons of eggs, and 1.52 million tons of milk. Belarus also produced 34,105 tons of cattle hide and 86 tons of raw wool. Belarus produces more dairy products than any other former Soviet republic except Russia, with 400 tons of butter and ghee and 80,800 tons of cheese produced in 2004. That year, honey production amounted to 3,100 tons.

24 FISHING

As a landlocked nation, fishing is confined to the system of rivers (Pripyat, Byarezina, Nyoman, Zach Dvina, Sozh, Dnieper) that cross Belarus. In 2008 the annual capture totaled 900 tons according to the FAO.

25 FORESTRY

About 43% of the total land area was covered by forests in 2009. Radioactive contamination of some forestland from the 1986 Chernobyl disaster has severely restricted output. The FAO estimated the 2009 roundwood production at 7.41 million cu m (261.7 million cu ft). The value of all forest products, including roundwood, totaled $258.4 million.

26 MINING

Potash is the one significant mineral resource possessed by Belarus, which accounted for 14% of world production in 2008. During the 1980s Belarus produced 5 million tons per year (calculated based on potassium oxide content), about 50% of the former Soviet Union's output. After the breakup of the Soviet Union, production fell to 1.95 million tons by 1993. A program was then undertaken to raise the quality of potash to world standards to increase exports. Total production in 2009 was 2.48 million tons, down from 4.97 million tons in 2007. Potash is mined in the Salihorsk region by the Belaruskaliy production association. Accumulated waste from the industry has raised environmental concerns. Two plants produced 4.35 million tons of cement in 2009.

27 ENERGY AND POWER

Domestic electricity is produced by four thermal plants. Belarus also imports electricity generated by nuclear and hydroelectric plants. The World Bank reported in 2008 that Belarus produced 35.1 billion kWh of electricity and consumed 33.2 billion kWh or 3,464 kWh per capita. Roughly 92% of energy came from fossil fuels, with the remainder from hydropower and other sources. In the same year, consumption of electricity totaled 31.07 million kWh. Per capita oil consumption was 2,907 kg. In 2008 Belarus imported 1.84 billion kWh of electricity and exported 5.245 billion kWh.

There are two major oil refineries: Mazyr and Navapolatsk. Although oil consumption has been cut roughly in half since the early 1990s, Belarus was still obliged to import 75% of its oil from Russia as of 2002. In December 2002 Belarus sold its 11% stake in Slavneft, a joint Belarusian-Russian state-run oil company, to Russia.

Belarus and Russia had another dispute over oil starting in December 2006. Russia decided to levy a duty on oil to Belarus in order to recoup profits from Belarus's processing of previously duty-free Russian-sourced crude oil. In January 2007 both countries agreed on a smaller duty than Russia had originally imposed. In January 2010 there was another dispute as Belarus and Russia could not come to an agreement on renewing the January 2007 agreement. A new accord was subsequently reached whereby Russia would export oil duty-free for Belarus's internal consumption, but oil to be processed for re-export would be subject to full export duties. As of 2008 oil production in Belarus totaled 30,000 barrels of oil a day.

In 2009 and 2010 Belarus accrued substantial debt to Russia, after Russia began to gradually inflate the price of the gas sold to Belarus. Before 2009 Belarus was accustomed to being charged $150 per 1,000 cu ft of Russian gas. By the end of the first quarter of 2010, however, Russia was charging Belarus $184.80, yet Belarus continued to pay the original price for the gas. The state-owned Russian energy giant, Gazprom, estimated that Belarus would owe between $500 and $600 million by the end of 2010 if no adjustment was made in Belarus's payment plan. Russian president Dmitry Medvedev ordered Gazprom to begin reducing supplies to Belarus on a day-by-day basis to squeeze the country into compliance. In June 2010 Belarus announced that it would take out a $200 million loan to pay off its gas debts to Russia.

28 INDUSTRY

Belarus's industrial base is relatively well-developed and diversified compared to other former Soviet states. Belarus's main industries are engineering, machine tools, agricultural equipment, fertilizer, chemicals, defense-related products, prefabricated construction materials, motor vehicles, motorcycles, textiles, threads, and some consumer products such as refrigerators, watches, televisions, and radios. The types of motor vehicles produced are off-highway dump trucks with up to 110-metric-ton load capacity, tractors, earth movers for construction and mining, and 25-metric-ton trucks for use in road-less and tundra areas.

While there had been an increase in industrial production as of 2002, a high volume of unsold industrial goods remain stocked in warehouses due to high overhead costs that make Belarusian products uncompetitive on the world market. Belarus has taken few steps to privatize state-owned industries, and most remain under state authority.

By 2004 the participation of industry in the overall economic output had decreased to 36.4%, while its share in the labor fell to 34.7%. Agriculture made up 11% of the GDP and employed 14% of the labor force; services came in first with 52.6%, and 51.3% respectively. The industrial production growth was less than half of the GDP growth rate, at 10.5 4%, but it recovered in the first nine months of 2005 (10%) and was well above the same rate in Russia and Ukraine (4% and 3.2% respectively).

In 2010 industrial production growth rate was 10.5%. As of 2010 agriculture shared 9.5% of the GDP, industry shared 44.8% and services made up to 45.8% of the GDP.

29 SCIENCE AND TECHNOLOGY

According to the World Bank there were 1,510 patent applications in science and technology in Belarus as of 2009. The Academy of Sciences of Belarus, founded in 1929 and headquartered in Minsk, has departments of physics, mathematics, informatics, physical and engineering problems of machine building and energetic, chemical and geological sciences, biological sciences, and medical-biological sciences. The academy also operates numerous research institutes.

The Belarusian State University, founded in 1921 at Minsk, has faculties of applied mathematics, biology, chemistry, geography, mechanics and mathematics, physics, and radiophysics and electronics. The Belarusian State Technological University, founded in 1930 at Minsk, has faculties of chemistry technology and engineering, forestry, and organic substances technology. In 1987–97 science and engineering students accounted for 48% of college and university enrollment.

The Belarusian State Scientific and Technical Library, located in Minsk, had more than 1.2 million volumes as of 1996. In 2007

Principal Trading Partners – Belarus (2010)				
(In millions of US dollars)				
Country	**Total**	**Exports**	**Imports**	**Balance**
World	60,167.9	25,283.5	34,884.4	-9,600.9
Russia	27,874.3	9,816.1	18,058.2	-8,242.1
Ukraine	4,439.9	2,562.3	1,877.6	684.7
Netherlands	3,091.7	2,773.3	318.4	2,454.9
Germany	2,849.1	461.0	2,388.1	-1,927.1
China	2,157.4	474.0	1,683.4	-1,209.5
Poland	1,963.8	886.3	1,077.4	-191.1
Venezuela	1,454.7	302.3	1,152.3	-850.0
United Kingdom	1,296.0	984.0	312.0	672.0
Latvia	1,026.4	930.6	95.8	834.7
Italy	963.2	191.7	771.5	-579.7

(…) data not available or not significant.

(n.s.) not specified.

SOURCE: *2011 Direction of Trade Statistics Yearbook*, New York: United Nations, 2011.

total research and development (R&D) expenditures in Belarus amounted to $348.3 million or 0.96% of GDP, of which 63.4% came from the government, 24.4% from business, 10.1% from foreign sources, and 2.2% from higher education. In that year, 1,870 researchers and 207 technicians per million people were actively engaged in R&D. In 2002 high technology exports totaled $212 million or 4% of manufactured exports. As of 2009 public financing of science was 0.96% of GDP.

30 DOMESTIC TRADE

In 1992 retail prices rose more than 1,000%. The same year a parallel national currency (called the ruble) was introduced and declared the only legal tender for purchasing goods such as food, alcohol, and tobacco. In 1998 the inflation rate was 182%. Though the government had initiated some capitalist reforms from 1991 to 1994, President Aleksandr Lukashenko (elected 1994) has significantly slowed efforts toward privatization through a program of "market socialism." The government has administrative control of prices and currency exchange rates and has also re-established certain management rights over private enterprises. As of early 2010 nearly 80% of industry was state-owned. Independent banks had also been re-nationalized. Normal business hours are from 9 a.m. to 6 p.m.

31 FOREIGN TRADE

Before the collapse of the Soviet Union, Belarus exported about 40% of its industrial output to other Soviet republics and imported 90% of its primary energy and 70% of its raw materials from them. Belarus has remained exceedingly dependant on Russia for economic support; a proposed EU-style partnership between the two nations threatens its economic independence. Belarus imported $29.79 billion worth of goods and services in 2008, while exporting $24.49 billion worth of goods and services.

In 2010 Belarus exported machinery and transport equipment, chemicals, petroleum products, mineral products, metals, textiles, foodstuff. Imports included mineral products, machinery and equipment, chemicals, foodstuff, and metals. As of 2010 its major

Balance of Payments – Belarus (2010)

(In millions of US dollars)

Current Account		**-8,316.8**
Balance on goods		-9,077.6
Imports	-34,482.7	
Exports	25,405.1	
Balance on services		1,619.5
Balance on income		-1,162.8
Current transfers		304.1
Capital Account		**144.9**
Financial Account		**6,140.2**
Direct investment abroad		-50.4
Direct investment in Belarus		1,402.8
Portfolio investment assets		-59.4
Portfolio investment liabilities		1,245.0
Financial derivatives		...
Other investment assets		-1,178.4
Other investment liabilities		4,780.6
Net Errors and Omissions		**593.9**
Reserves and Related Items		**1,437.8**

(...) data not available or not significant.

SOURCE: *Balance of Payment Statistics Yearbook 2011*, Washington, DC: International Monetary Fund, 2011.

Public Finance – Belarus (2009)

(In billions of rubels, central government figures)

Revenue and Grants	**48,452.5**	**100.0%**
Tax revenue	26,470.9	54.6%
Social contributions	15,799.4	32.6%
Grants	...	...
Other revenue	6,182.2	12.8%
Expenditures	**48,276**	**100.0%**
General public services	9,014.1	18.7%
Defense	1,350.4	2.8%
Public order and safety	2,400.7	5.0%
Economic affairs	12,613.1	26.1%
Environmental protection	410.8	0.9%
Housing and community amenities	330.2	0.7%
Health	1,483.8	3.1%
Recreational, culture, and religion	1,261.4	2.6%
Education	2,079.6	4.3%
Social protection	17,331.9	35.9%

(...) data not available or not significant.

SOURCE: *Government Finance Statistics Yearbook 2010*, Washington, DC: International Monetary Fund, 2010.

export partners were Russia, 38.9%; Netherlands, 11%; Ukraine, 10.2%. Major import partners were Russia 51.8%, Germany 6.8%, Ukraine 5.4%, China 4.8%.

Other important trading partners included the United Kingdom, Germany, the Netherlands, and Poland.

³²BALANCE OF PAYMENTS

The CIA reported that in 2010 the PPP of Belarus's exports was $25.35 billion, while imports totaled $34.47 billion, resulting in a trade deficit of $600 million. The same year Belarus had a foreign trade deficit of $5.5 billion, amounting to 0.2% of GDP.

The US State Department reported that in 2010 Belarus had exports of goods totaling $24.8 billion (refined petroleum, potash fertilizers, machinery and transport equipment, chemicals, foodstuff, metal, and textiles) and imports totaling $30.4 billion (mineral products, machinery and equipment, metals, crude oil and natural gas, chemicals, and foodstuff). As of 2011 the IMF reported that the services credit totaled $3.49 billion and debit $2.067 billion.

³³BANKING AND SECURITIES

The National Bank of Belarus is the central bank of the country, charged with regulating the money supply, circulating currency, and regulating the commercial banks of Belarus. The currency unit is the ruble. There are no current figures on the level of foreign currency reserves, but it is widely assumed that these have dwindled to perilously low levels because of the need for the National Bank of Belarus to maintain the local currency at its overvalued exchange rate on the Minsk Interbank Currency Exchange (MICE). The central bank has also had to turn to the street market to replenish reserves; in August 1996 it bought $25 million, paying effectively 10% more than it would have through MICE. Under Belarus's "currency corridor," the Belarusian ruble cannot fall

below BYB615,000 to $1 at its twice-weekly auctions at the MICE. The street market accounts for 70–80% of foreign exchange trading. The IMF reports that in 2001 currency and demand deposits—an aggregate commonly known as M1—were equal to $640.0 million. In that same year, M2—an aggregate equal to M1 plus savings deposits, small time deposits, and money market mutual funds—was $1.8 billion.

In 2010 the discount rate, the interest rate at which the central bank lends to financial institutions in the short term, was 10.5%. At the end of 2010 the nation's reserves of foreign exchange and gold estimated $3.431 billion.

³⁴INSURANCE

The Insurance Supervisory Department, part of the Ministry of Finance, regulates the insurance industry. No recent information about the insurance industry in Belarus is available.

³⁵PUBLIC FINANCE

Because it was formerly a part of the Soviet Union, Belarus has a well-established industrial base, but the transition from a centrally planned economy to a free market economy has not been easy. Privatization, although in progress, has been happening slowly, and foreign investment is discouraged by the "hostile" business climate.

In 2010 the budget of Belarus included $23.27 billion in public revenue and $24.32 billion in public expenditures. The budget deficit amounted to 2% of GDP. In total $25.04 billion of the debt was held by foreign entities.

Government outlays by function were as follows: general public services, 13.43%; defense, 2.5%; public order and safety, 4.28%; economic affairs, 23.22%; health, 8.97%; recreation, culture, and religion, 2.32%; education, 11.51%; and social protection, 27%.

36 TAXATION

Belarus imposes a wide array of taxes on business and citizens. In 2009 the corporate income tax for resident companies was 24%. Securities transactions are taxed at 40%. There are also local taxes of approximately 3%, creating an aggregate rate of profits tax of 26.3%. Foreign companies not registered for tax purposes in Belarus are subject to 15% with-holding tax. Joint ventures in which foreign participation is more than 30% are eligible for a three-year tax holiday.

The main indirect tax is the country's value-added tax (VAT) with a standard rate of 20%. VAT is payable on most goods in Belarus at 20% (2011). A reduced rate of 12% is placed upon certain foodstuffs, agricultural products, repair services, hairdressers, and laundries. Other consumption taxes include a 1% turnover tax and excise taxes ranging from 10–75%. There are also taxes on the use of natural resources. Individual income is taxed according to a progressive schedule of rates at 12% (up from 4.7%). There is a 64.8% employer payroll tax for social security and employment taxes. There are also direct taxes on property and land.

37 CUSTOMS AND DUTIES

A 1995 customs union with Russia allows goods to flow between the two countries duty-free. However, the union required Belarus to conform its customs rates to those of Russia, resulting in a tariff increase from 5–10% to 20–40%. In 1995 Belarus also introduced a 20% import VAT to be paid at the border on all incoming goods, except certain raw material used by local manufacturers.

38 FOREIGN INVESTMENT

Foreign direct investment (FDI) in Belarus was a net inflow of $1.88 billion according to World Bank figures published in 2009. FDI represented 3.84% of GDP.

The European Bank for Reconstruction and Development (EBRD) financed several major infrastructure improvement and commercial projects. The World Bank was financing construction and telecommunication projects, but these were discontinued in 1996 by President Lukashenko. At the end of the decade, President Lukashenko's steadfast refusal to implement market reforms continued to keep foreign investment levels low. In May 2002, however, the government announced a new program aimed at raising the share of foreign investment in GDP from 19% to 26–28%, with most investments coming from Russia. Several state-owned enterprises (SOEs), including oil refineries and chemical plants, were to be transformed into joint stock companies in preparation of selling 49.9% in blocks of 10%. Many restrictions are still tied to foreign investments and in June 2003, President Lukashenko announced that he had turned down proposals from foreign investors amounting to $10 billion because of unacceptable terms. The president stated that the government's goal was at least $1 billion in FDI in 2003.

FDI inflow for Belarus reached $444 million in 1999, up from $352 million in 1997 and $203 million in 1998. However, the inflow was reduced to a trickle in 2000 ($90 million) and 2001 ($169 million). During the time period 1993–2003, according to the Belarus government, foreign investment totaled $4 billion, $1.7 billion in FDI and $2.5 billion in credits guaranteed by the government. All but a small proportion of foreign investment has come from Russia. Other sources include the Netherlands, Germany, and the United States (McDonald's, Coca Cola, and Ford). However, McDonald's and Coca Cola have both had problems with the government and the Ford plant closed in 2000.

Investments regained strength in 2004, but they were still relatively low to the GDP. For the most part, investments are fueled by a high domestic demand (such as financing of new housing), and in Belarus only a small part went to productive assets. However, Belarus has been determined to capitalize on its domestic liberalization and privatization program by boosting its foreign investment. In 2008 it drew total overseas investment of $6.5 billion, of which $2.23 billion was direct investment, up 28.9% from 2007 which in turn saw a five-fold increase on 2006. In 2009 the total overseas investment amounted to $9.3 billion, of which $4.8 billion was direct investment, up 1.4 times compared to 2008.

As of 2008 nearly 4,800 companies had been started in Belarus with foreign backing, with investors from more than 77 countries. The majority of investment in 2008 came from EU states (43%) and Russia (33%). In 2009 among the major investors were Russia (82.5 %), Switzerland (7.3%), Cyprus (2.2%) and Germany (1.1%).

39 ECONOMIC DEVELOPMENT

In the summer of 1995 the Belarusian president announced the policy of "market socialism," after a period of economic liberalization and privatization that had taken place from 1991–94. The government still controls key market sectors as the private sector only makes up 20% of the economy. Most of the heavy industry in Belarus remains state-owned. Belarus offers easy credit to spur economic growth, but this comes at the price of high inflation. To combat spiraling wages and prices, President Lukashenko imposed price controls. These policies have driven away foreign investment and left Belarus economically isolated.

Bad harvests in 1998 and 1999 and continued trade deficits worsened the climate of economic development. The government resorted to inflationary monetary policies, including the printing of money, to pay salaries and pensions. In 2000 the government tightened its monetary policies, but in 2002 the IMF criticized Belarus for its economic performance and refused to resume loans to the country (IMF loans were last offered in 1995). The balance of payments situation remained weak from 2001–03 as the ruble rose against the US dollar and the Russian ruble. The current account deficit was 0.2% of GDP in 2009.

Through 2011, Belarus continued to rely on trade with and assistance from Russia, which made it vulnerable to the political and economic demands of Russia. Those demands typically favored Russia in the long term in order to meet short-term needs in Belarus.

40 SOCIAL DEVELOPMENT

Old age, disability, and survivors are protected by a social insurance system that was updated in 1999. Sickness, maternity, work injury, family allowance, and unemployment benefits are covered by the system. Employers contribute between 10–35% of payroll depending on the type of company. The government covers the cost of social pensions and subsidies as needed. Retirement is set at age 60 for men and age 55 for women. Workers' compensation laws were first instituted in 1939. Family allowances are available for families with one or more children.

The human rights record of Belarus has worsened in recent years, after President Lukashenko amended the constitution to extend his stay in office and handpick members of parliament. Reports of police brutality are widespread and prison conditions are poor. Arbitrary arrests and detention have been reported, as well as incidents of severe hazing in the military. As of 2004 political opponents and protests are met with a violent government response. The government abridges freedom of the press, speech, assembly, religion, and movement. Religious freedom and equality is provided for in the constitution, but religions other than Russian Orthodox are discriminated against. There were a number of right wing and skinhead groups active in 2012.

Domestic abuse and violence against women continued to be a significant problem in 2012. Although laws against rape exist, most women do not report the crime due to fear that the police will blame the victim. Spousal rape is not viewed as a crime. While there are no legal restrictions on women's participation in public life, social barriers are considerable, and women commonly experience discrimination when it comes to job opportunities. The law mandates equal pay for equal work, but few women reach senior management or government positions. The human trafficking of women remains a serious problem.

41 HEALTH

The Belarusian health system is free at the point of use. While there is equity in distribution of facilities and staff and receiving health services, there remains a disparity between urban and rural areas.

The Ministry of Health plays a key regulatory role at all levels of the highly centralized health system. Regional and district health authorities are considered to be important stakeholders, however due to their responsibility for local health care financing, their decision-making capacity is still limited.

The country spent 5.6% of its GDP on healthcare, amounting to $295 per person. Maternal and infant mortality have been steadily improving in recent years. According to the CIA, life expectancy in Belarus was 70 years in 2011.

Belarus is experiencing negative population growth as the birth rates are falling and death rates are increasing due to non-communicable diseases, external causes, and communicable diseases. The CIA calculated HIV/AIDS prevalence in Belarus to be about 0.3% in 2009.

There were 49 physicians, 126 nurses and midwives, and 112 hospital beds per 10,000 inhabitants. The fertility rate was 1.5, while the infant mortality rate was 11 per 1,000 live births. In 2008 the maternal mortality rate, according to the World Bank, was 15 per 100,000 births. It was estimated that 99% of children were vaccinated against measles.

42 HOUSING

The lack of adequate, affordable housing continues to be a problem for Belarus, but certain advances have been made. After the 1986 Chernobyl nuclear plant disaster, the government was forced to seal off 485 human settlement areas, displacing about 135,000 people. Over 65,000 apartments and homes have since been built to house these people. Since 1992 the government has been re-

forming housing laws to secure the constitutional right of citizens to acquire, build, reconstruct, or lease housing facilities.

In 1999 about 97% of the population were living in what was defined as conventional dwellings (primarily detached houses, separate or shared apartments or flats, and hostels). About 56% were living in separate flats. About 31% were in detached houses. Those living in flats had the greatest access to improved utilities, such as central heating, central piped hot water, and flush toilets. Nationwide, only about 68% of the population had flush toilets in the home (1999), and only 71% had piped water. About 26.5% of the total population were using stove heating. About 66% of the housing stock was built in the period 1961–90.

With gaining independence most housing stock in Belarus was privatized; as of 2008, 84% was in private hands, and the total housing stock consisted of 1,612,022 houses. The remaining 16% belongs to the state (National Housing Fund) or the municipalities (Municipal Housing Fund).

While individual housing units are more common in the suburbs and rural areas, apartment buildings are most common in the cities. Many new housing projects, especially in Minsk, have been constructed in Belarus since its independence. Most urban residents rent rather than own their apartments. Rents are subsidized and remain low, but the serious shortage of housing that existed during the Soviet period still remains a big issue in the 21st century. In 2008 nearly 717,500 families in the country were registered as in need of improvement of living conditions.

43 EDUCATION

Overall, the CIA estimated that Belarus had a literacy rate of 99.6%. Public expenditure on education represented 4.5% of GDP in 2009 with equal rates for men and women.

Education is compulsory for children between the ages of 6–15. The primary school program covers four years of study and basic education covers five years. General secondary programs are offered at gymnasiums (general studies), lyceums (affiliated with universities), and colleges (vocational studies); general secondary studies courses cover an additional two years. Students also have an option of attending a four-year technical school (technicum) or a three year trade school instead of the general programs.

Primary school enrollment in 2008 was estimated at about 94% of age-eligible children. The same year, secondary school enrollment was about 87% of age-eligible students. Tertiary enrollment was estimated at 77%. Of those enrolled in tertiary education, there were 100 male students for every 143 female students. As of 2007 school life expectancy was 15 years. It was estimated that about 99% of all students completed their primary education in 2010. Enrollment in primary school was 344,852 students in 2008, which declined from 470,986 in 2001. That same year female enrollment in primary school was 169,666 student and males students totaled 175,186. The academic year runs from September to July.

Education at public higher education institutes is free for students who pass the entrance competition. In 2005 there were 44 public higher education institutions, including 25 universities, 9 academies, 4 institutes, 5 colleges, and 1 technical school. There were also 13 private higher education institutions. Total enrollment at these institutions was about 545,800. The largest public institute is the Belarusian State University, which is located in Minsk and was founded in 1921.

The official languages of education are Belarusian, which is written in the Cyrillic script, and Russian. The government is now putting more emphasis on replacing Russian with Belarusian. The Ministry of Education and the National Institute for Higher Education are the primary administrative bodies.

44 LIBRARIES AND MUSEUMS

The country has an extensive public library system. Universities with significant library holdings include the Belarusian State Polytechnical Academy (over 2 million volumes), Belarusian State University (1.7 million volumes), and the Minsk Teacher Training Institute (1.2 million volumes). The presidential library holds 1.5 million volumes, and the Gomel Regional Library has 1.3 million volumes.

The country records 14,392 monuments and historic sites. The State Art Museum in Minsk houses the country's largest collection of fine arts. The Belarusian State Museum of the Great Patriotic War (World War II) in Minsk houses artifacts and memorials of the country's great travails during the war. There is a historical and archaeological museum in Grodno and a natural history museum in Belovezskaja Pusca.

45 MEDIA

The Ministry of Telecommunications controls all telecommunications through Beltelecom. Generally, Belarus's telecommunications system lags behind those of its neighbors, with modernization proceeding only slowly. In 2009 there were four million main phone lines; mobile cellular phone subscription averaged 100 per 100 people. International service is provided through analog lines to Russia; satellite ground stations belonging to Intersputnik, Eutelsat, and Intelsat; and through the country's membership in the Trans-European Line, the Trans-Asia-Europe fiber-optic line, and access to the Trans-Siberia Line. There are also fiber-optic connections to Russia, Latvia, Poland, and Ukraine.

The government operates the only nationwide television and radio stations. However, there are several local stations. Some Russian, Polish, and Lithuanian stations are received in various parts of the country, but the government has blocked certain programming and has removed some channels from local cable access. In 2009 there were 28 FM radio stations, 37 radio stations, and 11 shortwave radio stations.

In 2010 the country had about 147,311 internet hosts. As of 2009 there were some 2.6 million internet users in Belarus. All ISPs are controlled by the state.

The most widely read newspapers (with English title if applicable and 2010 circulation figures) are *Sovetskaya Belorussiya* (*Soviet Belorussia*, 330,000); *Narodnaya Hazeta* (*People's Newspaper*, 259,597); *Respublika* (*Republic*, 130,000); *Vechernii Minsk* (*Evening Minsk*, 111,000); *Svaboda* (90,000); *Zvyazda (Star, 90,000);* and *Belorusskaya Niva* (*Belarusian Cornfield*, 80,000).

Most of the higher circulation papers are controlled by the state in some way. Though freedom of the press is granted in the 1996 constitution, the government continues to restrict this right through a virtual monopoly over forms of mass communication and its desire to limit media criticism of its actions. The government controls the editorial content and policy of the largest circu-

lation daily newspapers and of radio and television broadcasts and places severe restrictions on the editorial content of independent publications or broadcasts. Local radio and television stations are pressured to refrain from reporting on national issues. Government authorities reserve the right to ban and censor publications presenting critical reports on national issues. In 2004 the government suspended publication of 25 privately owned newspapers.

46 ORGANIZATIONS

Belarus's important business and commercial organizations include the Chamber of Commerce and Industry of the Republic of Belarus. Important agricultural and industrial organizations include the Belarusian Peasants' Union, the Union of Entrepreneurs and Farmers, and the Union of Small Ventures. There are number of professional associations, particularly for members of medical professions.

The National Academy of Sciences and the Belarusian Physical Society promotes public interest and education in science. The Belarusian Think Tanks is a public policy center involved in developing and promoting ideas to create democracy, market economy, and respect for human rights in Belarus.

Political interest youth organizations include the Belarusian Patriotic Youth Union and the Youth Front of Belarus (est. 1993). The Belarus Youth Information Center (YIC) was founded in 1994 to encourage and support youth involvement in science, culture, and education. The Belarusian Students Association is an affiliate member of the National Union of Students in Europe (ESIB). There is an organization of Girl Guides in the country, the Young Men's Christian Association/Young Women's Christian Association (YMCA/YWCA), and a Junior Chamber Belarus. Several sports associations are active, representing such pastimes as baseball and softball, track and field, badminton, tennis, and air sports. The country sponsors a National Olympic Committee, a Paralympic Committee, and a Special Olympics chapter.

The International Association for Volunteer Effort serves to promote and provide a network for voluntary service organizations, including Lions Club International which is active in the country. There is also a League of Youth Voluntary Service. There are active chapters of the Red Cross, Caritas and United Nations Children's Fund (UNICEF).

47 TOURISM, TRAVEL, AND RECREATION

Scenery, architecture, and cultural museums and memorials are primary attractions in Belarus. The Belavaezhskaja Puscha Nature Reserve features a variety of wildlife and a nature museum. The city of Hrodna is home to the baroque Farny Cathedral, the Renaissance Bernadine church and monastery, and the History of Religion Museum which is part of a renovated 18th-century palace. There are also two castles in the area, both housing museums. A valid passport and visa are required of all visitors. An HIV test is required for visits longer than 90 days.

According to the *Tourism Factbook*, published by the UN World Tourism Organization, tourist arrivals to Belarus increased from 63,779 in 2003 to 95,000 in 2009. Of those incoming tourists, there were 92,000 from Europe. Tourism receipts totaled $562 million, much higher than the 2003 total of $339 million. There were 25,689 hotel beds available in Belarus, which had an occupancy rate of 46%.

Visitors should be prepared to demonstrate sufficient financial means to support their stay. The estimated daily cost to visit Minsk, the capital, was $393.

⁴⁸FAMOUS PERSONS

Frantsky Sharyna, who lived in the first quarter of the 16th century, translated the Bible into Belarusian. Symeon of Polatsk was a 17th-century poet who wrote in Belarusian. Maksim Bahdanovich (1891–1917) was an important 19th-century poet. Modern writers include Uladzimir Dubouka (1900–76) and Iazep Pushcha (1902–64), both poets. Kuzma Chorny (1900–44) and Kandrat Krapiva (1896–1991) were writers of fiction during the outpouring of Belarusian poetry and literature during the 1920s. Famous modern composers from Belarus include Dzmitry Lukas, Ryhor Pukst, and Yauhen Hlebau (1929–2000).

⁴⁹DEPENDENCIES

Belarus has no territories or colonies.

⁵⁰BIBLIOGRAPHY

Aleksievich, Svetlana. Keth Gessen, trans. *Voices from Chernobyl.* Normal, IL: Dalkey Archive, 2005.

Belarus Investment and Business Guide: Strategic and Practical Information. Washington, DC: International Business Publications USA, 2012.

Dean, Martin. *Collaboration in the Holocaust: Crimes of the Local Police in Belorussia and Ukraine, 1941–44.* New York: St. Martin's Press, 2000.

Korosteleva, Elena, Colin W. Lawson, and Rosalind J. Marsh, eds. *Contemporary Belarus: Between Democracy and Dictatorship.* London, Eng.: RoutledgeCurzon, 2003.

Kulik, Anatoly, and Susanna Pshizova. *Political Parties in Post-Soviet Space: Russia, Belarus, Ukraine, Moldova, and the Baltics.* Westport, CT: Praeger, 2005.

Levy, Patricia. *Belarus.* 2nd ed. New York: Marshall Cavendish Benchmark, 2010.

Mandel, David. *Labour after Communism: Auto Workers and Their Unions in Russia, Ukraine, and Belarus.* New York: Black Rose Books, 2004.

McElrath, Karen, ed. *HIV and AIDS: A Global View.* Westport, Conn.: Greenwood Press, 2002.

Opello, Walter C. *European Politics.* Boulder, CO: Lynne Rienner Publishers, 2009.

Political Chronology of Europe. London: Europa, 2001.

Silitski, Vitali, and Jan Zaprudnik. *Historical Dictionary of Belarus.* Lanham, MD: Scarecrow Press, 2007.

White, Stephen, Elena Korosteleva, and John Löwenhardt, eds. *Postcommunist Belarus.* Lanham, MD: Rowman and Littlefield, 2004.

BELGIUM

Kingdom of Belgium
Dutch: Koninkrijk België;
French: Royaume de Belgique

CAPITAL: Brussels (Brussel, Bruxelles)

FLAG: The flag, adopted in 1831, is a tricolor of black, yellow, and red vertical stripes.

ANTHEM: *La Brabançonne (The Song of Brabant).*

MONETARY UNIT: The euro replaced the Belgian franc in 2002. The euro is divided into 100 cents. There are coins in denominations of 1, 2, 5, 10, 20, and 50 cents and 1 euro; and 2 euros. There are notes of 5, 10, 20, 50, 100, 200, and 500 euros. €1 = US$1.2778 (or US$1 = €0.78246) as of 2012.

WEIGHTS AND MEASURES: The metric system is the legal standard.

HOLIDAYS: New Year's Day, 1 January; Labor Day, 1 May; Independence Day, 21 July; Assumption Day, 15 August; All Saints' Day, 1 November; Armistice Day, 11 November; Dynasty Day, 15 November; and Christmas, 25 December. Movable religious holidays are Easter Monday, Ascension, and Whitmonday.

TIME: 1 p.m. = noon GMT.

¹LOCATION, SIZE, AND EXTENT

Situated in northwestern Europe, Belgium has an area of 30,510 sq km (11,780 sq mi) and extends 280 km (174 mi) SE–NW and 222 km (137 mi) NE–SW. Comparatively, the area occupied by Belgium is about the same size as the state of Maryland. Belgium borders the Netherlands to the N, Germany and Luxembourg to the E, France to the S and SW, and the North Sea to the NW, with a total boundary length of 1,385 km (859 mi).

Belgium's capital city, Brussels, is located in the north-central part of the country.

²TOPOGRAPHY

The coastal region, extending about 16–48 km (10–30 mi) inland, consists of sand dunes, flat pasture land, and polders (land reclaimed from the sea and protected by dikes), and attains a maximum of 15 m (50 ft) above sea level. Eastward, this region gradually gives way to a gently rolling central plain, whose many fertile valleys are irrigated by an extensive network of canals and waterways. Altitudes in this region are about 60–180 m (200–600 ft). The Ardennes, a heavily wooded plateau, is located in southeast Belgium and continues into France. It has an average altitude of about 460 m (1,500 ft) and reaches a maximum of 694 m (2,277 ft) at the Signal de Botrange, the country's highest point. Chief rivers are the Schelde (Scheldt, Escaut) and the Meuse (Maas), both of which rise in France, flow through Belgium, pass through the Netherlands, and empty into the North Sea.

³CLIMATE

In the coastal region, the climate is mild and humid. There are marked temperature changes farther inland. In the high southeasterly districts, hot summers alternate with very cold winters.

Except in the highlands, rainfall is seldom heavy. The average annual temperature is 8°C (46°F); in Brussels, the mean temperature is 10°C (50°F), ranging from 3°C (37°F) in January to 18°C (64°F) in July. Average annual rainfall is between 70 and 100 cm (28 to 40 in).

⁴FLORA AND FAUNA

The World Resources Institute estimates that there are 1,550 plant species in Belgium. In addition Belgium is home to 92 mammal, 427 bird, 12 reptile, and 17 amphibian species. The calculation reflects the total number of distinct species residing in the country, not the number of endemic species.

The digitalis, wild arum, hyacinth, strawberry, goldenrod, lily of the valley, and other plants common to temperate zones grow in abundance. Beech and oak are the predominant trees. Among mammals still found in Belgium are the boar, fox, badger, squirrel, weasel, marten, and hedgehog. The many varieties of aquatic life include pike, carp, trout, eel, barbel, perch, smelt, chub, roach, bream, shad, sole, mussels, crayfish, and shrimp.

⁵ENVIRONMENT

The World Resources Institute reported that Belgium had designated 97,400 hectares (240,681 acres) of land for protection as of 2006. Water resources totaled 20.8 cu km (4.99 cu mi) while water usage was 7.44 cu km (1.78 cu mi) per year. Domestic water usage accounted for 13% of total usage, industrial for 85%, and agricultural for 2%. Per capita water usage totaled 714 cu m (25,215 cu ft) per year.

The UN reported in 2008 that carbon dioxide emissions in Belgium totaled 102,951 kilotons.

About 520 sq km (200 sq mi) of reclaimed coastal land is protected from the sea by concrete dikes. Belgium's most significant

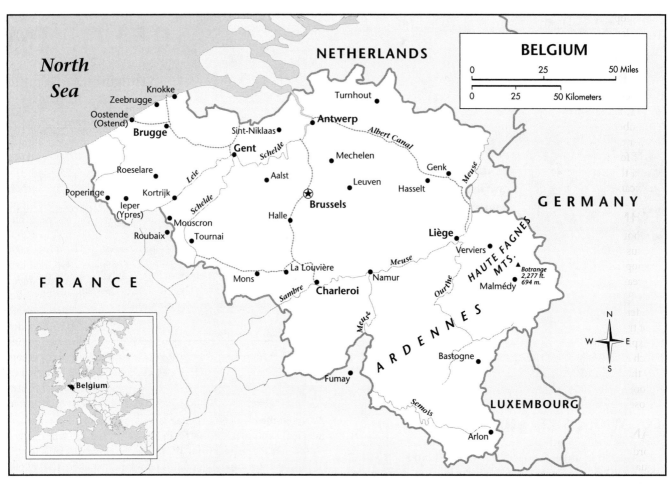

LOCATION: 49°29′52° to 51°30′21″N; 2°32′48° to 6°25′38° E. BOUNDARY LENGTHS: Netherlands, 450 kilometers (280 miles); Germany, 162 kilometers (101 miles); Luxembourg, 148 kilometers (92 miles); France, 620 kilometers (385 miles); North Sea, 66 kilometers (41 miles). TERRITORIAL SEA LIMIT: 12 miles.

environmental problems are air, land, and water pollution due to the heavy concentration of industrial facilities in the country. The sources of pollution range from nuclear radiation to mercury from industry and pesticides from agricultural activity. The country's water supply is threatened by hazardous levels of heavy metals, mercury, and phosphorous. Pollution of rivers and canals in Belgium was considered the worst in Europe until 1970, when strict water-protection laws were enacted.

Air pollution reaches dangerous levels due to high concentrations of lead and hydrocarbons. Belgium is among the 50 nations that emit the highest levels of carbon dioxide from industrial sources. In 2008 Belgium's carbon dioxide emission level was 9.8 metric tons per capita. A 2006 study by Yale and Columbia Universities ranked Belgium as the worst performing country in the EU, based on 16 environmental indicators. Belgium's problems with air pollution have also affected neighboring countries by contributing to the conditions that cause acid rain.

The Ministry of Public Health and Environment is Belgium's principal environmental agency, and there is also a Secretary of State for Public Health and Environment. The Belgian government has created several environmental policies to help eliminate the country's pollution problems.

According to a 2011 report issued by the International Union for Conservation of Nature and Natural Resources (IUCN),

threatened species included 3 types of mammals, 2 species of bird, 11 species of fish, 6 types of mollusks, and 7 other invertebrates. The Mediterranean mouflon, the Atlantic sturgeon, and the black right whale are listed as endangered. There are nine Ramsar wetland sites within the country.

⁶POPULATION

The US Central Intelligence Agency (CIA) estimates the population of Belgium in 2011 to be approximately 10,431,477, which placed it at number 80 in population among the 196 nations of the world. In 2011 approximately 18% of the population was over 65 years of age, with another 15.9% under 15 years of age. The median age in Belgium was 42.3 years. There were 0.96 males for every female in the country. The population's annual rate of change was 0.071%. The projected population for the year 2025 was 11,800,000. Population density in Belgium was calculated at 342 people per sq km (886 people per sq mi).

The UN estimates that 97% of the population live in urban areas, and that urban populations have an annual rate of change of 0.4%. The largest urban areas, along with their respective populations, include Brussels, 1.9 million; and Antwerp, 961,000.

The government has conducted a census every 10 years since 1848. Since 1984 the registration of births and deaths has been delegated to the Flemish and Walloon language communities. Belgium's population has distinctive language and ethnic divisions. The Ardennes region in the south is the least densely populated region.

7 MIGRATION

Estimates of Belgium's net migration rate, carried out by the CIA in 2011, amounted to 1.22 migrants per 1,000 citizens. The total number of emigrants living abroad was 455,000, and the total number of immigrants living in Belgium was 1.47 million. About 65% of foreigners were from other EU countries, primarily Italy, France, the Netherlands, and Spain; there were also a number of Moroccans and Turks living in Belgium.

8 ETHNIC GROUPS

Two thousand years ago the population of Belgium, as mentioned by Julius Caesar in his book on the Gallic wars, was of Celtic stock. This population was displaced or lost its identity, however, during the great invasions that brought down the Roman Empire. The Salian Franks, who settled there during the 4th century AD, are considered the ancestors of Belgium's present population. The origin of the language frontier in Belgium has never been satisfactorily explained. In the indigenous population, the ratio of Flemings (Dutch speakers) to Walloons (French speakers) is about 5 to 3. In 2010 the Flemings constituted about 58% of the total population; Walloons accounted for 31%. The remaining 11% was comprised of those with mixed ancestry or other groups.

9 LANGUAGES

According to a 1970 constitutional revision, there are three official languages in Belgium—French, Dutch (also called Flemish), and German. Dutch is the language of the four provinces of Antwerp, Limburg, East Flanders (Oost-Vlaanderen), and West Flanders (West-Vlaanderen), which form the northern half of the country. French is the language of the four southern Walloon provinces of Hainaut, Liège, Luxembourg, and Namur. The central province of Brabant is divided into three districts—one French-speaking (Nivelles, Nijvel), one Dutch-speaking (Leuven, Louvain), and one bilingual (composed of the 19 boroughs of the capital city, Brussels). The majority of people in the Brussels metropolitan area are French-speaking. According to 2010 estimates, 60% of the total population speak Dutch (Flemish), 40% speak French, less than 1% speak German, and 11% are legally bilingual in Dutch and French. The relationship between the two major language groups has been tense at times. For many years, French was the only official language. A series of laws enacted in the 1930s established equality between the two languages. Dutch became the language of administration, the schools, and the courts in the Flemish region (Flanders), while French continued to be the language of Wallonia. The use of German is regulated in the same way in the German-speaking municipalities in the province of Liège. As a rule, French is studied in all secondary schools in the Flemish region, while Dutch is a required secondary-school subject in Wallonia. In 1963 a set of laws created four linguistic regions (with bilingual status for Brussels), a decision incorporated into the constitution in 1970. Subsequent legislation in 1971–74 provided for cultural autonomy, regional economic power, and linguistic equality in the central government. Disagreement over the future status of bilingual Brussels intensified during the late 1970s. In 1980, after a political crisis, the Flemish and Walloon regions were given greater autonomy, but the issue of Brussels, a predominantly French-speaking territory surrounded by a Dutch-speaking region, remained intractable and was deferred.

10 RELIGIONS

According to an unofficial 2010 survey, about 60% of all citizens are nominally Roman Catholic, though earlier reports have placed the number as high as 75%. Less than 10% of Roman Catholics regularly attend religious services. The 2010 survey indicated that 4% of citizens are Muslim, 2% Protestant, 1% Jewish, and 31% nonbelievers. Some prominent Christian denominations include Greek and Russian Orthodox, Anglicanism, the Church of Jesus Christ of Latter-Day Saints (Mormons), Jehovah's Witnesses, and other independent Protestant congregations. According to a 2007 report, there were about 10,000 Buddhists, 5,000 Hindus, 3,000 Sikhs, 1,500 Hare Krishnas, and between 200 and 300 members of the Church of Scientology. Freedom of religion is guaranteed by the constitution and this right is generally respected in practice. The government gives "recognized" status to Roman Catholicism, Protestantism, Judaism, Anglicanism, Islam, and Orthodox Christianity. These groups are allowed to receive some funding from the government. Laic groups are also considered a recognized religion. Some social discrimination has been reported by Jews, Muslims, and members of "unrecognized" groups. Easter, Ascension, Pentecost, Assumption, All Saints' Day, and Christmas are all observed as national holidays.

11 TRANSPORTATION

The CIA reports that Belgium has a total of 152,256 km (94,607 mi) of roads, of which 119,079 km (73,992 mi) are paved. There are 543 vehicles per 1,000 people in the country. All major European highways pass through Belgium.

Railroads extend for 3,578 km (2,223 mi). As of 2008 Belgium had the densest railway network in the world.

Belgium has approximately 2,043 km (1,269 mi) of navigable waterways. Inland waterways, comprised of rivers and canals, are linked with those of France, Germany, and the Netherlands. The chief port, Antwerp (one of the world's busiest ports), on the Scheldt River, about 84 km (52 mi) from the sea, handles three fourths of the country's foreign cargo. Other leading ports are Gent and Zeebrugge. Liège is the third largest inland river port in Western Europe, after Duisburg, Germany, and Paris. In 2010 the Belgian merchant fleet was comprised of 81 vessels. The fleet numbered 101 ships (2.2 million GRT) in 2002, but offshore registry programs and so-called "flags of convenience" have enticed ship owners into foreign registry.

There are 43 airports (27 with paved runways), which transported 4.86 million passengers in 2009 according to the World Bank. Belgium has one heliport. The Belgian national airline Sabena, formed in 1923, is the third-oldest international airline. Brussels National Airport, an important international terminus, is served by more than 30 major airlines.

12 HISTORY

Belgium is named after the Belgae, a Celtic people whose territory was conquered in 57 BC by Julius Caesar and was organized by him as Gallia Belgica. In 15 BC, Augustus made Gallia Belgica (which at that time included much of present-day France) a province of the Roman Empire. In the 5th century AD, it was overrun by the Franks, and in the 8th century, it became part of the empire of Charlemagne. But this empire soon fell apart, and in the 10th century there emerged several feudal units that later would become provinces of Belgium. These included the counties of Flanders, Hainaut, and Namur, the duchy of Brabant, and the prince-bishopric of Liège. During the three following centuries, trade flourished in the towns of the county of Flanders. Antwerp, Bruges, Ypres (Ieper), and Ghent in particular became very prosperous. In the 15th century, most of the territory that currently forms Belgium, the Netherlands, and Luxembourg—formerly called the Low Countries and now called the Benelux countries—came under the rule of the dukes of Burgundy as the result of a shrewd policy of intermarriage. Through the marriage of Mary of Burgundy with Archduke Maximilian of Austria, those same provinces, then collectively known as the Netherlands, became part of the Habsburg Empire in the early 1500s. When Maximilian's grandson Emperor Charles V divided his empire, the Netherlands was united with Spain (1555) under Philip II, who dedicated himself to the repression of Protestantism. His policies resulted in a revolt led by the Protestants.

Thus began a long war, which, after a 12-year truce (1609–21), became intermingled with the Thirty Years' War. Under the Treaty of Westphalia (1648), which ended the Thirty Years' War, independence was granted to the northern Protestant provinces. The southern half remained Roman Catholic and under Spanish rule. By this time, the southern Low Countries (the territory now known as Belgium) had become embroiled in Franco-Spanish power politics. Belgium was invaded on several occasions, and part of its territory was lost to France.

Under the Peace of Utrecht (1713), which concluded the War of the Spanish Succession, Belgium became part of the Austrian Empire. The country was occupied by the French during the War of the Austrian Succession (1744) but was restored to Austria by the Treaty of Aix-la-Chapelle (1748). Belgium entered a period of recovery and material progress under Maria Theresa and her son Joseph II. The latter's administrative reforms created widespread discontent, however, which culminated in the Révolution Brabançonne of 1789. Leopold II, successor to Joseph II, defeated the Belgians and reoccupied the country, but his regime won little popular support. In 1792 the French army invaded the Belgian provinces, which were formally ceded to France by the Treaty of Campo Formio (1797). This French regime was defeated by the anti-Napoleonic coalition at Waterloo in 1815.

Belgium was united with the Netherlands by the Congress of Vienna in 1815. This action caused widespread discontent, culminating in a series of uprisings. The Dutch were compelled to retreat, and on 4 October 1830, Belgium was declared independent by a provisional government. The powers of the Congress of Vienna met again at London in June 1831 and accepted the separation of Belgium and the Netherlands. However, William I, King of the United Netherlands, refused to recognize the validity of this action. On 2 August 1831 he invaded Belgium, but the Dutch force was repulsed by a French army. In 1839 he was forced to accept the Treaty of the XXIV Articles, by which Belgian independence was formally recognized. The European powers guaranteed Belgium's status as "an independent and perpetually neutral state."

In 1831 the Belgian Parliament had chosen Prince Leopold of Saxe-Coburg-Gotha as ruler of the new kingdom, which was already in the process of industrialization. In 1865 Leopold I was succeeded by Leopold II (r. 1865–1909), who financed exploration and settlement in the Congo River Basin of Africa, thereby laying the foundations of Belgium's colonial empire. Leopold's nephew, Albert I, came to the throne in 1909. At the outbreak of World War I, German troops invaded Belgium (4 August 1914). The Belgian army offered fierce resistance, but by the end of November 1914, the only Belgian towns not occupied by the Germans were Nieuport (Nieuwpoort), Furnes (Veurne), and Ypres. Belgium, on the side of the Allies, continued to struggle to liberate the kingdom. Ypres, in particular, was the scene of fierce fighting: nearly 100,000 men lost their lives at a battle near there in April and May 1915 (during which the Germans used chlorine gas), and at least 300,000 Allied troops lost their lives in this region during an offensive that lasted from late July to mid-November 1917.

Under the Treaty of Versailles (1919), Germany ceded to Belgium the German-speaking districts of Eupen, Malmédy, St. Vith, and Moresnet. The country made a remarkable recovery from the war, and by 1923, manufacturing industries were nearly back to normal. After a heated controversy with Germany over reparations payments, Belgium joined France in the occupation of the Ruhr in 1923. In 1934 Leopold III succeeded Albert.

Belgium was again attacked on 10 May 1940, when, without warning, the German air force bombed Belgian airports, railroad stations, and communications centers, and Belgian soil was invaded. Antwerp fell on 18 May and Namur on 23 May. By the end of the month, British, French, and Belgian forces were trapped in northwestern Belgium. King Leopold III surrendered unconditionally on 28 May and was taken prisoner of war. The Belgian government-in-exile, in London, continued the war on the side of the Allies. With the country's liberation from the Germans by the Allies and the well-organized Belgian underground, the Belgian government returned to Brussels in September 1944. During the Allied landings in Normandy, King Leopold III had been deported to Germany. In his absence, his brother Prince Charles was designated by parliament as regent of the kingdom.

The country was economically better off after World War II than after World War I. However, a tense political situation resulted from the split that had developed during the war years between Leopold III and the exiled government in London, which had repudiated the king's surrender. After his liberation by the US 7th Army, the king chose to reside in Switzerland. On 12 March 1950, 57.7% of the Belgian electorate declared itself in favor of allowing Leopold III to return as sovereign. The general elections of 4 June 1950 gave an absolute majority to the Christian Social Party, which favored his return, and on 22 July 1950, Leopold came back from exile. But the Socialists and Liberals continued to oppose his resumption of royal prerogatives, and strikes, riots, and demonstrations ensued. On 1 August 1950 Leopold agreed to abdicate, and on 17 July 1951, one day after Leopold actually gave up his throne, his son Baudouin I was formally proclaimed king.

In 1960 the Belgian Congo (now the Democratic Republic of the Congo), a major vestige of Belgium's colonial empire, became independent. The event was followed by two years of brutal civil war, involving mercenaries from Belgium and other countries.

Another Belgian territory in Africa, Ruanda-Urundi, became independent as the two states of Rwanda and Burundi in 1962.

Belgium was transferred into a federal state in July 1993. The country is divided into three regions (Flanders, Wallonia, and Brussels) and three linguistic communities (Flemish, French, and German). Voters directly elect members to the regional parliaments. The French-speaking branch of the Socialist party dominates Wallonia while the Dutch-speaking faction of the Christian Democratic Party governs Flanders. As a participant in the Marshall Plan, a member of NATO, and a leader in the movement for European integration, Belgium shared fully in the European prosperity of the first three postwar decades. Domestic political conflict during this period centered on the unequal distribution of wealth and power between Flemings and Walloons. The Flemings generally contended that they were not given equal opportunity with the Walloons in government and business and that the Dutch language was regarded as inferior to French. The Walloons, in turn, complained of their minority status and the economic neglect of their region and feared being outnumbered by the rapidly growing Flemish population. In response to these conflicts, and after a series of cabinet crises, a revised constitution adopted in 1970 created the framework for complete regional autonomy in economic and cultural spheres. In July 1974, legislation provided for the granting of autonomy to Flanders, Wallonia, and Brussels upon a two-thirds vote in parliament. However, the necessary consensus could not be realized. In 1977 a Christian Social-Socialist coalition proposed to establish a federal administration representing the three regions, but could not obtain parliamentary approval for the proposal. In 1980, however, following several acts of violence as a result of the dispute, parliament allowed the establishment in stages of regional executive and legislative bodies for Flanders and Wallonia, with administrative control over cultural affairs, public health, roads, and urban projects.

Labor unrest and political violence has erupted in the past. In 1982, as a result of an industrial recession, worsened by rising petroleum prices and debt servicing costs, the government imposed an austerity program; an intensification of the austerity program, announced in May 1986, aimed to cut public sector spending, restrain wages, and simplify the taxation system. Vigorous trade-union protests have taken place to protest the freezing of wages and cuts in social security payments. Belgium has one of the largest national debts in Western Europe. Since 1995, however, unions have gone along with pay freezes to restore profitability and improve labor market performance.

Parliamentary elections were held on 18 May 2003, and the Flemish Liberals and Democrats (VLD) finished first in the Flemish elections, defeating the Socialists and Christian Democrats, and the far-right Vlaams Blok. In Wallonia, the Socialists came in first. In both elections, the Greens suffered. Prime Minister Guy Verhofstadt, in office since 1999, formed a center-left coalition of Liberals and Socialists after the May elections. Under Verhofstadt's leadership, Belgium legalized euthanasia and the use of marijuana, and approved gay marriages.

The European Union was divided over the use of military force by the United States and UK in the months leading up to the war in Iraq that began on 19 March 2003. Belgium stood with France and Germany in opposing a military response to the crisis. However, Belgium played a key role in helping to obtain EU-wide agreement on a European arrest warrant and in facilitating extradition of terrorist suspects. In support of Operation Enduring Freedom, Belgium contributed a navy frigate in the Mediterranean, AWAC crews for surveillance flights over the United States, and aircraft for humanitarian assistance to Afghanistan.

In 2004 the far-right Vlaams Blok increased its share of the vote in regional and European elections. However, the Belgian High Court ruled that the party was racist and stripped it of the right to state funding and access to television. The party was subsequently reorganized under a new name, the Vlaams Belang, or Flemish Interest.

In 20 March 2008 elections Yves Leterme took over as prime minister, replacing Guy Verhofstadt, who had led the country since 1999. The major issues before the government in 2008 included improving the climate for foreign investment, dealing with rising health care costs, and adjusting the federal social security system to a rapidly aging population. Belgium continued to increase its counter-terrorism capabilities by adding domestic legislative, judicial, intelligence, and law enforcement tools that increased its ability to prevent or respond to terrorism. The government also cooperated with other European states and the United States in investigating cases of international terrorism.

In April 2010 Prime Minister Yves Leterme offered his resignation following the withdrawal of the Flemish Open VLD party from his ruling coalition. The Open VLD pulled out of the government due to a failure to reach a resolution on a longstanding dispute over voting rights in the Brussels-Halle-Vilvoorde (BHV) voting district, a bilingual district in and around the country's capital. Under the constitution, voting districts are to be separated in Dutch-speaking and French-speaking regions. The BHV has been the only district that combines both groups. However, the constitutional court ruled that the district was unconstitutional in 2003, for violating the separation of Dutch and French-language regions. Attempts to negotiate a compromise between the two groups have been unsuccessful, thus leading to the formal resignation of the government.

The new elections held in June 2010 presented yet another major upset as the New Flemish Alliance (NVA), a prominent Flemish separatist party, became the largest party in parliament, capturing 27 of the 150 seats. Another separatist party, Vlaams Belang, earned 12 seats. The French Socialist (PS) party came in second with 26 seats and the Flemish Socialists (sp.a) came in with 13 seats. These results raised concerns that the already deep linguistic divide could lead to a fracture in the state if the Flemish separatist parties push for their own agenda with significant force. It also brought into question whether or not a successful coalition government would be formed anytime soon. It is not uncommon for the development of a coalition government to take several months of negotiations.

Following the election, Bart De Wever, the leader of the NVA, was charged with the task of negotiating a coalition government. However, the 18 October 2010 deadline for completing this task came and went with the French-speaking parties rejecting De Wever's draft proposals. As the leader of a party that seeks ultimate independence for Flanders, De Wever submitted proposals that would establish greater regional autonomy for the regions of Flanders, Wallonia, and Brussels, with particular focus on rights to regional tax revenues. Under such a plan, Flanders would receive the greatest benefit in tax revenues, a condition that representatives from other regions considered to be unacceptably divisive. With eight parties involved in the current government, all holding minority status, the formation of a coalition government posed a formidable challenge.

In December 2011, after a year and a half without a government, a six-party coalition government was formed and a new prime minister, French-speaking Socialist Elio Di Rupo, was appointed. Di Rupo's poor command of the Dutch language was a source of contention; he is Belgium's first French-speaking prime minister in three decades. Belgium's 541 days without a government was a modern-day world record.

A number of agreements between the Flemish and French sides contributed to the eventual formation of the government. The boundaries of the BHV were redrawn in response to Flemish concerns that the district was biased in favor of the French. Reforms to the constitution were also passed, giving the regions increased authority for tax collection, and phasing-out, over the next twenty years, revenue transfers from Flanders to the French region.

13 GOVERNMENT

Belgium is a hereditary monarchy governed under the constitution of 1831. This document has been frequently amended in recent years to grant recognition and autonomy to the Dutch- and French-speaking communities. Executive power is vested in the king, who appoints and removes ministers, civil servants, judges, and officers. In June 1991 parliament approved a constitutional amendment to allow female members of the royal family to succeed to the throne. The monarch, however, would continue to be known as king regardless of gender.

With approval of parliament, the king has the power to declare war and conclude treaties; he is commander-in-chief of the armed forces. According to the constitution, the king's rights include conferring titles of nobility, granting pardons, and administering the coinage of money. However, none of the king's acts becomes effective unless countersigned by a minister, who assumes responsibility for such acts before parliament. Therefore, the king must choose ministers who represent the majority in parliament. Each ministry is created in response to necessity, and there is no fixed number of ministers.

Legislative power is vested in the king and in the two-chamber parliament. The Chamber of Representatives has 150 members, who are elected for a four-year term through a system of proportional representation. The Senate has 71 members, with 40 directly elected and 31 indirectly elected or co-opted for a four-year term. All persons 18 years of age and older are entitled to vote in parliamentary elections, and those who fail to vote are subject to fines. In time of emergency, the king may convoke extraordinary sessions. The government and both chambers may introduce legislation, and both chambers have equal rights. When a bill is introduced, a committee examines it and appoints a rapporteur, who reports on it before the full assembly. The king may dissolve the chambers either simultaneously or separately, but an election must be provided for within 40 days and a session of the new parliament must meet within two months.

In accordance with the constitutional reform of 1980, there are three communities: the Dutch-, the French-, and the German-speaking communities. They have, in a wholly autonomous manner, responsibility for cultural affairs, education, and for matters concerning the individual. There are also three regions (Flanders, Wallonia, and Brussels), which are responsible for the regional aspects of a broad range of concerns, including the economy, energy, public works and housing, employment, and environmental policy. The institutions of the communities and regions are based on the same principles as those of the national political structure: each entity has a "regional parliament" (the council), whose decisions are implemented by a "regional government" (the executive). The council and the executive are directly elected and can only be brought down by a vote of no confidence.

On 14 July 1993 parliament approved a constitutional revision that changed Belgium from a unitary to a federal state.

14 POLITICAL PARTIES

Political parties in Belgium are organized primarily along ethno-linguistic lines, with each group in Flanders having its Walloon counterpart. The three major political alliances are the Christian Democratic parties, the Socialist parties, and the Liberal parties.

In 1968 the Christian Democratic Party divided into two independent parties in response to linguistic tensions in the country. These two parties are now known as the Center Democratic and Humanistic (CDH) in Francophone Wallonia and the Flemish Christian Democrats (CD&V) in Flanders. The two parties share similar policies, but not on institutional issues.

The modern Belgian Socialist parties are labor- and city-based parties. The Socialists also split along linguistic lines in 1978. The Social Progressive Alternative (SPA-Francophone Socialists) dominates the cities and towns of Wallonia's industrial basin. The Socialist Party (PS) represents Flemish concerns. The two parties are of almost equal strength.

The Liberal Parties in Belgium are primarily attractive to business people, property owners, shopkeepers, and the self-employed. The two major Liberal parties are the Flemish Liberals and Democrats (Open VLD) in Flanders and the Reform Movement (MR) in Wallonia. These parties were formed in 1971 by the division of the all-Belgium Liberal Party, which split along linguistic lines.

Under the category of Linguistic Parties, the Flemish Interest (Vlaams Belang-VB) is the most militant; it presents a separatist and anti-immigration platform. The much smaller far-right National Front (Front Nationale—FN) has been openly racist and xenophobic. The now-defunct Volksunie Party (VU) splintered into a traditional Flemish nationalist faction, the New Flemish Alliance (NVA—currently in alliance with the CD&V), and a more liberal faction, Spirit (in an electoral alliance with the Flemish Socialist Party).

Groen! (formerly AGALEV) is the Flemish Green Party and Ecolo represents francophone Greens.

The Flemish List Dedecker (LDD) party was founded in January 2007 by Senator Jean-Marie Dedecker as a right-liberal movement in Flanders. The party platform is primarily based on a drive for a more independent Flanders. The party's slogan is "Common Sense."

The 1999 election ended the political career of Prime Minister Jean-Luc Dehaene, the Flemish Christian Democrat who led a center-left coalition of francophone and Flemish socialists and his francophone Christian Democratic Party throughout the 1990s. Six parties (French-speaking and Dutch-speaking branches of the

Liberal, Socialist, and Green parties) reached a core agreement only three weeks after the election on forming a "blue-red-green" coalition government. It was Belgium's first government in 40 years not to include the Christian Democrats, the first to include the Greens, and the first since 1884 to be led by a Liberal prime minister (Guy Verhofstadt).

Following the legislative elections of 13 June 2010, the major parties in the house were the New Flemish Alliance (N-VA), 27 seats; Socialist Party (PS), 26 seats; Reform Movement (MR), 18 seats; Christian Democratic and Flemish (CD&V), 17 seats; Social Progressive Alternative (sp.a), 13 seats; Flemish Liberals and Democrats (Open VLD), 13 seats; Vlaams Belang (VB), 12 seats; Humanist and Democratic Center (CDH), 9 seats; Francophone Greens (Ecolo) 8 seats; Flemish Greens (Groen!) 5 seats; List Dedecker (LDD), 1 seat; and the Popular Party , 1 seat.

The new government formed in December 2011, and led by Walloon socialist prime minister Elio Di Rupo, was made of six parties—three Flemish and three French. The New Flemish Alliance was left out of the coalition.

[15]LOCAL GOVERNMENT

Belgium is divided into 10 provinces: Antwerp, East Flanders, West Flanders, and Limburg in the north, Hainaut, Liège, Luxembourg, and Namur in the south, Flemish Brabant, and Walloon Brabant. Each of the provinces has a council of 50 to 90 members elected for four-year terms by direct suffrage and empowered to legislate in matters of local concern. A governor, appointed by the king, is the highest executive officer in each province.

There are 482 communes. Each municipality has a town council elected for a six-year term. The council elects an executive body called the board of aldermen. The head of the municipality is the burgomaster, who is appointed by the sovereign upon nomination by the town council. Recently, the number of municipalities has been greatly reduced through consolidation.

In 1971 Brussels was established as a separate bilingual area, presided over by a proportionally elected metropolitan council. Linguistic parity was stipulated for the council's executive committee.

[16]JUDICIAL SYSTEM

Belgian law is modeled on the French legal system. The judiciary is an independent branch of government on an equal footing with the legislative and the executive branches. Minor offenses are dealt with by justices of the peace and police tribunals. More serious offenses and civil lawsuits are brought before district courts of first instance. Other district courts are commerce and labor tribunals. Verdicts rendered by these courts may be appealed before five regional courts of appeal or the five regional labor courts in Antwerp, Brussels, Gent, Mons, and Liège. All offenses punishable by prison sentences of more than five years must be dealt with by the 11 courts of assize (one for each province and the city of Brussels), the only jury courts in Belgium. The highest courts are five civil and criminal courts of appeal and the Supreme Court of Justice (Cour de Cassation in French). The latter's function is to verify that the law has been properly applied and interpreted. The constitutionality of legislation is the province of the Council of State, an advisory legal group.

When an error of procedure is found, the decision of the lower court is overruled and the case must be tried again. The death penalty was abolished for all crimes in Belgium in 1996.

A system of military tribunals, including appellate courts, handles both military and common-law offenses involving military personnel. The government is considering narrowing the jurisdiction of these courts to military offenses. All military tribunals consist of four officers and a civilian judge.

Detainees must be brought before a judge within 24 hours of arrest. Although there are provisions for bail, it is rarely granted. Defendants have the right to be present, to have counsel, to confront witnesses, to present evidence, and to appeal.

Under Belgium's "universal jurisdiction" law, enacted in 1993, Belgian courts can hear cases involving war crimes and crimes against humanity even if the crimes were not committed in Belgium and did not involve Belgian citizens. Amendments to the law in April 2003 made it harder to bring a case where neither the victim, nor the plaintiff, nor the accused were Belgian. Israeli Prime Minister Ariel Sharon and former U.S. president George H. W. Bush were charged with war crimes under the law, relating to the 1982 Sabra and Shatila massacres in Lebanon, and the bombing of a civilian shelter in the 1991 Gulf War, respectively. Due to pressure from the United States, Belgian courts now may try only cases which involve charges against Belgian citizens or people resident in Belgium.

[17]ARMED FORCES

The International Institute for Strategic Studies reports that armed forces in Belgium totaled 37,882 members in 2011. The force is comprised of 13,601 from the army, 1,590 from the navy, 6,814 from medical service staff, and 13,989 members of joint service forces. Armed forces represent .8% of the labor force in Belgium. Defense spending totaled $5.1 billion and accounted for 1.3% of GDP.

[18]INTERNATIONAL COOPERATION

Belgium is a charter member of the UN, having joined on 27 December 1945, and participates in nonregional specialized agencies. Paul-Henri Spaak of Belgium served as the UN General Assembly's first president (1946–47); from 1957 to 1961, he also served as the secretary-general of NATO, of which Belgium is also a member. The country has been partnered with Luxembourg in the Belgium-Luxembourg Economic Union (BLEU) since 1921. In 1958 Belgium signed a treaty forming the Benelux (Belgium-Netherlands-Luxembourg) Economic Union, following a 10-year period in which a customs union of the three countries was in effect. Belgium is also a member of the Asian Development Bank, Council of Europe, the European Union, the European Investment Bank, the Paris Club (G-10), G-9, the Western European Union, and OECD. It is also is a permanent observer of the OAS and a member of the OSCE (1973) and the WTO (1995).

Brussels, the seat of EU institutions, has become an important regional center for Western Europe. In 1967 the Supreme Headquarters Allied Powers Europe (SHAPE) was transferred from Rocquencourt, near Paris, to a site near Mons. On 16 October 1967 the NATO Council's headquarters were moved from Paris to Brussels. Belgium is a member of the Permanent Court of Arbitration.

Belgium is part of the Organization for the Prohibition of Chemical Weapons, Nuclear Suppliers Group (London Group), the Australia Group, the Nuclear Energy Agency, the European Space Agency, the Zangger Committee, and the European Organization for Nuclear Research. The country has offered support for UN peacekeeping efforts in several regions.

In environmental cooperation, Belgium is part of the Antarctic Treaty, the Basel Convention, the Conventions on Biological Diversity and Air Pollution, Ramsar, CITES, the London Convention, the International Tropical Timber Agreements, the Kyoto Protocol, the Montréal Protocol, MARPOL, the Nuclear Test Ban Treaty, and UN Conventions on the Law of the Sea, Climate Change, and Desertification.

¹⁹ECONOMY

The gross domestic product (GDP) rate of change in Belgium, as of 2010, was 2%. Inflation stood at 2.3%, and unemployment was reported at 8.5%.

In relation to its size and population, Belgium is among the most highly industrialized countries in Europe. Poor in natural resources, it imports raw materials in great quantity and processes them largely for export. About 75% of Belgium's foreign trade is with other EU countries.

With the exception of Luxembourg and Ireland, Belgium is the most open economy in the EU as measured by the value of exports and imports relative to GDP, and one of the most open in the world. Belgium's economy is highly integrated with that of its three main neighbors—Germany, France, and the Netherlands.

For a century and a half, Belgium maintained its status as an industrial country, not only by virtue of its geographical position and transport facilities but also because of its ability for most of this period to shape production to meet the changing requirements of world commerce. Since the 1950s, the Belgian parliament enacted economic expansion laws to enable long-established industries to modernize obsolete plant equipment. Belgium's highly developed transportation systems are closely linked with those of its neighbors. Its chief port, Antwerp, is one of the world's busiest. Belgium has a highly skilled and productive workforce, and the economy is diversified.

In 1993, when Belgium became a federal state with three distinct regions (Flanders, Wallonia, and Brussels), substantial economic powers were given to each region, such as jurisdiction over industrial development, research, trade promotion, and environmental regulation. Belgium has been seen as a "laboratory state," in that its federal system might stand as a precursor to a more unified EU based on regional divisions.

Economic growth in 2001–03 dropped sharply because of the global economic slowdown, with moderate recovery in 2004–07. Real GDP growth in 2003 was 1.1%. Growth picked up in 2004, to 2.7%. In 2004 Belgium had the fourth-highest standard of living in the world. However, being a highly taxed and indebted country, some businesses stated that Belgium stifles private enterprise.

Although the prominent banking center took a hit during the global financial crisis that began in late 2008, the overall economy seemed to remain relatively stable into 2009. The government lowered the budget deficit from 6% of GDP to 4.1% in 2010.

Services accounted for 77.4% of GDP in 2010. Industry accounted for 21.9% and agriculture less than 1%.

²⁰INCOME

The CIA estimated that in 2010 the GDP of Belgium was $394.3 billion. The CIA defines GDP as the value of all final goods and services produced within a nation in a given year and computed on the basis of purchasing power parity (PPP) rather than value as measured on the basis of the rate of the exchange based on current dollars. The per capita GDP was estimated at $37,800. The annual growth rate of GDP was 2%.

According to the World Bank, remittances from citizens living abroad totaled $10.4 billion or about $1,001 per capita and accounted for approximately 2.6% of GDP.

The World Bank reports that in 2009, household consumption in Belgium totaled $247 billion or about $23,677 per capita, measured in current US dollars rather than PPP. Household consumption includes expenditures of individuals, households, and nongovernmental organizations on goods and services, excluding the purchases of dwellings. It was estimated that household consumption was growing at an average annual rate of 0.2%.

²¹LABOR

As of 2010 Belgium had a total labor force of 5.114 million people. Within that labor force, the CIA estimated in 2007 that 2% were employed in agriculture, 25% in industry, and 73% in the service sector.

The law provides workers with the right to associate freely and workers fully exercise their right to organize and join unions. Approximately 63% of the country's workforce (employed and unemployed) are union members. Workers have a broad right to strike except in "essential" industries including the military. A single collective bargaining agreement, negotiated every other year, covers about 2.4 million private sector workers. This gives unions considerable control over economic policy. In addition, unions also freely exercise the right to strike.

Belgium has a five-day, 38-hour workweek. Overtime pay is time-and-a-half on Mondays through Saturdays, with double-time paid on Sundays. Overtime is limited to 11 hours daily and up to 50 hours weekly. In addition, an 11-hour rest period is required between two work periods. Children under the age of 15 years are prohibited from working. Those between the ages of 15 and 18 may engage in part-time work-study programs, or work during school vacations. Child labor laws and standards are strictly enforced. In 2010 the national minimum wage was $1,931 per month (for those age 22 and over who had worked at least one year), in addition to extensive social benefits. This minimum wage provides a decent standard of living for workers and their families.

²²AGRICULTURE

Roughly 28% of the total land is used in agriculture, and the country's major crops include sugar beets, fresh vegetables, fruits, grain, and tobacco. Cereal production in 2009 amounted to 3.3 million tons, fruit production 635,300 tons, and vegetable production 2 million tons.

Agriculture's role in the economy continues to decrease. In 2003 about 1.3% of the employed population worked on farms, compared with 3.7% in 1973. Agriculture's share in the GNP fell from

3.8% in 1973 to about 1.5% in 2002. By 2010 it was .7% of GDP. Only 2% of the labor force was employed in agriculture. Many marginal farms have disappeared; the remaining farms are small but intensively cultivated. Average farm size grew from 6.17 hectares (15.2 acres) in 1959 to 26.88 hectares (66.4 acres) in 2005, when there were 51,540 farms (down from 269,060 in 1959). The richest farm areas are in Flanders and Brabant. Over half the land cultivated is used for pastureland or green fodder; one-quarter is used for the production of cereals.

Belgium imports considerable quantities of bread and feed grains, fodder concentrates, and fruits. Its only agricultural exports are processed foods and a few specialty items such as endive, chicory, flower bulbs, sugar, and chocolates. Imports from other EU countries account for 85% of agricultural imports.

23 ANIMAL HUSBANDRY

The UN Food and Agriculture Organization (FAO) reported that Belgium dedicated 505,000 hectares (1.25 million acres) to permanent pasture or meadow in 2009. During that year, the country tended 33.2 million chickens, 2.6 million head of cattle, and 6.3 million pigs. The production from these animals amounted to 204,755 tons of beef and veal, 357,572 tons of pork, 264,321 tons of poultry, 137,346 tons of eggs, and 2.51 million tons of milk. Belgium also produced 23,600 tons of cattle hide and 215 tons of raw wool.

Livestock-raising is the most important single sector of Belgian agriculture. Belgian farmers breed some of the finest draft horses in the world, including the famous Percherons.

The country is self-sufficient in butter, milk, meat, and eggs. Some cheese is imported, mainly from the Netherlands.

24 FISHING

Belgium had 139 decked commercial fishing boats in 2008. The annual capture totaled 22,609 tons according to the UN FAO. The export value of seafood totaled $950.9 million.

The chief fishing ports are Zeebrugge and Ostend (Oostende, Ostende), from which boats sail the North Atlantic from the North Sea to Iceland. Principal species caught include plaice, sole, turbot, and cod.

25 FORESTRY

Approximately 22% of Belgium is covered by forest. The UN FAO estimated the 2009 roundwood production at 3.67 million cu m (129.6 million cu ft). The value of all forest products, including roundwood, totaled $5.27 billion.

Commercial production of timber is limited. Most common trees are beech and oak, but considerable plantings of conifers have been made in recent years. Belgium serves as a large transshipment center for temperate hardwood logs, softwood lumber, and softwood plywood. Large quantities of timber for the woodworking industry are typically imported from the Democratic Republic of the Congo. Belgium's wood processing industry is large and dominated by small-scale furniture manufacturers.

26 MINING

Belgium's only remaining active mining operations in 2009 were for the production of sand and gravel and the quarrying of some stone, including specialty marbles and the Belgian blue-gray lime-

stone called "petit granite." An important producer of marble for more than 2,000 years, Belgium is recognized for the diversity and quality of its dimension stone. All the marble quarries are in Wallonia, and red, black, and gray are the principal color ranges of the marble. The country is an important producer of such industrial materials as carbonates, including limestone, dolomite, silica sand, whiting, and sodium sulfate.

The mineral-processing industry is a significant contributor to the Belgian economy. The refining of copper, zinc, and minor metals, and the production of steel (all from imported materials), are the most developed mineral industries in Belgium. The country possesses Europe's largest electrolytic copper and zinc refineries, and one of the continent's largest lead refineries. In addition, Belgium retains its position as the world's diamond capital. Estimated production figures for 2009, in metric tons, included: secondary copper, 124,000 and primary zinc, 239,000. Hydraulic cement output in 2009 totaled 9.5 million tons, with lime and dead-burned dolomite at 2.4 million tons. Quarried stone totaled 19,000 metric tons in 2009. Petite granite, which is actually a dark blue-gray crinoidal limestone, is one of the most important facing stones the country produces.

27 ENERGY AND POWER

The World Bank reported in 2008 that Belgium produced 83.6 billion kWh of electricity and consumed 91.3 billion kWh, or 8,749 kWh per capita. Roughly 74% of energy came from fossil fuels, while 20% came from alternative fuels. Per capita oil consumption was 5,471 kg.

In 1981 only 25% of the nation's power was from nuclear sources. In October 2009 that percentage had risen to 55%. In that month, Belgium agreed to extend the life of its three oldest reactors into 2025, in exchange for large, annual fixed-payment sums by the nuclear producers in the country. At the same time, Belgium and GDF Suez—a French utility provider whose Belgian subsidiary, Electrabel, dominates Belgium's electric grid—reached agreement that GDF Suez would pay Belgium between €215 and 245 million per year between 2010–2014, and an unspecified amount for the years from 2015–2025. In 2010 Belgium's top court ruled that it was lawful for the government to levy a nuclear producer tax against GDF Suez. In response to reports in late 2011 that the Belgian government was considering charging GDF Suez higher amounts than had been previously agreed, GDF Suez said it would reevaluate its nuclear strategy in the country. Belgium plans to stop using nuclear power by 2025, as long as alternate energy sources can be secured.

With the exception of coal, the exploitation of which isn't economical, Belgium has no natural energy resources.

28 INDUSTRY

Industry, highly developed in Belgium, is devoted mainly to the processing of imported raw materials into semifinished and finished products, most of which are then exported. Industry accounted for 22% of GDP in 2010. Steel production is the single most important sector of industry, with Belgium ranking high among world producers of iron and steel. However, it must import all its iron ore, which comes principally from Brazil, West Africa, and Venezuela. About four fifths of Belgium's steel products and more than three quarters of its crude steel output are exported. In recent years, Belgian industry has been hampered by high labor costs, aging plant facilities, and a shrinking market for its products. Nevertheless, industrial production rose by nearly 11% between 1987 and 1991, as a result of falling energy costs (after 1985) and financial costs, and only a moderate rise in wage costs. Industrial production continued to rise in the late 1990s; 1997 registered a 4% growth rate, which slowed to 3.1% in 1998. The industrial growth rate in 2000 was 5.3%; it was -0.5% in 2001, due to the global economic downturn, and rebounded to an estimated 3.5% in 2004. By 2010 the growth rate was 7.1%, ranking Belgium 55th in the world in that category.

Production of crude steel declined from 16.2 million tons in 1974 to 11.3 million tons in 1991, while the output of finished steel dropped from 12.2 million tons to 8.98 million tons. By 1981, 60% of all Belgian steel production and 80% of all Wallonian steel (concentrated in Charleroi and Liège) came under the control of a single company, the government-owned Cockerill-Sambre. Government subsidies for this firm ended (in conformity with EC policy) in 1985. In 1998 French-owned Usinor agreed to take over Cockerill-Sambre, the last major steel making enterprise in Wallonia. As a result of this and other mergers, the Belgian steel industry is now dominated by one multinational company, Arcelor, based in Luxembourg. Arcelor, which was created in 2001, is the largest steel company in the world and is a merger of Usinor, Arbed, and Arcelia.

Belgium also produces significant amounts of crude copper, crude zinc, and crude lead. The bulk of metal manufactures consists of heavy machinery, structural steelwork, and industrial equipment. The railroad equipment industry supplies one of the most extensive railroad systems in Europe. An important shipbuilding industry is centered in Temse, south of Antwerp. Belgian engineering and construction firms have built steel plants, chemical works, power stations, port facilities, and office buildings throughout the world.

Belgium's automotive industry has always been one of the strongest components of its economy. Belgium is a world leader in the car assembly industry; with nearly 95% of its output designed for export, Belgium has the highest per capita production in the world. The industry took a hit in January 2010, when U.S.-based General Motors (GM) announced that it would close its Opel assembly facility in Antwerp. GM's move came as part of the company's plan to restructure its European operations, particularly the Opel division. The Antwerp plant, which began operations in 1924, employed 1,400 people at the time of GM's announcement. As of early 2012, GM was considering closing Opel plants in Germany and the United Kingdom.

The textile industry, dating from the Middle Ages, produces cottons, woolens, linens, and synthetic fibers. With the exception of flax, all raw materials are imported. Centers of the textile industry are Bruges, Brussels, Verviers, Gent, Courtrai (Kortrijk), and Malines (Mechelen). Carpets are made in large quantities at Saint-Nicolas (Sint-Niklaas). Brussels and Bruges are noted for fine linen and lace. Foreign competition has cut into the Belgian textile industry, however. Following the expiration of the World Trade Organization's longstanding system of textile quotas at the beginning of 2005, the EU signed an agreement with China in June 2005 imposing new quotas on 10 categories of textile goods, limiting growth in those categories to between 8% and 12.5% a year.

The agreement ran until 2007, and was designed to give European textile manufacturers time to adjust to a world of unfettered competition. Nevertheless, barely a month after the EU-China agreement was signed, China reached its quotas for sweaters, followed soon after by blouses, bras, T-shirts, and flax yarn. Tens of millions of garments piled up in warehouses and customs checkpoints, which affected both retailers and consumers. The agreement was not renewed.

The chemical industry manufactures a wide range of products, from heavy chemicals and explosives to pharmaceuticals and photographic supplies. The diamond-cutting industry in Antwerp supplies most of the United States's industrial diamond requirements. The majority of all rough diamonds are handled in Antwerp, and about half of all polished diamonds pass through Antwerp. The Antwerp World Diamond Center is concentrated in a two-square-mile area, comprising more than 1,500 diamond companies and four diamond bourses. Those working in the Belgian diamond industry are increasingly being pressured to refrain from buying "conflict diamonds" from Africa, whose proceeds have fueled civil wars in a number of African countries, including Sierra Leone, the Democratic Republic of the Congo, and Angola. Belgium has one of the largest glass industries in the world. Val St. Lambert is especially known for its fine crystal glassware. Belgian refineries (chiefly in Antwerp) turn out oil products.

29 SCIENCE AND TECHNOLOGY

Patent applications in science and technology totaled 669 in 2009, according to the World Bank. Public financing of science was 1.92% of GDP. As of 2008 there were 3,435 researchers per million people actively engaged in research and development.

The Royal Academy of Sciences, Letters, and Fine Arts, founded in Brussels in 1772, and since divided into French and Flemish counterparts, has sections for mathematics, physical sciences, and the natural sciences. There are, in addition, many specialized societies for the study of medicine, biology, zoology, anthropology, astronomy, chemistry, mathematics, geology, and engineering. The National Scientific Research Fund (inaugurated in 1928) in Brussels promotes scientific research by providing subsidies and grants to scientists and students. The Royal Institute of Natural Sciences (founded in 1846), also in Brussels, provides general scientific services in the areas of biology, mineralogy, paleontology, and zoology. From 1987 to 1997, science and engineering students accounted for 41% of college and university enrollment.

Among the nation's distinguished scientific institutions are the Center for the Study of Nuclear Energy in Mol (founded in 1952); the National Botanical Garden of Belgium in Meise (founded in 1870); the Royal Observatory of Belgium in Brussels (founded in 1826); the Institute of Chemical Research in Tervuren (founded in 1928); the Royal Meteorological Institute in Brussels (reorganized in 1913); the Von Karman Institute for Fluid Dynamics in Rhode-St-Genese (founded in 1956) and supported by NATO; and the Institute of Spatial Aeronomy in Brussels (founded in 1964). Belgium has 18 universities and colleges offering degrees in basic and applied sciences.

30 DOMESTIC TRADE

Brussels is the main center for commerce and for the distribution of manufactured goods. Other important centers include

Antwerp, Liège, and Ghent. Most large wholesale firms engage in import and export. Customary terms of sale are payment within 30–90 days after delivery, depending upon the commodity and the credit rating of the purchaser.

In 1994 the government began privatization efforts of several public sector corporations, including banks and airlines. The domestic market is relatively small. Instead, the economy relies heavily on trade as various industries have capitalized on the country's prime central European location, which serves as a regional transit and distribution center. The country also serves as a vital test market for many European goods and franchises.

Belgium's franchising sector has been expanding. According to the Belgian Franchise Federation, there were 3,500 franchises in Belgium in 2011. Some 30,000 people are directly employed by the franchising sector, which has an annual turnover of €2.4 billion. Although franchising is not new to Belgium, it currently represents only about 6% of the retail market in the country, compared to 40% in the United States, and 11% in the rest of Europe.

Direct marketing in Belgium has been steadily growing. Telemarketing calls at home, personalized mailings, and door-to-door letter drops are all increasingly being used. However, such techniques are increasingly falling out of favor with Belgian consumers.

Electronic commerce (e-commerce) is expanding in Belgium, although acceptance among consumers has been slow to materialize. One factor may be the close distance of retailers to consumers. Some 91% of all Belgian consumers are within a 10-mile radius of the nation's department stores and retail shops.

Business hours are mainly from 8 or 9 a.m. to 5 or 6 p.m., Monday through Friday, with an hour for lunch. Banks are open from 9 a.m. to between 3:30 and 5 p.m., Monday-Friday. Retail stores are generally open from 9 a.m. to 6 p.m., Monday through Saturday; some may close for lunch. Larger stores and shopping centers stay open until 9 p.m. on Fridays. Important international trade fairs are held annually in Brussels and Ghent. Advertising techniques are well developed, and the chief media are the press, radio, and television.

31 FOREIGN TRADE

Belgium relies heavily on foreign trade. The country imported $281.7 billion worth of goods and services in 2008, while exporting $279.2 billion worth of goods and services. Major import partners in 2009 were Netherlands, 17.9%; Germany, 17.1%; France, 11.7%; Ireland, 6.3%; the United States, 5.7%; UK, 5.1%; and China, 4.1% . Major export partners were Germany, 19.6%; France, 17.7%; Netherlands, 11.8%; UK, 7.2%; the United States, 5.4%; and Italy, 4.8%.

Foreign trade plays a greater role in the Belgian economy than in any other EU country except Luxembourg. Belgium's chief exports are machinery and equipment, chemicals, metals and metal products, finished diamonds, and foodstuffs. Its imports are raw materials, machinery and equipment, chemicals, raw diamonds, pharmaceuticals, foodstuffs, oil products, and transportation equipment. Since 1921 Belgium has been partnered with Luxembourg in the Belgium-Luxembourg Economic Union (BLEU).

Belgium's central location and multilingual, highly skilled work force are assets to foreign trade.

Principal Trading Partners – Belgium (2010)

(In millions of US dollars)

Country	Total	Exports	Imports	Balance
World	800,966.0	410,388.0	390,578.0	19,810.0
Germany	140,370.0	76,842.0	63,528.0	13,314.0
Netherlands	123,097.0	49,095.0	74,002.0	-24,907.0
France	112,557.0	68,552.0	44,005.0	24,547.0
United Kingdom	49,847.0	28,869.0	20,978.0	7,891.0
United States	42,012.0	21,278.0	20,734.0	544.0
Italy	30,975.0	18,933.0	12,042.0	6,891.0
Ireland	22,727.0	2,304.0	20,423.0	-18,119.0
China	22,022.0	6,288.0	15,734.0	-9,446.0
Australia	20,587.0	12,326.0	8,261.0	4,065.0
India	13,590.0	8,835.0	4,755.0	4,080.0

(…) data not available or not significant.

(n.s.) not specified.

SOURCE: *2011 Direction of Trade Statistics Yearbook,* New York: United Nations, 2011.

Balance of Payments – Belgium (2010)

(In millions of US dollars)

Current Account		**6,349.0**
Balance on goods		-4,730.0
Imports	-284,431.0	
Exports	279,701.0	
Balance on services		8,544.0
Balance on income		10,958.0
Current transfers		-8,420.0
Capital Account		**-857.0**
Financial Account		**-5,846.0**
Direct investment abroad		-47,867.0
Direct investment in Belgium		72,914.0
Portfolio investment assets		7,879.0
Portfolio investment liabilities		-9,025.0
Financial derivatives		1,800.0
Other investment assets		10,186.0
Other investment liabilities		-41,732.0
Net Errors and Omissions		**1,172.0**
Reserves and Related Items		**-819.0**

(…) data not available or not significant.

SOURCE: *Balance of Payment Statistics Yearbook 2011,* Washington, DC: International Monetary Fund, 2011.

32 BALANCE OF PAYMENTS

In 2010 Belgium had a foreign trade surplus of $5.8 billion, amounting to 5.1% of GDP.

Belgium ran deficits on current accounts each year from 1976 through 1984. Trade deficits, incurred consistently in the late 1970s and early 1980s, were only partly counterbalanced by invisible exports, such as tourism and services, and capital transfers. Belgium in the early 2000s had a high current account surplus—$14.3 billion in 2003, and averaging 4.2% of GDP from 2000–04. The current account surplus in 2004 was estimated at $11.4 billion.

Belgium in the early 2000s was attempting to meet the EU's Maastricht target of a cumulative public debt of not more than 60% of GDP. However, the public debt only fell below 100% of

Public Finance – Belgium (2008)

(In millions of euros, central government figures)

Revenue and Grants	142,756	100.0%
Tax revenue	88,018	61.7%
Social contributions	50,019	35.0%
Grants	657	0.5%
Other revenue	4,062	2.8%
Expenditures	146,270	100.0%
General public services	51,528	35.2%
Defense	3,726	2.5%
Public order and safety	3,794	2.6%
Economic affairs	8,260	5.6%
Environmental protection	154	0.1%
Housing and community amenities	47	<0.1%
Health	23,979	16.4%
Recreational, culture, and religion	307	0.2%
Education	4,366	3.0%
Social protection	50,109	34.3%

(…) data not available or not significant.

SOURCE: *Government Finance Statistics Yearbook 2010,* Washington, DC: International Monetary Fund, 2010.

GDP at the end of 2003, for the first time in nearly 30 years. In 2010 public debt stood at just under 100% of GDP.

33BANKING AND SECURITIES

Because Belgium is part of the European Monetary Union (the EMU), and uses the euro as its currency, the European Central Bank (ECB) acts as the nation's central bank, a function formally performed by the National Bank of Belgium (Banque Nationale de Belgique—BNB, founded in 1850). The BNB is now part of the ECB system and acts as the Belgian banking representative to the ECB.

Because Belgium uses the euro, the discount rate is set by the ECB. In 2010 the discount rate, the interest rate at which the ECB lends to financial institutions in the short term, was 1.75%.

At the end of 2010, the nation's reserves of foreign exchange and gold were valued at $26.81 billion.

By law, the name "bank" in Belgium may be used only by institutions engaged mainly in deposit bank activities and short-term operations. Commercial banks are not authorized to invest long-term capital in industrial or business enterprises.

The Bourse in Belgium is a very old institution. As early as the 13th century, merchants from the main commercial centers, particularly Genoa and Venice, used to gather in front of the house of the Van der Bourse family in Brugge, which was then the prosperous trading center of the low countries. The word "Bourse" is often considered to have originated in Brugge.

The Brussels Stock Exchange was founded in 1801 after Napoleon, then Consul of the Republic, issued a decree of the 13th Messidor in the 9th Year that "There shall be an exchange in Brussels, in the Department of the Dyle." The law of 30 December 1867 completely abolished the provisions then in force controlling the profession of broker, the organization of the exchanges and the operations transacted there. After the crisis of 1929 through 1933, a commission was created to assure investors of greater se-

curity. In September 2000 the Brussels Exchanges—comprised of the Belgian Futures and Options Exchange, the Bourse de Bruxelles, and the central securities depository—merged with the Paris Bourse and Amsterdam Exchanges to create Euronext. Euronext is the first pan-European exchange.

In October 2011 Belgium, France, and Luxembourg announced that they would partially nationalize Belgium's largest bank, Dexia, at a cost of four billion Euros. Dexia had also been bailed out in 2008, as a result of its large subprime mortgage loan portfolio.

34INSURANCE

Insurance transactions are supervised by the National Bank of Belgium and the Financial Services and Markets Authority. The latter is a federal body that in April 2011 replaced the Banking, Financial, and Insurance Commission.

In 1996 and 1997 a general pattern of mergers and acquisitions among European union insurers formed, as companies sought to strategically take advantage of the single market in insurance, which became effective in July 1994. Many insurance companies throughout the European Union (EU) were considered too small to operate effectively on an international scale, to meet the challenge of *bancassurance*, or to invest sufficiently in the new technology needed to survive in the increasingly competitive industry.

35PUBLIC FINANCE

In 2010 the budget of Belgium included $220.6 billion in public revenue and $242.6 billion in public expenditures. The budget deficit amounted to 4.1% of GDP. Public debt was 98.6% of GDP, with $1.241 trillion of the debt held by foreign entities.

The government's budgetary year coincides with the calendar year. In the final months of the year, the minister of finance places before Parliament a budget containing estimated revenues and expenditures for the following year, and a finance law authorizing the collection of taxes is passed before 1 January. Inasmuch as expenditure budgets generally are not all passed by then, "provisional twelfths" enable the government to meet expenditures month by month, until all expenditure budgets are passed. Current expenditures, supposedly covered by the usual revenues (including all tax and other government receipts), relate to the normal functioning of government services and to pension and public debt charges. Capital expenditures consist mainly of public projects and are normally covered by borrowings. Improvements in fiscal and external balances in the early 1990s and a slowdown in external debt growth enable the Belgian government to easily obtain loans on the local credit market. As a member of the G-10 group of leading financial nations, Belgium actively participates in the IMF, World Bank, and the Paris Club. Belgium is a leading donor nation, and it closely follows development and debt issues, particularly with respect to the DROC and other African nations.

36TAXATION

Belgian citizens have one of the highest tax burdens in Europe. The most important direct tax is the income tax. Since enactment of the tax law of 20 November 1962, this tax has been levied on the total amount of each taxpayer's income from all sources. In 2011 the top individual income tax rate was 50%, excluding local taxes. The lowest rate was 25%. Local taxes are levied at rates varying from 0–8.5%. Taxes are not paid in one lump sum, but rather by a series of prepayments on the various sources of income. There is a withholding tax on salaries that is turned over directly to the revenue officer. Self-employed persons send a prepayment to the revenue officer during the first half of July. Taxes on real estate are based on the assessed rental value.

Numerous tax exemptions are granted to promote investments in Belgium.

In 1971 a value-added tax system was introduced, replacing sales and excise taxes. A general rate of 21% was applied as of 1996 to industrial goods, with a reduced rate of 6% applying to basic necessities and an interim rate of 12% to certain other products, such as social housing and agricultural products.

Into 2010 there was growing concern over the tax burden imposed on Belgium-based companies. According to research conducted in 2010 by the World Bank, the corporate tax burden in Belgium was the third highest in Europe (after France and Italy), at an estimated 57% with taxes compared to profits. The average tax burden for companies worldwide was estimated at 48%. A few days after these figures were released, the government revealed that nearly 35,000 businesses registered in Belgium had failed to file tax returns for 2009. This was an 11% increase from the number of missing tax filings in 2008. Although some of the companies were no longer operational, a large number of businesses simply refused to file returns. The national tax service can impose a tax bill on companies that fail to file tax returns, but this rarely occurs.

37 CUSTOMS AND DUTIES

Customs duties are levied at the time of importation and are generally ad valorem. Belgium applies the EU common external tariff (CET) to goods imported from non-EU countries. There is a single duty system (the CET) among all EU members for products coming from non-EU members. Theoretically, no customs duties apply for goods imported into Belgium from EU countries. Value-added taxes are levied on the importation of foodstuffs, tobacco, alcohol, beer, mineral water, and fuel oils. There are no export duties.

38 FOREIGN INVESTMENT

Foreign direct investment (FDI) in Belgium was a net outflow of $38.9 billion according to World Bank figures published in 2009. FDI represented -8.25% of GDP.

Foreign investment in Belgium generally takes the form of establishing subsidiaries of foreign firms in the country. Belgium is the economic as well as the political center of Europe. The Belgian government actively promotes foreign investment. In recent years the government has given special encouragement to industries that will create new skills and increase export earnings. The government grants equal treatment under the law, as well as special tax inducements and assistance, to foreign firms that establish enterprises in the country. There is no regulation prescribing the proportion of foreign to domestic capital that may be invested in an enterprise. The foreign investor can repatriate all capital profits and long-term credit is available. Local authorities sometimes offer special assistance and concessions to new foreign enterprises in their area. Since the start of EU's single market, most, but not all, trade and investment rules have been implemented by Belgium in order to be in line with other EU member nations.

The corporation tax rate was reduced in 2003 to 33.99%. Small and medium-sized companies benefit from a reduced tax rate, determined on a scale according to taxable profit. The standard rate of value-added tax (VAT) is 21%. Overall, Belgium has strong competitive advantages, such as an excellent transportation infrastructure, high-quality industrial sites, and a skilled and productive workforce.

Countries with large investments in Belgium include the United States, Germany, United Kingdom, Netherlands, France, and Switzerland. Belgian investment abroad is substantial in the fields of transport (particularly in Latin American countries), nonferrous metals, metalworking, and photographic materials.

Belgium has well-developed capital markets to accommodate foreign finance and portfolio investment. More than half its banking activities involve foreign countries. The world's first stock market was opened in Antwerp in the 14th century.

Foreign direct investment in Belgium was more than $705 billion in 2009. About 6% of the country's work force was employed by US companies. US companies are found in the chemical, automotive, petroleum, and pharmaceutical industries.

In November 2011 Standard and Poor's (S&P) downgraded Belgium's credit rating by one level. The move by S&P acted as a major incentive for political parties to find consensus and form a government. The following month Moody's lowered Belgium's credit rating by two levels. Uncertainties around funding, economic growth, and the nation's public debt contributed to the downgrading.

39 ECONOMIC DEVELOPMENT

Belgian economic policy is based upon the encouragement of private enterprise, with very little government intervention in the economy. Also, as a country heavily dependent upon foreign trade, Belgium has traditionally favored the freest exchange of goods, without tariffs or other limitations. Restrictions on free enterprise and free trade have always been due to external pressure and abnormal circumstances, as in time of war or economic decline.

To meet increased competition in world markets and to furnish relief for areas of the country suffering from chronic unemployment, the government has taken measures to promote the modernization of plants and the creation of new industries. Organizations have been established to provide financial aid and advice, marketing and scientific research, studies on methods of increasing productivity, and nuclear research for economic utilization. Government policy aims at helping industry to hold costs down and to engage in greater production of finished (rather than semifinished) goods. Results have been mixed, with greater success in chemicals and light manufacturing than in the critical iron and steel industry.

In 1993 the government modified its policy of forbidding more than 49% private ownership in government banks, insurance companies, and the national telecommunications company. In 2000 the government enacted tax reform, reducing corporate, trade, and income taxes. The telecommunications sector has been liberalized, as have the gas and energy markets.

Belgium successfully attained a budget deficit of less than 3% by the end of 1997, as stipulated by the EU. A main economic policy priority has for many years been the reduction of the large public debt, which fell below 100% of GDP at the end of 2003, for the first time in nearly 30 years.

The 2011 unemployment rate of 8.5% doesn't reflect regional disparities within Belgium: Flanders' unemployment level is half that of Wallonia's. The southern part of the country has been harder hit by the decline of traditional industries (steel and coal), while the country's burgeoning industries, such as services and chemicals, are based in the north.

40 SOCIAL DEVELOPMENT

Belgium has a social insurance system covering all workers dating back to 1900 for old age and 1944 for disability. The age to receive full retirement benefits is 65 for both men and women, with 45 years of service. The law provides for disability and survivorship benefits as well. Sickness and maternity benefits were originally established in 1894 with mutual benefits societies. There is work accident and occupational disease coverage for all employed persons. Family allowances cover all workers, with special systems for civil servants and the self-employed.

The Belgian government has taken an active stance to protect and promote the rights of women and children. Domestic violence is a problem and in 2004 the government initiated a national plan to increase awareness. Belgium's equal opportunity law includes a sexual harassment provision, giving women a stronger legal basis for complaints. Child protection laws are comprehensive, and governmental programs for child welfare are amply funded. The government also attempts to integrate women at all levels of decision-making and women play an important role in both the public and private sectors.

Legislation prohibits discrimination based on race, ethnicity or nationality, and penalizes incitement of hate and discrimination. Denial of the Holocaust is forbidden by law. The constitution provides for the freedom of religion. Although minority rights are well protected in Belgium, extreme-right political parties with xenophobic beliefs have gained ground in recent years. In 2009 there were 109 reported anti-Semitic incidents, including attacks against Jewish persons and property; in 2010 there were 47 such reported incidents.

41 HEALTH

According to the CIA, life expectancy in Belgium was 81 years in 2011. The country spent 11.1% of its GDP on healthcare, amounting to $5,104 per person. There were 30 physicians, 3 nurses and midwives, and 66 hospital beds per 10,000 inhabitants. The fertility rate was 1.9, while the infant mortality rate was 4 per 1,000 live births. In 2008 the maternal mortality rate, according to the World Bank, was 5 per 100,000 births. It was estimated that 94% of children were vaccinated against measles. The CIA calculated HIV/AIDS prevalence in Belgium to be about 0.2% in 2009.

Every city or town in Belgium has a public assistance committee (elected by the city or town council), which is in charge of health and hospital services in its community. These committees organize clinics and visiting nurse services, run public hospitals, and pay for relief patients in private hospitals. There is a national health insurance plan, membership of which covers practically the whole population. A number of private hospitals are run by local communities or mutual aid societies attached to religious organizations. A school health program includes annual medical examinations for all school children. Private and public mental institutions include observation centers, asylums, and colonies where mental patients live in groups and enjoy a limited amount of liberty.

Nearly 100% of the Belgium population has access to health services. In 2007 the country immunized one-year-old children as follows: diphtheria, pertussis, and tetanus, 97%, and measles, 88%. Average life expectancy for 2011 was 79.51 years. The HIV/AIDS adult prevalence rate was 0.2% in 2009. The incidence of tuberculosis was 13 per 100,000 people in 2007.

42 HOUSING

Belgium no longer has a housing shortage. In the mid-1970s an average of over 60,000 new dwellings were built every year; by the early 1980s, however, the government tried to revitalize the depressed housing market by reducing the value-added tax on residential construction.

Belgium's housing market experienced a price boom between 2000 and 2008. However, the political stalemate that began in 2010 adversely affected the housing market. The average price of a home in Brussels in 2011 was €338,645 ($432,721). In the Flemish region the average home price was €197,415 ($252,257).

43 EDUCATION

In 2008 the World Bank estimated that 98% of age-eligible children in Belgium were enrolled in primary school. Secondary enrollment for age-eligible children stood at 87%. Overall, the CIA estimated that Belgium has a literacy rate of 99%. Public expenditure on education represented 6.0% of GDP.

Education is free and compulsory for children between the ages of 6 and 18. Belgium has two complete school systems operating side by side. One is organized by the state or by local authorities and is known as the official school system. The other, the private school system, is largely Roman Catholic. For a long time, the rivalry between the public and private systems and the question of subsidies to private schools were the main issues in Belgian politics. The controversy was settled in 1958, and both systems are presently financed with government funds along more or less identical lines.

Within the public system, there are also some variations in programming between the French community and the Flemish community. In both, the primary (elementary) school covers six years of study. In the French system, secondary school is divided into three levels, with each level lasting two years. Following this course of study, a student may choose to continue in a one-year program for professional development, technical training, or preparation for university studies. There are also programs for artistic development. In the Flemish system, secondary students may choose between four educational tracks: general, technical, artistic, or vocational. Each track covers a six-year course of study. Most children between the ages of three and five attend some type of preschool program. The academic year runs from September to July.

Higher education centers on the eight main universities: the state universities of Ghent, Liège, Antwerp, and Mons; the two branches of the Free University of Brussels, which in 1970 became separate private institutions, one Dutch (Vrije Universiteit Brussel) and the other French (Université Libre de Bruxelles);

the Catholic University of Brussels; and the Catholic University of Louvain, which also split in 1970 into the Katholicke Universiteit Leuven (Dutch) and the Université Catholique de Louvain (French). In 2009 tertiary enrollment was estimated at 67%. Of those enrolled in tertiary education, there were 100 male students for every 126 female students.

⁴⁴LIBRARIES AND MUSEUMS

There are large libraries, general and specialized, in the principal cities. Brussels has the kingdom's main reference collections, including the Royal Library (founded in 1837), with close to five million volumes, the Library of the Royal Institute of Natural Sciences, and the General Archives of the Kingdom, founded in 1794, with 350,000 documents from the 11th to the 20th centuries. Antwerp is the seat of the Archives and the Museum of Flemish Culture, which has an open library of 55,000 volumes. The university libraries of Louvain (1.2 million volumes), Gent (three million volumes), and Liège (1.7 million volumes) date back to 1425, 1797, and 1817, respectively. The library of the Free University of Brussels (1846) has 1.8 million volumes. Also in Brussels is the library of Commission of the European Communities. In addition, there are several hundred private, special, and business libraries, especially in Antwerp and Brussels, including Antwerp's International Peace Information Service (1981) with 25,000 volumes related to disarmament, and the library of the Center for American Studies in Brussels, with 30,000 volumes dealing with American civilization.

Belgium's 200 or more museums, many of them with art and historical treasures dating back to the Middle Ages and earlier, are found in cities and towns throughout the country. Among Antwerp's outstanding institutions are the Open-Air Museum of Sculpture in Middelheim Park, displaying works by Rodin, Maillol, Marini, Moore, and others; the Rubens House, containing 17th-century furnishings and paintings by Peter Paul Rubens; and the Folk Art Museum (1907) featuring popular music and crafts unique to Flemish Culture and mythology. Brussels' museums include the Royal Museum of Fine Arts (founded 1795), which has medieval, Renaissance, and modern collections; Royal Museum of Central Africa (1897), which has rich collections of African arts and crafts, natural history, ethnography, and prehistory; the Royal Museum of Art and History (1835), with its special collections of Chinese porcelain and furniture, Flemish tapestries, and of 18th- and 19th-century applied and decorative art; and the Museum of Modern Art, featuring 20th-century paintings, sculptures, and drawings. Museums in Bruges, Liège, Gent, Malines, and Verviers have important general or local collections.

In June 2009 the Stoclet House, built by the Vienna Secession movement architect Josef Hoffmann in 1905, was inscribed as a cultural UNESCO World Heritage Site. The home was commissioned by Adolphe Stoclet, a prominent banker and art collector. Belgium has nine additional UNESCO World Heritage Sites.

⁴⁵MEDIA

Belgium's international and domestic telegraph and telephone services are well developed, fully automated, and technologically advanced. In 2009 the CIA reported that there were 4.3 million telephone landlines in Belgium. There were 12.4 million mobile cellular phones in use, or 115 mobile phones per 100 people. International service that year was provided by five submarine cables and seven satellite ground stations.

There were 7 FM radio stations, 79 AM radio stations, and 1 shortwave radio station. In 2010 the country had about 4.4 million Internet hosts. In 2009 there were some 8.1 million Internet users.

National radio and television service is organized into Dutch and French branches. Commercial broadcasting is permitted, hence costs are defrayed through annual license fees on radio and television receivers. There are two national public stations, one broadcasting in French, the other in Dutch. There are also commercial stations; at least two of which are Dutch-language, one of which is French-language, and one German-language.

The Belgian press has full freedom of expression as guaranteed by the constitution of 1831. There are some restrictions on the press regarding slander, libel, and the advocating of racial or ethnic hate, violence, or discrimination. Newspapers are published in French and Dutch, and generally reflect the views of one of the major parties. Agence Belga is the official news agency.

Prominent newspapers in 2010, with circulation numbers listed parenthetically, included *La Capitale* (129,840), *Het Belang Van Limburg* (100,980), and *De Standard* (100,000), as well as 34 other major newspapers.

⁴⁶ORGANIZATIONS

Among Belgium's numerous learned societies are the Royal Academy of Sciences, Letters, and Fine Arts and the Royal Academy of Medicine; in addition, there are the Royal Academy of French Language and Literature and the Royal Academy of Dutch Language and Literature. There is a cultural council for each of the three official languages. Architects, painters, and sculptors are organized in the Association of Professional Artists of Belgium.

Business and industry are organized in the Belgium Business Federation (1885), the Chambers of Commerce, and the American Chamber of Commerce in Brussels, as well as on the basis of industrial sectors and in local bodies. Among the latter, the Flemish and Walloon economic councils and the nine provincial economic councils are the most important. There are a vast number of national professional, trade, and industry associations for a wide variety of occupations and professions.

There are numerous sports societies and soccer, cycling, archery, homing pigeon, tennis, hunting, boating, camping, and riding clubs. Youth organizations include branches of the World Organization of Scouting and an organization of Girl Guides.

Veterans' and disabled veterans' associations, voluntary associations to combat major diseases, and philanthropic societies are all active in Belgium.

There are active chapters of the Red Cross, UNICEF, CARE International, Greenpeace, Caritas, and Amnesty International.

⁴⁷TOURISM, TRAVEL, AND RECREATION

The *Tourism Factbook*, published by the UN World Tourism Organization, reported 6.82 million incoming tourists to Belgium in 2009; they spent a total of $11.1 billion. Of those incoming tourists, there were six million from Europe. There were 170,904 hotel beds available in Belgium. The estimated daily cost to visit Brussels, the capital, was $397. The cost of visiting other cities averaged $195.

Belgium has three major tourist regions: the seacoast, the old Flemish cities, and the Ardennes Forest in the southeast. Ostend is the largest North Sea resort; others are Blankenberge and Knokke. Among Flemish cities, Brugge, Gent, and Ypres stand out, while Antwerp also has many sightseeing attractions, including the busy port, exhibitions of the diamond industry, and the Antwerp Zoo, an oasis of green in the city center. Brussels, home of the European Community headquarters, is a modern city whose most famous landmark is the Grand Place. The capital is the site of the Palais des Beaux-Arts, with its varied concert and dance programs, and of the Théâtre Royal de la Monnaie, home of the internationally famous Ballet of the 20th Century. St. Michael's Cathedral and Notre Dame du Sablon are the city's best-known churches. The Erasmus House in the suburb of Anderlecht and the Royal Palace and Gardens at nearby Laeken are popular tourist centers. Louvain possesses an architecturally splendid city hall and a renowned university. Malines, seat of the Belgian primate, has a handsome cathedral. Liège, in the eastern industrial heartland, boasts one of the finest Renaissance buildings, the palace of its prince-bishops. Tournai is famous for its Romanesque cathedral. Spa, in the Ardennes, is one of Europe's oldest resorts and gave its name to mineral spring resorts in general. Namur, Dinant, and Huy have impressive fortresses overlooking one of the most important strategic crossroads in Western Europe, the Meuse Valley.

In November 2010 three traditional festivals were officially inscribed on the UNESCO Representative List of the Intangible Cultural Heritage of Humanity, an offshoot of the World Heritage program. To be added to the list, the festivals were deemed living traditions by UNESCO, meaning that the rituals involved in them are still passed from generation to generation and continue to create a sense of identity and community for those who participate. Such traditions have been approved by UNESCO for special consideration since 2001. For one that is inscribed, a special program is designed to protect and promote the practice and understanding of the tradition. The Belgian festivals added in 2010 were the three-day Aalst Carnaval in East Flanders (starting on the Sunday before Lent), the annual winter fair and livestock market in Sint-Lievens-Houtem (held on 11 and 12 November), and the bread and fire feast in the city of Geraardsbergen (held on the first Monday of March to celebrate the end of winter).

All travelers are required to have a valid passport; visas are issued for stays of up to 30 days. No visa is required for citizens of the United States or Canada.

48 FAMOUS PERSONS

Belgium has produced many famous figures in the arts. In the 15th century, one of the great periods of European painting culminated in the work of Jan van Eyck (1390?–1441) and Hans Memling (1430?–94). They were followed by Hugo van der Goes (1440?–82), and Pieter Brueghel the Elder (1525?–69), the ancestor of a long line of painters. Generally considered the greatest of Flemish painters are Peter Paul Rubens (1577–1640) and Anthony Van Dyck (1599–1641). In the 19th century, Henri Evenepoel (1872–99) continued this tradition. The 20th century boasts such names as James Ensor (1860–1949), Paul Delvaux (1897–1994), and René Magritte (1898–1967). Modern Belgian architecture was represented by Victor Horta (1861–1947) and Henry van de Velde (1863–1957).

Belgium made substantial contributions to the development of music through the works of such outstanding 15th- and 16th-century composers as Johannes Ockeghem (1430?–95), Josquin des Prés (1450?–1521), Heinrich Isaac (1450?–1517), Adrian Willaert (1480?–1562), Nicolas Gombert (1490?–1556), Cipriano de Rore (1516–65), Philippe de Monte (1521–1603), and Roland de Lassus (known originally as Roland de Latre and later called Orlando di Lasso, 1532–94), the "Prince of Music." Later Belgian composers of renown include François-Joseph Gossec (1734–1829), Peter Van Maldere (1729–68), André Ernest Modeste Grétry (1741–1813), César Franck (1822–90), and Joseph Jongen (1873–1953). Among famous interpreters are the violinists Eugène Ysaye (1858–1931) and Arthur Grumiaux (1921–86). André Cluytens (1905–67) was the conductor of the National Orchestra of Belgium. Maurice Béjart (Maurice Berger, 1927–2007), an internationally famous choreographer, was the director of the Ballet of the 20th Century from 1959 until 1999.

Outstanding Belgian names in French historical literature are Jean Froissart (1333?–1405?) and Philippe de Commynes (1447?–1511?), whereas early Dutch literature boasts the mystical writing of Jan van Ruysbroeck (1293–1381). The 19th century was marked by such important writers as Charles de Coster (1827–79), Camille Lemonnier (1844–1913), Georges Eeckhoud (1854–1927), and Emile Verhaeren (1855–1916) in French; and by Hendrik Conscience (1812–83) and Guido Gezelle (1830–99) in Flemish. Among contemporary authors writing in French, Michel de Ghelderode (1898–1962), Suzanne Lilar (1901–1992), Georges Simenon (1903–1989), and Françoise Mallet-Joris (b. 1930) have been translated into English. Translations of Belgian authors writing in Dutch include works by Johan Daisne (1912–78) and Hugo Claus (1929–2008).

Belgians have won the Nobel Prize in various fields. The poet and playwright Maurice Maeterlinck (1862–1949), whose symbolist dramas have been performed in many countries, received the prize for literature in 1911. Jules Bordet (1870–1961) received the physiology or medicine award in 1919 for his contributions to immunology. The same award went to Corneille J. F. Heymans (1892–1968) in 1938 and was shared by Albert Claude (1898–1983) and Christian de Duve (b. 1917) in 1974. Russian-born Ilya Prigogine (1917–2003) won the chemistry prize in 1977. Three Belgians have won the Nobel Peace Prize: Auguste Beernaert (1829–1912) in 1909, Henri Lafontaine (1854–1943) in 1913, and Father Dominique Pire (1910–69) in 1958.

Belgium's chief of state since 1951 had been King Baudouin I (1930–93), the son of Leopold III (1901–83), who reigned from 1934 until his abdication in 1951. Baudouin was succeeded by his younger brother Albert II (b. 1934) in 1993.

49 DEPENDENCIES

Belgium has no territories or colonies.

50 BIBLIOGRAPHY

Annesley, Claire, ed. *A Political and Economic Dictionary of Western Europe*. Philadelphia: Routledge/Taylor and Francis, 2005.

Arblaster, Paul. *A History of the Low Countries.* Basingstoke, Eng.: Palgrave Macmillan, 2006.

Belgium Investment and Business Guide: Strategic and Practical Information. Washington, DC: International Business Publications USA, 2012.

Coppieters, Bruno and Michel Huysseune, eds. *Secession, History and the Social Sciences.* Brussels, Belgium: VUB Brussels University Press, 2002.

De Vries, André. *Brussels: A Cultural and Literary History.* New York: Interlink Books, 2003.

Gagnon, Alain-G. and James Tully, eds. *Multinational Democracies.* New York: Cambridge University Press, 2001.

International Smoking Statistics: A Collection of Historical Data from 30 Economically Developed Countries. New York: Oxford University Press, 2002.

MacDonald, Mandy. *Belgium: A Quick Guide to Culture and Etiquette.* Portland, OR: Graphic Arts Books, 2005.

Murray, James M. *Bruges, Cradle of Capitalism, 1280–1390.* New York: Cambridge University Press, 2005.

Opello, Walter C. *European Politics.* Boulder, CO: Lynne Rienner Publishers, 2009.

Organization for Economic Cooperation and Development (OECD). *Belgium-Luxembourg.* OECD Economic Surveys. Paris (annual).

Political Chronology of Europe. London, Eng.: Europa, 2001.

Wessels, Wolfgang, Andreas Maurer, and Jürgan Mittag, eds. *Fifteen into One?: the European Union and Its Member States.* New York: Palgrave, 2003.

BOSNIA AND HERZEGOVINA

CAPITAL: Sarajevo

FLAG: Introduced in early 1998, the flag consists of a yellow triangle on a royal blue field, with a row of white stars running diagonally along the triangle's edge. The yellow triangle represents the country's three main ethnic groups, while the royal blue field and stars symbolize a possible future inclusion in the Council of Europe.

ANTHEM: *Državna himna Bosne i Hercegovine (National Anthem of Bosnia and Herzegovina).*

MONETARY UNIT: 1 convertible marka (BAM) = 100 convertible pfenniga. BAM1 = US$0.67 (or US$1 = BAM1.49) as of 2011.

WEIGHTS AND MEASURES: The metric system is the legal standard.

HOLIDAYS: New Year's Day, 1–2 January; Labor Days, 1–2 May. In addition, statehood days and various religious holidays are celebrated regionally in the Federation of Bosnia and Herzegovina (FBH) and Republika Srpska (RS).

TIME: 1 p.m. = noon GMT.

¹LOCATION, SIZE, AND EXTENT

Bosnia and Herzegovina is located in southeastern Europe on the Balkan Peninsula, between Croatia and Serbia and Montenegro. Comparatively, Bosnia and Herzegovina is slightly smaller than the state of West Virginia, with a total area of 51,129 sq km (19,741 sq mi). Bosnia and Herzegovina shares boundaries with Croatia on the N, W, and S, Serbia and Montenegro on the E, and the Adriatic Sea on the S, with a total boundary length of 1,459 km (906 mi). Bosnia and Herzegovina's capital city, Sarajevo, is located near the center of the country.

²TOPOGRAPHY

The topography of Bosnia and Herzegovina features hills, mountains, and valleys. Approximately 50% of the land is forested. The country has three main geographic zones: high plains and plateaus along the northern border with Croatia, low mountains in the center, and the higher Dinaric Alps which cover the rest of the country. Approximately 10% of the land in Bosnia and Herzegovina is arable. Bosnia and Herzegovina's natural resources include coal, iron, bauxite, manganese, timber, wood products, copper, chromium, lead, and zinc. Bosnia and Herzegovina is subject to frequent and destructive earthquakes.

³CLIMATE

The climate features hot summers and cold winters. In higher elevations of the country, summers tend to be short and cold while winters tend to be long and severe. Along the coast, winters tend to be short and rainy. In July, the mean temperature is 22.5°C (72.5°F). January's mean temperature is 0°C (32°F). Annual rainfall averages roughly 62.5 cm (24.6 in).

⁴FLORA AND FAUNA

The region's climate has given Bosnia and Herzegovina a wealth of diverse flora and fauna. Ferns, flowers, mosses, and common trees populate the landscape. Beech forests are found throughout the mountains, with spruce found at some higher altitudes. In addition to the many plant species, the World Resources Institute estimates that Bosnia and Herzegovina is home to 78 mammal species (including deer, brown bears, rabbits, fox, and wild boars), 312 bird species, 27 reptile species, and 8 amphibian species. These figures reflect the total number of distinct species residing in the country, not the number of endemic species.

⁵ENVIRONMENT

Bosnia and Herzegovina faces several environmental challenges. Ongoing inter-ethnic civil strife has seriously damaged the country's infrastructure and led to water shortages. The nation's metallurgical plants contribute to air pollution, and urban landfill sites are limited. The UN reported in 2008 that carbon dioxide emissions in Bosnia and Herzegovina totaled 29,001 kilotons.

According to a 2011 report issued by the International Union for Conservation of Nature and Natural Resources (IUCN), threatened species included 4 types of mammals, 5 species of birds, 2 types of reptiles, 1 amphibian species, 31 species of fish, 14 invertebrates, and 1 plant species. Endangered species include the slender-billed curlew, Danube salmon, and the field adder.

Deforestation is not a significant problem. Hutovo Blato is a Ramsar Wetland Site. The Sutjeska National Park in the south covers an area of about 17,500 hectares (43,250 acres). The World Resources Institute reported that Bosnia and Herzegovina had designated 23,600 hectares (58,317 acres) of land for protection as of 2006. Water resources totaled 37.5 cu km (9 cu mi).

⁶POPULATION

The US Central Intelligence Agency (CIA) estimated the population of Bosnia and Herzegovina in 2011 to be approximately 4,622,163, which placed it at number 121 in population among the 196 nations of the world. In 2011 approximately 15% of the population was over 65 years of age, with another 14% under 15 years of age. The median age in Bosnia and Herzegovina was 40.7 years. There were 0.97 males for every female in the country. The population's annual rate of change was 0.008%, with a projected population for the year 2025 of 3,700,000. Population density in Bosnia and Herzegovina was calculated at 90 people per sq km (233 people per sq mi). The UN estimated that 49% of the population lived in urban areas, and that urban populations had an annual rate of change of 1.1%. The largest urban area was Sarajevo, with a population of 392,000.

Civil strife greatly reduced the population through war, genocide, and emigration. In 1996 there were an estimated 25,000 more deaths than births, creating a population decrease of 1%. By 2006 the population was no longer declining.

⁷MIGRATION

Estimates of Bosnia and Herzegovina's net migration rate, carried out by the CIA in 2011, amounted to zero. The total number of emigrants living abroad was 1.46 million, and the total number of immigrants living in Bosnia and Herzegovina was 27,800. Bosnia and Herzegovina also accepted 7,269 Croatian refugees. Many people living in Bosnia and Herzegovina fled the war that followed independence. In other countries, their numbers were lumped together with other refugees from "Yugoslavia" or "former Yugoslavia." As of 2007, there were still 131,600 internally displaced persons (IDPs) living in Bosnia and Herzegovina.

⁸ETHNIC GROUPS

In 2002 about 48.3% of the people were Bosniak (Muslim) and 34% were Serbs. Croats made up about 15.4% of the populace.

⁹LANGUAGES

Croatian and Bosnian are official languages, but Serbian is also spoken.

¹⁰RELIGIONS

Throughout its history, ethnicity and religion have served as flash points for conflict and changes in government. Ethnic groups tend to be closely linked with distinct religious affiliations; however, the rate of active religious participation is considered to be low. The Bosniaks are generally Muslim. As such, nearly 45% of the population is Muslim. The Serbs are generally Serbian Orthodox, a faith practiced by about 36% of the population. Most of the Serbian Orthodox live in the Republika Srpska. The Croats are primarily Roman Catholic, a faith practiced by about 15% of the population. Protestants account for about 1% of the population. Missionary groups include Seventh-Day Adventists, Jehovah's Witnesses, Methodists, the Church of Jesus Christ of Latter-Day Saints (Mormons), and Krishna Consciousness. There is a Jewish community of about 1,000 members. Freedom of religion is guaranteed by the constitution and by the passage in 2004 of the Law on Religious Freedom which provided for greater freedom of religion and governed the legal licensing of religious groups. This right is generally respected in practice, although a 2009 US State Department report noted that local authorities continue to on occasion restrict the religious freedom of some minority groups. No religious holidays are officially observed as national holidays, but some Christian and Muslim holidays are observed at a local level

and the law requires employers to grant up to four days off per year for religious holidays.

¹¹TRANSPORTATION

The CIA reports that Bosnia and Herzegovina has a total of 22,926 km (14,246 mi) of roads, of which 19,426 km (12,071 mi) are paved. There are 135 vehicles per 1,000 people in the country. Railroads extend for 1,016 km (631 mi). There are 25 airports, which transported 79,977 passengers in 2009 according to the World Bank. Seven of the airports have paved runways; in addition, the nation is served by five heliports.

Bosnia has 795 km (494 mi) of electrified rail. A train route connecting the capitals of Bosnia and Herzegovina and Serbia began service again in December 2009, after a nearly two-decade hiatus. The Belgrade-Sarajevo train route was forced to shut down in 1992 when widespread ethnic violence erupted in the region.

Ports include those at Bosanska Gradiska, Bosanski Brod, Bosanski Samac, and Brčko. All are inland waterway ports on the Sava. None of these ports is fully operational, due to lack of investment, lack of maintenance, war-damaged infrastructure, and low economic development which has led to low demand. A study concluded in 2007 by the International Sava River Basin Commission found improvement of the Sava's navigation potential to be urgent.

There is no merchant marine.

¹²HISTORY

Origins

Bosnia and Herzegovina occupies the area between historical Croatia-Slavonia to the north, Dalmatia to the south, and Serbia and Montenegro to the east/southeast. Populated in ancient times by Thracians, Illyrians, Celts, with Greek colonies since 400 BC, the area was taken over by the Romans around 168 BC. However, it took the Romans some one hundred and fifty years to gain control of the entire area, which they called Dalmatia Province. The most difficult aspect of their occupation was getting past the coastal cities to build roads to rich mining sites in the interior, which still maintained its native, Illyrian character in resistance to pressures to Romanize. Eventually, many Romanized Illyrians became important leaders in the Roman armies and administration and some even became emperors. The division of the Roman Empire into the western and eastern halves in AD 395 found Bosnia as the frontier land of the western half, since the dividing line ran south from Sirmium on the Sava river along the Drina River to Skadar Lake by the Adriatic coast.

Slavic tribes have been raiding and settling in the Balkan area in large numbers since the 5th century AD, moving in slowly from their original lands east of the Carpathian Mountains. These early Slavic settlers were joined in the 7th century AD by Croatian and Serbian tribes invited by Byzantine Emperor Heraclius to help him fight the Avars. The area of Bosnia and Herzegovina became the meeting ground of Croats (western area) and Serbs (eastern area). As medieval Bulgarians, Croatians, and Serbians developed their first states, Bosnia became a battleground among them and the Byzantine Empire. Christianization of the area was completed by the 9th century, when most of the Bosnian area came under the influence of Rome and Croats became Catholic, while most Serbs fell under the influence of the Byzantine Empire and became Eastern Orthodox.

The Bosnian area between the 9th and 11th centuries was essentially under Croatian influence when not conquered by Bulgarians, Serbs, or Byzantium. After Hungary and Croatia effected their royal union in AD 1102, Hungary took over Bosnia and the Dalmatian cities in 1136. Bosnia was then ruled by Croatian "Bans" under joint Hungarian-Croatian sovereignty. When the soldiers supplied by Ban Borić (r. 1150–1167) to the Hungarian Army were defeated by Byzantium in 1167 at Zemun, Bosnia came under Byzantine rule. Hungary renewed its claim to Bosnia in 1185, during Ban Kulin's reign (1180–1204), which was marked by his independence from Hungary, partly due to the inaccessibility of its mountainous terrain.

Geography itself was an incentive to the local autonomy of Bosnia's individual regions of Podrina, Central Bosnia, Lower Bosnia, and Hum (today's Herzegovina). Each region had its own local hereditary nobility and customs, and was divided into districts (*Župas*). The typical Bosnian family of this period had possession of its land without dependence on a feudal relationship to prince or king, as was the case in much of Europe. Bosnia was nominally Catholic under the jurisdiction of the Archbishop of Dubrovnik, who would consecrate a Bishop of Bosnia, usually from local Bosnian priests. These Bosnian Catholics used a Slavic liturgy and a modified Cyrillic alphabet called "Bosanica" and had no knowledge of Latin. The region of Hum, on the other hand, was settled by Serbs in the interior, was mixed Orthodox and Catholic in the coastal area and mostly ruled by princes of the Serbian dynasty (Nemanja) until 1326.

The Catholic Church in Bosnia was isolated from the coastal areas and had developed its own Slavic liturgy and practices. These customs were suspect to the Latin hierarchy in both Hungary and the coastal cities. Ignorance of the language and customs of simple people and poor communications generated rumors and accusations of heresy against the Bosnian Church and Ban Kulin, its supposed protector. Kulin called a Church Council in 1203 at Bolino Polje that declared its loyalty to the Pope and renounced errors in its practices. Reports of heresy in Bosnia persisted, possibly fanned by Hungary, and caused visits by Papal legates in the 1220s. By 1225 the Pope was calling on the Hungarians to launch a crusade against the Bosnia heretics. In 1233, the native Bishop of Bosnia was removed and a German Dominican appointed to replace him. In spite of Ban Ninoslav's (1233–1250) renunciation of the "heresy," the Hungarians undertook a crusade in 1235–41, accompanied by Dominicans who were already erecting a cathedral in Vrhbosna (today's Sarajevo) in 1238. The Hungarians used the crusade to take control of most of Bosnia, but had to retreat in 1241 because of the Tartars' attack on Hungary. This allowed the Bosnians to regain their independence and in 1248 the Pope sent a neutral team (a Franciscan and a Bishop from the coastal town of Senj) to investigate the situation but no report is extant.

The Hungarians insisted that the Bosnian Church be subjected to the Archbishop of Kalocsa in Hungary, who it was thought would intervene to end its heretical practices. In 1252, the Pope obliged. However, no Bishop was sent to Bosnia itself, only to Djakovo in Slavonia, so this act had no impact on the Bosnian Church. The crusades against the Bosnian Church caused a deep animosity toward the Hungarians that in the long run weakened Bosnia's determination to resist the invasion of the Islamic Turks. Thus the Bosnian Church that professed to be loyal to Catholicism, even though it continued in its practice of ascetic and rather primitive rituals by its Catholic monastic order, was pushed into separation from Rome.

Around 1288, Stjepan Kotroman became Ban of the Northern Bosnia area. In his quest to consolidate all of Bosnia under his rule, though, he was challenged by the Šubić family of Croatia, who had taken over Western Bosnia. Paul I Šubić then expanded his family's area of control, becoming Ban of Bosnia and later, in 1305, Ban of All Bosnia. However, the power of the Šubić family declined in subsequent years, and Kotroman's son Stjepan Kotromanić was able to take control of Central Bosnia by 1318, serving as a vassal of the Croatian Ban of Bosnia, Mladen Šubić. Kotromanić then allied himself with Charles Robert, King of Hungary, to defeat Mladen Šubić, helping Kotromanić to consolidate his control over Bosnia, the Neretva River Delta, and over Hum, which he took in 1326 but lost in 1350 to Dušan the Great of Serbia. In recognition of the role the Hungarians had played in his consolidation of power in Bosnia, Ban Kotromanić gave his daughter Elizabeth into marriage to King Louis of Hungary in 1353, the year of his death.

Raised in the Orthodox faith, Kotromanić was converted to Catholicism by Franciscan fathers, an order he had allowed into Bosnia in 1342. The Franciscans concentrated their efforts at conversion on the members of the Bosnian Church (or Bogomili) and, by 1385, had built some 35 monasteries, four in Bosnia itself. Since most Franciscans were Italian and did not know the Slavic language, their effectiveness was not as great as it could have been and it was concentrated in the towns where numerous non-Bosnians had settled to ply their trades. During this period silver and other mines were opened which were administered by the townspeople of Dubrovnik. This influx of commerce helped in the development of prosperous towns in key locations and customs duties from increased trade enriched Bosnian nobles. A whole new class of native craftsmen developed in towns where foreign colonies also prospered and interacted with the native population, thus raising Bosnia's overall cultural level.

Kotromanić's heir was his nephew Tvrtko (r. 1353–91) who would become the greatest ruler of Bosnia. Tvrtko could not command the loyalty of the nobles at first, however, and he soon lost the western part of Hum (1357) to Hungary as the dowry promised to King Louis of Hungary when he married Elizabeth, Kotromanić's daughter. But by 1363, Tvrtko had grown powerful enough to repel Hungarian attacks into Northern Bosnia. In 1366 Tvrtko fled to the Hungarian Court, having been unable to repress a revolt by his own nobles, and with Hungarian help regained his lands in 1367. In 1373 he obtained the upper Drina and Lim Rivers region. In 1377 he was crowned King of Bosnia and Serbia (his grandmother was a Nemanja) at the Mileševo monastery where Saint Sava, the founder of the Serbian Orthodox Church, was buried. Between 1378 and 1385, Tvrtko also gained control of the coastal territory of Trebinje and Konavli near Dubrovnik, along with the port city of Kotor. In 1389, Tvrtko sent his troops to support the Serbian armies of Prince Lazar and Vuk Branković at the legendary Battle of Kosovo Polje. The battle itself was a draw but it exhausted the Serbs' capability to resist the further Turkish invasions. The Turks retreated, having suffered the death of Sultan Murad I, assassinated by a Serbian military leader, and Tvrtko's commander at Kosovo claimed victory. Having sent such a message to Italy, Tvrtko was hailed as a savior of Christendom. He had made a first step toward a possible unification of Bosnia and Serbian lands, but the Turks, and then his own death in 1391, made it impossible.

Bosnia did not disintegrate after Tvrtko's death, but was held together through a council of the key nobles. The Council elected weak kings to maintain their own power and privileges. Tvrtko had no legitimate descendants so his cousin Dabiša (r. 1391–95) was elected, followed by his widow Helen of Hum (r. 1395–98), and then Stjepan Ostoja (r. 1398–1404), opposed by Tvrtko II (r. 1404–09), probably Tvrtko I's illegitimate son. Between 1404 and 1443, Bosnia witnessed civil wars between factions of the nobles taking opposite sides in the Hungarian wars of succession. Thus Stjepan Ostoja was returned to the throne from 1409 to 1418, followed by Stjepan Ostojić (r. 1418–21), then Tvrtko II again (r. 1421–43). During this period the Turks participated in Bosnian affairs as paid mercenaries, through their own raids, and by taking sides in the struggles for the Bosnian throne. The Turks supported Tvrtko II, who managed to rule for over 20 years by recognizing the sovereignty of both the Hungarians and Turks, and playing one against the other. After the Turks' conquest of Serbia in 1439 made them direct neighbors of Bosnia along the Drina River, Turkish raids into Bosnia increased. The Ottomans assumed a key role in internal Bosnian affairs and became the mediator for Bosnian nobles' quarrels. The Bosnian nobles and their Council clung to their opposition to a centralized royal authority, even though it could have mounted a stronger defense against Hungarians and Turks. Thus Bosnia grew ever weaker with the skillful maneuvering of the Turks. Twenty years after Tvrtko II's death in 1443, the Turks conquered an exhausted Bosnia with a surprise campaign.

Herzegovina (named after the ruler of Hum, Stefan Vukčić who called himself Herzeg/Duke) was occupied by the Turks gradually by 1482, and the two regions were subject to the Ottoman Empire for the next 400 years until the 1878 takeover by Austria.

Under Ottoman Rule

The mass conversion of Bosnian Christians to Islam, a rather unique phenomenon in European history, is explained by two schools of thought. The traditional view recognizes the existence of a strong Bogomil heresy of dualism and social protest. These Bosnian Christians, having been persecuted by both Catholic and Orthodox Churches and rulers, welcomed the Ottomans and easily converted in order to preserve their land holdings. In doing so, they became trusted Ottoman soldiers and administrators. The other school of thought denies the existence of a strong and influential Bogomil heresy, but defines the Bosnian Christian church as a nativistic, anti-Hungarian, loosely organized religion with a Catholic theological background and simple, peasant-based practices supported by its monastic order. The rulers/kings of Bosnia were Catholic (with the single exception of Ostoja) and very tolerant of the Orthodox and so-called Bosnian religions. However, these religious organizations had very few priests and monks, and therefore were not very strong. The Bosnian Church was practically eliminated in 1459 through conversions to official Catholicism, or the forced exile of its leadership. Thus, by the time of the Turkish conquest, the Bosnian Church had ceased to exist and the

allure of privileged status under the Ottomans was too strong for many to resist.

Bosnia and Herzegovina was ruled by a Pasha or Vizier appointed by the Sultan and assisted by a Chancellor, supreme justice, and treasurer, each heading his own bureaucracy, both central and spread into eight districts (Sandžaks). Justice was administered by a *khadi* who was both prosecutor and judge using the Koran for legal guidance, thus favoring Muslim subjects. Catholics, who were outside the established Orthodox and Jewish communities represented by the Greek Orthodox patriarch and chief rabbi in Constantinople, were particularly exposed to arbitrary persecutions. In spite of all this, communities of followers of the Orthodox (Serbian) Church and Catholic (Croatian) Church survived into the late 19th century when in 1878 Austria obtained the authority to occupy Bosnia and Herzegovina, putting an end to four centuries of Ottoman rule. The Ottomans introduced in Bosnia and Herzegovina their administration, property concepts, and customs. The adherents to Islam were the ruling class, regardless of their national or ethnic backgrounds. Christian peasants practically became serfs to Muslim landlords, while in the towns civil and military administrators had control over an increasingly Muslim population. Large numbers of Bosnians fled the Turkish takeover and settled in Venetian-occupied coastal areas where many continued the fight against the Turks as "Uskoki" raiders. Others emigrated north or west into Slavonia and Croatia and were organized as lifetime soldiers along military regions (Krajina) in exchange for freemen status, land, and other privileges. On the Bosnian side, Christians were not required to enter military service, but the so-called "blood tax" took a heavy toll by turning boys forcibly into Muslim Janissaries—professional soldiers converted to Islam who would generally forget their origins and become oppressors of the Sultan's subjects. Girls were sent to harems. Taxation became more and more oppressive, leading to revolts by the Christian peasantry that elicited bloody repressions.

Under Austro-Hungarian Rule

Historically both Croats and Serbs have competed for control over Bosnia. The Croats, who had included Bosnia in their medieval kingdom, could not effectively continue their rule once joined with the more powerful Hungarians in their royal union. The Serbs, on the other hand, were assisted by Hungary in their expansion at the expense of the Byzantine Empire. Later, they also received Hungarian support in their resistance to Turkish inroads and therefore could not invest their energies in Bosnia, in their view a "Hungarian" territory. Thus Bosnia was able to assert its own autonomy and individuality, but did not evolve into a separate nation. With the Austrian occupation, however, a new period began marked by a search for a Bosnian identity, supported by Austria who had an interest in countering the national unification ambitions of both Croats and Serbs.

The population of Bosnia and Herzegovina was divided into three major religious-ethnic groups: Croatian Catholics, Serbian Orthodox, and Bosnian Muslims. With the disappearance of the Bosnian Church just before the Ottoman occupation in 1463, most Bosnians were Croatian and Catholic, with a Serbian Orthodox population concentrated in Eastern Herzegovina and along the Drina River frontier with Serbia. The Serbs were mostly peasants, many of whom became serfs to Muslim landlords. Their

LOCATION: 44°17′ N; 17°30′ E. BOUNDARY LENGTHS: Croatia, 932 kilometers (578 miles); Montenegro, 249 kilometers (155 miles); Serbia, 357 kilometers (222 miles); total coastline, 20 kilometers (12 miles).

priests, who were generally poorly educated, lived as peasants among them. Serbian urban dwellers, insignificant in number at first, grew to be an important factor by the late Ottoman period and developed their own churches and schools in the 19th century. Crafts and commerce were the main occupations of the new Serbian middle class.

Croats were also mostly peasants and, like the Serbs, became serfs to Muslim landlords. Members of the Franciscan order lived among the peasants, even though they also had built several monasteries in urban centers. There was almost no Croat middle class at the start of the Austrian period and the Catholic clergy was generally its advocate.

The Muslim group consisted of three social subgroups: the elites, the peasants, and urban lower classes. Most Muslims were free peasants with a standard of living not better than that of the Christian serf-peasants. The Muslim hodžas (priests) lived among the peasants as peasants themselves. The second subgroup consisted of merchants, craftsmen, and artisans and was mostly concentrated in towns. Together with the urban lower classes, these two groups made up the Muslim majorities in most towns by 1878. The members of the Muslim elites were mostly religious functionaries, landowners, and commercial entrepreneurs, all favored by Islamic laws and traditions. Following the 1878 occupation, Austria recognized the right of Turkish functionaries to keep their posts, the right of Muslims to be in communication with their religious leaders in the Ottoman Empire, the right of Turkish currency to circulate in Bosnia, and also promised to respect all traditions and customs of the Bosnian Muslims. The Austrian approach to the administration of Bosnia and Herzegovina was close to the British colonial model that retained the existing elites and cultural individuality while gradually introducing Western administrative and education models.

Bosnia and Herzegovina was divided by the Turks into six administrative regions that were confirmed by Austria: Sarajevo, Travnik, Bihać, Donja Tuzla, Banja Luka, and Mostar (Herzegovina). Each was headed by a regional supervisor. Participation in cultural and religious organizations was encouraged, while engaging in politics was prohibited. The Austrians promoted a policy of equality between Christians and Muslims, banned organizations of an open political purpose, and prohibited the use of national names (Serb and Croat) for public institutions. At the same time, educational institutions designed to promote loyalty to Bosnia (and Austria) as such were encouraged. Censorship and other means were used to insulate Bosnians from the influence of their Croatian and Serbian co-nationals across the borders. By terminating the earlier Muslim secular/religious unity, many administrative and judicial functions were no longer carried out by the Muslim elites, but were instead presided over by the Austrian bureaucracy and judiciary, though a separate Muslim judiciary was continued. The Muslim landowners lost some privileges but were able to retain their land and the system of serfdom was allowed to continue.

A widespread and important institution supporting Muslim cultural life was the Vakif (Vakuf in Serbian/Croatian). The Vakuf was a revenue-producing property set up and administered as a family foundation for the support of specified causes. Once set up, a Vakuf could not be sold, bequeathed, or divided and was exempt from normal taxes. In 1878 it was estimated that one-fourth to one-third of usable land in Bosnia was tied to Vakufs. The administration of Vakufs was lax and open to much manipulation and abuse. The Austrian administration was able to establish effective controls over the Vakuf system by 1894 through a centralized commission and the involvement of prominent Muslims in the administration of Vakuf revenues in support of Islamic institutions.

The continuation of serfdom by the Austrian authorities was a deep disappointment for the peasants eagerly expecting emancipation. Abuses led to peasant revolts until the Austrians introduced cash payments of the tithe (one-tenth of harvest due to the state) and the appraising of harvest value as basis for payment in kind (one-third) to the landlord. A land-registry system was instituted in 1884, and landowners that could not prove legal ownership lost title to some properties. This policy generated wide discontent among Muslim landowners. Another cause of frequent

disorders was cases of religious conversions. Under Muslim law, a Muslim convert to another faith was to be executed (this penalty was later eased to banishment). The Austrian policy of confessional equality required a freedom of religious conversion without any penalty and a conversion statute was issued in 1891.

The general aim of the Austrian administration was to guide the development of a coequal confessional society that would focus its efforts on cultural and economic progress without political and national assertiveness. Benjamin von Kallay, the first Austrian Chief Administrator for Bosnia and Herzegovina wanted to avoid anything that could lead to the creation of a separate Muslim nation in Bosnia. On the other hand, he was determined to insulate Bosnians from external developments in the South Slavic areas. Such a position was unrealistic, since all of the main groups—Serbs, Croats, and Muslims—identified themselves with their own national/religious groups in the neighboring areas and had developed intense cultural/political relationships with them. Serbs looked at Serbia's successes and hoped for unification with their motherland. Croats followed closely the Croatian-Hungarian tensions and hoped likewise for their unification. The Muslim community, meanwhile, struggled for its own cultural/religious autonomy within a Bosnia that still recognized the Ottoman Sultan's sovereignty and looked to him for assistance.

The unilateral annexation of Bosnia and Herzegovina to Austria in 1908 exacerbated Austria's relations with Serbia (and almost caused a war) and with the Hungarian half of the Hapsburg Crown that opposed the enlargement of the Slavic population of Austria-Hungary. Serbia's victories in the Balkan wars added fuel to the "Yugoslav" movement among the South Slavs of Austria, including Bosnia and Herzegovina. Here the Austrian administration countered the growing "Yugoslav" assertiveness with a "divide and rule" initiative of developing a separate "Bosnian" national consciousness which they hoped would tie together Serbs, Croats, and Muslims. All nationalist movements use elements of history to develop their own mythology to unite their members. Thus, the medieval Bosnian kingdom was the basis for development of a Bosnian national consciousness. It was opposed by most Serbs and Croats, who awaited unification with Serbia or Croatia, but gave some sense of security to the more isolated Muslim Bosnian community. Already by the beginning of the 20th century, separate ethnic organizations and related political associations had to be allowed. The 1908 annexation led to the promulgation of a constitution, legal recognition of political parties, and a Bosnian Parliament in 1910. The internal political liberalization then allowed the Austrian administration to concentrate on the repression of student radicals, internal and external terrorists, and other such perceived threats to their rule.

The Muslim community was split internally, with a leadership dominated by landowners and weakened by the forced emigration to Turkey of its top leaders. It finally came together in 1906 and formed the Muslim National Organization (Muslimanska Narodna Organizacija) as its political party, with the blessing of its émigré leaders in Istanbul. Intense negotiations with the Austrian administration produced agreements on religious and cultural autonomy as well as landowners' rights. The latter were a preeminent concern, and landowners were able to preserve their ownership rights based on Ottoman law and the peasants' payments of compulsory dues. The religious autonomy of the Muslim faith was assured by having the nominees for the top offices confirmed by the Sultan's religious head upon request by the Austrian Embassy in Istanbul. The same process was also used in matters of religious dogma and law.

Cultural autonomy for Muslims was affirmed through the streamlining of the preexisting Vakuf system into local, regional, and central assemblies responsible for the operation of the vakufs and the related educational system. Overall, the Muslims of Bosnia had achieved their objectives: preserving their large landholdings with peasants still in a quasi-serfdom condition; assuring their cultural autonomy; and retaining access to the Sultan, head of a foreign country, in matters of their religious hierarchies. Politically, the Muslim National Organization participated in the first parliament as part of the majority supportive of the Austrian government.

Serbs and Croats had also formed political organizations, the nature of which reflected Bosnia's peculiar ethnic and sociopolitical conditions. The Serbian National Organization (Srpska Narodna Organizacija) was founded in 1907 as a coalition of three factions. The Croatian National Community (Hrvatska Narodna Zajednica) was formed in 1908 by liberal Croat intellectuals, followed in 1910 by the Croatian Catholic Association (Hrvatska Katolička Udruga). A cross-ethnic Social Democratic party, formed in 1909, failed to win any seats in the Parliament. A Muslim Progressive Party, formed in 1908, found hardly any support even after changing its name to the Muslim Independent Party. The Muslims were more conservative and were opposed to the agrarian reform demanded by the Serbs and Croats, who each continued to favor an association or unification with their respective "Mother Country." Croats asserted the Croatian character of Bosnia based on its Croatian past, while Serbs just as adamantly claimed its Serbian character and supported Serbia's "Greater Serbia" policies.

Given the demographics of Bosnia and Herzegovina (1910 census: Serbian Orthodox, 43%; Croat Catholics, 23%; Muslims, 32%), each side needed the support of the Muslims who, though pressured to declare themselves Serbs or Croats, very seldom would do so, preferring to keep their own separate identity. Up until the Balkan wars, Muslims and Serbs would support one another hoping for some kind of political autonomy. Croats advocated unification with Croatia and a trialist reorganization of the Hapsburg Monarchy, giving the united South Slavs a coequal status with Austrians and Hungarians. Any cooperation by the Muslims was predicated on support for the continuation of serfdom. This stance prevented cooperation with the Croatian Catholic Association, which insisted on agrarian reform and the termination of serfdom.

With the Serbian victories and Ottoman defeat in the Balkan wars, Serbs became more assertive and Croats more willing to cooperate with them in the growing enthusiasm generated by the idea of "Yugoslavism." A parliamentary majority of Serbs and Croats could have affected the liberation of the peasants in 1913 but the Hungarians opposed it. The assassination of Archduke Ferdinand on 28 June 1914, and World War I, combined to make the issue moot when the Parliament was adjourned. The assassination of the Archduke was apparently the work of members of the "Young Bosnia" students association supported (unofficially) by Serbia through its extremist conspiratorial associations, the

"Black Hand" and the "Serbian National Defense." The Austrian ultimatum to Serbia was extremely harsh but Serbia met all the conditions that did not violate its sovereignty. Austria nevertheless declared war and immediately attacked Serbia. The Serbian community of Bosnia and Herzegovina was subjected to a regime of terror and indiscriminate executions by the Austrian authorities. Serbian leaders were subjected to trials, court martial proceedings, and infamous concentrations camps where internees died of epidemics and starvation.

First (Royal) Yugoslavia

Throughout World War I, Bosnians fought in Austrian units, particularly on the Italian front until Austria's surrender. The Bosnian National Council decided to unite with the Kingdom of Serbia, as Vojvodina did and the Montenegrin assembly did on 24 November 1918. On 27 November 1918 the delegation from the Zagreb-based National Council of the Slovenes, Croats, and Serbs also requested unification with Serbia of the Slovene, Croat, and Serbian lands of Austria-Hungary. Following the Declaration of Union on 1 December 1918, a provisional government was set, made up of representatives of Serbia and the National Council, with other groups added later. A provisional Assembly was also convened consisting of members of the Serbian Parliament, nominees from the National Council and other regional Assemblies such as Bosnia and Herzegovina and Vojvodina. In November 1920 a Constituent Assembly was elected and functioned as both the legislature and constitutional convention. Bosnian Serbs supported the Serbian Agrarian Party, while two Muslim parties, the National Muslim Organization from Bosnia and Herzegovina and the Džemijet Party of the Kosovo and Macedonia Muslims had seats in the assembly. Croats, on the other hand, joined the mainstream parties of Croatia.

By joining the Kingdom of Serbs, Croats, and Slovenes in 1918, Bosnia and Herzegovina ceased to exist as a distinct political/historical unit, particularly since the heads of local governments were appointed by and directly accountable to the central government in Belgrade. After 10 years of a tumultuous parliamentary history culminating in the assassination of Croatian deputies, King Alexander dissolved parliament and disbanded all political parties, establishing a royal dictatorship in 1929. He then reorganized the country into a "Yugoslavia" made up of nine administrative regions (*banovine*) named after rivers. What once was Bosnia and Herzegovina was split among four of the new units (Vrbaska, Drinska, Primorska, and Zetska). Serb and Croat peasants were finally freed from their feudal obligations to Muslim landlords through the agrarian reforms decreed in 1919 and slowly implemented over the next 20 years. Except for Bosnia and Herzegovina and Dalmatia, lands held by ex-enemies (Austrians, Hungarians, Turks) were expropriated without compensation and redistributed to the peasants—1.75 million of them plus 2.8 million dependents. As a result, the average size of agricultural holdings fell to 15 acres, causing inefficiencies and very low yields per acre. Peasants were forced to borrow even to buy food and necessities. They fell deeply in debt, both to local shopkeepers who charged 100–200% interest and to banks that charged rates up to 50%. In comparison, peasant cooperatives in Slovenia used single digit interest rates.

Politically, the Muslim Organization, as a small party, allied itself mostly with the Slovene People's Party and either the Serbian

Democratic or Radical parties in order to participate in a series of governments before the 1929 royal dictatorship was implemented. The Muslim Organization's main goals were to obtain the best possible compensation for land expropriated from Bosnia's Muslim landowners and to preserve the Muslims' cultural identity. In 1932, Muslim leaders joined the Croats, Slovenes, and some Liberal Serbs in issuing the Zagreb manifesto calling for an end to the King's dictatorship and for democratization and regional autonomies. For this the centralist regime interned and imprisoned several of the leaders and instituted wider repressions. Following the assassination of King Alexander in 1934 in Marseille, France, the Croat Peasants Party was joined by the Muslims, Serbian Agrarians, and Serbian Democrats in opposition to the Centralists, winning 38% of the votes in spite of the government's intimidating tactics. With the opposition refusing to take part in the parliament, a new government was formed by the Serbian Radicals with the inclusion of the Muslims and the Slovene People's Party.

This new coalition government lasted until 1939, but was never able to resolve the "Croatian" autonomy issue. In addition, while under the leadership of Milan Stojadinović, Yugoslavia's foreign policy moved the country closer to Italy and Germany. Meanwhile a growing consensus had developed that the "Croatian" question had to be solved, particularly in view of the aggressive ambitions of Yugoslavia's neighbors. Thus, the Regent Prince Paul and Dr. Vladimir Maćek, leader of the Croatian Peasant Party, worked with the Minister of Social Policy, Dragiša Cvetković, on an agreement establishing a Croatian Banovina made up of the historical regions of Croatia-Slavonia and Dalmatia along with parts of Vojvodina, Srem, and Bosnia. The president of the senate, Monsignor Anton Korošec (also leader of the Slovene People's Party), engineered the resignation of five ministers, two Slovenes, two Muslims, and Dragiša Cvetković. Regent Paul then called on Cvetković to form a new government. Dr. Maćek became vice-premier and Ivan Subašić was named Ban of the autonomous Croatian Banovina, which was given its own Sabor (parliament). The Croatian parties considered this development as a positive first phase toward their goal of an independent Croatia that would incorporate all of Bosnia and Herzegovina. The Serbian centralists, on the other hand, saw this phase as a threat to their own designs of incorporating Bosnia and Herzegovina (and Serb populated areas of Croatia) into a "Greater Serbia" unit of Yugoslavia. Thus, on the eve of World War II, the stage was set for a direct confrontation between the independent-minded Croatians and centralistic Serbs. The Muslims of Bosnia were caught in their crossfire.

World War II

Germany, Italy, and their allies Hungary, Romania, and Bulgaria, attacked Yugoslavia on 6 April 1941 and divided the country among themselves. The Croatian terrorist Ustaša organization collaborated with the aggressors and was allowed to proclaim an Independent State of Croatia on 10 April 1941. This new state incorporated the old Croatian Banovina in addition to all of Bosnia and Herzegovina. Of its total population of 6.3 million, one-third was Serbian and 750,000 were Muslim. Once entrenched in power, the Ustaša troops began implementing their plan for "cleansing" their Greater Croatia of the Serbian population by the use

of terror, mass deportations, and genocidal massacres later condemned by the Nürnberg Court.

The Serbian population responded in kind with its Cetnik formations and by joining the Partisan resistance movement led by Josip Broz-Tito, head of the Yugoslav Communist Party. Bosnia and Herzegovina suffered terrible losses in several German-led offensives against Bosnian resistance, and in the internecine civil war among Communist-dominated Partisans, nationalist Cetniks (mostly Serbs), and Croatian Ustaše and home guard units. The Muslim population in particular was caught in the middle between the Ustaše and the Serbian Cetniks. The Ustaše considered the Muslims of Croatian origin and expected them to collaborate with the Ustaša regime. The Serbian Cetniks, on the other hand, viewed most Muslims as the hated Turks and Ustaša collaborators, and therefore engaged in slaughters of Muslims, particularly in Eastern Bosnia around the cities of Foča and Goražde.

The political programs of the Cetniks and Partisans were a reflection of the old centralist (Serbian) hegemony and the Federalist positions of the prewar opposition parties. Thus the Partisan resistance, though aiming at a revolutionary power grab, offered a federated Yugoslavia made up of individual republics for each national group—Serbs, Croats, Slovenes, newly recognized Macedonians and Montenegrins. To avoid a battle over a Serbian-Croatian border issue, Bosnia and Herzegovina was resurrected as a buffer area between Serbia and Croatia. It would also allow (again) for the cultural autonomy of the Muslim population. The Allied and Soviet support the Partisans received enabled them to prevail, and they organized Socialist Yugoslavia as a Federative People's Republic with Bosnia and Herzegovina as one of the constituent republics approximately within the boundaries of the former Austrian province.

When Soviet armies entered Yugoslavia from Romania and Bulgaria in the fall of 1944, Marshal Tito with them, military units and civilians that had opposed the partisans had no choice but retreat to Austria or Italy to save themselves. Among them were the Cetnik units of Draža Mihajlović and "home guards" from Serbia, Croatia, and Slovenia that had been under German control but were pro-Allies in their convictions and hopes. Also in retreat were the units of the Croatian Ustaša that had collaborated with Italy and Germany in order to achieve (and control) an "independent" greater Croatia and in the process had committed terrible and large-scale massacres of Serbs, Jews, Gypsies, and others who opposed them. Of course, Serbs and Partisans counteracted and a fratricidal civil war raged over Yugoslavia, pitting Croats against Serbs, Communists against Nationalists. These skirmishes not only wasted countless lives, they used up the energy and property that could have been used instead against the occupiers. After the end of the war, the Communist-led forces took control of all of Yugoslavia and instituted a violent dictatorship that committed systematic crimes and human rights violations on an unexpectedly large scale. Thousands upon thousands of their former opponents were returned from Austria by British military authorities only to be tortured and massacred by Partisan executioners.

Second (Communist) Yugoslavia

Such was the background for the formation of the second Yugoslavia as a Federative People's Republic of five nations—Slovenes, Croats, Serbs, Macedonians, and Montenegrins—and Bosnia and

Herzegovina as a buffer area with its mix of Serb, Muslim, and Croat populations. The problem of large Hungarian and Muslim Albanian populations in Serbia was solved by creating the autonomous region of Vojvodina (Hungarian minority) and Kosovo (Muslim Albanian majority) to assure their political and cultural development. Tito attempted a balancing act to satisfy most of the nationality issues that were carried over unresolved from the first Yugoslavia, but failed to satisfy anyone.

Compared to pre-1941 Yugoslavia where Serbs enjoyed their controlling role, the numerically stronger Serbs in the new Yugoslavia had "lost" the Macedonian area they considered "Southern Serbia"; they had lost the opportunity to incorporate Montenegro into Serbia; they had lost direct control over the Hungarian minority in Vojvodina and Muslim Albanians of Kosovo (viewed as the cradle of the Serbian nation since the Middle Ages); they could no longer incorporate into Serbia the large Serbian populated areas of Bosnia; and they had not obtained an autonomous region for the large minority Serbian population within the Croatian Republic. The Croats, while gaining back from Hungary the Medjumurje area and from Italy the cities of Rijeka (Fiume), Zadar (Zara), some Dalmatian islands, and the Istrian Peninsula, had "lost" the Srem area to Serbia and Bosnia and Herzegovina, which had been part of the World War II "independent" Croatian state under the Ustaša leadership. In addition, the Croats were confronted with a deeply resentful Serbian minority that became ever more pervasive in public administrative and security positions. The Slovenes had obtained back from Hungary the Prekmurje enclave and from Italy most of the Slovenian lands taken over by Italy following World War I (Julian Region and Northern Istria). Italy retained control over the "Venetian Slovenia" area, the Gorizia area, and the port city of Trieste. (Trieste was initially part of the UN protected "Free Territory of Trieste," split in 1954 between Italy and Yugoslavia, with Trieste itself given to Italy.) Nor were the Slovenian claims to the southern Carinthia area of Austria satisfied. The "loss" of Trieste was a bitter pill for the Slovenes and many blamed it on the fact that Tito's Yugoslavia was, initially, Stalin's advance threat to Western Europe, thus making Western Europe and the United States more supportive of Italy.

The official position of the Marxist Yugoslav regime was that national rivalries and conflicting interests would gradually diminish through their sublimation into a new Socialist order. Without capitalism, nationalism was supposed to wither away. Therefore, in the name of their "unity and brotherhood" motto, any "nationalistic" expression of concern was prohibited and repressed by the dictatorial and centralized regime of the "League of Yugoslav Communists" acting through the "Socialist Alliance" as its mass front organization. As a constituent Republic of the Federal Yugoslavia, Bosnia and Herzegovina shared in the history of the second experiment in "Yugoslavism."

After a short postwar "coalition" government period, the elections of 11 November 1945, boycotted by the noncommunist "coalition" parties, gave the Communist-led People's Front 90% of the vote. A Constituent Assembly met on November 29 and abolished the monarchy, establishing the Federative People's Republic of Yugoslavia. In January 1946, a new constitution was adopted, based on the 1936 Soviet constitution. The Stalin-engineered expulsion of Yugoslavia from the Soviet-dominated Cominform Group in 1948 was actually a blessing for Yugoslavia after its leadership was able to survive Stalin's pressures. Survival had to be justified, both practically and in theory, by developing a "road to Socialism" based on Yugoslavia's own circumstances. This new "road map" evolved rather quickly in response to some of Stalin's accusations and Yugoslavia's need to perform a balancing act between the NATO alliance and the Soviet bloc. Having taken over all power after World War II, the Communist dictatorship under Tito pushed the nationalization of the economy through a policy of forced industrialization, to be supported by the collectivization of agriculture.

The agricultural reform of 1945–46 (limited private ownership of a maximum of 35 hectares (85 acres) and a limited free market after the initial forced delivery of quotas to the state at very low prices) had to be abandoned because of the strong passive, but at times active, resistance by the peasants. The actual collectivization efforts were initiated in 1949 using welfare benefits and lower taxes as incentives along with direct coercion. But collectivization had to be abandoned by 1958 simply because its inefficiency and low productivity could not support the concentrated effort of industrial development.

By the 1950s, Yugoslavia had initiated the development of its internal trademark: self-management of enterprises through workers councils and local decision-making as the road to Marx's "withering away of the state." Following the failure of the first five-year plan (1947–51), the second five-year plan (1957–61) was completed in four years by relying on the well-established self-management system. Economic targets were set from the local to the republic level and then coordinated by a Federal Planning Institute to meet an overall national economic strategy. This system supported a period of very rapid industrial growth in the 1950s. But a high consumption rate encouraged a volume of imports, largely financed by foreign loans, far in excess of exports. In addition, inefficient and low-productivity industries were kept in place through public subsidies, cheap credit, and other artificial protective measures that led to a serious crisis by 1961.

Reforms were necessary and, by 1965, "market socialism" was introduced with laws that abolished most price controls and halved import duties while withdrawing export subsidies. After necessary amounts were left with the earning enterprise, the rest of the earned foreign currencies were deposited with the national bank and used by the state, other enterprises, or were used to assist less developed areas. Councils were given more decision-making power on investing their earnings. They also tended to vote for higher salaries in order to meet steep increases in the cost of living. Unemployment grew rapidly even though "political factories" were still subsidized. The government thus relaxed its restrictions to allow labor migration particularly to West Germany where workers were needed for its thriving economy. Foreign investment was encouraged up to 49% in joint enterprises, and barriers to the movement of people and exchange of ideas were largely removed. The role of trade unions continued to be one of transmission of instructions from government to workers, allocation of perks along with the education/training of workers, monitoring legislation, and overall protection of the self-management system. Until the 1958 miners strike in Trbovlje, Slovenia, strikes were neither legally allowed nor forbidden, but they were suppressed and not publicly acknowledged. After 1958, strikes were tolerated as an indication of problems to be resolved. Unions, however, did not initiate strikes but were expected to convince workers to go back to work.

Having survived its expulsion from the Cominform in 1948 and Stalin's attempts to take control, Yugoslavia began to develop a foreign policy independent of the Soviet Union. By mid-1949 Yugoslavia ceased its support of the Greek Communists in their civil war against the then Royalist government of Greece. In October 1949, Yugoslavia was elected to one of the nonpermanent seats on the UN Security Council and openly condemned North Korea's aggression toward South Korea. Following the "rapprochement" opening with the Soviet Union initiated by Nikita Khrushchev and his 1956 denunciation of Stalin, Tito intensified his work on developing the movement of nonaligned "third world" nations. This would become Yugoslavia's external trademark, in cooperation with Nehru of India, Nasser of Egypt, and others. With the September 1961 Belgrade summit conference of nonaligned nations, Tito became the recognized leader of the movement. The nonaligned position served Tito's Yugoslavia well by allowing Tito to draw on economic and political support from the Western powers while neutralizing any aggressiveness from the Soviet bloc. While Tito had acquiesced, reluctantly, to the 1956 Soviet invasion of Hungary for fear of chaos and its liberalizing impact on Yugoslavia, he condemned the Soviet invasion of Dubček's Czechoslovakia in 1968, as did Romania's Ceausescu, both fearing their countries might be the next in line for "corrective" action by the Red Army and the Warsaw Pact. Just before his death on 4 May 1980, Tito also condemned the Soviet invasion of Afghanistan. Yugoslavia actively participated in the 1975 Helsinki Conference and agreements and the first 1977–78 review conference that took place in Belgrade, even though Yugoslavia's one-party communist regime perpetrated and condoned numerous human rights violations. Overall, in the 1970s and 1980s, Yugoslavia maintained fairly good relations with its neighboring states by playing down or solving pending disputes—such as the Trieste issue with Italy in 1975—and by developing cooperative projects and increased trade.

Ravaged by the war, occupation, resistance, and civil war losses and preoccupied with carrying out the elimination of all actual and potential opposition, the Communist government faced the double task of building its Socialist economy while rebuilding the country. As an integral part of the Yugoslav federation, Bosnia and Herzegovina was, naturally, impacted by Yugoslavia's internal and external political developments. The main problems facing communist Yugoslavia and Bosnia and Herzegovina were essentially the same as the unresolved ones under Royalist Yugoslavia. As the "Royal Yugoslavism" had failed in its assimilative efforts, so did the "Socialist Yugoslavism" fail to overcome the forces of nationalism. Bosnia and Herzegovina differs from the other republics because its area has been the meeting ground of Serbian and Croatian nationalist claims, with the Muslims as a third party, pulled to both sides. Centuries of coexistence of the three major national groups had made Bosnia and Herzegovina into a territorial maze where no boundaries could be drawn to clearly separate Serbs, Croats, and Muslims without resorting to violence and forced movements of people. The inability to negotiate a peaceful partition of Bosnia and Herzegovina between Serbia and Croatia doomed the first interwar Yugoslavia to failure. The Socialist experiment with "Yugoslavism" in post-World War II Yugoslavia

was particularly relevant to the situation in Bosnia and Herzegovina where the increasing incidence of intermarriage, particularly between Serbs and Croats, caused the introduction of the "Yugoslav" category with the 1961 census. By 1981 the "Yugoslav" category was selected by 1.2 million citizens (5.4% of the total population), a large increase over the 273,077 number in 1971. Muslims, not impacted much by intermarriage, have also been recognized since 1971 as a separate category, and numbered two million in 1981 in Yugoslavia. The 1991 census showed the population of Bosnia and Herzegovina consisting mainly of Muslims (43.7%), Serbs (31.4%), and Croats (17.3%), with 6% "Yugoslavs" out of a total population of 4,364,000.

Bosnia as a political unit has existed since at least 1150. Headed by a Ban in the Croatian tradition, Bosnia lasted for over 300 years with an increasing degree of independence from Hungary through King Tvrtko I and his successors until the occupation by the Ottoman Turks in 1463 (1482 for Herzegovina). Bosnia and Herzegovina was then ruled by the Turks for 415 years until 1878, and by Austria-Hungary for 40 years until 1918. Bosnia and Herzegovina ceased to be a separate political unit only for the 27 years of the first Yugoslavia (1918–1945) and became again a separate unit for 47 years as one of the republics of the Federal Socialist Republic of Yugoslavia until 1992. Yet, in spite of an 800-year history of common development, the Serbs, Croats, and Muslims of Bosnia and Herzegovina never assimilated into a single nation. Bosnia was initially settled by Croats who became Catholic and then by Orthodox Serbs escaping from the Turks. Under the Turks, large numbers converted to Islam and, in spite of a common language, their religious and cultural differences kept the Serbs, Croats, and Muslims apart through history so that Bosnia and Herzegovina has been more a geographic-political notion than a unified nation.

Consequently, while the resurgent nationalism was galvanizing Croatia into an intensifying confrontation with Serbia, the Bosnian leadership had to keep an internal balance by joining one or the other side depending on its own interests. Bosnia and Herzegovina was torn between the two opposing "liberal" and "conservative/centralist" coalitions. In terms of widening civil and political liberties, Bosnia and Herzegovina usually supported the liberal group. Its own economic needs as a less developed area, however, pulled it into the conservative coalition with Serbia in order to keep the source of development funds flowing.

The liberal group, centered in Slovenia and Croatia, grew stronger on the basis of the deepening resentment against forced subsidizing of less-developed areas of the federation and buildup of the Yugoslav army. Finally, the increased political and economic autonomy enjoyed by the republics after the 1974 constitution and particularly following Tito's death in 1980, assisted in turning Tito's motto of "unity and brotherhood" into "freedom and democracy" to be achieved through either a confederated rearrangement of Yugoslavia or by complete independence of the individual republics. Other issues of direct impact on Bosnia and Herzegovina fueled acrimony between individual nations, such as the 1967 Declaration in Zagreb claiming a Croatian linguistic and literary tradition separate from the Serbian one, thus undermining the validity of the "Serbo-Croatian" language. Also, Kosovo Albanians and Montenegrins, along with Slovenes and Croats, began to assert their national rights as superior to their rights as Yugoslav nationals.

The Eighth Congress of the League of Communists of Yugoslavia (LCY) in December 1964 acknowledged that ethnic prejudice and antagonisms existed in socialist Yugoslavia. Economic reforms were the other focus of the Eighth LCY Congress led by Croatia and Slovenia, with emphasis on efficiencies and local economic development decisions with profit criteria as their basis. The liberal bloc (Slovenia, Croatia, Macedonia, and Vojvodina) prevailed over the conservative group and the reforms of 1965 did away with central investment planning and political factories.

Meanwhile, as the result of a series of 1967–68 constitutional amendments that limited federal power in favor of the republics and autonomous provinces, the federal government was seen by liberals as an inter-republican problem-solving mechanism bordering on a confederacy. A network of inter-republican committees established by mid-1971 proved to be very efficient at resolving a large number of difficult issues in a short time.

By the summer of 1971, the Serbian party leadership was pressuring President Tito to put an end to the "dangerous" development of Croatian nationalism. While Tito wavered because of his support for the balancing system of autonomous republic units, the situation quickly reached critical proportions also in terms of the direct interests of Bosnia and Herzegovina. Croat nationalists, complaining about discrimination against Croats in Bosnia and Herzegovina, demanded the incorporation of Western Herzegovina into Croatia. Serbia countered by claiming Southeastern Herzegovina for itself.

Confronted with such intensive agitation, the liberal Croatian party leadership could not back down and did not try to restrain the public demands nor the widespread university students' strike of November 1971. At this point Tito intervened, condemned the Croatian liberal leadership on 1 December 1971 and supported the conservative wing. The liberal leadership group resigned on 12 December 1971. When Croatian students demonstrated and demanded an independent Croatia, the Yugoslav army was ready to move in if necessary. Leading Croatian nationalist organizations and their publications were closed.

By 1989, the relations between Slovenia and Serbia reached a crisis point, especially following the Serbian assumption of control in the Kosovo and Vojvodina provinces (as well as in Montenegro). Serbian President Slobodan Milošević's tactics were extremely distasteful to the Slovenians and the use of force against the Albanian population of the Kosovo province worried the Slovenes (and Croats) about the possible use of force by Serbia against Slovenia itself. The Slovenian leadership in September 1989 issued draft amendments to the constitution of Slovenia, which included the right to secession, the sole right of the Slovenian legislature to introduce martial law and to control the deployment of armed forces in Slovenia.

A last attempt at salvaging Yugoslavia was to be made as the extraordinary Congress of the League of Communists of Yugoslavia convened in January 1990 to review proposed reforms such as free multiparty elections and freedom of speech. The Slovenian delegation attempted to broaden the spectrum of reforms but was rebuffed and walked out on 23 January 1990. On 10 April 1990 the first free elections since before World War II were held in Slovenia. A coalition of six newly formed democratic parties, called Demos, won 55% of the votes and organized the first freely elected Slovenian government of the post-Communist era with Dr. Lojze Peterle as the prime minister.

These developments had a deep impact on Bosnia and Herzegovina. Bosnia and Herzegovina was included as one of the constituent republics of post-World War II Yugoslavia. Serbs claimed that Muslims were Islamized Serbs and Croats claimed that Muslims were descendants of the Croatian Bosnian Church that had converted to Islam. The Muslims themselves, meanwhile, claimed their own separate identity and were recognized as equal to Serbs and Croats.

The sense of Muslim identity grew stronger. Muslims began to demand the establishment of Muslim institutions parallel to the Serbian and Croatian ones. Muslims sought to define themselves as the only "true" Bosnians, and thus they called for Bosnia and Herzegovina to be defined as a Muslim Republic. Muslim activist groups multiplied during the 1970s and 1980s.

The Muslims' assertiveness as an ethnic community grew stronger and was viewed as a balancing element between Serbs and Croats. As the winds of change away from communism swept the western republics of Slovenia and Croatia in 1989 and 1990, Bosnia and Herzegovina also was preparing for multiparty elections to be held on 18 November 1990.

By July 1990, a Bosnia and Herzegovina branch of the Croatia-based Serbian Democratic Party had become very active in the 18 Bosnian communes with Serbian majorities adjacent to the border with Croatia. By the fall of 1990, the program of the Serbian Democratic Party in Croatia had advanced a plan to include the Bosnian Serbs into a joint Krajina state, which would have a federal arrangement with Serbia proper. This arrangement, it was hoped, would undercut any thoughts of a confederation of Slovenia, Croatia, and Bosnia and Herzegovina. On 1 August 1990, Bosnia and Herzegovina declared itself a "sovereign and democratic state." The Muslim Party, Serbian Party, and Croatian Democratic Union formed a coalition government with Alija Izetbegović of the Muslim Party as president of Bosnia and Herzegovina.

Independence and War

Slovenia declared its independence on 25 June 1991. On 27 June 1991, the Yugoslav Army tried to seize control of Slovenia and its borders with Italy, Austria, and Hungary under the pretext that it was its constitutional duty to assure the integrity of Socialist Yugoslavia. The war in Slovenia was ended in 10 days due to the intervention of the European Community (EC); a cease-fire was declared, which gave time to the Yugoslav Army to retreat from Slovenia by the end of October 1991.

The coalition government of Bosnia and Herzegovina had a very difficult time maintaining the spirit of ethnic cooperation won in its elections, while the situations in Slovenia and Croatia were moving to the point of no return. Yugoslav army units were being based in Bosnia and Herzegovina following their retreat, first from Slovenia and then from Croatia. In October 1991, the Serbian Democratic Party held a plebiscite in the two-thirds of Bosnian territory under Serbian control and announced the establishment of a Serbian Republic inside Bosnia and Herzegovina.

In December 1991, the Bosnian Parliament passed a Declaration of Sovereignty and President Izetbegović submitted to the European Community an application for international recognition of Bosnia and Herzegovina as an independent nation. A referendum on independence was held on 29 February 1992. With the Serbs abstaining in opposition to the secession from Yugoslavia, Muslims and Croats approved an independent Bosnia and Herzegovina by a vote of 99.7%. In reaction to the referendum, Serbs proceeded to prepare for war in close cooperation with the Yugoslav army.

On 1 March 1992 in Sarajevo a Serbian wedding party was fired upon. This was the spark that ignited armed confrontations in Sarajevo and other areas of Bosnia and Herzegovina. The Bosnian Serbs by late March of 1992 formally established their own "Serbian Republic of Bosnia and Herzegovina."

On 6 April 1992 Bosnia and Herzegovina was recognized (along with Slovenia and Croatia) by the European Community and the United States. This action was viewed as another affront to the Serbs and gave more impetus to Serbian determination to oppose the further splitting of Yugoslavia. The bond among the Serbs of Croatia and Bosnia with the Serbian government controlled by Slobodan Milošević and with the Yugoslav Army was firmly cemented. Serbia, along with the Serbs of Bosnia and Croatia, wanted to unite Serbian territories in Croatia and Bosnia and Herzegovina with Serbia proper. This decision precipitated war, first in Croatia and then in Bosnia and Herzegovina.

War spread in Bosnia in mid-1992 with the relentless bombardment of Sarajevo by Serbs and the brutal use of "ethnic cleansing," primarily by Serbs intent on freeing the areas along the Drina River of Muslim inhabitants. Croats and Muslims retaliated, while Serbs took over control of some 70% of the country and used concentration camps and the raping of women as systematic terror tactics to achieve their "cleansing" goals. Croats kept control of western Herzegovina, while their Muslim allies tried to resist Serbian attacks, and the world watched in horror. The European Community, the United States, the UN, and North Atlantic Treaty Organization (NATO) coordinated peacekeeping efforts, dangerous air deliveries to Sarajevo, airdrops of food and medicinal supplies to keep the people of Sarajevo from dying of starvation and sicknesses.

The various plans proposing the division of Bosnia and Herzegovina into three ethnic cantons were not acceptable to the winning Serbian side. At this time, the Muslim-Croatian alliance broke down, as the two sides began fighting over areas of mixed Croat and Muslim populations, such as the city of Mostar in Herzegovina. A truce was implemented by mid-February 1994 and was barely held while continuing negotiations were taking place. With support from the United States, Croats and Muslims were brought together in Washington, where they signed a confederation plan on 18 March 1994.

In July 1994, the EC, the United States, and Russia agreed on a partition plan, but the Bosnian Serbs' parliament rejected it and the Serbs resumed violent attacks on Sarajevo. After almost two-and-a-half years of war, destruction, and terrible suffering imposed on the people of Bosnia and Herzegovina, the efforts of the international community and its very cumbersome decision-making process had brought Bosnia and Herzegovina back to the partitioning plan originally agreed on at a Lisbon meeting in February 1992. In the fall of 1994, President Milošević of Serbia had closed the borders between Serbia and Bosnia and Herzegovina in order to stop any further assistance to the "Republika Srpska" that he himself helped establish. President Milošević agreed to "extri-cate" Serbia from its direct support for the Bosnian Serbs in the hope that a compromised partitioning plan that would allow each side to "confederate" with Croatia and Serbia respectively and would offer both sides the opportunity to turn their energies to positive efforts of physical and psychological reconstruction.

The quest to create a "Greater Serbia" continued into July 1995, when Bosnian Serbs overran the UN protected areas of Srebrenica and Zepa, extending their territory near the Croatian border. Over 8,000 Bosnian Muslim men and boys were summarily executed at Srebrenica. In retaliation, NATO forces initiated air raids on Bosnian Serb positions on 30 August 1995. Two weeks later, Bosnian Serb forces began lifting their siege of Sarajevo, and agreed to enter into negotiations on the future of Bosnia. Pressured by air strikes and diplomacy, Serb leaders joined authorities from Croatia and Bosnia in Dayton, Ohio, for US-sponsored peace talks.

The Dayton Accords

After three years of war, the General Framework Agreement for Peace in Bosnia and Herzegovina was completed on 21 November 1995 in Dayton, Ohio. Signed in Paris in mid-December, the agreement called for 60,000 NATO peacekeepers to oversee the disarming process. The agreement, known as the Dayton Accords, provided for the continuity of Bosnia and Herzegovina as a single state with two constituent entities: the Federation of Bosnia and Herzegovina (FBH) and the Republika Srpska (RS). The FBH occupies the 51% of the territory with a Bosniak (Muslim) and Croat majority, while the RS occupies the remaining 49% with a Bosnian Serb majority. Following the signing of the Dayton Accords, the UN economic sanctions against the Federal Republic of Yugoslavia and the Bosnian Serb party were suspended, and the arms embargo was lifted (except for heavy weapons). Elections were scheduled and conducted on 11 September 1996.

In March 1996, the International Criminal Tribunal for the former Yugoslavia filed its first charges against Serbian soldiers accused of committing atrocities in Bosnia. Among those cited were Serb generals Djordje Djukic and Ratko Mladic, and the former Bosnian Serb leader Radovan Karadzic. In May 1997, the tribunal completed its first trial with a conviction of a Bosnian Serb police officer for murdering two Muslim policemen and torturing Muslim civilians.

Casualty estimates from the war vary from as low as 25,000 to over 250,000 persons. Some three million people became refugees or internally displaced persons. About 320,000 Bosnians had taken refuge in Germany during the war. Refugees returned to find a significant housing shortage and massive unemployment.

Despite the Dayton Accords, outbreaks of violence persisted. The legacy of centuries of confrontations by the Austro-Hungarian, Russian, and Turkish empires in the Balkans continued to haunt the area. In June 1998 NATO peacekeeping forces decided to extend their stay until a more stable peace was achieved. Violent conflicts dissipated through the next year, as the International Court of Justice furthered reparations for crimes, and Yugoslavia agreed to a peace plan on 3 June 1999.

Bosnia and Croatia signed a border agreement in July 1999. The strategically located city of Brčko, previously Serb-ruled, and a main site of contention between the country's factions, received a Muslim-Croat/Serb coalition government in March 1999 from The Hague International Court of Justice. In 1999, NATO reduced the 25-nation peacekeeping force by one-third over a period of six months. Mass gravesites continued to be unearthed in northeastern Bosnia near Sarajevo and in Srebrenica, as numerous war criminals were arrested and brought to trial at The Hague.

Parliamentary, presidential, and municipal elections were held in October 2002, and nationalists strengthened their positions. The work of the International Criminal Tribunal for the former Yugoslavia (ICTY) in The Hague continued. In 2001, former Bosnian Serb President Biljana Plavsic surrendered to the tribunal, but pleaded not guilty to charges of genocide; however, in October 2002, she changed her plea to one of guilty of crimes against humanity and was sentenced to 11 years in prison. In early 2001, a guilty verdict against three Bosnian Serbs charged with torturing and raping Bosnian Muslim women marked the first time the tribunal called rape a crime against humanity. Later that year the tribunal found Bosnian Serb general Radislav Krstic guilty of genocide for his role in the massacre at Srebrenica; he was sentenced to 46 years in prison.

In May 1999, former Yugoslav President Milošević was indicted by the tribunal for war crimes committed in Kosovo; he was subsequently indicted for crimes committed in Bosnia and Herzegovina and Croatia, including charges of genocide carried out in Bosnia and Herzegovina from 1992–95. His trial began in February 2002. Milošević died in March 2006 in the The Hague, with just 50 hours of testimony left before the conclusion of his trial. In December 2004, the NATO-led Stabilization Force in Bosnia and Herzegovina (SFOR), whose goal was to deter renewed hostilities, concluded its mission. Peacekeeping operations were taken up by the European Union Force in Bosnia and Herzegovina (EUFOR). In June 2005, a Bosnian armed unit with members from all three main ethnic groups left for Iraq to support the US-led coalition at war there.

In November 2005, European Union (EU) foreign ministers declared that Stabilization and Association Agreement talks with Bosnia and Herzegovina could begin. This was the first step toward possible EU membership. In December 2006, Bosnia and Herzegovina joined NATO's Partnership for Peace program, after NATO overturned a decision to exclude the country because of its failure to catch war crimes suspect Radovan Karadzic. The Partnership for Peace program may lead to NATO membership for the country. With the prospect of EU membership on the horizon, the country stepped up efforts to catch Karadzic; in July 2008, after living in hiding for 13 years, Radovan Karadzic was arrested in Belgrade, Serbia.

In February 2006, the International Court of Justice (ICJ) in The Hague began hearings in a genocide case brought by Bosnia and Herzegovina against Serbia and Montenegro; the court ruled that Serbia was not responsible for genocide. In February 2007, the largest war crimes trial to date over the 1995 Srebrenica massacre ended with a verdict in The Hague confirming that the massacre was an act of genocide but assigned only passive blame to Serbia for its failure to prevent genocide.

In October 2006, general elections were held, reflecting sharp ethnic divisions. The Republika Srpska (RS) voted to maintain the split from the Federation of Bosnia and Herzegovina (FBH). In the run-up to the election, the Bosnian Serb leadership threatened to seek complete secession in the event of moves to end the autonomy of the RS. In January 2007, Nikola Spiric, a Bosnian Serb, was asked to form a government after party leaders agreed on a coalition.

Into 2009, talk among the nation's Serbs became increasing nationalistic, leading the Croats and Bosniaks to fear that the Republika Srpska was considering secession. In June 2009, the Republika Srpska parliament issued a declaration calling for the right to legislate its own rules over areas such as customs and immigration. The declaration was vetoed by the high representative, Valentin Inzko. At the July 2009 meeting of the Peace Implementation Council, the international body charged with the decision of when the post of high representative should be closed, Inzko expressed concern that the nation's politicians have been unable to work across ethnic divisions for the common good. This lack of teamwork, coupled with an unstable economy and still sharp ethnic divisions, has hindered the growth of the nation and raised concern that civil war might be renewed if differences cannot be resolved.

On 20 October 2009, the second round of joint EU-US talks with Bosnian leaders commenced in Sarajevo. The talks centered on the implementation of a new reform package that aimed to alter the political status of Bosnia—ending its status as a protectorate—and to streamline Bosnia's inclusion in the European Union. However, leaders from the main ethnic groups found the proposed reform package unacceptable. Serbs argued that the new reform package compromised the conditions of the Dayton Accords, which afforded a degree of autonomy for the Republika Srpska, while Muslim and Croat leaders believed that the reforms failed to unify the republic.

In the 3 October 2010 presidential election, Nebojša Radmanović from the Alliance of Independent Social Democrats took 48.9% of the votes for the Serb seat, while Zeljko Komsic of the Social Democratic Party took 60.6% of the votes for the Croat seat, and Bakir Izetbegovic of the Party of Democratic Action took 34.9% of the votes for the Bosniak seat. The three officials that compose the presidency were sworn in on 10 October 2010.

Results for the 3 October 2010 election indicated that political deadlock would continue to prevail in the nation, as voters seemed to adhere to ethnic lines in choosing members of parliament. Serbian voters primarily backed the Alliance of Independent Social Democrats, a nationalist alliance that promotes Serbian secession, while Muslims and Croats favored the multiethnic Social Democratic Party, which supports a united Bosnia. Valentin Inzko, the international high representative assigned to the nation, told reporters that, given such strong divisions, a new government was not likely to form before the end of 2010. In fact, it was not until late in December 2011 that an agreement was reached and the six main political parties of the nation agreed to give the Croatian Democratic Union (HDZ) and the Croatian Coalition (HDZ 1990—HSP Croatian Party of Rights) the prime minister spot and leadership of two ministries. Vjekoslav Bevanda was named prime minister on 29 December 2011, 15 months after the general election. Bevanda still faced confirmation by the three members of the presidency, investigation by the Central Election Commission, and state parliamentary approval. Bevanda was a member of parliament for the Federation of Bosnia and Herzegovina (FBH), served as its finance minister, and was vice president of the federal government from 2006–2010. The government consists of 10 ministries, of which four will be Bosniak, three Croat, and three Serb.

In May 2011, alleged war criminal Ratko Mladic was arrested in Serbia. Commander of Bosnian Serb forces during the 1992–1995 Bosnian war, he was indicted in 1995 for genocide related to the massacre in Srebrenica of thousands of Muslim men and boys. The remaining indicted suspect, Goran Hadzic, remained at large.

13 GOVERNMENT

Under the Dayton Accords, a constitution for Bosnia and Herzegovina was established that recognized a single state with two constituent entities. The Federation of Bosnia and Herzegovina (FBH) incorporated the 51% of the country with a Bosnian Muslim and Bosnian Croat majority, while the Republika Srpska (RS) occupied the 49% of the country with a Bosnian Serb majority. The constitution specified a central government with a bicameral legislature, a three-member presidency comprised of a member of each major ethnic group, a council of ministers, a constitutional court, and a central bank. The bicameral Parliamentary Assembly consists of a House of Peoples, with 15 delegates, and the House of Representatives, with 42 members. In each house, two-thirds of the representatives are from the Federation of Bosnia and Herzegovina and one-third from the Republika Srpska.

As a result of the Dayton Accords, Bosnia and Herzegovina is administered in a supervisory role by a High Representative chosen by the UN Security Council. As of January 2012, that representative was Valentin Inzko; he has held the office since March 2009.

The FBH government has a president and a bicameral parliament (House of Representatives and House of Peoples). The RS government has a president and a unicameral legislature (National Assembly). As a result of a 2002 constitutional reform process, an RS Council of Peoples was established in the RS National Assembly. In 2003, High Representative Paddy Ashdown abolished the Supreme Defense Council of the RS, and altered the constitutions of the RS and FBH, removing all reference to statehood from both.

Several proposals contributed to the current system of government, which was outlined through the Dayton Accords of 1995. The February 1992 Lisbon proposal first suggested the partitioning of Bosnia and Herzegovina into "ethnic cantons," but was rejected by the Muslim side. The Vance-Owen proposal of early January 1993 dividing Bosnia and Herzegovina, still a unified state, into nine "ethnic majority" provinces with Sarajevo as a central weak government district was accepted by Croats and Muslims on 7 January 1993 and ratified on 20 January 1993 by the Bosnian Serbs' Parliament with a 55-to-15 vote in spite of deep misgivings. However, two key events delayed the necessary detailed implementation discussions: Croat forces' attacks on Muslims in Bosnia and Herzegovina and on Serbs in Croatia, and the new administration of US President Bill Clinton, from whom the Bosnian Muslims hoped to obtain stronger support, even military intervention. Thus by mid-March 1993, only the Croats had agreed to the three essential points of the Vance-Owen proposal, namely the Constitutional Principles (10 provinces), the Military Arrangements, and the detailed map of the 10 provinces. On 25 March 1993 the Bosnian Muslims agreed to all the terms, but the Bosnian Serb legislature rejected the revised 10-province map on 2 April 1993, and the Vance-Owen plan was scuttled.

The Owen-Stoltenberg plan was based on a June 1993 proposal in Geneva by Presidents Tudjman and Milošević about partitioning Bosnia and Herzegovina into three ethnic-based "states." Owen-Stoltenberg announced the new plan in August 1993 indicating that the three ethnic states were realistically based on the acceptance of Serbian and Croatian territorial "conquests." At the same time the Croat Bosnian "parliament" announced the establishment of the "State of Herzeg-Bosnia" and the Croatian Democratic Alliance withdrew its members from the Bosnian Parliament. The Bosnian Parliament then rejected the Owen-Stoltenberg Plan while seeking further negotiations on the Muslim state's territory and clarifications on the international status of Bosnia and Herzegovina.

The next plan, developed with the more proactive participation of the United States and bringing together again the Croats and Muslims into a federation of their own, was signed in Washington on 18 March 1994 following the Sarajevo cease-fire of 17 March. On 31 March 1994 the Bosnian assembly in Sarajevo approved the new constitutional provisions establishing a Federation of Muslims and Croats with the presidency to alternate between Croats and Muslims. The Geneva contact group (United States, United Kingdom, France, Germany, and Russia) agreed on a new partition plan in July 1994 that divided Bosnia and Herzegovina: 51% to the joint Muslim-Croat federation and 49% to the Serbs.

Elections for central and federation-level canton offices were conducted on 14 September 1996 as specified by the Dayton Accords. Alija Izetbegović, Momcilo Krajisnik, and Kresimir Zubak were elected to the presidency representing respectively the Bosniaks (Muslims), Serbs, and Croats. Izetbegović was named Chair in accordance with the new constitution. Krajisnik, later accused of joining Karadzic in siphoning off million of dollars in potential tax revenue through gasoline and cigarette monopolies, boycotted the council after one meeting, paralyzing the government.

Izetbegović was reelected to the Muslim seat of the joint presidency in the September 1998 elections; Ante Jelavic won the Croat seat; and Zivko Radisic, the Serb seat. An eight-month chairpersonship rotates among the three joint presidents. Elections were held in 2002. Sulejman Tihić won the Muslim seat; Dragan Cović, the Croat seat; and Mirko Sarović, the Serb seat. In April 2003, Sarović resigned following a report by Western intelligence agencies regarding an affair involving illegal military exports to Iraq and allegations of spying on international officials. He was replaced by Borislav Paravac. In March 2005, High Representative Paddy Ashdown removed Dragan Cović, who faced corruption charges, from the presidency. He was replaced by Ivo Miro Jović. In the 1 October 2006 general elections, Haris Silajdžić won the Muslim presidential seat; Željko Komšić won the Croat seat; and Nebojša Radmanović won the Serb seat. In the 3 October 2010 general elections, Nebojša Radmanović again won the Serb seat, Zeljko Komsic kept the Croat seat, and Bakir Izetbegovic won the Bosniak seat.

14 POLITICAL PARTIES

Three main political parties wield significant political power at all levels of government. The Serb Democratic Party (SDS) dominates the Republika Srpska, the Party of Democratic Action (SDA) is the main Bosniak (Muslim) nationalist party, and the Croatian Democratic Union of Bosnia and Herzegovina (HDZ) represents Croat areas. However, a reformist party, the Social Democratic Party (SDP) in the FBH is gaining in popularity. Other parties include: Party for Bosnia and Herzegovina (SBIH); Civic Democratic Party (GDS); Croatian Peasants' Party of BIH (HSS); Croat Christian Democratic Union of Bosnia and Herzegovina (HKDU); Croat Party of Rights (HSP); Independent Social Democratic Party (SNSD); Liberal Bosniak Organization (LBO); Liberal Party (LS); Muslim-Bosniak Organization (MBO); Republican Party of Bosnia and Herzegovina (RP); Serb Civic Council (SGV); Socialist Party of Republika Srpska (SPRS); Serb Radical Party (SRS); Democratic Socialist Party (DSP); Social Democrats of Bosnia Herzegovina; Party for Democratic Progress (PDP); National Democratic Union (DNZ); Social Democratic Union (SDU): Serb National Alliance (SNS); and the Coalition for a United and Democratic BIH (coalition of SDA, SBIH, LS, and GDS).

Parliamentary elections were held on 1 October 2006. For the FBH, seats were allocated as follows: SDA, 8 seats; SBiH, 7 seats; SDP, 5 seats; HDZ BiH, 3 seats; the coalition Croats Together, 2 seats; BPS-Sefer Halilović, 1 seat; the People's Party Work for Betterment, 1 seat; and the Democratic People's Community, 1 seat. From the Republika Srpska, seats were allocated as follows: SNSD, 7 seats; SDS, 3 seats; PDP RS, 1 seat; SBiH, 1 seat; SDA, 1 seat; and the Democratic People's Alliance (DNS), 1 seat.

In the federal parliamentary election of 3 October 2010, the Social Democratic Party earned the highest percentage of votes for the FBH with 26%. The Party of Democratic Action earned 19.4%, followed by the Union for a Better Future of BiH with 12.1%, the Croatian Democratic Union with 10.9%, the Party for BiH with 7.2%, the Croatian Coalition with 4.86%, and the Progress through Work People's Party with 4.81%. For the Republika Srpska, the Union of Independent Social Democrats won the greatest percentage of votes with 43.3%, followed by the Serbian Democratic Party with 22.1%, the Party for Democratic Progress with 6.4%, the Democratic People's Union with 4.59%, the Social Democratic Party with 2.9% and the Party of Democratic Action with 2.64%.

In the 2010 elections for the local parliament of the FBH, the Social Democratic Party earned 24.5% of the vote, followed by the Party of Democratic Action with 20.2%, the Union for a Better Future of BiH with 11.89%, the Croatian Democratic Union (HDZ) with 10.64%, the Party for BiH (SBiH) with 7.63%, the Progress Through Work People's Party with 4.72%, and the Croatian Coalition (HDZ 1990–HSP Croatian Party of Rights) with 4.68%. For the local parliament Republika Srpska, the Union of Independent Social Democrats was ahead with 38% of the vote, followed by the Serbian Democratic Party with 18.97%, the Party for Democratic Progress (PDP) with 7.55%, the Democratic People's Union (DNZ BiH) with 6.09%, the Socialist Party/United Pensioners with 4.24%, the Democratic Party (Dragan Cavic) with 3.41%, and the Social Democratic Party with 3.05%.

In the presidential race, Nebojsa Radmanović from the Union of Independent Social Democrats won as the Serbian president with 48.9% of the vote, narrowly beating out Mladen Ivanci of the Coalition Together for Srpska who had 47.3% of the vote. Zeljko Komsic of the Social Democratic Party, representing the Croat presidency, won with 60.6% of the vote, and Bakir Izetbegovic of the Party of Democratic Action, representing the Bosniak presidency, won with 34.9%.

15 LOCAL GOVERNMENT

Bosnia and Herzegovina is divided into the Federation of Bosnia and Herzegovina (FBH) and the Republika Srpska (RS). The FBH is further divided into 10 cantons: Goražde, Livno, Middle Bosnia, Neretva, Posavina, Sarajevo, Tuzla Podrinje, Una Sana, West Herzegovina, and Zenica Doboj. There are also municipal governments. Brčko district, in northeastern Bosnia, is an administrative unit under the sovereignty of Bosnia and Herzegovina; it is not part of either the RS or the FBH, and the district remains under international supervision.

16 JUDICIAL SYSTEM

The 1995 Dayton Accords established a constitution including a Constitutional Court composed of nine members. The Constitutional Court's original jurisdiction lies in deciding any constitutional dispute that arises between the FBH and the RS or between Bosnia and Herzegovina and one or both of the FBH and the RS. The Court also has appellate jurisdiction within the territory of Bosnia and Herzegovina. The constitution provides for an independent judiciary, although it is subject to influence by nationalist elements, political parties, and the executive branch. Original court jurisdiction exists in both municipal and cantonal courts (10 in the FBH); the RS has 5 municipal courts and district courts. In addition, Brčko District has its own courts. Appeals in the FBH are taken to the Federation Supreme Court, and in the RS to the RS Supreme Court. The constitution provides for open and public trials. The legal system is based on civil law system.

17 ARMED FORCES

The International Institute for Strategic Studies reports that armed forces in Bosnia and Herzegovina totaled 10,577 members in 2011. The force was comprised of 9,205 from the army, 872 from aviation forces, and 500 members of joint forces. Armed forces represented .5% of the labor force in Bosnia and Herzegovina. Defense spending totaled $1.4 billion and accounted for 4.5% of GDP.

The country is composed of two political entities: the Muslim and Croat-based Federation of Bosnia and Herzegovina and the Serb-based Republika Srpska. As a result, the country's armed forces, as well as its equipment, are divided between the two entities. In December 2003, the Bosnian parliament passed a law that established a chain of command that went from the State Presidency to the Ministry of Defense, then to the Joint Staff, then to a joint Operational Command, and from there, down to the armed forces of each entity. Under the Dayton Peace Accord (1995) and the Common Defence Policy (2001) the armed forces have been reduced.

18 INTERNATIONAL COOPERATION

Bosnia and Herzegovina was admitted to the UN on 22 May 1992 and serves in several specialized agencies, such as the FAO, IAEA, UNESCO, UNIDO, and WHO. The country is an observer in the WTO. Bosnia and Herzegovina joined the OSCE on 30 April 1992. The country is also a member of G-77, the Council of Europe, the Southeast Europe Cooperation Initiative (SECI), and the Central European Initiative. Bosnia and Herzegovina is an observer in the OAS and the OIC. The country is part of the Nonaligned Movement and has supported UN efforts in Ethiopia and Eritrea (est.

2000) and the DROC (est. 1999). Diplomatic relations with Croatia, Albania, and Serbia and Montenegro have been stable since the signing of Dayton Accords (1995). In environmental cooperation, Bosnia and Herzegovina is part of the Basel Convention, the Convention on Long-Range Transboundary Air Pollution, Ramsar, the Montréal Protocol, the Nuclear Test Ban Treaty, and the UN Convention on the Law of the Sea and Climate Change.

19 ECONOMY

The GDP rate of change in Bosnia and Herzegovina, as of 2010, was 0.8%. Inflation stood at 3.1%, and unemployment was reported at 43.1%, although as many as half of those reported as unemployed may actually be part of the large gray economy.

Before the war, Bosnia and Herzegovina ranked next to Macedonia as the poorest republic of the former Yugoslav SFR; it remains one of the poorest nations in Europe. Although industry accounted for over 50% of GDP, Bosnia and Herzegovina was primarily agricultural. Farms were small and inefficient, thus necessitating food imports. Industry was greatly overstaffed, with Bosnia and Herzegovina accounting for much of the former Yugoslav SFR's metallic ore and coal production. Timber production and textiles also were important.

The destructive impact of the war on the economy led to a 75% drop in GDP. Since the Dayton Accords of 1995, trade increased in Croat areas, and significant growth began in Muslim areas. Reconstruction programs initiated by the international community financed the construction of infrastructure and provided loans to the manufacturing sector. External aid amounted to $5 billion between 1995 and 1999. This aid caused growth rates to increase to 30%, stabilizing to around 6% after 2000. Actual GDP growth by that year had reached half its prewar level.

In the early 2000s, privatization was slow, with the private sector accounting for only 35% of the economy. Western financial organizations increasingly called for reform in this area, especially in telecommunications and energy. Foreign direct investment remained low, due in part to corruption and many layers of bureaucracy. In 2002, the government adopted a poverty reduction strategy designed to create more jobs and increase exports. As foreign aid declines were scheduled to decline during the 2000s, Bosnia and Herzegovina sought to increase exports to generate hard currency revenues. Some progress was made in this area in 2001 with exports of clothing, furniture, and leather goods. Tax reform is also needed, as is reform of the banking industry and the financial services sector.

The GDP growth rate improved from 5.6% in 2002, to 7.0% in 2003, and to 8.3% in 2004. Growth diminished to 5.8% in 2007, but still remained healthy. Unemployment, similar to most former Yugoslav republics except Slovenia, remained a huge problem, although many of the officially jobless were thought to be working within the gray economy.

In 2007 Bosnia and Herzegovina became a full member of the Central European Free Trade Agreement. The estimated real GDP growth rate for 2008 was 5.5%. In March 2010, the International Monetary Fund (IMF) approved a $184.4 million aid package to Bosnia and Herzegovina, acknowledging the Balkan nation's progress in cutting recurrent social spending, amid the challenging economic times of the 2008–09 global financial crisis. Analysts predicted 0.5% growth for Bosnia and Herzegovina in 2010;

the actual results came in significantly higher, at 0.8% growth for 2010.

20 INCOME

The CIA estimated that in 2010 the GDP of Bosnia and Herzegovina was $30.33 billion. The CIA defines GDP as the value of all final goods and services produced within a nation in a given year and computed on the basis of purchasing power parity (PPP) rather than value as measured on the basis of the rate of the exchange based on current dollars. The per capita GDP was estimated at $6,600. The annual growth rate of GDP was 0.8%. The average inflation rate was 3.1%. It was estimated that agriculture accounted for 6.5% of GDP, industry 28.4%, and services 65.1%.

The World Bank estimates that Bosnia and Herzegovina, with 0.06% of the world's population, accounted for 0.05% of the world's GDP. By comparison, the United States, with 4.85% of the world's population, accounted for 22.51% of world GDP. As of 2011 the most recent study by the World Bank reported that actual individual consumption in Bosnia and Herzegovina was 101.0% of GDP and accounted for 0.07% of world consumption. By comparison, the United States accounted for 25.44% of world individual consumption. The World Bank also estimated that 36% of Bosnia and Herzegovina's GDP was spent on food and beverages, 20.8% on housing and household furnishings, 5.4% on clothes, 8.8% on health, 8.0% on transportation, 2.6% on communications, 4.4% on recreation, 6.9% on restaurants and hotels, and 2.7% on miscellaneous goods and services and purchases from abroad.

According to the World Bank, remittances from citizens living abroad totaled $2.1 billion or about $450 per capita and accounted for approximately 6.9% of GDP.

It was estimated that in 2007 about 18.6% of the population subsisted on an income below the poverty line established by Bosnia and Herzegovina's government.

21 LABOR

As of 2010, Bosnia and Herzegovina had a total labor force of 2.6 million people. Within that labor force, CIA estimates in 2008 noted that 20.5% were employed in agriculture, 32.6% in industry, and 47% in the service sector.

By law, all workers are legally entitled to form or join unions and to strike, but the government process for registering a union can be prohibitively cumbersome and strikes must be negotiated with management prior to taking place. Government authorities have in numerous cases failed to sanction employers who take punitive action against union organizers and leaders. High unemployment has also acted to limit labor activity.

The minimum employment age in the Bosnian-Croat Federation and the Republika Srpska entities is 15; however, many younger children often assist with family agricultural work. Minors between the ages of 15 and 18 must provide a valid health certificate in order to work. As of 2009, the minimum wage was BAM343 ($227.61) per month in the FBH and $320 ($212.35) per month in Republika Srpska. The legal workweek in both entities is 40 hours, although seasonal workers may work up to 60 hours per week. Laws in both entities require a 30-minute rest period during the work day. Safety and health regulations are generally ignored due to the economic devastation of war.

22 AGRICULTURE

During the disintegration of Yugoslavia, civil fighting in the major agricultural areas often interrupted harvests and caused considerable loss of field crops. The World Bank reported in 2007 that investment in small scale commercial agriculture had increased productivity and increased the area under horticulture by 25%; however, despite these improvements, the overall productivity of the nation's farms is low.

Roughly 22% of the total land is used in agriculture. The country's major crops include wheat, corn, fruits, and vegetables. Cereal production in 2009 amounted to 1.3 million tons, fruit production 325,612 tons, and vegetable production 771,366 tons.

23 ANIMAL HUSBANDRY

Because of the breakup of Yugoslavia and subsequent civil war, the livestock population fell significantly during the 1990s. Production of meat fell from 158,000 tons in 1990 to 32,300 tons in 2004. By 2009, this figure had rebounded to 78,442 tons, including 29,682 tons of beef and veal, 19,889 tons of pork, and 28,871 tons of poultry. Bosnia and Herzegovina also produced 20,090 tons of eggs, 743,051 tons of milk, 3,357 tons of cattle hide and 1,438 tons of raw wool.

The UN Food and Agriculture Organization (FAO) reported that Bosnia and Herzegovina dedicated 1 million hectares (2.55 million acres) to permanent pasture or meadow in 2009. During that year, the country tended 17.3 million chickens, 457,743 head of cattle, and 529,095 pigs.

24 FISHING

With no ports on its 20 km (12 mi) of Adriatic coastline, marine fishing is not commercially significant. Inland fishing occurs on the Sava, Una, and Drina Rivers. In 2008, the annual capture totaled 2,005 tons according to the UN FAO.

25 FORESTRY

Approximately 43% of Bosnia and Herzegovina is covered by forest. The UN FAO estimated the 2009 roundwood production at 2.1 million cu m (74.1 million cu ft). The value of all forest products, including roundwood, totaled $212.1 million.

26 MINING

Bosnia and Herzegovina's mineral resources include iron ore, lead, zinc, manganese, and bauxite. Iron ore production was centered in Varescaron, Jablanica, Ljubija, and Radovan; lead and zinc ore was mined at Olovo, Varescaron, and Srebrenica; manganese ore operations were centered at Bosanska Krupa; bauxite deposits were worked at Vlasenica, Zvornik, and Banja Luka; and substantial nickel deposits had been worked near Visegrad. Energoinvest operated a lead-zinc mine at Srebrenica, a manganese mine at Buzim, bauxite mines in many locations, alumina plants at Birac-Zvornik and Mostar, an aluminum smelter at Mostar, and a petroleum refinery at Bosanski Brod. Before the civil war, Bosnia and Herzegovina was a major center for metallurgical industries in the former Yugoslavia and a major producer of bauxite, alumina, and aluminum. Mineral production in 2009 were, in metric tons: iron ore, 678,000; bauxite, 550,820; lead, 2,100; zinc, 3,400; salt, 556,089; crude gypsum, 74,302; ceramic clay, 15,000; and granite,

18,755. Other nonfuel mineral resources included asbestos, barite, bentonite, kaolin, lime, magnesite, ammonia nitrogen, glass sand, sand and gravel, soda ash, caustic soda, and crushed and brown stone. Mining and quarrying accounted for 2% of GDP in 2009, and made up 1.9% of exports.

27 ENERGY AND POWER

The World Bank reported in 2008 that Bosnia and Herzegovina produced 13.3 billion kWh of electricity and consumed 9.31 billion kWh, or 2,014 kWh per capita. Roughly 93% of energy came from fossil fuels, while 7% came from alternative fuels. Per capita oil consumption was 1,588 kg.

Brown coal and lignite mines are located around Tuzla. Coal production rose steadily following a precipitous drop in 1994–1996, to a peak of 12,882 million short tons in 2008; however, production dropped 18.36% in 2009 to 10,516 million short tons. The coal produced is consumed primarily by the country's thermal electric power stations. The nation's only petroleum refinery, located at Bosanski Brod and under majority-Russian ownership, closed in 2005 after suffering heavy damages during the 1992–95 Balkan war. It reopened in 2009, and in 2010 received $139 million in Russian investments as part of a five-year plan to boost handling capacity to 3.0–4.2 million metric tons of crude oil per year.

28 INDUSTRY

Mining and mining-related activities make up the bulk of Bosnia and Herzegovina's industry. Steel production, vehicle assembly, textiles, tobacco products, wooden furniture, and domestic appliances are also important industries. Industrial capacity, largely damaged or shut down in 1995 because of the civil war, has increased since then. In 1998 alone, industrial production grew an estimated 35%. Nevertheless, in 2001, six years after the war ended, industrial production was still only about half its prewar level. The industrial growth rate has generally decreased since its peak in 1998, with growth standing at -3.3% in 2008, and 1.6% in 2010. In the Republika Srpska, the Serb Democratic Party controls every significant production facility, government department, and state institution. Privatization began in 1999. While only 7 of 138 strategic enterprises had been sold by 2001, the effort continues with, among others, the privatization of Telekom Srpske and the oil industry of Serbia (NIS) starting in 2006 and 2007. Exports increased steadily from $0.45 billion in 1997 to $5.18 billion in 2008, then dipped 21.6% in 2009, but recovered most of that loss in the following year.

In 2010 the services sector contributed 64.3% to the overall GDP; industry came in second with a 25.9% share in the GDP composition; agriculture contributed 9.8%.

29 SCIENCE AND TECHNOLOGY

Patent applications in science and technology as of 2009, according to the World Bank, totaled 59 in Bosnia and Herzegovina. Public financing of science was 0.03% of GDP. Scientific and engineering education is provided at the universities of Sarajevo, Banja Luka, and Tuzla (founded in 1948, 1975, and 1976, respectively). The Institute for Thermal and Nuclear Technology, founded in 1961, is located in Sarajevo. Leading professional groups include the Society of Mathematicians, Physicists and Astronomers, the

Principal Trading Partners – Bosnia and Herzegovina (2010)

(In millions of US dollars)

Country	Total	Exports	Imports	Balance
World	10,269.3	3,339.8	6,929.5	-3,589.7
Croatia	2,052.3	546.7	1,505.6	-958.8
Slovenia	1,584.4	671.0	913.4	-242.4
Germany	1,349.5	445.1	904.4	-459.3
Italy	1,321.8	544.5	777.4	-232.9
Austria	798.4	360.7	437.7	-77.1
Hungary	489.2	96.4	392.8	-296.4
Russia	384.6	33.2	351.5	-318.3
Turkey	312.5	65.8	246.7	-181.0
Czech Republic	216.1	40.8	175.3	-134.4
Netherlands	161.9	34.2	127.7	-93.5

(…) data not available or not significant.

(n.s.) not specified.

SOURCE: *2011 Direction of Trade Statistics Yearbook,* New York: United Nations, 2011.

Balance of Payments – Bosnia and Herzegovina (2010)

(In millions of US dollars)

Current Account		-1,008.5
Balance on goods	-4,293.2	
Imports	-9,230.2	
Exports	4,937.0	
Balance on services	695.1	
Balance on income	331.2	
Current transfers	2,258.3	
Capital Account		212.5
Financial Account		474.9
Direct investment abroad	-43.7	
Direct investment in Bosnia and Herzegovina	231.5	
Portfolio investment assets	-91.3	
Portfolio investment liabilities	…	
Financial derivatives	…	
Other investment assets	344.5	
Other investment liabilities	33.9	
Net Errors and Omissions		76.2
Reserves and Related Items		244.9

(…) data not available or not significant.

SOURCE: *Balance of Payment Statistics Yearbook 2011,* Washington, DC: International Monetary Fund, 2011.

Union of Engineers and Technicians, and the Medical Society of Bosnia and Herzegovina, all headquartered in Sarajevo.

³⁰ DOMESTIC TRADE

Bosnia and Herzegovina is still struggling with efforts to move from socialism to private sector, market-led capitalism. Retail establishments tend to be very small with limited inventories; however, some large shopping centers are gaining ground. Direct marketing and sales are also gaining in popularity. Installment plans and financing, even for very low cost items, is common, since credit is not widely available or accepted.

With the establishment of the Central Bank and currency board in 1997, inflation has since been brought under control; however, unemployment is still high, at about 47% in 2009, though as many as half of the officially unemployed may have some employment in the gray economy. As of 2007, government spending still accounted for about 50% of the economy.

³¹ FOREIGN TRADE

Bosnia and Herzegovina imported $9.22 billion worth of goods and services in 2008, while exporting $4.804 billion worth of goods and services. Major import partners in 2009 were Croatia, 22.1%; Germany, 14%; Slovenia, 13.4%; Italy, 11.8%; Austria, 6.6%; and Hungary, 5.7%. Its major export partners were Croatia, 19%; Slovenia, 18.5%; Italy, 16.8%; Germany, 13.4%; and Austria, 10.2%.

Before the war, manufactured goods accounted for 31% of exports; by 2008, this had increased to 64.0%, with the remaining exports made up of agricultural raw materials, 6.8%; food, 6.0%; fuel, 9.7%; and ores and materials, 12.9%. In 2008, manufactured goods made up 63.3% of imports, with the balance made up of agricultural raw materials, 1.3%; food, 15.8%; fuel, 16.5%; and ores and metals, 3.1%.

³² BALANCE OF PAYMENTS

In 2010 Bosnia and Herzegovina had a foreign trade deficit of $4 billion, amounting to 1.7% of GDP. The CIA reported that in 2010 Bosnia and Herzegovina had exports totaling $4.937 billion and imports totaling $9.23 billion. The national reserves of foreign exchange and gold were $4.383 billion in 2010.

³³ BANKING AND SECURITIES

The central bank of Bosnia and Herzegovina is the National Bank of Bosnia and Herzegovina. Commercial banks in the country include Privredna Banka Sarajevo, Hrvatsk A Banka d.d. Mostar, and Investiciono-Komercijalua Banka d.d. Zenica. Foreign ownership of banks in 2010 was 85%.

In April 1997, the presidential council agreed on a single currency, the convertible marka (BAM), for both the Muslim/Croat and Bosnian Serb parts of the country. The BAM is linked to the euro, making it one of the region's most stable currencies.

At the end of 2010, the stock of broad and narrow money was $9.442 billion. The commercial bank prime lending rate was 7.89%.

³⁴ INSURANCE

A variety of types of insurance are available in FBH. The Insurance Supervisory Agency of the Federation of Bosnia and Herzegovina regulates the industry in FBH. The insurance industry was still in development in RS in 2011.

³⁵ PUBLIC FINANCE

In 2010 the budget of Bosnia and Herzegovina included $7.75 billion in public revenue and $7.82 billion in public expenditures. The budget deficit amounted to 4.4% of GDP. Public debt was 39% of GDP, with $9.678 billion of the debt held by foreign entities.

³⁶ TAXATION

In 2012, individuals paid a 10% income tax in both FBH and RS. Employers withhold the tax from employees' paychecks. The corporate tax in both entities was also 10%. Sales tax and VAT are

Public Finance – Bosnia and Herzegovina (2009)

(In millions of convertible marka, central government figures)

Revenue and Grants	**9,359.9**	**100.0%**
Tax revenue	4,698.4	50.2%
Social contributions	3,638.4	38.9%
Grants	94.8	1.0%
Other revenue	927.4	9.9%
Expenditures	**10,396**	**100.0%**
General public services	...	...
Defense	...	...
Public order and safety	...	...
Economic affairs	...	...
Environmental protection	...	...
Housing and community amenities	...	...
Health	...	...
Recreational, culture, and religion	...	...
Education	...	...
Social protection	...	...

(…) data not available or not significant.

SOURCE: *Government Finance Statistics Yearbook 2010*, Washington, DC: International Monetary Fund, 2010.

17%. Capital gains are taxed at 10% in FBH, and 8% in RS. Real estate is taxed at 5% in FBH, and 3% in RS. In FBH, employers pay 10.5% of their employees' gross salaries into the social security systems, while the employees pay 31%. In the RS, both employers and employees pay 30.6% of the employees' gross salary into social security.

[37] CUSTOMS AND DUTIES

Bosnia and Herzegovina became a member of the Central European Free Trade Agreement (CEPTA) in 2006. CEPTA counts among its signatories Albania, Bosnia and Herzegovina, Croatia, Macedonia, Moldova, Montenegro, Serbia, and UNMIK/Kosovo, and had as its goal the creation of a free trade zone in the area by 31 December 2010. Bosnia and Herzegovina also has free trade agreement with Turkey and Slovenia. Tariff rates for imports from other countries are zero, 5% or 10%, depending on the good, with consumption and luxury goods generally receiving the higher rates.

[38] FOREIGN INVESTMENT

Foreign direct investment (FDI) in Bosnia and Herzegovina was a net inflow of $234.6 million according to World Bank figures published in 2009. FDI represented 1.38% of GDP.

Private investment plummeted during the civil war, when UN sanctions were in force. The conclusion of the Dayton Peace Accords in 1995 brought positive changes in the investment climate. In May 1998, a law on foreign direct investment (FDI) was passed and in June 1998, a law on privatization. While privatization of small and medium enterprises made good progress, the state of larger strategic firms progressed more slowly. As of spring 2002, only 7 of 138 large state-owned enterprises had been sold and only 35% of the economy had been privatized. The largest foreign sale was the Zenica Steel Mill, which became the BH Steel Company in a joint venture with Kuwait Consulting and Investment Com-

pany (KCIC). The privatization effort has continued with, among others, the privatization of Telekom Srpske and the oil industry of Serbia (NIS) starting in 2006 and 2007.

The overwhelming majority of foreign investment into Bosnia and Herzegovina comes from aid groups and international financial institutions.

Bosnia and Herzegovina has promoted itself as an investment opportunity, citing its availability of natural resources, low inflation rate, fast growing economy, free trade zones, stable currency, and the willingness of its government to facilitate privatization. In 2007, the nation received its highest total FDI in 15 years, with a total of EUR1.6 billion. In 2009, the global economic crisis took its toll, and FDI dropped to EUR452 million. Most of the FDI comes from other European countries. In 2009, the biggest investors were Austria, Serbia, Slovenia, Croatia, and Switzerland.

Previous years have seen Bosnia and Herzegovina take on major changes in an attempt to attract foreign investors. A liberal State Foreign Investment Policy Law, a common currency, and a more streamlined trade and customs policy were some of the most noteworthy attempts to increase capital inflows.

[39] ECONOMIC DEVELOPMENT

Following the 1995 peace agreement, economic assistance was expected to lay the groundwork for a revival of the economy. The actual distribution of assistance to particular entities or areas was tied to the government's compliance with the Dayton Accords. Into 2011, privatization and reconstruction were ongoing. The absence of a single market in Bosnia and Herzegovina is an obstacle to economic development, as is the high degree of bureaucratization. Successful debt negotiations have been held with the London Club and the Paris Club.

In the years following the Dayton Accords, Bosnia and Herzegovina has seen an overall increase in economic output. Apart from a series of systemic and political problems, the country has to fight rampant unemployment, a large underground economy, and an inflation level that was not helping the already low export levels. In 2011 Bosnia and Herzegovina continued to work toward its long-term goal of EU integration. A series of planned privatizations and restructurings in the energy, transportation, telecommunication, and construction sectors were expected to jump-start the economy and attract future investments.

In 2009, increased social spending and the global fiscal crisis pushed Bosnia and Herzegovina into an IMF standby arrangement, the aims of which were to reduce government spending and improve the nation's revenue collection.

[40] SOCIAL DEVELOPMENT

Social welfare systems in Bosnia and Herzegovina are under the control of each of the two entities: FBH and RS. Old age and disability pensions were originally regulated by the 1998 Pension and Disability Insurance Act. Since that time, the calculation of pensions and rules governing them have been reformed in an effort to sufficiently fund the pension system so that it can meet the population's needs. The age at which one can receive an old-age pension has been raised to 65 for both men and women, where it had been 55 for women and 60 for men. The pension base has been increased every year since 2005 and was to continue to rise until 2015.

Although gender discrimination is proscribed by the 2003 Law on Gender Equality, the extent of legal and social discrimination against women varies by region. Women in urban areas pursue professional careers in such areas as law, medicine, and academia, while their rural counterparts are often relegated to the margins of public life. Violence against women remains underreported and there are accounts of police inaction in domestic situations. It was estimated in 2008 that over 25% of the nation's women in relationships had experienced domestic violence. The problem is more significant in rural areas, and is exacerbated by poverty and alcoholism. Trafficking of women remains a major problem in the region.

All sides were guilty of human rights atrocities in the war and its aftermath. By 1995, it was estimated that up to two-thirds of the country's prewar population had become refugees or displaced persons. Women were targeted for cruel treatment during the war, with Serb forces systematically using rape as a tool to accelerate ethnic cleansing. The worst single incident of genocide in Europe since World War II occurred in the Bosnian "safe haven" of Srebrenica in 1995, when over 8,000 men and boys were massacred. In May 2011, alleged war criminal Ratko Mladic, under indictment for genocide in relation to the massacre in Srebrenica, was captured in Serbia. The remaining indicted suspect, Goran Hadzic, remained at large.

In December 2009, the European Court of Human Rights found Bosnia and Herzegovina's constitution to be in violation of the right to free and fair elections, in light of its stipulation that only members of the nation's three major ethnic groups may run for the nation's highest political offices. The court ruled that Bosnia and Herzegovina must modify its constitution to be in compliance with the European Convention for Human Rights. It was hoped this ruling, along with an anti-discrimination law adopted in 2009, would help end ethnic discrimination in the country.

While media legislation is regarded as good, there were numerous cases of threats against journalists and other members of the media. In 2008, there were 56 reported cases; in 2009 there were 40, six of which involved death threats and four involving physical attacks.

[41]HEALTH

According to the CIA, life expectancy in Bosnia and Herzegovina was 75 years in 2011. The country spent 10.3% of its GDP on healthcare, amounting to $495 per person. There were 14 physicians, 47 nurses and midwives, and 30 hospital beds per 10,000 inhabitants. The fertility rate was 1.2, while the infant mortality rate was 13 per 1,000 live births. In 2008 the maternal mortality rate, according to the World Bank, was 9 per 100,000 births. It was estimated that 93% of children were vaccinated against measles. The CIA calculated HIV/AIDS prevalence in Bosnia and Herzegovina to be about less than 0.1% in 2007.

[42]HOUSING

Bosnia and Herzegovina suffers from a housing shortage as a result of the 1992–1995 civil war which forced over two million people from their homes and destroyed or seriously damaged approximately 65% of the housing stock. In 2005 it was estimated that 58% of the damaged and destroyed houses had been rehabilitated. The cost of repairing the remaining housing stock was estimated to be €1.3 billion.

[43]EDUCATION

The war of the early 1990s resulted in the destruction of many schools and interrupted the education of many of the nation's children; however, in 2009 the World Bank estimated that 87% of age-eligible children in Bosnia and Herzegovina were enrolled in primary school. Tertiary enrollment was estimated at 37%. Overall, the CIA estimated that Bosnia and Herzegovina had a literacy rate of 96.7%.

Education is administered by the Ministry of Education, Science, Culture and Sports. Each of the FBH's 10 cantons also has its own education ministry, as do the RS and the Brĉko District; these entity-level ministries are responsible for approving the school curricula.

Education at the elementary level is free and compulsory for students between the ages of 6 and 15. Primary school is organized into three three-year cycles, with grades 1–3 being preparatory; grades 4–6, classroom instruction; and 7–9, subject instruction. In 2007, one year of preschool attendance became mandatory, but a UNICEF report showed that only roughly 10% of first graders had attended preschool. At the secondary level, children have the option to take up general education (gymnasium), vocational, or technical schooling. General secondary lasts for four years and qualifies the students for university education. The academic year runs from October to July. The languages of instructions are Croatian and Serbian.

Entrance to public universities is based on the results of an entrance exam. There are four main universities: the University of Banja Luka (founded in 1975); the University of Mostar (founded in 1977); the University of Tuzla (founded in 1976); and the University of Sarajevo (founded in 1949), which offers programs in the social sciences, humanities, sciences, medicine, law, and engineering.

[44]LIBRARIES AND MUSEUMS

Prior to the 1992 war, Sarajevo was a major cultural center in the Balkans. It still hosts nearly a dozen museums, including the Museum of the Old Orthodox Church, the Museum of Young Bosnia, the State Museum, and the Museum of the City of Sarajevo, as well as Bosnia's National Museum. The Museum of the National Struggle for Liberation is in Jajce and the Museum of Herzegovina is in Mostar.

Numerous historic sites were damaged by war, including the National and University Library of Bosnia and Herzegovina, which sustained major damage and the destruction of almost all its contents in a 1992 fire-bombing. Some 1.5 million books were lost. Outside groups, such as UNESCO, have since been working to rebuild the National Library. It currently is housed in a military barracks and two one-story buildings. Banja Luka has an important university and public library founded in 1936, and holding 226,000 volumes with an impressive collection of Eastern manuscripts. The University of Sarajevo also housed an impressive library, but it was badly damaged during the civil war. The National Museum of Bosnia and Herzegovina has a library with 162,000 volumes.

⁴⁵MEDIA

Postwar reconstruction of the telecommunications network has increased the number of fixed telephone lines available. The CIA reports there were 998,600 main phone lines in 2009, and 86 mobile phone subscriptions per 100 people. Internet users numbered 38 per 100 citizens. In 2010 the country had 95,234 Internet hosts.

 In 2009 there were 8 FM radio stations, 16 AM radio stations, and 1 shortwave radio station. Prominent newspapers in 2010 included *Oslobodjenje (Liberation)*, with a circulation of 56,000. Founded in 1943 as a Nazi resistance publication, *Oslobodjenje*, which is published in Serbo-Croatian, managed to publish continuously throughout the siege of that city despite power and phone line outages, newsprint shortages, and direct attacks on its offices.

The most influential radio and TV stations are those operated by the Public Broadcasting Service of Bosnia-Herzegovina and Serb Republic Radio-TV. In 2008, there were an estimated 243 radios for every 1,000 people. The number of television sets in use was unavailable in the same survey.

The constitution signed in Dayton, Ohio, on 21 November 1995, provides for freedom of speech and the press. However, the extreme ethnic segregation in various regions is said to put the media in each area under considerable regional restrictions. In 2008 and 2009, journalists received threats, including death threats and physical attacks, related to issues they reported. The development of independent media has been supported through the sponsorship of private organizations, cultural societies, and political parties, along with Western aid organizations.

⁴⁶ORGANIZATIONS

The Bosnia and Herzegovina Chamber of Commerce promotes trade and commerce in world markets. There are some professional associations, particularly those representing medical professionals in specialized fields.

There are over a dozen learned societies in Bosnia and Herzegovina. Research institutions in the country are concentrated in the areas of nuclear technology, meteorology, historical monument preservation, and language.

Youth organizations include the Student Union of Bosnia and Herzegovina and the Council of Scout Associations. There are a number of sports associations, including those dedicated to such favorite pastimes as tennis, skating, and handball. There is also an active committee of the Special Olympics.

There is a national chapter of UNICEF and the Red Cross Society. Volunteer service organizations, such as the Lions Clubs International, are also present.

⁴⁷TOURISM, TRAVEL, AND RECREATION

While civil war has limited the development of a tourism industry in Bosnia and Herzegovina, Sarajevo, the capital city, is growing as a tourist attraction. The city was the site of the 1984 Winter Olympics. Bosnia and Herzegovina promotes itself as a destination for eco-tourism and outdoor activities including hiking and whitewater rafting, as well as skiing and other winter sports.

The *Tourism Factbook*, published by the UN World Tourism Organization, reported 311,000 incoming tourists to Bosnia and Herzegovina in 2009; they spent a total of $761 million. Of those incoming tourists, there were 292,000 from Europe. There were 24,471 hotel beds available in Bosnia and Herzegovina. The estimated daily cost to visit Sarajevo, the capital, was $200.

⁴⁸FAMOUS PERSONS

Dr. Alija Izetbegović (1925–2003) was the president of Bosnia and Herzegovina from 1991 to 1996, and was a member of the three-man presidency from 1996 to 2000 until he stepped down due to illness. Dzemd Bijedic (1917–1977) was a leader of Yugoslavia from 1971 until 1977, when he was killed in a plane crash. The 1914 assassination of the Austrian Archduke Franz Ferdinand in Sarajevo led to World War I.

⁴⁹DEPENDENCIES

Bosnia and Herzegovina has no territories or colonies.

⁵⁰BIBLIOGRAPHY

Andjelic, Neven. *Bosnia-Herzegovina: The End of a Legacy.* London: Frank Cass, 2003.

Bose, Sumantra. *Bosnia after Dayton: Nationalist Partition and International Intervention.* New York: Oxford University Press, 2002.

Bosnia and Herzegovina Investment and Business Guide: Strategic and Practical Information. Washington, DC: International Business Publications USA, 2012.

Cousens, Elizabeth M. *Toward Peace in Bosnia: Implementing the Dayton Accords.* Boulder, CO: Lynne Rienner, 2001.

Cuvalo, Ante. *Historical Dictionary of Bosnia and Herzegovina.* Lanham, MD: Scarecrow, 1997.

Doubt, Keith. *Sociology after Bosnia and Kosovo: Recovering Justice.* Lanham, MD: Rowman and Littlefield, 2000.

Filipovic, Zlata. *Zlata's Diary: A Child's Life in Sarajevo.* New York: Penguin, 2006.

Frucht, Richard, ed. *Eastern Europe: An Introduction to the People, Lands, and Culture.* Santa Barbara, CA: ABC-CLIO, 2005.

Jones, Lynne. *Then They Started Shooting: Growing Up in Wartime Bosnia.* Cambridge, MA: Harvard University Press, 2004.

King, David C. *Bosnia and Herzegovina.* New York: Marshall Cavendish Benchmark, 2005.

Lovrenovic, Ivan. *Bosnia: A Cultural History.* New York: New York University Press, 2001.

Mahmutcehajic, Rusmir. *Bosnia the Good: Tolerance and Tradition.* New York: Central European University Press, 2000.

McElrath, Karen, ed. *HIV and AIDS: A Global View.* Westport, CT: Greenwood Press, 2002.

Opello, Walter C. *European Politics.* Boulder, CO: Lynne Rienner Publishers, 2009.

Pejanovic, Mirko. *Through Bosnian Eyes: The Political Memoir of a Bosnian Serb.* West Lafayette, IN: Purdue University Press, 2004.

Political Chronology of Europe. London: Europa, 2001.

Sacco, Joe. *War's End: Profiles from Bosnia, 1995–1996.* Montréal: Drawn and Quarterly, 2005.

Schuman, Michael. *Bosnia and Herzegovina.* New York: Facts On File, 2004.

Terry, Sara. *Aftermath: Bosnia's Long Road to Peace*. New York: Channel Photographics, 2005.

Velikonja, Mitja. *Religious Separation and Political Intolerance in Bosnia-Herzegovina*. College Station, TX: Texas A and M University Press, 2003.

Mahmutcehajic, Rusmir. *Bosnia the Good: Tolerance and Tradition*. New York: Central European University Press, 2000.

McElrath, Karen (ed.). *HIV and AIDS: A Global View*. Westport, Conn.: Greenwood Press, 2002.

Pinson, Mark (ed.) *The Muslims of Bosnia-Herzegovina: Their Historic Development from the Middle Ages to the Dissolution of Yugoslavia*. 2nd ed., Cambridge, Mass.: Harvard University Press, 1996.

Pejanovic, Mirko. *Through Bosnian Eyes: The Political Memoir of a Bosnian Serb*. West Lafayette, Ind.: Purdue University Press, 2004.

Sacco, Joe. *War's End: Profiles from Bosnia, 1995–1996*. Montréal: Drawn and Quarterly, 2005.

Schuman, Michael. *Bosnia and Herzegovina*. New York: Facts On File, 2004.

Terry, Sara. *Aftermath: Bosnia's Long Road to Peace*. New York: Channel Photographics, 2005.

Velikonja, Mitja. *Religious Separation and Political Intolerance in Bosnia-Herzegovina*. College Station, Tex.: Texas A and M University Press, 2003.

Yugoslavia, the Former and Future: Reflections by Scholars from the Region. Washington, D.C.: Brookings Institution, 1995.

BULGARIA

Republic of Bulgaria
Republika Bulgariya

CAPITAL: Sofia (Sofiya)

FLAG: The flag is a tricolor of white, green, and red horizontal stripes.

ANTHEM: *Mila Rodino (Dear Homeland).*

MONETARY UNIT: The lev (BGN) of 100 stotinki has coins of 1, 2, 5, 10, 20, and 50 stotinki and 1 and 2 leva, and notes of 1, 2, 5, 10, 20, 50, and 100 leva. BGN1 = US1$0.70423 (or US$1 = BGN1.42) as of November 2011.

WEIGHTS AND MEASURES: The metric system is the legal standard.

HOLIDAYS: New Year's Day, 1 January; Labor Days, 1–2 May; Education and Culture Day, 24 May; Christmas, 24–25 December.

TIME: 2 p.m.=noon GMT.

¹LOCATION, SIZE, AND EXTENT

Part of the Balkan Peninsula, Bulgaria has an area of 110,910 sq km (42,822 sq mi) and extends 330 km (205 mi) N–S and 520 km (323 mi) E–W. Comparatively, the area occupied by Bulgaria is slightly larger than the state of Tennessee. Bulgaria is bounded on the N by Romania, on the E by the Black Sea, on the SE by Turkey, on the S by Greece, and on the W by Macedonia and Serbia, with a total boundary length of 1,808 km (1,123 mi).

Bulgaria's capital city, Sofia, is located in the west central part of the country.

²TOPOGRAPHY

Bulgaria consists of a number of roughly parallel east-west zones. They are the Danubian tableland in the north, the Balkan Mountains (Stara Planina) in the center, and the Thracian Plain, drained by the Maritsa River, in the south. The Rhodope, Rila, and Pirin mountains lie in the southwestern part of the country. The average elevation is 480 m (1,575 ft), and the highest point, in the Rila Mountains, is the Musala, at 2,925 m (9,596 ft). The Danube (Dunav), Bulgaria's only navigable river, forms most of the northern boundary with Romania. Located along the Eurasian Tectonic Plate, the country does experience some low-level magnitude earthquakes.

³CLIMATE

Bulgaria lies along the southern margins of the continental climate of Central and Eastern Europe. Regional climatic differences occur in the Danubian tableland, exposed to cold winter winds from the north, and the Thracian Plain, which has a modified Mediterranean climate and is protected by the Balkan Mountains against the northern frosts. January temperatures are between 0°C and 2°C (32–36°F) in the lowlands but colder in the mountains; July temperatures average about 22°C to 24°C (72–75°F). Precipitation

is fairly regularly distributed throughout the year and amounts to an average of 64 cm (25 in).

⁴FLORA AND FAUNA

The World Resources Institute estimates that there are 3,572 plant species in Bulgaria. In addition, Bulgaria is home to 106 species of mammals, 379 species of birds, 33 species of reptiles, and 17 species of amphibians. This calculation reflects the total number of distinct species residing in the country, not the number of endemic species.

In the northeast lies the typical steppe grassland zone of the Dobrudja, merging into the wooded steppe of the Danubian tableland. Most trees in this area have been cut down to make room for cultivated land. The Balkan Mountains are covered by broadleaf forests at lower altitudes and by needle-leaf conifers at higher elevations. The vegetation of the Thracian Plain is a mixture of the middle-latitude forest of the north and Mediterranean flora. Deforestation has reduced the amount of wildlife, which includes bears, foxes, squirrels, elks, wildcats, and rodents of various types. Fish resources in the Black Sea are not extensive.

⁵ENVIRONMENT

The World Resources Institute reported that Bulgaria had designated 591,900 hectares (1.46 million acres) of land for protection as of 2006. The long-term average annual water resources totaled 21.3 cu km (5.11 cu mi), while water usage was 6.12 cu km (1.47 cu mi) per year. In 2009 municipal water usage accounted for 16% of total usage, industrial for 68%, and agricultural for 16%. Per capita water usage totaled 811 cu m (28,640 cu ft) per person.

The United Nations (UN) reported in 2008 that carbon dioxide emissions in Bulgaria totaled 51,739 kilotons.

Bulgaria's air pollution problem results from the combined influence of industry and transportation. In the mid-1990s, Bulgaria was among the 50 countries with the highest per capita industrial emissions of carbon dioxide, producing around 60,000 kilotons. In 1996, the total was 62,216 kilotons. Industrial pollutants, especially from metallurgical plants, are responsible for damage to 297 sq km (115 sq mi) of land in Bulgaria. Bulgaria's rivers and the Black Sea are seriously affected by industrial and chemical pollutants, raw sewage, heavy metals, and detergents.

Twenty-five percent of Bulgaria's forests have been significantly damaged by airborne pollutants. Protected land areas include Pirin National Park and the Srebarna Nature Reserve, which are both natural UNESCO World Heritage Sites. There are 11 Ramsar wetland sites.

According to a 2011 report issued by the International Union for Conservation of Nature and Natural Resources (IUCN), threatened species included 7 types of mammals, 11 species of birds, 2 types of reptiles, 19 species of fish, and 9 other invertebrates. Endangered species in Bulgaria include the Rosalia longhorn, Atlantic sturgeon, and slender-billed curlew.

6 POPULATION

The US Central Intelligence Agency (CIA) estimated the population of Bulgaria in 2011 to be approximately 7,093,635, which placed it at number 99 in population among the 196 nations of the world. In 2011 approximately 18.2% of the population was over 65 years of age, with another 13.9% under 15 years of age. The median age in Bulgaria was 41.9 years. There were 0.92 males for every female in the country. The population's annual rate of change was -0.781%. The projected population for the year 2025 is 6,900,000. Population density in Bulgaria was calculated at 66 people per sq km (165 people per sq mi).

In 2010 the UN estimated that 71% of the population lived in urban areas, and that urban populations had a projected annual rate of change of -0.3% for the next five years. The largest urban area was Sofia, with a population of 1.2 million.

7 MIGRATION

Estimates of Bulgaria's net migration rate, carried out by the CIA in 2011, amounted to -2.82 migrants per 1,000 citizens. The total number of emigrants living abroad was 1.2 million, and the total number of immigrants living in Bulgaria was 107,200. Emigration between 1948 and 1951 consisted mainly of Jews going to Israel and Turks going to Turkey. A high of 99,477 (of whom 98,341 were Turks) was reached in 1951. Most of the emigrants since the 1950s have been Turks bound for Turkey or other Balkan countries. A total of 313,894 emigrated to Turkey in 1989 because of government persecution. More than 100,000 had returned to Bulgaria by February 1990. Meanwhile, about 150,000 ethnic Bulgarians also emigrated. In 1991 about three million Bulgarians were living abroad. Of those emigrating 85% were under age 30.

According to *Migration News*, due to low fertility and emigration, Bulgaria's population is shrinking faster than any other nation in Europe. The majority of those leaving Bulgaria are moving to Germany, Spain, the Netherlands, and North America. Once the European Union (EU) lifted visa requirements for Bulgarians in 2001, Bulgarians illegally migrated to Western countries. Between April 2001 and October 2002, about 6,561 Bulgarians were arrested and expelled from EU counties, the United States, and Canada. The number of illegal foreigners in Bulgaria is low. Due to the high unemployment rate (12% in 2011), there are serious restrictions on foreign workers.

8 ETHNIC GROUPS

In 2001 Bulgarians accounted for an estimated 83.9% of the total population. The Turks, who constituted about 9.4% of the total, are settled mainly in southern Dobrudja and in the Rhodope Mountains. Romas account for about 4.7% of the population. Other groups, including Macedonians, Armenians, Tatars, and Circassians, make up the remaining 2% of the populace. Macedonians live mainly in the Pirin region of southwestern Bulgaria. Romanian-speaking Vlachs live in the towns and countryside of northwestern Bulgaria. Greek-speaking Karakatchans are nomadic mountain shepherds of Romanian origin. The Gagauzi of northeastern Bulgaria are a Turkish-speaking group of Christian Orthodox religion. Bulgaria's cities have small minorities of Russians, Jews, Armenians, Tatars, and Greeks.

9 LANGUAGES

Bulgarian is classified as a Slavic language of the southern group, which also includes Macedonian, Serbo-Croatian, and Slovenian. Old Bulgarian, also known as Old Church Slavonic, was the first Slavic language fixed in its own writing script (9th century). For this purpose, two monks, Cyril and Methodius, created a new alphabet, based partly on the Greek that became known as the Cyrillic alphabet. Both the grammar and the vocabulary of modern Bulgarian show Turkish, Greek, Romanian, and Albanian influences. According to a 2001 census, 84.5% of the population speak Bulgarian, 9.6% speak Turkish, 4.1% speak Roma, and 1.8% speak other languages or did not specify a primary language.

10 RELIGIONS

According to a 2010 report, about 85% of the population belonged at least nominally to the Bulgarian (Eastern) Orthodox Church. There were also an estimated 13% who were Muslims. Other religious groups include Roman Catholics, Jews, Uniate Catholics, evangelical Protestants, and Gregorian Armenians. After seizing power in 1946, the Communist regime, whose aim was eventually to establish an atheistic society, sought during the ensuing period to replace all religious rites and rituals with civil ceremonies. The new constitution of 1991 guaranteed freedom of religion to all, but named the Bulgarian Orthodox Church as a traditional religion of state. Orthodox Christmas, Good Friday, and Easter are observed as national holidays.

11 TRANSPORTATION

The CIA reports that Bulgaria has a total of 40,231 km (24,998 mi) of roads, of which 39,587 km (24,598 mi) are paved. There are 353 vehicles per 1,000 people in the country. Railroads extend for 4,150 km (2,579 mi). Bulgaria has approximately 470 km (292 mi) of navigable waterways.

The Bulgarian Railway Company (BDZ) oversees Bulgaria's railway system. Railroads are still the basic means of freight transportation in Bulgaria.

Road transportation has grown steadily in recent years. Bulgaria has many highway projects underway, including portions of the Trans-European Motorway (TEM), a route connecting Budapest with Athens via Vidin and Sofia and with Istanbul via eastern Bulgaria.

LOCATION: 41°14′ to 44°13′N; 22°22′ to 28°37′E. BOUNDARY LENGTHS: Romania, 608 kilometers (378 miles); Black Sea, 354 kilometers (220 miles); Turkey, 240 kilometers (149 miles); Greece, 494 kilometers (307 miles); Macedonia, 148 kilometers (92 miles); Serbia, 318 kilometers (198 miles). TERRITORIAL SEA LIMIT: 12 miles.

Water transportation is also significant. As of 2008, Bulgaria's maritime fleet was comprised of 74 ships. The major seaports are Burgas and Varna. Principal river ports are Ruse, Lom, and Vidin.

There are 210 airports, which transported 798,165 passengers in 2009 according to the World Bank. There are also three heliports. Sofia's Vrazhdebna Airport is the major air center, but there are also international airports at Varna and Burgas, as well as seven domestic airports. The current flag carrier, Bulgaria Air, was established in 2003, after the former Bulgarian Airlines (BALKAN) declared bankruptcy in 2002.

12 HISTORY

Ancient Thrace and Moesia, the areas that modern Bulgaria occupies, were settled in the 6th century AD by southern Slavs migrating from the area north of the Carpathian Mountains (modern-day Ukraine and Romania). The Thracian tribes, which had populated that territory since the middle of the 2nd century BC, were displaced or conquered. In the 7th century AD the Bulgars, a Central Asian Turkic tribe, crossed the Danube River to settle permanently in the Balkans. In alliance with the overpowered Slavs, the Bulgars formed the Bulgarian state, which was recognized by the Byzantine Empire in 681 AD. The name and initial political framework of the new state were taken from the Bulgars, but the language and the culture remained predominantly Slavic.

In the late 9th century, Bulgaria became an arena for political and cultural rivalry between the Byzantine Empire centered in Constantinople and the Roman Empire. The Bulgarians adopted Christianity from the Byzantine Empire and embraced the Cyrillic alphabet, named for St. Cyril. As a result, the integration of the disparate tribes into a Bulgarian people was more or less complete by the end of the 9th century.

The early Bulgarian state reached its territorial and cultural height under Simeon I (r.893–927). In 1018, Bulgaria, which had struggled to assert itself against Constantinople since its foundation, fell under Byzantine dominance. The country rose again as a major Balkan power in the 12th and 13th centuries, especially under Ivan Asen II (r.1218–41) whose rule extended over nearly the whole Balkan Peninsula except the Greek islands. However, by the end of the 14th century, Bulgaria was overrun by the Ottoman Turks, who ruled the country for nearly five centuries.

The Ottoman rule was often oppressive and sought to assimilate Bulgarian Christianity, culture, and language. Rebellions were frequent but sporadic and unorganized. However, in the early 19th century, under the influence of Western ideas such as liberalism and nationalism, a well-organized national liberation movement emerged. Its efforts culminated in the April uprising of 1876, which was brutally crushed. Russia, a rival of the Ottoman Empire at the time, insisted on a peaceful solution to the Bulgarian question. When diplomacy failed, Russia declared war on Turkey. The Bulgarian state was restored in the aftermath of the Russian-Turkish War of 1877–78.

Apprehensive of the existence of a big Bulgarian state under Russian influence, the Congress of Berlin (June–July 1878) divided the Bulgarian territories into three parts. Northern Bulgaria was given the status of an independent principality under Turkish suzerainty, with its capital at Sofia. Southern Bulgaria (then known as Eastern Rumelia) remained under Turkish rule as an autonomous province. Lastly, ethnic Bulgarians in the regions of Macedonia and Thrace were unconditionally returned to the Ottoman Empire. The decisions of the congress triggered first the Kresna-Razlog uprising (1878–79), which sought to unify the Principality of Bulgaria and Eastern Rumelia; and the Ilinden-Preobrazhenie Uprising (1903), which demanded the liberation of Macedonia. Neither rebellion was immediately successful.

In 1879 the First Grand National Assembly adopted the first constitution of Bulgaria and elected the German prince Alexander Battenberg as the prince of Bulgaria. In 1885 the continuing unrest in Eastern Rumelia culminated in a military coup, which annexed the province to Bulgaria. Stefan Stambolov, premier from 1887 to 1894, consolidated the country's administration and economy. In 1908 Bulgaria declared itself a kingdom completely independent of Turkey.

Striving to unite all Bulgarians, the country took part in the First Balkan War (October 1912–May 1913) and fought with the anti-Turkish coalition (Greece, Serbia, and Montenegro) against the Ottomans. Bulgaria gained most of Thrace including a long-desired outlet to the Aegean Sea. But as a result of a dispute over Macedonia, Bulgaria became pitted against Greece and Serbia. Turkey joined the Greece-Serbia coalition in the hope of winning back some of its territories. Romania also sided against Bulgaria in the Second Balkan War (June–July 1913), and Bulgaria was defeated. As a result, Bulgaria lost southern Dobrudja to Romania, a large part of Macedonia to Serbia, western Thrace to Greece and southeastern Thrace to Turkey. Having sided with the Central Powers in World War I in an attempt to recoup its losses, Bulgaria also lost its outlet to the Aegean Sea and additional parts of Mace-

donia and Dobrudja through the Treaty of Neuilly (27 November 1919).

At the end of World War I, Bulgarian ruler Tsar Ferdinand of Saxe-Coburg-Gotha abdicated in favor of his son, Boris III, who ruled Bulgaria until his death in 1943. After an early period of stability and initial progressive reform under the leadership of Premier Alexander Stamboliski (assassinated in 1923 after agreeing to recognize Yugoslav sovereignty in Macedonia), growing political rivalries allowed Tsar Boris to establish a military government in 1934 and then to personally assume dictatorial powers in 1935.

When World War II broke out, Bulgaria moved toward an alliance with Germany in the hope of recovering lost territories. In 1940 Romania was forced to return southern Dobrudja, and during the war, Bulgaria occupied Macedonia and western Thrace. By 1943 some 20,000 Jews were deported but protests from political and clerical leaders stopped further cooperation, thus saving all of the remaining 50,000 Jews in the country. Bulgaria did, however, actively deport Jews in all areas it conquered.

After Tsar Boris's sudden death in 1943, a cabinet, which was in most respects a German puppet, assumed power. Coordinated mainly by Communists, resistance to the Germans and the authoritarian Bulgarian regime was widespread by 1943. In September 1944, Soviet troops entered the country. At that time, the Bulgarian government withdrew from the occupied territories, severed relations with Germany, and intended to sign an armistice with the Western Allies. But Moscow declared war on Bulgaria and proceeded with the occupation of the country. A coalition government—the Fatherland Front (Otechestven Front)—was established, which, with the assistance of the Soviet army, came under the domination of the Communist Party. Subsequently, anti-Communist political activists were purged.

A plebiscite in September 1946 replaced the monarchy with the People's Republic of Bulgaria and the Communists openly took power. The 1947 peace treaty formally ending Bulgaria's role in World War II allowed the nation to keep southern Dobrudja but limited the size of its armed forces.

Shortly after coming to power, the Bulgarian Communist Party fell under increasing pressure from Moscow to demonstrate its loyalty by stepping up the "socialist transformation" in the country. The Bulgarian leadership moved to ascertain its effective monopoly on political power by eliminating political opposition in the country and "nationalist" elements within the party and to emulate the Soviet economic experience through the introduction of a planned economy. A new constitution in 1947 instituted the nationalization of industry, banking, and public utilities and the collectivization of agriculture. Centralized planning was introduced for the development of the national economy through a series of five-year plans, which stressed the expansion of heavy industry at the expense of agriculture and light industry. Subsequently, Bulgaria joined the Warsaw Pact and the Council for Mutual Economic Assistance (CMEA), thus placing itself firmly within the Soviet Bloc.

Under Todor Zhivkov, first secretary of the Communist Party since 1954 and chairman of the state council (head of state) since 1971, the Bulgarian government remained unquestionably loyal to the Soviet Union. This continued even after Soviet leader Joseph Stalin's death in 1953. While some freedom of expression was gradually restored, labor camps closed, and persecution of the

Christian church ended, upheavals like those in Poland and Hungary in 1956 or in Czechoslovakia in 1968 were not allowed in Bulgaria. Still, a cultural thaw took place in the late 1970s under the leadership of Zhivkov's daughter, Lyudmila Zhivkova. To further strengthen support for the regime, the party leadership devoted enormous resources to the celebration of the national past and culture. However, the period of the so-called "revival process" (with two peaks in 1972–74 and 1984–85) was marked by a campaign to assimilate members of Bulgaria's Turkish minority by forcing them to take Slavic names, prohibiting them from speaking Turkish in public, and subjecting them to other forms of harassment; more than 300,000 Bulgarian Turks crossed the border into Turkey to escape persecution.

The Communist regime drew its legitimacy by preserving the strong egalitarian and statist political traditions in the country. Additionally, the relatively good economic performance and impressive set of social policy achievements generated a considerable level of popular support. The developmental rise in mechanization, technical sophistication, and productivity was remarkable especially given the lack of natural resources and energy endowment and the very low initial material and cultural levels. However, despite these accomplishments, Bulgaria remained one of the countries with the lowest living standards in both Western and Eastern Europe. Moreover, the many and generous social policies were secured at the expense of economic efficiency.

Thus the radical changes introduced in the Soviet Union by Mikhail Gorbachev were welcomed and readily replicated in Bulgaria. A program of far-reaching political and economic changes was announced in July 1987, including an administrative overhaul meant to reduce the number of Communist Party functionaries by as much as two-thirds, the introduction of self-management for individual enterprises, and liberalization of rules for joint ventures with foreign investors. Economic and political restructuring throughout the Soviet Bloc empowered reformist elements within the Bulgarian Communist Party, which were growing increasingly restive under Zhivkov.

Although Zhivkov was never a despot in the Stalinist mold, by the early 1980s his regime was growing increasingly corrupt, autocratic, and erratic. The long-time ruler resisted attempts to change and moved into a pattern of direct confrontation with reformists, led by his foreign minister, Petar Mladenov. Mladenov, who had close ties to Gorbachev, wanted to change Bulgaria's image, which had been tarnished by Zhivkov's intensifying efforts to assimilate the country's ethnic Turks. Finally, in November 1989, Mladenov, backed by other reformists within the party, was able to take advantage of an international environmental conference convened in Sofia to press for Zhivkov's resignation. Mladenov was also successful in winning support from Defense Minister Dobri Dzhurov, thus leaving Zhivkov without resort to the military. Zhivkov had no choice but to resign.

Mladenov had intended to reform the Communist Party, not remove it from power. However, demonstrations on ecological issues in the streets of Sofia in November 1989 soon broadened into a general campaign for political reform. As the newly emergent opposition groups signaled their entry into the political arena by organizing the Union of Democratic Forces (UDF), the Communist leaders invited opposition leaders to roundtable negotiations meant to provide the elite with a safe channel against the antici-

pated popular backlash against communism. A new democratic constitution was negotiated and multiparty elections held in June 1990.

In something of a surprise, the Socialists led by Mladenov received nearly 53% of the 1990 vote, while the UDF got only about a third; the rest of the votes went to the Movement for Rights and Freedoms (MRF), which had emerged to represent the interests of the country's one million ethnic Turks. Popular hostility to Mladenov forced him to resign about a month after the election. Since the Socialists remained generally in charge of the government, there was little tangible progress with economic reform, and Bulgaria's economy, left in poor condition by Zhivkov, continued to decline. In addition, a great deal of effort was devoted to the attempt to prosecute Zhivkov and his prominent cronies for malfeasance, incompetence, and other failings. Zhivkov fought back vigorously, exposing the sins of former colleagues who had remained in power.

Although convictions were eventually obtained (in 1992, with additional charges brought in 1993), the exercise served to undermine public sympathy for the Socialists. That opened the way for the Narodno Sabranie (National Assembly) to appoint the leader of the UDF and famous dissident, Zhelyu Zhelev, as a president in August 1990. Moreover, the first Socialist government, led by Prime Minister Andrei Lukanov, a Mladenov ally, collapsed after a few months of its coming to power; in December 1990, the replacement government of Dimitar Popov, an unaffiliated technocrat, outlined an ambitious program of economic reform.

The Narodno Sabranie passed a new constitution in July 1991, making Bulgaria the first of the Eastern Bloc countries to adopt a new basic law. Among other things, this document called for new parliamentary elections to be held in October 1991. The UDF received 34%, the Socialists, 33%, and the MRF, 8%. The UDF adamantly refused to cooperate with the former Communists, instead taking the MRF as their coalition partner. Filip Dimitrov of the UDF led Bulgaria's first non-Communist government since World War II; however, most of his ministers were chosen for technical expertise rather than party affiliation and 60% of them were drawn from outside the Narodno Sabranie. In January 1992, there were direct presidential elections. Zhelev received 45% of the votes while his Socialist opponent, Velko Vulkanov, received 30%.

Dimitrov undertook an ambitious program of economic and political transformation: he invested his administration in returning property confiscated by the Communists and in the privatization of industry by issuing shares in government enterprises to all citizens. However, Bulgaria's economy continued to deteriorate and unemployment continued to grow as uncompetitive industries failed, exposing strains within the ruling coalition. In late 1992 the Dimitrov government was replaced by a minority coalition of the Socialists, the MRF, and some defecting UDF deputies. Widely seen only as a caretaker prime minister, Lyuben Berov defied predictions, remaining in power for more than 15 months.

The UDF was unrelenting in its hostility to Berov, accusing Berov of trying to "re-communize" Bulgaria; they submitted as many as six votes of no confidence in a single year. This increasing political deadlock and the continued deterioration of Bulgaria's economy led to new parliamentary elections in 1994.

Pledging to defend ordinary citizens against the excesses of the free market, the Bulgarian Socialist Party (BSP) and its two nominal coalition partners won an absolute majority in the 1994 elections. The BSP government, headed by Zhan Videnov, failed to move forward with economic reforms and by the end of 1996, Bulgaria had become the poorest country in Europe with average wages at only $30 a month. In the November 1996 presidential elections, Petar Stoyanov of the UDF was elected president by a wide margin over Socialist party candidate Ivan Marazov.

Fueled by a slow pace of structural reforms, rampant corruption, and a failure to establish market discipline, Bulgaria's problems culminated in a severe economic crisis in 1996–97. Without a stable government and with their economy in free fall, Bulgarians around the country demonstrated for new parliamentary elections. After a few months of chaos and hyperinflation, a major foreign exchange crisis, and the collapse of the banking sector, Bulgaria adopted a Currency Board Arrangement with the International Monetary Fund in July 1997. A conservative fiscal policy and a significant acceleration of structural reforms have underpinned the Currency Board Arrangement.

The elections held in April 1997 were won by a four-party alliance, United Democratic Forces (UtDF), anchored by the UDF. The new prime minister, Ivan Kostov, quickly instituted economic reforms, passed a tough budget, and clamped down on crime and corruption. The economy began to stabilize and popular discontent began to subside. New International Monetary Fund (IMF) loans were approved, and the government embarked on a campaign to attract foreign investment and speed up privatization. The battle against entrenched political corruption continued through 1999 and 2000 and included the dismissal of top government officials. The government increasingly embraced the West, declaring its interest in NATO membership and allowing access to its airspace during the NATO bombing of Serbia in the spring of 1999.

In 1999 Bulgaria also started the accession negotiations to become a member of the European Union (EU). Despite much economic and political progress achieved by the Kostov cabinet, the citizenry was nevertheless disillusioned with the party's corruption and its inability to address the high unemployment in the country.

In April 2001 Simeon Saxe-Coburg-Gotha, the exiled son of Tsar Boris, established a political party, the National Movement for Simeon II (NMS2), pledging to fight corruption, to improve Bulgaria's chances for EU membership, and to better the economy (through deregulation, privatization, and investment). Saxe-Coburg-Gotha was accused (both by the left and the right) of being an opportunist and a populist without competence and political experience, but he claimed his party's intent was not to restore the monarchy but to move ahead with reforms. As the elections came closer, Saxe-Coburg-Gotha's popularity kept growing. His NMS2 party won 120 of 240 assembly seats in the 2001 elections. Having failed to win an absolute majority, the NMS2 signed a coalition agreement with the Movement for Rights and Freedoms. Saxe-Coburg-Gotha's cabinet included two MRF and two BSP ministers.

Saxe-Coburg-Gotha pursued a strongly pro-Western course. Bulgaria sent a nearly 500-strong stabilization force patrol to Iraq. In November 2002, NATO officially invited Bulgaria to join the organization in 2004. Also in 2002, the European Union announced that Bulgaria was not ready to become a member in 2004, but

was expected to join in 2007. In Luxembourg on 25 April 2005, the Treaty of Accession of Republic of Bulgaria to the European Union was signed. At the time, EU member country support for Bulgaria's integration in the union was about 65%.

Four years after Saxe-Coburg-Gotha came to power, the government reported significant economic growth (5.3%), but corruption and organized crime continued to plague the country, and high unemployment, low standard of living, and increasing inequality continued to face Bulgarians. Moreover, for the first time in Bulgaria's post-communist history, ethnic tensions escalated into riots between the Bulgarian and Roma communities in several Bulgarian cities, including Sofia. Hopes for better social protection, disillusionment with Saxe-Coburg-Gotha's policies, and heightened ethnic tensions were all reflected in the results of the 25 June 2005 parliamentary elections. The Coalition for Bulgaria (CfB) won the elections but failed to muster a majority. The NMS2 came in second but received only half of the votes it got in the 2001 elections. The right was in disarray, as the conservative votes were divided among three parties. Lastly, the rising support for the MRF, the third-largest parliamentary group, was paralleled by the emergence of an ultranationalist coalition, Attack Coalition (ATAKA). After the elections, ATAKA was largely marginalized by other parties and soon began to crumble as its representatives began to defect.

In the political maneuvering that followed the elections, the Socialist bid for forming a government was immediately supported by the MRF but was blocked by the NMS2. The stumbling blocks in the negotiation process were the distribution of key posts and the head of the future cabinet. As negotiations dragged on, the EU urged a rapid resolution of the situation so the country could continue implementing the reforms required for accession in 2007. Ending weeks of postelection deadlock, the new Bulgarian government formally took office on 17 August, after the parliament approved the nominations of Prime Minister Sergey Stanishev of the Bulgarian Socialist Party and his 17 cabinet members. The new cabinet was finally elected following a coalition deal among the three leading parties—the BSP, the NMS2, and the MRF—that jointly controlled 169 out of 240 seats in the legislature.

Prime Minister Stanishev maintained that EU membership was his government's top priority and pledged to make up for lost time. He also promised to intensify the campaign against corruption and organized crime and confirmed that the 400 remaining Bulgarian troops deployed in Iraq would be withdrawn before the end of 2006. In fact, those troops were withdrawn in December 2005, but in February 2006 parliament agreed to send a noncombat guard unit to Iraq.

On 1 January 2007, Bulgaria and Romania formally joined the European Union, enlarging the body to 27 members. By the summer of 2008, however, the EU had issued sanctions against Bulgaria over the corruption and fraud that plagued the country and had become, by almost all measures, the worst in the European Union. The sanctions, which froze roughly $1.1 billion of transitional aid that had been promised to Bulgaria by the European Union, constituted the toughest sanctions ever imposed on any EU member.

The Citizens for the European Development of Bulgaria (GERB) won the July 2009 parliamentary. The GERB party was established by the former mayor of Sofia, Boyko Borissov, in 2006.

13 GOVERNMENT

The Bulgarian constitution of July 1991 provides for a multiparty presidential-parliamentary form of republican government, in which all the citizens of the Republic of Bulgaria take part with the right to vote. The document provides clear distinctions among the legislative, executive, and judicial branches of government.

The Council of Ministers is the main executive body, headed by the prime minister. The Council of Ministers conducts the internal and foreign policy of the state, secures public order and national security, and exercises control over the public administration and the military forces. The president, who is head of state, is popularly elected to a five-year term, and may serve a maximum of two terms. The president serves as commander-in-chief of the armed forces and appoints and dismisses their senior command. Among the president's duties is also setting the date for national referenda, scheduling parliamentary elections and naming of the prime minister, who must be confirmed by the Narodno Sabranie (National Assembly). Together with the prime minister or the respective minister, the president countersigns decrees to promulgate newly adopted laws.

The legislative branch of government is the Narodno Sabranie, with 240 members elected to four-year terms. Deputies are elected on a proportional voting basis in a mixed proportional/majoritarian system of elections, in which parties must receive at least 4% of the total national vote in order to receive seats. The largest parliamentary group constructs the cabinet. A simple majority is required to approve the Council of Ministers and to adopt regular legal acts. Amendments to the constitution, however, require approval by a three-quarters majority. Members of parliament represent not only their electoral regions but also the whole nation. The assembly elects temporary and permanent committees, where parliamentarians participate. Members of the assembly, as well as member of the Council of Ministers, have the right to introduce draft laws, but only the Council of Ministers develops draft laws on the state budget.

14 POLITICAL PARTIES

The Bulgarian Socialist Party (BSP) is the successor of the former Bulgarian Communist Party and combines various leftist factions. Some are of social democratic orientation while others remain attached to communism. The 1989 internal coup left the party with strong public support—53% of the vote in the 1991 elections. In 1994 the socialists won a majority in the parliamentary elections for the second time after the fall of state socialism but fell out of favor after two years of particularly disastrous economic policies, which had reduced their popular support to 10% by the end of 1996. The reputation of the BSP is still tied to its inability to deal with the problems of 1996 in the minds of the populace. The BSP remained in opposition after the 1997 and 2001 elections. In 2000, the socialists remaining in the BSP made a significant break with the past by changing their former negative attitude towards NATO membership (without, however, cooling down support for good relations with Russia). In December 2001, Sergey Stanishev was elected as the new party leader with a mission to not only redefine and reform the BSP but also to rejuvenate it by trying to attract younger supporters. In addition, BSP became a full member of the Socialist International. In its campaign for the 2005 parliamentary elections, the party chose to focus on the neglected social rights of the Bulgarian citizens, which helped it gain the greatest share of the vote, 31%.

The Union of Democratic Forces (UDF) was created in the final days of the Communist regime (1989) as a platform movement uniting 15 different formerly dissident political groups. When the UDF came to power in 1992, the divisions between these factions weakened the government, which lost a vote of confidence in parliament in 1994. Under the leadership of Ivan Kostov in early 1997, the UDF was transformed into a single party with liberal ideology. During the 1996–97 political and parliamentary crisis, the UDF dominated the conservative coalition United Democratic Forces (UtDF), which became the main opposition force to the Bulgarian Socialist Party and won a majority in the 1997 parliamentary elections. Kostov stepped down after the party lost in the 2001 parliamentary elections and was succeeded by his former foreign minister Nadezhda Mikhailova in June 2002. However, despite the party losing the 2003 local elections, Mikhailova was reelected as UDF chairwoman.

In February 2004 Ivan Kostov, together with about 2,000 party members (among them 29 members of parliament), left the party. In May 2004, the group around Kostov established a new right-wing party named Democrats for Strong Bulgaria (DSB), which vows to work for a country with strong democracy, capable state institutions, and wealthy society. The party won about 6% of the vote in the 2005 elections. In 2009 it ran as part of a coalition with UDF and together they gained less than 7%.

The Movement for Rights and Freedoms (MRF) primarily represents the interests of Bulgaria's large Turkish minority (about 10% of the population), which was harshly repressed during the Zhivkov years. In economic issues the MRF advocates neoliberal policies. For the 2001 parliamentary elections the MRF formed a coalition with two small parties and got in power together with the NMS2. Similarly, the so-called "triple coalition," which formed a government after the 2005 elections, was comprised of the BSP, NMS2 and the MRF. Yet nationalist antipathy among many Bulgarians towards the country's large Turkish minority makes the MRF an unpopular coalition partner for most political parties. In fact, in 1991 the MRF was accused of being an ethnic party and proved to be a costly partner in the majority of post-1989 governments. After the 2009 elections MRF had 38 seats in parliament.

While ethnic Turks have been represented in parliament since 1990, parties have included very few members of the Roma national minority. Still, compared with Roma in Slovakia and Romania for example, Bulgarian Roma are relatively successful in exercising influence on the government through the formation of an umbrella coalition. Nonetheless, Roma efforts are hampered by corruption and the lack of focused agendas among Roma organizations. Discrimination, unwillingness of mainstream political parties to encourage Roma participation, and the lack of political engagement within the Roma community itself are all obstacles to the political inclusion of the Roma.

The National Movement Simeon II, registered as a party in April 2002, was founded by Simeon Saxe-Coburg-Gotha, the exiled son of Tsar Boris. Simeon Saxe-Coburg-Gotha's advisors and top ministers were young Bulgarian emigrants who, having built careers abroad mostly in Western finance, returned to their homeland to affect economic change. The NMS2 proposed to bring about change to Bulgaria's economic and political outlook within 800 days. Thousands of Bulgarians hastened to join the NMS2 in what many saw as a protest against those who had ruled Bulgaria since the collapse of communism. In the 2001 elections the NMS2 took the lead in forming a new government but the popularity of the party quickly declined. The movement placed NATO and EU integration high on the political agenda. After the 2005 elections the party received only half of the seats it had in the previous assembly, and in 2009 it did not pass the threshold for entry in parliament.

In the 25 June 2005 parliamentary elections, the Coalition for Bulgaria (dominated by the Bulgarian Socialist Party) won 31.1% of the vote and received a total of 82 seats in the 240-seat assembly. The National Movement Simeon II (NMS2) garnered 19.9%, and 53 seats. The Movement for Rights and Freedoms (MRF) ranked third with 12.7% and 34 seats. The surprise in the 2005 elections was that the nationalist coalition ATAKA received 8.1% of the vote and 21 seats. The United Democratic Forces (UDF), which was supported by 7.7% of voters, received 20 seats, whereas the other rightist party, Democrats for Strong Bulgaria (DSB), won 6.4% and 17 seats. Lastly, the Bulgarian People's Union (BPU), a coalition of the Union of Free Democrats (UFD) and the Agrarian Party of Anastasia Mozer (BANU), won 5.2% and 13 seats.

Georgi Parvanov, a former member of both the Communist Party and the Socialist Party, has been an independent candidate since he first took office as president in 2002. He was reelected in 2006. After Parvanov completed his two terms allowed in the constitution, the 2011 presidential elections were won in a second-round vote by Rosen Plevneliev of the Citizens for the European Development of Bulgaria (CEDB) who took office in 2012.

In the July 2009 legislative elections, the socialist-led coalition was soundly defeated by the CEDB, which won 39.7% of the vote and 116 seats in the 240-seat assembly. The Bulgarian Socialist Party took 17.7% of the vote and 40 seats in the assembly, followed by the Movement for Rights and Freedom with 14.5% and 38 seats, the ATAKA (Attack party) with 9.4% and 21 seats, the Blue Coalition with 6.8% and 15 seats, and the new Order, Law, Justice party (OLJ) with 4.1% and 10 seats. Boyko Borissov of CEDB was elected as prime minister.

15 LOCAL GOVERNMENT

Bulgaria is divided into 262 municipalities (*obshtini*). The municipality is the main administrative territorial unit for local government and is governed by a mayor and an elected municipal council. Municipal councils determine the policy of every municipality, including economic development, environmental, and educational policies, as well as cultural activities. Mayors are in charge of the whole executive activity of their municipality, of keeping the public order, and of organizing distribution of the municipal budget.

Bulgaria is also divided into 28 regions (*oblasti*), which are larger administrative territorial units through which the government decentralizes its policies. The Council of Ministers appoints the regional governor for each province.

In preparation for EU accession, six planning regions were created in 1999 to fulfill the requirements for receiving cohesion funds. However, as of the end of the 2000s, those regions existed on paper only.

16 JUDICIAL SYSTEM

Bulgaria has an independent judicial system. The 1991 constitution provides for regional courts, district courts, a Supreme Court of Cassation (appeals), which rules on decisions by the lower courts, and a Supreme Administrative Court, which rules on the legality of actions by institutions of government. A constitutional court is responsible for judicial review of legislation and for resolving issues of competency of the other branches of government as well as impeachments and election law. Judges are appointed by the Supreme Judicial Council, which organizes and administers the judiciary. The constitutional court has 12 judges appointed to a nine-year term by parliament, the president, and judicial authorities.

Military courts handle cases involving military personnel and national security issues. Under the 1991 constitution, the judiciary is independent of the legislative and executive branches. The trials are public. Criminal defendants have the right to confront witnesses, the right to counsel, and the right to know the charges against them to prepare their defense. The constitution prohibits arbitrary interference with privacy, home, or correspondence.

Bulgaria accepts compulsory jurisdiction of the International Court of Justice.

17 ARMED FORCES

The International Institute for Strategic Studies reports that armed forces in Bulgaria totaled 31,315 members in 2011. The force is comprised of 16,304 from the army, 3,471 from the navy, 6,706 from the air force, and 4,834 members of central staff. Armed forces represent 2% of the labor force in Bulgaria. The defense budget totaled $1.04 billion in 2009 and $609 million in 2010, as the armed forces were being reduced in number after the 2007 end of conscription. In 2011 Bulgaria participated in seven multi-national missions abroad, including Afghanistan and Iraq.

18 INTERNATIONAL COOPERATION

Bulgaria joined the United Nations on 14 December 1955 and participates in the ECE group and all the nonregional specialized agencies. It belongs to the WTO (1996) and became a member of the European Union in 2007. The nation also belongs to NATO (2004), the Council of Europe, the Central European Initiative, the Central European Free Trade Agreement (CEFTA), and the OSCE. Bulgaria is part of the Australia Group, the Zangger Committee, the European Organization for Nuclear Research (CERN), and the Nuclear Suppliers Group (London Group). It is a guest in the Nonaligned Movement. In environmental cooperation, Bulgaria is part of the Antarctic Treaty, the Basel Convention, Conventions on Biological Diversity and Air Pollution, Ramsar, CITES, the Kyoto Protocol, the Montréal Protocol, MARPOL, the Nuclear Test Ban Treaty, and the UN Conventions on the Law of the Sea, Climate Change, and Desertification.

19 ECONOMY

The gross domestic product (GDP) rate of change in Bulgaria, as of 2010, was 0.2%. Inflation stood at 2.9%, and unemployment was reported at 11%.

Before World War II Bulgaria was an agricultural country, consisting mainly of small peasant farms; farming provided a livelihood for about 80% of the population. After the war, the Communist regime initiated an industrialization program. By 1947 a sizable portion of the economy was nationalized, and collectivization of agriculture followed during the 1950s. Until 1990 the country had a centrally planned economy, along Soviet lines, and its sequence of five-year economic plans, beginning in 1949, emphasized heavy industrial production. In 1956, according to official Bulgarian statistics, industry contributed 36.5% of national income, and agriculture and forestry, 32.9%; in 1992, the respective contributions were 42.5% and 12%.

Although Bulgaria has brown coal and lignite, iron ore, copper lead, zinc, and manganese, it lacks other important natural resources and must export in order to pay for needed commodities. Because it relied on the former USSR and other CMEA countries for essential imports and as the major market for its exports, and lacked large foreign exchange reserves, the Bulgarian economy was greatly influenced by the breakup of the Soviet Bloc and the switch to hard-currency foreign trade. In the 1970s the economic growth rate was quite high (6.8% annually), but the pace of growth slowed in the 1980s, mainly because of energy shortages. The average annual growth rate was only 2% in that decade.

With the disintegration of Soviet Bloc trade and payments arrangements, GDP declined by about 10% in 1990, 13% in 1991, 8% in 1992, and an estimated 4% in 1993. Meanwhile, Bulgaria began an economic reform program supported by the World Bank and the International Monetary Fund (IMF). But the economy remained largely state controlled, although there was progress in privatizing many smaller enterprises. The private sector accounted for only about 20% of GDP in 1993 and 45% in 1996. Efforts at economic reform stalled in 1994 as the Socialist government again failed to privatize state-owned industries and institute structural reforms aimed at creating a market economy. The economy was further plagued by wide-scale corruption among businessmen from the former Communist Party who stripped state enterprises of their assets and transferred the funds out of the country. By 1997 the Bulgarian economy was at the brink of collapse with inflation at 300%, the banking system in chaos, and the government on the verge of bankruptcy. Bulgaria became the poorest country in Europe with average monthly wages of $30 a month.

Angry with the governing Socialists, tens of thousands of Bulgarians demonstrated in all major cities calling for early elections. In April of 1997 a new government took power and instituted structural reforms designed to bring order to the economy. The government of Prime Minister Ivan Kostov quickly moved to implement market reforms. While operating under the direction of an IMF currency board, Bulgaria pegged the lev to the deutschmark (and later to the euro), and reduced inflation to 1%. In 1997 the private sector accounted for 65% of GDP. This milestone marked the first time in the post-Communist era that the private sector outperformed the public sector in production. In addition to structural reforms, the Kostov government also moved to combat corruption by becoming the first non-OECD country to ratify the anti-bribery convention.

Industry increasingly was being privatized, and agriculture was almost completely privatized. Bulgaria started accession talks with the European Union in 2000, but was not one of 10 new countries formally invited in December 2002 to join the body. Bulgaria did join the European Union in 2007, along with Romania. Bulgaria's laws were formally harmonized with EU laws, and customs barriers between them were repealed in preparation for Bulgaria's entry into the single market. By the end of 1999 more than 50% of Bulgaria's exports went to EU nations and in 2010 the figure passed 60%.

Following the 2001 elections that brought Simeon Saxe-Coburg-Gotha to office as prime minister, the stock market soared more than 100% (from 12.5% turnover in 2001 to 27.9% in 2002), but the government in 2002 was unable to live up to its pledge to improve living standards. Foreign direct investment rose modestly in 2002, and although economic growth slowed that year from its 5.8% high in 2000, it was higher than that of many other European countries. Tourism was strong in 2002, and although the weather was poor that year, Bulgaria's agricultural sector performed well. Taxes were lowered to 10% flat for individual income, corporate profit and capital gains.

Bulgaria's overall economic performance was positive over the mid-2000s. According to World Bank data, in 2004, the GDP grew by 6.7%. This six-plus percent growth continued through 2008, fueled by an increase in domestic demand (encouraged by higher real wages and remittances from abroad), a more dynamic job market, and bank credits. Inflation was rather high in the mid-2000s, peaking at 9.2% in 2007. At 9%, unemployment was on a downward path in 2006, and dropped even further by 2009, to 6.8%. This was the result of a more dynamic private job market, and government policies geared towards unemployment reduction. Corruption and organized crime, however, remain stumbling blocks to Bulgaria's economic success. Additionally, the 2008–09 global financial crisis and the euro troubles (Bulgaria is not a member of the eurozone, but its currency is pegged to the European currency) affected the economic outlook for the country negatively. In 2009 the GDP contracted by approximately 5% and stagnated further in 2010, despite a recovery in exports.

20 INCOME

The CIA estimated that in 2010 the GDP of Bulgaria was $96.78 billion. The CIA defines GDP as the value of all final goods and services produced within a nation in a given year and computed on the basis of purchasing power parity (PPP), rather than value as measured on the basis of the rate of the exchange based on current dollars. The per capita GDP was estimated at $13,500. The annual growth rate of GDP was 0.2% in 2010. The average inflation rate was 2.9% in 2010. It was estimated that agriculture accounted for 5.3% of GDP, industry 30.1%, and services 64.6%.

According to the World Bank, remittances from citizens living abroad totaled $1.39 billion in 2010 or about $185 per capita and accounted for approximately 3% of GDP.

The World Bank reports that in 2010, household consumption in Bulgaria totaled $32.2 billion or about $4,536 per capita, measured in current US dollars rather than PPP. Household consumption includes expenditures of individuals, households, and nongovernmental organizations on goods and services, excluding the purchases of dwellings. It was estimated that household consumption was declining at an average annual rate of 3% for two years in a row after the 2008 global crisis.

As of 2011 the most recent study by the World Bank reported that actual individual consumption in Bulgaria was 78.4% of GDP and accounted for 0.15% of world consumption. By comparison, the United States accounted for 25.44% of world individual consumption. The World Bank also estimated that18.8% of Bulgaria's GDP was spent on food and beverages, 17.8% on housing and household furnishings, 2.4% on clothes, 6.5% on health, 13.3% on transportation, 4.5% on communications, 4.3% on recreation, 6.6% on restaurants and hotels, and 0.5% on miscellaneous goods and services and purchases from abroad.

It was estimated that in 2008 about 21.8% of the population subsisted on an income below the poverty line established by Bulgaria's government.

21 LABOR

As of 2010 Bulgaria had a total labor force of 2.499 million people. Within that labor force, CIA estimates in 2009 noted that 7.1% were employed in agriculture, 35.2% in industry, and 57.7% in the service sector. Unemployment was officially reported at 1% in 2009, although actual rates were believed to be higher.

The constitution guarantees the right of all to form or join trade unions of their own choosing. The labor code recognizes the right to strike when all other means of conflict resolution have been exhausted. Essential employees, mainly military and law enforcement personnel, are forbidden to strike and political strikes are prohibited as well. About 20% of Bulgaria's workforce is unionized.

Minimum age for employment is 16 years, with 18 years the minimum for hazardous work. In the formal sector these regulations are generally observed, but children participate in work in certain industries, family operations, and illegal businesses. The law establishes a standard workweek of 40 hours with at least one 24-hour rest period per week. Overtime rates of no less than 150% during weekdays, 175% during weekends, and 200% during official holidays are mandated by law. The minimum wage was about $185 per month as of 2011, but is inadequate to support a worker and a family with a decent standard of living. Minimum health and safety standards exist and are effectively enforced in the public sector, but not effectively enforced in the largely unregulated and often informal private sector.

22 AGRICULTURE

Roughly 32% of the total land is farmed, and the country's major crops include vegetables, fruits, tobacco, grapes, wheat, barley, sunflowers, and sugar beets. In 2009 cereal production amounted to 6.2 million tons, fruit production 405,897 tons, and vegetable production 502,702 tons.

The average annual agricultural growth rate was -2.1% for 1980–90 and -0.4% for 1990–2000. By 2000 agricultural output was only two-thirds of what it was in 1990. However, during 2002–04, crop production averaged 2.9% higher than during 1999–2001. In 2005 agriculture accounted for 9.3% of GDP. In 2004 agriculture (including fishing and forestry) engaged about 11% of the economically active population.

Collectivized agriculture became the norm under the Communist government after 1958. In March 1991 the government adopted a land law which restored ownership rights to former owners of expropriated land. These owners were to receive 20–30 hectares (49–74 acres) each of land approximating the type and location of the former holdings, regardless of whether or not the owner cultivates that land. After February 1991 full price liberalization for producers and consumers was to occur. However, the

agricultural sector was still shrinking due to the lack of progress in the implementation of privatization and property restitution. A grain crisis developed when Bulgaria exported a million tons of wheat in 1995. Currency depreciations, increased taxes, and lack of funds exacerbated the disintegration of the agricultural sector in the mid-1990s.

The principal grain-growing areas are the Danube tableland and southern Dobrudja. The production of major crops in 2009 (in thousands of metric tons) was wheat, 3,976; corn, 1,291; barley, 859; sunflower seeds, 1,318; and rapeseed, 235.

Bulgaria is a major supplier of grapes, apples, and tomatoes to Europe and the former Soviet Union. Potatoes and paprika are also important crops. Production in 2009 included (in thousands of metric tons): grapes, 281; apples, 35; tomatoes, 104; and potatoes, 232. About 52 thousand tons of tobacco were also produced that year.

Machinery available to agriculture has increased significantly. Tractors rose from 25,800 units in 1960 to 53,800 units in 1985, before falling to 32,100 in 2002; combines increased from 7,000 to 16,000 in 1985, but by 2002 numbered only 9,000 in use. About 16% of the cultivated area is irrigated.

23 ANIMAL HUSBANDRY

The UN Food and Agriculture Organization (FAO) reported that Bulgaria dedicated 1.7 million hectares (4.77 million acres) to permanent pasture or meadow in 2009. During that year, the country tended 17.4 million chickens, 1.4 million sheep, 547,866 head of cattle, and 729,798 pigs. The production from these animals amounted to 37,976 tons of beef / veal and mutton, 73,660 tons of pork, 130,152 tons of poultry, 1,430,000 eggs, and 1.27 million tons of milk. Bulgaria also produced 4,427 tons of cattle hide and 7,353 tons of raw wool.

24 FISHING

Bulgaria had 41 decked commercial fishing boats in 2008. The annual capture totaled 8,861 tons according to the UN FAO. The export value of seafood totaled $10.59 million.

Fishing resources in the Black Sea are less than abundant. Before 1960 the annual catch was slightly above 5,000 tons. Fishing output reached a high of 167,100 tons in 1976, then fell to 115,607 tons in 1982. Prior to 1989 Bulgaria used to produce about 20,000 tons of fish from freshwater aquaculture. The fish farms and fish processing industries went through major restructuring and privatization during the 1990s. Only after 2000 did the fish industry register some growth. Fishing vessels are based at the ports of Varna and Burgas. The most popular river fish is sturgeon. Due to environmental limitations, the government sets an annual sturgeon quota; for 2003 it was 22 tons. The beluga caviar quota set that year was 1,720 kg (3,780 lb).

25 FORESTRY

Forests cover 3,927,000 hectares (9,703,828 acres), or 36.2% of Bulgaria's territory. The UN FAO estimated the 2010 roundwood production at 3 million cu m (106 million cu ft). The value of all forest products, including roundwood, totaled $371 million.

About 80% of the total forest area is wooded forestland. Forests are about 34% coniferous and 66% deciduous, and mainly occupy regions of higher altitudes. Over half of the forests in Bulgaria are situated on slopes of over 20°, making harvesting and reforestation very difficult. The principal lumbering areas are the Rila and western Rhodope Mountains in the southwest and the northern slopes of the Balkan Mountains in the center. Forestry and the forest industry contribute about 2% to the GDP.

Intensive exploitation and neglect before and during World War II (1939–45) and even more intensive exploitation following the war contributed to the deterioration of the forests. So during 1945–65, 860,000 hectares (2,125,000 acres) were reforested; the 20-year plan (1961–80) called for the planting of 1.4 million hectares (3.5 million acres). During the 1980s annual reforestation averaged 50,000 hectares (123,500 acres). Despite the intensive harvesting during 1950–73 (which exceeded the government's Forest Management Plan-FMP), the total timber volume increased from 165 million cu m (5.8 billion cu ft) in 1934 to 404 million cu m (14 billion cu ft) in 1995. The FMP decreased the amount of timber permitted to be cut from 6.8 million cu m (240 million cu ft) in 1955 to 6.2 million cu m (219 million cu ft) of roundwood in 1995 because fewer large trees are available. Roundwood production has decreased from 8.6 million cu m (304 million cu ft) in 1960 to 4.8 million cu m (522 million cu ft) in 2003. Forestry exports in 2003 totaled $139.3 million. Bulgaria exports logs to Turkey, Greece, Italy, and Macedonia; veneer to Greece and Syria; and particleboard to Greece, Macedonia, and Egypt. The main problems prohibiting greater roundwood production are diseases, drying of trees, and pests. Acid rain and heavy metals have not hurt the local forests. In 1998, the government began a forestry restitution and privatization program covering 3.6 million hectares (8.9 million acres). The average annual reforestation rate was 0.6% during 1990–2000.

26 MINING

As of 2011 Bulgaria was an important regional producer of non-ferrous metal ores and concentrates, and was mostly self-sufficient in mineral requirements. Mining and metalworking in the region was well documented by Roman times, when Bulgaria and Romania, known respectively as Thrace and Dacia, were important sources of base and precious metals. Small quantities of bismuth, chromite, copper, gold, iron, lead, magnesite, manganese, molybdenum, palladium, platinum, silver, tellurium, tin, uranium, and zinc are mined, as well as the industrial minerals anhydrite, asbestos fiber, barite, bentonite, common clays, refractory clays, dolomite, feldspar, fluorspar, gypsum, kaolin, industrial lime, limestone, nitrogen (in ammonia), perlite, pyrites, salt (all types), sand and gravel, silica (quartz sand), calcined sodium carbonate, dimension stone, sulfur (content of pyrite), sulfuric acid, and crushed stone. Most of the copper deposits are within a roughly 50 km-wide (30-mi) swath from Burgas in the east, to the former Yugoslavia in the west, and almost all is produced by two enterprises, Asarel-Medet, at Panagurishte, and Elatzite-Med, at Srednogorie; copper is also mined at Burgas and Malko Turnovo. Lead and zinc are mined chiefly in the Rhodope Mountains, at Madan and Rudozem. Production outputs for 2009 were: gold, 4,300 kg; gross copper, 27,800,000 tons; barite ore (run of mine), 14,300,000 metric tons; limestone and dolomite, 3,100,000 tons; industrial lime,

1,300,000 tons; and silica, 650,000 tons. Manganese ore production was zero in 2000, but totaled 39,100 metric tons in 2009.

In 1998 the National Program for Sustainable Development of Mining in Bulgaria was drafted and approved, and the Underground Resources Act was enacted. The latter, which aimed to promote private enterprise and foreign investment, stipulated that underground mineral wealth was the property of the state, and provided for claims by domestic and foreign companies for the development and operation of mineral deposits for up to 35 years with potential 15-year extensions. Improved economic performance at the end of the 1990s, the significant shift away from economic uncertainties during the transition from central economic planning, improving political stability in the Balkans, and greater investor confidence in the legal underpinnings of the growing privatization process combined to contribute to the $1 billion net foreign investment in 2000, one-third more than in 1999. As of 2007 mining and quarrying made up 4.4% of industrial activity and employed 26,800 people.

27 ENERGY AND POWER

The World Bank reported in 2008 that Bulgaria produced 44.6 billion kWh of electricity and consumed a little over 35 billion kWh, or 4,594 kWh per capita. Roughly 76% of energy came from fossil fuels, while 22% came from alternative fuels. Per capita oil consumption was 2,595 kg. Oil production totaled 2,925 barrels of oil a day in 2010, ranking 100th according to the CIA's list of oil-producing countries in the world.

Bulgaria has only modest reserves of oil and natural gas, but somewhat larger recoverable reserves of coal. But it is nuclear power that allows Bulgaria to be an exporter of electricity.

Bulgaria's nuclear power generating capability allows the country to be a power exporter. That capability is based upon its Kozloduy facility, which has six reactors, of which only two are working since 2004, under an agreement with the European Commission. Nuclear power generated about 35% of all electricity. In 2010 Bulgaria's electricity exports marked a record high of 7,500 GWh (21.6% of the total power produced domestically), almost doubling the 2009 figure of 3,700 GWh. The main markets were Serbia, Montenegro, Kosovo, Greece, Turkey, and Macedonia.

Bulgaria is heavily reliant on petroleum product imports. Consumption was estimated in 2009 at 91,000 barrels per day. Exploration for oil and natural gas is primarily centered in the Black Sea and in the northern part of the country. Bulgaria's sole refinery is located at Burgas, the country's main port.

Bulgaria's consumption of natural gas far exceeds its proven reserves and production, and it must rely on imports to meet almost its entire natural gas needs. As of 2011 Bulgaria's proven reserves of natural gas were estimated at 0.2 trillion cu ft. Output in 2010 was estimated at only 1.9 billion cu ft. Imports and consumption were both estimated to be around 90 billion cu ft for the same year.

Coal is the most important mineral fuel, with lignite accounting for nearly 90% and brown coal for around 10%. Bulgaria was estimated in 2004 to have recoverable coal reserves of 5,552 million short tons. Production, consumption and imports of coal are estimated at: 26.2 million short tons; 33.4 million short tons; and 4.0 million short tons, respectively

28 INDUSTRY

Before World War II, Bulgarian industry, construction, mining, and handicrafts contributed only 17% to the net national income and accounted for only 8% of employment. Handicrafts in 1939 contributed almost half the net industrial output, followed by textiles and food processing. In the postwar period, the Communist regime nationalized industry and, through economic planning, emphasized a heavy industrialization program that resulted in a substantial increase in the metalworking and chemical industries. Between 1950 and 1960 the annual rate of growth of output in industry (including mining and power production) was 14.8%, according to the official index of gross output. Official statistics indicate that industrial output grew by 1,100% between 1956 and 1980, with the production of capital goods increasing by 1,500% and the production of consumer goods by 658%. Industrial output increased by 9.1% annually during 1971–75, 6% during 1976–80, 6.8% during 1980–85, and 2.7% during 1985–90. Ferrous metallurgy was given special emphasis in the 1960s, machine-building and chemicals in the 1970s and early 1980s, and high technology in the mid-1980s.

Even after the collapse of communism, industrial and agricultural production fell annually until 1997 and 1998, respectively, when the Kostov reforms took effect. Although traditional industries remain the foundation of the industrial sector, Bulgaria expects high-technology production to post gains in the future as high-tech companies establish operation there.

Industry accounted for about 30% of GDP in 2010. The privatization of Bulgaria's industries was largely complete as of 2002, with the exception of a few large companies. For instance, Bulgartabac—after five aborted sale attempts—only seemed to be on its way to private ownership in 2011. The construction sector realized strong growth during the late 2000s, serving as a backbone of a general economic boom, due to the need to undertake major infrastructure projects. Even after the financial slump in 2008–09, its share of the GDP remained at 8.1% in 2010.

Primary industries include electricity, gas and water, food, beverages and tobacco, machinery and equipment, base metals, chemical products, coke, refined petroleum, and nuclear fuel. Bulgaria also produces electrical components and computers. The industrial production growth rate was 2% in 2010.

29 SCIENCE AND TECHNOLOGY

Patent applications in science and technology, as of 2009, according to the World Bank, totaled 242 in Bulgaria. Total financing of science was 0.49% of GDP, with the majority of resources coming from the public sector. As part of the European 2020 Strategy, the target for research and development investment was set to rise to 1.5% of the GDP. The Bulgarian Academy of Sciences (founded in 1869) is the main research organization. The Academy of Medicine (founded in 1972) has five higher medical institutes. In 2008 there were 1,149 researchers and 476 technicians per million people, actively engaged in research and development. High technology exports in 2009 totaled $714 million, accounting for 8% of the country's manufactured exports.

Bulgaria has 53 universities and colleges offering degrees in basic and applied sciences. In Sofia are the National Natural History Museum (founded in 1889) and the National Polytechnical Muse-

Principal Trading Partners – Bulgaria (2010)				
(In millions of US dollars)				
Country	Total	Exports	Imports	Balance
World	45,969.1	20,608.0	25,361.1	-4,753.1
Germany	5,156.1	2,198.0	2,958.1	-760.0
Russia	4,647.1	568.1	4,079.0	-3,510.9
Italy	3,874.3	1,997.7	1,876.6	121.0
Romania	3,673.6	1,903.7	1,769.9	133.8
Greece	3,143.8	1,634.1	1,509.8	124.3
Turkey	2,907.1	1,593.7	1,313.4	280.3
France	1,669.3	833.9	835.4	-1.6
Ukraine	1,309.6	258.7	1,050.8	-792.1
Austria	1,274.8	390.0	884.8	-494.8
Belgium	1,250.0	769.7	480.3	289.4

(…) data not available or not significant.

(n.s.) not specified.

SOURCE: *2011 Direction of Trade Statistics Yearbook*, New York: United Nations, 2011.

um (founded in 1968). In 2010 science and engineering students accounted for 21% of university enrollment.

30 DOMESTIC TRADE

Private shops and small supermarkets are open in many cities and local farmers' markets are still active. A few warehouse stores have opened in Sofia. The government has remained committed to privatization efforts. By the end of 2009 about 99.18% of state-owned assets subject to privatization had been privatized, which amounted to 65.49% of all state-owned assets. Bulgaria has also attracted a number of foreign investors, including US companies such as American Standard, McDonald's, Kraft Foods, and Hilton International. However, Germany is the top foreign investor.

Newspapers and magazines are the important means of advertising to the population at large. Radio advertisements are permitted for half an hour each day.

Generally, business office hours are from 9 a.m. to 6 p.m., Monday through Friday, although meetings in the afternoon are to be avoided. Normal banking hours are 9 a.m. to 3 p.m., Monday–Friday. Stores are usually open from 9 a.m. to 7 p.m. on weekdays.

31 FOREIGN TRADE

Bulgaria imported $23.86 billion worth of goods and services in 2010, while exporting $20.64 billion worth of goods and services. Major import partners in 2010 were Russia, 16.3%; Germany, 11.8%; Italy, 7.5%; Romania, 7.1%; Greece, 6%; Turkey, 5.2%; Ukraine, 4.2%. Its major export partners were Germany, 10.9%; Italy, 9.9%; Romania, 9.5%; Greece, 8.1%; Turkey, 7.9%; and France, 4.1%.

The principal imports were crude oil, natural gas, diesel fuel, fuel oil, coal, textiles, and machinery and equipment.

Geographic distribution of trade has changed radically twice: after World War II and following the collapse of the Soviet Bloc. Whereas before the war Bulgaria traded mainly with the countries of Western and Central Europe, after the war, trade shifted almost entirely to the countries of the Communist Bloc. In 1991 about 49.8% of all exports still went to the former USSR and 43.2% of all imports still came from the former USSR.

Balance of Payments – Bulgaria (2010)

(In millions of US dollars)

Current Account		-578.0
Balance on goods	-3,217.4	
Imports	-23,825.6	
Exports	20,608.2	
Balance on services	2,437.8	
Balance on income	-1,834.8	
Current transfers	2,036.3	
Capital Account		391.3
Financial Account		-41.1
Direct investment abroad	-236.0	
Direct investment in Bulgaria	2,167.5	
Portfolio investment assets	-738.8	
Portfolio investment liabilities	-19.9	
Financial derivatives	-32.9	
Other investment assets	482.7	
Other investment liabilities	-1,663.7	
Net Errors and Omissions		-377.5
Reserves and Related Items		605.3

(…) data not available or not significant.

SOURCE: *Balance of Payment Statistics Yearbook 2011*, Washington, DC: International Monetary Fund, 2011.

By the mid-1990s weak demand in the former Soviet bloc markets led to an increase in exports to European Union countries, which in 2011 accounted for about 60% of Bulgaria's exports. Other important export areas include Central and Eastern European, and other OECD countries.

32 BALANCE OF PAYMENTS

In 2010 Bulgaria had a foreign trade deficit of $3.9 billion, amounting to 3.3% of GDP.

During the postwar industrialization program, Bulgaria had a trade imbalance, made up largely by credits, particularly from the former USSR. From 1952 to 1958 the country had visible export surpluses, but another industrialization drive resulted in a trade imbalance during 1959–61, and there were persistent imbalances during the latter part of the 1960s. In the early 1970s export surpluses were reported for most years; there were also small surpluses in 1979, 1980, and 1984. With the collapse of COMECON trade, Bulgaria began exporting agricultural products and light manufactured products in exchange for consumer goods. During the first nine months of 1992, Bulgaria recorded its first surplus in many years. Failure of the government to institute economic reforms, however, led to severe economic hardship and trade deficits of $1.4 billion in 1993 and $1.6 billion in 1994. In 1994 the deficit was partially financed by almost $1.1 billion in aid from other countries and international financial institutions. According to the IMF, in 2010 the current account deficit was 5.5% of GDP, a drop from the 2009 level of 8.5%.

Bulgaria's total reserves (including gold) amounted to $17.78 billion in 2011.

33 BANKING AND SECURITIES

The Bulgarian National Bank (BNB) acts as the Central Bank of Bulgaria. Established in 1879, BNB has as its primary goal the stabilization of the national currency, the lev. It is also responsible for the minting and printing of the national currency, as well as being its sole issuer. As the national regulator and supervisor of the banking sector, it grants banking licenses and gathers and inspects data from the commercial banks. It also supervises and licenses the nation's non-bank financial institutions. The BNB also administers the Government Securities Depository and monitors the Central Depository. The bank is administered by a governor and three deputy governors.

All banks were nationalized in 1947 in accord with Soviet banking policies. In 1969 the BNB was renamed the Bulgarian Central Bank and remained the bank of issue. Two new banks—the Industrial Bank and the Agricultural and Trade Bank—assumed the functions of providing credit for industry and for agriculture and individuals, respectively. In 1968, the Bulgarian Foreign Trade Bank was established as a joint-stock company. The State Savings Bank was the chief savings institution.

In late January of 1997 the BNB announced that it would no longer be fixing a base interest rate. Instead, the BNB would set an indicative rate defined by the interest on short-term government bonds. Banks themselves would be able to set their own rates according to market principles, without interference from the central bank. In 2011 the lev remained pegged to the euro at a constant value of 1.955 levas for one euro, averaging about 1.45 levas to the dollar.

The history of the Bulgarian capital market dates back to the beginning of the 20th century, when in 1914 the first real stock exchange was established in Bulgaria under a 1907 Stock Exchange Act. Activity started in 1918, but trading was suspended between 1925 and 1928 and later, during the world Great Depression of 1929–33 the exchange worked on a very small scale due to the large number of company bankruptcies. In 1947, due to the new nationalized nature of the economy, the Sofia Stock Exchange ceased its operations.

The present-day exchange, the Bulgarian Stock Exchange-Sofia (BSE–Sofia), was officially licensed by the State Securities and Exchange Commission on 9 October 1997, after several years during which a number of regional exchanges operated in a completely unregulated environment. As of June 2007 BSE–Sofia has been a full member of the Federation of European Exchanges. Managed by a board of directors and two chief executive officers, BSE—Sofia publishes the SOFIX, BG40, BGTR30 and BGREIT indices. BSE's market capitalization as of December 2011 stood at $8.5 billion, with the SOFIX Index down 8.12% from the previous year at 361.01.

34 INSURANCE

Private insurance companies were nationalized in 1947 and absorbed into the State Insurance Institute. Property insurance and life insurance are compulsory for collective farms and voluntary for cooperatives, social organizations, and the population in general. Insurance policies and premiums have increased steadily for both. Third-party automobile liability and workers' compensation are also compulsory insurances. The insurance regulatory body is the Ministry of Finance. Since March of 1998 foreigners have been permitted to own a Bulgarian insurer.

35 PUBLIC FINANCE

In 2010 the budget of Bulgaria included $15.71 billion in public revenue and $17.52 billion in public expenditures. The budget deficit amounted to 4% of GDP. Public debt was 16.2% of GDP, with $47.15 billion of the debt held by foreign entities.

An annual budget for all levels of government, becoming effective on 1 January, is voted by parliament, after having been prepared by the Ministry of Finance. The disintegration of the communist system in November 1989 and the subsequent collapse of the Soviet trade bloc caused severe economic disruption, pushing the government's budget deficit to 8.5% of GDP in 1990 (not including interest payments on commercial foreign debt). However, by the late 1990s the country was seeing unprecedented growth (5.8% in 2000), due to aggressive market reforms put in place by the government during the prior decade.

36 TAXATION

Bulgaria revised much of its communist-era tax system first in 1996 and then most recently in 2007. As of 2011 individual income is subject to a 10% flat tax, as is standard corporate income. Special corporate rates apply for certain types of businesses, for example, shipping and gambling, as well as self-employment. Employers are required to contribute 17.8–18.5% of employees' gross salaries for social security insurance while the employees contribute an additional 12.9%. The value-added tax covers all goods, services and imports at a standard rate of 20%. However, exemptions include insurance and financial services, the transfer of or the renting of land, and educational and health-related services, which are taxed at 9%. Other taxes include a 5% tax on dividends, property tax at a variable rate but no more than 4.5%, and a vehicle tax (called "vignette) that is levied per year (month/week for visitors).

37 CUSTOMS AND DUTIES

The essential customs law was harmonized with European Commission *acquis* as of 2007. Most imports are subject only to declaration and registration. However, special licenses are required for imports of tobacco, alcoholic beverages, oils, military hardware, radioactive materials, jewelry, precious metals, pharmaceutical items, and narcotics. The National Customs Agency supervises the collection of customs duties.

Goods arriving from foreign (non-EU) points to be unloaded in Bulgaria must have customs manifests and other shipping documents as specified by law. Customs duties are paid ad valorem at a rate of 5–40% on industrial products and 5–70% on agricultural products. Duty must be paid on all goods except those specifically exempt, such as many foods products, farm machinery, toiletries, fertilizer and pesticide, mining equipment, and medical and dental supplies.

38 FOREIGN INVESTMENT

Foreign direct investment (FDI) in Bulgaria was a net inflow of $2.17 billion for 2010 according to World Bank figures, a sharp

Public Finance – Bulgaria (2009)		
(In millions of leva, central government figures)		
Revenue and Grants	**23,292**	**100.0%**
Tax revenue	14,358	61.6%
Social contributions	5,273	22.6%
Grants	1,167	5.0%
Other revenue	2,494	10.7%
Expenditures	**23,357**	**100.0%**
General public services	5,854	25.1%
Defense	1,116	4.8%
Public order and safety	1,767	7.6%
Economic affairs	1,644	7.0%
Environmental protection	269	1.2%
Housing and community amenities	103	0.4%
Health	2,403	10.3%
Recreational, culture, and religion	291	1.2%
Education	1,181	5.1%
Social protection	8,726	37.4%
(…) data not available or not significant.		

SOURCE: *Government Finance Statistics Yearbook 2010*, Washington, DC: International Monetary Fund, 2010.

drop from the 2007 peak of $13.21 billion. In 2010 FDI represented 5% of GDP.

In 2011 energy, information technology, transportation, telecommunications, and agriculture were all sectors of major investment potential in Bulgaria. Government bureaucracy has been sighted as an impediment to investment, as has a weak judicial system and corruption.

Under legislation from 1987 and since revised, Bulgaria has six free zones where companies with foreign participation can receive equal or preferential treatment. The most profitable free zone has been the one at Plovdiv. Others are on the Danube (at Ruse and Vidin), near the Turkish border (at Svilengrad), near the Serbia border (Dragoman), and on the Black Sea (at Burgas, which has the most advanced warehousing and trans-shipment facilities). With the establishment of free-market trade, the zones lost most of their economic significance and in 2011 were put up for privatization by the central government.

Capital markets are small and underdeveloped in Bulgaria. The new Bulgaria Stock Exchange opened in 1998 with 998 domestic companies listed and a total market valuation of $992 million. In December 2001 there were 399 listed companies with a market capitalization of $505 million, and since then the number has been closer to that, with 390 domestic companies listed in 2010. However, Bulgaria offers a favorable investment climate, boasting strong economic growth, political stability, a well-educated workforce and competitive costs. It is a good springboard to other markets in Europe and the Middle East, and after its EU accession in 2007 it serves as an entry point to otherwise well protected markets. In that year, the market capitalization value of the companies listed on BSE—Sofia reached a peak of close to $22 billion.

39 ECONOMIC DEVELOPMENT

Until 1990 when the post-Communist government began a program of privatization, the economy was almost entirely nationalized or cooperatively owned and operated on the basis of state plans. These were designed to expand the economy as a whole, with emphasis on the growth of heavy industry (fuels, metals, machinery, chemicals) and on the development of export goods. In 1971, productive enterprises were grouped into more than 60 state concerns responsible for almost all nonagricultural production.

Bulgaria's first five-year plan (1949–53) emphasized capital investment in industry. The period was marked by a slow pace in agricultural production (owing largely to collectivization and small investment), an inadequate supply of consumer goods, and a poor livestock output. The 1953–57 plan provided for a decrease in industrial investment, with a resultant improvement in agriculture, housing, and living conditions. The food-processing industry, important for export, began to receive greater attention in 1958, as did textiles and clothing. The lagging rate of growth during the early 1960s was due mainly to poor agricultural output and to a slower industrial pace. The third five-year plan (1958–62), with its "big leap forward" (1959–60), was claimed to have reached its goals by the end of 1960, but definite shortcomings remained. The fourth plan (1961–65) devoted 70% of total investment to industry, while agriculture received only 6.5%. Investments directed by the fifth plan (1966–70) adhered essentially to precedent, with some shift toward agriculture, and this trend continued under the sixth plan (1971–75). Of total investment during 1971–73, over 40% went to industry and 15% to agriculture. The 1976–80 plan resulted in a 35% increase in industrial output and a 20% increase in agricultural output. The overall growth rate began to slow down in the late 1970s, and the 1981–85 plan reflected the concept of a more gradual economic growth. Under the 1986–90 plan, it was projected that national income would grow by 22–25%, industrial output by 25–30%, and agricultural production by 10–12%. Priority was to be given to the development of high technology.

In the 1990s the post-Communist government began a program to reform the nation's economy. It rescheduled the foreign debt, abolished price controls, and became a member of the International Monetary Fund (IMF) and the International Bank for Reconstruction and Development (IBRD). The reforms, however, were not embraced by the Socialist government that took power in 1994 and by 1996 the economy was in a tailspin. The government, led by Prime Minister Ivan Kostov that took power in 1997, laid the financial groundwork for a market economy by selling off state firms, strengthening the currency (lev), and doing away with price controls, state subsidies, monopolies, and trade restrictions. As a result of its successful stabilization of the lev and inflation, as well as its achievement of EU membership in 2007, Bulgaria is viewed favorably by investors.

The government of Prime Minister Simeon Saxe-Coburg-Gotha, which came to power in 2001, took steps to reduce taxes, rein in corruption, and encourage foreign investment. Bulgaria nevertheless suffers from high unemployment and low standards of living. A $337 million stand-by arrangement with the IMF, approved in February 2002, expired in February 2004. The government, while pledging to the IMF that it would adhere to sound macroeconomic policies (including controlling spending, strengthening tax administration, curbing inflation, balancing the budget, and strengthening the country's external financing position), stated the improvement of Bulgarians' living standards was central to the country's economic development.

Although Bulgaria has registered some of the highest GDP growth rates in Europe, the real income of the population (and subsequently their living standards) have failed to develop as quickly. Policy makers in Bulgaria are therefore looking to match the macroeconomic boom with similar improvements at the population level, particularly in terms of lower unemployment and more job opportunities. The national elections from June 2005 were followed by political turmoil, none of the parties being able to gain a clear majority. Eventually, the socialist party managed to form a government around Prime Minister Sergei Stanishev and promised to continue economic reforms and market restructuring. His coalition government (with NMS2 and MRF) largely continued the earlier policies, additionally instituting flat taxes. Together with Romania, Bulgaria met the EU accession date of 2007. Corruption remains the main point of contention for both countries, and is an issue that still needs to be addressed comprehensively.

The government that came into power in 2009, under the premiership of a former Sofia city mayor, Boyko Borisov and his newly established party, declared that its highest priority would be fighting organized crime and corruption (including abuse and improper use of European funds), achieving energy independence and weathering the consequences for Bulgaria of the global and European economic crises.

40 SOCIAL DEVELOPMENT

The code for compulsory social insurance was revised in 2000. It provides for dual coverage by a social insurance system and mandatory private insurance. The program covers all employees, self-employed persons, farmers, artists, and craftsman. Old-age (pension) benefits began at age 61 and 6 months for men and 56 and 6 months for women; these were increased incrementally until 2009 when retirement became 63 for men and 60 for women. A 2010 agreement between the government, trade unions and employer associations envisioned further annual increases in the retirement age after 2021 until it reaches 65 for men and 65 for women. Survivors' and disability pensions are also provided, as well as work injury and unemployment benefits. All residents are provided with medical care. Parental benefits amount to 100% of earnings for the first year, and the possibility of a second year of leave paid at the minimum salary. The government provides family allowance benefits based on the age and number of children.

Although women have equal rights under the constitution, they have not had the same employment opportunities as men. Although many women attend university, they have a higher rate of unemployment, and are likely to work in low paid jobs. Violence against women remains a serious problem, and domestic violence is considered a family problem and not a criminal matter. The government provides no shelter or counseling for women. There exists societal stigma against rape victims, and while the criminal code prohibits some forms of sexual harassment, it is not comprehensive and is poorly implemented. Trafficking in women remains a huge problem.

A significant problem of discrimination against the Roma minority continued throughout the 2000s with episodic organized protests against and riots within Roma communities in various cities. Although freedom of speech is provided for by the constitution, the government maintains influence over the media and libel is a criminal offense. The government and public have limited tolerance for religious freedom.

41 HEALTH

According to the CIA, life expectancy in Bulgaria was 73 years in 2011. The country spent 7.1% of its GDP on healthcare in 2009, amounting to $475 per person. There were 36 physicians, 47 nurses and midwives, and 65 hospital beds per 10,000 inhabitants. The CIA calculated the HIV/AIDS prevalence rate in Bulgaria to be about 0.1% in 2009. The population has been declining since the end of communism, due both to mass emigration and worse living standards. In 2011 the rate of change was -0.78% which is the steepest decline of any state in the world.

The Ministry of Health is the controlling and policy-making agency for the health system in Bulgaria. The Bulgarian government passed a bill restoring the right of the private sector to practice medicine and permitting the establishment of private pharmacies, dentists, and opticians. Bulgaria is in the process of restructuring its health care system from one based on command and control to one founded on pluralism. Medical care has never been well funded, but the shift from a centrally planned to a private enterprise system has left the medical sector in disarray. Doctors continue to receive low wages and operate inadequate and outdated machinery and patients on the whole receive minimal health services.

Stroke mortality is among the highest in Europe and circulatory diseases account for more than half of all deaths. Smoking has always been high across genders and age groups and is on the increase; alcohol consumption is high; physical activity is low; and obesity is common (12.4% of adults in 2001). Improved maternal and childcare lowered infant mortality from 108.2 per 1,000 in 1951 to 13 per 1,000 in 2000. However, by 2011 the infant mortality rate increased to an estimated 16.68 per 1,000 live births. In 2009 there were 41 cases of tuberculosis per 100,000 people. In the same year Bulgaria immunized children up to one year old as follows: diphtheria, pertussis, and tetanus, 96%, and measles, 96%. An estimated 41.5% of married women used contraception. The fertility rate has decreased from 2.2 per woman in 1960 to 1.42 per woman by 2011. Bulgaria's maternal mortality rate was estimated at 13 per 100,000 live births in 2008. Approximately 99% of the population had access to safe drinking water.

42 HOUSING

There are two main types of housing environments in the country: street district and housing complexes. Most of the street district housing was built before World War II and consists of private lots built to follow a street regulation plan. Beginning in the 1950s, housing complexes were built on public property, though the homes themselves are privately owned. Over 120 complexes have been built since the 1960s, with a large number of prefab homes. Capital investment for housing construction during the period 1976–80 amounted to BGN3.5 billion. At the end of 1985 there were 3,092,000 dwelling units in the country, 24% more than in 1975; by 1991, this figure had risen to 3,406,000. In 2010 there were an estimated 3,804,081 dwellings; about 507 per 1,000 population. The average number of people per household was 2.09. About 11% of all housing stock are one-room dwellings; about

65% are two- or three-room units. About 63% of all dwellings are in urban areas.

43 EDUCATION

In 2009 the World Bank estimated that 97% of age-eligible children in Bulgaria were enrolled in primary school. Secondary enrollment for age-eligible children stood at 82%. Tertiary enrollment was estimated at 54%. Of those enrolled in tertiary education, there were 100 male students for every 132 female students. Overall, the CIA estimated that Bulgaria had a literacy rate of 98.2%, with fairly even rates among men and women. Public expenditure on education represented 4.1% of GDP.

Education is free and compulsory for ten years between the ages of 7 (or 6 at parents' discretion) and 16. Primary education is divided into two stages of four years in each stage. Secondary students then choose between a general studies and a either a vocational or professional training program, each of which lasts for four years. The academic year runs from September to June. The language of instruction is Bulgarian and all schools are coeducational.

The student-to-teacher ratio for primary school was at about 17.4:1 in 2009; the ratio for secondary school was about 9:1 that same year.

There are over 50 higher education institutions, including ten comprehensive universities. The most important is the University of Sofia, founded in 1888. Others include the University of Plovdiv (founded 1961), the University of Veliko Tarnovo (founded 1971), and the American University in Bulgaria (founded 1991). All higher level institutions had a total of 258,692 students and 18,060 teaching staff in 2007.

44 LIBRARIES AND MUSEUMS

The St. Cyril and St. Methodius National Library, established in 1878 in Sofia, is the largest in Bulgaria (7.75 million volumes). Other important libraries are the Bulgarian Academy of Sciences library (1.92 million volumes), the Sofia University Library (2 million volumes), and the Ivan Vazov National Library in Plovdiv (with 1.4 million volumes). The Pencho Slaveykov Public library in Varna has over 800,000 volumes. The Bulgarian Library and Information Association was established in Bulgaria in 1990.

Bulgaria has some 200 museums, of which the most important include the National Archaeological Museum (attached to the Academy of Sciences);the National Art Gallery, founded in 1892; and the National Gallery for Foreign Art, established as a separate entity in 1985. Other museums are devoted to history, science, and the revolutionary movement, and include the Bojana Church Museum in Sofia, the Museum of Wood Carvings and Mural Painting in Trijavna, with an important collection of artifacts from the Bulgarian National Revival Period in the 18th and 19th centuries, and the open-air Architectural Ethnographic Complex "Etar," operating since 1964 near Gabrovo.

45 MEDIA

In 2010 the CIA reported that there were 2.2 million telephone landlines in Bulgaria. In addition to landlines, mobile phone subscriptions averaged 140 per 100 people (or 10.6 million). There were 31 FM radio stations, 63 AM radio stations, and 2 shortwave radio stations. Internet users numbered 45 per 100 citizens. Prominent national dailies numbered 14 in 2009, and included, with circulation numbers listed parenthetically, *Telegraph* (100,000), *Trud* (80,000), *24 Chasa* (60,000), and *Standart* (35,000). Both the number of titles published and the regular readership have declined dramatically from the 1990s.

Bulgaria's telecommunications system is extensive but antiquated. Domestically, over two-thirds of all telephone landlines are residential. Most villages have telephone service and the switching centers in most of the country's regions are linked by a modern digital cable trunk line. International service is provided by a direct dialing system to 58 countries, as well as by satellite ground stations. In 2010 the country had 785,546 Internet hosts.

In Spring 2000, the government awarded a license for the first privately owned television station with nationwide coverage to the Balkan News Corporation (which in 2010 sold the license to BTV Media Group, part of Central European Media Corporation); in 2003, Nova TV became the second national commercial station. In 2010 there were 3 private stations with nation-wide coverage, though there are a number of privately operated regional stations. In 2003 there were an estimated 543 radios for every 1,000 people; the number of television sets was not available in the same survey. It is estimated that about 133 of every 1,000 people subscribe to cable television services.

The constitution of Bulgaria ensures freedom of speech and of the press, and the government is said to generally respect these rights. National television and radio broadcasting remain under supervision of the Council for Electronic Media and the Communications Regulation Commission.

46 ORGANIZATIONS

Bulgaria's important economic organizations include the Bulgarian Chamber of Commerce and Industry (1985) and organizations dedicated to promoting Bulgaria's exports in world markets. There are trade unions representing a wide variety of vocations. The Confederation of Independent Trade Unions of Bulgaria was founded in 1901 and taken over by the Communists after World War II. In 1990 it became an independent organization. It has about 75 member federations and four association members. There are professional and trade organizations representing a variety of fields.

The Bulgarian Medical Association serves as a national organization promoting high standards of healthcare, advancement in medical research, and the free dissemination of health information. There are also several similar medical organizations dedicated to promoting research and education concerning specific conditions and diseases.

There are several associations promoting a wide range of sports and leisure activities, including bobsledding, badminton, baseball, chess, yoga, and amateur radio. The National Federation of Sports in Schools was established in 1993 to promote and coordinate sport activities through the schools. There are national branches of the Olympic Committee, the Special Olympics, and the Paralympic Committee.

The Bulgaria Academy of Science promotes scientific study and advancement, conducts research projects, and maintains a museum. The Institute of Art Studies is cosponsored by the Academy of Science as an organization dedicated to promoting Bulgarian art and culture.

There are national chapters of the Red Cross Society, UNICEF, Helsinki Committee, Habitat for Humanity, and Caritas.

47 TOURISM, TRAVEL, AND RECREATION

The *Tourism Factbook*, published by the UN World Tourism Organization, reported 7.87 million incoming tourists to Bulgaria in 2009, who spent a total of $4.27 billion. Of those incoming tourists, there were 7.6 million from Europe. There were 249,193 hotel beds available in Bulgaria, which had an occupancy rate of 26%. The estimated daily cost to visit Sofia, the capital, was $271. The cost of visiting other cities averaged $151.

Bulgaria is rich in mineral waters and has numerous tourist spas. Visitors are attracted to the Black Sea resorts and the archaeological monuments. There are three national parks—Pirin, Rila, and Central Balkan—all rich in historic sites and self-regulating ecosystems. Lying between the slopes of the Balkan and the Sredna Gora mountain range is the Valley of Roses. Foreign visitors to Bulgaria must have a passport. Visas are not required for stays of up to 30 days.

48 FAMOUS PERSONS

The founders of modern Bulgarian literature, writing before the end of Turkish rule, were Georgi Rakovski (1821–67), Petko Slaveikov (1827–95), Lyuben Karavelov (1835–79), and Hristo Botev (1848–76), who was one of Bulgaria's greatest poets. The most significant writer after the liberation of 1878 was Ivan Vazov (1850–1921), whose *Under the Yoke* gives an impressive picture of the struggle against the Ottomans. Pentcho Slaveikov (1866–1912), the son of Petko, infused Bulgarian literature with philosophical content and subject matter of universal appeal; his epic poem *A Song of Blood* recalls an insurrection suppressed by the Turks in 1876. In the period between the two world wars, Nikolai Liliyev (1885–1960) and Todor Trayanov (1882–1945) were leaders of a symbolist school of poetry. Elin Pelin (1877–1949) and Iordan Iovkov (1880–1937) wrote popular short stories on regional themes. More recent writers and poets include Nikola Vaptzarov (1909–42), Christo Shirvenski, Dimiter Dimov (1909–65), Orlin Vassilev, and Georgi Karaslavov (1904–80). Elias Canetti (1905–94), who received the Nobel Prize for literature in 1981 was born in Bulgaria, although he spent the majority of his life abroad, in the UK, Austria and Switzerland. Tzvetan Todorov (b.1939), is a Bulgarian-born philosopher and literary theorist living in France; he is the author of *The Conquest of America* (1982). Julia Kristeva (b. 1941), is a philosopher, literary critic and sociologist who similarly was born in Bulgaria, but has lived in France most of her adult life becoming a major figure in the humanities and poststructuralist thought in particular.

Ivan Mrkvicka (1856–1938), a distinguished Czech-born painter who took up residence in Bulgaria, founded the Academy of Fine Arts in Sofia.

A prominent Bulgarian statesman was Alexander Stamboliski (1879–1923), leader of the politically influential Bulgarian Agrarian People's Union who was premier of Bulgaria from 1919 until his assassination in 1923. Another major politician, active before and after the establishment of the Communist regime, Georgi Dimitrov (1882–1949), was falsely charged in 1933 with burning the Reichstag building in Berlin; he became general secretary of Communist International (Comintern) from 1935 until its dissolution in 1943 and prime minister of Bulgaria in 1946. Traicho Kostov (1897–1949), an early revolutionary leader, was a principal architect of Bulgaria's postwar economic expansion. Caught up in the Tito-Stalin rift, he was expelled from the Politburo and executed in December 1949.

Todor Zhivkov (1911–98) was first secretary of the Bulgarian Communist Party between 1954 and 1989, the longest tenure of any Warsaw Pact leader. His was marked by ardent and steadfast support of Soviet policies and ideological positions. Zhivkov's daughter Lyudmila Zhivkova (1942–81) was regarded by Western observers as second only to her father in power and influence. Zhivkov was replaced by Dimitar Popov as premier of a coalition government headed by the Socialist Party (formerly the Communist Party). Simeon II (b. 1937) was the last tsar of Bulgaria from 1943–46, and was prime minister from 2001–05. He is also known as Simeon of Saxe-Coburg-Gotha.

49 DEPENDENCIES

Bulgaria has no territories or colonies.

50 BIBLIOGRAPHY

Anguelov, Zlatko. *Communism and the Remorse of an Innocent Victimizer.* College Station, TX: Texas A & M University Press, 2002.

Bulgaria Investment and Business Guide: Strategic and Practical Information. Washington, DC: International Business Publications USA, 2012.

Chary, Frederick B. *The History of Bulgaria.* Santa Barbara, CA: Greenwood, 2011.

Detrez, Raymond. *Historical Dictionary of Bulgaria.* 2nd ed. Lanham, MD: Scarecrow, 2006.

Dimitrov, Georgi. *The Diary of Georgi Dimitrov, 1933–1949.* New Haven: Yale University Press, 2003.

The Fragility of Goodness: Why Bulgaria's Jews Survived the Holocaust: A Collection of Texts. Princeton, NJ: Princeton University Press, 2001.

Frucht, Richard (ed.). *Eastern Europe: An Introduction to the People, Lands, and Culture.* Santa Barbara, CA: ABC-CLIO, 2005.

International Smoking Statistics: A Collection of Historical Data from 30 Economically Developed Countries. New York: Oxford University Press, 2002.

McElrath, Karen (ed.). *HIV and AIDS: A Global View.* Westport, CT: Greenwood Press, 2002.

Opello, Walter C. *European Politics.* Boulder, CO: Lynne Rienner Publishers, 2009.

Otfinoski, Steven. *Bulgaria.* 2nd ed. New York: Facts On File, 2004.

Petkov, Petko. *The United States and Bulgaria in World War I.* Boulder, CO: East European Monographs, 1991.

CROATIA

Republic of Croatia
Republika Hrvatska

CAPITAL: Zagreb

FLAG: Red, white, and blue horizontal bands with the Croatian coat of arms (red and white checkered).

ANTHEM: *Lijepa Nasa Domovina (Our beautiful Homeland).*

MONETARY UNIT: The Croatian kuna (HRK) was introduced in 1994, consisting of 100 lipa. HRK1 = $0.1801 (or $1 = HRK 5.55) as of November 2011.

WEIGHTS AND MEASURES: The metric system is the legal standard.

HOLIDAYS: New Year's Day, 1 January; Epiphany, 6 January; Labor Day, 1 May; Republic Day, 30 May; National Holiday, 22 June; Assumption, 15 August; Christmas, 25–26 December.

TIME: 7 p.m. = noon GMT.

¹LOCATION, SIZE, AND EXTENT

Croatia is located in southeastern Europe. Comparatively, the area occupied by Croatia is slightly smaller than the state of West Virginia with a total area of 56,542 sq km (21,831 sq mi). Croatia shares boundaries with Slovenia on the W, Hungary on the N, Serbia on the E, Bosnia and Herzegovina on the S and E, Montenegro on the E, and the Adriatic Sea on the W, and has a total boundary length of 8,020 km (4.983 mi), including 5,835 km (3,626 mi) of coastline. Croatia's capital city, Zagreb, is located in the northern part of the country. Croatia's territory includes 1,185 nearby islands in the Adriatic Sea, of which only 66 are inhabited.

²TOPOGRAPHY

The topography of Croatia is geographically diverse, with flat plains along the Hungarian border, as well as low mountains and highlands near the Adriatic coast. The country is generally divided into three main geographic zones: the Pannonian and Peri-Pannonian Plains in the east and northwest, the central hills and mountains, and the Adriatic coast. Approximately 24% of Croatia's land is arable. Croatia's natural resources include: oil, some coal, bauxite, low-grade iron ore, calcium, natural asphalt, silica, mica, clays, and salt. Croatia's natural environment experiences effects from frequent earthquakes, air pollution from metallurgical plants, coastal pollution from industrial and domestic waste, and forest damage.

³CLIMATE

Croatia's climate in the lowlands features hot, dry summers and cold winters. In Zagreb, the average annual temperature is 12°C (53°F) with average highs of 2°C (35°F) in January and 27°C (80°F) in July. In the mountains, summers are cool and winters cold and snowy. Along the coast, the climate is Mediterranean with mild winters and dry summers. In Split, the average annual temperature is 17°C (62°F). Annual average precipitation is about 94 cm (37 in).

⁴FLORA AND FAUNA

Ferns, flowers, mosses, and common trees populate the landscape. Along the Adriatic Sea there are subtropical plants. Native animals include deer, brown bears, rabbits, foxes, and wild boars. The World Resources Institute estimates that there are 4,288 plant species in Croatia. In addition, Croatia is home to 96 mammal, 365 bird, 34 reptile, and 10 amphibian species. The calculation reflects the total number of distinct species residing in the country, not the number of endemic species.

⁵ENVIRONMENT

Air pollution (from metallurgical plant emissions) and deforestation are inland environmental problems. In 2008 the United Nations (UN) reported that carbon dioxide emissions in Croatia totaled 24.8 million metric tons, up from 19.6 million in 2000 and 17.5 million in 1996. Coastal water systems have been damaged by industrial and domestic waste. Environmental management is becoming more decentralized, thereby empowering city and municipal administrations to determine environmental policy.

The World Resources Institute reported that Croatia had designated 314,700 hectares (777,641 acres) of land for protection as of 2006. Water resources totaled 105.5 cu km (25.31 cu mi). Croatia's 195 protected areas include the Plitvice Lakes National Park, a natural UNESCO World Heritage Site. There are four Ramsar wetland sites. According to the International Union for Conservation of Nature and Natural Resources (IUCN) Red List of Threatened Species, threatened species as of 2011 included 7 types of mammals, 10 species of birds, 2 types of reptiles, 2 species of amphibians, 60 species of fish, and 15 species of invertebrates. Endangered species included the Atlantic sturgeon, slender-billed curlew, and the Mediterranean monk seal.

⁶POPULATION

The US Central Intelligence Agency (CIA) estimated the population of Croatia in 2011 to be approximately 4,483,804, which placed it at number 123 in population among the 196 nations of the world. Approximately 16.8% of the population was over 65 years of age, with another 15.1% under 15 years of age. The median age in Croatia was 41.4 years. There were 0.93 males for every female in the country. The population's annual rate of change was -0.076%. The projected population for the year 2025 was 4,300,000. Population density in Croatia was calculated at 79 people per sq km (205 people per sq mi).

The UN estimated that 58% of the population lived in urban areas, with an annual rate of change of 0.4%. The largest urban area was Zagreb, with a population of 685,000.

⁷MIGRATION

Estimates of Croatia's net migration rate, carried out by the CIA in 2011, amounted to 1.55 migrants per 1,000 citizens. The total number of emigrants living abroad was 753,900, and the total number of immigrants living in Croatia was 699,900. In the early 1990s, some 160,000 people living in Croatia fled to neighboring countries to escape ethnic conflict, with another 120,000 fleeing to countries abroad. Total returns to Croatia by February 2000 numbered over 112,000, including 36,000 Croatian Serbs who repatriated from Serbia and Montenegro. Nearly 74,000 internally displaced people had returned to their homes within Croatia. During the 2000s, Croatia's immigration policies were geared toward enticing the rest of the displaced populations to return. Migration between the former Yugoslav republics remains high. In 2009, more than half of immigrants to Croatia came from Bosnia and Herzegovina, and almost half of all emigrants left for Serbia.

⁸ETHNIC GROUPS

As of the 2001 census, Croats made up about 89.6% of the population, and Serbs accounedt for 4.5%. The remainder included Bosniaks, Hungarians, Slovenians, Czechs, and Roma.

⁹LANGUAGES

Serbo-Croatian is the native language and is used by 96% of the populace. Since 1991, Croats have insisted that their tongue (now called Croat) is distinctive. The spoken language is basically the same, with very differences between Serbian and Croatian vocabulary. However, in written language, Croats use the Latin alphabet, whereas Serbs predominantly use Cyrillic. The Croatian alphabet has the special consonants č, ć, š, ž, dj, dž, and nj, representing sounds provided by the Cyrillic alphabet. The remaining 4% of the population speak various other languages, including Italian, Hungarian, Czech, Slovak, and German.

¹⁰RELIGIONS

The latest estimates record a Roman Catholic population of 87.8%, with 6% Serbian Orthodox. Muslims, Jews, and other faiths each constitute less than 5% of the population. The constitution provides for freedom of conscience and religion, and this right is generally respected in practice. Though there is no official state religion, the Roman Catholic Church, the Serbian Orthodox Church, the Islamic Community of Croatia, the Bet Israel Jewish Community, and 12 other Christian denominations have signed agreements with the government through which they qualify for state support. The government requires that religious training must be provided in public schools, but attendance is optional. A 2003 Regulation on Forms and Maintaining Records of Religious Communities in Croatia requires all religious organizations to register with the government in order to receive legal status under the Law on Religious Communities. As of 2010, there were 42 registered religious communities. Epiphany, Easter Monday, Corpus Christi Day, Assumption Day, All Saints' Day, Christmas, and St. Stephen's Day (Boxing Day) are all observed as national holidays.

¹¹TRANSPORTATION

The CIA reports that Croatia has a total of 29,343 km (18,233 mi) of roads. There are 388 vehicles per 1,000 people in the country. Railroads extend for 2,723 km (1,692 mi). Croatia has approximately 785 km (488 mi) of navigable waterways.

Croatia's railroads consist of two main routes. An east-west route originating in Serbia nearly parallels the Sava before reaching Zagreb and continuing on to Slovenia and Hungary. The north-south route connects the coastal cities of Split and Rijeka to Zagreb. Another railway connects Dubrovnik to Bosnia and Herzegovina.

Rijeka, Split, and Kardeljevo (Ploce) are the main seaports along the Adriatic. Vukovar, Osijek, Sisak, and Vinkovci are the principal inland ports. In 2010, Croatia had 75 ships of at least 1,000 GRT in the merchant marine fleet.

Croatia has 69 airports, which transported 1.68 million passengers in 2009 according to the World Bank. An estimated 23 of the airports have paved runways. There is one heliport. Principal airports include Dubrovnik, Split, and Pleso at Zagreb.

¹²HISTORY

Origins through the Middle Ages

Slavic tribes penetrated slowly but persistently into the Balkan area beginning in the 5th century. Their migration, and that of the Serbians, occurred upon the invitation of the Byzantine emperor Heraclius I (r. 610–641) in 626, to repel the destructive inroads of the Avars. A coalition of Byzantine and Croat forces succeeded in forcing the Avars out of Dalmatia first, and then from the remainder of Illirycum and the lands between the Drava and Sava rivers. The Croats settled on the lands that they had freed from the Avars and established their own organized units that included indigenous Slavic tribes.

By the year 1000, Venice, having defeated the Croatian fleet, controlled the entire Adriatic coast. The coastal cities, while welcoming the Italian cultural influence of Venice, feared potential Venetian domination over their trading interests with the enormous Balkan hinterland. Thus Dubrovnik (formerly called Ragusa), with its growing fleet, preferred to remain tied to the more distant Byzantine Empire.

Zvonimir, son-in-law of the Hungarian king Bela I, was crowned king of Croatia in 1075. Zvonimir died around 1089 without an heir, leaving his widow with the throne, but the nobles opposed her rule because of her Hungarian ancestry. The king of Hungary intervened to protect his sister's interests (and his own) by occupying Pannonian Croatia. The area was recovered in 1095 by Peter

LOCATION: 45°10′ N 15°30′ E. BOUNDARY LENGTHS: Serbia, 241 kilometers (150 miles); Montenegro, 25 kilometers (16 miles); Bosnia and Herzegovina, 932 kilometers (579 miles); Slovenia, 455 kilometers (283 miles); Hungary, 329 kilometers (204 miles). coastline: 5,790 kilometers (3,598 miles); mainland coastline, 1,778 kilometers (1,105 miles); islands coastline, 4,012 kilometers (2,493 miles).

Svacic from Knin (1093–97). Peter, the last independent king of Croatia, was killed in battle in 1096 by King Koloman of Hungary, who then conquered Croatia. After concluding a nonaggression pact with Venice, which had retained control of the coastal islands and cities, the Croats rebelled and drove the Hungarian forces back to the Drava River frontier between Croatia and Hungary.

Royal Union with Hungary

In 1102, Koloman regrouped and attacked Croatia. He stopped at the Drava River, however, where he invited the nobles representing the 12 Croatian tribes to a conference. They worked out the so-called Pacta Conventa, an agreement on a personal royal union between Hungary and Croatia (including Slavonia and Dalmatia). The overall administration of the state would be by a "ban" (viceroy) appointed by the king, while regional and local administration were to stay in the hands of the Croatian nobles. This legal arrangement, with some practical modifications, remained the basis of the Hungarian-Croatian personal royal union and relationship until 1918.

Internal warfare among Croatia's nobility weakened its overall ability to resist attack from Venice. In 1377, Tvrtko (1353–1390) proclaimed himself king of the Serbs, Bosnia, and the Croatian coast. Venice was defeated in 1385, and was forced to surrender all rights to the coastal cities all the way to Durazzo in today's Albania. Dubrovnik also gained its independence from Venice, recognizing the sovereignty of the Hungarian-Croatian king.

Defense against the Turks

By the mid-15th century the threat from both the Turks and Venice was growing more ominous, leading King Sigismund to establish three military defense regions in 1432. As these defensive regions were further developed, they attracted new, mostly Serbian, settlers/fighters who became the strong Serbian minority population in Croatia. The Ottoman threat brought about the appointment of Vladislav Jagiellon, the king of Poland, as king of Hungary and Croatia in 1440. Vladislav was succeeded in 1445 by Ladislas, son of Albert of Hapsburg, and therefore king of both Austria and Hungary/Croatia. Since Ladislas was a minor, John Hunyadi, a brilliant general, was appointed regent. Hunyadi had to protect the throne from the counts of Celje, who, in 1453, also claimed the title of ban of Croatia. Ulrich, one of the counts of Celje, fell victim to Hunyadi's assassins at the defense of Belgrade from the Turks in 1456. This murder was avenged by King Ladislas V, who had Hunyadi executed in 1456.

After 1520, the Turks began effective rule over some Croatian territory. In 1522, the Croatian nobility asked Austrian archduke Ferdinand of the Hapsburgs to help defend Croatia against the Turks, but by 1526, the Turks had conquered Eastern Slavonia and had advanced north into Hungary. On 29 August 1526, in a massive battle at Mohacs, the Turks defeated the Hungarian and Croatian forces, killing King Louis. By 1528, the Ottomans held the southern part of Croatia, and by 1541 had conquered Budapest. Dubrovnik, on the other hand, had accepted the Ottoman suzerainty in 1483, keeping its autonomy through extensive trade with the Turkish Empire. Most coastal towns were under the protection of Venice, with its good trade relations with the Turks.

In 1526, after King Louis's death at Mohacs, Ferdinand of Hapsburg was elected king of Hungary and Croatia. The Hapsburg rulers began to encroach on the rights of Croats by turning the throne from a traditionally elected position into a hereditary one, and by allocating Croatian lands as fiefs to their supporters, turning the Croatian peasants from free men into serfs.

King Ferdinand III (r. 1637–1657) consolidated Hungary and Croatia under Hapsburg rule. Under Ferdinand's son, Leopold I (who in 1658 had also become the German emperor), the status of Hungary and Croatia continued to deteriorate. All power was centralized in the hands of the king/emperor and his court. Leopold tried to emulate the absolutist model practiced by Louis XIV of France. The Turkish offensives of 1663 were successfully repelled by the Croatian brothers Nicholas and Peter Zrinski. Following the defeat of the Turks at Saint Gotthard in western Hungary in 1664, Leopold I unilaterally concluded a 20-year peace treaty with the Turks based essentially on the prewar situation.

The Peace of Vasvar proved to the Hungarians and Croats that the Hapsburg court was not interested in fighting the Turks for Hungary and Croatia. This situation led to a conspiracy by the Zrinski brothers and key Hungarian nobles against the Hapsburg Court. But the Turks warned the Hapsburgs of the conspiracy, and Peter Zrinski and his coconspirator Francis Frankopan were executed on 30 April 1671 (Nicholas Zrinski had died in 1664). Leopold I suspended for 10 years the office of the Croatian ban.

The last king of the male Hapsburg line was Charles III (r. 1711–1740). In 1722, during his reign, the Hungarian parliament agreed to extend the Hapsburg hereditary right to its female line (Charles had no son), something already agreed to by the Croatian parliament in 1712. At the same time the Hungarians obtained a legal guarantee on the indivisibility of the realm of the Crown of Saint Stephen, which included Croatia. Charles was thus followed by his daughter Maria Teresa (r. 1740–1780), who, by decree, divided Croatia into regions headed by her appointees. Joseph II, her son, emancipated the serfs, tried to improve education, tried to impose the German language as a unifying force, closed monasteries in an attempt to control the Roman Catholic Church, and decreed religious toleration. In the 1788 war against the Turks, Joseph II suffered a devastating defeat; he died two years later.

Leopold II, Joseph II's brother, succeeded him, and he recognized Hungary and Croatia as kingdoms with separate constitutions. Hungarian replaced Latin as the official language of the Hungarian parliament. Hungarians then began trying to establish the Hungarian language in Croatia, Slavonia, and Dalmatia, thus initiating a hundred-year struggle of the Croats to preserve their identity.

Napoleon and the Spring of Nations

With the peace treaty of Campoformio ending the war against Napoleon in 1797, Austria obtained the territories of the Venice Republic, including the Adriatic coast as far as Kotor. In 1806, Napoleon seized Dubrovnik, and in 1809 he obtained control of Slovenian and Croatian territories and created his Illyrian Provinces. The French regime levied heavy taxes and conscription into Napoleon's armies. With Napoleon's defeat, all of Dalmatia reverted back to direct Austrian administration until the end of World War I in 1918.

In 1825, Francis I called the Hungarian parliament into session, and the Hungarians resumed their pressure to introduce the Hungarian language into Croatian schools. Ljudevit Gaj became the leader of the movement, calling for the reassertion of the independent Kingdom of Croatia and advocating the introduction of "Illyrian" (Croatian) as the official language to replace Latin. Count Janko Draškovic, a member of the Illyrian movement, also promoted the idea of reorganizing the Hapsburg lands into a federation of political units with coequal rights. The Croatian parliament then nullified the previous agreement on using Hungarian and made Croatian the official language of parliament. In 1840, the Croatian Sabor voted for the introduction of Croatian as the language of instruction in all Croatian schools and at the Zagreb Academy.

The struggle over the Croatian language and national identity brought about the establishment of the first political parties in Croatia. The Croatian-Hungarian Party supported a continued Croat-Hungarian commonwealth. The Illyrian Party advocated an independent kingdom of Croatia comprised of all the Croatian lands including Bosnia and Herzegovina. The Austrian government banned the term "Illyrian," and the name of the Illyrian party of Ljudevit Gaj and Draskovic was changed to the National Party.

At the next session of the Hungarian parliament in 1843, the Croatian delegation walked out when not permitted to use Latin instead of Hungarian. The Croatian National Party submitted to the emperor its demands to reestablish an independent government of Croatia, elevate the Zagreb Academy to university status, and raise the Zagreb bishopric to the archbishopric rank. The lines were thus drawn between the Hungarian and Croatian nationalists. This situation came to a head in 1848 when great unrest and revolts developed in Austria and Hungary.

Autonomy or Independence

Francis Joseph I (r. 1848–1916) ascended to the Hapsburg throne on 2 December 1848 and ruled for a long time, favoring the Hungarians against the Croats. Croatian parties had split between the pro-Hungarian union and those advocating Croatian independence based on ancient state rights. The latter evolved into the "Yugoslav" (South Slavic Unity) movement led by Bishop Josip Juraj Strossmayer and the "Pravaši" movement for total Croatian independence led by Ante Starcevic. Austria and Hungary resolved their problems by agreeing on the "dual monarchy" concept. The Hungarian half of the dual monarchy consisted of Hungary, Transylvania, Croatia, Slavonia, and Dalmatia. A ban would be appointed by the emperor-king of Hungary upon the recommendation of the Hungarian premier, who would usually nominate a Hungarian noble. Croatia-Slavonia-Dalmatia was recognized as a nation with its own territory, the Croatian language was allowed, and it was granted political autonomy in internal affairs. Despite this, the Hungarians continued to dominate the political and economic life of Croatia.

Yugoslavism

In the 1870s, Ivan Mazuranic was appointed ban of Croatia. He implemented general administrative reform and a modern system of education. The Sabor instituted a supreme court and a complete judicial system. The 1878 Congress of Berlin allowed Austria's military occupation and administration of Bosnia and Herzegovina and the Sandzak area (lost by the Turks after their defeat by Russia in 1877). The Croatian Sabor then requested the annexation of those areas, but Austria and Hungary refused. Croatia and Serbia were deeply disappointed, and Serbia began supporting terrorist activities against the Austrians. In 1881, the military region was joined to Croatia, thus increasing the size of its Serbian Orthodox population. This offered the Hungarian ban Khuen Hedervary the opportunity to play Serbs against Croats in order to prevent their joint front. The relations between Croats and Serbs continued to deteriorate.

By 1893, there was a united Croatian opposition that called for equality with Hungary, unification of all Croatian lands, and the Slovenes to join Croatia in the formation of a new state within the framework of the Hapsburg monarchy. This united opposition took the name of Croatian Party of Right ("Stranka Prava"). National unification, however, had strong opposition from powerful forces: the Hungarians with their Great Hungary Drive; the Serbs, who wanted to annex Bosnia and Herzegovina into Serbia; the Italians, claiming Istria, Rijeka, and Dalmatia; and the Austrians and their Pan-Germanic partners.

The Croats and Serbs formed a Croat-Serbian coalition, winning a simple majority in the 1908 Croatian parliamentary elections, followed by the Party of Right and the Peasant Party, led by the brothers Anthony and Stephen Radic. Also in 1908, the direct annexation of Bosnia and Herzegovina by Austria took place. The Party of Right and the Peasant Party supported the annexation, hoping that the next step would be Bosnia and Herzegovina's incorporation into a unified Croatia. Serbia, conversely, was enraged by the annexation. Assassination attempts increased and led to the assassination of Archduke Ferdinand and his wife in Sarajevo on 28 June 1914. These tragedies followed the Serbian victories and territorial expansion in the wake of the 1912 and 1913 Balkan wars.

The idea of a separate state uniting the South Slavic nations ("Yugoslavism") grew stronger during World War I (1914–18). An émigré "Yugoslav Committee" was formed and worked for the unification of the South Slavs with the Kingdom of Serbia. In 1917, an agreement was reached on the formation of a "Kingdom of Serbs, Croats, and Slovenes" upon the defeat of Austro-Hungary.

Royal Yugoslavia

The unification of Croatia and the new "Kingdom of Serbs, Croats, and Slovenes" on 1 December 1918 was flawed by the inability to work out an acceptable compromise between the Serbs and Croat-Slovenes. The National Council for all Slavs of former Austro-Hungary was formed on 12 October 1918 in Zagreb (Croatia) and was chaired by Monsignor Anton Korošec, head of the Slovenian People's Party. On 29 October 1918, the National Council proclaimed the formation of a new, separate state of Slovenes, Croats, and Serbs of the former Austro-Hungary. The Zagreb Council intended to negotiate a federal type of union between the new state and the Kingdom of Serbia that would preserve the respective national autonomies of the Slovenes, Croats, and Serbs. Monsignor Korošec had negotiated a similar agreement in principle with Serbian prime minister Nikola Pašic in Geneva, but the Serbian government reneged on it. While Korošec was detained in Geneva, a delegation of the National Council went to Belgrade and submitted to Serbia a declaration expressing the will to unite with the Kingdom of Serbia, and Serbia readily agreed. On 1 December 1918, Prince Alexander of Serbia declared the unification of the "Kingdom of Serbs, Croats, and Slovenes."

The provisional assembly convened in 1918, with the addition to the Serbian parliament of representatives from the other southern Slavic historical regions, while the Croatian Sabor was deprived of its authority. The elections to the Constituent Assembly were held on 28 November 1920, but the 50-member delegation of the Croatian Republican Peasant Party refused to participate. The new Vidovdan Constitution was adopted on 28 June 1921 by a "simple majority" vote of 223 to 35, with 111 abstentions in the absence of the Croatian delegation with 50 votes.

The period between 1921 and 1929 saw a sequence of 23 governments, a parliament without both the Croatian delegation's 50 votes and the Communist Party's 58 votes (it continued its work underground). This situation assured control to the Serbian majority, but it was not possible to govern the new country effectively without the participation of the Croats, the second-largest nation.

Finally, in 1925, Prime Minister Pašic invited Stjepan Radic, head of the Croatian Peasant Party, to form a government with him. However, not much was accomplished and Pašic died just a few years later. On 20 June 1928, Radic was shot in parliament by a Serbian deputy and died the next month. Riots broke out as a result of his assassination.

Dr. Vlatko Macek, the new Croatian Peasant Party leader, declared that "there is no longer a constitution, but only king and people." A coalition government under Prime Minister Monsignor Anton Korošec, head of the Slovene People's Party, lasted only until December 1928. King Alexander dissolved the parliament on 6 January 1929, abolished the 1921 constitution, and established his own personal dictatorship as a temporary arrangement.

At first, most people accepted King Alexander's dictatorship as a necessity, which gave the country an opportunity to focus on building its economy from the foundation of postwar reconstruction. Royal decrees established penalties of death or 20 years in prison for terrorism, sedition, or Communist activities. All elected local councils and traditional political parties were dissolved. Freedom of the press was severely constrained and government permission was required for any kind of association. All power was centralized and exercised by the king through a council of ministers accountable only to him.

On 3 October 1929, the country was renamed the Kingdom of Yugoslavia, and the territorial regions (*banovinas*) were named after rivers to emphasize the king's opposition to national names. One of the consequences of the dictatorship and its harsh measures against political opposition and cultural nationalism was the emigration of some political opponents, among them some of the top leadership of the Croatian Peasant Party and the leader of the Ustaša movement, Ante Pavelic.

The new constitution, initiated by King Alexander on 3 September 1931, was in theory a return to civil liberties and freedoms of association, assembly, and expression. In reality, all such freedoms were limited by the king's decrees that remained in force. Parliament was to consist of two houses with a council of ministers still accountable directly to the king. The Croatian opposition grew stronger, and in the winter of 1932, their Zagreb Manifesto called for the removal of Serbian hegemony and for popular sovereignty. In reaction, the regime interned or imprisoned political opponents. Croatia was seething with rebellion, and the three-year prison sentence for opposition leader Macek would have sparked an open revolt, were it not for the danger of then-Fascist Italy's intervention.

The worldwide economic depression hit Yugoslavia hard in 1932. Opposition continued to grow to the king's dictatorship, which had not proffered any solutions to the so-called Croatian question. In late 1934, the king planned to release Macek from prison, reintroduce a real parliamentary system, and try to reach some compromise between the Serbs and Croats. Unfortunately, King Alexander was assassinated in Marseille on 9 October 1934 by agents of the Ustaša group, who were trained in terrorism in Hungary with Mussolini's support. Prince Paul, King Alexander's cousin, headed the interim government, releasing Macek and other political leaders but otherwise continuing the royal dictatorship. On 5 May 1935, the elections for a new parliament were so shamefully improper that a boycott of parliament began. Prince Paul consulted with Macek, and a new government of reconstruction was formed by Milan Stojadinovic. The new government initiated serious discussions with Macek on a limited autonomous Croatian entity that would be empowered on all matters except the armed forces, foreign affairs, state finance, customs, foreign trade, posts, and telegraphs.

Since 1937, the thorniest issue discussed had been the make-up of the federal units. Serbs wanted to unite with Macedonia, Vojvodina, and Montenegro. Croatia wanted Dalmatia and a part of Vojvodina. Slovenia was recognized as a separate unit, but Bosnia and Herzegovina posed a real problem, with both Croats and Serbs claiming ownership over a land that contained a substantial minority of Bosnian Muslims. Meanwhile, intense trade relations with Germany and friendlier relations with Italy were bringing Yugoslavia closer to those countries. Adolf Hitler's annexation of Austria and Czechoslovakia in 1938 made it imperative that Yugoslavia resolve its internal problem before Hitler and Mussolini attempted to destabilize and conquer Yugoslavia.

Stojadinovic resigned, and Prince Paul appointed Dragiša Cvetkovic as prime minister, charging him with the task of reaching a formal agreement with the Croatian opposition. The agreement was concluded on 26 August 1939. Macek became the new vice-premier, a territorial region of Croatia was established that included Dalmatia and western Herzegovina, and the traditional Sabor of Croatia was revived. But autonomy for Croatia was not received well by most of Serbia. Concerned with the status of Serbs in Croatia, Serbia was anxious to incorporate most of Bosnia and Herzegovina. Even less satisfied was the extreme Croatian nationalist Ustaša movement, whose goal was an independent greater Croatia inclusive of Bosnia and Herzegovina. For the Ustaša, this goal was to be achieved by any means and at any cost, including violence and support from foreign powers. Tensions between the extremes of the failed Yugoslavia had seemingly reached the boiling point.

World War II

The clouds of World War II had gathered with Italy's takeover of Albania and its war with Greece, and Hitler's agreement with Stalin followed by his attack on Poland in the fall of 1939, resulting in its partitioning. By 1940, Hungary, Romania, and Bulgaria had joined the Axis powers and England and France had entered the war against Germany and Italy. With the fall of France in 1940, Hitler decided to assist Mussolini in his war with Greece through Bulgaria, and therefore needed Yugoslavia to join the Axis so that Germany would be assured of ample food and raw materials.

The Yugoslav Government had limited choices—either accept the possibility of immediate attack by Germany, or join the Axis, with Hitler's assurance that no German troops would pass through Yugoslavia towards Greece. The regent was aware of Yugoslavia's weak defense capabilities and the inability of the Allies to assist Yugoslavia against the Axis powers, despite security agreements with Britain and France. Yugoslavia signed a treaty with Hitler on 26 March 1941, and on 27 March a coup d'état by Serbian military officers forced the regent to abdicate. The military declared Prince Peter the new king and formed a government with General Dušan Simovic as premier and Macek as vice-premier. The new government tried to temporize and placate Hitler, who was enraged by the deep anti-German feeling of the Yugoslav people who shouted in demonstrations, "Bolje rat nego pact" (Better war than the pact). Feeling betrayed, Hitler unleashed the German fury on Yugoslavia on 6 April 1941 by bombing Belgrade and other centers without any warning or formal declaration of war.

The war was over in 11 days, with the surrender signed by the Yugoslav Army Command while the Yugoslav government (with young King Peter II) fled the country for allied territory and settled in London. Yugoslavia was partitioned among Germany, Italy, Hungary, Bulgaria, and Italian-occupied Albania, while Montenegro, under Italian occupation, was to be restored as a separate kingdom. Croatia was set up as an independent kingdom with an Italian prince to be crowned Tomislav II. Ante Pavelic was installed by the Italians and Germans as head of independent Croatia (after Macek had declined Hitler's offer). Croatia was forced to cede part of Dalmatia, with most of its islands and the Boka Kotorska area, to Italy. In exchange, Croatia was given Bosnia and Herzegovina and the Srijem region up to Belgrade.

On 10 April 1941, the "resurrection of our independent State of Croatia" was proclaimed in Zagreb by Slavko Kvaternik for Ante Pavelic, who was still in Italy with some 600 of his Ustaše. With Pavelic's arrival in Zagreb five days later, the Ustaša regime was established, with new laws that expressed the basic Ustaša tenets of a purely Croatian state viewed as the bulwark of Western civilization against the Byzantine Serbs. Slavko Kvaternik explained how a pure Croatia would be built—by forcing one-third of the Serbs to leave Croatia, one-third to convert to Catholicism, and one-third to be exterminated. Soon Ustaša bands initiated the mass murders of Serbs unfortunate enough not to have converted or left Croatia on time. The enormity of such criminal behavior shocked even the conscience of German commanders, but Pavelic had Hitler's personal support for such actions, which resulted in the loss of lives of hundreds of thousands of Serbs in Croatia and Bosnia and Herzegovina. In addition, the Ustaša regime organized extermination camps, the most notorious one at Jasenovac, where Serbs, Jews, Gypsies, and other opponents were massacred in large numbers. The Serbs reacted by forming their own resistance groups ("Cetniks") or by joining with the Communist-led partisan resistance, striking back at the Ustaša in a terrible fratricidal war encouraged by the Germans and Italians.

The Ustaša regime organized its armed forces into the Domobrani, its Ustaša shock troops, and the local gendarmerie. Its attempt at organizing the Croatian people in the Fascist mode failed, however. Most Croats remained faithful to the Croatian Peasant Party Democratic principles, or joined the Partisan movement led by Josip Broz-Tito that offered a federal political program. With respect to Bosnia and Herzegovina, the Ustaša regime never attained real control. The continuous fighting generated by Cetniks and Partisans fighting one another while being pursued by the Ustaša, the Germans, and the Italians made it impossible for the Ustaša to dominate. Most Croats rejected (and deeply resented) the trappings of an imported Fascist mystique and the abuse of their Catholic faith as a cover or justification for the systematic slaughter of their Serbian neighbors.

By the spring of 1942, the Ustaša regime began to retreat from its policy and practice of extermination of Serbs. But the terrible harm was done, and one consequence was the deep split between the Serbian members and their Croatian colleagues within the cabinet of the Yugoslav government-in-exile. The Serbs held the entire Croatian nation accountable for the Ustaša massacres, and reneged on the 1939 agreement establishing the Croatian Banovina as the basis for a federative reorganization in a postwar Yugoslavia. This discord made the Yugoslav government-in-exile inca-

pable of offering any kind of leadership to the people in occupied Yugoslavia. The fortunes of war and diplomacy favored the Communist Partisans—after Italy's surrender in September 1943, it handed over to the Partisans armaments and supplies from some 10 Italian divisions. More and more Croats left their home guard, and even some Ustaša units, to join the Partisans. Some Ustaša leaders, on the other hand, conspired against Pavelic in order to negotiate with the allies for recognition of the "independent" state of Croatia; they were caught and executed in the summer of 1944.

With the entry of Soviet armies into Yugoslav territory in October 1944, the Communist Partisans swept over Yugoslavia in pursuit of the retreating German forces. Pavelic and his followers, along with the Croatian home guard units, moved north to Austria at the beginning of May 1945 to escape from the Partisan forces and their retaliation. The Partisans took over Croatia, launching terrible retaliation in the form of summary executions, people's court sentences, and large-scale massacres, carried out in secret, of entire home guard and other Ustaša units.

Communist Yugoslavia

Such was the background for the formation of the second Yugoslavia, led by Tito as a Federative People's Republic of five nations—Slovenia, Croatia, Serbia, Macedonia, Montenegro—with Bosnia and Herzegovina as a buffer area with its mix of Serbs, Muslims, and Croats. The problem of large Hungarian and Muslim Albanian populations in Serbia was solved by creating the autonomous regions of Vojvodina (Hungarian minority) and Kosovo (Muslim Albanian majority), which assured their political and cultural development. Tito attempted a balancing act to satisfy most of the nationality issues that were still unresolved from the first Yugoslavia, along with decades of ethnic and religious conflict.

In pre-1941 Yugoslavia, Serbs had enjoyed a controlling role. After 1945, the numerically stronger Serbs had lost the Macedonian area they considered Southern Serbia, lost the opportunity to incorporate Montenegro into Serbia, and had lost direct control over both the Hungarian minority in Vojvodina and the Muslim Albanians of Kosovo, which had been viewed as the cradle of the Serbian nation since the Middle Ages. They could no longer incorporate into Serbia the large Serbian-populated areas of Bosnia and had not obtained an autonomous region for the large minority of Serbian population within the Croatian Republic. The Croats—while gaining back from Hungary the Medjumurje area and from Italy the cities of Rijeka (Fiume), Zadar (Zara), some Dalmatian islands, and the Istrian Peninsula—had lost the Srijem area to Serbia, and Bosnia and Herzegovina. In addition, the Croats were confronted with a deeply resentful Serbian population that became ever more pervasive in public administrative and security positions.

The official position of the Marxist Yugoslav regime was that national rivalries and conflicting interests would gradually diminish through their sublimation into a new Socialist order. Without capitalism, nationalism was supposed to wither away. Therefore, in the name of unity and brotherhood, nationalistic expression of concern was prohibited, repressed by the dictatorial and centralized regime of the League of Yugoslav Communists acting through the Socialist Alliance as its mass front organization. After a short postwar coalition government, the elections of 11 November 1945, boycotted by the noncommunist coalition parties, gave the communist People's Front 90% of the votes. A constituent assembly met on 29 November, abolished the monarchy, and established the Federative People's Republic of Yugoslavia. In January 1946, a new constitution was adopted, based on the 1936 Soviet constitution.

The Communist Party of Yugoslavia took over total control of the country and instituted a regime of terror through its secret police. To destroy the bourgeoisie, property was confiscated, and the intelligentsia were declared "enemies of the people," to be executed or imprisoned. Large enterprises were nationalized, and forced-labor camps were formed. The church and religion were persecuted, properties confiscated, religious instruction and organizations banned, and education used for Communist indoctrination. The media was forced into complete service to the totalitarian regime, and education was denied to "enemies of the people."

The expulsion of Yugoslavia from the Soviet-dominated Cominform Group in 1948, engineered by Soviet leader Joseph Stalin, was actually a blessing for Yugoslavia. Yugoslavia's "road to Socialism" evolved quickly in response to Stalin's pressures and Yugoslavia's need to perform a balancing act between the North Atlantic Treaty Organization (NATO) and the Soviet bloc. Tito also pushed the nationalization of the economy through a policy of forced industrialization supported by the collectivization of agriculture.

By the 1950s, Yugoslavia had initiated the development of what would become its internal trademark: self-management of enterprises through workers' councils and local decision making as the road to Marx's "withering away of the state." Following the failure of the first five-year plan (1947–51), the second five-year plan (1957–61) was completed in four years by relying on the well-established self-management system. Economic targets were set from the local to the republic level and then coordinated by a federal planning institute to meet an overall national economic strategy. This system supported a period of very rapid industrial growth in the 1950s, but a high consumption rate encouraged a volume of imports financed by foreign loans that exceeded exports. In addition, inefficient and low productivity industries were kept in place through public subsidies, cheap credit, and other artificial protective measures, leading to a serious crisis by 1961. Reforms were necessary and, by 1965, market socialism was introduced with laws that abolished most price controls and halved import duties while withdrawing export subsidies. The agricultural reform of 1945–46 limited private ownership to a maximum of 35 hectares (85 acres). The limited free market (after the initial forced delivery of quotas to the state at very low prices) had to be abandoned because of resistance by the peasants. The actual collectivization efforts were initiated in 1949 using welfare benefits and lower taxes as incentives, along with direct coercion. But collectivization had to be abandoned by 1958 simply because its inefficiency and low productivity could not support the concentrated effort of industrial development.

The government relaxed its restrictions to allow labor migration, particularly from Croatia to West Germany, where workers were needed for its thriving economy. Foreign investment was encouraged (up to 49%) in joint enterprises, and barriers to the movement of people and exchange of ideas were largely removed. The role of trade unions continued to include transmission of instructions from government to workers, allocation of perks, the education/training of workers, monitoring of legislation, and overall protection of the self-management system. Strikes were legally allowed, but the 1958 miners' strike in Trbovlje, Slovenia, was not publicly acknowledged and was suppressed. After 1958, strikes were tolerated as an indication of problems to be resolved.

After the split from the Cominform, Yugoslavia began also to develop a foreign policy independent of the Soviet Union. By mid-1949, Yugoslavia ceased its support of the Greek Communists in their civil war against the then-Royalist government of Greece. In October 1949, Yugoslavia was elected to one of the nonpermanent seats on the UN Security Council and openly condemned Communist-supported North Korea's aggression toward South Korea. Following Nikita Khrushchev's 1956 denunciation of Stalin, Tito intensified his work on developing the movement of nonaligned "third world" nations. This became Yugoslavia's external trademark, in cooperation with Nehru of India, Nasser of Egypt, and others. With the September 1961 Belgrade summit conference of nonaligned nations, Tito became the recognized leader of the movement. The nonaligned position served Tito's Yugoslavia well by allowing Tito to draw on economic and political support from the Western powers while neutralizing aggressive behavior from the Soviet bloc.

While Tito had acquiesced, reluctantly, to the 1956 Soviet invasion of Hungary for fear of political chaos and its liberalizing impact on Yugoslavia, he condemned the Soviet invasion of Dubček's Czechoslovakia in 1968, as did Romania's Ceausescu, both fearing their countries might be the next in line for "corrective" action by the Red Army and the Warsaw Pact. Just before his death on 4 May 1980, Tito also condemned the Soviet invasion of Afghanistan. Yugoslavia actively participated in the 1975 Helsinki Conference and Agreements, and the first 1977–78 review conference that took place in Belgrade, even though Yugoslavia's one-party Communist regime perpetrated and condoned numerous human rights violations.

The debates of the 1960s led to a closer scrutiny of the Communist experiment. The 1967 Declaration in Zagreb, claiming a Croatian linguistic and literary tradition separate from the Serbian one, undermined the validity of the "Serb-Croatian" language and a unified Yugoslavian linguistic heritage. Kosovo Albanians and Montenegrins, along with Slovenes and Croats, began to assert their national rights as superior to the right of the Yugoslavian federation. The eighth congress of the League of Communists of Yugoslavia (LCY) in December 1964 acknowledged that ethnic prejudice and antagonism existed in socialist Yugoslavia, and that Yugoslavia's nations were disintegrating into a socialist Yugoslavism. Thus the republic, based on individual nations, became an advocate of a strong federalism that devolved and decentralized authority from the federal to the republic level. Yugoslav Socialist Patriotism was defined as a feeling for both national identity and for the overall socialist self-management framework of Yugoslavia, despite the signs of a deeply divided country.

As the Royal Yugoslavism had failed in its assimilative efforts, so did the Socialist Yugoslavism fail to overcome the forces of nationalism. In the case of Croatia, there were several key factors sustaining the attraction to its national identity: more than a thousand years of its historical development, the carefully nurtured tradition of Croatian statehood, a location bridging central Europe and the Balkan area, an identification with Western

European civilization, and the Catholic religion with the traditional role of Catholic priests (even under the persecutions by the Communist regime). In addition, Croatia had a well-developed and productive economy with a standard of living superior to most other areas of the Yugoslav Federation other than Slovenia. This generated a growing resentment against the forced subsidizing by Croatia and Slovenia of less developed areas, and for the buildup of the Yugoslav Army. Finally, the increased political and economic autonomy enjoyed by the Republic of Croatia after the 1974 constitution and particularly following Tito's death in 1980 added impetus to the growing Croatian nationalism.

Croatian Spring

The liberal bloc (Slovenia, Croatia, Macedonia, Vojvodina) prevailed over the conservative group, and the reforms of 1965 did away with central investment planning and political factories. The positions of the two blocs hardened into a national-liberal coalition that viewed the conservative, centrist group led by Serbia as the Greater Serbian attempt at majority domination. The devolution of power in economic decision making, spearheaded by the Slovenes, assisted in the federalization of the League of Communists of Yugoslavia as a league of quasi-sovereign republican parties. Under strong prodding from the Croats, the party agreed in 1970 to the principle of unanimity for decision making. In practice, this meant each republic had veto power. However, the concentration of economic resources in Serbian hands continued, with Belgrade banks controlling half of total credits and some 80% of foreign credits. Fear of Serbian political and cultural domination continued, particularly with respect to Croatian language sensitivities aroused by the use of the Serbian version of Serbo-Croatian as the norm, with the Croatian version as a deviation.

The language controversy exacerbated the economic and political tensions between Serbs and Croats, spilling easily into ethnic confrontations. To the conservative centrists, the devolution of power to the republic level meant the subordination of the broad Yugoslav and Socialist interests to the narrow nationalist interest of national majorities. With the Croat League of Communists taking the liberal position in 1970, nationalism was rehabilitated, and the "Croatian Spring" bloomed and impacted all the other republics of Yugoslavia. Meanwhile, through a series of constitutional amendments in 1967–68 that limited federal power in favor of republics and autonomous provinces, the federal government came to be viewed by liberals as an inter-republican problem-solving mechanism bordering on a confederalist arrangement. A network of inter-republican committees established by mid-1971 proved to be very efficient, resolving a large number of difficult issues in a short time. The coalition of liberals and nationalists in Croatia, however, also generated sharp condemnation in Serbia, where its own brand of nationalism grew stronger as part of a conservative-centrist alliance. Thus, the liberal/federalist versus conservative/centrist conflict became entangled in the rising nationalism within each opposing bloc.

The situations in Croatia and Serbia were particularly difficult because of their minorities' issues. Serbs in Croatia sided with the Croat conservatives and sought a constitutional amendment guaranteeing their own national identity and rights. In the process, the Serbs challenged the sovereignty of the Croatian nation. The conservatives prevailed, and the amendment declared that "the So-

cialist Republic of Croatia [was] the national state of the Croatian nation, the state of the Serbian nation in Croatia, and the state of the nationalities inhabiting it."

Slovenia, not burdened by large minorities, developed in a liberal and nationalist direction. This fostered an incipient separatist sentiment opposed by both the liberal and conservative party wings. Led by Stane Kavcic, head of the Slovenian Government, the liberal wing gained as much political local latitude from the federal level as possible during the "Slovenian Spring" of the early 1970s. By the summer of 1971, the Serbian Party leadership was pressuring President Tito to put an end to what was in their view the dangerous development of Croatian nationalism. While Tito wavered because of his support for the balancing system of autonomous republic units, the situation quickly reached critical proportions. Croat nationalists, complaining about discrimination against Croats in Bosnia and Herzegovina, demanded the incorporation of western Herzegovina into Croatia. Serbia countered by claiming southeastern Herzegovina for itself. Croats also advanced demands for a larger share of their foreign currency earnings, the issuance of their own currency, their own national bank that would directly negotiate foreign loans, the printing of Croatian postage stamps, a Croatian Army, recognition of the Croatian Sabor as the highest Croatian political body and, finally, Croatian secession and complete independence.

Confronted with such intensive agitation, the liberal Croatian Party leadership could not back down and did not restrain the public demands nor the widespread university students' strike of November 1971. This situation caused the loss of support from the liberal party wings of Slovenia and even Macedonia. Tito intervened, condemning the Croatian liberal leadership on 1 December 1971, while supporting the conservative wing. The liberal leadership group resigned on 12 December 1971. When Croatian students demonstrated and demanded an independent Croatia, the Yugoslav Army was ready to move in if necessary. A wholesale purge of the party liberals followed with tens of thousands expelled. Key functionaries lost their positions, several thousands were imprisoned (including Franjo Tudjman, who later became president of independent Croatia), and leading Croatian nationalist organizations and their publications were closed. On 8 May 1972 the Croatian Party expelled its liberal wing leaders, and the purge of nationalists continued through 1973.

The issues and sentiments raised during the "Slovene and Croat Springs" of 1969–71 did not disappear. Tito and the conservatives were forced to nominally satisfy some demands, and the 1974 Constitution was an attempt to resolve the strained inter-republican relations as each republic pursued its own interests over and above any conceivable overall Yugoslav interest. The repression of liberal-nationalist Croats was accompanied by the growing influence of the Serbian element in the Croatian Party (24% in 1980) and police force (majority). This influence contributed to the ongoing persecution and imprisonments of Croatian nationalists into the 1980s. Tito's widespread purges of the "Croatian Spring" movement's leadership and participants in 1971 had repressed the reawakened Croatian nationalism, but could not eliminate it. Croatian elites had realized the disadvantages of the Croatian situation and had expressed it in 1970–71 through the only channel then available—the Communist Party of Croatia and its liberal wing. With the purges, this wing became officially silent in order to survive, but it remained active under the surface, hoping for its turn. This came with the 1974 constitution and its devolution of power to the republic level, helped along by the growing role of the Catholic Church in Croatia. The Catholic Church, as the only openly organized opposition force in the country, became the outspoken defender of Croatian nationalism. As a result, Catholic leaders and priests were subjected to persecution and furious attacks by the government.

Yugoslavia—A House Divided

After Tito's death in 1980, relations between the Croatian majority and the Serbian minority became strained. Tito had set up a rotating presidency in which the leaders of each of the six republics and two autonomous regions of Serbia would have the Yugoslavian presidency for one year at a time. Unfortunately, the Serbian president that first held the office was not recognized by the Croats. Demands for autonomy by the half million Serbs in Croatia were brushed aside by the Croats, who pointed out the absence of such autonomy for Croats in Vojvodina and Bosnia and Herzegovina. The conservatives' control of the League of Communist of Croatia between 1972 and 1987 could not prevent the resurfacing of the Croat question, which led in a few years to Croatia's disassociation from Yugoslavia and to war.

As the Communist parties of the various republics kept losing in membership and control, the clamoring for multiparty elections became irresistible. The first such elections were held on 8 April 1990 in Slovenia, where a coalition of non-Communist parties (Demos) won and formed the first non-Communist Government since 1945. In Croatia, the Croatian Democratic Union (HDZ), under the leadership of Dr. Franjo Tudjman, had worked illegally since 1989 and had developed an effective network of offices throughout Croatia and in Vojvodina and Bosnia and Herzegovina. The HDZ had also established its branches abroad from where, particularly in the United States, it received substantial financial support. Thus, in the elections of late April–early May 1990 the Croatian Democratic Union was able to obtain an overwhelming victory with 205 of 356 seats won and a majority in each of the three chambers of the Croatian Assembly. In the most important Socio-Political Chamber, Dr. Tudjman's party won 54 of the 80 seats, with the Communists and their allies obtaining only 26 seats. On 30 May 1990, Dr. Tudjman was elected president of Croatia with 281 of 331 votes, and Stjepan Mesic became prime minister. Krajina Serbs voted either for the former Communists or for their new Serbian Democratic Party (SNS) led by Jovan Raškovic. The Serbian Democratic Party gained five delegates to the parliament and became the main voice of the Serbs in Croatia.

The overwhelming victory of Dr. Tudjman's party made the Serbs very uncomfortable. Their traditional desire for closer political ties to Serbia proper, the prospect of losing their overrepresentation (and jobs) in the Croatian Republic's administration, and fear of the repetition of the World War II Ustaša–directed persecutions and massacres of Serbs made them an easy and eager audience for Slobodan Miloševic's policy and tactics of unifying all Serbian lands to Serbia proper. Tensions between Croats and Serbs increased when Tudjman proposed constitutional amendments in June 1990 defining Croatia as the Sovereign State of the Croats and other nations and national minorities without specifically mentioning the Serbs of Croatia. The Serbs feared they would be

left unprotected in an independent Croatia and therefore strongly supported Miloševic's centralist policies. This fear, along with the anti-Croatian propaganda from Belgrade that claimed the revival of the Ustaša and called upon Serbs to defend themselves, caused Jovan Raškovic to reject the invitation from Tudjman to join the new government as its deputy prime minister. Instead, Raškovic ended the participation in legislative activities of the five Serbian Democratic Party deputies. At the end of August 1990, a new Serbian National Council adopted a "Declaration on the Sovereignty and Autonomy of the Serbian People," implying the need for cultural autonomy for the Serbs if Croatia were to remain a member of the Yugoslav Federation, but claiming political autonomy for the Serbs if Croatia were to secede from the Yugoslav Federation. A referendum held on 18 August 1990 by Serbs in Croatia gave unanimous support to their "Declaration on Sovereignty" as the foundation for the further development of their Knin Republic—the council of Serbian-majority communes, from the name of the Dalmatian city of Knin where it was based.

The Tudjman government refrained from taking any action against the Knin Republic in order to avoid any reason for interference by the Yugoslav Army, but Tudjman made very clear that territorial autonomy for the Serbs was out of the question. When, in December 1990, Croatia proclaimed its sovereignty and promulgated its new constitution, the Serbs of Croatia established a "Serbian Autonomous Region," immediately invalidated by the constitutional court of Croatia. In February 1991, Croatia and Slovenia declared invalid all federal laws regarding the two republics. On 28 February, the Krajina Serbs declared their autonomy in response to Croatia's call for disassociation from the Yugoslav Federation. Violence spread in many places with clashes between the Serbian paramilitary and special Croatian police units, and Yugoslav Army units were ordered to intervene. The Yugoslav Army was also used in Serbia in March 1991 to aid Serbian authorities against large Serbian opposition demonstrations in Belgrade. The sight of Yugoslav tanks in the streets of Belgrade, with two dead and some 90 wounded, signaled the decision of the Yugoslav Army to defend Yugoslavia's borders and oppose interethnic clashes that could lead to a civil war. The Serbian leadership and the Yugoslav Army top command (mostly Serbian) had cemented their alliance, with the goal of preserving Yugoslavia as a centralized state through pressuring Slovenia and Croatia into disarming their territorial defense units and by threatening forceful intervention in case of their refusal. Still, Slovenia and Croatia continued to buy arms for their defense forces and to proclaim their intentions to gain independence.

At the end of March 1991, there were again bloody armed clashes between the Krajina Serbs and Croatian police, and again the Yugoslav Army intervened around the Plitvice National Park, an area the Serbs wanted to join to their Knin Republic. For President Tudjman this Serbian action was the last straw—Croatia had been patient for eight months, but could wait no longer. The overall determination of Serbia to maintain a unitary Yugoslavia hardened, as did the determination of Slovenia and Croatia to attain their full independence. This caused the Yugoslav Army leadership to support Serbia and Slobodan Miloševic, who had made his position clear by the spring of 1991 on the potential unilateral separation of Slovenia, Croatia, and Bosnia and Herzegovina. Since there was no substantial Serbian population in Slovenia, its disassociation did not present a real problem for Miloševic. However, separation of Croatia and Bosnia and Herzegovina would necessitate border revisions in order to allow for lands with Serbian populations to be joined to Serbia.

Independence

A last effort to avoid Yugoslavia's disintegration was made by Bosnia and Herzegovina and Macedonia with their 3 June 1991 compromise proposal to form a Community of Yugoslav Republics. National defense, foreign policy, and a common market would be administered centrally while all other areas—other than armed forces and diplomatic representation—would fall into the jurisdiction of the member states. However, it was too late. Serbia opposed the federal nature of the proposal and this left an opening for the establishment of separate armed forces. In addition, Miloševic and the Yugoslav Army had already committed to the support of the Serbs' revolt in Croatia. In any case, both Miloševic and Tudjman were past the state of salvaging Yugoslavia. They met in Split on 12 June 1991 to discuss how to divide Bosnia and Herzegovina into ethnic cantons.

The federal government of Yugoslavia ceased to exist when its last president (Stjepan Mesic, Croatia's future president) and prime minister (Ante Markovic), both Croatian, resigned on 5 December 1991. Both Croatia and Slovenia reaffirmed their decision to disassociate from federal Yugoslavia after a three-month moratorium, in the Brioni Declaration of 7 July 1991. The European Community held a conference on Yugoslavia, chaired by Lord Carrington, where a series of unsuccessful cease-fires was negotiated for Croatia. The conference also attempted to negotiate new arrangements based on the premise that the Yugoslav Federation no longer existed, a position strongly rejected by Serbia, who viewed with great suspicion Germany's support for the independence of Slovenia and Croatia. Germany granted recognition to Slovenia and Croatia on 18 December 1991, while other European community members and the United States followed suit. The European community continued its efforts to stop the killing and destruction in Croatia, along with the UN special envoy, Cyrus Vance, who was able to conclude a peace accord on 3 January 1992 calling for a major UN peacekeeping force in Croatia. Part of the accord was also an agreement by the Serbian side to hand over their heavy weapons to the UN units and to allow the return of thousands of refugees to their homes. The international community stood firmly in support of the preservation of Yugoslavia. The United States and the European community had indicated that they would refuse to recognize the independence of Slovenia and Croatia if they unilaterally seceded. At the same time, Slovenia and Croatia defined their separation as a disassociation by sovereign nations, and declared their independence on 25 June 1991. Miloševic was prepared to let Slovenia go, but Croatia still held around 600,000 ethnic Serbs. Miloševic knew that a military attack on a member republic would deal a mortal blow to both the idea and the reality of a "Yugoslavia" in any form. Thus, following the Yugoslav Army's attack on Slovenia on 27 June 1991, Miloševic used the Yugoslav Army and its superior capabilities toward the goal of establishing the Serbian autonomous region of Krajina in Croatia. Increased fighting from July 1991 caused the tremendous destruction of entire cities (for example, Vukovar) and large-scale damage to medieval Dubrovnik. Croatia had been arming since 1990 with the financial aid of émigrés, and thus withstood fighting over a seven-month period, suffering some 10,000 deaths, 30,000 wounded, and over 14,000 missing, losing to the Krajina Serbs (and to the Yugoslav Army). Croatia also lost about one-third of its territory—from Slavonia to the west and around the border with Bosnia and south to northern Dalmatia.

By late 1992, rebel Serbs controlled about one-third of Croatia's territory. In 1993, the Krajina Serbs voted to integrate with Serbs in Bosnia and Serbia. Although the Croatian government and the Krajina Serbs agreed to a cease-fire in March 1994, further talks disintegrated. This portion of land was strategically important to Croatia because it held the land routes to the Dalmatian coast (supporting the once-thriving tourist industry), the country's petroleum resources, and the access route from Zagreb into Slavonia. Also in 1994, the Croatian government agreed to give up its plan to partition Bosnia with Serbia. In return for US political support (which included military training and equipment), Croatia began cooperating with the Bosnian Muslims and recognized the sovereignty of Bosnia and Herzegovina.

In May 1995, the Croatian Army—in a mission it called "Operation Storm"—quickly occupied western Slavonia, and by August 1995, the Krajina region was under Croatian control. International reaction to the military mission was mild, largely judged as vindication for earlier Serb aggression. An estimated 200,000 Serbs fled from the region their ancestors had occupied for 200 years. Before the Croatian Army could move into eastern Slavonia, the government halted the mission upon insistence by the United States. The cessation of the Croatian military campaign before it reached eastern Slavonia probably prevented a future round of killings.

Eastern Slavonia was put under UN control, with a force of about 5,500 military and police peacekeepers. With the signing of a basic agreement between the Croatian government and the Eastern Slavonia Serbs at the Dayton Peace Accords in Dayton, Ohio, in 1995, the UN had the support to establish the UN Transitional Administration for Eastern Slavonia (UNTAES) on 15 January 1996. The UNTAES established a Transitional Police Force, in which Serb and Croat police forces jointly administered the region, in order to prepare the area for reversion to Croatian control in July 1997. On 15 January 1998, any Serbs remaining in eastern Slavonia became Croatian citizens. Also, the Serbs that fled Croatia for fear of persecution were invited back into the country on 26 June 1998, when the Croatian parliament adopted the Croatian government's Return Program.

The 1997 elections that supported the reigning President Tudjman and his HDZ party were considered "fundamentally flawed." The tight grip that Tudjman kept on the Croatian nation through control of the media, police, and judicial system were considered not only undemocratic, but unconstitutional. In 1999, President Tudjman announced that "National issues are more important than democracy," alienating many Croatians and concerning international observers. Tudjman cooperated with some requests of the International Criminal Tribunal for the Former Yugoslavia (ICTY) but refused to comply with others, especially the insistence on field investigations into the military operations of the 1990s. The ruling party agreed in 1999 to hold new parliamentary elections in January 2000, but these were scheduled too late for Tudjman to organize his resistance. He died on 10 December 1999, and Speaker of Parliament Vlatko Pavletic assumed interim power. On 18 February 2000, Stjepan Mesic was elected president of Croatia, signaling a new era in Croatian history that promised to be more European and more peaceful. In February 2005, Mesic was elected for a second term, with 66% of the vote, over his main contender Jadranka Kosor.

The parliamentary elections held in early 2000 resulted in an end to the rule of the HDZ party, which won only 46 of 151 seats in the House of Representatives; Social Democratic Party (SDP) leader Ivica Racan led a center-left coalition government as prime minister. Constitutional reforms later that year reduced the powers exercised by the president and replaced the semi-presidential system of government with a parliamentary one. In 2001, parliament approved a constitutional amendment abolishing its upper house, the House of Counties. The HDZ branded the government's move as politically motivated, as it controlled the upper house and had been able to delay reform-minded legislation.

In November 2003, the parliamentary elections were won by the HDZ, which took 66 out of 152 seats in the House of Representatives. The SDP got only 34 seats, while other parties and representatives had to settle for 10 seats or less. Ivo Sanader, the leader of HDZ, was invited by president Mesic to form a government. Subsequently, the parliament gave its consent, and Sanader was appointed prime minister with 88 votes in favor. Sanader, a strong supporter of EU and NATO membership, promised that his party had undergone major changes since the death of Tudjman and pledged to uphold democracy and the rule of law.

In September 2001, the ICTY indicted Milošević for war crimes and crimes against humanity committed in the war in Croatia. He went on trial in The Hague in February 2002 and died there in March 2006, with only 50 hours of testimony left before the conclusion of the trial. In September 2002, under pressure from nationalists, the Croatian government declined to turn over to the Hague tribunal former Army Chief of Staff Janko Bobetko, indicted for war crimes. In March 2003, former Maj. Gen. Mirko Norac was sentenced in a Croatian court to 12 years in prison for orchestrating the killings of Serb civilians in 1991. He was the most senior Croatian Army officer to be convicted for war crimes in a Croatian court. Norac had given himself up to Croatian authorities in March 2001 on the understanding that he would not be extradited to the ICTY. In June 2004, wartime Croatian Serb leader Milan Babic was sentenced to 13 years in prison by the ICTY for his part in war crimes against non-Serbs in the self-proclaimed Krajina Serb republic where he was a leader in the early 1990s. In December 2005, fugitive Croatian General Ante Gotovina was arrested in Spain. He was sought by the ICTY for war crimes. In April 2011, Gotovina, along with Mladen Markač, a fellow Croatian officer accused of war crimes, received an extended prison sentence from the ICTY.

In February 2003, Croatia submitted its application for membership to the European Union; it had previously concluded its Stabilization and Association Agreement (SAA) with the EU in May 2001. Accession talks stalled from time to time over issues including government corruption, border disputes, and the status of war criminals in the country. After its summit in December of 2004, the European Council decided that EU accession negotiations were to commence on March 17th of the following year. However, on 16 March 2005, the EU postponed negotiations due to the ICTY's verdict that Croatia was not making a serious effort

to capture Ante Gotovina. Negotiations resumed following Gotovina's arrest in December of 2005.

Croatia's bid for EU accession was further set back by its long-standing border disputes with Slovenia. In December of 2008, Slovenia vetoed Croatia's bid for membership as a result of a border dispute in the Bay of Piran. Croatia favored a border line that split the bay directly in half. Slovenia claimed the entire bay as its own, arguing that any dissection would hinder its own access to the Adriatic Sea. An Arbitration Agreement between Croatia and Slovenia was finally signed in Stockholm on 4 November 2009, by both countries' prime ministers as well as the President of the EU. Croatia also became a full member of NATO in April of the same year. Croatia finished EU accession negotiations on 30 June 2011 and on 9 December 2011 signed the treaty to become the bloc's 28th member. The ratification process, by the Parliaments of all 27 EU member states, was expected to be concluded by the end of June 2013, with entry into force and accession of Croatia to the EU to take place on 1 July 2013. An EU accession referendum was held in Croatia on 22 January 2012.

Despite being generally friendly to EU accession, Croatian citizens have occasionally displayed Euroskeptic sentiments. Much of the opposition to accession has come as a result of the organization's request for the extradition of Croatian citizens to the ICTY. The convictions of Gotovina and Markač in 2011 caused a spike in Euroskepticism due to the perceived association between the ICTY and the EU. Despite these occasional spikes of Euroskepticism, most Croatian voters view EU accession favorably, and the 2012 referendum passed in favor of joining the EU.

The 2007 parliamentary elections saw another electoral victory for the HDZ, although by a less convincing margin than in 2003. The HDZ won 66 seats, the same as in 2003. However, the SDP won 56 seats, or 22 more than in the previous election. Ivo Sanader remained prime minister in a cabinet supported by the HDZ, HSS, and HSLS. However, in July of 2009, Sanader announced his resignation from politics The decision came as a surprise, because many had projected that he would be a top contender for the 2010 presidential race. Sanader was defined politically by his drive to move Croatia into NATO and the EU. To fill his place, the HDZ elected Jadranka Kosor as the head of the party. She was approved by parliament as the new prime minister a few days after Sanader stepped down. The appointment made Kosor the nation's first woman premier.

In January 2010, Croatian voters selected Social Democratic lawmaker Ivo Josipovic to succeed Stipe Mesic as the country's president. Mesic, a two-term, ten-year president with centrist inclinations, remained very popular in Croatia but could not run for reelection due to term limits. Josipovic defeated his lone rival, an independent, in the elections, capturing over 60% of the vote. The aspiration for European Union membership was a repeated motif throughout Josipovic's campaign.

On 22 and 24 February 2011, citizens gathered in Zagreb in anti-government protests, calling for the resignation of Kosor, whose government had been blamed for the nation's economic crisis. The second protest involved a march on the government building in St. Marc square. Since rallies and other protests have been banned from the square since 2005, police forces were called to disperse the crowds with tear gas. No injuries were reported, but eleven protestors were detained, presumably for violence against the police. Additional protests were organized largely through communication on Facebook. Several thousand activists responded to such a call for a march in Zagreb and three other major towns on 3 March. Protesters in the capital burned the flags of the European Union, the Social Democrats, and the Croatian Democratic Union. Some demonstrators also assembled at the Kosor residence.

The Croatian parliamentary elections held in December 2011 finally brought an end to the HDZ's dominance in parliamentary politics. Kukuriku, a political alliance of four center-left parties (including the SDP) formed in 2010, triumphed in the elections, receiving a majority (81) of the seats in Parliament. The election was the first in which the HDZ did not become the best-represented party in parliament; the center-right party won a paltry 47 seats to come in a distant second in the elections. Domestic policy and economy were the main themes of the campaign. The dethroning of the HDZ did not come as a surprise; the cabinets headed by Sanader and Kosor had poor approval ratings due to numerous corruption scandals, high unemployment, and a grim economic outlook. Zoran Milanović, who had failed in his bid to become prime minister four years earlier, headed the new cabinet.

13 GOVERNMENT

Croatia is a democratic republic with a president and parliamentary system of government. The parliament of Croatia, formed on 30 May 1990, adopted a new constitution on 22 December 1990. The executive authority is held by the president, elected for five years, and a government cabinet headed by the prime minister. Constitutional reforms in 2000 significantly reduced the powers exercised by the president. However, the president remains the supreme commander of the armed forces and participates in foreign and national security policy decision making. The constitutional court assures legality.

In March 2001, amendments to the constitution abolished the upper house of parliament (House of Counties) in what had been a bicameral legislature (also including the lower house, or House of Representatives). The unicameral parliament, known as the Sabor (Assembly), has 151 members elected for four-year terms.

The threshold that parties must cross for representation in parliament is 5% of the turnout in each of the 10 electoral districts. Croatian citizens that live outside the country's borders are counted in a distinct electoral unit, and their votes are weighed directly against the number of domestic votes to determine the number of parliamentary seats the Diaspora will receive. (Voters must be 18 or older, or 16 if employed.) The prime minister is nominated by the president, in line with the balance of power in the Assembly. Domestic policy making is the responsibility of parliament.

14 POLITICAL PARTIES

In the presidential elections of May 1997, Tudjman, founder of the Christian Democratic Union (HDZ) in 1988, won a second term as president of Croatia, with 61.2% of the vote. International monitors, however, condemned the elections as seriously biased in favor of the incumbent. Zdravko Tomac of the socialist Social Democrat Party won 21.1% of the vote, and Vlado Gotovac of the moderate Social Liberal Party received 17.7%. After the death of Tudjman at the end of 1999, presidential elections were held in January and February 2000. Thirteen candidates successfully reg-

istered for the election. Stjepan Mesic of the Croatian People's Party (HNS), supported by the Croatian Peasant Party (HSS)/Istrian Democratic Sabor (IDS)/LS liberal coalition, defeated rival Drazen Budiša of the Social Democratic Party (SDP)/Croatian Social Liberal Party (HSLS) coalition, 41.1% to 27.7% in the first round, with Croatian Democratic Union (HDZ) candidate Mate Granic gaining 22.5% of the vote, and 56% to 44% in the second round of the ballot. Mesic won in 17 out of 21 counties. Voter turnout in round one was 63% and 61% in round two. Mesic was reelected in 2005. He had the support of eight political parties and defeated his main contender, Jadranka Kosor, in the second round of the elections, with 66% of the popular vote.

In the parliamentary elections held 23 November 2003, HDZ garnered 66 seats in the House of the Representatives; the SDP won 34. The HDZ formed a minority government coalition with DC (Democratic Center), HSLS, HSU, and SDSS. The leader of HDZ, Ivo Sanader, became the new prime minister. The 2007 parliamentary elections saw another electoral victory for the HDZ, although by a less convincing margin than in 2003. The HDZ won 66 seats, the same as in 2003. However, the SDP won 56 seats, or 22 more than in the previous election. Ivo Sanader remained prime minister in a cabinet supported by the HDZ, HSS, and HSLS.

Jadranka Kosor was elected as the head of the Croatian Democratic Union and approved by parliament as the new prime minister in July 2009 following the resignation of Ivo Sanader amid allegations of corruption. The appointment made Kosor the nation's first female premier.

In January 2010, Croatian voters selected Social Democratic lawmaker Ivo Josipovic to succeed Stipe Mesic as the country's president. Mesic, a two-term, ten-year president with centrist inclinations, remained very popular in Croatia but could not run for reelection due to term limits. The next presidential elections were scheduled for December 2015.

In October 2010, the Social Democrats, Croatia's primary opposition party, called for a vote of no confidence against the ruling coalition, led by the Croatian Democratic Union. The Social Democrats cited continued allegations of corruption and economic problems as the reasons for the motion. The motion was rejected by a vote of 79 to 62, with 12 abstentions.

Kukuriku, a political alliance of four center-left parties (including the SDP) formed in 2010, triumphed in the 2011 elections, receiving a majority (81) of the seats in Parliament. The HDZ won only 47 seats. Zoran Milanović headed the new cabinet.

In the elections of December 2011, the Kukuriku coalition (including the Social Democratic Party, the Croatian People's Party, the Istrian Democratic Assembly, and the Croatian Party of Pensioners) won 81 of the 151 seats in the unicameral assembly. The conservative ruling Croatian Democratic Union (HDZ) won only 47 seats. The Croatian Labor Party and the Croatian Democratic Alliance of Slavonia and Baranja took six seats each. Other parties represented included the Croatian Party of the Right and the Croatian Peasant Party. Zoran Milanovic of the Social Democratic Party took the post of prime minister.

15 LOCAL GOVERNMENT

Local government in Croatia consists of municipalities that are grouped into 20 counties and 1 city. Citizens are guaranteed the right to local self-government with competencies to decide on matters, needs, and interest of local relevance. Counties consist of areas determined by history, transportation, and other economic factors. The 20 counties are: Zagreb, Kradina-Zagorje, Sisacko-Moslavacka, Karlovac, Varazdin, Koprivnica-Krizevci, Bjelovar-Bilogora, Hrvatsko Primorje-Gorski Kotar, Lika-Senj, Virovitica-Podravina, Pozega-Slavonija, Slavonski Brod-Posavina, Zadar-Knin, Osijek-Baranja, Šibenik, Vukovar-Srijem, Dalmatia-Split, Istria, Dubrovnik-Neretva, and Medjimurje, along with the City of Zagreb.

The mayor of Zagreb is elected by the city assembly and is approved by the president. In the local elections of 2009, the HDZ won a majority of prefects and councils, with the SDP coming in at a distant second. However, the SDP performed well in some of the larger cities. In Zagreb, socialist incumbent Milan Bandić won a convincing victory over HDZ challenger Josip Kregar. The SDP similarly dominated the Zagreb council elections. The 2009 elections were the first in which mayors and county prefects were elected directly by popular vote, rather than by a majority coalition in the council. The new system proved to be favorable for independent candidates, as many cities (including Split) elected independent mayors. Many cities and counties elected opposite lists for mayoral and council elections, causing a larger amount of cohabitation in local governments.

16 JUDICIAL SYSTEM

The judicial system is comprised of municipal and county courts, a Supreme Court, an Administrative Court, and a Constitutional Court. A High Judicial Council (made up of 11 members serving eight-year terms) appoints judges and public prosecutors. The judicial system, supervised by the justice and administration ministry, remains subject to ethnic bias and political influence, especially at the local level. Judges are prohibited constitutionally from being members of any political party.

A commercial court system handles all commercial and contractual disputes. The Supreme Court judges are appointed for an eight-year term by the Judicial Council. The Constitutional Court has 13 judges (11 prior to March 2001) who are also elected in the same manner. The military court system was abolished in November 1996. The constitution prohibits the arbitrary interference with privacy, family, home, or correspondence, but these freedoms are not always protected by the government.

17 ARMED FORCES

The International Institute for Strategic Studies reported that armed forces in Croatia totaled 18,600 members in 2011. The force was comprised of 11,390 from the army, 1,850 from the navy, 3,500 from the air force, and 1,860 members of joint forces. Armed forces represented 1.1% of the labor force in Croatia. Defense spending totaled $1.9 billion and accounted for 2.4% of gross domestic product (GDP).

The armed forces of Croatia are restricted by the Dayton Peace Accords. As of 2011, Croatia was involved in 12 foreign countries or regions as part of NATO, UN, and EU military and peacekeeping missions.

18 INTERNATIONAL COOPERATION

Croatia was admitted to the UN on 22 May 1992; it is part of the Economic Commission for Europe (ECE) and serves on several specialized agencies, such as the Food and Agriculture Organization (FAO), the International Atomic Energy Agency (IAEA), the International Civil Aviation Organization (ICAO), the International Monetary Fund (IMF), the UN Educational, Scientific and Cultural Organization (UNESCO), the UN Industrial Development Organization (UNIDO), the World Health Organization (WHO), and the World Bank. The nation was admitted to the World Trade Organization (WTO) on 30 November 2000. Croatia is a member of the Organization for Security and Cooperation in Europe (OSCE), the Council of Europe, the Central European Initiative, the Euro-Atlantic Partnership Council, and the European Bank for Reconstruction and Development. The nation joined NATO in April 2009.

Croatia has been a candidate for membership in the European Union since 2003. Accession talks have stalled a few times over issues such as government corruption and the status of war criminals in the nation. In 2008, Slovenia vetoed Croatia's bid for membership as a result of a border dispute in the Bay of Piran. The dispute had been ongoing since both countries declared independence in 1991. Croatia favored a border line that split the bay directly in half. Slovenia claimed the entire bay as its own, arguing that any dissection would hinder its own access to the Adriatic Sea. An Arbitration Agreement between Croatia and Slovenia was finally signed in Stockholm on 4 November 2009, by both countries' prime ministers as well as the President of the EU. Croatia finished EU accession negotiations on 30 June 2011 and on 9 December 2011 signed the treaty to become the bloc's 28th member. The ratification process, by the Parliaments of all 27 EU member states, was expected to be concluded by the end of June 2013, with entry into force and accession of Croatia to the EU on 1 July 2013. An EU accession referendum was held in Croatia on 22 January 2012. Despite occasional spikes of Euroskepticism, most Croatian voters view EU accession favorably and the referendum passed.

Croatia is an observer in the Nonaligned Movement and is part of the Organization for the Prohibition of Chemical Weapons. The UN sent peacekeeping troops to Croatia in the spring of 1992 to mediate an ongoing civil war in the region. In environmental cooperation, Croatia is part of the Basel Convention, Conventions on Biological Diversity and Air Pollution, Ramsar, CITES, the London Convention, the Montréal Protocol, MARPOL, the Nuclear Test Ban Treaty, and the UN Conventions on the Law of the Sea, Climate Change, and Desertification.

19 ECONOMY

The GDP rate of change in Croatia as of 2010 was -1.4%. Inflation stood at 1.3%, and unemployment was reported at 17.6%.

Before the dissolution of the Yugoslav SFR, Croatia was its second most prosperous and industrialized area (after Slovenia). Per capita output in Croatia was comparable to that of Portugal and about 33% above the Yugoslav average. Croatia's economic problems were largely inherited from a legacy of Communist mismanagement and a bloated foreign debt. Internal conflicts caused massive infrastructure and industrial damage to bridges, power lines, factories, buildings, and houses. Croatia's economy also had to grapple with a large population of refugees and internally displaced persons. As a result of the war and loss in output capacity, GDP fell by more than 40%.

Although unemployment remained high and the country had a growing trade deficit, Croatia in the early 2000s experienced a growth in tourism and an increase in remittances and investment from expatriate Croats. Many small and medium-sized businesses were privatized, and even larger state-owned industries were being restructured. Croatia joined the WTO in 2000 and in October 2001 signed a Stabilization and Association Agreement with the EU, which moved the country in the direction of integration with the EU. Major growth sectors included energy, tourism, construction, transportation, and telecommunications. In 2002, the GDP growth rate reached 5.2%, dropping to 4.3% in 2003 and 3.7% in 2004. In 2007, the economy experienced a resurgence as the GDP real growth rate increased to 5.8% and unemployment fell to 11.8%. A number of privatizations were completed by 2007, but government spending still accounted for as much as 40% of GDP, and many large businesses were still heavily subsidized by the state.

While Croatia weathered the 2008–09 global financial crisis better than some of its neighbors, a serious decline in tourism and a decreased demand for industrial exports, particularly wood and automobiles, led the country into a recession in 2009. GDP contracted by 5.9% and unemployment was estimated at 14.9%. Although the Croatian economy showed signs of recovery by the last quarter of 2010, GDP declined by 1.2% for the year and unemployment grew to 17.6%.

While the country is set to enjoy the economic benefits of joining the European Union by 2013, there is accession opposition among small business owners and local shopkeepers, who worry that they will have to spend more than they can afford to update their facilities to meet EU standards.

20 INCOME

The CIA estimated that in 2010 the GDP of Croatia was $78.09 billion. The CIA defines GDP as the value of all final goods and services produced within a nation in a given year, computed on the basis of purchasing power parity (PPP) rather than value as measured on the basis of the rate of the exchange based on current dollars. The per capita GDP was estimated at $17,400. The annual growth rate of GDP was -1.2%. The average inflation rate was 1.3%. It was estimated that agriculture accounted for 6.8% of GDP, industry 27.2%, and services 66%. Remittances from citizens living abroad totaled $1.5 billion, or about $329 per capita, and accounted for approximately 1.9% of GDP.

As of 2011, the most recent study by the World Bank reported that actual individual consumption in Croatia was 68.0% of GDP and accounted for 0.11% of world consumption. By comparison, the United States accounted for 25.44% of world individual consumption. The World Bank also estimated that 19.1% of Croatia's GDP was spent on food and beverages, 18.3% on housing and household furnishings, 3.8% on clothes, 7.8% on health, 7.5% on transportation, 2.4% on communications, 6.4% on recreation, 6.2% on restaurants and hotels, and -9.2% on miscellaneous goods and services and purchases from abroad. It was estimated that in 2008 about 17% of the population subsisted on an income below the poverty line established by Croatia's government.

21 LABOR

As of 2010, Croatia had a total labor force of 1.721 million people. Within that labor force, the CIA estimated in 2008 that 5% were employed in agriculture, 31.3% in industry, and 63.6% in the service sector. All workers, except the military and police, may form and join unions of their own choosing without prior authorization. Generally, unions are independent of political parties and of the government. About 35% of the workforce was unionized in 2009. The right to strike and bargain collectively is protected by law, although there are restrictions and limitations. Nonpayment of wages continues to be a serious problem.

As of 2010, Croatia had a national minimum wage of €385 (approximately $500), one of the highest among Central and Eastern European (CEE) states. Among CEE members of the EU, only Slovenia had a higher minimum wage. In 2002 the standard workweek was shortened from 42 to 40 hours. Workers are also entitled to a 30-minute break every day, one day off every seven days, and a minimum of eighteen days paid vacation per year. The minimum working age is 15 and this is generally enforced. In addition, workers under the age of 18 are prohibited from working overtime, at night, or under hazardous conditions. There are also occupational safety and health standards, but these are not routinely respected.

22 AGRICULTURE

The civil war reduced agricultural output in the years immediately following the breakup of the Yugoslav SFR. Roughly 23% of the total land is farmed, and the country's major crops include wheat, corn, sugar beets, sunflower seed, barley, alfalfa, clover, olives, citrus, grapes, soybeans, and potatoes. Cereal production in 2009 amounted to 3.4 million tons, fruit production to 419,483 tons, and vegetable production to 299,356 tons. Plums are used in the production of slivovitz, a type of plum brandy popular in the Balkan region.

23 ANIMAL HUSBANDRY

The UN Food and Agriculture Organization (FAO) reported that Croatia dedicated 342,000 hectares (845,100 acres) to permanent pasture or meadow in 2009. During that year, the country tended 6.7 million chickens, 447,000 head of cattle, and 1.3 million pigs. The production from these animals amounted to 38,237 tons of beef and veal, 119,188 tons of pork, 56,557 tons of poultry, 47,937 tons of eggs, and 963,380 tons of milk. Croatia also produced 3,294 tons of cattle hide and 659 tons of raw wool.

24 FISHING

With a mainland coastline of 1,778 km (1,105 mi) and island coastlines totaling 4,012 km (2,493 mi) on the Adriatic, Croatia is suited to the development of marine fishing. However, Croatia lacks adequate fishing vessels as well as the infrastructure to transport and process seafood. Sardine is the principal saltwater species caught; carp is the most common freshwater species. Croatia's annual catch has declined steadily due to overfishing for a variety of species. However, fish farming has resulted in an overproduction of freshwater species and a decline in prices. Croatia had 2,314 decked commercial fishing boats in 2008. The annual capture totaled 49,024 tons according to the UN FAO. The export value of seafood totaled $96.92 million.

25 FORESTRY

Approximately 34% of Croatia is covered by forest, and the country supplies small but good quality oak and beech. The wood industry has traditionally been oriented to the Italian market (accounting for over 35% of exports) and suffered damages during the civil war. Croatian exports of hardwood lumber typically consist of 50% beech, 30% oak, and 6% ash. Panels and veneer are also exported, and Croatia is starting to increase the output of value-added products such as veneer sheets, plywood, and particle board. The UN FAO estimated the 2009 roundwood production at 3.38 million cu m (119.4 million cu ft). The value of all forest products, including roundwood, totaled $444.2 million. The forestry sector, along with the whole of Croatian industry, is also attempting to produce in accordance with European standards and develop standardized contracts.

26 MINING

Aside from petroleum, the chief minerals industry, Croatia produces small quantities of ferrous and nonferrous metals and industrial minerals, mainly for domestic needs. In 2008, the mining and quarrying sector exported about $375 million of goods, while imports amounted to $3.5 billion. Cement output in 2009 was down 22% from 2008. The production of clays, lime, nitrogen, pumice, stone, and sand and gravel satisfied most of Croatia's demand for construction materials. Mineral production in 2009 included cement, 2.838 million tons; salt, processed at Pag Island, 32,500 metric tons; bentonite, 19,000 metric tons; crude gypsum, 234,300 metric tons; and quartz, quartzite, and glass sand, 150,000 metric tons. Bauxite production has ceased; it was 1,500 metric tons in 1996. Prior to the breakup of Yugoslavia, Croatia was the federation's chief producer of natural gas and petroleum, and a leading producer of iron and steel. The minerals sector was heavily hurt by the 1991–92 war, which damaged facilities, affected the market for raw materials, and disrupted normal commercial activities.

27 ENERGY AND POWER

The World Bank reported in 2008 that Croatia produced 12.2 billion kWh of electricity and consumed 17.2 billion kWh, or 3,835 kWh per capita. Roughly 85% of energy came from fossil fuels, while 5% came from alternative fuels. Per capita oil consumption was 2,047 kg. Oil production totaled 14,584 barrels of oil a day. In 2009, oil imports were 103,000 barrels per day, and in 2010, oil consumption was 98,000 barrels per day.

As of 1 January 2011, Croatia had proven natural gas reserves totaling 24.92 billion cu m (880 billion cu ft). Croatia imported 1.22 billion cu m (43.1 billion cu ft) of natural gas in 2009.

28 INDUSTRY

Light industry, especially for the production of consumer goods, is more advanced in Croatia than in the other republics of the former Yugoslav SFR. Croatia's main manufacturing industries include chemicals and plastics, machine tools, fabricated metal products, electronics, pig iron and rolled steel products, aluminum processing, paper and wood products (including furniture), building ma-

terials (including cement), textiles, shipbuilding, petroleum and petroleum refining, and food processing and beverages.

The collapse of Yugoslavia and the hostilities following Croatia's declaration of independence in 1991 damaged industrial production. Manufacturing employed about 335,000 people in 1995. The textile and clothing industry accounted for about 11% of total industrial output in 1995; the food industry, 17%. Industrial production increased 3.7% in 1998 and accounted for 24% of GDP. Industrial production increased to 33% of GDP in 2002. Subsequent years saw efforts by the government to privatize state-owned enterprises, which further aided the industrial sector.

Although industry is an important part of the Croatian economy, it suffered some setbacks due to the 2008–09 global financial crisis. In 2009 industrial output declined by 5.8%. In 2010, the industrial growth rate was estimated at -1.4%, and industry accounted for 25.7% of Croatia's economy, down from 30.8% in 2005. The percentage of the workforce employed in the industrial sector in 2010 was 31.3%, down slightly from 32.8% in 2005.

29 SCIENCE AND TECHNOLOGY

The Croatian Academy of Sciences and Arts (founded in 1866 and headquartered in Zagreb) has sections devoted to mathematical sciences and physics, natural sciences, and medical sciences. The Museum of Natural Sciences (founded in 1924) is located in Split and the Croatian Natural History Museum (founded in 1846) and the Technical Museum (founded in 1954) are in Zagreb. The universities of Zagreb (founded in 1669), Osijek (founded in 1975), Rijeka (founded in 1973), and Split (founded in 1974) offer degrees in basic and applied science.

As of 2008, Croatia had 1,514 researchers per million people engaged in research and development (R&D), down from 1,920 in 2002. Research and development spending for 2008 totaled $700 million, or 0.9% of Croatia's per capita GDP, down from 1.14% in 2002. In 2008, Croatia ranked 40th in the world in R&D spending as a percentage of the national economy. The government accounts for the majority of R&D spending.

30 DOMESTIC TRADE

Domestic trade occurs mainly between urban industry and rural agriculture. Civil strife and economic recessions during the 1990s severely weakened the domestic economy. The government has looked toward foreign investments to boost the economy. Privatization and anticorruption programs are likely to attract such foreign investments. A boost in the tourism industry has also aided the economy.

Normal working hours for public offices are 8:30 a.m. to 5:00 p.m., Monday through Friday. Banks are typically open from 7:00 a.m. to 7:00 p.m., Monday through Friday, and from 7:00 a.m. until noon on Saturdays. During the week, shops are open from 7:00 a.m. to 8:00 p.m., and from 7:00 a.m. until 3:00 p.m. on Saturdays. Summer holidays may translate into closed businesses during the months of July and August.

31 FOREIGN TRADE

Ships are Croatia's major export (13.6% of exports), while other commodities fall close behind, including refined petroleum products (8.1%), polymers (2.9%), men's outerwear (3.4%), and wom-

Principal Trading Partners – Croatia (2010)

(In millions of US dollars)

Country	Total	Exports	Imports	Balance
World	31,857.0	11,806.0	20,051.0	-8,245.0
Italy	5,224.0	2,179.0	3,045.0	-866.0
Germany	3,726.0	1,219.0	2,507.0	-1,288.0
Slovenia	2,096.0	924.0	1,172.0	-248.0
Russia	2,037.0	231.0	1,806.0	-1,575.0
Bosnia & Herzegovina	1,970.0	1,369.0	601.0	768.0
Austria	1,575.0	624.0	951.0	-327.0
China	1,477.0	38.0	1,439.0	-1,401.0
Hungary	822.0	264.0	558.0	-294.0
Serbia	767.0	463.0	304.0	159.0
United States	742.0	307.0	435.0	-128.0

(…) data not available or not significant.

(n.s.) not specified.

SOURCE: *2011 Direction of Trade Statistics Yearbook,* New York: United Nations, 2011.

Balance of Payments – Croatia (2010)

(In millions of US dollars)

Current Account		**-900.7**
Balance on goods		-7,877.2
Imports	-1,943.8	
Exports	12,066.6	
Balance on services		7,568.5
Balance on income		-2,045.9
Current transfers		1,453.9
Capital Account		**45.5**
Financial Account		**1,679.8**
Direct investment abroad		147.1
Direct investment in Croatia		334.2
Portfolio investment assets		-437.4
Portfolio investment liabilities		907.3
Financial derivatives		-333.6
Other investment assets		965.1
Other investment liabilities		97.2
Net Errors and Omissions		**-816.9**
Reserves and Related Items		**-7.7**

(…) data not available or not significant.

SOURCE: *Balance of Payment Statistics Yearbook 2011,* Washington, DC: International Monetary Fund, 2011.

en's outerwear (2.6%). Croatia's diverse export market also includes various chemicals, foodstuff, and raw materials.

Exports of goods and services totaled $23.3 billion in 2010, down from $29.1 billion in 2008, and down from 42% to 38% as a percentage of GDP. Imports decreased even more dramatically, from $34.9 billion in 2008 to $24.9% billion in 2010. In 2010, Croatia had a current account deficit of -$0.9 billion, a dramatic improvement from -$6.8 billion in 2008, and a foreign trade deficit of $2.3 billion, amounting to 3% of GDP.

Major import partners in 2009 were Italy, 15.5%; Germany, 13.6%; Russia, 9.3%; China, 6.8%; Slovenia, 5.7%; and Austria, 5%. Its major export partners were Italy, 19.1%; Bosnia and Herzegovina, 13%; Germany, 11.1%; Slovenia, 7.5%; and Austria, 5.4%.

[32]BALANCE OF PAYMENTS

Before the civil war, Croatia led the Yugoslav SFR in worker remittances, as thousands of Croats held factory jobs in Germany and elsewhere. In order to provide a framework for economic recovery, the government organized the Ministry for Reconstruction, which planned to rebuild war-damaged regions and infrastructure for tourism and bring in much needed foreign currency. Croatia had almost no foreign exchange reserves in 1991, but by the beginning of 1996 the National Bank of Croatia reported $1,386 million in foreign exchange reserves.

Croatia's balance of payments situation has been helped by tourism receipts, but its strong export sectors registered declines in the early 2000s. The textiles and apparel sectors were faced with competition from low-wage countries, and in wood product exports, Croatian producers competed with lower-priced Southeast Asian products. Croatian farmers complained they were unable to compete with subsidized farm products in the EU. Croatia reported a trade deficit of $4.6 billion in 2002. The current account balance was -$900.7 million in 2010 and -$1.027 billion in 2011.

[33]BANKING AND SECURITIES

The National Bank of Croatia was founded in 1992. It has the responsibility of issuing currency and regulating the commercial banking sector. The Croatian dinar was issued 23 December 1991 but was replaced in 1994 by the kuna. Currently, the kuna is allowed to float freely, although the nation's central bank periodically intervenes to ensure the kuna's stability.

The Croatian Bank for Reconstruction and Development (HBOR) was established in 1992 as a 100% government-owned institution, with the tasks of financing reconstruction and development and promoting exports through credits and credit guarantees. In 1995, Raiffeisenbank Austria d.d. Zagreb began operating in Croatia as the first bank with 100% foreign capital.

As of January 2011, Croatia had 32 licensed commercial banks and 6 savings banks. The Croatian banking sector has been marked by bad lending practices, whereby banks are willing to lend to local companies regardless of creditworthiness. Since independence, at least 15 Croatian banks have gone bankrupt. Another aspect of the nation's banking sector is the high proportion of assets held by foreign banks. Estimates are that 91% of all bank assets in the country are held by foreign banks.

The Zagreb Stock Exchange (ZSE) started operations in 1991. However, out of the entire portfolio of the Croatian Privatization Fund, only 2% was privatized through the exchange. The introduction of the new Privatization Act in 1996 was expected to increase the role of the stock exchange, as was the adoption of an Investment Funds Act and a Securities Act. The Securities Law regulates the public offer of securities, legal entities who are authorized to conduct business with securities, securities transactions, prohibitions regarding businesses with securities, and the protection of investors. As of April 2008, the ZSE included stocks of 376 companies, with market capitalization of $33.9 billion.

[34]INSURANCE

The Insurance Companies Supervision Directorate grants approvals for insurance companies' operations and supervises the operations of insurance companies doing business in Croatia. Insurance

Public Finance – Croatia (2009)

(In millions of kunas, budgetary central government figures)

Revenue and Grants	110,258	100.0%
Tax revenue	63,679	57.8%
Social contributions	39,995	36.3%
Grants	616	0.6%
Other revenue	5,968	5.4%
Expenditures	120,191	100.0%
General public services	12,177	10.1%
Defense	4,997	4.2%
Public order and safety	7,627	6.3%
Economic affairs	13,676	11.4%
Environmental protection	289	0.2%
Housing and community amenities	1,896	1.6%
Health	19,883	16.5%
Recreational, culture, and religion	1,715	1.4%
Education	10,396	8.6%
Social protection	47,536	39.6%

(…) data not available or not significant.

SOURCE: *Government Finance Statistics Yearbook 2010*, Washington, DC: International Monetary Fund, 2010.

companies may be established by domestic or foreign entities and may be formed as a joint-stock, mutual, private, or public company. Pension funds (divided between employees, self-employed, and independent farmers) controlled substantial financial assets in Croatia as of 1997. In the first eleven months of 2011, 26 insurance companies in Croatia charged a total gross premium of HRK8.3 billion, which was 1.1% less than in the same period last year. The premium in non-life insurance was HRK6.17 billion, or 1.2% less than 2009, accounting for 74.3 percent of the total premium charged. In 2010, the country's top insurer was Croatia Osiguranje with a 31.4% share. Allianz Zagreb was the runner-up with 11.4%.

35 PUBLIC FINANCE

The fiscal year follows the calendar year. The IMF and World Bank have granted Croatia $192 million and $100 million, respectively, to repair economic imbalances from war and to curb hyperinflation. The European Bank for Reconstruction and Development (EBRD) has approved financial support totaling $230 million for infrastructure, telecommunications, and energy projects that otherwise would be unobtainable by the Croatian government.

The CIA estimated that in 2010 Croatia's central government took in revenues of approximately $22 billion and had expenditures of $24.3 billion. Revenues minus expenditures totaled approximately -$2.3 billion. Public debt in 2010 amounted to 55% of GDP, up from 52% in 2005. Total external debt was $60.7 billion, up significantly from $29.3 billion in 2005.

36 TAXATION

In 2010, the corporate profits tax was reduced from 35% to 20%, where it remained as of December 2011. Reduced corporate tax rates of 5%, 10%, and 15% are available for companies locating in "special care areas" (62 municipalities and towns deemed to be undeveloped) and in the Vukovar area. The corporate tax rate is also reduced for larger new investments: 7% for investments of

at least HRK10 million ($1.56 million), 3% for investments of at least HRK20 million (about $3.12 million), and 0% on investments over HRK60 million ($9.3 million). Companies operating in one of Croatia's 12 free trade zones (FTZs) pay half the standard corporate tax rate (10%) or 0% if their investment is more than HRK1 million (about $156,000). There is no separate foreign investment law in Croatia, so branches of foreign companies are taxed the same as domestic companies, though only on profits made in Croatia.

Croatia's top income tax rate of 45% was reduced to 40% in 2010. Income taxes are progressive and range between 12% and 40%. Croatians are taxed 12% on income under HRK 43,200($7,438), 25% on income between HRK43,200 and HRK129,600 ($22,314), and 40% on income over HRK129,600. Croatians are taxed on their worldwide income while foreigners pay only on income realized in Croatia. Deductions from taxable income are allowed for medical and housing expenses. There is a 15% withholding tax on dividend, interest, and royalty income. Local surcharges on state income taxes range from up to 10% in small municipalities to up to 30% in Zagreb. The inheritance and gift tax is 5%, and there is a 5% real property transaction tax. Property taxes are assessed locally.

The employee's contribution to social security is 20%, of which 15% goes to the national pension fund and 5% to private pension funds. The pension system is mandatory for workers who were under 40 as of 1 January 2002, and optional for workers 40 to 50 years old on that date. The employers' contributions to social security, amounting to 17.2%, go for health and unemployment insurance: 15% for general health insurance, 0.5% for work-related accident insurance, and 1.7% for unemployment insurance.

The main indirect taxes in Croatia are the value-added tax (VAT), with a flat rate of 23%, and excise taxes. Specified goods and services, such as those from banks and insurance companies, are exempt from the VAT (0% rate). Slot machines are taxed at about $14.50 per month, while winnings from games of chance are subject to the 23% VAT. Per-unit excise taxes are assessed on petroleum products, tobacco, beer, alcoholic drinks, coffee, and nonalcoholic drinks. Luxury goods carry a 30% excise. Producers and importers of vehicles (cars, motorbikes, boats, and airplanes) pay excise taxes, while buyers of used vehicles pay a sales tax. Auto insurance premiums are taxed at 15% for liability insurance and 10% for comprehensive insurance. There are local consumption taxes on alcoholic drinks up to 3%.

37 CUSTOMS AND DUTIES

The Customs Law, Law on Customs Tariffs, and Law on Customs Services were implemented in 1991. Croatia adopted all of the international tariffs and protection agreements ratified by the former Yugoslav SFR that did not contravene Croatia's constitution. The customs system was considerably changed in 1996 with a new customs law that harmonized the system with that of the European Union. In 2000, customs laws were revamped yet again to allow the government to change tariff rates annually. Goods such as raw materials, semi-finished goods, spare parts, supplies used for repairing war damage, and the household possessions of returning Croatian refugees are exempted from customs duty and subject only to an administrative charge. The Customs Tariff lists all the goods specified, grouped into a system of 11 sections and 97 chapters with remarks on each chapter to simplify the customs declaration procedure. Croatia has free trade agreements with Bosnia and Herzegovina, Hungary, Macedonia, and Slovenia. Croatia was set to become a member of the European Union in 2013.

³⁸ FOREIGN INVESTMENT

Attracting foreign investment is a key goal of the comprehensive strategy for long-term development, "Croatia in the 21st Century," adopted 21 June 2001 with the aim of becoming a fully integrated member of the European Union. The day before, the bilateral investment treaty (BIT) with the United States entered into force. Croatia does not have a separate foreign investment law, so foreign firms generally receive national treatment under the 1995 Company Law. The Law on Free Trade Zones (FTZs) was adopted in June 1996. Companies making infrastructure investments of at least $125,000 are eligible for a five-year tax holiday, while others (except those in retail trade, which are excluded from FTZs) pay half of Croatia's corporate income tax rate (10% instead of 20%). Exported goods are fully exempt from custom duties and taxes. The government has designated 12 FTZ locations. The Croatian constitution states that rights acquired through capital investments cannot be withdrawn by law or any legal act and it also insures free repatriation of profits and capital upon disinvestment.

The total stock of FDI that entered into Croatia between 1993 and 2003 was $10.1 billion, averaging around $1 billion per year. Most foreign direct investment (FDI) in the period came through the privatization of government-owned assets and most was directed to trade, services, banking, and telecommunications, rather than industry. Outward investment by Croatian firms from 1993 through the first quarter of 2001 totaled $413 million, with 39% going to Poland and 28% to Bosnia and Herzegovina.

The total stock of FDI that entered Croatia between 2004 and 2010 was $24.2 billion, averaging $3.5 billion per year. In 2009, FDI in Croatia was a net inflow of $2.95 billion and represented 4.68% of GDP. For the period 1993 to 2010, the countries contributing the most FDI were Austria (25.3%), the Netherlands (14.9%), Germany (12.1%), and Hungary (9.4%). The areas attracting the greatest amounts of FDI were financial intermediation (35.3%), wholesale and commission trade (11%), manufacture of coke and refined petroleum products (6.5), and real estate activities (6.2).

Croatia's performance in terms of FDI inflow has been average if compared to other countries in Central and Eastern Europe. Most foreign capital was used for acquiring state-owned enterprises (or shares in those), and less was used for Greenfield investments. The situation was expected to change in future years, however, as the political system in the country has become more stable, and the government was gearing up for the EU accession.

³⁹ ECONOMIC DEVELOPMENT

While it was one of the wealthiest of the Yugoslav republics, Croatia's economy suffered badly during the 1991–95 war. Economic output collapsed and the country missed the early waves of investment enjoyed by other Central and Eastern European countries following the fall of the Berlin Wall. Economic development following 1995 has been closely tied with privatization. The process of privatization, although initially fraught with controversy amid allegations of government mishandling, has transformed Croatia's

economy from a largely state-owned to a largely privately owned one. As a result, the Croatian economy has made steady gains in the post-war period. Between 2000 and 2007, Croatia enjoyed moderate but steady GDP growth between 4% and 6%. Besides privatization, the economic turnaround has been also attributed to a rebound in tourism and credit-driven consumer spending. Moderate inflation levels and a stable currency further contributed to the positive economic climate of the 2000s. Although in 2009 the Croatian economy finally suffered the consequences of the global financial crisis, it did not fare as poorly as some European states, and there were signs that it was beginning to rebound in 2011.

Nevertheless, difficult problems still remain for the Croatian economy, including a stubbornly high unemployment rate, a growing trade deficit, and uneven regional development. Despite the past and ongoing process of privatization, the state retains a large role in the economy. Perhaps due to past controversies, privatization efforts often meet stiff public and political resistance. While macroeconomic stabilization has largely been achieved, structural reforms lag because of deep resistance on the part of the public and lack of strong support from politicians. The EU accession process should accelerate fiscal and structural reform. While long-term growth prospects for the economy remain strong, Croatia is expected to face significant pressure as a result of the global financial crisis. Croatia's high foreign debt, anemic export sector, strained state budget, and overreliance on tourism revenue will likely result in higher risk to economic stability over the medium term.

Croatia has done reasonably well in attracting FDI, but improvements can be made. Red tape, corruption, and problems posed by domestic companies have kept a lot of investors away. Nonetheless, the country boasts an educated workforce, a stable government, equality under the law, and the prospect of joining the EU in 2013—all factors that make it a very attractive market, with great future potential.

⁴⁰ SOCIAL DEVELOPMENT

The effects of the 1991 war, the great refugee burden, the disruptions of the Bosnian war, the absence of significant international aid, and other factors combined to strain the country's social fabric and economy. In 1993, the average standard of living stood at less than 50% of its level before 1991. Over 400,000 Croats were displaced by the war and its aftermath.

Croatia's first pension laws date back to 1922, with most recent changes in 2003. The law provides for a dual system of a social system and mandatory private insurance. Health and maternity benefits, workers' compensation, unemployment coverage, and family allowances are also provided. As of 2010, retirement is set at age 65 for men and age 60 for women. Early retirement is penalized by a cut in pension by 0.15% for every month up to 9% for five years.

Women hold lower paying positions in the work force than men even though gender discrimination is prohibited by law. Also, women are more likely to be unemployed. Rape and spousal rape are grossly underreported, and there are only four women's shelters. A 2007 survey revealed that domestic abuse affects 1 in 3 families in Croatia. The weak economic situation, the aftermath and uncertainty from the war, and alcohol abuse are considered aggravating factors.

The constitution states that all persons shall enjoy all rights and freedoms, regardless of race, color, sex, language, religion, political opinion, national origin, property, birth, education, or social status. However, ethnic tensions continue. Muslims and Serbs in Croatia face considerable discrimination. Arbitrary detention and torture, abuse of detainees, and other human rights violations continue. The Roma population also suffers discrimination.

^{41}HEALTH

Croatia is in the process of improving healthcare since the war years in the 1990s. Life expectancy in 2011 was estimated at 76 years. The infant mortality rate in 2011 was 5 per 1,000 live births. The total fertility rate in that year was estimated at 1.5 children born per woman. The maternal mortality was estimated at 14 per 100,000 live births in 2008. Total expenditure on healthcare in Croatia in 2009 was an estimated 7% of GDP.

The country is known for its spas, where patients receive preventive and rehabilitative care that makes use of spring water and other natural resources, as well as such treatments as massage. As of 2011, there were an estimated 26 physicians, 56 nurses and midwives, and 55 hospital beds per 10,000 inhabitants. It was estimated that 98% of children were vaccinated against measles. The incidence of tuberculosis was 41 per 100,000 people in 2007. The CIA calculated HIV/AIDS prevalence in Croatia to be about less than 0.1% in 2009.

^{42}HOUSING

After years of war, the country began the process of rebuilding not only homes for the thousands who were displaced by the conflict, but industries, businesses, and civic buildings as well. During the 1990s, hundreds of thousands of displaced persons and refugees from Bosnia and occupied Croat territories were in Croatia.

According to the 2011 census, there were a total of 2,257,515 housing units in the nation. Of these, approximately 1,923,522 dwellings were for permanent residents. Most dwellings had between two to four rooms. There were about 1,535,635 households representing 4,290,612 people. Most households had between two to four members.

^{43}EDUCATION

In 2008, the World Bank estimated that 91% of age-eligible children in Croatia were enrolled in primary school, up from 87% in 2005. Secondary enrollment for age-eligible children stood at 88%, up from 84% in 2005. Tertiary enrollment was estimated at 51%. Of those enrolled in tertiary education, there were 100 male students for every 125 female students. Overall, the CIA estimated that Croatia had a literacy rate of 98.1%. In 2009, public expenditure on education represented 4.6% of GDP.

Education at the elementary level is free and compulsory for children between the ages of 6 and 15 years. Primary education covers an eight-year course of study. Secondary education covers a four-year course of study in one of three tracks: grammar schools, technical and vocational schools, and art schools. The academic year runs from October to June. The primary language of instruction is Croatian. The student-to-teacher ratio for primary school was at about 15:1 in 2009.

In higher education, there are seven public universities: University of Osijek (founded in 1975), University of Rijeka (founded in 1973), University of Split (founded in 1974), University of Zadar (2002), University of Dubrovnik (founded in 2003), University of Pula (founded in 2006), and University of Zagreb (founded in 1669). There are three private universities: Croatian Catholic University, Dubrovnik International University, and Media University in Split. There are also 13 polytechnic schools and 17 professional schools. In 2009, about 49% of the tertiary age population was enrolled in some type of higher education program, up from 39% in 2003.

^{44}LIBRARIES AND MUSEUMS

The National and University Library of Croatia in Zagreb (founded in 1606) has about 2.5 million volumes. The Zagreb public library holds close to 300,000 volumes. The Information and Documentation Centre and Library of the Institute for International Relations is also in Zagreb, with holdings that include books, periodicals and journals, and official documents from various countries and in a variety of languages. The Croatia Library Association was founded in 1940.

Major museums in Zagreb include the Historical Museum of Croatia, Strossmeyer's Gallery of Old Masters, and the Gallery of Modern Art. Other major cultural centers include Split, which houses the Museum of Croatian Medieval Archeology, and Dubrovnik, with the Natural Sciences Museum among others. In all, the country boasts over 100 museums.

^{45}MEDIA

As of 2011, there were 10 nationwide and 21 regional television channels and more than 30 other channels produced in Croatia or produced for Croatian market broadcast by IPTV (Internet Protocol television), cable, or satellite television. The electronic communications market in Croatia is regulated by Croatian Post and Electronic Communications Agency, which issues broadcast licenses and monitors the market. Digital and satellite transmission infrastructure is developed and maintained by the government-owned Odašiljači i veze company. In 2009, there were 16 FM radio stations, 98 AM radio stations, and 5 shortwave radio stations. Internet users numbered 50 per 100 citizens.

Prominent newspapers, with 2010 circulation numbers listed parenthetically, include *Glas Slavonije* (25,000), *Nova List* (60,000), *La Voce del Popolo* (4,000), and *Vecernji List* (200,000). In addition to these there are several regional dailies that are available throughout the country even though they mainly present regionally focused content. Examples of these are *Glas Istre*, *Glas Slavoniie*, *Zadarski list*, and *Dubrovački vjesnik*. The most popular weekly news magazines are *Globus* and *Nacional*.

In 2009, the CIA reported that there were 1.9 million telephone landlines in Croatia, and 6 million mobile cellular phones in use. Mobile phone subscriptions averaged 136 per 100 people. In 2010 the country had 1.28 million Internet hosts. There were some 2.2 million Internet users in Croatia in 2009, accounting for 32.9% of the population.

In October 1996, a comprehensive Law on Public Information was passed in Parliament with general support from all parties to regulate the media. In general, government influence on media through state ownership of most print and electronic media outlets restricts constitutionally provided freedoms of speech and press.

46 ORGANIZATIONS

In 1852, the Chamber of Commerce and Crafts was first organized in Zagreb. In 1990, the Croatian Chamber of the Economy (CCE) was established as the authentic representative of the Croatian economy. The CCE consists of 20 county chambers and promotes trade and commerce in world markets along with the Association of Independent Businesses and the Zagreb Trade Fair.

Since 1994, over 30 professional organizations have been founded in the CCE. A number of organizations promoting research and education in various medical and scientific fields have also formed, including the Croatia Medical Association. The Rudjer Boskovic Institute is a national organization that conducts research and educational programs for the natural sciences. The Croatian Academy of Sciences and Arts has been active since 1861. The Croatian Physical Society formed in 1990.

There are many sports associations throughout the country, including the general Croatian Athletic Federation and a chapter of the Special Olympics. Youth organizations include the umbrella organization of the Croatian National Youth Council (NSMH), the Croatian Club for the UN (CCUN), and the Junior Chamber of Croatia (JCC), as well as scouting programs. Among many national women's organizations are the Croatian Association of University Women, the Women's Infoteka, and Be Active, Be Emancipated (BABE).

There are national chapters of the Red Cross Society and Amnesty International.

47 TOURISM, TRAVEL, AND RECREATION

The *Tourism Factbook*, published by the UN World Tourism Organization, reported 9.34 million incoming tourists to Croatia in 2009, who spent a total of $9.22 billion. Of those incoming tourists, there were 8.9 million from Europe. There were 152,260 hotel beds available in Croatia, which had an occupancy rate of 34%. The estimated daily cost to visit Zagreb, the capital, was $324. Tourist attractions include visits to Dubrovnik and Split to enjoy the climate, scenery, and excellent swimming from April to October. Beautiful historic churches and ancient palaces can be found in the major cities. Casinos and nudist camps are also popular attractions.

In November 2010, the gingerbread craft from Northern Croatia was officially inscribed on the UNESCO Representative List of the Intangible Heritage of Humanity, an offshoot of the World Heritage program. The craft was deemed a living tradition by UNESCO, meaning that it is still passed from generation to generation and continues to create a sense of identity and community for those who participate. Such traditions have been approved by UNESCO for special consideration since 2001. For one that is inscribed, a special program is designed to protect and promote the practice and understanding of the tradition. In Croatia, the tradition of baking gingerbread was elevated to a craft, in which each craftsperson molds and shapes the gingerbread in a unique way and decorates the finished pieces with an individual style. Today, both men and women practice the craft of gingerbread making, which has become a significant symbol to Croatian identity. Another addition to the list was the Sinjska Alka, a knights' tournament held in the town of Sinj. In this tournament, each competitor uses a lance to attempt to catch a ring hanging from a rope while riding a horse at a full gallop.

48 FAMOUS PERSONS

Dr. Franjo Tudjman was president of Croatia from May 1990 until his death in 1999. Stjepan Mesić (b. 1934) was president between 2000 and 2010. Two Nobel prize winners have come from Croatia, both chemists: Lavoslav Ružička (1887–1976) and Vladimir Prelog (1906–98).

Josip Broz-Tito (1892–1980) was the leader of Communist Yugoslavia for many years after World War II. In 1948, he led his country away from the Communist bloc formed by the Soviet Union. Tito served in the Red Army during the Russian Civil War and led the Yugoslav resistance movement during World War II.

There are several internationally known figures in literature and the arts: Ivan Gundulic (1589–1638) wrote about the Italian influences in Croatia in *Dubravka*. Count Ivo Vojnović (1857–1929) is best known for *A Trilogy of Dubrovnik*. Miroslav Krleya (1857–1981) captured the concerns of prerevolutionary Yugoslavia in his trilogy of the Glembay family (1928–32) and in novels like *Return of Philip Latinovicz* (1932) and *Banners* (1963).

Double-agent Duško Popov (1912–1981), who worked during World War II, was the model for Ian Fleming's James Bond. The wartime figure Andrija Artukovic (1899–1988), known as "Butcher of the Balkans" for his activities in support of Germany, was from Croatia. Religious leader Franjo Seper (1884–1981) was born in Croatia, as was inventor Nikola Tesla (1856–1943). Musician Artur Radzinski (1894–1958) became conductor of the New York Philharmonic in 1943 and of the Chicago Symphony in 1947. Zinka Kumc Milanov (1906–1989) was a dramatic opera soprano with the New York Metropolitan Opera in the 1950s and 1960s. Mathilde Mallinger (1847–1920) was a famous Croatian soprano who performed with Berlin Opera from 1869–1882.

49 DEPENDENCIES

Croatia has no territories or colonies.

50 BIBLIOGRAPHY

Ceriani, Conatella. *Croatia*. New York: DK Publishing, 2003.

Croatia Investment and Business Guide: Strategic and Practical Information. Washington, DC: International Business Publications USA, 2012.

Cvitanic, Marilyn. *Culture and Customs of Croatia*. Santa Barbara, CA: Greenwood, 2011.

Frucht, Richard, ed. *Eastern Europe: An Introduction to the People, Lands, and Culture*. Santa Barbara, CA: ABC-CLIO, 2005.

McElrath, Karen, ed. *HIV and AIDS: A Global View*. Westport, CT: Greenwood Press, 2002.

Opello, Walter C. *European Politics*. Boulder, CO: Lynne Rienner Publishers, 2009.

Political Chronology of Europe. London, UK: Europa, 2001.

Stallaerts, Robert. *Historical Dictionary of the Republic of Croatia*. Lanham, MD: Scarecrow, 2003.

Terterov, Marat, and Visnja Bojanic, eds. *Doing Business with Croatia*. 2nd ed. Sterling, VA: Kogan Page, 2004.

CZECH REPUBLIC

Czech Republic
Ceskaá Republika

CAPITAL: Prague (Praha)

FLAG: The national flag consists of a white stripe over a red stripe, with a blue triangle extending from hoist to midpoint.

ANTHEM: *Kde domov muj (Where is My Native Land).*

MONETARY UNIT: The koruna (CZK) is a paper currency of 100 haléru, which replaced the Czechoslovak koruna (KCS) on 8 February 1993. There are coins of 1, 5, 10, 20, and 50 heller and of 1, 2, 5, 10, 20, and 50 koruny, and notes of 50, 100, 200, 500, 1,000, 2,000, and 5,000 koruny. CZK1 = US$0.05605 (or US$1 = CZK17.84) as of 2011.

WEIGHTS AND MEASURES: The metric system is the legal standard.

HOLIDAYS: New Year's Day, 1 January; Labor Day, 1 May; Liberation Day, 8 May; Day of the Apostles, St. Cyril and St. Methodius, 5 July; Jan Hus Day, July 6; Day of Czech Statehood, 28 September; Foundation of the Independent Czechoslavak State, 28 October; Day of Students' Fight for Freedom and Democracy, 17 November; Christmas, 24–26 December. Easter Monday is a movable holiday.

TIME: 1 p.m. = noon GMT.

¹LOCATION, SIZE, AND EXTENT

The Czech Republic is a strategically located landlocked country in Eastern Europe. It sits astride some of the oldest and most significant land routes in Europe. Comparatively, the Czech Republic is slightly smaller than the state of South Carolina with a total area of 78,867 sq km (30,451 sq mi). It shares boundaries with Poland (on the NE), Slovakia (on the SE), Austria (on the S), and Germany (on the W and NW) and has a total boundary length of 1,989 km (1,236 mi). The capital city of the Czech Republic, Prague, is located in the north-central part of the country.

²TOPOGRAPHY

The topography of the Czech Republic consists of two main regions. Bohemia in the west is comprised of rolling plains, hills, and plateaus surrounded by low mountains. Moravia in the east is very hilly. The country's highest point is Mt. Snezka at 1,602 m (5,256 ft) in the Krkonose Mountains along the north central border with Poland. The Elbe River is the nation's longest with a distance of 1,165 km (724 mi); located in the northwest, it runs north into Germany.

³CLIMATE

The Czech Republic has a Central European moderate and transitional climate, with variations resulting from the topography of the country. The climate is temperate with cool summers and cold, cloudy, and humid winters. The average temperature in Prague ranges from about -1°C (30°F) in January to 19°C (66°F) in July. A generally moderate oceanic climate prevails in the Czech lands. Rainfall distribution is greatly influenced by westerly winds, and its variation is closely correlated to relief. Over three-fifths of the rain falls during the spring and summer, which is advantageous

for agriculture. The precipitation range is from 50 cm (20 in) to more than 127 cm (50 in); rainfall is below 58 cm (23 in) in western Bohemia and southern Moravia.

⁴FLORA AND FAUNA

Plants and animals are Central European in character. Almost 70% of the forest is mixed or deciduous. Some original steppe grassland areas are still found in Moravia, but most of these lowlands are cultivated. The World Resource Institute estimates that there are 1,900 plant species in the Czech Republic. In addition, the Czech Republic is home to 88 species of mammals, the most common of which include the fox, hare, deer, rabbit, and wild pig. There are also 386 species of birds, 11 species of reptiles, and 19 species of amphibians found in the country. Fish such as carp, pike, and trout appear in numerous rivers and ponds. This calculation of species reflects the total number of distinct species residing in the country, not the number of endemic species.

⁵ENVIRONMENT

The Czech Republic suffers from air, water, and land pollution caused by industry, mining, and agriculture. Lung cancer is prevalent in areas with the highest air pollution levels. In the mid-1990s, the nation had the world's highest industrial carbon dioxide emissions, totaling 135.6 million metric tons per year, which translates to a per capita level of 13.04 metric tons. However, the UN reported in 2008 that total carbon dioxide emissions had decreased to about 113.2 million metric tons. Like the Slovak Republic, the Czech Republic has had its air contaminated by sulfur dioxide emissions resulting largely from the use of lignite as an energy source in the former Czechoslovakia, which had the highest level of sulfur dioxide emissions in Europe, and instituted a program to reduce pollution in the late 1980s. Western nations have offered $1 billion to spur environmental reforms, but the pressure to continue economic growth has postponed the push for environmental action.

Airborne emissions in the form of acid rain, combined with air pollution from Poland and former East Germany, have destroyed much of the forest in the northern part of the former Czechoslovakia. Land erosion caused by agricultural and mining practices is also a significant problem. There are 12 Ramsar Wetland Iites in the country.

In 2008, water resources totaled 16 cu km (3.84 cu mi) while water usage was 1.91 cu km (.458 cu mi) per year. Domestic water usage accounted for 41% of total usage, industrial for 57%, and agricultural for 2%. Per capita water usage totaled 187 cu m (6,604 cu ft) per year. Both urban and rural dwellers have access to safe drinking water.

According to a 2011 report issued by the International Union for Conservation of Nature and Natural Resources (IUCN), threatened species included 2 types of mammals, 5 species of birds, 2 species of fish, 5 types of mollusks, 17 species of other invertebrates, and 11 species of plants. Endangered species include the Atlantic sturgeon, slender-billed curlew, and Spengler's freshwater mussel.

The World Resource Institute reported that the Czech Republic had designated 1.25 million hectares (3.08 million acres) of land for protection as of 2006.

6 POPULATION

The US Central Intelligence Agency (CIA) estimated the population of the Czech Republic in 2011 to be approximately 10,190,213, which placed it at number 82 in population among the 196 nations of the world. In 2011, approximately 16.3% of the population was over 65 years of age, with another 13.5% under 15 years of age. The median age in the Czech Republic was 40.8 years. There were 0.95 males for every female in the country. The population's annual rate of change was -0.12%. The projected population for the year 2025 was 10,900,000. Population density in the Czech Republic was calculated at 129 people per sq km (334 people per sq mi).

The UN estimated that 74% of the population lived in urban areas, and that urban populations had an annual rate of change of 0.3%. The largest urban area was Prague, with a population of 1.2 million.

7 MIGRATION

Estimates of Czech Republic's net migration rate, carried out by the CIA in 2011, amounted to 0.97 migrants per 1,000 citizens. The total number of emigrants living abroad was 370,600, and the total number of immigrants living in Czech Republic was 453,000. After World War II, nearly 2.5 million ethnic Germans were expelled from the Sudeten region, which was part of Czechoslovakia and Poland. The emigration wave from Czechoslovakia after the Communist takeover in February 1948 included some 60,000 people; another 100,000 left the country after the invasion of the Warsaw Pact countries in August 1968. Emigration slowed during the 1970s to about 5,000 annually, but during the 1980s, some

10,000 people (according to Western estimates) were leaving each year.

According to the Czech Statistical Office, 435,000 foreigners resided legally in the country in 2009. The foreign population consists mainly of Ukrainians (132,000), Slovakians (73,000), and Vietnamese (61,000). This was a strong increase from 229,000 legal foreign residents 10 years earlier.

The Czech Republic encountered its first refugee influx in 1990. From 1990–2000, there were more than 22,000 applicants. However, accession to the European Union in 2004 contributed to a decrease in the number of applicants for international protection. In 2009, 1,258 people sought asylum.

8 ETHNIC GROUPS

Between 1945 and 1948, the deportation of the Sudeten Germans altered the ethnic structure of the Czech lands. Since the late 1940s, most of the remaining Germans have either assimilated or emigrated to the West. In 2011, Czechs constituted 90.4% of the total population; Moravians accounted for 3.7%; and Slovaks made up 1.9%. Other ethnic groups include Germans, Roma, and Poles.

9 LANGUAGES

Czech, which belongs to the Slavic language group, is the major and official language. In addition to the letters of the English alphabet, the Czech language has both vowels and consonants with acute accents (indicating length) and háčeks: á, é, ě, í, ó, ú, č, dž, Ď (ď), ň, ř, š, Ť (ť), ž, as well as ů (the circle also indicates length). In Czech, q, w, and x are found only in foreign words. There are numerous dialects. Many older Czechs speak German; many younger people speak Russian and English. Slovak is also spoken.

10 RELIGIONS

Though the country has a strong tradition of Christianity, the Communist rule of 1948 to 1989 greatly repressed religious practice so that many citizens do not claim membership in any religious organizations. In 2009, only about 32% of the population claimed to believe in God. About 38% claimed to be atheist.

According to the 2001 census (the latest official data available), 27% of citizens were members of the Roman Catholic Church, but only about 5% attended services regularly. About 3% were Protestants, while 1% belonged to the Czech Hussite Church. Islam became an officially recognized religion in 2004. The Jewish community numbers about 3,000 people.

The constitution provides for religious freedom, and the government reportedly respects this right in practice. Religious affairs are handled by the Department of Churches at the Ministry of Culture. In 2002, the Religious Freedom and the Position of Churches and Religious Associations established a tiered registration system for religious organizations.

While registering is not mandatory, groups registered at the second-tier, meaning that they have a membership equal to at least 0.1% of the population, are eligible for state funding. Clergy from second-tier groups are able to perform officially recognized marriages. Religious groups registered prior to 2002, such as the Jewish community, are not required to meet the conditions for second-tier registration. First-tier registration provides some tax benefits. In 2010, there were 31 state-recognized religious organizations.

LOCATION: 49°26' to 51°3' N; 12°6' to 18°54' E. BOUNDARY LENGTHS: Poland, 658 kilometers (409 miles); Slovakia, 214 kilometers (133 miles); Austria, 362 kilometers (225 miles); Germany, 646 kilometers (401 miles).

Easter Monday, Christmas Eve, Christmas, and St. Stephen's Day (December 26) are observed as national holidays.

¹¹TRANSPORTATION

As a landlocked nation, the Czech Republic relies on coastal outlets in Poland, Croatia, Slovenia, and Germany for international commerce by sea. Navigable inland waterways exist on the Elbe, Vltava, and Oder rivers. The principal river ports are Prague on the Vltava and Děčín on the Elbe. The country has approximately 664 km (413 mi) of navigable waterways.

In 2010, there were 44 airports with paved runways. There was also one heliport. According to the World Bank, 5.05 million passengers were transported by the country's 122 airports in 2009. Principal airports include Turany at Brno, Mosnov at Ostrava, and Ruzyne at Prague. Ruzyne is the nation's primary commercial airlink.With the separation of Czechoslovakia, the new Czech Republic has rapidly replaced its former Eastern European trading partners with Western ones (primarily Germany and the rest of

the EU). This shift in the direction of transportation of goods into and out of the Czech Republic overloaded the infrastructure of roads, airports, and railroads. However, the country now is connected to the European rail network—including Western Europe's high-speed train system. Trains between Prague and most European cities run every day. In addition, railroads in the Czech Republic connect Prague with Plzen, Kutná Hora, and Brno.

The CIA reports that railroads extend for 9,539 km (5,927 mi). In 2010, about 83 million tons of cargo were transported by rail, as compared to 356 million tons shipped by truck. The Czech Republic has a total of 127,719 km (79,361 mi) of roads, of which 127,719 km (79,361 mi) are paved. There are 513 vehicles per 1,000 people in the country.

¹²HISTORY

The first recorded inhabitants of the territory of the present-day Czech Republic were the Celtic Boii tribe, who settled there about 50 BC. They were displaced in the early modern era by German tribes (Marcomanni, Quidi) and later by Slavs, who pushed in from the east during the so-called Migration of the Peoples. The new settlers kept the Roman version of the name Boii for that region, Boiohaemum, which later became Bohemia. The first unified state in the region was that of a Frankish merchant named Samo, who protected his lands from the Avar Empire in Hungary and the Franks of the West, reigning until his death in 658. This mercantile city-state lasted until the 9th century, when it grew into the Moravian Empire. The fidelity of this new empire had strategic importance to both the Eastern and the Western Church, who sent missionaries to convert the Moravian people. Beginning in 863, two Orthodox monks, Cyril and Methodius, succeeded in converting large numbers of people to the Byzantine church (introducing a Slavic alphabet named "Cyrillic" after one of the monks), but Roman Catholic missionaries gained the majority of converts.

The Moravian Empire was destroyed at the end of the 9th century (903–907) by invading Magyars (Hungarians), who incorporated the eastern lands into their own, while the Kingdom of Bohemia inherited the lands and peoples of the west. The Premyslid Dynasty took control of the Bohemian kingdom, allying with the Germans to prevent further Magyar expansion. In the year 1085, Prince Vratislave was the first Bohemian prince to receive royal status from the Byzantine Empire, gaining his title by supporting Henry IV against Pope Gregory VII. A century later, in 1212, Premysl Otakar I was given the Golden Bull of Sicily, proclaiming Bohemia a kingdom in its own right and the Bohemian princes the hereditary rulers of that land. During the 13th century, the powers gained by the Premyslid Dynasty through the German alliance waned as this relationship brought the substantial migration of Germans into Bohemia and Moravia. The next line to rule Bohemia, starting with John of Luxembourg (1310–46), came to power before a time of great social and religious strife. Charles IV of Luxembourg was not only king of Bohemia (1346–78), but Holy Roman Emperor as well, ushering in the Czech "Golden Age," but his ties to the Roman Catholic Church would later tear the kingdom apart. In 1348, he founded the Charles University in Prague, one of the first learning institutions to operate outside of the Catholic monasteries, which nourished the minds of Bohemian intellectuals. As the citizens of Prague began to learn of the intransigence of the Roman Catholic Church, Wenceslas IV, successor to Charles IV, experienced a series of economic and political crisis (1378–1419) that escalated with the Western Schism (or Papal Schism, 1378–1417). Bohemia became a center of passionate opposition to the Catholic Church, and to German domination, led by Jan Hus in the Hussite movement. Burned at the stake for heresy in 1415 by German Emperor Sigismund, Hus became a national martyr and hero, and the country was in open rebellion (1420–36). During this time, Sigismund conducted six crusades in Bohemia to end the revolution, until he finally succeeded in 1434. By 1436, tired of fighting, both sides signed the Compacts of Basle. These documents allowed the Hussite denomination, and became a model of religious tolerance, which did not last for long. In 1462 Hungary extended its control over Bohemia, ruling through the Jagellon Dynasty until 1526, when Ferdinand of Hapsburg was elected to the Crown of St. Wenceslas, making Bohemia the property of the House of Hapsburg.

The Czechs were predominantly Protestant, while their new rulers were bent on introducing the Roman Catholic faith to Bohemia, exacerbating civil tensions. Although Protestants were able to secure certain civil rights and the freedom to worship, peace was fragile. In 1618, two Protestant churches were closed, leading Protestants to throw two royal governors out of the windows of Prague Castle, an act known as the "Defenestration of Prague." At the same time, 27 Protestant nobles were executed by the Habsburgs. In the Thirty Years' War (1618–48) that followed, the Czechs deposed their Catholic king, replacing him with Frederick of the Palatinate, a Protestant. The Protestant forces of the Bohemian Estates were defeated by the Catholic Emperor in 1620 at the Battle of White Mountain, and the Catholics again took the throne. This represented a disaster for the Czechs, who had their lands seized and their leaders executed, while nearly 30,000 of their number fled. The war ended in 1648 with the Peace of Westphalia, which sanctioned the large-scale immigration of Germans, resulting in the gradual Germanification of Czech territory. Under Empress Maria-Theresa (1740–1780), Bohemia became part of Austria, and the most industrialized part of the Austrian Empire, but Czech culture and language were suppressed.

Political tranquility was ended by the riots that broke out across Europe in 1848. On 11 March 1848, a demonstration in Prague demanded freedom of the press, equality of language, a parliament to represent Czech interests, and an end to serfdom. A Pan-Slavic Congress was convened in Prague in June of the same year, under Francis Palacky, a Bohemian historian. The Austrian authorities responded by imposing a military dictatorship, which struggled to restrain a steadily rising tide of nationalist aspirations. When World War I began, thousands of Czech soldiers surrendered to the Russians rather than fight for the Austro-Hungarians. They were transformed into the Czech Legion, which fought for the Russians until the Russian Revolution of 1917. Although Austria retained nominal control of Bohemia until the war's end, a separate Czech National Council began functioning in Paris as early as 1916.

Formation of the Czechoslovak Republic

It was the members of that council, especially Eduard Beneš and Tomáš Garrigue Masaryk, who were instrumental in gaining international support for the formation of an independent Czech and Slovak state at war's end. The Czechoslovak Republic, established 28 October 1918 under President Masaryk, was a contentious mix of at least five nationalities—Czechs, the so-called Sudeten Germans, Slovaks, Moravians, and Ruthenians—who created one of the 10 most developed countries in the world during the interwar period. All these nationalities were granted significant rights of self-determination, but many groups wished for full independence, and some of the Sudeten Germans hoped for reunification with Germany. In 1938, Adolf Hitler demanded that the Sudeten German area, which was the most heavily industrialized part of the country, be ceded to Germany. A conference consisting of Germany, Italy, France, and Great Britain was convened without Czechoslovakian representation. Ignoring the mutual assistance pacts that Czechoslovakia had signed with both France and the USSR, this conference agreed on 30 September 1938 that Germany could occupy the Sudetenland. On 15 March 1939, Hitler took the remainder of the Czech lands, beginning an occupation that lasted until 9 May 1945.

Many prominent Czechs managed to escape the Germans, including Eduard Beneš, the president, who established a provisional government in London in 1940, and Klement Gottwald, the communist leader, who took refuge in Moscow. In 1945, negotiations between Benes, Gottwald, and Josef Stalin established the basis for a postwar government, which was formed in the Slovak city of Kosice in April 1945 and moved to Prague the following month.

The government was drawn entirely from the National Front, an alliance of parties oriented toward Soviet Russia, with whom Czechoslovakia now had a common border, after the USSR incorporated Ruthenia. Although deferring to the Communists, the National Front government managed to run Czechoslovakia as a democracy until 1948. The Communists had been the largest vote-getter in the 1946 elections, but it seemed likely that they might lose in 1948. Rather than risk the election, they organized a Soviet-backed putsch , forcing President Benes to accept a government headed by Gottwald. Beneš resigned in June 1948, leaving the presidency open for Gottwald, while Antonín Zápotocky became prime minister. In a repeat of Czech history, Jan Masaryk, foreign minister at the time, and son of Tomáš Garrigue Masaryk, was thrown from a window during the coup, a defenestration that was reported as a suicide.

Once Czechoslovakia became a People's Republic and a faithful ally of the Soviet Union, a wave of purges and arrests rolled over the country (1949–54). In 1952, a number of high officials, including Foreign Minister V. Clementis and R. Slansky, head of the Czech Communist Party, were hanged for "Tito-ism" (after the Yugoslavian president who had been dismissed from the Cominform) and "national deviation."

After an unsuccessful army coup on his behalf, Novotny resigned in March 1968, and Czechoslovakia embarked on a radical liberalization, which Dubček termed "socialism with a human face." The leaders of the other Eastern Bloc nations and the Soviet leaders viewed these developments with alarm. Delegations went back and forth from Moscow during the Prague Spring of 1968, warning of counterrevolution. By July, the neighbors' alarm had grown; at a July meeting in Warsaw they issued a warning to Czechoslovakia against leaving the socialist camp. Although Dubček himself traveled to Moscow twice, in July and early August, to reassure Soviet party leader Brezhnev of the country's fidelity, the Soviets remained unconvinced.

On the night of 20–21 August 1968, military units from all the Warsaw Pact nations, save Romania, invaded Czechoslovakia to "save it from counterrevolution." Dubček and other officials were arrested, and the country was placed under Soviet control. Repeated efforts to find local officials willing to act as Soviet puppets failed, so on 31 December 1968 the country was made a federal state, comprised of the Czech Socialist Republic and the Slovak Socialist Republic. In April Gustáv Husák, once a reformer, but now viewing harmony with the USSR as the highest priority, was named head of the Czech Communist Party. A purge of liberals followed, and in May 1970, a new Soviet-Czechoslovak friendship treaty was signed; in June, Dubček was expelled from the party.

Between 1970 and 1975, nearly one-third of the party was dismissed, as Husák consolidated power, reestablishing the priority of the federal government over its constituent parts and, in May 1975, reuniting the titles of party head and republic president. Civil rights groups formed within the country; including a group of several hundred in 1977 that published a manifesto called Charter 77, protesting the suppression of human rights in Czechoslovakia. These groups did not seriously impinge upon Husák's power, but his successors had difficulty suppressing the liberalization movement.

Once again, it was revolution in the USSR that set off political change in Czechoslovakia. Husák ignored Soviet leader Mikhail Gorbachev's calls for *perestroika* and *glasnost* until 1987, when Husák reluctantly endorsed the general concept of party reform but delayed implementation until 1991. Aging and in ill health, Husák announced his retirement in December 1987, declaring that Milos Jakes would take his post. Jakes had been a lifelong compromiser and accommodator unable to control dissenting factions within his party, which were now using the radical changes in the Soviet Union as weapons against one another.

Even greater pressure came in early autumn 1989, when the West German embassy in Prague began to accept East German refugees who were trying to go west. Increasingly, the East German government was being forced to accede to popular demand for change, which, in turn, emboldened Czech citizens to make similar demands. On 17 November 1989, a group of about 3,000 youths gathered in Prague's Wenceslas Square, demanding free elections. On Jakes's orders, they were attacked and beaten by security forces, igniting a swell of public indignation expressed in 10 days of nonstop meetings and demonstrations. This Velvet Revolution ended on 24 November, when Jakes and all his government resigned. Novotny resigned his presidency soon after. Although Alexander Dubček was put forward as a possible replacement, he was rejected because he was Slovak. The choice fell instead on Vaclav Havel, a playwright and dissident and founder of the Charter 77 group, who was named president on 29 December 1989.

Dismantling of the apparatus of a Soviet-style state began immediately, but economic change came more slowly, in part because elections were not scheduled until June 1990. In the interim, the old struggle between Czechs and Slovaks resulted in the country being renamed the Czech and Slovak Federal Republic. In the June elections, the vote went overwhelmingly to Civic Forum and its Slovak partner, and economic transformation was begun, although there were continued tensions between those who wished a rapid move to a market economy and those who wanted to find some "third way" between socialism and capitalism. Equally contentious was the sentiment for separation by Slovakia, the pressure for which continued to build through 1991 and 1992. In the June 1992 elections, the split between the two parts of the country became obvious, as Czechs voted overwhelmingly for the reform and anticommunist candidates of Vaclav Klaus' Civic Democratic Party (ODS), while Slovaks voted for Vladimir Meciar and his Movement for Democratic Slovakia, a leftist and nationalist party. Legislative attempts to strengthen the federative structure at the expense of the legislatures of the two constituent republics failed, and the republics increasingly began to behave as though they were already separate so that, for example, by the end of 1992, 25.2% of Czech industry had been privatized, as opposed to only 5.3% of Slovak industry. The prime ministers of the two republics eventually agreed to separate, in the so-called "velvet divorce," which took effect 1 January 1993.

Havel, who did not subscribe to any party in the interest of political tranquility, was reconfirmed as president by a vote of the Czech parliament on 26 January 1993. Klaus was successful in fostering growth in the newly formed Czech Republic, emerging from close 1996 elections with another term as prime minister, but after the first glow of liberation, major cracks in the system became visible. Milos Zeman of the Social Democratic Party (CSSD) challenged Klaus' policies during and after the 1996 elections, especially those relating to economic growth (which was slowing). 1996 also saw the first elections of an 81-member senate, the upper body of parliament, which reflected a major split in the attitude of Czech voters. Governmental democracy and a newly liberated economy had not brought about the immediate transformation that Czech citizens wanted to see, and they ended up blaming the ODS party for their woes. This and charges of corruption in the ODS party brought about the triumph of the opposition. In the 1998 elections, the majority of votes went to the Social Democratic Party, based on a platform that stressed economic regulation and socialist government. Milos Zeman was appointed as the prime minister by President Vaclav Havel on 17 July 1998. Havel had been reelected president the previous January for another five-year term.

In March 1999, the Czech Republic became a member of NATO. The Czech Republic was one of 10 new countries to be formally invited to join the European Union in December 2002, and its accession was completed in 2004.

Havel stepped down as president in February 2003 after his second five-year term expired. Havel's rival and former prime minister, Vaclav Klaus, was elected president by a slim majority of 142 votes in the 281-member parliament after two inconclusive elections and three rounds of balloting on 28 February. Although, when he left the presidency, opinions about his legacy were mixed in the Czech Republic, on the international scene, Havel remains eternally popular for being a voice for democracy.

In the 2004 European Parliament elections, the CSSD garnered only 8.8% of the votes, signaling that the party's popularity among voters was on a downward spiral. As a consequence, in July 2004, the Socialists decided to sack the prime minister, Vladimir Spidla, and replace him with the minister of interior, Stanislav Gross. Gross's reign was short-lived, though. Plagued by scandals and corruption, and faced with the dissolution of his own government, Gross resigned only nine months after his appointment. Jiri Paroubek, the regional development minister in Gross's government, was appointed as the new Czech prime minister on 25 April 2005. He faced the difficult task of cutting public spending in preparation for the eurozone membership while improving his party's popularity among voters.

The 2006 election resulted in a hung parliament: the ODS, Christian Democrats (KDU-ČSL) and Greens (SZ) took 100 seats, exactly half of the 200-seat chamber of deputies. The Social Democrats (ČSSD) and Communists (KSČM) comprised the other half of the chamber. In September, President Klaus appointed a center-right government led by Mirek Topolanek of the ODS. The government lost a vote of confidence in October. In November, Klaus appointed Topolanek as prime minister for a second time. Talks began on forming a grand coalition. On 9 January 2007, par-

liament narrowly approved a three-party, center-right coalition. The coalition was composed of the ODS, the KDU-ČSL, and the Green Party (SZ). Three members of the cabinet were women.

In January 2009, the Czech Republic assumed the six-month rotating presidency of the European Union.

As a result of the 2010 elections, President Klaus appointed Civic Democrat Petr Necas as the country's next prime minister.

13 GOVERNMENT

The Czech Republic has a democratic government, based on a bicameral parliamentary democracy and the free association of political parties. Human and civil rights are guaranteed by the Bill of Fundamental Rights and Freedoms, a part of the constitution. The constitution of the Czech Republic was adopted by the Czech legislature in December 1992. It mandates a parliament consisting of a senate with 81 members who are elected for six-year terms and a chamber of deputies or lower house of 200 members who are elected for four-year terms. Every two years, one third of the senate's seats come up for reelection. The first senatorial elections were held in November 1996. The chamber was first seated by popular vote in 1992. A resolution by parliament is passed by a clear majority, while a constitutional bill or an international treaty must be passed by at least a 60% majority. All citizens over the age of 18 can vote.

The head of the executive branch is the president, who is elected by parliament for a five-year term and may serve two terms successively. The president is the supreme commander of the armed forces and has the power to veto bills passed by parliament under certain conditions. The prime minister, or premier, comes from the majority party, or a coalition, and is appointed by the president. The president appoints the ministers of the government on the recommendation of the prime minister.

14 POLITICAL PARTIES

Before 1996, the strongest political party in the republic was the Civic Democratic Party (ODS), headed by former prime minister Vaclav Klaus; it is a right-wing conservative party supporting democracy and a liberal economy. Supporters of the ODS are, in general, highly educated business people who come from Prague or other major cities. The ODS right-wing coalition with the Civic Democratic Alliance (ODA), Christian Democratic Union, and Christian Democratic Party, lost its majority in Parliament by two seats in the 1996 elections. Klaus and his coalition governed in the minority with the blessing of the opposition Social Democrats (CSSD), a socialist left-wing party that focuses on economic reform and growth in a planned economy. Supporters of the CSSD are mainly blue-collar laborers from industrial areas.

In December 1997, the ODS coalition (ODS, Christian Democratic Union/Czechoslovak People's Party or KDU-CSL, and ODA) was forced to resign due to the collapse of the union, government scandals, and a worsening economy. A temporary government was formed in January 1998, led by Josef Tosovsky, which was given the task of preparing the country for new elections. These were held in June 1998, when the Czech Social Democratic Party gained the majority of votes (32.3%). After negotiating with the ODS, which gained 27.74% of the votes, the CSSD formed a minority government, creating the first left-oriented party since Communist rule.

In the 1998 elections, the CSSD took 74 seats in the chamber and 25 seats in the senate, while the ODS took 63 seats in the lower house and 29 in the senate. The Christian Democratic Union-Czechoslovak People's Party (KDU-CSL, Catholic-conservative) took 20 seats in the chamber and 13 in the senate, and the Freedom Union (US, break-off party from the ODS) won 19 seats in the lower house and 3 in the senate. Voters who became disillusioned with the ineffective policies of the ODS coalition took a significant number of seats away from the party and gave them to the Freedom Union. The Communist Party won 24 seats in the chamber and 2 seats in the senate.

President Havel, appointed Milos Zeman of the majority Social Democratic Party as prime minister on 17 July 1998.

In the 2002 elections, the CSSD took 70 seats in the chamber and 11 seats in the senate. The ODS took 58 seats in the chamber and 26 in the senate, and the Coalition, a grouping of the KDU-CSL and the Freedom Union (US), won 31 seats in the chamber and 31 seats in the senate. The Communist Party, in its strongest showing since the end of Communist rule, took 41 seats in the lower house and 3 seats in the senate. The CSSD formed a majority government (101 seats) in the chamber with the Coalition. Vladimir Spidla of the CSSD became prime minister; following disastrous results in the 2004 European Parliament elections, he was replaced with Stanislav Gross, the former minister of interior. Accusations of corruption and threats from the Christian Democrats to leave the coalition forced Gross to resign after only nine months in office. On 25 April 2005, he was replaced with Jiri Paroubek, his former regional development minister.

Vaclav Klaus of the ODS was inaugurated president on 7 March 2003, after parliament voted him into office in February following many rounds of voting. The next parliamentary elections were held on 2–3 June 2006. The ODS, Christian Democrats (KDU-ČSL) and Greens (SZ), took 100 seats, exactly half of the 200-seat Chamber of Deputies, with the Social Democrats (ČSSD) and Communists Party of Bohemia and Moravia (KSČM) comprising the other half of the chamber. In September, President Klaus appointed a center-right government led by Mirek Topolanek of the ODS. The government lost a vote of confidence in October. In November, Klaus appointed Topolanek as prime minister for a second time. Talks began on forming a grand coalition. On 9 January 2007 parliament narrowly approved a three-party, center-right coalition. The coalition was composed of the ODS, the KDU-ČSL, and the Green Party (SZ). Three members of the cabinet are women. Amidst the global financial crisis of 2008–09 and accusations of manipulation of the public press, the coalition government received a vote of no confidence in March 2009 and was replaced by an interim government under the administration of Jan Fischer, the head of the Czech Statistical Office. New parliamentary elections were originally scheduled for October 2009 but did not take place until May 2010, since the constitutional court did not make a ruling on the bill in time to ensure a valid election.

Following inconclusive elections on 8–9 February 2008, Vaclav Klaus was reelected president on 15 February 2008.

In February 2010, a Czech court banned the extreme right-wing Workers' Party, labeling the party's rhetoric xenophobic, homophobic, anti-Semitic, and racist. The court's decision marks the first time in the Czech Republic's seventeen-year history that a political party has been banned. The leader of the Workers' Party pledged to appeal the ruling. Lawyers who filed the petition to have the group banned said that the party maintained close ties to neo-Nazi groups and held an ideological platform similar to that of Adolf Hitler. The group has also been accused of running modern-day pogroms, organizing protest demonstrations in minority neighborhoods that have often turned violent.

In the Czech Republic's May 2010 election for the lower house of parliament, the left-wing Social Democrats took the most votes in the election, capturing 22.1% of the vote and 56 of the 200 seats in the chamber. The Civic Democrats followed with took 20.2% of the vote and 53 seats, and the conservative TOP09 (Tradition, Responsibility, Prosperity) party, attracted 16.7% of the vote and 41 seats. The remaining seats went to the KSČM with 26 and the Public Affairs (VV) party with 24. Petr Necas of the Civic Democrats was appointed as prime minister in June 2010.

In the first round of senate elections held on 15–16 October 2010, no single candidate gained the 50% vote necessary to win a seat outright. As a result, the top two finishers in each voting district progressed to the second round of elections scheduled for 22–23 October. Twenty-seven of the eighty-one senate seats were contested in this election. The Social Democrats won first or second place in 22 districts during the first round of voting. In the run-off, the Social Democrats proved victorious by adding 12 seats to their count, thus taking a total of 41 seats. This is the first time that the left-wing party has held a majority in the senate. The Civic Democrats ended with a total of 25 seats, followed by the TOP 09 with 5 seats, and the Christian Democrats, also with 5 seats. One seat was won by independents and two by Communists.

15 LOCAL GOVERNMENT

The Czech Republic is divided into 6,249 municipalities for local administration, 13 self-governing regions, popularly elected for a four-year period of office, and the capital city of Prague, with a mayor and city council elected for four-year terms. Under Communist rule, Czechoslovakia's government was so centralized that little to no local government existed. Such institutions have become more common since the formation of the 1992 constitution and democratic rule.

16 JUDICIAL SYSTEM

Under the 1992 constitution, the judiciary was completely reorganized to provide for a system of courts that includes a Supreme Court; a supreme administrative court; high, regional, and district courts; and a constitutional court. The Supreme Court, which is situated in Brno, is the highest appellate court and has national jurisdiction. The high courts, with seats in Prague and Olomouc, represent the second instance in the judicial system. The district courts deal with proceedings in the first instance and are situated in the capital towns of the administrative districts. The 15-member constitutional court created in 1993 rules on the constitutionality of legislation. Constitutional court judges are appointed by the president, subject to senate approval, for 10-year terms.

Military courts were abolished in 1993 and their functions transferred to the civil court system. The new judiciary is independent from the executive and legislative branches and appears to be impartial in its application of the law. Criminal defendants are entitled to fair and open public trials. They have the right to have counsel and enjoy a presumption of innocence.

[17]ARMED FORCES

The International Institute for Strategic Studies reports that armed forces in the Czech Republic totaled 23,441 members in 2011. The force is comprised of 7,026 from the army, 4,567 from the air force, and 11,848 members of other forces. Armed forces represent 0.5% of the labor force in the Czech Republic. Defense spending totaled $3.8 billion and accounted for 1.5% of GDP.

The Czech Republic provided support to NATO, UN, and other peacekeeping missions in nine countries in Asia, Europe, and Africa.

The Košice Agreement of 1945 provided for military organization, equipment, and training to be modeled after those of the former USSR. Czechoslovakia was a signatory to the Warsaw Pact of 14 May 1955, which provided for military cooperation with the USSR and other Soviet-bloc countries and for a joint command with headquarters in Moscow.

[18]INTERNATIONAL COOPERATION

Czechoslovakia was a charter member of the United Nations, admitted on 24 October 1945. The Czech Republic became a member of the UN on 8 January 1993; it is part of the ECE and serves on several specialized agencies, such as the IFC, IMF, WHO, the World Bank, and UNESCO. The Czech Republic was admitted to NATO on 12 March 1999 and became a member of the European Union on 1 May 2004. It is also a member of the OECD, the OSCE, the Central European Initiative, the Council of Europe, and the European Bank for Reconstruction and Development. The country is an observer in the OAS and an affiliate member of the Western European Union.

The country is part of the European Organization for Nuclear Research (CERN), the Nuclear Suppliers Group (London Group), and the Nuclear Energy Agency. It is also a part of the Australia Group and the Zangger Committee. In environmental cooperation, the Czech Republic is part of the Antarctic Treaty, Basel Convention, Conventions on Biological Diversity and Air Pollution, Ramsar, CITES, the Kyoto Protocol, the Montréal Protocol, MARPOL, the Nuclear Test Ban Treaty, and the UN Conventions on the Law of the Sea, Climate Change, and Desertification.

The Czech Republic was the last country to ratify the Lisbon Treaty, which was signed by president Klaus in November 2009.

[19]ECONOMY

Before World War II, Bohemia and Moravia were among the most agriculturally and industrially developed areas in Europe. In 1993, the Czech Republic emerged from 40 years of centralized economic planning in the Communist era (including the more balanced economic development of the 1960s) with a more prosperous and less debt-ridden economy than most other post-Communist countries. It has made great strides in developing industry and manufacturing and in privatizing banks and other institutions in its transition from communism. As a result, foreign investments have poured into the country. The primary industries include iron and steel production, automobiles, chemicals, electronics, textiles, and pharmaceuticals. The agricultural sector is fairly small, with

sugar beets, potatoes, wheat, and hops as the primary products. Beer brewing is a major agricultural-based industry.

After recovering from a recession following the 1993 separation from Slovakia, the republic enjoyed GDP growth of 4.8% in 1995. The thriving economy of the mid-1990s depended upon loans easily secured from state-owned banks to newly privatized companies that did not have effective managers. This method of fueling the economy collapsed in a 1997 currency crisis, which caused the economy to go into a three-year recession. Following this collapse, the government rescued and privatized the four largest banks in the Czech Republic, which stabilized the banking sector, now largely foreign-owned. The banks began to lend again by 2001.

The steel and engineering industries were struggling in the early 2000s, but growth in information technology and electronics diversified the economy. The telecommunications, energy, gas, and petrochemical sectors were due to be privatized by 2002. The Czech Republic became a member of the European Union (EU) in 2004, but the country is not a eurozone member. Leaders estimate that the country may not adopt the euro until after 2014.

The country entered a recession as a result of the 2008–09 global financial crisis. Unemployment rose to 8.4% in July 2009. In 2010 unemployment was reported at 7.1%, and the gross domestic product (GDP) rate of change was 2.3%. Inflation stood at 1.5%.

[20]INCOME

The CIA estimated that in 2010 the GDP of the Czech Republic was $261.3 billion. The CIA defines GDP as the value of all final goods and services produced within a nation in a given year and computed on the basis of purchasing power parity (PPP) rather than value as measured on the basis of the rate of the exchange based on current dollars. The per capita GDP was estimated at $25,600. The annual growth rate of GDP was 2.3%. The average inflation rate was 1.5%. It was estimated that agriculture accounted for 2.4% of GDP, industry 37.6%, and services 60%.

According to the World Bank, remittances from citizens living abroad totaled $1.2 billion or about $118 per capita and accounted for approximately 0.5% of GDP.

The World Bank reports that, in 2009, household consumption in the Czech Republic totaled $96.4 billion or about $9,456 per capita, measured in current US dollars rather than PPP. Household consumption includes expenditures of individuals, households, and nongovernmental organizations on goods and services, excluding the purchases of dwellings. It was estimated that household consumption was growing at an average annual rate of 0.2%.

As of 2011, the most recent study by the World Bank reported that actual individual consumption in the Czech Republic was 59.9% of GDP and accounted for 0.36% of world consumption. By comparison, the United States accounted for 25.44% of world individual consumption. The World Bank also estimated that 12.2% of Czech Republic's GDP was spent on food and beverages, 14% on housing and household furnishings, 2.5% on clothes, 6.6% on health, 5.8% on transportation, 1.8% on communications, 6.6% on recreation, 3.3% on restaurants and hotels, and 2.6% on miscellaneous goods and services and purchases from abroad.

In 2007, the World Bank estimated that the Czech Republic, with 0.17% of the world's population, accounted for 0.38% of the world's GDP. By comparison, the United States, with 4.85% of the world's population, accounted for 22.51% of world GDP.

21 LABOR

As of 2010, the Czech Republic had a total labor force of 5.449 million people. Within that labor force, CIA estimates in 2009 noted that 3.1% were employed in agriculture, 38.6% in industry, and 58.3% in the service sector.

The right to form and join unions is protected by law. As of 2006, about 21% of the Czech labor force was unionized, although union membership was on the decline. The major labor confederation is the Czech-Moravian Chamber of Trade Unions. Workers are freely allowed to organize and engage in collective bargaining. Striking is also allowed, but only after mediation efforts fail. However, workers in certain critical sectors cannot strike and are limited only to mediation. Collective bargaining is usually conducted on a company-by-company basis between unions and employers.

According to the Czech labor code, the standard workweek is 40 hours, with at least two days of rest. There is also a mandatory 30-minute rest period during the eight-hour day. Overtime is limited to eight hours per week and is subject to employee consent. The minimum working age is 15 years with some exceptions allowing legal employment to 14-year-old workers. There are strict standards for all workers under the age of 18, and these standards are routinely enforced. Occupational health and safety standards are prescribed and effectively enforced except in some industries still awaiting privatization. As of 2011, the minimum wage was $453 per month and was considered to provide a decent standard of living for a worker and a family.

22 AGRICULTURE

Agriculture is a small but important sector of the economy that has steadily declined since the Velvet Revolution of 1989. Roughly 42% of the total land is farmed. The country's major crops include wheat, potatoes, sugar beets, hops, and fruit. In 2009, cereal production amounted to 7.8 million tons, fruit production 304,272 tons, and vegetable production 241,590 tons.

The principal crops are grains, which support the Czech Republic's dozens of small breweries. At 166 liters (44 gallons) per person, the Czech Republic is the world's highest per capita beer-consuming nation. There is a long tradition of brewing in the Czech Republic; some of the world's oldest brands were invented there. After Germany, the Czech Republic is Europe's largest producer of hops.

Agriculture lags behind other sectors in the restoration of private properties seized after 1948. As of 1993 agricultural subsidies were restricted to the formation of new farms and the production of wheat, dairy products, and meat. Over the long term, the government estimates that over 250,000 agricultural workers will need to find employment in other sectors and that arable land in use will decrease by 9%.

23 ANIMAL HUSBANDRY

The UN FAO reported that the Czech Republic dedicated 980,000 hectares (2.42 million acres) to permanent pasture or meadow in 2009. During that year, the country tended 24 million chickens, 1.3 million head of cattle, and 1.9 million pigs. The production from these animals amounted to 82,165 tons of beef and veal, 480,128 tons of pork, 253,996 tons of poultry, 94,869 tons of eggs, and 2.01 million tons of milk. The Czech Republic also produced 9,427 tons of cattle hide and 312 tons of raw wool.

Although hogs, cattle, and poultry are the main income producers in the livestock sector, there were an estimated 172,800 sheep, 15,850 goats, and 27,820 horses in 2007.

Meat, poultry, and dairy production have been oriented toward quantity rather than quality.

24 FISHING

Fishing is a relatively unimportant source of domestic food supply. Production is derived mostly from pond cultivation and, to a lesser extent, from rivers. In 2008, the annual capture totaled 4,164 tons according to the UN FAO.

25 FORESTRY

The Forest Code (1852) of the Austro-Hungarian Empire was incorporated into the laws of the former Czechoslovakia and governed forest conservation until World War II (1939–45). Most forests were privately owned, and during the world wars, they were excessively exploited. The Czech Republic had an estimated 2,593,923 hectares (6,409,723 acres) of forestland in 2009, accounting for 34% of the total land area. As of 2009 forest, ownership was 60% state, 23% private, and 16% municipal. The UN FAO estimated the 2009 roundwood production at 14.3 million cu m (505.2 million cu ft). The value of all forest products, including roundwood, totaled $2.13 billion. Since the Czech government began property restitution, the need for wood products has far outstripped domestic supply, especially for furniture and construction materials.

26 MINING

The mining and processing sector's share of GDP in 2009 was 1%, down from 3.7% in 1993. Mining and processing of industrial minerals and the production of construction materials continued to be of regional and domestic importance. Economic resources of most metals have been depleted. As of the end of 2000 only gold-bearing and tin-tungsten ores were among the exceptions. All the raw materials consumed by the country's steel industry were imported, including iron ore and concentrate, manganese ore, copper, and unwrought lead and zinc. Lead and zinc have not been mined for about seven years, and the number of registered lead deposits declined from 17 in 1998 to 9 in 2002, none of which were being worked. The country's eight iron ore deposits were no longer worked. In 2009, kaolin production was 2.088 million metric tons, down from 3.83 million tons in 2008; common sand and gravel, 23.614 million cu m; foundry sand, 374,000 tons, compared to 850,000 tons in 2007; glass sand, 990,000 tons, compared to 1,151,000 tons in 2008; dimension stone, 704 million cu m, down from 927 million cu m in 2005; limestone and calcareous stones, 9.49 million tons; crushed stone, 38.2 million cu m; hydrated lime and quicklime, 1.0 million tons; feldspar, 431,000 metric tons, down from 514,000 metric tons in 2007; and dolomite, 337,000 metric tons, down from 440,000 metric tons in 2008. Output of crude gypsum and anhydrite went from 35,000 metric tons in 2008 to 13,000 metric tons in 2009. The Czech Republic also produced arsenic, hydraulic cement, bentonite, dolomite, crude gemstones and pyrope-bearing rock, illite, iron ore, nitrogen, quartz, salt, basalt (for casting), silver, sodium compounds, sulfuric acid, talc, uranium, wollastonite, and zeolites.

27 ENERGY AND POWER

The Czech Republic has only small proven reserves of oil and natural gas, but relatively abundant recoverable reserves of coal.

The World Bank reported in 2008 that the Czech Republic produced 83.2 billion kWh of electricity and consumed 67.4 billion kWh, or 6,613 kWh per capita. Roughly 81% of energy came from fossil fuels, while 16% came from alternative fuels. The electricity production market in the Czech Republic is dominated by Ceske Energeticke Zavody (CEZ), which is majority owned by the state.

The Czech Republic has two operational nuclear power plants: Dukovany and Temelin, the latter located 37 miles from the Austrian border. Temelin initially went online in December 2000, with a second reactor placed on trial operation 8 April 2003. The following month, both Temelin reactors became fully operational. Both plants are operated by CEZ. In 2009, electricity production from nuclear sources was estimated at 24.6 billion kWh.

The Czech Republic's crude oil reserves are limited, totaling an estimated 15 million barrels as of 2011. Oil production in 2008 came to an estimated 3,592 barrels per day. The consumption rate for all oil products was 211,400 barrels per day for that year. Per capita oil consumption was 4,282 kg. As a result, the Czech Republic is heavily dependent upon imported oil. In 2009, total crude and refined oil product imports totaled 208,800 barrels per day. While much of the Czech Republic's oil imports come from Russia, the country has been able to tap other sources via the Ingolstadt-Kralupy nad Vltavou-Litvinov (ILK) pipeline, which permits crude oil to be transported from Trieste by way of the Trans-Alpine pipeline. The ILK pipeline is operated by Mero CR.

As with oil, the Czech Republic has only limited reserves of natural gas. In 2010, consumption and production of natural gas was estimated at 9.3 billion cu m and 203 million cu m, respectively. Imports for that year came to 8.51 billion cu m. Estimated natural gas reserves have been placed at 3.964 billion cu m in 2010.

The Czech Republic has seen its demand for coal fall over time. In spite of this, coal remains an important source of energy. In 2010, coal accounted for 41% of the nation's primary energy demand. Estimated coal reserves in the Czech Republic amounted to 2.4 billion tons in 2010.

28 INDUSTRY

Before World War II, Czechoslovakia favored traditional export-oriented light industries, including food processing. Concentration on the production of capital goods since the war has been at the expense of consumer goods and foodstuffs, although there have been increases in the metalworking industry and in the production of glass, wood products, paper, textiles, clothing, shoes, and leather goods. Some of these and other consumer goods—such as the world-famous pilsner beer, ham, and sugar—had figured prominently in the pre-World War II export trade, but machinery was predominant under the Communist regime.

A final wave of privatization that began in 1995 resulted in an 80% private stake in industry. By 2010, industry accounted for 37.6% of GDP. As of 2009, industry employed 38.6% of the work force. Although the relative contribution of industry to the economy had begun to decline, the industrial base remained diversified.

Major industries in the Czech Republic include fuels, ferrous metallurgy, machinery and equipment, coal, motor vehicles, glass, and armaments. The country is particularly strong in engineering. Car manufacturing remains the main industrial driving force. The Czech Republic produced 1,072,263 automobiles in 2010, up 9.5% from 2009.

29 SCIENCE AND TECHNOLOGY

Patent applications in science and technology as of 2009, according to the World Bank, totaled 789 in the Czech Republic. Public financing of science was 1.47% of GDP. The Czech Academy of Science has divisions of life and chemical sciences, mathematics, and physical and earth sciences, and 43 attached medical, scientific, and technical research institutes. In addition, there are 28 specialized agricultural, medical, scientific, and technical learned societies. There are technology museums in Brno, Mladá Boleslav, and Prague, and the latter also has a natural history museum. The Czech Republic has 13 universities offering degrees in medicine, natural sciences, mathematics, engineering, and agriculture. In 1987–97, science and engineering students accounted for 28% of university enrollment. In 2009, 10% of all graduates from tertiary educational programs were awarded science degrees (natural sciences, mathematics and computers, and engineering).

2009 total expenditures for research and development (R&D) amounted to CZK55,350 million (about US$3 billion), of which 48.8% came from business, 43.9% came from government sources, and 9.2% came from foreign sources. High technology exports in 2009 accounted for 15.3% of manufactured exports that year.

30 DOMESTIC TRADE

In the Communist period, marketing and distribution, including price-fixing, were controlled by the federal government; administration on the lower levels was handled by the national committees. Cooperative farms sold the bulk of their produce to the state at fixed prices, but marginal quantities of surplus items were sold directly to consumers through so-called free farmers' markets. Starting in 1958, the government operated a program of installment buying for certain durable consumer goods, with state savings banks granting special credits.

The Velvet Revolution of 1989 brought rapid privatization program on an innovative voucher system. Each citizen was given an opportunity to purchase a book of vouchers to be used in exchange for shares in state-owned businesses. As a result, more than 20,000 shops, restaurants, and workshops in both the Czech and Slovak republics were transferred to private owners by public auction in a wave of small privatization and through distribution of ownership shares.

The commercial center of the country is Prague. Though there are numerous small shops throughout the city, American- and European-style supermarkets and department stores are developing and providing stiff competition. Shopping malls have also begun to develop. Though most transactions are still in cash, credit cards are gaining a wider acceptance within major cities. Direct marketing, particularly through catalog sales, has become more popular, particularly in areas outside of the major cities.

Franchising in the Czech Republic is only in its early stages. As of 2010, there were over 100 franchised brands in the country—with growth spurred by the country's accession to the EU in 2004.

US-based McDonald's, Burger King, and KFC have franchise operations in the Czech Republic.

Direct sales is well-developed in the Czech Republic. Major firms include Amway, Avon, Mary Kay, Lux, Just, and Tupperware. Retail sales totaled $223.5 million in 2009. There were 223,673 dealers, of which 95% were woman; 85% of sellers worked only part-time.

Electronic commerce (e-commerce) is growing in popularity among Czech consumers, although most still do not regularly shop online. In 2010, 4% of retail sales took place online. The growing e-commerce sector in the Czech Republic is being encouraged by rising credit card use and a lowering of telecommunications tariffs. As of 2010, there were 6 million Internet users in the Czech Republic.

Businesses generally adhere to a standard 40-hour workweek, although many may close early on Fridays. Most businesses do not keep weekend hours. Generally, government and business offices are open Monday through Friday from 8 a.m. to 4 p.m. Banks and shops are open Monday through Friday from 8 a.m. to 6 p.m. On Sunday all businesses are closed, although some restaurants, coffee bars, cinemas, and some shopping centers may be open.

31 FOREIGN TRADE

Czech foreign trade has traditionally involved the import of raw materials, oil and gas, and semi-manufactured products and the export of semi-finished products and consumer and capital goods. In 1989, trade with former Eastern Bloc nations accounted for 56% of Czechoslovakia's total foreign trade; by the end of 1992, their share had more than halved to 27%.

The Czech Republic engages in the export of numerous manufactured goods, such as automobiles, furniture, and electrical appliances. The CIA reported that, in 2010, the Czech Republic's exports totaled $126.4 billion, while imports totaled $123.5 billion, resulting in a trade surplus of $2.9 billion. Major import partners in 2009 were Germany, 25.6%; China, 11.9%; Poland, 6.5%; Russia, 5.4%; and Slovakia, 5.2%. Its major export partners were Germany, 31.7%; Slovakia, 8.7%; Poland, 6.2%; France, 5.5%; the United Kingdom, 4.9%; Austria, 4.7%; and Italy, 4.5%.

32 BALANCE OF PAYMENTS

The current account balance in 2010 stood at -$7.188 billion, a decline from the 2004 level of -$5.6 billion. These negative figures contrast with positive current account numbers in prior years, such as the 2001 current account balance of $3.5 billion. Nonetheless, strong inflows of foreign direct investment have historically led to surpluses in the financial account, which often cover the current account deficit.

33 BANKING AND SECURITIES

The Czech National Bank (CNB) is the country's central bank, charged with issuing currency and regulating the state's commercial banking sector. As of March 2007, there were 36 commercial and savings banks in the Czech Republic, as well as 20 credit unions.

In 2010, the money market rate, the rate at which financial institutions lend to one another in the short term, was 1.08%. The discount rate, the interest rate at which the central bank lends to financial institutions in the short term, was 0.25%.

Principal Trading Partners – Czech Republic (2010)

(In millions of US dollars)

Country	Total	Exports	Imports	Balance
World	259,620.0	133,020.0	126,600.0	6,420.0
Germany	79,964.0	42,832.0	37,132.0	5,700.0
Slovak Republic	19,513.0	11,503.0	8,010.0	3,493.0
Poland	16,826.0	8,127.0	8,699.0	-572.0
Austria	12,376.0	6,276.0	6,100.0	176.0
France	11,215.0	7,113.0	4,102.0	3,011.0
Italy	10,473.0	5,901.0	4,572.0	1,329.0
China	10,283.0	1,200.0	9,083.0	-7,883.0
United Kingdom	10,025.0	6,493.0	3,532.0	2,961.0
Russia	9,861.0	3,387.0	6,474.0	-3,087.0
Netherlands	9,549.0	4,941.0	4,608.0	333.0

(…) data not available or not significant.
(n.s.) not specified.

SOURCE: *2011 Direction of Trade Statistics Yearbook*, New York: United Nations, 2011.

Balance of Payments – Czech Republic (2010)

(In millions of US dollars)

Current Account		**-7,188.0**
Balance on goods		2,814.0
Imports	-123,600.0	
Exports	126,414.0	
Balance on services		3,444.0
Balance on income		-13,356.0
Current transfers		-90.0
Capital Account		**1,768.0**
Financial Account		**9,431.0**
Direct investment abroad		-1,758.0
Direct investment in Czech Republic		6,720.0
Portfolio investment assets		705.0
Portfolio investment liabilities		7,371.0
Financial derivatives		-219.0
Other investment assets		-4,512.0
Other investment liabilities		1,124.0
Net Errors and Omissions		**-1,935.0**
Reserves and Related Items		**-2,076.0**

(…) data not available or not significant.

SOURCE: *Balance of Payment Statistics Yearbook 2011,* Washington, DC: International Monetary Fund, 2011.

The origins of the first exchange in Prague go back to the 1850s when foreign exchange and securities were the principal trading products. An exchange trading securities and commodities was established in 1871. The volumes traded at the exchange fluctuated considerably, and in 1938, official trading was suspended. After World War II, the operation of the Prague Exchange was not restored, and in 1952, the exchange was officially abolished. In 1990, eight banks became members of the Preparatory Committee on Stock Exchange Foundation. In 1992, this institution transformed itself into a stock exchange. The Prague Stock Exchange has been trading debt securities (mostly government and bank issues) since April 1993. Volume in mid-1993 was CZK18 million, of which two-thirds were listed issues. Leading Czech banks include: Ceská sporitelna (Czech Savings Bank), Investicní a poštovní banka (Investment and Postal Bank), Komercní banka (Commercial Bank),

Public Finance – Czech Republic (2009)

(In billions of koruny, central government figures)

Revenue and Grants	**1,136.28**	**100.0%**
Tax revenue	488.18	43.0%
Social contributions	509.65	44.9%
Grants	80.85	7.1%
Other revenue	57.6	5.1%
Expenditures	**1,375**	**100.0%**
General public services	133.18	9.7%
Defense	50.2	3.7%
Public order and safety	71.32	5.2%
Economic affairs	206.2	15.0%
Environmental protection	24	1.7%
Housing and community amenities	35.87	2.6%
Health	229.6	16.7%
Recreational, culture, and religion	13.68	1.0%
Education	124.87	9.1%
Social protection	486.08	35.4%

(…) data not available or not significant.

SOURCE: *Government Finance Statistics Yearbook 2010,* Washington, DC: International Monetary Fund, 2010.

and the Ceskoslovenská obchodní banka (Czechoslovak Commercial Bank). As of 2011, a total of 28 companies were listed on the Prague Stock Exchange. Total capitalization that year totaled $35 billion. In 2010, the PX Index (of major stocks in the exchange) rose 9.62% from the previous year to 1,224.8.

34 INSURANCE

The pre-World War II insurance companies and institutions of the former Czechoslovakia were reorganized after 1945 and merged, nationalized, and centralized. Since 1952, the insurance industry has been administered by the State Insurance Office, under the jurisdiction of the Ministry of Finance. Two enterprises conducted insurance activities, the Czech and the Slovak Insurance Enterprises of the state.

Property insurance and car insurance are used by more than 80% of the population in the Czech Republic. Most insurance companies offer standard life and health insurance, as well as property coverage and commercial insurance. Third-party auto insurance, workers' compensation, employer's liability, and liability for lawyers, auditors, architects, civil engineers, airlines, and hunters are compulsory. As of 2009, the value of all technical provisions totaled $10.4 billion for life and $6.2 billion for non-life insurance. Ceska Pojistovna, a subsidiary of Generali PPF Holding, is the largest insurance provider in the country.

35 PUBLIC FINANCE

The CIA estimated that, in 2010, Czech Republic's central government took in revenues of approximately $77.9 billion and had expenditures of $87.87 billion. Public debt in 2010 amounted to 40% of GDP, with $86.34 billion of the debt held by foreign entities.

In 2009, government outlays by function were as follows: general public services, 10.3%; defense, 2.4%; public order and safety, 4.7%; economic affairs, 16.4%; environmental protection, 1.6%; housing and community amenities, 2.6%; health, 17.4%; recre-

ation, culture, and religion, 3.2%; education, 10.9%; and social protection, 30.5%.

The country's total reserves of foreign exchange (including gold) grew to $41.95 billion in 2010.

36 TAXATION

As of 2011, the standard corporate income tax rate in the Czech Republic was 19%. Personal income tax schedules were changed in 2008 and amount to 15% of super gross salary, which includes a worker's base salary plus employer contributions. Payroll taxes of 47.5% (35% paid by the employer and 12.5% paid by the employee) cover pension insurance, sickness insurance, and employment insurance. There is a real estate transfer tax of 3%; gift taxes of 1–40%; and inheritance taxes of 0.5–20%. The Czech Republic has bilateral tax treaties (BITs) with dozens of countries.

The main indirect tax is a system of value-added taxes (VATs), which replaced turnover taxes as of 1 January 1993. VAT rates include 20% on most goods and some services and 10% on basic foodstuffs, minerals, pharmaceuticals, medical equipment, paper products, books, newspapers, and public transport services.

37 CUSTOMS AND DUTIES

In 2004 the Czech Republic joined the European Union and is thus a member of the single market. Customs duties on imports and exports between EU member states are illegal. Regulations concerning customs and duties between EU member states and third parties are formulated at the EU level, not by national governments.

38 FOREIGN INVESTMENT

Moody's Investors Service gave the Czech Republic the first investment grade-A rating to be awarded to a former Soviet bloc country. As of 2001, foreign direct investment (FDI) stock per capita in the Czech Republic was $2,432, the highest among the Eastern European transitional economies. FDI has served Czech economic development in providing capital and managerial expertise to restructure its enterprises. National treatment is the general rule, with screening of foreign investment proposals required only in banking, insurance, and defense industries. A competitive exchange rate and low wages have been conducive to foreign investment, but, in 1998, a six-point incentive package approved by the Czech government helped ratchet annual FDI inflows to about double previous levels. Incentives—tax breaks up to 10 years, duty-free imports, rent reductions, benefits for job creation, training grants, and incentives for reinvestments and expansions—are available for investments above $10 million or above $5 million in regions where unemployment is over 25%.

FDI in the Czech Republic was a net inflow of $2.67 billion according to World Bank figures published in 2009. FDI represented 1.4% of GDP. Net inflows of FDI reached $6.7 billion in 2010. The country received a record $11.6 billion in FDI in 2005. As of 2009, the Czech Republic has accumulated $122.3 billion in FDI; 89.1% of total FDI originated in other EU member states, and 3% came from the United States. Overall, the Czech Republic has received more FDI per capita than any other country in Central and Eastern Europe, most of it going towards manufacturing, financial services, hotels and restaurants, transportation, and telecommunications.

39 ECONOMIC DEVELOPMENT

Post-communist economic recovery has been implemented by development of the private sector, particularly in the trade and services areas, increased exports to industrialized nations, control of inflation, and achievement of a positive trade balance. The most promising growth sectors are those involving advanced technology, environmental protection, biotechnology, and, generally, high value-added production. At the end of 1996, approximately 80% of the Czech Republic's large companies had been privatized, most via voucher privatization, through which nearly six million Czechs bought vouchers exchangeable for shares in companies that were to be privatized. By 1997, however, the recovery had petered out, and the Czech Republic plunged into a recession that lasted through 1999. Most analysts blamed the downturn on incomplete restructuring.

In 2011, the non-private sector accounted for less than 20% of business. All banks have been privatized. The EU contributed significant resources to prepare the country for accession, including speeding administrative, regulatory, and judicial reform; accession to the EU was completed in 2004. The government is faced with reform of the pension and healthcare systems and a transition from manufacturing to a knowledge-based economy. The government must also consider a solution to environmental problems. In 2010, the GDP real growth rate rebounded to 2.3% from -4.1% the previous year.

High investment rates have managed to expand productivity and helped create new jobs and increase real wages. Inflation remained fairly low over this period, strengthening the national currency but at the same time undermining the export sector. As part of the EU, the Czech Republic can tap into a large market, and its maturing economy allows it to compete with countries from Western Europe.

40 SOCIAL DEVELOPMENT

Social welfare programs in the former Czechoslovakia dated back to the Austro-Hungarian Empire. Work injury laws were first introduced in 1887 and sickness benefits in 1888. During the First Republic (1918–39), social insurance was improved and extended. After World War II, new social legislation made sickness, accident, disability, and old age insurance compulsory. The trade unions administered health insurance and family allowances. The government's Bureau of Pension Insurance administered the pension insurance program, which was funded by the government and employers. In 1960, social welfare committees were established within the regional and district national committees to exercise closer control.

Social welfare programs include old age pensions, disability, survivor benefits, sickness and maternity, work injury, unemployment, and family allowances. Employers are required to contribute 21.5% of payroll, while employees contribute 6.5% to the pensions program. The retirement age has been gradually increasing.

Women have played an increasingly greater role in Czech society and account for about half of the labor force. Although the principle of equal pay for equal work is generally followed, women hold a disproportionate share of lower-paying positions. The unemployment rate for women is greater than for men, and only a small number of women hold senior positions in the workforce.

Rape and domestic violence is underreported, although societal attitudes are slowly improving to help victims seek assistance from authorities. In 2004, the criminal code was amended to recognize domestic violence as a distinct crime. Crisis centers exist to help victims of sexual abuse and violence. Sexual harassment is prohibited by law. Trafficking in women and children is evident.

The Roma minority, officially estimated to number 150,000-200,000, face discrimination in housing, employment, and often are subject to harassment. Racially motivated crime is on the increase, as is skinhead activity. Religious freedom is generally tolerated. The Czech Republic's human rights record is fairly good, although judicial backlogs result in extended pretrial detention in some cases, and sporadic police violence has been reported.

41 HEALTH

The Czech health care system combines compulsory universal health insurance with mixed public and private care. Health insurance is funded by individuals, employers, and the government. A number of physicians have private practices and maintain contracts with the insurance system for reimbursement of their services. As of 2011, there were an estimated 36 physicians, 86 nurses and housewives, and 72 hospital beds per 10,000 inhabitants. Health care expenditure was estimated at 7.1% of GDP in 2011, amounting to $1,384 per person.

Health activities are directed by the Ministry of Health through the National Health Service. Factories and offices have health services, ranging from first-aid facilities in small enterprises to hospitals in the largest. All school children receive medical attention, including inoculations, X-rays, and annual examinations. In 2007, children up to one year of age were immunized for the following diseases: diphtheria, pertussis, and tetanus, 99%; and measles, 98%.

Special attention has been devoted to preventive medicine, with campaigns waged against tuberculosis, venereal diseases, cancer, poliomyelitis, diphtheria, and mental disturbances. Diseases of the circulatory system are the leading cause of death. Free guidance and care given to women and children have resulted in a low infant mortality rate of 3 deaths per 1,000 live births in 2011, one of the lowest in the world. The total fertility rate in 2011 was estimated at 1.5 children born per woman. According to the World Bank, the maternal mortality rate in 2008 was 8 maternal deaths per 100,000 live births. Average life expectancy in 2011, according to the CIA, was 77 years. The CIA calculated HIV/AIDS prevalence to be about less than 0.1% in 2009.

42 HOUSING

The lack of affordable housing, which inhibits labor mobility, is a major factor slowing economic growth in the Czech Republic. Problems include lack of financing, shortages of materials and labor, and a poorly developed infrastructure. In the mid-1990s, the government drafted a new housing policy, which, among other things, lifted existing restrictive legal provisions barring occupants from buying and reselling flats and differentiate rents according to quality and location of flats.

According to the Czech Statistical Office, of the 1.9 million houses in the country, 83% were permanently occupied in 2008. There was an average of 2.5 people per household in 2009.

43 EDUCATION

Education is under state control and free, up to and including the university level. Nine years of education are compulsory. There is a general primary school program that lasts for nine years. However, after the fifth year, some students may choose to enter more specialized programs that will include their secondary education studies as well. Secondary programs include general academic studies (gymnasium), vocational studies, technical programs, or art studies (music and drama). The academic year runs from September to June. The primary languages of instruction are Czech, German, and English.

In 2009, about 95% of children between the ages of 3 and 5 were enrolled in some type of preschool program. Primary school enrollment in 2009 was estimated at about 90% of age-eligible students. The student-to-teacher ratio for primary school was at about 19:1 in 2009; the ratio for secondary school was about 11:1 that year.

Universities in the Czech Republic include the world-famous Charles University at Prague (founded 1348); Palacky University at Olomouc (1576; reestablished 1946); and J. E. Purkyne University at Brno (1919; reestablished 1945). In 2009, about 58% of the tertiary age population were enrolled in some type of higher education program. Of those enrolled in tertiary education, there were 100 male students for every 132 female students. The adult literacy rate is estimated at about 99%.

As of 2009, public expenditure on education was estimated at 4.2% of GDP, or 10.9% of total government expenditures.

44 LIBRARIES AND MUSEUMS

The National Library of the Czech Republic (over six million volumes in 2011) in Prague is the result of a 1958 amalgamation of six Prague libraries, including the venerable University Library, founded in 1348. It holds a valuable expensive collection of Mozart's papers and manuscripts. Other collections of significance are the university libraries at Brno and Olomouc. The State Research Library, including all six of its branches, holds more than six million volumes. In 2007, the Czech Republic had around 6,000 public libraries. The Jiří Mahen Library in Brno, established in 1921, is the largest municipal library in the region of Moravia; the library holds about 800,000 books and operates a system of 35 branch locations. The Association of Library and Information Professionals of the Czech Republic had more than 1,200 members in 2011.

Castles, mansions, churches, and other buildings of historical interest are public property. Many serve as museums and galleries. The largest museum in the country is the world-famous National Museum in Prague. The National Gallery, also in Prague, contains outstanding collections of medieval art and 17th-century and 18th-century Dutch paintings. Other Prague museums of note include the Jewish Museum, the Antonin Dvorak Museum (celebrating the life of the Czech composer, 1841–1904), and the Museum of Toys, holding the world's second-largest exposition of toys. Other outstanding museums and galleries are located in Brno and Plzen. The Prague Botanical Gardens are among the finest in Europe.

45 MEDIA

Formerly, the Communist Party and the government controlled all publishing. Formal censorship, via the government's Office for Press and Information, was lifted for three months during the Prague Spring of 1968, but prevailed after that time until the late 1980s. As of 2011, the government was said to fully uphold the legally provided freedoms of free speech and a free press.

The Czech telecommunications system has been privatized. Growth in the use of mobile cellular telephones is particularly strong. In 2009, there were some 2 million main phone lines and 14.2 million mobile cellular phones in use, with mobile phone subscriptions averaging 136 per 100 people. International service is provided by two Intersputnik, one Intelsat, one Eutelsat, one Inmarsat, and one Globalstar satellite ground stations.

In 2009, there were 31 AM and 304 FM radio stations and 17 shortwave radio stations. In 2007, there were an estimated 128 television sets per 100 households. In 2010, the country had about 3.4 million Internet hosts. As of 2010, there were some 6 million Internet users in the Czech Republic.

Major newspapers and estimated 2009 circulation totals are: *Blesk* (420,000), *Mlada Fronta Dnes* (350,000), *Hospodarske Noviny* (130,000), and *Lidove Noviny* (68,230).

46 ORGANIZATIONS

The most important umbrella labor organization is the Czech and Slovak Confederation of Trade Unions, an organization that promotes democracy. The World Federation of Trade Unions has an office in Prague. The Confederation of Industry of the Czech Republic (est. 1990) is also in Prague. Professional societies representing a wide variety of careers are also active. Important political associations include the Czech Democratic Left Movements and the Civic Movement. The Center for Democracy and Free Enterprise (est. 1991) promotes development of democratic institutions and a free market economy.

The Academy of Sciences of the Czech Republic was founded in 1993 to support and encourage research and educational institutions involved in the fields of natural and technical sciences, social sciences, and humanities.

Youth organizations include the Czech Association of Scouts and Guides (CASG), YMCA and YWCA, and chapters of the Red Cross Youth. There are many sports associations in the country, some of which are affiliated with international organizations as well. National women's organizations include the Gender Studies Center in Prague and the Czech Union of Women.

Multinational organizations based in Prague include the International Association for Vehicle Systems Dynamics and the International Union of Speleology. There are national chapters of Amnesty International and the Red Cross.

47 TOURISM, TRAVEL, AND RECREATION

Prague, which survived World War II relatively intact, has numerous palaces and churches from the Renaissance and Baroque periods. There are many attractive mountain resorts, especially in northern Bohemia. The mineral spas in Prague are popular as well as the historic monuments. Football (soccer), ice hockey, skiing, canoeing, swimming, and tennis are among the favorite sports.

A passport is required for all foreign nationals, whether temporary visitors or transit passengers. Visas are not required for stays of up to 90 days.

The 2011 *Tourism Factbook*, published by the UN World Tourism Organization, reported 6.03 million incoming tourists to the Czech Republic in 2009, spending a total of $7.4 billion. Of those incoming tourists, there were 5.1 million from Europe. There were 260,736 hotel beds available in the Czech Republic, which had an occupancy rate of 33%.

In 2011, the estimated daily cost to visit Prague, the capital, was $416. The cost of visiting other cities averaged $218.

48 FAMOUS PERSONS

The founder of modern Czechoslovakia was Tomáš Garrigue Masaryk (1850–1937), a philosopher-statesman born of a Slovak father and a Czech mother. Eduard Beneš (1884–1948), cofounder with Masaryk of the Czechoslovak Republic, was foreign minister, premier, and president of the republic (1935–38 and 1940–48). Jan Masaryk (1886–1948), son of Tomáš G. Masaryk, was foreign minister of the government-in-exile and, until his mysterious death, of the reconstituted republic. Klement Gottwald (1896–1953) became a leader of the Czechoslovak Communist Party in 1929 and was the president of the republic from 1948 to 1953; Antonín Zápotocky (1884–1957), a trade union leader, was president from 1953 to 1957. Alexander Dubček (1921–92) was secretary of the Czechoslovak Communist Party and principal leader of the 1968 reform movement that ended with Soviet intervention. Gen. Ludvík Svoboda (1895–1979) was president of the republic from 1968 to 1975. Gustáv Husák (1913–91) was general secretary of the Communist Party from 1969 to 1987; he became president of the republic in 1975. Parliamentary elections at the end of 1989 saw the rise of the playwright Vaclav Havel (b. 1936) to power. The Czech and Slovak republics decided to split in 1992. Havel was elected first president of the Czech Republic in parliamentary elections. Vaclav Klaus (b. 1941) was elected the second president of the Czech Republic in 2003.

Perhaps the two most famous Czechs are religious reformer John Huss (Jan Hus, 1371–1415) and theologian, educator, and philosopher John Amos Comenius (Jan Amos Komensk, 1592–1670), an early advocate of universal education. *The History of the Czech People* by František Palack (1798–1876) inspired Czech nationalism. Karel Havliček (1821–56) was a leading political journalist, while Alois Jirásek (1851–1930) is known for his historical novels. The most famous woman literary figure is Božena Němcová (1820–62), whose Babička (The Grandmother), depicting country life, is widely read to this day. A poet of renown, Jaroslav Vrchlick (1853–1912) wrote voluminous poetry and translations. *The Good Soldier Schweik* by Jaroslav Hašek (1883–1923) is a renowned satire on militarism. Karel Capek (1890–1938), brilliant novelist, journalist, and playwright, is well known for his play *R.U.R.* (in which he coined the word robot). Jan Patočka (1907–77) was one of the most influential Central European philosophers of the 20th century. Bedrich Smetana (1824–84), Antonín Dvorák (1841–1904), Leoš Janáček (1854–1928), and Bohuslav Martinu (1890–1959) are world-famous composers. The leading modern sculptor, Jan Stursa (1880–1925), is best known for his often-reproduced *The Wounded*.

Prominent 20th-century Czech personalities in culture and the arts include the writers Vladislav Vančura (1891–1942) and Ladislav Fuks (1923–94), the painter Jan Zrzav (1890–1977), and the Czech filmmakers Jirí Trnka (1912–69) and Karel Zeman (1910–89). Leaders of the "new wave" of Czechoslovak cinema in the 1960s were Ján Kadár (1918–79) and Miloš Forman (b. 1932), both expatriates after 1968. Josef Koudelka (b. 1938) is a Czech photographer who resides in France. The best-known political dissidents in the 1970s and 1980s were the playwrights Pavel Kohout (b. 1928) and Vaclav Havel (b. 1936), and the sociologist Rudolf Battek (b. 1924). The novelist Milan Kundera (b. 1929), who has lived in France since 1975, is the best-known contemporary Czech writer. Czechs have become top world tennis players: Martina Navrátilová (b. 1956), expatriate since 1975, Ivan Lendl (b. 1960), Hana Mandlíková (b. 1962), Jana Novotná (b. 1968), and Martina Hingis (b. 1980) have thrilled audiences with their skills on the courts.

There have been only two Czechoslovak Nobel Prize winners: in chemistry in 1959, Jaroslav Heyrovsk (1890–1967), who devised an electrochemical method of analysis; and in literature in 1984, the poet Jaroslav Seifert (1901–86).

49 DEPENDENCIES

The Czech Republic has no territories or colonies.

50 BIBLIOGRAPHY

Andreyev, Catherine. *Russia Abroad: Prague and the Russian Diaspora, 1918–1938.* New Haven, CT: Yale University Press, 2004.

Appel, Hilary. *A New Capitalist Order: Privatization and Ideology in Russia and Eastern Europe.* Pittsburgh: University of Pittsburgh Press, 2004.

Boehm, Barbara Drake and Jiri Fajt, eds. *Prague: The Crown of Bohemia, 1347–1437.* New York: Metropolitan Museum of Art, 2005.

Burton, Richard D. E. *Prague: A Cultural and Literary History.* New York: Interlink Books, 2003.

Czech Republic Investment and Business Guide: Strategic and Practical Information. Washington, DC: International Business Publications USA, 2012.

Eckhart, Karl, et al., eds. *Social, Economic and Cultural Aspects in the Dynamic Changing Process of Old Industrial Regions: Ruhr District (Germany), Upper Silesia (Poland), Ostrava Region (Czech Republic).* Piscataway, NJ: Transaction Publishers, 2003.

Forey, Barbara, et al., eds. *International Smoking Statistics: A Collection of Historical Data from 30 Economically Developed Countries.* New York: Oxford University Press, 2002.

Frucht, Richard, ed. *Eastern Europe: An Introduction to the People, Lands, and Culture.* Santa Barbara, CA: ABC-CLIO, 2005.

Holy, Ladislav. *The Little Czech and the Great Czech Nation: National Identity and the Post-Communist Transformation of Society.* Cambridge: Cambridge University Press, 1996.

Hoshi, Iraj, Ewa Balcerowicz, and Leszek Balcerowicz, eds. *Barriers to Entry and Growth of New Firms in Early Transition: A*

Comparative Study of Poland, Hungary, Czech Republic, Albania, and Lithuania. Boston: Kluwer Academic Publishers, 2003.

Lawson, George. *Negotiated Revolutions: The Czech Republic, South Africa and Chile.* Burlington, VT: Ashgate, 2005.

McElrath, Karen, ed. *HIV and AIDS: A Global View.* Westport, CT: Greenwood Press, 2002.

Opello, Walter C. *European Politics.* Boulder, CO: Lynne Rienner Publishers, 2009.

Otfinoski, Steven. *The Czech Republic.* 2nd ed. New York: Facts On File, 2004.

Political Chronology of Europe. London, Eng.: Europa, 2001.

Reuvid, Jonathan, ed. *Doing Business with the Czech Republic.* London, Eng.: Kogan Page, 2002.

Vogt, Henri. *Between Utopia and Disillusionment: A Narrative of the Political Transformation in Eastern Europe.* New York: Berghahn Books, 2004.

DENMARK

Kingdom of Denmark
Kongeriget Danmark

CAPITAL: Copenhagen (København)

FLAG: The Danish national flag, known as the Dannebrog, is one of the oldest national flags in the world, although the concept of a national flag did not develop until the late 18th century when the Dannebrog was already half a millennium old. The design shows a white cross on a field of red.

ANTHEM: There are two national anthems—*Kong Christian stod ved hojen mast (King Christian Stood by the Lofty Mast)* and *Der er et yndigt land (There Is a Lovely Land)*.

MONETARY UNIT: The krone (DKK) of 100 øre is a commercially convertible paper currency with one basic official exchange rate. There are coins of 50 øre and of 1, 2, 5, 10, and 20 kroner, and notes of 50, 100, 200, 500, and 1000 kroner. DKK1 = US$0.1715 (or US$1 = DKK5.828) as of 2012.

WEIGHTS AND MEASURES: The metric system is the legal standard, but some local units are used for special purposes.

HOLIDAYS: New Year's Day, 1 January; Constitution Day, 5 June; Christmas Day, 25 December; Boxing Day, 26 December. Movable religious holidays include Holy Thursday, Good Friday, Easter Sunday, Easter Monday, Prayer Day (4th Friday after Easter), Ascension, Pentecost, Second Pentecost, and Whitmonday.

TIME: 1 p.m. = noon GMT.

¹LOCATION, SIZE, AND EXTENT

Situated in southern Scandinavia, the Kingdom of Denmark consists of Denmark proper, the Faroe Islands, and Greenland. Denmark proper, comprising the peninsula of Jutland (Jylland) and 406 islands (97 of them inhabited), has an area of 43,094 sq km (16,638 sq mi) and extends about 402 km (250 mi) N–S and 354 km (220 mi) E–W. Comparatively, the area occupied by Denmark is slightly less than twice the size of the state of Massachusetts. The Jutland Peninsula accounts for 29,767 sq km (11,493 sq mi) of the total land area, while the islands have a combined area of 13,317 sq km (5,142 sq mi). Except for the southern boundary with Germany, the country is surrounded by water—Skagerrak on the N; Kattegat, Øresund, and the Baltic Sea on the E; and the North Sea on the W. Denmark's total boundary length is 7,382 km (4,587 mi), of which only 68 km (42 mi) is the land boundary with Germany.

Bornholm, one of Denmark's main islands, is situated in the Baltic Sea, less than 160 km (100 mi) due E of Denmark and about 40 km (25 mi) from southern Sweden. It has an area of 588 sq km (227 sq mi) and at its widest point is 40 km (25 mi) across.

Denmark's capital city, Copenhagen, is located on the eastern edge of the country on the island of Sjaelland.

²TOPOGRAPHY

The average altitude of Denmark is about 30 m (98 ft), and the highest point, Yding Skovhoj in southeastern Jutland, is only 173 m (568 ft). In parts of Jutland, along the southern coast of the island of Lolland, and in a few other areas, the coast is protected by dikes. All of Denmark proper (except for the extreme southeast of the island of Bornholm, which is rocky) consists of a glacial deposit over a chalk base. The surface comprises small hills, moors, ridges, hilly islands, raised sea bottoms, and, on the west coast, downs and marshes. There are many small rivers and inland seas. Good natural harbors are provided by the many fjords and bays.

³CLIMATE

Denmark has a temperate climate, the mildness of which is largely conditioned by the generally westerly winds and by the fact that the country is virtually encircled by water. There is little fluctuation between day and night temperatures, but sudden changes in wind direction cause considerable day-to-day temperature changes. The mean temperature in February, the coldest month, is 0°C (32°F), and in July, the warmest, 17°C (63°F). Rain falls fairly evenly throughout the year, with the annual average amounting to approximately 61 cm (24 in).

⁴FLORA AND FAUNA

The World Resources Institute estimates that there are 1,450 plant species in Denmark. In addition, Denmark is home to 81 mammal, 427 bird, 8 reptile, and 15 amphibian species. The calculation reflects the total number of distinct species residing in the country, not the number of endemic species.

Plants and animals are those common to middle Europe. There are many species of ferns, flower, fungi, and mosses; common trees include spruce and beech. Few wild or large animals remain. Birds, however, are abundant; many species breed in Denmark and migrate to warmer countries during the autumn and winter.

⁵ENVIRONMENT

The World Resources Institute reported that Denmark had designated 246,500 hectares (609,115 acres) of land for protection as of 2006. Water resources total 6.1 cu km (1.46 cu mi), while water usage is 0.67 cu km (0.161 cu mi) per year. Domestic water usage accounts for 32% of total usage, industrial for 26%, and agricultural for 42%. Per capita water usage totals 123 cu m (4,344 cu ft) per year.

Denmark's most basic environmental legislation is the Environmental Protection Act of 1974, which entrusts the Ministry of the Environment, in conjunction with local authorities, with antipollution responsibilities. The basic principle is that the polluter must pay the cost of adapting facilities to environmental requirements; installations built before 1974, however, are eligible for government subsidies to cover the cost of meeting environmental standards.

Land and water pollution are two of Denmark's most significant environmental problems, although much of Denmark's household and industrial waste is recycled. Animal wastes are responsible for polluting both drinking and surface water. Nitrogen and phosphorus pollution threaten the quality of North Sea waters. A special treatment plant at Nyborg, on the island of Fyn, handles dangerous chemical and oil wastes.

Remaining environmental problems include air pollution, especially from automobile emissions; excessive noise, notably in the major cities; and the pollution of rivers, lakes, and open sea by raw sewage. In the early 1990s, Denmark ranked among 50 nations with the heaviest industrial carbon dioxide emissions. In 1996, emissions totaled 56.5 million metric tons per year. In 2000, the emissions total dropped to 44.6 million metric tons, but by 2008 it had increased again: the UN reported that carbon dioxide emissions in Denmark that year totaled 49.9 million metric tons.

Denmark has at least 220 protected environmental sites. The Ilulissat Icefjord is a natural UNESCO World Heritage Site and there are 38 Ramsar wetland sites. According to the International Union for Conservation of Nature and Natural Resources (IUCN) Red List of Threatened Species, threatened species as of 2011 included 2 mammals, 2 birds, 15 fish, 4 mollusks, 10 other invertebrates, and 3 plants. Endangered species included the coalfish whale, blue whale, loggerhead, leatherback turtle, and Atlantic sturgeon.

6 POPULATION

The US Central Intelligence Agency (CIA) estimated the population of Denmark in 2011 to be approximately 5,529,888, which placed it at number 110 in population among the 196 nations of the world. Approximately 17.1% of the population was over 65 years of age, with another 17.6% under 15 years of age. The median age in Denmark was 40.9 years. There were 0.98 males for every female in the country. The population's annual rate of change was 0.251%. The projected population for the year 2025 was 5,800,000. Population density in Denmark was calculated at 128 people per sq km (332 people per sq mi).

The UN estimated that 87% of the population lived in urban areas, with an annual rate of change of 0.4%. The largest urban area was Copenhagen, with a population of 1.2 million.

7 MIGRATION

Estimates of Denmark's net migration rate, carried out by the CIA in 2011, amounted to 2.41 migrants per 1,000 citizens. The total number of emigrants living abroad was 259,600, and the total number of immigrants living in Denmark was 483,700. Emigra-

tion is limited, owing mainly to the relatively high standard of living in Denmark. There are approximately 500 refugees accepted every year by Denmark for resettlement. Refugees are those who need an alternative place to their first country of asylum, usually for protection-related reasons. An Integration Act took effect 1 January 1999. Under this act, most foreign nationals, including refugees, must participate in a three-year integration program, during which their social assistance is reduced. In 2009, Denmark accepted 463 refugees for resettlement, which represented .55% of the total number of refugees resettled worldwide by UNHCR that year.

8 ETHNIC GROUPS

The population of Denmark proper is of indigenous northern European stock, and the Danes are among the most homogeneous peoples of Europe. The population is comprised of Scandinavian, Inuit (Eskimo), and Faeroese peoples. There is also a small German minority in southern Jutland and small communities of Turks, Iranians, and Somalis.

9 LANGUAGES

Danish is the universal language. In addition to the letters of the English alphabet, it has the letters ae, ø, and å. A spelling reform of 1948 replaced aa with å, but English transliteration usually retains the aa. There are many dialects, but they are gradually being supplanted by standard Danish. Modern Danish has departed further from the ancient Nordic language of the Viking period than have Icelandic, Norwegian, and Swedish (to which Danish is closely related), and there is a substantial admixture of German and English words. Danish may be distinguished from the other Scandinavian languages by its change of k, p, and t to g, b, and d, in certain situations, and by its use of the glottal stop. Faeroese and Greenlandic (an Eskimo dialect) are also used. Many Danes have a speaking knowledge of English and German, and many more are capable of understanding these languages.

10 RELIGIONS

As of 2010 about 80.7% of the people were nominally members of the official state religion, the Evangelical Lutheran Church, which is supported by the state and headed by the sovereign. However, only about 3% of these Evangelical Lutherans attended services on a regular basis. Between 40% and 60% only attended services on religious holidays and for religious rituals, such as baptism, confirmation, weddings, and funerals. Muslims were the next largest group with about 3.6% of the population. The following groups each claimed less than 1% of the population: Roman Catholics, Jehovah's Witnesses, Serbian Orthodox, Jews, Baptists, Buddhists, The Church of Jesus Christ of Latter-Day Saints (Mormons), and the Pentecostal Church. Smaller groups included Seventh-Day Adventists, the Salvation Army, Methodists, Anglicans, and Russian Orthodox. Copenhagen was the site of the European headquarters for the Church of Scientology, which was not officially recognized as a religion by the state. An indigenous religion known as Forn Sidr was officially recognized in 2003; followers worship the old Norse gods.

Religious freedom is provided by the constitution and this right is generally respected in practice. In 2010 there were over 116 approved religious communities, representing a wide range of faiths.

LOCATION: 54°33′31″ to 57°44′55″ N; 8°4′36″ to 15°11′59″ E. BOUNDARY LENGTHS: Germany, 68 kilometers (42 miles); total coastline, 7,314 kilometers (4,545 miles). TERRITORIAL SEA LIMIT: 3 miles.

As the official church of state, the Evangelical Lutheran Church was the only church that received state funding. A number of other religious groups have complained that this system is unfair and contrary to religious equality. A 2007 ruling from the Supreme Court found that state financing of the church does not constitute religious discrimination, since the church is involved in civil duties not directly related to religious activities, such as registration of births and deaths. Approved religions may perform marriage and baptism rites, establish their own cemeteries, and are eligible for certain tax benefits.

[11]TRANSPORTATION

Transportation is highly developed in Denmark. The road system is well engineered and adequately maintained. The CIA reports that Denmark has a total of 73,197 km (45,483 mi) of roads, of which 73,197 km (45,483 mi) are paved. There are 477 vehicles per

1,000 people in the country. Among the most important bridges are the Storstrom Bridge, linking the islands of Sjaelland and Falster, and the Little Belt Bridge, linking Fyn and Jutland. A train and auto link joins Sjaell and Fyn (18 km/11 mi); a series of bridges connecting Denmark to Sweden—spanning 7.9 km (4.9 mi) across the Oresund Strait and costing DKK13.9 billion—opened in July 2000. The link reduced transit time between the two countries to 15 minutes for cars and trucks and less than 10 minutes for high-speed trains. Cars travel on the upper tier and trains on the lower. Railroads extend for 2,131 km (1,324 mi). Electrified railways cover 640 km (397 mi).

Denmark has approximately 400 km (249 mi) of navigable waterways. The Danish merchant fleet as of 2010 was composed of 347 ships. The majority of these vessels belonged to the Danish International Registry, an offshore registry program allowing foreign-owned vessels to sail under the Danish flag. Denmark, which pioneered the use of motor-driven ships, has many well-equipped harbors, of which Copenhagen is the most important.

There are 92 airports, which transported 6.77 million passengers in 2009 according to the World Bank. Twenty-eight airports have paved runways. Kastrup Airport, near Copenhagen, is a center of international air traffic. Domestic traffic is handled by Danish Airlines in conjunction with SAS, a joint Danish, Norwegian, and Swedish enterprise.

12HISTORY

Although there is evidence of agricultural settlement as early as 4000 BC and of bronze weaponry and jewelry by 1800 BC, Denmark's early history is little known. Tribesmen calling themselves Danes arrived from Sweden around AD 500, and Danish sailors later took part in the Viking raids, especially in those against England. Harald Bluetooth (d. 985), first Christian king of Denmark, conquered Norway, and his son Sweyn conquered England. During the reign of Canute II (1017–35), Denmark, Norway, and England were united, but in 1042, with the death of Canute's son, Hardecanute, the union with England came to an end, and Norway seceded. During the next three centuries, however, Danish hegemony was reestablished over Sweden and Norway, and in the reign of Margrethe (1387–1412) there was a union of the Danish, Norwegian, and Swedish crowns. In 1523, the Scandinavian union was dissolved, but Norway remained united with Denmark until 1814.

The Reformation was established in Denmark during the reign of Christian III (1534–59). A series of wars with Sweden during the 17th and early 18th centuries resulted in the loss of Danish territory. Meanwhile, under Frederik III (r. 1648–70) and Christian V (r. 1670–99), absolute monarchy was established and strengthened; it remained in force until 1849. Freedom of the press and improved judicial administration, introduced by Count Johann von Struensee, adviser (1770–72) to Christian VII, were abrogated after his fall from favor. Having allied itself with Napoleon, Denmark was deprived of Norway by the terms of the Peace of Kiel (1814), which united Norway with Sweden, and as a result of the Prusso-Danish wars of 1848–49 and 1864, Denmark lost its southern provinces of Slesvig, Holstein, and Lauenburg. Thereafter, the Danes concentrated on internal affairs, instituting important economic changes (in particular, specialization in dairy production) that transformed the country from a nation of poor peasants into

one of prosperous smallholders. Denmark remained neutral in World War I, and after a plebiscite in 1920, North Slesvig was reincorporated into Denmark.

Disregarding the German-Danish nonaggression pact of 1939, Adolf Hitler invaded Denmark in April 1940, and the German occupation lasted until 1945. At first, the Danish government continued to function, protecting as long as it could the nation's Jewish minority and other refugees (some 7,200 Jews eventually escaped to neutral Sweden). However, when a resistance movement developed, sabotaging factories, railroads, and other installations, the Danish government chose to resign in August 1943 rather than carry out the German demand for the death sentence against the saboteurs. Thereafter, Denmark was governed by Germany directly, and conflict with the resistance intensified.

After the war, Denmark became a charter member of the UN and of NATO. In 1952 it joined with the other Scandinavian nations to form the Nordic Council, a parliamentary body. Having joined the European Free Trade Association (EFTA) in 1960, Denmark left that association for the European Economic Community (EEC) in 1973. Meanwhile, during the 1950s and 1960s, agricultural and manufacturing production rose considerably, a high level of employment was maintained, and foreign trade terms were liberalized. However, the expense of maintaining Denmark's highly developed social security system, growing trade deficits (due partly to huge increases in the price of imported oil), persistent inflation, and rising unemployment posed political as well as economic problems for Denmark in the 1970s and 1980s, as one fragile coalition government succeeded another.

Economic performance was strong after the mid-1990s. Annual growth of GDP was 3% between 1994 and 1998, although the rate dropped to 1.6% in 1999. Thanks to strong growth, unemployment fell from 12.2% in 1994 to 6% in 1999. In March 2000 the buoyant economic outlook prompted Prime Minister Poul Nyrup Rasmussen to announce a referendum on Economic and Monetary Union to take place on 28 September 2000; it was rejected by 53.2% of the electorate. Voters narrowly rejected the Maastricht Treaty on European Union in 1992, but later approved it in 1993 after modifications were made in Denmark's favor. One of the special agreements was that Denmark could opt not to join EMU. For all practical purposes, however, Danish monetary policy has closely followed that of the European Central Bank, and the Danish crown shadows the euro (the European single currency).

As with other European countries, Denmark in the 21st century sees illegal immigration as a major problem. The issue was a deciding one in the 20 November 2001 elections, with the right-wing xenophobic Danish People's Party (founded in 1995) gaining 12% of the vote and 22 seats to become the third-largest party in parliament. The new government composed of the Liberal Party and the Conservative Party, formed by Prime Minister Anders Fogh Rasmussen, depended upon the Danish People's Party for legislative support. In June 2002 parliament passed a series of laws restricting the rights of immigrants, including the abolition of the right to asylum on humanitarian grounds and cuts of 30%–40% in the social benefits available to refugees during their first seven years of residency. In February 2005 Fogh Rasmussen won a second term as prime minister as his Liberal Party again formed a coalition with the Conservative Party. Rasmussen became the first Danish Liberal leader to win a second consecutive term.

In September 2005 the Danish newspaper *Jyllands-Posten* published caricatures of the Prophet Mohammed. Islamic law forbids the visual depiction of Mohammed's image and Muslims worldwide were outraged. In response, Muslims launched a boycott of Danish products, and in early 2006 the Danish embassies in Beirut and Damascus came under attack.

In November 2008 the citizens of Greenland voted in favor of a plan that would grant them even greater autonomy. The new self-rule agreement granted Greenlanders control of nearly all aspects of government with the exception of defense and foreign affairs, which would still be negotiated through Denmark. While many Greenlanders saw the change of status as a giant step toward independence, Danish officials have noted that the island's financial dependency on Denmark is likely to last for at least another 30 to 40 years.

A left-of-center minority coalition government came to power in October 2011. Denmark's role in the EU remained an important political issue. The new government was more open to the EU than the previous government; nonetheless, many Danes were hesitant to become further integrated into the EU. The new government said that it would seek to ease Denmark's strict immigration laws.

13 GOVERNMENT

Denmark is a constitutional monarchy. Legislative power is vested jointly in the crown and a unicameral parliament (Folketing), executive power in the sovereign—who exercises it through his or her ministers—and judicial power in the courts. The revised constitution of 1953 provides that powers constitutionally vested in Danish authorities by legislation may be transferred to international authorities established, by agreement with other states, for the promotion of international law and cooperation.

The sovereign must belong to the Lutheran Church. The crown is hereditary in the royal house of Lyksborg, which ascended the throne in 1863. On the death of a king, the throne descends to his son or daughter, with son taking precedence.

Executive powers belong to the crown, which enjoys personal integrity and is not responsible for acts of government. These powers are exercised by the cabinet, consisting of a prime minister and a variable number of ministers, who generally are members of the political party or coalition commanding a legislative majority. No minister may remain in office after the Folketing has passed a vote of no confidence in him or her.

The single-chamber Folketing, which has been in existence since 1953, is elected every four years (more frequently, if necessary) by direct and secret ballot by Danish subjects 18 years of age and older. Under the 1953 constitution there are 179 members, two of whom are elected in the Faroe Islands and two in Greenland. Members are elected by popular vote on the basis of proportional representation.

A parliamentary commission, acting as the representative both of the Folketing and of the nation, superintends civil and military government administration.

14 POLITICAL PARTIES

Until 1849 the Danish form of government was autocratic. The constitution of 1849 abolished privileges, established civil liberties, and laid down the framework of popular government through a bicameral parliament elected by all men over 30. In 1866, however, the National Liberal Party, composed largely of the urban middle class, succeeded in obtaining a majority for a constitution in which the upper chamber (Landsting) was to be elected by privileged franchise, the great landowners gaining a dominant position. This proved the starting point of a political struggle that divided Denmark until 1901. Formally, it concerned the struggle of the directly elected chamber, the Folketing, against the privileged Landsting, but in reality it was the struggle of the Left Party (made up largely of farmers, but after 1870 also of workers) to break the monopoly of political influence by the Right Party (consisting of the landowning aristocracy and the upper middle class). Meanwhile, the workers established trade unions, their political demands finding expression in the Social Democratic Party. In 1901 Christian IX called on the Left to form a government, and thereafter it was the accepted practice that the government should reflect the majority in the Folketing.

In 1905 the Left Party split. Its radical wing, which seceded, became a center party, the Social Liberals, and sought to collaborate with the Social Democrats. In 1913 these two parties together obtained a majority in the Folketing, and a Social Liberal government led Denmark through World War I. A new constitution adopted in 1915 provided for proportional representation and gave the vote to all citizens, male and female, 25 years of age and older (changed in 1978 to 18 years). In an attempt to obtain a broader popular base, the old Right Party adopted the name Conservative People's Party, and thenceforth this party and the Moderate Liberals (the old Left Party), the Social Liberals, and the Social Democrats formed the solid core of Danish politics. The Social Democrats briefly formed governments in 1924 and in 1929, in association with the Social Liberals.

During the German occupation (1940–45), a coalition government was formed by the main political parties, but increasing Danish popular resistance to the Germans led the Nazis to take over executive powers. From 1945 to 1957, Denmark was governed by minority governments, influence fluctuating between the Social Democrats and the Moderate Liberals and Conservatives, depending on which of the two groups the Social Liberals supported. In 1953 a new constitution abolished the Landsting and introduced a single-chamber system in which parliamentarianism is expressly laid down.

Issues in the 1970s focused less on international matters than on policies affecting Denmark's economy. The general elections of December 1973 resulted in heavy losses for all the established parties represented in the Folketing and successes for several new parties, notably the center-left Democratic Center Party and the "Poujadist" Progress Party led by Mogens Glistrup, an income tax expert who reputedly became a millionaire by avoiding taxes and providing others with advice on tax avoidance. The Progress Party, established early in 1973, advocated the gradual abolition of income tax and the dissolution of over 90% of the civil service. The Social Democrats, who had been in power, lost significantly in this election, and their chairman, Anker Jørgensen, resigned as prime minister. In mid-December, Poul Hartling was sworn in as prime minister, with a Liberal Democratic cabinet. The 22 Liberal members in the Folketing made up the smallest base for any government since parliamentary democracy was established in Denmark.

When it became clear in December 1974 that the Folketing would not approve the drastic anti-inflation program the Hartling government had announced, general elections were again called for. In the January 1975 balloting, the Liberals almost doubled their representation in the Folketing. However, because most of the other non-Socialist parties had lost support and because three of the four left-wing parties simultaneously gained parliamentary seats, the pre-election lack of majority persisted, and Hartling resigned at the end of the month. After several attempts at a coalition by Hartling and Anker Jørgensen, the latter's alignment of Social Democrats and other Socialist-oriented minority parties finally succeeded in forming a new government. Jørgensen remained prime minister through general elections in 1977, 1979, and 1981. In September 1982, however, dissension over Jørgensen's plan to increase taxes in order to create new jobs, boost aid to farmers, and reduce the budget deficit led the government to resign. A four-party coalition led by Poul Schlüter, the first Conservative prime minister since 1901, took power as a minority government, controlling only 66 seats out of 179. After the defeat of his 1984 budget, Schlüter called for new elections, which were held in January 1984 and increased the number of seats controlled by the coalition to 79. Following elections in September 1987, however, the number of seats held by the coalition fell to 70.

The 1994 election brought to power a three-party coalition of Social Democrats, Center Democrats, and Radical Liberals (they commanded a total of 76 seats in the 179-seat parliament). The 1994 election produced significant difficulties for the political right. The Conservatives were usually the major right-wing force with a legacy of heading governments, but it saw its representation drop to 28 seats from 31 while the Liberal Party increased its share of the vote from 15.8% to 23.3% and became the largest opposition party. The center-left coalition survived the departure of the Center Democrats in 1996, which rejected Prime Minister Poul Nyrup Rasmussen's decision to seek support for the 1997 budget from the far left. The fragile two-party coalition stumbled from one crisis to another in 1997, and the 1998 election promised to bring a Liberal-Conservative cabinet back to power. In February 1998 the Social Democrats recovered in opinion polls and Nyrup Rasmussen called a snap election.

The election results were as follows: Social Democrats 35.9% (65 seats), Radical Liberals 3.9% (7 seats), Center Democrats 4.3% (8 seats), Christian People's Party 2.5% (4 seats), Socialist People's Party 7.6% (13), Unity Party 2.7% (5 seats), Liberals 23% (43), Conservatives 8.9% (17), Progress Party 2.4% (4), and Danish People's Party 7.4% (13 seats). Following the 1998 election, the Social Democratic and Radical Liberal coalition remained intact with Nyrup Rasmussen as prime minister. The Conservatives suffered a dramatic defeat and saw their share of the vote drop from 15% to 8.9%. The two far right parties—the Danish People's Party and the Progress Party—recorded the biggest gains by taking votes from the mainstream right-wing parties. In March 2000 Nyrup Rasmussen reshuffled his cabinet to breathe new life into government and to respond to the pressures coming from the Danish People's Party, which accused the government of being soft on immigration. Campaigning on the platform "Denmark for the Danes," the People's Party attracted a large number of sympathizers.

The issue of immigration remained primary in the early elections called for by Nyrup Rasmussen on 20 November 2001. Nyrup Rasmussen's Social Democrats suffered a major defeat, gaining only 29.1% of the vote and 52 seats. Center-right parties gained their largest majority since 1926. The Liberal Party (31.3% of the vote and 56 seats) and the Conservative People's Party (9.1% and 16 seats) formed a minority government headed by Anders Fogh Rasmussen (no relation to Poul Nyrup Rasmussen) that depended upon the anti-immigrant Danish People's Party (12% and 22 seats) for legislative support. Other parties represented in the Folketing following the 2001 elections were as follows: Socialist People's Party, 6.4% (12 seats); Radical Left, 5.2% (9 seats); Unity List— the Red Greens, 2.4% (4 seats); Christian People's Party, 2.3% (4 seats); and the 2 representatives each from the Faroe Islands and Greenland.

Elections for the Folketing were next held on 8 February 2005. The percentage of the vote won by each party and distribution of seats was as follows: Liberal Party, 29% (52 seats); Social Democrats, 25.9% (47 seats); Danish People's Party, 13.2% (24 seats); Conservative People's Party, 10.3% (18 seats); Social Liberal Party, 9.2% (17 seats); Socialist People's Party, 6% (11 seats); Unity List, 3.4% (6 seats); and the two representatives each from the Faroe Islands and Greenland. Anders Fogh Rasmussen led a Liberal-Conservative coalition for a second consecutive term as prime minister. After the election, Fogh Rasmussen pledged to continue a "fair and firm immigration policy."

Citing a need to "renew and extend" the mandate of the government in order to carry out a package of public sector reforms, Rasmussen called for snap elections in November 2007. The Liberal Party took 26.2% of the vote (46 seats), followed by the Social Democrats with 25.5% (45 seats); the Danish People's Party, 13.9% (25 seats); Socialist People's Party, 13% (23 seats); Conservative People's Party, 10.4% (18 seats); Social Liberal Party, 5.1% (9 seats); New Alliance, 2.8% (5 seats); and Red-Green Unity List, 2.2% (4 seats). Rasmussen retained his seat as prime minister until 2009, when he was appointed as the secretary general of NATO. Larks Lokke Rasmussen (no relation) of the Liberal Party was appointed as the new prime minister.

General elections were next held in September 2011. Helle Thorning-Schmidt, leader of the Social Democrats, formed a minority coalition government that brought together the Social Democrats, Social Liberal Party, and Socialist People's Party. Results of the elections were as follows: Liberal Party 26.7%, Social Democrats 24.9%, Danish People's Party 12.3%, Social Liberal Party 9.5%, Socialist People's Party 9.2%, Unity List 6.7%, Liberal Alliance 5%, Conservative People's Party 4.9%, other 0.8%. The minority government held a combined 77 seats, plus the support of 12 seats held by the far-left Unity List. The opposition parties held 86 seats between them.

¹⁵LOCAL GOVERNMENT

A major reform of local government structure took effect on 1 April 1970. Copenhagen, Fredericksberg, and the regional municipality of Bornholm enjoy dual status as both local and county authorities. The previous distinction between boroughs and urban and rural districts was abolished, and the number of counties was reduced from 25 to 14 (and later to 13). The primary local units (municipalities) were reduced from 1,400 to 275 (and later to 271). The municipalities are governed by an elected council *(kommunalbestyrelse)* composed of 9 to 31 members who, in turn, elect a mayor *(borgmester)* who is vested with executive authority.

A second major restructuring of local government went into effect on 1 January 2007. The reform measures were enacted to create a more efficient and effective public sector. Denmark's 13 counties were dissolved, and instead five regions were created. The regions are represented by directly elected assemblies, called regional councils. Each council is elected for four years and has 41 members. The regional councils are responsible for health care, social services, and regional development planning and growth. The country's 271 municipalities were reduced to 98.

The Faroe Islands and Greenland enjoy home rule, with Denmark retaining responsibility for foreign affairs, defense, and monetary matters. Representatives of the Faroe Islands announced plans to organize a referendum on independence from Denmark by fall 2000. The government's response was to threaten to cut off all aid to the Faroese if they opted for independence. The referendum planned for May 2001 was cancelled.

Transparency International, a group that monitors corruption globally, listed Denmark as one of the least corrupt nations in the world in 2009, giving the country the second-highest score, behind New Zealand. The Berlin-based advocacy group rated countries on a zero-to-ten scale, with zero representing extreme levels of corruption and ten indicating a commendably uncorrupt nation. Although Denmark fell one spot from the year before—in 2008 Transparency International listed Denmark as the least corrupt nation in the world—the country scored a respectable 9.3 in 2009.

16 JUDICIAL SYSTEM

As a rule, cases in the first instance come before one of 82 county courts. Certain major cases, however, come under one of the two High Courts (Landsrettes), in Copenhagen and Viborg, in the first instance; otherwise these courts function as courts of appeal. The High Courts generally sit in chambers of three judges. In jury trials (only applicable in cases involving serious crimes) three High Court judges sit with 12 jurors. The Supreme Court (Hojesteret) is made up of a president and 18 other judges, sitting in two chambers, each having at least five judges; it serves solely as a court of appeal for cases coming from the High Courts. Special courts include the Maritime and Commercial Court. An Ombudsman elected by and responsible to parliament investigates citizen complaints against the government or its ministers.

The judiciary is fully independent of the executive and legislative branches. Judges are appointed by the monarch on recommendation of the Minister of Justice and serve life terms. They may be dismissed only for negligence or for criminal acts. Denmark accepts compulsory jurisdiction of the International Court of Justice with reservations.

17 ARMED FORCES

The International Institute for Strategic Studies reported that armed forces in Denmark totaled 18,707 members in 2011. The force was comprised of 9,925 from the army, 2,959 from the navy, 3,358 from the air force, and 2,465 members of joint forces. Armed forces represented 0.6% of the labor force in Denmark. Defense spending totaled $2.6 billion and accounted for 1.3% of GDP.

Since 1849, Danish military defense has been based on compulsory national service. All young men must register at the age of 18 and are subject to 9–12 months' service. Voluntary military service is popular because of educational benefits. Danish forces participated in NATO, UN, and European Union missions in 13 countries/regions around the globe, including support for Operation Enduring Freedom.

In June 2009, the government approved a plan to create a special military Arctic Response Force to protect its Arctic territory interests. The new measures were adopted to address the economic and political concerns arising from the melting of Arctic ice caps. As Arctic ice sheets melt and retreat, potential oil and gas resources will become more easily accessible. Denmark planned to expand its military operations in Greenland and the Faroe Islands in order to protect its own claim to these resources.

18 INTERNATIONAL COOPERATION

Denmark became a charter member of the UN on 24 October 1945 and belongs to ECE and several nonregional specialized agencies. In association with WHO, Denmark has supported UN relief work by supplying medical personnel to assist developing countries. The European regional office of WHO is in Copenhagen. The country is a member of the WTO. Denmark participates actively in multilateral technical aid programs, and the Danish Council for Technical Cooperation provides additional aid to developing countries in Asia and Africa. The nation also assists the African Development Bank and the Asian Development Bank. Denmark is a member of NATO and of various inter-European organizations including the Council of Europe, the European Investment Bank, G-9, the Paris Club, and the OECD. Denmark is a member of the European Union and an observer in the Organization of American States (OAS).

As a member of the Nordic Council, Denmark cooperates with other northern countries—Finland, Iceland, Norway, and Sweden—in social welfare and health insurance legislation and in freeing its frontiers of passport control for residents of other Scandinavian countries. The nation also participates in the regional Council of the Baltic Sea States and the Barents Council. Denmark has observer status in the Western European Union.

Denmark belongs to the Australia Group, the Zangger Committee, the Nuclear Suppliers Group (London Group), the European Organization for Nuclear Research (CERN), and the Nuclear Energy Agency. In environmental cooperation Denmark is part of the Antarctic Treaty; the Basel Convention; Conventions on Biological Diversity, Whaling, and Air Pollution; Ramsar; CITES; the London Convention; International Tropical Timber Agreements; the Kyoto Protocol; the Montréal Protocol; MARPOL; the Nuclear Test Ban Treaty; and the UN Conventions on the Law of the Sea, Climate Change and Desertification.

Denmark held the European Council Presidency in the first half of 2012.

19 ECONOMY

The GDP rate of change in Denmark, as of 2010, was 2.1%. Inflation stood at 2.6%, and unemployment was reported at 4.2%.

Economically, Denmark is a very successful nation and boasts one of the highest standards of living in the world. It is also characterized by relatively high income equality. The nation was traditionally an agricultural country, but after World War II, manufacturing rapidly gained in importance. Denmark's industrialized market economy depends on imported raw materials and foreign trade. Within the European Union, Denmark advocates a liberal trade policy. Denmark is a net exporter of food and energy. Its principal exports are machinery and instruments, meat and meat products, dairy products, fish, pharmaceuticals, furniture, and windmills.

Important service sectors are communications and information technologies, management consulting, and tourism. Shipping remains the most important service sector in Denmark: Denmark has always been a prominent maritime nation, and since much Danish shipping operates entirely in foreign waters, it contributes considerably to the nation's economy.

From the mid-1990s, economic growth rates averaged close to 3%. The inflation rate averaged 2% over the 2001–05 period and in 2007 was down to 1.7%. In 2001, GDP growth was only 0.9%, down from 3% in 2000, largely due to the global economic slowdown and poor domestic demand. GDP growth recovered in 2004, helped by income tax cuts. While there was a moderate decline in exports as a result of the global financial crisis of 2008–09, the overall economy remained fairly strong. However, unemployment rose to 3.8% in June 2009, up from 1.7% in June 2008.

Although Denmark easily met all of the criteria for membership in the European Economic and Monetary Union (EMU), it opted to stay out of the euro zone. Denmark participates in the exchange-rate mechanism (ERM 2), which pegs the Danish krone to the euro.

Denmark's economy was affected by the global recession that began in 2008. Private consumption shrank and by 2011 had not fully rebounded. Increased government spending facilitated a modest recovery in 2010.

20 INCOME

The CIA estimated that in 2010 the GDP of Denmark was $201.7 billion. The CIA defines GDP as the value of all final goods and services produced within a nation in a given year, computed on the basis of purchasing power parity (PPP) rather than value as measured on the basis of the rate of the exchange based on current dollars. The per capita GDP was estimated at $36,600. The annual growth rate of GDP was 2.1%. The average inflation rate was 2.6%. It was estimated that agriculture accounted for 1.1% of GDP, industry 22.8%, and services 76.1%.

According to the World Bank, remittances from citizens living abroad totaled $894.3 million in 2008, or about $162 per capita and accounted for approximately 0.4% of GDP.

The World Bank reported that in 2009, household consumption in Denmark totaled $151.8 billion or about $27,444 per capita, measured in current US dollars rather than PPP. Household consumption includes expenditures of individuals, households, and nongovernmental organizations on goods and services, excluding the purchases of dwellings. It was estimated that household consumption was growing at an average annual rate of 4.2%.

As of 2011, the most recent study by the World Bank reported that actual individual consumption in Denmark was 65.6% of GDP and accounted for 0.31% of world consumption. By comparison, the United States accounted for 25.44% of world individual consumption. The World Bank also estimated that 7.1% of Denmark's GDP was spent on food and beverages, 15.5% on housing and household furnishings, 2.3% on clothes, 7.2% on health, 6.5% on transportation, 1.0% on communications, 6.1% on recreation, 2.4% on restaurants and hotels, and 11.5% on miscellaneous goods and services and purchases from abroad.

In 2011 Denmark had the second lowest relative income poverty rate—6.1%—of the 34 OECD-member countries. According to the OECD, only 6% of Danes find it difficult or very difficult to live on their income.

21 LABOR

Denmark had a total labor force of 2.852 million people in 2010. Within that labor force, CIA estimates in 2011 noted that 2.6% were employed in agriculture, 20.3% in industry, and 77.1% in the service sector.

With the aim of holding down unemployment, the government offers the option of early retirement, apprenticeship and trainee programs, and special job offerings for the long-term unemployed.

As of 2010, an estimated 76% of all wage earners belonged to trade unions. These unions are independent of the government or political parties. Most unions are limited to particular trades. Most workers are entitled to strike and that option is exercised often. Collective bargaining is practiced widely. Military personnel and the police are also allowed to form and join a union.

Although there is no nationally mandated minimum wage rate, the average net wage (excluding pension benefits) for public and private sector adult workers was $19 per hour in 2010, which was sufficient to provide a decent standard of living for a family. The typical private sector workweek, as set by contract, not law, was 37 hours in 2010. Overtime is not compulsory. The minimum age for full-time work is 15 years; children as young as 13 can work part-time, but there are limits imposed as to the tasks they can perform and the hours worked. Health and safety standards are set by law and cover school-age children in the workplace.

Women are highly represented in the labor force.

22 AGRICULTURE

Roughly 53% of the total land is arable, and the country's major crops include barley, wheat, potatoes, and sugar beets. Cereal production in 2009 amounted to 10.2 million tons, fruit production 70,446 tons, and vegetable production 269,874 tons.

Most land is cultivated for feed and root crops. Although agriculture is of great significance to the Danish economy, its relative importance declined from 19% of the GDP in 1961 to 2.1% in 2003.

The majority of farms are small and medium-sized; about 63% are smaller than 50 hectares (124 acres). Thousands of smallholdings have been established since 1899 under special legislation empowering the state to provide the land by partitioning public lands, by expropriation, and by breaking up large private estates. In the more newly established holdings, the farmer owns only the buildings (for which the state advances loans), with the land being owned by the state and the smallholder paying an annual rent fixed under the land-tax assessment. Comparatively few new holdings have been established since 1951.

Grain growing and root-crop production are the traditional agricultural pursuits, but considerable progress has been made in recent decades in apple growing and the production of field, forage, flower, and industrial seeds. Although the soil is not particularly fertile and holdings are kept deliberately small, intensive mechanization and widespread use of fertilizers and concentrated feeds result in high yields and excellent quality.

Farm products provide materials for industrial processing, and a significant share of industry supplies the needs of domestic agriculture. The Danish government devotes particular effort to maintaining the volume, price, quality, and diversity of agricultural products, but internal regulation is largely left to private initiative or exercised through private organizations, notably the cooperatives.

23 ANIMAL HUSBANDRY

The UN Food and Agriculture Organization (FAO) reported that Denmark dedicated 261,000 hectares (644,945 acres) to permanent pasture or meadow in 2009. During that year, the country tended 19.2 million chickens, 1.5 million head of cattle, and 12.4 million pigs. The production from these animals amounted to 145,314 tons of beef and veal, 270,820 tons of pork, 99,397 tons of poultry, 106,746 tons of eggs, and 1.61 million tons of milk. Denmark also produced 14,607 tons of cattle hide and 180 tons of raw wool.

Denmark is generally regarded as the world's outstanding example of intensive animal husbandry. It maintains a uniformly high standard of operations, combining highly skilled labor, scientific experimentation and research, modern installations and machinery, and versatility in farm management and marketing. The excellent cooperative system guarantees the quality of every product of its members. Meat, dairy products, and eggs contribute a most important share of Danish exports. There is a close relationship between cost of feed and export prices.

Some 50% of all eggs consumed domestically are produced by alternative methods, a phrase that generally refers to layers raised organically or in free range. The government's goal is for all eggs to ultimately be produced by noncaged layers. Organic milk is also a growing market. Organically produced feed's share of the domestic market is also increasing.

24 FISHING

Denmark had 4,375 decked commercial fishing boats in 2008. The annual capture totaled 690,202 tons according to the UN FAO. The export value of seafood totaled $3.67 billion.

The country's long coastline, conveniently situated on rich fishing waters, provides Denmark with excellent fishing grounds. Fishing is an important source of domestic food supply, and both fresh and processed fish are important exports. During 1990–95, the government financially supported fleet reduction in order to alleviate structural problems in the industry, and 605 vessels left the fleet during those years. The catch is composed mainly of herring and sprat, cod, mackerel, plaice, salmon, and whiting, but sole and other flatfish, tuna, and other varieties are also caught.

Denmark is one of the world's leading seafood exporters.

25 FORESTRY

Approximately 13% of Denmark is covered by forest. The UN FAO estimated the 2009 roundwood production at 1.68 million cu m (59.3 million cu ft). The value of all forest products, including roundwood, totaled $556 million.

A law of 1805 placing all forestland under reservation stated that "where there is now high forest there must always be high forest." Various measures were adopted to maintain forest growth. Later revisions of the law compelled all woodland owners to replant when trees are felled and to give adequate attention to drainage, weeding out of inferior species, and road maintenance. As a result, forests, which occupied only 5% of Denmark's land area and were actually in danger of extinction at the beginning of the 19th century, now make up 10% of the land and are in excellent condition. The total forest area in 2010 was 544,000 hectares (1.34 million acres). Spruce and beech are the most important varieties. The government would like to increase forest area to 800,000 hectares (1,977,000 acres), nearly 20% of Denmark's total area, during the next 80 years.

Denmark is a large importer of softwood lumber, especially from the other Scandinavian countries, and is a large particleboard consumer.

On 3 December 1999, the first hurricane ever recorded in Denmark destroyed large tracts of its forested areas. Estimated loss of trees amounted to 150% of Denmark's normal annual timber harvest.

26 MINING

Denmark's industrialized market economy depends on imported raw materials. Its mineral resources are mainly fossil fuels in the North Sea, and the nonfuel minerals industry includes mining and quarrying of chalk, clays, diatomite, limestone (agricultural and industrial), and sand and gravel (onshore and offshore). The industrial minerals sector is particularly active. There are some 90 pits in Denmark from which clay is mined; this material is used primarily by the cement, brick making, and ceramic tile industries. The production of sand, gravel, and crushed stone has become more important in recent years, not only in meeting domestic demand, but also as an export to Germany and other Scandinavian countries. Kaolin, found on the island of Bornholm, is used mostly for coarse earthenware, furnace linings, and as filler for paper; production was 2,500 metric tons in 2009, unchanged from 2000. There are important limestone, chalk, and marl deposits in Jutland. Chalk production totaled 1,446,000 tons in 2009. Limonite (bog ore) is extracted for gas purification and pig iron production. Large deposits of salt were discovered in Jutland in 1966; in 2009, 600,000 metric tons were mined. The country also produces fire clay, extracted moler, lime (hydrated and quicklime), nitrogen, peat, crude phosphates, dimension stone (mostly granite), and sulfur. According to the constitution, subsurface resources belong to the nation, and concessions to exploit them require parliamentary approval.

27 ENERGY AND POWER

The World Bank reported in 2008 that Denmark produced 36.4 billion kWh of electricity and consumed 35.5 billion kWh, or

6,417 kWh per capita. Roughly 80% of energy came from fossil fuels, while 3% came from alternative fuels.

Denmark's energy sector is marked by negligible sources of waterpower and no nuclear power plants. However, the country has significant oil and natural gas reserves located in the North Sea, and it is also turning to wind power as an important source of electrical power generation.

The Danish electrical generating sector is marked by its use of alternative or geothermal/other power sources—most notably, wind-driven generation. Generation of renewable energy sources has grown considerably: in 1990 renewable sources accounted for 3.2% of the country's gross energy production; by 2009 that number had increased to 27.6%.

Denmark's position flanking the North Sea has given the nation a share of the significant oil and natural gas reserves discovered there. As of 1 January 2011, Denmark had proven oil reserves of 812 million barrels. Oil production totaled 247,500 barrels of oil a day in 2010. Per capita oil consumption was 3,460 kg in 2008.

Denmark has proven reserves of natural gas, as of early 2011, of 58.13 billion cu m. In 2010 Denmark produced 8.171 billion cu m of natural gas, and consumed nearly 5 billion cu m.

Denmark has no proven coal reserves and must therefore import all the coal it consumes.

28 INDUSTRY

Manufacturing greatly expanded after World War II and now accounts for a greater share of national income than does agriculture. In the important food and drink industry, which tends to be relatively stable, the pattern differs for various branches, but meat packing has developed remarkably. The chemical, metalworking, and pharmaceutical industries have made notable progress. Handicrafts remain important, and Danish stone, clay, glass, wood, and silver products are world famous. Other important industries include: iron, steel, machinery and transportation equipment, textiles and clothing, electronics, construction, furniture, shipbuilding and refurbishment, and windmills.

In the world market, Danish manufacturers, having a limited supply of domestic raw materials, a relatively small home market, and a naturally advantageous geographic position, have concentrated on the production of high-quality specialized items rather than those dependent on mass production. For example, Denmark became the world's largest supplier of insulin, the raw materials for which come from livestock intestines; the Danish company Novo Nordisk is the world leader in insulin and diabetes care. Denmark by the early 2000s produced some 20%–25% of the world's hearing aids.

Machinery, by far the most important industrial export, includes cement-making machinery, dairy machinery, diesel engines, electric motors, machine tools, and refrigeration equipment. Other important exports include meat and meat products (especially pork and pork products—Denmark is the world's largest exporter of pork), fish, dairy products, chemicals, furniture, ships, and windmills.

As a result of the global economic crisis that began in 2008, Denmark's industrial production fell to its lowest levels in more than a decade.

29 SCIENCE AND TECHNOLOGY

There were 1,518 patent applications in science and technology in 2009, according to the World Bank. Public financing of science was 2.72% of GDP. In 2008 there were 2,166 technicians and 5,670 researchers per million people actively engaged in research and development (R&D).

The Ministry of Research is the central administrative unit for research policy. Among advisory bodies to it are the Danish Council for Research Policy, the Danish Natural Science Research Council, the Danish Medical Research Council, the Danish Agricultural and Veterinary Research Council, the Danish Technical Research Council, and the Danish Committee for Scientific and Technical Information and Documentation. The chief learned societies are the Royal Danish Academy of Science and Letters (founded in 1742) and the Danish Academy of Technical Sciences (founded in 1937). Denmark also has specialized learned societies in the fields of agricultural and veterinary science, medicine, natural sciences, and technology. Among the principal public research institutions are the universities Aalborg, Aarhus, Copenhagen, Odense, and Roskilde; the Royal Veterinary and Agricultural University at Frederiksberg; the Technological University of Denmark near Copenhagen; the National Hospital in Copenhagen; the Risø National Laboratory near Roskilde; the Danish Institute for Fisheries and Marine Research at Charlottenlund; and the Danish Meteorological Institute at Copenhagen. Many of the world's preeminent theoretical nuclear physicists have worked at the Niels Bohr Institute for Astronomy, Physics, and Geophysics of Copenhagen University. Copenhagen has museums of geology and zoology and botanical gardens.

30 DOMESTIC TRADE

Large units are becoming more common in wholesale as well as retail trade, ordering directly from local manufacturers and foreign suppliers. Retail operations now include purchasing organizations, various types of chains, cooperatives, self-service stores, supermarkets, and department stores. Chain stores are gaining dominance in the nonfood retail goods market.

Danish retail trade is marked by keen competition between independent retailers, manufacturers' chains, and consumer cooperatives. About 30% of all Danish retail establishments are in the greater Copenhagen area, and these account for almost 40% of all retail sales.

Electronic commerce (e-commerce) has grown more slowly in Denmark than in the United States. It is expected to become a key player in the country's domestic trade sector, but not in sales to the private individual. Instead, e-commerce is anticipated to see most of its growth in the business-to-business sector. Home banking has become popular and several pure electronic banks have entered the Danish marketplace.

Business opening hours vary between 8 and 9 a.m.; closing is between 5:30 and 7 p.m. for stores and 4 to 4:30 p.m. for offices. Early closing (1 p.m.) on Saturdays is now standard. Banking hours are from 9:30 a.m. to 4 p.m., Monday through Friday; also, 4 to 6 p.m. on Thursday.

General, trade, and technical periodicals are important media, and direct-mail, television, and film advertising are used extensively. The most important trade exhibition, the International Fair, takes place every spring in Copenhagen.

31 FOREIGN TRADE

Denmark imported $90.83 billion worth of goods and services in 2008, while exporting $99.37 billion worth of goods and services. Major import partners in 2009 were Germany, 21%; Sweden, 13.1%; Norway, 7%; Netherlands, 7%; China, 6.3%; and UK, 5.5%. Its major export partners were Germany, 17.5%; Sweden, 12.8%; UK, 8.5%; the United States, 6%; Norway, 6%; Netherlands, 4.8%; and France, 4.5%.

The Danish economy depends heavily on foreign trade. Denmark is a net exporter of food and energy. Commodity exports include meat, fresh fish, and cheese, each of which commands a substantial percentage of the world's food exports in their categories. The country also exports fine furniture and medicaments.

To curb domestic demand, the government introduced several fiscal restraint measures in 1986, resulting in a decline in imports. Such measures and a tight-money policy curbed inflation and made Danish exports more competitive, leading to trade surpluses in the late 1980s, 1990s, and early 2000s.

Exports fell by 20% in the wake of the 2008–2009 global economic crisis. In 2010 they began to rebound, growing by 10%, and by 2011 had exceeded pre-2008 levels.

32 BALANCE OF PAYMENTS

The decline in Denmark's trade balance since the end of World War II resulted in a serious deterioration in the balance-of-payments position, particularly after 1960. In the late 1960s, the course of Denmark's international economic activity paralleled trends in continental Europe, with high trade and capital flow levels being accompanied by a deteriorating current-account position; this condition continued into the early 1970s. The Danish government had hoped that Denmark's entry into the EC would reduce the country's persistent deficit and bring the balance on current account into a more favorable position, but this was not the case by the late 1970s. Although current account deficits were reduced somewhat in 1980–81, thanks to the devaluation of the krone and restrictive income and fiscal policies implemented in 1979–80, the deficit again increased in 1982 and by 1985 was at the highest level since 1979. In 1990, after a century of deficits, the balance of payments showed a surplus of $1.3 billion, and rose to $4.7 billion in 1993. In 1994 the surplus dropped to $2.7 billion, but by 2002 it stood at $8.4 billion. In 2010, Denmark had a foreign trade surplus of $13 billion, amounting to 2.1% of GDP.

33 BANKING AND SECURITIES

By an act of 7 April 1936, the Danish National Bank, the bank of issue since 1818, was converted from an independent to an official government corporation. Its head office is in Copenhagen, and it has branches in provincial towns. Danmarks Nationalbank (as it is called in Danish) performs all the usual functions of a central bank, and it holds almost all the nation's foreign exchange reserves. Commercial banks provide short-term money to business and individuals, almost always in the form of overdraft credits, which are generally renewable.

Although Denmark is a member of the European Union, the country does not use the euro. In 2010, the central bank discount

Principal Trading Partners – Denmark (2010)

(In millions of US dollars)

Country	Total	Exports	Imports	Balance
World	181,515.0	96,773.0	84,742.0	12,031.0
Germany	34,175.0	16,711.0	17,464.0	-753.0
Sweden	24,475.0	13,119.0	11,356.0	1,763.0
United Kingdom	12,830.0	7,769.0	5,061.0	2,708.0
Netherlands	10,688.0	4,596.0	6,092.0	-1,496.0
Norway	9,937.0	5,362.0	4,575.0	787.0
United States	8,048.0	5,651.0	2,397.0	3,254.0
China	7,886.0	2,244.0	5,642.0	-3,398.0
France	7,248.0	4,421.0	2,827.0	1,594.0
Italy	5,793.0	2,895.0	2,898.0	-3.0
Poland	4,889.0	2,393.0	2,496.0	-103.0

(…) data not available or not significant.

(n.s.) not specified.

SOURCE: *2011 Direction of Trade Statistics Yearbook,* New York: United Nations, 2011.

Balance of Payments – Denmark (2010)

(In millions of US dollars)

Current Account		**16,210.0**
Balance on goods	8,696.0	
Imports	-87,348.0	
Exports	96,044.0	
Balance on services	8,302.0	
Balance on income	25,278.0	
Current transfers	-5,766.0	
Capital Account		**116.0**
Financial Account		**8,088.0**
Direct investment abroad	-2,971.0	
Direct investment in Denmark	-680.0	
Portfolio investment assets	-17,186.0	
Portfolio investment liabilities	15,907.0	
Financial derivatives	4,805.0	
Other investment assets	-7,698.0	
Other investment liabilities	15,912.0	
Net Errors and Omissions		**-20,136.0**
Reserves and Related Items		**-4,279.0**

(…) data not available or not significant.

SOURCE: *Balance of Payment Statistics Yearbook 2011,* Washington, DC: International Monetary Fund, 2011.

rate, the interest rate at which the central bank lends to financial institutions in the short term, was 0.75%. The commercial bank prime lending rate was 4.3%. At the end of 2010 the nation's reserves of foreign exchange and gold were $76.52 billion, the 25th highest in the world.

Danish banks were hit particularly hard by the Nordic banking crisis of 1991–93 but had fully rebounded by the end of the decade. Their recovery was bolstered in large part by continuing capital gains in securities markets. At the end of 2009 there were 132 commercial and savings banks, eight mortgage credit institutions, and 46 investment companies.

Credit and mortgage societies are active in Denmark. Beginning in the late 1990s, the idea of venture capital had taken hold in Denmark, and it is seen as an established method of financing.

Public Finance – Denmark (2009)

(In millions of kroner, central government figures)

Revenue and Grants	664,479	100.0%
Tax revenue	572,284	86.1%
Social contributions	23,062	3.5%
Grants	...	...
Other revenue	...	...
Expenditures	698,796	100.0%
General public services	280,574	40.2%
Defense	23,745	3.4%
Public order and safety	17,810	2.5%
Economic affairs	32,572	4.7%
Environmental protection	3,949	0.6%
Housing and community amenities	6,131	0.9%
Health	2,898	0.4%
Recreational, culture, and religion	13,333	1.9%
Education	69,247	9.9%
Social protection	248,537	35.6%

(…) data not available or not significant.

SOURCE: *Government Finance Statistics Yearbook 2010*, Washington, DC: International Monetary Fund, 2010.

However, the use of venture capital has largely been applied to biotechnology and information technology firms.

The original stock exchange (or Bourse) in Copenhagen was built during 1619–30 by Christian IV. He subsequently sold it to a Copenhagen merchant, but it reverted to the crown and in 1857 was finally sold by Frederik VII to the Merchants' Guild. In 1970 the Stock Exchange was placed under the jurisdiction of the Ministry of Commerce with a governing committee of 11 members. In 1974 the stock exchange moved into more modern facilities, although the original building still stands and was converted into banquet and conference facilities. In 1980 Denmark took the initial step toward becoming the first country to convert the issuing of stock, share, and bond certificates into a computer account registration system. In 1996 the Stock Exchange became a limited company. In 2005 the exchange merged with OMX, an exchange that had been formed by Swedish and Finnish mergers. In 2006 the OMX Nordic Exchange was launched, encompassing Sweden, Finland, and Denmark's stock exchanges. That same year the Iceland Stock Exchange also merged with OMX. In 2007 NASDAQ acquired OMX. The name became NASDAQ OMX Nordic.

34 INSURANCE

The Danish insurance industry is regulated by the Danish Financial Supervisory Authority (Danish FSA). The Danish FSA is part of the Ministry of Business and Growth. Danish companies do most stock insurance business. Some government-owned insurance companies sell automobile, fire, and life insurance and handle the government's war-risk insurance program. In Denmark, third-party auto insurance, workers' compensation, nuclear power station insurance, hunter's liability, dog liability, third-party aircraft liability, and mortgaged property insurance are compulsory. The two primary pieces of legislation affecting the insurance industry are the Insurance Companies Act and the Insurance Contracts Act. The first contains regulations for establishing and operating insurance companies and describes the public supervision of the insurance business. The second governs relations between insurance companies, policy holders, and claimants. In 2009 there were 100 non-life insurance companies and 33 life insurance companies in Denmark.

35 PUBLIC FINANCE

In 2010 the budget of Denmark included $160.3 billion in public revenue and $175.9 billion in public expenditures. The budget deficit amounted to 2.8% of GDP. Public debt was 46.6% of GDP, with $559.5 billion of the debt held by foreign entities.

The finance bill is presented to the Folketing yearly; the fiscal year follows the calendar year. As a general rule, the budget is prepared on the "net" principle, the difference between receipts and expenditures—surplus or deficit—of public undertakings being posted to the revenue accounts. By far the largest amounts of public expenditure are for social security, health, education and research, unemployment insurance, pensions, allowances, and rent subsidies. Under a new tax reform plan, agreed upon by the government and the Danish People's Party in March 2003, Danish citizens received tax relief in 2004, although at a lesser rate than originally was hoped. As of early 2012, Denmark had yet to accept the euro as its currency, although it met all the criteria set forth by the European Monetary Union to do so.

36 TAXATION

Denmark's taxes are among the highest in the world. Danish residents are liable for taxes on global income and net wealth. Nonresidents are liable only for tax on certain types of income from Danish sources.

The corporate income tax in Denmark is 30%, which must be prepaid during the income tax year to avoid a surcharge. Capital gains are also taxed at the 30% rate.

Personal income tax is collected at state, county, and local levels. A tax ceiling ensures that combined income taxes do not exceed 59% of income. Income tax rates are progressive and begin at 11% for those in the lowest income bracket. Several kinds of deductions or reductions can be applied to taxable income. Dividends are taxed at 28% up to the amount of personal allowance, after which the rate goes to 43%. Royalties are subject to a 30% tax rate. There is also a voluntary church tax with an average rate of 0.8%. The social security contribution from employee earnings is 9%—8% for unemployment insurance and 1% for special pension scheme savings. The voluntary church tax and social security contributions do not count toward the 59% tax ceiling. Tax is withheld at the source. Foreign researchers and key employers may qualify for a gross tax of 25% on their salary instead of paying regular income tax. They are still liable for 9% social security contributions.

Denmark's main indirect tax is the value-added tax (VAT), first introduced in March 1967 with a standard rate of 10%. The current standard rate of 25% was introduced in January 1992. Daily newspapers and a few other goods and services are exempt from the VAT.

Denmark's combined tax burden, including income and property tax, corporation tax, and VAT, accounted for 48.3% of GDP, or DKK799 billion, in 2009.

37 CUSTOMS AND DUTIES

Denmark—a consistent advocate of free and fair conditions of international trade—once had the lowest tariff rate in Europe. However, owing to shortages of foreign currency, Denmark did impose quantitative restrictions on imports, and as late as 1959 about 64% of Danish industrial production was so protected. On joining the European Free Trade Association (EFTA) on 8 May 1960, Denmark began eliminating tariff rates and quantitative restrictions on industrial products from other EFTA countries. By 1 January 1970 those that remained were abolished. On 1 January 1973 Denmark ended its membership in EFTA and became a member of the European Community, which not only represents a free-trade area but also seeks to integrate the economies of its member states.

Denmark adheres to provisions of the General Agreement on Tariffs and Trade (GATT) on import licensing requirements, although certain industrial products must meet Danish and EC technical standards. Denmark converted to the Harmonized System of import duties on 1 January 1988. Most products from European countries are duty free. Duty rates for manufactured goods range from 5–14% of CIF value, and a 25% VAT is applied to imported as well as domestic, products. Denmark's VAT is one of the highest in Europe. Agricultural products are governed by the Common Agricultural Policy (CAP), a system of variable levies instead of duties.

38 FOREIGN INVESTMENT

Denmark is a rich, modern society with a state-of-the art infrastructure and distribution system. A highly skilled labor force and a northern location in Europe make it attractive to foreign investors wishing to have access to markets in Scandinavia, the Baltics, and other northern European destinations. Denmark is a firm advocate of liberal trade and investment policies and actively courts foreign investment.

Foreign investors are treated on equal footing with Danish investors; investment capital and profits may be freely repatriated. After the late 1950s, Denmark attracted a moderate amount of foreign investment. In 1998, however, annual FDI inflows jumped from $2.8 billion to $7.7 billion and then soared to $32.3 billion in 2000. In terms of success in attracting FDI, Denmark went from the 62nd-ranked country (out of 140 countries studied) on UNCTAD's Inward FDI Performance Index for the period of 1988–90 to the 12th-ranked country for the period 1998–2000. Denmark's ranking in terms of potential for inward FDI increased from 10th place in the world to 8th place. In the economic slowdown of 2001 and in decline in FDI inflows that followed the 11 September 2001 terrorist attacks in the United States, annual FDI inflow fell to about $14 billion in 2001 and to an estimated $7.7 billion in 2002. Foreign direct investment (FDI) in Denmark was a net inflow of $2.91 billion according to World Bank figures published in 2009. FDI represented 0.94% of GDP.

The largest foreign investors in Denmark are the United States, Sweden, and the United Kingdom. The United States is Denmark's largest non-European trading partner. There were more than 400 US companies operating in Denmark in 2008.

39 ECONOMIC DEVELOPMENT

For many years, Danish governments followed a full-employment policy and relied chiefly on promotion of private enterprise to achieve this end. Beginning in the late 1970s, however, the government increased its intervention in the economy, in response to rising unemployment, inflation, and budget deficits. Inflation has been curbed and budget deficits reduced. This bolstered the currency from devaluation, but at the cost of restraining growth, and unemployment continued to rise.

Government influence on private enterprise through the exercise of import and export licensing has diminished in recent years. The discount policy of the National Bank is of major importance to the business community. Control of cartels and monopolies is flexible. The government has in recent years sold part or whole interest in many business entities, including the national telecommunications company TDC, Copenhagen airports, and the government's computer services company. Most of the country's power stations are owned and operated by local governments and municipalities.

Capital incentives are available to assist new industries, mainly in the less developed areas of Denmark. Municipalities also provide infrastructure, industrial parks, and inexpensive land. Under a 1967 provision, the Regional Development Committee (composed of representatives of a number of special-interest organizations and central and local authorities) can grant state guarantees or state loans for the establishment of enterprises in less developed districts.

Denmark reached the UN target for official development assistance (ODA)—foreign aid to developing countries—in 1978: 0.7% of GNP. It reached 0.96% of GNP in 1991, second only to Norway, and 1.01% in 2001, when it led the world in ODA. A decade later, in 2010, Denmark spent .91% of gross national income (GNI) on development assistance. It was one of the few countries in the world that exceeded the UN's target. The government that came into power in 2011 said that it would like to raise ODA to 1% of GNI.

Denmark was not immune to the global recession that began in 2008. Gross unemployment increased by several percentage points, and length of unemployment also increased. Unemployment was not expected to decrease before the end of 2012. Industrial production decreased, and the country experienced a budget deficit for the first time in years.

Longer-term challenges to Denmark's economy include an aging workforce and one of the lowest productivity growth rates in the OECD.

40 SOCIAL DEVELOPMENT

Denmark was one of the first countries in the world to establish efficient social services with the introduction of relief for the sick, unemployed, and aged. Old age benefits date back to 1891. Social welfare programs include health insurance, health and hospital services, insurance for occupational injuries, unemployment insurance and employment exchange services, old age and disability pensions, rehabilitation and nursing homes, family welfare subsidies, general public welfare, and payments for military accidents.

Maternity benefits are payable up to 52 weeks. In 2004, the retirement age increased to 69 years for residents.

According to the constitution, any incapacitated person living in Denmark has a right to public relief. Benefits such as maintenance allowances for the children of single supporters, day care, and others involve neither repayment nor any other conditions; some others are regarded as loans to be repaid when possible. Family allowances are paid to families with incomes below a certain threshold; rent subsidies require a means test. Denmark has a dual system of universal medical benefits for all residents and cash sickness benefits for employees. All Danish citizens over 67 years of age may draw old age pensions. Disability pensions, equal in amount to old age pensions plus special supplements, are paid to persons with a stipulated degree of disablement.

Women make up roughly half of the work force. Laws guarantee equal pay for equal work, and women have and use legal recourse if they feel discriminated against. Spousal rape and spousal abuse are criminal offenses. There are crisis centers that counsel and shelter victims of domestic violence. Children's rights are well protected.

The constitution provides for freedom of the press and speech, assembly and association, and for religious freedom, and generally respects these rights. Discrimination based on sex, creed, race, or ethnicity is prohibited by law.

41 HEALTH

According to the CIA, life expectancy in Denmark was 79 years in 2011. The country spent 9.9% of its GDP on health care, amounting to $6,273 per person. There were 34 physicians, 145 nurses and midwives, and 36 hospital beds per 10,000 inhabitants. The fertility rate was 1.8. The CIA calculated HIV/AIDS prevalence in Denmark to be about 0.2% in 2009.

Denmark's health care system has retained the same basic structure since the early 1970s. The administration of hospitals and personnel is dealt with by the Ministry of the Interior, while primary care facilities, health insurance, and community care are the responsibility of the Ministry of Social Affairs. Anyone can go to a physician for no fee, and the public health system entitles each Dane to his/her own doctor. Expert medical/surgical aid is available, with a qualified nursing staff. Costs are borne by public authorities, but high taxes contribute to these costs.

Cardiovascular diseases and cancer are leading causes of death. Denmark's cancer rates are among the highest in the European Union. The incidence of tuberculosis was 8 per 100,000 people in 2007.

Danish citizens may choose between two systems of primary health care: medical care provided free of charge by a doctor whom the individual chooses for a year and by those specialists to whom the doctor refers the patient; or complete freedom of choice of any physician or specialist at any time, with state reimbursement of about two-thirds of the cost for medical bills paid directly by the patient. Most Danes opt for the former. All patients receive subsidies on pharmaceuticals and vital drugs; everyone must pay a share of dental bills.

Responsibility for the public hospital service rests with regional authorities. State-appointed medical health officers, responsible to the National Board of Health, are employed to advise local governments on health matters. Public health authorities have waged large-scale campaigns against tuberculosis, venereal diseases, diphtheria, and poliomyelitis. The free guidance and assistance given to mothers of newborn children by public health nurses have resulted in a low infant mortality rate of 4.24 per 1,000 live births as of 2011. In 2008 the maternal mortality rate, according to the World Bank, was 5 per 100,000 births. Medical treatment is free up to school age, when free school medical inspections begin. It was estimated that 84% of children were vaccinated against measles in 2009.

42 HOUSING

In recent decades, especially since the passage of the Housing Subsidy Act of 1956, considerable government support has been given to housing. For large families building their own homes, government loans have been provided on exceptionally favorable terms, and special rent rebates have been granted to large families occupying apartments in buildings erected by social building societies or in buildings built with government loans since 1950. Subject to certain conditions, housing rebates have been granted to pensioners and invalids. An annual grant is made to reduce householders' maintenance expenses. This extensive support helped to reduce the wartime and immediate postwar housing shortage.

In 2011 there were 2,574,988 occupied dwellings in Denmark. Of these, 1.15 million were detached homes or farmhouses and 979,037 were multi-family dwellings, Of the occupied dwellings, about 60% were owner occupied. Of occupied dwellings, nearly a quarter were built before 1929. Nearly 40% were built in the 1950s and 1960s. Only about 200,000 have been built since the year 2000.

43 EDUCATION

Public expenditure on education represented 7.8% of GDP in 2008. The CIA estimates that Denmark's literacy rate is 99%.

Primary, secondary, and most university and other higher education are free. Preschools are operated by private persons or organizations with some government financial aid. Education has been compulsory since 1814; currently, it is compulsory for nine years, for children ages 7 to 16. The Danish primary school system, known as the Folkeskole, covers the nine required years and many opt for an additional 10th year. English is included in the curriculum from the fifth grade. After basic schooling, two-thirds of the pupils apply for practical training in a trade or commerce at special schools. The remaining one-third enrolls in secondary schools, which finish after three years with student examination and pave the way for higher education at universities. Municipal authorities, with some financial aid from the central government, have been responsible for providing schools for these children.

In 2008 the World Bank estimated that 95% of age-eligible children in Denmark were enrolled in primary school. Secondary enrollment for age-eligible children stood at 90%. The student-to-teacher ratio for primary school was at about 10:1 in 2001; the ratio for secondary school was also about 10:1 in 2000. (More recent figures were not available as of January 2012.)

Adult education exists side by side with the regular school system. Founded as early as 1844, the folk high schools are voluntary, self-governing high schools imparting general adult education. In addition, there are hundreds of schools for higher instruction of pupils without previous special training. There are 12 universities, including the University of Copenhagen (founded in 1479), the University of Aarhus (founded as a college in 1928 and established as a university in 1933), the University of Odense (opened in 1966), and the University Center at Roskilde (founded in 1970). Attached to the various faculties are institutes, laboratories, and clinics devoted primarily to research, but also offering advanced instruction. There are about 100 specialized colleges with professional programs. Many specialized schools and academies of university rank provide instruction in various technical and artistic fields. All these institutions are independent in their internal administration. Tertiary enrollment was estimated at 78% in 2008. Of those enrolled in tertiary education, there were 100 male students for every 144 female students.

44 LIBRARIES AND MUSEUMS

Denmark's national library, the Royal Library in Copenhagen, founded by Frederik III in 1653, is the largest in Scandinavia, with over 4.6 million volumes. The manuscript department of the Royal Library holds an extensive collection of the manuscripts and correspondence of Hans Christian Andersen and the Søren Kierkegaard Archives (manuscripts and personal papers). The National Museum of Photography (over 25,000 pieces) and the Museum of Danish Cartoon Art are also housed at the Royal Library. Three other large libraries are the University Library in Copenhagen, Copenhagen Public Libraries, and the State Library at Aarhus. The Regional Library of Northern Jutland includes a central library, 17 branch locations and 3 mobile units. The public libraries have a total of more than 31 million volumes. The Danish Library Association was founded in 1905.

Among the largest museums are the National Museum (with rare ethnologic and archaeological collections), the Glyptotek (with a large collection of ancient and modern sculpture), the State Art Museum (containing the main collection of Danish paintings as well as other Scandinavian artists), the Thorvaldsen Museum, the Hirshsprung Collection, and the Rosenborg Palace, all in Copenhagen, and the National Historical Museum in Frederiksborg Castle, at Hillerod. Among the newer facilities is the Amalienborg Museum in Copenhagen, which opened in 1994 and houses treasures of the royal family. The National Museum of Science and Technology in Elsinore includes the Teknisk Museum (Museum of Technology) and the Trafikmuseum (Transport Museum); the Kommunikationsmuseum (Museum of Communications) in Aalborg is an extension of the Teknisk Museum.

45 MEDIA

Although the government telephone service owns and operates long-distance lines and gives some local service, the bulk of local telephone service is operated by private companies under government concession with government participation. The country's telephone and telegraph services are generally of excellent quality. International service is provided by satellite ground stations and submarine fiber-optic cables. In 2009 the CIA reported that there were 2.1 million telephone landlines in Denmark.

In addition to landlines, mobile phone subscriptions averaged 134 per 100 people.

The radio broadcasting services are operated by the Danish State Radio System, on long, medium, and short waves. In 2009 there were 2 FM radio stations and 355 AM radio stations. Television broadcasting hours are mainly devoted to current and cul-

tural affairs and to programs for children and young people. There is limited commercial advertising on radio and television; owners of sets pay an annual license fee.

In 2010 the country had about 4.1 million Internet hosts. Internet subscriptions users numbered 86 per 100 citizens. As of 2009 there were some 4.7 million Internet users in Denmark.

Prominent newspapers in 2010, with circulation numbers listed parenthetically, included *B.T.-Detailhandlere/Landsannoncorer* (144,910), *Berlingske Tidende-Detailhandlere/Landsannoncorer* (160,000), and *Ekstra Bladet-Vestudgave* (123,952) as well as 37 other major newspapers.

Complete freedom of expression, including that in print and electronic media, is guaranteed under the constitution. The media in Denmark are largely independently operated and are free from government interference.

46 ORGANIZATIONS

Nearly every Danish farmer is a member of at least one agricultural organization and of one or more producer cooperatives. The oldest agricultural organization, the Royal Agricultural Society of Denmark, was established in 1769, but most of the other organizations were founded after 1850. They promote agricultural education and technical and economic development. Local societies have formed provincial federations, which in turn have combined into two national organizations, the Federation of Danish Agricultural Societies and the Federation of Danish Smallholders Societies. The Cooperative Movement of Denmark comprises three groups: agricultural cooperatives, retail cooperatives, and urban cooperatives. Owners of estates and large farms belong to separate organizations specializing in the affairs of larger agricultural units. Most consumers' cooperative societies belong to the Danish Cooperative Wholesale Society, which makes bulk purchases for member societies and also manufactures various products.

The Federation of Danish Industries and the Industrialists' Association in Copenhagen represent industrial undertakings and trade associations, safeguard and promote the interests of industry, and deal with trade questions of an economic nature. The Danish Confederation of Trade Unions has also been influential. The Council of Handicrafts represents various crafts, trades, and industries, and gives subsidies to technical and trade schools. The leading organizations of the wholesale trade are the Copenhagen Chamber of Commerce and the Provincial Chamber of Commerce. There are also active professional societies representing a broad range of career fields.

The scholarly and cultural organization of the Royal Danish Academy of Sciences and Letters was founded in 1742. A wide variety of organizations exist to promote research and education in medical and scientific fields, such as the Danish Academy of Technical Sciences, the Danish Dental Association, the Danish Medical Society, and the Danish Cancer Society. The Danish Council of Ethics is appointed by the government to conduct research and offer legislative recommendations on bioethical issues.

A number of national and regional cultural organizations are active, as are associations representing popular sports and recreational activities. The Danish Athletic Federation represents about 30,000 athletes nationwide. The Danish Youth Council is an umbrella organization representing about 62 youth organizations with a combined membership of over one million youth. Youth organizations include the Conservative Youth of Denmark, Danish 4-H Youth, Danish Socialist Democratic, Faroe Islands Youth Council, Greenland Youth Council (SORLAK), scouting programs, and YMCA/YWCA.

Denmark has active chapters of The Red Cross, CARE, Caritas, Greenpeace, UNICEF, and Amnesty International.

47 TOURISM, TRAVEL, AND RECREATION

The *Tourism Factbook*, published by the UN World Tourism Organization, reported 8.55 million incoming tourists to Denmark in 2009, with 8 million being from Europe. Tourists spent a total of $5.68 billion. There were 74,733 hotel beds available in Denmark, which had an occupancy rate of 38%. The estimated daily cost to visit Copenhagen, the capital, was $448. The cost of visiting other cities averaged $400.

Dozens of castles, palaces, mansions, and manor houses, including the castle at Elsinore (Helsingør)—site of Shakespeare's *Hamlet*—are open to the public. Tivoli Gardens, the world-famous amusement park, built in 1843 in the center of Copenhagen, is open from May through mid-September. Copenhagen is an important jazz center and holds a jazz festival in July. The Royal Danish Ballet, of international reputation, performs in Copenhagen's Royal Theater, which also presents opera and drama. Greenland, the world's largest island, is part of the Kingdom of Denmark and attracts tourists to its mountains, dog sledges, and midnight sun.

A valid passport is required of all visitors except for Scandinavian nationals. Visas are not required for stays of up to 90 days.

48 FAMOUS PERSONS

Denmark's greatest classic writer and the founder of Danish literature is Ludvig Holberg (1684–1754), historian, philologist, philosopher, critic, and playwright, whose brilliant satiric comedies are internationally famous. Another important dramatist and poet is Adam Gottlob Oehlenschlaeger (1779–1850). The two most celebrated 19th-century Danish writers are Hans Christian Andersen (1805–75), whose fairy tales are read and loved all over the world, and the influential philosopher and religious thinker Søren Kierkegaard (1813–55). Nikolaj Frederik Severin Grundtvig (1783–1872), noted theologian and poet, was renowned for his founding of folk high schools, which brought practical education to the countryside. The leading European literary critic of his time was Georg Morris Brandes (Cohen, 1842–1927), whose *Main Currents in 19th-Century European Literature* exerted an influence on two generations of readers. Leading novelists include Jens Peter Jacobsen (1847–85); Martin Anderson Nexø (1869–1954), author of *Pelle the Conquerer* (1906–10) and *Ditte* (1917–21); and Johannes Vilhelm Jensen (1873–1950), who was awarded the Nobel Prize for literature in 1944 for his series of novels. Karl Adolph Gjellerup (1857–1919) and Henrik Pontoppidan (1857–1943) shared the Nobel Prize for literature in 1917. Isak Dinesen (Karen Blixen, 1885–1962) achieved renown for her volumes of gothic tales and narratives of life in Africa. Jeppe Aaksjaer (1866–1930), poet and novelist, is called the Danish Robert Burns. A great film artist is Carl Dreyer (1889–1968), known for directing *The Passion of Joan of Arc, Day of Wrath,* and *Ordet.* Famous Danish musicians include the composers Niels Gade (1817–90) and Carl Nielsen (1865–1931), the tenors Lauritz Melchior (1890–1973) and Ak-

sel Schiøtz (1906–75), and the soprano Povla Frijsh (d. 1960). Notable dancers and choreographers include August Bournonville (1805–79), originator of the Danish ballet style; Erik Bruhn (1928–86), who was known for his classical technique and was director of ballet at the Royal Swedish Opera House and of the National Ballet of Canada; and Fleming Ole Flindt (1936–2009), who has directed the Royal Danish Ballet since 1965. The sculptor Bertel Thorvaldsen (1770–1844) is the artist of widest influence. Jørn Utzon (1918–2008) was an architect best known for his design of the Sydney Opera House.

Notable scientists include the astronomers Tycho Brahe (1546–1601) and Ole Rømer (1644–1710); the philologists Ramus Christian Rask (1787–1832) and Otto Jespersen (1860–1943); the physicist Hans Christian Ørsted (1777–1851), discoverer of electromagnetism; Nobel Prize winners for physics Niels Bohr (1885–1962) in 1922 and his son Aage Niels Bohr (1922–2009) and Benjamin Mottelson (b. 1926) in 1975; and Niels Rybert Finsen (b. Faroe Islands, 1860–1904), August Krogh (1874–1949), Johannes A. G. Fibiger (1867–1928), and Henrik C. P. Dam (1895–1976), Nobel Prize-winning physicians and physiologists in 1903, 1920, 1926, and 1944, respectively. Jens Christian Skou (b. 1918) shared the Nobel prize in chemistry in 1997. Frederik Bajer (1837–1922) was awarded the Nobel Prize for peace in 1908. Knud Johan Victor Rasmussen (1879–1933), explorer and anthropologist born in Greenland, was an authority on Eskimo ethnology.

Queen Margrethe II (b. 1940) became sovereign in 1972.

49 DEPENDENCIES

Faroe Islands

The Faroe Islands (Faerøerne in Danish and Føroyar in the Faroese language), whose name stems from the Scandinavian word for sheep (får), are situated in the Atlantic Ocean, due N of Scotland, between 61°20′ and 62°24′ N and 6°15′ and 7°41′ W. The 18 islands, 17 of which are inhabited, cover an area of 1,399 sq km (540 sq mi). Among the larger islands are Streymoy (Strømø) with an area of 373 sq km (144 sq mi), Eysturoy (Østerø) with 286 sq km (110 sq mi), Vágar (Vaagø) with 178 sq km (69 sq mi), Suduroy (Syderø) with 166 sq km (64 sq mi), and Sandoy (Sandø) with 112 sq km (43 sq mi). The maximum length of the Faroe Islands is 112 km (70 mi) N–S and the maximum width is 79 km (49 mi) NE–SW. The total coastline measures 1,117 km (694 mi).

The estimated population in 2011 was 49,267. Most Faroese are descended from the Vikings, who settled on the islands in the 9th century. The Faroes have been connected politically with Denmark since the 14th century. During World War II (1939–45), they were occupied by the British, and in this period important political differences emerged. The Faroese People's party advocated independence for the islands; the Unionists preferred to maintain the status quo; and the Faroese Social Democrats wanted home rule. After the war, it was agreed to establish home rule under Danish sovereignty, and since 23 March 1948, the central Danish government has been concerned only with matters of common interest, such as foreign policy and foreign-currency exchange. The Faroes have their own flag, levy their own taxes, and issue their own postage stamps and banknotes. The Faroese language, revived in the

19th century and akin to Icelandic, is used in schools, with Danish taught as a first foreign language.

The Faroese parliament, or Logting, dates back to Viking times and may be Europe's oldest legislative assembly. Members are elected by popular vote on a proportional basis from seven constituencies to the 32-member Logting; representation has been fairly evenly divided among the four major parties. After the October 2011 election, the Union Party held 8 seats; People's Party, 8; Republican Party, 6; Social Democrats, 6; Progressive Party 2; Center Party, 2; and Self-Government Party, 1. The islands elect two representatives to the Folketing (Danish parliament).

In keeping with the islands' name, sheep-raising was long the chief activity, but in recent years the fishing industry has grown rapidly. In 2010 fishing accounted for 98% of all exports, and about half of the island's GDP. Exports go mainly to Denmark (33%), the United Kingdom (20%), Nigeria (12.5%), the United States (10%), Netherlands (5.4%), and Norway (5%). Imports were valued at $983 million in 2008. In 2010 imports came mainly from Denmark (51%), Norway (22%), Sweden (6.7%), and Iceland (4%). Main agricultural products were milk, potatoes, vegetables, sheep, and salmon. In 2007 agriculture accounted for 16% of GDP.

The economy is regulated by an agreement with Denmark whereby the central government facilitates the marketing of Faroese fisheries products and guarantees to some extent an adequate supply of foreign currency.

Greenland

Greenland (Grønland in Danish, Kalaallit Nunaat in Greenlandic) is the largest island in the world. Extending from 59°46′ to 83°39′ N and from 11°39′ to 73°8′ W, Greenland has a total area of 2,166,086 sq km (836,330 sq mi). The greatest N–S distance is about 2,670 km (1,660 mi), and E–W about 1,290 km (800 mi). Greenland is bounded on the N by the Arctic Ocean, on the E by the Greenland Sea, on the SE by the Denmark Strait (separating it from Iceland), on the S by the Atlantic Ocean, and on the W by Baffin Bay and Davis Strait. The coastline measures 44,087 km (27,394 mi). The ice-free strip along the coast, rarely exceeding 80 km (50 mi) in width, is only 410,449 sq km (158,475 sq mi) in area. The rest of the area, covered with ice measuring at least 2,100 m (7,000 ft) thick in some places, amounts to 1,755,637 sq km (677,855 sq mi). Greenland has a typically arctic climate, but there is considerable variation between localities, and temperature changes in any one locality are apt to be sudden. Rainfall increases from north to south, ranging from about 25 to 114 cm (10–45 in). Land transport is very difficult, owing to the ice and rugged terrain, and most local travel must be done by water. SAS operates flights on the Scandinavia-US route via Greenland, and tourists are being attracted by Greenland's imposing scenery.

The population, grouped in a number of scattered settlements of varying sizes, was estimated at 56,534 in 2010. Greenlanders are predominantly Eskimos, with some admixture of Europeans. The Greenlandic language, an Eskimo-Aleut dialect, is in official use. Most native Greenlanders were engaged in hunting and fishing, but a steadily increasing number are now engaged in administration and in private enterprises. The Europeans chiefly follow such pursuits as administration, skilled services, and mining.

The Vikings reached Greenland as early as the 10th century. By the time Europeans rediscovered the island, however, Norse culture had died out and Greenland belonged to the Eskimos. Danish colonization began in the 18th century, when the whale trade flourished off Greenland's western shore. In 1933 the Permanent Court of Arbitration at The Hague definitively established Danish jurisdiction over all Greenland. Up to 1953, the island was a colony; at that time it became an integral part of Denmark. Greenland held that status until 1979, when it became self-governing after a referendum in which 70% of the population favored home rule. The 31 members in the Landsting (parliament) are elected by popular vote on the basis of proportional representation. In the election held June 2009, Inuit Ataqatigiit, a leftist party that favors complete independence from Denmark, received 43.7% of the vote (14 seats); the left-wing Siumut Party won 9 seats; the Demokratiit, 4; the right-wing Atassut Party, 3; and the Katusseqatigiit, 1. Greenland elects two representatives to the Folketing; following the September 2011 election, the representatives were from the Siumut and Inuit Ataqatigiit parties.

Fishing, hunting (mainly seal, and to a lesser extent fox), and mining are the principal occupations. Agriculture is not possible in most of Greenland, but some few vegetables are grown in the south, usually under glass.

At Ivigtut, on the southwest coast, a deposit of cryolite has long been worked by a Danish government-owned corporation, but reserves are believed to be nearing depletion. The government has a controlling interest in the lead-zinc mine at Mestersvig, on the east coast. Production began in 1956 and has continued sporadically. Low-grade coal mined at Disko Islands, midway on the west coast, is used for local fuel needs. Mining activities ceased in 1990, but exploration activity has revealed the potential for economic exploitation of antimony, barite, beryllium, chromite, coal, columbium, copper, cryolite, diamond, gold, graphite, ilmenite, iron, lead, molybdenum, nickel, platinum-group metals, rare earths, tantalum, thorium, tungsten, uranium, zinc, and zirconium. Fish and fish products make up the bulk of exports. Raw materials are administered jointly by a Denmark-Greenland commission. Underground resources remain in principle the property of Denmark, but the Landsting has veto power over matters having to do with mineral development.

A US Air Force base is situated at Thule, in the far north along the west coast, only 14° from the North Pole; Greenland also forms part of an early-warning radar network. An international meteorological service, administered by Denmark, serves transatlantic flights. In 1960 a 1,500-kW atomic reactor was set up in northern Greenland to supply electric power to a new US scientific base built on the icecap, 225 km (140 mi) inland from Thule.

⁵⁰BIBLIOGRAPHY

Annesley, Claire, ed. *A Political and Economic Dictionary of Western Europe*. Philadelphia: Routledge/Taylor and Francis, 2005.

Decent Work in Denmark: Employment, Social Efficiency and Economic Security. Geneva, Switzerland: International Labour Office, 2003.

Denmark Investment and Business Guide: Strategic and Practical Information. Washington, DC: International Business Publications USA, 2012.

Kinze, Carl Christian. *Marine Mammals of the North Atlantic.* Princeton, NJ: Princeton University Press, 2002.

Opello, Walter C. *European Politics.* Boulder, CO: Lynne Rienner Publishers, 2009.

Pasqualetti, Martin J., Paul Gipe, and Robert W. Righter, eds. *Wind Power in View: Energy Landscapes in a Crowded World.* San Diego: Academic Press, 2002.

Political Chronology of Europe. London: Europa, 2001

Wessels, Wolfgang, Andreas Maurer, and Jürgan Mittag, eds. *Fifteen into One? The European Union and Its Member States.* New York: Palgrave, 2003.

ESTONIA

Republic of Estonia
Eesti Vabariik

CAPITAL: Tallinn

FLAG: Three equal horizontal bands of blue (top), black, and white.

ANTHEM: *Mu isamaa, mu õnn ja rõõm (My Native Land, My Pride and Joy).*

MONETARY UNIT: On January 1, 2011, Estonia adopted the euro as legal tender. The euro is divided into 100 cents. There are coins in denominations of 1, 2, 5, 10, 20, and 50 cents and 1 euro and 2 euros. There are notes of 5, 10, 20, 50, 100, 200, and 500 euros. €1 = $1.3635 (or $1 = €0.7334) as of 2011.

WEIGHTS AND MEASURES: The metric system is in force.

HOLIDAYS: New Year's Day, 1 January; Independence Day, 24 February; Labor Day, 1 May; Victory Day, anniversary of the Battle of Vonnu in 1919, 23 June; Midsummer Day, 24 June; Christmas, 25–26 December. A movable religious holiday is Good Friday, the Friday before Easter.

TIME: 2 p.m. = noon GMT.

¹LOCATION, SIZE, AND EXTENT

Estonia is located in northeastern Europe, bordering the Baltic Sea, between Sweden and Russia. Comparatively, the area occupied by Estonia is slightly smaller than the states of New Hampshire and Vermont combined, with a total area of 45,228 sq km (17,462 sq mi), which includes more than 1,000 islands in the Baltic Sea. Estonia shares boundaries with the Baltic Sea on the N and W, Russia on the E, and Latvia on the S. Estonia's land boundaries total 633 km (392 mi). Its coastline is 3,794 km (2,352 mi). Estonia's capital city, Tallinn, is located in the northern part of the coast.

²TOPOGRAPHY

The topography of Estonia consists mainly of marshy lowlands with a hilly region in the southeast. Over a third of the country is forest. The highest point is Suur Munamagi, located in the Haanja Uplands of the south, with an altitude of 318 m (1,043 ft). The lowest point is at sea level (Baltic Sea).

The country has more than 1,400 natural and artificial lakes. The largest lake is Lake Peipus, located along the border with Russia. The shared lake has a total area of 3,555 sq km (1,386 sq mi). The Pärnu is the longest river with a length of 144 km (89 mi). The Narva and Ema are also chief rivers.

³CLIMATE

The proximity of the Baltic Sea influences the coastal climate. At the most western point, Vilsandi Saar, the mean temperature is 6°C (42.8°F). At the country's most eastern points, the mean temperature is between 4.2°C and 4.5°C (36 to 40°F). Rainfall averages 50 cm (20 in) on the coast. Inland, rainfall averages 70 cm (28 in). Rainfall is heaviest during the summer and lightest in the spring.

⁴FLORA AND FAUNA

Calcareous soil and a relatively mild climate permit rich flora and fauna in western Estonia. The abundance of woodland and plant species provides a suitable habitat for elk, deer, wild boar, wolf, lynx, bear, and otter.

The World Resources Institute estimates that there are 1,630 plant species in Estonia. In addition, Estonia is home to 67 species of mammals, 267 species of birds, 6 species of reptiles, and 11 species of amphibians. This calculation reflects the total number of distinct species residing in the country, not the number of endemic species.

⁵ENVIRONMENT

Air, water, and land pollution rank among Estonia's most significant environmental challenges. The combination of 300,000 tons of dust from the burning of oil shale by power plants in the northeast part of the country and airborne pollutants from industrial centers in Poland and Germany poses a significant hazard to Estonia's air quality.

Estonia's water resources have been affected by agricultural and industrial pollutants, including petroleum products, which have also contaminated the nation's soil. Some rivers and lakes within the country have been found to contain toxic sediments in excess of 10 times the accepted level for safety. Yet Estonia has taken steps to reduce the amount of untreated wastewater released into bodies of water. In 2000, the levels discharged were only 20% of the levels discharged in 1980.

The nation's land pollution problems are aggravated by the 15 million tons of pollutants that are added yearly to the existing 250 million tons of pollutants. In 1994, 24,000 acres of the country's total land area were affected. Radiation levels from the nuclear accident at Chernobyl exceed currently accepted safety levels. However, in 2000, emissions of airborne pollutants dropped 80 percent from 1980 levels and continue to fall steadily.

There are 12 Ramsar Wetlands Sites. According to a 2011 report issued by the International Union for Conservation of Nature and Natural Resources (IUCN), threatened species included 1 type of mammal, 3 species of birds, 5 species of fish, and 3 species of

187

invertebrates. The European mink and the Atlantic sturgeon are among those listed as endangered.

The World Resources Institute reported that Estonia had designated 2 million hectares (4.93 million acres) of land for protection as of 2006. Water resources totaled 21.1 cu km (5.06 cu mi) while water usage was 1.41 cu km (0.338 cu mi) per year. Domestic water usage accounted for 56% of total usage, industrial for 39%, and agricultural for 5%. Per capita water usage totaled 1,060 cu m (37,434 cu ft) per year.

The United Nations (UN) reported in 2008 that carbon dioxide emissions in Estonia totaled 20,456 kilotons.

6 POPULATION

The US Central Intelligence Agency (CIA) estimated the population of Estonia in 2011 to be approximately 1,282,963, which placed it at number 151 in population among the 196 nations of the world. In 2011 approximately 17.7% of the population was over 65 years of age, with another 15.1% under 15 years of age. The median age in Estonia was 40.5 years. There were 0.84 males for every female in the country. The population's annual rate of change was -0.65%. The projected population for the year 2025 was 1,300,000. Population density in Estonia was calculated at 28 people per sq km (11 people per sq mi).

The UN estimates that 69% of the population lives in urban areas, and that urban populations have an annual rate of change of 0.1%. The largest urban area was Tallinn, with a population of 399,000 in 2009.

7 MIGRATION

Newly independent in 1918, Estonia was occupied and annexed in 1940 by the Soviet Union. It was occupied by German troops the following year. When the Soviet army returned in 1944, more than 60,000 Estonians fled to Sweden and Germany. Other Estonians were sent to Soviet labor camps. Many Russians migrated to Estonia under Soviet rule. Some left after Estonia became independent again. After the breakup of the Soviet Union in 1991, Estonia suffered from waves of transit migration.

The total number of migrants living in Estonia in 2000 was 365,000, approximately one-quarter of the population. Estimates of Estonia's net migration rate, carried out by the CIA in 2011, amounted to -3.31 migrants per 1,000 citizens.

8 ETHNIC GROUPS

According to a 2008 census, Estonians make up about 68.7% of the population, Russians 25.6%, Ukrainians 2.1%, Belarusians 1.2%, Finns 0.8%, and others 1.6%. Non-Estonians were found chiefly in the northeastern industrial towns, while rural areas were over 80% Estonian.

9 LANGUAGES

Estonian is a member of the Finno-Ugric linguistic family. It is closely related to Finnish and distantly related to Hungarian. Standard Estonian is based on the North Estonian dialect. Most of the sounds can be pronounced as either short, long, or extra long. Changing the duration of a sound in a word can alter the grammatical function of the word or change its meaning completely. The language is highly agglutinative, and there are no less than 14 cases of noun declension. Most borrowed words are from Ger-

man. The alphabet is Roman. The first text written in Estonian dates from 1525. Estonian is the official language and is spoken by about 67.3% of the population; however, Russian (29.7%), Ukrainian, English, Finnish, and other languages are also used.

10 RELIGIONS

Christianity was introduced into Estonia in the 11th century. During the Reformation much of the population converted to Lutheranism, although political events in the 18th and 19th century occasioned a strong Russian Orthodox presence. Independence from the Soviet Union, achieved in 1991, relieved the pressure under which religious groups had labored since 1940. As of 2010 about 13.6% of all citizens were Evangelical Lutherans, while 12.8% were Orthodox Christians. About 34% of the population listed as unaffiliated in the last census, while 32% listed as unspecified or other. Christian groups such as Methodists, Seventh-Day Adventists, Roman Catholics, and Pentecostals accounted for about 1.4% of the population.

Freedom of religion is guaranteed by the constitution, and this right is generally respected in practice. All religious organizations must register with the Religious Affairs Department of the Ministry of Interior Affairs. Basic Christian ecumenical religious instruction is available in public schools as an elective. Good Friday, Easter Sunday, Pentecost, and Christmas are observed as national holidays.

11 TRANSPORTATION

Tallinn, Haapsalu, Pärnu, Tartu, and Narva are provided rail access to Russia, Latvia, and the Baltic Sea. In order to overcome problems in rolling stock shortages and load fluctuations, a second line of tracks is being laid along the Tallinn-Narva route.

Motor vehicles dominate domestic freight transportation, carrying nearly 75% of all dispatched goods.

The Baltic Sea (with the Gulf of Finland and Gulf of Riga) provides Estonia with its primary access to international markets. The principal maritime ports and terminals are Kuivastu, Kunda, Muuga, Tallinn, and Virtsu. The merchant fleet had 29 vessels of at least 1,000 GRT in 2008. Sea transportation has increased, especially since the completion of Tallinn's new harbor and the acquisition of high capacity vessels. Ships carry grain from North America and also serve West African cargo routes. In 1990 a ferry service opened between Tallinn and Stockholm. During one of these commutes in September 1994, the ferry *Estonia* sank off the coast of Finland, resulting in about 900 deaths. The tragedy brought international attention to the safety design of roll-on/roll-off ferries in use worldwide.

The CIA reports that Estonia has a total of 58,034 km (36,061 mi) of roads, of which 34,936 km (21,708 mi) are paved. There are 477 vehicles per 1,000 people in the country. Railroads extend for 929 km (577 mi). There are 19 airports, which transported 395,532 passengers in 2009, according to the World Bank. Estonia has approximately 335 km (208 mi) of navigable waterways.

12 HISTORY

What is now Estonia was ruled in turn by the Danes, the Germans, and the Swedes from the Middle Ages until the 18th century. Russia annexed the region in 1721. During the 19th century, an Estonian nationalist movement arose, and by the early 20th century sought independence.

After the 1917 Bolshevik Revolution and the advance of German troops into Russia, Estonia declared independence on 24 February 1918. But after the German surrender to the Western powers in November 1918, Russian troops attempted to move back into Estonia. The Estonians, however, pushed out the Soviet forces by April 1919, and the following year Soviet Russia recognized the Republic of Estonia.

The Nazi-Soviet Pact of 1939 assigned Estonia to the Soviet sphere of influence. The Red Army invaded in June 1940 and "admitted" the Estonian Soviet Socialist Republic into the USSR in August 1940. However, Hitler's forces invaded the USSR in June 1941, and took control of Estonia shortly thereafter. The German army retreated in 1944, and Soviet forces once again occupied Estonia.

Taking advantage of the relatively greater freedom allowed under Mikhail Gorbachev in the late 1980s, an Estonian nationalist movement, the Popular Front, was launched in 1987. Estonia declared its independence from Moscow on 20 August 1991. A new constitution was adopted on 28 June 1992.

With much fanfare, the last Russian tanks and 2,000 troops were removed from Estonia on 17 August 1994, ending 50 years of military presence in Estonia. Russia also announced it would begin dismantling two nuclear reactors within Estonia. Estonia demanded the return of more than 1,942 sq km (750 sq mi) of land that Russia considered part of its territory, but that belonged to Estonia before World War II. When Estonia renewed its claim to those lands, the Russian government began constructing 680 border posts, many of which were guarded by armed soldiers and linked by fences.

The 1995 parliamentary vote reflected dissatisfaction among rural inhabitants and pensioners and signaled a change from the vigorous free-market reforms that dominated Estonia's transition from Soviet rule. The results of the election, however, didn't significantly alter Estonia's commitment to a balanced budget, a stable currency, or a good foreign investment climate. Following the March 1995 elections, Tiit Vähi was approved as prime minister, but he and his cabinet resigned in October 1995 amidst a scandal within the administration that involved telephone tapping and the clandestine sales of weapons. President Lennart Meri later appointed a new government, which reinstated Vähi as prime minister. In September 1996 Meri won a second presidential term, although the election was turned over to an electoral college after no candidate won the required two-thirds majority in parliamentary balloting in August. Following a no-confidence vote in February 1997, Prime Minister Vähi resigned and was replaced by Mart Siimann, who formed a minority government.

Reformers once again won control of Estonia's parliament in the March 1999 general elections, in which a coalition of center-right parties gained a slim majority, wining 53 out of 101 seats. (However, the left-leaning Center Party won 28 seats, the highest number for a single party.) Mart Laar was named prime minister. The new government was expected to emphasize political reforms as much as economic ones, focusing on the elimination of corruption and inefficiency in the civil service, courts, and police.

In September 2001 Arnold Rüütel was elected president, succeeding Meri, who was barred by the constitution from seeking

LOCATION: 57°30′ to 59°40′ N; 21°50′ to 28°10′ E. BOUNDARY LENGTHS: Latvia, 339 kilometers (211 miles); Russia, 294 kilometers (183 miles); total coastline, 3,794 kilometers (2,358 miles).

a third consecutive term. Rüütel's victory was seen as a reaction to popular dissatisfaction with the government and growing economic problems in small towns and rural areas, among other reasons. However, because none of the presidential candidates received the required two-thirds vote in parliament after three rounds of voting, an electoral college, composed of all members of parliament and 266 local government representatives, elected the president. In January 2002 Laar resigned as prime minister and Siim Kallas took his place.

Parliamentary elections held on 2 March 2003 resulted in the formation of a coalition government made up of the center-right Res Publica, the right-leaning Reform Party, and the rural party People's Union. Thirty-six-year-old Juhan Parts became prime minister on 10 April. On 24 March 2005 Parts resigned, and President Arnold Rüütel asked Reform Party chairman Andrus Ansip to form a new government. Ansip became prime minister on 12 April, representing the Reform Party, the Center Party, and the People's Union.

Since it gained its independence in 1991, Estonia's foreign has policy focused on integration with Western Europe. Estonia became a member of NATO on 29 March 2004 and a member of the European Union on 1 May 2004.

On 23 September 2006 Toomas Hendrik Ilves, a former foreign minister, was elected president. Ilves received 174 votes to incumbent Arnold Rüütel's 162. The remaining nine ballots were left blank or invalid. He was reelected in August of 2011.

Estonia became a member of the Organization for Economic Cooperation and Development (OECD) on 27 May 2010.

13 GOVERNMENT

Estonia adopted a new post-Soviet constitution on 28 June 1992. It declares Estonia a parliamentary democracy with a unicameral parliament. The parliament (Riigikogu) has 101 seats. Members of parliament serve four-year terms. The president (who is elected for a five-year term), prime minister, and the cabinet make up the executive branch of government. The president is the head of state while the prime minister is the head of government. Both the parliament and the president are elected by direct universal suffrage of citizens 18 years or older. Furthermore, noncitizens who are residents and citizens of the European Union may vote in municipal elections. In addition to traditional voting methods, Estonia has created the option to vote over the Internet in some elections.

14 POLITICAL PARTIES

The Independent Communist Party of Estonia split from the Communist Party of the Soviet Union in January 1991. The Pro Patria Party, the Estonian Social Democratic Party, the Christian-Democratic Union of Estonia, the Estonian National Independence Party, and Estonian Green Movement were among the many parties that emerged since the collapse of the Soviet Union. The Popular Front of Estonia, founded in 1988 to unite pro-independence forces, has lost much of its influence and role since the attainment of independence. The non-Estonian, mainly Russian, interests are represented by the Inter-Movement of the Working People of Estonia and the Union of Work Collectives, both founded in 1988. In addition, a Russian Democratic Movement has emerged that specifically represents the Russian-speaking population of Estonia.

In the parliamentary elections of March 1995, the Coalition Party and Rural Union (made up of four parties: Coalition Party, Country People's Party, Farmer's Assembly, and Pensioners' and Families' League) won 41 seats; Reform Party-Liberals, 19; Center Party, 16; Pro Patria, 8; Our Home is Estonia, 6; Moderates (consisting of the Social Democratic Party and Rural Center Party), 2; and Right-Wingers, 5.

The Pro Patria and the Estonian National Independence Party, which had allied themselves in the 1995 election, joined forces at the end of that year to form the Fatherland Union. In the March 1999 elections, the Fatherland Union and two other parties formed a broader coalition that won a narrow majority in parliament, garnering a total of 53 parliamentary seats (Fatherland Union, 18; Estonian Reform Party, 18; Moderates, 17). However, the party winning the single largest number of seats was the Estonian Center Party, with 28. The remaining seats were distributed as follows: the Estonian Coalition Party, 7; the Estonian Rural People's Union, 7; and the United People's Party, 6.

In the 2 March 2003 elections, the Center Party and Res Publica, a new political party, each won 28 seats in the Riigikogu; the Reform Party took 19; the People's Union won 13; the Fatherland Union took 7 seats; and the Moderates won 6. The Res Publica, Reform, and People's Union parties formed a coalition government, securing 60 of 101 seats in parliament.

Andrus Ansip of the Reform Party was appointed as prime minister in 2005. In the 2006 presidential election, Toomas Hendrik Ilves of the Social Democratic Party was elected by parliament with 174 votes in the first round.

Parliamentary elections took place on 4 March 2007. It was Estonia's and the world's first national Internet election. Voting was available from 26 to 28 February. About 1% of voters used Internet voting. The Reform Party came in first, with 31 seats, followed by the Center Party with 29. The Union of Pro Patria and Res Publica won 19 seats; the Social Democratic Party took 10; and the Greens and the People's Union each won six seats in parliament. Five other parties competed in the election but won no seats.

In the elections of March 2011, the Reform Party again came in first with 33 seats (28.6% of the vote), followed by the Center Party with 26 seats (23.3%), the Union of Pro Patria and Res Publica with 23 seats (20.5%), and the Social Democratic Party with 19 seats (17.1%). Ansip retained his post as prime minister.

15 LOCAL GOVERNMENT

Estonia's major administrative divisions are 15 counties (*maakond*). The counties are further subdivided into municipalities-rural communes (*vald*) and urban municipalities (*linn*). Since October 2005 there have been 227 municipalities in Estonia, 34 of them urban and 193 of them rural.

While only citizens are allowed to vote in Estonia's national elections, residents of Estonia, including noncitizens, are allowed to vote in local elections. Noncitizens, however, cannot be candidates in local (or national) elections. Office holders serve three-year terms. In the 2005 local elections, some 800,000 Estonians, or 80% of the eligible electorate, had access to a new e-voting system via the Internet, the largest run by any European country. In the end, only 1% of voters cast their vote online.

16 JUDICIAL SYSTEM

The 1992 constitution established a court system consisting of three levels of courts: (1) rural, city, and administrative courts, (2) circuit courts of appeal, and (3) the National Court. The National Court engages in constitutional review of legislation. At the rural and city courts, the decisions are made by a majority vote with a judge and two lay members. There are 2 city courts, 14 county courts, and 4 administrative courts in Estonia. There are three circuit courts of appeal, at Tallinn and Tartu, and the Viru circuit court located in the city of Jõhvi.

The constitution provides for an independent judiciary, and the judiciary is independent in practice. The Chief Justice of the National Court, nominated by the president and confirmed by the Riigikogu, nominates National Court judges, whose nominations need to be confirmed by the Riigikogu. The Chief Justice of the National Court also nominates the lower court judges who are then appointed by the president. Judges are appointed for life. The 1992 interim criminal code abolishes a number of political and economic crimes under the former Soviet Criminal Code. A new criminal procedural code was adopted in 1994.

The constitution provides for a presumption of innocence, access to prosecution evidence, confrontation and cross-examination of witnesses, and public trials.

[17]ARMED FORCES

Estonian forces were deployed in Afghanistan, Bosnia, Iraq, Serbia and Montenegro, and as UN observers in the Middle East in 2005.

The International Institute for Strategic Studies reports that armed forces in Estonia totaled 5,450 members in 2011. The force is comprised of 4,800 from the army, 400 from the navy, and 250 members of the air force. Armed forces represent 0.8% of the labor force in Estonia. Defense spending totaled $493.8 million and accounted for 2% of gross domestic product (GDP). This 2% matched the NATO expectation for such spending.

[18]INTERNATIONAL COOPERATION

Estonia was admitted to the UN on 17 February 1991 and belongs to several specialized UN agencies, such as the FAO, IAEA, World Bank, ICAO, ILO, IMF, IMO, UNESCO, and the WHO. The country is also a member of the OSCE, the European Bank for Reconstruction and Development, the Council of the Baltic Sea States, the Council of Europe, the European Investment Bank, and NATO. Estonia joined the WTO in 1999 and the European Union in 2004. It has observer status in the OAS and is an affiliate member of the Western European Union. Estonia became a member of the Organization for Economic Cooperation and Development (OECD) on 27 May 2010.

Estonia belongs to the Australia Group and the Nuclear Suppliers Group (London Group). In environmental cooperation, Estonia is part of the Antarctic Treaty, the Basel Convention, Conventions on Biological Diversity and Air Pollution, Ramsar, CITES, the Kyoto Protocol, the Montréal Protocol, MARPOL, and the UN Convention on Climate Change.

[19]ECONOMY

Estonia is thriving financially, boasting some of the highest income levels in Central Europe, thanks to the country's successful transition to a market-based economy. The country's strong telecommunications and electronics sector have benefited Estonians in the increasingly technological world. The Skype software application, offering free international calls over the Internet, was written by Estonian-based developers. The prevalence of wireless Internet connections in local businesses, bars, and cafes has earned the country the nickname of "E-stonia." The nation is placed at a crossroads for trade, with excellent trade relationships between fellow European Union members, Scandinavia, and Russia. The nation boasts a strong energy sector, supplying over 90% of its domestic electricity needs with locally mined oil shale. About 9% of primary energy production comes from alternative sources such as wood, peat, and biomass. However, all of the nation's natural gas is imported from Russia. Agriculture is based mainly on rearing livestock, but dairy farming is also significant. Estonia is self-sufficient in electrical power.

The economy started to revive after the 1992 monetary reform, reintroducing the pre-occupation quasi-convertible Estonian kroon. Estonia's economy quickly became one of the strongest post-Communist economies in Eastern Europe as successive governments remained committed to the implementation of market reforms. Growth continued until 1998, when Estonia underwent its first post-Soviet economic downturn. GDP growth slowed to 4% in 1998 and declined to -1.1% in 1999. The country became a member of the WTO in 1999. The economy began to improve the following year, and by 2007 the growth rate reached a new high.

Estonia's economic progress is linked to its liberal foreign trade regime (there are few tariffs or nontariff barriers), effective bankruptcy legislation, and swift privatization. Estonia also has a flat-rate income tax system, the first of its kind in the world. State subsidies were in the process of being abolished in the early 2000s, and all of these measures helped to stabilize and restructure the economy. As a result, Estonia received high levels of foreign direct investment. Although the global economy was in a downturn in the early 2000s, Estonia was able to maintain GDP growth rates of around 5%, higher than many other European countries. Major growth sectors include information technology, transportation, and construction services. The GDP growth rate in 2004 was 6.2%, up from 5.1% in 2003. By 2007 the real GDP growth was 7.1%.

The global financial crisis of 2008–09 had a significant impact on the nation's economy. In June 2009 unemployment was at about 17%. On 1 January 2011 Estonia became the seventeenth country to switch to euro as currency. The future success of the euro in Estonia will depend on domestic economic and regulatory policy. However, immediate benefits for the trade-dependent country were apparent as the majority of its trading partners had already adopted the euro. The GDP rate of change in Estonia, as of 2011, was 6.5%. Inflation stood at 5%, and unemployment was reported at 13%.

[20]INCOME

The CIA estimated that in 2011 the GDP of Estonia was $26.93 billion. The CIA defines GDP as the value of all final goods and services produced within a nation in a given year and computed on the basis of purchasing power parity (PPP) rather than value as measured on the basis of the rate of the exchange based on current dollars. The per capita GDP was estimated at $20,200. The annual growth rate of GDP was 6.5%. The average inflation rate was 5%. It was estimated that agriculture accounted for 2.6% of GDP, industry 29.2%, and services 68.2%.

In 2007 the World Bank estimates that Estonia, with 0.02% of the world's population, accounted for 0.04% of the world's GDP. By comparison, the United States, with 4.85% of the world's population, accounted for 22.51% of world GDP.

The World Bank reports that in 2009, household consumption in Estonia totaled $10.1 billion or about $7,875 per capita, measured in current US dollars rather than PPP. Household consumption includes expenditures of individuals, households, and nongovernmental organizations on goods and services, excluding the purchases of dwellings. It was estimated that household consumption was growing at an average annual rate of 18.5%.

As of 2011 the World Bank reported that actual individual consumption in Estonia was 63.9% of GDP and accounted for 0.04% of world consumption. By comparison, the United States accounted for 25.44% of world individual consumption. The World Bank also estimated that 15% of Estonia's GDP was spent on food and beverages, 14.1% on housing and household furnishings, 4.2% on clothes, 5.2% on health, 7.2% on transportation, 1.7% on communications, 6.0% on recreation, 3.9% on restaurants and hotels, and 1.5% on miscellaneous goods and services and purchases from abroad.

It was estimated that in 2008 about 19.7% of the population subsisted on an income below the poverty line. According to the World Bank, remittances from citizens living abroad totaled $324.6 million or about $253 per capita and accounted for approximately 1.3% of GDP.

21 LABOR

As of 2011 Estonia had a total labor force of 685,400 people. Within that labor force, CIA estimates in 2008 noted that 2.8% were employed in agriculture, 22.7% in industry, and 74.5% in the service sector. In the same year, unemployment was estimated at 17.5%.

The Estonian constitution guarantees the right to form and freely join a union or employee association. The Central Organization of Estonian Trade Unions (EAKL) was founded in 1990 as a voluntary and culturally Estonian organization to replace the Estonian branch of the Soviet labor confederation. In 2002 the EAKL claimed 58,000 members. A rival union, the Organization of Employee Unions, split off from the EAKL in 1993. In 2005 about 10% of the Estonian workforce was unionized. Workers had the right to strike, and of collective bargaining, both of which were freely practiced. About 15% of Estonia's workforce was covered under collective bargaining agreements as of 2005.

The statutory minimum employment age is 18, although children aged 15 to 17 years may work with parental permission. Children between the ages of 13 and 15 can also work, but in addition to parental or guardian approval, they must also have the approval of a labor inspector. Minors under the age of 18 are also prohibited from performing dangerous and hazardous work. The number of hours minors can work and when they can work are also limited. The standard workweek is legally set at 40 hours with a mandatory 11-hour rest period every 24 hours. The monthly minimum wage was about $391 in 2011, with around 87% of the nation's workforce earning more than the minimum rate.

22 AGRICULTURE

During the Soviet period, forced collectivization reduced the share of labor in agriculture from 50% to less than 20%. By 2003, however, there were 36,859 private farms, with an average size of 21.6 hectares (53.4 acres).

Roughly 19% of the total land is farmed. The country's major crops include grain, potatoes, and vegetables. In 2009 cereal production amounted to 873,466 tons, fruit production 8,471 tons, and vegetable production 70,724 tons.

23 ANIMAL HUSBANDRY

The UN Food and Agriculture Organization (FAO) reported that Estonia dedicated 197,000 hectares (486,798 acres) to permanent pasture or meadow in 2009. During that year, the country tended 1.8 million chickens, 237,900 head of cattle, and 364,900 pigs. The production from these animals amounted to 18,499 tons of beef and veal, 35,803 tons of pork, 23,222 tons of poultry, 14,224 tons of eggs, and 320,795 tons of milk. Estonia also produced 1,269 tons of cattle hide and 134 tons of raw wool. In 2005 there were 38,800 sheep in the nation.

Meat production is well developed and provides a surplus for export. Cattle breeding was the main activity during the Soviet era, and production quotas were set extremely high, which re-quired massive imports of feed. Pork production has risen since 2005 to offset the decline in the total cattle herd.

24 FISHING

Estonia's Baltic and Atlantic catch is marketed primarily in the Russian Federation and among other former Soviet states, in spite of the nation's own need for quality fish products. The fishing industry is seen as an important way to acquire access to the world market, but scarcity of raw materials currently limits its development. Nonetheless, it is one of Estonia's most important agricultural industries. Estonia had 239 decked commercial fishing boats in 2008. The annual capture totaled 101,037 tons according to the UN FAO. The export value of seafood totaled $128.1 million.

25 FORESTRY

Approximately 52% of Estonia is covered by forest. The production of wood and wood products is the second-largest industry after textiles; two cellulose plants (at Tallinn and Kehra) use local raw material, but have caused significant environmental problems. There is also a fiberboard processing plant (for furniture making) at Püssi. The UN FAO estimated the 2009 roundwood production at 3.71 million cu m (130.9 million cu ft). The value of all forest products, including roundwood, totaled $566.1 million.

26 MINING

Oil shale is the primary mineral of importance. The country also produces cement, clays, nitrogen, peat, sand and gravel, and industrial silica sand. Production figures for 2008 were: clays for brick, 138,106,000 cu m, down from 231,400,000 cu m in 2006; clays for cement, 33.5 million cu m, down from 56.7 million cu m in 2006; and sand and gravel, 4.75 million cu m. Phosphate quarrying at the Maardu deposit ceased because of environmental concerns.

27 ENERGY AND POWER

Per capita oil consumption was 4,026 kg in 2008. There are no natural gas reserves in Estonia, which relies on imports from Russia. Estonia is however, a net exporter of electricity, sending its surplus power to parts of northwest Russia and to Latvia. After 2006 Estonia began exporting electricity to Finland via cable. A second cable is scheduled to be added by 2014, allowing for greater capacity for export to Finland. The World Bank reported in 2008 that Estonia produced 10.6 billion kWh of electricity and consumed 8.51 billion kWh, or 6,633 kWh per capita. Roughly 88% of energy came from fossil fuels.

28 INDUSTRY

Estonian industrial production focuses on shipbuilding, engineering, electronics, wood and wood products, textiles, information technology, and telecommunications. Extractive industries include oil shale, phosphate, and cement production. The textile mills of Kreenholmi Manufacturer in Narva and Bălți Manufacturer in Tallinn are the country's largest industrial enterprises.

Between 1990 and 1995, industrial output shrank by an average of 14.9% per year, but most of the decline occurred in the years immediately after independence. In 2010 industry had a 28.7% share in the GDP.

Principal Trading Partners – Estonia (2010)				
(In millions of US dollars)				
Country	**Total**	**Exports**	**Imports**	**Balance**
World	23,888.8	11,606.8	12,282.0	-675.2
Finland	3,795.8	1,973.4	1,822.4	151.0
Sweden	3,158.2	1,818.7	1,339.5	479.2
Kosovo	2,371.8	1,043.2	1,328.6	-285.4
Germany	1,984.8	605.7	1,379.1	-773.5
Russia	1,639.1	1,114.6	524.5	590.2
Latvia	1,516.1	568.6	947.5	-379.0
Poland	975.7	188.8	787.0	-598.2
Netherlands	672.6	266.1	406.5	-140.4
Denmark	524.3	291.0	233.3	57.7
United Kingdom	476.6	228.2	248.5	-20.3

(…) data not available or not significant.

(n.s.) not specified.

SOURCE: *2011 Direction of Trade Statistics Yearbook,* New York: United Nations, 2011.

Balance of Payments – Estonia (2010)		
(In millions of US dollars)		
Current Account		673.2
Balance on goods		-330.7
Imports	-11,972.0	
Exports	11,641.3	
Balance on services		1,729.4
Balance on income		-1,066.5
Current transfers		341.1
Capital Account		693.8
Financial Account		-2,191.4
Direct investment abroad		-127.2
Direct investment in Estonia		1,539.1
Portfolio investment assets		-364.6
Portfolio investment liabilities		-193.0
Financial derivatives		40.8
Other investment assets		-1,736.2
Other investment liabilities		-1,350.2
Net Errors and Omissions		-287.7
Reserves and Related Items		1,112.1

(…) data not available or not significant.

SOURCE: *Balance of Payment Statistics Yearbook 2011,* Washington, DC: International Monetary Fund, 2011.

29 SCIENCE AND TECHNOLOGY

In 2008 expenditures for research and development (R&D) totaled 1.29% of GDP. Also, in 2008 Estonia had 2,966 researchers and 617 technicians per million people that were actively engaged in R&D. In 2009 high technology exports by Estonia totaled $655 million. Patent applications in science and technology as of 2009, according to the World Bank, totaled 76 in Estonia. Public financing of science remained at 1.29% of GDP.

The Academy of Sciences, founded in 1938, has divisions of astronomy and physics, informatics and technical sciences, and biology, geology, and chemistry, and research institutes devoted to biology, ecology, experimental biology, zoology and botany, environmental biology, marine sciences, astrophysics and atmospheric physics, chemical physics and biophysics, chemistry, geology, physics, computer research and design, cybernetics, and energy. Other research institutes in the country are devoted to preventive medicine and oil shale research. Tallinn Technical University (founded in 1918) offers science and engineering degrees. The University of Tartu, founded in 1632, has faculties of biology and geography, mathematics, medicine, and physics and chemistry, as well as an institute of general and molecular pathology. Estonian Agricultural University was founded in 1951.

30 DOMESTIC TRADE

Before the collapse of the Soviet Union, Estonia's domestic trade was underdeveloped by international standards. Most trading companies were owned either by the state or by cooperatives. After the collapse, many shops were privatized or municipalized, new private shops established, and the assortment of goods widened.

Open-air markets control a large segment of domestic food sales. Market prices are usually lower than those in grocery stores, making it difficult for them to compete. Most sales are subject to a value added tax of 18%, although there is a reduced 5% rate.

Business office hours are generally from 9 a.m. to 5 p.m., Monday through Friday. Bank hours are from 10 a.m. to 4 p.m., Mondays through Fridays. Shop hours are generally from 9 a.m. to 7 p.m. Mondays through Fridays, and from 9 a.m. to 4 p.m. on Sat-

urdays. Supermarkets and shopping centers are usually open between 9 a.m. to 11 p.m. every day.

31 FOREIGN TRADE

During the Soviet era, Estonia's foreign trade was characterized by large net imports, 80–85% of which came from other Soviet republics, which were also the destination of 95% of Estonian exports. Beginning in 1992, the value of exports began to surpass that of imports, and the share of trade with other former Soviet republics diminished.

Estonia imported $16.24 billion worth of goods and services in 2011, while exporting $15.64 billion worth of goods and services. Major import partners in 2010 were Finland, 15.7%; Germany, 11.9%; Sweden, 11.6%; Latvia, 11.5%; Lithuania, 8.2%; Poland, 6.8%and Russia, 4.5%. Major export partners were Finland, 18.5%; Sweden, 17%; Russia, 10.4%; Latvia, 9.8%; Germany, 5.7%; and Lithuania, 5.3%.

32 BALANCE OF PAYMENTS

Since independence, Estonia has dismantled a Soviet-era system of trade barriers and tariffs to become one of the world's most free-trading nations. In the early 1990s, exports to the West quadrupled, helping to generate a strong surplus in the current account. By the late 1990s and early 2000s, however, the balance of trade on goods became generally negative. Services and capital inflows produced income in the form of foreign direct investment, which remained strong

In 2010 Estonia had a foreign trade surplus of $1.1 billion, amounting to 1.3% of GDP.

33 BANKING AND SECURITIES

The Bank of Estonia serves as the nation's central bank. Established in January 1990, the bank merged two years later with the

Estonian branch of Gosbank (the Soviet State Bank), forming the country's current central bank. All links with the Soviet budget and financial system were severed in 1991.

In December 1988 the authorities established the first Estonian commercial bank, the Tartu Commercial Bank, and by September 1991 there were 20 commercial banks responsible for 27% of total credit extended by banks. The commercial banks include the Bank of Tallinn (1990), Estonian Commercial Bank of Industry (1991), Cand Bank of Estonia (1990), and South Estonian Development Bank. Savings banks include the Estonian Savings Bank, a bank with 432 branches.

Like those of other Eastern European countries, Estonia's banking sector has suffered from an excessive number of banks: there were 43 by the end of 1992. Consolidations took place in 1993, with the banks being merged in Eesti Uhispank (Estonian Unified Bank). Estonia's private banking system is dominated by two foreign banking groups: Hansabank (Swedbank) and Uhispank (Skandinaviska Enskilda Banken). A hallmark of Estonia's banking system is the high proportion of electronic transactions. More than 90% of all bank transactions are electronic, and over 75% of the country's Internet connected population banks via the Internet.

Since independence, Estonia's banks have played a major role in fostering a climate of economic stability. In 1997 they took the initiative in tightening credit in the wake of the Asian financial crisis. This action, which resulted in a rise in interest rates, checked fears of a too-rapid economic expansion, which would bring about inflation. At the end of 2010 the commercial bank prime lending rate was 7.759%, down from 9.385% in 2009.

The Tallinn Stock Exchange was inaugurated in May 1996.

34 INSURANCE

Since Estonia regained its independence, it has sought to develop a system of health insurance involving the decentralization of medical care. Third-party automobile liability insurance is compulsory.

35 PUBLIC FINANCE

The government exercises fiscal responsibility characterized by a strictly balanced budget. No transfers or preferential credits are given to public enterprises, and governmental borrowing from the central bank is forbidden. In January 1996 Estonia instituted a centralized treasury system for managing the government's budget.

The CIA estimated that in 2005 Estonia's central government took in revenues of approximately $5.1 billion and had expenditures of $5 billion. Revenues minus expenditures totaled approximately $109 million. Public debt in 2005 amounted to 3.8% of GDP. Total external debt was $10.09 billion.

In 2010 the budget of Estonia included $7.851 billion in public revenue and $8.21 billion in public expenditures. The budget surplus amounted to 0.1% of GDP. Public debt was 7.7% of GDP, with $22.21 billion of the debt held by foreign entities.

36 TAXATION

Estonia does not tax the income of resident or permanently established nonresident companies. Instead, they are subject only to a tax on distributions (dividends, fringe benefits, gifts, profit distributions, and those payments not related to the payer's busi-

Public Finance – Estonia (2009)		
(In millions of krooni, central government figures)		
Revenue and Grants	**77,993**	**100.0%**
Tax revenue	38,021	48.7%
Social contributions	29,913	38.4%
Grants	…	…
Other revenue	…	…
Expenditures	**83,334**	**100.0%**
General public services	10,405	12.5%
Defense	4,450	5.3%
Public order and safety	6,812	8.2%
Economic affairs	9,585	11.5%
Environmental protection	2,083	2.5%
Housing and community amenities	6	<0.1%
Health	12,369	14.8%
Recreational, culture, and religion	2,961	3.6%
Education	6,687	8.0%
Social protection	27,976	33.6%

(…) data not available or not significant.

SOURCE: *Government Finance Statistics Yearbook 2010*, Washington, DC: International Monetary Fund, 2010.

ness) to resident legal entities, resident and nonresident persons, and nonresident companies. As of 2011 those subject are taxed at 22%. Interest payments are subject to a 24% withholding tax that is paid to resident persons, and on that portion of interest paid to nonresident persons or companies that is over the market interest rate. Royalty payments made to nonresident firms and persons, are subject to a 15% withholding tax. Resident persons and companies are subject to a higher, 24%, withholding rate. Generally, capital gains received by resident persons and companies are taxed as income. For companies, the gains are taxed as part of the distribution, when it is made. Individuals do not pay a capital gains tax on the sale of their primary residence.

Personal income taxes, as of 2011, are assessed at the same flat rate of 22% as corporate profits. Some school fees, living allowances, and interest on loans for the purchase of residential housing are deductible from taxable income. A withholding tax of 22% is imposed on dividends paid to nonresidents that hold less than 20% of the share capital in the paying company. However, Estonia has double tax treaties with at least 22 countries in which withholding taxes are eliminated or substantially reduced. A new Law on Social Tax came into effect in January 1999. The rate of social tax is 33% payable by employers and self-employed individuals. There are relatively few allowable deductions from taxable income in the Estonian tax code. The annual land tax varies from 0.1–2.5% of assessed value.

Main indirect tax is a value-added tax (VAT) set at a standard rate of 20%. Reduced rates of 0% and 5% apply to some goods and services, including a 0% rate on exported goods and a specific list of exported services. Excise duties are levied on tobacco, alcoholic beverages, motor fuel, motor oil, and fuel oil (but not liquefied or compressed gas), motor vehicles, and packages (imposed to encourage recycling of package material). There is a gambling tax, and a customs processing fee on each customs declaration submitted. Rights of recording are taxed at 0.4%. Local governments have the authority to impose taxes, and municipal taxes range from 1–2%.

37 CUSTOMS AND DUTIES

Estonia has a liberal trade regime, with few tariff or nontariff barriers. Among the few items that have tariffs placed on them are agricultural goods produced in countries that are not among Estonia's preferred trading partners. There is also a value-added tax (VAT) levied ad valorem on everything except a few select commodities, including medicines and medical equipment, funeral equipment, and goods for nonprofit purposes.

38 FOREIGN INVESTMENT

Estonia has successfully attracted a large number of joint ventures with Western companies, benefiting from a well-developed service sector and links with Scandinavian countries. The foreign investment act passed in September 1991 by the Supreme Council (the legislative body of 1990–92) offers tax relief to foreign investors. Property brought into Estonia by foreign investors as an initial capital investment is exempt from customs duties, but is subject to value-added tax. A foreign investor is legally entitled to repatriate profits after paying income tax.

In 1998 foreign direct investment (FDI) inflows peaked at $580.6, up from $266.7 million in 1997. FDI inflow averaged $346 million in 1999 and 2000, but increased to $538 million in 2001. Estonia's share of world FDI flows from 1998 to 2000 were 2.3 times its share of world GDP, making it 16th among the 140 countries ranked on FDI performance by UNCTAD.

Since the early 2000s Estonia has been one of the best performing Central and Eastern European countries in terms of foreign investments attracted. Numerous foreign companies have considered Estonia to be an attractive market, and today companies partly or wholly owned by foreign nationals make up one-third of the country's GDP, and over 50% of its exports. Foreign direct investment (FDI) in Estonia was a net inflow of $1.75 billion according to World Bank figures published in 2009. FDI represented 9.18% of GDP.

Industry accounts for 46% of the total foreign investment, primarily in the pulp and paper, transportation, and services sectors. Wholesale and retail trade accounts for 27% of foreign investment; transport accounts for 14%. Estonian agribusiness is an area of growing interest to foreign investors.

39 ECONOMIC DEVELOPMENT

After passing an ownership act in June 1990, the government began a privatization program at the beginning of 1991. Most of the nearly 500 state-owned companies have since passed into new hands. The Estonian Privatization Agency (EPA) was established to oversee major privatization programs. In late 1995 EPA announced privatization plans for Estonian Railways, Estonian Energy, Estonian Oil Shale, Estonian Telekom, and Tallinn Ports. Estonian Gas, Estonian Tobacco, and Estonian Air were privatized in 1996.

Estonia has excellent intellectual property laws, has enacted modern bankruptcy legislation, and has seen the emergence of well-managed privately held banks. The constitution mandates a balanced budget, and the climate for foreign investment is positive. In 2003 the economy was vulnerable, and the size of the current account deficit was a particular concern. The government was urged by the International Monetary Fund (IMF) to pursue a fiscal surplus policy, to prepare for membership in the European Union (EU). The country joined the World Trade Organization (WTO) in 1999 and the European Union in 2004. Aside from a small increase in the VAT from 18 to 20%, the global economic crisis has done little to Estonia's economic development when compared to other countries that use the euro.

40 SOCIAL DEVELOPMENT

Social security programs were originally introduced in 1924. After independence from the Soviet Union, new social insurance systems were introduced. The current law was implemented in 2003. Pension systems are funded by contributions from employers and the government. Retirement is set at age 63 for men and 59 for women, and is set to increase to age 63 for both men and women. Other social welfare programs include worker's compensation, unemployment assistance, survivorship payments, maternity and sickness benefits, and family allowances. There is a family allowance for all children under 17 years of age.

Women constitute slightly more than half the work force, and in theory are entitled to equal pay. Although women on average achieve higher educational levels than men, their average pay is lower. Sexual harassment is not officially reported. Domestic violence is a widespread problem and is grossly underreported; spousal abuse is not a criminal offense. Public attention is focused increasingly on the welfare of children in the wake of family crises caused by economic displacement. Women make up about 20 percent of the national legislature.

Ethnic Russians sometimes face discrimination in housing and employment. Estonian language requirements make it difficult for many of them to find public sector employment. Citizenship has not automatically been extended to ethnic Russians living in Estonia, and a significant proportion of the population remains noncitizens. Discrimination based on race, sex, nationality, or religion is illegal under the constitution. Prison conditions remain poor, and police brutality is commonly reported.

41 HEALTH

A major reform of the primary care system was implemented in 1998, making family practitioners independent contractors with combined private and public-financed payment. The number of hospitals in Estonia decreased significantly during the 1990s, with the number of available beds cut by one-third between 1991 and 1995. As of 2011 there were 34 physicians, 68 nurses and midwives, and 57 hospital beds per 10,000 inhabitants.

According to the CIA, life expectancy in Estonia was 73.58 years in 2011. The country spent 6.1% of its GDP on healthcare, amounting to $1,004 per person. The fertility rate was 1.44 children born per woman, while the infant mortality rate was 6.94 deaths per 1,000 live births. In 2008 the maternal mortality rate, according to the World Bank, was 12 deaths per 100,000 births. It was estimated that 95% of children were vaccinated against measles. The CIA calculated the HIV/AIDS prevalence rate in Estonia to be about 1.2% in 2009. The incidence of tuberculosis was 30 per 100,000 people in that same year.

There is a medical school at the Tartu University.

42 HOUSING

According to 2000 census figures, the total number of dwellings in the country was at about 628,615. Of these 617,399 were described as conventional dwellings; 424,769 were apartments and 171,086 were single-family, detached dwellings. About 85% of all conventional dwellings were owned by private citizens residing in Estonia. About 3.8% of all conventional dwellings are owned by housing associations. Only about 3.7% of all conventional dwellings were built in 1991 or later; 59% of the housing stock was built during the period 1961–1990. The housing costs of low-income families are subsidized. Almost all Estonians (98%) have access to improved water supplies, and 95% have access to improved sanitation facilities.

43 EDUCATION

Prior to the 1990s the Soviet system of education was followed. This was modified after Estonia's separation from the USSR. Primary education (basic school) covers nine years. This is followed by a general secondary school (gymnasium) or a vocational school, both of which cover a three-year program. Students in vocational schools may choose to continue in an advanced program of another three years. The academic year runs from September through June. In 2008 the World Bank estimated that 94% of age-eligible children in Estonia were enrolled in primary school. Secondary enrollment for age-eligible children stood at 89%. The primary languages of instruction are Estonian, Russian, and English.

There are two well-known universities: the University of Tartu, founded in 1632, and the Talliva Technical University, founded in 1936, which mainly offers engineering courses. In 2008 tertiary enrollment was estimated at 64%. Of those enrolled in tertiary education, there were 100 male students for every 169 female students.

Overall, the CIA estimates that Estonia has a literacy rate of 99.8%. Public expenditure on education represented 4.8% of GDP in 2008.

44 LIBRARIES AND MUSEUMS

The National Library of Estonia in Tallinn, founded in 1918, contains over 3.2 million volumes. Other important libraries located in Tallinn include the Estonian Technical Library (11.8 million volumes) and the Estonian Academic Library (2.2 million). The Tartu State University Library is the largest academic library; it contains 3.7 million volumes. In 2004, there were 564 public libraries in the country, along with 512 school libraries and 75 research and special libraries.

The Estonian History Museum in Tallinn was established in 1864. It contains 230,000 exhibits that follow the history of the region's people from ancient times to the present. The Estonian National Museum in Tartu, established in 1909, features exhibits about the living conditions of Estonians. Also in Tallinn is the Art Museum of Estonia, the Estonian Open Air Museum, the Estonian Theater and Music Museum, and the Tallinn City Museum. Tartu University houses a Museum of Classical Antiquities.

45 MEDIA

Estonia's telecommunications system has gone through significant improvements as a result of foreign investment. Fiber-optic cable systems carry digital telephone, television, and radio traffic; Internet services are available through most of the country. In 2010 the CIA reported that there were 492,200 telephone landlines in Estonia. In addition to landlines there were 1.653 cellular phones; mobile phone subscriptions averaged more than 100 per 100 people.

Estonian Radio began regular broadcasting in 1926. In 1937 the highest radio tower in Europe was built in Türi. In the 1970s Estonian Radio was the first in the former Soviet Union to carry advertising. Estonian television began broadcasting in 1955, and started color broadcasts in 1972. It broadcasts on four channels in Estonian and Russian. In 2009, there were 98 AM radio stations.

As of 2005 Estonia had the most advanced information infrastructure of any country in the former Communist Eastern Bloc. Around 700,000 of Estonia's approximately 1.3 million people bank online, up from zero in 1997. Citizens use the Internet to access state services and to conduct any number of business transactions, and many people who never owned a landline telephone now rely on wireless phones. In March 2007 Estonia became the first country to allow Internet voting for national parliamentary elections. In 2011 the country had 848,009 Internet hosts. Internet users numbered 81 per 100 citizens.

Journalism was subject to varying degrees of censorship from the Russian occupation in 1940 until the late 1980s. Prominent newspapers in 2010, with circulation numbers listed parenthetically, included *Ohtuleht* (65,000), *Paevaleht* (40,000), and *Postimees* (59,200), as well as three other major newspapers.

Estonia has an active publishing industry, although it faced economic difficulties in the early 1990s. The ISBN code has been used in Estonia since 1988.

The government is said to respect constitutional provisions for free expression. Foreign publications are widely available, and private print and broadcast media operate freely.

46 ORGANIZATIONS

The Chamber of Commerce and Industry of the Republic of Estonia promotes trade and commerce with its neighbors. Also, there is a chamber of commerce in Tartu. Professional societies and trade unions have developed for a number of careers.

Research and educational organizations include the Estonian Academy of Sciences and the Estonian Medical Association. There are also several associations dedicated to research and education for specific fields of medicine and particular diseases and conditions.

The Estonian Institute, established in 1989, promotes the appreciation of Estonian culture abroad. Ars Baltica is a multination group based in Vilnius that promotes appreciation for regional arts and culture.

Most student organizations belong to the umbrella organizations of the Federation of Estonian Student Unions or the Federation of Estonian Universities. Other youth organizations include the Estonian Green Movement, YMCA/YWCA, Junior Chamber, the Estonian Scout Associations, and the Girl Guides. In 1989 Estonian sports were reorganized, and the Soviets reduced their control of Estonia's sports system. In the same year the National Olympic Committee was restored. Other sports associations have since formed, including groups for wind surfing, yachting, Frisbee, and football (soccer). The Estonian Association of University Women promotes educational and professional opportunities for women.

The Estonian Institute for Human Rights monitors actions concerning civil rights and offers legal aid and information to the public. Volunteer service organizations, such as the Lions Clubs and Kiwanis International, are also present. There is a national chapter of the Red Cross Society.

⁴⁷TOURISM, TRAVEL, AND RECREATION

Visitors are drawn to the country's scenic landscapes, Hanseatic architecture, music and dance festivals, regattas, and beach resorts. The ancient town of Tallinn, noted for its architectural preservation, is a major tourist attraction and is linked by regular ferries to Helsinki and Stockholm.

The *Tourism Factbook*, published by the UN World Tourism Organization, reported 1.9 million incoming tourists to Estonia in 2009, who spent a total of $1.44 billion. Of those incoming tourists, there were 1.3 million from Europe. There were 30,826 hotel beds available in Estonia, which had an occupancy rate of 31%. The estimated daily cost to visit Tallinn, the capital, was $238. The cost of visiting other cities averaged $161.

⁴⁸FAMOUS PERSONS

Lennart Meri (b. 1929), writer, filmmaker, and historian, became president of Estonia in 1992 and won a second term in 1996. He left office in 2001, and was succeeded by Arnold Rüütel (b. 1928). Writer Friedrich Reinhold Kreutzwald (1803–1882) wrote the epic *Kalevipoeg* (Son of Kalev), which was published by the Estonian Learned Society in 1857–61 and marked the beginning of Estonian national literature.

The revolution of 1905 forced many Estonian writers to flee the country. In 1906 a stable government was established in Estonia, and a literary movement took hold, Birth of Young Estonia. The movement was led by poet Gustav Suits (1883–1956). He fled to Finland in 1910 but returned after the Russian Revolution of 1917. Later, Suits became a professor of literature at Tartu University. His fellow writers and poets between the revolution of 1917 and 1940 included Friedbert Tuglas (1886–1971) and Marie Under (1883–1980). Writers who fled abroad during World War II include Karl Rumor (1886–1971) and Arthur Adson (1889–1977). Estonian writers banned or exiled during the Soviet period include the playwright Hugo Raudsepp (1883–1952). American Architect Louis Kahn (1901?–1974) was born in Estonia.

⁴⁹DEPENDENCIES

Estonia has no territories or colonies.

⁵⁰BIBLIOGRAPHY

Estonia Investment and Business Guide: Strategic and Practical Information. Washington, DC: International Business Publications USA, 2012.

Frucht, Richard, ed. *Eastern Europe: An Introduction to the People, Lands, and Culture.* Santa Barbara, CA: ABC-CLIO, 2005.

Kasekamp, Andres. *The Radical Right in Interwar Estonia.* New York: St. Martin's Press, 2000.

Miljan, Toivo. *Historical Dictionary of Estonia.* Lanham, MD: Scarecrow, 2004.

Opello, Walter C. *European Politics.* Boulder, CO: Lynne Rienner Publishers, 2009.

Raun, Toivo U. *Estonia and the Estonians.* Stanford, CA: Hoover Institution Press, 2001.

Terterov, Marat, ed. *Doing Business with Estonia.* Sterling, VA: Kogan Page, 2004.

Vogt, Henri. *Between Utopia and Disillusionment: A Narrative of the Political Transformation in Eastern Europe.* New York: Berghahn Books, 2004.

FINLAND

Republic of Finland

Suomen Tasavalta

CAPITAL: Helsinki

FLAG: The civil flag contains an ultramarine blue cross with an extended right horizontal bar on a white background.

ANTHEM: *Maamme* (in Swedish, *Vårt land; Our Land).*

MONETARY UNIT: The euro replaced the markka as the official currency in 2002. The euro is divided into 100 cents. There are coins in denominations of 1, 2, 5, 10, 20, and 50 cents and 1 euro and 2 euros. There are notes of 5, 10, 20, 50, 100, 200, and 500 euros. €1 = US\$1.33352 (or US\$1 = €0.749897) as of March 2012.

WEIGHTS AND MEASURES: The metric system is the legal standard.

HOLIDAYS: New Year's Day, 1 January; May Day, 1 May; Independence Day, 6 December; Christmas, 25–26 December. Movable holidays include Good Friday, Easter Monday, Whitsun, and Midsummer Day (late June). Epiphany, Ascension, and All Saints' Day are adjusted to fall always on Saturdays.

TIME: 2 p.m. = noon GMT.

¹LOCATION, SIZE, AND EXTENT

Finland has an area of 338,145 sq km (130,559 sq mi), of which 34,330 sq km (13,255 sq mi) is inland water. Comparatively, the area occupied by Finland is slightly smaller than the state of Montana. Its length, one-third of which lies above the Arctic Circle, is 1,160 km (721 mi) N–S; its width is 540 km (336 mi) E–W.

Finland borders on Russia to the E, the Gulf of Finland to the SE, the Baltic Sea to the SW, the Gulf of Bothnia and Sweden to the W, and Norway to the NW and N, with a total land boundary of 2,628 km (1,629 mi) and a coastline of about 1,126 km (698 mi, excluding islands and coastal indentations.

Finland's capital, Helsinki, is located on the country's southern coast.

²TOPOGRAPHY

Southern and western Finland consist of a coastal plain with a severely indented coastline and thousands of small islands stretching out to the Åland Islands. Central Finland is an extensive lake plateau with a majority of the country's 60,000 lakes.

Northern Finland is densely forested upland. The highest elevations are in the Norwegian border areas; northwest of Enontekiö rises Haltia, a mountain 1,328 m (4,357 ft) above sea level. Haltia is also referred to as Haltiatunturi. Extensive, interconnected lake and river systems provide important natural waterways.

³CLIMATE

Because of the warming influence of the Gulf Stream and the prevailing wind patterns, Finland's climate is comparatively mild for the high latitude. During the winter, the average temperature ranges from -14°C to -3°C (7°F to 27°F), while summer mean temperatures range from 13°C to 18°C (55°F to 65°F). Snow cov-

er lasts from about 90 days in the Åland Islands to 250 days in Enontekiö. Average annual precipitation (including both rain and snow) ranges from 40 cm (16 in) in northern Finland to 71 cm (28 in) in southern Finland. In 2012 the Finnish Meteorological Society reported some record-breaking warm winters, but also some rather cold and snowy winters, in the first years of the 21st century. In 2008, the country recorded the sixth warmest year on record. The annual mean temperature recorded at Helsinki Kaisaniemi was the highest since records began (1829), at 7.6°C (45.7°F).

⁴FLORA AND FAUNA

The World Resources Institute estimates that there are 1,102 plant species in Finland. In addition, Finland is home to 80 mammal, 421 bird, 5 reptile, and 6 amphibian species. The calculation reflects the total number of distinct species residing in the country, not the number of endemic species.

Forests, chiefly pine, spruce, and birch, are economically the most significant flora. Flora is richest in southern Finland and the Åland Islands. More than 75% of the total fauna are insects. Fur-bearing animals (otter, marten, ermine) are declining in number, while elk, fox, and beaver have increased. Of some 248 species of breeding birds, the best known is the cuckoo, the harbinger of spring. Of some 66 species of freshwater fish, 33 have some economic importance; in fresh waters, the perch, walleyed pike, great northern pike, and others are plentiful. Salmon remains the favorite of fly rod enthusiasts.

⁵ENVIRONMENT

The World Resources Institute reported that Finland had designated 2.95 million hectares (7.28 million acres) of land for protection as of 2006. Water resources totaled 110 cu km (26.39 cu mi) while water usage was 2.33 cu km (.559 cu mi) per year. The Finnish Environmental Ministry reported in 2012 that about 9% of the country's total area was protected under the Nature Conservation Act or the Act on the Protection of Wilderness Reserves.

Domestic water usage accounted for 14% of total water usage, industrial for 83%, and agricultural for 3%. Per capita water usage totaled 444 cu m (15,680 cu ft) per year.

The United Nations (UN) reported in 2008 that carbon dioxide emissions in Finland totaled 64,124 kilotons.

Finland's main environmental issues are air and water pollution, and the preservation of its wildlife. Finland's principal environmental agency is the Ministry of the Environment, established in 1983. Lead-free gasoline was introduced in 1985. Beginning in 1987, environmental protection boards were established for every community with more than 3,000 inhabitants. To preserve the shoreline profile, 30–50% of the shores suitable for recreational use may not be built on. Industrial pollutants from within the country and surrounding countries affect the purity of both the nation's air and water supplies.

In October 2009, the Climate and Energy Strategy took effect. It sets an ambitious goal to cut energy consumption 30% from 2010 levels by 2050 and emissions to 80% of 1990 levels by 2050. The policy report indicated a number of specific measures that would need to be put into place to meet such a goal. One such measure would be the revision of energy efficiency standards for new buildings and renovations of existing buildings. Creating more wind power facilities is also listed for consideration. The policy set a goal that, by 2020, as much as 38% of the country's energy would come from renewable sources, the largest share of which was likely to be from wood-based biofuels. As of 2012, about 25% of the country's energy came from renewable sources.

Acid rain from high concentrations of sulfur in the air damaged the nation's lakes in the 1980s and 1990s, but by 2011, there was evidence that the freshwater lakes of the country were recovering. Antipollution legislation and increased environmental awareness among Scandinavian nations has cut back on high-sulfur emissions that cause acid rain.

Care is taken to protect the flora and fauna of the forests, which are of recreational as well as economic importance. Closed hunting seasons, nature protection areas, and other game-management measures are applied to preserve threatened animal species. According to a 2011 report issued by the International Union for Conservation of Nature and Natural Resources (IUCN), threatened species included 1 mammal, 4 species of birds, 6 species of fish, 3 types of mollusk, 6 other invertebrates, and 2 species of plant. Endangered species include the Siberian sturgeon, European mink, and the Saimaa ringed seal. In 2010, the European Union's (EU) Habitats Directive law designated the Saimaa seal as being in need of priority protection. The EU asked Finland to take strong action to protect the seal and its habitat.

6 POPULATION

The US Central Intelligence Agency (CIA) estimated the population of Finland in 2012 to be approximately 5,262,930, which placed it at number 116 in population among the 196 nations of the world. In 2011, approximately 17.9% of the population was over 65 years of age, with another 16% under 15 years of age. The median age in Finland was 42.5 years. There were 0.96 males for every female in the country. The population's annual rate of change was 0.075%. The projected population for the year 2025 was 5,800,000. Population density in Finland was calculated at 16 people per sq km (41 people per sq mi).

The UN estimated that 85% of the population lived in urban areas in 2010, and that urban populations had an annual rate of change of 0.6%. The largest urban area was Helsinki, with a 2009 population of 1.107 million.

Rovaniemi, with a 2009 population of 59,850, is considered the capital of Finnish Lapland.

7 MIGRATION

Estimates of Finland's net migration rate, carried out by the CIA in 2011, amounted to 0.62 migrants per 1,000 citizens. The total number of emigrants living abroad was 329,500, and the total number of immigrants living in Finland was 225,600. From 1866 to 1930, a total of 361,020 Finns emigrated, mostly to the United States and, after the US restriction of immigration, to Canada. After World War II (1939–45), about 250,000 to 300,000 Finns permanently emigrated to Sweden. This migration ended by the 1980s because of a stronger Finnish economy.

More than 400,000 people fled the Soviet occupation of the Karelia region during World War II. There was also a heavy migration from rural areas, particularly the east and northeast, to the urban, industrialized south, especially between 1960 and 1975.

From 1990 to 2000, the number of foreign citizens in Finland increased from 21,000 to 100,000. In April 1990, it was declared that all Finns living within the former Soviet Union, many known as Ingrians, could be considered returning migrants to Finland. As of 2003, some 25,000 Ingrians had returned to Finland, with approximately the same number awaiting entry interviews. Finland's longstanding ethnic minorities include Swedes, Sami (indigenous population), Jews, Romani or Gypsies, Tartars, and Russians.

By 2004 its foreign-born population represented over 168 nations. Most of these foreign born were from the former Soviet Union, former Yugoslavia, Sweden, Iraq, Somalia, Turkey, the United States, China, Vietnam, Thailand, and returning Finns. As of 2010, 3% of families in Finland were composed of parents whose native language was not Finnish or Swedish. Some 30% of these families are Russian speakers.

Finland accepts 500 refugees each year for those who need an alternative to their first country of asylum. In 2010, Finland granted 1,784 of the 4,837 applications from asylum seekers.

8 ETHNIC GROUPS

The Finns are thought to be descended from Germanic stock and from tribes that originally inhabited west-central Russia. Excluding the Swedish-speaking minority, there are only two very small non-Finnish ethnic groups: Lapps and Gypsies. As of 2006, Finns constituted about 93.4% of the total population, Swedes made up 5.6%, Russians accounted for 0.5%, Estonians for 0.3%, Roma for 0.1%, and Sami (Lapps) for 0.1%. Several societies have been established to foster the preservation of the Lappish language and culture.

9 LANGUAGES

From the early Middle Ages to 1809, Finland was part of the Kingdom of Sweden, and its official language was Swedish. Finnish did not become an official language until 1863. In 2007, 91.2% of the population was primarily Finnish-speaking and 5.5% was primarily Swedish-speaking. Swedish-speaking Finns make up more than 95% of the population of the Åland Islands. Swedish, the second legal language, is given constitutional safeguards. Only a minority of individuals have another language as their mother tongue, principally Lapp, Russian, English, or German. Finnish belongs to the Finno-Ugric language group and is closely related to Estonian; more distantly to the Komi, Mari, and Udmurt languages spoken among those peoples living in Russia; and remotely to Hungarian.

10 RELIGIONS

Both the Evangelical Lutheran Church and the Orthodox Church are considered state churches. As of 2010, about 81% of the population belonged to the Evangelical Lutheran Church. However, some reports have indicated that less than 10% of Lutherans attend services on a regular basis. Approximately 1% of the inhabitants are members of the Orthodox Church in Finland. There are a growing number of Pentecostal churches in the nation, but since many of these communities are unregistered, exact data on membership is not available. Other religious bodies include the Free Church, Jehovah's Witnesses, Adventists, Roman Catholics, Methodists, Mormons, Baptists, Swedish Lutherans, and Jews. The number of Muslims has increased from an estimated 20,000 in 1999 to about 40,000 in 2010. Immigration and a high birth rate have both attributed to the increase.

11 TRANSPORTATION

The CIA reports that Finland has a total of 78,141 km (48,555 mi) of roads, of which 50,914 km (31,636 mi) are paved. There are 534 vehicles per 1,000 people in the country. Railroads extend for 5,919 km (3,678 mi). There are 148 airports, which transported 7.42 million passengers in 2009 according to the World Bank. Finland has approximately 7,842 km (4,873 mi) of navigable waterways.

Virtually all railways were operated by the Finnish State Railways, and some 3,067 km (1906 mi) were electrified as of 2009. In 2010, there were 93 ships in Finland's merchant fleet of 1,000 GRT or more. Import and export shipping is concentrated at Naantali, Helsinki, Kotka, and Porvoo, Raahe, and Rauma. Icebreakers are used to maintain shipping lanes during winter months. Navigable inland waterways include the 3,577 km (2,224 mi) Saimaa Canal System, of which the southern part was leased from Russia.

In 2010, there were 73 airports with paved runways. Helsinki-Vantaa is the principal airport, located at Helsinki. State-run Finnair is engaged in civil air transport over domestic and international routes.

12 HISTORY

Finland, a province and a grand duchy of the Swedish kingdom from the 1150s to 1809 and an autonomous grand duchy of Russia from 1809 until the Russian Revolution in 1917, has been an independent republic since 1917. Ancestors of present-day Finns—hunters, trappers, agriculturists—came to Finland by way of the Baltic regions during the first centuries AD, spreading slowly from south and west to east and north. Swedish control over Finnish territory was established gradually beginning in the 12th century in a number of religious crusades. By 1293, Swedish rule had extended as far east as Karelia (Karjala), with colonization by Swedes

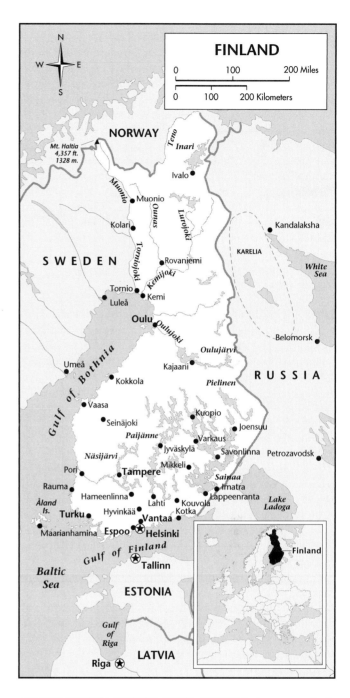

LOCATION: 59°30'10″ to 70°5'30″ N; 19°7'3″ to 31°35'20″ E. BOUNDARY LENGTHS: Russia, 1,313 kilometers (820 miles); Sweden, 586 kilometers (364 miles); Norway, 729 kilometers (445 miles); total coastline, 1,126 kilometers (694 miles). TERRITORIAL SEA LIMIT: 4 miles.

in the southwest and along the Gulf of Bothnia. As early as 1362, Finland as an eastern province of Sweden received the right to send representatives to the election of the Swedish king. On the basis of the Swedish constitution, Finland's four estates—nobles, clergy, burghers and peasant farmers—were also entitled to send representatives to the Diet in Stockholm. As a result of over six centuries of Swedish rule, Finnish political institutions and processes (marked by growing constitutionalism and self-government), economic life, and social order developed largely along

Swedish lines. Swedish colonization in Finland was concentrated in the southern and western regions of Finland.

When Sweden was a great power in European politics in the 17th century, Finland and the Finns bore a heavy military burden. Finland was a battleground between the Swedes and Russia, whose encroachments on southeastern Sweden were persistent as Swedish power declined in the 18th century. After Sweden's military defeat in the Napoleonic wars of 1808–09, sovereignty over Finland was transferred to Russia from Sweden after Napoleon and Tsar Alexander I concluded the Peace of Tilsit. Under the Russian rule of Alexander I, Finland was granted a privileged autonomous status that enabled Finland to continue the grand duchy's constitutional heritage. Alexander I, like his successors, took a solemn oath to "confirm and ratify the Lutheran religion and fundamental laws of the land as well as the privileges and rights which each class and all the inhabitants have hitherto enjoyed according to the constitution." Toward the end of the 19th century, a Russian drive to destroy Finland's autonomy ushered in several decades of strained relations and galvanized the burgeoning nationalist movement. Culturally, the nationalist movement in Finland was split linguistically between the Fennomen, who advocated Finnish language and culture, and the Svecomen, who promoted the continued dominance of Swedish. By the end of the 19th century, the Fennomen had gained the upper hand. In Russia's Revolution of 1905, Finland managed to extract concessions that included the creation of a modern, unicameral parliament with representatives elected through universal suffrage, including women. Thus, Finland was the first European country to offer women political suffrage at the national level. After the Bolshevik seizure of power in Russia in the late fall of 1917, Finland declared its independence on 6 December. A short civil war ensued (28 January-10 May 1918) between the Red faction supported by the Soviet Bolsheviks and the White faction supported by Germany. The White forces, led by General Mannerheim, were victorious, but Finland was forced to reorient its alliances toward the western allies when Germany was defeated in World War I.

In July 1919, Finland became a democratic parliamentary republic. In the nearly two decades of peace following the settlement of disputes with Sweden (over the Åland Islands) and the former USSR (East Karelia) there were noteworthy economic and social advances. Despite its neutral pro-Scandinavianism in the 1930s and support for the collective security provisions of the League of Nations, the country was unavoidably entangled in the worsening relations between the great powers. Negotiations with the former USSR, which demanded certain security provisions or territorial concessions, broke down in 1939, and two wars with the USSR ensued. The Winter War, lasting from 30 November 1939 to 13 March 1940, ended only when Finland ceded areas of southeastern Finland and the outer islands of the Gulf of Finland to the Soviets. However, Finland watched warily as the Soviets annexed the independent Baltic states of Estonia, Latvia, and Lithuania. After appeals to western allies went unfulfilled, Finland turned toward Germany for protection, and when Germany attacked the USSR on 26 June 1941, Finland entered the war on the German side. During the early part of the Continuation War, which lasted from 26 June 1941 to 19 September 1944, the Finns pushed the Soviets back to the old frontier lines and held that position for nearly three years. In 1944, a Russian counterattack forced Finland to ask for peace. The armistice terms of 1944, later confirmed by the Paris Peace Treaty of 10 February 1947, provided for cession of territory and payment of reparations to the Soviets and required Finland to expel the German troops on its soil; this resulted in German-Finnish hostilities from October 1944 to April 1945. Under the 1947 peace treaty Finland ceded some 12% of its territory to the USSR, imprisoned several prominent politicians, reduced its armed forces, and undertook to pay heavy economic reparations. A Soviet naval base was established only 25 km (15.5 miles) from Helsinki. A separate Treaty of Friendship, Cooperation, and Mutual Assistance, concluded in 1948 under heavy Soviet pressure, obligated Finland to resist attacks on itself or the USSR and in effect precluded Finland from undertaking any significant foreign policy initiative without the Kremlin's approval.

Finland's postwar policy, based on the Paasikivi Line named for the president that formulated the policy, has been termed dismissively as "Finlandization." It is true that Finland maintained a scrupulous and cautious policy of neutrality in foreign affairs. However, after 1955, when the Soviets withdrew from their Finnish base, Finland became an increasingly active member of the UN and the Nordic Council, as well as various Western economic organizations. Despite Soviet pressure, the Finnish Communist Party steadily declined in influence. Finland's standing was further enhanced by the signing of the 1975 Helsinki Treaty, which called for pan-European cooperation in security, economic, political, and human rights matters. The dominant figure of postwar politics was Urho Kekkonen, the Agrarian (later Center) Party leader who held the presidency from 1956 to 1981, when he resigned because of ill health. The cornerstone of his policy was maintenance of a center-left coalition (including the Communists), good relations with the USSR (which broke apart in 1991), and a foreign policy of "active neutrality."

Despite the negative connotations, "Finlandization" was something of a success. Unlike the Baltic states, Finland maintained sovereign independence and even managed to prosper in the post-WWII environment. Postwar political stability allowed a striking economic expansion and transformation in Finland. In 1950, nearly 70% of Finns worked on the land; as of 2009, less than 5% were engaged in agriculture or forestry. Following Kekkonen's resignation, the Social Democratic leader Mauno Koivisto, then prime minister, became acting president in October 1981. Koivisto was elected president in his own right in January 1982 and reelected in 1988.

Koivisto's tenure as president ended in 1994. In the presidential elections of February 1994, voters for the first time directly elected the president, Martti Ahtisaari, former UN mediator and leader of the Finnish Social Democratic Party, who defeated Elisabeth Rehn (defense minister) of the Swedish People's Party in a runoff election. Ahtisaari chose not to run for reelection in 2000, and in that contest no fewer than five candidates for the presidency were women. On 6 February 2000, Finns elected their first female president, Tarja Halonen, who won 51.6% of the vote in a runoff electoral contest with Esko Aho, leader of the Center Party.

Finland faced a deep recession brought about in part by the collapse of the Soviet market, which had accounted for 20% of Finnish exports. During 1991–94, the recession pushed unemployment up to nearly 20%. The collapse of the Soviet Union and the dissolution of the FCMA Treaty by mutual agreement of Finland

and the USSR prompted Finland to reassess its relationship with Europe. In March 1994, Finland completed negotiations for membership in the EU. Finland's relationship with the EU was a major issue of political debate even within the governing coalition. Following a referendum held in October 1994 with 57% approval, Finland formally joined the EU at the beginning of 1995. Finland also joined the European economic and monetary union in 1999, and adopted the euro as its currency in 2002.

Beyond Finlandization: Finland and the European Union

While a relative newcomer to European politics, Finland entered the political limelight as it took over the six-month rotating presidency of the EU in the second half of 1999. The priorities of the Finnish presidency included a number of pressing issues: preparing for institutional reform necessary prior to enlargement of the Union; increasing the transparency of the functioning of EU institutions; boosting employment and deepening the social dimension of European cooperation; environmental responsibility; and finally, in the area of foreign policy, the Finns championed the "Northern Dimension" which would extend a number of cooperative schemes to include the EU and non-EU countries along the Baltic, including increased ties with northwestern Russia. Though highly touted, this last initiative foundered as Europe continued to be preoccupied with ongoing NATO efforts in Kosovo. At the presidency's concluding summit (December 1999) of the European Council in Helsinki, the Finns could nonetheless point to a number of successes under their presidency. The groundwork for opening accession negotiations with six more applicant countries from Eastern Europe and recognizing Turkey's applicant status were approved by the 15 heads of state. In addition, the European Council approved the establishment of a rapid reaction force outside the structure of NATO, which would allow Europe to have an independent capacity to react in areas in which NATO was not engaged. This was an important accomplishment for Finland, whose neutral status makes participation in NATO actions problematic. Although Finland participates in NATO's "Partnership for Peace" program, the majority of Finns oppose NATO membership.

The issue of Finland's support for the US-led war in Iraq that began on 19 March 2003 was a deciding factor in the 16 March parliamentary elections. Opposition leader Anneli Jäätteenmäki accused sitting Prime Minister Paavo Lipponen of moving Finland too close to the US position on the use of military force to disarm Iraq, and her party went on to win the elections, albeit by a slim majority. Finland donated €1.6 million for humanitarian aid in Iraq. In June 2003, Prime Minister Jäätteenmäki resigned amid accusations that she used leaked confidential information on Iraq to help her party win the March elections; she was acquitted in March 2004 of inciting an aide to Lipponen to leak the documents.

Presidential elections were held on 15 January 2006. President Tarja Halonen came out ahead, with 46.3% of the vote, and Sauli Niinistö came in second with 24.1% of the vote. Since no candidate received a majority of the vote, a runoff election was held on 29 January. Results were Halonen, 51.8%, and Niinistö, 48.2% of the votes cast. In February 2012, Sauli Niinisto was elected president, becoming the first conservative to win in over 50 years. Prime Minister Jyrki Katainen had been elected in April 2011.

¹³GOVERNMENT

Finland's republican constitution combines a parliamentary system with a strong presidency. Legislative powers are vested in the Eduskunta (parliament), a unicameral body established in 1906. Members of parliament are elected for four-year terms by proportional representation from 15 multi-member electoral districts under universal suffrage at age 18. Finland was the first country in Europe to grant suffrage to women in national elections (1906).

The 1994 presidential election was the first direct presidential vote since the country gained independence in 1917. Previously voters selected slates of electors who then chose the president. Currently the president is elected directly in a two-stage vote. If no candidate gets a majority in the first round, a second round is held between the two candidates with the largest first round totals. The president is elected for a six-year term.

Finland's political system traditionally has been more like the French than most other European parliamentary democracies because of the division of executive power between the president and the prime minister. The president is the constitutionally designated head of state that appoints the cabinet and serves as commander-in-chief of the armed forces.

On 1 March 2000, a new Finnish constitution entered into force. The new constitution increased the power of the parliament in relation to the government (cabinet) and increased the power of the government in relation to the president. The power of the Finnish presidency was circumscribed in rather dramatic fashion while the power of the prime minister was increased. In the past, the Finnish president had the right to intervene in the formation of the government and to dissolve a government. Under the 2000 constitution, the president only formally appoints the prime minister and is bound by the decisions derived from negotiations among the parliamentary groups. Party leaders with the most seats in parliament select the prime minister in a complex bargaining process. The president appoints other ministers on the recommendation of the prime minister. The president may accept the resignation of a government or minister only in the event of a vote of no confidence by the parliament.

The government is responsible to the parliament. For example, the government must submit its program to parliament immediately after being appointed so that the parliament may take a vote of confidence in the government. Foreign and security policy are shared responsibilities between the president and the government, with the prime minister and foreign minister taking an active role in formulating a consensus approach to Finnish foreign policy. The government, not the president, now has responsibility over issues related to EU affairs, given the impact of much European law on domestic legislation. The parliament has created a Grand Committee, made up o f 25 members and 13 deputies, to scrutinize EU matters and to ensure parliament's influence on EU decision-making. Members are appointed based on political party representation in parliament.

Since 1945 no single party has ever held an absolute parliamentary majority, so all cabinet or governmental decisions involve coalitions. The cabinet is composed of the heads of government ministries and has as its primary responsibility the preparation of governmental budgets and legislation and the administration of public policies. The prime minister and cabinet serve only so long as they enjoy the support of a working majority in parliament, and there have been frequent changes of government.

Women are well represented in both the executive and legislative branches of government in Finland. Women have held top leadership positions, including defense minister (Elisabeth Rehn), foreign minister (Tarja Halonen), and speaker of parliament. In February 2000, Finns elected Tarja Halonen their first female president. (She was reelected in 2006.) Anneli Jäätteenmäki served as prime minister in 2003. Some 40% of the members of parliament as of 2011 were women.

14 POLITICAL PARTIES

The Finnish Social Democratic Party (Suomen Sosialidemokraattinen Puolue—SDP), still strongly represented as of 2011, was organized in 1899. It did not become a significant political force until 1907, following the modernization of the country's parliamentary structure. Swedish-speaking Socialists have their own league within the SDP. The party's program is moderate, and its emphasis on the partial nationalization of the economy has in recent decades given way to support for improvement of the condition of wage earners through legislation. The SDP has generally worked closely with the trade union movement and has been a vigorous opponent of communism.

The Center (or Centre) Party (Keskusrapuolue—KESK; until October 1965, the Agrarian League—Maalaisliitto) was organized in 1906, and it is still represented in political life as of the elections of 2011. While initially a smallholders' party, it won some support from middle and large landowners but virtually none from nonagricultural elements. In an effort to gain a larger following in urban areas, the party changed its name and revised its program in 1965.

The National Coalition Party (Kansallinen Kokoomus—KOK), also known as the Conservative Party, was established in 1918 as the successor to the conservative Old Finnish Party. Its program, described as "conservative middle-class," has traditionally emphasized the importance of private property, the established church, and the defense of the state. Sauli Niinisto, elected president in 2012, was the first person from this party to win the presidency since 1956.

The Christian Democratic League (Kristillisdemokraatit—KD), formerly known as the Finnish Christian League, was founded in 1958. It later became known as the Christian Democratic Party. The name was changed to the Christian Democratic League in 2001.

The Swedish People's Party (Svenska Folkpartiet—SFP), organized in 1906 as the successor to the Swedish Party, has stressed the need for protecting the common interests of Finland's Swedish-speaking population. It held 10 seats in parliament as of 2011.

The Finnish People's Democratic League (Suomen Kansan Demokraattinen Liitto—SKDL) represents the extreme left. Emerging in 1944, and illegal before then, the SKDL was a union of the Finnish Communist Party (organized in 1918) and the Socialist Unity Party. The SKDL had urged close relations with the former USSR and the Communist bloc, but it later moderated its demands for the establishment of a "people's democracy" in Finland. In 1986, a minority group within the SKDL was expelled; for the 1987 elections, it established a front called the Democratic Alternative (DEVA). Following the collapse of the Soviet Union, the

SKDL in May 1990 merged with other left parties to form the Left Alliance (Vasemmistoliitto—VAS).

The Greens, an environmentalist alliance, held 10 seats in the Eduskunta following the 2011 election.

In the 2006 presidential elections, Tarja Halonen of the Social Democratic Party was reelected in the second round of polls with 51.79% of the vote. Sauli Niinistö of the KOK won 48.2%. In the 2007 elections, the Center Party came in first with 51 seats (23% of the vote), followed by the KOK with 50 seats (22%), the Social Democrats with 45 (21%), the Left Alliance with 17 (8.8%), and the Green League with 15 seats (8.4%). The SFP won nine seats, followed by the Christian Democrats with seven, and the True Finns with five. Mari Kiviniemi of the Center Party was chosen as prime minister in 2010 following the resignation of Matti Vanhanen.

In the April 2011 parliamentary elections, the National Coalition Party (KOK) came in first with 20.4% of the vote and 44 seats, followed by the Social Democrats with 19.1% and 42 seats. The True Finns won 19% and 39 seats; the Center Party 15.8% and 35 seats; the Left Alliance, 8.1% and 12 seats; the Greens, 7.2% and 10 seats; the Swedish People's Party 4.3 % and 10 seats, including one representative from the Åland Islands; and the Christian Democrats 4% and 6 seats. There are also two independents, who had separated from the Left Alliance. The KOK formed a coalition government with other groups, and Jyrki Katainen was chosen as prime minister.

15 LOCAL GOVERNMENT

There is an ancient and flourishing tradition of local self-government extending back to the 14th century. Until 2009, there were six provinces (lääni), each headed by a governor appointed by the president. One of them, Ahvenanmaa (Åland Islands), has enjoyed increasing autonomy, including its own elected provincial council, and a statute effective 1 January 1952 enlarged the scope of its autonomy.

Provinces were abolished by a new law that took effect on 1 January 2010. They were replaced by six regional administrative agencies, plus the government of the Åland Islands. The tasks formerly handled by provincial offices were reorganized under two new regional state administrative bodies: the Regional State Administrative Agencies (AVI) and the Centres for Economic Development, Transport, and the Environment (ELY).

Below the provincial level, the local government units in 2011 included 342 municipalities. The number of municipalities has fluctuated over the years, but the trend has been downwards. (In 1955, there were 547 municipalities.) Each local government unit is self-governing and has a popularly chosen council. Local elections are held every four years; being partisan in nature, they are regarded as political barometers. The functions of local government include education, social welfare, health, culture, utilities, public transportation, water and wastewater management, and collection of local taxes.

In 2012, a report commissioned by Transparency International Finland indicated that the government should take action to address the close ties between politicians and business interests especially at the municipal level. Although corruption is not a significant problem in Finland, common practices of so-called "old boys' networks" at the local level were seen as having the potential to lead to corruption.

¹⁶JUDICIAL SYSTEM

There are three levels of courts: local (district), appellate, and supreme. The municipal courts of the first instance are staffed in each case by a magistrate and two councilors. Each of the six appellate courts is headed by a president and staffed by appellate judges. In certain criminal cases these courts have original jurisdiction. The final court of appeal, the Supreme Court (Korkeinoikeus), sits in Helsinki.

The judiciary is independent from the executive and legislative branches. Judges, who must be lawyers and Finnish citizens, are appointed to permanent positions by the president and are independent of political control. Retirement is mandatory at age 70.

The local (district) courts deal with criminal and civil cases. The decisions of these courts can be appealed. The decisions of the courts of appeal, in turn, can be appealed to the Supreme Court. The Supreme Court decides which cases it will hear. Some cases may also be referred to the courts of the EU, since Finland must adhere to European Community law and the European Convention on Human Rights.

There are certain special courts, including the Market Court, the Labour Court, the Insurance Court, and the High Court of Impeachment.

Like most other Nordic judicial systems, Finland's constitution calls for a Parliamentary Ombudsman. The Ombudsman is an independent official from the legal field, who is elected by the parliament and charged with "overseeing the courts of law, other public authorities and public servants in the performance of their official duties as well as public employees and other persons in the exercise of public functions...In discharging his or her duties, the Parliamentary Ombudsman shall also oversee the implementation of Constitutional rights and international human rights." The Ombudsman and Deputy Ombudsman investigate complaints by citizens regarding the public authorities, conduct investigations, and may intervene in matters of his or her own initiative. This important institution assists citizens in navigating the often Byzantine bureaucratic maze of the social welfare state and provides greater accountability and transparency in the enormous Finnish public sector.

¹⁷ARMED FORCES

The International Institute for Strategic Studies reports that armed forces in Finland totaled 22,250 members in 2011. The force is comprised of 16,000 from the army, 3,500 from the navy, and 2,750 members of the air force. Armed forces represent .9% of the labor force in Finland. Defense spending totaled $3.7 billion and accounted for 2% of gross domestic product (GDP).

Finland's armed forces also provided observers and troops to three UN-led operations as of 2012. In addition, Finland participates in NATO- and EU-led operations in Afghanistan, the Western Balkans, and the Horn of Africa. As of 2011, there were 260 Finnish peacekeepers participating in these efforts, nine of whom were women. Finland planned to join a UN-led mission in Lebanon in May 2012.

¹⁸INTERNATIONAL COOPERATION

Finland has been a UN member since 14 December 1955; it participates in several UN specialized agencies, such as the FAO, World Bank, IAEA, ILO, UNESCO, UNIDO, and the WHO. Finland is also a member of the OSCE, OECD, the WTO, G-9, and the Paris Club. The country joined the European Union in 1995. In addition, Finland plays a role in the African Development Bank and Asian Development Bank, and is involved in a number of bilateral projects, primarily in African countries.

Officially neutral, Finland seeks to maintain friendly relations with both the United States and Russia, its powerful eastern neighbor. Finland has hosted many major meetings and conferences, including rounds I, III, V, and VII of the Strategic Arms Limitation Talks (SALT) between the United States and USSR (1969–72). In November 1972, the multilateral consultations on the Conference on Security and Cooperation in Europe (CSCE, now the OSCE) began in Helsinki. These initial consultations were followed by the first phase of CSCE at the foreign ministerial level and then by the third phase at the highest political level, culminating with the signing of the Final Act in Helsinki on 1 August 1975.

Finland has a close relationship with the other Scandinavian (Nordic) countries. The main forum of cooperation is the Nordic Council, established in 1952; Finland joined in 1955. A common labor market was established in 1954, granting citizens of member states the right to stay and work in any other Scandinavian country without restrictions. Finland also belongs to the Council of the Baltic Sea States (est. in 1992).

Finland is part of the Australia Group, the Nuclear Suppliers Group (London Group), the European Organization for Nuclear Research (CERN), the Nuclear Energy Agency, the Zangger Committee, and the Organization for the Prohibition of Chemical Weapons. In environmental cooperation, Finland is part of the Antarctic Treaty; the Basel Convention; Conventions on Biological Diversity, Whaling, and Air Pollution; Ramsar; CITES; the London Convention; International Tropical Timber Agreements; the Kyoto Protocol; the Montréal Protocol; MARPOL; the Nuclear Test Ban Treaty; and the UN Conventions on the Law of the Sea, Climate Change and Desertification.

¹⁹ECONOMY

The GDP rate of change in Finland, as of 2011, was 2.7%. Inflation stood at 1.2%, and unemployment was reported at 7.8%.

Finland has a highly successful, modernized market economy. The country's manufacturing sector is very strong. Finland's abundance of forests has made the country home to a highly developed and profitable timber and paper industry. Metals and engineering, including high-tech electronics such as mobile phones, have become main industries too. Exports account for 37% of the GDP. The agricultural sector is small, focusing primarily on dairy, meat, and grains. A member of the European Union since 1995, Finland was one of the few Scandinavian nations to adopt the euro as its currency.

At the end of World War II, Finland's economy was in desperate straits. About 10% of the country's productive capacity had been lost to the former USSR, and over 400,000 evacuees had to be absorbed. Between 1944 and 1952, Finland was burdened with reparation payments to the USSR, rising inflation, and a large population growth. However, the GDP reached the prewar level by 1947, and since then the economy has shown consistent growth.

The 1990s saw Finland develop one of the world's leading high-tech economies. Finland has one of the highest rates in the world for per capita Internet connections and mobile phone ownership. Chief among Finnish companies is Nokia, the world's leading producer of mobile phones.

In the early 2000s, the global economic downturn affected Finland. Demand for Finnish exports declined, and industrial production shrank for the first time in 10 years. In 2004, the government cut taxes and tempered inflation in order to prod private consumption and promote GDP growth. GDP growth was estimated at 1.6% in 2005. In 2007 GDP growth accelerated to 4.4%. In 2008, exports of goods and services accounted for 32% of Finland's GDP. As a result of the 2008–09 global financial crisis, Finland's export-driven economy suffered the deepest recession in 80 years—contracting at a painful 7.8% in 2009. In March 2010, Finland's finance ministry forecast the country's economy to expand at 1.1% in 2010, revising figures released in December 2009, when it predicted 0.7% growth for the year. By 2011, the economy was growing at 2.7%.

20 INCOME

The CIA estimated that in 2011 the GDP of Finland was $196.7 billion. The CIA defines GDP as the value of all final goods and services produced within a nation in a given year and computed on the basis of purchasing power parity (PPP) rather than value as measured on the basis of the rate of the exchange based on current dollars. The per capita GDP was estimated at $38,380. The annual growth rate of GDP was 2.7%. The average inflation rate was 3.4%. It was estimated that agriculture accounted for 3% of GDP, industry 29.2%, and services 67.8%.

According to the World Bank, remittances from citizens living abroad totaled $859.4 million or about $163 per capita and accounted for approximately .5% of GDP.

The World Bank reports that in 2009, household consumption in Finland totaled $130.6 billion or about $24,840 per capita, measured in current US dollars rather than PPP. Household consumption includes expenditures of individuals, households, and non-governmental organizations on goods and services, excluding the purchases of dwellings. It was estimated that household consumption was growing at an average annual rate of 1.8%.

As of 2011, the most recent study by the World Bank reported that actual individual consumption in Finland was 66.3% of GDP and accounted for 0.27% of world consumption. By comparison, the United States accounted for 25.44% of world individual consumption. The World Bank also estimated that 8.7% of Finland's GDP was spent on food and beverages, 15.2% on housing and household furnishings, 2.4% on clothes, 7.8% on health, 6.4% on transportation, 1.4% on communications, 6.5% on recreation, 3.2% on restaurants and hotels, and 9.3% on miscellaneous goods and services and purchases from abroad.

21 LABOR

As of 2011, Finland had a total labor force of 2.682 million people. Within that labor force, CIA estimates for 2011 noted that 4.4% were employed in agriculture and forestry, 15.5% in indus-

try, 21.3% in commerce, 13.3% in finance, insurance, and business services, and 28.5% in the public services sector.

From the mid-1960s to the mid-1970s, the rate of unemployment fluctuated between 1.5% and 4% of the total workforce. Since then, however, the unemployment rate has crept upward, reaching 8.5% in 2002. By 2005, the unemployment had fallen slightly to an estimated 7.9%, a figure around which it is has remained. As of 2011, unemployment was 7.7%.

The law provides for the right to form and join unions. Unions are not regulated by the government or political parties. Labor relations are generally regulated by collective agreements among employers, employees, and the government. Finns with college degrees are likely to belong to unions. As of 2011, overall union membership was reported to be around 80%. Approximately 70% of all highly educated citizens were members of one of the unions affiliated with Akava, the Confederation of Unions for Professional and Managerial Staff, made up of unions whose members hold university or professional degrees.

Workers have the right to strike, but such actions are not common. Strikes that may involve national security are put before an official dispute board that can make nonbinding recommendations to the cabinet as to the strike's duration.

Child labor regulations are strictly enforced by the labor ministry. Minors under the age of 16 cannot work at night or more than six hours per day. In addition there are occupational health and safety restrictions applied to child labor. The law does not mandate minimum wages, as it is established by industry in collective bargaining negotiations for each sector of the workforce.

The workweek is legally set at 40 hours with five days of work and premium pay for overtime, which is limited to 250 hours annually and 138 hours in any four-month period. Health and safety standards are effectively enforced.

22 AGRICULTURE

Roughly 7% of the total land is arable, and the country's major crops include barley, wheat, sugar beets, and potatoes. Cereal production in 2009 amounted to 4.3 million tons, fruit production 18,803 tons, and vegetable production 252,108 tons.

Finnish farming is characterized by the relatively small proportion of arable land under cultivation, the large proportion of forestland, the small-sized landholdings, the close association of farming with forestry and stock raising, and the generally adverse climatic and soil conditions. Farming is concentrated in southwestern Finland; elsewhere, cultivation is set within the frame of the forest. Small-sized farms have been encouraged by a series of land reforms, which began with the Lex Kallio of 1922.

23 ANIMAL HUSBANDRY

The UN Food and Agriculture Organization (FAO) reported that Finland dedicated 33,000 hectares (81,545 acres) to permanent pasture or meadow in 2009. During that year, the country tended 4.9 million chickens, 918,268 head of cattle, and 1.4 million pigs. The production from these animals amounted to 98,340 tons of beef and veal, 181,016 tons of pork, 90,960 tons of poultry, 45,171 tons of eggs, and 1.91 million tons of milk. Finland also produced 9,000 tons of cattle hide and 95 tons of raw wool.

24 FISHING

Finland had 3,881 decked commercial fishing boats in 2008. The annual capture totaled 158,399 tons according to the UN FAO. The export value of seafood totaled $17.22 million.

The most important catch is Atlantic herring. Other important species are rainbow trout, perch, pike, salmon, and cod.

25 FORESTRY

Approximately 73% of Finland is covered by forest. The UN FAO estimated the 2009 roundwood production at 36.7 million cu m (1.3 billion cu ft). The value of all forest products, including roundwood, totaled $11.1 billion.

Forestry in Finland has been controlled since the 17th century. Since 1928, the government has emphasized a policy of sustainable yields, with production reflecting timber growth. The strategy for the Sustainable Use of Renewable Natural Resources was completed in 1997, with the government approving the Biodiversity Programme for Southern Finland (Metso Programme), a forest protection action plan that extends to 2016, in March 2008.

The most important varieties of forest trees for timber are pine (47% of the total growing stock), spruce (34%), birch (15%), aspen, and alder. About 52% of the productive woodland is privately owned; 35% is owned by the state; the remainder (12%) is owned by companies, communes, and religious bodies.

Forestry accounted for about 24% of net exports. Over 60% of forestry product exports are sent elsewhere in Europe; Finland supplies Europe with about 10% of its demand for forest products.

26 MINING

Finnish mining companies were producing at a level to make Finland the leader among EU countries in the mining sector in 2012. Nickel mines in eastern Finland had an estimated life of 60 years as of 2012; that year, they were producing 2.3% of the world's nickel. The nickel mines also contain recoverable quantities of zinc, copper, and cobalt. In 2011 the Geological Survey of Finland (GTK) reported that Finland had discovered gold deposits in Lapland in northern Finland. Some tests have shown that ores mined in that region contain from 4 to as much as 28 grams of gold per ton. As of 2011 Finland had five gold mines in operation, but that number was likely to grow; about 200 gold deposits have been test-drilled in various locations, with those in Lapland appearing to be the most promising.

Outokumpu Oyj was the third-largest zinc metal producer in Europe (15% share of the market and 5% share of world zinc production). In 2009, Finland mined chromite, copper, nickel, zinc, feldspar, lime, nitrogen, phosphate rock, pyrite, sodium sulfate, limestone and dolomite, quartz silica sand, sulfur, talc, and wollastonite. The Kemi mine, on the Gulf of Bothnia near the Swedish border, was the only chromium mine in Scandinavia and one of the largest in the world, with estimated reserves of 150 million tons and an annual capacity of one million tons. Mine output of zinc in 2009 was 56,415 metric tons, down from 72,118 metric tons in 2007; feldspar, 45,000 metric tons, down from 52,000 metric tons in 2005; chromite (gross weight of ore, concentrate, and foundry sand), 247,000 metric tons, down from 614,000 metric tons in

2008 and copper (mine output), 13,000 metric tons. Exploration activities were focused largely on diamond, gold, and base metals deposits (sulfide zinc, zinc, copper, chalcopyrite, pyrite, sphalerite, and platinum-group metals, or PGM). Finland also had capacities to mine mica, phophate-apatite, quartz, and quartzite, and to mine and produce 8 million tons per year of apatite.

Government involvement in the mineral industry was considerably higher in Finland than elsewhere in the EU. State-owned companies such as Finnminers Group, Kemira Oyj, Outokumpu, and Rautaruukki Oy dominated the domestic minerals industry, while institutions such as the State Geological Research Institute and the State Technological Research Center were active in exploration and research.

27 ENERGY AND POWER

The World Bank reported in 2008 that Finland produced 77.4 billion kWh of electricity and consumed 86.9 billion kWh, or 16,518 kWh per capita. Roughly 48% of energy came from fossil fuels, while 21% came from alternative fuels and 26% came from nuclear power. Per capita oil consumption was 6,635 kg.

About one-fifth of the electricity used in Finland is imported. Finland has been part of a joint electricity market with other Nordic countries since 1998. Imports of electricity from Nordic countries include hydroelectric power from Norway and Sweden and electricity from Russia. (Most of Finland's own hydropower resources are located along the Oulu and Kemi rivers.) Since 2007, Finland has also imported electricity from neighboring Estonia. Finland's first four nuclear power reactors, located in two plants, were constructed in the 1970s and 1980s. After the accident at the Chernobyl nuclear power plant in Ukraine in 1986, the Finnish parliament voted against further nuclear power plant construction. However, in 2002, the parliament voted to authorize construction of a new nuclear facility. Officials predicted that the plant would begin operation in 2013.

28 INDUSTRY

Since the end of World War II, industry in Finland has grown steadily. According to Statistics Finland, industrial output grew by 2% in 2011 over 2010 levels. According to preliminary data, industrial output grew by just short of one per cent in 2011. Experiencing growth were the metal, food, general manufacturing, electrical and electronics, and mining industries. Forest-related industries declined over the same period. The most important industrial regions center around Helsinki, Tampere, Turku, Lappeenranta, Lahti, Jyväskylä, and the valleys of the Kymi and Kokemäki rivers, and coastal towns like Kotka, Rauma, and Pori.

The growth in Finnish industry, from 25.8% of GDP in 1990 to 28.4% by 2000 and 29.2% in 2011, is atypical for developed countries, where the services sector has tended to increase more than industry. In 2009, industry employed 16.7% of the labor force. Finland is a world leader in the making of cellular telephone handsets, paper machinery, medical devices, and instruments for environmental measurements. Nokia, the largest company in the country, controlled about 25% of the mobile telephones market in 2011. (Nokia is nearly 90% foreign-owned; a large share of its stock is owned by American pension funds.) Finland is a leader in Europe in biotechnology and has a growing software industry.

The electrical engineering industry's roots go back to the late 19th century: the company founded by Finnish developer Gottfried Strömberg, who built generators and electric motors, is now a profitable arm of the ABB Group, which is based in Zurich, Switzerland. Finnish companies such as Neste Oil (oil and gas), Stora Enso and UPM-Kymmene (basic materials), and Fortum (utilities) are among the country's largest employers. Although certain fashion (Luhta and Marimekko) and footwear (Pertti Palmroth) design companies are important, the previously strong textile manufacturing industry, which produced cotton, woolen, and other fabrics, has disappeared due to foreign competition.

29 SCIENCE AND TECHNOLOGY

Scientific research is carried out at state research institutes, private research centers, and institutions of higher learning. The Finnish Science and Technology Information Service reported that the government targeted funding for research and development at 4% of GDP in both 2009 and 2010. Tekes, the Finnish Funding Agency for Technology and Innovation, was established as the Technology Development Center in 1983 under the Ministry of Trade and Industry. It oversees technological research and coordinates international research activities.

The Academy of Finland (founded in 1947), a central governmental organ for research administration, reports directly to the Ministry of Education. It promotes scientific research and develops national science policy by maintaining research fellowships, sponsoring projects, and publishing reports. Finland has 13 universities offering courses in basic and applied sciences. The University of Helsinki operates a natural history museum that has zoological, botanical, and geological components. The principal learned societies, all in Helsinki, are the Federation of Finnish Scientific Societies (founded in 1899), the Finnish Academy of Science and Letters (founded in 1908), and the Finnish Society of Sciences and Letters (founded in 1838); preeminent in technological development is the Finnish Technical Research Center (founded in 1942) at Espoo.

30 DOMESTIC TRADE

Domestic trade is carried on through the customary wholesale and retail channels. Kesko is Finland's largest retailer. The S-Group consists of cooperative societies and SOK with their subsidiaries. The S-Group's largest retail area is the grocery trade. Valio, a dairy company, is the leading food business company in terms of net turnover.

The Finnish Franchising Association was founded in 1988. Franchising opportunities in Finland have been governed by EU legislation since Finland joined the EU in 1995.

As of 2010, approximately 85% of Finns were active Internet users and online shopping was increasing. As of June 2010, there were 4.3 million Internet users, up from 3.25 million in 2005.

Most retail sales are subject to a value-added tax (VAT) of 23% as of 2012.

Government and business office hours are generally from 9 a.m. to 5 or 6 p.m., Mondays through Fridays. Stores and shops are open from 9 a.m. to 6 p.m., Monday through Friday, and 9 a.m. to 3 p.m. on Saturday, but department stores and shopping malls stay open until 8 p.m. on weekdays and until 4 p.m. on Saturday.

Principal Trading Partners – Finland (2010)

(In millions of US dollars)

Country	Total	Exports	Imports	Balance
World	138,711.0	70,022.0	68,689.0	1,333.0
Sweden	17,858.0	7,947.0	9,911.0	-1,964.0
Russia	17,614.0	5,806.0	11,808.0	-6,002.0
Germany	17,013.0	7,018.0	9,995.0	-2,977.0
Netherlands	10,292.0	4,693.0	5,599.0	-906.0
China	6,523.0	3,502.0	3,021.0	481.0
United States	6,185.0	4,802.0	1,383.0	3,419.0
United Kingdom	5,499.0	3,321.0	2,178.0	1,143.0
France	4,844.0	2,366.0	2,478.0	-112.0
Belgium	4,261.0	2,022.0	2,239.0	-217.0
Italy	3,639.0	1,816.0	1,823.0	-7.0

(…) data not available or not significant.

(n.s.) not specified.

SOURCE: *2011 Direction of Trade Statistics Yearbook,* New York: United Nations, 2011.

Balance of Payments – Finland (2010)

(In millions of US dollars)

Current Account		**4,459.0**
Balance on goods		3,947.0
Imports	-66,186.0	
Exports	70,132.0	
Balance on services		197.0
Balance on income		2,522.0
Current transfers		-2,207.0
Capital Account		**212.0**
Financial Account		**-3,997.0**
Direct investment abroad		-10,647.0
Direct investment in Finland		7,072.0
Portfolio investment assets		-29,520.0
Portfolio investment liabilities		20,967.0
Financial derivatives		-430.0
Other investment assets		-25,284.0
Other investment liabilities		-10,218.0
Net Errors and Omissions		**-2,847.0**
Reserves and Related Items		**2,173.0**

(…) data not available or not significant.

SOURCE: *Balance of Payment Statistics Yearbook 2011,* Washington, DC: International Monetary Fund, 2011.

31 FOREIGN TRADE

Finland imported $80.79 billion worth of goods and services in 2011, while exporting $85.4 billion worth of goods and services. Major import partners in 2010 were Russia, 17.4%; Germany, 14.7%; Sweden, 14.5%; Netherlands, 8.2%; and China, 4.4%. Its major export partners that year were Sweden, 11.6%; Germany, 10.2%; Russia, 8.5%; the United States, 7%; Netherlands, 6.9%; UK, 4.9%; and China, 5%.

32 BALANCE OF PAYMENTS

Since the 1990s, Finnish households and businesses have become more cautious in spending, due to the deep recession in the early 1990s, a slowdown in the global economy in 2001, and the

Public Finance – Finland (2007)

(In millions of euros, central government figures)

Revenue and Grants	**70,680**	**100.0%**
Tax revenue	38,959	55.1%
Social contributions	21,595	30.6%
Grants	1,156	1.6%
Other revenue	8,970	12.7%
Expenditures	**61,219**	**100.0%**
General public services	8,614	14.1%
Defense	2,507	4.1%
Public order and safety	1,804	2.9%
Economic affairs	5,792	9.5%
Environmental protection	349	0.6%
Housing and community amenities	322	0.5%
Health	6,456	10.5%
Recreational, culture, and religion	711	1.2%
Education	5,757	9.4%
Social protection	28,907	47.2%

(…) data not available or not significant.

SOURCE: *Government Finance Statistics Yearbook 2010*, Washington, DC: International Monetary Fund, 2010.

2008–09 global financial crisis. The 2008–09 global financial crisis weakened foreign trade—diminishing both export markets and domestic demand—and sent the government budget into deficit. However, by 2010, the economy had begun to recover worldwide. Income from exports and an increase in household spending helped to stimulated economic recovery. In 2010 Finland had a foreign trade surplus of $6.8 billion, amounting to 4.6% of GDP. The recovery of foreign trade markets was viewed as essential for the economy to avoid a recession during 2012.

33 BANKING AND SECURITIES

The Bank of Finland is the fourth-oldest central bank in Europe. Established in 1811, its headquarters were established in Helsinki in 1819. It has offices in Kuopio, Tampere, and Oulu. Until the country adopted the euro as its currency in 1999, the bank regulated the Finnish markka. Because Finland uses the euro as its currency, the bank discount rate, the rate at which the central bank lends to member banks in the short term, is set by the European Central Bank (ECB). The Bank of Finland is a member of the European System of Central Banks.

At the end of 2010, the nation's gold bullion deposits remained constant, totaling 1.58 million fine troy ounces.

Leading deposit banks in Finland include: Nordea (Merita Nordbanken, the result of a merger between Merita and Swedish Nordbanken, Danish Unidanmark, and Norwegian Christiania Bank) and OKO Bank (the Cooperative Bank Group, the first bank in the world to offer online banking transaction services, in 1996). Until 2006, the Sampo Group, (the result of a merger between Sampo Insurance Company and the Leonia bank group) was also involved in banking; since then, it has been dedicated exclusively to insurance. Eight major commercial banks and 40 savings banks serve the country. Ten foreign banks had branches in Finland as of 2012.

An exchange at Helsinki (established in 1912) is authorized to deal in stocks. As of 2008, the name of the stock exchange is NASDAQ OMX Helsinki. As of 2012, there were 126 companies listed on the NASDAQ OMX Helsinki. In addition, as of 2006, there are two exchange-traded funds listed.

34 INSURANCE

Insurance in Finland is highly developed and diversified. There are 76 Finnish insurance companies (including 64 insurance associations), 11 of them engaged in life insurance, as of 2010. That year, there were 65 companies and 199 individuals registered as insurance brokers, and 24 foreign insurance companies maintained agencies in Finland. Workers' compensation, hunter's liability, workers' pension, nuclear liability, ship owners' and employers' liability, and automobile third-party insurance are compulsory. Other forms of insurance include fire, burglary, water damage, maritime, funeral, livestock, fidelity guarantee, and credit.

35 PUBLIC FINANCE

In 2010 the budget of Finland included $66.58 billion in public revenue and $65.33 billion in public expenditures. The budget deficit amounted to 2.5% of GDP. Public debt was 45.4% of GDP, with $370.8 billion of the debt held by foreign entities. Budget estimates are prepared by the Ministry of Finance and submitted to the legislature.

36 TAXATION

As of 1 January 2011 the standard corporate income tax rate was 26%, which is also the capital gains tax rate. Branches of foreign companies are taxed equally. The Lutheran Church and the Orthodox Church receive a share of the corporate tax. Withholding taxes, reduced or eliminated through double taxation treaties that Finland has with about 60 countries, are otherwise 28% on dividends and on income from royalties. Interest paid to resident persons received from debentures, bonds, and bank deposits are subject to a 28% withholding tax. Generally, nonresidents are exempt from this tax. Dividends paid from one resident company to another resident company are also exempt.

A new personal income tax schedule went into effect in 2011. Taxes are assessed in a progressive schedule up to 30% on taxable income over €68,200 (about $91,000 in early 2012). Local income taxes vary from 16.25 to 21.5% as of 2011, depending upon the taxing municipality. Also at the municipal level is a religious tax with proportional rates ranging from 1 to 2% of taxable income. In Helsinki, the municipal tax is 18.5%, the Evangelical Lutheran Church income tax is 1%, and the Orthodox Church income tax is 1.6%. The amount of national, local, wealth, and health insurance taxes are limited to no more than 60% of taxable income.

Main indirect tax is a value-added tax (VAT) with a standard rate of 23% as of 2012. A reduced rate of 13% is charged on basic foodstuffs and animal feed. Medicines, books, public transportation, hotel services, and cultural events at subject to an 8% VAT. Exports, the sale or rental of immovable property, insurance, healthcare, educational and financial/bank services are exempt.

37 CUSTOMS AND DUTIES

Finland, as a member of the European Union, allows imports from EU and EFTA countries to enter duty-free. Finland is also a part of the European Economic Area, an agreement that eliminates trade barriers in Europe. Finland complies with trade agreements the EU has made with non-EU countries. Customs duties are levied based on the goods' CIF value (cost, insurance, and freight) at the time and place of importation.

³⁸ FOREIGN INVESTMENT

Foreign direct investment (FDI) in Finland was a net inflow of $60.1 million according to World Bank figures published in 2009. FDI represented 0.03% of GDP.

Finland is open to direct foreign investment, and there is in general no ban on wholly foreign-owned enterprises. Mergers and acquisitions are governed in large part by EU competition regulations. The Åland Islands are an exception to these open investment practices: based on international agreements dating from 1921, property ownership and the right to conduct business are limited to only those individuals with right of domicile in the Åland Islands.

The corporate tax rate stood at 26% in 2012. The net wealth tax was abolished in 2006. The Finnish labor force is highly skilled and well educated, which makes for an attractive investment climate.

Finland consistency ranks high in Transparency International's corruption perception index report. In 2011 it tied with Denmark as the second least corrupt country in the world, after New Zealand.

³⁹ ECONOMIC DEVELOPMENT

On the World Bank's 2012 list, "Ease of Doing Business," Finland ranked at number 11, up from number 14 in 2011. Finland has recovered from the loss of the Soviet market in the 1990s, after the breakup of the Soviet Union. The successful development of high tech industries placed Finland in the forefront of the communications boom. Finland joined the EU in 1995; as of 2011 it was one of the EU's strongest economies.

Economic activity is spread between the north and the south of the country, particularly in the information and communications technology sector. Oulu in northern Finland is a technology center, for example, as is the Helsinki region in the south. Agricultural activity is concentrated in the southern part of Finland, although reindeer husbandry is focused in the far north.

Finland's educational system is one of the best among OECD countries, and its highly developed welfare state allowed the country to convert easily to the euro. Early retirement has depressed the labor supply, however, and the population is aging rapidly. This could lower potential economic growth in the future.

Finland has put relatively more funds into research and development than most other Western countries, as demonstrated by the success of the electronics and other high-tech industries. Tekes, the Finnish Funding Agency for Technology and Innovation, reported that in 2010, it invested €633 million (about $843.5 million), 60% of which was invested in private enterprise and 40% in projects carried out by universities and research institutes.

⁴⁰ SOCIAL DEVELOPMENT

Social welfare legislation in Finland is patterned largely on Scandinavian models. The system has evolved gradually in response to social needs. Major benefits include employees' accident insurance, old age and disability pensions (pension reform was enacted in 2002), unemployment insurance, sickness insurance, compensation for war invalids, and family and child allowances. Finland had a standardized national electronic data system in place, with data on all citizens, by 2011.

The first social welfare laws were implemented in 1927, with the most recent update in 2003. Family allowance payments are based on number of children and marital status of the parents. There are also birth grants, and child home care allowances for parents who stay home to care for a child under age three. A universal pension system currently covers all Finnish citizens who have lived in the country for at least three years and foreign nationals with at least five years' residence. Payments begin at age 65.

Women have a high level of education and hold a large number of elective political posts. Finland has a comprehensive equal rights law. However, women seldom hold high-paying management positions in the private sector. There are strict criminal penalties for violence against women, and there are many shelters and programs to assist victims.

According to reports published by the World Economic Forum (WEF), Finland has consistently ranked among the top countries of the world for gender equality. The WEF considers equity in several areas of life, including employment, politics, health, and education. Finland was rated as third in the world (after Iceland and Norway) for 2010.

Indigenous Sami (Lapps) receive government subsidies, which enable them to maintain their traditional reindeer herding lifestyle. Minorities' rights and culture are traditionally protected by law. However, increasing hostility toward immigrants in recent years prompted the passage of a new law designed to facilitate the integration of immigrants into Finnish society and the granting of political asylum.

⁴¹ HEALTH

According to the CIA, life expectancy in Finland was nearly 80 years in 2012. The country spent 8.8% of its GDP on healthcare in 2011, amounting to $4,310 per person. There were 27 physicians, 155 nurses and midwives, and 65 hospital beds per 10,000 inhabitants. The fertility rate was 1.73, while the infant mortality rate was 3.4 per 1,000 live births, one of the world's lowest. In 2008 the maternal mortality rate, according to the World Bank, was 8 per 100,000 births. It was estimated that 98% of children were vaccinated against measles. The CIA calculated HIV/AIDS prevalence in Finland to be about 0.1% in 2009. Healthcare, safe water, and sanitation are available to 100% of the population.

In Finland, the local authorities are responsible for the majority of health services. The entire population is covered by health insurance, which includes compensation for lost earnings and treatment cost. This program is run by the Kela, the Social Insurance Institution of Finland, which also provides social security benefits and unemployment benefits, financial aid for students, and other benefits. A small number of Finns supplement their government health insurance with private insurance. In 1991 a Private Health Care Act took effect to enhance the quality of services provided. Electronic Patient Records (EPR) have been in almost universal use in Finland since the mid-2000s.

Finns are generally active, with more than 60% of the population reporting that they exercise three or more times per week.

While female health is good by international standards, male mortality in the over-25 age bracket is much higher in Finland than in most industrial countries. Heart disease among men was high relative to other European countries, and diseases of the circulatory system caused about half of all deaths in the country, with cancer being the second leading cause of death. Life expectancy for men is 75.94 years, compared to 83.02 years for women. Tobacco consumption was on the decrease, however. Smoking declined from 1978 to 2005 among men, from about 35% to 28%. Smoking by women, after increasing to more than 20% in the 1990s, has remained relatively constant, at about 18%. The incidence of tuberculosis was 9 per 100,000 people in 2009.

In 1994, Finland became the first country to eradicate indigenous cases of measles, German measles, and mumps. The diseases have disappeared except for a small number of cases brought in from abroad.

^{42}HOUSING

Housing in Finland is relatively new in general; about 60% of all housing has been constructed since 1970. About 93% of all housing had central heating as of 2010. Housing differs by region, but the most common style of housing comprises apartment buildings, called blocks of flats in Finland. These represent 44% of all housing stock. Detached houses make up 44%. Houses are generally small by international standards. Two-thirds of all housing was owner-occupied as of 2010. The remainder is rental housing; half of all rental housing is known as "social housing," which means it is subsidized by the government. Overall, there is one housing unit for every two Finns. In most areas there is adequate housing, except for Helsinki, where there is a housing shortage, and the average cost of housing is higher than the national average.

At the end of World War II, Finland faced a critical housing shortage. Dwellings had been severely damaged during the war, and only a modest amount of new housing was built from 1939 to 1944. Some 112,000 dwellings were lost to the ceded territories, and homes had to be found for the displaced persons. Government participation was inevitable in this situation. Two measures passed in the late 1940s, the Land Acquisition Act and the Arava Law, made large-scale credit available on reasonable terms. In the period 1949–59, a total of 334,000 dwellings were built, including 141,900 supported by the Land Acquisition Act and 89,400 supported by the Arava Law.

The migration into urban centers that continued throughout the 1950s and 1960s resulted in a constant urban housing shortage. During the period 1960–65, the number of new dwellings averaged about 37,000 annually. To stimulate housing construction, the government passed the Housing Act in 1966 providing for increased government support. In the period 1966–74, a total of 466,900 dwellings were completed, of which 214,700 were supported by government loans.

From 1974 through 1985, another 558,000 units were added to the housing stock. The total number of permanently occupied dwellings in 2010 was 2,537,000.

^{43}EDUCATION

In 2008 the World Bank estimated that 96% of age-eligible children in Finland were enrolled in primary school; about 66% of age-eligible children were enrolled in some type of preschool program. Nearly all students complete their primary education. Secondary enrollment for age-eligible children stood at 96%. Tertiary enrollment was estimated at 94%. Of those enrolled in tertiary education, there were 100 male students for every 124 female students. Overall, the CIA estimated that Finland had a literacy rate of 100%. Public expenditure on education represented 5.9% of GDP. The student-to-teacher ratio for primary school was at 15:1 in 2007.

The public school system unites the primary school and lower secondary school into a compulsory nine-year comprehensive school, with a six-year lower level and a three-year upper level. Instruction is uniform at the lower level. At the upper one, there are both required and elective courses. The upper secondary school (gymnasium) and vocational schools continue with three-year programs.

In the twenty-first century, Finnish students were routinely scoring at or near the top among students worldwide on standardized tests, notably on the Program for International Student Assessment (PISA) test administered by the Organization for Economic Cooperation and Development (OECD). From 2006 to 2009, Finnish students ranked at the top in performance on this test and educators from around the world began studying the Finnish education system to try to learn from its success. The Finnish system has few standardized tests, more time for recess, and rigorous standards for teacher certification. In addition, teachers' salaries are relatively high, making teaching a desirable profession.

People's high schools and workers' academies are evidence of the widespread interest in popular or adult education. Although they are owned by private foundations or organizations, these ventures also receive state subsidies. Higher education falls into three categories: universities and institutions of university status; people's high schools or colleges; and workers' academies. Entrance to the universities is through annual matriculation examinations. There are about 10 universities offering bachelor's, master's, and doctorate degrees in a variety of areas of study. Finland also has seven universities offering degrees in specialized subjects, such as art, economics, theater, and music. These universities are owned and operated by the state. In addition, since the 1990s, the network of polytechnical schools, which offer applied science degrees, has grown to number nearly 30 as of 2012. The polytechnic schools are co-funded by state and local governments.

Among the best known institutes are the University of Helsinki (founded 1640), Turku University (founded 1922), the Hanken School of Economics, and the University of Tampere (founded in 1925). University study is free of charge.

^{44}LIBRARIES AND MUSEUMS

The largest library in Finland is the Helsinki University Library, with more than 2.6 million volumes; it acts both as the general library of the university and as the national library. The Helsinki University Library began operating as an independent institution, with its own administrative board, on 1 January 2010. As of 2012, the collection included 16,000 electronic journals and 260,000 e-books.

Next in size are the Helsinki City Library (a regional library with 1.76 million volumes) and the libraries at Turku University (1.9 million) and Åbo Academy (1.7 million). Libraries in Finland may be located through a web portal, libraries.fi, which was established in 1995 to offer links to public and specialized libraries throughout the country. There are several hundred research and university libraries in Finland, most of which are small. There are regional libraries, such as the Espoo City Library with 14 branch locations, throughout the country.

The number of museums has grown rapidly since World War II. There are over 200 museums and 19,100 monuments and historic sites throughout the country. Many museums, which are accessible only from May to September, are open-air, depicting local or rural history. Among the better-known museums are the Finnish National Gallery and the National Museum of Finland (both in Helsinki), the Gallen-Kallela Museum (Espoo), the Mannerheim Museum (Helsinki), Ainola, the restored home of composer Jean Sibelius (Jarvenpaa), the Seurasaari Open-Air Museum, part of a national park on an island off the coast of Helsinki, the Turku Art Museum, and the Runeberg Museum (Porvoo).

45 MEDIA

In 2010 the CIA reported that there were 1.25 million telephone landlines in Finland. In addition to landlines, mobile phone subscriptions averaged 144 per 100 people. There were 2 FM radio stations, 186 AM radio stations, and 1 shortwave radio station. Internet subscriptions stood at 84 per 100 citizens. Prominent newspapers in 2010, with circulation numbers listed parenthetically, included *Helsigin Sanomat* (472,666), *Ilta-Sanomat* (218,185), and *Aamulehti* (132,952), as well as 39 other major newspapers.

Broadcasting is run by Oy Yleisradio Ab, a joint-stock company of which the government owns over 90%, and MTV, a commercial company. Regular television transmission began in 1958. In 2007, analog television broadcasts were shut down and replaced by digital broadcasts. The broadcast and print media enjoy independence and support from the government, which abides by legally provided free speech and press.

In 2010, the country had more than 4.39 million Internet users in Finland. That year, the Ministry of Transport and Communications passed a law that required telecommunications providers to make high-speed Internet connections available to all citizens; Finland became the first country in the world to make broadband internet access a legal right.

46 ORGANIZATIONS

The cooperative movement is highly developed in Finland. Cooperatives have developed extensive educational and informational programs, including a lively cooperative press and many training schools. According to Pellervo, a confederation of 340 Finnish cooperatives, there are some 6.9 million memberships in cooperatives (the total population of Finland is 5.2 million). Cooperatives include the Cooperative Dairy Association, Meat Producers' Central Federation, Central Cooperative Egg Export Association, a wholesalers' cooperative for farm inputs and products, and the forest products cooperative. The cooperative S-Group has a membership comprised of 62% of Finnish households.

Occupational and trade associations are numerous. In the agricultural sector the most influential is the Central Union of Agricultural Producers, a nonpolitical farmers' trade union. The Federation of Agricultural Societies concentrates on advisory and educational functions. Important in industry and commerce are the Confederation of Finnish Industries, Central Federation of Handicrafts and Small Industry, Central Board of Finnish Wholesalers' and Retailers' Associations, and the Finnish Foreign Trade Association. Professional associations are available for a wide variety of fields. The Central Chamber of Commerce of Finland has its headquarters in Helsinki.

Cultural and philanthropic organizations are also numerous; among the most influential are the Finnish Academy, the Finnish Cultural Fund, and the Wihuri Foundation. Other national cultural organizations include the Fine Arts Association of Finland and the Finnish Society of Sciences and Letters. There are also associations for a variety of hobbyists.

As of 2011, 94% of all doctors in Finland were members of the Finnish Medical Association, which promotes research and education on health issues and works to establish common policies and standards in healthcare. There are also several associations dedicated to research and education for specific fields of medicine and particular diseases and conditions, such as the Finnish Heart Association and the Finnish Diabetes Association.

National youth organizations exist for a variety of interests, including Finnish 4-H Federation, National Union of University Students in Finland, Guides and Scouts of Finland, and chapters of YMCA/YWCA. Some youth organizations are linked to political parties, such as the Youth League of the Coalition Party. The National Council of Women of Finland, an umbrella organization for women's rights groups throughout the country, celebrated the 100th anniversary of its founding in 2011. The Finnish White Ribbon Union works with groups dedicated to helping women and youth who are victims of drug and alcohol addictions.

The Finnish League for Human Rights is based in Helsinki. The Red Cross, Amnesty International, and Greenpeace also have active chapters.

47 TOURISM, TRAVEL, AND RECREATION

The *Tourism Factbook*, published by the UN World Tourism Organization, reported 5.7 million incoming tourists to Finland in 2009; they spent a total of $4.14 billion. Of those incoming tourists, 5.2 million were from Europe. There were 120,175 hotel beds available in Finland, which had an occupancy rate of 37%. The estimated daily cost to visit Helsinki, the capital, was $410. The cost of visiting other cities averaged $318.

Finland offers natural beauty and tranquility in forest cottages and on the tens of thousands of islands that dot the 60,000 lakes and the Baltic Sea. Winter offers cultural events and cross-country skiing; winter festivals feature sled and skating competitions, ice castles, and crafts. Finland is the original home of the sauna, a national tradition. Popular sports include skiing, cycling, fishing, golfing, running, rowing, and wrestling. A valid passport is required. Visits of over 90 days require a tourist/business visa.

48 FAMOUS PERSONS

Great Finnish literary figures include Elias Lönnrot (1802–84), compiler of the national epic, the *Kalevala;* Johan Ludwig Runeberg (1804–77), the most important of the 19th-century Finnish-Swedish writers, known for his *Elk Hunters* and *Songs of Ensign Stål;* Aleksis Kivi (1834–72), the founder of modern Finnish-language literature and author of *The Seven Brothers;* Juhani Aho (1861–1921), master of Finnish prose; Eino Leino (1878–1926), perhaps the greatest lyric poet to write in Finnish; Frans Eemil

Sillanpää (1888–1964), a Nobel Prize winner (1939), known to English-language audiences through his *Meek Heritage* and *The Maid Silja;* Toivo Pekkanen (1902–57), whose novels portray the impact of industrialization on Finnish life; Mika Waltari (1908–79), member of the Finnish Academy; Väinö Linna (1920–92), a Scandinavian Literature Prize winner (1963) and author of *The Unknown Soldier* (1954); and the antiwar novelist and playwright Veijo Meri (b. 1928).

Finnish architects who are well known abroad include Eliel Saarinen (1873–1950) and his son Eero Saarinen (1910–61), whose career was chiefly in the United States; Alvar Aalto (1898–1976); Viljo Revell (1910–64); and Aarne Ervi (1910–77). Leading sculptors include Wäinö Aaltonen (1894–1966), Eila Hiltunen (1922–2003), and Laila Pullinen (b. 1933). Five representative painters are Helena Schjerfbeck (1852–1946), Albert Edelfelt (1854–1905), Akseli Gallen-Kalléla (1865–1931), Pekka Halonen (1865–1933), and Tyko Sallinen (1879–1955). Arts and crafts hold an important place in Finnish culture: leading figures are Tapio Wirkkala (1915–85) and Timo Sarpaneva (1926–2006). Finnish music has been dominated by Jean Sibelius (1865–1957). Also notable are the composer of art songs Yrjö Kilpinen (1892–1957), the composer of operas and symphonies Aulis Sallinen (b. 1935), and opera and concert bass Martti Talvela (1935–89).

Scientists of international repute are A. I. Wirtanen (1895–1973), Nobel Prize winner for chemistry in 1945; Rolf Nevanlinna (1895–1980), mathematician; Pentti Eskola (1883–1964), geologist; V. A. Heiskanen (1895–1971), professor of geodesy; Aimo Kaarlo Cajander (1879–1943), botanist and silviculturist; Edward Westermarck (1862–1939), ethnographer and sociologist; and Yrjö Väisälä (1891–1971), astronomer. Ragnar Arthur Granit (1900–1991) shared the Nobel Prize in physiology or medicine in 1967. Linus Torvalds (b. 1969) is a software engineer best known for initiating the development of Linux.

Outstanding athletes include Hannes Kolehmainen (1890–1966) and Paavo Nurmi (1897–1973), who between them won 14 Olympic medals in track. Another distance runner, Lasse Viren (b. 1949), won four gold medals at the 1972 and 1976 games. Other Olympic gold medalists include skier Janne Lahtela (b. 1974) and Nordic combined athlete Samppa Lajunen (b. 1979).

Major political figures of the 19th century were Johan Wilhelm Snellman (1806–81) and Yrjö Sakari Yrjö-Koskinen (1830–1903). Inseparably linked with the history of independent Finland is Marshal Carl Gustaf Emil Mannerheim (1867–1951), and with the recent postwar period President Juho Kusti Paasikivi (1870–1956). Sakari Tuomioja (1911–64) was prominent in UN affairs. President Urho Kekkonen (1900–86) was instrumental in preserving Finland's neutrality. Mauno Henrik Koivisto (b. 1923) served as president from 1982 until 1994. Martti Oiva Kalevi Ahtisaari (b. 1937), a former president (1994–2000) and UN diplomat, is noted for his international peace work; he became Finland's first Nobel Laureate when he was awarded the Nobel Peace Prize in 2008. Tarja Kaarina Halonen (b. 1943) became Finland's first woman president in 2000; she won reelection in 2006.

⁴⁹DEPENDENCIES

Finland possesses no territories or colonies.

⁵⁰BIBLIOGRAPHY

Annesley, Claire, ed. *A Political and Economic Dictionary of Western Europe.* Philadelphia: Routledge/Taylor and Francis, 2005.

Finland Investment and Business Guide: Strategic and Practical Information. Washington, DC: International Business Publications USA, 2012.

Lavery, Jason E. The History of Finland. Westport, CT: Greenwood Press, 2006.

Maude, George. *Historical Dictionary of Finland.* 2nd ed., Lanham, MD: Scarecrow, 2007.

Nordstrom, Byron J. *Scandinavia since 1500.* Minneapolis: University of Minnesota Press, 2000.

Opello, Walter C. *European Politics.* Boulder, CO: Lynne Rienner Publishers, 2009.

Sahlberg, Pasi. *Finnish Lessons: What Can the World Learn from Educational Change in Finland?* New York: Teachers College Press, 2011.

FRANCE

French Republic
République Française

CAPITAL: Paris

FLAG: The national flag is a tricolor of blue, white, and red vertical stripes.

ANTHEM: *La Marseillaise (The Song of Marseille).*

MONETARY UNIT: The euro (€) replaced the franc as the official currency in 2002. The euro is divided into 100 cents. There are coins in denominations of 1, 2, 5, 10, 20, and 50 cents and 1 euro and 2 euros. There are notes of 5, 10, 20, 50, 100, 200, and 500 euros. €1 = US$1.33810 (or US$1 = €0.747329) as of 2011.

WEIGHTS AND MEASURES: The metric system is the legal standard.

HOLIDAYS: New Year's Day, 1 January; Labor Day, 1 May; World War II Armistice Day, 8 May; Bastille Day, 14 July; Assumption, 15 August; All Saints' Day, 1 November; World War I Armistice Day, 11 November; Christmas, 25 December. Movable holidays include Easter Monday, Ascension, and Pentecost Monday.

TIME: 1 p.m. = noon GMT.

¹LOCATION, SIZE, AND EXTENT

Situated in Western Europe, France is the second-largest country on the continent, with an area (including the island of Corsica) of 547,030 sq km (211,209 sq mi). Comparatively, the area occupied by France is slightly less than twice the size of the state of Colorado. It extends 962 km (598 mi) N–S and 950 km (590 mi) E–W. France is bounded on the N by the North Sea and Belgium, on the NE by Luxembourg and Germany, on the E by Switzerland and Italy, on the S by the Mediterranean Sea, on the SW by Andorra and Spain, on the w by the Bay of Biscay and the Atlantic Ocean, and on the NW by the English Channel, with a total boundary length of 2,889 km (1,795 mi), of which 3,427 km (2,130 mi) is coastline.

France's capital city, Paris, is located in the north-central part of the country.

²TOPOGRAPHY

France, topographically, is one of the most varied countries of Europe, with elevations ranging from 2 m (7 ft) below sea level at the Rhône River delta to the highest peak of the continent, Mont Blanc (4,807 m/15,771 ft), on the border with Italy. Much of the country is ringed with mountains. In the northeast is the Ardennes Plateau, which extends into Belgium and Luxembourg; to the east are the Vosges, the High Alps, and the Jura Mountains; and along the Spanish border are the Pyrenees, much like the Alps in ruggedness and height.

The core of France is the Paris Basin, connected in the southwest with the lowland of Aquitaine. Low hills cover much of Brittany and Normandy. The old, worn-down upland of the Massif Central, topped by extinct volcanoes, occupies the south-central area. The valley of the Rhône (813 km/505 mi), with that of its tributary the Saône (480 km/298 mi), provides an excellent passageway from the Paris Basin and eastern France to the Mediterranean.

There are three other main river systems: the Seine (776 km/482 mi), draining into the English Channel; the Loire (1,020 km/634 mi), which flows through central France to the Atlantic; and the Garonne (575 km/357 mi), which flows across southern France to the Atlantic.

³CLIMATE

Three types of climate may be found within France: oceanic, continental, and Mediterranean. The oceanic climate, prevailing in the western parts of the country, is one of small temperature range, ample rainfall, cool summers, and cool but seldom very cold winters. The continental (transition) type of climate, found over much of eastern and central France, adjoining its long common boundary with west-central Europe, is characterized by warmer summers and colder winters than areas farther west; rainfall is ample, and winters tend to be snowy, especially in the higher areas. The Mediterranean climate, widespread throughout the south of France (except in the mountainous southwest), is one of cool winters, hot summers, and limited rainfall. The mean temperature is about 11°C (53°F) at Paris and 15°C (59°F) at Nice. In central and southern France, annual rainfall is light to moderate, ranging from about 68 cm (27 in) at Paris to 100 cm (39 in) at Bordeaux. Rainfall is heavy in Brittany, the northern coastal areas, and the mountainous areas, where it reaches more than 112 cm (44 in).

⁴FLORA AND FAUNA

The World Resources Institute estimates that there are 4,630 plant species in France. In addition, France is home to 148 mammal, 517 bird, 46 reptile, and 39 amphibian species. The calculation reflects the total number of distinct species residing in the country, not the number of endemic species.

France's flora and fauna are as varied as its range of topography and climate. It has forests of oak and beech in the north and

LOCATION: 42°20′ to 51°5′N; 4°47′W to 8°15′E. BOUNDARY LENGTHS: Belgium, 620 kilometers (387 miles); Luxembourg, 73 kilometers (45 miles); Germany, 451 kilometers (280 miles); Switzerland, 573 kilometers (358 miles); Italy, 488 kilometers (305 miles); Andorra, 60 kilometers (37 miles); Spain, 623 kilometers (389 miles); total coastline (including islands), 3,427 kilometers (2,125 miles). TERRITORIAL SEA LIMIT: 12 miles.

center, as well as pine, birch, poplar, and willow. The Massif Central has chestnut and beech; the subalpine zone, juniper and dwarf pine. In the south are pine forests and various oaks. Eucalyptus (imported from Australia) and dwarf pines abound in Provence. Toward the Mediterranean are olive trees, vines, and mulberry and fig trees, as well as laurel, wild herbs, and the low scrub known as maquis (from which the French resistance movement in World War II took its name). The Pyrenees and the Alps are the home of the brown bear, chamois, marmot, and alpine hare. In the forests are polecat and marten, wild boar, and various deer. Hedgehog and shrew are common, as are fox, weasel, bat, squirrel, badger, rabbit, mouse, otter, and beaver. The birds of France are largely migratory; warblers, thrushes, magpies, owls, buzzards, and gulls are common. There are storks in Alsace, and elsewhere there are eagles and falcons in the mountains with pheasants and partridge in the south. Flamingos, terns, buntings, herons, and egrets are found in the Mediterranean zone. The rivers hold eels, pike, perch, carp, roach, salmon, and trout; lobster and crayfish are found in the Mediterranean.

5 ENVIRONMENT

The World Resources Institute reported that France had designated 5.56 million hectares (13.75 million acres) of land for protection as of 2006. Water resources totaled 189 cu km (45.34 cu mi), while water usage was 33.16 cu km (7.96 cu mi) per year. Domestic water usage accounted for 16% of total usage, industrial for 74%, and agricultural for 10%. Per capita water usage totaled 548 cu m (19,352 cu ft) per year.

The Ministry for the Environment is the principal environmental agency. France's basic law for the protection of water resources dates from 1964. The mid 1970s brought passage of laws governing air pollution, waste disposal, and chemicals. In general, environmental laws embody the "polluter pays" principle, although some of the charges imposed—for example, an aircraft landing fee—have little effect on the reduction of the pollutant (i.e., aircraft noise).

Water pollution is a serious problem in France due to the accumulation of industrial contaminants, agricultural nitrates, and waste from the nation's cities.

Air pollution is a significant environmental problem in France, which had the world's 11th-highest level of industrial carbon dioxide emissions in 1992, totaling 397 million metric tons, a per capita level of 6.34 metric tons. The total level of carbon dioxide emissions in 2008 had dropped to about 377 million metric tons. Official statistics reflect substantial progress in reducing airborne emissions in major cities: the amount of sulfur dioxide in Paris decreased from 122 micrograms per cu m of air in 1971 to 54 micrograms in 1985. An attempt to ban the dumping of toxic wastes entirely and to develop the technology to neutralize them proved less successful, however, and the licensing of approved dump sites was authorized in the early 1980s.

France has both national and regional parks, as well as 8 biosphere reserves, 4 natural and mixed UNESCO World Heritage Sites, and 36 Ramsar Wetlands of International Importance. According to a 2011 report issued by the International Union for Conservation of Nature and Natural Resources (IUCN), threatened species included 9 types of mammals, 6 species of birds, 4 types of reptiles, 2 species of amphibians, 44 species of fish, 90 types of mollusks, 29 species of other invertebrates, and 32 species of plants. Endangered or extinct species in France include the Corsican swallowtail, the gray wolf, the false ringlet butterfly, the Pyrenean desman, and the Baltic sturgeon. Perrin's cave beetle and the Sardinian pika are known to be extinct.

6 POPULATION

The US Central Intelligence Agency (CIA) estimates the population of France in 2011 to be approximately 65,312,249, which placed it at number 21 in population among the 196 nations of the world. In 2011, approximately 16.8% of the population was over 65 years of age, with another 18.5% under 15 years of age. The median age in France was 39.9 years. There were 0.96 males for every female in the country. The population's annual rate of change was 0.5%. The projected population for the year 2025 was 66,100,000. Population density in France was calculated at 118 people per sq km (306 people per sq mi).

The UN estimates that 85% of the population lived in urban areas, and that urban populations had an annual rate of change of 1.0%. The largest urban areas, along with their respective populations, included Paris, 10.4 million; Marseille-Aix-en-Provence, 1.5 million; Lyon, 1.5 million; Lille, 1 million; and Nice-Cannes, 977,000.

7 MIGRATION

Estimates of France's net migration rate, carried out by the CIA in 2011, amounted to 1.46 migrants per 1,000 citizens. The total number of emigrants living abroad was 1.74 million, and the total number of immigrants living in France was 6.68 million. A new law on immigration and asylum was passed by parliament in May 1998. The law included amendments to include the French constitution's provision to protect "those fighting for freedom" and those threatened with inhuman and degrading treatment in their country of origin. France hosted some 6,300 Kosovar Albanians who arrived in 1999 under the UNHCR/IOM Humanitarian Evacuation Programme. Refugees enjoy all the rights of regular immigrants.

Populations of concern to the United Nations High Commissioner for Refugees (UNHCR) in France numbered 151,452. Minorities are not recognized in France. They are expected to connect with "the Indivisible Republic," which is entitled in the French constitution. Nevertheless, in Paris environs between April and August 2005, rioting and fires killed immigrants. Police evacuated run-down buildings in which asylum seekers and irregular foreigners had been living in crowded conditions.

During the unrest in North Africa in the spring of 2011, France showed little support to refugees, even sending Tunisian migrants found in the south of France back to Italy, where they had entered Europe. This action, backed by President Sarkozy's government, went against the European Union open border policy.

Under French citizenship laws, immigrants seeking naturalization are expected to prove a willingness toward cultural integration. This has become a notable issue among Muslim immigrants. In 2008, a Moroccan woman was denied citizenship when her radical practice of Islam was deemed to be incompatible with French values. In February 2010, a Muslim man was denied citizenship when it was determined that he compelled his French wife to wear a full veil in public. French authorities fined women for wearing the veil in public during 2011.

8 ETHNIC GROUPS

The French are generally derived from three basic European ethnic stocks: Celtic, Latin, and Teutonic (Frankish). There are also small groups of Flemings, Catalans, Germans, Armenians, Roma, Russians, Poles, and others. The largest resident alien groups are Algerians, Portuguese, Moroccans, Italians, Spaniards, Tunisians, and Turks. Thousands of Roma, members of a widely dispersed European ethnic group, have migrated to France from European

Union countries such as Romania and Bulgaria. As EU citizens, the Roma can move freely within the countries of the EU. However, French laws require that immigrants have work permits and be able to support themselves. In August 2010, France began deporting Roma who did not have such permits, repatriating them mostly to Romania and Bulgaria. In justifying the widespread surge of deportations, the French government also claimed that members of some of the Roma camps have been linked to illegal activities such as prostitution and child exploitation. The European Parliament condemned the deportations as illegal under the laws of the European Union, which ban discrimination against ethnic or national groups, but no action was taken at that time.

9 LANGUAGES

Not only is French the national language of France, but it also has official status (often with other languages) throughout much of the former French colonial empire, including about two dozen nations in Africa. In all, it is estimated that more than 300 million people know French as their official language or mother tongue. Moreover, French is the sole official language at the International Court of Justice and Universal Postal Union and shares official status in most international organizations. Other languages spoken within France itself include Breton (akin to Welsh) in Brittany; a German dialect in Alsace and Lorraine; Flemish in northeastern France; Spanish, Catalan, and Basque in the southwest; Provençal in the southeast; and an Italian dialect on the island of Corsica.

10 RELIGIONS

The constitution provides for freedom of religion and a separation of state and religion. As such, official statistics on religious affiliation are not recorded by the government. An unofficial survey in 2009 reported that about 64% of respondents were Roman Catholic, though only 4.5% claimed to attend church services on a regular basis. Some estimates have placed the percentage of nominal Roman Catholics at a much higher 88%. Muslims, the second-largest religious group in the nation, account for about 10% of the population, with most adherents North African immigrants or the descendants of such immigrants. In an informal 2009 poll, about 33% of Muslims surveyed claimed to have a high level of observance, including the recitation of prayer five times daily. Protestants, Buddhists, Jews, Evangelicals, Jehovah's Witnesses, Orthodox Christians, Scientologists, Mormons, and Sikhs each account for less than 5% of the population.

11 TRANSPORTATION

The CIA reports that France has a total of 1.02 million km (633,798 mi) of roads. There are 598 vehicles per 1,000 people in the country. Railroads extend for 33,778 km (20,989 mi). There are 475 airports, which transported 58.32 million passengers in 2009, according to the World Bank. France has approximately 8,501 km (5,282 mi) of navigable waterways.

France has one of the most highly developed transportation systems in Europe. Its outstanding characteristic has long been the degree to which it is centralized at Paris—plateaus and plains offering easy access radiate from the city in all directions, and rivers with broad valleys converge on it from all sides.

All French railroads were nationalized in 1938 and are part of the national rail network Société Nationale des Chemins-de-Fer

Français, 51% of whose shares are controlled by the government. Standard-gauge track accounted for nearly the entire system, with narrow-gauge right of way accounting for only 167 km (104 mi). Le Train à Grande Vitesse (TGV), the fastest train in the world, averaging 250 km (155 mi) per hour over most of its run, entered service between Paris and Lyon in 1981. TGV service between Paris and Lausanne became fully operational in 1985. The TGV set another world speed record on 18 May 1990 with a registered speed of 515.2 km/h (320.2 mph). The Paris subway (métro), begun in the early 1900s but has since been extensively modernized, and the city's regional express railways cover a distance of 472 km (293 mi). The métro has over one million passengers a day. Parisian bus lines carry about 800,000 passengers daily. Other cities with subways are Marseille, Lille, Lyon, and Toulouse.

Two high-speed rail tunnels under the English Channel link Calais and Folkestone, England (near Dover). The 50-km (31-mi) project by Eurotunnel, a British-French consortium, was completed in 1993. From these terminals, people can drive their cars and trucks onto trains, which can make the underground trek in about 30 minutes. Rail lines that run through the tunnel include Le Shuttle, which provides both freight and passenger service, and Eurostar, a high-speed, passenger-only line.

France, especially in its northern and northeastern regions, is well-provided with navigable rivers and connecting canals, and inland water transportation is of major importance. The French merchant marine, as of 2010, had a total of 167 ships with 1,000 GRT or over. Kerguelen, an archipelago in the French Antarctic Territory, offers an offshore registry program that is less regulatory than official French registry. The leading ports are Marseille, Le Havre, Dunkerque, Rouen, Bordeaux, and Cherbourg. Other important ports include Boulogne, Brest, Fos-Sur-Mer, Sete, and Toulon. More than half of freight traffic to and from French ports is carried by French ships.

France's national airline, Air France, is government subsidized. It operates regularly scheduled flights to all parts of the world. The Concorde, jointly developed by France and the United Kingdom at a cost of more than £1 billion, entered regular transatlantic service in 1976. Both British Airways and Air France ceased operations of Concorde passenger flights in 2003.

There are two major private airlines: the Union des Transports Aériens, which provides service to Africa and the South Pacific, and Air Inter, which operates within metropolitan France. The two international airports of Paris, Charles de Gaulle and Orly, both located in Paris, lead all others in France in both passenger and freight traffic.

12 HISTORY

Cave paintings and engravings, the most famous of them at Lascaux, near Montignac in the southwest, attest to human habitation in France as early as 30,000 years ago. Relics from the period between 4000 and 1800 BC include some 4,500 dolmens (structures consisting of two vertical stones capped by a horizontal stone), nearly 1,000 of them in Brittany alone, and more than 6,000 menhirs (single vertical stones), measuring 1.5–21.3 m (5–70 ft) in height and weighing up to 350 tons. There may already have been

2–3 million people in France when Phoenician and Greek colonists founded cities on the southern coast around 600 BC.

Detailed knowledge of French history begins with the conquest of the region (58–51 BC) by Julius Caesar. The country was largely inhabited by Celtic tribes known to the Romans as Gauls. Under Roman rule, the Gallic provinces were among the most prosperous and civilized of the empire. Roman roads, traces of which still may be seen, traversed the land. Numerous cities were founded. Latin superseded the Celtic dialects. Christianity spread rapidly in Roman Gaul after its introduction in the 1st century, and, by the time the empire began to disintegrate a few hundred years later, the Gauls had become a thoroughly Romanized and Christianized people. Early in the 5th century, Teutonic tribes invaded the region from Germany, the Visigoths settling in the southwest, the Burgundians along the Rhône River Valley, and the Franks (from whom the French take their name) in the north. The Germanic invaders probably never constituted more than a dominant minority of the population.

The first leader to make himself king of all the Franks was Clovis (466–511), who began his reign in 481, routing the last forces of the Roman governors out of the province in 486. Clovis claimed that he would be baptized a Christian in the event of his victory against the Visigoths, which was said to have guaranteed the battle. Clovis regained the southwest from the Visigoths, was baptized in 496, and made himself master of western Germany, but, after his death, the kingdom disintegrated, and its population declined under the Merovingian dynasty. In 732, Charles Martel was able to rally the eastern Franks to inflict a decisive defeat on the Saracens—Muslim invaders who already controlled the Iberian Peninsula—between Poitiers and Tours. He spawned the Carolingian family, as well as his grandson, Charlemagne (r. 768–814), who was the greatest of the early Frankish rulers. Ruling "by the sword and the cross," he gave the kingdom an efficient administration, created a noteworthy legal system, and encouraged the revival of learning, piety, and the arts. He added to the territories under his rule through wide conquests, eventually reigning over an area corresponding to present-day France, the FRG, the Low Countries, and northern Italy. On Christmas Day in the year 800, he was crowned emperor of the West and ruler of the First Holy Roman Empire by the pope in Rome.

After the death of Charlemagne, the vast Carolingian Empire broke up during a century of feuding, and the title of emperor passed to German rulers in the east. The territory of what is now France was invaded anew, this time by pagan tribes from Scandinavia and the north, and the region that later became known as Normandy was ceded to the Northmen in 911 by Charles III ("the Simple," r. 898–923). At the end of the century, Hugh Capet (r. 987–996) founded the line of French kings that, including its collateral branches, was to rule the country for the next 800 years. Feudalism was by now a well-established system. The French kings were the dukes and feudal overlords of the Île de France, centered on Paris and extending roughly three days' march around the city. At first, their feudal overlordship over the other provinces of France was almost entirely nominal. Some of the largest of these, like the Duchy of Brittany, were practically independent kingdoms. The Duchy of Normandy grew in power when William II, duke of Normandy, engaged in the Norman Conquest of England (1066–70) and became king as William I ("the Conqueror"), introducing

the French language and culture to England. The powers of the French monarchy were gradually extended in the course of the 11th and early 12th centuries, particularly by Louis VI, who died in 1137. The power of his son Louis VII (r. 1137–80) was challenged by Henry of Anjou, who, upon his accession to the English throne as Henry II in 1154, was feudal master of a greater part of the territory of France, including Normandy, Brittany, Anjou, and Aquitaine. Henry's sons, Richard and John, were unable to hold these far-flung territories against the vigorous assaults of Louis's son Philip Augustus (r. 1180–1223). By 1215, Philip had not only reestablished the French crown's control over the former Angevin holdings in the north and west but also had firmly consolidated the crown's power in Languedoc and Toulouse. Philip's grandson Louis IX (St. Louis), in a long reign (1226–70), firmly established the strength of the monarchy through his vigorous administration of the royal powers. The reign of Louis's grandson Philip IV ("the Fair," 1285–1314) marks the apogee of French royal power in the medieval period. He quarreled with the papacy over fiscal control of the French clergy and other aspects of sovereignty. His emissaries arrested Pope Boniface VIII and, after Boniface's death, removed the seat of the papacy to Avignon, where the popes resided under French dominance (the so-called Babylonian Captivity) until 1377.

It is estimated that, between 1348 and 1400, the population dropped from 16 million to 11 million, mainly from a series of epidemics, beginning with the Black Death (bubonic plague) of 1348–50. In 1415, Henry V of England, taking advantage of civil war between the Gascons and Armagnacs and the growing insanity of Charles VI, launched a new invasion of France and won a decisive victory at Agincourt. Charles VI (r. 1380–1422) was compelled under the Treaty of Troyes (1420) to marry his daughter Catherine to Henry and to declare the latter and his descendants heirs to the French crown. Upon Henry's death in 1422, his infant son Henry VI was crowned king of both France and England, but in the same year, Charles's son, the dauphin of France, reasserted his claim, formally assumed the royal title, and slowly began the reconquest.

Philip the Fair was succeeded by three sons, who reigned briefly and who left no direct male heirs, ending the Capetian dynasty. In 1328, his nephew Philip VI (in accordance with the so-called Salic Law, under which succession could pass through a male line only) mounted the throne as the first of the Valois kings. The new king's title to the throne was challenged by Edward III of England, whose mother was the daughter of Philip the Fair. In 1337, Edward asserted a formal claim to the French crown, shortly thereafter quartering the lilies of France on his shield. The struggle that lasted from 1337 to 1453 over these rival claims is known as the Hundred Years' War, though it actually consisted of a series of shorter wars and skirmishes punctuated by periods of truce. Edward won a notable victory at Crécy in 1346, in a battle that showed the superiority of English ground troops and longbows against the French knights in armor. In 1356, the French royal forces were routed by the Prince of Wales at Poitiers, where the French king, John II, was taken prisoner. By terms of the Treaty of Brétigny (1360), the kingdom of France was dismembered, the southwest being formally ceded to the king of England. Under Charles V (r. 1364–80), also called "Charles the Wise," however, the great French soldier Bertrand du Guesclin, through a tenaciously conducted series of skirmishes, succeeded in driving the English from all French territory except Calais and the Bordeaux region.

1422–1789

The first part of the Hundred Years' War was essentially a dynastic rather than a national struggle. The English armies themselves were commanded by French-speaking nobles and a French-speaking king. Although the legitimate succession to the French crown was the ostensible issue throughout the war, the emerging forces of modern nationalism came into play with the campaign launched by Henry V, whose everyday language was English and who, after Agincourt, became an English national hero. France owed no small measure of its eventual success to the sentiment of nationalism that was arising throughout the country and that found its personification in the figure of Joan of Arc. Early in 1429, this young woman of surprising military genius, confident that she had a divinely inspired mission to save France, gained the confidence of the dauphin. She succeeded in raising the siege of Orléans and had the dauphin crowned Charles VII at Reims. Joan fell into English hands and, at Rouen, in 1431 was burned at the stake as a heretic, but the French armies continued to advance. Paris was retaken in 1436, and Rouen in 1453; by 1461, when Charles died, the English had been driven from all French territory except Calais, which was recaptured in 1558.

Louis XI (r. 1461–83), with the support of the commercial towns, which regarded the king as their natural ally, set France on a course that eventually destroyed the power of the great feudal lords. His most formidable antagonist, Charles the Bold, duke of Burgundy, who ruled virtually as an independent monarch, commanded for many years far more resources than the king of France himself. However, after the duke was defeated and killed in a battle against the Swiss in 1477, Louis was able to reunite Burgundy with France. When Louis's son Charles VIII united Brittany, the last remaining quasi-independent province, with the royal domain by his marriage to Anne of Brittany, the consolidation of the kingdom under one rule was complete.

Under Charles VIII (r. 1483–98) and Louis XII (r. 1498–1515), France embarked on a series of Italian wars, which were continued under Francis I (r. 1515–47) and Henry II (r. 1547–59). These wars developed into the first phase of a protracted imperialistic struggle between France and the house of Habsburg. Although the Italian wars ended in a French defeat, they served to introduce the artistic and cultural influences of the Italian Renaissance into France on a large scale. Meanwhile, as the Reformation gained an increasing following in France, a bitter enmity developed between the great families that had espoused the Protestant or Huguenot cause and those that had remained Catholic. The policy of the French monarchy was in general to suppress Protestantism at home while supporting it abroad as a counterpoise to Habsburg power. Under the last of the Valois kings, Charles IX (r. 1560–74) and Henry III (r. 1574–89), a series of eight fierce civil wars devastated France, called The Wars of Religion. Paris remained a stronghold of Catholicism, and, on 23–24 August 1572, a militia led by the Duke of Guise slaughtered thousands of Protestants in the Massacre of St. Bartholomew. The Protestant Henry of Navarre was spared because of his royal status and eventually, on the death of Henry III, he acceded to the throne, beginning the Bourbon dynasty. Unable to capture Paris by force, Henry embraced Catholicism in 1593

and entered the city peacefully the following year. In 1598, he signed the Edict of Nantes, which guaranteed religious freedom to the Huguenots. With the aid of his minister Sully, Henry successfully restored prosperity to France.

Assassinated in 1610 by a Catholic fanatic after 19 attempts on his life, Henry IV was succeeded by his young son Louis XIII, with the queen mother, Marie de Médicis, acting as regent in the early years of his reign. Later, the affairs of state were directed almost exclusively by Cardinal Richelieu, the king's minister. Richelieu followed a systematic policy that entailed enhancing the crown's absolute rule at home and combating the power of the Habsburgs abroad. In pursuit of the first of these objectives, Richelieu destroyed the political power of the Protestants by strictly monitoring the press and French language through the Academie Francaise; in pursuit of the second, he led France in 1635 into the Thirty Years' War, then raging in Germany, on the side of the Protestants and against the Austrians and the Spanish. Richelieu died in 1642, and Louis XIII died a few months later. His successor, Louis XIV, was five years old, and during the regency of his mother, Anne of Austria, France's policy was largely guided by her adviser Cardinal Mazarin. The generalship of the prince de Condé and the vicomte de Turenne brought France striking victories. The Peace of Westphalia (1648), which ended the Thirty Years' War, and the Peace of the Pyrenees (1659) marked the end of Habsburg hegemony and established France as the dominant power on the European continent. The last attempt of the French nobles in the Paris Parliament to rise against the crown, called the Fronde (1648–53), was successfully repressed by Mazarin even though the movement had the support of Condé and Turenne.

The active reign of Louis XIV began in 1661, the year of Mazarin's death, and lasted until his own death in 1715. Louis XIV had served in the French army against Spain before his accession and married the daughter of the King of Spain in order to bring peace to the region, despite his love for Mazarin's niece. Assisted by his able ministers Colbert and Louvois, he completed Mazarin's work of domestic centralization and transformed the French state into an absolute monarchy based on the so-called divine right of kings. Industry and commerce were encouraged by mercantilist policies, and great overseas empires were carved out in India, Canada, and Louisiana. By transforming the nobles into perennial courtiers, financially dependent on the crown, the king clipped their wings. Lavish display marked the early period of his reign, when the great palace at Versailles was built, beginning the era of French Classicism.

The reign of Louis XIV marked the high point in the prestige of the French monarchy. It was a golden age for French culture as well, as French fashions and manners set the standard for all Europe. Nevertheless, the Sun King, as he was styled, left the country in a weaker position than he had found it. In 1672, he invaded the Protestant Netherlands with his cousin Charles I of England, defeating Spain and the Holy Roman Empire as well in 1678. In 1685, he revoked the Edict of Nantes, and an estimated 200,000 Huguenots fled the country to escape persecution. Whole provinces were depopulated, and the economy was severely affected by the loss of many skilled and industrious workers. Louis undertook a long series of foreign wars, culminating in the War of the Spanish Succession (1701–14), in which England, the Netherlands, and most of the German states were arrayed against France, Spain, Bavaria, Portugal, and Savoy. In the end, little territory was lost, but the military primacy of the country was broken and its economic strength seriously sapped.

The reign of Louis XV (1715–74) and that of his successor, Louis XVI (1774–93), which was terminated by the French Revolution, showed the same lavish display of royal power and elegance that had been inaugurated by the Sun King. At the same time, the economic crisis that Louis XIV left as his legacy continued to grow more serious. A series of foreign wars cost France its Indian and Canadian colonies and bankrupted the country, including the French and Indian War (1755–1760). Meanwhile, the locus of the economic power in the kingdom had shifted to the hands of the upper bourgeoisie in the Enlightenment, who resented the almost wholly unproductive ruling class that espoused Classicism. The intellectual currents of the so-called Age of Reason were basically opposed to the old order. Voltaire attacked the Church and the principle of absolutism alike; Diderot advocated scientific materialism; Jean-Jacques Rousseau preached popular sovereignty. The writer changed from a royal servant into a revolutionary force.

1789–1900

In 1789, faced with an unmanageable public debt, Louis XVI convened, for the first time since the reign of Louis XIII, the States-General, the national legislative body, to consider certain fiscal reforms. The representatives of the third estate, the Commons, met separately on 17 June and proclaimed themselves the National Assembly. This action, strictly speaking, marked the beginning of the French Revolution, although the act that best symbolized the power of the revolution was the storming of the Bastille, a royal prison, by a Paris mob on 14 July—an event still commemorated as a national holiday. With the support of the mob, which forced the king, his wife Marie Antoinette, and his family from the palace at Versailles into virtual imprisonment in the Tuileries Palace in Paris, the Assembly was able to force Louis to accept a new constitution including The Declaration of the Rights of Man and the Citizen, providing for a limited monarchy, the secularization of the state, and the seizure of Church lands. War with Austria, which wished to intervene to restore the status quo ante in France, broke out in 1792. The Assembly's successor, the National Convention, elected in September 1792, proclaimed the First French Republic. Louis XVI was convicted of treason and executed. The radical group of Jacobins under Maximilien Robespierre's leadership exercised strict control through committees of public welfare and a revolutionary tribunal. The Jacobins attempted to remake France in the image of an egalitarian republic. Their excesses led to a Reign of Terror (1793–94), carried out indiscriminately against royalists and such moderate republican groups as the Girondins. Manifold opposition to the Jacobins and specifically to Robespierre combined to end their reign in the summer of 1794. In 1795, a new constitution of moderate character was introduced, and executive power was vested in a Directory of five men. The Directory, weakened by inefficient administration and military reverses, fell in turn in 1799, when the military hero Napoleon Bonaparte engineered a coup and established the Consulate. Ruling autocratically as the first consul, Bonaparte established domestic stability and decisively defeated the Austrian-British coalition arrayed against

France. In 1804, he had himself proclaimed emperor as Napoleon I and, until his downfall in 1814, he ruled France in that capacity.

Capitalizing on the newly awakened patriotic nationalism of France, Napoleon led his imperial armies to a striking series of victories over the dynastic powers of Europe. By 1808, he was the master of all Europe west of Russia with the exception of the British Isles. That year, however, the revolt in Spain—upon whose throne Napoleon had placed his brother Joseph—began to tax French military reserves. Napoleon's ill-fated attempt to conquer Russia in 1812 was followed by the consolidation of a powerful alliance against him, consisting of Russia, Prussia, Britain, and Sweden. The allies defeated Napoleon at Leipzig in 1813 and captured Paris in the spring of 1814. Napoleon was exiled to the island of Elba, just off the northwest coast of Italy, and Louis XVIII, a brother of Louis XVI, was placed on the French throne. In March 1815, Napoleon escaped from Elba, rallied France behind him, and reentered Paris in triumph behind the fleeing Louis XVIII. He was, however, finally and utterly crushed by the British and Prussian forces at Waterloo (18 June 1815) and spent the remaining years of his life as a British prisoner of war on the island of St. Helena in the South Atlantic.

After the final fall of Napoleon, Louis XVIII ruled as a moderate and peaceful monarch until 1824, when he was succeeded by his brother Charles X, an ultra royalist. Charles attempted to restore the absolute powers of the monarchy and the supremacy of the Catholic Church. In 1830, he was ousted after a three-day revolution in which the upper bourgeoisie allied itself with the forces of the left. Louis Philippe of the house of Orléans was placed on the throne as "citizen-king," with the understanding that he would be ruled by the desires of the rising industrial plutocracy. In 1848, his regime was overthrown in the name of the Second Republic. Four years later, however, its first president, Louis Napoleon, the nephew of Napoleon I, engineered a coup and had himself proclaimed emperor under the title Napoleon III. The Second Empire, as the period 1852–71 is known, was characterized by colonial expansion and great material prosperity. The emperor's aggressive foreign policy eventually led to the Franco-Prussian War (1870–71), which ended in a crushing defeat for France and the downfall of Napoleon III. France was stripped of the border provinces of Alsace and Lorraine (which once belonged to the Holy Roman Empire) and was forced to agree to an enormous indemnity. A provisional government proclaimed a republic on 4 September 1870 and took over the responsibility for law and order until a National Assembly was elected in February 1871. Angered at the rapid capitulation to Prussia by the provisionals and the conservative National Assembly, the national guard and radical elements of Paris seized the city in March and set up the Commune. During the "Bloody Week" of 21–28 May, the Commune was savagely dispatched by government troops.

Democratic government finally triumphed in France under the Third Republic, whose constitution was adopted in 1875. Royalist sentiment had been strong, but the factions backing different branches of the royal house had been unable to agree on a candidate for the throne. The Third Republic confirmed freedom of speech, the press, and association. It enforced complete separation of church and state. Social legislation guaranteeing the rights of trade unions was passed, and elections were held on the basis of universal manhood suffrage. The Third Republic, however, was characterized by an extremely weak executive branch. A long succession of cabinets was placed in power and shortly thereafter removed from office by the all-powerful lower house of the national legislature. Nevertheless, the republic was strong enough to weather an attempt on the part of the highly popular Gen. Georges Boulanger to overthrow the regime in the late 1880s, as well as the bitter dispute between the left-wing and right-wing parties occasioned by the trumped-up arrest and long imprisonment of Capt. Alfred Dreyfus, a scandal in which Dreyfus's being Jewish was as much an issue as the treason he had allegedly committed. The eventual vindication of Dreyfus went hand-in-hand with the decisive defeat of the monarchists and the emergence of a progressive governing coalition with Socialist representation.

The 20th Century

During World War I (1914–18), the forces of France, the United Kingdom, Russia, and, from 1917, the United States were locked in a protracted struggle with those of Germany, Austria-Hungary, and Turkey. Although France, under the leadership of Georges Clemenceau, could claim a major share in the final Allied victory, it was in many respects a Pyrrhic victory for France. Almost all the bitter fighting in the west was conducted on French soil, and among the Allies French casualties—including nearly 1,400,000 military deaths—were second only to those sustained by Russia. The heavily industrialized provinces of Alsace and Lorraine were restored to France under the Treaty of Versailles (1919), and Germany was ordered to pay heavy war reparations. Nevertheless, the French economy, plagued by recurrent crises, was unable to achieve great prosperity in the 1920s, and the worldwide economic depression of the 1930s (exacerbated in France by the cessation of German reparations payments) was accompanied in France by inflation, widespread unemployment, and profound social unrest. Right- and extreme left-wing elements caused major disturbances on 6 February 1934. In 1936, the left-wing parties carried the parliamentary elections and installed a so-called Popular Front government under a Socialist, Léon Blum. Blum nationalized certain war industries, carried out agricultural reforms, and made the 40-hour week mandatory in industry. Increasing conservative opposition forced the Popular Front government from power, however, and in the face of the growing menace of Adolf Hitler's Germany, the leftists accepted the conservative government of Édouard Daladier in 1938. In a futile attempt to secure peace, Daladier acquiesced in British Prime Minister Neville Chamberlain's policy of appeasement toward Hitler. Hitler was not to be appeased, however, and when Germany invaded Poland in September 1939, France joined the United Kingdom in declaring war on Germany.

On 10 May 1940, the Germans launched a great invasion of the west through the Low Countries and the heavily wooded and sparsely defended Ardennes region. In less than a month, German forces outflanked the French Maginot Line fortifications and routed the French armies between the Belgian frontier and Paris. Marshal Pétain, the aged hero of World War I, hastily formed a government and sued for peace. With the exception of a triangular zone with its northern apex near Vichy, all France was placed under the direct occupation of the Germans. The Vichy regime ended the Third Republic and proclaimed a constitution based on the slogan "labor, family, fatherland," as opposed to the traditional republican "liberty, equality, fraternity." While the Vichy

government did its best to accommodate itself to the German victory, French resistance gathered overseas around Gen. Charles de Gaulle, a brilliant career officer who had escaped to London on 18 June 1940 to declare that France had "lost a battle, not the war." De Gaulle organized the Provisional French National Committee, and this committee of the Free French later exercised all the powers of a wartime government in the French territories where resistance to the Germans continued. The Free French forces took part in the fighting that followed the Allied invasion of North Africa in 1942, and, in 1943, a provisional French government was established at Algiers. Regular French units and resistance fighters alike fought in the 1944 campaign that drove the Germans from France, and, shortly after the liberation of Paris, de Gaulle's provisional government moved from Algiers to the capital. It was officially recognized by the United States, the United Kingdom, and the former USSR in October 1944.

France's postwar vicissitudes have been political rather than economic. De Gaulle resigned as head of the government early in 1946 over the issue of executive powers, and, in spite of his efforts, the Fourth Republic, under a constitution that came into effect in December 1946, was launched with most of the weaknesses of the Third Republic. Almost all powers were concentrated in the hands of the National Assembly, the lower house of Parliament, and there were numerous warring political parties.

Although the people of metropolitan France overwhelmingly approved de Gaulle's program for eventual Algerian independence, some French army officers and units attempted to overthrow the government by terrorism, which de Gaulle suppressed by temporarily assuming emergency powers. Peace negotiations were successfully concluded with Algerian rebel leaders, and Algeria gained independence on 1 July 1962. By then, nearly all of France's former African territories had attained independence. France has continued to provide economic assistance, and its ties with most of the former colonies have remained close. Almost continuous fighting overseas in French colonies, first in Indochina, which was lost in 1954, and later in Algeria, the scene of a nationalist rebellion among the Muslims, placed a heavy burden on France and led, especially after the Suez expedition of 1956, to disillusionment on the part of elements in the French army, which felt that its work was being undermined by a series of vacillating parliamentary governments. In May 1958, extremists among the French settlers in Algeria, acting with a group of army officers, seized control of Algiers. Sympathetic movements in Corsica and in metropolitan France raised the specter of a right-wing coup. The government found itself powerless to deal with the situation, and on 1 June, Gen. de Gaulle, regarded as the only leader capable of rallying the nation, was installed as premier. He ended the threat peaceably, and, in the fall of 1958, he submitted to a national referendum a new constitution providing for a strong presidency; the constitution won overwhelming approval. Elections held in November swept candidates pledged to support de Gaulle into office, and, in December 1958, he was officially named the first president of the Fifth Republic.

During the mid-1960s, de Gaulle sought to distance France from the Anglo-American alliance. France developed its own atomic weapons and withdrew its forces from the NATO command; in addition, de Gaulle steadfastly opposed the admission of the United Kingdom to the European Economic Community

(EEC or EC), of which France had been a founding member in 1957. The Treaty of Rome in 1957 created the original European Economic Community that consisted of Germany, Belgium, France, Italy, and The Netherlands and formed EURATOM, which created an open forum for scientific exchange and nuclear arms regulation on the continent.

The political stability of the mid-1960s ended in the spring of 1968, when student riots and a month-long general strike severely weakened the Gaullist regime. In April 1969, Gen. de Gaulle resigned following a defeat, by national referendum, of a Gaullist plan to reorganize the Senate and regional government. In June, Georges Pompidou, a former premier in de Gaulle's government, was elected the second president of the Fifth Republic. Between 1969 and 1973, the Gaullist grip on the French populace continued to weaken, at the end of which time de Gaulle was forced to accept the United Kingdom, Ireland, and Denmark into the EC and to work within the economic constraints of the "Snake Mechanism," which, starting in 1972, linked EC currencies. In 1974, after President Pompidou died in office, the founder of the Independent Republicans, Valéry Giscard d'Estaing, narrowly won a national runoff election (with Gaullist help) and became the third president of the Fifth Republic. Giscard strengthened relations with the United States but continued to ply a middle course between the superpowers in world affairs. The European Currency Unit (ECU) was born in 1979 from the economic stresses of the 1970s, leading eventually to the introduction of the common currency, the euro, in 2002.

Although Giscard's center-right coalition held firm in the March 1978 legislative elections, Socialist François Mitterrand was elected president in May 1981, and the Socialists captured a parliamentary majority in June. Mitterrand launched a program of economic reforms, including the nationalization of many industrial companies and most major banks. However, three devaluations of the franc, high unemployment, and rising inflation led to the announcement of an austerity program in March 1983. In foreign policy, Mitterrand took an activist stance, opposing the US attempt in 1982 to halt construction of a natural gas pipeline between the former USSR and Western Europe, committing French troops to a peacekeeping force in Lebanon, and aiding the Chadian government against domestic insurgents and their Libyan backers.

In July 1984, Mitterrand accepted the resignation of Prime Minister Pierre Mauroy and named Laurent Fabius to replace him, signaling his intention to stress economic austerity and modernization of industry. In foreign affairs, the government attempted some retrenchment during 1984, withdrawing peacekeeping troops from Lebanon and announcing a "total and simultaneous" withdrawal of French and Libyan troops from Chad. However, Libyan troops did not actually withdraw as envisioned, and fighting there prompted a return of French troops in 1986. A major scandal was the disclosure in 1985 that French agents were responsible for the destruction in New Zealand, with the loss of a life, of a ship owned by an environmentalist group protesting French nuclear tests in the South Pacific.

In March 1986 elections, the Socialists lost their majority in the National Assembly, and Mitterrand had to appoint a conservative prime minister, Jacques Chirac, to head a new center-right cabinet. This unprecedented "cohabitation" between a Socialist president and a conservative government led to legislative conflict, as Chirac, with backing from the National Assembly, successfully instituted a program, opposed by Mitterrand, to denationalize 65 state-owned companies. Chirac encountered less success late in 1986 as he sought to deal with a wave of terrorist violence in Paris. In 1988, Chirac challenged Mitterrand for the presidency, but in the May runoff election, Mitterrand won a commanding 54% of the vote and a second seven-year term. Chirac then resigned, and Mitterand formed a minority Socialist government.

Economic and social problems as well as government scandals strained relations between the Socialist Mitterrand, the Conservative PM Eduard Balladur in the second cohabitation, and a center-right government. Unemployment remained high, and new legislation increased police powers to combat illegal immigration.

In May 1995, Jacques Chirac was elected president, winning 52.64% of the popular vote, compared to 47.36% for socialist Lionel Jospin, and Alain Juppé was appointed prime minister. The National Assembly had elected an RPR-Gaullist majority in 1993, setting the country firmly in the grips of the type of conservatism that had been ousting socialists and Social Democrats in much of Western Europe during the mid-to-late 1980s. Chirac immediately set about instituting austerity measures to rein in government spending in the hope of meeting certain rigid monetary guidelines so that France would be ready to join the European Monetary Union (EMU) in 1999. The EMU would create a single European currency, the "euro," to replace member countries' individual currencies. The idea of a monetary union had never been widely popular in France, and the Maastricht Treaty, which set down conditions for EMU membership passed by only a slim margin.

Many of Chirac's attempts to reduce public spending and limit—or even erode—France's welfare state met with stern resistance. With the signing of the Amsterdam Treaty of 1997, Chirac sensed the need for a reaffirmation of his commitment to meet austerity measures for EMU membership. Chirac dissolved the National Assembly, calling for parliamentary elections in 1997, one year earlier than constitutionally mandated. In doing so, the French president believed he would demonstrate that the majority of the population believed in responsible cutbacks in government spending and anti-inflammatory monetary policy, despite the adverse effects they might have on the country's already quite high inflation. In May and June of 1997, elections were held, and Chirac's plan badly backfired, with the Socialists winning a commanding majority, along with the Communists. After the elections, a demoralized Chirac appointed Socialist leader Lionel Jospin prime minister, beginning the third cohabitation government. Jospin, a halfhearted supporter of monetary union, called for a program of increased government spending to create 700,000 jobs, a reduction in the work week from 39 to 35 hours, and made a broad pledge to protect the welfare state. The euro was successfully launched in 1999, and the currency was circulated in January 2002.

Presidential elections were held on 21 April and 5 May 2002. In the first round, Chirac won 19.9% of the vote, National Front leader Jean-Marie Le Pen came in second with 16.9%, and Prime Minister Jospin finished third with 16.2% of the vote. The strong showing by Le Pen sent shock waves throughout France and Europe, as his extreme right-wing, anti-immigrant, xenophobic party demonstrated its popularity. Jospin announced he was retiring from politics; for the first time since 1969, the Socialists did not have a candidate in a presidential runoff, marking a major defeat for the French left.

In the second round of voting, Chirac overwhelmingly defeated Le Pen, taking 82.2% of the vote to Le Pen's 17.8%. It was the largest majority since direct presidential elections were first introduced, and was preceded by a major popular campaign against Le Pen. Chirac named centrist Jean-Pierre Raffarin to be prime minister. In elections for the National Assembly held in June 2002, the center-right coalition Union for the Presidential Majority (consisting of Chirac's Rally for the Republic and the Liberal Democracy party and created in the wake of the first round on the ashes of the short-lived Union en Mouvement) won a landslide victory, taking 33.7% of the vote and 357 of 577 seats in parliament. The Socialist Party finished second with 24.1% and 140 seats. Le Pen's National Front failed to win a single seat.

Jean-Pierre Raffarin started out by governing through ordinances, and eventually obtained a majority from his party that was large enough to carry him through the legislative elections. His political line exhibited a peculiar communicative style and enforced reforms with unflagging certainty; his adversaries would term this style "neo-liberalism." In 2003 alone, he led policies to reform the retirement system and to regionalize most administrative offices that were centralized in Paris, despite strong social unrest and demonstrations: in the summer of 2003, civil servants went on strike against the reform of the retirement benefits system, and part-time workers in entertainment went on strike, demanding higher salaries and improved benefits. Raffarin's popularity rate began to plummet; this, combined with the sharp electoral defeat sustained at the regional elections, was blamed on his social policies. As a consequence, the prime minister dissolved the government and handpicked Jean-Louis Borloo as minister of social affairs. However, the prime minister had to handle both the former's social agenda—sustaining rent-controlled housing, backed up by President Chirac—and then-finance minister Nicolas Sarkozy's extremely conservative managing of the finances. Jean-Pierre Raffarin then faced even more criticism, especially from Dominique de Villepin.

Raffarin's term of office came to a brisk end after the "no" vote to the referendum, held on 29 May 2005, on whether to adopt the project of the European Constitutional Treaty. He offered to resign on 31 May 2005 and was immediately replaced by Dominique de Villepin.

Dominique de Villepin had been named minister of foreign affairs in 2002, upon the reelection of President Chirac. In 2002–03, France was confronted with a major foreign policy dilemma. Throughout 2002, the United States and United Kingdom were committing troops to the Persian Gulf region, positioning themselves against Iraq and accusing its leader, Saddam Hussein, of possessing weapons of mass destruction (WMD). In the event that Iraq would not disarm itself of any WMD it might possess, it was evident that the United States and United Kingdom might use those troops to force a regime change in Iraq. The United Nations (UN) Security Council unanimously passed Resolution 1441 on 8 November 2002, calling for Iraq to disarm itself of chemical, biological, and nuclear weapons or weapons capabilities, to allow the immediate return of UN and International Atomic Energy Agency (IAEA) weapons inspectors, and to comply with all previous UN resolutions regarding the country since the end of the Gulf War in 1991. The United States and United Kingdom indicated that if Iraq would not comply with the resolution, "serious consequences" might result, meaning military action. The other three permanent members of the Security Council, France, Russia, and China, expressed their reservations with that position. France was the most vocal opponent of war and threatened to use its veto power in the Security Council if another Security Council resolution authorizing the use of force was called for. The United States and United Kingdom abandoned diplomatic efforts at conflict resolution in March 2003, and on 19 March, the coalition went to war in Iraq. Once coalition forces defeated Iraq and plans for reconstruction of the country were being discussed in April, France stressed the need for a strong role to be played by the UN in a postwar Iraq.

In May 2005, France, in a referendum, rejected the European Union constitution. It was a blow to the movement for further European integration. The "no" vote was followed by a rejection of the constitution by the Netherlands, dooming for the immediate future an EU constitution. The outcome of the referendum led to a political shakeup: Prime Minister Jean Pierre Raffarin resigned.

On 31 May 2005, Dominique de Villepin was chosen by President Chirac to become prime minister. In his inaugural speech, he gave himself 100 days to earn the trust of the French people and to give France its confidence back. He was increasingly perceived as a potential presidential candidate, an opinion reinforced by his acting as head of state during the cabinet meeting held on 7 September 2005 and for the 60th session of the UN General Assembly held on 14–15 September 2005 while President Chirac suffered from a cerebral vascular complication.

The eruption of rioting in many parts of France in fall 2005 posed the most serious challenge to government authority since the student riots that took place in Paris in 1968. The government imposed a state of emergency. Thousands of vehicles were set on fire in nearly 300 towns; more than 1,500 people had been arrested by mid-November 2005 when the violence began to subside. Areas with large African and Arab communities were most affected (France has Europe's largest Muslim population and over half the country's prison population is Muslim), where anger among many immigrant families over unemployment and discrimination has long been simmering. France's youth unemployment rate in 2005 was 23%, one of Europe's worst, and in "sensitive urban zones," youth unemployment reached 40%. The unrest caused politicians to rethink their social and economic policies. In June 2006, the upper house of parliament passed a bill setting strict new limits on immigration. The rules make it harder for low-skilled migrants to settle in France.

Conservative Nicolas Sarkozy defeated Socialist Ségolène Royal in the second round of presidential voting on 6 May 2007, 53% to 47%. The first round of voting had been held on 22 April 2007, but no candidate obtained an absolute majority. Sarkozy is the first French president born after World War II, an important generational change. In June 2007, the UMP was victorious in parliamentary elections, but with a reduced majority. The party maintained it still had a mandate to carry out its proposed reforms. Sarkozy fulfilled a promise to appoint women to 50% of the posts in the new cabinet, and brought in people from across the political divide. In his first few months as president, Sarkozy was characterized as something of a hyperactive president, keen to re-involve France in world affairs and reestablish good relations with the United States. He spent his August 2007 summer vacation in New Hampshire and visited President George W. Bush at the Bush retreat at Kennebunkport, Maine.

During the campaign, Sarkozy promised reforms to stimulate France's sluggish economic and address high unemployment. In September 2007, the government proposed a series of incentives for employers to allow overtime and proposed tax cuts for those in the highest wage categories. However, work rules and benefits are well-ingrained in France, and civil servants staged protests against proposed plans to cut pay rates in November 2007.

France entered a recession in early 2009 as a result of the global economic crisis. In January 2009, the government announced a $33 billion stimulus package to revitalize the economy. In 2010, the economy recovered somewhat, recording a growth rate of 1.5%. In August 2011, in response to growing concern over the nation's debt, the government agreed to levy an additional 3% annual income tax on French citizens making more than €500,000 ($721,000) per year. In November 2011, the government announced additional budget changes that could save the nation $9.6 billion in 2012 and $15.9 billion in 2013. Measures designed to reduce the deficit and protect the nation's credit rating included an increase in the value-added tax from 5.5% to 7% and accelerated pension reform.

In March 2009, the government announced its intentions to rejoin the NATO integrated military structure. While France has been a member of NATO since 1949, the nation withdrew its participation in the integrated military structure in 1966, claiming a desire for greater military independence.

Relations between France and Turkey were strained at the end of 2011 and into 2012 as the National Assembly of France considered a bill to make public denial of the Armenian genocide illegal. The facts concerning the Armenian genocide of 1915–16 at the hands of the Ottoman Turks have been somewhat controversial. According to some sources, nearly 1.5 million Armenians were killed or died from starvation and disease during this period of persecution by the Turks. The Turkish government rejects the term genocide and claims that only about 300,000 were killed during the time period. More than twenty countries have passed laws formally recognizing the actions of the Turks as genocide, including France, which passed its law in 2001. The bill was approved by the National Assembly in December 2011 and by the Senate in January 2012. As a result of the approval from the lower house, the Turkish government recalled its ambassador from France and accused the French parliament of fostering Islamophobia and discrimination against Turks. The French representative who authored the bill stated that it simply reflects European law, which calls for sanctions on those who deny the existence of the genocide. A similar law concerning those who publicly deny the Holocaust was passed in France in 1990. The bill was expected to be signed into law before the end of February 2012 but, on 28 February, the Constitutional Court of France ruled that the law was unconstitutional due to its infringement on free-speech rights. Sarkozy pushed parliament to draft a new Armenian genocide law, while Turkey, which applauded the ruling, announced that it would consider resuming foreign relations.

¹³GOVERNMENT

Under the constitution of the Fifth Republic (1958), as subsequently amended, the president of the republic is elected for a five-year term (changed from a seven-year term following a referendum on 24 September 2000) by direct universal suffrage. If no candidate receives an absolute majority of the votes cast, a runoff election is held between the two candidates having received the most votes. If the presidency falls vacant, the president of the Senate assumes the office until a new election can be held within 20–35 days. The president appoints the prime minister and, on the prime minister's recommendation, the other members of the cabinet. The president has the power to dissolve the National Assembly, in which event new elections must be held in 20–40 days. When the national sovereignty is gravely menaced, the president is empowered to take special measures after consulting the premier and other appropriate officials. The National Assembly, however, may not be dissolved during the exercise of exceptional powers. The president promulgates laws approved by the legislature, has the right of pardon, and is commander of the armed forces.

The bicameral parliament consists of two houses, the National Assembly and the Senate. Under a system enacted in 1986, the National Assembly is composed of 577 deputies, each representing an electoral district. If no candidate receives a clear majority, there is a runoff among those receiving at least 12.5% of the vote; a plurality then suffices for election. All citizens aged 18 or over are eligible to vote.

The deputies' term of office, unless the Assembly is dissolved, is five years. The Senate consisted of 348 members in 2011. Of the total, 328 represented metropolitan France; the remainder represent French territories and nationals living abroad. According to the provisions of the French constitutional reform, starting in 2008, the members of the Senate were to be indirectly elected by an electoral college to serve six-year terms with half elected every three years.

To become law, a measure must be passed by parliament. Parliament also has the right to develop in detail and amplify the list of matters on which it may legislate by passing an organic law to that effect. Regular parliamentary sessions occur once a year, lasting nine months each (amended in 1995 from two shorter sessions a year). A special session may be called by the prime minister or at the request of a majority of the National Assembly. Bills, which may be initiated by the executive, are introduced in either house, except finance bills, which must be introduced in the Assembly. These proceedings are open to the public, aired on television, and reported.

The prime minister and the cabinet formulate national policy and execute the laws. No one may serve concurrently as a member of parliament and a member of the executive. Under certain circumstances, an absolute majority in the National Assembly may force the executive to resign by voting a motion of censure. Under a 1993 law, members of the government are liable for actions performed in office deemed to be crimes or misdemeanors, and tried by the Court of Justice.

¹⁴POLITICAL PARTIES

French political life has long been ruled both by considerations of political theory and by the demands of political expediency. Traditional issues such as the separation of church and state help to distinguish between right and left, but otherwise the lines separating all but the extremist political parties are difficult to draw. One result of this has been the proliferation of political parties; another, the assumption by political parties of labels that seldom indicate any clear-cut platform or policy.

Broadly, since the late 1950s, French politics has been dominated by four political groups: the Gaullists, an independent center-right coalition, the Socialists, and the Communists. After the parliamentary elections of 23 and 30 November 1958, the first to be held under the constitution of the Fifth Republic, the largest single group in the Assembly was the Union for the New Republic (UNR), which stood for the policies of Gen. de Gaulle, elected president of the republic for a seven-year term in 1958. Independents of the right were the second-largest group, while the Christian Socialists (Mouvement Républicain Populaire) and several leftist groups followed. Only 16 members were elected by the center groups, and only 10 were Communists.

In the November 1962 elections, the Gaullist UNR scored an unparalleled victory, polling 40.5% of the total votes cast. As a result of the elections, several old parliamentary groups disappeared, and new groups emerged: the Democratic Center (Centre Démocratique) with 55 seats; the Democratic Rally (Rassemblement Démocratique), 38 seats; and the Independent Republicans (Républicains Indépendants–RI), 33 seats. The UNR and the Democratic Workers Union (Union Démocratique du Travail–UDT), left-wing Gaullists, agreed to a full merger of their parties and together controlled 219 seats.

In the first presidential elections held by direct universal suffrage in December 1965, President de Gaulle was reelected on the second ballot with 55.2% of the total vote. In the March 1967 general elections, the UNR-UDT gained 246 seats against 116 for the Socialists and 73 for the Communists. Following nationwide strikes and civil disturbances by workers and students in the spring of 1968, new parliamentary elections were held in June, in which de Gaulle's supporters won a sweeping victory.

The Union for the Defense of the Republic (Union pour la Défense de la République–UDR) emerged as the new official Gaullist organization. Political movements of the center joined to form the Progress and Modern Democracy group (Centre-PDM), while Socialists and the democratic left united under the Federation of the Left. Of the 487 Assembly seats, the UDR won 292 seats; RI, 61; Federation of the Left, 57; Communists, 34; Centre-PDM, 33; and independents, 10.

On 28 April 1969, following the defeat in a national referendum of a Gaullist plan to reorganize the Senate and regional government, President de Gaulle resigned. He was succeeded by former premier Georges Pompidou, a staunch Gaullist, who won 58% of the vote in elections held on 15 June 1969. During the Pompidou administration, Gaullist control was weakened by an alliance between the Communist and Socialist parties. In March 1973 elections, the Gaullist UDR lost 109 seats, falling to 183 of the 490 seats at stake. The Communists and Socialists increased their representation to 72 and 103, respectively. The remaining seats were won by the RI (55) and by centrists, reformists, and unaffiliated candidates (77).

On 2 April 1974, President Pompidou died. In elections held on 5 May, Gaullist candidate and former premier Jacques Chaban-

Delmas was defeated, receiving only 15% of the votes cast. The leader of the leftist coalition, François Mitterrand, received over 11 million votes, and Valéry Giscard d'Estaing, the leader of the RI, over 8 million. However, as neither had won a majority, a run-off election was held on 19 May. Giscard, with the help of Gaullist votes, defeated Mitterrand by a margin of 50.7% to 49.3%. Jacques Chirac of the UDR was made premier, with a cabinet made up mainly of RI and UDR members.

A new Gaullist party, the Rally for the Republic (Rassemblement pour la République–RPR), founded by Chirac in 1976, received 26.1% of the vote in the second round of the 1978 legislative elections, winning 154 seats in the National Assembly. That year, the centrist parties had formed the Union for French Democracy (Union pour la Démocratie Française–UDF). The federation, which included the Republican Party (Parti Républicain), the successor to the RI, won 23.2% of the vote in the second round of balloting, giving the centrist coalition 124 seats in the National Assembly. The Socialists and Communists, who ran on a common platform as the Union of the Left, together won 199 seats (Socialists 113, Communists 86) and 46.9% of the vote. Independents, with the remaining 3.8%, controlled 14 seats, for a total of 491.

In the presidential elections of 26 April and 10 May 1981, Mitterrand received 25.8% of the vote on the first ballot (behind Giscard's 28.3%) and 51.8% on the second ballot, to become France's first Socialist president since the 1930s. Within weeks, Mitterrand called new legislative elections: that June, the Socialists and their allies won 49.2% of the vote and 285 seats, the RPR 22.4% and 88 seats, the UDF 18.6% and 63 seats, the Communists 7% and 44 seats; independents won the remaining 2.8% and 11 seats. In return for concessions on various political matters, four Communists received cabinet portfolios, none relating directly to foreign affairs or national security. The sweeping victory of the left was, however, eroded in March 1983 when Socialist and Communist officeholders lost their seats in about 30 cities in municipal balloting. Meanwhile, the Communists had become disaffected by government policies and did not seek appointments in the cabinet named when a new Socialist prime minister, Laurent Fabius, was appointed in July 1984.

The National Assembly elections held in March 1993 represented a major defeat for the Socialist Party and their allies. The RPR and UDF won 247 and 213 seats, respectively, while the Socialists were reduced to 67 seats. The Communists also suffered losses, securing only 24 seats. Minor parties and independents won 26 seats. In cantonal elections held in March 1985, the candidates of the left won less than 40% of the vote, while candidates on the right increased their share by 10–15%. The Socialists lost 155 of the 579 Socialist seats that were at stake. As a result, the Socialists introduced a new system of proportional voting aimed at reducing their losses in the forthcoming general election of 16 March 1986. The Socialists and their allies nevertheless won only 33% of the vote and 216 seats out of 577 in the expanded National Assembly. The RPR, the UDF, and their allies received 45% of the vote and 291 seats. The Communists, suffering a historic defeat, split the remaining 70 seats evenly with the far-right National Front, which won representation for the first time. The Socialists remained the largest single party, but the coalition led by the RPR and UDF had a majority; on that basis, Mitterrand appointed RPR leader Chirac as prime minister, heading a center-right government. Following his defeat by Mitterrand in the May 1988 presidential election, Chirac resigned and a minority Socialist government was formed.

In 1995, Jacques Chirac was elected president, defeating Socialist Lionel Jospin. In 1997, one year before they were scheduled, Chirac called for new parliamentary elections, hoping to achieve a mandate to inaugurate his policy of fiscal austerity. Instead, the Gaullists suffered a stunning defeat by the Socialists and Communists, leading to the appointment of Jospin as prime minister. In those elections, held 25 May and 1 June 1997, the Gaullists saw their parliamentary presence decline from 464 seats to 249; the Socialists (and related splinter groups) went from 75 seats to 273; the Communists from 24 to 38; the Greens from no seats to 8; and the far-right National Front maintained its single seat.

The first round of presidential elections were held on 21 April 2002, with Jospin coming in third behind National Front leader Jean-Marie Le Pen and Jacques Chirac in the first round. Two days after these results, on 23 April 2002, the Union en Mouvement (Union in Motion–UEM) was dissolved and replaced by the Union pour la majorité présidentielle (Union for Presidential Majority–UMP) in order to create a major public support behind Chirac in his second round face-off with Le Pen. In May 2002, Jacques Chirac defeated Jean-Marie Le Pen in the second round, taking 82.2% of the vote to Le Pen's 17.8%.

In the National Assembly elections held in June 2002, Chirac's UMP (RPR united with the Liberal Democracy party, formerly the Republican Party) won an overwhelming majority of seats, taking 357 to the Socialists' 140. The National Front failed to win a single seat; the UDF held 29 seats, and the Communists took 21. The Greens held only three seats.

On 17 November 2002, the UMP changed its name to Union pour un Mouvement Populaire (Union for a Popular Movement), keeping the same acronym but modifying the out-of-date appellation. Its first test occurred in March 2004, during the cantonal and regional elections. While suffering a devastating loss, it managed, through alliances, to secure a relative majority of the votes.

Its second test was the European elections, also held in 2004. The UMP won only 17% of the votes, while the Socialist Party earned 29%, and the UDF (composed of members that refused to join in the UMP) reached 12%. The UDF's relative success was largely caused by the attractive alternative that it offered voters that were unhappy with the government's take on social and European issues.

The relative slump of the right can also be explained by the rise of popularity of the National Front and the unpopularity generated by the Raffarin governments.

However, on 6 May 2007, former minister of the interior conservative Nicolas Sarkozy of the UMP defeated Socialist Ségolène Royal in the second round of presidential voting, 53% to 47%. The first round of voting had been held on 22 April 2007, but no candidate obtained an absolute majority. Parliamentary elections were held in June 2007. The UMP won over 46% of the vote and 313 seats in the National Assembly; the Socialists took over 42% of the vote and 186 seats. In all, parties affiliated with the UMP and supporting President Sarkozy won 345 seats, and the United Left affiliated with the Socialists took 227 seats.

Sarkozy reshuffled his cabinet in March 2010 after his center-right Union for a Popular Movement (UMP) lost in regional elections in all but one of the twenty-two regions in mainland France and Corsica. The socialist-led opposition received about 54% of the votes.

15 LOCAL GOVERNMENT

In 1972, parliament approved a code of regional reforms that had been rejected when proposed previously by President de Gaulle in 1969. Under this law, the 96 departments of metropolitan France were grouped into 22 regions. Regional councils composed of local deputies, senators, and delegates were formed and prefects appointed; in addition, regional economic and social committees, made of labor and management representatives, were created. This system was superseded by the decentralization law of 2 March 1982, providing for the transfer of administrative and financial authority from the prefect to the general council, which elects its own president; the national government's representative in the department is appointed by the cabinet. The 1982 law likewise replaced the system of regional prefects with regional councils, elected by universal direct suffrage, and, for each region, an economic and social committee that serves in an advisory role; the national government's representative in each region, named by the cabinet, exercises administrative powers. The first regional assembly to be elected was that of Corsica in August 1982; the first direct assembly elections in all 22 regions were held in March 1986.

Each of the 96 departments (and four overseas: Martinique, Guadeloupe, Reunion and French Guiana) is further subdivided for administrative purposes into *arrondissements*, cantons, and communes (municipalities). The basic unit of local government is the commune, governed by a municipal council and presided over by a mayor. A commune may be an Alpine village with no more than a dozen inhabitants, or it may be a large city, such as Lyon or Marseille. The majority, however, are small. In 1990, only 235 communes out of 36,551 had more than 30,000 inhabitants; 84% of all communes had fewer than 1,500 inhabitants, and 43% had fewer than 300. Most recently, the trend has been for the smallest communes to merge and create larger urban communities or to come together as communal syndicates to share responsibilities. Municipal councilors are elected by universal suffrage for six-year terms. Each council elects a mayor who also serves as a representative of the central government. Several communes are grouped into a canton, and cantons are grouped into arrondissements, which have little administrative significance. As of 1 January 2008, France had 36,569 communes, with 212 overseas.

16 JUDICIAL SYSTEM

There are two types of lower judicial courts in France, the civil courts (471 *tribunaux d'instance* and 181 *tribunaux de grande instance* in 1985, including overseas departments) and the criminal courts (*tribunaux de police* for petty offenses such as parking violations, *tribunaux correctionnels* for criminal misdemeanors). The function of the civil courts is to judge conflicts arising between persons; the function of the criminal courts is to judge minor infractions (*contraventions*) and graver offenses (*délits*) against the law. The most serious crimes, for which the penalties may range to life imprisonment, are tried in assize courts (*cours d'assises*); these do not sit regularly but are called into session when necessary. They are presided over by judges from the appeals courts. In addition, there are special commercial courts (*tribunaux de commerce*), composed of judges elected among themselves by tradesmen and manufacturers, to decide commercial cases; conciliation boards (*conseils de prud'hommes*), made up of employees and employers, to decide their disputes; and professional courts with disciplinary powers within the professions. Special administrative courts (*tribunaux administratifs*) deal with disputes between individuals and government agencies. The highest administrative court is the Council of State (*Conseil d'État*).

From the lower civil and criminal courts alike, appeals may be taken to appeals courts (*cours d'Appel*), of which there were 35 in 2010. Judgments of the appeals courts and the courts of assize are final, except that appeals on the interpretation of the law or points of procedure may be taken to the highest of the judicial courts, the Court of Cassation in Paris. If it finds that either the letter or spirit of the law has been misapplied, it may annul a judgment and return a case for retrial by the lower courts. The High Court of Justice (*Haute Cour de Justice*), consisting of judges and members of parliament, is convened to pass judgment on the president and cabinet members if a formal accusation of treason or criminal behavior has been voted by an absolute majority of both the National Assembly and the Senate. The death penalty was abolished in 1981.

The Conseil Constitutionnel, created by the 1958 constitution, is now the only French forum available for constitutional review of legislation. Challenges to legislation may be raised by the president of the republic, the prime minister, the president of the Senate, the president of the National Assembly, 60 senators, or 60 deputies of the National Assembly during the period between passage and promulgation (signature of president). Once promulgated, French legislation is not subject to judicial review.

The French judiciary is fully independent from the executive and legislative branches. The judiciary is subject to European Union mandates, which guide national law. This has been the case in the Court of Cassation since 1975, in the Council of State since 1989, and now even in the civil courts.

17 ARMED FORCES

The International Institute for Strategic Studies reports that armed forces in France totaled 238,591 members in 2011. The force is comprised of 130,600 from the army, 40,353 from the navy, 52,669 from the air force, and 14,969 other staff members. Armed forces represent 1.2% of the labor force in France. Defense spending totaled $55.9 billion and accounted for 2.6% of GDP.

An additional 104,275 served in the Gendarmerie Nationale, which is heavily armed. Reserves totaled 21,650 from all services.

France maintains substantial forces abroad in a number of countries, current and former possessions, and protectorates. These forces are supported by aircraft and naval ships in the Indian and Pacific oceans, and in the Carribean. France has substantial garrisons in Antilles-Guyana, New Caledonia, Réunion Island, and Polynesia, and it provides military missions and combat formations to several African nations. Troops are also deployed on peacekeeping missions in several different regions and countries.

In November 2010, Sarkozy and British prime minister David Cameron signed two treaties that commit the countries to cooperation and shared resources in defense and nuclear testing. Under the defense treaty, the nations will create a combined joint expeditionary force of about 10,000 soldiers (5,000 from each country) to be deployed as deemed necessary under the leadership of a single military commander (to be chosen when necessary). Under the nuclear testing treaty, a research and testing center will be opened in each country, with the UK facility charged with the development of nuclear testing technology and the French facility charged with the actual testing operations. The treaties are expected to strengthen security in both countries while providing cost savings to each government in military and nuclear testing expenditures. The French nuclear test center is expected to open in Valduc in 2014.

18 INTERNATIONAL COOPERATION

France is a charter member of the United Nations, having joined on 24 October 1945, and actively cooperates in ECE, ECLAC, ESCAP, and most of the nonregional specialized agencies; it is one of the five permanent members of the Security Council. France joined the WTO in 1995. France is also a founding member of the European Union. In 1966, France withdrew its personnel from the two integrated NATO commands—Supreme Headquarters Allied Powers Europe (SHAPE) and Allied Forces Central Europe (AFCENT—claiming a desire for greater military independence. The government at the time also objected to what it believed to be the dominating forces of the United States and Britain within the organization. In December 1995, the country announced its intention to increase participation in the NATO military wing once again. In March 2009, the government announced its intentions to more fully integrate into NATO. France is a member of the Asian Development Bank, the African development Bank, the Central African States Development Bank (BDEAC), European Bank for Reconstruction and Development, Council of Europe, OAS (as a permanent observer), OECD, OSCE, G-5, G-7, G-8, the Association of Caribbean States (ACS), and the Paris Club.

Since 2003, France has supported four UN Security Council (UNSC) resolutions on Iraq. The country serves as a commissioner on the UN Monitoring, Verification, and Inspection Commission and has also offered support to UN missions in Kosovo (est. 1999), Lebanon (1978), the Western Sahara (1991), Ethiopia and Eritrea (2000), Liberia (2003), the DROC (1999), and Haiti (2004).

France belongs to the Australia Group, the Nuclear Suppliers Group (London Group), the Nuclear Energy Agency, the Zangger Committee, the Organization for the Prohibition of Chemical Weapons, and the European Organization for Nuclear Research (CERN). In environmental cooperation, France is part of the Antarctic Treaty; the Basel Convention; Conventions on Biological Diversity, Whaling, and Air Pollution; Ramsar; CITES; the London Convention; International Tropical Timber Agreements; the Kyoto Protocol; the Montréal Protocol; MARPOL; and the UN Conventions on the Law of the Sea, Climate Change and Desertification.

19 ECONOMY

The gross domestic product (GDP) rate of change in France, as of 2010, was 1.5%. Inflation stood at 1.5%, and unemployment was reported at 9.5%.

Generally a financially robust nation, France enjoys the world's sixth-largest economy. Long known for its fine food, wines, and cheeses, modern France has become a leader in telecommunications and aerospace technology, among other industries. The country's farms are highly successful, making France the European Union's (EU) largest exporter of agricultural products and the second-largest agricultural producer in the world (after the United States). Wine and beverages, wheat, meat, and dairy products are the principal agricultural exports. Most of France's trade is done with fellow member states, though the country retains strong economic ties with the United States. The service sector has become the primary growth sector, employing about 72% of the population and accounting for 77% of the gross domestic product (GDP).

After World War II, France's economy was stronger than it had been in the period between the two world wars. However, on the debit side were the extremely high costs of France's colonial campaigns in Indochina and North Africa; the periodic lack of confidence of French investors in the nation's economy, resulting in the large-scale flight of funds; and the successive devaluations of the franc.

Through most of the 1960s and early 1970s, the French economy expanded steadily, with GDP more than doubling between 1959 and 1967. However, the international oil crisis of 1974 led to a sharp rise in import costs; the resulting inflation eroded real growth to about 3% annually between 1977 and 1979. Further oil price increases in 1979–80 marked the beginning of a prolonged recession, with high inflation, high unemployment, balance-of-payments deficits, declining private investment, and shortages in foreign exchange reserves. However, GDP grew by an annual average of 2.5% between 1984 and 1991. During the early 1990s, GDP expanded by a modest average of 2%. By the late 1990s, however, the economy had begun to record higher growth rates. In 1998 the French economy grew by 3.3% in real terms. Unemployment, however, remained high at 11.5%. To combat this, the Socialist-led coalition of Lionel Jospin enacted legislation cutting the workweek to 35 hours in 2000. This measure, along with other incentives, resulted in unemployment falling under 10%, as over 400,000 new jobs were created in the first half of 2000. In 2002, GDP growth was low, due to the global economic slowdown and a decline in investment. However, France's exports increased at a greater rate than did imports, fueling the economy.

France joined 10 other European Union countries in adopting the euro as its currency in January 1999. Since then, monetary policy has been set by the European Central Bank in Frankfurt. On January 1, 2002, France, along with the other countries of the euro zone, dropped its national currency in favor of euro bills and coins.

The French social model, characterized by heavy state involvement in the economy, a tax on wealth, and generous benefits for workers, has proved to be a strong disincentive to growth and job creation. The pension system and rising health-care costs strain public finances. Attempts to liberalize the economy have met strong resistance from labor unions and the left. Pension reforms proposed by the government in early 2003 were met by huge protests and strikes. Discontent with the economy played a large role in France's rejection of the EU constitution in May 2005.

The 2008–09 global financial crisis led to a major slowdown of the economy. Real GDP fell by 2.5% in 2009. In the first quarter of 2010, the economic growth rate was only 0.1%, with a forecast of GDP growth between 1.3% and 1.7% by the end of 2010. The unemployment rate in metropolitan France was at 9.5% in the first quarter of 2010, up from 9.2% in the third quarter of 2009. The slowdown highlighted the ongoing problem of government spending, which accounted for about 55.6% of GDP in 2009. In one effort to cut costs, the government proposed a 2010 bill to increase the retirement age from 60 years to 62 years by 2018, with a full pension offered at 67 years instead of 65. The announcement of the proposal led to widespread protests in early September 2010, with more than 450,000 people marching in cities across the country. A 24-hour national strike was also staged, with schools closing and flight and rail service disrupted. As the assembly considers the bill, the government maintains that pension reform is a necessary measure that could save the government $88.9 billion (70 billion euros).

As of November 2011, the French economy still had excessively high public debt and was facing threats to its AAA credit rating. The unemployment rate remained high from the financial crisis, and labor productivity was low. The 2008 financial crisis evolved into an economic crisis for the members of the Eurozone (those under the single currency), and the French government responded to the need for more austerity measures by announcing a new plan in November 2011. The goal of the proposed plan was to reduce public debt, balance the budget, and stabilize the French economy.

20 INCOME

The CIA estimated that, in 2010, the GDP of France was $2.1 trillion. The CIA defines GDP as the value of all final goods and services produced within a nation in a given year and computed on the basis of purchasing power parity (PPP) rather than value as measured on the basis of the rate of the exchange based on current dollars. The per capita GDP was estimated at $33,100. The annual growth rate of GDP was 1.5%. The average inflation rate was 1.5%. It was estimated that agriculture accounted for 1.8% of GDP, industry 19.2%, and services 79%.

According to the World Bank, remittances from citizens living abroad totaled $15.6 billion or about $238 per capita and accounted for approximately 0.7% of GDP.

The World Bank reports that, in 2009, household consumption in France totaled $1.55 trillion or about $23,669 per capita, measured in current US dollars rather than PPP. Household consumption includes expenditures of individuals, households, and nongovernmental organizations on goods and services, excluding the purchases of dwellings. It was estimated that household consumption was growing at an average annual rate of 0.6%.

The World Bank estimates that France, with 1.03% of the world's population, accounted for 3.39% of the world's GDP. By comparison, the United States, with 4.85% of the world's population, accounted for 22.51% of world GDP.

As of 2011, the most recent study by the World Bank reported that actual individual consumption in France was 72.4% of GDP and accounted for 3.75% of world consumption. By comparison, the United States accounted for 25.44% of world individual consumption. The World Bank also estimated that 9.4% of France's GDP was spent on food and beverages, 17.7% on housing and household furnishings, 2.7% on clothes, 8.8% on health, 8.3% on transportation, 1.6% on communications, 6.4% on recreation, 3.5% on restaurants and hotels, and 8.8% on miscellaneous goods and services and purchases from abroad.

21LABOR

As of 2010, France had a total labor force of 29.32 million people. Within that labor force, CIA estimates in 2005 noted that 3.8% were employed in agriculture, 24.3% in industry, and 71.8% in the service sector.

Although only about 7% of the workforce was unionized as of 2010, trade unions have had significant influence in the country. Workers freely exercise their right to strike unless doing so is prohibited due to public safety. Many unions are members of international labor organizations. Collective bargaining is prevalent. It is illegal to discriminate against union activity.

The government determines the minimum hourly rate, which was the equivalent of $12.10 as of 2012. This amount provides a decent standard of living for a family. The standard legal workweek is set at 35 hours with restrictions on overtime. Children under age 16 are not permitted to work, and there are restrictions pertaining to employment of those under 18. Child labor laws are strictly enforced. The labor code and other laws provide for work, safety, and health standards.

The 2010 announcement of the proposal to increase both the retirement age and the years necessary to pay into social security led to widespread protests beginning in early September and continuing into October, with hundreds of thousands of people marching in cities across the country. Supported through numerous labor unions, the protests were accompanied by 24-hour strikes that involved several professions and industries, including teachers and daycare workers, public transportation, construction, and the oil industry. By mid October, a few unions, including those representing public transportation and energy sector workers, were considering a series of open-ended strikes as a means to force the government to back down.

Those opposed to the change believed, in part, that the new requirements place an unfair burden on those who have worked part-time or been unemployed for long periods of time, particularly women who have left the full-time workforce to raise children. Union officials and opposition leaders proposed that the government consider alternatives, such as taxes on certain salary bonuses and on higher incomes as a way to fund the pension system. However, the national assembly approved the reform bill on 27 October 2010 with a vote of 336 votes for and 233 against in the lower house and 177 votes for and 151 against in the senate.

22AGRICULTURE

Roughly 35% of the total land is farmed, and the country's major crops include wheat, cereals, sugar beets, potatoes, and wine grapes. Cereal production in 2009 amounted to 70 million tons, fruit production 9.2 million tons, and vegetable production 4.8 million tons.

France is the European Union's leading agricultural exporter and the second-largest agricultural producer in the world (after the United States). About 17% of all agricultural in the European Union is found in France. Most large grain farms are found in northern France. Dairy, pork, poultry, and apple production is found primarily in the western regions. Beef production takes place primarily in central France. Corn, fruits, vegetables, and wine are produced in central and southern France. French farmers have been extremely cautious about the cultivation of genetically modified crops. Wine and beverages, wheat, meat, and dairy products are the principal agricultural exports.

Although the most productive farms are in northern France, specialized areas such as the vegetable farms of Brittany, the great commercial vineyards of the Languedoc, Burgundy, and Bordeaux districts, and the flower gardens, olive groves, and orchards of Provence also contribute heavily to the farm economy.

There is large-scale production of fruits, chiefly apples, pears, peaches, and cherries.

23ANIMAL HUSBANDRY

The UN Food and Agriculture Organization (FAO) reported that France dedicated 9.9 million hectares (24.5 million acres) to permanent pasture or meadow in 2009. During that year, the country tended 183 million chickens, 19.2 million head of cattle, and 14.8 million pigs. The production from these animals amounted to 1.66 million tons of beef and veal, 1.96 million tons of pork, 1.3 million tons of poultry, 907,373 tons of eggs, and 16.1 million tons of milk. France also produced 138,694 tons of cattle hide and 8,646 tons of raw wool.

In 2009, farm animals included 10.2 million sheep and goats and 355,000 horses. Poultry and rabbits are raised in large numbers, both farm families and for city markets. Percheron draft horses are raised in northern France, range cattle in the central highlands and the flatlands west of the Rhône, and goats and sheep in the hills of the south. Meat production in 2009 included 117,500 tons of mutton. Meat exports in 2009 were valued at just under $3.3 billion.

Dairy farming flourishes in the rich grasslands of Normandy. France produces some 300 kinds of cheese; in 2009, production totaled about 1.8 million tons. Dairy and egg exports generated $5 billion in 2009.

24FISHING

France had 8,537 decked commercial fishing boats in 2008. The annual capture totaled 457,127 tons according to the UN FAO. The export value of seafood totaled $1.58 billion.

France's 4,716 km (2,930 mi) of coastline, dotted with numerous small harbors, has long supported a flourishing coastal and high-seas fishing industry. French aquaculture consists mainly of oyster and mussel production; most of the facilities are located along the English Channel and the Atlantic coasts.

Herring, skate, whiting, sole, mackerel, tuna, sardines, lobsters, and mussels make up the principal seafood catch, along with cod, mostly from the fishing banks off northern North America, where French fishing vessels have sailed for centuries.

The United Kingdom and Norway are France's leading seafood suppliers.

25FORESTRY

Approximately 29% of France is covered by forest. The UN FAO estimated the 2009 roundwood production at 28.6 million cu m (1.01 billion cu ft). The value of all forest products, including roundwood, totaled $6.23 billion.

Forestry production in France has been encouraged by the government since the 16th century, when wood was a strategic resource in building warships. Although much of the original forest cover was cut over the course of centuries, strict forest management practices and sizable reforestation projects during the last 100 years have restored French forests considerably. Since 1947, the government has subsidized the afforestation and replanting of 2.1 million hectares (5.2 million acres) of forestland along with thousands of miles of wood transport roads. The reforestation project in the Landes region of southwestern France has been particularly successful. About 66% of the forestland is covered with oak, beech, and poplar and 34% with resinous trees. France is the third-most-forested country in the EU, behind Sweden and Finland.

26 MINING

France was a major European mineral producer, despite significant declines in the production of traditional minerals in recent years. France was among the leading producers of coal, was Europe's only producer of andalusite, and counted iron among its top export commodities in 2009. France was also self-sufficient in salt, potash, fluorspar, and talc. Talc de Luzenac, a subsidiary of Rio Tinto, was the leading producer of talc in the world. In addition, France had sizable deposits of antimony, bauxite, magnesium, pyrites, tungsten, and certain radioactive minerals. One of the world's most developed economies, France had to make considerable changes in the structure of its industries, particularly those mineral industries controlled by the state. Prior to 2000, the state's heavy economic and political involvement was a main element of national mineral policy. Cessation of government subsidies to unprofitable operations, cheaper foreign sources, and depletion of mineral reserves have greatly affected the industry, particularly bauxite, coal, iron ore, lead, uranium, and zinc. The government has made efforts to promote the private sector, to proceed with a program of privatization, and to reduce the dependence of state-owned companies on subsidies. To encourage exploration, the government in 1995 passed a law expediting the granting of surveying and mining licenses.

Production figures for 2009 were agricultural and industrial limestone, 8,302,000 metric tons; hydraulic cement, 18.3 million tons; salt (rock, refined brine, marine, and in solution), 6.2 million tons; crude gypsum and anhydrite, 3.35 million tons (France was one of Europe's largest producers of gypsum, with two-thirds coming from the Paris Basin); marketable kaolin and kaolinitic clay, 519,000 tons; crude feldspar, 650,000 tons; kyanite, andalusite, and related materials, 65,000 tons; mica, 20,000 metric tons; and crude and powdered talc (significant to the European market), 420,000 metric tons. In 2009, France also produced copper; gold; silver; powder tungsten; uranium; elemental bromine; refractory clays; diatomite; lime; nitrogen; mineral, natural, and iron oxide pigments; Thomas slag phosphates; pozzolan and lapilli; and soda ash and sodium sulfate. No iron ore was produced in 2009; the iron ore basin, stretching from Lorraine northward, used to produce more than 50 million tons per year, but its high phosphorus and low iron content limited its desirability. Terres Rouges Mine, the last to operate in Lorraine, closed in 1998. France ceased producing bauxite (named after Les Baux, in southern France) in 1993. Mining of lead and zinc has completely ceased.

27 ENERGY AND POWER

The World Bank reported in 2008 that France produced 570.3 billion kWh of electricity and consumed 493.9 billion kWh, or 7,563 kWh per capita. Roughly 51% of energy came from fossil fuels, while 45% came from alternative fuels. Per capita oil consumption was 4,279 kg. Oil production totaled 18,085 barrels of oil a day.

France's energy and power sector is marked by modest reserves of oil, natural gas, and coal and a heavy reliance on nuclear energy to meet its energy needs.

As of 1 January 2011, France had estimated proven oil reserves of 91.63 million barrels, with the bulk of its oil production in the Paris and Aquitaine Basins. In 2010, total oil product output, including refinery gain, came to an estimated 84,820 barrels per day, of which 30% was crude oil. In 2010, domestic demand for oil came to an estimated total of 1.86 million barrels/day, making France the world's 9th-largest consumer of oil. As a result of the disparity between consumption and production, France has had to import crude oil. In 2010, net imports of crude oil came to 2.22 million barrels per day.

In October 2009, the president signed a series of business and energy deals with Kazakhstan that were met with some criticism from the international community. The largest of the deals secured a partnership between the French oil companies, Total and GDF Suez, and the Kazakh state energy firm, Kazmunaigaz, for the development of the Khvalynskoye Caspian Sea gas field. France and Kazakhstan will each take a 25% stake in the project. The remaining 50% will be controlled by the Russian firm Lukoil. A memorandum was also signed with the French firm Spie Capag for the construction of a pipeline to link the Kashagan oil field to the Caspian Sea, bypassing the Russian supply routes to Europe. The French government was criticized for dealing with a nation that has failed to meet international standards of protecting human rights. However, Kazakhstan's strategic location has led several Western nations to consider the potential for partnerships that would lessen Europe's dependence on Russia for oil.

Like its oil resources, France's coal and natural gas reserves are very limited. As of 1 January 2011, the country had an estimated 6.8 billion cu ft of proven natural gas reserves. Production and consumption of natural gas in 2010 totaled an estimated 721 billion cu ft and 49.78 billion cu ft, respectively.

France's electric power sector is marked by a heavy reliance on nuclear power. France has become the world's leading producer of nuclear power per capita, with the world's second-greatest nuclear power capacity (exceeded only by the United States). Nuclear power accounts for 78.5% of the electric power generated in France, followed by hydroelectric at 11.5% and conventional thermal at 9.3%.

All electric power generation and distribution is controlled by the state-owned monopoly Electricite de France (EdF). However, France has slowly begun to deregulate its electricity sector and to privatize EdF. France is also Europe's second-largest power market, exceeded only by Germany.

28 INDUSTRY

Industry has expanded considerably since World War II, with particularly significant progress in the electronics, transport, processing, and construction industries. As of 2010, France is the world's ninth-leading industrial power, after the United States, China, Japan, Germany, Brazil, Russia, Italy, and the UK. Manufacturing accounted for almost 80% of total exports of goods and services in 2010, and exports represent 18.6% of French GDP.

The state has long played an active role in French industry, but government involvement was greatly accelerated by a series of nationalization measures enacted by the Socialists in 1982. By 1983, about one third of French industry—3,500 companies in all—was under state control. However, there was some privatization during 1986–88, later resumed in 1993, with 21 state-owned industries, banks, and insurance companies scheduled to be sold. Although substantial progress had been made in privatization in the early 2000s, the government still held a majority stake in such industries as aeronautics, defense, automobiles, energy, and telecommunications. In July 2005, the government partially privatized Gaz de France, and in October gave the go-ahead for the partial privatization of Electricité de France.

Although France's industrial output has quadrupled since 1950, over 1.5 million jobs had been lost since the 1980s. This shrinkage reflects not only steadily rising productivity but also the major restructuring of industry due to globalization and the instability of oil markets. In this respect, French industry has seen a rapid concentration of its firms and a sharp rise in direct investment abroad. France is the third-largest destination of inward investment in the world, after the United States and the United Kingdom, above all in the fields of information technology, pharmaceuticals, machine tools, and precision instruments. In 2009, France attracted 529 inward investment projects.

The steel industry has suffered because of international competition and a general shift away from steel to aluminum and plastics. The French aluminum industry is dominated by a factory in Dunkirk owned by Pechiney, which was privatized at the end of 1995.

The two leading French automotive companies are PSA (which controls the Peugeot and Citroen brands) and Renault, with the latter state-owned. The domestic market, however, has fallen prey to foreign competitors, especially from Germany and Japan, forcing the French auto makers to make greater use of robots, lay off workers, and open plants abroad.

The French aircraft industry, not primarily a mass producer, specializes in sophisticated design and experimental development. Some of its models, such as the Caravelle and the Mirage IV, have been used in over 50 countries. Aérospatiale became a state company after World War II. Airbus, based in Toulouse and formed in 1970 following an agreement between Aérospatiale and Deutsche Aerospace (Germany), is the world's largest manufacturer of commercial aircraft. Airbus was incorporated in 2001 under French law as a simplified joint stock company.

The chemical industry, although not as strong as its rivals in Germany and the United States, ranks fourth in the world. The pharmaceuticals, perfume, and cosmetics industry is highly significant. France is the world's largest exporter of perfumes.

The textile industry is also important: France is the world's fourth-largest exporter of women's clothing. However, foreign competition has cut into the French textile industry. Following the expiration of the World Trade Organization's longstanding system of textile quotas at the beginning of 2005, the EU signed an agreement with China in June 2005 imposing new quotas on 10 categories of textile goods, limiting growth in those categories to between 8% and 12.5% a year for two years. The agreement was designed to give European textile manufacturers time to adjust to a world of unfettered competition. Nevertheless, barely a month after the EU-China agreement was signed, China reached its quotas for sweaters, followed soon after by blouses, bras, T-shirts, and flax yarn. Tens of millions of garments piled up in warehouses and customs checkpoints, which affected both retailers and consumers.

Agribusiness is an increasingly important industry, supplying France's vast number of restaurants and hotels. The food processing industry is a major force in the French economy. Cooperative ventures are particularly important to the food industry. France is the world's second-largest wine producer after Italy but generates the largest revenue from wine exports. It is the world's second-largest exporter of cheeses.

The great concentrations of French industry are in and around Paris, in the coal basin of northern France, in Alsace and Lorraine, and around Lyon and Clermont-Ferrand. French industry, in general, is strong on inventiveness and inclined toward small-scale production of high-quality items. The French government offers subsidies and easy credit to firms undertaking relocation, reconversion, or plant modernization.

29 SCIENCE AND TECHNOLOGY

Patent applications in science and technology as of 2009, according to the World Bank, totaled 14,295 in France. Public financing of science was 2.02% of GDP. French inventors played a pivotal role in the development of photography and the internal combustion engine. To French ingenuity the world also owes the first mechanical adding machine (1642), the parachute (1783), the electric generator (1832), the refrigerator (1858), and the neon lamp (1910). French industry has pioneered in the development of high-speed transportation systems, notably the supersonic Concorde and the TGV high-speed train, and French subway companies have built or provided equipment for mass-transit systems in Montréal, Mexico City, Río de Janeiro, and other cities.

France is a leading exporter of nuclear technology and has developed the first commercial vitrification plant for the disposal of radioactive wastes by integrating them in special glass and then encasing the glass in stainless steel containers for burial. In 1965, France was the third nation, after the USSR and the United States, to launch its own space satellite. The French no longer launch their own satellites, however, preferring instead to contribute to the European Space Agency.

The Académie des Sciences, founded by Louis XIV in 1666, consists of eight sections: mathematics, physics, mechanics, astronomy, chemistry, cellular and molecular biology, animal and plant biology, and human biology and medical sciences. The Centre National de la Recherche Scientifique (CNRS), founded in 1939, controls more than 1,370 laboratories and research centers. In 1996, the CNRS employed 19,391 researchers and engineers and 7,263 technicians and administrative staff. In addition, there are well over 100 other scientific and technological academies, learned societies, and research institutes. France has a large number of universities and colleges that offer courses in basic and applied sciences. The Palais de la Découverte in Paris (founded in 1937) is a scientific center for the popularization of science. It has departments of mathematics, astronomy, physics, chemistry, biology, medicine, and earth sciences and includes a planetarium

Principal Trading Partners – France (2010)

(In millions of US dollars)

Country	Total	Exports	Imports	Balance
World	1,117,825.0	514,124.0	603,701.0	-89,577.0
Germany	198,152.0	83,591.0	114,561.0	-30,970.0
Belgium	106,968.0	39,115.0	67,853.0	-28,738.0
Italy	89,634.0	41,826.0	47,808.0	-5,982.0
Spain	79,021.0	38,819.0	40,202.0	-1,383.0
Netherlands	66,455.0	21,541.0	44,914.0	-23,373.0
United Kingdom	64,471.0	34,861.0	29,610.0	5,251.0
United States	46,899.0	26,235.0	20,664.0	5,571.0
China	44,510.0	14,176.0	30,334.0	-16,158.0
Switzerland	30,658.0	14,605.0	16,053.0	-1,448.0
Russia	22,752.0	7,537.0	15,215.0	-7,678.0

(…) data not available or not significant.

(n.s.) not specified.

SOURCE: *2011 Direction of Trade Statistics Yearbook,* New York: United Nations, 2011.

Balance of Payments – France (2010)

(In billions of US dollars)

Current Account		**-44.5**
Balance on goods	-71.2	
Imports	-588.4	
Exports	517.2	
Balance on services	12.8	
Balance on income	48.9	
Current transfers	-35.0	
Capital Account		**0.1**
Financial Account		**31.8**
Direct investment abroad	-84.4	
Direct investment in France	33.7	
Portfolio investment assets	28.6	
Portfolio investment liabilities	128.9	
Financial derivatives	45.2	
Other investment assets	-159.7	
Other investment liabilities	39.5	
Net Errors and Omissions		**20.5**
Reserves and Related Items		**-7.8**

(…) data not available or not significant.

SOURCE: *Balance of Payment Statistics Yearbook 2011,* Washington, DC: International Monetary Fund, 2011.

and cinema. A similar Parisian facility is the Cité des Sciences et de l'Industrie (founded in 1986). The city also has the Musée National des Techniques (founded in 1794) and the Musée de l'Air et de l'Espace (founded in 1919).

In 2009, France's total research and development (R&D) expenditures amounted to 2.02% of GDP, of which business provided 52.1%, followed by the government at 38.4%, foreign sources at 8%, and higher education at 0.7%. In that same year, high-tech exports were valued at $83.8 billion and accounted for 23% of manufactured exports. R&D personnel in 2007 numbered 3,500 scientists and engineers per million people.

30 DOMESTIC TRADE

The heart of French commerce, both domestic and foreign, is Paris. One-third of the country's commercial establishments are in the capital, and, in many fields, Parisian control is complete. The major provincial cities act as regional trade centers. The principal ports are Marseille, for trade with North Africa and with the Mediterranean and the Middle East; Bordeaux, for trade with West Africa and much of South America; and Le Havre, for trade with North America and northern Europe. Dunkerque and Rouen are important industrial ports.

The French retail sector is diverse and comprehensive and increasingly resembles the US retail sector. Although the trend away from traditional small retailers is seen as a threat to tradition, in some areas of the country, government assistance is offered to small retailers. Even so, larger retail outlets and hypermarkets continue to gain ground. Mail order sales and specialty chain stores have also grown.

A rapidly growing sector is electronic commerce (e-commerce). As of 2010, the average yearly revenue for an e-commerce business was approximately $1.2 million. Business-to-consumer online retail sales in 2007 had 14.5 million users and accounted for $12.5 billion in sales. The most-searched products involved consumer electronics (26%), computers (21%), travel (19%), books, CDs, and DVDs (8%), and home appliances (6%).

Business hours are customarily on weekdays from 9 a.m. to noon and from 2 to 6 p.m. Normal banking hours are 9 a.m. to 4:30 p.m., Monday–Friday. Most banks are closed on Saturdays; to serve a particular city or larger district, one bank will usually open Saturday mornings from 9 a.m. to noon. Store hours are generally from 10 a.m. to 7 p.m., Monday–Saturday. Most businesses close for three or four weeks in August.

Advertising in newspapers and magazines and by outdoor signs is widespread. A limited amount of advertising is permitted on radio and television. Trade fairs are held regularly in Paris and other large cities.

31 FOREIGN TRADE

France imported $577.7 billion worth of goods and services in 2008 while exporting $508.7 billion worth of goods and services. Major import partners in 2009 were Germany, 19.4%; Belgium, 11.6%; Italy, 8%; Netherlands, 7.1%; Spain, 6.7%; UK, 4.9%; the United States, 4.7%; and China, 4.4%. Its major export partners were Germany, 15.9%; Italy, 8.2%; Spain, 7.8%; Belgium, 7.4%; UK, 7%; and the United States, 5.7%.

Leading French exports, by major categories, are capital goods (machinery, heavy electrical equipment, transport equipment, and aircraft), consumer goods (automobiles, textiles, and leather), and semifinished products (mainly chemicals, iron, and steel). Major imports are fuels, machinery and equipment, chemicals and paper goods, and consumer goods.

The French trade balance was favorable in 1961 for the first time since 1927, but, after 1961, imports rose at a higher rate than did exports. Trade deficits generally increased until the 1990s. From 1977 to 1985, the trade deficit nearly tripled. Among factors held responsible were heavy domestic demand for consumer products not widely produced in France, narrowness of the range of major exports, and a concentration on markets not ripe for expansion of exports from France, notably the EU and OPEC countries. In the following years, a growing change in the trade balance developed, and the deficit narrowed appreciably in 1992. By 1995, France had a trade surplus of $34 billion; deficits returned by the mid-2000s. In all, France is the world's fourth-largest exporter of goods and the third-largest provider of services. France is the largest producer and exporter of farm products in Europe.

Garnering the highest revenues of export commodities from France are transport machinery, including automobiles, vehicle parts, and aircraft. French wine, perfumes, and cosmetics represent about a quarter each of the world market in their respective categories.

32 BALANCE OF PAYMENTS

In 2010, France had a foreign trade deficit of $46 billion, amounting to 7.3% of GDP.

Between 1945 and 1958, France had a constant deficit in its balance of payments. The deficit was financed by foreign loans and by US aid under the Marshall Plan, which totaled more than $4.5 billion. A 1958 currency reform devalued the franc by 17.5%, reduced quota restrictions on imports, and allowed for repatriation of capital; these measures, combined with increased tourist trade and greater spending by US armed forces in the franc zone, improved France's payments position. With payments surpluses during most of the 1960s, gold and currency reserve holdings rose to $6.9 billion by the end of 1967. However, a massive deficit in 1968 led to another devaluation of the franc in 1969, and, by 31 December 1969, gold and reserve holdings had dropped to $3.8 billion. After surpluses in 1970–72 raised international reserves to over $10 billion, price increases for oil and other raw materials resulted in substantial negative balances on current accounts in 1973 and 1974; consequently, France required massive infusions of short-term capital to meet its payments obligations.

Huge surpluses on the services account led to positive payments balances during 1977–80, when reserves rose by nearly $9.7 billion. After that, France's trade position deteriorated sharply. To meet its payments obligation, France had to secure a $4 billion standby credit from international banks as well as loans from Saudi Arabia and the EC. During the mid-1980s, the trade deficit generally moderated; the current accounts balance recovered in 1985 from the heavy deficits of the past. In 1992, the merchandise trade account recorded a surplus after having recorded a significant deficit of 1990. Trade in industrial goods (including military equipment) and a surplus in the manufacturing sector (the first since 1986) were responsible for the boost in exports. Economic growth rose throughout 1994 due to exports to English-speaking countries and a strong economy in Europe.

33 BANKING AND SECURITIES

The Banque de France, founded in 1800, is one of Europe's oldest central banks. In 1945, it came completely under government control. Until France's began using the euro as its currency, the Banque de France was the bank of issue, setting discount rates and maximum discounts for each bank, regulating public and private finance, and operating as the Treasury depository. However, by virtue of the Banking Act of January 1984, the main regulatory authority for the banking sector was given to the Commission Bancaire, which is presided over by the governor of the Banque de France. In 1998, the Banque de France officially became a part of the European Central Bank (ECB) system. Because France is a member of the European Union and uses the euro, the discount rate is set by the ECB. In 2005, the discount rate, the interest rate at which the ECB lends to financial institutions in the short term, was 3.25%.

Beginning in 1945, when the provisional government headed by Gen. de Gaulle nationalized France's four largest commercial banks (Crédit Lyonnais, the Société Générale, the Banque Nationale pour le Commerce et l'Industrie, and the Comptoir National d'Escompte de Paris), the French banking system has been marked by a high degree of government control and ownership. The nationalizations in 1945 initially gave the state control of 55% of all deposits. This control increased in 1966 with the merger of the Banque Nationale and the Comptoir to form the Banque Nationale de Paris (BNP).

In 1982, Socialist president François Mitterrand nationalized 39 banks, bringing the state's control over deposits to 90%. Among leading banks nationalized in 1982 was the Crédit Commercial de France, but this bank and Société Générale were privatized in 1987 by the Chirac government.

France's biggest bank (and one of Europe's largest) is a curiosity. Crédit Agricole, founded at the end of the 19th century, was for most of its life a federation of rurally based mutual credit organizations. It has preserved its rural base and plays the leading role in providing farmers with state-subsidized loans. After 1982, it was allowed to pursue a policy of diversification so that farmers eventually accounted for only 15% of its customers. As of 2007, the bank had some 7,200 branch offices, 21 million customers, and operations in 60 countries.

La Poste, the postal service, which in France is an independent public entity, also offers financial services.

Public issues of stocks and bonds may be floated by corporations or by limited partnerships with shares. Publicly held companies that wish their stock to be traded on the exchange must receive prior authorization from the Stock Exchange Commission within the Ministry of Finance. In January 1962, the two principal Paris stock exchanges were merged. The six provincial exchanges specialize in shares of medium-size and small firms in their respective regions. In 2011, just under 600 companies were listed on EURONEXT Paris. Total market capitalization in December 2010 came to $2.93 trillion. In 2007, EURONEXT merged with NYSE Group and established the first "global" stock exchange. The CAC 40 sets the index for the French stock market and is one of the main indices used by EURONEXT.

Measured by stock market capitalization, the Paris Bourse is the third-largest in Europe after London and Frankfurt. The Lyon Bourse is the most active provincial stock exchange. MATIF (marché à terme des instruments financiers), the financial futures exchange, was opened in Paris in 1986 and has proven a success. The Société des Bourses Françaises (SBF), the operator of the French stock market, has been determinedly pursuing a policy of reform and modernization, and it expects to benefit from the liberalization of financial services brought about by the EU's Investment Services Directive (ISD). French legislation, providing for the liberalization of financial services, transposed the directive into national law.

34 INSURANCE

Insurance is supervised by the government directorate of insurance, while reinsurance is regulated by the Ministry of Commerce.

In 1946, a total of 32 major insurance companies were nationalized, and a central reinsurance institute was organized. All private insurance companies are required to place a portion of their reinsurance with the central reinsurance institute. In France, workers' compensation, tenants' property damage, third-party automobile, hunter's liability insurance, and professional indemnity for some professions are among those insurance lines that are compulsory.

However, as of 1996, the insurance sector was being shifted completely into private hands. Union des Assurances de Paris (UAP), which is France's largest insurance group, was privatized in 1994. The combining of insurance services with retail banking has become fashionable in recent years, hence the neologism *bancassurance*. Partners in this practice are UAP and BNP. Another development has been to forge alliances across the Rhine in Germany. Since July 1994, insurers registered in other European Union (EU) countries have been able to write risks in France under the EU Non-Life Directive.

In 2010, the value of direct premiums written totaled $224 billion, of which life premiums totaled $38.5 billion.

35 PUBLIC FINANCE

In 2010, the budget of France included $1.241 trillion in public revenue and $1.441 trillion in public expenditures. The budget deficit amounted to 6.9% of GDP. Public debt was 83.5% of GDP, with $4.698 trillion of the debt held by foreign entities.

The fiscal year runs from 1 January to 31 December. Deficits have been commonplace, but in recent years, efforts have been made to cut back on the growth of taxes and government spending and, since 1986, to remove major state enterprises from the expense of government ownership. Deficit reduction became a top priority of the government when France committed to the European Monetary Union (EMU). Maastricht Treaty targets for the EMU required France to reduce the government's budget deficit to 3% of GDP by 1997.

The global financial crisis, which began in 2008 in the United States, spread rapidly to the European markets and resulted in the need for significant cuts to public spending in France. The high unemployment and low labor productivity due to the financial crisis led the members of the Eurozone (those under the single currency), which included France, into a full-blown economic crisis by 2010. As public revenues dropped, further cuts to public spending were needed to balance the deficit in public finances. By 2011, the economic crisis led to excessive public debt in several nations of the Eurozone, most notably Greece, Italy, and Spain. As a response, the Eurozone members created a rescue package to stabilize the Eurozone economy. The deal was agreed on in October 2011 and included the European Financial Stability Facility, a rescue package of €1 trillion ($1.345 trillion), forgave 50% of Greek debt and required 9% capitalization of all European banks.

As of November 2011, the public debt in France was still very high. Rating agencies warned France that its AAA rating was under threat unless the public debt could be lowered. The French government responded by announcing a new austerity plan in November 2011, which included a 5% tax increase on businesses with $350 million in sales per year, implementing the minimum retirement age of 62 years by 2017 rather than 2018, raising the value added tax (VAT) from 5.5% to 7% and other cuts to tax deductions.

Public Finance – France (2008)

(In millions of euros, budgetary central government figures)

Revenue and Grants	**364,706**	**100.0%**
Tax revenue	292,647	80.2%
Social contributions	40,965	11.2%
Grants	...	...
Other revenue	...	...
Expenditures	**418,624**	**100.0%**
General public services	124,640	29.8%
Defense	34,586	8.3%
Public order and safety	18,135	4.3%
Economic affairs	57,243	13.7%
Environmental protection	1,963	0.5%
Housing and community amenities	5,353	1.3%
Health	3,796	0.9%
Recreational, culture, and religion	8,373	2.0%
Education	81,550	19.5%
Social protection	82,985	19.8%

(…) data not available or not significant.

SOURCE: *Government Finance Statistics Yearbook 2010*, Washington, DC: International Monetary Fund, 2010.

---

36 TAXATION

As with most industrialized democratic systems, France's tax system is complex and nuanced though also subject to recent movements to reductions and simplifications. The basic corporate income tax rate for filings in 2010 was 33.3%. Short-term capital gains are taxed according to the progressive individual income tax schedule. The main local tax is the business tax, charged on 84% of a value derived from the rental value of the premises, 16% of the value fixed assets, and 18% of annual payroll, and at rates set by local authorities each year. The business tax (*taxe professionelle*) varies significantly from place to place, with a range of 0–4%.

French tax law contains many provisions for exemptions and targeted reductions from taxable income, so that the actual income tax paid is highly individualized. Taxable capital gains for individuals include the sale of immovable property, securities and land (excluding bonds or the individual's primary residence).

The main indirect tax is the value-added tax first introduced in January 1968. The standard rate in 2010 was 19.6%, with a 5.5% on most foodstuffs and agricultural products, medicines, hotel rooms, books, water and newspapers. A 2.1% rate applies to certain medicines that are reimbursed by the social security system. Non-industrial businesses that do not pay the VAT on consumption (banks, insurance companies, the medical sector, associations, nonprofit organizations, etc.) pay a wage tax to cover social levies assessed according to a progressive schedule. Generally, social security contributions by employers range from range from approximately 35–45%, with the employee responsible for 18–23%. Inheritance taxes (succession duties) range from 5–60%, as do gift (donations) taxes. There is also a patrimonial tax of 3% on the fair market value of property owned in France, although foreign companies whose French financial assets are more than 50% are exempt. Also, foreign property holders may be exempt according to the terms of a bilateral tax treaty with France. (France is party to a numerous bilateral tax treaties with provisions that can greatly reduce tax liabilities for foreign investors.) Local taxes include a property tax, charged to owners of land and buildings, and a housing tax, charged to occupants of residential premises, assessed according to the rental value of the property. The social security system is operated separately from the general tax system, financed by contributions levied on earned income in accordance with four regimes: a general regime covering 80% of French citizens, a regime for agricultural workers, a special regime for civil servants and railway workers, and a regime for the self-employed. Tax levies have been used, however, to shore up the finances in the social security system.

In November 2011, the French government proposed a new austerity plan, which included raising the discounted VAT from 5.5% to 7%.

37 CUSTOMS AND DUTIES

Virtually all import duties are on an ad valorem CIF (cost, insurance, and freight) value basis. Minimum tariff rates apply to imports from countries that extend corresponding advantages to France. General rates, fixed at three times the minimum, are levied on imports from other countries. France adheres to the EU's common external tariff for imports. Most raw materials enter duty-free, while most manufactured goods have a tariff of 5–17%. The recession of the early 1980s gave rise to calls for protectionist measures (e.g., against Japanese electronic equipment), but the socialist government remained ostensibly committed to free trade principles. Observers noted, however, that cumbersome customs clearance procedures were being used to slow the entry of certain Japanese imports, notably videotape recorders, to protect French firms. There is a standard 19.6% VAT on most imports, with a reduced rate of 5.5% for basic necessities.

38 FOREIGN INVESTMENT

Foreign direct investment (FDI) in France was a net inflow of $60 billion according to World Bank figures published in 2009. FDI represented 2.26% of GDP.

Investment regulations are simple, and a range of financial incentives for foreign investors is available. France's skilled and productive labor force; central location in Europe, with its free movement of people, services capital, and goods; good infrastructure; and technology-oriented society all attract foreign investors. However, extensive economic regulation and taxation, high social costs, and a complex labor environment are all challenges for the investor.

All direct investments in France require advance notification of—and in some cases approval by—the Treasury Department. Investments from other EU countries cannot be refused, but the department may specify whether the investment is to be financed from French or foreign sources. High taxes dampen the investment climate: the standard rate of corporation tax in 2010 was 33.3%.

Major investors are the United States, the United Kingdom, the Netherlands, Germany, and Belgium. France invests most heavily in the United Kingdom, the United States, Germany, and Switzerland.

39 ECONOMIC DEVELOPMENT

Since World War II (1939–45), France has implemented a series of economic plans, introduced to direct the postwar recovery period but later expanded to provide for generally increasing governmental direction of the economy. The first postwar modernization and equipment plan (1947–53) was designed to get the machinery of production going again; the basic economic sectors—coal, steel, cement, farm machinery, and transportation—were chosen for major expansion, and productivity greatly exceeded the target goals. The second plan (1954–57) was extended to cover all productive activities, especially agriculture, the processing industries, housing construction, and expansion of overseas production. The third plan (1958–61) sought, in conditions of monetary stability and balanced foreign payments, to achieve a major economic expansion, increasing national production by 20% in four years. After the successful devaluation of 1958 and an improvement in the overall financial and political situation, growth rates of 6.3% and 5% were achieved in 1960 and 1961, respectively. The fourth plan (1962–65) called for an annual rate of growth of between 5% and 6% and an increase of 23% in private consumption; the fifth plan (1966–70), for a 5% annual expansion of production, a 25% increase in private consumption, and the maintenance of full financial stability and full employment; and the sixth plan (1971–75), for an annual gross domestic product (GDP) growth rate of between 5.8% and 6% and growth of about 7.5% in industrial production. The sixth plan also called for increases of 31% in private consumption, 34% in output, and 45% in social security expenditure.

The seventh plan (1976–80) called for equalization of the balance of payments, especially through a reduction of dependency on external sources of energy and raw materials; a lessening of social tensions in France by a significant reduction in inequalities of income and job hierarchies; and acceleration of the process of decentralization and deconcentration on the national level in favor of the newly formed regions. Because of the negative impact of the world oil crisis in the mid 1970s, the targets of the seventh plan were abandoned in 1978, and the government concentrated on helping the most depressed sectors and controlling inflation.

In October 1980, the cabinet approved the eighth plan (1981–85). It called for development of advanced technology and for reduction of oil in overall energy consumption. After the Socialists came to power, this plan was set aside, and an interim plan for 1982–84 was announced. It aimed at 3% GDP growth and reductions in unemployment and inflation. When these goals were not met, and France's international payments position reached a critical stage, the government in March 1983 announced austerity measures, including new taxes on gasoline, liquor, and tobacco, a "forced loan" equivalent to 10% of annual taxable income from most taxpayers, and restrictions on the amount of money French tourists could spend abroad. A ninth plan, established for the years 1984–88, called for reducing inflation, improving the trade balance, increasing spending on research and development, and reducing dependence on imported fuels to not more than 50% of total energy by 1990. The 10th plan, for 1989–92, identified increasing employment as its central objective. The main emphasis was on education and training and improved competitiveness through increased spending on research and development.

France adopted legislation for a 35-hour work week in 1998 that became effective in 2000. The object was to create jobs. Pension reform was being legislated in 2003, amid much popular protest. France's demography is changing, with the active population beginning to decline in 2007—this is due to reduce annual per capita GDP growth. Spending on health care increased in the early 2000s. The general government financial deficit exceeded the EU limit of 3% of GDP in 2004.

By the mid 1990s, and in line with European Union (EU) policy, French economic policy took a turn away from state dominance and moved toward liberalization. Large shares of utilities and telecommunications were privatized. Moreover, austerity came to the fore in budgetary planning as the government moved to meet the criteria for Economic and Monetary Union (EMU). France adopted the euro as its currency in 1999 and, in 2002, discontinued the franc in favor of euro bills and coins. Public debt, however, was estimated at 67.7% of GDP in 2004, among the highest of the G-8 nations. Despite privatization efforts, the state in the early 2000s still owned large shares in corporations in such sectors as banking, energy, automobiles, transportation, and telecommunications.

Economic policy challenges for France in 2011 included reducing the budget deficit and making inroads into the rate of unemployment, which remains high due to the effects of the global financial crisis of 2008–09. This requires reforming the tax and benefits system, as well as public administration and the legal framework for the labor market, but social resistance to such reforms is high.

French loans to its former African territories totaled XOF50 billion by November 1972, when President Pompidou announced that France would cancel the entire amount (including all accrued interest) to lighten these countries' debt burdens. In 2009, France's official and private flows for foreign development aid totaled $38.4 million.

40 SOCIAL DEVELOPMENT

France has a highly developed social welfare system. The social security fund is financed by contributions from both employers and employees, calculated on percentages of wages and salaries, and is partially subsidized by the government. Old age insurance guarantees payment of a pension when the insured reaches age 60. However, legislation passed in 2010 changed the retirement age from 60 to 62 by 2018, increasing in intervals of 4 months per year. Disability insurance pays a pension to compensate for the loss of earnings and costs of care. Unemployment insurance is provided for all workers. Workers' medical benefits are paid directly for all necessary care. Maternity benefits are payable for six weeks before and 10 weeks after the expected date of childbirth for the first and second child. There is a universal system of family allowances for all residents, including a birth grant, income supplements for reduced work, and child care benefits.

Equal pay for equal work is mandated by law, although this is not always the case in practice. Men continue to earn more than women, and unemployment rates are higher for women than for men. Sexual harassment is illegal in the workplace and is generally effectively enforced. In 2004, legislation was passed creating a High Authority to Fight Discrimination and Promote Equality. Rape and spousal abuse laws are strictly enforced and the penal-

ties are severe. Shelters, counseling, and hotlines are available to victims of sexual abuse and violence.

Religious freedom is provided for by the constitution. However, large Arab/Muslim, African, and Jewish communities have been subject to harassment and prejudice. Extremist anti-immigrant groups have increasingly been involved in racial attacks. Discrimination on the basis of race, sex, disability, language, religion, or social status is prohibited. In June 2010, France's parliament approved a law, unanimously, that made psychological violence a crime punishable by up to three years in prison and a fine of $90,000 (75,000 euros). The law defines psychological violence as "repeated acts, which could be constituted by words or other machinations, to degrade one's quality of life and cause a change to one's mental or physical state." Both men and women are protected under the new law; however, analysts say the bill is primarily designed to protect women, who are most often the victims of abuse in France. A number of critics, including some parliament members who supported the bill, expressed concerns about the application of the law, since it is difficult to prosecute a crime for which there is no physical evidence. Supporters of the bill, however, claimed that it was necessary to protect people from a form of prevalent but hidden abuse.

41 HEALTH

According to the CIA, life expectancy in France was 81 years in 2011. The country spent 11.2% of its GDP on healthcare, amounting to $4,798 per person. There were 35 physicians, 89 nurses and midwives, and 71 hospital beds per 10,000 inhabitants. The fertility rate was 2.0, while the infant mortality rate was 3 per 1,000 live births. Approximately 79% of France's married women used contraception in 2007. In 2008, the maternal mortality rate, according to the World Bank, was 8 per 100,000 births. It was estimated that 90% of children were vaccinated against measles. The CIA calculated HIV/AIDS prevalence in France to be about 0.4% in 2009.

Under the French system of health care, both public and private health care providers operate through centralized funding. Patients have the option of seeing a private doctor on a fee basis or going to a state-operated facility. Nearly all private doctors are affiliated with the social security system, and the patients' expenses are reimbursed in part. Many have private health insurance to cover the difference. Cost containment initiatives were introduced to increase patient contributions and establish global budgets for public hospitals. The social security system subsidizes approximately 75% of all health care costs. Pharmaceutical consumption in France is among the highest of all OECD member countries (exceeded only by Japan and the United States). The total expenditure on health care in France in 2009 was an estimated 11.7% of gross domestic product.

42 HOUSING

According to the 2004 French housing census, there were 30.3 million dwellings nationwide. About 25.4 million, or 84%, were primary residences, 2.9 million were second homes, and about 1.8 million, or 6.1%, were vacant. About 58% of all dwellings are detached homes. The average number of people per household was about 2.3.

After World War II, in which 4.2 million dwellings were destroyed and one million damaged, the government took steps to provide inexpensive public housing. Annual construction rose steadily through the 1950s and 1960s; in 1970–75, housing construction of all types increased by an annual average of more than 6%. In 1975, the total number of new dwellings completed was 514,300. Construction slowed thereafter, and, by 1996, the number had declined to 236,270.

In accordance with a law of 1953, industrial and commercial firms employing 10 or more wage earners must invest 1% of their total payroll in housing projects for their employees. These funds can finance either public or private low-cost housing. Concerns must undertake construction of low-cost projects either on their own responsibility or through a building concern to which they supply capital. Special housing allowances are provided for families who must spend an inordinately large share of their income on rent or mortgages.

43 EDUCATION

In 2008, the World Bank estimated that 98% of age-eligible children in France were enrolled in primary school. Secondary enrollment for age-eligible children stood at 98%. Tertiary enrollment was estimated at 55%. Of those enrolled in tertiary education, there were 100 male students for every 128 female students. Overall, the CIA estimated that France had a literacy rate of 99%. Public expenditure on education represented 5.6% of GDP.

The supreme authority over national education in France is the Ministry of Education. Free education starts at two years of age and is compulsory for children from the ages of 6 to 16. Education is free in all state primary and secondary schools. Higher education is not free, but academic fees are low, and more than half of students are excused from payment.

Since the end of 1959, private institutions have been authorized to receive state aid and to ask to be integrated into the public education system. In 2010, about 15% of elementary-school children and 20% of secondary-level students attended private schools, the majority of which are Roman Catholic. In Brittany, most children attend Catholic schools. Freedom of education is guaranteed by law, but the state exercises certain controls over private educational institutions, nearly all of which follow the uniform curriculum prescribed by the Ministry of Education.

Primary school covers five years of study. There are two levels of secondary instruction. The first, the collège, is compulsory; after four years of schooling are successfully completed, the student receives a national diploma (*brevet des collèges*). Those who wish to pursue further studies enter either the two-year *lycée d'enseignement professionel* or the three-year *lycée d'enseignement général et technologique*. The former prepares students for a certificate of vocational competence, the latter for the *baccalauréat*, which is a prerequisite for higher education. Choice of a *lycée* depends on aptitude test results. The academic year runs from September to June. The primary language of instruction is French.

In 2010, nearly all age-eligible children were enrolled in some type of preschool program.

There are 91 public universities and 175 professional schools within 26 *académies*, which now act as administrative units. Before the subdivision of these 26 units, the oldest and most important included Aix-Marseille (founded in 1409), Besançon (1691), Bordeaux (1441), Caen (1432), Dijon (1722), Grenoble (1339), Lille (1562), Montpellier (1180, reinstituted 1289), Nancy-Metz (1572), Paris (1150), Poitiers (1432), Rennes (1735, founded at Nantes 1461), Strasbourg (1538), and Toulouse (1229). The old University of Paris, also referred to as the Sorbonne, was the oldest in France and one of the leading institutions of higher learning in the world; it is now divided into 13 units, only a few of which are at the ancient Left Bank site. There are Catholic universities at Argers, Lille, Lyon, and Toulouse.

Besides the universities and specialized schools (such as École Normale Supérieure, which prepares teachers for secondary and postsecondary positions), higher educational institutions include the prestigious Grandes Écoles, which include the École Nationale d'Administration, École Normale Supérieure, Conservatoire National des Arts et Métiers, and École Polytechnique. Entrance is by competitive examination. Advanced-level research organizations include the Collège de France, École Pratique des Hautes Études, and École des Hautes Études en Sciences Sociales.

44 LIBRARIES AND MUSEUMS

Paris, the leader in all intellectual pursuits in France, has the largest concentration of libraries and museums. The Bibliothèque Nationale, founded in Paris in 1480, is one of the world's great research libraries, with a collection of over 10.4 million books, as well as millions of manuscripts, prints, maps, periodicals, and other items of importance (including 11 million stamps and photographs). The libraries of the 13-unit University of Paris system have collective holdings of more than six million volumes, and each major institution of higher learning has an important library of its own. The national archives are located in the Hôtel Rohan Soubise in Paris. There are dozens of libraries and historic sites dedicated to specific French writers and artists, including the Maison de Balzac in Paris, the Musée Calvin in Noyon, the Musée Matisse in Nice, the Musée Rodin in Meydon (there is also a National Museum of Rodin in Paris), and the Musée Picasso in Paris. Most provincial cities have municipal libraries and museums of varying sizes.

There are more than 1,000 museums in France. The Louvre, which underwent an extensive renovation and addition in the 1980s, including the construction of its now-famous glass pyramid, contains one of the largest and most important art collections in the world, covering all phases of the fine arts from all times and regions. The Cluny Museum specializes in the arts and crafts of the Middle Ages. The Museum of Man is a major research center as well. The Centre National d'Art et de Culture Georges Pompidou opened in 1977 on the Beaubourg Plateau (Les Halles). Primarily a museum specializing in contemporary art, it also houses several libraries (including the public library of Paris), children's workshops, music rooms, and conference halls. The Musée d'Orsay, a major new museum housing impressionist and postimpressionist paintings and many other works set in historical context, opened to the public in December 1986 in a former train station. Many of the 19th-century and 20th-century paintings in the Musée d'Orsay had previously been housed in the Musée du Jeu de Paume. Many of the great churches, cathedrals, castles, and châteaux of France are national monuments.

45 MEDIA

In 2009, the CIA reported that there were 35.5 million telephone landlines in France. In addition to landlines, mobile phone subscriptions averaged 95 per 100 people. There were 41 FM radio stations, about 3,500 AM radio stations, and 2 shortwave radio stations. Internet users numbered 71 per 100 citizens.

Postal, telephone, and telegraph systems are operated by the government under the direction of the Ministry of Post, Telegraph, and Telephones. France's telecommunications system is highly developed, with domestic services supplied through a mix of satellite, fiber-optic cable, coaxial cable, and microwave radio relay systems. International service is provided by high frequency radiotelephone communications, and by satellite ground stations.

The government-controlled Office de Radiodiffusion-Télévision Française was replaced in January 1975 by seven independent, state-financed companies. A law of July 1982 allowed greater independence to production and programming organizations. Under deregulation, many private radio stations have been established. Of the three state-owned television channels, TF-1, the oldest and largest, was privatized in 1987; a fourth, private channel for paying subscribers was started in 1984. Contracts were awarded in 1987 to private consortiums for fifth and sixth channels.

Traditionally, the French press falls into two categories. The *presse d'information,* with newspapers with the largest circulation, emphasizes news; the *presse d'opinion,* usually of higher prestige in literary and political circles but of much lower daily circulation, presents views on political, economic, and literary matters. Some of the important regional papers rival the Parisian dailies in influence and circulation.

Leading national newspapers (with their organizational affiliation and 2010 circulation totals) are: *Le Figaro* (moderate conservative, 318,909), *Le Monde* (independent, elite, 289,990), *Les Echos* (economics, 116,737), *Liberation* (115,952), *L'Humanité* (Communist, 46,238), and *La Croix* (Catholic, 93,480). Some leading regional dailies include *Ouest-France* (in Rennes, mass-appeal, 753,730), *La Voix du Nord* (in Lille, conservative, 263,947), *Sud-Ouest* (in Bordeaux, independent, 290,222), *Nice-Matin* (in Nice, radical independent, 103,589), *Les Dernieres Nouvelles D'Alsace* (in Strasbourg, 170,011), *La Dépêche du Midi* (in Toulouse, radical, 179,652), and *Le Telegramme* (in Morlaix, 204,888). *L'Express* and *Le Point* are popular news weeklies.

The Agence France-Presse is the most important French news service. It has autonomous status, but the government is represented on its board of directors. There are some 14,000 periodicals, of which the most widely read is the illustrated Paris-Match, with a weekly circulation (in 2010) of 626,178. Several magazines for women also enjoy wide popularity, including *Elle,* (2010 circulation 381,647). Also for women are magazines publishing novels in serial form. The most popular political weeklies are *L'Express* (left-wing), with a circulation of about 432,418; the satirical *Le Canard Enchaîné* (left-wing), circulation 500,000; *Le Nouvel Observateur* (left-wing), circulation 503,401; and the news-magazine *Le Point* (independent), circulation 410,996. Filmmaking is a major industry, subsidized by the state.

The law provides for free expression including freedom of speech and press, and these rights are supported by the government.

46 ORGANIZATIONS

The Confédération Générale d'Agriculture, originating in its present form in the resistance movement of World War II, has become the principal voice for farmers. The Société des Agriculteurs de France is considered the organization of landowners. Agricultural cooperatives, both producers' and consumers', are popular. There are also more than 44 large industrial trade organizations. Chambers of commerce function in the larger cities and towns. The International Chamber of Commerce has its headquarters in Paris, the national capital.

There are professional associations covering a wide variety of fields. The Association Medicale Francaise is a networking association for physicians that also promotes research and education on health issues and works to establish common policies and standards in healthcare. There are also several associations dedicated to research and education for specific fields of medicine and particular diseases and conditions. The World Medical Association has an office in Ferney-Voltaire.

The Institute of France (founded in 1795) consists of the famous French Academy (Académie Française), the Academy of Sciences, the Academy of Humanities, the Academy of Fine Arts, and the Academy of Moral Sciences and Politics. There are many scientific, artistic, technical, and scholarly societies at both national and local levels. The multinational organization of European Academy of Arts, Sciences, and Humanities is based in Paris. The United Nations Educational, Scientific, and Cultural Organization (UNESCO) has an office in Paris, as does the European Space Agency.

There are also many associations and organizations dedicated to various sports and leisure time activities. Youth organizations are numerous and range from sports groups, to volunteer and service organizations, religious and political organizations. Some groups with international ties include Junior Chamber, YMCA/YWCA, and the Guides and Scouts of France. Volunteer service organizations, such as the Lions Clubs and Kiwanis International, are also present. The Red Cross, the Society of St. Vincent de Paul, CARE, UNICEF, and Greenpeace have national chapters.

47 TOURISM, TRAVEL, AND RECREATION

The *Tourism Factbook*, published by the UN World Tourism Organization, reported 76.8 million incoming tourists to France in 2009, who spent a total of $59.4 billion. Of those incoming tourists, there were 65.3 million from Europe. There were 1.22 million hotel beds available in France. The estimated daily cost to visit Paris, the capital, was $598. The cost of visiting other cities averaged $345.

France has countless tourist attractions, ranging from the museums and monuments of Paris to beaches on the Riviera and ski slopes in the Alps. Haute cuisine, hearty regional specialties, and an extraordinary array of fine wines attract gourmets the world over; the area between the Rhone River and the Pyrenees contains the largest single tract of vineyards in the world. In 1992, Euro Disneyland, 20 miles east of Paris, opened to great fanfare but was plagued by the European recession, a strong French franc, bad weather, and difficulty marketing itself to the French.

The most popular French sport is soccer (commonly called "le foot"). The men's soccer team won the World Cup in 1998. Other favorite sports are skiing, tennis, rugby, water sports, and bicycling. Between 1896 and 1984, France won 137 gold, 156 silver, and 158 bronze medals in the Olympic Games. Paris hosted the Summer Olympics in 1900 and 1924; the Winter Olympics took place at Chamonix in 1924, Grenoble in 1968, and Albertville in 1992. Le Mans is the site of a world-class auto race.

In November 2010, the French gastronomic meal was officially inscribed on the UNESCO Representative List of the Intangible Heritage of Humanity, an offshoot of the World Heritage program. The listing was not simply based on specific foods or recipes, but in consideration of traditional meal rituals that include multiple courses, the pairing of wine with foods, the decoration of the table, the placement of dishware, glasses, and utensils, and food tasting gestures. Such an elaborate meal generally occurs at times of celebration, such as weddings, birthdays, and anniversaries, and serves to strengthen social and familial ties. This marked the first time that a nation's cuisine was added to the list. To be added, a tradition must be deemed a living tradition by UNESCO, meaning that it is still passed from generation to generation and continues to create a sense of identity and community for those who participate. Such traditions have been approved by UNESCO for special consideration since 2001. For one that is inscribed, a special program is designed to protect and promote the practice and understanding of the tradition. The needle lace-making technique known as point d'Alencon, originating in the town of Alencon in Normandy, was also added to the list.

Tourists need a valid passport to enter France. A visa is not necessary for tourist/business stays of up to 90 days.

⁴⁸ FAMOUS PERSONS

Principal figures of early French history include Clovis I (466?-511), the first important monarch of the Merovingian line, who sought to unite the Franks; Charles Martel ("the Hammer," 689?-741), leader of the Franks against the Saracens in 732; his grandson Charlemagne (742–814), the greatest of the Carolingians, crowned emperor of the West on 25 December 800; and William II, Duke of Normandy (1027–87), later William I of England ("the Conqueror," r. 1066–87). Important roles in theology and church history were played by St. Martin of Tours (b. Pannonia, 316?-97), bishop of Tours and founder of the monastery of Marmoutier, now considered the patron saint of France; the philosopher Pierre Abélard (1079–1142), traditionally regarded as a founder of the University of Paris but equally famous for his tragic romantic involvement with his pupil Héloise (d. 1164); and St. Bernard of Clairvaux (1090?-1153), leader of the Cistercian monastic order, preacher (1146) of the Second Crusade (1147–49), and guiding spirit of the Knights Templars. The first great writer of Arthurian romances was Chrétien de Troyes (fl. 1150?).

The exploits of famous 14th-century Frenchmen were recorded by the chronicler Jean Froissart (1333?-1401). Early warrior-heroes of renown were Bertrand du Guesclin (1320–80) and Pierre du Terrail, seigneur de Bayard (1474?-1524). Joan of Arc (Jeanne d'Arc, 1412–31) was the first to have a vision of France as a single nation; she died a martyr and became a saint and a national heroine. Guillaume de Machaut (1300?-1377) was a key literary and musical figure. François Villon (1431–63?) was first in the line of great French poets. Jacques Coeur (1395–1456) was the greatest financier of his time. Masters of the Burgundian school of composers were Guillaume Dufay (1400?-1474), Gilles Binchois (1400?-1467), Jan Ockeghem (1430?-95), and Josquin des Prez (1450?-1521). Jean Fouquet (1415?-80) and Jean Clouet (1485–1541) were among the finest painters of the period. The flag of France was first planted in the New World by Jacques Cartier (1491–1557), who was followed by the founder of New France in Canada, Samuel de Champlain (1567–1635).

The era of Louis XIV ("le Roi Soleil," or "the Sun King," 1638–1715) was in many respects the golden age of France. Great soldiers—Henri de La Tour d'Auvergne, vicomte de Turenne (1611–75), François Michel Le Tellier, marquis de Louvois (1639–91), and Louis II de Bourbon, prince de Condé, called the Grand Condé (1621–86)—led French armies to conquests on many battlefields. Great statesmen, such as the cardinals Armand Jean du Plessis, duc de Richelieu (1585–1642), and Jules Mazarin (1602–61), managed French diplomacy and created the French Academy. Great administrators, such as Maximilien de Bethune, duc de Sully (1560–1641), and Jean-Baptiste Colbert (1619–83), established financial policies. Noted explorers in the New World were Jacques Marquette (1637–75), Robert Cavalier, Sieur de La Salle (1643–87), and Louis Jolliet (1645–1700). Jean-Baptiste Lully (1632–87), Marc-Antoine Charpentier (1634–1704), and François Couperin (1668–1733) were the leading composers. Nicolas Poussin (1594–1665), Claude Lorrain (1600–1682), and Philippe de Champaigne (1602–74) were the outstanding painters. In literature, the great sermons and moralizing writings of Jacques Bénigne Bossuet, bishop of Meaux (1627–1704), and François Fénelon (1651–1715); the dramas of Pierre Corneille (1606–84), Molière (Jean-Baptiste Poquelin, 1622–73), and Jean Racine (1639–99); the poetry of Jean de La Fontaine (1621–95) and Nicolas Boileau-Despréaux (1636–1711); the maxims of François, duc de La Rochefoucauld (1613–80), and Jean de La Bruyère (1645–96); the fairy tales of Charles Perrault (1628–1703); the satirical fantasies of Savinien de Cyrano de Bergerac (1619–55); and the witty letters of Madame de Sévigné (1626–96) made this a great age for France. Two leading French philosophers and mathematicians of the period, René Descartes (1596–1650) and Blaise Pascal (1623–62), left their mark on the whole of European thought. Pierre Gassendi (1592–1655) was a philosopher and physicist; Pierre de Fermat (1601–55) was a noted mathematician. Modern French literature began during the 16th century, with François Rabelais (1490?-1553), Joachim du Bellay (1522–60), Pierre de Ronsard (1525–85), and Michel de Montaigne (1533–92). Ambroise Paré (1510–90) was the first surgeon, and Jacques Cujas (1522–90) the first of the great French jurists. Among other figures in the great controversy between Catholics and Protestants, Claude, duc de Guise (1496–1550), and Queen Catherine de Médicis (Caterina de'Medici, b. Florence, 1519–89) should be mentioned on the Catholic side, and Admiral Gaspard de Coligny (1519–72), a brilliant military leader, on the Protestant side. Two famous kings were Francis I (1494–1547) and Henry IV (Henry of Navarre, 1553–1610); the latter proclaimed the Edict of Nantes in 1598, granting religious freedom to his Protestant subjects. The poetic prophecies of the astrologer Nostradamus (Michel de Notredame, 1503–66) are still widely read today.

1700–1900

During the 18th century, France again was in the vanguard in many fields. Étienne François, duc de Choiseul (1719–85), and Anne Robert Jacques Turgot (1727–81) were among the leading statesmen of the monarchy. Charles Louis de Secondat, baron de La Brède et de Montesquieu (1689–1755), and Jean-Jacques Rousseau (b. Switzerland, 1712–78) left their mark on philosophy. Denis Diderot (1713–84) and Jean Le Rond d'Alembert (1717–83) created the Great Encyclopedia (*Encyclopédie ou Dictionnaire Raisonné des Sciences, des Artes et des Métiers*). Baron Paul Henri Thiery d'Holbach (1723–89) was another philosopher. Jeanne Antoinette Poisson Le Normant d'Etoiles, marquise de Pompadour (1721–64), is best known among the women who influenced royal decisions during the reign of Louis XV (1710–74). French explorers carried the flag of France around the world, among them Louis Antoine de Bougainville (1729–1811) and Jean La Pérouse (1741–88). French art was dominated by the painters Antoine Watteau (1684–1721), Jean-Baptiste Chardin (1699–1779), François Boucher (1703–70), and Jean Honoré Fragonard (1732–1806) and by the sculptor Jean Houdon (1741–1828). Jean-Philippe Rameau (1683–1764) was the foremost composer. French science was advanced by Georges Louis Leclerc, Comte de Buffon (1707–88), zoologist and founder of the Paris Museum, and Antoine Laurent Lavoisier (1743–94), the great chemist. In literature, the towering figure of Voltaire (François Marie Arouet, 1694–1778) and the brilliant dramatist Pierre Beaumarchais (1732–99) stand beside the greatest writer on gastronomy, Anthelme Brillat-Savarin (1755–1826).

The rule of Louis XVI (1754–93) and his queen, Marie Antoinette (1755–93), and the social order they represented, ended with the French Revolution. Outstanding figures of the Revolution included Jean-Paul Marat (1743–93), Honoré Gabriel Riquetti, comte de Mirabeau (1749–91), Maximilien Marie Isidore Robespierre (1758–94), and Georges Jacques Danton (1759–94). Napoleon Bonaparte (1769–1821) rose to prominence as a military leader in the Revolution and subsequently became emperor of France. Marie Joseph Paul Yves Roch Gilbert du Motier, marquis de Lafayette (1757–1834), was a brilliant figure in French as well as in American affairs. This was also the period of the eminent painter Jacques Louis David (1748–1825) and of the famed woman of letters Madame Germaine de Staël (Anne Louise Germaine Necker, baronne de Staël-Holstein, 1766–1817).

During the 19th century, French science, literature, and arts all but dominated the European scene. Among the leading figures were Louis Jacques Mendé Daguerre (1789–1851), inventor of photography, and Claude Bernard (1813–78), the great physiologist. Other pioneers of science included Jean-Baptiste Lamarck (1744–1829) and Georges Cuvier (1769–1832) in zoology and paleontology, Pierre Laplace (1749–1827) in geology, André Marie Ampère (1775–1836), Dominique François Arago (1786–1853), and Jean Bernard Léon Foucault (1819–68) in physics, Joseph Louis Gay-Lussac (1778–1850) in chemistry, Camille Flammarion (1842–1925) in astronomy, and Louis Pasteur (1822–95) in chemistry and bacteriology. Louis Braille (1809–52) invented the method of writing books for the blind that bears his name. Auguste (Isidore Auguste Marie François Xavier) Comte (1798–1857) was an influential philosopher. Literary figures included the poets Alphonse Marie Louis de Lamartine (1790–1869), Alfred de Vigny (1797–1863), Alfred de Musset (1810–57), Charles Baudelaire (1821–67), Stéphane Mallarmé (1842–98), Paul Verlaine (1844–96), and Arthur Rimbaud (1854–91); the fiction writers François René Chateaubriand (1768–1848), Stendhal (Marie Henri Beyle, 1783–1842), Honoré de Balzac (1799–1850), Victor Marie Hugo (1802–85), Alexandre Dumas the elder (1802–70) and his son, Al-

exandre Dumas the younger (1824–95), Prosper Merimée (1803–70), George Sand (Amandine Aurore Lucie Dupin, baronne Dudevant, 1804–76), Théophile Gautier (1811–72), Gustave Flaubert (1821–80), the Goncourt brothers (Edmond, 1822–96, and Jules, 1830–70), Jules Verne (1828–1905), Alphonse Daudet (1840–97), Emile Zola (1840–1902), and Guy de Maupassant (1850–93); and the historians and critics François Guizot (1787–1874), Jules Michelet (1798–1874), Charles Augustin Sainte-Beuve (1804–69), Alexis de Tocqueville (1805–59), Ernest Renan (1823–92), and Hippolyte Adolphe Taine (1828–93). Charles Maurice de Talleyrand (1754–1838), Joseph Fouché (1763–1820), Adolphe Thiers (1797–1877), and Léon Gambetta (1838–82) were leading statesmen. Louis Hector Berlioz (1803–69) was the greatest figure in 19th-century French music. Other figures were Charles François Gounod (1818–93), composer of *Faust*, Belgian-born César Auguste Franck (1822–90), and Charles Camille Saint-Saëns (1835–1921). Georges Bizet (1838–75) is renowned for his opera *Carmen,* and Jacques Lévy Offenbach (1819–80) for his immensely popular operettas.

In painting, the 19th century produced Jean August Dominique Ingres (1780–1867), Ferdinand Victor Eugène Delacroix (1789–1863), Jean-Baptiste Camille Corot (1796–1875), Honoré Daumier (1808–79), and Gustave Courbet (1819–77), and the impressionists and postimpressionists Camille Pissarro (1830–1903), Édouard Manet (1832–83), Hilaire Germain Edgar Degas (1834–1917), Paul Cézanne (1839–1906), Claude Monet (1840–1926), Pierre Auguste Renoir (1841–1919), Berthe Morisot (1841–1895), Paul Gauguin (1848–1903), Georges Seurat (1859–91), and Henri de Toulouse-Lautrec (1864–1901). Auguste Rodin (1840–1917) was the foremost sculptor; Frédéric Auguste Bartholdi (1834–1904) created the Statue of Liberty. The actresses Rachel (Elisa Félix, 1821–58) and Sarah Bernhardt (Rosine Bernard, 1844–1923) dominated French theater.

The 20th and 21st Centuries

In 20th-century political and military affairs, important parts were played by Georges Clemenceau (1841–1929), Ferdinand Foch (1851–1929), Henri Philippe Pétain (1856–1951), Raymond Poincaré (1860–1934), Léon Blum (1872–1950), Jean Monnet (1888–1979), Charles de Gaulle (1890–1970), Pierre Mendès-France (1907–82), François Maurice Marie Mitterrand (1916–96), and Valéry Giscard d'Estaing (b. 1926). Winners of the Nobel Peace Prize include Frédéric Passy (1822–1912) in 1901, Benjamin Constant (1852–1924) in 1909, Léon Victor Auguste Bourgeois (1851–1925) in 1920, Aristide Briand (1862–1932) in 1926, Ferdinand Buisson (1841–1932) in 1927, Léon Jouhaux (1879–1954) in 1951, and René Cassin (1887–1976) in 1968. Albert Schweitzer (1875–1965), musician, philosopher, physician, and humanist, a native of Alsace, received the Nobel Peace Prize in 1952.

Famous scientists include the mathematician Jules Henri Poincaré (1854–1912); the physicist Antoine Henri Becquerel (1852–1908), a Nobel laureate in physics in 1903; chemist and physicist Pierre Curie (1859–1906); his wife, Polish-born Marie Sklodowska Curie (1867–1934), who shared the 1903 Nobel Prize for physics with her husband and Becquerel and won a Nobel Prize again, for chemistry, in 1911; their daughter Irène Joliot-Curie (1897–1956) and her husband, Frédéric Joliot-Curie (Jean-Frédéric Joliot, 1900–1958), who shared the Nobel Prize for chemistry in 1935;

Jean-Baptiste Perrin (1870–1942), Nobel Prize winner for physics in 1926; the physiologist Alexis Carrel (1873–1944); and Louis de Broglie (1892–1987), who won the Nobel Prize for physics in 1929. Other Nobel Prize winners for physics include Charles Édouard Guillaume (1861–1938) in 1920, Alfred Kastler (1902–84) in 1966, Louis Eugène Néel (1904–2000) in 1970, Pierre-Gilles de Gennes (b. 1932) in 1991, and Georges Charpak (b. 1924) in 1992; for chemistry, Henri Moissan (1852–1907) in 1906, Victor Grignard (1871–1935) in 1912, Paul Sabatier (1854–1941) in 1912, and Yves Chauvin (b. 1930) in 2005. Also, in physiology or medicine: in 1907, Charles Louis Alphonse Laveran (1845–1922); in 1913, Charles Robert Richet (1850–1935); in 1928, Charles Jules Henri Nicolle (1866–1936); in 1965, François Jacob (b. 1920), André Lwoff (1902–94), and Jacques Monod (1910–76); and in 1980, Jean-Baptiste Gabriel Dausset (b. 1916).

The philosopher Henri Bergson (1859–1941) received the 1927 Nobel Prize for literature. Émile Durkheim (1858–1917) was a founder of modern sociology. Pierre Teilhard de Chardin (1881–1955), a Jesuit, was both a prominent paleontologist and an influential theologian. Claude Lévi-Strauss (b. Belgium, 1908) is a noted anthropologist, Pierre Bourdieu (1930–2002) was an important sociologist, and Fernand Braudel (1902–85) was an important historian. Twentieth-century philosophers included Louis Althusser (1918–1990), Raymond Aron (1905–1983), Gaston Bachelard (1884–1962), Georges Bataille (1897–1962), Jean Baudrillard (b. 1929), Gilles Deleuze (1925–1995), Jacques Derrida (1930–2004), Michel Foucault (1926–1984), Pierre-Félix Guattari (1930–1992), Philippe Lacoue-Labarthe (b. 1940), Henri Lefebvre (1901–1991), Emmanuel Lévinas (1906–1995), Jean-François Lyotard (1924–1998), Maurice Merleau-Ponty (1908–1961), and Paul Ricoeur (1913–2005).

Honored writers include Sully-Prudhomme (René François Armand, 1839–1907), winner of the first Nobel Prize for literature in 1901; Frédéric Mistral (1830–1914), Nobel Prize winner in 1904; Edmond Rostand (1868–1918); Anatole France (Jacques Anatole Thibaut, 1844–1924), Nobel Prize winner in 1921; Romain Rolland (1866–1944), Nobel Prize winner in 1915; André Paul Guillaume Gide (1869–1951), a 1947 Nobel laureate; Marcel Proust (1871–1922); Paul Valéry (1871–1945); Colette (Sidonie Gabrielle Claudine Colette, 1873–1954); Roger Martin du Gard (1881–1958), Nobel Prize winner in 1937; Jean Giraudoux (1882–1944); François Mauriac (1885–1970), 1952 Nobel Prize winner; Jean Cocteau (1889–1963); Louis Aragon (1897–1982); André Malraux (1901–76); Anaïs Nin (1903–1977); Jean-Paul Sartre (1905–80), who was awarded the 1964 Nobel Prize but declined it; Simone Lucie Ernestine Marie Bertrand de Beauvoir (1908–86); Simone Weil (1909–43); Jean Genet (1910–86); Jean Anouilh (1910–87); Albert Camus (1913–60), Nobel Prize winner in 1957; Claude Simon (1913–2005), a 1985 Nobel laureate; Marguerite Duras (1914–96); Roland Barthes (1915–80); and Georges Perec (1936–1982). Antoine de Saint-Exupéry (1900–1944) was a French writer and aviator. Romanian-born Eugene Ionesco (1912–94) and Irish-born Samuel Beckett (1906–89) spent their working lives in France. Significant composers include Gabriel Urbain Fauré (1845–1924), Claude Achille Debussy (1862–1918), Erik Satie (1866–1925), Albert Roussel (1869–1937), Maurice Ravel (1875–1937), Francis Poulenc (1899–1963), Olivier Messiaen (1908–92), Darius Milhaud (1892–1974), and composer-conductor Pierre Boulez (b. 1925). The sculptor Aristide Maillol (1861–1944) and the painters/artists Henri Matisse (1869–1954), Georges Rouault (1871–1958), Georges Braque (1882–1963), Spanish-born Pablo Picasso (1881–1974), Russian-born Marc Chagall (1887–1985), Marcel Duchamp (1887–1968), Fernand Léger (1881–1955), and Jean Dubuffet (1901–85) are world famous.

Of international renown are actor-singers Maurice Chevalier (1888–1972), Yves Montand (Ivo Livi, 1921–91), and Charles Aznavour (b. 1924); actor-director Jacques Tati (Jacques Tatischeff, 1907–82); actors Charles Boyer (1899–1978), Jean-Louis Xavier Trintignant (b. 1930), Jean-Paul Belmondo (b. 1933), and Gérard Depardieu (b. 1948); actresses Simone Signoret (Simone Kaminker, 1921–85), Jeanne Moreau (b. 1928), Leslie Caron (b. 1931), Brigitte Bardot (b. 1934), Catherine Deneuve (b. 1943), Isabelle Huppert (b. 1953), Isabelle Adjani (b. 1955), Juliette Binoche (b. 1964), Julie Delpy (b. 1969), and Audrey Tautou (b. 1978); singer Edith Piaf (1915–63); master of mime Marcel Marceau (b. 1923); and directors Georges Méliès (1861–1938), Abel Gance (1889–1981), Jean Renoir (1894–1979), Robert Bresson (1901–99), René Clément (1913–96), Eric Rohmer (Jean-Marie Maurice Scherer, b. 1920), Alain Resnais (b. 1922), Jean-Luc Godard (b. 1930), Louis Malle (1932–95), and François Truffaut (1932–84). One of the most recognizable Frenchmen in the world was oceanographer Jacques-Yves Cousteau (1910–97), who popularized undersea exploration with popular documentary films and books.

49 DEPENDENCIES

French overseas departments include French Guiana, Guadeloupe, Martinique, and Saint-Pierre and Miquelon (described in the *Americas* volume under French American Dependencies) and Réunion (in the *Africa* volume under French African Dependencies). French overseas territories and collectivities include French Polynesia, French Southern and Antarctic Territories, New Caledonia, and Wallis and Futuna (see French Asian Dependencies in the *Asia* volume). The inhabitants of French overseas departments and territories are French citizens, enjoy universal suffrage, and send elected representatives to the French parliament.

The island of Mayotte (in the *Africa* volume), which has been part of the French-administered overseas collectivity since the 1970s, gained status as an overseas department in April 2011. The change came about as a result of the 2009 referendum through which 95% of the voters on Mayotte approved the measure. The change in status makes the island a more integral part of France. Although the island is geographically a part of the Comoros archipelago, Mayotte voted against independence in 1974, when the other three islands of the chain became the independent nation of Comoros. While Mayotte remained under French administration, the Comoros has continued to claim the island as its own.

50 BIBLIOGRAPHY

Annesley, Claire, ed. *A Political and Economic Dictionary of Western Europe*. Philadelphia: Routledge/Taylor and Francis, 2005.

Cogan, Charles. *French Negotiating Behavior: Dealing with La Grande Nation*. Washington, DC: United States Institute of Peace Press, 2003.

France Investment and Business Guide: Strategic and Practical Information. Washington, DC: International Business Publications USA, 2012.

Gildea, Robert. *France Since 1945.* 2nd ed. Oxford: Oxford University Press, 2002.

Graham, Bruce Desmond. *Choice and Democratic Order: the French Socialist Party, 1937–1950.* New York: Cambridge University Press, 2006.

Haine, W. S. *Culture and Customs of France.* Westport, CT: Greenwood Press, 2006.

Hewitt, Nicholas, ed. *The Cambridge Companion to Modern French Culture.* New York: Cambridge University Press, 2003.

Illustrated Guide to France. New York: W. W. Norton, 2003.

International Smoking Statistics: A Collection of Historical Data from 30 Economically Developed Countries. New York: Oxford University Press, 2002.

Kaufmann, J. E., et al. *Fortress France: The Maginot Line and French Defenses in World War II.* Westport, CT: Praeger, 2005.

Kelly, Michael, ed. *French Culture and Society: The Essentials.* New York: Oxford University Press, 2001.

Political Chronology of Europe. London, Eng.: Europa, 2001.

Raymond, Gino. *Historical Dictionary of France.* 2nd ed. Lanham, MD: Scarecrow, 2008.

Wessels, Wolfgang, Andreas Maurer, and Jürgan Mittag, eds. *Fifteen into One?: the European Union and Its Member States.* New York: Palgrave, 2003

GEORGIA

Republic of Georgia
Sakartveld Respublika

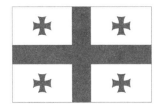

CAPITAL: T'bilisi (Tbilisi)

FLAG: White field with a red cross in the center; its arms extend horizontally and vertically to the edges of the flag. In each of the four corners against the white background are four smaller red crosses.

ANTHEM: *Tavisupleba (Liberty).*

MONETARY UNIT: The lari (GEL) was issued in 1995 to replace government coupons that were introduced in 1993. GEL1 = US$0.6034 (or US$1 = GEL1.657) as of October 2011.

WEIGHTS AND MEASURES: The metric system is in force.

HOLIDAYS: New Year's Day, 1–2 January; Christmas, 7 January; Independence Day, 26 May; St. George's Day, 22 November.

TIME: 4 p.m. = noon GMT.

¹LOCATION, SIZE, AND EXTENT

Georgia is located in southeastern Europe, bordering the Black Sea, between Turkey and Russia. Comparatively, the area occupied by Georgia is slightly smaller than the state of South Carolina, with a total area of 69,700 sq km (26,911 sq mi). Georgia shares boundaries with Russia on the N and E, Azerbaijan on the E and S, Armenia and Turkey on the S, and the Black Sea on the W. Georgia's land boundary totals 1,461 km (906 mi). Its coastline is 310 km (192 mi). Its capital city, T'bilisi, is located in the southeastern part of the country.

²TOPOGRAPHY

The topography of Georgia is mainly mountainous, with the great Caucasus Mountains in the north and lesser Caucasus Mountains in the south. The highest point in the nation is Mount Shkhara at a height of 5,201 m (17,064 ft) in the Greater Caucasus. The Kolkhida Lowland opens to the Black Sea in the west and the Kura River basin lies in the east. The Kura River is the nation's longest river with a length of 1,514 km (941 mi). Good soils occur in the river valley flood plains and in the foothills of the Kolkhida Lowland.

³CLIMATE

Georgia's climate along the Black Sea coast is similar to that along the Mediterranean: warm, humid, and almost subtropical. Farther inland the climate is continental, with warm summers and cold winters. July's mean temperature is 23°C (73.8°F). The mean temperature in January is -3°C (27.3°F). The annual rainfall in Georgia is 51 cm (20 in). In the mountains it is much cooler, with snow and ice all year in altitudes above 3,600 m (12,000 ft).

⁴FLORA AND FAUNA

The World Resources Institute estimates that there are 4,350 plant species in Georgia. In addition, Georgia is home to 98 mammal, 268 bird, 61 reptile, and 15 amphibian species. The calculation re-

flects the total number of distinct species residing in the country, not the number of endemic species.

The subtropical zone of the Black Sea coast of the Caucasus Mountains has distinctive vegetation: woods of black alder, oak, elm, and beech with a profusion of lianas and an admixture of evergreens. Mountain goats, Caucasian goats, Caucasian antelope, European wild boar, porcupine, and the leopard inhabit the Caucasus, and reptiles and amphibious creatures abound.

⁵ENVIRONMENT

The World Resources Institute reported that Georgia had designated 269,800 hectares (666,690 acres) of land for protection as of 2006. Water resources totaled 63.3 cu km (15.19 cu mi) while water usage was 3.61 cu km (0.866 cu mi) per year. Domestic water usage accounted for 20% of total usage, industrial for 21%, and agricultural for 59%. Per capita water usage totaled 808 cu m (28,534 cu ft) per year.

Georgia suffers from pollution of its air, water, and soil. The UN reported in 2008 that carbon dioxide emissions in Georgia totaled 6,027 kilotons. The Mtkvari River and the Black Sea are both heavily polluted. Pesticides from agricultural areas have significantly contaminated the soil.

Georgia is prone to earthquakes; however, they haven't occurred with great frequency. In September 2009 an earthquake measuring 6.2 in magnitude rattled northern Georgia, injuring one and severely damaging many buildings. While no deaths were reported, strong tremors were felt as far away as T'bilisi. In January 2011 a 5.7-magnitude earthquake was recorded in the western region of Imereti. No significant damage was reported.

There are two Ramsar wetland sites: one in central Kolkheti and the other at the Ispani II marshes. According to a 2011 report issued by the International Union for Conservation of Nature and Natural Resources (IUCN), threatened species included 10 types of mammals, 10 species of birds, 7 types of reptiles, 1 species of amphibian, 9 species of fish, and 9 species of invertebrates. Species on the endangered list include Atlantic sturgeon, slender-billed curlew, Mediterranean monk seals, Darevsky's viper, and the Armenian birch mouse.

6 POPULATION

The US Central Intelligence Agency (CIA) estimates the population of Georgia in 2011 to be approximately 4,585,874, which placed it at number 121 in population among the 196 nations of the world. In 2011 approximately 16.1% of the population was over 65 years of age, with another 15.6% under 15 years of age. The median age in Georgia was 39.1 years. There were 0.91 males for every female in the country. The population's annual rate of change was -0.326%. The projected population for the year 2025 was 4,300,000. Population density in Georgia was calculated at 66 people per sq km (170 people per sq mi).

The UN estimated that 53% of the population lived in urban areas, and that urban populations had an annual rate of change of -0.4%. The largest urban area was T'bilisi, with a population of 1.1 million.

7 MIGRATION

Estimates of Georgia's net migration rate, carried out by the CIA in 2011, amounted to -4.06 migrants per 1,000 citizens. The total number of emigrants living abroad was 1.06 million, and the total number of immigrants living in Georgia was 167,300. Georgia also accepted 1,100 refugees. With independence in 1991 came three secessionist movements in three autonomous areas and conflicts in two of them. The conflict in South Ossetia in 1991, followed by the conflict in Abkhazia in 1992 and 1993, resulted in the mass displacement of ethnic Georgians, Ossetians, and Abkhaz, as well as other ethnic minorities. As many as 200,000 Georgians may have fled the fighting in Abkhazia in 1993. By December 1996 Georgia had 280,000 internally displaced persons. In February of 1997 a voluntary repatriation plan was agreed upon for persons to return to South Ossetia. Hostilities resumed in Gali in May 1998, displacing some 40,000 residents. At the end of 2010, there were still 236,000 persons internally displaced in Georgia as a result of conflicts in South Ossetia and Abkhazia in the early 1990s, and an additional 22,000 displaced from the 2008 conflict with Russia over South Ossetia.

Repatriation of Meskhetian Turks began in 2003. Transit migration, trafficked migrants (primarily women from other former Soviet states), migrants from Asia and Africa, and irregular migrants were of increasing concern beginning in 2004 as Georgia looked to membership in the European Union (EU).

8 ETHNIC GROUPS

According to the 2002 census, 83.3% of the population are Georgian. The leading minorities are Azeris with 6.5%, Armenians with 5.7%, Russians with 1.5%, and others (including Ossetians and Abkhaz) with 2.5%. The census placed the number of Roma within the country at about 452; there have been reports of social discrimination against this group. Since 2008 there have been some legal efforts to repatriate the Muslim Meskhetian Turks who were deported by Joseph Stalin in 1944. By the end of 2009 more than 1,700 had applied for official repatriation; however, among the small number of those who had already resettled in the coun-

try, legally or otherwise, there were reports of discrimination and hostility from other groups.

9 LANGUAGES

Georgian is the official language and is spoken by about 71% of the population. Georgian is a South Caucasian language called Kartveli by its speakers. There is no article and a single declension with six cases. The alphabet is a phonetic one with 33 symbols. The literature dates from the 5th century AD. Russian is a second language for many Georgians, especially those whose schooling occurred prior to the fall of the Soviet Union.

10 RELIGIONS

In the 4th century AD Christianity briefly enjoyed the status of official religion, but successive conquests by Mongols, Turks, and Persians left Georgia with a complex and unsettled ethnic and religious heritage. According to the 2002 census, 83.9% of the population are nominally Georgian Orthodox. Other Orthodox groups include Russians, Armenians, and Greeks. A small number of ethnic Russians belong to dissident Orthodox groups such as the Molokani, Staroveriy (Old Believers) and the Dukhoboriy. There are also a few radical Georgian Orthodox factions that are not associated with the official church, including the Society of Saint David the Builder, Union of Orthodox Parents, and People's Orthodox Christian Movement. About 9.9% of the population are Muslims, most of whom are ethnic Azeris, Georgian Muslims of Ajara, and ethnic Chechen Kists. Less than 1% of the population are Roman Catholics. Smaller Christian denominations include Baptists, Seventh-Day Adventists, Pentecostals, Jehovah's Witnesses, the Armenian Apostolic Church, and the New Apostolic Church. There are also small numbers of Baha'is and Hare Krishnas. There are about 10,000 Jews in the country. In 2002 the parliament ratified a concordat with the Georgian Orthodox Church (GOC) granting them special recognition; however, the constitution has established a separation of church and state and freedom of religion. Some non-Orthodox groups have complained of the privileged status granted to the GOC. For instance, the GOC is allowed to review public school textbooks and to make suggestions on content. Registration of religious organizations is not required, but many do so in order to gain the legal status necessary to rent office or worship space and import written materials. Orthodox Christmas, Epiphany, Nowruz-Bairam (the Azeri Muslim spring and New Year festival), Good Friday, Orthodox Easter, Easter Monday, the Day of Apostle Andrew, the Day of the Virgin Mary, Svetitskhovloba, and Saint George's Day are observed as national holidays.

11 TRANSPORTATION

The CIA reports that Georgia has a total of 20,329 km (12,632 mi) of roads, of which 7,854 km (4,880 mi) are paved. Railroads extend for 1,566 km (973 mi). There are 22 airports, which transported 294,400 passengers in 2009 according to the World Bank.

Railways serve primarily as connections to the Black Sea for inland cities like T'bilisi, Chiat'ura, Jvari, and Tkvarcheli. The maritime fleet had 193 ships (of 1,000 GRT or over) in 2010. Batumi and Poti are the principal Black Sea ports. As of 2009 Georgia had 18 airports with paved runways and four heliports. Its only in-

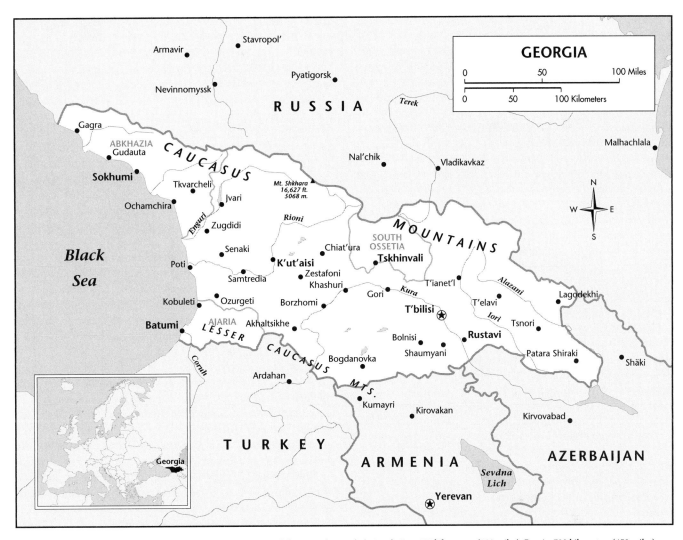

LOCATION: 42°0′ N; 44°0′ E. BOUNDARY LENGTHS: Armenia, 164 kilometers (102 miles); Azerbaijan, 322 kilometers (200 miles); Russia, 723 kilometers (450 miles); Turkey, 252 kilometers (157 miles); total coastline, 310 kilometers (193 miles).

ternational airport is T'bilisi which is capable of handling 1,000–1,200 passengers per hour.

Russia and Georgia reopened the Verkhny Lars border crossing in March 2010, marking the first time since 2006 that people and supplies were allowed to pass through the checkpoint. The Verkhny Lars checkpoint, located high in the Caucasus mountains, represents the only border crossing to connect Georgia directly with Russia; the others all go through the breakaway regions of South Ossetia and Abkhazia. Verkhny Lars was closed by Russia in 2006 as relations between the neighbors deteriorated. Still, Georgian officials remain adamant that the March 2010 Verkhny Lars reopening does not imply better relations between the neighbors. At the time of the decision, all Georgian exports remained under a Russian embargo, minimizing any economic windfall that could come from the move.

12 HISTORY

Georgia has existed as a state on a sporadic basis since classical times. The first Georgian state can be traced to the 4th century BC. Throughout its history Georgia has been conquered by the Ro-

mans, Iranians, the Arabs, the Turks, the Mongols, and the Hordes of Tamerlane. Georgia did enjoy independence for short periods of time from the 6th to the 12th centuries AD. The Mongols invaded and conquered Georgia by 1236. Later the Ottoman and Persian empires competed for control of the region. Western Georgia became a Russian protectorate in 1783. All of Georgia was absorbed directly into the Russian empire during the 19th century.

During the tumult of the Russian revolution, Georgia declared its independence on 26 May 1918. Twenty-two countries recognized this new state, including Soviet Russia. Nonetheless, the Soviet Red Army invaded in February 1921 and Georgia's brief independence came to an end. Georgia became one of the republics in the Soviet Union.

Many Georgians fell victim in the late 1920s and 1930s to Soviet collectivization, crash industrialization, and Joseph Stalin's purges (despite his Georgian-Ossetian ethnic origins). Nationalist riots were brutally suppressed in 1924 and 1956, and nationalist mass demonstrations occurred in 1978 and 1988. In April 1989 many Georgian demonstrators were murdered, some with shovels, by Soviet military and police forces during a peaceful protest against perceived Russian support for Abkhaz autonomy demands.

Georgia's first multiparty legislative elections, held in October 1990, resulted in a victory for the party coalition Round Table–Free Georgia, headed by academic and dissident Zviad Gamsakhurdia. He was subsequently selected by the deputies to serve as chairman of the legislature. Following a March 1991 referendum, a formal declaration of independence from the Soviet Union was unanimously approved by the legislature on 9 April 1991. Gamsakhurdia was popularly elected as president in May, but still faced opposition from, among others, parties belonging to the National Congress, a national liberation body formed in October 1990. The Mkhedrioni paramilitary group, led by Jaba Ioseliani, was allied with the National Congress. During 1991 Gamsakhurdia's erratic attempts to remake Georgian society and politics caused the head of the National Guard, Tengiz Kitovani, to also join the opposition. The National Guard and Mkhedrioni spearheaded a general assault to overthrow Gamsakhurdia in December 1991, forcing him to flee the country in early January 1992.

A military council formed by Ioseliani, Kitovani, and others assumed power. They suspended the constitution, replacing it with one from 1921, dissolved the legislature, and declared emergency rule. Former Georgian leader Eduard Shevardnadze (the Communist Party boss of Georgia from 1972 to 1985) was invited in early March 1992 to head a provisional government. He formed a civilian State Council to rule until elections could be held, and was elected head of its four-member presidium.

During legislative elections in October 1992 he was elected speaker in an uncontested race. The new legislature granted Shevardnadze wide-ranging powers as head of state pending completion of a new constitution. In May 1993 Shevardnadze moved to consolidate his power by securing the resignations of Kitovani and Ioseliani from government posts. Gamsakhurdia returned from exile in September 1993 to the western Georgian region of Mingrelia and led a revolt to unseat Shevardnadze. Pro-Shevardnadze forces, assisted by the Russian military, were able to put down the revolt by early November 1993. Gamsakhurdia's death was reported in early January 1994. In further moves by Shevardnadze to consolidate power, Kitovani was arrested in January 1995 for planning an illegal paramilitary attack on Abkhazia.

Several of Georgia's ethnic minorities stepped up their dissident and separatist actions in the late 1980s and early 1990s. South Ossetians in 1989 called for their territory to be joined with North Ossetia in Russia, or for independence. In June 1992 Russian president Boris Yeltsin brokered a cease-fire, and a predominantly Russian military "peacekeeping" force numbering about 500 was stationed in South Ossetia. A November 1999 OSCE Summit Declaration urged Georgia and South Ossetia to agree on resettling displaced persons and called for international aid for the region.

Georgia's southern Ajaria region is to a large extent self-governing. In 1992 it was formally declared an autonomous republic within Georgia; as such, its regional laws take precedence over Georgia's national laws.

The northwestern region of Abkhazia has sought independence since Georgia achieved its own independence in 1991. In July 1992 the Abkhaz Supreme Soviet declared its effective independence from Georgia. This prompted Georgian national guardsmen to attack Abkhazia. In October 1992 the UN Security Council (UNSC) approved the first UN observer mission to an NIS state, termed UNOMIG, to help reach a settlement. Abkhaz-Geor-

gian talks leading to a cease-fire were held under UN auspices. In April 1994 the two sides signed framework accords on a political settlement and on the return of refugees and displaced persons. The next month a cease-fire was signed by Georgia and Abkhazia, providing for Russian troops (acting as Commonwealth of Independent States or CIS peacekeepers) to be deployed in a security zone along the Enguri River, which divides Abkhazia from the rest of Georgia. The Russian Defense Ministry in 1999 reported the deployment of about 1,700 peacekeepers.

A major point of contention between the two sides is Georgia's demand that displaced persons be allowed to return to Abkhazia, after which an agreement on broad autonomy for Abkhazia may be negotiated. The Abkhazians have insisted upon recognition of their "equal status" with Georgia as a precondition to large-scale repatriation.

UN-sponsored peace talks were reconvened in mid-1997. In late 1997 the sides agreed to set up a Coordinating Council to discuss cease-fire maintenance and refugee, economic, and humanitarian issues. Abkhaz forces in mid-1998 reportedly expelled 30,000–40,000 ethnic Georgians. In 1999 Abkhazia declared independence, but this action was not recognized by Georgia or the international community.

Meanwhile, in November 1995, Eduard Shevardnadze had been elected to the re-created post of president, receiving 74.32% of the vote in a six-person race, and a new parliament was selected. International observers termed the elections generally free and fair nationwide except in the region of Ajaria.

Seven candidates were registered to run in Georgia's 9 April 2000 presidential election. The major challengers to Shevardnadze were Jumbar Patiashvili, former first secretary of the Georgian Communist Party (who ran in the 1995 presidential race), and Aslan Abashidze, chairman of the Ajarian Supreme Council. Both challengers were leaders of the Revival Bloc that contested the 1999 legislative races. Voting did not take place in Abkhazia or South Ossetia. The Georgian Central Election Commission (CEC) reported that Shevardnadze received 80% of 1.87 million votes and Patiashvili received 17% (less than he received in 1995). The 150 OSCE monitors reported on 10 April that the election did not meet OSCE standards, though "fundamental freedoms were generally respected during the election campaign and candidates were able to express their views." They stressed that the government aided the incumbent; state media were biased; vote counting and tabulation procedures lacked uniformity and, at times, transparency; ballot box stuffing had taken place; and some voting protocols reportedly had been tampered with.

In March 2001 officials from Georgia and Abkhazia signed an accord stating they would not use force against one another. However, meetings between the two sides were canceled later in the year due to continuing hostilities and hostage incidents. On 8 October 2001 a UNOMIG helicopter was shot down over Abkhazia, and all nine people on board were killed. In August 2002 Georgia and Abkhazia failed to come to an agreement on the withdrawal of Abkhaz fighters from the Kodori Gorge, the only enclave controlled by Georgia in Abkhazia. Georgia was concerned that Russians were supporting the Abkhaz fighters. In January 2003 UN Secretary-General Kofi Annan declared little progress had been made on talks to determine the future status of Abkhazia, and that the mandate for UNOMIG should be extended another six months, until 31 July 2003.

Upon coming into his second term in office, Shevardnadze claimed he would fight corruption and low living standards, undertake market reforms, and protect the territorial integrity of Georgia. Georgia desired NATO membership, and on 22 November 2002, Shevardnadze formally requested that Georgia be invited into the alliance.

In 1999 the OSCE demanded that Russia remove all of its troops from Georgia. In 2001 Russia vacated the Gudauta and Vaziani bases and the Marneuli military airfield, but did not agree to a time frame for a departure from the Akhalkalaki and Batumi military bases. One sore spot in Georgian-Russian relations remains the situation in Chechnya. Russian officials have accused Georgia of aiding Chechen rebels, especially in the Pankisi Gorge region of Georgia.

Russia regards the armed conflict in Chechnya as a part of the international campaign against terrorism, and has demanded that Georgia cooperate in combating Chechens in the region. Russia has warned Georgia that it would take military action if Georgia failed to deal with Chechen rebels in the Pankisi Gorge. The United States, since 11 September 2001, has claimed that members of the al-Qaeda organization are operating in the Pankisi Gorge and has enlisted Georgia's support in undertaking antiterror operations there.

In April and May 2002 US Special Forces arrived in Georgia to train and equip troops for counterterrorist operations. On 8 February 2003 Russia claimed that terrorists arrested in the UK and France had trained in the Pankisi Gorge, and used laboratories built there to produce the poisonous toxin ricin that can be used as an agent in chemical warfare.

The end of 2003 brought with it drastic changes for Georgians. The parliamentary elections that were held on 2 November 2003 were criticized by national and international organizations as being grossly rigged. Mikhail Saakashvili, who received a law degree from Columbia University and worked in the United States for a short while, denounced the election results and urged the population of Georgia to nonviolent civil disobedience against the authorities. People responded to Saakashvili's call and mounted protests in T'bilisi (the so-called "Rose Revolution"), crying for fair elections. (The "Rose Revolution" inspired similar movements in other parts of the world, most notably in Ukraine where the "Orange Revolution" brought about long-awaited change.)

President Shevardnadze eventually bowed under the pressure, and on 23 November 2003 resigned from his post, leaving parliamentary speaker Nino Burjanadze in charge until fresh presidential elections could be staged. This move was followed by a decision of the Supreme Court to annul the parliamentary elections results.

On 4 January 2004 Saakashvili emerged victorious in the presidential elections—he received support from all the opposition parties and garnered 96.3% of the votes. His party, the United National Movement, subsequently won 67.6% of the votes (and 135 out of 150 party list seats in parliament) in the re-run of the parliamentary elections; the Rightist Opposition got 7.6% (15 seats), while other parties received less than 7%. The new prime minister was Zurab Noghaideli.

This victory, however, came at a time when Georgia was very politically, socially, and economically unstable. Aslan Abashidze, the leader of the Ajarian Autonomous Republic in western Georgia, accused Saakashvili of planning to invade Ajaria and declared a state of emergency and the mobilization of armed forces. He failed to attract support from Russia though, and intense criticism from several foreign governments and international organizations forced him to resign and leave for Moscow in May 2004.

These events were followed by tensions in the other two problematic regions—South Ossetia and Abkhazia. Parliamentary elections in South Ossetia in May 2004 and troubled presidential elections in Abkhazia in October 2004 were not recognized by the government in T'bilisi. A proposal on autonomy for South Ossetia presented by Saakashvili was refused by the South Ossetian leaders, who sought full independence. Saakashvili remained firm in his goal to keep Abkhazia and South Ossetia within the territorial boundaries of Georgia. In November 2006 South Ossetians voted in favor of independence in an unrecognized referendum.

In May 2005 George W. Bush became the first US president to visit Georgia. That same month, the Baku-T'bilisi-Ceyhan pipeline was officially opened, with US Secretary of Energy Samuel Bodman joining the presidents of Kazakhstan, Azerbaijan, Georgia, and Turkey at the opening ceremony. A year later, oil began flowing through the pipeline.

In 2006 Georgia's relationship with Russia worsened amid tension over Georgia's breakaway regions and its ties with NATO. Russia imposed sanctions on Georgia and expelled hundreds of Georgians, whom it accused of being illegal immigrants. Russian restrictions included bans on Georgia's wine, mineral water, and fruits and vegetables, and a suspension of air, rail, and road transportation between the countries. Russia's Gazprom indicated that it would seek to more than double the price it charged Georgia for natural gas, beginning in January 2007. Georgia said that it was close to obtaining an alternative supply from a British Petroleum (BP)-run platform in the Caspian Sea off of Azerbaijan. Therefore, Gazprom would be deprived of its monopoly in the south Caucasus. Georgia said it would be mostly free of Russian gas by 2008. Azerbaijani gas would be sent through a pipeline that runs from Azerbaijan through Georgia to Turkey.

A political crisis evolved in late 2007. High unemployment, rising prices, and lingering poverty had eroded Saakashvili's popular support. In September the former defense minister, Irakli Okruashvili, accused Saakashvili of corruption and of planning a murder. The allegations led to mass antigovernment demonstrations in T'bilisi in November. The protesters demanded more political openness, and some demanded Saakashvili's resignation. President Saakashvili declared a state of emergency after sending in riot police to battle protesters; the police used clubs and fired tear gas into crowds. Opposition media were shut down. After declaring the state of emergency, Saakashvili backed down from the aggressive stance quickly, and called for early presidential elections to be held on 5 January 2008. Saakashvili, with 53.5% of the vote, won reelection.

Saakashvili also announced early parliamentary elections for May 2008. Saakashvili's National Movement-Democratic Front won nearly 60% of the vote and the majority of seats. (While the party is called the United National Movement, its parliamentary representation is called the National Movement-Democratic Front.)

By August 2008 relations with the separatists in South Ossetia reached a crisis point. Georgia launched attacks on South Ossetia, a region that lies along the border with Russia. Russia responded by sending thousands of troops into the region on the grounds that the attacks were threatening Russian citizens. Although a cease-fire and withdrawal of Russian troops was soon in effect, Russia officially recognized the independence of both South Ossetia and Abkhazia. Both the United Nations (UN) and the Organization for Security and Cooperation in Europe (OSCE) had observer missions in the region to monitor cease-fire agreements along the borders with the separatist regions. In June 2009, however, Russia vetoed the extension of the UN observers' mandate in Georgia, specifically calling for the removal of the UN team along the Georgia-Abkhazia border zone. The OSCE removed its observer mission in June 2009, after its member states also failed to reach agreement on extending its mandate. The withdrawal of UNOMIG and OSCE left the European Union Monitoring Mission as the only recognized international observation force to monitor the ceasefire agreements. Most of the international community condemned the military actions of both Georgia and Russia in the conflict. As of August 2011 Russia, Nicaragua, Nauru, and Venezuela were the only countries to recognize the independence of Abkhazia and South Ossetia.

13 GOVERNMENT

Until 1995 Georgia was governed according to a constitution dating back to 1921. Shevardnadze, though, pushed for the adoption of a new constitution giving the president added powers. A new constitution was approved by the legislature in August 1995. It reestablished a strong presidency, though affirming a balance of executive and legislative powers more equitable than those in most other new constitutions approved by former Soviet republics. The president is elected for a five-year term. The constitution establishes a unicameral, 150-member legislature. (The legislature was originally 235 members but was reduced in 2008.) Legislators serve four-year terms. Government ministers are responsible to the president, who is assisted by a state minister. Voting for the new legislature took place on 5 November 1995, simultaneous with the presidential race. Only three of the 54 parties running received at least 5% of the party list vote required to win seats, though other parties won representation through constituency races; they have formed eight legislative factions. The elections were judged "consistent with democratic norms" by international observers.

In 2004, after the Rose Revolution, the constitution was amended to give increased powers to the president.

In a move to address widespread corruption, Saakashvili's administration fired nearly all of the police force shortly after he was elected. Better training and higher salaries were provided to the new force.

Legislative elections were held in the spring of 2004 and again in 2008. Legislative elections were scheduled for spring 2012 and presidential elections for 2013. Under the constitution, Saakashvili cannot seek a third term.

In October 2010 the Parliament passed a number of amendments to the Constitution; effective after the 2013 presidential election, these measures reduce the power of the president and give more power to the prime minister and government.

The breakaway regions of South Ossetia and Abkhazia were not under the control of the central government as of October 2011.

14 POLITICAL PARTIES

The major political parties that won representation in the legislature in 1999 were Shevardnadze's Georgian Citizens' Union (gaining 891,000 of 2.1 million party list votes cast), Ajarian leader Abashidze's Revival Union (537,000 votes), and Industry Will Save Georgia (151,000 votes). The Georgian Labor Party failed to gain enough votes to win party list seats. Other parties that gained more than 1% of the party list vote included the opposition National Democratic Party (NDP), the People's Party, and the United Communist Party. Most of the minor political parties and groups characterized themselves as opposed to the government.

By November 2003, former President Eduard Shevardnadze had resigned from office in a bloodless "Rose Revolution" following protests against his rule and what were seen to be fraudulent parliamentary elections. The election results were later annulled. Elections held on 4 January 2004 resulted in Mikhail Saakashvili's election as president; he was reelected in January 2008. In elections held 21 May 2008, Saakashvili's party, the National Movement-Democratic Front, won 59.2% of the vote and 120 seats out of the 150 that are on the party lists; the National Council-New Rights won 17.7% of the vote and 16 seats. Other parties won 23.1% of the vote and the remaining seats.

The Organization for Security and Co-operation in Europe, which sent a team to monitor the 2008 presidential elections, reported afterward that, "while the election was in essence consistent with most OSCE and Council of Europe commitments and standards for democratic election, it also revealed significant challenges which need to be addressed urgently." Following the parliamentary elections later that year, the OSCE reported that, although deficiencies still existed, Georgian officials had made demonstrable efforts to correct election concerns.

15 LOCAL GOVERNMENT

Georgia's administrative subdivisions include the Abkhazian and Ajarian Autonomous Republics. The Georgian Supreme Soviet stripped South Ossetia of its autonomous status in late 1990, following its demands to secede and become a part of Russia. Abkhazia and South Ossetia consider themselves self-ruling, and Ajaria has substantial effective autonomy. There are 69 districts (rayons) and nine regions, whose governors or mayors are appointed by the president. The city of T'bilisi functions as a separate administrative entity. Local assembly (sakrebulo) elections were held for the first time under the new constitution in November 1998. Thirteen parties participated in the voting for more than 150,000 candidates for 10,000 municipal and district (rayon) assemblies or councils. In small towns and villages of fewer than 2,000 voters, 654 majoritarian elections were held, while elsewhere 377 proportional elections by party lists took place. The Citizen's Union Party won the largest number of seats, followed by the Revival bloc, the National Democratic Party, and the Labor Party, though 12 of the 13 parties won some seats. Inadequate funding and the absence of legislation limited the functions of the new locally elected governments. Opposition parties accused the government and the ruling Citizens' Union Party of retaining the effective power to appoint the mayors of the largest cities and the regional leaders. There remains considerable contention between the central government and the Autonomous Ajarian Republic over the scope of local powers.

Local elections were held in 2010. For the first time, the mayor of T'bilisi was directly elected. In all other cities in Georgia, the mayor is not directly elected. Giorgi ("Gigi") Ugulava, the incumbent mayor of T'bilisi and a member of the governing party, won the election with 55% of the vote. *Sakrebulo* seats were also up for election across the country. The governing party, the United National Movement, won the majority of seats in the city council elections.

¹⁶JUDICIAL SYSTEM

Before 1995, Georgia's legal system retained traces of the pre-Soviet era, the Soviet period, the Gamsakhurdia presidency, and the State Council period. Courts included district courts, a T'bilisi city court, a supreme court in each of the two autonomous republics, and at the highest level the Supreme Court of the Republic.

The 1995 constitution provides for an independent judiciary. The Law on Common Courts, passed in 1997, establishes a three-tier court system. District courts hear petty criminal and civil cases. Regional courts of appeal have original and appellate jurisdiction. They try major criminal and civil cases, review cases, and can remand cases to the lower court for retrial. The Supreme Court was envisioned as the highest appellate court, but it also hears some capital cases and appeals from the Central Electoral Commission.

A constitutional court was set up in September 1996. It arbitrates constitutional disputes between the branches of government and rules on individual claims of human rights abuses.

Administration of the court system was transferred from the Justice Ministry to a Council of Justice in 1997, to increase the independence of the courts from budgetary and other influence. The council consists of four members from each of the three branches of government.

The constitution provides for the rights to presumption of innocence, to have a public trial, to legal counsel, and to refuse to make a statement in the absence of counsel. A criminal procedures code was approved in November 1997, and a new criminal code was passed in June 1999. The criminal procedures code aimed at reducing the dominant power of prosecutors over arrests and investigations. Under the new procedures, judges issue warrants for arrest and detention orders, and detentions must follow correct legal procedures, including informing detainees of their rights, allowing visits by family members and lawyers, and treating detainees without brutality. In mid-1999, however, some of the liberal strictures on defendants' rights were reversed at the insistence of the prosecutors, who continued to have a major influence over the courts.

Under the Law on Common Courts, Georgia has launched a system of testing judges on basic legal principles; many of those who have taken the test have failed. Georgia's accession to the Council of Europe in April 1999 led to new legislation taking jurisdiction over the prison system away from the Interior (police) Ministry and giving it to the Ministry of Justice.

Since 2005 further judiciary reform efforts have been made. Amendments to the constitution were passed in 2006 to increase the independence of the judiciary. In 2007 legislation was passed that prohibits parties to a case from communicating with judges during the pre-trial and trial. Despite these measures, as of 2010 judiciary reform was still considered a priority. A sizeable percentage of the population, as well as observers, continued to assert that the judiciary lacks independence and professionalism, and that it is subject to pressures by the executive branch.

¹⁷ARMED FORCES

The International Institute for Strategic Studies reports that armed forces in Georgia totaled 20,655 members in 2011. The force is comprised of 17,767 from the army, 1,310 from the air force, and 1,578 members of a national guard. Armed forces represent 1.4% of the labor force in Georgia. Defense spending totaled $428.6 million and accounted for 1.9% of GDP.

Georgian armed forces were deployed to Iraq in a peacekeeping support role, and under NATO in Serbia and Montenegro. In 2010 Georgia sent troops to Afghanistan to serve alongside NATO forces. As of early 2011 there were slightly less than 1,000 Georgian troops in Afghanistan. That same year, Saakashvili offered to increase their number if needed.

¹⁸INTERNATIONAL COOPERATION

Georgia was admitted to the United Nations on 21 July 1992. The country is a member of several UN specialized agencies, such as the FAO, IAEA, ICAO, IFAD, ILO, IMF, UNCTAD, UNESCO, UNIDO, WHO, and the World Bank. Georgia joined the Commonwealth of Independent States (CIS) in 1993 and became a member of the WTO in 2000. The nation also belongs to the OSCE, the Council of Europe, the Black Sea Economic Cooperation Zone, the Euro-Atlantic Partnership Council, and the European Bank for Reconstruction and Development. Georgia has observer status in the OAS and is part of the NATO Partnership for Peace. In 2001 Georgia, Uzbekistan, Ukraine, Azerbaijan, and Moldova formed a social and economic development union known as GUAAM. Uzbekistan withdrew from the partnership in 2005.

In 1993 a UN Observer Mission (UNOMIG) was established in Georgia to monitor cease-fire agreements between the State of Georgia and the region of Abkhazia and to support ongoing CIS peacekeeping forces in that region. More than 30 countries contributed military personnel to UNOMIG during the course of its mandate.

In environmental cooperation, Georgia is part of the Basel Convention, Conventions on Biological Diversity and Air Pollution, Ramsar, CITES, the Kyoto Protocol, the Montréal Protocol, MARPOL, and the UN Conventions on the Law of the Sea, Climate Change and Desertification.

During the March 2011 talks concerning the accession of Russia to the World Trade Organization (WTO), Georgia stated that the only way it would allow the country in was if Russia ceded control of customs in the Georgian regions of South Ossetia and Abkhazia. Despite these demands, talks were seen as constructive, as other world powers noted their support for Russia's accession. Russia is the only major economy outside of the WTO.

¹⁹ECONOMY

The gross domestic product (GDP) rate of change in Georgia, as of 2010, was 6.4%. Inflation stood at 5.7%, and unemployment was reported at 16.4%.

For more than a decade after its emergence as an independent state, Georgia suffered from a host of economic problems, including hyperinflation, corruption, tax evasion, and a "shadow economy" larger than the legitimate one that stifled the country's economic progress. Shortfalls in revenues caused the government to turn to external as well as domestic financing to cover chronic budget deficits.

In 1996 the government embarked on a program for the privatization of land holdings. After low points in 1994 and 1995, there was sustained growth. Inflation fell from 163% (consumer prices) in 1995 to 39% in 1996 and 7% in 1997. The growth in GDP reached double digits, 11.2% (1996) and 10.6% (1997), stimulated in part by work on the Baku-Supsa pipeline (opened in April 1999). After 1998, however, GDP growth slowed to about 3% a year due to a combination of the effect of economic crises in Russia and Turkey (which together supply 40% of Georgia's imports and buy over 40% of its exports), an influx of refugees since 1999 from neighboring war-torn Chechnya, severe droughts affecting Georgia's agricultural output in 1998 and 2000, and, from 2001, the global economic slowdown. GDP growth was even lower (2%) in 2000, despite 11% growth in industrial production, due to a recurrence of drought which caused agricultural production to fall 15% in one year.

In 2001 agriculture recovered somewhat, growing 6%, but industrial production fell back 5%, reflecting in part an 11% decrease in exports to countries outside the CIS. Exports to CIS countries, by contrast, rose 23% in 2000 and 9% in 2001. Official government statistics reported that the GDP grew overall by 4.5% in 2001, while the US CIA estimated growth at 8.4%. Inflation, which spurted to 19% in 1999, then fell to moderate levels of between 4% and 5% in 2000 and 2001.

In 2002 Georgia's GDP levels were still only 40% of what they had been in the 1980s. The economy was hampered by the necessity of importing over 90% of the petroleum products consumed due to the shutting down of its only two remaining refineries. The larger 106,000-barrels-per-day refinery at Batumi was closed for modernization and expansion under an agreement with Japan's Mitsui Corp. A small 4,000 barrels-per-day refinery, built in 1998 and idle for much of 2001, was closed permanently in 2002 by its operation company, CanArgo, in favor of a plan to replace it with a larger 30,100-barrels-per-day facility. Georgia's future economic prospects were thought to have improved greatly in December 2002 however, with the announcement of an agreement on the Georgia portion of the Baku-T'bilisi-Ceyhan (BTC) pipeline, which opened in May 2005. In addition to the BTC project, which would pipe oil from the Caspian Sea to the Turkish port of Ceyhan on the Mediterranean to supply Western European markets, Georgia and Turkey concluded another agreement to build a railway from T'bilisi to Kars, Turkey. The railway would transport oil to Turkish refineries. The Baku-T'bilisi-Ceyhan oil pipe lines and the Baku-T'bilisi-Erzerum gas pipe lines brought much needed investment into the country and helped alleviate the chronic unemployment.

The "Rose Revolution" in 2003 brought hope that the economy would take a turn for the better by emulating a Western development pattern. This much needed change was key to healing the struggling economy. The new government promised to bring economic reforms, and throughout the mid-2000s these reforms took effect. The economy experienced an explosive expansion in 2003, with a GDP growth rate of 11.1%. The economy cooled down in 2004, growing by 6.2%, but by 2007, economic growth was flourishing at a GDP real growth rate of 12.4%.

In 2008 the World Bank recognized Georgia as the world's fastest reforming economy in its 2008 "Doing Business" report. In addition, foreign direct investment in the economy spurred new levels of growth.

Unfortunately, political instability returned in August 2008. Russia and Georgia began fighting over the territory of Ossetia, reminding investors that even though the economy was improving rapidly, the region was still dangerously unstable. To mitigate the effects of the conflict with Russia, and the 2008–09 global financial crisis, the IMF approved an 18-month, $750 million Stand-By Arrangement (SBA) with Georgia in September 2008. The following year, in August 2009, the amount of funds available was increased by $420 million. Against this agreement, Georgia drew more than $900 million. The arrangement expired in June 2011, having accomplished its objectives of restoring market confidence and making progress in returning Georgia's fiscal and external accounts to sustainable positions.

GDP growth was negative in 2009 as Georgia felt the effects of the 2008–09 global financial crisis, but it rebounded in 2010.

²⁰INCOME

The CIA estimated that in 2010 the GDP of Georgia was $22.44 billion. The CIA defines GDP as the value of all final goods and services produced within a nation in a given year and computed on the basis of purchasing power parity (PPP) rather than value as measured on the basis of the rate of the exchange based on current dollars. The per capita GDP was estimated at $4,900. The annual growth rate of GDP was 6.4%. The average inflation rate was 5.7%. It was estimated that agriculture accounted for 11% of GDP, industry 27.1%, and services 62%.

According to the World Bank, remittances from citizens living abroad totaled $714.3 million or about $156 per capita and accounted for approximately 3.2% of GDP.

The World Bank reports that in 2009, household consumption in Georgia totaled $8.8 billion or about $1,929 per capita, measured in current US dollars rather than PPP.

As of 2011 the most recent study by the World Bank reported that actual individual consumption in Georgia was 74.6% of GDP and accounted for 0.04% of world consumption. By comparison, the United States accounted for 25.44% of world individual consumption. The World Bank also estimated that 27.1% of Georgia's GDP was spent on food and beverages, 11% on housing and household furnishings, 1.9% on clothes, 8.3% on health, 9.4% on transportation, 3.1% on communications, 3.8% on recreation, 4.5% on restaurants and hotels, and 2.2% on miscellaneous goods and services and purchases from abroad.

It was estimated that in 2007 about 24% of the population subsisted on an income below the poverty line established by Georgia's government.

21 LABOR

As of 2007 Georgia had a total labor force of 1.918 million people. Within that labor force, CIA estimates in 2006 noted that 55.6% were employed in agriculture, 8.9% in industry, and 35.5% in the service sector.

Employees have the right to form or join unions freely. A confederation of independent trade unions has emerged with the abandonment of the old centralized Soviet trade unions. Georgia's main trade union is the Amalgamated Trade Unions of Georgia. Workers are permitted to engage in collective bargaining, but this practice is not extensive.

The minimum employment age is 16 except in unusual circumstances, and this minimum employment age is generally respected. In T'bilisi it is not uncommon to see children begging in the street, although their numbers have declined significantly since the 1990s. The government sets public-sector salaries dependent on the pay grade of the employee. In 2009 the minimum wage for public sector employees was GEL115 (US$68) per month. For private sector employees it was GEL20 (US$12) per month. In general, wages and salaries do not provide a decent standard of living for a family. The legal standard workweek is 41 hours with a 24-hour rest period weekly.

22 AGRICULTURE

In 2010, 10.4% of Georgia's GDP was attributed to the agricultural sector. Roughly 15% of the total land is farmed, and the country's major crops include citrus, grapes, tea, hazelnuts, and vegetables. Cereal production in 2009 amounted to 374,516 tons, fruit production 395,200 tons, and vegetable production 214,000 tons.

Since independence in April 1991, Georgian agriculture has become much more associated with the private sector; 99% of agricultural land is now privately held.

Georgia's mild climate makes it an important agricultural producer, raising a growing range of subtropical crops (including tea, tobacco, citrus fruits, and flowers) in the coastal region and exporting them to the northern republics in return for manufactured goods. During the Soviet era, Georgia supplied almost all of the former Soviet Union's citrus fruits and tea, and much of its grape crop.

23 ANIMAL HUSBANDRY

The UN Food and Agriculture Organization (FAO) reported that Georgia dedicated 1.9 million hectares (4.79 million acres) to permanent pasture or meadow in 2009. During that year, the country tended 6.2 million chickens, 1 million head of cattle, and 86,400 pigs. The production from these animals amounted to 38,740 tons of beef and veal, 36,152 tons of pork, 38,088 tons of poultry, 22,029 tons of eggs, and 659,449 tons of milk. Georgia also produced 7,725 tons of cattle hide and 1,800 tons of raw wool.

In mid-1993, a ban was placed on the export of dairy products (including milk), cattle and poultry, meat and meat products, and leather. Georgia does not produce enough meat and dairy products to satisfy domestic demand.

24 FISHING

Georgia had 30 decked commercial fishing boats in 2008. The annual capture totaled 26,512 tons according to the UN FAO. The export value of seafood totaled $1.4 million.

The Black Sea and Kura River are the main sources of the domestic catch. Commercial fishing is not a significant contributor to the economy.

25 FORESTRY

Approximately 40% of Georgia is covered by forest, but the mountainous terrain inhibits forestry production. Timber production is primarily for domestic use. The UN FAO estimated the 2009 roundwood production at 105,006 cu m (3.71 million cu ft). The value of all forest products, including roundwood, totaled $21.7 million.

26 MINING

Georgia had significant mineral deposits, but the future of the industry depended on a more secure climate for investment, through greater political and economic stability. Manganese was the country's foremost mineral commodity in the Soviet era, producing five million tons in the mid-1980s; production has since fallen precipitously, to 59,100 metric tons in 2000, but had increased to an estimated 102,000 metric tons in 2009. Manganese came from the Chiat'ura basin; reserves of high-grade ore were almost depleted.

The Madneuli region was a major site of barite, copper, lead-zinc, gold, and silver mining. Lead and zinc were mined at the Kvaisi deposit, and arsenic was mined from the Lukhumi and Tsansa deposits. In 1995 the Georgian State Geology Committee, Gruzgeologiya, stated that Georgia had gold reserves of 250 tons and silver reserves of 1,500 tons, with another 250 tons of prospective gold reserves.

In 1996 Georgia permitted foreign firms to manage metallurgical enterprises. The Zestafoni ferroalloy plant was signed over to the Russian-Georgian Bank for Reconstruction and Development in conjunction with a US partner, North Atlantic Research, to be managed for a period of 10 years.

Mine output of copper was 9,000 metric tons in 2009. In that same year, gold output was estimated at 2,000 kg, and for silver, an estimated 1,200 kg. Also produced in 2009 were mine lead, barite, bentonite, mine zinc, perlite, and cement.

27 ENERGY AND POWER

The World Bank reported in 2008 that Georgia produced 8.44 billion kWh of electricity and consumed 7.23 billion kWh, or 1,576 kWh per capita. Roughly 67% of energy came from fossil fuels, while 21% came from alternative fuels. Per capita oil consumption was 694 kg. Oil production totaled 1,000 barrels of oil a day.

Georgia must rely on imports for most of its energy needs. Its limited oil reserves were placed at about 35 million barrels in 2011. Oil exploration is actively being carried out both on land and along the Black Sea coast. Most of the oil comes primarily from Azerbaijan, and Russia. Natural gas reserves in 2011 were placed at 8.495 billion cu m, with production and consumption at 10 million cu m and at 1.71 billion cu m, respectively. As of 2010

Georgia had gas supply contracts with Azerbaijan for 10 and 20 years.

In 2010 the Georgian government was making strides to capitalize on its natural ability to produce hydroelectric power. It estimated that only 18% of its hydro capacity was being utilized. The government sought to replace its thermal and imported electric power with hydropower. Construction of two new hydropower plants was launched in 2009, and four more plants were planned. To foster growth, construction was deregulated.

From 2005 to 2011, the Millennium Challenge Corporation invested $36 million to rehabilitate Georgia's N–S natural gas pipeline (one of three gas pipelines in the country) and build the capacity of the Georgian Oil and Gas Corporation to better manage the pipeline.

28 INDUSTRY

Heavy industry, based on the country's mineral resources, includes metallurgy, construction materials, and machine building. Light industry includes food processing, beverage production, consumer durables, garments, and oil-processing. Hyperinflation in 1994 together with continuing political unrest severely affected industrial production. By 1995, industrial output of state enterprises was one-fifth of the 1990 level.

In 1996, although industrial production rose 6% for the year, less than 20% of the country's industries were operating, most at less than 15% of capacity. In 1997 another improvement of 7% was recorded, but in 1998, due mainly to the financial crisis in Russia, industrial production fell 2%. By the end of 1998, the privatization of small businesses was largely completed, with over 12,860 becoming privately owned. Among the large state enterprises, about 1,200 had been changed into joint stock companies, 910 of which have since been privatized.

Growth in industrial production returned in 1999 and 2000, at 7% and 11%, respectively, but in 2001, there was a decline of 5%, due, externally, to declining export demand in non-CIS countries, and, internally, to the shutdown of most of Georgia's refinery production. Before independence, Georgia had several refineries, but by 2001, it had only two: one at the Black Sea port of Batumi with a 106,000 b/d capacity, and the other, a small 4,000 b/d refinery built in 1998 near CanArgo's Ninotsminda oil field called the Georgian-American Oil Refinery (GAOR).

In 2001 the GAOR operated only between July and September, and at less than 50% capacity. In September 2001 CanArgo shut it down, announcing plans to build a $200 million refinery in its place that would have a 30,100 b/d capacity. In 2002 the Batumi refinery was also closed, undergoing a $250 million upgrade and expansion directed by the Mitsui Corporation. As a result, Georgia was obliged to import over 90% of its petroleum products. Mitsui undertook the work without Georgian government guarantees of its investment. The lack of such guarantees caused two other Japanese companies, Marubeni and JGC, to drop out of the project. Georgia's most promising industrial development came in December 2002, when agreement was announced for the construction of Georgia's part of the Baku-T'bilisi-Ceyhan (BTC) pipeline; the pipeline was officially opened on 25 May 2005.

In 2010 industry accounted for almost 29% of Georgia's GDP; 8.9% of the labor force was employed in the industrial sector. In 2010 Georgia's key industrial products included beverages (alcoholic and non-alcoholic), chemicals, metals, machinery, and aircraft. The annual percentage increase in industrial production was 4% in 2010.

29 SCIENCE AND TECHNOLOGY

Patent applications in science and technology as of 2009, according to the World Bank, totaled 250 in Georgia. The Georgian Academy of Sciences has departments of mathematics and physics, earth sciences, applied mechanics, machine building, and control processes, chemistry and chemical technology, agricultural science problems, biology, and physiology and experimental medicine. Georgia has 44 research institutes, many attached to the academy, conducting research concerning agriculture, fisheries, and veterinary science; and medicine, natural sciences, and technology. The academy's Sukhumi Botanical Garden is maintained at Chavchavadze. The Scientific and Technical Library of Georgia, with more than 10 million volumes, is located in T'bilisi.

In 2008 high technology exports totaled slightly less than $21 million, or 3% of all manufactured exports.

30 DOMESTIC TRADE

The war in Abkhazia severely disrupted domestic trade in 1993 and hyperinflation in 1994 led to widespread fighting in the nation and catastrophic economic decline. Economic conditions began to improve by the mid-1990s following the influx of foreign aid. Agriculture continues to be a primary basis for the domestic economy. The fastest growing segment of the economy, however, is in services, which accounted for about 60.9% of the GDP in 2010. Small privately owned shops are still more prevalent than supermarkets or larger retail establishments. Business hours are generally from 9 a.m. to 6 p.m., Monday through Friday.

31 FOREIGN TRADE

Georgia imported $4.828 billion worth of goods and services in 2008, while exporting $2.29 billion worth of goods and services. Major import partners in 2009 were Turkey, 18.2%; Ukraine, 9.7%; Azerbaijan, 8.7%; Germany, 7%; Russia, 6.7%; the United States, 5.2%; and China, 4% . Its major export partners were Turkey, 20.1%; Azerbaijan, 14.7%; Canada, 10.4%; Armenia, 7.9%; Ukraine, 7.5%; and Bulgaria, 7.3%.

Traditionally, Georgia was heavily dependent on Russia for power, bridges, roads, and other economic essentials. In return, Georgia sent Russia fruit, wine, and other agricultural products. Georgia's current government, however, began pursuing closer links with the EU and Turkey; the 2008 conflict with Russia over South Ossetia only worsened the relationship between the two countries.

Principal exports in 2010 were scrap metal, wine, mineral water, ores, vehicles, fruits, and nuts. Imports included oil, gas, electricity, vehicles, machinery and parts, grain and other foods, and pharmaceuticals.

32 BALANCE OF PAYMENTS

In 2010 Georgia had a foreign trade deficit of $2.1 billion, amounting to 7.8% of GDP.

Georgia's high level of imports, until 2000, was largely due to its capital account surplus, stemming from the inflows of invest-

Principal Trading Partners – Georgia (2010)

(In millions of US dollars)

Country	Total	Exports	Imports	Balance
World	6,678.2	1,581.0	5,097.2	-3,516.2
Turkey	1,102.6	214.8	887.8	-673.0
Azerbaijan	727.5	243.7	483.8	-240.0
Ukraine	663.5	103.3	560.1	-456.8
Germany	362.1	31.8	330.4	-298.6
Cambodia	359.4	24.3	335.1	-310.9
United States	357.8	180.5	177.3	3.2
Russia	324.7	34.3	290.4	-256.1
Armenia	205.9	159.7	46.2	113.5
Bulgaria	193.8	62.1	131.7	-69.6
United Arab Emirates	187.0	27.8	159.2	-131.4

(…) data not available or not significant.

(n.s.) not specified.

SOURCE: *2011 Direction of Trade Statistics Yearbook,* New York: United Nations, 2011.

Balance of Payments – Georgia (2010)

(In millions of US dollars)

Current Account		-1,464.8
Balance on goods		-2,586.3
Imports	-5,048.5	
Exports	2,462.2	
Balance on services		514.8
Balance on income		-360.0
Current transfers		966.7
Capital Account		206.1
Financial Account		1,112.7
Direct investment abroad		-5.9
Direct investment in Georgia		814.5
Portfolio investment assets		-0.6
Portfolio investment liabilities		252.7
Financial derivatives		0.8
Other investment assets		-408.0
Other investment liabilities		459.3
Net Errors and Omissions		-15.8
Reserves and Related Items		161.8

(…) data not available or not significant.

SOURCE: *Balance of Payment Statistics Yearbook 2011,* Washington, DC: International Monetary Fund, 2011.

ments, loans, and grants, rather than from weak export performance. Georgia's capital account subsequently fell into deficit.

The International Monetary Fund (IMF) reported that in 2000 Georgia had exports of goods totaling $459 million and imports totaling $971 million. The services credit totaled $206 million and debit $216 million.

A decade later, in 2010, exports totaled $2.46 billion. Imports were slightly more than $5 billion. Foreign exchange and gold reserves for the same year were estimated at $2.26 billion.

³³BANKING AND SECURITIES

The National Bank of Georgia (NBG), the state's central bank, was founded in 1991. The NBG has the functions of a central bank, namely issuing currency, managing the exchange rate, controlling monetary and credit aggregates, and regulating the activities of the banking sector.

The central bank's refinancing rate, as of 2008, was 8%. This rate is the monetary policy rate of NBG.

At the time of independence there were, in addition to the NBG, five specialized commercial banks, about 200 small domestic commercial banks, and the former Georgian branches of the Soviet Savings Bank and Vneshekonombank. During 1993 and 1994, a large number of small banks were set up, peaking at 227 by mid-1994. Several of these have since collapsed, leaving creditors bankrupt. In December 1994, the central bank stripped 28 commercial banks of their licenses on the ground that they had insufficient funds. In June 1995, the head of the central bank, Nodar Javakhishvili, moved to further stiffen capital requirements and stripped 22 more banks of the licenses. This was followed in July and August with similar measures that resulted in 58 additional banks losing their licenses. Also during 1995 was the merger of three state banks (Eximbank, Industrial Bank, and the Savings Bank) into the United Georgian Bank. State-owned banks accounted for some 75% of banking sector assets.

As of August 2011 there were 19 financial institutions in the country, down from 102 in 1995. Of these 19, 17 were foreign-controlled. The NBG reported 146 bank branches in the country and 523 service centers.

The Georgian Stock Exchange (GSE) is the country's sole stock market. It was established with the support of the US government. As of 2011, 138 companies were traded on GSE, with a total market capitalization of $1.1 billion dollars.

³⁴INSURANCE

Georgia's insurance system is largely inherited from government-controlled Soviet institutions.

³⁵PUBLIC FINANCE

In 2010 the budget of Georgia included $3.172 billion in public revenue and $3.915 billion in public expenditures. The budget deficit amounted to 6.6% of GDP. In total $3.381 billion of the debt was held by foreign entities.

In the initial years of post-Soviet independence, Georgia was notorious for mismanaging its budget. In 1999 the IMF put one of its programs in the country on hold because Georgia could not meet the conditional budgetary targets the IMF set forth. A more realistic budget in the second half of 2000 paved the way for a new IMF program beginning in January 2001. From 2008 to 2011, Georgia benefited from an IMF program that successfully helped the country weather the aftereffects of the 2008 conflict with Russia and the 2008–09 global financial crisis.

³⁶TAXATION

In 2005 the taxation system was reformed. Georgia now has six types of taxes, including a corporate profits tax of 15%, a flat personal income tax of 20%, a value-added tax (VAT) of 18% (reduced from 28%), and property taxes of up to 1% of the self-assessed value of property.

Georgia had one of the worst rates of tax compliance in the world. Chronic shortfalls in revenue collection meant that the state had to turn to external financing and loans from the National Bank of Georgia to make up for budget deficits. External borrow-

Public Finance – Georgia (2009)

(In millions of lari, central government figures)

Revenue and Grants	**4,917**	**100.0%**
Tax revenue	4,161.7	84.6%
Social contributions	...	...
Grants	387.7	7.9%
Other revenue	367	7.5%
Expenditures	**6,312.1**	**100.0%**
General public services	1,439.5	22.8%
Defense	1,043	16.5%
Public order and safety	853.1	13.5%
Economic affairs	767.3	12.2%
Environmental protection	28.7	0.5%
Housing and community amenities	2.3	<0.1%
Health	331.6	5.3%
Recreational, culture, and religion	137.4	2.2%
Education	459.6	7.3%
Social protection	1,249.6	19.8%

(...) data not available or not significant.

SOURCE: *Government Finance Statistics Yearbook 2010*, Washington, DC: International Monetary Fund, 2010.

ing to cover budget shortfalls had been the primary reason Georgia had to turn to the IMF and the Paris Club for stand-by credit agreements and rescheduling of sovereign debt. The high rate of tax evasion put legitimate business at a competitive disadvantage with a large "shadow economy," which was estimated officially to constitute 40–60% of the economy, but generally believed, according to the US State Department, to be much higher. Estimates of underpaying of taxes by enterprises had been close to 80%.

Since 2004 the government has made steady and considerable progress in the area of tax collection. For one, the taxation system was amended and simplified. Increased tax collection and the widespread privatization of state-owned assets further contributed to increased tax revenue. In 2001 tax revenue was 7% of GDP; by 2010 it was 28.2% of GDP.

37 CUSTOMS AND DUTIES

Georgia has an open trade regime, with most commodities carrying tariffs of either 5% or 12%, although automobiles have considerably higher rates. Some goods, such as grains, humanitarian goods, and aviation fuel, are exempt from carrying customs tariffs. Imported goods are also subject to a value-added tax (VAT) of 18%.

38 FOREIGN INVESTMENT

Foreign direct investment (FDI) in Georgia was a net inflow of $658.4 million according to World Bank figures published in 2009. FDI represented 6.13% of GDP.

Georgia was one of the first former Soviet republics to adopt market reforms on foreign investment. However, political instability initially hampered efforts to attract capital from abroad. Oil and gas pipeline projects and expanded privatization sales promised to reverse this trend. By the mid-1990s both GDP and total foreign investment began to grow steadily. In September 1998 the

decision was made to make all future economic regulations in full conformity with the norms of the European Community. Legislation in 2000 extended the scope of the privatization program, created a capital market, and provided for the registration of enterprise and agricultural land, all conducive to improving Georgia's investment climate. The main hindrances to foreign investment flows throughout the 1990s were not the legal framework but pervasive corruption and arbitrary and biased administration.

Annual foreign direct investment (FDI) inflow swelled to $242 million in 1997 and $265.3 million in 1998 mainly due to work on the Baku-Supsa pipeline and on the Supsa terminal. FDI flows fell to an annual average of $124.3 million 1999 to 2001. Total FDI stock from 1990 to 2000 was an estimated $672 million.

Investment levels soared in the first decade of the 21st century. Mainly due to work on the Baku-Tbilisi-Ceyhan pipeline and the Shah Deniz gas pipeline, FDI levels grew from $163 million in 2002, to $336 million in 2003, and $490 million in 2004. In 2010 the industrial sector had the highest level of direct foreign investment at $228.8 million, followed by transportation and communications at $215.1 million. Real estate and the financial sector each attracted investments of more than $100 million. With efforts to further liberalize the economy, the country hopes to attract increased foreign investment in the future.

39 ECONOMIC DEVELOPMENT

Despite its prosperity under the Soviet Union, the Georgian economy suffered dramatically in the initial post-independence years. Within five years of independence it was estimated that Georgia's GDP had shrunk to one-third of its previous size. When the new government came to power in 2004, it promised sweeping reforms to promote Georgia's economic development. In the intervening years considerable progress has been made toward that end. Georgia's 2010 GDP was more than double its 2004 GDP, and nearly triple its 2003 GDP.

At an international donors' conference held in Brussels in 2008, Georgia received pledges of a combined $4.5 billion dollars for the period from 2008 to 2010. The funds were earmarked largely for post-conflict reconstruction, infrastructure, and the banking sector.

In 2010 the World Bank ranked Georgia the 11th easiest country in which to do business. By comparison in 2005, it was ranked 115th. The World Bank has also recognized Georgia as one of the world's fastest-reforming economies.

40 SOCIAL DEVELOPMENT

All employees are eligible for old age benefits, which are funded primarily by employers, who contribute 20% of payroll. Disability and death are not covered. A special social pension exists for the aged and disabled who do not qualify for the employee pension system as determined by need. Paid maternity leave is provided for up to eight weeks, although it is reported that employers frequently withhold benefits. Furthermore, labor law does not protect women from having their employment terminated while on maternity leave. Temporary disability is only payable if the employer is responsible for the injury, although unemployment and permanent disability benefits are provided. Medical services are provided to needy residents by government health officials. Family allowances, initiated in 2002, provide for all needy residents and are funded by the government.

Women remain predominantly in low-skilled, low-paying jobs, regardless of qualifications. Female participation in politics has been discouraged, and women rarely fill leadership positions in the private sector. Discrimination and harassment in the workplace are common. Violence against women is a serious problem and there are virtually no mechanisms to assist victims. Societal bias discourages the reporting of domestic abuse or sexual violence. Kidnapping of women for marriage occurs in certain ethnic regions but is rare. It is said that in many cases the kidnappings are in fact elopements that have been pre-arranged.

Human rights abuses by the police and security forces have improved considerably since the 1990s; however, they do continue. There have been allegations that the law is not applied equally to all persons: supporters of opposition parties may face swifter and stricter sentencing than pro-government allies. Prison conditions are inhumane and there are accounts of prisoner abuse. In 2010 the construction of new prisons that meet international standards was underway.

There is some discrimination against ethnic minorities.

41 HEALTH

According to the CIA, life expectancy in Georgia was 72 years in 2011. The country spent 7.3% of its GDP on healthcare, amounting to $256 per person. There were 45 physicians, 39 nurses and midwives, and 33 hospital beds per 10,000 inhabitants. The fertility rate was 1.6, while the infant mortality rate was 26 per 1,000 live births. In 2008 the maternal mortality rate, according to the World Bank, was 48 per 100,000 births. It was estimated that 83% of children were vaccinated against measles. The CIA calculated HIV/AIDS prevalence in Georgia to be about 0.1% in 2009.

There have been wide-ranging reforms to the centralized system of health care inherited from the former Soviet Union. Staffed by a disproportionate number of specialists, and supporting a relatively high number of hospital beds, the system proved too costly and inefficient to maintain. In the period immediately following independence, financial shortages led to delayed payment, or even nonpayment, of medical staff salaries; a virtual halt to investment in new medical equipment and buildings; and the emergence of a black market in pharmaceuticals. Changes in health care policy since 1995 include introduction of a health insurance system and an end to free health care outside a basic package of health benefits, as well as new systems of provider payment. The network of rural and urban primary care centers is still largely a holdover from the Soviet era, but the payment structure for services has changed.

Immunization rates for the country in 2007 were as follows: children up to one year old were vaccinated against diphtheria, pertussis, and tetanus, 84%; polio, 98%; and measles, 92%.

An estimated 47% of women used contraceptives in 2007.

The incidence of tuberculosis was 82 per 100,000 people in 2007.

42 HOUSING

In the wake of the 2008 conflict with Russia, more than 100,000 Georgians were displaced. Many of these were subsequently able to return to their homes. For the more than 20,000 for whom there was not an immediate solution, the government acted to provide housing by building a large settlement of homes in Tserovani (approximately 12 miles from T'bilisi) and by using buildings originally intended for other purposes (including schools, hospitals, and hotels). These internally displaced persons added to the numbers of those who had been displaced since the early 1990s (through the conflicts in Abkhazia and South Ossetia), bringing the number of internally displaced to more than 200,000 by the end of 2010. In 2010, 40% were living in housing provided by the government. The remaining 60% were living with relatives, or in apartments they had rented or purchased.

Before independence, most urban housing was regulated by the government while most rural housing was privately owned. Beginning in the mid 1990s, legislation towards privatization led to the legalization of an open real estate market. Overcrowding became a problem as extended families stayed together in one household simply because of the lack of alternative housing.

Construction efforts in 1995 resulted in a total of 55,423 sq m of new dwellings; this represented a 4.4% increase in new dwelling area over 1987 figures. At the 2002 census there were 1.24 million private households, with the average size of a household at 3.5 persons.

In western Georgia, a typical older home is wooden, raised off the ground slightly in areas where flooding or very damp ground is problematic. In the drier climate of eastern Georgia, stone (later brick) houses with flat roofs were constructed along roads. In urban regions, two-story brick or cement block homes are not uncommon.

43 EDUCATION

In 2009 the World Bank estimated that 100% of age-eligible children in Georgia were enrolled in primary school. Secondary enrollment for age-eligible children stood at 81%. Tertiary enrollment was estimated at 25%. Of those enrolled in tertiary education, there were 100 male students for every 119 female students. Overall, the CIA estimated that Georgia had a literacy rate of 100%. Public expenditure on education represented 3.2% of GDP.

Georgia's educational system was based on the Soviet model until the late 1980s, when there was a de-emphasis of Soviet educational themes in favor of Georgian history and language. Georgian students are taught in a number of languages, including Georgian, Russian, Armenian, Azerbaijani, Abkhazian, and Ossetian. Education is compulsory for nine years, beginning at age seven. Elementary school covers six years of study. This is followed by either seven years of general secondary school or six years of technical school. The academic year runs from September to June.

In 2008 about 63% of age-eligible children were enrolled in some type of preschool program. The student-to-teacher ratio for primary school was 9:1 in 2009.

There are 24 state institutions of higher learning in the country and 73 private accredited institutions. These include the Iran Dzhavakhiladze University of T'bilisi, Georgian Technical University, Abkhazian State University, and State University of Batumi.

⁴⁴LIBRARIES AND MUSEUMS

The National Library in T'bilisi holds over six million volumes, while the Georgian State Public Library has eight million. The largest library in the country, however, is the Scientific and Technological Library of Georgia, which contains 10.1 million volumes. There are dozens of private libraries held by various scientific, cultural, and religious organizations and extensive university library holdings. Chief among the latter are T'bilisi State University, the Polytechnic University in T'bilisi, and the Pedagogical Institute in T'bilisi.

Most of the country's cultural institutions are in T'bilisi, including the State Art Museum, the Museum of Fine Arts, the State Museum of Georgia, the T'bilisi Museum of History and Ethnography, and the Georgian State Museum of Oriental Art. There are local or specialty museums in Gori, Suchumi, and Kútáisi.

⁴⁵MEDIA

In 2009 the CIA reported that there were 620,000 telephone landlines in Georgia. In addition to landlines, mobile phone subscriptions averaged 67 per 100 people; there were 2.8 million cellular phones in use. There were 7 FM radio stations, 12 AM radio stations, and 4 shortwave radio stations. Regular Internet users numbered 31 per 100 citizens. In 2010 the country had 110,680 Internet hosts.

Georgia has international telecommunications links via landline to other former Soviet republics and Turkey. There is also a low capacity satellite earth station and connections via Moscow.

There were dozens of independent television stations in the country in 2010, but only a few that provided national service. The latter included Rustavi 2 and Imedi. Though independently operated, most stations rely on some amount of support from the national or regional governments, leaving them open to allegations of bias in news reporting. There are at least 10 radio stations in operation, most of which are privately owned. News agencies include GHN, Media News, and Civil Georgia.

Newspapers included the dailies *Sakartvelos Respublika* (Republic of Georgia), *24 Saati* (24 Hours), and *Rezonansi* (Resonance).

The constitution and a 1991 press law provide for a free press, but in practice the government is said to restrict some press rights. Libel laws, as well as pressure from business and society leaders and government authorities, inhibit hard core investigative reporting.

⁴⁶ORGANIZATIONS

Georgia's Chamber of Commerce and Industry promotes trade and commerce with its fellow members of the CIS. The country belongs to the International Chamber of Commerce as well. Union organizations in Georgia include the Confederation of Independent Trade Unions, an umbrella organization. Important political organizations include the all-Georgian Mecrab Kostava Society and the Paramilitary group Mkhredrioni.

The Georgian Academy of Sciences, promoting research and education in all branches of science, was established in 1941. The Georgian Medical Association serves as a physician networking organization while also promoting research and education on health issues and working to establish common policies and standards in healthcare There are also associations dedicated to research and education for specific fields of medicine and particular diseases and conditions, such as Georgian Association of Cardiology.

Youth organizations include the National Youth Council of Georgia (through the Department of Youth and Sport), the United Nations of Youth: Georgia, YMCA/YWCA, and scouting programs. There are also several sports associations promoting amateur competition in such pastimes as baseball, track and field, badminton, and figure skating.

Volunteer service organizations, such as the Lions Clubs and Kiwanis International, are also present. There are national chapters of the Red Cross Society and Caritas.

⁴⁷TOURISM, TRAVEL, AND RECREATION

The *Tourism Factbook*, published by the UN World Tourism Organization, reported 1.5 million incoming tourists to Georgia in 2009 who spent a total of $531 million. Of those incoming tourists, there were 1.4 million from Europe.

There were 18,741 hotel beds available in Georgia. The estimated daily cost to visit T'bilisi, the capital, was $298. The cost of visiting other cities averaged $135.

Bounded by the Black Sea and the Caucasus Mountains, Georgia has been known for its lucrative tourist industry, but tourism declined after independence due to political and economic turmoil. Mtskheta, the ancient capital, is home to the Svetitskhoveli Cathedral, an 11th-century edifice that is the spiritual center of the Georgian Orthodox Church, and a major tourist attraction. The present-day capital, T'bilisi, is over 1,000 years old and offers historic citadels, cathedrals, and castles, as well as warm springs and dramatic mountain views.

⁴⁸FAMOUS PERSONS

Eduard A. Shevardnadze (b. 1928), a key figure in the Soviet government, was president of Georgia from 1992 until 2003, when he resigned in the midst of mounting criticism following disputed elections, known as the "Rose Revolution." Mikhail Saakashvili (b. 1967) was elected president in January 2004. Joseph Stalin (1879–1953), a key figure in the Soviet period, was born in Gori, Georgia. The medieval poet Shota Rustaveli, who was from Georgia, wrote the masterpiece *Knight in the Tiger's Skin*.

Nineteenth-century poets include Ilia Chavchavadze (1837–1907), Akaki Tsereteli (1840–1915), and Vazha Pshwda. Writers of that century include Titsian Tabidze (1895–1937), Giorgi Leonidze, and Irakli Abashidze. Painters include Niko Pirosmanashvili (1862–1918), and Irakli Toidze. Composers include Zakhari Paliashvili (1871–1933) and Meliton Balanchivadze (1862–1937).

⁴⁹DEPENDENCIES

Georgia has no territories or colonies.

⁵⁰BIBLIOGRAPHY

Gahrton, Per. *Georgia: Pawn in the New Political Game*. New York: Palgrave Macmillan, 2010.

George, Julie A. *The Politics of Ethnic Separatism in Russia and Georgia*. New York: Palgrave Macmillan, 2009.

Giannakos, S.A. (ed.). *Ethnic Conflict: Religion, Identity, and Politics*. Athens: Ohio University Press, 2002.

Mikaberidze, Alexander. *Historical Dictionary of Georgia*. Lanham, MD: Scarecrow Press, 2007.

Nasmuth, Peter. *Walking in the Caucasus: Georgia*. New York: I.B. Tauris, 2006.

Streissguth, Thomas. *The Transcaucasus*. San Diego, Calif.: Lucent Books, 2001.

GERMANY

Federal Republic of Germany
Bundesrepublik Deutschland

CAPITAL: Berlin

FLAG: The flag is a tricolor of black, red, and gold horizontal stripes--the flag of the German (Weimar) Republic from 1919 until 1933.

ANTHEM: *Einigkeit und Recht und Freiheit (Unity and Justice and Liberty).*

MONETARY UNIT: The euro replaced the deutsche mark as the official currency in 2002. The euro is divided into 100 cents. There are coins in denominations of 1, 2, 5, 10, 20, and 50 cents and 1 euro and 2 euros. There are notes of 5, 10, 20, 50, 100, 200, and 500 euros. €1 = US$1.356 (or US$1 = €0.738) as of November 2011.

WEIGHTS AND MEASURES: The metric system is the legal standard.

HOLIDAYS: New Year's Day, 1 January; Labor Day, 1 May; German Unity Day, 3 October; Repentance Day, Wednesday before the 3rd Sunday in November (except Bavaria); Christmas, 25–26 December. Movable religious holidays include Good Friday, Easter Monday, Ascension, and Whitmonday. In addition, the movable Carnival/Rose Monday holiday and various provincial holidays also are celebrated.

TIME: 1 p.m. = noon GMT.

¹LOCATION, SIZE, AND EXTENT

Germany is located in western Europe, bordering the North Sea between France and Poland. Germany is slightly smaller than the state of Montana, with a total area of 357,021 km sq (137,847 mi sq). Germany shares boundaries with Denmark and the Baltic Sea on the N, Poland and the Czech Republic to the E, Austria to the SE, Switzerland to the S, France to the SW, Luxembourg, Belgium, and the Netherlands to the W, and the North Sea to the NW. Germany's boundary length totals 6,010 km (3,734 mi), of which 2,389 km (1,484 mi) is coastline. Germany's capital city, Berlin, is located in the northeastern part of the country.

²TOPOGRAPHY

The topography of Germany is varied. The area along the Baltic coast is sandy, with dunes and small hills. Adjacent to the coast are forested ridges and numerous lakes of the Mecklenburg lake plateau. Around Berlin, the relief is less hilly. The southern limit of the lowland area is formed by a wide zone of fertile loess, reaching from Magdeburg to the highlands in the South. These highlands include the Harz Mountains, the densely wooded Thuringian Forest, and the Erzgebirge (Ore Mountains), where the Fichtelberg rises to 1,214 m (3,983 ft). In the northeast, the wide German lowland—characterized by sandy North Sea shores, heath and moor (in the south), and highest altitudes of about 300 m (1,000 ft)—rises slowly to the central Germany uplands. These low, eroded mountains (1,070–1,520 m/3,500–5,000 ft) extend from the Rhine to the former border of East Germany.

In the west are a wide rift valley and a narrow gorge carved by the Rhine River. A group of plateaus and low mountains, averaging 460 m (1,500 ft) in altitude and including the Black Forest and Odenwald Mountains (highest peak—the Feldberg, 1,493 m/4,898 ft), form the greater part of southern Germany. They merge gradually with the highest walls of the Bavarian Alps (2,440–2,740 m/8,000–9,000 ft), which form the boundary between Germany, Switzerland, and Austria; the Zugspitze (2,962 m/9,718 ft), on the Austrian border, is the highest point in Germany.

The only major lake is Lake Constance (Bodensee; within Germany, 305 sq km/118 sq mi), which is shared with Switzerland and Austria. Except in the extreme south, all of Germany is drained by rivers that empty into the North Sea. The Rhine, with its two main tributaries, the Mosel and the Main, dominates the western areas; farther east are the Ems, the Weser, the Elbe, and the Oder. These rivers have estuaries that are important for the ports located there. In the south, the Danube flows from west to east. The East Frisian Islands are off the northwest coast; the North Frisian Islands lie along the coast of Schleswig. The small island of Helgoland is opposite the mouth of the Elbe River.

³CLIMATE

The climate is temperate; rapid changes in temperature are rare. Average temperatures in January, the coldest month of the year, range from 1.5°C (35°F) in the lowlands to -6°C (21°F) in the mountains. July is the warmest month of the year, with average temperatures between 18°C (64°F) in low-lying areas to 20°C (68°F) in the sheltered valleys of the south. The upper valley of the Rhine has an extremely mild climate. Upper Bavaria experiences a warm alpine wind (Föhn) from the south. The Harz Mountains form their own climatic zone, with cool summers, cold wind, and heavy snowfalls in winter.

Precipitation occurs throughout the year: in the northern lowlands, from 51 to 71 cm (20–28 in); in the central uplands, from 69 to 152 cm (27–60 in); in the Bavarian Alps, to more than 200 cm (80 in). The higher mountains are snow covered from at least January to March.

[4] FLORA AND FAUNA

Plants and animals are those generally common to middle Europe. The World Resources Institute estimates that there are 2,682 plant species in Germany. Beeches, oaks, and other deciduous trees constitute one third of the forests; conifers are increasing as a result of reforestation. Spruce and fir trees predominate in the upper mountains, while pine and larch are found in sandy soil. There are many species of ferns, flowers, fungi, and mosses. In addition, Germany is home to 126 mammal, 487 bird, 15 reptile, and 20 amphibian species. This calculation reflects the total number of distinct species residing in the country, not the number of endemic species. Fish abound in the rivers and the North Sea. Wild animals include deer, wild boar, mouflon, fox, badger, hare, and small numbers of beaver. Various migratory birds cross Germany in the spring and autumn.

[5] ENVIRONMENT

Industrialization has taken its toll on Germany's environment, including that of the former German Democratic Republic (GDR), which, according to a 1985 UNESCO report, had the worst air, water, and ground pollution in Europe. Since 1976, the Petrol Lead Concentration Act has limited the lead content of gasoline; for control of other automotive pollutants, the government looked toward stricter enforcement of existing laws and to technological improvements in engine design. The Federal Emission Protection Act of 1974, based on the "polluter pays" principle, established emissions standards for industry, agriculture and forestry operations, and public utilities. Nevertheless, by 1994, 50% of Germany's forests had been damaged by acid rain resulting from sulfur dioxide emissions.

Water pollution is evident in virtually every major river of the Federal Republic of Germany (FRG), and the Baltic Sea is heavily polluted by industrial wastes and raw sewage from the rivers of eastern Germany. In the 1980s, the Rhine, from which some 10 million Germans and Dutch draw their drinking water, was 20 times as polluted as in 1949. The Effluency Levies Act, effective January 1978, requires anyone who discharges effluents into waterways to pay a fee reckoned in accordance with the quantity and severity of the pollutant; the proceeds of this act are allocated for the building of water treatment plants and for research on water treatment technology and reduced-effluent production techniques. In 2001, Germany's water resources totaled 188 cu km (45.1 cu mi), while water usage was 38.01 cu km (9.12 cu mi) per year. Domestic water usage accounted for 12% of total usage, industrial for 68%, and agricultural for 20%. Per capita water usage totaled 460 cu m (16,245 cu ft) per year.

Significant sources of air pollution include emissions from coal-burning utility plants and exhaust emissions from vehicles using leaded fuels. In 1996, industrial carbon dioxide emissions totaled 924 thousand metric tons but have decreased consistently since then due to governmental regulations. The UN reported that, in 2008, Germany's carbon dioxide emissions totaled 787,000 metric tons. The nation has set maximum levels for biocides in the soil to protect food supplies. Under the nation's basic waste disposal law of 1972, some 50,000 unauthorized dump sites have been closed down and 5,000 regulated sites established; provisions governing toxic wastes were added in 1976. Germany's principal environ-

mental agency is the Ministry of Environment, Nature Conservation, and Reactor Safety, created in June 1986.

The World Resources Institute reported that Germany had designated 7.58 million hectares (18.72 million acres) of land for protection as of 2006. The first German national park, with an area of 13,100 hectares (32,370 acres), was opened in 1970 in the Bavarian forest, and, in 1978, a second national park (21,000 hectares/52,000 acres) was opened near Berchtesgaden. The third national park, in Schleswig-Holstein (285,000 hectares/704,250 acres), opened in 1985, and a fourth, in Niedersachsen (240,000 hectares/593,000 acres), opened in 1986. The Messel Pit Fossil Site became a natural UNESCO World Heritage Site in 1995. There are also 34 Ramsar Wetland Sites.

According to a 2011 report issued by the International Union for Conservation of Nature and Natural Resources (IUCN), several animal species are threatened in nature. The species included 6 types of mammals, 5 species of birds, 23 species of fish, 30 types of mollusks, 24 species of other invertebrates, and 17 species of plants. Endangered species include Freya's damselfly, Atlantic sturgeon, slender-billed curlew, and the bald ibis. Species believed to be extinct include the Bavarian pine vole, Tobias' caddisfly, the wild horse, and the false ringlet butterfly.

[6] POPULATION

The US Central Intelligence Agency (CIA) estimates the population of Germany in 2011 to be approximately 81,471,834, which placed it at number 16 in population among the 196 nations of the world and made it the second most populous country in Europe. In 2011, approximately 20.6% of the population was more than 65 years of age, with another 13.3% less than 15 years of age. The median age in Germany was 44.9 years. There were 0.97 males for every female in the country. The population's annual population growth rate was -0.208%. The projected population for the year 2025 was 79,700,000. Population density in Germany was calculated at 228 people per sq km (591 people per sq mi).

The UN estimated that 74% of the population lived in urban areas. The largest urban areas, along with their respective populations, included Berlin, 3.4 million; Hamburg, 1.8 million; Munich, 1.3 million; and Cologne, 1 million.

Because of a low birthrate, an aging population, and emigration, Germany's population generally declined from the mid 1970s until around 1990. A heavy influx of immigrants in the 1990s more than compensated for the slight population loss due to more deaths than births. Although the annual growth rate in the 1980s was only 0.1%, immigration in the 1990s led to an annual growth rate in that decade of 0.8%. With immigration slowing, according to the UN, the annual population rate of change for 2005–10 was expected to be -0.1%, a rate the government viewed as too low.

[7] MIGRATION

Estimates of Germany's net migration rate, carried out by the CIA in 2011, amounted to 0.54 migrants per 1,000 citizens. The total number of emigrants living abroad was 3.54 million, and the total number of immigrants living in Germany in 2007 was 15.5 million, the majority of them of Turkish, Italian, or Polish origin. From 1946 to 1968, 475,505 Germans emigrated to the United States, 262,807 to Canada, and 99,530 to Australia and Oceania. During the same period, however, millions of people of German

LOCATION: 47°16′ to 55°4′N; 5°52′ to 15°2′ E. BOUNDARY LENGTHS: Denmark, 68 kilometers (42 miles); Poland, 456 kilometers (285 miles); Czech Republic, 646 kilometers (403 miles); Austria, 784 kilometers (487 miles); Switzerland, 334 kilometers (208 miles); France, 451 kilometers (281 miles); Luxembourg, 138 kilometers (86 miles); Belgium, 167 kilometers (104 miles); Netherlands, 577 kilometers (358 miles); total coastline, 2,389 kilometers (1,480 miles). TERRITORIAL SEA LIMIT: 12 miles.

origin and/or speech migrated to West Germany from eastern Europe, notably from the former Czechoslovakia and East Germany. Migration from East Germany to West Germany reached a climax just before the erection of the frontier wall in Berlin on 13 August 1961. It is estimated that about 4 million people—many of them skilled workers and professionals—crossed from East Germany to West Germany during the 40-year existence of East Germany. Immigration of ethnic Germans from Poland continued to be heavy after 1968, totaling about 800,000 between 1970 and 1989.

According to German law, persons who are not ethnic Germans are foreigners (except for the few granted citizenship) even if they were born and have spent their entire lives in Germany.

Conversely, ethnic Germans are not foreigners even if emigrating from birthplaces and homes in eastern Europe.

Under the UNHCR/IOM Humanitarian Evacuation Programm, 14,689 people had been evacuated from Macedonia to Germany as of 1999. The evacuees, as well as Kosovars who had already sought asylum in Germany but whose cases were still pending or already rejected, were granted temporary protection, renewable every three months. As of 20 August 1999, 4,147 evacuees had returned to their homeland. In 2005, Germany returned 51,000 Kosovars, including 34,000 Roma to the UN-administered province.

The main countries of origin were Serbia and Montenegro, Turkey, Iraq, Ukraine, Afghanistan, Russia, and Iran. Of these refugees 86,151—mainly from Serbia and Montenegro, Turkey, Iraq, Russia, Iran, India, and Pakistan—sought asylum.

8 ETHNIC GROUPS

Until the late 1950s, the population was 99% German; the Danes in Schleswig-Holstein were the sole national minority. The influx of foreigners as "guest workers" beginning in the late 1950s led to an upsurge in the number of permanent foreign residents. As of 2010, Germans account for about 91.5% of the total population. About 2.4% of the population is Turkish. Other minority groups include Italians, Greeks, Poles, Russians, Serbo-Croatians, and Spanish. Even persons born and reared in Germany are considered foreigners unless they are ethnically German or naturalized. The Roma (Sinti) were recognized as "national minorities" in 1995.

9 LANGUAGES

German is the official language, and although dialectical variations are considerable, High German is standard. Low German, spoken along the North and Baltic Sea coasts and in the offshore islands, is in some respects as close to Dutch as it is to standard German. Sorbian (also known as Wendish or Lusatian) is a Slavic language spoken by the Sorbian minority. Under the GDR, Sorbian was taught in schools in their settlement area. There was a daily newspaper in Sorbian and a publishing house for Sorbian literature. Many of Germany's sizable foreign-born population still speak their native languages, and there are numerous Turkish-speaking school children. Romani is spoken by the nation's small Roma population; the language has no written form, and the Roma generally restrict the use of the language to within their own community. In 1996, new rules were established reforming German orthography. Designed to eliminate the last vestiges of Gothic spelling, the rules, among other things, eliminated hyphens, restored some umlauts, and replaced the ß character after short vowels. The reform was met with so much criticism that, in 2000, Germany's leading newspaper the Frankfurter Allgemeine Zeitung decided to return to the old spelling rules; in 2004, the weekly news outlet Der Spiegel followed suit. The reform was revised and took full effect on August 1, 2005. From that day on, all official government publications and schools had to follow the new rules, while the media and publishers were encouraged to adhere to the revised spelling rules.

10 RELIGIONS

There are no official government statistics maintained on membership in religious groups. According to an unofficial 2010 report, the Roman Catholic Church has about 25.2 million members, and the Evangelical Church, a federation of several church bodies including Lutheran, Uniate, and Reformed Protestant Churches, has about 24.5 million members. Together, these churches account for about 60% of the population. Orthodox churches claim 1.4 million members. The Greek Orthodox Church is the largest division, with 450,000 members, followed by Serbian, Romanian, Russian (Moscow Patriarchate and Orthodox), Syrian, and Armenian Apostolic. Protestant Christian groups included the New Apostolic Church (363,300 members) and Baptists (75,000–184,000, including Evangelical Christian Baptists, International Baptist Convention, Reformed Baptists, Bible Baptists, independent Baptist congregations, and others). Smaller groups include Jehovah's Witnesses, the Church of Jesus Christ of Latter-Day Saints (Mormons), Seventh-Day Adventists, the Church of Scientology, Methodists, Mennonites, Quakers, and the Salvation Army. There are about 4 million Muslims, with about 2.6 million Sunnis, 400,000 Alevis, and 226,000 Shi'as. More than 200,000 Jews live in Germany. There were also small numbers of Unification Church members, Hare Krishnas, members of the Johannish Church, Buddhists, the International Grail Movement, Ananda Marga, and Sri Chinmoy. Approximately 28 million people, or about 33% of the population noted no religious affiliation or membership in small, unrecorded religious organizations. Freedom of religion is guaranteed under basic law, and this right is generally respected in practice. However, there have been reports of social discrimination against Muslims and Jews, as well as among some members of nontraditional religious groups, such as Scientologists and Jehovah's Witnesses. Some states have passed legislation banning the wearing of headscarves in public schools, a decree which primarily affects Muslim women. Religious organizations are not required to register with the government but often do in order to gain certain legal and tax benefits. While the law provides for separation of church and state, religious organizations may apply for recognition as a public law corporation at the state level, which allows for additional legal benefits. As of 2010, about 180 groups had obtained widespread status as public law corporations. However, the Jehovah's Witnesses were granted this recognition in only 12 states, and Muslim communities did not have this status within any states. The federal government has initiated negotiations between state governments and the Muslim Coordination Council, an umbrella organization of four major Muslim groups, to move toward greater legal recognition.

11 TRANSPORTATION

Although the German transportation network was heavily damaged during World War II, the system is now one of the best-developed in Europe (although much of the infrastructure in the former East Germany needs significant improvement). The CIA reports that Germany has a total of 644,480 km (400,461 mi) of roads, all of which are paved. There are 554 vehicles per 1,000 people in the country. Because of the country's central location, almost all continental surface traffic has to cross its terrain. The German railroad system extends for 33,706 km (20,944 mi), a majority of which is operated by the government-owned Federal Railways System.

According to the CIA, Germany has approximately 7,467 km (4,640 mi) of navigable waterways. Canals link the Elbe with the Ems, the Ems with the Dortmund, and the Baltic with the North Sea. The most important inland waterway consists of the Rhine and its tributaries, which carry more freight than any other European waterway. The Kiel Canal is an important connection between the Baltic Sea and North Sea. Major ports and harbors include Berlin, Bonn, Brake, Bremen, Bremerhaven, Cologne, Dresden, Duisburg, Emden, Hamburg, Karlsruhe, Kiel, Lubeck, Magdeburg, Mannheim, Rostock, and Stuttgart. In 2008, the FRG had a merchant fleet comprised of 393 ships of 1,000 GRT or more.

There are 549 airports, which transported 103.4 million passengers in 2009 according to the World Bank. Three hundred and thirty of these airports featured paved runways. Major airports include Schonefeld, Tegel, and Tempelhof at Berlin, Halle at Leipzig, Osnabruck at Munster, as well as those at Bremen, Dresden, Frankfurt, Düsseldorf, Hamburg, Hanover, Cologne-Bonn, Stuttgart, Nurenberg, and Munich. Lufthansa, organized in 1955, is the major air carrier; its route network includes both North and South America, the Near and Far East (including Australia), Africa, and Europe.

12 HISTORY

Hunting and gathering peoples roamed the land now known as Germany for thousands of years before the first farmers appeared in the sixth millennium BC. By the time these Indo-Europeans made contact with the Romans late in the 2nd century BC, the Teutons of the north had driven most of the Celts westward across the Rhine. During the succeeding centuries, Germanic tribes such as the Alemanni, Burgundians, Franks, Lombards, Vandals, Ostrogoths, and Visigoths gradually developed in the territory between the Rhine estuary in the west, the Elbe River in the east, and northern Italy in the south. Some of these peoples, whom the Romans called barbarians (from the Latin *barbari*, meaning "foreigners"), overran Italy and helped destroy the Roman Empire; others settled in Britain, France, and Spain. The area on either side of the Rhine was contested until Charlemagne, king of the Franks (r. 768–814), extended his domain to include most of Germany as far as the Elbe; he was crowned emperor at Rome in 800. Charlemagne's empire was eventually divided among his three grandsons, and the German sector itself was divided in the latter part of the 9th century.

Otto I, greatest of a new Saxon dynasty, united Germany and Italy and was crowned first Holy Roman emperor in 962. The strength of the rising Holy Roman Empire was undercut, however, by the two-pronged involvement in Italy and in Eastern Europe. Successive generations of Germanic emperors and of various ducal families engaged in constant struggles within Germany as well as with the papacy and dispersed their energies in many ventures beyond the confines of the empire. Frederick I (Barbarossa, r. 1152–90), of the Hohenstaufen family, overcame the last of the powerful duchies in 1180. His grandson Frederick II (r. 1212–50), the most brilliant of medieval emperors, reigned from Sicily and took little interest in German affairs. Four years after his death,

the empire broke up temporarily, and there followed a 19-year interregnum. In 1273, Rudolf of Habsburg was elected emperor, but neither he nor any of his immediate successors could weld the empire into a manageable unit.

The Holy Roman Empire's loose and cumbersome framework suffered from lack of strong national authority at the very time when powerful kingdoms were developing in England, France, and Spain. In the ensuing period, the Holy Roman emperors tended to ally themselves against the nobility and with the prosperous German cities and with such potent confederations of towns as the Hanseatic and Swabian leagues. During the 15th century and part of the 16th, Germany was prosperous: commerce and banking flourished, and great works of art were produced. However, the already weak structure of the empire was further undermined by a great religious schism, the Reformation, which began with Martin Luther in 1517 and ended in the ruinous Thirty Years' War (1618–48), which directly and indirectly (through disease and famine) may have taken the lives of up to two million people. Thereafter, Germany remained fragmented in more than 300 principalities, bishoprics, and free cities. In the 18th century, Prussia rose to first rank among the German states, especially through the military brilliance of Frederick II ("the Great," r. 1740–86).

During the French Revolution and the Napoleonic wars, German nationalism asserted itself for the first time since the Reformation. Although frustrated in the post-Napoleonic era, the nationalist and liberal movements were not eradicated, and they triumphed briefly in the Frankfurt parliament of 1848. Thereafter, a number of its leaders supported the conservative but dynamic Prussian chancellor Otto von Bismarck. After a series of successful wars with Denmark (1864), Austria (the Seven Weeks' War, 1866), and France (the Franco-Prussian War, 1870–71), Bismarck brought about the union of German states (excluding Austria) into the Second Empire, proclaimed in 1871.

Germany quickly became the strongest military, industrial, and economic power on the continent and joined other great powers in overseas expansion. While Bismarck governed as chancellor, further wars were avoided, and an elaborate system of alliances with other European powers was created. With the advent of Wilhelm II as German emperor (r. 1888–1918), the delicate international equilibrium was repeatedly disturbed in a series of crises that culminated in 1914 in the outbreak of World War I. Despite initial successes, the German armies—leagued with Austria-Hungary and Turkey against the United Kingdom, France, Russia, and eventually the United States—were defeated in 1918. As a consequence of the war, in which some 1,600,000 Germans died, the victorious Allies through the Treaty of Versailles (1919) stripped Germany of its colonies and of the territories won in the Franco-Prussian War, demanded the nation's almost complete disarmament, and imposed stringent reparations requirements. Germany became a republic, governed under the liberal Weimar constitution. The serious economic and social dislocations caused by the military defeat and by the subsequent economic depression, however, brought Adolf Hitler and the National Socialist (Nazi) Party to power in 1933. Hitler converted the republic into a dictatorship, consolidated Germany's position at home and abroad, and began a military expansion that, by 1939, had brought a great part of Europe under German control, either by military occupation or by alliance, leading to World War II.

Germany signed a military alliance with Italy on 22 May 1939 and a nonaggression pact with the former USSR on 23 August. Hitler's army then invaded Poland on 1 September, and France and Britain declared war on Germany two days later. France surrendered on 22 June 1940; the British continued to fight. On 10 December 1941, Germany declared war on the United States, three days after the attack on Pearl Harbor by its ally Japan. Hitler's troops were engaged on three major fronts—the eastern front (USSR), the North African front, and the western front (France). Hitler relied heavily on air power and bombed Britain continuously during 1941–42. However, by 1943, German forces were on the defensive everywhere, thus marking the beginning of the end of the Nazi offensive thrusts. Finally, on 7 May 1945, after Hitler had committed suicide, the Allies received Germany's unconditional surrender. It is estimated that more than 35 million people were killed during World War II. Of this number, at least 11 million were civilians. Among them were nearly 6 million Jews, mostly eastern Europeans, killed in a deliberate extermination by the Nazi regime known as the Holocaust; there were also about 5 million non-Jewish victims, including Romani (Gypsies), homosexuals, political dissidents, and the physically and mentally disabled.

From Division to Reunification

After the surrender in 1945, Germany was divided into four occupation zones, controlled respectively by the former USSR, the United States, the United Kingdom, and France. Berlin was likewise divided, and from April 1948 through May 1949, the USSR sought unsuccessfully to blockade the city's western sectors; not until the quadripartite agreement of 1971 was unimpeded access of the FRG to West Berlin firmly established. In 1949, pending a final peace settlement, Germany was divided into the Federal Republic of Germany, or West Germany, consisting of the former United Kingdom, French, and US zones of occupation, and the German Democratic Republic, or East Germany, consisting of the former Soviet zone of occupation. Territories in the east (including East Prussia), which were in German hands prior to 1939, were taken over by Poland and the former USSR.

The FRG's first chancellor (1949–63), Konrad Adenauer, the leader of the Christian Democratic Union (CDU), followed a policy of "peace through strength." During his administration, the FRG joined NATO in 1955 and became a founding member of the EC in 1957. That same year, the Saar territory, politically autonomous under the Versailles Treaty but economically tied to France after 1947, became a German state after a free election and an agreement between France and the FRG. A treaty of cooperation between those two nations, signed on 22 January 1963, provided for coordination of their policies in foreign affairs, defense, information, and cultural affairs. The cost of this program of cooperation with the West was further alienation from the GDR and abandonment, for the foreseeable future, of the goal of German reunification. Many citizens, including a significant number of skilled and highly educated persons, had been covertly emigrating through Berlin in the West, and, on 13 August 1961, East Berlin was sealed off from West Berlin by a wall of concrete and barbed wire. The Western Allies declared that they accepted neither the legality nor the potential practical consequences of the partition and reaffirmed their determination to ensure free access and the continuation of a free and viable Berlin.

On 16 October 1963, Adenauer resigned and was succeeded by former Finance Minister Ludwig Erhard, who is generally credited with stimulating the FRG's extraordinary postwar economic development—the so-called "economic miracle." Kurt George Kiesinger of the CDU formed a new coalition government on 17 November 1966 with Willy Brandt, leader of the Social Democratic Party, as vice-chancellor. Three years later, Brandt became chancellor, and the CDU became an opposition party for the first time. One of Brandt's boldest steps was the development of an "Eastern policy" (Ostpolitik), which sought improved relations with the Socialist bloc and resulted, initially, in the establishment of diplomatic ties with Romania and the former Yugoslavia. On 7 December 1970, the FRG signed a treaty with Poland reaffirming the existing western Polish boundary of the Oder and western Neisse rivers and establishing a pact of friendship and cooperation between the two nations. That August, the FRG concluded a nonaggression treaty with the former USSR; a 10-year economic agreement was signed on 19 May 1973. Throughout the late 1960s and early 1970s, tensions over the Berlin division in particular and between the two Germanys eased markedly, as did, in consequence, the intensity of pressures for reunification from both Allied and Soviet sides. In an effort to normalize inter-German relations, FRG Chancellor Willy Brandt and GDR Chairman Willi Stoph exchanged visits in March and May 1970, the first such meetings since the states were established. A basic treaty between the two Germanys was reached on 21 December 1972 and ratified by the Bundestag on 17 May 1973; under the treaty, the FRG recognized the sovereignty and territorial integrity of the GDR, and the two nations agreed to cooperate culturally and economically. Two years later, the GDR and FRG agreed on the establishment of permanent representative missions in each others' capitals. Relations with Czechoslovakia were normalized by a treaty initialed 20 June 1973. The early 1970s brought an upsurge of terrorism on West German soil, including the killing by Palestinians of Israeli athletes at the 1972 Summer Olympics in Munich. The terrorist wave, which also enlisted a number of German radicals, continued into the mid 1970s but declined thereafter.

Brandt remained chancellor until 6 May 1974, when he resigned after his personal aide, Günter Guillaume, was arrested as a spy for the GDR. Helmut Schmidt, Brandt's finance minister, was elected chancellor by the Bundestag on 16 May. Under Schmidt's pragmatic leadership, the FRG continued its efforts to normalize relations with Eastern Europe while also emphasizing economic and political cooperation with its West European allies and with the United States. Schmidt remained chancellor until the fall of 1982, when his governing coalition collapsed in a political party dispute. General elections in March 1983 resulted in a victory for the CDU, whose leader, Helmut Kohl, retained the chancellorship he had assumed on an interim basis the previous October. In January 1987 elections, Kohl was again returned to power, as the CDU and its coalition allies won 54% of the seats in the Bundestag.

The exodus of East Germans through Hungary in the summer of 1989 as well as mass demonstrations in several East German cities, especially Leipzig, led to the collapse of the German Democratic Republic in the fall of 1989. Chancellor Kohl outlined a 10-point plan for peaceful reunification, including continued membership in NATO and free elections in March 1990. Following these elections, the two Germanys peacefully evolved into a single state. Four-power control ended in 1991, and, by the end of 1994, all former Soviet forces had left the country, although British, French, and American forces remained for an interim period. Berlin became the new capital of Germany, although the shift from Bonn to Berlin took place over several years.

Unification has been accompanied by disillusionment and dissatisfaction with politics and the economy. A falling GDP and rising unemployment have raised concerns that the costs of unification were underestimated. By 1997, the German government had given more than $600 billion to eastern Germany through business subsidies, special tax breaks, and support payment for individuals, while private companies invested $500 million more. Even so, the eastern German economy was fundamentally bankrupt, with unemployment at about 20%. Some analysts predict that convergence of the two economies will not be complete for another 10 to 20 years. In the meantime, the financial drain imposed on the government by the east threatened to imperil Germany's other convergence project, European economic unification. However, Germany and 11 other EU countries introduced a common European currency, the euro, in January 2002.

By October 1996, Chancellor Helmut Kohl had been in office for 14 years, becoming the longest-serving postwar German chancellor. In 1998, German voters decided it was time for a change. In the September parliamentary elections, Kohl's CDU (Christian Democratic) coalition was defeated by the Social Democrats (SPD), and Gerhard Schröder became the first SPD member in 18 years to serve as Germany's chancellor. The following month, Schröder formed a center-left coalition with the Green Party. The new coalition inaugurated "Future Program 2000" to tackle the country's economic woes and in June 1999 pushed through the most extensive reform package in German history, which included major cuts in state spending as well as tax cuts. In April 1999, the German government was transferred from Bonn back to its prewar seat in Berlin, where the Bundestag moved into the renovated (and renamed) building formerly known as the Reichstag.

In July 1999, Johannes Rau became the first Social Democrat to be elected president of Germany in 30 years. However, continuing dissatisfaction with the nation's budget deficit and other problems resulted in a disappointing showing for the Social Democrats in local elections in September 1999.

In July 2000, government negotiators reached an agreement on the payment of compensation to people subjected to forced and slave labor under the Nazi regime. A total of dm 10 billion was to be paid out under the auspices of a specially created foundation. Official figures showed that racist attacks increased in 2000, a worrying trend that continued through 2011.

Following the 11 September 2001 terrorist attacks on New York and Washington, D.C., Germany agreed to deploy 4,000 troops to the US-led campaign in Afghanistan directed to oust the Taliban regime and al-Qaeda forces. It was Germany's largest deployment outside Europe since World War II, and, in November, Schröder survived a parliamentary confidence vote following his decision to deploy the troops.

Parliamentary elections were held on 22 September 2002. Schröder, unable to campaign on a strong economy, staked out a foreign policy position that ran counter to that of the United States. Schröder announced Germany unconditionally would not support a war in Iraq and that Germany was in favor of a peaceful settlement to the conflict.

Edmund Stoiber of the Christian Democratic Union (CDU) was Schröder's opponent in the September elections, and the race between them was exceedingly close. The SPD and CDU/CSU each won 38.5% of the vote, but the SPD emerged with 251 to 248 seats in the Bundestag (due to a peculiarity in the German voting system which awards extra seats to a party if it wins more constituency seats than it is entitled to under the party vote), and, in coalition with the 55 seats won by the Green Party, formed a government with Schröder remaining chancellor.

Although Schröder was popular for his position toward Iraq, he became increasingly criticized for Germany's economic underperformance. The high unemployment level became quite astonishing because Germany's low unemployment rate was, at one point, the envy of the industrial world. By the end of 2002, more than four million people were unemployed in Germany. The situation got worse in early 2005, when Germany's Federal Labor Agency announced that, come January 2005, more than five million Germans were unemployed, which was the highest number since 1932, when the economic devastation of the Great Depression brought the Weimar Republic to an end.

To deal with the economic challenges in 2003, Schröder launched a major reform package called "Agenda 2010." This policy aimed to reform health, education, labor training, social security, family welfare, unemployment benefits, and pensions. Agenda 2010's priority was labor-market reform. Neither these reforms nor reduced taxation did much to improve the slow economic growth or lower the unemployment that had reached especially great proportions since the Great Depression.

Following the protests on 1 January 2005, the government's controversial reform of unemployment benefits, also called "Hartz IV" reform, came into effect. Under this reform, those who have been unemployed for more than a year would qualify for a flat-rate benefit only if they could prove that they were actively looking for work. Schröder's inability to deal with the weak economy was thought to have contributed to his loss of the chancellery in the 2005 elections to Angela Merkel (CDU/CSU). A very tense election race followed by an alliance between the two opposing parties, the CDU/CSU and the SDP, became known as the Grand Coalition. On 22 November 2005 Merkel officially became not only the first female chancellor in the history of the country, but also the first former citizen of the GDR to take on the second-highest position in the German government.

Merkel defined the main goals of her government as reducing unemployment and improving GDP growth. It was her goal to improve the German economy by pursuing a mix of reforms including cutting public spending, lowering corporate tax rates, and accelerating labor-market and pushing through other reforms begun by Merkel's predecessor. She also intended to increase value-added tax, social insurance contributions, and the top rate of income tax.

During her first few months in office, Merkel attained an 85% approval rating. During the third quarter of 2005, the economy posted a 0.6% increase over the previous year's period, and it was forecasted that Germany's GDP would grow by 1.6–1.8% in 2006. Although Germany's unemployment rate was still at 11.3%, it had been gradually decreasing since mid 2005 and reached, according to the German government, 6,5% in October 2011.

Merkel presided over a fragile coalition government consisting of her conservative Christian Democratic Union party, the conservative Christian Social Union (CSU), and the left-leaning Social Democratic Party. Consequently, to push any reforms or programs through, she would have to be able to work together with the Social Democrats.

In the field of foreign policy, Merkel acknowledged the importance of Franco-German relations. She intended to maintain Germany's strong ties with France but not as exclusively as they used to be. Merkel was interested in working with the new EU member states and repairing relations with the United States. During Merkel's term, it was thought that Germany might become less involved with Russia due to her criticism of Russian President Vladimir Putin's policies in Chechnya and human rights abuses. Germany would continue to support Turkey in its desire to become a European Union member state and to support Iraq from outside. The next chancellery election was scheduled for November 2009.

The global economic crisis of 2008 hit the German economy hard. In early 2009, the nation's economic minister acknowledged the beginning of a recession, with the economy contracting by an estimated 5.6% by year-end.

In the September 2009 general elections, the center-right Christian Democratic Union/Christian Social Union (CDU/CSU) retained control in parliament by earning 239 of the 622 assembly seats. To obtain a parliamentary majority, Merkel agreed to form a coalition government with the pro-business Free Democrats Party, which earned 93 seats in the election. The new coalition government promised to make economic recovery a priority by tackling unemployment and initiating a program of tax cuts.

In May 2010, one day after the parliament of Greece approved tough and locally unpopular austerity measures designed to rein in the growing Greek deficit, German parliament approved a $28.6 billion bailout package for the fiscally troubled European state. German members of parliament voted 390–72 in favor of the bailout, with 139 members of parliament abstaining from the vote. The large German bailout was viewed by analysts as essential to ensuring the stability of the euro currency. In October 2011, European leaders agreed on additional measures in order to secure the financial stability of the Eurozone, including further financial support for Greece.

In May 2010, German president Horst Koehler resigned from his post after making controversial remarks that cast a shadow on the nature of Germany's military deployment in Afghanistan, already a deeply unpopular conflict for Germans. Following a brief visit to Afghanistan, Koehler said in a radio interview that, as an export-driven country, it was necessary for Germany to deploy troops "to protect [German] interests . . . for example free trade routes." The remark was heavily criticized by German politicians, who interpreted it as an affirmation of "gun-boat diplomacy." In June 2010, the German Federal Assembly chose Christian Wulff of the conservative Christian Democratic Union as the next German president.

13 GOVERNMENT

Germany is a federal republic founded in 1949. Germany's Basic Law (Grundgesetz) or its constitution, was promulgated on 23 May 1949. On 3 October 1990, the Federal Republic of Germany and the German Democratic Republic were unified in accordance with Article 23 of the Basic Law, under which the FRG is governed. German governmental structure consists of three branches: the executive branch represented by a president (titular chief of state) and a chancellor (executive head of government), a legislative branch composed of a bicameral parliament, and a judicial branch represented by the independent Federal Constitutional Court. The federal government exercises complete sovereignty and may be amended by a two-thirds vote of the legislature.

The federal chancellor and his or her cabinet ministers and the federal president compose a federal executive branch. This branch is situated at the center of the German political system, where the chancellor is the head of federal government, and an elected president performs the largely ceremonial functions of proposing the chancellor to the Bundestag, promulgating laws, formally appointing and dismissing judges and federal civil servants, and receiving foreign ambassadors. The president is elected for a five-year term by a federal convention composed of members of the Bundestag and an equal number of delegates elected by the provincial legislatures.

Every four years, after national elections and seating of the newly elected Bundestag members, the federal president nominates a chancellor candidate to that parliamentary body, and the chancellor is elected by majority vote in the Bundestag. Since a chancellor can only be elected by a coalition possessing a majority of the seats in parliament, each individual chancellor belongs to a particular party and represents the ideologies of that party. The Bundestag cannot remove the chancellor simply with a vote of no confidence. The Basic Law allows only for a "constructive" vote of no confidence; that is, the Bundestag can remove a chancellor only when it simultaneously agrees on a successor.

The chancellor's authority is drawn from the provisions of the Basic Law and from his or her status as leader of the party (or coalition of parties) holding a majority of seats in the Bundestag. The chancellor has powers of patronage and agenda-setting circumscribed by coalition government. Thus, the chancellor outlines federal policy and declares guidelines for cabinet ministers. Any formal policy guidelines issued by the chancellor are legally binding directives and must be implemented by the cabinet ministers. Guideline power allows the chancellor to interfere in any policy issue and to determine the government's approach to the problem.

Ministers are appointed and dismissed by the federal president with chancellor's approval; no Bundestag approval is needed. By and large, the chancellor and ministers are accountable to the Bundestag.

The bicameral legislature (the federal parliament) consists of a federal council (Bundesrat) and a federal diet (Bundestag).

The Bundestag is the principal legislative chamber in the parliament. Members of the Bundestag are the only federal officials directly elected by the public. The Bundestag had 497 voting deputies in 1987; 22 nonvoting deputies represented West Berlin. Following unification, Bundestag membership was raised to 662 deputies; as of November 2011 it stood at 622. Elections are held every four years (or earlier if a government falls from power). Candidates must be at least 18 years old. Bundestag members are elected for four-year terms by universal, free, and secret ballot, and may be reelected. The most important organizational structures within the Bundestag are parliamentary groups (Fraktionen), which are formed by each political party represented in the chamber. Among other things, the Bundestag may introduce federal bills. However, it usually responds to federal bills introduced by the federal government or by the federal council.

The Bundesrat is the body that represents the interests of the states (Länder) within the federal structure. It consists of 69 representatives appointed by the provincial governments according to the population of each province. Each state has three to six votes, depending on population, and is required to vote as a block. The federal council participates in the Federation's policy-making and thus acts as a counterweight to the federal diet (Bundestag). It also serves as a link between the federation and the federal states' delegations, representing the governments of the states. It can reject any federal bill and has an absolute veto power over any federal legislation that has an impact on the states.

Disagreements between the two chambers are handled by a conciliating committee.

¹⁴POLITICAL PARTIES

The "five percent clause," under which parties represented in the Bundestag must obtain at least 5% of the total votes cast by the electorate, has prevented the development of parliamentary splinter groups. In order to become a leading force in the parliament, parties have to win the local elections and become a majority by building coalitions. Since party elections happen on the regional level, consistency of the parliament depends on the outcome of the Länder's elections.

The chancellor of Germany always belongs to the coalition of the parties that received the largest number of seats in the Bundestag. The chancellor seemingly could push his reforms by counting on the support of his coalition. However, coalitions do not agree on everything and often are fragmented, and there is some fragmentation within each party. Additionally, after the German unification, there has been noticeable discrepancy between east and west because Western and Eastern Germany had different patterns of party developments.

Looking back, only three parties gained representation in the Bundestag following the elections of September 1965. The Christian Democratic Union and its Bavarian affiliate, the Christian Social Union, with 245 seats, remained the strongest group, as it had been since the first Bundestag was elected in 1949. The Social Democratic Party increased its seats to 202 and remained the major opposition party. The Free Democratic Party (Freie Demokratische Partei-FDP), winning 49 seats, joined with the CDU and the CSU to form the "small coalition" government of Chancellor Ludwig Erhard.

The coalition government was dissolved in October 1966, following a budgetary disagreement between the CDU/CSU and the FDP. In November 1966, the CDU/CSU joined with the SPD to form a new coalition government, but, following the general elections of September 1969, the SPD and FDP formed a coalition government with a combined strength of 254 seats. The elections of November 1972 resulted in a coalition composed of the SPD's 230 seats and the FDP's 42 to the CDU/CSU's 224 seats. Following the resignation of SPD leader Willy Brandt, Helmut Schmidt (SPD) was elected chancellor by the Bundestag in May 1974 by a 267–255 vote. The SPD/FDP coalition retained its majorities in the elections of 1976 (SPD 214, FDP 39) and 1980 (SPD 218, FDP 53).

In the general election of 25 January 1987, the results were as follows: CDU/CSU, 44.3% (223 seats); FDP, 9.1% (46 seats); SPD, 37% (186 seats); and the Greens, 8.3% (42 seats). The first all-Germany elections were held 2 December 1990. The results were as follows: CDU/CSU, 43.8% (319 seats); SPD, 33.5% (239 seats); FDP, 11.0% (79 seats); and Greens, 1.2% (8). The Party of Democratic Socialism (PDS), successor to the SED (Communist party), won 2.4% of the vote and 17 seats. East German parties were allowed to win seats if they received at least 5% of the vote in East Germany. After the breakup of the coalition in 1982, however, the CDU/CSU swept to victory in the voting of March 1983, winning 244 seats and 48.8% of the vote, compared with 226 seats (44.5%) in 1980 and 243 seats (48.6%) in 1976. The swing party, the FDP, took 34 seats (6.9%) and joined the CDU/CSU in a coalition behind Chancellor Helmut Kohl. The SPD polled 38.2% (down from 42.9% in 1980) and captured 193 seats, a drop of 25.

The CDU and CSU emphasize Christian precepts but are not denominational parties. They favor free enterprise and are supported by small business, professional groups, farmers, and Christian-oriented labor unions. In foreign policy, the CDU/CSU alliance supports European integration and the strengthening of NATO.

The SPD is the oldest and best organized of all German parties. In recent decades it has modified its traditional Marxist program and made an appeal not only to industrial workers but also to farmers, youth, professional people, and the petty bourgeoisie. Its revised Godesberg Program (1959) envisages a mixed economy, support for European integration and NATO, public ownership of key industries, a strong defense force, and recognition of religious values.

The FDP is a more heterogeneous organization, consisting of both classical liberals and strongly nationalistic groups. The party is supported mainly by business interests and Protestant groups. It rejects socialism or state capitalism in principle.

The Greens (Die Grünen) constitute a coalition of environmentalists and antinuclear activists; in 1983, they became the first left-wing opposition party to gain a parliamentary foothold since the Communists won 15 seats in 1949. In 1990, in cooperation with Alliance 90, a loose left-wing coalition, the Greens were able to clear the 5% hurdle and win Bundestag seats. From 1998 to 2005, they belonged to the governing coalition with the SPD. After the nuclear disaster in Fukushima, Japan, the party's strong opposition to nuclear power gained in popularity, resulting in large gains in state (Länder) election in 2011.

The Left Party was founded in June 2007 by the PDS (composed largely of former East German communists) and the WASG (western leftist). The party proposes to return to socialist economic principles and is rigidly opposed to foreign military deployments.

The October 1994 elections saw a weakening of the Free Democratic and Christian Democratic coalition and a strengthening of the Social Democrats and the Greens. The Christian Democrats won 41.5% of the vote and the Free Democrats 6.9%. This gave the governing coalition 341 seats in parliament and a majority of only 10 seats as compared to its previous 134-seat edge. The combined opposition alliance took 48.1% of the vote (331 seats): the Social Democrats took 36.4%; the Greens, 7.3%; and the former Communists in eastern Germany (now called the Party of Democratic Socialism), 4.4%.

Kohl's CDU-CSU coalition was weakened further in the September 1998 parliamentary elections, winning only 245 seats (35.1%), compared to 298 for the SDP (40.9%). Seats won by other parties were as follows: Greens, 47; Free Democrats, 44; and Party of Democratic Socialism, 35. Following the election, Germany's new chancellor Gerhard Schröder formed a center-left coalition government with the Green Party.

Elections held in September 2002 saw both the SPD and the CDU-CSU coalition each win 38.5% of the vote; however, the SPD came away with 251 seats to 248 for the CDU-CSU. The SPD renewed its coalition with the Greens, who took 8.5% of the vote and 55 seats, and Schröder remained chancellor. The Free Democrats took 7.4% of the vote and 47 seats, and the PDS won 4.3% of the vote and held 2 seats in the Bundestag. On 23 May 2004, Horst Koehler was elected president with the next election scheduled for May 2009.

In the 2005 elections, Gerhard Schröder (SPD/Greens coalition) lost the chancellery office to Angela Merkel (CDU/CSU-FDP coalition). It was the first time in German history that one of the two larger parties had nominated a woman for this position. The election campaign turned into a tense race of Merkel running against Schröder. Election polls fluctuated as did the predictions of the election results. Polls showed that right before the election day, at least a quarter of German voters were still undecided.

Germany held elections on 18 September 2005, except in a constituency in Dresden that held the elections on 2 October. Unsurprisingly, both candidates came close, with the Christian Democrats receiving only 1% more votes and four more seats than did the SPD. Exit polls showed that neither coalition group had won a majority of seats in the federal diet (Bundestag), and both parties lost seats compared to 2002. The SPD/Green coalition fell from 306 seats (in a house of 603) to 273 seats (in a house of 614). At the same time the CDU/CSU-FDP coalition fell from 295 seats to 286 seats. In the final distribution of seats in the federal diet, CDU got 180 seats, CSU received 46 seats, FDP gained 61 seats, SPD got 222 seats, the Greens remained with 51 seats, and the recently formed left-wing Left Party (or PDS/WASG alliance) climbed to 54 seats.

Neither of the coalitions (SPD-Greens and CDU/CSU-FDP) could achieve the majority of votes in the federal diet (Kandzlermehrheit) that is required to elect a chancellor. Both chancellors claimed a victory, but to make it functional, they had to negotiate with all the parties to form an appropriate winning coalition. On 10 October 2005, a round of negotiations ended with the Grand Coalition between the CDU/CSU and the SPD. Merkel officially became chancellor on the condition that 16 seats in the new cabinet would be equally divided between the CDU/CSU and the SPD and with the SPD controlling 8 out of the 14 ministries, including the ministries of foreign affairs and finance.

In the September 2009 general elections, the center-right CDU/CSU retained control in parliament by earning 239 of the 622 assembly seats. The Social Democratic Party won 146 seats, followed by the FDP with 93 seats, the Left Party with 76 seats, and the Greens with 68 seats. The CDU/CSU formed a coalition with the FDP, and Merkel was reelected as chancellor. Christian Wulff of the Christian Democratic Union was elected president by the assembly in 2010.

15 LOCAL GOVERNMENT

The Basic Law guarantees local self-government, and the states (Länder) are granted all powers not specifically reserved to the federal government. The Federal Republic consists of 13 Länder, and 3 free states (Freistaaten); Baden-Wuerttemberg, Bayern (Freistaat), Berlin, Brandenburg, Bremen, Hamburg, Hessen, Mecklenburg-Vorpommern, Niedersachsen, Nordrhein-Westfalen, Rheinland-Pfalz, Saarland, Sachsen (Freistaat), Sachsen-Anhalt, Schleswig-Holstein, and Thueringen (Freistaat).

Länder each have ministerial governments and legislatures. They have primary responsibility for the maintenance of law and order; jurisdiction over their own finances, taxes, and administration; and supreme authority in education and other cultural activities. Through the Bundesrat, the Länder have considerable influence in federal legislation and can prevent the central government from imposing radical reforms.

Communes (Gemeinden) are the basic units of local government, apart from the municipalities, and have the right to regulate such local matters as those involving schools, building, cultural affairs, and welfare. Halfway between the Länder and the communes are the counties (Landkreise), which have autonomy in such matters as road building, transportation, and hospitals. They are administered by a Landrat, the chief official, and a Kreistag (country legislature).

16 JUDICIAL SYSTEM

Cases of the first instance are tried by local or Landkreis courts and the superior courts in each of the Länder. The Federal Court of Justice in Karlsruhe, the court of last resort in regular civil and criminal cases, consists of members appointed by a committee that includes federal and Land ministers and several Bundestag members. A court of appeal and the several Land and Landkreis courts are subordinate to the Karlsruhe tribunal. Special courts handle administrative, labor, financial, and social welfare matters. The Federal Constitutional Court, the highest court in the land, has competence to decide problems concerning the Basic Law and to test the constitutionality of laws. The court has 16 members: one 8-member panel elected by a committee of the Bundestag, the other by the Bundesrat.

The judiciary is independent of the legislative and judicial branches and remains free from interference or intimidation. The Basic Law provides for the rights to a fair trial and prohibits arbitrary interference with privacy, family, home and correspondence. The government authorities generally respect these prohibitions.

17 ARMED FORCES

The International Institute for Strategic Studies reports that armed forces in Germany totaled 251,465 members in 2011. The force is comprised of 105,291 from the army, 19,179 from the navy, 44,565 from the air force, 57,495 from joint support services, and 24,935 from joint medical services. Armed forces represent .6% of the labor force in Germany. Defense spending totaled $44.2 billion and accounted for 1.5% of GDP.

The unification of Germany in 1991 brought the amalgamation of the People's Army of the German Democratic Republic and the Bundeswehr of the Federal Republic—on the Bundeswehr's terms, modified by political guidance. Essentially, West Germany abolished the East German Ministry of Defense and officer corps but kept much of the GDR's Russian equipment and a few of its career officers and noncommissioned specialists. The Bundeswehr occupied East German military installations and found many of them beyond repair for training and suitable housing. The Bundeswehr moved eastward with all deliberate speed, especially since six Russian divisions and a tactical air force still remained in German installations. With dependents, these dispossessed Russians numbered almost 500,000. Meanwhile, Germany's NATO allies still maintained an integrated ground and air force of almost 250,000 troops in western Germany, although this force shrank with the departure of the Canadian and Belgian forces and the reduction of the American and British contingents in the 1990s.

German armed forces are actively involved in peacekeeping and UN missions abroad. Germany has troops in France and Poland and trains with the United States military.

In January 2010, Chancellor Angela Merkel announced that Germany would send 500 additional troops to Afghanistan and double the reconstruction aid that Germany provides to the country. In terms of numbers, Germany's commitment to the NATO campaign was sizeable. With more than 4,000 troops, the German forces are the third-largest in Afghanistan, behind the United States and Great Britain. However, analysts noted that the fighting capabilities of German troops remained deliberately limited, in keeping with the nation's own laws concerning foreign military assistance. At the time of Merkel's announcement, the war in Afghanistan was deeply unpopular in Germany, and domestic polling showed that a majority of the population wanted Germany's troops pulled from the conflict. NATO's response to the German troop increase was not much more positive. Top NATO commanders said in mid 2009 that 40,000 more troops were needed to secure the country.

The constitutional mandate for conscription, calling all German men to serve in the military, was suspended in July 2011, at which time the government switched to a program of voluntary military service. The decision was made, in part, to reduce the Bundeswehr (German army) from 250,000 to about 185,000 troops who would be deployed on missions abroad. Mandatory military conscription was added to the constitution following World War II as a means of forming a military linked more closely to social and civilian national loyalty rather than political power. The restructuring plan was largely driven by economics, as reducing the military is expected to save billions of dollars.

18 INTERNATIONAL COOPERATION

The Federal Republic of Germany became a full member of the United Nations on 18 September 1973; it belongs to several nonregional specialized UN agencies. It is also an active participant in the Council of Europe, the European Union, NATO, OECD, OSCE, the Asian Development Bank, the African Development Bank, the Council of the Baltic Sea States, the Euro-Atlantic Partnership Council, the Caribbean Development Bank, G-5, G-7, G-8, and the Paris Club (G-10). Germany is a permanent observer of the OAS and a nonregional member of the West African Development Bank. The country is a member of the WTO. Germa-

ny held the presidency of the European Union in the first half of 2007.

Germany has supported UN operations and missions in Kosovo (1999), Ethiopia and Eritrea (2000), Sierra Leone (1999), and Georgia (1993). Germany is part of the Australia Group, the Zangger Committee, the Nuclear Suppliers Group (London Group), the Nuclear Energy Agency, the Organization for the Prohibition of Chemical Weapons, and the European Organization for Nuclear Research (CERN).

In environmental cooperation, Germany is part of the Antarctic Treaty; the Basel Convention; Conventions on Biological Diversity, Whaling, and Air Pollution; Ramsar; CITES; the London Convention; International Tropical Timber Agreements; the Kyoto Protocol; the Montréal Protocol; MARPOL; the Nuclear Test Ban Treaty; and the UN Conventions on the Law of the Sea, Climate Change, and Desertification.

In 2010, Germany was elected for a two-year term on the United Nations Security Council. The term began 1 January 2011.

19 ECONOMY

The German economy is one of the largest in Europe and the world. For many years, Germany has been the world's largest exporter, with sales concentrated in motor vehicles, machinery, chemicals, and heavy electrical equipment. France is its greatest partner in both importation and exportation of goods, but Germany also exports its products to the United States, the United Kingdom, and Italy.

Before unification in 1990, GNP in West Germany increased at an annual average rate of 7% between 1950 and 1960 and 5.4% between 1960 and 1970. This rate slowed to 3.1% between 1970 and 1980 and 2.3% between 1980 and 1990. However, the unification of Germany in October 1990 proved a heavy economic burden on the west. In 1992, the former East Germany accounted for only 8% of GDP. Transfer payments and subsidies for the east resulted in a large public deficit. Alarmed at the potential for inflation, the Bundesbank pursued a tight monetary policy. This boosted the value of the mark and had a recessionary effect on the European economy. The unemployment rate in 1993 was 7.3% in the west, but 15.8% in the east because so many antiquated, inefficient enterprises were unable to compete in a market economy. These factors led to the recession of 1992–93 with growth in the GDP dropping to 1.1%. The economy recovered in 1994, posting a growth rate of 2.9%, but declined to 1.9% in 1995 and 1% in 1996.

Strong exports in 1997 were expected to bring the growth rate back to 3.5% with sustained growth projected at 4–4.5% for 1998–2000. Such hopes failed to materialize, as the real growth rate for 1998 was 2.7%. The costs of reunification saddled the country with $300 billion in debt, forcing western Germans to pay a 7.5% "solidarity" surtax for reconstructing the eastern section. Even with the infusion of cash, the eastern sector was essentially bankrupt in the late 1990s with 25% unemployment and worker output at 50% of its western counterpart. However, high unemployment did not result in a drop in the hourly wage rate. High labor costs also plagued the west, where workers averaged a 38-hour work week and enjoyed six weeks of vacation per year. To remain competitive, German companies cut staff and relocated manufacturing jobs to lower-wage countries.

The coalition government of Social Democrats and Greens elected in 1998 pledged to combat Germany's economic sluggishness through a reform program dubbed "Future Program 2000." This program included budget cuts, tax reforms, and a major reform of the pension system. The government also tried to coordinate better labor-management cooperation in its effort to implement its reforms. This coalition government was returned to power in 2002, and Chancellor Gerhard Schröder called on citizens to "renew Germany" by pulling together during difficult economic times. Germany, on the brink of recession, saw a drop in the government's popularity. Schröder threatened to resign in 2003 if his reform package, called "Agenda 2010," was not passed by 2004. This program included a relaxation of job protections, reductions in unemployment and health care benefits, and an easing of the rules on collective bargaining. Indeed, the Social Democrats' traditional support from unions was compromised by the proposed reforms, including, as in France, pension reform—strikes broke out in Germany, France, Austria, and Italy in 2003 due to opposition to cuts in old-age benefits. Neither the reforms of "Agenda 2010" nor reduced taxation did much to improve consumer confidence for Germany's industrial workers, who were unemployed in large numbers. The unemployment rate in Germany stood at 10.6% in 2004 and at 12.4% for the first quarter of 2005.

As a result of elections held in September 2005, a "grand coalition" of the Christian Democratic Union and the Social Democratic Party, headed by Chancellor Angela Merkel, was faced with the task of implementing further economic reforms. Reforming business taxes was one item on the policy agenda. The federal corporation tax rate is 25%, with local taxes pushing the total tax burden on companies up to 38%. A 3% increase on the value added tax (VAT) enabled Germany to get its budget deficit well below the EU limit of 3% of GDP.

In 2006, Germany had its best year since 2000 with 2.7% growth; in 2007, growth was at 2.5%. While Germany's reliance on exports has generally led to strong economic growth and stability, it translated into a quick and sharp recession in the wake of the global financial crisis of 2008–09. In April 2009, industrial production in Germany fell by 21.6%, and exports dropped by 28.7% compared to figures from April 2008. The Bundesbank (German central bank) projected an overall decline in the economy of 6.2% for 2009, the worst drop experienced in the nation since World War II. While the government was initially reluctant to initiate any type of rescue plan, the German parliament approved two major stimulus packages of $40 billion and $62 billion in November 2008 and January 2009, respectively. Portions of the funds were earmarked for investment in highways, education, and tax cuts for businesses and individuals. A loan fund was also established to help struggling businesses. However, some of the relief measures did not go into effect until the end of 2009 and into 2010.

In January 2009, unemployment was estimated at about 3 million people. That rate was expected to rise to 4.4 million, representing over 10% of the workforce, by mid-2010. However, economic reports issued in August 2009 were promising. An overall second quarter growth of 0.3% was registered, making Germany one of the first European countries to officially pull out of recession. Analysts were quick to point out that such growth may have resulted from government stimulus efforts and expressed concern that the perceived economic recovery might not last once stimulus

programs were exhausted. In December 2009, Germany's cabinet approved a 2010 budget that included record levels of debt and significant increases in government spending. In total, government spending was set to rise 7.3% to $475 billion, while borrowing would jump by more than 50%, to $125 billion--the highest levels since World War II.

In 2010, the gross domestic product (GDP) grew by 3.5% in 2010. Inflation stood at 1.1%, and unemployment was reported at 7.4%. The Federal Government expected the upswing to continue, forecasting a GDP growth rate of 2.3.% for 2011.

²⁰INCOME

The World Bank reports that, in 2009, household consumption in Germany totaled $1.96 trillion or about $24,060 per capita, measured in current US dollars rather than in purchasing power parity (PPP). Household consumption includes expenditures of individuals, households, and nongovernmental organizations on goods and services, excluding the purchases of dwellings. It was estimated that household consumption was growing at an average annual rate of 0.2%.

The CIA estimated that, in 2010, the GDP of Germany was $2.9 trillion. The CIA defines GDP as the value of all final goods and services produced within a nation in a given year and computed on the basis of PPP rather than value as measured on the basis of the rate of the exchange based on current dollars. The per capita GDP was estimated at $35,700. The annual growth rate of GDP was 3.5%. The average inflation rate was 1.1%. It was estimated that agriculture accounted for 0.8% of GDP, industry 27.9%, and services 71.3%.

According to the World Bank, remittances from citizens living abroad totaled $10.9 billion or about $134 per capita and accounted for approximately .4% of GDP.

As of 2011 the most recent study by the World Bank reported that actual individual consumption in Germany was 70.1% of GDP and accounted for 4.80% of world consumption. By comparison, the United States accounted for 25.44% of world individual consumption. The World Bank also estimated that 8.3% of Germany's GDP was spent on food and beverages, 17.5% on housing and household furnishings, 3.0% on clothes, 8.7% on health, 7.7% on transportation, 1.5% on communications, 5.7% on recreation, 3.0% on restaurants and hotels, and 10.7% on miscellaneous goods and services and purchases from abroad.

It was estimated that, in 2010, about 15.5% of the population subsisted on an income below the poverty line established by Germany's government.

²¹LABOR

As of 2010, Germany had a total labor force of 43.44 million people. Within that labor force, CIA estimates in 2005 noted that 2.4% were employed in agriculture, 29.7% in industry, and 67.8% in the service sector.

Reports from 2011 showed that a shrinking percentage of Germany's workforce was occupied by women. Gender stereotypes have been shown to hold strong in the country, where only 14 percent of mothers with one child resume full-time work, and only 6 percent of those with two children do. Additionally, only 2 percent of German women serve on executive committees, as opposed to 14 percent in Great Britain.

The right to organize and to join trade unions is guaranteed by law. As of 2009 about 21% of the eligible labor force was unionized. In 1991, the western trade unions successfully expanded eastward, where they created western structures in the new states, totally dominating overall development so that no GDR trade union survived reunification. Disputes concerning the interpretation of labor agreements are settled before special labor courts. Wages and working conditions in virtually all commercial and industrial establishments are governed by collective bargaining agreements between employers' associations and trade unions. Germany in 2009 did not have an administratively or legislated minimum wage rate; however, binding minimum wages have been established in 14 branches or sectors covering 1.4 million workers.

As of 2009, children under the age of 15 were generally prohibited from employment, and these child labor laws were strictly enforced. Minors 13 and 14 years of age were permitted to work on a farm up to three hours per day or deliver newspapers up to two hours per day. Although the average full-time workweek ranges from 39 to 31 hours, the law allows a maximum workweek of 48 hours. Provisions for overtime, holiday, and weekend pay vary depending upon the applicable collective bargaining agreement. About 63% of workers in the western part of Germany and 54% in the east were covered by a collective bargaining agreement in 2009, which partly explains the relatively high wages in the absence of a minimum wage law and why working time and vacation provisions exceed legal requirements. Health and safety standards are stringently regulated.

22 AGRICULTURE

Agricultural production falls far short of satisfying industrial and consumer demand. The average size of Germany's 420,697 farms was about 40 hectares (100 acres).

Article 15 of the 1990 Treaty (for monetary, economic and social union) arranged for transitional price supports for GDR farmers until an integration within the EU agricultural market could occur. Before reunification, agriculture had engaged about 6.1% and 3% of the economically active populations of the former GDR and old FRG, respectively. The former GDR Länder contribute significantly to German agricultural production. Apples and pears as well as cherries and peaches are significant fruit crops. In 2003, apple production was the smallest since 1995 due to bad pollination and forest damage. Viticulture is important in the southwest, and Germany is a renowned producer of wines for world consumption. Germany is the world's second-largest importer of agricultural products (after the United States).

In 2008, roughly 34% of the total land was farmed, and the country's major crops include potatoes, wheat, barley, sugar beets, fruit, and cabbages. Cereal production in 2009 amounted to 49.7 million tons, fruit production 3 million tons, and vegetable production 3.7 million tons.

In January 2011, Germany stopped sales from 4,700 small farms and pulled millions of eggs from the shelves of grocery stores due to the discovery of dioxin in chicken and pig feed. Although levels of dioxin in meat and eggs were likely too low to affect human health, it was not a risk the government found acceptable. As a result, many countries banned the importing of German food products. Additionally, the German government began to crack down on food services and anti-dioxin plans.

23 ANIMAL HUSBANDRY

The government regulates the marketing of livestock, meat, and some dairy products; it also controls the distribution of livestock for slaughter and meat. The UN Food and Agriculture Organization (FAO) reported that Germany dedicated 4.8 million hectares (11.8 million acres) to permanent pasture or meadow in 2009. During that year, the country tended 118 million chickens, 12.9 million head of cattle, and 26.9 million pigs. The production from these animals amounted to 1.09 million tons of beef and veal, 4.59 million tons of pork, 1.28 million tons of poultry, 990,040 tons of eggs, and 20.4 million tons of milk. Germany also produced 132,000 tons of cattle hide and 5,868 tons of raw wool. Germany is the leading meat, milk, and honey producer in Europe.

24 FISHING

The importance of the fishing industry has declined. The main fishing areas are the North Sea, the Baltic Sea, and the waters off Greenland. Overfishing is a serious environmental problem. The government subsidizes capacity reduction and modernization measures. The fish varieties accounting for the greatest volume are herring, mackerel, cod, and sardines. In 2008, Germany had 2,309 decked commercial fishing boats, whose annual capture totaled 229,499 tons, according to the UN FAO. The export value of seafood totaled $1.5 billion that same year.

25 FORESTRY

Total forest area amounted in 2000 to more than 10.7 million hectares (26.5 million acres), about 32% of the total land area. Reforestation has resulted in a 6% increase in the forest area since the end of World War II (1939–45). Deciduous species (such as beech, oak, ash, maple, and alder) originally covered about two thirds of the area, and conifers were only predominant in higher elevations. Today, hardwood trees comprise only one third of the forests. Principal softwood species include silver fir, pine, spruce, and Douglas fir, which was introduced from the northwest United States late in the 19th century. The most thickly wooded of the federal Länder are Hessen and Rhineland-Pfalz. The wood products industry consists of about 185,000 companies employing more than 1.3 million people, larger than the German automotive industry. Almost half of the raw timber is used by sawmills for lumber production. The German sawmilling industry consists of about 2,500 sawmills producing around 17 million cu m (600 million cu ft) of softwood lumber and 1.2 million cu m (42.4 million cu ft) of hardwood lumber. The UN FAO estimated the 2009 roundwood production at 48.1 million cu m (1.7 billion cu ft). The value of all forest products, including roundwood, totaled $19.7 billion. High domestic labor costs compel Germany to import substantial quantities of value-added products, such as veneers and panels.

26 MINING

Germany's export-oriented economy is the largest in Europe. Approximately one-third of Germany's gross domestic product (GDP) depends on exports. Germany is also a major processing nation, relying on imports of raw materials for the metals processing industry and the manufacture of industrial mineral products. The country is a leader in the mining equipment manufacturing sector and is among the largest and most technologically advanced producers of iron, coal, and cement. Although the underground mining sector has steadily declined, certain minerals remain important domestically and worldwide. In 2009, Germany was the world's largest lignite producer, the world's sixth-largest producer of potash, third in kaolin, a major European producer of crude gypsum, and self-sufficient in feldspar and salt. The only metal mineral still mined in Germany is uranium.

Except for the very large lignite and potash operations, most of the producing and processing facilities in operation are small. Production figures for 2009 were, in million tons: potash, 2.208; kaolin, 4.5; marketable gypsum and anhydrite, 1.898, down from 2.112 in 2008; feldspar, 0.16; industrial dolomite and limestone, 19; and marketable salt (evaporated, rock, and other), 18.9, up from 15.8 in 2008. In 2009, Germany also produced barite; bromine; chalk; clays (bentonite, ceramic, fire, fuller's earth, brick); diatomite; fluorspar; graphite; lime; quicklime; dead-burned dolomite; nitrogen; phosphate materials, including Thomas slag; mineral and natural pigments; pumice; dimension stone; quartz; quartzite; slate; building sand; gravel; terrazzo splits; foundry sand; industrial glass sand; talc; and steatite. In terms of overseas developments, Süd-Chemie AG is the largest bentonite producer in Europe. Between 140 and 160 small- to medium-sized clay mines are in operation; about one half of the high-quality refractory and ceramic clays produced are from the Rhineland-Palatinate area. Iron ore mining produced 38,000 tons of metal in 2009; demand was met by imports of 44 million tons.

27 ENERGY AND POWER

Germany is the greatest consumer of electric power in Europe. The World Bank reported in 2008 that Germany produced 631.2 billion kWh of electricity and consumed 587 billion kWh, or 7,205 kWh per capita. Roughly 80% of energy came from fossil fuels, while 13% came from alternative fuels. Per capita oil consumption was 4,083 kg. Oil production totaled 28,134 barrels of oil a day.

While most of Europe is considering ways to eliminate the use of nuclear power, Germany made the decision to keep its own 17 nuclear plants up and running until more renewable energy sources have been developed. A law passed in 2002 had officially called for the closure of all nuclear plants in the nation by 2022. While many government officials believed that the 2022 goal was too soon, in the aftermath of the nuclear disaster in Fukushima Japan in March 2011, Germany formally announced plans to abandon nuclear energy within 11 years, thus confirming the 2022 deadline. Fukushima also prompted Germany to investigate the security standards in its 17 nuclear plants, with investigations leading to temporary shutdowns in March 2011.

Proven natural gas reserves were estimated at 175.6 billion cu m, as of 1 January 2010. Domestic production in 2010 accounted for slightly more than 13% of the natural gas consumed in the same year. Major natural gas suppliers to Germany are Russia, the Netherlands, and Norway. In 2000, production began at Germany's first offshore gas field in the North Sea. It is expected to produce 3.3 billion cu m (116 billion cu ft) of gas per day for 16 years. Production of oil was estimated at 147,200 barrels per day in 2010. Local production is not sufficient to cover consumption, which totaled an estimated 2.5 million barrels per day in 2009, resulting in estimated oil imports of 2.7 million barrels per day.

Germany has extensive coal reserves. Germany's hard coal (anthracite and bituminous) deposits lie deep underground and are difficult to mine economically. As a result, hard coal extraction is subsidized by the government. However, by 2012, coal subsidies are slated to fall to $2.3 billion, the result of a pact with the coal industry reached in 1997. Brown coal, or lignite, however, is easier to obtain and does not require subsidies from the government. It also accounts for the vast bulk of German coal output. The lignite industry, which is centered in the eastern part of the country, was drastically changed as a result of unification and the introduction of the strict environmental and safety laws of the pre-1991 FRG. In 2009, Germany produced about 204 million tons of coal.

Germany is also looking at renewable energy sources. Under the Renewable Energy Sources Act, Germany is looking to have 12.5% of its energy supplied by renewable sources by 2010 and 20% by 2020. During the 1990s, more than 5,000 electricity-generating windmills were installed in Germany, mostly along the North Sea coast, and wind power is expected to supply 3.5% of electricity by 2010. As of November 2005, Germany had 14,600 MW of installed wind power capacity and 390 MW of installed solar voltaic capacity.

28 INDUSTRY

Germany is the world's third-largest industrial power, behind the United States and Japan. The major industrial concentrations of western Germany are the Ruhr-Westphalia complex; the Upper Rhine Valley, Bremen and Hamburg, notable for shipbuilding; the southern region, with such cities as Munich and Augsburg; and the central region, with such industrial cities as Salzgitter, Kassel, Hanover, and Braunschweig. In the east, most of the leading industries are located in the Berlin region or in such cities as Dresden, Leipzig, Dessau, Halle, Cottbus, and Chemnitz.

The main industrial sectors in the former GDR were electrical engineering and electronics, chemicals, glass, and ceramics. The optical and precision industries were important producers of export items. Following unification, wages in the east were allowed to reach levels far exceeding productivity. As a result, many factories closed and industrial production plunged by two thirds before stabilizing.

German industry has been struggling with high labor costs, stiff international competition, and high business taxes. Large industrial concerns like Daimler-Benz have spun off unprofitable companies, cut staff, and are looking for ways to boost productivity. Policies such as these have led to a loss of some two million industrial jobs since 1991. Other companies, like the electronics giant Siemens, have moved plants abroad in search for lower labor costs and to secure positions in developing economies like China and Thailand.

Despite the costs of restructuring the former GDR, Germany had some of the largest and most successful companies in the world, from automobiles to advanced electronics, steel, chemicals, machinery, shipbuilding, and textiles. German industrial products are known for their high quality and reliability. Manufacturing remained at the heart of the German economy.

29 SCIENCE AND TECHNOLOGY

The reunification of East and West Germany has created great opportunities for the entire population but has also placed great strains on the nation. Perhaps nowhere is this more evident than in science, engineering and technical education, and vocational training. Germany maintains an excellent science and technology educational system and vocational training in many fields. About 140,000 science and engineering students graduated per year in the last years of the 20th century.

The German national science and technology budget is applied to many areas of science and technology, and leading fields include traditional areas of German strength, like chemical, automotive, and telecommunications research and development. Current policy emphasizes the application of science and technology to enhance Germany's economic and competitive standing while protecting the nation's health and the environment. Support for science and technology also occurs at other levels. There are independent laboratories, comprised of both the national laboratories and private research institutes like the Max Planck and Fraunhofer Societies. In addition, German industry supports many important types of research and development, and the German states provide still more resources for scientific research. The Ministry for Science and Technology (BMFT), an organization without parallel in the United States, both coordinates and sets priorities for the entire national science and technology program. Finally, Germany's participation in the European Union also has a significant science and technology component—Germany provides funding, scientists, and laboratories for broad European research and development. In 2009, 2.54 % of the GDP were used for expenditures in research and development (R&D), according to the World Bank and patent applications in science totaled 47,859 that same year.

In 2007, there were 3,532 scientists and engineers and 1,301 technicians per million people that were actively engaged in R&D. High-tech exports that same year accounted for 16% of manufactured exports. In February of 2010, the United States and Germany signed the first Science and Technology Agreement between the two nations that will provide a framework for future corporations.

Germany has numerous universities and colleges offering courses in basic and applied sciences. In 2009/10, science and engineering students accounted for 33% of university enrollment, according to the German Ministry for Education and Research (BMBF).

The Natural History Museum in Berlin (founded in 1889) has geological, paleontological, mineralogical, zoological, and botanical components. The country has numerous specialized learned societies concerned with agriculture and veterinary science, medicine, the natural sciences, and technology.

30 DOMESTIC TRADE

Wholesalers, retailers, mail-order houses, door-to-door salespersons, department stores, consumer cooperatives, and factory stores all engage in distribution. Chain stores are common, with the top 10 German retail organizations accounting for almost 80% of total German retail turnover. Convenience shops are a fast-growing market outlet in Germany.

Germany's franchising market is mature and sophisticated. The largest portion of franchising chains are in the services sector at 45%, followed by trade at 37%, fine dining at 10%, and building and handcrafts at 8%.

Principal Trading Partners – Germany (2010)

(In millions of US dollars)

Country	Total	Exports	Imports	Balance
World	2,339,409.0	1,271,354.0	1,068,055.0	203,299.0
Netherlands	225,185.0	83,689.0	141,496.0	-57,807.0
France	204,364.0	120,170.0	84,194.0	35,976.0
China	141,324.0	58,346.0	82,978.0	-24,632.0
Italy	135,761.0	77,510.0	58,251.0	19,259.0
Belgium	131,768.0	61,403.0	70,365.0	-8,962.0
United Kingdom	127,783.0	78,696.0	49,087.0	29,609.0
Austria	118,814.0	71,141.0	47,673.0	23,468.0
United States	103,116.0	65,474.0	37,642.0	27,832.0
Switzerland	95,677.0	54,547.0	41,130.0	13,417.0
Poland	90,348.0	50,393.0	39,955.0	10,438.0

(…) data not available or not significant.

(n.s.) not specified.

SOURCE: *2011 Direction of Trade Statistics Yearbook,* New York: United Nations, 2011.

Balance of Payments – Germany (2010)

(In billions of US dollars)

Current Account		187.9
Balance on goods	204.7	
Imports	-1,098.6	
Exports	1,303.3	
Balance on services	-25.6	
Balance on income	59.7	
Current transfers	-50.8	
Capital Account		-0.8
Financial Account		-184.8
Direct investment abroad	-108.4	
Direct investment in Germany	46.1	
Portfolio investment assets	-231.1	
Portfolio investment liabilities	61.4	
Financial derivatives	-22.9	
Other investment assets	-163.6	
Other investment liabilities	233.8	
Net Errors and Omissions		-0.2
Reserves and Related Items		-2.1

(…) data not available or not significant.

SOURCE: *Balance of Payment Statistics Yearbook 2011,* Washington, DC: International Monetary Fund, 2011.

Usual business hours for retail stores are from 9 a.m. to 6 or 6:30 p.m. on weekdays and from 9 a.m. to 4 p.m. on Saturday. Retail stores are not open on Sundays or holidays unless they have a special limited permit allowing them to be open. Twenty-four-hour shopping is available only at certain gas stations and at other sites related to travel. Wholesale houses and industrial plants usually have a half day (noon closing) on Saturday. Banks are open Monday–Friday from 8:30 a.m. to 1 p.m. and from 2:30 p.m. to 4 p.m. (6 p.m. on Thursday). Government and business office are open from 9 a.m. to 6 p.m., Mondays through Fridays.

31 FOREIGN TRADE

Germany is one of the world's great trading nations. In 2003 and 2004 it was the largest exporter in the world. In 2010, Germany's

Public Finance – Germany (2009)

(In millions of euro, general government figures)

Revenue and Grants	**1,066,040**	**100.0%**
Tax revenue	569,010	53.4%
Social contributions	409,900	38.5%
Grants	3,250	0.3%
Other revenue	83,880	7.9%
Expenditures	**1,138,710**	**100.0%**
General public services	146,590	12.9%
Defense	27,790	2.4%
Public order and safety	40,150	3.5%
Economic affairs	86,780	7.6%
Environmental protection	15,600	1.4%
Housing and community amenities	17,790	1.6%
Health	164,780	14.5%
Recreational, culture, and religion	15,800	1.4%
Education	104,700	9.2%
Social protection	518,730	45.6%

(…) data not available or not significant.

SOURCE: *Government Finance Statistics Yearbook 2010,* Washington, DC: International Monetary Fund, 2010.

exports were estimated to be $1.303 trillion, compared with the United States' estimated $1.289 trillion. Its major export partners were France, 10.1%; the United States, 6.7%; UK, 6.6%; Netherlands, 6.6%; Italy, 6.3%; Austria, 5.7%; Belgium, 5.2%; China, 4.7%; and Switzerland, 4.5%. German imports stood at $1.099 trillion, resulting in a trade surplus of $204 billion in 2010. Major import partners in 2009 were Netherlands, 13%; France, 8.2%; Belgium, 7.2%; China, 6.8%; Italy, 5.6%; UK, 4.7%; Austria, 4.4%; the United States, 4.2%; and Switzerland, 4.1%

Manufactured products are the leading exports. Germany supplies a large portion of the world with automobiles and car parts. Diverse machinery exports, including nonelectrical and electrical parts, also account for a large percentage of the world's exports in those commodities. Chemical products, telecommunications technology, in addition to devices for electricity production and distribution, are the next leading exports.

³²BALANCE OF PAYMENTS

After experiencing deficits during 1979–81, Germany's accounts balance rebounded to a surplus of about 9.9 billion deutsche marks in 1982 and then kept rising to 76.5 billion deutsche marks in 1986, primarily because of falling prices for crude oil and other imports combined with appreciation of the deutsche mark relative to other European currencies. By 1989, Germany's account surplus was nearly 5% of GNP. With reunification, however, this changed immediately. Imports rushed in as former GDR residents sought newly available consumer goods, and exports fell as goods and services were diverted to the east. As a result, Germany recorded current account deficits since 1991, created in part because of the substantial foreign borrowing undertaken to finance the cost of unification. From 1990 to 1996, Germany's share of world exports dropped from 12% to 9.8% due in large part to high labor costs which were making it hard for Germany to compete in the global economy. In 2010, Germany had a foreign trade surplus of $165 billion, amounting to 2.2% of GDP. Between January

and June 2011, Germany's foreign trade surplus had already reach $107 billion, according to the German Federal Statistical Office, indicating a continuous growth in this area.

³³BANKING AND SECURITIES

As Germany is a member of the European Monetary Union (EMU) and a user of the euro, the European Central Bank (ECB) now functions as the nation's central bank, a function formally performed by the German Federal Bank (Deutsche Bundesbank). Currently, the German Federal Bank is part of the ECB system, and acts as a representative to the ECB and as the ECB's representative to the German banking system. The Federal Bank also maintains a leading role in Germany's domestic banking sector. All German banks are subject to supervision by the German Federal Banking Supervisory Authority (Bundesaufsichtsamt für das Kreditwesen) in Berlin.

In 2009, the money market rate, the rate at which financial institutions lend to one another in the short term, was 1%. Because Germany uses the euro, the nation's discount rate—the interest rate at which the central bank lends to financial institutions in the short term—is set by the ECB. In 2008, the discount rate was 4.25%. At the end of 2010, the nation's gold holdings totaled 3.401 tonnes, the second-largest amount after the United States.

The largest commercial banks are the Deutsche Bank, Dresdner Bank, and Commerzbank. The German financial system includes just under 2,700 small industrial and agricultural credit cooperatives and allied institutions, in addition to four central institutions; 33 private and public mortgage banks that obtain funds from the sale of bonds; the postal check and postal savings system; and 34 building societies.

Under the constitution, the governments of the Länder regulate the operations of stock exchanges and produce exchanges. Eight stock exchanges operate in Berlin, Bremen, Düsseldorf, Frankfurt, Hamburg, Hannover, Munich, and Stuttgart. Germany has several other independent exchanges for agricultural items. There are no restrictions on foreign investments in any securities quoted on the German stock exchanges. However, a foreign (or domestic) business investor that acquires more than 25% of the issued capital of a German quoted company must inform the company of this fact. The most notable recent banking legislation is the January 2002 elimination of the capital gains tax on holdings sold by one corporation to another. In December 2010, a total of 765 companies were listed on the Deutsche Borse AG. Market capitalization in 2010 totaled $1.9 trillion. That year, the DAX closed at 6.914.1 on December 30.

In March 2010, Germany and Switzerland initialed a double-taxation agreement that would streamline information sharing on suspected tax evaders and would set benchmark tax rates that Germans must pay on interest earned in Swiss accounts. Germany has been one of the harshest critics of Switzerland's banking secrecy laws and angered the Swiss by purchasing stolen Swiss banking records earlier in the year. In signing the double-taxation agreement, Germany and Switzerland smoothed over what had been deeply strained relations.

³⁴INSURANCE

The insurance sector is highly regulated, and, despite the opening of the European Union (EU) market, it will be difficult for foreign companies to win the confidence of potential German customers. Worker's compensation, third-party automobile liability, legal liability for drug companies, airlines, hunters, auditors, tax advisors, security firms, architects, lawyers, nuclear power station operators, and accident and health insurance are compulsory.

35 PUBLIC FINANCE

The 1967 Law for the Promotion of Economic Stability and Growth requires the federal and state governments to orient their budgets to the main economic policy objectives of price stability, high employment, balanced foreign trade, and steady commensurate growth. The Financial Planning Council, formed in 1968, coordinates the federal government, states, municipalities, and the Bundesbank in setting public budgets. Income, corporate turnover, mineral oil, and trade taxes account for more than 80% of all tax revenue, with the federal government controlling just under half of it. Since the 1960s, social insurance provisions have accounted for the largest share of federal expenditures. Germany's reunification in 1990 raised special problems with regard to economic and financial assimilation. The Unification Treaty provided that the new states, as much as possible from the onset, should be incorporated in the financial system established by the Basic Law. Therefore, since 1991, the new states have basically been subject to the same regulations with regard to budgetary management and tax distribution as the western states. A "German Unity Fund" was initiated to provide financial support for the new states and their municipalities; it is jointly financed by the western states, with most of the money being raised in the capital market.

The CIA estimated that, in 2010, Germany's budget included $1.427 trillion in public revenue and $1.535 trillion in public expenditures. The budget deficit amounted to 3.3% of GDP. Public debt was estimated at 83.4% of GDP, with $4.713 trillion of the debt held by foreign entities.

The International Monetary Fund (IMF) reported that, in 2010, the most recent general government revenues were €1,082 billion, and expenditures were €1,164 billion. The value of revenues was $1,478 million and expenditures $1,590 million. According to the OECD, federal government outlays by function in 2006 were as follows: general public services 30.5%; defense, 7.6%; public order and safety, 1.0%; economic affairs, 8.9%; environmental protection, 0.1%; housing and community amenities, 1.6%; recreation, culture, and religion, 0.2%; education, 1.2%; and social protection, 48.7%.

36 TAXATION

In 2000, the German tax system underwent a major reform featuring a dramatic reduction in taxes on business (from a corporate income tax rate of 40% to 25% and the elimination altogether of a 53% tax on investment profits), as well as a scheduled reduction in the top income tax rate to 42% by 2005 from 56% in the 1980s, and 53% in 2000. As of 2008, Germany's corporate income tax rate was 15%, plus a 5.5% surcharge. There is also a 14% basic trade tax. A nonresident corporation, the headquarters and management of which are outside Germany, does not have to pay the surcharge. Business-related capital gains are taxed as income, with a 95% exemption on gains from the sale of most shareholdings by companies for tax years ending after 31 December 2003. Business

activities are also subject to municipal trade taxes of 12–20.5%, depending upon the municipality.

As of 2010, Germany's progressive individual income tax had a top rate of 45% plus a 5.5% surcharge. Although self-employed people are subject to the country's trade tax, the tax can be credited against a person's individual income tax. In 2010, the progressive schedule of income tax rates saw an increase in the 0%, tax-free base to €8,004, with decreases in other brackets. The threshold for the highest tax rate of 45% is a taxable income of €250,730. Rates and exemptions depend on the number of children, age, and marital status of the taxpayer. Individuals also pay an 8–9% church tax, although non-churchgoers and members of the Orthodox or Anglican Churches are exempt from paying any church tax. Other direct taxes include an inheritance and gift tax, a net worth tax, and real estate transfer tax.

The main indirect tax in Germany is a value-added tax (VAT) introduced in 1968 with a standard rate of 10%. By 2010, the standard rate had risen to 19%. A reduced rate of 7% applies to some basic foods, water supplies, medical care and dentistry, medical equipment for disabled persons, books, newspapers and periodicals, some shows, social housing, agricultural inputs, social services, and public transportation. Items exempt from the VAT include admissions to cultural events, building land, supplies for new buildings, TV licenses, telephones and faxes, basic medical and dental care, the use of sports facilities, and some waste disposal services. Exports are also zero-rated.

In January 2010, the government introduced an aviation tax that taxes all passenger flights departing from Germany. The tax amount depends on the distance to the final destination, with a minimum amount of €8 and a maximum amount of €45 per passenger.

37 CUSTOMS AND DUTIES

Germany is a member of the European Union and thus has a common import customs tariff and complies with trade agreements put in place by the EU. Germany is also a contracting party to the Harmonized System Convention. In regard to trade with non-EU countries, most raw materials enter duty-free, while most manufactured goods are subject to varying rates between 5% and 8%. Germany levies a 15% value-added tax on industrial goods.

38 FOREIGN INVESTMENT

All foreign investment must be reported to the German Federal Bank (Bundesbank), but there are no restrictions on the repatriation of capital or profits. Until the 1998 deregulation of Deutsche Telekom, telecommunications remained closed to foreign investment. There is no special treatment for foreign investors. Incentives for all investors included cash grants; tax incentives, such as capital reserve allowances and special depreciation allowances; investment grants; and credit programs, including low-interest loans. Foreign firms may also participate in government and/or subsidized research and development programs.

Although few formal barriers exist, high labor costs have discouraged foreign companies from setting up manufacturing plants in Germany. Nevertheless, the German government and industry enthusiastically encourage foreign investment in Germany. German law provides foreign investors national treatment.

There are eight free ports in Germany operated under EU Community law. Duty-free zones within the ports are open to both domestic and foreign entities.

Across the 10-year period 1991 to 2001, total foreign direct investment (FDI) totaled $393 billion, the third-highest total in the world. Half of this came in 2000, when FDI inflow reached over $195 billion. Annual FDI inflow had been $12 billion in 1997, rising to $24.5 billion in 1998, to $54.7 billion in 1999. With the bursting of the dot-com bubble in 2001, FDI inflow to Germany fell to about $21.1 billion in 2001 and was estimated at $36.2 billion in 2002. According to World Bank figures published in 2009, FDI in Germany was a net inflow of $39.2 billion, representing 1.18% of GDP.

39ECONOMIC DEVELOPMENT

Germany describes its economy as a "social market economy." Outside of transportation, communications, and certain utilities, the government has remained on the sidelines of entrepreneurship. Beginning in 1998, and in line with EU regulations, the German government began deregulating these fields, as well. It has, nevertheless, upheld its role as social arbiter and economic adviser. Overall economic priorities are set by the federal and Land governments pursuant to the 1967 Stability and Growth Act, which demands stability of prices, a high level of employment, steady growth, and equilibrium in foreign trade. In addition to the state, the independent German Federal Bank (Bundesbank), trade unions, and employers' associations bear responsibility for the nation's economic health. With the advent of the euro in 1999, much of the Federal Bank's authority in monetary matters was transferred to the European Central Bank (ECB). In the international arena, Germany has acted as a leader of European economic integration.

Government price and currency policies have been stable and effective. Less successful have been wage-price policies, which have been unable to control a continued upward movement. Inflationary pressures have increased and combined with a general leveling off in productivity and growth. Attempts to neutralize competition by agreements between competitors and mergers are controlled by the Law Against Restraints of Competition (Cartel Act), passed in 1957 and strengthened thereafter. The law is administered by the Federal Cartel Office, located in Bonn.

Unemployment remained at an average 9% in the early 2000s; it was twice as high in eastern Germany as in western Germany. In 2010, the unemployment rate stood at 10.8%. Although much effort has been expended to integrate the former East German economy with the West's (infrastructure has improved drastically and a market economy has been introduced), progress in fusing the two economies slowed in the late 1990s and early 2000s.

The aging population, combined with high unemployment, has pushed social security outlays to a level exceeding contributions from workers. Corporate restructuring and growing capital markets are setting the foundations allowing Germany to thrive globally and to lead the process of European economic integration, particularly if labor-market rigidities are addressed. However, in the short run, rising expenditures and lowered revenues have raised the budget deficit above the EU's 3% debt limit.

40SOCIAL DEVELOPMENT

The social security system of the FRG remained in place following unification with the German Democratic Republic. However, the GDR system continued to apply on an interim basis within the former GDR territory. The two systems were merged effectively 2 January 1992. The social insurance system provides for sickness and maternity, workers' compensation, disability, unemployment, and old age; the program is financed by compulsory employee and employer contributions. While old age pensions up until 2011 began at age 65 after five years of contribution, the government has raised this age to 67 starting in 2012. Workers' medical coverage is comprehensive, including dental care. Unemployment coverage includes all workers, trainees, apprentices, and at-home workers in varying degrees. The government funds a family allowance to parents with one or more children.

Equal pay for equal work is mandated by law, but women continue to earn less than men. Women continue to be underrepresented in managerial positions. Sexual harassment of women in the workplace is recognized and addressed. Although violence against women exists, the law and government provides protection. Victims of violence can receive police protection, legal help, shelter and counseling. Children's rights are strongly protected.

Freedom of religion is guaranteed by the Basic Law in Germany, although there have been reports of some discrimination against minority religions. Extremist right-wing groups continue to commit violent acts against immigrants and Jews, although the government is committed to preventing such acts. The Basic Law also provides for the freedom of association, assembly, and expression.

In June 2010, a German high court ruled that it is legal to passively assist the death of a terminally ill patient if the patient has given prior approval. The ruling applies principally to the removal of life support and feeding tubes from a patient who has fallen into a vegetative state but has previously given clear consent. In Germany, engaging in active forms of physician-assisted suicide remains a crime punishable by up to five years in prison.

41HEALTH

Health insurance in Germany is available to everyone. Benefits are broad and nationally uniform, with only minor variations among plans. They include free choice of doctors; unlimited physician visits; preventive checkups; total freedom from out-of-pocket payments for physician services; unlimited acute hospital care (with a nominal co-payment); prescription drug coverage (with a minimal co-payment); comprehensive dental benefits (with a 25–30% co-payment); vision and hearing exams, glasses, aids, prostheses, etc.; inpatient and psychiatric care (and outpatient psychiatric visits); monthly home care allowances; maternity benefits; disability payments; and rehabilitation and/or occupational therapy. The country spent 10.5% of its GDP on healthcare, amounting to $4,629 per person.

In 2010, there were 35 physicians, 108 nurses and midwives, and 82 hospital beds per 10,000 inhabitants, according to the CIA. In 2009, Germany immunized 93% of children up to one year old against diphtheria, pertussis, and tetanus and an estimated 96% of children were vaccinated against measles. The CIA calculated HIV/AIDS prevalence to be about 0.1%.

Average life expectancy was 80.07 years in 2011, according to the CIA. Infant mortality was 3.54 deaths per 1,000 live births in the same year, one of the lowest rates in the world. The total fertility rate in 2011 was estimated at 1.41 children born per woman. The maternal mortality rate was also low, 7 deaths per 100,000 live births in 2008.

⁴²HOUSING

More than half of the population lives in residential buildings of three or more dwelling units. Nearly 98% of all dwelling units are in such multi-unit residential buildings; of these, about 42.6% are owner occupied. About 69% of the dwelling units in residential buildings have central heating systems. Gas and oil are the most common energy sources. The average number of persons per household is 2.2.

⁴³EDUCATION

Overall, the CIA estimated that Germany had a literacy rate of 99%. In 2007, public expenditure on education represented 4.5% of GDP.

Most schools and kindergartens are the responsibility of the states, not of the federal government. Therefore, though the overall structure is basically the same, it is difficult for a pupil to transfer from one school to another. German teachers are civil servants. They are required to have teaching degrees and are paid according to a uniform salary scale. Attendance at all public schools and universities is free. In 2008, the World Bank estimated that 98% of age-eligible children in Germany were enrolled in primary school.

Children start school after their sixth birthdays and are required to attend on a full-time basis for nine or ten years, depending on the state of residence. After four years of primary or elementary school (*Grundschule*), students choose from three types of secondary school. The best pupils go to a gymnasium, which prepares them for the university matriculation examination, or *abitur*. A second option is the *realschule*, leading to technical job training and middle-management employment. The third type is the *hauptschule*, or general school.

However, a network of correspondence courses has developed, geared for those who wish to continue their studies while working. In Germany, vocational training is the rule. On-the-job training in an authorized company is combined with instruction in a vocational school. Vocational training is concluded by taking a theoretical and practical examination before a Board of the Chamber, and those who pass are given a certificate. This system of vocational training has clearly reduced youth unemployment, which is currently estimated at 11% for youth between the ages of 15–24.

Nearly all children between the ages of three and five were enrolled in some type of preschool program. Primary school enrollment in 2009 has been estimated at about 97% of age-eligible students. Nearly all students complete their primary education. The student-to-teacher ratio for primary school was at about 13:1 in 2009, according to the World Bank.

Higher education is represented by three types of institutions: universities (*universitäten*), colleges of art and music, and universities of applied sciences (*fachhochscchulen*). There are also several *fachschulen*, which offer continuing vocational training for adults.

⁴⁴LIBRARIES AND MUSEUMS

Germany had no national library until 1913, when the German Library (7.2 million volumes in 2002) in Leipzig brought together an extensive collection literature of the German language under one roof. The library also contains 3.9 million volumes of works written in exile by German authors during the Nazi era. In 1990, a further consolidation of German libraries was completed with the establishment of the German Library in Frankfurt, which had 18 million volumes in 2002. Other prominent libraries are the Bavarian State Library in Munich (7.6 million books) and the Prussian Cultural Property State Library (10 million books) in Berlin. The Herzog-August Library in Wolfenbüttel (848,000 volumes) has archives of 12,000 handwritten medieval books. One of the most important collections of German literature is at the Central Library of German Classics in Weimar. The Berlin Central and Regional Library, the public library network for the area, contains more than 3.1 million print and electronic sources. The German Library for the Blind in Leipzig was founded in 1894. It serves as a publishing house and production center for Braille texts and audio books, as well as a public lending library containing 40,000 book titles and 5,000 titles of sheet music in Braille.

Germany has more than 4,500 state, municipal, association, private, residential, castle, palace, and church and cathedral treasures museums, which annually attract more than 100 million visitors. Berlin has the Egyptian and Pergaman Museums, the Painting Gallery of Old Masters, and the National Gallery of Modern Art. The Jewish Museum opened in Berlin in 2001 offering exhibits on the history and culture of the Jewish people in the region. The Germanic National Museum in Nüremberg has the largest collection on the history of German art and culture from antiquity to the 20th century. The German Museum in Munich is one of the most well-known natural sciences and technology museums in Europe. The Pinakothek Moderne, opened in 2003, houses a huge modern art collection in Munich. In addition, there are hundreds of smaller museums, ethnological and archaeological institutions, scientific collections, and art galleries.

The Bach Archive in Leipzig contains a museum, research institute, and library dedicated to the life and work of the composer J.S. Bach, who once served as the city's music director. Beethoven Haus in Bonn and the Richard Wagner Museum Haus in Bayreuth honor two more famous German composers. Museums on the life and work of Goethe are located in Frankfurt (his birthplace) and Weimar. Lutherhaus in Wittenberg serves as a historical museum for both the life and work of Martin Luther and the Protestant Reformation that he ignited.

⁴⁵MEDIA

Since reunification, postal services have been under the jurisdiction of the Deutsche Bundespost Postdienst and telecommunications under Deutsche Bundespost Telekom. Intensive capital investments since reunification have rapidly modernized and integrated most of the obsolete telephone network of the GDR. Germany now has one of the most technologically advanced telecommunications systems in the world. In 2009, the CIA reported there were some 48.7 million main phone lines and 105 million mobile cellular phones in use.

There are 11 regional broadcasting corporations, including Zweites Deutsches Fernsehen, which operates Channel Two nationally. In 2004, 98% of the population owned at least one television set. As of 2009, there were 51 FM radio stations, 787 AM radio stations, and 4 shortwave radio stations. There were some 65.125 million Internet users in Germany, about 80% of the population, as well as 21.7 million Internet hosts in 2010.

There are about 305 national, regional, and local newspapers in Germany, as well as a large number of other periodicals. Of the newspapers sold on the street, the Bild has the largest circulation, at about 3.9 million in 2008. The Berliner Zeitung, founded in 1945 but completely redesigned in 1997, is a nationally prominent daily with a circulation in 2008 of about 207,800. Other influential daily national newspapers (with 2008 circulation rates unless noted) are the Frankfurter Allgemeine Zeitung (Frankfurt, 477,407), Die Welt (350,240), Frankfurter Rundschau (203,917), Suddeutsche Zeitung (Munich, 559,287), Der Tagesspiegel (184,830), and die tageszeitung, the name of which is intentionally not capitalized (80,262).

More than 20,000 periodicals are published in Germany. The best-known internationally is the news magazine *Der* Spiegel, which is modeled after the American Time magazine and distributes about 1 million copies. The German Press Agency, owned by German newspaper publishers and publishers' organizations, furnishes domestic and international news. There are hundreds of small press agencies and services.

The Basic Law provides for free press rights, and the government mostly supports these rights in practice, though propaganda of Nazi and certain other proscribed groups is illegal, as are statements endorsing Nazism.

46 ORGANIZATIONS

The Federation of German Industries, the Confederation of German Employers' Associations, the Federation of German Wholesale and Foreign Traders, and the Association of German Chambers of Commerce represent business in the FRG. There are about 14 regional associations of chambers of business and industry located in the largest cities; many maintain branch offices in smaller cities. The chambers are organized into provincial associations and are headed by the Permanent Conference of German Industry and Trade. The cooperative movement is well-developed. Consumer cooperatives are represented in the International Cooperative Alliance by the Central Association of German Cooperatives, founded in 1949; it also represents credit cooperatives. The central association of agricultural cooperatives, the German Raiffeisen Society, is located in Wiesbaden. The Association of German Peasants is the largest society of farmers. There is also a Central Association of German Artisan Industries. The private Association of Consumers operates more than 150 local advisory centers. Professional societies and associations are numerous and represent a wide variety of occupations and fields of study.

Civil action groups (Bürgerinitiativen) have proliferated in recent years. August 13 Working Committee serves in part as a human rights awareness organization. Deutscher Frauenring serves as an umbrella organization for national women's groups. The Red Cross is active. There are national chapters of Habitat for Humanity, CARE, and Caritas.

The German Academy of Arts in Berlin and the Academy of Fine Arts in Dresden are well-known arts organizations. There is a network of seven academies of science in Germany. The UNESCO Institute for Education has an office in Hamburg. A few cultural and learned associations particular to Germany include the International Gottfried Wilhelm Leibniz Society, the Alexander von Humboldt Foundation, and the International Hegel Gesellschaft Society. There are numerous organizations dedicated to research and education in scientific fields, particularly those relating to medicine. The German Academic Exchange Service is a vital organization dedicated to supporting international research and study as well as international exchange in higher education institutions.

There are about 80 youth associations, most of which belong to the Federal Youth Ring. The scouting movement is highly active, and political parties sponsor groups associated in the Ring of Political Youth. In total, there are about 90 national youth organizations and youth associations. Many of them are part of the umbrella organization known as the German Federal Youth Association.

There are thousands of groups and associations sponsoring various arts and cultural activities and special organizations for various hobbies and sports. The German Sports Confederation serves as an umbrella organization for more than 88,000 sports clubs nationwide. There are also many patriotic and religious organizations in the country.

47 TOURISM, TRAVEL, AND RECREATION

Germany is famous for its beautiful scenery, particularly the Alps in the south and the river valleys of the Rhine, Main, and Danube; the landscape is dotted with castles and medieval villages. Theater, opera, and orchestral music abound in the major cities. The area that was formerly the German Democratic Republic offers a number of Baltic beach resorts and scenic Rügen Island. Residents of the United States and Canada need only a valid passport to enter Germany for a period of no more than three months; citizens of other countries need a visa. All border formalities for residents of other European Community countries were abandoned with the lifting of trade barriers in 1993.

Facilities for camping, cycling, skiing, and mountaineering are abundant. Football (soccer) is the favorite sport; Germany hosted and won the World Cup competition in 1974, and hosted it again in 2006. Tennis has become more popular since Boris Becker won the Wimbledon Championship in 1985, and German Steffi Graf was inducted into the International Tennis Hall of Fame in 2004. The Olympic Games were held in Berlin in 1936, during the Hitler years, and in Munich in 1972.

The *Tourism Factbook*, published by the UN World Tourism Organization, reported 24.2 million incoming tourists to Germany in 2009 who spent a total of $47.5 billion. Of those incoming tourists, there were 18.8 million from Europe. The 1.81 million hotel beds available in Germany had an occupancy rate of 36%. The estimated daily cost to visit Berlin, the capital, was $454. The cost of visiting other cities averaged $364.

48 FAMOUS PERSONS

The roster of famous Germans is long in most fields of endeavor. The name of Johann Gutenberg (1398?–1468), who is generally regarded in the Western world as the inventor of movable precision-cast metal type, and therefore as the father of modern book printing, might well head the list of notable Germans. Martin Luther (1483–1546), founder of the Reformation, still exerts profound influence on German religion, society, music, and language.

The earliest major names in German literature were the poets Wolfram von Eschenbach (1170?-1220?), Gottfried von Strassburg (d. 1210?), and Sebastian Brant (1457-1521). Hans Sachs (1494–1576) wrote thousands of plays, poems, stories, and songs. Hans Jakob Christoffel von Grimmelshausen (1621–76) created a famous picaresque novel, *Simplicissimus.* The flowering of German literature began with such renowned 18th-century poets and dramatists as Friedrich Gottlieb Klopstock (1724–1803), Gotthold Ephraim Lessing (1729–81), Christoph Martin Wieland (1733–1813), and Johann Gottfried von Herder (1744–1803), and culminated with the greatest German poet, Johann Wolfgang von Goethe (1749–1832), and the greatest German dramatist, Johann Christoph Friedrich von Schiller (1759–1805). Leaders of the Romantic movement included Jean Paul (Jean Paul Friedrich Richter, 1763–1825), August Wilhelm von Schlegel (1767–1845), Novalis (Friedrich von Hardenberg, 1772–1801), Ludwig Tieck (1773–1853), E. T. A. (Ernst Theodor Wilhelm—the A stood for Amadeus, the middle name of Mozart) Hoffmann (1776–1822), and Heinrich Wilhelm von Kleist (1777–1811). The brothers Jakob Grimm (1785–1863) and Wilhelm Grimm (1786–1859) are world-famous for their collections of folk tales and myths. Heinrich Heine (1797–1856), many of whose poems have become folksongs, is generally regarded as the greatest German poet after Goethe. Other significant poets are Friedrich Hölderlin (1770–1843), Friedrich Rückert (1788–1866), Eduard Mörike (1804–75), Stefan Georg (1868–1933), and Rainer Maria Rilke (1875–1926). Playwrights of distinction include Friedrich Hebbel (1813–63), Georg Büchner (1813–37), Georg Kaiser (1878–1945), Ernst Toller (1893–1939), and Bertolt Brecht (1898–1957). Two leading novelists of the 19th century were Gustav Freytag (1816–95) and Theodor Storm (1817–88). Germany's 20th-century novelists include Ernst Wiechert (1887–1950), Anna Seghers (Netty Reiling, 1900–1983), and Nobel Prize winners Gerhart Johann Robert Hauptmann (1862–1946), Thomas Mann (1875–1955), Nelly Sachs (1891–1970), Heinrich Böll (1917–86), Günter Grass (b. 1927), and Herta Mueller (b. Romania, 1953). Other major writers of the 20th and 21st centuries include German-born Erich Maria Remarque (1898–1970), Christa Wolf (b. 1929), and Peter Handke (b. 1942).

Leading filmmakers include G. W. (Georg Wilhelm) Pabst (b. Czechoslovakia, 1885–1967), F. W. (Friedrich Wilhelm Plumpe) Murnau (1888–1931), Fritz Lang (b. Austria, 1890–1976), German-born Ernst Lubitsch (1892–1947), Max Ophüls (Oppenheimer, 1902–57), Leni (Helene Bertha Amalie) Riefenstahl (1902–2003), Volker Schlöndorff (b. 1939), Werner Herzog (b. 1942), Rainer Werner Fassbinder (1946–82), Wim Wenders (b. 1945), and Doris Dörrie (b. 1955). Outstanding performers include Emil Jannings (Theodor Friedrich Emil Janenz, b. Switzerland, 1886–1950), Marlene Dietrich (1901–1992), and Klaus Kinski (Claus Günther Nakszynski, 1926–91) and Armin Mueller-Stahl (b. 1930).

The two giants of German church music were Heinrich Schütz (1585–1672) and, preeminently, Johann Sebastian Bach (1685–

1750). Significant composers of the 18th century were German-born Georg Friedrich Handel (1685–1759), Carl Philipp Emanuel Bach (1714–88), and Christoph Willibald von Gluck (1714–87). The classical period and music in general were dominated by the titanic figure of Ludwig von Beethoven (1770–1827). Romanticism in music was ushered in by Carl Maria von Weber (1786–1826), among others. Outstanding composers of the 19th century were Felix Mendelssohn-Bartholdy (1809–47), Robert Schumann (1810–56), Richard Wagner (1813–83), and Johannes Brahms (1833–97). Major figures of the 20th and 21st centuries are Richard Strauss (1864–1949), Paul Hindemith (1895–1963), Carl Orff (1895–1982), German-born Kurt Weill (1900–50), Hans Werner Henze (b. 1926), and Karlheinz Stockhausen (b. 1928). Important symphonic conductors included Otto Klemperer (1885–1973), Wilhelm Furtwängler (1886–1954), Karl Böhm (1894–1981), and Eugen Jochum (1902–87). Among Germany's outstanding musical performers are singers Elisabeth Schwarzkopf (b. 1915) and Dietrich Fischer-Dieskau (b. 1925), and pianists Walter Gieseking (1895–1956) and Wilhelm Kempff (1895–91).

Veit Stoss (1440?-1533) was one of the greatest German sculptors and woodcarvers of the 15th century; another was Tilman Riemenschneider (1460?-1531). Outstanding painters, engravers, and makers of woodcuts were Martin Schongauer (1445?-91), Matthias Grünewald (1460?-1528?), Hans Holbein the Elder (1465?-1524), Lucas Cranach (1472-1553), Hans Holbein the Younger (1497?-1543), and, above all, Albrecht Dürer (1471-1528). More recent artists of renown are the painters Emil Nolde (1867–1956), Franz Marc (1880–1916), Max Beckmann (1884–1950), the US-born Lyonel Feininger (1871–1956), Otto Dix (1891–1969), Max Ernst (1891–1976), and Horst Antes (b. 1936); the painter and cartoonist George Grosz (1893–1959); the sculptors Ernst Barlach (1870–1938) and Wilhelm Lehmbruck (1881–1919); the painter-etcher-sculptor Käthe Kollwitz (1867–1945); the Dadaist Hannah Höch (1889–1978); the painter-sculptor-installation artist Joseph Beuys (1921–1986); the painter and sculptor Anselm Kiefer (b. 1945); and the architects Walter Gropius (1883–1969), leader of the Bauhaus School of Design, Ludwig Mies van der Rohe (1886–1969), Erich Mendelsohn (1887–1953), Gottfried Böhm (b. 1920), and Helmut Jahn (b. 1940).

Scholars and Leaders

German influence on Western thought can be traced back at least as far as the 13th century, to the great scholastic philosopher, naturalist, and theologian Albertus Magnus (Albert von Bollstädt, d. 1280) and the mystic philosopher Meister Eckhart (1260?-1327?). Philipp Melanchthon (Schwartzerd, 1497–1560) was a scholar and religious reformer. Gottfried Wilhelm von Leibniz (1646–1716) was an outstanding philosopher, theologian, mathematician, and natural scientist. The next two centuries were dominated by the ideas of Immanuel Kant (1724–1804), Moses Mendelssohn (1729–86), Johann Gottlieb Fichte (1762–1814), Friedrich Ernst Daniel Schleiermacher (1768–1834), Georg Wilhelm Friedrich Hegel (1770–1831), Friedrich Wilhelm Joseph von Schelling (1775–1854), Arthur Schopenhauer (1788–1860), Ludwig Andreas Feuerbach (1804–72), Karl Marx (1818–83), Friedrich Engels (1820–95), and Friedrich Wilhelm Nietzsche (1844–1900). In the 20th century, Edmund Husserl (1859–1938), Oswald Spengler (1880–1936), Karl Jaspers (1883–1969), Martin Heidegger

(1889–1976), and Hans-Georg Gadamer (1900–2002) are highly regarded. Figures of the Frankfurt School of social and political philosophy include Theodor Adorno (1903–1969), Max Horkheimer (1895–1973), Walter Benjamin (1892–1940), Herbert Marcuse (1898–1979), and Jürgen Habermas (b. 1929). Political theorist Hannah Arendt (1906–1975) is also highly regarded, as is Carl Schmitt (1888–1985). One of the founders of modern Biblical scholarship was Julius Wellhausen (1844–1918). Franz Rosenzweig (1886–1929) was one of the most influential modern Jewish religious thinkers, as was Gershom Scholem (1897–1982).

Among the most famous German scientists are Johann Rudolf Glauber (1694–1768), Justus von Liebig (1803–73), Robert Wilhelm Bunsen (1811–99), and Nobel Prize winners Hermann Emil Fischer (1852–1919), Adolf von Baeyer (1835–1917), Eduard Buchner (1860–1917), Wilhelm Ostwald (1853–1932), Otto Wallach (1847–1931), Richard Martin Willstätter (1872–1942), Fritz Haber (1868–1934), Walther Nernst (b. Poland, 1864–1941), Heinrich Otto Wieland (1877–1957), Adolf Otto Reinhold Windaus (1876–1959), Carl Bosch (1874–1940), Friedrich Bergius (1884–1949), Otto Hahn (1879–1968), Hans Fischer (1881–1945), Friedrich Bergius (1884–1949), Georg Wittig (1897–1987), Adolf Butenandt (1903–1995), Otto Diels (1876–1954), Kurt Alder (1902–58), Hermann Staudinger (1881–1965), Karl Ziegler (1898–1973), Manfred Eigen (b. 1927), Ernst Otto Fischer (b. 1918), Johann Deisenhofer (b. 1943), Robert Huber (b. 1937), and Hartmut Michel (b. 1948) in chemistry; Karl Friedrich Gauss (1777–1855), Georg Simon Ohm (1787–1854), Hermann Ludwig Ferdinand von Helmholtz (1821–94), Heinrich Rudolf Hertz (1857–1894), and Nobel Prize winners Wilhelm Konrad Röntgen (1845–1923), Max Karl Ernst Ludwig Planck (1858–1947), Albert Einstein (1879–1955), Gustav Ludwig Hertz (1887–1975), Werner Heisenberg (1901–76), Walter Bothe (1891–1957), Carl-Friedrich von Weizsäcker (b. 1912), Rudolf Mössbauer (b. 1929), Hans Bethe (1906–2005), Klaus von Klitzing (b. 1943), Ernst Ruska (1906–1988), Gerd Binnig (b. 1947), Johannes Georg Bednorz (b. 1950), Hans Georg Dehmelt (b. Germany 1922), Wolfgang Paul (1913–1993), Wolfgang Ketterle (b. 1957), and Theodor Wolfgang Hänsch (b. 1941) in physics; Rudolf Virchow (1821–1902), August von Wassermann (1866–1925), and Nobel Prize winners Robert Koch (1843–1910), Paul Ehrlich (1854–1915), Emil von Behring (1854–1917), Otto H. Warburg (1883–1970), Konrad Lorenz (Austria, 1903–89), Konrad Emil Bloch (1912–2000), Feodor Felix Konrad Lynen (1911–1979), Max Delbrück (b. Germany 1906–1981), Sir Bernard Katz (b. Germany 1911–2003), Georges Jean Franz Köhler (1946–1995), Erwin Neher (b. 1944), Bert Sakmann (b. 1942), Christiane Nüsslein-Volhard (b. 1942), and Günter Blobel (b. 1936), in physiology or medicine; earth scientists Alexander von Humboldt (1769–1859) and Karl Ernst Richter (1795–1863); and mathematician Georg Friedrich Bernhard Riemann (1826–66). Notable among German inventors and engineers are Gabriel Daniel Fahrenheit (1686–1736), developer of the thermometer; Gottlieb Daimler (1834–1900), Rudolf Diesel (b. Paris, 1858–1913), and Felix Wankel (1902–88), developers of the internal combustion engine; airship builder Count Ferdinand von Zeppelin (1838–1917); and rocketry pioneer Wernher von Braun (1912–77). Leading social scientists, in addition to Marx and Engels, were the historians Leopold von Ranke (1795–1886) and Theodor Mommsen (1817–1903), Nobel Prize winner in lit-

erature; the political economist Georg Friedrich List (1789–1846); the sociologists Georg Simmel (1858–1918) and Max Weber (1864–1920); and the German-born anthropologist Franz Boas (1858–1942). Johann Joachim Winckelmann (1717–68) founded the scientific study of classical art and archaeology. Heinrich Schliemann (1822–90) uncovered the remains of ancient Troy, Mycenae, and Tiryns; Wilhelm Dörpfeld (1853–1940) continued his work.

Outstanding figures in German political history are the Holy Roman emperors Otto I (the Great, 912–973), Frederick I (Barbarossa, 1123–90), Frederick II (1194–1250), and Spanish-born Charles V (1500–58); Frederick William (1620–88), the "great elector" of Brandenburg; his great-grandson Frederick II (the Great, 1712–86), regarded as the most brilliant soldier and statesman of his age; Otto Eduard Leopold von Bismarck (1815–98), the Prussian statesman who made German unity possible; Austrian-born Adolf Hitler (1889–1945), founder of Nazism and dictator of Germany (1933–45); and Konrad Adenauer (1876–1967), FRG chancellor (1948–63). Walter Ernst Karl Ulbricht (1893–1973), chairman of the Council of State (1960–73), and leader of the SED from 1950 to 1971, was the dominant political figure in the GDR until his death in 1973. Erich Honecker (1912–94) became first secretary of the SED in 1971 and was chairman of the Council of State and SED general secretary from 1976 until the FRG and GDR merged in 1990. Willi Stoph (1914–1999), a member of the Politburo since 1953, served as chairman of the Council of Ministers in 1964–73 and again from 1976 on. Willy Brandt (1913–1992), FRG chancellor (1969–74) won the Nobel Peace Prize for his policy of Ostpolitik. Other Nobel Peace Prize winners were Ludwig Quidde (1858–1941), Gustav Stresemann (1878–1929), Carl von Ossietzky (1889–1938), and Albert Schweitzer (1875–1965).

Baron Friedrich Wilhelm Ludolf Gerhard Augustin von Steuben (1730–94) was a general in the American Revolution. Karl von Clausewitz (1780–1831) is one of the great names connected with the science of war. Important military leaders were Hellmuth von Moltke (1800–1891); Gen. Paul von Hindenburg (1847–1934), who also served as president of the German Reich (1925–34); and Gen. Erwin Rommel (1891–1944).

Pope Benedict XVI (b. Joseph Alois Ratzinger, 1927) became the 265th pope in 2005. He is the ninth German pope, the last being the Dutch-German Adrian VI (1522–1523).

⁴⁹DEPENDENCIES

Germany has no territories or colonies.

⁵⁰BIBLIOGRAPHY

Annesley, Claire, ed. *A Political and Economic Dictionary of Western Europe*. Philadelphia: Routledge/Taylor and Francis, 2005.

Bernstein, Eckhard. *Culture and Customs of Germany*. Westport, CT: Greenwood Press, 2004.

Briel, Holger, ed. *German Culture and Society: The Essential Glossary*. London: Arnold, 2002.

Bullock, Alan Louis Charles. *Hitler and Stalin: Parallel Lives*. London: Harper-Collins, 1991.

Eckhart, Karl, et al., eds. *Social, Economic and Cultural Aspects in the Dynamic Changing Process of Old Industrial Regions: Ruhr*

District (Germany), Upper Silesia (Poland), Ostrava Region (Czech Republic). Piscataway, NJ: Transaction Publishers, 2003.

Germany Investment and Business Guide: Strategic and Practical Information. Washington, DC: International Business Publications USA, 2012.

International Smoking Statistics: A Collection of Historical Data from 30 Economically Developed Countries. New York: Oxford University Press, 2002.

Mercatante, Steven D. *Why Germany Nearly Won: A New History of the Second World War in Europe.* Santa Barbara, CA: Praeger, 2012.

Mitcham, Samuel W. *Retreat to the Reich: The German Defeat in France, 1944.* Westport, CT: Praeger, 2000.

Opello, Walter C. *European Politics.* Boulder, CO: Lynne Rienner Publishers, 2009.

Shirer, William L. *The Rise and Fall of the Third Reich.* New York: Simon and Schuster, 1960.

Summers, Randal W., and Allan M. Hoffman, ed. *Domestic Violence: A Global View.* Westport, Conn.: Greenwood Press, 2002.

Tipton, Frank B. *A History of Modern Germany Since 1815.* Berkeley: University of California Press, 2003.

Verhey, Jeffrey. *The Spirit of 1914: Militarism, Myth and Mobilization in Germany.* New York: Cambridge University Press, 2000.

Vogt, Henri. *Between Utopia and Disillusionment: A Narrative of the Political Transformation in Eastern Europe.* New York: Berghahn Books, 2004.

Wessels, Wolfgang, Andreas Maurer, and Jürgan Mittag, eds. *Fifteen into One?: the European Union and Its Member States.* New York: Palgrave, 2003.

GREECE

Hellenic Republic
Elliniki Dhimokratia

CAPITAL: Athens (Athínai)

FLAG: The national flag consists of nine equal horizontal stripes of royal blue alternating with white and a white cross on a royal-blue square canton.

ANTHEM: *Ýmnos is tin Eleftherían (Hymn to Liberty).*

MONETARY UNIT: The euro replaced the drachma as official currency in 2002. The euro is divided into 100 cents. There are coins in denominations of 1, 2, 5, 10, 20, and 50 cents and 1 euro and 2 euros. There are notes of 5, 10, 20, 50, 100, 200, and 500 euros. €1 = $1.371 (or $1 = €0.72939) as of September 2011.

WEIGHTS AND MEASURES: The metric system is the legal standard.

HOLIDAYS: New Year's Day, 1 January; Epiphany, 6 January; Independence Day, 25 March; Easter, March-April, based on Orthodox calendar; Labor Day, 1 May; Assumption, 15 August; National Day (anniversary of successful resistance to Italian attack in 1940), 28 October; Christmas, 25 December; Boxing Day, 26 December. Movable religious holidays include Shrove Monday, Good Friday, and Easter Monday.

TIME: 2 p.m. = noon GMT.

¹LOCATION, SIZE, AND EXTENT

Greece is the southernmost country in the Balkan Peninsula, with a total area of 131,947 sq km (50,945 sq mi); about a fifth of the area is composed of more than 1,400 islands in the Ionian and Aegean seas. Comparatively, Greece is slightly smaller than Alabama. Continental Greece has a length of 940 km (584 mi) N–S and a width of 772 km (480 mi) E–W. It is bounded on the N by Macedonia and Bulgaria, on the Ne by Turkey, on the E by the Aegean Sea, on the S by the Mediterranean Sea, on the SW and W by the Ionian Sea, and on the Nw by Albania, with a total land boundary length of 1,228 km (763 mi) and a coastline of 13,676 km (8,498 mi). The capital city of Greece, Athens, is located along the country's southern coast.

²TOPOGRAPHY

About four-fifths of Greece is mountainous, including most of the islands. The most important range is the Pindus, which runs down the center of the peninsula from north to south at about 2,650 m (8,700 ft) in average elevation. Mt. Olympus (Ólimbos; 2,917 m/9,570 ft) is the highest peak and was the legendary home of the ancient gods.

Greece has four recognizable geographic regions. The Pindus range divides northern Greece into damp, mountainous, and isolated Epirus (Ipiros) in the west and the sunny, dry plains and lesser mountain ranges of the east. This eastern region comprises the plains of Thessaly (Thessalía) and the "new provinces" of Macedonia (Makedonia) and Thrace (Thraki)—"new" because they became part of Greece after the Balkan wars in 1912–13. Central Greece is the southeastern finger of the mainland that cradled the city-states of ancient Greece and comprises such classical provinces as Attica (Atikí), Boeotia (Voiotia), Doris, Phocis,

and Locris. Southern Greece consists of the mountainous, four-fingered Peloponnesus (Pelopónnisos), separated from the mainland by the Gulf of Corinth (Korinthiakós Kólpos). Islands of the Aegean comprise the numerous Cyclades (Kikládes); the Dodecanese (Dhodhekánisos), including Rhodes (Ródhos); and the two large islands of Crete (Kríti) and Euboea (Évvoia).

Greek rivers are not navigable. Many dry up in the summer and become rushing mountain torrents in the spring. The longest river is the Maritsa, which runs along the northeast border a distance of 480 km (300 mi).

Greece is located above the convergence of the Eurasian and the African Tectonic Plates, a situation that causes frequent earthquakes and tremors. While many quakes are low-magnitude tremors with minimal damage and injury, stronger quakes are not entirely uncommon. More than 140 people died in 1999 in a 5.9 magnitude quake near Athens. On 14 August 2003, a 6.3 magnitude earthquake occurred in western Greece, causing injuries to about 50 people and damaging roads and buildings. In June 2008, two people died, at least 200 were injured, and hundreds of buildings were damaged when a 6.5 magnitude quake struck in the city of Patras, about 120 miles west of Athens.

³CLIMATE

The climate in southern Greece and on the islands is Mediterranean, with hot, dry summers and cool, wet winters. Winters are severe in the northern mountain regions. The summer heat is moderated by mountain and sea breezes. Precipitation is heaviest in the north and in the mountains. Average annual rainfall varies from 50 to 121 cm (20 to 48 in) in the north and from 38 to 81 cm (15 to 32 in) in the south. The mean temperature of Athens is 17°C

(63°F), ranging from a low of 2°C (36° F) in the winter to a high of 37°C (99°F) in the summer.

⁴FLORA AND FAUNA

The World Resources Institute estimates that there are 4,992 plant species in Greece. In addition, Greece is home to 118 species of mammals, 412 species of birds, 63 species of reptiles, and 21 species of amphibians. The calculation reflects the total number of distinct species residing in the country, not the number of endemic species.

About 742 species of flora are endemic to the country. Many pharmaceutical plants and other rare plants and flowers considered botanical treasures flourish in Greece. Vegetation varies according to altitude. From sea level to 460 m (1,500 ft), oranges, olives, dates, almonds, pomegranates, figs, grapes, tobacco, cotton, and rice abound. From 460 to 1,070 m (1,500 to 3,500 ft) are forests of oak, chestnut, and pine. Above 1,070 m (3,500 ft), beech and fir are most common.

Fauna are not plentiful, but bear, wildcat, jackal, fox, and chamois still exist in many sparsely populated areas. The wild goat (agrimi), which has disappeared from the rest of Europe, still lives in parts of Greece and on the island of Crete. There are more than 250 species of marine life. Natural sponges are a main export item.

⁵ENVIRONMENT

The World Resources Institute reported that Greece had designated 403,300 hectares (996,576 acres) of land for protection as of 2006. There are 10 national parks in Greece—a total area of 68.372 hectares or 0.5% of the total land area. Water resources totaled 72 cu km (17.27 cu mi) while water usage was 8.7 cu km (2.09 cu mi) per year. Domestic water usage accounted for 16% of total usage, industrial for 3%, and agricultural for 81%. Per capita water usage totaled 782 cu m (27,616 cu ft) per year. The UN reported in 2008 that carbon dioxide emissions in Greece totaled 98,038 kilotons.

Among Greece's principal environmental problems are industrial smog and automobile exhaust fumes in metropolitan Athens. Over half of all industry is located in the greater Athens area. From June to August 1982, the air pollution became so oppressive that the government closed down 87 industries, ordered 19 others to cut production, and banned traffic from the city center. In July 1984, the smog again reached a danger point, and 73 factories were ordered to cut production, and cars were banned from the city. In January 1988, the number of taxis in the center of Athens was halved, and private cars were banned from the city's three main thoroughfares. The smog regularly sends hundreds of Greeks to the hospital with respiratory and heart complaints. In 1992, Greece ranked 37th among the top 50 pollutors, with emissions totaling 73.8 million metric tons, a per capita level of 7.25. In 1996, the total rose to 80.6 million metric tons.

A series of anti-pollution measures in the 1990s, as well as substantial improvements to the city's infrastructure undertaken in preparation for the 2004 Olympic games, have improved urban air quality significantly.

Water pollution is a significant problem due to industrial pollutants, agricultural chemicals such as fertilizers and pesticides, and sewage. The Gulf of Saronikos is one of the most polluted areas because 50% of Greece's industrial facilities are located there.

Greece has been referred numerous times to the European Court of Justice for failing to respect the EU directives or to put in place adequate measures to protect the water environment. In May 2010, the European Commission pursued legal proceedings against Greece for failing to put in place adequate measures to protect one of Europe's most important wetlands. The case relates to the pollution and degradation of Lake Koronia in the region of Thessaloniki.

Greece's pollution problems are the result of almost complete disregard for environmental protection measures during the rapid industrial growth of the 1970s, compounded by unbalanced development and rapid, unregulated urban growth. Government policies have emphasized rational use of natural resources, balanced regional development, protection of the environment, and increased public participation in environmental matters. Four environmental and planning services were consolidated under the Ministry for Physical Planning, Housing, and the Environment.

As part of the Natura 2000 ecological network, created by the 1992 Habitat Directive and 1979 Birds Directive, Greece proposed 151 Special Protection Areas (SPAs) and 239 Sites of Community Importance (SCIs). Greece undertook a very difficult task: to protect and ensure that no significant deterioration or disturbance will occur in these sites. Natura 2000 in Greece is very ambitious, covering 21% of the land surface and 5.5% of territorial waters.

Meteora and Mount Athos are UNESCO World Heritage Sites. There are 10 Ramsar Wetland Sites in the country. According to a 2011 report issued by the International Union for Conservation of Nature and Natural Resources (IUCN), threatened species included 10 species of mammals, 10 species of birds, 8 species of reptiles, 5 species of amphibians, 75 species of fish, 63 species of mollusks, 27 species of other invertebrates, and 55 species of plants. Endangered species include the Mediterranean monk seal, the hawksbill turtle, Atlantic sturgeon, and the large copper butterfly.

⁶POPULATION

The US Central Intelligence Agency (CIA) estimates the population of Greece in 2011 to be approximately 10,760,136, which placed it at number 76 in population among the 196 nations of the world. In 2011, approximately 19.6% of the population was over 65 years of age, with another 14.2% under 15 years of age. The median age in Greece was 42.5 years. There were 0.96 males for every female in the country. The population's annual rate of change was 0.06% in 2012. The projected population for the year 2025 was 11,700,000. Population density in Greece was calculated at 82 people per sq km (212 people per sq mi).

The UN estimated that 61% of the population lived in urban areas, and that urban populations had an annual rate of change of 0.6%. The largest urban areas, along with their respective populations, included Athens, 3.3 million; and Thessaloniki, 834,000.

⁷MIGRATION

Estimates of Greece's net migration rate, carried out by the CIA in 2011, amounted to 2.32 migrants per 1,000 citizens. The total number of emigrants living abroad was 1.21 million, and the total number of immigrants living in Greece was 1.13 million. Under League of Nations supervision in 1923, more than one million Greek residents of Asia Minor were repatriated, and some 800,000 Turks left Greece. During the German occupation (1941–44) and the civil war (1944–49), there was a general movement of people from the islands, the Peloponnesus, and the northern border regions into the urban areas, especially the Athens metropolitan area, including Piraiévs. Between 1955 and 1971, about 1,500,000 peasants left their farms—about 600,000 going to the cities, the rest emigrating abroad. According to the 1981 census, 813,490 Greeks had migrated since 1975 to urban areas, and 165,770 had moved to rural areas. The growth rate of the Athens, Thessaloniki, Pátrai, Iráklion, and Vólos metropolitan areas during 1971–81 far exceeded the population growth rate for the nation as a whole.

Many Greeks leave the country for economic reasons. In the years after World War II (1939–45), the number of annual emigrants has varied from a high of 117,167 (in 1965) to a low of 20,330 (in 1975). The net outflow of Greek workers during the 1960s was 450,000; during the 1970s, however, there was a net inflow of 300,000. This mainly reflected declining need for foreign labor in western Europe.

In 1974, when the Greek military government collapsed, about 60,000 political refugees were living overseas; by the beginning of 1983, about half had been repatriated, the remainder being, for the most part, Communists who had fled to Soviet-bloc countries after the civil war of 1944–49. After the fall of Communism in 1989, slightly more than half of the migrants to Greece were Albanians, followed by other influxes from nearby countries.

In August 2005, Greece passed a new immigration law allowing for foreigners legally living in the country in 2004 to become permanent residents in 2006. However, the ethnic Greek Albanians and about 500,000 unauthorized foreigners were excluded from this policy change.

8 ETHNIC GROUPS

About 93% of the population is Greek. Minority groups include Turks, Macedonian Slavs, Albanians, Armenians, Bulgarians, Jews, and Vlachs. Though a number of citizens identify themselves as Pomaks, Romas, Macedonians, Slavomacedonians, and Arvanites, the government does not officially acknowledge these groups as minorities. Though some citizens describe themselves as Turks or Turkish, use of the term is prohibited in titles of organizations or associations. The Greeks also object to use of the term Macedonian by the Slavic-speaking inhabitants of that region. The nation's Roma population faces widespread social discrimination and marginalization by the government, with limited access to adequate permanent housing, employment, education, medical care, and social services. This is due, in part, to the nomadic lifestyle of most Roma, coupled with a law that requires a permit for all temporary settlements of "wandering nomads." The Roma are often forced to live in more remote rural areas or far on the outskirts of major towns or cities, and those without legal permits are subject to evictions. Those who identify themselves as ethnic Macedonian or Turkish (but not of these nationalities) have reported some incidences of discrimination and harassment, due in part to the fact that the government opposes the use of these terms by ethnic minorities on political grounds (having long-standing conflicts with Macedonia and Turkey). Some immigrants have faced discrimination and harassment within the nation, as well.

9 LANGUAGES

Modern Greek, the official language, is the first language of about 99% of the population. English, learned mostly outside the school system, and French are widely spoken. Turkish and other minority languages, such as Albanian, Pomakic, Kutzovalachian, and Armenian, also are spoken. The vernacular and the language of popular literature are called dimotiki (demotic). The official language dialect—katharevousa—generally used by the state, the press, and universities, employs classical terms and forms. In 1976, the government began to upgrade the status of dimotiki in education and government. The liturgical language is akin to classical Greek.

10 RELIGIONS

Though the government does not keep official statistics on membership in religious groups, unofficial estimates indicate that about 95% of the population are nominally Greek Orthodox, which is the state religion. About 30% of these members are regular participants in religious services. Official estimates place the number of resident Muslims between 110,000 people and 120,000, with most living in Thrace and consisting of the those who are ethnic Turkish, Pomak, or Roma. About 200,000 immigrants are also Muslim. There are also congregations of Jehovah's Witnesses, Roman Catholics, Protestants, Jews, the Church of Jesus Christ of Latter-Day Saints (Mormons), the Church of Scientology, and the Anglican church. There are small communities of Baha'is, Hare Krishnas, and followers of ancient polytheistic Hellenic religions. Freedom of religion is guaranteed by the constitution, and this right is generally respected in practice. However, under the constitution the Eastern Orthodox Church of Christ (Greek Orthodox) is the "prevailing" religion of Greece; the church is self-governing under the ecumenical patriarch resident in Istanbul, Turkey, and is protected by the government, which pays the salaries of the Orthodox clergy. The Orthodox Church is also allowed a significant influence in economic and political policies. The constitution prohibits proselytizing. The Orthodox Church, Judaism, and Islam are considered to be "legal persons of public law."

11 TRANSPORTATION

The CIA reports that Greece has a total of 117,533 km (73,032 mi) of roads, of which 107,895 km (67,043 mi) are paved. Railroads extend for 1,552 km (964 mi). There are 81 airports, which transported 8.8 million passengers in 2009 according to the World Bank. Greece has approximately 6 km (3.7 mi) of navigable waterways.

Greek transportation was completely reconstructed and greatly expanded after World War II. Toll highways connect Athens with Lamía and Pátrai.

The Hellenic State Railways, a government organ, operates the railroads, which consist of standard, narrow, and dual-gauge lines. Standard-gauge lines make up the bulk of the nation's railway system. The agency also operates a network of subsidiary bus lines connecting major cities. The privately owned Hellenic Electric Railways operates a high-speed shuttle service between Piraiévs and Athens.

Principal ports are Elevsís, Thessaloniki, Vólos, Piraiévs, Iráklion, and Thíra. In 2008, the Greek merchant fleet had 869 ships (down from 2,893 in 1982) of 1,000 GRT or over. In addition, Greek shipowners had many other ships sailing under Cypriot, Lebanese, Liberian, Panamanian, or other foreign registries. The Greek fleet was hard hit by the international shipping slump of the 1980s. The Corinth Canal, which crosses the isthmus of Corinth, stretches six km (3.7 mi).

Greece has an estimated 67 airports with paved runways. There are also nine heliports. Athens' main airport connects the capital by regular flights to major cities in Europe, the Middle East, and North America. The new Athens airport at Spata opened March 2001. Olympic Airways, nationalized in 1975, operates a large internal domestic network as well as international flights.

12 HISTORY

Civilization in Greece first arose on Crete in the 3rd millennium BC, probably as a result of immigration from Asia Minor (now Turkey). The Minoan civilization (c.3000-c.1100 BC), named after the legendary King Minos (which may have been a title rather than a name), was centered in the capital of Knossos, where it became known as Helladic (c.2700-c.1100 BC). During the 2nd millennium BC, Greece was conquered by Indo-European invaders: first the Achaeans, then the Aeolians and Ionians, and finally the Dorians. The Greeks, who called themselves Hellenes after a tribe in Thessaly (they were called Greeks by the Romans after another tribe in northwestern Greece), adapted the native culture to their own peasant village traditions and developed the characteristic form of ancient Greek political organization, the city-state *(polis)*. The resulting Mycenaean civilization (c.1600-c.1100 BC), named after the dominant city-state of Mycenae, constituted the latter period of the Helladic civilization.

The Mycenaeans, who were rivals of the Minoans, destroyed Knossos about 1400 BC and, according to legend, the city of Troy in Asia Minor about 1200 BC. The Minoan and Mycenaean civilizations both came to a relatively abrupt end about 1100 BC, possibly as a result of the Dorian invasion, but the foundations had already been laid for what was to become the basis of Western civilization. It was the Greeks who first tried democratic government; produced the world's first outstanding dramatists, poets, historians, philosophers, and orators; and made the first scientific study of medicine, zoology, botany, physics, geometry, and the social sciences.

In the 1st millennium BC, overpopulation forced the Greeks to emigrate and to colonize areas from Spain to Asia Minor. The Greeks derived their alphabet from the Phoenicians during the 8th century BC. By the 6th century BC, the two dominant *polises* (city-states) were Athens and Sparta. The 5th century BC, recognized as the golden age of Athenian culture, brought the defeat of the Persians by the Athenians in the Persian Wars (490–479 BC) and the defeat of Athens and its allies by Sparta and its allies in the Peloponnesian War (431–404 BC). The territory that is present-day Greece was under Spartan rule.

The inability of Greeks to unite politically led to the annexation of their territories by Philip II of Macedon in 338 BC and by his son Alexander the Great. Through Alexander's ambition for world empire and his admiration of Greek learning, Greek civilization was spread to all his conquered lands. The death of Alexander in 323 BC, the breakup of his empire, and the lack of national feeling among the Greeks prepared the way for their conquest by Rome at the close of the Macedonian Wars in 146 BC.

Greece was made a Roman province, but Athens remained a center of learning. To speak the Greek language was to speak the language of culture, commerce, art, and politics. Greeks were widely influential in Rome, in the Egyptian city of Alexandria, and elsewhere. For this reason, the period between the death of Alexander and the beginning of the Roman Empire is known as the Hellenistic period.

When the Roman Empire was officially divided in AD 395, Greece, by this time Christianized, became part of the Eastern Roman Empire, eventually known as the Byzantine Empire (so named from Byzantium, the former name of Constantinople, its capital). The Byzantine Empire lasted for more than a thousand years. During this period, Greek civilization continued to contribute to Byzantine art and culture.

The formal schism between Eastern Orthodox Christianity and Roman Catholicism came in 1054, when Pope Leo IX and Patriarch Michael Cerularius excommunicated each other. The continuity of Byzantine rule was broken by the fall of Constantinople in the Fourth Crusade in 1204. Under the Latin Empire of the East, which lasted until 1261, Greece was divided into feudal fiefs, with the Duchy of Athens passing successively under French, Spanish, and Florentine rulers.

The Ottoman Turks, who conquered Constantinople in 1453 and the Greek peninsula by the end of the decade, gave the Greeks a large degree of local autonomy. Communal affairs were controlled by the Orthodox Church, and Greek merchants ranged throughout the world on their business ventures, but Greece itself was poverty-stricken. Following an unsuccessful attempt to overthrow the Turks in 1770—an uprising aided by Russia, as part of Catherine the Great's plan to replace Muslim with Orthodox Christian rule throughout the Near East—the Greeks, led by the archbishop of Patras, proclaimed a war of independence against the Turks on 25 March 1821. The revolution, which aroused much sympathy in Europe, succeeded only after Britain, France, and Russia decided to aid the Greeks in 1827. These three nations recognized Greek independence through the London Protocol of 1830, and the Ottomans accepted the terms later in the year.

The same three powers also found a king for Greece in the person of Otto I of Bavaria. During his reign (1832–1844), Otto I faced a series of foreign and domestic problems. In March 1844, Otto's administration was pressured to draft a constitution to establish a new government. Under this document, the leader would reign as a constitutional monarch and the legislature would be elected by all property-holding males over the age of 25. Otto managed to hold onto power for another decade, until the outbreak of the Crimean War (1854–1856). Otto sent troops to occupy Ottoman territory with the pretense of protecting Christians in the Balkans, but the European powers sided against him. Otto, humiliated, was forced to give up his "Christian Cause" in the Balkans. He abdicated in 1862.

Next, Prince William George of Denmark, who ruled as King George I, took control of Greece until his assassination in 1913. During and after his rule, Greece gradually added islands and neighboring territories with Greek-speaking populations, including the Ionian Islands, ceded by the British in 1864; Thessaly,

LOCATION: 34°48′2″ to 41°45′1″N; 19°22′41 to 29°38′39″E. BOUNDARY LENGTHS: Macedonia, 228 kilometers (142 miles); Bulgaria, 494 kilometers (308 miles); Turkey, 206 kilometers (128 miles); Albania, 282 kilometers (176 miles); total coastline, 13,676 kilometers (8,496 miles). TERRITORIAL SEA LIMIT: 6 miles.

seized from Turkey in 1881; Macedonia, Crete, and some Aegean islands in 1913; and the Dodecanese Islands and Rhodes, ceded by Italy in 1947.

The first half of the 20th century for Greece was a period of wars and rivalries with Turkey; of republican rule under the Cretan patriot Eleutherios Venizelos; of occupation by Italy and Germany during World War II (in World War I, Greece had been neutral for three years and had then sided with the Allies); and of a five-year civil war (1944–49) between the government and the Communist-supported National Liberation Front, in which US aid under the Truman Doctrine played a significant role in defeating the insurgency. In September 1946, the Greeks voted back to the throne the twice-exiled George II (grandson of George I), who was succeeded upon his death in April 1947 by his brother Paul I. A new constitution took effect in 1952, the same year Greece joined NATO. For much of the decade, Greece backed demands by Greek Cypriots for *enosis*, or the union of Cyprus with Greece, but in 1959, the Greek, Turkish, and Cypriot governments agreed on a formula for an independent Cyprus, which became a reality in 1960.

King Paul died on 6 March 1964 and was succeeded by his son Constantine. Meanwhile, a parliamentary crisis was brewing, as rightist and leftist elements struggled for control of the army, and the government sought to purge the military of political influence. On 21 April 1967, a right wing military junta staged a successful coup d'etat. Leftists were rounded up, press censorship was imposed, and political liberties were suspended. After an unsuccessful countercoup on 13 December 1967, King Constantine and the royal family fled to exile in Italy. Lt. Gen. George Zoetakis was named regent to act for the king, and Col. George Papadopoulos was made premier. A constitutional reform was approved by 92% of the voters in a plebiscite held under martial law on 29 September 1968. Under the new constitution, individual rights were held to be subordinate to the interests of the state, many powers of the king and legislature were transferred to the ruling junta, and the army was granted extended powers as overseer of civil order. The constitution outlawed membership in the Communist Party. US military aid to Greece, suspended after the 1967 coup, was restored by President Richard M. Nixon in September 1970.

Following an abortive naval mutiny in 1973, Greece was declared a republic by the surviving junta. Papadopoulos became president, only to be overthrown by a group of officers following the bloody repression of a student uprising. The complicity of the junta in a conspiracy by Greek army officers on Cyprus against the government of Archbishop Makarios precipitated the final fall from power of Greece's military rulers in July 1974, when the Turkish army intervened in Cyprus and overwhelmed the island's Greek contingent. Constantine Karamanlis, a former prime minister and moderate, returned from exile to form a civilian government that effectively ended eight years of dictatorial rule.

General elections were held on 17 November 1974, the first since 1964, marking the recovery of democratic rule. In a referendum held on 8 December 1974, 69% of the electorate voted to end the monarchy and declare Greece a parliamentary republic. On 7 June 1975, a democratic constitution was adopted by the new legislature, although 86 of the 300 members boycotted the session. Karamanlis became Greece's first prime minister under the new system, and, on 19 June 1975, parliament elected Konstantinos Tsatsos as president.

Prime Minister Karamanlis, who had withdrawn Greece from NATO's military structure in 1974 to protest Turkey's invasion of Cyprus, resumed military cooperation with NATO in the fall of 1980—a few months after he was elected president of Greece—and brought his nation into the European Community (EC) effective 1 January 1981. With the victory of the Pan-Hellenic Socialist Movement (Panellinio Socialistikou Kinema-PASOK) in the elections of October 1981, Greece installed its first Socialist government. The new prime minister, Andreas Papandreou—the son of former prime minister George Papandreou and a man accused by rightists in 1967 of complicity in an abortive leftist military plot—had campaigned on a promise to take Greece out of the EC, although his government did not do so. In November 1982, he refused to allow Greek participation in NATO military exercises in

the Aegean, which were then canceled. In January 1983, the government declared a general amnesty for the Communist exiles of the 1944–49 civil war.

In mid-1982, in an attempt to deal with the deepening economic crisis, the government created a ministry of national economy, which embraced industrial and commercial affairs. The proposed "radical socialization" of the economy, however, provoked widespread opposition, which limited it to the introduction of worker participation in supervisory councils; state control was imposed only on the pharmaceutical industry (in 1982). Of Greece's largest enterprises, only the Heracles Cement Co. was nationalized (in 1983). Relations with labor were strained, as the government sought to balance worker demands that wages be indexed to inflation with the growing need for austerity; in late 1986, the government imposed a two-year wage freeze, which provoked widespread strikes and demonstrations.

In 1985, Prime Minister Papandreou unexpectedly withdrew his support for President Karamanlis's bid for a second five-year term and announced amendments to the constitution that would transfer powers from the president to the legislature and prime minister. Karamanlis resigned, and Papandreou proceeded with his proposed changes, calling an election in June and winning a mandate to follow through with them (parliament's approval was given in March 1986). Subsequently, however, the government began to lose power; the opposition made substantial gains in the 1986 local elections, and a 1987 scandal associated with Papandreou further weakened the government. In January 1988, Papandreou met with Turkish premier Turgut Ozal in Switzerland; they agreed to work toward solving the problems between the two countries.

Two rounds of parliamentary elections were held in 1989; neither was conclusive. After the June vote, the center-conservative New Democracy (ND) party, with 146 of 300 seats, formed a government with left-wing parties and concentrated on investigating scandals of the Papandreou government, including those of the former prime minister himself. That government resigned in the fall, and new elections were held in November. The ND and PASOK both improved their totals, and an all-party coalition was formed to address economic reform. That government, however, also failed. In April 1990 elections, the ND emerged victorious.

In the balloting of 10 October 1993, PASOK won 171 seats to 110 for the ND and Papandreou was again elected prime minister, despite repeated scandals of both personal and political nature. In 1995, parliament appointed Konstandinos Stephanopoulos president. Voters appeared dissatisfied with the ND's economic reforms while PASOK won support for its hard-line foreign policy demanding that the former Yugoslav Republic of Macedonia change its name. Many Greeks believe the name of the newly independent state implies territorial designs on the northern Greek region, which once formed part of historic Macedonia. In 1995, Papandreou became ill and was not able to adequately perform his duties. In January 1996, PASOK named Costas Simitis prime minister. In June of that year, Papandreou died at 77, ending the tumultuous political career of postwar Greece's most important—and controversial—politician.

In 1996, Simitis, facing strong resistance to austerity measures from labor and farmers, called on the president to dissolve parliament and hold early elections. Simitis had vowed not to call for a dissolution, but faced with mounting opposition to his austerity measures—taken to prepare the Greek economy for European monetary union in 1999—felt he needed a reinforced mandate. The election, held on 22 September 1996, returned PASOK and Simitis to power, giving them, in fact, a commanding majority in parliament.

The next four years were highlighted by continued Greek-Turkish tension, and Simitis's push for Greek entry into the monetary union. Relations with Turkey reached a new low in early 1999 when Turkey's most-wanted man, Kurdish terrorist leader Abdullah Ocalan, was captured by the Turkish secret services in Nairobi, Kenya. Ocalan had sought refuge in the Greek embassy and was seized while en route to the airport, apparently on the way to an asylum-granting country in Africa. Ocalan's capture led to subsequent Turkish charges that the Greek state sponsored international terrorism.

The outbreak of a war in Kosovo little over a month later also placed Greece in an awkward diplomatic position. Although the overwhelming majority of the Greek public opposed the war, the Simitis government maintained its ties to NATO and offered logistical, although not combat, support to its allies. Nevertheless, the widespread anti-Western backlash remained for some months. Rioting greeted US President Bill Clinton when he visited Greece in November 1999.

Unexpectedly, relations with Turkey began to significantly improve in August 1999 following a devastating earthquake in Turkey that killed over 20,000 Turkish citizens. Greece was among the first countries to offer aid to its traditional foe. When a smaller earthquake struck Greece the following month, Turkey reciprocated the Greek gesture. In the aftermath of the tragedies, Greece and Turkey continued a dialogue that resulted in cooperation accords in commerce and the fight against terrorism. In addition, Greece supported the decision of the December 1999 European Union (EU) summit in Helsinki to place Turkey as a candidate for EU membership, which also contributed to improving relations between Greece and Turkey. When the EU, in late 2002, announced Turkey would not be one of 10 new candidate countries invited to join the body as of 2004, Greece pressed the EU to set a date for the start of accession talks. Greece itself entered the euro zone on 1 January 2002. However, in December 2004, the European Commission issued a formal warning to Greece after the Commission found Greece to have falsified budget deficit data in the run-up to joining the euro zone. Nevertheless, in April 2005, the Greek parliament ratified the EU constitution.

Negotiations between the Greek and Turkish leaders in Cyprus were held in early 2003 to see whether they could agree on a plan to unify the island prior to Cyprus signing an EU accession treaty on 16 April. The talks failed, and the internationally recognized Greek government of Cyprus signed the accession treaty. However, later that month, Turkish-Cypriot leader Rauf Denktash opened the borders of northern Cyprus to Greeks, and, by 15 May 2003, about 250,000 Greek Cypriots and 70,000 Turkish Cypriots—40% of the island's combined population—had visited each other's side.

Approximately 90% of Greece's population was opposed to the US-led war in Iraq that began on 19 March 2003. Prime Minister Costas Simitis indicated that by waging war, the United States and United Kingdom were undermining the EU. Yet he gave the coalition permission to use Greek airspace to launch strikes against Iraq.

In February 2004, Simitis called for new elections in March; he stood down as leader of PASOK. George Papandreou took over as party chief. In the March parliamentary elections, the conservative New Democracy party led by Costas Karamanlis came in first, ending over a decade of PASOK rule.

Greece's international standing received a boost when the country hosted the 2004 Summer Olympics.

In February 2005, parliament elected Karolos Papoulias president by a vote of 279 out of 300 votes; he took office on 12 March 2005.

In March 2005, Greek trade unions began 24-hour strikes to protest rising unemployment and high inflation. In December, amid protest strikes by transportation workers, parliament approved changes to labor laws, including an end to jobs-for-life in the public sector. The plans had led to industrial action in June. In March 2006, public sector workers went on strike over wages and to protest government plans to eliminate job security laws and intensify privatization.

In September 2006, Greece, Russia, and Bulgaria supported a long-awaited agreement to build an oil pipeline to carry Russian oil to Europe via Alexandropoulis in Greece.

The conservative government in February 2007 survived a vote of no confidence. In the September 2007 general elections, the New Democracy party retained its lead in parliament with 41.8% of the vote. However, opposition leaders continued to criticize Prime Minister Costas Karamanlis for failed attempts to modernize the nation's economy and combat political corruption. Karamanlis called for early general elections in October 2009, hoping to establish a new mandate that would confront the country's growing economic problems. Instead, the opposition PASOK overtook the incumbent ND party with 44% of the vote. The ND party secured only 33.5% of the vote in the snap election, the lowest election result the party had ever had. George Papandreou of PASOK was sworn in as prime minister on 6 October 2009. He promised to address the immediate financial crisis with a stimulus package of up to $4.4 billion.

The global financial crisis that began in 2008 had devastating effects on Greece's economy. In 2011, Greece became the focus of international attention as it declared itself incapable of continuing payments on its foreign debt and, thus, became the first EU member country to threaten default on its financial obligations. For decades, consecutive Greek governments had relied on borrowing to hold down unemployment and boost public payrolls. An early retirement age (57), long paid vacations (25 business days), and a long history of tax evasion have been among the factors cited as root causes of the 2011 financial crisis. While awaiting EU action, the Greek government initiated an economic austerity program that included major cuts in public spending and a $50-billion sell-off of government assets. The proposed reforms were met with hostility by a sifnificant portion of the Greek population, particularly because PASOK had come to power on a social welfare platform. Street riots and violent clashes with police marked the summer of 2011. In October 2011, Greece secured a €130 billion financial bailout plan that restructured Greece's foreign debt and was predicated on the continued implementation of economic austerity measures. In early November 2011, there were signs that Prime Minister Papandreou's cabinet might weather the storm, but eventually he had to step down in favor of fellow Socialist Lucas Papademos, whose new cabinet included two ministers from the opposition ND party—a first-time alliance between Greece's two major parties since the country's return to democracy in 1974. Mr. Papandreou's finance minister—the public face of Greece's austerity program—kept his post in the new cabinet.

13 GOVERNMENT

Before the 1967 coup, executive power was vested in the crown but was exercised by a Council of Ministers appointed by the king and headed by a premier. The 1975 constitution abolished the 146-year-old Greek monarchy and created the office of president as head of state. If a majority in parliament fails to agree on the selection of a president, the office is filled in a general election. The president, who is limited to two five-year terms, appoints the prime minister, usually the leader of the party that has won plurality in a parliamentary election. The prime minister is head of government and requires the confidence of parliament to remain in power. The 1975 constitution was amended in 1986 to reduce the power of the president, limiting his right to dissolve parliament on his own initiative and depriving him of the right to dismiss the prime minister, veto legislation, or proclaim a state of emergency; basically, these powers were transferred to parliament. The prime minister selects a cabinet from among the members of parliament.

Legislative power is vested in a parliament (Vouli), a unicameral body of 300 deputies elected by direct, universal, secret ballot for maximum four-year terms. A proportional electoral system makes it possible for a party with a minority of the popular vote to have a parliamentary majority. In the 1974 elections, voting was made compulsory for all persons aged 21–70 residing within 200 km (124 mi) of their constituencies. Suffrage is now universal and compulsory at age 18.

14 POLITICAL PARTIES

After World War II, political parties in Greece centered more on leaders than platforms. The Greek Rally, founded and led by Field Marshal Alexander Papagos, won control of the government in the 1951 elections. About 10% of the vote was received by the Union of the Democratic Left, a left-wing party founded in 1951 as a substitute for the Communist Party, outlawed since 1947. When Papagos died in October 1955, Constantine Karamanlis formed a new party called the National Radical Union, which won the elections of 1956, 1958, and 1961 and held power until 1963, when Karamanlis resigned and the newly formed Center Union, comprising a coalition of liberals and progressives and led by George Papandreou, subsequently won a narrow plurality, with Papandreou becoming prime minister. In elections held in February 1964, the Center Union won 174 out of 300 seats; however, King Constantine dismissed Papandreou in July 1965, and Stephanos Stephanopoulos formed a new government. This government, too, was short-lived. Political conflict came to a head when Panayotis Kanellopoulos, leader of the National Radical Union, who had been appointed premier of a caretaker government, set new elections for 28 May 1967. On 21 April, however, a military coup

resulted in the cancellation of elections and suppression of political parties, which lasted until 1974.

On 28 September 1974, following his return from exile, Karamanlis formed the New Democracy Party (Nea Dimokratia-ND), advocating a middle course between left and right and promoting closer ties with Western Europe. The Center Union-New Forces (EKND), renamed the Union of the Democratic Center (EDHK) in 1976, rallied liberal factions of the former Center Union and announced a line that generally paralleled ND policies. The EDHK disintegrated following the 1981 elections. Other groups to emerge, most of them led by former opponents of the junta, including the Pan-Hellenic Socialist Movement (Panellinio Socialistiko Kinema-PASOK), led by Andreas Papandreou; the United Left (UL), which brought together elements of the Union of the Democratic Left and the Communist Party to oppose the upcoming elections; and the National Democratic Union (NDU), which represented an amalgam of various elements, including some royalists and right-wing activists. Also in 1974, the Communist Party (Kommounistiko Komma Ellados-KKE) was made legal for the first time since 1947; the party later split into two factions, the pro-Soviet KKE-Exterior and the Eurocommunist wing, called the KKE-Interior. In May 1986, the KKE-Interior changed its name to the New Hellenic Left Party.

In the general elections held on 17 November 1974, the ND won an overwhelming majority in parliament, with the EKND forming the major opposition. The ND was again the winner in 1977, although its parliamentary majority dropped from 220 to 172. After parliament elected Karamanlis president in 1980, George Rallis succeeded him as prime minister. In the elections of 18 October 1981, Papandreou's PASOK won 48% of the popular vote and commanded a clear parliamentary majority. Although PASOK won again in the election of 2 June 1985, its share of the total votes cast fell to 45.8%.

In the elections of 10 October 1993, PASOK had about the same percentage (46.9%) and a majority of 171 seats. The ND followed with 110 seats, and an offshoot party, Political Spring, had 10 seats. The Communists gained 9 places.

In the parliamentary elections of 22 September 1996, PASOK retained its majority, but lost 9 seats. ND emerged with 108 seats; the KKE, 11; Coalition of the Left and Progress, 10; and the Democratic and Social Movement Parties, 9. The Political Spring lost all its seats in the election, gaining only 2.95% of the popular vote.

PASOK continued its dominance of the post-1974 era with yet another victory at the polls on 9 April 2000. In a close election, PASOK won 158 seats (43.8% of the vote), ND earned 125 seats (42.7%), the KKE held steady at 11 (5.5%), while the Coalition of the Left and Progress saw its share of the seats drop to 6 (3.2%). The Democratic Social Movement failed to clear the 3% hurdle needed for representation, and Political Spring once again failed to win any seats.

Following the 7 March 2004 elections, ND increased its seats in parliament to 165 (45.5%), while PASOK's number declined to 117 (40.6%). The KKE gained one seat, winning 12 (5.9%), with the Coalition of the Left and Progress (Synaspismos) holding steady at 6 seats (3.3%). Costas Karamanlis was appointed as prime minister.

Following the September 2007 general elections, the ND presence in parliament decreased to 152 seats as the party gained

41.8% of the vote. PASOK earned 102 seats (38.1%), followed by the KKE with 22 seats (8.2%), the Synaspismos with 14 seats (5%), and the Popular Orthodox Rally (LAOS) with 10 seats (3.8%).

Following a series of corruption scandals and criticism against Karamanlis over failed promises, a snap election was held in October 2009. PASOK earned 160 seats (43.92%) while ND decreased its presence to 91 seats (33.48%). KKE took 21 seats (7.54%), followed by LAOS with 15 seats (5.63%), and Synaspismos with 13 seats (4.6%). George Papandreou was appointed as prime minister.

George Papandreou stepped down as prime minister in November 2011, in the wake of Greece's near financial collapse, and was replaced by fellow PASOK member Lucas Papademos. Mr. Papademos's cabinet includes appointees from both of the country's two major political parties, as well as the nationalist LAOS party—an unprecedented instance of political cooperation in the 37 years since Greece's return to democracy in 1974.

15LOCAL GOVERNMENT

The 1975 constitution restored the large measure of local self-government initially provided for in the constitution of 1952 and reemphasized the principle of decentralization, although local units must depend on the central government for funding. Under the military regime of 1967–74, local units were closely controlled by the central authorities.

Greece is divided into 13 regional governments (*periferiarchis*), which are subdivided into 51 prefectures or nomarchies (*nomoi*), in addition to the autonomous administration of Mt. Áthos (Aghion Oros) in Macedonia. Each prefecture is governed by a prefect (*nomoi*), who is elected. There are also 272 municipalities or *demoi* (cities of more than 10,000 inhabitants), administered by mayors; communes (with 300 to 10,000 inhabitants), each run by a president and a community council; and localities.

The rocky promontory of Mt. Áthos, southeast of Salonika, is occupied by 20 monasteries, of which 17 are Greek, one Russian, one Serbian, and one Bulgarian. Mt. Áthos is governed by a 4-member council and a 20-member assembly, which consists of one representative from each monastery. The special status of Mt. Áthos was first formalized in the 1952 constitution.

16JUDICIAL SYSTEM

The 1975 constitution (Syntagma) has been revised twice, in 1985 and in 2001. The constitution provides for an independent judiciary.

The constitution designates the Supreme Court (Areios Pagos) as the highest court of appeal. It consists of both penal and civil sections. The supreme court of the civil and penal justice is the Court of Cassation, while the supreme court of the administrative justice is the Council of State. The Council of State does not hear cases but decides on administrative disputes, administrative violations of laws, and revision of disciplinary procedures affecting civil servants. A Comptrollers Council (alternatively referred to as Chamber of Accounts or Court of Auditors) decides cases of a fiscal nature. The 1975 constitution also established a Special Supreme Tribunal as a final arbiter in disputes arising over general elections and referenda, in addition to exercising review of the constitutionality of laws. Other elements of the judicial system include justices of the peace, magistrates' courts, courts of first instance, courts of appeal, and various administrative courts. Judg-

es of the Supreme Court, the courts of appeal, and the courts of first instance are appointed for life on the recommendation of the Ministry of Justice. The president has the constitutional right, with certain exceptions, to commute and reduce sentences.

As in other EU member countries, the European Court of Justice considers the law of the EU superior to Greece's national laws in areas explicitly legislated by the EU.

17ARMED FORCES

The International Institute for Strategic Studies reports that armed forces in Greece totaled 138,936 members in 2011. The force is comprised of 78,836 from the army, 20,000 from the navy, 28,500 from the air force, and 11,600 members of joint forces. Armed forces represent 2.8% of the labor force in Greece. Defense spending totaled $13.7 billion and accounted for 4.3% of GDP.

The Greek field army has a large and varied combined arms structure, with units manned at three different levels of readiness: 85% are fully ready; 65% are ready within 24 hours; and 20% are ready within 48 hours. The 1,150 troops serving on Cyprus include a mechanized brigade. Greek military personnel have provided support to UN peacekeeping missions in several countries or regions around the world. The United States has one major naval base on Greek soil and several smaller installations.

18INTERNATIONAL COOPERATION

Greece is a charter member of the United Nations (UN), having joined on 25 October 1945, and participates in ECE and several nonregional specialized agencies. Greece was admitted to NATO in 1951 but suspended its military participation (1974–80) because of the Cyprus conflict. It belongs to the Council of Europe, the OECD, OSCE, WTO, G-6, the European Bank for Reconstruction and Development, the Black Sea Economic Cooperation Zone, and the Western European Union. Greece is also a permanent observer at the OAS. The country became a full member of the European Union as of 1 January 1981.

In August 1987, Greece and Albania signed a pact ending the state of war that had existed between them since World War II. The Greek government continues to be in dispute with the neighboring Republic of Macedonia over the name of the latter. In 1995, Greece agreed to recognize the country as the Former Yugoslav Republic of Macedonia. However, Greece vetoed Macedonia's bid for NATO membership in 2008, proving that the unresolved dispute is still a major issue for the government. Greece and Turkey have unresolved boundary disputes in the Aegean Sea, and there has historically been tension between the two countries has in connection with the Greek-Turkish disputes in the nation of Cyprus. Greece has guest status in the Nonaligned Movement.

Greece belongs to the Australia group, the Zangger Committee, the Nuclear Energy Agency, the Nuclear Suppliers Group (London Group), and the European Organization for Nuclear Research (CERN). In environmental cooperation, Greece is part of the Antarctic Treaty, the Basel Convention, Conventions on Biological Diversity and Air Pollution, Ramsar, CITES, the London Convention, International Tropical Timber Agreements, the Kyoto Protocol, the Montréal Protocol, MARPOL, the Nuclear Test Ban Treaty, and the UN Conventions on the Law of the Sea, Climate Change, and Desertification.

¹⁹ECONOMY

The gross domestic product (GDP) rate of change in Greece, as of 2011, was -6%. Inflation stood at 2.9%, and unemployment was reported at 17%.

The Greek economy suffers from a paucity of exploitable natural resources and a low level of industrial development relative to the rest of Western Europe. By 1992, Greece had fallen behind Portugal to become the poorest European Community (now European Union-EU) member; with the entrance into the EU of 10 primarily Eastern European nations in 2004, that was no longer the case. In 2010, agriculture generated about 4% of GDP but employed about 12.4% of the labor force. Agricultural exports include tobacco, cotton, wheat, raisins, currants, fresh fruits, tomato products, olive oil, and olives. In 2010, industry accounted for about 17.9% of GDP and 22.4% of the labor force. Services provided some 78.8% of GDP, employing 65.1% of the labor force.

Next to food processing, textile manufacturing used to be the most important industry, but chemicals, metals, and machinery have outstripped it in recent years. The paper products industry has been a fast-growing since 1980. Greece has stimulated foreign investments in the development of its mineral resources by constitutionally providing guarantees for capital and profits. The government has encouraged tourism, which has developed into a major source of revenue (15% of GDP in 2004). Greece continues to play a dominant role in the international shipping industry.

During the late 1950s and 1960s, the government took steps to reclaim land, develop new farms, increase credits and investments for agriculture, protect agricultural prices, improve the agricultural product, and utilize it to the best advantage; however, the country still depends on imports to meet its food needs. Industrial output contributed substantially to the rapid increase in national income after 1960, and manufacturing and service industries were the fastest-growing sectors in the 1970s. In the 1980s, however, the economy retracted sharply because of the worldwide recession, and growth in real terms was sluggish. In the best year of the decade, 1988, GDP grew by 4.9%. In 1993, GDP dropped by 0.5%, but rebounded in 1995. Inflation, which neared 20% in 1991, had been lowered to 8.1% in 1995, lower than the many European Union (EU) countries that struggled mightily with inflation in the mid-1990s. As Greece pursued an economic austerity program aimed at meeting the criteria for European economic and monetary union (EMU), inflation continued to fall, reaching less than 4% at the end of 1998. Greece entered into the EMU in 2001.

As of 2006, Greece had failed to meet the EU's Growth and Stability Pact budget deficit criteria of 3% of GDP since 2000. The criteria were met briefly, in 2007, to be exceeded again in 2009. Greece is a recipient of EU aid, amounting to 3.3% of annual GDP. The country's public debt burden is a major drag on economic growth and prosperity, at about 104% of GDP. Unemployment remained high in the mid 2000s, and the country was in need of introducing social insurance reform. Greece has a large public sector (some 40% of GDP) but is implementing privatization policies. Per capita GDP is about 70% that of other leading euro-zone economies. Public and private investment was strong in 2003 in preparation for the 2004 Olympic Games that were held in Athens; the Greek economy grew at a rate of approximately 4% from 2003 to 2007. Spending on the Olympic Games contributed to an estimated general government deficit of 6.6% of GDP in 2004.

The global financial crisis of 2008–09 took a heavy toll on the nation, as the growth rate dropped to 2.9% in 2008 and was -2.3% at year-end 2009. The CIA estimates real growth to have been 1% in 2008, -1% in 2009, -4.5% in 2010, and -6% in 2011. By January 2010, the nation's economy was in a major debt crisis, and the government began to seek help from the international community. In April 2010, Eurozone leaders announced the details of a long-awaited loan package for Greece, soothing concerns about the future of the country and the euro. The financial rescue plan provided Greece with up to $40 billion in 5% interest loans, significantly lower than the 7.5% interest that markets were demanding. Analysts expected the International Monetary Fund (IMF) to offer an additional $20 billion in loans for Greece, with interest rates even lower than the 5% offered by eurozone leaders. Together, these measures stabilized the markets but created concerns that other cash-strapped European countries, such as Spain, Portugal, and Italy, would plead for similar rescue packages.

The IMF and EU bailout package for Greece was contingent on Greek lawmakers implementing a tough and extremely unpopular three-year austerity program. As lawmakers began debating the austerity measures in May 2010, storms of protesters descended on Athens. Greek lawmakers voted on 6 May 2010 in favor of the austerity measures by wide margins, ushering in hikes in taxes and cuts in pensions and public sector bonuses. One day after the approval of the measures, the German parliament approved a $28.6 billion bailout package for Greece.

In the second quarter of 2010, the economy declined by 1.8%, with exports falling by 5% and gross capital investment dropping by 18.6%.

An unstable job market has made unemployment a major problem for youth and young adults just entering the workforce. According to an August 2010 survey, seven of ten Greek college graduates between the ages of 22 and 35 wanted to find work abroad. Four of ten were actively seeking for work abroad or were pursuing further education in order to be better qualified for work abroad. In June 2010, unemployment for those between the ages of 15 and 24 was at 29.8%. For those between the ages of 25 and 34, unemployment was at 16.2%. Overall unemployment in June 2010 was at 11.6% and had increased to 17% by 2011.

In October 2010, the government announced another round of austerity measures as part of its 2011 draft budget. The measures included higher taxes for businesses and an increase in the value-added tax (VAT). Officials hoped that such measures would reduce the budget deficit to 7% of GDP by the end of 2011, coming in below the 7.6% target set by eurozone countries and the IMF as part of the nation's bailout package.

Yet another round of public sector wage cuts and job eliminations was passed by the parliament in December 2010. Throughout 2010, each round of austerity measures was met by public protests and often violent demonstrators. Many protestors displayed anti-IMF slogans, expressing a general belief that the Greek government was bowing to the demands of the international community, thereby placing Greek citizens under the economic thumb of others.

In June 2011, the International Monetary Fund and European Central Bank released reports showing that Greece was making good progress, but needed to step up fiscal and structural reforms in order to promote economic growth. Later that month, parliament passed a five-year austerity plan to cut wages, increase taxes, and privatize $71 billion in state assets, thereby providing Greece with the assurance that it would receive a European Union $17 billion bailout.

While foreign financial markets continued to be wary of the nation's economic future, the OECD issued a report indicating general satisfaction with some of the tough reforms already implemented. The report concluded that with continued tax, labor, and market reforms, public debt will drop below 60% of GDP by 2031. As of 2010, the debt was at 140% of GDP.

Throughout 2010 and 2011, investors continued to demand ever higher interest rates for Greek borrowing as the market appeared to conclude that some sort of default was inevitable. In June 2011, Standard and Poor's downgraded Greece's international credit rating to CCC, the lowest in the world. Mass demonstrations turned violent in October 2011, as Parliament barely passed the additional austerity measures Europe demanded to keep the bailout money flowing. Later that month, the country received a measure of potential relief, as European leaders and the IMF obtained an agreement from banks to take a 50 percent loss on the face value of their Greek debt, the equivalent of €130 billion ($177 billion). The plan is expected to bring Greek debt down to 120% of GDP by 2020.

20 INCOME

The CIA estimated that, in 2010, the GDP of Greece was $318.1 billion. The CIA defines GDP as the value of all final goods and services produced within a nation in a given year and computed on the basis of purchasing power parity (PPP) rather than value as measured on the basis of the rate of the exchange based on current dollars. The per capita GDP was estimated at $29,600. The annual growth rate of GDP was -4.5%. The average inflation rate was 4.5%. It was estimated that agriculture accounted for 4% of GDP, industry 17.6%, and services 78.5%.

According to the World Bank, remittances from citizens living abroad totaled $2 billion or about $188 per capita and accounted for approximately .6% of GDP.

The World Bank reports that in 2009, household consumption in Greece totaled $242.3 billion or about $22,515 per capita, measured in current US dollars rather than PPP. Household consumption includes expenditures of individuals, households, and nongovernmental organizations on goods and services, excluding the purchases of dwellings. It was estimated that household consumption was growing at an average annual rate of 1.7%.

The World Bank estimates that Greece, with 0.18% of the world's population, accounted for 0.51% of the world's GDP. By comparison, the United States, with 4.85% of the world's population, accounted for 22.51% of world GDP.

As of 2011, the most recent study by the World Bank reported that actual individual consumption in Greece was 72.8% of GDP and accounted for 0.55% of world consumption. By comparison, the United States accounted for 25.44% of world individual consumption. The World Bank also estimated that 14.1% of Greece's GDP was spent on food and beverages, 15.4% on housing and household furnishings, 7.2% on clothes, 6.4% on health, 6.1% on transportation, 1.7% on communications, 4.4% on recreation, 13.2% on restaurants and hotels, and -.3% on miscellaneous goods and services and purchases from abroad.

It was estimated that, in 2009, about 20% of the population subsisted on an income below the poverty line established by Greece's government.

21 LABOR

As of 2010, Greece had a total labor force of 5.013 million people. Within that labor force, CIA estimates in 2005 noted that 12.4% were employed in agriculture, 22.4% in industry, and 65.1% in the service sector.

In 2011, about 30% of salaried, nonagricultural employees belonged to unions. Unions were organized on a territorial rather than a plant basis: all workers of a certain trade in a town usually belong to one union. On a nationwide scale, union members of the same trade or profession form a federation; the General Confederation of Greek Workers (GSEE) is the central core of the private sector union movement. Government plays an important role in labor-management relations. Collective bargaining and the right to strike are protected by law, although workers must give notice of an intent to strike (4 days for public utilities, 24 hours in the private sector). Because of a history of compulsory arbitration as a means to resolve labor disputes, unions successfully lobbied for new legislation, passed in 1992, which restricted the use of compulsory arbitration in favor of mediation procedures. Unions played a prominent role in the 2010 and 2011 protests against the Greek government's austerity program.

As of 2011, the maximum legal workweek was 40 hours in the private sector and 37.5 hours in the public sector. The minimum monthly salary was around $47 per day or $1,060 per month, but this amount did not provide a decent standard of living for families in high-cost urban areas. Annual vacations (of up to a month) with pay are provided by law. In general, employment of children under the age of 15 in the industrial sector was prohibited. The minimum age for children employed in cinemas, theaters and family businesses was 12. Industrial health and safety standards are set by law and regularly enforced.

22 AGRICULTURE

Roughly 29% of the total land is farmed, and the country's major crops include wheat, corn, barley, sugar beets, olives, tomatoes, wine, tobacco, and potatoes. Cereal production in 2009 amounted to 4.8 million tons, fruit production 3.2 million tons, and vegetable production 3.5 million tons.

Agriculture in Greece suffers not only from natural limitations, such as poor soils and droughts, but also from soil erosion, lack of fertilizers, and insufficient capital investment despite a number of subsidies granted by the European Union.

Cultivable land supports over half of the population. In recent decades, Greek agriculture has been characterized by an increasing diversification of fruit crops for export. Progress has been made toward modernization in machinery and cultivation techniques. Agricultural products, including processed foods, beverages, and tobacco, make up one-third of total exports. To expand agricultural production and encourage farm prosperity, the government exempts agricultural income from most taxes, extends liberal farm credits, and subsidizes agriculture. It also operates a service by which individual growers or cooperatives may hire heavy farm equipment at low prices, encourages the development of industries that use farm products, provides educational programs, and has sought to halt the trend toward ever-smaller farm holdings.

23 ANIMAL HUSBANDRY

The UN Food and Agriculture Organization (FAO) reported that Greece dedicated 1.4 million hectares (3.46 million acres) to permanent pasture or meadow in 2009. During that year, the country tended 31.8 million chickens, 620,000 head of cattle, and 942,000 pigs. The production from these animals amounted to 204,284 tons of beef and veal, 304,566 tons of pork, 152,960 tons of poultry, 97,154 tons of eggs, and 3.5 million tons of milk. Greece also produced 11,130 tons of cattle hide and 7,420 tons of raw wool.

Although production of milk, meat, and cheese has risen greatly since the end of World War II (1939–45), Greece still must import substantial quantities of evaporated and condensed milk, cheese, cattle, sheep, hides, and meat. Recent modernization in machinery has especially helped poultry and hog operations.

24 FISHING

Greece had 20,495 decked commercial fishing boats in 2008. The annual capture totaled 88,971 tons according to the UN FAO. The export value of seafood totaled $436.9 million.

The fishing industry has expanded and been modernized in recent years. In 2002, there were 33,992 people employed in small scale fisheries. A total of $317.2 million of fish and fish products were exported that year. In the north of Greece, freshwater fisheries have been restocked and developed, but the inland catch only accounted for 3% of total volume in 2003. During 2000–06, Greece benefited from EU support in the amount of €223,611,900. In 2008, the European Commission approved an operational program for Greek fisheries in the amount of to €274,105,143 for the period 2007–2013. As a result of the first plan, more than 1,330 new jobs were created, and over 2,350 jobs were maintained. The production of aquaculture units was increased by more than 12,500 tons (+18%), and the capacity of the processing industry was increased by 16,500 tons (+ 36.67%). Many new companies were created and a number of small ports (fishing shelters) were built.

Sponge fishing, once an important source of wealth in the Dodecanese and other regions, had virtually collapsed by 2003 but retains a cultural significance in the Greek islands. Its volume decreased from 135.5 tons of sponges in 1955 to 2.5 tons in 2003.

25 FORESTRY

Approximately 30% of Greece is covered by forest. The UN FAO estimated the 2009 roundwood production at 948,076 cu m (33.5 million cu ft). The value of all forest products, including roundwood, totaled $129.6 million.

Forests cover about 28% of the country's total area. Much of the forest area was destroyed during the 1940s, but the government's reforestation program planted more than 100 million trees during the 1970s and 1980s. Pine, fir, and oak are the most common trees, and resin and turpentine are the principal products.

26 MINING

The minerals industry, consisting of the mining, industrial minerals, and metal processing sectors, was a small but important part of the national economy. Greece, the only Balkan country in the EU, was the union's largest producer of bauxite, magnesium, nickel, and perlite, and was second to the United States in bentonite production (from Milos Island). Chromite (from Tsingeli Mines, near Volos) and zinc (from Kassandra Mines, in Olympias and Stratoni) were other important commodities. Greek marble, produced in all parts of the country, continued to play a leading role in the international dimension stone market because of its versatility and many colors (ash, black, brown, green, pink, red, and multicolored). With the exception of bauxite, Greece's mines operated far below their productive capacity. A relatively small industrial base, lack of adequate investment, and distance from EU markets, have restricted the export potential of the country. The emerging Balkan markets could offer opportunities for growth. About 50% of the country's mineral production was exported. Northern Greece was thought to contain a significant amount of exploitable mineral resources, and most new activities were directed toward gold. Since 1990, the significance of the mineral industry to the Greek economy has slowly declined.

Production in 2009 of bauxite was 1,935,000 metric tons, compared to 2,176,865 metric tons in 2008. Nickel (content of ferronickel) output in 2009 was estimated at 18,500 metric tons, while crude perlite production in that year was estimated at 1,100,000 metric tons. Other types of magnesite produced were dead-burned, caustic-calcined, and crude huntite/hydromagnesite, which had unique flame-retardant properties. Grecian Magnesite S.A., with its open-pit mine at Yerakini, was a leading magnesite producer in the western world. In 2009, Greece was the world's leading producer of perlite (30%) and the world's third-ranked producer of pumice (11%) after Turkey and Italy; it also produced 9% of the world's bentonite. Also produced in 2009 were alumina, lead, manganese, silver, barite, cement, kaolin, feldspar, gypsum (from Crete), anhydrite, nitrogen, pozzolan (Santorin earth, from Milos), pumice (from Yali), salt, silica, sodium compounds, dolomite, marble, flysch, quartz, sulfur, zeolite, and crude construction materials. No asbestos was produced in 2009. Other mineral deposits of commercial importance were antimony, gold (placer dredger), asbestos, emery, ceramic clay, talc, and limestone. Industrial processing of mineral ores was very limited until the 1960s and 1970s, when facilities for refining nickeliferous iron ore and bauxite were developed.

27 ENERGY AND POWER

The World Bank reported in 2008 that Greece produced 62.9 billion kWh of electricity and consumed 64.3 billion kWh, or 5,977 kWh per capita. Roughly 93% of energy came from fossil fuels, while 2% came from alternative fuels. Per capita oil consumption was 2,707 kg. Oil production totaled 2,334 barrels of oil a day. The CIA estimates 2009 electricity production at 51.5 kWh, and consumption at 59.6 kWh.

Coal and oil are imported to supply power for the many small generating plants spread over the country. Before World War II, the Athens-Piraiévs Electricity Co. operated the only modern plant in Greece, which ran on imported coal. In 1950, the government-organized Public Power Corp. was established to construct and operate electricity generating plants and power transmission and distribution lines; by 1955, it had erected four major power plants. In 1965, the first two units of the Kremasta hydroelectric station were opened; by 2001, installed capacity totaled 10.2

million kW. Production of electricity increased from 8,991 million kWh in 1970 to 50,400 million kWh in 2000, of which 91.5%; was provided by thermal power, 6.6%; by hydroelectric stations, and the rest by other sources. It has been estimated that 15%; of Greece's energy needs can be supplied by wind power by 2010, and there are wind farms on Crete, Andors, and a number of other Greek islands. As of 2002, solar water heaters were used in 20% of Greek homes.

In 2010 Greece produced 7,946 and consumed 371,300 barrels of oil per day. Although actively exploring offshore oil resources, it relies strongly on imported oil, mostly from Russia, Libya, OPEC, the Persian Gulf, and Egypt. A field off Thásos in the northern Aegean began operations in July 1981. Total production, however, fell from 25,000 to 6,000 barrels per day between 1986 and 1998. In 2004, oil production totaled an estimated 6,411 barrels per day, of which crude oil accounted for 2,836 barrels per day, from reserves estimated at 7 million barrels, as of 1 January 2005. In January 2011, Greece was estimated to have proved reserves of 10 million barrels. In 2010, natural gas production stood at 35 million cu ft with an estimated consumption of 135 billion cu ft. In comparison, in 2003 these numbers were 1.0 billion cu ft and 86 billion cu ft, respectively. Two-thirds of Greece's imports of natural gas come from Russia, with the remainder from Algeria. Greece's only substantial fossil fuel resource is brown coal, or lignite. In 2009, it produced 71,344 short tons of coal, making the country the 12th-largest coal producer in the world. In 2008, its lignite reserves totaled an estimated 6.7 billion tons, of which 3.2 were considered economically workable.

28 INDUSTRY

Manufacturing, which now ranks ahead of agriculture as an income earner, has increased rapidly, owing to a vigorous policy of industrialization. However, Greek industry must rely on imports for its raw materials, machinery, parts, and fuel. Greece has only a rudimentary iron and steel industry and does not manufacture basic transport equipment, such as cars and trucks. Industry is concentrated in the Athens area.

Chief industries in 2006 were food, beverages and tobacco; metals and metals manufactures; machinery and electrical goods; chemicals; textiles; and nonmetallic minerals. Although the government controls certain basic industries, such as electric power and petroleum refining, most industry is privately owned. The portion of government-controlled industries is declining as the state has divested itself of substantial control over key holdings such as Olympic Airways and the telecommunications company, OTE. There is substantial room for investment in tourism infrastructure.

Industrial production fell by 5.7% in 2010 and the industrial sector accounted for 17.9% of GDP, down from 22% of GDP in 2004 when it grew by 4.1%. High-technology equipment is a growth sector, as are the production of electrical machinery, office machinery and computers, defense products, building products and equipment, medical equipment, environmental engineering products and services, and certain agricultural products.

29 SCIENCE AND TECHNOLOGY

Patent applications in science and technology as of 2009, according to the World Bank, totaled 698 in Greece. Public financing of

science was $1.9 billion or 0.57% of GDP. The Academy of Athens, founded in 1926, oversees the activities of research institutes in astronomy and applied mathematics and in atmospheric physics and climatology. Greece has five other scientific research institutes. Specialized scientific learned societies include the Association of Greek Chemists, founded in 1924, and the Greek Mathematical Society, founded in 1918, both headquartered in Athens. Advanced scientific and technical training is provided at nine colleges and universities. The University of Athens has maintained a zoological museum since 1858. In the early 1980s, the government established a Ministry of Research and Technology to foster scientific and technological development.

30 DOMESTIC TRADE

Industry and trade are centered on about 20 seaports throughout the country. Athens, Piraeus, and Thessaloniki are the principal commercial cities; importers and exporters have offices in these cities and branches in other centers.

In general, the Greek retail and wholesale sectors are largely made up of small, family-owned and operated businesses, each of which specializes in particular lines of merchandise. Overall, there were some 800,000 businesses in Greece as of 2005. Of that total, 660,000 were personal businesses following the family-owned and operated pattern. In addition, out of that 800,000 only 100,000 were corporations or limited liability companies. Another 40,000, were general or limited partnerships.

In the retail sector, there are a small number of department stores and several supermarket chains. Many of them tend to operate like small shopping centers where the "shop-in-a-shop" mode of retailing is used. Small, specialized shops still account for most of the nation's retail sales. However, in recent years a number of major European chain store firms have begun to enter the Greek retail market, either by opening their own outlets or by acquiring existing large department stores and supermarkets.

Electronic commerce (e-commerce), both business-to-business (B2B) and business-to-consumer (B2C), have been slow to develop in Greece. Compared to other European Union (EU) countries, Greek e-commerce is still in its infancy. Few companies in Greece are willing to use the Internet as a basis for their communications. In addition, many businesses see a marketing presence on the Internet as expensive with little immediate benefit, even though Internet Service Providers' (ISPs) prices are relatively low due to competition. As of 2005, there were under 4 million Internet users in Greece out of a general population of over 11 million. Although in 2009 there were already 4.8 million, this number still accounted for barely 47% of the nation's population, well below the EU average of 69% in that year. E-commerce is expected to continue to grow, as the government liberalized its telecommunications sector in 2005.

There is a 19% value-added tax rate on most sales. However, a reduced rate of 9% is applied to food and medicine, while the rate for books and newspapers in 4.5%.

Usual private sector business hours are from 8 or 9 a.m. to 5 p.m. Monday through Friday. Banking hours are from 8:30 a.m. to 2 p.m. Monday through Thursday and from 8:30 a.m. to 1:30 p.m. on Friday. Stores are open from 9 a.m. to 6 p.m., Monday through Saturday, but some have longer evening hours. Businesses are of-

Principal Trading Partners – Greece (2010)

(In millions of US dollars)

Country	Total	Exports	Imports	Balance
World	71,613.0	20,919.0	50,694.0	-29,775.0
Germany	9,024.0	2,348.0	6,676.0	-4,328.0
Italy	8,597.0	2,330.0	6,267.0	-3,937.0
Russia	6,511.0	341.0	6,170.0	-5,829.0
China	3,990.0	205.0	3,785.0	-3,580.0
France	3,927.0	822.0	3,105.0	-2,283.0
Netherlands	3,855.0	506.0	3,349.0	-2,843.0
United Kingdom	3,027.0	1,119.0	1,908.0	-789.0
Turkey	2,672.0	1,128.0	1,544.0	-416.0
Bulgaria	2,657.0	1,388.0	1,269.0	119.0
Spain	2,433.0	515.0	1,918.0	-1,403.0

(…) data not available or not significant.

(n.s.) not specified.

SOURCE: *2011 Direction of Trade Statistics Yearbook,* New York: United Nations, 2011.

Balance of Payments – Greece (2010)

(In millions of US dollars)

Current Account		-32,335.0
Balance on goods		-37,537.0
Imports	-60,165.0	
Exports	22,628.0	
Balance on services		17,278.0
Balance on income		-12,195.0
Current transfers		118.0
Capital Account		2,776.0
Financial Account		15,722.0
Direct investment abroad		-1,262.0
Direct investment in Greece		2,250.0
Portfolio investment assets		17,078.0
Portfolio investment liabilities		-43,932.0
Financial derivatives		416.0
Other investment assets		10,245.0
Other investment liabilities		30,926.0
Net Errors and Omissions		-99.0
Reserves and Related Items		13,936.0

(…) data not available or not significant.

SOURCE: *Balance of Payment Statistics Yearbook 2011,* Washington, DC: International Monetary Fund, 2011.

ten closed for extended vacations throughout July and August, reopening in September after the annual trade fair.

Advertising is used widely in the towns and cities, and several advertising agencies are active in Athens and Thessaloniki. The most common media are television, newspapers, radio, films, billboards, neon signs, and window displays. The principal annual trade fair is the International Fair of Thessaloniki, held in September.

31 FOREIGN TRADE

Greece imported $60.19 billion worth of goods and services in 2010 while exporting $22.66 billion worth of goods and services. Major import partners in 2010 were Germany, 10.6%; Italy, 9.9%; Russia, 9.6%; China, 6.1%; the Netherlands, 5.3%; France, 4.9%; South Korea; and Austria, 4.5%. Its major export partners were Germany, 10.9%; Italy, 10.9%; Cyprus, 7.3%; Bulgaria, 6.5%; Turkey, 5.4%; the UK, 5.3%; Belgium, 5.1%; China, 4.8%; Switzerland, 4.5%; and Poland, 4.2%.

Garments and cotton have traditionally provided Greece with the most exports, followed by petroleum products; fruit, nuts, and vegetable oils; and tobacco. Tobacco exports from Greece are substantial on the world commodities export market. In 2010, the major exports were food and beverages, manufactured goods, petroleum products, chemicals, textiles. The imports were machinery, transport equipment, fuels, and chemicals. Trade is the second-largest services sub-sector, after property management. The transportation and communications sector has grown in importance following the liberalization of the telecommunications market, while the financial services sector also increased in the mid-2000s.

32 BALANCE OF PAYMENTS

In 2010 Greece had a foreign trade deficit of $25 billion, amounting to 15.2% of GDP.

Because it imports more than twice the value of its exports, Greece has registered chronic annual deficits in its balance of payments. The major contributors to Greece's foreign exchange earnings are tourism, shipping services, and remittances from Greek

workers abroad. Greece's relatively small industrial base and lack of substantial investment since the mid-1990s limited the country's export potential. Greece's productive base expanded in 1999 and 2000, however, in part due to a thriving stock exchange, and low interest rates. A devaluation of the drachma in 1998 and Greece's inclusion in the euro zone in 1999 restored Greek competitiveness. Merchandise exports amounted to $15.7 billion in 2004 and imports to $47.4 billion, while the current-account deficit was $13 billion. The current-account balance averaged -6.7% from 2001–05.

33 BANKING AND SECURITIES

Because Greece is part of the European Monetary Union (the EMU) and uses the euro as its currency, the European Central Bank (ECB) acts as the nation's central bank, a function formally performed by the Bank of Greece, which originally opened in 1927 and is government-controlled. Currently, the Bank of Greece is part of the ECB system (as of 2001) and acts as Greece's banking representative to the ECB and as the ECB's representative to the nation's domestic banks. It also acts as the depository for the Greek government's accounts, and supervises domestic commercial banks, and other financial institutions. It also grants approval to foreign banks wishing to do business in Greece.

Because Greece uses the euro, the nation's discount rate, the interest rate at which the central bank lends to financial institutions in the short term, is set by the ECB. In 2005, the discount rate was 3.25%; in december 2010, it was 1.75%. At the end of 2005, the nation's gold bullion deposits totaled 3.47 million fine troy ounces. According to the International Monetary Fund, Greece increased its reserves to 3.585 million ounces in June, from 3.584 million ounces in May and 3.583 million ounces in April of 2011. In 2010, Greece's reserves of foreign exchange and gold amounted to $6.37 billion.

As of 2009, there were 41 Greek commercial banks, 3 investment banks, a specialized bank (the Agricultural Bank of Greece), a postal savings bank, a consignments and loans bank, and 7 local cooperative banks. Of the commercial banks, 22 were foreign, including four American banks. The largest domestic commercial bank is the National Bank of Greece, which accounts for around 20% of the banking business in Greece. Specialized financial institutions and state-controlled banks together account for about 40% of all loans and 47% of all deposits. Greek-owned private banks accounted for 37% of all deposits and 45% of all loans. Foreign-owned banks accounted for the remaining loans and deposits.

The Currency Committee, composed of five cabinet ministers, controls the eight specialized credit institutions: the Agricultural Bank, National Investment Bank, National Investment Bank for Industrial Development, Hellenic Industrial Development Bank, National Mortgage Bank, Mortgage Bank, Postal Savings Bank, and Consignments and Loans Fund.

The Athens Stock Exchange (Chrimatisterion) was founded by royal decree in 1876. In 1967, significant reforms were instituted, including more stringent listing requirements, bringing about a rapid increase in the number of listed securities. New legislation was introduced in 1988 to expand and liberalize its activities. The rule changes provided for the establishment of brokerage companies, thus breaking the traditional closed shop of individual brokers. In 1997, there were 53 brokerage houses and just 6 private brokers. Computerized trading was implemented in 1992, and there has since been a rapid evolution of the market. The aim is to secure total dematerialization of shares and allow brokers to screen-trade from their offices. A satellite trading floor was established in Thessaloniki in 1995. In 1996, Greek law was harmonized with the European Union financial services directive, and banks may now be directly represented on the floor of the exchange instead of having to establish subsidiary brokerage houses. The late 1990s witnessed a boom on the exchange. In 1998, the index rose 85%, while the first five months of 1999 saw a further jump of 43.7%. However, this expansion did not continue into the new millennium. Between 2002 and 2003, the index lost 33.1% of its value. As of 2004, a total of 340 companies were listed on the Athens Stock Exchange (ASE), which had a market capitalization of $125.242 billion that year. In 2004, the ASE rose 23.1% from the previous year to $2,786.2 billion. Over the course of 2011, ASE's general index fell 45%. Overall, the Athens Stock Exchange lost 42% of its value between 2000 and 2010. The valuations of Greece's biggest fell dramatically since the onset of the financial crisis in 2008–2009. Shares of the National Bank of Greece, for example, lost 93% of their value from 2006–2011.

34 INSURANCE

Most of Greece's large insurance companies are partly or wholly owned by banks. In addition, insurers are required to join several unions, trade groups, and insurance pools. Brokers in Greece also must be accepted by the Ministry of Trade. In Greece, the social security scheme and third-party automobile liability insurance are compulsory. In 2003, the direct premiums written were valued at $3.668 billion, of which non-life premiums accounted for $2.040 billion. Ethniki was the country's largest non-life and life insurer in 2003, with total gross earned non-life premiums (including personal accident and inwards reinsurance) and gross written life

Public Finance – Greece (2008)		
(In millions of euros, central government figures)		
Revenue and Grants	**91,587**	**100.0%**
Tax revenue	47,421	51.8%
Social contributions	31,899	34.8%
Grants	930	1.0%
Other revenue	11,336	12.4%
Expenditures	**113,286**	**100.0%**
General public services	18,105	16.0%
Defense	4,873	4.3%
Public order and safety	2,822	2.5%
Economic affairs	18,659	16.5%
Environmental protection	290	0.3%
Housing and community amenities	447	0.4%
Health	12,266	10.8%
Recreational, culture, and religion	613	0.5%
Education	7,471	6.6%
Social protection	47,740	42.1%

(…) data not available or not significant.

SOURCE: *Government Finance Statistics Yearbook 2010,* Washington, DC: International Monetary Fund, 2010.

insurance premiums valued at $361.2 million and $258.3 million, respectively. In 2009, there were 81 insrurance enterprises, down from 110 at the beginning of the decade. The top five held 65% of the life insurance and 35% of the nonlife insurance market. The direct premiums written were valued at $7.4 billion, of which non-life premiums accounted for $4 billion.

Insurance companies have begun to develop private pension schemes and corporate pension schemes. However, most occupational pension funds remain under state control because they are partially financed by state-enacted levies. Insurance companies have also been responsible for the recent explosion in unit trusts (mutual funds), from two in 1989 to 152 in December 1995, when there were more than $2 trillion (7.8% of GDP) under management.

35 PUBLIC FINANCE

In 2010, the budget of Greece included $114.5 billion in public revenue and $142.9 billion in public expenditures. The budget deficit amounted to 10.5% of GDP. Public debt was 144% of GDP, with $532.9 billion of the debt held by foreign entities.

The state budget includes ordinary revenues and expenditures and a special investment budget administered by the Ministry of Coordination. The public sector, which employs 15% of the workforce, has many more civil servants than required for a country the size of Greece. Public payrolls, liberal social security benefits, and loss-generating state-owned companies have all contributed to a government deficit. Recent austerity measures implemented to meet the criteria for European Monetary Union membership significantly lowered the budget shortfall.

36 TAXATION

The corporate income tax rate in Greece in 2011 was 25%, down from 29% in 2006 and 32% in 2005. For a company, capital gain in Greece is added to regular income and is taxable at the same rate as regular income for a company, other than in specific instances as defined in law. For individuals, the capital gain tax is 0%-20%. A sale of goodwill or sale of business as a whole is taxed at 20% for companies and individuals. For individuals, rental income is taxed at the standard rates. There are deductions of 10%-15% for maintenace, 15% for documented expenses, and a 10% deduction for depreciation.

As of 2011, individuals were taxed at a rate of 18%-45%. Exemptions are granted to taxpayers with specific types of income. Various deductions or tax credits can be applied to taxable income for medical and hospitalization expenses, social security taxes, interest payments on home loans, and donations to charitable organizations, with special deductions for families whose income is derived primarily from their own work on agricultural enterprises. The withholding tax is 15% on interest income from banks and 10% on interest income derived from treasury bills and corporate bonds. There is a 20% tax on royalty payments, but these are often reduced or eliminated in bilateral double-tax prevention treaties, of which Greece has concluded more than 35. Gift and inheritance taxes, property taxes on large estates having a certain value, real estate transfer taxes, and taxes on urban property and rural property are also levied.

The main indirect tax in Greece is its value-added tax (VAT) introduced in January 1987. Since 2010, the standard VAT rate has been 23%, up from 19% in 2005. There is a reduced rate of 13% that applies, in the main to food and medicines. The VAT rate for hotel accommodation, books and newspapers is 6.5%. In specific areas of Greece, there is a reduction on the above rate of VAT.

37 CUSTOMS AND DUTIES

The import tariff protects domestic products and provides a source of government revenue. Many Greek industries are not yet large enough or sufficiently modern to compete in price with foreign products, either in markets abroad or in Greece itself. As a full member of the EU since 1981, Greece eliminated its remaining tariffs and quotas on imports from EU nations by 1986 and aligned its own tariffs on imports from other countries with those of EU members. Greek exports to EU countries are tariff-free. Imports from non-EU countries are subject to the EU's common customs tariff. Most raw materials enter duty-free, while manufactured goods have rates between 5% and 7%. Textiles, electronics, and some food products have higher rates. Motor vehicles, yachts, and motorcycles are subject to special duties. In addition, Greece imposes an 8–19% value-added tax and special consumption taxes on alcohol and tobacco.

38 FOREIGN INVESTMENT

The government encourages foreign capital investment and protects foreign investors against compulsory appropriation of their assets in Greece. Incentives include reduced tax rates and increased depreciation rates.

Foreign direct investment (FDI) in Greece was a net inflow of $2.42 billion according to World Bank figures published in 2009. FDI represented 0.73% of GDP.

Total direct foreign investment (FDI) was estimated at $3.78 billion in 1995. From 1995 to 1997, FDI inflow averaged about $1 billion a year. In the wake of the Russian financial crisis of 1998, FDI inflow fell to $700 million in 1998 and to $567 million in 1999. FDI inflow in 2000 reached over $1 billion and grew to a record $1.56 billion in 2001. In 2002, FDI inflow fell nearly 90% to $50.3 million. For the period 1999 to 2002, FDI inflow averaged about $833 million.

Outward FDI flow was $542 million in 1999, over $2 billion in 2000, and $611 million in 2001. Outward FDI increased to $655.3 million in 2002. For the period 1999 to 2002, average outward FDI from Greece was $993.3 billion.

From 2001–05, FDI inflows averaged 0.6% of GDP. The corporate tax rate was being cut from 35% to 32% on income earned in 2005, to 29% on income earned in 2006, and to 25% on income earned in 2007. Value-added tax (VAT) is levied at 19%, 8%, and 4.5%. Although there is no official estimate of total foreign investment in Greece, as of 2002, the total stock of FDI was estimated at $6 billion, or approximately 4.3% of GDP. Greece's investment abroad is directed primarily to the Balkans. Greek direct investment in the Balkans was estimated at $3.6 billion in 2002.

39 ECONOMIC DEVELOPMENT

Until the mid-1970s, Greek governments devoted themselves principally to expanding agricultural and industrial production, controlling prices and inflation, improving state finances, developing natural resources, and creating basic industries. In 1975, the Karamanlis government undertook a series of austerity measures designed to curb inflation and redress the balance-of-payments deficit. A new energy program included plans to expand exploitation of oil and lignite reserves, along with uranium exploration in northern Greece. Increased efforts at import substitution were to be undertaken in all sectors. On 7 March 1975, in an effort to strengthen confidence in the national currency, the government announced that the value of the drachma would no longer be quoted in terms of a fixed link with the US dollar but would be based on daily averages taken from the currencies of Greece's main trade partners.

The Socialist government that took office in 1981 promised more equal distribution of income and wealth through "democratic planning" and measures to control inflation and increase productivity. It imposed controls on prices and credit and began to restructure public corporations. But the government was cautious in introducing what it called "social control in certain key sectors" of the economy, and it ordered detailed studies to be made first. Its development policies emphasized balanced regional growth and technological modernization, especially in agriculture. The conservative government that came to power in 1990 adopted a 1991–93 "adjustment program" that called for reduction of price and wage increases and a reduction in the public-sector deficit from 13% to 3% of GDP. Twenty-eight industrial companies were to be privatized.

The chief goal of the Simitis government was admission to the European Monetary Union (EMU). As a consequence, his government instituted an austerity program aimed at tackling chronically high inflation, unemployment, and a bloated public sector. By 1998–99, these policies showed significant progress. Greece gained admission to the EMU in 2001 and adopted the euro as its new currency in 2002. Greece has been benefitting from EU aid, equal to about 3.3% of GDP. The Greek economy was growing at rates above EU averages from 2002–05; however, unemployment and inflation rates were still higher than those in most euro-area countries. In 2004, Greece's general government debt stood at approximately 112% of GDP. By 2011, it had exceeded 140% of GDP. The 2009–2011 financial crisis raised serious doubts as to Greece's future in the Eurozone. The success of the 2011 EU-IMF financial bailout plan was said to depend on major structural reforms and on Greece's ability to boost tax revenues and cut spending in the face of public discontent and global recession.

Privatization of state-owned enterprises has moved at a relatively slow pace, especially in the telecommunications, banking, aerospace, and energy sectors. In 2003, preparations for the 2004 Olympics drove investment, but spending on the Olympic Games contributed to a general government deficit of 6.6% of GDP in 2004. With the aid of EU grants, Greece will need to update its infrastructure, especially in the northern regions and on the islands. Improvements in road, rail, harbor, and airport links financed through the EU's Community Support Framework (CSF) programs have contributed to economic decentralization. In 2005, Greece liberalized the telecommunications market. Since then, the state-owned monopoly OTE, which controlled 76% of the market share in fixed telephony, has been losing market share to competing telecom operators.

40 SOCIAL DEVELOPMENT

The Social Insurance Foundation, the national social security system, is supported by contributions from employees, employers, and the government. It provides for old age, disability and survivorship. Work injury and unemployment benefits are also provided. Sickness and maternity benefits have been in place since 1922. Current benefits include medical care, hospitalization, medicine, maternity care, dental coverage, appliances, and transportation. Payments also include birth and funeral grants.

Although the law mandates equal pay for equal work, according to statistics in 2007 women's pay amounted to 84% of that of their male counterparts. Still, this number was up from 75.5% in 2004. Domestic violence and rape remain underreported, and the number of prosecutions and convictions is low. Women are beginning to enter traditionally male-oriented careers such as law and medicine but make up only 42.5% of the work force. Sexual harassment is specifically prohibited by law. There were three women In George Papandreou's 17-member cabinet (2009–2011) and 51 women in the 300-seat parliament. A quota system requires 30 percent of all local government candidates to be women. At the three highest courts, 14 of 61 Council of State justices, 28 of 59 Supreme Administrative Court justices, and 3 of 62 Supreme Court justices were women.

Occasional human rights abuses, involving residents, illegal aliens and persons in custody, have been reported. Government measures to improve prison conditions continue. The constitution prohibits discrimination on the basis of nationality, race, language, religion, or political beliefs; however, in practice the government does not always protect these rights. There have been repeated reports of physical abuse by the authorities of immigrants and asylum seekers. In 2010, Human Rights Watch reported on the deplorable conditions and inhumane treatment of undocumented migrants in detention centers in northern Greece.

The constitution and law generally provide for freedom of speech and of the press, and the government generally respected these rights in practice. However, the law prohibits speech that endangers the country's foreign relations; spreads false information or rumors causing fear, rivalry, or division among citizens; or incites citizens to disturb the peace or commit acts of violence. In practice these legal prohibitions are seldom invoked. In most criminal defamation cases, defendants are released on bail pending trial without serving time in jail. Individuals can criticize the government publicly or privately without reprisal, and the government does not impede criticism.

41 HEALTH

According to the CIA, life expectancy in Greece was 80 years in 2011. The country spent 10.1% of its GDP on healthcare, amounting to $3,041 per person. There were 60 physicians, 37 nurses and midwives, and 48 hospital beds per 10,000 inhabitants. The fertility rate was 1.5, while the infant mortality rate was 3 per 1,000 live births. In 2008, the maternal mortality rate, according to the World Bank, was 2 per 100,000 births. It was estimated that 99% of children were vaccinated against measles. The CIA calculated HIV/AIDS prevalence in Greece to be about 0.1% in 2009.

Since World War II, the government has broadened health services by building new hospitals and providing more clinics and medical personnel. Total healthcare expenditure was estimated at 7.9% of GDP. As of 2007 there were an estimated 438 physicians per 100,000 people. In addition, there were an estimated 386 nurses and 113 dentists per 100,000 people. Pulmonary tuberculosis, dysentery, and malaria, which were once endemic, have been controlled. Nearly 100% of the population has access to safe water. In 2011, the infant mortality rate was 5 deaths per 1,000 live births. The total fertility rate in 2011 was 1.38. The birth rate decline since World War II has been attributed to the legalization of abortion. In 2011, life expectancy averaged 79.92 years.

In 2007, 88% of children up to one year old were immunized against diphtheria, pertussis, and tetanus. The maternal mortality rate was estimated at 10 per 100,000 live births.

The HIV/AIDS adult prevalence rate was 0.1%; in 2009. The incidence of tuberculosis was 19 per 100,000 people in 2007.

42 HOUSING

Construction of new dwellings (including repairs and extensions) reached 88,477 units in 1985 and rose to 120,240 in 1990. Most new construction is in Athens or Thessaloniki, indicating the emphasis on urban development. Considerable amounts of private investment have been spent on the construction of apartment houses in urban areas. In 2001, the total number of dwelling units was 5,476,162. About 47.9% of all dwelling units are owner occupied. About 40% of all dwellings are single-household homes.

43 EDUCATION

In 2007 the World Bank estimated that 99% of age-eligible children in Greece were enrolled in primary school. Secondary enrollment for age-eligible children stood at 91%. Tertiary enrollment was estimated at 91%. Overall, the CIA estimated that Greece had a literacy rate of 96%.

Education is free and compulsory for nine years beginning at age six, and primary education lasts for six years. Secondary education is comprised of two steps: first, three years, followed by an additional three years of college preparation. At the upper-secondary levels, students may choose to attend a three-year vocational school. The central and local governments pay the cost of state schools, and private schools are state-regulated. The academic year runs from September to June. Greek is the primary language of instruction.

In July 1982, the Socialist government initiated a program to democratize the higher-education system; a law was approved that diminished the power of individual professors by establishing American-style departments with integrated faculties. Junior faculty members and representatives of the student body were granted roles in academic decision-making. The legislation also curbed university autonomy by establishing the National University Council to advise the government on higher-education planning and the Academy of Letters and Sciences to set and implement university standards.

Greece has six major universities: Athens, Salonika, Thrace, Ioánnina, Crete, and Pátrai, together with the National Technical University of Athens, the new University of the Aegean, and the Technical University of Crete, plus seven special institutions of higher education. There are several technological educational institutions, which offer nondegree programs of higher education. Private universities are constitutionally banned.

44 LIBRARIES AND MUSEUMS

The National Library traces its origins to 1828, when it was established on the island of Aíyina; the library was moved to its present site in Athens in 1903 and today has more than 2.5 million volumes. Both the National Library and the Library of Parliament (1.5 million volumes) act as legal depositories for Greek publications and are open to the public. Public libraries are located mainly in provincial capitals, and there are regional libraries with bookmobile services for rural areas.

Besides the libraries attached to the universities and other educational institutions, there are several specialized research libraries located in Athens. Outstanding special collections can be found at the Democritus Nuclear Research Center (91,000 volumes), the Center of Planning and Economic Research (30,000 volumes), the Athens Center of Ekistics (30,000 volumes), and the Gennadius Library (80,000 volumes), which houses a large collection on modern Greek history. Being at the crossroads of different civilizations and an important European country, there are several libraries attached to various cultural and ethnic studies centers. Notable among these are the libraries of the Institute for Balkan Studies in Thessaloniki, the British Council, the Society for Byzantine Studies in Athens, and the Center for Asia Minor Studies in Athens.

Most museums are devoted to antiquities and archaeology. One of the richest collections of Greek sculpture and antiquities is found at the National Archaeological Museum in Athens, which is also home to the Byzantine and Christian Museum, Benaki Museum, and Kanellopoulos Museum. The most impressive archaeological remains, of course, are the great temples and palaces at Athens (particularly the Parthenon and the Stoa of Attalos), Corinth, Salonika, Delphi, Olympia, Mycenae, the island of Delos, and Knossos, on Crete. There are also notable museums dedicated to the work of other cultures, including the Byzantine Museum and the Jewish Museum, both in Athens. Among the newer facilities are the Hellenic Children's Museum (1987), the Museum of Greek Popular Musical Instruments (1991), the Museum of Del-

phic Celebrations of Angelos and Eva Sikelianou (1991), the Nikolaos Parantinos Museum of Sculpture (1991), and the Maria Callas Museum (2003) all located in Athens.

45 MEDIA

In 2009, the CIA reported that there were 5.9 million telephone landlines in Greece. In addition to landlines, mobile phone subscriptions averaged 118 per 100 people. There were 26 FM radio stations, 88 AM radio stations, and 4 shortwave radio stations. Internet users numbered 44 per 100 citizens. Prominent newspapers in 2010, with circulation numbers listed parenthetically, included To Vima (250,000), Apoyevmatini (72,904), and Estia (60,000), as well as 76 other major newspapers.

The Greek Telecommunications Authority operates domestic telegraph and telephone communications. In general, the country's telecommunications system is adequate, with modern networks reaching all parts of Greece. International and mobile telephone service quality is good. In 2009, there were some 5.9 million main phone lines and 13.2 million mobile cellular phones in use.

Radio Athens broadcasts are carried by provincial relay stations located in various parts of the country; other stations are operated by the Greek armed forces and by the Hellenic National Radio and Television Institute. There are numerous independent radio and television stations. In 2003, there were an estimated 466 radios and 519 television sets for every 1,000 people. In 2010, the country had 2.5 million Internet hosts. As of 2009, there were some 4.9 million Internet users in Greece.

In 2010, there were 82 newspapers with national circulation in Greece. Sunday newspapers took the lead with 56.2 percent of annual sales. Evening and weekly newspapers shared the second place (11.9 percent and 11.4 percent respectively), followed by sports newspapers (7.7 percent), daily (5.5 percent), and financial (0.09 percent) newspapers. Among the morning daily newspapers, the market leaders were Kathimerini with 47,682 copies, and To Vima with 44,144 copies. The most popular evening newspapers were Ta Nea with 55,014 copies, followed by Eleftherotypia (40,848 copies) and Ethnos (39,843copies). In the Sunday market, Proto Thema and To Vima tis Kyriakis shared the majority of the Sunday readers (189,389 copies for To Proto Thema and 187,664 copies for To Vima tis Kyriakis), followed by Kyriakatiki Eleftherotypia (153,085 copies).

The constitution provides for freedom of speech and press, and, with a few exceptions, the government is said to respect these rights. On matters involving the politically sensitive subject of the recognition of certain ethnic minorities, it is reported that the government is restrictive. The constitution also allows for seizure of publications that insult the president, offend religious beliefs, contain obscene articles, advocate violent overthrow of the political system, or disclose military and defense information. However, such action is very rare.

46 ORGANIZATIONS

Most of the larger cities and towns have associations of commerce, industry, handicrafts, and finance. There are some consumers' and producers' cooperatives; chambers of commerce and industry function in Athens, Piraiévs, and Salonika. There are professional and trade organizations for a variety of occupations and industries, such as the Association of Greek Honey Processors and

Exporters, the Greek Association of Industries and Processors of Olive Oil, and the Pan-Hellenic Association of Meat-Processing Industries. The Federation of Greek Industries draws together many of these business and manufacturing organizations

The Academy of Athens serves to promote public interest in science and works to improve availability and effectiveness in science education programs. Artists, writers, musicians, educators, and journalists are organized into professional associations. Scholarly societies include those devoted to archaeology, anthropology, geography, history, political science, and sociology. Several professional associations also promote research and education in their fields.

National youth organizations in Greece include the Greek Democratic Socialist Youth, Girl Guides and Girl Scouts of Greece, the Association of Boy Scouts, YMCA/YWCA, the Greek Youth Federation, the Radical Left Youth, and the Student and Scientist Christian Association of Greece. There are several sports organization in Greece, including the historical societies of the Hellenic Federation of Ancient Olympic Games and the International Society of Olympic Historians. The World Chess Federation is based in Athens.

There are national chapters of the Red Cross Society, Caritas, and Amnesty International.

47 TOURISM, TRAVEL, AND RECREATION

The *Tourism Factbook*, published by the UN World Tourism Organization, reported 14.9 million incoming tourists to Greece in 2009 who spent a total of $14.8 billion. Of those incoming tourists, there were 13,884 from Europe. There were 732,279 hotel beds available in Greece, which had an occupancy rate of 51%. The estimated daily cost to visit Athens, the capital, was $352. The cost of visiting other cities averaged $351.

Principal tourist sites, in addition to the world-famous Parthenon and Acropolis in Athens, include Mt. Olympus (the home of the gods in ancient mythology), the site of the ancient oracle at Delphi, the Agora at Corinth, the natural spring at the rock of the Acropolis, and the Minoan ruins on Crete. Operas, concerts, ballet performances, and ancient Greek dramas are presented at the Athens Festival each year from July to September; during July and August, Greek classics also are performed in the open-air theater at Epidaurus, 40 km (25 mi) east of Árgos. Popular sports include swimming at the many beaches, sailing, water-skiing, fishing, golf, and mountain climbing.

The Greek government encourages tourists and facilitates their entry and accommodation. A passport is needed for admission; residents of the United States, Australia, Canada, and 37 other countries do not require visas for stays of up to 90 days.

48 FAMOUS PERSONS

The origins of Western literature and of the main branches of Western learning may be traced to the era of Greek greatness that began before 700 BC with the epics of Homer (possibly born in Asia Minor), the *Iliad* and the *Odyssey*. Hesiod (fl. 700 BC), the first didactic poet, put into epic verse his descriptions of pastoral life, including practical advice on farming, and allegorical myths. The poets Alcaeus (620?–580? BC), Sappho (612?–580? BC), Anacreon (582?–485? BC), and Bacchylides (fl.5th cent. BC) wrote of love, war, and death in lyrics of great feeling and beauty. Pin-

dar (522?–438? BC) celebrated the Panhellenic athletic festivals in vivid odes. The fables of the slave Aesop (b. Asia Minor, 620?–560? BC) have been famous for more than 2,500 years. Three of the world's greatest dramatists were Aeschylus (525–456 BC), author of the *Oresteia* trilogy; Sophocles (496?–406? BC), author of the Theban plays; and Euripides (485?–406? BC), author of *Medea, The Trojan Women,* and *The Bacchae.* Aristophanes (450?–385? BC), the greatest author of comedies, satirized the mores of his day in a series of brilliant plays. Three great historians were Herodotus (b. Asia Minor, 484?–420? BC), regarded as the father of history, known for *The Persian Wars*; Thucydides (460?–400? BC), who generally avoided myth and legend and applied greater standards of historical accuracy in his *History of the Peloponnesian War*; and Xenophon (428?–354? BC), best known for his account of the Greek retreat from Persia, the *Anabasis.* Outstanding literary figures of the Hellenistic period were Menander (342–290? BC), the chief representative of a newer type of comedy; the poets Callimachus (b.Libya, 305?–240? BC), Theocritus (b.Italy, 310?–250? BC), and Apollonius Rhodius (fl. 3rd cent. BC), author of the *Argonautica*; and Polybius (200?–118? BC), who wrote a detailed history of the Mediterranean world. Noteworthy in the Roman period were Strabo (b. Asia Minor, 64? BC-ad 24?), a writer on geography; Plutarch (AD 46?–120?), the father of biography, whose *Parallel Lives* of famous Greeks and Romans is a chief source of information about great figures of antiquity; Pausanias (b. Asia Minor, fl. AD 150), a travel writer; and Lucian (AD 120?–180?), a satirist.

The leading philosophers of the period preceding Greece's golden age were Thales (b. Asia Minor, 625?–547? BC), Pythagoras (570?–500? BC), Heraclitus (b. Asia Minor, 540?–480? BC), Protagoras (485?–410? BC), and Democritus (460?–370? BC). Socrates (469?–399 BC) investigated ethics and politics. His greatest pupil, Plato (429?–347 BC), used Socrates' question-and-answer method of investigating philosophical problems in his famous dialogues. Plato's pupil Aristotle (384–322 BC) established the rules of deductive reasoning but also used observation and inductive reasoning, applying himself to the systematic study of almost every form of human endeavor. Outstanding in the Hellenistic period were Epicurus (341?–270 BC), the philosopher of moderation; Zeno (b. Cyprus, 335?–263? BC), the founder of Stoicism; and Diogenes (b. Asia Minor, 412?–323 BC), the famous Cynic. The oath of Hippocrates (460?–377 BC), the father of medicine, is still recited by newly graduating physicians. Euclid (fl. 300 BC) evolved the system of geometry that bears his name. Archimedes (287?–212 BC) discovered the principles of mechanics and hydrostatics. Eratosthenes (275?–194? BC) calculated the earth's circumference with remarkable accuracy, and Hipparchus (190?–125? BC) founded scientific astronomy. Galen (AD 129?–199?) was an outstanding physician of ancient times.

The sculptor Phidias (490?–430? BC) created the statue of Athena and the figure of Zeus in the temple at Olympia and supervised the construction and decoration of the Parthenon. Another renowned sculptor was Praxiteles (390?–330? BC).

The legal reforms of Solon (638?–559? BC) served as the basis of Athenian democracy. The Athenian general Miltiades (554?–489? BC) led the victory over the Persians at Marathon in 490 BC, and Themistocles (528?–460? BC) was chiefly responsible for the victory at Salamis 10 years later. Pericles (495?–429? BC), the virtual ruler of Athens for more than 25 years, added to the political power of that city, inaugurated the construction of the Parthenon and other noteworthy buildings, and encouraged the arts of sculpture and painting. With the decline of Athens, first Sparta and then Thebes, under the great military tactician Epaminondas (418?–362 BC), gained the ascendancy; but soon thereafter, two military geniuses, Philip II of Macedon (382–336 BC) and his son Alexander the Great (356–323 BC), gained control over all of Greece and formed a vast empire stretching as far east as India. It was against Philip that Demosthenes (384–322 BC), the greatest Greek orator, directed his diatribes, the *Philippics*.

The most renowned Greek painter during the Renaissance was El Greco (Domenikos Theotokopoulos, 1541–1614), born in Crete, whose major works, painted in Spain, have influenced many 20th-century artists. An outstanding modern literary figure is Nikos Kazantzakis (1883–1957), a novelist and poet who composed a vast sequel to Homer's *Odyssey*. Leading modern poets are Kostes Palamas (1859–1943), Georgios Drosines (1859–1951), and Constantine Cavafy (1868–1933), as well as George Seferis (Seferiades, 1900–72), and Odysseus Elytis (Alepoudhelis, 1911–96), winners of the Nobel Prize for literature in 1963 and 1979, respectively. The work of social theorist Cornelius Castoriadis (1922–97) is known for its multidisciplinary breadth. Musicians of stature are the composers Nikos Skalkottas (1904–49), Iannis Xenakis (b. Romania, 1922–2001), and Mikis Theodorakis (b. 1925); the conductor Dmitri Mitropoulos (1896–1960); and the soprano Maria Callas (Calogeropoulos, b. United States, 1923–77). Filmmakers who have won international acclaim are Greek-Americans John Cassavetes (1929–89) and Elia Kazan (1909–2003), and Greeks Michael Cacoyannis (b. 1922) and Constantin Costa-Gavras (b. 1933). Actresses of note are Katina Paxinou (1900–73); Melina Mercouri (1925–94), who was appointed minister of culture and science in the Socialist cabinet in 1981; and Irene Papas (Lelekou, b. 1926).

Outstanding Greek public figures in the 20th century include Cretan-born Eleutherios Venizelos (1864–1936), prominent statesman of the interwar period; Ioannis Metaxas (1871–1941), dictator from 1936 until his death; Constantine Karamanlis (1907–98), prime minister (1955–63, 1974–80) and president (1980–85) of Greece; George Papandreou (1888–1968), head of the Center Union Party and prime minister (1963–65); and his son Andreas Papandreou (1919–96), the PASOK leader who became prime minister in 1981. Costas Simitis (b. 1936) was leader of PASOK and prime minister from 1996–2004. He was succeeded by Kóstas Karamanlís (b. 1956).

⁴⁹DEPENDENCIES

Greece has no territories or colonies.

⁵⁰BIBLIOGRAPHY

Brown, John Pairman. *Ancient Israel and Ancient Greece: Religion, Politics, and Culture.* Minneapolis: Fortress Press, 2003.

Camp, John M. *The World of the Ancient Greeks.* London: Thames and Hudson, 2002.

Cosmopoulos, Michael B., ed. *The Parthenon and Its Sculptures.* New York: Cambridge University Press, 2004.

Darling, Janina K. *Architecture of Greece.* Westport, CT: Greenwood Press, 2004.

Frucht, Richard, ed. *Eastern Europe: An Introduction to the People, Lands, and Culture.* Santa Barbara, CA: ABC-CLIO, 2005.

Greece Investment and Business Guide: Strategic and Practical Information. Washington, DC: International Business Publications USA, 2012.

Green, Sarah F. *Notes From the Balkans: Locating Marginality and Ambiguity on the Greek-Albanian Border.* Princeton, NJ: Princeton University Press, 2005.

Greene, Ellen, ed. *Women Poets in Ancient Greece and Rome.* Norman: University of Oklahoma Press, 2005.

Halkias, Alexandra. *Empty Cradle of Democracy: Sex, Abortion, and Nationalism in Modern Greece.* Durham: Duke University Press, 2004.

Hazel, John. *Who's Who in the Greek World.* New York: Routledge, 2000.

International Smoking Statistics: A Collection of Historical Data From 30 Economically Developed Countries. New York: Oxford University Press, 2002.

Leontis, Artemis. *Culture and Customs of Greece.* Westport, CT: Greenwood Press, 2009.

Morris, Ian. *The Greeks: History, Culture, and Society.* Upper Saddle River, NJ: Pearson Prentice Hall, 2006.

Opello, Walter C. *European Politics.* Boulder, CO: Lynne Rienner Publishers, 2009.

Sheehan, Sean. *Illustrated Encyclopedia of Ancient Greece.* Los Angeles, CA: The J. Paul Getty Museum, 2002.

Speake, Graham, ed. *Encyclopedia of Greece and the Hellenic Tradition.* Chicago: Fitzroy Dearborn, 2000.

Wessels, Wolfgang, Andreas Maurer, and Jürgan Mittag, eds. *Fifteen Into One?: The European Union and Its Member States.* New York: Palgrave, 2003.

HUNGARY

Republic of Hungary
Magyar Népköztársaság

CAPITAL: Budapest

FLAG: The national flag, adopted in 1957, is a tricolor of red, white, and green horizontal stripes.

ANTHEM: *Isten áldd meg a magyart (God Bless the Hungarians).*

MONETARY UNIT: The forint (HUF) is a paper currency with flexible rates of exchange. It consists of 100 fillérs, although the fillér is no longer in circulation. There are coins of 5, 10, 20, 100, and 200 forints, and notes of 200, 500, 1,000, 2,000, 5,000, 10,000, and 20,000 forints. HUF1 = US$0.00480 (or US$1 = HUF208.15) average for 2010.

WEIGHTS AND MEASURES: The metric system is the legal standard.

HOLIDAYS: New Year's Day, 1 January; Anniversary of 1848 uprising against Austrian rule, 15 March; Labor Day, 1 May; St. Stephen's Day—Founder of the Nation, 20 August; Day of the Proclamation of the Republic, 23 October; Christmas, 25–26 December. Easter Monday is a movable holiday.

TIME: 1 p.m. = noon GMT.

¹LOCATION, SIZE, AND EXTENT

Hungary is a landlocked country in the Carpathian Basin of Central Europe, with an area of 93,030 sq km (35,919 sq mi), extending 268 km (167 mi) N–S and 528 km (328 mi) E–W. Comparatively, Hungary is slightly smaller than Indiana. It is bounded on the N by Slovakia, on the NE by the Ukraine, on the E by Romania, on the S by Serbia and Croatia, on the SW by Slovenia, and on the W by Austria, with a total boundary length of 2,185 km (1,358 mi). Hungary's capital city, Budapest, is located in the north central part of the country.

²TOPOGRAPHY

About 84% of Hungary is below 200 m (656 ft) in altitude; its lowest point, at the Tisza River, is 78 m (256 ft) above sea level, and the highest is Mt. Kékes (1,014 m/3,327 ft) in the Mátra Mountains, northeast of Budapest. The country has four chief geographic regions: Transdanubia (*Dunántúl*), the Great Plain (*Alföld*), the Little Plain (*Kisalföld*), and the Northern Mountains. Hungary's river valleys and its highest mountains are in the northeast. Generally, the soil is fertile. The chief rivers are the Danube (*Duna*) and Tisza. The largest lake is Balaton, which has an area of 601 sq km (232 sq mi).

³CLIMATE

Hungary lies at the meeting point of three climatic zones: the continental, Mediterranean, and oceanic. Yearly temperatures vary from a minimum of -14°C (7°F) to a maximum of 36°C (97°F). The mean temperature in January is -4°C to 0°C (25° to 32°F) and in July 18° to 23°C (64° to 73°F). Rainfall varies, but the annual average is approximately 63 cm (25 in)—more in the west and less in the east—with maximum rainfall during the summer months. Severe droughts often occur in the summers.

⁴FLORA AND FAUNA

Plants and animals are those common to Central Europe. The World Resources Institute estimates that there are 2,214 plant species in Hungary. Oak is the predominant deciduous tree; various conifers are located in the mountains. In addition, Hungary is home to 88 mammal, 367 bird, 18 reptile, and 17 amphibian species. The calculation reflects the total number of distinct species residing in the country, not the number of endemic species. Among the abundant wildlife are deer, boar, hare, and mouflon. The Great Plain is a breeding ground and a migration center for a variety of birds. Fish are plentiful in rivers and lakes.

⁵ENVIRONMENT

In 1992, Hungary was one of 50 nations to lead the world in industrial carbon dioxide emissions, with a total of 59.9 million metric tons, a per capita level of 5.72 metric tons. However, the United Nations (UN) reported that the total carbon dioxide emissions dropped to 56.426 million metric tons by 2008. Hungary's principal environmental agency is the National Council for Environment and Nature Conservation, under the auspices of the Council of Ministers.

Water resources totaled 120 cu km (28.79 cu mi) while water usage was 21.03 cu km (5.05 cu mi) per year. Domestic water usage accounted for 9% of total usage, industrial for 59%, and agricultural for 32%. Per capita water usage totaled 2,082 cu m (73,525 cu ft) per year. Geothermal aquifers lie below most of Hungary. The water brought from these to the earth's surface ranges in temperature from 40°C (104°F) to 70°C (158°F). In the southwest, geothermal aquifers have produced water at 140°C (284°F). Some of these waters are cooled and used for drinking water, but many aquifers are used to heat greenhouses.

The World Resources Institute reported that Hungary had designated 521,300 hectares (1.29 million acres) of land for protection as of 2006.

According to a 2011 report issued by the International Union for Conservation of Nature and Natural Resources (IUCN), threatened species included 2 types of mammals, 8 species of birds, 1 type of reptile, 9 species of fish, 7 types of mollusks, 25 species of other invertebrates, and 9 species of plants. Endangered species included the longicorn, the alcon large blue butterfly, the dusky large blue butterfly, and the Mediterranean mouflon.

On 4 October 2010, a break in the wall surrounding a waste reservoir at the Ajkai Timföldgyár alumina plant in the town of Ajka led to a major spill of hazardous sludge that flooded streets and homes, causing at least eight deaths and more than 150 injuries. A state of emergency was declared in three adjacent western counties as the sludge made its way toward major waterways including the Marcal, Torna, Raba, and Danube Rivers. Police and military troops were deployed to assist in rescues and evacuations and to initiate measures to keep the sludge from further contaminating major water supplies. However, despite immediate efforts, the sludge poured into the Marcal, a major tributary of the Danube. By 7 October, officials reported that all life in the Marcal had been "extinguished." The sludge reached the Danube by that date, but reports indicated that the level of contamination was still within an acceptable range. The sludge mixture contained water and mining waste, which includes a number of heavy metals. On 11 October, the CEO of MAL Hungarian Aluminum was arrested amid allegations of negligence. The government announced that the plant would be brought under state control until the spill is cleaned up, the damage repaired, and those who have been affected fairly compensated.

6 POPULATION

The US Central Intelligence Agency (CIA) estimates the population of Hungary in 2011 to be approximately 9,976,062, which placed it at number 84 in population among the 196 nations of the world. In 2011, approximately 16.9% of the population was over 65 years of age, with another 14.9% under 15 years of age. The median age in Hungary was 40.2 years. There were 0.91 males for every female in the country. The population's annual rate of change was -0.17%. The projected population for the year 2025 was 9,800,000. Population density in Hungary was calculated at 107 people per sq km (278 people per sq mi).

The UN estimated that 68% of the population lived in urban area and that urban populations had an annual rate of change of 0.3%. The largest urban area was Budapest, with a population of 1.7 million.

7 MIGRATION

Estimates of Hungary's net migration rate, carried out by the CIA in 2011, amounted to 1.39 migrants per 1,000 citizens. The total number of emigrants living abroad was 462,700, and the total number of immigrants living in Hungary was 368,100.Sizable migration during the two world wars resulted from military operations, territorial changes, and population transfers. Peacetime emigration in the decades before World War I was heavy (about 1,400,000 between 1899 and 1913). Emigration of non-Magyars was prompted by the repressive policy of Magyarization; groups also left because of economic pressures, the majority going to the United States and Canada. In the interwar period, migration was negligible, but, after 1947, many thousands left, despite restrictions on emigration. As a result of the October 1956 uprising, approximately 250,000 persons fled Hungary. The largest numbers ultimately emigrated to the United States, Canada, the United Kingdom, Germany, France, Switzerland, and Australia. Emigration totaled 42,700 between 1981 and 1989. By the 1990s, emigration was virtually nonexistent; only 778 persons left in 1991, according to official statistics.

Between 1990 and 2003, some 115,000 immigrants acquired Hungarian citizenship, granted almost exclusively to ethnic Hungarians from neighboring countries. At the end of 2000, 3% of Hungary's population (294,000) was foreign-born, resulting from international migration, and as a consequence of historic events such as border changes or citizenship agreements. According to *Migration Information Source*, from 1990 to 2003, the border guards recorded 152,000 cases of foreigners attempting to enter illegally and 80,000 efforts to leave Hungary illegally. These activities indicate Hungary's transit role in illegal migration.

Since 1960, net migration from the villages to the cities has decreased, from about 52,000 that year to 20,814 in 1986. Since 1989, Hungary has received nearly 155,000 refugees, with major influxes from Romania in 1988–89 and the former Yugoslavia in 1991–92. About 5,400 asylum seekers have been recognized as refugees since 1989. In the 1990s, Hungary provided temporary protection for over 32,000 Bosnians. Most of these refugees resettled to another country or repatriated. The Temporary Protection status of some 480 Bosnian refugees, who remained in Hungary in the latter part of the 1990s, was withdrawn by the government in mid-1999. As a result of the Kosovo crisis, 2,800 Yugoslav asylum seekers arrived in Hungary, including 1,000 Kosovo Albanians. The organized voluntary repatriation of refugees began in August 1999, when the first 185 Kosovars returned to their homeland.

As a member of the European Union (EU) since 1 May 2004, Hungary's migration and illegal migration border controls have tightened. Changing waves of labor migration are also characterized by a new form of labor migration within the EU, termed "walk-over-the-border for employment," where workers seeking higher wages travel from one country to a neighboring one, such as from Slovakia to Hungary.

On 31 May 2010, Hungarian president Laszlo Solyom signed into law a bill that streamlined the citizenship process for ethnic Hungarians who do not reside in the country. The law, which analysts said was targeted at the roughly 2.6 million ethnic Hungarians who live in the countries surrounding Hungary, granted citizenship on a case-by-case basis to applicants who could prove their knowledge of the Hungarian language. The move immediately angered Slovakia, a nation in which 10% of the population is ethnically Hungarian. Other neighboring nations, such as Romania, Serbia, Ukraine, Austria, Croatia, and Slovenia, also have sizable ethnically Hungarian populations. This "proximate diaspora" can largely be attributed to the 1920 Treaty of Trianon, which cut off nearly two thirds of the land previously controlled by Hungary and left many ethnic Hungarians outside their homeland.

LOCATION: 45°48′ to 48°35′N; 16°5′ to 22°58′ E. BOUNDARY LENGTHS: Slovakia, 515 kilometers (320 miles); Ukraine, 103 kilometers (64 miles); Romania, 443 kilometers (275 miles); Serbia, 166 kilometers (103 miles); Croatia, 329 kilometers (204 miles); Slovenia, 102 kilometers (63 miles); Austria, 366 kilometers (227 miles).

8 ETHNIC GROUPS

Ethnically, Hungary is essentially a homogeneous state of Magyar extraction. The 2001 census indicates that Hungarians constitute about 92.3% of the total population. Roma account for about 1.9%. Ethnic Germans make up about 0.7% of the population. There are also small groups of Croats, Poles, Ukrainians, Greeks, Serbs, Slovenes, Armenians, Ruthenians, Bulgarians, Slovaks, and Romanians. The ethnic Roma (Gypsies) have been the target of discrimination for much of their history. While government estimates place the number of Roma at about 200,000, or 1.9% of the total population, unofficial estimates place the number between 500,000 and 800,000, since many Roma are afraid to publicly identify their heritage.

The Roma have suffered discrimination and marginalization in gaining adequate employment, housing, and education, and generally have had difficulties in obtaining health care and other social services. In some instances, Roma are denied access to public places, such as restaurants. In 2009, there were reports of a number of violent attacks and murders involving Roma victims. As the nation's economy faltered following the 2008–09 global economic crisis, Roma were increasingly stereotyped as petty criminals who also tax the limits of the welfare system. Some extreme right-wing Hungarian political leaders were criticized for using the Roma as scapegoats for the country's economic woes to gain support in elections.

9 LANGUAGES

Hungarian, also known as Magyar, is the universal language. In addition to the letters of the English alphabet, it has the following letters and combinations: á, é, í, ó, ö, ő, ú, ü, ű, cs, dz, dzs, gy, ly, ny, sz, ty, zs. Written in Latin characters, Hungarian (Magyar) belongs to the Finno-Ugric family, a branch of the Ural-Altaic language group. Hungarian (Magyar) is also characterized by an admixture of Turkish, Slavic, German, Latin, and French words. In addition to their native language, many Hungarians speak English, German, French, or (since World War II) Russian. In 2002, 98.2% of the population spoke Hungarian; 1.8% spoke various other languages.

¹⁰RELIGIONS

While the government does not officially record information on religious membership, according to a 2001 census (containing an optional question on religion), approximately 55% of the people are nominally Catholic (51.4% Roman Catholic, 2.6% Greek Catholic), 15% are members of the Calvinist Hungarian Reformed Church, 3% of the population are Lutheran, and less than 1% are Jewish. About 3% of the population describe themselves as Greek Catholics. About 15% of the population claims no religious affiliation. About one million Jews lived in Hungary before World War II, and an estimated 600,000 were deported in 1944 to concentration camps. A 2010 report places the number of Jews currently residing in Hungary between 80,000 and 100,000. Buddhism, Islam, and Orthodox Christian denominations are also represented. Freedom of religion is guaranteed by the constitution, and this right is generally respected in practice. A 1990 Law on the Freedom of Conscience provides for separation of church and state and safeguards the liberty of conscience of all citizens and the freedom of religious worship. However, the state does grant financial support to the four historical religious groups (Roman Catholics, Hungarian Reformed, Lutherans, and Jews) for religious practice, educational work, and maintenance of public collections. Other registered religious groups may qualify for smaller amounts of government funding. Registration is not mandatory but offers some legal benefits. Registration is handled at the county government level. This inequality in government subsidies has been the source of tension between some religions and the government. Despite government attempts to combat anti-Semitism, the nation's Jews continue to face discrimination and harassment. Anti-Semitic rhetoric increased in the political arena during 2009 and 2010 with an increase in support for the Jobbik Party (Movement for a Better Hungary). During that time, the party began publishing their official magazine on a weekly basis (increasing from monthly) and continued to post anti-Semitic content. In the April 2010 elections, Jobbik gained 47 seats (12%) in parliament. However, in 2010, parliament passed a legal amendment that criminalizes Holocaust denial.

¹¹TRANSPORTATION

The CIA reports that Hungary has a total of 197,519 km (122,733 mi) of roads, of which 74,993 km (46,598 mi) are paved. Railroads extend for 7,793 km (4,842 mi).

Transportation facilities have improved steadily since the 1960s. Budapest is the transportation center. Most freight is carried by trucks; railway transport is of lesser importance. The railroad and bus networks are state-owned.

Hungary has approximately 1,622 km (1,008 mi) of navigable waterways. Permanently navigable waterways were mostly on the Danube and Tisza rivers. In addition to the government shipping enterprises—which operate the best and largest ships and handle the bulk of water traffic—the Shipping Cooperative, an association of small operators, continues to function.

There are 43 airports (22 with paved runways), which transported 2.95 million passengers in 2009 according to the World Bank. There were also five heliports. Liszt Ferenc International Airport in Budapest is the most important center for domestic and international flights. All domestic traffic is handled by the nationalized Hungarian Air Transportation Enterprise (Magyar Légiközlekedési Vállalat-MALÉV).

¹²HISTORY

Ancient human footprints, tools, and a skull found at Vértesszőlős date the earliest occupants of present Hungary at a period from 250,000 to 500,000 years ago. Close to that site, at Tata, objects used for aesthetic or ceremonial purposes have been discovered, among the earliest such finds made anywhere in the world.

Celtic tribes settled in Hungary before the Romans came to occupy the western part of the country, which they called Pannonia and which the Roman Emperor Augustus conquered in 9 BC. Invasions by the Huns, the Goths, and later the Langobards had little lasting effect, but the two subsequent migrations of the Avars (who ruled for 250 years and, like the Huns, established a khanate in the Hungarian plain) left a more lasting impression.

The Magyars (Hungarians) migrated from the plains south and west of the Ural Mountains and invaded the Carpathian Basin under the leadership of Árpád in AD 896. For half a century, they ranged far and wide until their defeat by Otto the Great, king of Germany and Holy Roman emperor, near Augsburg in 955. They were converted to Christianity under King Stephen I (r. 1001–1038), who was canonized in 1083. The Holy Crown of St. Stephen became the national symbol, and a constitution was gradually developed. The Magna Carta of Hungary, known as the Golden Bull of 1222, gave the nation a basic framework of national liberties to which every subsequent Hungarian monarch had to swear fidelity. Hungary was invaded at various times during the medieval period; the Mongols succeeded in devastating the country in 1241–42.

Medieval Hungary achieved its greatest heights under the Angevin rulers Charles Robert and Louis the Great (r. 1342–82), when Hungarian mines yielded five times as much gold as those of any other European state. Sigismund of Luxembourg, king of Hungary, became Holy Roman emperor in 1410, largely on the strength of this national treasure. During the 15th century, however, Turkish armies began to threaten Hungary. The Balkan principalities to the south and southeast of Hungary developed as buffer states, but they did not long delay the advance of the Turks; nor could the victories of János Hunyadi, brilliant though they were, ultimately stem the Turkish tide. With the Turks temporarily at bay, the Hungarian renaissance flourished during the reign of Hunyadi's son, Matthias Corvinus (1458–90), but his successors in the 16th century overexploited the gold mines, brutally suppressed a peasant revolt, and allowed the Magyar army to deteriorate. Hungary's golden age ended with the rout by the Turks at Mohács in 1526, an event that is still regarded in Hungary as one of the nation's most enduring tragedies.

Thereafter, warring factions split Hungary, but power was gradually consolidated by the Habsburg kings of Austria. With the defeat of the Turks at Vienna in 1683, Turkish power waned, and that of the Habsburgs became stronger. The Hungarians mounted many unsuccessful uprisings against the Habsburgs, the most important insurrectionist leaders being the Báthorys, Bocskai, Bethlen, and the Rákóczys. In 1713, however, the Hungarian Diet accepted the Pragmatic Sanction, which, in guaranteeing the continuing integrity of Habsburg territories, bound Hungary to Austria.

During the first half of the 19th century, in the aftermath of the French Revolution and the Napoleonic wars, Hungary experienced an upsurge of Magyar nationalism accompanied by a burst of literary creativity. The inability of a liberal reform movement, led by István Széchenyi, to establish a constitutional monarchy led to the revolt of 1848, directed by Lajos Kossuth, which established a short-lived Hungarian republic. Although Hungarian autonomy was abolished as a result of intervention by Austrian and Russian armies, Austria, weakened by its war with Prussia, was obliged to give in to Magyar national aspirations. The Compromise (Ausgleich) of 1867 established a dual monarchy of Austria and Hungary and permitted the Magyars a degree of self-government.

After World War I, in which Austria-Hungary was defeated, the dual monarchy collapsed, and a democratic republic was established under Count Mihály Károlyi. This was supplanted in March 1919 by a Communist regime led by Béla Kun, but Romanian troops invaded Hungary and helped suppress it. In 1920, Hungary became a kingdom without a king; for the next 25 years, Adm. Miklós Horthy served as regent. The Treaty of Trianon in 1920 dramatically reduced Hungary's territory, forcing the nation to cede nearly two thirds of its land to neighboring states. This formally freed the non-Magyar nationalities from Hungarian rule but also left significant numbers of Magyars in Romania and elsewhere beyond Hungary's borders. The fundamental policy of interwar Hungary was to recover the "lost" territories, and, in the hope of achieving that end, Hungary formed alliances with the Axis powers and sided with them during World War II. Hungary temporarily regained territories from Czechoslovakia, Romania, and Yugoslavia. In March 1944, the German army occupied Hungary, but Soviet troops invaded the country later that year and liberated it by April 1945.

In 1946, a republican constitution was promulgated, and a coalition government (with Communist participation) was established. Under the terms of the peace treaty of 1947, Hungary was forced to give up all territories acquired after 1937. The Hungarian Workers (Communist) Party seized power in 1948 and adopted a constitution (on the Soviet model) in 1949. Hungarian foreign trade was oriented toward the Soviet bloc, industry was nationalized and greatly expanded, and collectivization of land was pressed. Resentment of continued Soviet influence over Hungarian affairs was one element in the popular uprising of October 1956, which after a few days' success—during which Hungary briefly withdrew from the Warsaw Treaty Organization—was summarily put down by Soviet military force. Many people fled the country, and many others were executed. From that time on, Hungary, led by János Kádár, was a firm ally of the USSR. In 1968, the New Economic Mechanism was introduced in order to make the economy more competitive and open to market forces; reform measures beginning in 1979 further encouraged private enterprise. The movement toward relaxation of tensions in Europe in the 1970s was reflected in the improvement of Hungary's relations with Western countries, including the reestablishment of diplomatic relations with The Federal Republic of Germany in 1973. A US-Hungarian war-claims agreement was signed that year, and, on 6 January 1978, the United States returned the Hungarian coronation regalia that had been seized following WWII and stored at Fort Knox.

The New Economic Mechanism that had been instituted in 1968 was largely abandoned, at Soviet and Comecon insistence, a decade later. This compounded the blows suffered by Hungary's economy during the energy crisis of the late 1970s, leading to a ballooning of the country's foreign indebtedness. By the late 1980s, the country owed $18 billion, the highest per capita indebtedness in Europe.

This indebtedness was the primary engine of political change. The necessity of introducing fiscal austerity was "sweetened" by the appointment of reform-minded Károly Grosz as prime minister in 1987. Faced with continued high inflation, the government took the step the following year of forcing János Kádár out entirely, giving control of the party to Grosz. In 1989, Grosz and his supporters went even further, changing the party's name to the Hungarian Socialist Party and dismantling their nation's section of the Iron Curtain. The action that had the most far-reaching consequences, however, came in October 1989, when the state constitution was amended so as to create a multiparty political system.

Although Hungarians had been able to choose among multiple candidates for some legislative seats since as early as 1983, the foundations of a true multiparty system had been laid in 1987–88, when large numbers of discussion groups and special interest associations began to flourish. Many of these, such as the Network of Free Initiatives, the Bajscy-Zsilinszky Society, the Hungarian Democratic Forum, and the Alliance of Free Democrats, soon became true political parties. In addition, parties that had existed before the 1949 imposition of Communist rule, such as the People's Party, the Hungarian Independence Party, and the Social Democrats, began to reactivate themselves.

All of these groups, or the parties they had spawned, competed in the 1990 general election, the first major free election to be held in more than four decades. No party gained an absolute majority of seats, so a coalition government was formed, composed of the Democratic Forum, Smallholders' Party, and Christian Democrats, with Forum leader József Antall as prime minister. Árpád Göncz, of the Free Democrats, was selected as president. An important indicator of Hungary's intentions came in June 1989, when the remains of Imre Nagy, hanged for his part in the events of 1956, were reentered with public honors; politicians and other public figures used the occasion to press further distance from Communism and the removal of Soviet troops. Another sign of public sentiment was the first commemoration in 40 years of the anniversary of the Revolution of 1848.

Under Antall, Hungary pursued a vigorous program of economic transformation, with the goal of transferring 30–35% of state assets to private control by the end of 1993. Hungary's liberal investment laws and comparatively well-developed industrial infrastructure permitted the nation to become an early leader in attracting Western investors. However, there were large blocs in society, and within the Democratic Forum itself, that found the pace of transition too slow, particularly since the government did not keep to its own time schedule.

In addition to economic demands, a far-right contingent also had a strongly nationalist, even xenophobic agenda, which tended to polarize Hungarian national politics. Approximately 10% of the Hungarian population is non-Hungarian, including significant populations of Jews and Roma (Gypsies). There are also large Hungarian populations in neighboring states, particularly in Romania, all of whom had been declared dual citizens of Hungary in 1988. The appeal to "Hungarian-ness" has been touted fairly frequently, widening preexisting tensions within the dominant Democratic Forum party, and weakening its coalition in parliament. The Smallholders Party withdrew from the coalition in 1992, and, in 1993, other elements were threatening to do the same.

The Democratic Forum's loss of popularity was vividly exposed in the parliamentary elections of May 1994, when the party, led by acting head Sándor Lezsák, lost almost one third of the seats it had controlled. In that election, voters turned overwhelmingly to the Hungarian Socialist Party, giving the former Communist party an absolute majority of 54%. Voter turnout in the two-tier election was as high as 70%, leaving little doubt that Hungarian voters had repudiated the Democratic Forum and its programs of forced transition to a market economy.

Hungary's international indebtedness remained very high—the country ran a $936 million trade deficit for the first two months of 1994 alone—obligating new prime minister Gyula Horn to continue most of the same economic reform programs that the Socialists' predecessors had begun. There was concern, however, that the Socialists' absolute majority could lead to a reversal of some of the important democratic gains of the recent past. Those concerns sharpened in July 1994, when Prime Minister Horn unilaterally appointed new heads for the state-owned radio and television, who immediately dismissed or suspended a number of conservative journalists.

On 8 January 1994 Hungary formally accepted the offer of a compromise on NATO membership. The offer involved a new defense partnership between Eastern Europe and NATO. By July 1997, NATO agreed to grant Hungary full membership (along with Poland and the Czech Republic) in the organization in 1999. In order to help qualify to join NATO and the EU, Hungary and Romania signed a treaty on 16 September 1996 ending a centuries-old dispute between the two neighbors. The agreement ended five years of negotiations over the status of Romania's 1.6 million ethnic Hungarians. On 12 March 1999, Hungary, Poland, and the Czech Republic were formally admitted to NATO, becoming the first former Warsaw Pact nations to join the alliance.

Although the economy was improving, the position of the Socialists was undermined by dissatisfaction among those negatively affected by privatization and austerity measures, as well as by financial scandals in 1997. The Socialist government was toppled in national elections held in May 1998, and a new center-right coalition government was formed in July by Viktor Orbán, leader of the victorious Federation of Young Democrats-Hungarian Civic Party (Fidesz).

In 1997, Hungary was invited to begin negotiations leading to membership in the European Union. It was formally invited to join the body in 2002 at the EU summit in Copenhagen. It was accepted as a full member on 1 January 2004. In 2000, parliament elected Ferenc Madl as president to replace Göncz.

Under Victor Orbán, Hungary experienced increasing prosperity but also increasing social division. Fidesz is a strong supporter of ethnic Hungarians in neighboring countries. Indeed, parlia-

ment in June 2001 passed a controversial law entitling Hungarians living in Romania, Slovakia, Ukraine, Serbia, Croatia, and Slovenia to a special identity document allowing them to temporarily work, study, and claim health care in Hungary. In June 2003, the law was amended by the parliament, with a majority of the Hungarian population agreeing with it. However, the referendum held in December 2004, in conjunction with this law, was invalidated due to low turnout.

Orbán's party was challenged in the April 2002 general elections by the Socialist Party, which chose Péter Medgyessy as its candidate for prime minister. Although Medgyessy characterized his party as patriotic, he stressed it was less extreme than Fidesz and supported diversity as well as traditional values of fairness and social justice.

The 2002 campaign was divisive and saw nationalists come out in force in favor of Fidesz. Although Fidesz won the largest bloc of seats in the National Assembly in the second round of voting (aligned with the Hungarian Democratic Forum), it was the Socialists in concert with the Alliance of Free Democrats that formed a coalition government with Medgyessy as prime minister.

In June 2002, allegations surfaced that Medgyessy had worked as a counterintelligence officer in the secret service under the Communist regime in the late 1970s and early 1980s. Medgyessy claimed he never collaborated with Moscow's KGB but instead sought out Soviet spies attempting to disrupt Hungary's efforts to join the IMF.

In the summer of 2004, internal problems within his own party, as well as growing opposition from the coalition partners, the Alliance of Free Democrats, led Medgyessy to resign. He was replaced with Ferenc Gyurcsány, the former sports minister and one of the government's most popular figures. Gyurcsány received 453 votes, while his main contender—Peter Kiss—got 166.

The new prime minister promised to strengthen the coalition, boost economic growth, and improve living conditions for Hungarians. However, strict budget controls (many imposed by the EU) and unfulfilled election promises dramatically decreased the popular support for his government, and party. In the 2004 European Parliament elections, the Fidesz (the main opposition party) led the pack.

In June 2005, opposition-backed László Sólyom was elected the new president of Hungary. He garnered 185 votes in the third round of elections, followed closely by the Socialist's nominee—Katalin Szili—with 182 votes.

In April 2006, general elections were held; the Socialist-led coalition under Prime Minister Gyurcsány was returned to power. However, violent protests erupted in September and October 2006 after the leak of a tape recording in which Gyurcsány told fellow party members that he had lied about the state of the economy to win the national elections in April. Thousands of Hungarians rallied in Budapest, demanding Gyurcsány's resignation. The anti-government protests in Budapest cast a pall on the 50th anniversary commemorations of the 1956 uprising against Soviet rule. In February 2007, a commission of inquiry into the violence that had broken out in September and October, in which 800 people were hurt, criticized the police, the government, and Hungary's entire political elite. By March 2007, Gyurcsány was attempting to convince Hungarians that he could be trusted again and that austerity measures would have to be followed to right the economy. Nevertheless, about 100,000 people protested in Budapest in March 2007, demanding the prime minister's resignation.

In February 2010, the Hungarian parliament approved a law to make denial of the Holocaust a crime punishable by up to three years in prison. The vote—197 in favor and 1 against, with 142 abstentions—came in the parliament's last session before the April 2010 elections. Roughly 450,000 Hungarian-Jews are believed to have been murdered under Hungary's Nazi-aligned World War II government. Roughly fifty thousand Jews still live in Hungary, representing the largest Jewish community among the European Union's eastern members.

Continued low approval ratings led to a vote of no confidence for Gyurcsány's government in early 2009. Gordon Bajnai, also of the Hungarian Socialist Party, briefly assumed the Prime Ministership before Viktor Orbán once again assumed the position after Fidesz won a super-majority in the 2010 parliamentary elections.

13 GOVERNMENT

Hungary's present constitution remains based upon the 1949 Soviet-style constitution, with major revisions made in 1972 and 1988. The 1988 revisions mandated the end of the Communist Party's monopoly on power, removed the word People's from the name of the state, and created the post of president to replace the earlier Presidential Council. As of 2011, implementation of a new constitution remained incomplete.

The present system is a unitary multiparty republic with a parliamentary government. There is one legislative house (the National Assembly) with 386 members who are elected to four-year terms. The head of state is the president, who is elected by the parliament for a five-year term.

The head of the government is the prime minister, leader of the largest party seated in the parliament. The prime minister is elected by the National Assembly on the recommendation of the president. In the Antall government, important ministerial and other posts were split among representatives of various parties.

14 POLITICAL PARTIES

Following the general elections of April 2002, four political parties were represented in the 386-member National Assembly, split into two coalitions. This situation raised fears that Hungary was drifting into a two-party state, divided by ideology and personalities, instead of reflecting other interests not represented in government.

One of the two largest parties was the Hungarian Socialist Party (MSZP), whose government was toppled in 1998 but returned to power in 2002, receiving 42.05% of the popular vote and garnering 178 seats in the National Assembly. The MSZP is the Hungarian Communist Party renamed and, to a certain extent, reoriented. The party's platform indicates strong support for the market economy system, albeit with a wide net of social services. It supports diversity in Hungarian society, as opposed to the center-right's more populist, nationalistic party, Fidesz. The party struggled under Gyurcsány to implement austerity measures, which were widely unpopular among the population.

The other principal, and, as of 2011, ruling party, was the Federation of Young Democrats-Hungarian Civic Party (also known as Fidesz), which held 164 seats. The party's leader, Viktor Orbán, was named prime minister in 1998; he was out of office in 2002

when the Socialists came to power but returned in 2010. Originally known as the Federation of Young Democrats, the party was formed on an anti-Communist platform by student activists and young professionals in 1988. During the 1990s, it evolved into a mainstream center-right party and was renamed in 1995.

The Alliance of Free Democrats (SzDSz), which formerly held numerous seats in the 1990s, was the coalition partner of the MSZP. This party was a liberal opposition party during the Antall government with positions strongly in favor of closer integration with Europe, cooperation with Hungary's neighbors, and support for alien Hungarians. In economic terms, their platform was very similar to that of the MSZP, which was the basis of their agreement to enter into a coalition. However, their alliance had frequent disputes that undermined their political strength, and they failed to gain any seats in the 2010 elections.

The Hungarian Democratic Forum (MDF), which was reduced to 24 seats, is a party of strong support for the ethnic minorities within Hungary. It has aligned itself with Fidesz. The Hungarian Justice and Life Party (MIEP), founded by István Csúrka, who was expelled from the MDF for his nationalist and anti-Semitic sentiments, first gained parliamentary representation in 1998, winning 14 seats. The party is populist in orientation, seeking to elevate "Hungarian values." It won 4.4% of the vote in 2002 in coalition with Fidesz. In 2010, it garnered 2.6%, thus losing all parliamentary seats.

The Independent Smallholders' Party (FKgP), which held 48 seats in the 1998 government but no seats in the government formed in 2002, is a center-right party that seeks to ensure Hungarian interests in the context of European integration. It is a historically strong party in Hungary. It draws particular support from rural districts and among farmers. Since 2010, when it lost all parliamentary seats, the party has essentially disappeared.

Other parties include the Politics Can Be Different Party (a green party) and the Communist Worker's Party. In 2010, the former gained 11 seats in parliament, and the latter lost all seats. Hungary also has a notable "skinhead" movement, which has provoked fights and other disturbances, especially with Roma people. In 2010, the far-right party Jobbik gained enough votes for 47 seats in parliament. Some European Union states have expressed concern over the more radical elements represented by the party, including anti-Semitism, aggressive nationalism, and anti-Roma sentiment.

In the general elections held in 2010, Prime Minister Viktor Orbán's Fidesz won a simple majority of the vote and formed a coalition with the Communist Workers Party totaling 262 seats, though the latter remained a minor coalition partner. The MSZP won 59 seats and Jobbik won 47. Sixteen seats were won by the Politics Can Be Different Party.

In 2010, Pál Schmitt was elected president by an absolute majority of the legislative vote. The next presidential elections were scheduled for June 2015.

15 LOCAL GOVERNMENT

Hungary is divided administratively into 19 counties, 23 urban counties, and the capital city of Budapest also has county status. At the local and regional level, legislative authority is vested in county, town, borough, and town precinct councils, whose members are directly elected for four-year terms. Members of the county councils are elected by members of the lower-level councils. Hungary also has provisions for minority self-government, which is not based territorially because minorities live dispersed throughout the country. Municipality councils must seek the approval of minority self-governments for matters affecting minority education and culture, among others.

16 JUDICIAL SYSTEM

Cases in the first instance usually come before provincial city courts or Budapest district courts. Appeals can be submitted to county courts or the Budapest Metropolitan Court. The Supreme Court is basically a court of appeal, although it may also hear important cases in the first instance. As of 2003, a new intermediate court of appeal was to be established between county courts and the Supreme Court, designed to alleviate the backlog of court cases.

The president of the Supreme Court is elected by the National Assembly. A National Judicial Council nominates judicial appointees other than those of the Constitutional Court. The state's punitive power is represented by the public prosecutor. Peter Polt was appointed to a second term as prosecutor general in 2006.

The Constitutional Court reviews the constitutionality of laws and statutes as well as compliance of these laws with international treaties the government has ratified. The 11 members of the Constitutional Court are elected by parliament for nine-year terms with a two-thirds majority; their mandates may be renewed in theory, but as of 2010, this had not happened in practice.

17 ARMED FORCES

The International Institute for Strategic Studies reports that armed forces in Hungary totaled 29,626 members in 2011. The force is comprised of 10,100 from the army, 5,806 from the air force, and 13,720 members of joint forces. Armed forces represent 1% of the labor force in Hungary. Defense spending totaled $3.3 billion and accounted for 1.8% of gross domestic product (GDP).

Hungary provides UN observers and peacekeepers to eight regions or countries.

18 INTERNATIONAL COOPERATION

Hungary has been a member of the UN since 14 December 1955 and participates in ECE and most of the non-regional specialized agencies except the IFAD. Hungary became a member of the OECD in 1996, a NATO member in 1999, and a member of the European Union in 2004. Hungary is also a member of the WTO, the Council of Europe, G-9, and the OSCE. The nation has observer status in the OAS and is a member affiliate of the Western European Union.

Hungary is part of the Australia Group, the Zangger Committee, the Nuclear Suppliers Group, the Organization for the Prohibition of Chemical Weapons, the European Organization for Nuclear Research (CERN), and the Nuclear Energy Agency. In environmental cooperation, Hungary is part of the Antarctic Treaty, the Basel Convention, Conventions on Biological Diversity and Air Pollution, Ramsar, CITES, the London Convention, International Tropical Timber Agreements, the Kyoto Protocol, the Montréal Protocol, MARPOL, the Nuclear Test Ban Treaty, and the UN Conventions on the Law of the Sea, Climate Change, and Desertification.

19 ECONOMY

The GDP rate of change in Hungary, as of 2010, was 1.2%. Inflation stood at 4.9%, and unemployment was reported at 10.7%.

Before World War II, industrial growth was slow because adequate capital was lacking. Since 1949, however, industry has expanded rapidly, and it now contributes a larger share than agriculture to the national income. The government has no capital investments abroad, but it participates in limited economic activities in developing countries. Substantial industrial growth continued through the 1960s and mid-1970s, but output in the socialized sector declined during 1979–80, and growth was sluggish in the 1980s.

After the fall of Communism in 1989, Hungary began a painful transition to a market economy. Between 1990 and 1992, GDP dropped by about 20%. Freed to reach their own level, consumer prices rose 162% between 1989 and 1993. The rate of unemployment was 12.2% at the end of 1992. By late 1998, private-sector output was over 85% of the GDP.

By 1994, Hungary was in an economic slump unknown since the reforms toward capitalism began. Export earnings were down, inflation was on the rise, and Hungary's gross debt rose to about $31.6 billion in mid 1995 (the highest per capita foreign debt in Europe). The IMF directed the government to curb social spending, but restricting social welfare during a period of high unemployment was unpopular with voters. The government began a stabilization plan in March 1995 designed to decrease the budget deficit by HUF170 billion (3–4% of the GDP) and to decrease the current account deficit to $2.5 billion from the record high of $4 billion in 1994. The government cut expenditures, increased its revenues, devalued the forint by 9%, introduced a crawling peg exchange rate policy, added an 8% surcharge on imports, and called for wage controls at state-owned companies. As a result of the program, inflation and GDP growth rose. In addition, the black market economy was estimated to be as much as 30% of GDP.

In the years since its implementation, the stabilization program has borne fruit. By 1999, the IMF assistance had been repaid. The Hungarian economy exhibited strong growth rates with GDP increases of 4.6% and 5.1% in 1997 and 1998, respectively. Although a hard winter and the Kosovo conflict appeared to hamper Hungarian efforts to match the prior years' growth rate levels, the economy performed well in 2000, led by an increase in foreign direct investment. Since then, manufacturing output and productivity increased, and export industries did well, although increases in wages and a rapid appreciation of the forint in 2002 moderated export growth. The global economic downturn that began in 2001 had an impact on the Hungarian economy, as GDP rose by only half the rate in 2002 as it had in 2000. Although this growth rate was higher than most European nations in 2002, it was below the rate needed for Hungary to reach the wealth levels of EU countries.

Due to government efforts at privatization, over 80% of the economy was privately owned by 2001, and Hungary stands as a model for countries undergoing market reforms. In December 2002, Hungary was formally invited to join the EU; it was accepted as a full member in May 2004 as one of the most advanced of the 10 candidate countries slated for accession.

As an EU member, Hungary maintained its position as one of the most dynamic and strong economies in Central and Eastern

Europe. Its position within the European Union and the fact that it is still comparatively cheaper to do business there than in other Western European countries make Hungary a prime target for investments. However, Hungary is being challenged by some of its neighbors that have managed to maintain lower labor costs and more attractive tax systems. Already some of the investments in the country have moved further east to countries like Romania and Ukraine, and some of the bids for new investments have been lost for the same reasons. Hungary's largest economic partner is Germany.

Although the GDP growth was slower in 2002 and 2003, it recuperated lost ground in 2004. Inflation decreased to 7% in 2004, and 4.9% in 2010. Unemployment, however, rose from 5.9% in the same time period to 11.2% in 2010. However, IMF specialists recommend that Hungary register annual growth rates of 5–5.25% in order to catch up with the developed economies in the EU. This means that Hungary must attract further investment in order to generate funds for the state. Consequently, the government sold Budapest Airport and Antenna Hungaria in 2005, though the airport was renationalized shortly thereafter. Attracting additional foreign investment is increasingly difficult, as the country has to fight with moderate budget deficits (4.3% in 2004) and increased competition from its neighbors.

In 2007, Hungary eliminated its trade deficit, which had existed for several years. The global financial crisis of 2008–09 hit Hungary hard, however, as the nation in debt faced a significant decline in foreign investment and trade. The International Monetary Fund presented a $25 billion rescue package for Hungary in October 2008, with the stipulation that the government should make significant changes in economic policies in order to secure a more stable and efficient economy and lower the national debt. In a July 2010 review of progress, the IMF noted that there was still much to be done to ensure that Hungary would meet its target deficits of 3.8% of GDP by year-end 2010 and 3% by 2011. Restructuring of state-owned companies to make them more efficient and less costly was cited as a primary need. The announcement of this less than favorable review caused a devaluation of the Hungarian forint by more than 3% against the euro. The Budapest Stock Exchange also fell by nearly 3% as a result.

20 INCOME

The CIA estimated that in 2010 the GDP of Hungary was $187.6 billion. The CIA defines GDP as the value of all final goods and services produced within a nation in a given year and computed on the basis of purchasing power parity (PPP) rather than value as measured on the basis of the rate of the exchange based on current dollars. The per capita GDP was estimated at $18,800. The annual growth rate of GDP was 1.2%. The average inflation rate was 4.9%. It was estimated that agriculture accounted for 2.4% of GDP, industry 37%, and services 60.5%.

According to the World Bank, remittances from citizens living abroad totaled $2.1 billion or about $214 per capita and accounted for approximately 1.1% of GDP.

The World Bank reports that, in 2009, household consumption in Hungary totaled $121 billion or about $12,200 per capita, measured in current US dollars rather than PPP. Household consumption includes expenditures of individuals, households, and nongovernmental organizations on goods and services, excluding the

purchases of dwellings. It was estimated that household consumption was growing at an average annual rate of 0.1%.

As of 2011, the most recent study by the World Bank reported that actual individual consumption in Hungary was 67.6% of GDP and accounted for 0.33% of world consumption. By comparison, the United States accounted for 25.44% of world individual consumption. The World Bank also estimated that 13.8% of Hungary's GDP was spent on food and beverages, 13.8% on housing and household furnishings, 2.0% on clothes, 7.5% on health, 8.7% on transportation, 2.5% on communications, 5.4% on recreation, 2.7% on restaurants and hotels, and 5.9% on miscellaneous goods and services and purchases from abroad.

It was estimated that, in 2010, about 13.9% of the population subsisted on an income below the poverty line established by Hungary's government.

21 LABOR

As of 2010, Hungary had a total labor force of 4.23 million people. Within that labor force, CIA estimates in 2010 noted that 4.7% were employed in agriculture, 30.9% in industry, and 64.4% in the service sector.

Before World War II, trade unions had not developed substantially; their combined membership was only about 100,000, principally craftsmen. After the war, the government reduced the number of the traditional craft unions, organized them along industrial lines, and placed them under Communist Party control. The Central Council of Hungarian Trade Unions (SZOT) held a monopoly over labor interests for over 40 years. Since wages, benefits, and other aspects of employment were state-controlled, the SZOT acted as a social service agency but was dissolved in 1990 with the shift away from centralization to democracy. The National Federation of Trade Unions is its successor, with 735,000 members in 1999. There are now several other large labor organizations in Hungary, including the Democratic League of Independent Trade Unions, with some 100,000 members, and the Federation of Workers' Councils, with 56,000 members. Labor disputes are usually resolved by conciliation boards; appeal may be made to courts. Since 1991, most unions have been hesitant to strike, preferring instead to act as a buffer between workers and the negative side effects of economic reform. Collective bargaining is permitted but is not widespread.

The eight-hour day, adopted in several industries before World War II, is now widespread. The five-day week is typical, but many Hungarians have second or third jobs. The law prohibits employment for children under the age of 15 and closely regulates child labor. The minimum wage in 2010 was $402 per month, which was not sufficient to provide a decent lifestyle for a family. Most workers earn more than this amount. Health and safety conditions in the workplace do not always meet international standards, and regulations are not enforced due to limited resources.

22 AGRICULTURE

Roughly 52% of the total land is currently farmed. Much of this land lies in the Great Plain where the soil is fertile; however, most of the region lacks adequate rainfall and is prone to droughts, requiring extensive irrigation, though lands along the Tisza and Danube rivers are also prone to decennial flooding. Major crops include wheat, corn, sunflowers, potatoes, sugar beets, and rape seed. In 2009, cereal production amounted to 13.6 million tons, fruit production 1.5 million tons, and vegetable production 1.6 million tons.

Before World War II (1939–45), Hungary was a country of large, landed estates and landless and land-poor peasants. In the land reform of 1945, about 35% of the land area was distributed, 1.9 million hectares (4.7 million acres) among 640,000 families and 1.3 million hectares (3.2 million acres) in state farms. In 1949, the government adopted a policy of collectivization based on the Soviet kolkhoz, and, by the end of 1952, 5,110 collectives, many forcibly organized, controlled 22.6% of total arable land. Peasant resentment led to a policy change in 1953, and many collectives were dissolved, but the regime returned to its previous policy in 1955. As a result of the 1956 uprising, collectives were again dissolved, but a new collectivization drive begun in 1959 was essentially completed by 1961. Meanwhile, the proportion of the economically active population employed in agriculture decreased steadily. In 1949, agricultural employees accounted for 55.1% of the total labor force.

Hungary has achieved self-sufficiency in temperate zone crops, and exports about one third of all produce, especially fruit and preserved vegetables. The traditional agricultural crops have been cereals, with wheat, corn (maize), and rye grown on more than half the total sown area. In recent years, considerable progress has been made in industrial crops, especially oilseeds and sugar beets. Fruit production (especially for preserves) and viticulture are also significant.

23 ANIMAL HUSBANDRY

The UN Food and Agriculture Organization (FAO) reported that Hungary dedicated 1 million hectares (2.5 million acres) to permanent pasture or meadow in 2009. During that year, the country tended 31.2 million chickens, 701,000 head of cattle, and 3.4 million pigs. The production from these animals amounted to 43,110 tons of beef and veal, 2,043,000 tons of milk (2005), 473,613 tons of pork, 276,447 tons of poultry, 158,396 tons of eggs. Hungary also produced 2,200 tons of cattle hide and 4,444 tons of raw wool. The country had 1,397,000 sheep and 68,000 horses in 2005.

Although animal husbandry is second only to cereal cultivation in agricultural production, the number and quality of animals are much lower than in neighboring countries. An inadequate supply of fodder is one of the chief deficiencies.

24 FISHING

Fishing was unimportant before World War II (1939–45), but production has increased in recent years. The best fishing areas are the Danube and Tisza rivers, Lake Balaton, and various artificial ponds. The catch is composed mainly of carp, catfish, eel, and perch. In 2008, the annual capture totaled 7,394 tons according to the UN FAO. Hungary annually imports $15–20 million in seafood to meet demand.

25 FORESTRY

Forests totaled 1,840,000 hectares (4,547,000 acres) or 23% of Hungary's total land area in 2009. The forest consists of the following main species: oak, 23%; black locust, 20%; pine and fir, 15%;

Austrian and turkey oak, 11%; poplars, 9%; beech, 6%; hornbeam (blue beech), 6%; and others, 10%.

Because of the relatively small forest area and the high rate of exploitation, Hungary traditionally has had to import timber. During the 1960s, a systematic reforestation program began. Reforestation affected about 440,000 hectares (1,087,000 acres) during 1960–68 but only about 65,000 hectares (161,000 acres) in 1970–74 and 64,322 hectares (158,942 acres) during 1975–81. From 1990–2000, some 136,000 hectares (336,000 acres) were annually reforested. The UN Food and Agriculture Organization (FAO) estimated the 2009 roundwood production at 2.36 million cu m (83.5 million cu ft). The value of all forest products, including roundwood, totaled $854.4 million.

Privatization of agricultural land, including forests, finished in 1996. According to estimates from the Ministry of Agriculture's Forestry Office, 55% of forests were under state control, 44.5% were owned by private individuals, and 0.5% belonged to municipalities.

26 MINING

In 2009, Hungary produced modest amounts of fossil fuels and industrial minerals, cement and coal being the dominant components of industrial minerals and metals. Although the country had significant output of alumina and bauxite, the output of primary aluminum was modest, due to limited domestic energy sources. Construction aggregates and cement continued to play an important role in Hungary's economy, especially in view of the modernization process necessary for the country's infrastructure. Mineral reserves were small and generally inadequate.

Bauxite mining and refining of alumina, as well as manganese mining, remained the only metal mining and processing operations in Hungary in 2009. Production of bauxite, found in various parts of western Hungary, was 317,000 tons in 2009, compared with 1 million tons in 2001. Total resources of bauxite were estimated to be 23 million metric tons, with commercial reserves at 16 million metric tons. Magyar Aluminum Ltd. operates the Bakony bauxite mine 5 km (3 mi) south of Ajka. Gallium production totaled 3,400 kg in 2009. Hungary also produced 50,000 metric tons of manganese ore concentrate (gross weight) in 2009, and 24,000 tons of gypsum and anhydrite in 2009. In addition, Hungary produced alumina (calcined basis), bentonite, common clays, diatomite, kaolin, nitrogen, perlite, sand (common, foundry, and glass) and gravel, dimension stone, dolomite, limestone, sulfuric acid, and talc. Although Hungary no longer mined copper, past surveys of the deep-lying Recsk copper ore body in the Matra mountains discovered 172–175 million tons of copper ore at a grade of 1.12% copper and about 20 million tons of polymetallic ore at a grade of 4.22% lead and 0.92% zinc, as well as smaller quantities of gold, molybdenum, and silver. After failing to attract foreign investment, the exploration shaft and adit at Recsk were closed, the equipment removed, and the facilities flooded in 1999.

27 ENERGY AND POWER

The World Bank reported in 2008 that Hungary produced 40 billion kWh of electricity and consumed 40 billion kWh, or 4,014 kWh per capita. Roughly 78% of energy came from fossil fuels, while 15% came from alternative fuels. Per capita oil consumption was 2,636 kg. Oil production totaled 14,408 barrels of oil a day.

Hungary has modest reserves of oil, natural gas, and coal. In addition, the country's electric power sector relies on nuclear power to provide a sizable portion of its electric power needs. By the end of 1963, all villages were supplied with electric power.

Hungary's sole nuclear power plant, at Pécs, consists of four second-generation, Soviet-designed, VVER-440/213 reactors, which began production in 1982. Modernization was planned to extend the operating life of the reactors by twenty years. The normal lifespan of the four units would end between 2012 and 2017. Legislation has consistently supported the extension of the plant's lifespan and, in 2009, the potential construction of another plant. Uranium, discovered in 1953 near Pécs, is expected to supply its nuclear station until 2020.

28 INDUSTRY

Hungary is poor in the natural resources essential for heavy industry and relies strongly on imported raw materials. Industry, only partially developed before World War II, has expanded rapidly since 1948 and provides the bulk of exports. Industrial plants were nationalized by 1949, and the socialized sector accounted for about 98.5% of gross production in 1985.

Hungary has concentrated on developing steel, machine tools, buses, diesel engines and locomotives, television sets, radios, electric light bulbs and fluorescent lamps, telecommunications equipment, refrigerators, washing machines, medical apparatuses and other precision engineering equipment, pharmaceuticals, and petrochemical products. Textile and leather production has decreased in relative importance since World War II, while chemicals grew to become the leading industry in the early 1990s. Food processing, formerly the leading industry, provides a significant portion of exports; meat, poultry, grain, and wine are common export items.

In 1993, industrial production was only two-thirds of the 1985 level. In 1997, industrial output increased in the manufacture of road vehicles, consumer electronics, insulated cables, office equipment and computers, steel products, aluminum metallurgy, household chemical products and cosmetics, rubber and plastic products, and paper and pulp production. In 1992, Suzuki and Opel began producing automobiles in Hungary, the first produced there since before World War II. Suzuki increased annual output at the Magyar Suzuki Corporation from 29,000 to 50,000 units starting in the 1995 fiscal year. Since 1990, Hungary has developed industrial strength in the automotive field as well as an expanding automotive sourcing industry in plastics and electronics. In 2001, Hungary produced 144,313 automobiles, a 5% increase over 2000. In 2000, it produced 1,621 heavy trucks, a 24% increase over 1999. According to the European Automobile Manufacturers Association, about 19.4% of total Hungarian industrial output was accounted for by the vehicle manufacturing industry in 2007.

The growth in manufacturing output and productivity in the early 2000s has been supported by a considerable amount of foreign investment. Successive Hungarian governments have pursued privatization policies and policies to restructure industry, so that by 2002, 80% of the economy was privately owned. High-tech equipment (computers, telecommunication equipment, and household appliances) showed the strongest industrial growth in 2001. Industries targeted for growth in 2003 were the automotive industry, the general industrial and machine tool industry, and the information technology industry. Housing construction was another growth sector in 2002.

In 2010, the share of the industrial output in the GDP was 37%, while its representation in the labor force was 30.9%. The industrial production growth rate was 9.6% in 2004, and most of this growth occurred in industries like motor vehicles, chemicals (especially pharmaceuticals), textiles, processed foods, construction materials, metallurgy, and mining.

29 SCIENCE AND TECHNOLOGY

In 2002, there were 486 technicians and 1,473 researchers per million people that were actively engaged in research and development (R&D). Total expenditures on R&D during that year amounted to $1.374 million, or 1.01% of GDP. Of that total, the government sector accounted for the majority of spending at 58.6%, followed by business at 29.7%, foreign investors at 10.4%, and higher education at 0.3%. Undistributed funds accounted for the remainder. Patent applications in science and technology as of 2009, according to the World Bank, totaled 757 in Hungary. Public financing of science was 0.96% of GDP. High-tech exports in 2002 were valued at $7.364 billion and accounted for 25% of manufactured exports.

Among major scientific organizations are the Hungarian Academy of Sciences (founded in 1825), the Association for Dissemination of Sciences (founded in 1841), and the Federation of Technical and Scientific Societies (founded in 1948), with 32 agricultural, medical, scientific, and technical member societies. In 1996, Hungary had 45 research institutes concerned with agriculture and veterinary science, medicine, natural sciences, and technology. There are 25 universities and colleges offering courses in basic and applied science. In 1987–97, science and engineering students accounted for 32% of university enrollment. In 2002, science degrees (natural sciences, mathematics and computers, and engineering) accounted for 11.9% of all bachelor's degrees awarded.

In addition to the National Museum of Science and Technology, Budapest has museums devoted to transport, electrical engineering, agriculture, natural history, foundries, and history.

30 DOMESTIC TRADE

Budapest is the business and trade center of the country, though most production facilities lie elsewhere. Over the past few years, the retail and wholesale sector has grown along Western standards.

Throughout most of the country, small, family-owned and -operated retail establishments predominate. However, there is an ongoing trend toward medium-size, financially sound companies operating a chain of shops, not only in Budapest, but also in the countryside. In Budapest, the retail sector is dominated by supermarkets, shopping centers, and superstores. Small family-run stores are most common in rural areas and tend to serve immediate needs. Indoor shopping malls have also appeared in Budapest and other major cities. By 2005, there were some 40 shopping malls operating in Budapest.

The Poles Center, the first American-style shopping mall in Central Europe, opened on the outskirts of Budapest in November 1996. West End City Center, the largest mall complex in Central Europe, was opened in Budapest in 1999. Retail purchases are still primarily cash-based, though some banks are beginning to issue credit and debit cards. Checks, however, are not used at all.

Principal Trading Partners – Hungary (2010)

(In millions of US dollars)

Country	Total	Exports	Imports	Balance
World	182,371.0	94,759.0	87,612.0	7,147.0
Germany	46,283.0	23,907.0	22,376.0	1,531.0
Russia	10,296.0	3,404.0	6,892.0	-3,488.0
China	10,263.0	1,561.0	8,702.0	-7,141.0
Austria	10,160.0	4,558.0	5,602.0	-1,044.0
Italy	8,977.0	5,281.0	3,696.0	1,585.0
Slovak Republic	8,355.0	4,930.0	3,425.0	1,505.0
France	7,997.0	4,769.0	3,228.0	1,541.0
Poland	7,206.0	3,483.0	3,723.0	-240.0
Romania	7,200.0	5,101.0	2,099.0	3,002.0
Portugal	7,018.0	3,153.0	3,865.0	-712.0

(…) data not available or not significant.

(n.s.) not specified.

SOURCE: *2011 Direction of Trade Statistics Yearbook*, New York: United Nations, 2011.

Balance of Payments – Hungary (2010)

(In millions of US dollars)

Current Account		**3,049.0**
Balance on goods	6,212.0	
Imports	-87,082.0	
Exports	93,294.0	
Balance on services	3,177.0	
Balance on income	-6,837.0	
Current transfers	497.0	
Capital Account		**2,295.0**
Financial Account		**2,078.0**
Direct investment abroad	45,187.0	
Direct investment in Hungary	-41,989.0	
Portfolio investment assets	-437.0	
Portfolio investment liabilities	604.0	
Financial derivatives	839.0	
Other investment assets	-906.0	
Other investment liabilities	-1,220.0	
Net Errors and Omissions		**-3,259.0**
Reserves and Related Items		**-4,162.0**

(…) data not available or not significant.

SOURCE: *Balance of Payment Statistics Yearbook 2011*, Washington, DC: International Monetary Fund, 2011.

Franchising is well established in Hungary. As of 2004, there were some 400 franchise operations doing business in the country, 50% of which were foreign-based. In Hungary, as well as in other Central European countries, US-based McDonald's is the leading fast-food franchise. Other US fast-food franchisers operating in Hungary were Burger King, Subway, Pizza Hut, and Kentucky Fried Chicken. In other service areas, Eastman Kodak, Avis, and Hertz also had well-established operations.

Direct marketing or selling is an accepted business format in Hungary. In 1993, the Association of Direct Selling (DSA) was founded to promote direct selling and to protect consumer interests. Since then, the DSA has adopted the European Codes of Conduct, which set guidelines designed to ensure consumer protection and satisfaction, and the promotion of fair competition.

Electronic commerce (e-commerce) has been slow to develop in Hungary. However, there has been steady growth in e-banking services. Hungarian banks, as of June 2005, had 96,000 business and 604,000 private online customers. Most business-to-consumer (B2C) e-commerce consists of computer products, CDs, DVDs, and book sales.

Business office hours are generally from 8 a.m. to 5 p.m. Mondays through Thursdays, and from 8 a.m. to 1 p.m. on Fridays. Bank hours are from 8 a.m. to 2 p.m. Mondays through Thursdays, and from 8 a.m. to 1 p.m. on Fridays. Shops are open from 10 a.m. to 6 p.m. weekdays, and from 9 a.m. to 1 p.m. on Saturdays. Sunday closing is general, although restaurants, coffee bars, cinemas, and some shopping centers remain open on Sundays.

Newspapers and general, trade, and technical magazines are used for advertising; there is also broadcast and outdoor advertising. A major industrial fair, held since 1906, takes place every spring and autumn in Budapest.

31 FOREIGN TRADE

Hungary imports raw materials and semi-finished products and exports finished products. Within that general framework, however, the structure, volume, and direction of Hungarian foreign trade have changed perceptibly over the years. The total trade volume expanded from HUF18.344 million (foreign exchange) in 1959 to HUF2.657 billion in 1994. In 2000, exports were estimat-

ed at $28.1 billion (up from $12.9 billion in 1995), while imports were estimated to be $32.1 billion (up from $15.4 billion in 1995).

Hungary imported $87.44 billion worth of goods and services in 2008, while exporting $93.74 billion worth of goods and services. Major import partners in 2009 were Germany, 26.1%; Russia, 7.7%; China, 6.8%; Austria, 5.9%; Netherlands, 4.4%; Poland, 4.3%; and Italy, 4.2%. Its major export partners were Germany, 25.5%; Italy, 5.5%; UK, 5.4%; Romania, 5.3%; Slovakia, 5.1%; France, 4.9%; and Austria, 4.7%.

The majority of Hungary's export market is concentrated in the manufacturing industry, including electrical machinery, motor vehicle parts, polymers, petroleum refining, telecommunications equipment, and aluminum. Manufactured goods make up 82% of all exports. Other important exports include apparel (4.4%), polymers (2.2%), and meat (2.1%).

32 BALANCE OF PAYMENTS

In 2010 Hungary had a foreign trade surplus of $6.7 billion, amounting to 4% of GDP.

Having scrapped central planning, the Hungarian government is engaged in stabilizing the economy and taming inflation. In 1992, exports had grown by 7.4%, but recession in export markets, Western Europe's protectionism, an appreciating forint, bankruptcies of firms producing one third of exports, and drought caused Hungarian trade to slow. In 1994, Hungary had a current account deficit of $4 billion, but it shrank to $2.5 billion in 1995 and to a further $1 billion in 2001. Strong private consumption growth was sustaining the growth of the economy in 2003, but the current account deficit was forecast at 4.3% of GDP in 2010.

33 BANKING AND SECURITIES

The National Bank of Hungary (Magyar Nemzeti Bank-NMB) is the central bank of Hungary. Beginning operations in June 1924 and replacing the Royal Hungarian State Bank (est. 1921), the

NMB was nationalized under the communist regime in 1947, functioning as a central and commercial bank. It was the bank of issue, and had a monopoly on credit and foreign exchange operations. Following the 1987 reform of the banking system, the NMB retained its central position as a bank of issue and its foreign exchange monopoly, but its credit functions were transferred to commercial banks. The NMB is responsible for setting the size of mandatory reserves and setting the base interest rate. The State Authority for Financial Institutions oversees the banking, capital, insurance and pensions fund systems.

In 2011, the discount rate, the interest rate at which the central bank lends to financial institutions in the short term, was 6%. At the end of 2005, the nation's gold bullion deposits totaled 0.10 million fine troy ounces.

In 1991, following the collapse of the Soviet Union and the dissolution of the communist system in Eastern Europe, there were 10 government-owned commercial banks, 16 joint-stock-owned commercial banks, 5 government-owned specialized financial institutions, one offshore bank, and 260 savings cooperatives in Hungary. By 1997, Hungary had over 30 commercial banks, about 10 specialized financial institutions, and 260 savings cooperatives. By 1998, around 75% of all banks had been privatized, and 70% of these shares had foreign owners. Upon joining the OECD in 1996, Hungary ceased its ban on the establishment of foreign branches, effective January 1998. More than two thirds of Hungary's banking sector is controlled by foreign investors.

Hungarian law allows for "universal banking," which means that licensed banks are permitted to engage in a full range of financial transactions, including those involving securities (stocks and bonds). Foreign financial institutions are also allowed to open branches or wholly-owned subsidiaries. Two US-based banks operate in Hungary. These are Citibank Rt and Budapest Bank Rt (an affiliate of GE Capital).

In Budapest, an authentic commodity and stock exchange functioned from 1867 until 1948, when it was closed down as the country transformed into a centralized socialist economy. The reorganization of the Hungarian securities market, after a pause of some 40 years, started at the beginning of the 1980s. The Exchange was founded eventually on 21 June 1990. The bull market on the Budapest Stock Exchange (BUX) continued during the final quarter of 1996. The BUX index closed 1996 at 4,125, up 170% compared with end 1995. The increase was the second-strongest in the world, following the Venezuelan market. By 7 February 1997, the BUX index had reached 5,657. By mid 2000, the index stood at over 8,800, but as of mid 2003, it had dropped to just over 8,000 amid the global recession. However, by the end of 2004, the BUX had recovered, rising 57.2% that year to close at 14,742.6. By 2010, it had reached a high of 24,531.

34 INSURANCE

Before World War II, 49 private insurance companies—25 domestic and 24 foreign—conducted business activities in Hungary. All insurance was nationalized in 1949 and placed under the State Insurance Institute, a government monopoly. A new institution, Hungária Insurance Co., was founded in 1986. As of 1997, the regulatory authority was the Insurance Supervisor (*allami Biztositasfeluegyelet*). Compulsory insurance in Hungary includes third-party auto liability, workers' compensation, and liability for

Public Finance – Hungary (2008)		
(In billions of forint, central government figures)		
Revenue and Grants	**10,945.1**	**100.0%**
Tax revenue	6,284	57.4%
Social contributions	3,662	33.5%
Grants	138.1	1.3%
Other revenue	861	7.9%
Expenditures	**11,969.2**	**100.0%**
General public services	2,532	21.2%
Defense	239.3	2.0%
Public order and safety	539.1	4.5%
Economic affairs	1,456.4	12.2%
Environmental protection	136.9	1.1%
Housing and community amenities	26	0.2%
Health	1,242.5	10.4%
Recreational, culture, and religion	260.9	2.2%
Education	945.2	7.9%
Social protection	4,590.9	38.4%

(…) data not available or not significant.

SOURCE: *Government Finance Statistics Yearbook 2010,* Washington, DC: International Monetary Fund, 2010.

aircraft, watercraft, and several professions. Allianz Hungaria was the country's leading non-life insurer in 2003, with gross written non-life premiums of $621.8 million. ING was Hungary's top life insurer, with gross written life premiums totaling $280.1 million.

35 PUBLIC FINANCE

In April 2011 Hungary's budget deficit hit $992.4 million, exceeding its year-end target by 8%. Despite the wide gap, Hungary's finance ministry said that it was still aiming to meet a 2.94% goal by the end of 2011.

In recent years, the government has presented its budget bill to the National Assembly sometime during the first several months of the year, but the budget itself becomes effective on 1 January, when the fiscal year begins. It is prepared by the Ministry of Finance. Although Hungary had one of the most liberal economic regimes of the former Eastern bloc countries, its economy still suffered the growing pains of any country trying to come out of communism and privatize its industries. During the last few years, however, Hungary has enjoyed a remarkable expansion, averaging annual GDP growth of 4.5% between 1996 and 2002. Inflation in that period dropped from 28% to 7%, and unemployment fell to 6%, less than that in most EU countries, though it had arisen to above 10% by 2011. Eighty percent of GDP is now produced by privately owned companies. Still, Hungary's foreign debts remain large, putting a damper on the economy's otherwise spectacular performance.

The CIA estimated that, in 2010, Hungary's central government took in revenues of approximately $63.1 billion and had expenditures of $67.31 billion. Revenues minus expenditures totaled approximately -$4.21 billion. Public debt in 2010 amounted to 79.6% of GDP. Total external debt was $152 billion.

36 TAXATION

In 2011, Hungary's corporate tax rate was raised to 19%, up from 18% in 2009 and 16% in preceding years. Capital gains are also taxed at the 16% rate. However, only 50% of capital gains generated from stock transactions are subject to the tax. Capital gains from the sale of business assets are treated as business income. The withholding tax on dividends paid to foreign companies is 20% unless recipients reinvest in Hungarian companies. Dividends paid to individuals are subject to a 25% withholding tax, and dividends that are in excess of 30% of the return on equity are subject to a 35% rate. However, most tax treaties with Hungary reduce the withholding tax to between 5% and 15%.

In 2010, the personal income tax rate was 16% for all income groups. The disabled are given an extra deduction. There are also partial deductions allowed for school fees, interest paid for the purchase of a house, and for donations to charity. Inheritance and gift taxes range from 11–15%. There is a 2–6% tax on the transfer of housing and a 10% tax on the transfer of large estates. Local authorities may levy individual income and corporate taxes.

Plans were accounted to combine the Tax and Financial Control Administration with the Hungarian Customs and Finance Guard, creating the National Tax and Customs Office.

[37] CUSTOMS AND DUTIES

In 2010, there were no customs free zones, though as many as 130 had existed prior to Hungary's membership in the EU. Permits in all customs free zones expired in 2003. The reformation of such zones was discussed but suffered from a perceived lack of demand. Customs duties are expressed as a percentage of the value of the goods being imported.

[38] FOREIGN INVESTMENT

Even before the repudiation of communism, Hungary sought to enter joint ventures with Western countries. By the end of 1996, Hungary had attracted $15 billion in foreign direct investment (FDI). Since 1989, Hungary has attracted nearly one third of all foreign direct investment in Central and Eastern Europe. In 1995–96, the government adopted a stringent economic reform program of liberalization and privatization, and by 2002, the private sector, which had been 20% of the economy in 1989, was about 80%.

In the period from 1988 to 1990, Hungary's share of world FDI inward flows was five and a half times its share of world GDP, the sixth-largest ratio in the world. Annual foreign direct investment inflows into Hungary reached a peak in 1995 at about $4.5 billion, from which point they declined steadily until 2001, when there was an upswing to $2.4 billion from $1.6 billion in 2000. In 2002, FDI inflow fell to less than $1.5 billion. The average FDI inflow from 1998 to 2001 was about $2 billion a year. Foreign direct investment in Hungary was a net inflow of $2.78 billion according to World Bank figures published in 2009. FDI represented 2.16% of GDP.

The largest single source of foreign investment has been the United States, followed by Germany, the Netherlands, Austria, the United Kingdom, and France.

[39] ECONOMIC DEVELOPMENT

During the first 20 years after World War II, Hungary had the following economic plans: the three-year plan (1947–49) for economic reconstruction; the first five-year plan (1950–54) which aimed at rapid and forced industrialization and which was slightly modified in 1951 and again in 1953; the one-year plan of 1955; the second five-year plan (1956–60), designed to further industrialization but discarded as a result of the October 1956 uprising; the three-year plan (1958–60), which also emphasized industrialization, although it allocated greater investment for housing and certain consumer goods; and the new second five-year plan (1961–65), which provided for a 50% increase in industrial production. These were followed by the third five-year plan (1966–70); the fourth five-year plan (1971–75), with greater emphasis on modernization of industrial plants producing for export and housing construction; the fifth five-year plan (1976–80), which called for amelioration of the gap in living standards between the peasantry and the working class; the sixth five-year plan (1981–85), emphasizing investment in export industries and energy conservation and seeking to curb domestic demand; and the seventh five-year plan (1986–90), which projected growth of 15–17% in NMP, 13–16% in industrial production, and 12–14% in agriculture.

Far-reaching economic reforms, called the New Economic Mechanism (NEM), were introduced on 1 January 1968. In order to create a competitive consumers' market, some prices were no longer fixed administratively but were to be determined by market forces. Central planning was restricted to essential materials, and managers of state enterprises were expected to plan and carry out all the tasks necessary to ensure profitable production. In the early years of the NEM, the growth rate of industrial output surpassed target figures; national income rose substantially, surpassing any previous planning periods; and productivity increased significantly in all sectors of the national economy. However, following the huge oil price increases of 1973–74, the government returned to more interventionist policies in an attempt to protect Hungary's economy from external forces. Beginning in 1979, the government introduced a program that included price reform aimed at aligning domestic with world prices; changes in wage setting, which were intended to encourage productivity; and decentralization of industry, including the breakup of certain large enterprises and the creation of small-scale private ones, especially in services. New measures introduced in 1985 and 1986 included the lifting of government subsidies for retail prices (which led to sharp price increases) and the imposition of management reform, including the election of managers in 80% of all enterprises. The 1991–95 economic program aimed to fully integrate Hungary into the world economy on a competitive basis. The program's main features were to accelerate privatization, control inflation, and institute measures to prepare the way for the convertibility of the forint.

Reforms slowed in 1993 and 1994, and the privatization of state firms stopped. However, privatization accelerated in 1995 as the result of new laws passed in May of that year, which made the process simpler and allowed for the rapid privatization of small firms. Some large utilities were privatized in 1995; the first wave of the electricity and gas company privatization totaled $3.2 billion, primarily from German, Italian, and French interests. Budapest Bank, one of the country's largest banks, was sold to GE Capital Services. Hungary is now one of the few countries in Eastern Europe to have privatized major portions of its telecommunications and energy sectors. In 1995, the government received $4.5 billion in privatization proceeds. From the mid 1990s, a massive amount of foreign investment flowed into the country, which stood at just under $23.5 billion by the end of 2001, equivalent to about 46% of GDP.

In 1994, the Development Assistance Committee of the OECD distributed $68.3 million in aid to Hungary. Net concession flows from multilateral institutions that year amounted to $132 million. With the adoption of an IMF-backed stabilization program in 1995, Hungary exhibited consistent GDP annual growth of 4% in the late 1990s. Moreover, Hungary has repaid its entire debt to the IMF, was formally invited to join the EU in 2002, and finally accepted in 2004, together with nine other countries.

The Hungarian economy improved as it joined the EU, but the rate of improvement was deemed unsatisfactory. The GDP growth rate was 4% in 2004, but IMF specialists consider that the economy needs to grow by 5–5.25% annually if Hungary is to catch up with Western Europe in the timeline that it set for itself. The Hungarian policymakers are trying to attract additional investments to the country as a way of fostering additional growth. This task is made difficult, however, by increasing competition from neighboring countries and the need to implement a leaner and more flexible tax system.

40 SOCIAL DEVELOPMENT

A national social insurance system was relatively well-advanced before World War II for the nonagricultural population. A 1972 decree of the Council of Ministers extended this system to cover virtually the entire population, including craftsmen; by 1974, 99% of the population enjoyed the benefits of social insurance. Coverage includes relief for sickness, accidents, unemployment, and old age and incapacity, and provides maternity allowances for working women, allowances for children, and payment of funeral expenses. Men can collect old age pensions at the age of 62 after 20 years of employment. The social insurance system also provides for disability and survivorship benefits. Medical care is provided directly to the insured through the public health service.

Women have the same legal rights as men, including inheritance and property rights. They hold a large number of the positions in teaching, medicine, and the judiciary but generally earn less than men. Women are underrepresented in senior positions in both the private and public sectors. Sexual harassment in the workplace is commonplace, and it is not prohibited by law. Spousal abuse is a huge problem; approximately 20% of women were victimized in 2004. Sexual abuse, rape, and domestic violence are underreported due to cultural prejudice.

Minority rights are protected by law, allowing for the creation of minority local government bodies for limited self-rule. The law also preserves ethnic language rights and encourages minorities to preserve their cultural traditions. Despite these efforts, the Roma minority continues to face discrimination and prejudice. There were also reports of excessive police force in certain cases, as well as pretrial detention.

41 HEALTH

According to the CIA, life expectancy in Hungary was 74 years in 2011. The country spent 7.2% of its GDP on healthcare, amounting to $938 per person. There were 31 physicians, 63 nurses and midwives, and 70 hospital beds per 10,000 inhabitants. The fertility rate was 1.3, while the infant mortality rate was 5 per 1,000 live births. In 2008, the maternal mortality rate, according to the

World Bank, was 13 per 100,000 births. It was estimated that 99% of children were vaccinated against measles. The CIA calculated HIV/AIDS prevalence in Hungary to be about less than 0.1% in 2009.

The Ministry of Health administers the state health service, with the counties and districts forming hospital regions. By the end of 1974, 99% of the population was covered by social insurance and enjoyed free medical services; those few not insured pay for medical and hospital care. Limited private medical practice is permitted. In 1992, the Ministry of Welfare proposed a compulsory health care scheme based on the German system, to be administered by the National Health Security Directorate. After the termination of socialism in 1989, the Hungarian health system was largely unchanged. About 5% of clinics were privatized, and health care was available to nearly all of Hungary's people.

42 HOUSING

The construction rate for new dwellings has been greater in smaller cities and towns than in Budapest, where, as of 1980, 17.3% of all housing units were built before 1900 and 56.3% before 1945. According to national statistics, in 2005 there were about 4,127,743 dwelling units nationwide. About 84% were owner occupied. Only about 130,208 units were owned by municipal governments. Most homes have an average of four rooms. It has been estimated that about 1.2 million people are affected by overcrowding.

Low-income residents and other private builders generally rely on the labor of family and friends, buying the essential materials little by little; they may apply for loans if necessary to complete the dwelling.

43 EDUCATION

In 2011 the CIA estimated that Hungary had a literacy rate of 99.4%. Public expenditure on education represented 5.2% of GDP. In 2008 the World Bank estimated that 90% of age-eligible children in Hungary were enrolled in primary school. Secondary enrollment for age-eligible children stood at 91%. Tertiary enrollment was estimated at 65%. Of those enrolled in tertiary education, there were 100 male students for every 143 female students.

Before education was nationalized in 1948, most schools were operated by religious bodies, especially the Roman Catholic Church. The educational system is under the control of the Ministry of Education and is supervised by the local councils, which receive financial assistance from the central government.

Education is free for 12 years of study and compulsory for 10 years. The state also pays the bulk of costs for higher education. Primary school covers eight years of study. Secondary schools are divided into academic schools (*gimnázium*) and vocational schools (*szakközépiskola*). Programs at academic schools run from four to six years. Vocational school programs generally cover four years of study. In addition to its regular primary education, Hungary has over 100 primary schools with special music programs based on the pedagogy of the 20th-century composer Zoltan Kodály; at these "music primary schools," music receives as much emphasis as all other subjects. The academic year runs from September to June.

Hungary has about 77 institutions of higher education, including 25 universities and 47 colleges. Adult education expanded after World War II, especially through workers' schools and correspondence courses. Although there are university fees, many students are exempt from payment or pay reduced fees.

44 LIBRARIES AND MUSEUMS

Hungary's National Archives were established in 1756; among its treasures are some 100,000 items from the period prior to the Turkish occupation (1526). Hungary's National Széchényi Library is the largest and most significant in the country. Founded in Budapest in 1802, it has more than 2.5 million books and periodicals and more than 4.5 million manuscripts, maps, prints, and microfilms. Other important libraries are the Lóránd Eötvös University Library (1.5 million volumes) and the Library of the Hungarian Academy of Sciences (2.1 million volumes), both in Budapest; and the Central Library of the Lajos Kossuth University in Debrecen (1.27 million volumes). There are numerous local and regional public libraries.

There are over 500 museums (about 70 in Budapest) and many zoological and botanical gardens. One of the largest institutions is the Hungarian National Museum, which displays relics of prehistoric times as well as artifacts reflecting the history of Hungary from the Magyar conquest through 1849, including the Hungarian coronation regalia. A branch of the National Museum is the Hungarian Natural History Museum. Other museums, all in Budapest, include the Ethnographical Museum, the Museum of History, the Hungarian National Gallery, and the Museum of Fine Arts. Many castles and monasteries throughout the country have been converted to museums. There is also a Bela Bartok Museum, a Chinese Museum, a House of Terror museum (2002), and a Franz Lizst Memorial Museum and Research Center, all in Budapest.

45 MEDIA

In 2009, the CIA reported that there were 3.1 million telephone landlines in Hungary. In addition to landlines, mobile phone subscriptions averaged 118 per 100 people. There were 17 FM radio stations, 57 AM radio stations, and 3 shortwave radio stations. Internet users numbered 62 per 100 citizens. Prominent newspapers in 2010, with circulation numbers listed parenthetically, included *Nepszabadsag* (316,000), *Zalai Hirlap* (71,000), *Kisalfold* (80,000), as well as 19 other major newspapers.

Budapest is the principle communications center. Although telecommunication services in Hungary were long underdeveloped, services improved significantly during the 1990s, and investment in value-added services, such as the Internet and VSAT, grew. Hungary now has a modern telecommunications system capable of meeting all service demands. The country's domestic system is digitized and highly automated, with fiber-optic cable and microwave radio relay systems in place. Mobile cellular telephone use is heavy. In 2009, there were some 3.1 million main phone lines, and cellular phone subscriptions averaged 118 per 100 citizens.

In 2004 there were two state-owned public service television stations and two national commercial television stations. The same year, there were one public service radio and two national commercial radio stations. There are some smaller regional stations amounting to 17FM and 57AM stations as well as 3 shortwave radio stations. In 2003, there were an estimated 690 radios and 475 television sets for every 1,000 people. About 190.7 of every 1,000 people were cable subscribers. In 2010, the country had 2.6 million Internet hosts. As of 2009, there were some 6.1 million Internet users, and Internet subscriptions stood at 62 per 100 people.

The constitution of Hungary provides for free speech and a free press, and the government is said generally to respect these rights. Although previously all means of communication had been government property, 1995 saw the beginning of the privatization process, with aims to put most print and broadcast media in private hands.

46 ORGANIZATIONS

There is a Chamber of Commerce in Budapest. The International Labour Organization has a sub-regional office in Budapest. Hungary is a member of the International Chamber of Commerce. Trade and professional associations exist representing a variety of occupations, including the steel and automotive workers, journalists, teachers, librarians, engineers, architects, and various medical professionals. There is a Confederation of Professional Unions based in Budapest.

Organizations promoting research and study of various medical and scientific fields also exist. Some of these are member organizations of the Federation of Hungarian Medical Societies and/or the Hungarian Academy of Sciences. A cultural organization particular to Hungary is the International Kodaly Society; named for the music composer, scholar, and teacher, this organization promotes appreciate and study of music, particularly for youth. The multinational scientific organization of the International Measurement Confederation is based in Budapest.

Notable national youth organizations include the Federation of Young Democrats of Hungary, the Goncol Environmental Youth Alliance, the National Union of Hungarian Students, and Young Musicians of Hungary. The Hungarian Scout Association is also active, as are various chapters of the YMCA/YWCA. There are several sports associations promoting amateur competition in such pastimes as tennis, badminton, skating, and baseball. There is a national chapter of the Paralympic Committee. National women's organizations include the Association of Hungarian Women and the National Council of Hungarian Women.

Volunteer service organizations, such as the Lions Clubs and International, are also present. The Red Cross, Caritas, and Amnesty International have active chapters in the country.

47 TOURISM, TRAVEL, AND RECREATION

The *Tourism Factbook*, published by the UN World Tourism Organization, reported 40.6 million incoming tourists to Hungary in 2009, who spent a total of $6.74 billion. Of those incoming tourists, there were 39.6 million from Europe. There were 157,464 hotel beds available in Hungary, which had an occupancy rate of 30%. The estimated daily cost to visit Budapest, the capital, was $253. The cost of visiting other cities averaged $133.

Among Hungary's diverse tourist attractions are Turkish and Roman ruins, medieval towns and castles, more than 500 thermal springs (some with resort facilities), and Lake Balaton, the largest freshwater lake in Europe. Budapest is a major tourist attraction and cultural capital, with 2 opera houses, over 200 monuments and museums, and several annual arts festivals.

Popular sports include handball, football (soccer), tennis, and volleyball. The Budapest Grand Prix, the only Formula-1 motor race in Eastern Europe, was inaugurated in August 1986. A valid passport is required of all foreign visitors.

⁴⁸FAMOUS PERSONS

The foundations for modern Hungarian literature begin with the movement known as the Period of Linguistic Reform, whose leaders were the versatile writer Ferenc Kazinczy (1759–1831) and Ferencz Kölcsey (1790–1838), lyric poet and literary critic. Among the outstanding literary figures was Dániel Berzsenyi (1772–1836) of the Latin School. Károly Kisfaludy (1788–1830) founded the Hungarian national drama. Mihaly Vörösmarty (1800–55), a fine poet, related the Magyar victories under Árpád in his *Flight of Zalán*. He was followed by Hungary's greatest lyric poet, Sándor Petöfi (1823–49), a national hero who stirred the Magyars in their struggle against the Habsburgs in 1848 with his *Arise Hungarians*. Another revolutionary hero was Lajos Kossuth (1802–94), orator and political author. János Arany (1817–82), epic poet and translator, influenced future generations, as did Mór Jókai (1825–1904), Hungary's greatest novelist. The outstanding dramatist Imre Madách (1823–64) is known for his *Tragedy of Man*. Endre Ady (1877–1919) was a harbinger of modern poetry and Western ideas; Attila József (1905–1937) is another well-known poet. Lyric poets of the contemporary era include László Nagy (1925–78), János Pilinszky (1921–81), and Ferenc Juhász (b. 1928). Gyula Illyés (1902–83), a poet, novelist, and dramatist, was one of the outstanding figures of 20th-century Hungarian literature. Ferenc Molnár (1878–1952) is known for his plays *Liliom, The Swan,* and *The Guardsman*. György Lukács (1885–1971) was an outstanding Marxist writer and literary critic. Hungarian-born Arthur Koestler (1905–83), a former radical, was a well-known anti-Communist novelist and writer. Imre Kertész (b. 1929) is a Jewish-Hungarian author, Holocaust concentration camp survivor, and winner of the Nobel Prize in literature in 2002.

János Fadrusz (1858–1903) and József Somogyi (1916–93) are among Hungary's best-known sculptors. The outstanding Hungarian painter Mihály Munkácsy (1844–1900) is best known for his *Christ before Pilate*. Victor Vasarely (1908–97), a world-famous painter of "op art," was born in Budapest and settled in France in 1930. Miklós Ybl (1814–91) was a leading architect; and Gyula Halasz (1899–1984), better known as Brassai, was a well-known photographer. The Hungarian-born Joseph Pulitzer (1847–1911) was a noted journalist and publisher in the United States. Hungarian musicians include the composers Franz (Ferenc) Liszt (1811–86), Ernst (Ernö) von Dohnányi (1877–1960), Béla Bartók (1881–1945), Zoltán Kodály (1882–1967), and György Ligeti (b. 1923); violinists Jeno Hubay (1858–1937) and Joseph Szigeti (1892–1973); cellist János Starker (b. 1924); and pianists Lili Kraus (1903–86) and Erwin Nyiregyhazi (1903–87). Renowned Hungarian-born conductors who became famous abroad include Fritz Reiner (1888–1963), George Széll (1897–1970), Eugene Ormándy (1899–1985), Antal Doráti (1906–88), and Ferenc Fricsay (1914–63). Miklós Jancsó (b. 1921) is a distinguished film director, and Vilmos Zsigmond (b. 1930) a noted cinematographer; Béla Lugosi (Blasko, 1882–1956) and Peter Lorre (Laszlo Loewenstein, 1904–64) were famous actors.

Notable scientists include Lóránd Eötvös (1848–1919), inventor of torsion balance; Ányos Jedlik (1800–95), known for his research on dynamos; and the psychoanalyst Sándor Ferenczi (1873–1933).

Ignaz Philipp Semmelweis (1818–65) pioneered in the use of antiseptic methods in obstetrics. Béla Schick (1877–1967) invented the skin test to determine susceptibility to diphtheria.

Hungarian-born Nobel Prize winners are Róbert Bárány (1876–1936) in 1914, Albert Szent-Györgyi (1893–1986) in 1937, and Georg von Békésy (1899–1972) in 1961 in physiology or medicine, Georg de Hevesy (1885–1966) in 1944 in chemistry, and Dénés Gábor (1900–79) in 1971 for physics. Budapest-born scientists who contributed to atomic research in the United States were Leó Szilárd (1898–1964), Eugene Paul Wigner (1902–95), John von Neumann (1903–57), and Edward Teller (1908–2003). Theodore van Karman (Todor Kármán, 1881–1963) is the father of aerodynamics. Paul Erdős (1913–1996) was an important mathematician, as was John von Neumann (Neumann János, 1903–1957). Eugene Paul Wigner (1902–1995), physicist and mathematician, received the 1963 Nobel Prize in physics. George Andrew Olah (b. 1927 as György Oláh), a Hungarian-American chemist, won the Nobel Prize in chemistry in 1994.

Imre Nagy (1895?–1958) served as prime minister from 1953 to 1955, but was removed from office because of his criticism of Soviet policy; the uprising of October 1956 briefly brought Nagy back to the premiership. Arrested after the Soviet military intervention, Nagy was tried and executed in 1958. János Kádár (1912–89), first secretary of the HSWP since 1956, initially aligned himself with Nagy but subsequently headed the government established after Soviet troops rolled in. Kádár, who held the premiership from late 1956 to 1958 and again from 1961 to 1965, was the preeminent political leader in Hungary until his removal in May 1988. Gyula Horn (b. 1932), a former communist, was named prime minister in 1994. He served in that post until 1998, when he was succeeded by Viktor Orbán (b. 1963), who was prime minister between 1998 and 2002. Péter Medgyessy (b. 1942) served as prime minister from 2002 until 2004, not completing his term. Ferenc Gyurcsány (b. 1961) succeeded him.

George Soros (b. 1930), philanthropist, was born in Budapest.

⁴⁹DEPENDENCIES

Hungary has no territories or colonies.

⁵⁰BIBLIOGRAPHY

Ardo, Zsuzsanna. *Hungary.* London: Marshall Cavendish, 2008.

Buranbaeva, Oksana. *Culture and Customs of Hungary.* Santa Barbara, CA: Greenwood Publishing Group, 2011.

Bedford, Neal, et al. *Hungary.* Footscray, Vic.: Lonely Planet, 2009.

Dent, Bob. Hungary. New York: W.W. Norton, 2002.

Frucht, Richard (ed.). *Eastern Europe: An Introduction to the People, Lands, and Culture.* Santa Barbara, CA: ABC-CLIO, 2005.

Hill, Raymond. *Hungary. 2nd ed.* New York: Facts On File, 2004.

Horvath, Michael J. *Hungarian Civilization: A Short History.* College Park, MD: University of Maryland, 2000.

Hoshi, Iraj, Ewa Balcerowicz, and Leszek Balcerowicz (eds.). *Barriers to Entry and Growth of New Firms in Early Transition: A Comparative Study of Poland, Hungary, Czech Republic, Albania, and Lithuania.* Boston: Kluwer Academic Publishers, 2003.

International Smoking Statistics: A Collection of Historical Data from 30 Economically Developed Countries. New York: Oxford University Press, 2002.

McElrath, Karen (ed.). *HIV and AIDS: A Global View.* Westport, CT: Greenwood Press, 2002.

Opello, Walter C. *European Politics.* Boulder, CO: Lynne Rienner Publishers, 2009.

Political Chronology of Europe. London, Eng.: Europa, 2001.

Roman, Eric. *Austria-Hungary and the Successor States: A Reference Guide from the Renaissance to the Present.* New York: Facts On File, 2003.

Rose-Ackerman, Susan. *From Elections to Democracy: Building Accountable Government in Hungary and Poland.* New York: Cambridge University Press, 2005.

Turp, Craig. *Hungary.* New York: Dorling Kindersley, 2007.

ICELAND

Republic of Iceland

Lveldi Ísland

CAPITAL: Reykjavík

FLAG: The national flag, introduced in 1916, consists of a red cross (with an extended right horizontal), bordered in white, on a blue field.

ANTHEM: *O Guð; vors lands (O God of Our Land).*

MONETARY UNIT: The new króna (ISK), introduced 1 January 1981 and equivalent to 100 old krónur, is a paper currency of 100 aurar. There are coins of 5, 10, and 50 aurar and 1, 10 and 50 krónur, and notes of 10, 50, 100, 500, 1,000 and 5,000 krónur. ISK1 = US$0.00832 (or US$1 = ISK118.51) as of October 2011.

WEIGHTS AND MEASURES: The metric system is used.

HOLIDAYS: New Year's Day, 1 January; Labor Day, 1 May; National Holiday, 17 June; Bank Holiday, August; Christmas, 25–26 December. Movable religious holidays include Holy Thursday, Good Friday, Easter Monday, Ascension, and Whitmonday. Half-holidays are observed on Christmas Eve, 24 December, and New Year's Eve, 31 December.

TIME: GMT.

¹LOCATION, SIZE, AND EXTENT

Iceland, the westernmost country of Europe, is an island in the North Atlantic Ocean, just below the Arctic Circle and a little more than 322 km (200 mi) E of Greenland, 1,038 km (645 mi) W of Norway, and 837 km (520 mi) NW of Scotland. It has an area of 103,000 sq km (39,769 sq mi), extending 490 km (304 mi) E–W and 312 km (194 mi) N–S. Comparatively, the area occupied by Iceland is slightly smaller than the state of Kentucky. The total length of coastline is about 4,988 km (3,099 mi). The republic includes many smaller islands, of which the chief are the Westman Islands (Vestmannaeyjar) off the southern coast.

Iceland's capital city, Reykjavík, is located on the country's southwest coast.

²TOPOGRAPHY

Iceland consists mainly of a central volcanic plateau, with elevations from about 700 to 800 m (2,297–2,625 ft), ringed by mountains, the highest of which is Hvannadalshnúkur (2,119 m/6,952 ft), in the Örfajökull glacier. Lava fields cover almost 11% of the country, and glaciers almost 12%. Among the many active volcanoes there is an average of about one eruption every five years. The largest glacier in Europe, Vatnajökull (about 8,400 sq km/3,200 sq mi), is in southeast Iceland. There are also many lakes, snowfields, hot springs, and geysers (the word "geyser" itself is of Icelandic origin).

The longest river is the Thjórsá (about 230 km/143 mi) in southern Iceland. Most rivers are short and none are navigable, but because of swift currents and waterfalls, Iceland's rivers have important waterpower potential. There are strips of low arable land along the southwest coast and in the valleys. Good natural harbors are provided by fjords on the north, east, and west coasts.

³CLIMATE

Despite Iceland's northern latitude, its climate is fairly mild because of the Gulf Stream, part of which almost encircles the island. There are no extreme temperature variations between seasons, but frequent weather changes are usual, particularly in the south, which experiences many storms and heavy precipitation. Temperatures at Reykjavík range from an average of 11°C (52°F) in July to -1°C (30°F) in January, with an annual mean of about 5°C (41°F). Humidity is high, and there is much fog in the east. Annual rainfall in the north ranges from 30 to 70 cm (12–28 in); in the south, 127 to 203 cm (50–80 in); and in the mountains, up to 457 cm (180 in). Winters are long and fairly mild, summers short and cool. Summer days are long and nights short; in winter, days are short and nights long.

⁴FLORA AND FAUNA

Although there are a few small trees (ash, aspen, birch, and willow), the chief forms of vegetation are grass, mosses, and small shrubs (heather, willow, dwarf birch). The World Resources Institute estimates that there are 377 plant species in Iceland. In addition, Iceland is home to 33 mammal, 305 bird, and 1 reptile species. The calculation reflects the total number of distinct species residing in the country, not the number of endemic species.

The fox, Iceland's chief indigenous animal, is common. Wild reindeer, introduced in the 18th century and once abundant, were almost exterminated and, therefore, have been protected in recent years; they are found chiefly in the northeastern highlands. The waters around Iceland abound in whales, many types of seals, and many kinds of fish. Dolphin, grampus, porpoise, and rorqual are numerous. Cod, haddock, and herring are particularly abundant, but there are also sole, shark, halibut, redfish, saithe, and other fish. Salmon abound in many rivers and trout in rivers and lakes. Most mating bird species are aquatic. The chief resident birds are eiderduck (raised commercially for their down) and ptarmigan. Other characteristic indigenous birds are swan, eagle, falcon, and gannet, all rare now and protected. Iceland has very little insect life.

5 ENVIRONMENT

Iceland historically has been a conservative user of hydrocarbon fuels, so its air is cleaner than that of most other industrialized nations. On the other hand, its water supply is polluted by extensive use of fertilizers. The most recent available data reported a yearly average usage rate of 2,500 lbs per acre. Water pollution is also attributed to population increases in larger cities. Protected lands include 4 national parks and 27 nature reserves. Responsibility for environmental regulation is entrusted to the Ministry of Social Affairs.

Iceland's location on the Atlantic's mid-oceanic ridge makes the island vulnerable to volcanic activity. The Eyjafjallajokull volcano, located in southern Iceland, ended its 200-year dormancy in March 2010, emitting both lava and volcanic ash. The enormous ash clouds swept over several northern European nations, leading to the grounding of commercial air services for several days. In May 2011, Iceland's Grimsvotn volcano erupted, setting off an ash cloud that affected flights from the United Kingdom. Though delays were reported, the volcano did not cause as many problems as the eruption of the Eyjafjallajokull (only 900 of 90,000 flights were cancelled).

Iceland has been criticized by environmental groups for its 2006 decision to resume commercial whaling. The country had abandoned the practice in 1989 in cooperation with a global moratorium on whaling. Officials in favor of the whale hunts claimed that they are sustainable and that market demand justifies the hunts. For commercial whaling, the government enacted a quota of 40 minke whales in 2008. However, in the same year, there was no quota in place for fin whales. In 2009, the quota was adjusted to 100 minke whales and 150 fin whales. In the first nine months of 2010, Iceland exported 600 tons of whale meat to Japan. As of 2011, this remained a highly contested issue.

According to a 2011 report issued by the International Union for Conservation of Nature and Natural Resources (IUCN), threatened species included one type of mammal and eight species of fish. Endangered species include the leatherback turtle, three species of whales, and three species of fish. The extremely endangered species list includes the European eel, blue skate, and Eskimo curlew). The great auk has become extinct.

The World Resources Institute reported that Iceland had designated 391,500 hectares (967,418 acres) of land for protection as of 2006. Water resources totaled 170 cu km (40.79 cu mi) while water usage was 0.17 cu km (0.041 cu mi) per year. Domestic water usage accounted for 34% of total usage and industrial usage for 66%. Per capita water usage totaled 567 cu m (20,023 cu ft) per year.

The United Nations (UN) reported in 2008 that carbon dioxide emissions in Iceland totaled 3,594 kilotons.

6 POPULATION

The US Central Intelligence Agency (CIA) estimated the population of Iceland in 2011 to be approximately 311,058, which placed it at number 179 in population among the 196 nations of the world. In 2011 approximately 12.7% of the population was over 65 years of age, with another 20.2% under 15 years of age. The median age in Iceland was 35.6 years. There was 1 male for every female in the country. The population's annual rate of change was 0.687%. The projected population for the year 2025 was 360,000. Population density in Iceland was calculated at 3 people per sq km (8 people per sq mi).

The UN estimated that 93% of the population lived in urban areas, and that urban populations had an annual rate of change of 1.5%. The largest urban area was Reykjavík, with a population of 198,000.

7 MIGRATION

Estimates of Iceland's net migration rate carried out by the CIA in 2011 amounted to 0.53 migrants per 1,000 citizens. The total number of emigrants living abroad was 42,700, and the total number of immigrants living in Iceland was 37,200. Little immigration has occurred since the original settlement in the 9th and 10th centuries. In the last quarter of the 19th century, because of unfavorable economic conditions, about 12,000 residents of Iceland emigrated to Canada and the United States. After 1900, net emigration decreased substantially. Between 1956 and 1997, just 375 refugees arrived in Iceland.

During the Kosovo crisis, Iceland offered to take up to 100 refugees under the UNHCR/IOM Humanitarian Evacuation Program. A total of 70 people were actually evacuated to Iceland, 16 of whom returned to Kosovo by 1999.

8 ETHNIC GROUPS

The population is almost entirely Icelandic (94%), many of whom descended from the Norse and Celtic settlers who came in the late 9th and early 10th centuries. The remaining 6% of the population is of foreign origin.

9 LANGUAGES

Icelandic, the national language, derives from the Old Norse language that was spoken throughout Scandinavia at the time of settlement. It has changed little through the centuries, partly because of the country's isolation and partly because of the people's familiarity with the classical language, as preserved in early historical and literary writings. There is comparatively little difference between the old language and the modern, or between the written language and the spoken. To this day, Icelanders are able to read the great 13th-century sagas without special study. English, the Nordic languages, and German are also widely spoken.

10 RELIGIONS

According to a 2010 report, about 79% of the population were nominally members of the state established Evangelical Lutheran Church (ELC). About 5.2% of the population belong to the Lutheran Free Churches, which are independent of the ELC. Most Lutherans do not attend services regularly; however, a majority of citizens turn to the ELC for baptisms, confirmations, and marriages. Another 6.2% (about 13,025 people) belong to one of 21 different denominations that are registered and recognized by the state. The largest of these groups is the Roman Catholic Church (9,672 members); the smallest is the Homechurch (11 members). The Reykjavik Catholic Church, Seventh-Day Adventists, Jehovah's Witnesses, Buddhists, Baha'is, Muslims, and Jews are also

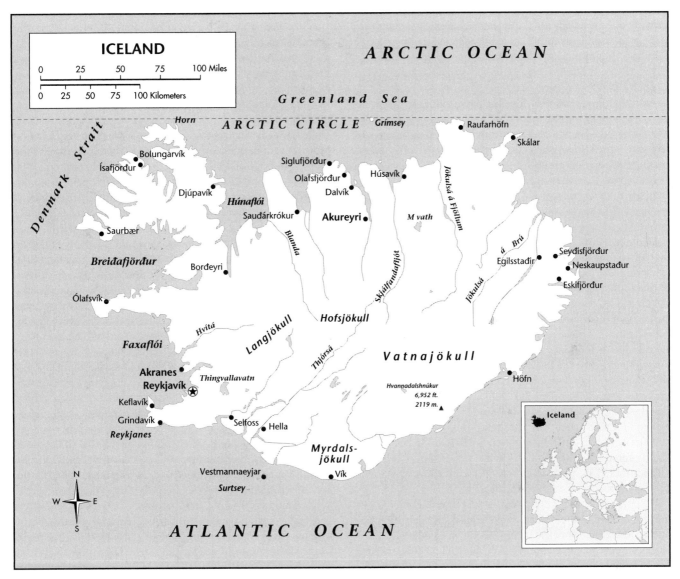

LOCATION: 63°19′ to 67°7′5″ N; 13°16′7″ to 24°32′3″ W. BOUNDARY LENGTHS: Total coastline, 4,970 kilometers (3,090 miles). TERRITORIAL SEA LIMIT: 12 miles.

represented by small congregations. Approximately 3.3% of the population are not affiliated with any religion.

Freedom of religion is guaranteed by the constitution and this right is generally respected in practice. Lutheranism is the nation's official religion, and the ELC is designated as the state church. As such, the government pays the salaries of at least 130 ELC ministers, who are considered to be public servants under the Ministry of Justice and Human Rights. By law, all taxpayers are required to pay a church tax; however, citizens may choose any officially registered church as the recipient of the tax and those not affiliated with any religion can designate that the tax be submitted to the state treasury. All public schools are required to include instruction in theology and Christian heritage from grades 1 through 10, though students may apply for exemptions. While registration is not required for religious groups, it allows for certain benefits. Registration is handled through the Ministry of Justice and Human Rights and consists of a fairly easy process. Maundy Thursday, Good Friday, Easter Monday, Ascension Day, Whit Monday,

Christmas Eve (afternoon only), Christmas Day, and Boxing Day are observed as national holidays.

¹¹TRANSPORTATION

All important towns and districts can be reached by bus and truck via interurban roads. The CIA reports that Iceland has a total of 12,869 km (7,996 mi) of roads. There are 767 vehicles per 1,000 people in the country.

In 2008, Iceland's merchant marine fleet consisted of two ships of 1,000 GRT or more. In addition, there are about 1,000 civilian vessels, mostly small fishing craft. Most of the import and export trade is handled in Reykjavík. Akureyri, on the north coast, is the largest port serving the outlying areas.

There are 99 airports, which transported 1.36 million passengers in 2009 according to the World Bank. As of 2010, six of the airports had paved runways. The principal airport is Keflavik at Reykjavík. In the 1950s, Icelandic Airlines was the first transatlantic airline to offer fares drastically lower than those of the major carriers. Icelandair, formed by a merger of Icelandic Airlines and Iceland Air in the early 1970s, operates domestic routes as well as international flights to the United Kingdom, Scandinavia, and Germany, and transatlantic flights with stopovers at Reykjavík.

12 HISTORY

Iceland's first known settler, Ingólfur Arnarson, sailed from his native Norway to Iceland and settled at what is now Reykjavík in 874. During the late 9th and early 10th centuries, the island was settled by other Norwegians, fleeing the oppressive rule of their king, and by smaller groups of Scottish and Irish emigrants. In 930, a central legislative and judicial assembly, the Althing, was established, and a uniform code of laws for the entire country was compiled. Christianity was introduced in 1000, but memories of the old pagan religion were preserved in 12th- and 13th-century Icelandic literature. Many of the early settlers were great seafarers and continued their westward voyages of discovery and exploration from Iceland. Most famous of these were Eric the Red (Eiríkur Thorvaldsson), who discovered and settled in Greenland in 982, and his son Leif Ericsson (Leifur Eiríksson), who around the year 1000 discovered the North American continent, which he called Vinland ("wineland") because of the grapes he found there.

Icelanders acknowledged the sovereignty of Haakon IV of Norway in a treaty of 1262, which established a purely personal union, ending the independent republic or commonwealth in Iceland. When all the Scandinavian countries came under the rule of Denmark at the end of the 14th century, Iceland became a Danish dominion. Lutheranism was introduced in the 1540s. Exclusive trading rights with Iceland were given in 1602 to a private Danish trading company. Danes had a complete monopoly of trade with Iceland until 1786, when trade was opened to all subjects of the kings of Denmark, including Icelanders.

The last decades of the 18th century were a period of economic ruin for Iceland, compounded by poor harvests, epidemics, and volcanic eruptions (notably that of 1783, the worst in Iceland's history); by 1800 the population had dwindled to 38,000, less than half the number in the period of independence. In that year, the king abolished the Althing, long since reduced in power. Within a few decades, however, a nationalist movement had attained considerable strength, winning the reestablishment of the Althing (but only as an advisory body) in 1843, followed by the opening of trade with all countries in 1854. After a long constitutional struggle—led by a national hero, Jón Sigurðsson, who was both statesman and scholar—limited home rule was granted in 1874, and almost complete home rule in 1903. By agreement with Denmark in 1918, Iceland was declared a free and independent state, but personal union with the Danish crown was retained. The Danish king continued to function as king of Iceland, and Denmark conducted Iceland's foreign affairs, but Iceland had the right to terminate this union after 25 years.

Cut off from Denmark during World War II by the German occupation of that country, Iceland established diplomatic relations with the United Kingdom and the United States. British forces took over the protection of the island in 1940 and were replaced the following year by US troops that remained in Iceland until early 1947. In a referendum held in May 1944, more than 97% of those participating voted to end the union with the king of Denmark and, on 17 June 1944, Iceland became an independent re-

public. In 1946, it was admitted to UN membership. Three years later, Iceland became a party to the Atlantic Pact (NATO). A bilateral defense agreement was signed in 1951 providing for a US military presence. In March 1970, Iceland joined the European Free Trade Association (EFTA), and a tariff agreement was ratified with the European Commission in February 1973. To protect its fishing industry, Iceland unilaterally extended its fishing zone in 1958, and again in 1972 and 1975, provoking conflict with the United Kingdom and other countries. Casualties resulted from the most serious outbreak of the "cod war" with the United Kingdom in late 1975 and in February 1976. An agreement ended the conflict in June 1976 and relations with the United Kingdom improved. Disputes over fisheries resources have also arisen with the Norwegians periodically, though both Norway and Iceland are united in their opposition to the international ban on whaling.

Depressed world fish prices weakened the economy in the early 1990s, resulting in a no-growth gross domestic product (GDP) and higher unemployment. The government launched an austerity program to trim the Icelandic welfare state, which included measures such as increasing the retirement age from 65 to 67 (with future increases to age 70 envisioned). Icelanders also were asked to pay for a greater portion of social services out of their own pockets. Demand in Europe and the United States for Icelandic fish rebounded. Liberalization of many sectors of the economy, such as telecoms and banking, required under the European Economic Area (EEA) agreement with the European Union (EU) in exchange for greater access to the EU market, reduced public expenditures and positively affected governmental finances. By 1999, Iceland had experienced four years of more than 5% GDP growth, and purchasing power was increasing at four times the Organization for Economic Co-operation and Development (OECD) average. The economic boom years from 1996 to 2001 slowed in 2002, and Iceland experienced a mild recession.

A major financial and political crisis rocked the nation beginning in October 2008 when three of the nation's largest banks failed. The government stepped in to take control of the banks, but the measure was not enough. The government itself faced bankruptcy as the króna depreciated by 90% and foreign banks denied credit to refinance loans. Iceland turned to the International Monetary Fund (IMF), which offered an initial loan of $2.1 billion. The government, led by Geir Haarde of the Independence Party, was highly criticized for its actions in the crisis. Citizen protests in January 2009 led to the resignation of the government and early parliamentary elections in April 2009. Jóhanna Sigurðardóttir of the Social Democratic Party was elected as prime minister as her party won 20 seats in parliament.

In July 2009, after days of heated debate, members of the Althing voted to submit a bid for application to the European Union. While Icelanders had been skeptical about EU membership in the past, the economic recession brought on by the collapse of the banks and the 2008–09 global financial crisis led many to consider membership as a means of stabilizing and strengthening the economy. The vote for the application was close, at 33 to 28 with 2 abstentions.

Accession talks kicked off in July 2010, but Iceland opened discussions with a tough negotiating stance, saying that it would not accept the EU's common fisheries policy. Fish and fish products account for roughly half of Iceland's exports, and the EU's common fisheries policy would open Iceland's exclusive economic zone, which covers 760,000 sq km (293,438 sq mi), to rival, non-Icelandic, EU fishing fleets. In response to Iceland's objections over the fisheries policy, the EU Enlargement Commissioner, Stefan Fuele, took a calculated but concessionary stance, saying that the EU grants no "permanent" exemptions.

According to a report by the European Commission, the screening process ended and formal negotiations began on 27 June 2011. Four chapters were opened: science and research; education and culture; public procurement; and information society and media. The first two were immediately closed, creating a first in accession history. Iceland expected to open half of the remaining chapters in the latter half of 2011 during the Polish presidency and the other half during the first part of 2012 under the Danish presidency.

13 GOVERNMENT

Iceland is an independent republic. Executive power is vested in the prime minister, who serves as chief of state, and the prime minister, serving as head of government. Legislative power is shared by the president and the legislative assembly (Althing). The president is elected by universal suffrage for a four-year term. The prime minister (typically the leader of the majority party or coalition) is appointed by the president, and the prime minister in turn selects a cabinet composed of ministers responsible to the Althing for their acts. The president must sign all legislation before it becomes law.

All citizens who have reached the age of 18 may vote, provided they have resided in Iceland for the five years immediately preceding an election. In 2009, according to the Institute for Democracy and Electoral Assistance, nearly 85% of Icelanders eligible to vote in the parliamentary elections did so. By a system of proportional representation, voters elect the 63 members of the unicameral Althing from eight constituencies at a general election held every four years, or sooner if the governing coalition loses its ability to command a legislative majority. Because of the widely varying populations of the constituencies (Reykjavík constitutes one-third of the nation's population), each constituency has a minimum of five seats, and more populous regions have more. Three-quarters of the seats in any constituency are divided by the parties according to proportional representation of that region, while the final quarter of the seats in each constituency are apportioned according to the national vote tally to ensure national proportional representation. Any citizen qualified to vote is eligible to run for a seat in the Althing. When any amendment to the constitution is brought up for a vote, the Althing is dissolved and new elections are held; if the new Althing accepts the proposed amendment, it becomes law when ratified by the president.

The institution of the Althing has parliamentary immunity and its members swear allegiance to the constitution. Government ministers are normally members of the Althing and enjoy full parliamentary privileges. The constitution and the rules of procedure of the Althing specify the rights and duties of parliamentarians. The legislative year of the Althing begins on 1 October. The legislative agenda of the Althing is divided among 12 standing committees. At the first meeting following the inauguration ceremony, the president of the Althing is elected. In addition to acting as the chief executive of Althing, the president sits on the five-person presidium along with the four vice presidents. The presidium is responsible for the organization of parliamentary activities. Sessions of the Althing are normally held four days a week.

14 POLITICAL PARTIES

No one major party in recent years has been able to command a majority of the electorate, and coalition governments have been the rule. Principal parties include the Independence Party (Sjálfstoeðisflokkurinn), a conservative grouping; the Progressive Party (Framsóknarflokkurinn), an agrarian, left-center party; the Progressive Alliance (Althýðubandalag), a formerly communist-oriented party, now a far-left party; and the Social Democratic People's Party (Althýðuflokkurinn), a center-left group. An Independence Party splinter group, the Citizens' Party (CP), lost its parliamentary representation by securing no seats. Iceland is unique among the Nordic states (which lead the OECD countries on all indicators of gender equality) in that it is the only one to have a women's party, which has gained a foothold in parliament. In 1995, the Icelandic Women's Alliance, a political party devoted to feminist issues, gained three seats in the Althing.

Of these parties, the Independence Party dates back to 1929 and the Progressive and Social Democratic People's (formerly Labor) parties to 1916; all three have been the source of various splinter groups. The People's Alliance became a distinct political party in 1970; it grew out of an alliance among communist-oriented elements in the SDP and other groups, and in effect replaced the earlier People's Union-Socialist Party (Sameiningarflokkur althyðu-Sósíalistaflokkurinn).

It was the issue of the North Atlantic Treaty Organization (NATO) and the US military presence that in March 1956 broke up an early alliance between Progressives and Independents, and the elections that year led to a new coalition of the Progressive, Labor, and People's Union-Socialist parties, all of which opposed the US military base on Iceland. After the Hungarian uprising of October 1956, however, the Progressive and Labor parties reversed their stand. That government fell because of Communist opposition to a proposed wage freeze, and after elections in October 1959, a government formed by the Independence and Labor parties came into office. This coalition endured for some time. But after the loss of four seats in the June 1971 general elections, a new government, composed of the Progressive Party, the People's Alliance, and the Liberal and Left Alliance (a party established in 1969 on a platform opposing Iceland's participation in NATO and its defense agreement with the United States) came into power under Prime Minister Olafur Jóhannesson. Then, on 29 August 1974, after gains by the Independence Party in June elections, a coalition of Independents and Progressives was sworn in under Geir Hallgrímsson of the Independence Party.

Two short-lived coalition governments followed. The first, a leftist coalition including the Social Democrats, People's Alliance, and Progressive Party, led by Jóhannesson, was dissolved when the Social Democrats left the coalition in October 1979. Following an election that December, a second coalition was eventually formed from members of the Independence Party, the People's Alliance, and the Progressives, with Gunnar Thoroddsen, deputy chairman of the Independence Party, as prime minister. After three unsuccessful attempts by party leaders to form a governing coalition following the April 1983 elections, Vigdís Finnbogadóttir—who in August 1981 had been elected president, becoming the first woman democratically elected as head of state—threatened to request the formation of a government of civil servants. Eventually, Progressive leader Steingrímur Hermannsson formed and headed a coalition of the Independence and Progressive parties. Following the 1987 elections, Thorsteinn Pálsson of the Independence Party replaced Hermannsson as prime minister.

The general election of April 1991 resulted in a new center-right coalition led by Davíð Oddsson of the Independence Party and members of the Social Democratic People's Party. Finnbogadóttir was reelected unopposed for a fourth four-year term in June 1992. The center-right coalition was dissolved after the elections of April 1995 when Oddsson formed a new coalition government composed of the Independence Party and the Progressive Party, chaired by Halldór Ásgrímsson, minister for foreign affairs and external trade. This coalition remained in power after the 1999 elections in which the Independence Party increased its share of the popular vote while the Progressives polled more poorly. Two new parties gained representation in the Althing in 1999, the environmental Left-Green Party (Vinstrihreyfing-Grænt framboð) and the Liberal Party (Frjáslyndi Flokkurin).

In the presidential elections of June 1996, Finnbogadóttir chose not to run and Dr. Ólafur Ragnar Grímsson won with 41.4% of the vote. In 2000, Grímsson was reappointed president, unopposed, to a second four-year term. Grímsson faced two opponents in the 2004 presidential election, but beat them soundly (with 85.6% of the vote).

In the May 2007 elections for the Althing, the Independence Party secured 36.5% of the vote and 25 seats in parliament. The opposition Social Democratic Alliance won 26.6% of the vote and took 18 seats. The Left-Green Movement came in next with 14.3% of the vote and nine seats. Following the election, Geir Haarde of the Independence Party was elected to the post of prime minister.

The 2008 presidential election was cancelled since there was no registered candidate to oppose Grímsson for his fourth term.

The economic crisis in late 2008 led to political crisis in January 2009, as citizens called for, and were granted, the resignation of the Haarde-led government. Jóhanna Sigurðardóttir of the Social Democratic Alliance temporarily stepped into the post of prime minister in January 2009. In the April 2009 elections, the Social Democratic Alliance won 29.8% of the vote, with 20 seats. The Independence Party kept 16 seats, followed by the Left-Green Movement with 14 seats. The Progressive Party won nine seats and the Citizens' Movement won four. Sigurðardóttir became the first woman elected to the position of prime minister in Iceland.

15 LOCAL GOVERNMENT

Iceland is divided into eight regions (landshluta), 23 counties (sýslur), and 23 independent towns (kaupstaðir). A magistrate or sheriff (sýslumaðour) administers each county. Within the counties are 79 municipalities (as of 2011), each governed by a council. Town councils are elected by proportional representation while rural councils are elected by a simple majority. The local government units supervise tax collections, police administration, local finances, employment, and other local affairs.

16 JUDICIAL SYSTEM

District courts are courts of first instance. The eight district courts have jurisdiction in both civil and criminal cases. Appeals are heard by the Supreme Court, consisting of nine justices (all appointed for life by the president), who elect one of their number as chief justice for a two-year term. There are special courts for maritime cases, labor disputes, and other types of cases.

The courts are free from political control. Although the Ministry of Justice administers the lower courts, the Supreme Court oversees independent and fair application of the law.

A special reform project transferred all judicial authority for criminal and civil cases from local officials (chiefs of police) to newly established district courts. This complete separation of judicial and executive power in regional jurisdictions was completed in 1992. Iceland did not accept compulsory International Court of Justice jurisdiction.

17 ARMED FORCES

The International Institute for Strategic Studies reported that armed forces in Iceland totaled 130 members in 2011, all of them belonging to a paramilitary force. Armed forces represent 0.1% of the labor force in Iceland. Defense spending totaled $591 million and accounted for 5% of GDP.

Iceland is the only NATO member with no military force of its own, although the government does maintain a coast guard with three patrols and one logistical/support vessels. US forces (1,658 personnel), along with Dutch forces, are stationed in Iceland.

18 INTERNATIONAL COOPERATION

Iceland became a member of the UN on 19 November 1946 and belongs to ECE and most of the nonregional specialized agencies, such as FAO, UNESCO, ILO, IFC, IFAD, the World Bank, and WHO. It belongs to the Council of Europe, the WTO, European Bank for Reconstruction and Development, the Euro-Atlantic Partnership Council, EFTA, NATO, the OECD, and the OSCE. The country is an associate member of the Western European Union. Iceland holds membership in the Council of the Baltic Sea States, the Nordic Council, the Nordic Investment Bank, the Arctic Council, and Barents Euro-Arctic Council. In 2001, the government established the Icelandic Crisis Response Unit (ICRU), which is designed to expand national support for cooperation in peacekeeping initiatives through the United Nations.

Iceland belongs to the Australia Group, the Nuclear Energy Agency, and the Organization for the Prohibition of Chemical Weapons. In environmental cooperation, Iceland is part of the Basel Convention, Conventions on Biological Diversity and Air Pollution, Ramsar, CITES, the London Convention, the Kyoto Protocol, the Montréal Protocol, MARPOL, the Nuclear Test Ban Treaty, and the UN Conventions on the Law of the Sea, Climate Change and Desertification.

19 ECONOMY

Marine products have generally accounted for the largest percentage of Iceland's export earnings. In 2008, however, aluminum exports exceeded marine products for the first time. Crop raising plays a small role, since most of the land is unsuitable for cultivation and the growing season is short. Sheep raising and dairying are the chief agricultural activities, with horse breeding also substantial. Iceland is generally self-sufficient in meat, eggs, and dairy products, but sugar and cereal products must be imported. The nation has been investing more of its resources in its own supply of geothermal energy. Because Iceland has almost no known mineral resources and has had no concentrations of population until recent decades, industry is small-scale and local, depends heavily on imported raw and semi-manufactured materials, and cannot compete favorably with foreign industry, especially with imports from low-income countries.

Although the economy is based on private ownership and operates mainly on a free-enterprise basis, public enterprises account for a sizable share of GDP. The cooperative movement is important in rural trade, and the national and local governments own some productive facilities in certain fields requiring large amounts of capital not available from private sources.

The economy developed rapidly after World War II, with a rate of capital investment so high at times as to strain available resources. Gross National Product (GNP) growth fell from 9% in 1977 to -3% in 1983 but recovered to 9% in 1987. After that, it averaged -0.4% through 1993. From 1992 to 2001, the economy grew impressively. Per capita GDP reached one of the highest levels among OECD countries. This performance was largely due to market liberalization, privatization, and other factors that spurred entrepreneurship and investment.

After 2001, the overheated economy slowed. The government tightened monetary policy and exercised fiscal restraint to reduce domestic demand. The króna went through a period of devaluation and inflation rose. However, the weak currency—along with increased production—resulted in a surge in exports.

In 2007, GDP growth was estimated at 3.8%, down from 5.2% in 2005. Industrial production grew at a rate of about 9% that year. The inflation rate stood at 5%, up slightly from previous years. With this increase in inflation, the international financial press began to question the stability of Iceland's major banks. The financial and banking sectors were particularly strong in the early 2000s, as Icelandic banks built up foreign assets and foreign debt. Icelandic businesses also made major investments abroad. In early 2008, the system began to falter with the development of a global credit crunch. The value of the króna decreased and banks were unable to secure the foreign credit needed to refinance existing loans. This led to economic meltdown in October 2008, as three of the largest banks in the nation collapsed. The government assumed control of the banks, but the measure was not enough. The government applied for and received loans exceeding $10 billion from the IMF in efforts to stabilize the króna. By early 2009, inflation was at about 18.6%, the currency had depreciated by 90%, and unemployment had reached 9.4% and was rising.

According to the OECD, by mid-2011 Iceland's financial position had progressively improved since the 2008–09 global financial crisis. The economic contraction and rise in unemployment appeared to have been halted by late 2010, and there were reports of impending growth in mid 2011. A major factor behind the resolution of the financial crisis was the pronouncement by the Icelandic government to apply for membership in the EU in July 2009. While views on the practicability of EU membership are quite mixed in Iceland, this action served to enhance the country's credibility on international financial markets. In 2010 GDP rate of change in Iceland was estimated at -3.5%. Inflation stood at 5.5% and unemployment was reported at 8.3%.

20 INCOME

The CIA estimated that in 2010 the GDP of Iceland was $11.82 billion. The CIA defines GDP as the value of all final goods and services produced within a nation in a given year, computed on the basis of purchasing power parity (PPP) rather than on the exchange rate based on current dollars. The per capita GDP was estimated at $38,300. The annual growth rate of GDP was -3.5%. The average inflation rate was 5.5%. It was estimated that agriculture accounted for 5.5% of GDP, industry 24.6%, and services 69.9%.

According to the World Bank, remittances from citizens living abroad totaled $23.5 million or about $75 per capita and accounted for approximately 0.2% of GDP.

The World Bank reported that in 2009, household consumption in Iceland totaled $6.2 billion or about $19,902 per capita, measured in current US dollars rather than PPP. Household consumption includes expenditures of individuals, households, and nongovernmental organizations on goods and services, excluding purchases of dwellings. It was estimated that household consumption was growing at an average annual rate of 15.5%.

The World Bank estimated that Iceland, with less than 0.01% of the world's population, accounted for 0.02% of the world's GDP. By comparison, the United States, with 4.85% of the world's population, accounted for 22.51% of world GDP.

As of 2011, the World Bank's most recent study reported that actual individual consumption in Iceland was 76.2% of GDP and accounted for 0.02% of world consumption. By comparison, the United States accounted for 25.44% of world individual consumption. The World Bank also estimated that 8.7% of Iceland's GDP was spent on food and beverages, 14.8% on housing and household furnishings, 2.5% on clothes, 9.2% on health, 9.8% on transportation, 1.4% on communications, 8.0% on recreation, 4.3% on restaurants and hotels, and 10.5% on miscellaneous goods and services and purchases from abroad.

21 LABOR

As of 2010, Iceland had a total labor force of 181,000 people. Within that labor force, CIA estimates in 2008 noted that 4.8% were employed in agriculture, 22.2% in industry, and 73% in the service sector.

In 2011, the Icelandic Confederation of Labor reported that more than 80% of workers are union members. Principal unions are the Icelandic Federation of Labor (associated with the International Confederation of Free Trade Unions, or ICFTU) and the Municipal and Government Employees' Association. Labor disputes are settled by direct negotiations or by special courts; however, strikes are permitted. Collective bargaining is used to negotiate pay, hours, and other conditions.

The customary workweek is 40 hours. Workers are entitled to overtime pay in excess of eight hours per day. There is no legal minimum wage, but wages are negotiated through collective bargaining. Even the lowest paid workers earn sufficient wages to provide a decent standard of living. Child labor standards are stringent and strictly enforced.

22 AGRICULTURE

In the 19th century and earlier, agriculture was the chief occupation, but by 1930, fewer than 36% of the people devoted their energies to farming, and the proportion has continued to fall. Into the 2000s, as is the case throughout the Nordic countries, less than 5% of Iceland's population is engaged in agriculture. Less than 1% of the total land is farmed. Fruit production amounted to 26 tons and vegetable production to 4,781 tons in 2009.

Hay is the principal crop; other crops are turnips, oats, and garden vegetables. In hot-spring areas, vegetables, flowers, and even tropical fruits are cultivated for domestic consumption in greenhouses heated with hot water from the springs. There are agricultural institutions in Borgarfjörður, Hjaltadalur, Hvanneyri, and Reykir; between 15 and 20% of all farmers have finished an agricultural degree program.

23 ANIMAL HUSBANDRY

Sheep raising is extensive, and mutton and lamb are primary meat products. Sheep are permitted to find their own grazing pasture during the warmer months and are rounded up toward the middle of September and put in shed for the winter. Cattle are raised mainly for dairying, and their number has been rising steadily; beef production is negligible. Sheep in 2005 numbered an estimated 454,000 and horses, 72,000.

The UN Food and Agriculture Organization (FAO) reported that Iceland dedicated 2.3 million hectares (5.62 million acres) to permanent pasture or meadow in 2009. During that year, the country tended 261,000 chickens, 73,498 head of cattle, and 43,286 pigs. The production from these animals amounted to 3,721 tons of beef and veal, 6,417 tons of pork, 7,958 tons of poultry, 2,654 tons of eggs, and 68,892 tons of milk. Iceland also produced 440 tons of cattle hide and 787 tons of raw wool.

Icelandic farm animals are directly descended from the sheep, cattle, goats, pigs, poultry, dogs, cats, and especially horses (that were an invaluable means of travel) brought by 10th century Scandinavian settlers. In sparsely populated areas, such as the western fjords and on the east coast, farming is chiefly limited to raising sheep, although sheep farming exists in all areas of the country. Milk is produced mostly in the south and north. Except for poultry, egg, and pig production, farms are small in acreage and usually family-run. About 2,000 farmers engage in full-time sheep farming, and 1,000 more in mixed farming. There also are about 1,800 dairy farms in operation; Icelanders consume on average 175 liters (46.2 gal) of milk per capita per year, one of the highest amounts in the world. Cheese consumption is fourth highest, after France, Germany, and Italy. Horse breeding is also a growing branch of animal husbandry in Iceland, as the popularity of the Icelandic horse (which has five gaits) grows at home and abroad.

Animal farming is a highly mechanized industry carried out by well-educated farmers; nearly one fifth of all farmers matriculate at one of three agricultural colleges in Iceland.

24 FISHING

Accounting for about 9% of Iceland's employment, fishing and fish processing provide the primary source of foreign exchange. Icelanders consume more fish per capita annually (over 91.5 kg/201 lb live weight equivalent) than any other people in Europe. Cod is caught during the first five months of the year off the southwest coast. Herring are taken off the north and northeast coasts from June to September and off the southwest from September to December.

Iceland had 799 decked commercial fishing boats in 2008. Most fishing vessels are now equipped with telecommunications devices, computers, and automated equipment. The annual capture totaled 1.28 million tons according to the UN FAO. The export value of seafood totaled $1.78 billion. In the first four months of 2011, the total commercial catch of Icelandic fishing vessels amounted to about $400 million. Fishing accounted for 12% of GDP in 2011 and 40% of total exports.

In 2010, the salmon rod fishery totals were the second-highest ever recorded, with a total of 74,961 salmon caught. About 53,485 were landed, with the remainder released. The total number of brown trout landed in rod fishery was 40,957 fish which the total number of Arctic char landed was reported at 31,117 fish.

The fishing industry came under international scrutiny in 2011 regarding the nation's self-imposed mackerel quotas. Since 2009, Iceland has opted out of the previously held agreements with the EU and Norway to set its own total allowable catch (TAC) for mackerel. In January 2011, Iceland and the Faroe Islands walked out on talks with the European Union and Norway as they were again unable to come to an agreement on appropriate fishing quotas. Iceland then set a 2011 TAC of 147,000 tons, up from 120,000 tons set in 2009 and 2010. Scottish officials condemned the move as a shortsighted attempt to make quick profits at the expense of catch sustainability. The EU was pressured to impose an import ban on all fish from Iceland and the Faroe Islands, but as of July 2011 no action had been taken.

Through the early 1980s, about 250 whales a year were caught off the coast, providing lucrative export products. Although Iceland had agreed to phase out whaling in order to comply with the 1982 ban by the International Whaling Commission, commercial whaling resumed in 2006. In 2009, quotas were set to allow of the capture of 100 minke whales and 150 fin whales. In the first nine months of 2010, Iceland exported 600 tons of whale meat to Japan.

Abundant quantities of pure water and geothermal heat give Iceland an advantage over other nations in fish farming. Aquaculture is being developed to offset lean years in the natural fish catch, and to produce more expensive and profitable species of fish.

25 FORESTRY

There are no forests of commercial value, and the existing trees (ash, birch, aspen, and willow) are small. The originally extensive birch forests were cut down for firewood and to clear land for grazing sheep. In recent years, the remaining woods have been protected and reforestation has begun.

26 MINING

Ferrosilicon production and geothermal power were Iceland's major mineral industries. Diatomite production, from Lake Myvatn, was estimated at 28,000 metric tons in 2004; production ceased in 2006. Iceland also produced hydraulic cement, nitrogen, pumice, salt, scoria, sand (basaltic, calcareous, and shell), sand and gravel, and crushed stone (basaltic and rhyolite); these minerals were used by local industries. Among Iceland's other mineral resources, spar and sulfur deposits, once mined, were no longer worked extensively. Peat was common, but little used and sulfur and lignite were being processed experimentally, the former with the use of subterranean steam. The country's aluminum plant and ferrosilicon plant relied on imported raw materials and inexpensive hydroelectric and geothermal energy.

27 ENERGY AND POWER

The World Bank reported in 2008 that Iceland produced 16.5 billion kWh of electricity and consumed 15.9 billion kWh, or 51,090 kWh per capita. Roughly 17% of energy came from fossil fuels, while 83% came from alternative fuels. Per capita oil consumption was 16,556 kg.

Iceland has no known reserves of oil, natural gas or coal. Thus, the country is entirely reliant upon imports to meet its demand for fossil fuels. However, the country does rely on hydroelectric power and geothermal sources to generate electric power and to provide heat. Hydroelectric power is the main source of electric power for Iceland, followed by geothermal and conventional thermal sources, respectively.

Hot springs are used for heating greenhouses in which vegetables, fruit, and flowers are raised, and for heating public buildings. Since 1943, most of Reykjavík has been heated by water from hot springs at Reykir, some 160 km (100 mi) from the city. About 85% of the population lives in homes heated with geothermal power. However, a significant decline in flow from geothermal drill holes has raised concern that the energy resource may not be as boundless as once thought.

28 INDUSTRY

Fish processing is the most important industry. Facilities for freezing, salting, sun-curing, and reducing to oil or fish meal are flexible enough to allow shifting from one process to another in accordance with demand. By-products include fish meal and cod-liver oil.

Although Iceland's industry is focused on fish processing, the country in the 21st century needs to diversify its economy, as fish stocks are declining. As a result, there has been an increase in energy-intensive manufacturing enterprises, particularly for aluminum. The ISAL (Alcan Iceland Ltd.) aluminum smelter has expanded its capacity, and in 2002, construction of another aluminum smelter was underway. Other projects include the construction of a magnesium plant and the enlargement of the ferro alloy plant.

Other industry is small-scale and designed to meet local needs. Chief manufactures include fishing equipment, electric stoves and cookers, paints, clothing, soaps, candles, cosmetics, dairy products, confectionery, and beer. Clothing factories are situated in Reykjavík and Akureyri. Icelandic ammonium nitrate needs are more than met by a fertilizer plant at Gufunes with an annual production capacity of 60,000 tons. A cement factory in Akranes with a capacity of 115,000 tons per year supplies most domestic cement requirements.

In 2010, industry accounted for 24.5% of GDP. In 2008, industry employed about 22.2% of labor force. The industrial production growth rate was -0.1% in 2010, indicating that industry was stagnating as a growth market in Iceland.

29 SCIENCE AND TECHNOLOGY

Patent applications in science and technology as of 2009, according to the World Bank, totaled 64 in Iceland. Public financing of science was 2.67% of GDP. The Icelandic Research Council coordinates science policy and advises the government on scientific matters. It has five research institutes devoted to marine science, technology, agriculture, the fish industry, and the construction and building industries. Other research institutes and learned societies include the Surtsey Research Society, the Icelandic Meteorological Office, the Association of Chartered Engineers in Iceland, the Agricultural Society of Iceland, the Iceland Glaciological Society, the Icelandic Natural History Society, and the Icelandic Society of Sciences, all located at Reykjavík.

The Icelandic Council of Science, an independent agency under the Ministry of Culture and Education, aims to stimulate and encourage scientific research. The University of Iceland has faculties of medicine, engineering, dentistry, and science. Two agricultural colleges are located in Hólum i Hjaltadal and Hvanneyri. The Icelandic College of Engineering and Technology is in Reykjavík. In 1987–97, science and engineering students accounted for 41% of university enrollment. In 2008, of all bachelor's degrees awarded, 16.4% were in the sciences (natural, mathematics and computers, and engineering).

In 2008, 7,315 researchers and 1,712 technicians per million people were actively engaged in research and development (R&D). In 2009, R&D expenditures totaled $46.5 billion, or 3.1% of GDP. Of that amount, health accounted for the largest slice.

30 DOMESTIC TRADE

Foreign firms do not have branches in Iceland. Instead, their business is conducted by Icelandic agents. Imports are handled by these agents, by wholesale or retail importers, or by the Federation of Iceland Cooperative Societies (Samband íslenskra samvinnufélaga, or SIS), and distribution is through private channels. Most advertising is translated and disseminated directly by agents. Foreign trade fairs are held from time to time.

Of the wholesale enterprises, 80 to 90% are concentrated in Reykjavík; more than half the retail establishments are likewise in the capital. Much trade is handled by cooperative societies, most of which belong to SIS. Retail prices tend to be high, a reflection of the need to ship goods to an isolated location and to import most industrial items.

Franchising is well established in Iceland, with many of the country's people very open to US-based fast-food franchises. The leaders are Burger King, McDonald's, KFC, Subway, Pizza Hut, and Domino's. Non-food US franchisers have yet to gain a significant presence in the country.

Direct marketing is carried out in Iceland but not to great extent. Telemarketing is permitted, but consumers can indicate whether they wish to be contacted. Books and magazines are the most frequently offered products by telemarketers.

A standard value-added tax (VAT) of 25.5% applies to most goods and services. A sales tax of 7% applies to hotel accommodations, food purchases, book sales, and residential electrical/hot water bills.

Standard business hours are from 9 a.m. to 6 p.m. on weekdays, and from 9 or 10 a.m. to noon on Saturdays. Banking hours are from 9:15 a.m. to 4 p.m., Monday–Friday, with an additional hour from 5 to 6 p.m. on Thursday.

<table>
<table>
<tr><td colspan="5">Principal Trading Partners – Iceland (2010)</td></tr>
</table>
</table>

Principal Trading Partners – Iceland (2010)				
(In millions of US dollars)				
Country	**Total**	**Exports**	**Imports**	**Balance**
World	8,523.9	4,604.4	3,919.5	684.9
Netherlands	1,890.9	1,555.9	335.0	1,221.0
Germany	939.2	645.8	293.5	352.3
United Kingdom	663.9	464.5	199.4	265.2
Norway	549.8	196.3	353.5	-157.3
United States	528.8	208.8	320.0	-111.2
Denmark	395.8	119.3	276.5	-157.2
Brazil	349.2	5.3	343.9	-338.6
China	265.1	28.1	237.0	-208.9
Spain	262.0	217.4	44.6	172.9
Sweden	225.6	22.8	202.7	-179.9

(…) data not available or not significant.

(n.s.) not specified.

SOURCE: *2011 Direction of Trade Statistics Yearbook,* New York: United Nations, 2011.

31 FOREIGN TRADE

In 2010, exports reached $5.61 billion (FOB—free on board), while imports grew to $4.408 billion (FOB). The bulk of exports went to the United Kingdom (10.1%), Germany (14.0%), the Netherlands (34.0%), the United States (4.5%), Spain (4.7%), and Denmark (2.7%). Imports included machinery and equipment, petroleum products, foodstuffs, and textiles, and mainly came from Germany (7.5%), the United States (7.9%), Norway (9.1%), Brazil (8.7%), Denmark (7.1%), the United Kingdom (5.1%), Sweden (5.2%), and the Netherlands (8.5%).

Iceland's fishing industry supports most of its commodity export market (39.3%). It supplies the world export market with 10.5% of its salted, dried, or smoked fish, second only to Norway in volume. Other important exports include agricultural products (1.6%) and manufacturing products (55.4%).

32 BALANCE OF PAYMENTS

In 2010 Iceland had a foreign trade surplus of $1.2 billion, amounting to 8.9% of GDP.

The difference between imports and exports since World War II has been met by drawing from large wartime reserves, by Marshall Plan aid, and, since 1953, by income from US defense spending at Keflavík, the NATO airbase. Widely fluctuating current account deficits, attributable mainly to the trade imbalance, averaged more than 6.5% of GNP during 1971–75. During the next four years, although still largely negative, the current account balance improved; in 1980–85, however, Iceland's current accounts position again deteriorated, this time because of large deficits in services.

Iceland suffered a prolonged recession during 1987–93 due to cuts in fish catch quotas necessitated in part by overfishing. Again, there was a significant deterioration in the balance of payments, especially on the current account and merchandise trade balances. In 1994 the economy recovered with the help of 6.3% growth in exports, due to a better than expected performance in the fishing sector. The external current account balance was positive for the first time since 1986. Iceland experienced successful economic performance in the 1990s but fell into recession in 2001, which had a negative impact on the current account deficit.

Balance of Payments – Iceland (2010)		
(In millions of US dollars)		
Current Account		**-1,417.0**
Balance on goods	983.0	
Imports	-3,620.0	
Exports	4,603.0	
Balance on services	281.0	
Balance on income	-2,610.0	
Current transfers	-71.0	
Capital Account		**-3.0**
Financial Account		**4,891.0**
Direct investment abroad	2,630.0	
Direct investment in Iceland	488.0	
Portfolio investment assets	-22.0	
Portfolio investment liabilities	-10,540.0	
Financial derivatives	…	
Other investment assets	2,438.0	
Other investment liabilities	9,898.0	
Net Errors and Omissions		**-1,811.0**
Reserves and Related Items		**-1,660.0**

(…) data not available or not significant.

SOURCE: *Balance of Payment Statistics Yearbook 2011,* Washington, DC: International Monetary Fund, 2011.

33 BANKING AND SECURITIES

In the first few years of the 21st century, Iceland's strong economy offered its country's citizens one of the highest standards of living in the world. The financial and banking sectors were particularly strong, as Icelandic banks built up foreign assets and foreign debt and Icelandic businesses made major investments abroad. In early 2008, the system began to falter with the development of a global credit crunch. The value of the Icelandic króna decreased and banks were unable to secure the foreign credit needed to refinance existing loans. This led to economic meltdown in October 2008, as three of the largest banks in the nation—Glitnir, Kaupthing, and Landsbanki—nearly collapsed. The government assumed control of the banks, but the measure was not enough. The government applied for and received loans exceeding $10 billion from the IMF in efforts to stabilize the króna. The governments of the United Kingdom and the Netherlands issued funds to compensate those who lost money from accounts with Icesave, an online Icelandic bank.

In December 2009, Iceland's Althing (parliament) approved its first controversial compensation bill. Opponents of the agreement questioned why the government would consider repaying debts that were incurred by a private bank. Many also feared that the repayment agreement would leave the nation bankrupt. The bill approved payment of up to $5 billion. After much public protest, the president refused to sign the bill into law and announced plans for a referendum to be held on the agreement. In the 6 March 2010 vote, an overwhelming majority of Icelandic voters (93%) rejected the bill. Starting over, the three nations reached a new agreement in December 2010 that called for the repayment of $5.3 billion with interest rates of 3.5% for the Netherlands and 3.3% for the UK. Under this agreement, payments would begin in 2016 and extend to 2046. The plan was moved to parliament, which approved the plan in February 2011. At the same time, parliament voted against the idea of another referendum, but President Grimsson insisted that public approval was necessary for the plan to move forward. In an April 2011 referendum, the Icelandic people rejected the repayment plan with a vote of nearly 60% against. However, a portion of the lost funds was still expected to be repaid by the end of the year through the sale of assets of Landsbanki. The governments of the Netherlands and the UK announced that they would take legal action through international courts to ensure full repayment of the lost funds.

The Central Bank of Iceland functions as the nation's central bank. Established in 1961, the bank is owned by the government of Iceland, but is under a separate administration. The bank's primary duty is the maintenance of price stability, although it is also charged with the implementation of monetary policy. The bank is responsible for maintaining the nation's foreign reserves, issuing bank notes and coins, and setting exchange rates. The bank is governed by a seven-member Supervisory Board elected by the Althing, and a three-person Board of Governors appointed by the prime minister.

As of 2011, there were 21 savings banks in Iceland; the Postal Giro system also accepts deposits. There are 11 other credit institutions in Iceland, three leasing companies, four investment banks, and four investment funds. No US banks operate in Iceland.

The whole basis on which the financial system is supervised and regulated was transformed by Iceland's accession to the European Economic Area (EEA) in 1994. Under the agreement, Iceland has been required to implement into national law the common minimum standards for the supervision of financial institutions-banks, insurance companies, and securities firms-developed at EU level.

The Securities Exchange of Iceland (SEI) was established in 1985 on the basis of rules set by the Central Bank. A new Act on the Icelandic Stock Exchange was passed in February 1993, granting a monopoly to the exchange. As of 2011, a total of 67 companies were listed on the stock exchange, which had a bond market capitalization that year of 75% of GDP.

OMX Iceland 15, a stock market index of 15 Icelandic countries, was discontinued in 2009 after suffering serious losses in the wake of the nation's 2008 banking crisis. It was replaced by the OMX Iceland 6, which in October 2011 consisted of the companies Atlantic Petroleum, Atlantic Airways, BankNordik, Icelandair Group, Marel, and Ossur.

34INSURANCE

There are many mutual insurance societies in addition to the national health and social insurance scheme. Almost all direct insurance is written by domestic companies that conduct business in various kinds of property and life insurance. Automobile liability insurance and homeowners' coverage against fire, floods, earthquakes, and volcanic eruptions are compulsory. The Ministry of Business Affairs is the principal supervisory body. In 2009, direct premiums written totaled 2.3% of GDP.

35PUBLIC FINANCE

Since 1984, Iceland's budget has shown a deficit averaging nearly 2% of GDP, raising its net indebtedness relative to GDP to almost 30% in 1994. Government attempts to balance the budget were frustrated by the economic downturn during 1987–93 and by fiscal concessions to expedite wage settlements. Consequently,

Public Finance – Iceland (2009)		
(In millions of kronur, central government figures)		
Revenue and Grants	**444,707**	**100.0%**
Tax revenue	321,362	72.3%
Social contributions	45,912	10.3%
Grants	3,137	0.7%
Other revenue	74,296	16.7%
Expenditures	**578,789**	**100.0%**
General public services	142,758	24.7%
Defense	652	0.1%
Public order and safety	22,992	4.0%
Economic affairs	74,436	12.9%
Environmental protection	5,470	0.9%
Housing and community amenities	2,192	0.4%
Health	123,701	21.4%
Recreational, culture, and religion	19,604	3.4%
Education	52,964	9.2%
Social protection	134,020	23.2%
(…) data not available or not significant.		

SOURCE: *Government Finance Statistics Yearbook 2010,* Washington, DC: International Monetary Fund, 2010.

the deficit has been larger than expected, reaching 34% of GDP in 1999. In 2010 Iceland's budget included $4.81 billion in public revenue and $5.673 billion in public expenditures. The budget deficit had lessened to 7.8% of GDP. Public debt was 123.8% of GDP, with $3.073 billion of the debt held by foreign entities.

Government outlays by function were as follows in 2009 (provided by the OECD): general public services, 14.5%; public order and safety, 4.5%; economic affairs, 14.8%; housing and community amenities, 0.1%; health, 25.8%; recreation, culture, and religion, 4.4%; education, 11.1%; defense, 0.2%; environmental protection, 1.1%; and social protection, 23.4%.

36TAXATION

The corporate income tax rate, at 50% in 1989, decreased from 30% in 2001 to 18% in 2002. The income tax on partnerships decreased from 38% in 2001 to 26% in 2002 and 20% in 2011. Since March 1999, Iceland has also offered an offshore corporate tax rate of 20% to international trading companies (ITCs) that exclusively trade in goods and services outside of Iceland. Capital gains are taxed as ordinary income at 18%, although gains may be offset by extraordinary depreciation. Dividends paid to nonresident companies are subject to a 18% tax rate, although all countries within the EEA are taxed as residents of the country in which they conduct business. Capital gains are taxed as income although a deduction is possible in certain cases. No tax is levied on capital gains from the corporate sale of shares in companies if the recipient owns at least 10% of the share capital of that company and current and carried for losses have been exhausted.

According to Deloitte in 2011, the personal income tax schedule in Iceland consists of a tax-free allowance (about ISK530,466/$4,605 in 2011); a total tax rate that is the sum of the central government's general rate (25.50% in 2011) and the municipal tax rate (14.41% on average). Iceland has created a three-bracket structure with maximum tax rate of 31.8% (if income is upwards of ISK8,166,601/$70,902). The other two levels are taxed at a rate of 22.9% (the lowest income tier) and 25.8%.

Seamen are entitled to a credit against calculated income tax. The credit is deducted from the calculated income tax before the personal tax credit and is limited to the amount of income tax computed on the basis of wages received from the employer (benefit started an annual 25% phase out in 2011 and is expected to be terminated by 2014).

Payments to a pension fund for private pensions insurance are deductible up to 8% of total employment income and presumptive employment income. The employer is liable for social security contributions on behalf of the employee. Since 1999, reductions in social security taxes have been offered to employers in exchange for their contribution to supplementary employee pension premiums. Gross individual interest income exceeding ISK100,000 ($868) is taxed at 20%.

The major indirect tax is Iceland's VAT, with a normal rate of 25.5% on domestic goods and services. A reduced rate of 7% is applied to most foodstuffs, books, newspapers and periodicals, subscriptions to radio and television, hotels, electricity, and geothermal heating. Exempted from VAT are exports of goods and services, as well as services connected with imports and exports. Other categories for exemption include health services, social services, education, libraries, the arts, sports, passenger transport, postal services, rental of property, insurance, and banking.

37 CUSTOMS AND DUTIES

More than 90% of imports are not subject to import restrictions or duties other than the same VAT applied to domestically produced goods. Special excise taxes are levied on sugar and some sugar products, potatoes, and motor vehicles. Agricultural products remain the most heavily taxed.

Duty rates generally range from 0 to 30% according to value, and the average weighted tariff of all products in 2007 was 1.1%. Some goods enter duty-free, such as meat, fish, and dairy products.

In March 1970, Iceland acquired full membership in EFTA. On 28 February 1973, Iceland ratified a trade agreement with the European Community (later named the European Union) leading to the elimination of tariffs on industrial goods. A law authorizing the establishment of free trade zones went into effect in 1992. Iceland's trade regime underwent considerable liberalization in the 1990s with accession to the EEA in 1993 and the Uruguay Round in 1994.

38 FOREIGN INVESTMENT

Icelanders have been reluctant to permit substantial foreign investment; nearly all such investment is limited to participation in joint ventures in which Icelandic interests hold a majority share. There is only one wholly foreign-owned industrial facility in the country, a Swiss aluminum-processing facility. Two others, a ferro-silicon plant and a diatomite plant, have foreign equity participation. Icelanders have been free to invest abroad since 1993.

Energy-intensive industrial activities is one of the main areas for foreign investments, due to the inexpensive energy resources available in Iceland. The national telephone company was expected to be privatized by the end of 2005, and the government has started discussing about opening part of the fishing industry to limited foreign investment. Biomedical and genetic research are two areas with future potential for investments.

For the period 1988–90, Iceland's share in world foreign direct investment (FDI) inflow was only 30% of its share in world GDP. For the period 1998–2000, its share of world FDI inflows was 40% of its share of world GDP, a marginal improvement. Except for a fall to $66 million in 1998, yearly FDI inflows to Iceland have in the range of $146 million (2001) to $158 million (2000). The total stock of FDI by Icelandic residents grew by 76% to €19 billion ($26 billion) in 2007 by over 61% per year on average over the prior 10 years. FDI in Iceland was a net inflow of $60.8 million according to World Bank figures published in 2009. FDI represented 0.5% of GDP.

39 ECONOMIC DEVELOPMENT

The national government and some local governments are involved in trawler fishing, herring processing, merchant shipping, electric power facilities, and certain other industries. To a considerable degree, the central government supervises the export-import trade and the fishing and fish-processing industries. It may set uniform prices of export commodities and may shift export and import trade to specific countries as balance-of-payments considerations require. It channels investment funds into fields it considers desirable.

The government supports farmers in the rebuilding or enlarging of their homes, livestock sheds, and barns, and assists them in the purchase of machinery. By providing crawler tractors and excavators, a government agency helps farmers enlarge cultivated areas and break, drain, and level new lands for the establishment of homesteads. Thousands of new acres have thus been brought under cultivation.

The government fixes prices of essential foods and other basic consumption items and subsidizes them, both to limit prices for the consumer and to maintain farm incomes. It also fixes mark-ups that manufacturers, wholesalers, retailers, and importers may place on a wide variety of products.

In the early 1990s, the government concentrated on maintaining the value of the króna by bringing down inflation, even at the cost of economic growth. Wage gains were restricted. In late 1992, plans were made public for a Fisheries Development Fund that would buy and scrap unneeded vessels and thereby promote efficiency. The fund would also be used to help firms establish joint ventures abroad and buy fishing rights. Plans were also under way to sell several state-owned companies, with the money used for research and development and reducing the deficit. Entry into the EEA in 1994 and the Uruguay Round brought increased trade liberalization and foreign investment. The country experienced rapid economic growth during the late 1990s, but high domestic spending led to a widening current account deficit that peaked at 10% of GDP in 2000.

The economy went into recession in 2001, and inflation rose. The government tightened monetary and fiscal policy to bring inflation down, but GDP growth remained negative in 2002. The government adopted a floating exchange rate for the króna in March 2001. Gross external debt amounted to 130% of GDP at the end of 2002. The government sought to diversify exports in order to stabilize the economy.

In 2008, about 32% of export revenues were contributed by the fishing industry in 2008, making the Icelandic economy susceptible to declining fish stocks and fluctuations in world prices for fish and fish products. To better equip for the future, Iceland began diversifying its economic base by branching out into software production, biotechnology, and financial services. It also began to expand its manufacturing and tourism sectors.

The country's economic development plan, known as Iceland 2020, was broad in scope. Pillars of the plan included infrastructure development, research and innovation, the development of human resources, and social welfare programs. While creating distinct regional and local plans was highlighted, national efforts centered on innovations in high technology through investment in scientific research.

40 SOCIAL DEVELOPMENT

There is a universal pension covering all residents and a mandatory occupational pension covering all employees and self-employed persons. Universal pensions are paid by employer and government contributions, while the cost of occupational pensions is shared by employees and employers. Benefits include old age, disability, and survivorship pensions. Sickness and maternity benefits are available to all residents. The first laws covering sickness and maternity were instituted in 1936. Medical benefits cover all residents.

The number of women in the work force is high, partially due to a comprehensive subsidized day care program. In 2008, 83% of women were actively engaged in the work force. Equal pay for equal work is required by law although men continue to earn more than women. The government takes serious measures to protect women against violence and sexual abuse; however, many cases remain unreported.

The constitution provides for freedom of speech and press, assembly and association, and religion. These rights generally are respected by the government. There is very little discrimination based on race, gender, religion, disability, language, or social status.

According to reports published by the World Economic Forum (WEF), Iceland consistently ranks among the top countries of the world for gender equality. The WEF considers equality in several areas of life, including employment, politics, health, and education. Iceland was rated as first in the world in 2008–10, taking over Norway's position.

41 HEALTH

According to the CIA, life expectancy in Iceland was 81 years in 2011. The country spent 9.2% of its GDP on healthcare, amounting to $3,130 per person. There were 39 physicians, 165 nurses and midwives, and 58 hospital beds per 10,000 inhabitants. The fertility rate was 1.89, while the infant mortality rate was 3.2 per 1,000 live births. In 2008 the maternal mortality rate, according to the World Bank, was 5 per 100,000 births. It was estimated that 92% of children were vaccinated against measles. The CIA calculated HIV/AIDS prevalence in Iceland to be about 0.3% in 2009.

42 HOUSING

In 2009, there were about 130,019 dwellings in Iceland, or about 409 dwellings for every 1,000 inhabitants. About 50% of all dwellings were one- or two-family houses; 49% were apartments. About 35% of all dwellings had five or more rooms and a kitchen. Most rural buildings were at one time made of turf, then of wood, and most recently of stone and concrete. In the towns, turf houses long ago gave way to wooden ones, but for some decades most new housing has been concrete. Virtually all dwellings have electricity, piped water, and central heating.

43 EDUCATION

Education is compulsory for 10 years of basic education (ages 6 to 16). Students may then choose to attend a general or technical secondary school, each offering four-year programs. Specialized vocational schools are also available to secondary students, including a commercial high school, a school of navigation, two schools of agriculture, and a health professions school. In some remote rural areas, a system of "alternate teaching" is in effect. This allows children to study intensively for a week or two at a boarding school, and then return home for the same period of time. The academic year runs from September to May.

Most children between the ages of three and five are enrolled in some type of preschool program. In 2008 the World Bank estimated that 98% of age-eligible children in Iceland were enrolled in primary school. Secondary enrollment for age-eligible children stood at 90%. Nearly all students complete their primary education. The student-to-teacher ratio for primary school was at about 10.5:1 in 2005 (last available data); the ratio for secondary school was about 11.3:1.

There are at least eight *háskóli*; a term that refers to both traditional universities and other institutions of higher education that do not have research programs. The University of Iceland in Reykjavík, founded in 1911, has faculties of law and economics, theology, medicine and dentistry, philosophy (art and humanities), and engineering. Tuition is free; only nominal registration and examination fees must be paid. In 2008, tertiary enrollment was estimated at 75%. Of those enrolled in tertiary education, there were 100 male students for every 191 female students. The adult literacy rate has been estimated at about 99.9%.

Public expenditure on education represented 7.4% of GDP.

44 LIBRARIES AND MUSEUMS

Founded in 1818, the National and University Library in Reykjavík serves as a national library as well as a public lending library with 900,000 items. Other leading libraries, in the Reykjavík include the City Library of Reykjavík, which sponsors seven branch locations and a bookmobile, and the National Archives, which contains a collection of documents covering 800 years of Icelandic history.

Important museums, also all in Reykjavík, are the Icelandic National Museum (founded in 1863), the Natural History Museum (1889), and a museum devoted to the sculptures and paintings of Einar Jónsson. The Arni Magnusson Institute contains Iceland literature and documents that were somewhat recently returned to the Icelandic government after being held by Denmark for centuries. Also in the capital are the National Gallery of Iceland, the Living Art Museum, and the Sigurjón Ólaffson Museum, among others. The Kopavogur Art Museum contains exhibits primarily on modern and contemporary art. The Icelandic Saltfish Museum opened in Grindavik in 2002 to commemorate the country's fishing industry.

45 MEDIA

Radio and radiotelephone communications are maintained with Europe and America and an underwater telegraph cable connects Iceland with Europe. International services are also provided by satellite ground stations. The country's domestic communications system includes microwave radio relay, and coaxial and fiber-optic cable systems. The telephone, telegraph, and radio systems are publicly owned and administered. In 2009 there were some 185,200 main phone lines and 349,000 mobile cellular phones in use. Mobile phone subscriptions averaged 109 per 100 people.

The government-owned Icelandic National Broadcasting Service (RUV) provides the primary national radio and television broadcasts. There are, however, several smaller private stations. As of 2011 there were 74 radio stations and 14 television stations. In 2011, there were 260,000 radios and 98,000 television sets throughout the country. In 2009, there were some 308,901 Internet users in Iceland (97.6% of the population).

There are five daily newspapers, four of which are published in Reykjavík. With their political orientation and average daily circulation in 2008, they were: *Morgunblaid* (from the Independence Party), 52,000; *DV Dagblaid,* 16,000; *Viðskiptablaðið,* 9,000; and the all popular *Fréttablaði,* circulation rate of 103,000, which is free for the public. Icelandreview.com is an English-language news site. Nondaily newspapers are published in Reykjavík and other towns. Various popular and scholarly periodicals are published in Reykjavík.

The law prohibits the production, showing, distribution, and/ or sale of violent movies, which are defined as containing scenes depicting the mistreatment or the brutal killing of humans or animals. The Motion Picture Review Committee, which includes six members, is appointed by the Minister of Education and Culture to review all movies before they are shown. The committee also rates the films based on their suitability for children. By their evaluation, the committee may ban a film or require edits before its release.

The constitution provides for freedom of speech and press, and the government is said to respect these rights in practice.

46 ORGANIZATIONS

The Iceland Chamber of Commerce and the Confederation of Icelandic Employers are based in Reykjavík. Organizations representing laborers, businesses, and industries include the Farmers Association of Iceland, the Federation of Icelandic Industries, and the Federation of Icelandic Trade.

Professional associations such as the Icelandic Teachers Union and the Icelandic Nurses' Association represent a variety of fields. Many organizations, including the Icelandic Medical Association and the Icelandic Heart Association, promote research and education.

Notable national youth organizations include the Federation of Young Progressives, Independence Party Youth Organization, National Council of Icelandic Youth, National Union of Icelandic Students, Social Democratic Youth Federation, Youth Movement of the People's Alliance, YMCA/YWCA, and The Icelandic Boy and Girl Scouts Association. There are several sports associations

in the country representing such pastimes as football (soccer), badminton, squash, mountain biking, skiing, skating, and track and field.

Learned societies include the Icelandic Archaeological Society, the Icelandic Historical Society, the Icelandic Literary Society, the Music Society, the Icelandic Natural History Society, and the Agricultural Association. There are also the Icelandic Artists' Association, the Iceland Association of Pictorial Artists, the Icelandic Actors' Association, the Icelandic Musicians' Association, the Icelandic Composers' Society, the Icelandic Architects' Association, and the Icelandic Writers' Association. Among other cultural organizations are the Icelandic-American Society, the Danish Society, the Danish-Icelandic Society, the Anglo-Icelandic Society, the Alliance Française, the Nordic Society, and the Union of Women's Societies.

The Salvation Army, Caritas, Amnesty International, and the Red Cross all have active chapters within the country. Volunteer service organizations, such as the Lions Clubs and Kiwanis International, are also present.

47 TOURISM, TRAVEL, AND RECREATION

Iceland offers such diverse and unusual natural attractions as active volcanoes, glaciers, and hot springs. Among popular participatory sports are swimming (possible year-round in geothermal pools), salmon fishing, pony trekking, bird-watching, skiing, river rafting, and golf. Tourists can stay in modern hotels, guesthouses, youth hostels, or on farms.

In March 2001, Iceland joined the Schengen Area, allowing citizens from all area countries unrestricted travel to and from Iceland. In addition, citizens of the Scandinavian countries do not require a passport when visiting Iceland. All other visitors need valid visas (good for up to 90 days), except residents of some 60 countries (including the United States, Australia, and Canada—although all visitors are required to have a valid passport). A certificate of vaccination against yellow fever is required if traveling from an infected country.

The *Tourism Factbook*, published by the UN World Tourism Organization, reported 1.24 million incoming tourists to Iceland in 2009 who spent a total of $555 million. Of those incoming tourists, there were 1 million from Europe. There were 18,937 hotel beds available in Iceland, which had an occupancy rate of 38%. The estimated daily cost to visit Reykjavik, the capital, was $337. The cost of visiting other cities averaged $238.

48 FAMOUS PERSONS

Famous early Icelanders were Eric the Red (Eiríkur Thorvaldsson), who discovered and colonized Greenland in 982, and his son Leif Ericsson (Leifur Eiríksson, b. 970), who introduced Christianity to Greenland and discovered the North American continent (c. 1000). Two famous patriots and statesmen were Bishop Jón Arason (1484–1550), who led the fight for liberty against the power of the Danish king, and Jón Sigurðsson (1811–79), Iceland's national hero and champion of the fight for independence. Vigdís Finnbogadottír (b. 1930) served four consecutive terms as president from 1980 to 1996, becoming the first female elected to the presidency of a republic.

Prominent writers include Ari Thorgilsson (1067–1148), father of Icelandic historical writing; Snorri Sturluson (1178–1241), author of the famous *Prose Edda*, a collection of Norse myths; and Hallgrímur Pétursson (1614–74), author of Iceland's beloved Passion Hymns.

Leading poets include Bjarni Thorarensen (1786–1841) and Jónas Hallgrímsson (1807–45), pioneers of the Romantic movement in Iceland; Matthías Jochumsson (1835–1920), author of Iceland's national anthem; Thorsteinn Erlingsson (1858–1914), lyricist; Einar Hjörleifsson Kvaran (1859–1939), a pioneer of realism in Icelandic literature and an outstanding short story writer; Einar Benediktsson (1864–1940), ranked as one of the greatest modern Icelandic poets; Jóhann Sigurjónsson (1880–1919), who lived much of his life in Denmark and wrote many plays based on Icelandic history and legend, as well as poetry; and the novelist Halldór Kiljan Laxness (1902–98), who received the Nobel Prize for literature in 1955.

Niels Ryberg Finsen (1860–1904), a physician who pioneered in the field of light (ray) therapy, received the Nobel Prize for medicine in 1903. Stefán Stefánsson (1863–1921) was a pioneering Icelandic botanist. Helgi Pjeturss (1872–1949), geologist and philosopher, was an authority on the Ice Age and the geology of Iceland. Einar Jónsson (1874–1954), Iceland's greatest sculptor, is represented in European and American museums.

Singer, songwriter, and composer Björk (b. 1965), formerly the lead singer of the Icelandic band The Sugarcubes, works in a variety of musical genres. The former world chess champion Bobby Fischer (b. 1943–2008) became an Icelandic citizen in 2005. Russian pianist and composer Vladimir Ashkenazy (b. 1937) has been a citizen since 1972.

⁴⁹ DEPENDENCIES

Iceland has no territories or colonies.

⁵⁰ BIBLIOGRAPHY

Evans, Andrew. *Iceland.* Chalfont St Peter, Eng.: Bradt Publications, 2012.

Iceland Investment and Business Guide: Strategic and Practical Information. Washington, DC: International Business Publications USA, 2012.

International Smoking Statistics: A Collection of Historical Data from 30 Economically Developed Countries. New York: Oxford University Press, 2002.

Jonsdottir, Johanna. *Europeanization and the European Economic Area: Iceland's Participation in the EU's Policy Process.* New York: Routledge, 2012.

Karlsson, Gunnar. *The History of Iceland.* Minneapolis: University of Minnesota Press, 2000.

Magnusson, Magnus. *The Icelandic Sagas.* London: Folio Society, 2002.

Opello, Walter C. *European Politics.* Boulder, CO: Lynne Rienner Publishers, 2009.

Political Chronology of Europe. London, Eng.: Europa, 2001.

Ross, Margaret Clunies (ed.). *Old Icelandic Literature and Society.* New York: Cambridge University Press, 2000.

Sullivan, Paul. *Waking Up in Iceland.* London, Eng.: Sanctuary, 2003.

Tulinius, Torfi H. *The Matter of the North: The Rise of Literary Fiction in Thirteenth-Century Iceland.* Odense, Denmark: Odense University Press, 2002.

IRELAND

Éire

CAPITAL: Dublin (Baile Átha Cliath)

FLAG: The national flag is a tricolor of green, white, and orange vertical stripes.

ANTHEM: *Amhrán na bhFiann (The Soldier's Song).*

MONETARY UNIT: The euro replaced the Irish punt as the official currency in 2002. The euro is divided into 100 cents. There are coins in denominations of 1, 2, 5, 10, 20, and 50 cents and 1 euro and 2 euros. There are notes of 5, 10, 20, 50, 100, 200, and 500 euros. €1 = $1.3242 (or $1 = €0.7552) as of 2012.

WEIGHTS AND MEASURES: Since 1988 Ireland has largely converted from the British system of weights and measures to the metric system.

HOLIDAYS: New Year's Day, 1 January; St. Patrick's Day, 17 March; Bank Holidays, 1st Monday in June, 1st Monday in August, and last Monday in October; Christmas Day, 25 December; St. Stephen's Day, 26 December. Movable religious holidays include Good Friday and Easter Monday.

TIME: GMT.

1 LOCATION, SIZE, AND EXTENT

An island in the eastern part of the North Atlantic directly west of the United Kingdom, on the continental shelf of Europe, Ireland covers an area of 70,273 sq km (27,133 sq mi). Comparatively, the area occupied by Ireland is slightly larger than the state of West Virginia. The island's length is 486 km (302 mi) N–S, and its width is 275 km (171 mi) E–W. The Irish Republic is bounded on the N by the North Channel, which separates it from Scotland; on the NE by Northern Ireland; and on the E and SE by the Irish Sea and St. George's Channel, which separate it from England and Wales. To the W, from north to south, the coast is washed by the Atlantic Ocean.

Ireland's capital city, Dublin, is located on the Irish Sea coast.

2 TOPOGRAPHY

Ireland is a limestone plateau rimmed by coastal highlands of varying geological structure. The central plain area, characterized by many lakes, bogs, and scattered low ridges, averages about 90 m (300 ft) above sea level. Principal mountain ranges include the Wicklow Mountains in the east and Macgillicuddy's Reeks in the southwest. The highest peaks are Carrantuohill (1,041 m/3,414 ft) and Mt. Brandon (953 m/3,127 ft), near Killarney, and, 64 km (40 mi) south of Dublin, Lugnaquillia (926 m/3,039 ft).

The coastline, 1,448 km (900 mi) long, is heavily indented along the south and west coasts where the ranges of Donegal, Mayo, and Munster end in bold headlands and rocky islands, forming long, narrow fjord-like inlets or wide-mouthed bays. On the southern coast, drowned river channels have created deep natural harbors. The east coast has few good harbors.

Most important of the many rivers is the Shannon, which rises in the mountains along the Ulster border and drains the central plain as it flows 370 km (230 mi) to the Atlantic, into which it empties through a wide estuary nearly 110 km (70 mi) long. Other important rivers are the Boyne, Suir, Liffey, Slaney, Barrow, Blackwater, Lee, and Nore.

3 CLIMATE

Ireland has an equable climate, because the prevailing west and southwest winds have crossed long stretches of the North Atlantic Ocean, which is warmer in winter and cooler in summer than the continental land masses. The mean annual temperature is 10°C (50°F), and average monthly temperatures range from a mild 4°C (39°F) in January to 16°C (61°F) in July. Average yearly rainfall ranges from less than 76 cm (30 in) in places near Dublin to more than 254 cm (100 in) in some mountainous regions. The sunniest area is the extreme southeast, with an annual average of 1,700 hours of bright sunshine. Winds are strongest near the west coast, where the average speed is about 26 kmph (16 mph).

4 FLORA AND FAUNA

The World Resources Institute estimates that there are 950 plant species in Ireland. In addition, Ireland is home to 63 species of mammals, 408 species of birds, 6 species of reptiles, and 4 species of amphibians. These calculations reflect the total number of distinct species residing in the country, not the number of endemic species.

Since Ireland was completely covered by ice sheets during the most recent Ice Age, all existing native plant and animal life originated from the natural migration of species, chiefly from other parts of Europe and especially from Britain. Early sea inundation of the land bridge connecting Ireland and Britain prevented further migration after 6000 BC. Although many species have subsequently been introduced, Ireland has a much narrower range of flora and fauna than Britain. Forest is the natural dominant vegetation, but the total forest area is now only 10.7% of the total area, and most of that remains because of the state afforestation program. The natural forest cover was chiefly mixed sessile oak woodland with ash, wych elm, birch, and yew. Pine was dominant on poorer soils, with rowan and birch. Beech and lime are notable natural absentees that thrive when introduced.

The fauna of Ireland is basically similar to that of Britain, but there are some notable gaps. Among those absent are weasel, polecat, wildcat, most shrews, moles, water voles, roe deer, snakes, and common toads. There are also fewer bird and insect species. Some introduced animals, such as the rabbit and brown rat, have been very successful. Ireland has some species not native to Britain, such as the spotted slug and certain species of wood lice. Ireland's isolation has made it notably free from plant and animal diseases. Among the common domestic animals, Ireland is particularly noted for its fine horses, dogs, and cattle. The Connemara pony, Irish wolfhound, Kerry blue terrier, and several types of cattle and sheep are recognized as distinct breeds.

5 ENVIRONMENT

Principal responsibility for environmental protection is vested in the Department of the Environment. The Department of Fisheries and Forestry, the Department of Agriculture, and the Office of Public Works also deal with environmental affairs. Local authorities, acting under the supervision of the Department of the Environment, are responsible for water supply, sewage disposal, and other environmental matters.

The World Resources Institute reported that Ireland had designated 77,500 hectares (191,507 acres) of land for protection as of 2006. Water resources totaled 46.8 cu km (11.23 cu mi), while water usage was 1.18 cu km (.283 cu mi) per year. Domestic water usage accounted for 23% of total usage and industrial usage for 77%. Per capita water usage totaled 284 cu m (10,029 cu ft) per year.

Protected lands included 45 Ramsar wetland sites. According to a 2011 report issued by the International Union for Conservation of Nature and Natural Resources (IUCN), threatened species included 5 types of mammals, 1 bird species, 20 species of fish, 1 type of mollusk, 1 species of other invertebrate, and 1 species of plant. Threatened species include the Baltic sturgeon, Kerry slug, and Marsh snail. The great auk has become extinct.

Ireland enjoys the benefits of a climate in which calms are rare and the winds are sufficiently strong to disperse atmospheric pollution. Nevertheless, industry is a significant source of pollution. In 2009 carbon dioxide emissions in Ireland totaled 45,370 kilotons. Water pollution is also a problem, especially pollution of lakes from agricultural runoff.

6 POPULATION

The US Central Intelligence Agency (CIA) estimated the population of Ireland in 2011 to be approximately 4,670,976, which placed it at number 119 in population among the 196 nations of the world. In 2011, approximately 11.6% of the population was over 65 years of age, with another 21.1% under 15 years of age. The median age in Ireland was 34.8 years. There were 0.99 males for every female in the country. The population's annual rate of change was 1.061%. The projected population for the year 2025 was 5,700,000. Population density in Ireland was calculated at 66 people per sq km (25 people per sq mi).

The United Nations (UN) estimated that 62% of the population lived in urban areas in 2010, and that urban populations had an annual rate of change of 1.8%. The largest urban area was Dublin, with a population of 1.1 million.

7 MIGRATION

Estimates of Ireland's net migration rate, carried out by the CIA in 2011, amounted to 0.86 migrants per 1,000 citizens. The total number of emigrants living abroad was 737,200, and the total number of immigrants living in Ireland was 898,600. The great famine in the late 1840s inaugurated the wave of Irish emigrants to the United States, Canada, Argentina, and other countries: 100,000 in 1846, 200,000 per year from 1847 to 1850, and 250,000 in 1851. Since then, emigration has been a traditional feature of Irish life, although it has been considerably reduced since World War II. The net emigration figure decreased from 212,000 for 1956–61 to 80,605 for 1961–66 and 53,906 for 1966–71. During 1971–81 Ireland recorded a net gain from immigration of 103,889. Between 1985 and 1995, more than 150,000 people left Ireland, unemployment being the main reason. The top two destinations were the United Kingdom and the United States.

During the 1990s there was a considerable rise in the number of asylum seekers, from 39 applications in 1992 to 4,630 in 1998. The main countries of origin were Nigeria, Romania, the Democratic Republic of the Congo, Libya, and Algeria. Also, during the Kosovo crisis in 1999 Ireland took in 1,033 Kosovar Albanians who were evacuated from Macedonia under the UNHCR/IOM Humanitarian Evacuation Programme. Between 2006 and 2010 asylum applications decreased steadily, from 4,310 in 2006 to 1,940 in 2010.

8 ETHNIC GROUPS

Ireland has been inhabited by Celts, Norsemen, French Normans, and English. Through the centuries, the racial strains represented by these groups have been so intermingled that no purely ethnic divisions remain. At the 2006 census about 87.4% of the population identified as Irish. About 7.5% of the population listed as other white, followed by Asians at 1.3%, blacks at 1.1%, mixed race at 1.1%, and 1.6% unspecified.

9 LANGUAGES

Two languages are spoken, English and Irish (Gaelic). During the long centuries of British control, Irish fell into disuse except in parts of western Ireland. Since the establishment of the Irish Free State in 1922, the government has sought to reestablish Irish as a spoken language throughout the country. It is taught as a compulsory subject in schools and all government publications, street signs, and post office notices are printed in both Irish and English. English, however, remains the language in common use. Only in a few areas (the Gaeltacht), mostly along the western seaboard, is Irish in everyday use. About 30% of the population claims some proficiency in Gaelic.

10 RELIGIONS

According to the 2006 census, about 86.8% of the population were nominally Roman Catholic. The next largest organization was the

Church of Ireland (Anglican), with a membership of about 2.9% of the population. Muslims, Presbyterians, Orthodox Christians, Methodists, other Christians, and Jews each accounted for less than 1% of the population. There are small communities Jehovah's Witnesses. For ecclesiastical purposes, the Republic of Ireland and Northern Ireland (UK) constitute a single entity. Both Roman Catholics and Episcopalian churches have administrative seats at Armagh in Northern Ireland. The Presbyterian Church has its headquarters in Belfast.

The constitutional right to freedom of religion is generally respected in practice. St. Patrick's Day (the country's national day), Good Friday, Easter Monday, Christmas, and St. Stephen's Day are observed as national holidays.

11 TRANSPORTATION

The CIA reports that Ireland has a total of 96,036 km (59,674 mi) of roads, 96,036 km of which (59,674 mi) are paved. There are 534 vehicles per 1,000 people in the country. Railroads extend for 1,919 km (1,192 mi). There are 39 airports which transported 77.75 million passengers in 2009, according to the World Bank. Ireland has approximately 956 km (594 mi) of navigable waterways.

The Irish Transport System (Córas Iompair Éireann—CIE), a state-sponsored entity, provides a nationwide coordinated road and rail system of public transport for goods and passengers. It is also responsible for maintaining the canals, although they are no longer used for commercial transport. Ireland's railroads, like those of many other European countries, have become increasingly unprofitable because of competition from road transport facilities.

A network of good main roads extends throughout the country, and improved country roads lead to smaller towns and villages. In 2006 the car share of inland passenger transport totaled 83.7%, and 98% of inland freight was conveyed by road. Bus routes connect all the major population centers and numerous moderate-sized towns.

The state-supported shipping firm, the British and Irish Steam Packet Co. (the B and I Line), was largely engaged in cross-channel passenger, car ferry, and freight services between Ireland and the United Kingdom until 1992, when it was privatized and taken over by the Irish Continental Group. The Ferries Division of the Group operates services to Britain and France, linking Dublin with Holyhead and Rosslare with Pembroke, Cherbourg, and Roscoff. Brittany Ferries operates a weekly service between Cork and Roscoff. Other shipping concerns operate regular passenger and freight services to the United Kingdom and freight services to the Continent. There are deepwater ports at Cork and Dublin and 10 secondary ports. Dublin is the main port. Most of Ireland's inland waterways are accessible only by pleasure craft.

Aer Lingus (Irish International Airlines), the Irish national airline, operates services between Ireland, the United Kingdom, and continental Europe as well as transatlantic flights. Many foreign airlines operate scheduled transatlantic passenger and air freight services through the duty-free port at Shannon, and most transatlantic airlines make nonscheduled stops there; foreign airlines also operate services between Ireland, the United Kingdom, and continental Europe. The three state airports at Dublin, Shannon, and Cork are managed by Aer Rianta on behalf of the Ministry for Transport and Power. A domestic airline, Aer Arann Teo, con-

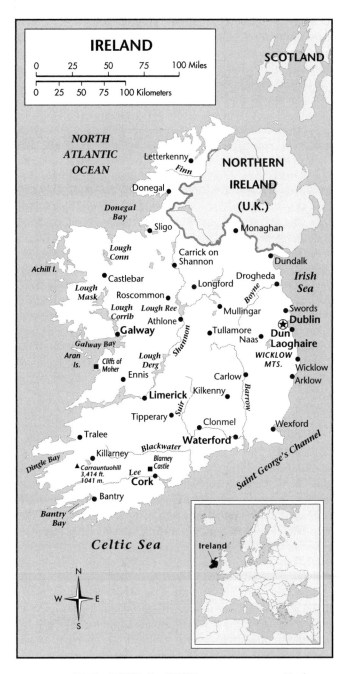

LOCATION: 51°30′ to 55°30′N; 6° to 10°30′W. BOUNDARY LENGTHS: Northern Ireland, 434 kilometers (270 miles); total coastline, 3,169 kilometers (1,969 miles). TERRITORIAL SEA LIMIT: 3 miles.

nects Dublin, Kerry, and Waterford with the Isle of Man and various cities in the United Kingdom.

12 HISTORY

The pre-Christian era in Ireland is known chiefly through legend, although there is archaeological evidence of habitation during the Stone and Bronze ages. In about the 4th century BC, the tall, red-haired Celts from Gaul or Galicia arrived, bringing with them the Iron Age. They subdued the Picts in the north and the Érainn tribe in the south, then settled down to establish a Gaelic civilization, absorbing many of the traditions of the previous inhabitants.

By the 3rd century AD, the Gaels had established five permanent kingdoms—Ulster, Connacht, Leinster, Meath (North Leinster), and Munster—with a high king, whose title was often little more than honorary, at Tara. After St. Patrick's arrival in AD 432, Christian Ireland rapidly became a center of Latin and Gaelic learning. Irish monasteries drew not only the pious, but also the intellectuals of the day, and sent out missionaries to many parts of Europe.

Toward the end of the 8th century, the Vikings began their invasions, destroying monasteries and wreaking havoc on the land, but also intermarrying, adopting Irish customs, and establishing coastal settlements from which have grown Ireland's chief cities. Viking power was finally broken at the Battle of Clontarf in 1014. About 150 years later, the Anglo-Norman invasions began. Gradually, the invaders gained control of the whole country. Many of them intermarried; adopted the Irish language, customs, and traditions; and became more Irish than the Gaels. However, the political attachment to the English crown instituted by the Norman invasion caused almost 800 years of strife, as successive English monarchs sought to subdue Gaels and Norman-Irish alike. Wholesale confiscations of land and large plantations of English colonists began under Mary I (Mary Tudor) and continued under Elizabeth I, Oliver Cromwell, and William III. Treatment of the Irish reached a brutal climax in the 18th century with the Penal Laws, which deprived Catholics and Dissenters (the majority of the population) of all legal rights.

By the end of the 18th century many of the English colonists had come to regard themselves as Irish, and like the English colonists in America, resented the domination of London and their own lack of power to rule themselves. In 1783 they forced the establishment of an independent Irish parliament, but it was abolished by the Act of Union (1800), which gave Ireland direct representation in Westminster. Catholic emancipation was finally achieved in 1829 through the efforts of Daniel O'Connell, but the great famine of the 1840s, when millions died or emigrated for lack of potatoes while landlords continued to export other crops to England, emphasized the tragic condition of the Irish peasant and the great need for land reform.

A series of uprisings and the growth of various movements aimed at home rule or outright independence led gradually to many reforms, but the desire for complete independence continued to grow. After the bloodshed and political maneuvers that followed the Easter Uprising of 1916, and the proclamation of an Irish Republic by Irish members of Parliament in 1919, the Anglo-Irish Treaty was signed in 1921, establishing an Irish Free State with dominion status in the British Commonwealth. Violent opposition to dominion status and to a separate government in Protestant-dominated Northern Ireland precipitated a civil war lasting almost a year. The Free State was officially proclaimed and a new constitution adopted in 1922, but sentiment in favor of a reunified Irish Republic remained strong, represented at its extreme by the terrorist activities of the Irish Republican Army (IRA). Powerful at first, the IRA lost much of its popularity after Éamon de Valera, a disillusioned supporter, took over the government in 1932. During the civil violence that disrupted Northern Ireland from the late 1960s on, the Irish government attempted to curb the "provisional wing" of the IRA, a terrorist organization that used Ireland as a base for attacks in the north. Beginning in 1976, the government assumed emergency powers to cope with IRA activities, but the terrorist acts continued, most notably the assassination on 27 August 1979 of Louis Mountbatten, the British earl.

The Irish government continued to favor union with Northern Ireland, but only by peaceful means. In November 1985, with the aim of promoting peace in Northern Ireland, Ireland and the United Kingdom ratified a treaty enabling Ireland to play a role in various aspects of Northern Ireland's affairs. On 10 April 1998 the Irish Republic jointly signed a peace agreement with the United Kingdom to resolve the Northern Ireland crisis. Ireland pledged to amend articles 2 and 3 of the Irish constitution, which lay claim to the territory of the North, in return for the United Kingdom promising to amend the Government of Ireland Act. On 22 May 1998, 94.4% of the electorate voted in a referendum to drop Ireland's claim to Northern Ireland. A year after the agreement, several key provisions of the Good Friday Agreement had been implemented.

The peace process witnessed long moments of gloom in spite of the ongoing involvement of the British and Irish prime ministers to resolve the situation in Northern Ireland. One of the largest obstacles was the disarmament of the IRA and the reservations on the part of the Ulster Unionists to share power with Sinn Feìn, the political arm of the IRA. Finally, in May 2000, the IRA proposed that outside observers be shown the contents of arms dumps and be permitted to reinspect them at regular intervals to ensure that weaponry had not been removed and was back in circulation. The Ulster Unionists agreed to power-sharing arrangements and to endorse devolution of Northern Ireland.

Decommissioning of the IRA did not progress in early 2001, however, and David Trimble, the first minister of the power-sharing government, resigned in July 2001. Sinn Feìn's offices at Stormont, the Northern Ireland parliament building, were raided by the police in October 2002, due to spying allegations. On 14 October 2002 devolution was suspended and direct rule from London returned to Northern Ireland. Elections planned for the assembly in May 2003 were indefinitely postponed by British Prime Minister Tony Blair, due to a lack of evidence of peaceful intentions on the part of the IRA. Talks aimed at restoring devolved government in 2004 failed due to the continued IRA possession of illegal arms and its refusal to disband and pull out of illegal activities. In 2006, the governments of Ireland and Britain made some progress with the implementation of the St. Andrews Agreement, an extension of the Good Friday Agreement of 1998. The agreement restored power-sharing to Stormont in May 2007, with Unionist Ian Paisley and Sinn Feìn's Martin McGuinness serving as Northern Ireland's first and deputy first ministers, respectively. In the last years of the 2000s, resurgence of violence by the IRA, including a number of bombing attacks, once again threatened the fragile Northern Irish peace process.

The years since the proclamation of the Irish Free State have witnessed important changes in governmental structure and international relations. In 1937, under a new constitution, the governor-general was replaced by an elected president, and the name of the country was officially changed to Ireland (Éire in Irish). In 1948 Ireland voted itself out of the Commonwealth of Nations, and on 18 April 1949 it declared itself a republic. Ireland was admitted to the United Nations in 1955 and became a member of the European Community in 1973. Ireland, unlike the United Kingdom, joined the European Economic and Monetary Union in

1999 without problem, and adopted the euro as its currency. However, Irish voters in June 2001 rejected the Treaty of Nice, which allowed for the enlargement of the European Union. The other 14 members of the EU all approved the treaty by parliamentary vote, but Ireland's adoption required amending the constitution, which stipulated a popular vote. Voter turnout was low (34.8%), and when the treaty was put to Irish voters once again in October 2002, the government conducted a massive education campaign to bring voters to the polls. This time, voter turnout was 48.5%, and 63% of voters in the October referendum approved the Nice Treaty. Ten new EU candidate countries joined the body on 1 May 2004, and Romania and Bulgaria acceded in 2007.

Ireland has also benefited from progressive leadership. Mary Robinson, an international lawyer, activist, and Catholic, was elected president in November 1990. She became the first woman to hold that office. In 1974, while serving in the Irish legislature, she shocked her fellow country people by calling for legal sale of contraceptives. Her victory came at a period in Irish history dominated by controversy over the major issues of the first half of the 1990s: unemployment, women's rights, abortion, divorce, and homosexuality. Robinson promoted legislation that enabled women to serve on juries and gave 18-year-olds the right to vote. In 1997 Mary McAleese, who lived in Northern Ireland, became the first British subject to be elected president of the Irish Republic. In March 2002 Irish voters rejected a referendum proposal that would further restrict abortion laws.

In October 2004 McAleese won a second seven-year term as president; however, this was in light of the fact that opposing parties didn't nominate alternative candidates. She will not be eligible for another reelection in the October 2011 elections. The May 2007 national elections brought the Fianna Fáil party and its leader Bertie Ahern back to power in a coalition government for an unprecedented third five-year term. Ahern appointed Finance Minister Brian Cowen as deputy prime minister. In April 2008 Ahern announced his intention to resign as leader of Fianna Fáil and *taoiseach* (prime minister). Cowen was elected leader of Fianna Fáil and assumed office on May 6. He was elected taoiseach on May 7. In the 2011 general election Fine Gael overtook opposition party Fianna Fáil in senate seats, and Enda Kenny, leader of Fine Gael since 2002, became taoiseach.

In a referendum held on 12 June 2008, Irish voters rejected the European Union Lisbon Treaty, which proposed amendments to the Treaty of Maastricht and other EU agreements, by 53.7% to 46.3%. The Lisbon Treaty calls for reforms in both the structure and operational procedures of EU administration that may promote more efficient and effective leadership. Irish voters are concerned that some of the proposed reforms could threaten national sovereignty. A second referendum was held in October 2009, following discussions about legal guarantees to protect national sovereignty for EU members. The treaty was finally approved by 67% of voters. All of the major political parties campaigned for approval of the treaty, with the exception of Sinn Fein. Voter turnout was about 58%.

13 GOVERNMENT

Constitutionally, Ireland is a parliamentary democracy. Under the constitution of 1937, as amended, legislative power is vested in the Oireachtas (parliament), which consists of the president and two houses—Dáil Éireann (house of representatives) and Seanad Éireann (senate)—and sits in Dublin, the capital city. The president is elected by popular vote for seven years. Members of the Dáil, who are also elected by popular suffrage, using the single transferable vote, represent constituencies determined by law and serve five-year terms. These constituencies, none of which may return fewer than three members, must be revised at least once every 12 years, and the ratio between the number of members to be elected for each constituency and its population as ascertained at the last census must be the same, as far as practicable, throughout the country. Since 1981 there have been 166 seats in the Dáil.

The Seanad consists of 60 members: 49 elected from five panels of candidates representing (a) industry and commerce, (b) agricultural and allied interests and fisheries, (c) labor, (d) cultural and educational interests, and (e) public administration and social services; 6 elected by the universities; and 11 nominated by the taoiseach (prime minister). Elections for the Seanad must be held within 90 days of the dissolution of the Dáil; the electorate consists of members of the outgoing Seanad, members of the incoming Dáil, members of county councils, and county borough authorities. The taoiseach is assisted by a *tánaiste* (deputy prime minister) and at least six but not more than 14 other ministers. The constitution provides for popular referendums on certain bills of national importance passed by the Oireachtas. Suffrage is universal at age 18.

The chief of state is the president, who is elected by universal suffrage to serve a seven-year term and may be reelected only once. The presidency is traditionally a figurehead role with limited powers. The president appoints a cabinet based upon a nomination from the taoiseach and approval from the Dáil. The head of government is the taoiseach, who is nominated by the Dáil and appointed by the president.

A number of amendments having to do with European integration, Northern Ireland, abortion, and divorce have been added to the 1937 constitution, which may only be altered by referendum. A recent referendum in 2004 ended in a 4-to-1 vote that native-born children could not be granted automatic citizenship.

14 POLITICAL PARTIES

The major political parties are the Fianna Fáil, the Fine Gael, Labour, and the Progressive Democrats. Because the members of the Dáil are elected by a proportional representation system, smaller parties have also at times won representation in the Oireachtas. In 1986 Sinn Feìn, the political arm of the Provisional IRA, ended its 65-year boycott of the Dáil and registered as a political party, winning one seat in the Dáil in the 6 June 1997 elections.

Fianna Fáil, the Republican Party, was founded by Éamon de Valera. It is the largest party since 1932 and has participated in government during 61 of the past 79 years, as of 2011. When the Anglo-Irish Treaty of 1921 was signed, de Valera violently opposed the dominion status accepted by a close vote of the Dáil. Until 1927, when the government threatened to annul their election if they did not fulfill their mandates, de Valera and his followers boycotted the Dáil and refused to take an oath of allegiance to the English crown. In 1932, however, de Valera became prime minister, a position he held continuously until 1947 and intermittently until 1959, when he became president for the first of two terms. From 1932 to 1973, when it lost its majority to a Fine Gael-Labour coalition, Fianna Fáil was in power for all but six years.

Fine Gael is the present name for the traditionally center-right party (of the Christian democratic type) and is the second-largest party in Ireland. It grew out of the policies of Arthur Griffith, first president of the Irish Free State, and Michael Collins, first minister for finance and commander-in-chief of the army. W. T. Cosgrave, their successor, accepted the conditions of the 1921 treaty as the best then obtainable and worked out the details of the partition boundary and dominion status. This party held power from the first general election of 1922 until 1932. Since 1948, as the principal opponent of Fianna Fáil, it has provided leadership for several coalition governments. The policies of Fine Gael traditionally have been far more moderate than those of Fianna Fáil, although it was an interparty coalition government dominated by Fine Gael and Labour that voted Ireland out of the Commonwealth in 1948.

The Labour Party incorporated the Democratic Left into its party in 1998, but still failed to increase its seats in the 2002 election (it is much smaller than Fine Gael). The party moved toward the center under the leadership of Pat Rabitte.

In 1985 a group of parliamentarians broke away from Fianna Fáil because of the autocratic leadership of Charles Haughey. They formed the Progressive Democrats (PDs) party, which supported liberal economic orthodoxy in the 1980s. It joined in a coalition with Fianna Fáil in 1997 and was influential in economic policy making until its disbandment in 2009.

In the general elections of 24 November 1982 (the third general election to be held within a year and a half), Fianna Fáil won 75 seats, Fine Gael 70, and the Labour Party 16. Two members of the Workers' Party and three independents were also elected. Garret FitzGerald was elected taoiseach (1983–1987), heading a Fine Gael-Labour coalition. It was the second time in a year that he had replaced Charles J. Haughey of the Fianna Fáil in that office. In December 1979 Haughey had replaced Jack Lynch as head of his party and become taoiseach. The 1987 elections saw Fianna Fáil raise its representation, despite a drop in its proportion of the vote compared to the 1982 elections. Fine Gael and Labour lost seats, while the Progressive Democrats and Workers' Party (which increased its representation from two to four seats) increased their seat holding. In a bitter contest, Charles Haughey was elected taoiseach (1987–1991) and formed a minority Fianna Fáil government. Albert Reynolds was taoiseach from 1991 to 1994.

An early general election in 1992 saw Fianna Fáil and Fine Gael lose seats to the Labour Party. Albert Reynolds of Fianna Fáil was reelected taoiseach of the Fianna Fáil-Labour Coalition. From 1994 to 1997, John Bruton, of the Fianna Gael-Labour-Democratic Left was taoiseach. However, a center-right alliance led by Bertie Ahern of Fianna Fáil defeated Bruton's three-party left-of-center coalition in the 6 June 1997 general election. Although Bruton's own party, Fine Gael, increased its share of the vote, its coalition partners, the Labour Party and the Democratic Left, both lost seats. Fianna Fáil won 77 seats outright, 6 shy of the 83 required for a majority. Other parties winning seats were Labor (17), Democratic Left (4), Progressive Democrats (4), Greens (2), Sinn Fein (1), Socialists (1), and Independents (6).

Fianna Fáil joined with the Progressive Democrats and Independents to form a new government with Bertie Ahern as taoiseach. In 1999 the Labour Party and the Democratic Left merged and the new party is called the Labour Party. The electoral significance of this realignment of the left is not yet clear, but the merger provides the Irish electorate with a more viable social democratic alternative to the governing coalition.

Bertie Ahern remained taoiseach after Fianna Fáil won 41.5% of the vote on 16 May 2002, capturing 81 seats in the Dáil. Fine Gael won 22.5% of the vote and 31 seats, its worst defeat in 70 years. The Labour Party took 10.8% of the vote and 21 seats. Other parties winning seats were the Progressive Democrats (8), the Greens (6), Sinn Fein (5), the Socialist Party (1), and Independents (13).

In the 24 May 2007 national elections Fianna Fáil party won 41.6% of the vote in the Dáil, earning 78 seats. Fine Gael won 27.3% of the vote with and 51 seats. The Labour Party earned 10.1% of the vote and 20 seats. Other parties winning seats were Sinn Fein (4), the Greens (6), and Progressive Democrats (2).

In May 2008 Ahern resigned as leader of Fianna Fail and Taoiseach. Brian Cowen was elected leader of Fianna Fail on 5 April and assumed office on 6 May. He was elected taoiseach on 7 May.

In the 25 February 2011 elections for the Dáil, Fine Gael won 76 seats with 45.8% of the vote, followed by the Labor Party with 37 seats (22.3%), Fianna Fail with 20 seats (12%), Sinn Fein with 14 seats (8.4%), United Left Alliance with 5 seats (3%), New Vision with one seat, and 13 seats to independents. Enda Kenny of Fine Gael was sworn in as the new taoiseach in March 2011.

As of 2011, Labour's Michael Higgins became Mary McAleese's successor in the presidential office, defeating independent Seán Gallagher and Sinn Féin's Martin McGuinness. As of March 2011, Enda Kenny replaced Bertie Ahern as taoiseach.

15 LOCAL GOVERNMENT

The provinces of Ulster, Munster, Leinster, and Connacht no longer serve as political divisions, but each is divided into a number of counties that do. Prior to the passage of the new Local Government Act of 2001 and its implementation in 2002, Ireland was divided into 29 county councils, 5 boroughs, 5 boroughs governed by municipal corporations, 49 urban district councils, and 26 boards of town commissioners. Under the new system, the county councils remain the same, but the corporations no longer exist. The cities of Dublin, Cork, Limerick, Waterford, and Galway are city councils, while Drogheda, Wexford, Kilkenny, Sligo, and Clonmel are the five borough councils. The urban district councils and town commissions are now one and the same and known as town councils, of which there are 75.

Local authorities' principal functions include planning and development, housing, roads, and sanitary and environmental services. Health services, which were administered by local authorities up to 1971, are now administered by regional health boards, although the local authorities still continue to pay part of the cost. Expenditures are financed by a local tax on the occupation of property (rates), by grants and subsidies from the central government, and by charges made for certain services. Capital expenditure is financed mainly by borrowing from the Local Loans Fund, operated by the central government, and from banking and insurance institutions.

16 JUDICIAL SYSTEM

Responsibility for law enforcement is in the hands of a commissioner, responsible to the Department of Justice, who controls an unarmed police force known as the civil guard (Garda Síochána). Justice is administered by the Supreme Court of Ireland, a high court with full original jurisdiction, eight circuit courts, and 23 district courts with local and limited jurisdiction. Judges are appointed by the president, on the advice of the prime minister and cabinet.

Individual liberties are protected by the 1937 constitution and by Supreme Court decisions. The constitution provides for the creation of "special courts" to handle cases that cannot be adequately managed by the ordinary court system. The Offenses Against the State Act formally established a special court to hear cases involving political violence by terrorist groups. In such cases, in order to prevent intimidation, the panel of judges sits in place of a jury.

The judiciary is independent and provides a fair, efficient judicial process based upon the English common law system. Judicial precedent makes it a vital check on the power of the executive in Ireland. It can declare laws unconstitutional before and after they have been enacted, as well. Typically, however, the relationship between the judiciary and the other two branches of government has been untroubled by conflict.

17 ARMED FORCES

The Irish army and its reservists, along with the air corps, and navy, constitute a small but well-trained nucleus that can be enlarged in a time of emergency. The International Institute for Strategic Studies reports that armed forces in Ireland totaled 10,460 members in 2011. The force is comprised of 8,500 from the army, 1,110 from the navy, and 850 members of the air force, representing a total of 0.5% of the labor force in Ireland. Defense spending in 2011 totaled $1.6 billion and accounted for 0.9% of gross domestic product (GDP) as Ireland provided support to UN, NATO and European Union peacekeeping or military operations in 10 countries or regions.

18 INTERNATIONAL COOPERATION

Ireland, which became a member of the United Nations on 14 December 1955, belongs to ECE and several nonregional specialized agencies, such as the FAO, UNESCO, UNHCR, IFC, the World Bank, and WHO. On 1 January 1973, Ireland became a member of the European Union. The country is also a member of the WTO, the European Bank for Reconstruction and Development, the Paris Club, the Euro-Atlantic Partnership Council, and the OSCE. Ireland is a founding member of OECD and the Council of Europe. The country also participates as an observer in the OAS and the Western European Union.

Irish troops have served in UN operations and missions in the Congo (est. 1999), Cyprus (est. 1964), Kosovo (est. 1999), Lebanon (est. 1978), Liberia (est. 2003), and Côte d'Ivoire (est. 2004), among others. Ireland is a guest of the Nonaligned Movement, It is also a part of the Australia Group, the Zangger Committee, the Nuclear Suppliers Group (London Group), the Organization for the Prohibition of Chemical Weapons, and the Nuclear Energy Agency. In environmental cooperation, Ireland is part of the Basel Convention; Conventions on Biological Diversity, Whaling, and Air Pollution; Ramsar; the London Convention; International Tropical Timber Agreements; the Kyoto Protocol; the Montréal Protocol; MARPOL; the Nuclear Test Ban Treaty; and the UN Conventions on the Law of the Sea, Climate Change and Desertification.

19 ECONOMY

Until the 1950s Ireland had a predominantly agricultural economy, with agriculture making the largest contribution to the GNP. However, liberal trade policies and the drive for industrialization stimulated economic expansion. In 1958 agriculture accounted for 21% of the GNP, industry 23.5%, and other sectors 55.5%. By 2002, however, agriculture accounted for only 5% of the total, industry 46%, and services 49%. The CIA estimated that in 2010 agriculture accounted for 2% of GDP, industry 29%, and services 70%.

Ireland's economy was initially slower in developing than the economies of other West European countries. The government carried on a comprehensive public investment program, particularly in housing, public welfare, communications, transportation, new industries, and electric power. Growth rose quickly in the 1960s and, since then, the government has tried to stimulate output, particularly of goods for the export market. Thus, manufactured exports grew from £78.4 million in 1967 to £11,510 million in 1992.

In the 1970s Ireland began to approach the income of the rest of Western Europe, until it lost fiscal control in the latter part of the 1970s due to the oil crisis. During the early 1980s Ireland suffered considerably from the worldwide recession, experiencing double-digit inflation and high unemployment. The economy continued to lag through 1986, but the GNP grew 30% between 1987 and 1992, and continued at a yearly pace of about 7.5% until 1996 when it was expected to slow to about 5.25%. However, the Irish economy grew faster than any other in the European Union during the so-called "Celtic Tiger" years of the second half of the 1990s, when growth rates were in double digits. The good economic performance was mainly due to strong consumer and investor confidence and strong export opportunities.

Ireland suffered from the global economic slowdown that began in 2001; however, the average growth rate between 1995 and 2007 remained 6%. According to the CIA, this dropped sharply in the wake of the global financial crisis of 2008–09, with GDP falling by over 3% in 2008, nearly 8% in 2009, and another 1% in 2010.

Although substantially lower than in 1986 when it topped 18%, unemployment remained high until 1998, when it dropped to 7.7%. The estimated unemployment rate in 2005 was 4.2%. The inflation rate stood at 2.4% in 1998 and was 2% in 2003 and 3% in 2004. Inflation fell steadily from a rate of 4.9% in 2000 to 2.2% in 2004, and price levels are among the highest in Europe. As of 2011 inflation stood at -1.6%, and unemployment was reported at 14.2%.

Ireland has depended on substantial financial assistance from the European Union designed to raise the per capita gross national product to the EU average. Almost $11 billion was allocated for the period 1993–99 from the EU's Structural and Cohesion Funds. During the 1990s living standards rose from 56% to 87% of the EU average. Per capita GDP is 40% above that of the four big European economies and second highest in Europe, after Luxembourg.

In the wake of the global financial crisis of 2008–09, the nation showed double-digit employment and, perhaps due to outlays in social services, a substantial increase in the national budget deficit. In December 2009 the government announced a new budget proposal to cut spending by about $5.8 billion. Such cuts are necessary, in part, to work toward the EU requirement of bringing the budget deficit to under 3% by 2014.

20 INCOME

The CIA estimated that in 2010 the GDP of Ireland was $172.3 billion. The CIA defines GDP as the value of all final goods and services produced within a nation in a given year, computed on the basis of purchasing power parity (PPP) rather than value as measured on the basis of the rate of exchange based on current dollars. The per capita GDP was estimated at $37,300, while the annual growth rate of GDP was -1%. As of 2011, inflation stood at -1.6%. he CIA estimated that in 2010 agriculture accounted for 2% of GDP, industry 29%, and services 70%. According to the World Bank, remittances from citizens living abroad totaled $575.7 million or about $123 per capita and accounted for approximately 0.3% of GDP.

The World Bank reports that in 2009, household consumption in Ireland totaled $112.5 billion or about $24,078 per capita, measured in current US dollars. Household consumption includes expenditures of individuals, households, and nongovernmental organizations on goods and services, excluding the purchases of dwellings. It was estimated that household consumption was growing at an average annual rate of 7.1%.

As of 2011, the most recent study by the World Bank reported that actual individual consumption in Ireland was 56.0% of GDP and accounted for 0.23% of world consumption. By comparison, the United States accounted for 25.44% of world individual consumption. The World Bank also estimated that 4.9% of Ireland's GDP was spent on food and beverages, 12.2% on housing and household furnishings, 2.3% on clothes, 5.6% on health, 5.4% on transportation, 1.5% on communications, 3.8% on recreation, 6.8% on restaurants and hotels, and 7.8% on miscellaneous goods and services and purchases from abroad.

It was estimated that in 2009 about 5.5% of the population subsisted on an income below the poverty line established by Ireland's government.

21 LABOR

As of 2010, Ireland had a total labor force of 2.14 million people. Within that labor force, CIA estimates in 2010 noted that 5% were employed in agriculture, 20% in industry, and 76% in the service sector. Unemployment was reported at 13.7% in 2011.

The right to join a union is protected by law, and as of 2010, about 35% of the labor force were union members. The Irish Congress of Trade Unions (ICTU) represents 55 unions and is independent of political parties and the government. The right to strike, except for police and military personnel, is exercised in both the public and private sectors. Employers are legally prohibited from discriminating against those who participate in union activity. Collective bargaining is used to determine wages and other conditions of employment.

Children under age 16 are legally prohibited from engaging in regular, full-time work. Under certain restrictions, some part-time or educational work may be given to 14- and 15-year-olds. Violations of child labor laws are not common. The standard workweek is 39 hours, and the legal limit on industrial work is nine hours per day and 48 hours per week. In July 2011 the national minimum wage was raised to €8.65 ($11.52) per hour.

22 AGRICULTURE

Roughly 17% of the total land is used for agriculture. The country's major crops include beef, dairy products, barley, potatoes, and wheat. In 2009 cereal production amounted to 2 million tons, fruit production 50,926 tons, and vegetable production 218,330 tons.

Most of the farmland is used to support livestock, the leading source of Ireland's exports. Most farms are small, although there has been a trend toward consolidation. Agriculture accounts for about 5% of Irish employment.

Over half of agricultural production, by value, is exported. The benefits of the EU's Common Agricultural Policy, which provides secure markets and improved prices for most major agricultural products, account in part for the increase of Ireland's agricultural income from £314 million in 1972 (before Ireland's accession) to £1,919.9 million in 1995. In 2010 Ireland's Department of Agriculture, Fisheries and Food reported a contribution of €24 billion ($31.9 billion) by the agri-food sector to the national economy.

The government operates a comprehensive network of services within the framework of the Common Agricultural Policy, including educational and advisory services to farmers. Under a farm modernization scheme, capital assistance is provided to farmers for land development, improvement of farm buildings, and other projects, with part of the cost borne by the European Union. In 1974, pursuant to an European Community directive, incentives were made available to farmers wishing to retire and make their lands available, by lease or sale, for the land reform program.

23 ANIMAL HUSBANDRY

The UN Food and Agriculture Organization (FAO) reported that Ireland dedicated 3.1 million hectares (7.65 million acres) to permanent pasture or meadow in 2009. With over 90% of Ireland's agricultural land devoted to pasture and hay, the main activity of the farming community is the production of grazing animals and other livestock, which account for about 53% of agricultural exports. In 2010 total livestock output was valued at €2.44 billion ($3.2 billion), up 9% from 2009.

In 2009 the country tended 13.5 million chickens, 6.7 million head of cattle, and 1.5 million pigs. The production from these animals amounted to 102,732 tons of beef and veal, 157,680 tons of pork, 111,025 tons of poultry, 29,733 tons of eggs, and 1.08 million tons of milk. Ireland also produced 59,000 tons of cattle hide and 13,711 tons of raw wool.

Since livestock is a major element in the country's economy, the government is particularly concerned with improving methods of operation and increasing output. A campaign for eradication of bovine tuberculosis was completed in 1965, and programs are under way for eradication of bovine brucellosis, warble fly, and sheep scab.

24 FISHING

Salmon, eels, trout, pike, perch, and other freshwater fish are found in Ireland's rivers and lakes; sea angling is good along the entire coast; and deep-sea fishing is done from the south and west coasts. The fishing industry has made considerable progress as a result of government measures to improve credit facilities for the purchase of fishing boats and the development of harbors, establishment of training programs for fishermen, increased emphasis on market development and research, establishment of hatcheries, and promotion of sport fishing as an attraction for tourists. In 2008 Ireland had 1,278 decked commercial fishing boats.

Leading varieties of saltwater fish are mackerel, herring, cod, whiting, plaice, ray, skate, and haddock. Lobsters, crawfish, and Dublin Bay prawns are also important. Aquaculture production value was €105.7 million ($140.8 million) in 2007, down 15% from 2006. Although the overall production volume decreased, gigas oysters, scallops, native oysters, and other finifish showed growth. According to the UN FAO, the annual capture totaled 205,342 tons and the export value of seafood totaled $437.4 million in 2008.

25 FORESTRY

Once well forested, Ireland was stripped of timber in the 17th and 18th centuries by absentee landlords, who made no attempt to reforest the denuded land, and later by the steady conversion of natural forest into farms and grazing lands. In an effort to restore part of the woodland areas, a state forestry program was inaugurated in 1903; since then, over 350,000 hectares (865,000 acres) have been planted. More than half the planting is carried out in the western counties. In 2009 approximately 11% of Ireland was covered by forest with roundwood production at 2.26 million cu m (79.9 million cu ft). The value of all forest products, including roundwood, totaled $425.1 million. The aim of the forestry program is to eliminate a large part of timber imports-a major drain on the balance of payments-and to produce a surplus of natural and processed timber for export.

26 MINING

Ireland was a leading EU producer of lead and zinc in 2009, and an important producer of lead, alumina, and peat. Mineral production in 2009 included zinc, 357,000 metric tons, compared to 425,756 metric tons in 2006; mined lead, 43,000 tons, compared to 61,800 tons in 2006; and an estimated 1.2 million metric tons of alumina. Other commercially exploited minerals were silver, hydraulic cement, clays for cement production, fire clay, granite, slate, marble, rock sand, silica rock, gypsum, lime, limestone, sand and gravel, shales, dolomite, diatomite, building stone, and aggregate building materials.

Zinc production centered on three zinc-lead mines, the Lisheen (a joint venture of Anglo American PLC and Ivernia West PLC), the Galmoy (Arcon International Resources PLC), and the Tara (Outokumpu Oyj), three of Europe's most modern mines. Outokumpu announced that because of low zinc prices, it was closing the Tara Mine (at Navan, County Meath), the largest lead-zinc field in Europe, and putting it on care and maintenance; the Tara came into production in the late 1970s. The Galmoy Mine was producing 650,000 tons per year of ore at target grades of 11.3% zinc and 1% lead, but closed in 2009 due to collapse of base-metal prices. The Lisheen Mine, which mined its first ore in 1999 and began commercial production in 2001, initially planned to produce 160,000 tons per year of zinc concentrate, to be increased to 330,000 tons per year of zinc concentrate and 40,000 tons per year of lead in concentrate at full production; both were on the Rath-

downey Trend mineralized belt, southwest of Dublin. Cambridge Mineral Resources PLC continues diamond and sapphire exploration work, identifying numerous diamond indicator minerals and recovering significant quantities of ruby and sapphire. Gold was discovered in County Mayo in 1989, with an estimated 498,000 tons of ore at 1.5 grams per ton of gold. There was a marked increase in mining exploration beginning in the early 1960s, resulting in Ireland becoming a significant source of base metals.

27 ENERGY AND POWER

Ireland's electric power generating sector is primarily based upon the use of conventional fossil fuels to provide electric power. Total production in 2009 stood at 25.537 billion kWh, with 3.872 billion kWh of this from renewable energy sources.

Ireland's energy and power sector is marked by a lack of any oil reserves, thus making it totally dependent upon imports. However, the country has modest natural gas reserves, and a small refining capacity.

In 2009 Ireland's imports of crude and refined petroleum products were 89% of supply. According to the CIA, demand for refined oil products averaged an estimated 159,700 barrels per day in 2010, with imports of 176,000 bbl/day and exports of 17,480 bbl/day for that year. Per capita oil consumption was 3,385 kg in 2008.

Ireland's proven reserves of natural gas were estimated at 9.911 billion cu m as of 1 January 2011. Production in 2010 was estimated at 388 million cu m, with consumption and imports estimated at 5.656 billion cu m and 5.261 billion cu m, respectively, for that year.

Ireland's coal production tapered off in the early 1990s, and 2.76 million short tons of coal were imported in 2008.

28 INDUSTRY

Since the establishment of the Irish Free State, successive governments encouraged industrialization by granting tariff protection and promoting diversification. Following the launching of the First Program for Economic Expansion by the government in 1958, considerable progress was made in developing this sector of the economy, in which foreign industrialists played a significant role. The Industrial Development Authority (IDA) administers a scheme of incentives to attract foreign investment. In addition, several government agencies offer facilities for consulting on research and development, marketing, exporting, and other management matters.

Official policy favors private enterprises. Where private capital and interest were lacking, the state created firms to operate essential services and to stimulate further industrial development, notably in the fields of sugar, peat, electricity, steel, fertilizers, industrial alcohol, and transportation. Although efforts have been made to encourage decentralization, about half of all industrial establishments and personnel are concentrated in Dublin and Cork.

Industry grew by an average annual rate of more than 5% from 1968 to 1981, and peaked at 12% in 1984 before subsiding to an annual rate of about 4%. The greatest growth was in high technology industries, like electronics and pharmaceuticals, where labor productivity also was growing substantially, thus limiting increases in the number of jobs. The most important products of manufacturing, by gross output, are food and drink, electrical and optical, chemicals and pharmaceuticals, and print and recorded media, as well as metals, nonmetallic minerals, and tobacco. The making of glass and crystal are also important industries. Industrial production continued to grow into the late 1990s, the "Celtic Tiger" years, and posted 14.6% growth from 2005 to 2011.

According to the CIA, industry employed 20% of the labor force in 2010, and accounted for 29% of GDP in 2010. Computer and pharmaceutical enterprises, largely owned by foreign companies, were responsible for high manufacturing output in 2000 prior to the outsourcing and downsizing of ICT companies in the following years. Although there is no formal governmental privatization plan, the government planned to privatize the state-owned natural gas distributor (Bord Gáis), the state-owned airline (Aer Lingus), and the state-owned electricity distributor (ESB). As of 2011 no steps had been taken to privatize Bord Gáis, but the government has privatized a portion of Aer Lingus and has agreed to do the same with ESB as a condition of the EU and IMF bailout.

Ireland is shifting attention away from industry and towards services. Activity was quickened by preferential corporation tax rates for manufacturers and manufactures were decreasing relative to services and agriculture.

29 SCIENCE AND TECHNOLOGY

Patent applications in science and technology as of 2009, according to the World Bank, totaled 908 in Ireland. Public financing of science was 1.42% of GDP. The major organizations doing scientific research in Ireland are the Agricultural Institute (established in 1958) and the Institute for Industrial Research and Standards (1946). The Dublin Institute of Advanced Studies, established by the state in 1940, includes a School of Theoretical Physics and a School of Cosmic Physics. The Royal Irish Academy, founded in 1785 and headquartered in Dublin, promotes study in science and the humanities and is the principal vehicle for Ireland's participation in international scientific unions. It has sections for mathematical and physical sciences and for biology and the environment.

The Royal Dublin Society (founded in 1731) promotes the advancement of agriculture, industry, science, and art. Ireland has 13 other specialized learned societies concerned with agriculture, medicine, science, and technology. Major scientific facilities include the Dinsink Observatory (founded in 1785) and the National Botanic Gardens (founded in 1795), both in Dublin.

Most scientific research is funded by the government; the government advisory and coordinating body on scientific matters is the National Board for Science and Technology. Medical research is supported by the Medical Research Council and Medico-Social Research Board. Veterinary and cereals research is promoted by the Department of Agriculture. The Department of Fisheries and Forestry and the Department of Industry and Energy have developed their own research programs. The UNESCO prize in science was awarded in 1981 for the development of clofazimines, a leprosy drug produced by the Medical Research Council of Ireland with aid from the Development Cooperation Division of the Department of Foreign Affairs.

Research and development (R&D) expenditures in 2009 totaled 1.42% of GDP. Of that amount, 67.7% came from the business sector, 6.3% from the government, and 26.1% from higher education. As of 2009, there were some 14,433 researchers actively engaged

Principal Trading Partners – Ireland (2010)

(In millions of US dollars)

Country	Total	Exports	Imports	Balance
World	178,925.0	118,274.0	60,651.0	57,623.0
United Kingdom	40,766.0	18,063.0	22,703.0	-4,640.0
United States	33,043.0	24,801.0	8,242.0	16,559.0
Belgium	19,734.0	18,120.0	1,614.0	16,506.0
Germany	12,582.0	8,016.0	4,566.0	3,450.0
France	8,197.0	5,918.0	2,279.0	3,639.0
Netherlands	7,460.0	4,080.0	3,380.0	700.0
Switzerland	5,811.0	4,662.0	1,149.0	3,513.0
Spain	5,236.0	4,443.0	793.0	3,650.0
China	4,541.0	2,066.0	2,475.0	-409.0
Italy	4,531.0	3,594.0	937.0	2,657.0

(…) data not available or not significant.

(n.s.) not specified.

SOURCE: *2011 Direction of Trade Statistics Yearbook*, New York: United Nations, 2011.

in R&D. According to the OECD, Ireland's Strategy for Science, Technology and Innovation 2006–13 has led to significant investments by the government in research infrastructure, including an increased R&D tax credit from 2006. Ireland has 21 universities and colleges that offer courses in basic and applied science. From 1987–97 science and engineering students accounted for 31% of university enrollment. In 2007, a total of 22.7% of all bachelor's degrees awarded were in the sciences (natural, mathematics and computers, and engineering).

30 DOMESTIC TRADE

Dublin is the financial and commercial center, the distribution point for most imported goods, and the port through which most of the country's agricultural products are shipped to Britain and the Continent. Cork, the second-largest manufacturing city and close to the transatlantic port of Cobh, is also important, as is Limerick, with its proximity to Shannon International Airport. Other important local marketing centers are Galway, Drogheda, Dundalk, Sligo, and Waterford.

The trend in retail establishments has been changing from small shops owned and operated by individuals, to larger department stores, outlets, and chain stores operated by management companies. This trend was helped by the Irish government's removal in January 2005 of a 6,000 sq m (64,583 sq ft) limit on the size of retail warehouse floor space in the country's major cities. A 21% value-added tax (VAT) applies to most goods and services. However, rates of 4.8% and 13.5% are applied to specific items. Medical and health services, children's clothing, food, banking and insurance services, exports, and agricultural fertilizers are exempt from the VAT.

The development of electronic commerce (e-commerce) has become a priority of the Irish government. A comprehensive strategy has been developed that includes world-class telecommunications connectivity, the passage of proactive e-commerce legislation, a 100-acre e-commerce campus, support for the development of e-commerce strategies by small and medium size firms, and for related educational programs in the schools. In addition, online reservation systems are in use by Ryanair and Aer Lingus, Ireland's two major airlines. Also, Internet companies such as

Google, Overture, eBay, Amazon, PayPal, and Yahoo have established a presence in Ireland.

Office business hours are usually 9 a.m. to 4 p.m. Shops are generally open from 9 a.m. to 6 p.m., although most stores are open until 8 p.m. on Thursdays and Fridays. In general, banking hours are 10 a.m. to 4 p.m., Monday through Friday, although banks in the major cities may remain open to 5 p.m. one day of the week. Most offices are closed on Saturday, and shops close on either Wednesday or Saturday afternoon. Businesses may close for extended periods during the months of July and August.

31 FOREIGN TRADE

Ireland began opening to free trade in the 1960s. It is now one of the most open and largest exporting markets (on a per capital level). Information communication technologies, chemicals and pharmaceuticals, and food and drink have become some of Ireland's most profitable export products. The country also manufactures and exports musical instruments.

Ireland imported $70.36 billion worth of goods and services in 2008, while exporting $115.7 billion worth of goods and services. Major import partners in 2009 were the United Kingdom at 35.4%, the United States at 16.8%, Germany at 6.8%, the Netherlands at 5.9%, and France at 4.8% . Major export partners were the United States at 21%, Belgium at 17%, the United Kingdom at 16.1%, Germany at 7%, and France at 5.4%. Imported commodities include data processing equipment, machinery and equipment, chemicals, petroleum and petroleum products, textiles, and clothing.

32 BALANCE OF PAYMENTS

The volume of Irish exports increased dramatically between 1995 and 2000, registering an average annual growth of 16.9%; the rate of import growth over the same period was only slightly lower at 16.6%. The year 2000 was the first since 1991 that the current account was not in surplus. The reduction of the balance of payments surplus in the early 2000s suggested that the level of Irish imports was increasing due to increased demand for luxury items and services, rather than from a decline in exports. In 2010 Ireland had a foreign trade surplus of $33 billion, amounting to 13.9% of GDP. A slowdown in the global economy and slower than predicted growth in the euro area has negatively impacted Irish exports over the last decade.

33 BANKING AND SECURITIES

In 1979 Ireland joined the European Monetary System, thus severing the 150-year-old tie with the British pound. The Central Bank of Ireland, established in 1942, is both the monetary authority and the bank of issue. Its role quickly expanded considerably, particularly in monetary policy. Commercial deposits with the Central Bank have strongly increased since 1964, when legislation first permitted it to pay interest on deposits held for purposes other than settlement of clearing balances. Since July 1969 the Central Bank has accepted short-term deposits from various institutions, including commercial and merchant banks. With the advent of the European Monetary Union (EMU) in 1999, authority over monetary policy shifted to the European Central Bank (ECB).

The commercial banking sector is dominated by two main Irish-owned groups, the Bank of Ireland Group and the Allied

Balance of Payments – Ireland (2010)		
(In millions of US dollars)		
Current Account		954.0
Balance on goods	48,273.0	
Imports	-61,583.0	
Exports	109,856.0	
Balance on services	-9,437.0	
Balance on income	-36,293.0	
Current transfers	-1,589.0	
Capital Account		-915.0
Financial Account		15,439.0
Direct investment abroad	-18,108.0	
Direct investment in Ireland	27,085.0	
Portfolio investment assets	28,611.0	
Portfolio investment liabilities	101,137.0	
Financial derivatives	-16,038.0	
Other investment assets	-21,004.0	
Other investment liabilities	-86,244.0	
Net Errors and Omissions		-15,520.0
Reserves and Related Items		42.0

(…) data not available or not significant.

SOURCE: *Balance of Payment Statistics Yearbook 2011*, Washington, DC: International Monetary Fund, 2011.

Irish Banks Group. Successive governments have indicated that they would like to see a third banking force (possibly involving a strategic alliance with a foreign bank). Other major banks include the National Irish Bank, a member of the National Australia Bank, and Ulster Bank, a member of the National Westminster Bank Group. The International Monetary Fund reports that in 2011 currency and demand deposits—an aggregate commonly known as M1—were equal to $93.9 billion. In that same year, M2—an aggregate equal to M1 plus savings deposits, small time deposits, and money market mutual funds—was $180 billion.

In 2010 the money market rate, the rate at which financial institutions lend to one another in the short term, was 1.5%. As a user of the euro, the nation's discount rate, the interest rate at which the central bank lends to financial institutions in the short term, is set by the ECB. In 2010 the discount rate was 1.75%, down from 3.25% in 2005, and the nation's gold reserves totaled $2,113,853,184.

A number of other commercial, merchant, and industrial banks also operate. Additionally, Ireland's post office operates the Post Office Savings Banks and Trustee Savings Banks. The Irish Stock Exchange has its trading floor in Dublin. All stockbrokers in Ireland are members of this exchange. The Irish Stock Exchange is small by international standards, with a total of 73 domestic companies listed at the end of 2007. Total market capitalization at the end of 2010 was €47.6 billion ($63.4 billion), down from €119 billion ($158.6 billion) at the end of 2006. In 2009 the ISEQ index rose 27% from the previous year after a 66% slump in 2008.

In August 2010 the nationalized Anglo Irish Bank announced a corporate loss of 8.2 billion euros ($10 billion) in the first half of 2010, representing the largest corporate loss in the history of the republic. The bank had been struggling since 2008, when a downturn in the housing market left it holding numerous debts. The government bailout to keep the bank afloat amounted to 25 billion euros ($32 billion), but poor performance since has left some

```
┌──────────────────────────────────────────────────────────┐
│  Public Finance – Ireland (2008)                           │
│                                                            │
│  (In millions of euros, central government figures)        │
│                                                            │
│  Revenue and Grants               58,357        100.0%     │
│    Tax revenue                    41,946         71.9%     │
│    Social contributions           12,061         20.7%     │
│    Grants                            ...            ...     │
│    Other revenue                     ...            ...     │
│                                                            │
│  Expenditures                     70,229        100.0%     │
│    General public services         7,074         10.1%     │
│    Defense                           895          1.3%     │
│    Public order and safety         3,084          4.4%     │
│    Economic affairs                8,051         11.5%     │
│    Environmental protection        1,013          1.4%     │
│    Housing and community amenities   871          1.2%     │
│    Health                         14,228         20.3%     │
│    Recreational, culture, and religion  753       1.1%     │
│    Education                       9,555         13.6%     │
│    Social protection              24,705         35.2%     │
│                                                            │
│  (…) data not available or not significant.                │
│                                                            │
│  SOURCE: Government Finance Statistics Yearbook 2010,      │
│  Washington, DC: International Monetary Fund, 2010.        │
└──────────────────────────────────────────────────────────┘
```

calling for a breakup of the bank. Uncertainty over the stability of banks pushed borrowing costs up, leading many of the eurozone nations to speculate that the debt crisis could lead to the same type of economic disaster that hit the Greek economy. In November expert analysts from the European Union and the International Monetary Fund met with Irish government officials to consider the possibility of an outside bailout package. That month, the British government, which remains outside of the eurozone, also offered to provide financial assistance to shore up the Irish banking system. Though Irish officials were originally steadfast in claims that such action was not needed, they soon relented to a proposal for a bailout of about $124 billion.

[34] INSURANCE

Insurance firms must be licensed by the Insurance Division of the Ministry of Industry, Trade, Commerce, and Tourism. The regulatory body is the Irish Brokers' Association. The Insurance Acts of 1936 and 1989 outline the monitoring of insurers, brokers, and agents.

In Ireland, workers' compensation, third-party automobile, bodily injury, and property damage liability are compulsory. In 1997 shareholders of Irish Life, Ireland's largest life assurance company, unanimously approved the company's £100 million ($163 million) takeover of an Illinois life assurance company, Guarantee Reserve. In 2009 the gross insurance premium income was €12.5 billion ($16.6 billion). Irish Life was the nation's leader in new life insurance as of 2009.

[35] PUBLIC FINANCE

Ireland's fiscal year follows the calendar year. Expenditures of local authorities are principally for health, roads, housing, and social welfare.

In 2010 the budget of Ireland included $68.7 billion in public revenue and $135.1 billion in public expenditures. The budget def-

icit amounted to 32.4% of GDP, with public debt at 94.2% of GDP, $2.253 trillion of the which was held by foreign entities.

Government outlays by function from greatest to least expenditure in 2010 were: societal protection; health; education; economic affairs; general public services; environmental protection; housing and community amenities; public order and safety; recreation, culture, and religion; and defense.

[36] TAXATION

To stimulate economic expansion and encourage investment in Irish industry, particularly in the area of industrial exports, tax adjustments have been made to give relief to export profits, expenditures for mineral development, shipping, plant and machinery, new industrial buildings, and investments in Irish securities. As of 1 January 2003, with Ireland's accession to the European Union, the government had mostly completed the transition of the tax regime from an incentive regime to a low, single-tax regime with 12.5% as the country's rate for most corporate profits. Passive income, including that from interest, royalties, and dividends, is taxed at 20%. Capital gains are also taxed at 20%. As of 2011 Ireland was party to double-taxation agreements with 64 countries, the terms of which provide for the reduction or elimination of many capital income tax rates and related withholding taxes. The incentive 10% corporation tax rate, applied to industrial manufacturing, to projects licensed to operate in the Shannon Airport area, and to various service operations, was phased out and has not been in place since 2006.

As of 2009 Ireland has a progressive personal income tax with a top rate of 41% on incomes above €36,400 ($48,518) for single taxpayers. Married taxpayers are subject to a higher income threshold level. For persons over 65 years old, tax exemptions are available for those with annual income under €20,000 ($26,661) per person. Deductions were available for mortgage payments and pension contributions. Since 1969 the government has encouraged artists and writers to live in Ireland by exempting from income tax their earnings from their works of art. Royalties and other income from patent rights are also tax-exempt. The gift and inheritance taxes are based upon the relationship of the beneficiary to the donor. Between a parent and child, the tax-free threshold in 2010 was €332,084 ($442,686); for any other lineal descendent, the tax-free threshold was one-tenth this amount, or €33,208 ($44,268); and for any other person, one-twentieth, or €16,604 ($22,134). Land taxes are assessed at variable rates by local governments, and there is a buildings transfer tax based on the price of the transfer.

The major indirect tax is Ireland's value-added tax (VAT) instituted 1 January 1972 with a standard rate of 16.37% plus a number of reduced, intermediate, and increased rates. As of 1 March 2002, the standard rate was increased to 21% from 20%, and the reduced rate of 12.5% increased to 13.5% as of 1 January 2003. The reduced rate applies to domestic fuel and power, newspapers, hotels and new housing. Ireland also has an extensive list of goods and services to which a 0% VAT rate is applied including, books and pamphlets, gold for the Central Bank, basic foodstuffs and beverages, agricultural supplies, medicines and medical equipment, and, more unusually, children's clothing and footwear, and wax candles. A 4.8% rate applies to livestock by unregistered farmers. Excise duties are charged on tobacco products, alcohol, fuel, and motor vehicles. Per unit and/or annual stamp taxes are assessed on checks, credit cards, ATM cards, and Laser cards.

³⁷CUSTOMS AND DUTIES

From the time of the establishment of the Irish Free State, government policy was to encourage development of domestic industry by maintaining protective tariffs and quotas on commodities that would compete with Irish-made products. Following Ireland's admission to the European Community (EC, now the European Union [EU]), the country's tariff schedule was greatly revised. The schedule vis-à-vis third-world countries and the United States was gradually aligned with EC tariffs and customs duties between Ireland and the EC were phased down to zero by July 1977. Duty rates on manufactured goods from non-EU countries range from 5–8%, while most raw materials enter duty-free. Certain goods still require import licenses and tariffs are based on the Harmonized System. The Shannon Free Trade Zone, the oldest official free trade area in the world, is located at the Shannon International Airport.

³⁸FOREIGN INVESTMENT

The Irish government has successfully attracted foreign direct investment (FDI) over the years with various policies and preferential tax rates. To stimulate economic expansion, the Industrial Development Authority encourages and facilitates investment by foreign interests, particularly in the development of industries with export potential. Special concessions include non-repayable grants to help establish industries in underdeveloped areas and tax relief on export profits. Freedom to take out profits is unimpaired. Engineering goods, computers, electronic products, electrical equipment, pharmaceuticals and chemicals, textiles, foodstuffs, leisure products, and metal and plastic products are among the items produced. Much of the new investment occurred after Ireland became a member of the European Union.

Annual FDI inflows into Ireland increased steadily through the 1990s. In the period 1988 to 1990, Ireland's share of world FDI inflows was only 70% of its share of world GDP, but for the period 1998 to 2000 Ireland's share of FDI inflows was over five times its share of world GDP. In 1998 annual FDI inflow reached $11 billion, up from $2.7 billion in 1997, and then jumped to almost $15 billion in 1999. FDI inflows to Ireland peaked in 2000, at over $24 billion, mainly from high-tech computer and pharmaceutical companies. FDI inflow dropped sharply to $9.8 billion in 2001 with the global economic slowdown, but has since recovered, with a net inflow of $25.2 billion according to World Bank figures published in 2009. This amounted to 11.11% of Ireland's GDP.

Leading sources of foreign investors in 2008 in terms of the funds invested in Ireland were the Netherlands ($42 billion), Luxembourg ($35 billion), the United Kingdom ($16 billion), and the United States ($12.3 billion). As of 2010 the primary destinations of foreign investment were the services industry, including software and customer support, as well as high quality manufacturing projects. As of 2011 Ireland was the second most attractive country for FDI globally.

³⁹ECONOMIC DEVELOPMENT

Government policies are premised on private enterprise as a predominant factor in the economy. Specific economic programs ad-

opted in the 1990s and 2000s have attempted to increase efficiency in agriculture and industry, stimulate new export industries, create employment opportunities for labor leaving the agricultural sector, and reduce unemployment and net emigration. In pursuit of these objectives, the government provides aids to industry through the Industrial Development Authority (IDA), the Industrial Credit Co., and other agencies. Tax concessions, information, and advisory services are also provided.

The IDA seeks to attract foreign investment by offering a 10% maximum corporation tax rate for manufacturing and certain service industries, generous tax-free grants for staff training, ready-built factories on modern industrial estates, accelerated depreciation, export-risk guarantee programs, and other financial inducements. IDA also administers industrial estates at Waterford and Galway. The Shannon Free Airport Development Co., another government-sponsored entity, administers an industrial estate on the fringes of Shannon Airport, a location that benefits from proximity to the airport's duty-free facilities. A third entity, Udaras Na Gaeltachia, promotes investment and development in western areas where Irish is the predominant language. As of 1986 there were some 900 foreign-owned plants in Ireland.

Price control legislation was introduced under the Prices Act of 1958, amended in 1965 and 1972. In general, manufacturers, service industries, and professions are required to obtain permission from the Ministry of Commerce and Trade for any increase. Price changes are monitored by a National Prices Commission, established in 1971. The economic plan for 1983–1987, called The Way Forward, aimed at improving the cost-competitiveness of the economy by cutting government expenditures and restraining the growth of public service pay, among other measures. The 1987–1990 Program for National Recovery is generally credited with creating the conditions to bring government spending and the national debt under control. The 1991–1993 Program for Economic and Social Progress was to further reduce the national debt and budget deficit and to establish a schedule of wage increases.

A 1994–1999 national development plan called for investment of £20 billion and aimed to achieve an average annual GDP growth rate of 3.5%. The government hoped to create 200,000 jobs through this plan, with funding by the state, the European Union, and the private sector. Half of the money was earmarked for industry, transport, training, and energy.

At the end of the 1990s, Ireland boasted the fastest growing economy in the European Union with a 9.5% GDP real growth rate in 1998. Total expenditures on imports and exports in 2000 were equivalent to 175% of GDP, far ahead of the EU average, which made Ireland's economy one of the most open in the world. Ireland became known as the "Celtic Tiger," to compare with the formerly fast-growing economies of East Asia prior to the Asian financial crisis of 1997. In 2000 the economy grew by 11.5%, the highest growth rate ever recorded in an OECD member country. Wage inequality grew, however, and spending on infrastructure failed to keep pace with social or industrial demands. Corporate taxes were as low as 12.5% in some circumstances in the early 2000s. Economic growth decelerated rapidly in 2001, to 6%. Inflation fell as did housing prices, but they rose again in 2002. Tax increases and spending growth began in 2003, and Ireland was severely affected by the 2008–09 financial crisis. The National Recovery Plan 2011–2014 aims to lower the deficit to the EU's 3% target by 2015, to cut public expenditures, and to increase VAT.

40 SOCIAL DEVELOPMENT

A social insurance program exists for all employees and self-employed persons, and for all residents with limited means. The system is financed through employee contributions, employer contributions, and government subsidies. Benefits are available for old age, sickness, disability, survivorship, maternity, work injury, unemployment, and adoptive services. There are also funds available for those leaving the workforce to care for one in need of full-time assistance. The system also provides bereavement and a widowed parent's grant. The universal medical care system provides medical services to all residents. The workmen's compensation act was first initiated in 1897. Parents with one or more children are entitled to a family allowance.

The predominance of the Roman Catholic Church has had a significant impact on social legislation. Divorce was made legal only in 1995. Contraceptives, the sale of which had been entirely prohibited, became available to married couples by prescription in the early 1980s. In 1985 the need for a prescription was abolished, and the minimum age for marriage was raised from 14 to 18 for girls and from 16 to 18 for boys. Abortion remains illegal, an issue which came under scrutiny toward the end of the 2000s.

Domestic abuse and spousal violence remain serious problems. The government funds victim support centers, and there are active women's rights groups to address these issues. The law prohibits gender discrimination in the workplace, but inequalities persist regarding promotion and pay. The government addresses the issue of child abuse, and funds systems to promote child welfare.

The government attempts to curb discrimination against foreign workers and the ethnic community known as "Travellers." There have been reports of racially motivated incidents including violence and intimidation. In general, the government respects the human rights of its citizens.

41 HEALTH

According to the CIA, life expectancy in Ireland was 80 years in 2011. The country spent 8.7% of its GDP on healthcare, amounting to $4,952 per person. While deaths from cancer, particularly lung cancer, and heart disease are rising, those from many other causes have been decreasing rapidly. Infant mortality has been reduced from 50.3 deaths per 1,000 live births in 1948 to 3.85 deaths per 1,000 live births in 2011. The fertility rate was 2.1 children for every woman of childbearing age in 2011. In 2008 the maternal mortality rate, according to the World Bank, was 3 deaths per 100,000 births. It was estimated that 89% of children were vaccinated against measles. The CIA calculated the HIV/AIDS prevalence rate in Ireland to be about 0.2% in 2009.

Health services in Ireland are provided by regional boards under the administration and control of the Department of Health. A comprehensive health service, with free hospitalization, treatment, and medication, is provided for low-income groups. The middle-income population is entitled to free maternity, hospital, and specialist services, and a free diagnostic and preventive service is available to all persons suffering from specified infectious diseases. Insurance against hospital and certain other medical expenses is available under a voluntary plan introduced in 1957.

Since World War II, many regional and county hospitals and tuberculosis sanatoriums have been built. As of 2011 there were 32 physicians, 157 nurses and midwives, and 52 hospital beds per 10,000 inhabitants.

42 HOUSING

The aim of public housing policy is to ensure, so far as possible, that every family can obtain decent housing at a price or rent it can afford. Government subsidies are given to encourage home ownership, and local authorities provide housing for those unable to house themselves adequately. Housing legislation has encouraged private construction through grants and loans. Projected and existing housing needs are assessed regularly by local authorities, and their reports are the basis for local building programs, which are integrated with national programs and reconciled with available public resources.

According to the 2006 census, there were 1,462,296 total private dwellings in permanent housing units. The number of households was listed as 1,469,521, with 42.8% of all households living in single-family detached homes. The average number of persons per household was 2.8.

43 EDUCATION

In 2008, the World Bank estimated that 97% of age-eligible children in Ireland were enrolled in primary school. Secondary enrollment for age-eligible children stood at 88%, with tertiary enrollment estimated at 58%. Of those enrolled in tertiary education, there were 100 male students for every 122 female students. Overall, the CIA estimated that Ireland had a literacy rate of 99%.

Ten years of education are compulsory. Primary school covers eight years of education, with most students entering at age four. This is followed by a three-year junior secondary school and a two-year senior secondary program. Some schools offer a transition year program between the junior and senior levels. This transition year is meant to be a time of independent study for the student, when he or she focuses on special interests, while still under the guidance of instructors, in order make a decision concerning the direction of their future studies. At the senior level, students may choose to attend a vocational school instead of a general studies school. While private, religious-based secondary schools were once the norm, there are now many multi-denominational, public schools available at all levels. Coeducational programs have also grown substantially in recent years. The academic year runs from September to June. The primary languages of instruction are Irish and English.

Ireland has two main universities: the University of Dublin (Trinity College) and the National University of Ireland, which consists of three constituent colleges in Dublin, Galway, and Cork. St. Patrick's College, Maynooth, is a recognized college of the National University. Universities are self-governing, but each receives an annual state grant, as well as supplementary grants for capital outlays. There are also various colleges of education, home economics, technology, and the arts.

As of 2008 public expenditure on education represented 4.9% of GDP.

In September 2010 the government of Ireland launched an education strategy to increase the amount of international students in Ireland. The goal is to increase the number of international students in higher education by 50% and English-language school attendance by 25% by 2015. The strategy includes attempts at government-education partnerships and new student immigration rules. Ireland would like to be known as a world leader in higher education.

44 LIBRARIES AND MUSEUMS

Trinity College Library, which dates from 1591 and counts among its many treasures the *Book of Kells* and the *Book of Durrow*, two of the most beautiful illuminated manuscripts from the pre-Viking period, is the oldest and largest library in Ireland, with a stock of 4.1 million volumes. The Chester Beatty Library, noted for one of the world's finest collections of Oriental manuscripts and miniatures, is also in Dublin. The National Library of Ireland, which also serves as a lending library, was founded in 1877 and houses over one million books, with special collections including works on or by Jonathan Swift and W. B. Yeats. The National Photographic Archive of over 600,000 photographs is also housed in the National Library. The University College Dublin library has more than one million volumes. The Dublin City Public Library system has about 31 branches and service points and holdings of over 1.5 million items.

Dublin, the center of cultural life in Ireland, has several museums and a number of libraries. The National Museum contains collections on Irish antiquities, folk life, fine arts, natural history, zoology, and geology. The National Gallery houses valuable paintings representing the various European schools from the 13th century to the present. The National Portrait Gallery provides a visual survey of Irish historical personalities over the past three centuries. The Municipal Gallery of Modern Art has a fine collection of works by recent and contemporary artists. There is a Heraldic Museum in Dublin Castle; the National Botanic Gardens are at Glasnevin; and the Zoological Gardens are in Phoenix Park. There is a James Joyce Museum in Dublin housing personal memorabilia of the great writer, including signed manuscripts. Yeats Tower in Gort displays memorabilia of W. B. Yeats. The Dublin Writers' Museum opened in 1991.

Public libraries and small museums, devoted mostly to local historical exhibits, are found in Cork, Limerick, Waterford, Galway, and other cities.

45 MEDIA

In 2009, the CIA reported there were some 2.1 million main phone lines and 4.8 million mobile cellular phones in use. In 2010, the country had 1.3 million Internet hosts, with some 3 million Internet users in Ireland, or about 68 Internet users per 100 citizens (in 2009).

An autonomous public corporation, Radio Telefís Éireann (RTE), is the Irish national broadcasting organization which operates both analogue and digital only television channels as well as radio. Ireland's second radio service, Raidio na Gaeltachta, an Irish language broadcast, was launched by RTE in 1972; it broadcasts VHF from County Galway. Ireland has a modern, digital telecommunications system that makes use of microwave radio relay and cable technologies. In 2009 there were 9 FM radio stations and 106 AM radio stations.

In 2011 there were fifteen independent national newspapers for Ireland, as well as many local newspapers. There were three major independent current affairs magazines along with hundreds of special interest magazines. Prominent newspapers in 2010, with circulation numbers listed parenthetically, included the *Irish Independent* (159,363), the *Irish Times* (118,259), and the *Irish Examiner* (54,191), as well as 12 other major newspapers. Waterford, Limerick, Galway, and many other smaller cities and towns have their own newspapers, most of them weeklies. The Censorship of Publication Board has the right to censor or ban publication of books and periodicals.

The constitution provides for free speech and a free press; however, government bodies may decree without public hearing or justification any material unfit for distribution on moral grounds. The Irish Film Classification Office, formerly the Irish Film Censor's Office, rates films and videos before they are distributed and can ban or require edits of movies which contain content considered to be "indecent, obscene, or blasphemous," or which expresses principles "contrary to public morality." Of 50,000 film censorship decisions to date, approximately 2,500 have been banned and 11,000 cut, most before 1965. In 2009, 307 cinema feature films were certified by IFCO.

46 ORGANIZATIONS

The Chambers of Commerce of Ireland in Dublin is the umbrella organization for regional chambers. The Irish Congress of Trade Unions is also based in Dublin. There are trade unions and professional associations representing a wide variety of occupations. The Consumers Association of Ireland is active in advocating consumer information services.

The oldest and best known of the learned societies are the Royal Dublin Society, founded in 1731, and the Royal Irish Academy, founded in 1785. The Royal Irish Academy of Music was added in 1856, the Irish Society of Arts and Commerce in 1911, the Irish Academy of Letters in 1932, and the Arts Council of Ireland in 1951. Many organizations exist for research and study in medicine and science, including the Royal Academy of Medicine in Ireland.

National youth organizations include the Church of Ireland Youth Council, Comhchairdeas (the Irish Workcamp Movement), Confederation of Peace Corps, Federation of Irish Scout Associations, Irish Girl Guides, Girls' Brigade Ireland, Junior Chamber, Student Christian Movement of Ireland, Voluntary Service International, Workers Party Youth, Young Fine Gael, and chapters of YMCA/YWCA. The Irish Sports Council serves as an umbrella organization for numerous athletic organizations both on amateur and professional levels.

Civil rights organizations include the Irish Council for Civil Liberties and the National Women's Council of Ireland. Several organizations are available to represent those with disabilities. International organizations with chapters in Ireland include the Red Cross, Habitat for Humanity, and Amnesty International.

47 TOURISM, TRAVEL, AND RECREATION

Among Ireland's numerous ancient and prehistoric sights are a restored Bronze Age lake dwelling (*crannog*) near Quin in County

Clare, burial mounds at Newgrange and Knowth along the Boyne, and the palace at the Hill of Tara, the seat of government up to the Middle Ages. Numerous castles may be visited, including Blarney Castle in County Cork, where visitors kiss the famous Blarney Stone. Some, such as Bunratty Castle and Knappogue Castle, County Clare, and Dungaire Castle, County Galway, offer medieval-style banquets, and some rent rooms to tourists.

Among Dublin's tourist attractions are the Trinity College Library, with its 8th-century illuminated *Book of Kells*; Phoenix Park, the largest enclosed park in Western Europe and home of the Dublin Zoo; and literary landmarks associated with such writers as William Butler Yeats, James Joyce, Jonathan Swift, and Oscar Wilde. Dublin has long been noted for its theaters, foremost among them the Abbey Theatre, Ireland's national theater, which was founded in 1904 by Yeats and Lady Gregory. Dublin was the European Community's Cultural Capital of Europe for 1991, during which time the National Gallery, Civic Museum, and Municipal Gallery were all refurbished and several new museums opened, including the Irish Museum of Modern Art.

Traditional musical events are held frequently, one of the best known being the All-Ireland Fleadh at Ennis in County Clare. Numerous parades, concerts, and other festivities occur on and around the St. Patrick's Day holiday of 17 March. Ireland has numerous golf courses, some of worldwide reputation. Fishing, sailing, horseback riding, hunting, horse racing, and greyhound racing are other popular sports. The traditional sports of Gaelic football, hurling, and camogie (the women's version of hurling) were revived in the 19th century and have become increasingly popular. The All-Ireland Hurling Final and the All-Ireland Football Final are held in September.

A passport is required of all visitors. Visas are not required for stays of up to 90 days, although an onward/return ticket may be needed.

The *Tourism Factbook*, published by the UN World Tourism Organization, reported 7.19 million incoming tourists to Ireland in 2009, who spent a total of $8.19 billion. Of those incoming tourists, there were 6 million from Europe. A total of 163,637 hotel beds were available in Ireland, with an estimated daily cost of $492 to visit Dublin, the capital, and an average of $327 to visit other cities.

48 FAMOUS PERSONS

A list of famous Irish must begin with St. Patrick (c. 385–461), who, though not born in Ireland, represents Ireland to the rest of the world. Among the "saints and scholars" of the 6th to the 8th centuries were St. Columba (521–97), missionary to Scotland; St. Columban (540?–616), who founded monasteries in France and Italy; and Johannes Scotus Erigena (810?–80), a major Neoplatonic philosopher.

For the thousand years after the Viking invasions, the famous names belong to warriors and politicians: Brian Boru (962?–1014), who temporarily united the kings of Ireland and defeated the Vikings; Hugh O'Neill (1547?–1616), Owen Roe O'Neill (1590?–1649), and Patrick Sarsfield (d. 1693), national heroes of the 17th century; and Henry Grattan (1746–1820), Wolf Tone (1763–98), Edward Fitzgerald (1763–98), Robert Emmet (1778–1803), Daniel O'Connell (1775–1847), Michael Davitt (1846–1906), Charles Stewart Parnell (1846–91), Arthur Griffith (1872–1922), Patrick

Henry Pearse (1879–1916), and Éamon de Valera (b. US, 1882–1975), who, with many others, fought Ireland's political battles. The politician and statesman Seán MacBride (1904–88) won the Nobel Peace Prize in 1974.

Irishmen who have made outstanding contributions to science and scholarship include Robert Boyle (1627–91), the physicist who defined Boyle's law relating to pressure and volume of gas; Sir William Rowan Hamilton (1805–65), astronomer and mathematician, who developed the theory of quaternions; George Berkeley (1685–1753), philosopher and clergyman; Edward Hincks (1792–1866), discoverer of the Sumerian language; and John Bagnell Bury (1861–1927), classical scholar. The nuclear physicist Ernest T. S. Walton (1903–95) won the Nobel Prize for physics in 1951.

Painters of note include Sir William Orpen (1878–1931), John Butler Yeats (1839–1922), his son Jack Butler Yeats (1871–1957), and Mainie Jellet (1897–1944). Irish musicians include the pianist and composer John Field (1782–1837), the opera composer Michael William Balfe (1808–70), the tenor John McCormack (1884–1945), and the flutist James Galway (b. Belfast, 1939).

After the Restoration, many brilliant satirists in English literature were born in Ireland, among them Jonathan Swift (1667–1745), dean of St. Patrick's Cathedral in Dublin and creator of *Gulliver's Travels*; Oliver Goldsmith (1730?–74); Richard Brinsley Sheridan (1751–1816); Oscar Fingal O'Flahertie Wills Wilde (1854–1900); and George Bernard Shaw (1856–1950).

Thomas Moore (1779–1852) and James Clarence Mangan (1803–49) wrote patriotic airs, hymns, and love lyrics, while Maria Edgeworth (1767–1849) wrote novels on Irish themes. Half a century later the great literary revival led by Nobel Prize-winning poet-dramatist William Butler Yeats (1865–1939), another son of John Butler Yeats, produced a succession of famous playwrights, poets, novelists, and short-story writers: the dramatists Lady Augusta (Persse) Gregory (1859?–1932), John Millington Synge (1871–1909), Sean O'Casey (1884–1964), and Lennox Robinson (1886–1958); the poets AE (George William Russell, 1867–1935), Oliver St. John Gogarty (1878–1957), Pádraic Colum (1881–1972), James Stephens (1882–1950); Austin Clarke (1890–1974), Thomas Kinsella (b. 1928), and Seamus Heaney (b. 1939), who won the 1995 Nobel Prize in literature; the novelists and short-story writers George Moore (1852–1932), Edward John Moreton Drax Plunkett, 18th baron of Dunsany (1878–1957), Liam O'Flaherty (1896–1984), Seán O'Faoláin (1900–91), Frank O'Connor (Michael O'Donovan, 1903–66), and Flann O'Brien (Brian O'Nolan, 1911–66). Two outstanding authors of novels and plays whose experimental styles have had worldwide influence are James Augustine Joyce (1882–1941), the author of *Ulysses*, and Samuel Beckett (1906–89), recipient of the 1969 Nobel Prize for literature.

The Abbey Theatre, which was the backbone of the literary revival, also produced many outstanding dramatic performers, such as Dudley Digges (1879–1947), Sara Allgood (1883–1950), Arthur Sinclair (1883–1951), Maire O'Neill (Mrs. Arthur Sinclair, 1887–1952), Barry Fitzgerald (William Shields, 1888–1961), and Siobhan McKenna (1923–1986). For many years Douglas Hyde (1860–1949), first president of Ireland (1938–45), spurred on the Irish-speaking theater as playwright, producer, and actor.

In addition to the genres of Irish folk and dance music, contemporary Irish popular and rock music has gained international attention. Van Morrison (b. 1945), is a singer and songwriter from

Belfast whose career began in the 1960s and was going strong in the 2000s. Enya (b. 1961), is Ireland's best-selling solo musician. The Irish rock band U2 is led by Bono (b. 1960): Bono has also spearheaded efforts to raise money for famine relief in Ethiopia, to fight world poverty, to campaign for third-world debt relief, and to raise world consciousness to the plight of Africa, including the spread of HIV/AIDS on the African continent.

⁴⁹DEPENDENCIES

Ireland has no territories or colonies.

⁵⁰BIBLIOGRAPHY

Aughey, Arthur. *The Politics of Northern Ireland: Beyond the Belfast Agreement.* New York: Routledge, 2005.

Gibbons, Luke, Richard Kearney, and Willa Murphy, eds. *Encyclopedia of Contemporary Irish Culture.* London: Routledge, 2002.

Hannigan, Dave. *De Valera in America: The Rebel President and the Making of Irish Independence.* New York: Palgrave Macmillan, 2010.

International Smoking Statistics: A Collection of Historical Data from 30 Economically Developed Countries. New York: Oxford University Press, 2002.

Kinealy, Christine. *War and Peace: Ireland since the 1960s.* London, Eng.: Reaktion, 2010.

Livesey, James. *Civil Society and Empire: Ireland and Scotland in the Eighteenth-century Atlantic World.* New Haven: Yale University Press, 2009.

Maillot, Agnes. *The New Sinn Féin: Irish Republicanism in the Twenty-First Century.* New York: Routledge, 2004.

McElrath, Karen, ed. *HIV and AIDS: A Global View.* Westport, CT: Greenwood Press, 2002.

O'Dowd, Mary. *A History of Women in Ireland, 1500–1800.* New York: Pearson Longman, 2005.

Roy, James Charles. *The Fields of Athenry: A Journey through Irish History,* Boulder, CO: Westview Press, 2001.

Wessels, Wolfgang, Andreas Maurer, and Jürgan Mittag (eds.). *Fifteen into One?: the European Union and Its Member States.* New York: Palgrave, 2003.

ITALY

Italian Republic
Repubblica Italiana

CAPITAL: Rome (Roma)

FLAG: The national flag is a tricolor of green, white, and red vertical stripes.

ANTHEM: *Il Canto degli Italiani (The Song of the Italians).*

MONETARY UNIT: The euro replaced the lira as the official currency in 2002. The euro is divided into 100 cents. There are coins in denominations of 1, 2, 5, 10, 20, and 50 cents and 1 euro and 2 euros. There are notes of 5, 10, 20, 50, 100, 200, and 500 euros. €1 = US$1.33750 (or US$1 = €0.74766) as of 2011.

WEIGHTS AND MEASURES: The metric system is the legal standard.

HOLIDAYS: New Year's Day, 1 January; Epiphany, 6 January; Liberation Day, 25 April; Labor Day, 1 May; Assumption, 15 August; All Saints' Day, 1 November; National Unity Day, 5 November; Immaculate Conception, 8 December; Christmas, 25 December; St. Stephen's Day, 26 December. Easter Monday is a movable holiday. In addition, each town has a holiday on its Saint's Day.

TIME: 1 p.m. = noon GMT.

¹LOCATION, SIZE, AND EXTENT

Situated in southern Europe, the Italian Republic, including the major islands of Sicily (Sicilia) and Sardinia (Sardegna), covers a land area of 301,225 sq km (116,303 sq mi). Comparatively, the area occupied by Italy is slightly larger than the state of Arizona. The boot-shaped Italian mainland extends into the Mediterranean Sea with a length of 1,185 km (736 mi) SE–NW and a width of 381 km (237 mi) NE–SW. It is bordered on the N by Switzerland and Austria, on the NE by Slovenia, on the E by the Adriatic and Ionian seas, on the W by the Tyrrhenian and Ligurian seas, and on the NW by France, with a total land boundary length of 1,932 km (1,200 mi) and a coastline of 7,600 km (4,712 mi).

Situated off the toe of the Italian boot, Sicily has a surface area of 25,708 sq km (9,926 sq mi). Sardinia, which is about 320 km (200 mi) NW of Sicily, covers an area of some 24,090 sq km (9,300 sq mi). Within the frontiers of Italy are the sovereign Republic of San Marino, with an area of 61.2 sq km (23.6 sq mi), and the sovereign state of Vatican City, which covers 44 hectares (108.7 acres).

A dispute over Trieste, a 518-sq-km (200-sq-mi) area situated at the head of the Adriatic Sea, was resolved in 1954 when Italy assumed the administration of the city and harbor of Trieste, while Yugoslavia controlled the rural hinterlands of the Istrian Peninsula. A treaty of October 1975 made the partition permanent. Today Trieste lies on the Italian border with Slovenia.

Italy's capital city, Rome, is located in the west-central part of the country.

²TOPOGRAPHY

Except for the fertile Po River Valley in the north and the narrow coastal belts farther south, Italy's mainland is generally mountainous, with considerable seismic activity. During Roman times, the city of Pompeii, near present-day Naples (Napoli), was devastated first by an earthquake in AD 63 and then by the famed eruption of Mt. Vesuvius (1,277 m/4,190 ft) in AD 79. In the last century, a 7.2 magnitude earthquake in the Calabrian-Sicilian region occurred in December 1908 that leveled the cities of Reggio di Calabria and Messina and left about 100,000 dead. A quake in the south on 23 November 1980 (and subsequent aftershocks) claimed at least 4,500 lives. On 5 April 2009, a 6.3 magnitude earthquake struck the Abruzzo region in central Italy, leaving about 55,000 people homeless and some 300 people dead.

The Alpine mountain area in the north along the French and Swiss borders includes three famous lakes—Como, Maggiore, and Garda—and gives rise to six small rivers that flow southward into the Po. Italy's highest peaks are found in the northwest in the Savoy Alps, the Pennines, and the Graian chain. They include Mont Blanc (4,807 m/15,771 ft), on the French border; Monte Rosa (Dufourspitze, 4,634 m/15,203 ft) and the Matterhorn (Monte Cervino, 4,478 m/14,692 ft), on the Swiss border; and Gran Paradiso (4,061 m/13,323 ft). Marmolada (3,342 m/10,965 ft), in northeast Italy, is the highest peak in the Dolomites. In 2009 the Dolomites were inscribed as a natural UNESCO World Heritage Site. The mountains feature a wide variety of rock formations, glacial landforms, and karst systems. The site is home to one of the best-preserved examples of a carbonate platform (a sedimentary rock formation containing fossil records) dating back to the Mesozoic period. The highest point in the Apennines is Corno Grande (2,912 m/9,554 ft). Vesuvius is the only active volcano on the European mainland.

At the foot of the Alps, the Po River, the only large river in Italy, flows from west to east, draining plains covering about 17% of Italy's total area and forming the agricultural and industrial heartland. The Apennines, the rugged backbone of peninsular Italy, rise to form the southern border of the Po Plain. Numerous streams and a few small rivers, including the Arno and the Tiber (Tevere), flow from the Apennines to the west coast.

While altitudes are lower in southern Italy, the Calabrian coast is still rugged. Among the narrow, fertile coastal plains, the Plain of Foggia in northern Apulia, which starts along the Adriatic, and the more extensive lowland areas near Naples, Rome, and Livorno (Leghorn) are the most important. The mountainous western coastline forms natural harbors at Naples, Livorno, La Spezia, Genoa (Genova), and Savona, and the low Adriatic coast permits natural ports at Venice (Venezia), Bari, Brindisi, and Taranto.

Sicily, separated from the mainland by the narrow Strait of Messina, has the Madonie Mountains, a continuation of the Apennines, and the Plain of Catania, the largest plain on the island. Mount Etna (3,369 m/11,053 ft) is an isolated and active volcano in the northeast.

Sardinia, in the Tyrrhenian Sea, is generally mountainous and culminates in the peak of Gennargentu (1,834 m/6,017 ft). The largest and most fertile plains are the Campidano in the south and the Ozieri in the north. The principal bay is Porto Torres in the Gulf of Asinara.

³CLIMATE

Climate varies with elevation and region. Generally, however, Italy is included between the annual isotherms of 11 and 19°C (52 and 66°F). The coldest period occurs in December and January, the hottest in July and August. In the Po Plain, the average annual temperature is about 13°C (55°F); in Sicily, about 18°C (64°F); and in the coastal lowlands, about 14°C (57°F). The climate of the Po Valley and the Alps is characterized by cold winters, warm summers, and considerable rain, falling mostly in spring and autumn, with snow accumulating heavily in the mountains. The climate of the peninsula and of the islands is Mediterranean, with cool, rainy winters and hot, dry summers. Mean annual rainfall varies from about 50 cm (20 in) per year, on the southeast coast and in Sicily and Sardinia, to over 200 cm (80 in), in the Alps and on some westerly slopes of the Apennines. Frosts are rare in the sheltered western coastal areas, but severe winters are common in the Apennine and Alpine uplands.

⁴FLORA AND FAUNA

Plants and animals vary with area and altitude. The World Resources Institute estimates that there are 5,599 plant species in Italy. Mountain flora is found above 1,980 m (6,500 ft) in the Alps and above 2,290 m (7,500 ft) in the Apennines. The highest forest belt consists of conifers; beech, oak, and chestnut trees grow on lower mountain slopes. Poplar and willow thrive in the Po Plain. On the peninsula and on the larger islands, Mediterranean vegetation predominates: evergreens, holm oak, cork, juniper, bramble, laurel, myrtle, and dwarf palm.

In addition, Italy is home to 132 mammal, 478 bird, 55 reptile, and 45 amphibian species. This calculation reflects the total number of distinct species, not the number of endemic species. Although larger mammals are scarce, chamois, ibex, and roe deer are found in the Alps, and bears, chamois, and otters inhabit the Apennines. Ravens and swallows are characteristic birds of Italy. Abundant marine life inhabits the surrounding seas.

⁵ENVIRONMENT

Italy has been slow to confront its environmental problems. Most of the burden of environmental planning and enforcement falls on regional authorities. According to the World Resources Institute, as of 2006 Italy had designated 1.94 million hectares (4.78 million acres) of land for protection. The principal antipollution statute is Law No. 319 of 1976 (the Merli Law), which controls the disposal of organic and chemical wastes; enforcement, however, has proved difficult.

Air pollution is a significant problem in Italy, especially for industrial cities in the north. The United Nations reported in 2008 that Italy's carbon dioxide emissions totaled 445,119 thousand metric tons, which was the twelfth-highest total in the world that year. Per capita emissions were 7.5 metric tons.

Water pollution is another important environmental issue in Italy. The nation's rivers and coasts have been polluted by industrial and agricultural contaminants and its lakes contaminated by acid rain. Facilities for the treatment and disposal of industrial wastes are inadequate. In 2006 the World Resources Institute reported that water resources totaled 175 cu km (41.98 cu mi), while water usage was 41.98 cu km (10.07 cu mi) per year. Agricultural water usage accounted for 45% of total use, industrial for 37%, and domestic water use for 18%. Per capita water usage totaled 723 cu m (25,533 cu ft) per year.

Long-term environmental threats were highlighted by a disastrous flood in November 1966, which damaged priceless art treasures and manuscripts in Florence (Firenze). The sinking of the island-city of Venice is another serious problem. The digging of artesian wells in the nearby mainland cities of Mestre and Marghera so lowered the water table that the Venetian islands sank at many times the normal annual rate of 4 mm (0.16 in) a year between 1900 and 1975; with the wells capped as a protective measure, Venice's normal sinkage rate was restored, although there is still danger. Rome has implemented a project designed to protect the Roman Forum and other ancient monuments from the vibration and pollution of motor vehicles.

According to a 2011 report issued by the International Union for Conservation of Nature and Natural Resources (IUCN), threatened species in Italy included 7 mammals, 7 birds, 4 reptiles, 9 amphibians, 47 fish, 72 mollusks, 47 species of other invertebrates, and 65 species of plants. Threatened species include the Sicilian fir, the black vulture, the spotted eagle, the wild goat, the great white shark, and the red-breasted goose. The Sardinian pika is extinct.

⁶POPULATION

The US Central Intelligence Agency (CIA) estimated the population of Italy in 2011 to be approximately 61,016,804, which placed it at number 23 in population among the 196 nations of the world. In 2011, approximately 20.3% of the population was over 65 years of age, with another 13.8% under 15 years of age. The median age in Italy was 43.5 years. There were 0.96 males for every female in the country. The population's annual growth rate was 0.42%. Population density in Italy was calculated at 202 people per sq km (525 people per sq mi).

The UN estimated in 2010 that 68% of the population lived in urban areas, and that urban populations had an annual rate of change of 0.5%. The largest urban areas, along with their respective populations, included Rome, 3.4 million; Milan, 3 million; Naples, 2.3 million; Turin, 1.7 million; and Palermo, 872,000.

LOCATION: 47°05′ to 36°38′N; 6°37′ to 18°31′ E. BOUNDARY LENGTHS: Switzerland, 744 kilometers (462 miles); Austria, 430 kilometers (267 miles); Slovenia, 209 kilometers (130 miles); total coastline including islands of Sicily and Sardinia, 7,458 kilometers (4,634 miles); France, 514 kilometers (320 miles). TERRITORIAL SEA LIMIT: 12 miles.

⁷MIGRATION

Emigration, which traditionally provided relief from overpopulation and unemployment, now represents only a fraction of the millions of Italians who emigrated during the two decades prior to 1914. From 1900 to 1914, 16 of every 1,000 Italians left their homeland each year; by the late 1970s, that proportion had declined to about 1.5 per 1,000. Estimates of Italy's net migration rate, carried out by the CIA in 2011, amounted to 4.86 migrants

per 1,000 citizens. The total number of emigrants living abroad was 3.48 million, and the total number of immigrants living in Italy was 4.46 million. The overall impetus to emigrate has been greatly reduced by economic expansion within Italy itself and by the shrinking job market in other countries, especially Germany.

In 2009 parliament approved a law that makes illegal immigration a criminal offense and increases the penalties imposed on those who are charged. Under the new law, illegal immigrants may be punished by a fine of up to $14,200 and may be detained for up to six months. Criminalizing illegal immigration allows police to make arrests more easily, which can accumulate to deportation. The most controversial measure of the law is one that allows for the organization of unarmed citizen patrols to assist police in maintaining order while tracking down illegal immigrants. People who knowingly house illegal immigrants can be sentenced to up to three years in prison. The law was passed as a response to the growing number of immigrants pouring into the country.

In early 2011, political unrest in Tunisia and Libya caused a number of North Africans to flee to the Italian island of Lampedusa. From January through March 2011, more than 6,000 refuges landed on the island.

8 ETHNIC GROUPS

Historically, Italy has been the home of various peoples: Lombards and Goths in the north; Greeks, Saracens, and Spaniards in Sicily and the south; Latins in and around Rome; and Etruscans and others in central Italy. For centuries, however, Italy has enjoyed a high degree of ethnic homogeneity. The chief minority groups are the German-speaking people in the Alto Adige (South Tyrol) region and the Slavs of the Trieste area.

9 LANGUAGES

Italian, the official language, is spoken by the vast majority of people. While each region has its own dialect, Tuscan, the dialect of Tuscany, is the standard dialect for Italian. French is spoken in parts of Piedmonte and in Valle d'Aosta, where it is the second official language; Slovene is spoken in the Trieste-Gorizia area. German is widely used in Bolzano Province, or South Tyrol (part of the Trentino-Alto Adige region), which was ceded by Austria in 1919, and under agreements reached between Italy and Austria in 1946 and 1969, the latter oversees the treatment of these German-speakers, who continue to call for greater linguistic and cultural autonomy.

10 RELIGIONS

An estimated 85% of native-born Italian citizens claim to be members of the Roman Catholic faith; however, only about one-third are active participants. Non-Catholic Christian groups, Muslims, Jews, Hindus, Baha'is, and Buddhists each account for less than 5% of the population. The most prominent non-Catholic Christian communities include Orthodox Christians, Jehovah's Witnesses, Assemblies of God, the Confederation of Methodist and Waldensian Churches, and The Church of Jesus Christ of Latter-Day Saints (Mormons). There are also other small Protestant groups represented. Freedom of religion is guaranteed by the constitution, and that right is generally respected in practice. Roman Catholicism, confirmed as the state religion under the Lateran Treaty of 1929, lost that distinction under a concordat with the Vatican ratified in 1984. However, the Catholic Church continues to hold a privileged status within the state and receives some government subsidies. Other religious groups may apply for an *intesa*, which allows for some state funding for those communities through a voluntary check-off on taxpayer returns. As of 2010, the Confederation of Methodist and Waldensian Churches, Adventists, Assemblies of God, Jews, Baptists, and Lutherans all utilized this funding process. All religious groups may apply for legal recognition, which comes with tax-exempt benefits. There have been some reports of social discrimination against Jews and Muslims.

11 TRANSPORTATION

The CIA reports that Italy has a total of 487,700 km (303,043 mi) of paved roads. Italy's highway system, considered one of the world's best, has expressways that carry heavy traffic along such routes as Milan-Como-Varese, Venice-Padua, Naples-Salerno, and Milan-Bologna-Florence-Rome-Naples. A major highway runs through the Mont Blanc Tunnel, connecting France and Italy. There are 673 vehicles per 1,000 people in the country.

The government owns and operates 80% of the rail system, the Italian State Railway (Ferrovie dello Stato Italiane SpA), including the principal lines. Railroads extend for 16,959 km (10,538 mi). Connections with French railways are made at Ventimiglia, Tenda, and Mont Cenis; with the Swiss, through the Simplon and St. Gotthard passes; with the Austrian, at the Brenner Pass and Tarvisio; and with the Slovenian, through Gorizia.

Italy has approximately 2,400 km (1,491 mi) of navigable waterways. The navigable inland waterway system is mainly in the north and consists of the Po River, the Italian lakes, and the network of Venetian and Po River Valley canals. There is regular train-ferry and automobile-ferry service between Messina and other Sicilian ports. Freight and passengers are carried by ship from Palermo to Naples. Sardinia and the smaller islands are served by regular shipping. Regular passenger service is provided by hydrofoil between Calabria and Sicily, and between Naples, Ischia, and Capri.

As of 2010, Italy had 667 merchant vessels of 1,000 gross registered tons (GRT) or more. Genoa and Savona on the northwest coast and Venice on the Adriatic handle the major share of traffic to and from the northern industrial centers. Second only to Genoa, Naples is the principal port for central and southern Italy, while Livorno is the natural outlet for Florence, Bologna, and Perugia. Messina, Palermo, and Catania are the chief Sicilian ports, and Cagliari handles most Sardinian exports.

There are 132 airports, which transported 33.19 million passengers in 2009 according to the World Bank. There are also six heliports. Italy's one national airline, Alitalia, which is almost entirely government-owned, maintains an extensive domestic and international network of air routes. Rome's Fiumicino (also known as Leonardo da Vinci) and Milan's Malpensa and Linate are among the most important airports, being served by nearly every major international air carrier.

12 HISTORY

The Italian patrimony, based on Roman antecedents—with a tradition that extends over 2,500 years—is the oldest in Europe, next to Greece's. The Ligurians, Sabines, and Umbrians were among the earliest known inhabitants of Italy, but in the 9th century BC they were largely displaced in central Italy by the Etruscans, a seafaring people probably from Asia Minor. Shortly thereafter, the Phoenicians and Greeks conquered parts of Sicily and southern Italy. By 650 BC, Italy was divided into ethnic areas, with the Umbrians in the north, Ligurians in the northwest, Latins and Etruscans in the central regions, and Greeks and Phoenicians in the south and Sicily. The Etruscan civilization, a great maritime, commercial, and artistic culture, reached its peak about the 7th century BC, but its control in Italy was in decline by 509 BC when the Romans overthrew their Etruscan monarchs. After a series of wars with both Greeks and Etruscans, the Latins, with Rome as their capital, gained the ascendancy by 350 BC, and they managed to unite the entire Italian peninsula by 272 BC.

This period of unification was followed by one of conquest, beginning with the First Punic War against Carthage (264–241 BC). In the course of their century-long struggle against Carthage, the Romans conquered Sicily, Sardinia, and Corsica. Finally, at the conclusion of the Third Punic War in 146 BC, with Carthage completely destroyed and its inhabitants enslaved, Rome became the dominant power in the Mediterranean. After overthrowing the last kings, Rome had become a republican city-state, but four famous civil conflicts destroyed the republic: Sulla against Marius and his son (88–82 BC), Julius Caesar against Pompey (49–45 BC), Brutus and Cassius against Mark Antony and Octavian (43 BC), and Mark Antony against Octavian. Octavian, the final victor (31 BC), was accorded the title of Augustus ("exalted") by the Senate and became the first Roman emperor. Under imperial rule, Rome undertook a series of conquests that brought Roman law, administration, and the Pax Romana ("Roman Peace") to an area extending from the Atlantic to the Rhine, from the British Isles to large parts of North Africa, and to the Middle East as far as the Euphrates.

In the 3rd century AD, after two centuries of successful rule, Rome was threatened by internal discord and menaced by Germanic and Asian invaders, commonly called barbarians (from the Latin word *barbari*, "foreigners"). The emperor Diocletian's administrative division of the empire into two parts in 285 provided only temporary relief. In 313 the emperor Constantine accepted Christianity, and the religion spread throughout the empire. He also moved his capital from Rome to Constantinople, greatly reducing the importance of the former. From the 4th to the 5th century, the Western Roman Empire disintegrated under the blows of barbarian invasions, finally falling in 476, and the unity of Italy came to an end. For a time, Byzantine emperors attempted to reconquer Italy but could not hold the peninsula. Continuing conflicts between the Western (Latin) and Eastern (Greek) Christian churches culminated in a schism in 1054, when the pope and eastern patriarch excommunicated one another.

From the 6th to the 13th century, Italy suffered a variety of invasions and rulers: the Lombards in the 6th century, the Franks in the 8th century, the Saracens in the 9th, and the Germans in the 10th. The German emperors of the Holy Roman Empire, the popes, and the rising Italian city-states vied for power from the 10th to the 14th century, and Italy was divided into several, often hostile, territories: in the south, the Kingdom of Naples, under Norman and Angevin rule; in the central area, the Papal States; and in the north, a welter of large and small city-states, such as Venice, Milan, Florence, and Siena.

By the 13th century, the city-states had emerged as centers of commerce and of the arts and sciences. Venice, in particular, had become a major maritime power, and many city-states acted as a conduit for goods and learning from the Byzantine and Islamic empires. In this capacity, they provided great impetus to developing the Renaissance, which between the 13th and 16th centuries led to an unparalleled flourishing of the arts, literature, music, and science. However, the emergence of Portugal and Spain as great seagoing nations at the end of the 15th century undercut Italian prosperity. After the Italian Wars (1494–1559), in which France tried unsuccessfully to extend its influence in Italy, Spain emerged as the dominant force in the region. Venice, Milan, and other city-states retained at least some of their former greatness during this period, as did Savoy-Piedmont, protected by the Alps and well defended by its vigorous rulers.

Economic hardship, waves of the plague, and religious unrest tormented the region throughout the 17th century and into the 18th. Napoleon brought the French Revolution to the Italian peninsula, and concepts such as nationalism and liberalism infiltrated everywhere. Short-lived republics and even a Kingdom of Italy (under Napoleon's stepson Eugene) were formed. But reaction set in with the Congress of Vienna (1815), and many of the old rulers and systems were restored under Austrian domination. Nationalistic sentiment remained strong, however, and sporadic outbreaks led by such inveterate reformers as Giuseppe Mazzini occurred in several parts of the peninsula until 1848–49. This Risorgimento ("resurgence") movement was brought to a successful conclusion under the able guidance of Count Camillo Cavour, prime minister of Piedmont. Cavour managed to unite most of Italy under the headship of Victor Emmanuel II of the house of Savoy, and on 17 March 1861, the Kingdom of Italy was proclaimed, with Victor Emmanuel II as king. Giuseppe Garibaldi, the popular republican hero of Italy, contributed much to this achievement and to the subsequent incorporation of the Papal States under the Italian monarch. Italian troops occupied Rome in 1870, and in July 1871, it formally became the capital of the kingdom, although Pope Pius IX, a longtime rival of Italian kings, considered himself a "prisoner of the Vatican" and refused to cooperate with the royal administration.

The 20th Century

The new monarchy aspired to great-power status but was severely handicapped by domestic social and economic conditions, particularly in the south. Political and social reforms introduced by Premier Giovanni Giolitti in the first decade of the 20th century improved Italy's status among Western powers but failed to overcome such basic problems as poverty and illiteracy. Giolitti resigned in March 1914 and was succeeded by Antonia Salandra. During World War I, Italy initially allied with the Central Powers, then declared itself neutral in 1914 and a year later, in April 1915, joined the British and French in exchange for advantages offered by the secret Treaty of London. Although Italy had suffered heavy losses on the Alpine front, at the Versailles Peace Conference it failed to obtain all the territories it claimed and felt slighted by its Western allies.

This disappointment, coupled with the severe economic depression of the postwar period, created great social unrest and led eventually to the rise of Benito Mussolini, who, after leading his Fascist followers in a mass march on Rome, became premier in 1922. He established a Fascist dictatorship that scored early successes in social welfare, employment, and transportation. In 1929, Mussolini negotiated the Lateran Treaties, under which the Holy See became sovereign within the newly constituted state of Vatican City (Città del Vaticano), and Roman Catholicism was reaffirmed as Italy's official religion, although the latter provision was abolished in 1984. The military conquest of Ethiopia (1935–36) added to Italy's colonial strength and exposed the inability of the League of Nations to punish aggression or keep the peace.

Italy allied with Germany in World War II, but defeats in Greece and North Africa, plus the Allied invasion of Sicily, toppled Mussolini's regime on 25 July 1943. Soon Italy was divided into two warring zones, one controlled by the Allies in the south and the other (including Rome) held by the Germans, who had rescued Mussolini and established him as head of the puppet "Italian Social Republic." When German power collapsed, Mussolini was captured and executed by Italian partisans.

The conclusion of the war left Italy poverty-stricken and politically disunited. In 1946, Italy became a republic by plebiscite; in the following year, a new constitution was drafted, which went into effect in 1948. Under the peace treaty of 10 February 1947, Italy was required to pay $360 million in reparations to the Soviet Union, Yugoslavia, Greece, Ethiopia, and Albania. By this time, the Italian economy, initially disorganized by Mussolini's dream of national self-sufficiency and later physically devastated by the war, was in a state of near collapse. By the early 1950s, however, with foreign assistance (including $1.517 billion from the United States under the Marshall Plan), Italy managed to restore its economy to prewar levels. From this point, the Italian economy experienced unprecedented development through the 1960s and 1970s.

Politically, postwar Italy was marked by a pattern of accelerating instability, with 48 different coalition governments through 15 March 1988. In May 1981, the coalition of Prime Minister Arnaldo Forlani was brought down after it was learned that many government officials, including three cabinet ministers, were members of a secret Masonic lodge, Propaganda Due (P-2), that had reportedly been involved in illegal right-wing activities. Left-wing terrorism, notably by the Red Brigades (Brigate Rosse), also plagued Italy in the 1970s and early 1980s. In January 1983, 23 Red Brigade members were sentenced to life imprisonment in connection with the kidnapping and murder of Prime Minister Aldo Moro in 1978; another 36 members received sentences of varying lengths for other crimes, including 11 murders and 11 attempted murders, committed between 1976 and 1980. By the mid-1980s, the Mafia actively engaged in extortion, government corruption, and violent crime, in addition to its central role in global heroin trafficking.

By 1986, however, internal security had improved. A major effort against organized crime was underway in the mid-1980s; over 1,000 suspects were tried and the majority convicted in trials that took place in Naples beginning in February 1985 and in Sicily beginning in February 1986.

Revelations of corruption and scandals involving senior politicians, members of the government administration, and business leaders rocked Italy in the early 1990s. Hundreds of politicians, party leaders, and industrialists were either under arrest or under investigation. The scandals discredited the major parties that had governed Italy since 1948, and the instability gave impetus to new reformist groups.

In August 1993, Italy made significant changes in its electoral system. Three-fourths of the seats in both the Chamber and the Senate would be filled by simple majority voting. The remainder would be allocated by proportional representation to those parties securing at least 4% of the vote. The first elections under the new system in March 1994 resulted in a simplification of electoral alliances and brought a center-right government to power. Silvio Berlusconi, founder of the "Go Italy" (Forza Italia) movement, emerged as prime minister. Berlusconi, a successful Italian businessman, was a newcomer to Italian politics. He was supported by the Alliance for Freedom coalition, which had received over 42% of the vote and 366 seats.

Berlusconi's government, however, became victim to charges of government corruption, and on 22 December 1994 he was forced to resign in the face of a revolt by the Northern League, one of the parties in his ruling coalition. Three weeks after Berlusconi's resignation, his treasury minister, Lamberto Dini was named prime minister. He formed a government of technocrats and set about to enact fiscal and electoral reforms. Pragmatism and a lack of viable alternatives kept him in power until supporters of Berlusconi, his main political rival, presented a motion that he step down. When Dini learned that two splinter groups in his center-left coalition (the Greens and the Communist Refounding party) would not vote in his favor, he resigned on 11 January 1996 rather than face a no-confidence vote.

The elections, held on 21 April 1996, saw a center-left coalition, dominated by the former communists (DS), take control of the country for the first time in 50 years. Romano Prodi, an economics professor with little political experience, was chosen to serve as prime minister on 16 May. His coalition government collapsed after it failed to win a vote of no-confidence over the budget. President Oscar Luigi Scalfaro asked Massimo D'Alema, the leader of the DS, to form a new administration. His cabinet retained the same members from the left and center as before. This government also continued to pursue fiscal consolidation to join European economic and monetary union in 1999. Prodi left for Brussels to take up the presidency of the European Commission in May 1999. D'Alema reshuffled his cabinet in 1999, but it finally fell in April 2000. The immediate cause was the dismal performance in regional elections. The center-left won 7 out of 15 regions while the right, under the leadership of Silvio Berlusconi, took 8 regions.

The coalition of 12 discordant political blocs backed the treasury minister, Giuliano Amato, to become the new prime minister (appointed by then-President Carlo Azeglio Ciampi). Prior to the fall of the D'Alema administration, the government had scheduled an important referendum to scrap the last remaining vestiges of direct proportional representation in the electoral system. Only one-third of the electorate bothered to vote on 21 May 2000, not enough to validate the referendum outcome.

Berlusconi's House of Liberties coalition, led by Go Italy, secured 368 seats in the Chamber of Deputies in the May 2001 parliamentary elections, to the Olive Tree coalition's 242 seats. (The House of Liberties coalition also won a majority in the senate.) After becoming Italy's 59th postwar prime minister, Berlusconi faced long-standing charges of criminal wrongdoing, including bribery; he became the first sitting Italian prime minister to appear at his own trial. It was not until December 2004 that Berlusconi was cleared of all charges.

Italy offered the use of its airspace and military bases to the U.S.-led coalition in its war with Iraq, which began on 19 March 2003, although Italy did not initially send troops to the region and did not allow coalition forces to launch a direct attack on Iraq from Italy. Some 75% of Italians opposed the use of military force against the Saddam Hussein regime, but Berlusconi adopted a position of solidarity with the U.S.-led coalition. Troops were later sent to Iraq. In January 2006, the Italian defense minister announced Italian troops would leave Iraq. The mission ended in September 2006.

In April 2005, Berlusconi's government coalition collapsed after suffering a crushing defeat in regional elections. Berlusconi resigned, but days later he formed a new government after receiving a presidential mandate. In April 2006, Romano Prodi, a leader of the center left, won closely-fought general elections. He was sworn in as prime minister in May. In February 2007, Prodi resigned after the government lost a senate vote on its foreign policy. The president, Giorgio Napolitano, asked Prodi to remain in office, and Prodi went on to win confidence votes in both houses of parliament. However, in January 2008 the Prodi government fell when small coalition partner UDEUR (the Union of Democrats for Europe) withdrew support. The president dissolved parliament and Berlusconi returned to power after defeating former Rome mayor Walter Veltroni in elections during April 2008. Berlusconi's winning coalition was composed of the People of Liberty (a union of Forza Italia and National Alliance), the Northern League, and the Movement for Autonomy. Berlusconi was sworn in as prime minister on 8 May 2008.

During his years in office, Berlusconi gained a reputation for his alleged involvement in numerous political and sexual scandals. Throughout his political career, he has been involved in nearly 2,500 legal hearings. While he had initially been found guilty in some cases regarding illegal party financing, corruption, bribery, tax fraud, and false accounting, he later won those cases on appeal. Other cases either ended in acquittal or were dropped as the case expired under the statute of limitations. Facing considerable political and public pressure due to Italy's burgeoning public debt, Berlusconi resigned on 12 November 2011 after the Italian parliament passed austerity measures intended to relieve the country's debt crisis. Berlusconi's replacement, Mario Monti, took office on 16 November 2011. Monti was chosen due to his considerable economic expertise and was charged with guiding the Italian economy through its fiscal crisis.

13 GOVERNMENT

In a plebiscite on 2 June 1946, the Italian people voted (12.7 million to 10.7 million) to end the constitutional monarchy, which had existed since 1861, and establish a republic. At the same time, a constituent assembly was elected, which proceeded to draft and approve a new constitution; it came into force on 2 January 1948. Under this constitution, as amended, the head of the Italian Republic is the president, who is elected for a seven-year term by an electoral college consisting of both houses of parliament and 58 regional representatives. Elections for a new president must be held 30 days before the end of the presidential term. Presidential powers and duties include nomination of the prime minister (referred to as president of the Council of Ministers) who, in turn, chooses a Council of Ministers (cabinet) with the approval of the president; the power to dissolve parliament, except during the last six months of the presidential term of office; representation of the state on important occasions; ratification of treaties after parliamentary authorization; and the power to grant pardons and commute penalties. Although the constitution limits presidential pow-

ers, a strong president can play an important political as well as ceremonial role.

Legislative power is vested in the bicameral parliament, consisting of the Chamber of Deputies and the Senate. Members of the 630-seat lower house, the Chamber of Deputies, must be at least 25 years old and are elected for five-year terms. The 315 elected members of the Senate must be at least 40 years old and are elected for five-year terms. Former presidents of the republic are automatically life senators, and the president may also appoint as life senators persons who have performed meritorious service. Citizens must be at least 25 years of age to vote for senators; otherwise, those over the age of 18 may vote in all other elections.

In August 1993, Italy made significant changes in its electoral system. Three-fourths of the seats in both the chamber and the senate would be filled by simple majority voting. The remainder would be allocated by proportional representation to those parties securing at least 4% of the vote. The new system simplified electoral alliances.

The constitution gives the people the right to hold referenda to abrogate laws passed by the parliament. On 21 May 2000, Italian voters were asked to decide on electoral reform by increasing the number of lower house seats filled on the basis of a nonproportional system to 100%, effectively scrapping the last remaining element of pure proportional representation. The referendum needed to secure a quorum of 50% of the electorate to gain validity. The final turnout of 32% was much lower than expected and was an alarming sign of voter fatigue and popular disaffection. In June 2006, voters in a national referendum rejected reforms intended to increase the powers of the prime minister and regions.

14 POLITICAL PARTIES

Italy has a complex system of political alignments in which the parties, their congresses, and their leaders often appear to wield more power than parliament or the other constitutional branches of government. Basic party policy is decided at the party congresses—generally held every second year—which are attended by locally elected party leaders. At the same time, the national party leadership is selected.

The most important political party traditionally had been the Christian Democratic Party (Partito Democrazia Cristiana—DC), which stood about midway in the political spectrum. From 1948 until 1981, the prime minister of Italy was consistently drawn from the ranks of the DC, whose religious and anti-class base constituted both its strength and its weakness. Its relationship with the Church gave it added strength but also opened it to criticism, as did its popular association with the mafia. In 1992, investigations uncovered widespread corruption, leading to many arrests and resignations of senior government officials. As a result of these scandals and corruption charges, the DC disbanded in 1994.

To the right and the left of the DC stood a wide range of parties, the most prominent of which was the Italian Communist Party (Partito Comunista Italiano—PCI), the largest Communist party in Western Europe at the time. The PCI had been second in power and influence only to the DC, but its electoral base declined in the 1980s, despite the fact that it effectively severed its ties with both the former Soviet Union and Marxism-Leninism.

Of all the parties of the mid to late 20th century, the most powerful, in addition to the DC and PCI, were the Italian Socialist Party

(Partito Socialista Italiano—PSI), the Italian Socialist Democratic Party (Partito Socialista Democratico Italiano—PSDI), the Italian Republican Party (Partito Repubblicano Italiano—PRI), the Italian Liberal Party (Partito Liberale Italiano—PLI), the Radical Party (Partito Radicale), the Italian Social Movement, (Movimento Sociale Italiano—MSI), the Proletarian Democracy (Democrazia Proletaria—DP), and the environmentalist Greens party. The end of the Cold War and the mafia crackdown in the 1990s led to an overhaul of the political party system so significant that, although there was little actual constitutional change, the post-1992 period is often referred to as the "Second Republic."

A rise in the number of political parties has led to the domination of coalition parties. The April 1996 election saw a resurgence of the left as the Olive Tree coalition, anchored by former communists calling themselves the Party of the Democratic Left (PDS), gained 284 seats in the 630-seat Chamber of Deputies and 157 seats in the 315-seat Senate. The domination of the center-left came to an end in the May 2001 election when Berlusconi's right-leaning coalition, Freedom House (formerly the House of Liberties), won 368 seats in the Chamber of Deputies, and 177 in the Senate. In elections held in April 2006, Berlusconi was narrowly defeated by Romano Prodi, leader of the center-left Union bloc. The Union bloc, composed of the Olive Tree coalition, the Rose in the Fist coalition, the Communist Refounding, and 11 other smaller parties, won 49.8% of the vote and secured 348 seats in the Chamber of Deputies. The Prodi government fell in January 2008 when the small coalition partner UDEUR (the Union of Democrats for Europe) withdrew support. In response, Silvio Berlusconi launched a coalition composed of the People of Liberty (PdL—a union of Forza Italia and National Alliance), the Northern League (LN), and the Movement for Autonomy (MpA); the parties ran together under the People of Liberty symbol in the 13–14 April 2008 elections. Berlusconi's coalition dominated in the April 2008 elections, earning 174 seats in the senate (PdL 147, LN 25, MpA 2) and 344 seats in the chamber (PdL 276, LN 60, MpA 8). The opposition coalition led by Walter Veltroni won 132 seats in the senate and 246 seats in the chamber. The election greatly simplified parliament, dramatically reducing the numbers of parties, and, for the first time since World War II, left communist parties out of parliament.

In the summer of 2010, the speaker of parliament, Gianfranco Fini, dropped out of Berlusconi's People of Liberty Party and established his own Future and Freedom for Italy party. Berlusconi managed to survive a vote of confidence in September 2010. But in November, the deputy minister and three other ministers who had aligned with Fini resigned from their posts.

These resignations signaled a lack of support from Berlusconi's coalition partners, who scheduled a vote of confidence in both the lower and upper houses of parliament for 14 December. Berlusconi survived the vote in the senate by a clear margin, but barely won the house vote with a count of 314 to 311. Following parliamentary passage of austerity measures to mitigate Italy's debt crisis, Berlusconi resigned on 16 November 2011. He was replaced by Monti on 16 November.

Giorgio Napolitano of the Democrats of the Left was elected president in 2006 after a fourth round of voting in the electoral college. The next presidential election was scheduled for May 2013.

15 LOCAL GOVERNMENT

Under the terms of the 1948 constitution, Italy is divided into 20 regions. Five of these regions (Sicily, Sardinia, Trentino-Alto Adige, Friuli-Venezia Giulia, and the Valle d'Aosta) have been granted semiautonomous status, although the powers of self-government delegated from Rome have not been sufficient to satisfy the militant separatists, especially in Alto Adige. Legislation passed in 1968 granted the remaining 15 regions an even more limited degree of autonomy. All the regions elect a regional council. The councils and president are elected by universal franchise under a proportional system analogous to that of the parliament at Rome.

The regions are subdivided into a total of 94 provinces, which elect their own council and president, and each region is in turn subdivided into communes—townships, cities, and towns—that constitute the basic units of local administration. Communes are governed by councils elected by universal suffrage for a four-year term. The council elects a mayor and a board of aldermen to administer the commune. A commissioner in each region represents the federal government.

16 JUDICIAL SYSTEM

Minor legal matters may be brought before conciliators, while civil cases and lesser criminal cases are tried before judges called *pretori*. There are 159 tribunals, each with jurisdiction over its own district; 90 assize courts, where cases are heard by juries; and 26 assize courts of appeal. The Court of Cassation in Rome acts as the last instance of appeal in all cases except those involving constitutional matters, which are brought before the special Constitutional Court (consisting of 15 judges). For many years, the number of civil and criminal cases has been increasing more rapidly than judicial resources.

The Italian legal system is based on Roman law, although much is also derived from the French Napoleonic model. The law assuring criminal defendants a fair and public trial is largely observed in practice. The 1989 amendments to the criminal procedure law both streamlined the process and provided for a more adversarial (as opposed to inquisitorial) system along the American model.

By law the judiciary is autonomous and independent of the executive branch. In practice, there has been a perception that magistrates were subject to political pressures and that political bias of individual magistrates could affect outcomes. Since the start of "clean hands" investigations of the government, including the judiciary, in 1992 for kickbacks and corruption, magistrates have taken steps to distance themselves from political parties and other pressure groups.

In October 2009 the Constitutional Court issued a landmark ruling that overturned the law granting legal immunity to the prime minister while serving in office. The immunity law had been pushed through parliament in 2008, largely at the urging of Prime Minister Silvio Berlusconi. Under the law, legal immunity was granted to the president, prime minister, and two parliamentary speakers while they served in office. Supporters claimed that the law was necessary to allow these officials to govern without the distraction of the judiciary. A group of prosecutors issued an appeal to the Constitutional Court, which declared the law unconstitutional in a vote of nine to six, stating that it violated the constitutional principle that all citizens are equal under the law.

17 ARMED FORCES

The International Institute for Strategic Studies reported that armed forces in Italy totaled 184,609 members in 2011. The force is comprised of 107,500 from the army, 34,000 from the navy, and 43,109 members of the air force. Armed forces represented 1.3% of the labor force in Italy. Defense spending totaled $32 billion and accounted for 1.8% of GDP. Since 1949 Italy, as a member of NATO, has maintained large and balanced modern forces. Italian armed forces were deployed among 19 countries or regions in various peacekeeping, training, or active military missions.

18 INTERNATIONAL COOPERATION

Italy has been a member of the United Nations since 14 December 1955 and participates in the ECE and several UN nonregional specialized agencies, such as FAO, UNESCO, UNIDO, UNHCR, IFC, WHO, and the World Bank. It is a member of the Council of Europe, the European Union, NATO, and the OECD. Italy held the EU presidency from July to December 2003. Italy also participates in the Asian, African, Caribbean, European, and the Inter-American development banks, and is a part of G-7, G-8, and G-10. The country holds observer status in the Black Sea Economic Cooperation Zone, the OAS, and the Latin American Integration Association (LAIA).

Italy is a guest in the Nonaligned Movement. The country has supplied troops for UN operations and missions in Kosovo (est. 1999), Lebanon (est. 1978), India and Pakistan (est. 1949), and Ethiopia and Eritrea (est. 2000), among others. Italy belongs to the Australia Group, the Zangger Committee, the Nuclear Suppliers Group (London Group), the Nuclear Energy Agency, the Organization for the Prohibition of Chemical Weapons, and the European Organization for Nuclear Research (CERN).

In environmental cooperation, Italy is part of the Antarctic Treaty; the Basel Convention; Conventions on Biological Diversity, Whaling, and Air Pollution; Ramsar; CITES; the London Convention; International Tropical Timber Agreements; the Kyoto Protocol; the Montréal Protocol; MARPOL; the Nuclear Test Ban Treaty; and the UN Conventions on the Law of the Sea, Climate Change and Desertification.

19 ECONOMY

As the Italian economy, one of the world's largest, has expanded since the 1950s, its structure has changed markedly. Agriculture, which in 1953 contributed 25% of the GNP and employed 35% of the labor force, contributed only 11% of the GNP and employed only 22% of the active labor force in 1968. Agriculture's contribution to the GDP further declined to only 1.8% in 2010. Conversely, the importance of industry has increased dramatically. Industrial output almost tripled between 1953 and 1968 and generally showed steady growth during the 1970s; in 2010, industry (including fuel, power, and construction) contributed 24.9% to the GDP. Precision machinery and motor vehicles have led the growth in manufacturing, and Italy has generally been a leader in Europe-

an industrial design and fashion. Apart from tourism and design, Italy is not internationally competitive in most service sectors.

Despite this economic achievement, a number of basic problems remain. Natural resources are limited, landholdings often are poor and invariably too small, industrial enterprises are of minimal size and productivity, and industrial growth has not been translated into general prosperity. Italy is almost totally dependent on energy imports. In addition, because economic activity is centered predominantly in the north, Italians living in the northern part of the country enjoy a substantially higher standard of living than those living in the south.

Partly because of increased energy costs, inflation increased from an annual rate of about 5% in the early 1970s to an annual average of 16.6% during 1975–81, well above the OECD average. Inflation was brought down to 14.6% in 1983 and to between 4 and 6% during most of the 1990s. The inflation rate was estimated at 1.4% in 2010.

From 1981 through 1983, Italy endured a period of recession, with rising budget deficits, interest rates above 20%, virtually no real GDP growth, and an unemployment rate approaching 10%. Unemployment hovered around the 10 to 12% range for most of the 1990s and at 9% into the 2000s. In 2010 it measured 8.4%. Between 1985 and 1995, GDP growth averaged 1.9% a year. Recessions in 2008 (GDP decline of -1.3%) and 2009 (-5.2%) gave way to modest growth in 2010 (1.3%).

Italy's large public debt, public sector deficit, low productivity growth, and burdensome and complex tax system are generally blamed for the poor state of the economy. A rigid labor market and generous pension system are also seen as responsible for a sluggish economy. The Berlusconi administration abolished an inheritance tax in 2002, a move popular among affluent Italians. Berlusconi also attempted to loosen labor laws to increase temporary work contracts and to ease hiring and firing practices.

With a reliance on export income, Italy's economy took a major hit during the 2008–09 global financial crisis. By 2010 the government had taken a number of cost-cutting measures. Cuts in public sector pay and pension plans were among the first unpopular measures taken by the government. The government approved austerity measures worth $31 billion for the 2011–12 budget.

20 INCOME

The CIA estimated that in 2010 the GDP of Italy was $1.8 trillion. The CIA defines GDP as the value of all final goods and services produced within a nation in a given year and computed on the basis of purchasing power parity (PPP) rather than value as measured on the basis of the rate of the exchange based on current dollars. The per capita GDP was estimated at $30,500. The annual growth rate of GDP was 1.3%. The average inflation rate was 1.4%. It was estimated that agriculture accounted for 1.8% of GDP, industry 24.9%, and services 73.3%. According to the World Bank, remittances from citizens living abroad totaled $2.7 billion or about $44 per capita and accounted for approximately 0.1% of GDP.

The World Bank reports that in 2009, household consumption in Italy totaled $1.27 trillion or about $20,753 per capita, measured in current US dollars rather than PPP. Household consumption includes expenditures of individuals, households, and nongovernmental organizations on goods and services, excluding the purchases of dwellings. It was estimated that household consumption was growing at an average annual rate of 1.7%.

As of 2011 the most recent study by the World Bank reported that actual individual consumption in Italy was 70.9% of GDP and accounted for 3.09% of world consumption. By comparison, the United States accounted for 25.44% of world individual consumption. The World Bank also estimated that 10.5% of Italy's GDP was spent on food and beverages, 16.9% on housing and household furnishings, 4.7% on clothes, 8.5% on health, 8.0% on transportation, 1.7% on communications, 4.5% on recreation, 5.9% on restaurants and hotels, and 5.7% on miscellaneous goods and services and purchases from abroad.

21 LABOR

As of 2010, Italy had a total labor force of 24.98 million people. Within that group, the CIA estimated in 2005 that 65.1% were employed in the service sector, 30.7% in industry, and 4.2% in agriculture. The law provides the right to form and join unions, and many workers exercise this right. According to union claims, between 35% and 40% of the nation's workforce was unionized as of 2010. About 47% of the labor force was covered by collective bargaining agreements. The right to strike is constitutionally protected. Employers may not discriminate against those engaged in union activity.

As of 2010, the legal workweek was set at 40 hours, with overtime not to exceed 2 hours per day or an average of 12 hours per week. However, in the industrial sector, maximum overtime was set at no more than 80 hours per quarter and 250 hours annually, unless limited by a collective bargaining agreement. Minimum wages in Italy are not set by law, but through collective labor contracts, which establish wages and salaries in every major field. In most industries these minimum rates offered a worker and family a decent standard of living. Labor contracts may also call for additional compulsory bonuses, and basic wages and salaries are adjusted quarterly to compensate for increases in the cost of living. With some limited exceptions, children under age 15 are prohibited by law from employment.

22 AGRICULTURE

Approximately 36% of Italy's total land is dedicated to agriculture. Major crops include fruits, vegetables, grapes, potatoes, sugar beets, soybeans, grain, and olives. Small, individually owned farms predominate, with the majority 3 hectares (7.4 acres) or less. Despite government efforts, the agricultural sector has shown little growth in recent decades. In 2009 cereal production amounted to 17.4 million tons, fruit production 18.2 million tons, and vegetable production 14.2 million tons.

The land is well suited for raising fruits and vegetables, both early and late crops, and these are the principal agricultural exports. Although yields per hectare in sugar beets, tomatoes, and other vegetable crops have increased significantly, both plantings and production of wheat declined between 1974 and 1981. Thus, although Italy remains a major cereal-producing country, wheat must be imported. The government controls the supply of domestic wheat and the import of foreign wheat.

23 ANIMAL HUSBANDRY

The UN Food and Agriculture Organization (FAO) reported that Italy dedicated 3.6 million hectares (8.96 million acres) to permanent pasture or meadow in 2009. During that year, the country tended 120 million chickens, 6.4 million head of cattle, and 9.3 million pigs. The production from these animals amounted to 1.43 million tons of beef and veal, 2.66 million tons of pork, 940,279 tons of poultry, 689,002 tons of eggs, and 15.2 million tons of milk. In addition, Italy produced 121,000 tons of cattle hide and 8,535 tons of raw wool. Meat production falls short of domestic requirements, and about half of all meat consumed must be imported. Dairy farming remains comparatively undeveloped. Both dairy and beef cattle are raised mainly in the north. Both a growing need for fodder and insufficient domestic production compel Italy to import large amounts of corn.

24 FISHING

Italy's geography provides abundant access to marine fishing. In 2008 the annual capture totaled 235,785 tons according to the UN FAO. Peninsular Italy and the islands of Sicily and Sardinia together have over 8,000 km (4,900 mi) of coastline and over 800 landing ports equipped for fishing boats. Italy had 18,779 decked commercial fishing boats in 2008. There are also 1,500 sq km (580 sq mi) of lagoons and 1,700 sq km (650 sq mi) of marine ponds.

Although coastal and deep-sea fishing in the Mediterranean engage over 50,000 fishermen, the fishing industry is unable to meet domestic needs. Since the extension of the 200-mile-limit zones and the consequent drop in the total catch, Italy's fishing industry has declined because their deep-sea vessels are not suited to Mediterranean fishing. Up to 50% of the Italian fish harvest is not officially recorded but sold directly to restaurants, wholesalers, and fishmongers. Anchovy, rainbow trout, sardine, and European hake are the main finfish species caught. Sponges and coral are also commercially important. The main commercial fishing ports are Mazara del Vallo, Palermo, San Benedetto del Tronto, Chioggia-Venezia, and Genoa.

There are over a thousand intensive production fish farms that belong to the Italian Fish Farming Association, with most located in northern Italy.

25 FORESTRY

Approximately 31% of Italy is covered by forest. The major portion of the 10 million hectares (24.7 million acres) of forest is in the Alpine areas of northern Italy; few extensive forests grow in central or southern Italy or on the islands. Italy has more softwood than hardwood growth and extensive coppice (thicket and small shrub) stands. The overall forest structure consists of 42% coppice stands, 26% softwoods, and 25% hardwood high stands. The only species that are commercially important are chestnut, beech, oak, and poplar. The UN FAO estimated the 2009 value of all forest products at $4.72 billion. Roundwood production was estimated at 2.6 million cu m (91.8 million cu ft). Poplar is the only species grown using managed forestry practices. Poplar plantations account for only 1% of the total forest area but about half of domestic wood output. Virtually all of Italian forest product exports consist of wooden furniture, semifinished wood products, and other finished wood products.

26 MINING

Although Italy is relatively poor in mineral resources, it is, nevertheless, a major producer of feldspar, pumice and related materials, as well as of crude steel, cement, and a leading producer of dimension stone and marble. The country also continued to supply a significant portion of its own need for some minerals. Industrial mineral production in 2009, including construction materials, is one of the most important sectors of the economy. Italy has been a significant processor of imported raw materials, and a significant consumer and exporter of mineral and metal semi-manufactured and finished products.

Production totals for the leading minerals in 2009 were feldspar, estimated at 4,700,000 metric tons; barite, estimated at 3,500 metric tons; hydraulic cement, estimated at 36.3 million tons; pumice and pumiceous lapilli, estimated at 30,000 tons (from Lipari Island, off the northern coast of Sicily); and pozzolan, estimated at 4 million tons (from Lipari). Alumina production (calcined basis) in 2009 was estimated at 752,853 metric tons. In addition, Italy produced antimony oxides, gold (from Sardinia), mine lead, mine manganese, bromine, crude clays (including bentonite, refractory, fuller's earth, kaolin, and kaolinitic earth), diatomite, gypsum, lime, nitrogen, perlite, mineral pigments, salt (marine, rock, and brine), sand and gravel (including volcanic and silica sands), soda ash, sodium sulfate, stone (alabaster, dolomite, granite, limestone, marble, marl, quartz, quartzite, sandstone, serpentine, and slate), sulfur, and talc and related materials.

Marble and travertine quarrying from the famous mines in the Massa and Carrara areas was still significant. Marble was quarried at hundreds of locations from the Alps to Sicily. The most important white-marble-producing area was in the Apuan Alps, near Carrara, and accounted for one-third of the country's 4.6 million metric tons of white marble. Important colored-marble-producing areas included the Lazio region, Lombardy, the Po Valley, Puglia, Sicily, Venice, and Verona-Vincenza. Reserves of several types were considered to be unlimited; half of the country's output was in block form, and half was exported.

27 ENERGY AND POWER

The World Bank reported that in 2008 Italy produced 313.5 billion kWh of electricity and consumed 338.7 billion kWh, or 5,551 kWh per capita. Roughly 90% of energy came from fossil fuels, while 5% came from alternative fuels. Italy must rely heavily on foreign sources to meet its energy needs.

According to the CIA, Italy has proven oil reserves estimated at 476.5 million barrels as of 2011. Oil production totaled 96,005 barrels of oil per day. However, domestic demand far outstrips production, with consumption in 2010 estimated at 1.528 billion barrels a day. Per capita oil consumption was 2,942 kg. Net imports were estimated at 1.8 million barrels a day in 2009.

Italy's National Hydrocarbon Agency (Ente Nazionale Idrocarburi), or ENI, is the country's largest oil and national gas company, in which the government holds a controlling 35% stake. More than 70% of ENI's production comes from the Val d'Agri project in the south of Italy, the Villafortuna project in the north, and from the Aquila project off the Adriatic coast in the southeast. Develop-

ment of the Tempa Rossa field, with an estimated 200 million barrels of oil, is being led by France's Total, with production expected to start in 2015.

Oil has been partly replaced by natural gas, whose consumption is expected to continue rising in the future, driven largely by the construction of combined-cycle, gas-fired turbines. Italy has proven natural gas reserves of 2.245 trillion cu ft, as of 2011. Natural gas production in 2010 totaled 293 billion cu ft. Combined with declining field output, Italy's reliance on natural gas imports has increased.

In 2001 Italy completely closed down its domestic coal production industry, when it shuttered its last production facility.

28 INDUSTRY

Characterized both by a few large industrial concerns controlling the greater part of industrial output and by thousands of small shops engaged in artisan-type production, Italian industry expanded rapidly in the postwar period. Industrial production almost tripled between 1955 and 1968 and has generally showed continued growth, although the global recession of 2001 slowed industrial production and the economy as a whole. The lack of domestic raw materials and fuels represents a serious drag on industrial expansion. Industry accounted for 24.9% of GDP in 2010, and employed 30.7% of the labor force.

Three state-holding companies have played a large role in industry: ENI, IRI (Industrial Reconstruction Institute), and EFIM (Agency for Participation and Financing of Manufacturing Industry). EFIM controlled armaments and metallurgy industries. Debt-ridden EFIM was liquidated, IRI became dismantled in 2002, and the state has continued to reduce its stake in ENI and Ente Nazionale per l'Energia Elettrica (Enel), the national electricity company. Major private companies are the Fiat automobile company; the Olivetti company (office computers and telecommunications); the Montedison chemical firm; and the Pirelli rubber company. The bulk of heavy industry continues to be concentrated in the northwest, in the Milan-Turin-Genoa industrial triangle, despite concerted government efforts to attract industry to the underdeveloped southeast.

Italy has become known for niche products, including fashion eye-wear, specialized machine tools, packaging, stylish furniture, kitchen equipment, and other products featuring high design. The "made in Italy" stamp is associated with quality and style. Traditional industries, still prominent in 2012, were iron and steel, machinery, chemicals, food processing (including olive oil, wine, and cheese), textiles, clothing, footwear, motor vehicles, and ceramics.

29 SCIENCE AND TECHNOLOGY

The still-standing aqueducts, bathhouses, and other public works of both ancient republic and empire testify to the engineering and architectural skills of the Romans. The rebirth of science during the Renaissance included the daring speculations of Leonardo da Vinci (including discoveries in anatomy, meteorology, geology, and hydrology, as well as a series of designs for a "flying machine"), advances in physics and astronomy by Galileo Galilei, and the development of the barometer by Evangelista Torricelli. To later Italian scientists and inventors, the world owes the electric bat-

Principal Trading Partners – Italy (2010)

(In millions of US dollars)

Country	Total	Exports	Imports	Balance
World	934,063.0	447,466.0	486,597.0	-39,131.0
Germany	135,293.0	58,086.0	77,207.0	-19,121.0
France	92,101.0	51,788.0	40,313.0	11,475.0
China	49,140.0	11,174.0	37,966.0	-26,792.0
Spain	47,621.0	26,005.0	21,616.0	4,389.0
United Kingdom	40,008.0	24,010.0	15,998.0	8,012.0
United States	38,264.0	25,370.0	12,894.0	12,476.0
Netherlands	36,930.0	11,093.0	25,837.0	-14,744.0
Switzerland	34,443.0	20,185.0	14,258.0	5,927.0
Belgium	29,239.0	11,497.0	17,742.0	-6,245.0
Russia	27,021.0	10,348.0	16,673.0	-6,325.0

(…) data not available or not significant.

(n.s.) not specified.

SOURCE: *2011 Direction of Trade Statistics Yearbook*, New York: United Nations, 2011.

tery (1800), the electroplating process (1805), and the radiotelegraph (1895).

According to UNESCO, in 2009 there were 1,701 Italians engaged in research and development (R&D) per million inhabitants. Patent applications in science and technology totaled 8,814 in 2009, according to the World Bank. Public financing of science was 1.18% of GDP.

The National Research Council (Consiglio Nazionale delle Ricerche—CNR), founded in 1923, is the country's principal research organization. CNR institutes and associated private and university research centers conduct scientific work in mathematics, physics, chemistry, geology, technology, engineering, medicine, biology, and agriculture. Especially noteworthy are the National Institute of Nuclear Physics, in Rome, and the Enrico Fermi Center for Nuclear Studies, in Milan.

Italy has 47 universities offering courses in basic and applied sciences. The Instituto e Museo di Storia della Scienza di Firenzo, founded in 1930, is located in Florence.

30 DOMESTIC TRADE

Milan is the principal commercial center, followed by Turin, Genoa, Naples, and Rome. Genoa, the chief port of entry for Milan and Turin, handles about one-third of Italy's trade; Naples is the principal entrepôt for central and southern Italy. Adriatic as well as Middle Eastern trade is carried through Ancona, Bari, and Brindisi.

Economics and geography play key roles in Italy's divided domestic trade sector. The northern part of the country has a greater number of commercial, industrial, and financial enterprises. The country's retail and wholesale distribution systems are highly fragmented, being tied to small, family-owned retail units that dominate the retail sector. In addition, there is an overly large number of point-of-sale outlets, which only adds to the system's inefficiency. This retail system has survived largely through the use of complex and protective government regulations. However this is starting to change, as department stores and supermarket operations are playing an increasing role in the retail sector. In addition, the use of franchising is increasing.

Advertising in all forms is well developed, and the usual mass media (billboards, neon signs, newspapers and magazines, radio, cinema, and television) are used extensively. Market research is handled by over 100 firms.

Usual business office hours in Italy generally are from 8:30 a.m. until 1 p.m. and from 3 to 6:30 p.m. Most firms are closed in August. In general, banking hours are 8:30 a.m. to 1:30 p.m. and 2:45 p.m. to 4:15 p.m., Monday through Friday. Store hours are from 9 a.m. to 1 p.m. and from 4:30 p.m. to 7:30 p.m. Monday through Saturday. Retail establishments are generally closed on Sundays.

31 FOREIGN TRADE

Trade deficits were substantial between the end of World War II and 1955, but between 1956 and 1968 the deficit gradually declined, and Italy's trade balance continued in relative equilibrium through 1972. Then, as prices of crude oil and other raw-material imports rose, Italy again began registering growing trade deficits. In 1993, however, a large surplus was recorded because of an export boom that followed the devaluation of the lira in September 1992. This surplus decreased and then vanished in the 2000s. Italy imported $459.7 billion worth of goods and services in 2008, while exporting $458.4 billion worth of goods and services.

The bulk of manufactured imports come from EU countries and the United States, which are also the leading customers for Italian exports. The big commodity exports from Italy in 2010 included industrial and automobile machinery and parts, textiles, clothing, transportation equipment, metal products, chemical products, and food and agricultural products. The textile industry has been hit hard by foreign competition, especially from China. The major imports included machinery and transportation equipment, food, metals, wool, cotton, and energy products. Major import partners in 2009 were Germany, 16.7%; France, 8.9%; China, 6.5%; Netherlands, 5.7%; Spain, 4.4%; Russia, 4.1%; and Belgium, 4%. Major export partners were Germany, 12.6%; France, 11.6%; the United States, 5.9%; Spain, 5.7%; UK, 5.1%; and Switzerland, 4.7%.

32 BALANCE OF PAYMENTS

Italy did not have serious balance of payments problems after the mid-1970s. Exports soared after 1992, turning Italy's balance of payments positive. The growth in exports was extremely strong in the northeast, where small and medium-sized companies produced high-quality and low-cost products-ranging from industrial machinery to ski boots-for French, German, Japanese, and Indian customers.

Italy had current account surpluses from 1993 to 1999, but in 2000 the country registered a $5.6 billion deficit, after an $8.2 billion surplus in 1999. Italy experienced weak economic growth in the period 2001–05, and the country was hard-hit by the 2008–09 global financial crisis. In 2010 Italy had a foreign trade deficit of $11 billion, amounting to 4.9% of GDP.

33 BANKING AND SECURITIES

The Banca d'Italia, the central bank, was the sole bank of issue and exercised credit control functions until Italy's accession to the European Central Bank, which now controls monetary policy and the euro, the EU's common currency (excepting the United King-

<table>
<tr><td colspan="2">Balance of Payments – Italy (2010)</td></tr>
</table>

Balance of Payments – Italy (2010)

(In billions of US dollars)

Current Account		**-71.2**
Balance on goods		-27.3
Imports	-475.7	
Exports	448.4	
Balance on services		-11.9
Balance on income		-10.7
Current transfers		-21.4
Capital Account		**-0.7**
Financial Account		**117.7**
Direct investment abroad		-20.4
Direct investment in Italy		9.6
Portfolio investment assets		-43.2
Portfolio investment liabilities		94.0
Financial derivatives		3.0
Other investment assets		57.7
Other investment liabilities		16.9
Net Errors and Omissions		**-44.4**
Reserves and Related Items		**-1.3**

(…) data not available or not significant.

SOURCE: *Balance of Payment Statistics Yearbook 2011*, Washington, DC: International Monetary Fund, 2011.

Public Finance – Italy (2008)

(In millions of euros, central government figures)

Revenue and Grants	**591,096**	**100.0%**
Tax revenue	352,712	59.7%
Social contributions	214,573	36.3%
Grants	1,396	0.2%
Other revenue	22,415	3.8%
Expenditures	**628,908**	**100.0%**
General public services	140,388	22.3%
Defense	21,712	3.5%
Public order and safety	25,263	4.0%
Economic affairs	26,912	4.3%
Environmental protection	2,885	0.5%
Housing and community amenities	4,746	0.8%
Health	58,765	9.3%
Recreational, culture, and religion	6,566	1.0%
Education	56,550	9.0%
Social protection	285,121	45.3%

(…) data not available or not significant.

SOURCE: *Government Finance Statistics Yearbook 2010*, Washington, DC: International Monetary Fund, 2010.

dom, Denmark, and Sweden). La Banca d'Italia is still responsible for controlling domestic inflation and balance of payments pressures.

In March 1979, Italy became a founder member of the European Monetary System (EMS) and its Exchange Rate Mechanism (ERM). During the first 10 years of its membership, the lira was allowed to diverge by up to 6% against other member currencies before action had to be taken, compared with 2.25% for other ERM currencies. Uncertainty about Italy's ability to meet the convergence targets of the 1992 Treaty for European Union (Maastricht) for inflation, interest rates, and participation to stabilize the rate, the lira was withdrawn from the ERM in September 1992, after which the lira declined. At the beginning of 1996 it began to appreciate again. The introduction of the euro in 2002, however, made all that irrelevant.

The most important stock exchange, known as the Borsa Italiana, is in Milan (established in 1808). Following a June 2007 agreement, it became part of the London Stock Exchange Group. Through most of the 2000s, the exchange index hovered between 31,700 and 31,800. However, since the 2008–09 global financial crisis, the index has dropped significantly. After dropping to 13,032 in September 2009, the index hovered around 16,000 as of October 2011. A total of 291 companies were listed as of 2010.

In 2009, the discount rate was 1.75%. In 2010, the nation's gold reserves totaled 2,451 tons, the fourth largest holding in the world.

34INSURANCE

The insurance industry is government-supervised, and insurers must be authorized to do business. Automobile insurance was made compulsory in 1971, and coverage is also required for aircraft, powerboats, hunters, auditors, yachts, nuclear facilities, and insurance brokers. The insurance regulatory body is the Instituto per Viglanza sulle Assicurazioni Private di Interesse Collettivo (Institute for Control of Private Insurance Companies—ISVAP). European Union reporting and other insurance directives have been implemented.

The Italian insurance market was traditionally characterized by a relatively large number of insurers with no one organization dominating the industry. In 2010 the top insurance companies were Poste Vita, Mediolanum Vita, Assicurazioni generali, Allianz, and UGF Assicurazioni. The volume of life products has increased as consumers have become aware that the Italian Social Security System benefits will have to be supplemented by individual savings and as insurance awareness has increased through advertising campaigns and the distribution of insurance products through the extensive branch banking system. The Italian insurance market grew by 6.9% in fiscal year 2009, buoyed almost exclusively by an 11% increase in life products. The Italian government has placed additional solvency requirements on companies that require an increase in insurer assets by 2013.

35PUBLIC FINANCE

Reflecting increasing economic activity and the pressures of inflation, the Italian budget has expanded continually since 1950. However, the Italian economy has traditionally run a high government debt, and the 2008–09 global financial crisis has only exacerbated the problem. In 2010 the CIA estimated that the Italian budget included $940.3 billion in public revenue and $1.042 trillion in public expenditures. The public deficit amounted to 4.6% of GDP. Public debt was 118.1% of GDP, with $2.223 trillion of the debt held by foreign entities. During 2011 Italy was embroiled in a eurozone debt crisis that, in addition to Italy, focused on the troubled public finances of both Greece and Portugal. The Italian government passed highly unpopular austerity measures in an effort to lower its budget deficit, which ultimately led to the resignation of Berlusconi. Monti, his replacement, was a technocrat and revered economist chosen specifically to resolve Italy's ongoing public finance concerns.

³⁶TAXATION

The Italian tax system is considered among the most complicated in the world. During the late 1990s and early 2000s, the government used tax cuts to stimulate economic growth. On 1 January 1998 the government introduced the Dual Income Tax (DIT) system designed to encourage investment by taxing income derived from the increase in equity capital in a company at a lower rate than the standard corporate income tax rate. In 2003, the corporate income tax rate (IRPEG), at 36% in 2002, was reduced to 34%. As of 2011, the standard corporate rate was 27.5%, excluding a 3.9% regional tax (IRAP) on productive activities. Capital gains realized by companies are taxable as business income under the IRPEG and IRAP, and capital losses are deductible.

The schedule of personal income tax rates was reformed in 2003 to reduce tax rates and to increase the amount covered by the lowest income band. As of 2012, the individual tax rate progressively increases to a top rate of 43%. On 25 October 2001 Italy's gift and inheritance taxes were abolished by the legislature; they were reintroduced in 2007 and applied at rates between 4 and 8%.

Italy's main indirect tax is its value-added tax (VAT) introduced on 1 January 1973 with a standard rate of 12%, replacing a turnover tax on goods and services. Beginning in 1997 and continuing in 2012, the standard rate was levied at 20% and is applicable to most goods and services. A reduced rate of 10% is applied to some foodstuffs, certain fuel supplies, some transport and some housing, consumers, catering services and live animals. A 4% rate is applied to some foodstuffs, books, newspapers and periodicals, agricultural inputs, and medical equipment. Basic medical and dental services, as well as financial and insurance services are exempt from VAT.

³⁷CUSTOMS AND DUTIES

Italy's membership in the European Union has greatly influenced its tariff structure. Duties on imports from then-European-Community members and their dependencies were gradually reduced following the Rome Pact in 1957 and disappeared by 1969, more than a year ahead of schedule. Duties on goods from Greece, which entered the European Community in 1981, were reduced gradually and eliminated by 1986. Italy's adjustment of its tariff structure to that of the current European Union also has resulted in a substantial reduction of duties on products imported from areas other than the European Union, including the United States. Import duties remain on manufactured goods from non-EU countries, while raw materials enter mostly duty-free. Other import taxes include a value-added tax (VAT) that ranges from 0–20% depending on the product and excise taxes on alcoholic beverages, tobacco, sugar and petroleum products.

³⁸FOREIGN INVESTMENT

The government encourages foreign industrial investment, although investment has been discouraged by extensive labor laws, a heavy tax burden, and an inefficient public sector. The extent of the state's direct involvement in the economy has been greatly reduced by the privatization programs carried out by successive governments since 1993, encouraged by the EU demand that companies from member countries receive treatment equal to domestic companies. The World Bank reported that for Italy, the net inflows of FDI were approximately $9.6 billion in 2010. This is a modest number compared to inflows during the preceding decade. In 2006, net inflows of FDI totaled $39 billion, which increased to $40 billion in 2007. This was followed by a negative inflow of -$9.5 billion in 2008 and a positive $16.6 billion in 2009.

³⁹ECONOMIC DEVELOPMENT

Under Mussolini, business and labor were grouped into corporations that, in theory at least, jointly determined economic policy. Also, under the Fascist regime, direct government control over the economy was increased through the creation of powerful economic bodies, such as the Institute for Industrial Reconstruction. Although the corporative system disappeared after the fall of Mussolini, the concept of economic planning remained firmly implanted among the large Marxist parties, as well as among Christian Democratic leaders, who—by different means and for different reasons—sought to create a society free from the class warfare associated with a strictly liberal economic system.

Principal government objectives following World War II were reconstruction of the economy; stabilization of the currency; and long-term, large-scale investment aimed at correcting the imbalance of the Italian economy and, in particular, the imbalance between northern and southern Italy. The first and second phases of this policy were accomplished by 1949. Then the government, supported by domestic financial and industrial groups and by foreign aid, principally from the United States, embarked on the third and most important phase, best known as the Vanoni Plan (after former finance minister Ezio Vanoni). Notable in this development effort was the Cassa per il Mezzogiorno, a government agency set up to develop southern Italy and attract private investment to the region. Between 1951 and 1978, government spending on infrastructure in the south was $11.5 billion; additional low-cost loans totaled $13 billion, and outright grants amounted to $3.2 billion.

Simultaneously, direct government control of the economy increased through such government agencies as ENI, whose activities expanded rapidly in the postwar era. The nationalization of the electric industry, in order to lay the industrial base for a more highly planned economy, and the creation of the National Economic Planning Board composed of leaders from government, industry, and labor, were further indications of the importance attached to the concept of a planned Italian economy.

The combined effects of inflation, increased energy prices, and political instability posed serious economic problems during the 1970s. With Italy mired in recession in the early 1980s, economic policy was directed at reducing the public sector deficit, tightening controls on credit, and maintaining a stable exchange rate, chiefly through a variety of short-term constraints. A period of recovery began in 1983, leading to expanded output and lower inflation but also to expanded unemployment. The economic policy aims in 1987 included the reduction of the public-sector deficit and unemployment. Furthermore, improvement in the external sector (due mainly to the fall of oil prices and depreciation of the dollar) led to liberalization of the foreign exchange market in 1987.

Priorities of the early 1990s were cutting government spending, fighting tax evasion to reduce public debt, and selling off state-owned enterprises. At the end of the decade, the results of these policies were mixed. Liberalization provided the impetus for greater foreign investment, while the funds generated from privatization eased the public debt. Italy qualified for the first round of Economic and Monetary Union (EMU) and entered the euro zone in 1999.

During the 2000s, the strength of the economy continued to rest on the back of small- and medium-sized family-owned companies, mostly in the north and center of the country. In 2011 the burden of Italy's public debt came to the forefront of country's economy. The focus of economic policy has been on cutting taxes, fighting unemployment, enhancing competitiveness, and reducing both the budget deficit and debt. Reform of the pension system continues to be a controversial policy issue. Balancing fiscal austerity and policies to promote growth pose a major economic policy challenge.

40 SOCIAL DEVELOPMENT

Social welfare legislation in Italy, begun in 1898, was redesigned by law in 1952 and has subsequently been expanded. All workers and their families are covered and receive old-age, disability, and survivor pensions, unemployment and injury benefits, health and maternity coverage. The system is primarily funded by employer contributions, along with employee payments and some government subsidies. Family allowances are paid for primarily by employer contributions, and are determined by the size and income of the family. Conditions for old age pensions have varying conditions. The first maternity coverage was initiated in 1912.

Despite full legal rights under law, women face some social discrimination in Italy. On average, women earn less than men and are underrepresented in management, the professions, and other areas. Sexual abuse and violence remain a problem, although when reported, the authorities prosecute perpetrators and assist victims. Increased public awareness of sexual harassment and violence has increased the number of reported abuses. The government is committed to protecting and promoting children's rights.

Human rights are generally respected in Italy. Lengthy pretrial detentions still occur due to the slow pace of the judicial system, and occasional cases of the mistreatment of prisoners were reported. Discrimination based on race, sex, religion, ethnicity, disability, and language is prohibited by law.

41 HEALTH

A national health plan, begun in 1980, seeks to provide free healthcare for all citizens, but certain minimum charges remain. It is financed by contributions from salaries, by employers, and by the central government. Patients are still able to choose their own healthcare providers. Reforms in 1999 sought to integrate primary care with other health care programs, including home care, social services, and health education. Consistent health reforms are hampered by frequent political changes in administration. Most private hospitals have contracts with the national plan, but healthcare services are more highly concentrated in the northern regions of Italy. The shortage of medical personnel and hospital facilities in Italy's rural areas remains serious. In 2009 healthcare expenditures were estimated at 8.7% of GDP, amounting to $3,328 per person.

As of 2009 Italy had an estimated 42 physicians, 65 nurses and midwives, and 37 hospital beds per 10,000 inhabitants. The in-

fant mortality rate was estimated at 3 per 1,000 live births in 2011, with average life expectancy estimated at 81 years, the tenth highest in the world. The total fertility rate in 2011 was estimated at 1.4 births per woman. Maternal mortality was estimated at 5 per 100,000 live births in 2008, according to the World Bank.

In 2009 some 91% of children were vaccinated against measles. The major causes of death are circulatory system diseases, cancers, respiratory diseases, and accidents and violence. The HIV/AIDS adult prevalence rate was 0.3% in 2009.

42 HOUSING

Italy's housing and public building program was a major item in the general program of postwar reconstruction. Between 1940 and 1945, almost 20% of the habitable rooms in the country were destroyed. From June 1945 to June 1953, however, of the 6,407,000 rooms destroyed or severely damaged, 354,100 were rebuilt and 4,441,000 were repaired. Under a special housing program, originally instituted with funds from UNRRA and subsequently financed by employer and employee contributions, a total of 15 million rooms were constructed between 1953 and 1961, alleviating the nation's immediate housing problems. In 2008, the World Bank reported that 100% of urban homes had access to an improved water source. According to a 2008 study by the European Central Bank, home ownership in Italy (70%) continued to outpace the EU average. Additionally, mortgage debt, which averaged 39% of GDP across the EU, was only 10% of GDP in Italy.

43 EDUCATION

Education is free and compulsory for eight years (for students age 6 through 15). This includes five years of elementary school and three years of lower secondary school. Next, students may choose to attend a technical school, a vocational school, or one of several academic secondary schools, which offer a choice of specialized programs in classical, scientific, linguistic, and artistic studies. All secondary programs generally cover a five-year course of study.

In 2008 nearly all age-eligible children were enrolled in some type of preschool program. Primary school enrollment that same year was estimated at about 98% of age-eligible students, while secondary school enrollment was about 95% of age-eligible students. Tertiary enrollment was estimated at 67%. Of those enrolled in tertiary education, there were 100 male students for every 142 female students. Overall, the CIA estimated that Italy has a literacy rate of 98.4%. Public expenditure on education represented 4.3% of GDP in 2009.

There are 55 state universities and 23 other universities, colleges, and higher learning institutes, including the University of Bologna (founded in the 11th century), the oldest in Italy, and the University of Rome, which is the country's largest.

44 LIBRARIES AND MUSEUMS

Italy, with its rich cultural heritage, is one of the world's great storehouses of books and art. Among its many of libraries, the most important are in the national library system, which contains two central libraries, in Florence (5.3 million volumes) and Rome (5 million), and four regional libraries, in Naples (1.8 million volumes), Milan (1 million), Turin (973,000) and Venice (917,000). The existence of two national central libraries, while most nations have one, came about through the history of the country, as Rome was once part of the Papal States and Florence was the first capital of the unified Kingdom of Italy. While both libraries are designated as copyright libraries, Florence now serves as the site designated for conservation and cataloging of Italian publications, and the site in Rome catalogs foreign publications acquired by the state libraries. All of the national libraries are public. The Estense Library in Modena holds 425,600 volumes, including illuminated manuscripts from the 14th to 18th centuries. The university libraries in Bologna (1.1 million volumes) and Naples (750,000 volumes) each hold important collections. The Medici-Laurentian and Marucelliana (544,000) libraries in Florence and the Ambrosiana Library in Milan are also important research centers. Italy's public library system has about 84 branches and holds a total of 41 million volumes.

Italy, a world center of culture, history and art, has more than 3,000 museums. Among the more important are the Villa Giulia Museum and the National Gallery in Rome; the National Archeological Museum and the National Museum of San Martino in Naples; the National Museum in Palermo; the Galleria dell'Academia, and Uffizi, Medici, Pitti, Bargello, and St. Mark's Museums in Florence; the National Museum in Cagliari, Sardinia; the Brera Museum in Milan; the Museum of Siena; the Archaeological Museum of Syracuse (Siracusa); the National Museum of Urbino; and the Guggenheim Museum and the Academy and Libreria Sansoviniana in Venice. Venice also has the Jewish Museum, the Diocesan Museum of Sacred Art, a Natural History Museum, an Archeological Museum, and the Museum of Byzantine Icons. The Campidoglio Museum, the Museum of Villa Borghese, and the Palazzo Barberini Museum, all in Rome, each contain important works of art by Italian masters. Naples hosts the Museum of Ethnoprehistory of Castel Dell'ovo and museums of paleontology, mineralogy, anthropology, and astronomy. The National Museum of Science and technology in Milan has an extensive exhibit on Leonardo da Vinci, including models of some of the machines designed by the Renaissance man. A Goethe museum, with manuscripts and illustrations describing Goethe's travels in Italy, opened in 1997 in Rome. In 2012, after nine years of construction, the Museo Casa Enzo Ferrari opened in Modena, featuring exhibits that detail the history of the Ferrari auto industry.

45 MEDIA

Communication systems in Italy, including telephone, telex, and data services, are generally considered to be modern, well developed, and fully automated. In 2009 there were some 21.3 million main phone lines, and mobile phone subscriptions averaged 150 per 100 people.

Radiotelevisione Italiana (RAI), a government corporation, broadcasts on three channels. The other major media group is the privately held Mediaset, which has three channels. As of 2007 there were about 1,300 commercial radio stations. In 2010 the country had 23.1 million Internet hosts, with 49 Internet users per 100 citizens.

Major daily newspapers (with their political orientations and estimated circulations) are: *La Repubblica* (Rome), left-wing, 700,000 in 2010; *Corriere della Sera* (Milan), independent, 700,000 in 2010; *La Stampa* (Turin), liberal, 536,233 in 2010; as well as some 67 other major newspapers. *Panorama* is the most popular news weekly. Among the most influential periodicals are the pictorial weeklies—*Oggi, L'Europeo, Epoca, L'Espresso,* and *Gente. Famiglia Cristiana* is a Catholic weekly periodical with a wide readership.

The law provides for freedom of speech and the press, and the government is said to respect these rights in practice.

46 ORGANIZATIONS

Italian society abounds with organizations of every description. Many of these are associated with or controlled by political parties, which have their ideological counterparts in labor organizations, agricultural associations, cultural groups, sports clubs, and cooperatives. Among the most important organizations are the National Confederation of Smallholders and the General Confederation of Italian Industry, which strongly influences economic policy. The General Confederation of Agriculture, the General Confederation of Trade, and the General Confederation of Master Craftsmen also are influential. There are chambers of commerce in most major cities. There are labor and trade unions and professional associations representing a wide variety of occupations. A large number of professional organizations are dedicated to research and education in specialized fields of medicine or for particular diseases and conditions.

Catholic Action and the Catholic Association of Italian Workers are the most prominent of the religious organizations. The international religious Order of St. Augustine and the Society of Jesus (Jesuits) are based in Rome.

A number of political and religious organizations sponsor youth chapters. Scouting programs and chapters of the YMCA/YWCA are also active for youth. Sports associations are plentiful. National women's organizations include the National Italian Women's Council, the Italian Association for Women in Development, and the Italian Women's Center, based in Rome.

International organizations within the country include Amnesty International, Caritas, and the Red Cross.

47 TOURISM, TRAVEL, AND RECREATION

Among Italy's tourist attractions are the artistic and architectural treasures of Rome and Florence; the thousands of historic churches and galleries in smaller cities; the canals and palaces of Venice; the ruins of ancient Pompeii; the Shroud of Turin, reputed to be the burial cloth of Jesus; and the delicacies of northern Italian cooking, as well as the heartier fare of the south. Tourists are also lured by Italy's many beaches and by excellent Alpine skiing. Italians enjoy a wide variety of sports, including football (soccer), bowling, tennis, track and field, and swimming. Italy won the World Cup in soccer four times, in 1934 (as host), 1938, 1982, and 2006. Cortina d'Ampezzo, in the Dolomites, was the site of the 1956 Winter Olympics. Rome hosted the Summer Olympics in 1960. Turin was the host the 2006 Winter Olympics.

Tourism is a major industry in Italy. The *Tourism Factbook*, published by the UN World Tourism Organization, reported 71.7 million incoming tourists to Italy in 2009; they spent a total of $41.9 billion. Of those incoming tourists, there were 37.9 million from Europe. There were 2.23 million hotel beds available in Italy, which had an occupancy rate of 39%.

The estimated daily cost to visit Rome, the capital, was $646. The cost of visiting other cities averaged $283.

⁴⁸FAMOUS PERSONS

The Italian peninsula has been at the heart of Western cultural development at least since Roman times. Important poets of the Roman republic and empire were Lucretius (Titus Lucretius Carus, 96?–55 BC), Gaius Valerius Catullus (84?–54 BC), Vergil (Publius Vergilius Maro, 70–19 BC), Horace (Quintius Horatius Flaccus, 65–8 BC), and Ovid (Publius Ovidius Naso, 43 BC–ad 18). Also prominent in Latin literature were the orator-rhetorician Marcus Tullius Cicero (106–43 BC); the satirists Gaius Petronius Arbiter (d.AD 66) and Juvenal (Decimus Junius Juvenalis, AD 60?–140?); the prose writers Pliny the Elder (Gaius Plinius Secundus, AD 23–79), his nephew Pliny the Younger (Gaius Plinius Caecilius Secundus, AD 61?–113?), and Lucius Apuleius (AD 124?–170?); and the historians Sallust (Gaius Sallustius Crispus, 86–34 BC), Livy (Titus Livius, 59 BC–ad 17), Cornelius Tacitus (AD 55?–117), and Suetonius (Gaius Suetonius Tranquillus, AD 69?–140). Gaius Julius Caesar (100?–44 BC), renowned as a historian and prose stylist, is even more famous as a military and political leader. The first of the Roman emperors was Octavian (Gaius Octavianus, 63 BC–ad 14), better known by the honorific Augustus. Noteworthy among later emperors are the tyrants Caligula (Gaius Caesar Germanicus, AD 12–41) and Nero (Lucius Domitius Ahenobarbus, AD 37–68), the philosopher-statesman Marcus Aurelius (Marcus Annius Verius, AD 121–180), and Constantine I (the Great; Flavius Valerius Aurelius Constantinus, b. Moesia, 280?–337), who was the first to accept Christianity. No history of the Christian Church during the medieval period would be complete without mention of such men of Italian birth as St. Benedict of Nursia (480?–543?), Pope Gregory I (St. Gregory the Great, 540?–604), St. Francis of Assisi (1182?–1226), and the philosopher-theologians St. Anselm (1033?–1109) and St. Thomas Aquinas (1225–74).

No land has made a greater contribution to the visual arts. In the 13th and 14th centuries there were the sculptors Niccolò Pisano (1220–84) and his son Giovanni (1245–1314); the painters Cimabue (Cenni di Pepo, 1240–1302?), Duccio di Buoninsegna (1255?–1319), and Giotto di Bondone (1276?–1337); and, later in the period, the sculptor Andrea Pisano (1270?–1348). Among the many great artists of the 15th century-the golden age of Florence and Venice-were the architects Filippo Brunelleschi (1377–1446), Lorenzo Ghiberti (1378–1455), and Leone Battista Alberti (1404–72); the sculptors Donatello (Donato di Niccolò di Betto Bardi, 1386?–1466), Luca della Robbia (1400–1482), Desiderio da Settignano (1428–64), and Andrea del Verrocchio (1435–88); and the painters Fra Angelico (Giovanni de Fiesole, 1387–1455), Sassetta (Stefano di Giovanni, 1392–1450?), Uccello (Paolo di Dono, 1397–1475), Masaccio (Tomaso di Giovanni di Simone Guidi, 1401–28?), Fra Filippo Lippi (1406?–69), Piero della Francesca (Pietro de' Franceschi, 1416?–92), Giovanni Bellini (1430?–1516), Andrea Mantegna (1431–1506), Antonio dei Pollaiuolo (1433–98), Luca Signorelli (1441?–1523), Perugino (Pietro Vannucci, 1446–1524), Sandro Botticelli (Alessandro Filipepi, 1447?–1510), Ghirlandaio (Domenico Currado Bigordi, 1449–94), and Vittore Carpaccio (1450–1522).

During the 16th century, the High Renaissance, Rome shared with Florence the leading position in the world of the arts. Major masters included the architects Bramante (Donato d'Agnolo, 1444?–1514) and Andrea Palladio (1508–80); the sculptor Benvenuto Cellini (1500–1571); the painter-designer-inventor Leonardo da Vinci (1452–1519); the painter-sculptor-architect-poet Michelangelo Buonarroti (1475–1564); and the painters Titian (Tiziano Vecelli, 1477–1576), Giorgione da Castelfranco (Giorgio Barbarelli, 1478?–1510), Raphael (Raffaelo Sanzio, 1483–1520), Andrea del Sarto (1486–1531), and Correggio (Antonio Allegri, 1494–1534). Among the great painters of the late Renaissance were Tintoretto (Jacopo Robusti, 1518–94) and Veronese (Paolo Cagliari, 1528–88). Giorgio Vasari (1511–74) was a painter, architect, art historian, and critic.

Among the leading artists of the Baroque period were the sculptor and architect Giovanni Lorenzo Bernini (1598–1680) and the painters Michelangelo Merisi da Caravaggio (1560?–1609), Giovanni Battista Tiepolo (1690–1770), Canaletto (Antonio Canal, 1697–1768), Pietro Longhi (1702–85), and Francesco Guardi (1712–93). Leading figures in modern painting were Umberto Boccioni (1882–1916), Amedeo Modigliani (1884–1920), Giorgio di Chirico (b. Greece, 1888–1978), and Giorgio Morandi (1890–1964). A noted contemporary architect was Pier Luigi Nervi (1891–1979).

Music, an integral part of Italian life, owes many of its forms as well as its language to Italy. The musical staff was either invented or established by Guido d'Arezzo (995?–1050). A leading 14th-century composer was the blind Florentine organist Francesco Landini (1325–97). Leading composers of the High Renaissance and early Baroque periods were Giovanni Pierluigi da Palestrina (1525–94); the madrigalists Luca Marenzio (1533–99) and Carlo Gesualdo, prince of Venosa (1560?–1613); the Venetian organists Andrea Gabrieli (1510?–86) and Giovanni Gabrieli (1557–1612); Claudio Monteverdi (1567–1643), the founder of modern opera; organist-composer Girolamo Frescobaldi (1583–1643); and Giacomo Carissimi (1605–74). Important figures of the later Baroque era were Arcangelo Corelli (1653–1713), Antonio Vivaldi (1678–1743), Alessandro Scarlatti (1660–1725), and his son Domenico Scarlatti (1683–1757). Italian-born Luigi Cherubini (1760–1842) was the central figure of French music in the Napoleonic era, while Antonio Salieri (1750–1825) and Gasparo Spontini (1774–1851) played important roles in the musical life of Vienna and Berlin, respectively. Composers of the 19th century who made their period the great age of Italian opera were Gioacchino Antonio Rossini (1792–1868), Gaetano Donizetti (1797–1848), Vincenzo Bellini (1801–35), and, above all, Giuseppe Verdi (1831–1901). Niccolò Paganini (1782–1840) was the greatest violinist of his time. More recent operatic composers include Ruggiero Leoncavallo (1853–1919), Giacomo Puccini (1858–1924), and Pietro Mascagni (1863–1945). Renowned operatic singers include Enrico Caruso (1873–1921), Luisa Tetrazzini (1874–1940), Titta Ruffo (1878–1953), Amelita Galli-Curci (1882–1963), Beniamino Gigli (1890–1957), Ezio Pinza (1892–1957), and Luciano Pavarotti (b.1935). Ferruccio Busoni (1866–1924), Ottorino Respighi (1879–1936), Luigi Dallapiccola (1904–75), Luigi Nono (1924–1990), and Luciano Berio (1925–2003) are major 20th-century composers. Arturo Toscanini (1867–1957) is generally regarded as one of the greatest operatic and orchestral conductors of his time; two noted contemporary conductors are Claudio Abbado (b. 1933) and Riccardo Muti (b. 1941). The foremost makers of stringed instruments were Gasparo da Salò (Bertolotti, 1540–1609) of Brescia, Niccolò Amati (1596–1684), Antonius Stradivarius (Antonio Stradivari, 1644–1737), and Giuseppe Bartolommeo Guarneri (del Gesù, 1687?–1745) of Cremona. Bartolommeo Cristofori (1655–1731) invented the pianoforte.

Italian literature and literary language includes such luminaries as Dante Alighieri (1265–1321), author of *The Divine Comedy*, Petrarch (Francesco Petrarca, 1304–74), Giovanni Boccaccio (1313–75), Lodovico Ariosto (1474–1533), Pietro Aretino (1492–1556), and Torquato Tasso (1544–95). An outstanding writer of the Baroque period was Metastasio (Pietro Trapassi, 1698–1782), and Carlo Goldoni (1707–93) was the most prominent playwright of the 18th century. The time of Italy's rebirth was heralded by the poets Vittorio Alfieri (1749–1803), Ugo Foscolo (1778–1827), and Giacomo Leopardi (1798–1837). Alessandro Manzoni (1785–1873) was the principal Italian novelist of the 19th century, and Francesco de Sanctis (1817–83) the greatest literary critic. Among the Italian literary figures of the late 19th and early 20th centuries, Giosuè Carducci (1835–1907; Nobel Prize winner, 1906), Giovanni Verga (1840–1922), Gabriele d'Annunzio (1863–1938), Luigi Pirandello (1867–1936; Nobel Prize winner, 1934), and Grazia Deledda (1875–1936; Nobel Prize winner, 1926) achieved international renown. Leading writers of the postwar era are Ignazio Silone (Secondo Tranquilli, 1900–78), Alberto Moravia (Pincherle, 1907–1990), Italo Calvino (1923–87), Umberto Eco (b.1932), and the poets Salvatore Quasimodo (1908–68; Nobel Prize winner, 1959) and Eugenio Montale (1896–1981; Nobel Prize winner, 1975). Outstanding film directors are Italian-born Frank Capra (1897–1991), Vittorio de Sica (1902–74), Luchino Visconti (1906–76), Roberto Rossellini (1906–77), Michelangelo Antonioni (1912–2007), Federico Fellini (1920–93), Sergio Leone (1929–1989), Pier Paolo Pasolini (1922–75), Franco Zeffirelli (b. 1923), Lina Wertmüller (Arcangela Felice Assunta Wertmüller von Elgg, b. 1928), and Bernardo Bertolucci (b. 1940). Famous film stars include Italian-born Rudolph Valentino (Rodolfo Alfonso Raffaele Pierre Philibert Guglielmi, 1895–1926), Marcello Mastroianni (1924–1996), and Sophia Loren (Scicoloni, b. 1934).

In philosophy, exploration, and statesmanship, Italy has produced many world-renowned figures: the traveler Marco Polo (1254?–1324); the statesman and patron of the arts Cosimo de' Medici (1389–1464); the statesman, clergyman, and artistic patron Roderigo Borgia (Lanzol y Borja, b. Spain, 1431?–1503), who became Pope Alexander VI (r.1492–1503); the soldier, statesman, and artistic patron Lorenzo de' Medici, the son of Cosimo (1449–92); the explorer John Cabot (Giovanni Caboto, 1450?–98?); the explorer Christopher Columbus (Cristoforo Colombo or Cristóbal Colón, 1451–1506); the explorer Amerigo Vespucci (1454–1512), after whom the Americas are named; the admiral and statesman Andrea Doria (1468?–1540); Niccolò Machiavelli (1469–1527), author of *The Prince* and the outstanding political theorist of the Renaissance; the statesman and clergyman Cesare Borgia (1475?–1507), the son of Rodrigo; the explorer Sebastian Cabot (1476?–1557), the son of John; Baldassare Castiglione (1478–1529), author of *The Courtier*; the historian Francesco Guicciardini

(1483–1540); the explorer Giovanni da Verrazano (1485?–1528?); the philosopher Giordano Bruno (1548?–1600); the political philosopher Giovanni Battista Vico (1668–1744); the noted jurist Cesare Bonesana Beccaria (1735–94); Giuseppe Mazzini (1805–72), the leading spirit of the Risorgimento; Camillo Benso di Cavour (1810–61), its prime statesman; and Giuseppe Garibaldi (1807–82), its foremost soldier and man of action. Notable intellectual and political leaders of more recent times include the Nobel Peace Prize winner in 1907, Ernesto Teodoro Moneta (1833–1918); the sociologist and economist Vilfredo Pareto (1848–1923); the political theorist Gaetano Mosca (1858–1941); the philosopher, critic, and historian Benedetto Croce (1866–1952); the educator Maria Montessori (1870–1952); Benito Mussolini (1883–1945), the founder of Fascism and dictator of Italy from 1922 to 1943; Carlo Sforza (1873–1952) and Alcide De Gasperi (1881–1954), famous latter-day statesmen; and the Communist leaders Antonio Gramsci (1891–1937), Palmiro Togliatti (1893–1964), and Enrico Berlinguer (1922–84).

Italian scientists and mathematicians of note include Leonardo Fibonacci (1180?–1250?), Galileo Galilei (1564–1642), Evangelista Torricelli (1608–47), Francesco Redi (1626?–97), Marcello Malpighi (1628–94), Luigi Galvani (1737–98), Lazzaro Spallanzani (1729–99), Alessandro Volta (1745–1827), Amedeo Avogadro (1776–1856), Stanislao Cannizzaro (1826–1910), Camillo Golgi (1843–1926; Nobel Prize winner, 1906), Guglielmo Marconi (1874–1937; Nobel Prize winner, 1909), Enrico Fermi (1901–54; Nobel Prize winner, 1938), Giulio Natta (1903–79; Nobel Prize winner, 1963), Italian-American Emilio Gino Segrè (1905–1989; Nobel Prize winner, 1959), Daniel Bovet (1907–1992; Nobel Prize winner, 1957), Renato Dulbecco (1914–2012; Nobel Prize winner, 1975), Carlo Rubbia (b. 1934; Nobel Prize winner, 1984), and Rita Levi-Montalcini (1909–1989; Nobel Prize winner, 1986), and Italian-American Riccardo Giacconi (b. 1931; Nobel Prize winner, 2002).

⁴⁹DEPENDENCIES

Italy has no territories or colonies.

⁵⁰BIBLIOGRAPHY

Andrews, Geoff. *Not a Normal Country: Italy after Berlusconi*. Ann Arbor, MI: Pluto Press, 2005.

Baranski, Zygmunt G. and Rebecca J. West (eds.). *The Cambridge Companion to Modern Italian Culture*. New York: Cambridge University Press, 2001.

Ben-Ghiat, Ruth. *Fascist Modernities: Italy, 1922–1945*. Berkeley: University of California Press, 2001.

Binda, Veronia. *The Dynamics of Big Business Structure, Strategy, and Impact in Italy and Spain*. New York: Routledge, 2012.

Findlen, Paula (ed.). *The Italian Renaissance: The Essential Readings*. Malden, MA: Blackwell, 2002.

Gardner, Richard N. *Mission Italy: On the Front Lines of the Cold War*. Lanham, MD: Rowan and Littlefield, 2005.

Hearder, Harry. *Italy: A Short History*. New York: Cambridge University Press, 2001.

International Smoking Statistics: A Collection of Historical Data from 30 Economically Developed Countries. New York: Oxford University Press, 2002.

Italy Investment and Business Guide: Strategic and Practical Information. Washington, DC: International Business Publications USA, 2007.

Moliterno, Gino (ed.). *Encyclopedia of Contemporary Italian Culture.* New York: Routledge, 2000.

Opello, Walter C. *European Politics.* Boulder, CO: Lynne Rienner Publishers, 2009.

Political Chronology of Europe. London, Eng.: Europa, 2001.

Torriglia, Anna Maria. *Broken Time, Fragmented Space: A Cultural Map for Postwar Italy.* Buffalo: University of Toronto Press, 2002.

Wessels, Wolfgang, Andreas Maurer, and Jürgan Mittag (eds.). *Fifteen into One?: the European Union and Its Member States.* New York: Palgrave, 2003.

KOSOVO

CAPITAL: Pristina

FLAG: The national flag consists of a dark blue field with a gold-colored geographical shape of Kosovo in the center, with six white five-pointed stars arrayed in an arc above it; each star represents one of the major ethnic groups of Kosovo: Albanians, Serbs, Turks, Gorani, Roma, and Bosniaks.

ANTHEM: *Europe.*

MONETARY UNIT: The euro (€) is the official currency. There are coins of 1, 5, 10, 20, and 50 cents and 1 euro and 2 euros. There are notes of 5, 10, 20, 50, 100, 200, and 500 euros. €1 = US$1.371 (or US$1 = €0.72939) as of September 2011. The Serbian dinar, while not an official currency, is used in Serb enclaves.

WEIGHTS AND MEASURES: The metric system is in force.

HOLIDAYS: New Year (1 and 2 January), Orthodox Christmas (7 January), Independence Day (17 February), Constitution Day (9 April), Labor Day (1 May), Europe Day (9 May), Roman Catholic Christmas (25 December). Movable holidays include Roman Catholic Easter Monday, Orthodox Easter Monday, Eid al-Fitr, and Eid al-Adha.

TIME: 1 p.m. = noon GMT.

¹LOCATION, SIZE, AND EXTENT

Kosovo is located in southeast Europe in the central region of the Balkan Peninsula. The total land area is approximately 10,887 sq km (4,203 sq mi). The entire country is slightly smaller than the state of Connecticut. The landlocked country is bordered by Serbia on the N and NE, by Macedonia to the S, by Albania on the SW, and by Montenegro to the W. The total boundary length is 702 km (436 mi). There have been ongoing territorial disputes with Serbia, which does not officially recognize the independence of Kosovo.

Kosovo's capital city, Pristina (Prishtina), is located northeast of the center of the country.

²TOPOGRAPHY

The nation is encircled by mountains and hills, with the Kopaonik to the north, the Albanian Alps (Prokletije) to the west, and the Sharr (Sar) Mountains along the southern border. The capital city of Pristina is located within the eastern Goljak range. Gjeravica (2,656 m/8,714 ft), the highest peak in Kosovo, is located within the Albanian Alps. The lowest point (297 m/974 ft) is found along the nation's longest river, the Drini i Bardhë (White Drin), near the border of Albania.

The Drini i Bardhë extends for about 122 km (75.8 mi) through the western Metohija plain before entering into Albania. The Plain of Kosovo covers the eastern portion of the country. The Metohija and Kosovo plains are roughly divided by the central mountains of Cicavica, Drenica, Crnoljeva, Goles, and Milanovac Planina.

Other major rivers include the Sitnica, Lumbardhi i Pejës, Morava e Binçës, Lepenci, Ereniku, Ibri, and Lumbardhi i Prizrenit. The largest lake is the Gazivodë (Gazivoda), a reservoir along the northwest border with Serbia that covers a total of 11.9 sq km

(4.6 sq mi), of which 9.1 sq km (3.5 sq mi) lie within Kosovo. The reservoir was formed by a dam along the Ibar River. Other lakes include the Radoniq, Batllavë, and Badovc.

³CLIMATE

The climate of Kosovo is generally characterized as continental with hot, dry summers and cold winters. In the Dukagjini region of the west (including the Drini i Bardhë river basin), the climate is influenced by warmer air masses from the Adriatic Sea. Cooler annual temperatures prevail in some mountain regions. Average temperatures throughout the country can range from 30°C (86°F) in the summer to -10°C (14°F) in the winter. Average temperatures in Pristina range from about -1°C (30°F) in January to 20°C (70°F) in July. Annual precipitation ranges from about 60 cm (23 in) to more than 90 cm (35 in) in some mountain regions.

⁴FLORA AND FAUNA

Approximately 1,800 vascular plant species have been documented in Kosovo, with between 150 and 200 of these found only in the Balkan regions and about 13 found only in Kosovo. The latter include *Aconitum pantheri* (a type of hay) and *Saxifraga scardica* (a wildflower). Some of the common trees found in Kosovo include the plane tree, beech, white mulberry, black mulberry, acacia, laurel, ash-tree, Japanese robita, juniper (red fir), white pine, black pine, and chestnut. There are more than 40 mammal species found in the nation. Brown bears, wolves, foxes, wild goats, and roebuck are found primarily in the mountain regions, while rabbits, squirrels, and other small rodent species are found along the plains. There are approximately 225 species of bird, including big and small wildfowl, forest hens, and partridges. Eagles, falcons, and griffin vultures are also present, but rare. Trout, carp, and perch are among the most common fish species. There are also several species of frogs, salamanders, snakes, turtles, and lizards.

5 ENVIRONMENT

As of 2003, about 5% of the total land area was protected. The only national park is the Sharr (Sar) Mountain National Park, established in 1986 and located along the border with Macedonia. The park has been nominated as a UNESCO World Heritage Site, but such a designation may not be possible while the official political status of the state is challenged by Serbia. A second national park has been proposed (Prokletije National Park) in the Albanian Alps. The Mirusha River Gorge and the Germia Mountains are classified as protected landscapes (or regional parks)—the former for its natural pools and waterfalls, and the latter for its floral diversity, including 610 higher plant species and 83 species of fungi. There are 82 natural monuments treated as protected sites. These include caves, water features, and trees that have significant histories.

About 41% of Kosovo is covered in forest, but less than one-third of these forests are considered to be ecologically healthy, due to the poor management practices of the socialist-era forest products industry. The current forest industry is under state regulation through the Kosovo Trust Agency.

The Kosovo Environmental Protection Agency was established under the 2003 Law on Environmental Protection. Other institutions involved in conservation and management efforts include the Kosovo Institute for Nature Protection; the Ministry of Environment and Spatial Planning; Ministry of Agriculture, Forestry and Rural Development; and Kosovo Forestry Agency. In general, conservation efforts have been hampered by a poor economy, which translates into a lack of sufficient investment funds for environmental protection, limited research and data on existing resources, and few trained professionals involved in conservation efforts.

Pollution from aging power plants has been a major concern for the government.

6 POPULATION

The population of Kosovo in 2011 was estimated at 1,825,632. Approximately 6.7% of the population was 65 years of age or older, and another 27.2% of the population was 14 years of age or younger. There were 106 males for every 100 females in the country. The population of the capital city of Pristina was estimated at 198,214 in 2011.

7 MIGRATION

In the years preceding and including the Kosovo conflict (1998–99), hundreds of thousands of Kosovars left the country, both voluntarily and by force, to escape discrimination and violence at the hands of the Serbian government. It has been estimated that more than 800,000 ethnic Kosovar Albanians were forced from their homes by Serbian troops during the conflict. While most returned following the nation's independence (2008), widespread poverty and unemployment have prompted new waves of emigrants, particularly young adults seeking employment or improved lifestyles abroad. In 2009, the government estimated that about 30% of all Kosovo families had one or more members living aboard. Nearly 40% of these emigrants were living in Germany and 23% in Swit-

zerland. Others were living in Italy, Austria, Great Britain, Sweden, the United States, France, Canada, and Croatia.

8 ETHNIC GROUPS

About 92% of the population is ethnic Albanian. Ethnic Serbs are the largest minority group (accounting for about half of all minorities), while the Gorani, from the Gora region at the southern tip of Kosovo, make up the smallest group. Other groups include Bosniaks (Bosnian Muslims), Turks, Roma, Ashkali, and Egyptians.

The Roma, Ashkali, and Egyptians are often referred to collectively by the government as the RAE community. All three groups share common Roma (gypsy) origins and generally similar traditions and cultures. The Ashkali are sometimes referred to as Albanized Roma, or those of the Roma who aligned themselves with Albania before and after the Kosovo conflict. The Egyptians, sometimes referred to as Balkan Egyptians, are those who are considered to be Roma by outsiders, but identify themselves as being of Egyptian (African) heritage. Many of the Egyptians are also aligned with Albania. While members of the Roma, Ashkali, and Egyptian communities are provided a voice in the national government (with four seats reserved in the assembly), these minorities have reported numerous incidents of social and economic discrimination. Their standard of living is generally lower than that of other Kosovars, with many lacking access to basic health care and education.

The Serbs have also reported incidents of discrimination from the Albanian majority in employment, education, and social services. There have been reports of violent clashes between Serbs and Albanians throughout the country.

The Gorani, though located along the border region with Albania, have been loyal to Serbia, which has inspired a certain amount of enmity against the group from the Kosovar Albanians.

On major attempt to reconcile the various ethnic communities is the constitutional provision for the establishment of the Consultative Council for Communities in Kosovo. This body, which meets on a regular basis, consists of members from the various ethnic communities and serves as an advisory council for the president in addressing the needs and concerns of the communities. The council members are typically leaders from civil and political organizations within their respective communities.

9 LANGUAGES

Albanian and Serbian are official languages throughout the nation, though Albanian is most widely known and used. The Gheg dialect of Albanian is widely used in common speech, while standard Albanian (based on the Tosk dialect) is most often used in official settings and by the media. Bosnian and Turkish are official languages in the municipalities of Prizren, Peja, Dragas, Pristina, and Gnjilane. Roma languages are also allowed official status at the municipal level.

10 RELIGIONS

Islam, the predominant religion, is practiced by a majority of the ethnic Albanians and many members of the minority communi-

LOCATION: 43°12′ to 41°55′ N; 20°4′ to 21°44′ E. BOUNDARY LENGTHS: Albania, 112 kilometers (70 miles); Macedonia, 159 kilometers (99 miles); Montenegro, 79 kilometers (49 miles); Serbia, 352 kilometers (219 miles).

ties. The ethnic Serbs, however, are primarily Serbian Orthodox, which is the largest Christian denomination in the nation.

The Hanafi school of Sunni Islam is the predominant sect. The largest and most famous Sufi group in Kosovo is the Bektashi Order, which is affiliated with Shi'a Islam but differs in some practices.

Roman Catholics and Protestants each constitute less than 5% of the population. Both Muslim and Christian holidays are officially observed. The constitution provides for freedom of religion.

11 TRANSPORTATION

In 2009, Kosovo had 1,926 km (1,197 mi) of roadways, of which 1,668 km (1,036 mi) were paved. Railways included 430 km (267 mi) of standard gauge track in 2007. In 2010, there were eight airports, four of which had paved runways. There were also two heliports.

12 HISTORY

The region that is now Kosovo was part of the Roman and Byzantine Empires before becoming a part of the Serbian Empire in the 14th century. The Serbs were soon defeated by the Ottomans at the Battle of Kosovo in 1389. During the next five centuries of Ottoman rule, the Albanians slowly but steadily migrated into the area, so that by the end of the 19th century, they were the dominant ethnic group. The region came under Serbian control again during the First Balkan War of 1912.

In 1943, Serbia joined with the republics of Bosnia and Herzegovina, Croatia, Macedonia, Montenegro, and Slovenia to form the Socialist Federal Republic of Yugoslavia. At that time, Kosovo gained status as an autonomous Muslim Albanian province of Serbia.

A few years later, after World War II, Kosovar Albanians became more assertive in their call for a republic of their own, since they comprised about 80% of Kosovo's population. At the same time, Serbian nationalists were striving for a more unified Serbia.

In 1989, Slobodan Milosevic, the head of the Communist Party in Serbia, rose to power as president of Serbia, in part on a promise to reign in the Albanian nationalists. He made good on this promise by pushing through a new constitution that stripped Kosovo of its autonomous status. But the fervor of Albanian nationalism persisted. As the federation of Yugoslavia began to unravel, the cause of Kosovar independence grew stronger. Kosovar Albanians began to organize their own political parties, with one of the strongest being the Democratic League of Kosovo led by Ibrahim Rugova. On 2 July 1990, the adjourned Kosovo assembly adopted a declaration proclaiming Kosovo an independent nation. Though this status was not internationally recognized at the time, Ibrahim Rugova was elected as the first president of the unofficial government in 1992.

Rugova's initial approach of passive resistance to gain international approval for the cause of independence was not widely accepted, particularly as Milosevic began his own campaign of repression against the Kosovar Albanians in efforts to keep them under control. This dissatisfaction with Rugova's administration led to the formation of the militant Kosovo Liberation Army. The civil war between the Serbs and the Kosovar Albanians (referred to as the Kosovo conflict or Kosovo War) began in 1998, as Milosevic (who had become president of Yugoslavia in 1997) initiated a brutal military campaign resulting in numerous deaths and the displacement of more than 800,000 Kosovar Albanians. The conflict drew international attention, resulting in military intervention by the North Atlantic Treaty Organization (NATO) beginning 24 March 1999. On 3 June, Milosevic accepted a peace plan that forced Serbian and Yugoslav troops from Kosovo. On 10 June, Kosovo was placed under the administration of the United Nations Interim Administration Mission in Kosovo (UNMIK) through Security Council Resolution 1244.

Under UNMIK administration, Kosovo held its first multiparty parliamentary elections in 2001, creating a coalition government between the Democratic Party of Kosovo (PDK) and the Democratic League of Kosovo (LDK). Bajram Rexhepi of the PDK was chosen as prime minister and Ibrahim Rugova of the LDK as president. Within the next few years, municipal and centralized government institutions were established, as was a multiethnic Kosovo Police Service.

In 2005, the UN appointed former Finnish president Martti Ahtisaari as a special envoy to work with leaders from Serbia and Kosovo to establish a process that would lead to Kosovar independence. The resulting Ahtisaari Process considered numerous issues involved in creating a sustainable democratic government and securing equal rights and protections for the Serbs and other ethnic minorities within Kosovo. The process was not approved by Serbia or by the Russian contingency of the UN Security Council. Regardless, Kosovo declared independence on 17 February 2008, with a promise to embrace the Ahtisaari Process in forming its new government. A new constitution was adopted in April and came into force on 15 June 2008.

Serbia continued to refuse to recognize Kosovo as a sovereign state and filed a lawsuit with the International Court of Justice, arguing that the Kosovar declaration of independence was a violation of international law. In July 2010, the court concluded that Kosovo's declaration of independence was not in violation of the law; however, the court's published decision was viewed as rather ambiguous by the international community. The court addressed only the issue of the declaration's legality, without making any final determination as to whether Kosovo could or should be recognized as an independent state. For the Serbian government, the court's assertion that the declaration of independence was not illegal was seen as a far cry from saying that the nation had earned the legal status of independence. When the decision was announced, the president of Serbia renewed his claim that the Serbian government would never recognize the independence of Kosovo.

That stand seemed to soften somewhat when the matter was brought before the UN General Assembly in September 2010, resulting in one resolution that acknowledged the ruling of the International Court of Justice and another unanimously adopted resolution that paved the way for direct negotiations between the governments of Serbia and Kosovo. In accepting this new resolution, Serbia agreed to drop its demand to continue negotiations concerning the status of Kosovo. In so doing, Serbia essentially ended, or at least suspended, its fight to nullify the declaration of independence made by Kosovo, while still refusing to accept the declaration outright.

In March 2011, it was announced that talks between Serbia and Kosovo would begin under the sponsorship of the European Union. The initial proceedings were expected to address issues such as trade and travel between the two nations, since Serbia has continually blocked trade from Kosovo and there have been disputes over the use of airspace. Kosovo was expected to push for dialogue on issues concerning its own right to membership in international organizations, since Serbia has adamantly opposed any such steps that would signal the acceptance of national independence. EU officials were expected to promote compromise by pointing toward the eventual goal of EU membership for both nations.

In April 2011, Serbia's chief negotiator suggested that Serbia might be open to accepting Kosovo's independence, if its northern territory, which is largely Serbian, remained part of Serbia. Kosovo's government rejected this idea, stating that Kosovo must be preserved within its current borders.

13 GOVERNMENT

The constitution of 15 June 2008 established a parliamentary republic with a president as chief of state and a prime minister as head of government. The president is elected by the national assembly to serve a five-year term and may be reelected once. The president holds most traditional executive powers, such as leadership in foreign policy and the responsibility to approve or veto legislation, but also has the right to introduce new legislation and amendments to the constitution. The president appoints a candidate to serve as prime minister, who must then be elected by the assembly.

The unicameral assembly consists of 120 seats, of which 100 are filled through direct elections under an open-list proportional representation system. Twenty seats are reserved for ethnic minorities, with ten seats reserved for ethnic Serbs; four seats for representatives from the Roma, Ashkali, and Egyptian (RAE) communities; three seats for representatives of the Bosniak community, two seats for the Turkish community, and one seat for the Gorani community. Electoral law also requires a 30% quota for female assembly members. All representatives serve four-year terms.

Suffrage is universal beginning at 18 years of age.

14 POLITICAL PARTIES

The Democratic League of Kosovo (LDK) was founded by the Albanian politician and author Ibrahim Rugova in 1989 in response to the removal of Kosovo's autonomy by President Slobodan Milosevic of Serbia. The party played a leading role in organizing a 1992 referendum for self-determination. The Democratic Party of Kosovo (PDK–formerly known as the Party for the Democratic Progress of Kosovo) was founded in 1999 as a political offshoot of the Kosovo Liberation Army (KLA), which was also instrumental in the nation's fight for independence. While the PDK was founded with some socialist ideals, it has since aligned itself more closely with the center-right. The PDK and LDK have been the largest and most politically prominent parties since independence.

Other leading political parties include the Alliance for the Future of Kosovo (AAK), founded in 2000 by former KLA commander Ramush Haradinjai; New Kosovo Alliance (AKR), founded in 2006 by businessman Behgjet Pacolli; the Democratic League of Dardania (LDD), established in 2007 by former speaker of the assembly Nexhat Daci as a splinter group of the LDK; and the Independent Liberal Party (SLS), a Serbian party established in 2006. The Movement for Self-Determination (Vetëvendosje!), a left-wing Albanian party, became active in 2007. There are several other parties representing the various ethnic communities.

In the first parliamentary elections in 2001 (under the administration of the UN Mission in Kosovo), the LDK gained 47 seats in the assembly with 45.6% of the vote, while the PDK gained 26 seats and 25.7% of the vote. After some difficult negotiations, the two parties agreed to a coalition government with Bajram Rexhepi of the PDK as prime minister and Ibrahim Rugova of the LDK as president.

The first elections administered by Kosovo's own central elections commission were held in 2004. The LDK prevailed again with 45% of the vote and 47 seats, followed by the PDK with 28.8% and 30 seats. This time the LDK formed a coalition with the AAK, which won nine seats with about 8.4% of the vote. Ramush Haradinaj of the AAK replaced Rexhepi as prime minister. President Rugova died in 2006 and was succeeded by Fatmir Sejdiu of the LDK.

The 2007 elections brought the PDK and LDK in coalition once again as the PDK won 37 seats with 34.3% of the vote and the LDK won 25 seats with 22.6% of the vote. A large number of Serbs boycotted this election. Hashim Thaci of the PDK was chosen as prime minster.

In September 2010, President Sejdiu resigned from office after the constitutional court ruled that he had violated the law by maintaining his post as head of the LDK after accepting the post of president, since the president is not permitted to actively lead a political party while in office. He was replaced by a caretaker president, Jakup Krasniqi. As a result of Sejdiu's resignation, however, Sejdiu's LDK withdrew from the government coalition, leaving the PDK without a parliamentary majority. In November 2010, opposition parties quickly made a motion for a vote of no confidence, which narrowly passed with 66 votes out of the 120-seat parliament.

Following the collapse of the government, general elections were rescheduled for 12 December 2010. Preliminary results from this election placed the PDK ahead with about 33.5% of the vote and the LDK trailing at 23.6%. Although the election was generally noted as calm and fair, there were serious allegations of fraud made against polling officials in two areas that were believed to be heavily populated by Thaci supporters. Voter turnout in those strongholds was reported as 95%, which many considered to be suspiciously high.

In response, the central elections commission held a rerun of the election in several municipalities on 9 January 2011. The certified results published in February 2011 gave the PDK 32 seats, while the LDK earned 27 seats. The Movement for Self-Determination, running for the first time, won 12 seats, and the New Kosovo Alliance (AKR) received 8 seats. The PDK formed a coalition government with the AKR, and Behgjet Pacolli of the AKR was elected president in proceedings that were boycotted by the LDK and the Alliance for the Future of Kosovo. As a result of the boycott, opposition parties argued that there had not been enough members of the assembly present to take a legitimate vote. In March 2011, the constitutional court agreed that the two-thirds quorum was not met, marking the election as invalid. In April 2011, Atifete Jahjaga, an independent candidate nominated through a consensus of the PDK, LDK, and AKR, was chosen as the nation's first female president.

15 LOCAL GOVERNMENT

As of mid-2011 Kosovo was divided into 30 municipalities. However, the government expected to delineate eight additional municipalities pursuant to recommendations presented by the UN mandated Ahtisaari Process. Each municipality is governed by its own elected mayor and legislative council.

16 JUDICIAL SYSTEM

A law that went into effect on 1 January 2011 established a process of reorganization for the justice system, which has, since independence, been considered ineffective and prone to corruption.

According to the constitution, the supreme court of Kosovo is the highest judicial authority. At least 15%, but no fewer than three, of the judges in the Supreme Court must be from minority communities. The president of the Supreme Court is appointed by the president of Kosovo from among the judges of the court to serve a seven-year non-renewable term.

In 2010 there were 5 district courts, 25 municipal courts, 25 minor offense courts, and one commercial court. At least 15%, but no fewer than two, of the judges in any court with appeal jurisdiction must be from minority communities. Judges for all courts are nominated by the 13-member independent Kosovo Judicial Council and appointed by the president. This council is responsible for the recruitment, promotion, transfer, and general oversight of the judges. Judges serve an initial term of three years and are eligible for reappointment. Once reappointed, each judge may serve until retirement age.

A separate independent constitutional court of nine judges has final authority over matters pertaining to the interpretation of the constitution and laws that must be in compliance with the constitution. Constitutional court judges are nominated by the assembly and appointed by the president to serve a nine-year nonrenewable term. The president of the court is elected by the members of the court to serve a three-year term; however, election to this post cannot extend the original mandate of the judge. The constitutional court only hears matters referred by the assembly, the president, and the ombudsperson. A municipality may present a matter before this court if it relates to a government ruling that infringes upon the municipalities rights and/or revenues.

The right to appeal is guaranteed by the constitution.

17 ARMED FORCES

The NATO-led Kosovo Force (KFOR) began its peacekeeping mission in Kosovo in June 1999. Following independence on 17 February 2008, KFOR remained in Kosovo in continuation of its peacekeeping mission, with additional responsibilities of providing training and development of the new Kosovo Security Force, which replaced the former Kosovo Protection Corps in January 2009. In 2010, KFOR consisted of about 6,300 troops from 31 countries.

The Kosovo Security Force (KSF) is a professional, voluntary, multiethnic, lightly armed force trained to handle civil protection operations and emergency responses that require a higher level of force and authority than the Kosovo Police. The KSF is subject to civilian control through the Ministry for the Kosovo Security Force.

The Kosovo Police are under the authority of the Ministry of Internal Affairs. As of 2010, the Kosovo Police consisted of more than 7,200 police officers.

Additional assistance for local law enforcement and judicial operations (including training for police, judges, and prosecutors) has been provided through the European Rule of Law Mission in Kosovo (EULEX Kosovo) since December 2008.

18 INTERNATIONAL COOPERATION

As of 2011, more than 70 countries had recognized Kosovo as an independent nation. Kosovo became a member of the International Monetary Fund and the World Bank in 2009. Kosovo's prospects for membership in other international bodies, including NATO and the European Union, have been hindered by Serbia's refusal to accept Kosovo as an independent nation.

19 ECONOMY

At the end of the conflict with Serbia (1999), Kosovo began a slow but steady process toward a free market economy. However, economic growth has not kept pace with other European countries, making Kosovo one of the poorest nations in Europe. Initial growth was made possible by large sums of foreign aid designated for reconstruction and development through private investments.

The real GDP growth rate of 6.9% in 2008 dropped to 2.9% in 2009 as a result of the global economic crisis of 2008–09, but rebounded to 4% in 2010.

With foreign aid, the government was able to privatize about 50% of its previously state-owned enterprises by 2010. In that year, economic growth was primarily attributed to continued international assistance for reconstruction and the development of private small-scale retail businesses. The service industry was the strongest sector of the economy, accounting for about 64.5% of gross domestic product (GDP).

20 INCOME

The CIA reported that in 2010 Kosovo's gross domestic product (GDP) was estimated at $11.9 billion. The CIA defines GDP as the value of all final goods and services produced within a nation in a given year. The numbers reported here were computed on the basis of purchasing power parity (PPP) rather than on the basis of the rate of exchange.

The per capita GDP was estimated at $6,600 in 2010. The annual growth rate of GDP was estimated at 4%. For 2009, it was estimated that agriculture accounted for 12.9% of GDP, industry 22.6%, and services 64.5%. However, remittances from Kosovars in Germany, Switzerland, and Nordic countries account for about 13% to 15% of GDP and the government still relies heavily on international donors for financial assistance. The average inflation rate in 2010 was 3.5%.

In 2010 it was estimated that 30% of the population lived on an income below the poverty level.

21 LABOR

In 2009, the labor force consisted of 310,000 people. That year, the unemployment rate was estimated at 45%.

Labor laws established in 2010 call for a 40-hour workweek with 20 days of paid leave per year. The law also provides for a 12-month maternity leave. The minimum age for general employment is 16, unless the work is considered likely to jeopardize the health, safety, or morality of the individual, in which case the minimum age is 18. Special regulations allow for children to work beginning at age 15, as long as the work schedule does not conflict with mandatory schooling. In practice, child labor continues to be a problem for the nation. Although there is no legal minimum wage, a memorandum of understanding between the government, chamber of commerce, and associations of trade unions was signed in 2004 to set an unofficial minimum wage of $161 (€120) per month. In 2010, the average monthly salary was estimated at $308 for the public sector and $375 for the private sector.

By law, workers have the right to form and join unions, but reports indicate that some companies have threatened employees who choose to exercise this right. In 2010, the largest unions were the Association of Independent Trade Unions of Kosovo and the Confederation of Free Unions.

22 AGRICULTURE

About 53% of the total land area is agricultural land, with a little more than half of this land under cultivation. In 2010, agriculture was the largest employment sector (23.6%) and accounted for about 12.9% of total GDP. More than 80% of the agricultural land is under private ownership, consisting of relatively small operations. For 2008, vegetables and horticultural products accounted for about 40.5% of total crop output, followed by cereals at 23.2%, forage crops at 21%, and fruit at 7.2%. Wheat and spelt, rye, grain maize, tomatoes and potatoes are all significant crops. Grapes are a primary fruit crop. Wild berries and wild herbs, including oregano, chamomile, and mint, are harvested from the nation's forests for use in teas and medicinal remedies.

The nation is not self-sufficient in food production.

23 ANIMAL HUSBANDRY

More than 30% of the nation's agricultural lands are used for pasture of livestock, including cattle, sheep and goats, poultry, and pigs. Milk is the most important animal product, accounting for more than 90% of the value of all animal products in 2008.

24 FISHING

There is no significant commercial fishing industry in the nation.

25 FORESTRY

About 41% of the total land area is covered in forests. The current forest industry is under state-regulation through the Kosovo Trust Agency. The forestry industry is relatively small, but includes wood for fuel, wood processing, and wood products, such as flooring and furniture. However, the hope is that proper management and investment might turn wood processing into a significant growth sector for the economy.

26 MINING

Mining was a prominent industry for the region into the early 1990s, but most mining operations were shut down or destroyed as a result of the conflict for independence. Revival of the industry has been slow, primarily due to a lack of investment and the decline in demand that stemmed from the global financial crisis of 2008–09. In 2009, production of lead and zinc decreased by about 25% from 2008. Production of silica sand decreased by 76%, sand

and gravel by 47%, and marl by 33%. However, in 2009, production of limestone increased by more than 140% from the previous year. Bentonite and pumice also saw increased production. In 2009, mineral products made up about 14.8% of total exports.

²⁷ENERGY AND POWER

In 2009, total electricity generation was estimated at 4.77 billion kWh, while total consumption was estimated at 5.39 billion kWh. In 2005, proven reserves of lignite coal were estimated at 14.7 billion metric tons. There are no proven oil or gas reserves.

²⁸INDUSTRY

Kosovo's leading manufacturing industries, including production of metals and minerals, food processing, automotive components, and textiles, declined drastically as a result of the conflict for independence. This occurred first as factories were destroyed during the war or forced to shut down, then as international trade declined due to the effects of the global financial crisis of 2008–09. As of 2011, the mining and food processing industries had started to recover, but not nearly to prewar levels. The government is working to attract private foreign investment to rebuild its industrial sector. Target growth industries include mining, energy, construction, information technology and telecommunications, wood processing, food processing, and textiles.

²⁹SCIENCE AND TECHNOLOGY

The Department of Science and Technology within the Ministry of Education, Science, and Technology is responsible for the execution of government policies relating to research and innovation. Within this department there is a Center for Innovation and Technology Transfer, which has a mandate to support relations between science and industry. The Center for International Higher Education, Research, and Technology Cooperation is mandated to support the participation of Kosovar researchers in international programs.

Since independence, most research and development activity has occurred at the university level. With a weak economy, government investment in science and technology has been relatively low. In 2008, general expenditures on research and development were estimated at 0.1%.

In 2008 the National Research Council (sometimes referred to as the National Science Council) was appointed by the assembly to design the nation's first five-year plan for the promotion of research and technological development. The result was the National Research Program 2010–15, which sets forth five key objectives for the future: development of human capacity for research activities, development of research infrastructure, internationalization of scientific research activity, strengthening the links between science and society and economy for enhancing economic and social development, and promoting excellence in research and scientific activity.

Other national institutions supporting growth in science and technology include the Kosovo Academy of Arts and Sciences, the Institute of Albanology, Kosovo Institute of History, Institute of Pedagogy, and the National and University Library.

³⁰DOMESTIC TRADE

Many local importers serve directly as distributors and retailers of goods throughout the nation. Before independence, most retail establishments were fairly small, family-owned businesses. However, since independence many such business have partnered with foreign companies to open larger supermarkets, shopping malls, and other retail centers. A number of foreign retail franchises have also been established within the country, including Nike (USA) and Benetton (Italy).

³¹FOREIGN TRADE

According to a report from the Statistical Office of Kosovo, for 2010 the total value of exports was estimated at more than $420 million while imports were listed at more than $3 billion. Manufactured goods accounted for about 56% of exports and 20% of imports. Other export commodities included scrap metals, mining and processed metal products, leather products, and appliance. Machinery and transport equipment accounted for about 20% of imports. Other import commodities included food and livestock, wood, petroleum, chemicals, and electrical equipment. The European Union serves as the largest export market, with Italy alone receiving about 27.1% of all exports. Export partners for 2010 included Albania (10.4%), Macedonia (8.9%), Switzerland (6%), China (5%), and Turkey (3.2%). Member states of the European Union are the primary import partners, with Germany alone providing 13% of imports. Import partners for 2010 included Albania (14.8%), Serbia (12.1%), Turkey (7%), and China (6.3%).

Kosovo signed on as a member of the Central Europe Free trade Area (CEFTA) in 2006. The nation has also been designated as a beneficiary under the Generalized System of Preferences (GSP) program, which allows for free trade of some products shipped to the United States.

³²BALANCE OF PAYMENTS

With a strong reliance on imports, the nation has maintained a significant deficit since independence. In 2009 the total deficit was estimated at -$2.77 billion. For 2010, the deficit was estimated at -$2.72 billion.

³³BANKING AND SECURITIES

Since 1999, Kosovo has had two tier banking system consisting of the Central Banking Authority of Kosovo and eight private banks. Six of the eight private banks are under foreign ownership. Pro Credit Bank and Raiffeisen Bank of Austria hold the largest market share in the sector. There are also two pension schemes under authority of the central bank.

³⁴INSURANCE

The legal provisions concerning the operation of insurance companies are primarily designed to insure transparency. The Central Banking Authority of Kosovo is responsible for oversight of the insurance industry. In 2009, there were nine insurance companies operating in Kosovo, six of which were foreign owned. In 2007, insurance companies accounted for about 5% of total financial sector revenues.

The primary product within the sector is third party liability insurance, specifically automobile insurance. As of 2010, there were no laws requiring the purchase of vehicle insurance, and there have been reports that those who do purchase auto insurance have had difficulties filing claims and receiving compensation. In 2010, it was estimated that only about 30% of the damages caused by vehicles were covered by insurance companies.

35 PUBLIC FINANCE

The U.S. Central Intelligence Agency (CIA) estimated that in 2010 Kosovo's central government took in revenues of $1.458 billion and had expenditures of $1.581 billion. Revenues minus expenditures totaled approximately –$123 million. Public debt in 2009 amounted to 7% of the GDP.

36 TAXATION

The Tax Administration of Kosovo (TAK) has the status of an executive agency within the Ministry of Economy and Finance. It is responsible for implementing all provisions for the law on tax administration.

Personal income tax rates are based on annual earned salary and implemented at the following rates: 0% for income up to €960 per year; 4% between €960 and €3,000 per year; 8% between €3,001 and €5,400 per year; and 10% over €5,401 per year.

Corporate tax is paid quarterly, in advance, based on quarterly net income predictions. The following rates apply: €37.5 per quarter for annual income up to €5,000; 3% for income between €5,001 and €50,000; and 10% over €50,000 income.

A value added tax (VAT) of 16% is applied to all importers and businesses with an annual turnover in excess of €50,000. There is an exemption for certain agricultural and capital good products. Exporters receive a full VAT reimbursement for goods exported.

Property tax is set and collected by municipal governments, and is usually within a range of 0.05% to 1% of the market value of the property.

37 CUSTOMS AND DUTIES

A 10% customs tariff applies to most imports from most countries. A 1% tariff is applied for goods from Macedonia and Albania under the terms of a free trade agreement. An excise tax between 10% and 50% is applied to a number of products, including coffee, tobacco products, alcoholic beverages, and motor fuel. Kosovo became a member of the Central European Free Trade Agreement in 2006.

There are no internal duties or taxes on exports.

38 FOREIGN INVESTMENT

The government of Kosovo strongly encourages foreign investment as a means of rebuilding the economy. In 2008, foreign direct investment was estimated at about $518 million. Germany, Slovenia, Italy, and Switzerland have provided the most prominent sources of foreign investment. As of 2010, Kosovo was host to more than 2,000 companies of foreign or mixed ownership.

39 ECONOMIC DEVELOPMENT

Since the conflict of 1999, the government has relied heavily on international intervention to maintain a functioning economy. With imports exceeding exports by a wide margin for several years in a row, the trade deficit is significant. Poverty and unemployment are widespread, and many families rely on remittances from members abroad to afford basic needs. These factors and more have placed the government in a challenging position of finding ways to supply the most drastic current needs, while considering ways to secure a sustainable economy in the future, all with very limited resources.

The European Union has become a primary partner for economic growth and development as Kosovo has been included in the Stabilization and Association Process (SAP) for the Western Balkans. The EU provides macro-financial assistance grants directly to the government and also provides financing for the economic development pillar of the UNMIK mission.

Private sector development and encouragement of foreign direct investment are seen as major keys in developing economic stability and sustainability.

40 SOCIAL DEVELOPMENT

A base pension program, funded by the government, is available for all permanent citizens over 65 years of age. Supplementing this base pension is a personal savings plan, through which all permanent resident employees are required to make monthly contributions of 5% of their salary. Employers are required to provide a 5% match. These personal contributions are maintained in an account under the employees' names and are invested under the Pension Trust of Kosovo. Voluntary individual retirement plans are available, with oversight from the Central Bank of Kosovo.

A wide array of financial assistance is available for the families of war casualties. Benefits to these families include pensions, payment of educational fees and scholarships, reduced utility costs, and certain tax exemptions. War invalids, including any civilians or members of the armed forces who were wounded as a result of conflict, are also eligible for many of these same benefits. Disability benefits are not dispersed specifically to an individual, but are designed as financial assistance for the families that care for those who are disabled. Families must apply for benefits through local social centers.

Although the constitution prohibits discrimination based on sexual orientation, traditional attitudes persist against lesbian, gay, bisexual, and transgender individuals. Reports indicate that many of these individuals simply hide their sexual orientation out of fear of social discrimination. In some segments of the media, homosexuality is often portrayed as a mental illness.

Widespread poverty and unemployment have led to reports of violations and abuses of labor laws. From those who are employed, there have been reports of forced overtime without appropriate pay. Reports also indicate that some private sector employment is conducted without contracts, regular pay, or required pension contributions, despite laws that provide these benefits for employees. Violation of these laws may go unreported as employees fear dismissal. Forced child labor continues to be a problem, despite the implementation of child labor laws. Infringement of these laws is most common in rural areas, where children are kept from school to work on family farms or where families are so poor that children are sent work to supplement the family's income.

While the law provides for gender equality in the workplace, there is no specific law against sexual harassment in the workplace. Though there have been many reports of sexual discrimination, harassment, and abuse against women in the workplace, women's rights organizations claim that numerous incidents are not reported, as women fear retaliation from their employers or loss of employment. The female unemployment rate (55% of those unemployed in 2010) is typically much higher than the male unemployment rate and very few women are found in upper management positions. There is no law prohibiting women from inheriting property, but traditional customs favor men in matters of inheritance.

Although the law prohibits domestic violence, violence against women is considered to be a significant problem, with far more occurrences than are actually reported to the authorities. Rape is a criminal offense, but the law does not specifically address spousal rape.

41 HEALTH

The University Clinical Center of Kosovo (QKUK) in Pristina provides care at all levels and supports the regional hospitals in Prizren, Peja, Gjakova, Ferizaj, Gjilan, Mitrovica, and Vushtri. In 2009, the University Clinical Center had a total of 2,757 employees. The regional hospitals, in total, employed 416 physicians, 981 nurses, and 159 additional health associates. Additionally, each municipality has its own public clinic, or health house, offering some level of basic health care services. There are many private hospitals and clinics as well. Nationwide, in 2009 there were about 1,037 physicians employed in family medicine and 165 dentists.

In 2009 the total fertility rate was estimated at 2.3 children born to every woman of childbearing age. Average life expectancy in 2009 was 70 years. In 2011, the infant mortality rate was estimated at 9.7 deaths for 1,000 live births.

Two types of health insurance programs are available for citizens. Basic medical insurance is mandatory for everyone employed in the formal job market and for all natural and legal citizens. A number of groups qualify for free health care services under the basic insurance plan. These include all children under the age of 15 and all students until the end of their regular education; citizens aged 65 and older; war invalids and close family members of war casualties and war invalids; disabled persons; and citizens enrolled in other social assistance programs (along with their close family members). Private medical insurance is also available on a voluntary basis.

42 HOUSING

As poverty prevails, living conditions in Kosovo continue to be among the worst in Europe. During the Kosovo conflict (1998–99), more than 800,000 ethnic Kosovar Albanians were forced from their homes by Serbian forces. A 1999 assessment estimated that more than 120,000 homes (nearly 50% of the existing housing stock) were destroyed or severely damaged during the conflict, leaving large numbers of homeless and displaced persons. Immediately following the conflict, many Kosovar Serbians were forced from their homes by returning Albanians claiming original ownership. Reconstruction of homes in the years following were hampered both by poverty, as many could not afford to rebuild, and by the lack of clear property ownership title to land. The UNMIK responded, in part, by establishing the Housing and Property Directorate, managed by staff from the UN Center on Human Settlements (UN Habitat), which worked from 1999 through 2006 to establish a fair land and property ownership regulatory system and to ensure restitution for those who lost property during the

conflict. Authority over claim resolution for private immovable property, including agricultural and commercial property was transferred to the Kosovo Property Agency in 2006.

Preliminary results from the 2011 national census placed the number of dwellings at 403,459. About 71% of all dwellings were inhabited. Approximately 295,070 households responded to the survey. The average household consisted of 5.8 people. The 2011 census did not include a number of Serbian households in the northern regions of the country, who boycotted the census out of loyalty to Serbia.

43 EDUCATION

Primary and secondary education in Kosovo is free and compulsory from ages 6 through 15. Primary education covers grades one through five and lower secondary covers grades six through nine. By law, students have a right to attend classes in their native language through ninth grade. As a result, classes have been made available in five languages: Albanian, Serbian, Bosnian, Turkish, and Croatian. Special education classes are also available for qualified students. For the 2009/10 school year, there were about 307,090 students enrolled in more than 950 primary and lower secondary schools. About 1,355 of these students attended a private school. In the same year, there were about 17,393 teachers at this level of education.

Higher secondary education, while still free, is not compulsory. Students at this level may opt for a general (gymnasium) education program or a professional (vocational) education curriculum. General secondary studies offer a three or four year curriculum primarily focused on general skills and college preparation. Professional or vocational programs last from three to four years depending on the chosen curriculum. Generally speaking, a three-year program qualifies a student for immediate entry into the skilled workforce, while a four-year program allows a student to enter the workforce at a higher level occupation or to proceed to university studies. For the 2009/10 year, there were about 104,900 students enrolled in higher secondary education programs. About 1,295 of these students attended private schools. In that same year, there were about 5,565 teachers at the higher secondary level.

Preschool programs are available for children from ages one through five. In the 2009/10 school year, 24,033 students were enrolled in preschool. The academic year begins in September and ends in June. The average number of students per classroom is 35.

The University of Pristina is the only public university. It supports 17 faculties and offers bachelor, masters, and doctorate programs. Government scholarships and loan programs are available for qualified students. Private universities include the American University in Kosovo, AAB University, and European Vision University.

As of the 2007 census, the adult literacy rate was estimated at nearly 92%. For 2008, public expenditure on education was estimated at 4.3% of GDP.

44 LIBRARIES AND MUSEUMS

In 2009 the country was home to about 158 libraries (with a total of about 641,905 titles) and 18 major museums. The National Library of Kosovo was originally established as part of the University of Kosovo in 1970. A 2006 law called for the administrative separation of the National Library from the University Library

Center, though both are still found on the same campus in Pristina. There are municipal and regional libraries in Pristina, Prizren, Gjilan, Peja, Mitrovica, Gjakova, Ferizaj, and Albanik/Leposaviq. A library for the blind is located in Pristina. The Association of Libraries of Kosovo was founded in 1971 and serves as the only nationwide union of library professionals.

Notable museums include the National Museum of Kosovo, the Railway Museum of Kosovo, Ethnographic Museum (Emin Gjiku), all in Pristina; the Albanian League of Prizren Museum; and the Center for Contemporary Art in Pristina.

45 MEDIA

The state-owned Post and Telecommunications of Kosovo (PTK) was established in 2005 to provide a full range of telecommunication services. In 2010, mobile cellular phone service was provided by two companies, Vala, a subsidiary of PTK, and IPKO, a company owned by Slovenian Telecom. In 2010 there were about 135,000 mainline telephones and 1.15 million cellular mobile phones in use. In 2010 there were four Internet hosts with 350,000 Internet users.

In 2010 there were nine daily Albanian-language newspapers. In that year there were four national radio stations: two public and two private. There was one public television station and three private stations.

The constitution provides for freedom of speech and press.

46 ORGANIZATIONS

A variety of political and professional associations have been established within Kosovo. Some of the organizations that have been the most prominent in the political arena are the Council for the Defense of Human Rights and Freedom, the Organization for Democracy, Anti-Corruption and Dignity Arise, the Serb National Council, and the Speak Up (FOL) Movement. The Kosovo Rehabilitation Center for Torture Victims is a prominent voice for human rights.

There are several local youth centers and many organizations for youth interested in charitable service and educational opportunities. The YMCA has at least six operating branches and was instrumental in establishing the Kosovo Special Olympics. Youth scout groups are also available, and local sports clubs are open to all ages.

The Centers for Protection of Women and Children in Pristina and Mitrovica and the Kosova Women's Network are important organizations for the promotion of women's rights and gender equality. Kosovo Mental Disability Rights International and HandiKos are prominent organizations in promoting the rights of the disabled. The Center for Social Group Development works to meet the health needs of the lesbian, gay, bisexual, and transgender communities.

47 TOURISM, TRAVEL, AND RECREATION

Tourist facilities are limited in Kosovo and most foreign tourists visit as part of a tour group organized by foreign operated travel agencies. Visitors interested in cultural heritage sites can see the Serbian Orthodox monasteries at Gracanica, Decani, and Peja; the Church of Our Lady of Ljevis (an UNESCO World Heritage Site); the Imperial Mosque; the Prizren Fortress; and the Gazi Mehmet Pasha Hamam (a Turkish bathhouse). Some hikers and skiers are drawn to the mountain regions, particularly Sharr/Sara Mountain National Park, located along the border with Macedonia, and the proposed Prokletije National Park in the Albanian Alps.

The National Theater of Kosovo is located in Prizren, while Pristina is home to the National Ensemble of Songs and Dances of Kosovo "Shota."

Sports clubs for soccer and basketball are popular with residents, as are small local cafes and music clubs.

A passport is needed to enter Kosovo. No visa is required. Travelers might be asked to provide documentation stating the purpose of their visit. Those who wish to remain in the country for 90 days or more must register with the Directorate for Migration and Foreigners, which is located in the Main Police Headquarters in Pristina.

In 2011, the U.S. Department of State estimated the daily expenses for staying in Pristina at $211.

48 FAMOUS PERSONS

Ibrahim Rugova (1944–2006), an Albanian politician and author, served as the nation's first president and was regarded as the "Father of the Nation." Bajram Rexhepi (b. 1954) was the nation's first elected prime minister. Atifete Jahjaga (b. 1975), a former deputy director of the Kosovo police, was elected as the nation's first female (and the youngest) president in 2011.

49 DEPENDENCIES

There are no dependencies.

50 BIBLIOGRAPHY

Buckley, William Joseph. *Kosovo: Contending Voices on Balkan Interventions.* Grand Rapids, MI: William B. Eerdmans Publishing, 2000.

Herscher, Andrew. *Violence Taking Place: The Architecture of the Kosovo Conflict.* Stanford, CA: Stanford University Press, 2010.

Higate, Paul. *Insecure Places: Peacekeeping, Power, and Performance in Haiti, Kosovo, and Liberia.* New York: Palgrave Macmillan, 2009.

Judah, Tim. *Kosovo: What Everyone Needs to Know.* New York: Oxford University Press, 2008.

Mertis, Julie. *Kosovo: How Myths and Truths Started a War.* Berkeley, CA: University of California Press, 1999.

Perritt, Henry H. *Kosovo Liberation Army: The Inside Story of an Insurgency.* Urbana, IL: University of Illinois Press, 2008.

Schwartz, Stephen. *Kosovo: Background to a War.* London, UK: Anthiem Press, 2000.

LATVIA

Republic of Latvia
Latvijas Republika

CAPITAL: Riga

FLAG: The flag consists of a single white horizontal stripe on a maroon field.

ANTHEM: *Dievs, svēti Latviju! (God bless Latvia!).*

MONETARY UNIT: The lat (LVL) was introduced as the official currency in May 1993; US$1 = LVL0.5422 as of 2010.

WEIGHTS AND MEASURES: The metric system is in force.

HOLIDAYS: New Year's Day, 1 January; Good Friday (movable); Midsummer Festival, 23–24 June; National Day, Proclamation of the Republic, 18 November; Christmas, 25–26 December; New Year's Eve, 31 December.

TIME: 2 p.m. = noon GMT.

¹LOCATION, SIZE, AND EXTENT

Latvia is located in northeastern Europe, bordering the Baltic Sea, between Sweden and Russia. Comparatively, Latvia is slightly larger than the state of West Virginia, with a total area of 64,589 sq km (24,938 sq mi). Latvia shares boundaries with Estonia on the N, Russia on the E, Belarus on the S, Lithuania on the SW, and the Baltic Sea on the W. Latvia's land boundary length totals 1,150 km (713 mi). Its coastline is 531 km (330 mi). Latvia's capital city, Riga, is located near the southern edge of the Gulf of Riga.

²TOPOGRAPHY

The topography of Latvia consists mainly of central and eastern lowland plains enclosed in areas of uplands consisting of moderate-sized hills. The highest point in the country is Gaizinkalns (312 m/1,024 ft), located near the edge of the Vidzme uplands. The nation's longest river is the Daugava (Dvina); which begins in Russia and passes through both Belarus and Latvia in its course to the Gulf of Riga. The total length of the Daugava is 1,020 km (632 mi).

³CLIMATE

The country's climate is influenced by geographical location and by its closeness to the North Atlantic Ocean. The average temperature in July is between 16.8°C and 17.6°C (62–64°F). In January the average temperature ranges between -2.8°C and 6.6°C (31–44°F). The rainfall in the country is between 56–79 cm (22–31 in).

⁴FLORA AND FAUNA

One-half of the forests consist of pines, birch, and firs. About 10% of the total land area is covered in marshes, swamps, or peat bogs. Species native to Latvia are the wild boar, Eurasian beaver, and brown bear. The Baltic Sea coast is home to a significant population of seals. The routes of migratory birds pass along the Black Sea and over the country. In addition, The World Resources Institute estimates that there are 1,153 plant species in Latvia and that Latvia is home to 68 species of mammals, 325 species of birds, 7 species of reptiles, and 13 species of amphibians. This calculation reflects the total number of distinct species residing in the country, not the number of endemic species. In 2009 the UN reported that there are 21 threatened species residing in Latvia.

⁵ENVIRONMENT

Air and water pollution are among Latvia's most significant environmental concerns and are largely related to a lack of waste treatment facilities. In 2008 carbon dioxide emissions in Latvia totaled 7,819 kilotons. Cars and other vehicles account for a majority of the country's air pollution. Acid rain has contributed to the destruction of Latvia's forests. Latvia's water supply is perilously polluted with agricultural chemicals and industrial waste. The Gulf of Riga and the Daugava River are both heavily polluted. Water resources totaled 49.9 cu km (11.97 cu mi) while water usage was 0.25 cu km (0.06 cu mi) per year. Domestic water usage accounted for 55% of total usage, industrial for 33%, and agricultural for 12%. Per capita water usage totaled 108 cu m (3,814 cu ft) per year.

According to a 2011 report issued by the International Union for Conservation of Nature and Natural Resources (IUCN), threatened species included 2 types of mammals, 8 species of birds, 9 species of fish, and 9 species of invertebrates. Threatened species include the black vulture, the asp, the Eurasian beaver, the medicinal leech, the marsh snail, and the Russian desman. The World Resources Institute reported that Latvia had designated 1.04 million hectares (2.58 million acres) of land for protection as of 2006.

In 2010 Latvia committed to full enforcement of European Union environmental directives.

⁶POPULATION

The US Central Intelligence Agency (CIA) estimated the population of Latvia in 2011 to be approximately 2,204,708, which placed it at number 139 in population among the 196 nations of the world. In 2011 approximately 17% of the population was over 65 years of age, with another 13.5% under 15 years of age. The median age in Latvia was 40.6 years. Life expectancy at birth had risen to 73 years by 2009. There were 0.86 males for every female in the country. The population's annual rate of change was -0.597%. The projected population for the year 2025 was 2,100,000. Population density in Latvia was calculated at 34 people per sq km (88 people per sq mi).

The UN estimated that 68% of the population lived in urban areas, and that urban populations had an annual rate of change of -0.4%. The largest urban areas was Riga, with a population of 711,000.

7 MIGRATION

Estimates of Latvia's net migration rate, carried out by the CIA in 2011, amounted to -2.33 migrants per 1,000 citizens. The total number of emigrants living abroad was 272,600, and the total number of immigrants living in Latvia was 335,000. Some 250,000 Latvians fled Soviet occupation during World War II, and others were sent to Soviet labor camps. After the war many Russians moved to Latvia.

With independence in 1991, citizenship issues surrounding the large non-Latvian ethnic population became a problem. Only 55% were ethnic Latvians, 32% were Russians, 3.9% Belarusians, and 9.1% other. Immigration from other former Soviet republics came to 4,590 in 1992. A breakthrough came in 1998 when the Citizenship Law was changed, abolishing the annual quota of naturalizations and entitling children born after independence to automatically acquire Latvian citizenship upon request from their parents. A total of 51,778 persons emigrated when Latvia gained independence in 1991; almost all of them went to Russia, Ukraine, or Belarus.

8 ETHNIC GROUPS

According to 2009 estimates, the percentage of ethnic Latvians is about 59.3% of the total population. Russians constitute about 27.8% of the population, Belarusians make up 3.6%, Ukrainians account for 2.5%, Poles for 2.4%, Lithuanians for 1.3%, and others 3.1%. The Roma (Romani) population is estimated at 0.4% of the population, or about 8,000 people. Nearly half the Russians and Ukrainians lived in Riga, where Russians formed a majority of the population.

9 LANGUAGES

Latvian (also called Lettish), a Baltic language written in the Roman alphabet, is the official language; it is spoken by about 58.2% of the population. It is highly inflected, with seven noun cases and six verb declensions. The stress is always on the first syllable. There are three dialects. The macron is used for long vowels, and there is a hacek for "h." A cedilla adds the y sound. Education is now available in both Latvian and Russian, the latter of which is spoken by about 37.5% of the population. Lithuania and other languages are spoken by about 4.3% of the population.

10 RELIGIONS

Christianity arrived in Latvia in the 12th century, and the Reformation made Lutheranism the primary religious persuasion after 1530. After declaring independence from the Soviet Union in 1991, freedom of religion and worship was restored for the first time since 1941. The three largest faiths are Catholicism, Lutheranism, and Orthodoxy.

According to a 2010 report, Roman Catholics accounted for 22.7% of the population, followed by Lutherans at 19.7% and Orthodox Christians t 16.8%. Baptists, Pentecostals, and evangelical Protestants were significant Christian minorities. There were approximately 9,900 Jews in the country. Other religious groups include Old Believer Orthodox, Seventh-Day Adventists, Dievturi, Jehovah's Witnesses, Methodists, Muslims, Hare Krishnas, and Buddhists.

Freedom of religion is guaranteed by the constitution and this right is generally respected in practice. Though there is no state religion, eight religions are recognized by the government as traditional religions: Lutheranism, Roman Catholicism, Christian Orthodoxy, Old Believers, the Baptist Church, Methodism, Seventh-Day Adventism, and Judaism. All other religions are categorized as "new" religions. The government does not require religious groups to register, but those that do are eligible for some legal rights and benefits. There are some rights and privileges enjoyed only by the traditional religions. Roman Catholic and Protestant Good Friday, Easter Monday, and Christmas are observed as national holidays.

11 TRANSPORTATION

The CIA reports that Latvia has a total of 73,074 km (45,406 mi) of roads, of which 14,459 km (8,984 mi) are paved. There are 474 vehicles per 1,000 people in the country. Latvia's railroad system that linked the country's port cities with Russia. Railroads extend for 1,885 km (1,171 mi). More than 80% of railway use is for daily commuting. Maritime ports include Riga, Ventspils, and Liepāja. Ventspils is the terminus of the 750 km (466 mi) oil pipeline from Polotsk, Belarus. Latvia has approximately 300 km (186 mi) of navigable waterways.

There are 42 airports, which transported 1.3 million passengers in 2009 according to the World Bank. The principal airport at Riga has international air links to Helsinki, Stockholm, Copenhagen, and New York, as well as direct flights to Austria, Germany, Israel, Russia, and Belarus.

12 HISTORY

Germans, Poles, Swedes, and Russians competed for influence in what is now Latvia from the Middle Ages until the 18th century, when it was incorporated into the Russian Empire. During the 19th century, a Latvian nationalist movement arose, which by the early 20th century sought independence. The political chaos in Europe following World War I provided the opportunity for Latvia to break away from Russia's control.

On 18 November 1918 the independent Republic of Latvia was proclaimed. Moscow recognized Latvian independence in the August 1920 Soviet-Latvian treaty, and the new republic joined the League of Nations in 1922. Latvia prospered economically during the 1920s, and began to export dairy and grain products to Europe. During the 1930s, as tensions in Europe escalated, the Soviet government allied itself with the United Kingdom and France, which in July 1939 granted the concession that Soviet troops could move into the Baltic States in case an indirect aggression was made by Germany. Sensing that an alliance between the United Kingdom, France, and the USSR would leave Germany politically

LOCATION: 57°0′ N; 25°0′ E. BOUNDARY LENGTHS: Belarus, 141 kilometers (88 miles); Estonia, 339 kilometers (211 miles); Lithuania, 453 kilometers (281 miles); Russia, 217 kilometers (135 miles).

and militarily surrounded, the Nazi government decided to reach its own agreement with the Soviet government in August 1939. A secret protocol to the 1939 Nazi-Soviet pact assigned Latvia to the Soviet sphere of influence.

Soviet forces invaded Latvia on 17 June 1940, and Latvia was incorporated into the USSR. Thousands of Latvia's military and law enforcement officials were executed; political and social leaders were imprisoned. Latvian civilians were deported en masse to Soviet camps in Siberia; 15,000 alone were expelled on the night of 14 June 1941. The Soviets, however, lost control of Latvia to the Germans in July 1941, shortly after Hitler launched his attack on the USSR. Soviet forces recaptured Latvia in 1944. During the Teheran Conference of November/December 1943 between US president Franklin D. Roosevelt and the Soviet leader Joseph Stalin, it was agreed that the USSR would maintain control of the Baltic States, and this agreement was confirmed at the Conference of Yalta in February 1945.

Following World War II, forced collectivization of agriculture began another round of deportations in 1949, bringing the total number of postwar deportees to more than 200,000. The Soviet

policy of russification sought to replace Latvian language and culture with those of Russia. Freedom of speech, press, and religion was denied. For most of the 50 years of Soviet rule, political dissent was strictly forbidden.

Soviet president Mikhail Gorbachev's policy of glasnost and perestroika allowed Latvians to voice their long-suppressed desire for national self-determination. In June 1987 an openly anti-Soviet demonstration took place in Riga. In 1988 political activists founded the Latvian National Independence Movement and the Latvian Popular Front (LPF). On 23 August 1989 Latvians, Lithuanians, and Estonians organized a massive demonstration of Baltic solidarity. The LPF united independence forces and gained a majority in the elections for the Latvian Supreme Council in the spring of 1990. On 4 May 1990 provisional independence and a period of transitional rule were proclaimed.

On 21 August 1991—shortly after the failure of a coup against Gorbachev—Latvia proclaimed its full independence. The first post-independence elections for the new Saeima (parliament) were held on 5–6 June 1993. On 30 April 1994 the Latvian and Russian governments signed a series of accords calling for the withdrawal of nearly all Russian armed forces from Latvia by the end of that year. On 12 June 1995 Latvia, Estonia, and Lithuania signed accords with the European Union that were to eventually lead to full membership. A second parliamentary election the same year resulted in a legislature that was strongly divided between pro-Western and pro-Russian contingents. At the end of 1995 Andris Shkele, a former government official and businessman, became prime minister, heading a broad-based coalition cabinet. Shkele, who retained his post until 1997, balanced the budget and sped up economic reform, although his leadership style alienated many other politicians.

The Russian economic decline of 1998 decreased the market for Latvian goods and services, seriously hurting its economy and increasing unemployment. In October of the same year, Shkele's People's Party won a plurality of the vote in new parliamentary elections, but the former prime minister's personal unpopularity resulted in the formation of a minority government by a coalition that opted to exclude him. Latvia elected its first female president in June 1999, when Vaira Vike-Freiberga, a Canadian psychology professor of Latvian birth known for promoting Latvian cultural interests internationally, was chosen as her homeland's new head of state. She was inaugurated on 8 July 1999. One of her first acts as president was to veto new legislation that could have required the use of the Latvian language in government and business communications, thus further disenfranchising Latvia's large Russian-speaking minority, whose rights and status remained a problematical issue for the country as the new century began. In May 2002 Latvia changed its election law to omit a clause requiring parliamentary candidates to be speakers of the Latvian language, a provision seen as discriminatory to Russian speakers. The change improved Latvia's chances for membership in the North Atlantic Treaty Organization (NATO). Latvia joined NATO and the European Union in the spring of 2004.

In 2004 the language controversy emerged again as the government issued reforms to restrict the use of Russian language in schools. Two years later, legislation was passed to tighten language requirements for those seeking Latvian citizenship. If a candidate for citizenship is unable to pass a Latvian language test, he or she is denied citizenship. Without citizenship, the person cannot vote or get a European Union (EU) passport.

In February 2004 Prime Minister Einars Repse resigned after the government collapses. Indulis Emsis of Greens and Farmers Union became prime minister in new coalition. By October 2004 Prime Minister Emsis was forced to resign when the government collapsed over lack of a budget. Aigars Kalvitis becomes prime minister in December. In June 2005 the Saeima ratified the proposed EU constitution.

October 2006 saw another change in government leadership, when Aigars Kalvitis became prime minister after the general elections. On 31 May 2007 the Saeima elected Valdis Zatlers president, with 58 votes; Aivars Endzins received 39 votes. Zatlers took office on 8 July 2007. In December 2007 Prime Minister Kalvitis resigned amid a controversy over government corruption. His four-party center-right coalition held onto power, however, with Ivars Godmanis as the new prime minister. Godmanis had previously served as prime minister after Latvia regained its independence from the Soviet Union in 1991.

In March of 2009 Vladis Dombrovski became prime minister, leading a coalition of five political parties. Under Dombrovski, Latvia cut approximately $2 billion from their budget in 2009 and 2010 in the face of economic instability. The global economic crisis was the source of Latvia's economic problems in 2008. However, their economy had stabilized, especially when compared to other EU nations such as Greece which faced dire economic conditions by the end of 2011. Dombrovski remained prime minister after the 2010 election, in part due to his handling of the economy.

13 GOVERNMENT

The 1990 declaration of provisional independence reinstated the 1922 constitution. From 1990 to 1993, Latvia was in a state of transition and authority was held by the Supreme Council. The new Saeima (parliament) consists of a single chamber with 100 deputies. A party must receive at least 5% of the national vote to hold a seat in parliament. Deputies are elected to a term of four years by citizens over the age of 18.

The executive branch of government is made up of the president, prime minister, and the cabinet. The Saeima elects the president for a four-year term. Executive power lies with the prime minister, who heads the council of ministers (cabinet).

Only citizens of Latvia at the time of the 1940 Soviet invasion and their descendants were allowed to vote in the 1993 elections. This meant that an estimated 34% of the country's residents (primarily Russians) were ineligible to vote. A citizenship law passed in June 1944 restricted naturalization to fewer than 2,000 resident aliens a year. On 22 July 1994, bowing to domestic and international pressure, the Saeima amended the citizenship law, eliminating the quota system. Applicants need a minimum of five years of continuous residence; basic knowledge of the Latvian language, history, and constitution; and a legal source of income; they must also take an oath of loyalty to Latvia and renounce any other citizenship. Thus, the new citizenship law accelerates the naturalization process for the several hundred thousand Russian-speakers living in Latvia.

14 POLITICAL PARTIES

The Latvian Popular Front, established in 1988 to unite pro-independence forces, split apart after independence was achieved, giving way to a number of new parties, many defined by their stance on the status of the country's Russian-speaking population.

Following the October 2002 parliamentary elections, New Era, a new party led by former central bank head Einars Repse, won the most seats in the Saeima (26), followed by the For Human Rights in a United Latvia Party with 24, the People's Party with 21, the Alliance of Greens and Farmers with 12, Latvia's First Party with 10, and the For Fatherland and Freedom Party with 7. Repse was named prime minister, leading a coalition of New Era, Latvia's First Party, the Alliance of Greens and Farmers, and the For Fatherland and Freedom Party.

The parliamentary elections held 7 October 2006 resulted in the People's Party (TP) winning 19.5% of the vote and 23 seats; The Union of Latvian Greens and Farmers Party (ZZS) 16.7% and 18 seats, New Era Party (JL) 16.4% and 18 seats, Harmony Center (SC) 14.4% and 17 seats, First Party of Latvia/Latvia's Way (LPP/LC) 8.6% and 10 seats, For the Fatherland and Freedom/Latvian National Independence Movement (TB/LNNK) 7% and 8 seats, and For Human Rights in a United Latvia (PCTVL) 6% and 6 seats.

Valdis Zatlers of the Reform Party was chosen as president in 2007. Seats in the Saeima are somewhat fluid. By February 2008 People's Party (TP) had lost 2 seats, to hold 21; The Union of Latvian Greens and Farmers Party (ZZS) had lost 1 seat, to hold 17, Harmony Center (SC) retained its 17 seats, New Era Party (JL) had lost 4 seats to hold 14, First Party of Latvia/Latvia's Way (LPP/LC) retained its 10 seats, For the Fatherland and Freedom/Latvian National Independence Movement (TB/LNNK) had lost 3 seats to hold 5 seats, and For Human Rights in a United Latvia (PCTVL) retained its 6 seats, and independents held 10 seats.

In the parliamentary elections of October 2010, the center-right Unity coalition led by Prime Minister Valdis Dombrovskis of the New Era party gained 33 of the 100 seats in parliament with 31.2% of the vote. The Unity coalition includes members of the New Era, Civic Union, and Society for Other Politics parties. The left-wing opposition coalition Harmony Center won 29 seats with 26% of the vote, followed by the Union of Greens and Farmers coalition with 22 seats and 19.6% of the vote. The National Alliance and the For a Good Latvia Party each gained 8 seats with about 7.6% of the vote.

One month before the scheduled presidential elections of 2011, the incumbent Zatlers accused parliamentary members of supporting government corruption when the body stopped the national anticorruption bureau from searching the home of a parliamentary deputy who was under investigation. Zatlers followed the accusation by scheduling a referendum on the dissolution of parliament. His outburst resulted in an early presidential election in June 2011, in which Andris Berzins of the Greens and Farmers Union was chosen by 53 of 100 votes.

However, the referendum took place as scheduled on 23 July 2011, resulting in a vote of 94.3% in favor of the dissolution of parliament. In the September 2011 snap elections, the ethnic Russian Harmony Center (SC) won 28.4% of the vote, taking 31 seats. This marked the strongest ethnic Russian presence in parliament since independence. The newly formed Zatlers' Reform Party (founded by Valdis Zatlers) came in second place with 20.8% of the vote and 22 seats, followed by the Unity Party with 18.8% of the vote and 20, the National Alliance with 13.9% and 14, and the Union of Latvian Greens and Farmers Party (ZZS) with 12.2% and 12 seats. Andris Berzins, an independent candidate, was elected as president in June 2011. Valdis Dombrovskis has served as prime minister since 2009.

15 LOCAL GOVERNMENT

Latvia's local governmental structure is divided into two levels, municipalities (novadi) and cities. As of 2011 there were 109 municipalities, and 9 cities. The cities recognized as administrative units are Daugavpils, Jekabpils, Jelgava, Jurmala, Liepaja, Rezekne, Riga, Valmiera, Ventspils.

16 JUDICIAL SYSTEM

A 1991 constitution, which supplements the reinstated 1922 constitution, provides for a number of basic rights and freedoms. The courts have been reorganized along democratic lines. Regional courts were added in 1995 to hear appeals of lower court decisions. There are now district courts, regional courts, a Supreme Court, and a constitutional court. Judges appointed to the Supreme Court or constitutional court must be confirmed by parliament.

More serious criminal cases are heard before a panel consisting of a judge and two lay assessors. There is a provision for a 12-member jury in capital cases. The judiciary is independent; however, it suffers from a lack of personnel and training. In 1996 a seven-member constitutional court was established with power to hear cases at the request of the president, the cabinet, prosecutors, the Supreme Court, local government, or one-third of parliament members. The constitutional court may also rule on the constitutionality of legislation or its conformity with Latvia's international obligations.

17 ARMED FORCES

The International Institute for Strategic Studies reports that armed forces in Latvia totaled 5,745 members in 2011. The force is comprised of 1,058 from the army, 587 from the navy, 319 from the air force, 579 from the national guard, and 3,202 members of joint staff. Armed forces represent .5% of the labor force in Latvia. Defense spending totaled $391.7 million and accounted for 1.2% of gross domestic product (GDP).

Military service in Latvia is open to both men and women at least 18 years of age. Conscription was abolished in 2007.

Latvia assisted in UN and NATO operations in Bosnia, Serbia and Montenegro, Iraq and Afghanistan.

18 INTERNATIONAL COOPERATION

Latvia was admitted to the United Nations on 17 September 1991 and serves in several specialized agencies, such as UNESCO, FAO, IFC, the World Bank, WHO, and the ILO. The country is a member of the WTO, the Council of Europe, Euro-Atlantic Partnership Council, the European Bank for Reconstruction and Development, the OSCE, and the Council of the Baltic Sea States. Latvia joined the European Union and NATO in 2004. Latvia is an observer in the OAS and a member affiliate of the Western European Union. In environmental cooperation, Latvia is part of the Basel Convention, Conventions on Biological Diversity and Air Pollution, CITES, the Kyoto Protocol, the Montréal Protocol, MARPOL, and the UN Conventions on the Law of the Sea and Climate Change.

19 ECONOMY

Latvia has a relatively well-developed infrastructure and a diversified industrial base, which accounts for about 22% of GDP. Agriculture constitutes approximately 4.2% of GDP and centers around the cultivation of potatoes, cereals, fodder, and other crops, as well as dairy farming. The largest sector of the economy is the service sector, with wholesale and retail trade, transportation, financial services, communications, and real estate management the most important industries.

Latvia's GDP fell about 30% in 1992 due to a steep decline in industrial exports to Russia. However, by 1994 GDP rose by 2%. A banking crisis caused by the collapse of Latvia's largest bank (and some smaller commercial banks) inhibited economic growth in 1995. Difficulties in revenue collection and inadequate control over governmental spending led to a high budget deficit. As a result, GDP fell by 1.6% in 1995. GDP growth improved markedly during the mid- to late-1990s, but it slowed somewhat in 1999, due to the Russian financial crisis of the previous year. By 2001 its growth rate stood at 7.7%.

Latvia joined the WTO in 1999 and the European Union in 2004. Latvian governments in the early 2000s implemented strict monetary policies and liberal trade policies, attempted to keep budget deficits low, and tried to provide for a more competitive economic environment. Though the nation's economy increased by 50% between 2004 and 2007, the global financial crisis of 2008–09 hit Latvia hard. GDP fell by 10.5% in the last quarter of 2008. The manufacturing sector took a major hit, dropping by some 11%, with decreased demand for export products.

The real estate and financial sectors, however, were at the head of the crisis as the worldwide credit crunch hit. While foreign banks in Sweden and Denmark were primarily blamed, a run on the domestic bank, Parex, resulted in a government bailout of $353 million in November 2008. In turn, the government received a rescue loan of $2.35 billion from the International Monetary Fund (IMF) in December 2008, primarily in an effort to keep the value of the lat pegged to the euro. An additional $1.7 billion was loaned by the European Commission in July, again in attempts to stabilize the struggling lat. The two loans were installments of a larger $10.5 billion financing package offered by the European Union, the IMF, and other international lenders. In accepting the loans, the government was forced to make budget cuts resulting in a 10% decrease in state pensions and a 20% decrease in public sector salaries. While the cuts were controversial, the prime minister stated that they were necessary to keep the nation from bankruptcy. The government also wants to keep the lat strong, with hopes of adopting the euro by 2012.

The Latvian economy was one of the hardest hit in the European Union as a result of the global financial crisis. In August 2009 unemployment was estimated at 18.3%. That figure soared to 22.3% in March 2010, the seventh month in a row that Latvia had the highest unemployment rate in the European Union. The average for EU countries at the time was 9.6%.

The GDP rate of change in Latvia, as of year-end 2010, was -0.3%. Inflation stood at -1.2%, and unemployment was reported at 14.3%.

20 INCOME

The CIA estimated that in 2010 the GDP of Latvia was $32.51 billion. The CIA defines GDP as the value of all final goods and services produced within a nation in a given year and computed on the basis of purchasing power parity (PPP) rather than value as measured on the basis of the rate of the exchange based on current dollars. The per capita GDP was estimated at $14,700. The annual growth rate of GDP was -0.3%. The average inflation rate was -1.2%. It was estimated that agriculture accounted for 4.2% of GDP, industry 20.6%, and services 75.2%.

According to the World Bank, remittances from citizens living abroad totaled $591.1 million or about $268 per capita and accounted for approximately 1.8% of GDP.

The World Bank reports that in 2009, household consumption in Latvia totaled $16 billion or about $7,235 per capita, measured in current US dollars rather than PPP. Household consumption includes expenditures of individuals, households, and nongovernmental organizations on goods and services, excluding the purchases of dwellings. It was estimated that household consumption was growing at an average annual rate of 22.4%. The World Bank estimates that Latvia, with 0.04% of the world's population, accounted for 0.06% of the world's GDP.

In 2011 the World Bank reported that actual individual consumption in Latvia was 71.0% of GDP and accounted for 0.06% of world consumption. The World Bank also estimated that 17.6% of Latvia's GDP was spent on food and beverages, 14.9% on housing and household furnishings, 4.3% on clothes, 5.3% on health, 6.8% on transportation, 2.5% on communications, 5.8% on recreation, 3.3% on restaurants and hotels, and 4.8% on miscellaneous goods and services and purchases from abroad.

21 LABOR

As of 2010 Latvia had a total labor force of 1.178 million people. Within that labor force, CIA estimates in 2005 noted that 12.1% were employed in agriculture, 25.8% in industry, and 61.8% in the service sector.

Latvian workers have the legal right to form and join labor unions. As of 2011 about 15% of the labor force was unionized. Unions are generally nonpolitical, have the right to strike (with some limits), are free to affiliate internationally, can bargain collectively, and are mostly free of government interference in their negotiations with employers.

The minimum employment age is 15, and the mandatory maximum workweek is set at 40 hours. Latvian labor regulations also provide workers with four weeks of annual vacation and special assistance to working mothers with small children. Certain minimum standards of labor conditions are defined by law, although they are not effectively enforced. The minimum wage was $408 per month as of June 2011.

22 AGRICULTURE

Agricultural output declined by an annual average of 7% during 1990–2000. Privatization of agriculture progressed rapidly after 1991. By the beginning of 1993, over 50,000 private farms had been established, and many agricultural facilities were being privatized.

Roughly 29% of the total land is farmed. The country's major crops include grain, rapeseed, potatoes, and vegetables. Cereal production in 2009 amounted to 1.7 million tons, fruit production 17,658 tons, and vegetable production 170,928 tons.

23 ANIMAL HUSBANDRY

Before World War II (1939–45), Latvia was a prominent dairy producer; in the postwar period, the number of cattle, poultry, and pigs rose steeply. Milk production stabilized in 1995, after four years of decreases in dairy cattle and milk production.

The UN Food and Agriculture Organization (FAO) reported that Latvia dedicated 648,000 hectares (1.6 million acres) to permanent pasture or meadow in 2009. During that year, the country tended 4 million chickens, 380,200 head of cattle, and 383,700 pigs. The production from these animals amounted to 19,139 tons of beef and veal, 71,266 tons of pork, 46,844 tons of poultry, 34,892 tons of eggs, and 473,456 tons of milk. Latvia also produced 2,145 tons of cattle hide and 42 tons of raw wool.

²⁴FISHING

Nearly all the landings are from marine fishing. Principal species include sprat, herring, sardines, cod, and mackerel. In February 2005 the Latvian government banned the retail sale of salmon caught in the Baltic Sea and Gulf of Riga, due to levels of dioxin detected in tested fish. Fish packing is an important industry in Latvia. Latvia had 251 decked commercial fishing boats in 2008. The annual capture totaled 157,934 tons according to the UN FAO. The export value of seafood totaled $133 million.

²⁵FORESTRY

Latvia's forests and woodlands covered 2.9 million hectares (7 million acres), or approximately 47% of the total land area in 2000 (up from 24.7% in 1923). Before World War II (1939–45), the timber and paper industries accounted for 29% of employment; by 1990 the number had fallen to 9%, where it remained in 2009. In 1939 the timber industry contributed 53.5% to total exports; in 1990 wood and paper exports accounted for 2.2% of total exports. The timber cut in 2004 was 12,419,000 cu m (438 million cu ft), with 8% used as fuel wood. Production amounts in 2004 included: sawn wood, 3,920,000 cu m (138 million cu ft); particleboard and plywood, 394,000 cu m (13.9 million cu ft); and paper and paperboard, 38,000 tons.

According to estimates from 2009, approximately 54% of Latvia is covered by forest. The UN FAO estimated the 2009 roundwood production at 8.67 million cu m (306.3 million cu ft). The value of all forest products in 2009, including roundwood, totaled $949.5 million.

²⁶MINING

Latvia is dependent on imports for raw materials. Limestone (for cement) and sand and gravel mines are spread throughout the country. Ceramic clays, dolomite, and gypsum also are produced. Peat (taken from 85 deposits, for fuel) covered approximately 10% of Latvia's territory, with the heaviest concentration in the eastern plains. Tonnage production figures for 2009 were: peat, 1,163,803 metric tons, compared with 2,153,000 metric tons in 2008; and sand and gravel, 2,292,848 metric tons, compared with 2,222,504 metric tons in 2008. Production figures for cement that year totaled 300,000 metric tons; gypsum, 230,000 metric tons; and dolomite, 929,070 metric tons.

²⁷ENERGY AND POWER

Hydroelectric generated power is the source for the bulk of the electric power Latvia produces. In 2002 hydroelectric sources accounted for 63% of the power produced. However, Latvia's heavy reliance upon hydropower, means that in a dry year, the country is estimated to be capable of producing only around 60% of the power it needs.

As of 2009 Latvia had no known reserves of oil or natural gas, and no oil refining capacity. Thus the country must import all required gas and petroleum products, most of which comes from Russia. However, Latvia' territorial waters in the Baltic Sea are thought to contain as many as 300 million barrels of oil.

The World Bank reported in 2008 that Latvia produced 5.27 billion kWh of electricity and consumed 7 billion kWh, or 3,173 kWh per capita. Roughly 64% of energy came from fossil fuels,

while 6% came from alternative fuels. Per capita oil consumption was 1,979 kg.

In 2009 refined petroleum was consumed at a rate of 38,000 barrels per day, with imports averaging the same amount. Demand for natural gas in 2009 came to 54 billion cu ft, all of which was imported. Although Latvia did have recoverable coal reserves, it did not produce any in 2009, and imported a relatively small 138,000 short tons.

²⁸INDUSTRY

Latvia's industrial base has centered mainly on heavy industries such as chemicals and petrochemicals, metal working, and machine building. Major manufactured items include railway carriages, buses, mopeds, washing machines, radios, electronics, and telephone systems. Since 1995 output of buses has fallen, but there has been an increase in the production of transport vehicles and passenger rail cars. Base chemical production has also declined slightly, as demand for household detergents and fibers has fallen. Other important industries include paper, petrochemicals, mechanical engineering, and communications.

Prior to 1998 the food processing sector provided the largest portion of the country's manufacturing output. Following the 1998 economic crisis in Russia, that sector declined, as Latvia depended upon Russia for exports. As of 2002, however, food processing showed potential for growth. Although some 50 enterprises are excluded from privatization (including ports, the railway company, and the postal service), only a few large state enterprises had not been privatized as of 2002, including the Latvian Shipping Company (Lasco), and the electricity utility company (Latvenergo). Ninety-eight percent of former state-owned enterprises had been sold as of 2002.

In 2010 industrial production growth was an estimated 14.3% according to the CIA World Factbook.

²⁹SCIENCE AND TECHNOLOGY

Patent applications in science and technology as of 2009 totaled 114 in Latvia, according to the World Bank. Public financing of science was 0.61% of GDP.

The Latvian Academy of Sciences has divisions of physical and technical sciences and of chemical and biological sciences. Fifteen research institutes, most attached to the academy, conduct medical, technical, and scientific research. The University of Latvia (founded in 1919) has faculties of physics and mathematics, chemistry, and biology. The Riga Technical University (founded in 1990) has various engineering faculties. Both are in Riga, as are the Latvian Academy of Medicine (founded in 1951), the Riga Aviation University (founded in 1919), and the Stradin Museum of the History of Medicine. The Latvian University of Agriculture (founded in 1939) is located in Jelgava, and the National Botanical Garden is situated in Salaspils.

In 1987–97 science and engineering students accounted for 23% of university enrollment. By 2008 Latvia had 1,935 scientists and engineers and 543 technicians per million people actively engaged in research and development (R&D). For that same year, Latvia's expenditures on R&D totaled .61% of GDP. High technology exports in 2009 totaled $363 million.

Principal Trading Partners – Latvia (2010)

(In millions of US dollars)

Country	Total	Exports	Imports	Balance
World	19,881.3	8,817.1	11,064.2	-2,247.1
Lithuania	3,338.2	1,437.1	1,901.1	-464.0
Russia	2,598.4	1,432.9	1,165.4	267.5
Germany	2,103.6	775.1	1,328.4	-553.3
Estonia	2,018.4	1,193.1	825.3	367.7
Poland	1,323.1	442.8	880.3	-437.6
Sweden	967.4	554.4	413.1	141.3
Finland	830.4	278.3	552.1	-273.8
Netherlands	656.9	200.8	456.0	-255.2
Italy	632.2	172.5	459.7	-287.3
Denmark	604.3	340.7	263.6	77.1

(…) data not available or not significant.

(n.s.) not specified.

SOURCE: *2011 Direction of Trade Statistics Yearbook*, New York: United Nations, 2011.

Balance of Payments – Latvia (2010)

(In millions of US dollars)

Current Account		731.0
Balance on goods	-1,691.0	
Imports	-10,799.0	
Exports	9,107.0	
Balance on services	1,467.0	
Balance on income	85.0	
Current transfers	871.0	
Capital Account		470.0
Financial Account		-745.0
Direct investment abroad	-20.0	
Direct investment in Latvia	369.0	
Portfolio investment assets	-178.0	
Portfolio investment liabilities	-34.0	
Financial derivatives	-220.0	
Other investment assets	-875.0	
Other investment liabilities	214.0	
Net Errors and Omissions		114.0
Reserves and Related Items		-570.0

(…) data not available or not significant.

SOURCE: *Balance of Payment Statistics Yearbook 2011*, Washington, DC: International Monetary Fund, 2011.

30 DOMESTIC TRADE

The traditional, small, privately owned farmer's markets, bakeries, and dairies are still prevalent throughout the country; however, large supermarkets are making their mark in larger cities. Latvia's center of domestic commerce is in Riga. One of the country's first malls opened with major investment from a Finnish department store chain. The most widely demanded domestic services include dressmaking and repair; house construction and repair; and automotive servicing. As of 2002 privatization of previously state-owned companies and industries was nearly complete.

Electronic commerce (e-commerce) is growing rapidly in Latvia. However, most of this growth is occurring through local e-shops which prefer payment by cash or bank transfers. The main obstacle to e-commerce in Latvia is the reluctance of consumers to send credit card information over the Internet.

A value-added tax (VAT) is levied on most sales and services, although reduced rates of 5% and 0% are applied to certain products and services.

Office hours in Latvia are usually from 8:30 a.m. to 5:30 p.m. Monday through Friday. Shops are generally open from 9 a.m. to 6 p.m., and from 9 a.m. to 4 p.m. on Saturday. Banks are open Mondays through Thursdays from 10 a.m. to 6 p.m.

31 FOREIGN TRADE

Like most of the former Soviet republics, Latvia's trade was formerly dominated by the other Soviet states, but it has been relatively successful in achieving a wider range of trade partners. Latvia's major commodity exports include wood and wood products, metals, machinery and equipment, and textiles.

Latvia imported $9.153 billion worth of goods and services in 2008, while exporting $7.894 billion worth of goods and services. Major import partners in 2009 were Lithuania, 16.4%; Germany, 11.3%; Russia, 10.6%; Poland, 8.1%; and Estonia, 7.8% . Major export partners were Lithuania, 15.2%; Estonia, 13.7%; Russia, 13.1%; Germany, 8.2%; and Sweden, 5.7%. Imports included machinery and equipment, consumer goods, chemicals, fuels and vehicles.

32 BALANCE OF PAYMENTS

In 2010 Latvia had a foreign trade deficit of $255 million, amounting to 6.4% of GDP. The external debt at the end of 2010 was estimated by the CIA to be $39.55 billion.

33 BANKING AND SECURITIES

In 1991 banking matters were transferred to the Bank of Latvia from Soviet bank officials. Previously, Latvia had its branch of the Soviet State Bank (Gosbank). The central bank had the authority to issue Latvian rubles and regulate the commercial banking sector. There are many banks in Latvia, including the Baltic Transit Bank, Banka Atmoda, Latgale Stocj Commercial Bank, Latvian Credit Bank, Investment Bank of Latvia, and the Latvian Land Bank.

Latvia effectively exited the ruble zone on 20 July 1992. By early 1993 the Bank of Latvia introduced a national currency, the lat. The lat is now fully convertible for capital and current account purposes.

Latvia's banking sector has proved one of the country's most successful industries and also its most controversial. Riga has developed into an offshore financial center, offering numbered accounts and related services, and drawing in a substantial chunk of flight capital from other former Soviet republics. Owing to fairly liberal banking laws in the early 1990s, a large number of banks (54 as of May 1995) were established. Subsequently, capital and other requirements were progressively tightened. For existing banks, the minimum reserve requirements was raised from LVL100,000 as of 1995 to LVL1.0 million by 31 March 1998. As of April 1995 all banks had to be audited by one of the recognized international accounting firms. The stricter capital regime led to an inevitable attrition, with 11 banks losing their licenses between 1992 and 1995. Only some 15 banks made profits in 1994 and had adequate reserves. The audits also revealed huge losses at Baltija

Bank (Latvia's largest institution, with some 200,000 private depositors), which had been incurred as a result of systematic fraud. Latvian banks suffered heavy losses in 1999 as a result of the Russian financial crisis.

In February 1997 the Bank of Latvia gave its approval to the proposed merger between the Latvian Savings Bank and the United Baltic Bank of Riga. As a result of the merger, the state owns 75% of shares in the Latvian Savings Bank. The government's plans are to privatize the entity. Total assets of Latvia's 23 commercial banks were $5 billion as of June 2001. A run on the domestic bank, Parex, resulted in a government bailout of $353 million in November 2008.

In 2010 the commercial bank prime lending rate was 9.56%. The discount rate, the interest rate at which the central bank lends to financial institutions in the short term, was 4% in 2009.

34 INSURANCE

All of Latvia's insurers, foreign and domestic, must be licensed by the Superintendent of Insurance. Foreign companies entering the Latvian market will find that licenses are relatively easy to obtain, although each class of insurance offered must be approved by the Superintendent of Insurance. In Latvia, third-party automobile liability insurance is compulsory. By 2003 Latvian insurance companies held policies worth over $200 million.

35 PUBLIC FINANCE

Privatization is generally considered to be near-finished; although the government still owns a few key companies, most are in private hands, even the utilities, and the government is working to sell off its ownership of what remains in order to satisfy its commitments to the IMF.

The US Central Intelligence Agency (CIA) estimated that in 2005 Latvia's central government took in revenues of approximately $5.6 billion and had expenditures of $5.8 billion. Revenues minus expenditures totaled approximately -$243 million. Public debt in 2005 amounted to 12% of GDP. Total external debt was $13.2 billion.

In 2010 the budget of Latvia included $8.028 billion in public revenue and $9.863 billion in public expenditures. The budget deficit amounted to 7.6% of GDP. Public debt was 46.2% of GDP, with $39.93 billion of the debt held by foreign entities.

36 TAXATION

In 1995 Latvia replaced its profits tax with a 25% business income tax (BIT). Under amendments in 2001, the BIT rate was reduced to 22% for 2002, and to 19% for 2003. As of 2011 it stood at 15%, which applies to all businesses. Reduced rates for small enterprises were eliminated in 2004. Branches of foreign companies are taxed at the same rate as Latvian companies, but are eligible for the same deductions and allowances. For companies operating in Latvia, capital gains are included in corporate income and are taxed at the corporate rate. There is a 2% withholding tax for nonresident companies on proceeds from the sale of Latvian real estate. The withholding rate on dividends is either 0% or 10% depending upon whether the payer and receiver meet certain guidelines regarding residency. Withholding taxes on various forms of capital income may be reduced or eliminated according to the terms of bilateral double tax prevention agreements. Shipping companies (cargo

Public Finance – Latvia (2009)

(In millions of lats, central government figures)

Revenue and Grants	**3,825**	**100.0%**
Tax revenue	1,662.9	43.5%
Social contributions	1,166.7	30.5%
Grants	527.1	13.8%
Other revenue	468.3	12.2%
Expenditures	**4,668.4**	**100.0%**
General public services	558.1	12.0%
Defense	152.1	3.3%
Public order and safety	256.5	5.5%
Economic affairs	854.9	18.3%
Environmental protection	78.2	1.7%
Housing and community amenities	6.7	0.1%
Health	468.9	10.0%
Recreational, culture, and religion	100.1	2.1%
Education	558.2	12.0%
Social protection	1,634.8	35.0%

(…) data not available or not significant.

SOURCE: *Government Finance Statistics Yearbook 2010*, Washington, DC: International Monetary Fund, 2010.

or passenger) engaged primarily in international commerce may choose to be taxed according to a tonnage tax introduced in 2002. There are no local taxes.

As of 1995 Latvians pay personal income tax at a flat rate of 25% of taxable income. Taxable income is determined by lump sum deductions, and specific allowances for social security payments, donations to charity, hospitalization and medical expenses, and some school fees. There is also a property tax and a land tax.

According to the Investment and Development Agency of Latvia, the main indirect tax is Latvia's value-added tax (VAT) which had standard rate of 22% for most goods and services in 2011. A reduced rate of 12% is applied to medical (including veterinary) and hotel services, and water and waste collection services. A 0% VAT applies to exports. Exempted from the VAT agricultural services, insurance, rent on dwellings, as well as certain financial services and royalties from copyrights. There are also excise taxes levied on luxury products at rates ranging from 10–100%, customs taxes, and stamp taxes.

In February 2011 the government announced plans to raise the real-estate tax in an effort to increase the country's 2012 budget after damages from the world-recession. The revenue service signed agreements with eleven business associations to ensure that the tax increase was implemented as easily as possible.

37 CUSTOMS AND DUTIES

Latvia imposes a standard 22% VAT on imports. However, certain items qualify for lower rates of 0–9%. Tariff rates depend on both the type of good imported and its origin. Goods from countries with most-favored nation (MFN) status receive lower rates, usually 15% (but up to 45% for agricultural products), while goods from non-MFN countries receive slightly higher rates, usually 20% (but up to 55% for agricultural products).

Latvia has free trade agreements with Sweden, Finland, Norway, Switzerland, and Kyrgyzstan. US products receive MFN status. Latvia has also formed a free trade area with Estonia and Lithuania. In January 1995 a free trade agreement went into effect with the European Union, which reduced tariffs on most industrial products to zero and set a schedule on tariff reductions over a course of five years for certain agricultural products. Latvia joined the World Trade Organization in February 1999.

38 FOREIGN INVESTMENT

In November 1991 a foreign investment act was passed permitting joint ventures in the form of either public or private limited companies. Businesses that are at least 30% foreign-owned receive a two-year tax holiday and a 50% tax abatement for the following two years.

At the end of 1995 foreign direct investment (FDI) in Latvia totaled $521 million, based on registered statutory capital. The largest investors were Denmark (26.1%), Russia (19.4%), the United States (13.5%), Germany (6.4%), the United Kingdom (5.2%), and the Netherlands (4.2%). Finland and Sweden were also significant investors. Industry accounted for only 17% of all foreign investment and there were approximately 5,200 firms with a foreign capital share.

FDI inflow into Latvia reached $521 million in 1997, averaging $400 million a year 1996 to 2000, but fell sharply in the global economic downturn of 2001 to less than $201 million. From 1995 to 2001 Latvia stock of FDI nearly quadrupled, reaching $2.3 billion in 2001. In the period 1988 to 1990 Latvia's share of world FDI inflows was almost five times its share of world GDP, but for the period 1998 to 2000 Latvia's share of FDI inflows was only 60% greater than its share of world GDP.

The leading sources of FDI from 1996 to 2001 were the United States (13%), Germany(11%), and Demark (11%). The primary destinations of foreign investment inflow were trade (22%), finance (16%), and business services, especially real estate (16%). The largest foreign affiliate is the telecommunications company Lattelekom SA of Finland. The largest foreign bank invested is Hansabanka SA of Estonia. FDI in Latvia was a net inflow of $93.5 million in 2009 according to World Bank figures. FDI represented 0.36% of GDP. However, FDI increased to $338.6 million in 2010, showing increased confidence in Latvia's economic status.

39 ECONOMIC DEVELOPMENT

The government began introducing economic reforms in 1990 to effect the transition to a market-driven economy. Individual and family-owned businesses, cooperatives, and privately and publicly held companies are now permitted. The privatization process was simplified with a 1994 law that created the Privatization Agency (PA) and the State Property Fund. Distribution of privatization vouchers was completed by March 1995, with certificates valued at LVL2.8 billion distributed to 2.2 million Latvians.

The privatization program focuses on international tenders and public offerings of shares. By mid-1994, 450 state enterprises had been transferred for privatization. The first international tender of 45 enterprises came in November 1994, followed by 80 more in 1995. Large-scale privatization began in 1996 and continued into the beginning of the 21st century, when privatization was almost complete (with the exception of large state utilities).

In 2001 Latvia negotiated a 20-month, $44-million stand-by arrangement with the International Monetary Fund (IMF). Real GDP growth was strong in 2001–02, led by investment and consumption. Inflation was low during those years. In 2003 per capita GDP stood around 50% above its level in 1995. Latvia's economy in 2003 was regarded as one of the best of the 10 countries slated for EU admission in 2004. The government took steps toward achieving a balanced budget by reducing government spending in 2003.

In anticipation of the 2006 election, the government sought to exploit the strong revenue growth and increase public spending. In addition, it planned to sell off its share in the Ventspils oil terminal, and thus give an extra boost to the overall economic growth. One of the biggest threats to economic expansion was the growing inflation rate. The global economic recession slowed economic development from 2008 to 2011.

40 SOCIAL DEVELOPMENT

Social insurance provides benefits for old age and disability, and survivorship pensions for employees and self-employed persons. The first laws were enacted in 1922 and were updated in 2001. Pensions are funded by contributions from employees and employers in most sectors. Age requirements for pensions are set at 62 for men and women. The government funds programs to provide for active military personnel, individuals caring for infants, and spouses of diplomatic staff. Sickness and maternity benefits are provided to employed persons, while medical benefits are provided to all permanent residents. A universal program of family allowances exists, as well as workers' compensation and unemployment programs.

Employment discrimination based on gender is legally banned, although women are barred from certain occupations considered dangerous. In practice, women face unequal treatment in terms of both pay and hiring, including discrimination stemming from the cost of legally mandated childbirth benefits if a woman is hired. Sexual harassment is common in the workplace, although prohibited by law. Few resources exist for victims of sexual assault.

Latvia's main human rights problem stems from the large number of minorities who were not granted citizenship after independence. These noncitizens, mainly ethnic Russians, do not have clear travel, property, and residency rights. Instances of excessive use of force by security forces were still reported, and prison conditions remained poor.

41 HEALTH

Primary care is provided at large urban health centers, hospital and walk-in emergency facilities, individual and group private practices, rural clinics staffed by midwives and physician's assistants, and workplace clinics run by large private employers and the military. According to the CIA, life expectancy in Latvia was 73 years in 2011. The country spent 6.6% of its GDP on healthcare, amounting to $750 per person. There were 30 physicians, 48 nurses and midwives, and 64 hospital beds per 10,000 inhabitants. The fertility rate was 1.3 children per woman, while the infant mortality rate was 7 deaths per 1,000 live births. In 2008 the maternal mortality rate, according to the World Bank, was 20 deaths per 100,000 births. It was estimated that 96% of children were vaccinated against measles. The CIA calculated HIV/AIDS prevalence in Latvia to be about 0.7% in 2009. Cardiovascular disease is a major cause of mortality in Latvia, with a rate of nearly 400 per

1,000 people over age 65. The incidence of tuberculosis was 68 per 100,000 people in 2007.

⁴²HOUSING

In the 1990s about 165,000 families (one out of five) were registered for new housing. Approximately 200,000 people lived in the 8% of existing housing stock that was in substandard condition. But the government has made some progress in reforms for the housing sector. In 1993 about 54% of housing was owned by state and municipalities. In 1999 the majority of property (70%) was privately owned.

At the 2000 census about 26% of all respondents lived in single-family houses; 68.5% lived in apartments. About 60% of all dwellings were owner occupied. About 52% of the population were living in housing units built in 1970 or earlier. About 43.7% of the population were in dwellings built during the period 1971–95.

Since 1996 the government has signed several agreements with international organizations for funds to improve housing projects. In 2000 the Housing Crediting Program was initiated to promote a new mortgage system.

⁴³EDUCATION

The modern Latvian educational system is based on the reforms introduced in 1991. Compulsory education lasts for nine years beginning at the age of seven. At this stage, students have a choice between basic vocational school (two or three years), general secondary school (three years), or vocational secondary school (four years, offering a diploma that may fulfill the prerequisite for university studies).

In 2005, about 84% of age-eligible children were enrolled in some type of preschool program. In 2009 the World Bank estimated that 93% of age-eligible children in Latvia were enrolled in primary school. Secondary enrollment for age-eligible children stood at 84%. Nearly all students complete their primary education. The student-to-teacher ratio for primary school was at about 12:1 in 2005.

Entrance examinations are a prerequisite for admission into universities. Higher education is offered by both private and public institutions. The state offers free higher education in some areas of specialized study. Latvia has a total of about 34 state-recognized institutions of higher learning, including two major universities: the University of Latvia and the Riga Technical University. In 2009 tertiary enrollment was estimated at 69%. Of those enrolled in tertiary education, there were 100 male students for every 189 female students.

The World Bank also indicated that in 2008 Latvia spent 5.7% of its GDP on public education, up slightly from previous years. Overall, the CIA estimated that Latvia had a literacy rate of 99.7% in 2009.

⁴⁴LIBRARIES AND MUSEUMS

The National Library in Riga holds about 2.1 million volumes; the main library site was designed by Gunnar Birkerts, who was born in Latvia but has an architectural firm in the United States. The Latvian Academic Library in Riga holds 1.2 million books and the University of Latvia holds about two million; both libraries also include large collections of periodicals. The Riga City Library (Bibliotheca Rigensis), established in 1524, was the first public library in the nation. In 2005 there were about 892 public libraries in the nation, including 7 branches of the Latvian Library for the Blind.

The larger museums are located in Riga, including the State Museum of Fine Arts, the History Museum of Latvia, The Latvian Photography Museum, and the Museum of Foreign Art. Riga also hosts the Museum of Natural History; the Riga Film Museum; the State Museum of Art; the Literature, Theater, and Music Museum; the Latvian Sports Museum, and the Latvian War Museum. In 1990 Bauska Castle was converted into a historic museum. The Bauska Art Museum holds over 8,000 works of art by Russian and Western European artists. With the end of the Soviet era, a number of new museums devoted to Latvian culture and history opened in the 1990s, including museums of architecture, photography, telecommunications, Jewish life in Latvia, and a museum chronicling 50 years of Soviet occupation. There are a local history museums in almost every region.

⁴⁵MEDIA

The constitution provides for free speech and a free press, and the government is said to respect these rights in practice. A 1991 Press Law prohibits censorship of the press or other mass media; however, a Law on the Media imposes regulations on the content and language of broadcasts.

Latvia's telecommunications system is marked by a decrease in the number of fixed land lines and an increase in wireless telephony. There are currently three domestic wireless service providers operating in Latvia, including Lattelekom, the national service provider. International service is provided by fiber-optic cable links to Sweden, Estonia, and Finland. In 2009 the CIA reported that there were 644,000 telephone landlines in Latvia. In addition to landlines, mobile phone subscriptions averaged 99 per 100 people.

The Committee for Television and Radio controls broadcasting. Domestic and international programming in Latvian, Russian, Swedish, English, and German is broadcast by Latvian Radio. There were 8 FM radio stations, 56 AM radio stations, and 1 shortwave radio station. Latvian State Television broadcasts on two channels, and there are several independent television stations with daily broadcasts. Cable and satellite services are available, and foreign broadcasts can also be seen. Internet users numbered 67 per 100 citizens in 2010. Prominent newspapers in 2010, with circulation numbers listed parenthetically, included *Diena* (110,000) and *Neatkariga Rita Avize* (30,000). Foreign language newspapers include the weekly *Baltic Times* in English.

⁴⁶ORGANIZATIONS

Important economic organizations in Latvia include the Latvian Chamber of Commerce, an organization that promotes trade and commerce with its Baltic neighbors, Europe, and The Russian Federation. There are five business and trade organizations including: the Latvia International Commerce Center, Latvian Small Business Association, and the World Latvian Businessmen's Association. The largest trade union in Latvia is the umbrella organization of the Association of Free Trade Unions, founded in 1990.

The Latvian Academy of Sciences promotes public interest and education for all branches of science. Several medical fields have professional associations. There are also several environmental protection and preservation organizations.

National youth organizations include the Student Council of the University of Latvia, United Nations Student Association of Latvia, YMCA/YWCA of Latvia, Junior Chamber, and the Scout and Guide Central Organization of Latvia. There are a wide variety of sports associations represented in the country. National women's organizations include the Women's National League of Latvia and the Latvian Association of University Women.

There are national chapters of the Red Cross Society and Caritas.

⁴⁷TOURISM, TRAVEL, AND RECREATION

Riga is the major tourism center of the Baltic states. Its historic architecture has undergone extensive restoration. The white sand beaches offer sailing and river rafting along with many spas. Latvia boasts 12,310 rivers and 3,000 lakes, which are popular for boating, as well as country castles and medieval towns. Tennis, horseback riding, fishing, hunting, sailing, water sports, and winter sports are available to visitors, as well as a ski marathon in February, the Sport Festival of Riga in May, and the International Riga Marathon in July.

All visitors need passports valid for at least three months after the planned stay. Visas are not required for stays of up to 90 days.

The *Tourism Factbook*, published by the UN World Tourism Organization, reported 4.73 million incoming tourists to Latvia in 2009, who spent a total of $1.01 billion. Of those incoming tourists, there were 4,611,000 from Europe. There were 25,392 hotel beds available in Latvia, which had an occupancy rate of 22%. The estimated daily cost to visit Riga, the capital, was $258. The cost of visiting other cities averaged $258.

⁴⁸FAMOUS PERSONS

Guntis Ulmanis (b. 1939) was president of Latvia from 1993 to 1999. Vaira Vike-Freiberga (b. 1937), Latvia's first female president, succeeded him in 1999, and was reelected in 2003. Famous writers include the poets Krisjanis Barons (1823–1923) and Atis Kronvalds (1837–75). Romantic literature in the 20th century was symbolized by Janis Rainis's (1865–1929) *Fire and Night*.

⁴⁹DEPENDENCIES

Latvia has no territories or colonies.

⁵⁰BIBLIOGRAPHY

Bousfield, Jonathan. *Eyewitness Travel Guide: Estonia, Latvia, and Lithuania*. New York: Dorling Kindersley, 2011.

Eglitis, Daina Stukuls. *Imagining the Nation: History, Modernity, and Revolution in Latvia*. University Park, PA: *Environmental Justice and Sustainability in the Former Soviet Union*. Cambridge, MA: MIT Press, 2009.

Environmental Justice and Sustainability in the Former Soviet Union. Cambridge, MA: MIT Press, 2009.

Estonia, Latvia & Lithuania. New York: DK Publishing, 2009.

Frucht, Richard, ed. *Eastern Europe: An Introduction to the People, Lands, and Culture*. Santa Barbara, CA: ABC-CLIO, 2005.

Opello, Walter C. *European Politics*. Boulder, CO: Lynne Rienner Publishers, 2009.

Political Chronology of Europe. London, Eng.: Europa, 2001.

Terterov, Marat. *Doing Business with Latvia*. Sterling, VA: Kogan Page, 2003.

Thompson, Wayne C. *Nordic, Central, and Southeastern Europe, 2010*. 10th ed. Harper's Ferry, WV: Stryker Post Publications, 2010.

LIECHTENSTEIN

Principality of Liechtenstein
Fürstentum Liechtenstein

CAPITAL: Vaduz

FLAG: The national flag is divided into two horizontal rectangles, blue above red. On the blue rectangle, near the hoist, is the princely crown in gold.

ANTHEM: *Oben am jungen Rhein (High Above the Young Rhine).*

MONETARY UNIT: The Swiss franc (CHF) of 100 centimes, or rappen, has been in use since February 1921. There are coins of 1, 5, 10, 20, and 50 centimes and 1, 2, and 5 francs, and notes of 10, 20, 50, 100, 500, and 1,000 francs. CHF1 = $1.10509 (or $1 = CHF.904906 as of October 2011).

WEIGHTS AND MEASURES: The metric system is the legal standard.

HOLIDAYS: New Year's Day, 1 January; Epiphany, 6 January; Candlemas, 2 February; St. Joseph's Day, 19 March; Labor Day, 1 May; Assumption, 15 August; Nativity of Our Lady (Mary), 8 September; All Saints' Day, 1 November; Immaculate Conception, 8 December; Christmas Eve, 24 December; Christmas, 25 December; St. Stephen's Day, 26 December. Movable religious holidays include Good Friday, Easter, Easter Monday, Ascension, Whitsunday, Whitmonday, and Corpus Christi.

TIME: 1 p.m. = noon GMT.

¹LOCATION, SIZE, AND EXTENT

Liechtenstein, roughly triangular in shape, is a landlocked country situated in the Rhine River Valley. The fourth-smallest country in Europe, it is bordered by the Austrian province of Vorarlberg to the N and E, the Swiss canton of Graubünden to the S, and the Rhine River and the Swiss canton of St. Gallen to the W, with a total boundary length of 76 km (47 mi).

The principality has an area of 160 sq km (62 sq mi) and extends 24.5 km (15.2 mi) N–S and 9.4 km (5.8 mi) E–W. Comparatively, the area occupied by Liechtenstein is about 0.9 times the size of Washington, DC.

Liechtenstein's capital city, Vaduz, is located in the western part of the country.

²TOPOGRAPHY

Liechtenstein is divided into a comparatively narrow area of level land bordering the right bank of the Rhine River and an upland and mountainous region occupying the remainder of the country; the level land occupies about two-fifths of the total surface area. The greatest elevation, Grauspitz (2,599 m/8,527 ft), is in the south, in a spur of the Rhaetian Alps.

³CLIMATE

Climatic conditions in Liechtenstein are less severe than might be expected from its elevated terrain and inland situation; the mitigating factor is a warm south wind called the Föhn. The annual lowland temperature varies between -4.5°C (24°F) in January and 19.9°C (68°F) in July. Late frost and prolonged dry periods are rare. Average annual precipitation is 105 cm (41 in).

⁴FLORA AND FAUNA

The World Resources Institute estimates that there are 1,410 plant species in Liechtenstein. In addition, Liechtenstein is home to 56 mammals species, 241 bird species, 5 reptile species, and 8 amphibian species. The calculation reflects the total number of distinct species residing in the country, not the number of endemic species.

The natural plant and animal life of Liechtenstein displays a considerable variety because of the marked differences in altitude. A number of orchid species are able to grow because of the warmth carried by the Föhn. In the higher mountain reaches are such alpine plants as gentian, alpine rose, and edelweiss. Common trees include the red beech, sycamore, maple, alder, larch, and various conifers. Indigenous mammals include the deer, fox, badger, and chamois. Birds include ravens and eagles.

In 2001 the government set several goals, including increasing the share of renewable energy to more than 10% by 2013, especially through expanded usage of domestic biomass, biogas, and solar energy. Liechtenstein aims at a reduction of greenhouse gas emissions of 50% from 1990 levels by 2050.

⁵ENVIRONMENT

The World Resources Institute reported that Liechtenstein had designated 6,400 hectares (15,815 acres) of land for protection as of 2006. The UN reported in 2008 that carbon dioxide emissions in Liechtenstein totaled 224 kilotons.

The Nature Conservation Act, adopted in 1933, was the nation's first major piece of environmental legislation; the Water Conservation Act dates from 1957, and air pollution laws were passed in 1973 and 1974. All wastewater is purified before being discharged into the Rhine. According to a 2011 report issued by the International Union for Conservation of Nature and Natural Resources (IUCN), threatened species included two types of mollusks and two species of invertebrates. Threatened species include the great horned owl, the Eurasian beaver, the hermit beetle, and the Apollo butterfly.

6 POPULATION

The US Central Intelligence Agency (CIA) estimated the population of Liechtenstein in 2012 to be approximately 36,713, which placed it at number 190 in population among the 196 nations of the world. In 2011, approximately 15% of the population was over 65 years of age, with another 16.1% under 15 years of age. The median age in Liechtenstein was 41.8 years. There was one male for every female in the country. The population's annual rate of change was 0.795% in 2012. The projected population for the year 2025 was 40,000. Population density in Liechtenstein was calculated at 226 people per sq km (585 people per sq mi).

The UN estimated that 14% of the population lived in urban areas, and that urban populations had an annual rate of change of 0.9%. The largest urban areas are Schaan (5,800 inhabitants) and Vaduz (5,200 residents).

7 MIGRATION

Liechtenstein's net migration rate was estimated by the CIA to be 4.48 migrants per 1,000 citizens in 2011. Several hundred Italian, Greek, and Spanish workers have migrated to the principality on a semi-permanent basis. In 1998 and 1999, Liechtenstein accepted a high number of Kosovo Albanian asylum seekers, granting them temporary protection.

8 ETHNIC GROUPS

The indigenous population is described as being chiefly of Alemannic stock, descendants of the German-speaking tribes that settled between the Main and Danube rivers. At the 2010 census 66.8% of the population identified themselves as Liechtensteiners. Austrians, Germans, Swiss, and various other groups account for the remaining 33.2%.

9 LANGUAGES

German is the official language. The population speaks an Alemannic dialect.

10 RELIGIONS

The national religion of Roman Catholicism is practiced by an estimated 78.4% of the population. About 8.3% of the population are Protestants, 4.5% are Muslims, and 1.1% are Orthodox Christians. Jews accounted for less than 1% of the population. According to a 2008 government survey, only about 40% of respondents claimed to participate in formal religious services at least once a month. The Muslims were the most active religious group, with 44% attending services at least once a week. Only about 23% of Roman Catholics claimed to attend weekly services.

Freedom of religion is guaranteed by the constitution and this right is generally respected in practice. Although the Roman Catholic Church is named as the national church by the constitution, the government provides some state funding for other Protestant denominations as well. Religious holidays, including Epiphany, Candlemas, Good Friday, Easter, Easter Monday, Ascension, Whitsunday, Whitmonday, the Nativity of Mary, All Saints' Day, Immaculate Conception, Christmas Eve, Christmas Day, and Saint Stephen's Day, are observed as national holidays. Most businesses are closed on Sundays.

11 TRANSPORTATION

Liechtenstein has approximately 28 km (17.4 mi) of navigable waterways.

The line of the Arlberg express (Paris to Vienna) passes through Liechtenstein at Schaan-Vaduz, extending for 18.5 km (11.5 mi), but few international trains stop. The main center for reaching Liechtenstein is Buchs, Switzerland, about 8 km (5 mi) from Vaduz.

Postal buses are the chief means of public transportation both within the country and to Austria and Switzerland. A tunnel, 740 m (2,428 ft) in length, connects the Samina River Valley with the Rhine River Valley.

In 2010, there were some 380 km (236 mi) of paved roadways. A major highway runs through the principality, linking Austria and Switzerland.

The nearest major airport is in Zürich, Switzerland.

12 HISTORY

The territory now occupied by the Principality of Liechtenstein first acquired a political identity with the formation of the sub-country of Lower Rhaetia after the death of Charlemagne in 814. The County of Vaduz was formally established in 1342 and became a direct dependency of the Holy Roman Empire in 1396. The area (to which, in 1434, was added the Lordship of Schellenberg, in the north) was ruled in turn by various families, such as the counts of Montfort, von Brandis, van Sulz, and von Hohenems.

During the Thirty Years' War (1618–48), the area was invaded first by Austrian troops and then, in 1647, by the Swedes. After the von Hohenems line encountered financial difficulty, Prince Johann Adam of Liechtenstein purchased from them first Schellenberg (1699) and then Vaduz (1712). The Liechtenstein family thus added to its vast holdings in Austria and adjoining territories.

The Principality of Liechtenstein as such was created on 23 January 1719 by act of Holy Roman Emperor Charles VI, who made it a direct fief of the crown and confirmed the rule of Prince Anton-Florian, Johann Adam's successor, under the title of Prince von und zu Liechtenstein.

During the Napoleonic wars, Liechtenstein was invaded by both the French and the Russians. Following the Treaty of Pressburg (1805), Liechtenstein joined the Confederation of the Rhine, which made the principality a sovereign state. In 1815, following the downfall of Napoleon, Liechtenstein joined the newly formed Germanic Confederation.

With Prussia's victory over Austria in the Seven Weeks' War (1866), the Confederation was dissolved and the constitutional ties of Liechtenstein to other German states came to an end. In the war, Liechtenstein had furnished Austria-Hungary with 80 soldiers; two years later, the principality disbanded its military force for all time.

From 1852, when the first treaty establishing a customs union was signed, until the end of World War I, Liechtenstein was closely tied economically to Austria. After the war, the collapse of the Austrian currency and economy inclined the principality to seek economic partnership with its other neighbor, Switzerland. A treaty concluded with Switzerland in 1923 provided for a customs union and the use of Swiss currency.

Liechtenstein (like Switzerland) remained neutral in World War II, as it had in World War I. After Germany was defeated in 1945, Nazi sympathizers in Liechtenstein who had supported incorporation of the principality into Adolf Hitler's Third Reich were prosecuted and sentenced. The postwar decades were marked by political stability and outstanding economic growth.

Prince Franz Josef II, who succeeded his granduncle, Franz I, in 1938, was the first reigning monarch actually to reside in Liechtenstein. On 26 August 1984, Franz Josef II handed over executive authority to his eldest son and heir, Crown Prince Hans-Adam. Hans-Adam II has been ruling prince since 13 November 1989, after Franz Josef II died.

Liechtenstein has sought further integration into the world community. The country was admitted to the United Nations (UN) in September 1991. In Europe, Liechtenstein joined EFTA in 1991 and became a member of the European Economic Area (EEA) in 1995.

Disagreements between Prince Hans-Adam II and parliament arose in the latter half of 1999. In September, the prince's assertion that he had the right to dissolve the government at his discretion raised tensions to the point where Hans-Adam threatened to go into exile in Austria. In October, the European Court of Human Rights ruled on a complaint filed by Dr. Herbert Wille, a senior judge whom the prince had refused to re-appoint because of Wille's assertion that the country's Supreme Court rather than its monarch should be the ultimate authority on constitutional issues. The court ruled that in depriving Wille of his judicial position because of his political views, the prince had violated the judge's freedom of speech. Wille was awarded 10,000 Swiss francs in compensation as well as payment of his legal costs.

Sixty-four percent of Liechtenstein's voters approved a new constitution for Liechtenstein in a referendum held in March 2003; the prince was granted near-absolute powers. Turnout was large, with 14,800 of Liechtenstein's 17,000 electorate casting votes. Under the new constitution, the prince has the right to dissolve government, control a committee appointing judges, and has veto power over legislation. The constitution also gives the people the power to call a referendum and abolish the monarchy. As a result of the changes, which many observers deemed undemocratic, Prince Hans-Adam II rescinded his pledge to leave the country. On 15 August 2004 Prince Hans-Adam II transferred the official duties of the ruling prince to his son and heir apparent, Alois, who was seen as less confrontational than his father. Prince Hans-Adam II retained the status of chief of state.

Liechtenstein ranks as one of the world's most prosperous countries with one of the world's highest living standards, while its people pay very low taxes. In 1999, the royal family itself was ranked as

LOCATION: 47°3′ to 47°14′N; 9°29′ to 9°38′ E. BOUNDARY LENGTHS: Austria, 34.9 kilometers (21.7 miles); Switzerland, 41.1 kilometers (25.5 miles).

the wealthiest in all of Europe and Prince Hans-Adam II personally was ranked as Europe's third-wealthiest monarch. However, in 2000 Liechtenstein ranked among the top 15 countries named by an international task force investigating countries whose banking laws make money laundering possible. Liechtenstein took steps in 2001 to make its banking system more transparent; however, a 2003 International Monetary Fund report concluded that although the banking sector had updated its banking regulations, there were not enough staff to fully enforce the regulations.

In March 2009, after nearly a year of international pressure, as Germany, the United States, the United Kingdom, and other countries all launched tax evasion investigations against wealthy citizens holding accounts in Liechtenstein, the government formally stated its commitment to initiate measures toward greater transparency. The country made good on its pledge. In December 2008, Liechtenstein signed a Tax Information Exchange Agreement with the United States and 11 other nations; by 2010, the country had agreements to share banking information with a total of 25 nations. In August 2009, it signed an agreement with the United Kingdom to release information on nearly 5,000 British account holders who were being accused of tax evasion.

The Organisation for Economic Co-operation and Development (OECD) maintains a list of countries that have not implemented the requirements of its tax conventions. In late 2009, the OECD removed Liechtenstein from that list, signifying that its programs had brought the country into alignment with international information sharing standards.

13 GOVERNMENT

Liechtenstein is a constitutional monarchy ruled by the hereditary princes of the house of Liechtenstein. The monarchy is hereditary in the male line. The constitution of 5 October 1921, as amended in 1987 and 2003, provides for a unicameral parliament (Landtag) of 25 members elected for four years. Election is by universal suffrage at age 18 and is on the basis of proportional representation. Women gained the right to vote in 1984.

Amendments to the constitution were approved in March 2003. The changes extended the ruling prince's powers, giving him the right to veto legislation and to control the appointment of judges.

The prince can call and dismiss the Landtag. On parliamentary recommendation, he appoints the prime minister, who must have been born in Liechtenstein, and the deputy prime minister for four-year terms. It is the regular practice for the prime minister to be of the majority party and the deputy prime minister to be selected from the opposition. The Landtag appoints four councilors for four-year terms to assist in administration. Any group of 1,000 persons or any three communes may propose legislation. Bills passed by the Landtag may be submitted to popular referendum. A law is valid when it receives majority approval by the Landtag and the prince's signed concurrence.

14 POLITICAL PARTIES

The principal parties are The Free List (FL, Die Freie Liste, also known as the Greens), Progressive Citizens' Party (FBP, Fortschrittliche Buergerpartei), and the Fatherland Union (VU, Vaterlaendische Union).

In the general elections of 1997, the VU, which has held a majority since 1978, won 13 seats in the Landtag and the FBP won 10. The general elections in 1993 resulted in a coalition government headed by Mario Frick of the VU. Frick was reelected as prime minister by the Landtag in 1997. Although the VU remains the largest single party, Liechtenstein had a coalition government from 1938 until 1997.

In the 2001 elections, the FBP won 49.9% of the vote and 13 seats in the Landtag, to the VU's 41.1% and 11 seats. The FL won 8.8% of the vote and 1 seat. Otmar Hasler was named prime minister. It was the first time since 1978 that the FBP held a majority in parliament. The 2005 elections saw the FBP retaining power with 48.7% of the vote and 12 seats, to the VU's 38.2% and 10 seats. The

minority party FL increased their following with 13% of the vote and 3 seats.

In the parliamentary elections of February 2009, the VU won 13 seats, followed by the FBP with 11, and the FL with just 1 seat. The next parliamentary elections were scheduled for February 2013. In March 2009, Klaus Tschütscher of the VU was appointed as prime minister. This new government was formed through a coalition agreement between the VU and the FBP.

15 LOCAL GOVERNMENT

The 11 communes (Gemeinden) are fully independent administrative bodies within the laws of the principality. They levy their own taxes. The communes are Balzers, Eschen, Gamprin, Mauren, Planken, Ruggell, Schaan, Schellenberg, Triesen, Triesenberg, and Vaduz.

16 JUDICIAL SYSTEM

The principality has its own civil and penal codes. Courts that function under sole Liechtenstein jurisdiction are the county court (Landgericht), presided over by one judge, which decides minor civil cases and summary criminal offenses; the juvenile court; and the Schöffengericht, a court for misdemeanors. The Supreme Court (Oberster Gerichtshof) is the nation's highest court. An administrative court of appeal hears appeals from government actions, and the Constitutional Court (Verfassungsgericht) determines the constitutionality of laws. In June 1986, Liechtenstein adopted a new penal code abolishing the death penalty.

The constitution provides for public trials and judicial appeal. The judiciary is separate from the executive and legislative branches. The 2003 referendum gave the prince the ultimate right to control the appointment of the country's judges.

The constitution provides for freedom of assembly, association, and religion. Crime is rare and Switzerland is responsible for Liechtenstein's defense. Liechtenstein retains a restrictive law on the availability of abortion; it is allowable only when the life or health of a woman is threatened.

17 ARMED FORCES

Since 1868, no military forces have been maintained in Liechtenstein.

18 INTERNATIONAL COOPERATION

Liechtenstein became a member of the United Nations on 18 September 1990; it belongs to the IAEA, ICRM, IFRCS, IOC, IPU, ITSO, ITU, OPCW, PCA, UNCTAD, UPU, and WIPO. Liechtenstein is also a member of the Council of Europe, the European Bank for Reconstruction and Development, EFTA, the OSCE, Interpol, and the WTO. It is a de facto member of the Schengen Convention, the treaty that eliminates internal border controls for travelers.

The principality joined the European Economic Area in 1995. Liechtenstein now has diplomatic relations with nearly 50 countries. In environmental cooperation, the country is part of the Basel Convention, Conventions on Biological Diversity and Air Pollution, Ramsar, CITES, the Kyoto Protocol, the Montréal Protocol, and the UN Conventions on Climate Change and Desertification.

¹⁹ECONOMY

The gross domestic product (GDP) rate of change in Liechtenstein was estimated at -0.5% in 2009. Inflation stood at 0.7% in 2010, and unemployment was reported at 2.8% in 2008.

Despite its small size and limited national resources, Liechtenstein is one of the richest countries in the world on a per capita GDP basis. According to CIA estimates in 2008, Liechtenstein ranked first in the world in per capita GDP. It has developed since the 1940s from a mainly agricultural to an industrialized country and a prosperous center of trade and tourism. Factories produce a wide range of high-technology products, including electronics and precision instruments. Liechtenstein is also a world leader in specialized dental products. Industrial products are manufactured almost exclusively for export.

Special economic advantages enjoyed by very small nations of Europe (e.g., the issuance of new postage stamps, free exchange of currencies, and liberal laws that provide incentives for the establishment of bank deposits and of nominal foreign business headquarters) also play a part in this prosperity.

In 1999 Liechtenstein became the subject of an international investigation into money laundering. Liechtenstein subsequently drafted legislation to combat money laundering and to increase transparency in its financial sector. As of 2009, the country was no longer included on the list of countries that fail to cooperate with international authorities on financial and tax matters.

The country has no central bank and does not print its own currency, but uses the Swiss franc instead. Liechtenstein is engaged in harmonizing its economic policies with those of the EU.

²⁰INCOME

The CIA estimated that in 2008 the GDP of Liechtenstein was $5.01 billion. The CIA defines GDP as the value of all final goods and services produced within a nation in a given year and computed on the basis of purchasing power parity (PPP) rather than value as measured on the basis of the rate of the exchange based on current dollars. The per capita GDP was estimated at $141,100. The average inflation rate was 0.7%. It was estimated that agriculture accounted for 6% of GDP, industry 36%, and services 58%.

²¹LABOR

As of 2009, Liechtenstein had a total labor force of 34,330, about 51% of whom commuted from outside the country daily. Within that labor force, CIA estimates in 2009 noted that 0.8% were employed in agriculture, 41.3% in industry, and 56% in the service sector.

Liechtenstein's workforce is highly skilled, but there are not enough native-born workers to meet industry's needs. Unemployment in 2009 was 2.8%. In 2009, it was estimated that women earned 80% of men's earnings for equal work.

All workers, including foreigners, are entitled to form and join unions. There is one trade union that represented about 3% of the workforce in 2009. Strikes are permitted but are not generally used. Most collective bargaining agreements, which covered an estimated 25% of workers as of 2009, are adapted from ones signed between Swiss workers and employers.

There is no minimum wage, although wages are among the highest in the world. The maximum legal workweek was 45 hours for white-collar workers and 48 hours for other workers, as of 2011. Overtime pay must be at least 25% above the standard rate and overtime is restricted to two hours per day. The actual workweek is usually 40 to 43 hours. Sunday work is not generally permitted. Occupational safety and health standards are set by the government and are rigorously enforced.

The minimum working age is 16, but exceptions to this may be made for children wishing to leave school at the age of 14. Children who are 14 or older may be employed for not more than nine hours per week during the school year and 15 hours per week at other times, as of 2011.

²²AGRICULTURE

Out of 16,000 hectares (39,537) of total land, there are 3,500 hectares (8,649 acres) of arable land. The country's major crops include wheat, barley, corn, potatoes, livestock, and dairy products. In 2009, agriculture accounted for 8% of GDP and employed about 0.8% of the total workforce.

Until the end of World War II (1939–45), the economy was primarily focused on agriculture. The Rhine Valley is the most productive area. On gradual mountain slopes, a variety of grapes and orchard fruits are grown. In 2008, the government reported that agriculture production was down by about 4% over average for the period 1999–2001.

The royal family's business interests include agriculture; they own vineyards in Vaduz and have invested in RiceTec, a company based in the US state of Texas that produces hybrid rice seeds.

²³ANIMAL HUSBANDRY

The UN Food and Agriculture Organization (FAO) reported that Liechtenstein dedicated 3,000 hectares (7,413 acres) to permanent pasture or meadow in 2009. During that year, the country tended 6,000 head of cattle.

Alpine pasture, particularly well suited for cattle grazing, covers over 35% of the total land area.

In 2005, hogs numbered 3,000 and sheep, 2,900.

²⁴FISHING

There is no commercial fishing in Liechtenstein. Rivers and brooks are stocked for sport fishing.

²⁵FORESTRY

Approximately 43% of Liechtenstein is covered by forest. The forests of Liechtenstein not only supply wood but also have an important function in preventing erosion, landslides, and floods. Forests cover about 7,000 hectares (17,200 acres).

More than 90% of all forestland is publicly owned; of the 474 hectares (1,171 acres) of private forest, 158 hectares (390 acres) are the property of the prince. The most common trees are spruce, fir, beech, and pine.

26MINING

There was no mining of commercial importance.

27ENERGY AND POWER

In 2009 Liechtenstein consumed some 1,354 million kWh of electricity. The country is committed to reducing its energy consumption and greenhouse gas emissions. Since domestic production does not meet the country's requirements, supplementary energy is imported from Switzerland, especially in winter.

28INDUSTRY

The industry of Liechtenstein, limited by shortages of raw materials, is primarily devoted to small-scale production of precision manufactures. The output includes optical lenses, dental products, high-vacuum pumps, heating equipment, electron microscopes, electronic measuring and control devices, steel bolts, knitting machines, and textiles. Pharmaceuticals, electronics, ceramics, and metal manufacturing are also important. The largest industrial companies in Liechtenstein are Hilti (construction services), Oerlikon Balzers (electro-optical coatings), Hilcona (frozen foods), and Ivoclar-Vivadent (dental medical technology). Liechtenstein's industry is completely geared to exports.

In 2009, industry contributed approximately 37% of the overall GDP and employed about 41.3% of the workforce.

29SCIENCE AND TECHNOLOGY

The World Bank reported in 2009 that there were no patent applications in science and technology in Liechtenstein. Still, the country invests in research and development; in 2009 approximately 5% of the country's revenue was allocated to this area.

Like Swiss industry, manufacturing in Liechtenstein entails a high degree of precision and technological sophistication. Oerlikon Balzers Coatings, the country's second-largest employer, is known for its leading role in providing equipment and thin film technology for the CD-ROM industry. Liechtenstein itself has no educational institutions offering advanced scientific training. The Liechtensteinische Gesellschaft für Umweltschutz, founded in 1973, is concerned with environmental protection.

30DOMESTIC TRADE

Liechtenstein and Switzerland are essentially linked in one common economic zone. The domestic economy is largely based on industry and financial services. The primary product industries are electronics, metal manufacturing, and medical precision instruments. About 51% of the workforce are foreigners, commuting from Switzerland, Austria, and Germany.

Vaduz and Schaan, the chief commercial centers, have specialty shops. Most smaller communities have only general stores. Regular business hours are generally from 8 a.m. to 6:30 p.m. Normal banking hours are from 8:15 a.m. to noon and from 1:30 p.m. to 4 or 5 p.m., Monday through Friday.

31FOREIGN TRADE

The US State Department reported that exports decreased by 27.4% in 2009, but recovered slightly (7.9%) in 2010. Imports declined by 21.8% in 2009 and by 2.3% in 2010. Major import part-

ners in 2009 were EU countries and Switzerland. Its major export partners were Western Europe, 61.72%; Asia, 12.49%; and North America, 12.07%.

Goods to and from Liechtenstein pass freely across the frontier with Switzerland, with which Liechtenstein maintains a customs union. Exports in 2009 were valued at $2.79–2.83 billion, while imports were valued at $1.73 billion.

Important exports include small specialty machinery, dental products, connectors for audio and video, stamps, hardware, electronic equipment, optical products, pottery, textiles, and pharmaceuticals. Liechtenstein imports mainly machinery, metal goods, textiles, foodstuffs, and motor vehicles.

32BALANCE OF PAYMENTS

The CIA reported that in 2009 the purchasing power parity of Liechtenstein's exports was $2.79 billion while imports totaled $1.73 billion, resulting in a trade surplus of $1.06 billion.

33BANKING AND SECURITIES

Although there is a national bank, the duties of the central bank are performed by the Swiss National Bank, a consequence of the currency union with Switzerland. Liechtenstein's banks form an important part of the economy, and they have experienced significant growth since the 1990s. In 2009 customer deposits were valued at $127.2 billion, up about 3.5% over 2008.

The National Bank of Liechtenstein (Liechtensteinische Landesbank), founded in 1861, is the state bank of issue; in addition, it deals in real estate mortgages and ordinary banking operations. Liechtenstein Global Trust (LGT), the country's largest financial institution (owned by the royal family), and the Private Trust Bank Corp., founded in 1956, play an important role in the finance and credit spheres of Liechtenstein's economy. Banking is linked with the Swiss banking system, as is securities trading. In 2007, the LGT reported that it had about half of all the money deposited in Liechtenstein under management.

Lichtenstein signed a European anti-corruption treaty in November 2009, continuing the country's efforts to allow for greater transparency in its financial system. Liechtenstein's foreign minister indicated that the country would also likely ratify the Council of Europe's Criminal Law Convention on Corruption in 2010. Under current Liechtenstein law, payments to private individuals and foreign officials are legal. The same transfer of payments would be called bribery in other countries. Europe's Criminal Law Convention on Corruption will require that signatories punish individuals who take bribes, whether in government or in private business. In ratifying the agreement, Liechtenstein moved toward a more widely accepted legal framework on corruption, taking another step away from the secretive financial world that drew the ire of international organizations.

34INSURANCE

Insurance activities in Liechtenstein are variously conducted by the government (old age and survivors' insurance), by private companies under government regulation (e.g., life, accident, health, and fire), and by farmers' associations. There were an estimated 37 insurance companies operating in the country as of 2007

(19 were in life insurance, 13 in indemnity, 5 in reinsurance.) Life insurance accounted for almost 96% of the revenue for the insurance sector.

In 1996, after Liechtenstein joined the European Economic Area (now the European Union), the country enacted a new insurance law to align with European standards and to attract insurance business from abroad.

35 PUBLIC FINANCE

In 2010 the budget of Liechtenstein included $943 million in public revenue and $820 million in public expenditures. The budget surplus amounted to 2.4% of GDP.

Liechtenstein's economy has experienced development and industrialization since World War II (1939–45). Since then, it has gone from a predominantly agricultural economy to a highly advanced industry-driven economy and has introduced transparency in its finance sector.

36 TAXATION

A new tax law was enacted in 2010 and took effect 1 January 2011. The main taxes are levied on personal income, business income, and principal. The main taxes include income tax, net worth tax, gift and estate tax, and property profits tax. A value-added tax (VAT) of 7.5% applies to most goods and services.

Corporate tax rates were progressive until the flat rate of 12.5% took effect on 1 January 2011.

In 2004 Liechtenstein (along with Switzerland) accepted the EU's Savings Tax Directive and imposed a withholding tax on interest and other savings returns paid to citizens of the member states of the EU. This took effect 1 July 2005. Initially, this tax was at the rate of 15%. It increased to 20% on 1 July 2008 and to 35% on 1 July 2011. About 75% of the revenues collected from the tax are paid out to the designated member states.

37 CUSTOMS AND DUTIES

There have been no customs between Switzerland and Liechtenstein since a customs treaty was ratified in 1924. The terms of the customs union between Switzerland and Liechtenstein allow Liechtenstein to participate in free trade agreements entered into by Switzerland elsewhere in the world. For example, in 2009, the Canada-European Free Trade Association Agreement (CEFTA) was signed by Switzerland (among other countries) and extends to Liechtenstein.

38 FOREIGN INVESTMENT

Foreign direct investment (FDI) in Liechtenstein was unreported according to World Bank figures published in 2009.

The Prince of Liechtenstein Foundation has established a number of ventures abroad, mainly in the field of investment management and counseling.

Several thousand foreign companies have established offices in Liechtenstein because taxes are very low and the principality is politically stable. Some industrial establishments are owned and managed by Swiss interests.

39 ECONOMIC DEVELOPMENT

The government generally encourages the increasing diversification of industry and the development of tourism. The principality's low taxes are attractive to foreign corporations wanting to safeguard patents and trademarks and to individuals who want to protect their wealth for the future. Thousands of corporations have established nominal headquarters in Liechtenstein. In 2002, the International Monetary Fund (IMF) conducted an Offshore Financial Center (OFC) Assessment of Liechtenstein, to evaluate the regulation and monitoring of the country's financial center. The IMF approved of Liechtenstein's efforts to fight money laundering and the financing of international terrorism. Liechtenstein has established the Financial Market Authority (FMA), which is responsible for the supervision and execution of legislation related to banking and financial information sharing.

Hilti, a manufacturer of power tools, and Oerlikon Balzers Coatins, (Unaxis Balzers until 2006), a supplier of industrial coatings, are among the major corporations headquartered in the country.

40 SOCIAL DEVELOPMENT

There is a universal pension system covering all residents, employed persons, and self-employed individuals. It is funded primarily by the government along with contributions from employees and employers. It provides benefits for old age, disability, and survivorship. A social insurance system and universal medical coverage provides sickness and maternity benefits. All residents and persons employed in Liechtenstein are entitled to medical coverage. Work injury and unemployment insurance are provided to all employed persons. There is a family allowance based on the number of children and a birth grant provided to all residents and nonresident workers.

Equality for women is protected by law, and several groups monitor and promote women's rights. An equal opportunity law addresses workplace discrimination and sexual harassment. In 2004 the government-sponsored mentoring classes to inspire women to run for seats in parliament. In 2009, there were six women in the 25-member parliament and two women in the five-seat cabinet.

Domestic violence laws have been enacted and are actively implemented. Human rights are fully respected in Liechtenstein.

In June 2011, 68% of voters approved a law passed by the parliament of Liechtenstein to provide the same rights and benefits to same-sex couples that are available to heterosexual couples.

41 HEALTH

According to the CIA, life expectancy in Liechtenstein was 81.5 years in 2012, with the average 79.37 years for men and 84.19 years for women. The fertility rate was 1.69 children born per woman, while the infant mortality rate was 4.39 deaths per 1,000 live births.

The government regulates the practice of medicine and subsidiary occupations, such as nursing and pharmacy. In 2006 Liechtenstein had an estimated 2.5 physicians per 1,000 people. There were approximately 8.3 hospital beds per 1,000 people. A program of preventive medicine, introduced in 1976, provides regular examinations for children up to the age of 10.

⁴²HOUSING

Houses in the countryside are similar to those found in the mountainous areas of Austria and Switzerland. Liechtenstein does not have a significant housing problem. Nearly all dwellings have central heating, a kitchen, a private bath, access to hot water, and adequate sewage systems.

⁴³EDUCATION

In 2008 the World Bank estimated that 90% of age-eligible children in Liechtenstein were enrolled in primary school. Secondary enrollment for age-eligible children stood at 66%. Tertiary enrollment was estimated at 37%. Overall, the CIA estimated that Liechtenstein had a literacy rate of 100% for those age 10 and over.

Education is based on Roman Catholic principles and is under government supervision. In 1974, the compulsory primary school attendance period was lowered from eight years to five, beginning at age seven. Kindergarten, offered to children ages five to seven, is optional, followed by five compulsory years of primary school. Secondary education is divided into three tracks: *oberschule* (general); *realschule* (which offers vocational and, in some cases, university preparatory education), and *gymnasium* (which provides an eight-year program to prepare students for a university education, with concentrations in either the classics and humanities or economics and mathematics). Liechtenstein also has an evening technical school, a music school, and a children's pedagogic-welfare day school.

Although there are no universities in Liechtenstein, gymnasium graduates may attend universities in Switzerland and Austria and the University of Tubingen in Germany without passing an examination.

⁴⁴LIBRARIES AND MUSEUMS

The Liechtensteinische Landesbibliothek (National Library), founded in 1961, serves as the public, academic, and national library. It is located in Vaduz and has over 200,000 volumes and e-resources. There are three specialized libraries maintained by private institutes and a small library attached to a state music school.

The National Museum, located in Vaduz, includes 42 exhibitions rooms displaying collections from six areas, including archaeology, history of the Middle Ages, the Modern Era, ethnic studies, modern history, and natural history. The Liechtenstein Museum and Princely Collections, located in a summer palace in Vienna, Austria, displays the artwork collected since the 1600s by the country's hereditary princes. Its collection provides the visitor with an understanding of the history of the House of Liechtenstein. The museum reopened in March 2004 after a renovation.

Also in Vaduz are a postage museum and a state historical museum. A ski museum opened in Vaduz in 1994, and there are also small museums in Schaan, Schellenberg, and Triesenberg.

⁴⁵MEDIA

In 2010 the CIA reported that there were 19,600 telephone landlines in Liechtenstein. In addition to landlines, mobile phone subscriptions numbered 35,500; with landline and mobile phone service widely available, it was estimated that there were 150 telephone subscriptions for every 100 people in the country.

Radio Liechtenstein operates several radio stations. The first television station to be based in the country began operation in August 2008. Internet users numbered 64 per 100 citizens.

Prominent newspapers in 2010, with circulation numbers listed parenthetically, included *Liechtensteiner Volksblatt* (9,000), which reflects the political outlook of the Progressive Citizen's Party; *Liechtensteiner Wochenzeitung* (5,000), a weekly; and *Liechtensteiner Vaterland* (9,584), which reflects the views of the Fatherland Union (VU) party.

The post office (including telegraph and telephone services) is administered by Switzerland. Liechtenstein, however, issues its own postage stamps.

The media is said to enjoy a large degree of autonomy and freedom from interference.

⁴⁶ORGANIZATIONS

Organizations include the Chamber of Industry and Commerce, the Historical Society of the Principality of Liechtenstein, three concert societies, and various other cultural organizations. There are professional organizations representing several fields and occupations. Kiwanis and Lion's clubs are active in the country. Charitable institutions include the Liechtenstein Caritas Society (founded in 1924) and the Liechtenstein Red Cross Society (1945). Youth organizations include the Scouts and Guides of Liechtenstein. There are also several organizations devoted to sports and leisure activities.

⁴⁷TOURISM

The *Tourism Factbook*, published by the UN World Tourism Organization, reported 52,300 incoming tourists to Liechtenstein in 2009. Of those incoming tourists, there were 48,200 from Europe. There were 1,127 hotel beds available in Liechtenstein, which had an occupancy rate of 30%. The estimated daily cost to visit Vaduz, the capital, was $488.

Attractions include mountaineering and nature walks, the castles of Vaduz and Gutenberg (overlooking Balzers), the ruins of several fortresses, the numerous local brass bands and choirs, as well as the operetta societies of Vaduz and Balzers. The most popular sports are swimming, golf, tennis, hiking, and skiing. The ski resort of Malbun has 12 hotels and 7 ski lifts.

Modern, comfortable buses offer regular service throughout Liechtenstein, connecting with Austria and Switzerland. In Vaduz, the lower country, and the Alpine regions there are hotels and guest houses.

⁴⁸FAMOUS PERSONS

Joseph Rheinberger (1839–1901), an organist and composer who lived in Munich, was the teacher of many famous composers. Prince John II (r. 1858–1929) was admired for donating some CHF75 million to the struggling country after World War I. Prince Franz Josef II (1906–89), whose rule began in 1938, was Europe's longest-reigning sovereign. Liechtenstein's head of state is Prince Hans Adam II (b. 1945), who first was given executive power in

1984 and assumed control in 1989. Prince Alois (b. 1968) manages the daily operations of the government.

In 1980, Hanni Wenzel (b. 1956) and her brother Andreas (b. 1958) won the World Cup international skiing championships.

⁴⁹DEPENDENCIES

Liechtenstein has no territories or colonies.

⁵⁰BIBLIOGRAPHY

Annesley, Claire, ed. *A Political and Economic Dictionary of Western Europe.* Philadelphia: Routledge/Taylor and Francis, 2005.

Beattie, David. *Liechtenstein: A Modern History.* New York: I.B. Tauris, 2004.

Eccardt, Thomas M. *Secrets of the Seven Smallest States of Europe.* New York: Hippocrene Books, 2005.

Opello, Walter C. *European Politics.* Boulder, CO: Lynne Rienner Publishers, 2009.

Palan, Ronen. *Tax Havens: How Globalization Really Works.* Ithaca, NY: Cornell University Press, 2010.

Political Chronology of Europe. London, UK: Europa, 2001.

LITHUANIA

Republic of Lithuania
Lietuvos Respublika

CAPITAL: Vilnius

FLAG: Three equal horizontal bands of yellow (top), green, and red.

ANTHEM: *Tautiška Giesme (The National Song).*

MONETARY UNIT: The Lithuanian lita (LTL) of 100 cents has replaced the transitional system of coupons (talonas) which had been in force since October 1992, when the Soviet ruble was demonetized. There are coins of 1, 2, 5, 10, 20, and 50 cents and 1, 2, and 5 litas, and notes of 10, 20, 50, and 100 litas; LTL1 = US$0.378648 (US$1 = LTL2.64097) as of 2011.

WEIGHTS AND MEASURES: The metric system is in force.

HOLIDAYS: New Year's Day, 1 January; Day of the Re-establishment of the State of Lithuania, 16 February; Easter (movable); Statehood Day of Lithuania, 6 July; National Day of Hope and Mourning, 14 June; All Saints' Day, 1 November; Christmas, 25–26 December.

TIME: 2 p.m. = noon GMT.

¹LOCATION, SIZE, AND EXTENT

Lithuania is located in eastern Europe between Latvia and Poland, bordering the Baltic Sea. Comparatively, it is slightly larger than the state of West Virginia with a total area of 65,200 sq km (25,174 sq mi). Lithuania shares boundaries with Latvia on the N and NE, Belarus on the S and SE, Poland on the SW, Russia-Kaliningrad Oblast on the W, and the Baltic Sea on the NW. Lithuania's land boundary length totals 1,273 km (791 mi). Its coastline is 99 km (62 mi).

Lithuania's capital city, Vilnius, is located in the southeastern part of the country.

²TOPOGRAPHY

The topography of Lithuania features a central lowland terrain with many scattered small lakes and fertile soil. Moderate highlands lie to the east and south, with a few hilly regions in the west. The main hill regions are the Zemaical Uplands of the northwest and the Baltic Highlands of the southeast. The highest point in the country is Aukstojas, located in the Medininkai Highlands. It has an elevation of 293 m (961 ft). The lowest point is at sea level (Baltic Sea).

There are about 758 rivers in the country that are longer than 10 km (6.2 mi); but very few are navigable. The Neman, which cuts through the center of the country from Belarus to the Baltic Sea, is the longest river, with a length of 936 km (582 mi). There are over 2,500 lakes in the country, most of which are in the eastern central regions. The largest is Lake Druksiai, which is located on the northeast border with Belarus and covers an area of 44.5 sq km (17.2 sq mi).

³CLIMATE

Lithuania's climate is transitional between maritime and continental; wet, moderate winters and summers. January tempera-

tures averages -5°C (23°F); the mean temperature in July is 17.1°C (63°F). Rainfall averages from 49 cm (24 in) to 85 cm (33 in) depending on location.

⁴FLORA AND FAUNA

Lithuania is located in the mixed forest zone. The country's vegetation is a mixture of coniferous, broadleaf woodlands, arctic, and steppe species. The country has rabbit, fox, red deer, roe, elk, wild boar, badger, raccoon dog, wolf, lynx, and gallinaceous birds. Roach, ruff, bream, and perch can be found in Lithuania's lakes and streams.

The World Resource Institute estimates that there are 1,796 plant species in Lithuania. In addition, it is home to 71 species of mammals, 227 species of birds, 6 species of reptiles, and 12 species of amphibians. The calculation reflects the total number of distinct species residing in the country, not the number of endemic species.

⁵ENVIRONMENT

Lithuania's environmental problems include air pollution, water pollution, and the threat of nuclear contamination. In 2008 the total of carbon dioxide emissions was at 15.268 kilotons. Water resources total 24.5 cu km (5.88 cu mi) while water usage is 3.33 cu km (0.799 cu mi) per year. Domestic water usage accounts for 78% of total usage, industrial for 15%, and agricultural for 7%. Per capita water usage totals 971 cu m (34,291 cu ft) per year. Water pollution results from uncontrolled dumping by industries and the lack of adequate sewage treatment facilities.

After the nuclear accident at Chernobyl (1986), in nearby Ukraine, that contaminated much of Lithuania with excessive radiation, Lithuanians are concerned about nuclear energy development, especially the use of nuclear power generated by plants of the same kind as the one at Chernobyl.

Lithuania's pollution problems have also affected the nation's wildlife. Many of the country's original animal and plant species are now extinct. According to a 2011 report issued by the International Union for Conservation of Nature and Natural Resources (IUCN), threatened species included 3 types of mammals, 4 species of birds, 6 species of fish, and 5 species of invertebrates. Threatened species include the European bison, the asp, the red wood ant, the marsh snail, and the Russian desman. The wild horse has become extinct. According to World Resource Institute Lithuania had designated 355,500 hectares (878,460 acres) of land for protection as of 2006.

6POPULATION

The US Central Intelligence Agency (CIA) estimated the population of Lithuania in 2011 to be approximately 3,535,547, which placed it at number 129 in population among the 196 nations of the world. In 2011 approximately 16.5% of the population was over 65 years of age, with another 13.8% under 15 years of age. The median age in Lithuania was 40.1 years. There were 0.89 males for every female in the country. The population's annual rate of change was -0.276%. The projected population for the year 2025 is 3,100,000. As of 2007 the population density in Lithuania was calculated at 51.8 people per sq km.

The UN estimated that 67% of the population lived in urban areas in 2010, and that urban populations had an annual rate of change of -0.5%. The largest urban area is Vilnius, with a population of 546,000 as of 2009.

7MIGRATION

Estimates of Lithuania's net migration rate, carried out by the CIA in 2011, amounted to -0.72 migrants per 1,000 citizens. The total number of emigrants living abroad was 440,400, and the total number of immigrants living in Lithuania was 128,900. Many Lithuanians unable to accept Soviet occupation in 1940 were deported to Siberia. However, Russian immigration to Lithuania was never as heavy as to the other Baltic republics. Lithuania has been used as a transit country to western Europe for many years. Government policy was to return asylum seekers to their homelands or detain them indefinitely. However, a Lithuanian refugee law passed on 27 July 1997 established an asylum procedure.

8ETHNIC GROUPS

According to 2009 estimates, Lithuanians account for about 84% of the population. Poles make up 6.1%, followed by Russians at 4.9%, and Belarusians at 1.1%. The remaining minority ethnic groups include Ukrainians, Tatars, Karaites, and others. There are about 3,000 in the Romani community.

9LANGUAGES

Lithuanian, the official language, is noted for its purity in retaining ancient Indo-European language forms and has some remarkable similarities with Sanskrit. It is highly inflected, with seven noun cases. Like Latvian, it has rising, falling, and short intonations. Its Roman alphabet has many special symbols, including the hacek, dot, and cedilla. The majority (82%) speak Lithuanian for their first tongue. Polish (5.6%) and Russian (8%) are also widely used.

Minorities have the right to official use of their languages where they form a substantial part of the population.

10RELIGIONS

The country witnessed extensive suppression of religious activities during the Soviet period, but the number of religiously active citizens seems to have increased since then. According to a 2007 government survey, 80.2% of respondents are nominally Roman Catholic. The next largest denomination, the Russian Orthodox Church, account for about 4% of the population. The Old Believers (an Orthodox sect) have about 27,000 members. About 20,000 people are Lutherans, 7,000 are Evangelical Reformed, 4,000 are Jewish, 2,700 are Sunni Muslim, and about 300 are Greek Catholic.

Lithuania is one of a few countries to have an active community of Karaites. The faith is a branch of Judaism, with tenets based exclusively on a literal interpretation of the Hebrew scriptures. The Karaites have two centers of worship in the country, in Vilnius and Trakia, with a total of about 250 members. The Karaites are considered to be an ethnic community as well. They speak a Turkic-based language and use the Hebrew alphabet. Other groups that are referred to as "nontraditional" by the government include Full Gospel Word of Faith Movement, Pentecostals/Charismatics, Jehovah's Witnesses, Baptists, Seventh-Day Adventists, the Church of Jesus Christ of Latter-Day Saints (Mormons), and the New Apostolic Church.

The constitution allows for freedom of religion and this right is generally respected in practice, but the government reserves the right to place restrictions on religious organizations with practices that might contradict the constitution or public law. The government recognizes nine groups as "traditional" faiths: Latin Rite Catholics, Greek Rite Catholics, Evangelical Lutherans, the Evangelical Reformed Church, Orthodox Christians, Old Believers, Jews, Sunni Muslims, and Karaites. These religions are eligible for state assistance and are accorded a number of rights, such as legal registration of marriages and the right to provide religious instruction in public schools. "Nontraditional" religious communities may apply for state recognition, which allows them to receive some funding from the government for various social or cultural programs. As of 2010 there were 181 nontraditional religious associations registered, but only two—the Evangelical Baptist Union of Lithuania and the Seventh-Day Adventists—were state-recognized.

There have been some reports of anti-Semitism within the country, primarily in the form of vandalism against property and anti-Semitic comments made in the media (primarily on the Internet).

Easter Monday, Assumption Day, All Saints' Day, and Christmas (25 and 26 December) are observed as national holidays.

11TRANSPORTATION

The CIA reports that Lithuania has a total of 81,030 km (50,350 mi) of roads, of which 71,563 km (44,467 mi) are paved. There are 546 vehicles per 1,000 people in the country. Lithuania's railroads extend for 1,767 km (1,098 mi). Railroad system provides rail access to the Baltic Sea for Vilnius, Kaunas, and other major urban areas. Of that total, broad gauge lines accounted for the bulk at 1,807 km (1,124 mi) of which, 122 km (76 mi) was electrified. Narrow gauge accounted for another 169 km (105 mi), with

LOCATION: 56°0′ N; 24°0′ E. BOUNDARY LENGTHS: Latvia, 453 kilometers (282 miles); Belarus, 502 kilometers (312 miles); Poland, 91 kilometers (57 miles); Russia, 227 kilometers (141 miles); Baltic Sea coastline, 99 kilometers (62 miles).

standard gauge accounting for the remainder. Lithuania has approximately 441 km (274 mi) of navigable waterways.

Sea routes link Klaipėda on the Baltic Sea with 200 foreign ports. Kaunas is the principal inland port. In 2010 the merchant fleet consisted of 42 ships of 1,000 gross registered tons or over. A railway sea ferry from Klaipėda to Mukran (Germany) began in 1986. As of 2010 there were an estimated 81 airports, which transported 616,514 passengers in 2009 according to the World Bank, of which 26 had paved runways. Principal airports include Palanga, Vilnius, and Kaunas International at Kaunas, and one commercial airport in Siauliai. Two international airlines serve Lithuania: Lithuanian Airlines and Lietuva.

12 HISTORY

Lithuanians are a branch of the Balts, whose permanent and lasting settlement of modern-day Lithuania dates back to 200 BC, much earlier than most of Europe whose people and cultures were still in flux well into the 5th century AD. Lithuanian, along with Latvian, is thus one of the oldest languages in Europe.

The first Lithuanian state was established by the grand duke and later king Mindaugas in 1236. Grand Duke Gediminas, who ruled from 1316-41, is credited with founding the capital of Vilnius and the Jagiellionian dynasty, whose members would become figures of power in Lithuania, Poland, and Hungary for the next 200 years.

In the late 14th century Lithuania ruled a vast area covering much of modern-day Belarus and Ukraine and stretching to the Black Sea. However, the country was constantly threatened by the German Teutonic Order, which occupied the southern Baltic coast. The power struggle had a religious element, since outside of a brief eight-year period, Lithuania remained devoutly pagan until 1386. That year Grand Duke Jogaila (Polish: Jagiello) wed the Polish queen Jadwiga and thereby converted to Christianity the last remaining European pagans. The combined Polish-Lithuanian armies led by Jogaila and his cousin Vytautas (Polish: Witold) decisively beat the Teutonic Knights at the battle of Grunwald in 1410.

The marriage of Jogaila to Jadwiga and his ascension to the Polish throne marked the beginning of a political union with Poland, intertwining the histories of the two nations for 400 years. The union was made formal in the 1569 Lublin Agreement, which created a Polish-Lithuanian Commonwealth with an elected monarch chosen by the gentry of both states. Although in principle it was a union of two equals, the Polish influence on the culture and politics of the commonwealth was stronger, due among other things simply to the larger size and population of the Polish state. Lithuania prospered and developed during the commonwealth's golden age in the 16th century with the founding of the region's first university in Vilnius in 1579 and the development of a distinct Lithuanian baroque artistic style.

The 18th century saw the decline of the commonwealth and occupation by foreign powers. What is now Lithuania was annexed to the Russian Empire in the final partition in 1795. During the 19th century, a Lithuanian nationalist movement arose leading to uprisings against Russian rule and, in turn, to Russian persecutions including the outlawing of the Lithuanian language.

On 16 February 1918 Lithuania proclaimed its independence after the defeat of both Germany and Russia in World War I. The new Bolshevik government in Moscow attempted to establish Soviet power in Lithuania, but failed. After a series of armed border conflicts between Lithuania, Russia, and Poland, in 1920 Moscow recognized Lithuanian independence, but Poland annexed Vilnius, and the Lithuanian capital had to be moved to Kaunas. A secret protocol to the 1939 Nazi-Soviet pact assigned Lithuania to the Soviet sphere of influence. Wishing to avoid conflict, the Lithuanian government allowed Soviet forces to be stationed on its territory. The local government was forced to resign in June 1940. Rigged elections created a parliament which proclaimed Lithuania to be a Soviet Socialist Republic in July 1940. Moscow lost control of Lithuania soon after Germany attacked the USSR in June 1941.

Lithuania suffered heavily at the hands of both powers. While the Nazis succeeded in exterminating most of Lithuania's 240,000 Jews, the Soviets deported tens of thousands of Lithuanians to Siberia. Soviet forces recaptured Lithuania in 1944, although armed resistance against Soviet rule continued for several years after World War II.

Forty-five years of Soviet occupation did not erase the Lithuanian national identity. The first open protests against Soviet rule occurred in 1987 and in 1988. Vytautas Landsbergis established the Sajudis anti-communist political movement which strove to create an autonomous republic and later an independent state. With the crumbling of the Eastern Bloc and fall of the Berlin Wall in 1989, Soviet pressure eased, and opposition parties were allowed to participate in elections to the Lithuanian Supreme Soviet held on 24 February 1990. Sajudis won a clear majority and Lithuania became the first Soviet republic to proclaim independence on 11 March 1990.

Although Soviet president Mikhail Gorbachev's policy of glasnost and perestroika had intended to allow a greater voice to Lithuanian self-determination, full Lithuanian independence from the Soviet Union was not what many in the Kremlin had in mind. The August 1991 coup by hardliners in Moscow was accompanied by a crackdown in Vilnius, with Soviet troops storming the TV Tower, killing 14 civilians and injuring 700. It was not until the failure of the coup and collapse of the Soviet Union that the government in Moscow fully recognized Lithuanian independence.

Since independence, Lithuania has been preoccupied with reforming its economic and political institutions. Privatization has transformed its economy to a market-oriented one. Politically, a thriving press and open democracy have been established. Former Communists won the first postindependence elections in 1992, but conservatives took back the Seimas (parliament) in 1996 elections, in response to growing allegations of government corruption. Presidential elections the following year were surrounded by controversy over the eligibility for office of candidate Valdas Adamkus, who had lived in the United States for over 30 years following World War II. Adamkus was elected in runoff elections in January 1998.

Parliamentary elections were held on 8 October 2000, resulting in a win for former president Algirdas Brazauskas' Social Democratic Coalition, which won 31.1% of the vote, taking 51 of 141 seats in the Seimas. However, a grouping of four smaller parties formed a new centrist government with Rolandas Paksas as prime minister. Presidential elections were held on 22 December 2002, and Adamkus took the lead in the first round of voting, with 35.3% of the vote, to 19.7% for Paksas. In what surprised many experts, Paksas campaigned vigorously for the run-off vote held on 5 January 2003, and won the second round with 54.9% to 45.1% for Adamkus.

Paksas did not serve out his entire term. When he was impeached in April 2004 for having ties with Russian organized crime and participating in influence peddling, the country was temporarily thrown into disarray. In the early election that followed, the constitutional court did not allow Paksas to run again despite his continued popularity, especially in rural regions. Adamkus seized the opportunity to return to office and beat Kazimira Prunskiene, the country's first post-Soviet prime minister, who was supported by those loyal to Paksas.

Given the history of Russian domination of Lithuania, it is understandable that Lithuania's primary foreign policy objective has been to improve relations with the West and especially to gain entrance into NATO and the EU. Lithuania became a member of both organizations in 2004.

On 12 July 2009 Dalia Grybauskaite was inaugurated as the first female president of Lithuania. Before her election, Grybauskaite served as the European Union budget commissioner. While concern for the lagging economy was a prominent issue during the election, the president of Lithuania is primarily responsible for foreign affairs, with very little oversight of economic policy.

^{13}GOVERNMENT

On 25 October 1992 Lithuanian voters approved a new constitution, which called for a 141-member unicameral parliament (Seimas) and a popularly elected president. The constitution requires whoever is elected as president to sever his or her formal party ties. All who were permanent residents of Lithuania in November 1989 have been granted the opportunity to become citizens, irrespective of their ethnic origins. Members of the Seimas are elected for four-year terms, and the president is directly elected for a five-year term. The prime minister is appointed by the president; all others ministers are nominated by the prime minister and appointed by the president. All ministerial appointments must be approved by the Seimas. Suffrage is universal at age 18.

^{14}POLITICAL PARTIES

The majority party in the Seimas after the 1996 parliamentary elections was the conservative Homeland Union Party, or TS, led by Vytautas Landsbergis, which won 70 out of 141 seats. Overall, 28 parties competed for the 141 parliamentary seats in elections held on 20 October 1996 (first round) and 10 November 1996 (second round). The other party of the right wing, the Christian Democrats, also did well, winning 16 seats, and entered into a coalition government with the TS and the Lithuanian Center Union, which won 13 seats. The Democratic Labor Party (composed mostly of ex-Communists), which had been the majority party in the previous parliament, won only 12 seats. Other parties with parliamentary representation included the Lithuanian Social Democratic Party and the Lithuanian Democratic Party.

The Homeland Union-Conservative coalition suffered in the October 2000 parliamentary elections, capturing only nine seats. Former president Algirdas Brazauskas led four leftist parties in a Social Democratic Coalition, winning 51 of the 141 seats in parliament. However, the New Policy coalition composed of the ideologically diverse Liberal Union (33 seats), New Alliance (28), Center Union (2), Modern Christian Democratic Union (3), and two smaller parties formed a new government, bypassing the Social Democratic Coalition. Rolandas Paksas was named prime minister.

In the elections of October 2004 the Labor Party—a political formation led by Russian millionaire Voktor Uspaskich—won 39 seats, Homeland Union 25, the Social Democrats 20, Liberal and Center Union 18, Social Liberals 11, Union of Farmers and New Democracy 10, Liberal Democrats 10, Electoral Action 2, and independents claimed 6 seats. In the presidential elections held in June 2004 Valdas Adamkus beat Kazimiera Prunskiene with 52.2% of the vote.

Following the 2008 parliamentary elections, the Homeland Union-Lithuanian Christian Democrats (TS-LKD), Liberal Movement (LRLS), Liberal and Center Union (LCS), and National Revival (TPP) formed a ruling coalition. Together these parties controlled 71 seats in parliament. The Social Democratic Party won 24 seats, followed by the Order and Justice Party with 18 seats, the Christian Party with 10 seats, and the Labor Party with 10 seats. There were seven unaffiliated seats and one seat was left vacant. Andrius Kubilius of TS-LKD was appointed as prime minister. The next elections were scheduled for October 2012.

On 12 July 2009 Dalia Grybauskaite was inaugurated as the first female president of Lithuania. Running as an independent candidate, Grybauskaite won the May 2009 presidential election with 68.1% of the vote. Social Democrat Algirdas Butkevicius came in second with 12% of the vote.

^{15}LOCAL GOVERNMENT

For administrative purposes, Lithuania's 10 provinces are divided into 60 municipalities; there are also urban districts, towns, and rural administrative units called *apylinkes*. Each level of local government has its own elected officials.

^{16}JUDICIAL SYSTEM

After Lithuania broke away from the Soviet Union, its legal system was transformed from that of the old Soviet regime to a democratic model. The system now consists of a constitutional court and a Supreme Court, whose members are elected by the Seimas, as well as district and local courts, whose judges are appointed by the president. A court of appeals hears appellate cases from the district courts. A new civil and criminal procedure code and a court reform law were enacted in 1995. The government has reviewed its laws to bring them into accord with the European Convention on Human Rights. The judiciary is independent.

^{17}ARMED FORCES

In 2011 the International Institute for Strategic Studies reported that armed forces in Lithuania totaled 10,640 members. The force is comprised of 8,200 from the army, 530 from the navy, 980 from the air force, and 1,804 members of joint forces. Armed forces represent 1.6% of the labor force in Lithuania. Defense spending totaled $683 million and accounted for 1.2% of GDP. Lithuanian forces have served in Afghanistan, Iraq, Bosnia, and Serbia and Montenegro.

^{18}INTERNATIONAL COOPERATION

Lithuania was admitted to the UN on 17 September 1991; it is a member of several specialized agencies, such as the FAO, IAEA, World Bank, ILO, IMF, UNCTAD, UNESCO, UNIDO, and the WHO. Lithuania is also a member of the WTO, the OSCE, the Council of Europe, the European Bank for Reconstruction and Development, the Euro-Atlantic Partnership Council, and the Council of the Baltic Sea States. It is a member affiliate of the Western European Union. Lithuania joined the European Union and NATO in 2004.

As of 2011 Lithuania had foreign diplomatic missions in 98 countries. The country has offered support to UN missions and operations in Kosovo (est. 1999). It is part of the Australia Group, the Nuclear Suppliers Group (London Group), and the Organization for the Prohibition of Chemical Weapons. In environmental cooperation, Lithuania is part of the Basel Convention, Conventions on Biological Diversity and Air Pollution, Ramsar, CITES, the Kyoto Protocol, the Montréal Protocol, MARPOL, and the UN Conventions on the Law of the Sea and Climate Change.

^{19}ECONOMY

Due to modernization that occurred during Soviet dominance, Lithuania built up a large, if somewhat inefficient, industrial sector that as of 2010 accounted for 27.6% of the country's economy. The service sector accounted for 68.2%, while agriculture accounts for about 4.3% of the economy.

In 1992 Lithuania's GDP fell 21.6%. In that year the government adopted an IMF-directed program aimed at privatizing the economy, controlling inflation, eliminating price controls, and lowering the budget deficit. In June 1993 Lithuania's convertible currency, the lita, was introduced, setting off another round of inflation, while GDP continued to decline, by 16.2% in 1993 and 9.8% in 1994. In 1994 the government entered into a three-year arrangement with the IMF under its Extended Fund Facility (EFF) aimed primarily at bringing inflation under control. The first year of positive growth (3.3%) since independence was 1995, although unemployment remained high, at 16.4% in that year. Inflation, which was still in double digits in 1996 (23%), fell to single digits (5.1%) by 1998 and unemployment fell to 6.4%. The economy registered real growth until 1999—4.7% in 1996, 7.3% in 1997 and 5.1% in 1998—but then was overtaken by the effects of the August 1998 financial crisis in Russia, still one of Lithuania's largest trading partners. Real GDP declined 3.9% in 1999 as unemployment jumped to 8.4%. Inflation remained under control, however, at 0.3%.

Growth returned in 2000, with real GDP up 3.3%, but unemployment continued to soar, peaking at 13.2% in March 2001. Growth in 2001 was 5.9%, above expectations, and in the first half of 2002, growth averaged about 5.6%. In February 2002, the government repegged the lita from the US dollar to the euro, at a rate of LTL3.4528 per euro. Inflation was about 1% for the year and by December 2002, unemployment had moderated to 10.9%. The unemployment rate continued to decrease and stood at just 3.2% in 2007. Between independence and 2008, about 80% of Lithuania's enterprises were privatized and over 25% of its trade was with countries outside the old Soviet Bloc. Lithuania was admitted to the World Trade Organization in 2001 and was admitted to the European Union in 2004.

The Lithuanian economy was hit hard by the global financial crisis of 2008–09. Decreased demand for exported goods led to a decrease in industrial output. Demand also dropped in construction, textiles, and retail industries, resulting in Lithuania's largest contraction in GDP since 1995. The government projected a decline in GDP of 15% by the end of 2009. Those projections materialized in January 2010. In that month Statistics Lithuania reported that the 2009 drop in GDP was 15%, marking the worst economic year since the country gained independence in 1990. A more detailed look at the statistics, however, left room for hope. The 2009 quarterly contractions moved from 19.5% in the second, to 14.2% in the third, and finally to 13% in the fourth.

More positive economic news arrived in July 2010, when Lithuania's statistics office reported that the Lithuanian economy had experienced its first quarterly growth in seven quarters in the second quarter of 2010. During the second quarter, April through June, the Lithuanian economy expanded at an annualized rate of 1.1%, driven by strong exports and rising industrial output. The economy's performance topped most economic forecasts, which had predicted it would contract. As of 2010 the GDP rate of change in Lithuania was 1.3%. Inflation stood at 0.9%, and unemployment was reported at 17.9%.

20 INCOME

In 2010 the CIA estimated that the GDP of Lithuania was $56.59 billion. The CIA defines GDP as the value of all final goods and services produced within a nation in a given year and computed on the basis of purchasing power parity (PPP) rather than value as measured on the basis of the rate of the exchange based on current dollars. Per capita GDP was estimated at $16,000. The annual growth rate of GDP was 1.3%. It was estimated that agriculture accounted for 4.3% of GDP, industry 27.6%, and services 68.2%. The average inflation rate was 0.9%.

According to the World Bank, remittances from citizens living abroad totaled $1.2 billion or about $331 per capita and accounted for approximately 2.1% of GDP.

In 2007 the World Bank estimated that Lithuania, with 0.06% of the world's population, accounted for 0.09% of the world's GDP. By comparison, the United States, with 4.85% of the world's population, accounted for 22.51% of world GDP.

A study by the World Bank from 2011 reported that actual individual consumption in Lithuania was 75.2% of GDP and accounted for 0.10% of world consumption. The household consumption was growing at an average annual rate of 3.6%. By comparison, the United States accounted for 25.44% of world individual consumption. The World Bank also estimated that 21.8% of Lithuania's GDP was spent on food and beverages, 13% on housing and household furnishings, 5.4% on clothes, 6.9% on health, 9.8% on transportation, 1.7% on communications, 4.9% on recreation, 2.0% on restaurants and hotels, and 4.5% on miscellaneous goods and services and purchases from abroad.

21 LABOR

As of 2010 Lithuania had a total labor force of 1.635 million people. Unemployment was reported at 17.9%. Within that labor force, CIA estimates in 2005 noted that 14% were employed in agriculture, 29.1% in industry, and 56.9% in the service sector.

The constitution recognizes the right for workers to form and join trade unions. Approximately 13% of employees are union members. There are four major trade union organizations. The law also provides the right of workers to strike, except those in essential services in the public sector. Collective bargaining is permitted but only utilized on a limited basis.

The legal minimum wage is periodically adjusted by the government for inflation, but these adjustments lag behind the inflation rate. The minimum wage was $320 per month as of 2011, but it is not universally enforced. The legal minimum age for employment is 16 years without parental consent, or 14 years with written parental consent. The 40-hour workweek is standard for most workers. The law stipulates occupational health and safety standards, but these are not effectively enforced and many industrial plants are unsafe.

22 AGRICULTURE

Roughly 43% of the total land is farmed. The country's major crops include grain, potatoes, sugar beets, flax, vegetables beef, milk, eggs, and fish. In 2009 cereal production amounted to 3.8

million tons, fruit production 188,000 tons, and vegetable production 188,000 tons.

Privatization in agriculture rapidly advanced after 1991; over 70,000 private farms had been established by 1996. In 2007 there were 230,000 agricultural holdings, which represented a 9% decrease from 2005. Due to a lack of financial resources and inefficiency in the crediting system, many of these new farmers were only operating at subsistence levels. Agricultural output decreased by a yearly average of 1.1% during 1990–2000. However, during 2002–04, crop production was up 9.5% from 1999–2001.

²³ANIMAL HUSBANDRY

The UN Food and Agriculture Organization (FAO) reported that Lithuania dedicated 783,200 hectares (1.94 million acres) to permanent pasture or meadow in 2009. During that year, the country tended 8.8 million chickens, 770,900 head of cattle, and 897,100 pigs. The production from these animals amounted to 24,929 tons of beef and veal, 150,075 tons of pork, 84,028 tons of poultry, 37,686 tons of eggs, and 919,118 tons of milk. Lithuania also produced 3,872 tons of cattle hide and 80 tons of raw wool. Livestock in 2011 included 58,500 sheep and 44,700 horses.

²⁴FISHING

Lithuania had 112 decked commercial fishing boats in 2008. Klaipeda's fishing port is the center of the fishing industry of Lithuania. There are two aquacultural facilities, consisting primarily of carp. Principal species include mackerel, sardines, and hairtail. The annual capture totaled 182,763 tons in 2008, according to the UN FAO. Fisheries exports were valued at $187.3 million in 2008.

²⁵FORESTRY

Forests cover about 35% of Lithuania. The forestry, wood products, and paper industries are some of Lithuania's oldest. Furniture, matches, and timber products were manufactured in Kaunas and Vilnius in the mid-1800s, and furniture making prevailed from 1919–40. Chemical timber processing, and the production of furniture, pulp, paper, wood fiber, wood chips, joinery articles, and cardboard, are the main activities of the modern forestry sector. Intensive timber processing, as well as the recycling of industrial waste are being expanded. The UN FAO estimated the 2009 roundwood production at 3.68 million cu m (129.8 million cu ft). The value of all forest products, including roundwood, totaled $328.2 million. The exports of forest products amounted to $335.7 million in 2004.

²⁶MINING

Lithuania's production of nonfuel minerals in 2009 included cement, limestone, nitrogen (from ammonia) and peat. Other industrial minerals produced include clays, and sand and gravel. Lithuania remains dependent on imports for its metals and fuel needs. Peat is extracted in the Siauliai, Ezherelis, Paraistis, and Baltoyi-Boke regions. Mineral production figures in 2009 included: limestone, 858,411 metric tons, down from 1,625,089 metric tons in 2008; cement, 583,100 metric tons, compared to 1,075,581 metric tons in 2008; and peat, 557,500 metric tons, up from 536,000 metric tons in 2008.

²⁷ENERGY AND POWER

Lithuania has no reserves of natural gas, but it does have a small amount of recoverable coal reserves. Lithuania had 12 million barrels of proven oil reserves in 2010, but potential onshore and offshore reserves could be much greater. As of 2010 the oil production totaled 2,000 barrels of oil a day. Per capita oil consumption was 2,733 kg. Lithuania imports the bulk of its oil, mostly from Russia.

Lithuania also operates the only petroleum refinery among the Baltic States. The Mazheikiai oil refinery has a production capacity of 15 million tons of crude per year.

The World Bank reported in 2008 that Lithuania produced 13.3 billion kWh of electricity and consumed 11.9 billion kWh, or 3,379 kWh per capita. The same year, reports indicated that roughly 61% of energy came from fossil fuels, while 29% came from alternative fuels.

²⁸INDUSTRY

Lithuania underwent rapid industrialization during the Soviet era and has developed significant capacity in machine building and metalworking, as well as in the textile and leather industries, and agro-processing (including processed meat, dairy products, and fish). The country's diverse manufacturing base also includes an oil refinery and high-tech minicomputer production. Other industrial products include refrigerators and freezers, electric motors, television sets, metal-cutting machine tools, small ships, furniture, fertilizers, optical equipment, and electronic components.

Due to a rapid program of privatization, more than 80% of Lithuania's enterprises were privately owned by 2008. Most capital investment has gone into the industrial sector, including upgrading the oil refinery, the nuclear power plant, construction of a main highway, and the modernization of seaport facilities.

²⁹SCIENCE AND TECHNOLOGY

The Lithuanian Academy of Science, founded in 1941, has departments of mathematical, physical, and chemical sciences; biological, medical, and agricultural sciences; and technical sciences. In 1987-97, science and engineering students accounted for 31% of university enrollment. Ten research institutes concerned with medicine, natural sciences, and technology, mostly in Vilnius, and a botanical garden in Kaunas are attached to the academy. Four other institutes conduct research in medicine and forestry. Seven universities and colleges offer degrees in basic and applied sciences.

Patent applications in science and technology as of 2009 totaled 91 in Lithuania, according to the World Bank. In 2009 Lithuania had one of the highest shares of highly-qualified professionals with 60% of its population engaged in research and development (R&D). In 2008 Lithuania spent 0.80% of GDP on R&D.

³⁰DOMESTIC TRADE

Vilnius, Klaipėda, and Kaunas each have shopping areas and several markets; many smaller towns have a central market. Several supermarkets have also opened and there are a number of newer privately owned import businesses taking root. There is little interest in franchising by local companies. With the exception of one or two companies, those that have tried it, found it to be unprofitable. However, as Lithuanian consumers become more brand-conscious, the demand for franchising may increase. An 18% value-added tax is applied to most sales and services in Lithuania, although there is a 9% rate on heating services and a 5% rate on transport services.

Business office hours are generally from 9 a.m. to 5 p.m. Monday through Friday. Banks are usually open from 8 a.m. to 3 p.m. Mondays through Fridays, although some banks are open on weekends. Shops are open Mondays through Saturdays from 9 a.m. to 7 p.m., although many stores are open on Sundays as well.

³¹FOREIGN TRADE

In the mid- to late-1990s Lithuania began trading more with Western nations, reducing its reliance on trade with former Soviet republics. Trade with the West increased from 15% to 60% between 1990 and 1995, while trade with former Soviet republics fell from 78% in 1990 to 40% in 1995. Since Lithuania's independence in 1990, growing disruptions in trade with Russia and the other former Soviet republics have resulted in a steep decline in import volumes and numerous domestic shortages.

Lithuania imported $20.34 billion worth of goods and services in 2008, while exporting $19.29 billion worth of goods and services. Mineral products make up Lithuania's most beneficial export commodity (23%), followed by textiles and clothing (16%), and machinery and equipment (11%). Other export commodities include chemicals (6%), wood and wood products (5%), and foodstuffs (5%). The main import commodities were mineral products, machinery and equipment, transport equipment, chemicals, textiles and clothing, and metals. Major import partners in 2009 were Russia, 29.9%; Germany, 11.3%; Poland, 10%; Latvia, 6.4%; and Netherlands, 4%. Major export partners were Russia, 13.3%; Latvia, 10.1%; Germany, 9.7%; Poland, 7.2%; Estonia, 7%; Netherlands, 5.1%; Belarus, 4.7%; and the United Kingdom, 4.4%.

³²BALANCE OF PAYMENTS

The CIA reported that in 2010 Lithuania had a foreign trade deficit of $297 million, amounting to 9% of GDP. That year Lithuania had exports of goods totaling $20.82 billion and imports totaling $22.38 billion. The services credit totaled $3,434.34 billion and debit $-2,515.50 million.

The current account has been negative and increased up to -$318.99 million in 2010, and -$884.29 million in 2011. However, the total reserves (including gold) increased since 2010 from $346.59 million $592.11 million in 2011.

³³BANKING AND SECURITIES

Since 1991 Lithuania has reorganized its banking sector numerous times. A myriad of banks emerged after independence, most of them weak. Consequently, consolidations, mergers, and collapses became a regular feature of the country's banking system.

On 3 July 1992 the government adopted a new currency unit, the lita, to replace the ruble. Between 1992 and 1995 six banks lost their licenses and two were merged; as of mid-1996, 16 were either suspended or facing bankruptcy procedures. The first serious crisis centered on Aurasbankas, the eighth-largest bank in the country, and the deposit bank for many ministries. The Bank of

---

Principal Trading Partners – Lithuania (2010)

(In millions of US dollars)

Country	Total	Exports	Imports	Balance
World	44,111.2	20,726.4	23,384.8	-2,658.4
Russia	10,811.4	3,195.4	7,616.0	-4,420.6
Germany	4,514.2	2,052.1	2,462.2	-410.1
Poland	3,684.0	1,608.0	2,076.0	-467.9
Kosovo	3,415.5	1,938.7	1,476.8	461.9
Netherlands	2,194.2	1,152.0	1,042.2	109.8
Estonia	1,715.4	1,046.6	668.8	377.8
Sweden	1,517.1	750.3	766.8	-16.5
Belarus	1,446.7	1,063.6	383.1	680.6
United Kingdom	1,389.8	1,016.9	372.9	644.0
France	1,292.5	687.3	605.2	82.1

(…) data not available or not significant.

(n.s.) not specified.

SOURCE: *2011 Direction of Trade Statistics Yearbook,* New York: United Nations, 2011.

Balance of Payments – Lithuania (2010)

(In millions of US dollars)

Current Account		667.2
Balance on goods	-1,560.0	
Imports	-22,375.7	
Exports	20,815.8	
Balance on services	1,295.5	
Balance on income	-902.7	
Current transfers	1,834.5	
Capital Account		985.8
Financial Account		-957.7
Direct investment abroad	-132.3	
Direct investment in Lithuania	622.2	
Portfolio investment assets	-532.6	
Portfolio investment liabilities	2,456.7	
Financial derivatives	0.9	
Other investment assets	-158.8	
Other investment liabilities	-3,124.0	
Net Errors and Omissions		4.0
Reserves and Related Items		-699.3

(…) data not available or not significant.

SOURCE: *Balance of Payment Statistics Yearbook 2011,* Washington, DC: International Monetary Fund, 2011.

Lithuania suspended Aurasbankas's operations in mid-1995 because of liquidity problems caused by bad lending and deposit-taking practices. In July 1995 the minimum capital requirement for existing banks was raised from LTL5 million to LTL10 million, the level already established for new banks.

Operations at Lithuania's largest bank, the Joint-Stock Innovation Bank, were suspended on 20 December 1995, and those of the Litimpeks bank, the country's second-largest, two days later. The two were in the process of merging to create the Lithuania United Bank and the fraud was uncovered during pre-merger audits. Due to rumors of a devaluation of the currency, a shortage of foreign exchange throughout the whole banking sector was created.

The International Monetary Fund reports that in 2010 currency demand deposits were equal to $171.23 billion. M2-an aggregate

Public Finance – Lithuania (2009)

(In millions of litai, central government figures)

Revenue and Grants	**28,161**	**100.0%**
Tax revenue	12,794	45.4%
Social contributions	11,750	41.7%
Grants	1,976	7.0%
Other revenue	1,640	5.8%
Expenditures	**36,446**	**100.0%**
General public services	8,839	24.3%
Defense	1,195	3.3%
Public order and safety	1,665	4.6%
Economic affairs	3,166	8.7%
Environmental protection	166	0.5%
Housing and community amenities	113	0.3%
Health	4,182	11.5%
Recreational, culture, and religion	623	1.7%
Education	2,257	6.2%
Social protection	14,240	39.1%

(…) data not available or not significant.

SOURCE: *Government Finance Statistics Yearbook 2010*, Washington, DC: International Monetary Fund, 2010.

equal to M1 plus savings deposits, small time deposits, and money market mutual funds-was $2.89 million in 2008.

The discount rate was 3% in 2011; the commercial bank prime lending rate was 5.5% that year. As of 2010 the nation's gold bullion deposits totaled $304 million.

The National Stock Exchange, NASDAQ OMX Vilnius, was established in September 1993. As of 2009, there were a total of 38 companies listed on the NASDAQ OMX Vilnius, with a market capitalization of $2.5 billion.

34 INSURANCE

Lithuania's health insurance system is reminiscent of the Soviet era, with a state-run system of coverage for all residents. In 2010 about 6.1% of GDP was spent on health, the plan was to increase the expenditure up to 10.3% by 2050. As of 2011 Lithuania's leading life insurer was ERGO LIETUVA.

35 PUBLIC FINANCE

The US Central Intelligence Agency (CIA) estimated that in 2010 Lithuania's central government took in revenues of approximately $12.5 billion and had expenditures of $15.07 billion. Revenues minus expenditures totaled approximately -$2.57 billion. Public debt in 2010 amounted to 38.7% of GDP. External debt represented about 57% of GDP.

36 TAXATION

Lithuania has one of the most liberal tax regimes in Europe. The corporate income tax rate as of 2009 was 20%. Capital gains are considered part of corporate income and are taxed at the corporate rate. Dividends are generally taxed at 15%, but if paid to a nonresident company that owns more than 10% of its voting shares (i.e., its parent company), there is no tax. This provision is not applicable to companies operating in free economic zones (FEZs), which offer 80% reduction in the corporate income tax rate for the first five years, and a 50% reduction for an additional five years.

Personal income as of 2011 was taxed at a flat rate of 15% and 5% from individual activity. Individual activities include income from distributed profits, the sale or rental of property, creative activities, and other types of activities. Individuals receiving capital gains from either the sale of property or shares are taxed at 15% on the gains. However, capital gains from shares held for more than a year may be exempt if certain conditions are met. If the gains are derived from the sale of immovable property in Lithuania, they are exempt if the property was held for more than three years. Deductions from income for the primary flat tax include a nontaxable minimum which is higher for disabled persons, single parents, and other specified groups, plus all social security and social assistance payments, death benefits, court awards, gifts, allowances for insurance payments, charity donations, and most payments to pension accounts. As of 2006 Lithuanian companies and individuals, pay 0.3%-1% annual tax on real estate tax was introduced. Gifts and inheritances are taxed at 0%, 5%, and 10% depending on the amount involved.

The main indirect tax is Lithuania's VAT, enacted 22 December 1993 and revised in 1 July 2002 for application in 2003. The VAT standard rate increased in 2011 from 19% to 21%, applicable to most goods and services, and three reduced rates of 9%, 5%, and 0%. The 9% rate is applied to the renovation and construction of buildings financed from certain sources. The 5% rate is applied to certain foodstuffs, newspapers, books, passenger and luggage transport, drugs and medicines, and hotel accommodations. Exports and some export related services, international transport, ships, and aircraft, and European Union related trade or supplies are zero-rated. Exempted from the VAT are educational, healthcare, insurance and financial services, the leasing, sale or transfer of immovable property (including dwellings), and social, sports, cultural, radio and television services, if provided by nonprofit organizations.

There are also excise duties on ethyl alcohol and alcoholic beverages, tobacco, and fuels. However, by the Law on Excise Duties of 1 July 2002, excise taxes on jewelry, electrical energy, coffee, chocolate, and other food products were abolished, while turnover taxes replaced excises on sugar, luxury cars, liquid cosmetics containing ethyl alcohol, and publications of an erotic and/or violent nature. In 1999 the government introduced a pollution tax on packages to encourage the recycling of packaging material.

37 CUSTOMS AND DUTIES

Most foreign imports, including all raw materials, are duty-free. Exceptions include food products (5-10%), fabrics (10%), electronics (10%), cement (25%), and window glass (50%). The average tariff on consumer products is 15%. Alcoholic beverages are subject to duties ranging from 10% for beer to 100% for some liquor. A 21% VAT is also placed on imports. In 1993 Lithuania, Estonia, and Latvia formed a free trade area, which eliminated customs duties and quotas between the three Baltic States. In accordance with Lithuania's participation in the European Union, some duties on EU goods have been lowered.

38FOREIGN INVESTMENT

In May 1991 a foreign investment law was passed permitting majority holdings by nonresidents and guaranteeing the full transfer of profits. Various tax benefits may be granted to foreign investors depending on the type and size of the investment. When purchasing privatized Lithuanian companies or forming joint ventures, foreign investors are usually expected to provide employment guarantees.

Foreigners from the European Union and NATO-member nations may own land, while foreigners from all other nations may not. The provision is aimed primarily at foreigners from former Soviet republics, who are the main non-Western investors in Lithuania. Foreigners not eligible to own land may rent it for a period of up to 99 years.

Foreign direct investment (FDI) inflow into Lithuania reached $230.1 million according to World Bank figures published in 2009. FDI represented 0.62% of GDP. On 1 July 2010 total foreign direct investment in Lithuania reached $15.8 billion, with most of it coming from the European Union. As of 2006 the largest chunk of this capital inflow went to the following sectors: manufacturing (39.6%), trade (11.0%), transportation and communication (13.7%), and financial mediation (12.3%).

Lithuania continues, despite its small size, to be an attractive location for FDI and a competitive center for product sourcing. It boasts a highly skilled labor force, competitive costs, a stable political and economic environment, a strong currency, and the region's most developed infrastructure.

39ECONOMIC DEVELOPMENT

In 1990 the Lithuanian government began a comprehensive economic reform program aimed at effecting the transformation to a market-driven economy. Reform measures included price reform, trade reform, and privatization. By mid-1993 about 92% of housing and roughly 60% of businesses slated for privatization had been privatized. By 1996 about 36% of state enterprises and about 83% of all state property had been privatized. International aid agencies committed about $765 million of assistance in 1992–95. Most international aid went either to infrastructure construction or loan credits to business. Citing continued progress toward democratic development, in 1999 the United States announced that it was terminating economic assistance to Lithuania. Having established itself as a democratic society with a market economy, Lithuania was invited to join the European Union in 2002, and it became a member in 2004.

In 2001 Lithuania negotiated a 19-month, $119-million standby arrangement with the International Monetary Fund (IMF). In 2002 the country's GDP grew at a rapid pace (6-6.7%), unemployment declined, the inflation rate fell to near zero, and there was a lower-than-expected general government deficit. In 2002 the tax system was aligned with EU requirements, the financial situation of municipalities and the Health Insurance Fund were improved, privatization moved forward, and the financial sector was strengthened. The privatization program for 2003 included the sale of a second 34% stake in Lithuania Gas, one or two electricity distribution companies, and four alcohol producers.

In 2003 Lithuania was one of the most dynamic economies in Europe, with a 9.7% growth of the GDP, and it continued strongly through 2004 and 2005. However, in 2009 the growth of GDP dropped down to -14.7%. In 2010 it went up again to an estimated 1.3%. Income levels still lag behind the rest of the European Union, and greenfield investments need to be attracted to counteract the effects of a more expensive future market. An inflow of structural funds from the European Union is expected to trigger a short-term economic boom.

40SOCIAL DEVELOPMENT

A national system of social insurance covers all of Lithuania's residents. Old age (pension), sickness, disability, and unemployment benefits are paid on an earnings-related basis, from contributions by both employers and employees. Retirement is set at age 62.5 for men, and age 60 for women, with at least 30 years of contribution at the normal pensionable age. The pension may be deferred from 1 to 5 years. Family allowance benefits are provided by states and municipalities to families with low incomes. There is a universal system of medical care, and a dual social insurance and social assistance program for maternity and health payments.

Legally, men and women have equal status, including equal pay for equal work, although in practice women are underrepresented in managerial and professional positions. Discrimination against women in the workplace persists. Violence against women, especially domestic abuse, is common. As of 2009 there was no law specifically prohibiting violence against women. In 2009 an estimated 56% of divorced women and 15% of married women had suffered domestic violence, and 20% experienced sexual harassment. Child abuse is also a serious social problem. Authorities link the upsurge in abuse to alcoholism.

Human rights are generally respected in Lithuania, and human rights organizations are permitted to operate freely and openly. Prolonged detention still occurs in some cases, and poor prison conditions persist.

In July 2009 the government passed a controversial child censor bill that raised concern among prominent international human rights organizations. The law officially bans public dissemination of material that is considered to be harmful to minors. Such harmful material includes media that is deemed to promote violence, gambling, bad eating habits, paranormal phenomena, hypnosis, and, more directly, homosexuality, bisexuality, and polygamy. The issue of homosexuality is a heated one in Lithuania, where a predominantly Catholic population is opposed to the practice. International human rights groups argue that the law is a clear infringement on the right of freedom of expression, but are more adamantly concerned that the ban on materials concerning homosexuality could prohibit legitimate discussion on the topic and lead to greater discrimination against homosexuals, bisexuals, and transgendered individuals. In 2009 a faction of parliament had begun to seek an outright ban of homosexuality within the nation, claiming that such a measure is necessary in defense of traditional family values, although no such law had been passed by April 2012.

41HEALTH

In 2011 Lithuania had approximately 37 physicians, 73 nurses and midwifes, and 68 hospital bed per 10,000 inhabitants. Most primary care providers are women. In 1994 the Public Health Surveillance Service was established to oversee control of communicable diseases, environmental and occupational health, and some other areas. As of 2009 the country spent 7.8% of its GDP on healthcare, amounting to $730 per person.

One-year-old children were immunized as follows: diphtheria, pertussis, and tetanus, 94%; polio, 89%; and measles, 96%. The HIV/AIDS adult prevalence rate was 0.1% in 2009. The incidence of tuberculosis was 75 per 100,000 people in 2007.

According to the CIA, life expectancy in Lithuania was 73 years in 2011. The total fertility rate in 2011 was estimated at 1.25 children born per woman. The infant mortality rate for that year was 5 deaths per 1,000 live births. In 2008 the maternal mortality rate, according to the World Bank, was estimated at 13 deaths per 100,000 live births.

42 HOUSING

In 2011 national statistics indicated that there were about 1,415,000 dwelling units in the country. About 32% of all housing units were individual houses; 61% were apartments. About 97% of these units are privately owned. The average living space is about 21.5 square meters per person. About 79% of all conventional dwellings are equipped with piped water, 72% had bath and shower facilities, and 52% had central heating. The next housing survey was scheduled for 2013. City governments are being encouraged to take more responsibility for social housing projects. Homeowners associations are being encouraged and new laws are being drafted for residential building associations. The Housing Loan Insurance Company was established in 2000 to provide insurance of loans and to promote housing loans with a low (5%) down payment.

43 EDUCATION

Education is free and compulsory for all children between the ages of 7 and 16 years (for 10 years). While Lithuanian is the most common medium of instruction, children also study Polish, Russian, and Yiddish. Primary school covers four years of study, followed by six years of basic or lower secondary school. Students then move on to either two years of senior secondary school or vocational schools, which offer two- to three-year programs. The academic year runs from September to June.

In 2008 the World Bank estimated that 92% of age-eligible children in Lithuania were enrolled in primary school. Secondary enrollment for age-eligible children stood at 92%. Tertiary enrollment was estimated at 77%. Of those enrolled in tertiary education, there were 100 male students for every 156 female students.

The four main universities are: Kaunas University of Technology (founded in 1950); Vilnius Technical University (founded in 1961); Vilnius University (founded in 1579); and Vytautas Magnus University (founded in 1922). The adult literacy rate for 2009 was at 100%. Public expenditure on education represented 4.7% of GDP as of 2007.

44 LIBRARIES AND MUSEUMS

The National Library at Vilnius has about 9.2 million volumes. Founded in 1570, the Vilnius University Library has over 5.3 million volumes. Vilnius also has the Central Library of the Academy of Sciences, with about 3.66 million volumes. There are dozens of other special collections in the country, including libraries maintained by the Union of Lithuanian Writers, the State Institute of Art, and the Institute of Urban Planning. The Institute of Lithuanian Literature and Folklore in Vilnius contains over 240,000 printed items. The Lithuanian Librarians' Association was established in 1931, disbanded under German occupation in 1941, and reorganized in 1989.

The majority of Lithuania's museums are in Vilnius, and these include the Lithuanian Art Museum (1941), the National Museum (1856), the Museum of Lithuanian Religious History, and, founded in 1991 just after gaining independence from the Soviet Union, the Lithuanian State Museum, dedicated to the country's suffering under and resistance to Soviet occupation. The Mikalojus Konstantinas Ciurlionis National Art Museum, named for a famous native composer and painter, is located in Kaunas; special branches of this museum include the Devil's Museum, a collection of artwork depicting devils, and a Ceramics Museum. The Museum of the Center of Europe, an open-air museum displaying large-scale works by European artists, was opened in Vilnius in 1994. There is also a Park of Soviet Sculptures in Druskininkai. The Lithuanian Theater, Music and Film Museum in Vilnius was founded by the Ministry of Culture. There are several other specialized museums, including the Museum of Genocide Victims (Vilnius), Museum of the History of Lithuania Medicine and Pharmacy (Kaunas), Museum of Ancient Beekeeping (Ignalina), and the Museum of Vilnius Sport History. There are several regional museums associated with secondary schools; these contain materials on local arts and history, as well as the history of the school to which the museum is linked.

45 MEDIA

Lithuania's telecommunications system remains inadequate, but modernization is moving ahead. Mobile cellular systems are also being installed, and access to the Internet is available. International service is provided through landlines and submarine cable connections to satellite ground stations. As of 2009, there were some 747,400 main phone lines and 4.9 million mobile cellular phones in use. The mobile phone subscriptions averaged 149 per 100 people.

Broadcasting is controlled by Lithuanian Television and Radio Broadcasting. Radio Vilnius broadcasts in Lithuanian, Russian, Polish, and English. As of 2009 there were 29 AM and 142 FM radio stations and 1 shortwave radio station. In 2009 every household had at least one TV set and 98.1% of Lithuania's population were television viewers. In 2010 the country had 1.17 million Internet hosts. Internet users numbered 59 per 100 citizens.

The most popular daily newspapers are *Lietuvos Rytas* (*Lithuania's Morning*, in Russian), with a 2010 circulation of 50,000; *Respubliká* (55,000); *Lietuvos Aidas* (*The Echo of Lithuania*, 20,000); and *Kauno Diena* (*Kaunas Daily*, 38,000). There are also several periodicals available.

The constitution provides for free speech and a free press, and the government is said to uphold these provisions. Since independence, the independent print media have flourished, producing some 2,000 newspapers and periodicals, and plans for a number of private radio and television stations are underway.

⁴⁶ORGANIZATIONS

Important economic organizations include the Association of Chamber of Commerce and Industry, an organization that coordinates the activities of all the chambers of commerce in Lithuania. There are three umbrella trade union organizations in the country: the Lithuania Confederation of Free Trade Unions, the Lithuania Union of Trade Unions, and the Lithuanian Workers' Union. Professional associations exist for a number of fields and occupations.

The Lithuanian Academy of Sciences promotes education and research in a wide variety of scientific fields. The Lithuanian Medical Association promotes research and education on health issues and works to establish common policies and standards in healthcare. There are several other associations dedicated to research and education for specific fields of medicine and particular diseases and conditions, such as the Lithuanian Heart Association.

There are a number of sports associations in the country, representing such pastimes as speed skating, squash, tae kwon do, tennis, badminton, weightlifting, and baseball. There are also branches of the Paralympic Committee. The Council of Lithuanian Youth Organizations helps organize and support a variety of youth groups. Scouting programs and chapters of the YMCA/YWCA are also active for youth. Volunteer service organizations, such as the Lions Clubs and Kiwanis International, are also present. The Red Cross is also active.

⁴⁷TOURISM, TRAVEL, AND RECREATION

The capital city of Vilnius has one of the largest historic districts in Eastern Europe, distinguished primarily by its Baroque churches, many of which have been reclaimed since independence by money and missionaries from abroad. Kaunas, Lithuania's second-largest city, offers the tourist old merchants' buildings and museums. The seaside resort towns are active in the summer. The traveler can participate in tennis, fishing, sailing, rowing, and winter sports. Lithuanians have long distinguished themselves at basketball, and have contributed top players to former Soviet teams. Seven Lithuanians have Olympic gold medals, and the national basketball team won a bronze medal in Barcelona in 1992 and again in Sydney in 2000.

All visitors need a valid passport. Visas are not required for nationals of the European Union states, the United States, Canada, Japan, Australia, and some South American and South Asian countries for traveling to Lithuania for up to 90 days. Travelers of non-European Union countries must carry proof of medical insurance to cover travel in Lithuania.

In November 2010 the traditional multipart song form known as sutartines was officially inscribed on the UNESCO Representative List of the Intangible Heritage of Humanity, an offshoot of the World Heritage program. The musical form was deemed a living tradition by UNESCO, meaning that it is still passed from generation to generation and continues to create a sense of identity and community for those who participate. Such traditions have been approved by UNESCO for special consideration since 2001. For one that is inscribed, a special program is designed to pro-

tect and promote the practice and understanding of the tradition. The sutartines are polyphonic in form, involving the use of several simple melodic lines that can be sung at staggered intervals, in a canon-form, at parallel seconds, or as a call and response between groups of singers. The poetic texts usually cover a wide variety of themes, with some designated for weddings or other family events and others based on historic themes, such as war. The performance of the sutartines promotes a sense of cultural identity.

The *Tourism Factbook*, published by the UN World Tourism Organization, reported 1.34 million incoming tourists to Lithuania in 2009. These tourists spent a total of $1.18 billion. There were 23,839 hotel beds available in Lithuania, which had an occupancy rate of 25%.

In 2011 the US Department of State estimated the daily cost of visiting Vilnius at $266. The cost of visiting other cities averaged $224.

⁴⁸FAMOUS PERSONS

President Valdas Adamkus (b. 1926) was chief of state from 1998 to 2003, and then again from 2004 to 2009.

⁴⁹DEPENDENCIES

Lithuania has no territories or colonies.

⁵⁰BIBLIOGRAPHY

Bousfield, Jonathan. *Eyewitness Travel Guide: Estonia, Latvia, and Lithuania.* New York: Dorling Kindersley, 2011.

Donskis, Leonidas. *Identity and Freedom: Mapping Nationalism and Social Criticism in Twentieth-Century Lithuania.* New York: Routledge, 2002.

Environmental Justice and Sustainability in the Former Soviet Union. Cambridge, MA: MIT Press, 2009.

Frucht, Richard, ed. *Eastern Europe: An Introduction to the People, Lands, and Culture.* Santa Barbara, CA: ABC-CLIO, 2005.

Hoshi, Iraj, Ewa Balcerowicz, and Leszek Balcerowicz, eds. *Barriers to Entry and Growth of New Firms in Early Transition: A Comparative Study of Poland, Hungary, Czech Republic, Albania, and Lithuania.* Boston: Kluwer Academic Publishers, 2003.

McElrath, Karen. ed. *HIV and AIDS: A Global View.* Westport, CT: Greenwood Press, 2002.

Opello, Walter C. *European Politics.* Boulder, CO: Lynne Rienner Publishers, 2009.

Otfinoski, Steven. *The Baltic Republics.* New York: Facts On File, 2004.

Petersen, Roger Dale. *Resistance and Rebellion: Lessons from Eastern Europe.* New York: Cambridge University Press, 2001.

Suziedelis, Saulius. *Historical Dictionary of Lithuania.* 2nd ed. Lanham, MD: Scarecrow Press, 2011.

Thompson, Wayne C. *Nordic, Central, and Southeastern Europe, 2010.* 10th ed. Harper's Ferry, WV: Stryker Post Publications, 2010.

LUXEMBOURG

Grand Duchy of Luxembourg
[French] *Grand-Duché de Luxembourg;*
[German] *Grossherzogtum Luxemburg*

CAPITAL: Luxembourg

FLAG: The flag is a tricolor of red, white, and blue horizontal stripes.

ANTHEM: *Ons Hémecht (Our Motherland).*

MONETARY UNIT: The Luxembourg franc was replaced by the euro as official currency as of 2002. The euro is divided into 100 cents. There are coins in denominations of 1, 2, 5, 10, 20, and 50 cents and 1 euro and 2 euros. There are notes of 5, 10, 20, 50, 100, 200, and 500 euros. €1 = US$1.31887 (or US$1 = €0.758671) as of 2011.

WEIGHTS AND MEASURES: The metric system is the legal standard.

HOLIDAYS: New Year's Day, 1 January; Labor Day, 1 May; public celebration of the Grand Duke's Birthday, 23 June; Assumption, 15 August; All Saints' Day, 1 November; Christmas, 25–26 December. Movable religious holidays include Shrove Monday, Easter Monday, Ascension, and Pentecost Monday.

TIME: 1 p.m. = noon GMT.

¹LOCATION, SIZE, AND EXTENT

A landlocked country in Western Europe, Luxembourg has an area of 2,586 sq km (998 sq mi), with a length of 82 km (51 mi) N–S and a width of 57 km (35 mi) E-W. Comparatively, the area occupied by Luxembourg is slightly smaller than the state of Rhode Island. The eastern boundary with Germany is formed by the Our, Sûre (Sauer), and Moselle rivers. Luxembourg is bordered on the S by France and on the W and N by Belgium, with total border length of 359 km (223 mi).

Luxembourg's capital city, Luxembourg, is located in the south central part of the country.

²TOPOGRAPHY

The country is divided into two distinct geographic regions: the rugged uplands (Oesling) of the Ardennes in the north, where the average elevation is 450 m (1,476 ft) with the highest point, Buurgplaatz, at 559 m (1,834 ft); and the fertile southern lowlands, called Bon Pays (Good Land), with an average altitude of 250 m (820 ft).

The entire area is crisscrossed by deep valleys, with most rivers draining eastward into the Sûre, which in turn flows into the Moselle on the eastern border. The northern region, comprising one-third of the country, is forested and has poor soil.

³CLIMATE

Luxembourg's climate is temperate and mild. Summers are generally cool, with a mean temperature of about 17°C (63°F); winters are seldom severe, average temperature being about 0°C (32°F). The high peaks of the Ardennes in the north shelter the country from rigorous north winds, and the prevailing northwesterly winds have a cooling effect. Rainfall is plentiful in the extreme southwest; precipitation throughout the country averages about 75 cm (30 in) annually.

⁴FLORA AND FAUNA

The World Resources Institute estimates that there are 1,246 plant species in Luxembourg. In addition Luxembourg is home to 66 species of mammals, 284 species of birds, 9 species of reptiles, and 16 species of amphibians. These figures reflect the total number of distinct species residing in the country, not the number of endemic species.

The principal trees are pine, chestnut, spruce, oak, linden, elm, and beech, along with fruit trees. There are many shrubs, such as blueberry and genista, and ferns; a multitude of lovely flowers; and many vineyards. Only a few wild animal species (deer, roe deer, and wild boar) remain, but many varieties of fish are found in the rivers, including perch, carp, bream, trout, pike, and eel.

⁵ENVIRONMENT

The Ministry of the Environment is the main environmental agency. Government statistics indicate considerable improvement in pollution control over the past few decades. Emissions of particles of sulfur dioxide declined substantially from 1972 to 1983. As of 1994, emissions of smoke, sulfur dioxide, nitrogen dioxide, and lead were well within EU acceptable limits. The UN reported in 2008 that carbon dioxide emissions in Luxembourg totaled 10,834 kilotons.

Water resources totaled 1.6 cu km (0.384 cu mi) while water usage was 0.06 cu km (0.014 cu mi) per year. Domestic water usage accounted for 42% of total usage, industrial for 45%, and agricultural for 13%. Per capita water usage totaled 121 cu m (4,273 cu ft) per year. Water pollution of rivers and streams has posed some problems. In 2009 only 7% of the rivers were rated with an ecological status of good by the government. About 52% were rated as moderate, while 26% were noted as poor and 16% as bad.

Forest reserves have been severely depleted since 1800, when three-fourths of the country was forest; today forest and woodland cover only one-fifth of Luxembourg. During World War II, German requisitions and heavy demands for fuel contributed to this depletion.

The World Resources Institute reported that Luxembourg had designated 43,000 hectares (106,255 acres) of land for protection as of 2006. According to a 2011 report issued by the International Union for Conservation of Nature and Natural Resources (IUCN), threatened species included three types of mammals, five types of mollusks, and two species of other invertebrates. Threatened species included the spotted eagle, the southern damselfly, and the great snipe.

6 POPULATION

In 2011 the US Central Intelligence Agency (CIA) estimated the population of Luxembourg to be approximately 503,302, which placed it at number 166 in population among the 196 nations of the world. Approximately 14.9% of the population was over 65 years of age, with another 18.2% under 15 years of age. About 43% of the population were foreigners. The median age in Luxembourg was 39.4 years. There were 1.07 males for every female in the country. The population's annual rate of change was 1.145%. The projected population for the year 2025 was 600,000. Population density in Luxembourg was calculated at 196 people per sq km (508 people per sq mi).

The UN estimated that 85% of the population lived in urban areas, and that urban populations had an annual rate of change of 1.4%. The largest urban area was Luxembourg, with a population of 90,000.

7 MIGRATION

According to the CIA, Luxembourg's net migration rate in 2011 amounted to 8.24 migrants per 1,000 citizens. The total number of emigrants living abroad was 57,800, and the total number of immigrants living in Luxembourg was 173,200. During the 19th century, thousands of Luxembourgers emigrated, chiefly to the United States. In 1870, however, rich deposits of iron ore were uncovered in southern Luxembourg, and during the period of industrialization and prosperity that followed, many people from neighboring countries migrated to Luxembourg.

With the adoption of national asylum legislation in April 1996, there was a significant increase in the number of asylum seekers. In 1997, 431 people applied for asylum. By 1998, 1,709 people applied. Between January and July 1999, as many as 2,404 people submitted asylum applications. The number of applicants dropped during the 2000s. In 2011 there were about 696 asylum seekers residing in the country.

8 ETHNIC GROUPS

The indigenous inhabitants of Luxembourg consider themselves a distinct nationality, with a specific ethnic character. A strong indication of that character is the national motto, "Mir woelle bleiwe wat mir sin" ("We want to remain what we are"), for despite a history of long foreign domination, Luxembourgers have retained their individuality as a nation. There are also native-born residents of Celtic, French, Belgian, or German ancestry, as well as a substantial immigrant population of Portuguese, Italian, and other Europeans (guest and worker residents). According to government estimates for 2011, 57% of the population identified themselves as Luxembourger. About 16% were noted as Portuguese, followed by the French at 6%, Italians at 3%, Belgians at 3%, Germans at 2%, and other nationals of the European Union at about 5%.

9 LANGUAGES

Luxembourgers speak Luxembourgian, or Letzeburgesch, the original dialect of the country, as well as French and German. All three are official languages. Letzeburgesch is a Germanic dialect related to the Moselle Frankish language that was once spoken in western Germany. It rarely appears in written form. Letzeburgesch, French, and German are all languages of instruction in primary schools, while French is the most common language of instruction in secondary schools. Government publications are generally in French. English is also spoken.

10 RELIGIONS

The country is historically Roman Catholic. Though the government does not maintain statistics on religious affiliation, it is estimated that over 90% of the population are nominally Roman Catholic. The largest Protestant denominations are Lutheranism and Calvinism. Other prominent Protestant churches include the Anglican Church, the Reformed Protestant Church of Luxembourg, and the Protestant Church of Luxembourg. About 9,000 people are Muslim, about 5,000 are Orthodox Christians (Greek, Serbian, Russian, and Romanian), and about 1,000 are Jewish. There are also small communities of the Baha'is, Mormons, Jehovah's Witnesses, and members of the Universal Church. Freedom of religion is guaranteed by the constitution, and this right is respected in practice. A special Concordat of 1801 allows certain religious groups to receive financial support. For instance, the state pays salaries for Roman Catholic and Greek and Russian Orthodox priests, Jewish rabbis, and pastors of some Protestant denominations. The state also supports some private religious schools. Certain Shrove Monday, Easter Monday, Ascension Day, Whitmonday, Assumption Day, All Saints' Day, All Souls' Day, Christmas, and the second day of Christmas are observed as national holidays.

11 TRANSPORTATION

Transportation facilities are excellent. The railways are consolidated into one organization, the Société Nationale des Chemins de Fers Luxembourgeois (CFL), with the government of Luxembourg controlling 51% of the stock and the remaining 49% divided between the French and Belgian governments. Railway lines provide direct links with Belgium via Arlon, with France via Metz and Longwy, and with Germany via Trier. There is through-train service to Paris and various other points in France. As of 2011, the railroads covered 275 km (171 mi) of track.

Direct roads connect all important towns, and the main arteries are suitable for heavy motor traffic. The CIA reports that Luxembourg has a total of 5,227 km (3,248 mi) of roads, of which 5,227 km (3,248 mi) are paved. There are an estimated 747 vehicles per 1,000 people in the country.

The only river available for industrial transport is the Moselle, which for 37 km (23 mi) allows navigation of barges of up to 1,500 tons. In 2010 the merchant fleet comprised 47 ships of 1,000 GRT or more. There were two airports, one of which had a paved runaway. There was also a single heliport. The principal airport is Findel, located near the city of Luxembourg. Regular flights to other European cities are operated by Luxair, the national carrier, and by foreign airlines. Luxembourg's largest airline, Cargolux, ranks among Europe's top 10 cargo carriers. Luxembourg and the United States have shared open sky aviation rights since a 1995 agreement.

12 HISTORY

The land now known as Luxembourg fell under the successive domination of the Celts, the Romans, and the Riparian Franks before its founding as the County of Luxembourg in 963 by Sigefroid, count of the Ardennes, who reconstructed a small ruined fortress called Lucilinburhuc (Little Burg) on the site of the present capital. The area tripled in size during the reign of Countess Ermesinde (1196–1247). John, count of Luxembourg (r. 1309–46) and king of Bohemia, became the national hero; although blind for many years, the inveterate knight-errant laid the foundations for a powerful dynasty before he fell in the Battle of Crécy, in northern France, during the Hundred Years' War. His son Charles (1316–78) was the second of four Luxembourg princes to become Holy Roman emperor. He made Luxembourg a duchy, but under his successors the country was ruined financially.

Luxembourg came under Burgundian rule in 1443 and remained in foreign hands for more than 400 years. Successively it passed to Spain (1506–1714, excepting 1684–97, when it was ruled by France), Austria (1714–95), and France (1795–1815). The Congress of Vienna in 1815 made Luxembourg a grand duchy and allotted it as an independent state to the king of the Netherlands, after ceding to Prussia its territory east of the Moselle, Sûre, and Our. Luxembourg lost more than half its territory to Belgium in 1839, but gained a larger measure of autonomy, although Dutch kings continued to rule as grand dukes. By the Treaty of London in 1867, Luxembourg was declared an independent and neutral state under the protection of the Great Powers but was required to dismantle its mighty fortress. In 1890, the house of Nassau-Weilbourg, through the Grand Duke Adolphe (r. 1890–1905), became the ruling house of Luxembourg. The country was occupied by German troops in World War I. In 1919, Grand Duchess Charlotte succeeded to the throne, and on 28 September 1919, in a referendum held to decide the country's future, a plurality supported her.

The Germans again invaded the country in May 1940, but the grand ducal family and most members of the government escaped to safety. Under the Nazi occupation, the people suffered severely, particularly when their 1942 revolt, in protest of compulsory service in the German army, was savagely repressed. Luxembourg was liberated by Allied forces in September 1944.

That year, while still in exile, the government agreed to form an economic union with Belgium and the Netherlands; the first phase, the Benelux Customs Union, was put into effect in 1948. In February 1958, a treaty of economic union, which became effective in 1960, was signed by representatives of the three countries. During the postwar decades, Luxembourg also became an active member of NATO (1949) and the European Coal and Steel Com-

LOCATION: 49°26′52″ to 50°10′58″ N; 5°44′10″ to 6°31′53″ E. BOUNDARY LENGTHS: Germany, 135 kilometers (84 miles); France, 73 kilometers (45 miles); Belgium, 148 kilometers (92 miles).

munity (1950), the latter of which served as the first seed for the formation of the European Union.

On 12 November 1964, Grand Duchess Charlotte abdicated in favor of her son, Jean. The Grand Duke announced on Christmas Day 1999 that he planned to abdicate in favor of his eldest son Prince Henri in September 2000. (Prince Henri took the throne on 7 October 2000.) Jean's reign was marked by continued prosperity, as Luxembourg's economy shifted from dependence on steel to an emphasis on services, notably finance and telecommunications. Luxembourg is now among the world's top ten financial centers.

13 GOVERNMENT

Luxembourg is a constitutional monarchy, governed by the constitution of 1868 as revised in 1919 when universal suffrage and proportional representation were introduced. The grand ducal crown is hereditary in the house of Nassau-Weilbourg. Executive power rests jointly in the sovereign, who may initiate legislation, and a prime minister, appointed by the monarch, who in turn selects a council of ministers to serve as a cabinet. The prime minister, who serves as head of government, is typically the leader of the majority party or coalition of the legislature.

Legislative power is vested in the Chamber of Deputies, the 60 members of which are elected by popular vote for five-year terms. In addition the Council of State, composed of 21 members appointed by the grand duke with the advice of the prime minister, acts as a consulting body in the drafting of legislation. The opinions of the council are not binding.

Voting is compulsory, and eligibility begins at age 18.

14 POLITICAL PARTIES

Since 1947, shifting coalitions among the three largest parties have governed the country. The Christian Social People's Party (CSV) is Catholic and similar to Christian democratic parties found in other European countries. It is a promonarchist movement favoring progressive labor legislation and government protection for farmers and small business. Except for the period 1974–79, the CSV has been the dominant partner in all ruling coalitions since World War I. The Socialist Party (LSAP) is similar to other social democratic parties in Europe. It supports improvement and extension of the present system of social welfare programs and approves of state intervention in the economy. The LASP served a major role in the government from 1984 through 1999. The third major group, the center-right Democratic Party (DP), favors social reforms and minimal government activity in the economy. In addition, the ecologist Green Party was formed in 1983 and has gained in support since. The Alternative Democratic Reform Party (ADR), a pensioners' party, gained seats in the legislature in 2004, when it was known as the Action Committee for Democracy and Pension Rights. The Left, formerly the Marxist and Reformed Communist Party, also remains active in government.

In 2009 elections the CSV gained 26 seats with 38% of the vote, followed by the LSAP with 13 seats (21.6%), the DP with 9 seats (15%), the Green Party with 7 seats (11.7%), ADR with 4 seats (8.1%), and the Left with 1 seat (3.3%). Jean-Claude Juncker of CSV has served as prime minister since 1995. The next legislative elections will be held in June 2014.

Grand Duke Henri ascended to the throne in 2000 at the abdication of his father, Jean. Henri's son Guillaume is the heir apparent.

15 LOCAL GOVERNMENT

Luxembourg is divided into three districts (Luxembourg, Diekirch, and Grevenmacher) comprising 12 cantons, which in turn make up 118 communes (municipalities). The districts are headed by commissioners⊠civil servants responsible to the central government. Each commune elects an autonomous communal council headed by a burgomaster; the councils elect government officials at the local level. Local elections are held every six years.

16 JUDICIAL SYSTEM

The legal system combines elements of the French, Belgium, and German systems, along with local traditions and practices. The judicial system consists of two main branches of jurisdiction: the judicial order (including the magistrates' courts or justices of the peace, the district courts, and the Supreme Court of Justice) and the administrative order (including the administrative tribunal and the administrative court). The Supreme Court of Justice includes a court of appeal and a court of cassation. There is also constitutional court.

Luxembourg is home to the European Court of Justice.

17 ARMED FORCES

In 1967 Luxembourg abolished conscription and created a volunteer military force. Responsibility for defense matters is vested in the Ministry of Public Force, which also controls the police and gendarmerie. As of 2011 there were 1,038 soldiers, 896 enlisted recruits, and 142 civilians employed in the Luxembourg Army. According to a 2011 report from The International Institute for Strategic Studies, defense spending in Luxembourg totaled $371.9 million and accounted for 0.9% of GDP.

Luxembourg has contributed troops to a variety of EU, NATO, and UN missions abroad. More than 5,000 American soldiers, including Gen. George S. Patton, are buried at the American Military Cemetery near the capital.

18 INTERNATIONAL COOPERATION

Luxembourg is a founding member of the UN, having joined the organization on 24 October 1945, and participates in ECE and several nonregional specialized agencies, such as the FAO, IAEA, the World Bank, UNESCO, UNIDO, the ILO, IMF, and the WHO. Since 1921 it has been joined with Belgium in the Belgium-Luxembourg Economic Union (BLEU). It is also a partner with Belgium and the Netherlands in the Benelux Economic Union. Luxembourg is a member of the Council of Europe, the Asian Development Bank, NATO, OECD, OSCE, WTO, the Euro-Atlantic Partnership Council, the European Bank for Reconstruction and Development, the Western European Union, and the European Union. Luxembourg held the EU presidency for the first half of 2005. The country is the home site of the European Court of Justice, the European Court of Auditors, European Investment Bank, and other EU organizations. The Secretariat of the European Parliament is also located in Luxembourg.

Luxembourg belongs to the Australia Group, the Zangger Committee, the Nuclear Energy Agency, and the Nuclear Suppliers Group (London Group). In environmental cooperation, the country is part of the Basel Convention, Conventions on Biological Diversity and Air Pollution, Ramsar, CITES, the London Convention, International Tropical Timber Agreements, the Kyoto Protocol, the Montréal Protocol, MARPOL, the Nuclear Test Ban Treaty, and the UN Conventions on the Law of the Sea, Climate Change, and Desertification.

¹⁹ECONOMY

In relation to its size and population, Luxembourg is one of the most highly industrialized countries in the world. Its standard of living rivals that of any country in Europe. While the iron and steel industry has declined since the 1970s, it is still considered to form the backbone of the economy. In 2011 the steel industry contributed an estimated 7% to the overall economy. Other industries, including plastics, rubber, chemicals, and other light industries, have been successfully developed, and the service industries, most notably banking, have expanded rapidly. Into the 2000s the government has made considerable efforts to promote the development of its information technology and e-commerce sectors. Agriculture is generally small-scale, with livestock and vineyards comprising the most important segment.

The country's growth rate has been among the highest in the European Union and averaged over 4% annually between 1994 and 2000, though the nation did suffer due to the global economic downturn and the turmoil in international stock markets that began in 2001. The GDP rate of change in Luxembourg for 2010 was 3.4%. Inflation stood at 2.1%, and unemployment was reported at 5.5%.

Luxembourg has used the euro as its currency since the euro's inception in 1999.

²⁰INCOME

The CIA estimated that in 2010 the GDP of Luxembourg was $41.09 billion. The CIA defines GDP as the value of all final goods and services produced within a nation in a given year and computed on the basis of purchasing power parity (PPP) rather than value as measured on the basis of the rate of the exchange based on current dollars. The per capita GDP was estimated at $82,600. The annual growth rate of GDP was 3.4%. The average inflation rate was 2.1%. In 2007 it was estimated that agriculture accounted for 0.4% of GDP, industry 13.6%, and services 86%.

According to the World Bank, remittances from citizens living abroad totaled $1.6 billion or about $3,149 per capita and accounted for approximately 3.9% of GDP.

As of 2011 the most recent study by the World Bank reported that actual individual consumption in Luxembourg was 48.5% of GDP and accounted for 0.04% of world consumption. By comparison, the United States accounted for 25.44% of world individual consumption. The World Bank also estimated that 6.2% of Luxembourg's GDP was spent on food and beverages, 8.9% on housing and household furnishings, 1.2% on clothes, 4.5% on health, 5.8% on transportation, 0.4% on communications, 3.2% on recreation, 2.3% on restaurants and hotels, and 11.7% on miscellaneous goods and services and purchases from abroad.

²¹LABOR

As of 2010 Luxembourg had an estimated total resident labor force of 205,900 people. Within that labor force, CIA estimates in 2007 noted that 2.2% were employed in agriculture, 17.2% in industry, and 80.6% in the service sector. More than 100,000 foreign workers cross the border from France, Belgium, and Germany.

Labor relations have been generally peaceful since the 1930s. Foreign investors are attracted by the positive relationship between employers and the labor force. There is a strong trade union movement. About 50% of the labor force was organized into unions as of 2010. Although independent, the two largest labor organizations are associated with major political parties. Workers may strike only after their dispute is submitted to the national conciliation office and all mediation efforts have failed. Collective bargaining is widely practiced, with about 66% of workers under collective bargaining agreements in 2010.

As of 2011, unskilled workers over 18 years of age are entitled to a minimum wage of €1,757.56 ($2,337.90) per month, while the minimum for skilled workers was €2,2109 ($2,571) per month. These totals were insufficient to provide a worker and family with a decent living standard; however, most workers earned more than the minimum rate. Wage agreements are generally arrived at by industry-wide bargaining between labor and management. The maximum workweek is legally set at 40 hours, with a maximum daily limit of 10 hours. Overtime is paid at premium rates. Work on Sunday must be voluntary with compensation at double the normal wage or compensatory time off on another day. Children under the age of 16 are prohibited from employment except in some special circumstances. The law mandates a safe working environment, and this is effectively enforced by the Ministry of Labor.

²²AGRICULTURE

The majority of agricultural land consists of meadows and pastures. Farms are generally small and highly mechanized, although average farm size has been increasing. While the number of farms of 2 hectares (5 acres) or more fell from 10,570 in 1950 to 2,242 in 2009, the average holding increased from 13.16 to about 64.9 hectares (from 32.52 to 160.3 acres) over about the same period.

Vineyards including Ehnen, Stadtbredmis, and Bech-Kleinmacher are located in the Moselle River Valley. Wine production totaled about 11 million liters in 2010, including rivaner, elbling, auxerrois, riesling, pinot blanc, pinot gris, chardonnay, and pinot noir. Wine and clover seeds are the important agricultural exports. In addition, millions of rosebushes, a major specialty crop, are exported annually. Chief fruits produced include apples, plums, and cherries. Other major crops include Wheat, spelt, rye, colza, potatoes, and wheat. Cereal production in 2009 amounted to 188,562 tons, fruit production 28,293 tons, and vegetable production 863 tons.

²³ANIMAL HUSBANDRY

Livestock breeding is relatively important, particularly because of Luxembourg's dairy product exports. The UN Food and Agriculture Organization (FAO) reported that Luxembourg dedicated 67,000 hectares (165,561 acres) to permanent pasture or meadow in 2009. During that year, the national livestock totals amounted to about 97,000 chickens, 196,470 head of cattle, and 80,217 pigs. The production from these animals amounted to 20,820 tons of beef and veal, 21,626 tons of pork, 18,955 tons of poultry, and 4,095 tons of eggs in 2009. Luxembourg also produced 2,390 tons of cattle hide and 15 tons of raw wool. In 2010 the country produced 295,300 tons of milk. In 2009 livestock included 8,824 sheep and 4,562 equines.

24 FISHING

There is some commercial fishing for domestic consumption and much private fishing for sport. The rivers teem with perch, carp, trout, pike, eel, and bream.

25 FORESTRY

About 89,785 hectares (221,863 acres) were covered by forests in 2003, of which 52% was private forest. The UN FAO estimated the 2009 roundwood production at 257,274 cu m (9.09 million cu ft). The value of all forest products, including roundwood, totaled $285.5 million. Chief commercial woods are spruce and oak. In 2004 forest product imports exceeded exports by $13.7 million.

26 MINING

In 2009 Luxembourg's mineral sector consisted primarily of raw materials processing, information systems, and mineral trading. Metals produced included crude and semi-manufactured steel, while industrial minerals consisted of hydraulic cement, crude gypsum and anhydrite, and Thomas slag phosphates. The iron and steel industry was the most important mineral industry sector, with steel products as the country's main export commodity. Mining in Luxembourg was represented by small industrial mineral operations that produced material for domestic construction, including cement manufacture. In 2009 Luxembourg produced 2.2 million metric tons of crude steel and 2.8 million metric tons of semi-manufactured steel. Hydraulic cement production in 2009 was estimated at 700,000 metric tons. Production of Thomas slag phosphates (by gross weight) totaled an estimated 475,000 metric tons in 2009. Luxembourg's traditional source of mineral wealth was iron ore, concentrated between Redange and Dudelange. Because of mine depletion, production declined from 2.08 million tons in 1976 to 429,000 tons in 1981, when the last iron mines were closed.

27 ENERGY AND POWER

Luxembourg imports all the petroleum products, natural gas, and coal it requires; it has no oil, natural gas or coal reserves. In 2009 oil imports amounted to 51,930 barrels per day. In 2010 oil consumption was estimated at 60,500 barrels per day. Natural gas imports and consumption in 2010 each totaled about 1.36 billion cu m.

Total electric generating capacity in 2002 was 128 MW, of which nearly 52% used fossil fuels, 31% was hydroelectric, and the remainder geothermal/other. Production of electrical energy in 2009 amounted to 2.667 billion kWh. Roughly 88% of energy came from fossil fuels. Consumption of electricity in 2008 was 6.453 billion kWh. The steel industry consumes about 80% of total industrial energy demand.

28 INDUSTRY

The steel industry in Luxembourg was launched in 1911 through the founding of the Arbed company. While production has declined considerably since the 1970s, the industry continues to provide a solid base for the economy. In 2001 Arbed merged with France's Usinor and Spain's Aceralia to form Arcelor. In 2005 Arcelor acquired Dofasco, Canada's largest steel manufacturer. Then in 2006, Arcelor merged with Mittal Steel of the Netherlands to form ArcelorMittal. It is now the largest steelmaker in the world, producing 8% of the world's supply. In 2011 the company was also the second-largest employer in the nation after the government. The steel industry in Luxembourg accounts for about 7% of the overall economy.

As overall steel production has declined, Luxembourg has diversified its industrial production to include chemicals, medical products, rubber, tires, glass, aluminum, textiles, food processing, and pulp and paper. According to the CIA, industry accounted for 13.6% of the GDP and 17.2% of the workforce in 2007. The industrial production growth rate for 2010 was estimated at 7.9%.

29 SCIENCE AND TECHNOLOGY

The University of Luxembourg, established in 2003, conducts research in biomedicine systems, information technology, environmental resources and technologies, and the interface-induced properties of condensed matter, among other areas. The university is home to the Luxembourg Center for Systems Biomedicine, which fosters collaboration between biologists, medical doctors, physicists, mathematicians, and computer scientists in indentifying and studying the principal mechanisms of disease pathogenesis and the working to develop new diagnostic tools and therapies for diseases. The Integrated BioBank of Luxembourg (IBBL), opened in 2010, is an independent, not-for-profit biobanking and biotechnology foundation dedicated to medical research and focused on investigating new treatments for diseases. With members of the Luxembourg Personalized Medicine Consortium, the IBBL has selected four focus areas for research: cancer, type 2 diabetes, Parkinson's disease, and normal population cohort.

Luxinnovation, the National Agency for Innovation and Research in Luxembourg, was founded in 1984 as part of a greater European reference network. Its primary mission is to promote and support research and development activities. The Center for Research of Public Health (Centre de Recherche Public de la Santé) is the nation's leading public institution for clinical research in life sciences. Center for Public Research–Gabriel Lippman was founded in 1987 and is dedicated to research in applied science and technological development. The Center for Public Research–Henri Tudor is dedicated to strengthening the innovation capacity of businesses and public organizations, with activities that include applied and experimental research. The Grand Ducal Institute, serving as the national academy of arts and science, includes medical and scientific sections.

Sociéte Européenne des Satellites at Betzdorf (est. 1985) is the control center for a group of satellites important to Europe's broadcasting industry.

In 2007 the research and development sector in Luxembourg support 2,218 full-time researchers. The total number of full-time personnel involved in some type of research and development activity was estimated at 4,624.

30 DOMESTIC TRADE

The commercial code is similar to that of Belgium, and trade practices are nearly identical. The capital city of Luxembourg is the headquarters for the distribution of imported goods within the country, and Antwerp in Belgium is the principal port of entry. Consequently, manufacturers' agents and importers generally maintain offices in one or both of those cities. The Cactus Group, which supports a variety of shopping centers and malls, supermarkets, restaurants, and specialty shops, is among the nation's largest employers. A wide variety of other retail shops can be found throughout the country. In 2008 there were an estimated 6,857 wholesale and retail trade enterprises, with 568 new enterprises that year.

Advertising is extensive, particularly in newspapers and on Radio-Télé-Luxembourg. Most shops and stores are open 10 a.m. to 6 p.m. Monday through Saturday. Some shops are closed on Sunday or have reduced hours. Banking hours are on weekdays, 8:30 a.m. to 4:30 p.m. Private business hours are usually from 8 a.m. to 5 p.m.

31 FOREIGN TRADE

Luxembourg remains dependent on foreign trade, even though domestic demand has become increasingly important to the economy. Primary import commodities include minerals, metals, food and beverages, and other consumer goods. Steel products continue to be a major export commodity, along with machinery and equipment, chemicals, rubber products, and glass. Major import partners in 2010 were Belgium 31.4%, Germany 25.1%, France 11.6%, China 9.2%, and the Netherlands 5.2%. Its major export partners were Germany 22.3%, France 15.5%, Belgium 12.1%, UK 9.2%, Italy 7.2%, and the Netherlands 4.1%.

Luxembourg is a member of the Belgium-Luxembourg Economic Union (BLEU) and the Belgium Luxembourg and Netherlands Economic Union (BENELUX). Free trade policies between members of the European Union apply. The nation also maintains preferential trade agreements with a number of non-European countries.

32 BALANCE OF PAYMENTS

As steel exports have declined, the nation has often experienced an annual trade deficit. Luxembourg imported $21.24 billion worth of merchandise in 2010 while exporting $16.3 billion, creating a deficit of $4.94 billion. The overall balance of payments has, however, tended to show a surplus, mainly because of income from banking services.

33 BANKING AND SECURITIES

Banking and financial services have become increasingly important to the national economy. The banking sector has benefited from favorable laws governing holding companies. In addition, a strict 1992 law aimed at combating money laundering reinforced Luxembourg's reputation as a corruption-free environment. The nation's strict banking secrecy laws, which contributed to its reputation as a tax haven, were highly criticized by the international community in the wake of the 2008–09 global financial crisis. As a result, some of these secrecy laws have been eased to offer greater cooperation with governments seeking tax evaders.

The principal bank and the sole bank of issue is the International Bank of Luxembourg (Banque Internationale à Luxembourg), founded in 1856. The Belgium-Luxembourg monetary agreement provided for the establishment of the Luxembourg Monetary Institute to represent the nation at international monetary conferences and institutions. The European Investment Bank, the Euro-

pean Court of Auditors (both EU institutions), and the European Monetary Fund are headquartered in Luxembourg.

The euro-markets have made Luxembourg the home of Clearstream, an international clearinghouse and central securities depository created in 2000 by the merger of Cedel International and Deutsche Börse Clearing.

The discount rate, the interest rate at which the central bank lends to financial institutions in the short term, is set by the European Central Bank (ECB). In 2010 the discount rate was 1.75%. The commercial bank prime lending rate in December 2010 was 2.283%. In 2010 there were 146 banks nationwide. Most of them were foreign-owned.

The Luxembourg Stock Exchange (Bourse de Luxembourg), created in 1927 in the city of Luxembourg, serves as a major listing center of international bonds, equities, and investment funds.

Principal Trading Partners – Luxembourg (2010)

(In millions of US dollars)

Country	Total	Exports	Imports	Balance
World	38,228.0	14,155.0	24,073.0	-9,918.0
Germany	10,378.0	4,356.0	6,022.0	-1,666.0
Belgium	9,899.0	2,370.0	7,529.0	-5,159.0
France	5,804.0	3,027.0	2,777.0	250.0
China	2,382.0	170.0	2,212.0	-2,042.0
United Kingdom	2,128.0	1,807.0	321.0	1,486.0
Netherlands	2,053.0	808.0	1,245.0	-437.0
Italy	1,914.0	1,404.0	510.0	894.0
United States	1,220.0	346.0	874.0	-528.0
Switzerland	882.0	734.0	148.0	586.0
Spain	617.0	460.0	157.0	303.0

(…) data not available or not significant.

(n.s.) not specified.

SOURCE: 2011 Direction of Trade Statistics Yearbook, New York: United Nations, 2011.

Balance of Payments – Luxembourg (2010)

(In millions of US dollars)

Current Account		**4,122.0**
Balance on goods	-5,443.0	
Imports	-22,105.0	
Exports	1,662.0	
Balance on services	30,089.0	
Balance on income	-19,625.0	
Current transfers	-900.0	
Capital Account		**-306.0**
Financial Account		**-3,493.0**
Direct investment abroad	-185,132.0	
Direct investment in Luxembourg	207,871.0	
Portfolio investment assets	-135,253.0	
Portfolio investment liabilities	195,646.0	
Financial derivatives	24,083.0	
Other investment assets	-166,008.0	
Other investment liabilities	55,301.0	
Net Errors and Omissions		**-290.0**
Reserves and Related Items		**-33.0**

(…) data not available or not significant.

SOURCE: Balance of Payment Statistics Yearbook 2011, Washington, DC: International Monetary Fund, 2011.

Public Finance – Luxembourg (2009)

(In millions of euros, budgetary central government figures)

Revenue and Grants	**10,476.1**	**100.0%**
Tax revenue	9,168.8	87.5%
Social contributions	421	4.0%
Grants	254.6	2.4%
Other revenue	631.8	6.0%
Expenditures	**11,478.4**	**100.0%**
General public services	1,954.6	17.0%
Defense	114	1.0%
Public order and safety	350	3.0%
Economic affairs	1,529.2	13.3%
Environmental protection	187.6	1.6%
Housing and community amenities	227.9	2.0%
Health	207.5	1.8%
Recreational, culture, and religion	488.4	4.3%
Education	1,566.3	13.6%
Social protection	4,853	42.3%

(...) data not available or not significant.

SOURCE: *Government Finance Statistics Yearbook 2010*, Washington, DC: International Monetary Fund, 2010.

The exchange migrated its securities to the NYSE Euronext UTP platform in 2009. In 2010 there were 1,701 investment companies nationwide.

34 INSURANCE

Third-party liability insurance is compulsory for all automobile owners, as is insurance for nuclear operators, hunters, hotel operators, boats and aircraft, windsurfers and parachutists. Domestic insurance companies issue both life and nonlife policies. The Third European Life Directive has permitted life insurance companies to operate in any European Union (EU) country while being controlled by domestic regulations. In 2010 there were 96 insurance companies and 261 reinsurance companies nationwide. The total amount of gross premiums written in 2008 totaled €13.18 billion, with life insurance premiums accounting for €10.81 billion. The exchange rate in that year was US$1 = €0.6827.

The Commissariat aux Assurances regulates insurance companies in Luxembourg.

35 PUBLIC FINANCE

The budget of the Luxembourg government is presented to the Chamber of Deputies late in each calendar year and becomes effective the following year. In 2010 the budget of Luxembourg included $21.87 billion in public revenue and $22.67 billion in public expenditures. The budget deficit amounted to 1.4% of GDP. Public debt was 15.2% of GDP, with $1.892 trillion of the debt held by foreign entities. Taxes and other revenues totaled about 39.8% of GDP.

36 TAXATION

Luxembourg has come under pressure to share information on the interest paid to nonresidents' previously secret savings accounts. In 2003 the EU Commissioners issued a directive that would allow Luxembourg (as well as Belgium and Austria) to apply increased withholding taxes in lieu of directly sharing information on the interest tax paid on these accounts. Withholding rates of 15–20% would be applied from 2004 to 2007, rising to 25% from 2007 to 2009, and to 35% after 2009. The US government opposed the EU initiatives to deal with tax evasion on the grounds that they would eliminate useful "tax competition."

Luxembourg's corporate income tax (IRC) rate is 22%. In addition, there is a 4% employment fund surtax. Companies are also subject to municipal taxes levied at 6.75% for residents of Luxembourg city and 7.5% for all other cities. Companies must also pay an annual net worth tax of 0.5% on their total assets.

Dividends paid to nonresidents are subject to 25% withholding unless the payments are to a parent company resident in the EU that owns at least 10% of the subsidiary paying dividends. Subsidiaries of foreign companies are considered resident companies ("capital societies") and are taxed at the same rate.

Personal income in Luxembourg is taxed according to a progressive schedule with a top rate of 38%. Social security contributions amount to 23% of gross salary. Other taxes include a wealth tax, gift taxes, local real estate taxes, and registration taxes.

The main indirect tax is Luxembourg's value-added tax (VAT), with most goods and services taxed at 6% or 15%. A rate of 3% is applied to foodstuffs, newspapers, books, and periodicals, medicines and medical equipment, medical and dental care, and other basic goods and services. A rate of 12% applies to items such as heating oil, intellectual services, advertising, wine, and certain other service. There is a standard 16% service charge.

37 CUSTOMS AND DUTIES

Luxembourg adheres to the trade regulations of the European Union and the Common External Tariff regime. The standard VAT on imports of goods and services in 15%. Excise duties apply to alcoholic beverages, manufactured tobacco products, and energy products. Nontariff barriers exist also in the form of health, safety, and packaging regulations.

38 FOREIGN INVESTMENT

The nation offers a favorable investment climate, with no restrictions on foreign investment and a number of incentives, including financial aid, available to qualified small- and medium-sized enterprises. US firms are among the most prominent foreign investors, with a total of about $153 billion in US direct investment in 2008. Major firms include Goodyear Dunlop Tires, DuPont (chemicals), and Guardian Industries (glass and glass products). According to a 2009 report from the World Bank, FDI represented 372.58% of GDP.

In 2009 Luxembourg was the EU's largest investor outside the boundaries of the union, with FDI outflows of €112 billion, or 42% of the EU27 total. Luxembourg was the main recipient of FDI inflows for the European Union, receiving €88 billion, or 40% of the EU27 total. Statistics on Luxembourg's inward and outward foreign investment are calculated and published in conjunction with those of Belgium.

39 ECONOMIC DEVELOPMENT

The keystone of the economic system is free enterprise, and the government has attempted to promote the wellbeing of private industry by every means short of direct interference. The full-employment policy pursued by every postwar government has produced a high ratio of economically active population to total population. Not only is the population economically active, it is also highly skilled, a fact not overlooked by foreign companies seeking to invest. The government encourages the diversification of industry by tax concessions and other means.

The *Luxembourg Stability and Growth Program*, initiated in 1999 at the time the eurozone was established, set a basic development goal to promote prudent budgetary policies to ensure the stability of public finances, with a particular focus on keeping increases in general government expenditure within the limits of the average growth of gross domestic product, or rather, linking the increase in government expenditures to economic growth. While the economy was generally strong at the time, annual decreases in exports and increases in imports soon created trade deficits. As the 2008–09 global financial crisis brought unexpected change for both trade and financial services, the balance of the government budget switched from surplus to deficit.

Having pulled out of its recession in 2009 with a growth rate of 3.4% in 2010 and projected growth of 3.2% for 2011, the 12th Update of the Luxembourg Stability and Growth Program (2011–2014) set a goal to restore a balanced budgetary position at the general government level by 2014 at the latest. Budgetary consolidation measures were expected to play an important role in achieving this goal. A series of reforms for the pension system was also expected, as the government projected a sharp increase in public expenditures toward social security linked to demographic ageing.

40 SOCIAL DEVELOPMENT

An extensive system of social insurance covers virtually all employees and their families. Sickness, maternity, old age, disability, and survivors' benefits are paid, with both employee and employer contributing and the government absorbing part of the cost. Normal retirement is set at age 65 for both men and women, with early retirement possible at age 57 with 40 years of contributions. Birth, maternity, child, and education allowances are also provided to all residents. There is a choice for medical service providers. Parental leave and child-rearing allowances are available as well. The government covers the total cost for family allowances. Work injury compensation is also available. In 2009 about 14.9% of the population was considered to be at risk of poverty, up from 11.9% in 2003.

Women are well represented in politics and the professions. Although legally entitled to equal pay for equal work, a 2010 report indicated that women were paid 14% to 16% less than men for comparable work. However, the number of women in the workplace increased in 2004. The Ministry for the Promotion of Women is charged with ensuring equal opportunities for women. Violence against women is taken seriously by the authorities, and most abusers are prosecuted. Children's rights are fully protected, and the government amply funds systems providing education and health care. The law prohibits discrimination against persons with disabilities.

Human rights are fully respected in Luxembourg.

41 HEALTH

According to the CIA, life expectancy in Luxembourg was 79.61 years in 2011. The country spent 6.8% of its GDP on healthcare, amounting to $8,183 per person. There were about 29 physicians, 113 nurses and midwives, and 56 hospital beds per 10,000 inhabitants.

Luxembourg has an advanced national health service, supervised by the Ministry of Public Health. Public health facilities are available to physicians and treatment of patients is on a private basis. Hospitals are operated either by the state or by the Roman Catholic Church.

Public health officials have waged efficient national campaigns against contagious diseases and infant mortality has been reduced from 56.8 deaths per 1,000 live births in 1948 to an estimated 4.44 as of 2011. The fertility rate was estimated at 1.77. In 2008 the maternal mortality rate, according to the World Bank, was 17 per 100,000 births.

It was estimated that 96% of the country's children were immunized against measles. Leading causes of death are circulatory/heart diseases, cancer, road accidents, and suicide. The HIV/AIDS adult prevalence rate was 0.3% in 2009. In 2010 there were 28 reported cases of tuberculosis.

42 HOUSING

The immediate post-World War II housing shortage created by the considerable war damage has been alleviated by substantial construction of private homes and apartment buildings. The government has helped by making home loans at low interest rates available to buyers. In 1981 there were 128,281 private households in Luxembourg. At the 2001 census, there were about 171,953 private households. About 169,198 households were living in single-family units. Of these, 67% were living in owner-occupied dwellings. A new housing census was scheduled for 2011. Housing satisfaction is one of the highest in the European Union.

43 EDUCATION

School attendance is compulsory between the ages of 6 and 15. Pupils attend primary schools for six years and then enter a general secondary or technical school for a period of up to seven years. The school year runs from October to July. The primary languages of instruction are French and German. In 2005 about 86% of age-eligible children were enrolled in some type of preschool program. In 2008 the World Bank estimated that 96% of age-eligible children in Luxembourg were enrolled in primary school. Secondary enrollment for age-eligible children stood at 84%. In 2005 the student-to-teacher ratio for primary school was at about 11:1; the ratio for secondary school was about 10:1.

The University of Luxembourg, the country's first and only university, opened in 2003. Enrollment for the 2009–10 academic year included about 5,000 students of 96 different nationalities. Many advanced students attend institutions of higher learning in Belgium and France. High-level vocational training programs are available at the Center for Public Research–Henri Tudor, a public research institute dedicated toward strengthening the innovation capacity of businesses and public organizations. In 2003 about 12% of the tertiary age population was enrolled in some type of higher education program. The CIA estimated that Luxembourg had a literacy rate of 100%.

As of 2003 public expenditure on education was estimated at 3.6% of GDP, or 8.5% of total government expenditures.

⁴⁴LIBRARIES AND MUSEUMS

The National Library in Luxembourg is the largest in the country, with over 650,000 volumes. There are four libraries associated with the University of Luxembourg. Other libraries include the European Community Court of Justice (120,000), the Abbey of St. Maurice at Clervaux (100,000), the Seminary of Luxembourg (110,000), and the European Parliament (150,000). The Grand Ducal Institute maintains a few specialized collections in the city of Luxembourg, as does the government. In Esch-sur-Alzette the public library has close to 66,000 volumes and features a special collection of Luxembourgensia. The Association of Luxembourgish Librarians, Archivists, and Documentalists (ALBAD) was founded in 1991.

The National Museum of History and Art (founded in 1845) exhibits fine arts as well as the history of Luxembourg. The city of Luxembourg also hosts the Museum of Natural History, founded in 1988 and moved to a new building in 1996, the year that the Museum of the History of Luxembourg opened in the same city. The home where the 19th-century French writer Victor Hugo lived as an exile is in Vianden, and there is a museum of wine in Ehren. In 2010 there were 44 museums throughout the country.

⁴⁵MEDIA

Luxembourg's telecommunications system is highly developed, modern, and fully automated. The country's mobile cellular phone system operates nationwide. International service is provided by three leased channels on the TAT-6 coaxial submarine cable, which links Europe to America. In 2009 there were some 273,600 main phone lines and an additional 719,000 mobile cellular phones in use, with mobile phone subscriptions averaged at 144 per 100 people.

Radio-Télé-Luxembourg broadcasts on five radio channels (in Letzeburgesch, French, German, English, and Dutch) and two television channels (Letzeburgesch and French). The powerful commercial network reaches not only the domestic audience but millions of French, Germans, and other Europeans. The country is home to the Sociéte Européenne des Satellites at Betzdorf, the largest satellite television operator in Europe. In 2010 there were two FM radio stations, nine AM radio stations, and two short-wave radio stations. In 2010 the country had 244,225 Internet hosts. In 2009 there were some 424,500 Internet users in Luxembourg. An estimated 90% of all households have a computer and access to the Internet. About 78% of all households use a broadband connection.

The daily press is small in circulation but has high standards. Luxembourg does not have an independent news agency of its own but relies on foreign news agencies for information. Prominent newspapers in 2010, with circulation numbers listed parenthetically, included *Luxemburger Wort* (81,000), *Tageblatt/Zeitung fir Letzebuerg* (29,469), and *Le Republicain Lorrain* (15,000), as well as 2 other major newspapers.

The law provides for freedom of speech and the press, and the government is said to uphold these provisions in practice.

⁴⁶ORGANIZATIONS

The principal agricultural organization is Centrale Paysanne Luxembourgeoise; it is the umbrella organization for all producer cooperatives and other farmers' societies. Organizations promoting the interests of industry include federations of artisans, manufacturers, merchants, and winegrowers. The Luxembourg Chamber of Commerce is active in representing local business interests. The Luxembourg Confederation of Christian Trade Unions promotes workers' rights.

Several professional associations are active in supporting a wide variety of occupations and fields. The Association of Doctors and Dentists serves as a professional networking organization while also promoting research and education on health issues and working to establish common policies and standards in healthcare. There are several other associations dedicated to research and education for specific fields of medicine and particular diseases and conditions.

The Christian Social Women organization promotes women's rights and encourages political participation. Scouting programs are active for youth. There are also several sports associations active within the country, including the multinational European Table Tennis Union.

Kiwanis and Lions clubs also have programs in the country. International organizations with active chapters include the Red Cross, Amnesty International, UNICEF, and Greenpeace.

⁴⁷TOURISM, TRAVEL, AND RECREATION

Picturesque Luxembourg, with approximately 130 castles, has long been a tourist attraction. Among the points of greatest attraction are Vianden; Clervaux, with its castle of the De Lannoi family, forebears of Franklin Delano Roosevelt; the famous abbey of Clervaux; Echternach, an ancient religious center; the Moselle region; and the fortifications of the capital. Popular sports for both residents and visitors include fishing, rowing, swimming, hiking, rock climbing, cycling, and golf. More than 5,000 American soldiers are buried at the American Military Cemetery near the capital, including Gen. George S. Patton.

In 2010 the hopping procession of Echternach was officially inscribed on the UNESCO Representative List of the Intangible Heritage of Humanity, an offshoot of the World Heritage program. The traditional procession was deemed a living tradition by UNESCO, meaning that it is still passed from generation to generation and continues to create a sense of identity and community for those who participate. Such traditions have been approved by UNESCO for special consideration since 2001. A special program is designed to protect and promote the practice and understanding of the tradition. The hopping procession takes place each year on the Tuesday of Pentecost in honor of Saint Willibrord, the monk who founded the Abbey of Echternach. Thousands of residents participate in the annual procession, which starts at the courtyard of the abbey and ends at the basilica of Saint Willibrord.

Luxembourg is one of the 25 European countries that are part of the Schengen Group. By special agreement, citizens of member countries are allowed free movement among other member countries. Once a traveler enters a Schengen country, he or she may travel within the member countries continuously for up to 90 days without a visa. Citizens from countries outside the Schengen Group must have a passport for initial entry. Luxembourg receives more than 500,000 visitors each year, primarily from other European countries. The *Tourism Factbook*, published by the UN World Tourism Organization, reported that there were 14,709 hotel beds available in Luxembourg in 2009, which had an occupancy rate of 26%. The estimated daily cost to visit Luxembourg, the capital, was $520.

⁴⁸FAMOUS PERSONS

Count Sigefroid founded the nation in 963, and Countess Ermesinde (r. 1196–1247) tripled the extent of the country. Other outstanding historical personages are Henry VII of Luxembourg (c. 1275–1313), who became Holy Roman emperor in 1308; his son John the Blind (1296–1346), count of Luxembourg (1309–46) and king of Bohemia (1310–46), a national hero; and the latter's son Charles (1316–78), who became Holy Roman emperor as Charles IV (1346–78). Grand duke from 1890 to 1905 was Adolphe (1817–1905), one-time duke of Nassau (1839–66) and the founder of the present dynasty, the house of Nassau-Weilbourg, whose origins go back to 1059.

Joseph Bech (1887–1975), prime minister from 1926 to 1937 and from 1953 to 1958, served as foreign minister for 33 years. Luxembourg-born Robert Schuman (1886–1963), French premier (1947–48) and foreign minister (1948–53), was a key figure in the postwar movement for West European integration. Grand Duchess Charlotte (1896–1985) abdicated in 1964 in favor of her son Grand Duke Jean (b. 1921), ruled from 1964–2000. The current ruler is his son Grand Duke Henri (b. 1955).

An artist of note was painter Joseph Kutter (1894–1941). Gabriel Lippmann (1845–1921) was awarded the Nobel Prize in physics (1908) for his pioneering work in color photography. Jules Hoffman (b. 1941), shared the 2011 Nobel Prize in medicine with Bruce Beutler (b. United States, 1957) and Ralph Steinman (Canada, 1943–2011) for discoveries made in immunology. Hoffman was recognized for his 1996 discovery of the Toll gene in fruit flies, which appears to be essential in the activation of the innate immune system (that which initiates an immediate response to infection). Since this discovery, more than a dozen Toll-like receptors have been discovered in humans.

⁴⁹DEPENDENCIES

Luxembourg has no territories or colonies.

⁵⁰BIBLIOGRAPHY

Annesley, Claire (ed.). *A Political and Economic Dictionary of Western Europe.* Philadelphia: Routledge/Taylor and Francis, 2005.

Eccardt, Thomas M. *Secrets of the Seven Smallest States of Europe.* New York: Hippocrene Books, 2005.

Kelly, Mary, Gianpietro Mazzoleni, and Denis McQuail (eds.). *The Media in Europe.* 3rd ed. Thousand Oaks, CA: Sage, 2004.

Littler, Alan, et al. *In the Shadow of Luxembourg: EU and National Developments in the Regulation of Gambling.* Boston: Martinus Nijhoff, 2011.

Luxembourg Investment and Business Guide: Strategic and Practical Information. Washington, DC: International Business Publications USA, 2012.

Political Chronology of Europe. London, Eng.: Europa, 2001.

Opello, Walter C. *European Politics.* Boulder, CO: Lynne Rienner Publishers, 2009.

Wessels, Wolfgang, Andreas Maurer, and Jürgan Mittag (eds.). *Fifteen into One?: the European Union and Its Member States.* New York: Palgrave, 2003.

MACEDONIA

Former Yugoslav Republic of Macedonia
Republika Makedonija

CAPITAL: Skopje

FLAG: The flag consists of a gold sun with eight rays on a red field.

ANTHEM: *Denec Nad Makedonija (Today over Macedonia).*

MONETARY UNIT: The currency in use is the Macedonian denar (MKD). Bank notes are available in 10, 50, 100, 500, 1000 and 5000 denars. US$1 = MKD0.0214 (or MKD1 = US$46.43) as of 2010.

WEIGHTS AND MEASURES: The metric system is in effect in Macedonia.

HOLIDAYS: Orthodox Christmas, 7 January; national holiday, 2 August; Independence Day, 8 September (also known as National Day).

TIME: 1 p.m. = noon GMT.

¹LOCATION, SIZE, AND EXTENT

Macedonia is a landlocked nation located in southeastern Europe. Macedonia is slightly larger than the state of Vermont with a total area of 25,333 sq km (9,781 sq mi). Macedonia shares boundaries with Kosovo and Serbia to the N, Bulgaria to the E, Greece to the S, and Albania to the W, and has a total boundary length of 766 km (476 mi). Macedonia's capital city, Skopje, is located in the northwestern part of the country.

²TOPOGRAPHY

The topography of Macedonia features a mountainous landscape covered with deep basins and valleys. There are three large lakes, each divided by a frontier line and the country is bisected by the Vardar River. Approximately 22% of Macedonia's land is arable. Natural resources include copper, chromium, lead, zinc, manganese, tungsten, gold, silver, nickel, low-grade iron ore, gypsum, asbestos, and timber. Located above a thrust fault line of the Eurasian Tectonic Plate, the nation experiences frequent tremors and occasional severe earthquakes. In 1963, 6.0 magnitude quake at Skopje caused the death of about 1,100 people and destroyed much of the city.

³CLIMATE

Macedonia's climate features warm, dry summers and autumns. In July the average temperature is between 20 and 23°C (68 and 73°F). The average temperature in January is between -20 and 0°C (-4 and 32°F). Rainfall averages 51 cm (20 in) a year. Snowfalls can be heavy in winter.

⁴FLORA AND FAUNA

The World Resources Institute estimates that there are 3,500 plant species in Macedonia. In addition, Macedonia is home to 89 mammal, 291 bird, 29 reptile, and 5 amphibian species. The calcu-

lation reflects the total number of distinct species residing in the country, not the number of endemic species.

Deep basins and valleys are populated by European bison, fox, rabbits, brown bears, and deer. Ducks, turtles, frogs, raccoons, and muskrats inhabit the country's waterways. Pine trees are common in the higher mountain regions while beech and oak cover some of the lower mountain regions.

⁵ENVIRONMENT

The World Resources Institute reported that Macedonia had designated 180,700 hectares (446,519 acres) of land for protection as of 2006. Water resources totaled 6.4 cu km (1.54 cu mi) while water usage was 2.27 cu km (0.545 cu mi) per year. Per capita water usage totaled 1,118 cu m (39,482 cu ft) per year. All 100% of urban dwellers and 99% of rural residents have access to safe drinking water.

Air pollution from metallurgical plants is a problem in Macedonia, as in the other former Yugoslav republics. The UN reported in 2008 that carbon dioxide emissions in Macedonia totaled 11,267 kilotons.

Macedonia has one World Heritage Site and two Ramsar Wetlands of International Importance. According to a 2011 report issued by the International Union for Conservation of Nature and Natural Resources (IUCN), threatened species included 5 types of mammals, 9 species of birds, 2 types of reptiles, 8 species of fish, and 61 species of mollusk. Threatened species include the field adder, Apollo butterfly, and noble crayfish.

⁶POPULATION

The US Central Intelligence Agency (CIA) estimates the population of Macedonia in 2011 to be approximately 2,077,328, which placed it at number 144 in population among the 239 nations of the world. In 2011, approximately 11.5% of the population was over 65 years of age, with another 18.5% under 15 years of age. The median age in Macedonia was 35.8 years. There were 1.00 males for every female in the country. The population's annual rate of change was 0.248%. The projected population for the year 2025 was 2,100,000. According to the State Statistical Office Population reported a population density of 80 people per sq km (207 people per sq mi).

The UN estimated that 59% of the population lived in urban areas, and that urban populations had an annual rate of change of 0.3%. The largest urban area was Skopje, with a population of 480,000.

7 MIGRATION

Estimates of Macedonia's net migration rate, carried out by the CIA in 2011, amounted to -0.48 migrants per 1,000 citizens. The total number of emigrants living abroad was 447,100, and the total number of immigrants living in Macedonia was 129,700. In February 1999, violence in Kosovo forced more than 10,000 refugees to flee to Macedonia. The situation reached an emergency level when hundreds of thousands of refugees were arriving in late March and early April. By early June, the refugee population had grown to some 260,000. Macedonia did not have sufficient resources to cope with an emergency of this magnitude. At the government's request, some third-country asylum nations enacted bilateral evacuation programs, independently of the UN High Commissioner for Refugees (UNHCR). Also, a joint UNHCR/IOM Humanitarian Evacuation Programme was established, under which more than 90,000 refugees were evacuated from Macedonia to 29 countries. In 2011, the UNHCR reported that three-quarters of the nearly three million people displaced by conflict in South-Eastern Europe during the 1990s have since returned home, or found other durable solutions. Despite this, UNHCR continues to operate a refugee program in Macedonia.

8 ETHNIC GROUPS

According to the 2002 census, Macedonians comprise about 64.2% of the population. Another 25.2% are ethnic Albanians, mostly living in the west, particularly the northwest. Other groups include Turks (3.9%), Roma (2.7%), Serbs (1.8%), and others (including Bosniaks and Vlachs, 2.2%).Relations between the Macedonian majority and the ethnic Albanians have been strained for many years, and Albanians have made several claims of social, economic, and political discrimination. Ethnic Turks have also reported discrimination, particularly through unequal representation in the government. The nation's Roma community has also experienced widespread social discrimination.

9 LANGUAGES

Macedonian is a southern Slavic tongue that was not officially recognized until 1944, and is the primary language of 66.5% of the population. Bulgarians claim it is merely a dialect of their own language. As in Bulgarian, there are virtually no declensions and the definite article is suffixed. Also as in Bulgarian—and unlike any other Slavic language—an indefinite article exists as a separate word. It is written in the Cyrillic alphabet, but with two special characters—r and k. Albanian, a second official language, is spoken by about 25.1% of the population. Turkish is spoken by about

3.5%, Roma by 1.9%, Serbian by 1.2%, and various other languages by 1.8%.

10 RELIGIONS

About 65% of the population are nominally Macedonian Orthodox; another 33% are Muslim. Other common faiths are Roman Catholicism and various Protestant denominations. Islam is primarily practiced among the ethnic Albanian community in the western part of the country and in the capital of Skopje. The Roman Catholic community is centered in Skopje, as is a small Jewish community.

While there is no state religion, a 2001 amendment to the constitution names five recognized religious groups—Macedonian Orthodox Church (MOC), Islamic Community of Macedonia (ICM), Roman Catholic Church, Judaism, and Evangelical Methodist Church. Orthodox Easter, Christmas, and Ramazan Bajram (end of Ramadan) are observed as national holidays. The constitution and the 2007 Law on the Legal Status of Churches, Religious Communities, and Religious Groups provide for freedom of religion, and other laws and policies contributed to the generally free practice of religion. In April 2010, parliament passed an antidiscrimination law to protect against discrimination based on religious beliefs.

11 TRANSPORTATION

Macedonia had a total of 13,736 km (8,535 mi) of roads as of 2010. There were 144 vehicles per 1,000 people in the country. Railroads extend for 699 km (434 mi). There were 14 airports, which transported 86,868 passengers in 2009 according to the World Bank. A major rail line connects Skopje with Serbia to the north and the Greek port of Salonika to the south, while 2 other rail lines run east to west. A 2009 World Bank report assessed that the rail system suffered from declining usage and is fragile, with reforms necessary to improve financial stability and operating performance.

12 HISTORY

Origin and Middle Ages

Macedonia is an ancient name, historically related to Philip II of Macedon, whose son became Alexander the Great, founder of one of the great empires of the ancient world. As a regional name, Macedonia, the land of the Macedons, has been used since ancient Greek times for the territory extending north of Thessaly and into the Vardar River Valley and between Epirus on the west and Thrace on the east. In Alexander the Great's time, Macedonia extended west to the Adriatic Sea over the area then called Illyris, part of today's Albania. Under the Roman Empire, Macedonia was extended south over Thessaly and Achaia.

Beginning in the 5th century AD Slavic tribes began settling in the Balkan area, and by 700 they controlled most of the Central and Peloponnesian Greek lands. The Slavic conquerors were mostly assimilated into Greek culture except in the northern Greek area of Macedonia proper and the areas of northern Thrace populated by "Bulgarian" Slavs. That is how St. Cyril and Methodius, two Greek brothers and scholars who grew up in the Macedonian city of Salonika, were able to become the "Apostles of the

Slavs," having first translated Holy Scriptures in 863 into the common Slavic language they had learned in the Macedonian area.

Through most of the later Middle Ages, Macedonia was an area contested by the Byzantine Empire, with its Greek culture and Orthodox Christianity, the Bulgarian Kingdom, and particularly the 14th century Serbian empire of Dušan the Great. The Bulgarian and Serbian empires contributed to the spread of Christianity through the establishment of the Old Church Slavic liturgy.

After Dušan's death in 1355 his empire collapsed, partly due to the struggle for power among his heirs and partly to the advances of the Ottoman Turks. Following the defeat of the Serbs at the Kosovo Field in 1389, the Turks conquered the Macedonian area over the next half century and kept it under their control until the 1912 Balkan war.

Under Ottoman Rule

The decline of the Ottoman Empire brought about renewed competition over Slavic Macedonia between Bulgaria and Serbia. After the Russo-Turkish war of 1877 ended in a Turkish defeat, Bulgaria, an ally of Russia, was denied the prize of the Treaty of San Stefano (1878) in which Turkey had agreed to an enlarged and autonomous Bulgaria that would have included most of Macedonia. Such an enlarged Bulgaria—with control of the Vardar River Valley and access to the Aegean Sea—was, however, a violation of a prior Russo-Austrian agreement. The Western powers opposed Russia's penetration into the Mediterranean through the port of Salonika and, at the 1878 Congress of Berlin, forced the "return" of Macedonia and East Rumelia from Bulgaria to Turkey. This action enraged Serbia, which had fought in the war against Turkey, gained its own independence, and hoped to win control of Bosnia and Herzegovina, which had been given over to Austrian control, for itself.

In this situation both Serbia and Bulgaria concentrated their efforts on Macedonia, where Greek influence had been very strong through the Greek Orthodox Church. The Bulgarians obtained their own Orthodox Church in 1870, that extended its influence to the Macedonian area and worked in favor of unification with Bulgaria through intensive educational activities designed to "Bulgarize" the Slavic population. Systematic intimidation was also used, when the Bulgarians sent their terrorist units (komite) into the area. The Serbian side considered Macedonia to be Southern Serbia, with its own dialect but using Serbian as its literary language. Serbian schools predated Bulgarian ones in Macedonia and continued with their work.

While individual instances of Macedonian consciousness and language had appeared by the end of the 18th century, it was in the 1850s that "Macedonists" had declared Macedonia a separate Slavic nation. Macedonian Slavs had developed a preference for their central Macedonian dialect and had begun publishing some writings in it rather than using the Bulgaro-Macedonian version promoted by the Bulgarian Church and government emissaries. Thus, Macedonia, in the second half of the 19th century, while still under the weakening rule of the Turks, had become the object of territorial and cultural claims by its Greek, Serb, and Bulgarian neighbors.

The most systematic pressure had come from Bulgaria and had caused large numbers of "Bulgaro-Macedonians" to emigrate to

LOCATION: 41°50′ N; 22°0′ E. BOUNDARY LENGTHS: Albania, 151 kilometers (94 miles); Bulgaria, 148 kilometers (92 miles); Greece, 228 kilometers (142 miles); Serbia, 62 kilometers (39 miles); Kosovo, 159 kilometers (99 miles).

Bulgaria—some 100,000 in the 1890s—mainly to Sophia, where they constituted almost half the city's population and an extremely strong pressure group.

Struggle for Autonomy

More and more Macedonians became convinced that Macedonia should achieve at least an autonomous status under Turkey, if not complete independence. In 1893, a secret organization was formed in Salonika aiming at a revolt against the Turks and the establishment of an autonomous Macedonia. The organization was to be independent of Serbia, Bulgaria, and Greece and was named the Internal Macedonian Revolutionary Organization (IMRO), a group that became Socialist, revolutionary, and terrorist in nature. Much like Ireland's IRA, IMRO spread through Macedonia and became an underground paragovernmental network active up to World War II.

A pro-Bulgarian and an independent Macedonian faction soon developed, the first based in Sophia, the second in Salonika. Its strong base in Sophia gave the pro-Bulgarian faction a great advantage and it took control and pushed for an early uprising in order to impress the Western powers into intervening in support of Macedonia.

The large scale uprising took place on 2 August 1903 (Ilinden—"St. Elijah's Day") when the rebels took over the town of Kruševo and proclaimed a Socialist Republic. After initial defeats of the local Turkish forces, the rebels were subdued by massive Ottoman attacks using scorched earth tactics and wholesale massacres of the population over a three-month period. Europe and the United States paid attention and forced Turkey into granting reforms to be supervised by international observers. However, the disillusioned IMRO leadership engaged in factional bloody feuds that weakened the IMRO organization and image. This encouraged both Serbs and Greeks in the use of their own armed bands—Serbian Cetniks and Greek Andarte—creating an atmosphere of gang warfare in which Bulgaria, Serbia, and Greece fought each other (instead of the Turks) over a future division of Macedonia. In the meantime, the Young Turks movement had spread among Turkish officers and military uprisings began in Macedonia in 1906. These uprisings spread and Turkish officers demanded a constitutional system. They believed that Turkey could be saved only by Westernizing. In 1908 the Young Turks prevailed, and offered to the IMRO leadership agrarian reforms, regional autonomy, and introduction of the Macedonian language in the schools. However, the Young Turks turned out to be extreme Turkish nationalists bent on the assimilation of other national groups. Their denationalizing efforts caused further rebellions and massacres in the Balkans. Serbia, Greece, Bulgaria, and Montenegro turned for help to the great powers, but to no avail. In 1912 they formed the Balkan League, provisionally agreed on the division of Turkish Balkan territory among themselves, and declared war on Turkey in October 1912 after Turkey refused their request to establish the autonomous regions of Macedonia—Old Serbia, Epirus, and Albania—already provided for in the 1878 Treaty of Berlin.

Balkan Wars

The quick defeat of the Turks by the Balkan League stunned the European powers, particularly when Bulgarian forces reached the suburbs of Istanbul. Turkey signed a treaty in London on 30 May 1913 giving up all European possessions with the exception of Istanbul. However, when Italy and Austria vetoed a provision granting Serbia access to the Adriatic at Durazzo and Alessio and agreed to form an independent Albania, Serbia demanded a larger part of Macedonia from Bulgaria. Bulgaria refused and attacked both Serbian and Greek forces. This caused the second Balkan War that ended in a month with Bulgaria's defeat by Serbia and Greece with help from Romania, Montenegro, and Turkey. The outcome was the partitioning of Macedonia between Serbia and Greece. Turkey regained the Adrianople area it had lost to Bulgaria. Romania gained a part of Bulgarian Dobrudja while Bulgaria kept a part of Thrace and the Macedonian town of Strumica. Thus Southern Macedonia came under the Hellenizing influence of Greece while most of Macedonia was annexed to Serbia. Both Serbia and Greece denied any Macedonian "nationhood." In Greece, Macedonians were treated as "Slavophone" Greeks while Serbs viewed Macedonia as Southern Serbia and Serbian was made the official language of government and instruction in schools and churches.

First and Second Yugoslavia

After World War I, the IMRO organization became a terrorist group operating out of Bulgaria with a nuisance role against Yugoslavia. In later years, some IMRO members joined the Communist Party and tried to work toward a Balkan Federation where Macedonia would be an autonomous member. Its interest in the dissolution of the first Yugoslavia led IMRO members to join with the Croatian Ustaša in the assassination of King Alexander of Yugoslavia and French Foreign Minister Louis Barthou in Marseille on 9 October 1934. During World War II, Bulgaria, Hitler's ally, occupied the central and eastern parts of Macedonia while Albanians, supported by Italy, annexed western Macedonia along with the Kosovo region. Because of Bulgarian control, resistance was slow to develop in Macedonia; a conflict between the Bulgarian and Yugoslav Communist parties also played a part. By the summer of 1943, however, Tito, the leader of the Yugoslav Partisans, took over control of the Communist Party of Macedonia after winning its agreement to form a separate Macedonian republic as part of a Yugoslav federation. Some 120,000 Macedonian Serbs were forced to emigrate to Serbia because they had opted for Serbian citizenship. Partisan activities against the occupiers increased and, by August 1944, the Macedonian People's Republic was proclaimed with Macedonian as the official language and the goal of unifying all Macedonians was confirmed. But this goal was not achieved. However, the "Pirin" Macedonians in Bulgaria were granted their own cultural development rights in 1947, and then lost them after the Stalin-Tito split in 1948. The Bulgarian claims to Macedonia were revived from time to time after 1948.

On the Greek side, there was no support from the Greek Communist Party for the unification of Macedonian Slavs within Greece with the Yugoslav Macedonians, even though Macedonian Slavs had organized resistance units under Greek command and participated heavily in the postwar Greek Communists' insurrection. With Tito's closing the Yugoslav-Greek frontier in July 1949 and ending his assistance to the pro-Cominform Greek Communists, any chance of territorial gains from Greece had dissipated. On the Yugoslav side, Macedonia became one of the co-equal constituent republics of the Federal Socialist Republic of Yugoslavia under the Communist regime of Marshal Tito. The Macedonian language became one of the official languages of Yugoslavia, along with Slovenian and Serbo-Croatian, and the official language of the Republic of Macedonia where the Albanian and Serbo-Croatian languages were also used. Macedonian was fully developed into the literary language of Macedonians, used as the language of instruction in schools as well as the newly established Macedonian Orthodox Church. A Macedonian University was established in Skopje, the capital city, and all the usual cultural, political, social, and economic institutions were developed within the framework of the Yugoslav Socialist system of self-management. The main goals of autonomy and socialism of the old IMRO organization were fulfilled, with the exception of the unification of the "Pirin" (Bulgarian) and "Greek" Macedonian lands.

All of the republics of the former Federal Socialist Republic of Yugoslavia share a common history between 1945 and 1991, the year of Yugoslavia's dissolution. The World War II Partisan resistance movement, controlled by the Communist Party of Yugoslavia and led by Marshal Tito, won a civil war waged against nationalist groups under foreign occupation, having secured the assistance, and recognition, from both the Western powers and the Soviet Union. Aside from the reconstruction of the country and its economy, the first task facing the new regime was the establishment of its legitimacy and, at the same time, the liquidation of its internal enemies, both actual and potential. The first task was accomplished by the 11 November 1945 elections of a constitutional assembly on the basis of a single candidate list assembled by the People's Front. The list won 90% of the votes cast. The three members of the "coalition" government representing the Royal Yugoslav Government in exile had resigned earlier in frustration and did not run in the elections. The Constitutional Assembly voted against the continuation of the Monarchy and, on 31 January 1946, the new constitution of the Federal People's Republic of Yugoslavia was promulgated. Along with state-building activities, the Yugoslav Communist regime carried out ruthless executions, massacres, and imprisonments to liquidate any potential opposition.

The Tito-Stalin conflict that erupted in 1948 was not a real surprise considering the differences the two had had about Tito's refusal to cooperate with other resistance movements against the occupiers in World War II. The expulsion of Tito from the Cominform group separated Yugoslavia from the Soviet Bloc, caused internal purges of pro-Cominform Yugoslav Communist Party members, and also nudged Yugoslavia into a failed attempt to collectivize its agriculture. Yugoslavia then developed its own brand of Marxist economy based on workers' councils and self-management of enterprises and institutions, and became the leader of the nonaligned group of nations in the international arena. Being more open to Western influences, the Yugoslav Communist regime relaxed somewhat its central controls. This allowed for the development of more liberal wings of Communist parties, particularly in Croatia and Slovenia, which agitated for the devolution of power from the federal to the individual republic level in order to better cope with the increasing differentiation between the more productive republics (Slovenia and Croatia) and the less developed areas. Also, nationalism resurfaced with tensions particularly strong between Serbs and Croats in the Croatian Republic, leading to the repression by Tito of the Croatian and Slovenian "Springs" in 1970–71.

The 1974 constitution shifted much of the decision-making power from the federal to the republics' level, turning the Yugoslav Communist Party into a kind of federation (league) of the republican parties, thus further decentralizing the political process. The autonomous provinces of Vojvodina and Kosovo were also given a quasi-sovereign status as republics, and a collective presidency was designed to take over power upon Tito's death. When Tito died in 1980, the delegates of the six republics and the two autonomous provinces represented the interests of each republic or province in the process of shifting coalitions centered on specific issues. The investment of development funds to assist the less developed areas became the burning issue around which nationalist emotions and tensions grew ever stronger, along with the forceful repression of the Albanian majority in Kosovo.

The economic crisis of the 1980s, with runaway inflation, inability to pay the debt service on over $20 billion in international loans that had accumulated during Tito's rule, and low productivity in the less-developed areas became too much of a burden for Slovenia and Croatia, leading them to stand up to the centralizing power of the Serbian (and other) Republics. The demand for a reorganization of the Yugoslav Federation into a confederation of sovereign states was strongly opposed by the coalition of Serbia, Montenegro, and the Yugoslav army. The pressure towards political pluralism and a market economy also grew stronger, leading to the formation of non-Communist political parties that, by 1990, were able to win majorities in multiparty elections in Slovenia and then in Croatia, thus putting an end to the era of the Communist Party monopoly of power. The inability of the opposing groups of centralist and confederalist republics to find any common ground led to the dissolution of Yugoslavia through the disassociation of Slovenia, Croatia, Bosnia and Herzegovina, and Macedonia, leaving only Serbia and Montenegro together in a new Federal Republic of Yugoslavia.

The years between 1945 and 1990 offered the Macedonians an opportunity for development in some areas, in addition to their cultural and nation-building efforts, within the framework of a one-party Communist system. For the first time in their history the Macedonians had their own republic and government with a very broad range of responsibilities. Forty-five years was a long enough period to have trained generations for public service responsibilities and the governing of an independent state. In addition, Macedonia derived considerable benefits from the Yugoslav framework in terms of federal support for underdeveloped areas (Bosnia and Herzegovina, Kosovo, Macedonia, Montenegro). Macedonia's share of the special development funds ranged from 26% in 1966 to about 20% in 1985, much of it supplied by Croatia and Slovenia.

In the wake of developments in Slovenia and Croatia, Macedonia held its first multiparty elections in November–December 1990, with the participation of over 20 political parties. Four parties formed a coalition government that left the strongest nationalist party (IMRO) in the opposition. In January 1991 the Macedonian Assembly passed a declaration of sovereignty.

Independence

While early in 1989 Macedonia supported Serbia's Slobodan Milošević in his recentralizing efforts, by 1991, Milošević was viewed as a threat to Macedonia and its leadership took positions closer to the confederal ones of Slovenia and Croatia. A last effort to avoid Yugoslavia's disintegration was made 3 June 1991 through a joint proposal by Macedonia and Bosnia and Herzegovina, offering to form a "community of Yugoslav Republics" with a centrally administered common market, foreign policy, and national defense. However, Serbia opposed the proposal.

On 26 June 1991—one day after Slovenia and Croatia had declared their independence—the Macedonian Assembly debated the issue of secession from Yugoslavia with the IMRO group urging an immediate proclamation of independence. Other parties were more restrained, a position echoed by Macedonian president Kiro Gligorov in his cautious statement that Macedonia would remain faithful to Yugoslavia. Yet by 6 July 1991, the Macedonian Assembly decided in favor of Macedonia's independence if a confederal solution could not be attained.

Thus, when the process of dissolution of Yugoslavia took place in 1990–91, Macedonia refused to join Serbia and Montenegro and opted for independence on 20 November 1991. The unification issue was then raised again, albeit negatively, by the refusal of Greece to recognize the newly independent Macedonia for fear that its very name would incite irredentist designs toward the Slav Macedonians in northern Greece. The issue of recognition became a problem between Greece and its NATO allies in spite of the fact that Macedonia had adopted in 1992 a constitutional amendment forbidding any engagement in territorial expansion or interference in the internal affairs of another country. In April 1993, Macedonia gained membership in the UN, but only under the name of "Former Yugoslav Republic of Macedonia." Greece also voted against Macedonian membership in the Conference on Security and Cooperation in Europe on 1 December 1993. However, on 16 December 1993, the United Kingdom, Germany, Denmark, and the Netherlands had announced the initiation of the recognition process for Macedonia and other countries joined the process, which resulted in recognition of Macedonia by the United States on 8 February 1994. In April 1994 the EU began to take legal action in the European Court of Justice against Greece for refusing to lift a trade blockade against Macedonia that it initiated two months earlier. However, by October 1995, Greece agreed to lift the embargo, in return for concessions from Macedonia that included changing its national flag, which contained an ancient Greek emblem depicting the 16-pointed golden sun of Vergina. The dispute over the name of Macedonia remained, but the agreement defused the threat of violence in the region.

On 3 October 1995, Macedonian president Kiro Gligorov narrowly survived a car-bomb attack that killed his driver. The next day, parliament named its speaker, Stojan Andov, as the interim president after determining that Gligorov was incapable of performing his functions. Gligorov resumed his duties in early 1996. As tensions between majority Albanians and minority Serbs in the neighboring Yugoslav province of Kosovo heated up from 1997 to 1999, fears mounted that full-scale fighting would spread to Macedonia. Ethnic violence erupted in the town of Gostivar in July 1997 after the Macedonian government sent in special military forces to remove the illegal Albanian, Turkish, and Macedonian flags flying outside the town hall. Several thousand protesters, some armed, had gathered and were in a stalemate with police. During the skirmish, police killed three ethnic Albanians and several policemen were shot. The Albanian nationalist Kosovo Liberation Army also claimed attacks against two police stations in Macedonia in December 1997 and January 1998. As the violence mounted the UN Security Council voted unanimously on 21 July 1998 to renew the UN Preventive Deployment Force (UNPREDEP) mandate another six months and to bolster the contingent with 350 more soldiers.

When full-scale fighting in Kosovo erupted in early 1999 and NATO responded with air strikes against Serbia, Macedonia became the destination for tens of thousands of Kosovar Albanian refugees fleeing from Serbian ethnic cleansing. For a while the situation in Macedonia remained tense as the government, fearful of a spillover of the fighting into its territory, closed its frontiers to refugees. Nonetheless, the presence of NATO forces and pledges of international aid prevented (aside from errant bombs and a couple of cross-border incursions) a spread of the fighting and maintained domestic stability in Macedonia.

However, in 2000, violence on the border with Kosovo increased, putting Macedonian troops in a state of high alert. In February 2001, fighting broke out between government forces and ethnic Albanian rebels, many of who were from the Kosovo Liberation Army, but some were also ethnic Albanians from within Macedonia. The insurrection broke out in the northwest, where rebels took up arms around the town of Tetovo, where ethnic Albanians make up a majority of the population. NATO deployed additional forces along the border with Kosovo to stop the supply of arms to the rebels; however, the buffer zone proved ineffective. As fighting intensified in March, the government closed the border with Kosovo. The UN High Commissioner for Refugees estimated that 22,000 ethnic Albanians had fled the fighting by that time. Fears in Macedonia of the creation of a "Greater Albania," including Kosovo and parts of Macedonia, were fueled by the separatist movement, and mass demonstrations were held in Skopje urging tougher action against the rebels. The violence continued throughout the summer, until August, when the Ohrid Framework Agreement was signed by the government and ethnic Albanian representatives, granting greater recognition of ethnic Albanian rights in exchange for the rebels' pledge to turn over weapons to the NATO peacekeeping force.

In November 2001, parliament amended the constitution to include reforms laid out in the Ohrid Framework Agreement. The constitution recognizes Albanian as an official language, and increases access for ethnic Albanians to public-sector jobs, including the police. It also gives ethnic Albanians a voice in parliament, and guarantees their political, religious and cultural rights. In March 2002, parliament granted an amnesty to the former rebels who turned over their weapons to the NATO peacekeepers in August and September 2001. By September 2002, most of the 170,000 people who had fled their homes in advance of the fighting in 2001 had returned.

Parliamentary elections were held on 15 September 2002, which saw a change in leadership from the nationalist VMRO-DPMNE party of Prime Minister Ljubco Georgievski to the moderate Social Democratic League of Macedonia (SDSM)-led "Together for Macedonia" coalition. Branco Crvenkovski became prime minister. At that time Boris Trajkovski was president; he had been elected from the VMRO-DPMNE party in 1999. In the September 2002 elections, former ethnic Albanian rebel-turned-politician Ali Ahmeti saw his Democratic Union for Integration party (DUI) claim victory for the Albanian community, which makes up more than 25% of the Macedonian population. Ahmeti, former political leader of the National Liberation Army (NLA), delayed taking his seat in parliament until December, for fear it would ignite protests among Macedonians who still regarded him as a terrorist. Indeed, in January 2003, the DUI headquarters in Skopje came under assault from machine-gunfire and a grenade, the fourth such attack on DUI offices.

The year 2004 was a rather tumultuous one for Macedonia, and Macedonians. In February, President Trajkovski, who was on his way to a conference in Mostar, Bosnia, died in a plane crash. Two months later, elections were staged to replace him. Branko Crvenkovski, the acting prime minister and the leader of the ruling Social Democratic Union of Macedonia, won the second round of the election, with 62.7% of the vote; his main opponent—Sasko Kedev of the VMRO-DPMNE—got 37.3%. In June 2004, Hari Kostov, the former minister of interior, became prime minister following approval by the parliament. His reign was to be chaotic and short lived though—ethnic protests took place around the country as parliament implemented legislation that gave Albanians more autonomy in the areas where they predominated. In November 2004, Kostov resigned and his place was taken by the defense minister, Vlado Buckovski (who also took over the leadership of the Social Democratic Union). In summer 2005, parliament passed a law that allowed ethnic Albanians to fly the Albanian flag in the areas where they comprise the majority.

General elections were held in July 2006. Nikola Gruevski, leader of VMRO-DPMNE, formed a government after reaching a coalition agreement with Democratic Party of Albanians and three small parties. Gruevski's party won 45 seats in the 120-seat parliament. There were protests in some areas after the largest Albanian party, the Democratic Union of Integration, which was part of the outgoing coalition, was left out.

In April 2007, former Interior Minister Ljube Boskovski went on trial at the International Tribunal for the former Yugoslavia in The Hague. He was charged with war crimes during the 2001 ethnic Albanian rebellion, and acquitted in July 2008.

In the 2009 presidential elections, Gjorge Ivanov of the conservative VMRO-DPMNE party won the post of president with 64% of the vote. Ivanov announced that resolving the dispute with Greece and joining NATO were important goals for his presidency. Kosovo and Macedonia completed demarcation of their boundary in September 2008, but a resolution with Greece remained elusive.

Macedonia has worked diligently toward membership in NATO for a number of years through a NATO Membership Action Plan. In 2008 Greece blocked Macedonia's bid for membership as a result of the ongoing name dispute. In November of that year, Macedonia filed a suit against Greece in the International Court of Justice, claiming that the Greek veto was a violation of the interim accord of 1995. The dispute was elevated to the UN where an official negotiator has facilitated numerous rounds of talks. On 5 December 2011 the International Court of Justice ruled that Greece violated the 1995 Interim Accord and was wrong to interfere with Macedonia's path to NATO membership. In 2009, the European Commission recommended that Macedonia become a candidate for EU membership and begin negotiations. The negotiations had not started as of 2011. Neither EU nor NATO membership could move forward until the issue with Greece was resolved.

¹³ GOVERNMENT

Macedonia achieved its independence from the former Yugoslavia on 20 November 1991, having adopted its constitution on 17 November 1991. Macedonia's unicameral assembly of 120 seats is called the Sobranje. Eighty-five members are elected in single-seat constituencies, and 35 are elected by proportional representation. The executive branch consists of the president (elected by popular vote for a five-year term) and the Council of Ministers (elected by the majority vote of all the deputies in the Sobranje). The prime minister is elected by the assembly. In November 2001, parliament amended the constitution to include greater recognition of ethnic Albanian political, religious, and cultural rights.

¹⁴ POLITICAL PARTIES

In the July 2006 parliamentary elections, the Internal Macedonian Revolutionary Organization-Democratic Party for Macedonian Unity (VMRO-DPMNE) coalition won 45 seats, while the Together for Macedonia coalition (composed of 10 parties led by the Social Democratic League of Macedonia and the Liberal Democratic Party-SDSM-LDP) won 35. VMRO-DPMNE put together a government with four smaller parties, under the leadership of Nikola Gruevski. Gruevski announced that the new government would be composed of VMRO-DPMNE, Democratic Party of Albanians (DPA), New Social Democratic Party (NSDP), Democratic Renewal of Macedonia (DOM), and Party for European Integration (PEI). The Democratic Union for Integration (DUI) and Democratic Prosperity Party (PDP) coalition revolted because they were not invited to join the government; the coalition started protests throughout Albanian-dominated regions of the country. The DUI, DPA, and PDP are ethnic Albanian parties.

In 2008, as Greece blocked the nation's bid to join NATO due to the ongoing name dispute with Macedonia, Prime Minister Gruevski accused opposition parties of blocking reforms designed to boost the nation's chances at membership in both NATO and the European Union. As a result, 70 of the 120 parliamentary deputies voted to dissolve the assembly in favor of new elections in June 2008. In that race, the VMRO-DPMNE coalition won 63 seats with 49% of the vote. A coalition led by the Social Democratic Union of Macedonia (SDSM) won 27 seats, followed by the Democratic Union for Integration (BDI/DUI) with 18 seats, the Democratic Party of the Albanians (PDSh/DPA) with 11 seats, and the Party for European Integration (PEI) with 1 seat.

In the 2009 presidential election, Gjorge Ivanov of the conservative VMRO-DPMNE party won with 63% of the vote. Although the elections seemed to be peaceful and fair overall, some observers reported localized incidents of intimidation and irregularities. Voter turnout was just above the 40% requirement for the results to be official. Ivanov succeeded Branko Crvenkovski of the Social Democratic Union. The next presidential election was expected to take place in March 2014.

Parliamentary elections were held in June 2011. The VMRO-DPMNE-led block won 39% (63 seats), the SDSM-led block won 32.8% (27 seats), BDI/DUI won 10.2% (18 seats), PDSh/DPA won 5.9% (11 seats), and others received 12.1%. As of 2011, the cabinet was formed by the government coalition parties VMRO-DPMNE, BDI/DUI, and several small parties. The next parliamentary elections were scheduled to take place by June 2015.

¹⁵ LOCAL GOVERNMENT

Macedonia's 84 municipalities form the structure of local government. (Out of these municipalities, 10 represent the greater Skopje area.) The municipality is the basic self-managed sociopolitical community. Council members are directly elected for four-year terms, as are the mayors of the municipalities. Citizens may form neighborhood (village and suburb) governing bodies. Where the number of members of a particular nationality exceeds 20% of the total number of inhabitants in a municipality, the language and alphabet of that nationality shall be in official use, in addition to Macedonian and the Cyrillic alphabet.

The local elections held in April 2005 went without ethnic tensions, although international observers drew attention to irregularities during all of the three voting rounds. Despite criticism, Prime Minister Buckovski considered the local election process to be a "model" for the future. The ruling Together for Macedonia coalition won 36 mayoral races; the Albanian Democratic Union of Integration (a coalition partner of the former) won 15; the VMRO-DPMNE, 21; the VMRO-People's Party, 3; the Democratic Party of Albanians/Party of Democratic Prosperity, 2; the Macedonian Roma Alliance, 1; the rest of the seven mayoral seats were won by mayors supported by a voter's bloc. Trifun Kostovski won the city of Skopje race over the candidate of the SDSM-led coalition—Risto Penov.

In local election held in June 2011, the VMRO-led coalition won 39%, and the Social Democrats won 33%. Although the VMRO won 55 seats, they lost 8 seats. The election was called after the opposition boycotted Parliament in protest of the arrest of TV station leader Velija Ramkovski.

[16] JUDICIAL SYSTEM

The judicial system is comprised of three tiers: municipal courts, district courts, and the Supreme Court. A Constitutional Court handles issues of constitutional interpretation, including protection of individual rights. The constitution directs the establishment of a people's ombudsman to defend citizens' fundamental constitutional rights; the office became functional in 1997. An independent Republican Judicial Council appoints judges, who are confirmed by parliament. The constitution guarantees the autonomy and independence of the judiciary. Changes to the Macedonian Law on Civil Court Procedure, which took effect in September 2011, increases the information a plaintiff must provide when filing an intellectual property lawsuit, enables the plaintiff to present expert witnesses, and places a minimum on the damages in cases eligible for appeal.

[17] ARMED FORCES

As of 2010, the Army of the Republic of Macedonia (ARM) is composed of the Joint Operational Command, with subordinate Air Wing (Makedonsko Voeno Vozduhoplovstvo, MVV, Special Operations Regiment, Logistic Support Command and Training Command. Conscription was abolished by Parliament in 2006, and volunteers must be 18 years of age.

The International Institute for Strategic Studies reports that armed forces in Macedonia totaled 8,000 members in 2011, all of which are members of joint forces. Armed forces represented 0.9% of the labor force in Macedonia. Defense spending totaled $1.2 billion and accounted for 6% of gross domestic product (GDP).

[18] INTERNATIONAL COOPERATION

The Former Yugoslav Republic of Macedonia was admitted to the UN on 8 April 1993; it is a part of ECE and a member of several nonregional specialized agencies, such as FAO, IAEA, IMF, UNESCO, UNIDO, WHO, and the World Bank. Macedonia is also a member of the Council of Europe, the Euro-Atlantic Part-

nership Council, the European Bank for Reconstruction and Development, the NATO Partnership for Peace, and the OSCE.

In February 1994 Macedonia's sovereignty was recognized by the United States and EU countries. Greece objected to the use of the name Macedonia by the nation and imposed a trade embargo for this and other issues. Greece and Macedonia signed an interim agreement in 1995 ending the embargo and opening negotiations for diplomatic recognition.

In 1995, Macedonia ratified the European Convention on Human Rights and accepted the jurisdiction of the European Court of Human Rights. The convention includes several Eastern and Central European nations that see membership as a precursor to possible admission to the European Union in the future. While the nation was confirmed as a candidate for membership in the European Union in 2005, as of July 2009, no date had been set for membership talks to begin. The European Commission claims that, due to widespread corruption, the nation does not meet the political criteria necessary for membership. The issue with Greece over the name of Macedonia is an additional hurdle on the path to membership. As of 2011, Macedonia remains an EU candidate country.

As of 2011, Macedonia was a party to international environmental agreements on air pollution, biodiversity, climate change, climate change (the Kyoto Protocol), desertification, endangered species, hazardous wastes, law of the sea, ozone layer protection, and wetlands.

[19] ECONOMY

Macedonia's small size and integration with European markets made it particularly vulnerable during the economic downturn in the late 2000s. The immediate effects were a reduction in foreign direct investment, decreased access to credit and a growing trade deficit. Macedonia proved resilient, however, due to conservative fiscal policies and a monetary policy, which the currency pegged to the euro. By 2010, Macedonia received higher credit ratings and experienced modest GDP growth.

In August 1992, because it resented the use of "Macedonia" as the republic's name and feared a hidden ambition to lay claim to the Greek province with the same name, Greece imposed a partial blockade on Macedonia. Greece later imposed a full trade embargo against Macedonia in February 1994. This blockade, combined with the UN sanctions on Serbia and Montenegro, cost the economy an estimated $2 billion by the end of 1994. Macedonia's per capita GNP fell from $1,800 to less than $760 because of the sanctions and the Greek blockade. After threats of legal action by the EU, in October 1995 Greece ceased the embargo and promised not to interfere with Macedonia's commerce.

After inter-ethnic conflict in 2001 and a contraction in 2002, growth continued, averaging 4–6% per year until 2009. Although Macedonia proved relatively resilient, its real GDP growth rate fell from 6.1% in 2007 and 5.0% in 2008 to only 1.8% in 2010. Unemployment, however, remains a serious problem. The official estimate for 2002 was almost 32%, with some 70% of 15- to 24-year-olds without work. In 2007, overall unemployment rose to 35%, and by 2009, overall unemployment dropped to 32% and youth unemployment to 55%. Even with the economic growth, many skilled workers find work in other countries, contributing to the high unemployment rates, mostly among non-skilled workers.

20 INCOME

As of 2010, Macedonia's GDP was an estimated $20 billion, and the per capita GDP was estimated at $9,700. The average inflation rate was 1.6%. It was estimated that agriculture accounted for 8.7% of GDP, industry 22.1%, and services 69.2%.

It was estimated that in 2008 about 28.7% of the population subsisted on an income below the poverty line established by Macedonia's government. According to the World Bank, remittances from citizens living abroad totaled $381.1 million or about $183 per capita and accounted for approximately 1.9% of GDP.

As of 2011 the most recent study by the World Bank reported that actual individual consumption in Macedonia was 85.9% of GDP and accounted for 0.03% of world consumption. By comparison, the United States accounted for 25.44% of world individual consumption. The World Bank also estimated that 28.8% of Macedonia's GDP was spent on food and beverages, 18.5% on housing and household furnishings, 4.7% on clothes, 5.8% on health, 7.6% on transportation, 5.6% on communications, 2.0% on recreation, 2.9% on restaurants and hotels, and 5.4% on miscellaneous goods and services and purchases from abroad.

21 LABOR

As of 2010, Macedonia had a total labor force of 934,800 people. Within that labor force, CIA estimates in 2010 noted that 19.9% were employed in agriculture, 22.1% in industry, and 58% in the service sector.

The constitution guarantees citizens the right to form labor unions with restrictions on the military, police, and government workers. Approximately 50% of the legal workforce is organized. The Confederation of Trade Unions of Macedonia (SSM) is the labor confederation which is the successor to the old Communist Party labor confederation, and is still the government's primary negotiating partner on social issues. The right to strike is also guaranteed in the Constitution.

Macedonian law establishes a 40-hour workweek, with a 24-hour rest period (minimum) plus vacation and sick leave. The minimum employment age by law is 15 years, with minors under the age of 18 limited by the number of hours they can work and by the types of work they can perform. The law provides that workplaces must meet minimum occupational health and safety standards but reports indicate that these are not effectively enforced. On 1 October 2011 Prime Minister Gruevski's government passed a law to set the first minimum wage at €130 per month, effective January 2012.

22 AGRICULTURE

According to the World Bank, approximately 24 percent of the total land is farmed, and the country's major crops include grapes, tobacco, vegetables, and fruits. In 2009 cereal production amounted to 603,255 tons, fruit production 437,062 tons, and vegetable production 665,594 tons.

Most private farms are very small; 80% of private farmers own at most two three hectares, sometimes scattered in five or six locations. Wheat production is concentrated in south central Macedonia and in public farms. Corn and barley are produced throughout the country, mostly by the private sector. About 80% of agricultural land is held by the private sector. The remaining 20% is held by state-owned enterprises known as Kombinats, which are mostly not operating due to difficulties with privatization.

23 ANIMAL HUSBANDRY

The UN Food and Agriculture Organization (FAO) reported that Macedonia dedicated 603,000 hectares (1.49 million acres) to permanent pasture or meadow in 2009. During that year, the country tended 2.2 million chickens, 252,521 head of cattle, and 193,840 pigs. The production from these animals amounted to 27,558 tons of beef and veal, 31,283 tons of pork, 39,805 tons of poultry, 17,100 tons of eggs, and 279,667 tons of milk. Macedonia also produced 1,080 tons of cattle hide and 927 tons of raw wool.

Meadows and pastures accounted for about 25% of the total land area. Cattle numbers have increased slightly since 1992 due mainly to the increase in cows. Over 90% of cattle, are in private hands, with most farmers rarely having more than three cows because of limited land. Cow milk accounts for 74% of milk production; sheep milk, 26%. The rapidly growing goat sector is also contributing to increasing milk production. The raising of goats was prohibited during the socialist era in order to protect forestry resources.

24 FISHING

Inland fishing occurs primarily on Lake Ohrid, Lake Prespa, and the Vardar River, with a valid permit. Macedonia has no direct access to the sea for marine fishing. The total catch in 2006 was 646 tons (primarily trout and carp), down from a high in 2000 of 1,834 tons. According to a 2008 report from the Ministry of Environment and Physical Planning, the decrease was due to fishing companies losing their licenses and several sports fishing clubs closing.

25 FORESTRY

Approximately 40% of Macedonia is covered by forest. The UN FAO estimated the 2009 roundwood production at 109,000 cu m (3.85 million cu ft). The value of all forest products, including roundwood, totaled $7.93 million.

26 MINING

In 2008 the mining industry made up 1.1% of Macedonia's GDP. According to the State Statistical Office, mineral fuels, lubricants, and related materials made up 16.1% of the value of Macedonian imports and 7.5% of the value of exports in 2009. The world economic crisis impacted the production of Macedonian mineral exports, due to a decline in demand. Production of marl, decreased by 48%; gypsum, by 36%; bentonite, by 33%; feldspar, by 33%; sand and gravel by 23%; limestone flux, by 16%; and silica sand, by 15%.

The 2009 production output (in thousand metric tons) was: 694,968 limestone flux; 560,170 marl; 154,550 gypsum; 35,430 copper ore; 52,000 lead, and 32,000 zinc. Exported industrial minerals are primarily sold to Balkan countries, the EU, and Russia.

27 ENERGY AND POWER

In 2010, 6.819 billion kWh of electricity were generated, with 8.189 kWh consumed. In the same year, 84% of energy came from fossil fuels, while 3% came from alternative fuels; primarily hydropower. Per capita oil consumption was 1,520 kg. The only oil refinery is OKTA, located outside of Skopje. In 2009, 77% of total electricity production was from coal, 19% from hydroelectric, 4% from oil, and 0.02% from natural gas. Macedonia has no electricity production from nuclear sources. Some 42% of energy used in 2009 was imported.

28 INDUSTRY

Industrial production was recently eclipsed by the services industry as the dominant sector in Macedonia's economy. As of 2010, services accounted for more than 45% of GDP, and the industrial production growth rate was -4.9%.

Macedonia's industries are centered around Skopje. Steel, iron and chemical production, along with food processing, beverages, textiles, cement, energy, and pharmaceuticals are important industries.

Privatization began in 1989, under the Law on Social Capital of the former Yugoslav Federation, which privatized over 600 enterprises by giving shares to employees. The process gained momentum in 1993, with the adoption of the Law on Transformation of Enterprises with Social Capital. The privatization transformation was considered essentially complete by 2002.

29 SCIENCE AND TECHNOLOGY

In 2006, Macedonia spent 0.21% of its GDP on research and development (R&D), the second lowest in Southeast Europe. Of the gross domestic expenditure on R&D, 12.3% came from businesses, 47.9% from government, and 39.8% from higher education. Patent applications in science and technology as of 2009, according to the World Bank, totaled 34 in Macedonia, the lowest in Southeast Europe.

Between 2002 and 2008, the number of undergraduates in math and science increased by 209.5% and postgraduates increased by 70.6%. However, during the same period, the number of researchers actually decreased by 8.8%. According to UNESCO, Macedonia suffers from brain drain because of low R&D demand. The country is in the process of modernizing its science system. In 2006, the government approved the first national program related to developing the country's R&D capacities.

The Macedonian Academy of Sciences and Arts, founded in 1967 at Skopje, has sections of biological and medical sciences and of mathematical and technical sciences. The country also has an Association of Sciences and Arts, founded in 1960 at Bitola, as well as specialized learned societies concerned with physics, pharmacy, geology, medicine, mathematics and computers, veterinary surgery, engineering, forestry, and agriculture. Macedonia has research institutes dealing with geology, natural history, cotton, animal breeding, tobacco, animal husbandry, and water development.

The University of Skopje (founded in 1949) has faculties of civil engineering, agriculture, veterinary medicine, forestry, medicine, pharmacy, mechanical engineering, electrotechnical engineering, technology and metallurgy, natural and mathematical sciences, stomatology, and geology and mining. The Natural History Museum of Macedonia (founded in 1926) is located in Skopje.

30 DOMESTIC TRADE

Macedonia's small size and equally small population limits the size of the country's domestic trade sector. In addition, efforts to es-

Principal Trading Partners – Macedonia (2010)

(In millions of US dollars)

Country	Total	Exports	Imports	Balance
World	8,740.0	3,290.6	5,449.4	-2,158.8
Germany	1,302.6	692.5	610.1	82.4
Greece	693.7	245.1	448.7	-203.6
Serbia	690.2	271.8	418.4	-146.6
Russia	579.3	26.7	552.5	-525.8
Italy	561.9	234.6	327.3	-92.7
Kosovo	459.8	437.8	22.1	415.7
China	375.3	87.9	287.4	-199.5
United Kingdom	342.9	59.3	283.6	-224.3
Slovenia	234.2	69.1	165.1	-96.0
Romania	180.5	54.3	126.2	-71.9

(…) data not available or not significant.

(n.s.) not specified.

SOURCE: *2011 Direction of Trade Statistics Yearbook*, New York: United Nations, 2011.

tablish free trade zones to serve a larger Balkan market have yet to materialize.

Franchising is a new concept for the Macedonian business community. Although it has seen limited success there, franchises from Western European and US companies remain uncommon. However in the capital of Skopje, three McDonald's restaurants were opened between 1997 and 1999, while Holiday Inn opened a hotel there in 2000, followed by Best Western in 2002.

A 2010 USAID report on e-commerce reports that the number of payment cards in circulation in the Macedonia is approximately 1.4 million. The e-commerce turnover (buying from Macedonian online merchants) in the first 10 months of 2011 was MKD4 million. The turnover when buying from foreign online merchants with payment cards issued in Macedonia is 20 times higher. Whether a card can be used for online payment depends on the bank's policy and whether the bank obtained a license from the international payment card organization. The bank does not open a separate account for the Internet merchant to perform e-commerce, but to allow the trader to conduct e-commerce (to gain revenues through Internet transactions) it requires fulfillment of number of conditions. Most important of all is the bank's assessment whether the potential internet merchant has a serious and professional attitude. A large number of interested traders have given up on opening e-store, after the bank has introduced them with all aspects of e-commerce, which traders themselves had not taken into account in the elaboration of the idea.

Business hours are generally from 8 a.m. to 4 p.m.

31 FOREIGN TRADE

Macedonia is an open economy, highly integrated into international trade. In 2010, the country imported $5.241 billion worth of goods and services and exported $3.296 billion worth of goods and services. Major import partners in 2010 were Germany, 11.5%; Russia, 11.1%; Greece, 8.3%; Bulgaria, 8.2%; UK 7%; Turkey 5.1%; and Italy 5.1%. Macedonia's major export partners were Germany 20.2%; Italy 7.1%; Bulgaria 7.1%; and Greece 6.4%.

According to the US State Department, Macedonia has bilateral free trade agreements with Ukraine, Turkey, and the Europe-

Balance of Payments – Macedonia (2010)		
(In millions of US dollars)		
Current Account		-261.8
Balance on goods		-1,945.4
Imports	-5,241.0	
Exports	3,295.6	
Balance on services		78.3
Balance on income		-198.0
Current transfers		1,803.3
Capital Account		12.0
Financial Account		302.9
Direct investment abroad		-2.0
Direct investment in Macedonia		295.8
Portfolio investment assets		-29.0
Portfolio investment liabilities		-54.4
Financial derivatives		...
Other investment assets		-209.4
Other investment liabilities		301.9
Net Errors and Omissions		-0.1
Reserves and Related Items		-53.1

(…) data not available or not significant.

SOURCE: *Balance of Payment Statistics Yearbook 2011*, Washington, DC: International Monetary Fund, 2011.

Public Finance – Macedonia (2008)		
(In millions of denars, central government figures)		
Revenue and Grants	136,456	100.0%
Tax revenue	78,617	57.6%
Social contributions	39,471	28.9%
Grants	891	0.7%
Other revenue	17,477	12.8%
Expenditures	139,573	100.0%
General public services	...	...
Defense	...	...
Public order and safety	...	...
Economic affairs	...	...
Environmental protection	...	...
Housing and community amenities	...	...
Health	...	...
Recreational, culture, and religion	...	...
Education	...	...
Social protection	...	...

(…) data not available or not significant.

SOURCE: *Government Finance Statistics Yearbook 2010*, Washington, DC: International Monetary Fund, 2010.

an Free Trade Association (EFTA—Switzerland, Norway, Iceland, and Liechtenstein). Bilateral agreements with Albania, Bosnia and Herzegovina, Croatia, Serbia, Montenegro, UN Mission in Kosovo (UNMIK), and Moldova were replaced by membership in the Central European Free Trade Agreement (CEFTA). Macedonia also has concluded an "Agreement for Promotion and Protection of Foreign Direct Investments" with Albania, Austria, Bosnia and Herzegovina, Bulgaria, Belarus, Belgium, Luxembourg, Germany, Egypt, Iran, Italy, India, Spain, Serbia, Montenegro, People's Republic of China, Republic of Korea, Malaysia, Poland, Romania, Russia, Slovenia, Turkey, Ukraine, Hungary, Finland, France, the Netherlands, Croatia, Czech Republic, Switzerland, and Sweden.

³²BALANCE OF PAYMENTS

In 2010, Macedonia had a foreign trade deficit of $2.1 billion. The CIA reported that the purchasing power parity of Macedonia's exports was $20 billion while imports totaled $5.241 billion.

Macedonia has had a foreign trade deficit since 1994, which reached a record high of $2.873 billion in 2008, or 30.2% of GDP. Total trade in 2010 (imports plus exports of goods and services) was $8.752 billion, and the trade deficit amounted to $2.149 billion, or 23.4% of GDP. In the first 8 months of 2011, total trade was $7.470 billion and the trade deficit was $1.778 billion. A significant 56.5% of Macedonia's total trade was with EU countries. In 2010, total trade between Macedonia and the United States was $116.6 million, and in the first 8 months of 2011 it was $65 million.

³³BANKING AND SECURITIES

In 1992, the National Bank of Macedonia was created to issue currency, conduct monetary policies, and regulate the banking sector of the country.

Commercial banks in Macedonia include the Komercijalna Banka and Scopanska Banka, both in Skopje. The currency unit is the Macedonia denar (DEN) introduced on 10 May 1993, at a rate of 1:1,000 against the coupon. The central bank also introduced a floating rate for the denar against major currencies. There are no security exchanges in the country.

Under a five-year stabilization program agreed with the IMF, the government focused on reducing inflation, overhauling the financial system, and launching structural reforms. Despite the Greek blockade, the program met its fiscal targets in 1994 with the state deficit declining to 2.5% of GDP in 1994. Reform of the state banking system made progress in 1996, although banks are still lending to inefficient state enterprises. Privatization has made some progress with the privatization agency raising $8 million in revenue in 1994 through the sale of four large companies and 14 medium-sized and small companies.

In 2020, the deposit interest rate was 7.067% and the lending interest rate was 9.483%. Total reserves were valued at $2.28 billion.

³⁴INSURANCE

In 1995, the Makedonija Insurance and Reinsurance Company was offering the following types of insurance: property, liability, life, accident, motor, fire, and marine. As of 2011, there were 13 insurance companies, 12 insurance broker companies and 5 insurance representation companies.

³⁵PUBLIC FINANCE

In 2010 the budget of Macedonia included $2.772 billion in public revenue and $3.011 billion in public expenditures. The budget deficit amounted to 2.5% of GDP. Public debt was 34.2% of GDP, with $5.821 billion of the debt held by foreign entities.

³⁶TAXATION

As of 2011, Macedonia had a 10% corporate tax rate, which was also applied to branch operations. Capital gains, interest and royalties are considered income and are taxed at the corporate rate.

Dividends paid to resident companies are not considered income, if the dividends were paid out of taxable income. Dividends paid to individuals are taxed at the corporate rate, but are applied to only 50% of the gross dividend amount. Personal income taxes range from 1.28 to 2.17%. Payroll taxes include a 21.2% rate for the pension fund, a 9.2% rate for the health fund, a 1.6% employment tax, and a 0.5% additional health fund contribution. On 1 April 2000 a value-added tax (VAT) was introduced. As of 2011, the standard VAT rate was 18%. There is also a reduced rate of 5% applied to basic goods and services. Other taxes include excise taxes on petrol, fuel oil, alcoholic beverages, tobacco, and property taxes.

37 CUSTOMS AND DUTIES

As of 2011, importers pay $1,380 per container and exporters pay $1,376 per container, including document and other fees. Tariffs, as of 2005, ranged from 0 to 30%, with the average at 10.5%, and were based on the item's cost, insurance and freight (CIF) value. However, products such as beverages, cereals, vegetables and fruit were subject to a 60% rate. The VAT is also applied to imports based on the CIF plus duty value. Corruption in the customs system discourages trade.

38 FOREIGN INVESTMENT

In the 1990s, Macedonia's isolation, technological disadvantages, and penchant for political instability created a poor climate for potential foreign investors. In 1995, the government began restructuring and privatizing its largest state-owned companies. After 1997, inflows of foreign investment increased substantially.

After hitting a peak in 2001 (with capital in-flows totaling $445 million), when Hungary was the largest source of foreign direct investment (FDI), the rate of foreign investments slowed down in subsequent years, totaling $82 million in 2002, $98 million in 2003, and $104 million in the first three quarters of 2004. The biggest investing countries in 2004 were Switzerland (with $7.1 million invested), Greece ($6.6 million), and Slovenia ($1 million).

The global economic crisis also reduced the flow of FDI into Macedonia. In 2009, FDI accounted for 2.69% of GDP, or $247.9 million. Macedonia's external trade struggled in 2010 due to the slow recovery from the economic crisis of its main trading partners, particularly EU members. Starting from a very low base, export growth in the first 8 months of 2011 reached 41.7%, topping import growth of 36.8%. The trade deficit has widened to 18.3% of GDP, approaching the end-year target of 21.9% of GDP. At the same time, the current account balance deficit significantly improved and the end-year projection was revised upward to 5.5% of GDP. This was due primarily to a 4.4% higher inflow of current transfers, mostly during the summer, and came despite a poor level of foreign direct investment (FDI) of only $237.2 million by end-July 2011. Foreign currency reserves remained at about $2.6 billion, a level that comfortably covers 4 months of imports and about 110% of the country's short-term debt.

39 ECONOMIC DEVELOPMENT

In May 1994, the EBRD established a $10 million facility to guarantee Komercijalna Banka's designated correspondent banks against nonpayment under confirmed letters of credit. By securing credit facilities, the bank's clients are able to stimulate production and increase exports. In 1995, net resource flows from international financial institutions consisted of $43 million from the World Bank, $37 million from the International Monetary Fund (IMF), and $16 million from other institutions.

In 1995, the government began privatizing its largest state-owned industries. A total of 1,200 enterprises were to be privatized, 65% of them classified as small (fewer than 50 employees). The portion of a company's share capital, which is community-owned, is known as social capital; this forms the basis of the privatization process. In theory, social capital is owned by the company's employees. However, there are severe restrictions that make it nontransferable and hence valueless to the individual.

The Kosovo crisis of 1999 placed severe burdens on Macedonia's already-strained economy as an influx of Kosovar refugees flooded across the border and trade routes were disrupted. Fighting between government forces and ethnic Albanian rebels that began in February 2001 further disrupted the economy. Real GDP declined by 4.5% in 2001, and government spending mushroomed. Spending on security raised the general government deficit to 7.2% of GDP, compared with a surplus of 1.8% in 2000.

In 2003, the IMF approved a $28 million standby arrangement for Macedonia, which expired in June 2004. The loan was geared to support the government's economic program for fiscal stability following the 2001 crisis, to promote growth, improve the business climate, and improve living standards for Macedonians.

Although Macedonia's economy has been improving steadily, there still are a number of problems that need to be dealt with. Two of the most important issues are the rampant unemployment and an inflation rate that discourages exports. A 2005 World Bank report that looked at the business climate in 155 countries ranked Macedonia 81st in terms of the ease of conducting commercial operations. The government responded promptly to the results of this report and implemented a package of laws that would make it easier for entrepreneurs or investors to start a business. However, the 2006 business climate still had numerous weak spots that needed to be addressed through a concerted effort by the legislative.

In 2010, the World Bank initiated a Country Partnership Strategy (CPS) with Macedonia for the period 2011–2014 period. This program provides $100 million over 2 years to improve competitiveness, strengthen employability and social protection, and increase the use of sustainable energy. This assistance also includes a commitment of $30 million in direct budget support in the form of a policy-based guarantee by the World Bank to the government to facilitate its access to financing from international capital markets, a process that had been started as of November 2011. In 2011, Macedonia became the first country eligible for the IMF's Precautionary Credit Line (PCL), which gave the country access to a $675 million credit line for a 2 year time period. The PCL is intended for emergency need brought about by external shocks.

40 SOCIAL DEVELOPMENT

Macedonia, historically the poorest of the former Yugoslav republics, has suffered further from the imposition of international sanctions against Serbia, the rising tide of refugees, and increasing unemployment. Social care is funded by the government to assist the disabled, elderly, unemployed, and poor. Persons with disabilities faced discrimination in employment, education, and access to health care and other state services. The law requires persons with physical or mental disabilities to obtain approval from a medical commission of the government to serve in supervisory positions in both the private sector and the government.

Although women have the same legal rights as men, the traditional cultures of both Christian and Muslim communities have limited their advancement in society. There are some professional women but generally women are not represented in the higher levels of professional or public life. Sexual harassment in the workplace is prevalent, especially in the private sector. Widespread violence against women in the home remains unpunished by authorities, and it is extremely rare for criminal charges to be filed against abusive husbands. Maternity benefits are available for nine months, and women are guaranteed the right to return to work within two years after childbirth. Children, like adults, have been victims of internal conflict and ethnic violence. Resources are scarce to fund programs to benefit children.

Ethnic minorities, including Albanians and Turks, complain of widespread discrimination. Restrictive naturalization policies have left many Albanians without Macedonian citizenship, and therefore without voting rights. Abuse by police of prisoners and suspects is widespread, with most cases involving Roma, ethnic Albanians, or Kosovar refugees.

41HEALTH

According to the CIA, life expectancy in Macedonia was 75.14 years in 2011. The country spent 6.9% of its GDP on healthcare, amounting to $314 per person. There were 26 physicians, 43 nurses and midwives, and 46 hospital beds per 10,000 inhabitants. The total fertility rate in 2011 was estimated at 1.58 children born per woman. The infant mortality rate has been reduced from 54 per 1,000 live births in 1980 to 8.54 in 2011.

The immunization rates for children under the age of two have increased in the late 2000s. In 2006, 93% and 94% of children were immunized against DPT and measles, respectively. In 2010, the immunization rates had risen to 95% and 98%. The incidence of tuberculosis decreased from 30 per 100,000 people in 2005 to 21 per 100,000 people in 2010. The HIV/AIDS adult prevalence rate was less than 0.1% in 2007.

Following the breakup of the former Yugoslavia, the availability of health care statistics for Macedonia was hampered by internal hostilities. Separate health care data was slowly emerging from the new independent regions. Physicians in Macedonia are adequately trained, but there is a shortage of pharmaceuticals and medical equipment. Patients who are seriously ill will often go abroad for medical help.

42HOUSING

During the years of the former Yugoslav SFR, there was a chronic shortage of housing in Macedonia and the other republics. Since independence, the ability to find an available apartment or condominium has improved. Between 1994 and 2002, the number of dwellings increased from 580,342 to 698,143, while the average number of people per household decreased from 3.85 to 3.58 people.

43EDUCATION

Public education at the primary level is compulsory for eight years, generally for students between the ages of 7 and 15. Elementary school covers these first eight years of study. This is followed by a four-year secondary program of general, technical, vocational, or special (arts) studies. The country's schools suffer from chronic underfunding and insufficient classroom space. Many schools hold classes in shifts, usually divided along ethnic lines, but boys and girls generally have equal access to education.

The 2010 literacy rate was 97% and approximately equal among men and women. In 2008 the World Bank estimated that 86% of age-eligible children in Macedonia were enrolled in primary school. Secondary enrollment for age-eligible children stood at 82%. Tertiary enrollment was estimated at 40%. Of those enrolled in tertiary education, there were 100 male students for every 120 female students. The student-to-teacher ratio for primary schools was 16:1 in 2010. For primary and secondary students, instruction is given in Macedonia, Albanian, Serbian and Turkish. The number of students receiving instruction in their native language is growing, according to the State Department.

At the postsecondary level, there are four accredited public universities, located in Skopje, Bitola, Tetovo and Stip. There are at least 15 private colleges and universities, including campuses of MIT and New York University, both located in Skopje. In 2005, approximately 25% of college-aged men and 35% of college-aged women were enrolled in a higher education program. By 2010 enrollment had increased to 36% of men and 44% of women.

44LIBRARIES AND MUSEUMS

The Kliment Ohridski National and University Library in Skopje (1944) holds over 1.5 million items and is the largest collection in the country. The District of Skopje Public Library has 953,000 volumes.

In Skopje are the Fine Arts Museum, the Museum of Contemporary Art, and the Museum of the City of Skopje. There are also several archaeological and historical museums. The National Museums, specializing in archeology and ethnology, are in Ohrid and Stip, and there is an Islamic Art museum in Bitola. In Strumica is the Institute for Protection of Cultural Monuments, Natural Rarities, and Museum.

In March 2011, Macedonia opened a memorial center for Holocaust victims in the capital city of Skopje. The center is only the fourth such memorial in the world, following Jerusalem, Washington, DC, and Berlin. Around 66,000 of 80,000 Jews in Yugoslavia were killed during the Holocaust. The site has a multimedia center with everything from photos to narratives memorializing those who suffered.

45MEDIA

In 2010, there were 413,100 landlines in Macedonia, a decrease from 442,200 only the year before. By contrast, mobile phone subscriptions increased from 1.9 million in 2009 to 2.153 in 2010, an average of more than 95% of the population. In 2010, the country had 60,533 Internet hosts. As of 2009, there were 1.057 million Internet users in Macedonia.

As of 2010, there were 70 commercial radio stations, and 75 commercial TV stations. Though most media are government owned, an independent television station, A-1, broadcasted from Skopje until 2011. Macedonian Radio and Television (MRTV) is the only public broadcaster in the country and has the widest range, reaching about 90% of the population. This government-owned station operates three national TV networks and one satellite network, as well as one radio station.

As of 2010, the most prominent newspapers, Dnevnik, had a circulation of 120,000. Several daily newspapers are published in Skopje, as well as a number of periodicals. Newspapers in Albanian and a Turkish language paper are available nationally and subsidized by the government, including the Albanian-language Flaka e Vlazermit (Flame of Brotherhood) and the Turkish-language Birlik. In 1994 Delo, a new weekly with reportedly nationalistic leanings, began publication. Other newspapers included Nova Makedonia and Vecer.

The constitution forbids censorship and the government is said to respect this in practice. However, the government has restricted certain parts of the media during civil conflicts and has arrested contentious media figures. In December 2010, Velija Ramkovski, the owner of A1 TV was arrested, and the station's accounts were frozen. On 31 July 2011, the government announced that the station has been dissolved following a bankruptcy proceeding due to over €30 million accumulated in debt.

46 ORGANIZATIONS

The Chamber of Economy of Macedonia coordinates trade and commerce with the world.

The Macedonian Academy of Science, founded in 1967, coordinates and finances scientific research conducted in Macedonia. Macedonian Medical Association promotes research and education on health issues and works to establish common policies and standards in healthcare. There are several other associations dedicated to research and education for specific fields of medicine and particular diseases and conditions. There are professional associations representing other fields as well.

There are youth organizations affiliated with major political parties. There is also an active scouting association. The National Student Union of Macedonia is an umbrella organization representing youth groups involved in cultural, educational, and social activities. National women's organizations include Journalism About Women's and Children's Rights and Environment in Macedonia and the Union of Women's Organizations of the Republic of Macedonia.

There are national chapters of the Red Cross Society, Caritas, and Habitat for Humanity.

47 TOURISM, TRAVEL, AND RECREATION

The Tourism Factbook, published by the UN World Tourism Organization, reported 259,000 incoming tourists to Macedonia in 2009, who spent a total of $232 million. Of those incoming tourists, there were 240,000 from Europe. There were 11,904 hotel beds available in Macedonia, which had an occupancy rate of 17%. The estimated daily cost to visit Skopje, the capital, was $254. Macedonia has very modest levels of tourist activity. Medieval monasteries and Orthodox churches are primary attractions. Turkish baths and bazaars can also be found. In the winter tourists are attracted to Popova Shapka, one of the most popular ski resorts in Macedonia. The city of Mavrovo, home to the Mavrovo National Park, has over 140 different bird species and over 45 different species of other animals making it attractive to hunters worldwide. The ski resorts, monasteries, and beautiful topography make Mavrovo one of the most visited cities in Macedonia.

48 FAMOUS PERSONS

Kiro Gligorov (1917–2012) was president of Macedonia from 1991 to 1999. Boris Trajkovski (1956–2004) was president from 1999 to 2004. Trajovski died in a plane crash and was succeeded by Branko Crvenkovski (b. 1962). Mother Teresa (Agnes Gonxha Bojaxhiu, 1910–1997) was from Skopje but left at age 17 to join a convent in Calcutta, India. In 1948, Mother Teresa left the convent to found the Missionaries of Charity. She won the Nobel Peace Prize in 1979.

Phillip II (382 BC–336 BC) was the father of Alexander the Great. During Philip II's reign of 359–336 BC, he established a federal system of Greek States. Macedonian Alexander the Great (356 BC–323 BC) founded an enormous empire that extended from Greece to northern India. Cassandar (353 BC–297 BC) succeeded Alexander the Great, and was king of Macedonia between 316 BC and 297 BC. To consolidate his power, Cassandar murdered Alexander's mother, widow, and son. Philip V (237 BC–179 BC) warred against the Romans and tried to rebuild the kingdom.

49 DEPENDENCIES

Macedonia has no territories or colonies.

50 BIBLIOGRAPHY

Ackermann, Alice. *Making Peace Prevail: Preventing Violent Conflict in Macedonia.* Syracuse, NY: Syracuse University Press, 2000.

Allcock, John B. *Explaining Yugoslavia.* New York: Columbia University Press, 2000.

Bechev, Dimitar. *Historical Dictionary of the Republic of Macedonia.* Lanham, MD: Scarecrow, 2009.

Frucht, Richard, ed. *Eastern Europe: An Introduction to the People, Lands, and Culture.* Santa Barbara, CA: ABC-CLIO, 2005.

Macedonia Investment and Business Guide: Strategic and Practical Information. Washington, DC: International Business Publications USA, 2012.

Opello, Walter C. *European Politics.* Boulder, CO: Lynne Rienner Publishers, 2009.

Pearson, Brenda. *Putting Peace into Practice: Can Macedonia's New Government Meet the Challenge?* Washington, DC: U.S. Institute of Peace, 2002.

Phillips, John. *Macedonia: Warlords and Rebels in the Balkans.* London: I. B. Tauris, 2002.

Political Chronology of Europe. London: Europa, 2001.

Shea, John. *Macedonia and Greece: The Struggle to Define a New Balkan Nation.* Jefferson, NC: McFarland, 2008.

MALTA

The Republic of Malta
Repubblika Ta' Malta

CAPITAL: Valletta

FLAG: The national flag consists of two equal vertical stripes, white at the hoist and red at the fly, with a representation of the Maltese Cross, edged with red, in the canton of the white stripe.

ANTHEM: *L'Innu Malti (The Maltese Hymn).*

MONETARY UNIT: Malta joined the eurozone in 2008. The euro is divided into 100 cents. There are coins in denominations of 1, 2, 5, 10, 20, and 50 cents and €1 and €2. There are notes of 5, 10, 20, 50, 100, 200, and 500 euros. €1 = US$1.31887 (or US$1 = €0.758671) as of 2011.

WEIGHTS AND MEASURES: The metric system is the legal standard, but some local measures are still in use.

HOLIDAYS: New Year's Day, 1 January; National Day, 31 March; May Day, 1 May; Assumption, 15 August; Republic Day, 13 December; Christmas, 25 December. Movable holidays include Good Friday.

TIME: 1 p.m. = noon GMT.

¹LOCATION, SIZE, AND EXTENT

Malta lies in the central Mediterranean Sea, 93 km (58 mi) south of Sicily and 290 km (180 mi) from the nearest point of the North African mainland. There are three main islands-Malta, Gozo to the NW, and Comino between them—as well as two small, uninhabited islands, Cominotto and Filfla. Extending for 45 km (28 mi) SE–NW and 13 km (8 mi) NE–SW, Malta's total area is 316 sq km (122 sq mi): Malta, 245.7 sq km (94.9 sq mi); Gozo, 67.1 sq km (25.9 sq mi); Comino, 2.8 sq km (1.1 sq mi). Comparatively, the area occupied by Malta is slightly less than twice the size of Washington, DC. The total coastline is 252.81 km (157 mi).

Malta's capital city, Valletta, is located on the east coast of the island of Malta.

²TOPOGRAPHY

The islands of Malta are a rocky formation (chiefly limestone) running from east to northeast, with clefts that form deep harbors, bays, creeks, and rocky coves. The highest point is Ta'Dmejrek (253 m/803 ft), located on the southwest shore of Malta. Beaches range from rocky to sandy terrain. The northern beach of Ramla Bay is known for its red sands.

³CLIMATE

The climate is typically Mediterranean, with fairly hot, dry summers and rainy, mild winters. The average winter temperature is 9°C (48°F); the average summer temperature is 31°C (88°F). Rain-

fall occurs mostly between November and January and averages about 56 cm (22 in) per year.

⁴FLORA AND FAUNA

The World Resources Institute estimates that there are 914 plant species in Malta. In addition Malta is home to 34 species of mammals, 357 species of birds, 16 species of reptiles, and 1 species of amphibian. These figures reflect the total number of distinct species residing in the country, not the number of endemic species.

The islands are almost treeless. Vegetation is sparse and stunted. Carob and fig are endemic, and the grape, bay, and olive have been cultivated for centuries. There are some rock plants.

The weasel, hedgehog, and bat are native to Malta. White rabbits and mice have been introduced. Many types of turtles, tortoises, and butterflies and several varieties of lizard also are found. Common varieties of Mediterranean fish, as well as the seal and porpoise, inhabit the surrounding waters.

⁵ENVIRONMENT

Malta's most significant environmental problems include inadequate water supply, deforestation, and the preservation of its wildlife. The country's extremely limited fresh water resources have led to increasing dependence on desalination. The nation's agriculture lacks adequate water for crops due to limited rainfall. Water resources in 2006 totaled 0.07 cu km (0.02 cu mi) while water usage was 0.02 cu km (0.005 cu mi) per year. Domestic water usage accounted for 74% of total usage, industrial for 1%, and agricultural for 25%. Per capita water usage totaled 50 cu m (1,766 cu ft) per year. The UN reported in 2008 that carbon dioxide emissions in Malta totaled 2,722 kilotons.

Malta was one of the first countries to ratify the 1976 Barcelona Convention for the protection of the Mediterranean from pollution. Malta's government has made efforts to control environmental damage, including passage of the Environmental Protection Act of 1991 and the creation of a Ministry for the Environment. The Ministry of Health and Environment belongs to the International Union for the Conservation of Nature and Natural Resources. In cooperation with the World Wildlife Fund, the Ghadira wetland area was made a permanent nature reserve in 1980. In 1988 Ghadira was listed as a Ramsar Wetland of International Importance. The Is-Simar Nature Reserve was designated as a Ramsar site in 1996. The World Resources Institute reported that Malta had designated 4,500 hectares (11,120 acres) of land for protection as of 2006.

According to a 2011 report issued by the International Union for Conservation of Nature and Natural Resources (IUCN), threatened species included 3 types of mammals, 2 species of birds, 17 species of fish, and 3 types of mollusks. Endangered species include the slender-billed curlew, Mediterranean monk seal, hawksbill turtle, and Atlantic ridley turtle.

6 POPULATION

In 2011 the US Central Intelligence Agency (CIA) estimated the population of Malta to be 408,333, which placed it at number 168 in population among the 196 nations of the world. In 2011 approximately 15.8% of the population was over 65 years of age, with another 15.7% under 15 years of age. The median age in Malta was 40 years. There were 0.99 males for every female in the country. The population's annual rate of change was 0.375%. The projected population for the year 2025 was 420,000. Population density in Malta was calculated at 1,292 people per sq km (3,346 people per sq mi).

The UN estimated that 95% of the population lived in urban areas, and that urban populations had an annual rate of change of 0.5%. The largest urban area was Valletta, with a population of 199,000.

7 MIGRATION

Estimates of Malta's net migration rate, carried out by the CIA in 2011, amounted to 2.01 migrants per 1,000 citizens. The total number of emigrants living abroad was 107,500, and the total number of immigrants living in Malta was 15,500. High population density and unemployment have led to emigration. Most foreigners living in Malta are British nationals and their dependents. Malta has no national refugee law and all recognized refugees in Malta are resettled in third countries.

The continual influx of refugees from Africa has been a major issue for the government and a source of tension between Malta and Italy. The African refugees generally attempt to cross the Mediterranean by boat and often end up stranded at sea. Maltese search and rescue crews are responsible for patrolling the waters that stretch south of Sicily and between Tunisia and the island of Crete. While crews once rescued about 500 refugees a year, the number increased to about 3,400 from 2008 to 2009. While most refugees seek Italy as their final destination, Italy has refused to accept them. They then end up in Maltese detention centers or refu-

gee camps. Most of these centers are ill-equipped to handle such large numbers of people, leading some human rights groups to criticize the Maltese government for inhumane treatment. Malta argues that it is unable to accept so many new residents and has called upon other European nations to accept the refugees.

8 ETHNIC GROUPS

Most Maltese are believed to have descended from the ancient Carthaginians and Phoenicians, but there are strong elements of Italian and other Mediterranean stock. A few thousand people are of Arab, African, or Eastern European origin.

9 LANGUAGES

Maltese, a Semitic language with Romance-language assimilations, is spoken by about 90.2% of the population. It is the national (and official) language and the language of the courts. English is also an official language, though it is only spoken by about 6% of the population. About 3% of the population are multilingual.

10 RELIGIONS

An estimated 95% of the population is Roman Catholic, with about 53% actively practicing. Most of the Protestants in the country are not Maltese; British retirees and vacationers from other countries tend to form the Protestant population. Jehovah's Witnesses, the Church of Jesus Christ of Latter-Day Saints (Mormons), Seventh-Day Adventists, the Fellowship of Evangelical Churches, and the Bible Baptist Church have active groups on the island. There are approximately 6,000 Muslims, most of whom are foreigners. The Jewish community consists of about 100 people. Zen Buddhism and the Baha'i Faith are also represented. Roman Catholicism is the official state religion, and most of the principal political leaders in the nation are practicing Catholics. However, freedom of religion is guaranteed by the constitution, and this right is generally respected in practice. Religious groups are not required to register to with the government, and all religious groups have the same legal rights. The Motherhood of Our Lady, the Feast of Saint Paul's Shipwreck, the Feast of Saint Joseph, Good Friday, Easter Sunday, the Feast of Saint Peter and Saint Paul, the Feast of the Assumption, the Feast of the Immaculate Conception, and Christmas are observed as national holidays.

11 TRANSPORTATION

In 2008 the CIA reported that Malta had a total of 3,096 km (1,923 mi) of roads, of which 2,710 km (1,683 mi) are paved. In 2009 there were 721 vehicles per 1,000 people. Malta has no railways. Ferry and hydrofoil services connect Malta and Gozo.

The harbors of Valletta, among the finest in the Mediterranean, are a port of call for many lines connecting northwestern Europe and the Middle and Far East. Roughly 3,000 ships dock at Valletta each year. In 2010 the merchant marine fleet consisted of 1,571 vessels of 1,000 GRT or over. Of these, 1,401 were foreign-owned. The only airport is located in Luqa. A new terminal is designed to handle 2.2 million passengers per year (or 2,000 at any given moment). The national air carrier is Malta Airlines.

12 HISTORY

The strategic importance of the island of Malta was recognized in the time of the Phoenicians, whose occupation of Malta was followed by that of the Greeks, the Carthaginians, and the Romans. The apostle Paul was shipwrecked at Malta in AD 58, and the islanders were converted to Christianity within two years. With the official split of the Roman Empire in 395, Malta was assigned to Byzantium, and in 870 it fell under the domination of the Saracens. In 1090 it was taken by Count Roger of Normandy, and thereafter it was controlled by the rulers of Sicily-Norman and, later, Aragonese. The Emperor Charles V granted it in 1530 to the Knights of St. John, who had been driven from Rhodes by the Turks. The Knights surrendered Malta to Napoleon in 1798. Two years later, the British ousted the French garrison, with the aid of a revolt by the Maltese people. British possession of Malta was confirmed in 1814 by the Treaty of Paris.

During almost the entire 19th century, a British military governor ruled the colony. After World War I, during which the Maltese remained loyal to Britain, discontent and difficulties increased. The 1921 constitution granted a considerable measure of self-government, but political tensions reemerged, and the constitution, after having twice been suspended, was revoked in 1936. A new constitution in 1939 reinstated Malta as a British crown colony. In World War II the Maltese again remained loyal to the United Kingdom, and for gallantry under heavy fire during the German-Italian siege (1940–43), the entire population was awarded the George Cross.

Substantial self-government was restored in 1947. The Maltese, however, carried on negotiations with the United Kingdom for complete self-government, except in matters of defense and foreign affairs. In 1962 Prime Minister Borg Olivier requested that the United Kingdom grant Malta independence, and Malta became a sovereign and independent nation within the Commonwealth of Nations on 21 September 1964. At the same time, mutual defense and financial agreements were signed with the United Kingdom. Under subsequent accords negotiated between 1970 and 1979, British troops withdrew from Malta, and the NATO naval base on the main island was closed.

On 13 December 1974, Malta formally adopted a republican form of government, and the former governor-general, Sir Anthony Mamo, became the first president. Dom Mintoff, leader of the Malta Labor Party and prime minister from 1971 through 1984, instituted socialist measures and initiated a nonaligned policy in foreign affairs.

Since then, Maltese politics have revolved around foreign policy issues, especially Malta's relationship with Europe. The Nationalist Party government has been a strong proponent of EU membership. In 1990 Malta applied for full membership in the European Union. However, after the Labor Party won the 1996 elections, the government's stance shifted toward maintaining neutrality. The Labor government also adopted economic policies, such as raising utility rates, which alienated both the electorate and elements within its own party. In the early elections of September 1998, the Nationalist Party won a majority. The party soon moved to reactivate Malta's EU membership application and adopted policies—such as the reimposition of a controversial value-added tax—intended to pave the way for membership approval. Malta became one of 10 new candidate countries formally invited to join the European Union in December 2002. In the referendum on EU membership held on 8 March 2003, 53.6% voted in favor of joining the

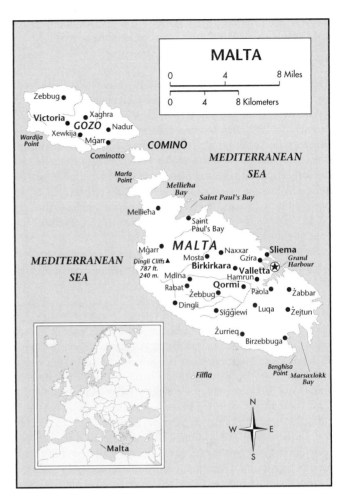

LOCATION: 35°48′ to 36°N; 14°10′30″ to 14°35′E. TERRITORIAL SEA LIMIT: 12 miles.

body versus 46.4% against. Malta became an official member on 1 May 2004 and joined the eurozone in January 2008.

13 GOVERNMENT

Malta's government is a parliamentary democracy within the Commonwealth of Nations. The unicameral House of Representatives generally consists of 65 members elected for a five-year term by universal adult suffrage (18 years of age and over) on the basis of proportional representation under a single transferable vote system. Under such a system, a voter gets one vote but is allowed to designate a first preference and a second preference of candidates. If the first preference choice appears unlikely to meet the necessary quota of votes to gain election, the vote is transferred to the second preference candidate. Under this voting system, the number of seats in the house may exceed 65. In an election where only two parties are represented, if the political party winning an absolute majority of first-preference votes does not win an absolute majority of seats, the winning party is awarded the number of seats necessary to guarantee an absolute majority. If more than two parties are represented in the house, but none have gained an absolute majority, the party with the majority of seats prevails.

The house elects the president, who serves a five-year term as head of state. The president appoints the prime minister and, on the latter's advice, the other members of the cabinet. The prime minister, who is typically the leader of the majority party, is responsible for general direction and control of the government.

14 POLITICAL PARTIES

There are two major political parties, the Nationalist Party (NP) and the Labor Party (LP, formerly the Malta Labor Party), which have alternated in political power. The NP was returned to government in 1987 after 16 years of LP rule and won reelection in February 1992 with a three-seat majority (34 to 31) in parliament. The LP regained control in October 1996 but lost it again following early elections held in September 1998, which the NP won by a five-seat margin. Elections held in April 2003 returned the NP to power; it took 35 seats in the House of Representatives to the LP's 30. In the 2008 elections the NP took 35 seats with 49.3% of the vote, and the LP took 34 seats with 48.8%.

Parties not represented in parliament include Democratic Alternative (AD, a Green Party), Malta Democratic Party (PDM), and the Malta Communist Party (PKM).

15 LOCAL GOVERNMENT

Local government was established by the Local Councils Act of 1993. There are 68 local councils in Malta, with 54 on the main island of Malta and 14 on Gozo. Councilors are elected under the system of proportional representative using the single transferable vote. As of 2011 councilors were elected every three years. The term is eventually expected to increase to four years. Each local council is headed by a mayor, who serves as the chief representative for the council. Each council also appoints an executive secretary who serves as the executive, administration, and financial head of the council. Communities within a locality are permitted to from their own representative groups and to elect a chairperson to attend local council meetings.

16 JUDICIAL SYSTEM

The court system consists of a constitutional court (with the power to review laws and executive acts), a court of appeal, a civil court, a criminal court, a court of criminal appeal, and a variety of special tribunals. There are a number of magistrate courts as well, and a special juvenile court. The president, on the advice of the prime minister, appoints the chief justice and 20 judges. Retirement is at age 65 for judges. The judiciary operates in an independent manner. Defendants in criminal cases have the right to counsel of choice. Indigent defendants are afforded court-appointed counsel at public expense.

17 ARMED FORCES

The International Institute for Strategic Studies reports that Armed Forces of Malta totaled 1,954 members in 2011. The combined force includes both a maritime and an air unit. Armed forces represented 1.2% of the labor force in Malta. Defense spending totaled $73.5 million and accounted for 0.7% of GDP. Military service is voluntary with a minimum age of 17 years and 6 months.

18 INTERNATIONAL COOPERATION

Malta joined the UN on 1 December 1964 and participates in ECE and several nonregional specialized agencies, such as the FAO, IAEA, World Bank, ILO, UNESCO, UNIDO, and the WHO. Malta is also a member of the Commonwealth of Nations, the Council of Europe, the European Bank for Reconstruction and Development, the Alliance of Small Island States (AOSIS), the NATO Partnership for Peace, and the OSCE. Malta joined the European Union in 2004 and the eurozone in 2008. The country is an observer affiliate in the Western European Union. Malta is a part of the Nonaligned Movement. The nation also participates in the Nuclear Suppliers Group (London Group) and the Organization for the Prohibition of Chemical Weapons.

In environmental cooperation, Malta is part of the Basel Convention, Conventions on Biological Diversity and Air Pollution, Ramsar, CITES, the London Convention, the Kyoto Protocol, the Montréal Protocol, MARPOL, the Nuclear Test Ban Treaty, and the UN Conventions on the Law of the Sea, Climate Change, and Desertification.

19 ECONOMY

Malta has few natural resources. Agriculture is limited by the rocky nature of the islands, and most food must be imported. Likewise, industrial raw materials are lacking and also must be imported. Malta's economy now relies heavily on its tourist industry, which has been greatly developed since the 1990s. The global financial crisis of 2008–09 led to a decline in the number of tourist arrivals by 8.4% in 2009. But figures for 2010 indicated an increase of 13% over 2009, marking an all-time high for the industry. The industrial sector, consisting primarily of light manufacturing, contributes significantly to the economy as well. The agricultural sector is very small.

Malta became a full member of the European Union in May 2004. At the beginning of 2008, Malta adopted the euro as its currency. The gross domestic product (GDP) rate of change in Malta, as of 2010, was 3.7%. Inflation stood at 3.3%, and unemployment was reported at 7%.

20 INCOME

The CIA estimated that in 2010 the GDP of Malta was $10.41 billion. The CIA defines GDP as the value of all final goods and services produced within a nation in a given year and computed on the basis of purchasing power parity (PPP) rather than value as measured on the basis of the rate of the exchange based on current dollars. The per capita GDP was estimated at $25,600. The annual growth rate of GDP was 3.7%. The average inflation rate was 3.3%. It was estimated that agriculture accounted for 1.9% of GDP, industry 17.2%, and services 80.9%.

According to the World Bank, remittances from citizens living abroad totaled $45.7 million or about $112 per capita and accounted for approximately 0.4% of GDP.

The World Bank reports that in 2009, household consumption in Malta totaled $5.1 billion or about $12,370 per capita, measured in current US dollars rather than PPP. Household consumption includes expenditures of individuals, households, and nongovernmental organizations on goods and services, excluding the purchases of dwellings. It was estimated that household consumption was growing at an average annual rate of less than 0.1%.

As of 2011 the most recent study by the World Bank reported that actual individual consumption in Malta was 76.6% of GDP and accounted for 0.02% of world consumption. By comparison, the United States accounted for 25.44% of world individual consumption. The World Bank also estimated that 14.4% of Malta's

GDP was spent on food and beverages, 14.7% on housing and household furnishings, 4.5% on clothes, 6.9% on health, 10.3% on transportation, 3.5% on communications, 8.5% on recreation, and 9.8% on restaurants and hotels.

21 LABOR

As of 2010, Malta had a total labor force of 163,100 people. Within that labor force, CIA estimates noted that 1.3% were employed in agriculture, 24.8% in industry, and 73.9% in the service sector.

Labor is highly organized in Malta, and about 55% of Malta's workers were unionized in 2010. Uniformed military and police personnel are not permitted to join unions. The largest union, the General Workers' Union, although independent, is informally associated with the Labor Party. The General Workers' Union was integrated with the Socialist Labor Party until 1992, when this affiliation was formally ended. Although certain compulsory arbitration and mediation provisions limit the right to strike, workers still enjoy a broad right to strike including antidiscrimination provisions to protect striking workers' employment. Comprehensive collective bargaining is practiced. As of 2008 about 26.7% of private sector employees were covered by collective bargaining agreements, as were 40,500 public sector employees.

The legal minimum working age is 16, and this is effectively enforced by the government. The standard workweek is 40 hours but workers in some occupations, including healthcare providers and civil protection services, can work up to 45 hours per week. Occupational safety and health standards are set by law but enforcement is uneven and accidents remain frequent. In 2010 the weekly minimum wage was €152.59 (US$201). The minimum wage may be revised annually based on changes in cost of living. However, changes in cost of living are sometimes covered by the implementation of a mandatory annual bonus or a one-time cost-of-living payment for employees.

22 AGRICULTURE

As of 2006, about 47.5% of the total land area was identified as agricultural land with significant areas of natural vegetation. Agriculture is carried out in small fields, usually consisting of strips of soil between rocks, and is characterized to a large extent by terracing. Most farms are small. Wheat, barley, and grapes are the principal crops for domestic consumption, while potatoes, onions, wine, cut flowers, seeds, and fruit are the chief export crops. According to government statistics, there were 39,800 tons of marketed vegetables produced in 2009, along with 3,100 tons of marketed fruit and 2,000 tons of potatoes for exports.

23 ANIMAL HUSBANDRY

In 2009 the country tended 500,000 chickens, 17,777 head of cattle, and 65,511 pigs. The production from these animals amounted to 8,678 tons of beef and veal, 15,173 tons of pork, 10,071 tons of poultry, 6,250 tons of eggs, and 76,586 tons of milk. Malta also produced 272 tons of cattle hide and 26 tons of raw wool. Malta's livestock population in 2005 included 14,900 sheep and 5,400 goats.

24 FISHING

In 2009 the government reported total fish landings at about 1,234 metric tons, including 332 metric tons of dorado, 237 metric tons

of swordfish, and 185 metric tons of blue-fin tuna. Other species included gilthead seabream, European sea bass, and dolphinfish. Exports of fish products were valued at $11.77 million in 2008, according to the UN Food and Agriculture Organization (FAO).

25 FORESTRY

Approximately 1% of Malta is covered by forest. This does not allow for an adequate supply of forest products to meet domestic needs. In 2004, $85 million in forest products were imported.

26 MINING

In 2009 Malta produced 6,000 cu m of salt, obtained in the desalination of sea water; 20 hard limestone quarries yielded 1.2 million cu m of limestone. The country also produced small amounts of cement, fertilizer, lime and plaster. The mining sector accounted for less than 0.5% of GDP, and the broader mineral industry economy depended mainly on trade and the storage of crude oil, refinery products, and other nonfuel mineral commodities for transshipment.

27 ENERGY AND POWER

The nation has no proven reserves of oil and natural gas and is therefore highly dependent on imported fuels to supply the demand for energy. In 2009 oil imports were estimated at 18,420 barrels per day. The World Bank reported in 2008 that Malta produced 2.31 billion kWh of electricity and consumed 1.98 billion kWh, or 4,849 kWh per capita. All energy came from fossil fuels. Per capita oil consumption was 1,988 kg.

28 INDUSTRY

Malta's manufacturing sector is substantial, with more than 200 international manufacturing and distribution companies in 2009. Manufactured products include electronics, pharmaceuticals, plastics, appliances, food and beverages, and clothing and footwear. In 2011 manufactured goods accounted for about 78% of total exports. Other operations in the industrial sector include shipbuilding and maintenance and repair of machinery. The construction industry has shown some signs of growth. In 2010 industry accounted for about 17.2% of the GDP and about 24.8% of employment. In 2009 construction accounted for about 7.2% of employment.

29 SCIENCE AND TECHNOLOGY

The Malta Council for Science and Technology was established in 1988 to advise the government in science and technology policies and provide leadership and support for the development and implementation of research and innovation strategies. The council was responsible for the launch of the *National Strategy for Research and Innovation 2007–2010* and the *National Research and Innovation Programme 2011*, the latter of which provides state financing in the form of grants for research, development, and innovation in science and technology, as directed by the national strategy guidelines. The government allocated at least €1.1 million (US$1.49 million) to fund such grants in 2011.

The Euro-Mediterranean Initiative for Technology and Innovation (EuroMedITI) is a Malta-led European initiative for innovation and economic growth in the Mediterranean. The goal of the program is to promote business-driven services in applied re-

Principal Trading Partners – Malta (2010)

(In millions of US dollars)

Country	Total	Exports	Imports	Balance
World	7,489.7	2,861.2	4,628.5	-1,767.3
Italy	1,098.5	111.4	987.1	-875.7
Germany	658.8	310.8	348.0	-37.2
France	601.8	265.8	336.0	-70.3
United Kingdom	504.3	153.3	351.0	-197.6
United States	211.4	96.0	115.5	-19.5
Singapore	175.6	6.3	169.4	-163.1
Netherlands	173.3	25.2	148.1	-122.9
China	163.6	16.9	146.6	-129.7
Switzerland	154.0	20.6	133.4	-112.7
Spain	146.9	24.8	122.1	-97.4

(…) data not available or not significant.

(n.s.) not specified.

SOURCE: *2011 Direction of Trade Statistics Yearbook,* New York: United Nations, 2011.

Balance of Payments – Malta (2010)

(In millions of US dollars)

Current Account		-415.3
Balance on goods	-1,229.3	
Imports	4,317.3	
Exports	3,088.0	
Balance on services	1,362.8	
Balance on income	-586.2	
Current transfers	37.5	
Capital Account		106.3
Financial Account		-92.7
Direct investment abroad	-86.2	
Direct investment in Malta	998.6	
Portfolio investment assets	-4,248.1	
Portfolio investment liabilities	1.0	
Financial derivatives	31.1	
Other investment assets	623.2	
Other investment liabilities	2,587.8	
Net Errors and Omissions		432.0
Reserves and Related Items		-30.3

(…) data not available or not significant.

SOURCE: *Balance of Payment Statistics Yearbook 2011,* Washington, DC: International Monetary Fund, 2011.

search and development and occupational training in the Malta and throughout the Mediterranean region.

Faculty and students at the University of Malta participate in a number of research endeavors sponsored by sixteen hosted institutes, including the Mediterranean Institute, the International Environment Institute, the Institute for Sustainable Development, the Institute for Sustainable Energy, and the Institute of Health Care.

In 2009 general government employment in research and development included 956 people, of whom 64 were full-time. Four hundred and one were PhD researchers, and 90 were technicians. That year, total general government expenditures on research and development were reported at more than €11.9 million (US$16.4 million), marking an increase from €10.5 million (US$13.2 million) in 2006.

Patent applications in science and technology as of 2009, according to the World Bank, totaled 8 in Malta. Public financing of science was 0.59% of GDP.

30 DOMESTIC TRADE

Valletta is the commercial center of Malta. Most large importers prefer to distribute goods through their own shops. Small retail establishments predominate, with a few larger supermarkets, malls, and outlet stores appearing during the 2000s. Shops selling traditional handicrafts, including hand-blown glass, lace, ceramics, silver and gold jewelry, pottery, and tiles are particularly popular with tourists. Billboards, newspapers, radio, and television are the main advertising media.

Electronic commerce (e-commerce) has been slow to take hold in Malta. One reason is that more than 96% of the country's 33,000 commercial businesses in 2010 had fewer than 10 employees. Also, there is a lack of familiarity and few intermediary operators, all of which have worked to slow e-commerce acceptance. However, as of 2010, over 96% of companies made use of computers, and about 90% of all businesses had access to the Internet. In addition, 66% of all companies in Malta had a website, while 63% had broadband connectivity. In a 2007 survey of Internet users in Malta, 60% stated that they participated in online shopping.

Some bank branches are open on Saturdays from 8:30 a.m. to 12 noon. Businesses and industries are open on weekdays from 8:30 a.m. to 5:30 p.m. and on Saturdays from 8 a.m. to 1 p.m. Generally, most establishments are closed on Sundays and many places have shorter hours during the summer months. However, several businesses that cater to the tourist trade are open on Sundays and on public holidays.

31 FOREIGN TRADE

Because it depends on external sources for much of its food, fuel, raw materials, and manufactured articles, Malta imports considerably more than it exports. Most of Malta's commodity exports are electronic microcircuits (62%). Other export commodities include clothes (5.9%), refined petroleum products (4.4%), and toys (4.3%).

Major import partners in 2009 were Italy, 25.2%; UK, 12.2%; France, 10.2%; Germany, 9%; and the Netherlands, 5.1%. Its major export partners were Germany, 13.8%; Singapore, 11.7%; France, 11.6%; the United States, 9.4%; Hong Kong, 6.5%; UK, 6.1%; Italy, 5.5%; and Libya, 5%.

According to the CIA, Malta imported $4.461 billion worth of merchandise in 2010, while exporting $3.124 billion worth of merchandise.

32 BALANCE OF PAYMENTS

Traditionally, Malta has had a large trade deficit because it must import most of its food and raw materials. The expansion of industry and improvements in living standards have further increased the deficit, which is made up by other foreign receipts in the form of tourist revenues, transfers, and financial assistance.

According to the CIA, Malta imported $4.461 billion worth of merchandise in 2010, while exporting $3.124 billion worth of merchandise, resulting in a trade deficit of $1.337 billion. The current account balance in 2010 (representing net trade in goods and services, plus all net earnings, expenditures, and transfer of payments) was estimated at -$361.5 million. Reserves of foreign exchange and gold were estimated at $540.2 million that year. The total external debt was $5.9 billion.

33 BANKING AND SECURITIES

In 1968, activities of the Currency Board were transferred to the new Central Bank of Malta. The bank joined the European System of Central Banks in 2004 and became part of the Eurosystem in 2008. HSBC (Malta) Ltd. and the Bank of Valletta are the leading banks, together accounting for more than 80% of the banking market activities in the nation. Other leading banks include Lombard Bank (Malta), Banif Bank, and APS Bank.

In 2010 the discount rate, the interest rate at which the central bank lends to financial institutions in the short term, was 1.75%.

The Malta Stock Exchange was established in 1993. In 2002 the Financial Market Act replaced the Malta Stock Exchange Act of 1990 as the law regulating the exchange. The Malta Financial Services Authority, established in 1994, is responsible for the regulation and registration of all financial services provided in and from Malta.

34 INSURANCE

All customary types of insurance are available. Many foreign insurance companies have representatives in Malta. In 2009 there were 14 insurance management companies in the nation. Middlesea Valletta is the nation's leading insurance provider. Insurance companies are licensed and regulated by the Malta Financial Services Authority.

35 PUBLIC FINANCE

The principal sources of recurrent revenues are income taxes and customs and excise taxes. In 2010 the budget of Malta included $4.455 billion in public revenue and $3.322 billion in public expenditures. The budget deficit amounted to 3.8% of GDP. Public debt was 69.1% of GDP, with $5.978 billion of the debt held by foreign entities.

36 TAXATION

As of 2011, individual incomes were taxed according to a progressive schedule with rates of 15%, 25%, and 35% (as the top rate). The chargeable amount related to each rate differs for single taxpayers and married taxpayers, with the top rate applied to single taxpayers earning €19,501 (US$26,224) or more, and married taxpayers earning €28,701 (US$38,587) or more. Social security taxes totaled about 20%, 10% paid by the employer and 10% by the employee.

The standard corporate tax rate is 35%. Reduced rates were available under certain circumstances on both corporate and individual income taxes. The main indirect tax was the VAT, set at a standard rate of 18%. There were also stamp taxes.

37 CUSTOMS AND DUTIES

Customs are collected mainly in the form of ad valorem duties; there are specific duties on petroleum, spirits, and tobacco. As a

Public Finance – Malta (2009)		
(In millions of euros, central government figures)		
Revenue and Grants	**2,292.71**	**100.0%**
Tax revenue	1,622.26	70.8%
Social contributions	434.87	19.0%
Grants	56.43	2.5%
Other revenue	179.15	7.8%
Expenditures	**2,510.64**	**100.0%**
General public services	427.94	17.0%
Defense	51.8	2.1%
Public order and safety	88.13	3.5%
Economic affairs	287.47	11.5%
Environmental protection	95.38	3.8%
Housing and community amenities	16.88	0.7%
Health	323.32	12.9%
Recreational, culture, and religion	34.24	1.4%
Education	320.91	12.8%
Social protection	864.56	34.4%

(…) data not available or not significant.

SOURCE: *Government Finance Statistics Yearbook 2010*, Washington, DC: International Monetary Fund, 2010.

member of the European Union, Malta imposes customs tariffs on imports only. Importers generally pay the 18% VAT as well.

38 FOREIGN INVESTMENT

Malta encourages foreign investment by offering incentives to companies involved in the fields of healthcare, medical equipment, and pharmaceuticals; logistic-based services; information and communications technology, including electronic components; front and back office knowledge-based operations, and high-precision engineering. As of 2009, firms involved in these five target sectors accoutered for more than 85% of Malta's business output. In total, there were more than 200 successful foreign companies with operations in Malta. There are very few restrictions on foreign investment. In 2006 Malta ranked sixth in the world in inward foreign direct investment (World Investment Report 2007, UNCTAD). According to World Bank figures published in 2009, the net inflow of FDI was $895.5 million, representing 11.21% of GDP.

39 ECONOMIC DEVELOPMENT

The government initiated the Malta Stability Program in 2007 with a focus on aligning the economy and government operations with EU standards. This program was updated in 2008 and in 2009. The program for 2009–2012 was designed to support continuing efforts toward sustainable economic growth and to bring the economy closer to average EU income levels. Increasing productivity, improving competitiveness, and encouraging private sector growth were all seen as essential steps for improving employment levels and creating a more stable economy. Under the plan, the government also pledged to adopt a more restrictive fiscal stance with hopes of reducing the deficit to 2.8% of GDP by 2012. This included efforts toward enacting and implementing policies to eliminate tax evasion and abuses of the social welfare system. At the same time, the plan promoted goals of strengthening the pension system and improving the efficiency of the healthcare system. The 2009–2012 update included provisions for continuing the work of the Malta National Reform Program 2008–2010, which focused on five strategic elements of structural reform: the sustainability of public finances, competitiveness, employment, education and training, and the environment.

40 SOCIAL DEVELOPMENT

Malta has a social security system that includes social insurance—through benefits for sickness, unemployment, old age, widowhood, disability, and industrial injuries—and social assistance for those in need. Pensions and other social security benefits are funded by contributions from employers, employees, and the government. The primary regulations for the system were set by the Social Security Act (1987), which consolidated and updated three primary welfare acts issued previously. In 2009 social benefits payments under the Social Security Act amounted to about €661.8 million (US$913 million). As of 2004, employers were required to provide 14 weeks of maternity leave with pay set at a flat weekly rate. Work injury laws have been in place since 1929.

Women make up a growing portion of the labor force due to changing social patterns and economic necessity. However, they are often channeled into traditionally female occupations or work in family-owned businesses, remaining underrepresented at the management level. Working women generally earn less than men. According to a 2008 national report, men earned about 17% more than women in comparable jobs. Unemployment for women also remains higher than that for men. Domestic violence against women remains a problem but is addressed by the government through specialized police units, legal assistance, shelters, and legislation. The efforts led to a decrease in domestic violence in 2004. Women have equality in matters of family law.

Malta is considered both a source and destination country for sex trafficking of European women and children. There have also been reports of human trafficking in forced labor, particularly among the nation's African immigrant population. According to a 2011 report from the US Department of State, the government has shown minimal efforts toward prosecuting and punishing those promoting human trafficking and has done little to protect trafficking victims.

In 2011, Maltese citizens passed a referendum to allow divorce, and the nation's first divorce laws were enacted that same year. Before the new law, Malta was the only EU country that did not allow divorce.

Maltese law mandates protection of all groups against economic, social, and political discrimination. There are also laws prohibiting discrimination against the disabled. Antidiscrimination laws concerning sexual orientation are only applicable in employment. Same sex couples are not granted legal recognition. In 2009 the Malta Gay rights movement hosted a Gay Pride Week and the International Lesbian and Gay Association–Europe Conference.

The government is committed to protecting human rights, and human rights organizations are free to operate in Malta.

41 HEALTH

According to the CIA, life expectancy in Malta was 82.12 years in 2011. The country spent 7.3% of its GDP on healthcare, amount-ing to $1,446 per person. The fertility rate was 1.52, while the infant mortality rate was 3.69 deaths per 1,000 live births. In 2008 the maternal mortality rate, according to the World Bank, was 8 per 100,000 births. The CIA calculated HIV/AIDS prevalence in Malta to be about 0.1% in 2009.

In 2009 there were six acute care hospitals in the nation and a total of 1,541 physicians, 200 dentists, 659 pharmacists, and 2,712 nurses and midwives. That year, about 81.8% of all children were immunized for measles, mumps, and rubella. About 91.4% of all children received vaccinations for diphtheria, tetanus, pertussis, and polio.

42 HOUSING

Malta has the somewhat unusual situation of having a large surplus of housing stock. At the 2005 census, there were 192,314 dwellings. Of these, 53,136 dwellings (27%) were vacant. About 19% of vacant homes are considered to be holiday dwellings or second homes in private ownership. About 35.7% of all housing units consisted of terraced houses, 31% were flats and penthouses, and 21% were maisonettes. At least 55.9% of the dwellings were listed as in good state of repair, while only a little more the 6% were dilapidated or in need of serious repair. Most of the occupied dwellings were built between 1971 and 1990. About 75.1% of all occupied dwellings were owner-occupied. Nearly all occupied dwellings had a kitchen or kitchenette, installed bath or shower, flush toilets, and a connection to the public sewage system.

43 EDUCATION

Maltese law requires that the teachings of the Roman Catholic Church be included in the public school curriculum, and legislation passed in 1983 requires all schools to provide free education. Education is compulsory for 11 years for children between the ages of 5 and 16 and is free in public schools. Primary school covers six years of study, followed by five years of junior lyceum (lower secondary). Students then have an option of attending a two-year high school or a four-year vocational school. State schools are organized as colleges, with each college hosting several levels of primary and secondary schools, including separate sections for boys and girls at the secondary level. In 2011 there were 10 state colleges. Private independent and church secondary schools may have more specialized curriculums. The academic year runs from October to June.

Most children between the ages of three and four are enrolled in some type of preschool program. In 2008 the World Bank estimated that 91% of age-eligible children in Malta were enrolled in primary school. Secondary enrollment for age-eligible children stood at 80%. Nearly all students complete their primary education. The student-to-teacher ratio for primary school was 11:1 in 2005; the ratio for secondary school was about 10:1. In 2005, private schools accounted for about 36.7% of primary school enrollment and 29% of secondary enrollment.

Institutes of higher education include the University of Malta and the Malta College of Arts, Science, and Technology (MCAST). The International Maritime Law Institute is also located in Malta. In 2008 tertiary enrollment was estimated at 32%. Of those enrolled in tertiary education, there were 100 male students for every 144 female students. Overall, the CIA estimated that Malta had a literacy rate of 92.8%. Public expenditure on education represented 6.4% of GDP in 2008.

⁴⁴LIBRARIES AND MUSEUMS

The National Library of Malta (founded in 1555) is located in Valetta and holds more than 380,000 volumes. The National Archives is housed in Rabat. The University of Malta Library (1769) is in Msida and contains over 700,000 volumes. The Malta Public Libraries consist of the main Central Public Library at Floriana, 7 regional libraries and 38 branch libraries. There is also a Gozo Public Library. There are over 50 school libraries throughout Malta.

Valletta is the site of the National Museum of Archaeology, the National Museum of Fine Arts, the Palace Armory, the National War Museum, and the St. John's Museum. The Folk Museum and the Museum of Political History are at Vittoriosa, where the Malta Maritime Museum also opened in 1992. There is an archeological museum located in a Copper Age temple in Mgarr and a museum of Zomon antiquities in Rabat.

⁴⁵MEDIA

Malta's telecommunications system is fully automated. The domestic system relies on microwave radio relay and submarine cable systems for inter-island communications. International service is through submarine cables and satellite ground stations. In 2009 there were some 252,700 main phone lines and 422,100 mobile cellular phones in use throughout the country, with mobile phone subscriptions numbered at about 102 per 100 people.

Malta's government radio service transmits on two channels (one Maltese, one English). The Labor Party and the Nationalist Party both own one radio and one television station. The Catholic Church also sponsors a radio station; there are additional private stations. Television programs are received primarily from a local service and from Italy. As of 2010 there was 1 FM radio station, 18 AM radio stations, and 6 shortwave radio stations. In 2006 there were five broadcast television stations. In 2010 the country had 24,941 Internet hosts. In 2009 Internet users numbered 27 per 100 citizens.

Prominent newspapers in 2010, with circulation numbers listed parenthetically, included *In-Nazzjon* (20,000), the *Malta Independent* (14,500), *L'Orizzont* (25,000), and the *Times* (23,000).

The constitution provides for freedom of speech and press, and the government is said to respect these rights in practice.

⁴⁶ORGANIZATIONS

The Chamber of Commerce is located in Valletta. There are several professional and trade organizations representing a variety of occupations. The largest independent private business organization is the General Retailers and Traders' Union-Malta. The Malta Federation of Industry also has some influence. The Medical Association of Malta represents the interests of doctors and patients. Other professional unions and associations are active on a national level.

The Malta Cultural Institute promotes primarily the arts of music and dance. Sports associations include organizations for cricket, football (soccer), weightlifting, and badminton. National youth

organizations include the Malta Youth Labor Brigade, Nationalist Party Youth Movement, Scout Association of Malta, Student Democrats of Malta, University Student Council of Malta, University Students' Catholic Movement, and the Young Christians. The National Council of Woman of Malta encourages equal opportunity for women in business and education. The Malta Gay Rights Movement promotes the rights of the gay, lesbian, bisexual, and transgendered population.

Multinational organizations based in Malta include the International Ocean Institute and Greenpeace Mediterranean. There is a national chapter of the Red Cross Society.

⁴⁷TOURISM, TRAVEL, AND RECREATION

Tourism, a major industry, has played a large role in developing the Maltese economy since the 1990s. Malta has many scenic and historical attractions, especially in Valletta, plus excellent beaches. Football (soccer) is the national sport; hockey, badminton, darts, and rugby are also popular as well as billiards and snooker.

Malta is one of the 25 European countries that are part of the Schengen Group. By special agreement, citizens of member countries are allowed free movement among other member countries. Once a traveler enters a Schengen country, he or she may travel within the member countries continuously for up to 90 days without a visa. Citizens from countries outside the Schengen Group must have a passport for initial entry.

In 2010 there were about 1.3 million inbound tourists to Malta, representing an all-time high for the nation. According to the *Tourism Factbook*, published by the UN World Tourism Organization, there were 39,138 hotel beds available in Malta, which had an occupancy rate of 51%. The estimated daily cost to visit Valletta, the capital, was $285.

⁴⁸FAMOUS PERSONS

The city of Valletta derives its nomenclature from Jehan Parisot de la Vallette (1494–1568), Grand Master of the Knights of St. John, who successfully withstood a great Turkish siege in 1565. Dominic (Dom) Mintoff (b. 1916), a founder of Malta's Labor Party, was prime minister during 1955–58 and 1971–84. Agatha Barbara (1923–2002), a former cabinet minister, was elected the first woman president of Malta on 16 February 1982. Edward Fenech-Adami (b. 1934), who served as prime minister from 1987 to 1996 and from 1998 to 2004, became president in 2004. Tony Drago (b. 1965) is a professional snooker and pool player who won the 2003 World Pool Masters Tournament. Jo Jo Zep (b. Joseph Vincent Camilleri, 1948) was a vocalist, songwriter, and saxophonist with the groups Jo Jo Zep & the Falcons and The Black Sorrows.

⁴⁹DEPENDENCIES

Malta has no territories or colonies.

⁵⁰BIBLIOGRAPHY

Ataurz, Alyse Devrim. *Eight Thousand Years of Maltese Maritime History: Trade, Piracy, and Naval Warfare in the Central Mediterranean.* Gainesville, FL: University Press of Florida, 2008.

Balbi, Francesco. Trans. by Ernle Bradford. *The Siege of Malta, 1565.* Rochester, NY: Boydell Press, 2005.

Cavialiero, Roderick. *The Last of the Crusaders: The Knights of St John and Malta in the Eighteenth Century*. London, UK: Tauris Parke Paperbacks, 2009.

Greene, Molly. *Catholic Pirates and Greek Merchants: A Maritime History of the Mediterranean*. Princeton, NJ: Princeton University Press, 2010.

Holland, James. *Fortress Malta: An Island under Siege, 1940–1943*. New York: Miramax Books/Hyperion, 2003.

Horsler, Val. *A Portrait of the Sovereign Order of Malta*. London, Eng.: Third Millennium, 2011.

Malta Investment and Business Guide: Strategic and Practical Information. Washington, DC: International Business Publications USA, 2012.

Opello, Walter C. *European Politics*. Boulder, CO: Lynne Rienner Publishers, 2009.

Political Chronology of Europe. London, Eng.: Europa, 2001.

Sheehan, Sean and Jui Lin Yong. *Malta*. New York: Marshall Cavendish Benchmark, 2010.

Vasileiou, Giorgos. *The Accession Story: The EU from Fifteen to Twenty-five Countries*. Oxford: Oxford University Press, 2007.

MOLDOVA

Republic of Moldova
Republica Moldoveneasca

CAPITAL: Chisinau

FLAG: Equal vertical bands of blue (hoist side), yellow, and red; emblem in center of yellow stripe is the coat of arms of Moldova, which represents a Roman eagle holding a shield charged with an aurochs head.

ANTHEM: *Limba noastra (Our Language).*

MONETARY UNIT: The leu is a paper currency, replacing the Soviet Union ruble. MDL1 = US$0.08496 (or US$1 = MDL11.77) as of 2011.

WEIGHTS AND MEASURES: The metric system is in force.

HOLIDAYS: Independence Day, 27 August.

TIME: 2 p.m. = noon GMT.

¹LOCATION, SIZE, AND EXTENT

Moldova is a landlocked nation located in Eastern Europe, sandwiched between Ukraine and Romania. Comparatively, it is slightly larger than the state of Maryland with a total area of 33,851 sq km (13,067 sq mi). Moldova shares boundaries with Ukraine on the N, E, and S; and Romania on the W. Moldova's border length totals 1,390 km (864 mi).

Its capital city, Chisinau, is located in the south central part of the country.

²TOPOGRAPHY

Moldova consists mostly of a hilly plain that is cut by deep valleys with many rivers and streams. The terrain slopes gradually southward. The Codri Hills run through the center of the country and contain the nation's highest point of Mount Balanesti, at 430 m (1,410 ft). The lowest point is along the Dniester River, with an elevation of 2 m (6.6 ft).

The Dniester, along the eastern border, is the longest river with a total length of 1,400 km (870 mi). The second longest river, the Prut, is a major tributary of the Danube. There are no major lakes, but saline marshes are found along the lower reaches of the Prut and in river valleys of southern Moldova.

³CLIMATE

The climate is of the humid continental type. The country is exposed to northerly cold winds in the winter and moderate westerly winds in the summer. The average temperature in July is 23°C (73°F). The average temperature in January is -4°C (24°F). Rainfall averages 58 cm (22.8 in) a year.

⁴FLORA AND FAUNA

A 2011 Moldovan Ministry of Environment report estimated that there are 5,568 plant species in Moldova, among which there are 2,044 species of higher plants and 3,524 species of lower plants. In addition, animal species in Moldova include 70 mammals, 281 birds, 14 reptiles, 14 amphibians, and 82 fish.

Three-fourths of the country's terrain features chernozem (black soil), which supports the natural vegetation of steppe-like grasslands. The central part of the country is densely forested, with forests occupying 336,600 hectares (831,757 acres). Common trees include oak, maple, linden, hornbeam, and beech. Badgers, polecats, ermines, wild boar, foxes, and hares are common animals. Larks, blackbirds, and jays are common birds. Carp, bream, trout, and pike populate the lakes and streams.

⁵ENVIRONMENT

The World Resources Institute reported that Moldova had designated 47,300 hectares (116,881 acres) of land for protection as of 2006. Water resources totaled 11.7 cu km (2.81 cu mi) while water usage was 2.31 cu km (.554 cu mi) per year. Domestic water usage accounted for 10% of total usage, industrial for 57%, and agricultural for 33%. Per capita water usage totaled 549 cu m (19,388 cu ft) per year.

The natural environment in Moldova is affected by the use of agricultural chemicals (including banned pesticides such as DDT), which was very widespread during the Soviet period. That practice contaminated soil and groundwater. Poor farming methods have caused widespread soil erosion. According to the Moldovan government, there were 114,200 hectares (282,194 acres) of heavily eroded land in 2010. The US Energy Information Administration reported that in 2009 carbon dioxide emissions totaled 7.1 million metric tons.

According to a 2011 report issued by the International Union for Conservation of Nature and Natural Resources (IUCN), threatened species included 4 mammals, 8 birds, 2 reptiles, 8 fish, and 3 invertebrates. Among those were the European bison, European souslik, and the great bustard.

6 POPULATION

The US Central Intelligence Agency (CIA) estimates the population of Moldova in 2011 to be approximately 4,314,377, which placed it at number 124 in population among the 196 nations of the world. This estimate includes the Moldovan population from its eastern secessionist Transdniester region, which the latest Moldovan 2004 census did not consider. In 2011, approximately 10.5% of the population was over 65 years of age, with another 15.5% under 15 years of age. The median age in Moldova was 35.4 years. There were 0.91 males for every female in the country. The population's annual rate of change was -0.072%. The projected population for the year 2025 was 4,000,000. Population density in Moldova was calculated at 127 people per sq km (329 people per sq mi).

The UN estimated that in 2010 about 47% of the population lived in urban areas, and that urban populations had an annual rate of change of 0.9%. The largest urban area was Chisinau, with a population of 650,000.

7 MIGRATION

Estimates of Moldova's net migration rate, carried out by the CIA in 2011, amounted to -1.13 migrants per 1,000 citizens. The total number of emigrants living abroad was 770,300, and the total number of immigrants living in Moldova was 408,300. There was a net emigration of 6,000 in 1979–88 to other Soviet republics. This grew to 16,300 in 1989 and 29,800 in 1990. Since independence in 1991, Moldova has experienced difficulties. A short but violent civil war in 1992—the Transdniester conflict—resulted in the internal displacement of some 51,000 people and the external displacement of some 56,000 refugees, who fled to the Ukraine.

8 ETHNIC GROUPS

The 2004 population census did not cover the secessionist Transdniester region in the East of the country. Nonetheless, according to that census, 78% are Moldovan/Romanian, 8.4% Ukrainian, 5.9% Russian, 4.4% Gagauz, 1.9% Bulgarian, and 1.4% other. The Gagauz are a Christian Turkic minority that live primarily in the south. The government estimates the number of Roma to be about 11,600; however, nongovernmental organizations have placed the estimated Romani population at 250,000, noting that many Roma do not identify themselves as such on government surveys for fear of harassment and discrimination.

9 LANGUAGES

Moldovan, the official language, is considered a dialect of Romanian rather than a separate language. It is derived from Latin but, unlike the other Romance languages, preserved the neutral gender and a system of three cases. There are a large number of Slavonic-derived words. Under Soviet rule the language was written in the Cyrillic alphabet, but Latin script was restored in 1989. This switch has caused problems, particularly in the separatist Transdniester region where the unofficial constitution forbids the use of the Latin alphabet. Though officials in Transnistria have since allowed a few Romanian-language schools to use the Latin script, Romanian speakers are subject to discrimination and harassment

in this region. Russian and Gagauz, a Turkish dialect, are also spoken within the country. Government officials are expected to know both Moldovan and Russian.

10 RELIGIONS

An overwhelming majority of the population belongs to either the Moldovan Orthodox Church (which claims to represent some 86% of the population) or the Bessarabia Orthodox Church (reportedly 7%). The Moldovan Orthodox Church is an autonomous church under the Russian Orthodox Church, whose canonic territory includes the Republic of Moldova. The Bessarabian Orthodox Church is an autonomous church under the Romanian Orthodox Church. Other Christian denominations include the Old Rite Russian Orthodox Church (Old Believers), Roman Catholics, Baptists, Pentecostals, Seventh-Day Adventists, Jehovah's Witnesses, Lutherans, Presbyterians, Molokans, and the Church of Jesus Christ of Latter-Day Saints (Mormons). There are also communities of Muslims, Jews, Baha'is, and members of the Unification Church.

Although the 2004 population census noted that some 93% of citizens were Christian Orthodox, church attendance is very low, with only 2–5% of the population being regular churchgoers. However, the Church does organize a small but politically active group of conservative clergy and their flock. The Moldovan Orthodox Church took a very aggressive stance in 2011 against an antidiscrimination bill, claiming it reflected the intention of the West to impose "homosexuality and Islamization" on Moldova.

11 TRANSPORTATION

The CIA reported that Moldova had a total of 9,343 km (5,805 mi) of roads as of 2008, of which 8,810 km (5,474 mi) were paved. There are 139 vehicles per 1,000 people in the country. Railroads extend for 1,190 km (739 mi). Broad gauge railway accounted for nearly all of Moldova's railway.

Moldova has 11 airports, among which five have paved runways and six are equipped with unpaved runways. Three of them were certified for major commercial flights as of 2009—Balti, Marculesti, and Chisinau, which is the country's international hub. Air travel transported 402,423 passengers in 2009 according to the World Bank. Moldova's two autochthonous air companies are the state-owned Air Moldova and the private carrier Moldavian Airlines. A large number of foreign air carriers also operate flights in Moldova.

Moldova has approximately 558 km (347 mi) of navigable fluvial waterways. As of 2008, Moldova's merchant fleet consisted of 39 cargo vessels of 1,000 gross registered tons or more. Moldova has had access to the sea mainly through Ukraine or Romania. In 2007 it opened the Giurgiulesti International Free Port on the Lower Danube with available water depths of up to 7 m (22.96 ft), and capable of receiving both inland and sea-going vessels.

12 HISTORY

The region that is now Moldova (also called Bessarabia) has historically been inhabited by a largely Romanian-speaking population. The region was part of the larger Romanian principality of Moldova in the 18th century, which in turn was under Ottoman suzerainty. In 1812, the region was taken over by the Russian Empire, which controlled it until March 1918 when it became part of

Romania. Moscow laid the basis for reclaiming Moldova by establishing a small Moldovian Autonomous Soviet Socialist Republic on Ukrainian territory in 1924.

The 1939 Nazi-Soviet pact assigned Moldova to the Soviet sphere of influence. Soviet forces seized Moldova in June 1940. After the Nazi invasion of the USSR, Germany helped Romania to regain Moldova. Romania held it from 1941 until Soviet forces reconquered it in 1944.

Moldova declared its independence from the USSR on 27 August 1991. In December, Mircea Snegur was elected the first president of the new nation. Moldova's new constitution was adopted on 28 July 1994, replacing the old Soviet constitution of 1979. The Agrarian Democratic Party, composed largely of former Communist officials, won a majority of seats in the new parliament elected the same year.

Petru Lucinschi, former speaker of the parliament, who was backed by Moscow, defeated Snegur in a December 1996 presidential runoff election (54% to 46%) and became Moldova's new president early in 1997. The following year, Moldova's Communist Party won a parliamentary majority in legislative elections. By 1999 Lucinschi was seeking to strengthen the nation's presidency in order to overcome an extended stalemate between the executive branch and parliament that was preventing the government from effectively addressing the nation's pressing economic problems. In a referendum, voters approved constitutional changes proposed by Lucinschi, but they were rejected by the parliament.

In July 2000, parliament cancelled the direct election of the president, who is now elected by parliament for a four-year term. Parliament failed to chose a new president by December 2000, and early parliamentary elections were held in February 2001. Communists took 71 of 101 seats, and in April, Vladimir Voronin, head of the Communist Party, became president. Voronin campaigned on a platform of providing public order and improving social welfare programs, by ensuring that citizens had adequate food, employment, and medical care.

In the March 2005 elections the Communist Party managed to hold onto power by garnering 46.1% of the votes. The Communist Party was not as popular as it was in 2001—it won only 56 parliamentary seats out of the 101 available—but the party still managed to vote President Voronin in for a second term. Its victory was partly due to the successful political appropriation of the European Union (EU) integration message used by the opposition, thus diminishing its appeal to the voters.

There is an ongoing ethnic and political conflict within the nation over the separatist region of Transnistria (or Transdniester region), which lies between the Dniester River and the Ukrainian border. Under Soviet rule, the region, formerly a part of the Ukraine, was home to many Russian-speaking citizens. This trend emerged as a result of a Moscow-directed ethnic policy, achieved through the planned movement of ethnic Russians to that region. They were mostly employed in the industrial sector, which in the Soviet Moldova was concentrated mainly in this eastern region. Bessarabia, formerly a part of Romania, was home to ethnic Romanians. As Moldovan nationalism grew and an independent Moldova began to take shape, the Dniester region, under the leadership of local industrial elites, declared its own independence as "Transdniester Republic" in 1990. This claim of sovereignty has not been recognized internationally. Violent conflicts ensued fol-

LOCATION: 47°0′ N; 29°0′ E. BOUNDARY LENGTHS: Romania, 450 kilometers (280 miles); Ukraine, 939 kilometers (584 miles).

lowing Moldovan independence, with the Russian military taking the side of the Transdniester separatist authorities. A ceasefire signed in 1992 established a 6-mile (10 kilometer) demilitarized security zone, enforced by Russian military forces.

In March 2006, the Transnistria leadership reacted angrily to new regulations requiring goods entering Ukraine from Transnistria to carry Moldovan customs stamps. Moldova held that the rules—supported by the EU, the United States, and the Organization for Security and Cooperation in Europe (OSCE)—are geared to halt smuggling. In a September 2006 referendum, which was reportedly run with the assistance and guidance of the Russian government, Transnistria reasserted its demand for independence and also supported a plan to eventually join Russia. Neither Moldova nor the international community recognized the referendum, which has been repeatedly used by Russian officials as leverage against Moldova's European integration policies. Even though Transdniester region contains most of the Moldova's post-Soviet industrial infrastructure, its economic potential is limited by its international isolation and lack of investment. It has its own currency, constitution, parliament, flag, and anthem. However, the region is plagued by corruption, organized crime, and smuggling. It has been accused of conducting illegal arms sales and of money laundering. Poverty is widespread.

In the April 2009 parliamentary elections, the Communist Party gained 60 of the 101 seats in parliament, falling one seat short of the three-fifths majority necessary for an immediate election of the president. There was disagreement among international OSCE-led observers about the fairness of elections. The main opposition parties accused authorities of fraud, and thousands of students gathered to protest against what they viewed as rigged elections in the capital city of Chisinau. The protests turned violent, resulting in the protesters storming and setting ablaze the buildings of the presidency and the parliament. A small number of the protesters called for reunification with Romania. A recount was called and the results, in favor of the Communist Party, were confirmed a few days later. A presidential election was initially scheduled for June 2009. However, members of the opposition threatened to boycott it and demanded a rerun of parliamentary elections instead. After the Communists failed to secure the one vote necessary to elect the president, a new parliamentary election was held in July 2009. The Communist Party won 44.7% of the vote, the Liberal Democratic Party earned 16.5% of the vote, the Liberal Party 14.6%, the Democratic Party 12.5 %, and the Our Moldova alliance 7.3%.

The opposition formed a coalition in the new parliament, obtaining an aggregated majority of votes. This parliament also failed to agree on a presidential candidate. However, since the constitution stipulates that parliament cannot be dissolved more than once in a 12-month period, new parliamentary elections could not be held until July 2010.

In lieu of those elections, the government offered Moldovan voters a chance to change the manner in which the president is elected by staging a September 2010 referendum to institute direct elections for the presidential office. In that poll, more than 87% of voters said yes to the referendum, but voter turnout was only 30%. Voter turnout must be at least 33% in order for the results of a referendum to be approved. After the new parliamentary elections on November 2010, the opposition was again just short of the three-fifths majority required to elect the president. A compromise with the Communists could not be reached, pushing the country into an extended political crisis. The Moldovan parliament had not held successful presidential elections as of February 2012.

¹³GOVERNMENT

Elections to Moldova's first postindependence parliament were held on 27 February 1994. The parliament consists of a single chamber of 101 seats, and members are elected for four-year terms on the basis of proportional representation. In order to enter the parliament, according to the latest 2010 modifications to the electoral code, parties must garner at least 4% of the votes; blocks of two parties need 7%, blocks of three or more parties need 9%, while independent candidates must poll at least 2%.

Prior to 2000, the president was directly elected. As of July 2000, however, the president is elected by parliament for a four-year term and may serve no more than two consecutive terms. The president nominates the prime minister upon consultation with parliament. The cabinet is selected by the prime minister, subject to approval by parliament.

The July 1994 constitution and the law provide for freedom of speech, press, assembly, and religion; however, the law requires that religious groups register with the government. Peaceful assembly is allowed; however, permits for demonstrations must be approved and political parties and private organizations are required to register with the government. Reforms approved in 1995 authorized the creation of a court to deal with constitutional issues and a system of appeals courts.

¹⁴POLITICAL PARTIES

Although 26 parties or coalitions of parties participated in the February 1994 elections, only four received more than the 4% of the national vote (then) required to gain seats.

The Agrarian Party had been the largest political group in the parliament with a plurality of 46 seats, following the departure of 10 deputies in 1995. They left to join a new party, the Party of Renewal and Conciliation, headed by then-president Mircea Snegur. The Socialist-Edenstro bloc had 26 seats, while the pro-Romanian parties, the Popular Front and the Peasants and Intellectuals bloc, had 11 and 9 seats, respectively.

Although the Party of Moldovan Communists won the single largest number of parliamentary seats (40) in the elections held on 22 March 1998, they had insufficient support to form a governing coalition and thus remained an opposition party, while the governing coalition consisted of the Democratic Convention of Moldova (26 seats), the Bloc for a Democratic and Prosperous Moldova (24), and the Party of Democratic Forces (11).

Twelve political parties or blocs participated in the parliamentary elections held on 25 February 2001. Three of them gained seats in parliament: the Communist Party, 71; the centrist Braghis Alliance (led by Dumitru Braghis) of the Social-Democratic Alliance of Moldova, 19; and the conservative Christian Democratic Popular Party, 11.

In 2005, 9 parties, 2 alliances, and 12 independent candidates entered the electoral race. The Communist Party (PCRM) won 56 of 101 parliamentary seats, the centrist and pro-Russian Democratic Moldova Block (BMD)—led by Dumitru Braghis and Chisinau mayor Serafim Urechean—won 34, while the rightist and pro-Romanian Christian Democratic Popular Party (PPCD) won 11. Despite their fragile majority, the Communists managed to vote former president Vladimir Voronin in for a second term—he received 75 of the 101 parliamentary votes. Vasile Tarlev was the designated prime minister.

In the parliamentary elections of July 2009, the Communist Party won 44.69% of the vote and 48 of the 101 seats in the assembly. The Liberal Democratic Party came in with 16.7% of the vote and 18 seats, followed by the Liberal Party with 14.6% and 15 seats, the Democratic Party with 12.5% and 13 seats, and the Moldova Nostra Alliance with 7.3% and 7 seats. Because no single party gained enough seats to form a government, the four minority parties formed a coalition government as the Alliance for European Integration. However, the coalition needed at least eight Communist votes to secure their choice for the presidency, and by December 2009, all attempts for a successful presidential vote failed. Such a failed vote could have led to the dissolution of parliament and new elections. However, the law did not allow the dissolution of parliament until the legislative has served for one full year, meaning the new parliament had to operate until June 2010.

As that date approached, the ruling coalition announced that it would hold a referendum on election reform that would allow the direct election of the president by popular vote. Unfortunately, the vote held on 5 September 2010 failed due to low turnout. Voter participation of 33.33% is necessary for the passage of such a referendum. In this vote, turnout was only 30.29%. Parliament was dissolved and elections were set for 28 November 2010.

In the November 2010 elections, the Communist Party won 42 seats (32.3% of the vote), followed by the Liberal Democrats with 31 seats (29.3%), the Democratic Party with 15 seats (12.7%), and the Liberal Party with 12 seats (9.9%). Without a majority government, the political deadlock continued. In December 2010, Marian Lupu, the speaker of parliament, was chosen to serve as acting president. The three opposition parties agreed to the formation of a coalition known as the Alliance for European Integration (AEI). As part of this agreement, Vladimir Filat of the Liberal Democratic Party was reinstated as prime minister in January 2011. Political deadlock continued through 2011, and final presidential elections had not occurred as of February 2012.

15 LOCAL GOVERNMENT

Following administrative reforms, Moldova's 40 districts, or *raions,* have been reorganized into nine counties, one municipality (Chisinau), and two territorial units (Transdniestria and Gagauzia). After their victory in the parliamentary elections of 2001, the Communist Party reverted back to the Soviet-style of administrative division of *raions.*

Following the June 2011 municipal elections, the Liberal Party won 31.8% of the vote in the capital's city hall, following the Communist Party which won 46.07% of the votes. The Liberal Party vice-president Dorin Chirtoaca was reelected as mayor of the capital city of Chisinau, only marginally defeating the Communist Party nominee Igor Dodon in a second round (50.6% vs. 49.4%). These results were contested by the Communist Party, with allegations of voting irregularities.

The Moldovan government has often proposed a large degree of political and economic autonomy to the secessionist Transdniester authorities. That proposal was declined by the latter, on the grounds that the offer was not genuine and that the region preferred independence or joining Russia. The predominantly Turkish Gagauz region in the south of the Republic of Moldova was granted autonomy in 1994 and has local legislative and executive bodies.

16 JUDICIAL SYSTEM

There are courts of first instance, an appellate court, a Supreme Court, and a Constitutional Court. The Supreme Court is divided into civil and criminal sections. A 1995 judicial reform law also provided for a system of appeals courts.

The Constitutional Court was created in 1995. Its six judges are appointed for a six-year term. Two of them are appointed by the Parliament, two are appointed by the government, and the last two are appointed by the Superior Council of the Magistracy.

There are district courts of the first instance and five regional tribunals. The higher appeals court and the Supreme Court are both in Chisinau. However, as of 2003, there was a backlog of cases at the tribunal and the higher appeals court levels, due to lack of funding.

The Superior Council of Magistrates nominates and the president appoints judges for an initial period of five years. The judges may be reappointed for a subsequent 10 years, and finally, on their third term, they serve until retirement age. The judiciary is more independent now than when it was subject to the Soviet regime. The Constitutional Court made several rulings in 1996 that demonstrated its independence. For example, in April 1996 the Constitutional Court found that the attempted dismissal of Defense Minister Creanga by President Snegur was unconstitutional. The Constitutional Court also overturned a Central Electoral Commission decision to exclude a presidential candidate from competing in the November 1996 election. And in 2000, the court ruled that legislation requiring political parties to be registered for two years prior to participating in elections was unconstitutional. The importance of the Constitutional Court has increased—in 2011 the court judged a number of cases defusing conflicts among the governing AIE and the opposition Communist Party.

During 2005–2009 the democratic process in Moldova continued to erode under the rule of the Communist Party, and the corruption level was assessed as among the highest in the post-Soviet area. While the constitution states that the judiciary is independent, there were multiple reports of political interference in the judicial process, and corruption among underpaid judges was believed to be pervasive.

17 ARMED FORCES

The International Institute for Strategic Studies reports that armed forces in Moldova totaled 5,354 members in 2011. The force is comprised of 3,231 from the army, 826 from the air force, and 1,297 members of logistical support. Armed forces represented 0.5% of the labor force in Moldova. Defense spending totaled $44.5 million and accounted for 0.4% of GDP.

Moldova contributed to the UN peacekeeping missions in Sudan, Côte d'Ivoire, and Liberia, sending predominantly military observers. It also contributed with peacekeepers to the tripartite peacekeeping forces deployed in its Transdniester region, along with Russia and the secessionist Transdniester administration. Russia has an estimated 1,500 troops stationed in Moldova, which in addition to the peacekeeping troops include a military unit guarding the former Soviet ammunition depot at Cobasna.

In June 2010 Moldova's interim president, Mihai Ghimpu, issued a decree ordering the 1,500 Russian troops stationed in the separatist Transnistria region out of the country. Russian troops have been in Transnistria since Soviet times, but have refused to leave the territory despite pledging under a 1999 international agreement to do so. Transnistria, sandwiched between Moldova and Ukraine, declared independence from Moldova in 1990 and with the assistance of the Russian military fought a short but bloody war with Moldovan forces soon after. Russian troops stationed in the region subdued that war in 1992, serving as a de facto protection force for the separatist administration.

18 INTERNATIONAL COOPERATION

Moldova was admitted to the UN on 2 March 1992, and is a member of the ECE and several nonregional specialized agencies, such as the IAEA, ICAO, ILO, IMF, UNCTAD, UNESCO, UNIDO, WHO, and the World Bank. Moldova joined NATO's Partnership for Peace on 16 March 1994. It is also a member of the Council of Europe, the WTO, the Black Sea Economic Cooperation Zone, the Commonwealth of Independent States (CIS), the Euro-Atlantic Partnership Council, the European Bank for Reconstruction and Development, and the OSCE. In 2001, Georgia, Uzbekistan, Ukraine, Azerbaijan, and Moldova formed a social and economic development union known as GUAAM. Uzbekistan withdrew from the partnership in 2005.

In May 2009 Moldova signed an agreement with the EU as part of a new Eastern Partnership Initiative (EPI), designed to establish greater economic ties with EU members, without the prospect of EU membership. Through the EPI, the EU promises economic aid and technical and security consultations in return for a commitment to democratic reform. The EU invitation to sign the partnership agreement was extended to five other former Soviet states, with an ultimate goal to establish free-trade areas within the region.

In environmental cooperation, Moldova is part of the Basel Convention, Conventions on Biological Diversity and Air Pollution, CITES, the Kyoto Protocol, the Montréal Protocol, and the UN Conventions on Climate Change and Desertification.

19 ECONOMY

Moldova is one of the poorest countries in Europe and has faced many economic problems relative to the rapid modernization of most economies on the continent. Moldova is landlocked and has few natural resources or mineral deposits, but its climate is ideal for farming; therefore, much of the country's economy still relies on agricultural output. Despite being well-known for its wine, along with sunflowers seeds, walnuts, and apples, Moldova's economy historically relied heavily on the Soviet Union—and later Russia—for energy resources. Russia remains the country's most important trading partner. Such reliance has proved to be the crux of some of the country's economic woes, leaving the small nation at the mercy of the greater power's political and economic whims.

Moldova has no major mineral deposits and must import all of its supplies of coal, oil, and natural gas. Since the breakup of the Soviet Union in 1991, energy shortages have contributed to sharp production declines. Moldova is seeking alternative energy sources and working to develop its own energy supplies including solar power, wind, and geothermal. The country is implementing a national energy conservation program.

In 1998 the Moldovan economy experienced an 8.6% decline due primarily to fallout from the financial crisis in Russia, by far

its biggest export market. Continuing financial turmoil in Ukraine and Romania hurt Moldova's exports, which were needed to pay for imports of fuel from these countries. About one-fourth of Moldova's external debt burden, which peaked at 75% of GDP in 2000, is traceable to energy imports from Russia, which has on occasion suspended gas supplies, and from the Ukraine and Romania, both of which have on occasion suspended electrical power to Moldova. Further isolation occurred in 1999 when the IMF halted loans following the refusal of the Moldovan parliament to carry out privatization plans. By year's end, the Moldovan economy had contracted to roughly one-third of its 1989 level, with end of period inflation soaring to 45.8%. In 2000 the contraction was halted with real GDP growth of 2.2%, and in December, the government entered into a three-year arrangement with the IMF under its Poverty Reduction and Growth Facility (PRGF).

The economy continued to expand in the following years, registering GDP growth rates of 6.3% in 2003, and 7.3% in 2004. The growth rate fell back down to 5% in 2007. Because of the country's poverty, many Moldovans work abroad and send their income to family members back home. It is estimated that around 25% of the country's workforce is employed in other countries. Because many of those countries slipped into recession in early 2009, remittances coming into Moldova declined, leading to a decrease in income for many Moldovans. The average wage within the country is only $250 per month. Such poverty has begun to take its toll on some younger urban dwellers, who have begun to blame the Communist government for their woes. However, the general mood among the working population has been one of indifference toward the government, as long as it did not interfere with their endeavors to make a living, either through private entrepreneurship or temporary labor migration abroad.

In May 2009, Moldova signed an agreement with the EU as part of a new EPI, designed to establish greater economic ties with EU members, without the prospect of EU membership. Through the EPI, the EU promises economic aid and technical and security consultations in return for a commitment to democratic reform. The EU invitation to sign the partnership agreement was extended to five other former Soviet states, with an ultimate goal to establish free-trade areas within the region.

The combination of its domestic political crisis and global economic downfall resulted in a drop 6% in GDP in 2009. However, Moldova posted GDP growth of 6.9% in 2010. Inflation stood at 7.3%, and unemployment was reported at 6.5%. GDP growth was 7% in 2011.

20 INCOME

The CIA estimated that in 2010 the GDP of Moldova was $10.99 billion. The CIA defines GDP as the value of all final goods and services produced within a nation in a given year and computed on the basis of purchasing power parity (PPP) rather than value as measured on the basis of the rate of the exchange based on current dollars. The per capita GDP was estimated at $2,500. The annual growth rate of GDP was 7% in 2011. The average inflation rate was 7.3%. It was estimated that agriculture accounted for 16.3% of GDP, industry 20.1%, and services 63.6%.

According to the World Bank, remittances from citizens living abroad totaled $1.2 billion or about $281 per capita and accounted for approximately 11% of GDP. In 2007 the World Bank estimated that Moldova, with 0.06% of the world's population, accounted for 0.02% of the world's GDP. By comparison, the United States, with 4.85% of the world's population, accounted for 22.51% of world GDP.

As of 2011 the most recent study by the World Bank reported that actual individual consumption in Moldova was 102.3% of GDP and accounted for 0.03% of world consumption. By comparison, the United States accounted for 25.44% of world individual consumption. The World Bank also estimated that 32.3% of Moldova's GDP was spent on food and beverages, 22.6% on housing and household furnishings, 4.5% on clothes, 4.9% on health, 10.0% on transportation, 4.7% on communications, 6.3% on recreation, 1.7% on restaurants and hotels, and 7.7% on miscellaneous goods and services and purchases from abroad.

The World Bank reports that in 2009, household consumption in Moldova totaled $4.7 billion or about $1,092 per capita, measured in current US dollars rather than PPP. Household consumption includes expenditures of individuals, households, and nongovernmental organizations on goods and services, excluding the purchases of dwellings. It was estimated that household consumption was growing at an average annual rate of 13.5%. According to other estimates in 2009 about 26.3% of the population subsisted on an income below the poverty line established by Moldova's government.

21 LABOR

As of 2010, Moldova had a total labor force of 1.235 million people. Within that labor force, a national Labor Force Survey estimated that in 2007 about 32.8% were employed in agriculture, 12.7% in manufacturing, 6.1% in construction, 15.9% in wholesale, retail trade and services sectors, 5.5% in transportation and communications, 20.1% in public administration, education, health and social work, and 7% in other sectors.

The law provides workers with the right of association, including the right to form and join labor unions. The General Federation of Trade Unions of Moldova (GFTU) is the successor to the previously existing Soviet trade union system. Various industrial unions still maintain voluntary membership in the GFTU, and there have been no attempts to form alternate trade union structures. Government workers do not have the right to strike, nor do those in essential services such as health care and energy. Unions in the private sector may strike if two-thirds of their membership assents. Collective bargaining is used to negotiate workers' pay and benefits.

The unrestricted minimum working age is 18, with restrictions as to the number of hours that may be worked for those between 16 and 18 years of age. Children generally do not work except in agriculture on family farms. The labor code stipulates a standard workweek of 40 hours, with at least one day off weekly. By the end of 2011, the monthly average wage was $209 in the public sector and $364 in private firms.

Because of the country's poverty level and increased opportunities for travelling, many Moldovans work abroad and send their income to family members back home. It is estimated that around 25% of the country's workforce is employed in other countries. When many of those countries slipped into recession in early 2009, remittances coming into Moldova dropped slightly, but increased in subsequent years. Remittances from Moldovan foreign workers have contributed to a significant boost of internal consumption in Moldova during 2008–2011, affecting mostly the construction and services sectors of the economy.

22 AGRICULTURE

Agriculture is an important sector of the Moldovan economy and, according to the CIA, represented 16.1% of Moldova's GDP in 2011. This figure is a significant decline from the 33% in 1995. However, when combined with the agro-processing sector, the two sectors account for 30% of the GDP.

Roughly 62% of the total land is farmed, and the country's major crops include vegetables, fruits, grapes, grain, sugar beets, sunflower seed, and tobacco. In 2008 Moldova produced 370,000 tons of fruits and 647,000 tons of vegetables.

Wine and tobacco products are important agricultural exports. In 2009 Moldova produced an estimated 3.976 million hectoliters (hl) of wine, which placed it 14th in the world by production volume. About 86% of its wine exports went either to Russia (41%), Kazakhstan (13%), Ukraine (11%), Belarus (11%), or Poland (10%). Wine exports in 2009 amounted to 1.2 million hl, down from 2.3 million hl in 2005, mainly due to Russian trade embargoes. During 2003–2007 Russia used trade sanctions against the Moldovan government in an attempt to influence Moldova's stance on the Transdniester conflict and European integration. Top Moldovan wine companies include Acorex Wine Holding, Chateau Vartely, Cricova Winery, DK-Intertrade, Dionysos-Mereni, LionGri, Milestii, Mici, and Purcari Winery.

Tobacco is grown mostly on privately owned farms. In 2010 the large agricultural enterprises produced 6,100 tons of tobacco leaves, farmers provided 1,300 tons of tobacco leaves, and households sold 200 tons of tobacco leaves to cigarette producers. There were 4,400 hectares (10,873 acres) of land dedicated to the tobacco crop in 2010. The value of Moldova's tobacco exports was estimated at $27.2 million.

23 ANIMAL HUSBANDRY

The UN Food and Agriculture Organization (FAO) reported that Moldova dedicated 360,000 hectares (889,579 acres) to permanent pasture or meadow in 2009, which represented some 10% of the total land area. During that year, the country tended 18.2 million chickens, 218,000 head of cattle, and 284,000 pigs. The production from these animals amounted to 4,875 tons of beef and veal, 46,416 tons of pork, 44,187 tons of poultry, 37,220 tons of eggs, and 598,184 tons of milk. Moldova also produced 1,753 tons of cattle hide and 1,996 tons of raw wool.

24 FISHING

In 2008, the annual capture totaled 1,407 tons according to the UN FAO. With no direct connection to the Black Sea, fishing is limited to the Dniester River and ponds, both natural and artificial. Commercial fishing is not a significant part of the national economy.

25 FORESTRY

Approximately 13.3% of Moldova is covered by forest. The UN FAO estimated the 2009 roundwood production at 43,000 cu m (1.52 million cu ft). The value of all forest products, including roundwood, totaled $25.9 million. Production is largely domestically consumed.

26MINING

Moldova did not possess significant mineral resources. More than 100 deposits of gypsum, limestone, sand, and stone were exploited. Production totals for 2009 were gypsum, 250,000 metric tons; sand and gravel, 150,000 metric tons; lime, 800 metric tons; and cement, 700,000 metric tons. Moldova also produced crude steel, peat, oil, and natural gas.

27ENERGY AND POWER

Moldova has no proven reserves of oil or natural gas and no estimated recoverable reserves of coal. As a result, Moldova must rely upon imports of refined oil products and natural gas from Russia, Ukraine, and Belarus to meet its fossil fuel needs.

In 2010 consumption of refined oil each came to an estimated 20,000 barrels per day. In 2008 the Republic of Moldova imported 1.227 trillion cu m of natural gas. Also, Moldova imported and consumed 206,000 short tons of coal, 213,000 tones of gasoline, and 371,000 tons of diesel fuel in 2008.

Electric power generating capacity has declined since Moldova gained its independence in 1992 due to lack of funds, civil disturbances, and a general economic downturn in the 1990s. The World Bank reported in 2008 that Moldova produced 3.63 billion kWh of electricity and consumed 4.68 billion kWh, or 1,085 kWh per capita. Roughly 89% of energy came from fossil fuels. Moldova imported another 2.958 billion kWh in 2008, according to the National Statistics Bureau.

28INDUSTRY

Moldova's industry, including processed food, is composed of approximately 600 major and mid-sized enterprises and associations. It accounted for 20.1% of Moldova's GDP in 2010.

In the wake of the economic downturn in 1998, Moldova's industrial production declined 11% from the previous year. Growth in industrial output was a component of improved economic performance in 2001, as industrial output registered a 3.1% growth rate that year. This growth expanded to 17% in 2004, but industrial representation in GDP and labor force remained low in 2004, at 24.8% and 14% respectively. Most of Soviet-inherited industry is situated in the secessionist region of Transnistria, which makes industrial strategy exceedingly difficult.

In 2010 the most prominent industries were food and beverages processing (40.2%); production of electric and thermal energy (13.2%); engineering and metal processing (8.3%); chemical industry (4.6%); production of construction materials (7.5%); light industry (16.8%); and forestry, wood processing, pulp and paper (3.1%). Other industrial products include pharmaceutical equipment, furniture, and tobacco.

29SCIENCE AND TECHNOLOGY

The Moldovan Academy of Sciences, founded in 1961, has faculties of physical and mathematical sciences, biological and chemical sciences, technical sciences, agricultural sciences, and medical sciences, and 14 research institutes concerned with the natural sciences. Four scientific institutes conduct medical and agricultural research. Moldovan State University, founded in 1945, has facul-

Principal Trading Partners – Moldova (2010)				
(In millions of US dollars)				
Country	Total	Exports	Imports	Balance
World	5,396.8	1,541.5	3,855.3	-2,313.8
Russia	990.5	404.0	586.5	-182.5
Romania	633.1	246.4	386.7	-140.3
Ukraine	620.1	91.6	528.5	-436.9
Italy	421.5	150.8	270.7	-120.0
Germany	370.2	75.4	294.7	-219.3
China	322.5	2.3	320.2	-317.9
Turkey	273.3	67.5	205.8	-138.4
Belarus	199.4	80.3	119.1	-38.8
Poland	151.8	46.7	105.1	-58.4
United Kingdom	134.8	82.1	52.6	29.5

(…) data not available or not significant.

(n.s.) not specified.

SOURCE: *2011 Direction of Trade Statistics Yearbook*, New York: United Nations, 2011.

ties of physics, mathematics and cybernetics, chemistry, biology, and soil science. The Technical University of Moldova, founded in 1964, and the Chisinau Medical Institute and State Agricultural University of Moldova, founded in 1932, are located in Chisinau. M.V. Frunze Agricultural Institute is another educational institution in the sciences. In 2010–2011, science and engineering students accounted for 20% of university enrollment. Patent applications in science and technology as of 2009, according to the World Bank, totaled 134 in Moldova. Public financing of science was 0.4% of GDP in 2010 according to the Moldovan government.

30DOMESTIC TRADE

Chisinau is the main commercial center, with a well-developed system for product distribution. Both national and foreign firms have a strong presence within the retail sector. Since two-thirds of Moldova is rural, local farm markets play an important role in the domestic economy. A great deal of progress had been made in liberalizing and privatizing the economy. With US assistance, nearly all of the nation's farmlands were under private ownership as of 2000. Most of the household consumption is fueled by remittances sent home by Moldovans working abroad.

31FOREIGN TRADE

A trade agreement between the United States and Moldova providing reciprocal most-favored-nation tariff treatment became effective in 1992. The same year, an overseas Private Investment Corporation agreement—encouraging US private investment by providing direct loans and loan guarantees—was signed. In 1993 a bilateral investment treaty was signed between the United States and Moldova; a general system of preferences status was granted in 1995, which included EX-IM bank coverage. Wine tops the list of Moldova's export commodities (24%), followed by apparel (16%). Other exports include tobacco (6.5%), glassware (5.7%), and meat (5.4%).

Moldova imported $3.66 billion worth of goods and services in 2008, while exporting $1.45 billion worth of goods and services. Major import partners in 2009 were Ukraine, 14%; Russia, 11.4%; Romania, 9.5%; Germany, 7.7%; China, 7.5%; Italy, 7.1%; Turkey,

```
┌─────────────────────────────────────────────────────┐
│ Balance of Payments – Moldova (2010)                  │
│                                                        │
│ (In millions of US dollars)                            │
└─────────────────────────────────────────────────────┘
```

Balance of Payments – Moldova (2010)		
(In millions of US dollars)		
Current Account		**-591.6**
Balance on goods		-2,219.5
Imports	-3,810.0	
Exports	1,590.4	
Balance on services		-69.8
Balance on income		486.6
Current transfers		1,211.0
Capital Account		**-28.4**
Financial Account		**414.5**
Direct investment abroad		-3.5
Direct investment in Moldova		192.8
Portfolio investment assets		-0.2
Portfolio investment liabilities		5.8
Financial derivatives		-0.6
Other investment assets		75.5
Other investment liabilities		144.8
Net Errors and Omissions		**62.8**
Reserves and Related Items		**142.6**

(…) data not available or not significant.

SOURCE: *Balance of Payment Statistics Yearbook 2011,* Washington, DC: International Monetary Fund, 2011.

Public Finance – Moldova (2009)		
(In millions lei, central government figures)		
Revenue and Grants	**21,034**	**100.0%**
Tax revenue	10,687	50.8%
Social contributions	6,972	33.1%
Grants	1,159	5.5%
Other revenue	2,216	10.5%
Expenditures	**24,445**	**100.0%**
General public services	6,653	27.2%
Defense	242	1.0%
Public order and safety	1,280	5.2%
Economic affairs	1,719	7.0%
Environmental protection	126	0.5%
Housing and community amenities	54	0.2%
Health	3,774	15.4%
Recreational, culture, and religion	275	1.1%
Education	1,761	7.2%
Social protection	8,561	35.0%

(…) data not available or not significant.

SOURCE: *Government Finance Statistics Yearbook 2010,* Washington, DC: International Monetary Fund, 2010.

5.3%; Kazakhstan, 5.1%; and Belarus, 4.2%. Its major export partners were Russia, 22.3%; Romania, 18.7%; Italy, 10.8%; Ukraine, 6.3%; Belarus, 6.3%; Germany, 5.9%; and United Kingdom, 4.7%. Main import categories were fuel and energy, capital goods, and foods.

The EU became Moldova's main trade partner since 2004 and consumed 47.3% of Moldovan exports in 2010. Russia and the Ukraine represented of 26.2% and 6% in overall trade, respectively.

³²BALANCE OF PAYMENTS

In 2010 Moldova had a foreign trade deficit of $2.22 billion, amounting to 37.87% of nominal GDP. Its current account deficit of $483.6 million in 2010 was more favorable, representing only 8.3% of GDP. Moldova's current account balance in 2010 was an improvement over the 2008 figure of -$979 million, although it also reflected a slight deterioration from the previous year (-$465 million). Guaranteed public debt stood at $1.349 billion in 2010. Moldova also had an additional $3.44 billion in private foreign debt.

The government took the dramatic step of handing 50% of ownership of its gas lines to Russia's Gazprom, one of its largest creditors. In 2010 the IMF approved a $574 million loan to Moldovan government, aiming to help reduce growing public deficit. In April 2011 the IMF agreed to offer Moldovan another $77 million loan.

³³BANKING AND SECURITIES

Moldova's banking sector has played a key role in the country's transition from a managed economy to a market economy. The banking system was reformed in 1991. The National Bank of Moldova (NBM, the central bank) is charged with implementing monetary policy and issuing currency. The only state-owned bank is the State Savings Bank (Banca de Economii), with 37 branches and 537 representative offices around the country. Holdovers from the old Soviet system include three regional banks, which have been changed to joint-stock companies whose shares are owned by state enterprises. There were 15 commercial banks in the country in 2011 with licenses to perform international transactions.

November 1993 was a turning point for Moldova's financial stability. The NBM became a fully independent central bank with its own administrative council and was no longer required to finance industrial and agricultural funding shortfalls. As the leu was introduced, the NBM started phasing out credit emissions. As of January 1994, the NBM became fully responsible for monetary policy.

The NBM uses four policy instruments: reserve requirement—which were raised progressively throughout 1994—interest rates, money market operations, and foreign exchange interventions. The required reserve ratio from attracted funds in both leu and foreign currency was 14% in 2011. The discount rate reached a peak of 377% in February 1994, and was kept high despite the subsequent dramatic fall in inflation. As of 2011, the money market rate was 10%, while the NBM interest rate was 7%.

Moldova's 15 voucher funds have played an important role in the privatization program. Most citizens have opted to invest their vouchers in the funds rather than directly acquire shares in newly privatized companies.

The Chisinau-based Moldovan Stock Exchange opened for business in June 1995. Trading is electronic and is based on an order-driven system.

At the end of 2011 the foreign currency reserves at the NBM reached $1.952 billion, which is a slight increase over the $1.72 billion the bank had at the end of 2010. Substantial inflows of funds from multilateral institutions, notably the World Bank and the European Bank for Reconstruction and Development, were primarily responsible for the increase in bank holdings.

34 INSURANCE

The demand for insurance services continues to rise. Twenty-four insurance companies and 63 insurance brokers operated in the Moldovan insurance market in 2010. Their aggregated insurance reserves totaled $41.7 million.

35 PUBLIC FINANCE

In 1993, following independence, Moldova undertook a massive privatization program. By January 2003, 80% of all housing units were in private hands, as were nearly all small, medium, and large businesses. Agriculture was privatized by 2000 through a US-sponsored program called "Pamint" (land). In line with its previous agreements with international donors, the Moldovan government undertook privatization of the large state-owned Moldtelecom, Air Moldova, and Savings Bank in 2011.

The 2010 budget of Moldova included $2.164 billion in public revenue and $2.462 billion in public expenditures. The budget deficit amounted to 2.48% of GDP. Government expenditures by share of budget were general public services, $713.5 million (32%); defense, $18.34 million (0.82%); public order and safety, $109.32 million (4.9%); economic affairs, $38 million (11.5%); environmental protection, $16.25 million (0.72%); health, $201 million (9%); culture, arts, and sport, $47.7 million (2.14%); education, $153.5 million (6.9%); and social protection, $284 million (12.8%).

36 TAXATION

The personal income tax rate ranges from 10 to 55%. The corporate rate is a standard 18%. Capital gains derived from the sale, exchange, or transfer of capital assets are taxed at an effective rate of 9%. Dividends are subject to a 10% withholding tax if paid to nonresidents, and 18% if paid to resident legal entities. Dividends received by resident individuals from resident and nonresident companies are considered part of taxable income. Dividends paid to Moldovan citizens by resident firms are exempt from taxation. Payroll taxes are charged at rates of 4.7–30%. Also levied is a 20% value-added tax (VAT). A reduced rate applies to bread, milk and other dairy products. For five years, 2002 to 2007, a number of housing projects were exempt from the VAT.

37 CUSTOMS AND DUTIES

Moldova's foreign trade environment is characterized by extensive export and import tariffs, exhaustive license requirements, and export quotas. Under the provisions of a 2001 budget law, all imports are assessed a 5% tax of their customs cost regardless of their country of origin. Moldova also levies customs tariffs on all imports except those from the former Soviet Union, Romania, the EU, and a select group of countries with which Moldova has free-trade agreements. Excise taxes apply to automobiles (30%), alcoholic beverages (50%), electronics (50%), and cigarettes (70%). Since 1998 most imports are subject to a value-added tax (VAT) that amounts to 20% of the customs value of the goods. Grain and medical supplies may be imported duty free.

38 FOREIGN INVESTMENT

With the exception of certain state-controlled enterprises, current legislation does not restrict foreign capital participation in Moldovan enterprises. Some foreign equity participation in privatization of government-owned enterprises is also possible. Land under privatized enterprises can be owned by the enterprise owners. Barriers in Moldova to foreign investment involve the underdeveloped banking, insurance, legal, and trade services.

In 1997 and 1998, average annual foreign direct investment (FDI) inflows into Moldova had reached $77 million, up from about $24 million in 1996. In 1998, the financial crisis in Russia, which accounts for a 30% share of Moldova's inward FDI, helped reduce inflows to $40.6 million for the year, but in 2000 and 2001, record levels of FDI inflows of $143 million and $160 million, respectively, were attained. Total FDI stock has increased 22 times over since independence. The total stock of FDI in Moldova reached $620 million in 2001, equivalent to 36% of GDP and about 82% of gross fixed capital formation (compared to the world average of 22%). Moldova's share of world inflows of FDI from 1998 to 2000, while small in absolute terms, was 1.7 times its share of world GDP. Foreign investment was $110.8 million in 2003, and by 2004 total investments made up 17.1% of the GDP. In 2009, foreign direct investment in Moldova reached a net inflow of $127.8 million according to World Bank figures. It represented about 2.37% of GDP. MNB reported that in 2010 Moldova received about $182.63 million in FDI.

Moldova remains a relatively unattractive market for investors, mainly due to its small distribution markets, unclear legal framework, and inefficient law implementation. It has, however, a significant future potential due to its highly educated population, low wages, and competitive costs.

39 ECONOMIC DEVELOPMENT

In March 1993, the Moldovan government inaugurated the Program of Activity of the Government 1992–95 to make the transition to a market-oriented economy. The first stage focused on stabilization, including price liberalization, and the second stage concentrated on economic recovery and growth, including privatization, agrarian reform, infrastructure development, social protection, and trade reform. However, the government was slow to institute privatization in the agricultural sector. Although the government backed privatization, freed prices and interest rates, and removed export controls, economic growth was difficult. By 1998, Moldova's economy stood at one-third its 1989 level. In large part, the decline was due to unfavorable circumstances: the Transnistrian conflict, the collapse of the Soviet Union, the near-total loss of the grape crop in 1997, and the 1998 Russian financial crisis.

Close to 2,000 small, medium, and large enterprises as well as 80% of all housing units were privatized by 2002. Nearly all of Moldova's agricultural land is privatized as well. In 2000, Moldova negotiated a three-year $147 million Poverty Reduction and Growth Facility (PRGF) Arrangement with the IMF. Moldova joined the WTO in 2001. That year, the government adopted laws to combat money laundering and the financing of terrorism. The economy had turned around—spurred by industrial growth and a good harvest in 2001, real GDP growth increased by 6%. GDP growth during 2010 reached 6.9%, and growth in 2011 was 7%. Nevertheless, Moldova carries a heavy external debt burden and depends on international financial support from the public and private sector.

⁴⁰SOCIAL DEVELOPMENT

A social insurance system provides benefits for old age, disability, and survivorship in addition to worker's compensation for injury and unemployment, and family allowances. Benefits are available to salaried citizens, agricultural workers, the self-employed, and public officials. The government contributes the whole cost of social pensions for those who are excluded from coverage from the national social security system. Medical care is available to all residents. Moldova has comprehensive legislation for the protection of children, including programs for paid maternity leave, a birth grant, and family allowances. Sickness and maternity benefits were first implemented in 1993, and were updated in 2003.

Although women are accorded equal rights under the law, they are underrepresented in government and other leadership positions. Nevertheless, the president of the country's largest bank is a woman, and women constitute a growing percentage of public-sector managers. Several women's organizations participate in political or charitable activities. Domestic violence remains a problem and is rarely prosecuted. The government has worked to increase public awareness of the problem.

The constitution provides for equality under the law regardless of race, sex, disability, religion, or social origin, but discrimination persists. The minority Roma population continues to suffer violence and harassment. Human rights are generally observed and respected, although there were reports of mistreatment of prisoners and detainees. Prison conditions remain harsh.

⁴¹HEALTH

Moldova has been working on developing its own standards for healthcare. In 2009 the country spent 10.7% of its GDP on healthcare, amounting to $181 per person. There were 27 physicians, 67 nurses and midwives, and 61 hospital beds per 10,000 inhabitants. The fertility rate was 1.5, while the infant mortality rate was 15 per 1,000 live births. In 2008 the maternal mortality rate, according to the World Bank, was 32 per 100,000 births. It was estimated that 90% of children were vaccinated against measles. The CIA calculated HIV/AIDS prevalence in Moldova to be about 0.4% in 2009. Life expectancy in Moldova, according to the CIA, was 69 years in 2011.

⁴²HOUSING

Though the government has encouraged privatization of housing and individual home ownership, most residents, particularly in urban areas, find home ownership to be far too expensive in a poor economy. The existing housing stock is in serious disrepair and overcrowding is an issue. Most structures were built before 1980 and maintenance has been poor. Only about 28.9% of all dwellings have an indoor bathroom; only 31% have access to a sewage system. About 62% of all households use wells as a primary source of water. Most new housing is built with brick or stone and concrete frames. The average number of rooms per dwelling is about 2.8.

⁴³EDUCATION

While Moldova was a part of the Soviet Union, its education system was based on the Soviet pattern. Both Romanian (with a Cyrillic alphabet) and Russian were languages of instruction. How-

ever, after it gained independence, Moldova introduced extensive changes in the education system. Education is compulsory for 11 years, between the ages of 6 and 17. Primary school covers four years of study. This is followed by five years of general secondary studies. Upper secondary studies may cover two or three years, depending on a student's interests. The academic year runs from September to July.

In 2009 the World Bank estimated that 88% of age-eligible children in Moldova were enrolled in primary school. Secondary enrollment for age-eligible children stood at 80%. Tertiary enrollment was estimated at 38%. About 92% of all students complete their primary education. Of those enrolled in tertiary education, there were 100 male students for every 145 female students. Overall, the CIA estimated that Moldova had a literacy rate of 99.1%. Public expenditure on education represented 6.9% of GDP in 2010.

The Moldovan State University was founded in 1945 and uses predominantly Moldovan as the language of instruction. The adult literacy rate for 2006 was estimated at about 98.4%. The primary administrative body is the Ministry of Education, Youth and Sports.

⁴⁴LIBRARIES AND MUSEUMS

The National Library at Chisinau—the largest library in the country—held 2.5 million volumes in 2011. The Scientific and Technical Library of Moldova holds about 600,000 volumes. The library at the State University of Moldova owned over 1.82 million volumes, including a valuable rare books collection. The Technical University of Moldova has over 1.04 million volumes. The country had a public library system of over 1,300 branches.

Chisinau is home to several museums, including the National Museum of Fine Arts, the National History Museum, the Museum of Ethnography and Archaeology, and the Alexander Pushkin House and Museum. The Museum of Popular Art is in Ivancea.

⁴⁵MEDIA

The Moldovan constitution provides for free speech and a free press, and the AIE government generally has respected these rights. A wide variety of political views and commentaries are expressed through a number of newspapers and periodicals. National and city governments sponsor newspapers, as do political parties, professional organizations, and trade unions. Prominent newspapers in 2010 included *Flux*, *Jurnal de Chisinau*, *Moldavskie Vedomosti*, *Ziarul de Garda*, *Moldova Suverana*, and *Nezavisimaya Moldova*. It is difficult to obtain objective circulation numbers for Moldovan newspapers, as they only provide general numbers without the period of distribution. This is done to create an inflated perception of their popularity.

The state-operated Teleradio-Moldova operates one television and one radio station. Many stations are independent. There were some 50 radio stations in operation in 2007, including 33 FM radio stations. In 2010, the country had 492,181 Internet hosts. As of 2009, there were some 1.3 million Internet users in Moldova.

In 2009 the CIA reported that there were 1.1 million telephone landlines in Moldova. In addition to landlines, mobile phone subscriptions averaged 77 per 100 people. Telecommunications links are via land line to the Ukraine and through Moscow's switching center to countries beyond the former USSR.

46 ORGANIZATIONS

The Chamber of Commerce and Industry of the Republic of Moldova handles the internal and external economic affairs of the country. The Central Union of Consumers Co-operatives of the Republic of Moldova serves farmers as well as a variety of food producers and retailers. There are trade and professional associations throughout the country as well.

Political associations and organizations in the country include the Union of Council of Labor Collectives (ULC), Ecology Movement of Moldova (EMM), the Christian Democratic League of Women of Moldova, and the Alliance of Working People of Moldova.

The Academy of Sciences of Moldova works to promote public interest and education in scientific fields. A number of non-governmental think-tank organizations emerged after the collapse of the Soviet Union, providing high quality public policy analysis. The most prominent are the Institute for Development and Social Initiatives (IDIS) "Viitorul," the Institute for Public Policies, the "Expert" Group, and the Foreign Policy Association of Moldova.

The NGO Club was formed to assist in the development and consolidation of various organizations, as well as to serve as an informational network between groups. National women's organizations include the Women's Organization of Moldova (est. 1996) and the Gender in Development (GID) Project (est. 1994). International organizations with national chapters include Save the Children, Caritas, and the Red Cross.

There are several sports associations within the country, including branches of the Special Olympics and the Paralympics Committee. The National Scout Organization of Moldova offers programs for youth.

47 TOURISM, TRAVEL, AND RECREATION

Picturesque scenery, several casinos, and wineries are the primary attractions of Moldova, including Cricova, the underground wine city. The tourists sector was in need of greater infrastructure development. The *Tourism Factbook*, published by the UN World Tourism Organization, reported that incoming tourists to Moldova spent a total of $289 million in 2009. There were 59,563 registered foreign visitors that year; there were 63,593 in 2010. Moldova had 95 hotels in 2010, among which 14 were rated with four or five stars; 22 were rated three stars; 9 were rated two stars; and 2 were rated with one star. There were 2,695 available rooms with 5,112 beds. The occupancy rate in 2010 was 22.1%.

Tourists need a valid passport to enter Moldova. Citizens of Canada, Japan, the United States, and EU member countries do not need a visa to enter Moldova for stays of up to 90 days. In 2011 the US Department of State estimated the daily cost of staying in Moldova at $234. However this cost is based on maximum estimates, and most daily costs are significantly lower.

48 FAMOUS PERSONS

Petru Lucinschi (b. 1940) was elected president in 1996, and served until 2001. He succeeded Mircea Snegur (b. 1940), the first president of the Republic of Moldova. Vladimir Nicolae Voronin (b. 1941) became president in 2001.

49 DEPENDENCIES

Moldova has no territories or colonies.

50 BIBLIOGRAPHY

Brezianu, Andrei. *Historical Dictionary of the Republic of Moldova.* Lanham, MD: Scarecrow Press, 2000.

Dannreuther, Roland. *European Union Foreign and Security Policy: Towards a Neighbourhood Strategy.* London: Routledge, 2006.

King, Charles. *The Moldovans: Romania, Russia, and the Politics of Culture.* Stanford, CA: Hoover Institution Press, 2000.

Lobell, Steven E., and Philip Mauceri, eds. *Ethnic Conflict and International Politics: Explaining Diffusion and Escalation.* New York: Palgrave Macmillan, 2004.

McElrath, Karen, ed. *HIV and AIDS: A Global View.* Westport, Conn.: Greenwood Press, 2002.

Mitrasca, Marcel. *Moldova: A Romanian Province under Russian Rule: Diplomatic History from the Archives of the Great Powers.* New York: Algora, 2002.

Moldova Investment and Business Guide: Strategic and Practical Information. Washington, DC: International Business Publications USA, 2012.

Opello, Walter C. *European Politics.* Boulder, CO: Lynne Rienner Publishers, 2009.

Political Chronology of Europe. London: Europa, 2001.

MONACO

Principality of Monaco
Principauté de Monaco

CAPITAL: The seat of government is at Monaco-Ville

FLAG: The national flag consists of a red horizontal stripe above a white horizontal stripe.

ANTHEM: *A Marcia de Muneghu (The March of Monaco).*

MONETARY UNIT: The euro replaced the French franc as the official currency in 2002. The euro is divided into 100 cents. There are coins in denominations of 1, 2, 5, 10, 20, and 50 cents and 1 euro and 2 euros. There are notes of 5, 10, 20, 50, 100, 200, and 500 euros. €1 = $1.371 (or $1 = €0.72939) as of September 2011.

WEIGHTS AND MEASURES: The metric system is the legal standard.

HOLIDAYS: New Year's Day, 1 January; St. Dévôte, 27 January; Labor Day, 1 May; Assumption, 15 August; All Saints' Day, 1 November; National Day, 19 November; Immaculate Conception, 8 December; Christmas, 25 December. Movable religious holidays include Easter Monday, Ascension, Pentecost Monday, and Fête-Dieu.

TIME: 1 p.m. = noon GMT.

¹LOCATION, SIZE, AND EXTENT

The second-smallest country in Europe and the world after the Vatican, Monaco is situated in the southeastern part of the French department of Alpes-Maritimes. The area, including recent reclamation, is 195 hectares (482 acres), or 1.95 sq km (0.75 sq mi). Comparatively, the area occupied by Monaco is about three times the size of the National Mall in Washington, DC. The principality's length is 3.18 km (1.98 mi) E–W, and its width is 1.1 km (0.68 mi) N–S. Bounded on the N, NE, SW, and W by France and on the E and SE by the Mediterranean Sea, Monaco has a total border length of 8.5 km (5.3 mi), of which 4.1 km (2.5 mi) is coastline.

²TOPOGRAPHY

There are four main areas (determined more by economic activity than geographic difference): La Condamine, the business district around the port; Monte Carlo, the site of the famous casino, which is at a higher elevation; Monaco-Ville, on a rocky promontory about 60 m (200 ft) above sea level; and Fontvieille, a 22 hectare (54 acre) industrial area of La Condamine that was reclaimed by landfill in the 1960s and 1970s. There are plans to create more new land in Fontvieille because of increases in population growth. The extension is scheduled to be finished by 2015.

³CLIMATE

Winters are mild, with temperatures rarely falling below freezing and with a January average of about 8°C (46°F). Summer heat is tempered by sea breezes; the average maximum in July and Au-

gust is 26°C (79°F). Rainfall averages about 77 cm (30 in) a year, and some 300 days a year have no precipitation whatsoever.

⁴FLORA AND FAUNA

Monaco is home to 4 mammal, 12 bird, 5 reptile, and 1 amphibian species, none of which are unique to Monaco. The calculation reflects the total number of distinct species residing in the country, not the number of endemic species. Palms, aloes, carobs, tamarisks, mimosas, and other Mediterranean trees, shrubs, and flowers are abundant.

⁵ENVIRONMENT

Monaco is noted for its beautiful natural scenery and mild, sunny climate. The principality has sponsored numerous marine conservation efforts. Its own environment is entirely urban. According to UN reports, Monaco's environmental circumstances are very good. The nation has consistently monitored pollution levels in its air and water to ensure the safety of its citizens. Two marine areas are protected by environmental statutes.

The government has also instituted a system of air pollution control facilities controlled by the Environmental Service. Citizens are encouraged to use public transportation to limit the amount of gas emissions. Carbon dioxide emissions in 2008 totaled 92 kilotons. Similar techniques have been applied to the protection of Monaco's water supply. Noise levels from industry and transportation are also monitored to ensure safe levels.

Monaco is known for its activity in the field of marine sciences. The Oceanographic Museum, formerly directed by Jacques Cousteau, is renowned for its work and exhibits on marine life. The Direction for the Environment, a government arm established in

2008, managed Monaco's natural resources and operated within the Ministry of Public Works, the Environment, and Urban Development.

According to a 2011 report issued by the International Union for Conservation of Nature and Natural Resources (IUCN), threatened species included 11 species of marine life. Threatened species included the great white shark, the blue shark, the striped dolphin, albacore tuna, and swordfish.

6 POPULATION

The US Central Intelligence Agency (CIA) estimates the population of Monaco in 2011 to be approximately 30,539, which placed it at number 192 in population among the 196 nations of the world. In 2011 approximately 26.9% of the population was over 65 years of age, with another 12.3% under 15 years of age. The median age in Monaco was 49.4 years. There were 0.95 males for every female in the country. The population's annual rate of change was -0.066% in 2012. The projected population for the year 2025 was 40,000. Population density in Monaco was calculated at 15,270 people per sq km (39,549 people per sq mi).

The UN stated that 100% of the population lived in urban areas.

7 MIGRATION

Estimates of Monaco's net migration rate, carried out by the CIA in 2011, amounted to 0.10 migrants per 1,000 citizens. There is a long waiting list for Monégasque citizenship. A 1992 law allowed Monégasque women to confer citizenship on their children.

8 ETHNIC GROUPS

On the evidence of certain place names, the native Monégasques are said to be of Rhaetian stock; they make up only 16% of the population. The foreign residents are a highly cosmopolitan group: 47% are French; 16% are Italian; and various other groups comprise the remaining 21%.

9 LANGUAGES

French is the official language. English and Italian are also widely spoken. Many inhabitants speak the Monégasque language, which has its origins in the Genoese dialect of Italian and the Provençal language of southern France.

10 RELIGIONS

About 90% of the population adheres to Roman Catholicism, which is the official state religion. There are five Catholic churches and one cathedral in the principality, two Protestant churches, one Greek Orthodox Church, and one Jewish synagogue. Though there are a small number of Muslims, there are no mosques.

11 TRANSPORTATION

The CIA reported that Monaco had a total of 77 km (47.8 mi) of roads. There were 863 vehicles per 1,000 people in the country. French national roads join Monaco to Nice toward the west, and to Menton and the Italian Riviera toward the east. There is frequent bus service. The principality itself is served by motorbuses and taxicabs. The southeastern network of the French national railroad system serves Monaco with about 1.7 km (1 mi) of track.

Express trains on the Paris-Marseille-Nice-Ventimiglia line pass through the principality.

Monaco is only 10 km (6 mi) from the international airport at Nice and is connected with it by bus and by a helicopter shuttle service. Air service transported 63,876 passengers in 2009 according to the World Bank.

The harbor provides access by sea. There were 68 ships registered in other countries in 2010, with the majority registered in the Marshall Islands, the Bahamas, Panama, and Liberia.

12 HISTORY

The ruling family of Monaco, the house of Grimaldi, traces its ancestry to Otto Canella (c. 1070–1143), who was consul of Genoa in 1133. The family name, Grimaldi, was adapted from the Christian name of Canella's youngest son, Grimaldo. The Genoese built a fort on the site of present-day Monaco in 1215, and the Grimaldi family secured control late in the 13th century. The principality was founded in 1338 by Charles I, during whose reign Menton and Roquebrune were acquired. Claudine became sovereign upon the death of her father, Catalan, in 1457. She ceded her rights to her husband and cousin, Lambert, during whose reign, in 1489, the duke of Savoy recognized the independence of Monaco. The first Monégasque coins were minted in the 16th century. Full recognition of the princely title was obtained by Honoré II in 1641.

The last male in the Grimaldi line, Antoine I, died in 1731. His daughter Louise-Hippolyte in 1715 had married Jacques-François-Léonor de Goyon-Matignon, Count of Thorigny, who adopted the name Grimaldi and assumed the Monégasque throne. France annexed the principality in 1793, but independence was reestablished in 1814. The following year, the Treaty of Stupinigi placed Monaco under the protection of the neighboring kingdom of Sardinia. In 1848, the towns of Roquebrune and Menton, which constituted the eastern extremity of Monaco, successfully rebelled and established themselves as a republic. In 1861, a year after the Sardinian cession of Savoy and Nice to France, Roquebrune and Menton also became part of that nation.

The economic development of Monaco proceeded rapidly with the opening of the railroad in 1868 and of the gambling casino. Since that time, the principality has become world famous as a tourist and recreation center. Gambling operations are managed by Société des Bains de Mer, a state controlled group. Monaco had no unemployment in 2011 and provided jobs for 25,000 Italian and French commuters. More than half of government revenues, however, come from value-added tax. The rate levied by France is also in effect in Monaco. France has the highest VAT in the European Union and has come under pressure to adjust its rate downward in conformity with the rest of the EU. However, Monaco is not an EU member. Light industry and banking have also become important. Monaco joined the United Nations on 28 May 1993. Monaco is the second-smallest independent state in the world, after the Holy See, and is almost entirely urban.

Prince Rainier III, married to the American actress Grace Kelly until her death in 1982, led the country from 1949–2005 and is often credited for the country's impressive economic growth. Tourism, banking and other types of financial services augment the economy's former dependence on gambling. Rainier died in early 2005 and in July 2005, Prince Albert II, son of Rainier and Kelly, assumed the throne. The event was somewhat overshadowed by his admission of having illegitimate children. His illegitimate son and daughter are not eligible to inherit the throne, although Prince Albert has acknowledged paternity and assumed his financial responsibilities in both cases.

In 2010 Prince Albert II announced his engagement to Charlene Wittstock, a 32-year-old Olympic swimmer and former teacher from South Africa. They married in 2011.

¹³GOVERNMENT

Monaco is a constitutional monarchy ruled, until 2002, by the hereditary princes of the Grimaldi line. Prior to constitutional changes made in 2002, if the reigning prince were to die without leaving a male heir, Monaco, according to treaty, would be incorporated into France. Because Prince Rainier III's son Albert was a 43-year-old bachelor in 2002, without male heirs, and his own health was failing, Rainier changed Monaco's constitution to allow one of his two daughters, Caroline or Stephanie, to inherit the throne and preserve the Grimaldi dynasty.

On 7 January 1911, Monaco's first constitution was granted by Prince Albert I. On 29 January 1959, Prince Rainier III temporarily suspended part of the constitution because of a disagreement over the budget with the National Council (Conseil National), and decreed that the functions of that body were to be assumed temporarily by the Council of State (Conseil d'État). In February 1961, the National Council was restored and an economic advisory council established to assist it.

A new constitution was promulgated on 17 December 1962. It provides for a unicameral National Council of 18 (later changed to 24) members elected every five years (16 by majority vote and 8 by proportional representation); it shares legislative functions with the prince. Executive operations are conducted in the name of the prince by a minister of state (a French citizen) with the assistance of the Council of Government, consisting of three civil servants who are in charge of finances, public works, and internal affairs, respectively. All are appointed by the prince.

Women were enfranchised for municipal elections in 1945, and participated in elections for the National Council for the first time in February 1963. In 2011, about 25 percent of the National Council was female. Until 2003, suffrage was exercised only by true-born Monégasques of 21 and over. Naturalized Monégasques were granted voting rights in 2003 and the voting age was reduced to 18.

¹⁴POLITICAL PARTIES

Major political groups include Monaco Together, the Rally and Issues for Monaco (REM), and the Union for Monaco (UPM). In the February 2008 legislative elections, the UPM won 21 of the 24 seats in the National Council with 52.2% of the vote. The REM took the remaining three seats with 40.5% of the vote. The next elections are set for February 2013.

¹⁵LOCAL GOVERNMENT

Municipal government is conducted by an elected council *Conseil Communal* of 15 members, headed by a mayor. The council members are elected by universal suffrage for four-year terms, and the mayor is chosen by the Communal Council. The three communes that made up Monaco before 1917—Monaco-Ville, La Condamine, and Monte Carlo—each had its own mayor from 1911 to

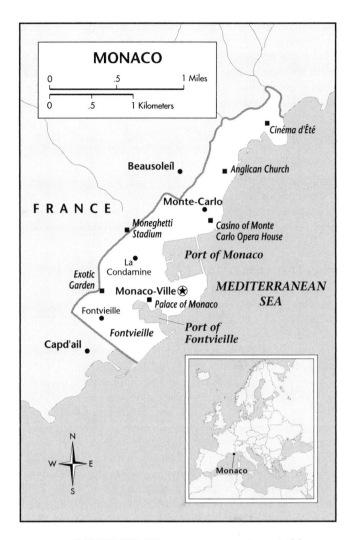

LOCATION: 43°43′49″ N; 7°25′36″ E. BOUNDARY LENGTHS: France, 5.4 kilometers (3.4 miles); Mediterranean coastline, 7.3 kilometers (4.5 miles).
TERRITORIAL SEA LIMIT: 12 miles.

1917. Since that date, they have formed a single commune, together with Fontvieille.

Anne Marie Campora became mayor of Monte Carlo in 1991, succeeding Jean-Louis Médecin who had served as mayor since 1971. Georges Marsan was elected mayor of Monte Carlo in 2003; he was reelected in 2011.

¹⁶JUDICIAL SYSTEM

A justice of the peace tries petty cases. Other courts are the court of first instance, the court of appeal, the court of revision, and the criminal court. The highest judicial authority is vested in the Supreme Court, established as part of the 1962 constitution, which interprets the constitution and sits as the highest court of appeals. It has five full members and two assistant members, named by the prince on the basis of nominations by the National Council and other government bodies.

The Code Louis, promulgated by Prince Louis I (1642–1701) and based on French legal codes, was formally adopted in 1919. Under the 1962 constitution the prince delegates his authority to the judiciary to render justice in his name.

The legal guarantee of a fair and public trial for criminal defendants is respected in practice. Defendants have the right to counsel at public expense if necessary.

The constitution provides for freedom of speech, although the penal code prohibits denunciations of the royal family. The constitution differentiates between the rights of nationals and those of noncitizens; only about 7,000 of the nation's residents are actual Monégasques.

17 ARMED FORCES

France assumed responsibility for the defense of Monaco as part of the Versailles Treaty in 1919. There is no army in the principality. A private guard protects the royal family, and a police force of 390 ensures public safety. The Palace Guard performs ceremonial duties.

18 INTERNATIONAL COOPERATION

Monaco joined the United Nations on 28 May 1993 and is a member of the ECE and several nonregional specialized agencies, such as the FAO, IAEA, ICAO, IMO, ITU, UNCTAD, UNESCO, WHO, and WIPO. Monaco is also a member of the Council of Europe and the OSCE. The headquarters of the International Hydrographic Bureau (IHB) is located in Monaco.

A treaty providing in detail for mutual administrative assistance between France and Monaco became operative on 14 December 1954. Fiscal relations between the two countries are governed by a convention signed on 18 May 1963. France may station troops in Monaco and make use of Monaco's territorial waters. As a result of a customs union with France and French control of Monaco's foreign policy, the principality operates within the European Union.

In environmental cooperation, Monaco is part of the Basel Convention; Conventions on Biological Diversity, Whaling, and Air Pollution; Ramsar; CITES; the London Convention; the Montréal Protocol; MARPOL; and the UN Conventions on the Law of the Sea, Climate Change, and Desertification.

19 ECONOMY

The gross domestic product (GDP) rate of change in Monaco, as of 2010, was 2.5%. Inflation stood at 1.5%. The principality does not publish statistics on its economy, and compiled statistics are rough estimates.

Economically, Monaco depends chiefly on income from tourism (25% of revenue), real estate, financial services, and small, high value-added, nonpolluting industry. A substantial part of the principality's revenue from tourist sources comes from the operations of Sea-Bathing Co. (Société des Bains de Mer—SBM), in which the government holds a 69% interest. The SBM operates the gambling casino at Monte Carlo as well as four hotels, 19 restaurants, a cabaret, and the Thermos Margins spa. The government also retains monopolies in telephone services, postal services and tobacco. A 22-hectare landfill project at Fontvieille increased Monaco's total land area, with plans for future expansion. Land reclamation since Prince Rainier's accession to the throne in 1949 has increased Monaco's territory by 23%.

Monaco also serves as a tax refuge for foreign non-French residents. Although it was removed from the Organisation for Economic Co-operation and Development (OECD) grey list in 2009, it has yet to fully disclose its banking procedures.

20 INCOME

The US State Department estimated that in 2010 the GDP of Monaco was $5.47 billion. The annual growth rate of GDP was 2.5%. The average inflation rate was 1.5%. It was estimated that industry accounted for 4.9% of GDP and services for 95.1%.

21 LABOR

As of 2010 Monaco had a total labor force of 49,300 people. There is virtually no unemployment in Monaco, as the Prince guarantees all his subjects lifetime employment. The major employer of the working population is the SBM; others work in industry or in service establishments.

Owners and workers are each grouped in syndicates. Less than 10% of the workforce in 2005 was unionized. However, most of these union workers commute from outside the principality. About two-thirds of all employees commute from France and Italy. Unions operate independently of the government and political parties. The rights to strike, organize, and bargain collectively are protected by law, although public government workers may not strike. Labor disruptions are infrequent.

The minimum working age is 16, although special restrictions apply until the age of 18. Employers who violate the minimum age laws can be criminally prosecuted. The standard workweek is 39 hours. The minimum wage is the French minimum ($11.87 per hour in 2011) plus an additional 5% to adjust for travel costs for commuters. This provides a family with a decent standard of living, and most workers earn more than the minimum. Health and safety standards are rigorously enforced.

22 AGRICULTURE

There is no agriculture.

23 ANIMAL HUSBANDRY

There is a dairy industry serving local needs.

24 FISHING

In 2008, the annual capture totaled 1 ton according to the UN FAO. Fishing is carried on to meet domestic requirements. Monaco was actively engaged in marine science research, and in marine life preservation. The Oceanographic Institute has studied the effects of radiation in the ocean since 1961.

25 FORESTRY

There are no forests.

26 MINING

There is no mining.

27 ENERGY AND POWER

Services are provided by the Monégasque Electric Co. and Monégasque Gas Co.

28 INDUSTRY

The tourist industry dominates Monaco's economic life, but small-scale industries produce a variety of items for domestic use and for export. Industrial production in 2010 employed 2,967 people across nearly 100 businesses, generating $1.13 billion in revenue. Most industrial plants are located on Fontvieille. Small businesses make pottery and glass objects, paper and cards, jewelry, perfumes, dolls, precision instruments, plastics, chemicals and pharmaceuticals, machine tools, watches, leather items, and radio parts.

There are flour mills, dairies, and chocolate and candy plants, as well as textile mills and a small shipyard. The chemicals, pharmaceuticals, and cosmetics industries are present as well. Monaco's industries were forced to expand their facilities upward; some industrial buildings rise as high as 13 stories.

Monaco's industrial production is marked by its skilled labor force and tightly regulated pollution standards.

29 SCIENCE AND TECHNOLOGY

According to the World Bank in 2009, there were three patent applications in science and technology in Monaco. Marine sciences have been the focus of scientific inquiry in the principality for several decades. Prince Albert (1848–1922), who reigned in Monaco during the early 1900s, was well-known internationally for his work as an oceanographer, and he inaugurated the Oceanographic Museum of Monaco at Monaco-Ville in 1910. His interest led to the establishment of a focus on oceanography for scientific pursuits in Monaco. Jacques-Yves Cousteau, a famous oceanographer and activist, was involved with Monaco's activities in marine life research.

In March 1961, in its first research agreement concluded with a member government, the International Atomic Energy Agency, with the government of Monaco and the Oceanographic Institute in Monaco, undertook to research the effects of radioactivity in the sea. The Oceanographic Institute put at the disposal of the project a number of valuable facilities, including marine-biology laboratories, oceanographic vessels, specialized fishing equipment, and a wide variety of electronic and monitoring equipment.

The Scientific Center of Monaco, founded in 1960 at Monte Carlo, conducts pure and applied research in oceanography and the environment. The Museum of Prehistoric Anthropology, founded in 1902 at Monte Carlo, is concerned with prehistory and quaternary geology.

AIR Worldwide, a private company with offices in Monaco, develops sophisticated models for assessing European vulnerability to natural disasters.

30 DOMESTIC TRADE

Domestic trade practices are similar to those in other towns along the French Riviera. Specialty shops deal primarily in tourist souvenirs. The SBM controls most of the amusement facilities and owns most major hotels, sporting clubs, workshops, a printing press, and various retail shops. There is no personal income tax. Business taxes are low, especially for businesses that generate a 75% majority of profits within Monaco. Tourism and related services account for about 25% of revenues.

Advertising media include magazines, billboards, and motion pictures. General business hours are from 8:30 AM to 12:30 PM and from 2 to 6 PM, Monday–Friday. Banking hours are 9 AM to 12 noon and 2 to 4 PM, Monday–Friday.

31 FOREIGN TRADE

Monaco has full customs integration with France, and records of Monaco's foreign trade transactions are, as a result, speculative. Estimates suggest that Monaco imported $882.6 million worth of goods and services in 2010, while exporting $711 million worth of goods and services. Main imports included food and natural resources and are imported primarily from Italy and France. Exports were pharmaceuticals, perfumes, and clothing.

32 BALANCE OF PAYMENTS

Monaco had a trade deficit of roughly $200 million in 2008, though it incurred substantial tourist revenues to partially offset the imbalance.

33 BANKING AND SECURITIES

The most important local bank is Crédit Foncier de Monaco, founded in 1922. The banking industry grew in the 1990s and 2000s. In 2009 Monaco's banking industry had approximately 350,000 accounts, more than ten times its number of residents—the vast majority of customers were nonresidents.

Under international pressure, the government has considered reforms to the banking system that would lead to greater transparency and change the nation's reputation as a tax haven for foreign investors. Once blacklisted by the OECD as an uncooperative tax haven, Monaco issued a declaration in 2009 formally stating its commitment to initiate measures toward greater transparency in its banking systems. The commitment came as a result of several years of pressure from the international community as governments began to launch aggressive tax evasion investigations against wealthy citizens holding foreign accounts.

34 INSURANCE

Branches of French insurance companies provide life, fire, accident, and other forms of insurance. They include: CGRM-Compagnie Générale de Réassurance de Monte Carlo; Concorde; Mutuelle de Marseille Assurances Compagnie Générale de Réassurance; and the Shipowners' Mutual Strike Insurance Association (Bermuda)—all located in Monte Carlo.

35 PUBLIC FINANCE

In 2010 the budget of Monaco included $863 million in public revenue and $920.6 million in public expenditures. Public debt totaled $18 billion, all of which was held by foreign entities.

36 TAXATION

There are no personal income taxes. Indirect taxes included a value-added tax of nearly 20% in 2011. There is a tax of up to 33.3% on the profits of businesses that obtain more than 25% of their gross profits from operations outside Monaco. Corporations whose income is derived from royalties, licenses, trademarks, or other industrial or artistic property rights are subject to this tax, whether or not the income arises outside Monaco. Qualifying new companies may be assessed at reduced rates. Spouses, parents, and children were exempt from inheritance taxes.

37 CUSTOMS AND DUTIES

By treaty, France and Monaco form a customs union that treats the Monaco coast as part of France. The French customs service collects the duties on cargoes discharged in Monaco and pays a share to the principality.

Monaco imposes a duty on all exports to places other than France; the levy applies whether the transfer of goods is actual or fictitious.

38 FOREIGN INVESTMENT

Monaco permits foreign businesses to establish their headquarters in its territory; ownership and management must be made a matter of public record. Although both corporations and limited partnerships with shares are allowed, in fact only corporations are in existence. Two persons may form a corporation; the minimum capital must be fully subscribed and at least one-fourth paid up front. Foreign companies may establish subsidiaries in Monaco.

Low taxes on company profits, strong pollution controls, and a high standard of living are all incentives for locating in Monaco.

39 ECONOMIC DEVELOPMENT

The government strenuously promotes Monaco as a tourist and convention attraction. A government-financed International Convention Center offers large conference rooms, projection equipment, television and radio recording studios, telex communications, and simultaneous translation into five languages.

Two major development and reclamation projects were undertaken under Prince Rainier. They were the major landfill and reclamation project at Fontvieille, and the Monte Carlo Bord de Mer. At Fontvieille, the government financed the reclamation of 220,000 sq m (2,368,000 sq ft) of inundated shore, creating a "platform" for residential construction and new port facilities. Another expansion is planned to be completed by 2015.

The Monte Carlo seashore scheme, also government-financed, involved the relocation of railroad tracks underground in order to create a man-made beach, with a boardwalk and other tourist attractions. The beach lies between two other land reclamation projects: the Larvotto, a sports complex financed by SBM, and the Portier, an entertainment complex developed by the government.

Roughly half of government revenues come from the VAT tax, and the banking sector has become one of the most important economic realms, alongside tourism. In 2011 the government continued to promote development in those sectors as well as its high end industrial production.

40 SOCIAL DEVELOPMENT

The social insurance system provides old age, survivorship and disability pensions. It is funded through employee and employer contributions. Sickness and maternity benefits are available to all employed persons with a special program for the self-employed. Workers and their dependents are reimbursed for medical expenses, including primary and specialized care, pharmaceuticals, hospitalization, transportation, dental care and appliances. Employers are required to provide workers' compensation through private insurance plans. Unemployment benefits are provided

through the French system. There is also a family allowance, a prenatal allowance, and an education grant.

Women have become increasingly visible in public life, and are well represented in the professions. Equal pay for equal work is prevalent, although women are underrepresented in business and finance. Reports of violence against women are rare, and domestic abuse is a criminal offense. Human rights are respected in Monaco.

41 HEALTH

According to the CIA, life expectancy in Monaco was 90 years in 2011, the longest of any country. The country spent 15.8% of its GDP on healthcare, amounting to $7,137 per person. There were 6 physicians per 1,000 inhabitants. The fertility rate was 1.5, while the infant mortality rate was 1.8 per 1,000 live births. It was estimated that 99% of children were vaccinated against measles.

The entire population has access to safe water and sanitation. AIDS cases, although present, are not considered a major problem.

42 HOUSING

About 31% of the housing stock was built 1915–61. Another 26% was built 1968–81, and an additional 21% was constructed 1982–2000. About 25% of all dwellings are owner occupied.

In recent years, the government has stressed the construction of luxury housing. The government allows rental rate freedom and numerous legal alternatives to purchasing property.

43 EDUCATION

Monaco had an estimated literacy rate of 97.8% in 2010. Education is offered in Monaco from the preschool to the secondary and technical levels and is compulsory from age 6 to 16. There are five years of primary school and seven years of secondary school. More than 98% of secondary students in the public school system passed their final year exams in 2008.

The University of Southern Europe was renamed the International University of Monaco in 2002. The university offers undergraduate and graduate degrees in business-centered programs. Students may travel abroad for higher education.

44 LIBRARIES AND MUSEUMS

The palace archives include the private collections of the princes of Monaco, as well as a collection of money minted since 1640. The Louis Notari Library in Monaco (1909) has a collection of over 285,000 volumes. There is a Princess Grace Irish Library in Monaco featuring 1,500 pieces of Irish folk music and personal papers of Princess Grace and Prince Rainier.

The Oceanographic Museum in Monaco-Ville, founded in 1910 by Prince Albert I and previously directed by the noted Jacques-Yves Cousteau, contains a library of 50,000 volumes, an aquarium, and displays of rare marine specimens. In addition to the museum, the Oceanographic Institute conducts research in various marine areas, including the effects of radiation on the sea and its life forms.

The Exotic Gardens include thousands of varieties of cacti and tropical plants. The National Museum in Monte Carlo was established 1972. There is a Museum of Prehistoric Anthropology in Monte Carlo; the Museum of Stamps and Coins opened in 1996 to display the private collection of Prince Rainier.

⁴⁵MEDIA

In 2010 the CIA reported that there were 35,100 telephone land-lines in Monaco. In addition to landlines, there were 26,300 mobile phones, and subscriptions averaged 75 per 100 people. There was 1 FM radio station and 8 shortwave radio stations. Internet users numbered 75 per 100 citizens. Prominent newspapers in 2010 included *Monaco-Matin*. Postal and telegraphic services are operated by France, but Monaco issues its own postage stamps. Local telephone service is controlled by Monaco, while France is responsible for international service.

Radio Monte Carlo and TV Monte Carlo provide radio and television services and have had broadcast programs since 1954. Radio Monte Carlo's home service is broadcast in French. The system also provides overseas service in 12 foreign languages and is majority owner of the Cyprus-based Radio Monte Carlo relay station, a privately funded religious broadcasting service in 35 languages under the name Trans World Radio.

Freedom of expression is legally guaranteed. However, a Penal Code prohibition on public denunciations of the ruling family was still in place in 2010. Otherwise, the government is said to uphold free speech and a free press.

⁴⁶ORGANIZATIONS

The International Hydrographic Bureau, which sponsors international conferences in its field, has its headquarters in Monaco. The following international organizations also have their headquarters in Monaco: International Commission for Scientific Exploration of the Mediterranean Sea, International Center for Studies of Human Problems, and the International Commission for Legal-Medical Problems.

National youth organizations include the Association of Scouts and Guides of Monaco, the Princess Stephanie Youth Center, and Catholic Youth of Monaco. There are several sports associations in Monaco; the country is home to the International Association of Athletics Federations.

Other organizations include the Monégasque Red Cross, Caritas, the St. Vincent de Paul Society, the Society of Monégasque Traditions, the Commission for the Monégasque language (established 1985), and the Union of French Interests.

⁴⁷TOURISM

The *Tourism Factbook*, published by the UN World Tourism Organization, reported 265,000 incoming tourists to Monaco in 2009. Of those incoming tourists, there were 216,000 from Europe. There were 5,665 hotel beds available in Monaco, which had an occupancy rate of 61%. The estimated daily cost to visit Monaco was $418.

In addition to overnight stays, there were 189 cruise ship stopovers in 2007 and a total of more than five million day tourists. About 79% of tourist visits were designated as leisure tourism, compared to 21% dedicated to business tourism.

Monaco has been famous for attracting wealth and titled tourists since its gambling casino was established at Monte Carlo in 1856. In 2005 gambling accounted for almost 25% of the annual revenue, though it was less economically important by 2011. Among the many attractions are the Louis II Stadium, the many museums and gardens, and the beach. The Monte Carlo opera house was the site of many world premiere performances, including Massenet's *Le Jongleur de Notre Dame* (1902) and *Don Quichotte* (1910), Fauré's *Pénélope* (1913), and Ravel's *L'Enfant et les sortilèges* (1925). It was also the home of Serge Diaghilev's Russian Ballet (founded in 1911), later known as the Ballet Russe de Monte Carlo.

In 2009, the tourist board launched a new program called Monaco Private Label, designed to attract the ultra-rich to the small nation. Private Label guests will be invited on private shopping tours and enjoy fine dining experiences. Private helicopters will be available to transport guests quickly to other nearby locations.

The principality has excellent sports facilities. The Monte Carlo Rally, a world-famous driving championship, ends with a finish line in Monaco.

No restriction is placed on the entrance of French nationals into Monaco. A valid passport is required for citizens of other countries who visit. Visas are not required for tourist/business stays of up to 90 days.

⁴⁸FAMOUS PERSONS

Prince Albert (1848–1922), who reigned from 1889 to 1922, was famous as an oceanographer. In 1956, his great-grandson Rainier III (1923–2005), reigning monarch from 1949–2005, married Grace Patricia Kelly (1929–82), a US motion picture actress, whose death on 14 September 1982 following an automobile accident was mourned throughout Monaco. Their son, Prince Albert (b. 1958) became Prince Albert II upon his father's death; Princess Caroline (b. 1957) and Princess Stéphanie (b. 1965) are the daughters of Rainier III and Grace.

⁴⁹DEPENDENCIES

Monaco has no territories or colonies.

⁵⁰BIBLIOGRAPHY

Annesley, Claire, ed. *A Political and Economic Dictionary of Western Europe*. Philadelphia: Routledge/Taylor and Francis, 2005.

Duursma, Jorri. *Self-Determination, Statehood, and International Relations of Micro-States: The Cases of Liechtenstein, San Marino, Monaco, Andorra, and the Vatican City*. New York: Cambridge University Press, 1996.

Eccardt, Thomas M. *Secrets of the Seven Smallest States of Europe*. New York: Hippocrene Books, 2005.

Opello, Walter C. *European Politics*. Boulder, CO: Lynne Rienner Publishers, 2009.

Political Chronology of Europe. London: Europa, 2001.

Stahl, Christiane. *Albert II de Monaco*. [French] Mocado: Editions du Rocher, 2009.

Taraborrelli, J. Randy. *Once Upon a Time: Behind the Fairy Tale of Princess Grace and Prince Rainier*. New York: Warner Books, 2003.

MONTENEGRO

Republic of Montenegro

CAPITAL: Podgorica

FLAG: The flag, initially adopted in 2004 and constitutionally sanctioned in 2007, is a red banner with a gold border bearing the gold coat of arms of Montenegro.

ANTHEM: *Oj svijetla majska zoro (Oh, Bright Dawn of May).*

MONETARY UNIT: The euro is the official currency. The euro is divided into 100 cents. There are coins in denominations of 1, 2, 5, 10, 20, and 50 cents and 1 euro and 2 euros. There are notes of 5, 10, 20, 50, 100, 200, and 500 euros. €1 = US$1.34 (or US$1 = €0.75) as of December 2011.

WEIGHTS AND MEASURES: The metric system is in force.

HOLIDAYS: New Year's Day, 1 and 2 January; Orthodox Christmas Eve, 6 January; Orthodox Christmas Day, 7 and 8 January; Good Friday (varies); Easter (varies), Labor Day, 1 May; Independence Day, 21 May; Statehood Day, 13 July.

TIME: 1 p.m. = noon GMT.

¹LOCATION, SIZE, AND EXTENT

Montenegro is situated in southeastern Europe along the Adriatic Sea. The total area is 13,812 sq km (5,333 sq mi). Montenegro is bordered on the NW by Bosnia and Herzegovina, on the E by Serbia, on the SE by Kosovo, on the S by Albania, and on the SW by the Adriatic Sea and a narrow strip of Croatia; total land boundary length is 614 km (302 mi) and the coastline is 294 km (183 mi). Montenegro's capital is Podgorica, located in the lowland plain region of the south.

²TOPOGRAPHY

The shoreline of southwestern Montenegro is highly elevated, with no offshore islands. The limestone mountains of Rumija, Sutorman, Orjen, and Lovcen separate the narrow strip of land that is the coastline from the inland regions. Of the 294 km (183 mi) of coastline, 52 km (32 mi) are beaches. The largest bay is the Bay of Kotor, which is the world's southernmost fjord. In the limestone area bordering the coastline, plants and animals are scarce, and patches of fertile land can be found in karst depressions and crater-like hollows. Lake Scutari (Skadarsko Jezero) is the largest lake in the country, covering an area of about 400 sq km (150 sq mi). The Zeta plain and Zeta River valley region on which Lake Scutari (Skadarsko) is found is a lowland region. Northern Montenegro is composed of limestone mountains. The highest peak in Montenegro is Mt. Durmitor (Bobotov kuk), at 2,522 m (8,274 ft). Other high peaks are Bjelasica, Komovi, and Visitor. These mountain ranges are rich in pasturelands, forests, and mountain lakes. The Piva, Tara, Moraca, and Cehotina rivers and their tributaries

have carved deep canyons: the Tara Canyon, at a depth of 1,300 m (4,265 ft), is the deepest canyon in Europe.

Located on the Eurasian Tectonic Plate, there are several fault lines running through the country which are seismically active. Earth tremors are fairly common and destructive earthquakes have occurred.

³CLIMATE

The Adriatic climate along the south brings hot and dry summers and relatively cold winters with heavy snowfall inland. Podgorica is the warmest city, with an average July temperature of 26°C (80° F) and an average January temperature of 5°C (41°F). In the mountainous regions, the climate is sub-alpine. Snow on Mt. Durmitor can reach up to 5 m (16 ft). Annual precipitation ranges from 56 to 190 cm (22 to 75 in).

⁴FLORA AND FAUNA

There are 2,833 plant species and subspecies, which comprise nearly one quarter of European flora. The animals found in Montenegro include types of hare, pheasant, deer, stag, wild boar, fox, chamois, mouflon, crane, duck, and goose.

⁵ENVIRONMENT

Coastal waters are polluted from sewage outlets, especially in resort areas such as Kotor. The United Nations (UN) reported in 2008 that carbon dioxide emissions in Montenegro totaled 460 kilotons. Destructive earthquakes are a natural hazard.

National parks in Montenegro include Durmitor, Lovcen, Biogradska gora, and Lake Skadar. Mt. Durmitor and the old city of Kotor are UNESCO World Heritage sites.

According to a 2011 report issued by the International Union for Conservation of Nature and Natural Resources (IUCN), the number of threatened species in Montenegro included 6 types of mammals, 10 species of birds, 2 types of reptiles, 1 species of amphibian, 25 species of fish, and 11 species of invertebrates. Threatened species include Atlantic sturgeon, slender-billed curlew, black vultures, asps, bald ibis, several species of shark, the red wood ant, and beluga. At least one type of mollusk has become extinct.

6 POPULATION

The US Central Intelligence Agency (CIA) estimates the population of Montenegro in 2011 to be approximately 661,807, which placed it at number 167 in population among the 196 nations of the world. In 2011, approximately 13.5% of the population was over 65 years of age, with another 15.5% under 15 years of age. The median age in Montenegro was 37.8 years. There were 1.07 males for every female in the country. The population's annual rate of change was -0.705%. The projected population for the year 2025 was 640,000. Population density in Montenegro was calculated at 47 people per sq km (122 people per sq mi).

The UN estimated that 61% of the population lived in urban areas, and that urban populations had an annual rate of change of 0.1%. The largest urban area was Podgorica, with a population of 144,000.

7 MIGRATION

The following information on refugees and internally displaced persons (IDPs) pertains to the Union of Serbia and Montenegro, prior to the 2006 independence of Montenegro. The breakup of the Yugoslav SFR in the early 1990s and the ethnic hostilities that came in its aftermath resulted in enormous population movements between the various former republics. According to the UNHCR, The total number of refugees and IDPs living in Serbia and Montenegro in 2000 was 751,891. At the end of 2005, UNHCR reported a total of 394,655 IPDs and refugees. In 2004, over 204,000 citizens of Serbia and Montenegro were refugees in Germany, the United Kingdom, Sweden, Switzerland, Canada, France, and Australia. Also, in that same year over 29,000 citizens of Serbia and Montenegro sought asylum in 18 countries primarily in Europe, and in the United Kingdom and the United States.

The bulk of the individuals mentioned in the above figures resided in, or originated from, Serbia. Thus, with independence, refugee and IDP issues became less relevant for Montenegro. In 2011, UNHCR reported that there were 16,364 refugees from Bosnia and Herzegovina, Croatia and Serbia (including Kosovo) registered in Montenegro. UNHCR also reported 3,246 refugees and 184 asylum seekers abroad with origins in Montenegro.

Reliable data on non-refugee immigration patterns has not been collected since the 2003 census. At that time, there were 53,433 Montenegrin emigrants abroad mostly in Europe and the United States. According to 2007 International Organization for Migration Report, there were 38,958 foreign citizens with work permits in Montenegro from January–July 2007. In 2006, there were 1,482 foreign citizens with temporary resident permits. Most foreign residents came from other countries in the Western Balkans, many to work in the tourist and agricultural sectors.

8 ETHNIC GROUPS

According to a 2011 census, 45% of the population of Montenegro are Montenegrins, 29% Serbs, 9% Bosniaks, 5% ethnic Albanians, 3% other Muslim Slavs, 1% Croatians, 1% Roma, and 6% other population.

9 LANGUAGES

According to the 2011 census Serbian remains the common language, spoken by about 42.9% of the population. There is disagreement regarding the Montenegrin dialect of Serbian as some Montenegrins claim it as a separate language. According to the 2011 census, 37% of the population claimed Montenegrin as its native language (22% claimed it as their native language in the 2003 census). Smaller numbers of individuals claimed Albanian (5.3%) and Bosnian (5.3%) as their native tongues.

10 RELIGIONS

The ancestors of the Serbs converted to Christianity in the 9th century and sided with Eastern Orthodoxy after the Great Schism of 1054 that split Christendom between the Eastern and Roman Churches. Islam came to the area from the Ottoman Turks in the 15th century. About 74% of the total population are Serbian Orthodox; the Montenegrin Orthodox Church also exists but is canonically unrecognized. Muslims account for 18% of the population, with smaller numbers of Roman Catholics and Protestants. Protestant denominations include Baptists, Adventists, Reformed Christians, Evangelical Christians, Evangelical Methodists, Jehovah's Witnesses, the Church of Christ, Mormons, and Pentecostals. There is a small Jewish community in the country. Freedom of religion is guaranteed by the constitution and that right is generally respected in practice. While there is no state religion, there are four main religious communities recognized by law: the Serbian Orthodox Church (SPC), the Montenegrin Orthodox Church (CPC), the Roman Catholic Church, and the Islamic community. All registered religious communities are eligible for some government funding, but these four communities generally receive the largest percentage of funding. Orthodox Christmas and Easter are observed as national holidays for all. Roman Catholics, Muslims, and Jews are permitted leave work to observe their own religious holidays. After Montenegro's independence in 2006, conflicts arose between the Montenegrin Orthodox Church and Serbian Orthodox Church over church property and the right of succession to the autocephalous Montenegrin Metropolitanate.

11 TRANSPORTATION

The Belgrade-Bar rail line links Serbia to Montenegro and terminates at the Adriatic Sea. Other major rail lines in Montenegro are Podgorica-Niksic and Podgorica-Skandar (Albania). Rail service is provided by locomotives manufactured in the 1950s and 1960s. The total length of standard-gauge tracks is 250 km (155.35 mi), most of which are electrified.

There were 7,624 km (4,737 mi) of roads in Montenegro in 2010, of which 5,097 km (3,167 mi) were paved. While there are no motorway-standard roads currently open, main roads include European Route E65/E80 (locally M2) from Herceg Novi to Rožaje, E762 (locally M18) from Božaj to Šćepan Polje, E763 (lo-

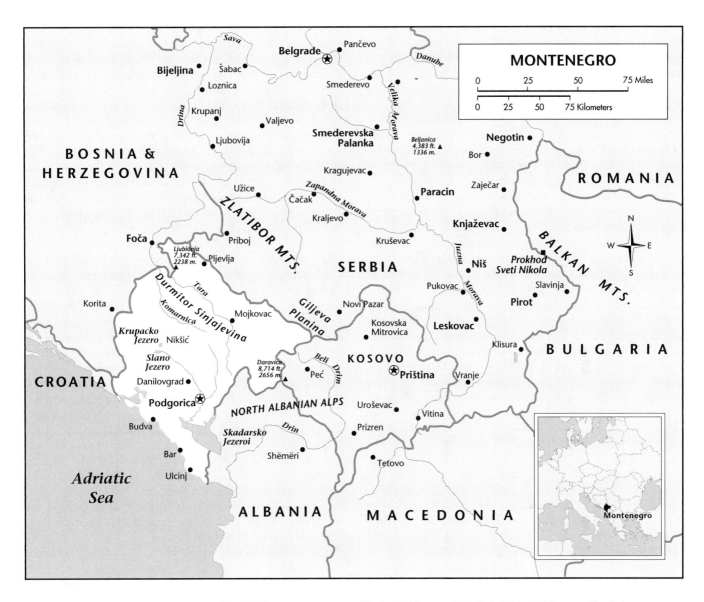

LOCATION: 41°50′ to 43°35′ N; 18°30′ to 20°30′ E. BOUNDARY LENGTHS: Albania, 172 kilometers (108 miles); Serbia, 124 kilometers (77 miles); Croatia, 25 kilometers (16 miles); Bosnia and Herzegovina, 225 kilometers (140 miles); Kosovo, 79 kilometers (49 miles); Adriatic Sea coastline, 199 kilometers, (124 miles).

cally M21) from Biljeo Polje to Dobrakovo and E851 from Zgrade to Sukobin. Sections of E65-E80 and E851 make up the Adriatic Highway. The Montenegrin portions of the Adriatic–Ionian and Bar–Boljare motorways were in the planning phase as of 2011.

Important ports are Bar, Kotor, Zelenika, Risan and Tivat. In 2010, the merchant marine fleet consisted of two vessels of 1,000 gross registered tons or more. The port of Bar is the largest port and is equipped to handle around five million metric tons of cargo per year.

In 2010, there were 5 operating civilian airports the largest of which are located in Podgorica and Tivat. International service is provided by Montenegro Airlines, Turkish Airlines, Croatian Airlines, Austrian Airlines, Malev, JAT and Adria Airways. Because the two main airports are only 80 km (50 mi) apart, no regularly scheduled domestic passenger service is offered.

12 HISTORY

Montenegro's early history is as part of the medieval development of Serbia, known as Duklja or Zeta, north of Lake Scutari (Skadarsko). The Serbs, one of the large family of Slavic nations, first began settling in the Balkans around the 7th century in the areas now known as Bosnia, Kosovo, and Montenegro, straddling the line that since AD 395 had divided the Eastern and Western halves of the Roman Empire.

Tracing the origins of the Serbs (and Croats) has fueled many debates among historians, but there seems to be a consensus on their Sarmatian (Iranian) origin. Having assimilated into the Slavic tribes, the Serbs migrated with them west into central Europe (White Serbia) in the Saxony area and from there moved to the Balkans around AD 626 upon an invitation by the Byzantine emperor Heraclius to assist him in repelling the Avar and Persian attack on Constantinople. Having settled in the Balkan area, the Serbs organized several principalities of their own, made up of a number of clans headed by leaders known as *zupans*. Both the Byzantine Empire and the Bulgars tried to conquer them, but the Serbs were too decentralized to be conquered.

Between the 9th and 12th centuries, several Serbian principalities evolved, among them Raška in the mountainous north of Montenegro and southern Serbia, and Zeta (south Montenegro along the Adriatic coast), whose ruler Mihajlo (Michael) was anointed king by Pope Gregory VII in 1077.

In the late 10th century the Bulgarian khan (leader) Samuilo extended his control over Bosnia, Raška, and Zeta, north to the Sava River, and south over Macedonia. Raška became the area from where the medieval Serbian empire developed. Stephen Nemanja, grand zupan of Raška, fought against the Byzantines in AD 1169, and added Zeta to his domain in 1186. He built several Serbian monasteries, including Hilandar on Mount Athos. His son, Rastko, became a monk (Sava) and the first Serbian archbishop of the new Serbian Autocephalous Church in 1219. The second son, Stephen, received his crown from Pope Innocent IV in 1202. Stephen developed political alliances that, following his death in 1227, allowed Serbia to resist the pressure from Bulgaria and, internally, keep control over subordinate zupans. Archbishop Sava (later Saint Sava) preferred the Byzantine Church and utilized the Orthodox religion in his nation-building effort. He began by establishing numerous Serbian-Orthodox monasteries around Serbia. He also succeeded in turning Zeta from Catholicism to Serbian Orthodoxy.

The medieval Serbian empire, under Stephen Dušan the Mighty (1331–55) extended from the Aegean Sea to the Danube (Belgrade), along the Adriatic and Ionian coasts from the Neretva River to the Gulf of Corinth and controlled, aside from the central Serbian lands, Macedonia, Thessaly, the Epirus, and Albania. The Serbian Church obtained its own patriarchate, with its center in Peć. Serbia became an exporting land with abundant crops and minerals. Dušan, who was crowned tsar of "the Serbs and Greeks" in 1346, gave Serbia its first code of laws based on a combination of Serbian customs and Byzantine law. His attempt to conquer the throne of Byzantium failed, however, when the Byzantines called on the advancing Ottoman Turks for help in 1345. Even though Dušan withstood the attacks from the Turks twice (in 1345 and 1349), the gates to Europe had been opened, and the Ottoman Turks had initiated their campaign to subjugate the Balkans.

Dušan's heirs could not hold his empire together against the Turks and the Nemanja dynasty ended with the death of his son Stephen Uroš in 1371, the same year his brothers Vukašin and Ivan Ugleš were killed at the battle of Marica. The defeat of the Serbs at Kosovo Polje in 1389 in an epochal battle that took the lives of both Sultan Murad I and Serbian prince Lazar left Serbia open to further Turkish conquest. Following a series of wars, the Turks succeeded in overtaking Constantinople in 1453 and all of Serbia by 1459. For the next three-and-a-half centuries, Serbs and others had to learn how to survive under Ottoman rule.

The Turks did not make any distinctions based on ethnicity, but only on religion. Turkish Muslims were the dominant class while Christians and Jews were subordinated. While maintaining their religious and cultural autonomy, the non-Turks developed most of the nonmilitary administrative professions and carried on most of the economic activities, including internal trade and trade with other countries of the Christian world. There was no regular conscription of non-Turks into the sultan's armies, but non-Turks were taxed to pay for defense. Christian boys between the age of eight and twenty were forcibly taken from their families to be converted to Islam and trained as "Janissaries" or government administrators. Some these former Christians became administrators and even became grand viziers (advisers) to sultans.

Urban dwellers under Ottoman rule, involved in crafts, trade, and the professions, fared much better than the Christian peasantry, who were forced into serfdom. Heavy regular taxes were levied on the peasants, with corruption making the load so unbearable that the peasants rebelled.

Two distinct cultures lived side by side—Turkish Muslim in cities and towns as administrative centers and Christian Orthodox in the countryside. The numerous Serbian monasteries built around the country since the Nemanja dynasty became the supportive network for Serbian survival. The Serbian Church was subjected after 1459 to the Greek patriarchate for about a century until a Serbian patriarchate emerged again. The Serbian patriarchate covered a large area from north of Ohrid to the Hungarian lands north of the Danube and west through Bosnia.

Montenegro was subjected to continuous fighting for 400 years, from the mid-1400s to the mid-1800s. Living in a very harsh mountain territory, the Montenegrins were natural and fierce fighters, and not even the large Turkish armies could conquer them. Until 1851, Montenegro was ruled by bishops. The bishops' role strengthened the Montenegrins' loyalty to the Orthodox Church and prevented their conversion to Islam, except in the lowlands and coastal areas occupied by the Turks. In 1696, Danilo Petrović Njegoš (1696–1737) was elected Vladika (bishop), and his dynastic family ruled Montenegro until its unification with Serbia into the first Yugoslavia.

The Montenegro area was an almost impregnable mountain fortress with some limited access from the Adriatic coast where the Turks had taken hold. In 1714 the Turks were able to occupy the capital of Cetinje, but they could not sustain their hold because of difficulties in getting supplies and constant guerrilla attacks by the Montenegrins.

Meanwhile, Peter the Great of Russia had recognized Montenegro's independence in 1715, viewing it as an allied Orthodox country valuable in his struggle against the Ottoman Empire. Having gained a greatly supportive ally in Russia, Danilo was successful in opposing the Turks with occasional support from Venice until his death in 1737. His successors had to struggle with the blood feuds among key Montenegrin families. Peter I (1782–1830) was able to bring together the feuding factions, reorganize his administration, issue the first Montenegrin Code of Laws in 1798, and defeat the Turks in 1799. Peter also obtained from the Turks a formal recognition of Montenegro's independence. During the Napoleonic wars, Montenegro, Russia's ally, fought the French over Dubrovnik and, in 1806, occupied the Gulf of Kotor, thus gaining access to the Adriatic sea. But Montenegro had to relinquish Kotor to Austria following the Congress of Vienna decisions in 1814–15.

Peter I died in 1830, having again repelled Turkish attacks in 1819–21 and 1828–29. Peter II, considered by many to be the greatest Serbian poet, established a senate of 12 members and centralized his authority by abolishing the office of civil governor, which had existed since 1516. However, his successor, Danilo II (1851–60), effected a radical change by proclaiming himself hereditary prince in 1852. Danilo II introduced a new legal code in 1855 that guaranteed civil and religious freedoms based on the constitution of 1852. Danilo died in 1860 of a wound inflicted by an exiled Montenegrin rebel.

Danilo's nephew Nicholas took over as the last independent ruler of Montenegro from 1860 until the 1918 unification with Serbia and the first Yugoslavia. During his 58-year reign Nicholas gained the nickname of "Father-in-Law of Europe" by marrying six daughters into Italian, Russian, Serbian, and German royal families. Through a series of wars with Turkey (1862, 1876, 1912, and 1913), Nicholas succeeded in more than doubling Montenegro's territory. Following the 1913 Balkan War, Montenegro and Serbia divided the Sandžak area and became neighbor states, both primarily populated by Serbs. Montenegro also gained access to the Adriatic Sea south of Lake Scutari (Skadar), which was divided in 1913 between Montenegro and the newly formed Albanian state.

Between 1880 and 1912, Montenegro took advantage of an era of relative peace to develop roads, education, agriculture, postal services, and banks, mostly with foreign investment especially from Italy, whose queen was Nicholas's daughter Elena.

The first Montenegrin parliament met in 1905, with 62 elected and 14 *ex officio* members. Following the successful Balkan wars, Serbian-Montenegrin relations grew closer, and by 1914, the two Serbian kingdoms proposed a union in which they would share their armed forces, foreign policy, and customs while maintaining their separate royal dynasties. World War I (1913–18) interrupted this process. Montenegro's poor defense led to Austrian occupation for the better part of the war; thus Montenegro ceased to officially participate in the war.

A Montenegrin Committee for National Union was formed by exiles in Paris who supported the 20 July 1917 Corfu Declaration on the establishment of a Kingdom of Serbs, Croats, and Slovenes. The Montenegrin Committee felt the time had come to unite with the Kingdom of Serbs, Croats, and Slovenes. King Nicholas opposed such a move and was deposed. On 24 November 1918, a resolution was passed in favor of Montenegro's union with the Kingdom of Serbia. Thus, Montenegro became part of the first Yugoslavia on 1 December 1918. Montenegrins participated very actively in political life, mostly supporting the centralist Serbian positions.

During World War II (1939–45), Italy controlled Montenegro and attempted unsuccessfully to revive the old kingdom. In the post-World War II Socialist Federative Yugoslavia, Tito reestablished Montenegro as a separate republic due to strong Montenegrin representation in the circle of his closest collaborators.

Montenegro entered the turbulent 1990s under the effective control of the Slobodan Milošević regime via the republic's largely pro-Milošević president, Momir Bulatović. However, the political transformation of Bulatović's formerly loyal Prime Minister, Milo Đukanović, set the stage for confrontation between Montenegro and Serbia which would ultimately end with Montenegro's independence in 2006. Đukanović first began distancing himself from Serbia following the Dayton Agreement (1995) in an attempt to gain Montenegro's exemption from outer wall sanctions against the FRY. In subsequent years, Đukanović pulled Montenegro further away from Serbia by effectively cutting economic ties between the republics, adopting the German Deutsche Mark and promoting media policy highly critical of the Milošević regime. In 1998 Bulatović was ousted from the ruling Democratic Party of Socialists and Đukanović went on to defeat him in subsequent presidential elections. Montenegro was largely spared in the 1999 NATO bombardment of the FRY and Serbia and Montenegro entered the post-Milošević era as practically separated political entities embedded in increasingly irrelevant federal structures.

On 14 March 2002, under mediation by the European Union (EU), Serbia and Montenegro agreed to form a new federal union, called "Serbia and Montenegro." Montenegro's prime minister, Milo Djukanović, was reluctant to sign the agreement, being the leader of the drive for independence of Montenegro's population of 660,000. However, the union of Serbia and Montenegro came into existence in 2003. The constitution provided for either of the two constituent republics to vote for independence in three years (2006). In February 2005, officials from Montenegro asked their Serbian counterparts for early secession, claiming the union was inefficient and squandered money. Serbian Prime Minister Vojislav Kostunica refused the proposal and indicated that European integration and economic development should be the main focus of Serbia and Montenegro.

A referendum on full independence for Montenegro was held on 21 May 2006. To be accepted internationally, a 55% majority was required for a "yes" vote to the question: "Do you want the Republic of Montenegro to be an independent state with full international and legal subjectivity?" The Montenegrin diaspora had the right to vote, with the exception of Montenegrins living in Serbia, who were barred from voting in the referendum. The vote on independence was 55.5% in favor. Voter turnout was 86.3%. A demand by pro-Serbian unionist parties for a recount was rejected. Serb politicians, Orthodox church leaders, and Montenegrins from the mountainous inland regions bordering Serbia opposed secession. However, ethnic Montenegrins and Albanians from the coastal area favored independence. Serbian President Boris Tadic recognized the independence of Montenegro. Serbia became the successor state to the union of Serbia and Montenegro, inheriting its seat in the UN and seats in other international institutions: Montenegro had to apply for UN and EU membership on its own once it was granted recognition by other states. Montenegro became the UN's 192nd member in June 2006.

The first national elections after independence were held in September 2006. The governing coalition—the Coalition for European Montenegro—headed by Prime Minister Milo Djukanovic, took the most seats (39) in the 81-member parliament. Zeljko Sturanovic of the leading Democratic Party of Socialists (DPS) was appointed as prime minister.

In December 2006, NATO admitted Montenegro to its Partnership for Peace pre-membership program. In January 2007, Montenegro was admitted to the IMF and the World Bank. In March 2007, Montenegro took its first step towards EU membership by entering into a stabilization and association agreement.

The country's first post-independence constitution was adopted on 19 October 2007. The constitution, among other things, changed the country's official name to Montenegro. European and Euro-Atlantic integration has been one of the driving forces behind the reform process that led to the signing of a Stabilization and Association Agreement with the European Union (EU) on 15 October 2007.

In February 2008, Prime Minister Sturanovic resigned because of health reasons. President Vujanović nominated and parliament approved Milo Djukanović, who was still the leader of the DPS, as head of the government. When presidential elections were held on 6 April 2008, Vujanović was reelected for a second five-year term with 52% of the vote. Following the March 2009 legislative elections, Djukanović was reelected for a sixth term as prime minister.

Montenegro's Stabilization and Association Agreement (SAA) with the European Union officially took effect on 1 May 2010. The SAA streamlines the process for the country to achieve full EU membership. The SAA essentially makes Montenegro an associate member of the EU, with greater responsibilities to act in compliance with EU laws and standards.

In November 2010, the European Commission agreed that Montenegro had made significant progress in efforts toward membership and recommended that the European Union grant candidate status to the nation.

In December 2010, one month after Montenegro was accepted as a candidate for the European Union, Djukanović announced his resignation. Djukanović, one of the leaders involved in the successful campaign for independence from Serbia, told reporters that achieving candidacy with the EU created the conditions for him to step down in favor of new leadership. Djukanović was the longest-serving leader in the Balkans.

13 GOVERNMENT

Prior to Montenegro's independence in 2006, a constitutional charter for the state of Serbia and Montenegro was ratified by both parliaments in January 2003 and the constitution for the unified state was approved on 4 February 2003. The constitution allowed the member republics to hold independence referendums in 2006, which Montenegro did. Following the "yes" vote on independence in mid-2006, Montenegro became independent.

Montenegro's existing constitution was proclaimed on 22 October 2007. It established a parliamentary republic with a prime minister as head of government and a president as chief of state. Elections for parliament must be held at least every four years and presidents are elected for five year terms.

According to the constitution, the president of Montenegro represents the country abroad, promulgates laws, proposes candidates for prime minister to the parliament, announces parliamentary elections, proposes the president and justices of the Constitutional Court, grants pardons and proposes referendums. The government (made up of the prime minister, deputy prime ministers and other ministers) formulates and carries out foreign policy, adopts decrees and regulations, implements laws, concludes treaties, and oversees government administration. The 81-member parliament is responsible for passing laws, ratifying treaties, appointing the prime minister and other ministers, appointing justices and adopting the budget.

In principle, the constitution establishes a division of powers between the judicial, legislative, and executive branches with an autonomous and independent judiciary.

14 POLITICAL PARTIES

The first parliamentary elections in the newly independent Republic of Montenegro took place on 10 September 2006. The main contenders were the DPS/SDP/HGI Coalition for European Montenegro, headed by Prime Minister Djukanović's Democratic Party of Socialists. The party supported Montenegrin independence and integration into the EU and NATO. In second place was the SNP/NS/DSS coalition, headed by the main opposition party, the Socialist People's Party (SNP), led by Predrag Bulatovic, who led the anti-independence campaign in the May 2006 referendum. However, Bulatovic has said Montenegrin integration with the EU and NATO is an important policy. Third, the Serb List, led by the Serbian People's Party (SNS), is a conservative party that claims to represent the interests of the Serb community in Montenegro. The SNS rejected the referendum result and seeks to renew the union with Serbia. Its chairman is Andrija Mandic. The other main party in the alliance was the Serbian Radical Party, headed by Vojislav Seselj (SRP-VS), which is the Montenegrin branch of Serbia's hard-line nationalist party of the same name. As of April, 2012, Seselj was awaiting verdict in his trial at the international war crimes tribunal in The Hague. The Movement for Change (PZP) was created out of the Group for Change, a non-party social movement that supported the pro-Serb alliance in the referendum on independence. The PZP is led by Nebojsa Medojeva, who has claimed the party aims to "topple the Djukanović regime" and tackle crime and corruption. The final seat allocation for the 10 September elections was as follows: Coalition for European Montenegro 39 seats, Serbian List 12, Coalition SNP/NS/DSS 11, PZP 11, Liberals and Bosniaks 3, and Albanian minority parties, 5.

The first presidential election since the country's independence was held on 6 April 2008, Filip Vujanović was elected with 51.89% of the vote. Voter turnout was 68.2%.

In 2011, there were over 20 political parties operating in Montenegro. Major parties include the ruling Democratic Party of Socialists (DPS), which continues to position itself as a pro-EU party dedicated to achieving Montenegro's EU membership; the Social Democratic Party (SDP), which has historically aligned itself with the DPS; the Socialist People's Party (SNP), which was initially established by the pro-Serbian wing of the DPS, currently acts as the main opposition to DPS and has recently adopted a more civic, social democratic and pro-EU agenda; New Serbian Democracy (NOVA), which emerged in 2009 as a more moderate version of the Serbian List; The Movement for Changes (PZP), an NGO-turned-political party which maintains a strong pro-EU stance along with strong opposition to the DPS; the Bosniak party (BS), which was formed from four smaller parties in 2006 to represent the interests of Montenegro's Bosniak community; and the Democratic Union of Albanians (DUA), which is one of four parties (the others being FORCA, the Democratic League of Montenegro and the Albanian Alternative) established to represent the interests of Montenegro's Albanian community.

[15] LOCAL GOVERNMENT

Montenegro has 21 municipalities (opštine).

[16] JUDICIAL SYSTEM

The republic of Montenegro followed the system of separation of powers: the judicial, legislative, and executive branches are independent of one another. The judiciary is autonomous and independent. The Constitutional Court has the power of judicial review. Appointments to the judiciary are for life.

[17] ARMED FORCES

Shortly after independence, compulsory national military service was abolished in favor of a fully professional standing military. The International Institute for Strategic Studies reports that armed forces in Montenegro totaled 3,127 members in 2011. The force is comprised of 2,500 from the army, 401 from the navy, and 226 members of the air force. Some 10,100 personnel are organized into various paramilitary forces including special police and Ministry of Interior units. Defense spending totaled $35 million. Montenegro has been a member of NATO's Partnership for Peace since 2006 and was granted a NATO Membership Action Plan in 2009. In 2011, Montenegrin troops were involved in the NATO ISAF mission in Afghanistan, the UNMIL mission in Liberia, and the OSCE mission in Kosovo.

[18] INTERNATIONAL COOPERATION

The Socialist Federal Republic of Yugoslavia was an original member of the UN (1945) until its dissolution and the establishment of Bosnia and Herzegovina, Croatia, Slovenia, the Former Yugoslav Republic of Macedonia, and the Federal Republic of Yugoslavia as new states. The Federal Republic of Yugoslavia was admitted to the UN on 1 November 2000. Following the adoption and promulgation of the Constitutional Charter of Serbia and Montenegro on 4 February 2003, the name of the Federal Republic of Yugoslavia was changed to Serbia and Montenegro. Serbia and Montenegro participated in several nonregional specialized UN agencies, such as the FAO, UNESCO, UNHCR, UNIDO, the World Bank, IAEA, and the WHO.

Serbia and Montenegro was a member of the Council of Europe, the Black Sea Economic Cooperation Zone, the European Bank for Reconstruction and Development, and the OSCE. It had observer status in the OAS and the WTO. In environmental cooperation, the country was part of Basel Convention, Ramsar, the London Convention, the Montréal Protocol, and the UN Conventions on the Law of the Sea and Climate Change.

Since Serbia was recognized as the successor state to the former union of Serbia and Montenegro, Montenegro needed to apply for membership in the UN and other international bodies. By 2011 it was a member of the Council of Europe, Central European Initiative, Euro-Atlantic Partnership Council, European Bank of Reconstruction and Development, Food and Agricultural Organization, International Atomic Energy Agency, World Bank, International Civil Aviation Organization, International Development Association, International Finance Corporation, International Federation of Red Cross and Red Crescent Societies, International Labor Organization, International Monetary Fund, International Maritime Organization, International Mobile Satellite Organiza-

tion, Interpol, International Olympic Committee, International Organization for Migration, Inter-parliamentary Union, International Organization for Standardization (correspondent), International Telecommunications Satellites Organization, International Telecommunications Union, International Trade Union Confederation, Multilateral Investment Geographic Agency, Nonaligned Movement (observer), Organization of Prohibited Chemical Weapons, Organization for Security and Cooperation in Europe, Permanent Court of Arbitration, Partnership for Peace, Southeast European Cooperative Initiative, UN, UN Conference on Trade and Development, UNESCO, UNHCR, UN Industrial Development Organization, UN Mission in Liberia, World Tourism Organization, Universal Postal Union, World Customs Organization, WHO, World Intellectual Property Organization, World Meteorological Organization, and the WTO (observer).

[19] ECONOMY

During the UN economic sanctions that lasted from 1992 to 1995, economic activity in the former Yugoslavia was extremely limited. Formal lifting of these sanctions occurred in October 1996. However, the United States sponsored an "Outer Wall" of sanctions, which prevented Yugoslavia from joining international organizations and financial institutions. Taken together, the "Outer Wall," the Kosovo war, and continuing corruption continue to stifle Yugoslav economic development. In October 2000, the coalition government began implementation of stabilization and market-reform measures. Real growth in 2000 was reported as 5%. A donors' conference in June 2001 raised $1.3 billion in pledges for help in infrastructural rebuilding.

In March of 2002, Montenegro began using the euro as its official currency even though it did not gain approval from the European central bank. Economic output was positive, but volatile after 2002, dropping to 2.1% in 2003 and jumping to 8% in 2004. Economic reforms were launched in 2003 and were driven by the goal of EU integration. In 2005 the gross domestic product (GDP) growth rate in Serbia and Montenegro was estimated at 4%.

After Montenegro and Serbia declared independence from one another in 2006, the economy of Montenegro showed three years of unexpected growth. In 2006, GDP growth was about 8.6%, followed by 10.7% in 2007, and 6.9% in 2008. Most growth, however, was in property development and housing construction, markets that sharply declined with the onset of the global financial crisis at the end of 2008. As a result, Montenegro's GDP contracted by 5.7% in 2009 (the sharpest decline of the SEE6 countries) and returned to a tepid 2.5% growth rate in 2010. The government has created a business-friendly investment climate with the lowest corporate tax rate in the region. While the banking, telecommunication, and oil industries have been fully privatized, the government still has ownership in some major companies. Tourism is seen as a major growth industry, as the government seeks investment in high-end travel resorts along the country's Adriatic Coast. A major actor in the Montenegrin economy was the Russian-owned aluminum-processing factory in Podogorica and its related industries. In early 2009, however, the factory faced a number of problems, as the price of aluminum declined and the cost of the massive amounts of electricity needed for the plant rose. The factory also produces high levels of pollutants. In October 2010, the government regained partial ownership in the plant and associated bauxite mine as well as membership on the boards of both companies.

[20] INCOME

The CIA estimated that in 2010 the GDP (PPP) of Montenegro was $6.724 billion with per capita GDP estimated at $10,100. The average inflation rate was 3.4%. It was estimated that agriculture accounted for 8.3% of GDP, industry 11.3%, and services 80.4%.

In 2007 the World Bank estimated that Montenegro, with 0.01% of the world's population, accounted for 0.01% of the world's GDP. By comparison, the United States, with 4.85% of the world's population, accounted for 22.51% of world GDP.

The World Bank reported that in 2009, household consumption in Montenegro totaled $3.5 billion or about $5,256 per capita, measured in current US dollars. As of 2011 the most recent study by the World Bank reported that actual individual consumption in Montenegro was 79.6% of GDP and accounted for 0.01% of world consumption. By comparison, the United States accounted for 25.44% of world individual consumption. The World Bank also estimated that 27.9% of Montenegro's GDP was spent on food and beverages, 20.8% on housing and household furnishings, 4.0% on clothes, 5.5% on health, 5.1% on transportation, 3.4% on communications, 2.2% on recreation, 1.0% on restaurants and hotels, and 6.1% on miscellaneous goods and services and purchases from abroad.

It was estimated that in 2007 about 7% of the population subsisted on an income below the poverty line established by Montenegro's government.

[21] LABOR

As of 2004, Montenegro had a total labor force of 259,100 people. Within that labor force, CIA estimates in 2004 noted that 2% were employed in agriculture, 30% in industry, and 68% in the service sector. Unemployment in 2009 was reported at 19.1%.

With the exception of the military, all workers are entitled to form unions. However, the majority of unions are government-sponsored or affiliated: independent unions are rare. Therefore, unions have not been effective in improving work conditions or wage structure increases. Virtually all of the workers in the formal economy are union members. Strikes are permitted and are utilized especially to collect unpaid wages. Collective bargaining is still at rudimentary levels.

As of 2009, the minimum employment age was 15 although younger children frequently work on family farms. The minimum wage was $77 per month. On average, the full-time monthly wage was $596. This wage rate did not offer a decent living wage for a family. The official workweek was set at 40 hours, with 30 minute required rest periods. There are no limits on overtime, however labor laws require an unspecified wage premium for hours worked in excess of 40 per week. Health and safety standards are not a priority due to harsh economic circumstances.

[22] AGRICULTURE

Agricultural land accounts for 15% of Montenegro's total territory. The largest share of agricultural land resources is pasture and grassland (88%), Montenegro has a high level of biodiversity and, despite its size, is rich in genetic resources of both agricultural plants and forest fruits (blueberries, edible mushrooms and wild medicinal herbs). Meadows and pastures prevail in the land structure. Arable land, orchards and vineyards occupy only 12% of the total agricultural area with growth of predominantly tobacco, vegetables (tomatoes, peppers, cucumbers, plums) and fruits (plums, apples, grapes, citrus fruits, and olives). Cereal production in 2009 amounted to 16,768 tons, fruit production 77,877 tons, and vegetable production 139,338 tons. Other food products include high-quality wines (Vranac, Krstac, among others), honey and natural water. Food production and agriculture play a significant role in Montenegro's economy, with agriculture, hunting and forestry providing 10% of total GDP (2007). More than 60,000 rural households obtain their income partly or entirely from agriculture. The agricultural production is structured by traditional vegetable markets and small privately-owned family farms, the average size of which is estimated to be less than 5 ha of agricultural land.

[23] ANIMAL HUSBANDRY

The UN Food and Agriculture Organization (FAO) reported that Montenegro had 324,000 hectares (800,621 acres) of permanent pasture or meadow in 2009. During that year, the country tended 417,000 chickens, 100,835 head of cattle, and 12,377 pigs. The production from these animals amounted to 5,235 tons of beef and veal, 19,595 tons of pork, 3,342 tons of poultry, 3,585 tons of eggs. Montenegro also produced 296 tons of raw wool. Between 2006 and 2009, overall livestock production decreased by 14%.

[24] FISHING

In 2008 the annual capture totaled 900 tons according to the UN FAO. The fishery sector accounts for only about 0.5% of Montenegro's GDP.

[25] FORESTRY

Forests and woodlands cover 718,000 hectares (1,774,217 acres) in Montenegro, accounting for 52% of the total surface area of the republic. Of this figure, the major part (572,000 hectares/1,413,469 acres) is in the northern region of the country. The UN FAO estimated the 2009 roundwood production at 208,001 cu m (7.35 million cu ft). The value of all forest products, including roundwood, totaled $17.3 million.

[26] MINING

Mining accounts for a very small portion of economic activity in Montenegro and produced only 0.6% of the country's GDP in 2009. Since independence, production of most metals, industrial minerals and fuels has remained steady or declined. Production of bauxite was 659,370 metric tons in 2006, 667,053 in 2007, 671,811 in 2008, 45,779 in 2009 and 61,205 in 2010. Lime production fell from 9,239 metric tons in 2008 to 839 metric tons in 2010. Gravel production fell from 146,381 cubic meters in 2008 to 49,517 in 2010. Lignite coal production in 2008 was 1,740,076 metric tons. It fell to 957,164 metric tons in 2009 and then returned to 1,937,847 metric tons in 2010. The outlook in 2010 was that Montenegro's industry would remain a modest producer with little prospect for new exploration or the development of new deposits.

[27] ENERGY AND POWER

According to Montenegrin government sources, three power plants—the Perucica and Piva hydroelectric plants and the Pljevlja

Principal Trading Partners – Montenegro (2010)

(In millions of US dollars)

Country	Total	Exports	Imports	Balance
World	1,381.4	338.3	1,043.1	-704.8
Italy	189.5	32.3	157.2	-124.9
Slovenia	184.7	42.2	142.5	-100.3
Greece	127.9	70.3	57.6	12.7
Austria	98.1	6.1	92.0	-85.9
Egypt	96.5	96.1	0.4	95.7
Germany	89.9	6.2	83.7	-77.5
Hungary	81.3	33.0	48.3	-15.3
China	80.8	2.6	78.2	-75.6
Brazil	70.4	…	70.4	-70.4
Netherlands	51.7	10.8	40.9	-30.1

(…) data not available or not significant.

(n.s.) not specified.

SOURCE: *2011 Direction of Trade Statistics Yearbook,* New York: United Nations, 2011.

Balance of Payments – Montenegro (2010)

(In millions of US dollars)

Current Account		**-1,031.0**
Balance on goods		-1,745.0
Imports	-2,217.0	
Exports	472.0	
Balance on services		591.0
Balance on income		-28.0
Current transfers		152.0
Capital Account		**-1.0**
Financial Account		**513.0**
Direct investment abroad		-29.0
Direct investment in Montenegro		760.0
Portfolio investment assets		-5.0
Portfolio investment liabilities		254.0
Financial derivatives		…
Other investment assets		-447.0
Other investment liabilities		-21.0
Net Errors and Omissions		**540.0**
Reserves and Related Items		**-22.0**

(…) data not available or not significant.

SOURCE: *Balance of Payment Statistics Yearbook 2011,* Washington, DC: International Monetary Fund, 2011.

thermoelectric plant—produce approximately 3 billion kWh per year. Montenegro has the capacity to produce 2,700,000 metric tons of coal. The World Bank reported in 2008 that Montenegro produced 2.66 billion kWh of electricity.

28 INDUSTRY

Industry was the primary engine of economic development in Montenegro in the second half of the 20th century. During that period, the growth of the power and energy sector, metallurgy (steel and aluminum), and transportation infrastructure formed the basis for overall economic growth and development. Approximately 90% of Montenegro's industrial products were marketed outside the republic.

In the early 2000s, Montenegro had facilities for producing 400,000 metric tons of crude steel; 1,000,000 metric tons of bauxite; 280,000 metric tons of alumina; 100,000 metric tons of aluminum; and 75,000 metric tons of sea salt.

Industries in Montenegro include metal processing, engineering, wood-processing, textile manufacture, chemicals, leather and footwear, apparel, household appliances, construction, and machinery.

Montenegro processes and finishes agricultural products. The country has fish-processing plants, flour mills, dairies, slaughterhouses, bakeries, breweries, juice factories, fruit processing factories, grape processing plants and wine cellars, medicinal herb processing plants, tobacco and cigarette factories, and confectioners, among other industries.

At the start of independence, the industrial sector was in poor shape due to the lingering effects of war and isolation in the former Yugoslavia. In 2009 manufacturing accounted for only 4.8% of total GDP. The country's largest enterprise, the Podgorica Aluminum Plant (KAP) and associated mining facilities, was hard hit by increases in energy costs and the fall in world aluminum prices. The company had been privatized in 2005 with a majority of its shares sold to a Russian Company owned by Russian tycoon Oleg Deripaska. However, in 2010 the government regained a share in the plant and associated mine following a series of strikes and law-

suits. Montenegro's construction sector has been active since independence developing housing and infrastructure related to the tourism industry. Activity in this sector has also been highly vulnerable to fluctuations in the world economy.

29 SCIENCE AND TECHNOLOGY

Scientific and technological policies are developed and implemented by the Ministry of Education and Science of the Republic of Montenegro. There are 13 registered research institutions in Montenegro and one university (the University of Montenegro, located in Podgorica). Patent applications in science and technology as of 2009, according to the World Bank, totaled 3 in Montenegro. Public financing of science was 1.10% of GDP.

30 DOMESTIC TRADE

Podgorica serves as the economic and commercial center of the country. However major tourist areas are also strong players in the domestic economy. Due to the country's size, the domestic market is quite small and highly responsive to economic fluctuations in Europe and elsewhere.

31 FOREIGN TRADE

Montenegro imported $601.7 million worth of goods and services in 2008, while exporting $171.3 million worth of goods and services. Major import partners in 2009 were Italy, 17.2%; Slovenia, 14.4%; Germany, 9.9%; China, 7.8%; Austria, 7.7%; Russia, 6.1%; Greece, 4%; and Hungary, 4%. Its major export partners were Italy, 27.9%; Greece, 21.6%; Slovenia, 11.3%; Hungary, 8.5%; the United States, 7.6%; and Egypt, 4.8%.

32 BALANCE OF PAYMENTS

Montenegro, both as its own republic and as a constituent republic of Serbia and Montenegro until mid-2006, maintained a relatively high current account deficit. For Serbia and Montenegro, exports of goods and services totaled $5.9 billion in 2004, up from $4.2 billion in 2003. Imports grew from $8.7 billion in 2003, to $12.8 billion in 2004. Consequently, the resource balance was on a negative upsurge, growing from -$4.5 billion in 2003, to -$7.1 billion in 2004. A similar trend was registered for the current account balance, which deteriorated from -$2.0 billion in 2003, to -$3.1 billion in 2004. The national reserves of Serbia and Montenegro (including gold) were $3.6 billion in 2003, covering less than 6 months of imports; by 2004, they increased to $4.3 billion.

After independence, Montenegro continued to run substantial current account deficits. According to World Bank data, in 2009 it had a current account deficit of $1.2 billion. In that year, exports of goods and services totaled $1.4 billion. Imports of goods and services totaled $2.7 billion. Reserves amounted to $785 million.

33 BANKING AND SECURITIES

Montenegro has its own independent central bank. As of 2010, the banking system was 100% privately owned and there were 11 licensed banks in Montenegro in 2011.

34 INSURANCE

Health insurance is compulsory and is administered by the Health Insurance Fund of Montenegro (HIF). Insurance of public transport passengers, motor vehicle insurance, aircraft insurance, and insurance on bank deposits are also compulsory.

Before independence, in 2003, the value of all direct insurance premiums written in Serbia and Montenegro totaled $436 million, of which nonlife premiums accounted for $420 million. In that same year, the top nonlife insurer was Dunav, which had gross written nonlife premiums of $138.6 million, while the country's leading life insurer was Zepter, which had gross written life insurance premiums of $7.1 million.

Independence brought a smaller, but more active, market and new players. At the end of 2009, there were 10 insurance companies registered in Montenegro with the Slovenian controlled "Lovcen Osiguranje" holding 61% of the market. During the same year insurance accounted for 3% of the country's GDP. Total premiums were estimated at €54 million ($77.7 million). The car insurance segment constituted the largest part of the insurance market.

35 PUBLIC FINANCE

The CIA estimated that in 2005 Serbia and Montenegro's central government took in revenues of approximately $11.4 billion and had expenditures of $11.1 billion. Revenues minus expenditures totaled approximately $330 million. Public debt in 2005 amounted to 53.1% of GDP. Total external debt was $15.43 billion.

In 2010 the projected budget of Montenegro included €1.4 billion ($1.9 billion) in public expenditures and €1.3 billion ($1.7 billion) in revenue. The government budget deficit as a percentage of GDP was 5.7% in 2009 and 3.9% in 2010. Public debt amounted to €1.2 billion ($1.6 billion) or 42.3% of GDP. External debt accounted for €917.7 million ($1.2 billion) of the total public debt.

In 2011 Moody's rated Montenegrin government bonds as Ba3 with a stable outlook.

36 TAXATION

Montenegro has a flat corporate tax rate of 9% and introduced a flat 9% income tax rate in 2010. In 2003 a VAT tax of 17% was adopted, with a lower rate of 7% on tourism and staple food items.

37 CUSTOMS AND DUTIES

Montenegrin customs rates range from 0 to 30% with an average of 6.11%. Montenegro has one authorized free trade zone (FTZ) that is located in the Port of Bar.

38 FOREIGN INVESTMENT

Foreign investment was severely restricted during the years of the economic embargo. Since the sanctions were lifted, foreign investors from neighboring countries, Russia, and Asia have expressed an interest in capital investment. The main sectors attracting the interest of foreign investors are metal manufacturing and machinery, infrastructure improvement, agriculture and food processing, and chemicals and pharmaceuticals. Foreign investors may hold majority shares in companies.

In 1997, foreign direct investment (FDI) inflows into the former Yugoslavia reached $740 million, but dried up with the onset of the conflict in Kosovo. FDI inflows averaged $122.5 million in 1998 and 1999, then fell to $25 million in 2000. In 2001, FDI inflow reached $125 million.

In the following years, Serbia and Montenegro undertook an aggressive program of reforms aimed at both reestablishing the area as a major transportation hub, and at attracting foreign investment. These policies seem to have paid off as in 2004, capital inflows jumped to $3.4 billion. While Serbia and Montenegro was considered to be a risky place for doing business, the political and economic climate was steadily improving as of 2005.

After independence Montenegro continued to place a great deal of importance upon attracting new foreign investment. In 2009, foreign direct investment (FDI) inflows totaled $1.32 billion. FDI represented 31.99% of GDP. In 2008, foreign investment originated from 86 countries with the most significant investors from Norway, Austria, Russia, Hungary and Great Britain. 28% of investments went into finance, 22% into tourism, 14% into construction, 11% into services, 10% into industry, 5% into transportation and logistics, 2% into agriculture and the remaining 8% into other sectors. In 2009, Montenegro was ranked 71st out of 183 countries surveyed by the World Bank Group's "Doing Business 2010."

39 ECONOMIC DEVELOPMENT

In an effort to promote foreign investment and spur economic growth, Montenegro strove to create a business friendly environment by introducing the lowest corporate tax rate (9%) in the region privatizing over 90% of the Montenegrin economy. A VAT tax was introduced in April of 2003 that established lower rates for tourism and staple food items in order to encourage development in the crucial tourist sector. The government also decreased the personal income tax and introduced a flat (9%) income tax in 2010. Net foreign investment in Montenegro reached $935.1 million in 2010 and investment per capita was among the highest in Europe. Nonetheless, corruption, organized crime, economic disparities, the troubled Podgorica Aluminum Plant and failed efforts to privatize Montenegro Airlines all presented continued challenges for Montenegro's future economic development.

The three years after independence produced significant rates of growth (8.6% in 2006, 10.7% in 2007 and 6.9% in 2008) as a result of a boom in several sectors: trade, financial services and transport and communications. However, the global economic crisis hit Montenegro's economy particularly hard and the country registered the steepest decline in GDP (5.7%) in the region for 2009. Construction and industry led the decline with decreases in output of 15.3% and 12.4%. Data for 2010 indicated a return to weak growth at 2.5%.

The US Agency for International Development (USAID) remains the primary foreign aid donor in Montenegro. The European Agency for Reconstruction (EAR), Germany, and the United Kingdom have smaller budgets and, like USAID, work in the areas of economic policy reform and enterprise development, among other programs such as civil society, independent media development, and the rule of law. The International Finance Corporation (IFC) focuses on small and medium enterprise development. The World Bank and EBRD focus on economic growth and infrastructure investments. The UN Development Program (UNDP), with funding from EAR, Germany, Canada, and the Netherlands, works in the environment, enterprise development, and civil society development areas. Montenegro has implemented an Economic Reform Agenda. In 2010 Montenegro issued its first Eurobond financing $255 million. It was also in talks with the World Bank for a $85 million development loan to support the state budget.

40 SOCIAL DEVELOPMENT

The Ministry of Health, Labor and Social Welfare (MHLSW) is the main institution responsible for providing social programs in Montenegro. Its areas of responsibility include family and child protection, pension and disability insurance, health insurance and employment insurance. As reported in the 2007 European Commission Report, *Social Protection and Social Inclusion in Montenegro*, Montenegro's system of social protections can be broken down into two types of benefits: Contributory benefits paid by the insured and non-contributory benefits paid from the central budget. Contributory benefits include pensions and disability, health and unemployment insurance. Non-contributory benefits include prevention, counseling, therapy and advice, institutional and non-institutional care and social welfare benefits. The Commission's report pointed to a number of challenges facing the social welfare, pension and health care programs in terms of the allocation and use of resources, administrative capacity, transparency and over-reliance on public providers.

Traditional gender roles keep women from enjoying equal status with men and few occupy positions of leadership in the private sector. However, women are active in human rights and political organizations. High levels of domestic abuse persist and social pressures prevent women from obtaining protection against abusers.

41 HEALTH

According to the CIA, life expectancy in Montenegro was 74 years in 2011. The country spent 13.6% of its GDP on healthcare, amounting to $617 per person. There were 20 physicians, 55 nurses and midwives, and 40 hospital beds per 10,000 inhabitants. The fertility rate was 1.6, while the infant mortality rate was 8 per 1,000 live births. In 2008 the maternal mortality rate, according to the World Bank, was 15 per 100,000 births. It was estimated that 86% of children were vaccinated against measles.

The government provides obligatory health care to citizens for preventive, diagnostic, therapeutic, and rehabilitative services.

The HIV/AIDS prevalence was 0.20 per 100 adults in 2007. The incidence of tuberculosis was 33 per 100,000 people in 2007.

42 HOUSING

At the beginning of 1996, there were 3,124,000 dwellings in Serbia and Montenegro, with an average of 3.4 persons per dwelling. Housing area at that time averaged 20 sq m (215 sq ft) per person. New housing completions during 1995 totaled 14,337 units, of which 11,847 were in the public sector, and 2,490 were in the private sector. In 2002, Serbia and Montenegro counted about 2,790,411 households with an average of 2.89 people per household.

In 2003 (Montenegro's last housing census) there were 125,000 dwellings in Montenegro with a total area of 8.3 million sq m (89.3 million sq ft). The average size of a dwelling was 67 sq m (721 sq ft), which came to 21.7 sq m (233 sq ft) per person. On average there were 3.1 individuals per dwelling. In 2010 there were 4,093 housing completions in Montenegro for a total increase in housing area of 293,000 sq m (3.15 million sq ft). The average cost of new housing was €1,272 ($1,704) per sq m.

43 EDUCATION

As of 2010, education is compulsory for nine years of primary school with a compulsory starting age of 6. This may be followed by three years of secondary school, with students having the option to attend general, vocational, or professional schools. The academic year runs from September to June.

The CIA estimated that Montenegro had a literacy rate of 96.4%. According to UNESCO data, in 2009, 30% of children younger than 6 were enrolled in preschool programs. UN data for 2010 indicates that 83% of age-eligible students were enrolled in primary school. Gross enrollment ratios for secondary education indicate that practically all age-eligible students are enrolled in secondary schools. It is estimated that about 96% of all students complete their primary education. Official Montenegrin statistics indicate that, in 2009–2010, there were 15.8 primary school students for every primary school teacher and 13.1 secondary school students for every secondary school teacher. In the same year there were 439 public primary schools and 49 public secondary schools operating in the country.

In Montenegro, elementary and secondary schools are managed by school boards, while principals are responsible for day-to-day administration. School boards and principals are appointed by the Ministry of Education and Science for four-year terms. Teachers must have a university degree and pass a professional (state) examination.

Montenegro currently has two universities including the public University of Montenegro (20 faculties) and private University Mediteran (6 faculties). In 2001, it was estimated that about 36% of the tertiary age population in Serbia and Montenegro was enrolled in tertiary education programs.

44 LIBRARIES AND MUSEUMS

According to Montenegro's Registry of Cultural Monuments, the country currently has 357 immovable (towns, buildings, monuments and other structures) cultural monuments. 22 museums contain 145 collections consisting of 92,513 objects of cultural importance. The Central National Library of Montenegro has 1.5 million volumes.

Culturally, Montenegro has been shaped by Mediterranean, middle European, Eastern European, and Asian civilizations. Archaeological treasures include Crvena Stijena (Red Rock), Bioce okapine (shelters) in the Moraca Canyon, and Malisina pecina (cave) and Medena stijena (rock) in the Cehotina Canyon.

Pre-Roman, Roman, Gothic, and Baroque architectural styles may be found. The city of Kotor is a UNESCO World Heritage site. The region of Lake Scutari (Skadarsko) has many monasteries built on goricas (small islands), including Beska, Moracnik, Starcevo, Kom, and Vranjina, along with the fortresses of Zabljak and Lesendro.

Islamic culture is evidenced in the Mosque of Husein-pasha Boljanic in Pljevlja, as well as in residential architecture (such as the Redzepagics' Manor in Plav).

Montenegro has a long literary and printing history, beginning in the 12th century. The town of Cetinje, which features a monastery of Cetinje and museum complex and Biljarda, built by Njegos as a residence in 1838, is recognized as a cultural capital. Other buildings in Cetinje include King Nikola's Palace, numerous embassies, Prince Heir's Palace, the Zetski dom theater, and the house of parliament.

Montenegro has a rich heritage of theater, film, poetry, prose, and painting.

45 MEDIA

In 2009 the CIA reported that there were 366,600 telephone landlines in Montenegro. In addition to landlines, mobile phone subscriptions averaged 120 per 100 people (752,000 cell phones in use). Internet users numbered 45 per 100 citizens. In 2010 there were 6,247 Internet hosts in the nation. In 2009, there were some 280,000 Internet users in Montenegro. According to official state statistics, in 2010, 32% of all households had a personal computer, 97% had a television and 64% had a radio.

According to the Agency for Electronic Media of Montenegro, in 2011 there were 23 television stations, 53 radio stations and a single news agency operating in the country. Commercial television stations included 777 TV Lutrija, NTV Orion, Srpska TV, TV APR, TV Boin, TV Ehoo, TV Glas Plava, TV Mojkovac, TV Pink M, TV Teuta, NTV Montena, PRO TV, TV IN, TV Atlas, TV Corona, TV Elmag, TV MBC, TV Panorama, TV Suna and TV Vijesti. Publicly owned stations included TV Budva, TV Nikšić and TV Pljevlja. Montenegro had 39 private and 14 publicly-owned radio stations. The news agency MNNews-Mina is private.

Print media in 2011 included 3 daily, 4 weekly and 40 monthly publications. The top three circulating newspapers were *Vijesti* (a private firm with a circulation of 26,000), *Dan* (private with a circulation of 25,000), and *Pobjeda* (state-owned with a circulation of 8,000).

In 2011 Montenegro held a USAID Media Sustainability score of 2.28 which placed it in the "Near Sustainability" range on a 0 (unsustainable, anti-free press) to 4 (sustainable) point scale. While media legislation met most international standards, enforcement remained selective and slow. Montenegro scored low on the professionalism of journalism with issues of bias and the sourcing of information at the forefront. The market remained varied in terms of alternative news sources, but financial constraints accompanying economic challenges was slowly shrinking the number of outlets. Finally trade associations were weak and fragmented thus undermining the ability of mass media to promote its interests.

46 ORGANIZATIONS

In 2009 there were close to 4,500 NGOs registered in Montenegro but only a few hundred were active. USAID reports that 2009 was marked by both setbacks and improvements in the local NGO environment. On the one hand, state harassment of NGOs increased as state officials utilized increasingly hostile rhetoric and sometimes resorted to legal action against NGOs critical of the government. Libel actions against media outlets and NGOs sometimes proved costly for resource-strapped civil society organizations. At the same time, NGOs took advantage of an increasing array of legal tools to force greater government transparency and protect themselves against government pressure. USAID noted further improvements in the NGO environment in 2010 indicating that the government and NGO were increasingly viewing one another as partners in the country's development. Financial sustainability is a continuing challenge as the majority of active NGOs remain dependent on foreign financial assistance. Sectoral infrastructure and public trust in the NGO sector is well developed but could be improved by establishing organizations to represent the sector as a whole and expanding the range of NGO-advocated issues which the public supports. Montenegro's 2007–2010 sustainability scores of 4.1 (on a scale from 0 [best] to 7 [worst]) placed it in second to last place for the Southern Tier countries (Albania, Bosnia, Bulgaria, Croatia, Kosovo, Macedonia, Montenegro, Romania and Serbia), just ahead of lowest-ranking Serbia.

47 TOURISM, TRAVEL, AND RECREATION

Rich architecture, museums, galleries, cathedrals, parks, rivers, and the many beaches are just some of the attractions that bring visitors to Montenegro. Montenegro has four national parks; the largest are the Lake of Skadar (Skadarsko) Basin (40,000 hectares/98,800 acres) and Durmitor (39,000 hectares/96,300 acres). Montenegro has two UNESCO natural area and heritage sites: Mt. Durmitor and the old city of Kotor. Popular sports in Montenegro are tennis, football, volleyball, water sports, bocanje (a kind of bowling), skiing, and rafting. The Ministry of Sports of the Montenegrin government was founded in 1993. There are numerous sand and pebble beaches on the Montenegrin coastline. It is one of the warmest and sunniest tourist regions in Europe. Although classified as a Mediterranean country, Montenegro is a mountainous region in which areas of 1,000 m (3,280.8 ft) or higher comprise 60.5% of the nation's territory.

Nationals from most European Countries, North America and Oceania may travel and stay in Montenegro for up to 90 days without a visa. Nationals of the Republic of Albania, the Russian Federation and the Republic of Ukraine may enter and stay in Montenegro with a tourist visa issued at the border. These visas are free of charge, and are valid for 30 days. Serbian nationals can enter and stay in Montenegro under the same conditions as Montenegrin citizens.

After independence, Montenegro continued to focus on its tourism industry. The *Tourism Factbook*, published by the UN World Tourism Organization, reported 1.04 million incoming tourists to Montenegro in 2009, who spent a total of $705 million. Of those incoming tourists, there were 1 million from Europe. There were 43,786 hotel beds available in Montenegro, which had an occupancy rate of 17%. The estimated daily cost to visit Podgorica, the capital, was $381. In 2008, it was estimated that 26.4% of Montenegro's GDP came from tourism and tourism related industries.

⁴⁸FAMOUS PERSONS

Prince Danilo II of Montenegro (r. 1851–60) introduced a new legal code in 1855 that guaranteed civil and religious freedoms. King Nikola I Petrović Njegoš (1841–1921) was the only king of Montenegro, reigning as a king from 1910 to 1918 and as a prince from 1860 to 1910. He was also a poet who wrote "Onamo, 'namo," the popular anthem of Montenegro. King Alexander of Yugoslavia (1888–1934) was assassinated in Marseille, France. Prince Paul of Yugoslavia (1893–1976) ruled as a regent for Peter II (1923–70) from 1934 to 1941 and was forced into exile after signing a secret pact with the Nazi government.

Important Montenegrin poets of the 20th century include Risto Ratkovic and Radovan Ziogovic. Important prose writers include Mihailo Lalic, whose realistic novels portray Montenegro's place in World War II. Painters include Petar Lubarda, Milo Milunovic, Dado Djuric, Branko Filipovic-Filo, Vojo Stanic, and Uros Toskovic.

⁴⁹DEPENDENCIES

Montenegro has no dependencies or territories.

⁵⁰BIBLIOGRAPHY

Bennett, Christopher. *Yugoslavia's Bloody Collapse: Causes, Course and Consequences*. London: Hurst and Company, 1995.

Deliso, Christopher. *Culture and Customs of Serbia and Montenegro*. Westport, CT: Greenwood Press, 2009.

Fleming, Thomas. *Montenegro: The Divided Land*. San Francisco: Chronicle Books, 2002.

Frucht, Richard, ed. *Eastern Europe: An Introduction to the People, Lands, and Culture*. Santa Barbara, CA: ABC-CLIO, 2005.

Houston, Marco. *Nikola and Milena, King and Queen of the Black Mountain: The Rise and Fall of Montenegro's Royal Family*. London: Leppi Publications, 2003.

International Smoking Statistics: A Collection of Historical Data from 30 Economically Developed Countries. New York: Oxford University Press, 2002.

Judah, Tim. *The Serbs: History, Myth, and the Destruction of Yugoslavia*. New Haven, CT: Yale University Press, 1997.

Klemencic, Matjaz. *The Former Yugoslavia's Diverse Peoples: A Reference Sourcebook*. Santa Barbara, CA: ABC-Clio, 2003.

Lampe, John R. *Yugoslavia as History: Twice There Was a Country*. New York: Cambridge University Press, 1996.

Malešević, Siniša. *Ideology, Legitimacy, and the New State: Yugoslavia, Serbia, and Croatia*. Portland, OR: Frank Cass, 2002.

Ramet, Sabrina P. *Balkan Babel: The Disintegration of Yugoslavia from the Death of Tito to Ethnic War*. 4th ed. Boulder, CO: Westview, 1996.

Schuman, Michael. *Serbia and Montenegro*. 2nd ed. New York: Facts On File, 2004.

Stevenson, Francis Seymour. *A History of Montenegro*. Boston: Adamant Media Corporation, 2002.

Terterov, Marat, ed. *Doing Business with Serbia and Montenegro*. Sterling, Va.: Kogan Page, 2004.

International Smoking Statistics: A Collection of Historical Data from 30 Economically Developed Countries. New York: Oxford University Press, 2002.

Judah, Tim. *The Serbs: History, Myth, and the Destruction of Yugoslavia*. New Haven, Conn.: Yale University Press, 1997.

Klemencic, Matjaz. *The Former Yugoslavia's Diverse Peoples: A Reference Sourcebook*. Oxford, Eng.: ABC-Clio, 2003.

Lampe, John R. *Yugoslavia as History: Twice There Was a Country*. New York: Cambridge University Press, 1996.

Malešević, Siniša. *Ideology, Legitimacy, and the New State: Yugoslavia, Serbia, and Croatia*. Portland, Ore.: Frank Cass, 2002.

Pavkovic, Aleksandar. *The Fragmentation of Yugoslavia: Nationalism in a Multinational State*. New York: St. Martin's, 1997.

Ramet, Sabrina P. *Balkan Babel: The Disintegration of Yugoslavia from the Death of Tito to Ethnic War*. Boulder, Colo.: Westview, 1996.

Schuman, Michael. *Serbia and Montenegro*. 2nd ed. New York: Facts On File, 2004.

Stevenson, Francis Seymour. *A History of Montenegro*. Boston: Adamant Media Corporation, 2002.

Terterov, Marat (ed.). *Doing Business with Serbia and Montenegro*. Sterling, Va.: Kogan Page, 2004.

Treadway, John D. *The Falcon and the Eagle: Montenegro and Austria-Hungary, 1908-1914*. West Lafayette, Ind: Purdue University Press, 1983.

West, Richard. *Tito: And the Rise and Fall of Yugoslavia*. New York: Carroll and Graf, 1995.

NETHERLANDS

Kingdom of the Netherlands
Koninkrijk der Nederlanden

CAPITAL: Constitutional capital: Amsterdam. Seat of government: The Hague (*'S Gravenhage; Den Haag*).

FLAG: The national flag, standardized in 1937, is a tricolor of red, white, and blue horizontal stripes.

ANTHEM: *Wilhelmus van Nassouwen (William of Nassau)*.

MONETARY UNIT: The guilder was replaced by the euro as official currency in 2002. The euro is divided into 100 cents. There are coins in denominations of 1, 2, 5, 10, 20, and 50 cents and 1 euro and 2 euros. There are notes of 5, 10, 20, 50, 100, 200, and 500 euros. €1 = US$1.3802 (or US$1 = €0.7245) as of 2011.

WEIGHTS AND MEASURES: The metric system is the legal standard.

HOLIDAYS: New Year's Day, 1 January; Queen's Day, 30 April; National Liberation Day, 5 May; Christmas, 25–26 December. Movable religious holidays include Good Friday, Holy Saturday, Easter Monday, Ascension, and Whitmonday.

TIME: 1 p.m. = noon GMT.

¹LOCATION, SIZE, AND EXTENT

Situated in northwestern Europe, the Netherlands has a total area of 41,543 sq km (16,040 sq mi), of which inland water accounts for more than 7,650 sq km (2,954 sq mi). The land area is 33,893 sq km (13,086 sq mi). Comparatively, the Netherlands is slightly less than twice the size of New Jersey. The Netherlands extends 312 km (194 mi) N–S and 264 km (164 mi) E–W. The land area increases slightly each year as a result of continuous land reclamation and drainage. The Netherlands is bounded on the E by Germany, on the S by Belgium, and on the W and N by the North Sea, with a total boundary length of 1,027 km (638 mi), of which 451 km (280 mi) is coastline.

The capital city of the Netherlands, Amsterdam, is in the western part of the country.

²TOPOGRAPHY

The country falls into three natural topographical divisions: the dunes, the lowlands or *"polders"* (low-lying land reclaimed from the sea and from lakes and protected by dikes), and the higher, eastern section of the country. About 27% of the land lies below sea level. A long range of sand dunes on the western coast protects the low alluvial land to the east from the high tides of the North Sea, and farther east and southeast are found diluvial sand and gravel soil. The highest point of land, the Vaalserberg, is situated in the extreme south and is 322 m (1,056 ft) above sea level; the lowest point, 7 m (23 ft) below sea level, is Zuidplaspolder, an area of reclaimed land situated to the west of Gouda. The most extensive polder is that of East Flevoland in the province of Flevoland; it has an area of nearly 55,000 hectares (136,000 acres). Many dikes have been constructed along the lower Rhine and Meuse (Maas) rivers, as well as on a portion of the North Sea coast and along nearly the whole of the coast of the former Zuider Zee (formally called the Ijsselmeer since its enclosure by a dike in 1932). There are many canals in the country, most of which have numerous locks.

³CLIMATE

The Netherlands has a maritime climate, with cool summers and mild winters. The average temperature is 2°C (36°F) in January and 17°C (62°F) in July, with an annual average of about 9°C (49°F). Clouds generally appear every day, and in the winter months fog often abounds, while rainfall occurs frequently. Average annual rainfall is about 76.5 cm (30 in). The mild, damp climate is ideal for dairying and livestock raising, but the limited sunshine restricts the growing of food crops.

⁴FLORA AND FAUNA

Plants and animals that thrive in temperate climates are found in the Netherlands. The World Resources Institute estimates that there are 1,221 plant species in the Netherlands. The most common trees are oak, elm, pine, linden, and beech. The country is famous for its flowers, both cultivated varieties (best known among them the Dutch tulip) and wild flowers such as daisies, buttercups, and the purple heather that blooms on the heaths in September. In addition, the World Resources Institute approximates that the Netherlands is home to 95 mammal, 444 bird, 13 reptile, and 17 amphibian species. The calculation reflects the total number of distinct species residing in the country, not the number of endemic species. Birds are those characteristic of Western and Central Europe, with large numbers of seagulls swarming over the coastal areas from time to time. Many kinds of fish abound along the North Sea coast and in the lakes and rivers. Wild or large animals are practically nonexistent.

⁵ENVIRONMENT

In recent years, as a result of rapid population and economic growth, the government has placed increased emphasis on pres-

LOCATION: 50°45' to 53°52'N; 3°21' to 7°13' E. BOUNDARY LENGTHS: Germany, 577 kilometers (358 miles); Belgium, 450 kilometers (280 miles); North Sea coastline, 451 kilometers (280 miles). TERRITORIAL SEA LIMIT: 12 miles.

ervation of the natural environment. One key concern is the pressure put on the countryside, traditionally the domain of the smallholder, by the demands of modern mechanized agriculture and the needs of a large urban population for recreational areas and waste disposal. To help solve this environmental problem, the government has instituted comprehensive land-use planning by means of a system of zoning that indicates the priorities for land use in each zone. Air and water pollution are significant environmental problems in the Netherlands.

The nation has one of the world's highest levels of industrial carbon dioxide emissions, which, according to the United Nations (UN), totaled 173,102 kilotons in 2008. Efforts to control air pollution reduced sulphur dioxide emissions between 1980 and 1990 from 490,000 tons to 240,000 tons. Severe pollution of the country's rivers results from industrial and agricultural pollution, including heavy metals, organic compounds, nitrates, and phosphates.

Solid waste in the nation's cities has been reported at an average of 7.6 million tons yearly. Aggravating the situation are the prevailing southwesterly winds, which carry the pollutants from coastal industries inland, and the great rivers that carry pollution into the Netherlands from originating countries farther inland.

Water resources in the Netherlands totaled 89.7 cu km (21.52 cu mi) in 2008, while water usage was 8.86 cu km (2.13 cu mi) per year. Domestic water usage accounted for 6% of total usage, industrial for 60%, and agricultural for 34%. Per capita water usage totaled 544 cu m (19,211 cu ft) per year.

In 1971, the Ministry of Health and Environment was established; a countrywide system of air pollution monitoring by the National Institute of Public Health has been in place since 1975. Since the mid-1970s, discharges of heavy metals into industrial wastewater and emissions of most major air pollutants from industrial use of fossil fuels have been substantially reduced. Progress has also been recorded in reducing automotive emissions. An excise tax surcharge on gasoline and diesel fuel was imposed to abate pollution in 1981.

The World Resources Institute reported that the Netherlands had designated 430,000 hectares (1.06 million acres) of land for protection as of 2006. Protected areas included 49 Ramsar Wetland Sites. According to a 2011 report issued by the International Union for Conservation of Nature and Natural Resources (IUCN), threatened species included 4 mammals, 2 birds, 13 fish, 4 mollusks, and 5 other invertebrates. Endangered species include Atlantic sturgeon, slender-billed curlew, Atlantic ridley, and Spengler's freshwater mussel.

6 POPULATION

The US Central Intelligence Agency (CIA) estimated the population of the Netherlands in 2011 to be approximately 16,847,007, which placed it at number 60 in population among the 196 nations of the world. Approximately 15.6% of the population was over 65 years of age, with another 17% under 15 years of age. The median age in the Netherlands was 41.1 years. There were 0.98 males for every female in the country. The population's annual rate of change was 0.371%. According to the UN, the projected population for the year 2025 was 16,571,000. Population density in the Netherlands was calculated at 494 people per sq km (1,279 people per sq mi).

The UN estimated that 83% of the population lived in urban areas, with an annual rate of change of 0.8%. The largest urban areas, along with their respective populations, included Amsterdam, 1 million; Rotterdam, 1 million; and The Hague, 629,000.

7 MIGRATION

Estimates of the Netherlands's net migration rate, carried out by the CIA in 2011, amounted to 2.33 migrants per 1,000 citizens. The total number of emigrants living abroad was 993,400, and the total number of immigrants living in the Netherlands was 1.75 million. In the past, although the government encouraged emigration to curb overpopulation, more people migrated to the Neth-

erlands than have left the country. Rapid economic growth in the 1960s drew many unskilled laborers from Mediterranean countries, and, during the 1970s, many people left Suriname for the Netherlands when the former Dutch colony became independent. At first, both groups settled mainly in the western region, but, after 1970, the pattern of internal migration changed, as increasing numbers left the western provinces to settle in the east and south. The traditional pattern of migration from the countryside to the cities has likewise been altered, and, since the 1970s, the trend has been largely from the larger cities to small towns and villages. By 2003, it was becoming harder for asylum migrants to find work. In addition, in 2004, employer groups asked that the admission of skilled foreigner workers be streamlined.

In 2010, some 121,351 persons left the Netherlands. In the same year, 154,432 immigrants arrived in the Netherlands. In 2003, for the first time since 1982, there were more emigrants (104,800) than immigrants (104,500). In that same year, the percent of foreign-born was distributed as follows: 17.6% from Africa (mainly Morocco); 21.2% from the Americas (mainly from the Netherlands Antilles and South America); 34.3% from Asia (mainly from Indonesia); and 26.1% from Europe (with Germans the largest group). However, the large numbers of migrants from the Antilles has been decreasing, while emigration to these countries has increased.

After the election of a conservative government in 2002, the Dutch integration policy of multiculturalism (where all cultures were considered of equal value and there was no need for foreigners to integrate into Dutch society) was eroded with new policies requiring that immigrants pass a test of Dutch language and culture. After the death of filmmaker Theo Van Gogh in 2004 at the hands of a Dutch-born man of Moroccan descent, a law was passed that made being a member of a "terrorist" organization a crime. By 2005, new policies included integration exams for foreign residents under age 65 with less than eight years of schooling in the Netherlands. Mandatory Dutch language exams were also instituted. As of 2012, the Dutch government continued to push strong anti-immigration policies, which included the introduction of a quota for deportations—4,800 illegal immigrants in 2012, a 10% increase over the 2011 quota. Many local authorities voiced opposition to the quota, arguing that it would disrupt the fabric of their communities by breaking apart families.

At the beginning of 1996, there were 72,000 recognized refugees and 23,000 applications for asylum. In 1999, 4,060 people were evacuated from Macedonia to the Netherlands. Following the trend in the 25 countries of the European Union (EU), the Netherlands, in 2004, had the lowest number of asylum seekers since 1988. In 2011, as many as 11,030 asylum applications were submitted.

8 ETHNIC GROUPS

The Dutch are an ethnically homogeneous people descended from Frankish, Saxon, and Frisian tribes. Ethnic homogeneity slightly changed as a result of the arrival of some 300,000 repatriates and immigrants from Indonesia, mostly Eurasian, and more than 140,000 from Suriname. The influx of Turks and other workers from the Mediterranean area has further added to the ethnic mix. Estimates from 2008 indicate that about 80.7% of the total population are Dutch; the principal minority groups are Indonesian

(2.4%), Turkish (2.2%), Moroccan (2%), Surinamese (2%), and Antillean (Caribbean, 0.8%).

9 LANGUAGES

Dutch and Frisian are the official languages. Frisian, the native language of about 300,000 people, is closely related to the Anglo-Saxon tongue but has many points in common with Dutch, which belongs to the Germanic language group. There are six Dutch dialects. Many Netherlanders speak and understand English, French, and German, which are taught in secondary schools.

10 RELIGIONS

Dutch society is becoming increasingly secular. According to the Social Cultural Planning Bureau, church membership steadily declined from 76% in 1958 to 30% in 2006. Only about 16% of those claiming a religious affiliation attended services regularly. A 2006 report from the national Scientific Council for government policy indicated that an estimated 43.4% of the population were nominally Christians (including Roman Catholics, Dutch Reformed, Baptists, Lutherans, Anglicans, and Remonstrants), 5.7% were Muslim, and 2.3% other (Hindu, Jewish, or Buddhist).

11 TRANSPORTATION

Merchant shipping has always been of great economic importance to the seagoing Dutch. The Netherlands Maritime Institute is internationally famous, and the Dutch ship-testing station at Wageningen is known for its research in marine engineering. The Dutch merchant marine had 706 ships of 1,000 gross register tonnage (GRT) or over in 2011. Emphasis has been placed on the development of new vessels suitable for container transport and on improving the Dutch tanker fleet. Rotterdam is the Netherlands' chief port and Europe's largest. There are also ports and harbors at Amsterdam, Delfzijl, Dordrecht, Eemshaven, Groningen, Haarlem, Ijmuiden, Maastricht, Terneuzen, and Utrecht.

Out of all of the Netherlands' navigable waterways, 6,214 km (3,861 mi) are canals and are capable of handling vessels of up to 50 tons.

The CIA reports that the Netherlands has a total of 136,827 km (85,020 mi) of roads. There are 515 vehicles per 1,000 people in the country. Railroads extend for 2,886 km (1,793 mi). This railway system in 2011 consisted in part of 2,195 km (1,364 mi) of electrified rail. Passenger transport on railways is subsidized as part of the national policy for promoting public transport. Public transport is provided for urban areas by municipal and regional transport companies, and minibus service in rural areas ensures public transport for all towns with 1,000 residents or more. The state subsidizes the construction of urban and rural cycle paths.

In 2011, there were 27 airports (20 with paved runways). There was also one heliport. Principal airports include Schiphol at Amsterdam, Reina Beatrix at Aruba, and Hato at Curaçao. Dutch airports transported 29.11 million passengers in 2009, according to the World Bank. The world's first airline from the standpoint of continuous corporate existence and operation is Royal Dutch Airlines (Koninklijke Luchtvaart Maatschappij—KLM), which began regularly scheduled operations in 1920. The Netherlands government owns a large part of the outstanding capital stock. KLM serves some 115 cities in 70 countries.

12 HISTORY

In about 55 BC, Julius Caesar conquered a large part of the lowlands near the mouths of the Rhine and Meuse (Maas) rivers that was populated by Celtic and Germanic tribes. To the north of the Rhine delta, several Germanic tribes had settled, among which the Batavi and the Frisians were the most important. The Batavi served with the Roman legions until they rebelled in AD 70, but even after the revolt was quelled, Batavian soldiers fought for Rome. About 300 years later, successive waves of powerful Germanic tribes, such as the Salic or West Franks, invaded this region, called the Low Countries, and gradually pushed the Frisians back to the east coast of the North Sea except in the extreme northern section of the mainland where Saxons had settled. By the time of Charlemagne (742–814), the Saxons and Frisians had been completely conquered by the West Franks, and the Frankish language had replaced the languages of the Germanic tribes.

Soon after the death of Charlemagne and the disintegration of his realm, several duchies and counties were founded in the Low Countries by local leaders. With the coming of the Middle Ages, Holland (now the North and South Holland provinces) became the most important region and extended its power and territory under Count Floris V (r. 1256–96). The ancient bishopric of Utrecht was another important principality. As the Middle Ages drew to a close, individual cities such as Amsterdam, Haarlem, and Groningen rose to eminence, together with the Duchy of Gelderland. In the 15th century, the dukes of Burgundy acquired, by various means, most of the Low Countries. Upon the extinction of the male line of the Burgundian dynasty and the marriage of Mary of Burgundy and Archduke (later Emperor) Maximilian I in 1477, however, the Austrian house of Habsburg fell heir to the lands.

The Habsburgs

Mary's son, Philip of Habsburg, married Joanna of Castile, heiress to the Spanish throne. Their son, Charles, became King Charles I of Spain in 1516 and Holy Roman Emperor Charles V in 1519. In 1547, he decreed the formal union of the Netherlands and Austria, and in 1549, the union of the Netherlands and Spain. By the end of his reign in 1555, he was master of the Low Countries. His son, Philip II, concentrated his efforts to aggrandize Spain. To bring the Low Countries under his direct control, he tried to stamp out the rising force of Protestantism and suppressed the political, economic, and religious liberties long cherished by the population. As a result, both Roman Catholics and Protestants rebelled against him under the leadership of William the Silent, prince of Orange, who by marriage had acquired large properties in the Netherlands.

For 10 years, the 17 provinces comprising the Low Countries united in a common revolt. Much of the area was freed in 1577, with William as the acknowledged ruler, but not even his moderation and statesmanship sufficed to keep the northern and southern provinces united. In 1578, the southern region (now Belgium) began to turn against William. In 1579, the northern provinces concluded the Union of Utrecht, in which the province of Holland was the most prominent. The Union, or United Provinces, carried on the fight against Spain, and William was the soul of the resistance until his assassination in 1584. William's son Maurits, governor (*stadtholder*) of the republic from 1584 to 1624, carried on a successful campaign against Spain, but final recognition of Dutch independence by the Spanish government was not obtained until the end of the Eighty Years' War with the Treaty of Westphalia (1648). Meanwhile, the southern provinces remained loyal to Spain and to the Roman Catholic Church and were thereafter known as the Spanish Netherlands.

Independence brought mixed success in the 17th century for the United Provinces. Dutch prosperity was nourished by settlements and colonies in the East Indies, India, South Africa, the West Indies, South America, and elsewhere. The government was oligarchic but based on republican and federative principles. The Dutch were noted for their religious freedom, welcoming religious refugees—Spanish and Portuguese Jews, French Huguenots, and English Pilgrims.

While the Netherlands became a leading commercial and maritime power, external economic and military threats and controversy over the leadership complicated political and economic stability. Trade and territory disagreements with England resulted in the First Anglo-Dutch War, which began in 1652 but ended with the Treaty of Westminster in 1654. The English were quick to attack again, beginning the Second Anglo-Dutch War, which ended with successful Dutch attacks but also in the loss of colonial possession in North America—the area that now surrounds New York City—via a trade-off under the 1667 Treaty of Breda.

Arts, sciences, literature, and philosophy flourished alongside trade and banking during the Dutch "golden era." In 1672, however, England declared war on the Republic, igniting the Third Anglo-Dutch War; France, Münster, and Cologne soon followed in their own attack. The new *stadtholder* William III rose out of what is known as the "Disastrous Year" to triumphantly end the war with England in 1674 and lead a coalition against the aggressive France of Louis XIV. William III (r. 1672–1702), great-grandson of William the Silent and grandson of the English King Charles I and his English wife, Mary, were invited by the English Parliament to occupy the British throne in 1688, but they continued to take a keen interest in Dutch affairs. The Dutch republic of which William had been governor survived for nearly a century after his death. Its position was continually threatened, however, by intense rivalries among and within the provinces. Four naval wars with Britain from the middle of the 17th century to the end of the 18th also sapped Dutch strength. In 1795, a much-weakened republic was overrun by revolutionary French armies.

After the brief Napoleonic occupation, the great powers of Europe at the Congress of Vienna (1814–15) set up a new kingdom of the Netherlands, composed of the former United Provinces and the former Spanish or Austrian Netherlands, and installed a prince of the house of Orange as King William I. The constitution that was founded in 1814 was last revised in 1983. In 1830, a revolt by the southern provinces resulted in the establishment of the kingdom of Belgium. Thereafter, the much-reduced kingdom was mainly concerned with domestic problems, such as the school conflict over secular versus religious instruction, social problems stemming from the industrialization of the country, and electoral reforms.

In foreign affairs, relations with Belgium were gradually improved after a decade of war and tension following Belgian independence, and Dutch claims to the principality of Luxembourg ended with the death of William III in 1890.

The World Wars to the Present

Foreign policies based on neutrality successfully met their test in World War I. Although the Netherlands mobilized their army, the country remained neutral, even as the Germans invaded Belgium and all the surrounding states were at war.

The Netherlands again declared their neutrality when World War II erupted in 1939. Neutrality was preserved until the German World War II war machine overran the country in May 1940. Queen Wilhelmina (r. 1890–1948) refused to surrender to the Germans and instead fled to Britain with other officials of her government. Although Dutch resistance lasted only five days, destruction was widespread: nearly the whole of downtown Rotterdam was wiped out, and the cities of Arnhem and Nijmegen suffered great damage. In addition, Dutch factory equipment was carried away to Germany, bridges and railroads were blown up or removed, cattle were stolen, and part of the land was flooded. The Dutch withstood severe repression until their liberation by Allied forces in May 1945. Wilhelmina abdicated in 1948 and was succeeded by her daughter, Juliana (r. 1948–80).

The East Indies, most of which had been under Dutch rule for over 300 years, were invaded by Japanese forces in January 1942. After Japanese troops continued through the territory, the Dutch surrendered in March when the Japanese arrived in Java. In 1945, a group of Indonesians proclaimed an independent republic and resisted Dutch reoccupation. After four years of hostilities and following UN intervention, the Netherlands recognized the independence of Indonesia in December 1949. Suriname (formerly Dutch Guiana), controlled by the Netherlands since 1815, became an independent nation on 25 November 1975. This Dutch colonial legacy was the root cause of several violent outbreaks during the late 1970s, as a group of South Moluccans, a few of the 40,000 Moluccans living in the Netherlands, used terrorism on Dutch soil to dramatize their demand for the independence of the South Molucca Islands from Indonesia. The Netherlands continues to hold several Caribbean possessions.

As they did for many western countries, the 1960s and 1970s brought extensive cultural and social change. Traditional class and religious lines that had supported separate education and social status were erased, leading to significant change for women's rights, sexuality, economic, and environmental issues.

Reform of the social security system was the major political issue in the 1990s, along with efforts to reduce public spending. Years of administrative tinkering with the social security system reduced the number of claimants, increased labor force participation, and generated a central government budget surplus of 1% of gross domestic product (GDP) in 2000. The budget surplus prompted heated cabinet discussions as the Labor Party wished to use the extra money for redistribution while the neo-liberal conservatives hoped to lower tax rates. Buoyant growth rates of more than 3% in the period during 1996–2001 brought down the official unemployment level to 2.7%. However, the global economic downturn that began in 2001 contributed to the Netherlands' shrinking economy in late 2002 and early 2003. The government also passed a number of radical social measures that received parliamentary approval in recent years, including conditions for administering euthanasia, legalization of prostitution, legalization of gay marriages, and laws banning discrimination.

A founder of the European Coal and Steel Community, the Netherlands became part of the Economic and Monetary Union and strongly supports an independent European central bank, low inflation, and stable currency. It hosted two different intergovernmental conferences of the European Union and chaired the finalization of the Treaty of European Union (Maastricht Treaty) in 1991 and the Amsterdam Treaty in 1997. However, in a referendum held on 1 June 2005, Dutch voters rejected the proposed European Union constitution days after French voters in a referendum rejected the treaty. The Dutch vote was 61.5% against and 38.5% for the constitution.

In May 2002, Pim Fortuyn, an anti-immigration political party leader, was assassinated by a single gunman. His party, List Pim Fortuyn, came in second in the 15 May 2002 parliamentary elections. The conservative Christian Democrats, led by Jan Peter Balkenende, came in first, and Balkenende became prime minister of a center-right coalition government. In October, Balkenende's government collapsed following disagreements within the List Pim Fortuyn Party. Elections were held on 22 January 2003, and the Christian Democrats narrowly defeated the Labor Party in the Second Chamber. After 125 days, a coalition government was formed comprising the Christian Democrats, the free-market liberal People's Party for Freedom and Democracy, and the socially liberal Democrats.

The Netherlands gave political support to the military action taken by the United States and United Kingdom against Saddam Hussein's regime in Iraq in 2003. Although the Netherlands has a history of open immigration and integration, the increased controversies in Europe surrounding Islamic fundamentalism and immigration have plagued it as well. On 2 November 2004, a member of a Dutch-Moroccan Islamic youth group assassinated filmmaker and publicist Theo van Gogh. In November 2006, the Dutch cabinet supported plans to outlaw the burka—the full body and face covering for women—in public places; legislation was still pending as of early 2012.

Queen Juliana abdicated in 1980 in favor of her daughter, Beatrix. Juliana died on 20 March 2004. In 1966, Beatrix married Claus von Amsberg, a German diplomat, and his title remained Prince of the Netherlands when Beatrix became Queen. Their firstborn son and Crown Prince, Willem-Alexander, was born in 1967. Beatrix and Claus von Amsberg had two other sons, Johan Friso and Constantijn, before Prince Claus's death in 2002. Prince Willem-Alexander has two daughters with his wife, Princess Máxima: Princess Catharina-Amalia was born 7 June 2003, and Princess Alexia was born 26 June 2005.

In February 2006, the Dutch parliament agreed to send an additional 1,400 troops to join NATO-led forces in southern Afghanistan. The decision came after weeks of negotiations and international pressure. In November 2006, the government ordered an inquiry into reports that its troops had tortured prisoners in Iraq in 2003. In 2010, after much debate, the Dutch ended their mission in Afghanistan.

In June–July 2006, Prime Minister Balkenende formed a temporary minority government after his coalition collapsed in a disagreement over immigration, precipitating early elections in November. In February 2007, Balkenende was sworn in as head of a three-party centrist coalition after the general elections in November.

In the midst of the 2008–09 global financial crisis, the Dutch bank DSB came under national scrutiny for its money-lending policies. In a televised interview in October 2009, an official representing the Mortgage Grievances Foundation encouraged account holders with DSB to close their accounts in protest of the bank's aggressive lending practices, through which many customers were reportedly offered loans in excess of what they could afford to repay. Within hours after the broadcast, a run on the bank began. A few days later, over a quarter of the bank's assets had been withdrawn by customers, leading the bank first into receivership, then bankruptcy. The Dutch government deposit guarantee program covers account holders for about $147,860 (€100,000), but payments to customers were not expected to be immediately available. Bank owner Dick Sheringa claimed foul play and called for a parliamentary inquiry into the matter. A few days before the run, Scheringa's Museum of Realist Art, displaying a collection of over 130 paintings, was seized by ABN Amro Bank as collateral for $48 million in unpaid loans made to Scheringa. Scheringa also lost his ownership of the Alkmaar football club AZ.

In February 2010, Prime Minister Balkenende's fourth cabinet collapsed in a disagreement over the Dutch presence in Afghanistan, precipitating early elections in June. In October 2010, Mark Rutte was sworn in as head of a two-party minority coalition, with symbolic support from Geert Wilders' far-right "Party for Freedom".

¹³GOVERNMENT

The Netherlands is a constitutional monarchy, under the house of Orange-Nassau. The monarch and the Council of Ministers together are called the Crown and are the center of executive power. The prime minister is the active head of government, a member of the Council of Ministers, the head of the cabinet, and usually the leader of the largest party within the ruling party coalition. Executive power is also shared with the cabinet, which must have majority support in the parliament. Cabinet ministers may not be members of the parliament. The Council of State, instituted as an advisory body for the government in 1532, is appointed by and presided over by the monarch. It is composed of a vice president, councilors (28 maximum), and honorary members (25 maximum). The council considers all legislation proposed by the sovereign or the cabinet before it is submitted to the parliament. While functioning in an advisory capacity, the council has executive powers when it implements orders of the sovereign, and it has judiciary powers when it acts in disputes and citizen appeals concerning the government.

Legislative power is exercised jointly by the crown and the States-General (Staten-Generaal), a bicameral parliament. The upper house (Eerste Kamer) consists of 75 members elected for four years by the provincial representative councils on the basis of proportional representation. The lower house (Tweede Kamer) has 150 members elected for four years directly by the people, also on the basis of proportional representation. Only the lower house has the right to introduce bills and to move amendments, but the upper house can accept or reject bills passed by the other chamber.

All Dutch citizens who have reached the age of 18 years and reside within the Netherlands have the right to vote. All citizens who have reached the age of 18 years are eligible for election to the States-General.

Every year on the third Tuesday in September, the session of the States-General is opened at the Hague by the monarch. In the speech from the throne, the government's program for the year is announced. The monarch acts as an adviser to the cabinet, may propose bills, and signs all bills approved by the legislature. Theoretically, she could refuse to sign a bill, but this never occurs in practice because the cabinet is responsible for the actions of the ruler. Thus, if the queen should refuse to sign a bill, the cabinet must resign and she must then find a new cabinet acceptable to the parliament.

Immediately following elections, the monarch appoints a formateur to help determine the program and composition of the new cabinet and to form the Council of Ministers. If the formateur fails to bring together a new ministry, a new formateur is appointed, and so on, until a new cabinet has been formed.

¹⁴POLITICAL PARTIES

Throughout the political history of the Netherlands, religion has played an important role. During World War II, strenuous efforts were made to reduce this role, but denominational parties continued to exercise considerable influence. However, since the mid-1960s, the general trend has been toward the polarization of politics into conservative and progressive parties, and denominational parties have lost voter support.

The religious political party with the largest membership throughout the postwar period was the Catholic People's Party (Katholieke Volkspartij—KVP), which favored democratic government and a middle-of-the-road social policy. It began to lose votes in the 1960s, and the KVP joined the Anti-Revolutionary Party (Anti-Revolutionaire Partij—ARP) and the right-wing Christian Historical Union (Christelijk-Historische Unie—CHU) to form the Christian Democratic Appeal (Christen-Democratisch Appèl—CDA) and contest the 1977 elections; the CDA has since been a major political force. The Labor Party (Partij van de Arbeid—PvdA) vied for political leadership with the KVP in the first decades of the postwar period, polling about the same number of votes in national elections until 1972, when the PvdA won a plurality of nearly 25% of the total vote and emerged as the dominant member of a centrist coalition government. A social democratic party that resulted from the merger of three socialist and liberal parties, the Labor Party has appealed mainly to national interests rather than to socialist ones, although it does favor redistribution and solidarity. Since 1986, it has pursued de-radicalization and has moved to the political center. The conservative People's Party for Freedom and Democracy (Volkspartij voor Vrijheid en Democratie—VVD) advocates free enterprise, separation of church and state, and individual liberties.

Since 1965, discontent with the major political parties and erosion of party discipline have led to the establishment of change-oriented parties like Democrats 66 (Democraten 66—D66), which pushes for greater democratic accountability, political transparency, and involvement of the citizen in the policy process. Smaller parties include the left-wing Green Left (GroenLinks—GL), which is the product of a merger of socialist and ecology parties in 1991. Three small social conservative Calvinist parties have been at the heart of much political debate and change in the end of the 20th and beginning of the 21st century: the Political Reformed Party (Staatkundig Gereformeerde Partij—SGP), which was de-

nied state funding in 2005 for prohibiting women from becoming full members, and the Reformed Political Union (Gereformeerd Politiek Verbond—GPV) and the Reformatorian Political Federation (Reformatorische Politieke Federation—RPF), which merged in 2001 to form the far-right Christian Union (ChristenUnie), a party that combines fundamental religious values on abortion, gay marriage, and euthanasia with socially democratic views on economic, immigration, and environmental issues.

As no single party commands a majority in the States-General, the governing cabinet is a coalition of various party representatives, according to their numerical strength. In 1994, for the first time in 80 years, a coalition emerged that did not include a confessional party. The Labor Party won a plurality of votes in spite of an absolute loss of votes. Its closest ally, D66, absolutely refused to join a coalition government with the Christian Democrats. In 1994 the first "purple" cabinet emerged, led by Wim Kok of the Labor Party, and was composed of D66 and the VVD. In 1998, the government fell after D66 failed to push through parliament a bill to make more use of referendums. A month later, in June 1998, voters brought back the purple coalition and Kok led another government of VVD, D66, and PvdA.

Willem Kok initially let it be known in various interviews that he would stand again in the 2002 election, greatly increasing the likelihood of another four years of Labor Party leadership. However, in April 2002, Kok's government resigned following an official report criticizing its role in the 1995 Srebrenica massacre in the former Yugoslavia, when some 100 lightly armed Dutch peacekeepers failed to stop Bosnian Serb forces from murdering around 7,000 Muslims.

Elections were held on 15 May 2002 and resulted in a victory for the Christian Democrats. A surprise showing was made by the List Pim Fortuyn (LPF), a political party formed just a month earlier by the anti-immigrant politician Pim Fortuyn. Fortuyn was assassinated just prior to the election, but his party came in second. Labor, the VVD, and D66 all suffered losses. Christian Democratic leader Jan Peter Balkenende became prime minister; however, his government collapsed in October 2002, and new elections were held on 22 January 2003.

Following the January 2003 elections, the 150 seats in the lower house of the legislature were distributed as follows: CDA, 28.6% (44 seats); PvdA, 27.3% (42 seats); VVD, 17.9% (28 seats); SP, 6.3% (9 seats); LPF, 5.7% (8 seats); GL, 5.1% (8 seats); D66, 4.1% (6 seats); the Christian Union (CU), 2.1% (3 seats); and the conservative Calvinist party Political Reformed Party (SGP), 1.6% (2 seats). The PvdA scored an increase of 19 seats over the May 2002 elections, and the LPF suffered a loss of 18 seats. After prohibitive disagreement in the formation of a CDA-PvdA cabinet, the center-right CDA, the conservative VVD, and the center-left D66 formed a coalition with Balkenende again as prime minister.

The next general elections were scheduled for May 2007 but were held earlier, on 22 November 2006, because the governing coalition had collapsed that summer. In the elections for the lower house, the CDA won 26.5% of the vote and 41 seats; the PvdA took 21.2% of the vote and 33 of the 150 seats; the Socialist Party won 16.6% of the vote and 25 seats; the VVD took 14.6% of the vote and 22 seats; the Party for Freedom won 5.9% of the vote and 9 seats; the Green Party won 4.6% and 7 seats; the CU took 4.0% of the vote and 6 seats; and other parties secured 6.6% of the vote and 7 seats. In the upper house, the CDA won 21 of the 75 seats, followed by the PvdA with 14 seats, the VVD with 14, the Socialist party with 11, the CU with 4, the GL with 4, Democrats 66 with 2, and others with 5 seats. Jan Pieter Balkenende returned as prime minister.

Elections for the lower house took place again in June 2010. In that election, the VVD won 31 of the 150 seats, followed by the PvdA with 30 seats, the Party for Freedom (PVV) with 24, the Christian Democratic Appeal (CDA) with 21, the Socialist Party with 15, Democrats 66 with 10, the Green Left with 10, and the CU with 5. The remaining four seats went to smaller parties or independents. Mark Rutte of the VVD was selected prime minister.

¹⁵LOCAL GOVERNMENT

Through 2005, the country was divided into 12 provinces, each governed by a locally direct-elected representative provincial council (provinciale staten). The size of the council depends on the number of inhabitants in the province. Members are elected for four-year terms. From among their members, the councils elect provincial executives (gedeputeerde staten) with six to eight members. Each province has a commissioner appointed by and representing the Crown.

The smaller municipalities (421 in 2011) are administered by municipal councils, which are elected directly for four-year terms by the local inhabitants to make local bylaws. The executive powers of the municipality are entrusted to a corporate board consisting of a burgomaster (mayor) and two to six aldermen; the latter are elected from and by the council, while the burgomaster is appointed by the Crown. The important function of flood control and water management is exercised by autonomous public authorities, some of which date as far back as the 13th century.

¹⁶JUDICIAL SYSTEM

The judiciary is independent and the judges irremovable except for malfeasance or incapacity. Roman law still is basic, but the judicial system is largely patterned on that of France. There is no jury system, and the state rather than the individual acts as initiator of legal proceedings. Administrative justice is separate from civil and criminal justice and is not uniform in dispensation.

The supreme judiciary body is the Supreme Court of the Netherlands (Court of Cassation). As of 2011, it was staffed by 41 justices. Its principal task is to supervise administration of justice and to review the judgments of lower courts. There are five courts of appeal (gerechtshoven), which act as courts of first instance only in fiscal matters. They are divided into chambers of three justices each. The 19 district courts (arrondissementsrechtsbanken) deal as courts of first instance with criminal cases and civil cases not handled by the 61 subdistrict courts. Most of these courts are manned by single magistrates. In 2002, the subdistrict courts were incorporated administratively into the district courts; a subdistrict court section is now formed at these courts. There also are juvenile courts and special arbitration courts (for such institutions as the Stock Exchange Association and professional organizations).

Normally appointed for life, judges are usually retired at age 70.

¹⁷ARMED FORCES

In 2011, the International Institute for Strategic Studies reported that there were 37,368 active personnel in the Netherlands' armed forces, with reservists numbering 3,189. The Army numbered 20,836. Equipment included 60 main battle tanks, 151 armored infantry fighting vehicles, 16 armored personnel carriers, and 67 artillery pieces. The Navy had 8,502 personnel including 2,854 marines. Its fleet included four tactical submarines and six surface combatants (four destroyers and two frigates). The Air Force had 8,030 active personnel plus 421 reservists subject to immediate recall. The Air Force had 72 combat-capable aircraft and 29 attack helicopters. A paramilitary force known as the Royal Military Constabulary numbered 5,911 persons. The United States stationed about 477 personnel in the Netherlands. The Netherlands participated in UN, NATO, EU, Organization for Security and Co-operation in Europe (OSCE), and peacekeeping missions in five other countries, including Iraq and Afghanistan. The military budget in 2011 totaled $10.9 billion and accounted for 1.6% of GDP. Armed forces represented 0.5% of the labor force in the Netherlands.

¹⁸INTERNATIONAL COOPERATION

The Netherlands is a founding member of the UN, having joined on 10 December 1945. It participates in the Economic Commission for Europe (ECE), the Economic Commission for Latin America and the Caribbean (ECLAC), the Economic and Social Commission for Asia and the Pacific (ESCAP), and several nonregional specialized agencies, such as the Food and Agriculture Organization (FAO), the World Bank, the International Atomic Energy Agency (IAEA), the International Labour Organization (ILO), the UN Educational, Scientific and Cultural Organization (UNESCO), the UN High Commissioner for Refugees (UNHCR), the UN Industrial Development Organization (UNIDO), and the World Health Organization (WHO). In addition, the Netherlands is a member of the World Trade Organization (WTO), the Asian Development Bank, the African Development Bank, the Council of Europe, the Euro-Atlantic Partnership Council, G-10 (Paris Club), the Western European Union, the European Union, NATO, OSCE, and the Organization for Economic Co-operation and Development (OECD). The Netherlands is a permanent observer at the Organization of American States (OAS). The Netherlands is the home site of the International Court of Justice, Eurojust, Europol, the Organization for the Prohibition of Chemical Weapons, and the International Criminal Court.

On 1 January 1948, Belgium, the Netherlands, and Luxembourg established a joint customs union, Benelux; since that time, the three countries have freed nearly all of their mutual imports from quantitative restrictions. On 3 February 1958, the Benelux Economic Union was established to make it possible for each participating country to apply itself more intensively to the production for which it is best suited as well as to extend the total market for the member countries.

The Netherlands is a part of the Australia Group, the Zangger Committee, the European Organization for Nuclear Research (CERN), the Nuclear Suppliers Group (London Group), the Organization for the Prohibition of Chemical Weapons, and the Nuclear Energy Agency. In environmental cooperation, the Netherlands is part of the Antarctic Treaty; the Basel Convention; Conventions on Biological Diversity, Whaling, and Air Pollution; Ramsar; CITES; the London Convention; International Tropical Timber Agreements; the Kyoto Protocol; the Montréal Protocol; MAR-

POL; the Nuclear Test Ban Treaty; and the UN Conventions on the Law of the Sea, Climate Change and Desertification.

The Hague agreed to host the Special Court for Sierra Leone in its trial of Charles Taylor, the former president of Liberia. Mr. Taylor's trial was originally slated to begin in 2007; however, after four successive postponements that year, it moved forward in January 2008. The trial continued into July 2009, when the former Liberian president took to the stand in his own defense. Mr. Taylor, the first African leader to be tried for war crimes by an international court, faced down charges including torture, murder, rape, and terrorism. In March 2011, closing arguments for his case ended, with the verdict expected to be delivered in April 2012.

The trial aimed to address the atrocities committed in Sierra Leone amidst its 1991–2002 civil war. Mr. Taylor stands accused of commanding and arming the brutal Revolutionary United Front (RUF) rebels during the war in an attempt to gain access to Sierra Leone's vast diamond riches.

19 ECONOMY

The Netherlands has an advanced economy, which combines high per capita income with a fairly even income distribution. An industrial nation with limited natural resources, the Netherlands bases its economy on the importation of raw materials for processing into finished products for export. Food processing, metallurgy, chemicals, manufacturing, and oil refining are the principal industries. Agriculture is particularly important to the economy, as about 60% of total agricultural production is exported.

Because of its geographic position on the sea, outstanding harbor facilities, and numerous internal waterways, the Netherlands became a trading, transporting, and brokerage nation. A major role in the economy has always been played by the service industries, such as banks, trading companies, shipping enterprises, and brokerage and supply firms. The economy, involved in international trade, is sharply affected by economic developments abroad—including fluctuations in prices of primary goods—over which the Netherlands has little or no control.

Growth in GDP averaged just under 3% per year during 1988–95 with exceptionally strong growth occurring in 1989 and particularly slow growth in 1993. Inflation was low, averaging about 2% a year between 1986 and 1998. The unemployment rate fell from 10.5% in 1985 to 8.4% in 1995 and has continued to fall steadily, reaching an estimated 6% in 2004. For the four years from 1997 to 2000, real GDP growth averaged 4%, well ahead of most of Europe. Growth slowed due to the global economic slowdown of 2001 to 2.8% and was brought close to a standstill in 2002. Real GDP growth averaged 1.2% over the 2000–04 period. The economy experienced a slowdown in 2005, but picked back up in 2006 and 2007. GDP rate of change in the Netherlands as of 2010 was 1.7%.

Inflation jumped from 2.2% in 1999 to a yearly average of 4.5% in 2001 due mainly to a hike in the value-added tax (VAT) rate and increases in gasoline and food prices. The inflation rate averaged 2.7% over the 2000–04 period. In 2010, inflation stood at 1.1%, and unemployment was reported at 5.5%.

The Netherlands was one of the first countries to qualify for the Economic and Monetary Union of the EU. The country's fiscal policy is a combination of reductions in public spending and low-er taxes and social security contributions. In 2007, the job growth rate reached a 10-year high.

20 INCOME

The CIA estimated that in 2010 the GDP of the Netherlands was $676.9 billion. The CIA defines GDP as the value of all final goods and services produced within a nation in a given year, computed on the basis of purchasing power parity (PPP) rather than value as measured on the basis of the rate of the exchange based on current dollars. The per capita GDP was estimated at $40,300. The annual growth rate of GDP was 1.7%. The average inflation rate was 1.1%. It was estimated that agriculture accounted for 2.6% of GDP, industry 24.9%, and services 72.4%.

The World Bank estimated that the Netherlands, with 0.27% of the world's population, accounted for 1.03% of the world's GDP. By comparison, the United States, with 4.85% of the world's population, accounted for 22.51% of world GDP.

As of 2011, the most recent study by the World Bank reported that actual individual consumption in the Netherlands was 62.5% of GDP and accounted for 0.99% of world consumption. By comparison, the United States accounted for 25.44% of world individual consumption. The World Bank reported that in 2009, household consumption in the Netherlands totaled $364.8 billion or about $21,653 per capita, measured in current US dollars rather than PPP. Household consumption includes expenditures of individuals, households, and nongovernmental organizations on goods and services, excluding the purchases of dwellings. It was estimated that household consumption was growing at an average annual rate of 2.3%. The World Bank also estimated that 6.5% of the Netherlands's GDP was spent on food and beverages, 14% on housing and household furnishings, 2.5% on clothes, 6.7% on health, 5.5% on transportation, 2.2% on communications, 5.5% on recreation, 2.5% on restaurants and hotels, and 12.6% on miscellaneous goods and services and purchases from abroad.

According to the World Bank, remittances from citizens living abroad totaled $3.7 billion or about $219 per capita and accounted for approximately 0.5% of GDP.

21 LABOR

As of 2010, the Netherlands had a total labor force of 7.816 million people. Within that labor force, CIA estimates in 2005 (most recent available information as of April 2012) noted that 2% were employed in agriculture, 18% in industry, and 80% in the service sector. As of 2011, workers in the Netherlands were allowed to organize and join unions, engage in collective bargaining, and exercise the right to strike, though strikes are rare. Labor unions in 2009 accounted for about 22% of the country's workforce. However, collective bargaining agreements covered about 85% of the labor force. Antiunion discrimination is prohibited.

The law stipulates a 48-hour legal-maximum workweek, but in 2007, the average workweek was 32.5 hours (46.0 hours for full-time employees). The five-day workweek has been generally adopted. Workers receive workers' compensation, unemployment insurance, sick pay, payment for legal holidays, and paid vacations. The employment of women and adolescents for night work is forbidden. The minimum wage for adults in 2011 was $2,002 per month and was capable of providing a worker and family with a decent living standard. However, most workers earn more. There is a reduced minimum wage for workers under 23, which uses a sliding scale ranging from 30% of the adult minimum wage for a 16-year-old to 85% for those 22 years of age. The minimum age for employment is 15 years. These laws are effectively enforced.

22 AGRICULTURE

Roughly 22% of the total land is arable, and the country's major crops include grains, potatoes, sugar beets, fruits, and vegetables. Grasslands account for about 54% of all agricultural lands. In 2009, cereal production amounted to 2 million tons, fruit production to 772,040 tons, and vegetable production to 4.6 million tons. Most farms are effectively managed and worked intensively with mechanical equipment. The many cooperatives have added to the efficiency of production and distribution.

Although agricultural production has decreased in recent years, labor productivity in Dutch agricultural and horticultural industries has risen sharply. The number of holdings declined by over 17% from the mid-1970s to the mid-1980s; in 2007, there were 76,700 agricultural holdings. The crop output in 2010 was valued at almost €12.3 billion, accounting for 6.7% of the EU-27's total crop output.

Much of the soil in the east and southeast is poor. Moreover, large regions are so moist because of their low altitude that only grass can be grown profitably, a condition that has led to the enormous development of the dairy industry. The best land is found in reclaimed polders.

The Netherlands is famous for its bulbs grown for export, principally tulip, hyacinth, daffodil, narcissus, and crocus. Flower growing is centered at Aalsmeer (near Amsterdam), and nurseries are situated mainly at Boskoop. Bulb growing, done principally at Lisse and Hillegom, between Haarlem and Leiden, has been extended in recent years to areas of North Holland.

Since the beginning of the 20th century, the government has been helping the agrarian sector through extension services, the promotion of scientific research, and the creation of specific types of agricultural education. In the 1930s, an extensive system of governmental controls of agricultural production was introduced, and, after World War II (1939–45), an even more active policy was initiated, which evolved into integrated planning covering practically every aspect of rural life. In recent years, the government has actively encouraged the consolidation of small landholdings into larger, more efficient units.

23 ANIMAL HUSBANDRY

World-renowned Dutch dairy products outrank all other agricultural produce, and livestock provides 43.4% of the nation's total agricultural value. The UN Food and Agriculture Organization (FAO) reported that the Netherlands dedicated 827,800 hectares (2.05 million acres) to permanent pasture or meadow in 2009. During that year, the country tended 97 million chickens, 4 million head of cattle, and 12.1 million pigs. The production from these animals amounted to 303,208 tons of beef and veal, 538,144 tons of pork, 245,750 tons of poultry, 295,255 tons of eggs, and 5.27 million tons of milk. The Netherlands also produced 45,501 tons of cattle hide and 3,036 tons of raw wool.

Friesland is the most important region for the production of milk and butter. Excellent grazing lands and a long growing season have greatly helped the Frisian dairy industry, the main support of which is the famed Frisian strain of cows. The making of cheese is connected with such famous brands as those named for Edam and Gouda, towns in the province of South Holland, and Alkmaar in North Holland.

In 2011 the value of animal products was €9.42 billion. The Netherlands regularly imports calves from the United Kingdom.

24 FISHING

Although no longer as important as it was in the 16th and 17th centuries, fishing still contributes substantially to the food supply. Annual fish consumption in the Netherlands is 23.8 kg (54.2 lbs) per person. About half of the fish catch is landed at the ports of Scheveningen and Ijmuiden. The Dutch fishing industry faces declining fish stocks and quota cuts from the EU that make profitability difficult because of excess capacity.

The Netherlands had 1,053 decked commercial fishing boats in 2008. The total catch in 2008 totaled 416,748 tons according to the UN FAO. The export value of seafood totaled $2.82 billion. Dutch catches consist primarily of mackerel, mussels, sardines, herring, plaice, and whiting. Shrimp, oysters, sole, and other saltwater fish are also caught.

25 FORESTRY

One of the least forested countries in Europe, the Netherlands produces only about 8% of its wood requirements. Woodland, chiefly pine, covers about 375,000 hectares (927,000 acres), or only 11% of the total land area, of which state forest areas comprise some 37%; private owners, 31%; provincial and local governments, 14%; and nature conservation organizations, 18%. The UN FAO estimated the 2009 roundwood production at 726,133 cu m (25.6 million cu ft). The value of all forest products, including roundwood, totaled $3.68 billion. The Netherlands imports about 95% of its softwood lumber needs, mostly from Sweden, Finland, and Russia. Domestic sources of temperate hardwood lumber usually meet 20%–30% of annual demand.

The Dutch wood industry is focused on the furniture, construction, packing, and pulp and paper sectors. The Netherlands is a major European producer of pulp and paper, producing 3.1 million tons of paper and paperboard in 2010, with over 73% exported to neighboring countries at a total value of $2.54 billion.

Afforestation has not kept pace with increasing consumption. The Dutch government would like to become at least 25% self-sufficient in wood fiber by 2025. In order to meet this goal, some 3.9 million cu m (137.7 million cu ft) of fiber would need to be produced annually (assuming current consumption trends). During 1990–2000, only 1,000 hectares (2,500 acres) of forest were planted. The government established a goal in 1994 of increasing forested land by 3,000 hectares (7,400 acres) annually until 2020.

26 MINING

The Netherlands is an important regional producer of natural gas and petroleum and plays a major role as a transshipment center for mineral materials entering and leaving Europe—Rotterdam is Europe's largest container port. The only other mineral of commercial importance is salt, and the only other mining operations left in the country are involved in the extraction of limestone, peat, sand, and gravel. The production of salt from the mines at Hengelo and Delfzijl is one of the oldest industries in the country; an estimated 6.0 million tons were produced in 2009 (various types), unchanged since 2007. Akzo Nobel Salt BV is a leading producer of salt. Magnesium chloride and oxide are produced in a plant at Veendam from extracted salt brines. Also produced are hydraulic cement, nitrogen, industrial sand, sodium compounds, and sulfur. No metals were mined in 2009, but an estimated 3 million tons of iron ore was sintered from imported ore in 2009. Coal was mined in Limburg until 1974. Among the country's leading industries in 2009 were metal production, chemical production, petroleum refining, and construction; chemicals and fuels were top export commodities.

27 ENERGY AND POWER

The Netherlands, which has little waterpower, depends mostly on natural gas and petroleum as energy sources. Natural gas is the Netherlands' most abundant fossil fuel, with major fields located in the North Sea. As of 2011, the Netherlands had proven natural gas reserves of 49 trillion cu ft. In 2010, production of natural gas totaled 3.01 trillion cu ft. However, natural gas output has fallen as a result of government policy. The country's Natural Gas Law capped production at 2.68 trillion cu ft annually between 2003 and 2007. From 2008 through 2013, production was further limited to 2.47 trillion cu ft per year. This policy was instituted so that the country's natural gas reserves would be maintained for future use. In 2010, domestic consumption of natural gas totaled 1.878 trillion cu ft.

The Netherlands' second principal energy source is oil. As of 1 January 2011, the country's proven reserves of oil totaled 310 million barrels. In 2010, total oil production included 59,490 barrels per day of crude oil. Although oil output continued to increase, the nation was still dependent on imported petroleum. In 2009, imports of crude and refined oil products averaged 2.577 million barrels per day. Consumption of refined petroleum products in that year averaged 1.009 million barrels per day. Exports of all petroleum products that year averaged 1.871 million barrels per day. The Netherlands also re-exports two-thirds of all its imported petroleum in the form of refined oil products. Refinery capacity in 2009 averaged 1.208 million barrels per day. In 2008, per capita oil consumption was 4,845 kg. Per capita oil production totaled 7,764 barrels of oil a day.

The Netherlands's demand for coal came to 13.3 million short tons in 2009, all of it imported. Imports that year totaled 22 million short tons.

The World Bank reported in 2008 that the Netherlands produced 107.7 billion kWh of electricity and consumed 118.8 billion kWh, or 7,054 kWh per capita. Roughly 93% of energy came from fossil fuels, while 2% came from alternative fuels. Nuclear generating capacity is provided chiefly by a 485 MW station in Borssele, Zeeland. As of 2002, the Netherlands was one of five EU countries that had declared a moratorium on building new nuclear facilities. However, by 2008 the government had relented due to its focus on energy independence and the reduction of carbon dioxide emissions, and policy papers suggested that, under certain circumstances, the issuance of new construction permits would be considered. Construction of a second facility in Borssele, which was to be subject to stringent regulations and the highest safety standards, was expected to begin in 2013, with a completion date of

2018. Consumption of electricity in 2008 was 112.5 billion kWh. Installed capacity in 2008 was 24.88 million kW.

28 INDUSTRY

Because of World War II and its consequences (the high rate of population increase and the severing of economic ties with Indonesia), drastic structural changes took place in the Dutch economy, and the further development of industry became important. Industry increased to such an extent that it produced 32% of GDP in 1990. Since then, however, industrial production has declined, accounting for 24.9% of GDP in 2010.

Since World War II, the metallurgical industry in particular has made tremendous progress. Philips, the Dutch electronics giant, has become the greatest electrical products firm in Europe as well as one of the world's major exporters of electric bulbs and appliances. Unilever, the British-Dutch consumer products company, has grown to become one of the world's largest corporations. The Heineken brewing company is one of the world's largest brewing companies in terms of sales volume and profitability. More phenomenal has been the success of Royal Dutch/Shell, which began as a small concern in 1890 and grew to become one of the world's largest income producers. Rotterdam's suburb of Pernis has the largest oil refinery in Europe. Akzo Nobel produces healthcare products, coatings, and chemicals. DSM produces nutritional and pharma ingredients, performance materials, and industrial chemicals.

Pig iron is exported, produced from imported ore at the Velsen-Ijmuiden plant, situated where the canal from Amsterdam reaches the North Sea. The chemical industry has grown increasingly important, but the once-prosperous textile industry in Enschede has declined because of foreign competition.

Industrial products include petroleum, metal and engineering products, and pharmaceutical products. The Netherlands produces electrical machinery and equipment (including computers and computer parts) and microelectronics. Agroindustries are important: the Netherlands is one of the world's three largest exporters of agricultural produce. Dairy farming and market gardening are the major agricultural industries. The Netherlands also produces cigarettes, beer, canned fish, cocoa and cocoa products, coffee, tea, sugar, candies, biscuits, and potato flour.

29 SCIENCE AND TECHNOLOGY

Advanced scientific research and development (R&D) has provided the technological impetus for the Netherlands' economic recovery since World War II. Dutch universities have traditionally carried out fundamental scientific research, and the government has promoted research activities through the Netherlands Organization for Scientific Research, established in 1988, and the Netherlands Organization for Applied Scientific Research, established in 1930. It also has supported scientific organizations such as the Energy Development Corp. and Energy Research Foundation, Aerospace Development Agency, National Aerospace Laboratory, and Netherlands Maritime Institute.

The highly developed electrotechnical industry produces computers, telecommunications systems, electronic measurement and control equipment, electric switching gear and transformers, and medical and scientific instruments. Dutch firms designed and constructed the Netherlands' astronomical satellites and play a major

Principal Trading Partners – Netherlands (2010)

(In millions of US dollars)

Country	Total	Exports	Imports	Balance
World	932,887.0	492,267.0	440,620.0	51,647.0
Germany	227,668.0	148,353.0	79,315.0	69,038.0
Belgium	116,571.0	73,879.0	42,692.0	31,187.0
United Kingdom	75,205.0	43,660.0	31,545.0	12,115.0
France	72,102.0	52,488.0	19,614.0	32,874.0
China	71,828.0	6,887.0	64,941.0	-58,054.0
United States	56,103.0	21,271.0	34,832.0	-13,561.0
Italy	37,725.0	28,069.0	9,656.0	18,413.0
Russia	36,232.0	7,641.0	28,591.0	-20,950.0
Spain	29,386.0	19,686.0	9,700.0	9,986.0
Norway	20,636.0	4,773.0	15,863.0	-11,090.0

(…) data not available or not significant.

(n.s.) not specified.

SOURCE: *2011 Direction of Trade Statistics Yearbook,* New York: United Nations, 2011.

Balance of Payments – Netherlands (2010)

(In millions of US dollars)

Current Account		51,635.0
Balance on goods		51,877.0
Imports	-428,419.0	
Exports	480,296.0	
Balance on services		10,692.0
Balance on income		886,100.0
Current transfers		-14,504.0
Capital Account		**-5,836.0**
Financial Account		**-24,303.0**
Direct investment abroad		-49,267.0
Direct investment in Netherlands		-15,597.0
Portfolio investment assets		10,988.0
Portfolio investment liabilities		48,352.0
Financial derivatives		-15,531.0
Other investment assets		-41,746.0
Other investment liabilities		38,498.0
Net Errors and Omissions		**-21,315.0**
Reserves and Related Items		**-181.0**

(…) data not available or not significant.

SOURCE: *Balance of Payment Statistics Yearbook 2011,* Washington, DC: International Monetary Fund, 2011.

role in the European Space Agency. The important aerospace industry is led by the world-famous firm of Fokker, which produced Europe's best-selling passenger jet aircraft, the F-27 Friendship, and has been active in the consortium that developed the European Airbus. In 2009, high-tech exports were valued at $58.450 billion and accounted for 24.07% of manufactured exports.

Expenditures on scientific R&D in 2007 totaled $9.6 billion, or 1.7% of GDP. Of that amount, 48.8% came from the business sector, followed by government sources at 36.8%. Foreign sources accounted for 10.6%, with higher education at 0.2%. In that same year, there were 3,021 scientists and engineers engaged in R&D. Patent applications in science and technology as of 2009, according to the World Bank, totaled 2,575 in the Netherlands. Public financing of science was 1.63% of GDP.

Among the Netherlands' 39 scientific and technical learned societies, the most prominent is the Royal Netherlands Academy of Sciences, founded in 1808. The country also has 37 scientific and technical research institutes. In Leiden are located the National Museum of Natural History and the National Museum of History of Science and Medicine. The Netherlands has 15 universities offering courses in basic and applied sciences.

30 DOMESTIC TRADE

A considerable but declining part of Dutch retail business is still conducted by small enterprises, which are usually owner-operated. Some of the larger department stores in the cities have branches in small towns, and there are several nationwide supermarket chains. Cooperatives and associations are important in both purchasing and producing.

Amsterdam is the chief center for commerce and trade, with Rotterdam and the Hague next. Many companies use the Netherlands as a distribution center for European markets. Terms of sale usually call for payment within 90 days. A value-added tax (VAT) of 19% applies to most goods.

As of 2009, there were 679 franchise operations in the Netherlands with 28,475 outlets, which generated €29.23 billion ($21.04 billion) in sales that year. Although few US-based franchisers operate in the Netherlands, a number do have operations there.

Electronic commerce (e-commerce) is well-developed in the Netherlands, owing to the nation's large number of broadband connections and the highest rate of Internet penetration of any country in the European Union. In 2009, some 12 million Dutch citizens spent time on the Internet. In 2005, an estimated 4.7 million citizens purchased products online. For all of 2008, an estimated $7 billion was spent by consumers shopping online.

Business offices are generally open from 8:30 a.m. to 5:30 p.m. on weekdays. Retail stores are usually open between 9 a.m. and 6 p.m. on weekdays, with one late evening per week. On Saturdays, stores are usually open from 9 a.m. to 5 p.m. Bank hours are from 9 a.m. to 4 p.m. Monday through Friday.

The country's most important trade fair is held at Utrecht, twice each year, in the spring and fall.

31 FOREIGN TRADE

The Dutch have traditionally been a powerful force in international trade. The Netherlands is the world's seventh-largest exporting nation. As exports and imports of goods and services both account for well over 60% of GDP, the backbone of Dutch prosperity is foreign trade. Rotterdam is Europe's largest port and one of the largest ports in the world. The Netherlands' geographical position as a key hub of Europe's transportation system and the small size of its domestic market have made the Dutch economy one of the most open and outward-looking in the world.

The Netherlands imported $408.4 billion worth of goods and services in 2008, while exporting $451.3 billion worth of goods and services. Major import partners in 2009 were Germany, 16.8%; China, 11.7%; Belgium, 8.7%; the United States, 7.8%; UK, 6%; Russia, 4.5%; and France, 4.4%. Its major export partners were Germany, 25.8%; Belgium, 12.6%; France, 9.2%; UK, 8.1%; and Italy, 5.1%. Principal Dutch exports in the early 2000s were manufactured goods, machines, electronics, chemicals, petroleum products, natural gas, and foods. Chief imports are manufactured products, machines, crude petroleum, chemicals, and clothing. From 1981 through 2011, the Netherlands experienced trade surpluses each year.

³²BALANCE OF PAYMENTS

Dutch merchandise and services exports have grown to represent more than 65% of GDP, making the Dutch economy one of the most internationally oriented in the world. Economic expansion of the Netherlands in the period immediately after World War II paralleled a generally favorable balance of payments. After occasional and minor deficits on current accounts during the mid-1960s, a major deficit occurred in 1970. Since then, the current account balance has generally registered a surplus, despite increased costs of oil imports during the 1970s and beginning in 2005. The Netherlands' reliance on exports that are resistant to recessions (such as some food and agricultural products and semifinished products, such as chemicals) has protected the Dutch economy from weaker demand from Germany and other EU countries during recessions. In 2010, exports totaled $485.9 billion and imports $429 billion, resulting in a trade surplus of $30.7 billion. In 2010, the Netherlands had a foreign trade surplus of $59 billion, amounting to 4.8% of GDP.

³³BANKING AND SECURITIES

The Netherlands Bank, nationalized in 1948, is the central bank. It issues the currency and supervises the privately owned banks. Since the 1950s, the Netherlands Bank had used reserve regulations and the central bank discount rate as instruments of monetary policy, but with the introduction of the European Central Bank, those responsibilities are now more centralized for all of the EU. The Dutch financial services industry has a long, distinguished history and has introduced many banking innovations to the world. Since the late 1980s, the sector has undergone a revolution. A common strategic desire to expand and to gain more financial strength, combined with deregulation of the financial market, prompted several bank mergers and the formation of financial conglomerates of banks and insurance groups. As a result, the number of dominant participants in the market has diminished to a handful, each providing the full range of financial services. The Netherlands Middenstands-bank (NMB) and the state-owned Postbank merged to form the NMB Postbank in 1989, which in turn merged again with the Nationale Nederlanden insurance group to form the International Nederlanden Groep (ING) in 1991. The large ABN and Amro commercial banking groups joined up to form ABN-Amro in 1990. VSB-bank, a conglomerate of savings banks, teamed up with the Ameu insurance group and Belgium's AG insurance group in 1990 to form the Dutch-Belgian Fortis group. Rabobank, a large cooperative group that specializes in the provision of agricultural credits and mortgage facilities but has been rapidly expanding its product portfolio in recent years, took a 50% share in the Robeco investment group in 1996. The robust nature of the Dutch banking industry came to the forefront once again in December 1999. Although it ultimately failed, ING made headlines through its attempted takeover of the French Crédit Commercial de France (CCF). Had ING's bid succeeded, it would have been the first successful merger of a French bank with another European financial institution.

The CIA World Factbook reported that in 2010, currency and demand deposits—an aggregate commonly known as M1—were equal to $385.5 billion. In that same year, the World Bank reported that the Netherlands's M2—an aggregate equal to M1 plus savings deposits, small-time deposits, and money-market mutual funds—was $1.325 trillion.

Because the nation's currency is the euro, the nation's discount rate, the interest rate at which the central bank lends to financial institutions in the short term, is set by the European Central Bank (ECB). In 2010, the discount rate was 1.75%.

By August 2011, the nation's gold bullion deposits totaled 19.69 million fine troy ounces.

The Netherlands lays claim to the oldest stock exchange in the world, the Amsterdam Stock Exchange, which was founded in the early 17th century. On 1 January 1997, the Amsterdam Exchanges (AEX) was formed by the merger of the Amsterdam Stock Exchange (ASE) and the city's European Options Exchange (EDE). AEX became Euronext in 2000, through a merger with exchanges in Brussels and Paris; a merger with the New York Stock Exchange (NYSE) created NYSE Euronext in 2007.

Historically, the comparatively large share of foreign security listings and capital supply gave the ASE an international importance disproportionate to its size. Its strong international orientation was also reflected in the fact that its share of Europe's total market capitalization far outweighed the relative importance of the Dutch economy. The multinational nature of the major Dutch companies (which include Royal Dutch Shell, Unilever, and ArcelorMittal) led to their shares being quoted on a number of international stock markets, and meant that stock price levels on the ASE were heavily influenced by developments elsewhere.

As of 2010, a total of 153 companies were listed on the NYSE EURONEXT's Amsterdam exchange, which had a market capitalization of $559 billion.

³⁴INSURANCE

Before 2006, there were two sectors of the insurance industry in the Netherlands: the companies operating under control laws set down by the European Commission (EC) and supervised by the government and the companies (mutuals, reinsurance, marine, and aviation) not under official supervision. In 2006, the Dutch government abolished this distinction. Compulsory third-party motor insurance has been in effect since 1935. In addition, insurance for workers, hunters, nuclear facilities, and pensions are compulsory. In 2009, the value of all direct insurance premiums written totaled $78.3 billion, of which life insurance premiums accounted for $24.3 billion.

³⁵PUBLIC FINANCE

In 2010, the budget of Netherlands included $356 billion in public revenue and $399.3 billion in public expenditures. The budget deficit amounted to 5.3% of GDP. Public debt was 64.6% of GDP in 2010. An estimated $3.73 trillion of debt was held by foreign entities in 2009. Under the Maastricht Treaty, the Netherlands Central Bank was abolished in 1994. Although the private sector is the cornerstone of the economy, the government plays a vital role in the Netherlands' economy. It decides microeconomic policy

Public Finance – Netherlands (2009)

(In millions of euros, central government figures)

Revenue and Grants	**234,498**	**100.0%**
Tax revenue	129,238	55.1%
Social contributions	81,284	34.7%
Grants	729	0.3%
Other revenue	23,247	9.9%
Expenditures	**261,885**	**100.0%**
General public services	50,302	19.2%
Defense	8,357	3.2%
Public order and safety	10,814	4.1%
Economic affairs	20,267	7.7%
Environmental protection	1,393	0.5%
Housing and community amenities	1,849	0.7%
Health	37,657	14.4%
Recreational, culture, and religion	1,893	0.7%
Education	28,317	10.8%
Social protection	101,006	38.6%

(…) data not available or not significant.

SOURCE: *Government Finance Statistics Yearbook 2010*, Washington, DC: International Monetary Fund, 2010.

and tax laws, as well as working toward structural and regulatory reforms.

As in many European countries, stimulus spending by the government during the 2008–09 global financial crisis increased the public debt burden. As of 2011, the Dutch government was aiming to reduce government spending $26 billion by 2015. The reduction was to be achieved through a general downsizing of government and a decrease in "income transfers," subsidies for social benefits such as childcare.

36 TAXATION

Principal taxes raised by the central government are income and profits taxes levied on individuals and companies, a VAT on goods and services, and a tax on enterprises of public bodies (except agricultural enterprises). There is a wealth tax of 1.2% also levied on nonexempt taxable capital of individuals. Provinces and municipalities are not authorized to impose income taxes and may impose other taxes only to a limited extent. The most important tax levied by municipalities is a real estate tax paid partly by owners and partly by occupants. Residents are taxed on both their local and foreign incomes, but nonresidents pay taxes only on income earned in the Netherlands.

The tax on the net profits of corporations in 2011 was 20% for annual profits up to €20,000 and 25% on the increment of profits above that. Depreciation and other business deductions are permitted. Capital gains were taxed at the same rates, although some capital gains were tax-exempt. Withholding taxes up to a maximum of 20% were applied to dividends, although there is no withholding if the dividends are being paid by a subsidiary to a nonresident parent company owning more than 25% of the payer. Companies can qualify for tax exemptions and tax reductions under investment incentive regimes. Branches of foreign companies are treated the same as Dutch companies in accordance with the fiscal regime under which they qualify.

Incomes are taxed on a graduated scale, with a top rate of 52%. There are also liberal deductions for dependents. Taxes are withheld by the state on the incomes of wage earners. In the tax reforms of 2001, marginal income tax rates were set in a course of increases in the lower rates and decreases in the higher ones. The progressive schedule consists of four brackets, not counting a tax-exempt base for each individual taxpayer. Gift and inheritance taxes range from 5%–63%, depending on the family relationship of the donor or deceased.

The Netherlands' main indirect tax is its VAT, which was introduced 1 January 1969 with a standard rate of 12% and a reduced rate of 4% on basics. Effective 1 January 2001, the standard rate was increased from 17.5% to 19% with a reduced rate of 6%; the latter applied to basic foodstuffs, books, newspapers and periodicals, public ground and sea transport, water supplies, sports centers, and pharmaceuticals. Exempted from VAT are exported goods; medical, cultural, and educational services; and credit and insurance transactions. Other taxes include excise taxes, energy taxes, taxes on legal transactions, and taxes on motor vehicles.

37 CUSTOMS AND DUTIES

The Dutch government has a traditionally liberal policy on tariffs, and its membership in the Benelux Economic Union, the European Union, and other international trade organizations has resulted in comparatively low import duties. Tariffs on imports from the dollar area have also been liberalized, and about 90% of imports from the United States are unrestricted quantitatively. Manufactured goods from the United States are generally subject to a duty ranging from 5%–8% based on the cost, insurance, and freight (CIF) value of the goods. Raw materials are usually not subject to import duties.

Imports are subject to EU customs regulations and tariff rates, plus VAT and other charges levied at entry through customs.

38 FOREIGN INVESTMENT

The Netherlands has favorable tax structures for investors, which has made the country one of the top recipients of foreign direct investment (FDI) in the European Union. The Netherlands has consistently been ranked as one of the most attractive destinations for FDI in the world, ranking seventh among the ten largest foreign investors in the world, as well as the ninth-largest global recipient of FDI (2010).

The government has encouraged foreign corporations to set up branch plants in the Netherlands and to establish joint ventures with Dutch companies in order to benefit from the introduction of new production techniques and improved methods of management that outside firms often bring. The government does not discriminate between foreign and domestic companies; foreign entrepreneurs have the same business privileges and obligations as Dutch businessmen and women. As a result, foreign companies operate in virtually all industries, including high-technology electronics, chemicals, metals, electrical equipment, textiles, and food processing. The labor force is largely well-educated and multilingual.

The corporation tax in 2011 was 20% for the first €200,000 (approximately $276,000) and 25% on profits after that. The corporate taxation regime was reformed in 2006–07. The Corporation Tax Act provided for a participation exemption, applicable to both foreign and domestic shareholdings, thus preventing double taxation when the profits of a subsidiary are distributed to its parent company.

Annual foreign direct investment inflows were $11 billion in 1997, down from $16.6 billion in 1996, but then soared to $37.6 billion in 1998. The peak was reached in 2000 and 2001, when total inflows reached $52 billion and $50 billion, respectively. In 2002, FDI inflow fell to an estimated $30 billion, and to $19.3 billion in 2003. By 2004, the total stock of FDI had reached $387 billion, about 75% of GDP. FDI in the Netherlands was a net inflow of $33.3 billion according to World Bank figures published in 2009. FDI represented 4.2% of GDP. In 2010, total domestic stock of FDI was $589.8 billion.

Overall, the United States, the United Kingdom, Germany, Belgium, and France are the primary sources of and destinations for FDI with the Netherlands.

Foreign companies established in the Netherlands account for roughly one-third of industrial production and employment in industry. At the end of 2009, an estimated 36% of foreign establishments in the Netherlands came from the United States, 11% from Germany, 11% from the United Kingdom, 17% from Scandinavia, 3% from the rest of Europe, 19% from Asia, and the remaining 3% from other non-OECD and non-EU countries.

39 ECONOMIC DEVELOPMENT

For nearly four decades after World War II, the Dutch government aimed at increased industrialization. During the 1990s, however, industrial growth slowed, while the service sector continued to expand. In this regard, the Netherlands has made the transition to a more liberalized high-technology economy quite successfully.

In an effort to encourage industrialization after the Second World War, the maintenance of internal monetary equilibrium was vitally important, and the government largely succeeded in this task. Successive governments pursued a policy of easy credits and a "soft" currency, but after the Netherlands had fully recovered from the war by the mid-1950s, a harder currency and credit policy came into effect. In the social sphere, stable relationships were maintained by a deliberate governmental social policy seeking to bridge major differences between management and labor. The organized collaboration of workers and employers in the Labor Foundation has contributed in no small measure to the success of this policy, and, as a result, strikes are rare.

Successive wage increases helped bring the overall wage level in the Netherlands up to that of other EC countries by 1968. The Dutch government's policy, meanwhile, was directed toward controlling inflation while seeking to maintain high employment. In 1966, the government raised indirect taxes to help finance rising expenditures, particularly in the fields of education, public transportation, and public health. Further attempts to cope with inflation and other economic problems involved increased government control over the economy. Wage and price controls were imposed in 1970–71, and the States-General approved a measure granting the government power to control wages, rents, dividends, health and insurance costs, and job layoffs during 1974.

During the mid-1980s, the nation experienced modest recovery from recession: the government's goal was to expand recovery and reduce high unemployment, while cutting down the size of the annual budget deficit. The government generally sought to foster a climate favorable to private industrial investment through such measures as preparing industrial sites, subsidizing or permitting allowances for industrial construction and equipment, assisting in the creation of new markets, granting subsidies for establishing industries in distressed areas, and establishing schools for adult training. In 1978, the government began, by means of a selective investment levy, to discourage investment in the western region (Randstad), while encouraging industrial development in the southern province of Limburg and the northern provinces of Drenthe, Friesland, and Groningen.

The Netherlands' largest economic development projects have involved the reclamation of land from the sea by construction of dikes and dams and by the drainage of lakes to create polders for additional agricultural land. The Zuider Zee project closed off the sea and created the freshwater Ijsselmeer by means of a 30 km (19-mi) barrier dam in 1932 and subsequently drained four polders enclosing about 165,000 hectares (408,000 acres). After a storm washed away dikes on islands in Zeeland and South Holland in 1953, killing some 1,800 people, the Delta project was begun. This project, designed to close estuaries between the islands with massive dams, was officially inaugurated in 1986; the cost was $2.4 billion. The Delta works include a storm-surge barrier with 62 steel gates, each weighing 500 tons, that are usually left open to allow normal tidal flow in order to protect the natural environment. Another major engineering project was the construction of a bridge and tunnel across the Western Schelde estuary in the south to connect Zeeland Flanders more directly with the rest of the country.

Beginning in the 1980s, Dutch governments began stressing fiscal discipline by reversing the growth of the welfare state and ending a policy of inflation-based wage indexing. The latter policy represented a spirit of consensus among labor and management. At a time when other labor unions fought losing battles with management, Dutch unions agreed to a compromise on this cherished issue in return for a business promise to emphasize job creation. By the late 1990s, these reforms had paid off as Dutch unemployment plummeted to below 5%. As of the early 2000s, the Netherlands had among the lowest unemployment rates in the industrialized world. By 2005, the Dutch economy was being heralded around the world for its combination of strong employment growth, low inflation, falling public budget deficits, low inequality, and strong social welfare policies.

In January 2004, the government launched its Innovation Partnerships Grant Program to promote cooperation in research and development. The program encourages businesses and public-sector knowledge institutes to study and launch national and international partnerships. Some 5,000 Dutch companies are conducting research to develop new products and to boost quality and efficiency. The country's five largest multinationals—Philips, Shell, Akzo Nobel, DSM, and Unilever—are at the forefront of industrial research and development.

The Netherlands' commitment to the project of further European integration was stalled in 2005, when, on 1 June, Dutch voters rejected the EU constitution by a wide margin (62% to 38%). This vote directly followed the French rejection of the constitution. Many Dutch "no" voters, however, said they were pro-European but feared that small countries were losing influence in an EU dominated by larger ones. The Dutch treasure their sound money and liberal social policies and do not want to see these eroded.

Like most European economies, the Dutch economy was weakened as a result of the 2008–09 global financial crisis. However, even before the crisis, the economy was losing its competitiveness due to increased labor costs. Despite efforts to control costs, a small labor market continued to push labor costs higher. The problem of a limited labor market transformed into a focus on job creation following economic contractions in 2009. Government stimulus spending softened the fall from the recession but also increased government debt, compelling the government to adopt mild austerity measures through 2015.

⁴⁰SOCIAL DEVELOPMENT

A widespread system of social insurance and assistance is in effect. The first laws were implemented in 1901. All residents are provided with old-age and survivorship benefits. Disability pensions are available to all employees, self-employed workers, students, and those disabled since childhood. Unemployment, accidents, illness, and disability are covered by insurance, which is compulsory for most employees and voluntary for self-employed persons. Maternity grants and full insurance for the worker's family are also provided, as are family allowances for children. The government covers the total cost for family allowances. Women receive one month of maternity leave with full pay. Exceptional medical expenses are covered for all residents.

Legislation mandates equal pay for equal work and prohibits dismissal due to marriage, pregnancy, or motherhood. However, cultural factors and lack of day care discourage women from employment. Many women work in part-time positions and are underemployed, and, on average, women earn less than men. Sexual harassment in the workplace is an issue, and, in 2004, the government funded an awareness campaign to combat the problem. Domestic violence is an issue, especially among ethnic minorities. The government provides programs to reduce and prevent violence against women.

Human rights are fully respected in the Netherlands. There are incidents of discrimination against religious minorities and some immigrant groups.

⁴¹HEALTH

The Netherlands has a social insurance system similar to Germany's. About two-thirds of workers are covered by the social insurance program; the remainder are covered by private insurance. Under the Health Insurance Act, lower-income workers pay a monthly contribution, in return for which they receive medical, pharmaceutical, and dental treatment and hospitalization. People who earn more have to take out private medical insurance. The state also pays for preventive medicine including vaccinations for children, school dental services, medical research, and the training of health workers. Preventive care emphasizes education, a clean environment, and regular exams and screenings. There were 39 physicians, 2 nurses and midwives, and 43 hospital beds per 10,000 inhabitants in 2009.

The total fertility rate in 2011 was estimated at 1.8 children born per woman. Approximately 69% of women used contraception in 2008. The infant mortality was 4 deaths per 1,000 live births in 2011. The maternal mortality rate was 9 per 100,000 live births that same year These low rates were attributed to a rise in the standard of living; improvements in nutrition, hygiene, housing,

and working conditions; and the expansion of public health measures. Immunization rates for children up to one year old were as follows: diphtheria, pertussis, and tetanus, 95%; polio, 97%; and measles, 96%. The average life expectancy was 81 years.

Most doctors and hospitals operate privately. A system of hospital budgeting, which was introduced in 1983, helps contain costs. In 1990, a proposal to increase competition among insurers, eliminating the distinction between public and private insurers, was developed. In 2010, the country spent 9.9% of its GDP on healthcare, amounting to $5,164 per person.

The Ministry of Public Health and Environment is entrusted with matters relating to healthcare, but health services are not centrally organized. There are numerous local and regional health centers and hospitals, many of which are maintained by religious groups.

Major causes of death are attributed to cardiovascular problems and cancer. The HIV/AIDS adult prevalence rate was 0.2% in 2009. The incidence of tuberculosis was 8 per 100,000 people in 2007.

⁴²HOUSING

During World War II, more than 25% of the nation's two million dwellings were damaged: 95,000 dwellings were completely destroyed, 55,000 were seriously damaged, and 520,000 were slightly damaged. The housing shortage remained acute until 1950, when an accelerated program of housing construction began, and in 1953, the government decided to increase the house-building program to a level of 65,000 dwellings a year. Since then, the production rate has far exceeded both the pre-war rate and yearly forecasts. From 1945 to 1985, nearly four million dwellings were built. In 1985 alone, 98,131 dwellings were built, bringing the total housing stock to 5,384,100 units by the end of the year. Most of the new units were subsidized by the national government. Subsidies are granted to municipalities, building societies, and housing associations, which generally build low-income, multi-unit dwellings. Government regulations, which are considerable, are laid down in the Housing Act of 1965 and the Rental Act of 1979.

The government determines on an annual basis the scope of the construction program. On the basis of national estimates, each municipality is allocated a permissible volume of construction. Within this allocation, the municipalities must follow certain guidelines: central government approval is required for all construction projects exceeding a specific cost, and all construction must conform to technical and aesthetic requirements, as established by the government.

In 2010, the total number of dwellings was about 7.2 million. In 2009, there was an average of 2.2 residents per dwelling. The number of residents per dwelling has nearly halved since WWII. Approximately 46,893 new dwellings were constructed in 2010. About 62% of the dwellings built in 2010 were owner-occupied.

⁴³EDUCATION

Overall, the CIA estimates that the Netherlands has a literacy rate of 99%. Public expenditure on education represented 5.9% of GDP or 11.2% of total government expenditures.

The present Dutch education system has its origins in the Batavian Republic, which was constituted after the French Revolution. The role of education gained importance in the Civil and Constitutional Regulations of 1789, and the first legislation on education was passed in 1801. After 1848, the municipalities, supported by state funds, were responsible for managing the schools. Private schools were not originally supported by the government; however, after 1917, private and state schools received equal state funding.

School attendance between the ages of 5 and 18 is compulsory. Apart from play groups and crèches (which do not come under the Ministry of Education), there are no schools for children below the age of four. Children may, however, attend primary school from the age of four. Primary school covers eight years of study. Secondary school is comprised of three types: (1) general secondary school, with two options—the four-year junior general secondary school (MAVO) or the five-year senior general secondary school (HAVO); (2) preuniversity—the athenaeum or the gymnasium—both lasting for six years in preparation for university education; and (3) vocational secondary schools with four-year programs. Special education is provided to children with physical, mental, or social disabilities at special primary and secondary schools. Whenever possible, these children are later transferred into mainstream schools for continued education. The academic year runs from September to June.

In 2008 the World Bank estimated that 99% of age-eligible children in the Netherlands were enrolled in primary school. The same year, secondary school enrollment was about 88% of age-eligible students. It is estimated that about 98% of all students complete their primary education.

Facilities have been opened in various municipalities for adult education. Open schools and open universities have also been introduced. Vocational and university education is provided at the 15 universities. There is also a much larger system of technical schools (Hogescholen), which are not accredited to give out doctoral degrees. All universities and technical schools are funded entirely by the government. There are also seven theological colleges. In 2011, about 61% of the tertiary-age population was enrolled in some type of higher education program. Of those enrolled in tertiary education, there were 100 male students for every 111 female students.

44 LIBRARIES AND MUSEUMS

The largest public library is the Royal Library at the Hague, which has about six million items (including books, newspapers, and journals); this also serves as the national library. Outstanding libraries are found in the universities: Amsterdam, with over 2.6 million volumes; Leiden, 2.7 million volumes; Utrecht, 2 million volumes; Groningen, 2.7 million volumes; and Erasmus of Rotterdam, 800,000 volumes. The technical universities at Delft, Wageningen, and Tilburg also have excellent collections. Libraries of importance are found in some provincial capitals, such as Hertogenbosch, Leeuwarden, Middelburg, and Maastricht. Also noteworthy are the International Institute of Social History at Amsterdam, which houses important collections of historical letters and documents, such as the Marx-Engels Archives; and the Institute of the Netherlands Economic-Historical Archive, which has its library in Amsterdam and its collection of old trade archives at the Hague. There are about 500 public libraries across the country. The Netherlands Public Library Association was founded in 1972. In 2007, the Amsterdam Public Library became Europe's largest public library in terms of square feet, occupying 301,389 ft² and maintaining a collection of 1.7 million books.

Among Amsterdam's many museums, particularly outstanding are the Rijksmuseum (1800), the Stedelijk Museum (1895) with special collections of modern art, the Van Gogh Museum (1979), the Museum of the Royal Tropical Institute (1910), and the Jewish Historical Museum (1932). Other museums include the Huis Marseille (1999), which has historic and modern photography exhibits; the hands-on New Metropolis Interactive Science and Technology Museum (1997); and the Tattoo Museum (2011). The Boymans-Van Beuningen Museum in Rotterdam has older paintings as well as modern works and a fine collection of minor arts. The Hague's Mauritshuis and the Frans Hals Museum at Haarlem have world-renowned collections of old masters. Other collections of national interest are in the Central Museum in Utrecht, the National Museum of Natural History in Leiden, Teyler's Museum in Haarlem, and the Folklore Museum in Arnhem. In the past, the most important art museums were found mainly in the large population centers of western Holland, but there are now museums of interest in such provincial capitals as Groningen, Leeuwarden, Arnhem, and Maastricht. The government stimulates the spread of artistic culture by providing art objects on loan and by granting subsidies to a number of privately owned museums. There are dozens of museums dedicated to the work of individual Dutch artists.

45 MEDIA

The Netherlands has a well-maintained and highly developed telecommunications system. Domestic services are provided by an extensive fixed-line, fiber-optic network, while the nation's cellular phone system is one of Europe's largest and is served by five major operators employing third-generation Global System for Mobile Communications (GSM) technology. International service is provided by submarine cables and satellite ground stations operated by Inmarsat, Eutelsat, and Intelsat. In 2009, there were some 7.32 million main phone lines and 21.2 million mobile cellular phones in use. Mobile phone subscriptions averaged 128 per 100 people.

There are several radio networks. The Netherlands Broadcasting Foundation, a joint foundation, maintains and makes available all studios, technical equipment, record and music libraries, orchestras, and other facilities. Broadcasting to other countries is carried on by the Netherlands World Broadcasting Service, which is managed by a board of governors appointed by the minister of cultural affairs. As of 2009, there were 4 FM, 246 AM, and 3 shortwave radio stations. According to the CIA World Factbook, there were also about 342 television stations in the Netherlands. Shortwave programs are transmitted in Dutch, Afrikaans, Arabic, English, French, Indonesian, Portuguese, and Spanish. Annual license fees are charged to radio and television set owners. Commercial advertising was introduced in 1967–68 and limited to fixed times before and after news broadcasts. In 2010, the country had about 12.6 million Internet hosts. In 2009, there were some 14.8 million Internet users in the Netherlands. Internet subscriptions stood at 90 per 100 citizens.

The Dutch were among the first to issue regular daily newspapers. The oldest newspaper, the *Oprechte Haarlemsche Courant*, was founded in 1656 and is published today as the *Haarlemsche Courant*. The Dutch press is largely a subscription press, depending for two-thirds of its income on advertising. Editorial boards, however, are usually completely independent of the commercial management.

In 2010, the largest national and regional newspapers, with daily circulations, were: *De Telegraaf* (Amsterdam), 649,000; *Algemeen Dagblad* (Amsterdan), 490,000; *De Volkskrant* (Amsterdam), 262,000; *NRC Handelsblad* (Rotterdam), 200,000; *De Gelderland-er* (Gelderland), 149,000; *Dagblad van het Noorden* (Groningen), 138,000; *Noordhollands Dagblad* (Alkmaar), 137,000; *De Sten-toor* (Apeldoorn), 131,000; *Brabants Dagblad* (North Brabant), 129,200; *Dagblad de Limburger* (Sittard),129,100; *De Twentsche Courant Tubantia* (Enschede), 114,000; *De Stem* (Breda), 112,000; *Eindhovens Dagblad* (Eindhoven), 108,000; and *Trouw* (Amsterdam), 106,000.

Complete freedom of speech and press is guaranteed by the constitution, and the government is said to fully support free expression in practice.

46 ORGANIZATIONS

Associations established on the basis of economic interests include the Federation of Netherlands Industries, the Netherlands Society for the Promotion of Industry and Commerce, the Federation of Christian Employers in the Netherlands, the National Bankers Association, and chambers of commerce in Amsterdam, Rotterdam, the Hague, and other cities.

Learned societies include the Royal Netherlands Academy of Arts and Sciences, the Royal Antiquarian Society, the Netherlands Anthropological Society, the Historical Association, the Royal Netherlands Geographical Society, and similar bodies in the fields of botany, zoology, philology, mathematics, chemistry, and other sciences. The Royal Netherlands Association for the Advancement of Medicine, the General Netherlands Society for Social Medicine and Public Health, the Royal Dutch Medical Association, and the Netherlands Association for Psychiatry and Neurology are some of the organizations active in the field of medicine. The International Statistical Institute is based in the Netherlands. The International Esperanto Institute and the International Montessori Association are also located in the country.

In the arts, groups include the Society for the Preservation of Cultural and Natural Beauty in the Netherlands, the Society of Netherlands Literature, the St. Luke Association, the Society for the Advancement of Music, the Royal Netherlands Association of Musicians, Holland Society of Arts and Sciences, and national societies of painters, sculptors, and architects. The Netherlands Center of the International Association of Playwrights, Editors, Essayists and Novelists (PEN); the Netherlands Branch of the International Law Association; and the Netherlands Foundation for International Cooperation are among the organizations active internationally in their fields.

National youth organizations include the Evangelical Students of the Netherlands, Dutch UN Student Association, Junior Chamber, Youth Organization for Freedom and Democracy, The Netherlands Scouting Association, and YMCA/YWCA. There are numerous sports associations for all ages. The Netherlands is home to the International Korfball Federation. Women's organizations include the Netherlands Association for Women's Interests, Women's Work and Equal Citizenship, and the Netherlands Council of Women.

International organizations with national chapters include Amnesty International, Defence for Children International, Greenpeace International, Habitat for Humanity, and the Red Cross.

47 TOURISM, TRAVEL, AND RECREATION

Travel in the Netherlands by public railway, bus, and inland-waterway boat service is frequent and efficient. Principal tourist attractions include the great cities of Amsterdam, Rotterdam, and the Hague, with their famous monuments and museums, particularly the Rijksmuseum in Amsterdam; the flower gardens and bulb fields of the countryside; and North Sea beach resorts. Modern hotels and large conference halls in the large cities are the sites of numerous international congresses, trade shows, and other exhibitions.

Recreational opportunities include theaters, music halls, opera houses, cinemas, zoos, and amusement parks. Popular sports include football (soccer), swimming, cycling, sailing, and hockey. Foreign visitors need only a valid passport for stays of up to 90 days. Proof of sufficient funds, health insurance coverage, return/onward ticket, and lodging reservations may be required upon arrival. Within eight days of arrival, visitors staying long term must register with the local police.

The *Tourism Factbook*, published by the UN World Tourism Organization, reported 9.92 million incoming tourists to the Netherlands in 2009, who spent a total of $12.4 billion. Of those incoming tourists, there were 8.1 million from Europe. There were 203,852 hotel beds available in the Netherlands, which had an occupancy rate of 42%. The estimated daily cost to visit Amsterdam, the capital, was $481. The cost of visiting other cities averaged $387.

48 FAMOUS PERSONS

The Imitation of Christ, usually attributed to the German Thomas à Kempis, is sometimes credited to the Dutch Gerhard Groote (1340–84); written in Latin, it has gone through more than 6,000 editions in about 100 languages. Outstanding Dutch humanists were Wessel Gansfort (1420?–89), precursor of the Reformation; Rodolphus Agricola (Roelof Huysman, 1443–85); and Renaissance humanist Desiderius Erasmus (Gerhard Gerhards, 1466?–1536). Baruch (Benedict de) Spinoza (1632–77), the influential pantheistic philosopher, was born in Amsterdam.

The composers Jacob Obrecht (1453–1505) and Jan Pieterszoon Sweelinck (1562–1621) were renowned throughout Europe; later composers of more local importance were Julius Röntgen (1855–1932), Alfons Diepenbrock (1862–1921), and Cornelis Dopper (1870–1939). Bernard van Dieren (1887–1936), a composer of highly complex music of distinct individuality, settled in London. Henk Badings (b. Bandung, Java, 1907–87) was a prolific composer of international repute. Outstanding conductors of the Amsterdam Concertgebouw Orchestra include Willem Mengelberg (1871–1951), Eduard van Beinum (1901–59), and Bernard Haitink (b. 1929), who also was principal conductor of the London Philharmonic from 1967 to 1979; music director of the Royal Opera House, Covent Garden, from 1987–2002; and principal conductor of the Dresden Staatskapelle from 2002.

Hieronymus Bosch van Aken (1450?–1516) was a famous painter. Dutch painting reached its greatest heights in the 17th century, when Rembrandt van Rijn (1606–69) and Jan Vermeer

(1632–75) painted their masterpieces. Other great painters of the period were Frans Hals (1580–1666), Jan Steen (1626–69), Jacob van Ruisdael (1628–82), and Meindert Hobbema (1638–1709). Two more recent painters, Vincent van Gogh (1853–90) and Piet Mondrian (1872–1944), represent two widely divergent artistic styles and attitudes. Maurits C. Escher (1898–1972) was a skilled and imaginative graphic artist.

Hugo Grotius (Huig de Groot, 1583–1645), who is often regarded as the founder of international law, is famous for his great book, *On the Law of War and Peace*. An outstanding figure in Dutch literature was Joost van den Vondel (1587–1679), poet and playwright. Another noted poet and playwright was Constantijn Huygens (1596–1687), father of the scientist Christian. Popular for several centuries were the poems of Jacob Cats (1577–1660). Distinguished historians include Johan Huizinga (1872–1945) and Pieter Geyl (1887–1966). Anne Frank (b. Germany, 1929–45) became known throughout the world with the publication of the diary and other material that she had written while hiding from the Nazis in Amsterdam.

Jan Pieterszoon Coen (1587–1630), greatest of Dutch empire builders, founded the city of Batavia in the Malay Archipelago (now Jakarta, the capital of Indonesia). Two Dutch naval heroes, Maarten Harpertszoon Tromp (1597–1653) and Michel Adriaanszoon de Ruyter (1607–76), led the Dutch nation in triumphs in sea wars with France, England, and Sweden. Peter Minuit (Minnewit, 1580–1638) founded the colonies of New Amsterdam (now New York City) and New Sweden (now Delaware). Peter Stuyvesant (1592–1672) took over New Sweden from the Swedish and lost New Netherland (now New York State) to the British.

Leading scientists include the mathematician Simon Stevinus (1548–1620); Christian Huygens (1629–95), mathematician, physicist, and astronomer; Anton van Leeuwenhoek (1632–1723), developer of the microscope; Jan Swammerdam (1637–80), authority on insects; and Hermann Boerhaave (1668–1738), physician, botanist, and chemist. Among more recent scientists are a group of Nobel Prize winners: Johannes Diderik van der Waals (1837–1923), authority on gases and fluids, who received the award for physics in 1910; Jacobus Hendricus van 't Hoff (1852–1911), chemistry, 1901; Hendrik Antoon Lorentz (1853–1928) and Pieter Zeeman (1865–1943), who shared the 1902 award for physics; Heike Kamerlingh Onnes (1853–1926), physics, 1913; Willem Einthoven (1860–1927), physiology, 1924; Christiaan Eijkman (1858–1930), physiology, 1929; Petrus Josephus Wilhelmus Debye (1884–1966), chemistry, 1936; Frits Zernike (1888–1966), physics, 1953; Jan Tinbergen (1903–94), economic science, 1969; Dutch-born Tjalling Koopmans (1910–85), who shared the 1975 prize for economic science; Simon van der Meer (b. 1925), cowinner of the physics prize in 1984; Paul J. Crutzen (b. 1933), who shared the 1995 chemistry prize; and Gerardus 't Hooft (b. 1946) and Martinus J.G. Veltman (b. 1931), who shared the 1999 physics prize. The 1911 Nobel Prize for peace was awarded to Tobias Michael Carel Asser (1838–1913). Dutch national Andrei Geim (b. 1958) and his colleague Konstantin Novoselov were awarded the 2010 Nobel Prize in physics for research on graphene, a flat, one-atom-thick layer of carbon that is nearly transparent, extremely strong, and a good conductor of electricity. The material has potential for a wide variety of uses in electronics and computer systems. Novoselov and Geim were among the first to isolate the material from graphite, which is widely used in pencils. Novoselov holds British and Russian citizenship.

The head of state since 1980 has been Queen Beatrix (b. 1938).

⁴⁹DEPENDENCIES

Until 1986, all of the Netherland's island possessions in the Caribbean were grouped under the umbrella of the Netherlands Antilles. However, Aruba seceded from the Netherlands Antilles in 1986, and in 2010 Curaçao and Sint Maarten seceded, leaving Bonaire, Sint Eustatius, and Saba as public entities in the Rijksdienst Caribisch Nederland.

⁵⁰BIBLIOGRAPHY

Annesley, Claire, ed. *A Political and Economic Dictionary of Western Europe*. Philadelphia: Routledge/Taylor and Francis, 2005.

Fuykschot, Cornelia. *Hunger in Holland: Life During the Nazi Occupation*. 2nd ed. Amherst, NY: Prometheus Books, 2005.

Gelauff, George, ed. *Fostering Productivity: Patterns, Determinants, and Policy Implications*. Boston: Elsevier, 2004.

Houben, Marc. *International Crisis Management: The Approach of European States*. New York: Routledge, 2005.

International Smoking Statistics: A Collection of Historical Data from 30 Economically Developed Countries. New York: Oxford University Press, 2002.

Leijenaar, Monique. *Political Empowerment of Women: The Netherlands and Other Countries*. Boston: Martinus Nijhoff, 2004.

McElrath, Karen, ed. *HIV and AIDS: A Global View*. Westport, CT: Greenwood Press, 2002.

Netherlands Investment and Business Guide: Strategic and Practical Information. Washington, DC: International Business Publications USA, 2012.

Roney, John B. *Culture and Customs of the Netherlands*. Santa Barbara, CA: Greenwood Press, 2009.

Vuijsje, Herman. *The Politically Correct Netherlands: Since the 1960s*. Westport, CT: Greenwood Press, 2000.

Wessels, Wolfgang, Andreas Maurer, and Jürgan Mittag (eds.). *Fifteen into One? The European Union and Its Member States*. New York: Palgrave, 2003.

NORWAY

Kingdom of Norway
Kongeriket Norge

CAPITAL: Oslo

FLAG: The national flag has a red field on which appears a blue cross (with an extended right horizontal) outlined in white.

ANTHEM: *Ja, vi elsker dette landet (Yes, We Love This Country).*

MONETARY UNIT: The krone (NOK) of 100 øre is the national currency. There are coins of 50 øre and 1, 5, and 10 kroner, and notes of 20, 50, 100, 200, 500, and 1,000 kroner. NOK1 = US$0.18409 (or US$1 = NOK5.432) as of 2011.

WEIGHTS AND MEASURES: The metric system is the legal standard.

HOLIDAYS: New Year's Day, 1 January; Labor Day, 1 May; National Independence Day, 17 May; Christmas, 25 December; Boxing Day, 26 December. Movable religious holidays include Holy Thursday, Good Friday, Easter Monday, Ascension, and Whitmonday.

TIME: 1 p.m. = noon GMT.

¹LOCATION, SIZE, AND EXTENT

Norway occupies the western part of the Scandinavian peninsula in northern Europe, with almost one-third of the country situated N of the Arctic Circle. It has an area of 323,802 sq km (125,021 sq mi). Comparatively, the area occupied by Norway is slightly larger than the state of New Mexico. Extending 1,752 km (1,089 mi) NNE–SSW, Norway has the greatest length of any European country; its width is 430 km (267 mi) ESE–WNW. Bounded on the N by the Arctic Ocean, on the NE by Finland and Russia, on the E by Sweden, on the S by the Skagerrak, on the SW by the North Sea, and on the W by the Norwegian Sea of the Atlantic Ocean, Norway has a land boundary length of 2,544 km (1,581 mi) and a total coastline estimated at 21,925 km (13,624 mi).

Norway's capital city, Oslo, is in the southern part of the country.

²TOPOGRAPHY

Norway is formed of some of the oldest rocks in the world. It is dominated by mountain masses, with only one-fifth of its total area less than 150 m (500 ft) above sea level. The average altitude is 500 m (1,640 ft). The Glittertinden (2,472 m/8,110 ft, including a glacier at the summit) and Galdhøpiggen (2,469 m/8,100 ft), both in the Jotunheimen, are the highest points in Europe north of the Alpine-Carpathian mountain range. The principal river, the Glåma, 611 km (380 mi) long, flows through the timbered southeast. Much of Norway has been scraped by ice, and there are 1,700 glaciers totaling some 3,400 sq km (1,310 sq mi). In the Lista and Jaeren regions in the far south, extensive glacial deposits form agricultural lowlands. Excellent harbors are provided by the almost numberless fjords, deeply indented bays of scenic beauty that are never closed by ice and penetrate the mainland as far as 182 km

(113 mi). Along many coastal stretches is a chain of islands known as the skjærgård.

³CLIMATE

Because of the North Atlantic Drift, Norway has a mild climate for a country so far north. With the great latitudinal range, the north is considerably cooler than the south, while the interior is cooler than the west coast, influenced by prevailing westerly winds and the Gulf Stream. Oslo's average yearly temperature ranges from about 5°C (41°F) in January to 28°C (82°F) in July. The annual range of coastal temperatures is much less than that of the continental interior. The eastern valleys have less than 30 cm (12 in) of rain yearly, whereas at Haukeland in Masfjord the average rainfall is 330 cm (130 in).

Norway is the land of the midnight sun in the North Cape area, with 24-hour daylight from the middle of May to the end of July, during which the sun does not set. Conversely, there are long winter nights from the end of November to the end of January, during which the sun does not rise above the horizon and the northern lights, or aurora borealis, can be seen.

⁴FLORA AND FAUNA

The World Resources Institute estimates that there are 1,715 plant species in Norway. In addition, Norway is home to 83 mammal, 442 bird, 7 reptile, and 5 amphibian species. The calculation reflects the total number of distinct species residing in the country, not the number of endemic species.

The richest vegetation is found in the southeast around Oslofjord, which is dominated by conifers (spruce, fir, and pine); at lower levels, deciduous trees such as oak, ash, elm, and maple are common. Conifers are seldom found at altitudes above 1,000 m (3,300 ft). Above the conifer zone extends a zone of birch trees;

511

above that, a zone of dwarf willow and dwarf birch, and a zone of lichens and arctic plants. In areas exposed to salt sea winds, there is little tree growth. Of the larger wild animals, elk, roe deer, red deer, and badger survive, as do fox, lynx, and otter. Bird life includes game birds such as capercaillie (cock of the woods) and black grouse. In the rivers,trout, salmon, and char are found.

5 ENVIRONMENT

Norway's plentiful forests, lakes, flora, and wildlife have suffered encroachment in recent years from the growing population and consequent development of urban areas, roads, and hydroelectric power. The forest floor and waterways have been polluted by Norway's own industry and by airborne industrial pollution from central Europe and the British Isles in the form of acid rain. The acid rain problem has affected the nation's water supply over an area of nearly 18,130 sq km (7,000 sq mi).

Since its creation in 1972, the Ministry of the Environment has been Norway's principal environmental agency. Between 1962 and 1985, 15 national parks and more than 150 nature reserves were established. The West Norwegian Fjords—Geirangerfjord and Naerofjord—were named as a natural UNESCO World Heritage site in 2005. The country has 51 Ramsar Wetland Sites.

By the early 1980s, the government enacted stringent regulations to prevent oil spills from wells and tankers operating on the Norwegian continental shelf. Coastal protection devices have since been installed, and new technologies to prevent oil damage have been developed.

In 1992, Norway was among the 50 nations with the world's heaviest emissions of carbon dioxide from industrial sources, which totaled 60,200 kilotons, a per capita level of 14.03 metric tons. In 2000, however, total carbon dioxide emissions had decreased to 49,900 kilotons. By 2008, the UN reported that carbon dioxide emissions in Norway totaled 42,722 kilotons. Transportation vehicle emissions are also a significant source of air pollution.

Pollution control laws operate on the premise that the polluter must accept legal and economic responsibility for any damage caused and for preventing any recurrence; the state makes loans and grants for the purchase of pollution control equipment. Municipal authorities supervise waste disposal.

The World Resources Institute reported that Norway had designated 1.55 million hectares (3.84 million acres) of land for protection as of 2006. Water resources totaled 381.4 cu km (91.5 cu mi) while water usage was 2.4 cu km (0.576 cu mi) per year. Domestic water usage accounted for 23% of total usage, industrial for 67%, and agricultural for 10%. Per capita water usage totaled 519 cu m (18,328 cu ft) per year.

According to a 2011 report issued by the International Union for Conservation of Nature and Natural Resources (IUCN), threatened species included 7 mammals, 2 birds, 19 fish, 4 mollusks, 6 other invertebrates, and 4 plants. Threatened species include the Baltic sturgeon, marsh snail, and freshwater pearl mussel.

6 POPULATION

The US Central Intelligence Agency (CIA) estimates the population of Norway in 2011 to be approximately 4,691,849, which placed it at number 118 in population among the 196 nations of the world. In 2011, approximately 12.916% of the population was over 65 years of age, with another 25.318% under 15 years of age.

The median age in Norway was 40 years. There were 0.98 males for every female in the country. The population's annual rate of change was 0.329%. The projected population for the year 2025 was 5,600,000. Population density in Norway was calculated at 14 people per sq km (36 people per sq mi).

The UN estimated that 79% of the population lived in urban areas, and that urban populations had an annual rate of change of 1.2%. The largest urban area was Metropolitan Oslo, with a population of 1,442,318. With an annual growth rate of 1.64%, Oslo was the fastest-growing city in Europe, largely due to immigration.

7 MIGRATION

Estimates of Norway's net migration rate, carried out by the CIA in 2011, amounted to 1.70 migrants per 1,000 citizens. The total number of emigrants living abroad was 184,000, and the total number of immigrants living in Norway was 485,400. Beginning in 1866, North America received great waves of immigration from Norway, including an estimated 880,000 Norwegian immigrants to the United States by 1910. The United States and Canada still provide residence for many of the estimated 400,000 Norwegians living abroad. Emigration in recent years has not been significant.

Norway is an important resettlement country. Main countries of origin included Russia, Poland, Lithuania, Eritrea, Somalia, Serbia and Montenegro, Nigeria, the Philippines, and Afghanistan.

8 ETHNIC GROUPS

For centuries, the Norwegians have been a highly homogeneous people of Germanic (Nordic, Alpine, and Baltic) stock, generally tall and fair-skinned, with blue eyes. As of 2010, about 94.4% of the population was Norwegian. Other Europeans account for about 3.6% of the population. The Sami (Lapp) population has been estimated at approximately 50,000 people, primarily in the northern portion of the country.

9 LANGUAGES

Norwegian, closely related to Danish and Swedish, is part of the Germanic language group. In addition to the letters of the English alphabet, it has the letters æ, å, and ø. Historically, Old Norse was displaced by a modified form of Danish for writing, but in the 19th century there arose a reaction against Danish usages. Many dialects are spoken. There are two language forms, Bokmål and Nynorsk; the former (spoken by a large majority of Norwegians) is based on the written, town language, the latter on country dialects. Both forms of Norwegian have absorbed many modern international words, particularly from British and American English, despite attempts to provide indigenous substitutes. While Norwegian is the official language, English is spoken widely in Norway, especially in the urban areas. The Sami (Lapps) in northern Norway have retained their own language, which is of Finno-Ugric origin. There is also a small Finnish-speaking minority.

10 RELIGIONS

Citizens are generally considered to be members of the Evangelical Lutheran Church of Norway, which is the state church, unless they specifically indicate other affiliations. As such, a 2010 report indicates that about 79.2% of the population are nominally affiliated with the Evangelical Lutheran Church. The Roman Catholicism is the next largest Christian denomination, with about

57,000 registered members. The Pentecostal Church has 40,000 registered members. At 2% of the population, the Muslim community is the largest non-Christian faith, increasing from 84,000 members in 2009 to 93,000 members in 2010. There are small communities of Buddhists, Jews, Orthodox Christians, Sikhs, and Hindus. The Norwegian Humanist Association, an organization for atheists and the nonreligious, claims about 78,000 adults as registered members. The constitution provides for religious freedom for all faiths, even though the religion of state is designated as the Evangelical Lutheran Church of Norway. The king nominates the Lutheran bishops and the Lutheran church receives an endowment from the state. The constitution states that the king and half of the cabinet must be members of this church. There are a number of interfaith groups within the country, including the Cooperation Council for Faith and Secular Society, the Oslo Coalition for Freedom of Religious Beliefs, and the Ecumenical Council of Christian Communities.

11 TRANSPORTATION

In spite of Norway's difficult terrain, the road system has been well engineered, with tunnels and zigzags, particularly in the fjordlands of the west; however, there are problems of maintenance because of heavy rain in the west and freezing in the east. Road transport accounts for a vast majority of inland passenger transport. The state railway operates bus routes and has been steadily increasing its activities in this field, which is heavily subsidized by the government. In 2009, there were 2,552 km (1,586 mi) of electrified rail.

With a merchant fleet of 688 vessels of 1,000 gross registered tons or more, Norway has one of the world's largest fleets. The sale of Norwegian ships and their registration abroad, which increased considerably during the mid-1980s, severely reduced the size of the fleet. In 1988, the Norwegian International Ship Register program began, whereby ships could be registered offshore, thus allowing foreign vessels to operate under the Norwegian flag while reducing costs to shipowners. Oslo and Bergen have excellent harbor facilities, and several other ports are almost as fully equipped. The CIA reported that Norway has a total of 92,946 km (57,754 mi) of roads as of 2008, of which 72,033 km (44,759 mi) were paved. There are 575 vehicles per 1,000 people in the country. Railroads extend for 4,114 km (2,556 mi).

There are 98 airports, which transported 8.79 million passengers in 2009 according to the World Bank. Norway had 67 airports with paved runways. There was also one heliport. Flesland at Bergen, Sola at Stavanger, and Fornebu and Gardermoen at Oslo are the main centers of air traffic. External services are operated by the Scandinavian Airlines System (SAS), which is 21% Norwegian-owned. Braathens Air Transport operates most of the domestic scheduled flights. Important internal air services include those linking Kirkenes, Tromsø, and Bodø; 2,000 km (1,240 mi) long, this air route is reputed to be the most difficult to operate in western Europe.

12 HISTORY

Humans have lived in Norway for about 10,000 years, but only since the early centuries of the Christian era have the names of tribes and individuals been recorded. This was the period when small kingdoms were forming; the name Norge ("Northern Way") was in use for the coastal district from Vestfold to Hålogaland before AD 900. The Viking period (800–1050) was one of vigorous expansion, aided by consolidation of a kingdom under Olav Haraldsson.

From the death of Olav in 1030, the nation was officially Christian. During the next two centuries-a period marked by dynastic conflicts and civil wars-a landed aristocracy emerged, displacing peasant freeholders. A common legal code was adopted in 1274–76, and the right of succession to the crown was fixed. Shortly before, Iceland (1261) and Greenland (1261–64) came under Norwegian rule, but the Hebrides (Western Isles), also Norwegian possessions, were lost in 1266. Before 1300, Hanseatic merchants of the Baltic towns secured control of the essential grain imports, weakening the Norwegian economy.

Norway lost its independence at the death of Haakon V in 1319, when Magnus VII became ruler of both Norway and Sweden. The Black Death ravaged the country in the middle of the 14th century. In 1397, the three Scandinavian countries were united under Queen Margrethe of Denmark. Sweden left the union in 1523, but for nearly 300 more years Norway was ruled by Danish governors. Although the loss to Sweden of the provinces of Bohuslän (1645), Härjedalen (1658), and Jämtland (1645) was a disadvantage, gradual exploitation of the forest wealth improved Norwegian status. Denmark's alliance with France during the Napoleonic Wars resulted in the dissolution of the union.

With the Peace of Kiel (1814), Norway was ceded to Sweden, but the Faroe Islands, Iceland, and Greenland were retained by Denmark. However, Norwegians resisted Swedish domination, adopted a new constitution on 17 May 1814, and elected the Danish Prince Christian Frederick as king of Norway. Sweden then invaded Norway, but agreed to let Norway keep its constitution in return for accepting union with Sweden under the rule of the Swedish king. During the second half of the 19th century, the *Storting* (parliament) became more powerful; an upsurge of nationalist agitation, both within the Storting and among Norway's cultural leaders, paved the way for the referendum that in 1905 gave independence to Norway. Feelings ran high on both sides, but once the results were announced, Norway and Sweden settled down to friendly relations. The Danish Prince Carl was elected king of Norway, assuming the name Haakon VII.

Although Norway remained neutral during World War I, its merchant marine suffered losses. Norway proclaimed its neutrality during the early days of World War II, but Norwegian waters were strategically too important for Norway to remain outside the war. Germany invaded on 9 April 1940. National resistance was led by King Haakon, who in June escaped with the government to England where he established Norway's government-in-exile, representing the legally elected Storting. Governmental affairs in Oslo fell to Vidkun Quisling, a Fascist leader and former Norwegian defense minister who had aided the German invasion and whose name subsequently became a synonym for collaborator; after the German surrender, he was arrested, convicted of treason, and shot. During the late 1940s, Norway abandoned its former neutrality, accepted Marshall Plan aid from the United States, and joined NATO. King Haakon died in 1957 and was succeeded by Olav V. King Harald V succeeded his father who died on 17 January 1991.

The direction of economic policy has been the major issue in Norwegian postwar history, especially as related to taxation and the degree of government intervention in private industry. Economic planning was introduced, and several state-owned enterprises were established. Prior to the mid-1970s, Labor Party-dominated governments enjoyed a broad public consensus for their foreign and military policies. A crucial development occurred in November 1972, when the Norwegian electorate voted in a referendum to reject Norway's entry into the European Community (EC), despite a strong pro-EC stance adopted by the minority Labor government. After the 1973 general elections, the Labor Party's hold on government policies began to erode, and in the 1981 elections the party lost control of the government to the Conservatives. Although the non-Socialists retained a small majority in the 1985 elections, disagreements among them permitted Labor to return to office in 1986.

Norway reaffirmed its rejection of the European Union (EU) on 28 November 1994, when the vote was cast with the results 52% against and 47.8% for joining Europe. Public opinion polls in June 2003 registered 51.9% of the electorate in favor of joining the EU; 38.2% were opposed and 9.9% were undecided.

Norway was forthright in its support for the US-led war on terror following the 11 September 2001 terrorist attacks. It supported the NATO decision to invoke Article 5 of the alliance's constitution, pledging all members to collective security in the event of an attack on one. However, Norway did not support the US-led war in Iraq that began on 19 March 2003. Prime Minister Bondevik held that international weapons inspectors authorized by UN Security Council Resolution 1441 to inspect Iraq's weapons programs should have been given more time to do their work, and that military action should not be taken without an express Security Council resolution authorizing it. Eight out of ten Norwegian voters agreed in March 2003 that Norway should not support the US and British decision to go to war against Iraq.

In April 2010, Russia and Norway resolved its longstanding border dispute within the Barents Sea by somewhat evenly dividing the 175,000-sq-km (68,000 sq-mi) region. The Barents Sea is thought to hold a tremendous amount of oil and gas. Ice shrinkage has improved accessibility to the region's mineral wealth, causing dispute over the area.

In July 2011, Norway suffered one of the most violent attacks in its history. A lone assailant, Anders Behring Breivik, detonated a car bomb outside of government buildings in Oslo, which killed 8 people. This was followed by a massacre on Utoeya Island, where dressed as a police officer, Breivik spent over an hour on a violent rampage, shooting and killing 69 people. The majority of those killed on Utoeya Island were teenagers attending a camp hosted by the Labour Party's youth wing. Breivik declared that he was on a crusade against multiculturalism and the "Muslim invasion" of Europe. As of January 2012, Breivik was found to be criminally insane due to paranoid schizophrenia, but was awaiting a second psychological evaluation.

13 GOVERNMENT

Norway is a constitutional monarchy. The constitution of 17 May 1814, as subsequently amended, vests executive power in the king and legislative power in the Storting. Prior to 1990, the eldest son of the monarch was next in line to the throne. A constitutional amendment in May 1990 allowed females to succeed to the throne as well. The amendment only affects those born after 1990. The king or queen must be a member of the Evangelical Lutheran Church of Norway, which he/she heads. Royal power is exercised through a cabinet (the Council of State), consisting of a prime minister and various ministers of state. Since the introduction of parliamentary rule in 1884, the Storting has become the supreme authority, with sole control over national budgets and the power to override the king's veto under a specified procedure. While the king is theoretically free to choose his own cabinet, in practice the Storting selects the ministers, who must resign if the Storting votes no confidence.

The Storting is made up of 169 representatives from 19 counties. Election to a four-year term is determined by direct, universal suffrage at age 18, on the basis of proportional representation. After election, the Storting divided into two sections by choosing one fourth of its members to form the upper chamber Lagting, with the rest constituting the lower chamber Odelsting. The Odelsting dealt with certain types of bills after the committee stage and passed them onto the Lagting, which, after approval, sent them to the king for the royal assent. Financial, organizational, political, and other matters were dealt with in plenary session. While the constitution states that the Storting may not be dissolved, in 2007 a vote successfully dissolved the division between the Odelsting and Lagting. This took effect in 2009 with the election of a new Storting.

A special parliamentary ombudsman supervises the observance of laws and statutes as applied by the courts and by public officials. His main responsibility is to protect citizens against unjust or arbitrary treatment by civil servants.

14 POLITICAL PARTIES

The present-day Conservative Party (Høyre) was established in 1885. The Liberal Party (Venstre), founded in 1885 as a counterbalance to the civil servant class, became the rallying organization of the Agrarian Friends' Association. The party's political program stresses social reform. Industrial workers founded the Labor Party (Arbeiderparti) in 1887 and, with the assistance of the Liberals, obtained universal male suffrage in 1898 and votes for women in 1913. The Social Democrats broke away from the Labor Party in 1921–22, and the Communist Party (Kommunistparti), made up of former Laborites, was established in 1923. The moderate Socialists reunited and revived the Labor Party organization in 1927. The Agrarian (Farmers) Party was formed in 1920; it changed its name to the Center Party (Senterparti) in 1958. The Christian People's Party (Kristelig Folkeparti), founded in 1933, and also known as the Christian Democratic Party, supports the principles of Christianity in public life.

For several decades, the Liberals were either in office or held the balance of power, but in 1935, as a result of the economic depression, an alliance between the Agrarian and Labor parties led to the formation of a Labor government. During World War II, the main parties formed a national cabinet-in-exile. Political differences between right and left sharpened in the postwar period. Attempts to form a national coalition among the four non-Socialist parties proved unsuccessful until the 1965 elections, when they gained a combined majority of 80 seats in the Storting. Per Borten, who was appointed in October 1965 to form a non-Socialist coalition

LOCATION: 57°57′31″ to 71°11′8″ N; 4°30′13″ to 31°10′4″ E. BOUNDARY LENGTHS: Finland, 729 kilometers (455 miles); Russia, 167 kilometers (104 miles); Sweden, 1,619 kilometers (1,011 miles); total coastline, 21,925 kilometers (13,703 miles). TERRITORIAL SEA LIMIT: 4 miles.

government, retained office in the 1969 elections, although with a majority of only two seats.

In the 1973 general elections, the Labor Party received only 35.3% of the national vote; its representation in the Storting shrank to 62 seats, but with its Socialist allies, it was able to form a minority government. The Christian People's Party, meanwhile,

registered gains, as did the Socialist Electoral League, a new coalition, which was able to take a number of votes away from the Labor Party. In 1975, the Socialist Electoral League was transformed into a single grouping known as the Socialist Left Party, comprising the former Socialist People's Party, the Norwegian Communist Party, and the Democratic Socialist Party (formed in 1972). The transformation, which resulted in a platform that voiced criticism neither of the former USSR nor of Leninist ideology, marked the first occasion when a Western Communist Party voted to dissolve its organization and merge into a new grouping with other parties.

In the 1977 elections, Labor expanded its representation to 76 seats, but its Socialist Left ally won only two seats, and their coalition commanded a single-seat majority in the Storting. Odvar Nordli, who became prime minister in January 1976, succeeding the retiring Trygve Bratteli, formed a new cabinet and remained in office until February 1981, when he quit because of ill health. His successor was Gro Harlem Brundtland, Norway's first woman prime minister. Her term in office lasted only until September, when the non-Socialist parties obtained a combined total of more than 56% of the vote and a Conservative, Kåre Willoch, became prime minister of a minority government. In April 1983, the government was transformed into a majority coalition.

Following the loss of a vote of confidence, the coalition was replaced in May 1986 by a Labor minority government led by Brundtland, who formed a cabinet of eight female ministers out of 18. With an average age of 47, her cabinet was the youngest ever in Norway.

Labor increased its support in the 1993 election, winning 67 seats. The Center Party became the second-largest party while the Conservatives and other right-wing parties suffered a decline.

The September 1997 election brought to power a coalition of Christian People's party, Liberals, and Center party and was headed by the Lutheran minister, Kjell Magne Bondevik. The coalition claimed only 42 seats in parliament and Bondevik was forced to seek compromises with opposition parties to pass legislation. In March 1999 his government lost a vote of confidence after Bondevik refused to weaken antipollution laws to allow the construction of gas-fired power plants.

Because the next legislative elections could only be held in September 2001, Jens Stoltenberg, the elected leader of the Labor party, became prime minister at the age of 41, becoming Norway's youngest leader. Stoltenberg pledged to seek strong ties to Europe and favored European Union membership. He also announced the privatization of Statoil, the state's oil company, and Telenor, the state-owned telecommunication group. The partial sell-off of Statoil was of huge symbolic significance because of its role as the guardian of the nation's oil and gas wealth.

In the September 2001 parliamentary elections, the Labor Party came in first, although it suffered its worst defeat since 1924, taking only 24.3% of the vote, compared with 35% in 1997. Voters were disgruntled with high tax rates-in some cases 50%-and inadequate public services, including hospitals, schools, and public transportation. The far-right Progress Party gained seats. Bondevik was returned to power as prime minister, putting together a coalition of the Christian People's Party, the Liberals, and the Conservatives, with support from the Progress Party.

In the September 2005 parliamentary elections, the Labor Party came in first, taking 32.7% of the vote (61 seats), an increase of 8.4% (18 seats) over the 2001 elections. The Progress Party came in second with 22.1% of the vote (38 seats), an increase of 7.4% of the vote (and 12 seats) over the 2001 elections. Jens Stoltenberg, leader of the Labor Party, claimed he would devote more of the country's oil wealth to jobs, schools, and care for the elderly. Stol-

tenberg was to form a coalition government with the Socialist Left and Center parties.

In the 2009 elections, the Labor Party won 35.4% of the vote (64 seats), followed by the Progress Party with 22.9% (41 seats), the Conservative Party with 17.2% (30 seats), Socialist Left Party with 6.2% (11 seats), Center Party with 6.2% (11 seats), Christian People's Party with 5.5% (10 seats), and the Liberal Party with 3.9% (2 seats). Stoltenberg retained his post as prime minister. Furthermore, with the newly elected Storting, the 2007 decision to end the division between the Odelsting and Lagting went into effect.

15 LOCAL GOVERNMENT

Norway has 435 municipalities (*kommuner*) of varying size, each administered by an elected municipal council. They are grouped into 19 counties (*fylker*), each governed by an elected county council. Each county is headed by a governor appointed by the king in council. Oslo is the only urban center that alone constitutes a county; the remaining 18 counties consist of both urban and rural areas. County and municipal councils are popularly elected every four years. The municipalities have wide powers over the local economy, with the state exercising strict supervision. They have the right to tax and to use their resources to support education, libraries, social security, and public works such as streetcar lines, gas and electricity works, roads, and town planning, but they are usually aided in these activities by state funds.

16 JUDICIAL SYSTEM

Each municipality has a conciliation council (*forliksråd*), elected by the municipal council, to mediate in lesser civil cases so as to settle them, if possible, before they go to court; under some conditions the conciliation councils also render judgments. The courts of first instance are town courts (*byrett*) and rural courts (*herredsrett*), which try both civil and criminal cases. Their decisions may be brought before a court of appeals (*lagmannsrett*), which also serves as a court of first instance in more serious criminal cases. There are six such courts: Borgarting, Eidsivating, Agder, Gulating, Frostating and Hålogaland. Appeals may be taken to the Supreme Court (Høyesterett) at Oslo, which consists of a chief justice and 18 judges. Special courts include a Social Insurance Court and a Labor Disputes Court who mediates industrial relations disputes.

The judiciary is independent of both the legislative and the executive branches. In criminal cases, defendants are afforded free legal counsel. Indigent persons are granted free legal counsel in certain civil cases as well.

17 ARMED FORCES

The International Institute for Strategic Studies reports that armed forces in Norway totaled 26,450 members in 2011. The force is comprised of 8,900 from the army, 3,750 from the navy, 5,550 from the air force, 7,750 from central support, and 500 members of the home guard. Armed forces represent 1% of the labor force in Norway. Defense spending totaled $4.9 billion and accounted for 1.9% of GDP. Norway is the host nation for the NATO Allied

Forces North headquarters and provides troops or observers for eight peacekeeping operations.

18 INTERNATIONAL COOPERATION

Norway has been a member of the UN since 27 November 1945; the country participates in the ECE and several nonregional specialized agencies, such as the FAO, IAEA, the World Bank, UNSECO, UNHCR, UNIDO, and the WHO. Norwegian experts serve in many countries under the UN Technical Assistance program. Norway has participated in at least 30 UN peacekeeping operations. The Norwegian Peace Corps, launched as an experiment in 1963, was made a permanent part of Norway's program of international aid in 1965.

Norway is a member of the WTO, the African Development Bank, the Asian Development Bank, the Council of the Baltic Sea States, the Euro-Atlantic Partnership Council, the Inter-American Development Bank, the Council of Europe, EFTA, the OSCE, the Paris Club, NATO, the Nordic Council, the Nordic Investment Bank, and OECD.

Norway is part of the Australia Group, the Zangger Committee, the Nuclear Suppliers Group (London Group), the Nuclear Energy Agency, the European Organization for Nuclear Research (CERN), and the Organization for the Prohibition of Chemical Weapons. In environmental cooperation, Norway is part of the Antarctic Treaty, the Basel Convention, the Convention on Biological Diversity, Ramsar, CITES, the London Convention, International Tropical Timber Agreements, the Kyoto Protocol, the Montréal Protocol, MARPOL, the Nuclear Test Ban Treaty, and the UN Conventions on the Law of the Sea, Climate Change and Desertification.

Despite Norway twice applying for EU membership, its electorate blocked accession by voting against EU membership in referendums held in 1972 and again in 1994.

19 ECONOMY

The prosperous Norwegian economy is credited to the country's successful balance of government ownership and free market activity. Norway was formerly dependent on fishing and lumbering as its main industries, but has been taking advantage of its oil reserves in the North Sea since the 1970s. It is one of the world's leading exporters of oil and gas, which account for one-third of the nation's exports. This oil wealth served as a buffer for the nation during the 2008–09 global financial crisis. High consumer confidence and growth in the labor market are only two of the many factors that continue to strengthen Norway's economy. However, Norwegian competitiveness in the global economy is hampered by a small population (4.6 million), a strict immigration policy, and an expensive social welfare system that places high tax burdens on the population.

From 1949 to 1989, the real GDP rose on the average by 3.9% per year. The GDP fell in 1988 for the first time in 30 years. Since 1989, however, incremental growth has continued. In 1999, low world oil prices led to a reduced growth rate of 1.1%, while the recovery of oil prices in 2000 helped raise GDP growth moderately. GDP growth fell in 2002 and 2003, largely due to the global economic slowdown of 2001–02. The GDP rate of change in Norway, as of 2010, was 0.4%. Inflation stood at 2.4%, and unemployment was reported at 3.6%.

Norwegian voters rejected European Union membership in 1994. However, Norway is a member of the European Economic Area (EEA), which consists of the EU member countries together with Norway, Iceland, and Liechtenstein. Membership gives Norway most of the rights and obligation of the EU single market but very little ability to influence EU decisions. Norway adopts and implements most EU directives.

20 INCOME

Norway is one of the richest countries in the world, in per capita terms. The World Bank estimates that Norway, with 0.08% of the world's population, accounted for 0.40% of the world's GDP. By comparison, the United States, with 4.85% of the world's population, accounted for 22.51% of world GDP.

The CIA estimated that in 2010 the GDP of Norway was $255.3 billion. The CIA defines GDP as the value of all final goods and services produced within a nation in a given year and computed on the basis of purchasing power parity (PPP) rather than value as measured on the basis of the rate of the exchange based on current dollars. The per capita GDP was estimated at $54,600. The annual growth rate of GDP was 0.4%. The average inflation rate was 2.4%. It was estimated that agriculture accounted for 2.1% of GDP, industry 40.1%, and services 57.8%.

According to the World Bank, remittances from citizens living abroad totaled $631.5 million or about $135 per capita and accounted for approximately 0.2% of GDP.

The World Bank reports that in 2009, household consumption in Norway totaled $161.5 billion or about $34,411 per capita, measured in current US dollars rather than PPP. Household consumption includes expenditures of individuals, households, and nongovernmental organizations on goods and services, excluding the purchases of dwellings. It was estimated that household consumption was growing at an average annual rate of 0.4%.

As of 2011 the most recent study by the World Bank reported that actual individual consumption in Norway was 55.1% of GDP and accounted for 0.30% of world consumption. By comparison, the United States accounted for 25.44% of world individual consumption. The World Bank also estimated that 6.9% of Norway's GDP was spent on food and beverages, 10.5% on housing and household furnishings, 2.2% on clothes, 7.3% on health, 5.8% on transportation, 1.3% on communications, 5.9% on recreation, 2.2% on restaurants and hotels, and 8.9% on miscellaneous goods and services and purchases from abroad.

21 LABOR

As of 2010, Norway had a total labor force of 2.602 million people. Within that labor force, CIA estimates in 2008 noted that 2.9% were employed in agriculture, 21.1% in industry, and 76% in the service sector.

As of 2011, about 55% of the labor force was unionized. Under Norwegian law, workers can organize and join unions, engage in collective bargaining, and strike. Government employees, including military personnel, can also organize unions and bargain collectively. Antiunion discrimination is prohibited by law.

In 1919, the eight-hour day was established, together with paid holiday periods. As framed by the Norwegian Working Environment Act, the work week consists of a maximum of 40 hours; any time exceeding this warrants overtime pay of a minimum of 40%

over an employee's standard hourly pay. The typical Norwegian works approximately 37.5 hours per week. There are also 25 days of paid leave, with 31 days for those 60 and older. There is no legal minimum wage. Wages scales are set through negotiations involving local government, employers and workers. Children between the ages of 13 and 18 years may engage in light work that will not negatively affect their health or education, but only on a part-time basis.

22 AGRICULTURE

While the production of wheat and mixed grains has dropped sharply since 1949, production for rye, oats, and barley has more than doubled. The greater part of these crops is used to supplement potatoes and hay in the feeding of livestock.

Because of the small size of the holdings, many farm families pursue additional occupations, mainly in forestry, fishing, and handicrafts. Norway imports most of its grain and large quantities of its fruits and vegetables. With steep slopes and heavy precipitation, Norway requires substantial quantities of fertilizers to counteract soil leaching. Smallholders and those in marginal farming areas in the north and in the mountains receive considerable government assistance for the purchase of fertilizers. Mechanization of agriculture is developing rapidly.

Since 1928, the state has subsidized Norwegian grain production; a state monopoly over the import of grains maintains the price of Norwegian-grown grains. The Ministry of Agriculture has divisions dealing with agricultural education, economics, and other aspects. Each county has an agricultural society headed by a government official. These societies, financed half by the district and half by the state, implement government schemes for improving agricultural practices.

Roughly 3% of the total land was farmed, and the country's major crops included barley, wheat, and potatoes. Cereal production in 2009 amounted to 946,500 tons, fruit production 31,971 tons, and vegetable production 187,976 tons.

23 ANIMAL HUSBANDRY

The UN Food and Agriculture Organization (FAO) reported that Norway dedicated 175,000 hectares (432,434 acres) to permanent pasture or meadow in 2009. During that year, the country tended 3.8 million chickens, 877,711 head of cattle, and 839,346 pigs. The production from these animals amounted to 96,667 tons of beef and veal, 108,863 tons of pork, 70,228 tons of poultry, 50,565 tons of eggs, and 1.23 million tons of milk. Norway also produced 7,832 tons of cattle hide and 4,584 tons of raw wool.

Norway is self-sufficient in farm animals and livestock products. It is also well known for its working horses. By careful breeding, Norway has developed dairy cows with very good milk qualities; artificial insemination is now widely used. Norwegian production of milk, cheese, and meat also satisfies local demand. However, at the end of 2011, Norway suffered a butter shortage, calling into question whether Norway should ease import tariffs on agricultural products.

24 FISHING

Seafood is Norway's third-largest export item, after petroleum products and metals. The main commercial species are herring, cod, mackerel, and sardines. Cod spawn in March and April off the Lofoten Islands. The Lofoten fisheries are coastal, permitting the use of small craft, but there has been increased use of large trawlers that fish in the waters of Greenland, the Norwegian Sea, and the Barents Sea. Cod roe and liver (yielding cod-liver oil) are valuable by-products. In recent years there has been concern about declining wild fish stocks in the sea, but for Norway the wild fish catches seem to increase almost every year. According to the Norwegian Institute of Marine Research, the most important fish stocks in northern Norwegian waters have stabilized, and will remain at a high level in the years to come. The traditional wage system is on a share-of-the-catch basis. In view of the seasonal nature of the fisheries, many men work also in agriculture or forestry, and the supplementary income from part-time fishing is important to small farmers.

Aquaculture is important in Norway, with over 3,500 workers and 700 facilities located along the entire coast from the Swedish border in the south to Finnmark far north of the Arctic Circle. Norway had 8,464 decked commercial fishing boats in 2008. The annual capture totaled 2.43 million tons according to the UN FAO. Seafood exports in 2011 totaled 2.3 million tons, valued at just over $8.5 billion, showing a slight decrease in seafood exports for the first time in seven years.

Norway was one of the four countries that did not agree to phase out whaling by 1986, having opposed a 1982 resolution of the International Whaling Commission to that effect. In 2006, the Norwegian parliament increased the whaling quota, which allows for hunting of the Minke whale, by 30% (or 1,052 Minke whales per year).

25 FORESTRY

Approximately 33% of Norway is covered by forest. Norway's forestland totals 8,868,000 hectares (21,913,000 acres), of which over 80% is owned by individuals, 9% by the state, and 7% by local governments; the remainder is held by institutions, companies, and cooperatives. The UN FAO estimated the 2009 roundwood production at 6.63 million cu m (234.2 million cu ft). The value of all forest products, including roundwood, totaled $1.68 billion. The state subsidizes silviculture and the building of forest roads. The Norwegian Forest Research Institute has centers near Oslo and Bergen.

26 MINING

Mining was Norway's oldest major export industry. In 2008, non-fuel mining and quarrying employed 4,332 persons in 638 enterprises, with production valued at over €1.1 billion. Some working mines were established more than 300 years ago and, for a time, silver, iron, and copper were important exports. Iron pyrites and iron ore were still mined in considerable quantities. Petroleum and gas comprised Norway's leading industry in 2009, and metals, chemicals, and mining were among other leading industries. Among export commodities, petroleum and petroleum products ranked first, while metals and chemicals followed close behind. Known deposits of other minerals were small; they included limestone, quartz, dolomite, feldspar, and mica (flake). In 2009, production of iron ore and concentrate (metal content) was 896,000 metric tons, up from 477,000 metric tons in 2008. Titanium (metal content) production in 2009 was 671,000 metric tons (7% of world total). Norway also produced nickel, hydraulic cement, dolomite, feldspar, graphite, lime (hydrated, quicklime), limestone, flake mica, nepheline syenite, nitrogen, olivine sand, quartz, quartzite, soapstone, steatite, sulfur (as a by-product), and talc. No lead or zinc was mined from 1998 through 2008, and no pyrite from 1999 through 2009. The largest titanium deposit in Europe was at Soknedal. A large plant at Thamshavn used half the Orkla mines' output of pyrites for sulfur production. Reserves of minerals have generally been depleted, except for olivine, which was abundant. There has been recent gold exploration, and a zinc exploration program in the Roros district confirmed the existence of extensive stratiform sulfide mineralization with dimensions of a type that could host commercial deposits.

27 ENERGY AND POWER

Norway has Western Europe's largest proven reserves of oil, which are located on the country's continental shelf. Norway is also the second-largest supplier of natural gas to continental Europe and one of the largest producers in the world. In spite of its oil and gas reserves, hydropower is the primary source of electric power for Norway since all of the gas and most of the oil produced is exported.

Norway is the fifth-largest exporter of oil in the world. In 2011, 28% of the state's revenues were generated from petroleum and petroleum products. As of 2010, Norway's proven reserves of oil amounted to 5.67 billion barrels. Domestic consumption for oil averaged 221,300 barrels of oil per day. There are two major refining facilities: the 200,000 barrel-per-day Mongstad plant, which is operated by 71% government owned Statoil; and the 110,000 barrel-per-day Slagen plant, which is operated by ExxonMobil.

Norway's natural gas reserves are mainly in the North Sea, although the Barents and Norwegian Seas are known to have significant reserves. As of 2011, Norway's proven reserves of natural gas were estimated at 2.039 trillion cu ft. In 2010, natural gas production was estimated at 106.3 billion cu ft, with domestic consumption that year estimated at 6.6 billion cu ft.

Norway's reserves of coal, unlike its reserves of oil and natural gas, are very modest.

The World Bank reported in 2008 that Norway produced 141.7 billion kWh of electricity and consumed 118.6 billion kWh, or 25,272 kWh per capita. Roughly 59% of energy came from fossil fuels, while 41% came from alternative fuels.

28 INDUSTRY

In 2010, industry made up 39.3% of Norway's GDP. The most important export industries are oil and gas extraction, metalworking, pulp and paper, chemical products, and processed fish. Products traditionally classified as home market industries (electrical and nonelectrical machinery, casting and foundry products, textiles, paints, varnishes, rubber goods, and furniture) also make an important contribution. Electrochemical and electrometallurgical products-aluminum, ferroalloys, steel, nickel, copper, magnesium, and fertilizers-are based mainly on Norway's low-cost electric power. Without any bauxite reserves of its own, Norway has thus been able to become a leading producer of aluminum. Industrial output is being increasingly diversified.

About half of Norway's industries are situated in the Oslofjord area. Other industrial centers are located around major cities along the coast as far north as Trondheim. Norway has two oil

refineries. In the early 2000s, despite an improvement in world oil prices, investment in offshore oil and natural gas remained in decline, in part due to the completion of major projects, such as the Aasgard field. Norway's oil and gas reserves have been on a declining trend. As of 2010, proven oil reserves were 5.67 billion barrels. Oil reserves were projected to last until 2050, while natural gas reserves were projected to last until 2095. The state oil company is Statoil. Norway's price support level for the oil industry is low, at around $20 per barrel of oil. Norway's oil economy employs more than 100,000 Norwegians. By 2020, natural gas production in Norway was expected to exceed its oil production.

As Norway's economy will not be able to depend indefinitely upon oil, it must diversify. In addition to developing its knowledge-based economy (biotechnology, nanotechnology, the Internet, and knowledge-services), Norway may look to further develop its mineral resources.

29 SCIENCE AND TECHNOLOGY

A highly advanced industrialized nation, Norway invested 1.62% of its GDP on research and development (R&D) in 2008. High-tech exports amounted to approximately $4.7 billion in 2009 and made up 16% of all manufactured exports. According to the World Bank, there were 1,140 patent applications in science and technology in Norway as of 2009. Norway employed 5,468 researchers in R&D per million people in 2008. Public funds come either as direct grants from the central government or as proceeds from the State Football Pool, whose net receipts are divided between research and sports.

The four principal research councils are the Agricultural Research Council of Norway, the Norwegian Research Council for Science and the Humanities, the Royal Norwegian Council for Scientific and Industrial Research, and the Norwegian Fisheries Research Council, each attached to separate government ministries. The councils recruit researchers by means of fellowship programs and allocate research grants to universities. They are part of the Science Policy Council of Norway, an advisory board to the government on all research matters. Principal areas of current study are arctic research, specifically studies of the northern lights; oceanography, especially ocean currents; marine biology, with special attention to fish migration; and meteorology.

The Royal Norwegian Society of Sciences and Letters, founded in 1760, has a Natural Sciences section. The country has 12 other scientific and technical learned societies and 24 scientific and technical research institutes. Located in Oslo are the Botanical Garden and Museum (founded in 1814), the Norwegian Museum of Science and Industry (founded in 1914), and other museums devoted to mineralogy-geology, paleontology, and zoology. The country has six universities and colleges offering courses in basic and applied sciences.

30 DOMESTIC TRADE

Oslo, the principal merchandising center, handles the distribution of many import products; Bergen and Stavanger are other west coast distribution centers. Trondheim is the chief northern center; Tromsø and Narvik are also important. The largest numbers of importers, exporters, and manufacturers' agents are in Oslo and Bergen. Most retailers and distributors are small by US standards and there are only a few countrywide, multi-store chains outside of the grocery store, apparel, and sporting goods sectors.

Cooperative societies are an important distribution factor, with local groups operating retail stores for many kinds of consumer goods, especially in the food sector. Food market chains have developed rapidly in recent years. The Norwegian Cooperative Union and Wholesale Society represents a large number of societies, with over half a million members. Agricultural cooperatives are active in produce marketing and cooperative purchasing societies (*Felleskjöp*) do much of the buying of farm equipment, fertilizer, and seed.

After a relatively slow start, franchising has gained in popularity and begun to grow. Although US-based companies such as McDonald's, Avis, and 7-Eleven are active in Norway, about 75% of operating franchises are of Norwegian origin, followed by 10% from the United States, 4% each from Sweden and Denmark, and 2% from Britain.

The Norwegian Consumer Council (established by the Storting in 1953) advances and safeguards the fundamental interests of consumers. It publishes comprehensive reports on accepted standards for key consumer goods, conducts conferences and buying courses in various parts of Norway, arranges consumer fairs, and cooperates closely with other organizations and institutions interested in consumer protection. Newspapers provide an important medium for advertisements; trade and other journals carry advertising, but the state-owned radio and television do not. However, in 1992, a national commercial television channel, TV2, was established in competition with the noncommercial Norwegian Broadcasting Corporation (NRK). TV2 currently has the sole right to broadcast advertising via Norwegian Telecom's terrestrial broadcasting network. Advertising is not permitted on NRK, but the growth of foreign-based commercial television channels broadcasting by satellite, and commercial television channels broadcasting via cable, opened the way for nationwide advertising on television. The advent of commercial television and radio advertising in Norway has led to new official control systems. Freedom of the press is provided for in the constitution.

Shopping hours are usually from 9 a.m. to 5 p.m. on weekdays (often until 7 p.m. on Thursdays) and from 9 a.m. to 1 or 3 p.m. on Saturdays. Banks stay open from 9 a.m. to 3:30 p.m. Mondays, Tuesdays, Wednesdays, and Fridays, and until 5 p.m. on Thursdays. Some manufacturers and major businesses will close for three to four weeks in July and/or August for a summer vacation.

31 FOREIGN TRADE

Foreign trade plays an exceptionally important role in the Norwegian economy. Imports of goods and services accounted for 29% of GDP in 2010 while exports accounted for 42% of GDP. Exports are largely based on oil, natural gas, shipbuilding, metals, forestry (including pulp and paper), fishing, and electrochemical and electrometallurgical products. As of 2010, Norway was the world's fifth-largest exporter of oil. The manufacture of oil rigs, drilling platforms, and associated equipment has developed into a sizable export industry. Norway imports considerable quantities of motor vehicles and other transport equipment, raw materials, and industrial equipment.

Exports tripled between 1974 and 1981, largely on the strength of the petroleum sector, which accounted for a negligible percent-

Principal Trading Partners – Norway (2010)				
(In millions of US dollars)				
Country	**Total**	**Exports**	**Imports**	**Balance**
World	208,647.0	131,395.0	77,252.0	54,143.0
United Kingdom	40,028.0	35,484.0	4,544.0	30,940.0
Germany	24,394.0	14,887.0	9,507.0	5,380.0
Sweden	20,020.0	9,170.0	10,850.0	-1,680.0
Netherlands	18,589.0	15,703.0	2,886.0	12,817.0
France	11,389.0	8,645.0	2,744.0	5,901.0
United States	10,784.0	6,567.0	4,217.0	2,350.0
Denmark	9,027.0	4,220.0	4,807.0	-587.0
China	8,805.0	2,240.0	6,565.0	-4,325.0
Italy	5,396.0	3,302.0	2,094.0	1,208.0
Belgium	4,883.0	3,468.0	1,415.0	2,053.0
(…) data not available or not significant.				
(n.s.) not specified.				

SOURCE: *2011 Direction of Trade Statistics Yearbook,* New York: United Nations, 2011.

age of exports in 1974 but half the total export value in 1981. During the same period, imports advanced by 93%. Following years of trade deficits, Norway had surpluses from 1980 through 1985. However, the drastic fall in oil prices caused a decline in export value resulting in deficits between 1986 and 1988. Since 1989, Norway has once again consistently recorded trade surpluses.

Norway imported $74.02 billion worth of goods and services in 2008, while exporting $137 billion worth of goods and services. Major import partners in 2009 were Sweden, 13.9%; Germany, 12.9%; China, 7.8%; Denmark, 6.8%; the United States, 6.2%; and the United Kingdom, 6%. Major export partners were the United Kingdom, 24.3%; Germany, 13.4%; Netherlands, 10.9%; France, 8.5%; Sweden, 5.8%; and the United States, 4.8%.

32 BALANCE OF PAYMENTS

Norway's foreign exchange reserves have been built up to meet adverse developments in the balance of payments without the necessity of a retreat from the liberalization of imports. Until the oil boom of the late 1970s, imports regularly exceeded exports, but large deficits on current account were more than offset by the capital account surplus, giving a net increase in foreign exchange reserves. In 2010 Norway had a foreign trade surplus of $56 billion, amounting to 10.7% of GDP. According to the CIA, its current account balance was $53.46 billion in 2010. Although Norway is a member of the European Economic Area, it is less trade-friendly than the Western European average.

33 BANKING AND SECURITIES

The Bank of Norway was founded as a commercial bank in 1816; in 1949, all its share capital was acquired by the state. It is the central bank and the sole note-issuing authority. The bank discounts treasury bills and some commercial paper; trades in bonds, foreign exchange, and gold and silver; and administers foreign exchange regulations. The bank also receives money for deposit on current account but generally pays no interest on deposits. The head office is in Oslo, and there are 20 branches.

In 1938 there were 105 commercial banks, but mergers brought the total down to only 31 in 1974 and 21 in 1984. As of 2009, the

<table>
<tr><td colspan="3">Balance of Payments – Norway (2010)</td></tr>
</table>

Balance of Payments – Norway (2010)

(In millions of US dollars)

Current Account		**51,444.0**
Balance on goods		58,391.0
Imports	-74,300.0	
Exports	132,691.0	
Balance on services		-3,108.0
Balance on income		872.0
Current transfers		-4,710.0
Capital Account		**-213.0**
Financial Account		**-42,181.0**
Direct investment abroad		-12,251.0
Direct investment in Norway		11,747.0
Portfolio investment assets		-52,712.0
Portfolio investment liabilities		32,647.0
Financial derivatives		...
Other investment assets		-27,202.0
Other investment liabilities		5,590.0
Net Errors and Omissions		**-4,832.0**
Reserves and Related Items		**-4,218.0**

(…) data not available or not significant.

SOURCE: *Balance of Payment Statistics Yearbook 2011,* Washington, DC: International Monetary Fund, 2011.

Public Finance – Norway (2009)

(In billions of kroner, central government figures)

Revenue and Grants	**1,135.72**	**100.0%**
Tax revenue	608.68	53.6%
Social contributions	234.8	20.7%
Grants	2.35	0.2%
Other revenue	289.89	25.5%
Expenditures	**878.99**	**100.0%**
General public services	166.44	18.9%
Defense	41.18	4.7%
Public order and safety	20.82	2.4%
Economic affairs	84.45	9.6%
Environmental protection	2.28	0.3%
Housing and community amenities	1.32	0.2%
Health	133.85	15.2%
Recreational, culture, and religion	12.72	1.4%
Education	48.23	5.5%
Social protection	367.58	41.8%

(…) data not available or not significant.

SOURCE: *Government Finance Statistics Yearbook 2010,* Washington, DC: International Monetary Fund, 2010.

total was down to 19. The three largest—the Norske Creditbank, Bergen Bank, and Christiania Bank og Kreditkasse—account for more than half of the total resources of the commercial banks. In 1988, a number of small savings banks and one medium-sized commercial bank, Sunnmorsbanken, became illiquid or insolvent. Most were rescued by merging with larger banks. After a slight improvement in 1989, however, banks' positions deteriorated again in 1990 following heavy losses sustained in the securities markets. As commercial property prices continued to fall, the position of the country's second and third-largest commercial banks, Christiania and Fokus, became increasingly precarious. To prevent a loss of confidence in the banking system, the government established a Government Bank Insurance Fund in March 1991. Within months this was called upon to provide capital to support the country's three largest banks, two of which—Christiania and Fokus—were by then insolvent. By the late 1990s, increasing pressure fell upon Norway to shed its nationalistic protection of its banking industry and allow for foreign investment, particularly from its Nordic neighbors.

Ten state banks and other financial institutions serve particular industries or undertakings, including agriculture, fisheries, manufacturing, student loans, mortgages, and others. Although savings banks also began to merge, there were still 133 private savings banks and many credit associations in 1993.

A 1961 law included measures to implement the principle that banking policies are to be based on social as well as economic and financial considerations. The government appoints 25% of the representatives on the board of every commercial bank with funds of over NOK100 million. Guidelines for these banks are worked out cooperatively with public authorities.

In 2010, the commercial bank prime lending rate was 4.6%. The central bank discount rate was 6.25%, an increase from only 1.75% in 2009.

The stock exchanges of Norway are at Oslo (the oldest, founded 1818), Trondheim, Bergen, Kristiansund, Drammen, Stavanger, Ålesund, Haugesund, and Fredrikstad. Amid the increasing consolidation among European stock exchanges in the late 1990s, calls increased for the Norwegian markets to merge. As of 2010, there were 195 companies listed on the Oslo exchange, whose market value equaled $250.9 billion.

34 INSURANCE

Norwegian insurance can be undertaken only by joint-stock companies of mutual assistance associations. Foreign life insurance companies have practically ceased to operate in Norway. Life insurance policies and those for pension schemes are exempt from income tax and cannot be written by firms doing other insurance work.

The crown in 1767 initiated compulsory fire insurance in towns and this fund still exists. Workers' compensation, third-party auto liability, pharmaceutical product liability, and aircraft liability are all compulsory insurances as well.

For marine insurance, stock companies now are more important than mutual associations. While a number of foreign insurance underwriters transact business in Norway, there is considerable direct insurance of Norwegian vessels abroad, especially in London. Most other insurance, such as automobile and burglary, is underwritten by Norwegian concerns. The insurance regulatory authority is the Banking, Insurance, and Securities Commission (BISC). The insurance sector is highly regulated, deeply influenced by the failure of a nonlife insurance company, Dovre, which spurred the Insurance Activities Act of 1988, which became effective in April 1989. The Insurance Activities Act of 1988 allows the BISC to control premium rates and monitor the financial position of insurance companies, as well as the risks that the insurance company writes. The BISC has wide powers of intervention. Companies may engage in insurance business after special permission has been granted and a license is obtained from the government.

Recent liberalization throughout Europe promises to radically change the structure of the Norwegian insurance industry as foreign firms tap into the market. Direct gross insurance premiums of life and non-life premiums were 5.6% of GDP in 2009.

35 PUBLIC FINANCE

Norway's fiscal year coincides with the calendar year. As one of the per capita richest countries in the world, Norway has a great deal of money to spend on investment, focusing especially on the offshore oil sector. The government maintains a Petroleum Fund worth $570 billion as of 2010. The Fund is to be used to finance government programs once oil and gas resources are depleted.

The US Central Intelligence Agency (CIA) estimated that in 2010 the budget of Norway included $226.8 billion in public revenue and $187 billion in public expenditures. The budget surplus amounted to 10.5% of GDP. Public debt was 47.7% of GDP, with $2.232 trillion of the debt held by foreign entities.

36 TAXATION

Both the central government and the municipal governments levy income and capital taxes. There is also a premium payable to the National Insurance Scheme. For individual taxpayers, income taxes and premiums adhere to the pay-as-you-earn system.

Taxes on corporations are paid in the year following the income year. As of 2010, corporate income taxes were levied at a flat rate of 28% of aggregate income. Companies involved in oil or gas pay a special oil tax of 50% in addition to the standard 28%. All income from capital is taxable at 28%. Although dividends received by resident shareholders from Norwegian counties are taxed at the corporate rate, a credit for the tax already paid by the distributing company on income effectively negates the tax. Dividends paid to nonresident shareholders are taxed at 25%. Interest and royalty income are not subject to a withholding tax.

Norway's personal income tax rate consists of a few different payees that affect the total tax rate paid by each employee. A flat 28% rate is paid for national and municipal taxes; the employee's national insurance contribution of 7.8% (3% for pensioners, and 11% for the self-employed), and a surtax of 0%, 9%, or 12%. A number of additional deductions from taxable income are available including allowance for some travel expenses, insurance payments, mortgage interest payments, living allowances, and deductions for contributions to capital investments. A withholding tax on wages can be credited against income taxes. There is also a municipal wealth tax, ranging from 0 to 1.1% and a land tax with rates from 0.2 to 0.7%. Gifts and inheritances are taxed according to progressive schedules with a maximum rate of 30%.

The main indirect tax is Norway's value-added tax (VAT), with a standard rate that has increased from 20% in 1999 to 25% as of 2011. A reduced rate of 14% is applied to basic foodstuffs, and there is an extensive list of VAT-exempt goods and services, including health and social services, education, passenger transport, hotel accommodations, travel agents, and government supplies, among other items.

37 CUSTOMS AND DUTIES

Heavily dependent on foreign trade, Norway has traditionally supported abolition of trade barriers. During the 1950s, direct control of imports was gradually abolished. Tariff rates on industrial raw materials and most manufactured goods are low. Duties on finished textile products are levied at 15–25%.

A signatory of GATT and a member of EFTA, Norway has bilateral trade agreements with many countries in every part of the world. In 1973, Norway signed a Special Relations Agreement with the European Community (now the European Union), whereby both sides abolished all tariffs on industrial goods over the 1973–77 period. Other trade goods receiving gradual tariff reductions were fish, agricultural products, and wine.

Although Norwegian voters rejected EU membership in a 1994 referendum, Norway is a member of the European Economic Area (EEA) and maintains a free trade agreement with the European Union.

38 FOREIGN INVESTMENT

Norway welcomes foreign investment as a matter of policy and in general grants national treatment to foreign investors. Investment is encouraged particularly in the key offshore petroleum sector, mainland industry (including high-technology and other advanced areas), and in less developed regions such as northern Norway. Corporate taxation is levied at a flat rate of 28%, which is low by European standards.

Foreign capital has traditionally been largely centered in Norway's electrochemical and electrometallurgical industries, the primary iron and metal industry, and mining. The discovery of oil and natural gas in the North Sea area spurred foreign investments. The Ekofisk oil field was discovered in 1969 by an American Phillips Petroleum Co. consortium, including Petrofina of Belgium, ENI of Italy, and Norway's Petronord. A joint Norwegian-Phillips group company, Norpiepe, was formed in 1973 to construct the pipelines and to operate them for 30 years. Another US company, McDermott International, was awarded a $150-million contract in 1982 to lay pipe from the Statfjord gas field in the North Sea to the Norwegian mainland. In 1995, 11 international oil and gas companies announced plans for a $1.2-$1.35 billion gas pipeline from Norway's North Sea production area to the European continent. That same year, Fokus, Norway's third-largest commercial bank, fell under foreign control as foreign investors captured more than half the shares for sale in the bank's privatization.

Norway's share in world FDI flows has been approximately equal to its share of world GDP. FDI in Norway was a net inflow of $11.3 billion according to World Bank figures published in 2009. FDI represented 2.95% of GDP.

39 ECONOMIC DEVELOPMENT

The government holds shares in a number of large enterprises: a minority of shares in most industrial establishments and all or controlling shares in some armaments factories, as well as in chemical and electrometallurgical companies, power stations, and mines. The government also participates in joint industrial undertakings with private capital, in enterprises too large or risky for private capital, and in establishments with shares formerly held by German interests. Government policy also aims at attracting foreign investment.

Rapid industrial development and exploitation of resources are major governmental goals, with special emphasis on northern Norway, where development has lagged behind that of the southern areas. The Development Fund for North Norway, established in 1952, together with a policy of tax concessions, resulted in progress there at a rate more rapid than that of the rest of the country. The exploitation of offshore oil and natural gas reserves has had a profound effect on Norway's economy. Increased oil revenues have expanded both domestic consumption and investment. The government has used oil revenues to ease taxes and increase public investment in regional development, environmental protection, social welfare, education, and communications. Although the expansion of innovative oil development projects continues (one of which was the $4.2 billion Heidrun oil project), Norway is looking to produce more natural gas than oil. The $5 billion Troll gas field was one such project.

A tax law permits industry and commerce to build up tax-free reserves for future investment, foreign sales promotion, and research. Designed to provide a flexible tool for influencing cyclical developments, the law's intent is to help ensure that total demand at any given time is sufficient to create full employment and strong economic growth. In the late 1970s, the government introduced combined price and wage agreements in an effort to restrain inflation and ensure real increases in buying power for consumers.

To stimulate industry, incentives are available for undertakings in the north as well as in other economically weak regions; companies may set aside up to 25% of taxable income for tax-free investment. Tariff incentives are available for essential imports. A Regional Development Fund grants low-interest, long-term loans to firms to strengthen the economy of low-income, high-unemployment areas anywhere in the country.

Although Norwegians rejected EU membership in a 1994 referendum, Norway's economy is largely integrated with that of the EU. Norway has a free trade agreement with the EU as part of its membership in the European Economic Area. Its currency is generally kept on par with the euro. Yet despite these elements of association, Norway retains extensive control over its own economic development policies.

Norway has been active in aiding developing nations under the Norwegian Agency for International Development (Norad). The leading recipients have been Tanzania, Mozambique, Zambia, Bangladesh, Nicaragua, and Ethiopia. Norway is one of the few countries meeting the UN international aid target for donor countries, 0.7% of national income. Norway gave 0.88% of GDP in 2008, more than any other country, second only to Sweden.

The country's Petroleum Fund reached a milestone of over $500 billion in assets in October 2010. The fund will be used to finance government programs once Norway's oil and gas resources run out. Despite the difficult global economic environment spurred by the 2008 global financial crisis, Norway has been able to remain relatively stable thanks to its financial regulation and high prices in world markets for its energy and fisheries exports. In 2011, unemployment climbed to 3.4%, but was still well below average unemployment rates throughout the EU. Norway was expected to continue to experience moderate growth and recovery throughout 2011 and into 2012.

⁴⁰SOCIAL DEVELOPMENT

Norway has been a pioneer in the field of social welfare and is often called a welfare state. Accident insurance for factory workers was introduced in 1894, unemployment insurance in 1906, compulsory health insurance in 1909, and accident insurance for fishermen in 1908 and for seamen in 1911. In the 1930s, further social welfare schemes were introduced: an old-age pension scheme; aid for the blind and crippled; and unemployment insurance for all workers except fishermen, whalers, sealers, civil servants, domestic servants, self-employed persons, salesmen, and agents. In the postwar period, health insurance became compulsory for all employees and available to self-employed persons; coverage includes dependents, with medical treatment including hospital and other benefits. Sickness benefits, family allowances during hospitalization, and grants for funeral expenses are paid. Costs of this scheme are met by deductions from wages and contributions by employers and by state and local authorities. Public assistance, available in Norway since 1845, supplements the foregoing programs. Social welfare has long included maternity benefits with free prenatal clinics.

The National Insurance Act, which came into effect in 1967, provides old-age pensions, rehabilitation allowances, disability pensions, widow and widower pensions, and survivor benefits to children. Membership is obligatory for all residents of Norway, including noncitizens, and for Norwegian foreign-service employees. Pensions begin at the age of 67. As of 2004, the system of varying rates for employers was reformed to eliminate intermediate levels. The source of funds is divided between employees, employers, and the government funds any deficit.

Workers' compensation covers both accidents and occupational diseases. Compensation is paid to a widow until she remarries, and to children up to the age of 18 (or for life if they are unemployable). Dependent parents and grandparents also are eligible for life annuities. Family allowance coverage, in force since 1946, is provided for children under the age of 16.

The law mandates equal wages for equal work by men and women. An Equal Rights Ombudsman addresses complaints of sexual discrimination. A provision protecting against sexual harassment is outlined in the Working Environment Act. A resolution mandated that 40% of publicly held companies be directed by women by 2005, with noncompliance resulting in removal from the stock exchange. Violence against women persisted but is seriously investigated and prosecuted by authorities. Victim's assistance programs and battered women's shelters are available.

According to reports published by the World Economic Forum (WEF), Norway has consistently ranked among the top countries of the world for gender equality. The WEF considers equality in several areas of life, including employment, politics, health, and education. Norway was rated as second in the world (after Iceland) for 2010.

In May 2011, a report issued by the organization Save the Children ranked Norway as the best country for motherhood. Among the reasons that pushed Norway to the top spot include the almost 100 percent attendance of a medical professional at every birth, the availability of child services, formal education, and quality of life.

Human rights are fully respected and protected in Norway. Provisions exist to protect the rights and cultural heritage of minority peoples. The Sami (Lapps) located in the northeast are entitled to schooling in their local language, and also receive radio and television broadcast subtitled in Sami. The Sami also have a constituent assembly that acts as a consultative body on issues that affect them.

41 HEALTH

Since 1971 there has been a tax-based National Insurance system. The public health service and the hospitals are the responsibility of the government at the central, county, and municipal levels. There are very few private hospitals in Norway. Hospital care is free of charge, but a minor fee is charged for medicine and primary health care. As of 1984 there has been a ceiling on the total amount one must pay for medical services. There is a three-part system made up of regional hospitals serving parts of the country, central hospitals serving the various counties, and local hospitals, also run by the counties. The country is in need of more nursing homes for the elderly.

On the local level, health councils are responsible for public health services, including tuberculosis control and school health services, and for environmental sanitation. Only in densely populated areas are public health officers appointed on a full-time basis; otherwise they engage in private practice as well. In some areas, they are the only physicians available.

According to the CIA, life expectancy in Norway, among the highest in the world, was 81 years in 2011. Infant mortality was 3.52 deaths per 1,000 live births, one of the lowest rates in the world. The total fertility rate was estimated at 1.77 children born per woman. The country spent 8.5% of its GDP on healthcare, amounting to $7,662 per person. There were 41 physicians, 148 nurses and midwives, and 35 hospital beds per 10,000 inhabitants. In 2008 the maternal mortality rate, according to the World Bank, was 7 per 100,000 births. It was estimated that 92% of children were vaccinated against measles. The CIA calculated HIV/AIDS prevalence in Norway to be about 0.1% in 2009.

42 HOUSING

Before World War II, responsibility for housing rested mainly with the municipalities, but the state has since assumed the major burden. Loans and subsidies keep rents under a certain percentage of a family's income. Cooperative housing has made great progress in such densely populated areas as Oslo, where the Oslo Housing and Savings Society pioneered the practice for Norway. With housing problems compounded by wartime destruction and postwar increases in marriages and in the birthrate, Norway built more dwellings per 1,000 inhabitants than any other European country, completing between 31,000 and 42,000 units annually from 1967 through 1981. Home construction financing has come principally from two state loan organizations, the Norwegian Smallholdings and Housing Bank and the Norwegian State Housing Bank, but one-fourth of the nation's housing is still privately financed.

43 EDUCATION

Elementary school education has been compulsory since the middle of the 18th century. As of 1997, education is compulsory for 10 years of study, with students entering school in the year that they reach the age of six. Primary school covers seven years of study, followed by three years of lower secondary school. At this stage,

students may choose to continue in a three-year general secondary school (gymnasium), which prepares students for the university. Since 1976, the upper secondary school system has also included vocational schools of various types, operated by the state, by local authorities, and by the industrial sector. A three-year trade apprenticeship program is also available for some secondary students.

Local authorities generally provide school buildings and equipment and the central government contributes funds towards teachers' salaries and covers a considerable proportion of the cost of running the schools. Although there are private schools, government authorities bear a major share of the financial responsibility for these through a system of grants.

In 2008 the World Bank estimated that 99% of age-eligible children in Norway were enrolled in primary school. Secondary enrollment for age-eligible children stood at 96%. Tertiary enrollment was estimated at 73%. Of those enrolled in tertiary education, there were 100 male students for every 162 female students. Overall, the CIA estimates that Norway has a literacy rate of 100%. Public expenditure on education represented 6.8% of GDP.

Norway's institutions of higher education include 130 colleges and four universities. The four major universities include the University of Oslo (founded in 1811), the University of Bergen (1948), the University of Trondheim (1969), and the University of Tromsø (1969). Representing fields not covered by the universities, there are also specialized institutions, such as the Agricultural University of Norway (near Oslo); the Norwegian School of Economics and Business Administration (Bergen); and the Norwegian College of Veterinary Medicine (Oslo). Universities and colleges in Norway serve a dual function: both learning and research. At the four universities, degrees are granted at three levels: Lower degree (a four-year study program); higher degree (five to seven-year course of study); and doctorate degree. There are also courses lasting from five to seven years in law, medicine, agriculture, or engineering.

With a goal of placing adults on an equal standing with the educated youth and giving them access to knowledge and job skills, a program of adult education was introduced in August 1977. An official administrative body for adult education exists in all municipalities and counties. However, the Ministry of Education and Research has the highest administrative responsibility for adult education. Folk high schools are associated with a long Scandinavian tradition of public enlightenment. There are more than 80 folk schools in Norway geared toward providing personal growth and development rather than academic achievement.

44 LIBRARIES AND MUSEUMS

The National Library of Norway in Oslo has over two million volumes in its central library. Since 1882, copies of all Norwegian publications have had to be deposited in the national library; since 1939, copies have been deposited at Bergen and Trondheim as well. Bergen University Library has over one million volumes, largely devoted to the natural sciences. Oslo University Library (founded in 1811), has the largest academic library system in the country, with four libraries and a central administrative unit. A special collection at the Oslo University Library includes the world's largest collection of materials on the life and works of Henrik Ibsen as part of the Centre for Ibsen Studies. The library of the Scientific Society in Trondheim, founded in 1760, is the country's oldest research library and has over one million volumes, including 330,000 pictures and UNESCO and GATT (General Agreement on Tariffs and Trade) documents. The Tromsø Museum Library has been organized to make it the research library for the north. There are technical and specialized libraries at many research institutes and higher educational centers. State archives are kept in Oslo, and there are record offices for provincial archives at Oslo, Kristiansund, Stavanger, Bergen, Hamar, Trondheim, and Tromsø.

The first municipal libraries were founded in the late 18th century. By law every municipality and every school must maintain a library; each such library receives financial support from state and municipality. Regional libraries also have been created. A special library service is provided for ships in the merchant navy, and a floating library service provides books to fishermen-farmers living in the sparsely populated regions.

There are natural history museums in Oslo, Stavanger, Bergen, Trondheim, and Tromsø. Oslo, Lillehammer, and Bergen have notable art collections. A traveling "national gallery" was established in 1952. The most important museums in Norway are those dealing with antiquities and folklore, such as the Norwegian Folk Museum in Oslo. Oslo has a unique collection of ships from the Viking period. Open-air museums in Oslo and elsewhere show old farms and other buildings, as well as objects of Norwegian historical and cultural interest. Also in Oslo are the International Museum of Children's Art; the Munch Museum, displaying the works of Edvard Munch, Norway's most famous artist; Norway's Resistance Museum, detailing the country's occupation during World War II; and the Viking Ship Museum. Among Norway's newer museums are the Astrup Fearnley Fine Arts Museum (1993), which features modern art; the National Museum of Contemporary Art (1990); and the Stenerson Museum (1994), which exhibits paintings from the 19th and 20th centuries. All three museums are in Oslo. There are at least three museums in the country that are dedicated to Henrik Ibsen. Additionally, the Astrup Fearnley Museum of Modern Art was scheduled to be moved to a newly constructed building in 2014.

45 MEDIA

In 2010 the CIA reported that there were 1.702 million main telephone lines in use in Norway. In addition to landlines, mobile phone subscriptions were at 5.525 million. There were 3 nationwide radio stations, 16 regional stations, 2 privately owned stations broadcast nationwide, and 240 private local stations. As for new media, Norway had 4.431 million Internet users in 2009. Prominent newspapers in 2010, with circulation numbers listed parenthetically, included *Verdens Gang* (484,131), *Aftenposten* (283,915), and *Adresseavisen* (130,000), as well as 74 other major newspapers.

Norway has one of the most advanced telecommunications networks in Europe and is completely modern in all respects. Domestic service is provided by a domestic satellite system and the country's large rural areas have worked to boost the use of mobile cellular phones, instead of fixed wire systems. International services are provided by land-based and submarine coaxial cable systems, and satellite ground stations.

The first private broadcasting stations launched in 1981. The public Norwegian Broadcasting Corp. continues to operate two television channels, three national radio stations, and a number of local radio stations. Educational broadcasts supplement school facilities in remote districts. Radio license fees have not been required since 1977. Television programming on an experimental basis was initiated in 1958 and full-scale television transmission began in July 1960.

The constitution provides for freedom of speech and of the press and the government generally respects these rights.

46 ORGANIZATIONS

Cooperative societies are numerous and important in Norway. About 2,500 agricultural cooperatives are active; these include purchasing, processing, and marketing organizations. Some 528 retail cooperatives are affiliated with the Norwegian Cooperative Union and Wholesale Society.

Doctors are organized in the Norwegian Medical Association and in local associations. Farming organizations and agricultural cooperatives are represented in the Federation of Agriculture. There are associations of small and large forest owners, fur breeders, and employers' organizations in most sectors of industry, as well as a central Norwegian Employers' Confederation.

The Norwegian Academy of Science and Letters, the Royal Norwegian Society of Science and Letters, the Norwegian Academy of Technological Sciences, and the Society for the Advancement of Science are leading learned society. Other learned and professional organizations include the Nobel Committee of the Storting, which awards the Nobel Peace Prize; the Norwegian Research Council for Science and the Humanities; and various legal, scientific, economic, literary, historical, musical, artistic, and research societies.

National youth organizations include the Norwegian Student Union, Christian Democratic Party Youth, En Verden Youth, European Democratic Students, European Good Templar Youth Federation, Federation of Young Conservatives, Norwegian Union of Social Democratic Youth, Norwegian YWCA/YMCA, and the Norwegian Guides and Scouts Association. There are numerous sports associations and clubs.

Health and relief organizations include the Norwegian Red Cross, the Norwegian Women's Health Organization, and societies to combat a variety of conditions and diseases. Volunteer service organizations, such as the Lions Clubs International, are also present. International organizations with national chapters include Amnesty International and CARE Norge.

47 TOURISM, TRAVEL, AND RECREATION

The *Tourism Factbook*, published by the UN World Tourism Organization, reported 6.06 million incoming tourists to Norway in 2009; they spent a total of $4.44 billion. Of those incoming tourists, there were 3.9 million from Europe. There were 169,245 hotel beds available in Norway, which had an occupancy rate of 35%. The estimated daily cost to visit Oslo, the capital, was $420. The cost of visiting other cities also averaged $420.

Norway's main tourist attractions are the cities of Oslo, Bergen, and Trondheim, which are connected by road, rail, and daily flights; the marvelous scenery of the fjord country in the west; and the arctic coast with the North Cape and "midnight sun." In 2005, UNESCO named two Norwegian fjords, the Geirangerfjord and the Naeroyfjord to its World Heritage List.

A favorite method of tourist travel is by coastal steamer (*hurti-gruten*), sailing from Bergen northward to Kirkenes, near the Soviet frontier. Many cruise ships ply the Norwegian fjords and coastal towns as far north as Spitsbergen. Notable outdoor recreational facilities include the Oslomarka, a 100,000 hectare (247,000 acre) area located near Oslo, with ski trails and walking paths. To compensate for the shortness of winter days, several trails are illuminated for evening skiing. Other popular sports include ice skating, freshwater fishing, mountaineering, hunting (grouse, reindeer, and elk), and football (soccer). In 1994, Norway hosted the XVII Olympic Winter Games in Lillehammer, and the women's soccer team won the World Cup in 1995.

There are major theaters in Oslo and Bergen, as well as six regional theaters; Den Norske Opera in Oslo; and four symphony orchestras. International musical events include the Bergen Festival, held annually in late May or early June, and several jazz festivals in July.

No passport is required of visitors from the Nordic area, but travelers arriving in Norway directly from non-Nordic countries are subject to passport control. A visa is not required for visits of up to 90 days. Norway is also part of the Schengen Zone, which eliminates all border control between participating countries. As of 2011, 25 European countries cooperate with the Schengen Agreement. Once in the Schengen Zone, one can travel continuously for up to 90 days within the member countries.

48 FAMOUS PERSONS

Ludvig Holberg (1684–1745), the father of Danish and Norwegian literature, was a leading dramatist whose comedies are still performed. Henrik Wergeland (1808–45), Norway's greatest poet, was also a patriot and social reformer; his sister Camilla Collett (1813–95), author of the first Norwegian realistic novel, was a pioneer in the movement for women's rights. Henrik Ibsen (1827–1906), founder of modern dramas, placed Norway in the forefront of world literature. Bjørnstjerne Bjørnson (1832–1910), poet, playwright, and novelist, received the Nobel Prize for literature in 1903. Other noted novelists are Jonas Lie (1833–1908); Alexander Kielland (1849–1906); Knut Hamsun (1859–1952), Nobel Prize winner in 1920; Sigrid Undset (1882–1949), awarded the Nobel Prize in 1928; and Johan Bojer (1872–1959).

Ole Bull (1810–80) was a world-famous violinist. Edvard Grieg (1843–1907) was the first Norwegian composer to win broad popularity. His leading contemporaries and successors were Johan Svendsen (1840–1911), Christian Sinding (1856–1941), Johan Halvorsen (1864–1935), and Fartein Valen (1887–1953). Kirsten Flagstad (1895–1962), world-renowned soprano, served for a time as director of the Norwegian State Opera. In painting, Harriet Backer (1845–1932), Christian Krohg (1852–1925), and Erik Werenskiold (1855–1938) were outstanding in the traditional manner; leading the way to newer styles was Edvard Munch (1863–1944), an outstanding expressionist, as well as Axel Revold (1887–1962) and Per Krohg (1889–1965). Norway's foremost sculptor is Gustav Vigeland (1869–1943). The Frogner Park in Oslo is the site of a vast collection of Vigeland's work in bronze and granite.

Outstanding scientists are Christopher Hansteen (1784–1873), famous for his work in terrestrial magnetism; Niels Henrik Abel (1802–29), noted for his work on the theory of equations; Armauer (Gerhard Henrik) Hansen (1841–1912), discoverer of the leprosy bacillus; Vilhelm Bjerknes (1862–1951), who advanced the science of meteorology; Fridtjof Nansen (1861–1930), an oceanographer and Arctic explorer who won the Nobel Peace Prize in 1922 for organizing famine relief in Russia; Otto Sverdrup (1854–1930), Roald Amundsen (1872–1928), and Bernt Balchen (1899–1973), polar explorers; Johan Hjort (1869–1948), a specialist in deep-sea fishery research; Regnar Frisch (1895–1978), who shared the first Nobel Prize in Economic Science in 1969 for developing econometrics; Odd Hassel (1897–1981), co-winner of the 1969 Nobel Prize in chemistry for his studies of molecular structure; and Thor Heyerdahl (1914–2002), explorer and anthropologist.

The first secretary-general of the UN was a Norwegian, Trygve (Halvdan) Lie (1896–1968), who served from 1946 to 1953. The historian Christian Louis Lange (1869–1938) was co-winner of the Nobel Peace Prize in 1921.

Sonja Henie (1913–69) was the leading woman figure skater of her time, and Liv Ullmann (b. 1939) is an internationally known actress. Linn Ullmann (b. 1966), daughter of Liv Ullman and Ingmar Bergman, is a respected novelist and journalist. Grete Waitz (b. 1953) is a champion long-distance runner.

49 DEPENDENCIES

Svalbard

The Svalbard group includes all the islands between 10° and 35° E and 74° and 81° N: the archipelago of Spitsbergen, White Island (Kvitøya), King Charles' Land (Kong Karls Land), Hope Island, and Bear Island (Bjørnøya), which have a combined area of about 62,700 sq km (24,200 sq mi). The largest islands are Spitsbergen, about 39,400 sq km (15,200 sq mi); North-East Land (Nordaustlandet), 14,530 sq km (5,610 sq mi); Edge Island (Edgeøya), 5,030 sq km (1,940 sq mi); and Barents Island (Barentsøya), 1,330 sq km (510 sq mi). The population is 55.4% Norwegian and 44.3% Russian and Ukrainian.

Discovered by Norwegians in the 12th century and rediscovered in 1596 by the Dutch navigator Willem Barents, Svalbard served in the 17th and 18th centuries as a base for British, Dutch, Danish, Norwegian, German, and other whalers, but no permanent sovereignty was established. Russian and Norwegian trappers wintered there, and coal mining started early in the 20th century. Norway's sovereignty was recognized by the League of Nations in 1920, and the territory was taken over officially by Norway in 1925. Much of the high land is ice-covered; glaciers descend to the sea, where they calve to produce icebergs. The west and south coasts have many fjords, while the western coastal lowland is up to 10 km (6 mi) broad.

The most important mineral, coal, occurs in vast deposits in Spitsbergen. The west coast is kept clear of ice for six months of the year by the relatively warm water of the North Atlantic Drift, but an air temperature as low as -62°C (-80°F) has been recorded. In this region there are 112 days without the sun's appearance above the horizon.

The chief official, a governor, lives at Longyearbyen; his administration is controlled by the Ministry of Industry. Coal mining is the main industry, with Norwegian-worked mines at Longyearbyen, Sveagruva, and Ny Ålesund, and Russian worked mines at

Barentsburg, Grumantbyen, and elsewhere. Russia has extraterritorial rights in the areas where they mine. Cod fishing takes place around Bear Island, but whaling has virtually ceased. Norwegian sealers hunt seals, polar bears, and walrus in the summer. For centuries, trappers wintered in Spitsbergen to catch fox and bear while the pelts were in the best condition, but few trappers have wintered there in recent years.

Communications are maintained during the summer months by ships from Tromsø carrying goods and passengers, while colliers put in frequently at the mine piers. There are no roads and no local ship services.

Jan Mayen

Located in the Norwegian Sea at 70°30′N and 8°30′W, 893 km (555 mi) from Tromsø, the island of Jan Mayen has an area of about 380 sq km (150 sq mi). The island is dominated by the volcano Beerenberg, 2,277 m (7,470 ft) high, which is responsible for its existence; a major eruption occurred in September 1970. Jan Mayen was discovered by Henry Hudson in 1607 and was visited in 1614 by the Dutch navigator Jay Mayen, who used it subsequently as a whaling base. In 1929, the island was placed under Norwegian sovereignty. It is the site of a meteorological station and an airfield.

Bouvet Island

Bouvet Island (Bouvetøya), situated at 54°26′S and 3°24′E in the South Atlantic Ocean, was discovered in 1739, and in 1928 was placed under Norwegian sovereignty. An uninhabited volcanic island of 59 sq km (23 sq mi), Bouvet is almost entirely covered by ice and is difficult to approach.

Peter I Island

Peter I Island (Peter I Øy), an uninhabited Antarctic island of volcanic origin, is located at 68°48′S and 90°35′W. It has an area of 249 sq km (96 sq mi), rises to over 1,233 m (4,045 ft), and is almost entirely ice-covered. The island was discovered in 1821 by a Russian admiral. In 1931, it was placed under Norwegian sovereignty, and by a parliamentary act of 1933 became a dependency.

Queen Maud Land

Queen Maud Land (Dronning Mauds land) consists of the sector of Antarctica between 20°W and 45°E, adjoining the Falkland Islands on the W and the Australian Antarctic Dependency on the E. It was placed under Norwegian sovereignty in 1939, and has been a Norwegian dependency since 1957. The land is basically uninhabited, except for several stations operated by Japan, South Africa, and Russia.

50 BIBLIOGRAPHY

Annesley, Claire, ed. *A Political and Economic Dictionary of Western Europe.* Philadelphia: Routledge/Taylor and Francis, 2005.

Fredman, Peter. *Frontiers in Nature-Based Tourism: Lessons from Norway and Sweden.* New York: Routledge, 2011.

Houben, Marc. *International Crisis Management: The Approach of European States.* New York: Routledge, 2005.

International Smoking Statistics: A Collection of Historical Data from 30 Economically Developed Countries. New York: Oxford University Press, 2002.

Jochens, Jenny. *Women in Old Norse Society.* Ithaca, NY: Cornell University Press, 1995.

Kemp, Graham and Douglas P. Fry, eds. *Keeping the Peace: Conflict Resolution and Peaceful Societies Around the World.* New York: Routledge, 2004.

March, Linda Davis. *Norway: A Quick Guide to Customs and Etiquette.* Portland, OR: Graphic Arts Books, 2005.

Norway Investment and Business Guide: Strategic and Practical Information. Washington, DC: International Business Publications USA, 2012.

O'Leary, Margaret H. *Culture and Customs of Norway.* Santa Barbara, CA: Greenwood, 2010.

Opello, Walter C. *European Politics.* Boulder, CO: Lynne Rienner Publishers, 2009.

POLAND

Republic of Poland
Rzeczpospolita Polska

CAPITAL: Warsaw (Warszawa)

FLAG: The national flag consists of two horizontal stripes, the upper white and the lower red.

ANTHEM: *Jeszcze Polska nie zginela (Poland Is Not Yet Lost).*

MONETARY UNIT: The zloty (PLN) is a paper currency of 100 groszy. The Polish National Bank currently issues nine circulating coins of 1, 2, 5, 10, 20, and 50 groszy and 1, 2, 5 zlotys, and five circulating notes of 10, 20, 50, 100, 200 zlotys. There are also collector coins and notes of other denominations. A currency reform on 1 January 1995 replaced 10,000 old zlotys with 1 new zloty. PLN1 = US$0.317474 (or US$1 = PLN3.15) as of 2011.

WEIGHTS AND MEASURES: The metric system is the legal standard.

HOLIDAYS: New Year's Day, 1 January; Labor Day, 1 May; Constitution of the Third of May Day, 3 May; Victory Day, 9 May; The Assumption of the Virgin Mary, 15 August; All Saints' Day, 1 November; Independence Day, 11 November; Christmas, 25–26 December. Movable holidays are Easter Monday and Corpus Christi.

TIME: 1 p.m. = noon GMT.

¹LOCATION, SIZE, AND EXTENT

Situated in East Central Europe, Poland has an area of 312,680 sq km (120,726 sq mi), extending 689 km (428 mi) E–W and 649 km (403 mi) N–S. It is bounded on the N by the Baltic Sea, on the N and E by Russia, Lithuania, Belarus, and Ukraine, on the S by Slovakia and the Czech Republic, and on the W by Germany, with a total land boundary of 2,788 km (1,794 mi) and a coastline of 491 km (305 mi). Comparatively, Poland is slightly smaller than New Mexico.

Before World War II, Poland encompassed a territory of nearly 390,000 sq km (150,600 sq mi). On 11 July 1920, an armistice mediated by Britain in a Polish-Soviet conflict established the "Curzon line" (named for George Nathaniel Curzon, the British statesman who proposed it), conferring the former Austrian territory of Galicia to the Soviet side. However, under the Treaty of Riga (1921), all of Galicia was assigned to Poland, and a boundary well to the east of the Curzon line prevailed until World War II. At the Yalta Conference in February 1945, the Allies accepted Soviet claims to eastern Poland, with a border running approximately along the Curzon line.

On 21 April 1945, a Polish-Soviet treaty of friendship and cooperation was signed, followed by a new agreement on the Polish-Soviet border. To compensate for the loss of 46% of Poland's territory to the USSR, the Potsdam Conference of July-August 1945 placed former German territories east of the Oder (Odra) and western Neisse rivers under Polish administration, pending a final determination by a German peace treaty. On 6 August 1950, an agreement was signed between Poland and the German Democratic Republic (GDR) according to which both parties recognized the frontier on the Oder-Neisse line. The Federal Republic of Germany (FRG) recognized this boundary under the terms of a treaty signed with Poland on 7 December 1970 and ratified by the FRG on 23 May 1972.

Poland's capital city, Warsaw, is located in the east-central part of the country.

²TOPOGRAPHY

Poland's average altitude is 173 m (568 ft); 75.4% of the land is less than 200 m (656 ft) above sea level. The highest point, Mount Rysy (2,499 m/8,199 ft), is located in the Tatra Mountains on the Slovakian border. The principal topographic regions are an undulating central lowland with a crystalline platform and warped bedrock; the Baltic highland in the north, a glaciated region with many lakes and sandy soils; and the coastland, a narrow lowland with promontories, bays, and lakes. The southern uplands are marked by rich loam and mineral deposits.

Several important navigable rivers drain into the Baltic Sea, among them the Vistula (Wisła), the Odra (Oder), the Bug, and the Warta. There are over 6,000 lakes in the northern lake region. Good harbors have been developed on the Baltic Sea.

³CLIMATE

Poland has a continental climate, conditioned especially by westerly winds. Only the southern areas are humid. Summers are cool, and winters range from moderately cold to cold. The average mean temperature is about 7°C (45°F); temperatures in Warsaw range, on average, from -6° to -1°C (21–30°F) in January and from 13° to 24°C (55–75°F) in July. Precipitation is greatest during the summer months, lasting 85 to 100 days. Annual rainfall ranges from about 50 cm (20 in) in the lowlands and 135 cm (53 in) in the mountains; the overall average is about 64 cm (25 in).

⁴FLORA AND FAUNA

The World Resource Institute estimates that there are 2,450 plant species in Poland. In addition, Poland is home to 110 mammal, 424 bird, 11 reptile, and 18 amphibian species. The calculation reflects the total number of distinct species residing in the country, not the number of endemic species.

Coniferous trees, especially pine, account for 70% of the forests; deciduous species include birch, beech, and elm. Lynx, wildcat, European bison (żubr), moose, wild horse (tarpan), and wild goat are among the few remaining large mammals. Birds, fish, and insects are plentiful.

⁵ENVIRONMENT

The World Resource Institute reported that Poland had designated 7.54 million hectares (18.64 million acres) of land for protection as of 2006. Water resources totaled 63.1 cu km (15.14 cu mi) while water usage was 11.73 cu km (2.81 cu mi) per year. Domestic water usage accounted for 13% of total usage, industrial for 79%, and agricultural for 8%. Per-capita water usage totaled 304 cu m (10,736 cu ft) per year.

Poland's environmental situation has improved since the ousting of its communist regime, which has been accompanied by decreased emphasis on heavy industry and increased government awareness of environmental issues. However, Poland has yet to recover from the overexploitation of forests during World War II and the loss of about 1.6 million hectares (4 million acres) of forestland after the war. As of the mid-1990s, 75% of Poland's forests have been damaged by airborne contaminants and acid rain. The United Nations (UN) reported in 2008 that carbon dioxide emissions totaled 317,119 kilotons.

Pollution of air, water, and land was the most significant environmental problem facing Poland in the 1990s. Air pollution results from hazardous concentrations of airborne dust and chemicals, including carbon dioxide, nitrogen compounds, fluorine, formaldehyde, ammonia, lead, and cadmium. In 1992, Poland had the world's 12th-highest level of industrial carbon dioxide emissions, which totaled 341.8 million metric tons, a per capita level of 8.9 metric tons. In 1996, the total rose to 356 million metric tons. However, some measures for reduction must be working, since in 2000, the total of carbon dioxide emissions was at 301.3 million metric tons. Industry-related pollution affects particularly the Katowice region, where dust and sulfur dioxide emissions exceed acceptable levels. Water pollution in the Baltic Sea is 10 times higher than in ocean water. As of 2010, the total emission of the main air pollutants in Poland was one of the higher (absolute levels) among the European Union (EU) countries. The Economist Intelligence Unit reported that during its European Union accession negotiations, Poland was granted ten transition periods in areas such as municipal sewage, which were to be fulfilled over 2008–15. It also reported that since 2004 Poland had made substantial progress in bringing its environmental legislation in line with EU standards and requirements.

The nation's wildlife has also suffered from degeneration of its habitats. As of 2010, 32.4% of Poland's total area was protected, in-

cluding 23 areas designated as national parks. According to a 2011 report issued by the International Union for Conservation of Nature and Natural Resources (IUCN), threatened species included 5 types of mammals, 6 species of birds, 7 species of fish, 6 types of mollusks, 15 species of other invertebrates, and 11 species of plants. The cerambyx longicorn and rosalia longicorn are among the endangered species. The wild horse has become extinct. As of 2010, major protected animals included 1,224 European bison, 770 wolves, 147 bears, and 285 lynxes.

⁶POPULATION

The US Central Intelligence Agency (CIA) estimates the population of Poland in 2011 to be approximately 38,441,588, which placed it at number 33 in population among the 196 nations of the world. In 2011, approximately 13.7% of the population was over 65 years of age, with another 14.7% under 15 years of age. The median age in Poland was 38.5 years. There were 0.94 males for every female in the country. The population's annual rate of change was 0.062%. The projected population for the year 2025 was 37,400,000. Population density in Poland was calculated at 123 people per sq km (319 people per sq mi). As of 2010, male life expectancy at birth was 72.1 years, and female life expectancy at birth was 80.6 years.

The UN estimated that 61% of the population lived in urban areas and that urban populations had an annual rate of change of -0.1%. The largest urban areas, along with their respective populations, included Warsaw, 1.7 million; and Kraków, 756,000.

⁷MIGRATION

Estimates of Poland's net migration rate, carried out by the CIA in 2011, amounted to -0.47 migrants per 1,000 citizens. The total number of emigrants living abroad was 3.1 million, and the total number of immigrants living in Poland was 827,500. Large-scale emigration from Poland took place before World War II, with the heaviest exodus in the decades before World War I. Between 1871 and 1915, a total of 3,510,000 Poles, Polish Jews, and Ukrainians emigrated, about half of them to the United States. Emigration diminished greatly during the interwar period, when France became the chief country of destination. From 1921 to 1938, some 1,400,000 Poles emigrated, while 700,000 returned. Poland suffered a net population loss of nearly 11,000,000 between 1939 and 1949 through war losses, deportations, voluntary emigrations, and population transfers arising out of territorial changes. An estimated 6,000,000 Germans left the present western territories of Poland when these territories came under Polish jurisdiction, and since the end of World War II more than 7,500,000 Poles have settled in the area. From the 1950s through the 1980s, Germans leaving for Germany constituted the bulk of emigrants; Jews also left in substantial numbers for Israel, both in the immediate postwar years and during the 1950s and 1960s. Another emigration wave occurred after the imposition of martial law in December 1981. In 2005, the Polish Ministry of Labor reported that 500,000 Poles were legally employed in 15 EU countries. Amongst these, Germany was the chief destination for Polish migrant labor, 350,000 legally admitted workers, including 90% employed seasonally in agriculture. In 2011, the Polish Ministry of Labor reported that after 2004, when most EU states opened their labor markets for the citizens of new EU members and former Soviet bloc countries, as

LOCATION: 14°7′ to 24°8′E; 49° to 54°50′N. BOUNDARY LENGTHS: Baltic coastline, 491 kilometers (304 miles); Russia, 432 kilometers (268 miles); Lithuania 91 kilometers (56 miles); Belarus, 605 kilometers (378 miles); and Ukraine, 428 kilometers (265 miles); Czech Republic, 658 kilometers (408 miles); Slovakia, 444 kilometers (275 miles); Germany, 456 kilometers (286 miles). TERRITORIAL SEA LIMIT: 12 miles.

many as two million Polish workers migrated west. The main destination countries for Polish workers were the United Kingdom, Ireland, and Germany. In 2011, as the external environment deteriorated due to turbulence in the euro zone, the migration largely stopped and was unlikely to return to the previous record levels.

Since 1989, Poland has been open to refugees. However, while tens of thousands of foreigners enter Poland every year, the number of recognized refugees has been rather limited. In 2009, the main country of origin of migrant workers in Poland was Ukraine, with smaller numbers from China, Belarus, Vietnam, and Turkey. While the Russian Federation was the main origin country of asylum seekers, the number of asylum seekers from Georgia rose from less than 100 in 2008 to more than 4,200 in 2009.

8 ETHNIC GROUPS

Before World War II, over 30% of the people living within the boundaries of Poland were non-Poles. As a result of World War II and of the boundary changes and population transfers that

followed, Poland today is a predominantly homogeneous state with only about 3% of the population being non-Polish. According to the 2002 census, Poles constitute about 96.7% of the total population. Germans make up 0.4%, Ukrainians account for 0.1%; and Belarusians, 0.1%. There are about 50,000 Lithuanians in the country. There is also a significant number of Roma. The Roma population is subject to social discrimination and harassment and its members continue to be politically and economically marginalized.

9 LANGUAGES

Polish is one of the western Slavic languages using the Latin alphabet and the only major Slavic language to preserve the old Slavic nasal vowels. It is easily distinguishable from other Slavic languages by the frequent accumulation of consonants. Polish uses the Roman alphabet, plus letters with diacritics for specific Polish sounds: ą, ć, ę, ł, ń, ó, ś, ź, and ż. It also has seven consonantal diphthongs (a combination of two consonants in one syllable). It has no q, v, or x, except for foreign words. Among the several dialects are Great Polish (spoken around Poznań), Kuyavian (around Inowroclaw), Little Polish (around Cracow), Silesian (around Katowice and Wrocław), and Mazovian (around Warsaw and extending north and east). Some philologists consider that Kashubian, spoken along the Baltic, is not a Polish dialect but a separate language. Many Poles speak English, French, German, or Russian, and understand other Slavic languages to varying degrees. By law, ethnic minorities have the right to be taught in their own language.

10 RELIGIONS

It is estimated that over 94% of Poles are nominally Roman Catholics. Other groups (each of which constitute less than 5% of the population) include Polish Orthodox, Greek Catholics (Byzantine-Ukrainian), Jehovah's Witnesses, and Lutherans (Augsburg). Other established Christian denominations include Old Catholic Mariavits, Polish-Catholics, Pentecostals, Baptists, Methodists, the Church of Christ, Reformed Lutherans, Mormons, and the New Apostolic Church. The Muslim community has been estimated at about 25,000 by Muslim organizations. On the eve of World War II, an estimated 3,351,000 Jews lived in Poland, more than in any other country; they constituted about 10% of the Polish population and nearly 20% of world Jewry. During the course of the Nazi occupation (1939–45), nearly 3,000,000 Polish Jews were killed, many of them in extermination camps such as Auschwitz (Oświęcim), near Cracow. Most of the survivors fled to the former Soviet Union; at the end of the war, only about 55,000 Jews remained in Poland. Repatriation raised the total Jewish population to 250,000 in 1946. However, the establishment of the State of Israel in 1948, combined with a series of anti-Semitic outbreaks in Poland (including a government-led campaign in 1968–69), induced most Jews to emigrate. As of 2010, Poland had only about 20,000–25,000 Jews living in the country. There have been some reports of social discrimination and harassment against Jews. During the 2000s, there were efforts underway to revive Jewish cultural and religious life, especially in Cracow and Warsaw.

Poland has historically been one of the world's most strongly Roman Catholic countries. During the period of Communist domination that began in 1945, that church suffered extensive repression by the state. A change in party leadership in October 1956, however, brought about a new relationship between church and state, which included voluntary religious instruction in schools and other guarantees to the Roman Catholic Church. In 1974, the Polish government established permanent working contacts with the Holy See. The position of the Church was further enhanced when the archbishop of Cracow, Karol Cardinal Wojtyła, became Pope John Paul II in 1978. In 1989, the Roman Catholic Church was finally granted legal status and control of its schools, its hospitals, and its university in Lublin. A concordat was signed with the Vatican in 1993 and ratified by parliament in 1998. Freedom of religion is guaranteed by the constitution, and this right is respected in practice. Religious groups are not required to register with the government, but those that do obtain certain tax benefits. After the fall of Communism, the government restored the communal property (nationalized by Communist governments) of religious denominations to their rightful owners, including Roman Catholic Church, Protestant churches, and Jewish religious communi-

ties (*gminy*). Easter Monday, Corpus Christi Day, Assumption of the Virgin Mary, All Saints' Day, Christmas, and St. Stephen's Day are observed as national holidays.

11 TRANSPORTATION

The CIA reports that Poland has a total of 423,997 km (263,460 mi) of roads, of which 295,356 km (183,526 mi) are paved. There are 495 vehicles per 1,000 people in the country. Railroads extend for 19,764 km (12,281 mi). There are 129 airports, which transported 4.28 million passengers in 2009, according to the World Bank. Poland has approximately 3,997 km (2,484 mi) of navigable waterways.

In terms of line length, the Polish State Railways (PKP) is the third-largest railway system in Europe. In 2000, PKP began privatization of passenger, cargo, and infrastructure. From 2000 to 2010, the length of railroad lines operated by PKP decreased by almost 11 %. During the same period of time, the number of electric and diesel locomotives (engines) increased by 7% and 10%, respectively, but the number of passenger and freight cars decreased by 35% and 9%, respectively, reflecting the modernization of PKP's rolling stock and the noticeable decrease in the number of goods and passengers transported by rail (2010 saw a slight increase in transporting freight and passengers).

There is a dense road and highway network. From 2000 to 2009, the average length of hard-surface public roads per 100 sq km (network density) increased from 79.9 km (49.6 mi) to 85.8 km (53.3 mi). During the same period of time, the total length of expressways (divided highways) in Poland increased from 358 km (222.5 mi) to 849 km (527.5 mi) but remains relatively modest by EU standards.

Before World War II, Polish merchant marine operations were mainly with the Western countries, especially the United States, but much of the current traffic is with Asian and African countries. The major ports are Szczecin, Gdynia, Gdánsk, and Świnoujście. The ports were badly damaged during World War II but have since been rehabilitated and enlarged. The principal inland waterways are the Odra (Oder), with Szczecin near its mouth, the Wisła, and the Warta.

Polish Air Transport (Polskie Linie Lotnicze-LOT), organized in 1922 and reorganized after World War II, is a state enterprise, with Warsaw's Okęcie International Airport as the center.

12 HISTORY

The land now known as Poland was sparsely populated in prehistoric times. The oldest preserved settlements, most notably at Biskupin in northwest Poland, date back to 1000 BC. A lack of Roman conquest and settlement delayed early urbanization in relation to the territories of Western Europe, such as Germany and France. Slavic tribes, from whom modern Poles are descendants in terms of language and culture, began settling Poland in the fourth and fifth centuries AD after the Hunnic invasions and mass migrations of peoples from Asia to Europe. By AD 800, the population was probably around one million and stabilized into permanent settlements. Rulers of the Piast dynasty united the Polish tribes of the Vistula and Oder basins about the middle of the 10th century. In 966, Mieszko I, a member of this dynasty, was baptized, and consequently Poland became a Christian nation. Thirty-three years later, his eldest son and successor, Bolesław I "the

Brave" (992–1025), whose military campaigns took him as far east as Kiev, secured recognition of Polish sovereignty and received a royal crown from Holy Roman Emperor Otto III, becoming the first king of Poland.

During the next three centuries, Poland was continually embroiled in conflicts with the Germans to the west and with the Eastern Slavs and Mongol invaders to the east while developing cultural relations with Western civilizations. Foreign penetration and internal difficulties led to the division of Poland among members of the Piast dynasty. Under Casimir III "the Great" (1333–1370), the last of the Piast rulers, Poland was restored to unity and greatness. Casimir made peace with the Teutonic Knights, added Galicia to the realm, and welcomed Jewish refugees from the west; internally, law was codified, administration centralized, and a university was established in Kraków in 1364. In 1386, a Polish-Lithuanian federal union was created through a dynastic marriage, which also gave birth to the Jagiellonian dynasty, named for Jagiello, grand duke of Lithuania, who ruled Poland as Ladislas II (1386–1434). The union extended from the Baltic to the Black Sea and held control over other territories in Central Europe, notably West Prussia and Pomerania. The combined forces of the union annihilated the Teutonic Knights in 1410 in the Battle of Grunwald. The 16th century, known as Poland's Golden Age, saw the flourishing of the arts, scholarship, and architecture. The most notable examples of the Golden Age are the poetry of Jan Kochanowski, the revolutionary astronomical work of Nicolaus Copernicus, and the Renaissance architecture of old Kraków. During this time, Poland was the largest state in Europe and a regional military power. In order to preserve the union during the reign of Sigismund II (1548–72), the last of the Jagiellonians, provisions were made for an elective monarch and a single parliament (Sejm) for Poland and Lithuania. The fact that kings were elected by the Polish/Lithuanian gentry (*szlachta*) and the ratification of the first constitution in Europe in 1792 are often mentioned to support the claim that Poland is a pioneer of European democracy.

Unfortunately, many of the political reforms contributed to the nation's subsequent decline. The *szlachta* had progressively gained influence and power at the expense of the king. Meeting in the Sejm, the gentry adopted the legislative practice whereby a single dissenting voice was sufficient to block passage. Such policies prevented any decisive action by the government with the gentry cementing their position of power in an economy based on agricultural serfdom. The nobility imposed such far-reaching limitations on the monarchy that national unity and integrity could not be maintained. Internal disorders, including the Cossack and peasant uprising (1648–49) led by Bogdan Chmielnicki against Polish domination of the Ukraine—a revolt that struck with particular ferocity against Polish Jews, many of whom had served as agents of the nobility in administering Ukrainian lands—further weakened the nation, as did the very destructive Swedish invasion in 1655–60. In 1683, Polish troops led by John III Sobieski (1674–96) rescued Vienna from a Turkish siege, but this was perhaps the last great military victory of an increasingly weakened and war-weary state.

The decline of Poland's power was taken advantage of by its neighboring states. A Russian, Prussian, and Austrian agreement led to the first partitioning of Poland in 1772; the second (1793) and third (1795) partitions led to the demise of Poland as a sovereign state. Galicia was ruled by Austria-Hungary, northwestern Poland by Prussia, and the Ukraine and eastern and central Poland by Russia, which extended its domains to include the Duchy of Warsaw, reconstituted as the Kingdom of Poland (under Russian imperial rule) at the Congress of Vienna in 1815. The Poles rebelled in 1830 and 1863 against the tsarist rulers, but each insurrection was suppressed. However, the peasants were emancipated by Prussia in 1823, by Austria in 1849, and by Russia in 1864. Galicia, which won partial autonomy from Austria following the Habsburg monarchy's constitutional reforms, became the cultural center of the Poles.

With the Russian Revolution of 1917 and the defeat of the Central Powers in World War I, Poland regained its independence. On 18 November 1918, Jozef Pilsudski, leader of the prewar anti-Russian independence movement, formed a civilian government. Dispute over the eastern borders of the reborn state led to a military clash with the Soviet Union. The conflict, in which the Bolshevik hope of spreading socialist revolution beyond Poland to Germany and France was dashed by a fortuitous Polish counterattack near Warsaw, ended with the Treaty of Riga in 1921, under which Galicia was restored to Poland.

In the next two decades, Poland was plagued by economic difficulties, political instability, and increasingly menacing pressures from its Soviet and German neighbors. Following the Nazi-Soviet Pact in 1939, Germany invaded Poland on 1 September, occupying Warsaw four weeks later. Meanwhile, the USSR began occupation of the eastern half of the country on 17 September despite nonaggression treaties Poland had signed with both the USSR and Germany. Almost immediately, Nazi forces began to brutally oppress large segments of the Polish population and loot Poland's industrial sector and major resources such as timber, coal, and wheat. Ghettos for Jews were set up in Warsaw and other cities, and numerous concentration camps were established on Polish territory, including the extermination camp at Auschwitz, where at least one million people perished between 1940 and 1944. Poland suffered tremendous losses of life and property during World War II. An estimated six million Poles were killed, half of them Jews; 2.5 million were deported for compulsory labor in Germany; more than 500,000 were permanently crippled; and the remaining population suffered virtual starvation throughout the Nazi occupation. Losses in property were evaluated at Z258 billion (more than US$50 billion). Poles under the Soviet occupation faced a similar fate. Close to 26,000 Polish prisoners, including about 15,000 soldiers and officers, were executed by the NKVD. About 350,000 Polish civilians were placed in Soviet prisons and labor camps, and about 1,700,000 Polish citizens were deported to Siberia and Soviet Central Asia from eastern Poland. The undetermined number perished during the deportation, during which many were deported in cattle cars.

The seeds of Poland's postwar political history were sown long before the war ended. A Polish government-in-exile was set up in France and later in the United Kingdom. Units of the Polish army fought together with the Allies while in Poland underground groups, organized along political lines, and maintained resistance activities. The Home Army (*Armia Krajowa*) was the major non-Communist resistance group and took its orders from the government-in-exile in London. Although formally allied to the Soviet Union, relations between Moscow and the London-based Polish government continued to deteriorate, especially after the discovery of mass graves of thousands of Polish officers murdered by the Soviets in 1940. In July 1944, the Polish National Council, a Soviet-backed resistance group, set up the Polish Committee of National Liberation as a provisional government in liberated Lublin, declaring the émigré Polish government illegal. In August 1944, the Home Army in Warsaw rose against the Nazis in hopes of liberating the capital in step with the Soviet military advance. In the events that followed, and that still breed controversy to this day, the Red Army halted its advance and allowed the Nazis to use their remaining forces to brutally suppress the uprising and completely destroy the city, killing almost 180,000 civilians. It was not until 17 January 1945 that the Red Army entered Warsaw and installed the provisional pro-Soviet government. At Yalta, the Allies agreed to accept the Curzon line, thereby awarding the USSR nearly half of former Polish territory (including Galicia) in return for a Soviet agreement to broaden the political base of the provisional government with the addition of non-Communist Polish leaders. After subsequent negotiations, the Provisional Government of National Unity was formally recognized by the United States and Britain in July 1945.

Despite Stalin's promises of free elections, a bloc of four parties dominated by the Communists emerged victorious in the elections of January 1947. The results were falsified and the opposition parties eliminated. Consequently, Stanisław Mikołajczyk, the leader of the democratic opposition, escaped from Poland and sought political asylum in the United States. The Communists and the Socialists merged in December 1948 to form the Polish United Workers' Party (PZPR). The PZPR consistently followed a pro-Soviet policy. Domestically, the party pursued a reconstruction program stressing agriculture and industrial development. It shunned the Marshall Plan and, in its first two decades, renounced all dealings with the Western powers.

The first decade of Communist rule was dominated by Stalinist repressions, tensions with the Roman Catholic Church, and a strong-handed Soviet influence, as practiced by Konstantin Rokossovsky, a Soviet general of Polish birth, who became Poland's defense minister in 1949 and served as deputy prime minister from 1952 until his resignation four years later. Rising nationalist sentiment, heightened by stagnating economic conditions, led to worker riots in Poznań on 28–29 July 1956. In response to the unrest, a new Polish Politburo, headed by Władysław Gomułka (who had been purged from the PZPR in 1949 and subsequently imprisoned because of his nationalist leanings), improved relations with the Church and introduced liberalizations, including the abolition of farm collectivization. Conditions improved from those immediately after the war, but, by the late 1950s, the reform movement had been halted, and the government took a harder line against dissent. In 1968, there were student demonstrations against the government in the university centers; the Gomułka regime countered with a political offensive in which many government officials and party members accused of anti-Socialist or pro-Zionist sentiments were removed from office, and an estimated 12,000 Polish Jews left Poland.

Two years later, following a drought in 1969 and an exceptionally severe winter, shipyard workers in Gdańsk demonstrated on 16 December 1970 to protest economic conditions, the privileges of the Communist party elite, and an announced rise in food prices.

The government responded with military force, and after widespread violence, with soldiers firing on striking workers, at least 44 people were killed. The unrest led to the removal from power of Gomułka and the installation of Edward Gierek as the first secretary of the *politburo* on December 20. Under continued pressure from strikes, Gierek's government postponed the controversial incentive system and froze prices at their new levels. After receiving a substantial long-term Soviet grant (estimated at $100 million), the Polish government rolled back prices to their pre-December 1970 levels, and labor peace was restored. In a move to bolster his support, Gierek reinstated Church control over thousands of religious properties in northwestern Poland to which the government had held title since 1945.

During the 1970s, Gierek's government vigorously pursued a policy of détente with the West. Three US presidents visited Poland, and Gierek himself traveled to the United States and to several West European countries. Peace agreements governing the Oder-Neisse line and formally recognizing Polish sovereignty in former German territories were concluded with West Germany, and trade pacts were signed with the United States, Britain, France, Italy, Austria, and other nations. With a bold plan of creating a "second Japan," Gierek secured huge loans (several billion dollars) from the West in hopes of building an industrial export economy and improving living conditions, which were at this point glaringly inferior to those in the capitalist world. Although many ambitious projects were undertaken, including the building of an oil refinery in Gdańsk and a new steel works plant in Katowice, mismanagement and the inefficiency of the socialist economy crippled real economic output, and the prospects of repaying the foreign debts became increasingly dim. In 1976, the government announced food price increases but had to rescind them after the workers responded by striking. During the next several years, the economic situation kept deteriorating, and Polish nationalism, buoyed in 1978 by the election of the archbishop of Kraków to the papacy as John Paul II, continued to rise. In July 1980, new meat price increases were announced, and within a few weeks, well-organized workers all over Poland demanded a series of economic and political concessions, including the right to organize independent trade unions outside the Communist party. The center of labor activity was the Lenin Shipyard in Gdańsk, where, in a public ceremony on 31 August, government officials agreed to allow workers the rights to organize and strike. The independent labor movement Solidarity, headed by Lech Wałęsa, the leader of the Gdańsk workers, and strongly supported by the Roman Catholic clergy, soon claimed a membership of about 10 million (about a fourth of the population), with its ranks filled not only with workers but also intellectuals. That month, Stanisław Kania replaced Gierek as first secretary.

For more than a year, the government and Solidarity leaders negotiated, with Catholic Church officials often acting as mediators. As Solidarity became more and more overtly political—demanding, for example, free parliamentary elections—Poland's Communist leaders came under increasing pressure from the USSR to stop the "anti-Socialist" and "anti-Soviet" forces. On 18 October 1981, Gen. Wojciech Jaruzelski, prime minister since February, replaced Kania as first secretary. On 13 December, after union leaders in Gdańsk called for a national referendum on forming a non-Communist government in Poland, Jaruzelski set up the Military Council for National Salvation and declared martial law. To what extent Jaruzelski's abrupt crackdown was carried out to prevent direct Soviet military intervention is still unclear, although evidence suggests that the Kremlin had not drawn up any plans for a military intrusion into Poland. Almost the whole leadership of Solidarity, including Wałęsa, was arrested, and the union was suspended. Despite further strikes and rioting, which resulted in several deaths, the military had soon gained complete control. More than 10,000 people were arrested and detained for up to 12 months, and all rights and freedoms gained in the preceding year and a half were abolished. In January 1982, the United States imposed sanctions against Poland, including withdrawal of most-favored-nation status, veto of Poland's entry into the IMF, and suspension of fishing rights in US waters and of LOT Polish Airline flights to the United States. Protests and rioting continued sporadically into 1983, and some Solidarity leaders remained active underground, but these disturbances did not seriously threaten the military regime. On 22 July 1983, the government formally ended martial law and proclaimed an amnesty, but a series of legislative measures had meanwhile institutionalized many of the powers the government had exercised, including the power to dissolve organizations, forbid public meetings, and run universities.

The internal political situation stabilized to such a degree that, in July 1984, the government proclaimed a general amnesty, and the United States began to lift its sanctions the following month (the last sanctions were lifted in early 1987). When an outspoken priest, Father Jerzy Popiełuszko, was kidnapped and subsequently murdered by two secret police officers, the government, in an unprecedented step, permitted a trial to take place in February 1985, which resulted in four security officers' conviction and sentencing. Another amnesty was proclaimed in September 1986, leading to the release of all remaining political prisoners. Economically, however, the country was spiraling out of control. Continued declines in standards of living and shortages of even basic necessities led to waves of strikes throughout Poland in spring and fall 1988, essentially paralyzing the nation. By November 1987 public antipathy had been so widespread that the government called for the first public referendum to be held in Poland in more than 40 years; this was also the first open election to be held within the Warsaw Pact. Although the ballot itself asked only for public support of an accelerated economic reform package, the people of Poland understood the referendum to be a vote of confidence in the government itself. The final tally was approximately two-thirds in support of the government, but because of a Solidarity-inspired voter boycott, only 67% of the eligible voters cast their ballots, which meant that the referendum failed to pass, a first-ever defeat for the government.

In autumn 1988, the entire government resigned, and it became clear that talks with labor activists were inevitable. The negotiations leading up to the so-called "round-table talks," which finally opened in February 1989, were as delicate and prolonged as the talks themselves. However, in April 1989, agreement was reached on a number of unprecedented concessions: Solidarity was recognized as a legal entity; the post of president was created, to be filled by legislative appointment; some independent media were permitted to operate; and the Catholic Church was given full legal status. In June 1989 came perhaps the most far-reaching change, the establishment of a senate, complementing the existing *Sejm*, with the seats to be filled by open election. In addition, 35% of the seats in the *Sejm* were also made subject to direct election.

The government did all it could to make it difficult for opposition candidates to run: only two months were allowed in which candidates could gather the petitions necessary to get on the ballot, and the ballots themselves listed candidates alphabetically, with no indication of party affiliation. Despite those efforts, Solidarity won a decisive victory; 99 of the 100 seats in the Senate went to Solidarity members. Moreover, many government candidates in the *Sejm* lost seats because voters crossed out the names of unopposed government candidates, thus denying them the necessary 50% of the total votes cast.

In June 1989, the newly elected parliament named General Wojciech Jaruzelski Poland's president by the slenderest of margins. Two months later, Solidarity pressed to balance Jaruzelski's post of president with a non-Communist prime minister, at which point the discredited PZPR could do little but comply. Although it was widely expected that Lech Wałęsa might lead the first Solidarity government, he demurred, instead putting forward Tadeusz Mazowiecki, who took office on 24 August 1989, as the first non-Communist prime minister in the Eastern Bloc. That autumn, motivated at least in part by the events unfolding in Poland, a wave of "velvet revolutions" spread across Eastern Europe culminating in the fall of the Berlin Wall. These events further accelerated the de-Sovietization of Polish government. In September 1990, Jaruzelski resigned, opening the way for new elections.

The election of Wałęsa as president was the formal end to Poland's Communist rule, with Poland rejoining the community of democratic nations. In what would become known as "shock therapy," the previously Socialist economy was abruptly opened to free market forces. Although initially inflation skyrocketed and economic output continued to fall, by 1997, Poland was attracting large amounts of foreign investment and enjoying the highest growth rates in Europe. At the same time, not everyone enjoyed economic prosperity, and political discord continued to grow. The number of political parties ballooned, making it difficult to undertake such complex and contentious issues as large-scale privatization, economic rationalization of Soviet-era giant industry, and fundamental constitutional revision. The October 1991 election saw 69 parties competing, with 29 actually winning seats, none with more than 14% of the vote. Inevitably, this resulted in coalition governments without clear mandates, giving Poland five prime ministers and four governments in 1991–93. This proliferation of parties reflected disparities among the electorate that emerged once the Communists had been removed as a unifying focus for opposition.

In the September 1993 election, the two most popular parties, the Polish Peasant Party (PSL) and the Democratic Left Alliance (SLD) were made up largely of ex-Communists or other figures from the governments of the past. The apparent rejection of the gains of Solidarity and the return of the vanquished ex-Communists was interpreted variously as a rejection of "shock-therapy" economic transformation, as the electorate's nostalgia for the more ordered life of the past, and as a vote against the Catholic Church, or at least against its social agenda of asserting close control on social issues such as abortion, school curriculum, and women's role in society.

Fears associated with the return of the many ex-Communists to power proved unfounded. Although differing from their predecessors on the pace of Poland's economic transformation, the government of Polish Peasant Party (PSL) leader Waldemar Pawlak, and his Democratic Left Alliance (SLD) partner, Aleksander Kwaśniewski, remained generally committed to Poland's course of democratization and economic transition. The Constitution Commission proposed a new constitution that passed the National Assembly in April 1997 and was approved in a national referendum on 23 May 1997. Kwaśniewski of the SLD beat Wałęsa to be elected president in 1995 and won a second term in 2000.

The parliamentary elections of 1997 saw the return to power of centrist and right-of-center Solidarity legacy parties, with Solidarity Electoral Action (AWS) and the Freedom Union (UW) forming a coalition with Jerzy Buzek as prime minister. The Buzek government presided over many successful reforms, including reorganization of local and regional administration, but an economic downturn and rising unemployment caused the voters to resoundingly return the reigns of power to the post-Communist SLD in 2001.

In 2005, the power pendulum swung again to the right with the scandal-ridden SLD winning less than 12% of the vote and the right-of-center Law and Justice (PiS) and centrist Civic Platform (PO) parties gaining the majority. The constant and almost predictable shift of power can either be interpreted as the political maturation of the young democracy or as the failure of either side to address the main economic issue of unemployment, which reached 20% in December 2004. In 2005, Law and Justice candidate Lech Kaczyński won the presidential election, and a minority government led by Prime Minister Kazimierz Marcinkiewicz of Law and Justice was sworn in. In May 2006, the Law and Justice Party reached a majority coalition agreement with the Self-Defense Party and the League of Polish Families. That July, Marcinkiewicz resigned as prime minister. President Lech Kaczyński's twin brother, Jarosław, became prime minister.

It has been on the international scene that Poland has made its most visible strides since the end of Communist rule. In 1997, NATO invited Poland, the Czech Republic, and Hungary to join the alliance, and the three countries became members in March 1999. In May 2004, Poland became a member of the European Union (EU) and is now the organization's sixth-most-populous member. Poland asserted itself as a close American ally by being one of the few countries to participate in the 2003 invasion of Iraq and subsequently administering an Iraqi-occupied zone with the initial involvement of 2,400 of its own troops. Poland has also attempted to play a leading role in the politics of eastern and central Europe and has invested its political capital in encouraging democratization in Belarus and supporting the Orange Revolution in Ukraine in December 2004.

Since joining the EU, investment and economic growth picked up, with new manufacturing jobs coming from Western Europe. However, corruption, inefficient bureaucracy, and weak infrastructure continued to be problems and slowed economic growth. Unemployment began to drop, but, at 17.9%, it still remained the highest in the European Union in mid-2006.

In 2007, the United States ramped up its plans for an anti-ballistic missile (ABM) defense system. This time, plans were made for radar and missile interceptor installations to be placed in the Czech Republic and Poland, respectively. The US said the defense shield was aimed at rogue states such as Iran and North Korea. However, another nation, Russia, saw the plans for the defense shield as directed toward itself and, in February 2007, warned the Czech Republic and Poland that Russia might aim nuclear weapons at them should they adopt Washington's plans. Russia had already been stung by the further expansion of NATO onto the territory of the former Soviet Union. The US tried to quell Russia's concerns and, in April 2007, even invited Russia to share ABM defense technology. Russia flatly condemned the notion, calling any ABM system a destabilizing factor that would have a great impact on global and regional security. On 26 April 2007, Russia announced it would suspend its compliance with the Treaty on Conventional Armed Forces in Europe (CFE Treaty), signed in 1990 by the members of NATO and the Warsaw Pact, including Russia. The CFE Treaty required the reduction and relocation of much of the main battle equipment that was then located along the East-West dividing lines, including tanks, artillery pieces, armored vehicles, and attack aircraft. Russia's decision to end compliance with the CFE was seen as a move on its part to bargain with the United States and NATO. In April 2007, the Polish government told the United States that it supported proposals to base 10 American missile interceptors on its soil, but only so long as Poland's security was enhanced along with that of Western Europe. In June 2007, Russia's President Vladimir Putin proposed locating an anti-missile defense system in Azerbaijan, and invited the US to join it. Poland and the United States reached a long-delayed deal in August 2008 to place an American missile defense base in Polish territory, prompting an angry and threatening response from Moscow. The move was widely understood to reflect the growing alarm and concern over Russia's invasion of Georgia that month.

After months of political turmoil, in August 2007 the governing coalition collapsed, and the government announced that elections would be held two years early, by November 2007. Analysts said that the vote might pave the way for a coalition government led by the opposition Civic Platform, a center-right party that has called for better relations with Germany and the EU. Prime Minister Jaroslaw Kaczynski had for months been at odds with his two small, radical coalition partners, the populist Self-Defense Party and the nationalist League of Polish Families. The two parties had demanded the introduction of the death penalty, a complete ban on abortion, and more independence from the EU. In 2009, former Polish prime minister Jerzy Buzek was elected president of the European Parliament. While the post is primarily ceremonial, the election was seen as symbolic of the growing strength and presence of the former communist countries within the European Union. These deepening ties with the West have often strained Poland's relationship with Russia, a major trading partner and energy supplier.

On 10 April 2010, President Lech Kaczyński, his wife Maria, and 94 others were killed in a plane crash as the pilot attempted to land in dense fog around the Smolensk airbase in western Russia. Several members of the Polish parliament and other key government officials, including top army generals and commanders, were aboard the plane when it crashed, leaving no survivors. The Polish delegation was traveling to Russia for a ceremony honoring the victims of the Soviet massacre of 22,000 Poles in the Smolensk district during World War II. Preliminary investigations showed no technical or mechanical malfunctions aboard the plane or with air traffic control, marking pilot error as the cause of the crash.

While the nation mourned, the parliamentary speaker Bronisław Komorowski scheduled the required emergency presidential elections for 20 June 2010, and Jarosław Kaczyński, the twin brother of the late Polish president and leader of the Conservative Law and Justice Party, announced his candidacy to succeed his brother as president. The elections were held as scheduled, with Kaczyński and Komorowski as primary rivals. Komorowski won the seat in the run-off election by a margin of 53% to 47% over Kaczyński. Representing the center-right Civic Platform party, Komorowski is pro-European Union and pro-free market, and favors increased cooperation with Russia as a key to providing stable regional development.

13 GOVERNMENT

Until 1997, the form of government in Poland was in the midst of a protracted transformation, which left a number of its important features unclear. Without a formal constitution, Poland had been functioning on a much-amended form of its Communist-era constitution. The most important modifications were the Jaruzelski government's concessions of April 1989, which created both the Senate and the office of president, and a package of amendments passed in October 1992 which are collectively called the "Little Constitution." Another important modification was the agreement of 1990, which made the presidency a popularly elected post rather than parliamentarily appointed.

The president is directly elected for a term of five years. The post has traditional executive obligations and powers, such as the duty to sign into law or veto legislations, but also retains substantial legislative powers, including the right to introduce bills and draft legal amendments.

During his tenure, Lech Wałęsa fought to widen the powers of the presidency, arguing that, at least during the transition period, Poland required a strong president able to resolve impasses and disputes on the basis of "practical experience" rather than on points of legal niceties.

Wałęsa's successor, Aleksander Kwaśniewski, succeeded in putting forth a new constitution in 1997.

The parliament consists of two houses, the *Sejm*, or lower house, with 460 seats, and the Senate, with 100 seats. The members of both houses serve four-year terms. Seats are filled on the basis of party lists; there is a minimum national vote threshold of 5% for parties, or 8% for coalitions, with the votes for parties that fail to reach those minimums assigned to victorious parties. The prime minister proposes, the president appoints, and the *Sejm* approves the Council of Ministers or cabinet. The president, who is elected by popular vote for a five-year term, appoints the prime minister, who is then confirmed by the *Sejm*.

14 POLITICAL PARTIES

After the political poverty of its Communist past, Poland initially saw a proliferation of political parties ranging across the full political spectrum, from the rabidly xenophobic nationalism of the Polish National Front (whose leader, Janusz Bryczkowski, invited Russian extremist Vladimir Zhirinovsky to Poland in 1994) to the socialist party, Union of Labor (UP). In between were special interest and even quirky parties, of which the best example may be the Polish Beerdrinkers' Party. Overall, 69 parties participated in the 1991 parliamentary elections, of which 29 gained seats, none with more than 14% of the total vote. By 1993, however, the political scene was stabilizing. Only 35 parties participated in that election; perhaps more significantly, only five received seats.

The local elections of 1994 showed the emergence of three basic political orientations shaped by shifting coalitions of parties, with the parties themselves often dissolving and reorganizing under new names. The Polish political spectrum slightly deviates from the traditional notions of right and left in part because, in contrast to most countries where labor movements are associated with the political left, the Polish right has its roots in the Solidarity labor movement.

The Polish far right was initially represented by several coalitions: the Alliance for Poland, which included the Christian National Union, the Center Alliance, the Movement for the Republic, Peasant Alliance, and the Conservative Coalition; and the 11 November Agreement, which included the Conservative Party, the Party of Christian Democrats, the Christian-Peasant Alliance, and the Real Politics Union (a radical *laissez-faire* party). These parties generally favored a major role for the Catholic Church and tended to draw their support from Poland's rural sectors; in 1994, they did best in the eastern districts. The religious right is represented by the League of Polish Families (LPR), which has a social platform based on traditional Catholic values and was not in favor of Polish membership in the EU. LPR won 7.97% of the vote in the October 2005 elections.

The mainstream right was represented during the years 1997–2001 by Elective Action Solidarity (AWS). AWS led the government in coalition with UW. However, after a resounding defeat in 2001, AWS dissolved, and its members eventually migrated to either the centrist Civic Platform (PO) or the right-of-center Law and Justice (PiS) party. PiS supports continuous but careful economic reforms, is in favor of raising retirement benefits, and remains socially conservative, as evidenced by the prohibition of a gay pride parade in Warsaw by its leader Lech Kaczynski in 2005. Another important PiS position is a strong stand against corruption. In the parliamentary elections of October 2005, PiS was the most popular party with 26.99% of the vote.

The center was dominated by Freedom Union (UW), which was formed in April 1994, when the Liberal Democratic Congress merged with the Democratic Union. The centrist position derives largely from the intellectual wing of the original Solidarity, favoring radical economic transformation while being less concerned with immediate impact on workers. UW formed a coalition with AWS as the junior partner in 1997–2000. UW's most prominent member was Leszek Balcerowicz, the architect of the "shock therapy" economic reform and president of Poland's National Bank. After the elections of 1997, UW largely dissolved, with its members joining the newly formed Civic Platform (PO), which also absorbed politicians from AWS. Both the UW and PO draw much of their support from smaller cities and university centers, such as Kraków, and the prosperous regions of western Poland. In the parliamentary elections of October 2005, PO's platform included a proposal for a 15% flat tax. PO was the second-most-popular party with 24.14% of the vote and was set to rule in a coalition with PiS.

The left, which was almost entirely discredited in 1991, has shown remarkable resilience. Through the 1990s, the two major parties were the Democratic Left Alliance (SLD) and the Polish Peasant Party (PSL), both descendants of elements of the old Communist party and its affiliates. The far left is dominated by Self-Defense (SO) headed by Andrzej Lepper. Lepper's party is in favor of protectionist agriculture and sometimes anti-western isolationist foreign policy. In 2001 the Democratic Left Alliance (SLD) in coalition with the Labor Union (UP), a minor left-wing party, won a decisive victory and formed a government under Leszek Miller. Although Miller's government presided over Poland's entry into the European Union, it became increasingly unpopular due to a series of scandals involving corruption and bribery and failed to accelerate economic growth. When Miller himself was forced to resign amid scandal in May 2005, the SLD continued to rule as a minority government under Marek Belka until the elections of October 2005. Unhappy with Miller's leadership of the party, many members withdrew from the SLD in 2004 and formed a new leftist party called Polish Social Democracy (SDPL). In the October 2005 elections, SLD won 11.31%, SO 11.41%, and PSL 6.96%. SDPL failed to make the 3% threshold to enter the parliament. The governing coalition led by Prime Minister Jaroslaw Kaczynski collapsed in August 2007; early elections were scheduled for October.

In the October 2007, elections, the Civic Platform won 209 seats in the *Sejm* (lower house) and 60 seats in the Senate. The Law and Justice Party won 166 seats in the *Sejm* and 39 in the Senate. There was one independent candidate elected to the Senate. The Democratic Left Alliance won 53 *Sejm* seats, while the Polish Peasant Party won 31. In the October 2011 elections, the Civic Platform won 39.18%, the Law and Justice Party 29.89%, a newly formed party—Palikot Movement 10.02%, the Polish Peasant Party (PSL) 8.36%, and the Democratic Left Alliance (SLD) 8.24%. The turnout was 48.92%.

In the 1995 presidential elections, Aleksander Kwaśniewski of SLD beat Lech Wałęsa by a small margin (51.7% to 48.3%) to become president for a five-year term. He was reelected in 2000 with 53.9% of the vote to nonparty candidate Andrzej Olechowski's 17.3% and AWS chairman Marian Krzaklewski's 15.6%. In a striking reversal, Wałęsa finished seventh with 0.8% of the vote.

Constitutionally limited to two terms, Kwaśniewski did not run again in 2005. The October 2005 presidential elections saw 14 candidates compete. In the first round, the top four contenders were Donald Tusk (PO) with 36.33% of the vote, Lech Kaczyński (PiS) with 33.10%, Andrzej Lepper (SO) with 15.11%, and Marek Borowski (SDPL) with 10.33%. The SDL candidate withdrew from the election due to a scandal. In the second round, which included only the top two candidates, Tusk and Kaczyński, Kaczyński won with 54.04% of the vote to Tusk's 45.96%.

Kaczyński died in a plane crash in April 2010, leading to an emergency presidential election on 20 June 2010. Jarosław Kaczyński, the twin brother of the late Polish president and leader of the Conservative Law and Justice Party, announced his candidacy to succeed his brother as president. The elections were held as scheduled, with Kaczyński and Bronisław Komorowski as primary rivals. Komorowski won the seat in the run-off election by a margin of 53% to 47% over Kaczyński. Representing the center-right Civic Platform party, Komorowski is pro-European Union

and pro-free market and favors increased cooperation with Russia as a key to providing stable regional development.

15 LOCAL GOVERNMENT

Poland had been divided into 49 administrative districts, or *voivodships,* which were the basic administrative units under the Communists. In 1989, Solidarity government replaced that system with one in which the basic unit was the *gmina,* or local authority, which owned property and had responsibility for its own budget. The *gmina* elected a council, which appointed the executive officials actually responsible for day-to-day administration of the locality.

In 1994, there were 2,383 such local councils, with a mixed system of election. In districts containing more than 40,000 people, of which there were 110 in 1994, council representation was proportionally determined based on party affiliation. In the smaller districts, council representatives were elected by direct majority vote.

Originally, these *gmina* councils were similar in makeup to the Solidarity Citizens Committees from which they originated. Increasingly, however, the councils differentiated themselves, some becoming controlled by national parties, others remaining dominated by personalities who responded primarily to local issues.

Changes in local government structure were introduced in 1999, transforming Poland's 49 provinces into 16 new ones. A three-tier division of government was established: municipalities/communes, 308 counties (*powiaty*), and 16 provinces (*województwa*). Each of these divisions is governed by a council. Council members are directly elected and appoint and dismiss the heads of the municipalities/communes (*wójt*), the town mayors, the *starosta* or head of the county, and the speaker of the provincial councils.

16 JUDICIAL SYSTEM

There is a four-tiered court system in Poland: regional, provincial, appellate divisions, and a Supreme Court. The Supreme Court, the highest judicial organ, functions primarily as a court of appeal. The Supreme Court and lower courts are divided into criminal, civil, military, labor, and family chambers. Judges are nominated by the National Judicial Council and are appointed for life by the president.

There is also a Constitutional Tribunal which offers opinions on legislation and exercises authority of judicial review. Constitutional Tribunal judges are appointed to nine-year terms by the *Sejm*.

Defendants enjoy a presumption of innocence and have the right to appeal. Although the judiciary is independent, it suffers from inefficiency, lack of resources, and lack of public confidence.

17 ARMED FORCES

The International Institute for Strategic Studies reports that armed forces in Poland totaled 100,000 members in 2011. The force is comprised of 47,300 from the army, 8,000 from the navy, 17,500 from the air force, 1,650 from special forces, and 25,550 members of joint forces. Armed forces represent .7% of the labor force in Poland. Defense spending totaled $12.3 billion and accounted for 1.7% of gross domestic product (GDP).

Poland provides troops and observers to several nations or regions as part of UN, NATO, or European Union missions.

¹⁸INTERNATIONAL COOPERATION

Poland is a charter member of the UN, having signed on 24 October 1945; it participates in ECE and several non-regional specialized agencies, such as the FAO, IAEA, the World Bank, UNESCO, UNIDO, and the WHO. Poland was admitted to NATO on 12 March 1999. The nation is also a member of the Council of Europe, the Council of the Baltic Sea States, the Euro-Atlantic Partnership Council, the European Bank for Reconstruction and Development, the OECD, and the OSCE. Poland became a member of the European Union in 2004. The country has observer status in the OAS.

Polish troops have supported UN missions and operations in Kosovo (est. 1999), Lebanon (est. 1978), Western Sahara (est. 1991), Ethiopia and Eritrea (est. 2000), Liberia (est. 2003), Georgia (est. 1993), and the DROC (est. 1999), among others. In 2003, Poland assumed command of a division of multinational forces working on peacekeeping and stabilization efforts in Iraq.

Poland is part of the Australia Group, the Zangger Committee, the European Organization for Nuclear Research (CERN), the Nuclear Suppliers Group (London Group), and the Organization for the Prohibition of Chemical Weapons. In environmental cooperation, Poland is part of the Antarctic Treaty, the Basel Convention, Conventions on Biological Diversity and Air Pollution, Ramsar, CITES, the London Convention, the Kyoto Protocol, the Montréal Protocol, MARPOL, the Nuclear Test Ban Treaty, and the UN Conventions on the Law of the Sea, Climate Change and Desertification.

¹⁹ECONOMY

According to the Central Statistical Office (Główny Urząd Statystyczny—GUS) the GDP increased by 3.8% in 2010 in real terms, compared with 1.7% in 2009. In 2011, the Economist Intelligence Unit expected GDP to remain at the 2010 level and slow to 3.2% in 2012. Consumer-price inflation stood at 2.6% in 2010 and was expected to increase to 4% in 2011. Poland's unemployment rate was expected to remain among the highest in the European Union in 2011. In December 2010, the unemployment rate increased to 12.3%, up from 11.9% in 2009.

Until 1990, Poland had a centrally planned economy that was primarily state-controlled. Agriculture, however, was only partly socialized, with state farms and cooperatives accounting for 23% of the country's total farmland in 1984. Since World War II, agriculture's predominance in the economy has been waning; in 1990, it accounted for 16.2% of the NMP, compared to 22.7% in 1970. In 2004, its contribution to GDP was an estimated 2.9%, although it continued to employ about 24% of the labor force. Poland, with its sizable coastline, has become a maritime nation of some note, having developed three major ports on the Baltic and a greatly expanded shipbuilding industry, which in 1991 produced 53 ships. In 2003, yearly production was reported as 50 ships, about one-tenth of the number of ships produced by South Korea and Japan, the industry leaders. However, in June 2002, the Szczecin Shipyards, considered an example of successful privatization, declared bankruptcy. Poland has rich coal deposits, but it lacks some important natural resources, such as petroleum and iron ore.

During 1971–75, Poland's NMP increased by about 12.8% annually; the growth was, to a substantial degree, the result of loans from the West. After 1975, however, Poland's economic performance deteriorated because of excessive investments, internal market problems, several bad harvests, the worldwide recession, and the political upheaval of 1980–81. An economic growth rate of 2.5% annually during 1976–78 was followed by declines of 2% in 1979, 4% in 1980, 12% in 1981, and 5.5% in 1982, while the debt to Western governments reached nearly $25 billion by 1983, rising to $33 billion in 1991, when the total hard-currency debt reached $52.5 billion. During 1980–91, the GNP grew at an annual average rate of only 1.2%. Inflation averaged 54.3% annually in the 1980s.

With Poland subjected to the "shock therapy" of a transition to a market economy, GDP fell 31.5% from 1990–92, and consumer prices shot up almost sixfold. However, the economy did not stay down long, and it soon became one of the most robust in Eastern and Central Europe thanks to the government's tight fiscal and monetary policies. The economy grew by just under 7% in 1995, and by 5.5% in 1996 and 1997, for an average of over 5% a year 1994 to 1997. Most of the growth since 1991 came from the booming private sector, by 1997 accounting for about 70% of GDP (up from 50% in 1992), due in large part to the creation of new private firms. Poland's pace of growth declined after 1998, as the economy was impacted by the Russian financial crisis and then the global economic slowdown in 2001. In 1998, growth fell to 4.8%; in 1999, 4.1%; in 2000, to 4%; and in 2001, to 1%. Signs of economic recovery began to be seen in 2003. In 2002, GDP grew at 1.4%, then in 2003 at 3.8% and reached an impressive 5.3% in 2004, when Poland joined the EU. The growth rate continued to improve in 2007, reaching a rate of 6.5%. Similarly, inflation shot up to 10.1% in 2000 with the recovery of oil prices, but in 2001 moderated to 5.5%. In 2002, inflation was only 1.9%, in 2003 0.8%, in 2004 3.6% and in 2005 3.2%. In 2007, the inflation rate was firmly under control at 2.5%. The growth of the economy was accompanied by privatization. Much of the economy had been privatized by 2007, and the government has continued to privatize state-owned industries in recent years by successfully utilizing the Warsaw Stock Exchange to this end. From 1990 to 2010, 7,534 state owned enterprises were included in the privatization process, resulting in the privatization of 2,115 companies (others were liquidated, incorporated, or commercialized into sole-shareholder companies of the State Treasury). The goal is to achieve the ownership structure similar to that of other EU member states, where private ownership is close to 80%.

The major problems facing the economy are unemployment and persistently high fiscal deficits. The budget deficit is the major factor blocking Poland from becoming a country in the euro zone. According to the Economist Intelligence Unit, Poland needs to narrow its budget deficit to stay within the European Union limit of 3% of GDP in order to meet the EU's Maastricht Treaty criteria and adopt the euro. In 2010, Poland's budget deficit amounted to about 8% of GDP, and the country's public debt stood at 53% of GDP. Consequently, the Polish government postponed the adoption of the euro until at least 2015. Unemployment increased to 13% in 1999, to 15% in 2000, to 16% in 2001, and reached 20% in 2002 before it started to fall again, to 19% in 2004 and 17.3% in 2005. In 2007, significant progress was made, and the number of unemployed workers fell to 12.8%. Still, much further improvement needs to occur before Poland's economy can be as healthy as that of its neighbors. Poland's economy suffered from the global recession of 2008–09, with projected economic growth falling to near-zero for 2009. By April of that year, worry was spreading in Poland over the price volatility of the zloty, the country's currency, increasing the desirability of the euro. Although the price stability of the euro remained attractive to Polish businesses, the move to the euro would also restrict the financial instruments available to the Polish government, complicating the decision. The International Monetary Fund (IMF) granted Poland a $20.5 billion non-emergency credit line in April as part of a new program designed to help insulate countries with sound economic policies against the global downturn. Poland, after Mexico, was the second country to participate in the IMF's new program. The 2011 Greece debt crisis decreased the attraction of the euro and increased the support for the zloty.

20 INCOME

The CIA estimated that, in 2010, the GDP of Poland was $721.3 billion. The CIA defines GDP as the value of all final goods and services produced within a nation in a given year and computed on the basis of purchasing power parity (PPP) rather than value as measured on the basis of the rate of the exchange based on current dollars. The per capita GDP was estimated at $18,800. The annual growth rate of GDP was 3.8%. The average inflation rate was 2.6%. It was estimated that agriculture accounted for 4% of GDP, industry 32%, and services 64%.

According to the World Bank, remittances from citizens living abroad totaled $8.1 billion, about $211 per capita, and accounted for approximately 1.1% of GDP.

The World Bank reports that in 2009, household consumption in Poland totaled $260.6 billion or about $6,780 per capita, measured in current US dollars rather than PPP. Household consumption includes expenditures of individuals, households, and non-governmental organizations on goods and services, excluding the purchases of dwellings. It was estimated that household consumption was growing at an average annual rate of 2.3%.

The World Bank estimates that Poland, with 0.62% of the world's population, accounted for 0.94% of the world's GDP. By comparison, the United States, with 4.85% of the world's population, accounted for 22.51% of world GDP.

As of 2011, the most recent study by the World Bank reported that actual individual consumption in Poland was 73.1% of GDP and accounted for 1.05% of world consumption. By comparison, the United States accounted for 25.44% of world individual consumption. The World Bank also estimated that 17.2% of Poland's GDP was spent on food and beverages, 17.6% on housing and household furnishings, 3.0% on clothes, 6.4% on health, 5.4% on transportation, 2.1% on communications, 5.2% on recreation, 1.8% on restaurants and hotels, and 8.6% on miscellaneous goods and services and purchases from abroad.

21 LABOR

As of 2010, Poland had a total labor force of 17.66 million people. CIA estimates in 2005 noted that, within that labor force, 17.4% were employed in agriculture, 29.2% in industry, and 53.4% in the service sector. The number of people employed in a private sector of the economy increased from 69.5% in 2002 to 74.5% in 2010.

Unions have the right to strike and bargain collectively, although union officials report that workers in the private sector are encouraged not to join unions by their employers and that workers organizing unions often face discrimination. About 15% of Poland's workforce was unionized in 2010.

The labor code prohibits employment for children under the age of 15. There are strict rules governing the work standards for those between 15 and 18 years old; however, these are not regularly enforced. The minimum wage in state-owned enterprises was around $300 per month as of 1 January 2006. However, a large number of construction and seasonal agricultural workers earn less than the minimum wage. The legal standard workweek is 40 hours with 35 hours of uninterrupted rest per week. Overtime is subject to premium pay rates. The labor code defines occupational safety and health standards, but they are not consistently enforced.

22 AGRICULTURE

Roughly 41% of the total land is arable or under permanent crops, and the country's major crops include potatoes, fruits, vegetables, and wheat. Cereal production in 2009 amounted to 29.8 million tons, fruit production 3.7 million tons, and vegetable production 5.8 million tons.

Overall agricultural output during 1980–90 fell by nearly 0.4% annually. Between 1990 and 2000, agricultural production dropped by 0.2% annually. Crop output was valued at nearly €5.76 billion in 2003. During 2002–04, crop output was down 8.5% compared with 1999–2001. In 2010, agriculture accounted for 4% of GDP, down from 14.5% in 1985.

The transition from an agricultural economy is due partly to territorial changes resulting from World War II (1939–45); largely agricultural areas were transferred to the USSR, whereas the areas acquired in the west were predominantly industrial. During the war, approximately one-third of the Polish farms were completely or partly laid waste, and five-sixths of the hogs and two-thirds of the cattle and sheep were destroyed, leaving farmers almost without draft animals and fertilizer. At the same time, population transfers delayed cultivation in the areas of resettlement.

Land redistribution followed both world wars but was much more extensive after World War II. A 1944 decree expropriated all holdings larger than 100 hectares (247 acres); land belonging to Germans or collaborators was also expropriated. Attempts at collectivization were generally resisted; after 1956, most collective farms were disbanded and their land redistributed. During the 1990s, about 3.7 million Poles were engaged in small-plot farming (with an average farm size of 6 hectares/15 acres) on 2.1 million private farms, which produced about 75% of agricultural output. In 2003, Poland had over 2,172,000 agricultural holdings and the largest number of full-time agricultural employment in the 25-nation EU at over 1,048,000 full-time workers and another 3,248,000 part-time agricultural workers that year. As of 2010, private farms used 88.1% of the total agricultural land.

Yields have been poor because of infertile soil, insufficient use of fertilizers, and inadequate mechanization, in addition to drought. There were 1,310,500 tractors in 1997, up from 620,724 during 1979–81. By 2010, the number of tractors had increased to 1.47 million. Although grain production has been Poland's traditional agricultural pursuit, since World War II, Poland has become an importer—instead of an exporter—of grains, particularly wheat.

23 ANIMAL HUSBANDRY

The UN Food and Agriculture Organization (FAO) reported that Poland dedicated 3.2 million hectares (7.87 million acres) to permanent pasture or meadow in 2009. During that year, the country tended 124.1 million chickens, 5.7 million head of cattle, and 14.3 million pigs. The production from these animals amounted to 179,030 tons of beef and veal, 1.96 million tons of pork, 774,937 tons of poultry, 440,430 tons of eggs, and 7.57 million tons of milk. Poland also produced 30,800 tons of cattle hide and 968 tons of raw wool. In 2010, there were 268,000 sheep, 15.3 million pigs, 151 million chickens , 5 million geese, 10 million turkeys (the number of turkeys doubled since 2005), 4.6 million ducks, and 5.75 million head of cattle.

The government has encouraged the development of livestock production through increased fodder supply and improvement in breeding stock and partial tax relief for hog raising. Emphasis has been placed on the raising of hogs and sheep.

Butter production in 2005 was 170,000 tons; cheese, 285,000; and honey, 12,500. In 2010, butter production was 175,000 tons; and cheese, 360,00.

24 FISHING

Poland had 456 decked commercial fishing boats in 2008. The annual capture totaled 142,496 tons, according to the UN FAO. The export value of seafood totaled $632.7 million. In 2010, the annual capture of fish totaled 170,800 tons of sea (saltwater) fish and 48,400 tons of freshwater fish.

Most of the fishing industry has been brought under state ownership. Sea fishing is conducted in the Baltic and North seas and in the Atlantic (Labrador, Newfoundland, and African waters), and there are inland fisheries in lakes, ponds, and rivers. The 2003 saltwater catch was predominantly sprat, herring, and cod. Aquaculture in 2003 produced 54,000 tons. Exports of fish products amounted to $313.2 million in 2003, with processed and preserved fish and caviar accounting for $100 million.

25 FORESTRY

Approximately 31% of Poland is covered by forest. The UN FAO estimated the 2009 roundwood production at 30.5 million cu m (1.08 billion cu ft). The value of all forest products, including roundwood, totaled $2.47 billion.

Pine, larch, spruce, and fir are the most important varieties of trees. Polish forests are subject to difficult growing conditions, such as wide temperature fluctuations in winter, hurricane-strength winds, and unusually high temperatures in summer. Most Polish forests grow on highly degraded sandy soils that hold little moisture. Moreover, much of Poland suffered from drought during the 1990s. Almost 50% of forests are young trees; only 17% of the stand can be cut. The Wielkopolski National Forest, a reservation in Rogalin, is famous for its thousand-year-old oak trees. In 2009, Poland was in the group of European countries with moderate forest damage—the share of trees of defoliation exceeding 25% amounted to 17.7%.

Despite the adversity, the forest products industry was one of the most rapidly growing sectors of the Polish economy in the 1990s. Wood processing occurs in the Biala Podlaska region, while large areas of forest in the Zamosc region foster development in the furniture industry.

The government has been attempting to offset losses from territorial redistribution and wartime destruction by afforestation. During 1990–2000, the forested area increased in size by an annual average of 18,000 hectares (44,500 acres) per year. Although land is being returned to forests, industrial pollution and pests are still causing deterioration.

26 MINING

In 2009 Poland ranked ninth globally in silver, seventh in coal and sulfur (a major export commodity), and tenth in mine copper (3% of world output, and second in Europe and Central Eurasia), and was a leading producer in Central Eurasia and Europe of lead, lime, nitrogen, and salt. Poland had 9% of world sulfur reserves, about 6% of world copper ore reserves, and had significant resources of bituminous coal, salt, silver, and lead and zinc ores. The mining and quarrying sector, which included mineral fuels and processing, accounted for around 2.2% of Poland's GDP in 2009, which grew by 1.7% in that year from 2008. In 2008, Poland had 1,201 non-fuel mining and quarrying enterprises, employing 40,187 workers with production valued at over €4.9 billion.

Mine output of metals in 2009 included mined zinc, 115,000 metric tons, down from 136,300 in 2008; silver (refined, primary), 1,206 metric tons; copper (ore and concentrate by metal content), 439,000 metric tons; and lead (by total mine content), 68,000 metric tons, down from 87,700 metric tons in 2008. All copper ore was mined by KGHM S.A., in the Lubin area; the government's share in KGHM's stock was 42%. Total copper reserves were 2,300 million tons containing 44 million tons of metal. Lead and zinc resources totaled 184 million tons; limestone and marl, 17,450 million tons; and gravel aggregates, 14,600 million tons. Gold mining yielded 814 kg in 2009. Important industrial minerals produced in 2009 included hydraulic cement (15.537 million metric tons), glass sand (2.7 million tons), and sulfur (native [Frasch]), by-product, and from gypsum), 263,000 million tons. Also produced in 2009 were palladium, platinum, selenium, anhydrite, diatomite, feldspar, fuller's earth, fire clay, kaolin, gypsum, magnesite ore (crude), nitrogen, foundry sand, filing sand, lime sand, quartz, quartz crystal, sodium compounds, dolomite, limestone, and crushed and dimension stone. Barite mining, at Boguszow, stopped in 1997 because of large-scale flooding; production has resumed but has been negligible since 2007.

The acquisition of former German territories in 1945 enriched Poland with hard coal and, to a lesser extent, zinc and lead. Iron ore was found in deposits of low metal content around Czestochowa, in south-central Poland. Uranium deposits occurred in Lower Silesia.

27 ENERGY AND POWER

The World Bank reported in 2008 that Poland produced 155.6 billion kWh of electricity and consumed 142.3 billion kWh, or 3,701 kWh per capita. Roughly 94% of energy came from fossil fuels. Per capita oil consumption was 2,567 kg.

Poland has only modest reserves of crude oil and natural gas. The country's main domestic energy sources are coal, lignite, and peat. Rivers remain a largely untapped source of power.

As of 2011, Poland had proven reserves of crude oil estimated at 96 million barrels and proven natural gas reserves estimated at 5.82 trillion cu ft. Oil production totaled 12,910 barrels of oil a day in 2010. As a result, Poland is a net importer of oil, most of which comes from Russia. Poland has a crude oil refining capacity estimated at 493,000 barrels per day as of 2011. In 2010, Poland produced an estimated 215 billion cu ft of natural gas.

Coal is Poland's most abundant energy source. Proven coal reserves in 2008 amounted to 6.29 billion tons (of which about two-thirds are anthracite and bituminous). In 2010, production of all types of coal was estimated at 146.2 million short tons. Poland's hard coal reserves are concentrated in Upper Silesia, near the border with the Czech Republic. Other major coal basins are located in Lower Silesia and Lublin. Although the coal industry has been one of the country's largest employers, a major restructuring of the industry has significantly lowered employment figures.

Poland has been gradually deregulating its power market since 1998. Each year, an increasing number of companies are allowed to choose their own electricity provider. By 2006, the sector was completely open

28 INDUSTRY

Leading industries in Poland include food processing, fuel, metals and metal products, automotive parts, chemicals, coal mining, glass, shipbuilding, and textiles. Industrial production increased by 14.5% annually during 1971–75, but in the late 1970s, the growth rate began to fall. During the 1980s, it grew at an annual rate of 1.1%. With the destabilizing effects of the dissolution of the Soviet bloc and central planning, industrial production initially fell by 26% in 1990 before returning to positive growth between 1991–98. The industrial production growth rate was 7% in 2011.

Light industries were long relegated to a secondary position, but, since the 1970s, Poland has increased its production of durable household articles and other consumer goods. Poland is a major world producer of coal, copper and sulphur, and, to a lesser extent, of sulphuric acid, cement, television sets, passenger cars, buses and trucks, and power engineering. Poland is also a leading world producer of some foodstuffs such as rye, sugar beets, meat, milk barley, wheat, sugar, and eggs.

Since the accession to the EU, there has been a rapid increase in exports as well as in relocation of production facilities, such as car and truck assembly plants and household appliances plants, from Western Europe to Polish commercial zones such as Lódz and Wroclaw. In addition, there have been many investments from non-European countries, such as plans to build an LCD factory near Wroclaw by the South Korean concern LG Electronics.

29 SCIENCE AND TECHNOLOGY

Patent applications in science and technology as of 2009, according to the World Bank, totaled 2,899 in Poland. Public financing of science was 0.61% of GDP. There were 75,309 people employed in research and development as of 2007, representing 0.8% of total employment.

Destruction of the Polish scientific community, buildings, and equipment during World War II was nearly total, requiring a tremendous rebuilding program. Attached to the various university faculties and government bodies are institutes, laboratories, and clinics devoted primarily to research, but some offer advanced instruction. In 1952, the Polish Academy of Sciences, established in Warsaw, replaced the old Polish Academy of Sciences and Letters of Cracow; it encompasses biological sciences; mathematical, physical, and chemical sciences; technical sciences; agricultural and forestry sciences; medical sciences; and earth and mining sciences. As of 1996, 54 scientific and technological research institutes were affiliated with the Polish Academy of Sciences, and there were 101 scientific and technological research institutes attached to government ministries. By 2009, the number of technological research institutes affiliated with the Polish Academy of Sciences had increased to 77. In Warsaw are located a botanical garden and museums devoted to zoology, technology, and the earth. The Polish Maritime Museum is located in Gdańsk. The Mikołaj Kopernik (Copernicus) Museum in Frombork includes exhibits on the history of medicine and astronomy.

In 1996, Poland had 50 universities offering courses in basic and applied sciences. In 1987–1997, science and engineering students accounted for 28% of university enrollment. In 2011, there were 42 universities located in 18 cities, including Kraków, Poznań, and Warsaw. In 2011, there were about 1.9 million university/college-level students in Poland, which represented a five-fold increase since the early 1990s.

30 DOMESTIC TRADE

By the end of 1996 ,Poland's retail sector had been more than 90% privatized. Since the 1990s, the trend in retail establishments, particularly in major cities, has moved from small, independent shops to international supermarket chains, hypermarkets, and large Western European specialty stores such as Aldi, Carrefour, Real, and Tesco. However, small business owners have been forming associations aimed at promoting and preserving local, independent retailing.

Franchising in Poland, initially introduced in the early 1990s, is well-established and flourishing. At the end of 2011, there were 750 franchise systems operating in Poland, with some 44,250 outlets. The majority of the country's franchises (73%) were of Polish origin as of 2009. The largest foreign systems came from the United States, France, and Germany.

Electronic commerce (e-commerce) is rapidly growing in Poland, in both size and sophistication. In 2004, e-commerce transactions reached nearly $2 billion, up from $1 billion the previous year. Internet usage by business is well-developed and has begun to significantly penetrate the consumer and household sectors. According to the Centre for Retail Research, a British retail and service researcher, the estimated online share of retail trade in Poland was just 2.5% in 2010 (compared with 10.7% in the UK and 8% in Germany). As of 2007, there were an estimated 11.4 million Internet users in Poland, or almost 30% of the population. According to Internet World Stats, the number of Internet users in Poland exceeded 22 million in June 2010, representing about 58% of the country's total population. About 80% of all businesses in Poland use the Internet on a daily basis, while 57% have their own web sites. Some 320 Polish companies are selling through the Internet.

Until the end of 2013, most goods and services are subject to a 23% value-added tax (VAT), although preferential rates of 8% and 5% were applied to certain basic goods and services.

Principal Trading Partners – Poland (2010)

(In millions of US dollars)

Country	Total	Exports	Imports	Balance
World	337,821.0	159,758.0	178,063.0	-18,305.0
Germany	88,882.0	40,473.0	48,409.0	-7,936.0
Russia	20,838.0	6,222.0	14,616.0	-8,394.0
Italy	19,180.0	9,543.0	9,637.0	-94.0
France	18,157.0	10,645.0	7,512.0	3,133.0
Netherlands	16,420.0	6,481.0	9,939.0	-3,458.0
Czech Republic	16,330.0	9,285.0	7,045.0	2,240.0
United Kingdom	14,772.0	9,650.0	5,122.0	4,528.0
China	10,919.0	1,625.0	9,294.0	-7,669.0
Belgium	9,459.0	3,642.0	5,817.0	-2,175.0
Slovak Republic	8,476.0	4,187.0	4,289.0	-102.0

(…) data not available or not significant.

(n.s.) not specified.

SOURCE: *2011 Direction of Trade Statistics Yearbook,* New York: United Nations, 2011.

Balance of Payments – Poland (2010)

(In millions of US dollars)

Current Account		-20,982.0
Balance on goods	-11,414.0	
Imports	-173,681.0	
Exports	162,267.0	
Balance on services	3,493.0	
Balance on income	-16,703.0	
Current transfers	3,642.0	
Capital Account		8,668.0
Financial Account		37,713.0
Direct investment abroad	-5,646.0	
Direct investment in Poland	9,056.0	
Portfolio investment assets	-965.0	
Portfolio investment liabilities	26,371.0	
Financial derivatives	-572.0	
Other investment assets	-4,254.0	
Other investment liabilities	13,723.0	
Net Errors and Omissions		-10,291.0
Reserves and Related Items		-15,108.0

(…) data not available or not significant.

SOURCE: *Balance of Payment Statistics Yearbook 2011,* Washington, DC: International Monetary Fund, 2011.

Offices are generally open from 8 a.m. to 4 p.m. Monday through Friday. Food stores are usually open from 6 or 7 a.m. to 7 p.m.; other stores, from 11 a.m. to 7 or 8 p.m.; and banks, from 8 a.m. to 4 p.m. Monday through Friday, and 9 a.m. to 1 p.m. on Saturday. The hours vary by location, with some food stores and supermarkets in big cities operating 24/7.

31 FOREIGN TRADE

Poland imported $167.4 billion worth of goods and services in 2008, while exporting $160.8 billion worth of goods and services. Major import partners in 2009 were Germany, 22.4%; China, 9.3%, Russia, 8.5%; Italy, 6.6%; Netherlands, 5.7%; China, 5.2%; France, 4.6%; and Czech Republic, 4%. Its major export partners were Germany, 26.2%; France, 6.9%; Italy, 6.9%; UK, 6.4%; Czech Republic, 5.9%; and Netherlands, 4.2%. Germany had the dominant position in Polish trade since 1990. In 2010, it accounted for 26.1% of Poland's total exports and 21.9% of imports (compared to 26.2% and 22.4%, respectively, in 2009). In 2010, Poland's second trading partners were Russia (10.2% of imports) and France (6.8% of exports), and third were China (9.4% of imports) and the UK (6.3% of exports). Poland's main imports included mineral fuels, consumer goods (especially electronics), machinery, and transport equipment. Poland's natural resources, such as copper and coal, were among the biggest exports as well as passenger cars manufactured in Poland for Fiat (Italy) and Opel (Germany). Since the mid 1990s, Poland has been running trade deficits.

Until recently, foreign trade was a state monopoly under the control of the Ministry of Foreign Trade. After World War II, the orientation of Polish trade shifted from Western and Central European countries to Eastern Europe. This changed with the dissolution of the Soviet-bloc CMEA in 1991. In December of that year, Poland signed an association agreement with the EC (now the EU), and by 2000, 70% of its exports and 61% of its imports were going to EC members. Poland also fosters trade through its membership in the Central European Free Trade Agreement (CEFTA), which includes Hungary, the Czech Republic, and the Slovak Republic. Since gaining full membership in the EU in 2004, Polish exports to the West have continued to increase. Trade with the countries to the east has recently recovered to the levels from before the 1998 Russian financial crisis, although it is often stifled by minor frictions with Russia and Belarus, for example the controversial restrictions on Polish meat exports to Russia in the fall of 2005. In 2010, Russia regained its position as Poland's second-largest import partner.

Poland's export commodities are a mixture of manufactured goods, including furniture (7.0%), garments (6.1%), motor vehicles (4.6%), iron and steel (3.9%), and ships (3.3%). Export commodities formed from natural resources include wood (2.5%); coal, lignite, and peat (2.3%); and copper (2.3%).

32 BALANCE OF PAYMENTS

According to Eurostat, the statistical office of the European Union, in 2010, Poland had the sixth-largest trade deficit (intra-EU and extra-EU) among the EU member states, with Germany having the largest trade surplus. In 2009, Poland's trade deficit was estimated at €8.4 billion (circa $11.3 billion). In 2010, it increased to €11.9 billion ($16.1 billion). By May 2011, Poland's total trade deficit (intra-EU and extra-EU) stood already at €5.6 billion ($7.5 billion).

Measured in terms of commodity trade figures, negative balances have been the rule in Poland in the post-World War II period. In 1991, the collapse of exports to the Soviet Union dealt a sharp blow to overall export performance. The requirement to exchange by means of hard currency for Soviet raw materials and energy prevented a repeat of the 1990 trade surplus. Poland attracted approximately $50 billion of foreign direct investment between 1990 and 2000. Net official reserves have increased in recent years, due to large capital surpluses from foreign direct investment and portfolio inflows. According to a survey by the UN Conference on Trade and Development, Poland ranked 12th worldwide in attracting FDI in 2010, up by one place from 2009. In 2010, net inflows of FDI reached $9.7 billion.

33 BANKING AND SECURITIES

The Banking Law of 1 July 1982 substantially reformed the Polish banking system by giving banks an effective role in setting monetary and credit policy, thereby allowing them to influence economic planning. The Council of Banks, consisting of top bank officers and representatives of the Planning Commission and the Ministry of Finance, is the principal coordinating body.

The National Bank of Poland (Narodowy Bank Polski—NBP), created in 1945 to replace the former Bank of Poland, is a state institution and the bank of issue. It also controls foreign transactions and prepares financial plans for the economy. On 1 January 1970, the National Bank merged with the Investment Bank and has since controlled funds for finance and investment transactions of state enterprises and organizations. The function of the Food Economy Bank and its associated cooperative banks is to supply short and long-term credits to rural areas. The national commercial bank, Bank Handlowy w Warszawie (BH), finances foreign trade operations. The General Savings Bank (Bank Polska Kasa Opieki—PKO), a central institution for personal savings, also handles financial transfers into Poland of persons living abroad.

In March 1985, two types of hard-currency accounts were introduced: "A" accounts, bearing interest, for currency earned in an approved way; and "B" accounts, for other currency, bearing no interest. "B" accounts can be converted into "A" accounts after one year. Major enterprises in Poland conduct their business by inter-account settlements through the National Bank rather than by check, and wages are paid in cash. Banking laws in 1989 opened the country's banking system to foreign banks.

A fundamental reorganization of the banking sector took place between 1990 and 1992. The NBP lost all its central planning functions, including holding the accounts of state enterprises, making transfers among them, crediting their operations, and exercising financial control of their activities. The NBP thus became only a central bank, and state enterprises competed with other businesses for the scarce credits available from commercial banks. Nine independent (so-called commercial), although state-owned, regional banks were created.

In 1993, the first of these, the Poznań-based Wielkopolski Bank Kredytowy (WBK), was privatized. A second highly controversial privatization took place in early 1994 with the sale of the Silesian Bank (Bank Slaski). Also, the Krakow-based Bank Przemyslowo-Handlowy (BPH) was disposed of at the start of 1995, and Bank Gdanski was sold in late 1995. With four major banks privatized, five remained to be sold off in a process that was supposed to have been completed by 1996. With no real hope of meeting this deadline, the Polish government returned in 1996 to proposals for "bank consolidation" prior to privatization. A major round of privatization was due to begin in 1998–99 beginning with the sale of Pekao, the country's largest commercial bank. This sale finally put over half of the industry's holdings in private hands. At the same time, foreign investment in Polish banks continued to increase. Citibank, ING, Commerzbank, Allied Irish Bank, and J.P. Morgan were leading foreign investors in 1998. In 2001, Bank Handlowy w Warszawie SA merged with Citibank (Poland) SA, but retained its historic name. By 2011, foreign mother banks controlled more than two-thirds of the banking sector in Poland.

The International Monetary Fund reports that, in 2001, currency and demand deposits—an aggregate commonly known as M1—were equal to $23.0 billion. In that same year, M2—an aggregate equal to M1 plus savings deposits, small-time deposits, and money-market mutual funds—was $82.8 billion.

In 2005, the money-market rate, the rate at which financial institutions lend to one another in the short term, was 5.34%. The discount rate, the interest rate at which the central bank lends to financial institutions in the short term, was 4.5%. At the end of 2005, the nation's gold bullion deposits totaled 3.31 million fine troy ounces. According to the World Bank, in June 2010, the capital adequacy ratio for the banking sector in Poland amounted to 13.5%, up from 11.1% in 2008. Unlike most European Union countries, the Polish banking sector remained profitable throughout the crisis, with some $2.5 billion of net profit in 2009 and projected more than $3.0 billion of net profits in 2010, translating into ROE and ROA ratios close to pre-crisis (2008) levels. Loan-to-deposit ratio improved from 113% in 2008 to below 110% in early 2010, as banks increased the share of local deposits in total financing.

In early 1991, important legislation was introduced to regulate securities transactions and establish a stock exchange in Warsaw. At the same time, a securities commission was formed for consumer protection. A year later, the shares of 11 Polish companies were being traded weekly on the new exchange. Restructuring the financial market not only was necessary for increasing the overall efficiency of the economy and accelerating privatization but also was a precondition for the rapid influx of Western capital critical to economic development.

When the Warsaw Stock Exchange (WSE) opened in April 1991, it had only five listed companies, but, by September 1996, that figure had increased to 63. Into 1998, the market still suffered growing pains similar to those afflicting other emerging markets. In particular, the high liquidity of Polish stocks made Poland particularly vulnerable to panic selling. Market capitalization in 2001 was $26 billion, down 17% from the $31.3 billion level of 2000. The WIG All Share Performance Index was at 13,922.2 in 2001, down 22% from 17.847.6 in 2000. As of 2004, a total of 225 companies were listed on the Warsaw Stock Exchange, which had a market capitalization of $71.102 billion. In 2004, the WIG All Share Performance Index rose 27.9% from the previous year to 26,636.2. In recent years, WSE became one of Europe's most dynamic IPO markets with 383 companies, including 23 foreign companies, listed on its Main Market, and 136 companies listed on NewConnect as of June 2010. In 2010, the market capitalization of WSE was estimated at $152 billion.

34 INSURANCE

In 1948, all insurance other than social insurance was included in a centralized State Insurance Bureau, with the former reinsurance organization Warta continuing its activity. In 1994, Warta was privatized and was one of three major insurers who together controlled over 90% of Poland's insurance market. In 1999, 54 licensed insurance companies competed in the Polish market.

Insurance is dominated by PZU, a state concern, but a number of Western companies, including the United Kingdom's Commercial Union (CU), have been tempted into joint ventures in the life insurance end of this underdeveloped market. CU began its Polish operations in cooperation with the Wielkopolski Bank Kredytowy (WBK) bank. It sold around 130,000 policies in its first four years.

Public Finance – Poland (2009)

(In billions of zlotys, central government figures)

Revenue and Grants	412,753	100.0%
Tax revenue	219,519	53.2%
Social contributions	152,085	36.8%
Grants	9,456	2.3%
Other revenue	31,693	7.7%
Expenditures	494,842	100.0%
General public services	74,390	15.0%
Defense	12,621	2.6%
Public order and safety	24,310	4.9%
Economic affairs	42,465	8.6%
Environmental protection	1,161	0.2%
Housing and community amenities	1,869	0.4%
Health	62,575	12.6%
Recreational, culture, and religion	4,327	0.9%
Education	53,169	10.7%
Social protection	217,955	44.0%

(…) data not available or not significant.

SOURCE: *Government Finance Statistics Yearbook 2010*, Washington, DC: International Monetary Fund, 2010.

PZU began to be privatized in 1999. In 2005, the Polish parliament investigated the privatization of PZU and found the process flawed and corrupt. According to the Economist Intelligence Unit, the initial public offering (IPO) of PZU, through which the state and Eureko (a Dutch financial group) sold a minority stake for 8.1 billion zloty (circa $2.5 billion) in 2010, was the largest IPO by a Polish company since the creation of the Warsaw Stock Exchange in 1991. That seemed to be the closing chapter in the saga of the privatization of Poland's largest insurance company. In Poland, third-party auto liability, farmer's liability, fire insurance, workers' compensation, and nuclear liability are all compulsory.

35 PUBLIC FINANCE

In 2010, the budget of Poland included $91.23 billion in public revenue and $128.4 billion in public expenditures. The budget deficit amounted to 3.2% of GDP. According to the Economist Intelligence Unit, in 2010, Poland's public debt reached 52.8% of GDP, according to local calculations, and to 54.9% of GDP using the EU's European System of Accounts (ESA 95) methodology. The Economist Intelligence Unit was predicting that public debt would peak in 2012–13 but would still exceed 50% in 2016.

The annual budget is presented to the *Sejm* in December and becomes effective for the fiscal year beginning on 1 January. Privatization in the former Eastern bloc nation has been fairly successful, with approximately two-thirds of GDP now coming from the private sector. By the early 1990s, Poland was the first formerly planned economy in Eastern Europe to come out of recession and experience economic growth.

The CIA estimated that, in 2005, Poland's central government took in revenues of approximately $52.7 billion and had expenditures of $63.2 billion. Revenues minus expenditures totaled approximately -$10.4 billion. Public debt in 2005 amounted to 47.3% of GDP. Total external debt was $123.4 billion. According to the World Bank, the general government deficit doubled to 7.2% of

GDP in 2009 from 3.6 % GDP in 2008. In 2010, the general government deficit increased further to 7.9 % of GDP. In 2011, the government started fiscal consolidation, and the fiscal deficit was set to decline to some 2.9% of GDP in 2012.

36 TAXATION

According to the Eurostat, the Statistical Office of the European Communities, in 2008 the overall tax burden in Poland stood at 34.3 % of GDP, almost three percentage points below the EU-27 average (37.0%). On January 1 2009, Poland introduced new personal income tax rates of 18% and 32%, replacing the previous three of 19%, 30%, and 40%. In 2010, the lowest rate applied to the vast majority of taxpayers. Some individuals (such as the self-employed) may opt to be taxed at a flat rate of 19% if certain conditions are met.

Poland has a general corporate profits tax rate of 19%. The corporate tax rate was significantly reduced from 40% in 1996 to 19% in 2011. In 2011, Poland's corporate tax rate was among the lowest rates in Europe. In 2011, the corporate income tax rate of 19% was applicable to income and capital gains. Capital gains and branch operations are each taxed at the corporate rate. Capital gains are treated as regular income. Dividends and interest paid to residents and nonresidents are taxed at a flat 19% rate. Income from interest, fees and royalties are subject to a 20% withholding rate unless other rates have been agreed to in bilateral tax treaties (BITs). Poland has BITs with at least 66 countries. In the BIT with the United States, withholding rates are 0% on interest income, 10% on income from royalties, and 5% on dividend income if the receiving company owns at least 10% of voting shares.

The main indirect tax is a system of value-added taxes (VATs), which Poland adopted in 1993. Until the end of 2013, most goods and services are subject to a 23% VAT, although preferential rates of 8% and 5% are applied to certain basic goods and services. A 5% VAT applied to agricultural products such as bread, eggs, meat, cereals as well as books and magazines. An 8% VAT applied to sales of various products and services, including medicines used in healthcare, hotel services, and construction and repair services. "VAT-exempt" applied to several groups of services, including financial services, insurance and healthcare. Excise taxes are charged on alcohol, cars, petroleum, and tobacco products. There is also a civil transactions tax.

37 CUSTOMS AND DUTIES

Poland uses the Harmonized System of Classification. Products are divided into three categories to determine which rate they receive: developing nations, WTO members, and countries with which Poland has a special trade relationship, such as a bilateral preferential trade agreement. Under the terms of a 1992 agreement, Poland uses the EU Nomenclature System of Tariff classification and has granted duty-free status to over 1,000 line items from EU countries. On January 1, 2008, Poland joined the so-called Schengen zone. Consequently, all border posts and checkpoints between Poland and the 24 other European countries that belong to the zone were removed. According to the Eurostat, the Statistical Office of the European Union, and the Directorate-General for Taxation and Customs Union of the European Commission, on March 1 2009, Poland implemented a new excise duties law. The law introduced, among other things, a new definition of excise goods, namely energy products, electricity, alcohol, manufactured tobacco and passenger vehicles. In 2008, the revenues from indirect taxes (such as VAT, excise duties, and import duties) amounted to 14.4% of GDP adding up to €52.3 billion (circa $70.8 billion).

38 FOREIGN INVESTMENT

Prior to World War II, considerable foreign capital was invested in the Polish economy, particularly in petroleum and mining, which were mostly foreign-owned. A nationalization decree in 1946 confiscated foreign properties and nationalized Poland's industries, eliminating foreign investments completely. The decree provided for no compensation procedures, and foreign governments involved negotiated directly with Poland. The first joint venture with Western counterparts (one Austrian and one US company) was formed in early 1987 to build a new airport terminal in Warsaw. In mid-1991, there were 4,100 foreign registrations, worth $506 million, and in 1993 another $2 billion in foreign investment entered Poland. Among the industrial companies sold to Western interests were Polam-Pila (lightbulbs) to Phillips, Polkolor (TV sets) to Thomson, Pollena-Bydgoszcz (detergents) to Unilever, and Wedel (confectioneries) to Pepsico Foods.

In 1996–97, Poland continued to invite foreign investors to help the government turn some of its banks and oil, arms, and telecommunications companies over to the private sector. In October 1996, President Aleksander Kwasniewski stated that the government's campaign to shed costly state-owned enterprises had been successful, with the private sector now accounting for about 70% of the goods and services produced in the economy. Total FDI reached nearly $27.3 billion in 1998. FDI inflow in 1998 was $6.3 billion, up from nearly $5 billion in 1997, and increased to $7.2 billion in 1999, undeterred by the effects of the Russian financial crisis. Annual FDI inflow reached over $9.3 billion in 2000, having grown at an average annual rate of 44% from 1991 to 2000. FDI in Poland was a net inflow of $13.8 billion according to World Bank figures published in 2009 and represented 3.21% of GDP. According to a survey by the UN Conference on Trade and Development, Poland ranked 12th worldwide in attracting FDI in 2010, up by one place from 2009. In 2010, net inflows of FDI decreased to $9.7 billion.

39 ECONOMIC DEVELOPMENT

After World War II, the economy of Poland was centrally planned and almost completely under state control, especially in nonagricultural sectors. The nationalized industries and businesses operated within the national economic plan and were governed by the directives issued by the pertinent ministries. After 1963, however, centralized planning and management were somewhat relaxed, and state-owned enterprises gained more freedom in the design and implementation of their programs. Private undertakings were confined to personal crafts, trades, and agriculture.

Under the three-year plan for 1947–49, principal emphasis was placed on the reconstruction of war-devastated areas and industries in order to raise production and living conditions at least to their prewar levels. Economic planning followed Soviet lines, setting production goals that determined tasks for each sector on a long-term basis. Under the six-year plan for 1950–55, the emphasis continued to be on heavy industry, and the housing, transport,

agriculture, and consumer sectors lagged. The five-year plan for 1956–60, originally cast along the same lines, was modified after the 1956 disturbances. It called for a lessened rate of industrial expansion and for increases in agricultural output, housing, consumer goods, and social services. Under a long-range plan for 1961–75, which governed the three five-year plans falling within that period, emphasis was placed on a direct improvement in living standards. The first and second of these plans (1961–65 and 1966–70) were oriented toward investments intended to (1) develop the raw-material base of the country, especially the newly discovered resources of sulfur, copper, and lignite; (2) secure employment opportunities for the rapidly growing population of working age; and (3) improve Poland's international trade balance. The five-year plan for 1961–65 reached its industrial targets but fell short in the areas of agriculture and consumer goods. The period 1966–70 witnessed two poor agricultural years in addition to export lags, and there were shortages of basic food commodities in 1969–70.

In late 1970, violent protests erupted over the government's increased efforts to spur production. After the change in political leadership from Gomulka to Gierek, government emphasis shifted from heavy industry to light, consumer-oriented production. In addition, through a concentration of investment in mechanization, fertilizers, and other farm improvements, the government sought and achieved a 50% increase in food production. Overall, the 1971–75 five-year plan achieved its main targets by a wide margin, with industrial production up about 73%. The 1976–80 plan, which aimed at a 50% increase in industrial production and a 16% increase in agricultural output, ran into difficulty almost from the beginning, and, by 1979, the economy had entered a period of decline and dislocation that continued into 1982. An economic reform stressing decentralization of the economy was introduced in January 1982, but it failed to produce any significant improvements. With price rises and consumer goods shortages continuing to fuel popular discontent, the government in March 1983 announced a three-year austerity plan for 1983–85. Its aims included a general consolidation of the economy, self-sufficiency in food production, and increased emphasis on building housing and producing industrial consumer goods. By 1986, the economy had rebounded. The 1986–90 plan expected the national income to grow 3–3.5% annually, industrial output to increase by 3.2% each year, and exports to grow by 5% (in fixed prices) annually. These goals were not reached. A "second stage," proclaimed in 1986, called for more autonomy for individual enterprises and for more efficient management with top jobs filled without regard to political affiliations.

The Economic Transformation Program adopted in January 1990 aimed to convert Poland from a planned to a market economy. Measures were aimed at drastically reducing the large budget deficit, abolishing all trade monopolies, and selling many state-owned enterprises to private interests.

The slow pace of privatization picked up somewhat in 1995, as 512 smaller state enterprises were transferred to private National Investment Funds under the Mass Privatization Program, but large-scale industry remained largely under state control. However, the government subsequently made an attempt to privatize such large-scale sectors of the economy as banks, oil, arms, and telecommunications. Poland in the early 2000s was in the process of bringing its economic policies in line with EU standards. These policies resulted in further liberalization and foreign investment into the Polish economy. Poland officially joined the EU in May 2004. Poland's real GDP growth was 3.8% in 2010 (up from 1.7% in 2009). The Economist Intelligence Unit's forecast for Poland's economic growth in 2012 was revised from 4% to 3.2%. According to a survey by the UN Conference on Trade and Development, Poland ranked 12th worldwide in attracting FDI in 2010, up by one place from 2009. In 2010, net inflows of FDI stood at $9.7 billion. Poland's economic development was negatively affected by the 2011 euro zone crisis and the government deficit and public debt. In 2010, the latter reached 52.8% of Poland's GDP (54.9% of GDP according to other calculations), threatening to breach the constitutionally set limit of 55% of GDP.

40 SOCIAL DEVELOPMENT

A social insurance institute, under the provision of new legislation passed in 1998 and implemented in 1999, administers social security programs through a network of branch offices. Social security, including social insurance and medical care, covers virtually the entire population. Old age, disability, and survivors' pensions are provided, as well as family allowances, sickness benefits, maternity benefits, workers' compensation, and unemployment. The system is funded by contributions from employers and employees and government subsidies. In 2004, a revised universal system of family allowances funded by the government covered all residents.

The constitution establishes that all citizens are equal, regardless of gender, but discrimination persists. Women participate actively in the labor force but are concentrated in low-paying professions and earn less than men on average. Also, women are more likely to be fired and less likely to be promoted than men. However, the highest political and government offices in the country are no longer closed to women. Hanna Suchocka became Poland's first female prime minister, serving from July 1992 thorugh October 1993. Hanna Gronkiewicz-Waltz was appointed president of the Polish National Bank (Central Bank), serving from 1992 through 2000, and later elected mayor of Warsaw, in 2006. Violence against women and domestic abuse still remain a problem. The law does not provide restraining orders, and even convicted abusers generally go unpunished.

The Romani minority living in Poland faces discrimination by local authorities. Anti-Semitic harassment, vandalism, and violence persist. The judicial system is hampered by inefficiency and budget constraints, and there are marginal restrictions on freedoms of speech and press.

41 HEALTH

According to the CIA, life expectancy in Poland was 76 years in 2011. The country spent 7.0% of its GDP on healthcare, amounting to $804 per person. There were 21 physicians, 57 nurses and midwives, and 66 hospital beds per 10,000 inhabitants. The fertility rate was 1.4, while the infant mortality rate was 6 per 1,000 live births. In 2008, the maternal mortality rate, according to the World Bank, was 6 per 100,000 births. It was estimated that 98% of children were vaccinated against measles. The CIA calculated HIV/AIDS prevalence in Poland to be about 0.1% in 2009.

As of 2007, there were an estimated 247 physicians, 490 nurses, and 30 dentists per 100,000 people. The same year, the total health care expenditure was estimated at 6.2% of GDP. As of 2007, Poland had an estimated 53 hospital beds for every 10,000 people.

The total fertility rate in 2011 was estimated at 1.3 children born per woman. Approximately 75% of women used contraception. Poland immunized children up to one year of age against diphtheria, pertussis, and tetanus, 99%; polio, 96%; and measles, 98%.

42 HOUSING

Almost 40% of all urban dwelling space was destroyed during World War II. Although investment in public housing has increased, and credits have been assigned for cooperative and private construction, the housing shortage remains critical five decades later. The average wait for an apartment ranges from 10 to 15 years. In 1984, there were 10,253,000 dwelling units; an additional 193,000 dwelling units were constructed in 1985. In 2002, there were about 12.5 million dwelling units registered in the census, serving about 13.3 million households; about 93.9% of these were occupied dwellings. About 67.6% of all dwellings were in urban areas. About 55.2% of all dwellings were owned by private individuals. The average number of persons per dwelling was 3.25. At least 76.2% of all dwellings were built after 1944. The housing deficit in 2007 was estimated at about 2.5 million units, one of the largest deficits in Europe.

43 EDUCATION

In 2008, the World Bank estimated that 95% of age-eligible children in Poland were enrolled in primary school. Secondary enrollment for age-eligible children stood at 94%. Tertiary enrollment was estimated at 69%. Of those enrolled in tertiary education, there were 100 male students for every 141 female students. Overall, the CIA estimated that Poland had a literacy rate of 99.8%. Public expenditure on education represented 4.9% of GDP.

Primary, secondary, and most university and other education is free. State and local expenditure on education is, therefore, substantial. Lower schools are financed by local budgets, higher and vocational schools from the state budget.

Since 1999, the school system, which is centralized, consists of a six-year primary school followed by a three-year lower secondary general education school. Students then have an option to enroll in a four-year technical school, a three-year upper secondary school, or a two- to three year vocational school. Vocational schools are attended by students studying technology, agriculture, forestry, economy, education, health services, and the arts. The school year runs from September to June and the academic year from October to May.

Higher learning is under the jurisdiction of the Ministry of Higher Education and other ministries. A matriculation examination, which is common for all students, is required for admission to institutions of higher learning. As of 2004, there were 128 state institutions of higher learning and 304 non-state institutions. Jagiellonian University, among the oldest in Europe, was established at Cracow in 1364. Other prominent universities are the Warsaw University; the Central School of Planning and Statistics (Warsaw); the Higher Theater School (Warsaw); the Academy of Fine Arts (Cracow); and the Adam Mickiewicz University (Poznań). During the communist era, the Roman Catholic University at Lublin was the only free private university in the Socialist bloc. Evening and extramural courses are available for anyone who is interested and is not a part of the school system. Foreign students are also welcome to study in Poland, either as regular students or at their summer schools.

⁴⁴LIBRARIES AND MUSEUMS

The National Library, established in Warsaw in 1928, is the largest in Poland, with about 8.7 million volumes and items, including periodicals, manuscripts, maps, illustrations, and music. Other important libraries are the Public University and the government departmental libraries in Warsaw; Poland's second-largest library, the Jagiellonian University Library in Cracow, which has 6.8 million volumes and items; and the Ossolineum Library in Wroclaw. There are 8,400 public and 1056 research and college libraries in the country.

Of the more than 780 museums in Poland, the foremost is the National Museum in Warsaw, which has an extensive and important art collection as well as a collection of Polish art from the 12th century to present day. Other important museums are the National Museum in Cracow, notable for its collection of Far Eastern Art, and the National Museum in Poznań, which has a celebrated collection of musical instruments. Cracow also has an important collection of European decorative arts at the Wawel Royal Castle, housed in a 16th century manor house, the Czartoryski Museum, a world-class collection of antiquities and contemporary artifacts including 35,000 prints, drawings, and paintings, and the Oskar Schindler Museum. Warsaw has dozens of museums, including the Center for Contemporary Art, founded in 1986, in Ujazdowski Castle; the Museum of Independence, founded in 1990, chronicling Poland's pivotal role in the collapse of the Soviet Empire; the Museum of Polish Emigration to America; the Museum of the Warsaw Uprising of 1944; the Frederick Chopin Museum, chronicling the life of one of the country's best-known composers; the Marie Curie Museum, housed at her birthplace; and the Museum of the Jewish Historical Institute. The Warsaw Museum of the History of Polish Jews was expected to open in 2012 or 2013.

⁴⁵MEDIA

In 2009, the CIA reported that there were 9.6 million telephone landlines in Poland. In addition to landlines, mobile phone subscriptions averaged 117 per 100 people. There were 14 FM radio stations, 77 AM radio stations, and 1 shortwave radio station. Internet users numbered 59 per 100 citizens. Prominent newspapers in 2010, with circulation numbers listed parenthetically, included *Gazeta Poznanska* (320,000), *Rzeczpospolita* (280,000), and *Gazeta Lubuska* (165,000), as well as 32 other major newspapers.

Modernization of Poland's telecommunications system has accelerated following the final adoption in 2003 of market-based competition. Wireless telephony now dominates the country's telecommunications scene. Domestic wireless service is provided by three country-wide networks, whose growth has been spurred by the nation's limited fixed-line coverage. Universal Mobile Telecommunications System (UMTS) service is available in urban areas. Although cellular coverage is generally rated as good, gaps exist in the eastern part of the country. Fixed-line growth is slow, and coverage lags in rural areas. International service is provided by satellite ground station access to the Intelsat, Eutelsat, Inmarsat, and Intersputnik networks. International direct-dialing service is also available through automated exchanges. In 2009, there were some 9.5 million main phone lines and 44.5 million mobile cellular phones in use.

In 2010, the country had 10.5 million Internet hosts. As of 2009, there were some 22.4 million Internet users in Poland. In 2010, 59% of the population between the ages 16 and 74 used the Internet. Almost 70% of all households had a computer, and 62% of all households had a computer with Internet access (58 percent had broadband Internet access).

The largest Polish daily newspapers, with circulation as noted, are: *Fakt Gazeta Codzienna,* 570,000 in 2011; *Gazeta Wyborcza,* 450,000 in 2011, *Super Express,* 300,000 in 2011; *Rzeczpospolita,* 195,000 in 2011; and *Dziennik Gazeta Prawna,* 155,000 in 2011.

Though the constitution provides for free speech and a free press, there are some restrictions on these rights. The Penal Code prohibits speech which publicly insults or ridicules the Polish state or its principal organs; it also prohibits advocating discord or offending religious groups. Though the media are not censored, they may be subject to prosecution under these and other penal codes.

⁴⁶ORGANIZATIONS

The Polish Chamber of Commerce and the Chamber of Foreign Trade promote foreign trade by furnishing information, establishing or extending commercial relations, and arranging for Polish participation in trade fairs and exhibitions abroad. The most important worker's organization in Poland is Solidarity (Solidarność), founded in 1980 by Lech Wałęsa. There are a number of professional associations and trade unions representing a wide variety of occupations.

The P.E.N. Club-Poland is based in Warsaw. The Frederick Chopin Society is a multinational organization promoting the life and works of this Polish composer and pianist. Several professional associations, such as the Polish Medical Association, also serve to promote research and education in specific fields.

There are also many cultural, sports and social organizations in Poland. National youth organizations include the European Federalist Youth, Junior Chamber, Polish Students' Union, Polish Environmental Youth Movement, Union of Young Christian Democrats, The Polish Scouting and Guiding Association, and YMCA/YWCA. There are numerous sports associations promoting amateur competitions in a wide variety of sports for athletes of all ages. There are organizations affiliated with the Special Olympics and the Paralympic Committee, as well as the Olympic Committee.

National women's organizations include the Democratic Women's Union and the Polish Association of University Women. Other social action groups include the Helsinki Human Rights Foundation and Fundacja Stefana Batorego, a group which promotes a democratic and open society. There are national chapters of the Red Cross Society, Habitat for Humanity, UNICEF, and Amnesty International.

⁴⁷TOURISM, TRAVEL, AND RECREATION

The *Tourism Factbook*, published by the UN World Tourism Organization, reported 53.8 million incoming tourists to Poland in 2009, who spent a total of $9.85 billion. Of those incoming tourists, there were 53.2 million from Europe. There were 221,633 hotel beds available in Poland, which had an occupancy rate of 32%.

The estimated daily cost to visit Warsaw, the capital, was $285. The cost of visiting other cities averaged $226.

The main tourist attractions include the historic city of Cracow, which suffered little war damage; the ancient Wieliczka salt mine near Cracow, the resort towns of Zakopane, in the Tatras, and Sopot, on the Baltic; and the restored Old Town in Warsaw, as well as the capital's museums and Palace of Science and Culture. Camping, hiking, and football (soccer) are among the most popular recreational activities.

Foreign visitors to Poland must have a valid passport. All visitors are required to carry a visa except citizens of over 30 nations including the United States and members of the European Union.

There were approximately 52 million visitors who arrived in Poland in 2003, about 99% of whom came from Europe. Hotel rooms numbered 68,588 with 134,323 beds and an occupancy rate of about 36%. The average length of stay was three nights. That year, tourism receipts totaled $4.7 billion.

[48] FAMOUS PERSONS

Figures prominent in Polish history include Mieszko I (fl. 10th century), who led Poland to Christianity; his son and successor, Bolesław I Chrobry ("the Brave," c. 967–1025), the first king of sovereign Poland; Kazimierz III Wielki ("the Great," 1310–70), who sponsored domestic reforms; and John III Sobieski (1629–96), who led the Polish-German army that lifted the siege of Vienna in 1683 and repelled the Turkish invaders. Tadeusz Andrzej Bonawentura Kościuszko (1746–1817), trained as a military engineer, served with colonial forces during the American Revolution, and then led a Polish rebellion against Russia in 1794; he was wounded, captured, and finally exiled. Kazimierz Pułaski (1745–79) fought and died in the American Revolution, and Haym Salomon (1740–85) helped to finance it. The reconstituted Polish state after World War I was led by Józef Piłsudski (1867–1935), who ruled as a dictator from 1926 until his death. Polish public life since World War II has been dominated by Bolesław Bierut (1892–1956), the leading figure of the Stalinist troika with Jakub Berman (state security) and Hilary Minc (economy) that ruled Poland from 1948 to 1956, and by Władysław Gomułka (1905–82), Edward Gierek (1913–2001), and Gen. Wojciech Jaruzelski (b. 1923), Communist leaders, respectively, during 1956–70, during 1970–80, and after 1981. Important roles have also been played by Stefan Cardinal Wyszyński (1901–81), Roman Catholic primate of Poland, archbishop of Gniezno and Warsaw, and frequent adversary of the postwar Communist regime; Karol Wojtyła (1920–2005), archbishop of Cracow from 1963 until his elevation to the papacy as John Paul II in 1978; and Lech Wałęsa (b. 1943), leader of the Solidarity movement during 1980–81, Nobel Peace Prize laureate in 1983, and President of Poland from 1990 to 1995.

The father of Polish literature is Mikołaj Rej (1505–69), one of the earliest Polish writers to turn from Latin to the vernacular. Poland's golden age is marked by the beginning of literature in Polish; its greatest poet was Jan Kochanowski (1530–84). Notable among 19th-century poets and dramatists was Adam Mickiewicz (1798–1855), whose *The Books of the Polish Nation and of the Polish Pilgrimage, Pan Tadeusz*, and other works exerted a paramount influence on all future generations. Other leading literary figures were the poets and dramatists Juliusz Slowacki (1809–49), Cyprian Kamil Norwid (1821–83), and Zygmunt Krasiński (1812–59),

whose *Dawn* breathed and inspired patriotism. Józef Kraszewski (1812–87), prolific and patriotic prose writer, is considered the father of the Polish novel. The leading late–19th-century novelists were the realists Aleksander Głowacki (1847–1912), who wrote under the pseudonym of Bolesław Prus, and Henryk Sienkiewicz (1846–1916), Poland's first Nobel Prize winner (1905), whose *The Trilogy* described the 17th-century wars of Poland; he is internationally famous for *Quo Vadis*. Another Nobel Prize winner (1924) was the novelist Władysław Reymont (1867–1925), acclaimed for *The Peasants*. A Pole who achieved stature as an English novelist was Joseph Conrad (Józef Teodor Konrad Korzeniowski, 1857–1924). Other important literary figures around the turn of the century were the playwright and painter Stanisław Wyspiański (1869–1907), the novelist Stefan Żeromski (1864–1926), and the novelist Stanislaw Ignacy Witkiewicz (1885–1939). The best-known modern authors are novelist and short-story writer Isaac Bashevis Singer (1904–91), a Nobel Prize winner in 1978 and a US resident after 1935; the satirist Witold Gombrowicz (1904–69); science-fiction writer Stanislaw Lem (1921–2006); the dissident novelist Jerzy Andrzejewski (1909–83); the poet Czesław Miłosz (1911–2004), a Nobel Prize winner in 1980 and resident of the United States after 1960; novelist Jerzy Kosinski (1933–91), who lived in the United States after 1957 and wrote in English; and poet Wisława Szymborska (1923–2012), a Nobel Prize winner in 1996.

The greatest Polish composer Frédéric Chopin (1810–49), was born in Warsaw but lived in Paris after 1831. Popular composer Stanisław Moniuszko (1819–72) founded the Polish national opera and composed many songs; he influenced such later composers as Władysław Żeleński (1837–1921), Zygmunt Noskowski (1846–1909), and Stanisław Niewiadomski (1859–1936). Other prominent musicians include the pianist Ignacy Jan Paderewski (1860–1941), also his country's first prime minister following World War I; the great harpsichordist Wanda Landowska (1877–1959); the renowned pianist Arthur Rubinstein (1887–1982); the violinist Wanda Wiłkomirska (b. 1929); the conductor Stanisław Skrowaczewski (b. 1923); and the composers Mieczysław Karłowicz (1876–1909) and Karol Szymanowski (1883–1937). Witold Lutosławski (1913–94) and Krzysztof Penderecki (b. 1933) are internationally known contemporary composers.

The first Polish painters of European importance were Piotr Michałowski (1800–55) and Henryk Rodakowski (1823–94). In the second half of the 19th century, Polish realism reached its height in the historical paintings of Jan Matejko (1838–93), Artur Grottger (1837–67), Juliusz Kossak (1824–99), and Józef Brandt (1841–1915), as well as in genre painting and the landscapes of Wojciech Gerson (1831–1901), Józef Szermentowski (1833–76), Aleksander Kotsis (1836–77), Maksymilian Gierymski (1846–74), Aleksander Gierymski (1849–1901), and Józef Chełmoński (1849–1914). Feliks Topolski (1907–89), who lived in London after 1935, is well-known for his oil paintings, watercolors, and drawings. Andrzej Wajda (b. 1926), Roman Polański (b. 1933), an expatriate since the mid-1960s, Krzysztof Zanussi (b. 1939), and Krzysztof Kieślowski (1941–1996) are famous film directors, and Jerzy Grotowski (1933–1999) was a well-known stage director.

The outstanding scientist and scholar Nicolaus Copernicus (Mikołaj Kopernik, 1473–1543) is world renowned. Among Poland's brilliant scientists are Maria Skłodowska-Curie (1867–1934), a co-discoverer of radium and the recipient of two Nobel

Prizes, and Casimir Funk (1884–1967), the discoverer of vitamins. Oskar Lange (1904–66) achieved renown as an economist.

⁴⁹DEPENDENCIES

Poland has no territories or colonies.

⁵⁰BIBLIOGRAPHY

Biskupski, Mieczysław B. *The History of Poland.* Westport, CT: Greenwood Press, 2000.

Eckhart, Karl, et al., eds. *Social, Economic and Cultural Aspects in the Dynamic Changing Process of Old Industrial Regions: Ruhr District (Germany), Upper Silesia (Poland), Ostrava Region (Czech Republic).* Piscataway, NJ: Transaction Publishers, 2003.

Frucht, Richard, ed. *Eastern Europe: An Introduction to the People, Lands, and Culture.* Santa Barbara, CA: ABC-CLIO, 2005.

Hoshi, Iraj, Ewa Balcerowicz, and Leszek Balcerowicz, eds. *Barriers to Entry and Growth of New Firms in Early Transition: A Comparative Study of Poland, Hungary, Czech Republic, Albania, and Lithuania.* Boston: Kluwer Academic Publishers, 2003.

McElrath, Karen, ed. *HIV and AIDS: A Global View.* Westport, CT: Greenwood Press, 2002.

Opello, Walter C. *European Politics.* Boulder, CO: Lynne Rienner Publishers, 2009.

Otfinoski, Steven. *Poland.* 2nd ed. New York: Facts On File, 2004.

Poland Investment and Business Guide: Strategic and Practical Information. Washington, DC: International Business Publications USA, 2012.

Political Chronology of Europe. London: Europa, 2001.

Reuvid, Jonathan, and Marat Terterov, eds. *Doing Business with Poland.* Sterling, VA: Kogan Page, 2003.

Rose-Ackerman, Susan. *From Elections to Democracy: Building Accountable Government in Hungary and Poland.* New York: Cambridge University Press, 2005.

Sanford, George. *Historical Dictionary of Poland.* 2nd ed. Lanham, MD: Scarecrow, 2003.

Steinlauf, Michael. *Bondage to the Dead: Poland and the Memory of the Holocaust.* Syracuse, NY: Syracuse University Press, 2006.

Walesa, Lech. *The Struggle and the Triumph: An Autobiography.* New York: Arcade, 1992.

PORTUGAL

Portuguese Republic
República Portuguesa

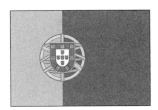

CAPITAL: Lisbon (Lisboa)

FLAG: The national flag, adopted in 1911, consists of a green field at the hoist and a larger red field. At the junction of the two, in yellow, red, blue, and white, is the national coat of arms.

ANTHEM: *A Portuguesa (The Song of the Portuguese).*

MONETARY UNIT: The escudo was replaced by the euro (€) as official currency as of 2002. The euro is divided into 100 cents. There are coins in denominations of 1, 2, 5, 10, 20, and 50 cents and 1 euro and 2 euros. There are notes of 5, 10, 20, 50, 100, 200, and 500 euros. €1 = US$1.3270 (or US$1 = €0.7536) as of April 2012.

WEIGHTS AND MEASURES: The metric system is the legal standard.

HOLIDAYS: New Year's Day, 1 January; Anniversary of the Revolution, 25 April; Labor Day, 1 May; National Day, 10 June; Assumption, 15 August; Republic Day, 5 October; All Saints' Day, 1 November; Independence Day, 1 December; Immaculate Conception, 8 December; Christmas, 25 December. Religious holidays with fluctuating dates include Carnival, Good Friday, Easter, and Corpus Christi.

TIME: GMT.

¹LOCATION, SIZE, AND EXTENT

The westernmost country of Europe, Portugal occupies the greater portion of the western littoral of the Iberian Peninsula. Portugal has an area of 92,090 sq km (57,222 sq mi), including the Azores (Açores) and Madeira archipelagos. Comparatively, Portugal is slightly smaller than Indiana. Bordered on the N and E by Spain and on the S and W by the Atlantic Ocean, Portugal has a total land boundary of 1,214 km (754 mi), and a coastline that stretches 1,793 km (1,114 mi).

Portugal's capital city, Lisbon, is located on Portugal's west coast.

²TOPOGRAPHY

Portugal exhibits diverse topographic features. The north is mostly rugged while the south features rolling hills and cliff-lined beaches. The north-easternmost region of Portugal is Trás-os-Montes (meaning across the mountains), the most mountainous part of the country. The geographic area between the two main rivers in Portugal, the Douro River and Rio Tejo (Tagus River), is the central region of Portugal (south of the Douro River and north of the Rio Tejo). Within the central region lies Serra da Estrela, mainland Portugal's highest mountain range peaked by Estrêla at 1,991 meters (6,532 ft). However, at 2,351 meters (7,714 ft), the tallest peak in Portugal is actually Ponta do Pico located in Pico, one of the Azores islands.

South of the Rio Tejo, the longest river in Portugal meandering 999 km (621 mi), is known as the Alentejo and is characterized by expansive open land and rolling hills. Beyond these hills is the Algarve, the southernmost coastal region of Portugal. It is separated from the Alentejo by the Serra de Monchique and Serra de Calde-

irao mountain ranges. The Algarve invites many tourists with its sandy beaches and steep cliffs in the background.

Portugal is a seismically active country, but fortunately, most earthquakes within the last century have been fairly moderate and primarily affected the northern part of the country. One of the most destructive earthquakes in Portuguese history struck Lisbon on 1 November 1755. The 8.7 magnitude earthquake was felt throughout the country and triggered a tsunami. The destruction from these events caused the deaths of about 70,000 people.

³CLIMATE

Marked seasonal and regional variations within temperate limits characterize Portugal's climate. In the north, an oceanic climate prevails: cool summers and rainy winters (average rainfall 125–150 cm/50–60 in annually), with occasional snowfall in the northern mountains. Winter temperatures average 10–12°C (50–54°F). Central Portugal has hot summers and cool, rainy winters, with 75–120 cm (30–47 in) average annual rainfall. The southern climate is very dry, with rainfall not exceeding 65 cm (25 in) along the coast. Summer temperatures in Lisbon and the Algarve average 28°C (82°F) while winter temperatures average around 17°C (63°F).

As for Portugal's island territories, the Azores have a mild temperature year-round averaging around 17°C (63°F) in the winter and 24°C (75°F) in the summer. Madeira has a subtropical climate whose average temperatures closely mimic those of the Azores.

⁴FLORA AND FAUNA

The World Resources Institute estimates that there are 5,050 plant species in Portugal. In addition, Portugal is home to 105 mammal, 501 bird, 38 reptile, and 20 amphibian species. The calculation reflects the total number of distinct species residing in the country, not the number of endemic species.

Three types of vegetation can be distinguished in Portugal: green forests of eucalyptus, pine, and chestnut in the north; open dry grasslands, interrupted by stands of cork and other types of evergreen oak in the central areas; and dry grasslands and evergreen brush in the south. Few wild animals remain in Portugal. The coastal waters abound with fish, with sardines and tuna among the most common species.

5 ENVIRONMENT

The World Resources Institute reported that Portugal had designated 459,900 hectares (1.14 million acres) of land for protection as of 2006. Water resources totaled 73.6 cu km (17.66 cu mi) while water usage was 37.22 cu km (8.93 cu mi) per year. Domestic water usage accounted for 10% of total usage, industrial for 12%, and agricultural for 78%. Per capita water usage totaled 1,056 cu m (37,292 cu ft) per year.

Air and water pollution are significant environmental problems especially in Portugal's urban centers. Industrial pollutants include nitrous oxide, sulfur dioxides, and carbon emissions. The UN reported in 2008 that carbon dioxide emissions in Portugal totaled 58,063 kilotons. Since the enactment of the Kyoto Protocol in 1997, Portugal and other participating countries have made an effort to reduce the emission of greenhouse gases including carbon dioxide.

The nation's water supply, especially in coastal areas, is threatened by pollutants from the oil and cellulose industries. The nation's wildlife and agricultural activities are threatened by erosion and desertification of the land. The Portuguese Environmental Agency addresses policies regarding the environment, sea, and agriculture. In 1994, the government approved the National Environmental Plan, which established objectives for sustainable development.

According to a 2011 report issued by the International Union for Conservation of Nature and Natural Resources (IUCN), threatened species included 11 types of mammals, 8 species of birds, 3 types of reptiles, 53 species of fish, 75 types of mollusks, 13 species of other invertebrates, and 81 species of plants. The number of threatened species grew to 167 according to 2009 UN Data statistics. In 2010, the Portuguese Parliament hosted its first conference on biodiversity to address challenges to and methods of conservation.

The Berlengas archipelago and the city of Peniche located on the central coast of Portugal became part of the United Nations Educational, Scientific, and Cultural Organization (UNESCO) Biosphere Reserve Program in July 2011. The archipelago is regularly visited by tourists, fishermen, and scientists who explore the unique geophysical and ecological settings of the Berlengas.

6 POPULATION

The 2011 US Central Intelligence Agency (CIA) World Factbook reported Portugal's population to be approximately 10,760,305, ranking it 75th in world population. The population growth rate was 0.212%. 2011 CIA data also showed that approximately 18% of the population was over 65 years of age, 65.8% were 15 to 64 years of age, and 16.2% were under 15 years of age. The median age in Portugal was 40 years. There were 0.95 males for every female in the country.

2011 CIA data also estimated that 61% of the Portuguese population lived in urban areas, and that urban populations had an annual rate of change of 1%. The largest urban areas, along with their respective populations, included Lisbon, 2.8 million; and Porto, 1.3 million.

7 MIGRATION

An estimate of Portugal's net migration rate, reported in the 2011 CIA World Factbook, equaled 2.98 migrants per 1,000 citizens. The total number of emigrants living abroad was 2.23 million, and the total number of immigrants living in Portugal was 918,600. Portuguese emigration, which decreased from an annual average of 48,000 persons in 1904–1913 to 37,562 in 1961, increased sharply after 1963 as a result of acute labor shortages in other European countries, especially in France and the Federal Republic of Germany (FRG). By 1970, it was estimated that more than 100,000 Portuguese were emigrating annually. Due to the loss of Portugal's African colonies (Angola, Cape Verde, Guinea Bissau, Mozambique, and São Tomé and Príncipe) in 1975, an estimated 800,000 Portuguese settlers returned to Portugal. Since then, at least 25,000 generally return from abroad each year, mostly from other European countries or America. According to World Bank country data, Portugal's net migration (total immigrants less total emigrants) in 2010 was 150,000, a figure that reflects a gradual decrease in net migration throughout the 2000s.

8 ETHNIC GROUPS

The Portuguese people represent a mixture of various ethnic strains. In the north are traces of Celtic influence; in the south, Arab and Berber influence is considerable. Other groups—Lusitanians, Phoenicians, Carthaginians, Romans, Visigoths, and Jews—also left their mark on the Portuguese people. The present-day Portuguese population is one of the most homogeneous in Europe. Minority groups are primarily made up of immigrants, both legal and illegal, from Brazil, former African colonies, and Eastern Europe. Legal immigrants account for about 5% of the total population. There are about 50,000 Roma in the country.

9 LANGUAGES

Portuguese, the national language, is a romance language that evolved from Latin. Portuguese is also the official language of Angola, Brazil, Cape Verde, Guinea Bissau, Mozambique, São Tomé, and Príncipe. Furthermore, it is recognized as one of the official languages in East Timor and Macau. Mirandese is the second official language of Portugal, spoken to a much lesser extent in the north. In 2009, the Orthographic Agreement of 1990 went into effect in Brazil and Portugal. This spelling reform standardized written Portuguese in the two countries.

10 RELIGIONS

The official number of Roman Catholics in Portugal is 84.5% as reported in the 2011 CIA World Factbook. According to a 2009 report by the US Department of State, over 80% of the population aged 12 or older identified themselves as Roman Catholic, though many claimed that they are not active participants in the church. Other Protestant denominations and non-Christian reli-

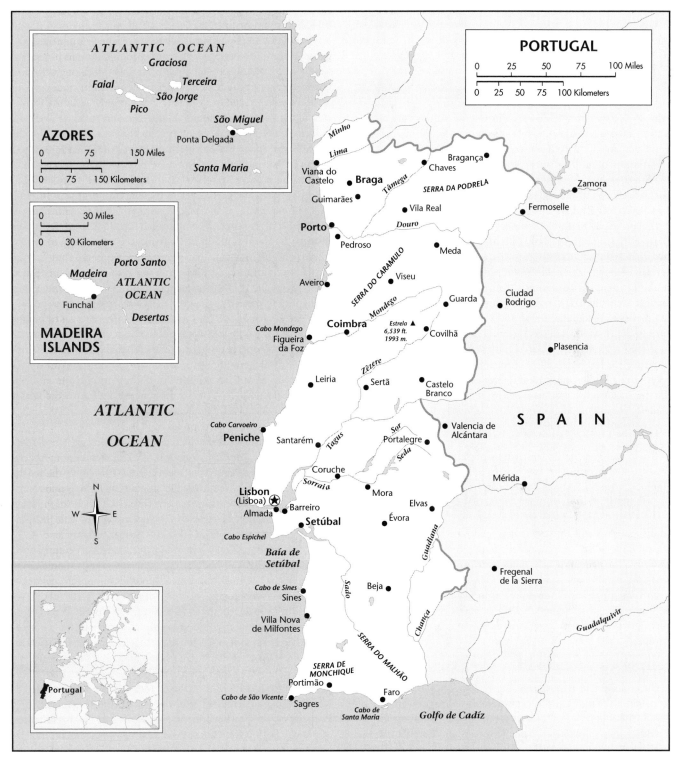

LOCATION: 36°57′39″ to 42°9′8″ N; 6°11′10″ to 9°29′45″ W. BOUNDARY LENGTHS: Spain, 1,214 kilometers (755 miles); Atlantic coastline, 1,793 kilometers (1,113 miles).
TERRITORIAL SEA LIMIT: 12 miles.

gious groups each constitute less than 5% of the population. There are also congregations of the Igreja Universal do Reino de Deus (the Universal Church of the Kingdom of God), which originated in Brazil. The Church of Scientology is also represented. Freedom of religion is guaranteed by the constitution. While the government is secular, the Catholic Church has maintained a special sta-

tus with the government through a 1940 concordat, which was amended in 2004. In 2001, the Religious Freedom Act was passed to extend benefits, previously granted only to the Roman Catholic Church, to minority religious groups. However, the law only applies to groups that have been established within the country for 30 years or more or that have been internationally recognized for at least 60 years. Good Friday, Easter, Corpus Christi, Assumption Day, All Saints' Day, the Feast of the Immaculate Conception, and Christmas are observed as national holidays.

¹¹TRANSPORTATION

The CIA reports that Portugal has a total of 82,900 km (51,512 mi) of roads, of which 71,294 km (44,300 mi) are paved. Railroads extend for 2,842 km (1,766 mi). Portuguese railways are almost entirely owned and operated by the state-owned Portuguese Railway Company, though the early 2000s saw the beginnings of the privatization of railways, such as the private Eixo Norte Sul suburban line and Porto light railway in 2002. As of 2008, broad-gauge rail track accounts for 2,603 km (1,617 mi), and 1,351 km (839 mi) have been electrified.

The principal highways connect Lisbon and Porto with La Coruña in Spain, and Lisbon with Madrid via Badajoz. Bus service links all Portuguese cities, towns, and principal villages.

As of 2008, the Portuguese merchant fleet had 117 oceangoing vessels of 1,000 GRT or more. The main shipping firm is the Portuguese Maritime Transport Co., created after the private shipping companies were nationalized in 1975. It maintains scheduled services to the Azores, Madeira, Macao, and the former overseas territories in Africa. There is also regular service to Brazil and North America. The largest ports—Aveiro, Leixões, Lisbon, Setúbal, and Sines—are all fully equipped and have adequate warehousing facilities. Portugal has created a captive register of convenience on Madeira for Portuguese-owned ships, allowing for taxation and crew benefits. Portugal's navigable waterways stretch 210 km (130 mi).

There are 65 airports, which transported 9.9 million passengers in 2009 according to the World Bank. Because of their geographical position, Lisbon's Portela Airport and Santa Maria in the Azores are of great importance in international aviation. Portela is one of the principal airports for overseas flights to North and South America and to western and central Africa. Santa Maria is a stopping point for transatlantic flights from Europe to North America. The primary aviation company in Portugal is TAP Portugal, which was originally known simply as TAP (Transportes Aereos Portugueses). It was founded in 1945 and later nationalized in 1975. According to the 2011 JACDEC AIrliner Safety Report, TAP Portugal was recognized as the safest airline in Western Europe.

¹²HISTORY

Portugal derives its name from ancient Portus Cale (now Porto), at the mouth of the Douro River, where the Portuguese monarchy began. The country's early history is indistinguishable from that of the other Iberian peoples. Lusitanians were successively overrun by Celts, Romans, Visigoths, and Moors. In 1094, Henry of Burgundy was given the county of Portugal by the king of Castile and León for his success against the Moors; his son, Alfonso I (Alfonso Henriques), became king and achieved independence for Portugal in 1143, beginning the Burgundy dynasty. By the mid-13th century, the present boundaries of Portugal had been established, and Lisbon had become the capital.

During the reign of King John (João) I, the founder of the powerful Aviz dynasty and husband of the English princess Philippa of Lancaster, the Portuguese defeated the Spanish in a war over the

throne (1385), established a political alliance with England (by the Treaty of Windsor in 1386) that has endured to the present day, and inaugurated their most brilliant era. Prince Henry the Navigator (Henrique o Navegador), a son of John I, founded a nautical school at Sagres, where he gathered the world's best navigators, cosmographers, geographers, and astronomers and commenced a series of voyages and explorations that culminated in the formation of the Portuguese Empire. In the 15th and 16th centuries, the golden age of Portugal, Portuguese explorers sailed most of the world's seas; made the European discovery of the Cape of Good Hope, Brazil, and Labrador; founded Portugal's overseas provinces in western and eastern Africa, India, Southeast Asia, and Brazil; and poured the vast riches of the empire into the homeland. In 1580–81, Philip II of Spain, claiming the throne, conquered Portugal and acquired its empire, but national sovereignty was restored by the revolution of 1640 and the accession of John IV, founder of the Bragança dynasty, to the Portuguese throne. John IV ushered in Portugal's silver age, the 17th and 18th centuries, when the wealth of Brazil once more made Lisbon one of the most brilliant of European capitals. The city was largely destroyed by a great earthquake in 1755 but was subsequently rebuilt. During the Napoleonic wars, Portugal, faithful to its British alliance, was the base of British operations against the French in the Iberian Peninsula. The royal family, however, withdrew to Brazil, and from 1807 to 1821, Río de Janeiro was the seat of the Portuguese monarchy. In 1822, Brazil, ruled by Pedro, the son of King John VI of Portugal, formally declared its independence; Pedro became Emperor Pedro I of Brazil but was deposed in 1831.

The Bragança dynasty, which had ruled Portugal since 1640, came to an end with the revolution of 1910, when the monarchy was replaced by a republican regime. Lack of stability under the new republic led to a military dictatorship in 1926. Marshal António Carmona served as president from 1926 to 1951. António de Oliveira Salazar, brought to the government in 1928 as minister of finance, emerged as Portugal's prime minister in 1932. In 1933, Salazar proclaimed a new constitution, which consolidated his regime and established Portugal as a corporative state. During World War II, Portugal supported the Allies but did not take part in combat; it subsequently became a member of NATO.

Despite its reduced status as a European power, Portugal attempted to maintain its overseas empire, especially its resource-rich African provinces. In 1961, Portugal surrendered Goa, Daman, and Diu to India. In the same year, uprisings in Angola began, organized by the Union of Angolan Peoples to protest Portugal's oppressive policies in the territory. These uprisings led to serious disagreements between the UN and Portugal; following Portugal's refusal to heed its recommendations for liberalization of policies with a view toward eventual self-government, the UN General Assembly passed a resolution in 1965 calling for a worldwide economic and arms boycott of Portugal in order to force it to grant independence to its African dependencies. Subsequently, the Assembly passed a number of resolutions condemning Portugal for its policies in its African territories. Meanwhile, guerrilla movements in Angola, Mozambique, and Guinea-Bissau were met by a steadily increasing commitment of Portuguese troops and supplies.

Salazar, who served as prime minister of Portugal from 1932 to 1968, died in July 1970 at the age of 81. When he was incapacitated in September 1968, he was succeeded by Marcello Caetano. The unwillingness of the Caetano regime to institute democratic and economic reforms, coupled with growing discontent over the continuance of the ever more costly colonial war in Africa, led to a military coup by the left-wing Armed Forces Movement in April 1974. Broad democratic liberties were immediately granted and opposition political parties legalized, while the corporate state apparatus was gradually dismantled. A decolonization program was also begun, resulting by November 1975 in the independence of all of Portugal's African provinces.

The first provisional coalition government came to power in May 1974, with Gen. António Sebastião Ribeiro de Spínola, whose book *Portugal and the Future* had played a key role in focusing antiwar sentiment among the military, as president. In September 1974, after a power struggle with the leftist forces, Gen. Spínola resigned and was replaced by Gen. Francisco da Costa Gomes. Following an unsuccessful right-wing coup attempt in March 1975, Gen. Spínola was forced to flee the country, along with a number of officers. The continued dissension between right and left—and between Communist and Socialist factions on the left—was evidenced by the numerous provisional governments that followed the coup. In April 1975, general elections were held for a Constituent Assembly, whose task was to draw up a new constitution. Legislative elections were held in April 1976 and presidential elections in June. Gen. António dos Santos Ramalho Eanes was elected president, and the leader of the Portuguese Socialist Party, Mário Alberto Nobre Lopes Soares, became prime minister. Mainly as a result of policy differences within the governing coalition, this administration fell in July 1978 and was replaced by a caretaker cabinet.

After a succession of different coalitions, the Socialist Party won a 35% plurality in the parliamentary elections of April 1983, and Soares was again named prime minister, forming a coalition government with the center-right Social Democratic Party (Partido Social Democratico—PSD). Political turbulence increased after the election, and in 1984, urban terrorism appeared. In the following year, Portugal entered the EC, boosting the economy. Political instability continued, however, and a general election was called in October 1985. The vote brought the PSD to power with a slim plurality; Prof. Aníbal Cavaço Silva was able to form a minority government. In 1986, four candidates ran for president; none was able to win a majority, and in the ensuing runoff election, former Prime Minister Soares won a narrow victory to become the nation's first civilian president in 60 years. In 1987, the government lost a vote of confidence, and Soares called a general election; the PSD under Silva won a majority in the Assembly, achieving the first such government since democracy was restored in 1974.

The PSD was returned to power in 1991, and Mário Soares was reelected president for a second five-year term on 13 January 1991. Economic recession, government deficits, and regional development initiatives were major concerns in the 1990s.

Following the success of the Socialist Party (Partido Socialist—PS) in the legislative elections held in October 1995, Socialist Jorge Sampaio defeated Silva to succeed Soares as president on 14 January 1996. (Sampaio won reelection for a second five-year term in January 2001.) Antonio Guterres was reappointed prime minister. The goal of the Guterres government was to prepare Portugal for entry into the European economic and monetary union.

Successive austerity measures were legislated, with the support of the center-right PSD, to guarantee Portugal's participation in the euro zone (this took place in 1999). The socialist government at the same time presided over a remarkable economic recovery after 1996. Thanks to strong economic growth and a real drop in unemployment, the PS retained power after the 10 October 1999 Assembly elections. Its program for the succeeding four years was to speed up Portugal's economic and bureaucratic modernization in order to attract investment and promote export-led growth.

The Socialist government's ability to manage a slowing economy deteriorated in Guterres' second term, and the PS suffered a major defeat in local elections held in December 2001. Guterres resigned, and early elections were held in March 2002. They resulted in a change in government, with the center-right PSD forming a coalition with the conservative Popular Party. PSD leader José Manuel Durão Barroso was named prime minister. Durão Barroso experienced his own troubles with the economy, as Portugal headed into a recession at the end of 2002 and into 2003. Portugal's economy was forecast to grow by 0.4% in 2003, the worst performance in the euro currency zone. As well, Portugal's budget deficit in 2002 was far above the 3% of GDP limit established by the EU's Growth and Stability Pact, putting it in jeopardy of punitive sanctions from the EU. In 2005, GDP growth was forecast at just 0.5%, and the budget deficit was 6.8% of GDP.

Portugal's overseas possession, Macau, was turned over to Chinese administration on 20 December 1999. Portugal supported independence for its former colony of East Timor; this was achieved in May 2002. Portugal took steps to normalize relations with Indonesia following the independence of East Timor.

Barroso supported the United States in its war in Iraq, which began in 2003. The prime minister faced criticism from within parliament and among the Portuguese electorate for his stance. In July 2004, Barroso resigned as prime minister to become president of the European Commission. Pedro Santana Lopes, his successor as leader of the PSD, formed a new government. Four months into Lopes's government, President Sampaio called for early elections amidst growing public dissent over the center-right government's inability to tackle the country's economic problems. The general elections were held in February 2005; the Socialists swept to victory, and José Sócrates became prime minister. The Socialists secured their first absolute majority in parliament since democracy returned to Portugal in 1974. Sócrates said his primary objective would be to boost the economy by investing in training and technology. His government had to face the task of bringing the budget deficit under control and putting a stop to rising unemployment.

The government declared a national calamity in August 2003 as forest fires swept across vast areas of woodlands; an area the size of Luxembourg was lost to the fires. At least 18 people were killed, and the damages were estimated at €1 billion. Portugal was plagued by deadly wildfires once again in August 2005. They were said to be the worst in recent times. Portugal appealed to the EU for emergency financial aid to cover the costs to farmers of lost harvests in the wake of the fires.

In January 2006, Social Democratic Party candidate and former Prime Minister Aníbal Cavaco Silva won the presidential election with 50.54% of the vote. Independent candidate Manuel Alegre Duarte came in second with 20.74% of the vote. In the September

2009 legislative elections, the Socialists retained the highest percentage of assembly seats by gaining 36% of the vote. However, at only seven points ahead of the center-right Social Democrat Party, the Socialists lost an absolute majority in parliament. Entering his second-term as prime minister, Socialist José Sócrates was considering the options of forming a coalition government with rivals or attempting to rule with a minority government. Sócrates promised to continue his plans for large-scale public works programs in order to boost the economy.

13 GOVERNMENT

Following authoritarian rule, Portugal created a parliamentary democracy when it adopted a new constitution on 2 April 1976. It stipulated that the Armed Forces Movement maintain governmental responsibilities as the guarantor of democracy and defined Portugal as a republic "engaged in the formation of a classless society." The document provided for a strong, popularly elected president, empowered to appoint the prime minister and cabinet. The constitution was revised in 1982, in which it placed the military under civilian control, limited presidential powers, and laid the groundwork for a pluralistic liberal democracy. Further revisions in 1989 privatized firms and media that had been nationalized under the 1976 constitution. Further amendments to the constitution were added in 1992 to accommodate the Maastricht Treaty on European Union (EU); in 1997, to allow referendums; and in 2001, to facilitate extradition; and in 2004, to accommodate referendums on international treaties.

The president, who is also commander in chief of the armed forces, is elected by popular vote for a five-year term. The president confirms the prime minister, who is nominated by the Assembly of the Republic, and Council of Ministers, which is named by the Prime Minister. The Council of State advises the president. The main lawmaking body is the unicameral Assembly of the Republic to which members are elected based on proportional representation. It is comprised of 230 members directly elected to four-year terms, subject to dissolution. Suffrage is universal from age 18.

14 POLITICAL PARTIES

Under the Salazar regime, although the constitution did not prohibit political activity, the National Union (União Nacional) was the only political party represented in the legislature. Candidates of the old Center parties, which had been active prior to 1926–28, were allowed to participate in national elections starting in 1932, although none was ever elected.

After the 1974 Carnation Revolution, several right-wing parties were banned, and various left-wing parties that had functioned underground or in exile were recognized. Among these was the Portuguese Communist Party (Partido Comunista Português—PCP), which was founded in 1921 and is Portugal's oldest political party. It is especially strong among industrial workers and southern farm workers. The government also recognized the Portuguese Socialist Party (Partido Socialista—PS), founded in exile in 1973, and the Popular Democratic Party (Partido Popular Democrático—PPD), formed during the Caetano regime. Both the PSP and the PPD favored the establishment of a Western European-style social democracy. Tied to the policies of the Caetano regime was the Social Democratic Center (Centro Democrático e

Social—CDS), founded in 1974, which held its first conference in January 1975 and became a target for left-wing disruptions.

In 1979, the right-of-center Democratic Alliance (Aliança Democrática—AD) was a coalition of the Social Democratic Party (Partido Social Democrático—PSD), the CDS, and the People's Monarchist Party (Partido Popular Monárquico—PPM). The leftist United People's Alliance (Aliança Povo Unido), also formed in 1979, included the Portuguese Democratic Movement (Movimento Democrático Português—MDP), dating from 1969, and the PCP.

The Republican and Socialist Front (Frente Republicana e Socialista—FRS), formed in 1980, consists of the PS, the Union of the Socialist and Democratic Left (União da Esquerda Socialista Democrática—UESD), founded in 1978, and Social Democratic Independent Action (Acção Social Democrata Independente—ASDI), founded in 1980. The People's Democratic Union (União Democrática Popular—UDP), dating from 1974, comprises political groups of the revolutionary left.

António Guterres served as Prime Minister starting in 1995. In December 2001, during a downturn in the global economy, Guterres resigned from his second term following a defeat for the PS in municipal elections. In the 17 March 2002 elections, the PSD led by José Manuel Durão Barroso, won 40.1% of the vote and took 105 seats in parliament to the PS's 37.9% and 96 seats. The Popular Party (PP) won 8.8% of the vote and secured 14 seats; the PSD formed a coalition government with the PP. Also winning seats were the CDU (Unitarian Democratic Coalition, comprised of the Portuguese Communist Party and the Greens), with 7% of the vote and 12 seats; and the Left Bloc (BE—comprised of the communist Democratic People's Union, the Revolutionary Socialist Party, and the extreme left party Politics XXI), with 2.8% of the vote and 3 seats.

Jorge Sampaio, the eighteenth president, dissolved Parliament in November 2004 because he lacked confidence in the center-right government of Pedro Santana Lopes (who became prime minister in July 2004 after Barroso stepped down to become president of the European Commission). The subsequent elections were held in February 2005. The results were as follows: PS, 45.1% of the vote (121 seats); PSD, 28.8% (75 seats); CDU, 7.6% (14 seats); PP, 7.2% (12 seats); BE, 6.3% (8 seats). Jóse Sócrates took the position of Prime Minister. In January 2006, Anibal Cavaco Silva was elected president with 50.6% of the vote. He was a Social Democrat, and his election marked him as Portugal's first center-right head of state to take office in three decades.

The Socialists retained the highest percentage of assembly seats following the September 2009 elections by gaining 36.6% of the vote and 97 seats. However, at only seven points ahead of the center-right Social Democrat Party, the Socialists lost an absolute majority in parliament. The PSD won 81 seats and 29.1% of the vote, followed by the Democratic and Social Center-People's Party (CDS-PP) with 21 seats (10.4%), the BE with 16 seats (9.9%), and CDU with 15 seats (7.9%).

In January 2011, Anibal Cavaco Silva of the Social Democratic Party was elected to a second term as president. Silva won by about 53% of the vote, while his nearest rival, Manuel Alegre of the Socialist Party, won about 20%. In June 2011, general elections were held, which shifted political power from the Socialists to the Social Democratic Party (PSD). While the PSD came just short of obtaining a parliamentary majority, it won 108 seats with 38.7% of the vote. The remaining seats were filled by the Socialists with 74 seats (28.1%), the CDS-PP with 24 seats (11.7%), the CDU with 16 seats (7.9%) and the BE with 8 seats (5.2%). Sócrates resigned as party leader of the Socialists. As leader of the PSD, Pedro Passos Coelho became the next Prime Minister and established a coalition government with the CDS-PP to secure a right-wing majority in Parliament.

15 LOCAL GOVERNMENT

Portugal is grouped into districts, including 18 on the mainland plus two additional autonomous regions of the Azores and Madeira islands. Each district has a governor, appointed by the Minister of the Interior, and an assembly. There are more than 300 municipalities, subdivided into parishes.

16 JUDICIAL SYSTEM

Justice is administered by ordinary and special courts, including a Constitutional Tribunal; the Supreme Court of Justice in Lisbon, consisting of a president and some 60 judges; five courts of appeal, at Lisbon, Porto, Coimbra, Évora and Guimarães; courts of first instance in every district; and special courts. The jury system was reintroduced in 1976, but it is used only when requested by either the prosecutor or the defendant. Supreme Court judges are appointed for life by the Conselho Superior da Magistratura.

The judiciary is independent and impartial. Citizens enjoy a wide range of protections of fundamental civil and political rights, which are outlined in the constitution with specific reference to the Universal Declaration of Human Rights. An Ombudsman, elected by the Assembly of the Republic (legislature) to a four-year term, serves as the nation's chief civil and human rights officer.

The legal system is based on the civil law system. Portugal accepts compulsory jurisdiction of the International Court of Justice with reservations.

17 ARMED FORCES

The International Institute for Strategic Studies reports that armed forces in Portugal totaled 43,340 members in 2011. The force is comprised of 26,700 from the army, 10,540 from the navy, and 7,100 members of the air force. Armed forces represent 1.6% of the labor force in Portugal. Defense spending accounted for 2% of GDP according to the 2010 World Bank military expenditure indicator.

The United States maintains a military presence with 1,008 personnel. Armed forces personnel are deployed to eight different countries either in a support role or as part of UN, European Union, or NATO missions.

18 INTERNATIONAL COOPERATION

Portugal joined the United Nations on 14 December 1955 and participates in ECE and several non-regional specialized agencies, such as the FAO, IAEA, the World Bank, ILO, UNESCO, UNIDO, and the WHO. The nation is one of the 12 original signatories to NATO. Portugal is a member of the WTO, the OECD, the African Development Bank, the Asian Development Bank, the Council of Europe, the Euro-Atlantic Partnership Council, the European Bank for Reconstruction and Development, the OSCE, and the Western European Union. Portugal joined the European Union in

1986. It also has observer status in the OAS and the Latin American Integration Association (LAIA).

Portugal belongs to the Australia Group, the Zangger Committee, the European Organization for Nuclear Research (CERN), the Nuclear Suppliers Group (London Group), the Nuclear Energy Agency, and the Organization for the Prohibition of Chemical Weapons. In environmental cooperation, Portugal is part of the Basel Convention, Conventions on Biological Diversity and Air Pollution, Ramsar, CITES, the London Convention, International Tropical Timber Agreements, the Kyoto Protocol, the Montréal Protocol, MARPOL, and the UN Conventions on the Law of the Sea, Climate Change, and Desertification.

In addition to the various international organizations Portugal is a member of and participates in, it is a key member of the Community of Portuguese-Speaking Countries, domestically known as Comunidade dos Países de Língua Portuguesa (CPLP). Other members include the former Portuguese colonies of Angola, Brazil, Cabo Verde, Guinea Bissau, Mozambique, São Tomé and Príncipe, and East Timor. The purpose of CPLP is to unite Lusophone countries through mutual friendship and cooperation. Its objectives are cooperation among members in education, health, science and technology, defense, agriculture, public administration, justice, public security, culture, sport, and social communication. It also works to promote the diffusion of the Portuguese language.

Portugal has offered support to UN missions and operations in Kosovo (est. 1999), East Timor (est. 2002), and Burundi (est. 2004). In 2010, Portugal was elected for a two-year term on the United Nations Security Council. The term ended 31 December 2012, during which Portugal served as the Security Council Presidency in November of 2011.

19 ECONOMY

Following the Carnation Revolution of 1974, Portugal experienced fluctuating economic growth. GNP growth in 1974 dropped to 2.3% from 8.1% the previous year. GDP growth rose to 5.5% in 1980 before it began to decline again. In mid-1983, the Soares government implemented an IMF stabilization plan of drastic internal tightening, which brought steady economic improvement. The persistent current account deficits ended in 1985, partially as a result of the decline in world oil prices and entry into the EC. The Silva government's economic liberalization emphasized competitiveness and accountability. From 1987 to 1999 Portugal was the net recipient of financial inflow from the EU of about $27 billion, most disbursed through the European Regional Development Fund. The money was spent on infrastructural improvements, most notably the highway system. With the accession into the EU of ten central and east European countries in 2004, Portugal lost its historic competitive advantage in Europe due to low labor costs in the new EU member states.

Through the 1990s, until the beginning of 2001, Portugal enjoyed strong economic growth partially due to its entry into the European Economic Community in 1986. The economy grew from 3% to 4.5% between 1998 and 2000. Unemployment lulled between 4% and 5% in this period. Even as growth slowed to 2.2% in 2001, unemployment in Portugal remained below that of most of its neighbors. In 2002, the economic growth rate continued to decline, and unemployment increased to 5.05%. Inflation in Portugal was moderate but increased from 1998 to 2000.

The Socialist government pledged its dedication both to meeting the Maastricht monetary convergence criteria and to increasing social spending, including provision of a guaranteed minimum income. This policy was realized when Portugal qualified for the first round of entry into the Economic and Monetary Union (EMU) in 1999. As of January 2002, the euro was circulated and became Portugal's official currency.

In 2003, the economy officially entered into a recession as unemployment shot up to 6.5%. In 2004, real GDP growth was in the positive figures once again, albeit estimated at a paltry 1.1%. Unemployment that year remained at 6.5%. The GDP per capita was roughly two-thirds of the EU average. Portugal was the first EU country to breech the 3% of GDP deficit agreement when the nation's deficit reached 6% in 2005, which was reduced to 2.6% by 2007. A poor educational system and a rigid labor market have been obstacles to greater productivity and growth.

The global financial crisis of 2008–09 dropped the nation into recession once again. According to 2009 World Bank indicators Portugal reported a fiscal deficit of 8.7% of gross domestic product (GDP) and a federal debt of 83.9% of GDP. International economists did not foresee improvement for 2010. The International Monetary Fund (IMF) urged Portugal to take measures to cut federal spending, asserting that relying on stimulus measures alone was unacceptable. In November 2009, the European Commission proposed a 2013 deadline for Portugal to reduce its deficit within the 3% of GDP stricture of the European Union.

Portugal's economic situation improved little in 2010 with GDP growth at .91%. As of 2010, its gross domestic product (GDP) rate of change was 1.4% and inflation stood at 1.1%. CIA reports showed that 2010 Portuguese unemployment was 10.8%, the budget deficit was 9.2% of GDP, and federal debt was 93% of GDP. In November 2010, parliament passed an austerity budget designed to reduce the deficit to 4.6% in 2011. The budget included measures to cut public spending and to increase the value-added tax. Many of the measures were unpopular with voters and members of opposition parties, including the Social Democrats. Budget talks leading up to the vote were tense, with many believing that the opposition would effectively block passage of the budget through the vote. The budget passed through parliament, primarily due to the fact that the opposition parties agreed to abstain from the vote.

In March 2011, Portugal continued to struggle with its economy as Prime Minister Sócrates announced a series of cuts to health and welfare budgets as well as a 5% public salary cut and 2% increase in the value-added tax. The austerity package faced strong opposition as government officials speculated Portugal would need an international bailout if the plan did not work. As the eurozone crisis continued to plague the EU in 2011, Portugal continued to address its own economic woes to avoid an economic catastrophe akin to that of Greece (which, as of November 2011, was pending the acceptance of a bailout plan proposed by the EU). In March 2011, a European Commission report stated that Portugal had presented the EU with its plan of fiscal consolidation, which included measures to reduce Portugal's budget deficit to 4.6% of GDP in 2011, 3% in 2012, and 2% in 2013. By May of 2011, Portugal had accepted a three-year bailout package proposed by the EU, IMF, and European Central Bank, which provided financial assistance of 78 billion euros. The loan came with the conditions of implementing comprehensive austerity measures and privatizing state-owned enterprises, as well as adjusted the aforementioned benchmarks for the reduction of the budget deficit. The more conservative budget deficit benchmarks were 5.9% of GDP by 2011, 4.5% in 2012, and 3% in 2013.

20 INCOME

The CIA estimated that, in 2010, the GDP of Portugal was $247 billion. The CIA defines GDP as the value of all final goods and services produced within a nation in a given year and is computed on the basis of purchasing power parity (PPP) rather than value, as measured on the basis of the rate of the exchange based on current dollars. The per capita GDP was estimated at $23,000. The annual growth rate of GDP was 1.4%. The average inflation rate was 1.1%. It was estimated that agriculture accounted for 2.6% of GDP, industry 23%, and services 74.5%.

The World Bank reported in 2009 that household consumption in Portugal totaled $155.5 billion or about $14,450 per capita, measured in current US dollars rather than PPP. Household consumption includes expenditures of individuals, households, and nongovernmental organizations on goods and services, excluding the purchases of dwellings. It was estimated that household consumption was growing at an average annual rate of 0.9%. According to the World Bank, remittances from citizens living abroad totaled $3.6 billion or about $333 per capita and accounted for approximately 1.5% of GDP.

The CIA estimated that, in 2006, about 18% of the population subsisted on an income below the poverty line established by Portugal's government.

21 LABOR

The service sector labor force rose from 39% of the total labor force in 1971 to 59.8% in 2009 and accounted for about 74.7% of GDP in 2010. The industrial sector employed approximately 28.5% of the labor force and generated 23% of Portugal's GDP in 2009. Portugal's main industries are clothing, textiles, footwear, wood and cork, paper, auto-parts manufacturing, base metals, chemicals, dairy products, wine and other foods, porcelain and ceramics, glassware, technology, telecommunications, ship construction and refurbishment, and tourism. Agriculture, forestry, hunting, and fishing employed 11.7% of the work force (down from 26.2% in 1971) and contributed only about 2% of GDP in 2009.

As of 2005, workers in Portugal could form and join unions, as well as engage in collective bargaining and strike. About 35% of the nation's workforce was unionized as of 2005. Armed forces and police personnel are banned from striking, but they have unions and have legal mechanisms to settle grievances. The government approves all collective bargaining contracts and regulates such matters as social insurance, pensions, hours of labor, and vacation provisions. Strikes are generally resolved quickly through negotiations.

A minimum wage was established in 1975. In 2009, the minimum monthly salary was 485 euros. This is paid out 14 times over the year, as employees are paid for two extra months of work per year to compensate for holiday and summer vacations. However, a salary cut was implemented in January 2011 as part of the austerity measures. Rent controls and subsidized food and utilities increase the standard of living. In addition, most workers earn more than this amount. The maximum legal workday is 10 hours, with the workweek set at 40 hours with a minimum of 12 hours between workdays. Overtime is limited to two hours per day up to 200 hours annually. Minimum standards of occupational safety and health are set by law, but they are not adequately enforced, and workplace accidents do occur, particularly in the construction industry. The minimum working age is 16 years.

22 AGRICULTURE

Roughly 25% of the total land is currently farmed, and the country's major crops include grain, potatoes, tomatoes, olives, and grapes. Cereal production in 2009 amounted to 1.1 million tons, fruit production 1.5 million tons, and vegetable production 2.7 million tons.

Wine, particularly port and Madeira from the Douro region and the Madeira islands, is an important agricultural export. Portugal is the world's ninth-largest producer of wine, although Portugal's wines are mostly unknown internationally apart from port, rosé, and vinho verde. Under the influence of EU policies, vineyard areas have been reduced in recent years.

Agriculture has been one of the problem areas in Portugal's economy. Yields per hectare are less than one-third of the European average, with a severe drought in 1991/92 only exacerbating the problem. The situation has been deteriorating since the mid-1970s, with many yields falling and arable and permanent crop areas declining. By 1999, crop output was only 87% of what it had been on average from 1989 to 1991. However, during the years 2002 to 2004, crop output declined a further 1.8%. Reform of the EU's Common Agriculture Policy (CAP), which included a significant reduction in the number of producers through consolidation (especially in the north), resulted in the end of traditional, subsistence-like based agriculture. The CAP was scheduled to undergo further reforms in 2013 that would affect the Portuguese agriculture sector. Between 1995 and 2003, the number of agricultural holdings decreased from 450,600 to 359,200, while the value of crop output increased from €3.7 billion to €4.33 billion during that time.

23 ANIMAL HUSBANDRY

The UN Food and Agriculture Organization (FAO) reported that Portugal dedicated 1.8 million hectares (4.51 million acres) to permanent pasture or meadow in 2009. During that year, the country tended 39 million chickens, 1.4 million head of cattle, and 2.3 million pigs. The production from these animals amounted to 194,172 tons of beef and veal, 478,122 tons of pork, 269,066 tons of poultry, 102,983 tons of eggs, and 2.37 million tons of milk. Portugal also produced 11,603 tons of cattle hide and 6,980 tons of raw wool.

The Alentejo region is Portugal's grazing heartland. Mules and donkeys, as well as horses and oxen, often provide draft power for the farms. The main districts for cattle are northern and north-central Portugal; most of the sheep, goats, and pigs are raised in the central and southern sections.

24 FISHING

Portugal had 17,521 decked commercial fishing boats in 2008. The annual capture totaled 240,192 tons according to the UN FAO. The export value of seafood totaled $2.58 billion.

Three main fields of activity make up the Portuguese fishing enterprise: coastal fishing, especially that of sardines; trawl fishing on the high seas; and cod fishing on the Grand Banks off Newfoundland. Dominant species are sardines, mackerel, red fish, scabbardfish, and octopus. These species accounted for nearly half the landings. Virtually all of the total catch is sold fresh, but small amounts of sardines and octopus are frozen. The average annual catch from 1995 to 1999 was 318,600 tons. According to OECD (Organization for Economic Cooperation and Development) statistics, 196,000 tons of fish were landed in domestic and foreign ports in 2007. The annual catch declined throughout the 1990s because Portugal was affected by internationally set limits (Total Allowable Catches) that restrict fishing access for certain species in the international waters of the North Atlantic and by EU fishing quotas. The fishing potential has also been affected by a reduction in the national fleet in association with EU fleet reduction incentives. The Portuguese fishing fleet was reduced by 40% from 1990 to 2000. There was an additional 5% reduction in fleet tonnage from 2000 to 2004.

25 FORESTRY

Approximately 38% of Portugal is covered by forest. The UN FAO estimated the 2009 roundwood production at 8.96 million cu m (316.6 million cu ft). The value of all forest products, including roundwood, totaled $2.19 billion.

Portugal is an important producer of forestry products. The country is the world's leading producer of cork, harvested exclusively from cork oak (Quercus suber) found predominantly in the Mediterranean region. Portugal ordinarily supplies around 175,000 tons of cork per year (about half of world output) from some 725,000 hectares (1,791,000 acres) of cork forests. Wine stoppers account for 55% of cork export value. Cork demand has fallen in recent years, and production is limited by the fact that a single tree can only be stripped once every nine years. Eucalyptus logs (the crux of the pulp industry) are exported as well; forestation of eucalyptus is a major national controversy, with opponents charging that it displaces traditional farmers and damages the soil and water table. Pine accounts for most lumber exports. Portugal is also an important producer of resin and turpentine.

26 MINING

Portugal's mineral wealth is significant, but the deposits are scattered and are not easily exploitable on a large scale. The country's most important metallic mineral resources are copper, tin, and tungsten. In 2009, Portugal was the world's fifth-largest producer of lithium, sixth in tungsten, and eleventh in tin. Portugal is a leading producer of mined copper in the European Union (EU), as well as being an important producer of dimension stone and tungsten concentrates. In 2008, Portugal had 1,463 nonfuel mineral and quarrying enterprises, employing 13,274 workers, with a production valued at €1.2 billion. Exports of base metals and minerals respectively accounted for 9.1% and 4.6% of exports in 2009. Minerals were one of the country's dynamic industrial sectors, mainly because of the discovery and development of the Neves-Corvo copper and tin deposits. The Panasqueira mine was one of the world's largest producers of tungsten concentrates.

In 2009, the output of mined copper (metal content) was 86,500 metric tons, down slightly from 89,504 metric tons in 2008. Output of mined tungsten (metal content) was 823 metric tons, compared to 982 metric tons in 2008. Tin mine output (metal content) in 2009 totaled 34 metric tons, down from 243 metric tons in 2005. Production of iron ore and concentrates (gross weight) in 2009 totaled was estimated at 14,000 metric tons, unchanged since 2002. Portugal also produced white arsenic, manganese, silver, uranium, anhydrite, hydraulic cement, refractory clays, diatomite, feldspar, gypsum, kaolin, hydrated lime, quicklime, lepidolite (a lithium mineral), nitrogen, pyrite and pyrrhotite (including cuprous), rock salt, sand, soda ash, sodium sulfate, stone (basalt, dolomite, diorite, gabbro, granite, both crushed and ornamental, graywacke, calcite marl limestone, marble, ophite, quartz, quartzite, schist, slate, and syenite), sulfur, and talc. Marble, mainly from the Evora District, was the most valuable of the stone products. A new deposit, at the Aljustrel mine/mill complex, encompassing five massive sulfide deposits, could be brought into production relatively quickly as a low-cost zinc producer; the most significant deposit, at Feitais, had 12 million tons of proven and probable minable zinc reserves with an average grade of 5.67% zinc, 1.7% lead, and 64 grams per ton of silver, and 1.6 million tons of proven and probable copper ore reserves with an average grade of 2.2% copper, 0.97% zinc, and 14 grams per ton of silver.

The southern Iberian Peninsula, known as the Iberian Pyrite Belt (IPB), was one of the most mineralized areas of Western Europe and was geologically very complex. The IPB's internationally well-known volcanogenic massive sulfide (VMS) deposits in the southwestern part of the peninsula dated to the Upper Devonian and the Lower Carboniferous ages. Clusters of deposits occurred around individual volcanic centers, and the largest individual deposit located to date may have held an original reserve of 500 million tons out of IPB's total resource of 1,725 million tons. Sulfide deposit resources in 1999 were 1,100 million tons.

The government continued its privatization program and was proceeding with legislation to privatize many public companies, part of a broader program to make the economy more market-driven. The structure of the mineral industry could change in the near future because of significant mining exploration by several foreign companies, particularly for copper, gold, kaolin, lead, lithium, pyrites, and tin. The IPB was the prime area for exploration activity and had an above-average potential for success based on an unusually high number of large VMS deposits.

27 ENERGY AND POWER

Portugal operates two refineries, which allows the country to meet a portion of its refined petroleum product needs. However, the country must import all of the crude oil it refines in addition to all of the natural gas and coal the country consumes, as well as additional amounts of refined petroleum products.

In 2010, the CIA estimated Portugal's production of oil to be 4,721 barrels per day. Domestic demand for refined oil in that year averaged 277,400 barrels per day. Imports of refined and crude petroleum averaged 294,600 barrels per day, although the country did export an average of 49,650 barrels per day. Natural gas

imports and consumption for 2010 totaled 5.122 billion cu m and 5.161 billion cu m, respectively.

Since 2005, the government has sponsored aggressive national policies for the development of renewable energy, particularly in wind, solar, and hydropower. Those policies seem to have worked, although at a great cost to consumers. In 2010, nearly 45% of the country's electricity came from renewable energy, up from 17% in 2005. In the same period, the cost of electricity, which has usually been higher than that of some other developed countries, rose by 15%. In 2011, the government sought to make Portugal the first nation to launch a national network of charging stations for electric cars.

The World Bank reported in 2008 that Portugal produced 45.5 billion kWh of electricity and consumed 51.2 billion kWh, or 4,760 kWh per capita. Roughly 78% of energy came from fossil fuels, while 5% came from alternative fuels. Per capita oil consumption was 2,274 kg. The CIA reported that, in 2009, Portugal imported 4,776 billion kWh of electricity and exported 2.822 billion kWh.

28 INDUSTRY

Industry (including construction, energy, and water) employs about one-third of the labor force, and its contribution to the national economy has grown significantly in recent decades. It accounted for 28.5% of GDP in 2009. Industrial production in 2010 had a growth rate of 1.6%. Portuguese industry is mainly light as the development of heavy industry has been hampered by a shortage of electric power. Textiles—especially cottons and woolens—are the oldest and most important of Portugal's manufactures. Other principal industries are automotive parts manufacturing, technology, glassware, porcelain and ceramics, footwear, clothing, paper, chemicals, base metals, wood and cork, dairy products, wine and other food, telecommunications, ship construction and refurbishment, and tourism. Small artisan industries, such as jewelry and homespun, hand-embroidered clothing are of local importance.

Foreign competition has cut into Portugal's textile industry. Following the expiration of the World Trade Organization's long-standing system of textile quotas at the beginning of 2005, the EU signed an agreement with China in June 2005. It imposed new quotas on 10 categories of textile goods, limiting growth in those categories to between 8% and 12.5% a year. The agreement ran until 2007, and was designed to give European textile manufacturers time to adjust to a world of unfettered competition. Nevertheless, barely a month after the EU-China agreement was signed, China reached its quotas for sweaters, followed soon after by blouses, bras, t-shirts, and flax yarn. Tens of millions of garments piled up in warehouses and customs checkpoints, which affected both retailers and consumers.

29 SCIENCE AND TECHNOLOGY

In 1996, Portugal had 18 scientific and technological learning societies and 20 scientific and technological research institutes. The leading scientific academy is the Lisbon Academy of Sciences, founded in 1779. In 1996, Portugal had 27 universities and colleges offering courses in basic and applied sciences. Attached to the University of Lisbon is the Museum and Laboratory of Mineralogy and Geology, founded in 1837. From 1987 to 1997, science and engineering students accounted for 36% of university enrollment.

Total government expenditures on research and development (R&D) in 2008 totaled 1.5% of GDP, an increase from the 0.84% of GDP invested in 2001. Also in 2008, there were 3,799 researchers engaged in R&D per million people. In 2009, high technology exports, those with high R&D intensity, totaled $1.288 billion, equal to 4% of the country's manufactured exports. Patent applications in science and technology as of 2009, according to the World Bank, totaled 381 in Portugal. Public financing of science was 1.51% of GDP. The World Bank also reported that in 2008, 15,508 resident trademark applications were filed.

30 DOMESTIC TRADE

Lisbon and Porto are the two leading commercial and distribution centers. Larger retail stores, shopping malls, and supermarkets have become well-established in many areas. The World Bank reported that in 2009, 27,759 new businesses were registered in Portugal, a decline in the 31,883 businesses registered in 2008. Franchising has also gained ground, particularly in the clothing and fast-food markets.

Electronic commerce (e-commerce) has had rapid growth. The World Bank reported that in 2009, Portugal had 5,168,842 million Internet users (those with access to the worldwide network), which is approximately 49% of the country's population.

Direct marketing through television and mail order sales has also grown considerably. The most common advertising media are newspapers, outdoor billboards, radio, television, and websites. Movie theaters also display advertisements on their screens.

The typical business hours are from 9 a.m. to 6 p.m., Monday through Friday. Banking hours are generally 8:30 a.m. to 3 p.m., Monday through Friday. Store hours are generally from 9 a.m. to 7 p.m., Monday through Friday, and from 9 a.m. to 1 p.m. on Saturdays. Shopping malls operate from 10 a.m. to 11 p.m., every day of the week, except for Christmas and New Year's day.

31 FOREIGN TRADE

Portugal's foreign trade balance has regularly shown a heavy deficit, which it finances through net receipts from tourism, remittances from Portuguese workers abroad, and net transfers from the EU. According to OECD statistics, Portugal's goods trade deficit in 2008 was $34.2 billion, while it had a trade surplus in services of $9.5 billion. Portugal imported $68.22 billion worth of goods and services in 2008, while exporting $46.27 billion worth of goods and services. Major import partners in 2009 were Spain, 32.6%; Germany, 13.2%; France, 8.3%; Italy, 5.8%; and the Netherlands, 5.5%, all of which are EU member states. Its major export partners were Spain, 27.3%; Germany, 12.9%; France, 12.4%; Angola, 7%; and UK, 5.7%

32 BALANCE OF PAYMENTS

Despite the current trend of chronic trade deficits, until 1973 Portugal managed to achieve a balance-of-payments surplus through tourist revenues and remittances from emigrant workers. With the economic dislocations of 1974, net tourist receipts fell 30%; the trade deficit almost doubled; and emigrant remittances stagnated. Thus, the 1973 payments surplus of $255.7 million became a $647.7 million deficit in 1974. Emigrant remittances grew

Principal Trading Partners – Portugal (2010)

(In millions of US dollars)

Country	Total	Exports	Imports	Balance
World	124,332.0	48,742.0	75,590.0	-26,848.0
Spain	36,570.0	12,945.0	23,625.0	-10,680.0
Germany	16,782.0	6,348.0	10,434.0	-4,086.0
France	11,247.0	5,758.0	5,489.0	269.0
Italy	6,170.0	1,860.0	4,310.0	-2,450.0
Netherlands	5,757.0	1,856.0	3,901.0	-2,045.0
United Kingdom	5,525.0	2,672.0	2,853.0	-181.0
Belgium	3,556.0	1,400.0	2,156.0	-756.0
Angola	3,249.0	2,501.0	748.0	1,753.0
United States	2,674.0	1,671.0	1,003.0	668.0
China	2,386.0	307.0	2,079.0	-1,772.0

(…) data not available or not significant.

(n.s.) not specified.

SOURCE: *2011 Direction of Trade Statistics Yearbook,* New York: United Nations, 2011.

Balance of Payments – Portugal (2010)

(In millions of US dollars)

Current Account		**-22,850.0**
Balance on goods	-24,111.0	
Imports	-73,016.0	
Exports	48,905.0	
Balance on services	8,825.0	
Balance on income	-10,423.0	
Current transfers	2,591.0	
Capital Account		**2,591.0**
Financial Account		**22,060.0**
Direct investment abroad	8,164.0	
Direct investment in Portugal	1,476.0	
Portfolio investment assets	-3,756.0	
Portfolio investment liabilities	-8,423.0	
Financial derivatives	505.0	
Other investment assets	-8,937.0	
Other investment liabilities	33,032.0	
Net Errors and Omissions		**-530.0**
Reserves and Related Items		**-1,271.0**

(…) data not available or not significant.

SOURCE: *Balance of Payment Statistics Yearbook 2011,* Washington, DC: International Monetary Fund, 2011.

steadily between 1976 and 1980, when they peaked at $2.946 million. Because of this, Portugal's balance of payments improved and even achieved a surplus of $761 million in 1979. Subsequently, increasing trade deficits resulted in balance-of-payments deficits that reached $3.2 billion in 1982. By 1985, however, the deficit had become a surplus of $0.4 billion, which rose to $1.1 billion in 1986. One of the main contributing factors to Portugal's increase in surplus was the weakening dollar, which boosted the value of tourism earnings and remittances. The 1990 Portuguese external payments surplus stabilized at the previous year's record level of nearly $4 billion. After a few years of surplus boom, mainly due to the enormous influx of foreign capital and transfers to Portugal following EC membership in 1986, measures were taken in July 1990 to restrict foreign credit and investment, thereby helping the authorities obtain better control over monetary aggregates. These measures, along with the hiatus in international investment caused by the 1990/91 Persian Gulf crisis and some deterioration in the merchandise trade account contributed to the halting growth of the total non-monetary balance.

Although foreign direct investment (FDI) in new manufacturing projects, such as the automotive and electronics sectors, increased in the 1990s, in the early 2000s FDI flowed to lower-cost manufacturing locations in central and eastern Europe, away from Portugal. Since the enlargement of the EU to eastern European countries, Portugal has had a difficult time attracting foreign investors since eastern European countries tend to offer even lower labor costs than Portugal.

According to the World Bank, Portugal's current account balance was a deficit of $22.605 billion in 2010. In 2010, Portugal had a foreign trade deficit of $16 billion, amounting to 8.7% of GDP.

33 BANKING AND SECURITIES

All 22 banks in Portugal, except for three foreign-owned ones (Banco do Brasil, Credit Franco-Portugais, and the Bank of London and South America), were nationalized in 1975. A 1983 law, however, permitted private enterprise to return to the banking industry. The Bank of Portugal, (the central bank founded in 1846), functions as a bank of issue, while the European Central Bank controls monetary policy.

During the late 1990s, Portugal's banking industry underwent significant restructuring due to foreign investment and consolidation. A major series of consolidations in 1996 left Banco Comercial Português (BCP), Banco Pinto and Sotto Mayor, and Banco Português de Investimento as the three largest private banks. Further consolidation came in 1999 when Spain's Banco Santander Central Hispano (BSCH) merged with Champalimaud. Fearing increased Spanish influence in the Portuguese banking industry, the Portuguese government sought to block the deal, and the dispute appeared to be headed for the European Court. Ultimately, Portugal's finance minister, Joaquim Pina Moura, forged a compromise in which BSCH acquired two banks in the Champalimaud group.

The International Monetary Fund reports that in 2001, currency and demand deposits—an aggregate commonly known as M1—were equal to $47.0 billion. In that same year, M2—an aggregate equal to M1 plus savings deposits, small-time deposits, and money market mutual funds—was $111.7 billion.

Because the nation's currency is the euro, the nation's discount rate, the interest rate at which the central bank lends to financial institutions in the short term, is set by the European Central Bank (ECB). In 2010, the discount rate was 1.75%.

Portugal's two stock exchanges, located in Lisbon and Porto, were closed after the coup of April 1974. The Lisbon exchange reopened in 1976 and the Porto exchange in 1981. In January 1992, the market was split into three tiers, of which the first is the major liquid market. This included the 11 firms whose shares are traded regularly and which have a minimum market capitalization of €500 million. Trading outside of the stock exchanges is still widespread. Into the late 1990s, trade on the exchange continued to grow as continued privatization led to greater amounts of Initial Public Offerings (IPOs). In 2007, Euronext merged with the New York Stock Exchange (NYSE), at which point Euronext Lisbon joined the NYSE Euronext group. In 2010, the NYSE Euronext Lisbon had 53 companies listed of which 48 were domestic and 5 foreign. It had a market capitalization of 57,236,000 euros, a decrease of 2.5% from 2009. The CIA reported that the market value of publicly traded shared was $82 billion at the end of 2010.

34 INSURANCE

Portugal's domestic insurance companies were nationalized in 1975. Foreign companies were required to accept government representatives among their directors. A new law, approved in 1983, allowed the private sector to reenter the domestic insurance industry. Almost all Portuguese companies sell life and non-life insurance, although some specialize in reinsurance only. Life insurance is its largest insurance segment, accounting for 74.5% of the gross insurance premium in 2010. Motor insurance comprises the largest non-life insurance segment accounting for 40.1% of market share in the non-life insurance market. In the wake of the reprivatization of the insurance industry, many insurance companies have sought alliances with banks. This position, in turn, serves as an impediment to new entrants into the insurance field, particularly from foreign countries. However, the market is opening, and brokers from any European Union (EU) country can operate in Portugal. Third-party auto insurance and workers' compensation are compulsory in Portugal. Contractors, travel agents, insurance brokers, and other professionals are also required to carry liability insurance. According to the Associação Portuguesa de Seguradores (Portuguese Association of Insurers), in 2008, the value of direct insurance premiums written totaled 15.336 billion euros, of which life insurance premiums accounted for 11.012 billion euros.

35 PUBLIC FINANCE

Portugal's budgets (accounting for the effects of loans and transfers) have been in deficit since 1974. Major factors contributing

Public Finance – Portugal (2009)

(In millions of euros, central government figures)

Revenue and Grants	**58,197**	**100.0%**
Tax revenue	32,950	56.6%
Social contributions	19,443	33.4%
Grants	...	...
Other revenue	...	...
Expenditures	**72,813**	**100.0%**
General public services	11,891	16.3%
Defense	2,416	3.3%
Public order and safety	3,648	5.0%
Economic affairs	4,417	6.1%
Environmental protection	212	0.3%
Housing and community amenities	19	<0.1%
Health	11,100	15.2%
Recreational, culture, and religion	677	0.9%
Education	9,932	13.6%
Social protection	28,501	39.1%

(…) data not available or not significant.

SOURCE: *Government Finance Statistics Yearbook 2010*, Washington, DC: International Monetary Fund, 2010.

to the deficits included spending on health and education programs, funding for major public investment projects, and large state-owned enterprise payrolls. To finance the deficit, the government issued bonds in the domestic market, which also serves the monetary policy purpose of absorbing excess liquidity. The government's objective to join the Economic and Monetary Union (EMU) was achieved in 1999. Since then, monetary policy responsibilities have been absorbed by the European Central Bank. Public debt exceeded 3% of GDP in 2001, exceeding EU limits and opening the country up to sanctions from the rest of the EU. By 2009, Portugal's budget deficit had reached 9.3% of GDP. After accepting a bailout package in May 2011 from the EU, European Central Bank, and IMF, it implemented measures to reduce the budget deficit to 5.9% of GDP in 2011, 4.5% in 2012, and 3% in 2013. These benchmarks were set so that Portugal could meet the bailout package terms of reducing its budget deficit below the 3% eurozone limit by 2014.

In 2010, the budget of Portugal included $93.61 billion in public revenue and $110.2 billion in public expenditures. The budget deficit amounted to 9.2% of GDP. Public debt was 83.2% of GDP, with $497.8 billion of the debt held by foreign entities.

³⁶TAXATION

The national corporate tax rate in Portugal as of 2011 was 25%, although rates in Madeira were 20% and 17.5% in the Azores. In addition, the corporate tax rate can be levied at 25%. Allowable deductions in calculating taxable corporate income include depreciation, interest payments, executives' salaries, and royalties. Capital gains are taxed at 25%. Dividends paid to parent companies by subsidiaries (owned at least 25% by the payee) are excluded from taxable income to avoid double taxation. Otherwise, dividends are taxed at general income tax rates.

The progressive personal income tax schedule has seven bands, not including a tax-exempt base. The schedule bands as of 2008 were 10.5% (up to €4,755); 13% on the next increment of income to €7,192; 23.5% on the next increment to €17,836; 34% on the next increment to €41,021; 36.5% on the next increment to €59,450; 40% on the increment of income up to €64,110; and 42% on the increment above €64,110. Social security taxes amount to 23.75% of nominal income. There are also municipal taxes on the value of real estate. Taxes on personal income totaled 5.6% of GDP in 2008 according to OECD statistics.

The main indirect tax in Portugal is the value-added tax (VAT), known as IVA in Portugal, which was introduced January 1, 1986 with a standard rate of 16%. This was raised to 19% in May 2002 and, as of September 2010, had been raised even further to 23%, reflecting the tough economic times. There is also a reduced rate of 5% (applied to basic foodstuffs, water supplies, books, newspapers and periodicals, social housing, some medical equipment and drugs, hotel accommodations, repair and domestic services); an intermediate "parking" rate of 8% (applied to some foodstuffs, catering, and some fuels and lubricants); and exemptions from VAT (for social services, some medical and dental services, waste collection and disposal, transportation services, gold transfers to the central bank, and cremation.). For the Azores and Madeira, the standard VAT rate is 15%, the reduced rate 4%, and the parking rate 8%. Other transactions taxes include stamp duties and transfer fees.

³⁷CUSTOMS AND DUTIES

Portugal uses the Harmonized Nomenclature and Classification System (HS) to organize imports into tariff categories. Almost all tariffs are levied on an ad valorem basis according to the EU Customs Code, except for luxury goods and petroleum, which have special, higher rates. Portugal adheres to all EU trade policies, including multilateral trade agreements, and conforms to WTO regulations. It also levies a value-added tax (VAT) of up to 21% on most imports, although there is a lower rate of 5%. In Madeira and the Azores, the lower rates of 4% and 13% apply. The VAT on imports from EU countries is not collected until the product is sold.

³⁸FOREIGN INVESTMENT

Foreign direct investment (FDI) in Portugal was a net inflow of $2.81 billion according to World Bank figures published in 2009. FDI represented 1.21% of GDP.

The government actively promotes foreign investment as an integral part of its economic development policy and specifically through the government agency API (Agency for Investment in Portugal). As a member of the European Union, Portugal abides by the investment rules that govern the rest of the union. New foreign investment legislation was enacted in 1986. The Institute of Foreign Investment (ICEP) is the supervising agency. Foreign investment is permitted in all sectors except ports, water management, rail services, public service telecommunications operators, and the arms industry. Portugal limits non-EU investment in regular air transport to 49% and non-EU investment in television operations to 15%. Even in these areas, however, deregulation is under way. The foreign investment code contains liberal profit remittance regulations and tax incentives.

In 1998, foreign direct investment (FDI) inflows reached $3.1 billion but fell to $1.2 billion in 1999. FDI inflows later soared to $6.4 billion in 2000, and were still above $6 billion in 2001, despite the global economic slowdown. However, FDI in Portugal has since fallen and was a net inflow of $2.81 billion according to World Bank figures published in 2009. FDI represented 1.21% of GDP.

Portugal invests most heavily in Brazil and Spain, followed by Germany and other EU countries. Low labor costs, combined with unrestricted access to the EU market, have attracted foreign investment in new manufacturing projects, especially in the automotive and electronics sectors. However, FDI has slowed as low-cost manufacturing locations in central and Eastern Europe have become increasingly appealing to investors, especially since the admission of 10 new EU members in 2004. Therefore, Portugal cannot rely solely on low wage costs to attract foreign investment.

³⁹ECONOMIC DEVELOPMENT

In 1975, radical economic transformations were accomplished through a series of decrees that nationalized the domestically owned companies of major sectors of the national economy. These decrees affected the leading banks, insurance companies (representing 99% of insurance companies' capital), petroleum refineries, the transportation sector, the steel industry, and eventually Portugal's leading privately owned industrial monopoly, Companhia União Fabril. At the same time, large-scale agrarian reform measures led to expropriation of many of the country's privately owned large landholdings; other holdings were seized illegally by peasants. In an attempt to stimulate agricultural production, the government decreed a 30% reduction in the price of fertilizer to farm workers and small and medium farmers. When the nationalization and agrarian reform measures met with only limited success, partly because of liquidity problems, an emergency austerity plan was approved by the Council of Ministers in October 1975. The program included wage and import controls and the reduction of subsidies on consumer goods.

As a result of Portugal's entry into EU, the highly protected, unresponsive, and inefficient economy was transformed. State intervention was reduced, and the physical infrastructure was modernized. Privatization expanded in 1989, which was reflected in the share of gross domestic product (GDP) for non-financial public enterprises being reduced from 17.9% (1985) to 10.7% (1991). In 1992, $3.6 billion was raised as banks, insurance companies, and a 25% interest in Petrogal—the state oil company—were sold. The government estimated that privatized companies would represent half of stock market capitalization by the end of 1994.

In 1996 and 1997, a series of important investments and acquisitions were made by companies such as Sonae and Jernimo Martins, Portugal's leading retail distributors; Cimpor, a cement producer; and Portugal Telecom and Electricidade de Portugal, the last of which was privatized. The big banks were developing new overseas operations as well. The best indicator of Portugal's economic progress was Portugal's acceptance into the European Economic and Monetary Union in 1999.

During the 1990s and into the 2000s, the economy grew at rates well above EU averages. However, growth slowed in 2002 and 2003, and fell below the euroarea average for the first time in close to a decade. In 2002, the external current account deficit remained one of the largest (in relation to GDP) among industrialized countries. The unemployment rate also increased sharply. Nonetheless, an inflow of capital funds continued to finance infrastructure projects.

In 2001, Portugal became the first country to breach the eurozone's Stability and Growth pact budget deficit target of 3%, with a gap equal to 4.2% of GDP. Portugal's government met the 3% target in 2002 and 2003, but despite a hiring freeze and other measures, the country had a structural budget deficit in 2004 projected at 4.9%. Public spending was expected to equal 47.9% of GDP in 2004. The 2005 budget projected a structural deficit in excess of 3% and violated the 60% limit on public debt.

As Portugal's budget deficit remained high at 9.1% of GDP in 2011, the EU, European Central Bank, and IMF offered Portugal a bailout package including set benchmarks to reduce the deficit back down to 3% by 2013. The Portuguese government accepted the package and was obligated to implement strict austerity measures. Fundamental changes to its economic model were needed as a long-term strategy to avoid a similar economic situation in the future. Portugal made aims to modify its economic development model from one based on public consumption and public investment to one focused on exports and private investment.

40 SOCIAL DEVELOPMENT

A social insurance and social assistance program has been frequently updated since 1935. The program provides old-age, disability, sickness, and unemployment benefits, family allowances, and health and medical care. The system is funded by payroll contributions from employers and employees. The government subsidizes social pensions for those persons not employed. Retirement is set at age 65, when the social pension is then payable. Medical benefits are provided to all residents, and cash sickness and maternity benefits are provided to employees. Maternity benefits of 100% of earnings and benefits are paid for 120 days for all employed persons. Paternity and adoption benefits are also available. There is a need based family allowance, a special education allowance, and a funeral grant.

Women have full rights and protections under both the constitution and civil code. According to law, women must receive equal pay for equal work. In practice, however, a salary gap still exists between men and women. Spousal abuse and other violence against women are widespread problems and remain underreported. The judicial system is supportive when cases are brought forward. Sexual harassment in the workplace is considered a crime, but only if committed by a superior.

Immigrants from Portugal's former African colonies face social prejudice and discrimination. There were reports of right-wing groups carrying out racially motivated attacks against immigrants and other non-ethnic Portuguese. Human rights are generally respected in Portugal. Prison conditions are poor, but the government is engaging in dialogue with human rights organizations on this and other issues.

In May 2010, the president signed the law approved by parliament that legalizes same-sex marriage. The law has been extremely controversial, with numerous conservative opponents in a country where Roman Catholicism is the dominant faith. In a visit to the country a few days before the president's announcement, Pope Benedict cited both same-sex marriage and abortion as "insidious and dangerous threats to the common good" and called for citizens to oppose the law. While the president was concerned over the controversy, he noted that an official veto would only send the bill back to parliament, where continued debate would only deepen existing divisions. The law does not allow same-sex couples to adopt children. In ratifying the law, Portugal became the sixth country in Europe to legalize same-sex marriage.

41 HEALTH

According to the CIA, life expectancy in Portugal was 78.54 years in 2011. The country spent 10.6% of its GDP on healthcare, amounting to $2,410 per person. There were 38 physicians, 53 nurses and midwives, and 34 hospital beds per 10,000 inhabitants. The fertility rate was 1.5, while the infant mortality rate was 4.66 per 1,000 live births. In 2008, the maternal mortality rate, according to the World Bank, was 7 per 100,000 births. It was estimated that 95% of children were vaccinated against measles. The CIA calculated HIV/AIDS prevalence in Portugal to be about 0.6% in 2009.

The leading natural causes of death are circulatory disorders, cancer, and respiratory disorders. The cancer and heart disease rates in Portugal are well below the industrialized countries average.

42 HOUSING

According to the 2001 census, Portugal had about 5,054,922 dwelling units. However, about 65% of all families lived in dilapidated structures and nearly 8.5% lived in shacks. While the Government Social Housing Program made some progress in rehousing families into more adequate structures, there were not enough programs to help those households rise above the poverty level. Traditional Portuguese houses are made of brick walls and tile roofs.

⁴³EDUCATION

In 2008 the World Bank estimated that 99% of age-eligible children in Portugal were enrolled in primary school. Secondary enrollment for age-eligible children stood at 88%. The student-to-teacher ratio for primary school was 11:1 in 2009. Overall, the CIA estimated that Portugal had a literacy rate of 93.3%. Public expenditure on education represented 4.4% of GDP in 2008.

Basic education is compulsory for nine years comprised of three cycles. The first cycle is four years; the second is two years; and the third is three years. Secondary level education covers a three-year program; students choose between general secondary, professional, and specialized technical or vocational schools. The academic year runs from September to July.

Coimbra University, founded in 1290, is Portugal's oldest institution of higher learning, and the universities of Lisbon and Porto are two of the largest. There are also art schools, music schools, and a school of tropical medicine. The Portuguese Catholic University was instituted by decree of the Holy See. In 2009, 61% of the population (of relevant age to tertiary education) was enrolled in some type of higher education program. Of those enrolled in tertiary education, there were 100 male students for every 120 female students.

⁴⁴LIBRARIES AND MUSEUMS

The leading libraries of Portugal are the National Library, founded in 1796 (about 2.3 million volumes) and the Library of the Academy of Sciences (400,000) in Lisbon, the University Library in Coimbra (one million), and the Municipal Library in Porto (1.27 million). The Public Libraries Programme in Portugal was launched in 1987 with a goal of providing public library services in each of the country's 275 municipalities. By 1999, about 166 libraries had been established.

There are some 300 museums in Portugal. Most feature exhibits relating to Portuguese history. Lisbon has the National Museum of Ancient Art, the Museum of Decorative Arts, the Calouste Gulbenkian Museum, the Center for Modern Art, as well as the National Museum of Natural History. The Abbey of the Friars of St. Jerome in Belém and the Battle Abbey in Batalha contain some of the finest examples of Portuguese architecture. There are dozens of municipal ethnographic and historic museums, as well as many finely restored castles and manors. One of the most popular castles is the Palacio Pena in Sintra.

⁴⁵MEDIA

Portugal has a state-of-the-art telephone system that offers high-speed and broadband capabilities. Domestic service is provided by an integrated mix of coaxial cables, microwave relay, open-wire, and satellite-based ground stations. International service is provided by submarine cable and satellite ground stations. Communications with Azores is by tropospheric scatter radio. In 2009, the CIA reported that there were over 4 million telephone landlines in Portugal. In addition to landlines, mobile phone subscrip-

tions averaged 143 per 100 people. Internet users numbered 49 per 100 citizens.

The government broadcasting network, Radiodifusão Portuguesa, and Radio Renascenca, a religious network, operate AM and FM stations. CIA reports indicate that in 2009, there were 47 FM radio stations, 172 AM radio stations, and 2 shortwave radio stations. The state-owned television network, Radiotelevisão Portuguesa, offers color broadcasts on two channels.

The constitution of 1976 guaranteed freedom of the press. Prominent newspapers in 2010, with circulation numbers listed parenthetically, included *Correio da Manha* (85,000), *Publico* (75,000), and *Jornal de Noticias* (90,000), as well as 13 other major newspapers.

⁴⁶ORGANIZATIONS

The principal current organizations are syndicates, the majority of which are linked to the national trade union confederation, residents' commissions, workers' commissions, and popular assemblies. Many of these associations, particularly in rural areas, are involved in local community improvement projects as well as political and cultural activities. There are four chambers of commerce and three main industrial organizations, the oldest of which is the Industrial Association of Porto and dates back to 1849.

The Academy of Sciences Lisbon is primarily a scholarly and research organization. Several professional associations also promote research and public education in a variety of fields, particularly in medicine and healthcare. There are organizations for hobbyists, including the multinational Federation of European Philatelic Associations.

National youth organizations include the Association of Young Farmers of Portugal, Communist Youth of Portugal, International Friendship League of Portugal, Monarchist Youth of Portugal, the Scout Federation of Portugal, and YMCA/YWCA. There are several sports associations in the country, representing a variety of pastimes such as soccer, tae kwon do, badminton, tennis, track and field, and more. There is a national chapter of the Special Olympics.

The Kiwanis and Lion's Clubs also have active programs. Amnesty International, Habitat for Humanity, and the Red Cross have national chapters.

⁴⁷TOURISM, TRAVEL, AND RECREATION

Portugal's historic cities—Lisbon, Porto, Coimbra, and others—offer numerous museums, old churches, and castles. Most villages still celebrate market days with dances and other festivities. The Algarve in the south is a popular beach destination lined with resorts. There are more than 800 km (500 mi) of beaches. The Portuguese bullfight (differing from the Spanish variety in that the bulls are not killed) is a popular spectator sport. The season lasts from Easter Sunday to October. Football (soccer) is popular as both a participant and a spectator sport.

Tourism has become a major contributor of foreign exchange earnings and a stimulus to employment and investment in the hotel industry and related services. The *Tourism Factbook*, published by the UN World Tourism Organization, reported 12.3 million incoming tourists to Portugal in 2007 who spent a total of $12.3 billion. Of those incoming tourists, there were 10.7 million from Europe. There were 273,804 hotel beds available in Portugal, which had an occupancy rate of 42%. The estimated daily cost to visit Lisbon, the capital, was $298. The cost of visiting other cities averaged $210. A valid passport is required; visas are needed for stays of more than 90 days.

⁴⁸FAMOUS PERSONS

During Portugal's golden age, the 15th and 16th centuries, the small Portuguese nation built an overseas empire that stretched halfway around the globe. Prince Henry the Navigator (Henrique Navegador, 1394–1460) laid the foundations of the empire. Among the leaders in overseas exploration were Bartholomeu Dias (1450?–1500), the first European to round the Cape of Good Hope; Vasco da Gama (1469–1524), who reached India and founded Portuguese India in 1498; and Pedro Alvares Cabral (1460?–1526), who took possession of Brazil for Portugal in 1500. Ferdinand Magellan (Fernão de Magalhães, 1480?–1521) led a Spanish expedition, the survivors of which were the first to sail around the world, although Magellan himself was killed after reaching the Philippines. Afonso de Albuquerque (1453–1515) was foremost among the builders of Portugal's Far Eastern empire.

Famous literary figures of the golden age include the historians Diogo do Couto (1542–1616) and João de Barros (1496–1570); Portugal's greatest writer, Luis Vas de Camões (1524?–80), the author of *Os Lusiadas,* the Portuguese national epic, and of lyric and dramatic poetry; the dramatists Gil Vicente (1465?–1537?) and Francisco de Sá de Miranda (1482–1558); the poets Bernardim Ribeiro (1482?–1552) and Diogo Bernardes (1532?–96?); and the travel writer Fernão Mendes Pinto (1509–83). Portugal's leading painter was Nuno Gonçalves (fl. 1450–80).

Among the noted Portuguese of more recent times are Sebastião José de Carvalho e Mello, marquis de Pombal (1699–1782), the celebrated prime minister of King Joseph Emanuel (José Manuel, 1715–77); the novelists Camilo Castelo Branco, viscount of Correia-Botelho (1825–90), and José Maria Eça de Queiróz (1843–1900); the poets João Baptista da Silva Leitão, viscount of Almeida-Garrett (1799–1854), Antero Tarquinio de Quental (1842–91), João de Deus Nogueira Ramos (1830–96), Teófilo Braga (1843–1924), and Abilio Manuel Guerra Junqueiro (1850–1923); the satirist José Duarte Ramalho Ortigão (1836–1915); and the painter Domingos António de Sequeira (1768–1837). António Caetano de Abreu Freire Egas Moniz (1874–1955) won the Nobel Prize in physiology in 1949.

António de Oliveira Salazar (1889–1970), prime minister for more than 30 years, was Portugal's best-known modern leader. Gen. (later Marshal) António Sebastião Ribeiro de Spínola (1910–96) played a key role in the revolution of April 1974. Gen. António dos Santos Ramalho Eanes (b. 1935) became president in 1976 and was reelected in 1980. Other political leaders include Mário Alberto Nobre Lopes Soares (b. 1924), Francisco Sá Carneiro (1934–80), Jorge Fernando Branco de Sampaio (b. 1939), Aníbal António Cavaco Silva (b. 1939), António Manuel de Oliveira Guterres (b. 1949)—a former prime minister who became the United Nations High Commissioner for Refugees, and José Manuel Durão Barroso (b. 1956), a former prime minister who became president of the European Commission.

⁴⁹DEPENDENCIES

Between 1974 and 1976, all of Portugal's overseas possessions in Africa–including Angola, the Cape Verde Islands, Portuguese Guinea (now Guinea-Bissau), Mozambique, and São Tomé and Príncipe–became independent countries in accordance with the Armed Forces Movement's decolonization policy. After the Portuguese withdrew from East Timor, in the Indonesian archipelago, the former colony was invaded by Indonesian forces in 1975 and became a province of Indonesia in 1976; East Timor became an independent nation in 2002. Macau, on the south coast of China, was a "Chinese territory under Portuguese administration" from 1975–99.

⁵⁰BIBLIOGRAPHY

Anderson, James M. *The History of Portugal.* Westport, CT: Greenwood Press, 2000.

Annesley, Claire, ed. *A Political and Economic Dictionary of Western Europe.* Philadelphia: Routledge/Taylor and Francis, 2005.

Birmingham, David. *A Concise History of Portugal.* 2nd ed. Cambridge: Cambridge University Press, 2009.

Cunha, Carlos A, and Rhonda Cunha. *Culture and Customs of Portugal.* Santa Barbara, CA: Greenwood, 2010.

International Smoking Statistics: A Collection of Historical Data from 30 Economically Developed Countries. New York: Oxford University Press, 2002.

Ortiz Griffin, Julia. *Spain and Portugal.* New York: Facts On File, 2006.

Wessels, Wolfgang, Andreas Maurer, and Jürgan Mittag, eds. *Fifteen into One?: the European Union and Its Member States.* New York: Palgrave, 2003.

Wheeler, Douglas L. *Historical Dictionary of Portugal.* Lanham, MD: Scarecrow Press, 2002.

Wiarda, Howard J., and Margaret M. L. Mott. *Catholic Roots and Democratic Flowers: Political Systems in Spain and Portugal.* Westport, CT: Praeger, 2001.

ROMANIA

Romania

CAPITAL: Bucharest (Bucuresti)

FLAG: The national flag, adopted in 1989, is a tricolor of blue, yellow, and red vertical stripes.

ANTHEM: *Deşteaptă-te, române! (Awaken, Romanian!).*

MONETARY UNIT: The Romanian new leu (RON) was introduced in 2005 and is a paper currency of 100 bani. There are coins of 1, 5, 10, and 50 bani, and notes of 1, 5, 10, 50, 100, 200, and 500 lei. RON1 = US$0.313 (US$1 = RON3.2) as of 2010. Romania was scheduled to adopt the euro in 2015.

WEIGHTS AND MEASURES: The metric system is the legal standard.

HOLIDAYS: New Year's Day, 1–2 January; Easter Sunday and Monday (April/May); Pentecost (May/June: 50th and 51stdays after the Orthodox Easter); International Labor Day, 1 May; Assumption, 15 August; Unification/National Day, 1 December; Christmas, 25–26 December.

TIME: 2 p.m. = noon GMT.

¹LOCATION, SIZE, AND EXTENT

Situated in Eastern Europe, north of the Balkan Peninsula, Romania has a total area of 238,391 sq km (92043 sq mi). Comparatively, Romania is slightly smaller than Oregon. The dimensions of the country are 789 km (490 mi) E–W and 475 km (295 mi) N–S. It is bounded on the N and NE by Ukraine and Moldova, on the E by the Black Sea, on the S by Bulgaria, on the SW by Serbia, and on the W by Hungary, with a total boundary length of 2,733 km (1,698 mi), of which 225 km (140 mi) is coastline. Romania's capital city, Bucharest, is located in the south-central part of the country.

²TOPOGRAPHY

The backbone of Romania is formed by the Carpathian Mountains, which swing southeastward and then westward through the country. The southern limb of this arc-shaped system is known as the Transylvanian Alps, whose compact, rugged peaks rise to 2,543 m (8,343 ft) in Mt. Moldoveanu, Romania's highest. The eastern Carpathians have an average elevation of 1,000 m (3,300 ft) and exceed 1,900 m (6,200 ft) only in the highest ranges.

On the eastern and southern fringes of the Carpathian arc are the low plateaus and plains of Walachia, extending to the Prut River (Moldovan border) in the east and to the Danube (Bulgarian border) in the south. On the inside of the Carpathian arc is the Transylvanian Basin, a hilly region dissected by the wide, deep valleys of the Mures and Somes rivers.

The Dobruja, located between the lower Danube and the Black Sea, is an eroded plateau with average elevations of 400 to 600 m (1,310–1,970 ft). Except for the low-lying, swampy Danube Delta in the north, the Black Sea coast of the Dobruja is steep, facing the sea with almost vertical cliffs.

Romania is susceptible to severe earthquakes. An earthquake that struck Romania on 4 March 1977 destroyed or severely damaged some 33,000 buildings and left more than 34,000 families homeless. The shock, measuring 7.2 on the open-ended Richter scale, was the most severe in Europe since a series of shocks in October-November 1940, also in Romania.

³CLIMATE

Romania's climate is of the moderate, humid continental type, exposed to predominant northerly cold winds in the winter and moderate westerly winds from the Atlantic in the summer. Average January temperatures range from -4°C to 0° C (25–32°F). During the summer, the highest temperatures are recorded in the Danube Valley (24°C/75°F). Temperatures decrease toward the high elevations in the northwest and toward the southeast, where the Black Sea exerts a moderating influence. Precipitation decreases from west to east and from the mountains to the plains, with an annual average of between 100 and 125 cm (about 40 and 50 in) in the mountains and about 38 cm (15 in) in the delta.

⁴FLORA AND FAUNA

The World Resources Institute estimates that there are 3,400 plant species in Romania. In addition, Romania is home to 101 mammal, 365 bird, 22 reptile, and 19 amphibian species. The calculation reflects the total number of distinct species residing in the country, not the number of endemic species.

Natural vegetation consists mainly of steppe-like grasslands in the Moldavian and Walachian lowlands, with tall, deep-rooted grasses in the more humid sections and short, shallow-rooted grass in the drier parts. The Carpathian system is covered with forests, with deciduous trees at lower elevations and conifers at altitudes above 1,070–1,220 m (3,500–4,000 ft). Alpine meadows occupy the highest parts of the mountains.

Wild animals, including the black chamois, Carpathian deer, wolves, hares, marten, brown bear, lynx, boar, and fox, have sought refuge in the sparsely inhabited and forested Carpathians. Water birds flourish in the Danube Delta, and sturgeon abound in the waters of the lower Danube. Carp, bream, and pike populate the lakes; dace, barbel, and trout are found in rivers and streams.

⁵ENVIRONMENT

Rapid industrialization since World War II has caused widespread water and air pollution, particularly in Prahova County, an oil-refining region.

Air pollution is heaviest in the nation's cities, where industry produces hazardous levels of sulphur dioxide. In 1992, Romania had the world's 28th-highest level of industrial carbon dioxide emissions, which totaled 122.1 million metric tons, a per-capita level of 5.24 metric tons. However, by 2009, Romania ranked 43rd in the world as the total of carbon dioxide emissions had dropped to 80.52 million metric tons, a per-capita level of 3.66 metric tons.

Damage to the nation's soils from erosion and pollution has decreased agricultural production by 50% in some areas. Acid rain originating in Hungary is another environmental problem. Some water conservation programs were initiated in the mid-1980s, but the Environmental Protection Law of 1972 has not been strictly enforced.

Romania's forests and natural steppes have been encroached on by farmers. Two floods, two earthquakes, and radioactivity from the Chernobyl nuclear site have also contributed to the nation's environmental problems. Moreover, intensive exploitation of forests before, during, and immediately after World War II necessitated a reforestation program that, between 1950 and 1964, resulted in the replanting of 1,159,600 hectares (2,865,400 acres).

According to a 2011 report issued by the International Union for Conservation of Nature and Natural Resources (IUCN), threatened species included 7 types of mammals, 11 species of birds, 2 types of reptiles, 19 species of fish, 24 species of invertebrates, and 4 species of plant. The Romanian bullhead perch, Atlantic sturgeon, slender-billed curlew, and Mediterranean monk seals are among those listed as endangered.

The World Resources Institute reported that Romania had designated 515,100 hectares (1.27 million acres) of land for protection as of 2006. Water resources totaled 42.3 cu km (10.15 cu mi), while water usage was 6.5 cu km (1.56 cu mi) per year. Domestic water usage accounted for 9% of total usage, industrial for 34%, and agricultural for 57%. Per capita water usage totaled 299 cu m (10,559 cu ft) per year.

In 2005, a revised environmental protection law brought environmental policy in Romania in line with European Union (EU) standards. Since Romania's accession to the EU in 2007, €5.6 billion from European funds have been allocated to environmental projects for the period 2007–2013. Among the notable developments since 2007 have been a nation-wide urban-waste-management program and a program to support the development and use of renewable energy sources.

⁶POPULATION

The US Central Intelligence Agency (CIA) estimates the population of Romania in 2011 to be approximately 21,904,551, which placed it at number 54 in population among the 196 nations of the world. In 2011, approximately 14.8% of the population was over 65 years of age, with another 14.8% under 15 years of age. The median age in Romania was 38.7 years. There were 1.06 males for every female in the country. The population's annual rate of change was -0.252%. The projected population for the year 2025 was 20,600,000. Population density in Romania was calculated at 93 people per sq km (241 people per sq mi).

The United Nations (UN) estimated that 57% of the population lived in urban areas and that urban populations had an annual rate of change of 0.6%. The largest urban area was Bucharest, with a population of 1.9 million.

⁷MIGRATION

Estimates of Romania's net migration rate, carried out by the CIA in 2011, amounted to -0.26 migrants per 1,000 citizens. The total number of emigrants living abroad was 2.77 million, and the total number of immigrants living in Romania was 132,800. Population shifts numbering in the millions occurred as a result of the two world wars—because of territorial changes, deportation and extermination of Jews by the Nazis, flight before the Soviet military forces, deportations to the USSR, expulsion of the Volksdeutsche (ethnic Germans), and departures following the Communist takeover and before stringent security measures halted the flow. About 117,950 Jews emigrated to Israel between 1948 and 1951; another 90,000 were permitted to emigrate during 1958–64. Some 120,000 ethnic Germans left Romania between 1978–88, and some 40,000 ethnic Hungarians fled in 1987 alone. In 1990, 80,346 people left, 78% to Germany, 9% to Hungary. Some 44,160 Romanians emigrated in 1991 and 31,152 in 1992. In 1992, 103,787 Romanians were given asylum in Germany, but, in September of that year, Germany returned 43,000 refugees, over half of whom were Gypsies. According to *Migration News*, in 2005, the Romanian government discouraged illegal migration by preventing some 1–4 million Romanians from leaving to travel to EU countries on the grounds that they had insufficient funds or could not prove that they were merely visiting abroad. In addition, returning Romanians who overstay 90 days abroad have their passports confiscated.

During the Kosovo crisis in 1999, Romania offered to accept 6,000 Kosovar refugees from Macedonia under the UNHCR/IOM Humanitarian Evacuation Programme. It only actually hosted about 100; by the end of July 1999, all but one had returned to Kosovo.

From 1991–2003, some 10,000 Romanians per year were permanent emigrants. In 2011, the CIA estimated Romania's net migration rate at -0.26 migrant(s)/1,000 population, or a loss of approximately 5,700 persons.

⁸ETHNIC GROUPS

According to the 2002 census, Romanians constitute about 89.5% of the total population. Hungarians make up the largest minority group with about 6.6% of the total population. Roma account for about 2.5% of the population according to census figures; how-

LOCATION: 48°15′06″ to 43°37′07″ N; 20°15′44″ to 29°41′24″ E. BOUNDARY LENGTHS: Ukraine, 531 kilometers (329 miles); Moldova, 450 kilometers (279 miles); Black Sea coastline, 234 kilometers (145 miles); Bulgaria, 608 kilometers (377 miles); Serbia, 476 kilometers (295 miles); Hungary, 445 kilometers (277 miles). TERRITORIAL SEA LIMIT: 12 miles.

ever, international groups estimate that the actual number of Roma may include up to 10% of the population. Lesser minority groups include Ukrainians (0.3%), Germans (0.3%), and Russians (0.2%). Others include Turks, Serbs, Croats, Jews, Poles, Bulgarians, Czechs, Greeks, Armenians, Tatars, and Slovaks. As of 2010, government statistics indicated that at least 530,000 people identified themselves as Roma (gypsies), members of a widely dispersed European ethnic group with significant presence in Romania and Bulgaria. Non-government sources place the number of Roma in Romania higher, at more than 2 million. The Roma are severely disadvantaged, with most living together in rural villages in extreme poverty. Literacy rates are low, as a majority do not attend or never complete primary schooling. Life expectancy among this group is lower than the national average. The government has of-

ten been criticized for a failure to provide adequate educational and health programs for the Roma and for the lack of programs to integrate them into Romanian society. Since Romania joined the European Union in 2007, the Roma have become EU citizens and thus can move freely within the countries of the EU. As a result, many have moved in search of better opportunities in countries such as France, Spain, Italy, and the United Kingdom, but such migration has also caused trouble in these new countries. In August 2010, France began deporting Roma people, repatriating them mostly to Romania and Bulgaria. Those who were sent back to Romania went right back to the same situations of poverty that they had originally experienced.

Hungarians, Czechs, Slovaks, Roma, and other minorities were represented in both chambers of the parliament elected in 2008, although Roma representatives had fewer seats in relation to their proportion of the population.

⁹LANGUAGES

Romanian is the official language. As Romanian is a Romance language derived from the Latin spoken in the Eastern Roman Empire, Latin word elements make up 85–90% of the modern Romanian vocabulary. In the 2,000 years of its development, the language was also influenced by contacts with Slavonic, Albanian, Hungarian, Greek, and Turkish. Of the loanwords, Slavonic elements are the most numerous. Earliest Romanian written texts still extant date from the 16th century. In addition to letters of the English alphabet, Romanian has the letters ţ, î, â, ă, and ş. Hungarian and German are spoken by a large percentage of the inhabitants of Transylvania.

¹⁰RELIGIONS

According to the 2002 census, about 86.8% of the population were members of the Romanian Orthodox Church, one of the autocephalous Eastern Orthodox churches. Roman Catholics account for about 4.7% of the population. Officials from the Greek Catholic Church claim a membership of about about 3.6% of the population, though the government places membership counts at less than 1%. Protestant denominations make up about 7.5% of the population. Some of the Christian groups represented include Old Rite Russian Christian (Orthodox) Church, Protestant Reformed Church, Christian Evangelical Church, Romanian Evangelical Church, Evangelical Augustinian Church, Lutheran Evangelical Church, Unitarian Church of Romania, Baptist Church, Apostolic Church of God (Pentecostal Church), Seventh-day Adventist Church, Armenian Church, Jehovah's Witnesses, The Church of Jesus Christ of Latter-Day Saints (Mormons), the Methodist Church, and the Presbyterian Church. There are also communities of Jews, Muslims, Baha'is, Zen Buddhists, and members of the Unification Church, along with members of the Society for Krishna Consciousness.

Under Bulgarian influence, the Slavonic rite was maintained in the Romanian Church until the 17th century, when Romanian became the liturgical language. The Romanian Church enjoyed a large measure of autonomy in the Middle Ages and, after Romania achieved full independence from the Turks in 1878, was formally declared independent of the Patriarchate of Constantinople; it is now headed by its own patriarch. The Greek Catholic (Uniate) Church was formed in 1698 by the Transylvanian Orthodox, who acknowledged the jurisdiction of the Holy See. In October 1948, the new Communist regime compelled the Uniate Church to sever its ties with Rome and to merge with the Romanian Orthodox Church. The constitution provides for religious freedom, but the government retains a great deal of legal control over religious groups and activities. The Romanian Orthodox Church holds substantial influence in political and social venues. All religious groups must register with the government. Those that are granted official recognition are eligible for state support. As of 2010, there were 18 officially recognized religions: Romanian Orthodox Church, Orthodox Serb Bishopric of Timisoara, Roman Catholic Church, Greek Catholic Church, Old Rite Russian Christian (Orthodox) Church, Reformed (Protestant) Church, Christian Evangelical Church, Romanian Evangelical Church,

Evangelical Augustinian Church, Lutheran Evangelical Church, Unitarian Church, Baptist Church, Pentecostal Church, Seventh-day Adventist Church, Armenian Church, Judaism, Islam, and Jehovah's Witnesses. Proselytizing is not illegal, but minority religions engaging in such activities have reported restrictions and harassment by local government officials. Some tension does exist between religious groups, particularly between the Romanian Orthodox and minority groups. Christmas (December 25) and Orthodox Easter are observed as national holidays.

¹¹TRANSPORTATION

Romania is strategically located at the crossroads of Europe and Asia. As of 2008, Romania's railroad network included 3,965 km (2,464 mi) of electrified rail. Standard-gauge railways predominate, totaling 10,731 km (6,668 mi).

The CIA reports that Romania has a total of 81,713 km (50,774 mi) of roads, of which 66,632 km (41,403 mi) are paved. There are 219 vehicles per 1,000 people in the country. Railroads extend for 10,776 km (6,696 mi). There are 54 airports, which transported 3.27 million passengers in 2009, according to the World Bank.

There were 25 airports with paved runways in 2009. There were also two heliports. Otopeni International Airport, near Bucharest, was opened in 1970 and remains the nation's principal international air terminal. Baneasa Airport, also near Bucharest, handles local traffic. Other important airports include M. Kogalniceanu at Constanţa and Giarmata at Timişoara. Romanian Air Transport (Transporturile Aeriene Române—TAROM) and Romanian Air Lines (Liniile Aeriene Române—LAR) are the primary air carriers.

Romania has approximately 1,731 km (1,076 mi) of navigable waterways. Only the Danube and, to a lesser extent, the Prut rivers are suitable for inland navigation, which accounts for only about 1% of the total freight traffic. The main Danube ports include Galati, Brăila, and Giurgiu. At Giurgiu, on the main transportation line between Romania and Bulgaria, a road-and-rail bridge was completed in 1954, replacing the former Danube ferry to Ruse, Bulgaria. A major project, the Danube-Black Sea Canal, designed to bypass the shallow, silted arms of the Danube Delta, was started in 1949 but abandoned in 1953. It was revived in the early 1980s and opened in 1984. The canal is 64 km (40 mi) long and connects Cernavoda with Constanţa. The Romanian merchant fleet consisted of 17 vessels of 1,000 GRT or more in 2008, and was based in Constanţa, the nation's chief Black Sea port.

¹²HISTORY

Archaeological excavations show that the land now known as Romania has been inhabited for thousands of years. Agriculture was introduced in the 6th century BC. By the 3rd century BC, the Cucuteni civilization had produced polychrome pottery. The Dacians, of Thracian stock, had become a distinct people by the end of the 1st century BC. The kingdom of Dacia reached the highest stage of its development toward the end of the 1st century AD, in the reign of Decebalus (87–106), but after four years of war, Dacia fell to the Roman Emperor Trajan in AD 106. The withdrawal of the Romans in AD 271 left the Romanians a partly Christianized Dacian-Roman people, speaking Latin and living in towns and villages built on the Roman pattern. In the following centuries, as Dacia was overrun by successive waves of invaders, the early Romanians are believed to have sought refuge in the mountains or to have migrated south of the Danube River. There the Dacian-Romanians, assimilating Slavic influences, became known by the 7th century as Vlachs (Walachians). The Vlachs apparently remained independent of their neighbors but came under Mongol domination in the 13th century.

The establishment of the two principalities of Walachia and Moldavia in the late 13th and early 14th centuries opened one of the most important chapters in the history of Romania. Walachia came under Turkish suzerainty in 1476 and Moldavia in 1513; 13 years later, Transylvania, which had been under Hungarian control since 1003, also passed into Turkish hands. The tide of Ottoman domination began to ebb under Russian pressure in the second half of the 17th century; in 1699, under the Treaty of Karlowitz, Transylvania was taken by Austria (later Austria-Hungary), and, in 1812, Russia obtained Bessarabia, a section of Moldavia, from the Turks. The Congress of Paris in 1856, which ended the Crimean War, guaranteed the autonomy of the principalities of Walachia and Moldavia and forced Russia to return the southernmost part of Bessarabia to Moldavia. The two principalities formed a union in 1859, with Alexandru Ioan Cuza as its first prince, but he was replaced in 1866 by Carol I of the house of Hohenzollern-Sigmaringen under a new governing document that proclaimed Romania a constitutional monarchy. At the Congress of Berlin in 1878, Romania obtained full independence from Turkey but returned southern Bessarabia to Russia. Under the rule of Carol I, Romania developed into a modern political and economic unit.

As a result of the Balkan Wars in 1912–13, Romania gained southern Dobruja from Bulgaria. Carol I died in 1914 and was succeeded by Ferdinand I. In World War I, Romania joined the Allies and, as a result, acquired Bessarabia from Russia, Bukovina from Austria, and Transylvania from Hungary. The establishment of a greatly expanded Romania was confirmed in 1919–20 by the treaties of St. Germain, Trianon, and Neuilly. In the early postwar period, Ion Bratianu (son of a 19th-century premier) instituted agrarian and electoral reforms. Both Ferdinand and Bratianu died in 1927. A brief regency period under Iuliu Maniu, Peasant Party leader, was followed in 1930 by the return to Romania of Carol II, who, having earlier renounced his right of succession, now deposed his nine-year-old son, Michael (Mihai), and established a royal dictatorship.

As economic conditions deteriorated, Fascism and anti-Semitism became increasingly powerful, and Carol II sought to appease both Germany and the USSR, which, by August 1939, had concluded their nonaggression agreement. In 1940, Romania ceded Bessarabia and northern Bukovina to the USSR, northern Transylvania to Hungary, and southern Dobruja to Bulgaria. In the same year, Carol II abdicated in favor of his son Michael, and German troops entered the country. Romania joined the Axis in war against the Allies in 1941. As Soviet forces drove into Romania in 1944, a coup overthrew the wartime regime of Gen. Ion Antonescu on 23 August, and Romania joined the Allies against Germany. A Communist-led coalition government under Premier Petru Groza was set up in March 1945. King Michael was forced to abdicate on 30 December 1947, and the Romanian People's Republic was proclaimed. The Paris Peace Treaty of 1947 fixed Romania's frontiers as of 1 January 1941, with the exception of the border with Hungary, which was restored as of 1 January 1938, so northern Transylvania was once again part of the Romanian state.

The Communist constitution of 1948 was superseded in 1952 by a constitution patterned more directly on that of the USSR. In international affairs, Romania followed a distinctly pro-Soviet line, becoming a member of CMEA and the Warsaw Pact. Internally, the regime nationalized the economy and pursued a policy of industrialization and the collectivization of agriculture. During the 1960s, however, and especially after the emergence of Nicolae Ceausescu as Communist Party and national leader, Romania followed a more independent course, increasing its trade with Western nations and avoiding a definite stand in the Sino-Soviet dispute. In 1967, Romania was the only Communist country that did not break diplomatic relations with Israel following the Six-Day War. In 1968, Romania denounced the Soviet intervention in Czechoslovakia, and the USSR-Romania treaty of friendship and cooperation expired; a new accord was not signed until 1970. Further examples of Romania's independent foreign policy in the 1970s were the gradual improvement of relations with China, numerous bilateral agreements with the nations of Western Europe, and President Ceausescu's state visit in December 1973 to Washington, where he signed a joint declaration on economic, industrial, and technical cooperation with the United States. In the 1970s and early 1980s, Romania also became increasingly involved in the nonaligned movement. In 1982, Ceausescu called on the USSR to withdraw from Afghanistan.

In contrast to some other East European countries, there was relatively little political and cultural dissent in Romania during the first 30 years of Communist rule. In 1977, however, about 35,000 miners in the Jiu Valley, west of Bucharest, went on strike because of economic grievances. Afterwards, the Romanian Communist Party hierarchy was frequently reshuffled, ostensibly to improve economic management, with Ceausescu and several members of his family (particularly his wife, Elena) increasing their power.

In the early and mid-1980s, there were a number of work stoppages and strikes caused by food and energy shortages. In early 1987, Ceausescu indicated that Romania would not follow the reform trend initiated by Mikhail Gorbachev in the USSR.

The progress of *perestroika* (restructuring) in the Soviet Union, intensified by the wave of "velvet revolutions" that rolled across Eastern Europe in autumn 1989, only served to highlight the repressiveness of the Ceausescu regime, which had all but starved and frozen the country to death in its attempt to repay international indebtedness, which Ceausescu said in April 1989 had been $10 billion. The regime was also single-mindedly pushing ahead with the "systemization plan" begun in March 1988, which intended to force about half the country's peasants into urbanized "agro-industrial" complexes by bulldozing their villages.

The policy was especially offensive to the 2.5 million Hungarians in Romania's western regions, who understood the policy to be an attempt to further undercut their cultural autonomy. In mid-December 1989, abysmal economic conditions and ethnic tension led to spontaneous demonstrations in the western city of Timişoara. When the Securitate, Romania's secret police, attempted to deport Laszlo Toekes, a popular clergyman who had been a leading spokesperson for the local Hungarians, thousands of people took to the streets. Troops were summoned, and two days of rioting ensued, during which several thousand citizens were killed.

News of the riot and of the government's handling of it fanned further demonstrations around the country. Probably unwisely, President Ceausescu went ahead with a planned three-day visit to Iran. Upon his return, he convened a mass rally at which he attempted to portray his opponents as fascists. However, the rally turned into an antigovernment demonstration in which the army sided with the demonstrators.

Ceausescu and his wife attempted to flee the country but were apprehended, tried, and summarily executed on 25 December 1989. Several days of fighting raged as the Securitate and the army battled for power. A hastily assembled Council of National Salvation took power, repealing a number of Ceausescu's most hated policies and laws. The Council's president was Ion Iliescu, a former secretary of the Communist Party, who had been one of several signatories to a letter that accused Ceausescu of gross mismanagement of Romania's economy, which was made public in March 1989. The prime minister, Peter Roman, was also a prominent Communist.

Although the Council contained some non-Communists, the majority had been prominent officials in Ceausescu's regime, which prompted almost continuous public protests. Despite a continued government monopoly on media, political opposition groups managed to rally public support to demand the banning of the Communist Party and the widening of the government. In February 1990, Iliescu agreed, replacing the 145-member Council of National Salvation with a 241-member Council of National Unity, which included members of opposition parties, national minorities, and former political prisoners; it also contained the full membership of the former Council. Iliescu remained president.

Parliamentary elections were held in May 1990 against a background of continued civil unrest, especially in the Hungarian west. Although international observers considered the elections to have been generally fair, the National Salvation Front—now a political party—made ruthless use of its media monopoly to take about two-thirds of the parliamentary seats from a divided, disorganized, and inexperienced opposition. Iliescu was elected president with about 85% of the votes in a contest in which there had been more than 94% voter turnout.

The conviction that ex-Communists had "stolen" the election brought continued demonstrations in Bucharest and elsewhere. In April 1990, in a move that was criticized internationally, the Iliescu government trucked in miners from the northern part of the country, urging them to beat and disperse the demonstrators, ending what threatened to become a coup d'etat against Iliescu.

After the failure of those demonstrations, the opposition began to link up into parties, hoping to challenge Iliescu and his party in the next parliamentary elections, to be held in 1992. Popular discontent, however, continued to find more direct expression. Angry that the promises which had brought them to Bucharest in June had not been kept, the miners returned in September 1991, this time to link up with many of the opposition figures that they earlier had attacked to mount a mass attack on the government. Iliescu had no choice but to dismiss Prime Minister Roman, replacing him with Theodor Stolojan, an economist who managed to contain popular discontent until the general elections of September 1992, largely by delaying implementation of economic reforms. The parliamentary elections demonstrated a wide diffusion of political support. Iliescu's National Salvation Front won 28% of

the seats, making it the largest party, but the Democratic Convention, an anti-Communist opposition coalition with a strong monarchist wing, took 20%, while former Prime Minister Roman's National Salvation Front, now opposed to Iliescu, took 10%. The remaining 42% of the seats were divided among five other parties.

The popular vote for president showed that Iliescu still had support, although it had dropped to just above 60% of the electorate. The success of his opponent, Emil Constantinescu, a former rector of Bucharest University, demonstrated the continuing hostility to Iliescu and the other ex-Communists who had managed to retain power.

Iliescu's dismissal of Stolojan in November 1992 was widely seen as a recognition of that significant minority's opposition. Iliescu chose Nicolae Vacaroiu as prime minister, who had no earlier ties to the Ceausescu or Iliescu governments. However, the move was addressed as much to the International Monetary Fund (IMF) as the rest of the international financial community, which had emerged as Romania's chief source of support. Continued political instability and the fitful pace of privatization, combined with a strong nationalist bloc in the parliament that warned against "selling out" Romania to foreigners, all kept foreign investment quite low, a total of only about $785 million for all of 1990–94. As a consequence, Romania has had to rely upon loans from Western sources, especially the IMF, piling up foreign debt at the rate of about $1 billion a year. In return for this infusion of cash, the foreign donors have set stringent requirements of economic reform, which Romania is not finding easy to meet.

Romania's fitful progress toward democratization exacerbates the social pressures of its continued economic decline. Romanians began the post-Ceausescu period as among the poorest people in Europe, and their economy worsened for several years. Inflation for 1992 was 210% and more than 300% for 1993, while unemployment was almost 10%. Most significantly, production fell for the first couple of years after the anti-Communist revolution. Beginning in 1994, however, Romania began slowly turning its economy around. In 1996, it even applied for membership in the European Union (EU), although it knew that admission before 2000 was doubtful.

In November 1996, presidential and parliamentary elections were held as the economy, while still fairly grim, continued to improve in several sectors. Popular opposition to the ex-Communist Iliescu had grown strong leading up to the elections, mainly due to broken promises of economic security and widespread corruption that saw the enrichment of a small clique of ex-Communist insiders amid general economic hardships across the country. Iliescu also failed to deliver on many privatization schemes, angering the middle-class merchants. In the election's first round on 3 November, the Democratic Convention Alliance of Opposition Groups, led by Emil Constantinescu, Iliescu's 1990 opponent, earned the highest percentage of votes (30%) followed by Iliescu's Party of Social Democracy (PDSR) and the Social Democratic Union (22%), then former prime minister Peter Roman's center-left party (13%). In the presidential election, neither Iliescu nor Constantinescu received a majority, so a runoff was held on 17 November in which Constantinescu took 54% of the vote, becoming Romania's first true post-Communist leader. The West was thrilled with the victory, as Constantinescu was seen as significantly more pro-free market and pro-international investment than Iliescu. The new government immediately began imposing austerity measures, vowing to reduce the deficit significantly by the end of 1997. However, it was hobbled by disagreements among coalition members, and, in March 1998, the prime minister, Victor Ciorbea, was replaced by Radu Vasile. The government's position was weakened even further in January 1999 when it backed down in the face of demands by striking coal miners in order to avert potential violence. In December 1999, in order to save face and boost the popularity of the coalition for the upcoming elections, President Constantinescu forced Radu Vasile to resign and replaced him with Mugur Isarescu, the governor of the Romanian National Bank.

By the first half of 2000, the failure of the reformist government to bring about the promised economic recovery had led to widespread disenchantment. Inflation, unemployment, and debt remained serious problems, and Romania had also failed to achieve its major foreign policy objectives—admission to NATO and the EU. Public discontent had led to a resurgence in the popularity by Iliescu's ex-Communists, who won a decisive victory in the June local elections. At midyear, it was widely expected that the November general elections would bring a change in both the government and the presidency, and it was considered possible that Iliescu himself might stage a political comeback.

Presidential and parliamentary elections were held on 26 November 2000, which were won by Iliescu's PDSR. Iliescu became president after a second round of voting was held on 10 December, defeating extreme right-wing candidate Corneliu Vadim Tudor of the xenophobic Greater Romania Party (PRM). Tudor has been compared to France's Jean-Marie Le Pen, Russia's Vladimir Zhirinovsky, Austria's Jörg Haider, and the late Pym Fortuyn of the Netherlands.

Romania joined NATO in 2004. Although between 2000 and 2004 Romania registered some of the highest economic growth rates in Europe, endemic corruption and internal problems within the ruling PDSR led to a surprise victory by the Truth and Justice Alliance in the November 2004 elections. Traian Basescu, a former sea captain who served as the minister of transportation from 1996 to 2000, and as the mayor of Bucharest from 2000 to 2004, won the presidential elections. The Alliance formed by the National Liberal Party (PNL) and the Democratic Party (PD) maintained a fragile parliamentary majority with the backing of the UDMR, the Humanist Party (PUR), and several ethnic minority groups.

Internal problems within the Alliance, the kidnapping of three Romanian journalists in Iraq, and massive floods that covered most of Romania in the spring and summer of 2005 threatened to break the coalition apart. President Basescu and the new prime minister, Calin Popescu Tariceanu, agreed to put their differences aside in order to achieve one of the most important goals for Romania—the accession to the EU.

Romania and Bulgaria joined the European Union on 1 January 2007, raising membership to 27 nations.

In April 2007, parliament voted to suspend President Basescu on the grounds of abuse of office. Basescu decided against resigning. An impeachment referendum was held on 23 May 2007, and Basescu remained in office by popular vote. The ruling PNL was upset in the November 2008 elections, coming in third, behind the Democratic Liberal Party (PDL), which had 37% of the vote, and the PSD, which had 34%. A majority PDL-PSD coalition was formed in December 2008, and Emil Boc was named prime minister. This partnership was short-lived. These international partnerships have not ensured greater stability within the government itself. In October 2009, the PSD resigned from the coalition government after the dismissal of the PSD interior minister Dan Nica, who was fired by Boc after making public comments about the potential for fraud in upcoming presidential elections. The PDL regarded the comments as accusations of imminent fraud, suggesting that the PDL was already planning to compromise the elections. Ten days after the mass resignation, parliament issued a vote of no confidence against the now-minority government, and Boc was ousted as prime minister. President Basescu nominated Lucian Croitoru, a monetary policy advisor linked to the PDL, for the post of prime minister, but opposition parties rejected the nomination, calling for the appointment of Klaus Johannis of the Democratic Forum of Germans in Romania as prime minister instead. Amidst this controversy, a caretaker government was established, pending presidential elections scheduled for November. However, in the first round of those elections, none of the twelve candidates received an absolute majority. Basescu reportedly received about one third of the votes, followed by Mircea Geoana of the Social Democrat party. In the December 2009 run-off, Basescu was reelected with only 50.3% of the vote, defeating Mircea Geoana, who came in with 49.7%.

In 2011, the European Parliament approved Romania and Bulgaria's entry into the Schengen Area, a no-internal-border-control area comprised of 22 other members of the the European Union, as well as Iceland, Norway, and Switzerland. Although the two countries have fulfilled all technical entry criteria, their expected accession in 2012 was blocked indefinitely by the European Council of Ministers of home affairs on account of their alleged failure to demonstrate sufficient capacity to ensure the security of their external borders. Romania and Bulgaria's Schengen membership has faced political opposition by key EU member states such as France, Germany, and the Netherlands on account of persistent allegations of pervasive corruption and inconsistency in enforcing the rule of law. In 2011, under pressure from the European Union, Romania launched a series of high-profile investigations into magistrates and other public officials.

13 GOVERNMENT

Romania has been a republic since 1947.

The Council for National Unity enacted a new constitution for Romania in November 1991, and the document carried many of the hallmarks of Soviet-era constitutions, granting rights in some articles and revoking them in others. In October 2003, the constitution was revised, following a national referendum. The legal system is generally based on Romania's old 1923 constitution and on the constitution of France's Fifth Republic.

The present arrangement has a directly elected president who serves for a maximum of two five-year terms; he is head of state. The president, in consultation with the parliament, names the prime minister. The prime minister, in turn, chooses his governing body, which has to be approved by the parliament. The government, together with the president, represents the executive power in the country.

As of 2011, the legislature was made up of two houses: the Senate, with 137 seats (one senator for 160,000 inhabitants), and the

Chamber of Deputies, with 334 seats (approximately one deputy for 65,000 inhabitants). Members of both bodies were directly elected on a proportional representation basis to serve four-year terms. A referendum on modifying the bicameral parliament to a unicameral one and on the reduction of the number of representatives to a maximum of 300 seats was held concurrently with the first round of the November 2009 presidential election. Both propositions were approved with 77.78% and 88.84%, respectively, of the votes cast. In October 2011, the Romanian government adopted revisions to the country's electoral law that were to take effect at the time of the next parliamentary election in November 2012.

14 POLITICAL PARTIES

After the coup against Ceausescu, some 80 political parties appeared; some were new, while others, like the Liberals and the Peasant Party, revived prewar parties that the Communists had outlawed. The dominant party in the 1990 elections, however, proved to be the National Salvation Front (NSF), which took two-thirds of the seats in the National Assembly.

By 1992, the NSF had split over the issue of whether or not to support Iliescu. The main party renamed itself the Party of Social Democracy in Romania (PDSR), while a pro-Iliescu wing became the Democratic National Salvation Front, and an anti-Iliescu wing, headed by ex-Prime Minister Roman, became the Front for National Salvation (FSN). The PDSR took 28% of the vote and the FSN, 10%.

The second-largest party in the 1992 elections was a coalition called the Democratic Convention of Romania (DCR), which incorporated such parties as the National Peasant Party Christian Democratic (PNTCD), the Movement of Civic Alliance, the Party of Civic Alliance, Liberal Party '93, and the Social Democratic Party. There are also small ultra-nationalist parties, the Party of Romanian National Unity and the Greater Romania Party (PRM), and the Communists have been reborn as the Socialist Labor Party. Despite superficial political differences, all three parties are anti-Hungarian, anti-Gypsy, and anti-Semitic, as well as anti-democratic.

In the parliamentary elections held on 3 November 1996, the PDSR lost its majority standing, and the DCR won a strong majority. The DCR became the ruling party with 53 seats in the Senate and 122 in the Chamber of Deputies; the PSDR held 41 and 91, respectively; the Social Democratic Union, 23 and 53; Hungarian Democratic Union, 8 and 19; Greater Romania Party, 8 and 19; and National Union Party, 7 and 18. Victor Ciorbea, a trade union leader and former mayor of Bucharest, became prime minister, and Emil Constantinescu became president.

Parliamentary and presidential elections were held on 26 November 2000, which were won by the PDSR. The PDSR merged with the Romanian Social Democratic Party to form the Social Democratic Party (PSD), and, with the Humanist Party of Romania, formed the Democratic Social Pole of Romania. This coalition won 155 of 346 seats in the Chamber of Deputies and 65 of 143 seats in the Senate. The PRM took 84 seats in the Chamber of Deputies and 37 in the Senate; the Democratic Party took 31 and 13 seats, respectively; the National Liberal Party won 30 and 13; the Hungarian Democratic Alliance (UDMR) won 27 and 12; and

19 ethnic parties were represented with 1 seat each in the Chamber of Deputies.

On 28 November 2004, the Truth and Justice Alliance, comprised of the National Liberal Party (PNL) and the Democratic Party (PD), scored a surprise victory over the ruling PSD. The Alliance formed a fragile coalition with UDMR, the Humanist Party (which recently changed its name to the Conservative Party—PC), and several ethnic minorities. The coalition won 169 of 332 seats in the Chamber of Deputies and 71 of 137 seats in the Senate, while PSD won 110 and 45 respectively, and PRM 32 and 19. At that time there were also 19 deputies with no political affiliation.

The ruling PNL was upset in the November 2008 elections, coming in third, behind Democratic Liberal Party (PDL) at 37% and the PSD-PC (an alliance of PSD and the Conservative Party) at 34% of the vote. A majority PDL-PSD coalition was formed in December 2008, and Emil Broc was named prime minister. The PSD-PC alliance gained 49 seats in the Senate and 114 in the Chamber of Deputies. The PDL took 51 seats in the Senate and 115 in the Chamber. The PNL with, only about 18% of the votes in both houses, retained 28 seats in the Senate and 65 seats in the Chamber. UDMR held 9 and 22 seats in the Senate and Chamber respectively. Ethnic minorities held 18 seats in the Chamber.

15 LOCAL GOVERNMENT

Romania is divided into 41 counties (*judete*), as well as the municipality of Bucharest, which has separate status. Counties are administered by directly elected municipal councils. Below the counties, there are three other categories of local authority: approximately 2,800 communes (with populations up to 5,000), 280 *orase* (towns with populations of approximately 5,000–20,000) and 86 municipalities. In the Ceausescu era, the counties were administered by appointees of the central government, whose responsibility was solely to Bucharest. The Iliescu government attempted to reshape local government, but most sources agree that the result was to further remove authority from the countryside. Much of Romania is deeply rural, with almost no contact between localities or with the central government.

While more than 40% of the Romanian population lives in the rural countryside, attending to a highly fragmented agricultural system, almost 40% of the national wealth is concentrated in Bucharest. As a result, prominent figures from all of Romania's main provinces have pleaded for a more decentralized government system. To date, all 41 counties are led by a prefect who is appointed by the government. The prefects respond directly to the Ministry of Public Administration.

16 JUDICIAL SYSTEM

Under the provisions of the 2004 reorganizaton of the judiciary, the highest judicial authority in Romania rests with the Supreme Court (High Court of Justice and Cassation). Its 11 members are appointed for three-year terms by the president in consultation with the Superior Council of Magistrates, which is comprised of the minister of justice, the prosecutor general, two civil society representatives appointed by the Senate, and 14 judges and prosecutors elected by their peers.

Below the supreme court in the judicial hierarchy are 15 courts of appeal, 42 county-level tribunals (including Bucharest), and 188 first-instance courts (of which only 177 are functioning). In addition, there is a three-tier military court hierarchy comprised of tribunals, the Bucharest Territorial Tribunal, and the Bucharest Military Court of Appeal.

A separate Constitutional Court oversees elections and rules on the constitutionality of laws, treaties, ordinances, and the internal rules of parliament. Its 9 members serve 9-year terms, with three members each appointed by the prresident, the Senate, and the Chamber of Deputies.

Under the law, the courts are independent of the executive branch.

The death penalty was abolished in 1989 and prohibited by the 1991 constitution.

As in other EU member countries, the European Court of Justice considers the law of the EU superior to Romania's national laws in areas explicitly legislated by the EU.

17 ARMED FORCES

The Romanian armed forces have been reorganized in the wake of the revolution of 1989–90, which destroyed the Communist armed forces and security establishment.

Formerly a member of the Warsaw Pact, Romania joined NATO in 2004. As part of a wide-reaching plan for the reorganization of the army, Romania suspended compulsory military service in October 2006.

Romania participated in Operation Enduring Freedom in Afghanistan and was part of the multi-national forces in Iraq (2003–2009). Romanian troops served in EU, NATO, OSCE, and UN peacekeeping or military missions in 10 other countries or regions.

The International Institute for Strategic Studies reports that armed forces in Romania totaled 71,745 members in 2011. The force is comprised of 42,500 from the army, 7,345 from the navy, 8,400 from the air force, and 13,500 members of joint forces. Armed forces represent 1.6% of the labor force in Romania. Defense spending totaled $4.8 billion and accounted for 1.9% of gross domestic product (GDP).

18 INTERNATIONAL COOPERATION

Romania, which became a member of the UN on 14 December 1955, participates in ECE and several non-regional specialized agencies, such as the World Bank, the ILO, the FAO, UNESCO, UNIDO, and the WHO. Romania served on the UN Security Council from 2004–05. The Romanian government has supported UN missions and operations in Kosovo (est. 1999), Ethiopia and Eritrea (est. 2000), Liberia (est. 2003), Burundi (est. 2004), and Côte d'Ivoire (est. 2004), among others.

Romania is also a member of the WTO, G-9, G-77, the Council of Europe, the Black Sea Economic Cooperation Zone, the Euro-Atlantic Partnership Council, the European Bank for Reconstruction and Development, and the OSCE. Romania became a member of NATO in 2004. The country has observer status in the OAS and the Latin American Integration Association (LAIA). Romania joined the European Union in 2007.

Romania is part of the Australia Group, the Zangger Committee, the Organization for the Prohibition of Chemical Weapons, and the Nuclear Suppliers Group (London Group). In environmental cooperation, Romania is part of the Antarctic Treaty, the Basel Convention, Conventions on Biological Diversity and Air Pollution, Ramsar, CITES, the Kyoto Protocol, the Montréal Protocol, MARPOL, the Nuclear Test Ban Treaty, and the UN Conventions on the Law of the Sea, Climate Change, and Desertification.

The relationship between Romania and neighboring Moldova has been strained, primarily as a result of the political and economic instability within Moldova. Because many Moldovans have ethnic ties to Romania, comparisons between the two countries are often brought into play. Many Moldovans believe that democracy and participation in the European Union have been key factors in the prosperity of Romania, where the average worker earns five times more than the average Moldovan. This has sparked political unrest, particularly among younger Moldovans. When the Communist Party gained a majority in the Moldovan parliamentary elections of April 2009, violent protests took place in Chisnau, with some protestors carrying Romanian flags and calling for reunification with Romania. Both the Moldovan government and its Russian ally accused the Romanian government of instigating the riots and attempting to inspire a coup, allegations that Romania promptly denied. The Romanian ambassador was expelled from Moldova, and the Moldovan government announced new visa restrictions on Romanians crossing into Moldova. In response, the Romanian government announced a streamlined citizenship application process that would allow nearly one million Moldovans with Romanian ancestry to become Romanian citizens in about six months. Nearly one week after the announcement, the Romanian government announced the receipt of about 650,000 applications. The Moldovan government condemned the action as a threat to the sovereignty and integrity of the country. Officials from the European Union criticized the actions of both governments.

19 ECONOMY

Once one of the poorest nations in the region, Romania has slowly developed a more stable economy with modest annual growth. Since the overthrow of Romania's long-standing oppressive communist regime, the government has initiated programs of free market reform, liberalization of the economy, and privatization of industry. Major industries include electric machinery and equipment, textiles and shoes, mining, timber, and petroleum refining. Romania's natural resources are abundant, including a plethora of energy sources and fertile farmland.

The basic organization of economic management in Romania was once highly centralized, like its original Soviet model, with few of the modifications introduced elsewhere in Eastern Europe. During the late 1970s and in the 1980s, the continued emphasis on industrial expansion and consequent neglect of agriculture led to food shortages and rationing. Romania's economic problems in the 1980s were exacerbated by the government's program to reduce foreign debt. The debt was indeed reduced, from $10.5 billion in 1981 to $6.6 billion at the end of 1987 but at the cost of reduced industrial development.

The transition to a market economy also proved extremely painful. By 1992, GDP had fallen by 30%, industrial production had fallen 47%, and inflation had reached 300%. Growth returned weakly in 1993, with GDP increasing 1%, but then gained some momentum, rising 3.9% in 1994, 6.9% in 1995, and 4% in 1996. In 1997, the government entered into an arrangement with the IMF for a standby agreement (SBA) supported by a credit line of

$430 million. The agreement was suspended, however, because of the government's slowness to implement agricultural reform. The effects of the Russian financial crisis in 1998, which came to a head in August, spread quickly to Romania, helping to produce a further contraction of 7.3% of GDP for the year. In August 1999, the government entered into another SBA with the IMF. In October 2001, the government entered into its third SBA arrangement with the IMF, which was successfully completed in October 2003. In July 2004, a standby agreement was signed with the IMF. The agreement is to be completed in two years and is aimed at decreasing the account deficit and the inflation rate through a mix of monetary policies and structural reforms.

In 2007, Romania joined the European Union, and the nation counts fellow member states as its most important trading partners, the largest being Germany and Italy. A reliance on foreign investment and the export market resulted in recession beginning in late 2008 with the onset of the global financial crisis. In 2008, the real GDP growth rate was 7.1%, which was the highest growth rate in the European Union. With a decline in demand for exports and job losses resulting from decreased production, the economy is expected to decline by 2.8% in 2009.

In March 2009, the IMF and other lenders agreed to a loan package of up to $27 billion. In June 2010, as Romania continued to struggle with budget deficits and a sluggish global economy, Prime Minister Boc proposed austerity measures that would cut public-sector job salaries by 25% and public pensions by 15%. Of the roughly 22 million people in Romania, 1.36 million are public-sector employees. The government indicated that, in addition to the salary and pension cuts, 125,000 of those jobs would need to be slashed in 2011 to ease pressure on Romania's budget.

In November 2010, a new wave of international bailout funds was released to the Romanian government. Rocky politics and constantly changing tax policies in Romania have made it difficult to incorporate previous funds. However, recent agreements made with the IMF and the European Commission show some hope for Romania's recession-hit economy.

The GDP rate of change in Romania, as of 2010, was -1.3%. Inflation stood at 6%, and unemployment was reported at 8.2%.

In April 2011, Romania's industrial production increased during the first quarter of the year. By February, industrial output had advanced by 12.7%. These numbers showed promise for the country that had been suffering due to the global economic crisis.

20 INCOME

The CIA estimated that. in 2010, the GDP of Romania was $254.2 billion. The CIA defines GDP as the value of all final goods and services produced within a nation in a given year and computed on the basis of purchasing power parity (PPP) rather than value as measured on the basis of the rate of the exchange based on current dollars. The per capita GDP was estimated at $11,600. The annual growth rate of GDP was -1.3%. The average inflation rate was 6%. It was estimated that agriculture accounted for 12.8% of GDP, industry 36%, and services 51.2%.

According to the World Bank, remittances from citizens living abroad totaled $4.9 billion in 2009, or about $225 per capita and accounted for approximately 1.9% of GDP.

The World Bank reports that, in 2009, household consumption in Romania totaled $102.1 billion or about $4,663 per capita, measured in current US dollars rather than PPP. Household consumption includes expenditures of individuals, households, and nongovernmental organizations on goods and services, excluding the purchases of dwellings. It was estimated that household consumption was growing at an average annual rate of 2.6%.

As of 2011, the most recent study by the World Bank reported that actual individual consumption in Romania was 78.5% of GDP and accounted for 0.42% of world consumption. By comparison, the United States accounted for 25.44% of world individual consumption. The World Bank also estimated that 23.1% of Romania's GDP was spent on food and beverages, 19% on housing and household furnishings, 2.4% on clothes, 6.5% on health, 11.6% on transportation, 1.4% on communications, 3.4% on recreation, 3.5% on restaurants and hotels, and 2.9% on miscellaneous goods and services and purchases from abroad.

It was estimated that, in 2005, about 25% of the population subsisted on an income below the poverty line established by Romania's government.

21 LABOR

As of 2010, Romania had a total labor force of 9.345 million people. Within that labor force, CIA estimates in 2006 noted that 30% were employed in agriculture, 20.2% in industry, and 49.8% in the service sector.

The Romanian economy is in the process of privatization. Private firms accounted for 64.5% of the workforce in 2001. The UN Economic Commission for Europe reports that in 2008 this number had risen to 81.6%.

Labor legislation adopted in 1991 guarantees the right of private sector employees to associate freely, organize and join unions, bargain collectively, and carry out strikes. In 2005, there were about 18 nationwide trade confederations, plus smaller independent unions. Unions are permitted to strike, but only after all attempts at arbitration have failed and a 48-hour advance notice is given to employers. However there have been complaints that the courts are biased towards ruling strikes illegal. Also, while the law protects the right to bargain collectively, contracts arising from collective bargaining have not been consistently enforced. However, at the branch and unit level, collective bargaining contracts covered around 40% of Romania's workforce in 2011.

Most employees work a five-day, 40-hour week with overtime pay rates for weekends, holidays and work over 40 hours. While the minimum wage has increased from $105 per month in 2005 to $220 in 2011, and while the government also subsidizes necessities such as housing and healthcare, this does not provide a decent standard of living for a worker and family. Children under the age of 16 years are not permitted to work, although 15-year-olds may be employed with parental consent. Minors are also banned from working under hazardous conditions. However, child labor remains a problem in Romania. Neither the government nor industry has the resources to enforce safety and health standards in the workplace.

22 AGRICULTURE

Although, under Communism, the emphasis had been on industrialization, Romania is still largely an agricultural country. Grain growing has been the traditional agricultural pursuit, but the acreage has been reduced since World War II, and more area has been assigned to industrial and fodder crops.

The government began forming collective farms in 1949 and had largely completed the collectivization process by 1962. By 1985, of a total of 15,020,178 hectares (37,115,460 acres) of agricultural land, 29.7% was in state farms, with another 60.8% in large cooperative farms. The socialized sector consisted of 3,745 collectives, 419 state farms, and 573 farming mechanization units by 1985. The Land Reform of 1991 returned 80% of agricultural land to private ownership. Of the 14.8 million acres of agricultural land in 1996, some 2.6 million private producers farmed 44.6%; 20,400 associations of private producers farmed 25%; 1,171 state farms operated 12.8%; and public land accounted for the remaining 17.6%. Average farm size for private producers that year was 2.5 hectares (6.2 acres); for associations, 180 hectares (445 acres); and for state farms, 1,620 hectares (4,003 acres). In 2003, Romania had 4,484,890 agricultural holdings, the highest in the European Union.

By 2007, the number of agricultural holdings had dropped to 3,931,350, a 7.6% decrease compared to 2005 and a 12.5% decrease compared to 2003. Eurostat reports that, in 2007, 64% of Romanian farms produced mainly for own consumption (agricultural land farmed by its owners). Another telling statistic is that 71% of the sole holders of farmland were 55 years old or older.

The country's major crops include wheat, corn, barley, sugar beets, sunflower seed, potatoes, and grapes. Yet the area used for cereals decreased by 18% between 2005 and 2007: common wheat and spelt decreased by 22%, barley by 23% and maize by 12%. In the same time, fallow land increased by 20%.

23 ANIMAL HUSBANDRY

Animal production in Romania has developed somewhat more rapidly than crop production. The 1970 value of total livestock production, including the increase in herds and flocks as well as livestock products, was slightly more than double the level of 1938, and the 1974 value was 34% above that of 1970. In view of the initially low level of Romanian livestock production, development has been slow, however. The major reasons for the inadequate increases had been lack of economic incentives, insufficient fodder, and inadequate shelter. Since the overthrow of the Ceausescu regime in 1989, privatization of much of the grazing land has begun. In order to improve livestock raising, the government continues to stress agricultural modernization. Livestock productivity during 2002–04 was 10.8% higher than during 1999–2001.

After several years of livestock reduction, the hog and poultry inventories rose at the end of 1995, due to increases in the private sector. Sheep numbers have dropped because of exports. State farms were also forced to cut their flocks due to reduced grazing land and financial difficulties.

Production of livestock food products for 2005 included 344,000 tons of sheep's milk, 37,900 tons of cheese, and 7,154 tons of butter. In 2004, exports of meat amounted to $37.2 million.

The UN Food and Agriculture Organization (FAO) reported that Romania dedicated 4.5 million hectares (11 million acres) to permanent pasture or meadow in 2009. During that year, the country tended 84.4 million chickens, 2.7 million head of cattle, 6.2 million pigs, and 9.8 million sheep and goats. The production from these animals amounted to 165,869 tons of beef and veal, 690,306 tons of pork, 418,058 tons of poultry, 275,116 tons of eggs, and 5.71 million tons of milk. Romania also produced 20,944 tons of cattle hide and 18,038 tons of raw wool.

24 FISHING

Romania lost an important fishing region and nearly all its caviar-producing lakes with the cession of Bessarabia to the USSR in 1940. However, the Black Sea, the Danube and its floodlands, as well as other rivers, lakes, and ponds, are favorable to the development of the fishing industry, which expanded rapidly during the early 1970s. About 90% of the fish comes from the Danube floodlands and delta and 10% from the Black Sea.

Romania had 33 decked commercial fishing boats in 2008. The annual capture totaled 5,410 tons, according to the UN FAO. The export value of seafood totaled $6.17 million.

25 FORESTRY

Approximately 29% of Romania is covered by forest. The UN FAO estimated the 2009 roundwood production at 8.59 million cu m (303.3 million cu ft). The value of all forest products, including roundwood, totaled $1 billion.

In 2004, forests covered 6.5 million hectares (16 million acres), representing about 27% of the total area of Romania, with 68% of forests state-owned. The forests are found mainly in the Carpathian Mountains and in Transylvania and are 70% hardwood (mostly beech and oak) and 30% softwood (mainly spruce and pine). Commercial forests account for 98% of the total forest area. About 40% of Romania's forests are damaged, and up to 25% are defoliated. Insects, air pollution, and fires are the main causes of tree damage. The amount of timber permitted to be cut is approved annually by the Romanian parliament, and was set at 18 million cu m (643 million cu ft) for 2005 (63% from state-owned forests). Roundwood production in 2004 was estimated at 17,500,000 cu m (618 million cu ft). Domestic lumber production is estimated at 5 million cu m (175 million cu ft) with more than half coming from small factories. Romania's furniture industry consists of about 2,400 furniture producers employing about 100,000 people, with exports of around €850 million in 2004. Forestry accounts for 3.5% of GDP and 9% of exports.

Between 1976 and 1985, 580,000 hectares (1,433,200 acres) were reforested. After the collapse of the Communist regime, domestic demand, exports, and reforestation plummeted. During 1990–2000, some 15,000 hectares (37,000 acres) were annually reforested. Since trade liberalization in 1997, Romania's wood industry has expanded; there are nearly 7,000 small- and medium-sized firms.

26 MINING

Romania's production of metals, industrial minerals, and mineral fuels was mainly of regional importance. The country produces aluminum, copper, lead, zinc, manganese, steel and ferroalloys.

Mining and quarrying employed about 73,000 people in 2009, including 40,000 in the manufacture of base metals.

Mined copper production (gross weight) totaled 1,000 metric tons in 2009, down from 15,000 metric tons in 2005. Bismuth (metal) output in 2009 was estimated at 40 metric tons, while gold mine output (metal content) in that year came to 400 kg. Silver mine production (metal content) totaled 18 metric tons in 2009. Among industrial minerals in 2009, Romania produced barite, bentonite, diatomite, feldspar, fluorspar, graphite, gypsum (600,000 tons), kaolin, lime (1.6 million tons), nitrogen (content of ammonia), pyrites, salt, sand and gravel, caustic soda, soda ash, sulfur, and talc.

Metals and metalworking in the region were well-documented by Roman times when Romania and Bulgaria, respectively known as Dacia and Thrace, were important sources of base and precious metals. Gold and nonferrous metals mined in the region remained attractive investment opportunities.

In October 2011, Romania launched the sale of its biggest copper mine, Copru Min SA Abrud, which sits on 60% of the country's copper reserves, or about 900,000 tonnes.

27 ENERGY AND POWER

The World Bank reported in 2008 that Romania produced 65 billion kWh of electricity and consumed 53.5 billion kWh, or 2,443 kWh per capita. Roughly 79% of energy came from fossil fuels, while 11% came from alternative fuels. Per capita oil consumption was 1,830 kg. Oil production totaled 88,139 barrels of oil a day.

Although Romania dominates the downstream petroleum industry in Southeastern Europe and is the largest producer of oil in Central and Eastern Europe, it is a net importer of oil.

As of May 2011, Romania's oil reserves were 600 million barrels, down from an estimated 956 million barrels in January 2005. Still, Romania holds the third-largest oil reserves in Europe after the UK and Denmark. Romania's oil production averaged an estimated 114,000 barrels per day in 2004, yet domestic demand for that year averaged an estimated 277,000 barrels per day, making the country a net importer, that year averaging 163,000 barrels per day. In 2009, the estimated daily oil production was 112,000 barrels per day, and the domestic demand exceeded production by 88,000 barrels per day.

Romania is also the region's largest producer of refined petroleum products. Of the 11 refineries located in Southeastern Europe, 10 are located in Romania.

In 2009, Romania had proven reserves of 2 trillion cu ft of natural gas, down from an estimated 3.6 trillion cu ft in 2005. Production of natural gas in 2010 was 374 billion cu ft, down from 470 billion cu ft in 2002, and demand outstripped production by 81 billion cu ft.

In 2009, Romania produced 33.7 million short tons of coal and imported an additional 2.4 million short tons to meet domestic demand. Romania's coal production consists of low-quality brown coal (lignite), while imports consist of anthracite for use in thermal power plants.

Romania's electric power is mostly generated by conventional thermal fuel plants, followed by hydroelectric and a single nuclear power plant. In 2008, Romania generated 62 billion Kilowatthours of electricity, and consumed 50.6 billion Kilowatthours.

Romania's Cernavoda nuclear plant has two operating reactors. The first one has been in operation since 1996 and the second one since 2007.

28 INDUSTRY

Industrial development received about half of all investment during the 1951–80 period. As officially measured, the average annual growth rate in gross industrial production between 1950 and 1980 was 12.3%, one of the highest in Eastern Europe. In 1993, however, industrial production was at only 47% of the 1989 level. The next year, industrial production increased by 3.3%. In 1995, it increased by 9.4% in absolute volume and was 13% higher than the 1992 output. In 1996, industrial production increased by 9.9% with the largest increases coming in the processing industry (12.5%) and machine and electronics (27.3%). After the Russian collapse of 1997, however, the industrial growth rate for 1998 was -17%. Industrial production picked up after Romania began to recover from its recession in 2000, and, in 2001, the industrial growth rate was 6.5%.

The industrial sector is in need of modernization and restructuring. Key industries in 2004 included textiles and footwear, light machinery and automobile assembly, construction materials, metallurgy, chemicals, food processing, and petroleum refining. While in 2001 all of Romania's car manufacturers produced 68,761 automobiles, by 2004, Dacia alone had produced 94,720.

Romania has been fairly successful in privatizing its industrial base—in 2005, less than 5% of the industrial assets were still in the hands of the state. While some privatizations have been plagued by corruption accusations, and while some of the newly privatized companies are not yet economically viable, the rest have benefited from switching leadership. Some of the success stories include the privatization of Dacia (Romania's main car manufacturer), and of Petrom (the national oil company), which were acquired by Renault and OMV, respectively. Among the industrial giants that have passed into private hands are RAFO (one of the largest oil refineries in Romania and Eastern Europe), acquired by the British Balkan Petrolium in 2003, and Sidex Galati (a major iron steel plant), bought by Mittal Steel in 2001. The privatization of the bank sector has also been hailed as an important step towards a functional market economy. Banca Comerciala Romana (BCR), one of Romania's largest state-owned banks, was acquired by Erste Bank in 2006.

In July 2011, European Aerospace and Defense Company (EADS) opened a large plant in Romania to produce parts for Airbus. The plant added 500 jobs to the town of Ghimbav after a $56 million investment to open it.

29 SCIENCE AND TECHNOLOGY

There has been a slow but steady increase in funds allocated to research and development (R&D) in Romania. The percentage of GDP dedicated to R&D has risen from 0.38% to 0.59% in the period 2001–2009.

Among Romania's primary research institutions are the Romanian Academy, founded in 1866, which has sections of mathematical sciences, physical sciences, chemical sciences, biological sciences, economical sciences, technical sciences, agricultural sciences and forestry, medical sciences, and science and technology of information; and the Academy of Medical Sciences and Academy of Agricultural and Forestry Sciences, both founded in 1969. All three organizations are located in Bucharest, and, in 1996, had 67 research institutes attached to them.

Patent applications in science and technology as of 2009, according to the World Bank, totaled 1,054 in Romania. Public financing of science was 0.59% of GDP, and, in 2007, researchers accounted for 0.3% of the workforce, the lowest percentage in the European Union.

In 2007, total research and development expenditures amounted to €653 million (around $900 million) or 0.58% of GDP, up from $555.266 million or 0.38% of GDP in 2002. Of that amount, 48.4% came from the government, while the business sector accounted for 41.6%. Foreign sources provided 7.1%, while higher education accounted for 3%. In that same year, there were 286 technicians and 910 scientists and engineers engaged in R&D per one million people. High technology exports in 2002 were valued at $390 million, or 3% of the country's manufactured exports.

In 2011 Romania had 56 public and 32 accredited private institutions of higher education.

30 DOMESTIC TRADE

The distribution of industrial goods is similar to that which exists in most European countries. The chief seaport is at Constanța. Cluj-Napoca, Timișoara, Iași, Craiova, and Brașov serve as regional industrial centers and railroad hubs. Oradea serves as a regional marketing and shipping center for livestock and agriculture. Arad is a regional commercial and industrial center in the west, while Pitesti serves as a hub for the south-central region. Turgu-Mures serves as a regional industrial and agricultural center for central Romania.

Romania's retail trade sector remains highly fragmented and dominated by many small independent outlets. Retail outlets include specialty shops, supermarkets, hypermarkets, cash and carry vendors, department stores, gas station convenience stores, kiosks, street vendors, open-air markets, and wholesale centers. Although supermarkets and shopping malls have begun to appear in Romania, kiosks remain the largest type of retail outlet. About 15,000 are located throughout the country. Specialized shops are usually found in the large cities.

The franchising system has been slow to develop in Romania, due mainly to the large amount of initial capital required for start-up. However, The number of franchisers in the country continues to grow. In 2000, there were 18 franchise chains doing business in Romania. By 2003, that number had risen to 60, and, by 2004, there were 124 franchise networks in operation. As of September 2005, there were 210 franchise companies in Romania. US-based franchise operations in Romania include McDonald's, Pizza Hut, KFC, Hertz, Budget, and the American Life Insurance Company.

Electronic commerce (e-commerce) has only begun to appear in Romania. Major obstacles to e-commerce include the low rate of Internet usage, limited use of credit cards, and a lack of legal support. In addition, merchandise sold through the country's e-commerce system generally consists of artifacts, CDs, books, and toys. Payment is made offline as either as cash to the supplier, through a payment order, or by post office transaction. Business-to-business (B2B) e-commerce appears to have better prospects, since three major Romanian banks have developed online systems that support B2B e-commerce. Most large banks in Romania offer

their clients (especially business) e-banking services. Some also offer Internet banking. As of March 2005, there were 4.9 million Internet users in Romania.

Romania has a standard 19% value added tax (VAT) rate on most goods and services, although a lower rate of 7% is applied to books, newspapers, hotel services, medicines and certain financial services.

Stores are generally open daily, except Sunday, from 9 a.m. to 6 p.m., although some supermarkets are open later. Banks are open from 9 a.m. to 5 p.m. Monday through Friday. Office hours are generally from 9 a.m. to 6 p.m. Monday through Friday.

31 FOREIGN TRADE

Before 1990, foreign trade was a state monopoly carried out through export-import agencies under the administration of the Ministry of Foreign Trade. Since World War II, the orientation and structure of Romanian foreign trade have shifted. Before the war, cereals, oil, timber, livestock, and animal derivatives accounted for over 90% of total exports, while consumer goods (60%) and raw materials (20%) accounted for the bulk of the imports. Under the Communist industrialization program, structural changes were particularly striking in exports, with machinery and nonedible consumer goods emerging as important export items. Foreign trade was in surplus throughout the 1980s but fell into deficit in the 1990s. Romania's increasing trade deficit after 1994 was due in large part to the depreciation of its currency, large energy imports (despite large domestic reserves), and the loss of two important export markets due to international sanctions: Iraq and the former Yugoslavia (Serbia and Montenegro). The low quality of Romania's export products has also contributed to its large trade deficits. Additionally, with 80% of all imports taking the form of raw materials—principally oil, natural gas, and minerals—the country has little foreign exchange for to import the equipment and technology needed to modernize its sluggish industrial sector.

Exports in 2010 were estimated at $49.41 billion, up from $10.4 billion in 2000 and $40.67 in 2009. The major export categories were machinery and equipment, textiles and footwear, metals and metal products, minerals and fuels, chemicals, and agricultural

Principal Trading Partners – Romania (2010)

(In millions of US dollars)

Country	Total	Exports	Imports	Balance
World	106,478.0	49,357.0	57,121.0	-7,764.0
Germany	18,336.0	8,923.0	9,413.0	-490.0
Italy	13,353.0	6,836.0	6,517.0	319.0
France	7,453.0	4,115.0	3,338.0	777.0
Hungary	7,253.0	2,363.0	4,890.0	-2,527.0
Turkey	5,417.0	3,358.0	2,059.0	1,299.0
Russia	3,509.0	1,062.0	2,447.0	-1,385.0
Bulgaria	3,496.0	1,770.0	1,726.0	44.0
China	3,454.0	403.0	3,051.0	-2,648.0
Austria	3,447.0	1,140.0	2,307.0	-1,167.0
Poland	3,407.0	1,301.0	2,106.0	-805.0

(…) data not available or not significant.

(n.s.) not specified.

SOURCE: *2011 Direction of Trade Statistics Yearbook*, New York: United Nations, 2011.

Balance of Payments – Romania (2010)

(In millions of US dollars)

Current Account		**-6,480.0**
Balance on goods		-7,805.0
Imports	-57,216.0	
Exports	49,411.0	
Balance on services		-836.0
Balance on income		-2,361.0
Current transfers		4,522.0
Capital Account		**294.0**
Financial Account		**6,135.0**
Direct investment abroad		-190.0
Direct investment in Romania		3,453.0
Portfolio investment assets		-165.0
Portfolio investment liabilities		1,779.0
Financial derivatives		4.0
Other investment assets		-554.0
Other investment liabilities		1,808.0
Net Errors and Omissions		**-922.0**
Reserves and Related Items		**973.0**

(…) data not available or not significant.

SOURCE: *Balance of Payment Statistics Yearbook 2011,* Washington, DC: International Monetary Fund, 2011.

products. Romania's main export partners were Germany (18.4%), Italy (14.1%), France (8.5%), Turkey (6.9%), and Hungary (4.9%).

Imports stood at $57.22 billion, up from $13.1 billion in 2000 and $50.28 billion in 2009. The major import categories were machinery and equipment, fuels and minerals, chemicals, textiles and products, metals, and agricultural products. Romania's main import partners were Germany (16.8%), Italy (11.6%), Hungary (8.7%), France (6%), China (5.5%), Russia (4.4%), and Austria (4.1%).

Trade with the EU countries, especially Germany, has increased substantially in recent years, largely because of Romania's expanding need for advanced Western technology and equipment.

32 BALANCE OF PAYMENTS

In 2010, Romania had a foreign trade deficit of $7.81 billion.

Trade with Western countries has involved growing amounts of credit in recent years. As a result of a series of devaluations of the Romanian leu dating from February 1990, Western imports became increasingly costly, while the quality of Romania's exports significantly declined. Romania's poor performance was additionally due to its reliance on the importation of raw materials—such as oil, natural gas and minerals—which accounted for as much as 80% of imports in 1995, leaving little exchange currency for equipment and technology.

The country's international risk ratings have made it difficult for Romania to borrow from the private international credit market. Current account deficits have been financed in large measure by loans and grants from international financial institutions, but Romania has attempted to diversify its sources of external financing. In December 2010, Romania's external debt stood at $122.8 billion, up from $11.6 billion in 2001.

In July 2011, Fitch Ratings raised Romania's credit rating to the lowest safe investment grade (BBB-) for the first time. It was also the first upgrade for Romania in almost three years.

33 BANKING AND SECURITIES

Romanian banks were nationalized in 1948. Established in 1880, the bank of issue is the National Bank of the Socialist Republic of Romania, which also extends short-term loans to state enterprises and supervises their financial activities. The Romanian Bank for Development (1990) finances investments of state enterprises and institutions and grants long-term credit. As investments increased in volume, this bank was required to intensify its control over the use of funds allocated for investment. The Romanian Bank for Foreign Trade conducts operations with foreign countries. Savings are deposited with the Loans and Savings Bank. In 1974, New York's Manufacturers Hanover Trust opened an office in Bucharest, the first such instance for a Western commercial bank in a communist nation.

Romania has generally been very cautious in its approach to banking reform. Since 1990, the financial sector has undergone a fundamental overhaul, although the pace of change has been slower than elsewhere in the region. The number of banks rose from 5 in December 1990 to 41 by the end of 2000—including 4 branches of foreign banks, 4 branches of joint ventures based abroad, and 33 domestic banks. The foreign specialized banks—for development, agriculture, and foreign trade—still handle almost all of the business in these areas. The Romanian Commercial Bank is still the banker to most Romanian firms, while the Savings Bank retains a virtual monopoly on personal savings deposits. At decade's end, Romania's financial institutions, like the rest of its economy, remained in severe and protracted crisis. Despite repeated calls from the IMF to privatize, the seven state-owned banks still controlled 70% of all assets in Romania's banks. Moreover, these banks continued to be plagued by bad debt.

The International Monetary Fund reports that in 2001, currency and demand deposits—an aggregate commonly known as M1—were equal to $2.1 billion. In that same year, M2—an aggregate equal to M1 plus savings deposits, small-time deposits, and money market mutual funds—was $9.3 billion. The discount rate, the interest rate at which the central bank lends to financial institutions in the short term, was 35%.

As of December 2010, Romania's reserves of foreign exchange and gold stood at $48.08 billion. The share of gold bullion was 9.1% of total reserves, or 103.7 tons.

Romania set up its first postwar stock exchange in 1995, after the enabling legislation had been delayed for several years. The RASDAQ (Romanian Association of Securities Dealers Automatic Quotation), an over-the-counter securities market, opened in 1996. As of 2001, the total market capitalization of the RASDAQ was $2.1 billion, up 98% from the previous year. By 2004, a total of 4,030 companies were listed on the combined Bucharest Stock Exchange and RASDAQ exchanges, which had a combined market capitalization of $11.786 billion. In 2004, the BET Index rose 101% from the previous year to 4,364.7. By 2010, the combined market capitalization of BET and RASDAQ was $33 billion.

34 INSURANCE

During the Communist era, all commercial insurance was nationalized. Since 1991, casualty, automobile, and life insurance have been made available through private insurers with foreign partners. Private insurers are only legally permitted as joint-stock or limited liability companies. Policies available include life, automobile, maritime and transport, aircraft, fire, civil liability, credit and guarantee, and agricultural insurance, with third-party auto insurance compulsory. Foreign insurance companies and agencies are now allowed to set up representative offices within Romania, under certain regulations.

³⁵PUBLIC FINANCE

The annual budget is presented to the Grand National Assembly around December and becomes effective for the fiscal year on 1 January. The state budget, prepared by the Ministry of Finance, is a central part of the financial plan for the whole economy. The reduction of the growth rate of expenditures during the early 1980s was in keeping with an economic stabilization program designed to hold down domestic investment and consumption. As a result of fiscal reforms begun since the fall of the Ceausescu regime in December 1989, adherence to IMF fiscal targets, and an unanticipated inflation-fed revenue windfall during the first half, the central government unofficially recorded a relatively modest deficit for 1991. Privatization of industry was accomplished in 1992 with the transfer of 30% of the shares of about 6,000 state-owned businesses to five private ownership funds, in which each adult citizen received certificates of ownership. As of the first decade of the 21st century, the government's priorities included reigning in of its fiscal policy, continuing to develop its relationship with the IMF, and continuing the process of privatization.

In 2010, the budget of Romania included $55.5 billion in public revenue and $65.91 billion in public expenditures. The budget deficit amounted to 6.4% of GDP. Public debt was 33.8% of GDP, with $118.9 billion of the debt held by foreign entities.

³⁶TAXATION

Romania's taxation system in the 1990s was notable for its erratic and confusing nature, but with reforms in late 1999, there has been movement towards uniformity and simplicity. As of 2010, the standard corporate income tax rate in Romania was 16%. Profits from nightclubs, casinos, and discotheques were taxed at the standard corporate rate with the stipulation that total tax could not be lower than 5% of qualifying gross revenue earnings. Capital gains are taxable at the normal corporate income tax rate of 16%, although a lower rate of 10% applies to the sale of corporate shares held in Romanian companies and the sale of Romanian real estate if the seller owned the real estate or shares for more than two years and if the buyer is not related to the seller. Dividends paid to either residents or resident companies by Romanian firms are subject to 10% withholding. Dividends paid to nonresident companies or individuals by Romanian firms are subject to a 15% withholding tax. Interest and royalties earned through nonresident companies are subject to withholding tax rates of 5% and 15%, respectively.

As part of the tax reform, Romania's top marginal rate for personal income tax was dropped from 60% to 40% in 2003. In 2005, Romania adopted a flat-tax set at 16% for all personal income.

The main indirect tax is Romania's value-added tax (VAT), with a standard rate of 19% as of 2005. Many basic services are exempt from VAT including banking and financial services. There are reduced VAT rates of 9% and 5%. The reduced 9% VAT rate applies to hotel services, books, newspapers and medicines. The reduced

Public Finance – Romania (2007)		
(In millions of lei, central government figures)		
Revenue and Grants	**106,905**	**100.0%**
Tax revenue	48,752	45.6%
Social contributions	43,162	40.4%
Grants	2,431	2.3%
Other revenue	12,561	11.7%
Expenditures	**116,721**	**100.0%**
General public services	14,766	12.7%
Defense	3,970	3.4%
Public order and safety	10,198	8.7%
Economic affairs	18,087	15.5%
Environmental protection	443	0.4%
Housing and community amenities	2,177	1.9%
Health	15,349	13.2%
Recreational, culture, and religion	1,727	1.5%
Education	8,318	7.1%
Social protection	41,686	35.7%

(…) data not available or not significant.

SOURCE: *Government Finance Statistics Yearbook 2010*, Washington, DC: International Monetary Fund, 2010.

5% rate applies to buildings supply. Other taxes include excise and stamp taxes.

³⁷CUSTOMS AND DUTIES

Romania joined the European Free Trade Association (EFTA) in December 1992 and, early in 1993, signed an association agreement with the European Union that provided for Romania to adapt to EU economic-commercial standards over a 10-year period. Under an interim collaborative agreement effective 1 May 1993, a revised Romanian import tariff schedule was introduced with preferential tariffs for imports from European Union and EFTA member nations.

Since joining the European Union in 2007, Romania uses the single external tariff—or Common Customs Tariff (CCT)—applied by all member states to imports coming from third countries.

³⁸FOREIGN INVESTMENT

Foreign investment was negligible before the overthrow of the Communist regime. A new foreign investment law was enacted in 1991. Incentives to foreign investors include tax holidays and reduction, full foreign ownership of an enterprise, and full conversion and repatriation of after-tax profits. However, the latter is a drawn-out process because of the central bank's shortage of hard currency.

In 1997, the inflow of foreign direct investment (FDI) reached $1.2 billion and then rose to a record of over $2 billion in 1998. Affected by the Russian financial crisis of August 1998, FDI inflow fell to a little over $1 billion in 1999. Annual FDI inflow averaged about $1.1 billion from 2000 to 2002. The FDI inflow continued to grow, reaching $1.6 billion in 2003 and $5.1 billion in 2004.

According to World Bank figures, in 2009, foreign direct investment in Romania was a net inflow of $6.31 billion. FDI represented 3.92% of GDP.

France, Austria, the Netherlands, Germany, the United States, and Italy have been the largest sources of FDI. The largest foreign operations are in the automobile, steel, oil and banking industries.

39 ECONOMIC DEVELOPMENT

The economy of Romania before 1990 was centrally planned and, for the most part, under complete state control. The nationalized industries and other economic enterprises operated within the state economic plan and were governed by the directives issued by the pertinent ministries. Economic planning, conducted by the State Planning Commission, emulated the Soviet example.

Nationalization of industry, mining, transportation, banking, and insurance on 11 June 1948 was followed by one-year economic plans in 1949 and 1950. These were succeeded by the first five-year plan (1951–55), which laid the groundwork for rapid industrialization, with emphasis on heavy industry, primarily machine-building. The state's second five-year plan (1956–60) provided for an increase of industrialization by 60–65%. Greater attention was given to consumer goods and to agriculture. A subsequent six-year plan (1960–65) envisaged an overall industrial increase of 110%, especially in producer goods. The five-year plan for 1966–70 realized an overall industrial increase of 73%. The five-year plans for 1971–75, 1976–80, and 1981–85 called for further industrial expansion, and, according to official figures, during 1966–85 industrial production grew by 9.5% annually. The eighth five-year plan, for 1986–90, projected a 13.3–14.2% annual increase in Romania's net industrial production.

In the farming sector, the government has assiduously pursued a policy of collectivization. By virtue of the 22 March 1945 land reform, most farms over 50 hectares (123 acres)—a total of about 1.5 million hectares (3.7 million acres)—were confiscated without compensation. In 1949, the remaining large private farms were seized, and their 500,000 hectares (1,236,000 acres) organized into state farms. Various pressures, including coercion, were used to force peasants into joining. In April 1962, collectivization was announced as virtually completed, although there were farms, especially in remote areas, that were left in the hands of their rightful owners. Agricultural development in following years was comparatively neglected.

As of 1 January 1979, Romania began implementing the "new economic-financial mechanism," an attempt to introduce into the Romanian economy the principle of workers' self-management as previously developed elsewhere in Eastern Europe, notably in the former Yugoslavia and Hungary. Accordingly, autonomous production units were expected to plan for their own revenues, expenditures, and manpower needs. These separate plans were, however, to be harmonized with the national economic plan, so that Romania's centralized system of goal and price setting was not significantly altered.

One of the major economic targets in the 1980s was the reduction of foreign debt, which was achieved but at the cost of drastic austerity measures and reduced industrial growth. After the fall of Communism, a major objective was the privatization of 6,200 state enterprises. The economy was to be completely restructured, with the emphasis on private ownership and adherence to the market for the allocation of resources. By late 1996, nearly all the country's agricultural land had been returned to private ownership, but only 65% of all eligible recipients had been officially given title. By

2002, Romania had privatized many major state-owned enterprises, with the help of the World Bank, IMF, and the EU. The private sector in 2002 accounted for an estimated 65% of GDP.

Economic growth declined in the late 1990s but picked up in the early 2000s. Inflation, once a problem (it stood at 18% at the end of 2002), had been reduced to single figures in 2004 and was predicted to drop to 5% by 2006. In 2004, the foreign direct investment in Romania reached $5.1 billion (second only to the Czech Republic in Europe), while the GDP registered a whopping 8.3% increase (second only to Latvia in Europe). The economy is expected to grow at a rate of around 7% in the coming years.

In December 2004 Romania closed the pre-accession negotiation with the European Union. In October 2004 it received the "functionally market economy" status, and, in 2007, it joined the European Union.

However, Romania has struggled to respond to EU market pressures. Along with its southern neighbor, Bulgaria, Romania remains the poorest EU member country. While some sectors have registered significant progress, others are still lagging. For example, Romania's main car manufacturer, Dacia—now owned by Renault—has been very successful in acquiring an important share of the internal and external market. The information technology (IT) industry is one of the most vibrant in Europe. The agriculture sector, on the other hand, suffers from fragmentation, lack of economic cohesion (economies of scale are hard to achieve on small parcels of land that are owned by people with different interests), and a lack of future perspective.

While EU membership made Romania eligible for economic assistance through the Union's Structural and Cohesion Funds, aimed at reducing regional disparities in terms of income, wealth and opportunities, the country has been slow to absorb funds made available by the EU for various economic development programs. The allocation and use of such funds has been predicated on an efficient public administration, reliable contract enforcement, and low levels of corruption—areas in which Romania has not demonstrated sufficient capacity.

Along with other European countries, Romania was affected by the late-2000s global financial crisis. In 2009, the country took a two-year, €20 billion-euro loan from the IMF, the EU, and the World Bank as its economy shrank by 7.1 percent. Romania imposed harsh austerity measures under the agreement, reducing public wages by one-fourth and increasing sales tax by five percent.

40 SOCIAL DEVELOPMENT

A social insurance system has been in place since 1912. Social security covers most wage earners, and a voluntary system is in place for persons wishing additional coverage. Old-age pensions are granted at age 65 for men and at 60 for women. Those engaged in hazardous or arduous work are eligible for retirement earlier. The program is funded by contributions from employers and employees, with deficits covered by the government. Workers who do not meet the conditions of duration of employment at retirement age are provided with social assistance. Survivors' benefits are payable to the spouse, fathers and mothers, brothers and sisters who are dependents of the deceased, and to children up to age 16. Workers' compensation and unemployment insurance are also provided, as well as maternity benefits and family allowances. In the past decade, a number of private Romanian and foreign companies have supplemented the traditional state insurance market.

All residents are entitled to medical care, although human rights organizations report that representatives of certain groups (Roma, prisoners, and persons with HIV/AIDS) may be illegally denied or provided inadequate medical care. Families with children under age 16 receive family allowances and a birth grant for each child. In addition to state social insurance, other schemes cover members of artisans' cooperatives, the clergy, and the professions.

The constitution guarantees equal pay for equal work, but women are still concentrated in low-paying professions. As of the 2008 parliamentary election, only 38 of the 334 members of the Chamber of Deputies were women (11.4%), and only 8 of the 137 members of the Senate (5.8%). Few women are in senior management positions in the private sector. Women also face considerable employment discrimination in Romania's harsh economic climate and suffer from a higher rate of unemployment than do men. Violence against women, including rape, is a serious problem. It is difficult to bring rape cases to trial because the victim's testimony is not considered sufficient evidence; medical evidence and witnesses are required. Domestic abuse is widespread. In 2010, public awareness of sexual harassment remained low, and no effective programs existed to educate the public about it.

Ethnic Hungarians are the largest minority and are subject to discrimination. The Roma population continues to be harassed, and there are reports of anti-Semitic activity. Human rights are generally respected, although there were continued reports of the mistreatment of detainees. The government has improved prison conditions and instituted vocational training, but prisons are still overcrowded, and the conditions remain poor. Human rights organizations also report incidences of verbal abuse and occasionally violence, including by the authorities, based on sexual orientation and gender identity.

41 HEALTH

As part of a broader social and economic transition, Romania's health care system underwent major reforms in the 1990s as it was transformed from a centralized, tax-based system to a pluralistic one based on contractual relationships between health care providers and insurance funds. As of 2007, there were an estimated 190 physicians, 389 nurses, and 22 dentists per 100,000 people. Total healthcare expenditure was estimated at 5.1% of GDP and has registered a slow growth since.

According to the CIA, life expectancy in Romania was 73 years in 2011. The government spent 5.4% of its GDP on healthcare, amounting to $408 per person. There were 19 physicians, 42 nurses and midwives, and 65 hospital beds per 10,000 inhabitants. The fertility rate was 1.4, while the infant mortality rate was 10 per 1,000 live births. In 2008, the maternal mortality rate, according to the World Bank, was 27 per 100,000 births. It was estimated that 97% of children were vaccinated against measles.

The infant mortality rate in 2011 was estimated at 11.02 deaths for every 1,000 live births. The general health of the population has improved, with several previously serious diseases eliminated or greatly reduced (e.g., diphtheria, tuberculosis), although proper sanitation was available to only 53% of the population and safe drinking water to 58%. Leading causes of death were cardiovascular disease, cancer, and respiratory diseases. Average life expectan-

cy in 2011 was 73.98 years. The total fertility rate was 1.29 children per woman during her childbearing years. Maternal mortality was estimated at 58 per 100,000 live births in 2007. About 48% of women used contraception. Immunization rates for children up to one year old were: tuberculosis, 100%; diphtheria, pertussis, and tetanus, 97%; polio, 97%; and measles, 97%.

The HIV/AIDS adult prevalence rate was 0.1% in 2009. The incidence of tuberculosis was 146 per 100,000 people that year and was disproportionately high among the prison population. In 2009, Romania's representative in the World Health Organization reported that, after a successfully implemented control program, the proportion of prisoners with tuberculosis had fallen to 2%.

42 HOUSING

Inadequate housing has been a serious problem since World War II. Romanian housing suffered from the 1940 earthquake, war damage, neglect, and inadequate repair and maintenance after the war. An increase in the urban population caused by industrialization and emphasis on capital construction exacerbated the problem. Since 1965, the government has encouraged private construction by state support in the form of credits and expertise. However, an uncertain economy means that maintenance for existing properties has been somewhat poor.

In 1999, the total housing stock was at about 7.88 million units. At the 2002 census, there were 8,107,114 dwellings serving 21.6 million people. About 56.8% of all dwellings were single-family detached houses of two or three rooms. About 97% of all units are under private ownership. About 47% of all residential buildings were built in the period 1945–70.

Between 2002 and 2007, as Romania prepared the join the EU, the Romanian housing market experienced a dramatic increase in property prices by a factor of 10. In 2007 only, the year of its accession, property prices jumped by 20%. As a result, Romania has an unusually high housing-price-to-income ratio.

43 EDUCATION

Education is compulsory for students between the ages of 6 and 16. The general course of study includes four years of primary school followed by four years of lower secondary school. Students may attend art or trade school after their primary education is complete. At the upper secondary level, students may choose between schools offering general studies, vocational programs, or technical studies. Upper-secondary programs generally last from three to four years. The academic year runs from October to June.

In 2008, the World Bank estimated that 90% of age-eligible children in Romania were enrolled in primary school, down from 90% in 2005. Secondary enrollment for age-eligible children stood at 81%, up from 80% in 2005. Tertiary enrollment was estimated at 66%. Of those enrolled in tertiary education, there were 100 male students for every 134 female students. Overall, the CIA estimated that Romania had a literacy rate of 98%. Public expenditure on education represented 4.3% of GDP.

Over 99% of all students complete their primary education. The student-to-teacher ratio for primary school was about 17:1 in 2005; the ratio for secondary school was about 13:1. Also in 2005, UNICEF estimated that 94.5% of all male and 95.4% of all female students complete their secondary education.

In 2005, about 45% of the tertiary age population was enrolled in some type of higher education program. The adult literacy rate for 2005 was estimated at about 97.3%. As of 2007, public expenditure on education was estimated at 4.3% of GDP, up from 3.5% in 2003.

Admission to an advanced institution depends on a variety of factors, including the student's social background. Over half the students receive government assistance. Yearly quotas are established by the Ministry of Education according to manpower needs. Students in some fields must first complete six months of practical work in industry or agriculture.

Like other formerly Communist countries, Romania has emphasized polytechnic education in recent years. This "link of education with life" in the early grades means studying practical subjects; however, beginning in the upper grades, there are work programs, often directly in enterprises, in workshops, or on collective farms, depending on the locality.

Romania's leading universities are those in in Bucharest (founded in 1864), Brașov (1971), Craiova (1966), Galati (1948), Iași (1860), Timișoara (1962), and the Babes-Bolyai University in Cluj-Napoca. The latter is the product of the 1959 merger of the Romanian Victor Babes University (founded 1919) and the János Bolyai University (1945) for Hungarian minority students, whose goal was to strengthen "socialist patriotism."

44 LIBRARIES AND MUSEUMS

The National Library in Bucharest holds over 8.7 million items. The Romanian Academy Library in Bucharest is also a national library. It holds about 10 million items, mainly on the history and culture of the Romanian people. The next-largest public libraries are the university libraries at Bucharest (1.4 million volumes), Iași (3 million), and Cluj-Napoca (3.6 million).

Romania has some 400 museums. Bucharest is home to many of the most important museums, including the National History Museum of Romania, the National Museum of Art, and the newer Historical Museum of Bucharest (founded in 1984) and Cotroceni National Museum (1991), featuring Romanian fine art, architecture, and decorative art. Also in the capital are the Cecilia and Frederick Storck Museum, highlighting the works of Karl Storck, a great Romanian sculptor, and his family, also prominent artists; the Curteo Veche Museum, featuring archaeological exhibits and housed in a 15th-century palace; and the Museum of Romanian Literature.

45 MEDIA

Romania's telecommunications network is experiencing rapid growth in both the domestic and international sectors. Growth in wireless telephony has been especially significant. Domestic service is provided by fixed-line and wireless systems. Since the implementation of liberalization in 2003, the number of fixed lines in use has grown by 20%, with connections to 58% of all households. Wireless is growing even faster. There are four major service providers with 32% of all households subscribing. International service is provided by ten satellite ground stations, while there are digital, international, and direct-dial exchanges operating in Bucharest.

In 2009, the CIA reported that there were 5.3 million telephone landlines in Romania. In addition to landlines, there were 25.377 million mobile phone subscriptions, or an average of 118 per 100 people. There were 698 FM radio stations, shortwave radio stations. Internet users numbered 36 per 100 citizens. Prominent newspapers in 2010, with circulation numbers listed parenthetically, included Romania Libera (100,000), Adevarul (85,000), and Libertatea (75,000), as well as 38 other major newspapers.

As of 2011, the state-owned Romanian Public Television, commonly known as TVR, controlled six national stations along with six regional studios in Bucharest, Cluj-Napoca, Iași, Timișoara, Craiova and Târgu Mureș. Radio Romania, the state-owned public radio broadcaster, operates 4 national networks and regional and local stations, as well as an international service. There are multiple privately owned commercial stations in both television and radio. The most popular privately-owned television stations are PRO TV and Antena 1. A 1995 report indicated that there were 48 television stations. In 2008, the number had risen to 100. About 172.5 of every 1,000 people are cable subscribers (79%). In 2005, there were 11.35 million television sets. In 2010, the country had 2.4 million Internet hosts. In 2009, there were some 7.7 million Internet users in Romania.

The leading daily newspapers (with 2010 circulation figures) are the tabloids Click (236,000) and Libertatea (Liberty, 150,000); Adevarul (Truth, 130,000); Romania Libera (Free Romania, 45,000); and Evenimentul Zilei (Events of the Day, 150,000).

Though the constitution provides for freedom of expression and prohibits censorship, it is illegal to "defame" the country. Insulting the state insignia (the coat of arms, national flag, or national anthem) is an offense punishable by imprisonment. In 2010, there were no prosecutions or convictions under this statute. Journalists are generally free to criticize the government, including at senior levels. There have been isolated instances when authorities intimidated or censored the press or verbally attacked journalists.

46 ORGANIZATIONS

Economic organizations concerned with Romania's internal and external economic activities include the Romanian Chamber of Commerce and Industry. In 1992, the Council for National Minority Affairs was formed to discuss minority issues. The organization helps the government formulate policies favorable to the minorities of the country. The body is headed by the Secretary General of the government. Representatives from 16 officially recognized minority groups and 12 government ministries make up the organization.

There are also many cooperatives in key sectors of the economy. Many Romanian farmers belong to the private Farmers' Federation. There are about 4,000 farming cooperatives and 41 district unions. A large cooperative located in the manufacturing and consumers sectors of the economy is the Central Union of Commerce and Credit Cooperative. There are over 2,500 production and 850 credit cooperatives. Another important cooperative is the Central Union of Handicraft Cooperatives. The National Union of the Consumers' Cooperatives is based in Bucharest. There is also an active Association for the Protection of Consumers.

The Romanian Academy was founded in 1866 to promote public interest, education, and research in scientific fields. Several professional associations also promote research and public education in specific fields, such as the Romanian Medical Association.

Serving a very specific cultural niche, the Transylvania Society of Dracula, based in Bucharest, promotes the study of the Bram Stoker novel *Dracula* and the life of Prince Vlad Dracula, on whom the book is loosely based. It has an American and a Canadian chapter.

National youth organizations include the Free Youth Association of Bucharest, the League of Students, National Union of Independent Students of Romania, Junior Chamber, Romanian Council of Churches–Youth Unit, the National Scout Organization of Romania, and YMCA/YWCA. There are several sports associations representing a variety of pastimes, such as tennis, skating, track and field, baseball and softball, and badminton.

Civitas Foundation for the Civil Society, established in 1992, sponsors community development and social programs promoting an open, democratic society. Other social action groups include the League for the Defense of Human Rights in Romania and the Women's Association of Romania. There are national chapters of the Red Cross Society, UNICEF, and Habitat for Humanity.

47 TOURISM, TRAVEL, AND RECREATION

The Carpathian Mountains, the Black Sea coast, and the Danube region were developed to attract large numbers of tourists. Major attractions include many old cities and towns (Brașov, Constanța, Sibiu, Sighisoara, Suceava, Timișoara, and others) and more than 120 health resorts and spas. The monasteries in Bukovina are famous for their exterior frescoes. Castle Dracula, the castle of Prince Vlad of Walachia, has been a tourist attraction since the 1970s.

The *Tourism Factbook*, published by the UN World Tourism Organization, reported 7.58 million incoming tourists to Romania in 2009, who spent a total of $1.67 billion. In comparison, in 2003 these numbers were 5,594,828 and $523 million, respectively. Some 7.3 million tourists were from Europe. There were 248,424 hotel beds available in Romania (compared to 201,636 in 2003), which had an occupancy rate of 28% (compared to 34% in 2003). The estimated daily cost to visit Bucharest, the capital, was $302—up from $228 in 2004. The cost of visiting other cities averaged $190 (compared to $152 in 2004).

A valid passport is required to enter Romania of all foreign nationals except those of the countries of the European Union who only need an identity card. Citizens of the United States, Canada, and most European countries do not need a visa for stays of up to 90 days.

Popular sports are football (soccer), skiing, hiking, swimming, canoeing, wrestling, handball, and gymnastics. Between 1965 and 1984, Romanian athletes won 176 Olympic medals (48 gold, 52 silver, and 76 bronze). Romania was the only Socialist country to send athletes to the 1984 games in Los Angeles; all the others, following the USSR's lead, boycotted these games.

48 FAMOUS PERSONS

Perhaps the most famous historical figure in what is now Romania was Vlad (1431?–76), a prince of Walachia who resisted the Turk-ish invasion and was called Tepes ("the impaler") and Dracula ("son of the devil") because of his practice of impaling his enemies on stakes; he was made into a vampire by Bram Stoker in his novel *Dracula*. The first leader of Communist Romania was Gheorghe Gheorghiu-Dej (1901–65), who held the office of premier from 1952 to 1955 and of president of the State Council from 1961 until his death. Nicolae Ceausescu (1918–89) was general secretary of the Communist Party between 1965 and 1989 and head of state from 1967 to 1989; his wife, Elena (1919–89), was a member of the Permanent Bureau of the Executive Committee of the Communist Party.

Ion Heliade-Radulescu (1802–72) founded the Bucharest Conservatory and the National Theater and became first president of the Romanian Academy. Mihail Kogalniceanu (1817–91), a leading statesman in the early Romanian monarchy, inaugurated modern Romanian historiography. Vasile Alecsandri (1821–90) was a leader of the traditionalist school of writers, which sought its inspiration in the Romanian past rather than in imitations of foreign writers. Mihail Eminescu (1850–89) is regarded as an outstanding poet, famous for romantic lyricism. His friend Ion Creanga (1837–87) drew from folklore and wrote with a gaiety and gusto recalling Rabelais. The nation's greatest playwright was Ion Luca Caragiale (1852–1912), who excelled in social comedy. An internationally famous Romanian-born playwright, Eugène Ionesco (1912–94), settled in Paris in 1938. Mihail Sadoveanu (1880–1961) was an important novelist in the period between the two world wars. Romanian-born Elie Wiesel (b. 1928), in the United States from 1956, is a writer on Jewish subjects, especially the Holocaust, and a winner of the Nobel Peace Prize in 1986. The Romanian-born German novelist Herta Mueller (b. 1953) was awarded the 2009 Nobel Prize in Literature. Romanian-born Mircea Eliade (1907–86) was a scholar in comparative religion and comparative mythology and lived in the United States from 1948. Romanian-born Tristan Tzara (1896–1963), a literary and artistic critic who settled in Paris, was one of the founders of Dadaism. Nicolae Grigorescu (1838–1907) and Ion Andreescu (1850–82) were leading painters, as was Theodor Aman (1831–91), a modern artist and founder of the School of Fine Arts in Bucharest. Saul Steinberg (1914–1999) was a cartoonist and illustrator, best known for his work for *The New Yorker* magazine; he emigrated to the United States in 1942. Sculpture was greatly advanced by Constantin Brâncusi (1876–1957). Perhaps the greatest names Romania has given to the musical world are those of the violinist and composer Georges Enescu (1881–1955), known for his *Romanian Rhapsodies,* and the pianist Dinu Lipatti (1917–50). A prominent tennis player was Ilie Nastase (1946–94). Gymnast Nadia Comaneci (b. 1961) won three gold medals at the 1976 Olympics and two gold medals at the 1980 games.

49 DEPENDENCIES

Romania has no territories or colonies.

50 BIBLIOGRAPHY

Achim, Viorel. *The Roma in Romanian History*. New York: Central European University Press, 2004.

Carey, Henry F., ed. *Romania since 1989: Politics, Economics, and Society.* Lanham, MD: Lexington Books, 2004.

Frucht, Richard, ed. *Eastern Europe: An Introduction to the People, Lands, and Culture.* Santa Barbara, CA: ABC-CLIO, 2005.

Gallagher, Tom. *Modern Romania: The End of Communism, the Failure of Democratic Reform, and the Theft of a Nation.* New York: New York University Press, 2005.

Gross, Peter. *Mass Media in Revolution and National Development: The Romanian Laboratory.* Ames, Iowa: Iowa State University Press, 1996.

International Smoking Statistics: A Collection of Historical Data from 30 Economically Developed Countries. New York: Oxford University Press, 2002.

McElrath, Karen, ed. *HIV and AIDS: A Global View.* Westport, CT: Greenwood Press, 2002.

Opello, Walter C. *European Politics.* Boulder, CO: Lynne Rienner Publishers, 2009.

Political Chronology of Europe. London: Europa, 2001.

Romania Investment and Business Guide: Strategic and Practical Information. Washington, DC: International Business Publications USA, 2012.

Sanborne, Mark. *Romania.* 2nd ed. New York: Facts On File, 2004.

Thompson, Wayne C. *Nordic, Central, and Southeastern Europe, 2010.* Harpers Ferry, WV: Stryker-Post Publications, 2010.

RUSSIA

Russian Federation

Rossiyskaya Federatsiya

CAPITAL: Moscow

FLAG: Equal horizontal bands of white (top), blue (middle), and red (bottom).

ANTHEM: Gimn Rossiyskoy Federatsii (National Anthem of the Russian Federation).

MONETARY UNIT: The ruble (RUB) is a paper currency of 100 kopecks. There are coins of 1, 2, 3, 5, 10, 15, 20, and 50 kopecks and 1 ruble, and notes of 100, 200, 500, 1000, and 5000 rubles. RUB1 = US$0.032 (or US$1 = RUB31.5) as of November 2011.

WEIGHTS AND MEASURES: The metric system is the legal standard.

HOLIDAYS: New Year's Day and Bank Holiday, 1–2 January; Orthodox Christmas, 7 January; Defense of the Motherland, 23 February; Women's Day, 8 March; Labor Day, 1–2 May; Victory Day, 9 May; Russia Day, 12 June; Day of Unity, 4 November. Cities have their own holidays.

TIME: 3 p.m. Moscow = noon GMT.

¹LOCATION, SIZE, AND EXTENT

The Russian Federation (Rossiiskaya Federatsiya) is located in northeastern Europe and northern Asia and stretches to the Pacific Ocean. It is the largest country in the world by area, occupying about one-sixth of the earth's land surface with a total of 17,098,242 sq km (6,601,668 sq mi). Russia shares boundaries on the Arctic Ocean with Norway to the N; on northern Pacific Ocean and with North Korea to the E; China, Mongolia, Kazakhstan, the Caspian Sea, Azerbaijan, and Georgia to the S; and the Black Sea, Ukraine, Belarus, Latvia, Estonia, Finland, Lithuania, and Poland (the last two bordering the Russian enclave Kaliningrad Oblast) to the W, with a total land boundary of 20,211 km (12,558 mi) and a coastline of 37,653 km (23,396 mi). Russia's capital city, Moscow, is located in the western part of the country.

For decades, Russia and North Atlantic Treaty Organization (NATO) member Norway disputed the 173,529 sq km (67,000 sq mi) area in the Barents Sea along the curved border between the countries. That border includes areas thought to hold vast amounts of oil and gas, and the melting of ice has increased accessibility to the region's mineral wealth. Fishing rights in this region have also been an issue between the two countries. In 2010 Russia and Norway announced that they had decided to divide the area evenly and signed an agreement delineating the maritime border between the countries.

²TOPOGRAPHY

From west to east, the country can be roughly divided into five large geographic regions: the Great European Plain, the Ural Mountains, the West Siberian Plain, the Central Siberian Plateau, and the mountains of the northeast and southeast. The Great European Plain and West Siberian Plain both contain a variety of terrain, including grasslands and farmlands in the south as well as forests, swamps, and large regions of tundra in the north and east. There is a desert in the southwest. Two parallel chains of the Caucasus Mountains are located between the Black Sea and the Caspian Sea in the southwest of the Great European Plain. The larger of these forms the Russian Federation border with Azerbaijan and Georgia. The highest peak in Russia (Kabardino-Balkaria) is the extinct volcano Mt. El'brus (5,642 m/18,510 ft); this Caucasian peak is also the highest in Europe. Between the Caucasian ridges are two lowlands. The lowest point in Russia is at the Caspian Sea, 28 m (92 ft) below sea level, which is the world's largest inland sea. Besides Russia, several other littoral countries claim shares of that sea and its underwater resources.

The plains are divided by the Ural Mountains, which form a traditional boundary between Asia on the east and Europe on the west. The Urals extend about 4,200 km (2,500 mi) from the Arctic Ocean to the northern border of Kazakhstan. The highest point in the Urals is Mt. Narodnaya at 1,894 m (6,212 ft). The Central Siberian Plateau ranges in height from 500 to 700 m (1,600 to 2,300 ft). A number of rivers and deep canyons stretch across this area; they flow northwards, limiting their use for civil navigation. The highest mountains of the eastern region are the Altay Shan, which reach a peak of 4,619 m (15,157 ft) at Mt. Pelukha. The other eastern mountain regions average less than 3,048 m (10,000 ft) in height.

The longest river in Russia is the Ob, which stretches through the West Siberian Plain to the Arctic Ocean at a length of 5,410 km (3,362 mi). The most important river commercially is the Volga, which stretches for 3,689 km (2,293 mi) through the Great European Plain to the Caspian Sea. The Volga is the longest river in Europe. The Dnieper (2,253/1,400 mi) is another important river

587

in this region; it flows from Smolensk to the Black Sea through Ukraine. The Amur River flows along the southeast border with China to the Pacific Ocean. The largest freshwater lake in Russia is Lake Baikal (Ozero Baykal—30,510 sq km/11.870 sq mi), located in the southern plateau region.

Most of western Russia is located on the Eurasian Tectonic Plate, with seismic activity occurring frequently in the Caucasus Mountains. The eastern coast lies on the North American Plate near the boundary with the Pacific Plate. This eastern coast is part of the "Ring of Fire," a seismically active band surrounding the Pacific Ocean. While many of the resulting earthquakes are moderate (below 6.0 magnitude on the Richter scale), more severe quakes are not uncommon. The largest earthquake (7.5 in magnitude) in recent years occurred in 1995 on Sakhalin Island, causing some 1,989 deaths. In July 2003 a 6.8 magnitude quake occurred near Primorye. In October that same year a 6.7 magnitude quake hit in southwestern Siberia; the same region was also struck by a 6.6 magnitude quake on 27 December 2011. A 6.8 magnitude quake occurred in Tuva, near the Mongolian border, on 26 February 2012.

³CLIMATE

Most of the country has a continental climate, with long cold winters and brief summers. There is a wide range of summer and winter temperatures and relatively low precipitation. Average January temperatures reach a high of 6°C (45°F) on the southeastern shore of the Black Sea. A record low temperature of -71°C (-96°F) was recorded in 1974 at the northeast Siberian village of Oymyakon, the lowest temperature ever recorded anywhere in the world for an inhabited region. In many areas of Siberia, especially east of the Ob River, the soil never thaws below the first foot of the taiga surface. The tundra has long winters and summers lasting one or two months; it receives 8–12 months of snow or rain. The far northern forest, like most of the country, has long severe winters, short summers, and extremely short springs and autumns.

Precipitation is low but falls throughout the year, varying from 53 cm (21 in) at Moscow to 20–25 cm (8–10 in) in eastern Siberia. Annual precipitation decreases from about 64 to 76 cm (25 to 30 in) in the European region to less than 10 cm (4.1 in) a year near the semi-desert city of Astrakhan.

In late July and early August of 2010 excessive heat and drought-like conditions in and around the Moscow area sparked numerous forest fires. The resulting smoke and airborne pollutants descended on the city, making health conditions difficult for residents already dealing with intense heat as daily temperatures reached 38°C (100°F). Russian health officials reported a death toll of up to 700 people a day from heat-related illnesses. El Nino was blamed by experts for the abnormal summer conditions.

⁴FLORA AND FAUNA

Russia has several soil and vegetation zones, each with its characteristic flora and fauna. Northernmost is the so-called arctic desert zone, which includes most of the islands of the Arctic Ocean and the seacoast of the Taymyr Peninsula. These areas are characterized by the almost complete absence of plant cover; only mosses and lichens are to be found. Birds and mammals associated with the sea (sea calf, seal, and walrus) are typical of this zone.

The tundra, which extends along the extreme northern part of Asia, is divided into arctic, moss-lichen, and shrubby tundra subzones. Only dwarf birches, willows, lichens, and mosses grow in the thin layer of acidic soil. Indigenous fauna include the arctic fox, reindeer, white hare, lemming, and common and willow ptarmigan.

South of the tundra is the vast forest zone, or taiga, covering half the country. Russia has the largest forested areas on the globe—some 8 million sq km (3.09 million sq mi)—and contains 25% of the world's forested area. Some 20% of the world's forests are in Siberia. The northern areas of this zone alternate between tundra landscape with sparse growth of birches, spruce, and other deciduous trees. Farther south are spruce, pine, fir, cedar, and some deciduous trees. There are subzones of mixed and broadleaf forests on the Great Russian Plain in the southern half of the forest zone. Mammalian wildlife in the taiga includes moose, Russian bear, reindeer, lynx, sable, and squirrel and among the birds, capercaillie, hazel-grouse, owl, and woodpecker. In the broadleaf woods are European wild boar, deer, roe deer, red deer, mink, and marten.

Farther south is the forest-steppe zone, a narrow band of the Great Russian plain and the West Siberian low country. Steppes with various grasses alternate with small tracts of oak, birch, and aspen. Still farther south, the forest-steppe changes to a region of varied grasses and small plants. The black (chernozem) and chestnut soils of this zone produce the best agricultural land in Russia. Here grain yields are 0.3 to 1 ton per hectare. Typical mammals are various rodents (hamsters and jerboas); birds include skylarks, cranes, eagles, and the great bustard.

In the semi-desert zone, plant cover includes xerophytic grasses and shrubs. Typical animals are the wildcat and saiga antelope; lizards, snakes, and tortoises are common.

The World Resources Institute estimates that there are 11,400 plant species in Russia. In addition, Russia is home to 296 mammal, 645 bird, 95 reptile, and 32 amphibian species. The calculation reflects the total number of distinct species residing in the country, not the number of endemic species.

⁵ENVIRONMENT

Russia has abundant water resources, and total rainfall has increased in many areas. However, rainfall is unreliable and too often remote from cultivable land. Consequently, only 89% of the rural population has access to an improved water source, though almost all urban residents do. Water resources totaled 4,498 cu km (1079.1 cu mi) while water usage was 76.68 cu km (18.4 cu mi) per year in 2007. Per capita water usage totaled 535 cu m (18,893 cu ft) per year. Domestic water usage accounted for 19% of the total, industrial for 63%, and agricultural for 18%.

Decades of Soviet mismanagement resulted in catastrophic pollution of Russian land, air, rivers, and seacoasts. Air pollution is especially a problem in the Urals and Kuznetsk, where local populations are exposed to hazardous emissions from metal-processing plants, as well as in the Volga and Moscow regions. In 1992 Russia had the world's third-highest level of industrial carbon dioxide emissions, totaling 2.1 billion metric tons, outpaced only by the United States and China. However, by 2007–08 this had dropped to 1.5 billion metric tons, a decrease of 35%.

LOCATION: 60°0′ N; 30°0′ E. BOUNDARY LENGTHS: Azerbaijan, 284 kilometers (177 miles); Belarus, 959 kilometers (596 miles); China (SE), 3,605 kilometers (2,240 miles); China (S), 40 kilometers (25 miles); Estonia, 290 kilometers (180.2 miles); Finland, 1,313 kilometers (816 miles); Georgia, 723 kilometers (450 miles); Kazakhstan, 6,846 kilometers (4,254 miles); North Korea, 19 kilometers (12 miles); Latvia, 217 kilometers (135 miles); Lithuania, 227 kilometers (141 miles); Mongolia, 3,441 kilometers (2,138 miles); Norway, 167 kilometers (104 miles); Poland 432 kilometers (268 miles); Ukraine, 1,576 kilometers (980 miles); total coastline 37,653 kilometers (23,398 miles).

The Volga River has been damaged through rash exploitation of hydroelectric power. Lake Baikal, the most voluminous freshwater reservoir in the world, has been heavily polluted through agricultural and industrial waste.

Protected areas included nine natural United Nations Educational, Scientific and Cultural Organization (UNESCO) World Heritage Sites and 35 Ramsar Wetland Sites. The World Resources Institute reported that Russia had designated 111.34 million hectares (275.12 million acres) of land for protection as of 2006, or about 7% of its total land area (2009).

According to a 2011 report issued by the International Union for Conservation of Nature and Natural Resources (IUCN), threatened species included 32 mammals, 49 birds, 8 reptiles, 35 fish, 8 mollusks, 24 invertebrates, and 13 plants. The threatened species included Atlantic sturgeon, beluga, crested shelduck, Amur leopard, Siberian tiger, Mediterranean monk seal, Wrangel lemming, and the Oriental stork. The great auk, Pallas's cormorant, and Steller's sea cow have become extinct.

6 POPULATION

The US Central Intelligence Agency (CIA) estimated the population of Russia in 2011 to be 138,739,892, which placed it 9 in size among the 196 countries of the world. Population density in Russia was calculated at 8.5 people per sq km (21.9 people per sq mi) overall, but population density falls off greatly from west to northeast. About one-sixth of the far-east Russian population have moved out since 1989. In 2011 approximately 13% of the population were over 65 years of age, with another 15% under 15 years of age. The median age in Russia was 38.7 years. There were 0.85 males for every female in the country. The population's annual rate of change was -0.2% from 1990 to 2009; this decline may accelerate somewhat in the period 2015–25 as the crude death rate of 14 per 1,000 exceeds the crude birth rate of 12 per 1,000.

The United Nations (UN) estimated that 73% of the Russian population lived in urban areas, and that urban populations had an annual rate of change of -0.2%. The largest urban areas are Moscow (10.5 million), Saint Petersburg (4.6 million), Novosibirsk (1.4 million), Yekaterinburg (1.3 million) and Nizhniy Novgorod (1.3 million).

7 MIGRATION

Estimates of Russia's net immigration rate by the CIA amounted to 0.29 migrants per 1,000 citizens in 2011. About 250,000 people migrated to Russia during 2005–10, according to the UN, many of them Russian-speaking citizens of independent former Soviet republics, such as Kazakhstan, where many had been born or sent during World War II. This was not a new phenomenon. During 1979–88, Soviet Russia gained 1,747,040 people through net migration from other Soviet republics. From 1989 to 1995, 169,000 Russians repatriated from Azerbaijan and 296,000 from Kyrgyzstan. From 1991 to 1995, 50,000 Great Russians exited from Belarus; 614,000 came from Kazakhstan; and 300,000 from Tajikistan. After 1991, 400,000 Slavic nationalities came to Russia from Uzbekistan, and 100,000 returned from Turkmenistan from 1993 to 1995. Following the military conflicts in Chechnya of 1994, 220,000 people fled to the neighboring Russian republics of Dagestan, Ingushetia, and North Ossetia. By 1999 the Russian Federation had 173,000 internally displaced people (mainly from Chechnya and Ingushetia) and an estimated total of 3.5–4 million forced migrants. As of 2009 there were 109,500 Russian refugees and 4,900 people seeking asylum in the country. The UN reported that Russia had 12.27 million international migrants within the country in 2010, up some 500,000 in 1995.

After the end of the Union of Soviet Socialist Republics (USSR) in 1991, Germany took in 156,299 former Soviet, ethnic Germans. Emigration from Russia to the West has become more common. An estimated 1.2 million former Russian citizens or their offspring reside in Israel.

Russia is a major source of women trafficked globally for the purpose of sexual or commercial exploitation. It is also a significant destination and transit country for people trafficked for similar exploitation from regional and neighboring countries into Russia. Internal trafficking from rural areas and Ukraine to urban areas of Russia remains a serious problem. Many women are then taken on to the Gulf States, Europe, Asia, and North America. In addition, the International Labour Organization estimated that of the five million illegal immigrants in Russia, 20% are victims of forced labor. Trafficking of children for sex and sex tourism involving children are also reported.

8 ETHNIC GROUPS

About 80% of the Russian population are ethnic Russians. Tatars constitute 4%, Ukrainians make up 2%, Bashkir account for 1%, and Chuvash form 1%. Armenians, Belarusians, Jews, Moldovans, and several other Caucasian, Turkic, and Siberian nationalities each make up less than 1% of the population. The Romani population, according to the 2002 census, was reported at about 182,000 people; however, unofficial estimates place the number at about 1.2 million. Small communities of indigenous groups include the Buryats in Siberia and the Enver, Tafarli, and Chukchi in the North.

Ethnic relations are problematic. A majority of Russian citizens said in a 2007 survey that non-Russian ethnic groups should be confined to their parts of the country. In that same year, hundreds

of racist attacks and some 52 murders were reported by the Russian nonprofit organization Sova. In 2007–08 thousands of Georgians were deported and their businesses closed as a result of conflict with the Republic of Georgia.

9 LANGUAGES

Russian is the official language of the country and one of the six official languages of the UN. About 90% of the population speaks Russian, an East Slavic language similar to Ukrainian and Belorussian. The Russian language is highly inflected, with nouns, pronouns, and adjectives declined in six cases with three grammatical genders. Versions of Russian or its predecessor Old Church Slavonic have been written since about AD 1000 in a Cyrillic alphabet of 33 letters. Joseph Stalin imposed the Cyrillic alphabet on Russia's minority groups in an effort to make Russian the national language.

A wide variety of other Slavic, Finno-Ugric, Turkic, Mongol, Tungus, and Paleo-Asiatic languages are also spoken in the Federation. In the southern republic of Dagestan alone, two million people speak 28 distinct languages, 14 of which are unwritten. With the breakup of the Soviet Union, several autonomous republics are considering their own language policies. Tatarstan, for example, may reintroduce the Latin script for Tatar as an official language in that region, while Buriatia may restore Old Mongol lettering for Buriat.

10 RELIGIONS

The Russian Federation has no official religion. The Russian Orthodox Church (ROC), which was the official faith of the Tsarist Empire, dates back to the Kievan period. In AD 988 Prince Vladimir the Saint, in order to gain an alliance with the powerful Byzantine Empire, declared Christianity as the religion of his realm and mandated the baptism of Kiev's population and the construction of cathedrals. Organized on the Greek pattern, the Russian church was then considered under the canonical authority of the Patriarch of Constantinople. During the Mongol occupation, the Metropolitan (headquarters of the ROC) was moved to Moscow, where the patriarchate was established in 1589. Orthodoxy and its Holy Synod (established 1721) allied itself with tsarist autocracy and identity.

After the Bolshevik Revolution of 1917, the Marxist-Leninist government imposed a policy of militant atheism and subordinated the ROC through fear and persecution. Other Christians, Muslims, and Jews were also oppressed. Anti-Semitism was widespread before and after the 1917 revolution. Since 1985, however, thousands of churches, mosques, and synagogues have been reopened. Freedom of religion was incorporated into the draft constitution of 1993.

The 1997 Law on Freedom of Conscience recognizes Russian Orthodoxy, Judaism, Islam, and Buddhism as traditional religions. Theoretically, no special privileges are granted to these traditional religions; however, the ROC has made special agreements with the Russian government that seem to place the church in a preferred status. Many Russian citizens consider Russian Orthodoxy and its rituals and national holidays to be forms of nationalism. Though religious registration is not required, many groups do so in order to enjoy certain tax and legal benefits.

According to the Russian Ministry of Justice, there were 23,494 registered religious organizations in the country at the beginning of 2010. The ROC had the largest number with 12,586 registered groups. It is estimated that about 53% of the population consider themselves to be Russian Orthodox, although only a much smaller percentage (15–20%) are active church members. Other Orthodox denominations include the Russian Orthodox Autonomous Church, the Russian Orthodox Church Abroad, the True Orthodox Church, the Russian Orthodox Free Church, and the Ukrainian Orthodox Church.

Islam is the largest minority religion, at an estimated 10–15% of the population (2006), concentrated in the Caucasian and Turkic republics. Officially though, they numbered 8.2% (2005) in about 3,815 registered groups. Protestants, the third-largest group of the country, compose a variety of denominations including Pentecostals, Baptists, Lutherans, Methodists, Presbyterians, and the Church of Christ. Altogether there were 3,410 Protestant organizations registered in 2010. There were also registered groups of Jehovah's Witnesses (some 402), the Church of Jesus Christ of Latter-day Saints, Mennonites, and the Salvation Army. The Molokane and Dukhobor are Christian-based movements that originated in Russia. There were about 286 registered Jewish groups, with between 250,000 and 1,000,000 ethnic Jews remaining in the country. Some synagogues are staffed and supported by worldwide Jewish organizations. There were 240 registered Roman Catholic groups representing a population of about 600,000. Hare Krishnas. Hindus, Scientologists, Taoists, Baha'is, Zoroastrians, Buddhists, Karaites, and shamanists are also represented. About 5% of Russians are declared atheists.

11 TRANSPORTATION

Because of its vast area, Russia's transportation system must be extensive. However, its roads, railroads, and airport facilities have fallen into disrepair from the climate and overuse. The CIA reports that Russia has a total of 982,000 km (610,187 mi) of roads, of which 776,000 km (482,184 mi) are paved. There were 29.2 million passenger cars and 5.7 million trucks and buses (about 250 vehicles per 1,000 people) in 2010. About 1.2 million passenger cars were manufactured within the country in 2010, but foreign models, new and used, are increasingly seen. Russian roads, especially in and around the capital cities, are seriously congested and polluted.

Railroads have long been an important means of transportation in Russia. One of the first lines built was that between St. Petersburg and Moscow, using the 1.52-m broad gauge track. In the 1890s a state-sponsored expansion of railway construction quickened, with foreign financing, to exploit natural resources in the southeast, expand Russia's metallurgical industry, and promote private trade. Intended to allow rapid movement of troops, the Trans-Siberian Railroad was the cornerstone of this development. From 1898 to 1901 more than 3,000 km (1,900 mi) of track was constructed per year. Railroad development also figured prominently during the Soviet era. As of 2011 railroads extended for 87,350 km (54,157 mi).

There are 1,213 airports, of which 595 have paved runways. Some 34.4 million passengers were transported through air travel in 2009, according to the World Bank. There are also 48 heliports. The largest international airport is Moscow's Sheremetevo. Principal airports also include Vnukovo and Domodedovo outside Moscow, Novy at Khabarovsk, Rostov-on-Don Airport, Tolmachevo at Novosibirsk, Pulkovo at St. Petersburg, Sochi Adler at Sochi, Koltsovo at Yekaterinburg, and Vladivostok International Airport. There are more than a dozen military airfields all over the country as well.

Russia has approximately 102,000 km (63,380 mi) of navigable waterways, of which the Volga and its tributaries are the most important. Out of all of Russia's waterways, 72,000 km (44,784 mi) were in European Russia and linked the Black Sea, the White Sea, the Baltic Sea, the Caspian Sea, and the Sea of Azov. Major inland ports include Nizhniy Novgorod, Kazan, Khabarovsk, Krasnoyarsk, Samara, Moscow, Rostov, and Volgograd.

International marine access has been important to Russia ever since the construction of St. Petersburg, ordered by Peter the Great on the marshland adjoining the Gulf of Finland to provide imperial Russia with a "window on the West." Other important ocean ports include Kaliningrad, on the Baltic Sea; Murmansk and Arkhangel'sk, both on the Barents Sea; Novorossiysk and Primorsk, on the Black Sea; Vladivostok and Nakhodka, both on the Sea of Japan; Tiksi on the Laptev Sea; and Magadan and Korsakov (Sakhalin) on the Sea of Okhotsk. In 2008 the merchant fleet consisted of 1,074 ships of at least 1,000 gross tons. Total port container traffic in 2009 reached 2.2 million twenty-foot-equivalent units (TEU).

12 HISTORY

Stone Age people inhabited southern Russia before 3000 BC. Scythian culture developed in the 6th century BC. Eastern Slavs inhabited the area of present-day Russia from the 5th century AD and accepted the protectorate of the Turkic Khazars (said to have accepted Judaism) on the lower Volga in the 8th century; the Khazars were defeated by Sviatoslav in 965. Starting from the end of the 8th century Vikings (also known as Varangians or Rus) penetrated the Slavic area southward and reached as far as Constantinople by 860. Contact with Greek culture and commerce began then.

The history of Russia is usually dated from the 9th century AD, when a loose federation of the eastern Slavic tribes was achieved under the legendary Scandinavian Riurik at Novgorod. Under Prince Oleg (d. 912), Kiev became the political and cultural center of a loose confederation. Vulnerable due to the flat land that surrounded them, the Kievan rulers sought security through city walls and expansion—a policy that subsequent Russian leaders frequently pursued.

By the 11th century, Kievan Rus under Iaroslav had united all the eastern Slavs, codified the "Russian Law" under Byzantine influence, and built the cathedral of St. Sophia. However, over the next two centuries, Kievan dominance was eroded by dynastic struggles and other Slavic and non-Slavic powers (Patzinaks and Cumans). New principalities arose, including Novgorod and Suzdal-Vladimir, precursor of the Duchy of Moscow, marking the eclipse of Kiev as a center of power. The Mongol Tatar conquest (1223–37) took Kiev in 1240; their Golden Horde levied tribute and conscripts on the Russians, but interfered little with the Russian Church. During that century Germans established settlements on the Baltic Sea coast, though Prince Alexander Nevski of Novgorod halted their advance by defeating the Teutonic Knights in 1242. When Mongol suzerainty declined and collapsed in the 14th and 15th centuries, Moscow emerged as the new Russian center of power; its grand dukes granted military fiefs to those who fought the Tatars, along with authority over the peasants. The latter often responded by running off to join the Cossacks in the southeast. The military victories of Grand Duke Ivan III (r. 1462–1505) in particular established Moscow's predominance over almost all other Russian principalities and ended Lithuanian influence. In 1547 Grand Duke Ivan IV ("the Terrible") was crowned as the first "Tsar of All the Russians." He tried to limit the power of the boyar nobles through terror and by taking half the realm as his personal property. Peace with Sweden and Poland was achieved in 1582, but these domestic and foreign groups reasserted their interests in the "Time of Troubles" (1604–13), and even afterwards. The new Romanov dynasty arose in 1613 under Tsar Michael. Local and noble self-government and peasant serf independence weakened under Tsar Alexis. During this period Russia expanded by incorporating the Smolensk region of the west, Siberia to the Pacific Ocean, and part of the Ukraine. The tsar's successor had soon to confront rising Turkish power in the south.

During the reign of Peter I ("the Great," r. 1682–1725), Russian power was extended to the Baltic Sea in the early 18th century. In 1703 the Russian capital was moved from Moscow to St. Petersburg. At the Battle of Poltava in 1709, Peter defeated Charles XII and the Cossack Mazeppa, and Russia replaced Sweden as the dominant power in the north, which was later commemorated in the Treaty of Nystadt (1721). As an early mercantilist interested in the means to power, Peter promoted the cast-iron, textile, and copper industries to supply his state. During the subsequent reign of Catherine the Great (r. 1762–96), victories against the Turks led to the first partition of Poland (1772) by which Russia acquired White Russia and the left bank of the Dnieper River. Russia also took part of Crimea and retook Azov about this time, in addition to gaining access to Turkish waters. Two further partitions of Poland with Austria and Prussia in 1793–95 gave Russia more territory in the west up to the Bug and Dniester rivers.

In alliance with Hapsburg Austria, Napoleon attacked Russia in 1812 with 600,000 men of diverse nationalities. Despite considerable advances and managing to occupy Moscow, by October Napoleon was famously forced by resistance and winter weather to withdraw in disarray from Russia. By the end of the Napoleonic wars in 1815 and the Congress of Vienna, Russia had acquired Bessarabia (Moldova), Finland, and eastern Poland.

During the 19th century Russia completed its conquest of the Caucasus by taking Georgia, part of Armenia, and Dagestan from Persia (1813–28); Bessarabia and some of the Black Sea coast from Turkey; Finland from Sweden; Central Asia from native khanates; and what became its Maritime Province (including Vladivostok) from China. However, as a result of the Crimean War (1853–56) with France, Russia lost control of the mouth of the Danube and southern Bessarabia (until 1878). The Black Sea was neutralized. In 1867 Russia sold Alaska to the United States, where it had abandoned California settlements earlier. In 1875 Russia exchanged the Kurile Islands to Japan for southern Sakhalin. Russian advances to the border of Afghanistan in 1885 almost led to war with England. Unexpected defeats in the 1904–05 Russo-Japanese War revealed the tsarist regime's material weakness and overextension.

In 1907 Russia left the Reinsurance Treaty (1887) with Germany to join England and France.

The autocratic nature of tsarist rule generated growing opposition in Russia, beginning with the abortive "Decembrist" uprising of 1825. Only a few domestic reforms were enacted until Tsar Alexander II (r. 1855–81) emancipated the serfs of Russia in 1861. The peasant communes received land in exchange for redemption payments over 49 years. Even though Russia suppressed the 1863 Polish revolution and imposed Russian administration, Alexander II appeared to be embarking on a course of political reform involving self-government, the courts, the army, and municipal elections when he was assassinated by radical populists in 1881. In response Alexander III (r. 1881–94) ended political reform efforts, silenced liberal opposition, and persecuted religious dissenters and minorities, particularly Jews. Under Minister of Finance Sergei Witte, industrialization was accelerated with a protective tariff, subsidies to native firms, adoption of the gold standard (1897), and extension of railroads financed by French loans. The new urban proletariat was still inadequately protected, however, and a growing peasantry suffered a great famine in 1891–92. By the reign of the last tsar, Nicholas II (r. 1894–1917), many opposition and revolutionary groups had arisen. Under the leadership of the socialists, revolutionary "soviets," or councils, seized power in parts of St. Petersburg and Moscow but were suppressed by the army and the "Black Hundreds." Small concessions were made, and there was a formation of a duma in 1905 with limited powers. During these years, marked by economic growth as well as strikes, Prime Minister Peter Stolypin made progress in agrarian reform, social insurance, and education. Dumas were convened with restricted suffrage, but the tsar and his ministers retained firm control over budgets.

Russia's disastrous involvement in World War I led to the end of the monarchy. By early 1917 Russia had suffered a number of defeats in its struggle with Austria and superior German forces. Defeats at Tannenberg and Masurian Lakes in 1914, further losses in Galicia and the south in 1915–16, and growing hardship at home led to discontentment with autocratic rule. Riots broke out in the major cities in March 1917. Soviets again rose up in Petrograd (as St. Petersburg had been renamed) and Moscow. Nicholas II was forced to abdicate on 15 March 1917, and a provisional government led by Prince Georgi Lvov took over. It proclaimed extensive civic liberties, future distribution of imperial and monastery lands, and independence for Finland and Poland, but promised to prosecute the war against the Central Powers.

Over the course of 1917, democrats and then socialists under Alexander Kerensky and Mensheviks (Marxist socialists) increasingly gained control over the provisional government but lost control over the Soviets to the Bolsheviks. Their leader, Vladimir Ulyanov (Lenin), had been transported back to Russia by the Germans. On the night of 6 November 1917, the Bolsheviks, supported by soldiers and sailors, seized control of St. Petersburg. Elections for a promised Constituent Assembly were held on 25 November and convened in January. The Bolsheviks had gained only 220 of the 703 deputies compared to the 420 seats held by the Social Revolutionaries, but their armed proponents dispersed the democratic assembly, never to meet again.

Lenin moved quickly to end Russia's involvement in the war. In March 1918 he agreed to the Treaty of Brest-Litovsk, which established peace with Germany; as a result, Russia gave up the Ukraine, Poland, and the non-Russian borderlands. These set up independent governments. To protect the Bolshevik government from the Germans, their satellites, and counter-revolutionaries, Lenin moved the capital from Petrograd to Moscow. From 1918 to 1920 the Bolsheviks fought against the Cossacks, Ukrainian Socialists, White armies, Japan, Poland, and several Western states. Gradually organized by Commissar of War Leon Trotsky and fighting for its homeland on inside lines, the Red Army defeated all of these opponents by 1921. After the German surrender, Bolshevik forces took back all the territory it had given up, except for Finland, Poland, the Baltic states, and Bessarabia (Moldova). The USSR was formed in 1922 and extended to Central Asia by 1925.

The Bolshevik regime, based on Marxist-Leninist ideology, sought to overthrow the rule of the aristocracy and bourgeois capitalists and replace it by a dictatorship of proletariats, expressed by "democratic centralism" of the Communist Party. That doctrine allowed debate within the party but imposed stern discipline once the line had been decided. Power in the Communist Party was to be vested in a periodically elected party congress, its Central Committee, and a smaller Politburo to run day-to-day affairs. In practice, Lenin and his chosen colleagues established policy and maintained control by party cadres and the Cheka secret police.

In March 1921, mutiny of the Kronstadt sailors, together with numerous peasant and worker riots, and the general collapse of the economy, forced Lenin to relent on his radical plans to control the entire economy. He ushered in the New Economic Policy (NEP), which allowed peasants to own land, sell their produce at markets, and permitted small private businesses to operate. However, the state retained control of banks, large enterprises, and the railroad. Lenin died on 21 January 1924, whereupon a power struggle for succession among the top Communist leaders broke out. By 1926–28 the Georgian Joseph Stalin had eliminated all rivals and achieved full power. He then began forced industrialization and brutal collectivization of agriculture, together with forced exile of richer peasants and non-Russian minorities. Out of fear of war with the openly hostile Nazis, he ordered the ambitious Five Year Plans beginning in 1928, which pushed rapid development of metallurgical industries and armaments. Despite some heroic achievements, as many as 20 million Soviet citizens died during the 1928–38 period either because of indiscriminate purges (including many Old Bolsheviks and army officers) or famine, caused in part by grain sequestration for export.

Despite ideological differences, the infamous Molotov-Ribbentrop non-aggression pact was signed in August 1939 dividing Eastern Europe into spheres of influence between Russia and Hitler's Germany. Under this agreement, the USSR regained control of most of Poland, the three Baltic states, and Bessarabia (Moldova). On 22 June 1941 Hitler's forces suddenly invaded the USSR and penetrated as far as the outskirts of Leningrad and Moscow and eastward to Stalingrad on the Volga by 1942. The two million Soviet forces were able to rally and drive the Germans and Romanians (three million with their allies) back. They were aided by credits, foodstuffs, steel, machinery, 4,100 planes, and 138,000 vehicles from the United States and other Western countries. By the end of the war in May 1945, the USSR had regained everything it had lost, but at the cost of 22–25 million military deaths and near-

ly twice that number of civilians. The number of Soviet casualties far exceeded those of all the other Allies.

With Red Army victories in Eastern Europe and Western acquiescence at the Yalta Conference, Stalin was able to establish Communist regimes in Poland, Czechoslovakia, Hungary, Romania, Bulgaria, and East Germany (part of the zones of occupation). Having declared war on Japan late in 1945, Russia gained the Kurile Islands and the southern half of Sakhalin, as provided in Japan's terms of surrender. By the peace treaties signed in 1947, Finland ceded the port of Petsamo to Russia, along with a lease on Porkala naval base. Russia joined the UN in 1945 as one of the five permanent members of the Security Council. The USSR did not prevent UN forces from defending South Korea from an invasion by the Communist North Korea in June 1950, though historians believe that Stalin and China's Mao were likely consulted in advance.

Stalin's rule was especially harsh during the last years of his life. When the United States offered Marshall aid to the Soviet-bloc countries, Stalin refused and continued to promote Communist parties in western Europe. Instead, Russia organized the Council of Mutual Economic Assistance (COMECON) for its East European satellite states. Before Stalin could launch further persecutions against Jewish writers and doctors, he died in 1953. The ensuing power struggle was eventually won by Nikita Khrushchev. Khrushchev ended the terror of the Stalin years, but the basic features of the Soviet system—Communist Party monopoly on power, a command economy with little private property, and ideologically controlled public expression—remained. Two of his successors, Premiers Alexei Kosygin and Leonid Brezhnev, tried to introduce market incentives into enterprise planning with little effect. The USSR suppressed the Polish and Hungarian uprisings in 1956 and the Czechoslovak rebellion in 1968. In 1979 Soviet forces entered Afghanistan to support the pro-Soviet government there against an Islamic (*mujahedeen*) resistance, which was aided by American arms. The Soviets withdrew in frustration in 1988.

Realizing that the Stalinist system had led to a stagnant economy and might undermine the USSR's ability to remain a superpower, Mikhail Gorbachev (b. 1931), the new general secretary of the Communist Party of the Soviet Union (CPSU), sought to reform the Communist system (*perestroika*) with more cooperatives and other devices. Despite greater freedom of expression (*glasnost*), Gorbachev was unwilling to replace socialism with a free-market democracy. Meanwhile, multicandidate elections in 1990, economic stagnation, intense competition for power by Russian Republic president Boris Yeltsin, and rising hopes for independence in the western Soviet republics led to the ultimate dissolution of the USSR. Twelve of its 15 constituent union republics formed the Commonwealth of Independent States (CIS). The core Russian Soviet Federative Socialist Republic (RSFSR) was renamed Russia. An attempted coup against Yeltsin by some conservative hard-liners in August 1991 was repulsed when most army generals refused to join, but Gorbachev soon resigned and CPSU activities were suspended. The Soviet Union officially ended on 26 December 26 1991.

In early 1992 Yeltsin and his acting prime minister, Egor Gaidar, sought to introduce rapid economic reform. Price controls were lifted on all but a few items. Prices rose rapidly and production dropped off, leading to growing public opposition to the reforms. The Yeltsin government's relations with the legislature be-came increasingly acrimonious, particularly when Yeltsin agreed with the United States on a policy of dramatic arms reduction. Many of the deputies had close ties with the state-run economy and bureaucracy that were threatened by economic reform. After much argument, Yeltsin unilaterally dissolved the Supreme Soviet in September 1993 and introduced rule by presidential decree. Many of the anti-Yeltsin legislators refused to accept this and barricaded themselves inside the legislature building. On 3 October loyalists of the legislature briefly occupied the office of the mayor of Moscow and attempted to seize the Ostankino television center. Forces loyal to Yeltsin, backed by the military, attacked and seized the legislature building. A state of emergency and press censorship were briefly introduced. Yeltsin banned several opposition parties, purged opponents from the government, and reaffirmed his intention to serve out his full term.

The constitutional referendum and legislative elections of December 1993 approved Russia's first post-Communist constitution; it provided for a strong presidency. In the subsequent legislative elections, Communist and ultra-nationalist candidates did well, owing to popular suspicion with economic reforms, corruption, and widespread poverty. But with the help of loans from rising oligarchs, Yeltsin won reelection in 1996, though with only 54% of the vote. Aleksandr I. Lebed, a retired law-and-order general, threw his support behind the president. Communist Party candidate Gennadiy A. Zyuganov received 32%.

When the north Caucasian Republic of Chechnya asserted its independence in December 1994, war ensued to break the rebellion. The weakened Russian military failed to subdue the Muslim-majority region and had to withdraw in late 1996. Yeltsin had to sign a peace treaty putting off a decision on the region for five years. On 23 September 1999, however, a series of Chechen terrorist attacks made Yeltsin resume military action there. The next year, Vladimir Putin became prime minister and a head of the Federal Security Service (FSB), formerly the Committee for State Security (KGB). He replaced most of the military troops in Chechnya with civilian intelligence forces and local police to fight the separatists. Despite holding elections there, the conflict was not resolved. Not long after, a bomb attack in a Moscow subway killed 11 and wounded many others. The conflict with Chechnya again intensified in 2002, when Chechen separatist rebels seized a theater in Moscow and held some 800 hostages for three days. Putin ordered an early-morning raid on the theater in which 117 hostages and all 50 of the hostage-takers died from the gas used. Despite the continuance of lethal attacks, a new constitution for Chechnya was approved in 2003, stipulating that Chechnya would remain a part of the Russia. In September 2004 the ongoing conflict with Chechnya took the form of a major terrorist attack on a public school in Beslan, Northern Ossetia. This stimulated President Putin to strengthen his control over regional officeholders. Two prominent Chechen rebel leaders were killed by Russian police and border guard forces during the next two years, but unrest continued. Suicide bombers from Dagestan attacked two Moscow subway stations in March 2010, killing 40 and injuring many more. Another bombing at a Moscow airport in January 2011 killed 37 bystanders. Despite the control exercised on Moscow's behalf by Ramzan Kadyrov, disorder in and from Chechnya

and neighboring Caucasian republics is still considered the largest Russian internal security problem.

Russia was initially opposed to any extension of NATO to its former Warsaw Pact allies and the Baltic states, but when Russia signed a pact for mutual cooperation with NATO in 1997 establishing a NATO-Russia council for consultation on security issues, most of the East European states were admitted to the Western collective security pact. Yeltsin called for the removal of NATO from Yugoslavia in early 1999 to no avail. On 31 May that year Yeltsin also signed a treaty of "friendship, cooperation, and partnership" with independent Ukraine. The agreement affirmed that the Crimean peninsula was indeed part of Ukraine, but allowed the Russian Black Sea Fleet to rent the naval port at Sevastopol.

The Russian Central Bank had been using ruble credits to prop up defunct enterprises, and Russian mobsters had been sending their hard currency abroad. In 1998 a global financial crisis and an abrupt fall in oil prices negatively affected the Russian economy. With the country also experiencing its worst harvest in 45 years, the Russian ruble value collapsed in August. The government defaulted on $40 billion in ruble bonds, and the banking system and economy experienced a swift decline. In February 1999 Prime Minister Y. Primakov met with International Monetary Fund (IMF) officials to reschedule debt payments.

Failing in health, President Yeltsin resigned in December 1999 amid allegations of financial improprieties, promoting Putin to the acting presidency on 31 December 1999. Putin was then elected to the presidency in the first round of elections held on 26 March; among the 11 candidates, Putin won 53% of 75.2 million votes, surpassing his nearest rival, the Communist Zyuganov, by a margin of 23.7%. Putin was formally inaugurated on 7 May. Putin then issued a decree granting Yeltsin and his family complete immunity from prosecution. Putin managed to organize strong support for unity and cooperation with Fatherland-All Russia (OVR). Reelected in 2004 with more than 70% of the vote, Putin endeavored to make Russia even more centralized by limiting the power of regional leaders and appointing them himself. He also brought energy monopolies such as Gazprom and arms exports under majority state control and cut the oligarchs' access to the decision-making process in favor of ex-security colleagues. Other laws deprived the republican governments of their seats in the upper house of parliament. Reorganization of the Federation Council substituted appointed senators and governors, who previously had been directly elected. State Duma elections were based solely on party ballots, therefore eliminating elections in one-mandate districts. A public chamber—a public body on a federal level created to act as an intermediary between society and the state—was created. These new amendments were not well-received. Strengthening Putin's hand further, a 2006 law gave authorities extensive new powers to monitor the activities of non-governmental organizations (NGOs) and to suspend them if they were found to pose a threat to Russia. Nevertheless, Russia became a member of the Council of Europe and began to strengthen its civil society and rule of law, designed to bring it into the good graces of the European Union (EU).

Following the 11 September 2001 terrorist attacks on the United States, Putin briefly turned Russian foreign policy towards the West. He acquiesced to a NATO presence in neighboring Central Asia to oust the Taliban and al-Qaeda from Afghanistan. Russia also tacitly accepted the arrival of US Special Forces into Georgia in 2002 to fight terrorists in the Pankisi Gorge region of Georgia. In May 2002 Russia and the United States announced a new agreement to reduce deployed strategic nuclear warheads on each side to a level of 1,700–2,200 over the next 10 years. This treaty was counterbalanced, however, when the Bush Administration announced that the United States would withdraw from the 1972 Anti-Ballistic Missile Treaty (ABM Treaty). Russia subsequently pulled out of the Strategic Arms Reduction Treaty (START) II.

On 19 March 2003 the United States launched air strikes against Iraq, citing UN Security Council resolution 144, requiring Saddam Hussein's regime to rid itself of all weapons of mass destruction. Russia sided with France and Germany in their opposition to armed intervention. During 2003–04 "color revolutions" occurred in Georgia, Kyrgyzstan, and—most threatening to Russia—Ukraine. Worried that Western powers were promoting these movements, Putin began a counter-offensive including a major military exercise to practice intervention in some unnamed CIS country. In Georgia, Russian "peacekeepers" gave South Ossetians passports and launched cyber-attacks on the new Georgian reformist government of Mikheil Saakashvili, who had eagerly solicited NATO interest and American arms.

Russia has increasingly relied on its energy resources for political advantage. In 2005 Russia and Germany signed an agreement to build a gas pipeline under the Baltic Sea between the two countries, bypassing the Baltic nations and Ukraine. Nordstream, as the pipeline is known, came on line in 2011. In January 2006 Russia briefly cut the supply of gas to Ukraine in a disagreement over gas prices. Ukrainian leaders blamed Russia's negative reaction to Ukraine's Orange Revolution of 2004. Tension rose when pro-Western Viktor Yushchenko defeated Moscow-backed Prime Minister Viktor Yanukovych in a disputed presidential election. In March 2006 Putin visited China and signed a range of economic agreements, including one on a future supply of Russian gas to China. In December 2006 Russia cut its supply line to Belarus until the Minsk government cancelled a disputed transit tax. Russia has purchased energy facilities in a number of East European states, a move opposed by the EU.

Prominent dissidents suffered in this period. The former KGB spy Aleksandr Litvinenko, who had been investigating the murder of a Russian journalist, died in November 2006 of radioactive polonium-210 in London, presumably poisoned by the Russian government. Anna Politkovskaya, a critic of Chechnya policy, and several other dissident journalists were assassinated in Russia. The billionaire Mikhail Khodorkovsky was detained in 2003 on questionable charges of fraud in the sale of Yukos and tax evasion. He had backed several liberal oppositionists to the Putin regime. Khodorkovsky was due to be released from jail in 2014.

In August 2007 Russia sent an expedition to the Arctic apparently aimed at expanding its territorial claims there. Two submersible vessels planted a Russian flag on the seabed under the North Pole. This demonstration was to enhance Moscow's disputed claim to nearly half of the floor of the Arctic Ocean and potential oil or other resources there.

Russia remained angered by the Bush administration's 2001 decision to withdraw unilaterally from the ABM Treaty of 1972. Early in the year 2007, the United States announced plans for an anti-ballistic missile defense system. Radar and missile interceptor installations were to be placed in the Czech Republic and Poland for "purely defensive" purposes against possible Iranian attacks. Warning of a new arms race, Russian authorities said the defense shield could be directed towards Russia. They warned the Czechs and Poles that Russia might aim nuclear weapons at their countries should they adopt the plans proposed by the United States. The United States tried to quell Russia's concerns by inviting Russia to share anti-ballistic missile defense technology, an idea rejected by the Kremlin. On 26 April 2007 Russia announced it would suspend its compliance with the Treaty on Conventional Armed Forces in Europe (CFE Treaty), signed in 1990 by the members of NATO, Russia, and the rest of the Warsaw Pact. The CFE Treaty had required the reduction and relocation of much of the main battle equipment then located along the East-West dividing lines including tanks, artillery pieces, armored vehicles, and attack aircraft. In June 2007 Putin again suggested Russia and the United States resolve this dispute by developing a joint anti-missile defense shield at the Russian-run radar station in Azerbaijan. Late in 2008 Putin threatened to pull out of the treaty limiting intermediate-range missiles if the United States persisted in its missile defense facilities in the Czech Republic and Poland. After taking office in 2009, US president Barack Obama decided to drop the idea but later planned to place 24 anti-missile batteries in Romania plus a radar station in Turkey. President Medvedev objected to this placement. In April 2009 Russia and the new US administration began a series of nuclear talks directed toward establishing a replacement to the START of 1991, which was set to expire on 5 December 2009. The new START was signed with President Medvedev on 4 April 2010 and ratified later that year. The agreement intended to reduce nuclear warheads to 1,550 for each country and improve verification procedures. Russia supported limited sanctions against the Iranian nuclear program but refused to authorize additional sanctions proposed by President Obama in 2011. However, Russia has cooperated with the Nunn-Lugar program for safeguarding the world from weapons of mass destruction. Hundreds of warheads have been destroyed in Russia and Kazakhstan.

In August 2008 Russian troops were deployed to repel Georgian troops that had entered its separatist South Ossetia region. Russia had recognized South Ossetia and Abkhazia as independent nations, the only country to do so. After a ceasefire, Russian troops remained in Georgian territory contrary to an internationally brokered agreement. Most of the international community condemned the actions of both Russia and Georgia in this conflict, and NATO suspended relations with Russia until April 2009. One day after formal contact with NATO resumed, Russian president Dmitry Medvedev signed border defense pacts with the separatist governments of South Ossetia and Abkhazia, pledging to offer military assistance whenever needed. The Obama administration, hoping for a positive "reset" of relations with Russia, continued to support Georgia's claims on the two regions diplomatically but cautioned against use of force.

Legislative elections were held on 2 December 2007. The pro-government party, United Russia, won a constitutional majority in a landslide victory that Western observers described as neither free nor democratic. Of the three other parties that won seats in the Duma, two of them were considered to have a pro-Kremlin orientation. The Communist Party was the only opposition party left in the Duma. United Russia won held a slimmer majority following 2011 Duma elections. Despite charges by international observers of ballot stuffing and governmental manipulation, this result was interpreted as a significant loss of support for Putin's (and Medvedev's) policies. Entitled to only 238 seats in the parliament, United Russia would be unable to amend the constitution without agreement from other parties.

With Putin barred from another term in succession by the constitution, Medvedev, running as United Russia's candidate, was elected to a four-year term as president on 2 March 2008 with 70.28% of the vote. Vladimir Putin was immediately appointed prime minister. In 2011 Putin announced he would again run for president in 2012, an election he won despite significant claims of voter fraud.

In late 2011 Putin again promoted his project for a comprehensive Eurasian economic union (EurAsEc) to include Belarus, Kazakhstan, Kyrgyzstan, and other CIS members. A limited customs union with Belarus and Kazakhstan had begun in 2010 amid complaints from Kazakh citizens about increased prices for automobiles and medicine. Ukraine, however, remained a holdout. Russian accession to the World Trade Organization (WTO), negotiated for 18 years, occurred in late 2011 after Swiss negotiators found a compromise that induced Georgia to lift its veto on Russian membership in the 153-member WTO. Membership required Russia to lower tariffs on many agricultural and manufactured goods; to stop subsidizing exports or import substitutes; and not to use dubious health or safety concerns to impose quotas on food imports.

13 GOVERNMENT

The Russian Federation is a democratic state with constitutional division of power among the legislative, executive, and judicial branches. The bicameral legislature is known as the Federal Assembly. Its lower house (the State Duma) consists of 450 deputies elected by popular vote for four-year terms. Beginning in 2007, single-mandate districts for the State Duma deputies were abolished in favor of a proportional party list system. Bills proposed by the upper house must first be considered by the Duma. The 176-member upper house (Council of the Federation or Federation Council) is composed of appointed representatives and officials of the 85 provinces and autonomous republics. Members are elected by proportional representation from party lists winning at least 7% of the vote. The Federation Council has jurisdiction over issues affecting the provinces and autonomous republics, including border changes and the use of force within Russia. It also confirms justices of the constitutional court, Supreme Court, and Superior Court of Arbitration. The upper house deals with finance and treaty ratifications.

The executive branch of the presidential administration consists of three bodies: the President's Administration or Presidential Executive Office, generally responsible for domestic political issues; Government, usually in charge of economic development; and the Security Council of the Russian Federation, chiefly responsible for the foreign policy, security and defense of the country. Responsibilities of the three centers in the executive branch often overlap.

The president is elected by popular vote for a six-year term. The president heads the executive branch, serves as head of state, and the supreme commander in chief of the armed forces. According to the constitution of 1993, the president issues legal regulations, settles disputes, and ensures that the constitution is observed. The president is also responsible for ensuring the state's mechanisms for protecting and respecting citizen's rights and liberties as well as the peaceful and democratic development of the country. The president is also charged to protect the nation's independence, sovereignty, and integrity, and prevent aggression against Russia or its allies. Presidential appointments of prime minister, deputy prime ministers, cabinet, other top posts, and chairman of the central bank are subject to confirmation by the State Duma. Appointments of high court judges and the prosecutor general are subject to confirmation by the Security Council of the Russian Federation. The president can refuse to accept the State Duma's rejection of an appointment to the prime ministership. If the State Duma refuses three times to confirm a new prime minister, the president may dissolve the lower house and order new elections. If the State Duma votes a no-confidence motion against the prime minister and cabinet twice within three months, the president may respond either by dismissing the cabinet or dissolving the State Duma. The president, however, cannot dissolve the State Duma for passing a no-confidence motion during the first year of the State Duma's term of office. The president may declare war or a state of emergency on his own authority.

Removal of the president, as provided for in the constitution, is very difficult. Two-thirds of the State Duma must vote to initiate the impeachment process. Both the Constitutional Court, established to arbitrate any disputes between the executive and legislative branches, and the Supreme Court must review the charges. The findings of all three organizations are then submitted to the Security Council of the Federation, which can remove the president by a two-thirds majority vote. The whole process must be completed within three months.

The Presidential Executive Office prepares the president's drafts of bills, decrees, orders, instructions, presidential speeches, and other documents for submission to the State Duma. It also coordinates all of the president's interactions with various political parties and leaders, NGOs, nonprofit organizations, unions, and foreign governments. A chief of staff manages the Executive Office, which is overseen by the president. During his presidency, Putin concentrated power within the executive branch to the Executive Office.

The Government, headed by the prime minister, is responsible for financial, credit, and monetary policies. It also develops state policies regarding culture, science, education, health, social welfare, ecology, and all other areas of social life. The president presides over Government meetings and gives instructions to the Government and other federal bodies.

The Security Council of the Russian Federation is responsible for national issues including defense, information, and the military, as well as international affairs. It advises the president, who serves as chair. It consults with an expert council made up of representatives of the Russian Academy of Science, the specialized academies of science and educational institutions, and other experts.

The State Council, composed of the leaders of the local governments, is an advisory body that deals with issues related to economic and social reforms. The president also acts as chairman; the secretary of state can be acting secretary.

14 POLITICAL PARTIES

In the elections to the State Duma held in 1993, the radical reformist Russia's Choice led by Boris Yeltsin's former acting prime minister, Egor Gaidar, received the largest number of seats (76). The centrist New Regional Policy group, formed by non-aligned deputies, won 65. Vladimir Zhirinovsky's ultranationalist, antidemocratic Liberal Democratic Party won 63. The pro-Communist Agrarian Party won 55 seats, and the Communist Party of the Russian Federation won 45. Six other parties or blocs won between 12 and 30 seats each. Of the 171 seats that were filled for the Security Council of the Federation, only 27 identified themselves with a particular party.

In the December 1995 elections the Communist Party won 149 of the 450 seats and was supported by two left-wing factions, Power to the People (37 seats) and the Agrarian Party (35). The center-right party Our Home Is Russia, won 50 seats, as did Vladimir Zhirinovsky's far-right Liberal Democratic Party and Yabloko, the moderate-reformist bloc led by Grigoriy Yavlinsky.

In the December 1999 Duma elections, six parties surmounted the 5% threshold, three of which were formed just prior to the election: Unity ("The Bear") created in late September by the Yeltsin government, the Union of Right-Wing Forces, and OVR, a liberal group associated with Yevgeni Primakov. In this election, the Communist Party won 120 seats, Unity 73, OVR 70, Union of Right-Wing Forces 29, Yabloko 20, and the Zhirinovskiy bloc 19. Unaffiliated candidates won 95 seats. Our Home, headed by presidential aspirant and former Prime Minister Viktor Chernomyrdin, fell below the 5%. Zhirinovsky's and Yavlinsky's parties lost more than half their seats. When the Duma convened, Unity and the Communist Party temporarily joined forces to win the largest number of leadership posts and committee chairmanships.

Parliamentary elections were held again on 7 December 2003, with Putin's Unity party using state resources and media control to win 37.1% of the vote. The Communist Party came in second with 12.7% of the vote, and Vladimir Zhirinovsky's ultranationalist Liberal Democratic Party took 11.6%. The pro-Western liberal parties—Union of Right Forces (SPS) and Yabloko—fared poorly. Another leftist-nationalist party, Rodina, was formed.

In the 2 December 2007 parliamentary elections Putin's party, United Russia, received 64.1% of the vote. His 315 seats in the 450-seat Duma would be enough to amend the constitution. Far behind was the Communist Party, with 11.6% of the vote or 57 seats. Two other parties allied with President Putin—the Liberal Democrats and A Just Russia—also won seats. Western observers again criticized the vote as neither free nor democratic.

In the December 2011 Duma elections United Russia (Putin's party) won less than 50% of the vote. The Communist Party earned 19%, A Just Russia 13%, and the Liberal Democratic Party of Russia 12%.

Prime Minister Dmitriy Medvedev, running as United Russia's candidate, was elected to a four-year term as president on 2 March 2008 with 70.28% of the vote. Vladimir Putin was appointed as prime minister on 8 May 2008, one day after Medvedev was sworn into office. United Russia nominated Putin to stand for president in the 2012 elections, and Putin won the 2012 presidential election with 63.6% of the vote.

15 LOCAL GOVERNMENT

The Russian Federation has a complicated patchwork of regional and local governments. Of 89 federal constituencies, there are 7 federal districts that include 49 provinces (oblasts), 21 autonomous republics (where non-Russian minorities predominate), 6 territories (krai), 1 autonomous region, 10 autonomous territories (okrugs), and 2 federal cities (Moscow and St. Petersburg). The secessionist Chechen Republic of Ichkeria is not recognized as sovereign by the federal authorities.

All but the 21 autonomous republics have a system of local government with an elected legislature, mostly unicameral. In the 1990s popular elections of regional governors took place. Heads (presidents) of the 21 autonomous republics are selected as prescribed by their individual constitutions. The regional and republic executive and legislative heads become ex officio members of the Security Council of the Federation, where they typically endeavor to preserve local power against encroachment from Moscow.

In 2000 Putin set out to reorganize center-regional relations by grouping Russia into seven administrative districts: Northwest, Central, Volga, North Caucasus, Ural, Siberia, and Far East. A presidential representative is appointed to each. Putin also appointed seven presidential representatives to coordinate the activities of federal organs. By a law passed in February 2001, the president is allowed to dismiss governors. Furthermore, prompted by 2004 Beslan School tragedy, Putin was freed to abolish popular elections for Russia's regional governors.

16 JUDICIAL SYSTEM

The judicial system is divided into three branches. There are courts of general jurisdiction (including military courts), which are subordinated to the Supreme Court; the arbitration (commercial) court system under the Superior Court of Arbitration; and the Constitutional Court, which arbitrates any disputes between the executive and legislative branches and determines questions pertaining to constitutional issues. Civil and criminal cases are tried in courts of primary jurisdiction (municipal and regional), courts of appeals, and higher courts.

Procurators (prosecutors) are also organized at the district, regional, and federal levels. The head of the procurators, the procurator general, is nominated by the president and confirmed by the Security Council of the Russian Federation. Trials are inquisitorial, not adversarial, and procurators are quite influential in non-jury trials.

17 ARMED FORCES

In 1992 Russia established a separate ministry of defense and military establishment out of the remains of the Soviet armed forces. Still formidable in terms of weapons and equipment, the Russia's armed forces nevertheless soon declined to a lower state of morale and readiness owing to failure of draft calls and lack of training and discipline. Military reforms were then undertaken. By 1998 the military command structure was rebuilt. Troop reductions and redistricting followed. A second phase focused on equipment modernization and operational readiness, prompted by Russia's objections to the NATO bombing of Belgrade, Serbia. Russia has assumed the treaty responsibility of the Soviet Union to reduce its strategic arsenal and conventional forces in Europe, though it remains the world's second-most nuclear armed nation. (The United States is first.)

The International Institute for Strategic Studies (IISS) reported that armed forces in Russia totaled 1.05 million members in 2011. The force is comprised of 360,000 members from the army, 35,000 from an airborne division, 161,000 of the navy, 160,000 in the air force, 80,000 from strategic deterrent forces, and 250,000 members serving in command and support. There are also 750,000 in active reserve. About half a million paramilitary personnel were assigned to the railways, special construction sites, and border and interior guard units. Conscripts serve a one-year minimum at low pay, though there are plans for an all-volunteer force. Armed forces represented 2% of the labor force in Russia. Defense spending totaled $95 billion (a disputed figure, with $38.3 billion reported by the IISS for 2009) and accounted for 4.3% of the $2.2 trillion gross domestic product (GDP) at world prices in 2009. Next to the United States, Russia's armed forces are rated the second-most powerful in the world. In 2011 the Putin administration announced a further military build-up.

The Russian army is equipped with 2,800 main battle tanks and some 70,000 other ground-based weapons. The independent ex-Soviet republics inherited Red Army bases and equipment, but the Navy remained almost wholly Russian, except for 20% of the Black Sea fleet, which went to Ukraine. The Russian fleet, deployed in the North Atlantic Ocean, the Pacific Ocean, and the Black Sea, possesses 233 ships: 1 aircraft carrier, 7 frigates, 18 destroyers, 67 submarines of several types (including nuclear armed), and more than 100 other naval craft.

Russia's Air Force consists of a long-range aviation command, a tactical aviation command, military transport aviation command, training schools, and operational combat units. The long-range aviation command was responsible for the country's strategic bomber force of 80 aircraft. According to the CIA, the Russian Air Force also possesses about 1,400 ground attack and fighter aircraft of several types, plus 588 helicopters and some 200 support airplanes.

The Strategic Defense Forces are responsible for the operation of the nation's land-based Intercontinental Ballistic Missiles (ICBMs), of which there are around 570 launchers carrying 2,035 nuclear warheads. Russia has a total of 4,000 active nuclear warheads, according to the *Bulletin of the Atomic Scientists* and another 7,000 inactive or stored.

[18] INTERNATIONAL COOPERATION

Russia has essentially assumed and expanded upon the foreign relations ties established by the former Soviet Union. It has embassies or consulates in nearly every country of the world. Besides its permanent seat in the UN Security Council, Russia participates in several global specialized agencies, such as IAEA, ICAO, ILO, UNHCR, UNIDO, and the World Health Organization (WHO). The nation is also member of APEC, the Commonwealth of Independent Nations, the Black Sea Economic Cooperation Zone, the Council of the Baltic Sea States, the Council of Europe, the Euro-Atlantic Partnership Council, the European Bank for Reconstruction and Development, G-8, the Paris Club (G-10), and the OSCE. In June 2001 leaders of Russia, China, Kazakhstan, Kyrgyzstan, Tajikistan and Uzbekistan met to initiate the Shanghai Coopera-

tion Organization (SCO) to fight terrorism and ethnic and religious militancy while promoting trade; this group has met several times with mostly rhetorical results. Russia joined the WTO in 2011. Russia holds observer status in the OAS and the Latin American Integration Association (LAIA). Russia is also dialogue partner in ASEAN and part of the ASEAN Regional Forum. Russia participates in the Middle East Peace Process "Quartet" and the Minsk group on the Armenian-Azerbaijani dispute over the Karabakh region, with no positive results through 2011.

Russia is part of the Zangger Committee, the Organization for the Prohibition of Chemical Weapons, and the Nuclear Suppliers Group (London Group). It is an observer in the European Organization for Nuclear Research (CERN). In environmental cooperation Russia is part of the Antarctic Treaty; the Basel Convention; Conventions on Biological Diversity, Whaling, and Air Pollution; Ramsar; CITES; the London Convention; International Tropical Timber Agreements; the Kyoto Protocol; the Montréal Protocol; MARPOL; the Nuclear Test Ban Treaty; and the UN Conventions on the Law of the Sea and Climate Change.

The Vatican and the Russian Federation upgraded their relationship to full diplomatic ties in December 2009 after a long period of Soviet hostility to religious authorities.

[19] ECONOMY

Since tsarist times, the Russian economy has earned its way internationally by exporting natural resources such as furs, cotton, lumber, petroleum and gas, and non-ferrous metals including gold. Aside from poor harvest years, the Soviet regime occasionally exported grain as well, in order to import machinery such as tractors. But as a large and relatively undeveloped economy, Russia has mostly been self-sufficient in food and materials for clothing and shelter. After World War II, Soviet Russia became a major source of armaments for its allies, including the famous MiG fighter jets, T-54 tanks, and Kalashnikov automatic rifles. With outside help, the economy also produced automobiles, trucks, and nuclear facilities. However, with the decline of oil prices and depletion of older wells, Soviet growth rates began to decelerate in the 1980s, and the USSR fell behind the growth and product developments in the West, Japan, and the newly industrializing countries of Southeast Asia. That put great pressure on the Communist government to maintain its military power and to satisfy an increasingly discriminating public.

After the breakup of the Soviet Union and its domestic and foreign trade links, the economy fell into a serious transitional recession, as did every other ex-Soviet country. Russia's GDP declined by over 12% in 1994 and 4% in 1995. By then, 25% of the population was living in poverty, corruption was rampant, and segments of the economy had gone "underground" to escape backbreaking taxes and bureaucratic regulation. President Yeltsin's 1992 reform program, led by Yegor Gaidar, had slashed defense spending, eliminated the old centralized distribution system, established private financial institutions, decentralized foreign trade, and began a program of privatizing state-owned enterprises. Recovery was slow, however. Subsidizing failing enterprises rather than allowing them to go bankrupt kept reported unemployment at the relatively low rate of 8%. With little spare tax money to pay salaries and pensions, inflation accelerated. Rising consumer prices (at a rate of some 26% yearly) were something new for Russia, as

Stalin and his successors had kept prices very stable at the consequence of chronic shortages. A stabilization program enacted in 1995 tightened the budget, liberalized trade, and lowered inflation through noninflationary financing of the budget deficit. Although the economy declined by another 3.6% in 1996, segments of the economy showed signs of recovery. In 1997 overall GDP registered its first positive growth, albeit only 0.9%. Inflation moderated to 11.3% and unemployment fell from 9.3% to 9%. In a major privatization program, the government turned thousands of enterprises over to private owners at bargain prices. In the upshot, many of the new oligarchs became billionaires by exporting scrap and raw materials and by monopolizing key sectors of industry and mining. Overall, during the decade 1990–2000, GDP fell about 35% in real terms while the population fell only 4%.

From 2000 to 2009 recovery occurred, with recorded growth rates of 6% per year. Agriculture (5% of output) and industry (33%, including 15% manufacturing) both declined somewhat, and by 2009 services comprised the largest sector of the economy (62%). Manufacturing centers around Moscow and St. Petersburg are the most important, as they were for the entire duration of the former USSR, although attempts have been made to open high-technology centers elsewhere.

Also during the 2000s, new luxury restaurants, shops, and hotels appeared—as well as open prostitution and gambling. Energy and consumption goods companies that sought to invest in Russia soon discovered commercial rules often changed and contracts capriciously applied. An unwieldy and corrupt bureaucracy has often protected influential domestic enterprise and enriched the commercial elite. Ownership structures are opaque, not transparent. Capital flight has persisted, allowing Russian citizens to buy luxurious real estate and even sports teams in the West. More than $24 billion left the country in 2010, according to official figures. In 2011 capital flight rose to $64 billion.

The sharp fall in energy prices during the global economic crisis of 2008–09 sent the nation into another recession. The government took some expensive measures to stabilize the country's banking sector and save jobs, but by the end of 2009 the economy had lost 7.9% in its GDP. Inflation had risen to 11.7%, and 8.4% of the labor force were reported as unemployed. Higher food prices hurt ordinary consumers. Amid this decline, President Medvedev called for diversification of the economy and modernization of business and industry. Oil output provided about 19% of Russia's GDP and was worth $255 billion in 2010. Medvedev also called for reforms to introduce greater accountability and transparency in business and industry, particularly in inefficient state companies. But his anti-corruption efforts had largely failed toward the end of his term.

At the beginning of 2011 Russia had $483 billion in gold and foreign currency reserves and a gross national debt of only 6% of GDP, the lowest of all the G20 states. By end of the year, the growth rate of Russia's GDP was 4.3%, with industrial production rising at 5.7%. Inflation of consumer prices stood at 8.9%, having risen from 5.8% in 2010, and unemployment was reported at 6.1%. Stimulus spending and better demand from China aided the Russian economy. The Russian Trading System (RTS) stock average had risen 11.6% from the end of 2010 in dollar terms, and stood at 1,976 on 30 July 2011. The European debt crisis was expected to reduce growth in 2012 by about one point.

However, Russia's long-term economic prospects have deteriorated. Without major substantial reforms and privatization, economists say growth is unlikely to resume at government target rates of 6 to 7%. Two-thirds of Russia's hard-currency exports still come from oil and gas markets, where prices are notoriously volatile. Taxes on those energy exports provide half of its budget revenues, and budget deficits of 8–9% appeared early in 2009 when oil prices fell to $50 per barrel. Despite high average oil prices in 2011, the IMF reported that Russia's trade surplus and the ruble both declined. Additionally, the gas, electricity, and railway industries are dominated by inefficient state-owned monopolies. Oil and gas production volumes are stable or decreasing, and world competition from liquefied natural gas (LNG), Qatar, and new oil fields is cutting into Russian demand. As a place to do business, Russia is rated less free than nearly all other European economies according to the *Wall Street Journal*, owing to its weak protection of property rights, heavy regulation and licensing requirements for entrepreneurs who wish to open a business, restrictions on payments, and distorted prices. Transparency International's Corruption Perceptions Index for 2011 ranked Russia 143rd out of 163 countries, about the same as Nigeria, Azerbaijan, or Belarus.

20 INCOME

The World Bank classifies Russia as an "upper middle income country." The CIA estimated that the GDP of Russia was $2.2 trillion in 2010. The CIA defines GDP as the value of all final goods and services produced within a nation in a given year and the GDP is computed on the basis of purchasing power parity (PPP) rather than value as measured on the basis of the rate of the exchange based on current dollars. The PPP-adjusted GDP was estimated at $18,330 per capita, ranking 68th in the world, about the same as Hungary or Portugal. Remittances from citizens living abroad totaled $5.4 billion or about $39 per capita and added about 0.2% to GDP. Gross national income was distributed very unequally. The top 10% received 33.5% according to a survey in 2008. Based on the national poverty standard in rubles, the poverty rate was 11.9% in 2005, but twice that in rural areas. By the same standard, the recession-troubled 2009 rate was 13.1%.

The World Bank reports that in 2009 household final consumption on goods and services in Russia totaled $671.7 billion (54% of GDP) or about $4,841 per capita. Such consumption was growing at an unsustainable average annual rate of 10.3% per capita from 2000 through 2009. Some 17.7% of GDP was spent on food and beverages, 7.7% on housing rent and household furnishings, 5.2% on clothes, 4.3% on health, 6.1% on transportation, 2.4% on communications, 3.5% on recreation, 1.6% on restaurants and hotels, and 5.8% on miscellaneous goods and services and purchases from abroad.

21 LABOR

As of 2010 Russia had a total labor force of 75 million people. Within that labor force, about 10% were employed in agriculture, 31.9% in industry, and 58.1% in the service sector. The labor force participation rate in 2009 was 69% of all males age 15 and older, as compared to 58% of females, many of them part-time. The official unemployment rate in 2011 was 6.1%, though a considerable number of workers were underemployed or out of the labor force.

The work-related illness rate was 16 per 100,000. The work-related rate of death was 11.8 per 100,000.

The Federation of Independent Trade Unions of Russia (FNPR) claims to represent 80% of all workers. In particular, the mining and air transport industries (along with the state sector) are highly unionized. Overall, according to more reliable estimates, about 46% of the workforce is at least nominally organized, and around 90% of the organized workforce is part of the FNPR. The legal right to strike is hindered by complex requirements; collective bargaining rights are not enforced. Only 2 per 1,000 employee-days have been lost to strikes. Court rulings have determined that nonpayment of wages, the most prevalent labor complaint, is an individual issue and cannot be addressed by the union. The cost of hiring and firing workers is high, discouraging new employment. Forty hours of work is the standard per week, yet reportedly quite a few employees work 10 or 12 hours each day. The minimum wage was set at 4,611 rubles per month (about $1,600) in 2011. Many workers earn more than this amount, but about one-fifth earn less, not to mention the rural labor force.

Children under the age of 16 are banned from most employment, but 14-year-old minors can work under certain conditions with the approval of a parent or guardian. In such cases, the health and the welfare of the child must not be threatened. While these provisions are generally enforced through government action, prevailing social norms, and a large pool of low-wage adult workers, child labor remains a problem, especially in the informal economy. The law establishes minimum standards of workplace safety and worker health, but these are not effectively enforced.

22 AGRICULTURE

Owing to the short growing season (120–180 days) in much of Russia, at most 13% of the total land area is farmed. Much of Russia's land lies too far north for cultivation. The country's major crops include grains, potatoes, sugar beets, sunflower seeds, vegetables (cabbages, corn, tomatoes, carrots, turnips, and onions), and fruits (currants, cherries, and berries). Except for drought years and attendant fires, Russia produces about 100 million tons of wheat a year and exports a fifth of it to Europe and elsewhere (2.8 million tons in 2009). Corn production was 4 million tons in 2009. Despite a good harvest season in 2011, grain exports were reduced to 3.5 million tons. August–October shipments were delayed by insufficient unloading from freight trains and handling at the ports. Much of the fresh crops and slaughtered meat is sold at open-air markets by growers themselves.

Agricultural production dropped by an average of 6% annually during 1990–2000, though it has recovered more recently. The 2009 crop index was 136 (1999–2001=100). Cereal yields per hectare improved 31% from 1990 to 2009, and overall agricultural productivity per worker rose more than 50% during that period. Nevertheless, a surge in imports of food products from 1990 to 2010 has been the direct result of difficulties faced by domestic farmers and processors, together with rising income and consumer demand for quality food. The country regularly imports meat, sugar, and tropical fruit. Russia's agricultural trade deficit persistently has been one of the highest in the world.

Agricultural policy has changed several times since market reforms began. Low interest loans were initially offered to the old state farms, but the government's budget soon could not afford all the demands made by farmers. The low-interest loans were replaced by in-kind loans to suppliers, which were then modified to in-kind loans from the federal government to local governments. To protect food security, the government is promoting the expansion of small-plot farming; about 150,000 new farms have begun operating since 1991, primarily in the south.

23 ANIMAL HUSBANDRY

Russia's livestock production fell from 1990 to 1999 because of insufficient infrastructure and distribution. As was true of field crops, livestock production continued to decline until the mid-2000s. Russian dairy farms have been unprofitable because of low-productivity milk cows, limited supplies of quality feed, and lack of support services. In addition, poultry output declined in the face of import competition. Continued decline in livestock production, especially poultry, as well as the rapid growth of imports, has been a source of trade friction. After a severe reduction of one-third of livestock production during the 1990s, the production index had recovered 18% by 2009 compared with figures from 2000, according to the World Bank.

Russia dedicated 92.1 million hectares (227.5 million acres) to permanent pasture or meadow in 2009, according to the UN Food and Agriculture Organization (FAO). In 2009 the livestock population included 21.5 million head of cattle, 15.8 million pigs, and 366.3 million chickens. These animals yielded 2.52 million tons of beef and veal, 2.57 million tons of pork, 3.17 million tons of poultry, 2.03 million tons of eggs, and 24.5 million tons of milk. Russia also produced 178,557 tons of cattle hide and 54,658 tons of raw wool.

24 FISHING

Russia had 2,502 decked commercial fishing boats in 2008, about 24% of the world's fishing fleet capacity, even though the fleet has many old vessels and worn equipment. Fuel shortages are common as well. Despite its limited ice-free shoreline, Russia's fish production ranks eighth in the world, with 3.38 million tons in 2009, according to the UN FAO. Only 3% of the total came from aquaculture (fish-farming). Of the catch, 91% was maritime, while 9% came from inland waters. Russia is authorized under international agreements to catch up to five million tons of fish outside its territorial waters, but typically the fleet brings in much less. Overfishing and pollution of territorial waters have forced fishermen farther away from traditional fishing grounds. The main species of the commercial catch are white fish, herring, cod, and salmon. Russia is a leading producer of crabmeat, fish roe, whole groundfish, and salmon products. More than half of Russian fish product exports consist of frozen products, filets, and roe. The export value of seafood totaled $1.95 billion.

Russia is renowned for its sturgeon and caviar, but excessive and illegal trade of sturgeon and caviar has resulted in a decline of all 11 of Russia's commercial sturgeon species. Russia does protect 9% of its territorial waters. Even so, pollutants like mercury had already caused the decline of 50% to 90% in the sturgeon and pike perch catches in the Caspian Sea during the last years of the Soviet Union from 1974 to 1987. Despite the effects of pollution, the total harvested volume expanded during the 1980s with intensified fishing in dam reservoirs, substitution of nontraditional fish varieties, and consumer acceptance of higher levels of contaminants.

Since the fall of the Soviet Union, however, the production of fish and fish products has declined, in part because subsidies from the federal government ceased in 1994 and in part owing to the loss of fishing grounds in the Baltic states, Ukraine, and Georgia.

25 FORESTRY

Nearly half of Russia's surface land is classified as forested-area. Most of this area is in Siberia where weather retards the trees' rates of growth. Only half of this area is commercially accessible, and only 7–10% is exploited. The forest stock in Russia is 80% coniferous, consisting mainly of spruce, fir, larch, and pine in subarctic areas; these stands account for 52% of the world's coniferous areas. Farther south, deciduous trees (birch, oak, beech, ash, maple, and elm) grow and account for 13% of the world's deciduous forests.

The UN FAO estimated the 2009 roundwood production at 112.9 million cu m (3.99 billion cu ft). The value of all forest products, including roundwood, totaled $7.76 billion. After the dissolution of the USSR, the forest products industry underwent massive changes, as hundreds of inexperienced people were attracted to the business of buying logs from newly unregulated *leskhozes*, the villages legally entitled to manage and harvest forests. Widespread privatization in the forest products industry began in 1993. The 40 different taxes payable by wood processing companies and weak enforcement the federal forest service prompted some to act outside the official system. During the 1990s about 50% of all forestry firms went out of business. Poaching, unsustainable logging, and fire damage are ongoing problems. Much of the forestry equipment is too old or expensive to operate.

26 MINING

Russia has a significant percentage of the world's mineral resources and mineral production. Russia is the world's largest producer of nickel, vanadium, asbestos, diamonds, and palladium. Russia is one of the largest producers of aluminum, potash, gold, and mined copper. Russia also produces bauxite, coal, cobalt, diamond, lead, mica, natural gas, oil, tin, zinc, and many other metals, industrial minerals, and mineral fuels. In 2009 Russia had 16,100 enterprises engaged in mining and quarrying.

More than half of Russia's mineral resources are east of the Urals. The most significant regions for mining are Siberia, particularly East Siberia for cobalt, columbium (niobium), copper (70% of Russia's reserves), gold, iron ore, lead (76% of the country's reserves), molybdenum, nickel (becoming depleted), platinum group metals (PGMs), tin, tungsten, zinc, asbestos, diamond, fluorspar, mica, and talc; the Kola Peninsula for cobalt, columbium, copper, nickel, rare-earth metals, phosphate (the majority in the form of apatite), and tantalum; North Caucasus for copper, lead, molybdenum, tungsten, and zinc; the Russian Far East for gold, lead, silver, tin, tungsten, and zinc; the Urals, for bauxite, beryllium, cobalt, copper, iron ore, lead, magnesite, nickel, titanium, vanadium, zinc, asbestos, bismuth, potash (96% of the country's reserves), soda ash, talc, and vermiculite; and the region near the Arctic Circle for cobalt, gold, mercury, nickel, tin, phosphate, and uranium. The Kaliningrad region contains 95% of the world's amber deposits, and Russia possesses 10% of the world's copper reserves. Metallurgical enterprises in Kola, North Caucasus, and the Urals are operating on rapidly depleting resource bases and are experiencing raw material shortages.

A large percentage of Russian reserves are in remote northern and eastern regions that lack transport, are distant from major population and industrial centers, and experience severe climates. Enterprises built there in the Soviet era have sharply curtailed operations. Efforts to develop new large deposits of nonferrous metals near the eastern Baikal-Amur railroad are not progressing. One researcher proposed the creation of small mining enterprises to develop the rich small deposits of eastern Russia. Reserves of iron ore are sufficient to last 15–20 years; those of nonferrous metals, 10–30 years. Reserves of major minerals included potash, 1.8 billion tons; magnesite, 585 million tons; bauxite, 250 million tons; phosphate rock, 240 million tons; asbestos, 100 million tons; fluorspar, 60 million tons; manganese, 15 million tons; nickel, 6.3 million tons; vanadium, 5 million tons; zinc, 4 million tons; antimony, 3 million tons; and lead, 3 million tons.

Output of iron ore (gross weight) was 92 million tons in 2009, down from 99.9 million metric tons in 2008. The largest producer was Kursk Magnetic Anomaly, at Zheleznogorsk and Gubkin, with a 50 million ton per year capacity.

Output of copper was 675,000 metric tons in 2009. The Noril'sk complex, in East Siberia, produced 70% of the country's copper and planned to increase output of cuprous ore from its Oktyabr'skiy underground mine, from 100,000 tons per year to 1.6 million tons, because the cuprous ores were 40% higher in copper content than the nickel-rich ores. The Oktyabr'skiy mine supplied 70% of Noril'sk's copper output and was planning to decrease production of the nickel-rich ores.

PMG production included 79,520 kg (175,311 lb) of palladium and 18,739 kg (41,312 lb) of platinum. Sixty percent of PGM output came from the Oktyabr'skiy mine, and a plan to expand output at the mine of cuprous ores by a factor of 16 was projected to yield more PGMs. Barrick Gold and OJSC Pava are developing the Fyodorova Tundra deposit in the Murmansk region.

The output of other metals in 2009 was bauxite, 5.77 million metric tons; mined nickel, 261,900 metric tons; mined zinc, 225,000 metric tons; mined lead, 78,000 metric tons; magnesite, 2.6 million metric tons (estimated); mined tin, 1,200 metric tons; molybdenum, 4,800 metric tons (estimated); and mined cobalt, 2,352 metric tons. Gold mine output was 205,236 kg (452,467 lb), fourth in the world. Russia also produced the metal minerals alumina, nepheline concentrate, antimony, white arsenic, bismuth, chromium, manganese, mercury, silver, tungsten, and baddeleyite zirconium. Russia stopped mining beryllium in the mid-1990s and continued producing cobbed beryl.

Industrial mineral production in 2009 included phosphate rock (apatite concentrate and sedimentary rock), 9.5 million metric tons; marketable potash, 3.7 million metric tons; mica, 9,000 metric tons (estimated); fluorspar concentrate, 210,000 metric tons (estimated); and gem and industrial diamonds, 34,759,400 carats. Russia also produced the industrial minerals amber, asbestos, barite, boron, hydraulic cement, kaolin clay, feldspar, graphite, gypsum, iodine, lime, lithium minerals, nitrogen, salt, sodium compounds, sulfur (including native and pyrites), sulfuric acid, talc, and vermiculite. Russia's only producer of amber, Kaliningrad Amber Works, was the world's largest producer, yielding 341 tons in 2010.

Despite some decreased metal output compared with the Soviet period, Russia was producing more aluminum, lead, and zinc by

2000 than during the Soviet era. However, only 10% of the technology employed in the nonferrous mining and metallurgy sector is rated as world class, labor productivity is one-third below that of advanced industrialized countries, and energy expenditures are 20–30% higher. Another problem is that the resource base for metallurgical enterprises is not competitive in terms of quality, with the exception of antimony, copper, nickel, and molybdenum. More than one-half of industrial mineral output is exported, depriving the domestic sector of needed supplies, especially barite, bentonite, crystalline graphite, and kaolin. Russia has not been successful in attracting foreign investment for developing its mineral deposits because of high and unpredictable taxes, an unreliable legal system, insecure licensing, unequal treatment between domestic and foreign partners, a weak banking system, and the inability to directly export commodities.

²⁷ENERGY AND POWER

The World Bank reported in 2008 that Russia produced 1.25 billion tons of oil equivalent in energy. Per capita use was 4,838 kg (10,665 lb), down about 18% since 1990, but still high by European standards. Roughly 91% of energy came from fossil fuels, while 8% came from alternative or nuclear fuels. The country produced 1.04 trillion kWh of electricity and consumed 913.5 billion kWh, or 6,584 kWh per capita. Much of the electricity is generated by coal-fired plants. Nuclear power provides 17% of electricity in Russia. As of 2011, the country had 32 reactors operating (3rd in the world) with 11 under construction.

Russia possesses enormous reserves of oil, natural gas, and coal. Russia possesses the world's largest natural gas reserves, the second largest coal reserves, and the eighth largest proven oil reserves (3.7 billion tons). These reserves amount to about 13% of the world's oil resources and a quarter of its conventional natural gas deposits. Gazprom, the state-backed gas monopoly, controls more than 20 billion tons of oil equivalent in proven oil and gas reserves according to *The Economist*. The publicly traded petroleum company Rosneft (75% state owned) and private LukOil have another 1 billion tons in reserve. Russia has a crude oil processing capacity estimated at 5.43 million barrels per day as of 2009. However, many facilities are inefficient, old, and in need of being modernized. Exports are handled by pipeline, rail, and barge transport.

In 2009 the Russian and Chinese governments finalized a series of agreements to forge a co-op program for shared oil resources. The agreements include plans for construction of a new branch of the Eastern Siberia-Pacific Ocean oil pipeline and a long-term crude oil trade deal with a finance plan between the Russia Oil Transport Company and the China Development Bank.

²⁸INDUSTRY

Industrial branches, including manufacturing, have been growing at a rate of 4.6% annually from 2000 through 2009 and at a rate of 3.9% in 2011. Manufacturing value added was $161.8 billion in 2009, according to the World Bank. Products include iron and crude steel; cars and trucks; aircraft; machines and equipment; chemicals (including fertilizers); plastics; cement, bricks, and other building materials; medical and scientific instruments; textiles; handicrafts; paper; television sets and other appliances; and food-

stuffs. In the years 2005–08, according to the World Bank, industry provided 38% of male and 24% of female employment.

Steel production remains a key industry, though this branch fell behind competitors during the 1980s, owing to inferior quality. Russian plants continue to operate, although less than half use updated equipment. Aluminum and nickel production continue, particularly in mineral-rich Siberia. European Russia and the Ural region continue to serve as the center for the production of textiles and machine industry. Chemical production is scattered throughout the country.

The automobile industry has expanded and modernized since Soviet times, though foreign makers and imports are also important. In 2009 the industry produced 595,000 light vehicles and 91,000 trucks. This represented about a 60% drop in units from 2008 because of the recession. In 2010 production doubled to 1.3 million vehicles, including 124,000 trucks. The industry benefited from about $5 billion in bailouts and credits and is protected behind 50–100% tariff walls. AvtoVaz of Togliatti, begun with Fiat of Italy, is the largest producer; its Lada brand is the most popular in the country. KAMAZ is the biggest truck producer. KIA of Korea and GM-Chevrolet are leading foreign producers.

Much of Russia's industrial base is outmoded and must be restructured or replaced. Industrial expansion in consumer goods and food processing sometimes takes place in enterprises converting from military production, once the priority industry of the USSR. Fixed-capital investments increased about 8.5% in 2011 over the same period in 2010.

Russia concluded $72.3 billion in arms agreements from 2003 to 2010, according to the Congressional Research Service. That amounted to about three-quarters of the US total, which was the largest in the world. In 2010 the Russian figure was $7.6 billion, just over half the US total of $14.9 billion.

²⁹SCIENCE AND TECHNOLOGY

Russia has a long history in science and mathematics. The Russian Academy of Sciences, founded in 1725, is the chief coordinating body for scientific research in Russia through its science councils and commissions. It has departments of physical, technical, and mathematical sciences; chemical, technological, and biological sciences; and earth sciences, and it controls a network of nearly 300 research institutes. The Russian Academy of Agricultural Sciences, founded in 1929, has departments of plant breeding and genetics; arable farming and the use of agricultural chemicals; feed and fodder crops production; plant protection; livestock production; veterinary science; mechanization, electrification, and automation in farming; forestry; the economics and management of agricultural production; land reform and the organization of land use; land reclamation and water resources; and the storage and processing of agricultural products. It controls a network of nearly 100 research institutes, experimental and breeding stations, dendraria, and arboreta. The Russian Academy of Medical Sciences, founded in 1944, has departments of preventive medicine, clinical medicine, and medical and biological sciences; it controls a network of nearly 100 research institutes. Russian scientists and technologists employed in the priority military sector were renowned for their work during the Soviet period.

As of 2009, according to the World Bank, patent applications in science and technology by Russian residents totaled 25,598. How-

Principal Trading Partners – Russia (2010)

(In millions of US dollars)

Country	Total	Exports	Imports	Balance
World	673,856.0	400,242.0	273,614.0	126,628.0
China	58,842.0	19,783.0	39,059.0	-19,276.0
Netherlands	57,679.0	53,240.0	4,439.0	48,801.0
Germany	42,481.0	15,861.0	26,620.0	-10,759.0
Italy	34,404.0	24,376.0	10,028.0	14,348.0
Ukraine	27,612.0	13,609.0	14,003.0	-394.0
Japan	22,750.0	12,494.0	10,256.0	2,238.0
United States	21,769.0	11,927.0	9,842.0	2,085.0
Poland	20,043.0	14,216.0	5,827.0	8,389.0
Turkey	18,856.0	13,977.0	4,879.0	9,098.0
South Korea	17,690.0	10,408.0	7,282.0	3,126.0

(…) data not available or not significant.

(n.s.) not specified.

SOURCE: *2011 Direction of Trade Statistics Yearbook*, New York: United Nations, 2011.

ever, Russian scientific performance in most fields has been disappointing, given its illustrious history. Over the period 1995–2010, barely 0.1% of worldwide patents awarded by the US Patent and Trademark Office went to Russians; a similarly miniscule share was reported by the UN World Intellectual Property Organization for out-of-country applications. The Russian Federation in 2000–08 had 3,191 scientists and engineers and 493 technicians engaged in research and development per million people. They published 13,953 articles in scientific and medical journals during 2007, a rate about the same as in 1990, though the global output has risen significantly. There were 49,000 trademark applications filed in 2009. Public financing of science was 1.03% of GDP during 2000–08, less than comparable European or East Asian countries. Of that spending, more than half came from government sources, while business accounted for 31% and foreign sources 8%. Higher education institutions were a negligible source of funding, although Russia has nearly 250 universities and institutes offering courses in basic and applied sciences.

High technology exports in 2009 totaled $4.6 billion, or 9% of the country's manufactured exports, a decline in the share relative to the early 2000s. Russia paid $4.1 billion in royalty fees during 2009 and received only $494 million in receipts.

Between 1957 (the first sputnik) and 2010 Russia launched 3,391 missions into space, twice the number for the United States according to NASA. In 2010 there were 38 successful Russian launches as compared with 24 US launches. Russia has been an important partner in the International Space Station venture.

About 15 Russian-born or Russian citizens have won Nobel prizes in chemistry or physics since 1956. The latest Russian-born Nobelists were André Geim and Vladimir Novoselov in physics in 2010.

30 DOMESTIC TRADE

A central marketplace is a common feature of Russian cities. Western-style stores have appeared in major cities supplied by regular distribution channels, despite occasional demands for protection money. Large shopping malls have opened up on the ring road that circles Moscow. Outside of Moscow and St. Petersburg, small open markets and kiosks are still common retail outlets. Distri-

bution and trade through informal and outdoor channels is still common, and national brands are advertised on billboards, buses, magazines, and other media. Foreign-made articles, often traded via the black market during the Soviet era, are now available for a price.

From the first MacDonald's and Pizza Huts in Soviet times, franchising has developed in the fast-food sector, coffee shops , and tea rooms. Other consumer-oriented franchise operations are in retail, healthcare, entertainment, travel and lodging, and automotives. Business-to-business franchising occurs in such areas as logistics, express mail services, cleaning and maintenance services, transportation, management training, and consulting. Electronic commerce (e-commerce) in the business-to-business sector is growing in Russia, as the number of Internet users has risen significantly. However, growth in the business-to-consumer sector and catalogue sales remain hampered by a lack of reliable Internet payment mechanisms.

Business hours are generally 9 a.m. to 6 p.m., Monday–Friday, but many shopping centers and supermarkets are open from 10 a.m. to 8 p.m. Banks are generally open from 9 a.m. to 6 p.m., Monday–Friday.

31 FOREIGN TRADE

Russia's principal exports have long been oil, natural gas, wood and wood products, minerals, military equipment and weapons, and gold. The main imports are machinery and equipment, consumer goods, medicines, meat, grain, sugar, and semi-finished metal products. Trade is carried on by rail, truck, railroads, and sea freight.

Largely because of the 170% rise in energy prices from 2000 to 2008, Russian exports totaled $301 billion (freight on board) by 2006. Crude and refined petroleum products represented 47% of this, natural gas another 14%. Non-ferrous metals exports were 6%, mostly aluminum, nickel, and copper. Imports totaled $137.7 billion (cost, insurance, and freight) in 2006, composed of 27.6% machinery (communications equipment, specialized and general machinery, electrical and electronics machinery, and motor vehicles and parts); chemical products including pharmaceuticals, 12%; and food products, 12%. Russia's main suppliers that year were Germany, China, Ukraine, Japan, Belarus, South Korea, United States, France, Italy, and Finland. Total merchandise and service trade was 48.6% of GDP in 2009, somewhat more than other large high-income countries such as the United States or Japan. Russia's current account (merchandise plus services) was $86.3 billion in 2010–11, or 12% of GDP. Exports totaled $498.6 billion in 2011, and imports totaled $310.1 billion.

Russia, Belarus, and Kazakhstan launched a customs union on 1 July 2010, and Russia joined the WTO in 2011. Freer trade was likely to hamper inefficient Russian enterprises, like some of those in pharmaceuticals, textiles, construction materials, and food processing. However, foreign competition was also expected to force Russian producers to match the quality of imports and to innovate. The World Bank has estimated that WTO membership could increase Russian GDP by 11% between 2010 and 2020.

32 BALANCE OF PAYMENTS

Foreign trade was largely deregulated in early 1992, and the trade balance contracted throughout the early Yeltsin years. Deficits in

Balance of Payments – Russia (2010)

(In millions of US dollars)

Current Account		**70,253.0**
Balance on goods		151,681.0
Imports	-248,738.0	
Exports	400,419.0	
Balance on services		-29,212.0
Balance on income		-48,616.0
Current transfers		-3,599.0
Capital Account		**73.0**
Financial Account		**-25,956.0**
Direct investment abroad		-52,476.0
Direct investment in Russia		42,846.0
Portfolio investment assets		-3,470.0
Portfolio investment liabilities		1,810.0
Financial derivatives		-1,841.0
Other investment assets		-22,834.0
Other investment liabilities		10,010.0
Net Errors and Omissions		**-7,621.0**
Reserves and Related Items		**-36,749.0**

(…) data not available or not significant.

SOURCE: *Balance of Payment Statistics Yearbook 2011,* Washington, DC: International Monetary Fund, 2011.

the current account created a shortage of hard currency that severely limited importation possibilities of consumer and capital goods. Since 1993, however, Russia has run a surplus on the current account. The current account balance averaged 10% of GDP over the 2001–05 period. In 2010 Russia had a foreign trade surplus of $92 billion, amounting to 5.3% of GDP. During 2010–11 (June to June) the merchandise trade balance was $167.3 billion, according to the Economist Intelligence Unit, and the current account (which includes a deficit on services) was $76.0 billion. During this time, owing to the current account surpluses and foreign investments, the ruble appreciated against the US dollar by about 10%.

33 BANKING AND SECURITIES

The Central Bank of the Russian Federation was created in January 1992 out of the Soviet mono-banking system headed by Gosbank. In the new two-tier banking system, the Central Bank regulates the commercial banking sector, handles foreign exchange transactions, and implements monetary policy by setting the reserve requirements and the discount rate. Sberbank (the Savings Bank) is by far the largest banking institution in the country with more than 2,000 branches; it holds most of the population's ruble savings. Sberbank became a joint-stock company in 1991, with the Central Bank taking a 20% shareholding. Russia has four other specialized banks: the Foreign Trade Bank (Vneshtorgbank), which is now more concerned with retail and corporate banking; the Bank for Construction and Industry (Promstroibank); the Agriculture Bank (Agroprombank); and the Social Sector Bank (Zhilotsbank). The other important state-owned bank is the Rosevneshtorgbank (Bank for Foreign Trade of the Russian Federation). State-owned banks together control more than one-third of all banking assets. Around 1,000 commercial banks also operate in Russia; one-third of them are former specialized state banks while the rest are new. Commercial banks include the Commer-

cial Bank Industriaservis, the Commercial Credit Bank, the Commercial Conservation Bank, the Commercial Innovation Bank, the International Moscow Bank, St. Petersburg's Investment Bank, and the Construction Bank. The International Bank is owned by Western banks interested in doing business in the country

In August 1998 government defaults led to collapse of Russia's financial markets as the government abandoned support for the ruble and ceased bond payments. With many banks insolvent, the Central Bank had to intervene to allow depositors to rescue a portion of their funds. Sberbank took over individual accounts from banks liquidated by the government. Following the 1998 crisis, a group of new banks flourished, having avoided speculation on defaulted short term government loans. These modern banks include the Bank of Moscow, Alfa-Bank, Rosbank, Mezhprombank, MDM Bank, Sobinbank, National Reserve Bank, and Gazprom Bank. Banking regulations were improved in 2006 and capital requirements raised in 2010. The government has intervened to prevent some 60 insolvent banks from closing. However, the banking system still suffers from widespread lack of trust.

The IMF reported that at the end of 2008, currency and demand deposits (M1) were RUB7.6 trillion ($306 billion) in Russia. M2—an aggregate equal to M1 plus savings deposits, small time deposits, and money market mutual funds—was RUB13.5 trillion ($549 billion). Broad money, which includes securities issued by the central government, was RUB16.8 trillion ($676 billion). The money market rate was 5.5%; the discount rate, the interest rate at which the central bank lends to financial institutions in the short term, was 5.8%, but the lending rate was 12%. Consumer prices had been rising at about 11% between 2005 and 2008, so the real lending rate, allowing for inflation, was barely positive.

At the end of 2008, the nation's gold bullion holdings were 16.7 million fine troy ounces, valued then at $14.5 billion. Russia also held $411 billion in foreign exchange.

The first Russian stock market opened in Moscow in 1991; a Commission for Securities and Stock Market was established in late 1994. Over 100 different securities were traded by 1996. The range, as well as the volume, of securities traded has been rapidly expanding, despite inadequate regulation and custody registration. Subsequent adoption of a tight monetary policy has contributed to the ongoing recovery. Stock market valuations rose and, by 2004, the exchange had a combined market capitalization of $268 billion. A number of foreign mutual funds have invested in the Russian stock exchange. As of mid-2011 the RTS market index stood at 1,976, up 0.7% in ruble terms (11.6% in dollar terms) over the end of 2010.

34 INSURANCE

In 1993 officials reported that 1,524 Russian companies were licensed to sell insurance and another 750 companies had applied for licenses. They began small—premium volume for the first nine months of 1993 amounted to only 1.3% of the GDP, compared with volume of 2.9% during the last full year of the former Soviet Union. As in the commercial banking sector, however, various insurance companies have gradually consolidated into groups. There were about 1,000 insurance companies operating in Russia in 2005, and that number had dropped to 786 by year-end 2008. Most analysts believed that 500 companies were sufficient to serve the Russian insurance market. During the 2008–09 global finan-

Public Finance – Russia (2009)

(In billions of rubles, central government figures)

Revenue and Grants	**14,151.8**	**100.0%**
Tax revenue	5,028	35.5%
Social contributions	2,354.7	16.6%
Grants	292.6	2.1%
Other revenue	6,476.5	45.8%
Expenditures	**11,621.3**	**100.0%**
General public services	3,122.4	26.9%
Defense	1,427.2	12.3%
Public order and safety	938.4	8.1%
Economic affairs	1,031.3	8.9%
Environmental protection	11.1	0.1%
Housing and community amenities	52.7	0.5%
Health	853.9	7.3%
Recreational, culture, and religion	100	0.9%
Education	417.7	3.6%
Social protection	3,666.6	31.6%

(…) data not available or not significant.

SOURCE: *Government Finance Statistics Yearbook 2010*, Washington, DC: International Monetary Fund, 2010.

cial crisis, as automotive sales declined and banking sector activity stalled, the insurance market suffered. Yet by 2011, the insurance industry in Russia was growing rapidly, with predicted growth of 12.3% during 2011–14. Total premiums were estimated to be worth $41 billion in 2010.

Compulsory insurance includes third-party automobile liability, medical insurance, pension, social insurance, and fire and accident insurance. Minimum capital requirements have been modest. Private firms are allowed to deduct their insurance premiums as a business expense for tax purposes.

35 PUBLIC FINANCE

In 2010 the budget of Russia included $262 billion in public revenue and $341.1 billion in public expenditures. The budget deficit of $79 billion amounted to 5.4% of GDP. Public debt was 9.5% of GDP (down from 16% in 2005), with $405.7 billion of the debt held by foreign entities. Public debt was an estimated 6% of GDP by early 2011. According to the Economist Intelligence Unit, the budget deficit was only 1.5% in 2011. As a result of this and a decline in global interest rates, the 10-year bond interest yield in Russia was 4.7%, compared to 2.7% in the European area. Debt payment was 2% in 2009. By type of payment in 2009, 68% was transfers, 16% salaries, 12% goods and services, 1% interest payment, and 3% other.

36 TAXATION

Historically, Russia's tax system has been inefficient and unfair to many. The Tsarist Empire taxed land, imports, vodka, and even beards. Businesses and individuals routinely failed to pay their taxes on time, if at all. This unfortunate pattern has continued. The current Russian government draws 18% of its tax revenue from international trade, though this was expected to decline following WTO accession in 2011. Royalties on export of raw materials, oil, and gas are very important. According to the World Bank,

the state managed to extract only 1% of its revenue from income, profits, and capital gains levies in 2009. Taxes on goods and services (gasoline, natural gas, alcohol, tobacco, cars, motorcycles, and jewelry) yielded 16%. Social contributions were 17%, and "other taxes (presumably royalties) and grants" were 48%. According to the World Bank's survey, in 2009 Russia's central government collected 12.9% of its GDP in taxes, somewhat below the average in Europe. The total tax rate was 46.5% of commercial profits, very similar to the United States and the European area. Overall, Russia's tax burden was 34.1% of GDP in 2009.

Since 1999 the tax system has been the focus of a major reform effort aimed at reducing tax loads, improving collection rates, and bringing the system in line with those of advanced market economies. The new tax code cut the number of official taxes from over 200 to about 40 and sought to close many loopholes. Taxes are levied at three levels of government: federal, regional, and local. The principal taxes collected at the federal level are the profits tax on organizations (divided among all three levels of government), a capital gains tax, a flat personal income tax, the Unified Social Tax (replacing payroll contributions to four separate social benefit funds), a value-added tax (VAT—18% in 2012) on most goods and services (10% on certain foods and children's clothing; pharmaceuticals and certain financial services are exempt), luxury excise taxes from 20% up to 570%, a securities tax (0.8% on nominal value with exemptions for initial issues), customs duties and customs fees, and federal license fees.

The labor tax took about 32% of commercial profits, according to the World Bank in 2010. As of 2011 the corporate income tax was 20% with payments split 5% to the federal budget, 13–17% payable to the regional governments, and 2% to the local level. Exceptions to the 13% flat rate include a 15% rate on dividend income and income of nonresidents from Russian sources. Gambling winnings, lottery prizes, constructive income from low-interest or interest-free loans, some insurance payments, and excessive bank interest are all considered income.

Foreign companies pay withholding of 20%. Non-residents are subject to a 30% rate on their regular incomes, but 15% on dividends. Residents are subject to a 9% withholding rate on payroll income. Though the trade-weighted tariff in 2009 was only 5.9%, non-transparent regulations and standards, discriminatory licensing, and service market barriers make importing time-consuming and unpredictable. Foreign investors can be exempted from import duties and export taxes, and there is limited relief from profits tax, varying by sector and region.

At the regional level the principal taxes are an assets tax (2.2%), a real estate tax, a transport tax, sales taxes, a tax on gambling, and regional license fees. Two turnover taxes exist at the regional level. The social infrastructure maintenance tax (Housing Fund Tax) and a road users' tax, considered to be among the most onerous under the previous tax system, were abolished in 2001–03. At the local level there are land taxes, individual property taxes, taxes on advertising expenses, inheritance and gift taxes, and local license fees. Although tax rates are low by international standards for a developed country, informal hassles and bureaucratic interference make the process more burdensome.

37 CUSTOMS AND DUTIES

In 1992 Russia eliminated many of the import restrictions imposed by the former Soviet Union. Beginning in 2001 Russia put into effect a new and simpler tariff structure consisting of four basic rates: 5%, 10%, 15%, and 20%. This effectively lowered the tariff ceiling from 30% to 20%. A VAT of 18% applies to most imported goods, except for food products, which carry a VAT of only 10%. These duties (if paid), in addition to excise taxes on luxury goods, alcohol, tobacco, and autos, have made imported goods essentially noncompetitive for all but the richest Russian consumers.

Under the accession agreement with the WTO, average Russian tariffs were slated to fall to 12%, with a general rate of 15%. The WTO estimated that the average tariff rate in 2011 was 11.5%; this is to fall to 7.8%. Administrative barriers in the customs service may also be reduced.

38 FOREIGN INVESTMENT

Foreign investment was carefully limited during Soviet times. In 1991 a new foreign investment law promoting the transfer of capital, technology, and know-how went into effect. Privatization was pursued in the Yeltsin years and, by 2011, most of the economy had been privatized, though many firms' ownership included significant state-held blocks of shares. Nonresidents may acquire partial shareholdings or form wholly owned subsidiaries in Russia. Foreign firms must obtain licenses to exploit natural resources. Although foreign and domestic capitalists are legally equal, the government prefers joint ventures with a foreign entity as minority stockholder, particularly in energy ventures. Foreign ownership is capped in some areas, and in 42 "strategic sectors" control by a foreign entity must be pre-approved by the government. Vague business laws, a bureaucratic tax and regulatory system, crime and corruption in commercial transactions, inadequate infrastructure and financial services, and a weak commitment to reform continue to deter investors. Russia's 2011 accession to the WTO had the potential to improve these conditions.

Foreign direct investment (FDI) in 2005–07 averaged $32.6 billion, while Russians invested $27 billion per year outside the country. According to World Bank figures published in 2009, FDI in Russia was a net inflow of $36.8 billion or 3% of GDP; however, net outflows slightly exceeded the net inflows. Russia's disappointing share of world FDI has persistently been only about 30% of its share of world GDP, an indication of its lack of success in attracting foreign investment. The top foreign investors in Russia have been Germany, the United Kingdom, Luxembourg, the Netherlands, the United States, France, and Switzerland. Turkish businessmen are also active, as Russia has become Turkey's second-leading trade partner. Russia also supplies gas to Turkey over the Blue Stream pipeline project under the Black Sea.

39 ECONOMIC DEVELOPMENT

In 1991 Russia's parliament enacted legislation that provided for full privatization of the commercial and service sectors by 1994, placing about half the medium and large companies in private hands by 1995. By the end of 1992, about 6,000 firms had applied to become joint-stock companies and 1,560 had completed the process. By mid-decade almost one-third of Russia's approximately 250,000 small businesses had been privatized. In 1996 the government asserted that the non-state sector produced approximately 70% of GDP, up from 62% in 1995.

The privatization process was often hasty and inconsistent. The *nomenklatura* of ex-officials somehow gained much of the resulting wealth and economic power. Communist parliamentarians were quick to criticize the Yeltsin-Gaidar privatization efforts, which they blamed for the economic decline, but Yeltsin's government was committed to privatization and largely ignored the parliament and large public demonstrations in the capitals. Many enterprises, even if private, operate like company towns, as they did in Soviet times, and have not changed their paternalistic employment practices. Job security and company housing are expected. Russians also demand cheap utilities and transportation, as well as free education and medical care. Housing privatization began late in 1992. In 1998 the government passed an improved bankruptcy code, and in 2001 the Duma passed a deregulation package and a lower corporate tax rate to improve the business and investment sector.

Russia's reforms in taxation and deregulation made considerable progress in Putin's first administration. As a result, in 2002 the US Department of Commerce designated Russia a "market economy." Russian officials were invited by the G-7 nations to take part in negotiations, causing the group to be renamed the G-8. Progress in utilities pricing and restructuring, together with housing, was slower. The large, unwieldy, and corrupt bureaucracy remains a problem for reform. Oil and gas revenues, however, allowed Russia to improve its international financial position over this period. Financial strengthening raised business and investor confidence in Russia's economy, though the manufacturing base remained in serious need of modernization.

By the end of his second term in 2008, President Putin had taken a number of steps to shore up presidential power by increasing ownership and/or indirect control of major banks, natural resource conglomerates, shipbuilding, aerospace, and construction. President Medvedev's efforts to invigorate the technology sector—he wanted to create a Russian "silicon valley" east of Moscow—were slow to show results. He was able, however, to raise fines against bribery and signed the Organisation for Economic Co-operation and Development (OECD) convention on bribery late in 2011.

40 SOCIAL DEVELOPMENT

Russia's first laws governing sickness benefits were implemented in 1912. A social insurance system now provides pensions for old-age, survivorship, and disability. All citizens and refugees are entitled to medical care; employed people receive cash benefits for sickness. There is also a benefit provided to those caring for a sick child. Maternity benefits cover 100% of earnings from between 10 and 12 weeks before the expected date of childbirth and 10 to 16 weeks after childbirth. A universal system of family allowances provides a birth grant, a funeral grant, and a monthly benefit for each child under the age of 16.

The constitution prohibits discrimination based on race, sex, religion, language, social status or other circumstances. Despite these constitutional provisions, employment discrimination against women and minorities occurs. On average women earn significantly less than men and cluster in the lower-paid jobs and professions. The high cost of maternity care benefits leads some employers to hire men rather than women. Women suffer disproportionately in situations of worker layoffs.

There is no law against sexual harassment, and abuses in the workplace are common. Spousal abuse is also widespread and is treated as a domestic matter by the police, rather than as a criminal offense. Sexual violence and other crimes against women are underreported. In 2009 the murder rate was 15.6 per 100,000. Criminal drug abuse crimes were 162.6 per 100,000; robberies 31.9 per 100,000. Russia has 584 prisoners per 100,000, the second highest rate in the world, though less than half the rate in the United States. Prisoners are subject to mistreatment, unhealthy living conditions, and lack of medical care.

In general, human rights are respected, but serious violations occur in relation to the struggle against rebels in Chechnya. Ethnic minorities are subjected to harassment, searches, and arrest by police, and are sometimes denied permission to reside in Moscow. Anti-Semitic rhetoric is increasing and several instances of intimidation and violence have been reported. Muslims continue to face discrimination as well.

41 HEALTH

According to the CIA, overall life expectancy in Russia was estimated at 69 years in 2011. Excessive drinking and poor diet have been cited as leading causes for the fall in life expectancy for males compared to 1959. The rates in the United States and European area were 77 and 79, respectively. In Russia in 2009 there were 43 physicians, 85 nurses and midwives, and 97 hospital beds per 10,000 inhabitants. The fertility rate was 1.6 (below population replacement levels), while the infant mortality rate was 11 per 1,000 live births. In 2008 the maternal mortality rate, according to the World Bank, was 39 per 100,000 births. This level—and the estimated lifetime risk of maternal death in Russia—is about five times that of the European area. Despite immigration from the former Soviet states, the Russian population has shrunk since the end of the Soviet era.

As of 2008 it is estimated that about 60% of Russian adult males smoke and 22% of females. The rate for males is about twice that in high income countries. In the United States only about 25% of adult males smoke and 19% of females. It was estimated that 98% of children were vaccinated against measles and diphtheria-tetanus-pertussis (DTP3). An estimated 57% of the tuberculosis cases (10.6 per 1,000, several times higher than in the Euro area) are successfully treated, as compared with 69% in high income countries. The CIA calculated HIV/AIDS prevalence in Russia to be about 1% in 2009.

The country spent 4.8% of its GDP on healthcare in 2009, amounting to $475 per person. Public expenditure on healthcare totaled 64% of total health expenditures, as healthcare finance in Russia has become increasingly private.

42 HOUSING

The right to housing is guaranteed to all citizens by the constitution, but providing for adequate housing for all has become a problem in a time of major economic reforms. Since 2002 many residents have begun paying more of the costs for rent, maintenance, and utilities. The government still allows somewhat generous subsidies for low-income families. However, the main housing problem occurs in maintenance and renovation of buildings in

urgent need of both structural repairs and upgrades in utility systems. The government viewed aging housing structures as a major inefficiency in the country's energy policy. As of 2012, high-rise apartment buildings absorbed 35% of Russian energy production, but an estimated 30% of heat and 11% of electricity was lost in transmission. The cost of upgrading Russia's energy infrastructure was estimated at $320 billion, although these costs could be recouped within four years due to energy savings.

43 EDUCATION

As in the latter Soviet era, education is mostly free and compulsory for 10 years. Primary school covers four years, followed by another five years of basic school. Senior secondary schools offer two-year programs. Vocational secondary schools offer a four-year course of study. Although Russian is the most common medium of instruction, other languages are also taught, especially at the secondary level. In the early 1990s many privately owned institutions were opened, and the education system was modified with the introduction of a revised curriculum. The academic year runs from September to June.

The student-to-teacher ratio for primary school was about 17:1 in 2009; the ratio for secondary school was about 10:1. In 2009 the World Bank estimated that 92% of age-eligible children in Russia were enrolled in primary school, and most enrolled children go on to finish primary school. Gross enrollment in secondary school was 85% of the relevant age group. Tertiary enrollment was estimated at 77%. Of students enrolled in tertiary education, 136 were female for every 100 male students. As of 2006–09, graduates of tertiary educational institutions composed 32% of the unemployed, considerably more than in high-income European countries.

St. Petersburg State University, which was founded in 1724, is well-known for its education. The internationally supported New Economic School in Moscow has eclipsed all pre-existing Russian institutions in that field.

The general level of Russian education has deteriorated. The Programme for International Student Assessment (PISA) score for Russia was 468 in 2009, as compared with 487 for the United States and a high of 561 for Singapore. The Trends in International Mathematics and Scientific Study (TIMSS) quality survey found that eighth-grade Russian students scored 512 in mathematics, down 12% between 1995 to 2007. The global average was 500. However, in science Russian children scored 530, up 7% over the same period.

The overall literacy rate, according to the 2002 census, was 99.4%. Public expenditure for mostly state-funded education represented 3.9% of GDP or 12.9% of total government expenditures in 2009. Private tutoring is common.

44 LIBRARIES AND MUSEUMS

The Russian State Library in Moscow serves as the national library as well as a public one, with the largest collection in the country (about 45 million volumes). The Russian National Library in St. Petersburg, which is one of the oldest public libraries in Eastern Europe, holds over 34 million volumes. There are also over 50,000 public libraries throughout the country. Some of the larger collections include the Gorky Moscow Institute of Literature Library in Moscow (over 13.2 million volumes), the State University of Technology Library in St. Petersburg (more than 2.9 million volumes), the Bauman Moscow State Engineering University Library (some three million volumes), the Moscow M. V. Lomonosov State University (over 7.27 million volumes), the State University at Petersburg (over 6.4 million volumes), and dozens of other massive collections throughout the country. The Russian Library Association was established in 1994.

Russia has over 1,000 museums. Russian museums house some of the finest collections of European art in the world. The best known is the Hermitage in St. Petersburg. Also in St. Petersburg are Dostoevsky Memorial House-Museum, the Literary Museum of the Institute of Russian Literature, the State Russian Museum, and the State Museum of Sculpture, housing the country's largest collection of sculpture. Among the dozens of important museums in Moscow are the State Historical Museum, the State Literature Museum, the Tolstoy House Museum, the Pushkin Museum, the Chekhov House Museum, the Paleontological Museum of the Academy of Sciences, and the Cathedral of the Assumption, a religious arts museum housed in a 15th-century cathedral.

45 MEDIA

Russia's telephone system has undergone significant improvements since the end of the USSR. In 2009 the CIA reported that there were 44.8 million telephone landlines in Russia, or about 31.5 per 100 people. Domestic service is provided by cross-country trunk lines stretching from St. Petersburg to Khabarovsk and from Moscow to Novorossiysk. However, in rural areas telephone service continues to lag behind. The growth in mobile subscribers has been particularly significant. Mobile phone subscriptions averaged 162 per 100 in 2009. Internet and e-mail services also continue to improve. Russia had 47 million personal computers in 2010, or about 33.7 per 100 people, and 49.6 million Internet users, some 2% of the world total. In 2009 the country had about 7.6 million internet hosts.

In 2009 there were 323 FM radio stations, about 1,500 AM radio stations, and 62 shortwave radio stations. The government maintains ownership of the largest radio stations, Radio Mayak and Radio Rossiya, and the news agencies ITAR-TASS and RIA Novosti.

Among more than 400 daily newspapers in circulation in 2010, Russia's major daily newspapers (all published in Moscow) were: *Moskovskii Komsomolets* (circulation 2,035,049), *Gudok* (*The Honk*, 500,000), and *Stroitelnaya Gazeta* (*Construction Journal*, 439,700), as well as *Moskovski Komsomolets* (*Moscow Communist Youth*); *Komsomolskaya Pravda* (686,000); *Trud* (*Labor*, 613,000); *Rossiiskaya Gazeta* (374,000); *Izvestia* (*The News*, 209,000); *Kommersant* (*Commerce*, 94,000); and *Nezarisimaya Gazeta* (*The Independent*, 27,000). *Argumenty I Fakty* (*Discussions and Facts*) is a popular weekly. *Novaya Gazeta* is published twice a week. *Vedomosti* is a business daily owned as a joint venture of *The Wall Street Journal*, *The Financial Times*, and the Independent Media group (a Dutch organization).

The constitution provides for freedom of the press and mass information. The government says it respects these provisions, though pro-government information dominates the electronic media. The law does contain provisions giving broad interpretive authority to government at all levels to enforce secrecy of sensitive information. Nevertheless, Russians are enjoying a freer media than at any other time in recent history.

46 ORGANIZATIONS

A chamber of commerce that promotes the economic and business activities of the country to the rest of the world operates in Moscow. The Russian Academy of Entrepreneurship assists business owners. There are several professional associations representing a wide variety fields, such as the Health Workers Union of the Russian Federation and the Association of Russian Automobile Dealers. Some professional associations also promote public education and research in specific technical or scientific fields, such as the Russian Medical Society.

National youth organizations include the Girl Guides and Girl Scouts of Russia, The All-Russia Scout Organizations, the Youth Agrarian Union of Russia, the Siberian Youth Initiative, and Young Men's Christian Association/Young Women's Christian Association (YMCA/YWCA). Sports associations are popular as well. There are active chapters of the Paralympics Committee and the Special Olympics. In late 2010 Russia was chosen to host the World Cup soccer tournament in 2018.

The Gaia International Women's Center promotes the advancement of women in business and politics. Several women's groups are organized under the umbrella of the Women's Union of Russia.

Volunteer service organizations, such as the Lions Clubs and Kiwanis International, are also present. The All-Russian Society for Disabled represents the concerns of over 2.5 million people. The International Red Cross and the Red Crescent operate branches throughout the federation. There are also branches of Amnesty International, Greenpeace, United Way, United Nations Children's Fund (UNICEF), and Habitat for Humanity.

47 TOURISM, TRAVEL, AND RECREATION

In September 1992 Russia lifted its travel restrictions on foreigners, opening the entire country to visitors and tourists with necessary passports and visas. Moscow is a major tourist destination with many attractions including Red Square, the Kremlin, St. Basil's Cathedral, and many other monasteries, churches, museums, and other cultural attractions. The most famous of Moscow's parks and gardens is Gorky Park. St. Petersburg is a beautifully preserved neoclassical city with palace-lined waterways. Attractions include the State Hermitage Museum, Peter and Paul Fortress, and the Nevsky Prospekt.

The *Tourism Factbook*, published by the UN World Tourism Organization, reported 23.7 million incoming tourists to Russia in 2009. They spent an estimated total of $12.3 billion. Of those incoming tourists, 21.2 million were from Europe. There were 499,956 hotel beds available in Russia, which had an occupancy rate of 35%. The estimated daily cost to visit Moscow, the capital, was $441. The cost of visiting other cities averaged $276.

48 FAMOUS PERSONS

Notable among the rulers of prerevolutionary Russia were Ivan III ("the Great," b. 1440–d. 1505), who established Moscow as a sovereign state; Peter I ("the Great," b. 1672–d. 1725), a key figure in the modernization of Russia; Alexander I (b. 1777–d. 1825), prominent in both the war against Napoleon and the political reaction that followed the war; Alexander II (b. 1818–d. 1881), a social reformer who freed the serfs; Minister of Finance Sergei Iul'evich Witte (b. 1849–d. 1915); and Petr Arkad'evich Stolypin (b. 1862–d. 1911), activist prime minister under the last two tsars. A famous revolutionary and Red Army leader was Leon (born Bronstein) Trotsky (b. 1879–d. 1940). An important conservative was Constantine Pobeddinostsev (b. 1827–d. 1907), procurator of the Holy Synod.

Mikhail Lomonosov (b. 1711–d. 1765) was a poet and grammarian and also a founder of natural science in Russia. The poet Gavrila Derzhavin (b. 1743–d. 1816) combined elements of topical satire with intimate, lyrical themes. Aleksandar Radishchev (b. 1749–d. 1802) criticized both religion and government absolutism. Nikolay Karamzin (b. 1766–d. 1826), an early translator of Shakespeare, was the founder of Russian Sentimentalism. The fables of Ivan Krylov (b.1768/69?–d. 1844) exposed human foibles and the shortcomings of court society. Russia's greatest poet, Aleksandr Pushkin (b. 1799–d. 1837), was also a brilliant writer of prose. Other outstanding poets were Fyodor Tyutchev (b. 1803–d. 1873), Mikhail Lermontov (b. 1814–d. 1841), and Afanasy Fet (Shen-shing, b. 1820–d. 1892). Nikolay Gogol (b. 1809–d. 1852), best known for his novel *Dead Souls* and his short stories, founded the realistic trend in Russian literature. Vissarion Belinsky (b. 1811–d. 1848) and Nikolay Dobrolyubov (b. 1812–d. 1891) were influential critics. Noted populists were Aleksandr Herzen (b. 1812–d. 1870) and Nikolay Chernyshevsky (b. 1828–d. 1889). Ivan Turgenev (b. 1818–d. 1883) is famous for his sketches, short stories, and the novel *Fathers and Sons*. Fyodor Dostoyevsky (b. 1821–d. 1881) wrote outstanding psychological novels (*Crime and Punishment, The Brothers Karamazov*). Count Leo (Lev) Tolstoy (b. 1828–d. 1910), perhaps the greatest Russian novelist (*War and Peace, Anna Karenina*), also wrote plays, essays, and short stories. Aleksandr Ostrovsky (b. 1823–d. 1886) was a prolific dramatist. The consummate playwright and short-story writer Anton Chekhov (b. 1860–d. 1904) was an outstanding prose writer of the late 19th century. Leonid Nikolayevich Aandreyev (b. 1871–d. 1919) wrote plays and short stories. The novels, stories, and plays of Maksim Gorky (Aleksey Peshkov, b. 1868–d. 1936) bridged the tsarist and Soviet periods. Ivan Bunin (b. 1870–d. 1953) received the Nobel Prize in 1933 for his novels and short stories. Mikhail Sholokhov (b. 1905–b. 1984) wrote *And Quiet Flows the Don*, a famous example of socialist realism which won the Stalin Prize and the Nobel Prize for Literature in 1965.

Georgy Plekhanov (b. 1856–d. 1918), a moderate Marxist philosopher and propagandist, also was a literary critic and art theorist, as was culture official Anatoly Lunacharsky (b. 1875–d. 1933).

Russian composers of note include Mikhail Glinka (b. 1804–d. 1857), Aleksandar Borodin (b. 1833–d. 1887), who was also a distinguished chemist, Mily Balakirev (b. 1837–d. 1910), Modest Mussorgsky (b. 1839–d. 1881), Pyotr Ilyich Tchaikovsky (b. 1840–d. 1893), Nikolay Rimsky-Korsakov (b. 1844–d. 1908), Aleksandr Scriabin (b. 1871–d. 1915), Sergei Rachmaninoff (b. 1873–d. 1943), Igor Stravinsky (b. 1882–d. 1971), Sergei Prokofiev (b. 1891–d. 1953), Aram Ilyich Khachaturian (b. 1903–d. 1978), Dmitry Kabalevsky (b. 1904–d. 1987), and Dmitry Shostakovich (b. 1906–d. 1975). Two of the greatest bassos of modern times are the Russian-born Fyodor Chaliapin (b. 1873–d. 1938) and Alexander Kipnis (b. 1891–d. 1978). Serge Koussevitzky (b. 1874–d.

1951), noted conductor of the Boston Symphony Orchestra, was important in Russian musical life before the Revolution.

Outstanding figures in the ballet were the impresario Sergey Diaghilev (b. 1872–d. 1929); the choreographers Marius Petipa (b. 1819–d. 1910), Lev Ivanov (b. 1834–d. 1901), and Mikhail Fokine (b. 1880–d. 1942); the ballet dancers Vaslav Nijinsky (b. 1890–d. 1950), Anna Pavlova (b. 1881–d. 1931), Tamaara Karsavina (b. 1885–d. 1978), Galina Ulanova (b. 1909–d. 1998), and Maya Plisetskaya (b. 1925); and the ballet teacher Agrippina Vaganova (b. 1879–d. 1951).

Outstanding figures in the theater include Kostantin Stanislavsky (Alekseyev, b. 1863–d. 1938), director, actor, and theorectician; Vladimir Nemirovich-Danchenko (b. 1858–d. 1943), director, playwright, and founder, with Stanislavsky, of the Moscow Art Theater; and Vsevolod Meyerhold (b. 1873–d. 1942), noted for innovations in stagecraft. Important film directors were Vsevolod Pudovkin (b. 1893–d. 1953), Aleksandr Dovzhenko (b. 1864–d. 1956), Sergey Eisenstein (b. 1898–d. 1948), Vasily Shiksin (b. 1929–d. 1974), and Andrei Tarkovsky (b. 1932–d. 1987).

Varfolomey (Bartolomeo Francesco) Rastrelli (b. 1700–d. 1771) designed many of the most beautiful buildings in St. Petersburg. Other important Russian architects include Vasily Bazhenov (b. 1737–d. 1799), Matvey Kazakov (b. 1733–d. 1812), Andreyan Zakharov (b. 1761–d. 1811), Ivan Starov (b. 1806–d. 1858), Vasily Perov (b. 1833/34–d. 1882), Vasily Vereshchagin (b. 1842–d. 1904), Ilya Repin (b. 1844–d. 1930), Mikhail Vrubel (b. 1856–d. 1910), Leon (Lev) Bakst (Rosenberg, b. 1866–d. 1924), and Aleksansr Benois (b. 1870–d. 1960). Modern Russian artists whose work is internationally important include the Suprematist painters Kasimir Malevich (b. 1878–d. 1935) and El (Lazar) Lissitzky (b. 1890–d. 1941), the "Rayonist" painters Natalya Goncharova (b. 1881–d. 1962) and Mikhail Larionov (b. 1881–d. 1964), the Constructivist artist Vladimir Tatlin (b. 1885–d. 1953), and the Spatial sculptor Aleksandar Rodchenko (b. 1891–d. 1956). Famous Russian-born artists who left their native country to work abroad include the painters Alexei von Jawlensky (b. 1864–d. 1941), Vasily Kandinsky (b. 1866–d. 1944), Marc Chagall (b. 1897–d. 1985), and Chaim Soutine (b. 1894–d. 1943) and the sculptors Antoine Pevsner (b. 1886–d. 1962), his brother Naum Gabo (b. 1890–d. 1977), Alexander Archipenko (b. 1887–d. 1964), and Ossip Zadkine (b. 1890–d. 1967).

Prominent Russian scientists of the 19th and 20th centuries include the chemist Dmitry Ivanovich Mendeleyev (b. 1834–d. 1907), inventor of the periodic table; Aleksandr Mikhailovich Butlerov (b. 1828–d. 1886), a creator of the theory of chemical structure; Nikolay Yegorovich Zhukovsky (b. 1847–d. 1921), a founder of modern hydrodynamics and aerodynamics; Pyotr Nikolayevich Lebedev (b. 1866–d. 1912), who discovered the existence of the pressure of light; Nikolay Ivanovich Lobachevsky (b. 1792–d. 1856), pioneer in non-Euclidean geometry; Ivan Petrovich Pavlov (b. 1849–d. 1936), creator of the behaviorist theory on the higher nervous systems of animals and man who received the Nobel Prize in 1904 for his work on digestive glands; Ilya Ilyich Mechnikov (Elie Metchnikoff, b. 1845–d. 1916), who received the Nobel Prize in 1908 for his Phagocyte theory; Kliment Arkadyevich Timiryazev (b. 1843–d. 1920), biologist and founder of the Russian school of plant physiology; and Aleksandr Stepanovich Popov (b. 1859–d. 1906), pioneer in radio transmission. Among later scientists and inventors are Ivan Vladimirovich Michurin (b. 1855–d. 1935), biologist and plant breeder; Konstantin Eduardovich Tsiolkovsky (b. 1857–d. 1935), scientist and the inventor in the field of the theory and technology of rocket engines, interplanetary travel, and aerodynamics; Vladimir Petrovich Filatov (b. 1875–d. 1956), ophthalmologist; Ivan Pavlovich Bardin (b. 1883–d. 1960), metallurgist; Yevgeny Nikanorovich Pavlovsky (b. 1884–d. 1965), parasitologist; Nikolay Ivanovich Vavilov (b. 1887–d. 1943), geneticist; and Leon Theremin (Lev Termen, b. 1896–d. 1993), pioneer of electronic music. Cosmonaut Yuri Alekseyevich Gagarin (b. 1934–d. 1968) was the first person to ever venture into space.

Russian nationals Konstantin Novoselov (b. 1974) and Andrei Geim (b. 1958), professors at Manchester University, were awarded the 2010 Nobel Prize in physics for research on graphene, a flat one-atom thick layer of carbon that is nearly transparent, extremely strong, and a good conductor of electricity.

The "Russian Adam Smith," who opposed the mercantilism of the Petrine period, was Ivan Pososhkov (b. 1652–d. 1726). Among the many excellent Russian economists was Leonid Vital'evich Kantorovich (b. 1912–d. 1986), mathematical economist who discovered linear programming, an important planning tool. Kantorovich was the sole Soviet Nobel prize winner in Economic Science, though Moscow-born Leonid Hurwicz (b. 1917–d. 2008), winner in 2007, emigrated in 1940. Evengenii Evgen'evich Slutskii (b. 1880–d. 1948), is famous for his analysis of consumer behavior;

Among premiers and presidents of the USSR and Russia were Vladimir Ulyanov Lenin (b. 1870–d. 1924); Joseph Stalin (b. 1878–d. 1953); Nikita S. Khrushchev (b. 1894–d. 1971), credited with the relaxation of Stalinist totalitarianism; and Mikhail Gorbachev (b. 1931), who came to power in 1985, initiated reforms of the old Communist system, allowed freedom for Communist satellite regimes in Eastern Europe, and won the Nobel Peace Prize in 1990. Gorbachev resigned and ceded power to Boris Yeltsin (b. 1931–d. 2007), who agreed to the breakup of the USSR in 1991 and served as president until 1999.

⁴⁹DEPENDENCIES

The Russian Federation has no territories or dependencies.

⁵⁰BIBLIOGRAPHY

Appel, Hilary. *A New Capitalist Order: Privatization and Ideology in Russia and Eastern Europe*. Pittsburgh, PA: University of Pittsburgh Press, 2004.

Brown, Archie. *The Rise and Fall of Communism*. NY: HarperCollins, 2009.

Cohen, Stephen F. *Soviet Fates and Lost Alternatives*. New York: Columbia University Press, 2009.

George, Julie A. *The Politics of Ethnic Separatism in Russia and Georgia*. New York: Palgrave Macmillan, 2009.

Gorbachev, Mikhail. *Memoirs*. NY: HarperCollis, *1996*.

Howe, Sonia E., ed. *A Thousand Years of Russian History*. New York: Nova Science, 2005.

Hunter, Robert Edwards. *Engaging Russia as Partner and Participant: The Next Stage of NATO-Russia Relations*. Santa Monica, CA: RAND, 2004.

International Smoking Statistics: A Collection of Historical Data from 30 Economically Developed Countries. 2nd ed. New York: Oxford University Press, 2003.

Mandel, David. *Labour after Communism: Auto Workers and Their Unions in Russia, Ukraine, and Belarus*. New York: Black Rose Books, 2004.

McCann, Leo, ed. *Russian Transformations: Challenging the Global Narrative*. New York: RoutledgeCurzon, 2004.

Miller, Steven E. and Dmitri Trenin, eds. *The Russian Military: Power and Policy*. Cambridge, MA: MIT Press, 2004.

Nove, Alec. *An Economic History of the USS.R.,* revised ed. London: Penguin, 2004.

Opello, Walter C. *European Politics*. Boulder, CO: Lynne Rienner Publishers, 2009.

Peterson, D. J. *Russia and the Information Revolution*. Santa Monica, CA: RAND, 2005.

Riasanovsky, Nicholas, and Steinberg, Mark. *A History of Russia*, 8th ed., 2 vols. NY: Oxford, 2010.

Russia Investment and Business Guide: Strategic and Practical Information. Washington, DC: International Business Publications USA, 2012.

Sheets, Lawrence. *Eight Pieces of Empire: A 20-year Journey Through the Soviet Collapse*. New York: Crown, 2011.

Shleifer, Andrei. *A Normal Country: Russia after Communism*. Cambridge, MA: Harvard University Press, 2005.

Shoemaker, Merle Wesley. *Russia and the Commonwealth of Independent States, 2005*. 36th ed. Harpers Ferry, WV: Stryker-Post Publications, 2005.

Summers, Randal W., and Allan M. Hoffman, eds. *Domestic Violence: A Global View*. Westport, CT: Greenwood Press, 2002.

Terterov, Marat, ed. *Doing Business with Russia: A Guide to Investment Opportunities and Business Practice*. 4th ed. Sterling, VA: Kogan Page, 2005.

SAN MARINO

Republic of San Marino
Repubblica di San Marino

CAPITAL: San Marino

FLAG: The flag is divided horizontally into two equal bands, sky blue below and white above. The national coat of arms is superimposed in the center of the flag.

ANTHEM: *Onore a te, onore, o antica repubblica (Honor to You, O Ancient Republic).*

MONETARY UNIT: The Italian lira was replaced by the euro as the official currency as of 2002. The euro is divided into 100 cents. There are coins in denominations of 1, 2, 5, 10, 20, and 50 cents and 1 euro and 2 euros. There are notes of 5, 10, 20, 50, 100, 200, and 500 euros. €1 = $1.371 (or $1 = €0.72939) as of September 2011. The country issues its own coins in limited numbers as well. Coins of San Marino may circulate in both the republic and in Italy.

WEIGHTS AND MEASURES: The metric system is the legal standard.

HOLIDAYS: New Year's Day, 1 January; Epiphany, 6 January; Anniversary of St. Agatha, second patron saint of the republic, and of the liberation of San Marino (1740), 5 February; Anniversary of the Arengo, 25 March; Investiture of the Captains-Regent, 1 April and 1 October; Labor Day, 1 May; Fall of Fascism, 28 July; Assumption and August Bank Holiday, 14–16 August; Anniversary of the Foundation of San Marino, 3 September; All Saints' Day, 1 November; Commemoration of the Dead, 2 November; Immaculate Conception, 8 December; Christmas, 24–26 December; New Year's Eve, 31 December. Movable religious holidays include Easter Monday and Ascension.

TIME: 1 p.m. = noon GMT.

¹LOCATION, SIZE, AND EXTENT

San Marino is the third-smallest country in Europe. With an area of 60 sq km (23 sq mi), it extends 13.1 km (8.1 mi) NE–SW and 9.1 km (5.7 mi) SE–NW. Comparatively, the area occupied by San Marino is about one third the size of Washington, DC. It is a landlocked state completely surrounded by Italy, with a total boundary length of 39 km (24 mi).

²TOPOGRAPHY

The town of San Marino is on the slopes and at the summit of Mt. Titano (755 m/2,477 ft), and much of the republic is coextensive with the mountain, which has major limestone pinnacles. Each of the peaks is crowned by old fortifications; on the north by a castle and the other two by towers. Level areas around the base of Mt. Titano provide land for agricultural use. The San Marino River begins in Italy and flows northward through the western portion of the country, forming part of the nation's western border. The Ausa River in the northwest and the Marano River of the east central region both drain into the Adriatic Sea.

³CLIMATE

The climate is that of northeastern Italy: rather mild in winter, but with temperatures frequently below freezing, and warm and pleasant in the summer, reaching a maximum of 26°C (79°F).

Winter temperatures rarely fall below 7°C (19°F). Annual rainfall averages between 56 and 80 cm (22 to 32 in).

⁴FLORA AND FAUNA

San Marino is home to 3 mammal species, 6 bird species, and 2 reptile species. The calculation reflects the total number of distinct species residing in the country, not the number of endemic species. The republic has generally the same flora and fauna as northeastern Italy. The hare, squirrel, badger, fox, and porcupine are among the more common animals seen. Most of the landscape has been cultivated with orchards, vineyards, and olive groves.

⁵ENVIRONMENT

The UN reported in 2008 that carbon dioxide emissions in San Marino totaled 232 kilotons. Urbanization is the primary concern for the environment; however, the country has shown great care for environmental protection and preservation both within its own borders and in the global arena.

San Marino has no endangered species, though the lesser horseshoe bat and the common otter are listed as near threatened. The country is party to international agreements on biodiversity, climate change, desertification, and whaling; in 2011 it had ratified but not yet signed an agreement on air pollution.

LOCATION: 12°27′ E and 43°56′ N.

6 POPULATION

The US Central Intelligence Agency (CIA) estimates the population of San Marino in 2012 to be approximately 32,140, which placed it at number 213 in population among the 196 nations of the world. In 2011, approximately 18% of the population was over 65 years of age, with another 16.6% under 15 years of age. The median age in San Marino was 42.5 years. There were 0.94 males for every female in the country. The population's annual rate of change was 0.98% in 2012. The projected population for the year 2025 was 40,000. Population density in San Marino was calculated at 522 people per sq km (202 people per sq mi).

The UN estimated that 94% of the population lived in urban areas, and that urban populations had an annual rate of change of 0.6%. The largest urban area, along with its respective populations, was San Marino, 4,377; other urban areas included Serravalle, Borgo, Maggiore, and Domagnano.

7 MIGRATION

Estimates of San Marino's net migration rate, carried out by the CIA in 2012, amounted to 8.96 migrants per 1,000 citizens. The total number of emigrants living abroad was 3,100, and the total number of immigrants living in San Marino was 11,700. Immigrants come chiefly from Italy; emigration is mainly to Italy, the United States, France, and Belgium. Foreigners who have been residents in San Marino for 30 years can become naturalized citizens.

8 ETHNIC GROUPS

The native population is predominantly of Italian origin.

9 LANGUAGES

Italian is the official language.

10 RELIGIONS

It has been estimated that over 90% of the population is Roman Catholic; however, while Roman Catholicism is dominant, it is not the state religion. The Catholic Church does receive direct benefits from the state, but so do other charities. Other religious groups represented include the Waldensian Church, Jehovah's Witnesses, Baha'is, Jews, and Muslims. Some Eastern European immigrants are Orthodox Christians. Epiphany, Saint Agatha, Easter, Corpus Domini, All Saints' Day, Commemoration of the Dead, Immaculate Conception, and Christmas are observed as national holidays.

11 TRANSPORTATION

Streets and roads within the republic totaled about 292 km (181 mi) in 2006, and there is regular bus service between San Marino and Rimini. Such roads are paved.

An electric railroad, 32 km (20 mi) long, between Rimini and San Marino was inaugurated in 1932. It was damaged and rendered unserviceable by a British air raid on 26 June 1944 during World War II. A 1.5-km (0.9-mi) cable-car service from the city of San Marino to Borgo Maggiore is operated by the government. There is helicopter service between San Marino and Rimini in summer.

12 HISTORY

San Marino, the oldest republic in the world, is the sole survivor of the independent states that existed in Italy at various times from the downfall of the Western Roman Empire to the proclamation of the Kingdom of Italy in 1861. (The Vatican City State, which is also an independent enclave in Italy, was not constituted in its present form until the 20th century.)

According to tradition, the republic was founded in AD 301 by Marinus, a Christian stonecutter who fled from Dalmatia to avoid religious persecution; later canonized, St. Marinus is known in Italian as San Marino. If founded at the time asserted by tradition, San Marino is the oldest existing national state in Europe. There was a monastery in San Marino in existence at least as early as 885.

Because of the poverty of the region and the difficult terrain, San Marino was rarely disturbed by outside powers, and it generally avoided the factional fights of the Middle Ages. For a time, it joined the Ghibellines and was therefore interdicted by Pope Innocent IV in 1247–49. It was protected by the Montefeltro family, later dukes of Urbino, and in 1441, with Urbino, it defeated Sigismondo Malatesta and extended the size of its territory. It was briefly held by Cesare Borgia in 1503, but in 1549 its sovereignty was confirmed by Pope Paul III. In 1739, however, a military force under a papal legate, Cardinal Giulio Alberoni, occupied San Marino and unsuccessfully attempted to get the Sammarinese to acknowledge his sovereignty over them. In the following year, Pope Clement II terminated the occupation and signed a treaty of friendship with the tiny republic. Napoleon allowed San Marino to retain its liberty; the Sammarinese are said to have declined his offer to increase their territory on the grounds that smallness and poverty alone had kept them from falling prey to larger states.

In 1849, Giuseppe Garibaldi, the liberator of Italy, took refuge from the Austrians in San Marino; he departed voluntarily shortly before the Austrians were to invade the republic to capture him. San Marino and Italy entered into a treaty of friendship and customs union in 1862. This treaty was renewed in March 1939 and amended in September 1971.

During the period of Benito Mussolini's rule in Italy, San Marino adopted a Fascist type of government. Despite the country's claim to neutrality in World War II, Allied planes bombed it on 26 June 1944. The raid caused heavy damage, especially to the railway line, and killed a number of persons. San Marino's resources were sorely taxed to provide food and shelter for the over 100,000 refugees who obtained sanctuary during the war.

The elections of 1945 put a coalition of Communists and left-wing Socialists in control of the country. In 1957, some defections from the ruling coalition were followed by a bloodless revolution, aided by Italy, against the government. The leftists surrendered, and some were imprisoned. The rightists, chiefly Christian Democrats, won the election of 1959 and remained in power until 1973, chiefly in coalition with the Social Democrats. In March 1973, after splitting with the Social Democrats, the Christian Democrats formed an unstable coalition with the Socialists. After new elections in May 1978, the Communists, the Socialists, and the Socialist Unity Party, who together commanded a one-seat majority in the legislature, formed a governing coalition; San Marino thus became the only West European country with a Communist-led government. This coalition governed until 1986, when a Communist–Christian Democratic coalition replaced it; this was the first coalition government formed by these two parties in San Marino's history.

San Marino's high standard of living makes Sammarinese citizenship a valuable commodity. With the only ways for foreigners to obtain citizenship being to reside in San Marino for 30 years or marry a male citizen, the government passed a law in August 1999 prohibiting female household servants under 50 because of the potential for elderly men to fall for their young female help who may have suspicious motives.

Also in 1999, San Marino joined the European Monetary Union and adopted the euro as its currency. The Europe-wide single currency was forecast to boost tourism but simultaneously hurt Sammarinese bank revenues as the banks would no longer be able to charge fees for currency exchange.

In December 2003, Fabio Berardi was named secretary of state for foreign and political affairs, the equivalent of the office of a prime minister. In 2006 Fiorenzo Stolfi replaced Berardi in the post; Stolfi was followed by Antonella Mularoni in 2008.

A 2005 act established a constitutional court charged with validating the constitutionality of new laws and referendums; settling conflicts between constitutional institutions; and monitoring the actions of the Captains Regent.

Because San Marino has a customs union with Italy, it enjoys all of the benefits that flow from European Union (EU) membership. San Marino has stated its eventual goal is to become a full-fledged member of the EU.

13 GOVERNMENT

Legislative power is exercised by the Grand and General Council (Consiglio Grande e Generale) of 60 members, regularly elected every five years by universal suffrage (which begins at age 18). The council elects from among its members a State Congress (Congresso di Stato) of 10 members (3 secretaries of state and 7 ministers of state), which makes most administrative decisions and carries them out. In 1960, universal male suffrage was established in place of the previous system, whereby only heads of families voted. Women also received the franchise effective in 1960 and were first permitted to run for office in 1974 (they voted in national elections for the first time in 1964). Nearly 100% of eligible voters participate in elections.

Two members of the council are named every six months to head the executive branch of the government; one represents the town of San Marino and the other the countryside. The terms of these officials, called captains-regent (capitani reggenti), begin on 1 April and 1 October. The captains-regent, who must be native-born citizens, are eligible for reelection after three years. As of April 2012, the captains-regents were Maurizio Rattini and Italo Righi. The secretary of state for foreign and political affairs serves the function of a prime minister. Antonella Mularoni assumed the office in 2008. The next election for captains-regent was scheduled for September 2012 and for secretary of state for foreign and political affairs by 2013.

14 POLITICAL PARTIES

The political parties in San Marino have close ties with the corresponding parties in Italy. Major parties in 2011 included the Christian Democratic Party (PDCS), the Communist Refoundation (RC), Democrats of the Center (DdC), Freedom List (NS), New Socialist Party (NPS), Party of Socialists and Democrats (PDS), Popular Alliance (AP), Union of Moderates (ANS), and San Marino Populars (POP).

In June 2008, the Popular Alliance dropped out of the government coalition, leading to snap elections in November 2008. These were the first elections under a new electoral law that required an electoral threshold of 3.5%. As a result a number of new coalitions emerged. The Pact for San Marino (including the Christian Democrats, Popular Alliance, Freedom List, and the San Marino Union of Moderates) won 54% of the vote and 35 seats in the assembly. The Reforms and Freedom coalition (including the Party of Socialists and Democrats, United Left, and Democrats for the Center) won 45.8% of the vote and 25 seats. Antonella Mularoni was chosen as secretary of state for foreign and political affairs (head of government).

15 LOCAL GOVERNMENT

San Marino consists of nine administrative divisions or castles (castelli): Acquaviva, Borgo Maggiore, Chiesanuova, Domagnano,

Faetano, Fiorentino, Montegiardino, San Marino Citta, and Serravalle. Each castle has an auxiliary council, elected for a four-year term. It is headed by an official called the captain of the castle, who is elected every two years. The nomenclature of local governance references the literal castles annexed into the republic in 1463.

16 JUDICIAL SYSTEM

There is a civil court, a criminal court, and a superior court, but most criminal cases are tried before Italian magistrates. Until a 2004 reform, judges in Sammarinese cases were not allowed to be citizens of San Marino; following the reform, nationals could serve as lower court judges, though most were Italian citizens in 2011.

The reform also established the final court of review as the judge of the last appeal. The rights of the accused, including the rights to a public trial, legal counsel, and other procedural safeguards, are guaranteed by law and observed in practice.

A 2002 act established a constitutional court, called the College of Guarantors, to validate laws and referendums and check executive authority. The court consisted of three standing judges and three alternate judges selected by the Great and General Council to four-year terms.

One third of the judges are reselected every two years. It replaced the Council of XII, one of the original bodies of the San Marino judicial order.

17 ARMED FORCES

The San Marino militia nominally consists of all able-bodied citizens between the ages of 16 and 55, but the armed forces actually maintained are principally for purposes of ceremonial display; these include the *Corpi Militari* used in various functions. Comprehensive defense responsibilities are delegated to Italy.

18 INTERNATIONAL COOPERATION

San Marino became a member of the United Nations on 2 March 1992; it belongs to several nonregional specialized agencies, such as the FAO, the World Bank, ILO, UNCTAD, UNESCO, and the WHO.

San Marino is also a member of the OSCE and the Council of Europe. In environmental cooperation, the nation is part of the Convention on Biological Diversity, the Nuclear Test Ban Treaty, and the UN Conventions on Climate Change and Desertification.

19 ECONOMY

The gross domestic product (GDP) of San Marino declined 13% in 2009. Inflation stood at 2.8%, and unemployment was reported at 3.8%. The economy contracted by 5% in 2009 and an estimated 1.8% in 2010. Farming was formerly the principal occupation, but it has been replaced in importance by light manufacturing; industry accounted for one third of San Marino's GDP in 2009. Other major revenue sources include tourism, which in some years has accounted for as much as 50% of GDP, and banking. Natural resources include building stone and agricultural products (wheat, grapes, maize, olives, cattle, pigs, horses, meat, cheese, and hides).

San Marino's prosperity has been tempered by a money laundering scandal, a 2009 tax repatriation effort in Italy (leading to $4.5 billion in outflows from San Marino), and a 2008 global economic recession that truncated tourism revenues and manufacturing exports. The downturn has caused budgets deficits, but San Marino has a small debt burden.

In economic consultations with the government, the International Monetary Fund (IMF) warned that San Marino would continue to suffer economically if the territory failed to meaningfully fortify its efforts to adjust to the new global economic framework of greater transparency.

San Marino was removed from an Organisation for Economic Co-operation and Development (OECD) list of tax havens in 2009; it signed Tax Information Exchange Agreements with most countries by 2010.

Close links with the Italian economy make San Marino dependent on Italian investment and economic prosperity.

20 INCOME

The US State Department estimated that in 2009 the GDP of San Marino was $1.54 billion. The per capita Gross National Product (GNP) was estimated at $34,830 for that same year.

The annual growth rate of GDP was -13%. The average inflation rate was 2.8%. It was estimated that agriculture accounted for 0.1% of GDP, industry 39.2%, and services 60.7%.

21 LABOR

As of 2011, San Marino had a total labor force of 22,050 people. In 2010, the CIA reported the division of labor as: 0.2% were employed in agriculture, 36.3% in industry, and 63.5% in the service sector.

Labor federations include the Democratic Federation of Sammarinese Workers, affiliated with the International Confederation of Free Trade Unions, and the General Federation of Labor. About 50% of the workforce is unionized. The minimum working age is 16 without any exceptions.

In 2011 the minimum wage was set at $12.98 per hour, an amount deemed insufficient to maintain a decent living standard. Most wages, however, were significantly higher than the minimum. The workweek ranged from 36 to 37.5 hours. In 2011 an increasing number of foreign workers operated in the informal sector without consistent regulation.

22 AGRICULTURE

Out of 6,000 hectares (14,826 acres) of land in San Marino, 1,000 hectares (2,471 acres) are arable. Roughly 17% of the total land is currently farmed, and the country's major crops include wheat, grapes, corn, and olives. Agriculture accounted for only 0.1% of GDP in 2009.

23 ANIMAL HUSBANDRY

Cattle, pigs, and horses are raised; meat, cheese, and animal hides are commercially produced.

24 FISHING

There is no fishing.

25 FORESTRY

Land not under cultivation is largely wooded. Small quantities of wood are cut for local use.

26 MINING

San Marino had no commercial mineral resources.

27 ENERGY AND POWER

Electric power is imported from Italy.

28 INDUSTRY

Manufacturing is limited to light industries such as textiles, bricks and tiles, leather goods, clothing, and metalwork. Cotton textiles are woven at Serravalle; bricks and tiles are made in La Dogana, which also has a dyeing plant; and cement factories and a tannery are located in Acquaviva, as well as a paper-making plant. Synthetic rubber is also produced. The pottery of Borgo Maggiore is well known. Gold and silver souvenirs are made for the tourist trade. Other products are Moscato wine, olive oil, and baked goods. A significant source of revenue is the selling of stamps to foreign collectors.

29 SCIENCE AND TECHNOLOGY

The World Bank reported in 2009 that there were no patent applications in science and technology in San Marino. Sammarinese students generally pursue their scientific and technical training abroad, since science and technology resources are domestically limited. The Universita Degli Studi, founded in 1985, focuses on scientific research through its Department of Biomedical Studies and the Department of Economics and Technology.

30 DOMESTIC TRADE

There are small general stores in the capital and the smaller towns. Billboards and newspapers are the main advertising outlets. A weekly market is held at Borgo Maggiore, which also sponsors an annual fair for the sale of cattle and sheep. Most retail trade within the country is focused on goods and services that support the tourism industry.

Because of San Marino's low tax burden, several products such as clothing and cosmetics are inexpensive relative to Italian prices. Two large shopping outlets in Rovereta and Dogana opened in 2007 and act as discount retailers for upscale clothing and household items.

Public Finance – San Marino (2006)		
(In thousands of euros, central government figures)		
Revenue and Grants	**547,025**	**100.0%**
Tax revenue	261,954	47.9%
Social contributions	123,222	22.5%
Grants	14,627	2.7%
Other revenue	147,221	26.9%
Expenditures	**474,425**	**100.0%**
General public services	...	...
Defense	...	...
Public order and safety	...	...
Economic affairs	...	...
Environmental protection	...	...
Housing and community amenities	...	...
Health	...	...
Recreational, culture, and religion	...	...
Education	...	...
Social protection	...	...

(…) data not available or not significant.

SOURCE: *Government Finance Statistics Yearbook 2010,* Washington, DC: International Monetary Fund, 2010.

31 FOREIGN TRADE

Exports in 2009 were valued at $2.44 billion, while imports totaled $2.165 billion. Major import partners were Italy, Western Europe, Eastern Europe, South America, China, and Taiwan. The major export partner was Italy, which absorbs 90% of Sammarinese exports.

Principal exports are building stone, lime, wood, chestnuts, wheat, wine, baked goods, hides, and ceramics. The chief imports are food and a wide variety of consumer goods. San Marino has a customs union with Italy. In 1999, San Marino joined the European Monetary Union (EMU), further strengthening its ties to the EU.

32 BALANCE OF PAYMENTS

Receipts from tourism, remittances from Sammarinese working abroad, and sales of postage stamps to foreign collectors are principal sources of foreign exchange.

33 BANKING AND SECURITIES

The tiny nation is home to dozens of banks and financial institutions, making up a banking and insurance sector that accounts for 17.4% of the GDP. The country was under pressure from Italy and the European Union to initiate a greater amount of transparency in its banking industry. In 2009 the Sammarinese government conducted an emergency population census to weed out those who claimed to be permanent residents of San Marino but resided in Italy or other countries.

Also in 2009, San Marino built greater transparency in the structure of its banking sector by sharing information with other concerned nations. A bank sharing agreement with Argentina made tax evasion more difficult for the citizens of both countries. The reforms, though welcomed by the international community, have diminished financial revenues. An agreement with Italy alone resulted in the outflow of 10% of capital stored in San Marino's banks. In 2011 Italy declared an amnesty tax that allowed Italians to repatriate capital from San Marino. This tax caused the San Marino bank a loss of at least $4.5 billion.

When San Marino joined the European Monetary Union (EMU) in 1999, it adopted the euro.

³⁴INSURANCE

Several major Italian insurance companies have agencies in San Marino.

³⁵PUBLIC FINANCE

In 2009 the budget of San Marino included $882.1 million in public revenue and $940.4 million in public expenditures. The budget deficit amounted to 3.8% of GDP. The government derived its revenues mainly from tourism, banking, the worldwide sale of postage stamps, direct and indirect taxes, and yearly subsidies by the Italian government.

Public debt remained small in 2011 and was a new phenomenon—San Marino was debt free in earlier years. Nonetheless, a significant decline in GDP pressured the government to stem economic losses and the corresponding growth of its debt.

³⁶TAXATION

Legislation introducing San Marino's first income tax was passed by the Grand and General Council in October 1984. A general income tax is applied progressively to individuals (12–50% in 1992) and a flat rate of 24% to corporations. Also levied are a stamp duty, registration tax, mortgage tax, and succession duty.

³⁷CUSTOMS AND DUTIES

San Marino's trade policy is governed by its customs union with Italy. In 2008 the World Bank estimated that 21.7% of exports were duty free.

³⁸FOREIGN INVESTMENT

Much of the foreign investment flowing into San Marino comes from Italy.

³⁹ECONOMIC DEVELOPMENT

The tourist industry is a main source of revenue for the country, so economic development strategies are coiled around this sector. Tourists constitute the primary market for all of San Marino's other industries. Stamps are one of the country's main export goods. The reformation of the banking sector both aided and hindered its development: enhanced regulation gave it international credibility while stripping it of billions in capital.

A 2008 global recession and 2009 banking reforms exposed San Marino's limited diversification. Its close economic relationship with Italy bound the two nations together economically, a concern due to Italy's debt crisis in 2011.

⁴⁰SOCIAL DEVELOPMENT

A social insurance system provides pensions for old age and disability. Employers, employees, and the government all contribute to the system. Self-employed contributions vary. There is universal medical coverage and maternity benefits of 100% of earnings for five months. All employees and self-employed persons have work injury insurance. Unemployment is only available to salaried employees and excludes civil servants.

The law mandates that women have equal access to employment opportunities, and in practice women face little or no discrimination in employment and in pay. Women actively participate in all careers including high public office. Laws protect women from violence, and instances of spousal abuse are infrequent.

The government is committed to protecting human rights. Prisons meet international standards and are open for inspection by human rights monitors.

⁴¹HEALTH

According to the CIA, life expectancy in San Marino was 83 years in 2012. The government spent 13.6% of its GDP on healthcare, amounting to $4,089 per person. The fertility rate was 1.48 children born per woman, while the infant mortality rate was 4.65 deaths per 1,000 live births. It was estimated that 92% of children were vaccinated against measles.

Public health institutions include the State Hospital (opened in 1975), a dispensary for the poor, and a laboratory of hygiene and prophylaxis. All citizens receive free, comprehensive medical care. In 2006 there were an estimated 251 physicians, 506 nurses, 26 midwives, 41 dentists, and 52 pharmacists per 100,000 people.

⁴²HOUSING

San Marino has over 7,000 dwellings, virtually all with electricity and piped-in water. Most new construction is financed privately. The housing stock for the nation is generally adequate to supply the population. Government concerns are primarily focused on preventing over-construction of rural areas. Over 90% of Sammarinese own their homes.

⁴³EDUCATION

In 2009 the World Bank estimated that 92% of age-eligible children in San Marino were enrolled in primary school. The CIA estimated that San Marino had a literacy rate of 96% among those age 10 and over.

Primary education is compulsory for all children between the ages of 6 and 16. The program of instruction is patterned after the Italian curriculum, and Sammarinese school certificates are recognized by Italy. Children go through five years of primary education followed by three years of secondary education at the first stage and a further three years of senior secondary school. At the secondary level, students may choose to attend technical or vocational programs instead of general (classical) studies. The academic year runs from October to July.

There are a few postsecondary programs offering degrees in a variety of fields, though many students attend postsecondary facilities outside of San Marino.

⁴⁴LIBRARIES AND MUSEUMS

In the capital city is the Biblioteca di Stato, founded in 1839. It contains a library of some 110,000 books, documents, and pamphlets. The Palazzo del Valloni also houses the state archives, as well as a collection of rare coins and medals. The State University has a small collection of 23,000 volumes.

The Palazzo del Governo (built in 1894) and most other large buildings in the capital are of comparatively recent date, but many monuments have been rebuilt in an earlier style. There were five national museums and at least seven private museums in San Marino in 2011; there were also four playhouses. One of the museums is devoted to the postage stamps of San Marino and other countries. The Gallery of Modern and Contemporary Art is also in San Marino. The 14th-century church of San Francesco has paintings by several minor masters.

Three historic fortresses, Guaita, Fratta, and Montale, are situated on the three pinnacles of Mt. Titano. There is also a museum in Borgia Maggiore devoted to objects connected with Giuseppe Garibaldi's stay in the republic.

45 MEDIA

In 2010 the CIA reported that there were 21,700 telephone landlines in San Marino. In addition to landlines, mobile phone subscriptions averaged 75 per 100 people. Internet subscriptions stood at 54 per 100 citizens.

San Marino RTV was the state-owned national TV and radio broadcaster. It operated one television station and two radio stations in 2008. Newspapers and other publications are protected by laws guaranteeing freedom of speech and of the press; the government generally respects these rights in practice.

46 ORGANIZATIONS

Business and labor organizations include the National Association for Industry of San Marino, National Small Enterprise Association of San Marino, Autonomous Workers Association of San Marino, Labour Confederation of San Marino, and the Democratic Workers Confederation of San Marino.

National youth organizations include the Young Christian Democrats and The Catholic Guide and Scout Association of San Marino. There are sports associations representing athletes in a variety of pastimes, such as weightlifting, tennis, football (soccer), and track and field. Many sports clubs are affiliated with the national Olympic Committee and other international organizations.

Volunteer service organizations, such as the Lions Clubs and Kiwanis International, are also present. The Red Cross and UNICEF have national chapters.

47 TOURISM, TRAVEL, AND RECREATION

The *Tourism Factbook*, published by the UN World Tourism Organization in 2011, reported 2.1 million incoming tourists to San Marino. Of those incoming tourists, there were 2 million from Europe. There were 1,674 hotel beds available in San Marino, which had an occupancy rate of 54%. The estimated daily cost to visit San Marino, the capital, was $275.

The government has promoted tourism so successfully that in the summer during the 1980s the number of San Marino residents was often exceeded by the number of visitors (20,000–30,000 daily). Growth in the tourist industry has increased the demand for San Marino's stamps and coins, gold and silver souvenirs, handicrafts, and pottery. Principal attractions are the three medieval fortresses at the summit of Mt. Titano and the magnificent view from there of Rimini and the Adriatic Sea.

48 FAMOUS PERSONS

Giambattista Belluzzi, a 16th-century military engineer in the service of Florence, was born in San Marino. Well-known Italians who were associated with San Marino include Cardinal Giulio Alberoni (1664–1752), who attempted to subject the republic to papal domination in 1739–40; Count Alessandro Cagliostro (Giuseppe Balsamo, 1743–1795), a Sicilian adventurer, imposter, and alchemist; Bartolommeo Borghesi (1781–1860), an antiquarian, epigrapher, and numismatist, who resided in San Marino from 1821 to 1860; and Giuseppe Garibaldi (1807–1882), the great Italian patriot, who obtained refuge from the Austrians in San Marino in 1849.

49 DEPENDENCIES

San Marino has no territories or colonies.

50 BIBLIOGRAPHY

Duursma, Jorri. *Self-Determination, Statehood, and International Relations of Micro-states: The Cases of Liechtenstein, San Marino, Monaco, Andorra, and the Vatican City.* New York: Cambridge University Press, 1996.

Eccardt, Thomas M. *Secrets of the Seven Smallest States of Europe.* New York: Hippocrene, 2005.

Opello, Walter C. *European Politics.* Boulder, CO: Lynne Rienner Publishers, 2009.

Political Chronology of Europe. London, UK: Europa, 2001.

SERBIA

Republic of Serbia

CAPITAL: Belgrade

FLAG: The flag has three equal horizontal stripes of red (top), blue, and white, with the coat of arms set slightly to the hoist side.

ANTHEM: *Boze Pravde (God of Justice).*

MONETARY UNIT: The currency of Serbia is the dinar (RSD). RSD1 = US$0.0135 (or US$1 = RSD74.1842; as of November 2011).

WEIGHTS AND MEASURES: The metric system is in force.

HOLIDAYS: New Year's Day, 1 and 2 January; Orthodox Christmas, 7 January; Orthodox New Year, 13 January; Unification of Serbia, 28 March; FR Yugoslavia Day, 27 April; Labor Day, 1 May; Victory Day, 9 May; St. Vitus Day, 28 June; Serbian Uprising, 7 July.

TIME: 1 p.m. = noon GMT.

¹LOCATION, SIZE, AND EXTENT

Serbia is situated on the central part of the Balkan Peninsula. The total area was approximately 77,474 sq km (29,913 sq mi). The country is slightly smaller than South Carolina. Serbia is bordered on the N by Hungary, on the NE by Romania, on the E by Bulgaria, on the S by Macedonia and Kosovo, on the SW by Montenegro, on the W by Bosnia and Herzegovina, and on the NW by Croatia; total land boundary length is 2,026 km (1,259 mi). There are territorial disputes with Bosnia and Herzegovina over Serbian-populated areas.

Serbia's capital is Belgrade, situated in north central Serbia.

²TOPOGRAPHY

Rich fertile plains are found in the Serbian north, while in the east there are limestone ranges and basins. Nearly half of Serbia is mountainous, with the Dinaric Alps on the western border, the North Albanian Alps (Prokletija) and the Sar Mountains in the south, and the Balkan Mountains along the southeast border. The highest point is Midzor at 2,169 m (7,116 ft).

The Danube is the longest river. With a total length of 2,783 km (1,729 mi), about 588 km (365 mi) flows from west to east through the northern region of Serbia. The Tisa, Sava and Morava rivers are major tributaries of the Danube.

Located on the Eurasian Tectonic Plate, there are several fault lines running through the country which are seismically active. Earth tremors are fairly common and destructive earthquakes have occurred.

³CLIMATE

In the north, winters are cold and summers are hot and humid. In the central and southern regions, the climate is more continental.

Annual precipitation in most of the country is 56 to 190 cm (22 to 75 in).

⁴FLORA AND FAUNA

The forests of Serbia contain about 170 broadleaf species of trees and shrubs, along with about 35 coniferous species. The animals found in Serbia include types of hare, pheasant, deer, stag, wild boar, fox, chamois, mouflon, crane, duck, and goose.

⁵ENVIRONMENT

Industrial wastes are dumped into the Sava, which flows into the Danube. Air pollution is a problem around Belgrade and other industrial cities. Thermal energy plants utilize technology from the 1950s and mostly burn lignite; since combustion is inefficient, air pollution is a major problem in Kosovo. Destructive earthquakes are a natural hazard. The UN reported in 2008 that carbon dioxide emissions in Serbia totaled 13,510 kilotons.

Serbia's water resources totaled 208.5 cu km (50.02 cu mi). There are four Wetlands of International Importance in Serbia and four UNESCO World Heritage Sites. According to a 2011 report issued by the International Union for Conservation of Nature and Natural Resources (IUCN), the number of threatened species in Serbia included 6 types of mammals, 9 species of birds, 11 species of fish, 15 species of invertebrates, and 4 plant species. Threatened species include Atlantic sturgeon, slender-billed curlew, black vultures, asps, bald ibis, Danube salmon, several species of shark, the red wood ant, and beluga. At least one type of mollusk has become extinct.

⁶POPULATION

The US Central Intelligence Agency (CIA) estimates the population of Serbia in 2011 to be approximately 7,310,555, which placed it at number 98 in population among the 196 nations of the world. In 2011, approximately 16.4% of the population was over 65 years of age, with another 15.1% under 15 years of age. The median age in Serbia was 41.3 years. There were 0.95 males for every female in the country. The population's annual rate of change was -0.467%. The projected population for the year 2025 was 6,800,000. Population density in Serbia was calculated at 94 people per sq km (243 people per sq mi).

The UN estimated that 58% of the population lived in urban areas, and that urban populations had an annual rate of change of 0.2%. The largest urban area was Belgrade, with a population of 1.1 million.

7 MIGRATION

Estimates of Serbia's net migration rate, carried out by the CIA in 2011, amounted to zero. The total number of emigrants living abroad was 196,000, and the total number of immigrants living in Serbia was 525,400. Serbia also accepted 71,111 refugees from Croatia, 27,414 from Bosnia and Herzegovina and 206,000 from Kosovo.

The following information on migration pertains to the union of Serbia and Montenegro based on statistics gathered prior to Montenegro's independence in 2006. During the 1960s and 1970s, many Serbs fled from the Yugoslav Socialist Federal Republic, seeking political and economic freedom. The breakup of the Yugoslav SFR in the early 1990s, and the ethnic hostilities that came in its aftermath, resulted in enormous migrations to and from its various former republics. During the first half of 1999, the situation of refugees and internally displaced people deteriorated even further. As of 30 June 1999, the UN High Commissioner for Refugees (UNHCR) reported 508,000 refugees from Bosnia and Herzegovina and Croatia; 770,000 returnees to Kosovo, and 500,000 other refugees remained; 220,000 Serb, Montenegrin, and Roma internally displaced persons from Kosovo were living in other parts of the former Yugoslavia. The total number of migrants in 2000 was 626,000. By the end of 2004, these numbers were still rising; UNHCR reported a total of 627,476 persons of concern. There were 276,683 refugees, 180,117 Croatians and over 95,000 from Bosnia and Herzegovina. In addition, in that same year there were 248,154 internally displaced persons, 85,000 local residents at risk, 8,143 refugees who returned primarily to Croatia, and another 9,456 refugees who returned to other places of origin during the year.

8 ETHNIC GROUPS

There are 37 different ethnicities in Serbia. Ethnic Serbs constitute a majority of the population, at about 82.9%. Ethnic Hungarians make up about 3.8% of the population and live in northern Serbia near the Hungarian border. The number of Roma in the country has been estimated at between 1.4% and 5.4% by various official sources. The Roma population is subject to social and legal discrimination and harassment, as well as political and economic marginalization. The remaining population consists primarily of Bosniaks, Bulgarians, Slovaks, Macedonians, Croats, Montenegrins, Ruthenians, Romanians, Vlachs, Bunjevci, and Turks.

9 LANGUAGES

Serbian, the official language, is spoken by about 88.3% of the population. The script in official use is Cyrillic, while the Latin script is also used. In the areas inhabited by ethnic minorities, the languages and scripts of the minorities are in official use, as provided by law. Hungarian is spoken by about 3.8% of the population, while Bosniak is spoken by 1.8% and Romany by 1.1%. Other languages include Romanian, Slovak, Ukrainian, and Croatian, all of which (along with Hungarian) are official languages in Vojvodina.

10 RELIGIONS

The ancestors of the Serbs converted to Christianity in the 9th century and sided with Eastern Orthodoxy after the Great Schism of 1054 that split Christendom between the Eastern and Roman Churches. The Serbian Orthodox Church has been autonomous since 1219. Islam came to the area from the Ottoman Turks in the 15th century. About 85% of all citizens are Serbian Orthodox. Muslims account for 3.2% of the total population, Roman Catholics for 5.5%, and Protestants 1.1%. Protestant denominations include Baptists, Adventists, Reformed Christians, Evangelical Christians, Evangelical Methodists, Jehovah's Witnesses, the Church of Christ, Mormons, and Pentecostals. There is a small Jewish community in the country. Although the constitution provides for freedom of religion, the government has implemented laws that restrict the activities of some minority religious groups. Though there is no state religion, the Serbian Orthodox Church enjoys preferential treatment by the government. Along with the Serbian Orthodox Church, there are six other religious communities recognized by law as traditional religions—the Serbian Orthodox Church, Roman Catholic Church, Slovak Evangelical Church, Reformed Christian Church, Evangelical Christian Church, Islamic Community, and Jewish community. These are granted some legal benefits. Religious groups are not required to register with the government, but must do so in order to enjoy some legal and economic benefits, such as the right to purchase property or open a bank account. Some minority religious groups have complained of difficulties in the registration process. Orthodox Good Friday, Easter, and Christmas are observed as national holidays.

11 TRANSPORTATION

The CIA reported that Serbia had a total of 36,884 km (22,919 mi) of roads as of 2009, of which 31,938 km (19,845 mi) are paved. There are 227 vehicles per 1,000 people in the country.

Railroads extend for 4,058 km (2,522 mi). They connect Belgrade with Budapest and Zagreb. The Belgrade–Bar line links Serbia to Montenegro and terminates at the Adriatic Sea. Rail service is provided by locomotives manufactured in the 1950s and 1960s. In 2010 the national infrastructure council adopted a master plan for the transportation sector in Serbia that calls for around €22.2 billion in investments through 2027.

Serbia has approximately 587 km (365 mi) of navigable waterways. The Danube, Sava, and Tisa are important commercial rivers, with ports at Belgrade, Novi Sad, Sabac, Pancevo, Smederevo, and Prahovo. Serbia's river fleet has a large transport capacity in Europe.

SERBIA

| 0 | 25 | 50 | 75 Miles |
| 0 | 25 | 50 | 75 Kilometers |

HUNGARY

Subotica

Bajmok

Senta

Sivac

Kula

Veliki

Kanal

Kikinda

Jimbolia

CROATIA

Danube

Bačka Palanka

Novi Sad

Zrenjanin

Giera

ROMANIA

FRUSKA GORA

Orlovat

Vršac

Sava

Belgrade

Pančevo

Oşarva

Bijeljina

Šabac

Loznica

Smederevo

Danube

Požarevac

Brza

Drina

Krupanj

Valjevo

Smederevska Palanka

Velika Morava

Beljanica 4,383 ft. ▲ 1336 m.

Bor

Negotin

BOSNIA & HERZEGOVINA

Ljubovija

Kragujevac

Paracin

Zaječar

Užice

Zapandna Morava

Čačak

Kraljevo

Knjaževac

ZLATIBOR MTS.

Kruševac

Foča

Priboj

Ljubionja 7,342 ft. 2238 m.

Pljevlja

Mojkovac

Juzna

Niš

Moravа

Prokhod Sveti Nikola

Tara

Novi Pazar

Pukovac

Slavinja

BALKAN MTS.

Korita

Durmitor Sinjajevina

Komarnica

Giljeva Planina

Kosovska Mitrovica

Leskovac

Pirot

Krupacko Jezero

Nikšić

MONTENEGRO

KOSOVO

Klisura

BULGARIA

Slano Jezero

Daravica 8,714 ft. 2656 m. ▲

Beli

Peć

Drin

Priština

Vranje

CROATIA

Danilovgrad

Podgorica

NORTH ALBANIAN ALPS

Uroševac

Vitina

Budva

Skadarsko Jezeroi

Drin

Prizren

Bar

Shëmëri

Tetovo

Ulcinj

Adriatic Sea

ALBANIA

MACEDONIA

N W E S

Serbia

LOCATION: 41°50′ to 46°10′ N; 19°5′ to 23° E. BOUNDARY LENGTHS: Romania, 476 kilometers (296 miles); Bulgaria, 318 kilometers (198 miles); Macedonia, 62 kilometers, (39 miles); Montenegro, 124 kilometers (77 miles); Bosnia and Herzegovina, 302 kilometers (187 miles); Croatia, 241 kilometers (150 miles); Hungary, 151 kilometers (94 miles); Kosovo, 352 kilometers (219 miles).

There were 11 airports with paved runways in 2010. In addition, there were two heliports. Yugoslav Aero Transport (YAT) operates from Belgrade. Air travel transported 926,618 passengers in 2009 according to the World Bank.

12 HISTORY

The Serbs, one of the large family of Slavic nations, first began settling in the Balkans around the 7th century in the areas now known as Bosnia, Kosovo, and Montenegro, straddling the line that since AD 395 had divided the Eastern and Western halves of the Roman Empire.

Tracing the origins of the Serbs (and Croats) has fueled many debates among historians, but there seems to be a consensus on their Sarmatian (Iranian) origin. Having assimilated into the Slavic tribes, the Serbs migrated with them west into central Europe (White Serbia) in the Saxony area and from there moved to the Balkans around AD 626 upon an invitation by the Byzantine emperor Heraclius to assist him in repelling the Avar and Persian attack on Constantinople. Having settled in the Balkan area the Serbs organized several principalities of their own, made up of a number of clans headed by leaders known as *zupans*. Both the Byzantine Empire and the Bulgars tried to conquer them, but the Serbs were too decentralized to be conquered.

Between the 9th and 12th centuries, several Serbian principalities evolved, among them Raška in the mountainous north of Montenegro and southern Serbia, and Zeta (south Montenegro along the Adriatic coast), whose ruler Mihajlo (Michael) was anointed king by Pope Gregory VII in 1077.

In the late 10th century the Bulgarian khan (leader) Samuil extended his control over Bosnia, Raška, and Zeta, north to the Sava River, and south over Macedonia. Raška became the area from where the medieval Serbian empire developed. Stephen Nemanja, grand zupan of Raška, fought against the Byzantines in AD 1169, and added Zeta to his domain in 1186. He built several Serbian monasteries, including Hilandar on Mount Athos. His son, Rastko, became a monk (Sava) and the first Serbian archbishop of the new Serbian Autocephalous Church in 1219. The second son, Stephen, received his crown from Pope Innocent IV in 1202. Stephen developed political alliances that, following his death in 1227, allowed Serbia to resist the pressure from Bulgaria and, internally, keep control over subordinate zupans. Archbishop Sava (later Saint Sava) preferred the Byzantine Church and utilized the Orthodox religion in his nation-building effort. He began by establishing numerous Serbian-Orthodox monasteries around Serbia. He also succeeded in turning Zeta from Catholicism to Serbian Orthodoxy.

The medieval Serbian empire, under Stephen Dušan the Mighty (1331–55) extended from the Aegean Sea to the Danube (Belgrade), along the Adriatic and Ionian coasts from the Neretva River to the Gulf of Corinth and controlled, aside from the central Serbian lands, Macedonia, Thessaly, the Epirus, and Albania. The Serbian Church obtained its own patriarchate, with its center in Peć. Serbia became an exporting land with abundant crops and minerals. Dušan, who was crowned tsar of "the Serbs and Greeks" in 1346, gave Serbia its first code of laws based on a combination of Serbian customs and Byzantine law. His attempt to conquer the throne of Byzantium failed, however, when the Byzantines called on the advancing Ottoman Turks for help in 1345. Even though Dušan withstood the attacks from the Turks twice (in 1345 and 1349), the gates to Europe had been opened, and the Ottoman Turks had initiated their campaign to subjugate the Balkans.

Under Ottoman Rule

Dušan's heirs could not hold his empire together against the Turks and the Nemanja dynasty ended with the death of his son Stephen Uroš in 1371, the same year his brothers Vukašin and Ivan Ugleš were killed at the battle of Marica. The defeat of the Serbs at Kosovo Polje in 1389 in an epochal battle that took the lives of both Sultan Murad I and Serbian prince Lazar left Serbia open to further Turkish conquest. Following a series of wars, the Turks succeeded in overtaking Constantinople in 1453 and all of Serbia by 1459. For the next three-and-a-half centuries, Serbs and others had to learn how to survive under Ottoman rule.

The Turks did not make any distinctions based on ethnicity, but only on religion. Turkish Muslims were the dominant class while Christians and Jews were subordinated. While maintaining their religious and cultural autonomy, the non-Turks developed most of the nonmilitary administrative professions and carried on most of the economic activities, including internal trade and trade with other countries of the Christian world. There was no regular conscription of non-Turks into the sultan's armies, but non-Turks were taxed to pay for defense. Christian boys between the age of eight and twenty were forcibly taken from their families to be converted to Islam and trained as "Janissaries" or government administrators. Some these former Christians became administrators and even became grand viziers (advisers) to sultans.

Urban dwellers under Ottoman rule, involved in crafts, trade, and the professions, fared much better than the Christian peasantry, who were forced into serfdom. Heavy regular taxes were levied on the peasants, with corruption making the load so unbearable that the peasants rebelled.

Two distinct cultures lived side by side-Turkish Muslim in cities and towns as administrative centers and Christian Orthodox in the countryside of Serbia. The numerous Serbian monasteries built around the country since the Nemanja dynasty became the supportive network for Serbian survival. The Serbian Church was subjected after 1459 to the Greek patriarchate for about a century until a Serbian patriarchate emerged again. The Serbian patriarchate covered a large area from north of Ohrid to the Hungarian lands north of the Danube and west through Bosnia.

The Serbian Diaspora

Over the two centuries 1459–1659 many Serbs left their lands and settled north of the Sava and Danube Rivers where Hungary had promised their leader ("Vojvoda") an autonomous arrangement in exchange for military service against the Turks. The region is called "Vojvodina" by Serbs, even though the Hungarians had reneged on their promise of autonomy. Fleeing the Turkish conquest, many Serbs and Croats settled in Venetian- occupied Dalmatia and continued fighting against the Turks from fortified areas. The wars between Austria and the Turks in the late 17th through the mid-18th centuries caused both mass migrations from Serbia and the hardening of Ottoman treatment of their Christian subjects.

Following the defeat of the Turks in 1683 at the gates of Vienna by a coalition led by Poland's king Jan Sobieski, the Christian armies pursued the Turks all the way to Macedonia and had a good chance to drive the Turks off the European continent. Turk reprisals were violent and many Serbs fled, leaving Serbian lands, particularly Kosovo, unpopulated. Albanians, whom the Turks favored because they were mostly Muslims, moved in. Conversion to Islam increased considerably.

A second large-scale migration took place 50 years later, after the 1736–39 Austrian defeat by the Turks. All these movements of population resulted in the loss of the Kosovo area—the cradle of Serbian nationhood—to Albanians. As a result, the Serbs were unable to give up control over an area to which they felt a tremendously deep emotional attachment, even though they represent only about 10% of its population. This situation has persisted and remained unresolved as of the early 21st century.

Serbian Revolts and Independence

Meanwhile, two areas of active Serbian national activity developed, one under the Turks in the northern Šumadija region and the other in Hungary. Šumadija, a forested region, became the refuge for many *hajduks* (Serbian "Robin Hoods") that raided Turkish establishments. These hajduks were legendary heroes among the Serbian people.

In 1805, the Serbs defeated the Turks and gained control of the Belgrade region. The sultan agreed to Serbian terms for political autonomy in September 1806. A partially elected government structure was established, and by 1811 the Serbian assembly confirmed Karadjordje as supreme leader with hereditary rights. The drive of Serbia for complete independence was thwarted, however, because Serbia was still under Ottoman rule. The Turks reoccupied Serbia by 1813, retaliating against the Serbs by pillaging, looting, enslaving women and children, while killing all males over age 15, and torturing any captured leader.

A second uprising by the Serbs occurred in 1815 and spread all over Šumadija. It was led by Miloš Obrenović, who had participated in the first revolt. Successful in repelling Turkish forces, Obrenović gained the support of the Russian tsar, and after some six months he negotiated an agreement giving Serbia a *de facto* autonomy in its internal administration. By 1830, Serbia had gained its full autonomy and Miloš was recognized as a hereditary prince of Serbia. Serbia was internationally accepted as a virtually independent state.

Miloš Obrenović was an authoritarian ruler who had to be forced to promulgate a constitution for Serbia, establishing a council of chiefs sharing power with him. In 1838, a council was appointed to pass laws and taxes, a council of ministers was created, and provisions were formulated for an eventual assembly. A succession of rulers were installed and deposed over the next decade until, in 1848, the Serbian assembly demanded the incorporation of Vojvodina into Serbia.

The 1858 assembly restored Miloš Obrenović to power, but he died in 1860 and was succeeded, again, by his son Mihajlo. Mihajlo built up the Serbian army to fight a war of liberation against the Turks as a first step towards the goal of a Greater Serbia. Mihajlo developed a highly centralized state organization, a functioning parliament, two political parties, a judicial system, and urban educational institutions prior to his murder in 1868. Mihajlo's cousin, Milan, succeeded him, and accomplished total independence from the Ottomans in 1882. Despite this success, during the same period Austria conquered Bosnia and Herzegovina, badly wanted by Serbia. Milan became dependent on Austria when that country saved Serbia from an invasion by Bulgaria.

Milan Obrenović abdicated in 1889 in favor of his son Alexander, who abolished the constitution, led a corrupt and scandalous life, and was murdered along with his wife, the premier, and other court members by a group of young officers in June 1903. The assembly then called on Peter, Alexander Karadjordjević's son, to take the crown. Under Peter Karadjordjević, a period of stable political and economic development ensued, interrupted by the 1908 Austrian annexation of Bosnia and Herzegovina, the 1912 and 1913 Balkan wars, and World War I (1913–18).

The Balkan Wars

Austria's annexation of Bosnia and Herzegovina was carried out in 1908 with the full backing of Germany. The Serbs saw Austria's move as a serious blow to their goal of a Greater Serbia with an outlet to the Adriatic Sea through Bosnia and Herzegovina. They turned to the only other possible access routes to the sea-Macedonia, with its port city of Salonika, and the northern coast of Albania. The Balkan countries (Serbia, Bulgaria, Montenegro, and Greece) formed the Balkan League and attacked Turkey in 1912, quickly defeating them and driving them to the gates of Constantinople. Austria and Italy opposed a Serbian outlet to the Adriatic in Albania, supporting instead an independent Albanian state, assisting its establishment in 1913. Serbia, deprived of access to the sea, requested it from Bulgaria. Bulgaria responded by attacking Serbia and Greece, hoping to obtain all of Macedonia. The resulting second Balkan War ended with the defeat of Bulgaria by Serbia, Montenegro, Greece, Romania, and Turkey, which gained back Adrianople and Thrace. Romania gained northern Dobrudja, Serbia kept central and northern Macedonia, and Greece was given control over the southern part with Salonika and Kavalla in addition to southern Epirus.

Austria viewed Serbian expansion with great alarm, and the "Greater Serbia" plans became a serious threat to the Austro-Hungarian empire. The Austro-Hungarians felt Serbia had to be restrained by whatever means, including war. They needed only a spark to ignite a conflagration against the Serbs.

World War I and Royal Yugoslavia

The spark was provided by the 28 June 1914 assassination in Sarajevo of Austria's Archduke Ferdinand and his wife. The archduke's visit to Sarajevo during large-scale maneuvers was viewed as a provocation by Bosnian Serbs, and they conspired to assassinate him with the assistance of the Serbian secret organization, Black Hand, which had also been behind the murder of Serbian king Miloš and his wife in 1903.

Austria presented an ultimatum to Serbia on 23 July with 10 requests, all of which were accepted by Serbia in a desperate effort to avoid a war. Austria, however, declared war on Serbia on 28 July 1914. They began bombing Belgrade the same day and sent armies across the Danube and Sava rivers to invade Serbia on 11 August 1914, taking the Serbs by surprise. The Serbian army twice repelled the Austrian forces in 1914, with tremendous losses in men and materials and civilian refugees. In addition, a typhus epidemic exacted some 150,000 victims among Serbian soldiers and civilians throughout Serbia, where there were almost no doctors or medical supplies. Still, an army of some 120,000 men joined the Allied forces holding the Salonika front in the fall of 1916. From there, after two years, they were successful in driving the Austrian forces out of Serbia in October 1918.

The Serbian elite's political goal for the outcome of World War I was a greater Serbia, with the liberation of their South Slavic brethren, particularly Serbs, from the Austro-Hungarian yoke. The dissolution of the Austro-Hungarian empire was not yet an operational concept. On 20 July 1916 the Corfu Declaration delineated the future joint state of Serbs, Croats, and Slovenes, while treating both Macedonians and Montenegrins as Serbs.

But Austro-Hungary was losing the war and disintegrating from the inside. In May 1917, the "Yugoslav Club" in the Vienna parliament, consisting of deputies from Slovenia, Istria, and Dalmatia, issued a declaration demanding the independence of all Slovenes, Croats, and Serbs united in one national state. (The phrase "under the scepter of the Hapsburgs" was added to their declaration for safety reasons, to avoid prosecution for treason.) Poles, Czechs, and Slovaks were also agitating for independence, and they all had received support from their communities in the United States. On 20 October 1918, US President Woodrow Wilson declared his support for the independence of all the nation subjects of the Austro-Hungarian monarchy.

Under the leadership of Monsignor Anton Korošec, a council of Slovenes, Croats, and Serbs was formed in Zagreb, Croatia, to negotiate a union with the Kingdom of Serbia. The Serbian army entered Belgrade on 1 November 1918 and proceeded to take over the Vojvodina region. The armistice ending World War I was signed on 3 November 1918, and on 6–9 November a conference was held in Geneva by Serbia's prime minister Nikola Pašić, Monsignor Korošec, and the Yugoslav Committee.

The conference was empowered by the Zagreb Council to negotiate with the Allies. Prime Minister Pašić could not ignore the provisional government set up by elected representatives of the Slovenes, Croats, and Serbs. Thus, Pašić signed a declaration setting up a joint provisional government with the right of the National Council in Zagreb to administer its territories until a constitutional assembly could be elected to agree on the form of government for the new state. However, the Serbian government reneged on Pašić's commitment. The National Council delegation with Monsignor Korošec was detained abroad and, given the pressures from the ongoing Italian occupation of Slovene and Croat territories and the urgent need for international recognition, the National Council sent a delegation to Belgrade on 27 November 1918 to negotiate terms for unification with Serbia. But time was running out and the unification was proclaimed on 1 December 1918 without any details on the nature of the new state, since Bosnia and Herzegovina, Vojvodina, and Montenegro had already voted for their union with Serbia.

The Corfu Declaration of 1917 had left open the issue of the unitarist or federalist structure of the new state. It provided for a constitutional assembly to decide the issue on the basis of a "numerically qualified majority." Serbs interpreted this to mean a simple majority whereas others advocated a two-thirds majority. Following the 28 November 1920 elections, the simple majority prevailed, and a constitution (mirroring the 1903 constitution of Serbia) for a unitary state was approved on 28 June 1921 by a vote of 223 to 35, with 111 abstentions out of a total of 419 members. The 50 members of the Croatian Peasant Party refused to participate in the work of the assembly, advocating instead an independent Croatian Republic.

After 10 years of a contentious parliamentary system that ended in the murder of Croatian deputies and their leader Stjepan Radić, King Alexander abrogated the 1921 constitution, dissolved the parliament and political parties, took over power directly, renamed the country "Yugoslavia," and abolished the 33 administrative departments.

A new policy was initiated with the goal of creating a single "Yugoslav" nation out of the three "tribes" of Serbs, Croats, and Slovenes. In practice, this meant the Serbian king's hegemony over the rest of the nation. The reaction was intense, and King Alexander himself was assassinated in Marseille, France, in 1934. Alexander's cousin, Prince Paul, assumed power and managed to reach an agreement in 1939 with the Croats. An autonomous Croatian *banovina* (territory headed by a leader called a *ban*) headed by Ivan Subašić was established; it included most Croatian lands outside of the Bosnia and Herzegovina area. Strong opposition developed among Serbs and there was no time for further negotiations, since Prince Paul's government was deposed on 27 March 1941 and Germany's Adolf Hitler and his allies (Italy, Hungary, Bulgaria) attacked Yugoslavia on 6 April 1941.

World War II

Yugoslavia was divided up and occupied by Germany and its allies. Serbia was put under the administration of General Milan Nedić, who was allowed to organize his own military force for internal peacekeeping purposes. In Serbia the resistance was led by the "Cetniks," the "Yugoslav army in the homeland." The Cetniks recognized the authority of the Yugoslav government-in-exile, which, in fact, promoted Draža Mihajlović to general and appointed him its minister of war. In the fall of 1941 Mihajlović and Josip Broz Tito, who led the Communist partisan movement, met to seek agreement on a common front against the Nazis. However, Mihajlović saw that Tito's goal was to conquer Yugoslavia for Communism. Mihajlović could not go along with this, nor could he accept Tito's request that he subordinate his command to Tito.

A civil war between the two movements (under foreign occupation) followed. Meanwhile, large numbers of Serbs fled Croatia, either to join the partisans or to seek refuge in the Dalmatian areas under Italian control. British leader Winston Churchill, convinced by reports that Mihajlović was collaborating with the Germans, decided to recognize Tito as the legitimate Yugoslav resistance. Though aware of Tito's Communist allegiance to Stalin, Churchill threw his support to Tito.

When Soviet armies, accompanied by Tito, entered Yugoslavia from Romania and Bulgaria in the fall of 1944, military units and civilians that had opposed the partisans had no choice but to retreat to Austria or Italy. After the end of the war, the Communist-led forces took control of Serbia and Yugoslavia and instituted a violent dictatorship that committed systematic crimes and human rights violations. Thousands upon thousands of their former opponents who were returned from Austria by British military authorities were tortured and massacred by partisan executioners. General Mihajlović was captured in Bosnia in March 1946 and publicly tried and executed on 17 July 1946.

Communist Yugoslavia

Such was the background for the formation of the second Yugoslavia as a Federative People's Republic of five nations (Slovenes, Croats, Serbs, Macedonians, Montenegrins) with their individual republics and Bosnia and Herzegovina as a buffer area with its mix of Serb, Muslim, and Croat populations. The problem of large Hungarian and Muslim Albanian populations in Serbia was solved by creating for them the autonomous region of Vojvodina (Hungarian minority) and Kosovo (Muslim Albanian majority), which assured their political and cultural development.

Tito attempted a balancing act to satisfy most of the nationality issues that were carried over, unresolved, from the first Yugoslavia. However, he failed to satisfy anyone. The numerically stronger Serbs had lost the Macedonian area they considered Southern Serbia; lost the opportunity to incorporate Montenegro into Serbia; lost direct control over the Hungarian minority in Vojvodina and Muslim Albanians of Kosovo (viewed as the cradle of the Serbian nation since the Middle Ages); were not able to incorporate into Serbia the large Serbian-populated areas of Bosnia; and had not obtained an autonomous region for the large minority Serbian population within the Croatian Republic. The official position of the Marxist Yugoslav regime was that national rivalries and conflicting interests would gradually diminish through their sublimation into a new Socialist order. Without capitalism, nationalism was supposed to wither away. Therefore, in the name of their unity and brotherhood motto, any nationalistic expression of concern was prohibited.

After a short post-war coalition government, the elections of 11 November 1945--boycotted by the non-Communist coalition parties--gave the Communist-led People's Front 90% of the vote. A Constituent Assembly met on 29 November, abolished the monarchy and established the Federative People's Republic of Yugoslavia. In January 1946, a new constitution was adopted based on the 1936 Soviet constitution.

Yugoslavia was expelled from the Soviet-dominated Cominform Group in 1948, and was forced to find its own road to Socialism, balancing its position between the North Atlantic Treaty Organization (NATO) alliance and the Soviet bloc. Tito quickly nationalized the economy through a policy of forced industrialization, supported by the collectivization of agriculture.

The agricultural reform of 1945–46 included limited private ownership of a maximum of 35 hectares (85 acres) and a limited free market (after the initial forced delivery of quotas to the state at very low prices) but was abandoned because of resistance by the peasants. Collectivization was initiated in 1949 but was abandoned by 1958 because its inefficiency and low productivity could not support the concentrated effort of industrial development.

By the 1950s, Yugoslavia had initiated the development of its internal trademark: self-management of enterprises through workers councils and local decision-making. Following the failure of the first five-year plan (1947–51), the second five-year plan (1957–61) was completed in four years by relying on the well-established self-management system. Economic targets were set from the local to the republic level and then coordinated by a federal planning institute to meet an overall national economic strategy. This system supported a period of very rapid industrial growth in the 1950s. But public subsidies, cheap credit, and other artificial measures led to a serious crisis by 1961, leading to the introduction of market socialism in 1965. Laws abolished most price controls and halved import duties while withdrawing export subsidies. Councils were given more decision-making power on investing their earnings, and they also tended to vote for higher salaries to meet steep increases in the cost of living. Unemployment grew rapidly even though political factories were still subsidized. The government responded by relaxing restrictions on labor migration, particularly to West Germany, encouraging up to 49% foreign investment in joint enterprises and removing barriers to the exchange of ideas.

Yugoslavia began to develop a foreign policy independent of the Soviet Union. In October 1949, Yugoslavia was elected to one of the nonpermanent seats on the UN Security Council and openly condemned North Korea's aggression in South Korea. Tito intensified his commitment to the movement of nonaligned "third world" nations in cooperation with Jawaharlal Nehru of India, Gamal Abdel-Nasser of Egypt, and others.

With the September 1961 Belgrade summit conference of nonaligned nations, Tito became the recognized leader of the movement. The nonaligned position served Tito's Yugoslavia well by allowing Tito to draw on economic and political support from the Western powers while neutralizing any aggression from the Soviet bloc. Tito condemned all Soviet aggression. Just before his death on 4 May 1980, Tito condemned the Soviet invasion of Afghanistan. In the 1970s and 1980s, Yugoslavia maintained fairly good relations with its neighboring states by playing down or solving pending disputes and developing cooperative projects and increased trade.

As an integral part of the Yugoslav federation, Serbia naturally was impacted by Yugoslavia's internal and external political developments. The main problem facing communist Yugoslavia was the force of nationalism.

As nationalism was on the rise in Yugoslavia, particularly in Croatia and Slovenia, Serbs were facing a real dilemma with the rising of Albanian nationalism in Kosovo. After World War II, Tito had set up Kosovo as an autonomous province and the Albanians were able to develop their own political and cultural autonomy, including a university with instructors and textbooks from Albania. Immigration from Albania also increased and after Tito's death in 1980, Albanians became more assertive and began agitating for a republic of their own, since by then they comprised about 80% of Kosovo's population.

The reverberations of the Kosovo events were very serious throughout Yugoslavia since most non-Serbs viewed the repression of the Albanians as a possible precedent for the use of force elsewhere. Serbs were accused of using a double standard-one for themselves in the defense of Serbs in Kosovo by denying the Albanians' political autonomy and violating their human rights, and a different standard for themselves by demanding political autonomy and human rights for Serbs in Croatia.

In 1986, the Serbian Academy of Arts and Sciences issued a draft manifesto that called for the creation of a unified Serbia whereby all lands inhabited by Serbs would be united with Serbia while bringing Kosovo under control to be eventually repopulated by Serbs. To accomplish this goal, the 1974 constitution would need to be amended into an instrument for a recentralizing effort of both the government and the economy.

Recentralization vs. Confederation

In 1986, work was begun on amendments to the 1974 constitution that, when submitted in 1987, created a furor, particularly in Slovenia and Croatia. The main points of contention were the creation of a unified legal system, the establishment of central control over the means of transportation and communication, the centralization of the economy into a unified market, and the granting of more control to Serbia over its autonomous provinces of Kosovo and Vojvodina. These moves were all viewed as coming at the expense of the individual republics. Serbia also proposed replacing the bicameral federal Skupština (assembly) with a tricameral one where deputies would no longer be elected by their republican assemblies but through a "one person, one vote" nationwide system. Slovenia, Croatia, and Bosnia and Herzegovina strongly opposed the change, just as they opposed the additional Chamber of Associated Labor that would have increased the federal role in the economy.

Meanwhile, Slobodan Milošević had become the head of the Communist Party in Serbia in early 1987. An ardent advocate of the Serbs in Kosovo (and elsewhere) and a vocal proponent of the recentralizing constitutional amendments, he was able to take control of the leadership in Montenegro and Vojvodina and impose Serbian control over Kosovo.

The Slovenian Communist Party had taken leadership in opposing the recentralizing initiatives and in advocating a confederate reorganization of Yugoslavia. Thus a political dueling took place between Slovenia and Serbia. Slobodan Milošević directed the organization of mass demonstrations by Serbs in Ljubljana, the capital city of Slovenia. Serbs began a boycott of Slovenian products, withdrew savings from Slovenian banks, and terminated economic cooperation and trade with Slovenia. The tensions with Serbia convinced the Slovenian leadership of the need to undertake protective measures and, in September 1989, draft amendments to the constitution of Slovenia were published that included the right to secession, the sole right of the Slovenian legislature to introduce martial law, and the right to control deployment of armed forces in Slovenia. The latter seemed particularly necessary since the Yugoslav Army was largely controlled by a Serbian and Montenegrin officer corps.

A last attempt at salvaging Yugoslavia was made when the League of Communists of Yugoslavia convened in January 1990 to review proposed reforms. The Slovenian delegation walked out on 23 January 1990 when their attempts to broaden the reforms were rebuffed.

Yugoslavia's Dissolution

In October 1990, Slovenia and Croatia published a joint proposal for a confederation of Yugoslavia as a last attempt at a negotiated solution, to no avail. The Slovenian legislature also adopted a draft constitution proclaiming that "Slovenia will become an independent state. . . ." It became clear that no negotiated agreement was possible, so Slovenia declared its independence on 25 June 1991.

The collapse of Communist regimes in Eastern Europe in 1989 had a deep impact in Yugoslavia. Communist leaders there realized that, in order to stay in power, they needed to embrace the goals of the various nationalistic movements.

Suppression of Kosovo and Revolt in Croatia

On 2 July 1990, Albanian members of the Yugoslav legislature declared Kosovo a separate territory within the Yugoslav federation. Three days later, on 5 July 1990, the Serbian parliament countered the Albanian move by suspending the autonomous government of Kosovo. The next month (August 1990), an open Serb insurrection against the Croatian government was initiated apparently with the support of Slobodan Milošević. On 17 March 1991, Milošević declared that Krajina, a region in Croatia, was a Serbian autonomous region. Clashes between the Serbian militia and Croatian police required the use of Yugoslav army units to keep the peace.

The Serbian determination to maintain a united Yugoslavia hardened, while the determination of the Slovenes and Croats to

gain their independence grew stronger. This caused the closing of ranks by the Yugoslav army command in support of the Serbian leadership and Slobodan Milošević. Since there was no substantial Serbian population in Slovenia, its secession did not present a real problem to Milošević, but secession by Croatia and Bosnia and Herzegovina would necessitate border revisions to allow land with Serbian populations to be joined to Serbia.

The new constitution promulgated by Serbia in September 1990 provided for a unicameral legislature of 250 seats and the elimination of autonomy for Vojvodina and Kosovo. The first elections were held on 9 December 1990. More than 50 parties and 32 presidential candidates participated. Slobodan Milošević's Socialist Party of Serbia received two-thirds of the votes and 194 out of the 250 seats. The Movement for Renewal, headed by Vuk Drašković, received 19 seats, while the Democratic Party won 7 seats. With the mandate from two-thirds of the electorate, Slobodan Milošević had complete control of Serbia.

Having gained control of Serbia, Montenegro, Kosovo, and Vojvodina, Milošević controlled four of the eight votes in the collective presidency of Yugoslavia. With the collective presidency stalemated, the top army leadership became more independent of the normal civilian controls and was able to make its own political decisions on rendering support to the Serbs in Croatia and their armed rebellion.

On 3 June 1991 Bosnia and Herzegovina and Macedonia proposed the formation of a Community of Yugoslav Republics as a compromise. In this community, national defense, foreign policy, and a common market would be centrally administered while all other areas would fall to the jurisdiction of the member states. But it was already too late. Serbia disliked the confederate nature of the proposal and objected to leaving an opening for the establishment of separate armed forces. In addition, Milošević and the army had already committed to the support of the revolt of the Serbs in Croatia. At their meeting in Split on 12 June 1991, Milošević and Croatia's president Tudjman were past the stage of salvaging Yugoslavia.

The international community stood firmly in support of the preservation of Yugoslavia, of the economic reforms initiated by the Marković government, and of the peaceful solution to the centralist vs. confederate conflict. The United States and the European Community had indicated that they would not recognize the independence of Slovenia and Croatia if they unilaterally seceded from the Yugoslav Federation. With the then-Soviet Union also supporting Socialist Federal Yugoslavia, Milošević was assured of strong international backing. Slovenia and Croatia proceeded with their declarations of independence on 25 June 1991.

As a shrewd politician, Slobodan Milošević knew that a military attack on a member republic would deal a mortal blow to both the idea and the reality of a Yugoslavia in any form. Thus, following the Yugoslav army's attack on Slovenia on 27 June 1991, Milošević and the Serbian leadership concentrated on the goal of uniting all Serbian lands to Serbia.

This position led to the direct use of the Yugoslav army and its superior capabilities in establishing the Serbian autonomous region of Krajina in Croatia. Increased fighting from July 1991 caused tremendous destruction of entire cities (such as Vukovar), and large scale damage to the medieval city of Dubrovnik. Croatia, which was poorly armed and caught by surprise, over a seven-month period. Croatia suffered some 10,000 dead, 30,000 wounded, over 14,000 missing, and lost about one-third of its territory, from Slavonia to the west and around the border with Bosnia and south to northern Dalmatia.

The intervention of the European Community (as earlier in the case of Slovenia) and the UN brought about a cease-fire on 3 January 1992. UN peacekeepers were stationed by March 1991 to separate the Serb-controlled areas from Croatian army and paramilitary forces. Milošević had very good reasons to press the Krajina Serbs and the Yugoslav army to accept the cease-fire because the Serb forces had already achieved control of about one-third of Croatian territory. He was confident that the UN forces would actually protect the Serb-occupied territories from the Croats.

Aggression in Bosnia and Herzegovina

In the meantime, a far worse situation was developing in Bosnia and Herzegovina. In 1991, Bosnia and Herzegovina was about 44% Muslim, 31% Serbian, 17% Croatian, and 6% Yugoslav. Milošević's goal of unifying all Serbian lands would become impossible with an independent Bosnia and Herzegovina. Therefore, Bosnian Serbs abstained from voting, while 64% of eligible voters approved of an independent Bosnia and Herzegovina by an almost unanimous 99.7%.

At the same time, a provisional agreement had been reached at a conference in Lisbon in late February 1992 on dividing Bosnia and Herzegovina into three ethnic units, with related central power sharing. This agreement was rejected by the Muslim side, and the Bosnian Serbs, who had earlier organized their territory into the Serbian Republic of Bosnia and Herzegovina, prepared for hostilities with the support of the Yugoslav army and volunteers from Serbia and Montenegro.

International recognition of Bosnia and Herzegovina came on 6 April 1992, the anniversary of the 1941 Nazi invasion of Yugoslavia. The fear of another genocidal orgy against Serbs steeled the Serbs' determination to fight for their own survival. On 1 March 1992 a Serbian wedding party was attacked in the Muslim section of Sarajevo. This was the spark that ignited the fighting in Bosnia and Herzegovina. Serbs pounded Sarajevo for two years, reducing it to rubble. They took control of two-thirds of the territory, and carried out ferocious "ethnic cleansing" of Muslims in areas they intended to acquire. Under international pressure, the Yugoslav army moved to Serbia, leaving to the Bosnian Serbs an abundance of weaponry and supplies.

Serbia and Montenegro formed their own Federal Republic of Yugoslavia on 27 April 1992. Despite the lack of international support, Milošević was elected president in December with 56% versus 34% for his opponent, Milan Panić. Inflation, unemployment, and savage corruption convinced Milošević to support the various plans for bringing about peace to Bosnia and Herzegovina. Even with the eventual settlement of hostilities in Bosnia and Herzegovina, Yugoslavia faced serious internal political problems.

Kosovo

Kosovo was the center of the Serbian kingdom in the Middle Ages. Firmly attached to their Christian faith and opposed to conversion into Islam, large numbers of Serbs were forced to leave the Kosovo region because of Turkish persecutions. In their place Muslim Albanians were settled in increasing numbers so that liberation of Serbian Kosovo in 1912 actually liberated an almost en-

tirely Albanian area. By the end of World War II, the Kosovo area was already about 70% Albanian. Tito granted Kosovo a special autonomous status, keeping Serbian hopes alive that eventually Serbs could repopulate Kosovo.

In a street meeting on 2 July 1990, the adjourned Kosovo Assembly adopted a declaration proclaiming Kosovo a separate republican entity. Serbs reacted by suspending the Kosovo Assembly on 5 July 1990. Most of the Albanian delegates had to flee the country to avoid imprisonment.

Serbia found itself in a very peculiar and dangerous situation. Through several past centuries the Serbian people expanded their reach by forced mass migrations and wars that have contributed to the depopulation of its own cradle area-Kosovo. The Serbian claims to these lands were contested by neighboring states or other older populations. Serbia and Montenegro became isolated and were facing adversary states.

The Ongoing Conflict

The quest to create a "Greater Serbia"—that is, to unite the Serbs under a single Serbian government--resulted in continued fighting, particularly in Bosnia and Herzegovina. Over 8,000 Bosnian Muslim men and boys were summarily executed at Srebrenica in July 1995.

In October 1995, Bosnia and Herzegovina accused the Bosnian Serbs of war crimes, leading to international suspicion that Serbian soldiers had massacred thousands of Muslims. Pressured by air strikes and diplomacy, Serb authorities joined leaders from Bosnia and Herzegovina and Croatia on 31 October 1995 in Dayton, Ohio, for a round of peace talks sponsored by the United States. On 21 November 1995, the three presidents of Bosnia and Herzegovina, Croatia, and Serbia finally agreed to terms that would end the fighting in Bosnia and Herzegovina after four years and an estimated 250,000 casualties. The agreement, formally signed in Paris in mid-December, called for 60,000 UN peacekeepers. The United States then ended its economic sanctions against Serbia.

Enforcement of the peace was difficult and problems arose over the exchange of prisoners. The United States ordered the leaders of the former warring parties to meet in Rome in February 1996 to recommit themselves to the Dayton agreement. Meanwhile, the International Criminal Tribunal for the former Yugoslavia at The Hague set out to find and prosecute Serbian soldiers accused of atrocities. In March 1996, the UN Tribunal filed its first charges. Among those cited were Serb generals Djordje Djukic and Ratko Mladić, and Bosnian Serb leader Radovan Karadzic. The latter two remained at large, spurring accusations by the United States and Europe that the Serbian government was protecting the international outlaws. In May 1996, Serbian President Milošević pledged that Karadzic would be removed from power. The presidents of Serbia, Croatia, and Bosnia and Herzegovina agreed to hold Bosnian elections in mid-September 1996.

While international suspicion swirled about him for his role in the Bosnian conflict, Serbian President Milošević was not very successful in delivering promised reforms for Serbia. In March 1996, a demonstration in Belgrade brought out 20,000 protestors against the Milošević regime, which opponents charged with starting the Bosnian conflict and devastating the Serbian economy.

Mass demonstrations against Milošević flared later in 1996 when he voided local elections won by the opposition. In December, the Milošević administration shut down Belgrade's independent radio station, which further alienated Serb citizens. Thousands of protesters met in the streets of Belgrade, hoping to topple the Milošević administration. In February 1997, Milošević relented and agreed to recognize the results of the previous local elections, in which opposition parties won majorities in 14 of Serbia's 19 largest cities. In July 1997, Milošević was appointed to the presidency of Yugoslavia by the federal parliament, allowing him to maintain control for another four years.

During early March of 1999, Albanian moderates led by Ibrahim Rugova (president of the self-proclaimed Republic of Kosovo) and representatives of the Yugoslav government held talks in Ramboullet, France; they came up with a plan to give Kosovo back its autonomy under a three-year NATO occupational guarantee. The Serbs refused to sign the accord, and Yugoslav forces grew to 40,000 in Kosovo, continuing hostilities. Beginning 24 March 1999 NATO forces bombed Serbia and Kosovo, in an attempt to check human rights violations and end fighting. NATO bombs and cruise missiles fell on military targets in Belgrade and Pristina. Fears ran high that other European nations would get involved in the conflict and take sides, resulting in a third world war. Russia disagreed with the NATO bombing runs, attempting its own peace process. After 11 weeks of bombing, casualties reported by the Yugoslav government amounted to 462 soldiers and 114 police officers, but NATO estimates claimed 5,000 had died including 2,000 civilians. On 3 June, the Yugoslav government accepted a peace plan that involved removing Yugoslav troops from Kosovo, and giving some autonomy to the province. NATO troops entered Kosovo on 12 June to enforce the peace plan. Some 170,000 Kosovar Serbs were thrown out of Kosovo by the ethnic Albanian majority during the conflict, adding to an already large refugee population.

On 29 June 1999, 10,000 Serbian protestors gathered in Čačak, in northern Serbia, to demand the resignation of Milošević. In August, more than 100,000 Serbians called for an end to his rule in a march on Belgrade. The UN began the unwieldy task of reconciliation in the region during the fall of 1999. Kosovo was to remain under the sovereignty of Yugoslavia as a Serbian province, but with some future determination of further self-government (scheduled to follow the fall of the Milošević regime). Sweeping constitutional changes in July 2000 changed the presidential term so that Milošević could run for two additional four-year terms. They also made the weight of the Montenegrin vote in the Yugoslav parliament equal to its population, or only 7%. Milošević called presidential elections early, for 24 September 2000; most believed that they would be rigged in his favor, and were planning to boycott the elections.

Milošević banned international observers from monitoring the 24 September elections. The opposition to Milošević was strong and a crowd of 150,000 turned out for the final pre-election rally against him. The opposition claimed victory in the election, with Vojislav Kostunica proclaiming himself the "people's president." The Federal Election Commission called for a second vote, stating that neither candidate had won an outright majority; this plan was met with worldwide opposition.

On 27 September 2000, 250,000 people took to the streets to demand that Milošević step down. On 28 September, the Electoral Commission announced that while the Democratic Opposition group had won the largest single block of seats, the Socialists and their coalition partners had won an absolute majority. By 2 October, protesters had called a general strike, were blocking Belgrade's main streets, and had caused a halt to economic activity in other Yugoslav cities. On 4 October 2000, the Constitutional Court annulled the election results and ruled that Milošević should serve out his last term in office.

Tens of thousands of opposition supporters stormed and burned the parliament building on 5 October and captured the state television service; police joined the crowds. Kostunica told approximately 500,000 supporters at a rally in Belgrade that Serbia had been liberated. On 6 October, Milošević conceded defeat, and Kostunica was sworn in as president on 7 October. He stated his first objective as president would be to right the economy and lead reconstruction efforts. Milošević was indicted for atrocities in Kosovo by the UN war crimes tribunal in The Hague.

The European Union (EU) and United States lifted their economic sanctions against Yugoslavia, and in November the country rejoined the UN; Kostunica indicated that the country wanted to join the EU as soon as possible. In January 2001, Yugoslavia and Albania reestablished diplomatic relations after they had been broken off during the crisis in Kosovo in 1999.

On 1 April 2001, Milošević was arrested at his home in Belgrade after a tense standoff in which shots were fired; he had been charged with corruption and abuse of power within Yugoslavia. Kostunica had originally ruled out extraditing Milošević to the war crimes tribunal at The Hague. Milošević was formerly indicted by the tribunal in May 1999 for alleged war crimes in Kosovo; other, later, indictments included war crimes carried out in Bosnia and Herzegovina and Croatia, including charges of genocide carried out in Bosnia and Herzegovina from 1992–95. In June, then-Serbian prime minister Zoran Djindjic authorized the extradition of Milošević to the tribunal, exacerbating a rift between him and Kostunica, who favored a trial for Milošević in Belgrade. Milošević's trial at The Hague began in February 2002; Milošević died of a heart attack in prison in The Hague on 11 March 2006 with just 50 hours of testimony left before the conclusion of the trial.

Serbia and Montenegro

On 14 March 2002, in an agreement mediated by the EU, Serbia and Montenegro agreed to consign the Yugoslav Republic to history and create a loose federation called "Serbia and Montenegro." Both republics would share defense and foreign policies, but would maintain separate economies, currencies (the dinar for Serbia and the euro for Montenegro), and customs services for the immediate future. Each republic would have its own parliament with a central 126-member parliament located in Belgrade.

Montenegrin president Milo Djukanovic reluctantly agreed to the union, committing Montenegro to a three-year moratorium on an independence referendum, but in April, the Montenegrin government collapsed over differences on the new union. Kosovo, which remained under UN administration, remained part of Serbia. This angered many Kosovo activists, although the agreement looked to some as possibly accelerating the process of independence for the province. The parliament of the Federal Republic of Yugoslavia voted to disband itself on 4 February 2003, dissolving the country and introducing the new state of Serbia and Montenegro.

Serbian presidential elections were held on 29 September 2002, with 55.5% of registered voters casting ballots. Kostunica won 30.9% of the vote, and his opponent Miroljub Labus finished second with 27.4%. The second round of voting was held two weeks later, with Kostunica winning 66.8% of the votes, to 30.9% for Labus. However, voter turnout failed to reach a mandated 50% (it was 45.5%) and the elections were declared to be invalid. Natasa Micic, formerly the speaker of parliament, became acting president. She stated that Serbian presidential elections would be held after the adoption of the new Serbian constitution. Montenegrin general elections were held in October 2002, and in November, Djukanovic resigned as president to take on the job of prime minister. Presidential elections held in Montenegro in December 2002 and February 2003 were invalidated due to low voter turnout. Filip Vujanovich was finally elected president of Montenegro in the third round of voting.

On 7 March 2003, Svetozar Marovic, deputy leader of the Montenegrin Democratic Party of Socialists, was elected the first president of Serbia and Montenegro after Kostunica stepped down as president of the former Yugoslavia.

On 12 March 2003, Serbian prime minister Zoran Djindjic was assassinated outside the main government building in Belgrade. Members of criminal organizations were suspected of carrying out the assassination; Djindjic had declared war on organized crime in Serbia, which was said to flourish under Milošević. After the assassination, Serbia was placed under a state of emergency and police arrested some 1,000 people, including members of Serbia's secret service and police force. Zoran Zivkovic, a leading official of the ruling Democratic Party, was elected prime minister to replace Djindjic.

While the Montenegrins managed to elect a president for their small republic, the Serbs failed to do so, even after the third voting round (in November 2003), due to low voter turnout. In addition, the indecisive parliamentary elections results from December 2003 led to a crisis within the Serbian parliament. The crisis was ended on March 2004 when former Yugoslav president, Vojislav Kostunica, was appointed the new prime minister of Serbia. In June 2004, the Serbs also got a new president, Boris Tadic. Tadic, the leader of the Democratic Party, managed to defeat his main contender, the nationalist Tomislav Nikolic, taking 52.34% of the tally in the second voting round. Tadic was reelected in the second round of voting in February 2008, with 51.2% of the vote.

In February 2005, officials from Montenegro asked their Serbian counterparts for an early vote on independence, claiming the union was inefficient and that it squandered money. Vojislav Kostunica refused the proposal and indicated that European integration and economic development should be the main focus of Serbia and Montenegro. A referendum on full independence for Montenegro was held on 21 May 2006; to be accepted internationally, a 55% majority was required for a "yes" vote. The vote on independence was 55.5% in favor. Voter turnout was 86.3%.

Serb politicians, Orthodox church leaders, and Montenegrins from the mountainous inland regions bordering Serbia opposed secession. However, ethnic Montenegrins and Albanians from the coastal area favored independence. Serbian President Boris Tadic recognized the independence of Montenegro. Serbia became the successor state to the union of Serbia and Montenegro, inheriting its UN seat and seats in other international institutions. In June 2006, the newly independent Montenegro became the 192nd member of the UN.

Republic of Serbia

A new Serbian constitution was ratified by a referendum held on 28–29 October 2006, and declared in the Second Special Session of the National Parliament on 8 November 2006. On 14 December 2006 Serbia became part of NATO's Partnership for Peace program, opening the possibility for the country's admission to the alliance in the future. In February of 2007, the International Court of Justice ruled that Serbia was not directly responsible for the Bosnian 1992–95 genocide. In a 13–2 vote, the court decided that Serbia had "not committed genocide, through its organs or persons whose acts engage its responsibility under customary international law." However, the Court decided in a 12–3 vote that Serbia had "violated obligation to prevent genocide."

In February 2006, UN-sponsored talks on the future status of Kosovo began. In February 2008, Kosovo achieved independence. Serbia did not recognize the independence of Kosovo and filed a lawsuit with the International Court of Justice, arguing that the Kosovar declaration of independence was a violation of international law. In July 2010, the court concluded that Kosovo's declaration of independence did not violate general international law. However, this decision was viewed as rather ambiguous by the international community, since the court addressed only the issue of the declaration's legality, without making any final determination as to whether or not Kosovo could or should be recognized as an independent state. For those who support the Serbian government, asserting that the declaration of independence was not illegal was seen as a far cry from saying that the nation had earned the legal status of independence. Immediately after the court's decision was announced, the president of Serbia renewed his claim that the government would never recognize the independence of Kosovo.

The matter was brought before the UN General Assembly in September 2010, resulting in a resolution that acknowledged the ruling of the International Court of Justice and a unanimously adopted resolution that paved the way for direct negotiations between the governments of Serbia and Kosovo. In accepting the new resolution, Serbia agreed to drop its demand to continue negotiations concerning the status of Kosovo. In so doing, Serbia essentially ended, or at least suspended, its fight to nullify the declaration of independence made by Kosovo, while still refusing to accept the declaration outright. The compromise resolution was viewed by government officials as a necessary step in seeking membership in the European Union. In October 2010, the European Commission began to formally assess Serbia's suitability for membership. Serbia was officially confirmed as an EU candidate on 1 March 2012.

Serbia's path toward EU accession faced several obstacles toward the end of the first decade of the 21st century. On 3 May 2006, the European Union suspended Stabilization and Association Agreement talks with Serbia over its failure to arrest war criminal Ratko Mladić, stating that Serbia failed to fulfill its commitment to fully co-operate with the International Criminal Tribunal for the Former Yugoslavia. Serbia's subsequent efforts to locate and arrest Mladić, along with arrests of other war criminals, prompted the EU to reopen accession negotiations on 13 June 2007. Further negotiation difficulties ensued following the decision by most EU states to recognize Kosovo as an independent state at the beginning of 2008. This development led to heated debate within Serbia's governing coalition as to the merits of EU accession. However, the new parliamentary majority and government formed after the 2008 election left EU accession opponents with no political power. On 9 September 2008, the Serbian parliament ratified the Stabilization and Association Agreement (SAA). On 26 May 2011, Ratko Mladić was arrested by Serbian authorities.

In July 2011, tension mounted between the Serbian government and Serbian nationals along the border as a violent clash resulted in the death of an ethnic Albanian Kosovar police officer. The skirmish grew from tension over the implementation of import bans between the two countries. On the Kosovar side of the border, ethnic Serb police officers have been responsible for upholding the government's ban on the importation of Serbian goods. (The Serbian government also maintains a ban on Kosovar imports.) But the Kosovar government suspected that the ban was not being properly enforced, and replaced the gatekeepers at two border crossings with ethnic Albanian security force members. Local Serbian nationalists responded by constructing road blocks, restricting all traffic at the crossings, and setting fire to one of the border posts, resulting in one death and four injuries. NATO responded by sending additional troops to boost border security as part of its existing Kosovo Force operation. In August, after a deal was made to allow NATO forces to remain in control of the border crossings, the Serbians dismantled the roadblocks.

13 GOVERNMENT

Serbia is a democratic parliamentary republic. The province of Vojvodina is nominally autonomous and has enjoyed increasing independence since the fall of Milošević.

Serbia has a unicameral legislature (National Assembly) of 250 deputies chosen in direct general elections for a period of four years. The deputies in the National Assembly elect the government of the Republic of Serbia, which, together with the president, represents the country's executive authority. The current Serbian government was restructured on 14 March 2011.

14 POLITICAL PARTIES

Boris Tadić of the Democratic Party was elected president in 2008 with 51.2% of the vote, over Tomislav Nikolić of the Serbian Progressive Party, with 48.8%. The next presidential election is scheduled for 2013. The Republic of Serbia held parliamentary elections on 11 May 2008. The following political parties won seats in the 250-seat National Assembly: For A European Serbia won 38.6% of the vote and 103 seats; Serbian Radical Party (SRS) won 29.1% and 77 seats; Democratic Party of Serbia and New Serbia coalition (DSS-NS) won 11.3% and 30 seats; coalition led by the Socialist Party of Serbia (SPS) won 7.9% and 20 seats; Movement for Dem-

ocratic Progress (LPD) won 5.2% and 13 seats; and others won 7.8% and 7 seats. The next election was scheduled for May 2012.

15 LOCAL GOVERNMENT

The Republic of Serbia is made up of 29 districts and the city of Belgrade. Each district is, in turn, divided into several municipalities.

Serbia's ethnic diversity often makes local governance a burdensome task. Besides Serbs and Albanians, there are considerable populations of Romanians, Hungarians, Roma, Bulgarians, Bosnians, Croats, Slovaks, and Montenegrins.

16 JUDICIAL SYSTEM

Serbia has a civil law legal system. The Serbian Constitutional Court determines whether Serbian laws, regulations and other enactments are in conformity with the Serbian constitution. Any citizen may begin an initiative in the Court. The Supreme Court is the highest appellate court. It also has an administrative law department with jurisdiction over all appeals of final decisions by administrative organs. In 2002, a new intermediate appellate body, the Court of Appeals, became effective. It has jurisdiction over appeals from the municipal and district courts. Its decisions may be appealed to the Supreme Court. The Administrative Court provides first instance review of all final administrative organ decisions. The decisions of the Administrative Court may be appealed to the Supreme Court.

The district courts' jurisdiction is limited to first instance matters. The courts have jurisdiction to try criminal offenses punishable by ten years' imprisonment or more, and other specified offenses, juvenile offenses, civil disputes of substantial value and in other specified areas, labor disputes, and certain other matters. There are 30 district courts in Serbia. The 138 municipal courts are the principal first instance courts. The courts have first instance jurisdiction over all criminal and civil cases that do not fall within the first instance jurisdiction of the district courts.

Commercial courts have jurisdiction over a wide range of commercial disputes, including copyright, privatization, foreign investment, unfair competition, maritime and other matters. These courts are also responsible for the registration of commercial enterprises. There are 16 commercial courts, and their decisions may be appealed to the High Commercial Court, located in Belgrade. Decisions of the latter court may be appealed to the Supreme Court.

17 ARMED FORCES

The International Institute for Strategic Studies reports that armed forces in Serbia totaled 29,125 members in 2011. The force is comprised of 12,260 from the army, 4,262 from the air force and air defense, 6,212 from training command, and 6,391 members of the ministry of defense. Defense spending totaled $918 million.

18 INTERNATIONAL COOPERATION

The Socialist Federal Republic of Yugoslavia was an original member of the UN (1945) until its dissolution and the establishment of Bosnia and Herzegovina, Croatia, Slovenia, the Former Yugoslav Republic of Macedonia, and the Federal Republic of Yugoslavia as new states. The Federal Republic of Yugoslavia was admitted to the UN on 1 November 2000. Following the adoption and promulgation of the Constitutional Charter of Serbia and Montenegro on 4 February 2003, the name of the Federal Republic of Yugoslavia was changed to Serbia and Montenegro. Following Montenegro's referendum on independence, Serbia became the successor state to the union of Serbia and Montenegro on 5 June 2006, and thus retained its membership in international bodies, including the UN and the specialized UN agencies, such as the FAO, UNESCO, UNHCR, UNIDO, the World Bank, IAEA, and the WHO.

Serbia is a member of the Council of Europe, the Black Sea Economic Cooperation Zone, the European Bank for Reconstruction and Development, and the OSCE. It has observer status in the OAS and the WTO. In environmental cooperation, the country is part of Basel Convention, Ramsar, the London Convention, the Montréal Protocol, and the UN Conventions on the Law of the Sea and Climate Change.

The controversy surrounding the status of Kosovo has led to protracted tensions in the Balkans. In 2011, talks between Serbia and Kosovo began under the sponsorship of the European Union. The initial proceedings were expected to address issues such as trade and travel between the two nations, since Serbia has continually blocked trade from Kosovo and there have been disputes over the use of airspace. Kosovo was expected to push for dialogue on issues concerning its own right to membership in international organizations, since Serbia has adamantly opposed such steps that would signal the acceptance of national independence. EU officials were expected to promote compromise by pointing toward an eventual goal of EU membership for both nations.

19ECONOMY

The GDP rate of change in Serbia, as of 2010, was 1.8%. Inflation stood at 10.3%, and unemployment was reported at 19.2%.

During the UN economic sanctions that lasted from 1992 to 1995, economic activity was extremely limited. By 1994, hyperinflation had brought formal economic activity to a virtual halt. By 1996, GDP had fallen to only 50.8% of 1990s total. Industry declined to just 46.6% of 1990s output; agriculture, 94.4%; construction, 37.5%; transportation, 29.3%; trade, 60.6%; and services, 81.1%. Formal lifting of these sanctions occurred in October 1996. However, the United States sponsored an "Outer Wall" of sanctions, which prevented Yugoslavia from joining international organizations and financial institutions. Taken together, the "Outer Wall," the Kosovo war, and corruption continued to stifle economic development. In October 2000, the coalition government began implementation of stabilization and market-reform measures. Real growth in 2000 was reported as 5%. A donors' conference in June 2001 raised $1.3 billion in pledges for help in infrastructural rebuilding. Real GDP growth was 5.5% in 2000 and 4% in 2002. The average lending rate, at 79.6% in 2000 dropped to 33.2% in 2001, reflecting some improvement in economic security.

Economic output was positive but volatile after 2002, dropping 2.1% in 2003 and jumping to 8% in 2004; in 2005 it was estimated at 5.5%. Inflation was on a downward spiral, reaching 9.8%, but grew again in 2005 (to 15.5%) as a result of the increase of service and oil derivatives prices. Unemployment remained unusually high, hovering around 30%, but a large chunk of the unemployed are considered to work in the informal economy. One of Serbia's main tasks was to bring about fiscal and monetary stability, and create a legal framework that will allow the market economy to flourish.

2007 showed more marked improvement of the economy. The banking sector was completely privatized, and GDP real growth rate stood at a robust 7.3%. Still, 26% of workers were employed by the state, the unemployment rate was 18.8% and GDP was only 65% of what it was in 1989.

At the beginning of 2009, it was estimated that Serbia's economy would register a decline of at least 2% by year-end as a result of the global economic crisis. As a result, in March 2009 the government secured a loan agreement with the International Monetary Fund (IMF) for a bailout package of $4.1 billion. As part of the agreement, the government was required to cut public spending, in part by initiating wage and hiring freezes in the state sector. A 6% tax on salaries and pensions was also added to address a budget deficit. The economy grew modestly in 2010 at 1.7%, along with a 16% growth in exports. Serbia adopted an economic growth plan in 2010 calling for a quadrupling of exports over ten years and heavy investments in basic infrastructure. As of 2011, unemployment has remained high and household incomes have remained stagnant. Serbia remains a transitional economy with a flawed and unfinished privatization, and incomplete structural reforms.

20INCOME

The CIA estimated that in 2010 the GDP of Serbia was $80.1 billion. The CIA defines GDP as the value of all final goods and services produced within a nation in a given year and computed on the basis of purchasing power parity (PPP) rather than value as measured on the basis of the rate of the exchange based on current dollars. The per capita GDP was estimated at $10,900. The annual growth rate of GDP was 1.8%. The average inflation rate was 10.3%. It was estimated that agriculture accounted for 12.6% of GDP, industry 21.9%, and services 65.5%.

In 2009 the World Bank reported that household consumption in Serbia totaled $31.7 billion or about $4,333 per capita, measured in current US dollars rather than PPP. Household consumption includes expenditures of individuals, households, and nongovernmental organizations on goods and services, excluding the purchases of dwellings. It was estimated that household consumption was growing at an average annual rate of 3%. According to the World Bank, in 2010 remittances from citizens living abroad totaled $3.35 billion or about $458 per capita, accounting for approximately 4.2% of GDP.

In 2011 the World Bank reported that actual individual consumption in Serbia was 80.7% of GDP and accounted for 0.13% of world consumption. By comparison, the United States accounted for 25.44% of world individual consumption. The World Bank also estimated that 24.5% of Serbia's GDP was spent on food and beverages, 21% on housing and household furnishings, 3.1% on clothes, 6.6% on health, 6.7% on transportation, 2.7% on communications, 3.6% on recreation, 1.9% on restaurants and hotels, and 6.1% on miscellaneous goods and services and purchases from abroad.

It was estimated that in 2010 about 8.8% of the population subsisted on an income below the poverty line established by Serbia's government.

21LABOR

As of 2010, Serbia had a total labor force of 3.25 million people. Within that labor force, CIA estimates in 2009 noted that 23.9%

were employed in agriculture, 20.5% in industry, and 55.6% in the service sector.

With the exception of the military, all workers are entitled to form unions. However, the majority of unions are government-sponsored or affiliated: independent unions are rare. Therefore, unions have not been effective in improving work conditions or wage structure increases. Virtually all of the workers in the formal economy are union members. Strikes are permitted and are utilized especially to collect unpaid wages. Collective bargaining is still at a rudimentary level.

The minimum employment age is 16 although younger children frequently work on family farms. As of 2008, the minimum monthly wage was RSD13,579 ($183.65). In 2011, the average monthly gross salary was estimated at RSD 64285 ($901). The official workweek is set at 40 hours, with required rest periods and overtime limited to 20 hours per week or 40 hours per month. Health and safety standards are not a priority due to harsh economic circumstances.

22 AGRICULTURE

Roughly 57% of the total land is used in agriculture, and the country's major crops include wheat, maize, sugar beets, sunflowers, and raspberries. Cereal production in 2009 amounted to 8.9 million tons, fruit production 1.8 million tons, and vegetable production 1.3 million tons. Vojvodina is the major agricultural region. Serbia has a network of agrarian organizations in the form of chambers, farmers' cooperatives, and unions.

23 ANIMAL HUSBANDRY

The UN Food and Agriculture Organization (FAO) reported that Serbia dedicated 1.5 million hectares (3.59 million acres) to permanent pasture or meadow in 2009. During that year, the country tended 22.4 million chickens, 1 million head of cattle, and 3.6 million pigs. The production from these animals amounted to 83,708 tons of beef and veal, 637,527 tons of pork, 68,590 tons of poultry, and 65,552 tons of eggs. Serbia also produced 11,200 tons of cattle hide and 2,403 tons of raw wool.

24 FISHING

In 2008, the annual capture totaled 3,197 tons according to the UN FAO. Common carp accounts for much of the inland catch.

25 FORESTRY

Approximately 31% of Serbia is covered by forest. The UN FAO estimated the 2009 roundwood production at 1.36 million cu m (48 million cu ft). Sawnwood production amounted to 428,000 cu m (15.1 million cu ft). The value of all forest products, including roundwood, totaled $190.7 million.

26 MINING

In 2009 mining and quarrying operations made up 1.3% of GDP, with exports totaling $42 million. The country had significant capacities to produce refined aluminum, lead, silver, and zinc. Mining in Serbia dates back to the Middle Ages, when silver, gold, and lead were extracted.

Mine output of metals in 2009 were: lead ore (gross weight), 225,000 metric tons, up from 202,000 metric tons in 2008 and 198,000 metric tons in 2007; and copper ore (gross weight),

10,014,000 tons, up from 8,680,000 tons in 2008 and from 6,867,000 tons in 2007. Production of silver in 2009 totaled 4,000 kg. Output of refined gold in 2009 was estimated at 500 kg. In 2009, the country also produced alumina, magnesium, palladium, platinum, and selenium. Among the industrial minerals produced were asbestos, bentonite, ceramic clay, fire clay, feldspar, pumice, lime, magnesite, mica, kaolin, gypsum, quartz sand, salt, nitrogen, caustic soda, sodium sulfate, sand and gravel, and stone.

27 ENERGY AND POWER

The World Bank reported in 2008 that Serbia produced 34.7 billion kWh of electricity and consumed 31.5 billion kWh, or 4,307 kWh per capita. Roughly 90% of energy came from fossil fuels, while 5% came from alternative fuels.

The Electric Utility Company of Serbia (EPS) has control over coal mines, electric power sources (hydroelectric power plants, thermal power plants, heating plants) and grid distribution systems. Serbia has abundant hydroelectric potential, but there are frequent electrical blackouts and brownouts during the peak winter months. In the 1990s, energy supplies were interrupted by UN and US sanctions. Hydroelectric projects are located on the Danube, Drina, Vlasina, and Lim rivers. Thermal plants are located at Kostolac and in Kosovo.

Serbia is the only Balkan country with substantial coal deposits. Proven reserves as of 2008 totaled 15.2 billion tons, 95.5% of which was lignite. The country's largest lignite mine has an annual capacity of 14,000 tons. Total coal output in 2010 was 41,169,000 short tons, while total consumption was 42,085,000 short tons. Coal imports totaled 946,000 short tons.

Serbia has limited proven reserves of oil and natural gas. As of 2010, these reserves totaled 77.5 million barrels and 48.14 billion cu m, respectively. Production of crude oil in Serbia in 2010 averaged 14,310 barrels per day. Refined petroleum product output in 2010 averaged 53,000 barrels per day. Imports of petroleum products in 2010 averaged 78,600 barrels per day, which included an average of 45,000 barrels per day of crude oil. Demand for refined oil products in 2009 averaged 90,000 barrels per day. Natural gas production totaled 356 million cu m in 2010. Dry consumption totaled 2.35 billion cu m.

28 INDUSTRY

Serbia contributed 35% to the total industrial production of the former Yugoslav SFR. Between 1989 and 1996, total industrial output fell by 60%. Production declines by sector during that time were as follows: metals and electrical products, 85%; textiles, leather, and rubber products, 75%; wood products, 63%; nonmetals, 56%; and chemicals and paper, 54%. In the mid-1990s, industry accounted for approximately 50% of the country's GDP.

By 2000, the industry's share of the economy had fallen to 36%. However, the industrial production growth rate that year was a promising 11%. The Law on Privatization passed in 2001 established conditions for reform of the industrial sector.

Large industrial enterprises with financial difficulties were obliged to undertake restructuring, which, it was hoped, would attract more foreign investment. However, subsequent years saw modest growth in the industrial sector. For instance, the industrial production growth rate in 2002 was only 1.2%, well under the real GDP growth rate-an indication that industry plays an increasing marginal role in the economy. In 2005, the industry of Serbia and Montenegro made up only 25.5% of the GDP, and by 2010 its share of the economy had dropped down to 22.5%, with an industrial production growth rate of 2.4%. In 2009, there were 666,250 workers employed in industrial and mining companies in the Republic of Serbia, comprising 20.5% of the total active labor force.

Principal industries in Serbia include machine building (aircraft, trucks, automobiles, tanks and weapons, electrical equipment, agricultural machinery), base metals, furniture, food processing, chemicals, sugar, tires, clothes and pharmaceuticals.

29 SCIENCE AND TECHNOLOGY

Patent applications in science and technology as of 2009, according to the World Bank, totaled 319 in Serbia. Public financing of science was 0.35% of GDP. A large communications satellite station became operational in Ivanica during the 1970s. Scientific and technological policies are developed and implemented by the Ministry of Science and Technology of the Republic of Serbia. As of 2011, Serbia had seven public and seven private universities.

A nationwide scientific and technological development policy formulated in 1994 created 250 five-year basic research projects in all scientific disciplines.

30 DOMESTIC TRADE

Belgrade serves as the economic and commercial center of the country. Pristina and Subotica serve as regional market centers. The domestic economy has been held back for the past few years due to the lack of major privatization reforms and trouble in the general European economy. Hours of business are usually between 8 a.m. and 4 p.m.

31 FOREIGN TRADE

The UN imposed sanctions on international trade with Yugoslavia in May 1992 and lifted them in December 1995. During the war, when sanctions were in force, dozens of Cypriot companies, set up by senior Serbian officials and businessmen, trafficked millions of dollars in illegal trade.

Trade started to catch up in subsequent years, and by 2004 exports in the union of Serbia and Montenegro reached $3.2 billion. In the same year, imports were almost triple that amount, at $9.5 billion, indicating that the economy in the two republics was in disarray, but that the union was trying to renew its industrial base. Most of the import commodities included machinery and transport equipment, fuels and lubricants, manufactured goods, chemicals, food and live animals, and raw materials.

Serbia imported $15.78 billion worth of goods and services in 2008, while exporting $9.7 billion worth of goods and services. Major import partners in 2009 were Russia, 12.8%; Germany, 10.6%; Italy, 8.5%; China, 7.2%; and Hungary, 4.9%. Its major export partners were Italy, 11.5%; Bosnia and Herzegovina, 11.2%; Germany, 10.5%; Montenegro, 8.4%; Romania, 6.3%; Russia, 5.4%; Macedonia, 4.9%; and Slovenia, 4.4%.

Imports were expected to be constrained by tight fiscal and monetary policies, while exports will be encouraged through targeted policy measures, and as a result of a restructured and more competitive economic base.

Principal Trading Partners – Serbia (2010)

(In millions of US dollars)

Country	Total	Exports	Imports	Balance
World	25,111.0	8,720.0	16,391.0	-7,671
Germany	2,597.6	817.1	1,780.5	-963.4
Italy	2,345.7	964.8	1,380.9	-416.1
Bosnia and Herzegovina	1,719.0	1,179.0	540.0	639
Hungary	1,638.6	374.0	1,264.6	-890.6
Slovenia	1,582.8	551.9	1,030.9	-479
Austria	1,127.5	405.8	721.7	-315.9
Romania	1,041.5	302.9	738.6	-435.7
Bulgaria	1,008.9	215.2	793.7	-578.5
Russia	783.5	516.8	266.7	250.1
Slovakia	697.2	170.8	526.4	-355.6

(…) data not available or not significant.

(n.s.) not specified.

SOURCE: *2011 Direction of Trade Statistics Yearbook,* New York: United Nations, 2011.

Balance of Payments – Serbia (2010)

(In millions of US dollars)

Current Account		-3,115.0
Balance on goods	-6,344.3	
Imports	-16.2	
Exports	9,818.8	
Balance on services	6.6	
Balance on income	-898.8	
Current transfers	4,121.6	
Capital Account		1.3
Financial Account		1,047.2
Direct investment abroad	-188.4	
Direct investment in Serbia	1,340.2	
Portfolio investment assets	-41.7	
Portfolio investment liabilities	130.1	
Financial derivatives	-30.1	
Other investment assets	-1,077.6	
Other investment liabilities	914.7	
Net Errors and Omissions		82.9
Reserves and Related Items		1,938.7

(…) data not available or not significant.

SOURCE: *Balance of Payment Statistics Yearbook 2011,* Washington, DC: International Monetary Fund, 2011.

32 BALANCE OF PAYMENTS

The US Central Intelligence Agency (CIA) reported that the current account balance was -$2.81 billion in 2010, a slight improvement from -$2.86 billion in 2009 and a dramatic improvement rom -$10.39 billion in 2008. The national reserves (including gold) were $13.3 billion in 2010, down from $15.2 billion in 2009.

33 BANKING AND SECURITIES

Serbia's banking system is still hampered by the history of international sanctions. Banks are severely hampered by a lack of liquidity, a result of the tight monetary policy prevalent in the country.

34 INSURANCE

Insurance of public transport passengers, motor vehicle insurance, aircraft insurance, and insurance on bank deposits are compulsory. Only domestic insurance companies may provide insurance.

35 PUBLIC FINANCE

In 2010 the budget of Serbia included $16.47 billion in public revenue and $18.48 billion in public expenditures. The budget deficit amounted to $2.01 billion, or 4.9% of GDP. Public debt was 41.5% of GDP, with $33.32 billion of the debt held by foreign entities.

36 TAXATION

As of 2011 Serbia had a salary income tax rate of 12% and a standard corporate tax rate of 10%. Capital gains derived from the sale of industrial property rights, real estate, shares and other securities, and capital participations are considered taxable income, and are taxed at the corporate rate. However, gains arising from certain government bonds or from bonds issued by the national bank are excluded from the tax. Dividends, interest and royalties are subject to a 20% withholding tax. Other taxes includes a value-added tax (VAT), with a standard rate of 18% and a lower rate of 8%, property taxes, transfer taxes, a tax on financial transactions, payroll taxes, and social security contributions. In Serbia, the republic government, rather than the city governments, collects local taxes and then disperses part of the funds to city officials. Local factories pay no city taxes in Serbia.

37 CUSTOMS AND DUTIES

Serbia has six tariff rates that range from 1 to 30%, with a weighted duty average of 9.37%. Serbia applies a VAT of 18%, with an 8% reduced rate for basic foodstuffs, medicines, published materials, public utilities and certain services. Serbia imposes excise taxes on certain luxury goods.

Serbia has established free trade zones (FTZ) in Smederrevo, Kovin, Nis, Belgrade, Novi Sad, Šabac, Pahovo, Sombor, Sremska Mitrovica, Subotica, and Zrenjanin.

38 FOREIGN INVESTMENT

Foreign investment was severely restricted during the years of the economic embargo. Since the sanctions have been lifted, foreign investors from neighboring countries, Russia, and Asia have expressed an interest in capital investment. The main sectors attracting the interest of foreign investors are metal manufacturing and machinery, infrastructure improvement, agriculture and food processing, and chemicals and pharmaceuticals. Foreign investors may hold majority shares in companies.

In 1997, foreign direct investment (FDI) inflows into the former Yugoslavia reached $740 million, but dried up with the onset of the conflict in Kosovo. FDI inflows averaged $122.5 million in 1998 and 1999, then fell to $25 million in 2000. In the following years, Serbia and Montenegro undertook an aggressive program of reforms aimed at both re-establishing the area as a major transportation hub, and at attracting foreign investment. These policies paid off as capital inflows jumped to $3.4 billion in 2004. According to World Bank figures published in 2009, FDI in Serbia was a net inflow of $1.9 billion. FDI represented 4.47% of GDP.

Public Finance – Serbia (2009)		
(In millions of Serbian dinars, central government figures)		
Revenue and Grants	**1,061,499**	**100.0%**
Tax revenue	610,574	57.5%
Social contributions	373,073	35.1%
Grants	5,956	0.6%
Other revenue	71,896	6.8%
Expenditures	**1,137,162**	**100.0%**
General public services	93,940	8.3%
Defense	70,861	6.2%
Public order and safety	68,109	6.0%
Economic affairs	97,432	8.6%
Environmental protection	1,792	0.2%
Housing and community amenities	1,237	0.1%
Health	180,630	15.9%
Recreational, culture, and religion	9,748	0.9%
Education	111,658	9.8%
Social protection	501,754	44.1%

(…) data not available or not significant.

SOURCE: *Government Finance Statistics Yearbook 2010,* Washington, DC: International Monetary Fund, 2010.

39 ECONOMIC DEVELOPMENT

Most officials see revitalization of the infrastructure (roads, rail and air transport, telecommunications, and power production) as one step toward economic recovery. Another important aspect of economic reconstruction will be the revival of former export industries such as agriculture, textiles, furniture, pharmaceuticals, and nonferrous metallic ores.

The Kosovo war in 1999 left much of Serbia's infrastructure in ruins, but reconstruction efforts were proceeding slowly in the early 2000s. Inflation decreased sharply from 113% at the end of 2000 to 23% in April 2002. In 2002, the International Monetary Fund (IMF) approved a three-year $829 million Extended Arrangement to support Serbia and Montenegro's (then Yugoslavia's) 2002–05 economic program. In 2002, the dinar became convertible. While foreign direct investment lagged in the early 2000s, government reforms prompted foreign investors, as well as several international financial institutions (EBRD, IMF, and the World Bank) to increase their capital transfers to the region.

In 2005 there was a boom in several sectors: trade, financial services and transport and communications. The growth is to be sustained by continued investment in newly privatized companies, by strong local demand, and by an expansion of the services sector. Like most European states, Serbia was adversely affected by the 2008 financial crisis. The main economic problems facing Serbia at the end of the 2000s were the high unemployment rate (19.2% in 2010) and a large trade deficit ($7.2 billion in 2009).

40 SOCIAL DEVELOPMENT

A social insurance system, updated in 2003, provides old age, disability, and survivorship benefits. The pension plan is funded by contributions from both employers and employees. The retirement varies depending on years of insurance; retirement from insured employment is necessary. Each Republic provides its own system for sickness and maternity benefits. Medical services are provided directly to patients through government facilities. Workers' compensation, unemployment benefits, and family allowances are also available. Family allowances vary according to the number of children in the family and are adjusted periodically for cost of living changes.

Traditional gender roles keep women from enjoying equal status with men and few occupy positions of leadership in the private sector. However, women are active in human rights and political organizations. High levels of domestic abuse persist and social pressures prevent women from obtaining protection against abusers.

While Serbia is a liberal democracy, its human rights record has been far from spotless. Commonly reported human rights problems include physical mistreatment of detainees by police; inefficient and lengthy trials; harassment of journalists, human rights advocates, and others critical of the government; limitations on freedom of speech and religion; lack of durable solutions for large numbers of internally displaced persons (IDPs); corruption in legislative, executive, and judicial branches of government; government failure to apprehend fugitive war crimes suspects under indictment of the International Criminal Tribunal for the former Yugoslavia (ICTY); societal violence against women and children; societal violence and discrimination against minorities, particularly Roma and the lesbian, gay, bisexual, transgender (LGBT) population; and trafficking in persons.

The Serbian government successfully apprehended war criminal Ratko Mladić in 2011.

[41]HEALTH

According to the CIA, life expectancy in Serbia was 74 years in 2011. The country spent 10.0% of its GDP on healthcare, amounting to $419 per person. There were 20 physicians, 44 nurses and midwives, and 54 hospital beds per 10,000 inhabitants. The fertility rate was 1.4, while the infant mortality rate was 6 per 1,000 live births. In 2008 the maternal mortality rate, according to the World Bank, was 8 per 100,000 births. It was estimated that 95% of children were vaccinated against measles. The CIA calculated HIV/AIDS prevalence in Serbia to be about 0.1% in 2009. The incidence of tuberculosis was estimated at 21 per 100,000 people in 2009. The University Clinical Center in Belgrade conducts about nine million examinations and 46,000 emergency operations per year and functions as one of the World Health Organization's largest diagnostic and referral centers.

[42]HOUSING

The Serbian housing market flourished in the 2000s, and house prices soared by 265% between 2000 and 2010. The Serbian residential market was very active as a result of construction activity in Serbia's three largest cities: Belgrade, Nis, and Novi Sad. Around 17,000 dwellings were completed annually from 2004 to 2006. In 2005, there was a shift toward developing low- and medium-priced apartments, rather than elite apartments or houses offering three or more bedrooms. The share of one- to two-bedroom apartments as a percent of total development activity has consistently grown, whereas the stock of four bedroom and larger apartments is growing at the lowest rate. Serbia's house prices rose 6.4% between June and December of 2010. The average price of new dwellings in 2010 stood at RSD144,294 ($1,913) per square meter,

up 12% from a year earlier. A total of 3,442 housing units intended for the purpose of accommodating refugees, internally displaced persons, and socially vulnerable families from the local population, had been constructed according to recorded statistics dating from December of 2009.

[43]EDUCATION

As of 2011 education was compulsory for nine years of primary school. This may be followed by three years of secondary school, with students having the option to attend general, vocational, or art schools. The academic year runs from October to July. Primary school enrollment in 2009 was estimated at about 94% of age-eligible students. The same year, secondary school enrollment was about 90% of age-eligible students. Public expenditure on education in 2010 represented 4.7% of GDP, an increase from past years but slightly lower than the average for EU members.

Serbia has seven public universities (at Belgrade, Novi Sad, Pristina, Nis, Novi Pazar and Kragujevac) and seven private universities. In 2009, it was estimated that about 50% of the tertiary age population were enrolled in tertiary education programs. The adult literacy rate for 2010 was estimated at about 96.4%. Serbia has implemented the Bologna Process, adopting the common academic degrees and standards of the European Higher Education Area. Consequently, there has been a reorganization of tertiary education and universities, which now offer bachelor's, master's and doctoral degrees.

[44]LIBRARIES AND MUSEUMS

The National Library of Serbia contains 1.6 million volumes and is located in Belgrade. The Matica Srpska Library has over 3 million volumes in holdings. The Serbian Academy of Arts and Sciences in Belgrade has about one million volumes and the library system at the University of Belgrade has 1.45 million volumes. The Belgrade City Library is the largest public lending library system in the country; the network contains 14 branches and over 1.7 million items in collection.

Serbia has over 2,500 cultural monuments, including about 100 museums and 37 historical archives libraries. The Belgrade National Museum, founded in 1844, includes exhibits featuring national history, archaeology, medieval frescoes, and works by Yugoslavian and other European artists. Belgrade also has the Museum of Modern Art, the Museum of the Serbian Orthodox Church, the Museum of Natural History, and the Museum of Science and Technology, which opened in 1989.

[45]MEDIA

Replacements of, and upgrades to, telecommunications equipment damaged during the 1999 war has resulted in a modern telecommunications system that is more than 95% digitalized in 2009, up from 65% in 2005. Wireless service, available through multiple providers with national coverage, is growing very rapidly. Domestically, the best telecommunications services are in the country's urban areas. There are two Global System for Mobile communications (GSM) wireless service providers that offer national coverage. A 3G mobile network launched in 2007. In 2009, there were some 3.1 million telephone landlines and 9.9 million mobile cellular phones in use. Mobile phone subscriptions averaged 135 per 100 people. In 2010, Serbia had 528,253 Internet hosts. In 2009, there were 4.1 million Internet users; Internet users numbered 56 per 100 citizens.

Television is by far the most widespread and most popular medium in Serbia. About 96 percent of households own a TV, making an average daily audience of 5.5 million people (73 percent of the population over the age of 4). A typical Serbian TV viewer spends more time in front of a TV set than any other European citizen. In 2009, the average viewing time was more than five hours per day. Serbia has two public broadcasters—the national public service Radio Television Serbia (RTS) and a regional service in the ethnically mixed province of Vojvodina, Radio Television Vojvodina (RTV). Of privately owned TV networks, TV B92 is most popular for current affairs and TV Pink leads in entertainment.

Radio is a widely available source of information and entertainment in Serbia. An average Serbian household has more than one radio set, while 73 percent of automobiles have a receiver. According to 2009 data by Strategic Marketing, 11 percent of people said they listen to radio on the Internet. The most popular radio stations are Radio S and Radio B92, each accounting for 18 percent of the audience. The former focuses on music, while the latter offers more diverse radio programs.

According to the May 2010 data of the Serbian Business Registers Agency there are 523 print media in Serbia. Out of that number, there are 20 daily papers, 84 weekly publications, 186 monthlies, seven biweeklies, 74 bimonthlies, and 67 quarterlies. It is estimated that between 800,000 and 1 million copies of papers are sold in Serbia daily. In 2010, approximately 41.4 percent of people aged between 12 and 65 read at least one daily paper. Most people read Blic (14.5 percent), Vecernje Novosti (9.0 percent), Kurir (7.3 percent), Press (6.6 percent), Alo! (5.1 percent), 24 Sata (4.2 percent) and Politika (2.5 percent).

The press is generally free and operates with little government interference, although most media outlets are thought to be aligned with specific political parties. Libel is a criminal offense punishable by fines, but not imprisonment. The Law on Electronic Communications, adopted by the parliament in June 2010, allows police and security services to view personal electronic communications, which press freedom groups criticized as a threat to the confidentiality of journalists' sources. Journalists continue to encounter threats and physical violence.

46 ORGANIZATIONS

The Chamber of Commerce and Economy of Serbia is located in Belgrade.

The Matica Srpska was founded in Novi Sad in 1824 as a literary and cultural society. The Serbian Academy of Science and Art was founded in Belgrade in 1886. There are several organizations for professional journalists, including the Journalists' Federation of Yugoslavia, the Journalists' Association of Serbia, the Independent Journalists' Association, and the Association of Private Owners of the Media.

National youth organizations include the Bureau of International Cooperation of Youth of Serbia, the Union of Socialist Youth of Yugoslavia, and the Junior Chamber. Scouting organizations are also active. The Child Rights Centre and Child to Child are national groups working to promote the rights of children and youth. Creative Youth of Novi Sad offers a variety of educational, volunteer, and development programs for youth as well. There are

a variety of sports associations that promote amateur competition among athletes of all ages. There are active chapters of the Paralympics Committee, as well as a national Olympic Committee.

There is a national chapter of the Red Cross Society.

47 TOURISM, TRAVEL, AND RECREATION

Rich architecture, museums, galleries, cathedrals, parks, and rivers, are just some of the attractions that bring visitors to Serbia. The largest two of Serbia's five national parks are Djerdap (64,000 hectares/158,000 acres) and Sar planina (39,000 hectares/96,000 acres). Serbia has dozens of spa resorts such as Vrnjacka Banja, Mataruska Banja, and Niska Banja. Serbia has three UNESCO heritage sites. Popular sports in Serbia are rafting, hunting, fishing, skiing, and cycling.

The Tourism Factbook, published by the UN World Tourism Organization, reported 645,000 incoming tourists to Serbia in 2009; they spent a total of $986 million. Of those incoming tourists, there were 603,000 from Europe. There were 55,650 hotel beds available in Serbia, which had an occupancy rate of 19%. The estimated daily cost to visit Belgrade, the capital, was $356. The cost of visiting other cities averaged $164.

All visitors need a valid passport to enter Serbia. Serbia requires an onward/return ticket, sufficient funds for the stay, and a certificate showing funds for health care. Visas are required for all nationals except those of 41 countries including the United States, Australia, and Canada.

48 FAMOUS PERSONS

Sava Rastko Nemanjic (c. 1174–1235) was the first Serbian archbishop and a writer who became one of Serbia's most prominent figures of the Middle Ages. Vuk Stefanovic Karadzic (1787–1864) reformed the Serbian language by clarifying grammar, standardizing spelling, and compiling a dictionary. Dositej Obradovic (1742–1811) was a famous writer, philosopher, and teacher.

Djordje Petrovic Karadjordje (1768–1817) led a rebellion against the Turks in 1804. Zivojin Misic (1855–1921) was a distinguished military leader during World War I. Prince Miloš Obrenović (r. 1815–1839) founded the Obrenović dynasty and ruled Serbia as an absolute monarch. King Alexander of Yugoslavia (1888–1934) was assassinated in Marseille, France. Prince Paul of Yugoslavia (1893–1976) ruled as a regent for Peter II (1923–70) from 1934 to 1941 and was forced into exile after signing a secret pact with the Nazi government.

Slobodan Milošević (1941–2006) was elected president of Serbia in 1990 and 1992 before being elected president of Yugoslavia in July 1997. He came before the UN's International Criminal Tribunal for the Former Yugoslavia in 2002 for genocide, crimes against humanity, and war crimes, and died of a heart attack in his cell just months before the trial was due to end.

Ibrahim Rugova (1944–2006) was president of Kosovo and its leading political party, the Democratic League of Kosovo (LDK). During the many conflicts in Kosovo, Rugova was regarded as a moderate ethnic Albanian leader, and later by some as "Father of the Nation."

Ivo Andrić (1892–1975) received the Nobel Prize for Literature in 1961. Danilo Kiš (1935–89) established his reputation with his work A Tomb for Boris Davidovich (1976). Other notable Serbian authors include Meša Selimović (1910–82), Miloš Crnjanski (1893–1977), Milorad Pavić (1929–2009), Dobrica Ćosić (b. 1921), and David Albahari (b. 1948). Anastas Jovanović (1817–99) was a pioneering photographer. Kirilo Kutlik (1847–1900) set up the first school of art in Serbia in 1895. Nadežda Petrović (1873–1915) was influenced by Fauvism while Sava Šumanović (1896–1942) worked in Cubism. Other Serbian artists include Milan Konjović (1898–1993), Marko Čelebonović (1902–86), Petar Lubarda (1907–74), Milo Milunović (1897–1967), and Vladimir Veličković (b. 1935).

⁴⁹DEPENDENCIES

Serbia has no dependencies or territories.

⁵⁰BIBLIOGRAPHY

Cevallos, Albert. *Whither the Bulldozer? Nonviolent Revolution and the Transition to Democracy in Serbia*. Washington, DC: US Institute of Peace, 2001.

Cox, John K. *The History of Serbia*. Westport, CT: Greenwood Press, 2002.

Deliso, Christopher. *Culture and Customs of Serbia and Montenegro*. Westport, CT: Greenwood Press, 2009.

Frucht, Richard, ed. *Eastern Europe: An Introduction to the People, Lands, and Culture*. Santa Barbara, CA: ABC-CLIO, 2005.

International Smoking Statistics: A Collection of Historical Data from 30 Economically Developed Countries. New York: Oxford University Press, 2002.

Judah, Tim. *The Serbs: History, Myth, and the Destruction of Yugoslavia*. 3rd ed. New Haven, CT: Yale University Press, 2009.

Klemencic, Matjaz. *The Former Yugoslavia's Diverse Peoples: A Reference Sourcebook*. Oxford, UK: ABC-Clio, 2003.

Maleševic, Siniša. *Ideology, Legitimacy, and the New State: Yugoslavia, Serbia, and Croatia*. Portland, OR: Frank Cass, 2002.

Opello, Walter C. *European Politics*. Boulder, CO: Lynne Rienner Publishers, 2009.

Political Chronology of Europe. London: Europa, 2001.

Ramet, Sabrina P. *Balkan Babel: The Disintegration of Yugoslavia from the Death of Tito to Ethnic War*. 2nd ed. Boulder, CO: Westview, 2002.

Schuman, Michael. *Serbia and Montenegro*. 2nd ed. New York: Facts On File, 2004.

Sell, Louis. *Slobodan Milosevic and the Destruction of Yugoslavia*. Durham, NC: Duke University Press, 2002.

Serbia Investment and Business Guide: Strategic and Practical Information. Washington, DC: International Business Publications USA, 2012.

Terterov, Marat, ed. *Doing Business with Serbia and Montenegro*. Sterling, VA: Kogan Page, 2004.

SLOVAKIA

Slovak Republic
Slovenska Republika

CAPITAL: Bratislava

FLAG: Horizontal bands of white (top), blue, and red superimposed with a crest of a white double cross on three blue mountains.

ANTHEM: *Nad Tatru sa blyska (Over Tatra it lightens).*

MONETARY UNIT: The currency of the Slovak Republic is the euro (€), which replaced the Slovak Koruna (SKK) on 1 January 2009. There are coins of 1, 5, 10, 20, and 50 cents and 1 euro and 2 euros. There are notes of 5, 10, 20, 50, 100, 200, and 500 euros. €1 = US$1.371 (or US$1 = €0.72939) as of September 2011.

WEIGHTS AND MEASURES: The metric system is the legal standard.

HOLIDAYS: New Year's Day and Establishment of Independent Slovakia, 1 January; Feast of the Epiphany, 6 January; May Day, 1 May; Anniversary of Liberation, 8 May; Day of the Slav Apostles, 5 July; Anniversary of the Slovak National Uprising, 29 August; Constitution Day 1 September; Feast Day of the Virgin Mary, 15 September; All Saints' Day, 1 November; Struggle for Freedom and Democracy Day 17 November; Christmas, 24–26 December. Movable holidays are Good Friday, Easter, and Easter Monday.

TIME: 1 p.m. = noon GMT.

¹LOCATION, SIZE, AND EXTENT

Slovakia is a landlocked country located in Eastern Europe. Comparatively, it is about twice the size of the state of New Hampshire with a total area of 48,845 sq km (18,859 sq mi). Slovakia shares boundaries with Poland to the N, Ukraine to the E, Hungary to the S, and Austria and the Czech Republic to the W, and has a total boundary length of 1,474 km (916 mi). Slovakia's capital city, Bratislava, is located on the southwestern border of the country.

²TOPOGRAPHY

The topography of Slovakia features rugged mountains in the central and northern part of the country, and lowlands in the south. The High Tatras (Vysoke Tatry) mountain range along the Polish border is interspersed between many lakes and deep valleys. The highest peak in the country, Gerlachovsy, is found in the High Tatras with an elevation of 2,655 m (8,711 ft). Bratislava is situated in Slovakia's only substantial region of plains, where the Danube River forms part of the border with Hungary.

³CLIMATE

Slovakia's climate is continental, with warm summers and cold winters. In July the mean temperature is 21°C (70°F). January's mean temperature is -1°C (30°F). Rainfall averages between 50 and 70 cm (19.6 to 27.5 in) a year and can exceed 200 cm (80 in) annually in the High Tatras.

⁴FLORA AND FAUNA

Some original steppe grassland areas can be found in the southwestern lowland region, where marsh grasses and reeds are also abundant. While oak is a primary tree found in the lowlands; beech, spruce, pine, and mountain maple are found on mountain slopes. Alpine meadows include carnations, glacial gentians, and edelweiss. The High Tatras support the growth of many types of moss, lichens, and fungi. The World Resources Institute estimates that there are 3,124 plant species in Slovakia. Slovakia is home to 87 mammal, 332 bird, 14 reptile, and 17 amphibian species. This calculation reflects the total number of distinct species residing in the country, not the number of endemic species. Mammals found in the country include foxes, rabbits, and wild pigs. A wide variety of birds inhabit the valleys of Slovakia. Carp, pike, and trout are found in the country's rivers, lakes, and streams.

⁵ENVIRONMENT

Like the Czech Republic, Slovakia's air has been contaminated by sulfur dioxide emissions resulting from the use of lignite as an energy source by the former Czechoslovakia, which once had the highest levels of sulfur dioxide emissions in Europe. The UN reported in 2008 that carbon dioxide emissions in Slovakia totaled 36,955 kilotons. Air pollution by metallurgical plants endangers human health as well as the environment, and lung cancer is prevalent in areas with the highest pollution levels. Airborne emissions in the form of acid rain, combined with air pollution from Poland and the former German Democratic Republic, have damaged Slovakia's forests.

Land erosion caused by agricultural and mining practices is also a significant problem. The World Resources Institute reported that Slovakia had designated 961,900 hectares (2.38 million acres) of land for protection as of 2006. Water resources totaled 50.1 cu km

(12.02 cu mi) while water usage was 1.04 cu km (0.25 cu mi) per year. Per capita water usage totaled 193 cu m (6,816 cu ft) per year.

There are 14 Ramsar wetland sites in the country and two natural UNESCO World Heritage sites. According to a 2011 report issued by the International Union for Conservation of Nature and Natural Resources (IUCN), threatened species included 3 types of mammals, 6 species of birds, 5 species of fish, 5 types of mollusks, 15 species of other invertebrates, and 6 species of plants. Threatened species include the Danube salmon, marsh snail, and false ringlet butterfly.

6 POPULATION

The US Central Intelligence Agency (CIA) estimates the population of Slovakia in 2011 to be approximately 5,477,038, which placed it at number 111 in population among the 196 nations of the world. In 2011, approximately 12.8% of the population was over 65 years of age, with another 15.6% under 15 years of age. The median age in Slovakia was 37.6 years. There were 0.94 males for every female in the country. The population's annual rate of change was 0.117%. The projected population for the year 2025 was 5,400,000. Population density in Slovakia was calculated at 112 people per sq km (290 people per sq mi).

The UN estimated that 55% of the population lived in urban areas, and that urban populations had an annual rate of change of 0.1%. The largest urban area was Bratislava, with a population of 428,000.

7 MIGRATION

Estimates of Slovakia's net migration rate, carried out by the CIA in 2011, amounted to 0.29 migrants per 1,000 citizens. The total number of emigrants living abroad was 520,100, and the total number of immigrants living in Slovakia was 130,700. Slovakia receives about 400 refugees every year. In April 1999 Slovakia granted temporary protection to 90 refugees from Kosovo. Of these, 70 left Slovakia in July 1999 and returned home.

8 ETHNIC GROUPS

The population is about 85.8% Slovak according to the latest census (2001). Hungarians, heavily concentrated in southern border areas, total 10.6%. While the census reported a Roma population of about 90,000, unofficial estimates place the number between 350,000 and 500,000. It is believed that many Roma identify themselves as other nationalities, such as Hungarian or Slovak, perhaps to escape social discrimination and harassment. Czechs, Ruthenians, Ukrainians, Germans, Poles, and various other groups account for the remainder.

The Hungarian minority is the only ethnic group with official representation in the Slovak parliament. Arguments for greater autonomy and rights for the Hungarian minority in Slovakia led to diplomatic conflict between Hungary and Slovakia in 2009 and 2010.

9 LANGUAGES

Slovak is the official language, spoken by about 83.9% of the population. It belongs to the western Slavic group and is written in the Roman alphabet. There are only slight differences between Slovak and Czech, and the two are mutually intelligible. Slovak lacks the *ď, ě ů* and *ř* in Czech but adds *ä, ľ, ô*, and *r*. As in Czech, *q, w*, and *x* are found only in foreign words. A minority language like Hungarian may be used for official business if its speakers make up at least 20% of the population at the local level. Hungarian is spoken by about 10.7% of the total population. Roma is spoken by about 1.8% of the population, while Ukrainian is spoken by 1%.

10 RELIGIONS

According to the 2001 census, about 68.9% of the population were Roman Catholics. About 10.8% of the population were Augsburg Lutheran, 4.1% were Greek (Byzantine) Catholics, 2% were members of the Reformed Christian Church, and 1% were Orthodox. 13% of the population reported no religious affiliation. Other registered groups include Jehovah's Witnesses, Baptists, Brethren Church members, Seventh-Day Adventists, Apostolic Church members, Evangelical Methodists, and members of the Christian Corps in Slovakia and the Czechoslovak Hussite Church. There are small communities of Muslims and Jews. Small, unregistered groups within the country include Hare Krishnas, Shambaola Slovakia, Shri Chinmoy, Zazen International Slovakia, Zen Centermyo Sahn Sah, the Church of Scientology, the Baha'i Faith, the Society of Friends of Jesus Christ (Quaker), Nazarenes, and the Church of Jesus Christ of Latter-Day Saints (Mormon). There are some links between religious affiliation and ethnicity. Many ethnic Hungarians in the south are members of the Reformed Christian Church while many Ruthenians are Greek Catholics.

Freedom of religion is guaranteed by the constitution and this right is generally respected in practice. There is no single State Church with special privileges and the state claims neutrality concerning religion and ideology. In the preamble of the Constitution the Cyril-Methodius spiritual heritage is acknowledged and Section 24 guarantees freedom of thinking, conscience, religious confession and beliefs. Churches and religious communities are independent from the State. They establish their own institutions, appoint clergy and provide religious instruction. However, the State supports registered churches and religious communities financially. Churches also benefit from certain tax exemptions. Religious groups are not required to register with the government, but must do so to receive certain benefits. Epiphany, Easter, the Day of the Virgin Mary of the Seven Sorrows, All Saints' Day, Christmas, and St. Stephen's Day are observed as national holidays.

11 TRANSPORTATION

The CIA reported that Slovakia had a total of 43,761 km (27,192 mi) of roads as of 2008, of which 38,085 km (23,665 mi) were paved. Railroads extend for 3,623 km (2,251 mi). Most railway runs along the Bratislava–Žilina–Košice route through the north of the country. Transportation networks in southern Slovakia are underdeveloped and represent a source of tension between the Hungarian minority living in the area and the central government. There are 36 airports, which transported 3.44 million passengers in 2009 according to the World Bank. Air service in Slovakia is conducted primarily through M. R. Stefanik Airport at Bratislava.

As an inland country, Slovakia relies on the Danube River, which runs for 172 km (45 mi) in the south of the country, for transportation of goods. Bratislava and Komárno are the major ports on the Danube, which connects with the European waterway system to Rotterdam and the Black Sea. In 2008, Slovakia's

LOCATION: 47°44′ to 49°37′; 16°51′ to 22°34′E. BOUNDARY LENGTHS: Austria, 91 kilometers (57 miles); Czech Republic, 215 kilometers (134 miles); Hungary, 515 kilometers (320 miles); Poland, 444 kilometers (275 miles); Ukraine, 90 kilometers (56 miles).

merchant fleet was comprised of 51 ships of 1,000 gross registered tons or more.

12 HISTORY

The first known peoples of the territory of present-day Slovakia were Celts, who lived in the region about 50 BC. The Celts were pushed out by Slavs, who moved in from the east at the beginning of the modern era. A Frankish merchant named Samo formed the first unified state in the region in the mid-7th century. The Great Moravian Empire appeared in the 9th century, incorporating parts of present-day Slovakia. Although the first Christian missionaries active in the area were Orthodox, including the monks Cyril and Methodius who introduced an alphabet of their own invention (still called Cyrillic) in which to write the Slavic languages, it was the Roman church that eventually established dominance. At the end of the 9th century the Magyars (Hungarians) moved into Slovakia, incorporating the territory into the Kingdom of Hungary. The territory of present-day Slovakia began to develop after the Tatar invasions in the 13th century. Košice (Kaschau/Kassa) received privileges as a royal free town in 1347 and Bratislava (Pressburg/Pozsony) in 1405. Some contact with the Czechs, who speak a closely related language, began in the early 15th century, as refugees from the Hussite religious wars in Bohemia moved east.

After the Turkish victory at Mohács in 1526, the Kingdom of Hungary was divided into three parts; so-called "Royal Hungary,"

which included Slovakia, was passed to the rule of the Habsburg dynasty. Bratislava became the capital of Hungary during Turkish occupation. The Hungarian parliament met in Bratislava until 1848 and the capital was officially transferred to Budapest only in 1873. Although there was some religious spillover of Protestantism from the west, the Catholic Counter-Reformation was very effective in maintaining Roman Catholicism in Slovakia, establishing the long tradition of strong church influence in the region.

In the late 18th century reform attempts of the Hapsburg rulers, especially Josef II (1765–1790), led to a rise in Hungarian nationalism. This in turn stimulated a rise in Slovak national self-consciousness in the 19th century. Slovak national leaders issued the "Demands of the Slovak Nation," during the Revolution of 1848. It called for the use of Slovak in schools, courts, and other settings, and demanded the creation of a Slovak assembly. These demands were rejected by the Hungarian revolutionaries, who continued their efforts to suppress Slovak nationalism. When the Austro-Hungarian Empire was formed in 1867, the autonomous Hungarian government began a program of intense Magyarization. In the absence of a Slovak intellectual elite, nationalist ideals were largely maintained by the local clergy.

During the First World War, Slovaks joined with Czechs and other suppressed nationalities of the Austro-Hungarian Empire in pushing for their own state. Czech and Slovak immigrants in the United States of America were united in their efforts to encourage the United States to recognize a postwar combined Czech and Slovak state. The Czechs declared independence on 28 October 1918, and the Slovaks seceded from Hungary two days later, to create the Czechoslovak Republic.

The relationship between the two parts of the new state was never firmly established. The Czech lands were more developed economically and Czech politicians dominated the political debate. Although the Czechoslovak project was supported by a portion of Slovak society, a large constituency of Slovak nationalists, led by Catholic priest Andrej Hlinka, advocated for increased autonomy for Slovakia.

The First Czechoslovak Republic contained large minority groups, including 3 million ethnic Germans in the Sudetenland area and 900,000 Hungarians in southern Slovakia. In 1938 Adolf Hitler demanded that the Sudetenland, in the Czech part of the country, be ceded to Germany. Representatives of Germany, Italy, France, and the United Kingdom met in Munich and decided that in order to achieve "peace in our time" Germany should occupy the Sudetenland. The Munich Agreement also stipulated that border disputes with Poland and Hungary must be resolved within three months. Czechoslovak representatives were not allowed to participate in the Munich negotiations. In October 1938, Germany took over the Sudetenland. Shortly thereafter, Poland seized the Ciezyn region. Hungarian demands were addressed in Vienna Arbitration of November 1938, which awarded a strip of territory in southern Slovakia to Hungary. Slovak nationalists debated seceding from Czechoslovakia, and when Hitler's forces seized Prague in March 1939, they declared an independent Slovak Republic, led by Josef Tiso. Although nominally independent, Slovakia was largely considered a Nazi puppet state. The Tiso government deported the majority of Slovak Jews during the war. An estimated 85% of Slovakia's Jews perished in Nazi death camps.

During the war, Slovak leaders like Stefan Osusky and Juraj Slavik cooperated with Edvard Benes' Czechoslovak government-in-exile, headquartered in London. There was also a small group of Slovak communists who took refuge in Moscow. With the Nazi defeat eminent, the Slovak National Uprising began in August 1944. The territory of Slovakia was liberated by Soviet troops. When the war ended, the Slovak National Council took control of the country and Czechoslovakia was re-established under President Benes. The country's pre-war borders were restored, with the exception of Carpathian Ruthenia, which was annexed by the Soviet Union. Tens of thousands of Hungarians and Germans were forced to leave Slovakia after the war, under the terms of the Benes decrees, collectively accused of collaborating against Czechoslovakia. Tiso was tried for treason and executed in 1947.

The communists were the largest vote-getters in the 1946 Czechoslovak elections, but by 1948 they had lost much of their popularity. Rather than risk the election, they organized a Soviet-backed coup, forcing President Benes to accept a government headed by Klement Gottwald, a communist. Benes resigned in June 1948, leaving the presidency open for Gottwald.

Once Czechoslovakia became a People's Republic, and a faithful ally of the Soviet Union, a wave of purges and arrests rolled over the country, from 1949 to 1954. In 1952 a number of high officials, including Rudolf Slansky, head of the Czech Communist Party, were tried and executed for "Titoism" and "national deviation."

Gottwald died in March 1953, a few days after Stalin, setting off the slow erosion of communist control. Antonin Zapotocky succeeded to the presidency, while Antonin Novotny became head of the party. Neither had Gottwald's authority, and so they clung even more tightly to the Stalinist methods, which, after Nikita Khrushchev's secret denunciation of Stalin in 1956, had begun to be discredited even in the USSR. Novotny became president upon Zapotocky's death in 1957, holding Czechoslovakia in a tight grip until well into the 1960s.

Khrushchev's liberalization in the USSR encouraged liberals within the Czechoslovak party to try to emulate Moscow. Past abuses of the party, including the hanging of Slansky, were repudiated, and Novotny was eventually forced to fire many of his most conservative allies, including Karol Bacilek, head of the Slovak Communist Party, and Viliam Siroky, premier for more than a decade. Slovaks detested both men because of their submission to Prague's continued policies of centralization, which in practice subordinated Slovak interests to those of the Czechs.

Alexander Dubček, the new head of the Slovak Communist Party, attacked Novotny at a meeting in late 1967, accusing him of undermining economic reform and ignoring Slovak demands for greater self-government. Two months later, in January 1968, the presidency was separated from the party chairmanship, and Dubček was named head of the Czechoslovak Communist Party, the first Slovak ever to hold the post.

Novotny resigned in March 1968, and Czechoslovakia embarked on a radical liberalization, which Dubček termed "socialism with a human face." The leaders of the other eastern bloc nations and the Soviet leaders viewed these developments with alarm. Delegations went back and forth from Moscow during the "Prague Spring" of 1968, warning of "counter-revolution." By July the neighbors' alarm had grown; at a meeting in Warsaw they issued a warning to Czechoslovakia against leaving the socialist camp. Although Dubček himself traveled to Moscow twice, in July and early August, to reassure Soviet party leader Brezhnev, the Soviets remained unconvinced.

Finally, on the night of 20–21 August 1968, military units from all the Warsaw Pact nations except Romania invaded Czechoslovakia, to "save it from counter-revolution." Dubček and other officials were arrested, and the country was placed under Soviet control. Difficulties in finding local officials willing to act as Soviet puppets caused the Soviets to play on Czech and Slovak antagonisms. On 31 December 1968 the country was made into a federative state, comprised of the Czech Socialist Republic and the Slovak Socialist Republic, each with its own legislature and government. In April Gustav Husak, once a reformer, but now viewing harmony with the USSR as the highest priority, was named head of the Czech Communist Party. A purge of liberals followed, and in May 1970 a new Soviet-Czechoslovak friendship treaty was signed; in June Dubček was expelled from the party.

Between 1970 and 1975 nearly one-third of the party was dismissed, as Husak consolidated power, re-establishing the priority of the federal government over its constituent parts and, in May 1975, reuniting the titles of party head and republic president.

In the late 1980s, once again it was liberalization in the USSR which set off political change in Czechoslovakia. Husak ignored Soviet leader Mikhail Gorbachev's calls for perestroika and glasnost until 1987, when he reluctantly endorsed the general concept of Party reform, but delayed implementation until 1991. Aging and in ill health, Husak announced his retirement in December 1987, declaring that Milos Jakes would take his post; Jakes had been a life-long compromiser and accommodator who was unable to control dissenting factions within his party, which were now using the radical changes in the Soviet Union as weapons against one another.

Enthusiasm for political change was not as great in Slovakia as it was in the Czech west, where in November 1989 people had begun to gather on Prague's Wenceslas Square, demanding free elections. The so-called "velvet revolution" ended on 24 November, when Jakes and all his government resigned. Novotny resigned his presidency soon after.

Alexander Dubček was brought out of exile and put forward as a potential replacement, but the hostility of Czech intellectuals and activists, who felt that they had to drag unwilling Slovaks into the new era, made it impossible to choose a Slovak as president. The choice fell instead on Vaclav Havel, a Czech playwright and dissident, who was named president by acclamation on 29 December 1989, while Dubček was named leader of the National Assembly.

Dismantling the apparatus of a Soviet-style state began immediately, but economic change came more slowly, in part because elections were not scheduled until June 1990. The old struggle between Czechs and Slovaks intensified, as Slovaks grew increasingly to resist the programs of economic and political change being proposed in Prague. Slovak demands led to an almost immediate renaming of the country, as the Czech and Slovak Federal Republic.

In the June elections the Slovaks voted overwhelmingly for Public Against Violence, the Slovak partner of the Czech Civic Forum, which meant that economic transformation was begun. Again there was much greater enthusiasm for returning to private ownership in the west than there was in the east, intensifying Slovak separatism. In December 1990 the country's Federal Assembly attempted to defuse the problem by increasing the roles of the Czech and Slovak regional governments, but it also gave President Havel extraordinary powers, to head off attempts at Slovak secession. The nationalists found an articulate and persuasive voice for growing separatist sentiments in Vladimir Meciar, the Slovak premier.

During a visit to Bratislava in March 1991, President Havel was jeered by thousands of Slovaks, making obvious the degree of Slovak discontent. Meciar was replaced in April 1991, by Jan Carnogursky, but the easing of tensions was only temporary, since Carnogursky, too, favored an independent Slovakia.

By June 1992 matters had reached a legislative impasse, so new federal elections were called. Slovakia chose to hold elections for its National Council at the same time. In July the new Slovak legislature issued a declaration of sovereignty and adopted a new constitution as an independent state, to take effect 1 January 1993. A struggle took place throughout 1991 and 1992, with the Federal Assembly and president on one side, trying to devise ways of increasing the strength of the federal state, and the Czech and Slovak National Councils on the other, seeking to shore up their own autonomy at the expense of the central authorities. Although polls indicated that most Slovaks continued to favor some form of union with the Czechs, the absence of any national figure able or

willing to articulate what form that union might take, left the field to the separatists and the charismatic Meciar.

In the federal election the vote split along national and regional lines, with the Czechs voting for right-of-center, reformist candidates, especially Vaclav Klaus's Civic Democratic Party, while the Slovaks voted for leftist and nationalist parties, especially Vladimir Meciar's Movement for a Democratic Slovakia (MDS). Although the federal government and President Havel continued to try to hold the state together, Czech Prime Minister Klaus made it clear that the Czechs would offer no financial incentives or assistance to induce the Slovaks to remain in the union. Increasingly the republics began to behave as though they were already separate so that, for example, by the end of 1992, 25.2% of Czech industry had been privatized, while only 5.3% of Slovak industry had. By the end of 1992 it was obvious that separation was inevitable. The two prime ministers, Klaus and Meciar, agreed to the so-called "velvet divorce," which took effect 1 January 1993. Czechs and Slovaks alike have objected that this move was never put to a popular referendum.

The new constitution created a 150-seat National Assembly, which elects the head of state, the president. Despite the strong showing of his party, Prime Minister Meciar was unable to get his first candidate through, and so put up Michal Kovac, a Dubček supporter and former finance minister in Slovakia, who had served as the last chairman of Czechoslovakia's federal parliament.

The Meciar government rejected the moves toward political and economic liberalization which the Czechs were pursuing, attempting instead to retain a socialist-style government, with strong central control. Swift economic decline, especially relative to the Czech's obviously growing prosperity, combined with Meciar's own erratic and autocratic manner, caused him to lose a vote of no-confidence in March 1994. However, Meciar's party, Movement for a Democratic Slovakia (MDS) held on to power and ruled Slovakia for its first five years as an independent state. His authoritarian style as Prime Minister created international concerns about the democratic development of Slovakia. During the MDS era, opportunities to privatize state-owned property were used to reward political loyalty, and election laws were changed in a way that favored the MDS. Much of the legislation introduced by the Meciar government was found to be unconstitutional. The MDS-led coalition government managed to remain in power until the September 1998 elections.

Under the new election laws, the Slovak Democratic Coalition (SDC) was formed by five small political groups in 1997. Mikulas Dzurinda was its leader. Elections held in September 1998 saw the SDC gain 26.33% of the vote. On 30 October 1998, SDC formed a coalition government with Dzurinda as prime minister. The first Dzurinda government enabled Slovakia to enter the Organization for Economic Cooperation and Development (OECD), begin accession negotiations with the European Union (EU), and make the country a strong candidate for North Atlantic Treaty Organization (NATO) accession. However, the popularity of the governing parties declined sharply, and several new parties gained relatively high levels of support in public opinion polls.

In January 1999, parliament passed a new law allowing for the direct election of the president. Presidential elections were held on 15 and 29 May, and in the second round, Rudolf Schuster of the small centrist Party of Civic Understanding (SOP) was elected with 57.2% of the vote over Meciar (42.8%). The Organization for Security and Cooperation in Europe (OSCE) found the elections to be free and fair. In July 1999, a law was passed improving the status of minority languages. In February 2001, parliament amended the constitution as a step toward gaining membership in the EU and NATO. Among the 85 amendments bringing the 1992 constitution in line with EU judiciary and financial standards were the creation of an ombudsman as a public protector of human rights, and an initiative to have the government support the aspirations of ethnic Slovaks living abroad to preserve their national identity and culture.

In the September 2002 parliamentary elections, Dzurinda received a mandate for a second term. He formed a government with three other center-right parties: the Hungarian Coalition Party (SMK), Christian Democrats (KDH), and Alliance of New Citizens (ANO). The main priorities of the coalition were to ensure a strong performance within NATO and the EU, fight government corruption, attract foreign investment, and reform social services, such as the health care system. Following a summer 2003 parliamentary shake-up, the government lost its narrow parliamentary majority and controlled only 69 of the 150 seats; however, because of conflicts among the opposition parties, the coalition was able to remain in power.

At a NATO summit in Prague held in November 2002, Slovakia was formally invited to join the organization, and in December, it was one of 10 new countries invited to join the EU. In the spring of 2004, it became a member of both organizations. In May 2005, Slovakia ratified the EU constitution. Slovakia joined the eurozone on 1 January 2009.

In the 2006 elections, the center-left party Direction-Social Democracy (Smer-SD) was the largest vote getter. The party formed a coalition government along with the Slovak National Party (SNS) and People's Party-Movement for a Democratic Slovakia (LS-HzDS). Robert Fico was appointed prime minister. Fico's government came under fire for weak economic performance and poor relations with neighboring Hungary. Several of the Fico's cabinet ministers became well-known for their anti-Hungarian statements and concerns about worsening ties between the two countries became a flashpoint for the 2010 elections.

The most recent parliamentary elections were held on 12 June 2010. Although Smer-SD gained the largest share of parliamentary seats, four center-right parties—Slovak Democratic and Christian Union (SDKU), Freedom and Solidarity (SaS), Christian-Democratic Movement (KDH), and Bridge (Most-Hid)—formed a narrow governing coalition with the stated principal aim of attacking corruption, enhancing transparency, and returning to a more free-market economic agenda. SDKU's Iveta Radicova leads the government; she is the first female prime minister in Slovakia's history.

13 GOVERNMENT

The constitution that the Slovak National Assembly adopted in July 1992 calls for a unicameral legislature of 150 members (the National Council of the Slovak Republic). Voting is by party slate, with proportional seat allotment affecting the gains of the winner. The government is formed by the leading party, or coalition of parties, and the prime minister is head of the government. The head of state is the president, who, after 1999, was directly elected

by popular vote for a five-year term. A cabinet is appointed by the president on the recommendation of the prime minister. Rudolf Schuster was Slovakia's first directly elected president; Ivan Gasparovic was elected president in 2004, defeating Meciar in the second round of voting. Gasparovic was reelected in April 2009 with 55% of vote and the support of the Social Democrats and the Nationalists. He is the first person to serve two terms as president.

A 2010 referendum on a set of six reforms was declared void by state officials due to a low voter turnout of only 22.84%. In order for the results of a referendum to be valid, more than 50% of registered voters must take part. The six reforms in question included a proposal to reduce the number of parliament members from 150 to 100, a measure to limit immunity from prosecution for parliament members, and a cap to limit the amount of money that public officials can spend on the purchase of official vehicles, particularly limousines. Most of the voters who participated were in favor of these measures.

14 POLITICAL PARTIES

There were 18 parties contesting the 150 seats of the National Council in the 1994 election, but only 7 or 8 were considered to be serious contenders, because of the necessity of receiving 5% of the total vote in order to take a seat. In 2010, 18 parties participated in the election and 6 parties won seats in the National Council. The single most popular party in 1994 was the Movement for a Democratic Slovakia (HZDS), which won 35% of the vote. By 2010, HZDS had failed to meet the 5% threshold required to win seats in the parliament.

In the elections of 2006, The Direction party came in with 29.1% of the vote and 50 seats, followed by the SDKU-DS with 18.3% of the vote and 31 seats. The Slovak National Party and the Hungarian Coalition Party each earned 20 seats. Another 15 seats went to the People's Party-Movement for Democratic Slovakia and 14 seats went to the Christian Democratic Union.

In the presidential election of 2009, incumbent Ivan Gasparovic of the Movement for Democracy was reelected with 55.5% of the vote. In the legislative elections of June 2010, a coalition of four center-right parties led by the Democratic and Christian Union-Democratic Party (SDKU-DS) out-seated the incumbent center-left Direction-Social Democracy (Smer-SD), led by Prime Minister Robert Fico, by winning 79 of 150 seats. The Smer-SD received the largest number of seats of any single party (62 seats with 34.8% of the vote), but was trumped by the coalition, which campaigned on a platform of austerity and economic recovery. The SDKU-DS won 28 seats (15.2%), followed by the Freedom and Solidarity party (SaS) with 22 seats (12.1%), the Most-Hid party with 14 seats (8.1%), and the Slovak National Party (SNS) with 9 seats (5.1%). Iveta Radicova of SDKU-DS was chosen as the nation's first female prime minister.

In the 2010 elections a center-right coalition came to power, led by the Slovak Democratic and Christian Union Party (SDKU). The coalition partners included SaS, the KDH, and Bridge (Most-Hid). Iveta Radicova was sworn in as Slovakia's first female prime minister in July 2010.

15 LOCAL GOVERNMENT

Slovakia is currently divided into 79 districts and 8 regions (kraje), and each region has a parliament and governor. In February 2001, in an effort to speed up Slovakia's EU accession process, the parliament implemented a series of constitutional changes aimed at decentralizing the country's power structure. Thus, the state audit office, the judiciary, and the minorities gain in independence and authority. In January 2002, Slovakia was divided into eight Upper-Tier Territorial Units—self-governing entities, named after their principal city. These changes responded to one of the EU's key requirements for increased decentralization and flexibility of the administrative apparatus.

16 JUDICIAL SYSTEM

The judicial system consists of a republic-level Supreme Court as the highest court of appeal; 8 regional courts seated in regional capitals; and 55 local courts seated in some district capitals. The courts have begun to form specialized sections, including commercial, civil, and criminal branches.

The 13-member constitutional court reviews the constitutionality of laws as well as the constitutional questions of lower level courts and national and local government bodies. Until 2002, parliament nominated and the president appointed the constitutional court and Supreme Court judges, and parliament chose all other judges based on the recommendations from the Ministry of Justice. In 2002, however, parliament passed legislation creating a judicial council, composed of judges, law professors, and other legal experts, to nominate judges. All judges except those of the constitutional court are now appointed by the president from a list proposed by the 18-member council. The president still appoints the constitutional court judges from a slate of candidates nominated by parliament.

The constitution declares the independence of the judiciary from the other branches of government. Judges are appointed for life, but constitutional court judges serve seven-year terms. There is also a military court system, and appeals may be taken to the Supreme Court and the constitutional court. Defendants in criminal cases have the right to free legal counsel and are guaranteed a fair and open public trial.

17 ARMED FORCES

The International Institute for Strategic Studies reports that armed forces in Slovakia totaled 16,531 members in 2011. The force is comprised of 7,322 from the army, 4,190 from the air force, 1,462 from central support, and 3,557 members of a training force. Armed forces represent .6% of the labor force in Slovakia. Defense spending totaled $2.2 billion and accounted for 1.9% of GDP.

18 INTERNATIONAL COOPERATION

Slovakia is a member of the UN, which it joined in 1993 when Czechoslovakia agreed to split into two parts. Slovakia serves on several nonregional specialized agencies, such as the FAO, UNESCO, UNIDO, the World Bank, ILO, and the WHO. The country is also a member of the Council of Europe, the European Bank for Reconstruction and Development, the OECD, OSCE, the Euro-Atlantic Partnership Council, and the WTO. Slovakia became an official member of NATO and the European Union in 2004. The country has observer status in the OAS and is an affiliate member of the Western European Union.

The government has actively participated in US- and NATO-led military actions in Iraq and Afghanistan. The country also partici-

pates in a joint Czech-Slovak peacekeeping force in Kosovo and supports UN missions and operations in Sierra Leone (est. 1999) and Cyprus (est. 1964).

Slovakia serves on the Australia Group, the Zangger Committee, the European Organization for Nuclear Research (CERN), the Nuclear Energy Agency, the Nuclear Suppliers Group (London Group), and the Organization for the Prohibition of Chemical Weapons. In environmental cooperation, is part of the Antarctic Treaty, the Basel Convention, Conventions on Biological Diversity and Air Pollution, Ramsar, CITES, the Kyoto Protocol, the Montréal Protocol, MARPOL, the Nuclear Test Ban Treaty, and the UN Conventions on the Law of the Sea, Climate Change, and Desertification. Slovakia is also a member of the Visegrad 4 for regional cooperation in Central Europe.

19 ECONOMY

The GDP rate of change in Slovakia, as of 2010, was 4%. Inflation stood at 1%, and unemployment was reported at 13.5%. Slovakia's GDP was $120.2 billion in 2010 and GDP per capita was $22,000.

Slovakia has made significant economic reforms since its separation from the Czech Republic in 1993. Reforms to the taxation, healthcare, pension, and social welfare systems helped Slovakia consolidate its budget in order to join the EU in 2004 and adopt the euro in January 2009. Major privatizations are nearly complete, the banking sector is almost entirely in foreign hands, and the government has helped facilitate a foreign investment boom with business-friendly policies. Slovakia's economic growth exceeded expectations in 2001–08 despite a general European slowdown. Unemployment, at an unacceptable 18% in 2003–04, dropped to 7.7% in 2008 but remains the economy's Achilles heel at nearly 14% in early 2012.

Foreign direct investment (FDI) accounted for much of the growth until 2008. Cheap and skilled labor, low taxes, a 19% flat tax for corporations and individuals, no dividend taxes, a relatively liberal labor code and a favorable geographical location are Slovakia's main advantages for foreign investors. Foreign investment in the automotive and electronic sectors has been especially strong. To maintain a stable operating environment for investors, the European Bank for Reconstruction and Development advised the Slovak government to refrain from intervening in important sectors of the economy. However, Bratislava's approach to mitigating the economic slowdown has included substantial government intervention and the option to nationalize strategic companies.

A decline in production of primary exports occurred as a result of the global economic crisis beginning in 2008, leading the nation into a steep recession. During the first four months of 2009, the economy contracted by 11.2%, one of the most dramatic declines in the European Union. Some recovery was managed through the strength of the euro, as Slovakia adopted the common currency on 1 January 2009. By mid-2009, this strength was a cause of concern for small businesses and the domestic consumer market, however, as many Slovaks were traveling across the borders into Poland, Hungary, and the Czech Republic to purchase lower-cost goods. The switch to the euro helped retain confidence from foreign investors. In April 2009, despite the initial decline in automobile production, Volkswagen chose Slovakia as the site for its $436 million factory to produce the new low-cost family vehicle, Up. Slovakia counts Germany and the Czech Republic as its largest trading partners.

20 INCOME

The CIA estimated that in 2010 the GDP of Slovakia was $120.2 billion. The CIA defines GDP as the value of all final goods and services produced within a nation in a given year and computed on the basis of purchasing power parity (PPP) rather than value as measured on the basis of the rate of the exchange based on current dollars. The per capita GDP was estimated at $22,000. The annual growth rate of GDP was 4%. The average inflation rate was 1%. It was estimated that agriculture accounted for 2.7% of GDP, industry 35.6%, and services 61.8%.

The World Bank estimates that Slovakia, with 0.09% of the world's population, accounted for 0.16% of the world's GDP. By comparison, the United States, with 4.85% of the world's population, accounted for 22.51% of world GDP.

As of 2011 the most recent study by the World Bank reported that actual individual consumption in Slovakia was 65.0% of GDP and accounted for 0.16% of world consumption. By comparison, the United States accounted for 25.44% of world individual consumption.

The World Bank also estimated that 13.1% of Slovakia's GDP was spent on food and beverages, 17.5% on housing and household furnishings, 2.4% on clothes, 6.0% on health, 4.9% on transportation, 2.0% on communications, 5.6% on recreation, 3.8% on restaurants and hotels, and 5.9% on miscellaneous goods and services and purchases from abroad. The World Bank reports that in 2009, household consumption in Slovakia totaled $58.1 billion or about $10,605 per capita, measured in current US dollars rather than PPP. Household consumption includes expenditures of individuals, households, and nongovernmental organizations on goods and services, excluding the purchases of dwellings. It was estimated that household consumption was growing at an average annual rate of 5.2%.

21 LABOR

As of 2010, Slovakia had a total labor force of 2.707 million people. Within that labor force, CIA estimates in 2009 noted that 3.5% were employed in agriculture, 27% in industry, and 69.4% in the service sector.

Unions are freely allowed to organize in Slovakia as well as engage in collective bargaining. Strikes are legal only if they meet certain stringent requirements. Between 10 and 17% of the workforce was unionized in 2010.

Children may not work until the age of 15. After age 16, minors may work without restrictions as to hours or condition of work. These provisions are effectively enforced by the government. The minimum wage was $412 per month in 2010.

The standard workweek was 42.5 hours, although under collective bargaining agreements, many workweeks are 40 hours. The government sets minimum occupational health and safety standards and it effectively monitors them.

22 AGRICULTURE

Roughly 40% of the total land is farmed, and the country's major crops include grains, potatoes, sugar beets, hops, and fruit.

Cereal production in 2009 amounted to 3.3 million tons, fruit production 129,051 tons, and vegetable production 313,394 tons. Barley and hops are important agricultural exports; fruit, wine, and seed oil are also produced for export.

23 ANIMAL HUSBANDRY

The UN Food and Agriculture Organization (FAO) reported that Slovakia dedicated 532,000 hectares (1.31 million acres) to permanent pasture or meadow in 2009. During that year, the country tended 13.2 million chickens, 483,810 head of cattle, and 740,862 pigs. The production from these animals amounted to 32,963 tons of beef and veal, 179,797 tons of pork, 97,790 tons of poultry, 57,944 tons of eggs, and 701,746 tons of milk. Slovakia also produced 1,950 tons of cattle hide and 820 tons of raw wool.

24 FISHING

Fishing is only a minor source of the domestic food supply. Production comes mostly from mountain streams and stocked ponds. Some of the rivers and ponds near Bratislava are polluted with chemicals and petrochemical seepings, impairing the growth of fish stocks regionally. Common carp and rainbow trout are the dominant species. In 2008 the annual capture totaled 1,655 tons according to the UN FAO.

25 FORESTRY

Approximately 40% of Slovakia is covered by forest. The UN FAO estimated the 2009 roundwood production at 8.5 million cu m (300.2 million cu ft). The value of all forest products, including roundwood, totaled $1.33 billion. Forests have been severely damaged by acid rain from coal-fired power stations. Slovak forest product exports include paper, wood, and furniture.

26 MINING

Metal and metal products, particularly aluminum and steel, comprised Slovakia's leading industries in 2009, each of which was heavily dependent upon imports of raw materials. Iron, steel, and ferroalloys made up 5% of exports in 2009.

Gas, coke, oil, nuclear fuel, and chemicals were other top industries. Industrial mineral production in 2009 included: dolomite, 908,000 metric tons, down from 1,249,000 tons in 2008; lime (hydrated and quicklime), 867,000 tons; magnesite concentrate, 800,000 metric tons, down from 957,000 metric tons in 2007; crude gypsum and anhydrite, 150,000 metric tons; salt, 100,000 metric tons; barite concentrate, 130,000 metric tons; bentonite, 145,000 metric tons; kaolin, 44,000 metric tons; perlite, 25,000 metric tons; and zeolites, 85,000 metric tons. The Košice magnesite mines were put on care-and-maintenance.

Also produced in 2009 were asbestos, basalt, feldspar, gold, iron ore, refractory clays, nitrogen, sand and gravel, sodium compounds, limestone and other calcareous stones, and crushed stone. No zinc, lead, silver, or copper was mined in 2009.

Other mineral resources included antimony ore, mercury, brick soils, ceramic materials, and stonesalt. All mining companies were government owned.

27 ENERGY AND POWER

The World Bank reported in 2008 that Slovakia produced 28.8 billion kWh of electricity and consumed 28.5 billion kWh, or 5,204 kWh per capita. Roughly 70% of energy came from fossil fuels, while 26% came from alternative fuels. Two new nuclear reactors came on line between 1998 and 2000, reducing Slovakia's dependence on fossil fuels and allowing it to become a net exporter of electricity.

Coal mining produced some 2,836,000 short tons in 2009. In 2009, Slovakia imported 5,787,000 short tons of coal. As of 2011, Slovakia had crude oil reserves of 9 million barrels, natural gas reserves of 14.6 billion cu m, and a crude oil refining capacity of 115,000 barrels per day. Production of oil in 2010 was estimated at 8,281 barrels per day. Natural gas output in 2010 was estimated at 103 million cu m. Domestic demand for oil averaged 83,000 barrels per day in 2010. Natural gas consumption in 2010 was estimated at 6.4 billion cu m.

28 INDUSTRY

In 2010, industry accounted for 34.5% of Slovakia's GDP. Foreign firms such as US Steel and Whirlpool are major investors in Slovak industry. Foreign Direct Investment (FDI) to Slovakia was estimated at $3.07 billion in 2010. FDI in Slovakia accounted for much of the growth in the period 2000–08. Cheap and skilled labor, low taxes, a 19% flat tax for corporations and individuals, no dividend taxes, a relatively liberal labor code, and a favorable geographical location are Slovakia's main advantages for foreign investors. FDI inflow cumulatively reached $39.4 billion in 2008; the total inflow of FDI in 2008 was $1.39 billion. Volkswagen, Peugeot-Citröen, and Kia Motors all produce motor vehicles in Slovakia. In 2009, Slovakia produced 510,000 motor vehicles.

In 2011, Slovakia's industrial production growth rate was estimated at 9%. The industrial sector employed 27% of Slovakia's labor force according to 2009 estimates. Agriculture made up 3.9% of the GDP and employed 3.5% of the working population; services came in first with 61.46% of the GDP and 55.9% of the labor force. Major industries in 2010 were: metal and metal products; food and beverages; electricity, gas, coke, oil, nuclear fuel; chemicals and manmade fibers; machinery; paper and printing; earthenware and ceramics; transport vehicles; textiles; electrical and optical apparatus; and rubber products.

29 SCIENCE AND TECHNOLOGY

Patent applications in science and technology as of 2009, according to the World Bank, totaled 176 in Slovakia. Public financing of science was 0.47% of GDP. The Slovak Academy of Sciences, founded in 1953, has departments of exact and technical sciences and of natural sciences and chemistry, and 36 affiliated research institutes. The Council of Scientific Societies, headquartered in Bratislava, coordinates the activities of 16 societies concerned with specific scientific and technical fields. Natural history exhibits are displayed in the Slovak National Museum in Bratislava, the Central Slovak Museum in Banská Bstrica, and the Museum of Eastern Slovakia in Košice. The Slovak Mining Museum, founded

in 1900, is located in Banská Stiavnica. Eight universities offer scientific and technical degrees.

In 2008, research and development (R&D) expenditures totaled 0.47% of GDP. In that same year, there were 2,331 per one million people that were engaged in R&D. 5% of manufactured exports were considered high-technology exports in 2008.

30 DOMESTIC TRADE

Bratislava is the primary commercial center of the country. Other major centers include Košice, Trencin, Zilina, and Poprad. Nitra is a primary distribution center for agricultural products.

The Slovak retail sector has been 98% privatized. Initially, most establishments were small, family-owned shops specializing in one type of product, such as groceries, flowers, books, clothing, music, etc. However, retail has since moved towards larger Western-style stores and hypermarkets that offer a wider variety of products under one roof. This has caused many small retailers to either consolidate or liquidate. According to the Statistics Office of the Slovak Republic, retail sales declined by 10% in 2009. Franchising in Slovakia has been growing and includes hotels, fast food operations, gas stations, and business services.

Electronic commerce (e-commerce) has been rapidly growing. The most commonly bought products are computers, audio-video equipment, books, CDs, DVDs, office supplies, food, and financial services. As of 2010, there were 4 million Internet users in Slovakia.

Slovakia imposes a 19% value added tax on most goods and services.

Retail shops are generally open from 9 a.m. to 6 p.m., Monday through Friday. New chain stores are open seven days a week from about 7 a.m. to 8 p.m. Grocery stores often operate from 6 a.m. to 7 p.m. Many stores will open for half a day on Saturdays, but most businesses and shops are closed on Sundays. Generally banks and offices are open from 9 a.m. to 6 p.m. Monday through Friday.

31 FOREIGN TRADE

Slovakia imported $62.43 billion worth of goods and services in 2008, while exporting $64.18 billion worth of goods and services.

Principal Trading Partners – Slovakia (2010)				
(In millions of US dollars)				
Country	Total	Exports	Imports	Balance
World	132,280.0	64,620.0	67,660.0	-3,040.0
Germany	24,357.0	12,463.0	11,894.0	569.0
Czech Republic	20,932.0	9,107.0	11,825.0	-2,718.0
Hungary	9,191.0	4,545.0	4,646.0	-101.0
Poland	8,528.0	4,885.0	3,643.0	1,242.0
Russia	7,865.0	1,660.0	6,205.0	-4,545.0
Austria	7,558.0	4,413.0	3,145.0	1,268.0
France	6,943.0	4,442.0	2,501.0	1,941.0
Italy	6,295.0	3,603.0	2,692.0	911.0
United Kingdom	3,703.0	2,356.0	1,347.0	1,009.0
Netherlands	3,484.0	1,875.0	1,609.0	266.0

(…) data not available or not significant.

(n.s.) not specified.

SOURCE: *2011 Direction of Trade Statistics Yearbook,* New York: United Nations, 2011.

Balance of Payments – Slovakia (2010)

(In millions of US dollars)

Current Account		**-3,009.0**
Balance on goods		182.0
Imports	-64,484.0	
Exports	64,665.0	
Balance on services		-988.0
Balance on income		-1,658.0
Current transfers		-544.0
Capital Account		**1,372.0**
Financial Account		**-644.0**
Direct investment abroad		-319.0
Direct investment in Slovakia		553.0
Portfolio investment assets		-3,393.0
Portfolio investment liabilities		1,866.0
Financial derivatives		-142.0
Other investment assets		-461.0
Other investment liabilities		1,252.0
Net Errors and Omissions		**2,317.0**
Reserves and Related Items		**-37.0**

(…) data not available or not significant.

SOURCE: *Balance of Payment Statistics Yearbook 2011,* Washington, DC: International Monetary Fund, 2011.

Public Finance – Slovakia (2009)

(In billions of euros, central government figures)

Revenue and Grants	**18,583**	**100.0%**
Tax revenue	7,814	42.0%
Social contributions	7,993	43.0%
Grants	583	3.1%
Other revenue	2,194	11.8%
Expenditures	**23,241**	**100.0%**
General public services	4,307	18.5%
Defense	800	3.4%
Public order and safety	1,313	5.6%
Economic affairs	2,955	12.7%
Environmental protection	255	1.1%
Housing and community amenities	101	0.4%
Health	4,681	20.1%
Recreational, culture, and religion	376	1.6%
Education	1,014	4.4%
Social protection	7,439	32.0%

(…) data not available or not significant.

SOURCE: *Government Finance Statistics Yearbook 2010,* Washington, DC: International Monetary Fund, 2010.

Germany is Slovakia's largest trading partner, purchasing 20.1% of Slovakia's exports and supplying 16.8% of its imports in 2009. Other major partners include the Czech Republic (12.9% of Slovakia's exports and 12.3% of Slovakia's imports); Italy (6.1% and 3.7%); Russia (3.8% and 9.0%); Austria (5.8% and 2.9%); Hungary (6.3% and 5.3%); Poland (7.2% and 3.9%); and France (7.8% and 4.0%). Slovakia imports nearly all of its oil and gas from Russia and its export markets are primarily OECD and EU countries. More than 85.1% of its trade in 2008 was with EU members and with OECD countries (86.2%).

In 2009, export commodities included machinery and electrical equipment (35.9%), vehicles (21%), base metals (11.3%), chemicals and minerals (8.1%), plastics (4.9%). Import commodities included machinery and transport equipment (31%), mineral products (13%), vehicles (12%), base metals (9%), chemicals (8%), and plastics (6%).

32 BALANCE OF PAYMENTS

In 2010 Slovakia had a foreign trade deficit of $13 million, amounting to 7.3% of GDP. Exports of goods and services totaled $67.97 billion in 2010. Imports were estimated at $67.77 billion for the same year. The reserves of foreign exchange and gold were $2.16 billion in 2010.

33 BANKING AND SECURITIES

In January 1992 the banking system of Czechoslovakia was split. From that point on the National Bank of Slovakia was charged with the responsibility of circulating currency and regulating the banking sector. The National Bank of Slovakia is part of the Eurosystem and the European Central Bank. At the end of 2011, there were 24 commercial banks operating in the Slovak Republic. The commercial bank prime lending rate in 2010 was 3.39%.

Slovakia entered into the European Exchange Rate Mechanism in November 2005, and joined the European Monetary Union on January 1, 2009. Headline consumer price inflation dropped from a high of 26% in 1993 to 1.4% in 2009. The current account deficit, including the cost of the second pension pillar, reached 5.0% in 2008 then moved considerably higher. The general government deficit for 2010 was forecast at 5.5%, although private sector analysts expected it to be as high as 7.0%. Government debt was estimated at 37.1% of GDP at the end of 2009.

The Bratislava Stock Exchange (BSE) opened on 8 July 1990 and acts as a share holding company formed by all Slovak financial institutions, banks and savings banks, and companies authorized to trade securities. Brokers and other mediators are not permitted in the trading system. The market value of publicly traded shares in Slovakia was $4.15 billion in 2010. The Bratislava Option and Futures Exchange opened in 1994.

34 INSURANCE

The pre-World War II insurance companies and institutions of the former Czechoslovakia after 1945 were reorganized, merged, nationalized and centralized. Since 1952, the insurance industry has been administered by the State Insurance Office, under the jurisdiction of the Ministry of Finance, and two enterprises conducted insurance activities, the Czech and the Slovak Insurance Enterprises of the State. The Slovak Insurance Company remains the only company authorized to write the compulsory third-party automobile liability insurance. Lawyers, architects and dentists are also required to carry liability insurance. There are no restrictions on foreign ownership of companies. In 2009, direct gross insurance premiums were 3.3% of GDP.

35 PUBLIC FINANCE

Since the dissolution of Czechoslovakia, the Slovak government has implemented several measures to compensate for the large loss of fiscal transfers it received from the Federation, which were equivalent to between SKK20 and 25 billion in 1992. The Slovak government's initial budget was balanced at the beginning of

1992, with revenues and expenditures equivalent to SKK159 billion. Since that time, however, Slovakia's budget has fallen into deficit. Privatization efforts have been successful, attracting a large amount of foreign direct investment (FDI).

In 2010 the budget of Slovakia included $28.45 billion in public revenue and $35.01 billion in public expenditures. The budget deficit amounted to 7.9% of GDP. Public debt was 41% of GDP, with $59.33 billion of the debt held by foreign entities.

The Slovak government devotes relatively large shares of expenditures toward public order and safety, economic affairs (including infrastructure), and health. In 2008, 29% of government expenditure went toward social protection, 19.7% to health, and 14.4% on economic affairs.

36 TAXATION

The principal taxes are corporate income tax, personal income tax, and value-added tax. Individuals are liable for tax on all sources of worldwide income. Corporate income tax is levied on joint stock companies, limited liability companies, and limited partnerships. In 2010, the corporate tax rate for resident companies was 19%. Capital gains were also taxed at 19%. Dividends paid out of after-tax profits are not taxed. Interest income from loans or bands are taxed at the corporate rate, as is income from royalties. Other taxes include a road tax, excise duties, import duties, and taxes on property.

As of 2010, individual income was taxed at a flat 19% rate. Dividends paid to individuals are not taxed. Income from interest and capital are included in total income.

The principle indirect tax is Slovakia's value-added tax (VAT). As of 2010, the standard rate was 19% and was applied to most transactions. However, exports are zero-rated, and financial, broadcasting, insurance and educational services are exempt.

37 CUSTOMS AND DUTIES

As a WTO member, Slovakia uses the Brussels Tariff Nomenclature. Goods imported into Slovakia are subject to three kinds of charges: customs duties, value-added tax (VAT) of 10% or 19%, and an excise tax. A 3% import surcharge was eliminated on 1 January 2001. However, Slovakia imposes surcharges on approximately 80% of its imports. Slovakia is also a member of the Central European Free Trade Area (CEFTA) along with Bulgaria, the Czech Republic, Hungary, Poland, Romania, and Slovenia. There are no import duties for EU member states.

38 FOREIGN INVESTMENT

Prior to the defeat of Prime Minister Vladimir Meciar, Slovakia experienced difficulty attracting foreign investment due to perceived political uncertainty and vacillations in its privatization policy. The government successfully introduced tax incentives to attract more capital from abroad.

Annual foreign direct investment (FDI) inflow was $220 million in 1997 and rose to $648 million in 1998. Affected by the Russian financial crisis, FDI inflow fell to $390 million in 1999, but then recovered sharply in 2000 to reach a peak of over $2 billion. FDI inflow to Slovakia in 2008 was $1.39 billion.

Foreign Direct Investment (FDI) to Slovakia was estimated at $3.07 billion in 2010. Cheap and skilled labor, low taxes, a 19% flat tax for corporations and individuals, no dividend taxes, a rela-

tively liberal labor code, and a favorable geographical location encourage foreign investment in Slovakia. FDI inflow cumulatively reached $39.4 billion in 2008. Volkswagen, Peugeot-Citröen, and Kia Motors all produce motor vehicles in Slovakia. In 2009, Slovakia produced 510,000 motor vehicles.

39 ECONOMIC DEVELOPMENT

The government in the early 1990s slowed economic reforms due to the social burden imposed by the transformation to a market economy. Measures included stimulation of demand through price subsidies and public spending. Slovakia's most successful structural reform has been privatization. The first stage of large-scale privatization included 751 companies, and a second stage, which involved 650 medium- and large-scale enterprises, was implemented in late 1993.

However, the Meciar government was slow to implement the $1.5 billion privatization program after he regained power in 1994 and the country continued to rely heavily on foreign aid. Western investors cheered his defeat and replacement by reformer Mikulas Dzurinda in 1998. The Dzurinda government quickly earned praise for its implementation of reforms. The renewed liberalization measures, combined with a new attitude toward Slovakia's Roma (Gypsy) population, caused the EU to place Slovakia back on its list of candidate members. In December 2002, Slovakia was officially invited to join the EU, and accession took place in May 2004.

Slovakia's external debt at the beginning of 2002 was about $11 billion, approximately 55% of GDP. The current account deficit was high, largely due to a shortfall in foreign trade. Foreign direct investment (FDI) grew slowly in the 1990s, however FDI in 2000 alone was greater than cumulative investment received by Slovakia in the preceding 10 years. Although growth was strong and inflation relatively low in the early 2000s, the unemployment rate remained high. By 2002, the main banks and utilities had been privatized; but further corporate restructuring and labor market reform, improved banking supervision, and strengthening state administration and the judicial system remained structural reforms to be implemented.

A strong economic expansion followed in 2003 and 2004, with GDP growth rates of 4.5% and 5.5% respectively. In 2004, Slovakia joined NATO and the EU, which greatly improved the stability of the political and economic climate. In addition, an investment-friendly environment was created, which led to a dramatic increase in the inflow of foreign capital. In 2005, Slovakia was considered by the World Bank the world's top performer in improving its business climate over the last year; in the same year it was deemed one of the top 20 countries in the world for ease of doing business. As of 2006, Slovakia was able to boast a highly skilled and relatively low-cost labor force, an attractive tax system (19% flat tax), a liberal labor code, and a favorable geographic location. However, with the world economic downturn starting in 2008, Slovakia's economy faltered. In 2011, the ranking for ease of doing business in Slovakia had plummeted to 43rd.

40 SOCIAL DEVELOPMENT

Slovakia's social security system was first introduced in 1906. The current program was implemented in 2004. Old age, disability and survivor's pensions are funded by employee and employer contributions as well as government subsidies. Retirement is set at age 62 for both men and women. The first laws covering sickness benefits were instituted in 1888. A family allowance system provides benefits for all residents funded totally by the government. There are also sickness and maternity benefits, a workers' compensation program, and unemployment benefits.

Women and men are equal under the law, enjoying the same property, inheritance, and other rights, however discrimination persists. Women on the average earn 30% less than men. Despite legal safeguards, the small number of women in private and public leadership roles is evidence of continuing cultural barriers to full equality. The Coordinating Committee for Women's Affairs has not been successful in protecting women against violence, health risks, or economic disadvantages. Domestic abuse and sexual violence against women remains an extensive and underreported problem. Human rights are generally well respected, but some democratic freedoms are not respected. There have been reports of intimidation of political opponents and interference with the media. There are also reports of police abuse of Roma.

Roma minorities suffer from high levels of unemployment and housing discrimination. Racially motivated attacks against Roma and other minorities by extremists have been reported.

41 HEALTH

Since 1995 general public health services have been organized into a system of state health institutes. However, primary health care services, formerly operated by the state, are now separate from the public health sector and reimbursed through a compulsory insurance program. According to the CIA, life expectancy in Slovakia was 75 years in 2011. The country spent 8.0% of its GDP on healthcare, amounting to $1,373 per person. There were 30 physicians, 66 nurses and midwives, and 66 hospital beds per 10,000 inhabitants. The fertility rate was 1.4, while the infant mortality rate was 6 per 1,000 live births. In 2008 the maternal mortality rate, according to the World Bank, was 6 per 100,000 births. Immunization rates for children up to one year old were impressively high: tuberculosis, 90%; diphtheria, pertussis, and tetanus, 99%; polio, 98%; and measles, 98%. The CIA calculated HIV/AIDS prevalence in Slovakia to be about less than 0.1% in 2009.

42 HOUSING

In 1992, the Slovak Association of Towns and Villages, comprised of some 2,000 towns, was engaged in recovering all housing units from former state administration authorities. In 2009 the number of total housing starts amounted to 20,325 units and the number of dwelling completions amounted to 18,834 units. Most of these were detached houses. About 88% of all dwellings were permanently occupied. About 11% of all dwellings were unoccupied. Of the permanently occupied units, the average number of rooms per unit was 3.2; nearly 73% of all dwellings had 3 rooms or more. The average number of people per dwelling was also 3.21. About 76.3% of all dwellings had central heating and 92.8% had a separate bathroom or shower facility.

43 EDUCATION

Education is compulsory for nine years, approximately up to the age of 15. This basic schooling is accomplished in two stages of four years and five years. At the secondary level, there are a variety of general, vocational, professional, and art school programs to choose from. Most secondary programs last about four years.

In 2009 about 73.4% of four-year-old children were enrolled in some type of preschool program. That year, secondary school enrollment was about 83% of age-eligible students. The student-to-teacher ratio for primary school was at about 18:1 in 2009. The average number of foreign languages per pupil among Slovak secondary students was 1.2 in 2009.

Tertiary enrollment was estimated at 54%. In 2009, 235,000 students were enrolled in tertiary education programs. Of those enrolled in tertiary education, there were 100 male students for every 158 female students. Overall, the CIA estimated that Slovakia had a literacy rate of 99.6%. Public expenditure on education represented 3.6% of GDP and 7.5% of total government expenditure.

Slovakia has 20 public universities, with the oldest being Cornenius (Komensky) University in Bratislava, founded in 1919. In 2004, the first Hungarian language university in Slovakia, János Selye University, was founded in Komárno.

44 LIBRARIES AND MUSEUMS

The most important library in Slovakia is the Slovak National Library (4.4 million volumes), founded in 1863 and located at Martin. The State Scientific Library in Banská Bstrica (1926) holds almost two million volumes, and the Comenius University in Bratislava has the country's largest university collection of 2.2 million volumes. In total there are over 450 libraries in universities and other higher-educational institutions and about 2,600 public library branches nationwide.

The Slovak National Gallery (1948), the Slovak National Museum (1924), the Natural History Museum (1948), and the History Museum (1924), are all in Bratislava. The administrators of the Slovak National Museum also sponsor the branch museums of the Museum of Archaeology, the Museum of Ethnography, the Museum of Music, the Museum of Puppetry and Toys, and the Museum of Jewish Culture. The State Gallery of Art is in Banská Bstrica. There are dozens of regional museums throughout the country.

45 MEDIA

Slovakia's telecommunications system is modern and has seen dramatic growth, due in large part to cellular services. Domestically, the country's analog-based telecommunications network is being replaced by digital equipment, with fiber-optic cable used to expand the system, particularly in large urban areas. Nationwide cellular service is provided by three companies. International service is supplied by three international service exchanges. Efforts are currently underway to increase international service availability. In 2009, there were about 1 million main phone lines and 5.4 million mobile cellular phones in use. There were 15 FM radio stations, 78 AM radio stations, and 2 shortwave radio stations. In 2010, the country had 1.1 million Internet hosts. As of 2009, there were some 4 million Internet users in Slovakia. Internet users numbered 75 per 100 citizens. Prominent newspapers in 2010, with circulation numbers listed parenthetically, included *Pravda* (165,000), *Republika* (50,000), and the Hungarian-language *Uj Szo* (42,000).

There are three government boards appointed by a majority vote of parliament to supervise radio and television broadcasting: The Slovak Television Council and the Slovak Radio Council establish broadcasting policy for state-owned television and radio. The Slovak Council for Radio and Television Broadcasting issues broadcast licenses for nongovernment groups and administers advertising laws and other regulations. The privately owned TV Markiza has the widest broadcast audience. In 2008, there were 37 broadcast television stations. The public broadcaster, Slovak TV and Radio, sponsored three national television networks and five national radio networks. In 2010, 40% of households were connected to multi-channel cable or satellite television systems.

46 ORGANIZATIONS

The Slovak Chamber of Commerce and Industry is located in Bratislava. There are professional associations for a number of occupations, including teaching, and a number of medical professions.

The Slovak Academy of Sciences promotes public interest, education, and research in various scientific fields. Cultural and educational associations include the Organization of Slovak Writers. The Slovak Medical Association promotes research and education on health issues and works to establish common policies and standards in healthcare. There are several other associations dedicated to research and education for specific fields of medicine and particular diseases and conditions.

National youth organizations include the Association of Slovak Students, Civic Democratic Youth, YMCA/YWCA, and Slovak Scouting. There are several sports associations promoting amateur competition in a variety of pastimes, such as Frisbee, aikido, badminton, baseball, figure skating, floorball, and track and field; many sports associations are affiliated with international groups as well. There are national chapters of the Paralympics Committee and the Special Olympics, as well as a national Olympic Committee.

Kiwanis and Lion's Clubs have programs in the country. Women's organizations include the Alliance of Women in Slovakia. Greenpeace, Habitat for Humanity, and the Red Cross have national chapters.

The Hungarian minority has a number of organizations in Slovakia, including the Hungarian Workers' Cultural Association of Slovakia, the Hungarian Students' Association, the Hungarian Students' Network, and the Civic Association of Young People for the Future. There is also a Society of Hungarian Writers in Slovakia as well as the Hungarian Teachers' Association.

47 TOURISM, TRAVEL, AND RECREATION

Slovakia's outdoor tourist attractions include mountains (the most famous being the High and Low Tatras), forests, cave formations, and over 1,000 mineral and hot springs. In addition, tourists can visit ancient castles, monuments, chateaux, museums, and galleries. Slovakia is also home to many health spas. Horse racing is a national pastime. Golf, skiing, mountaineering, and rafting are popular sports among tourists. All visitors are required to have valid passports, onward/return tickets and sufficient funds for their stay.

The *Tourism Factbook*, published by the UN World Tourism Organization, reported 6.64 million incoming tourists to Slovakia in 2008; they spent a total of $2.54 billion. There were 109,555 hotel beds available in Slovakia, which had an occupancy rate of 22%. The estimated daily cost to visit Bratislava, the capital, was $342. The cost of visiting other cities averaged $225.

48 FAMOUS PERSONS

Ján Kollár (1793–1852), writer, poet, Slavist, and archaeologist, was a Slovak patriot who championed the Slav struggle against foreign oppression. Ludovít Stúr (1815–56) is the founder of the Slovak literary language and modern Slovak literature. The founder of scientific Slavic studies was Pavel Josef Safačrík (1795–1861), whose *Slavonic Antiquities* had great scholarly influence. Andrej Hlinka (1864–1938) led the Slovak Catholic autonomist movement. The greatest Slovak poet, Pavel Hviezdoslav (1849–1921), translated foreign poetry, refined the language, and contributed to Slovak awakening. The Robin Hood of the Slovaks, Juraj Jánošík (1688–1713), fought the Hungarians. Milan Rastislav Stefánik (1880–1919), military leader, astronomer, and ally of Tomáš Masaryk, represented the Slovaks in their struggle for liberty. Alexander Dubček (1921–92) was first secretary of the Czechoslovak Communist Party (1968–69). His attempt to increase civil liberties led to the invasion of Czechoslovakia by the Warsaw Pact in 1968. In 1989 he was elected the Federal Assembly's first speaker. The most famous Hungarian minority leader from Slovakia was János Esterházy (1901–57), leader of the United Hungarian Party in inter-war Czechoslovakia.

49 DEPENDENCIES

Slovakia has no territories or colonies.

50 BIBLIOGRAPHY

Cravens, Craig S. *Culture and Customs of the Czech Republic and Slovakia*. Westport, CT: Greenwood Press, 2006.

Frucht, Richard, ed. *Eastern Europe: An Introduction to the People, Lands, and Culture*. Santa Barbara, CA: ABC-CLIO, 2005.

Johnson, Lonnie. *Central Europe: Enemies, Neighbors, Friends*, 3rd ed. New York: Oxford University Press, 2010.

Kirschbaum, Stanislav J. *Historical Dictionary of Slovakia*. 2nd ed. Lanham, MD: Scarecrow, 2007.

Kirschbaum, Stanislav J. *A History of Slovakia: The Struggle for Survival*. 2nd ed. New York: St. Martin's Press, 2005.

Mahoney, William M. *The History of the Czech Republic and Slovakia*. Santa Barbara, CA: Greenwood, 2011.

Mikus, Joseph A. *Slovakia: A Political and Constitutional History: With Documents*. Bratislava: Slovak Academy Press, 1995.

Opello, Walter C. *European Politics*. Boulder, CO: Lynne Rienner Publishers, 2009.

Political Chronology of Europe. London: Europa, 2001.

Reuvid, Jonathan. *Doing Business with Slovakia*. Sterling, VA: Kogan Page, 2004.

Slovakia Investment and Business Guide: Strategic and Practical Information. Washington, DC: International Business Publications USA, 2012.

Wandycz, Piotr Stefan. *The Price of Freedom: A History of East Central Europe from the Middle Ages to the Present*, 2nd ed. New York: Routledge, 2001.

SLOVENIA

Republic of Slovenia
Republika Slovenije

CAPITAL: Ljubljana

FLAG: Equal horizontal bands of white (top), blue, and red with seal superimposed on upper hoist side.

ANTHEM: *Zdravljica (A Toast).*

MONETARY UNIT: The currency of Slovenia is the euro, as of 1 January 2007. Previously, Slovenia's currency was the tolar. The euro itself consists of 100 euro cents. There are coins of 1, 2, 5, 10, 20 and 50 euro cents, 1 and 2 euros, and bills of 5, 10, 20, 50, 100, 200 and 500 euro. €1 = US$1.356 (or US$1 = €0.738) as of November 2011.

WEIGHTS AND MEASURES: The metric system is in force.

HOLIDAYS: New Year, 1–2 January; Prešeren Day, Day of Culture, 8 February; Resistance Day, 27 April; Labor Days, 1–2 May; National Statehood Day, 25 June; Assumption, 15 August; Reformation Day, 31 October; All Saints' Day, 1 November; Christmas Day, 25 December; Independence Day, 26 December. Movable holidays are Easter Sunday and Monday.

TIME: 1 p.m. = noon GMT.

¹LOCATION, SIZE, AND EXTENT

Slovenia is located in central Europe. It is slightly larger than the state of New Jersey with a total area of 20,273 sq km (7,827 sq mi). Slovenia shares boundaries with Austria on the N, Hungary on the E, Croatia on the S, and the Adriatic Sea and Italy on the W, and has a total land boundary of 1,334 km (829 mi) and a coastline of 46.6 km (29 mi). Its capital city Ljubljana is located near the center of the country.

²TOPOGRAPHY

The topography of Slovenia features a small coastal strip on the Adriatic, the Julian Alps adjacent to Italy, the Karawanken Mountains of the northern border with Austria, and mixed mountains and valleys with numerous rivers in the central and eastern regions. The highest point of Mt. Triglav is found in the Julian Alps with an elevation of 2,864 m (9,396 ft). The longest river is the Sava, which flows through the center of the country for 221 km (137 mi). A unique feature of Slovenia is the presence of over 6,500 karst formed caves, the most well-known being the Skocjan caves in the southwest, which are designated as a natural UNESCO World Heritage Site.

³CLIMATE

Slovenia's coastal climate is influenced by the Mediterranean Sea. Its interior climate ranges from mild to hot summers, with cold winters in the plateaus and valleys to the east.

In Ljubljana, July's mean temperature is 20°C (68°F). The mean temperature in January is -1°C (30°F). Rainfall in the capital averages 139 cm (59 in) a year.

⁴FLORA AND FAUNA

The region's climate has given Slovenia a wealth of diverse flora and fauna. Ferns, flowers, mosses, and common trees populate the landscape. There are subtropical plants along the Adriatic Sea. The World Resources Institute estimates that there are 3,200 plant species in Slovenia.

Slovenia is home to 87 mammal, 350 bird, 29 reptile, and 18 amphibian species. The calculation reflects the total number of distinct species residing in the country, not the number of endemic species. Wild animals include deer, brown bear, rabbit, fox, and wild boar. Farmers plant vineyards on the hillsides and raise livestock in the fertile lowlands of the country.

⁵ENVIRONMENT

The World Resources Institute reported that Slovenia had designated 134,100 hectares (331,368 acres) of land for protection as of 2006. Water resources totaled 32.1 cu km (7.7 cu mi) while water usage was 0.9 cu km (0.216 cu mi) per year. Per capita water usage totaled 457 cu m (16,139 cu ft) per year.

Slovenia's natural environment suffers from damage to forests by industrial pollutants, especially chemical and metallurgical plant emissions and the resulting acid rain. Water pollution is also a problem. The Sava River is polluted with domestic and industrial waste; heavy metals and toxic chemicals can be found in the coastal waters. The country is subject to flooding and earthquakes. The UN reported in 2008 that carbon dioxide emissions in Slovenia totaled 15,096 kilotons.

One of the largest protected areas is Triglav National Park. According to a 2011 report issued by the International Union for

Conservation of Nature and Natural Resources (IUCN), threatened species included 4 types of mammals, 2 species of birds, 2 species of amphibians, 29 species of fish, and 41 species of invertebrates. Threatened species include the Italian agile frog, slender-billed curlew, beluga, Danube salmon, the garden dormouse, and the great snipe.

6 POPULATION

The US Central Intelligence Agency (CIA) estimated the population of Slovenia in 2011 to be approximately 2,000,092, which placed it at number 143 in population among the 196 nations of the world. In 2011 approximately 16.8% of the population was over 65 years of age, with another 13.4% under 15 years of age. The median age in Slovenia was 42.4 years. There were 0.95 males for every female in the country. The population's annual rate of change was -0.163%. The projected population for the year 2025 was 2,100,000. Population density in Slovenia was calculated at 99 people per sq km (256 people per sq mi).

The UN estimated that 50% of the population lived in urban areas in 2009, and that urban populations had an annual rate of change of 0.2%. The largest urban area was Ljubljana, with a population of 260,000. At the end of 2007, 12.8 percent of the Slovene population lived in Ljubljana.

7 MIGRATION

Estimates of Slovenia's net migration rate, carried out by the CIA in 2011, amounted to 0.39 migrants per 1,000 citizens. The total number of emigrants living abroad was 132,000, and the total number of immigrants living in Slovenia was 163,900. In 1995, Slovenia was harboring 29,000 refugees from the former Yugoslav SFR. Of the 5,000–10,000 that remained in 1999, most had opted not to take Slovene citizenship during a six-month window of opportunity in 1991–92 and had been living in the country as stateless persons ever since. In 1999, parliament passed legislation that offered these persons permanent resident status; a six-week window for applications closed at the end of the year.

8 ETHNIC GROUPS

According to the 2002 census, the total population at that point was 83.1% Slovene. Minority groups included Serbs (2%), Croats (1.8%), and Bosniaks (1.1%). There were about 10,467 Muslims, 6,243 Hungarians, 6,186 Albanians, 3,246 Roma and 2,254 Italians. Several minority groups faced social and governmental discrimination, including the Roma and those considered by the government to be "new" minorities (Serbs, Croats, Bosnians, and Kosovo Albanians).

9 LANGUAGES

Like Bosnian, Serbian, Croatian, Macedonian, and Bulgarian, Slovenian is a language of the South Slavonic group. Its closest linguistic relatives are those of the former Yugoslavia, but they are generally not mutually intelligible. Slovenian is written in the Roman alphabet and has the special letters č, š, and ž. The letters q, w, x, and y are missing. As of the 2002 Slovenian census, 91.1% of the populace spoke Slovenian (the official language); 4.5% spoke Serbo-Croatian and 4.4% used various other languages. Italian and Hungarian are considered official languages in a few communities with large populations of these minority groups.

10 RELIGIONS

According to the 2002 census, the largest denominational group in the country was the Roman Catholic Church, representing about 58% of the population. There was also a Slovenian Old Catholic Church and some Eastern Orthodox that made up about 2% of the population. Although Calvinism played an important role during the Reformation, the only well-established Protestant group was the Evangelical Lutheran Church of Slovenia, which had about 14,736 members. Muslims made up about 2% of the population. Jews accounted for less than 1% of the population. About 10% of the people responded as atheists or non-believers and 3% responded as believers that are not affiliated with any religion. Freedom of religion is guaranteed in the constitution. Religious organizations register with the Office of Religious Communities in order to secure legal status and conduct business. Easter Sunday and Monday, Pentecost, the Assumption, Reformation Day, and Christmas are observed as national holidays.

11 TRANSPORTATION

The Slovene government reported a total of 39,052 km (24,187 mi) of roads in 2009, all of which were paved. There were 565 vehicles per 1,000 people in the country. Slovenia had two expressways: one connecting Ljubljana, Postojna, and Razdrto with the coastal region; the other linking Ljubljana with Kranj and the Gorenjska region in the northwest and with the Karawanken tunnel to Austria.

Railroads extended for 1,228 km (763 mi). Emanating from Ljubljana, railroads connected the capital to Kranj and Jesenice, Postojna and Novo Gorica, Celje and Maribor, and Nova Mesto before continuing to Austria, Italy, and Croatia. There were 499 km (310 mi) of electrified rail. With over 150 passenger stations and 140 freight stations, almost every town in Slovenia can be reached by train. Slovenian Railways used high-speed trains and container transports.

There were 16 airports, which transported 953,378 passengers in 2009 according to the World Bank. The principal marine port was Koper. Technically there was no merchant fleet, but Slovenian owners had registered their respective vessels in other countries.

12 HISTORY

Slovenia is located in the central European area where Latin, Germanic, Slavic, and Magyar peoples have come into contact with one another. The historical dynamics of these four groups have impacted the development of this small nation.

Until the 8th–9th centuries AD, Slavs used the same common Slavic language that was codified by St. Cyril and Methodius in their AD 863 translations of Holy Scriptures into the Slavic tongue. Essentially an agricultural people, the Slovenes settled from around AD 550 in the eastern Alps and in the western Pannonian Plains. The ancestors of today's Slovenes developed their own form of political organization in which power was delegated to their rulers through an "electors" group of peasant leaders/soldiers (the "Kosezi"). Allies of the Bavarians against the Avars, whom they defeated in AD 743, the Carantania Slovenes came un-

LOCATION: 46°15′ N; 15°10′ E. BOUNDARY LENGTHS: Austria 262 kilometers (163 miles); Croatia, 455 kilometers (283 miles); Italy, 199 kilometers (124 miles); Hungary, 83 kilometers (52 miles).

der control of the numerically stronger Bavarians and both were overtaken by the Franks in AD 745.

In 863, the Greek scholars Constantine (Cyril) and Methodius were sent to Moravia, having first developed an original alphabet (called "Glagolitic") and translated the necessary Holy Scriptures into the Slavic tongue of the time. The work of the two "Apostles of the Slavs" was opposed by the Frankish Bishops who accused them of teaching heresy and using a nonsacred language and script. Invited by Pope Nicholas I to Rome to explain their work, the brothers visited with the Slovene Prince Kocelj in 867 and took along some 50 young men to be instructed in the Slavic scriptures and liturgy that were competing with the traditionally "sacred" liturgical languages of Latin and Greek. Political events prevented the utilization of the Slavic language in Central European Churches with the exception of Croatia and Bosnia. However, the liturgy in Slavic spread among Balkan and Eastern Slavs.

Slovenes view the installation of the Dukes of Carinthia with great pride as the expression of a nonfeudal, bottom-up delegation of authority by the people's "electors" through a ceremony inspired by old Slavic egalitarian customs. All the people assembled would intone a Slovene hymn of praise—"Glory and praise to God Almighty, who created heaven and earth, for giving us and our land the Duke and master according to our will."

This ceremony lasted for 700 years with some feudal accretions and was conducted in the Slovenian language until the last one in 1414. The uniqueness of the Carinthian installation ceremony is confirmed by several sources, including medieval reports, the writing of Pope Pius II in 1509, and its recounting in Jean Bodin's *Treatise on Republican Government* (1576) as "unrivaled in the entire world." In fact, Thomas Jefferson's copy of Bodin's *Republic* contains Jefferson's own initials calling attention to the description of the Carinthian installation and, therefore, to its conceptual impact on the writer of the American Declaration of Independence.

The eastward expansion of the Franks in the 9th century brought all Slovene lands under Frankish control. Carantania then lost its autonomy and, following the 955 victory of the Franks over the Hungarians, the Slovene lands were organized into separate frontier regions. This facilitated their colonization by German elements while inhibiting any effort at unifying the shrinking Slovene territories. Under the feudal system, various families of mostly Germanic nobility were granted fiefdoms over Slovene lands and competed among themselves bent on increasing their holdings.

The Bohemian King Premysl Otokar II was an exception and attempted to unite the Czech, Slovak, and Slovene lands in the second half of the 13th century. Otokar II acquired the Duchy of

Austria in 1251, Styria in 1260, and Carinthia, Carniola, and Istria in 1269, thus laying the foundation for the future Austrian empire. However, Otokar II was defeated in 1278 by a Hapsburg-led coalition that conquered Styria and Austria by 1282. The Hapsburgs, of Swiss origin, grew steadily in power and by the 15th century became the leading Austrian feudal family in control of most Slovene lands.

Christianization and the feudal system supported the Germanization process and created a society divided into "haves" (German) and "have nots" (Slovene), which were further separated into the nobility/urban dwellers versus the Slovene peasants/serfs. The Slovenes were deprived of their original, egalitarian "Freemen" rights and subjected to harsh oppression of economic, social, and political nature. The increasing demands imposed on the serfs due to the feudal lords' commitment in support of the fighting against the Turks and the suffering caused by Turkish invasions led to a series of insurrections by Slovene and Croat peasants in the 15th to 18th centuries, cruelly repressed by the feudal system.

Reformation

The Reformation gave an impetus to the national identity process through the efforts of Protestant Slovenes to provide printed materials in the Slovenian language in support of the Reformation movement itself. Martin Luther's translation of the New Testament into German in 1521 encouraged translations into other vernaculars, including the Slovenian. Thus Primož Trubar, a Slovenian Protestant preacher and scholar, published the first *Catechism* in Slovenian in 1551 and, among other works, a smaller elementary grammar (*abecedarium*) of the Slovenian language in 1552. These works were followed by the complete Slovenian translation of the Bible by Jurij Dalmatin in 1578, printed in 1584. The same year Adam Bohorič published, in Latin, the first comprehensive grammar of the Slovenian language which was also the first published grammar of any Slavic language. The first Slovenian publishing house (1575) and a Jesuit College (1595) were established in Ljubljana, the central Slovenian city, and between 1550 and 1600 over 50 books in Slovenian were published. In addition, Primož Trubar and his co-workers encouraged the opening of Slovenian elementary and high schools. This sudden explosion of literary activity built the foundation for the further development of literature in Slovenian and its use by the educated classes of Slovenes. The Catholic Counter-Reformation reacted to the spread of Protestantism very strongly within Catholic Austria, and slowed down the entire process until the Napoleonic period. Despite these efforts, important cultural institutions were established, such as an Academy of Arts and Sciences (1673) and the Philharmonic Society in 1701 (perhaps the oldest in Europe).

The Jesuits, heavily involved in the Counter-Reformation, had to use religious literature and songs in the Slovene language, but generally Latin was used as the main language in Jesuit schools. However, the first Catholic books in Slovenian were issued in 1615 to assist priests in the reading of Gospel passages and delivery of sermons. The Protestant books in Slovenian were used for such purposes, and they thus assisted in the further development of a standard literary Slovenian. Since Primož Trubar used his dialect from the Carniola region, it heavily influenced the literary standard. From the late 17th and through the 18th century the Slovenes continued their divided existence under Austrian control.

Standing over trade routes connecting the German/Austrian hinterland to the Adriatic Sea and the Italian plains eastward into the Balkan region, the Slovenes partook of the benefits from such trade in terms of both economic and cultural enrichment. Thus by the end of the 18th century, a significant change occurred in the urban centers where an educated Slovene middle class came into existence. Deeply rooted in the Slovene peasantry, this element ceased to assimilate into the Germanized mainstream and began to assert its own cultural/national identity. Many of their sons were educated in German, French, and Italian universities and thus exposed to the influence of the Enlightenment. Such a person was, for instance, Baron Ziga Zois (1749–1819), an industrialist, landowner, and linguist who became the patron of the Slovene literary movement. When the ideas of the French Revolution spread through Europe and the Napoleonic conquest reached the Slovenes, they were ready to embrace them.

During the reign of Maria Teresa (1740–80) and Joseph II (1780–90), the influence of Jansenism—the emancipation of serfs, the introduction of public schools (in German), equality of religions, closing of monasteries not involved in education or tending to the sick—weakened the hold of the nobility. On the other hand, the stronger Germanization emphasis generated resistance to it from an awakening Slovene national consciousness and the publication of Slovene nonreligious works, such as Marko Pohlin's *Abecedika* (1765), a *Carniolan Grammar* (1783) with explanations in German, and other educational works in Slovenian, which include a Slovenian-German-Latin dictionary (1781). Pohlin's theory of metrics and poetics became the foundation of secular poetry in Slovenian, which reached its zenith only 50 years later with France Prešeren (1800–49), still considered the greatest Slovene poet. Just prior to the short Napoleonic occupation of Slovenia, the first Slovenian newspaper was published in 1797 by Valentin Vodnik (1758–1819), a very popular poet and grammarian. The first drama in Slovenian appeared in 1789 by Anton Tomaž Linhart (1756–95), playwright and historian of Slovenes and South Slavs. Both authors were members of Baron Zois' circle.

Napoleon and the Spring of Nations

When Napoleon defeated Austria and established his Illyrian Provinces (1809–13), comprising the southern half of the Slovenian lands, parts of Croatia, and Dalmatia all the way to Dubrovnik with Ljubljana as the capital, the Slovene language was encouraged in the schools and also used, along with French, as an official language in order to communicate with the Slovene population. The four-year French occupation served to reinforce the national awakening of the Slovenes and other nations that had been submerged through the long feudal era of the Austrian Empire. Austria, however, regained the Illyrian Provinces in 1813 and reestablished its direct control over the Slovene lands.

The 1848 "spring of nations" brought about various demands for national freedom of Slovenes and other Slavic nations of Austria. An important role was played by Jernej Kopitar with his influence as librarian/censor in the Imperial Library in Vienna, as the developer of Slavic studies in Austria, as the mentor to Vuk Karadžić (one of the founders of the contemporary Serbo-Croatian language standard), as the advocate of Austro-Slavism (a state for all Slavs of Austria), and as author of the first modern Slovenian grammar in 1808. In mid-May 1848, the "United Slovenia" manifesto demanded that the Austrian Emperor establish a Kingdom of Slovenia with its own parliament, consisting of the then-separate historical regions of Carniola, Carinthia, Styria, and the Littoral, with Slovenian as its official language. This kingdom would remain a part of Austria, but not of the German Empire. While other nations based their demands on the "historical statehood" principle, the Slovenian demands were based on the principle of national self-determination some 70 years before American President Woodrow Wilson would embrace the principle in his "Fourteen Points."

Matija Kavčič, one of 14 Slovenian deputies elected to the 1848–49 Austrian parliament, proposed a plan of turning the Austrian Empire into a federation of 14 national states that would completely do away with the system of historic regions based on the old feudal system. At the 1848 Slavic Congress in Prague, the Slovenian delegates also demanded the establishment of the Slovenian University in Ljubljana. A map of a United Slovenia was designed by Peter Kozler based on then available ethnic data. It was confiscated by Austrian authorities, and Kozler was accused of treason in 1852 but was later released for insufficient evidence. The revolts of 1848 were repressed after a few years, and absolutistic regimes kept control on any movements in support of national rights. However, recognition was given to equal rights of the Slovenian language in principle, while denied in practice by the German/Hungarian element that considered Slovenian the language of servants and peasants. Even the "minimalist" Maribor program of 1865 (a common assembly of deputies from the historical provinces to discuss mutual problems) was fiercely opposed by most Austrians that supported the Pan-German plan of a unified German nation from the Baltic to the Adriatic seas. The Slovenian nation was blocking the Pan-German plan simply by being located between the Adriatic Sea (Trieste) and the German/Austrian Alpine areas; therefore, any concessions had to be refused in order to speed up its total assimilation. Hitler's World War II plan to "cleanse" the Slovenians was an accelerated approach to the same end by use of extreme violence.

Toward "Yugoslavism"

In 1867, the German and Hungarian majorities agreed to the reorganization of the state into a "Dualistic" Austro-Hungarian Monarchy in order to be better able to control the minority elements in each half of the empire. The same year, in view of such intransigence, the Slovenes reverted back to their "maximalist" demand of a "United Slovenia" (1867 Ljubljana Manifesto) and initiated a series of mass political meetings, called "Tabori," after the Czech model. Their motto became "Umreti nočemo!" ("We refuse to die!"), and a movement was initiated to bring about a cultural/political coalition of Slovenes, Croats, and Serbs of Austria-Hungary in order to more successfully defend themselves from the increasing efforts of Germanization/Magyarization. At the same time, Slovenes, Croats, and Serbs followed with great interest several movements of national liberation and unification, such as those in Italy, Germany, Greece, and Serbia, and drew from them much inspiration. While Austria lost its northern Italian provinces to the Italian "Risorgimento," it gained, on the other hand, Bosnia and Herzegovina through occupation (1878) and annexation (1908). These actions increased the interest of Slovenes, Croats, and Serbs of Austro-Hungary in a "Trialistic" arrangement that would allow the South Slavic groups ("Yugoslavs") to form their own joint (and "Third") unit within Austro-Hungary. A federalist solution, they believed, would make possible the survival of a country to which they had been loyal subjects for many centuries. Crown Prince Ferdinand supported this approach, called "The United States of greater Austria" by his advisers, also because it would remove the attraction of a Greater Serbia. But the German leadership's sense of its own superiority and consequent expansionist goals prevented any compromise and led to two world wars.

World War I and Royal Yugoslavia

Unable to achieve their maximalist goals, the Slovenes concentrated their effort at the micro-level and made tremendous strides prior to World War I in introducing education in Slovenian, organizing literary and reading rooms in every town, participating in economic development, upgrading their agriculture, organizing cultural societies and political parties, such as the Catholic People's Party in 1892 and the Liberal Party in 1894, and participating in the Socialist movement of the 1890s. World War I brought about the dissolution of centuries-old ties between the Slovenes and the Austrian Monarchy and the Croats/Serbs with the Hungarian Crown. Toward the end of the war, on 12 August 1918, the National Council for Slovenian Lands was formed in Ljubljana. On 12 October 1918, the National Council for all Slavs of former Austro-Hungary was founded in Zagreb, Croatia, and was chaired by Msgr. Anton Korošec, head of the Slovenian People's Party. This Council proclaimed on 29 October 1918 the separation of the South Slavs from Austro-Hungary and the formation of a new state of Slovenes, Croats, and Serbs.

A National Government for Slovenia was established in Ljubljana. The Zagreb Council intended to negotiate a Federal Union with the Kingdom of Serbia that would preserve the respective national autonomies of the Slovenes, Croats, and Serbs. Msgr. Korošec had negotiated a similar agreement in Geneva with Nikola Pašić, his Serbian counterpart, but a new Serbian government reneged on it. There was no time for further negotiations due to the Italian occupation of much Slovenian and Croatian territory and only Serbia, a victor state, could resist Italy. Thus, a delegation of the Zagreb Council submitted to Serbia a declaration expressing the will to unite with The Kingdom of Serbia. At that time, there were no conditions presented or demand made regarding the type of union, and Serbia immediately accepted the proposed unification under its strongly centralized government; a unitary "Kingdom of Serbs, Croats, and Slovenes" was declared on 1 December 1918. Because of the absence of an initial compromise between the Unitarists and Federalists, what became Yugoslavia never gained a solid consensual foundation. Serbs were winners and viewed their expansion as liberation of their Slavic brethren from Austria-Hungary, as compensation for their tremendous war sacrifices, and as the realization of their "Greater Serbia" goal. Slovenes and Croats, while freed from the Austro-Hungarian domination, were nevertheless the losers in terms of their desired political/cultural autonomy. In addition, they suffered painful territorial losses to Italy (some 700,000 Slovenes and Croats were denied any national rights by Fascist Italy and subjected to all kinds of persecutions) and to Austria (a similar fate for some 100,000 Slovenes left within Austria in the Carinthia region).

After 10 years of a contentious parliamentary system that ended in the murder of Croatian deputies and their leader Stjepan Radić, King Alexander abrogated the 1921 constitution, dissolved the parliament and political parties, took over power directly, and renamed the country "Yugoslavia." He abolished the 33 administrative departments that had replaced the historic political/national regions in favor of administrative areas named mostly after rivers. A new policy was initiated with the goal of creating a single "Yugoslav" nation out of the three "Tribes" of Serbs, Croats, and Slovenes. But in practice this policy meant the King's Serbian hegemony over the rest of the nations. The reaction was intense, and King Alexander himself fell victim of Croat-Ustaša and Macedonian terrorists and died in Marseille in 1934. A regency ruled Yugoslavia, headed by Alexander's cousin, Prince Paul, who managed to reach an agreement in 1939 with the Croats. An autonomous Croatian "Banovina" headed by "Ban" Ivan Subašić was established, including most Croatian lands outside of the Bosnia and Herzegovina area. Strong opposition developed among Serbs because they viewed the Croatian Banovina as a privilege for Croats while Serbs were split among six old administrative units with a large Serbian population left inside the Croatian Banovina itself. Still, there might have been a chance for further similar agreements that would have satisfied the Serbs and Slovenes. But there was no time left—Hitler and his allies (Italy, Hungary, Bulgaria) attacked Yugoslavia on 6 April 1941, after a coup on 27 March 1941 had deposed Prince Paul's government, which had yielded to Hitler's pressures on 25 March. Thus the first Yugoslavia, born out of the distress of World War I, had not had time to consolidate and work out its problems in a mere 23 years and was then dismembered by its aggressors. Still, the first Yugoslavia allowed the Slovenes a chance for fuller development of their cultural, economic, and political life, in greater freedom and relative independence for the first time in modern times.

World War II

Slovenia was divided in 1941 among Germany, Italy, and Hungary. Germany annexed northern Slovenia, mobilized its men into the German army, interned, expelled, or killed most of the Slovenian leaders, and removed to labor camps the populations of entire areas, repopulating them with Germans. Italy annexed southern Slovenia but did not mobilize its men. In both areas, particularly the Italian, resistance movements were initiated by both nationalist groups and by Communist-dominated Partisans, the latter particularly after Hitler's attack on the Soviet Union on 22 June 1941. The Partisans claimed monopoly of the resistance leadership and dealt cruelly with anyone that dared to oppose their intended power grab. Spontaneous resistance to the Partisans by the non-Communist Slovenian peasantry led to a bloody civil war in Slovenia under foreign occupiers, who encouraged the bloodshed. The resistance movement led by General Draža Mihajlović, appointed minister of war of the Yugoslav government-in-exile, was handicapped by the exile government's lack of unity and clear purpose (mostly due to the fact that the Serbian side had reneged on the 1939 agreement on Croatia). On the other hand, Winston Churchill, convinced by rather one-sided reports that Mihajlović was "collaborating" with the Germans while the Partisans under Marshal Tito were the ones "who killed more Germans," decided to recognize Tito as the only legitimate Yugoslav resistance.

Though aware of Tito's communist allegiance to Stalin, Churchill threw his support to Tito, and forced the Yugoslav government-in-exile into a coalition government with Tito, who had no intention of keeping the agreement and, in fact, would have fought against an Allied landing in Yugoslavia along with the Germans.

When Soviet armies, accompanied by Tito, entered Yugoslavia from Romania and Bulgaria in the fall of 1944, military units and civilians that had opposed the Partisans retreated to Austria or Italy. Among them were the Cetnik units of Draža Mihajlović and "homeguards" from Serbia, Croatia, and Slovenia that had been under German control but were pro-Allies in their convictions and hopes. Also in retreat were the units of the Croatian Ustaša that had collaborated with Italy and Germany in order to achieve (and control) an "independent" greater Croatia and, in the process, had committed terrible and large-scale massacres of Serbs, Jews, Gypsies, and others who opposed them. Serbs and Partisans counteracted, and a fratricidal civil war raged over Yugoslavia. After the end of the war, the Communist-led forces took control of Slovenia and Yugoslavia and instituted a violent dictatorship that committed systematic crimes and human rights violations on an unexpectedly large scale. Thousands upon thousands of their former opponents that were returned, unaware, from Austria by British military authorities were tortured and massacred by Partisan executioners.

Communist Yugoslavia

Such was the background for the formation of the second Yugoslavia as a Federative People's Republic of five nations (Slovenes, Croats, Serbs, Macedonians, Montenegrins) with their individual republics and Bosnia and Herzegovina as a buffer area with its mix of Serb, Muslim, and Croat populations. The problem of large Hungarian and Muslim Albanian populations in Serbia was solved by creating for them the autonomous region of Vojvodina (Hungarian minority) and Kosovo (Muslim Albanian majority) that assured their political and cultural development. Tito attempted a balancing act to satisfy most of the nationality issues that were carried over unresolved from the first Yugoslavia, but failed to satisfy anyone.

Compared to pre-1941 Yugoslavia where Serbs enjoyed a controlling role, the numerically stronger Serbs had lost both the Macedonian area they considered "Southern Serbia" and the opportunity to incorporate Montenegro into Serbia, as well as losing direct control over the Hungarian minority in Vojvodina and the Muslim Albanians of Kosovo, viewed as the cradle of the Serbian nation since the Middle Ages. They further were not able to incorporate into Serbia the large Serbian populated areas of Bosnia and had not obtained an autonomous region for the large minority of Serbian population within the Croatian Republic. The Croats, while gaining back the Medjumurje area from Hungary, and from Italy, the cities of Rijeka (Fiume), Zadar (Zara), some Dalmatian islands, and the Istrian Peninsula had, on the other hand, lost other areas. These included the Srem area to Serbia, and also Bosnia and Herzegovina, which had been part of the World War II "independent" Croatian state under the Ustaša leadership.

In addition, the Croats were confronted with a deeply resentful Serbian minority that became ever more pervasive in public administrative and security positions. The Slovenes had regained the Prekmurje enclave from Hungary and most of the Slovenian lands that had been taken over by Italy following World War I (Julian region and Northern Istria), except for the "Venetian Slovenia" area, the Gorizia area, and the port city of Trieste. The latter was initially part of the UN protected "Free Territory of Trieste," split in 1954 between Italy and Yugoslavia with Trieste itself given to Italy. Nor were the Slovenian claims to the southern Carinthia area of Austria satisfied. The loss of Trieste was a bitter pill for the Slovenes and many blamed it on the fact that Tito's Yugoslavia was, initially, Stalin's advance threat to Western Europe, thus making the Allies more supportive of Italy.

The official position of the Marxist Yugoslav regime was that national rivalries and conflicting interests would gradually diminish through their sublimation into a new Socialist order. Without capitalism, nationalism was supposed to wither away. Therefore, in the name of their "unity and brotherhood" motto, any nationalistic expression of concern was prohibited and repressed by the dictatorial and centralized regime of the "League of Yugoslav Communists" acting through the "Socialist Alliance" as its mass front organization.

After a short postwar "coalition" government period, the elections of 11 November 1945, boycotted by the non-communist "coalition" parties, gave the Communist-led People's Front 90% of the vote. A Constituent Assembly met on 29 November, abolishing the monarchy and establishing the Federative People's Republic of Yugoslavia. In January 1946 a new constitution was adopted, based on the 1936 Soviet constitution. The Stalin-engineered expulsion of Yugoslavia from the Soviet-dominated Cominform Group in 1948 was actually a blessing for Yugoslavia after its leadership was able to survive Stalin's pressures. Survival had to be justified, both practically and in theory, by developing a "Road to Socialism" based on Yugoslavia's own circumstances. This new "road map" evolved rather quickly in response to some of Stalin's accusations and Yugoslavia's need to perform a balancing act between the North Atlantic Treaty Organization (NATO) alliance and the Soviet bloc. Tito quickly nationalized the economy through a policy of forced industrialization, to be supported by the collectivization of the agriculture.

The agricultural reform of 1945–46 (limited private ownership of a maximum of 35 hectares/85 acres, and a limited free market after the initial forced delivery of quotas to the state at very low prices) had to be abandoned because of the strong resistance by the peasants. The actual collectivization efforts were initiated in 1949 using welfare benefits and lower taxes as incentives along with direct coercion. But collectivization had to be abandoned by 1958 simply because its inefficiency and low productivity could not support the concentrated effort of industrial development.

By the 1950s Yugoslavia had initiated the development of its internal trademark: self-management of enterprises through workers councils and local decision-making as the road to Marx's "withering away of the state." The second five-year plan (1957–61), as opposed to the failed first one (1947–51), was completed in four years by relying on the well-established self-management system. Economic targets were set from the local to the republic level and then coordinated by a Federal Planning Institute to meet an overall national economic strategy. This system supported a period of very rapid industrial growth in the 1950s from a very low base. But a high consumption rate encouraged a volume of imports far in excess of exports, largely financed by foreign loans. In addi-

tion, inefficient and low productivity industries were kept in place through public subsidies, cheap credit, and other artificial measures that led to a serious crisis by 1961.

Reforms were necessary and, by 1965, "market socialism" was introduced with laws that abolished most price controls and halved import duties while withdrawing export subsidies. After necessary amounts were left with the earning enterprise, the rest of the earned foreign currencies were deposited with the national bank and used by the state, other enterprises, or were used to assist less-developed areas. Councils were given more decision-making power in investing their earnings, and they also tended to vote for higher salaries in order to meet steep increases in the cost of living. Unemployment grew rapidly even though "political factories" were still subsidized. The government thus relaxed its restrictions to allow labor migration, particularly to West Germany where workers were needed for its thriving economy. Foreign investment was encouraged up to 49% in joint enterprises, and barriers to the movement of people and exchange of ideas were largely removed.

The role of trade unions continued to be one of transmission of instructions from government to workers, allocation of perks along with the education/training of workers, monitoring legislation, and overall protection of the self-management system. Strikes were legally neither allowed nor forbidden, but until the 1958 miners strike in Trbovlje, Slovenia, were not publicly acknowledged and were suppressed. After 1958, strikes were tolerated as an indication of problems to be resolved. Unions, however, did not initiate strikes but were expected to convince workers to go back to work.

Having survived its expulsion from the Cominform in 1948 and Stalin's attempts to take control, Yugoslavia began to develop a foreign policy independent of the Soviet Union. By mid-1949 Yugoslavia withdrew its support from the Greek Communists in their civil war against the then-Royalist government. In October 1949, Yugoslavia was elected to one of the nonpermanent seats on the UN Security Council and openly condemned North Korea's aggression toward South Korea. Following the "rapprochement" opening with the Soviet Union, initiated by Nikita Khrushchev and his 1956 denunciation of Stalin, Tito intensified his work on developing the movement of nonaligned "third world" nations as Yugoslavia's external trademark in cooperation with Nehru of India, Nasser of Egypt, and others. With the September 1961 Belgrade summit conference of nonaligned nations, Tito became the recognized leader of the movement. The nonaligned position served Tito's Yugoslavia well by allowing Tito to draw on economic and political support from the Western powers while neutralizing any aggression from the Soviet bloc. While Tito had acquiesced, reluctantly, to the 1956 Soviet invasion of Hungary for fear of chaos and any liberalizing impact on Yugoslavia, he condemned the Soviet invasion of Dubček's Czechoslovakia in 1968, as did Romania's Ceausescu, both fearing their countries might be the next in line for "corrective" action by the Red Army and the Warsaw Pact. Just before his death on 4 May 1980, Tito also condemned the Soviet invasion of Afghanistan. Yugoslavia actively participated in the 1975 Helsinki Conference and agreements and the first 1977–78 review conference that took place in Belgrade, even though Yugoslavia's one-party Communist regime perpetrated and condoned numerous human rights violations. Overall, in the 1970s–80s Yugoslavia maintained fairly good relations with its neighboring states by playing down or solving pending disputes such as the Trieste issue with Italy in 1975, and developing cooperative projects and increased trade.

Compared to the other republics of the Federative People's Republic of Yugoslavia, the Republic of Slovenia had several advantages. It was 95% homogeneous. The Slovenes had the highest level of literacy. Their prewar economy was the most advanced and so was their agriculture, which was based on an extensive network of peasant cooperatives and savings and loans institutions developed as a primary initiative of the Slovenian People's Party ("clerical"). Though ravaged by the war, occupation, resistance and civil war losses, and preoccupied with carrying out the elimination of all actual and potential opposition, the Communist government faced the double task of building its Socialist economy while rebuilding the country. As an integral part of the Yugoslav federation, Slovenia was, naturally, affected by Yugoslavia's internal and external political developments. The main problems facing communist Yugoslavia/Slovenia were essentially the same as the unresolved ones under Royalist Yugoslavia. As the "Royal Yugoslavism" had failed in its assimilative efforts, so did the "Socialist Yugoslavism" fail to overcome the forces of nationalism. In the case of Slovenia there were several key factors in the continued attraction to its national identity: more than a thousand years of historical development; a location within Central Europe (not part of the Balkan area) and related identification with Western European civilization; the Catholic religion with the traditional role of Catholic priests (even under the persecutions by the Communist regime); the most developed and productive economy with a standard of living far superior to most other areas of the Yugoslav Federation; and finally, the increased political and economic autonomy enjoyed by the Republic after the 1974 constitution, particularly following Tito's death in 1980. Tito's motto of "unity and brotherhood" was replaced by "freedom and democracy" to be achieved through either a confederative rearrangement of Yugoslavia or by complete independence.

In December 1964, the eighth Congress of the League of Communists of Yugoslavia (LCY) acknowledged that ethnic prejudice and antagonisms existed in socialist Yugoslavia and went on record against the position that Yugoslavia's nations had become obsolete and were disintegrating into a socialist "Yugoslavism." Thus the republics, based on individual nations, became bastions of a strong Federalism that advocated the devolution and decentralization of authority from the federal to the republic level. "Yugoslav Socialist Patriotism" was at times defined as a deep feeling for both one's own national identity and for the socialist self-management of Yugoslavia. Economic reforms were the other focus of the Eighth LCY Congress, led by Croatia and Slovenia with emphasis on efficiencies and local economic development decisions with profit criteria as their basis. The "liberal" bloc (Slovenia, Croatia, Macedonia, Vojvodina) prevailed over the "conservative" group and the reforms of 1965 did away with central investment planning and "political factories." The positions of the two blocs hardened into a national-liberal coalition that viewed the conservative, centralist group led by Serbia as the "Greater Serbian" attempt at majority domination. The devolution of power in economic decision-making spearheaded by the Slovenes assisted in the "federalization" of the League of Communists of Yugoslavia as a league of "quasi-sovereign" republican parties. Under strong prodding from the Croats, the party agreed in 1970 to the principle of unanimity for decision-making that, in practice, meant a veto power for each republic. However, the concentration of economic resources in Serbian hands continued with Belgrade banks controlling half of total credits and some 80% of foreign credits. This was also combined with the fear of Serbian political and cultural domination, particularly with respect to Croatian language sensitivities, which had been aroused by the use of the Serbian version of Serbo-Croatian as the norm, with the Croatian version as a deviation. The debates over the reforms of the 1960s led to a closer scrutiny, not only of the economic system, but also of the decision-making process at the republic and federal levels, particularly the investment of funds to less developed areas that Slovenia and Croatia felt were very poorly managed, if not squandered. Other issues fueled acrimony between individual nations, such as the 1967 Declaration in Zagreb claiming a Croatian linguistic and literary tradition separate from the Serbian one, thus undermining the validity of the Serbo-Croatian language. Also, Kosovo Albanians and Montenegrins, along with Slovenes and Croats, began to assert their national rights as superior to the Federation ones.

The language controversy exacerbated the economic and political tensions between Serbs and Croats, which spilled into the easily inflamed area of ethnic confrontations. To the conservative centralists the devolution of power to the republic level meant the subordination of the broad "Yugoslav" and "Socialist" interests to the narrow "nationalist" interest of republic national majorities. With the Croat League of Communists taking the liberal position in 1970, nationalism was rehabilitated. Thus the "Croatian Spring" bloomed and impacted all the other republics of Yugoslavia. Meanwhile, through a series of 1967–68 constitutional amendments that had limited federal power in favor of the republics and autonomous provinces, the federal government came to be seen by liberals more as an inter-republican problem-solving mechanism bordering on a confederative arrangement. A network of inter-republican committees established by mid-1971 proved to be very efficient at resolving a large number of difficult issues in a short time. The coalition of liberals and nationalists in Croatia also generated sharp condemnation in Serbia whose own brand of nationalism grew stronger, but as part of a conservative/centralist alliance. Thus the liberal/federalist versus conservative/centralist opposition became entangled in the rising nationalism within each opposing bloc. The situation in Croatia and Serbia was particularly difficult because of their minorities' issues—Serbian in Croatia and Hungarian/Albanian in Serbia.

Serbs in Croatia sided with the Croat conservatives and sought a constitutional amendment guaranteeing their own national identity and rights and, in the process, challenged the sovereignty of the Croatian nation and state as well as the right to self-determination, including the right to secession. The conservatives won and the amendment declared that "the Socialist Republic of Croatia (was) the national state of the Croatian nation, the state of the Serbian nation in Croatia, and the state of the nationalities inhabiting it."

Slovenian "Spring"

Meanwhile, Slovenia, not burdened by large minorities, developed a similar liberal and nationalist direction along with Croatia. This fostered an incipient separatist sentiment opposed by both the liberal and conservative party wings. Led by Stane Kavčič, head of the Slovenian government, the liberal wing gained as much local political latitude as possible from the federal level during the early 1970s "Slovenian Spring." By the summer of 1971, the Serbian party leadership was pressuring President Tito to put an end to the "dangerous" development of Croatian nationalism. While Tito wavered because of his support for the balancing system of autonomous republic units, the situation quickly reached critical proportions.

Croat nationalists, complaining about discrimination against Croats in Bosnia and Herzegovina, demanded the incorporation of Western Herzegovina into Croatia. Serbia countered by claiming Southeastern Herzegovina for itself. Croats also advanced claims to a larger share of their foreign currency earnings, to the issuance of their own currency, the creation of their own national bank that would directly negotiate foreign loans, the printing of Croatian postage stamps, the creation of a Croatian army, and recognition of the Croatian Sabor (assembly) as the highest Croatian political body, and, finally, to Croatian secession and complete independence. Confronted with such intensive agitation, the liberal Croatian party leadership could not back down and did not try to restrain the maximalist public demands nor the widespread university students' strike of November 1971. This situation caused a loss of support from the liberal party wings of Slovenia and even Macedonia. At this point Tito intervened, condemned the Croatian liberal leadership on 1 December 1971, and supported the conservative wing. The liberal leadership group resigned on 12 December 1971. When Croatian students demonstrated and demanded an independent Croatia, the Yugoslav army was ready to move in if necessary. A wholesale purge of the party liberals followed with tens of thousands expelled, key functionaries lost their positions, several thousand were imprisoned (including Franjo Tudjman, who later became president in independent Croatia), and leading Croatian nationalist organizations and their publications were closed.

On 8 May 1972, the Croatian party also expelled its liberal wing leaders and the purge of nationalists continued through 1973 in Croatia, as well as in Slovenia and Macedonia. However, the issues and sentiments raised during the "Slovene and Croat Springs" of 1969–71 did not disappear. Tito and the conservatives were forced to satisfy nominally some demands. The 1974 constitution was an attempt to resolve the strained inter-republican relations as each republic pursued its own interests over and above an overall "Yugoslav" interest. The repression of liberal-nationalist Croats was accompanied by the growing influence of the Serbian element in the Croatian Party (24% in 1980) and police force (majority) that contributed to the continued persecution and imprisonments of Croatian nationalists into the 1980s.

Yugoslavia—A House Divided

In Slovenia, developments took a direction of their own. The purge of the nationalists took place as in Croatia but on a lesser scale, and after a decade or so, nationalism was revived through the development of grassroots movements in the arts, music, peace, and environmental concerns. Activism was particularly strong among young people, who shrewdly used the regime-supported youth organizations, youth periodicals—such as *Mladina* (in Ljubljana) and *Katedra* (in Maribor)—and an independent student radio sta-

tion. The journal *Nova Revija* published a series of articles focusing on problems confronting the Slovenian nation in February 1987; these included such varied topics as the status of the Slovenian language, the role of the Communist Party, the multiparty system, and independence. The *Nova Revija* was in reality a Slovenian national manifesto that, along with yearly public opinion polls showing ever higher support for Slovenian independence, indicated a definite mood toward secession. In this charged atmosphere, the Yugoslav army committed two actions that led the Slovenes to the path of actual separation from Yugoslavia. In March 1988, the army's Military Council submitted a confidential report to the federal presidency claiming that Slovenia was planning a counter revolution and calling for repressive measures against liberals and a *coup d'état*. An army document delineating such actions was delivered by an army sergeant to the journal *Mladina*; before the document could be published, the editor and two journalists were arrested by the army on 31 March 1988. Meanwhile, the strong intervention of the Slovenian political leadership succeeded in stopping any army action. But the four men involved in the affair were put on trial by the Yugoslav army.

The second army *faux pas* was to hold the trial in Ljubljana, capital of Slovenia, and to conduct it in the Serbo-Croatian language, an action declared constitutional by the Yugoslav presidency, claiming that Slovenian law could not be applied to the Yugoslav army. This trial brought about complete unity among Slovenians in opposition to the Yugoslav army and what it represented, and the four individuals on trial became overnight heroes. One of them was Janez Jansa who had written articles in *Mladina* critical of the Yugoslav army and was the head of the Slovenian pacifist movement and president of the Slovenian Youth Organization. (Ironically, three years later Janša led the successful defense of Slovenia against the Yugoslav army and became the first minister of defense of independent Slovenia.) The four men were found guilty and sentenced to jail terms from four years (Janša) to five months. The total mobilization of Slovenia against the military trials led to the formation of the first non-Communist political organizations and political parties. In a time of perceived national crisis, both the Communist and non-Communist leadership found it possible to work closely together. But from that time on the liberal/nationalist vs. conservative/centralist positions hardened in Yugoslavia and no amount of negotiation at the federal presidency level regarding a possible confederal solution could hold Yugoslavia together any longer.

Since 1986, work had been done on amendments to the 1974 constitution that, when submitted in 1987, created a furor, particularly in Slovenia, due to the proposed creation of a unified legal system, the establishment of central control over the means of transportation and communication, centralization of the economy into a unified market, and the granting of more control to Serbia over its autonomous provinces of Kosovo and Vojvodina. This all came at the expense of the individual republics. A recentralization of the League of Communists was also recommended but opposed by liberal/nationalist groups. Serbia's President Slobodan Milošević also proposed changes to the bicameral Federal Skupština (Assembly) by replacing it with a tricameral one where deputies would no longer be elected by their republican assemblies but through a "one person, one vote" national system. Slovenia, Croatia, and Bosnia and Herzegovina strongly opposed the change as they opposed the additional Chamber of Associated Labor that would have increased the federal role in the economy. The debates over the recentralizing amendments caused an even greater focus in Slovenia and Croatia on the concept of a confederative structure based on self-determination by "sovereign" states and a multiparty democratic system as the only one that could maintain some semblance of a "Yugoslav" state.

By 1989 and the period following the Serbian assertion of control in the Kosovo and Vojvodina provinces, as well as in the republic of Montenegro, relations between Slovenia and Serbia reached a crisis point: Serbian President Milošević attempted to orchestrate mass demonstrations by Serbs in Ljubljana, the capital city of Slovenia, and the Slovenian leadership vetoed it. Then Serbs started to boycott Slovenian products, to withdraw their savings from Slovenian banks, and to terminate economic cooperation and trade with Slovenia.

Serbian President Milošević's tactics were extremely distasteful to the Slovenians and the use of force against the Albanian population of the Kosovo province worried the Slovenes (and Croats) about the possible use of force by Serbia against Slovenia itself. The tensions with Serbia convinced the Slovenian leadership of the need to take necessary protective measures.

In September 1989, draft amendments to the constitution of Slovenia were published that included the right to secession, and the sole right of the Slovenian legislature to introduce martial law. The Yugoslav army particularly needed the amendment granting control over deployment of armed forces in Slovenia, since the Yugoslav army, controlled by a mostly Serbian/Montenegrin officer corps dedicated to the preservation of a Communist system, had a self-interest in preserving the source of their own budgetary allocations of some 51% of the Yugoslav federal budget.

A last attempt at salvaging Yugoslavia was to be made at the extraordinary Congress of the League of Communists of Yugoslavia convened in January 1990 to review proposed reforms such as free multiparty elections and freedom of speech. The Slovenian delegation attempted to broaden the spectrum of reforms but was rebuffed and walked out on 23 January 1990, pulling out of the Yugoslav League. The Slovenian Communists then renamed their party the Party for Democratic Renewal.

The political debate in Slovenia intensified and some 19 parties were formed by early 1990. On 10 April 1990 the first free elections since before World War II were held in Slovenia, where there still was a three-chamber Assembly: political affairs, associated labor, and territorial communities. A coalition of six newly formed democratic parties, called *Demos*, won 55% of the votes, with the remainder going to the Party for Democratic Renewal, the former Communists (17%), the Socialist Party (5%), and the Liberal Democratic Party—heir to the Slovenia Youth Organization—(15%). The *Demos* coalition organized the first freely elected Slovenian government of the post-Communist era with Dr. Lojze Peterle as the prime minister.

Milan Kucan, former head of the League of Communists of Slovenia, was elected president with 54% of the vote in recognition of his efforts to affect a bloodless transfer of power from a monopoly by the Communist party to a free multiparty system and his standing up to the recentralizing attempts by Serbia.

Toward Independence

In October 1990, Slovenia and Croatia published a joint proposal for a Yugoslavian confederation as a last attempt at a negotiated solution, but to no avail. The Slovenian legislature also adopted in October a draft constitution proclaiming that "Slovenia will become an independent state." On 23 December 1990, a plebiscite was held on Slovenia's disassociation from Yugoslavia if a confederate solution could not be negotiated within a six-month period. An overwhelming majority of 89% of voters approved the secession provision and a declaration of sovereignty was adopted on 26 December 1990. All federal laws were declared void in Slovenia as of 20 February 1991, and since no negotiated agreement was possible, Slovenia declared its independence on 25 June 1991. On 27 June 1991, the Yugoslav army tried to seize control of Slovenia and its common borders with Italy, Austria, and Hungary under the pretext that it was the army's constitutional duty to assure the integrity of Socialist Yugoslavia. The Yugoslav army units were surprised and shocked by the resistance they encountered from the Slovenian "territorial guards," who surrounded Yugoslav army tank units, isolated them, and engaged in close combat, mostly along border checkpoints that ended in most cases with Yugoslav units surrendering to the Slovenian forces. Fortunately, casualties were limited on both sides. Over 3,200 Yugoslav army soldiers surrendered and were well treated by the Slovenes, who scored a public relations coup by having the prisoners call their parents all over Yugoslavia to come to Slovenia and take their sons back home.

The war in Slovenia ended in 10 days due to the intervention of the European Community, who negotiated a cease-fire and a three-month moratorium on Slovenia's implementation of independence, giving the Yugoslav army time to retreat from Slovenia by the end of October 1991. Thus Slovenia was able to "disassociate" itself from Yugoslavia with a minimum of casualties, although the military operations caused considerable physical damages estimated at almost US$3 billion. On 23 December 1991, one year following the independence plebiscite, a new constitution was adopted by Slovenia establishing a parliamentary democracy with a bicameral legislature. Even though US Secretary of State James Baker in his visit to Belgrade on 21 June 1991 had declared that the United States opposed unilateral secessions by Slovenia and Croatia and that the United States would therefore not recognize them as independent countries, such recognition came first from Germany on 18 December 1991, from the European Community on 15 January 1992, and finally from the United States on 7 April 1992. Slovenia was accepted as a member of the UN on 23 April 1992 and has since become a member of many other international organizations, including the Council of Europe in 1993 and the NATO related Partnership for Peace in 1994.

On 6 December 1992, general elections were held in accordance with the new constitution, with 22 parties participating and eight receiving sufficient votes to assure representation. A coalition government was formed by the Liberal Democrats, Christian Democrats, and the United List Group of Leftist Parties. Dr. Milan Kucan was elected president, and Dr. Janez Drnovšek became prime minister. In 1997 a compromise was struck which allowed Poland, the Czech Republic, and Hungary to join the NATO alliance in 1999 while Romania and Slovenia were identified as prime candidates for future nomination into the alliance. Also in 1997, Slovenia signed an association agreement with the European Union (EU) and was invited to talks on EU membership.

In the 1970s, Slovenia had reached a standard of living close to the one in neighboring Austria and Italy. However, the burdens imposed by the excessive cost of maintaining a large Yugoslav army, heavy contributions to the Fund for Less Developed Areas, and the repayments on a US$20 billion international debt, caused a lowering of its living standard over the 1980s. The situation worsened with the trauma of secession from Yugoslavia, the war damages suffered, and the loss of the former Yugoslav markets. In spite of all these problems Slovenia made progress by improving its productivity, controlling inflation, and reorienting its exports to Western Europe. The Slovenian economy remained quite strong past 1994, growing at an annual rate of about 4% during the late 1990s.

Although governed from independence by centrist coalitions headed by Prime Minister Janez Drnovšek, the coalition collapsed in April 2000. Economist and center-right Social Democrat Party leader Andrej Bajuk became prime minister, until elections on 15 October 2000 saw Drnovšek return to power at the head of a four-party coalition. Drnovšek ran for president in elections held on 1 December 2002, and emerged with 56.5% of the vote in the second round, defeating Barbara Brezigar, who took 43.5%. Both supported EU and NATO membership for Slovenia. Liberal Democrat Anton Rop took over as prime minister when Drnovšek was elected president.

In the spring of 2004, Slovenia became a member of NATO and the EU. Later that year it held parliamentary elections, which were won by the center-right Slovenian Democratic Party—the first time in 13 years that a party other than the Liberal Democrats took power. In December 2004, Janez Jansa, who served as defense minister in previous governments, became, with the support of the parliament, prime minister. Jansa promised to reduce state administrative costs and to speed up the euro adoption process. Leftist Danilo Turk won the presidential runoff elections in November 2007.

In February 2005, Slovenia ratified the EU constitution. The country adopted the euro in January 2007, becoming the first former communist bloc country to do so. In December 2007, Slovenia was invited to begin the accession process for joining the OECD. On 1 January 2008, Slovenia became the first former communist state to take on the EU presidency, which it held through June 2008.

In December 2008, Slovenia vetoed the EU membership bid of Croatia as a result of an ongoing border dispute concerning the Bay of Piran. In November 2009, the two nations moved one step closer to resolving the dispute as the prime ministers of both countries met in Sweden to sign a border arbitration agreement. The agreement called for international negotiators to draw a new Adriatic border that dictates a fair distribution for both Slovenia and Croatia. In order to be finalized, however, the deal requires ratification from the parliaments of both countries. The Croatian parliament approved the agreement by the end of November 2009. In Slovenia, the matter went first to the constitutional court, which finally approved the legality of the agreement in March 2010, paving the way for parliamentary ratification. However, opposition leaders called for a national referendum to be held on the matter instead. At the time of the court's decision, polls showed that a majority of Slovenia's population supported the arbitration agreement. Still, high unemployment was contributing to rising frustration and disapproval with the government, and analysts noted that a pervasive anti-government sentiment could jeopardize the passage of the referendum, which was scheduled for 6 June 2010. On 25 May 2011, Croatia and Slovenia submitted their arbitration agreement to the UN. A final resolution was expected to take up to three years. The coastal border between Italy and Croatia is only 25.7 km (16 mi) long. Slovenia wants a sovereign shipping corridor established so that it can freely access the seas. Croatia has only agreed to offer Slovenia free access to its waters.

13 GOVERNMENT

Slovenia is a republic based on a constitution adopted on 23 December 1991, one year following the plebiscite that supported its independence.

The constitution provides for a National Assembly as the highest legislative authority with 90 seats. Deputies are elected to four-year terms of office. The National Council, with 40 seats, has an advisory role, and councilors represent social, economic, professional, and local interests. They are elected to five-year terms of office and may propose laws to the National Assembly, request the latter to review its decisions, and may demand the calling of a constitutional referendum.

The executive branch consists of a president of the republic who is also Supreme Commander of the Armed Forces, and is elected to a five-year term of office, limited to two consecutive terms. The president calls for elections to the National Assembly, proclaims the adopted laws, and proposes candidates for prime minister to the National Assembly. A Council of Ministers to advise the president is nominated by the prime minister and elected by the National Assembly.

14 POLITICAL PARTIES

Parliamentary elections were held on 21 September 2008, with the Slovene Democratic Party (SDS) garnering the highest number of seats—29; the Liberal Democratic Party (which dominated the political scene since Slovenia's independence, in 1991) got 23; the United List of Social Democrats (ZLSD), 10 seats; New Slovenia (NSi), 9 seats; Slovene People's Party (SLS), 7 seats; Slovenian National Party (SNS), 6 seats; Democratic Party of Retired People of Slovenia (DeSUS), 4 seats; Italian Minority, 1 seat; and the Hungarian Minority, 1 seat. The SDS forged a coalition with two center-right parties—NSi and SLS—and a center-left party—DeSUS. In November 2004, the National Assembly elected Janez Jansa prime minister, with 57 votes in favor.

In the 2007 presidential election, Danilo Turk, an independent, was elected with 68.2% of the vote. Alojz Peterle of the SLS won 31.8% of the vote. In the September 2008 elections, the Social Democrats (formerly the ZLSD) won 30.5% of the vote (29 seats), followed by the SDS with 29.3% (28 seats), ZARES with 9.4% (9 seats), DeSUS with 7.5% (7 seats), SNS with 5.5% (5 seats), the coalition SLS+SMS with 5.2% (5 seats), and the Liberal Democracy of Slovenia (LDS) with 5.2% (5 seats). One seat was taken by a Hungarian minority and one seat by an Italian minority. Borut Pahor of the Social Democrats was elected as prime minister.

In the December 2011 parliamentary elections, Positive Slovenia won 28.6% of the vote (28 seats), the SDS won 26.2% (26 seats), the Social Democrats (formerly the ZLSD) 10.5% (10 seats), the Civic List Party 8.4% (8 seats), DeSUS 6% (6 seats), SLS 6% (6 seats), and NSi 4.8% (4 seats). Other parties won the remainder. Jansa was chosen to return to the prime ministership in January 2012.

Party candidates are elected by each district. A candidate is elected only when votes for each party reach a given threshold. A new electoral code was passed in 2000, raising the threshold for securing seats from 3.2% to 4% and ending the use of preferential party lists for allocating seats to candidates who did not win direct mandates.

15 LOCAL GOVERNMENT

The commune or municipality (občina) is the basic self-managed sociopolitical community. There are 200 municipalities and 11 urban municipalities in Slovenia, which have directly elected councils as their representative bodies. A municipality must have at least 5,000 inhabitants. An urban municipality must have at least 20,000 inhabitants, be the place of employment for at least 15,000 people, and be the geographic, economic, and cultural center of the area. There are 58 state administrative units in Slovenia, which have jurisdiction over one or several municipalities. Advisory committees are formed to ensure cooperation between municipal bodies and administrative units. Members of these committees are appointed by the municipal councils. There are also local, village, and ward communities in Slovenia.

16 JUDICIAL SYSTEM

The judicial system consists of local and district courts and a Supreme Court, which hears appeals from these courts. A nine-member Constitutional Court resolves jurisdictional disputes and rules on the constitutionality of legislation and regulations. The Constitutional Court also acts as a final court of appeal in cases requiring constitutional interpretation.

Judges are elected by parliament after nomination by a Judicial Council composed of 11 members—six judges selected by their peers and five persons elected by the National Assembly on nomination of the president. The constitution guarantees the independence of judges. Judges are appointed to permanent positions subject to an age limit.

The constitution affords criminal defendants a presumption of innocence, open court proceedings, the right to an appeal, prohibition against double jeopardy, and a number of other procedural due process protections.

17 ARMED FORCES

The International Institute for Strategic Studies reports that armed forces in Slovenia totaled 7,600 members in 2011, all of which were members of the army. Armed forces represented 1.2% of the labor force in Slovenia. Defense spending totaled $964.7 million and accounted for 1.7% of GDP. Slovenia participated in UN, NATO, and European Union peacekeeping or military missions in four regions or countries.

18 INTERNATIONAL COOPERATION

Slovenia was admitted to the UN in 1992; it is part of several non-regional specialized agencies, such as the FAO, IAEA, UNCTAD, UNESCO, UNIDO, ILO, the World Bank, and the WHO. Slovenia is also a member of the Council of Europe, OSCE, the WTO, the European Bank for Reconstruction and Development, the Inter-American Development Bank, NATO, the Euro-Atlantic Partnership Council, and the European Union. The country holds observer status in the OAS and is a member affiliate of the Western European Union. Slovenia held the chairmanship of the Council of Europe from May to November 2009. Slovenia became a member of the Organization for Economic Cooperation and Development (OECD) in May 2010.

Slovenia is part of the Australia Group, the Zangger Committee, and the Nuclear Suppliers Group (London Group). In environmental cooperation, the nation is part of the Basel Convention, Conventions on Biological Diversity and Air Pollution, Ramsar, CITES, the London Convention, the Kyoto Protocol, the Montréal Protocol, MARPOL, the Nuclear Test Ban Treaty, and the UN Conventions on the Law of the Sea, Climate Change, and Desertification.

Slovenia became a member of both the North Atlantic Treaty Organization (NATO) and the European Union (EU) in 2004. The government has since become a strong advocate for the inclusion of other former Yugoslav republics into Euro-Atlantic institutions. However, in December 2008, Slovenia vetoed the EU membership bid of Croatia as a result of an ongoing border dispute concerning the Bay of Piran. The coastal border between Italy and Croatia is only 25.7 km (16 mi) long. Slovenia wants to have a sovereign shipping corridor established so that it can freely access the seas. Croatia has agreed to offer Slovenia only free access to its waters. In November 2009, both countries met in Sweden to sign a border arbitration agreement. The agreement called for international negotiators to draw a new Adriatic border that dictates a fair distribution for both Slovenia and Croatia. In order to be finalized, the deal required ratification from the parliaments of both countries. In Slovenia, the opposition parties in parliament pushed to have the matter decided by a national referendum. That vote occurred in June 2010 and narrowly passed with a yes vote of 51.6%.

19 ECONOMY

Before its independence, Slovenia was the most highly developed and wealthiest republic of the former Yugoslav SFR, with a per capita income more than double that of the Yugoslav average and nearly comparable to levels in neighboring Austria and Italy. The painful transition to a market-based economy was exacerbated by the disruption of intra-Yugoslav trade. However, Slovenia's economy has not suffered as much as was predicted during the breakup of the Yugoslav SFR, due to strong ties with Western Europe, and during the late 1990s and throughout the 2000s was a model of stability and economic progress in the region.

Under the Communists, large parts of the economy were nationalized, with most restructuring involving the infrastructure, electricity, telecommunications, utilities, major banks, insurers, and the steel industry. Subsequent reforms enabled managers and workers to purchase up to 60% of their companies. As a result, nearly 70% of manufacturing firms in Slovenia are owned by their employees.

Slovenia freed prices and implemented a privatization law in November 1992, which has enabled private businesses to expand. The Slovene privatization program began in 1993 and involved 1,500 companies, 1,000 of which had completed privatization by mid-1997, including most small and medium-sized enterprises.

Whereas GDP fell by 9% in 1991 and 6% in 1992, the 1993 GDP grew by 1.3%. Since then real GDP growth has averaged 4% a year, and the growth rate increased to 6.1% in 2007. Until 1991 to 1999, Slovenia's budget deficit rarely exceeded 1% of GDP. The unemployment rate (ILO definition) has fallen from 7.6% in 1999 to 6.4% in 2001 and an estimated 6.3% in 2002. Inflation as measured by consumer prices (end of period) rose from 8% in 1998 and 1999 to 8.9% in 2000, but then fell to 7% in 2001 and 7.2%(est.) in 2002. By 2002 the country's real GDP per capita had risen to about 70% the EU average, and in May 2004 Slovenia was accepted as a full member of the EU.

Moderate growth rates were registered in 2003 and 2004 (2.5% and 3.9% respectively). Inflation continued on its downward spiral, reaching 5.6% in 2003, and 3.3% in 2004. In 2007, the unemployment rate was at 4.8%, reflecting an ever expanding economy. The GDP growth rate of 6.1% in 2007 was very good too. Dependence on trade translated into an economic recession in early 2009 as a drop in demand for major exports resulted in a contraction of the economy by 8.5% in the first quarter. Slovenia banks felt the downturn even sooner, as they relied heavily on foreign financial markets to finance the credit boom at home. While riding out the economic storm, the government looked toward research and development in the automobile industry as a potential growth sector. Specifically, industry leaders were working to develop more efficient hybrid and electric vehicles. The GDP rate of change in Slovenia, as of 2010, was 1.2%. Inflation stood at 2.1%, and unemployment was reported at 10.6%.

In its 2011 annual review, the International Monetary Fund noted that Slovenia must take additional measures to narrow the budget deficit, which increased to 5.8% of GDP in 2011 from 5.6% in 2010. In particular, the country is expected to concentrate on the sustainability of public finances, financial sector resilience, and market competition.

20INCOME

The CIA estimated that in 2010 the GDP of Slovenia was $56.58 billion. The CIA defines GDP as the value of all final goods and services produced within a nation in a given year and computed on the basis of purchasing power parity (PPP) rather than value as measured on the basis of the rate of the exchange based on current dollars. The per capita GDP was estimated at $28,200. The annual growth rate of GDP was 1.2%. The average inflation rate was 2.1%. It was estimated that agriculture accounted for 2.4% of GDP, industry 31%, and services 66.6%.

According to the World Bank, remittances from citizens living abroad totaled $279.1 million in 2009, or about $140 per capita and accounted for approximately 0.5% of GDP.

The World Bank reports that in 2009, household consumption in Slovenia totaled $26.6 billion or about $13,283 per capita, measured in current US dollars rather than PPP. Household consump-

tion includes expenditures of individuals, households, and non-governmental organizations on goods and services, excluding the purchases of dwellings. It was estimated that household consumption was growing at an average annual rate of 2%.

As of 2011 the most recent study by the World Bank reported that actual individual consumption in Slovenia was 65.5% of GDP and accounted for 0.08% of world consumption. By comparison, the United States accounted for 25.44% of world individual consumption. The World Bank also estimated that 11% of Slovenia's GDP was spent on food and beverages, 14.1% on housing and household furnishings, 3.2% on clothes, 7.4% on health, 8.9% on transportation, 2.0% on communications, 6.2% on recreation, 3.7% on restaurants and hotels, and 3% on miscellaneous goods and services and purchases from abroad.

It was estimated that in 2008 about 12.3% of the population subsisted on an income below the poverty line established by Slovenia's government.

21LABOR

As of 2010, Slovenia had a total labor force of 935,500 people. Within that labor force, CIA estimates in 2009 noted that 2.2% were employed in agriculture, 35% in industry, and 62.8% in the service sector.

The constitution provides that the establishment, activities, and recruitment of members of labor unions shall be unrestricted. There are two main labor federations, with constituent branches throughout the society, as well as a smaller regional union. Virtually all workers except for police and military personnel are eligible to form and join unions. The right to strike is also guaranteed by the constitution. Collective bargaining is still undergoing development, and the government still has the principal role in setting labor conditions.

The minimum wage was $984 monthly in 2010, although increasingly, private businesses are setting pay scales directly with their employees' unions or representatives. The workweek is 42 hours, and the minimum working age is 16. Occupational health and safety standards are set by the government and regularly enforced.

A nine-day public sector general strike took place in September 2010 as public sector workers demanded the implementation of a significant wage increase that had been promised by the government prior to the financial crisis. Government officials claimed that the increase is not possible in the current economic climate. The strike had serious economic consequences for the nation, as transportation workers, public health and social care workers, customs officers, and police officers (among other) participated in the strike. Workers from the energy sector threatened to strike for four days, a move which would have resulted in power blackouts, but this motion was called off just one day before it was scheduled to begin. The strike ended as the government agreed to continue negotiations with the public sector in the hope of coming to a fair compromise, although it was understood that there would be a delay of promised wage increases for potentially several years, as the government waited for the economy to stabilize.

22AGRICULTURE

Roughly 10% of the total land is farmed, and the country's major crops include potatoes, hops, wheat, sugar beets, corn, and grapes.

Cereal production in 2009 amounted to 535,278 tons, fruit production 240,493 tons, and vegetable production 85,016 tons. Slovenia was the least agriculturally active of all the republics of the former Yugoslav SFR.

23 ANIMAL HUSBANDRY

The UN Food and Agriculture Organization (FAO) reported that Slovenia dedicated 296,000 hectares (731,432 acres) to permanent pasture or meadow in 2009. During that year, the country tended 4.4 million chickens, 469,983 head of cattle, and 432,011 pigs. The production from these animals amounted to 43,085 tons of beef and veal, 82,452 tons of pork, 40,026 tons of poultry, 17,895 tons of eggs, and 495,349 tons of milk. Slovenia also produced 4,133 tons of cattle hide and 150 tons of raw wool.

Sheep and cattle breeding, as well as dairy farming, dominate the agricultural sector of the economy. Productivity rates for livestock and dairy farming are comparable to much of Western Europe. Poultry and eggs are some of the few agricultural products where Slovenia's domestic production still exceeds domestic demand.

24 FISHING

Slovenia had 12 decked commercial fishing boats in 2008. The annual capture totaled 869 tons according to the UN FAO. The export value of seafood totaled $32.93 million. The freshwater catch is dominated by rainbow trout and common carp. The fishing sector accounts for only a small fraction of foreign investment.

25 FORESTRY

Approximately 62% of Slovenia is covered by forest. The UN FAO estimated the 2009 roundwood production at 1.95 million cu m (68.8 million cu ft). The value of all forest products, including roundwood, totaled $962.4 million. The furniture-making industry is a prominent consumer of forest products.

26 MINING

Slovenia's output of metals in 2009 included refined and secondary lead, aluminum ingot, and crude steel. The country's mining and quarrying sector accounted for around 0.4% of Slovenia's GDP in 2009. Apart from being a substantial producer of quartz, quartzite and glass sand (326,636 metric tons in 2009), Slovenia was also a modest producer of common clay, coke and petroleum products. In 2009 output of aluminum ingot (primary and secondary) totaled 45,148 metric tons; crude steel, 436,000 metric tons; and lead (refined and secondary), 14,000 metric tons. Industrial mineral production in 2009 included: cement, 1.0 million tons; bentonite, 130 metric tons; salt (all sources) 200 metric tons; and dimension stone, 15,000 metric tons. Also produced were pumice, sand and gravel.

27 ENERGY AND POWER

The World Bank reported in 2008 that Slovenia produced 16.4 billion kWh of electricity and consumed 14 billion kWh, or 6,994 kWh per capita. Roughly 69% of energy came from fossil fuels, while 26% came from alternative fuels. Per capita oil consumption was 3,827 kg. Oil production totaled 5 barrels of oil a day. Slovenia, with miniscule reserves of oil and no natural gas reserves, is

Principal Trading Partners – Slovenia (2010)

(In millions of US dollars)

Country	Total	Exports	Imports	Balance
World	50,559.0	24,189.0	26,370.0	-2,181.0
Germany	10,507.0	5,646.0	4,861.0	785.0
Italy	8,236.0	3,530.0	4,706.0	-1,176.0
Austria	5,366.0	2,177.0	3,189.0	-1,012.0
France	3,457.0	2,007.0	1,450.0	557.0
Croatia	3,282.0	1,888.0	1,394.0	494.0
Hungary	2,276.0	1,210.0	1,066.0	144.0
Poland	1,623.0	1,069.0	554.0	515.0
Bosnia & Herzegovina	1,568.0	830.0	738.0	92.0
Serbia	1,544.0	937.0	607.0	330.0
Czech Republic	1,512.0	841.0	671.0	170.0

(…) data not available or not significant.

(n.s.) not specified.

SOURCE: *2011 Direction of Trade Statistics Yearbook*, New York: United Nations, 2011.

heavily reliant upon imports to meet its petroleum and natural gas needs.

Addressing issues of sustainable energy, the government opened its third new biogas power plant (in Dubrovnik) in 2009. The plant, which runs on cow manure and corn and grass silage, was expected to produce 8,500 MW hours of electricity and an equal amount of heat energy per year.

In March 2011, Slovenia's nuclear power plant in Krsko invested $42 million into security systems that would strengthen levies, reduce flooding, and lower the risk of damage from earthquakes. The decision immediately followed the March 2011 tsunami and earthquake in Japan that caused radiation leaks from nuclear power plants.

28 INDUSTRY

Manufacturing is widely diversified. Important manufacturing sectors include: electrical and nonelectrical machinery, metal processing, chemicals, textiles and clothing, wood processing and furniture, transport equipment, and food processing. Industrial production, which fell by about 25% in the early 1990s due in part to the international sanctions against Serbia, grew by an estimated 1% in 1996 and increased by 3.3% in 2001. It stood at 4.5% in 2011. The recovery of industrial production was slowed by the shift from parastatal to private enterprise.

29 SCIENCE AND TECHNOLOGY

Patent applications in science and technology as of 2009, according to the World Bank, totaled 373 in Slovenia. Public financing of science was 1.66% of GDP. The Slovenian Academy of Sciences and Arts, founded in 1938, has institutes conducting research in biology, paleontology, and medicine. Headquartered in Ljubljana are the Association of Engineers and Technicians of Slovenia; the Association of Mathematicians, Physicists, and Astronomers of Slovenia, and the Society for Natural Sciences of Slovenia. The Ljubljana Geological Institute was founded in 1946, and the Institute for Karst Research a year later in Postojna. The University of Ljubljana has faculties of arts and sciences; natural sciences and technology; architecture, civil engineering, and geodesy; electrical and computer engineering; mechanical engineering; medicine; and veterinary medicine. The University of Maribor has a college of agriculture, a faculty of technical sciences, and a center for applied mathematics and theoretical physics.

30 DOMESTIC TRADE

Slovenia's domestic economy has historically been small, thus necessitating an emphasis on exports. New legislation in 1994 regarding tax exemptions on imported inputs was expected to help domestic companies compete with foreign firms. More recent reforms are aimed at encouraging and increasing both local and foreign investment.

There are a number of wholesalers and retailers throughout the country. American and European franchises have been established within the country. Installment financing, even for small ticket items, is common. Consumer prices are generally high due to the high cost of labor and transportation. The government maintains price controls on certain goods and services, such as gasoline, railway travel, telecommunications, and milk.

Retail hours are generally between 9 a.m. and 7 p.m. on weekdays. Stores may be open for a half-day on Saturdays. Banks are generally open from 7 a.m. to 7 p.m. Monday through Friday. Large banks may also be open Saturday mornings. Office hours are generally from 9 a.m. to 5 p.m. Monday through Friday.

31 FOREIGN TRADE

Slovenia imported $25.96 billion worth of goods and services in 2008, while exporting $24.97 billion worth of goods and services. Major import partners in 2009 were Germany, 16.5%; Italy, 15.9%; Austria, 11.8%; France, 5%; and Croatia, 4.3%. Its major export partners were Germany, 19.4%; Italy, 11.4%; Croatia, 7.8%; France, 7.4%; and Austria, 7.3%. Slovenia has reoriented much of its trade away from its former Yugoslav neighbors toward Western Europe.

32 BALANCE OF PAYMENTS

In 2010 Slovenia had a foreign trade surplus of $5.6 billion, amounting to 5.5% of GDP. However, the current account balance was -$394.3 million in 2010. The deficit increased to -$764.9 million in 2011.

33 BANKING AND SECURITIES

The Bank of Slovenia is the country's central bank, and it is independent of the government. It has pursued a tight monetary and credit policy, aimed at the gradual reduction of inflation, since the introduction of the tolar in October 1991. The bank ended some of the worst abuses of the banking system under the Yugoslavian federation, such as enterprises setting up their own banks from which they borrowed freely.

At the end of 1996, the Bank of Slovenia changed its method of calculating the revalorization rate for other banks. From January 1997, the rate is derived from price increases over the preceding six months, instead of four months as before.

Yet not until 1999 did Slovenia move to reform its banking sector by privatizing some of its largest banks and permitting foreign investment. Two of the largest state-owned banks, Nova Ljubljanska Banka (NLB) and Nova Kreditna banka Maribor, were prime

Balance of Payments – Slovenia (2010)

(In millions of US dollars)

Current Account		**-388.0**
Balance on goods	-1,602.0	
Imports	-25,961.0	
Exports	24,359.0	
Balance on services	1,730.0	
Balance on income	-662.0	
Current transfers	146.0	
Capital Account		**11.0**
Financial Account		**356.0**
Direct investment abroad	73.0	
Direct investment in Slovenia	366.0	
Portfolio investment assets	-532.0	
Portfolio investment liabilities	3,165.0	
Financial derivatives	-153.0	
Other investment assets	950.0	
Other investment liabilities	-3,514.0	
Net Errors and Omissions		**26.0**
Reserves and Related Items		**-5.0**

(…) data not available or not significant.

SOURCE: *Balance of Payment Statistics Yearbook 2011,* Washington, DC: International Monetary Fund, 2011.

Public Finance – Slovenia (2009)

(In billions of euros, central government figures)

Revenue and Grants	**13,655**	**100.0%**
Tax revenue	6,381	46.7%
Social contributions	5,637	41.3%
Grants	565	4.1%
Other revenue	1,073	7.9%
Expenditures	**15,595**	**100.0%**
General public services	1,627	10.4%
Defense	533	3.4%
Public order and safety	632	4.1%
Economic affairs	1,585	10.2%
Environmental protection	179	1.1%
Housing and community amenities	106	0.7%
Health	2,396	15.4%
Recreational, culture, and religion	415	2.7%
Education	1,880	12.1%
Social protection	6,242	40.0%

(…) data not available or not significant.

SOURCE: *Government Finance Statistics Yearbook 2010,* Washington, DC: International Monetary Fund, 2010.

candidates for privatization. Analysts also expected large-scale consolidation to follow in the wake of the banking divestment.

In May 2001, the government initiated the privatization of NLB. By September 2002, a 34% stake was acquired by Belgian-based KBC, with a 5% stake taken by the European Bank for Reconstruction and Development.

In 2010 the discount rate, the interest rate at which the central bank lends to other financial institutions, was 1.75%. The commercial bank prime lending rate, the rate at which banks lend to customers, was 5.9% in 2011.

The Ljubljana Stock Exchange, abolished in 1953, was reopened in December 1989. As of 2001, it listed 38 securities and had 60 members. In 2011 a total of 138 securities were listed. Market capitalization was €6.6 billion ($8.8 billion) in 2011. Slovenia took advantage of its favorable credit rating in January 2010 and issued €1.5 billion euros ($2.1 billion) of ten-year bonds. The yield on the bonds was 4.125%, considerably higher than German or US bonds with similar maturities.

34 INSURANCE

There were at least 15 companies operating in Slovenia. The value of all direct insurance premiums written exceeded $1.4 billion. Triglav was one of Slovenia's top nonlife and life insurer and posted net profits of €35 ($46.6) million from January to September 2011.

35 PUBLIC FINANCE

In 2010 the budget of Slovenia included $22.56 billion in public revenue and $25.53 billion in public expenditures. The budget deficit amounted to 5.3% of GDP. Public debt was 35.5% of GDP, with $51.57 billion of the debt held by foreign entities. In 2011 an annual IMF report cited Slovenia's high budget deficit as a long-term concern for stable economic growth.

Economic management is fairly good in Slovenia. Privatization has been relatively successful, although some of the business practices of the Yugoslav brand of communism have carried over to the newly private enterprises.

36 TAXATION

As of 2011, Slovenia had a flat 20% tax rate on corporate income. Capital gains are included as business income and taxed at the same corporate rate. The resident branches of foreign companies were taxed at the same rate as Slovenian companies.

A sales tax of 20% on consumer products and 10% on services was replaced as of 1 July 1999 with Slovenia's value-added tax (VAT) introduced at a standard rate of 19% and a reduced rate of 7.5%. The standard rate was increased to 20% in 2002, where it stood as of 2011. The reduced rate applies to food, medicines and agricultural products. Exports, insurance, banking and financial services are exempt. There are also excise taxes on alcohol, tobacco, and fuel.

37 CUSTOMS AND DUTIES

Slovenia is a member of the EU and thus has a common import customs tariff and complies with trade agreements put in place by the EU.

38 FOREIGN INVESTMENT

Foreign direct investment (FDI) in Slovenia was a net outflow of $578.8 million according to World Bank figures published in 2009. FDI represented -1.19% of GDP.

Since independence, the foreign investment climate has steadily improved in Slovenia, despite constraints that have inhibited investment. The small domestic economy has been viewed by many prospective investors as the least risky of the former Yugoslav republics, but to date Slovenia's share of world foreign direct investment (FDI) flows have been well below its share of world GDP. From 1988 to 1990, its share of world FDI was 60% of its share of world GDP, and from 1998 to 2000, it was only 30% of its share of world GDP.

Until the late 1990s Slovenia retained several barriers to foreign investment. Any company incorporated in Slovenia was required to have a majority of Slovenes on its board of directors, or a managing director or proxy of Slovene nationality. Foreign companies and individuals of foreign nationality were prohibited from owning land in Slovenia. However, any company incorporated in Slovenia was permitted to purchase real estate, regardless of the origin of its founding capital. Liberalization laws enacted in 1999 lowered the threshold of foreign direct investment from 50% to 10%. This allowed more foreign investors to avert the custody account regime.

Despite its overall attractiveness, Slovenia has not managed to attract significant levels of FDI, as compared to some other Central and Eastern European Countries (like Hungary or the Czech Republic). Privatization has occurred slowly, and Slovenia retained one of the highest levels of state control in the EU as of 2011.

39 ECONOMIC DEVELOPMENT

The most productive of the former Yugoslav republics, Slovenia enjoys a relatively high degree of prosperity and stability, and has made a successful transition to a market economy. It has become a member of the International Monetary Fund (IMF) as well as the World Bank; it obtained an $80 million loan for financial rehabilitation from the latter. The EBRD loaned Slovenia $50 million for the improvement of the railway sector. In March 2004, Slovenia became the first donor partner at the World Bank of the transition countries. The country is a founding member of the WTO. Unlike the rest of the former communist states of Eastern Europe, Slovenia never received assistance from the International Monetary Fund. Its per capita GDP is comparable to EU members Portugal and Greece.

Slovenia's economy is heavily dependent upon foreign trade, with trade equaling around 120% of GDP. The budgets for 2003 and 2004 restricted the public deficit to 1% of GDP. Inflation fell from 200% in 1992 to 7.5% in 2002. Further privatizations—especially in the telecommunications, financial, and energy sectors—were planned as of 2003 but were put on hold indefinitely.

On 1 May 2004 Slovenia joined the European Union, which further strengthened the aura of political and economic stability it already had. It was one of the first 10 newly accepted countries and introduced the euro by 2007. Slovenia registered steady growth rates since 1993 and is now behaving like a fully developed economy, boasting a modern and extensive infrastructure, a highly educated work force, and a prime geographic location. However, the levels of foreign investment remained under the capacity of the Slovenian economy, due in part to protectionist measures by the government. Corruption, although lower than in other Central and Eastern European countries, remains an issue that has to be addressed.

A recession in 2009—the product of the 2008–09 global financial crisis—returned to growth by 2010, which continued in 2011. Unemployment, however, continued to rise, a major point of concern for the government. The comparative inflexibility of the labor market has damaged domestic industries. Expanding foreign investment was viewed a central tenet for continued economic growth.

40 SOCIAL DEVELOPMENT

Slovenia's first social insurance programs were established in 1922, and were updated in 2003. The system provides old age, disability, survivor's pensions, sickness, work injury, and unemployment benefits. The pension system covers most employed persons. Funds are provided by employee and employer contributions, with any unforeseen deficit covered by the government. The government funds the total cost for some groups of insured including veterans. The age of retirement is variable, depending upon the numbers of years worked. A universal system of family allowances provides benefits to families with children with incomes below a specified monthly amount. There is a maternity grant available to all permanent residents in Slovakia to purchase clothing and other necessities for a newborn child.

Women and men have equal status under the law. Discrimination against women or minorities in housing, jobs, or other areas is illegal. Officially, both spouses are equal in marriage, and the constitution asserts the state's responsibility to protect the family. Women are well represented in business, academia, and government, although they still hold a disproportionate share of lower-paying jobs. On average, women earn less than men. Violence against women is underreported, but awareness has been increasing. There have been improved efforts to assist victims. The constitution provides for special protection for children.

The constitution ensures minority participation in government by mandating that Italian and Hungarian minorities each receive at least one representative in the National Assembly. The Roma population continues to experience discrimination. Human rights are generally respected by the government and upheld by the legal and judicial systems.

41 HEALTH

According to the CIA, life expectancy in Slovenia was 79 years in 2011. The country spent 8.3% of its GDP on healthcare, amounting to $2,175 per person. There were 25 physicians, 82 nurses and midwives, and 47 hospital beds per 10,000 inhabitants. The fertility rate was 1.5, while the infant mortality rate was 2 per 1,000 live births. In 2008 the maternal mortality rate, according to the World Bank, was 18 per 100,000 births. It was estimated that 95% of children were vaccinated against measles. The CIA calculated HIV/AIDS prevalence in Slovenia to be about less than 0.1% in 2009.

42 HOUSING

According to the 2002 census, there were 777,772 dwelling units. About 92% of all dwellings were privately owned by a citizen and 82% of all dwellings were owner occupied. About 44% of all households were living in single-family detached homes and 52% of all dwellings were in urban areas. About 94,635 dwellings, or 12% of the housing stock, had been built since 1991. The average household had 2.8 people.

Since the 1991 Housing Act, the State is no longer directly responsible for housing provisions. Municipalities have responsibility for social housing projects. The State does, however, offer subsidized loans for the construction of individual private homes and nonprofit rental housing.

43 EDUCATION

In 2008 the World Bank estimated that 97% of age-eligible children in Slovenia were enrolled in primary school. Secondary enrollment for age-eligible children stood at 91%. Tertiary enrollment was estimated at 87%. Of those enrolled in tertiary education, there were 100 male students for every 146 female students. Overall, the CIA estimated that Slovenia had a literacy rate of 99.7%. Public expenditure on education represented 5.7% of GDP.

Between 1999 and 2009, Slovenia gradually replaced an eight-year basic schooling program with a nine-year program, which contained three cycles of three years each, and covered primary and lower secondary studies. Upper secondary studies generally covered an additional three to four years with students given the options of attending general, technical, or vocational schools. The academic year runs from October to June.

Higher education at public institutions is free for native, full-time students and students from other European Union countries. Slovenia has 3 universities, 3 art academies or professional colleges, and 10 private higher education institutions. The University of Ljubljana, founded in 1919, has 25 faculties. The University of Maribor has a faculty for teaching, a faculty for economics and business, and a faculty for technology. There are also two colleges attached to it.

44 LIBRARIES AND MUSEUMS

The National and University Library of Slovenia is located in Ljubljana and holds 2.3 million items. The University of Ljubljana maintains 39 faculty libraries. The University of Maribor Library maintains eight faculty libraries and serves as a legal depository for all Slovenica materials printed in the Slovene language. The Slovenian Academy of Sciences and Arts, also in the capital, holds 450,000 volumes. There are about 60 public library systems, with over 280 branch locations and nine mobile library services. One of the largest, the Oton Župančič Public Library in Ljubljana, maintains six locations and a mobile service. There are about 138 special libraries in the country, including the Slovene National Museum Library that holds about 200,000 printed materials.

Ljubljana hosts the National Gallery, Museum of Modern Art, Museum of Architecture, National Museum of Slovenia, Slovene Sports Museum, and the Slovene Ethnographic Museum, among others. The Technology Museum of Slovenia is in Vrhnika. The National Liberation Museum is in Maribor, a city which also hosts several smaller art and history museums. The Slovene Religious Museum is in Gorica. There are dozens of other regional museums throughout the country, including several in restored historical houses and castles. Many of these smaller museums are located in and around Celje, Kranj and Novo mesto.

45 MEDIA

In 2009, the CIA reported that there were 1 million telephone landlines in Slovenia. In addition to landlines, mobile phone subscriptions averaged 103 per 100 people, for a total of over 2.1 million mobile phones in use. There were over 75 radio stations. Internet users numbered 64 per 100 citizens. Prominent newspapers in 2010, with circulation numbers listed parenthetically, included *Delo* (90,000), *Dnevnik* (62,000), *Slovenske Novice* (80,000), and *Vecer* (70,000).

Minority language television and radio broadcasts were available. The constitution provides for free expression, including freedom of speech and the press; however, it is said that lingering self-censorship and some indirect political pressures do continue to influence the media.

46 ORGANIZATIONS

The Slovenia Chamber of Commerce (Chamber of Economy of Slovenia) coordinates all economic activities within and outside the country. In the 1990s, two large associations of trade unions were formed: the Confederation of New Trade Unions of Slovenia and the Association of Independent Trade Unions. There are professional associations for the advancement of research and education in a variety of medical fields.

The Slovenian Academy of Sciences and the Arts was founded in 1938.

National youth organizations include the UN Student Club of Slovenia, the Catholic Student Movement of Slovenia, the Students Union of Slovenia, Girl Guides, and the Scout Association of Slovenia. There are sports associations promoting amateur competition among athletes of all ages; many of these groups are affiliated with international counterparts as well. Women's organizations include The Center for Gender and Politics at the Peace Institute and Soroptimist International.

International organizations with national chapters include Amnesty International, the Society of St. Vincent de Paul, UNICEF, and the Red Cross.

47 TOURISM, TRAVEL, AND RECREATION

The *Tourism Factbook*, published by the UN World Tourism Organization, reported 1.82 million incoming tourists to Slovenia in 2009 who spent a total of $2.73 billion. Both the number of tourists and the total receipts from tourism increased between 2006 and 2009. Of those incoming tourists, there were 1.7 million from Europe. There were 48,627 hotel beds available in Slovenia, which had an occupancy rate of 40%. The estimated daily cost to visit Ljubljana, the capital, was $297.

The rich architecture, museums, caves, and springs are some of Slovenia's main tourist attractions. Health resorts are popular, many in the north where there are mineral and thermal springs. The 10 casinos also attract visitors each year, making entertainment a major part of the tourism industry. Slovenia has convention centers in Ljubljana and three other cities and international airports in Ljubljana, Maribor, and Portoroz. Popular recreational activities include skiing, snowboarding, tennis, golf, mountain climbing, canoeing, and fishing. Visitors from Europe and most other countries can enter Slovenia without visas.

48 FAMOUS PERSONS

Milan Kučan (b. 1941) was president from 1991–2002, when he was succeeded by Janez Drnovšek (b. 1950), who had previously served as prime minister. In 1551, Primož Trubar translated the New Bible into Slovene. The poet, Valentin Vodnik (1754–1819), wrote poems in praise of Napoleon; literature in praise of the French flourished during the French occupation of Slovenia in 1813. Slovenian tennis star Mima Jausovec (b. 1956) won the Italian Open in 1976 and the French Open in 1977.

49 DEPENDENCIES

Slovenia has no territories or colonies.

50 BIBLIOGRAPHY

Frucht, Richard, ed. *Eastern Europe: An Introduction to the People, Lands, and Culture.* Santa Barbara, CA: ABC-CLIO, 2005.

Gottfried, Ted. *Slovenia.* New York: Benchmark Books, 2005.

McElrath, Karen, ed. *HIV and AIDS: A Global View.* Westport, CT: Greenwood Press, 2002.

Opello, Walter C. *European Politics.* Boulder, CO: Lynne Rienner Publishers, 2009.

Plut-Pregelj, Leopoldina, and Carole Rogel. *Historical Dictionary of Slovenia.* 2nd ed. Lanham, MD: Scarecrow Press, 2007.

Political Chronology of Europe. London: Europa, 2001.

Šabič, Zlatko, and Charles J. Bukowski. *Small States in the Post-Cold War World: Slovenia and NATO Enlargement.* Westport, CT: Praeger, 2002.

Slovenia Investment and Business Guide: Strategic and Practical Information. Washington, DC: International Business Publications USA, 2012.

Summers, Randal W., and Allan M. Hoffman, eds. *Domestic Violence: A Global View.* Westport, CT: Greenwood Press, 2002.

SPAIN

Kingdom of Spain
España

CAPITAL: Madrid

FLAG: The national flag, adopted in 1785, consists of three horizontal stripes: a yellow one-equal in size to the other two combined-between two red ones, with the coat of arms on the yellow stripe.

ANTHEM: *Marcha Real Granadera (March of the Royal Grenadier).*

MONETARY UNIT: The peseta was replaced by the euro as official currency as of 2002. The euro is divided into 100 cents. There are coins in denominations of 1, 2, 5, 10, 20, and 50 cents and 1 euro and 2 euros. There are notes of 5, 10, 20, 50, 100, 200, and 500 euros. €1 = \$1.3462 (or \$1 = €0.7428) as of 2011.

WEIGHTS AND MEASURES: The metric system is the legal standard.

HOLIDAYS: New Year's Day, 1 January; St. Joseph's Day, 19 March; Epiphany, 31 March; Day of St. Joseph the Artisan, 1 May; St. James's Day, 25 July; Assumption, 15 August; National Day and Hispanic Day, 12 October; All Saints' Day, 1 November; Immaculate Conception, 8 December; Christmas, 25 December. Movable religious holidays include Holy Thursday, Good Friday, Easter Monday, and Corpus Christi.

TIME: 1 p.m. = noon GMT.

¹LOCATION, SIZE, AND EXTENT

Occupying the greater part of the Iberian Peninsula, Spain is the third-largest country in Europe, with an area of 504,782 sq km (194,897 sq mi). Comparatively, the area occupied by Spain is slightly more than twice the size of the state of Oregon. This total includes the Balearic Islands (Islas Baleares) in the western Mediterranean Sea and the Canary Islands (Islas Canarias) in the Atlantic Ocean west of Morocco; both island groups are regarded as integral parts of metropolitan Spain. The Spanish mainland extends 1,085 km (674 mi) E–W and 950 km (590 mi) N–S. Bordered by the Bay of Biscay, France, and Andorra on the N, by the Mediterranean on the E and S, by Gibraltar and the Strait of Gibraltar on the S, by the Gulf of Cádiz on the SW, and by Portugal and the Atlantic on the W, Spain has a total land boundary of 1,918 km (1,192 mi) and a coastline of 4,964 km (3,084 mi). Spain also holds Ceuta, Melilla, and other "places of sovereignty" in the north of Morocco.

Spain has long claimed Gibraltar, a narrow peninsula on the south coast, which was taken by a British-Dutch fleet in 1704 and became a British colony under the Treaty of Utrecht (1713). In 2003, Gibraltar residents voted to remain a British colony and demanded greater participation in talks between the United Kingdom and Spain concerning the future of Gibraltar. The United Kingdom plans to grant Gibraltar greater autonomy, but Spain does not agree with this plan.

Spain's capital city, Madrid, is located in the center of the country.

²TOPOGRAPHY

Continental Spain is divided into five general topographic regions: (1) The northern coastal belt is a mountainous region with fertile valleys and large areas under pasture and covered with forests. (2) The central plateau, or Meseta, with an average altitude of about 670 m (2,200 ft), comprises most of Castilla y León, Castilla-La Mancha, and the city of Madrid. (3) Andalucía, with Sevilla its largest city, covers the whole of southern and southwestern Spain and, except for the flat fertile plain of the Guadalquivir River, is a mountainous region with deep fertile valleys. (4) The Levante is on the Mediterranean coastal belt, with Valencia its chief city. (5) Catalonia (Cataluña) and the Ebro Valley comprise the northeastern region.

Spain has six principal mountain ranges-the Pyrenees, the Cordillera Cantábrica, the Montes de Toledo, the Sierra Morena, the Serranías Penibéticas, and the Sistema Ibérico. The principal peaks are Pico de Aneto (3,404 m/11,168 ft) in the Pyrenees and Mulhacén (3,478 m/11,411 ft) in the Penibéticas. The main rivers are the Tagus (Tajo), Duero, Guadiana, and Guadalquivir, which flow to the Atlantic, and the Ebro, which flows to the Mediterranean. The Duero and the Guadalquivir form broad valleys and alluvial plains and at their mouths deposit saline soils, creating deltas and salt marshes. The coastline has few natural harbors except the estuaries (rías) in the northwest, formed by glaciers, and those in the Levante and the south, created by sandbars during the Quaternary period.

The Canary Islands are a group of 13 volcanic islands, of which six are barren. They have a ruggedly mountainous terrain interspersed with some fertile valleys. Spain's highest mountain, Pico de Teide (3,718 m/12,198 ft), is on Tenerife. The Balearic Islands are a picturesque group with sharply indented coastlines; they combine steep mountains with rolling, fertile ranges.

³CLIMATE

The climate of Spain is extremely varied. The northern coastal regions are cool and humid, with an average annual temperature of

14°C (57°F); temperatures at Bilbao range from an average of 10°C (50°F) in January-March to 19°C (66°F) during July-September. The central plateau is cold in the winter and hot in the summer; Madrid has a winter average of about 8°C (46°F) and a summer average of 23°C (73°F). In Andalucía and the Levante, the climate is temperate except in summer, when temperatures sometimes reach above 40°C (104°F) in the shade. The northern coastal regions have an average annual rainfall of 99 cm (39 in); the southern coastal belt has 41–79 cm (16–31 in); and the interior central plain averages no more than 50 cm (20 in) annually.

⁴FLORA AND FAUNA

Because of its wide variety of climate, Spain has a greater variety of natural vegetation than any other European country. In total, the World Resources Institute estimates that there are 5,050 plant species in Spain. Nevertheless, vegetation is generally sparse. In the humid areas of the north there are deciduous trees (including oak, chestnut, elm, beech and poplar), as well as varieties of pine. Pine, juniper, and other evergreens, particularly the ilex and cork oak, and drought-resistant shrubs predominate in the dry southern region. Much of the Meseta and of Andalucía has steppe vegetation. The Canaries, named for the wild dogs (*Canariae insulae*) once found there, support both Mediterranean and African flora. A small, yellow-tinged finch on the islands has given the name "canary" to a variety of yellow songbirds widely bred as house pets.

Animal life in Spain is limited by the pressure of population, and few wild species remain. That said, the World Resources Institute estimated that Spain is home to 132 species of mammals, 515 of birds, 67 of reptiles, and 32 of amphibians. The calculation reflected the total number of distinct species residing in the country, not the number of endemic species.

⁵ENVIRONMENT

The World Resources Institute reported that Spain had designated 4.14 million hectares (10.23 million acres) of land for protection as of 2006. Water resources totaled 111.1 cu km (26.65 cu mi) while water usage was 37.22 cu km (8.93 cu mi) per year. Domestic water usage accounted for 13% of total usage, industrial for 19%, and agricultural for 68%. Per capita water usage totaled 864 cu m (30,512 cu ft) per year.

Extensive forests are now limited to the Pyrenees and the Asturias-Galicia area in the north because centuries of unplanned cutting have depleted stands. Government reforestation schemes meet with difficulties where sheep and goats graze freely over large areas. Erosion affects about 18% of the total land mass of Spain.

Air pollution is also a problem in Spain. In 1995 industrial carbon dioxide emissions totaled 223.2 million metric tons (a per capita level of 5.72 metric tons), ranking Spain 20th compared to the other nations of the world. In 2000, the total of carbon dioxide emissions was at 282.9 million metric tons. In 2000 Spain's total carbon dioxide emissions totaled 282.9 million metric tons. By 2008 the UN reported that Spain's carbon dioxide emissions had increased further to 358.9 million metric tons, which made Spain the 19th largest emitter (1.09% of the global total). Industrial and agricultural sources contribute to the nation's water pollution problem. Spain is also vulnerable to oil pollution from tankers which travel the shipping routes near the nation's shores. Spain's cities produce about 13.8 million tons of solid waste per year.

The Spanish government's economic recovery plan in response to the 2008–09 global financial crisis included various measures to combat climate change, in areas such as waste and manure management, sustainable mobility, sustainable construction, energy efficiency and renewable energy, forest policy and urban drainage systems, and innovation. For example, in August 2008 the Spanish government launched the VIVE Plan (Innovative Vehicle-Ecological Vehicle) to subsidize the purchase of vehicles emitting less carbon dioxide and to encourage the recycling and dismantling of polluting vehicles more than 10 years old.

Principal environmental responsibility is vested in the Directorate General of the Environment, within the Ministry of Public Works and Urban Affairs. Protected areas included 4 natural UNESCO World Heritage sites and 68 Ramsar wetland sites. According to a 2011 report issued by the International Union for Conservation of Nature and Natural Resources (IUCN), threatened species included 16 types of mammals, 9 species of birds, 19 types of reptiles, 6 species of amphibians, 71 species of fish, 140 types of mollusks, 39 species of other invertebrates, and 214 species of plants. Threatened species included the Spanish lynx, Pyrenean ibex, Mediterranean monk seal, northern bald ibis, Spanish imperial eagle, Cantabrian capercaillie, dusky large blue and Nevada blue butterflies, and on the Canary Islands, the green sea turtle and Hierro giant lizard. The Canarian black oystercatcher and the Canary mouse have become extinct.

⁶POPULATION

The US Central Intelligence Agency (CIA) estimated the population of Spain to be approximately 46,754,784 (as of 2011), which placed it at number 27 in population among the 196 nations of the world. In 2011, approximately 17.1% of the population was over 65 years of age, with another 15.1% under 15 years of age. The median age in Spain was 40.5 years. There were 0.96 males for every female in the country. The population's annual rate of change was 0.574%. The projected population for the year 2025 is 48,400,000. Population density in Spain was calculated at 93 people per sq km (241 people per sq mi).

According to the CIA World Factbook, 77% of the population lived in urban areas, and that urban populations had an annual rate of change of 1.0% (as of 2010). The largest urban areas, along with their respective populations, included Madrid, 5.8 million; Barcelona, 5 million; and Valencia, 812,000.

⁷MIGRATION

Estimates of Spain's net migration rate, carried out by the CIA in 2011, amounted to 3.89 migrants per 1,000 citizens. The total number of emigrants living abroad was 1.37 million, and the total number of immigrants living in Spain was 6.9 million. Emigration of Spanish workers to the more industrialized countries of Western Europe, notably to the Federal Republic of Germany (FRG), France, Switzerland, and Belgium, increased markedly during the 1960s, but since 1973 the number of Spaniards returning to Spain has been greater than the number of those leaving.

A gateway into Europe, Spain receives large numbers of non-European migrants through Ceuta and Melilla. In August and September 2006, Spain attempted to rally international support regarding illegal immigration from Africa. Officials from the Canary Islands declared more than 22,000 immigrants had arrived

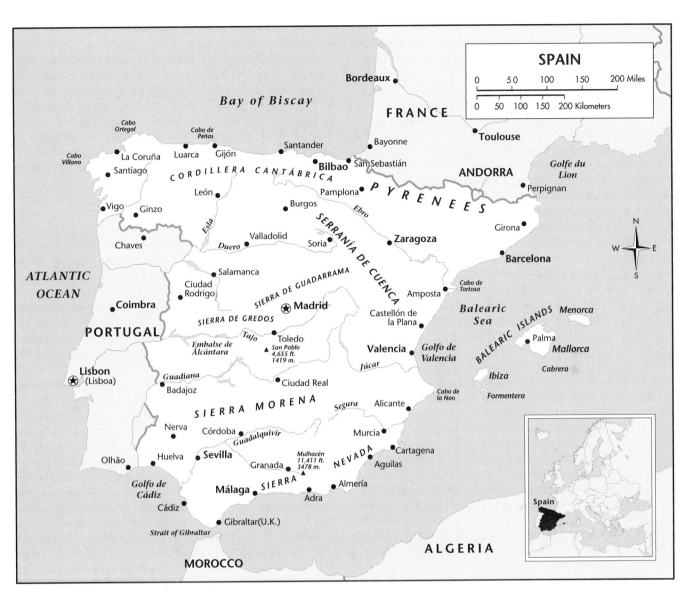

LOCATION: 36° to 43°47′N; 3°19′E to 9°30′W. BOUNDARY LENGTHS: France, 623 kilometers (387 miles); Andorra, 65 kilometers (40 miles); Mediterranean coastline, 1,670 kilometers (1,038 miles); Gibraltar, 1 kilometer (0.6 miles); Portugal, 1,214 kilometers (754 miles); Atlantic and Bay of Biscay coastlines, 2,234 kilometers (1,388 miles). The Balearic Islands extend from 1°12′ to 4°19′ E and 38°38′ to 40°5′N; coastline, 910 kilometers (565 miles). The Canary Islands, 1,400 kilometers (900 miles) to the southwest, extend from 13°20′ to 18°19′W and 27°38′ to 29°25′ N; coastline, 1,126 kilometers (700 miles). TERRITORIAL SEA LIMIT: 12 miles.

on the islands since the start of the year, and hundreds had died while attempting the sea crossing.

Placed into practice in 2001, Plan Greco was a scheme to regularize the immigration process; it was paralleled by a labor quota system aimed at responding to short and long-term labor shortages. However, both employers and labor unions agreed that the 2002 labor quota was a failure, falling short of the necessary workers. Between 1995and 2004, Spain's legal foreign-born population quadrupled from 500,000 to 2,000,000. In 2005, Spain had its fifth and largest legalization program with 690,679 unauthorized foreign workers applying. The global financial crisis of 2008–09 was particularly difficult on immigrant workers, who were among the first to lose their jobs in layoffs. In an effort to ease the overall unemployment situation, the government initiated a plan to pay Latin American immigrants to leave the country for at least three years. By June 2009, more than 25,000 Latin American immi-

grants had left Spain in search of jobs, but only about 4,000 took advantage of the government's offer, retaining the right to return whenever possible.

8 ETHNIC GROUPS

Ethnological studies reveal a homogeneous Latin stock in three-fourths of the country. The greatest contrasts are found between those of Celtic, Iberic, and Gothic antecedents in the north and those of southern lineage. The great mobility of the population toward the urban centers, the coast, and the islands has contributed to the diffusion of ethnic characteristics. Cultural groups, but not properly distinct ethnic groups, include the Castilians of central Spain, the Asturians and the Basques of Vizcaya, Álava, Guipúzcoa, and (in part) Navarra provinces in the north, the Catalans of Catalonia, the Galicians of the far northwest, and the Andalusians of the south. The Basques, Galicians, and Catalans consider themselves separate nations within Spain; they enjoy considerable cultural, economic, and political autonomy. Estimates of the Roma population are usually given as several hundred thousand.

9 LANGUAGES

According to the 1978 constitution, Spanish is the national language. Castilian, the dialect of the central and southern regions, is spoken by most Spaniards (74%) and is used in the schools and courts. Regional languages-Catalan (spoken by 17% of the population), Galician (7%), Basque (2%), Bable, and Valencian-are also official in the respective autonomous communities, where education is bilingual. Regional languages are spoken by over 16 million persons in Spain. A majority of those who live in the northeastern provinces and the Balearic Islands spoke Catalan, a neo-Latin tongue. Galician, close to Portuguese, was used in Galicia, in the northwest corner of Spain. The Basques in northern Spain spoke Basque, a pre-Roman language unrelated to any other known tongue and using an ancient script. Bable, a form of Old Castilian was spoken in Asturias (northwest), and Valencian, a dialect of Catalan, was used by inhabitants of the eastern province of Valencia.

10 RELIGIONS

In 2010, the Center for Sociological Investigations reported that about 73.2% of respondents were nominally Catholic, but 53.1% admitted that they don't usually attend Mass. Membership in all other Christian groups accounted for about 10% of the total population. These include Eastern Orthodox Christians, Protestants and evangelicals, Christian Scientists, Jehovah's Witnesses, Seventh-Day Adventists, and Mormons (members of The Church of Jesus Christ of Latter-day Saints). Muslims, Jews, Buddhists, Hindus, and Baha'is together account for less than 10% of the population. In 2009, there were approximately 1.4 million Muslims in the nation and 48,000 Jews. Roman Catholicism was once the official religion of Spain, but the constitution of 1978 established the principles of religious freedom and separation of church and state. The Roman Catholic Church does, however, continue to maintain certain privileges, as well as monetary support, from the state. There have been some reports of social discrimination against Muslims and Jews. Epiphany, Holy Thursday, Good Friday, Assumption, All Saints' Day, Immaculate Conception, and Christmas are observed as national holidays.

11 TRANSPORTATION

The CIA reports that Spain had a total of 681,298 km (423,339 mi) of roads in 2008, of which 681,298 km (423,339 mi) were paved. The Mediterranean and Cantábrico roadways are the most important. There are 606 vehicles per 1,000 people in the country. Railroads extend for 15,043 km (9,347 mi).

Spain has approximately 1,000 km (621 mi) of navigable waterways. Of Spain's 200 ports, 26 are of commercial significance. The largest are Barcelona, Tarragona, and Cartagena on the Mediterranean, Algeciras on the Strait of Gibraltar, La Coruña on the Atlantic, and Las Palmas and Santa Cruz de Tenerife in the Canaries. The port of Bilbao, on the Bay of Biscay, can accommodate tankers of up to 500,000 tons. Substantial improvements were made during the 1970s at Gijón, Huelva, and Valencia. Scheduled ferry services connect Spain with neighboring countries and North Africa.

In 2008, the merchant fleet was comprised of 158 vessels of 1,000 gross registered tons or more.

Spain had 95 airports with paved runways in 2009. Air travel transported 49.29 million passengers that year according to the World Bank. There were also nine heliports. Principal airports include Alicante, Prat at Barcelona, Ibiza, Lanzarote, Gran Canaria at Las Palmas, Barajas at Madrid, Málaga, Menorca, Son San Juan at Palma Mallorca, and Valencia. The state-owned Iberia Air Lines has regular connections with 50 countries and 89 cities in Europe, Africa, Asia (including the Middle East), and the Western Hemisphere.

12 HISTORY

Archaeological findings indicate that the region now known as Spain has been inhabited for thousands of years. A shrine near Santander, discovered in 1981, is believed to be over 14,000 years old, and the paintings discovered in the nearby caves of Altamira in 1879 are of comparable antiquity. The recorded history of Spain begins about 1000 BC, when the prehistoric Iberian culture was transformed by the invasion of Celtic tribes from the north and the coming of Phoenician and Greek colonists to the Spanish coast. From the 6th to the 2nd century BC, Carthage controlled the Iberian Peninsula up to the Ebro River; from 133 BC, with the fall of Numantia, until the barbarian invasions of the 5th century AD, Rome held Hispania, from which the name Spain is derived. During the Roman period, cities and roads were built, and Christianity and Latin, the language from which Spanish originated, were introduced. In the 5th century, the Visigoths, or western Goths, settled in Spain, dominating the country until 711, when the invading Moors defeated King Roderick. All of Spain, except for a few northern districts, knew Muslim rule for periods ranging from 300 to 800 years. Under Islam, a rich civilization arose, characterized by prosperous cities, industries, and agriculture and by brilliant writers, philosophers, and physicians, including Jews as well as Muslims. Throughout this period (711–1492), however, Christian Spain waged intermittent and local war against the Moors. The most prominent figure in this battle was El Cid, who fought for both Christians and Moors in the 11th century. By the 13th century, Muslim rule was restricted to the south of Spain. In 1492, Granada, the last Moorish stronghold on Spanish soil, fell, and Spain was unified under Ferdinand II of Aragón and Isabella I of Castile, the "Catholic Sovereigns." Until then, Aragón (consisting of Aragón, Catalonia, Valencia, and the Balearic Islands) had been an independent kingdom, which had expanded toward the eastern Mediterranean, incorporating Sicily and Naples, and had competed with Genoa and Venice. In order to strengthen the unity of the new state, Moors and Jews were expelled from Spain; Catholic converts who chose to stay were subject to the terrors of the Inquisition if suspected of practicing their former religions. The year 1492 also witnessed the official European discovery of the Americas by Christopher Columbus, sailing under the Castilian flag. In 1519, Ferdinand Magellan, a Portuguese in the service of Spain, began the first circumnavigation of the world, completed in 1522 by Juan Sebastián Elcano.

The 16th century, particularly under Charles I, who was also Holy Roman Emperor Charles V, was the golden age of Spain: its empire in the Americas produced vast wealth; its arts flourished; its fleet ruled the high seas; and its armies were the strongest in

Europe. By the latter part of the 16th century, however, under Philip II, the toll of religious wars in Europe and the flow of people and resources to the New World had drained the strength of the Spanish nation; in 1588, the "invincible" Spanish Armada was defeated by England. Spain's continental power was ended by wars with England, the Netherlands, and France in the 17th century and by the War of the Spanish Succession (1701–14), which also established the Bourbon (Borbón) dynasty in Spain. In 1808, the enfeebled Spanish monarchy was temporarily ended, and Napoleon Bonaparte's brother Joseph was proclaimed king of Spain. On 2 May 1808, however, the Spanish people revolted and, later assisted by the British, drove the French from Spain. In the post-Napoleonic period, the Bourbons were restored to the Spanish throne, but a spirit of liberalism, symbolized by the 1812 Constitution of Cádiz, remained strong.

Much of the 19th and early 20th centuries were consumed in passionate struggles between radical republicanism and absolute monarchy. Abroad, imperial Spain lost most of its dominions in the Western Hemisphere as a result of colonial rebellions in the first half of the 19th century; Cuba, Puerto Rico, and the Philippines were lost as a result of the Spanish-American War in 1898. Spain remained neutral in World War I but in the postwar period engaged in extensive military action to maintain its colonial possessions in Morocco. Early defeats in the Moroccan campaign paved the way in 1923 for the benevolent dictatorship of Primo de Rivera, who successfully ended the war in 1927 and remained in power under the monarchy until 1930. In 1931, after municipal elections indicated a large urban vote in favor of a republic, Alfonso XIII left Spain and a republic was established.

The constitution of December 1931 defined Spain as a "democratic republic of workers," with "no official religion," respecting the "rules of international law . . . renouncing war as an instrument of national policy and recognizing the principle of regional autonomy." Neither right nor left had a parliamentary majority, and on the whole the coalition governments were ineffective. On 17 July 1936, an army revolt against the republic took place in Spanish Morocco. On the following day, Gen. Francisco Franco landed in Spain, and for the next two and a half years, until 31 March 1939, Spain was ravaged by civil war. The two contending parties were the Republicans, made up partly of democrats and partly of antidemocratic left-wing groups, and the rebels (Nationalists), who favored the establishment of a right-wing dictatorship. Almost from the beginning, a number of foreign countries intervened. Germany and Italy furnished manpower and armaments to the Nationalists, while the USSR, Czechoslovakia, and Mexico supported the Republicans. Finally the Republicans were defeated, and General Franco formed a corporative state. Under the Franco regime, Spain gave aid to the Axis powers in World War II but was itself a nonbelligerent.

The Postwar Years

Diplomatically isolated following the end of World War II, Spain in succeeding decades improved its international standing, in part by signing economic and military agreements with the United States in 1953 and 1963. Spain was admitted to the UN in 1955. While relations with its European neighbors approached normality, the repressive nature of the Franco regime kept Spain apart from the main social, political, and economic currents of postwar Western Europe.

On 22 July 1969, Juan Carlos de Borbón y Borbón was officially designated by Franco as his successor, to rule with the title of king; formally, Franco had been ruling as regent for the prince since 1947. On 20 November 1975, Gen. Franco died at the age of 82, thus ending a career that had dominated nearly four decades of Spanish history. Two days later, Juan Carlos I was sworn in as king. He reconfirmed Carlos Arias Navarro as prime minister on 5 December. Despite Juan Carlos I's announcement, in early 1976, of a program of moderate political and social reform, the new government was received with widespread demonstrations by labor groups and Catalan and Basque separatists. Continued political unrest, coupled with a sharp rise in living costs, led ultimately to the king's dismissal of Arias Navarro, who was replaced, on 7 July, by Adolfo Suárez González.

On 15 June 1977, the first democratic elections in Spain in 40 years took place, with the Union of the Democratic Center (Unión de Centro Democrático—UCD), headed by Suárez, winning a majority in the new Cortes. The Cortes prepared a new constitution (in many respects similar to that of 1931), which was approved by popular referendum and sanctioned by the king in December 1978. In the elections of March 1979, the UCD was again the victor, and in the April local elections it captured more than 75% of the municipalities.

When Suárez announced his resignation in January 1981, the king named Leopoldo Calvo Sotelo y Bustelo to the premiership. As the Cortes wavered over the appointment, a group of armed civil guards stormed parliament on 23 February and held more than 300 deputies hostage for 17 hours. The attempted coup was swiftly neutralized by the king, who secured the loyalty of other military commanders. The plotters were arrested, and Sotelo was swiftly confirmed. A year of political wrangling followed; by mid-1982 the UCD was in disarray, and Sotelo called new elections. In October 1982, the Spanish Socialist Worker's Party (Partido Socialista Obrero Español—PSOE), headed by Felipe González Márquez, won absolute majorities in both houses of parliament. The new government was characterized by its relative youthfulness-the average age of cabinet ministers was 41-and by the fact that its members had no links with the Franco dictatorship. In the 1986 and 1989 elections, the PSOE again won majorities in both houses of parliament. The PSOE failed to win a majority in 1993 but governed with the support of the Basque and Catalan nationalist parties.

A continuing problem since the late 1960s has been political violence, especially in the Basque region. Political murders and kidnappings, mainly perpetrated by the separatist Basque Nation and Liberty (Euzkadi ta Askatasuna), commonly known as ETA, by the Antifascist Resistance Groups (GRAPO), and by several right-wing groups, abated only slightly in recent years. Another uncertainty in Spain's political future was the role of the military. Several army officers were arrested in October 1982 on charges of plotting a preelection coup, which reportedly had the backing of those involved in the February 1981 attempt. Spain joined NATO in 1982, but the membership question became so controversial that a referendum on it was held in March 1986; about two-thirds of the electorate voted, and 53% chose continued NATO membership. On 1 January of that year, Spain became a full member of the EC (now EU). In January 1988, the United States, acceding to Spain's demands, agreed to withdraw 72 jet fighters based near Madrid.

Spain received considerable recognition when they hosted the 1992 Summer Olympics in Barcelona, and Expo 92, a world's fair, in Sevilla. Other notable events included the designation of Madrid as the culture capital of Europe in 1992.

Throughout 1995–2000 Basque terrorists continued their attacks on civilian, police, and military targets and began to target more visible political targets. In August of 1995, the terrorists came close to assassinating King Juan Carlos while he was vacationing on the island of Majorca, off the southeastern coast of Spain. In 1997 Basque terrorists killed an important Socialist official of one of the Basque regions. In 2000, Jose Luis Lopez de la Calle, a Madrid newspaper columnist who was outspoken in his criticism of the Basque group, ETA, was shot to death outside his home. Thousands marched in the streets to protest his killing.

In 1995 information came to light revealing that from 1983 to 1987 government officials in cooperation with the Civil Guard (Spain's national police force) formed death squads to hunt down and kill Basque terrorists living in France. The squads were disbanded after France agreed to greater cooperation with Spanish authorities, but not before 27 suspected Basque terrorists had been killed. The existence of the death squads may have remained a secret, but two death squad members were caught in the course of an attack and prosecuted for murder. At first government officials secured the silence of these two men by agreeing to make yearly payments to their wives, but by 1994 they felt that the story should no longer be hidden and revealed it to the world from their jail cells. Initially, Prime Minister Gonzalez had been charged with having knowledge of the attacks but an official inquiry into the charges concluded that they were groundless and he was completely exonerated.

Although French and Spanish security officials worked together to combat terrorism, violence attributed to the Basque terrorists continued into the 2000s. However, public support for Basque terrorists had waned nearly completely. A 1996 Basque execution of a kidnapped university professor brought out almost a half-million protesters in Madrid alone denouncing the Basque terrorists. A year later and again in 2000, assassinations allegedly carried out by Basque terrorists triggered large protests as well. The ETA was suspected of being behind bombings in several tourist resorts in June 2002 as an EU summit was held in Seville. In February 2003, Basque Socialist Party activist Joseba Pagazaurtundua was assassinated; the shooting was attributed to the ETA. Batasuna, the separatist Basque political party believed to be the political arm of the ETA, was banned by the Supreme Court in 2003. This ban prevented Batasuna candidates from running in municipal elections that year. In February 2005, a car bomb exploded in Madrid, injuring about 40 people: ETA was suspected of being responsible for the attack. In May 2005, the government offered to hold peace talks with the ETA if the group disarmed. In March 2006, ETA declared a cease-fire. In June, Prime Minister José Luis Rodríguez Zapatero said the government would hold peace talks with the group. However, in December 2006, Zapatero suspended moves to seek dialogue with ETA after a car bomb attack at a Madrid airport. In June 2007, ETA called off the cease-fire. That August, the ETA was blamed for a car bomb in Basque country.

In September 2007, a leading ETA bomb maker was arrested near Toulouse, France.

As Spain attempted to hold itself together against regional separatism, it joined with seven other nations in 1995 to create a passport-free zone that allowed much greater mobility between them to implement the Schengen Agreement, which created the EU's passport-free Schengen Area. Spain also rejoined the NATO Military Command in the mid-1990s, making it once again a full member of the alliance. The adjustments to Spain's economy carried out in the mid- and late-1990s were successful. As a result, Spain was one of the 11 countries that joined together in launching the euro, the European Union's single currency, on 1 January 1999. (Greece joined shortly thereafter, bringing the number of countries in the euro zone to 12).

On 11 July 2002, 12 Moroccan frontier guards landed on the island of Perejil, which is claimed by Spain, and claimed it as Moroccan territory. Spain's Prime Minister José María Aznar opposed the occupation, and sent troops to evacuate the Moroccan guards. Diplomatic relations between Spain and Morocco improved in December 2002, when plans were made for the return of each state's ambassadors.

During 2002 and into 2003, Aznar affirmed Spain's support for the United States and British position on the use of military force to force Iraq to disarm itself of weapons of mass destruction. More than 90% of Spain's citizens were against a war in Iraq, which began on 19 March 2003. Spain's pro-US stance alienated France and Germany, among other nations opposing the use of military force. Spain did not commit combat troops to fight alongside US and British forces, but it sent 900 troops trained in medical support and anti-mine specialties to assist the coalition forces.

On 11 March 2004, Madrid suffered a major terrorist attack as four rush-hour trains were bombed simultaneously in 10 explosions, killing 191 people and wounding more than 1,400. An Islamic group with links to the al-Qaeda organization was later blamed for the attacks. The attacks took place three days prior to general elections. On 12 March, massive demonstrations in many Spanish cities were held (some 11.4 million people took part, more than a fourth of the Spanish population), which denounced terrorism, and in part the Aznar administration for its support of the war in Iraq and the presence of Spanish troops there. In the general elections held on 14 March, the Socialists, led by José Luis Rodríguez Zapatero, defied earlier public opinion polls and won nearly 43% of the vote for a gain of 39 seats in the Congress of Deputies. When Zapatero was sworn in as president of the government and prime minister in April, he ordered the withdrawal of all Spanish troops from Iraq. The next presidential elections were scheduled for March 2008.

In February 2005, Spanish voters approved the EU constitution in a referendum by 77%. However, the French and Dutch rejections of the constitution in May and June 2005 indefinitely shelved plans for the EU to adopt such a document for itself.

In June 2005, the Spanish parliament defied the Roman Catholic Church by legalizing gay marriage and granting homosexual couples the same adoption and inheritance rights as heterosexual couples. As of 2007, five countries in the world-Spain, the Netherlands, Belgium, Canada, and South Africa-had legalized same-sex marriages. As of 2011, 10 countries in the world—Argentina, Belgium, Canada, Iceland, the Netherlands, Norway, Portugal, South Africa, Spain, and Sweden—had legalized same-sex marriages.

In June 2006, voters in Catalonia supported proposals to give the region greater autonomy as well as the status of a nation within Spain.

In August and September 2006, Spain attempted to rally international support regarding illegal immigration from Africa. Officials from the Canary Islands declared more than 22,000 immigrants had arrived on the islands since the start of the year, and hundreds had died while attempting the sea crossing.

In March 2008 José Luis Rodríguez Zapatero's Socialist party gained five additional seats in the Congress of Deputies. Nevertheless, it still fell seven seats short of an overall majority.

The global recession of 2008–09 ravaged Spain's economy, sending the unemployment rate to 17.9% by May 2009. Spain's unemployment figures, the highest in the European Union (EU), affected immigrant and young workers disproportionately. Spain introduced public policy programs that incentivized the return migration of Latin American and Romanian workers, although the effectiveness of the programs remained unclear. By June 2009, youth unemployment was estimated at more than 36%.

The economic crisis spurred a political crisis as well, and the ruling Socialist Party was blamed for the nation's woes. In response, José Luis Rodríguez Zapatero called for early elections to be held on 20 November 2011, with the hope that a change in government would provide a fresh start toward recovery in 2012 and boost market confidence. The opposition Popular Party, led by Mariano Rajoy, won a resounding victory, with 44% of the vote compared to 29% for the Socialists, amidst concern over the country's continued debt, slow growth, and high unemployment rates.

In January 2011, ETA announced in a video statement to the local media that it would initiate a permanent ceasefire in its violent fight for Basque independence. The Spanish government rejected the ETA's statement as invalid, since similar promises made in the past have been broken. The ETA statement did not include any reference to disarmament, which has been one of the demands set forth by the Spanish government.

13 GOVERNMENT

Between 1966 and 1978, Spain was governed under the Organic Law of the Spanish State. A new constitution, approved by the Cortes on 31 October 1978 and by the electorate in a national referendum on 6 December, and ratified by King Juan Carlos I on 27 December 1978, repealed all the laws of the Franco regime and confirmed Spain as a parliamentary monarchy. It also guaranteed the democratic functioning of all political parties, disestablished the Roman Catholic Church, and recognized the right to autonomy of distinct nationalities and regions.

According to the constitution, the king is the head of state, symbolizing its unity. Legislative power is vested in the Cortes Generales (General Courts), consisting of two chambers: the Congreso de los Diputados (Congress of Deputies) with 350 members (deputies); and the Senado (Senate) with 264 members (senators). All deputies and 208 of the senators are popularly elected to four-year terms under universal adult suffrage. The remaining senators (56) are chosen by the assemblies in the 17 autonomous regions. The government, which answers to the congress, consists of the president (prime minister), vice president, and ministers, all ap-

pointed by the king. The supreme consultative organ of government is the Council of State. Also established by the constitution is the function of "defender of the people," inspired by medieval tradition and by the Scandinavian ombudsman. Suffrage is universal at age 18.

14 POLITICAL PARTIES

The Falange, known officially as the Nationalist Movement, was the only legally functioning party in Spain during the Franco regime. Founded in 1933 by José Antonio Primo de Rivera, it dated in its later form from 1937, when various right-wing groups were united under Gen. Franco. Nationalists, monarchists, and national syndicalists (Fascists) were the leading groups within the Falange. It lost some of its former power and much of its prestige during the last decades of Franco's regime. On 21 December 1974, the Franco government passed a law conferring a limited right of political association. On 9 June 1976, after Franco's death, the Cortes voted to legalize political parties; by the 1977 parliamentary elections, no fewer than 156 political parties were organized into 10 national coalitions and 12 regional alliances.

The Spanish political scene is characterized by changing parties and shifting alliances. The Union of the Democratic Center (Unión de Centro Democrático—UCD) was formed as an electoral coalition of smaller moderate parties. From 1977 to 1982, the UCD was the governing political body, headed first by Adolfo Suárez González and then by Leopoldo Calvo Sotelo y Bustelo. In late 1981, the UCD began to disintegrate; it won only 8% of the vote in the 1982 elections and was dissolved in February 1983. A new centrist party, the Democratic and Social Center (Centro Democrático y Social—CDS), was created in 1982. The Spanish Socialist Worker's Party (Partido Socialista Obrero Español— PSOE), which traces its lineage to the late 19th century, won absolute majorities in both chambers of the Cortes in October 1982 and June 1986.

The right is represented by the Popular Party or PP, embracing the Alianza Popular, the Christian Democratic Partido Demócrata Popular, and the Partido Liberal; the coalition took 26% of the 1986 vote. An extreme rightist party, New Force (Fuerza Nueva), lost its only seat in parliament in 1982 and thereupon dissolved. The Communist Party (Partido Comunista—PC), legalized in 1977, was one of the most outspoken "Eurocommunist" parties in the late 1970s, harshly criticizing the former USSR for human rights abuses. In the 1986 election, the PC formed part of the United Left coalition (Izquierda Unida—IU), which included a rival Communist faction and several socialist parties; the IU's share of the vote was 4.6%. Nationalist parties function in Catalonia, Andalucía, the Basque Provinces, and other areas. The most powerful are the Catalan Convergence and Union (CIU), the Basque Nationalists (PNV), and the Canaries Coalition (CC).

Despite charges of corruption and economic mismanagement, the PSOE secured electoral victories in 1989 and 1993; however, the party finished 17 seats short of a parliamentary majority in 1993. A noticeable shift toward the conservative PP was evident with a 34-seat gain between 1989 and 1993. PSOE secretary-general Felipe Gonzalez Marquez received endorsement for a fourth term as prime minister, receiving support from the small Basque and Catalan nationalist parties.

In 1996, however, Gonzalez was turned out of power by José María Aznar, a young conservative leader with little international visibility. Aznar, as leader of PP, won reelection as prime minister in the March 2000 election, the first in which a center-right party won majority control of the government outright. In the March 2004 election, which was held three days after the 11 March Madrid train bombings, Aznar's PP lost 39 seats in the Congress of Deputies and the PSOE gained 35 seats to hold 164 seats in the chamber. The PSOE victory was seen to have been a reaction to the train bombings, which were blamed in part on the Aznar administration for its support of the US-led war in Iraq. José Luis Rodríguez Zapatero of the PSOE became prime minister.

The distribution of seats in the Congress of Deputies following the March 2004 election was as follows: PSOE, 164; PP, 148; CIU, 10; ERC (a Catalan party), 8; PNV, 7; CC, 3; IU, 2; and others, 8. Election results for the Senate were as follows: PP, 102; PSOE, 81; Entesa Catalona de Progress, 12; PNV, 6; CIU, 4; and CC, 3.

In the 2008 senate elections, the Popular Party won 101 seats, followed by the Spanish Socialist Workers Party with 88 seats, the Entesa Catalona de Progress coalition (including four Catalan parties) with 12 seats, Convergence and Union (a coalition of the Democratic Convergence of Catalonia and the Democratic Union of Catalonia) with 4 seats, the Basque Nationalist Party with 2 seats, and the Canarian Coalition with 1 seat. In the elections for the Congress of Deputies, the Spanish Socialist Workers Party won 169 seats, followed by the Popular Party with 154 seats, Convergence and Union with 10 seats, the Basque Nationalist Party with six seats, and the Republican Left of Catalonia with three seats. Jose Luis Rodriguez Zapatero was reelected as president of the government with 46.9% of the vote from the national assembly.

In October 2009, authorities arrested ten senior members of Batasuna, a banned political party of the Basque separatist movement. The arrests resulted from allegations that the members have been meeting secretly since the beginning of the year while planning to rebuild the party in cooperation with ETA (Euskadi Ta Azkatasuna—Basque Homeland and Freedom), an armed separatist group that has also been officially banned from politics. Batasuna was banned in 2003 because of its affiliation with ETA. The interior minister has stated that any attempts to reestablish the party will be blocked, as long as the Basque separatist movement links violence to its political aspirations. ETA was established in the 1960s as a student resistance movement. Since then, it has grown significantly while promoting its sometimes violent campaign for a Basque homeland that would include seven regions of northern Spain and southwest France. Since its founding, ETA has been responsible for over 820 deaths; its primary targets have been members of the Spanish civil guard and police force, and local and national politicians opposed to Basque independence.

King Juan Carlos I has reigned since November 1975. Jose Luis Rodriguez Zapatero of the Spanish Socialist Workers Party (Partido Socialista Obrero Español—PSOE) was first elected as president in 2004 and then reelected in 2008. On 20 November 2011, the opposition Popular Party, led by Mariano Rajoy, won a resounding victory, with 44% of the vote compared to 29% for the Socialists, amidst concern over the country's continued debt, slow growth, and high unemployment rates.

¹⁵LOCAL GOVERNMENT

Spain is divided into 17 autonomous regions, each of which has an elected assembly and a governor appointed by the central government. Municipalities are gradually becoming consolidated; their number had declined to about 8,000 by the early 2000s. Each municipality has a mayor (*alcalde*) and councilmen (*concejales*); the councilmen, directly elected by the people, elect the mayors. Fifty-six of the 264 members of the Senate are chosen by the regional assemblies.

The statutes governing the Basque and Catalan autonomous communities, providing for regional high courts and legislative assemblies, were approved by referendum in October 1979; the statutes for Galicia in December 1980; and those for Andalucía in October 1981. Autonomy statutes for the other 11 historic regions of continental Spain and the Balearic and Canary Islands were subsequently approved and a regular electoral process begun.

¹⁶JUDICIAL SYSTEM

According to the 1978 constitution, the judiciary is independent and subject only to the rule of law. The highest judicial body is the Supreme Court (Tribunal Supremo), the president of which is nominated by the 20 judges of the General Council of the Judiciary and appointed by the king.

Territorial high courts (*audiencias*) are the courts of last appeal in the 17 regions of the country; provincial audiencias serve as appellate courts in civil matters and as courts of first instance in criminal cases. On the lowest level are the judges of the first instance and instruction, district judges, and justices of the peace.

The National High Court (Audiencia Nacional), created in 1977, has jurisdiction over criminal cases that transgress regional boundaries and over civil cases involving the central state administration. The constitution of 1978 also established the 12-member Constitutional Court (Tribunal Constitucional), with competence to judge the constitutionality of laws and decide disputes between the central government and the autonomous regions. The European Court of Human Rights is the final arbiter in cases concerning human rights.

Defendants in criminal cases have the right to counsel at state expense if indigent. The constitution prohibits arbitrary arrest and detention. Suspects may be held for no more than three days without a judicial hearing.

A jury system was established in 1995, and a new penal code was enacted in 1996.

The constitution provides for the right to a fair public trial and the government respects this provision in practice.

¹⁷ARMED FORCES

The International Institute for Strategic Studies reported that the Spanish Armed Forces consisted of armed forces in Spain totaled 142,212 members in 2011. The force is comprised of 78,121 from the army, 21,606 from the navy, 21,172 from the air force, and 21,313 members of joint forces. Armed forces represent 1% of the labor force in Spain. Defense spending totaled $16.5 billion and accounted for 1.2% of GDP.

In December 2009, Spain announced that it would send 511 more troops to Afghanistan to bolster the International Security Assistance Force (ISAF), the North Atlantic Treaty Organization's

(NATO) efforts in the country. The December announcement followed US president Barack Obama's commitment of an additional 30,000 troops to Afghanistan. As of 2011, Spain's total deployment in Afghanistan numbered 1,523 troops, almost double the country's commitment to Afghanistan in January 2009. Spain also provided troops to UN peacekeeping and other EU and NATO military missions.

[18] INTERNATIONAL COOPERATION

Spain joined the UN on 14 December 1955; it participates in ECE, ECLAC, and several nonregional specialized agencies, such as the FAO, UNESCO, UNHCR, UNIDO, ILO, the World Bank, and the WHO. Spain is also a member of the Council of Europe, the African Development Bank, the Asian Development Bank, the European Bank for Reconstruction and Development, the Inter-American Development Bank, NATO, OECD, the WTO, OSCE, the Paris Club, the Western EU, and the EU. The nation holds observer status in the OAS and the Latin American Integration Association (LAIA).

Spain has supported UN missions and operations in Kosovo (est. 1999), Ethiopia and Eritrea (est. 2000), Burundi (est. 2004), Haiti (est. 2004), and the DROC (est. 1999). The nation is part of the Australia Group, the Zangger Committee, the Nuclear Suppliers Group (London Group), and the Nuclear Energy Agency. In environmental cooperation, Spain is part of the Antarctic Treaty; the Basel Convention; Conventions on Biological Diversity, Whaling, and Air Pollution; Ramsar; CITES; the London Convention; International Tropical Timber Agreements; the Kyoto Protocol; the Montréal Protocol; MARPOL; the Nuclear Test Ban Treaty; and the UN Conventions on the Law of the Sea, Climate Change, and Desertification.

[19] ECONOMY

The GDP rate of change in Spain, as of 2010, was -0.1%. Inflation stood at 1.3%, and unemployment was reported at 20%, which rose to 21.5% by the third quarter of 2011.

Agriculture, livestock, and mining—the traditional economic mainstays—no longer occupy the greater part of the labor force or provide most of the exports. In order to offset the damage suffered by the industrial sector during the Civil War and to cope with the problems created by Spain's post-World War II isolation, the Franco regime concentrated its efforts on industrial expansion. Especially after 1953, the industrial sector expanded rapidly.

From 1974 through the early 1980s, the Spanish economy was adversely affected by international factors, especially oil price increases. Tourism is a major source of foreign exchange, and in 2000 was generating 10% of GDP (up from 3.3% in 1995) and employing, directly or indirectly, one eighth of the labor force. Spain is one of the world's most popular tourist destinations. Spain had 53.6 million tourists in 2004, an increase over 2003, despite the terrorist attacks on Spain's commuter trains on 11 March 2004, which killed 191 people and injured 1,500. The annual GDP growth rate during 1974–77 was 3%, higher than that in other OECD countries, but the inflation rate reached 24% in 1977. Real GDP growth slowed during 1980–85. Following peak growth year in the late 1980s, Spain entered a recession in 1992. By 1998, however, growth had increased, and in 1999 and 2000, averaged

over 4%. The global economic slowdown after 2001 helped reduce GDP growth an averaged 3.3% over the period 2000–04.

Consumer prices rose 37% between 1989 and 1995, and unemployment rose from 17.3% to 21.3%, the highest in the EU. Macroeconomic improvements from 1995 to 1998, however, were sufficient for Spain to be included in the first group of EU members to enter the Economic and Monetary Union (EMU) in 1999. Under the Aznar administration unemployment fell steadily, although still remained high and increase somewhat in 2002. By 1998 inflation had been reduced and averaged 3.3% from 2000–04. The Rodriguez Zapatero government pursued job creation upon coming into power in April 2004. Joblessness is among the highest in the EU, and profound changes to labor market regulations have been called for to reduce unemployment further. Spain has continued to fight a battle against loss of competition under the new currency and a loss of structural funds from the EU.

The economy grew each year from 1994 through early 2008, but suffered significantly during the global recession of 2008–09, primarily as a result of a major decline in the construction and housing industries. By May 2009, Spain's unemployment rate had reached a soaring 17.9%, the highest in the EU. Many economists worried that Spain was in the early grips of a deflationary spiral. A stimulus package announced in May 2009 offered tax cuts for small businesses and a plan to boost sales of unsold new homes. Government subsidies for new car buyers were also promised as a means to shore up the nation's auto industry, which is the third largest in Europe.

The recession has been particularly difficult on immigrant workers, who are among the first to lose their jobs in layoffs, and youth just entering the job market. In an effort to ease the overall unemployment situation, the government initiated a plan to pay Latin American immigrants to leave the country for at least three years. By June 2009, more than 25,000 Latin American immigrants had left Spain in search of jobs, but only about 4,000 took advantage of the government's offer, retaining the right to return whenever possible. In June, the government began to consider a similar plan for the nation's 70,000 unemployed Romanian workers, but with the bleak economic situation in their home country, Spanish unemployment benefits are a more attractive offer than a Romanian salary.

In June 2009, youth unemployment was estimated at 36%. As a result, record numbers of the country's youth enlisted in the military in an effort to secure a stable paycheck, along with other benefits. Some new immigrant recruits have joined for both a job and as a means of gaining Spanish citizenship. Overall, the economy grew by about 3.6% for 2009. Into 2010, Spain remained in recession even as other European countries were showing signs of recovery. The International Monetary Fund predicted a year-end contraction in the economy of 0.6% and public debt was expected to rise from 55.2% of GDP in 2009 to 74.3% by 2012.

By April 2010, Spain's unemployment rate was 20%, the highest rate of unemployment for Spain in nearly thirteen years. The announcement, which was released by Spain's national statistics agency, came as official EU statistics showed unemployment across the eurozone to remain constant at 10%.

In May 2010, the IMF issued a stark warning to Spain, calling for "urgent and decisive action" to address the challenges that threatened to unravel the country's recovery. The IMF's warning came just weeks after the IMF joined the EU to launch a massive $975 billion bailout package for Greece. With a deficit that amounted to 11% of its economic output, many worried that Spain could need massive international assistance. Among the difficult challenges Spain faced, the IMF included a dysfunctional labor market, a large fiscal deficit, heavy private sector and external indebtedness, anemic productivity growth, weak competitiveness, and a banking sector with pockets of weakness.

To address the deficit, the government initiated an $18 billion austerity package in May 2010 that included a 5% cut in pay for nearly 2.5 million public sector workers and a freeze on some pensions, with a freeze on salaries until 2011. The move led to large, nationwide protests and a day-long strike of public workers in June 2010. Despite these and additional measures, government borrowing costs continued to rise into 2011, leading to a sharp decline in consumer and investor confidence. The financial crisis spurred a political crisis as well, as the ruling Socialist Party was blamed for the nation's woes. In response, the prime minister called for early elections to be held on 20 November 2011, with the hope that a change in government would provide a fresh start toward recovery in 2012 and boost market confidence. The opposition Popular Party won a resounding victory in these amidst concern over the country's continued debt, slow growth, and high unemployment rates.

20 INCOME

The CIA estimated that in 2010 the GDP of Spain was $1.4 trillion. The CIA defines GDP as the value of all final goods and services produced within a nation in a given year and computed on the basis of purchasing power parity (PPP) rather than value as measured on the basis of the rate of the exchange based on current dollars. The per capita GDP was estimated at $29,400, and the annual growth rate of GDP was -0.1%. The average inflation rate was 1.3%. It was estimated that Agriculture accounted for an estimated 2.9% of GDP, industry 25.5%, and services 71.6%. The World Bank estimated that Spain, with 0.71% of the world's population, accounted for 2.15% of the world's GDP. By comparison, the United States, with 4.85% of the world's population, accounted for 22.51% of world GDP.

The World Bank reports that in 2009, household consumption in Spain totaled $828.5 billion or about $17,721 per capita, measured in current US dollars rather than PPP. Household consumption includes expenditures of individuals, households, and nongovernmental organizations on goods and services, excluding the purchases of dwellings. It was estimated that household consumption was growing at an average annual rate of 4.2%. In 2011, the World Bank reported that actual individual consumption in Spain was 68.3% of GDP and accounted for 2.23% of world consumption. By comparison, the United States accounted for 25.44% of world individual consumption. The World Bank also estimated that 10.1% of Spain's GDP was spent on food and beverages, 13% on housing and household furnishings, 3.3% on clothes, 7.5% on health, 7.1% on transportation, 1.6% on communications, 6.2% on recreation, 11.2% on restaurants and hotels, and 3.7% on miscellaneous goods and services and purchases from abroad.

According to the World Bank, remittances from citizens living abroad totaled $9.9 billion or about $212 per capita and accounted for approximately .7% of GDP.

On 20 October 2011, the National Statistics Institute, or INE, reported that 21.8 percent of Spain's population lives under the poverty line, exceeding the poverty rate of 20.7 percent in 2010 and 19.5 percent in 2009.

21 LABOR

As of 2010, Spain had a total labor force of 23.09 million people. Within that labor force, the CIA estimated in 2009 that 4.2% were employed in agriculture, 24% in industry, and 71.7% in the service sector. Employment in agriculture has been in steady decline; many farm workers have been absorbed by construction and industry.

The constitution of 1978 guarantees the freedom to form unions and the right to strike. The law provides for the right to bargain collectively, and unions exercise this right in practice. Discrimination against union activity is illegal. According to Spain's Social and Economic Council, as of 2007 approximately 60.3% of employees were covered by collective agreements. The Ministry of Work and Immigration reported that in 2007 about 17% of all employees in dependent employment were union members.

An expansive labor reform package was passed in 2010 to address Spain's high unemployment rate. It included measures to measures to promote more flexibility in the labor market, such as cutting the costs of firing workers and reducing severance payouts. These reforms, however, were protested by some Spanish unions, youths, and others.

As of July 2011, the monthly minimum wage was about $1,008. This wage provides a decent standard of living for a family. The regular workweek was 40 hours, with a mandated 36-hour rest period. In addition, workers receive 12 paid holidays per year and one month's paid vacation. The legal minimum age for employment was 16 years, and this is enforced by the Ministry of Labor and Social Affairs.

22 AGRICULTURE

During 1970–2003, the proportion of the GDP from agriculture fell from 11.3% to 3%, and the proportion of workers employed in agriculture decreased from 26% to about 7%. Roughly 37% of the total land is farmed, and the country's major crops include grain, vegetables, olives, wine grapes, sugar beets, and citrus. Cereal production in 2009 amounted to 17.8 million tons, fruit production 14.5 million tons, and vegetable production 13.4 million tons.

According to Eurostat, Spain's crop output in 2010 totaled €24.354 billion ($32.4 billion), the third greatest national yield among EU member-states. In 2003, Spain's crop output was valued third highest among the EU nations, at more than €27.1 billion ($36.1 billion). Grapes are cultivated in every region; the most important olive groves are in Andalucía. After France and Italy, Spain is the world's leading wine producer. According to the UN FAO, in 2009 Spain produced 3,250,610 tons of wine. Within the domestic market, the use of sunflower oil and soybean oil has grown considerably.

Agricultural mechanization has been increasing steadily. The use of fertilizers has also increased. The Institute for Agrarian Development and Reform directly or indirectly regulates some 10 million hectares (25 million acres) of land, promoting intensive cultivation and irrigation to improve productivity.

23 ANIMAL HUSBANDRY

The UN Food and Agriculture Organization (FAO) reported that Spain dedicated 10.6 million hectares (26.2 million acres) to permanent pasture or meadow in 2009. Spain's pastures cover about 23% of the total area. Because much of Spain is arid or semiarid, sheep are by far the most important domestic animals. The sheep population numbered 19.7 million in 2009; production totaled 124,424 tons of lamb and mutton. In 2009, Spain's livestock population also included 142,000 asses, 6 million head of cattle, 138 million chickens, 2.26 million goats, 250,000 horses, 110,000 mules, 26.3 million pigs, and 19.7 million sheep. The production from these animals amounted to 666,116 tons of beef and veal, 2.72 million tons of pork, 1.22 million tons of poultry, 655,716 tons of eggs, and 7.82 million tons of milk. Spain also produced 66,600 tons of cattle hide and 28,500 tons of raw wool.

24 FISHING

Fishing is important, especially along the northern coastline. The Spanish fishing fleet is the largest within the EU. Spain had 17,521 decked commercial fishing boats in 2008. The annual capture totaled 917,188 tons according to the UN FAO. The export value of seafood totaled $2.58 billion. The most common species processed by the Spanish canning industry are: tuna, mussels, sardines, white tuna, cephalopod, mackerel, and anchovy.

The main aquacultural commodities are mussels, trout, oysters, clams, and gilthead bream. Mussel production began in 1940 in northwestern Spain, and today there are thousands of floating mollusk beds found in many Spanish bays. Trout farming began in 1960, and is located in the north and northwest. Spain is the world's second leading producer of mussels after China.

25 FORESTRY

Approximately 36% of Spain is covered by forest. The northern Cantabrian range accounts for about one third of the timberland. In addition, Spain has 2.5 million hectares (6.2 million acres) of woodlots typically comprised of oaks and cork trees, located mostly in the west (especially in Estremadura and Salamanca). The UN FAO estimated roundwood production in 2009 at 11.9 million cu m (420.3 million cu ft), with about 13% used as fuel wood. Spain is one of the largest producers of cork, its most important commercial forest product. Spain's annual production of cork amounts to about 110,000 tons, or 32% of world production. Scotch and maritime pine, as well as radiata pine, are the main softwood lumber species produced in Spain; eucalyptus and poplar are the principal hardwood species. The value of all forest products in 2009, including roundwood, totaled $4.34 billion.

26 MINING

Spain had some of the most mineralized territory in Western Europe, including the volcanic-hosted massive sulfide (VMS) deposits of the Iberian Pyrite Belt (IPB) of southern Spain. The IPB alone was estimated to have yielded 1.7 billion tons of sulfides, and more than 80 VMS deposits have been recorded in which individual tonnages were in excess of one million tons. Spain had the largest known reserves of celestite (Europe's sole producer, ranking second in world production, behind China); was home to the richest mercury deposit in the world and one of the biggest open-pit zinc mines in Europe; and remained the leading producer of sepiolite, with 70% of world reserves (around Madrid). Spain was the largest EU producer of mine lead and zinc, and a major producer of pyrites, among other nonferrous and precious metals. Production far exceeded domestic consumption for most nonmetallic minerals, and Spain was a net exporter to other EU countries of lead, mercury, nonmetallic-mineral manufactured products, slate, other crude industrial minerals, and zinc. In terms of value, Spain was one of the leading EU countries, with one of its highest levels of self-sufficiency in mineral raw materials. Spain's nonfuel mineral production was valued at €4.8 billion in 2008, fourth in the EU after France, Germany, and Poland. In 2009, Spain was the world's third largest producer of gypsum, sixth in fluorspar, and ninth in cement. Almost all known minerals were found in Spain, and mining was still a notable, though much diminished, factor in the economy. Of the 100 minerals mined, 18 were produced in large quantities—bentonite, copper, fluorspar, glauberite, gold, iron, lead, magnetite, mercury, potash, pyrites, quartz, refractory argillite, sea and rock salt, sepiolitic salts, tin, tungsten, and zinc. The output of lead, zinc, and copper ores, all once important to the Spanish economy, has been declining. The number of active operations has halved in recent years, with copper production a notable casualty. In 2008, Spain had 2,549 enterprises in the nonfuel minerals sector. Quarried mineral products, particularly quarried stone, accounted for a significant share of the value of all minerals produced.

Lead mine output was 125,000 metric tons in 2009. Zinc mine output totaled 500,770 metric tons in 2009, up from 456,050 metric tons in 2008. Copper mine production in 2009 was estimated at 6,987 metric tons, down from 7,067 metric tons in 2008 and from 9,748 metric tons in 2001. Gold mine output in 2009 totaled 3,400 kg. Silver mine output in 2009 totaled 3,400 kg. Germanium oxide, tin, titanium dioxide, and uranium also were mined. Because of market conditions, iron mining was halted in 1997, after 588,000 tons (metal content) was produced in 1996. Iron ore was one of Spain's principal mineral assets, with 6 million tons of total reserves in the north (Basque provinces, Asturias, León) and in Andalucía; the Alquife mine, in Granada, which was closed for maintenance, had a capacity of 4 million tons per year.

Among industrial minerals, Spain in 2009 produced an estimated: 10 million tons of marl; 15 million tons of dolomite; 2.6 million tons of ornamental marble; 270 million tons of limestone; 770,007 metric tons (reported) of meerschaum sepiolite; 435,000 metric tons of potash (reported); and 169,930 metric tons of calcined magnesite (from deposits in Navarra and Lugo). Spain also produced barite, bromine, calcium carbonate, hydraulic cement, clays (including attapulgite, bentonite, and washed kaolin), diatomite, tripoli, feldspar, fluorspar (acid-grade and metallurgical grade), gypsum, anhydrite, andalusite kyanite, hydrated lime and quicklime, mica, nitrogen, mineral pigments (ocher and red iron oxide), pumice, salt (including rock, marine, and by-product from potash), silica sand (including as by-product of feldspar and kaolin production), soda ash, natural sulfate (including glauberite and thenardite), large quantities of all stone (including basalt, chalk, ornamental granite, ophite, phonolite, porphyry, quartz, quartzite, sandstone, serpentine, slate), strontium minerals, sulfur, talc, and steatite.

Historically, minerals belonged to the state, with the industry comprising a mix of state-owned, state-and-privately owned, and privately owned companies. However, the Spanish government has been moving rapidly toward privatization and changed laws regarding financing of industrial participation in 2006. The economic development of certain areas, such as the Asturias and the Basque regions, was based on their mineral wealth, and mining continued to be an important current and potential source of income in these and other mineral-rich areas. The independent government of Andalucía completed its first mining development plan (1996–2000). Several old and new prospects were being evaluated, and exploration activity was high, particularly for feldspar (in Badajoz, Toledo, and Salamanca), garnet (Galicia), pyrites (Badajoz), and rutile and zircon (Cuidad Real). The main polymetallic deposits included Tharsis, Scotiel, Rio Tinto, and Aznalcollar.

27 ENERGY AND POWER

Spain has only small reserves of oil and natural gas, with coal being the country's most abundant energy source. As of 1 January 2011, the CIA World Factbook estimated that Spain's proved reserves of crude oil and natural gas totaled 150 million barrels and 2,548 million cu m, respectively. As a result, Spain had to rely heavily on imports to meet its petroleum needs. Spain has seven active oil fields, all of them operated by Repsol-YPF. Spain's refining sector has a combined capacity of 1.27 million barrels and is spread among seven refineries, of which the largest is the Cadiz plant operated by Cepsa, with a capacity of 240,000 barrels per day. However, Repsol-YPF has the largest total capacity at 520,000 barrels per day.

According to the CIA, in 2010 Spain produced 48 million and consumed 35,820 million cubic meters of natural gas. Spanish demand for natural gas has risen sharply, driven in large part by the introduction of gas-fired power plants. Algeria was the main source of natural gas imports, followed by Norway, Qatar, Nigeria, and Oman, as well as other countries.

According to the US Energy Information Administration, in 2010 Spain produced 8.737 million short tons of coal and consumed 18.240 million short tons. In 2009 Spain imported 18.915 million short tons and exported 1.734 million short tons. As of 2008, Spain's coal reserves totaled 584 million short tons.

Spain is the EU's fifth-largest electricity market. The World Bank reported in 2008 that Spain produced 311.1 billion kWh of electricity and consumed 287.7 billion kWh, or 6,154 kWh per capita. Roughly 82% of energy came from fossil fuels, while 15% came from alternative fuels.

As of 2010, Spain had eight operational nuclear power plants, which the OECD estimates produced 20.1% of its total electricity supply (compared to 144 nuclear power plants in operation across European OECD countries, which produced 24.7% of their electricity supply). According to the OECD's Nuclear Energy Agency, the policy of the Spanish government was to reduce the usage of nuclear energy in an orderly and progressive way, by shutting down nuclear power plants at the end of their lifetime, advancing the use of renewable energy sources, and assisting in the development of new technologies to optimize power savings and efficiency.

28 INDUSTRY

The CIA estimated that, as of 2010, industry accounted for 26% of Spain's GDP, and that the sector had a 0.8% growth rate. As of 2009, industry employed 24% of Spain's labor force. The chief industrial sectors are food and beverages, textiles and footwear, energy, and transport materials. Chemical production, particularly of superphosphates, sulfuric acid, dyestuffs, and pharmaceutical products, is also significant. Of the heavy industries, iron and steel, centered mainly in Bilbao and Avilés, is the most important. The International Organization of Motor Vehicle Manufacturers reported that 2,387,900 motor vehicles were produced in Spain in 2010, a 10% increase from 2009. Automobiles are Spain's leading manufacturing industry, accounting for about 5% of GDP and exporting more than 80% of output.

Prior to the 1990s wave of privatization, government participation in industry was through the National Industrial Institute (INI), which owned mining enterprises, oil refineries, steel and chemical plants, shipbuilding yards, and artificial fiber factories, or through Patrimonio. Telefónica, Gas Natural, and the petrochemical company Repsol had been privatized by 2005.

Industries demonstrating significant growth in the early 2000s were metalworking industries, due to increased production in shipbuilding, data-processing equipment, and other transportation equipment. Other growth sectors included food processing, medical products and services, chemicals, computer equipment, electronics, footwear, construction and security equipment, cosmetics and jewelry, and industrial machinery. In the early 2000s, the construction industry was aided by such public works projects as a high-speed train link between Madrid and Barcelona, and an increase in property development on the Mediterranean coast.

29 SCIENCE AND TECHNOLOGY

According to the World Bank, high-technology exports (products with high research and development intensity, such as in aerospace, computers, pharmaceuticals, scientific instruments, and electrical machinery) accounted for 5% of Spain's manufactured exports in 2008. Patent applications in science and technology as of 2009, according to the World Bank, totaled 3,596 in Spain. Public financing of science was 1.34% of GDP.

The Council for Scientific Research, founded in 1940, coordinates research in science and technology and operates numerous constituent research institutes in a wide variety of disciplines. The Royal Academy of Exact, Physical, and Natural Sciences, founded in 1916, is the nation's chief scientific academy. The National Science Museum and the National Railway Museum are located in Madrid, and two geology museums are located in Barcelona. Spain has 32 universities, colleges, and polytechnics offering courses in basic and applied sciences.

30 DOMESTIC TRADE

Madrid and Barcelona are the primary commercial hubs for distribution of goods throughout the country. Spain has no free ports, but free-zone privileges are granted at Barcelona, Bilbao, Cádiz, Vigo, and the Canary Islands. There are bonded warehouses at the larger ports. The government has established a market distribution program to regulate the flow of goods to and from the producing and consuming areas. Since 1972, wholesale market

Principal Trading Partners – Spain (2010)

(In millions of US dollars)

Country	Total	Exports	Imports	Balance
World	561,822.0	246,274.0	315,548.0	-69,274.0
France	80,927.0	45,061.0	35,866.0	9,195.0
Germany	64,891.0	25,779.0	39,112.0	-13,333.0
Italy	44,172.0	21,610.0	22,562.0	-952.0
Portugal	33,675.0	21,986.0	11,689.0	10,297.0
United Kingdom	30,431.0	15,238.0	15,193.0	45.0
Netherlands	24,986.0	7,715.0	17,271.0	-9,556.0
China	24,435.0	3,391.0	21,044.0	-17,653.0
United States	17,429.0	7,846.0	9,583.0	-1,737.0
Belgium	17,428.0	6,920.0	10,508.0	-3,588.0
Russia	10,511.0	2,503.0	8,008.0	-5,505.0

(…) data not available or not significant.

(n.s.) not specified.

SOURCE: *2011 Direction of Trade Statistics Yearbook*, New York: United Nations, 2011.

Balance of Payments – Spain (2010)

(In millions of US dollars)

Current Account		-64,342.0
Balance on goods		-62,350.0
Imports	-315,323.0	
Exports	252,974.0	
Balance on services		36,500.0
Balance on income		-28,985.0
Current transfers		-9,508.0
Capital Account		8,358.0
Financial Account		60,265.0
Direct investment abroad		-20,557.0
Direct investment in Spain		24,658.0
Portfolio investment assets		91,209.0
Portfolio investment liabilities		-43,510.0
Financial derivatives		9,752.0
Other investment assets		-20,644.0
Other investment liabilities		19,357.0
Net Errors and Omissions		-3,218.0
Reserves and Related Items		-1,061.0

(…) data not available or not significant.

SOURCE: *Balance of Payment Statistics Yearbook 2011*, Washington, DC: International Monetary Fund, 2011.

networks have been established in cities with more than 150,000 inhabitants. The National Consumption Institute promotes consumer cooperatives and credit unions.

A wide variety of shops are available in Spain, from small specialty boutiques to large department stores, shopping centers, and outlet stores. The franchise sector in Spain is considered to have matured.

A 16% value-added tax applies to most goods and services. This rate is reduced for some products, such as food, books, and medical supplies. Advertising is largely through newspapers, magazines, radio, and motion picture theaters.

Normal business hours are from 9 a.m. to 6 p.m., Monday through Friday. Banks are open from 8:30 a.m. to 2:30 p.m., Monday through Friday, and until 1 p.m. on Saturday. Department stores are often open from 10 a.m. to 8 p.m., Monday through Saturday. Many small shops and businesses are often closed in the afternoons, from 2 p.m. to 4 or 5 p.m.

[31] FOREIGN TRADE

Spain imported $324.6 billion worth of goods and services in 2008, while exporting $268.3 billion worth of goods and services. Major import partners in 2009 were Germany, 14%; France, 12.8%; Italy, 7.4%; China, 5.7%; Netherlands, 5.4%; UK, 4.9%; and Portugal, 4.1% . Its major export partners were France, 19.5%; Germany, 11.4%; Portugal, 9.2%; Italy, 8.5%; and UK, 6.4%.

Traditionally, exports consisted mainly of agricultural products (chiefly wine, citrus fruits, olives and olive oil, and cork) and minerals. While agricultural products and minerals remain important, they have, since the 1960s, been overtaken by industrial exports. Imports habitually exceed exports by a large margin.

Of Spain's export commodities, transport-related items make up more than 20% of the total. Fruits, nuts, and vegetables are also exported in sizable amounts. Spain is the world's largest producer of olive oil; the country supplies about one-third of the olive oil in the world. Footwear and chemicals (chiefly pharmaceuticals) are other important exports. The liberalization of product markets and more effective antitrust mechanisms have been cited as ways to boost Spain's economic growth potential.

[32] BALANCE OF PAYMENTS

Tourism, remittances from Spaniards living abroad, investment income, and loans to the private sector have been the principal factors that help to offset recurrent trade deficits, especially deficits in merchandise trade and net investment income. In 2000 Spain experienced a large increase in its trade deficit due in large measure to increased petroleum prices, the weakness of the euro, and decreased competitiveness. By 2010 Spain's foreign trade deficit had grown further, to $27 billion, which amounted to 8.6% of its GDP. The current account balance was -$64.34 million that year.

[33] BANKING AND SECURITIES

The banking and credit structure centers on the Bank of Spain, the government's national bank of issue since 1874. The bank acts as the government depository as well as a banker's bank for discount and other operations. The European Central Bank (ECB) determines monetary policy for the EU. Other "official" but privately owned banks are the Mortgage Bank of Spain, the Local Credit Bank of Spain, the Industrial Credit Bank, the Agricultural Credit Bank, and the External Credit Bank.

The liberalization of the banking system and Spain's entry into the EC raised the number and presence of foreign banks. During the process of financial liberalization required by the EU, the government tried to promote a series of mergers within the banking industry, which it hoped could enable the banks to compete more effectively. As a result, there were two major mergers: Banco de Vizcaya and Banco de Bilbao formed Banco Bilbao Vizcaya (BBV), and Banco Central and Banco Hispanoamericano merged to form Banco Central Hispanoamericano (BCH). The government also brought together all the state-owned banking institutions to form Corporación Bancaria de España, better known by its trade name Argentaria, whose most important component is

Public Finance – Spain (2009)

(In millions of euros, central government figures)

Revenue and Grants	239,697	100.0%
Tax revenue	89,745	37.4%
Social contributions	139,470	58.2%
Grants	3,856	1.6%
Other revenue	6,626	2.8%
Expenditures	**329,936**	**100.0%**
General public services	118,621	36.0%
Defense	10,951	3.3%
Public order and safety	12,865	3.9%
Economic affairs	24,494	7.4%
Environmental protection	964	0.3%
Housing and community amenities	508	0.2%
Health	4,632	1.4%
Recreational, culture, and religion	3,299	1.0%
Education	1,544	0.5%
Social protection	152,058	46.1%

(...) data not available or not significant.

SOURCE: *Government Finance Statistics Yearbook 2010,* Washington, DC: International Monetary Fund, 2010.

Banco Exterior (BEX). The government subsequently privatized a 50% stake in Argentaria in 1993 and a further 25% in early 1996. Ultimately, the state sold its remaining 25% share in Argentaria, thereby leaving the banking sector entirely in private hands. In October 1999, BBV took over Argentaria to create Spain's largest banking group.

In light of the 2008–09 global financial crisis, Spain's savings banks underwent a thorough restructuring, and by 2011, complex mergers to cut costs shrunk their number from 45 to 17. The CIA World Factbook estimates that Spain's commercial bank prime lending rate was 7.223% in 2010. Because Spain's currency is now the euro, the discount rate, the rate at which the central bank lends to other financial institutions is set by the ECB. In 2010, the discount rate was 1.75%. Spain's reserves of foreign exchange and gold was estimated at $31.91 billion at the end of 2010.

Spain has major stock exchanges in Madrid, Barcelona, Bilbao, and Valencia. These exchanges are open for a few hours a day, Tuesday through Friday. Since 1961, foreign investment in these exchanges has increased rapidly. The major commercial banks invest in the equity and debt securities of private firms and carry on brokerage businesses as well. Latibex, a Madrid-based stock exchange providing a market for the trading (in euros) of Latin American stocks, opened in late 1999. The exchange lists companies based in Latin American nations such as Argentina, Brazil, Chile, Columbia, and Venezuela. As of 2004, there were 3,272 companies listed on the BME Spanish Exchanges, which had a market capitalization of $941 billion. As of June 2011, there were 3,288 companies listed on the BME Spanish Exchanges, which had a combined market capitalization of $1.35 trillion.

34 INSURANCE

Insurance companies are supervised by the government through the Direccion General de Seguros. The Spanish insurance market is characterized by a relatively large number of insurers with one organization dominating the industry. Latest information available indicates an insurance market in Spain with moderate penetration when compared to North America and Europe, especially for life products. Recently, however, Spanish insurance firms such as Euroseguros are taking advantage of linguistic, cultural, and historical ties and are expanding operations to Latin America. Compulsory insurance includes third-party automobile liability, workers' compensation, hunters', nuclear and professional liability, and personal injury insurance. Workers' compensation and property insurance can only be obtained through the government. Spain's insurance market is made up of both local and foreign insurers, with the local insurers often owned by Spanish banks.

35 PUBLIC FINANCE

Because of Spain's desire to enter the European Monetary Union, it had to meet stringent limits on its public debt and finances, including a 3% debt-to-GDP ratio. The government trimmed the budget by reducing the civil service payroll and limiting transfers to government-owned companies.

In 2010 the budget of Spain included $515.8 billion in public revenue and $648.6 billion in public expenditures. The budget deficit amounted to 9.2% of GDP. Public debt was 63.4% of GDP, with $2.166 trillion of the debt held by foreign entities.

36 TAXATION

Total taxes and other revenues collected by Spain's government totaled 35.7% of its GDP in 2010. In 2010 Spain's combined corporate tax rate was 30%. A reduced rate of 30% is applied to companies with annual turnover of less than €6 million ($8 million) in the preceding tax year on initial profits of €90,151 ($119,865). Generally, capital gains are taxed at the corporate rate, while dividends, interest and royalties are subject to withholding taxes of 15%, 15% and 25%, respectively.

Tax is imposed on aggregate income and includes dividends, interest and royalties received. However, dividends received from a resident company may be subject to an imputation credit. There is also a wealth tax with a maximum rate of 2.5%. In 2011 the Spanish government created new tax brackets for higher income earners, thereby raising top rates to 45%.

The main indirect tax is Spain's value-added tax (VAT), introduced 1 January 1986 as a condition for membership in the EU. As of 2005, the VAT had a standard rate of 16%. Since July 2010, the VAT had a standard rate of 18% with two reduced rates: 4% on basic necessities; and 7–8% on food, dwellings, tourism and certain transport services. Indirect taxes include levies on inheritances, documents, sales, special products (alcohol, petroleum, and others), luxury items, and fiscal monopolies. An exception is the Canary Islands, where the standard VAT rate is 5%, with reduced rates of 0–2%

37 CUSTOMS AND DUTIES

Spain, a member of the EU and the World Trade Organization, adheres to EU and GATT trading rules. Spain determines customs duties based on cost, insurance, and freight (CIF), and applies the EU Common External Tariff to non-EU imports. Most customs costs amount to 20–30% of CIF (cost, insurance, freight), including the duty, the VAT, and customs agent and handling fees.

38 FOREIGN INVESTMENT

In keeping with the rest of the EU, in recent years the Spanish government has instituted a wholesale revision of its previously restrictive foreign investment laws. With the exception of strategic sectors, up to 100% foreign investment is permitted in all sectors of the Spanish economy.

By 2009, FDI inflow into Spain totaled $6.45 billion, according to the World Bank, which represented 0.44% of Spain's GDP.

39 ECONOMIC DEVELOPMENT

After 1939, Spanish economic policy was characterized by the attempt to achieve economic self-sufficiency. This policy, largely imposed by Spain's position during World War II and the isolation to which Spain was subjected in the decade following 1945, was also favored by many Spanish political and business leaders. In 1959, following two decades of little or no overall growth, the Spanish government acceded to reforms suggested by the International Monetary Fund (IMF), OECD, and IBRD, and encouraged by the promise of foreign financial assistance, announced its acceptance of the so-called Stabilization Plan, intended to curb domestic inflation and adverse foreign payment balances.

Long-range planning began with Spain's first four-year development plan (1964–67), providing a total investment of 355 billion pesetas. The second four-year plan (1968–71) called for an investment of 553 billion pesetas, with an average annual growth of 5.5% in GNP. The third plan (1972–75) called for investments of 871 billion pesetas; drastic readjustments had to be made in 1975 to compensate for an economic slump brought on by increased petroleum costs, a tourist slowdown, and a surge in imports. A fifth plan (1976–79) focused on development of energy resources, with investments to increase annually by 9% increments. A stabilization program introduced in 1977 included devaluation of the peseta and tightening of monetary policy. The economic plan of 1979–82 committed Spain to a market economy and rejected protectionism.

Accession to the EU generated increased foreign investment but also turned Spain's former trade surplus with the EU into a growing deficit: the lowering of tariffs boosted imports, but exports did not keep pace. The government responded by pursuing market liberalization and deregulation, in hopes of boosting productivity and efficiency to respond to EU competition. A number of projects, such as the construction of airports, highways, and a high-speed rail line between Madrid and Seville, received EU funding. To prepare Spain for European economic and monetary union, the government in 1992 planned to cut public spending. The currency was devalued three times in 1992–93. Additionally, Spain was a principal beneficiary of the EU's "harmonization fund." This fund provides financial support to poorer EU nations to attempt to reduce the disparities in economic development.

After an economic downturn in the early and mid-1990s, the Spanish economy turned around to register a new dynamism characterized by strong growth rates and a rise in foreign investment sparked by increased liberalization. Moreover, unemployment dropped and inflation remained in check. Spain capped its success by entering the Economic and Monetary Union (EMU) in 1999. Reducing the public sector deficit, decreasing unemployment, reforming labor laws, lowering inflation, and raising per capita GDP were all goals in the early 2000s.

Spain cushioned the effects of the 2001–03 global economic slowdown on its economy through effective management of fiscal policy, but the constraints of the European Stability and Growth Pact-which requires EU members to keep their budget deficits within 3% of GDP-continued to limit freedom to maneuver. After coming to power in April 2004, the Socialist government made little change in economic policy. Expansion of the services sector, including retailing, tourism, banking, and telecommunications, led to growth. Spain has developed a greenhouse industry in the southeast region of the country, which has become one of the most competitive suppliers of fresh produce to the main European markets.

However, after almost 15 years of above average GDP growth, the Spanish economy began to slow in late 2007, entering a recession in the second quarter of 2008. GDP contracted by 3.7% in 2009, ending a 16-year growth trend, and by another 0.2% in 2010. As a result, Spain was the last major economy to emerge from the global recession. The reversal in Spain's economic growth reflected a significant decline in construction amid an oversupply of housing and falling consumer spending, while exports actually have begun to grow. Government efforts to boost the economy through stimulus spending, extended unemployment benefits, and loan guarantees failed to prevent a sharp rise in the unemployment rate, which rose from a low of approximately 8% in 2007 to 21.5% as of the third quarter of 2011.

40 SOCIAL DEVELOPMENT

The social insurance system provides pensions for employees in industry and services, with a special system for the self-employed, farmers, domestic workers, seamen and coal miners. The system is funded through employee and employer contributions, and an annual government subsidy. The fund provides for health and maternity benefits, old age and incapacity insurance, a widow and widower pension, orphan pension, a family subsidy, workers' compensation, job-related disability payments, unemployment insurance and a funeral grant. Retirement is set at age 65, but is allowed at age 64 under certain conditions. Maternity benefits are payable for 16 weeks, and is applicable to adoption as well. Fathers may also take parental leave. Work injury legislation was first instituted in 1900 and covers all employed persons. It is funded solely by the employer.

Discrimination against women in the workplace persists although it is prohibited by law. The female rate of unemployment is about twice that for men, and the median salary for women was lower than that of men. There are a growing number of women entering the medical and legal professions. Women take an active role in politics. The law prohibits sexual harassment in the workplace but it is not effectively enforced. The government takes steps to address the problems of domestic abuse and violence against women. The Integral Law Against Gender Violence enacted in 2005 provides harsher penalties to those convicted of domestic violence. The government is strongly committed to children's welfare and rights.

Roma ethnic minorities suffer from housing, education, and employment discrimination. The government provides mechanisms for legal redress for discrimination and harassment for Roma and other minorities. In addition, a growing number of right-wing extremist attacks against minorities have been reported in recent years. Human rights abuses have been committed by both the government and Basque (ETA) separatist groups. The ETA has carried out killings and kidnapping, while the government has failed to prevent the mistreatment of prisoners.

In June 2010, the city of Barcelona announced a new law that prohibited the use of headwear in public places. Although the law is viewed by many as simply a prohibition against the use of the Islamic veil worn by the most conservative Muslim women, the rule actually applies to all types of headwear that would hide the identity of an individual, such as ski masks and motorbike helmets. The ban is in effect for municipal offices, public markets, and libraries, but not on public streets.

⁴¹HEALTH

Following the adoption of the country's constitution, Spain's health care system underwent major reforms. Instead of being organized directly as part of the social security system, it was transformed to the more decentralized National Health System. Coverage was extended further than before and the primary care network was reorganized. Spanish officials say that public contributions to the cost of health care must be limited in the face of potentially unlimited demand. In 2011 the country spent 9.0% of its GDP on healthcare, amounting to $3,075 per person.

The public sector in health care was the largest and continued to grow. There were 354 public hospitals, 149 private hospitals, and 312 private business hospitals. As of 2011, there were 37 physicians, 52 nurses and midwives, and 32 hospital beds per 10,000 inhabitants. Recent programs have created special residences for elderly and retired people, eye clinics, a network of government health centers in the principal cities, and more than a dozen human tissue and organ banks for transplantation and research.

The total fertility rate in 2011 was estimated at 1.47. Average life expectancy in 2011 was 81.17 years. That year the infant mortality rate was 3.39 deaths per 1,000 live births. Immunization rates for children up to one year old were: diphtheria, pertussis, and tetanus, 96%; polio, 88%; and measles, 98%. In 2008 the maternal mortality rate, according to the World Bank, was 6 per 100,000 births.

Leading causes of death were communicable diseases and maternal/perinatal causes, noncommunicable diseases, and injuries. The CIA calculated HIV/AIDS prevalence in Spain to be about 0.4% in 2009.

The smoking rates for both men and women in Spain are above the average of "high human development" countries as defined by the World Bank. However, the likelihood of dying after the age of 65 of heart disease was below the highly industrialized country average at 235 (male) and 277 (female) per 1,000 people.

⁴²HOUSING

As of 2011, approximately 85% of Spaniards were homeowners, while only about 15% were renters. A housing boom beginning around 1998–2001 saw the creation of more than two million new houses with about 600,000 new houses built in 2000. In 2000, about 20–25% of the housing market was attributed to those building second homes/vacation homes. At the 2001 census,

there were about 20,946,554 dwellings nationwide. About 31.9% were single-family dwellings; 35% were dwellings in multi-family buildings. About 16% of the existing stock was built in the period 1991–2001; with an average of about 307,000 units per year. Some 52% of all dwellings were owned by private individuals; 46% were owned by communities. Nearly 90% of all dwellings were listed in good condition; 195,910 dwellings were listed as in ruin.

However, Spain's severe economic recession, which began in mid-2008, reflected in part a significant decline in construction amid an oversupply of housing. Spanish housing prices rose 155% between 1995 and 2007, at an annual growth rate of 8%, but after peaking in 2007 prices fell 24% by 2011, and were expected to decline between 35 and 40% by 2020. Residential construction accounted for 4.7% of Spain's GDP in 2010 versus 9.3% in 2006, and economists expected that investment in residential construction would decline by nearly 50% between 2007 and 2013.

⁴³EDUCATION

Since 1990, schooling has been compulsory for ten years, including six years of primary school and four years of secondary school. Many students continue on for an additional two years of higher secondary school. Vocational programs are available at the secondary level. The academic year runs from October to July. Most children between the ages of three and five are enrolled in some type of preschool program. Primary school enrollment in 2005 was estimated at about 100% of age-eligible students. The same year, secondary school enrollment was about 98% of age-eligible students. In 2008 the World Bank estimated that 100% of age-eligible children in Spain were enrolled in primary school. Secondary enrollment for age-eligible children stood at 95%. Of those enrolled in tertiary education, there were 100 male students for every 124 female students. It is estimated that nearly all students complete their primary education.

The Pontifical University of Salamanca, founded in 1254, is the oldest university, while the University of Madrid has the largest student body. According to the World Bank, in 2008 about 71% of the tertiary age population were enrolled in tertiary education programs; 60% for men and 74% for women. Overall, the CIA estimated that Spain had a literacy rate of 97.9%. Public expenditure on education represented 4.3% of GDP.

⁴⁴LIBRARIES AND MUSEUMS

The National Library in Madrid (four million volumes), the Library of Catalonia in Barcelona (one million volumes), the university libraries of Santiago de Compostela (one million volumes), Salamanca (906,000 volumes), Barcelona (two million volumes), and Sevilla (777,000 volumes), Valladolid (500,000 volumes), and the public library in Toledo (with many imprints from the 15th to the 18th centuries) are among the most important collections. Spain also has 61 historical archives, among them the Archivo General de Indias in Sevilla, with 60,000 volumes and files, and the archives of Simancas, with 86,000 volumes and files. In total, Spain's public library collection holds more than 32.8 million volumes. There are over 2,500 public libraries nationwide. In the province of Barcelona there are about 143 public libraries and 8 mobile services.

The Prado, in Madrid, with its extensive collection of Spanish art, is the most famous museum of Spain and one of the best in the world, featuring Picasso's world-famous *Guernica*. The National Archaeological Museum, also in Madrid, contains the prehistoric cave paintings of Altamira. The Museum of Modern Art, in Barcelona, houses excellent cubist and surrealist collections. There are also important art collections in the Escorial and Aranjuez palaces, near Madrid. Also in Madrid are the Museum of America, with artifacts from Spain's colonial holdings; the African Museum, with exhibits of many African cultures, especially Makonde art from Mozambique; and the Antiquities Collection of the Academy of History, founded in 1738, which houses Iberian and Visigoth artifacts, Islamic art, 4th century relics, including the Silver Dish of Theodosius, general European art, and 11th century documents. Barcelona also has the Museum of Ceramics, the Museum of Decorative Arts, a Picasso museum, the National Museum of Catalonian Art, and the Museum of Perfume. The Guggenheim Museum Bilbao, designed by American architect Frank Gehry, opened in 1997 as a joint project of the Guggenheim Foundation and the Basque regional government. The innovative design of the 24,000-sq-m (257,000 sq-ft) metal-and-stone structure has won worldwide attention and acclaim.

45 MEDIA

Spain's telecommunications system is modern and capable of meeting the country's telecommunication needs. International services are provided by 22 coaxial submarine cables, and Intelsat and Eutelsat satellite ground stations. Tropospheric scatter radio is used for communications to neighboring countries. In 2009, there were some 20 million main phone lines and In 2009, the CIA reported that there were 20.1 million telephone landlines in Spain. Mobile phone subscriptions averaged 111 per 100 people. Some 50.9 million mobile cellular phones were in use.

RadioTelevision Espanola operates public radio and television broadcasts. There are hundreds of privately owned stations as well. There are 208 FM radio stations, 715 AM radio stations, and 1 shortwave radio station. In 2010 the country had about 3.8 million Internet hosts. There were 61 internet users for every 100 citizens.

There are about 100 daily papers published in Spain, but very few have a circulation exceeding 100,000. Prominent newspapers in 2010, with circulation numbers listed parenthetically, included La Vanguardia (208,029), ABC (334,696), and El Diario Vasco (80,714), as well as more than 100 other major newspapers. Sunday newspaper editions have become increasingly common, with circulations often double the weekday runs. English-language papers are now printed in Madrid and Palma de Mallorca. There are also over 3,000 magazines, bulletins, and journals.

Formerly, the Falange published the newspapers in all provincial capitals and controlled some 35% of the total national circulation; censorship was obligatory. In 1966, a new press law abolished censorship but established stiff penalties for editors who published news "contrary to the principles of the national interest;" offending newspapers could be seized. The 1978 constitution guarantees freedom of the press and the government is said to uphold this freedom in practice.

46 ORGANIZATIONS

Under the Falangist system of corporate organization, all branches of society were required to participate in business and in agricultural or professional syndicates. Despite this system, coopera-

tives emerged in various sectors of Spanish society, among them agricultural, consumer, credit, industrial, maritime, fishing, rural, housing, and educational organizations. Chambers of commerce function in all provincial capitals, and there are numerous industrial and trade associations. The Association of Mediterranean Chambers of Commerce and Industry is based in Barcelona. Trade and professional associations exist representing a broad range of occupations.

Cultural and educational organizations include the Royal Academy of Belles Lettres, the Scientific and Literary and Art Society, the Association of Spanish Artists and Sculptors, The Royal Society of Physics, Institute of Catalan Studies, and the Society of Natural Sciences.

National youth organizations include Christian Democratic Youth of Spain, Socialist Youth, Junior Chamber, a national students' union, the Counting Federation of Spain, Girl Guides, and chapters of YMCA/YWCA. There are sports associations representing a wide variety of pastimes.

National women's organizations include University Women of Spain and the National Council of Women in Spain. International organizations with national chapters include Save the Children, Amnesty International, Greenpeace, and the Red Cross.

47 TOURISM, TRAVEL, AND RECREATION

Many are attracted to the country by its accessibility, warm climate, beaches, and relatively low costs. Among the principal tourist attractions are Madrid, with its museums, the Escorial Palace, and the nearby Valley of the Fallen (dead in the civil war); Toledo, with its churches and its paintings by El Greco; the Emerald Coast around San Sebastián; the Costa Brava on the coast of Catalonia, north of Barcelona; Granada, with the Alhambra and the Generalife; Sevilla, with its cathedral and religious processions; and the Canary and Balearic islands.

Fútbol (soccer) is the most popular sport in Spain, and many cities have large soccer stadiums; Spain was host to the World Cup competition in 1982. On 11 July 2010, Spain won its first World Cup in Johannesburg, South Africa, defeating the Netherlands 1–0 in extra time. Barcelona was the site of the 1992 Summer Olympics, and in the same year, an International Exposition was held in Sevilla. Among traditional attractions are the bullfights, held in Madrid from April through October, and pelota, an indoor ball game in which spectators bet on the outcome. However, lawmakers in the Spanish region of Catalonia, located in the far northeast of the country, voted in July 2010 to ban bullfighting, a practice considered by many Spaniards to be an essential part of their cultural heritage.

In November 2010, the Spanish flamenco dance was officially inscribed on the UNESCO Representative List of the Intangible Heritage of Humanity, an offshoot of the World Heritage program. The dance was deemed a living tradition by UNESCO, meaning that it is still passed from generation to generation and continues to create a sense of identity and community for those who participate. Such traditions have been approved by UNESCO for special consideration since 2001. For one that is inscribed, a special program is designed to protect and promote the practice and understanding of the tradition. Castells, the human towers created by acrobats as part of the annual festivities in Catalonian towns, were also placed on the list. The creation of the castells is always accompanied by music that sets the rhythm for the formation of the tower. Another addition to the list was the chant of Sybil, performed at matins on Christmas Eve in churches throughout Majorca. The chant is sung by a boy or girl who walks through the church carrying a sword held upright before his or her face. At the end of the song, the sword is used to make the sign of the cross.

The *Tourism Factbook*, published by the UN World Tourism Organization, reported 52.2 million incoming tourists to Spain in 2009, who spent a total of $58.6 billion. Of those incoming tourists, there were 47.7 million from Europe. There were 1.73 million hotel beds available in Spain, which had an occupancy rate of 49%. The estimated daily cost to visit Madrid, the capital, was $453. The cost of visiting other cities averaged $313.

Passports are required to enter Spain. Citizens of many countries, including the United States, may stay up to 90 days without a visa.

⁴⁸FAMOUS PERSONS

The Hispanic-Roman epoch produced the philosopher and dramatist Marcus (or Lucius) Annaeus Seneca (54 BC–AD 39), while the Gothic period was marked by the encyclopedist Isidore of Seville (560?–636), author of the *Etymologies*. Important Spanish thinkers of the Middle Ages included Averroës (Ibn Rushd, or Abu al-Walid Muhammad ibn Ahmad ibn Rushd, 1126–98), philosopher; Maimonides (Moses ben Maimon, also known as the Rambam, 1135–1204), the great Jewish physician and philosopher; Benjamin de Tudela (d. 1173), geographer and historian; King Alfonso X (the Wise, 1226?-84), jurist, historian, musician, and astronomer; Juan Ruiz (1283?–1351?), archpriest of Hita, the greatest Spanish medieval poet; and Fernando de Rojas (1475?–1538?), a dramatic poet. El Cid (Rodrigo Díaz de Vivar, 1043?–99) has become the national hero of Spain for his fight against the Moors, although he also fought for them at times.

The golden age of Spanish exploration and conquest began with the Catholic Sovereigns, Ferdinand (1452–1516) and Isabella (1451–1504), in the late 15th century. The first great explorer for Spain was Christopher Columbus (Cristoforo Colombo or Cristóbal Colón, 1451–1506), a seaman of Genoese birth but possibly of Judeo-Catalán origin, who made four voyages of discovery to the Americas, the first landing occurring on 12 October 1492 on the island of Guanahaní (probably on the island now called San Salvador) in the Bahamas. Among the later explorers, Alvar Núñez Cabeza de Vaca (1490?–1557?), Hernando de Soto (d. 1542), and Francisco Vázquez de Coronado (1510–54) became famous for their explorations in the southern and southwestern parts of the present US; Juan Ponce de León (1460?–1521), for his travels in Florida; Vasco Núñez de Balboa (1475–1517), for his European discovery of the Pacific Ocean and claim of it for Spain; Francisco Pizarro (1470?–1541), for his conquest of Peru; and Hernán Cortés (1485–1547) for his conquest of Mexico. Juan de la Costa (1460?–1510) was a great cartographer of the period. Spanish power was at its greatest under Charles I (1500–1558), who was also Holy Roman Emperor Charles V. It began to decline under Philip II (1527–98).

In Spanish art, architecture, and literature, the great age was the 16th century and the early part of the 17th. Among the painters, El Greco (Domenikos Theotokopoulos, b. Crete, 1541–1614), Lo Spagnoletto (Jusepe de Ribera, 1589?–1652?), Francisco de Zurba-

rán (1598?–1660), Diego Rodriguez de Silva y Velázquez (1599–1660), and Bartolomé Esteban Murillo (1617–82) were the leading figures. In architecture, Juan de Herrera (1530–97), the designer of the royal palace, monastery, and tomb of the Escorial, and the baroque architect José Churriguera (1650–1723) are among the most important names. In literature, the dramatists Lope Félix de Vega Carpio (1562–1635) and Pedro Calderón de la Barca (1600–1681) and the novelist Miguel de Cervantes y Saavedra (1547–1616), author of *Don Quixote*, are immortal names. Other leading literary figures include the great poet Luis de Góngora y Argote (1561–1627), the satirist Francisco Gómez de Quevedo y Villegas (1580–1645), and the playwrights Tirso de Molina (Gabriel Téllez, 1571?–1648) and Mexican-born Juan Ruiz de Alarcón y Mendoza (1580?–1639). Outstanding personalities in the annals of the Roman Catholic Church are St. Ignatius de Loyola (Iñigo de Oñez y Loyola, 1491–1556), founder of the Jesuit order; St. Francis Xavier (Francisco Javier, 1506–52), Jesuit "apostle to the Indies"; and the great mystics St. Teresa of Ávila (Teresa de Cepeda y Ahumada, 1515–82) and St. John of the Cross (Juan de Yepes y Álvarez, 1542–91). The phenomenon of pulmonary blood circulation was discovered by Michael Servetus (Miguel Servet, 1511–53), a heretical theologian, while he was still a medical student.

The 16th century was also the golden age of Spanish music. Cristóbal de Morales (1500?–53) and Tomás Luis de Vittoria (1549?–1611) were the greatest Spanish masters of sacred vocal polyphony. Important composers include Luis Milán (1500?–1565?), Antonio de Cabezón (1510–66), Alonso Mudarra (1510–80), and Miguel de Fuenllana. Juan Bermudo (1510?–55?), Francisco de Salinas (1513–90), and Diego Ortiz (c. 1525-c. 1570) were theorists of note. Two leading 18th-century composers in Spain were the Italians Domenico Scarlatti (1685–1757) and Luigi Boccherini (1743–1805). Padre Antonio Soler (1729–83) was strongly influenced by Scarlatti. Leading modern composers are Isaac Albéniz (1860–1909), Enrique Granados y Campina (1867–1916), Manuel du Falla (1876–1946), and Joaquín Turina (1882–1949). World-famous performers include the cellist and conductor Pablo Casals (1876–1973), the guitarist Andrés Segovia (1894–1987), operatic singers Victoria de los Angeles (Victoria Gómez Cima, 1923–2005), José Carreras (b. 1946), and Placido Domingo (b. 1941), and the pianist Alicia de Larrocha (b. 1923).

Francisco Goya y Lucientes (1746–1828) was the outstanding Spanish painter and etcher of his time. Pablo Ruiz y Picasso (1881–1973) was perhaps the most powerful single influence on contemporary art; other major figures include Juan Gris (1887–1927), Joan Miró (1893–1983), and Salvador Dali (1904–89), who, like Picasso, spent most of his creative life outside Spain. The sculptor Julio González (1876–1942) was noted for his work in iron. A leading architect was Antonio Gaudí (1852–1926); an influential modern architect was José Luis Sert (1902–83), dean of the Graduate School of Design at Harvard University for 16 years.

Miguel de Unamuno y Jugo (1864–1936) and José Ortega y Gasset (1883–1955) are highly regarded Spanish philosophers. Benito Pérez Galdos (1843–1920) was one of the greatest 19th-century novelists. Other Spanish novelists include Pedro Antonio de Alarcón (1833–91), Emilia Pardo Bazán (1852–1921), Vicente Blasco Ibáñez (1867–1928), Pío Baroja y Nessi (1872–1956), Ramón Pérez de Ayala (1880–1962), and Ramón José Sender (1902–82). Prominent dramatists include José Zorrilla y Moral (1817–93),

José de Echegaray y Eizaguirre (1832–1916), and Jacinto Benavente y Martínez (1886–1954). The poets Juan Ramón Jiménez (1881–1958) and Vicente Aleixandre (1900–84) were winners of the Nobel Prize for literature in 1956 and 1977, respectively. Other outstanding poets are Gustavo Adolfo Bécquer (1836–70), Antonio Machado Ruiz (1875–1939), Pedro Salinas (1891–1951), Jorge Guillén (1893–1984), Dámaso Alonso (1898–1990), Federico García Lorca (1899–1936), Luis Cernuda (1902–63), and José Angel Valente (1929–2000). Ramón María del Valle-Inclán (1866–1936) was a novelist, dramatist, poet, and essayist. A noted novelist, essayist, and critic was Azorín (José Martínez Ruiz, 1876–1967). Salvador de Madariaga y Rojo (1886–1978) was an important cultural historian and former diplomat. Luis Buñuel (1900–83), who also lived in Mexico, was one of the world's leading film directors. Pedro Almodóvar (b. 1951) is a contemporary film director, and Antonio Banderas (b. 1960) is a Spanish film actor who has had success in Hollywood.

Santiago Ramón y Cajal (1852–1934), histologist, was awarded the first Nobel Prize for medicine in 1906. The physicians Gregorio Marañón (1887–1960) and Pedro Laín Entralgo (1908–2001) were scholars and humanists of distinction. Juan de la Cierva y Codorniu (1896–1937) invented the autogyro. Severo Ochoa (1905–93), who lived in the United States, won the Nobel Prize for medicine in 1959.

Francisco Franco (1892–1975), the leader of the right-wing insurgency that led to the Spanish Civil War (1936–39), was chief of state during 1939–47 and lifetime regent of the Spanish monarchy after 1947. After Franco's death, King Juan Carlos I (b. 1938) guided Spain through the transitional period between dictatorship and democracy.

49 DEPENDENCIES

Spanish "places of sovereignty" on the North African shore, which are part of metropolitan Spain subject to special statutes owing to their location, include Alborán Island (at 35°56′ N and 3°2′ W), Islas de Alhucemas (at 35°13′ N and 3°52′ W), Islas Chafarinas (at 35°10′ N and 2°26′ W), and Perejil (at 35°54′ N and 5°25′ W). The two major places of sovereignty are Ceuta and Melilla. Ceuta (19 sq km/7.3 sq mi; population 71,403 in 1993) is a fortified port on the Moroccan coast opposite Gibraltar. Melilla (12.3 sq km/4.7 sq mi; resident population 55,613 in 1993), on a rocky promontory on the Rif coast, is connected with the African mainland by a narrow isthmus. Melilla has been Spanish since 1496; Ceuta since 1580. Since 1956, Morocco has repeatedly advanced claims to these areas. Under the 1978 constitution, Ceuta and Melilla are represented in the Cortes by one deputy and two senators each.

50 BIBLIOGRAPHY

Alexander, Yonah, ed. *Combating Terrorism: Strategies of Ten Countries*. Ann Arbor: University of Michigan Press, 2002.

Annesley, Claire, ed. *A Political and Economic Dictionary of Western Europe*. Philadelphia: Routledge/Taylor and Francis, 2005.

Binda, Veronia. *The Dynamics of Big Business Structure, Strategy, and Impact in Italy and Spain*. New York: Routledge, 2012.

Bowen, Wayne H, and José E. Alvarez. *A Military History of Modern Spain: From the Napoleonic Era to the International War on Terror*. Westport, CT: Praeger Security International, 2007.

Gagnon, Alain G., and James Tully, eds. *Multinational Democracies*. New York: Cambridge University Press, 2001.

Grabowski, John F. *Spain*. San Diego: Lucent Books, 2000.

McElrath, Karen, ed. *HIV and AIDS: A Global View*. Westport, CT: Greenwood Press, 2002.

Opello, Walter C. *European Politics*. Boulder, CO: Lynne Rienner Publishers, 2009.

Ortiz Griffin, Julia. *Spain and Portugal*. New York: Facts On File, 2006.

Political Chronology of Europe. London: Europa, 2001.

Pritchett, V S. *The Spanish Temper*. London: Bloomsbury Reader, 2011.

Smith, Angel. *Historical Dictionary of Spain*. 2nd ed. Lanham, MD: Scarecrow, 2009.

Spain Investment and Business Guide: Strategic and Practical Information. Washington, DC: International Business Publications USA, 2012.

Stanton, Edward F. *Culture and Customs of Spain*. Westport, CT: Greenwood Press, 2002.

Summers, Randal W., and Allan M. Hoffman, eds. *Domestic Violence: A Global View*. Westport, CT: Greenwood Press, 2002.

Wessels, Wolfgang, Andreas Maurer, and Jürgen Mittag, eds. *Fifteen into One?: The European Union and Its Member States*. New York: Palgrave, 2003.

SWEDEN

Kingdom of Sweden

Konungariket Sverige

CAPITAL: Stockholm

FLAG: The national flag, dating from 1569 and employing a blue and gold motif used as early as the mid-14th century, consists of a yellow cross with extended right horizontal on a blue field.

ANTHEM: *Du gamla, du fria, du fjallhöga nord (O Glorious Old Mountain-Crowned Land of the North).*

MONETARY UNIT: The krona (SEK) is a paper currency of 100 öre. There are coins of 50 öre and 1, 2, 5, and 10 kronor, and notes of 5, 10, 20, 50, 100, 500, and 1,000 kronor. SEK1 = US$0.144630 (or US$1 = SEK6.91386) as of 2011.

WEIGHTS AND MEASURES: The metric system is the legal standard, but some old local measures are still in use, notably the Swedish mile (10 kilometers).

HOLIDAYS: New Year's Day, 1 January; Epiphany, 6 January; Labor Day, 1 May; Midsummer Day, Saturday nearest 24 June; All Saints' Day, 5 November; Christmas, 25–26 December. Movable religious holidays include Good Friday, Easter Monday, Ascension, and Whitmonday.

TIME: 1 p.m. = noon GMT.

¹LOCATION, SIZE, AND EXTENT

Fourth in size among the countries of Europe, Sweden is the largest of the Scandinavian countries, with about 15% of its total area situated north of the Arctic Circle. Extreme length N–S is 1,574 km (978 mi) and greatest breadth E–W is 499 km (310 mi). Sweden has a total area of 449,964 sq km (173,732 sq mi): land area, 410,934 sq km (158,663 sq mi); water area, 39,030 sq km (15,070 sq mi), including some 96,000 lakes. Comparatively, the area occupied by Sweden is slightly larger than the state of California. Sweden is bounded on the N and NE by Finland, on the E by the Gulf of Bothnia, on the SE by the Baltic Sea, on the SW by the Öresund, the Kattegat, and the Skagarrak, and on the W by Norway, with a total boundary length of 5,423 km (3,370 mi), of which 3,218 km (2000 mi) is coastline. The two largest Swedish islands in the Baltic Sea are Gotland and Öland. Sweden's capital city, Stockholm, is located on the southeast Baltic Sea coast.

²TOPOGRAPHY

Northern Sweden (Norrland) slopes from the Kjölen Mountains along the Norwegian frontier (with the high point at Kebnekaise, 2,111 m/6,926 ft) to the coast of the Gulf of Bothnia. The many rivers—notably the Göta, the Dal, the Ångerman, the Ume, and the Lule—flow generally toward the southeast and have incised the plateau surface; waterfalls abound. Central Sweden, consisting of a down-faulted lowland, has several large lakes, of which Vänern (5,584 sq km/2,156 sq mi) is the largest in Europe outside the former USSR. To the south of the lake belt rises the upland of Småland and its small but fertile appendage, Skåne. The lowlands were once submerged and so acquired a cover of fertile, silty soils. Much of Sweden is composed of ancient rock; most ice erosion has resulted in generally poor sandy or stony soils. The best,

most lime-rich soils are found in Skåne, and this southernmost district is the leading agricultural region; it resembles Denmark in its physical endowments and development.

³CLIMATE

Because of maritime influences, particularly the warm North Atlantic Drift and the prevailing westerly airstreams, Sweden has higher temperatures than its northerly latitude would suggest. Stockholm averages -3°C (26°F) in February and 18°C (64°F) in July. As would be expected from its latitudinal extent, there is a wide divergence of climate between northern and southern Sweden: the north has a winter of more than seven months and a summer of less than three, while Skåne in the south has a winter of about two months and a summer of more than four. The increasing shortness of summer northward is partly compensated by comparatively high summer temperatures, the greater length of day, and the infrequency of summer cloud; the considerable cloud cover in winter reduces heat loss by radiation.

Annual rainfall averages 61 cm (24 in) and is heaviest in the southwest and along the frontier between Norrland and Norway; the average rainfall for Lapland is about 30 cm (12 in) a year. The maximum rainfall occurs in late summer, and the minimum in early spring. There is considerable snowfall, and snow remains on the ground in the north for about half the year. Ice conditions in the surrounding seas, especially the Gulf of Bothnia, often are severe in winter and seriously interfere with navigation.

⁴FLORA AND FAUNA

The World Resources Institute estimates that there are 1,750 plant species in Sweden. In addition, Sweden is home to 85 mammal, 457 bird, 7 reptile, and 13 amphibian species. The calculation reflects the total number of distinct species residing in the country, not the number of endemic species.

Vegetation ranges from Alpine-Arctic types in the north and upland areas to coniferous forests in the central regions and deciduous trees in the south. Common trees include birch, aspen, beech elm, oak, and Norway spruce. Black cock, woodcock, duck, partridge, swan, and many other varieties of birds are abundant. Fish and insects are plentiful.

5 ENVIRONMENT

The World Resources Institute reported that Sweden had designated 4.24 million hectares (10.47 million acres) of land for protection as of 2006. Water resources totaled 179 cu km (42.94 cu mi) while water usage was 2.68 cu km (0.643 cu mi) per year. Domestic water usage accounted for 37% of total usage, industrial for 54%, and agricultural for 9%. Per capita water usage totaled 296 cu m (10,453 cu ft) per year.

The United Nations (UN) reported in 2008 that carbon dioxide emissions in Sweden totaled 49,208 kilotons.

Sweden has been at the forefront of international efforts to protect the environment since hosting the first UN environmental conference in 1972. In its favor, Sweden's relatively slow population growth and an effective conservation movement have helped preserve the nation's extensive forest resources. By the end of 2011 there were 29 national parks covering 731,589 hectares (1,807,796 acres), with another six parks scheduled to open by 2013. Sweden also has 1,215 nature reserves of 870,748 hectares (2,151,653 acres), and 2,016 other protected landscape areas of 540,064 hectares (1,334,520 acres), along with 51 Ramsar Wetland Sites. Principal responsibility for the environment is vested in the National Environmental Protection Agency.

Pollution of the nation's water supply constitutes a significant environmental threat. Factory effluents have endangered water quality, and airborne sulfur pollutants have so acidified more than 16,000 lakes that fish can no longer breed in them. According to a 2011 report issued by the International Union for Conservation of Nature and Natural Resources (IUCN), threatened species include 5 types of mammals, 3 species of birds, 9 species of fish, 1 species of mollusk, 12 species of other invertebrates, and 3 species of plants. Threatened species include the blue ground beetle and cerambyx longhorn. Protected fauna include the wild reindeer, golden eagle, and crane.

Each year, Sweden kills thousands of rabbits as part of a program designed to protect its public shrubs, parks, and green space from foraging hares. In October 2009, reports emerged that indicated another use for the culling of rabbits: heating homes. Stockholm, Sweden's capital, piloted a program in which the killed rabbits were frozen and burned to form bioenergy.

By 2011, the government had adopted 16 environmental quality objectives to achieve by 2020, including clean air and protection of the ozone layer.

6 POPULATION

The US Central Intelligence Agency (CIA) reported the population of Sweden in 2011 to be approximately 9,088,728, which placed it at number 90 in population among the 196 nations of the world. In 2011, approximately 19.8% of the population was over 65 years of age, with another 15.4% under 15 years of age.

The median age in Sweden was 42 years. There were 0.98 males for every female in the country. The population's annual rate of change was 0.163%. The projected population for the year 2025 was 10,200,000. Population density in Sweden was calculated at 20 people per sq km (52 people per sq mi).

The UN estimated in 2009 that 85% of the Swedish population lived in urban areas, and that urban populations had an annual rate of change of 0.6%. The largest urban area was Stockholm, with a population of 1.3 million.

7 MIGRATION

During the period 1865–1930, nearly 1,400,000 Swedes, or about one-fifth of the country's population, emigrated; over 80% went to the United States, and about 15% to other Nordic countries. The exodus ended by the 1930s, when resource development in Sweden started to keep pace with the population growth. In the 1960s there was a flood of immigration—especially by Finns—that increased the number of aliens in Sweden from 190,621 to 411,280. The number remained steady in the 1970s but increased, though at a slower rate, in the 1980s.

Estimates of Sweden's net migration rate, reported by the CIA in 2011, amounted to 1.65 migrants per 1,000 citizens. The total number of emigrants living abroad was 317,900, and the total number of immigrants living in Sweden was 1.31 million.

As of January 2011, Sweden's population of concern numbered 110,608, of which 82,629 were refugees, 18,635 were asylum seekers, and 9,344 were stateless persons. Sweden's policy of generosity toward refugees and asylum seekers results in as many as 31,000 asylum applications annually. However, rising opposition to minority groups such as Muslims has resulted in appeals for stricter immigration laws. In 2011 Sweden was the world's fourth-largest contributor to the budget of the United Nations High Commissioner for Refugees.

8 ETHNIC GROUPS

The Swedes are primarily Scandinavians of Germanic origin. There are about 20,000 Sami (Lapps) within the country. The Roma population is estimated at about 50,000 people. The remaining 12% of the population is comprised of foreign-born or first-generation immigrants, including Finns in the north, Danes, Iraqis, Iranians, Norwegians, Greeks, and Turks.

9 LANGUAGES

Swedish is a national language. In addition to the letters of the English language, it has å, ä, and ö. Swedish is closely related to Norwegian and Danish. Many Swedes speak English and German, and many more understand these languages. The Sami speak their own language. There are also a number of Finnish-speaking people in Sweden.

10 RELIGIONS

For hundreds of years, the Church of Sweden, an Evangelical Lutheran church, represented the religion of state. However, in 2000, the Church and government placed into effect a formal separation of church and state, with a stipulation that the Church of Sweden will continue to receive a certain degree of state support. This agreement triggered a decline in membership for this church. According to a 2010 report, about 71.3% of the population belonged to the Church of Sweden, down 14% from 2000. Some members who separated from the church did so for economic reasons, since members were required to pay a special income tax in support of the church. Protestant groups other than the Church of Sweden accounted for about 4.4% of the population. Other Christian groups in Sweden include Roman Catholics, Christian Orthodox, Pentecostals, the Missionary (or Missions) Church, Jehovah's Witnesses, and The Church of Jesus Christ of Latter-Day Saints (Mormons).

As of 2009, a growing but small Muslim population accounted for about 5% of the total population in Sweden. The Sunni and Shi'a branches represented the primary practices. There were also about 20,000 Jews (Orthodox, Conservative, and Reform), with about half being active. There were small communities of Buddhists, Hindus, Sikhs, Zoroastrians, Hare Krishnas, Scientologists (Church of Scientology), and members of the Unification Church.

The constitution provides for freedom of religion. Since the separation of church and state, all religions have been eligible for financial support from the government through the church tax. Individuals can designate which organization they wish to receive their contribution, or they can receive a tax reduction. The Commission for State Grants to Religious Communities is the government body that oversees religious funding, in cooperation with the Swedish Free Church Council. Religious groups are not required to register with the government. Epiphany, Good Friday, Easter Sunday, Easter Monday, Ascension Day, Whit Sunday, All Saints' Day, Christmas, and Boxing Day are observed as national holidays.

The Muslim and Jewish communities have protested government laws which they believe interfere with religious practice. For instance, a 1930 law requires the use of anesthesia before slaughter of animals in order to minimize suffering. This practice interferes with Jewish dietary laws on foods that may be considered kosher. A 2001 law requires that mohels (who perform circumcisions according to Jewish customs) must be certified by the National Board of Health and the procedure must be completed in the presence of a medical doctor or an anesthesia nurse. Some Jews (and Muslims) claim that this regulation interferes with their religious ceremony.

Local government reports indicate a significant increase in social discrimination, harassment, and physical abuse against Muslims, with anti-Islamic sentiments mostly directed toward immigrants. Intolerance toward Muslims was reflected in gains by the right-wing Swedish Democratic Party, which won seats in the Riksdag for the first time in 2010. There continue to be reports of discrimination against the nation's Jews.

11 TRANSPORTATION

The CIA reported that Sweden had a total of 572,900 km (355,984 mi) of roads in 2009. There were 521 vehicles per 1,000 people in the country at that time. Railroads extended for 9,946 km (6,180 mi), and 249 airports transported 5.82 million passengers in 2009 according to the World Bank. Sweden also has approximately 2,052 km (1,275 mi) of navigable waterways.

Since the 1960s, the number of ships in the merchant navy has decreased because of competition from low-cost shipping nations and, more recently, the slump in world trade. Sweden has an increasing number of special-purpose vessels, such as fruit tramps, ore carriers, and oil tankers. Most of the larger vessels, representing the majority of Sweden's commercial tonnage, were engaged in traffic that never touched home ports, and less than half of Swedish foreign trade was carried in Swedish ships. Göteborg, Stockholm, and Malmö, the three largest ports, and a number of smaller ports were well-equipped to handle large oceangoing vessels. In 2008, the Swedish merchant fleet consisted of 195 ships of 1,000 GRT or more. Canals in central Sweden have opened the lakes to seagoing craft; inland waterways added up to 2,052 km (1,275 mi), navigable by small steamers and barges.

In 2009 there were 152 airports with paved runways. There were also two heliports. Arlanda international airport at Stockholm received its first jet aircraft in 1960; other principal airports are Sturup at Malmö and Landvetter at Göteborg. The Scandinavian Airlines System (SAS) was operated jointly by Sweden, Denmark, and Norway, each of which owned a 50% share of the company operating in its own territory; the other half in Sweden was owned by private investors. Linjeflyg, a subsidiary of SAS, operated a domestic service to most of the larger cities and resorts.

12 HISTORY

Sweden and the Swedes are first referred to in written records by the Roman historian Tacitus, who, in his Germania (AD 98), mentions the Suiones, a people "mighty in ships and arms." These people, also referred to as Svear, conquered their southern neighbors, the Gotar, merged with them, and extended their dominion over most of what is now central and southern Sweden. In the 9th and 10th centuries when Vikings from the Norwegian homeland traveled west to Iceland, Greenland and farther afield to Newfoundland, Vikings from eastern Sweden raided areas southeastward across Russia to Constantinople. Archeologists and historians hold that the descendants of one of their chieftains, Rurik, founded the Kievan Russian state. Some other settled regions and place-names in various parts of Europe also show Swedish influence through rune-stones found across Eastern Europe.

In the Viking era, the Swedish kingdom took shape but was not very centralized. Political power became more centralized with the advent of Christianity between the 9th and 11th centuries. During the 12th century, the Swedish kingdom consolidated internally, and under the guise of the crusades began to expand into the Baltic, incorporating Finland, between 1150 and 1300. Among the institutions established in Sweden during the 12th and 13th centuries were Latin education, new modes and styles of architecture and literature, town life, and a more centralized monarchy with new standards in royal administration—all with significant economic, legal, and social implications.

Norway and Sweden were united in 1319 under the infant king Magnus VII, but Waldemar IV, King of Denmark, regained Skåne, the southern part of Sweden, and all the Scandinavian countries were united in the Kalmar Union under his daughter Margaret (Margrethe) in 1397. For over a century, Sweden resisted Danish rule, and the union was marked by internal tensions.

In 1523, following a war with Denmark that is remembered in part for the Stortorget (Great Square) massacre in Stockholm, when hundreds of Swedish nobles were executed, the Swedes elected Gustavus Vasa (Gustaf I) to the Swedish throne. A great king and the founder of modern Sweden, Gustavus made Lutheranism the state religion, established a hereditary monarchy, and organized a national army and navy. His successors incorporated Estonia and other areas in Eastern Europe. The growth of nationalism and Protestantism, along with the decline of the Hanseatic League's control of Baltic trade, contributed to the rise of Sweden in the following century.

Another great king and one of the world's outstanding military geniuses, Gustavus Adolphus (Gustaf II Adolf, r. 1611–32), is generally regarded as the creator of the first modern army. He defeated Poland and conquered the rest of Livonia, and by winning a war with Russia acquired Ingermanland and Karelia. During the period of the Thirty Years' War (1618–48), Sweden was the foremost Protestant power on the Continent, and for the following half century the Baltic Sea became a Swedish lake. Although the king was killed at Lützen in 1632, his policies were carried on during the reign of his daughter Christina by the prime minister, Axel Oxenstierna. By terms of the Peace of Westphalia (1648) Sweden gained Pomerania and the archbishopric of Bremen, part of the Holy Roman Empire. Swedish expansionism resulted, in 1658, in the recapture of the southern Swedish provinces that Denmark had retained since the early 16th century. Renewed wars extended the Swedish frontier to the west coast while reducing Danish control over trade by taking away the eastern shore of the Öresund.

Under young Charles XII (r. 1697–1718), Sweden fought the Great Northern War (1700–1721) against a coalition of Denmark, Poland, Saxony, and Russia. Sweden at first was militarily successful, but after a crushing defeat by Russian forces under Peter the Great (Peter I) in 1709 at the Battle of Poltava, the nation lost territories to Russia, Prussia, and Hannover. Thereafter Sweden was a second-rate power. Throughout the 18th century there was internal dissension between those who favored increased political liberties and constitutionally shared political power and those who favored monarchical absolutism. In 1770, a power struggle between the nobility and the commoner estates, including the clergy, burghers and farmers, ended when Gustav III carried out a bloodless coup and restored absolutism. Gustavus III (r. 1771–92), a poet, playwright, and patron of the arts and sciences, and founder of the Swedish Academy, was eventually assassinated by a group of disgruntled nobles.

Sweden entered the Napoleonic Wars in 1805, allying itself with Great Britain, Austria, and Russia against France. Russia switched sides in 1807, however, and the ensuing Russo-Swedish conflict (1808–9) resulted in the loss of Finland. King Gustavus IV was then overthrown by the army, and a more democratic constitution was adopted. In 1810, one of Napoleon's marshals, a Frenchman from Pau named Jean Baptiste Jules Bernadotte, was invited to become the heir to the Swedish throne. Three years later, he brought his adopted country once again over to the side of the allies against Napoleon in the last full-scale war fought by Sweden. His reward for being on the winning side of the Napoleonic wars was to wrest a reluctant Norway from Danish control. After a show of Swedish force, Norway was forced into political union with Sweden that lasted until 1905 when the union was largely peacefully dissolved.

Bernadotte assumed the name Charles John (Carl Johan) and succeeded to the Swedish throne in 1818 as Charles XIV John. The Bernadotte dynasty, which has reigned successively since 1818, gradually relinquished virtually all of its powers, which were assumed by the Riksdag, Sweden's parliament. Sweden has become one of the most progressive countries in the world. Industry was developed, the cooperative movement began to play an important part in the economy, and the Social Democratic Labor Party gained a dominant position in political life.

Carl XVI Gustaf has been king since the death of his grandfather, Gustav VI Adolf, in 1973. In September 1976, a coalition of three non-Socialist parties won a majority in parliamentary elections, ending 44 years of almost uninterrupted Social Democratic rule that had established a modern welfare state. The country's economic situation worsened, however, and the Social Democrats were returned to power in the elections of September 1982. Prime Minister Olof Palme, leader of the Social Democratic Party since 1969, was assassinated in February 1986. In the ensuing years, investigators have been unable to establish a motive for the killing or to find the assassin.

In April 2009, the Swedish parliament passed a law to legalize same-sex marriages in a vote of 226 to 22. The law went into effect on 1 May 2009, making Sweden the fifth European nation to legalize same-sex marriage. Though such unions will now be considered legal, churches will not be required to perform the marriage ceremonies. The Lutheran Church, which is the largest in Sweden, has allowed for the blessing of same-sex partnerships since 2007, but individual pastors are still permitted to refuse to officiate at same-sex weddings.

Sweden assumed the European Union (EU) presidency for a six-month term beginning on 1 July 2009.

Sweden and Neutrality

Sweden remained neutral in both world wars; during World War II, however, the nation had difficulty maintaining neutrality as its Nordic neighbors were drawn into the conflict. Sweden served as a haven for refugees from the Nazis, allowed the Danish resistance movement to operate on its soil, and sent volunteers to assist Finland's fight against the Russians. On the other hand, Sweden was compelled to comply with German demands to transport its troops through Sweden to and from Nazi-occupied Norway. After the war, Sweden did not join NATO, as did its Scandinavian neighbors Norway and Denmark, but it did become a member of the UN in 1946 and participated in some of the European Recovery Program benefits. In 1953, Sweden joined with Denmark, Norway, Iceland, and, later, Finland to form the Nordic Council, and was instrumental in creating EFTA in 1960. Subsequently Sweden declined an invitation to join the EEC with Denmark, Ireland, and the United Kingdom; a free-trade agreement with the EEC was signed 22 July 1972. Sweden's post-WWII foreign policy has been termed "active neutrality." Neutral Sweden tried to mediate in the Cold War confrontation between the Western and Soviet blocs and sought a major role in development assistance toward newly independent countries in the Third World.

Sweden's traditional policy of neutrality was strained in late October 1981 when a Soviet submarine ran aground inside a restricted military zone near the Swedish naval base at Karlskrona. The Swedish government protested this "flagrant violation of territorial rights" and produced reasons for believing that the submarine had been carrying nuclear weapons. Swedish naval vessels raised the damaged submarine and permitted it to return to the Soviet fleet in early November. In 1984, a Swedish military report stated that at least 10 "alien" submarines had been detected in Swedish waters.

The environment and nuclear energy were major political issues in Sweden during the 1980s. Since that time, the major concerns have been conflicts over immigration policies, the economy, and Sweden's relationship to the European Communities. Sweden's economic crisis of the early 1990s led to large-scale public spending cuts by a center-right government. In 1991, Sweden applied for membership in the EC against a background of considerable opposition. In May 1993, the Riksdag altered Sweden's long-standing foreign policy of neutrality. In the future, neutrality would only be followed in time of war. The Riksdag also opened up the possibility of Sweden's participation in defense alliances, which remains a hotly debated issue in Sweden.

In 1994, Swedes voted to join the EU and the country officially became a member on 1 January 1995. Nevertheless, Sweden did not join the 11 EU countries participating in the launch of the new European currency, the euro, on 1 January 1999. Public opinion over the succeeding years softened on the issue of euro membership, however, and a referendum on joining the monetary union was held on 14 September 2003. The ruling Social Democratic Party supported euro membership, but its coalition partners in 2003, the ex-communist Left Party and the Greens, were strongly opposed, as those parties feared Sweden would lose not only its currency, but its status as an advanced welfare state. On 10 September, Swedish Foreign Minister Anna Lindh was stabbed in a Stockholm department store by an assailant unknown to her; she died the next day. Lindh was one of the primary spokespersons for the "yes" campaign for the euro, and was one of the country's best-loved politicians; many thought she could have become prime minister. The referendum was defeated by a margin of 56.1% to 41.8% with a turnout of 81.2%.

Following the 11 September 2001 terrorist attacks on the United States, Sweden pledged support for US-led retaliation against terrorists. At the same time, Sweden relaxed further its policy of neutrality, leading some to speculate that it will eventually join NATO. Sweden since 1992 has been a member of NATO's Partnership for Peace program, and in 1999, the first Swedish troops were sent to Kosovo in the Balkans.

In February 2002, Prime Minister Göran Persson's government made the decision for Sweden to enter into military alliances and defensive pacts with other nations. The Swedish government has devoted particular attention to issues of disarmament, arms control, and nuclear nonproliferation and has contributed importantly to UN and other international peacekeeping efforts, including those of the NATO-led peacekeeping forces in the Balkans (KFOR). Sweden also contributed to the International Security Assistance Force (ISAF) in Afghanistan and assumed leadership of the Provincial Reconstruction Team in Mazar e-Sharif in March 2006.

The September 2006 elections marked a major change in leadership for the country. The Alliance for Sweden, a center-right coalition of parties, narrowly unseated the Social Democrat Party that had held the majority for 12 years. Campaigning on a platform of welfare reform and tax cuts to create new jobs, the Alliance gained a narrow seven-seat majority in parliament. Frederik Reinfeldt, leader of the Moderate Party, replaced Persson as prime minister.

LOCATION: 55°20′ to 69°4′N; 10°58′ to 24°10′ E. BOUNDARY LENGTHS: Finland, 586 kilometers (364 miles); coastline, 2,746 kilometers (1,706 miles); Norway, 1,619 kilometers (1,006 miles); Gotland Island coastline, 400 kilometers (249 miles); Öland Island coastline, 72 kilometers (45 miles). TERRITORIAL SEA LIMIT: 12 miles.

On 19 June 2010, Crown Princess Victoria married commoner Daniel Westling, her former personal trainer, at Stockholm Cathedral. Her parents, King Carl XVI Gustaf and Queen Silvia, were married in the same place on the same date in 1976. Princess

Victoria was designated as the heiress apparent by the passage of equal primogeniture in 1980, which allowed for the eldest child to be designated as heir, regardless of gender. Sweden was the first country in Europe to pass such a law.

At the end of 2011, Julian Assange, the founder of WikiLeaks, was awaiting a decision on his appeal against extradition from the UK to Sweden on charges of rape and sexual assault. Assange was being detained under a European Arrest Warrant issued by a Swedish public prosecutor over allegations that he sexually assaulted two women during a visit to Sweden in August 2010, claims which he denied.

13 GOVERNMENT

Sweden has been a constitutional monarchy since 1809. The 1809 constitution was replaced by a new Instrument of Government on 1 January 1975. Legislative authority is vested in the parliament (Riksdag). The monarch ceded involvement in power-brokering among the parties as early as 1917 when the Liberals and Social Democrats entered into a coalition. Today, the monarch performs only ceremonial duties as the official head of state; the monarch's last political duty, regular participation in cabinet meetings, was taken away under the most recent constitution. The king must belong to the Lutheran Church; the throne was hereditary only for male descendants until 1980, when female descendants were granted the right to the throne. In 2012, Crown Princess Victoria remained the heiress apparent. Fredrik Reinfeldt has served as Prime Minister since 2006, and Jan Bjorklund as Deputy Prime Minister since October 2010.

The Riksdag was bicameral until 1971, when a unicameral body of 350 members serving three-year terms was established; the 1975 constitution provided for 349 members, and the parliamentary term was lengthened to four years in 1994. All members of the Riksdag are directly elected by universal suffrage that begins at age 18. Voter turnout has traditionally been very high in Sweden, averaging well over 80%, and occasionally more than 90%, for all elections since 1960. Foreign nationals are allowed to vote in regional and municipal elections. Elections at all levels are simultaneous and are held on the third Sunday of September every fourth year. The parties' share of the national vote translated directly into seats in Riksdag. Interim national elections can be called by the government between regular elections, but the mandate of the interim election is valid only for the remaining portion of the regular four-year parliamentary term of office.

In Sweden's parliamentary system, executive power lay with the government, or cabinet, that is formed by the majority party in parliament or by a coalition of parties. Sweden has also functioned with a minority government in which the largest party does not enjoy a majority in parliament and has to form ad-hoc coalitions with other parties in the Riksdag. The cabinet as a whole is responsible for all government decisions and has to defend their legislative agenda in the plenary sessions of the Riksdag. A vote of no confidence by an absolute majority of the Riksdag allows for the forced resignation of individual ministers or of the entire cabinet. A vote of no confidence becomes moot if within one week of the vote the government calls for new elections for the entire Riksdag.

Chief executive power is wielded by the prime minister, who is formally proposed by the speaker of the Riksdag and confirmed by vote of the parliamentary parties. The prime minister appoints a cabinet usually consisting of 18–20 members reflecting the party or coalition of parties in power. Once a week the government takes decisions in a formal meeting presided over by the prime minister. The cabinet as a whole discusses all-important decisions prior to taking action. After a decision had been taken by the cabinet, the ministers practice collective responsibility in which all support the decision taken by the government. Ministers can issue directives, but administrative decisions are taken by central boards, which have their respective spheres of activity delimited by the Riksdag.

National referenda on policy questions of national importance are permitted by the constitution. Sweden ranked first in the world on the 2007 Gender Gap Index, which measures economic participation and opportunities, health and survival, political empowerment and educational attainment. In 2008 Sweden's parliament had the highest level of political representation of women in the world with 47% of 349 Riksdag seats held by women. Women also held 52% of ministerial positions in government.

14 POLITICAL PARTIES

The unicameral system and the electoral system of proportional representation have allowed almost exact equality in proportional representation among the constituencies on the national level and have produced a multiparty system. The constitution requires, however, that a party must gain at least 4% of the national popular vote or 12% in a constituency to be represented in the Riksdag. Sweden has for many years utilized the party list system in which the candidates for office from any given party are listed in order of party preference. If a party won 10 seats in the Riksdag, the top 10 candidates from that party would be represented in parliament. In 1998, voters for the first time had the option of indicating which candidates on the party list they preferred to see elected to parliament and to local councils. A given candidate must receive at least 8% of his or her party's ballots in any electoral district to be moved to the top of the party's nomination list. If no candidate attains the 8% threshold, the party's nomination list remains in force.

The Social Democratic Party represents a large portion of blue-collar workers and public sector employees. It derives much of its power from strong links with the National Swedish Confederation of Trade Unions (LO). The party platform is based on a commitment to social welfare programs and government direction of the economy.

The Moderate Party platform focuses on personal freedom and free enterprise, while still supporting most of the social benefits introduced since the 1930s. The party also supports a strong defense and Sweden's membership in the European Union (EU). Its voter base is urban business people and professionals, but the party also attracts young voters, main-street shop owners, and, to some extent, blue-collar workers.

The Center Party maintains close ties to rural Sweden. The main priorities of the party include providing a sound economic climate for business and job creation, climate change and environmental concerns (including nuclear power), and health and welfare issues. The Left Party, formerly the Communist Party, focuses on feminist issues, employment in the public sector, and the environment. It opposes privatization, cuts in public expenditure, Swedish participation in NATO activities, and EU membership. Its voter base consists mainly of young people, public sector employees, feminists, journalists, and former social democrats.

The Christian Democrat Party is conservative and value-oriented. Its voter base is primarily among members of conservative churches and rural populations. Christian Democrats seek government support for families and better ethical practices to improve care for the elderly. The Liberal Party's platform emphasizes a commitment to a free-market economy combined with comprehensive Swedish social welfare programs. Foreign aid, education and women's equality also are popular issues. The Liberal Party base is mainly centered in educated middle-class voters. The Green Party is a leftist environmentalist party that supports a phasing-out of nuclear energy in Sweden, to be replaced with alternative, environmentally friendly energy sources.

Except for a brief period in 1936, the Social Democratic Labor Party was in power almost uninterruptedly from 1932 to 1976, either alone or in coalition. In 1945, the Social Democrats dissolved the wartime Grand Coalition Cabinet representing every party except the Left Party Communists and launched a program of social reform. Although inflation and other difficulties slowed the Social Democratic program, steadily mounting production encouraged the government to push through its huge social welfare program, which was sanctioned in principle by all major parties.

The Social Democrats held or controlled all parliamentary majorities until the elections of September 1976 when a non-Socialist coalition including the Center Party, the Moderates, and the Liberals won 180 of the 349 seats at stake. The center-right coalition retained control in the 1979 election with a reduced majority of 175 seats and a stronger showing for the Moderates. In the election of September 1982, however, the Social Democrats returned to power. Olof Palme, who had been the Social Democratic prime minister from 1969 to 1976, was able to put together a new coalition cabinet. His party remained in power following the 1985 election. Palme was assassinated in February 1986; he was succeeded by Ingvar Carlsson.

The 1988 election was a watershed that registered political discontentment. The Social Democrats lost seats as the Moderates' and Liberals' share of the vote continued to increase. More remarkably, for the first time in 70 years, a new party gained representation in the Riksdag—the Green Party (MP), which obtained 20 seats. The Social Democrats were narrowly defeated in September 1991, and the government of Ingvar Carlsson gave way to that of Carl Bildt (Moderate Party), who headed a minority four-party, center-right coalition composed of the Moderates, the Liberals, the Center Party, and the Christian Democratic party, which together controlled 170 seats.

The 1991 election represented a gain for two previously unrepresented parties—Christian Democrats (26 seats) and New Democracy (25 seats)—who managed to exceed the 4% threshold while the Greens fell below the threshold and lost representation in the Riksdag. New Democracy emerged prior to the 1991 general election as a party of discontent urging tax cuts and reduced immigration. The Left Party-Communists were renamed the Left Party (VP) in 1990.

The Moderate Coalition, which promised to end Sweden's deepening recession in the early 1990s, found itself unable to address the country's problems, largely because of Social Democrat and popular opposition to its cost-cutting measures. In 1994, the So-

cial Democrats were returned to office by a population reluctantly willing to bear austerity if initiated and directed by the party that created the welfare state. The Social Democratic Coalition government under Prime Minister Ingvar Carlsson navigated Sweden through the referendum on Swedish membership in the EU in late 1994. Carlsson was replaced as prime minister by the former finance minister, Göran Persson.

The September 1998 election represented a protest vote against the mainstream parties and perhaps greater voter polarization in Sweden. The mainstream party of the left, the Social Democrats, had their worst election showing in over 70 years but maintained power in a minority government dependent upon support from a formal alliance from the Left and Green parties. The Social Democrats slipped from 45.3% of the vote in 1994 to 36.4% in 1998, while the Left Party advanced from 6.2% in 1994 to 12% in 1998 and the Greens returned to the Riksdag with 4.5% of the national vote. Similarly on the right, the Christian Democrats advanced from 4.1% of vote in 1994 to 11.8% in 1998 at the expense of the more centrist Center and Liberal parties, which narrowly passed the 4% threshold. The Moderates' share of the vote held basically steady.

The 2002 general election campaign focused largely on the issues of immigration and membership in the euro zone. The Liberals and Moderates supported a plan to import large numbers of guest workers, who would be classed as noncitizens. The Social Democrats and the Left Party denounced this plan. The Social Democrats registered a strong showing in the elections, winning 39.8% of the vote (up from 36.4% in 1998) and taking 144 of 349 seats in the Riksdag. The Social Democrats under Göran Persson formed a government with the Left Party (8.3% of the vote and 30 seats) and the Greens (4.6% and 17 seats). However, the Liberal Party, with its immigration plan, increased its strength in parliament, with 13.3% of the vote (up from 4.7% in 1998) and 48 seats.

In the election of September 2006, the center-right Alliance for Sweden—a coalition of the Moderate Party, the Liberal Party, the Christian Democrat, and the Center Party—won 178 of the 349 seats. Fredrik Reinfeldt, leader of the Moderate Party, took the position of prime minister. The Social Democratic Party gained 34.99% of the vote and 130 seats. The Left Party gained 5.85% of the vote and 22 seats while the Green Party won 5.24% of the vote and 19 seats.

The 19 September 2010 election resulted in the far-right Sweden Democrats winning seats in parliament for the first time. The party campaigned on an anti-immigration platform, calling for a cut in immigration by 90% and pointing to the growth of Sweden's Muslim population as a threat to the nation. The Sweden Democrats won 20 of 349 seats with 5.7% of the vote. The center-right Alliance, led by Prime Minister Fredrik Reinfeldt, retained 172 seats and the opposition, made up of the Green Party and the Social Democrats, held the remaining 157 seats in parliament. With no single alliance or party holding a majority, Reinfeldt intended to turn to the Green Party for support in forming a new government that could effectively counter the influence of the Sweden Democrats. The day after the vote, about 6,000 people took part in demonstrations against the Sweden Democrats with shouts of "No to Racism."

15 LOCAL GOVERNMENT

Local self-government has a long tradition in Sweden as the civil role of the Lutheran Church has been gradually reduced. The first legislation establishing municipal governance was the Local Government Ordinances of 1862 that separated religious tasks from civil tasks, which were given to cities and rural municipal districts. On 1 January 2000, the Church of Sweden separated from the central government, and local parishes lost their local government status.

Decentralization is markedly characteristic of Sweden's governmental structure. With the most recent reforms there are two main types of local governance in Sweden: the municipality, or *kommun*, as the local unit, and the county council as the regional unit. The country is divided into 21 counties, 2 regions, 289 municipalities, and one "county council-free municipality" on the island of Gotland, each with an elected council. Local government is administered by county councils and municipalities consisting of at least 20 members popularly elected, on a proportional basis, for four years. Under each council is an executive board with various committees. In addition, there is a governor (prefect), the government-appointed head of the administrative board in each of Sweden's counties, who holds supreme police and other supervisory authority. Local authorities are responsible for most social welfare services, including hospitals, elementary education, certain utilities, and the police force. It is up to the Swedish cabinet and parliament to decide on the overall framework of public sector activities, but within these wide parameters, local governments have a large measure of freedom to implement public programs.

16 JUDICIAL SYSTEM

Swedish law is a system of civil law influenced by Roman-Germanic law, and customary law. Ordinary criminal and civil cases are tried in a local court (*tingsrätt*), consisting of a judge and a panel of lay assessors appointed by the municipal council. Above these local courts are six courts of appeal (*hovrätter*). The highest tribunal is the Supreme Court (*Högsta Domstolen*), made up of at least 16 justices. Special cases are heard by the Supreme Administrative Court and other courts. The Swedish judicial procedure uses a jury of the Anglo-US type only in press libel suits. Capital punishment, last employed in 1910, is expressly forbidden by the constitution.

The judiciary is independent of executive control or political influence. The right to counsel of criminal defendants is restricted to cases in which the maximum penalty possible is six-month imprisonment or greater.

Sweden originated the judicial practice of the ombudsman when its first ombudsman was designated in 1766. The office has been in continuous existence since 1809. The institution has also been enshrined by the constitution and provides parliamentary control over the executive. The Riksdag elects four ombudsmen representing various interests such as consumers, gender equality, the press, children, the disabled, those experiencing ethnic and/or sexual orientation discrimination. The ombudsmen are charged with supervising the observance of laws and statutes as applied by the courts and by public officials, excluding cabinet ministers, members of the Riksdag, or directly elected local government officials. The ombudsmen are concerned especially with protecting the civil rights of individual citizens and of religious and other groups. There are some 5,000 complaints lodged with the office of the ombudsman annually, though about 40% are dismissed immediately for a variety of reasons. Only about 20–25% of these complaints are investigated fully and usually reflect an individual caught on a bureaucratic "merry-go-round." Ombudsmen may admonish or prosecute offenders, although prosecutions are relatively rare.

17 ARMED FORCES

The International Institute for Strategic Studies reported that armed forces in Sweden totaled 21,070 members in 2011. The force was comprised of 7,332 from the army, 3,423 from the navy, 3,770 from the air force, and 6,545 staff members. Armed forces represented 0.4% of the labor force in Sweden at that time. Defense spending totaled $5.3 billion and accounted for 1.5% of gross domestic product.

Sweden's policy of neutrality and nonalignment required a strong, modern, and independent defense establishment. The Swedish Navy maintained naval stations at Stockholm, Karlskrona, and Göteborg. Major naval units included seven tactical submarines, 36 patrol and coastal vessels, and 21 mine warfare vessels. The Air Force operated 170 combat capable aircraft, including 13 fighter ground attack aircraft and 151 JAS-39 Gripen multirole aircraft. A 600-person paramilitary force acted as the nation's coast guard and more than 35,000 people belonged to voluntary auxiliary organizations. A civil defense service could call to service persons between the ages of 16 and 25. Sweden participated in UN and peacekeeping missions in 11 countries or regions.

18 INTERNATIONAL COOPERATION

Sweden joined the UN on 19 November 1946, and takes part in ECE and several nonregional specialized agencies, such as UNESCO, UNCTAD, UNHCR, the FAO, the World Bank, IAEA, ILO, and the WHO. The country served on the UN Security Council from 1997–98. The first UN Conference on the Human Environment was held in Stockholm in June 1972. Together with Denmark, Finland, Iceland, and Norway, Sweden has been a member of the advisory Nordic Council since 1953 and cooperates with these other Scandinavian countries in social welfare and health insurance and in freeing frontiers of passport control. The nation is also a member of the Asian Development Bank, the African Development Bank, the Council of the Baltic Sea States, G-6, G-9, the Paris Club (G-10), the Inter-American Development Bank, the Nordic Investment Bank, OECD, OSCE, the NATO Partnership for Peace, and the Council of Europe. In 1995, Sweden became a member of the European Union. It has observer status in the OAS and the Western European Union.

Sweden has offered support to UN missions and operations in Kosovo (est. 1999), India and Pakistan (est. 1949), Ethiopia and Eritrea (est. 2000), Liberia (est. 2003), Sierra Leone (est. 1999), East Timor (est. 2002), Georgia (est. 1993), and the DROC (est. 1999), among others. Sweden is part of the Australia Group, the Zangger Committee, the European Organization for Nuclear Research (CERN), the Nuclear Suppliers Group (London Group), Organization for the Prohibition of Chemical Weapons, and the Nuclear Energy Agency.

In environmental cooperation, Sweden is part of the Antarctic Treaty; the Basel Convention; Conventions on Biological Diversity, Whaling, and Air Pollution; Ramsar; CITES; the London Convention; International Tropical Timber Agreements; the Kyoto Protocol; the Montréal Protocol; MARPOL; the Nuclear Test Ban Treaty; and the UN Conventions on the Law of the Sea, Climate Change, and Desertification.

Sweden assumed the European Union presidency for a six-month term beginning on 1 July 2009.

19 ECONOMY

In 2011 Sweden had one of the most vibrant economies in Europe, if not in the world. The GDP rate of change was 5.5% in 2010, inflation stood at only 1.4%, and unemployment was reported at 8.3%, and expected to decline. Sweden's economy was one of the world's most open, ranked 22nd out of 179 economies on the World Bank and Heritage Foundation's 2011 Index of Economic Freedom.

Sweden began to shift from agriculture to industry in the 1930s and developed rapidly during the postwar period. Sweden began to produce the goods and specialized products for which it became world renowned: ball bearings, high-grade steel, machine tools, automobiles, chemicals and glassware—items in world demand. Close cooperation among trade, industry, and finance was a feature of the economy, as was the building of factories in rural districts.

Although the country experienced a long period of decline from 1960–1990, in 1994 the economy rebounded. From then until 2008 strong exports and rising domestic demand fueled economic growth. With the onset of global recession in 2008, Sweden fell victim to contracting world markets. GDP fell 4.9% in 2009. However, a strong financial base and sound fiscal policy insulated the country from crises besetting other EU members. In 2011 government projected GDP growth of 4.4% and expected to show a budget surplus by 2012.

20 INCOME

Sweden enjoys a highly even distribution of wealth: in 2010 Sweden had the world's lowest Gini coefficient at 0.22. In 2011, most income was generated by the services sector. It was estimated that agriculture accounted for 1.7% of GDP, industry 26.1%, and services 72.2%. In 2010 the GDP of Sweden was $354.7 billion with per capita GDP estimated at $39,100. The annual GDP growth rate was 5.5%, with an average inflation rate of 1.4%. GDP was defined as the value of all final goods and services produced within a nation in a given year and computed on the basis of purchasing power parity (PPP) rather than value as measured on the basis of the rate of the exchange based on current dollars. In 2007 the World Bank estimated that Sweden, with 0.15% of the world's population, accounted for 0.53% of the world's GDP. By comparison, the United States, with 4.85% of the world's population, accounted for 22.51% of world GDP. According to the World Bank, remittances from citizens living abroad totaled $651.5 million or about $72 per capita and accounted for approximately .2% of GDP.

The World Bank reported that in 2009, household consumption in Sweden totaled $198.1 billion or about $21,792 per capita, measured in current US dollars rather than PPP. Household consumption includes expenditures of individuals, households, and nongovernmental organizations on goods and services, excluding the purchases of dwellings. It was estimated that household consumption was growing at an average annual rate of 0.7%.

As of 2011 the most recent study by the World Bank reported that actual individual consumption in Sweden was 67.6% of GDP and accounted for 0.53% of world consumption. By comparison, the United States accounted for 25.44% of world individual consumption. The World Bank also estimated that 7.2% of Sweden's GDP was spent on food and beverages, 15.4% on housing and household furnishings, 2.5% on clothes, 7.9% on health, 6.2% on transportation, 1.5% on communications, 6.6% on recreation, 2.4% on restaurants and hotels, and 11% on miscellaneous goods and services and purchases from abroad.

21 LABOR

As of 2010, Sweden had a total labor force of 4.961 million people. Within that labor force, CIA estimates in 2008 noted that 1.1% were employed in agriculture, 28.2% in industry, and 70.7% in the service sector. Labor is highly unionized with more than 80% of Swedish wage earners members of trade unions. The trade union movement is based on voluntary membership, and there is neither a closed shop nor a union shop. Although workers have the right to strike, employers also have the right to use the lockout.

Agreements between employers and trade unions are generally the product of negotiation. Public mediators or mediation commissions intervene if necessary. A labor court, made up of three impartial members and five representing employers, workers, and salaried employees, has jurisdiction over the application and interpretation of collective agreements already signed and can impose damages on employers, trade unions, or trade union members violating a contract. For many years, an overwhelming majority of the court's decisions were unanimous, and since the end of the 1930s peace between management and labor has generally prevailed. In 1997, management and labor agreed to a new negotiating framework that decreased strikes and increased wages. Swedish law requires employee representation on company boards of directors. A law passed in 1983 introduced employee funds, partly funded by contributions from profits of all Swedish companies, which gives unions and employees equity in companies, while providing the companies with investment capital.

The legal minimum age for full-time employment is 16 years old, but only under the supervision of local authorities. In addition, minors under 18 can only work in the daytime and have to be supervised. The regular workweek cannot exceed 40 hours, and overtime is limited to 48 hours over a four-week period and a total of 200 hours a year. However, these regulations can be modified with a collective bargaining agreement, as can minimum wages. A minimum of five weeks of holiday with pay is stipulated by law. There is no national minimum wage. Workers, even at the lowest end of the pay scale, are able to provide a decent standard of living for their families. Health and safety standards are very high and are stringently enforced.

22 AGRICULTURE

Roughly 8% of the total land in Sweden is farmed; the country's major crops include barley, wheat, and sugar beets. Cereal production in 2009 amounted to 5.2 million tons, fruit production 40,522 tons, and vegetable production 325,750 tons.

Only slightly more than 1% of Sweden's labor force earned its living in agriculture in 2011, compared with more than 50% at the beginning of the 20th century and about 20% in 1950. Production in major crops exceeds domestic consumption, but given the short growing season and climatic limitations, a considerable amount of food is imported.

In 2010 the country comprised 71,091 land holdings of which 3,785 were smaller than two hectares (five acres); 13, 943 between 5 and 10 hectares (12 and 25 acres), and 6,457 greater than 100 hectares (247 acres). Farm holdings are intensively tilled; fertilizers are used heavily and mechanization is increasing. Most farmers are elderly, and support themselves through supplemental forestry and fishing. By 1995, government had harmonized Swedish agriculture with EU policies, and has gradually sought to merge small, unprofitable farms into larger units of 10–20 hectares (25–50 acres) with some woodland, the size estimated to be able to support a family at the same living standard as an industrial worker. Sweden also was implementing a plan to convert 10% of the country's arable land to ecological, or organic, agriculture by increasing taxes on energy, fertilizers, and biocides. The government had also introduced incentives to promote the production of biomass for energy production.

23 ANIMAL HUSBANDRY

The UN Food and Agriculture Organization (FAO) reported that Sweden dedicated 458,000 hectares (1.13 million acres) to permanent pasture or meadow in 2009. During that year, the country tended 7.2 million chickens, 1.5 million head of cattle, and 1.5 million pigs. The production from these animals amounted to 219,735 tons of beef and veal, 333,835 tons of pork, 135,384 tons of poultry, 102,333 tons of eggs, and 3.26 million tons of milk. Sweden also produced 10,500 tons of cattle hide and 148 tons of raw wool.

Although Sweden's long winters require indoor feeding from October to May, pastoral farming is important, and about 80% of farm income derives from animal products such as cheese and butter. Agricultural reform in the early 1990s dismantled many of the price regulations and subsidies for products like milk and meat in favor of market-oriented pricing. As these adjustments were made, the number of dairy producers fell. Sweden's beef industry in 2011 was supported by direct EU subsidies.

Fur farms bred large numbers of mink and a declining number of fox. Reindeer were raised by 51 Sami (Lapp) communities in the north, and between 1970 and 2003 the reindeer population in Lapp villages increased from 166,200 to 238,800.

24 FISHING

Sweden had 2,123 decked commercial fishing boats in 2008. The annual capture totaled 231,336 tons according to the UN FAO. The export value of seafood totaled $1.22 billion.

Fish is important to the Swedish diet; Sweden is both a major importer of fish products and a principal supplier to other countries. Göteborg, Bohus, and Halland are the principal fishing districts, but large quantities of fish are caught all along the coasts. Herring, cod, plaice, flounder, salmon, eel, mackerel, and shellfish are the most important saltwater varieties. Freshwater fish includ-

ed trout, salmon, and crayfish, a national delicacy. According to FAO statistics, in 2003 there were 360 aquacultural enterprises, yielding 4,585 tons of fish. By tradition, a large part of the annual catch was landed in Denmark. Fish for feed was the largest single commodity, accounting for 65% of the 2003 catch.

25 FORESTRY

Approximately 69% of Sweden is covered by forest, making Sweden one of the world's most heavily forested countries. Around 55% of the land area consists of productive forestry land totaling 22.7 million hectares (56.1 million acres). The percentage has varied little, between 55.5% and 58.1%, since the first National Forestry Inventory of 1923–29. The UN FAO estimated the 2009 roundwood production at 59.2 million cu m (2.09 billion cu ft). The value of all forest products, including roundwood, totaled $14.1 billion.

Economically, forest wealth ranked second in importance after metal-based industry. Sweden competed with Canada for world leadership in the export of wood pulp and was the world's leading exporter of cellulose. About 60% of Sweden's annual forestry production was exported every year. Sweden was the third-largest exporter of paper and board, supplying 10% of the export market, with production amounting to 3% of the world's total.

Virtually all of Sweden's forests were regrowth; virgin forests covered 788,000 hectares (1,947,000 acres) and were almost exclusively found in national parks and nature reserves. The growing stock was estimated at 3 billion cu m (106 billion cu ft). The annual growth amounted to about 101 million cu m (3.5 billion cu ft). Important varieties included spruce (46% of commercial stands), pine (38%), birch (11%), and oak, beech, alder, and aspen (5% combined).

Forestry and farming are interdependent everywhere except in the most fertile plains; in northern Sweden, almost one of every two men worked in the woods for at least part of the winter. However, since the early 1970s, the number of employees in the forestry sector has fallen by over 40%. The government has attempted through forestry policies to provide incentives and regulations that improve efficiencies in forest management, cutting and use. In the early 1990s, the government eliminated subsidies to commercial forestry to strengthen Sweden's position in a strongly competitive international market. Between 1994 and 2003, Sweden's government negotiated 1,750 agreements with landowners compensating them with $11.2 million to develop and preserve natural areas.

In January 2005 a severe storm raged through southern Sweden and caused major damage to forests. About 75 million cu m (2.6 billion cu ft) of timber, nearly the total annual cut for all of Sweden, was damaged by the storm, 80% Norway spruce.

26 MINING

Since ancient days, mining and the iron industry have been of great importance in the economic life of Sweden, which is among the most active mining countries in Europe. In addition to iron ore, Sweden also is a producer of primary metals such as zinc, copper and lead, as well as industrial minerals such as dolomite, feldspar, granite, kaolin, quartz and limestone. Sweden accounts for a large percentage of Western Europe's iron output, and is home to one of the region's largest gold mines.

Iron-ore production in 2009 (concentrate and pellets) was estimated at 17,700,000 metric tons, down from an estimated 23,800,000 metric tons in 2008. The Bergslagen region, in central Sweden, yielded high-grade ores for quality steel. Gold mine output in 2009 totaled 5,600 kg, down from 5,530 kg in 2008, while silver mine output in 2009 totaled 290,000 kg, down from 293,100 kg in 2008. Lead mine output in 2009 totaled 65,000 metric tons, while copper mine output, in that year, totaled 46,019 metric tons. Zinc mine output in 2009 totaled 192,538 metric tons. Lead, copper, zinc, gold, and silver were produced in the rich Skellefte (Boliden) region, where bismuth, cobalt, and huge quantities of arsenic were also found. The open-pit Björgal gold mine upgraded its facility, to increase production capacity to 3,000 kg per year, from 2,600 kg per year in 1996. Further south, phosphate, tungsten, kyanite, and pyrite were found. Sweden also produced hydraulic cement, kaolin clay, feldspar, fertilizer, graphite, lime, quartz, quartzite, dimension and crushed stone (including dolomite, granite—for domestic use and for export, limestone, sandstone, and slate), sulfur, and soapstone talc. Marble (in Askersund) and ilmenite were also found in Sweden. In 2008 mineral production of Sweden's 517 nonfuel mining and quarrying enterprises was valued at €3.4 billion.

27 ENERGY AND POWER

The World Bank reported in 2008 that Sweden produced 149.9 billion kWh of electricity and consumed 137.1 billion kWh, or 15,084 kWh per capita. Roughly 33% of energy came from fossil fuels, while 46% came from alternative fuels. Per capita oil consumption was 5,379 kg. The CIA reported that Sweden imported on average 546,500 bbl/day of crude oil in 2009, 1.626 billion cu meters of natural gas, and approximately 3.5 million short tons of coal. The country refined some 434,000 barrels per day of crude oil. With no proven oil and gas reserves and only small deposits of coal, Sweden's many rivers, waterfalls, and lakes offered favorable conditions for waterpower.

Since the oil shocks of the 1970s, Sweden has been working to reduce petroleum imports. The share of oil in the primary energy supply declined from nearly 70% in 1979 to 31.6% in 2002. In the same year, nuclear energy accounted for 29.6% of primary energy, hydroelectricity 30%, coal 4.1%, natural gas 1.5%, and renewable sources for the rest.

In June 2010, parliament narrowly approved a plan to replace the country's aging nuclear reactors. The vote proved controversial because it reversed plans to phase out the reactors. The new scheme allowed for reactors to be built only on three existing sites, not to exceed the existing number of ten plants. The vote passed 174 to 172, with three abstentions. Because of environmental considerations, high production costs, and low world market prices, Sweden's substantial uranium reserves—some 250,000–300,000 tons (or about 20% of the known world reserves)—have not been exploited.

The practice of culling rabbits for bioenergy also remained controversial in Sweden. Supporters touted the policy as a utilization of an otherwise wasted resource. Animal rights groups on the other hand protested the practice on humanitarian grounds.

28 INDUSTRY

The basic resources for industrial development in Sweden are forests, iron ore, and waterpower. Forest products, machinery, and motor vehicles are primary exports. Industrial production accounted for 29% of GDP in 2001. From 1990 to 1992, Swedish industry suffered as a result of the deep national recession as well as an overpriced labor pool. In those years, manufacturing output fell by 10%. Between 1989 and 1992, 260,000 Swedes lost jobs in manufacturing. As the economy rebounded, especially from 1994–96, industrial output grew. From 2001 to 2004 industrial growth averaged 5.0% , and in 2010 it reached 8.7%

Since the end of World War II, emphasis has shifted from production of consumer goods to manufactures for export. Swedish-made ships, airplanes, automobiles, machinery, precision equipment and chemicals are considered outstanding in quality. In 1990 General Motors Corporation made a successful bid for half of Saab's automotive operations and bought the remaining 50% in 2000. Saab was sold to Dutch automotive company Spyker in 2010, after General Motors announced its intention to sell the company in 2009. A controlling stake in Spyker and Saab was then sold to a Chinese company, Youngman Automobile Group, in 2011. In 1999, the Ford Motor Co. purchased Sweden's Volvo car operations (excluding its heavy truck operations). Ford later sold Volvo to Zhejiang Geely Holding Group, a Chinese conglomerate, in 2010. IKEA, a company that originated in Sweden in the 1940s, was composed of subsidiaries held in other countries, and by end of 2011 operated some 330 stores in nearly 40 countries. In fiscal year 2010 IKEA sold over $23 billion worth of goods.

Sweden remains a world leader in telecommunications, computers, electronics, robotics, pharmaceutical and medical products, and biotechnology. Sweden's Ericsson is the world's largest telecommunications service provider. Sweden has the largest number of biotechnology companies per capita in the world.

29 SCIENCE AND TECHNOLOGY

Sweden's scientific and technological development is renowned throughout the world. Patent applications in science and technology as of 2009, according to the World Bank, totaled 2,549 in Sweden. Technological products invented or developed by Swedish firms include the self-aligning ball bearing, the cream separator, the three-phase electric motor, and a refrigerator without moving parts. Sweden's more recent applications of sophisticated technology ranged from powder metallurgy to the Hasselblad camera and the Viggen jet fighter. Six of Sweden's largest industrial corporations were engineering companies: Volvo, SAAB-Scania, ASEA, Electrolux, SKF, and L. M. Ericsson. In 2010, high-tech exports were valued at $17.06 billion and accounted for 14% of manufactured exports.

Public financing of research and development accounted for 3.75% of GDP in 2008. In addition, companies largely funded their own research, and other funding came from private sources, foundations, fundraising, and abroad. State-financed research, centering on the universities, was directed by the Council for Planning and Coordination of Research. Long-term industrial research and development was the responsibility of the government through the National Board for Technological Development. Local governments and municipalities funded research mainly in health care and social services. In 2008, research in basic and applied science was conducted at 14 universities and 25 institutions of higher learning in Sweden, enrolling some 385,000 students, 17,000 postgraduates, and employing 27,800 teachers and researchers.

Sweden is known for several research institutions including the Nobel Foundation, which sponsors annual awards in chemistry, physics, and physiology or medicine, as well as for peace, literature, and economic science; the Royal Academy of Sciences, founded in 1739 in Stockholm; the Royal Swedish Academy of Engineering Sciences, founded in 1919 at Stockholm; and the Karolinska Institute, founded in 1810 in Stockholm, specializing in medical research.

30 DOMESTIC TRADE

Stockholm, Gothenburg, and Malmö are the nation's primary distribution centers. Stockholm, the nation's capital, is also the country's business center. The head offices of most of Sweden's industrial and commercial associations, and most of its large corporations, are located in Stockholm. Gothenburg is the country's second-largest city and the nation's leading port. Malmo and Helsingborg are also important ports. Located at the southern tip of Sweden, these ports offer access to continental Europe.

Most of the country's retail business is in private hands, but the consumer cooperative movement has long been one of the strongest in Europe. The Cooperative Union and Wholesale Society, a central buying and manufacturing organization, operate factories, department stores, supermarkets, and specialized shops. Competition between the cooperatives and private enterprise has improved selling methods, so that Sweden's self-service shops are among the most modern in Europe. The nation's three major trade fair/exhibition sites are the Stockholm International Fair, the Swedish Exhibition and Congress Center, and the Sollentuna Fair.

Offices and stores are open on weekdays from 9 a.m. to 5 or 6 p.m. (in summer, sometimes to 3 or 4 p.m.). Many businesses are closed, or management generally unavailable, for extended vacations in the summer and around the Christmas holidays.

31 FOREIGN TRADE

Sweden imported $187.4 billion worth of goods and services in 2010, while exporting $202.4 billion worth of goods and services. Major import partners in 2009 were Germany, 18%; Denmark, 8.9%; Norway, 8.7%; Netherlands, 6.1%; UK, 5.5%; Finland, 5.2%; France, 5%; and China, 4.8%. Its major export partners were Norway, 10.6%; Germany, 10.2%; UK, 7.4%; Denmark, 7.3%; Finland, 6.4%; the United States, 6.4%; France, 5%; and Netherlands, 4.7%.

Sweden is one of the world's leading free-trading nations, ranked 22nd out of 179 economies on the 2011 Index of Economic Freedom. About half the economy is dependent upon trade, and businesses operate largely free of political influence. The volume of Sweden's foreign trade has increased very rapidly since World War II, mainly as a result of the gradual liberalization of trade restrictions within the framework of the OECD, EFTA, and the EU. Telecommunications equipment, automobile manufacturing, and logging dominates export commodities from Sweden. Sweden is home to more multinational corporations per capita than any other nation in the world. It is at the economic center of the Nordic and Baltic world, a market of over 27 million consumers.

Major exports in 2009 included machinery (35%), automobiles, paper, iron and steel, and chemicals. Major imports were machinery and transportation equipment (45.8% of all imports), petroleum products, chemicals, iron and steel, foodstuffs and clothing.

32 BALANCE OF PAYMENTS

In 2010 Sweden had a foreign trade surplus of $29 billion. From 1974 through 1985, Sweden ran annual current-account deficits (except in 1984) owing to increases in world oil prices and a decline in the competitiveness of Swedish export products on the world market. Until 1977, deficits were financed mainly through long-term foreign private borrowing by the private sector. Thereafter, central government borrowing expanded rapidly.

In the 1990s current account deficits increased, but a turnaround began in 1996 when the deficit declined from a high of 12%

Principal Trading Partners – Sweden (2010)

(In millions of US dollars)

Country	Total	Exports	Imports	Balance
World	306,587.0	158,114.0	148,473.0	9,641.0
Germany	42,574.0	15,768.0	26,806.0	-11,038.0
Norway	27,116.0	14,643.0	12,473.0	2,170.0
Denmark	22,589.0	10,343.0	12,246.0	-1,903.0
United Kingdom	20,055.0	11,676.0	8,379.0	3,297.0
Finland	17,707.0	9,801.0	7,906.0	1,895.0
Netherlands	17,001.0	7,821.0	9,180.0	-1,359.0
France	14,611.0	7,752.0	6,859.0	893.0
United States	14,142.0	9,620.0	4,522.0	5,098.0
Belgium	12,166.0	6,430.0	5,736.0	694.0
China	11,737.0	4,488.0	7,249.0	-2,761.0

(…) data not available or not significant.

(n.s.) not specified.

SOURCE: *2011 Direction of Trade Statistics Yearbook,* New York: United Nations, 2011.

Balance of Payments – Sweden (2010)

(In millions of US dollars)

Current Account		**30,408.0**
Balance on goods	10,894.0	
Imports	-149,514.0	
Exports	160,408.0	
Balance on services	17,938.0	
Balance on income	101,341.0	
Current transfers	-6,205.0	
Capital Account		**-828.0**
Financial Account		**-42,699.0**
Direct investment abroad	-32,135.0	
Direct investment in Sweden	5,847.0	
Portfolio investment assets	-18,657.0	
Portfolio investment liabilities	40,408.0	
Financial derivatives	4,187.0	
Other investment assets	-30,548.0	
Other investment liabilities	-11,802.0	
Net Errors and Omissions		**12,042.0**
Reserves and Related Items		**1,078.0**

(…) data not available or not significant.

SOURCE: *Balance of Payment Statistics Yearbook 2011,* Washington, DC: International Monetary Fund, 2011.

of GDP in 1993 to 2% of GDP. A rebounding trade balance surplus and a turnaround in direct investment aided in the improvement. The lifting of controls on foreign direct investment, combined with improved competitiveness accruing from greater wage restraint and rising productivity also brought continued interest in investing in Sweden. Sweden's liberal international investment policy, allowing 100% foreign ownership of virtually any sector, other than certain types of transportation and arms manufacture, figured significantly in its favorable balance of payments.

33 BANKING AND SECURITIES

The Central Bank of Sweden (Sveriges Riksbank), founded in 1656, is the oldest central bank in the world. It is the bank of issue and regulates domestic banking operations. The European Central Bank is responsible for determining monetary policy and setting interest rates. The banking sector in Sweden is highly concentrated; four bank groups of a total of 114 banks hold about 75% of the assets. The largest commercial bank is the Skandinaviska Enskilda Banken. Smaller banks serve provincial interests.

In the early 1990s, Swedish banks suffered severe losses; the government was forced to intervene and support two of the five largest commercial banks, Nordbanken and Gota Bank, by taking them over and eventually merging them, and the savings bank Forsta Sparbanken. By the end of 1996, Swedish banks showed improved results, with reduced credit losses and a stricter control of costs.

The deregulation of financial markets in the latter 1990s paved the way for foreign banks to open offices in Sweden. In 1997, Sweden's banking sector saw a series of mergers and acquisitions as Svenska Handelsbanken, the nation's largest bank, acquired the country's largest mortgage lender, Stadshypotek. Swedbank and Föreningsbanken merged, creating the second-largest bank. ForeningsSparbanken and Skandinaviska Enskilda Banken (SEB) broke off a contemplated merger in 2001 for lack of synergies. Den Donske Bank, based in Denmark, made the first incursion by a foreign bank into the Swedish retail sector when it purchased Ostgöta Enskilda Bank. All Swedish banks passed summer 2010 EU stress tests with wide margins.

Mortgage banks of various types met the needs of property owners, home builders, farmers, and shipbuilders. Credit also was extended by some 500 local rural credit societies and by about an equal number of agricultural cooperatives. There were four semi-governmental credit concerns, organized as business companies and created in cooperation with private commercial banks to facilitate long-term lending to agriculture, industry, small industry, and exports. Although the Riksbank's note issue was not tied to its gold reserves, there was an adjustable legal limit. On December 31, 2010 the Central Bank's discount rate was 5.5%, and the commercial bank prime lending rate was 3.386%. At the end of 2010, foreign exchange and gold reserves totaled $48.36 billion.

The Stockholm Stock Exchange (Stockholmsbörsen) was founded in 1863. In 1997, the Stockholm Stock Exchange entered into a joint equity trading union with the Danish bourse and in 2003 operations were merged with those of the Helsinki stock exchange. In 2011, 310 companies were listed on the Exchange with a total market capitalization of $14.55 billion.

34 INSURANCE

Swedes were more life-insurance conscious than the world average. Life insurance was an $878.62 million industry in 2010 with defined contributions making up 53% of the total. Of non-life insurance premiums in the country in 2010, motor vehicle insurance accounted for 24% of the trade; homeowners insurance 21%; business 19%; motor vehicle third party insurance 16%; and health and accident insurance 11%. The five largest life insurance companies held almost 80% of total insurance assets. Automobile liability insurance was compulsory, as was nuclear liability and workers' compensation.

Since the deregulation of financial markets in the late 1980s, insurance companies such as Skandia have created their own banks. The National Insurance Pension Fund and private insurance funds are among the largest single domestic investors on the Stockholm Stock Exchange. The insurance regulatory authority was the Financial Supervisory Authority, an independent state agency.

35 PUBLIC FINANCE

In 2010 the budget of Sweden included $230.1 billion in public revenue and $236.6 billion in public expenditures. The budget deficit amounted to 0.3% of GDP. Public debt was 40.8% of GDP, with $853.3 billion of the debt held by foreign entities. Assuming a projected GDP growth rate of 4.4% for end of year 2011, government expected a budget surplus.

Government outlays by function were as follows: general public services, 23.5%; defense, 5.7%; public order and safety, 3.2%; economic affairs, 9.4%; environmental protection, 0.5%; housing and community amenities, 0.6%; health, 2.9%; recreation, culture, and religion, 0.8%; education, 6.4%; and social protection, 47.2%.

36 TAXATION

Sweden's personal income tax rates are among the highest in the world. As of 2011, Sweden's highest income tax rates stood at

Public Finance – Sweden (2008)

(In billions of kronor, budgetary central government figures)

Revenue and Grants	971.8	100.0%
Tax revenue	693.8	71.4%
Social contributions	184.2	19.0%
Grants	8.3	0.9%
Other revenue	85.5	8.8%
Expenditures	909.9	100.0%
General public services	233	25.6%
Defense	46.9	5.2%
Public order and safety	36.6	4.0%
Economic affairs	85.9	9.4%
Environmental protection	4.8	0.5%
Housing and community amenities	3.6	0.4%
Health	40.7	4.5%
Recreational, culture, and religion	9.6	1.1%
Education	55	6.0%
Social protection	393.8	43.3%

(…) data not available or not significant.

SOURCE: *Government Finance Statistics Yearbook 2010*, Washington, DC: International Monetary Fund, 2010.

57.77%, which, depending on the locality, comprised municipal income taxes on employment income averaging 31% (including contributions to church and funeral fees), and national income tax rates averaging 25%. In addition, capital income was taxed at a flat rate of 30%. Income of nonresidents was subject to a flat rate of 25%. Personal deductions varied between 8,600 and 18,100 krona ($6,364 and $13,400). A health tax was levied at 1.5%. There was also a real estate tax.

Corporations were taxed relatively lightly compared with other OECD countries. The national income tax rate on corporations was 26.3% in 2011 (separate municipal income tax on corporations was abolished as of 1985), with no distinction between distributed and undistributed profits. Capital gains were taxed like other corporate income, although capital gains on shares held for business purposes were tax exempt. The withholding tax on dividends was 30%, applied to nonresidents. Royalties paid to residents were not taxed, but those paid to nonresidents were subject to the corporate rate. These rates were often reduced or eliminated in bilateral tax treaties. Interest income was not subject to withholding.

Tax liability was determined according to a firm's books so long as these were properly kept. Companies were allowed considerable discretion in determining their net income for any particular year; they could take advantage of the flexible rules governing the valuation of stocks and the depreciation of equipment and machinery. Swedish companies could set aside an investment reserve in boom years and use this reserve in years of slack production.

Profits from the sale of securities were taxable provided they had been owned for less than five years. The capital gain was wholly taxable for securities held less than two years, but only 40% of the gain was taxable if the shares had been held more than two years. For machinery and equipment a minimum write-off period of three years was prescribed.

The general VAT tax was 25%, with reduced rates of 12% on food and 6% on items including books, magazines, and personal transportation. A zero VAT rate applied to printing services, ship and airplane building and repair, sea rescue services, prescription medicine, aircraft fuel, and gold supplied to the Central Bank. In general, output VAT was levied on all domestic sales, but not on export or EU sales. Returns for input and output VAT needed to be settled each month with the Swedish tax authorities.

37 CUSTOMS AND DUTIES

With the exception of tariffs in the 19th century to protect the development of Swedish industry, customs duties in Sweden have been among the lowest in the world. Sweden subscribes to the OECD trade liberalization program, and imports are not generally subject to controls. As a member of EFTA, Sweden abolished customs duties against other EFTA countries by the end of 1966. Some 90% of imports from developing countries were duty-free, including most raw materials.

Import duties were based on freight, insurance and handling costs, broker fees, package costs, royalties or license fees, and the seller's yield if sale was to a third party. Import restrictions applied mainly to protected agricultural products, automobiles, and trade with Eastern Europe and the Far East. Sweden applied common external European Union tariffs to imports from the United States at rates ranging from 2–14% for industrial products. Other import taxes included a 25% value-added tax (VAT). A lower 12% VAT applied for food and selected services, and a 6% rate for periodicals and books.

38 FOREIGN INVESTMENT

Sweden had one of the world's most liberal foreign investment regimes, and was one of the biggest magnets for foreign investment in 2011. Besides offering low corporate income tax rates, Sweden was open to nearly all foreign investment, allowed 100% foreign ownership, except in the air and maritime transportation sectors and in arms manufacture, offered highly skilled labor, a multi-lingual workforce, excellent infrastructure, and access to capital. On the negative side, labor costs were high and labor laws were rigid.

Foreign Direct Investment (FDI) in Sweden slowed in 2009, due to the global recession, and then recovered with the resumption of trade. The country was exceeded only by Ireland, Belgium and Hong Kong in terms of per capita FDI receipt. In 2009, FDI in Sweden registered a net inflow of $11.5 billion according to World Bank figures, representing 2.84% of GDP. In 2010, the countries with the largest FDI in Sweden were the Netherlands (15.2%); Luxembourg (14.5%), and the UK (13.4%). The US, which had some 1,100 companies doing business in Sweden, was the seventh largest investor at 6.9%.

39 ECONOMIC DEVELOPMENT

Sweden had one of the world's hottest economies in 2010, growing at 5.5%, with an anticipated growth rate of 4.4% in 2011. That figure was expected to hold into 2012. The Swedish government's liberal foreign trade policy, strong public sector finance and a solid export-led business climate were key factors in this growth, especially when foreign companies were hard-pressed to find attractive investments in a global recession. Exports were expected to grow by 8% annually through 2013.

Central Bank policy supported growth by keeping the Consumer Price Index (CPI) at or around 2% annually. The country also respected a budget process that established Parliamentary-designated spending ceilings. The ceilings allowed spending up to $144.7 billion in 2010, $150.3 billion in 2011, $153.1 billion in 2012, and $154.5 billion in 2013. While the ceilings could be surpassed, they symbolized the trust between government and the people—an important plank in Sweden's social contract.

Sweden's entry into the EU in 1995 constituted a major step in modernizing the economy. As a result of EU membership, Sweden harmonized its trade laws with those of its fellow members and continued to privatize and liberalize its economy. Sweden also qualified for membership in the Economic and Monetary Union (EMU) but decided to opt out—a decision that in 2011 appeared to have been vindicated. In a referendum held in September 2003 Swedes decided not to join the euro zone by a vote of 56% to 42%.

Since 2007, government has controlled spending, generated revenues and encouraged profitability through the sale of state assets. Major sales have included V&S (Vin & Sprit AB) to French Pernod Ricard for about $8.3 billion, and the Swedish OMX stock exchange to Borse Dubai/Nasdaq for $318 million. Additionally, the government eliminated its monopoly on pharmacies, and approved the sale of Svensk Bilprovning (the Swedish Motor Vehicle Inspection Company).

In 2011 the government crafted a conservative budget aimed at reestablishing a surplus and consolidating economic recovery. The budget offered new funding to create jobs, to maintain public welfare, to promote exports and to address climate change. Lowering taxes on low and middle income earners was also proposed to stimulate economic activity.

Going into 2012 the key challenge for the economy was to maintain the core of Sweden's social-welfare system in the face of an aging population. By 2015, the number of people 65 years of age and older was projected to increase by 25% over 2005, while other age categories were expected to remain largely unchanged. This trend was not unique to Sweden, but it required continued economic development to pay for ever-greater demands on medical care and social services.

40 SOCIAL DEVELOPMENT

Sweden is the archetypal welfare state where every citizen is guaranteed a minimum subsistence income and medical care. In 2011 Sweden ranked 10th out of 187 countries worldwide on the UNDP Human Development Index (HDI). The HDI measures prospects for a long, healthy life and quality education.

Social welfare legislation was introduced in the 1930s and was greatly expanded after World War II. The system was financed partly by insurance premiums and partly by state and local taxes. Basic benefits increased periodically by cost-of-living supplements. Employers and employees contributed to the program, with government funding certain aspects of the system. All residents were covered by sickness and maternity benefits. There was also a universal system for family allowances completely funded by the government.

Old-age pensions were paid to all residents 65 years of age or older, but an earlier retirement was possible, with a reduction in pension benefits. Under the new system, there was a flexible retirement age, starting from 61, and funded by 6.95% of employee earnings and 6.4% of employer payroll. Unemployment insurance was administered by the trade unions and provided benefits according to salary to those who voluntarily enrolled. Unemployment relief, through monetary assistance or public works, was provided by the central government or by state-subsidized municipalities.

Compulsory health service was introduced in 1955. In 2011, hospital care was free for up to two years. Medical services and medicines were provided at substantially reduced rates or, in some cases, without charge. In the event of illness, employed persons and women staying at home to raise children received cash payments and further benefits according to income. Costs of confinement and maternity allowances for women were covered by health insurance. There was also a national program of dental insurance.

Workers' compensation was coordinated with the national health service scheme. Financed entirely by employers, this scheme covered work time and travel to and from work for all employees. Benefits included free medical treatment, medicines, and appliances. Annuities were paid to persons permanently disabled, and funeral benefits and pensions to dependents in case of death. Public assistance was provided for blind or infirm persons confined to their homes and to people who were in sanitariums, special hospitals, or charitable institutions.

Sweden ranked best in the world on the 2007 Gender Gap Index, which measured economic participation and opportunities, health and survival, political empowerment and educational attainment of women. The government had adopted a national objective for equality of women with men on key indicators, and laws required equal opportunities and equal pay for women. The Equal Opportunity Ombudsman, a government official, reviewed equality plans required by employers and investigated allegations of gender discrimination. Notwithstanding these efforts, women were underrepresented in higher-paying jobs, and often received less pay for equal work. Violence against women, primarily spousal abuse, persisted, despite laws prohibiting such practices. Government provided shelters and other assistance to victims. Strict laws protecting children from abuse were also in effect.

Swedes have traditionally been highly tolerant of religious differences and ethnic minorities, although right-wing and neo-Nazi activities were on the rise. The government protected and supported minority languages.

41 HEALTH

Sweden has one of best set of health indicators in the world. According to the CIA, life expectancy in Sweden was 81 years in 2011. The country spent 9.4% of its GDP on healthcare, amounting to $4,252 per person. There were 36 physicians, 116 nurses and midwives, and 24 hospital beds per 10,000 inhabitants. The fertility rate was 1.9, while the infant mortality rate was 2 per 1,000 live births. In 2008 the maternal mortality rate, according to the World Bank, was 5 per 100,000 births. It was estimated that 97% of children were vaccinated against measles. The CIA reported that the HIV/AIDS adult prevalence rate in Sweden was 0.1% in 2009.

The national health insurance system, financed by the state and employer contributions, was established in January 1955 and covers all Swedish citizens and alien residents. Total expenditure for health care insurance was 9.1% of the GDP as of 2007. Principal health care reform issues include universal and equal access to services and equitable funding of health care. For rural medical attention, doctors are supplemented by district nurses. Only about 5% of all physicians are in full-time private practice. Swedish hospitals are well known for their high standards.

Cardiovascular disease accounts for about half of all deaths in Sweden; cancer is the next leading cause of death. Many health problems are related to environment and lifestyle (including tobacco smoking, alcohol consumption, and overeating). Periodic campaigns have been conducted to reduce tuberculosis (with a nationwide X-ray survey), cancer, rheumatism, and venereal diseases.

Immunization rates for children under age one are as follows: diphtheria, pertussis, and tetanus, 99% and measles, 94%. There is a well-developed prenatal service. Children receive free dental care until the age of 20.

42 HOUSING

In 2010, there were 4.45 million dwellings nationwide. Of these, about 2.4 million (52%) were multi-family dwellings and the remainder were one- or two-family homes (48%). It was estimated that 22% of disposable household income was spent on housing and that an annual increase of about 9–13% in units would be required annually to meet rising demand.

Nearly all of Sweden's housing stock was modernized during a mass housing improvement program in the 1980s. Most houses were built by private contractors, but more than half of new housing was designed, planned, and financed by nonprofit organizations and cooperatives. NPOs and cooperatives provided dwellings for members who were designated as tenant-owners of their dwellings.

The government subsidized new construction and reconditioning, helped various groups to obtain better housing, and extended credit at interest rates lower than those obtainable in the open market. A system of rent controls, introduced in 1942 and designed to freeze rents at the existing rate, was abolished in 1975. It was replaced by a policy known as a utility-value provision, through which the rent of a flat could not be higher than that of a similar flat in the same area which was of the same general value to the occupant. Many tenant organizations negotiated rental agreements with landlords and rent increases could be reviewed by a tribunal. The National Board of Housing, Building, and Planning estimated that 250,000 new dwellings would be built from 2000–2010. About 30,000 dwellings per year would be renovated or rebuilt during the same period.

43 EDUCATION

In 2008 the World Bank estimated that 95% of age-eligible children in Sweden were enrolled in primary school. Nearly all pupils completed their primary schooling. Secondary enrollment for age-eligible children stood at 99%. Tertiary enrollment was estimated at 71%. Of those enrolled in tertiary education, there were 100 male students for every 159 female students. Overall, the CIA estimated that Sweden had a literacy rate of 99%. Public expenditure on education represented 6.6% of GDP. In 2005, private schools accounted for about 7% of primary school enrollment and some 10% of secondary enrollment.

Education was free and compulsory between ages 7 and 15. A nine-year comprehensive course was introduced in 1962. All pupils received the same course of instruction for six years; beginning in the seventh year the curriculum was differentiated, and students could choose between a classical and a vocational course. About 80% of all students then entered gymnasium (senior high school) or continuation schools. The gymnasium specialized in classical or modern languages or science; after the three-year course, students could take a final graduating examination. The continuation schools offered a two-year curriculum that was more practical and specialized than that of the gymnasium and led more quickly to the practice of a trade. Both comprehensive schools and secondary schools were administered by local authorities, while the central government provided grants-in-aid to cover the greater part of the costs.

Sweden's six universities, all largely financed by the state, are at Uppsala (founded in 1477), Lund (1666), Stockholm (1877), Göteborg (1891), and Umea and Linköping (both completed in 1963). Uppsala and Lund have four faculties each—law, theology, medicine, and philosophy (arts and sciences). Stockholm has faculties of humanities, law, mathematics, and science; Göteborg,

medicine and humanities. There are also more than two dozen specialized schools and institutions of university rank for such subjects as medicine, dentistry, pharmacology, veterinary science, music, economics, commerce, technology, agriculture, and forestry. Tuition is free, except for some special courses; most university students receive government loans to help them meet their living expenses.

Sweden has an active adult general education movement in which some three million persons participate each year. People's schools and other educational institutions give courses for all those who want to study. All the universities have extension divisions for general studies. There are 130 state-subsidized folk high schools for working adults that provide courses ranging in length from a few days to 80 weeks.

44 LIBRARIES AND MUSEUMS

The four major libraries, the Royal Library (also known as the National Library) at Stockholm (three million volumes) and the university libraries of Uppsala (5.4 million), Lunds (3.2 million), and Göteborg (2.7 million), receive free copies of all Swedish publications. There are technical and other special libraries, all of which have an interlibrary loan scheme with the university libraries, the state-aided municipal libraries, and the 24 county libraries. The largest public library is the Stockholm Public Library, which holds over 2.1 million books and over 150,000 materials of other media. The Stockholm Public Library supports 44 city branches, 60 hospital branches, 90 lending points in workplaces and correctional facilities, and bookmobile services. The Göteborg Public Library holds 1.6 million volumes. Altogether, the public library systems have a combined total of about 46.3 million volumes. The Swedish Library of Talking Books and Braille is a government program that works through local public libraries; founded in 1955, the library has over 86,500 talking book titles (in 50 languages) and over 12,000 books in Braille. The Swedish Authors' Fund administers a library loan compensation system that pays an author royalties each time a book is borrowed.

Most of the outstanding museums are in Stockholm. Especially renowned are the rich art collections of the Swedish National Art Museum and the sculptures of Carl Milles in the artist's former home at Millesgarden in Lidingö. In Stockholm are located the Swedish Museum of Natural History (founded 1739) and the National Museum of Science and Technology (founded 1924). The Aquaria Vatten Museum, opened in 1991, was a natural history museum that included a shark aquarium, salmon ladder, and living rain forest. The Nobel Museum celebrates the life and work of Alfred Nobel and many of the Nobel Prize laureates; the Nobel Museum also houses the 15,000-volume private library of Alfred Nobel. Göteborg has a number of museums including the Göteborg Art Gallery and a maritime museum reflecting the interests of that city. The finest Swedish folk museum is in Skansen, near Stockholm. Göteborg also has a public affairs museum including an exhibit of the history of the East India Tea Company of Sweden. Lund has the Museum of Cultural History and the Museum of Zoology. The Victoria Museum for Egyptian Antiquities is in Uppsala.

45 MEDIA

In 2009 the CIA reported that there were 5.1 million telephone landlines in Sweden, and an average of 123 mobile phone subscriptions per 100 people totaling some 11.4 million mobile cellular phones in use. There were five commercial radio networks, some of which had internet streaming and had as many as 30 stations. In addition, more than 900 non-commercial community and neighborhood radio stations operated in the country along with 265 AM radio stations, and 1 shortwave radio station. Five stations were broadcasted in Swedish outside of Sweden. In 2010, the country had 4.3 million Internet hosts. Internet users numbered 90 per 100 citizens. Sveriges Radio and Television operated three national and 25 regional public broadcasting channels. There were several private TV commercial stations, including satellite and cable networks. Prominent newspapers in 2010, with circulation numbers listed parenthetically, included *Sydsvenskan* (155,600), *Aftonbladet* (381,200), and *Expressen* (374,200), as well as 77 other major newspapers.

Sweden's telecommunications system is fully automated, with facilities rated as excellent. Most domestic voice traffic is carried through multiconductor and coaxial cables, while some additional telephone channels are carried by microwave radio relay systems. International service is provided by submarine coaxial cables, satellite ground stations allowing access to the Inmarsat, Eutelsat, and Intelsat networks.

The Swedish press is said to be the oldest in which censorship was legally forbidden. The first regular newspaper, *Post-och Inrikes Tidningar,* appeared in 1645 and is still published. The first daily was *Norrköpings Tidningen* (1758). News was drawn largely from the Swedish News Agency (Tidningarnas Telegrambyra—TT), an agency owned by the Swedish press. Owing partly to its press freedoms, Sweden scored the highest marks for political rights and civil liberties on Freedom House's "Freedom in the World 2011" index.

46 ORGANIZATIONS

Sweden has a rich tapestry of cultural, sports, youth, faith-based, professional, trade, business and academic associations. Almost all farmers are members of agricultural cooperatives, which buy supplies and sell products for farmers and represent their interests to state agencies. Over 300,000 farmers belong to the Federation of Swedish Farmers, which provide farmers with legal and tax advice as well as educational services on agricultural matters. There are two farm credit institutions, a dairies association, a meat marketing association, and an egg marketing association. The National Union of Swedish Farmers (formed in 1905) supplies its members with fertilizer, seeds, feeds, and other supplies and buy their crops.

The Federation of Swedish Industries (founded 1910) is active in promoting trade. Chambers of commerce operate in all the principal cities and towns. There are specialist industrial and trade associations such as those of the glass exporters and wood exporters. There are professional organizations in agriculture, archaeology, art, education, engineering, ethnology, geography, geology, law, literature, mathematics, medicine, music, science, and other fields. The Swedish Medical Association is a major physicians union.

The three most distinguished scholarly organizations are the Swedish Academy (founded 1786), the Royal Academy of Letters, History, and Antiquities (founded 1753), and the Royal Academy of Arts and Sciences (founded 1776). The Nobel Foundation administers the trust fund established by Swedish scientist and inventor Alfred Nobel (1833–96) and presents the annual Nobel Prizes. The Royal Swedish Academy of Sciences assists in awarding the annual Nobel Prizes for physics, chemistry, and economic sciences. The Swedish National Council for Cultural Affairs helps promote study in arts and culture, in part by serving as an advisory council for the national cultural budget. The Swedish P.E.N. Centre was based in Stockholm. There were several clubs and associations available for hobbyists and amateur participants in a variety of fields, such as the Gothenburg Ornithological Society.

Numerous national youth organizations include the Association of Young Catholics in Sweden, Center Party University Students Federation, Christian Democratic Youth Union, Good Templar Youth of Sweden, Liberal Student Federation, Swedish 4-H Youth, Junior Chamber, Swedish National Union of Students, Young Left of Sweden, YMCA/YWCA, and the Swedish Guide and Scout Council. Some youth councils are organized under the National Council of Swedish Youth Organizations. There are numerous sports associations promoting amateur competitions for athletes of all ages.

The Women's Front served as an umbrella organization for groups campaigning for equal rights. There are strong women's groups within political parties. International organizations with national chapters include Greenpeace, Save the Children, Amnesty International, and the Red Cross.

47 TOURISM, TRAVEL, AND RECREATION

Tourism, a major industry in Sweden, was stagnant in the 1990s due to a value-added tax on hotels, restaurants, and travel services. Since 2000, however, the industry has steadily grown. The *Tourism Factbook*, published by the UN World Tourism Organization, reported 4.68 million incoming tourists to Sweden in 2009, who spent a total of $12.1 billion. Of those incoming tourists, 4 million were from Europe. There were 221,767 hotel beds available in Sweden at that time, with an occupancy rate of 35%. The estimated daily cost to visit Stockholm, the capital, was $459.

Principal tourist sites include the Royal Palace in Stockholm, the "garden city" of Göteborg, the resort island of Öland off the Baltic coast, and the lake and mountain country in the north. Cultural centers in Stockholm include the Royal Opera, Royal Dramatic Theater, and Berwald Concert Hall. Popular recreational activities include football (soccer), polo, skiing, ice skating, swimming, mountain climbing, and gymnastics.

All visitors had to have a valid passport as well as sufficient funds for their stay and an onward/return ticket. Citizens of 133 countries including the United Kingdom, Russia, and China were required to carry an entry visa. Citizens of Canada, the United States, Western European countries, and some other nations could enter Sweden with a valid passport and did not require a visa.

48 FAMOUS PERSONS

Esaias Tegnér (1782–1846), considered the national poet of Sweden, and Erik Gustaf Geijer (1783–1847), historian and poet, are the best-known Swedish writers of the early 19th century. A new impulse was given to literature by August Strindberg (1849–1912), a major literary figure whose powerful, socially oriented plays and stories reflected the advanced thought of the age. Selma Lagerlöf (1858–1940), who won the Nobel Prize for literature in 1909, showed in her novels a depth of narrative genius reminiscent of the Norse sagas. Other Swedish winners of the Nobel Prize for literature were the novelist and poet Karl Gustav Verner von Heidenstam (1859–1940), in 1916; the novelist and short-story writer Pär Lagerkvist (1891–1974), in 1951; and the novelists Eyvind Johnson (1900–1976) and Harry Edmund Martinson (1904–78), who shared the 1974 award. A noted contemporary novelist is Vilhelm Moberg (1889–1974).

The painter, etcher, and sculptor Anders Leonhard Zorn (1860–1920) and the sculptor Carl Milles (1875–1955) are the greatest figures in Swedish art. The outstanding Swedish musician of the 19th century was Franz Adolf Berwald (1796–1868), composer of symphonies, operas, and chamber music. August Johan Söderman (1832–76) is considered the leading Swedish operatic composer. Two famous sopranos were Jenny Lind (1820–87), the "Swedish nightingale," and Christine (Kristina) Nilsson (1843–1921). Outstanding 20th-century musicians are the composers Wilhelm Stenhammar (1871–1927), Hugo Alfvén (1872–1960), Ture Rangström (1884–1947), Kurt Atterberg (1887–1974), Hilding Constantin Rosenberg (1892–1985), and the singers Jussi Björling (1910–60) and Birgit Nilsson (1918–2006).

Famous 18th-century scientists were the astronomer and physicist Anders Celsius (1705–44), who devised the temperature scale named after him; the chemist Karl Wilhelm Scheele (1742–86); and the botanist Carolus Linnaeus (Carl von Linné, 1707–78), who established the classification scheme of plants and animals that is named after him. Emanuel Swedenborg (1688–1772) was a scientist, philosopher, and religious writer whose followers founded a religious sect in his name.

Svante August Arrhenius (1859–1927), a great pioneer in physical chemistry, is renowned for his theory of electrolytic dissociation and his speculations in the field of cosmic physics; in 1903, he was awarded the Nobel Prize for chemistry. Other Swedish Nobel Prize winners in science or medicine are Gustaf Dalén (1869–1957), for his work in automatic beacons for coast lighting (1912); Allvar Gullstrand (1862–1930), for work on dioptics of the eye (1911); Karl Manne Georg Siegbahn (1886–1978), for work on X-ray spectroscopy (1924); The (Theodor) Svedberg (1884–1971), for work in colloidal chemistry (1926); Hans Karl August Simon von Euler-Chelpin (b. Augsburg, 1873–1964), for work in enzyme chemistry (1929); George Karl de Hevesy (b. Budapest, 1885–1966), for work on isotopes (1943); Arne Wilhelm Kaurin Tiselius (1902–71), for investigations in electrophoresis (1948); Axel Hugo Theodor Theorell (1903–82), for work on enzymes (1955); Ragnar Arthur Granit (Finland, 1900–91), for "discoveries in primary physiological and chemical visual processes in the eye" (1967); Hannes Olof Gösta Alfvén (1908–95), for work in magnetohydrodynamics (1970); and Ulf von Euler-Chelpin (1905–83), for work on the treatment of nervous and mental disorders (1970). In addition, Kai M. Siegbahn (1918–2007) shared the 1981 Nobel Prize in physics for developing spectroscopy; and Sune Karl Bergström (1916–2004) and Bengt Ingemar Samuelsson (b. 1934) shared the 1982 prize in medicine for their research on prostaglandins. Bergström also served as chairman of the Nobel Foundation.

Three distinguished political economists are Karl Gunnar Myrdal (1898–1987), who was awarded the 1974 Nobel Prize in economic science for work in the theory of money and economic fluctuations and whose 1944 book An American Dilemma contributed to the overthrowing of legally sanctioned racial segregation in the United States; Bertil Gotthard Ohlin (1899–1979), who shared the 1977 prize for his contribution to international trade theory; and Dag Hammarskjöld (1905–61), who was secretary-general of the UN from 1953 until his death and was posthumously awarded the 1961 Nobel Prize for peace. Other Swedish winners of the Nobel Peace Prize were Klas Pontus Arnoldson (1844–1916), in 1908; Karl Hjalmar Branting (1860–1925), in 1921; Nathan Söderblom (Lars Olof Jonathan, 1866–1931), in 1930; and Alva Reimer Myrdal (1902–86), the wife of Gunnar Myrdal, in 1982. Swedish inventors who have done much to promote manufacturing and technical advances include the Swedish-American John Ericsson (1803–89), who pioneered the screw propeller and designed the first Western armored-turret warship, the Monitor; Alfred Nobel (1833–96), inventor of dynamite and progenitor of the Nobel Prizes; Lars Magnus Ericsson (1846–1926), who contributed much to the development of telephones; and Gustaf de Laval (1845–1913), who developed steam turbines and invented a centrifugal cream separator.

One of the most noted film directors of our times is Ingmar Bergman (1918–2007); other noted directors were Victor Seastrom (Sjöström, 1879–1960) and Mauritz (Moshe) Stiller (b.Finland, 1883–1928). Famous screen personalities have included Greta Garbo (Greta Louisa Gustafsson, 1905–90) and Ingrid Bergman (1917–82). More recent stars of Swedish theater and films include Erland Josephson (b. 1923), Max Von Sydow (b. 1929), Ingrid Thulin (1929–2004), Harriet Andersson (b. 1932), and Bibi Andersson (b. 1935). Sweden's sports stars include five-time Wimbledon tennis champion Björn Borg (b. 1956); Alpine skiing champion Ingemar Stenmark (b. 1956); and golfer Annika Sörenstam (b. 1970).

⁴⁹DEPENDENCIES

Sweden has no territories or colonies.

⁵⁰BIBLIOGRAPHY

Annesley, Claire, ed. A Political and Economic Dictionary of Western Europe. Philadelphia: Routledge/Taylor and Francis, 2005.

International Smoking Statistics: A Collection of Historical Data from 30 Economically Developed Countries. New York: Oxford University Press, 2002.

Nordstrom, Byron J. Culture and Customs of Sweden. Santa Barbara, CA: Greenwood, 2010.

Nordstrom, Byron J. The History of Sweden. Westport, CT: Greenwood Press, 2002.

Opello, Walter C. European Politics. Boulder, CO: Lynne Rienner Publishers, 2009.

Political Chronology of Europe. London: Europa, 2001.

Scobbie, Irene. *Historical Dictionary of Sweden.* 2nd ed. Lanham, MD.: Scarecrow, 1995.

Sejersted, Francis. *The Age of Social Democracy: Norway and Sweden in the Twentieth Century.* 2005. Translated by Richard Daly, ed. by Madeleine B. Adams. Princeton: Princeton University Press, 2011.

Sweden Investment and Business Guide: Strategic and Practical Information. Washington, DC: International Business Publications USA, 2012.

Wessels, Wolfgang, Andreas Maurer, and Jürgan Mittag, eds. *Fifteen into One?: the European Union and Its Member States.* New York: Palgrave, 2003.

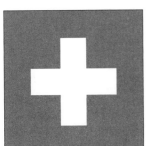

SWITZERLAND

Swiss Confederation

[French] *Suisse; (Confédération Suisse);* [German] *Schweiz; (Schweizerische Eidgenossenschaft);* [Italian] *Svizzera; (Confederazione Svizzera);* [Romansch] *Svizra (Confederaziun Helvetica)*

CAPITAL: Bern

FLAG: The national flag consists of an equilateral white cross on a red background, each arm of the cross being one-sixth longer than its width.

ANTHEM: *Schweizerpsalm* (German), *Cantique Suisse* (French), *Salmo svizzero* (Italian), *Psalm svizzer* (Romansch), *Swiss Psalm* (English).

MONETARY UNIT: The Swiss franc (CHF) of 100 centimes, or rappen, is the national currency. There are coins of 1, 5, 10, 20, and 50 centimes and 1, 2, and 5 francs, and notes of 10, 20, 50, 100, 500, and 1,000 francs. CHF1 = US$1.1337 (or US$1 = CHF8821) as of November 2011.

WEIGHTS AND MEASURES: The metric system is the legal standard.

HOLIDAYS: New Year, 1–2 January; Labor Day, 1 May; Christmas, 25–26 December. Movable religious holidays include Good Friday, Easter Monday, Ascension, and Whitmonday.

TIME: 1 p.m. = noon GMT.

¹LOCATION, SIZE, AND EXTENT

A landlocked country in central Europe, Switzerland has an area of 41,290 sq km (15,942 sq mi), extending 348 km (216 mi) E–W and 220 km (137 mi) N–S. Comparatively, the area occupied by Switzerland is slightly less than twice the size of New Jersey. Bounded on the N by Germany, on the E by Liechtenstein and Austria, on the SE and S by Italy, and on the W and NW by France, Switzerland has a total boundary length of 1,852 km (1,151 mi).

Switzerland's capital city, Bern, is located in the western part of the country.

²TOPOGRAPHY

Switzerland is divided into three natural topographical regions: (1) the Jura Mountains in the northwest, rising between Switzerland and eastern France; (2) the Alps in the south, covering three-fifths of the country's total area; and (3) the central Swiss plateau, or Mittelland, consisting of fertile plains and rolling hills that run between the Jura and the Alps. The Mittelland, with a mean altitude of 580 m (1,900 ft), covers about 30% of Switzerland and is the heartland of Swiss farming and industry; Zürich, Bern, Lausanne, and Geneva (Genève) are on the plateau. The central portion of the Alps, around the St. Gotthard Pass, is a major watershed and the source of the Rhine, which drains into the North Sea; of the Aare, a tributary of the Rhine; of the Rhône, which flows into the Mediterranean; and of the Ticino, a tributary of the Po, and of the Inn, a tributary of the Danube, which flow into the Adriatic and the Black seas, respectively.

The highest point in Switzerland is the Dufourspitze of Monte Rosa at 4,634 m (15,203 ft); the lowest is the shore of Lake Maggiore at less than 195 m (640 ft). The second highest and most cel-ebrated of the Swiss Alps is the Matterhorn (4,478 m/14,692 ft), long a challenge to mountaineers and first scaled in 1865.

Switzerland has 1,484 lakes, more than 12,900 smaller bodies of water, and many waterfalls. Lake Geneva (Léman), with an area of 581 sq km (224 sq mi), is considered the largest Swiss lake, though its southern shore is in France. Lake Neuchâtel, the largest lake totally within Switzerland, has an area of 218 sq km (84 sq mi). Switzerland also contains more than 1,000 glaciers, many the relics of Pleistocene glaciation. The largest area of permanent ice is in the Valais.

³CLIMATE

The climate of Switzerland north of the Alps is temperate but varies with altitude, wind exposure, and other factors; the average annual temperature is 9°C (48°F). The average rainfall varies from 53 cm (21 in) in the Rhône Valley to 170 cm (67 in) in Lugano. Generally, the areas to the west and north of the Alps have a cool, rainy climate, with winter averages near or below freezing and summer temperatures seldom above 21°C (70°F). South of the Alps, the canton of Ticino has a warm, moist, Mediterranean climate, and frost is almost unknown. The climate of the Alps and of the Jura uplands is mostly raw, rainy, or snowy, with frost occurring above 1,830 m (6,000 ft).

⁴FLORA AND FAUNA

Variation in climate and altitude produces a varied flora and fauna. The World Resources Institute estimates that there are 3,030 plant species in Switzerland. In the lowest zone (below 550 m/1,800 ft), chestnut, walnut, cypress, and palm trees grow, as well as figs, oranges, and almonds; up to 1,200 m (3,940 ft), forests of beech, maple, and oak; around 1,680 m (5,500 ft), fir and pine; around 2,130 m (7,000 ft), rhododendron, larches, dwarf and cembra pine, and whortleberries; and above the snow line, more than 100 species of flowering plants, including the edelweiss.

Wild animals include the chamois, boar, deer, otter, and fox. There are large birds of prey, as well as snipe, heath cock, and cuckoo. Lakes and rivers teem with fish. In all, Switzerland is home to 93 mammal, 382 bird, 17 reptile, and 21 amphibian species. The calculation reflects the total number of distinct species residing in the country, not the number of endemic species.

⁵ENVIRONMENT

The World Resources Institute reported that Switzerland had designated 1.18 million hectares (2.92 million acres) of land for protection as of 2006. Water resources total 53.3 cu km (12.79 cu mi) while water usage is 2.52 cu km (0.605 cu mi) per year. Domestic water usage accounts for 24% of total usage, industrial for 74%, and agricultural for 2%. Per capita water usage totals 348 cu m (12,290 cu ft) per year.

The Swiss have long been aware of the need to protect their natural resources. Switzerland's federal forestry law of 1876 is among the world's earliest pieces of environmental legislation. Since 1953, provisions for environmental protection have been incorporated in the federal constitution. A measure creating a federal role in town and rural planning by allowing the central government to set the ground rules for the cantonal master plans took effect in January 1980.

Air pollution is a major environmental concern in Switzerland; automobiles and other transportation vehicles are the main contributors. The UN reported in 2008 that carbon dioxide emissions in Switzerland totaled 37,963 kilotons. Strict standards for exhaust emissions were imposed on new passenger cars manufactured after October 1987. Additional regulations were adopted by the Federal Council in 2006. Water pollution is also a problem due to the presence of phosphates, fertilizers, and pesticides in the water supply. Annually, municipal solid waste disposal in Switzerland has been on the increase. By 2009, they had reached 700 kg per person, according to a UN report.

Chemical contaminants and erosion damage the nation's soil and limit productivity. In 1986, the Swiss Federal Office of Forestry issued a report stating that 36% of the country's forests had been killed or damaged by acid rain and other types of air pollution. Between 1990 and 2010, Switzerland continued to lose 0.39% of their forest cover per year.

Important environmental groups include Pro Natura/Friends of the Earth Switzerland, formerly the Swiss League for the Protection of Nature, founded in 1909; the Swiss Foundation for Landscape Conservation, founded in 1970; and the Swiss Society for the Protection of the Environment, founded in 1971. The principal federal agency is the Federal Office for the Environment (FOEN).

According to a 2011 report issued by the International Union for Conservation of Nature and Natural Resources (IUCN), threatened species included 2 types of mammals, 1 species of bird, 1 species of amphibian, 9 species of fish, 28 species of invertebrate, and 5 species of plants. The northern bald ibis and the Italian spadefoot toad are extinct; the false ringlet butterfly, Italian agile frog, and marsh snail are threatened. The bear and wolf were exterminated by the end of the 19th century, but the lynx, once extinct in Switzerland, has been reestablished. There has been a complete loss of six species of animals that are native to its deep lakes.

⁶POPULATION

The US Central Intelligence Agency (CIA) estimates the population of Switzerland in 2011 to be approximately 7,639,961, which placed it 95th in population among the 196 nations of the world. In 2011, approximately 17% of the population was over 65 years of age, with another 15.2% under 15 years of age. The median age in Switzerland was 41.7 years. There were 0.97 males for every female in the country. The population's annual rate of change was 0.21%. The projected population for the year 2025 was 8,300,000. Population density in Switzerland was calculated at 185 people per sq km (479 people per sq mi).

The UN estimated that 74% of the population lived in urban areas in 2009, and that urban populations had an annual rate of change of 0.5%. The largest urban areas, along with their respective populations, included Zürich, 359,000; and Bern, 123,000.

⁷MIGRATION

Foreign residents in Switzerland comprised 22.4% of the total population in 2010. The largest group of foreigners were of Italian nationality; Germany, Portugal, and Serbia were the next-leading countries of origin. In April 1987, Swiss voters approved a government plan to tighten rules on immigration and political asylum. In comparison, Estimates of Switzerland's net migration rate, carried out by the CIA in 2011, amounted to 1.29 migrants per 1,000 citizens. The total number of emigrants living abroad was 407,800, and the total number of immigrants living in Switzerland was 1.76 million.

From the beginning of the civil war in Bosnia, Switzerland took in some 27,000 Bosnian refugees by 1997, granting most only temporary protection. In 1997, 8,000 singles and couples without children returned to Bosnia; another 2,800 returned voluntarily. Nonetheless, as a result of the drastic increase in the number of asylum seekers, Switzerland suspended its resettlement policy in mid-1998.

As a result of the Kosovo conflict, Switzerland again faced a major increase in asylum seekers in 1999. The Swiss government offered temporary protection to about 65,000 Kosovars living in the country. Main countries of origin for refugees included Bosnia and Herzegovina, Serbia and Montenegro, and Turkey. Asylum applications came from 19 countries of origin, the largest numbers from Bulgaria and Belarus.

In 2010 Swiss voters passed a referendum that calls for the deportation of foreign citizens who are convicted of crimes ranging from benefit fraud to murder. The plan was spearheaded by the right-wing Swiss People's Party (SVP), which was also responsible for the development of a 2009 referendum that banned the construction of Islamic minarets in the country. The SVP reported that more than 60% of the inmates in Swiss prisons do not hold Swiss citizenship and pushed for the measure, which requires convicts to serve their sentences in Switzerland and then be deported without appeal. Many Swiss government officials asked voters to adopt a more lenient alternative measure that would call for deportation on certain crimes, with each case assessed individually. Opponents of the measure were particularly concerned that mandatory deportation could bring Switzerland in violation of international law by sending people back to countries that al-

LOCATION: 5°57′24″ to 10°29′36″ E; 45°49′8″ to 47°48′35″ N. BOUNDARY LENGTHS: Germany, 334 kilometers (208 miles); Liechtenstein, 41 kilometers (25 miles); Austria, 164 kilometers (103 miles); Italy, 740 kilometers (460 miles); France, 573 kilometers (355 miles).

low torture or execution. The measure in favor of deportation was passed by nearly 53% of the vote.

Throughout 2010 and 2011, the SVP lost votes in parliament, signaling waning support for their immigration policies. In October 2011, the party won only 25.3% of the parliamentary vote. This was the first time in two decades that the SVP did not boost its popularity in the federal election. It is also important to note that the SVP is against EU membership and foreign military involvement.

8 ETHNIC GROUPS

The four ethnolinguistic groups (Germanic, French, Italian, and Rhaeto-Romansch) that make up the native Swiss population have retained their specific characteristics. Originally, the country was inhabited by Celtic tribes in the west and south and by Rhaetians

in the east. With the collapse of Roman rule, Germanic tribes poured in, among them the Alemanni and Burgundians. The Alemanni ultimately became the dominant group, and the present Alemannic vernacular (Schwyzertütsch, or Schweizerdeutsch) is spoken by nearly two-thirds of the total population as their principal language. About 65% of the population is German, 18% is French, 10% is Italian, 1% is Romansch, and 6% are of various other groups. There are between 30,000 and 35,000 Jenisch (Swiss gypsies) in the nation.

9 LANGUAGES

Switzerland is a multilingual state with four national languages—German, French, Italian, and Rhaeto-Romansch. About 63.7% of the resident population speaks German as their principal language, predominantly in northern, central, and western Switzerland; 20.4% speak French, mainly in the west and southwest; 6.5% Italian, primarily in the southern region closest to Italy; and 0.5% Rhaeto-Romansch, used widely only in the southeastern canton of Graubünden (Grisons). The remaining 8.9% speak various other languages. There are numerous local dialects.

10 RELIGIONS

According to a 2010 report, more than 75% of the population are nominal Christian. Roman Catholics account for about 41.8% of the population whereas Protestant groups account for about 35.3%. Muslims account for 4.3% of the population. Most Muslims are Sunni, though Shi'as and Alawites are also present. Members of the Jewish community are primarily located in Zürich, Geneva, Basel, and Bern. About 11.1% of the population claimed no religious affiliation. There is no official state church, and religious freedom is guaranteed. However, all but two of the cantons (Geneva and Neuchâtel) financially support at least one of three traditional denominations—Roman Catholic, Old Catholic, or Protestant—with money collected through taxes. Some cantons allow church taxes to be pledged to Jewish communities. The payment of church tax is voluntary in many cantons, but in some cases, those who do not wish to pay the tax must formally give up their church membership. As a result, since the 1970s there has been a trend of individuals formally resigning their church membership in order to avoid church taxation. Religious organizations must register with the government to obtain tax benefits.

Switzerland has seen an increase in ant-Muslim sentiment at social and political levels. In November 2009, Swiss voters approved a constitutional referendum banning the construction of minarets, the towering spires that often adjoin mosques, Islamic houses of worship. The ban, which passed with a clear majority of 57.5%, caused great concern in various religious communities and was seen by some as perhaps a sign of rising intolerance or Islamophobia in Switzerland. Beginning in 2010, local and national debates occurred on whether or not the government should ban the wearing of burqas, the loose fitting, full body-covering garment worn by some Muslim women. There have been some reports of harassment against women wearing the hijab, or headscarf, as well. As of 2011, the ban had yet to be instituted and was often protested. Jews have also reportedly been the targets of social discrimination and harassment. Good Friday, Easter, Easter Monday, Ascension, Whit Sunday, Whit Monday, Christmas Day, and St. Stephen's Day are observed as national holidays.

11 TRANSPORTATION

Because of its geographical position, Switzerland is an international railway center, with traffic moving from France, Germany, Austria, and northern Europe through the Simplon, Lötschberg, and St. Gotthard tunnels to Italy and southern Europe. The CIA reports that Switzerland has a total of 71,454 km (44,399 mi) of roads as of 2010, of which 71,454 km (44,399 mi) are paved. There are 567 vehicles per 1,000 people in the country. Railroads extend for 3,544 km (2,202 mi). There are total 65 airports (43 paved runways and one heliport), which transported 14.7 million passengers in 2009 according to the World Bank. Switzerland has approximately 1,299 km (807 mi) of navigable waterways. Swissair, partially owned by the federal and local governments, is the flag line of Switzerland. It has flights from the principal international

airports at Zürich, Geneva (Cointrin), and Basel to major European cities, North and South America, the Middle East, Asia, and West Africa.

Inland waterway (65 km/40 mi) traffic is an important component of Swiss transportation. Basel, the only river port, has direct connections to Strasbourg, the German Rhineland, the Ruhr, Rotterdam, and Antwerp. The Rhine-Rhône canal provides an alternative link between Basel and Strasbourg. There are 12 navigable lakes. During World War II, the Swiss organized a merchant marine to carry Swiss imports and exports on the high seas. In 2008, it consisted of 35 ships of 1,000 gross registered tons (GRT) or more. Switzerland's merchant fleet is larger than that of any other landlocked nation.

The longest road tunnel in the world, the 17-km (10.6-mi) St. Gotthard, in the Ticino, opened in September 1980. In October 2010, Swiss engineers completed the final stage of drilling for this tunnel. The 57-kilometer (35-mile) Gotthard rail tunnel was constructed for high-speed rail trains to go under the Swiss Alps, resulting in significantly quicker travel times between Zürich and Milan. The tunnel took 14 years to drill and involved the work of 2,500 people. Eight people were killed during the construction period. The $10.3 billion rail project is not expected to be operational until the end of 2016. Once fully operational, up to 300 trains can pass through the tunnel each day.

Solar Impulse, a design team based in Switzerland, reached a milestone in solar aviation in 2010, when one of its solar-powered airplanes flew for twenty-six hours with a man on board. Analysts hailed the achievement as the first time a manned solar-powered aircraft flew through the night and indicated that it showed the possibility of solar flight in perpetuity. The plane was retrofitted with some 12,000 solar cells, which extended across its 207-feet (63-meter) wingspan. Solar Impulse hoped to have one of its solar planes circumnavigate the globe by 2013, and is a wide proponent of programs aimed at promoting global sustainability.

12 HISTORY

The Helvetii, a Celtic tribe conquered by Julius Caesar in 58 BC, were the first inhabitants of Switzerland (Helvetia) known by name. A Roman province for 200 years, Switzerland was a prosperous land with large cities (Avenches was the capital) and a flourishing trade. In AD 250, however, Switzerland was occupied by the Alemanni, a Germanic tribe, and in 433 by the Burgundians. The Franks, who defeated the Alemanni in 496 and the Burgundians in about 534, incorporated the country into the Frankish Empire. Under Frankish rule, new cities were founded; others, such as Zürich and Lausanne, were rebuilt; and Christianity was introduced.

In 1032, some 200 years after the death of Charlemagne, king of the Franks, and the defeat of his weak successors, Switzerland became part of the Holy Roman Empire. In the 13th century, it was placed under the House of Habsburg. Harsh domination resulted in the rebellion of several cities and the formation on 1 August 1291 of the "eternal alliance" between the three forest cantons of Schwyz, Uri, and Unterwalden, the first step toward the Swiss Confederation. The Habsburgs invaded the three provinces, but with their defeat at Morgarten Pass on 15 November 1315, the Swiss secured their independence. By 1353, five other cantons, Luzern (1332), Zürich (1351), Glarus and Zug (1352), and Bern

(1353), had joined the confederacy. All these allies were called Swiss (Schwyzer), after the largest canton. Four victories over Austria (1386, 1388, 1476, and 1499) confirmed the confederation. The Swiss also defeated Charles of Burgundy, whose ambitions threatened their independence until his death in 1477. Complete independence was secured by the Treaty of Basel (1499) with the Holy Roman Empire. Switzerland thereafter remained unmolested by foreign troops until the French Revolution of 1789. Such legendary or real heroes as William Tell, Arnold von Winkelried, and Nikolaus von der Flüe symbolized Swiss bravery and love of freedom. The Helvetian Confederation (Eidgenossenschaft) continued to grow with the inclusion of Aargau (1415), Thurgau (1460), Fribourg and Solothurn (1481), Basel and Schaffhausen (1501), and Appenzell (1513). As of 1513, there were 13 cantons and several affiliated cities and regions. Swiss sovereignty reached south of the crest of the Alps into the Ticino. The Swiss also controlled many of the vital mountain passes linking southern and northern Europe.

The power of the Confederation was, however, undermined by conflicts stemming from the Reformation, led by Ulrich Zwingli in Zürich and John Calvin in Geneva. Seven cantons resisted the Reformation, and a prolonged conflict resulted. In its first round, Zwingli was killed in action (1531). The Catholic cantons later allied with Savoy and Spain. The struggle with the Protestant cantons centered during the Thirty Years' War (1618–48) on control of the Valtelline pass. The Treaty of Westphalia ending that war granted the Swiss Confederation formal recognition of independence by all European powers.

In the following centuries, the Catholic-Protestant conflict continued with varying success for each side. Apart from this struggle, a number of abortive uprisings against oligarchic control occurred in such places as Geneva and the canton of Vaud. The oligarchs were still in power in most cantons when the French Revolution broke out. With the progress of the revolution, radical groups gained the upper hand in several cities. In 1798, the Helvetic Republic was proclaimed, under French tutelage, and during the Napoleonic imperial era Switzerland was governed as an appendage of France. Boundaries were partly redrawn, and six new cantons were added to the original 13.

In 1815, the Congress of Vienna reconstituted the independent Swiss Confederation with three additional cantons (for a total of 22) and recognized its perpetual neutrality. Switzerland, however, did not remain untouched by the great conflict between liberalism and conservatism that affected all of Europe in the first half of the 19th century. Many revolutionaries found temporary refuge in Switzerland and influenced some of its citizens. Under their goading, several cantons introduced more progressive governments and liberalized their old constitutions.

In 1848, a new federal constitution, quite similar to that of the US Constitution, was promulgated. Meanwhile, the struggle between Protestants and Catholics had culminated in the Secession (Sonderbund) War of 1847, in which the Protestant cantons quickly overcame the secessionist movement of the seven Catholic cantons. As a result of the war, federal authority was greatly strengthened.

In 1874, the constitution was again revised to enlarge federal authority, especially in fiscal and military affairs. Since the last quarter of the 19th century, Switzerland has been concerned primarily with domestic matters, such as social legislation, communications, and industrialization. In foreign affairs, it remained rigidly neutral through both world wars, resolutely determined to protect its independence with its highly reputed militia. In 1978, Switzerland's 23rd sovereign canton, Jura, was established by nationwide vote. In 1991, Switzerland celebrated the 700th anniversary of Confederation.

Despite its neutrality, Switzerland has cooperated wholeheartedly in various international organizations, offering home and hospitality to such diverse bodies as the League of Nations, the Red Cross, and the University Postal Union (UPU). Switzerland has long resisted joining the UN, however, partly on the grounds that imposition of sanctions, as entailed in various UN resolutions, is contrary to a policy of strict neutrality. In a March 1986 referendum, a proposal for UN membership approved by the Federal Assembly was rejected by Swiss voters. Switzerland is a member of most specialized UN agencies and is a party to the Statute of the International Court of Justice. Swiss attitudes toward UN membership changed at the beginning of the 21st century, as citizens decreasingly saw participation in the UN as jeopardizing the country's neutrality. In a referendum held on 3 March 2002, nearly 55% of Swiss voters approved of joining the UN, but approval by the country's 23 cantons received a narrower 12 to 11 vote. On 10 September 2002 Switzerland became a full member of the UN.

Foreign governments have targeted Switzerland's tight bank secrecy laws as providing a haven for tax evasion and money laundering. The EU maintains that if Switzerland were to join the body, such laws would have to be reformed. Switzerland suffered from the global economic downturn that began in 2001, as its workforce is focused heavily in the banking sector. The Swiss have also expressed ambivalence toward Europe. In December 1992, the Swiss rejected participation in the two major European organizations—the European Economic Area (EEA) of the European Union (EU). Fearing adverse effects from nonparticipation, the Swiss government has taken steps to bring the country's laws and economy into harmony with the EEA. Because of the fact that all legislation can be subjected to referenda, however, the government is finding it difficult to alter certain protectionist policies and to lower certain barriers. Officially, the government is committed to eventually joining the EU, although in order to do so it will have to convince a majority of voters it is the correct path.

In a blow to Euro skeptics, in June 2005, voters, in a referendum endorsed by a 55% majority, planned to join the other European Union members then in the Schengen passport-free travel zone. Voters also approved joining the EU's Dublin agreement on handling asylum seekers and participating in further coordination of policing and crime-fighting. In September 2005, a bilateral accord on the free movement of labor to the 10 newest EU member states was approved in a referendum.

In October 2003, the right-wing Swiss People's Party (SVP) became the largest force in the National Council after winning 26.6% of the vote in general elections. That December, parliament decided to grant the SVP the second post in the seven-seat government at the expense of the Christian Democrats, altering the "magic formula" that had brought stability to Swiss politics since 1959. On 1 January 2004, Christoph Blocher of the Swiss People's Party was placed in the Federal Council as the second SVP representative.

Blocher turned out to be an extremely controversial choice, primarily for his strong stand against immigration and foreigners. The SVP had made several anti-immigrant, anti-foreigner stands after the 2003 elections. For instance, the SVP gained the criticism of the United Nations in 2007 by distributing an election campaign poster that called for immigrants charged with crimes to be deported along with their families. The poster featured three white sheep on a background of the Swiss flag kicking a black sheep out of its group. Another poster featured a veiled Muslim woman with the words "Where are we living, Baden or Baghdad?" Blocher himself was criticized for publicly calling two Albanian asylum-seekers criminals, even though they had not been convicted of a crime. In the elections of 2007, the SVP once again gained a majority of seats in parliament; however, parliament refused to re-elect Blocher to his seat on the council. The more moderate SVP member, Eveline Widmer-Schlumpf, was elected in his place.

Despite a dearth of natural resources, the Swiss economy is among the world's most advanced and prosperous. Per capita income is virtually the highest in the world, as are wages. Trade has been the key to prosperity in Switzerland. Switzerland was ranked as the second most competitive economy in the World Economic Forum's 2007 Global Competitiveness Report, reflecting the country's sound institutional environment, excellent infrastructure, efficient markets, competent macroeconomic management, world-class educational attainment, and high levels of technological innovation, which boost Switzerland's competitiveness in the global economy.

Switzerland's legendary banking system came under fire in 2009, as the issue of banking secrecy and tax havens became major points of contention in world politics. In February 2009, the US Justice Department filed a lawsuit against UBS AG, a major Swiss bank, ordering it to release the identities of 52,000 US clients suspected of tax evasion. By order of the Swiss Financial Markets Supervisory Authority (FINMA), UBS also entered into a deferred prosecution agreement with the Justice Department, agreeing to disclose the names of many of their US customers and pay $780 million in fines, penalties, interest, and restitution.

13 GOVERNMENT

The Swiss Confederation is a federal union and was governed, until 2000, under the constitution of 1874, which vested supreme authority in the legislative body, or Federal Assembly, and executive power in the Federal Council. On 1 January 2000, a new federal constitution entered into force, replacing the 1874 constitution. The new constitution formally separates and codifies four pillars of Swiss constitutional law: democracy; the rule of law; social welfare; and federalism. Fundamental rights, such as freedom of speech and assembly, which had not been explicitly mentioned in the 1874 constitution, now received their formal expression.

The Federal Assembly consists of two chambers. The National Council (*Nationalrat*) of 200 members is elected by direct ballot for four-year terms by citizens 18 years of age or older. The Council of States (*Ständerat*) consists of 46 members, two appointed by each of the 20 cantons and one from each of the six half-cantons, and is paid by the cantons; deputies are elected according to the laws of the cantons. Legislation must be approved by both houses.

The Federal Council of seven members is elected for four-year terms by joint session of the Federal Assembly. The president and

vice president of the Federal Council and of the Confederation are elected by the assembly for one-year terms and cannot be reelected to the same office until after the expiration of another year. The seven members of the Federal Council, which has no veto power, are the respective heads of the main departments of the federal government. In September 2010, the election of Simonetta Sommaruga to a newly opened spot in the Federal Council marked the first time in history that women outnumbered men in the council (four to three).

The cantons are sovereign in all matters not delegated to the federal government by the constitution and may force federal law to a plebiscite by the right of referendum. In addition, by popular initiative, 50,000 citizens may demand a direct popular vote on any legislation or regulation proposed by the federal government, and 100,000 citizens may demand a referendum on a constitutional revision. Any proposed amendments to the constitution must be submitted for public approval.

In 1971, Swiss women were granted the right to vote in federal elections. In November 1990, the Federal Court ruled in favor of female suffrage in the half-canton of Appenzell-Inner Rhoden, the last area with male-only suffrage.

14 POLITICAL PARTIES

Swiss politics are generally stable and the strengths of the chief political parties varied little over the past several decades. The conduct of national-level politics is generally calm and is marked by mutual esteem and cooperation. On the cantonal and municipal levels, however, the give-and-take of political life is more lively and unrestrained, as well as more partisan.

Until 2003, the ruling Federal Council was made up of what the Swiss referred to as the "magic formula" coalition, an informal, but strictly adhered to, arrangement whereby the four largest political parties filled the seven positions on the Federal Council with two seats for the Christian Democrats, two for the Social Democrats, two for the Free Democrats, and one for the Swiss People's Party. As of 1 January 2004, the magic formula switched to allow one seat for the Christian Democrats and two seats for the other three parties.

The four strongest parties are the Swiss People's Party (SVP), a right-wing, xenophobic and anti-EU party; the Social Democratic Party (SPS), similar to the Scandinavian Social Democrats, which advocates wider state participation in industry and strong social legislation; FDP.The Liberals—formed in 2009 when the radical Free Democratic Party merged with the smaller Liberal Party—a progressive middle-class party, which favors increased social welfare, strengthening of national defense, and a democratic federally structured government; and the Christian Democrat People's Party (CVP), a clerical federalist party, which opposes centralization of power. The SVP was formed in 1971 by a union of the Farmers', Traders', and Citizens' Party, which favored agrarian reform, protective tariffs, and a stronger national defense, and the Democratic Party, a leftist middle-class group.

Other parties include the Green Party, the Green Liberal Party, the Conservative Democratic Party, the Christian Social Party, and the Evangelical People's Party, which is Protestant, federalist, and conservative.

National elections typically produce only marginal changes in party representation. In recent years, Switzerland has seen a gradual shift in the party landscape. Following the October 1999 elections, the Social Democratic Party took 51 seats in the National Council; the Swiss People's Party took 44; the Radical Free Democratic Party, 43; and the Christian Democrats, 35. In the Council of States after the 1999 elections, the Radical Democratic Party held 18 seats; the Christian Democrats held 15; the Swiss People's Party had 7; and the Social Democrats held 6.

Following the 2003 elections, in the National Council the Swiss People's Party took 55 seats; the Social Democratic Party took 54; the Radical Free Democratic Party took 36; the Christian Democrats took 28.

The rightist Swiss People's Party (SVP), traditionally the junior partner in the four-party coalition government, has more than doubled its share of the popular vote for the National Council from 11% in 1987 to 22.5% in 1999, to 26.6% in 2003, to 29% in October 2007, and back to 26.6% in 2011, thus overtaking its three major rivals.

In the 2007 parliamentary elections, the SVP picked up an additional seven seats in the 200-seat National Council (lower house), bringing the SVP to 62 seats total. The SPS held 19.5% of the vote and 43 seats. The Greens gained more than 2% points and seven seats in the National Council, bringing their total shares to 9.6% and 20 respectively. They also for the first time gained seats in the Council of States. The Christian Democratic Party (CVP) booked modest gains of 0.2% and three seats, for a total of 14.6% and 31 seats in the National Council. This halted a downward trend that had cost the CVP a seat on the Federal Council to the SVP in 2003. The FDP lost 1.7% and five seats in the National Council, dropping to 15.6% of the votership and 31 seats in the National Council. Total voter turnout was 48%, a gain of 2.8% over the 2003 elections. In the Council of States, the CVP took 16 seats, the FDP, 14; SVP, 7; and SPS, 9; as of December 2007.

Soon after the 2007 elections, moderates within the SVP split off to form the Conservative Democratic Party (BDP). In January 2009, the Free Democratic Party (FDP) and the smaller Liberal Party combined to create the center-right party FDP.The Liberals. In 2010, FDP boasted the highest membership of any party with 130,000 members.

In the 2010 presidential election, Micheline Calmy-Rey of the Social Democratic Party was elected by the assembly with 108 out of 189 votes. Eveline Widmer-Schlumpf was selected to replace Calmy-Rey in December 2011; her term began on 1 January 2012. In the 2011 election, two smaller parties—BDP and Green Liberal Party (GLP)—were successful, in that each received 5.4% of the popular vote. Both the GLP and the BDP have gained the required five seats to form their own parliamentary groups. This suggested a split of the current power party coalition. The Swiss People's Party (SVP) lost votes for the first time in over 20 years. Although the SVP is still the strongest party, having 26.6% of the vote, the viability of anti-immigration policies had waned. The Social Democratic Party and the FDP came in second and third with 18.7% and 15.1% of the vote, respectively.

15 LOCAL GOVERNMENT

The Swiss Confederation consists of 23 sovereign cantons, three of which are divided into half-cantons (i.e., 20 cantons and six half-cantons). The most recent of these, Jura, was formed from six French-speaking districts in the German-speaking area of Bern Canton in 1978. In 1993, the German-speaking Laufental district of Beru joined the canton of Basel-Land. This was the first time a political unit in Switzerland left one canton to join another. Swiss cantons are highly autonomous and exercise wide administrative control, with the weak federal government controlling only foreign affairs, national security, customs, communications, and monetary policy. The cantons have their own constitutions and laws and are responsible for their own public works, education, care of the poor, justice, and police forces. Local forms of government vary, but each canton has a legislative council (called Grand Conseil, Grosser Rat, Kantonsrat, or Gran Consiglio), which appoints a chief executive. In a few of the small cantons, the general assembly of all voting citizens, or Landesgemeinde, decides on major matters by voice vote; in the majority of the cantons, this ancient institution has been replaced by referendum. Communes, numbering over 3,000, are the basic units of local government. For the most part, Swiss districts (Bezirke), constituting a middle level of organization between the cantons and communes, are little more than judicial circuits.

16 JUDICIAL SYSTEM

The Federal Court of Justice in Lausanne is composed of 30 permanent members appointed for six-year terms by the Federal Assembly. Until 2000, the court had both original and final jurisdiction in the majority of cases where a canton or the federal government was involved and was the highest appeals court for many types of cases. Judicial reforms carried out in 2000 reduced the caseload of the Federal Court by creating a federal criminal court and federal administrative bodies with judicial competence. Now, the Federal Court exists as a pure appellate court.

Each canton has its own cantonal courts. District courts have three to five members and try lesser criminal and civil cases. Each canton has an appeals court and a court of cassation, the jurisdiction of which is limited to reviewing judicial procedures. Capital punishment was abolished in 1942. Minor cases are tried by a single judge, difficult cases by a panel of judges, and murder and other serious crimes by a public jury.

The judiciary is independent and free from interference by other branches of government. The trials are fair and the judicial process is efficient. The judicial system is based on civil law influenced by customary law. Switzerland accepts compulsory jurisdiction of the International Court of Justice.

17 ARMED FORCES

The International Institute for Strategic Studies reports that armed forces in Switzerland totaled 25,620 members in 2011, all of whom are members of joint forces. Armed forces represent 0.6% of the labor force in Switzerland. Defense spending totaled $3.2 billion and accounted for 1% of GDP.

The country has universal compulsory military service for males age 19–20, followed by varied annual training requirements until age 42 (55 for officers), with exemption only for physical disability. Initial basic training of 15 weeks is followed by regular short training periods. In addition, there is also a paramilitary civil defense force. Women may volunteer to join in all services, including combat, but make up less than 1% of the total armed forces.

Swiss fighters are world famous, and from the 16th to the 19th century some two million Swiss served as mercenaries in foreign armies. The modern Swiss citizen-soldier is trained only for territorial defense in prepared mountain positions, which is his or her only mission. A continuing legacy of Swiss mercenary service is the ceremonial Vatican Swiss Guard. Switzerland has military personnel deployed to eight countries or regions under UN, NATO, European Union, or other auspices.

18 INTERNATIONAL COOPERATION

Although it was a member of and served as the site for the League of Nations, Switzerland was not a member of the United Nations until 10 September 2002, partly from a fear of compromising traditional Swiss neutrality. The country participates in ECE and in several nonregional specialized agencies, such as the FAO, UNESCO, UNHCR, UNIDO, the World Bank, ILO, IAEA, and the WHO. Switzerland has actively participated in the OSCE. The nation is also a member of the Asian Development Bank, the African Development Bank, the Euro-Atlantic Partnership Council, the European Bank for Reconstruction and Development, the Council of Europe, the Paris Club, the Inter-American Development Bank, OSCE, EFTA, the WTO, and the OECD. Switzerland holds observer status in the OAS and the Latin American Integration Association (LAIA). The headquarters of the International Committee of the Red Cross is located in Geneva. Switzerland is also the repository of the Geneva Convention, governing treatment of civilians, prisoners, and the wounded in wartime.

Switzerland is part of the NATO Partnership for Peace and a guest of the Nonaligned Movement. The nation has supported UN missions and operations in Kosovo (est. 1999), Ethiopia and Eritrea (est. 2000), and the DROC (est. 1999). Switzerland is part of the Australia Group, the Zangger Committee, the European Organization for Nuclear Research (CERN), the Nuclear Suppliers Group (London Group), the Organization for the Prohibition of Chemical Weapons, and the Nuclear Energy Agency.

In environmental cooperation, Switzerland is part of the Antarctic Treaty; the Basel Convention; Conventions on Biological Diversity, Whaling, and Air Pollution; Ramsar; CITES; the London Convention; International Tropical Timber Agreements; the Kyoto Protocol; the Montréal Protocol; MARPOL; the Nuclear Test Ban Treaty; and the UN Conventions on Climate Change and Desertification.

19 ECONOMY

Because of the paucity of its minerals and other raw materials and its limited agricultural production, Switzerland depends upon imports of food and fodder and industrial raw materials, which it finances with exports of manufactured goods. Agriculture is important (in agriculture, Switzerland is about 60% self-sufficient) though limited by a scarcity of level and fertile land, but manufacturing engages more than five times as many workers as farming. Swiss manufacturers excel in quality of workmanship rather than quantity of output. Other important branches of the economy include international banking, insurance, tourism, and transportation. Switzerland ranks among leading countries in research and development (R&D), and is among the world's top five countries for R&D for biotech and nanotechnology.

Switzerland was less affected than most other nations by the worldwide recession of the early 1980s and experienced a strong recovery beginning in 1983. However, between 1986 and 1992,

GNP grew by an annual average of only 0.7% and it fell in 1991, 1992, and 1993. From 1993–95, growth averaged barely 1% a year and decreased once again in 1996. In 1998 and 1999, however, the economy grew moderately before soaring, relatively speaking, to 3.4% in 2000. Switzerland's economy was in recession in 2002: the global international slowdown in 2001 and the appreciation of the Swiss franc brought small contractions in 2001 and 2002. The financial sector was particularly affected by the slowdown in the economy. However, by 2004, the economy grew again, thanks to eastern and Asian export markets. The 2008–09 global financial crisis of 2008 and the resulting economic downturn in 2009 (with -1.9% growth) led to a recession in Switzerland. The independent Swiss National Bank (SNB) effectively implemented a zero-interest rate policy, and Switzerland was able to recover in 2010, achieving 2.7% growth. However, the strength of the franc continued to lessen the demand for exported goods, and growth slowed to an estimated 2.1% in 2011.

From 1990 to 1992, the annual inflation rate averaged 5.1%. By 1994 inflation had plummeted to 0.9% and has remained low since. The inflation rate rose slightly to 2.4% in 2008 but fell again soon after. By 2011 concerns over deflation led the Swiss National Bank to adopt measures to weaken the franc in the hopes of maintaining a fair value.

Unemployment in Switzerland has remained consistently low, often less than 1%, in comparison with other countries, although it reached an unusually high 5.7% in 1997. However, after the boom of the late 1990s, unemployment fell to an average annual rate of 2.3%, from 1999 to 2002. The unemployment rate in 2004 had risen to 3.4%, and young workers (ages 15–25) were particularly hard hit, as were restaurant and hotel industry workers. Nonetheless, unemployment rates remain less than half the EU average. Meanwhile, the Swiss GDP per capita continued to be among the highest in the world.

The Swiss have been well known for the banking industry because of its secrecy and the long-term external value of the franc. It has been a safe haven for investors. However, the Swiss have been conforming to EU economic practices in order to stay competitive internationally and allow EU countries full access to its Swiss market. Switzerland agreed to extend this access to the 2004 new members with restrictions until 2011.

The gross domestic product (GDP) rate of change in Switzerland, as of 2010, was 2.6%. Inflation stood at 0.7%, and unemployment was reported at 3.9%.

20 INCOME

The CIA estimated that in 2011 the GDP of Switzerland was $340.5 billion. The CIA defines GDP as the value of all final goods and services produced within a nation in a given year and computed on the basis of purchasing power parity (PPP) rather than value as measured on the basis of the rate of the exchange based on current dollars. The per capita GDP was estimated at $43,400. The annual growth rate of GDP was 2.1%. The average inflation rate was 0.4%. It was estimated that agriculture accounted for 1.2% of GDP, industry 27.5%, and services 71.3%.

According to the World Bank, remittances from citizens living abroad totaled $2.5 billion or about $330 per capita and accounted for approximately .8% of GDP.

The World Bank reports that in 2009, household consumption in Switzerland totaled $285.3 billion or about $37,345 per capita, measured in current US dollars rather than PPP. Household consumption includes expenditures of individuals, households, and nongovernmental organizations on goods and services, excluding the purchases of dwellings. It was estimated that household consumption was growing at an average annual rate of 1%.

In 2007, the World Bank estimated that Switzerland, with 0.12% of the world's population, accounted for 0.48% of the world's GDP. By comparison, the United States, with 4.85% of the world's population, accounted for 22.51% of world GDP.

As of 2011 the most recent study by the World Bank reported that actual individual consumption in Switzerland was 66.9% of GDP and accounted for 0.46% of world consumption. By comparison, the United States accounted for 25.44% of world individual consumption. The World Bank also estimated that 8.3% of Switzerland's GDP was spent on food and beverages, 16.5% on housing and household furnishings, 2.4% on clothes, 8.9% on health, 4.7% on transportation, 1.6% on communications, 5.7% on recreation, 4.7% on restaurants and hotels, and 8.9% on miscellaneous goods and services and purchases from abroad.

In 2010, an estimated 6.9% of the population lived below the poverty level.

21 LABOR

Swiss law provides for and regulates union organization and collective bargaining. Most labor disputes are settled on the basis of a so-called peace agreement existing since 1937 between the head organizations of employers and employees. Other collective disputes are dealt with by the various cantonal courts of conciliation. Strikes are rare and Switzerland generally records the lowest number of days lost to strikes in the OECD. As of 2010, Switzerland had a total labor force of 4.218 million people. Within that labor force, CIA estimates in 2010 noted that 3.4% were employed in agriculture, 23.4% in industry, and 73.2% in the service sector.

The legally mandated maximum workweek is set at 45 hours for blue- and white-collar workers in the services, industrial, and retail sectors. A 50-hour workweek covers the rest. Minors as young as 13 may perform light work for up to nine hours per week during the school year and 15 hours otherwise. There are severe restrictions on the hours and conditions of employment of workers until the age of 20. There is no government mandated minimum wage. The Federal Labor Act and the Code of Obligations mandate various other workplace requirements.

According to government directive, foreign citizens are granted relatively free access to the Swiss labor market, granted they are well qualified and pose minimal financial/security risk. Although Switzerland has been characterized by tough immigration laws, the foreign population is surprisingly significant in the Swiss labor market. According to EURES, over one-fifth of those who claim permanent employment were foreign citizens (870,000) in 2011. Additionally, an estimated two-thirds are European citizens. The most notable foreign populations in the labor market in 2011 were Italians and western Balkans at 4%, Germans at 2.7%, and the Portuguese at 2.6%.

22 AGRICULTURE

Most of the cultivable land is in the Mittelland, or central plateau, and the cantons regularly producing the largest quantities of wheat are Bern, Vaud, Fribourg, Zürich, and Aargau. Soil quality is often poor, but yields have been increasing as a result of modern technology. Roughly 10% of the total land is farmed, and the country's major crops include grains, fruits, and vegetables. Cereal production in 2009 amounted to 1 million tons, fruit production 507,170 tons, and vegetable production 367,134 tons.

Agricultural production provides only about 60% of the nation's food needs. Although productivity per worker has been increasing steadily, the proportion of the total labor force engaged in agriculture has fallen from 30% in 1900 to about 4.6% in 2011. Between 1955 and 2011, the number of farm holdings fell from 205,997 to 62,000.

Swiss agricultural policy is highly regulated, with fixed prices and quota restrictions maintained on several products. Domestic production is encouraged by the imposition of protective customs and duties on imported goods and by restrictions on imports. The Federal Council has the authority to fix prices of bread grains, flour, milk, and other foodstuffs. Production costs in Switzerland, as well as international exchange rates favorable to the Swiss franc, make competition with foreign products difficult. This highly protectionist system has led to excess production and mounting costs associated with the management of surpluses. The Uruguay Round and subsequent Swiss implementation of its provisions in July 1995 (along with rising costs in the agricultural sector) has forced the government to begin reforming its agricultural support system.

23 ANIMAL HUSBANDRY

The UN Food and Agriculture Organization (FAO) reported that Switzerland dedicated 1.1 million hectares (2.79 million acres) to permanent pasture or meadow in 2009. During that year, the country tended 8.7 million chickens, 1.6 million head of cattle, and 1.6 million pigs. The production from these animals amounted to 154,539 tons of beef and veal; 257,873 tons of pork; 112,503 tons of poultry; 78,915 tons of eggs; and 2.37 million tons of milk. Switzerland also produced 16,800 tons of cattle hide and 490 tons of raw wool.

More than half of Switzerland's productive area is grassland exploited for hay production and/or grazing. Livestock production contributes about 2% to GDP. Dairying and cattle breeding are practiced, more or less intensively, in all but the barren parts of the country and, during the summer months, even at altitudes of more than 1,200 m (4,000 ft). Swiss cheeses are world famous; production grew 1.6% to 62,000 tons in 2009.

While home production almost covers or exceeds the domestic requirements for milk and dairy products, substantial quantities of eggs and meat must be imported. New agricultural reforms for 2004–07 entailed the progressive abolition of the milk quota system and changes in import tariffs for meat. Selective cattle breeding, research, and improvement of production standards are promoted by the federal government and by farmers' cooperatives. Exports of dairy products amounted to 21% of total agricultural export in 2011.

24FISHING

Fishing is relatively unimportant but is carried on in many Swiss rivers and on lakes Constance, Neuchâtel, and Geneva. Rainbow trout, whitefish, and perch are the main species. Local fish supply about 12% of domestic needs. In 2008, the annual capture totaled 1,582 tons according to the UN FAO.

25FORESTRY

About one-third of Switzerland is covered in forest. The UN FAO estimated the 2009 roundwood production at 3.25 million cu m (114.9 million cu ft). The value of all forest products, including roundwood, totaled $1.41 billion. About two-thirds of the forested land is owned by communes; most of the remainder is owned privately. Federal and cantonal governments account for about 8%. About 80% of the wood in Swiss forests is coniferous, primarily spruce; the remaining 20% is deciduous, predominantly red beech. Approximately 31% of Switzerland is covered by forest.

As of 2011, only half of the timber produced is used effectively, according to the Swiss Forest Agency. Around 64% of Switzerland's forest enterprises reported a loss in 2010 even though they were subsidized by local and federal governments.

26MINING

Mining, exclusively of industrial minerals for construction, played a minor role in Switzerland's economy. Metal mining has ceased, reserves of the small deposits of iron, nickel-cobalt, gold, and silver were mostly depleted, and new mining activities were discouraged for environmental reasons. Industrial minerals produced in 2009 included hydraulic cement, common clay, gravel, gypsum, lime, nitrogen, salt, sand, stone, and sulfur (from petroleum refining). Metal processing, restricted to primary and secondary aluminum, secondary lead, and steel, depended on imported raw materials or scrap. Environmental concerns have led to a policy to curtail or gradually cease smelting activities. The production and export of chemicals were among the nation's leading industries. Steel was another leading export commodity. A large diamond center, Switzerland was actively involved in cutting and polishing diamonds and played a big role in international trade activities.

27ENERGY AND POWER

The World Bank reported in 2008 that Switzerland produced 67.1 billion kWh of electricity and consumed 63.5 billion kWh, or 8,316 kWh per capita. Roughly 53% of energy came from fossil fuels, while 40% came from alternative fuels. Per capita oil consumption was 3,491 kg. Switzerland is heavily dependent on imported oil, natural gas, and coal to meet its hydrocarbon needs, although it does have the refining capacity to permit a modest amount of refined petroleum products to be exported.

28INDUSTRY

Manufacturing industries contributed 93.43% of merchandise exports in 2011. The industrial growth rate in 2010 was 6.2%. Swiss industries are chiefly engaged in the manufacture, from imported raw materials, of highly finished goods for domestic consumption and for export. Most of the industrial enterprises are located in the plains and the Swiss plateau, especially in the cantons of Zürich, Bern, Aargau, St. Gallen, Solothurn, Vaud, Basel (Baselstadt and

Baselland), and Thurgau. Some industries are concentrated in certain regions: the watch and jewelry industry in the Jura Mountains; machinery in Zürich, Geneva, and Basel; chemical industries (dyes and pharmaceuticals) in Basel; and the textile industry in northeastern Switzerland. In 1993, the industrial sector was targeted for assistance by a government-initiated revitalization program; in 1995, the sector again benefited from government policy when the turnover tax was replaced by a value-added tax system. Switzerland, along with Germany and Japan, is at the forefront of the emerging industry of environmental technology.

The textile industry, using wool, cotton, silk, and synthetics, is the oldest Swiss industry and, despite foreign competition resulting from the elimination of textile quotas by the World Trade Organization in 2005, remains important. The machine industry, first among Swiss industries today, produces goods ranging from heavy arms and ammunition to fine precision and optical instruments. Switzerland is the world's largest exporter of watches and watch products (followed by Hong Kong and China). For the first half of 2011, Swiss watch exports were up 20% over the same period in 2010 and exceeding forecasts. Chemicals, especially dyes and pharmaceuticals, also are important. As of 2011, Switzerland had a 4% share of the world export of chemical and pharmaceutical products, and ranked 7th among the largest export nations. Pharmaceutical exports as a percentage of total chemical industry exports increased from 40% in 1980 to 70.3% in 2003, with sustained comparable rates in 2011. Switzerland has also developed a major food industry, relying in part on the country's capacity for milk production. Condensed milk was first developed in Switzerland, as were two other important processed food products: chocolate and baby food. The Swiss company Nestlé S. A., headquartered in Vevey, is one of the world's largest food companies. In addition to Switzerland's major industries, such as textiles, nonmetallic minerals, and watchmaking and clockmaking, others, such as chemicals, plastics, and paper, have grown rapidly.

29SCIENCE AND TECHNOLOGY

Patent applications in science and technology as of 2009, according to the World Bank, totaled 1,684 in Switzerland. The major scientific learned societies, headquartered in Bern, are the Swiss Academy of Sciences, founded in 1815, and the Swiss Academy of Engineering Sciences, founded in 1981. About two-thirds of the funds for Swiss research and development (R&D), a high proportion by world standards, are supplied by industry and the rest by federal and cantonal governments. In 2008, expenditures for R&D totaled $16.3 billion, or 3% of GDP. Of that amount, the business sector accounted for 68.2%, followed by the government at 22.8%, foreign sources at 6.0%, higher education at 2.3%, and private nonprofit organizations at 0.7%. For that same year, there were 3,594 scientists and 2,315 technicians per million people engaged in R&D. The Swiss National Science Foundation was established in 1952 to finance noncommercial research for which funds would not otherwise be available. Most such spending is in the important chemicals sector. The Ministry of Public Economy, the center for federal agricultural research, has six research stations. In 2009, high-tech exports were valued at $38 billion and accounted for 24.96% of manufactured exports. In 2007, of all bachelor's

Principal Trading Partners – Switzerland (2010)

(In millions of US dollars)

Country	Total	Exports	Imports	Balance
World	352,685.0	185,775.0	166,910.0	18,865.0
Germany	94,074.0	37,750.0	56,324.0	-18,574.0
Italy	33,286.0	15,324.0	17,962.0	-2,638.0
France	29,985.0	14,975.0	15,010.0	-35.0
United States	29,237.0	19,823.0	9,414.0	10,409.0
United Kingdom	18,344.0	11,491.0	6,853.0	4,638.0
Austria	13,847.0	6,207.0	7,640.0	-1,433.0
Netherlands	13,558.0	5,557.0	8,001.0	-2,444.0
China	13,062.0	7,206.0	5,856.0	1,350.0
Spain	10,849.0	6,123.0	4,726.0	1,397.0
Japan	10,005.0	6,462.0	3,543.0	2,919.0

(…) data not available or not significant.

(n.s.) not specified.

SOURCE: *2011 Direction of Trade Statistics Yearbook,* New York: United Nations, 2011.

Balance of Payments – Switzerland (2010)

(In millions of US dollars)

Current Account		76,901.0
Balance on goods	12,291.0	
Imports	-246,229.0	
Exports	258,521.0	
Balance on services	44,020.0	
Balance on income	32,854.0	
Current transfers	-12,263.0	
Capital Account		-4,364.0
Financial Account		44,027.0
Direct investment abroad	-38,940.0	
Direct investment in Switzerland	5,513.0	
Portfolio investment assets	7,823.0	
Portfolio investment liabilities	22,141.0	
Financial derivatives	1,169.0	
Other investment assets	62,194.0	
Other investment liabilities	-15,874.0	
Net Errors and Omissions		8,818.0
Reserves and Related Items		-125,382.0

(…) data not available or not significant.

SOURCE: *Balance of Payment Statistics Yearbook 2011,* Washington, DC: International Monetary Fund, 2011.

degrees awarded, 23.0% were for the sciences (natural, mathematics and computers, engineering).

[30] DOMESTIC TRADE

Zürich, the largest city, is the commercial, financial, and industrial center of Switzerland. Basel is the second most important commercial city, followed by Geneva and Lausanne. Most Swiss wholesale firms are importers as well, specializing in one commodity or a group of related commodities.

The trend in retail trade is moving from independent establishments to larger supermarkets, department stores, and discount chains. As such, many small retailers have joined together to form purchasing cooperatives. Most of these cooperatives are in the foodstuffs business but can also be found in textiles, leather goods, sports articles, pharmaceuticals, toys, and hardware. Overall, the majority of Switzerland's retailers are department stores, chain stores, discount stores, supermarkets, and consumer cooperatives.

However, Switzerland is a challenging market for franchising, due to Switzerland's limited market size, high salaries, and high costs of services; also, consumer preference for high quality and authentic products or a new innovative idea over already existing products is another challenge facing potential franchisees. A number of well-known US-based franchisers have either closed or scaled back their respective operations in Switzerland. These included Pizza Hut, which has left the market, and Starbucks which closed an outlet in Bern. McDonald's owns most of its restaurants in Switzerland (199 restaurants in 2011). Only 40% are franchised.

Home shopping is gaining in popularity as the preferred method of direct marketing. Products include Tupperware and other household articles, Mary Kay Cosmetics, lingerie, jewelry and apparel, cleansing agents, and food and nutritional items.

Advertising, mostly entrusted to firms of specialists, uses as media billboards, movie theaters, television, local transportation facilities, railroads, newspapers, and magazines.

Switzerland imposes a 8% value added tax on most goods and services. However, there is a reduced rate of 2.5% on food, medicine, newspapers, and books, and a 3.8% rate on lodging services (these values indicate a slight rise in taxes from 2010 to 2011).

Usual business hours are from 8 or 9 a.m. to 5 or 6 p.m. Shops are normally open from 9 a.m. to 6:30 p.m. on weekdays but only to 5 p.m. on Saturdays; some shops close from 12 p.m. to 2 p.m. at lunchtime. In larger cities, shops generally extend their hours until 8 p.m. on one evening of the week, usually Thursday. Banks are open to the public from 8:30 a.m. to 4:30 p.m. Monday-Friday.

[31] FOREIGN TRADE

Switzerland imported $226.3 billion worth of goods and services in 2008, while exporting $232.6 billion worth of goods and services. Major import partners in 2009 were Germany, 32.6%; Italy, 10.7%; France, 9.3%; the United States, 5.8%; Netherlands, 4.5%; and Austria, 4.3%. Its major export partners were Germany, 19.3%; the United States, 10.1%; Italy, 8.4%; France, 8.4%; and UK, 5%.

Switzerland's export commodities are split into two categories: machinery sold to other manufacturers and commodities used by consumers. The country exports a large number of the world's watches and clocks.

Although Switzerland is not a member of the EU, it has been seeking ways to adopt some of the advantages of membership without relinquishing sovereignty.

[32] BALANCE OF PAYMENTS

In 2010, Switzerland had a foreign trade surplus of $36 billion, amounting to 1.3% of GDP. In the past, Switzerland typically had a foreign trade deficit. More recently, however, this imbalance was more than compensated for by income from services, investments, insurance, and tourism. Restructuring of enterprises in the 1990s, due to the strength of the Swiss franc, caused the export-oriented manufacturing sector to become highly successful. Exports of goods and services amounted to some 52% of GDP in 2009.

The current account surplus amounted to $84 billion, equivalent to 15.8% of GDP in 2010, making Switzerland a net creditor nation.

³³BANKING AND SECURITIES

In 2009, Switzerland had two major banks, 24 cantonal banks, and numerous foreign-owned banks, savings banks, and other banks and finance companies. There were a total of 325 banks in the country in that year. The bank balance-sheet total per capita in Switzerland is higher than that of any other nation in the world. Total assets of the Swiss banking system amounted to CHF$3.1 billion by 2008. Moreover, registered banks and bank-like finance companies have increased from 2006 (331) to 2009 (325) to offer the Swiss, on average, the greatest access to banking services in the world.

The government-supervised Swiss National Bank, incorporated in 1905 and the sole bank of issue, is a semiprivate institution owned by the cantons, by former banks of issue, and by the public. The National Bank acts as a central clearinghouse and participates in many foreign and domestic banking operations. The two big banks, United Bank of Switzerland (UBS) and Credit Suisse Group, dominate the Swiss banking scene and are expanding aggressively overseas. They are universal banks, providing a full range of services to all types of customers.

Regional banks specialize in mortgage lending and credits for small businesses. Since 1994, most of the country's regional banks have been linked in a common holding company providing back-office operations and other services to members in a bid to cut costs.

Foreign banks make up about a third of banks active in Switzerland. In contrast to domestic banks, their numbers have risen over the last decade but their business is increasingly focused on asset management, mostly of funds from abroad. On 1 January 1995, a new banking law came into effect allowing for foreign banks to open subsidiaries, branches, or representative offices in the country without first getting approval of the Federal Banking Commission.

The transactions of private and foreign banks doing business in Switzerland traditionally play a significant role in both Swiss and foreign capital markets; however, precise accounting of assets and liabilities in this sector are not usually made available as public information. Switzerland's strong financial position and its tradition (protected by the penal code since 1934) of preserving the secrecy of individual bank depositors have made it a favorite depository with persons throughout the world. (However, Swiss secrecy provisions are not absolute and have been lifted to provide information in criminal investigations.) The Swiss Office for Compensation executes clearing traffic with foreign countries.

In 1997, Swiss banks came under heavy criticism for losing track of money, gold, and other valuables belonging to Jewish Holocaust victims and held by the banks during World War II. Records also showed the banks had closed thousands of victims' accounts without notice after the war. The banks claimed they had lost the old records, but a group of journalists found the records archived in Lausanne in April of that year.

Also in 1997, an embarrassed Swiss government selected four members to a panel empowered to run a fund for Holocaust victims. Nobel laureate, Elie Weisel, a concentration camp survivor, turned down an invitation to serve as one of the three foreign members on the board. The fund, intended to help impoverished Holocaust victims and their families, is supported by funds appropriated by Nazis from Jews sent to concentration camps. Much of the gold, jewels, bonds, and currency taken by the Nazis had been placed in Swiss banks. In March 1998, Switzerland's banks agreed to create a $1.25 billion fund designed to compensate Holocaust survivors and their families.

Swiss banks were also under fire in 1997 for possibly facilitating money laundering of drug money accrued by a former Mexican president's brother and for failing to adequately recover the billions of dollars supposedly plundered by former Zairian dictator Mobutu Sese Seko, who was overthrown that year. All the negative publicity has caused some to question the usefulness of Swiss banks' much-lauded secrecy.

In 2011, the money market rate, the rate at which financial institutions lend to one another in the short term, was -.65%. The discount rate, the interest rate at which the central bank lends to financial institutions in the short term, was a record low of 0.04% in 2010.

Stock exchanges operate in Geneva (founded 1850), Basel (1875), and Zürich (1876). The Zürich exchange is the most important in the country. The open outcry stock exchanges in Zürich, Geneva, and Basel closed in 1994 when a national electronic stock exchange for all securities trading began operations in August. In 2010, a total of 282 companies were listed on the SWX Swiss Exchange, which had a market capitalization of $1.229 billion.

The country is most famously known for its banking and financial services, and the Swiss franc is regarded as one of the world's most stable currencies. This legendary banking system came under fire in 2009, however, as the issue of banking secrecy and tax havens became points of contention in world politics. In March 2009, Switzerland bowed to international pressures and signed an agreement with the Organization for Economic Cooperation and Development (OECD) to institute international standards for bank data sharing. One major reform was the release of information in cases of suspected tax evasion, which is defined under Swiss law as the deliberate concealment of assets and is considered to be a civil offense. In the past, the Swiss government would release information only for the criminal offense of tax fraud, which involved lying on official documents. In July 2009, however, the UBS, a major Swiss bank, refused to release information on 52,000 American accounts to the US Internal Revenue Service. UBS claimed that there was insufficient evidence against the clients named and that the release of the information would be illegal under current Swiss law. Earlier in the year, however, the bank did release information on about 300 US clients.

In March 2010, Germany and Switzerland initialed a double-taxation agreement that would streamline information sharing on suspected tax evaders and set benchmark tax rates that Germans must pay on interest earned in Swiss accounts. Germany has been one of the harshest critics of Switzerland's banking secrecy laws and angered the Swiss by purchasing stolen Swiss banking records earlier in the year. In signing the double-taxation agreement, Germany and Switzerland smoothed over what had been deeply strained relations.

Many Swiss banks suffered significant losses in the global financial crisis, leading to a recession as the economy declined in the last quarter of 2008 and again in the first three quarters of 2009. However, the rate of decline for each quarter was less than one percent. Growth returned in 2010 and continued in 2011.

34 INSURANCE

The Swiss people are the most heavily insured in the world, although this reflects social insurance such as health insurance, as well as more commercial types of business. Nevertheless, Swiss insurers now rely on foreign business for two-thirds of their premium income. The insurance sector has been steadily deregulated during the 1990s. One of the last set of controls was scrapped in 1996 when the fixed tariff regime for third-party vehicle insurance was abolished. As of 1999, Swiss insurance companies numbered over 100 and were rapidly declining in pervasiveness.

Switzerland controls an estimated one-third of the world's reinsurance, and insurance income represents a major item in the Swiss balance of payments. Insurance investments are represented heavily in the Swiss capital market, and Swiss insurance firms have invested widely in foreign real estate. About half the domestic insurance business is in the hands of the state. The Swiss Reinsurance Co. in Zürich is the largest of its kind in the world. There are several types of compulsory insurance in Switzerland, including workers' compensation, third-party automobile liability, fire, pension, hunters', aircraft, nuclear power station, old age, unemployment, and disability insurance. In 2010, the total income of the Swiss domestic insurance market was 48 million, making it the 12th largest insurance market globally. In 2010, the value of all direct insurance premiums written generated about 4.2% of GDP, of which life insurance premiums accounted for $31.5 billion. In 2010, there was a premium volume growth of 0.7% in the non-life insurance business. Private insurers paid $476 million to cover damages. The insurance industry employed just under 50,000 Swiss, approximately 1% of the working population.

35 PUBLIC FINANCE

The Swiss government has been known historically for maintaining a relatively high degree of austerity in comparison to its European neighbors. In 1991, the federal government incurred a budget deficit of over CHF1.5 billion, the first budget discrepancy in seven years. Cantonal budgets also were in deficit. These deficits continued throughout the 1990s and into the 2000s, prompting governments at all levels to take further cost-cutting steps. As an international creditor, debt management policies are not relevant to Switzerland, which participates in the Paris Club debt reschedulings and is an active member of the OECD.

In 2011, the budget of Switzerland included $222 billion in public revenue and $216.8 billion in public expenditures. The budget surplus amounted to 0.8% of GDP. Public debt was 52.4% of GDP, with $1.2 trillion of the debt held by foreign entities (2010).

Government outlays by function in 2008 were as follows: general public services, 12.0%; defense, 2.6%; public order and safety, 5.1%; economic affairs, 12.8%; environmental protection, 1.6%; housing and community amenities, 0.6%; health, 5.4%; recreation,

Public Finance – Switzerland (2008)

(In millions of francs, central government figures)

Revenue and Grants	100,207.2	100.0%
Tax revenue	59,275.1	59.2%
Social contributions	36,405.4	36.3%
Grants	270.9	0.3%
Other revenue	4,255.7	4.2%
Expenditures	93,055.6	100.0%
General public services	23,253.1	25.0%
Defense	4,319.4	4.6%
Public order and safety	852	0.9%
Economic affairs	7,702.8	8.3%
Environmental protection	521.8	0.6%
Housing and community amenities	51.8	0.1%
Health	350.7	0.4%
Recreational, culture, and religion	344.1	0.4%
Education	2,655.6	2.9%
Social protection	53,004.4	57.0%

(…) data not available or not significant.

SOURCE: *Government Finance Statistics Yearbook 2010,* Washington, DC: International Monetary Fund, 2010.

culture, and religion, 2.3%; education, 17.1%; and social protection, 40.7% (according to the OECD).

36 TAXATION

The Swiss Confederation, the cantons, and the communes all levy taxes on income or profits. Periodic federal, cantonal, and communal taxes also are charged against capital values belonging to corporations and other corporate entities. The cantons all levy wealth taxes based on individual net assets, stamp duties, taxes on entertainment or admissions, and special charges for educational, social, and sanitary services. Most cantons also levy a tax surcharge on members of certain major churches for the support of those religions. Localities may impose taxes on land, rents, and entertainment, as well as a head tax and a dog tax.

The statutory tax rate on corporate income was 21.3% in 2010. Generally, capital gains received by a company are taxed as ordinary business income at regular business rates. However, different rules may apply to gains received from real estate or to real estate companies at the cantonal/communal level. Generally, dividends distributed by Swiss companies are taxed as ordinary income, to which a withholding rate of 35% is applied. However, applicable participation exemption rules may lower the federal tax liability for the recipient. Interest income from banks, publicly offered debentures, bonds, and other debt instruments issued by a Swiss borrower are subject to a withholding rate of 35%. However, loans from a foreign parent company to Swiss subsidiaries and commercial loans generally are exempt.

Federal tax is levied on personal income at rates up to 11.5%. However, cantonal rates can range from 10% to around 30%. Various deductions and personal allowances are granted according to circumstances. Those between the ages of 20 and 50 who do not fulfill their military obligation are liable for an additional tax. Cantonal and communal taxes are generally imposed at progressive rates.

In 1995, Switzerland replaced its old system of taxing turnover with a value-added tax (VAT) similar to those of its European neighbors. As of 2010, the VAT was 7.6% and was levied on all deliveries of goods and services, including investments, consumer goods, animals and plants, consulting and entertainment services, license fees, and the sale of rights. The VAT is also levied on imported goods and services. However, hotel and lodging services are subject to a lower rate of 3.6%, while items such as foodstuffs, medicines, newspapers, farming supplies, and agricultural products were subject to a 2.4% rate. Exports were zero-rated. There are also miscellaneous federal taxes, such as stamp duties, payroll and excise taxes.

37 CUSTOMS AND DUTIES

Switzerland joined EFTA in 1960 and became a full member of the GATT group in 1966. In 1973, Switzerland entered into an industrial free trade agreement with the European Community (now the European Union). Duties on industrial imports from the European Community were eliminated by 1977. Although it generally favors free trade, Switzerland protects domestic agriculture for national defense reasons and its customs tariff, established in 1921, is primarily a revenue-raising instrument. Specific duties, low for raw materials, moderate for semifinished goods, and high for manufactured goods, are levied by weight of import. Import duties average 3.2% on industrial goods. Switzerland gives preferential treatment to imports from developing nations. Other import taxes include a 3% statistical tax, a standard 7.6% VAT, and an environmental tax. Specific luxuries like cigarettes and spirits are subject to an excise tax. Quotas regulate the importation of certain agricultural items such as white wine.

38 FOREIGN INVESTMENT

In 1997, total foreign direct investment (FDI) stock in Switzerland exceeded $56.58 billion (22% of GDP). US companies accounted for 23% of that total. By 1999, FDI stock had risen to over $83 billion (32% of GDP), and the United States share to 26.6%. FDI inflows were $6.6 billion in 1997, climbing to a peak of $16.3 billion in 2000, before falling back to about $10 billion in 2001. In 2003, FDI inflows amounted to $12.2 billion. Foreign direct investment (FDI) in Switzerland was a net inflow of $27.6 billion according to World Bank figures published in 2009. FDI represented 5.61% of GDP. Switzerland is generally open to foreign investment and grants foreign investors national treatment. However, the government restricts investment in vacation real estate, utilities, and other sectors considered essential to national security (such as hydroelectric and nuclear power plants, operation of oil pipelines, operation of airlines and marine navigation, and the transportation of explosive materials). There are no restrictions on repatriation of profits. Federal grants are offered for investments in depressed areas. The cantonal governments offer tax and non-tax incentives for new investments or extensions of existing investments on a case-by-case basis.

Stocks of Swiss FDI abroad totaled $170 billion (62.3% of GDP) in 1997, rising to $205.2 billion (79% of GDP) in 1999. In 2008, the largest holders of Swiss outward FDI stock were the United States (with $140 billion USD); the United Kingdom ($47.7 billion); Germany ($52.7 billion); the Netherlands ($32.8 billion); and France ($33.1 billion). FDI outward stock in 2008 amounted

to $760.1 billion (rates according to the Swiss National Bank report for 2010).

39 ECONOMIC DEVELOPMENT

Private enterprise is the basis of Swiss economic policy. Although government intervention has traditionally been kept to a minimum, the international monetary crises from late 1974 to mid-1975 led to imposition of various interim control measures; in 1982, with inflation rising, a constitutional amendment mandating permanent government price controls was approved by popular referendum. The Swiss National Bank has followed a general policy of limiting monetary growth. To further raise the standard of living, the government also grants subsidies for educational and research purposes, promotes professional training, and encourages exports. Although certain foreign transactions are regulated, there is free currency exchange and a guarantee to repatriate earnings of foreign corporations.

The cause of the remarkable stability of Switzerland's economy lies in the adaptability of its industries; in the soundness of its convertible currency, which is backed by gold to an extent unmatched in any other country; and in the fact that the particular pattern of Swiss democracy, where every law may be submitted to the popular vote, entails taking into account the wishes of all parties whose interests would be affected by a change in legislation.

Switzerland's development assistance program takes the form of technical cooperation, preferential customs treatment for certain third-world products, and a limited number of bilateral aid arrangements.

The question of future European Union (EU) membership remains a point of contention among the Swiss. The French-speaking minority overwhelmingly favors EU membership, while the German-speaking majority strongly opposes it. In a 2000 referendum, Swiss voters approved closer ties to the EU. Some of the key provisions of the deal included agreement to allow EU trucks transit rights through Switzerland, as well as granting Swiss freedom of movement in the EU. Full access to the Swiss market by the original 15 EU member countries was achieved in a June 2004 agreement, ending as a result the "national preference." Switzerland approved another pact, the Schengen-Dublin agreement with the EU, in June 2005, which allows for the free movement of peoples, although fears of cheap labor coming from new EU member nations remained. However, voters approved by a referendum held on 25 September 2005 a measure to extend the provision of free movement of peoples to the 10 predominantly eastern European nations that joined the EU in 2004. A possible population shift was predicted with the fall of popularity of the Swiss People's Party in 2011, the party in power that was against EU membership.

The strength of the Swiss franc made exports less competitive through 2011, despite efforts by parliamentarians to weaken the currency. The future of the Swiss banking industry hinged upon the effects of several bank reform agreements that were signed in the late 2000s, including agreements with Germany and the United Kingdom signed in 2011.

40 SOCIAL DEVELOPMENT

Switzerland has a social insurance system and mandatory occupational pension system financed by employer and employee contributions as well as governmental subsidies. Old-age pensions are paid at age 65 for men and 63 for women. Disability and survivorship pensions are also available to qualified recipients. Sickness and maternity benefits were first implemented in 1911. Medical care is available to all persons living in Switzerland, and there is a voluntary insurance plan for all employees to provide cash benefits. Maternity benefits are payable up to 16 weeks. Work injury insurance is compulsory, with contribution rates varying according to risk. Unemployment and disability is also covered. Family allowances are provided by the cantons, but there is a federal program covering agricultural workers. Some cantons provide birth grants.

The law provides for equal pay and prohibits gender discrimination, but there is significant bias against women in the workplace. Women earn less than men and are less likely to receive training. There are few women in managerial positions, and they are also promoted less than men. Sexual harassment in the workplace continues, although laws and advocacy groups work to eradicate the problem. The Federal Office for Equality Between Women and Men and the Federal Commission on Women are charged with eliminating all types of gender discrimination. Physical and sexual violence against women and domestic abuse persist.

Extremist organizations continue physical and verbal attacks on religious, racial, and ethnic minorities. The government is taking some action to curtail the activities of these groups. Human rights are generally respected in Switzerland.

41 HEALTH

According to the CIA, life expectancy in Switzerland was 82 years in 2011. The country spent 10.7% of its GDP on healthcare, amounting to $7,141 per person. There were 41 physicians, 160 nurses and midwives, and 53 hospital beds per 10,000 inhabitants. The fertility rate was 1.46, while the infant mortality rate was 4.08 per 1,000 live births. In 2008 the maternal mortality rate, according to the World Bank, was 10 per 100,000 births. It was estimated that 90% of children were vaccinated against measles. The CIA calculated HIV/AIDS prevalence in Switzerland to be about 0.4% in 2009.

Health standards and medical care are excellent. The pharmaceuticals industry ranks as one of the major producers of specialized pharmaceutical products. Managed-care systems are widely used, especially with a "gatekeeper" component to control costs. Tobacco consumption has dramatically decreased. Voters in Zürich approved a government plan to supply heroin addicts with free access to their drug, which resulted in a decline of new users.

42 HOUSING

Although housing standards are comparatively high, there are shortages in certain areas. In the mid-1990s, less than 40,000 new dwellings per year were constructed in communities of 2,000 or more inhabitants, down from 44,228 in 1985. In 2000, there were about 3,115,399 private households and about 1,377,552 residential buildings. In 2009, the number of residential use was 1,623,000 with a total of 4,008,400 dwellings. About 30% of all residential buildings were designed for two or more households. There has been a steady decrease in unoccupied dwellings. In June of 2009,

around 34,760 dwellings (0.90%) of the estimated total housing stock were unoccupied.

43 EDUCATION

Education at all levels is first and foremost the responsibility of the cantons. Thus, Switzerland has 26 different systems based on differing education laws and varied cultural and linguistic needs. The cantons decide on the types of schools, length of study, teaching materials, and teachers' salaries. Education is compulsory in most cantons for nine years and in a few for eight. An optional 10th year has been introduced in several cantons. Church schools in some cantons are tax supported. After primary school, students complete the compulsory portion of their education in various types of secondary Grade I schools, which emphasize vocational or academic subjects to varying degrees. Secondary Grade II schools, which are not compulsory, include trade and vocational preparatory schools and gymnasiums, which prepare students for the university and lead to the *matura*, or higher school-leaving certificate.

Switzerland has a large number of private schools attracting primarily foreign students. These schools, most of them located in the French-speaking cantons, are known for their high-quality education, of either the academic or "finishing school" variety.

In 2010, about 99% of age-eligible children were enrolled in some type of preschool program. Primary school enrollment that year was estimated at about 99% of age-eligible students (535,577), while secondary school enrollment was about 99% of age-eligible students (555,505). It is estimated that about 95% of all students complete their primary education. The student-to-teacher ratio for primary school was at about 13.6:1 in 2011; the ratio for secondary school was also about 10:8. In 2011, private schools accounted for about 3.77% of primary school enrollment and about 6.99% of secondary enrollment.

Switzerland has 10 cantonal universities, including four in French-speaking areas and four in German-speaking ones. The universities' expenditures are largely financed by the cantons, with a 53% contribution from the Confederation. Approximately one-third of all higher-level educational funding goes to research and development. The largest universities are those of Zürich, Geneva, and Basel; others include those of Lausanne, Bern, Fribourg, and Neuchâtel. The Federal Institute of Technology in Zürich, the Economics College at St. Gallen, and the Federal Institute of Technology in Lausanne are also important. In 2011, it was estimated that about 46.99% of the age-eligible population was enrolled in some type of higher education program; 52.38% for men and 46.99% for women. The adult literacy rate has been estimated at about 99%.

As of 2011, public expenditure on education was estimated at 6.06% of GDP, or 12.96% of total government expenditures according to the World Bank.

44 LIBRARIES AND MUSEUMS

The library of Basel University (3 million volumes) and the Swiss National Library in Bern (3.6 million volumes) are the largest in Switzerland. The University of Geneva has 1.8 million volumes; the University of Lausanne has about 1.7 million; and the University of Fribourg has two million. Switzerland has an extensive public library system with about 2,344 service points holding over 28 million volumes in total. The Library and Archives of the United Nations is located in Geneva, as is the library of the International Labor Organization (over 580,000 items).

The National Museum, a federal institution in Zürich, houses historic objects; other historical museums are located in Basel, Bern, and Geneva. Basel houses both the Museum of Ancient Art and the Basel Museum of Fine Arts, which has a fine collection of 15th- and 16th-century German masterworks, paintings by Dutch artists of the 17th and 18th centuries, and a survey from Corot to Picasso. The Museum of Fine Arts in Bern contains paintings by old masters and impressionists (Klee Foundation). The Zürich Art Museum houses modern Swiss paintings, as well as works by Dutch and Flemish masters of the 17th century. Geneva houses the Museum of the Voltaire Institute, the Museum of the Institute of Henri Dunant, founder of the International Red Cross, the Jean-Jacques Rousseau Museum, and the Museum of Modern and Contemporary Art, which opened in 1994. The League of Nations (United Nations) Museum is in Geneva. There are arts and crafts museums in most of the larger cities, and Neuchâtel has an ethnographic museum. Many fine examples of Romanesque, Gothic, and Baroque architecture are found in Switzerland.

45 MEDIA

In 2009, the CIA reported that there were 4.7 million telephone landlines in Switzerland. In addition to landlines, mobile phone subscriptions averaged 120 per 100 people. There were 4 FM radio stations, 113 AM radio stations, and 2 shortwave radio stations. Internet users numbered 71 per 100 citizens. In 2010, the country had 4.8 million Internet hosts. Prominent newspapers in 2010, with circulation numbers listed parenthetically, included *Berner Zeitung BZ* (131,515), *Blick* (270,000), and *Tages-Anzeiger Zurich* (210,000), as well as 60 other major newspapers.

Switzerland's telephone system is fully automated, and the quality of domestic and international services are rated as excellent. Domestic service is provided by an extensive network of cables and microwave radio relay stations. International service is provided by satellite ground stations.

Broadcasting is controlled by the Swiss Broadcasting Corp. (SBC), an autonomous corporation under federal supervision. A number of independent local radio stations have been operating since 1983. Radio programs are broadcast in German, French, Italian, and Romansch. Agence Télégraphique Suisse (Schweizerische Depeschenagentur), co-owned by some 40 newspaper publishers, is Switzerland's most important national news agency.

The constitution provides for freedom of speech and a free press, and the government is said to uphold these freedoms in practice.

46 ORGANIZATIONS

Both agricultural and consumer cooperatives are numerous. The Swiss Office for Commercial Expansion is an important foreign trade promotion organization. The Swiss Federation of Commerce and Industry also promotes commerce, trade, and industry. The Swiss Confederation of Trade Unions serves the interests of workers/employees. The International Labour Organization has a base office in Geneva. There are chambers of commerce in all the major cities. Trade unions and professional associations exist for most occupations.

Geneva serves as home to a variety of international organizations including the International Red Cross and Red Crescent Society, the World Council of Churches, the Lutheran World Federation, the World Alliance of Reformed Churches, The World Health Organization, and the World Scout Foundation. Several United Nation's committee offices are based here as well, the UN Economic Commission for Europe, UN Environment Programme, UN High Commission for Refugees, the UN Institute for Training and Research, and the UN Research Institute for Social Development. Other international organizations with national chapters include Amnesty International, Defence for Children International, Caritas, and Greenpeace.

There are numerous cultural and educational organizations. A few with national interest include the Swiss Academy of Humanities and Social Sciences, the Swiss Academy of Medical Sciences, and the Swiss Academy of Sciences. The European Center for Culture is a multinational organization promoting understanding and cooperation between cultures.

Active youth groups within the country include Junior Chamber, YMCA/YWCA, and the Swiss Guide and Scout Movement. There are a large number of sports associations nationwide, including several international organizations such as the International Baseball Federation, the International Basketball Federation, and the International Gymnastic Federation. The International Olympic Committee is based in Lausanne.

Several human rights, social justice, and social action organizations exist, including the Association of International Consultants on Human Rights, the Berne Declaration, Green Cross, The National Council of Women of Switzerland, and the Women's International League for Peace and Freedom. The International Alliance for Women and the Women's World Summit Foundation both focus on health and equal rights for women. Soroptimist International of Europe is a multinational organization of businesswomen working toward the causes of peace, justice, health, and equal rights.

47 TOURISM, TRAVEL, AND RECREATION

The *Tourism Factbook*, published by the UN World Tourism Organization, reported 8.29 million incoming tourists to Switzerland in 2009; they spent a total of $16.3 billion. Of those incoming tourists, there were 6.3 million from Europe. There were 273,974 hotel beds available in Switzerland, which had an occupancy rate of 43%. The estimated daily cost to visit Bern, the capital, was $527. The cost of visiting other cities averaged $457.

Switzerland has long been one of the most famous tourist areas in the world, and Swiss hospitality and the Swiss hotel industry are justly renowned. Scenic attractions are manifold, and in the Swiss Alps and on the shores of the Swiss lakes there are features of interest for the skier, the swimmer, the hiker, the mountain climber, and the high alpinist. There are approximately 50,000 km (31,000 mi) of marked footpaths and 500 ski lifts. The hotels are among the best in the world; Switzerland pioneered in modern hotel management and in specialized training for hotel personnel. Central Switzerland and the Geneva region attract the largest number of foreign tourists.

48 FAMOUS PERSONS

World-famous Swiss scientists include the physician and alchemist Philippus Aureolus Paracelsus (Theophrastus Bombastus von Hohenheim, 1493?–1541); the outstanding mathematicians Johann Bernoulli (1667–1748) and Leonhard Euler (1707–83); the geologist Louis Agassiz (Jean Louis Rodolphe Agassiz, 1807–73), who was active in the United States; the physiologist, pathologist, and surgeon Emil Theodor Kocher (1841–1917), who received the Nobel Prize for medicine in 1909; Charles Édouard Guillaume (1861–1938) and the German-born Albert Einstein (1879–1955, a naturalized Swiss citizen), Nobel Prize winners in physics in 1920 and 1921, respectively; and Paul Karrer (b. Russia, 1889–1971), authority on vitamins, who shared the 1937 Nobel Prize in chemistry. Other Nobel Prize winners in the sciences include Alfred Werner (1866–1919; chemistry, 1913); Yugoslav-born Leopold Ruzicka (1887–1976; chemistry, 1939); Yugoslav-born Vladimir Prelog (1906–1998; chemistry, 1975); Austrian-born Wolfgang Pauli (1900–1958; physics, 1945); Paul Hermann Müller (1899–1965), Walter Rudolf Hess (1881–1973), and Polish-born Tadeus Reichstein (1897–1996), Nobel laureates for medicine in 1948, 1949, and 1950, respectively; Werner Arber (b. 1929; medicine, 1978); Heinrich Rohrer (b. 1933; physics, 1986); and K. Alex Müller (b. 1927) and German-born J. Georg Bednorz (b. 1950), for physics in 1987.

Jean-Jacques Rousseau (1712–78), a Geneva-born philosopher, musician, novelist, and diarist in France, was a great figure of the 18th century whose writings exerted a profound influence on education and political thought. Swiss-born Mme. Germaine de Staël (Anne Louise Germaine Necker, 1766–1817) was acclaimed the world over as defender of liberty against Napoleon. Other noted Swiss writers include Albrecht von Haller (1708–77), also an anatomist and physiologist; the novelists and short-story writers Johann Heinrich David Zschokke (1771–1848) and Jeremias Gotthelf (Albert Bitzius, 1797–1854), also a clergyman and poet; and the poets and novelists Gottfried Keller (1819–90), Conrad Ferdinand Meyer (1825–98), and Carl Spitteler (1845–1924), the last of whom won the Nobel Prize for literature in 1919. The diaries of the philosopher, poet, and essayist Henri-Frédéric Amiel (1821–81) are famous as the stirring confessions of a sensitive man's aspirations and failures. Charles Ferdinand Ramuz (1878–1947) is often regarded as the most powerful Swiss writer since Rousseau. The German-born novelist and poet Hermann Hesse (1877–1962) was awarded the Nobel Prize for literature in 1946. Other recent and contemporary Swiss writers include Robert Walser (1878–1956), a highly individualistic author, and the novelists and playwrights Max Rudolf Frisch (1911–91) and Friedrich Dürrenmatt (1921–90), whose psychological dramas have been performed throughout Europe and the United States.

Ludwig Senfl (1490–1543) was an outstanding Renaissance composer. The *Dodecachordon* (1547) of Henricus Glareanus (Heinrich Loris, 1488–1563) was one of the most important music treatises of the Renaissance period. Swiss-born composers of more recent times include Ernest Bloch (1880–1959), Othmar Schoeck (1886–1957), Arthur Honegger (1892–1955), Frank Martin (1890–1974), Ernst Lévy (1895–1981), Conrad Beck (1901–89), and Paul Burkhard (1911–77). Ernest Ansermet (1883–1969) was a noted conductor. Renowned Swiss painters include Konrad Witz (1400–1447), Henry Fuseli (Johann Heinrich Füssli, 1741–1825), Arnold Böcklin (1827–1901), Ferdinand Hodler (1853–1918), and Paul Klee (1879–1940). In sculpture and painting, artist Alberto Giacometti (1901–66) won world acclaim for his hauntingly elongated figures. Le Corbusier (Charles Édouard Jeanneret, 1887–1965) was a leading 20th-century architect.

Swiss religious leaders include Ulrich Zwingli (1484–1531), French-born John Calvin (Jean Chauvin, 1509–64), and Karl Barth (1886–1968). Other famous Swiss are Johann Heinrich Pestalozzi (1746–1827), an educational reformer who introduced new teaching methods; Ferdinand de Saussure (1857–1913), the founder of modern linguistics; Auguste Henri Forel (1848–1931), psychologist and entomologist; the noted art historians Jakob Burckhardt (1818–97) and Heinrich Wölfflin (1864–1945); the psychiatrists Eugen Bleuler (1857–1939), Carl Gustav Jung (1875–1961), and Hermann Rorschach (1884–1922); Jean Piaget (1896–1980), authority on child psychology; and the philosopher Karl Jaspers (1883–1969). Swiss winners of the Nobel Prize for peace are Henri Dunant (1828–1910) in 1901, founder of the Red Cross, and Elie Ducommun (1833–1906) and Charles Albert Gobat (1843–1914), both in 1902.

49 DEPENDENCIES

Switzerland has no territories or colonies.

50 BIBLIOGRAPHY

Annesley, Claire, ed. *A Political and Economic Dictionary of Western Europe*. Philadelphia: Routledge/Taylor and Francis, 2005.

International Smoking Statistics: A Collection of Historical Data from 30 Economically Developed Countries. New York: Oxford University Press, 2002.

Linder, Wolf. *Swiss Democracy: Possible Solutions to Conflict in Multicultural Societies*. 3rd ed. New York: Palgrave, 2010.

McElrath, Karen, ed. *HIV and AIDS: A Global View*. Westport, CT: Greenwood Press, 2002.

Opello, Walter C. *European Politics*. Boulder, CO: Lynne Rienner Publishers, 2009.

Political Chronology of Europe. London: Europa, 2001.

Switzerland Investment and Business Guide: Strategic and Practical Information. Washington, DC: International Business Publications USA, 2012.

Turk, Eleanor L. *Issues in Germany, Austria, and Switzerland*. Westport, CT: Greenwood Press, 2003.

UKRAINE

Ukraina

CAPITAL: Kiev (Kyiv)

FLAG: Equal horizontal bands of azure blue (top) and yellow.

ANTHEM: *Sche ne vmerla Ukraina (Ukraine Has Not Yet Perished).*

MONETARY UNIT: The official currency, introduced in September 1996, is the hryvnia (UAH), which consists of 100 kopiyka. UAH1 = US$0.1247 (or US$1 = UAH8.016) as of 2011.

WEIGHTS AND MEASURES: The metric system is used.

HOLIDAYS: New Year's Day, 1–2 January; Christmas, 7 January; Women's Day, 8 March; Spring and Labor Day, 1–2 May; Victory Day, 9 May; Ukrainian Independence Day, 24 August.

TIME: 2 p.m. = noon GMT.

¹LOCATION, SIZE, AND EXTENT

Ukraine, the second-largest country in Europe, is located in Eastern Europe, bordering the Black Sea, between Poland and Russia. Comparatively, Ukraine is slightly smaller than Texas with a total area of 603,700 sq km (233,090 sq mi). Ukraine shares boundaries with Belarus to the N, Russia to the E, the Black Sea to the S, Romania, Moldova, Hungary, and Slovakia to the W, and Poland on the NW. Ukraine's location is one of strategic importance at the crossroads between Europe and Asia. Its land boundary totals 4,663 km (2,897 mi) and its coastline is 2,782 km (1,729 mi). Ukraine's capital city, Kiev, is located in the north-central part of the country.

²TOPOGRAPHY

The topography of Ukraine consists mainly of fertile plains (steppes) and plateaus. True mountains (the Carpathians) are found only in the west and in the Crimean Peninsula in the extreme south. The Dnieper Uplands run through the central region of the country. The Donets Hills and Azov Uplands are located along the eastern border.

The coastal region of the Black Sea is a lowland area. The indent of Karkint Bay nearly separates the Crimean Peninsula from the mainland. The Kerch Strait connects the Black Sea to the Sea of Azov, which lies between Ukraine and Russia covering an area of 37,599 sq km (14,517 sq mi). An area of wetlands, the Polesye Marshes, is located near the northwest border.

The most important river in Ukraine is the Dnipro (Dnieper), the third longest river in Europe. It serves as a major source of hydroelectric power. Other major rivers include the Danube, Western Buh, the Tisza, the Pripyat, and the Desna. There are over 20,000 small lakes throughout the country, but the largest lakes are artificial, created by dams along the Dnipro.

³CLIMATE

The climate is subtropical on the Crimean Peninsula. Precipitation is disproportionately distributed: highest in the west and north, lowest in the east and southeast. Winters vary from cool along the Black Sea to cold farther inland. Summers are warm across the greater part of the country, except for the south where it becomes hot.

The rest of the country's climate is temperate. The mean temperature in July is about 10°C (66°F). In January, however, the mean temperature drops to -6°C (21°F). Average rainfall is 50 cm (20 in) a year with variations in different regions.

⁴FLORA AND FAUNA

There are an estimated 5,100 plant species in Ukraine with a variety of mixed shrubs, grasses, and evergreens found along the Mediterranean-like zone of the Crimean coast. Forest regions in Ukraine include such tree species as beech, linden, oak, and spruce. Additionally, Ukraine is home to some 120 mammal, 325 bird, 25 reptile, and 20 amphibian species. Notably, European bison, fox, and rabbits can be found living on the vast steppes of the country. These numbers reflect the total number of distinct species residing in the country, not the number of endemic species.

⁵ENVIRONMENT

Ukraine's environmental problems include the nuclear contamination that resulted from the 1986 Chernobyl accident. One-tenth of Ukraine's land area was affected by the radiation. According to United Nations (UN) reports, approximately 1 million people were exposed to unsafe levels of radiation through the consumption of food. Approximately 3.5 million hectares (8.6 million acres) of agricultural land and 1.5 million hectares (3.7 million acres) of forest were also contaminated.

Pollution from other sources also poses a threat to the environment. Ukraine releases polluted water, heavy metals, organic compounds, and oil-related pollutants into the Black Sea. The water supply in some areas of the country contains toxic industrial chemicals up to 10 times the concentration considered to be within safety limits. These pollution levels have resulted in large-scale elimination of the fish population, particularly in the Sea of Azov.

In all, Ukraine's water resources total 139.5 cu km (33.47 cu mi), while water usage is 37.53 cu km (9 cu mi) per year. Domestic water usage accounts for 13% of total usage, industrial for 35%, and agricultural for 52%. Per capita water usage totals 807 cu m (28,499 cu ft) per year.

Air pollution is also a significant environmental problem in Ukraine. In 1992, Ukraine had the world's seventh-highest level of industrial carbon dioxide emissions, which totaled 611.3 million metric tons, a per capita level of 11.72. By 2000, that number had dropped to 342.8 million metric tons, and reports from 2008 show that carbon dioxide emissions in Ukraine to be approximately 317.2 million metric tons.

Ukraine has 33 Wetlands of International Importance. According to a 2011 report issued by the International Union for Conservation of Nature and Natural Resources (IUCN), threatened species included 11 types of mammals, 11 species of birds, 1 types of reptiles, 21 species of fish, 15 species of invertebrates, and 16 species of plants. Threatened species include the European bison, the Russian desman, and the Dalmatian pelican. The wild horse has become extinct. The World Resources Institute reported in 2006 that Ukraine had designated 1.94 million hectares (4.79 million acres) of land for protection.

6 POPULATION

The US Central Intelligence Agency (CIA) estimates the population of Ukraine in 2011 to be approximately 45,134,707, which placed it at number 28 in population among the 196 nations of the world. In 2011, approximately 15.5% of the population was over 65 years of age, with another 13.7% under 15 years of age. The median age in Ukraine was 39.9 years. There were 0.85 males for every female in the country. The population's annual rate of change was -0.622%. The projected population for the year 2025 was 41,900,000. Population density in Ukraine was calculated at 75 people per sq km (194 people per sq mi).

The UN estimated that 69% of the population lived in urban areas and that urban populations had an annual rate of change of -0.1%. The largest urban areas, along with their respective populations, included Kyiv, 2.8 million; Kharkiv, 1.5 million; Dnipropetrovsk, 1 million; Odessa, 1 million; and Donetsk, 971,000.

7 MIGRATION

Estimates of Ukraine's net migration rate, carried out by the CIA in 2011, amounted to -0.09 migrants per 1,000 citizens. The total number of emigrants living abroad was 6.56 million, and the total number of immigrants living in Ukraine was 5.26 million. Since the breakup of the former Soviet Union, tens of thousands of Ukrainians have returned to Ukraine. Between 1989 and 1995, 15,000 returned from Azerbaijan, and 39,000 returned from Kyrgyzstan. Between 1991 and 1995, 15,000 returned from Belarus; 82,000 returned from Kazakhstan; and 30,000 returned from Tajikistan. There were still 150,000 ecological migrants internally displaced from the 1986 Chernobyl accident. As of February 1996, 250,000 Tatars had returned from Central Asia, mostly from Uzbekistan. These Tatars belong to the 500,000 Tatars who were

forcibly deported from the Crimean peninsula under the Stalin regime. The signing of an agreement between Ukraine and Uzbekistan in 1998 on the simultaneous release from Uzbek citizenship and acquisition of Ukrainian citizenship enabled more than 38,000 Crimean Tatars to obtain Ukrainian citizenship. Many of the rest of the Crimean Tatars in Central Asia wish to return to the Crimea.

Due to a series of amendments to the Law of Citizenship and a naturalization campaign, all formerly deported stateless people residing in Ukraine acquired Ukrainian citizenship by 1999.

8 ETHNIC GROUPS

According to the latest census (2001), 77.8% of the total population is Ukrainian. Russians form 17.3%, mainly in eastern Ukraine. Belarussians, Moldovans, Crimean Tatars, Bulgarians, Hungarians, Romanians, Poles, and Jews each account for less than 1% of the population. About 700,000 Rusyns (Ruthenians) live within the country, but they are not an officially recognized ethnic group. The Roma population is estimated between 200,000 and 400,000, though the official census placed the number at only 47,600.

9 LANGUAGES

Like Russian, Ukrainian is an eastern Slavic language. However, it has several distinctive vowel and consonant sounds. It is written in the Cyrillic alphabet but has three extra letters. Ukrainian began to emerge as a separate language from Russian in the late 12th century. Ukrainian is the official language and is spoken by about 67% of the population. Russian is spoken by about 24% of the population. Other languages include Romanian, Polish, and Hungarian.

10 RELIGIONS

Ukraine was Christianized by St. Volodymyr in 988. Under Soviet rule, churches and religion were subject to suppression and political manipulation, a situation that ended with the declaration of independence in 1991. According to a 2010 report, the nation is predominantly Christian, with Orthodox Christians accounting for 52% of the population. The largest is Ukrainian Orthodox Church of the Moscow Patriarchate, followed by the Ukrainian Orthodox Church of the Kyiv Patriarchate and the Ukrainian Autocephalous Orthodox Church. The Ukrainian Greek Catholic Church has the largest number of non-Orthodox members. An estimated 27% of the population is Protestant, with the Evangelical Baptist Union of Ukraine serving as the largest group at more than 300,000 members. Other Christian groups represented include Baptists, Pentecostals, Jehovah's Witnesses, Mormons (The Church of Jesus Christ of Latter-Day Saints), Anglicans, Lutherans, Methodists, Calvinists, and Evangelicals. The Roman Catholic Church claims 1 million members. Islamic leaders claim there are about 2 million Muslims in the nation. There are an estimated 103,600 Jews in the country. Small communities of Buddhists, Baha'is, and Hare Krishnas are also present. Approximately 10% of the population claims to be either atheist or agnostic. The constitution provides for freedom of religion, and this right is generally respected. Religious groups must register to obtain status as a juridical entity with the government in order to conduct financial and business activities. Some smaller and nontraditional religious groups have reported problems in meeting government registration require-

LOCATION: 49°0′ N; 32°0′ E. BOUNDARY LENGTHS: Belarus, 891 kilometers (554 miles); Hungary, 103 kilometers (64 miles); Moldova, 939 kilometers (584 miles); Poland, 428 kilometers (266 miles); Romania (SE), 169 kilometers (105 miles); Romania (W), 362 kilometers (225 miles); Russia 1,576 kilometers (980 miles); Slovakia, 90 kilometers (56 miles).

ments. Christmas, Easter Monday, and Holy Trinity Day (all according to the Julian calendar) are observed as national holidays.

11 TRANSPORTATION

The CIA reports that Ukraine has a total of 169,496 km (105,320 mi) of roads. Of this number, 165,844 km (103,051 mi) are paved, and there is an estimated 152 vehicles per 1,000 people in the country.

The total length of railway track in Ukraine is reported at 21,678 km (13,470 mi), which, according to a 2008 report, is broad-gauge.

The main marine ports in Ukraine are Berdyans'k, Illichivs'k, Kerch, Kherson, Mariupol', Mykolayiv, Odessa, and Sevastopol'. The merchant marine fleet had 189 ships of 1,000 GRT or over in 2008. The Dnipro River is the primary inland waterway, but the Danube, western Pivd Buh, Pryp'yat', and Desna are also used for import-export traffic. In all, Ukraine has approximately 2,185 km (1,358 mi) of navigable waterways.

As of 2010, 425 airports were reported in Ukraine with the largest being those in Kiev, Kharkiv, Donetsk, Odessa, and Simferopol. This number includes 189 airports with paved runways, while the remaining 236 are unpaved. In all, these airports transported some 3.43 million passengers in 2009. Ukraine is also home to seven heliports.

12 HISTORY

Ukrainians, Russians, and Belarussians belong to the eastern branch of the Slavic peoples, all of whom trace their origins to medieval Kievan Rus. Kievan Rus was established in the 9th century AD. St. Volodymyr the Great, one of the most celebrated rulers of Kievan Rus, adopted Christianity as the national faith in 988. Internal strife in the 12th century and the Mongol invasion in the 13th led to the ultimate destruction of Kievan Rus as a major power. Halych-Volhynia in Western Ukraine, however, became the new political center until it fell to Polish-Lithuanian rule in the 14th century. During the following centuries, Ukraine found itself the object of power struggles among its more powerful neighbors.

In a protracted struggle against Poland, Ukrainian Cossacks were able to establish an independent state in the 16th and 17th centuries. To safeguard Ukrainian independence from the Poles, Ukraine concluded the Treaty of Pereyaslav in 1654 with Moscow. The nature of this agreement has generated much historical controversy: Russian historians claim that, as part of the agreement, Ukraine accepted Moscow's rule, while Ukrainians claim that Ukraine was to retain its autonomy. The ensuing war between Russia and Poland resulted in the partition of Ukraine. Most of the rest of Ukraine's territory was incorporated into the Russian Empire with the partition of Poland in 1795. Small parts of Ukrainian territory to the west were absorbed by the Hapsburg Empire.

A Ukrainian national movement arose in the 19th century. Later, the collapse of the Tsarist regime and the chaos of the Russian revolution in 1917 allowed Ukraine to assert its independence. In April 1917, the National Ukrainian Assembly met in Kiev and, in November, proclaimed the creation of the Ukrainian People's Republic. When the Bolsheviks formed a rival Ukrainian Communist government, the National Assembly proclaimed the independence for Ukraine on 22 January 1918.

On 1 November 1918, an independent Republic of Western Ukraine was declared after the disintegration of the Austro-Hungarian Empire. On 22 January 1919, the Ukrainian People's Republic and the Republic of Western Ukraine united and established an independent Ukrainian state, recognized by over 40 other nations.

The new government, however, could not maintain its authority in the face of civil strife and the threat of the approaching Bolshevik, pro-Tsarist, and Polish forces. By 1920, eastern Ukraine fell to the Bolsheviks and became the Ukrainian Soviet Socialist Republic, while Poland occupied most of western Ukraine. Small areas of the west went to Romania, Hungary, and Czechoslovakia.

Early Soviet policy allowed for cultural autonomy and local administration by Ukrainian Communists, but Stalin changed this liberal policy in the 1930s when he initiated strict Russification and persecution of Ukrainian nationalists. This policy culminated in the Soviet-engineered famine of 1932–33 that resulted in the death of 7 to 10 million Ukrainians.

The 1939 Nazi-Soviet pact assigned Poland's Ukrainian territory to the Soviet sphere of influence. When Germany invaded the Soviet Union in 1941, Ukrainian nationalists in L'vin proclaimed the restoration of the Ukrainian state. The Germans arrested these nationalists and turned Ukraine into a German colony. When it became clear that the Nazis wanted to enslave them and not liberate them, a resistance movement led by nationalists fought both the Soviet and German armies. During World War II, Ukraine lost six million people through death or deportation, and a total of 18,000 villages were destroyed.

The Ukrainian resistance movement continued to fight in Soviet Ukraine (the western Ukraine, formerly part of Poland, that had been incorporated into the Ukrainian S.S.R.). It was not until the 1950s that they were completely defeated by the better-equipped Soviet Red Army.

In March 1990, semi-free elections for parliament were held. The Communist-dominated parliament declared Ukraine a sovereign state on 16 July 1990. On 24 August 1991, following the failed coup in Moscow, the parliament proclaimed the independence of Ukraine and declared that only the constitution and laws of Ukraine were valid in its territory. On 1 December 1991, the citizens of Ukraine confirmed this proclamation with a 90.3% vote in favor of independence. At the time of this referendum, Leonid Kravchuk was elected the first president.

Ukraine joined Russia and Belarus in creating the Commonwealth of Independent States (CIS) in December 1991. This agreement was meant to facilitate coordination of policy in various fields, but despite their efforts, Ukrainian-Russian differences arose in several areas, including the command and control of nuclear weapons, the formation of a unified military command, and the character and pace of economic reform.

In light of the 1986 Chernobyl nuclear power plant accident, Ukraine declared its intention to become a nuclear-free state. However, this process progressed much more slowly than expected. The lack of fuel resources and disagreements with Russia over pricing induced the government to keep the Chernobyl plant running. The START I agreement received the Ukrainian parliament's conditional ratification in November 1993 and unconditional ratification in February 1994, but the transfer of nuclear weapons to Russia did not occur as smoothly as planned. On 6 May 1992, it was announced that all Ukrainian tactical nuclear weapons had been shipped to Russia for dismantling. However, Ukraine cited Russia's failure to dismantle these weapons, inadequate compensation, and security concerns as the reasons for not turning over its entire strategic arsenal.

The CIS countries agreed to a unified nuclear command, but Ukraine declared its intent to create its own national conventional military and opposed any efforts to create a unified CIS conventional force. President Kravchuk declared all conventional forces on Ukrainian territory the property of Ukraine. This has given rise to disputes and disagreements about the Black Sea fleet, to which Russia has also laid claim.

Since its independence, Ukraine has experienced unrest in some of the predominantly Russian areas in the east and southeast. Crimea is the most notable example; it declared independence on 6 May 1992. At the same time, the Russian parliament approved a resolution that declared the 1954 Soviet grant of the Crimea to Ukraine unconstitutional and void. This resolution, however, was rejected by Russian president Boris Yeltsin. Demands for secession in Crimea have continued to complicate Ukrainian-Russian relations.

Ukraine adopted a new constitution in June 1996, establishing a presidency (elected for a five-year term) and a one-chamber parliament called the Supreme Council (elected for a four-year term). Under transitional provisions, President Leonid Kuchma, elected over incumbent Leonid Kravchuk in 1994, was to serve until elections in 1999. The Supreme Council adopted a new civil code in June 1997. In the same year, Ukraine signed a 10-year friendship treaty with Russia and an agreement with Western nations to shut down the Chernobyl nuclear plant by 2005. It was shut down in 2000. Public discontent with the slow pace of economic reforms was evident in the strong showing by the Communist party in the 1998 legislative elections, in which it won 25% of the vote (116 of 450 seats). However, support for the party did not translate into support for union with Russia, proposed by Petro Symonenko, the party's candidate in the 1999 presidential elections. Leonid Kuchma was reelected in a November 1999 runoff election with 56% of the vote and nominated central bank chairman Viktor Yushchenko to be prime minister. Soon after taking office, Yushchenko reached a restructuring agreement with foreign bondholders to avoid default on the nation's $2.6 billion foreign debt. As the new century began, Ukraine's much-needed economic reforms remained stalled by longstanding corruption and political stalemate between reformists and their parliamentary opponents.

In November 2000, the body of Ukrainian journalist Georgiy Gongadze was found decapitated: opposition demonstrators alleged Kuchma was involved in the murder of the journalist who was critical of the administration, and there were calls for Kuchma's impeachment. Kuchma denied the allegations, but, in February 2001, the EU called for an inquiry into the journalist's murder. In September 2002, an ad-hoc commission set up by parliament to investigate Gongadze's murder recommended that criminal charges be brought against the president and other top officials, based on tape recordings of a meeting at which Kuchma allegedly asked security officials to "take care" of the journalist. Anti-Kuchma protests were held throughout the country to call for the president's resignation. All six national television stations were off the air on the morning of the 16 September demonstrations, purportedly for "maintenance." Many protesters were beaten and arrested. In October, the Kiev Court of Appeals opened a criminal case against Kuchma based on the allegations of his involvement in the murder.

In parliamentary elections held on 30 March 2002, Ukrainians voted for many opposition parties, although parties opposed to Kuchma alleged widespread fraud. In April, Yushchenko's government was dismissed following a no-confidence vote in parliament; he was replaced with Viktor Yanukovych—the governor of the eastern province of Donetsk Oblast.

Although Yushchenko is respected in the West for fighting corruption and furthering economic reforms, he is unpopular with many Ukrainian businessmen, who are seen as corrupt. Presidential elections were scheduled for 2004, and Kuchma was constitutionally barred from running for a third term. In 2002, he announced plans to amend the constitution and weaken his executive powers. This was seen as a move to transfer power to parliament in the event that a reformer such as Yushchenko would be elected president. Kuchma's plans also included splitting parliament into two chambers. In March 2003, Yushchenko stated he feared the new amendments would postpone presidential elections for two years and extend Kuchma's rule until 2006. Tens of thousands of protesters nationwide took to the streets in March, calling once again on Kuchma to resign for abuse of office, arms dealing, vote-rigging, corruption, the involvement in Gongadze's murder, and for impoverishing the country.

For the 2004 presidential elections, Yushchenko announced that he would be running as an independent. His main contender was the current prime minister Viktor Yanukovych. Since the latter was backed by Kuchma and by most Ukrainian TV channels, Yushchenko relied heavily on direct interaction with the people to convey his message.

The initial vote was held on 31 October 2004, but neither of the two candidates obtained a decisive lead—Yushchenko won 39.87% of the votes, while Yanukovych won 39.32%. A second voting round was therefore staged on 21 November, with the final vote tally showing Yanukovych as the winner. However, observers noted several cases where the voting process was rigged to Yanukovych's favor. The suspicion that loomed over the October elections was strengthened by the major discrepancies between the exit poll results conducted by the observers and the official vote count. As a result, Yushchenko called for the people from all over the country to take to the streets and protest. After 13 days, the so-called Orange Revolution (named so after the orange ribbons worn by Yushchenko's supporters) led the Supreme Court to nullify the election results and order a re-run, to be held on 26 December 2004. This time, Yushchenko emerged victorious by an 8% margin. Yanukovych contested the results but eventually stepped down from his post.

In January 2005, Yushchenko was sworn in as president, and in February 2005 he nominated Yulia Tymoshenko—one of his former deputies, and an ardent supporter of the Orange Revolution—as prime minister. Although there had been some controversy regarding her "oligarch status" (she is one of the wealthiest people in Ukraine), her nomination was accepted by the parliament with 373 out of 450 possible votes. On 8 September 2005, after only a couple of months as prime minister, and following several resignations and accusations of corruption, Tymoshenko and her government were ousted by Yushchenko. Yuriy Yekhanurov, head of the Dnipropetrovsk Oblast state administration, was appointed the new prime minister.

Drawing on the political capital he garnered in the West after winning the troubled 2004 elections, during which he was allegedly poisoned with dioxins that led to severe facial disfigurements, Yushchenko pressed for EU and NATO integration. Both organizations cautioned, however, that the pace of political, economic, and military reforms would have to be stepped up before Ukraine's candidacy could be seriously considered. Constitutional reforms went into effect on 1 January 2006.

In January 2006, Russia briefly cut the supply of natural gas to Ukraine in a disagreement over gas prices. Russia said its reasons for doing so were purely economic, but Ukraine said they were political and related to the Orange Revolution. An agreement between Russia and Ukraine was reached over the gas issue, but concerns that the agreement had yielded too much to Russia led parliament to sack Yekhanurov's government. Parliamentary elections were held in March 2006, and Yanukovych's party came out on top. Tymoshenko's party came in second, leaving President Yushchenko's party trailing in third. After months of negotiations, in June and July 2006, the backers of the Orange Revolution—the Yushchenko and Tymoshenko blocs and the Socialists—agreed on a coalition, but the deal collapsed. The Socialists instead decided to enter into a coalition with Yanukovych's Party of Regions and the Communists. Yanukovych was nominated prime minister. In August, Yushchenko was faced with a deadline to accept Yanukovych's nomination or call new elections. President Yushchenko agreed that his rival could become prime minister. By March 2007, the political crisis had deepened, with the president and prime minister vying for power. Both sides held rallies in Kiev. In April 2007, Yushchenko dissolved parliament and called a snap election after talks with parliamentary leaders failed to resolve the struggle with Yanukovych.

Parliamentary elections were held in September 2007. President Yushchenko urged all parties to hold coalition talks after no clear winner emerged. On 15 October 2007, after official results had been announced, Yushchenko's and Yulia Tymoshenko's blocs stated they would form a coalition government, after they emerged with a combined 228 seats out of 450 in parliament. Yanukovich's Party of Regions won the most seats in the election, 175. Tymoshenko was expected to once again become prime minister.

In January 2009, a dispute erupted between the Russian Federation and Ukraine over natural gas pricing. The dispute prompted Russia to cut gas supplies to Ukraine and Ukraine to respond by doing the same to Europe. The crisis was resolved only after intense European diplomatic pressure. Although the precipitating factor seemed to be energy prices, the crisis underscored the delicate and complex geopolitical situation that has developed between Ukraine, Russia, and the West.

In the January 2010 presidential elections, the incumbent Viktor Yushchenko was eliminated in the first round. Former prime minister Viktor Yanukovych and the incumbent prime minister Yulia Tymoshenko received enough votes to be placed on the ballot for the second round, which took place in February 2010. Yanukovych won that election.

Not long after the elections, beginning in May 2010, Yulia Tymoshenko was the target of criminal cases stemming from alleged corruption. Officially charged a year later, Tymoshenko was subsequently found guilty of abuse of power on October 11, 2011. She was sentenced to seven years in prison and to paying substantial reparations.

¹³GOVERNMENT

Ukraine is governed by a constitution adopted in June 1996, which allows for an elected parliament and president. The constitution was amended in December 2004 as a response to the presidential election crisis.

The Ukrainian parliament consists of a single chamber with 450 seats called the Rada (Supreme Council). Seats are allocated proportionally to the parties that acquire more than 3% of the electoral votes. Members of parliament currently serve four-year terms, while the president serves a five-year term. Following the 2006 elections, members of parliament will serve five-year terms. The prime minister and cabinet are nominated by the president and confirmed by the Supreme Council. Although many parties participate in the elections, many candidates run as independents as well.

Ukraine's first post-independence presidential elections were held in two rounds on 26 June and 10 July 1994. In this election, the incumbent Leonid Kravchuk was defeated by his former prime minister, Leonid Kuchma, who was reelected in November 1999. In December 2004, following massive popular protests and after the Supreme Court ordered a re-run of the allegedly rigged November 2004 elections, Kuchma's former prime minister—Viktor Yushchenko—was elected president.

¹⁴POLITICAL PARTIES

There are some 120 political parties active in Ukraine. They fall roughly into four different categories: radical nationalist, democratic nationalist, liberal-centrist, and Communist-socialist.

The radical nationalist parties are fearful of Russia and advocate a strong presidency. Their commitment to democracy—particularly if regions of Ukraine seek to secede—is not firm. The democratic nationalist parties are also fearful of Russia, but also appear strongly committed to democracy, individual rights, and the protection of private property. The influential Rukh Party (Ukrainian Popular Movement), which won 43 seats in the 1998 elections, belongs to this group. The liberal-centrist parties are particularly concerned with promoting free market economic reform. They

are also committed to democracy and individual rights. The communist-socialist parties oppose privatization and seek continued state control of the economy. They generally favor close relations with Russia. The most important party in this group, the Communist Party of Ukraine, won 116 seats in 1998.

In the March 2002 parliamentary elections, many parties grouped together into voting blocs. Winning the most seats in the Rada was the "Our Ukraine" coalition, led by Viktor Yushchenko, which took 23.6% of the vote and 112 of 450 seats. The coalition was registered in January 2002, and then included the Ukrainian People's Rukh Party (registered in 2003 as the Ukrainian People's Party), the People's Rukh of Ukraine, the Congress of Ukrainian Nationalists, the Reforms and Order Party, Solidarity, the Liberal Party, the Youth Party of Ukraine, the Christian People's Union, the Go Forward, Ukraine! Party, and the Republican Christian Party. In March 2003, Yushchenko announced a "new political force" would be created that would form the basis for a European-style political party.

Also gaining seats in parliament in the 2002 elections were the "For a United Ukraine" bloc, 101; the Communist Party, 67; the United Social-Democratic Party of Ukraine, 24; the Socialist Party of Ukraine, 23; the Yuliya Tymoshenko bloc, 21; the Democratic Party of Ukraine/Democratic Union liberal bloc, 4; the "Unity" bloc, 3; and independents and others held 95 seats.

On 8 September 2005, the government led by Yuliya Tymoshenko was ousted by Yushchenko after allegations of corruption made their way into the media.

Parliamentary elections were held on 26 March 2006. Yanukovych's Party of Regions won the most seats, taking 186 of 450 (32.1%). Tymoshenko's Bloc won 129 seats (22.3%); Our Ukraine, 81 seats (13.9%); the Socialist Party of Ukraine, 33 seats (5.7%); and the Communist Party of Ukraine, 21 seats (3.7%). The next parliamentary elections were scheduled for March 2011. However, in April 2007, Yushchenko dissolved parliament and called a snap election after talks with parliamentary leaders failed to resolve a power struggle with Yanukovych. In the September 2007 elections, Yanukovich's Party of Regions won the most seats, with 175, followed by Tymoshenko's party, Bloc Tymoshenko, with 156, and Yushchenko's party, Our Ukraine, with 72. The two pro-Western parties, Our Ukraine and Bloc Tymoshenko, decided in October 2007 to enter into a coalition government with 228 seats. The coalition as of that time still had the potential to attract 20 more seats from one of the smaller parties.

In the January 2010 presidential elections, incumbent Viktor Yushchenko was eliminated in the first round, receiving only 5% of the votes. With voter turnout of about 69%, Viktor Yanukovych received 48.95% of the vote in the second round, which took place in February. Yulia Tymoshenko followed at 45.47%. Tymoshenko and her supporters called for a recount at some polling stations, but international observers called the election free and fair. In March 2010, the parliament was dissolved because the members of the ruling coalition failed to produce enough signatures to prove that they maintained the 226-member majority needed to run the 450-member parliament. A coalition government was formed later that month through an agreement signed by the Party of the Regions, the Communist Party, and the Lytvyn People's Bloc. The coalition is represented by 235 deputies. The agreement was made possible, in part, by the approval of a legal amendment that allowed parties to form coalitions by recruiting individual deputies instead of larger parliamentary blocs. The new coalition government approved ex-finance minister Mykola Azarov as the new prime minister.

15 LOCAL GOVERNMENT

Ukraine is divided into 24 administrative regions (*oblasts*) plus the autonomous Republic of Crimea. In addition, the cities of Kiev, the capital of Ukraine, and Sevastopol, capital of Crimea, enjoy *oblast* status. The *oblast* is divided into districts, each of which has a representative in the *Rada* (Supreme Council).

A strong secessionist movement has risen up in Crimea. In a nonbinding referendum held in 1994, over 78% of the 1.3 million people who voted supported greater autonomy from Ukraine. In 1995 Ukraine's parliament and President Leonid Kuchma moved to contain secessionist elements in the region. Kuchma temporarily took direct control over the area and afterward decreed that he must approve all candidates for premier of the region. The Crimea adopted a new constitution in 1999 providing for additional budgetary autonomy from the rest of Ukraine.

In spite of the election of the reform-oriented Yushchenko in 2004, Ukrainian local government officials complained that budget expenditures were still done in a centralized and inefficient fashion. On 13 September 2005 the Constitutional Court of Ukraine enforced a series of constitutional amendments that shift most of the presidential clout to the parliament. The new laws came in effect on 1 January 2006 and were expected to give more power to local governments.

16 JUDICIAL SYSTEM

The court system, until 2001, remained similar to that which existed under the former Soviet regime. In July 2001, a series of laws were passed designed to bring existing legislation regarding the judiciary and the administration of justice more in line with the requirements for an independent judiciary. The three levels of courts are *rayon* (also known as regional or people's courts), *oblast* (provincial) courts, and the Supreme Court. All three levels serve as courts of first instance, the choice of level varying with the severity of the crime. A case heard in first instance at the *rayon* level can be appealed through the next two higher stages. A case heard in first instance in the Supreme Court is not subject to appeal or review. A 1992 law added a Constitutional Court to the existing system. The Constitutional Court consists of 19 members appointed for nine-year terms. It is the final interpreter of legislation and the constitution, and it determines the constitutionality of legislation, presidential edicts, cabinet acts, and acts of the Crimean autonomous republic.

The *Rada* selects judges on recommendation from the Ministry of Justice based partly upon government test results. *Oblast* and Supreme Court judges must have five years of experience in order to be appointed and may not be members of political parties.

A new constitution, adopted in 1996, and amended in 2004, provides that the judiciary is funded separately from the Ministry of Justice to ensure an independent judiciary. Because the courts are funded by the Ministry of Justice, however, they have been subject to executive influence, and have suffered from corruption and inefficiency.

17 ARMED FORCES

The International Institute for Strategic Studies reports that armed forces in Ukraine totaled 129,925 members in 2011. The force was comprised of 70,753 from the army, 13,932 from the navy, and 45,240 members of the air force. Armed forces represent .9% of the labor force in Ukraine. Defense spending totaled $4.3 billion and accounted for 1.4% of gross domestic product (GDP), which ranks 109 worldwide.

Of greatest international concern has been the fate of the ICBMs and strategic bombers on Ukrainian soil, which are supposed to return to Russia for dismantling. As of 2000, the number of ICBMs had been reduced from 174 to 44, while numbers from 2005 show the number of strategic bombers being cut to 26.

18 INTERNATIONAL COOPERATION

Ukraine became a member of the UN on 24 October 1945; the country is part of the ECE and several non-regional specialized agencies, such as the IAEA, the FAO, the World Bank, UNCTAD, UNESCO, UNIDO, and the WHO. It is a member of the Commonwealth of Independent States (CIS), the Council of Europe, the Black Sea Economic Cooperation Zone, the Euro-Atlantic Partnership Council, the European Bank for Reconstruction and Development, and the OSCE. The nation has observer status in the WTO, the OAS, and the Nonaligned Movement. In 2001, Georgia, Uzbekistan, Ukraine, Azerbaijan, and Moldova formed a social and economic development union known as GUUAM. Uzbekistan withdrew from the partnership in 2005.

Ukraine is an active member of the NATO Partnership for Peace. The government has supported UN missions and operations in Kosovo (est. 1999), Ethiopia and Eritrea (est. 2000), Liberia (est. 2003), Sierra Leone (est. 1999), Georgia (est. 1993), and the Democratic Republic of the Congo (est. 1999). Ukraine is a member of the Zangger Committee and the Nuclear Suppliers Group (London Group).

In environmental cooperation, Ukraine is part of the Basel Convention, the Conventions on Biological Diversity and Air Pollution, Ramsar, CITES, the London Convention, the Kyoto Protocol, the Montréal Protocol, MARPOL, and the UN Conventions on the Law of the Sea and Climate Change.

19 ECONOMY

Ukraine was central to the Soviet agricultural and industrial system. The rich agricultural land of this region (commonly called the "breadbasket" of the former Soviet Union) provided 46% of Soviet agricultural output in the 1980s and also accounted for 25% of the USSR's coal production. Ukraine's economic base is dominated by industry, which accounts for over 33% of GDP (2005 est.). However, agriculture continues to play a major role in the economy, representing about 9% of GDP.

Real GDP declined 3% in 1990, 11% in 1991, and an estimated 15% in 1992. Recovery in 1997 was cut short by the effects of the Russian financial crisis of 1998. Real GDP fell -1.7% in 1998 and -0.2% in 1999. However, the economy has registered strong positive growth since 2000. Official unemployment since 1999 has averaged about 4.2%. Inflation, averaging 21.67% from 1998 to 2000, was reduced to a single-digit rate (6%) in 2001 and reached 0.8% in 2002. Although still high, this is a marked improvement over the 400% hyperinflation that plagued the country in 1994. In response to the hyperinflation, the government introduced a new currency and instituted mass privatization in 1995. However, the country remained plagued by a slow economic decline. A new civil code adopted by parliament in 1997 was expected to stabilize the country's business climate. Economic recovery beginning in 2000 is attributable to a number of factors: double-digit growth in industrial output in 2001; a good grain harvest resulting from good weather and reduced governmental controls; improved export competitiveness from the depreciation of the currency in 1998–99; the clearance of many wage and pension arrears; increased domestic demand as a result of wage and pension increases granted in 2000 and 2001; considerable idle capacity; and the expansion of export markets.

This economic expansion continued in the following years, with GDP growth rates of 5.2% in 2002, 9.6% in 2003, and an astonishing 12.1% in 2004; but in 2005, it fell sharply to only an estimated 2.4%. In 2007, the growth rate rebounded to 7.3% as a result of high steel prices, which is Ukraine's main export, and rising domestic consumption as a result of growing pensions and wages. Inflation started growing again after 2002, reaching 12% in 2004 and remaining high at 12.8% in 2007. Reports from 2010 show inflation to have dropped off a bit to 9.8%, while unemployment was reported at 8.4%.

Ukraine's economic dynamism was driven mainly by exports. The most effective growth engines in 2003–04 were manufactured goods, construction, oil and gas transport, services, private consumption, and government spending. The end of 2004 saw a hampering of this trend as three rounds of presidential elections and weeks of protesting throughout the country (the Orange Revolution), took their toll on the Ukrainian economy. The newly elected president has openly stated that Ukraine will take a clear course towards an open market economy, and that the mid-term goal is EU integration.

Ukraine became the 152nd member of the WTO in 2008 and looks to expand its economy further as it establishes itself as a regional economic superpower.

Ukraine's steel sector is robust and vital to the country's economy. Steel products account for some 40% of Ukraine's exports. When the 2008 global recession hit and global construction slowed dramatically, demand for Ukrainian steel plummeted, and Ukraine's economy took a significant hit. In response, the Ukrainian government implemented a series of significant subsidies to that sector, ordering state-owned companies to reduce their tariffs to steel companies. The International Monetary Fund (IMF) strongly criticized this move and threatened to withhold funding if the subsidies were not ended. In July 2010, Ukraine announced that it would scrap the subsidies, which had totaled roughly $190 million since November 2008.

20 INCOME

The CIA estimated that in 2010 the GDP of Ukraine was $305.2 billion, which was 40th worldwide. GDP is defined as the value of all final goods and services produced within a nation in a given year and computed on the basis of purchasing power parity (PPP) rather than value as measured on the basis of the rate of the exchange based on current dollars. An estimated breakdown of Ukraine's economy reported that agriculture accounted for 9.8%

of GDP, industry 32.3%, and services 57.9%. As of 2010, Ukraine's per capita GDP was estimated at $6,700, while the GDP annual growth rate was 4.2%. Ukraine's average inflation rate was listed at 9.8%.

The World Bank reported that remittances from citizens living abroad totaled $5.1 billion or about $112 per capita and accounted for approximately 1.7% of GDP. Further reports show that in 2009, household consumption in Ukraine totaled $74.3 billion or about $1,647 per capita, measured in current US dollars rather than PPP. Household consumption includes expenditures of individuals, households, and nongovernmental organizations on goods and services, excluding the purchases of dwellings. It was estimated that household consumption was growing at an average annual rate of 14.2%.

A 2011 study by the World Bank reported that actual individual consumption in Ukraine was 69.5% of GDP and accounted for 0.59% of world consumption. By comparison, the United States accounted for 25.44% of world individual consumption. The World Bank also estimated that 26% of Ukraine's GDP was spent on food and beverages, 8.5% on housing and household furnishings, 3.0% on clothes, 6.1% on health, 7.6% on transportation, 2.6% on communications, 3.7% on recreation, 1.9% on restaurants and hotels, and 3.4% on miscellaneous goods and services and purchases from abroad.

In 2007, the World Bank estimated that Ukraine, with 0.77% of the world's population, accounted for 0.48% of world GDP. By comparison, the United States, with 4.85% of the world's population, accounted for 22.51% of world GDP. In 2009, it was reported that approximately 35% of the population subsisted on an income below the poverty line established by Ukraine's government.

21 LABOR

As of 2010, Ukraine had a total labor force of 22.02 million people. Within that labor force, CIA estimates in 2008 noted that 15.8% were employed in agriculture, 18.5% in industry, and 65.7% in the service sector.

Labor unions have played an important role in post-Soviet Ukraine. Upon independence in 1991, the Federation of Independent Trade Unions of Ukraine was founded which then began to operate independently from the government. They were later renamed simply the Federation of Trade Unions (FPU). Since that time, many independent unions have been formed, providing an alternative to the official unions in most sectors of the economy. Estimates placed independent union membership at three million. Membership in the FPU was thought to be around 14 million. The right to strike is protected, except for the military, police, and continuing process plants.

The minimum employment age is 17, although children aged 15 to 17 can be employed by businesses with governmental permission. However, child labor remains a problem. In 2009, increases brought the minimum wage to approximately $77 per month. The maximum workweek is set at 40 hours; the law also provides for a minimum of 24 days of vacation per year. Ukraine's laws set forth occupational health and safety standards, but these are frequently ignored in practice and are not sufficiently enforced by the government.

22 AGRICULTURE

As in other former Soviet republics, total agricultural production dramatically declined after 1990. The average annual decline during 1990–2000 was 5.8%. By 1999, the agricultural sector was only producing 47% as much as it had during 1989–91. However, during 2002–04, crop production was 12.8% higher than during 1999–2001. An estimated 55% of the total land in Ukraine is arable or under permanent crops, and the country's major crops include grain, sugar beets, sunflower seeds, and vegetables. Cereal production in 2009 amounted to 45.4 million tons, fruit production 2 million tons, and vegetable production 9 million tons.

Foreign investment in agriculture began to increase in the late 2000s, with developers investing millions of dollars in new machinery and improvements to infrastructure. Although the new developments were welcomed by many farmers, some fear that foreign land-grabs will be detrimental to the nation's own agricultural needs. Most Ukrainian farms consist of small, family-owned plots. Foreign investors, such as Landkom from the United Kingdom, have negotiated lease deals to consolidate many small farms into larger enterprises. The state-of-the art technology that is implemented to make the farms more productive is viewed as a step forward by many in the agricultural sector, but critics believe that investors should be called in as backers for Ukrainian farmers, not as the primary owners of foreign enterprises.

Ukraine's steppe region in the south is possibly the most fertile region in the world. Ukraine's famous humus-rich black soil accounts for one-third of the world's black soil and holds great potential for agricultural production. However, the soil is rapidly losing its fertility due to improper land and crop management. Ukraine typically produced over half of the sugar beets and one-fifth of all grains grown for the former USSR. In addition, two of the largest vegetable-oil research centers in the world are at Odessa and Zaporizhzhya. Agroindustry accounts for one-third of agricultural employment. To some extent, however, agro-industrial development has been hampered by the deteriorating environment as well as a shortage of investment funds due to the aftermath of the nuclear power plant disaster at Chernobyl. According to estimates, nearly 60,000 hectares (148,250 acres) of arable land in the Chernobyl vicinity are now unavailable for cultivation.

Out of 33 million hectares (81.5 million acres) of total arable land, more than 17 million hectares (42 million acres) are depleted, 10 million hectares (24.7 million acres) are eroded, and another 10 million have excessive acidity. Furthermore, 17% of arable land is located in areas where there is risk of drought.

23 ANIMAL HUSBANDRY

Between 1990 and 2000, livestock production in Ukraine declined by 50%. Lack of finances for buying fuel pushed farmers in the public sector to sell their cattle abroad, mostly to Asian buyers. During 2002–04, livestock production was up 7.2% compared to the period 1999–2001. There are several factors involved in Ukraine's declining meat production: decentralization of meat processing with greater use of processing facilities at the farms; lack of cheap credits to buy animals; and antiquated meat process-

ing equipment. Prior to 2009, nearly 14% of Ukraine's total land area was composed of permanent pasture or meadowland.

In 2009, however, the UN Food and Agriculture Organization (FAO) reported that Ukraine dedicated some 7.9 million hectares (19.6 million acres) strictly for the purpose of permanent pasture and meadowland. During that year, the country tended 158.8 million chickens, 5.1 million head of cattle, and 6.5 million pigs. The production from these animals amounted to 525,676 tons of beef and veal, 706,595 tons of pork, 806,447 tons of poultry, 674,540 tons of eggs, and 8 million tons of milk. Ukraine also produced 67,000 tons of cattle hide and 4,111 tons of raw wool.

24 FISHING

The fishing industry in Ukraine is centered mainly on the Sea of Azov and Black Sea. As of 2008, the UN FAO reported that Ukraine had 197 decked commercial fishing boats and that the annual capture from these boats was totaled at 195,449 tons. The export value of seafood was reported at an estimated $23.47 million.

25 FORESTRY

Approximately 17% of Ukraine is covered by forest. While the radioactive contamination of forestland from the 1986 Chernobyl disaster is well-known, there is also widespread land, water, and air pollution from toxic wastes, which has also adversely affected timberlands. In 2009, the UN FAO estimated roundwood production at 7.36 million cu m (260.1 million cu ft). The value of all forest products, including roundwood, totaled $980.6 million.

26 MINING

In 2009, mining and quarrying accounted for 3.87% of GDP. Ukraine is one of the world's leading producers of iron ore, as well as a major world producer of ferroalloys, ilmenite, steel, and manganese ore (with 75% of the former Soviet Union's reserves). The mining and metallurgical industry employed 500,000 persons; 270,000 worked in ironmaking, steelmaking, and ferroalloys enterprises. Ferrous and nonferrous metals were Ukraine's top export commodities in 2009, valued at $12.2 billion, or 30.7% of total exports. Fuel and petroleum products were the country's second-leading export commodities.

Production outputs for 2009 included marketable iron ore (gross weight), 66.4 million metric tons; manganese, mined in the Nikopol' and Bol'shoy Tokmak basins (metal content), 932,000 metric tons; rock salt, 5.39 million metric tons (estimated); and potash (at the Stebnik and Kalush mines), 12,000 metric tons. In addition, Ukraine produced alumina, mercury, titanium (ilmenite and rutile concentrates), zirconium (fifth in the world), cement, clays (bentonite and kaolin), graphite, nitrogen, and sulfur (from the Rozdol and Yavoriv deposits). Iron ore production, concentrated at seven mining and beneficiation complexes in the Krivyy Rih (Krivoy Rog) Basin, and at the Poltavskiy complex, fell by 50% from 1990 through 1995. Explored iron ore reserves totaled 33 billion tons, including 28 billion tons of industrial reserves; total capacity was 108.5 million tons per year. Manganese reserves totaled 2.2 billion tons, and annual capacity was 6 million tons. No antimony, cadmium lead, nickel, tin, zinc, zircon, dolomite, limestone fluxes, quartz, soda ash, talc, or uranium was mined in the past several years, Ukraine having sharply reduced or ceased producing a number of these commodities as a result of the large reduction in demand following the breakup of the Soviet Union.

At the end of the 1980s, Ukraine mined 5% of the world's output of mineral products. After the breakup of the Soviet Union, production fell precipitously, and recovery of the mining sector was considered critical for the country's economic recovery. A 1999 law provided tax benefits for mining and metal industry firms for two and a half years. By 2000, the privatization of small-scale enterprises was virtually completed. The mining industry was a major source of waste, having accumulated 30 billion tons of mineral wastes.

27 ENERGY AND POWER

The World Bank reported in 2008 that Ukraine produced 192.5 billion kWh of electricity and consumed 163.5 billion kWh, or 3,622 kWh per capita. Roughly 82% of energy came from fossil fuels, while 18% came from alternative fuels.

Though the country has only modest reserves of oil and natural gas, it has more robust reserves of coal.

Of the oil reserves located in Ukraine, most are in the eastern Dnieper-Donetsk basin. As of 1 January 2011, the country had proven oil reserves estimated at 395 million barrels, according to the CIA. Estimates from 2009–2010 place oil production in Ukraine at approximately 82,000 barrels per day, which is far less than the 296,000 barrels per day the country consumed. Per capita oil consumption, according to a World Bank 2008 report, was 2,943 kg. Because of this, Ukraine imported an estimated 301,900 barrels per day. Production has dipped slightly since 2004 by approximately 4,000 barrels per day, and consumption has dropped from 422,000 barrels per day since the same period. Imported oil came primarily from Russia.

Ukraine, as of 1 January 2011, had proven natural gas reserves estimated at 1.104 billion cu m, according to the CIA. In 2009, natural gas production was estimated at 20.26 billion cu m, with consumption that year estimated at 44.16 billion cu m. As a result, Ukraine has had to resort to imports to make up the difference. In 2009, net imports of natural gas were estimated at 26.7 billion cu m. Turkmenistan became Ukraine's primary source for natural gas imports, following an agreement signed in 2001 that calls for 8.8 trillion cu ft per year to be provided from 2002 to 2006. To reach the European market, Russian natural gas and oil often flows through Ukraine as well, increasing the country's strategic importance.

According to 2009 reports, Ukraine's coal production was an estimated 60.6 million short tons, which ranked 16 worldwide. This number includes anthracite, bituminous, and lignite. Coal consumption, however, was estimated at close to 64 million short tons, making Ukraine a net importer of coal. Most of the country's coal comes from the eastern region in the Donetsk/Donbas basin.

28 INDUSTRY

Ukraine, with strong scientific and technological sectors, is a major producer of heavy machinery and industrial equipment for sectors including mining, steelmaking, and chemicals. Significant products also include non-numerically controlled machine tools, large electrical transformers, and agricultural machinery. Ukraine's industries are important suppliers of products—including automobiles, clothing, foodstuffs, timber, and paper—to oth-

er former Soviet republics. The country also retains much of the industry associated with the space program of the former USSR. Industrial sectors slated for growth in the early 2000s were food processing and packing, textiles, woodworking, furniture and building materials, automotive parts, pharmaceuticals, medical equipment, and aerospace. The construction sector experienced growth during that period; construction spending grew by 9% in the first quarter of 2001. Ukraine produced 31,824 automobiles in 2001 and 1,417 heavy trucks in 2000, a 74% increase over 1999.

Numbers have dipped since 2004 when industry accounted for 45.1% of the GDP and was represented by 32% of the labor force. Reports from 2010 showed 33.6% of GDP with the labor force represented by 18.5%. Industrial production growth also saw a decrease from 16.5% in 2004 to 11.2% in 2010. The decrease in production growth can perhaps be attributed to the fact that several industrial sectors in Ukraine saw rapid growth during the 2004 year. These included machine building (which registered a 30.7% growth as opposed to the previous year), construction (23.8%), wood processing, paper and printing (26%), processing industry (15.5%), and light industry (14%).

29 SCIENCE AND TECHNOLOGY

Patent applications in science and technology as of 2009, according to the World Bank, totaled 2,434 in Ukraine. Public financing of science was 0.85% of GDP. The Ukrainian Academy of Sciences, founded in 1919, has sections of physical engineering and mathematical sciences, and chemical engineering and biological sciences; it has 66 scientific and technical research institutes attached to it. The Ukrainian Academy of Agrarian Sciences has 13 research institutes, and the Ukrainian Academy of Medical Sciences has six research institutes. All three academies are headquartered in Kiev. A botanical museum is located in Kiev. Ukraine has 92 universities, polytechnics, and institutes that offer courses in basic and applied sciences. In 1987–97, science and engineering students accounted for 42% of university enrollment. In 2002, research and development (R&D) expenditures totaled $2,805.687 million, or 1.18% of GDP. Of that amount, government provided the largest portion at 37.4%, followed by the business sector at 33.4%, foreign sources at 26.2%, higher education and private nonprofit organizations at 0.4% each, with 2.3% listed as undistributed. In that same year, there were 1,749 scientists and engineers, and 456 technicians engaged in R&D per million people. High technology exports in 2002 were valued at $572 million, accounting for 5% of the country's manufactured exports.

30 DOMESTIC TRADE

As of 2002, nearly all of the previously state-owned retail establishments have been privatized. Chain stores, supermarkets, and brand-name specialty stores, many of which are owned by Ukrainians, have become more common in major cities. Department stores, smaller grocery and specialty stores, and bazaars are more common, since prices at these establishments are more in line with lower and middle-class spending capabilities. Retail superstore chains have also begun to appear in Ukraine. These chains tend to specialize in consumer electronics or food. Retailers in Ukraine tend to target either rich or poor customers, leaving the growing number of middle class consumers to choose between open markets or fashion boutiques. Discount superstores have

Principal Trading Partners – Ukraine (2010)

(In millions of US dollars)

Country	Total	Exports	Imports	Balance
World	112,389.0	51,478.0	60,911.0	-9,433.0
Russia	35,630.0	13,432.0	22,198.0	-8,766.0
Germany	6,102.0	1,499.0	4,603.0	-3,104.0
China	6,017.0	1,317.0	4,700.0	-3,383.0
Poland	4,576.0	1,787.0	2,789.0	-1,002.0
Belarus	4,467.0	1,899.0	2,568.0	-669.0
Turkey	4,325.0	3,027.0	1,298.0	1,729.0
Italy	3,803.0	2,413.0	1,390.0	1,023.0
United States	2,585.0	812.0	1,773.0	-961.0
India	2,107.0	1,426.0	681.0	745.0
Hungary	2,075.0	860.0	1,215.0	-355.0

(…) data not available or not significant.

(n.s.) not specified.

SOURCE: *2011 Direction of Trade Statistics Yearbook,* New York: United Nations, 2011.

Balance of Payments – Ukraine (2010)

(In millions of US dollars)

Current Account		**-3,018.0**
Balance on goods	-8,388.0	
Imports	-60,579.0	
Exports	52,191.0	
Balance on services	4,404.0	
Balance on income	-2,009.0	
Current transfers	2,975.0	
Capital Account		**187.0**
Financial Account		**6,508.0**
Direct investment abroad	-736.0	
Direct investment in Ukraine	6,495.0	
Portfolio investment assets	-17.0	
Portfolio investment liabilities	4,334.0	
Financial derivatives	…	
Other investment assets	-10,748.0	
Other investment liabilities	7,180.0	
Net Errors and Omissions		**1,368.0**
Reserves and Related Items		**-5,045.0**

(…) data not available or not significant.

SOURCE: *Balance of Payment Statistics Yearbook 2011,* Washington, DC: International Monetary Fund, 2011.

31 FOREIGN TRADE

Ukraine exports products to 140 countries of the world. Its main export products are ferrous metals and metal products, engines, transport and mechanical equipment, chemicals, and vehicles. Top import items include mineral products, automobiles, transportation equipment, chemicals, and textiles. Ukraine relies heavily on trade, particularly with the other former Soviet republics, although not nearly as much as it had before the breakup. Inter-republic trade accounted for 73% of its total imports in 1988 and 85% of its total exports.

In 1991–92, inter-republic trade contracted severely, partly due to a breakdown in payment mechanisms, and trade with other countries dropped as well. Much of Ukraine's foreign trade has been carried out in the context of intergovernmental agreements. However, the government has since stabilized its foreign trade. In 2000, total imports were valued at $14 billion, and total exports at $14.6 billion. Ukraine has had extensive trade ties with China since 1993.

Reports from 2008 indicate that Ukraine imported $53.54 billion worth of goods and services while exporting $49.71 billion worth of the same. Ukraine's major import partners in 2009 were Russia, 29.1%; Germany, 8.5%; China, 6%; Poland, 4.8%; and Kazakhstan, 4.5%. Its major export partners were Russia, 21.4%; and Turkey, 5.4%.

In May 2009, Ukraine signed an agreement with the European Union (EU) as part of a new Eastern Partnership Initiative (EPI), designed to establish greater economic ties with EU members without the prospect of EU membership. Through the EPI, the EU promises economic aid and technical and security consultations in return for a commitment to democratic reform. The EU invitation to sign the partnership agreement was extended to five other former Soviet states, with an ultimate goal of establishing free trade areas within the region.

32 BALANCE OF PAYMENTS

The financial crisis of 1998 caused a large outflow of capital, and reserves fell to less than a third of their level in 1997. Due to a major exchange rate adjustment that made Ukrainian products more competitive in both external and internal markets, reserves recovered somewhat in 1999. From June 2000 to July 2001, reserves increased dramatically, back to pre-1998 levels. This growth is surprising in light of the fact that the country received almost no external funding since 1998, when foreign investors began avoiding Ukraine. Following the 1998 devaluation of the hryvnia, trade surpluses drove the growth in reserves, and the balance of payments situation improved. Reserve growth also improved due to Ukraine's default on its sovereign debt. As of the early 2000s, Ukraine's balance of payments position was expected to be heavily influenced by its trade with Russia.

In 2010, Ukraine had a foreign trade deficit of $2 billion, amounting to 5.6% of GDP. The CIA reported that, in 2010, Ukraine exported an approximated $52.19 billion worth of goods, up from $40.39 billion the year previous. Estimates of imports from 2010 totaled $60.9 billion, up from $44.7 billion the year previous.

Ukraine's primary exports include goods such as metals, fuel and petroleum products, chemicals, mechanical transport equip-

yet to appear. About 40–60% of consumer goods are domestically produced. There are some successful foreign franchises, but the practice of franchising has not become widespread.

Electronic commerce (e-commerce) in Ukraine is basically viewed by businesses and customers as a form of entertainment rather than a serious business model. As a result, the business-to-business and business-to-consumer e-commerce segments are both in their initial developmental phases. Most Ukrainian Internet shops are essentially advertising sites or price lists that offer the option of placing an order for a product or service that would be delivered upon receipt of a cash payment, a bank transfer, or a credit or debit card payment. As of June 2010, there were nearly 15.3 million Internet users in Ukraine.

A value-added tax (VAT) of 20% applies to most goods and services. Normal business hours are usually from 9 a.m. to 6 p.m.

ment, and food products. Their major trade partners include Russia, Turkey, and Italy. These three countries received nearly 35% of all of Ukraine's exports in 2010.

The country's imports primarily include energy, machinery and equipment, and chemicals. Russia is Ukraine's largest import partner providing roughly 34% of the goods entering the country. Russia is followed by China, Germany, Poland, and Belarus as Ukraine's largest import partners.

33 BANKING AND SECURITIES

The National Bank of Ukraine (NBU) is the country's national bank and was established in June 1991. It has since assumed the function of a central bank. The commercial banking sector is dominated by the big five banks of Prominvest Bank, Ukrania, Ukreximbank, Eximbank and Oshadbank. As of 2009 there were 3.3 commercial banks per 100,000 inhabitants.

The NBU implements monetary control through reserve requirements and the interest rates it charges banks on funds transferred from the state savings bank. Before November 1992, the NBU was able to obtain additional rubles by running a surplus on transactions with other republics in the ruble zone. However, with inflation accelerating since early 1991, the supply of rubles proved insufficient to meet the economy's needs, and Ukraine consequently resorted to the use of coupons. The resulting rise in inflation was the main factor behind Ukraine's enforced departure from the ruble zone in November 1992.

Ukraine's money market rate, the rate at which financial institutions lend to one another in the short term, has seen dramatic fluctuation since 2007. Reported at 2.72% that year, the rates for 2008 and 2009 were reported at 13.7% and 12.6%, respectively. The 2009 number has dropped, however, and the money market rate in 2010 was 3.4%. The discount rate, the interest rate at which the central bank lends to financial institutions in the short term, was 7.75% in 2010. As of September 2011, the nation's gold bullion deposits totaled 0.896 million fine troy ounces.

The Law on Securities and the Stock Exchange came into effect in January 1992. There are seven stock exchanges and seven commodities exchanges, although these are more like the auction houses that sprang up after the collapse of the Soviet Union in 1991 as conduits for goods rather than the securities exchanges found in the West. Capital markets are undeveloped even by the standards of countries such as Russia. The stock market in Ukraine is comprised of two main trading entities, the Ukrainian Stock Exchange (USE) and the PFTS, or, First Stock Trade System. These two bodies were established in 2008 and 2006, respectively. The larger of the two, the PFTS, lists approximately 220 companies as of 2011. Their daily trading volume is between $30 and $60 million with a market capitalization of around $140 billion.

34 INSURANCE

Among the insurance companies operating in Ukraine in 1997 were Asko-Kiev Central Insurance Co.; Factotum Joint-Stock Insurance Co., First International Insurance Group; Ometa-Inster Joint-Stock Insurance Co.; Skide Insurance Co.; and Slavia. Beginning in August 1998, the Ukrainian government required that foreign visitors purchase mandatory "emergency medical insurance" from the Ukrainian State Insurance Company. In addition, personal accident insurance is required for all passengers on public

Public Finance – Ukraine (2009)

(In millions of hryvnias, central government figures)

Revenue and Grants	**324,236**	**100.0%**
Tax revenue	149,888	46.2%
Social contributions	118,802	36.6%
Grants	8,446	2.6%
Other revenue	47,101	14.5%
Expenditures	**376,492**	**100.0%**
General public services	87,031	23.1%
Defense	10,463	2.8%
Public order and safety	21,560	5.7%
Economic affairs	34,128	9.1%
Environmental protection	1,529	0.4%
Housing and community amenities	412	0.1%
Health	9,857	2.6%
Recreational, culture, and religion	3,409	0.9%
Education	23,808	6.3%
Social protection	184,295	49.0%

(…) data not available or not significant.

SOURCE: *Government Finance Statistics Yearbook 2010*, Washington, DC: International Monetary Fund, 2010.

transportation. Foreign shareholders in insurance companies may not exceed 49%. In 2003, the value of all direct insurance premiums written totaled $1.712 billion, of which non-life premiums accounted for $1.699 billion. In that same year, Lemma was the top non-life insurer, with gross written non-life premiums for direct business only of $124.8 million, while Grawe Ukraina was the country's leading life insurer, with gross written life insurance premiums of $4.8 million.

35 PUBLIC FINANCE

Ukraine has displayed positive growth in recent years, but long-term growth will require certain market reforms. The economy is burdened by excessive government regulation, and major sectors such as energy and telecommunications are yet to be privatized. Corporate governance is weak, and corruption is rampant. In the early 2000s, the government sought ways to reform the tax code to eliminate corruption and legitimize economic activity. Ukraine receives aid from the IMF, although the relationship between those two entities has not always been successful; Ukraine has had problems adhering to IMF monetary conditions.

The CIA estimated that, in 2010, Ukraine's central government took in revenues of approximately $39.62 billion and had expenditures of $46.79 billion. Revenues minus expenditures totaled approximately -$7.1 billion. Public debt in 2010 amounted to 40.1% of GDP up from 34.7% in 2009. Total external debt was $99.47 billion, an increase from $93.15 billion reported the year previous. This debt represented 38.4% of GDP.

36 TAXATION

According to a 2010 estimate, taxes and other revenues in Ukraine comprise 29% of the GDP.

The Ukrainian Parliament adopted a new tax code in 2010, which became effective 1 January. As of 2011, the standard corporate tax rate was 25%, although preferential rates are available for special economic zones. Capital gains for companies are taxed at the corporate rate. Withholding taxes on income from royalties and interest is 15%. Companies distributing dividends to residents and nonresidents are required to pay a 25% advance tax on the dividends. The tax can then be credited against the company's profits.

Personal income tax ranges from 0% on income such as that received as inheritance or the sale of a house all the way up to 30% on income from prizes won or that paid to nonresidents. The standard tax rate on salary income is 15%. Salary income of over 10 times the minimum is subject to an increased rate of 17%. Dividends, interest, and royalties received by nonresident individuals are subject to a 15% withholding tax.

The Ukraine's main indirect tax is its value-added tax (VAT), with a standard rate of 20%. A 0% VAT rate applies to exports and international transportation services. Some medicines, baby food, educational, medical and insurance services, and the sale of land are also exempt.

37 CUSTOMS AND DUTIES

Though few goods are subject to export duties in Ukraine, import licenses are required for all foreign trade activities. Ukraine has signed trade agreements with the United States, Russia, Iran, Turkmenistan, the United Arab Emirates, and several other former Soviet republics. As of 2011, all imported goods are subjected to customs fees, import duties of up to 200%, excise taxes up to 300% and a 20% value-added tax. Tariffs on imports range from 0–20%, with those on automobiles being the highest. Preferential tariffs are given to developing countries, and privileged tariffs are given to countries that have trade agreements with Ukraine. The number of categories of goods eligible for excise tax was reduced from 20 to 5: alcohol, automobiles, jewelry, oil products, and tobacco.

38 FOREIGN INVESTMENT

Among the transitional economies of Eastern Europe, nowhere has the gap between economic potential and economic performance been wider than in Ukraine, and nowhere has the gap been more glaring than in foreign investment statistics. By 2000, total foreign direct investment (FDI) in Ukraine was still less than $1 billion, compared with $9.3 billion that had flowed into Poland and $2.7 billion into Hungary during the same period.

Independence was first greeted by a rush of inward investment. The number of joint ventures operating in Ukraine rose from 76 in October 1990 to 189 in October 1991. Following the enactment in March 1992 of a more favorable foreign investment law, joint ventures jumped to 1,400 early in 1993. Most of these ventures were in industry, with a few engaged in foreign trade. The government's 1993 economic plan included tax incentives and other benefits for investors in specific areas including agro-industrial enterprises, energy, and production of consumer goods. However, by 1996 and 1997, rampant official graft and corruption were crippling foreign investment. Several significant multinational corporations withdrew from Ukraine after government decrees were issued that steered business to state-owned firms in which government officials were stakeholders. This action occurred despite President Kuchma's pledge to battle corruption and the Foreign Investment Law of 1996, which purported to put foreign investors on an equal footing with Ukrainian nationals. The government had declared a need for $40 billion in foreign investment, but only $2.8 billion was invested between 1992 and 1998.

In 1997, the law "On Special (Free) Economic Zones" was adopted, establishing three types of special investment zones: free economic zones (FEZs), territories with a special investment regime (SEZs), and territories of priority development (TPDs). As of 2002, there were 9 TPDs and 11 FEZs and SEZs. In 2002, the special zones attracted investment totaling $909 million, both domestic and foreign, but pressure has been brought by the IMF to either eliminate the special zones or curb their tax and regulatory exemptions.

Annual foreign direct investment (FDI) inflow was $496 million in 1999 in the wake of the Russian financial crisis. Contrary to the worldwide trend of reduced FDI flow after the 11 September 2001 terrorist attacks, however, Ukraine had its best year since independence in 2001 and saw steady increases thereafter, surpassing the $1 billion mark in 2003.

In 2004, Ukraine was a much more attractive market for foreign investments, receiving $1.7 billion of direct FDI—an increase of 22% from the previous year. Most of this investment went to production machinery and equipment, with food processing, agricultural processing, machine building, coal, oil and gas, and light industry the other important recipients of foreign funds. This growth however was well under the potential of the Ukrainian market, especially if one considers that in the same year, its neighbor, Romania, received over 5 billion in direct FDI. At the end of 2004, the level of foreign investment since 1992 rose to 7.7 billion—10 times lower than the figure in Poland for the same time period. Major investors in 2004 included: Cyprus (14.1%), the United States (13.6%), the United Kingdom (10.4%), Germany (7.1%), the Netherlands (6.8%), Virgin Islands (6.1%), Russia (5.5%), Switzerland (4.9%), and Austria (4%).

After Ukraine's successful 2004 year, the FDI skyrocketed to $7.8 billion and continued to climb. FDI reached $9.8 billion in 2007 and peaked a year later at almost $11 billion. Though it dropped significantly in 2009 (to $4.6 billion), FDI was reported at approximately $6.5 billion in 2010.

39 ECONOMIC DEVELOPMENT

In 1993, Ukraine's parliament tentatively approved a new economic reform plan to stabilize the republic's economy, attract more capital from abroad, and lay the groundwork for a market economy. Measures proposed included stricter monetary and banking regulation and the elimination of monopolies in industries. A privatization program was underway in sectors including retail trade, services, the food industry, agriculture, and housing.

Since the election of President Kuchma in 1994, the government has implemented a far-reaching economic reform program. Almost all price and trade controls have been abolished in an effort to stabilize the new market economy. Privatization began in earnest in 1995, and a new convertible currency was adopted in 1996. In the 1990s, Ukraine continued to register negative growth. By the end of the 1990s, real GDP declined to 40% of its pre-independence level. In late 1998, the International Monetary Fund (IMF) loaned Ukraine another $2.2 billion after Ukraine promised to exercise more fiscal discipline.

The economy started to grow in 2000; GDP growth in 2002 was over 4.5%. Small- and medium-sized enterprises were privatized by 2002, but the energy and telecommunications sectors had yet to be privatized. The government passed a foreign investment law, but bureaucratic hurdles, poor corporate governance, corruption, and the weak enforcement of contract law by courts all hampered investment. At the end of October 2002, total foreign direct investment into the country amounted to around $4.9 billion, which was one of the lowest figures in the region. In 2002, land reforms were ongoing, supporting growth in the agricultural sector.

The economy took off in 2003 and 2004 and was deemed one of the most dynamic in Europe (the GDP growth rate in 2004 was 12.1%). The 2004 election of Viktor Yushchenko and the political turmoil that preceded it hampered this expansive pulse. The new president stated however that the country is on the right path and that the economy will start booming again. Since then, the economy has slowed. By 2008, GDP growth rate had fallen to 1.9% and the following year witnessed a staggering fall to -14.8%. The economy rebounded in 2010 posting a GDP growth rate of 4.2%

Ukraine boasts a highly qualified work force, cheap labor and competitive costs, a relatively well-developed transportation and communications infrastructure, and a strategic geographic location. In addition, the large market—an estimated 45.6 million people as of 2011—makes it a prime location for foreign investment.

40 SOCIAL DEVELOPMENT

The social security system provides all employees with old age, disability, and survivor's pensions. The program is funded primarily from employer contributions, with a small contribution from employees and government subsidies as needed. Retirement is normally at age 60 for men and 55 for women, although this is reduced by five years for those engaged in arduous work and for mothers with five or more children. There is a dual system of medical benefits. Cash benefits for sickness are provided for employed people, while a universal medical care system exists for all residents. Maternity benefits of 100% of wages for 70 days before and 56 days after the expected date of childbirth are payable to all employed women. Workers' compensation and unemployment benefits are also provided. Special provisions exist for Chernobyl victims. Family allowances are provided to families with large numbers of children.

The law provides women with the same employment rights as men, although they rarely attain high-level managerial or political positions. Women who are employed mostly work in low-paying jobs or in industries that have trouble paying their employees on time. Help wanted ads often specify gender. Violence against women, domestic abuse, and sexual harassment in the workplace are pervasive.

Human rights violations continue. Harassment of racial minorities and religious intolerance are increasing problems. Anti-Semitic incidents and societal discrimination of ethnic minorities are commonplace. The Roma population is subject to abuse by police and general intolerance by the public. Prisoners are mistreated by authorities and live in substandard conditions. The government interferes with freedom of the press and with the electoral process.

41 HEALTH

Deterioration of the economy and declining living standards have had a negative impact on birth and mortality rates and women's and children's health standards need much improvement. Although safe water was available to 96.5%, proper sanitation was available to only 70% of the urban population and 8% of the rural population in the mid-1990s. Poor nutrition is another major problem in Ukraine, and a shortage of basic supplies exacerbates the health care situation.

Ukraine spent 6.8% of its GDP on healthcare in 2009, which amounted to $180 per person. The country has established 156 independent children's hospitals as well as 6,500 outpatient policlinical institutions. There were an estimated 31 physicians, 85 nurses and midwives, and 87 hospital beds per 10,000 people in Ukraine.

Life expectancy in Ukraine, according to a 2011 CIA report, was reported at 69 years. The same report showed a fertility rate of 1.5 while infant mortality was estimated at 13 deaths per 1,000 live births. A 2008 World Bank report showed maternal mortality rates in Ukraine to be 26 per 100,000 births. Immunization rates for children up to one year old were tuberculosis, 95%; diphtheria, pertussis, and tetanus, 96%; polio, 97%; and measles, 94%.

The leading causes of death were cardiovascular and respiratory diseases, cancer, traumas, and accidents. The HIV/AIDS adult prevalence rate was 1.1% in 2009. The incidence of tuberculosis was 101 per 100,000 people in 2007.

The likelihood of dying after age 65 of heart disease in Ukraine was below the average for medium human development as defined by the World Bank.

42 HOUSING

Before 1994, most housing and utility costs were covered by the government through a policy that was causing major federal debt. Through an IMF-approved program of economic reforms put in place in October 1994, residents were asked to contribute a much greater amount toward their own rent and utilities. Unfortunately, many households were unable to do so. In 1995, the government put in place a subsidy program to assist low-income families in meeting rising housing costs, but funding for housing continues to be a problem.

Though a census was to be carried out in Ukraine during the 2011 year, it was postponed until 2012. In the 2001 census, the first since 1989, there were 18,200,567 households counted representing 47,726,518 people. As of January 2011, that number fell to an estimated 45,668,028 people. Of this number, 31,359,194 people were identified as living in urban areas, while the remainder were identified as living in rural areas. As of the 2001 census about 44% of all Ukrainians lived in individual houses; another 44.6% lived in separate apartment units.

43 EDUCATION

Most schools in Ukraine are state-run, and education is compulsory for nine years, with students usually beginning at age six or seven. These compulsory years of education include four years of elementary school and five years of lower secondary school. Students may continue in general secondary schools, offering two- or three-year courses of study, or a specialized education secondary program of about three years. Vocational programs of four or five years are also available at the secondary level. While Ukrainian is the most commonly taught language and medium of instruction, other languages, such as Russian, Hungarian, Polish, Moldovan, or Crimean-Tatar, are offered based on the ethnic composition of the particular school district. The academic year runs from September to June.

There are over 900 colleges, technical schools, vocational schools, universities, and other institutes of higher education. The National University of Kyiv-Mohyla Academy, one of the oldest in eastern Europe, was originally founded in 1632. Other universities include Lviv University (1795), Kharkiv University (1804), Taras Shevchenko National University (1834), and Odessa University (1868).

In 2009, the World Bank estimated that 89% of age-eligible children in Ukraine were enrolled in primary school. Secondary enrollment for age-eligible children stood at 85%, while tertiary enrollment was estimated at 79%. Of those enrolled in tertiary education, there were 100 male students for every 125 female students. As of 2011, Ukraine's literacy rate, defined as anyone aged 15 years or older able to read and write, was 99.4%.

⁴⁴LIBRARIES AND MUSEUMS

The largest library in the country is the Vernadsky National Library of Ukraine in Kiev, which holds over 15 million items, including the collection of the Presidents of Ukraine, archive copies of Ukrainian printed documents from 1917, and the archives of the National Academy of Sciences of Ukraine. The National Parliamentary Library of Ukraine in Kiev holds 65,000 volumes. Also in Kiev, the National Library of Ukraine for Children has a collection of over 440,000 volumes. Other large collections include the V.G. Korolenko State Scientific Library with 6.7 million volumes and the libraries at Lviv Polytechnic University (3 million), Franko State University in Lviv (2.5 million), Shevchenko Kiev University (2.7 million), and Kiev Polytechnic Institute (2.5 million). There are reported to be about 21,857 public libraries operating in Ukraine with an overall stock of about 336.7 million books.

Located in Kiev are the Kiev State Museum of Russian Art, the Kiev State Museum of Ukrainian Art, the State Historical Museum, the Museum of Cultural Heritage, the National Museum of Medicine, the State Museum of Ukrainian Decorative Folk Art, and the Soros Center for Contemporary Art. There are also several small house museums in Kiev. There is a Museum of Fine Arts in Lugansk. Lviv houses the State Museum of Ethnography and Arts and Crafts and the Literary Museum of Ivan Franko. Odessa is home to the Odessa Museum of Fine Arts, the Museum of Literature, the Naval Museum, the Odessa Museum of Western and Oriental Art, the Odessa Archaeological Museum, and the Pushkin Museum.

⁴⁵MEDIA

Ukraine's telecommunications system is still overcoming the shortcomings of the ex-Soviet system it inherited at independence in December 1991. Telephone density continues to increase, but at a slow pace, while improvements are being made to the national trunk line system. However, the country's mobile cellular telephone system is expanding at a rapid pace. International service is provided by land-based and submarine fiber-optic cables, in addition to ground stations operated by the Intersputnik, Intelsat, and Inmarsat satellite systems. In 2009, the CIA reported some 13 million telephone landlines in Ukraine. In addition, mobile phone subscriptions averaged 120 per 100 people.

Most broadcast media is state-owned or controlled by political parties or other powerful business interests. In 2006, there were 647 television stations and 524 FM radio stations. While there are many privately owned radio and television stations, they are generally heavily influenced by the government and political parties. In 2010, Ukraine had close to 1.1 million Internet hosts, and Internet users numbered 33 per 100 citizens.

Prominent newspapers in 2010, with circulation numbers listed parenthetically, included *Donbass* (39,000), *Vechirniy Kyiv* (90,000), and *Vysokiy Zamok* (90,000). Though the constitution and a 1991 law provide for free speech and a free press, some journalists continue to practice self-censorship due to occasional pressures from the government.

⁴⁶ORGANIZATIONS

The Ukraine Chamber of Commerce and the Congress of Business Circles of Ukraine promote the commercial and business activities of the country to the rest of the world. Many of Ukraine's trade unions belong to the umbrella organization called the Federation of Independent Trade Unions. Professional associations are active in several different fields. There is an active Ukrainian Consumers' Association.

National cultural organizations include the Ukrainian Cultural Educational Organization and Flamenko, which promotes cultural exchange programs. National youth organizations include the Council of Ukrainian Students, the Ukrainian Fund of International Youth Cooperation, Junior Chamber, Ukrainian Girl Guides and Girl Scouts Association, the Compass Club, and YMCA/YWCA. There are several sports associations promoting amateur competition for athletes of all ages.

National social action organizations include the Ukrainian Center for Human Rights, the Ukrainian Environmental Association, the Ukrainian Legal Foundation, Freedom House (advocating the development of democratic institutions), The Children's Fund, and Zhinocha Hromada, an organization focused on encouraging women to be active in economic and community development. International organizations with national chapters include Caritas, UNICEF, Amnesty International, and the Red Cross.

⁴⁷TOURISM, TRAVEL, AND RECREATION

Kyiv (Kiev), Ukraine's capital and major cultural center, is known for its beautiful churches and golden-domed cathedrals, although much of its classic architecture was destroyed or obscured by Communist planners in the 1930s. The cathedral of St. Sophia, built in the 11th century, is one of the finest examples of Russo-Byzantine architecture. Another major tourist attraction is the Golden Gate, an 11th-century fortification restored in 1982. Lviv (formerly Lvov) offers architectural sights ranging from late-13th-century Russian to 16th-century Gothic structures.

According to the *Tourism Factbook*, published by the UN World Tourism Organization, there were approximately 20.8 million incoming tourists to Ukraine in 2009, who spent a total of $4.35 billion. Of those incoming tourists, 20.5 million were from Europe. The organization also reported a total of 77,610 hotel beds available in Ukraine, which had an occupancy rate of 33%. A valid passport is required for all travelers to enter Ukraine. Visas are not required for citizens of Japan, Canada, Switzerland, Liechtenstein, the United States, and the EU countries for stays of up to 90 days. To visit the nation, all other travelers need visas. Medical insurance that includes Ukraine coverage is required for all US citizens.

The estimated daily cost to visit Kyiv was $374. The cost of visiting other cities averaged $237.

⁴⁸ FAMOUS PERSONS

Leonid M. Kravchuk and Vitold P. Fokin were respectively the first president and prime minister of Ukraine. Leonid Brezhnev (Dneprodzershinsk, Ukraine, 1906–82) led the Soviet Union from 1966–82. Outstanding representatives of the culture and literature of Ukraine include poet Taras Shevchenko (1814–61) and the Jewish writer Sholom Aleichem (Solomon Rabinowitz, 1859–1916).

⁴⁹ DEPENDENCIES

Ukraine has no territories or colonies.

⁵⁰ BIBLIOGRAPHY

Dean, Martin. *Collaboration in the Holocaust: Crimes of the Local Police in Belorussia and Ukraine, 1941–44*. New York: St. Martin's Press, 2000.

Helbig, Adriana, Oksana Buranbaeva, and Vanja Mladineo. *Culture and Customs of Ukraine*. Westport, CT: Greenwood Press, 2009.

Kohut, Zenon E., Bohdan Y. Nebesio, and Myroslav Yurkevich. *Historical Dictionary of Ukraine*. Lanham, MD: Scarecrow, 2005.

Mandel, David. *Labour after Communism: Auto Workers and Their Unions in Russia, Ukraine, and Belarus*. New York: Black Rose Books, 2004.

McElrath, Karen, ed. *HIV and AIDS: A Global View*. Westport, CT: Greenwood Press, 2002.

Opello, Walter C. *European Politics*. Boulder, CO: Lynne Rienner Publishers, 2009.

Otfinoski, Steven. *Ukraine*. 2nd ed. New York: Facts On File, 2004.

Political Chronology of Europe. London: Europa, 2001.

Terterov, Marat, ed. *Doing Business with Ukraine*. Sterling, VA: Kogan Page, 2005.

Ukraine Investment and Business Guide: Strategic and Practical Information. Washington, DC: International Business Publications USA, 2012.

Yeltsin, Boris Nikolayevich. *The Struggle for Russia*. New York: Times Books, 1994.

UNITED KINGDOM

United Kingdom of Great Britain and Northern Ireland

CAPITAL: London

FLAG: The Union Jack, adopted in 1800, is a combination of the banners of England (St. George's flag: a red cross with extended horizontals on a white field), Scotland (St. Andrew's flag: a white saltire cross on a blue field), and Ireland (St. Patrick's flag: a red saltire cross on a white field). The arms of the saltire crosses do not meet at the center.

ANTHEM: *God Save the Queen.*

MONETARY UNIT: The pound sterling (£) is a paper currency of 100 pence. Before decimal coinage was introduced on 15 February 1971, the pound had been divided into 20 shillings, each shilling representing 12 pennies (p) or pence; some old-style coins are still in circulation. Under the new system, there are coins of 1, 2, 5, 10, 20, and 50 pence and 1 and 2 pounds, and notes of 5, 10, 20, and 50 pounds. £1 = US$1.5590 (or US$1 = £0.64) as of 2011.

WEIGHTS AND MEASURES: Although the traditional imperial system of weights and measures is still in use (sample units: of weight, the stone of 14 pounds is equivalent to 6.35 kilograms; of length, the yard is equivalent to 0.914 meter; of capacity, a bushel is equivalent to 36.37 liters), a changeover to the metric system was in progress as of 2011.

HOLIDAYS: New Year's Day, 1 January; Good Friday; Easter Monday (except Scotland); Late Summer Holiday, last Monday in August or 1st in September (except Scotland); Christmas, 25 December; and Boxing Day, 1st weekday after Christmas. Also observed in Scotland are bank holidays on 2 January and on the 1st Monday in August. Northern Ireland observes St. Patrick's Day, 17 March; and Orangeman's Day, 12 July, commemorating the Battle of the Boyne in 1690.

TIME: GMT.

¹LOCATION, SIZE, AND EXTENT

The United Kingdom is situated off the northwest coast of Europe between the Atlantic Ocean on the N and NW and the North Sea on the E, separated from the Continent by the Strait of Dover and the English Channel, 34 km (21 mi) wide at its narrowest point, and from the Irish Republic by the Irish Sea and St. George's Channel. Its total area of 244,820 sq km (94,526 sq mi) consists of the island of Great Britain—formed by England, 130,439 sq km (50,363 sq mi); Wales, 20,768 sq km (8,018 sq mi); and Scotland, 78,783 sq km (30,418 sq mi)—and Northern Ireland, 14,120 sq km (5,452 sq mi), on the island of Ireland, separated from Great Britain by the North Channel. Comparatively, the area occupied by the United Kingdom is slightly smaller than the state of Oregon.

There are also several island groups and hundreds of small single islands, most of them administratively part of the mainland units. The United Kingdom extends about 965 km (600 mi) N–S and about 485 km (300 mi) E–W. Its total boundary length is 12,789 km (7,947 mi), of which 12,429 km (7,723 mi) is coastline. The Isle of Man, 588 sq km (227 sq mi), and the Channel Islands, comprising Jersey, Guernsey, Alderney, and Sark, with a combined area of 194 sq km (75 sq mi), are not part of the United Kingdom but are dependencies of the crown. The 0° meridian of longitude passes through the old Royal Observatory, located at Greenwich in Greater London. The United Kingdom's capital city, London, is located in the southeast part of Great Britain.

²TOPOGRAPHY

England is divided into the hill regions of the north, west, and southwest and the rolling downs and low plains of the east and southeast. Running from east to west on the extreme north Scottish border are the Cheviot Hills. The Pennine Range runs north and south from the Scottish border to Derbyshire in central England. The rest of the countryside consists mainly of rich agricultural lands, occasional moors, and plains. South of the Pennines lie the Midlands (East and West), a plains region with low, rolling hills and fertile valleys. The eastern coast is low-lying, much of it less than 5 m (15 ft) above sea level; for centuries parts of it have been protected by embankments against inundation from gales and unusually high tides. Little of the south and east rises to higher than 300 m (1,000 ft).

The highest point in England is Scafell Pike (978 m/3,210 ft) in the famed Lake District of the northwest. The longest of the rivers flowing from the central highlands to the sea are the Severn (about 340 km/210 mi) in the west and the Thames (about 320 km/200 mi) in the southeast. Other rivers include the Humber, the Tees, the Tyne, and the Tweed in the east; the Avon and Exe in the south; and the Mersey in the west.

Scotland has three distinct topographical regions: the Northern Highlands, occupying almost the entire northern half of the country and containing the highest point in the British Isles, Ben Nevis (1,343 m/4,406 ft), as well as Loch Ness, site of a fabled "monster"; the Central Lowlands, with an average elevation of about 150 m (500 ft) and containing the valleys of the Tay, Forth, and Clyde rivers, as well as Loch Lomond, Scotland's largest lake; and the Southern Uplands, rising to their peak at Merrick (843 m/2,766 ft), with moorland cut by many valleys and rivers.

Wales is largely mountainous and bleak, with much of the land suitable only for pasture. The Cambrian Mountains occupy almost the entire area and include Wales's highest point, Mt. Snowdon (1,086 m/3,563 ft). There are narrow coastal plains in the south and west and small lowland areas in the north, including the valley of the Dee.

Northern Ireland consists mainly of low-lying plateaus and hills, generally about 150 to 180 m (500–600 ft) high. The Mourne Mountains in the southeast include Slieve Donard (852 m/2,796 ft), the highest point in Northern Ireland. In a central depression lies Lough Neagh, the largest lake in the United Kingdom.

The United Kingdom's long and rugged coastline, heavily indented, has towering cliffs and headlands and numerous bays and inlets, among them the deep and narrow lochs and the wide firths of Scotland. Many river estuaries serve as fine harbors.

3 CLIMATE

Despite its northern latitude, the United Kingdom generally enjoys a temperate climate, warmed by the North Atlantic Drift, a continuation of the Gulf Stream, and by southwest winds. Mean monthly temperatures range (north to south) from 3°C to 5°C (37–41°F) in winter and from 12°C to 16°C (54–61°F) in summer. The mean annual temperature in the west near sea level ranges from 8°C (46°F) in the Hebrides to 11°C (52°F) in the far southwest of England. Rarely do temperatures rise in summer to over 32°C (90°F) or drop in winter below -10°C (14°F).

Rainfall, averaging more than 100 cm (40 in) throughout the United Kingdom, is heaviest on the western and northern heights (over 380 cm/150 in), and lowest along the eastern and southeastern coasts. Fairly even distribution of rain throughout the year, together with the prevalence of mists and fogs, results in scanty sunshine, averaging from half an hour to two hours a day in winter and from five to eight hours in summer.

4 FLORA AND FAUNA

The World Resources Institute estimates that there are 1,623 plant species in the United Kingdom. With its mild climate and varied soils, the United Kingdom has a diverse pattern of natural vegetation. Originally, oak forests probably covered the lowland, except for the fens and marsh areas, while pine forests and patches of moorland covered the higher or sandy ground. Fairly extensive forests remain in east and north Scotland and in southeast England. Oak, elm, ash, and beech are the most common trees in England. Pine and birch are most common in Scotland. Almost all the lowland has varied, seminatural vegetation of grasses and flowering plants. Wild vegetation consists of the natural flora of woods, fens and marshes, cliffs, chalk downs, and mountain slopes, the

most widespread being the heather, grasses, gorse, and bracken of the moorlands.

The fauna is similar to that of northwestern continental Europe, although there are fewer species. Total animal species number 103 mammals, 557 birds, 16 reptiles, and 12 amphibians. The calculation reflects the total number of distinct species residing in the country, not the number of endemic species. Some of the larger mammals—wolf, bear, boar, and reindeer—are extinct, but red and roe deer are protected for sport. Common smaller mammals are foxes, hares, hedgehogs, rabbits, weasels, stoats, shrews, rats, and mice; otters are found in many rivers, and seals frequently appear along the coast.

Most numerous among bird species are the chaffinch, blackbird, sparrow, and starling. The number of large birds is declining, however, except for game birds—pheasant, partridge, and red grouse—which are protected. With the reclamation of the marshlands, waterfowl are moving to the many bird sanctuaries. The rivers and lakes abound in salmon, trout, perch, pike, roach, dace, and grayling. There are more than 21,000 species of insects.

5 ENVIRONMENT

Government officials and agencies with principal responsibility for environmental protection are the Department of the Environment, the Department of the Environment for Northern Ireland, and the secretaries of state for Scotland and Wales. The World Resources Institute reported that the United Kingdom had designated 4.75 million hectares (11.74 million acres) of land for protection as of 2006. The National Trust (for Places of Historic Interest or Natural Beauty), an organization of more than 1.3 million members, has acquired some 750 km (466 mi) of coastline in England, Northern Ireland, and Wales. In addition, 127 km (79 mi) of coastline in Scotland are protected under agreement with the National Trust of Scotland. Two countryside commissions, one for England and Wales and one for Scotland, are charged with conserving the beauty and amenities of rural areas. By 1982, the former had designated 10 national parks, covering 13,600 sq km (5,250 sq mi), or 9% of the area of England and Wales. An additional 36 areas of outstanding beauty have been designated, covering 17,000 sq km (6,600 sq mi). Scotland has 40 national scenic areas, with more than 98% of all Scottish lands under the commission's jurisdiction. Northern Ireland has eight designated areas of outstanding natural beauty, seven country parks, and one regional park. There are also seven forest parks in Great Britain and nine in Northern Ireland. England and Wales have 600,000 hectares (1,500,000 acres) of common land, much of which is open to the public. The Nature Conservancy Council manages 214 national nature reserves in Great Britain and 41 in Northern Ireland.

Air pollution is a significant environmental concern for the United Kingdom. The UN reported in 2008 that carbon dioxide emissions in the United Kingdom totaled 539,176 kilotons, or 8.5391 metric tons per capita. This was the world's ninth-highest level of carbon dioxide emissions. In addition, its sulphur contributes to the formation of acid rain in the surrounding countries of Western Europe. Air quality abatement has improved greatly in the United Kingdom as a result of the Control of Pollution Act of 1974 and other legislation. London is no longer densely smog ridden, and winter sunlight has been increasing in various industrial cities.

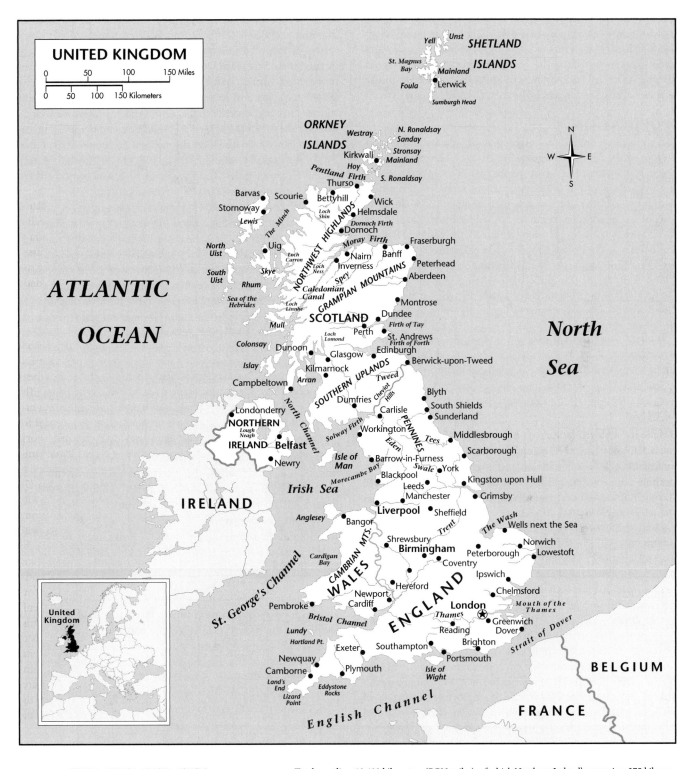

LOCATION: 49°56' to 60°50'N; 1°45'E to 8°10'W. BOUNDARY LENGTHS: Total coastline, 12,429 kilometers (7,722 miles), of which Northern Ireland's comprises 375 kilometers (233 miles); Irish Republic, 360 kilometers (225 miles). TERRITORIAL SEA LIMIT: 3 miles.

Water resources totaled 160.6 cu km (38.53 cu mi) in 2008, while water usage was 11.75 cu km (2.82 cu mi) per year. Domestic water usage accounted for 22% of total usage, industrial for 75%, and agricultural for 3%. Per capita water usage totaled 197 cu m (6,957 cu ft) per year. Water pollution from agricultural sources is a problem. The United Kingdom's cities produce an average of 22 million tons of solid waste per year. Pollution of the Thames has been reduced to one-quarter of its level in the 1950s, and more than 80% of the population is served by sewage treatment plants.

Protected areas include 168 Ramsar wetland sites and 5 natural UNESCO World Heritage Sites. According to the International Union for Conservation of Nature and Natural Resources (IUCN)

Red List of Threatened Species, the number of threatened species as of 2011 included 5 types of mammals, 2 species of birds, 43 species of fish, 5 types of mollusks, 9 species of other invertebrates, and 15 species of plants. The European otter, Atlantic sturgeon, Atlantic ridley, Eskimo curlew, and Spengler's freshwater mussel were classified as endangered. The great auk had become extinct.

6 POPULATION

The US Central Intelligence Agency (CIA) estimated the population of the United Kingdom in 2011 to be approximately 62,698,362, which placed it at number 22 in population among the 196 nations of the world. Approximately 16.5% of the population was over 65 years of age, with another 17.3% under 15 years of age. The median age in the United Kingdom was 40 years. There were 0.98 males for every female in the country. Population density in the United Kingdom was calculated at 257 people per sq km (666 people per sq mi). The population's annual rate of change was 0.557%. The projected population for the year 2025 was 68,600,000. In 2009, a UN report predicted that the United Kingdom will surpass Germany by becoming the most-populated European country by 2050.

The UN estimated that 80% of the population lived in urban areas, with an annual rate of change of 0.7%. The largest urban areas, along with their respective populations, included London, 8.6 million; Birmingham, 2.3 million; Manchester, 2.2 million; West Yorkshire, 1.5 million; and Glasgow, 1.7 million.

7 MIGRATION

Estimates of the United Kingdom's net migration rate, carried out by the CIA in 2011, amounted to 2.60 migrants per 1,000 citizens. The total number of emigrants living abroad was 4.67 million, and the total number of immigrants living in the United Kingdom was 6.96 million. From 1815 to 1930, the balance of migration was markedly outward as well over 20 million persons left Britain, settling mainly within the British Empire and in the United States. Since 1931, however, the flow has largely been inward. From 1931 to 1940, when emigration was very low, there was extensive immigration from Europe, including a quarter million refugees seeking sanctuary; during the 1950s, immigration from the Commonwealth, especially from the Caribbean countries, India, and Pakistan, steadily increased. The net influx of some 388,000 people (chiefly from the Commonwealth) during 1960–62 led to the introduction of the Commonwealth Immigrants Act of 1962, giving the government power to restrict the entry of Commonwealth citizens lacking adequate prospects of employment or means of self-support. Effective 1 January 1983, a new law further restricted entry by creating three categories of citizenship, two of which—citizens of British Dependent Territories and "British overseas citizens"—entail no right to live in the United Kingdom. Those in the last category, consisting of an estimated 1.5 million members of Asian minorities who chose to retain British passports when Malaysia and Britain's East African lands became independent, may not pass their British citizenship to their children without UK government approval.

Migration became a political issue in the 5 May 2005 elections. Conservative Party leader Michael Howard declared that if he were elected the United Kingdom would stop recognizing the 1951 UN Conventions on Refugees and an annual limit of

20,000 would be placed on immigration. The Labour Party stayed in power and Prime Minister Tony Blair proposed a tiered-point system to control immigration. In July 2005 the Home Office estimated that there were 570,000 unauthorized foreigners. A five-tiered guest worker system was introduced: tier one, for highly skilled migrants and investors; tier two, for skilled workers in shortage occupations; tier three, for unskilled workers via accredited recruiters; tier four, for foreign students; and tier five, for cultural exchange workers. After the death of 52 people in the 2 July 2005 bombings in London tubes and buses by British-born South Asians, tension increased and the far-right British National Party called for revamped laws to restrict immigration.

A 2009 government report indicated that migration was the main factor in the nation's rapid population growth. That year, the United Kingdom had the third-highest annual net migration rate in the world (after the United States and Canada), a fact that caused concern in what was already one of the most crowded countries in Europe. As a result, the government initiated a new point-based system in 2009 to regulate the number of economic migrants granted citizenship and/or permanent residency in the United Kingdom. Under the old system, immigrants who worked legally within the nation for five years could apply for a British passport and were generally granted citizenship. Under the new system, migrants must spend five years working as temporary residents before becoming probationary citizens. They can then begin to earn points toward full citizenship. Points are earned through such activities as volunteering in a local community or joining a political party or trade union. Those who relocate to Scotland earn extra points, since the region is considered to be in need of further immigration. Additionally, the citizenship test was expanded to include more in-depth topics on history and politics. The process toward full citizenship under this system may take between six and ten years to complete.

Despite these changes, there was a 37% rise in the number of people granted settlement in the UK from June 2009 through June 2010. The number of student visas issued during that timeframe, up by 35%, was a particular concern for some officials, who believed that too many would-be immigrants were seeking student visas as an easy way to slip through the system and bring their families to the country. However, the number of work visas issued to EU citizens dropped by 22%, with the decline attributed to the new system and the recession. Of those granted settlement in 2009, about 68% were dependants of someone already living in the country. The statistics report also indicated that 24.6% of all UK births in 2009 were to mothers born outside of the United Kingdom.

8 ETHNIC GROUPS

The present-day English, Welsh, Scots, and Irish are descended from a long succession of early peoples, including Iberians, Celts, Romans, Anglo-Saxons, Danes, and Normans, the last of whom invaded and conquered England in 1066–70. According to the 2001 census, about 83.6% of UK residents were English. The Scottish formed about 8.6% of the population, Welsh accounted for 4.9%, and the Northern Irish made up 2.9%. About 1.8% of the population were Indian, and 1.3% were Pakistani. There were about 300,000 persons who belonged to a group known as Travellers, a blend of Roma, Irish, and other ethnic groups who maintain an itinerant lifestyle.

⁹LANGUAGES

Spoken throughout the United Kingdom and by hundreds of millions of people throughout the world, English is second only to Mandarin Chinese in the number of speakers in the world. In northwestern Wales, Welsh, a form of Brythonic Celtic, is the first language of most of the inhabitants. Approximately 26% of those living in Wales speak Welsh (up from 19% in 1991). Some 60,000 or so persons in western Scotland speak the Scottish form of Gaelic (down from 80,000 in 1991), and a few families in Northern Ireland speak Irish Gaelic. On the Isle of Man, the Manx variety of Celtic is used in official pronouncements; in the Channel Islands some persons still speak a Norman-French dialect. French remains the language of Jersey for official ceremonies.

¹⁰RELIGIONS

Christians account for about 72% of the population. The Church of England (Anglican) claims about 29% of the population. The Church of Scotland (Presbyterian) and the Methodist Church in Britain (originally established as a type of revival movement by the Church of England minister John Wesley, 1703–91) both have significant membership, as does the Roman Catholic Church. Many immigrants have established community religious centers in the United Kingdom. Such Christian groups include Greek, Russian, Polish, Serb-Orthodox, Estonian and Latvian Orthodox, and the Armenian Church; Lutheran churches from various parts of Europe are also represented. There are active communities of Jehovah's Witnesses, Mormons (The Church of Jesus Christ of Latter-Day Saints), Christian Scientists, and Unitarians. The Anglo-Jewish community, with an estimated 300,000 members, is the second-largest group of Jews in Western Europe. Muslims account for about 3% of the population. Sikhs, Hindus, and Buddhists are also present. In Northern Ireland, about 53% of the population are nominally Protestants and 44% are nominally Catholics, though only about 30%–35% of all Northern Irish are active participants in religious services.

Protestants and Catholics in Northern Ireland tend to live in self-segregated communities. There is complete religious freedom in the United Kingdom. All churches and religious societies may own property and conduct schools. The Church of England and the Church of Scotland are considered to be established (state) churches. The Church of England is uniquely related to the crown in that the sovereign must be a member and, on accession, promise to uphold the faith; it is also linked with the state through the House of Lords, where the archbishops of Canterbury and York have seats. The archbishop of Canterbury is primate of all England. The monarch appoints all officials of the Church of England. The established Church of Scotland has a Presbyterian form of government: all ministers are of equal status and each of the congregations is locally governed by its minister and elected elders. Good Friday, Easter Monday, and Christmas are observed as national holidays.

¹¹TRANSPORTATION

The CIA reports that the United Kingdom has a total of 394,428 km (245,086 mi) of roads, of which 394,428 km (245,086 mi) are paved. There are 526 vehicles per 1,000 people in the country.

In Great Britain, railways, railway-owned steamships, docks, hotels, road transport, canals, and the entire London passenger transport system—the largest urban transport system in the world—were nationalized on 1 January 1948 under the control of the British Transport Commission (BTC). In 1962, the BTC was replaced by the British Railways Board, the London Transport Board, the British Transport Docks Board, and the British Waterways Board. Under the 1968 Transport Act, national transport operations were reorganized, with the creation of the National Freight Corp., the Freight Integration Council, and the National Bus Co. Organization of public transport in Northern Ireland is autonomous.

The Humber Bridge, the world's longest single-span suspension bridge, with a center span of 1,410 m (4,626 ft), links the city of Hull with a less developed region to the south. Eurotunnel, a British-French consortium, built two high-speed 50-km (31-mi) rail tunnels beneath the seabed of the English Channel. The project, referred to as the "Chunnel," links points near Folkestone, England (near Dover), and Calais, France. In November 1996, a truck aboard a freighter entering the tunnel caught fire, causing serious damage to the tunnel but no loss of life. Partial operations were resumed within a few weeks, and all repairs were completed by May 1997.

There are 5,248 km (3,261 mi) of electrified rail track in the United Kingdom. Standard gauge accounts for nearly all of the nation's railway system. Railroads extend for 16,173 km (10,049 mi). Underground railway systems operate in London, Glasgow, and Liverpool. In London, the Underground consists of some 3,875 cars that operate over about 408 km (254 mi) of track, 167 km (104 mi) of which is underground. The Underground, the oldest part of which dates to 1863, operates 20 hours per day and is comprised of 248 stations on 11 lines that provide 2.7 million rides per day. Capital investment has been diminished since the 1960s, resulting in increasing failures of signals and rolling stock and the deterioration of stations and track.

Great Britain has about 3,200 km (1,988 mi) of navigable inland waterways, mainly canals dating back to the pre-railroad age that are still in commercial use. Great Britain has some 300 ports, including the Port of London, one of the largest in the world. Other major ports are Liverpool, Southampton, Hull, Clydeport (near Glasgow), the inland port of Manchester, and Bristol. The British merchant fleet, privately owned and operated, consisted of 518 ships of 1,000 gross registered tons or more as of 2008. In an effort to curb the flagging of British merchant ships to less regulatory foreign nations, a British offshore registry program was initiated in the late 1980s. Under this program, merchant ships registered to the Isle of Man, Gibraltar, the Cayman Islands, and the Turks and Caicos Islands are entitled to fly the Red Ensign as if under the administration of the United Kingdom.

The Civil Aviation Authority was created in 1971 as an independent body responsible for national airline operations, traffic control, and air safety. There are 505 airports, which transported 102.46 million passengers in 2009 according to the World Bank. There are also 11 heliports. International flights operate from London's Heathrow; Gatwick, London's second airport; Glasgow, in Scotland; Ringway (for Manchester); Aldergrove (for Belfast); and Elmdon (for Birmingham). The two government-owned airlines, British European Airways and British Overseas Airways Corp., were amalgamated in 1974 to form British Airways (BA). In 1984, BA was reestablished as British Airways PLC, a public limited company under government ownership, soon thereafter to be sold wholly to the public. There are a number of privately operated airlines, some of which operate air taxi services. British Caledonian, which maintained scheduled flights on both domestic and international routes, merged with British Airways in 1988. The Concorde, a supersonic jetliner developed jointly in the 1960s by the United Kingdom and France at a cost exceeding £1 billion, entered service between Heathrow and the United States in 1976.

In June 2009, the Pontcysyllte Aqueduct and Canal, located in northeast Wales, was inscribed as a UNESCO World Heritage Site. Built in the early 19th century with a design by the celebrated civil engineer Thomas Telford, the canal is considered to represent one of the most amazing engineering feats of the Industrial revolution. The canal was built without locks over a very difficult geographic setting. The use of cast and wrought iron in the aqueduct allowed for the construction of arches that were lighter and stronger than those typical of the time.

12 HISTORY

The earliest people to occupy Britain are of unknown origin. Remains of these early inhabitants include the stone circles of Avebury and Stonehenge in Wiltshire. Celtic tribes from the Continent, the first known settlers in historical times, invaded before the 6th century BC. The islands were visited in ancient times by Mediterranean traders seeking jet, gold, pearls, and tin, which were being mined in Cornwall. Julius Caesar invaded in 55 BC but soon withdrew. In the 1st century AD, the Romans occupied most of the present-day area of England, remaining until the 5th century.

With the decline of the Roman Empire and the withdrawal of Roman troops (although many Romans had become Britonized and remained on the islands), Celtic tribes fought among themselves, and Scots and Picts raided from the north and from Ireland. Early raids by Angles, Saxons, and Jutes from the Continent soon swelled into invasions, and the leaders established kingdoms in the conquered territory while the native Celts retreated into the mountains of Wales and Cornwall. Although the Welsh were split into a northern and a southern group, they were not permanently subdued. In the 10th century, a Welsh king, Howel the Good (Hywel Dda), united Wales, codified the laws, and encouraged the Welsh bards.

Among the new English kingdoms, that of the West Saxons (Wessex) became predominant, chiefly through the leadership of Alfred the Great, who also had to fight a new wave of invasions by the Danes and other Norsemen. Alfred's successors were able to unify the country, but eventually the Danes completed their conquest, and King Canute (II) of Denmark became ruler of England by 1017. In 1042, with the expiration of the Scandinavian line, Edward the Confessor of Wessex became king. At his death in 1066, both Harold the Saxon and William, duke of Normandy, claimed the throne. William invaded England and defeated Harold in the Battle of Hastings, beginning the Norman Conquest (1066–70).

William I instituted a strong government, which lasted through the reigns of his sons William II and Henry I. The latter's death in 1135 brought a period of civil war and anarchy, which ended with the accession of Henry II (1154), who instituted notable constitutional and legal reforms. He and succeeding English kings expanded their holdings in France, touching off a long series of struggles between the two countries.

The Magna Carta

Long-standing conflict between the nobles and the kings reached a climax in the reign of King John with the victory of the barons, who at Runnymede in 1215 compelled the king to grant the Magna Carta. This marked a major advance toward the parliamentary system. Just half a century later, in 1265, Simon de Montfort, earl of Leicester, leader of the barons in their opposition to Henry III, summoned the first Parliament, with representatives not only of the rural nobility but also of the boroughs and towns. In the late 13th century, Edward I expanded the royal courts and reformed the legal system; he also began the first systematic attempts to conquer Wales and Scotland. In 1282, the last Welsh king, Llewellyn ap Gruffydd, was killed in battle, and Edward I completed the conquest of Wales. Two years later, the Statute of Rhuddlan established English rule. The spirit of resistance survived, however, and a last great uprising against England came in the early 15th century, when Owen Glendower (Owain ap Gruffydd) led a briefly successful revolt.

Scotland United

Scotland was inhabited in early historic times by the Picts and by roaming bands of Gaels, or Celts, from Ireland. Before the Romans left Britain in the 5th century, Scotland had been converted to Christianity by St. Ninian and his disciples. By the end of the following century, four separate kingdoms had been established in Scotland. Norsemen raided Scotland from the 8th to the 12th century, and some settled there. Most of the country was unified under Duncan I (r. 1034–40). His son, Malcolm III (r. 1059–93), who gained the throne after defeating Macbeth, the murderer of his father, married an English princess, Margaret (later sainted), and began to anglicize and modernize the lowlands.

Under David I (r. 1124–53), Scotland was united, responsible government was established, walled towns (known as burghs) were developed, and foreign trade was encouraged. William the Lion (r. 1165–1214) was captured by Henry II of England in 1174 and forced to accept the Treaty of Falaise, by which Scotland became an English fief. Although Scotland purchased its freedom from Richard I, the ambiguous wording of the agreement allowed later English kings to revive their claim.

When Alexander III died in 1286, Edward I of England, who claimed overlordship of Scotland, supported the claims of John Baliol, who was crowned in 1293. Edward began a war with Philip of France and demanded Scottish troops, but the Scots allied themselves with Philip, beginning the long relationship with France that distinguishes Scottish history. Edward subdued the Scots, put down an uprising led by William Wallace, executed Wallace in 1305, and established English rule. Baliol's heir was killed by Robert the Bruce, another claimant, who had himself crowned (1309), captured Edinburgh, and defeated Edward II of England decisively at Bannockburn in 1314. In 1328, Edward III signed a treaty acknowledging Scotland's freedom.

Hundred Years War and Wars of the Roses

Under Edward III, the Hundred Years' War (1337–1453) with France was begun. Notable victories by Edward the Black Prince (son of Edward III), Henry IV, and Henry V led to no permanent gains for England, and ultimately the English were driven out of France. The plague, known as the Black Death, broke out in England in 1348, wiping out a third of the population; it hastened the breakdown of the feudal system and the rise of towns. The 14th century was for England a time of confusion and change. John Wycliffe led a movement of reform in religion, spreading radical ideas about the need for churchly poverty and criticizing many established doctrines and practices. A peasant rebellion led by Wat Tyler in 1381 demanded the abolition of serfdom, monopolies, and the many restrictions on buying and selling.

In 1399, after 22 years of rule, Richard II was deposed. He was succeeded by Henry IV, the first king of the house of Lancaster. The war with France continued, commerce flourished, and the wool trade became important. The Wars of the Roses (1455–85), in which the houses of Lancaster and York fought for the throne, ended with the accession of Henry VII, a member of the Tudor family, marking the beginning of the modern history of England.

The Tudors

Under the Tudors, commerce was expanded, English seamen ranged far and wide, and clashes with Spain (accelerated by religious differences) intensified. Earlier English dominance had not had much effect on Wales, but the Tudors followed a policy of assimilation, anglicizing Welsh laws and practices. Finally, under Henry VIII, the Act of Union (1536) made English the legal language and abolished all Welsh laws "at variance with those of England." In 1531, Henry separated the Anglican Church from Rome and proclaimed himself its head. After his death (1547), the succession to the throne became a major issue during the reigns of Edward VI (1547–53), Mary I (1553–58), and Elizabeth I (1558–1603).

In Scotland, James I (r. 1406–37) had done much to regulate Scottish law and improve foreign relations. His murder in 1437 began a century of civil conflict. James IV (r. 1488–1513) married Margaret Tudor, sister of Henry VII of England, a marriage that was ultimately to unite the crowns of England and Scotland.

French influence in Scotland grew under James V (r. 1513–42), who married Mary of Guise, but the Scottish people and nobility became favorably inclined toward the Reformation, championed by John Knox. After James's death, Mary ruled as regent for her daughter, Mary, Queen of Scots, who had married the dauphin of France, where she lived as dauphiness and later as queen. By the time Mary returned to Scotland (1561), after the death of her husband, most of the Scots were Protestants. A pro-English faction had the support of Queen Elizabeth I against the pro-French faction, and Mary, who claimed the throne of England, was imprisoned and executed (1587) by Elizabeth. Under Elizabeth, England in 1583 acquired its first colony, Newfoundland, and in 1588 defeated the Spanish Armada; it also experienced the beginning of a golden age of drama, literature, and music, among whose towering achievements are the plays of William Shakespeare.

Oliver Cromwell and the Commonwealth

Elizabeth was succeeded by Mary's son, James VI of Scotland, who became James I of England (r. 1603–25), establishing the Stuart line. Under James and his son, Charles I (r. 1625–49), the rising middle classes (mainly Puritan in religion) sought to make Parliament superior to the king. In the English Civil War, which broke out in 1642, Charles was supported by the Welsh, who had remained overwhelmingly Catholic in feeling, but most Scots opposed him. Charles was tried and executed in 1649, and Oliver Cromwell ruled the new Commonwealth as Protector until his death in 1658. Cromwell ruthlessly crushed uprisings in Ireland and suppressed the Welsh. In 1660, Charles II, eldest son of the executed king, regained the throne. The Restoration was marked by a reaction against Puritanism, by persecution of the Scottish Covenanters (Presbyterians), by increased prosperity, and by intensified political activity; during this period, Parliament managed to maintain many of its gains. Charles II's younger brother, James II (r. 1685–88), who vainly attempted to restore Roman Catholicism, was overthrown in 1688 and was succeeded by his daughter, Mary II, and her Dutch husband, William III, who were invited to rule by Parliament. By this transfer of power, known to English history as the Glorious Revolution, the final supremacy of Parliament was established in the Bill of Rights, enacted in 1689. Supporters of James II (Jacobites) in Scotland and Ireland, aided by France, sought to restore the deposed Stuart line, but their insurrection was suppressed in 1690 at the Battle of the Boyne, fought on the banks of the Irish river of that name.

In Wales, after Cromwell and the Commonwealth, the people began to turn to Calvinism; dissent grew, and such ministers as Griffith Jones, a pioneer in popular education, became national leaders. Most Welsh were won to the Calvinistic Methodist Church, which played a large part in fostering a nonpolitical Welsh nationalism. A long struggle to disestablish the Church of England in Wales culminated successfully in a 1914 act of Parliament.

Colonial Expansion

English colonial expansion developed further in the 17th and 18th centuries, in competition with France and the Netherlands, while at the same time the English merchant marine gained commercial supremacy over the Dutch. The wars of the Grand Alliance (1688–97) and of the Spanish Succession (1701–14) consolidated Britain's overseas possessions. At home, to ensure Scottish allegiance to England and prevent possible alliances with inimical countries, the Act of Union of Scotland and England was voted by the two parliaments in 1707, thereby formally creating the kingdom of Great Britain under one crown and with a single Parliament composed of representatives of both countries. This union held, despite Jacobite uprisings in 1715 and 1745–46, the latter under Prince Charles (Bonnie Prince Charlie, or the Young Pretender, grandson of James II); his defeat at Culloden Moor was the last land battle fought in Great Britain. Scottish affairs eventually became the province of the secretary of state for Scotland, a member of the British cabinet. Nevertheless, a nationalist movement demanding independence for Scotland persists to this day.

The accession of George I of the House of Hanover in 1714 (a great-grandson of James I) saw the beginning of the modern cabinet system, with the king leaving much of the governing to his ministers. The 18th century was a time of rapid colonial and mercantile expansion abroad and internal stability and literary and artistic achievement at home. Britain won control of North America and India in the Seven Years' War (ended in 1763 by the Treaty of Paris), which also established British supremacy over the seas; however, the American Revolution (1775–83) cost Britain its most important group of colonies. A few years later, British settlement of Australia and then of New Zealand became key elements in the spreading British Empire. Britain increased its power further by its leading role in the French Revolutionary Wars and in the defeat of Napoleon and French expansionist aims.

Birth of the United Kingdom

In 1800, with the Act of Union of Great Britain and Ireland, the United Kingdom formally came into being. The conquest of Ireland had never been consolidated; the Act of Union followed an Irish rebellion in 1798 after the failure of a demand for parliamentary reform. But although the act established Irish representation in Parliament, the Irish question continued to cause trouble throughout the 19th century. Absentee landlordism, particularly in the 26 southern counties, fostered poverty and hatred of the English. Moreover, there was a growing division of interest between these counties and the six counties of the north, popularly called Ulster, where, early in the 17th century, Protestant Scots and English had settled on land confiscated by the British crown after a rebellion. While the north gradually became Protestant and industrial, the rest of Ireland remained Catholic and rural. With the introduction of the first Home Rule Bill in 1886, the northern Irish, fearing domination by the southern Catholic majority, began a campaign that ended in the 1920 Government of Ireland Act, which established separate domestic legislatures for the north and south, as well as continued representation in the UK Parliament. The six northern counties accepted the act and became Northern Ireland. The 26 southern counties, however, did not accept it; in 1921, the Anglo-Irish Treaty was signed, by which these counties left the United Kingdom to become the Irish Free State (now the Irish Republic, or Éire), which was officially established in 1922.

Queen Victoria's Reign

The Industrial Revolution, beginning in the second half of the 18th century, provided the economic underpinning for British colonial and military expansion throughout the 1800s. However, the growth of the factory system and of urbanization also brought grave new social problems. The enclosure of grazing land in the Scottish highlands and the industrialization of southern Wales were accompanied by extensive population shifts and led to large-scale immigration to the United States, Canada, and Australia. Reform legislation came slowly, although the spirit of reform and social justice was in the air. Slavery was abolished throughout the British Empire in 1834. The great Reform Acts of 1832, 1867, and 1884 gradually enfranchised the new middle class and the working class. Factory acts, poor laws, and other humanitarian legislation did away with some of the worst abuses, and pressure mounted for eliminating others. The long reign of Queen Victoria (1837–1901) saw an unprecedented commercial and industrial prosperity. This was a period of great imperial expansion, especially in Africa, where at the end of the century Britain fought settlers of predominantly Dutch origin in the South African (or Boer) War.

The labor movement grew strong, education was developed along national lines, and a regular civil service was established.

The 20th Century

The vast economic and human losses of World War I, in which nearly 800,000 Britons were killed, brought on serious disturbances in the United Kingdom as elsewhere, and the economic depression of the 1930s resulted in the unemployment of millions of workers. In 1931, the Statute of Westminster granted the status of equality to the self-governing British dominions and created the concept of a British Commonwealth of Nations. During the late 1930s, the government of Prime Minister Neville Chamberlain, seeking to avoid another major war, followed a policy of appeasement toward the aggressive Nazi Germany, but after Hitler invaded Poland, the United Kingdom declared war on Germany on 3 September 1939. Prime Minister Winston Churchill led the United Kingdom during World War II in a full mobilization of the population in the armed services, in home defense, and in war production. Although victorious, the United Kingdom suffered much destruction from massive German air attacks, and the military and civilian death toll exceeded 900,000. At war's end, a Labour government was elected; it pledged to carry out a full program of social welfare "from the cradle to the grave," coupled with the nationalization of industry. Medicine was socialized, other social services were expanded, and several industries were put under public ownership. Complete nationalization of industry, however, was halted with the return to power of the Conservatives in 1951. During Labour's subsequent terms in office, from 1964 to 1970 and from 1974 to 1979, little further nationalization was attempted.

Post-World War II Era

To a large extent, the United Kingdom's postwar history can be characterized as a prolonged effort to put the faltering economy on its feet and to cope with the economic, social, and political consequences of the disbandment of its empire. Decolonization was a complex and often violent process, particularly in Kenya, where the Mau Mau uprising was suppressed by British and local anti-Mau Mau forces. By early 1988, all that remained of what had been the largest empire in the world were 14 dependencies, many of them small islands with tiny populations and few economic resources. The United Kingdom has remained firmly within the Atlantic alliance since World War II. A founding member of the North Atlantic Treaty Organization (NATO) and European Free Trade Association (EFTA), the United Kingdom overcame years of domestic qualms and French opposition when it entered the European Community (EC) on 1 January 1973. After a Labour government replaced the Conservatives in March 1974, the membership terms were renegotiated, and United Kingdom voters approved continued British participation by a 67.2% majority in an unprecedented national referendum.

The principal domestic problems in the 1970s were rapid inflation, labor disputes, and the protracted conflict in Northern Ireland. Long-smoldering tensions between Protestants and Catholics erupted into open warfare after civil rights protests in 1969 by Catholics claiming discrimination and insufficient representation in the government. The Protestant reaction was violent, and the Irish Republican Army (IRA), seeking the union of Ulster with the Irish Republic, escalated the conflict by committing terrorist acts in both Northern Ireland and England. British troops, first dispatched to Belfast and Londonderry in August 1969, have remained there since.

On 30 March 1972, Northern Ireland's parliament (Stormont) was prorogued, and direct rule was imposed from London. Numerous attempts to devise a new constitution failed, as did other proposals for power sharing. In 1982, legislation establishing a new 78-member Northern Ireland Assembly was enacted. Elections were held that October, but the 19 Catholic members chosen refused to claim their seats. Meanwhile, the violence continued, one of the victims being the British war hero Earl Mountbatten of Burma, who was murdered while vacationing in Ireland on 27 August 1979. In October 1980, IRA members imprisoned in Ulster began a series of hunger strikes; by the time the strikes ended the following October, 10 men had died. In November 1985, the United Kingdom and the Irish Republic signed an agreement committing both governments to recognition of Northern Ireland as part of the United Kingdom and to cooperation between the two governments by establishing an intergovernmental conference concerned with Northern Ireland and with relations between the two parts of Ireland.

In 1979, a Conservative government, headed by Margaret Thatcher, came to power with a program of income tax cuts and reduced government spending. Thatcher, who won reelection in 1983 and 1987, embarked on a policy of "privatizing"—selling to the private sector—many of the UK's nationalized businesses. In foreign policy, the government's most dramatic action was sending a naval task force to the Falkland Islands following Argentina's occupation of the islands on 2 April 1982. After intense fighting, British administration was restored to the Falklands on 14 June.

Thatcher's leadership was challenged by Conservative MPs in November 1990, and she failed to win the necessary absolute majority. Thatcher withdrew and was replaced by John Major. The Conservatives were returned to power in April 1992 with a reduced majority. Major's government sought to redefine Conservative values with a renewed emphasis on law and order.

The "Downing Street Declaration" of December 1993 between British Prime Minister John Major and Irish Prime Minister Albert Reynolds over the future of Northern Ireland suggested that undisclosed contacts had been maintained for some time between the Irish Republican Army (IRA), Sinn Féin (the political wing of the IRA), and the British government. Tony Blair, who became prime minister in May 1997, also invested in normalization of relations between Ireland and the United Kingdom and in a long-term solution to the sectarian strife in Northern Ireland. In 1998, Ireland and the United Kingdom signed a peace agreement (Good Friday agreement) in which Ireland pledged to amend Articles 2 and 3 of the Irish constitution, which lay claim to the territory in the North. In return, the United Kingdom promised to amend the Government of Ireland Act.

Labour Party leader Tony Blair was elected prime minister on 2 May 1997, ending 18 years of Conservative Party rule and signaling a major shift in British domestic policy (he was reelected in 2001 and 2005). Blair, who moved his party to the center of the political spectrum during the campaign, pledged initiatives to modernize Britain's political structures. To that effect, he organized the creation of regional assemblies for Scotland and Wales and a municipal government for London. The regional parliaments were ratified by a referendum in late 1997 and began their first session in 1998. The city council for greater London came into being in mid-2000 and London's first mayor in 15 years was Ken Livingstone (reelected 2004), a left-wing Labourite not much liked by the middle-of-the-road Blairites.

As promised, Blair's government restructured the House of Lords to do away with the large number of hereditary peers. Only 75 of the 650 hereditary peers now sit in the House of Lords alongside 500 life peers, several senior judges, 26 bishops of the Church of England, and 15 deputy speakers.

The Blair government also spent much time tackling the Northern Ireland problem. The Good Friday Accord of 1998 envisioned a Catholic-Protestant administration and the gradual decommissioning of the IRA. The power-sharing government came into being in December 1999 but was suspended 11 weeks later because the IRA refused to make disarmament commitments. A breakthrough occurred in May 2000 when the IRA agreed to allow leading international figures to inspect arms dumps and to begin the process of complete and verifiable disarmament. The Protestant party voted to revive the power-sharing arrangements on 27 May 2000, and the UK government promised to restore substantial authority to the new Northern Irish cabinet (this was accomplished on 29 May). However, decommissioning of the IRA did not progress in early 2001. In October 2002, Sinn Féin's offices at Stormont (the Northern Ireland Assembly) were raided due to a large police investigation into intelligence-gathering operations on behalf of Irish republicans. On 14 October, devolution was suspended due to the spying allegations, and direct rule from London was reimposed on Northern Ireland. Blair announced in May 2003 that elections for the National Assembly would be postponed, due to the lack of evidence of peaceful intentions on behalf of the IRA. Elections were held on 26 November 2003, however, with the pro-British Democratic Unionist Party (DUP) and Sinn Féin forming the two largest parties. On 28 July 2005, the IRA announced it would halt its armed campaign to oust British rule. The statement was received with skepticism by the DUP, but in May 2006, the UK passed legislation paving the way for the recall of the Northern Ireland Assembly. Assembly leaders missed an initial November deadline to form a power-sharing executive, but assembly elections in March 2007 ultimately led to the swearing-in of the leaders of the power-sharing government on 8 May 2007, ending five years of direct rule from London. DUP leader Ian Paisley and Sinn Féin's Martin McGuinness took office as first and deputy first ministers, respectively. Prime Minister Blair and Ireland's Bertie Ahern witnessed the creation of the new executive.

Prime Minister Blair offered strong support for the US-led war on terrorism that began after the 11 September 2001 attacks on the United States; British forces took part in the campaign in Afghanistan to oust the Taliban regime. The United Kingdom in 2002–03 also stood with the United States in its diplomatic and military efforts to force Saddam Hussein's regime in Iraq to disarm itself of any weapons of mass destruction it might possess. The war in Iraq began on 19 March 2003, and British forces fought side-by-side with US forces, especially in southern Iraq. In the aftermath of the war, Blair indicated that the UN needed to play a central role in the reconstruction of Iraq, and other European leaders stood in agreement. In October 2004, the Iraq Survey Group (ISG) concluded there had been no weapons of mass destruction in Iraq for some time before the war. British intelligence withdrew a controversial claim that Saddam Hussein could have used WMDs with 45 minutes' notice. Blair acknowledged that the intelligence had been flawed, but denied having misrepresented it in making the case for war. Another controversy related to the Iraq War was the publication by *The London Times* on 1 May 2005 of a memo (subsequently labeled the "Downing Street memo") containing an overview of a secret 23 July 2002 meeting among British intelligence, government, and defense leaders discussing the build-up to the Iraq War. The memo included direct reference to classified US policy of the time and indicated that "intelligence and facts were being fixed" around the policy of removing Saddam Hussein from power. This was taken by some to show that US intelligence prior to the war had been deliberately falsified, and not just mistaken. The memo suggested that the UN weapons inspections that began after 8 November 2002 were manipulated to provide a legal pretext for the war, and that the removal by force of the Iraq regime had been planned prior to the date of the secret British meeting. In the United States, demands for an explanation of the revelations contained in the memo and calls for a formal Congressional inquiry were ignored by the Bush administration. In February 2007, Blair announced the first large-scale withdrawal of British troops from Iraq.

In mid-2005 the United Kingdom was wracked by terrorist violence. On 7 July 2005 four suicide bombers struck London's transit system, killing 52 people and injuring more than 700. Three underground trains were bombed, as was one double-decker bus. Two weeks later, on 21 July, bombings of three underground trains and one bus were attempted, but the suicide bombers' bombs failed to fully detonate. On 22 July, a Brazilian man, Jean Charles de Menezes, was shot to death at the Stockwell underground station by British police who believed him to be implicated in the bombing attempts. He was found not to have played any role in the 21 July attacks.

In May 2005, Blair became the first Labour Party leader to win a third successive term; however, he had a greatly reduced majority in parliament. Blair acknowledged that the war in Iraq had been a divisive issue and he promised to respond wisely to the election result. However, in November 2005, Blair suffered his first House of Commons defeat as prime minister when members of parliament voted against increasing from 14 to 90 days the length of time terrorist suspects can be held without charge. Instead, they supported increasing it to 28 days. In 2006, Tony Blair announced he would retire in 2007. Gordon Brown, Blair's chancellor of the exchequer, was primed to take his place as Labour Party leader and prime minister. Indeed, Blair stepped down and Gordon Brown became prime minister on 27 June 2007. Brown was the only candidate for the premiership when Blair stood down. In February 2007, Prime Minister Blair announced the first large-scale withdrawal of British troops from Iraq. Upon coming to power, Prime Minister Gordon Brown continued to move toward British troop withdrawal. The official withdrawal was completed on 1 January 2009. Brown was replaced by David Cameron following the Conservative Party victory in May 2010 elections.

In July 2008, the ruling General Synod of the Church of England approved by majority vote a controversial decision to allow the ordination of women as bishops. The traditional patriarchal Church began ordaining women as deacons in 1984 and priests in 1994. The decision had many dissenters among traditionalist members, who threatened to consider joining the Roman Catholic Church rather than accept the rule of a woman bishop. The General Synod submitted a draft code in February 2009 containing the amendments necessary to make the decision final. The earliest time for the potential consecration of the first woman bishop was projected for 2015.

During a European banking crisis in 2011, the British government was an outlier in EU efforts to strengthen the EU treaty—it was the only EU country to veto the proposed enhancement of fiscal controls imposed on member states. UK officials were reluctant to sign an agreement that lessened national sovereignty.

¹³GOVERNMENT

The United Kingdom is a monarchy in form but a parliamentary democracy in substance. The sovereign—Elizabeth II since 1952—is head of state and as such is head of the legislature, the executive, and the judiciary, commander-in-chief of the armed forces, and temporal head of the established Church of England. In practice, however, gradually evolving restrictions have transmuted the sovereign's legal powers into instruments for affecting the popular will as expressed through Parliament. In the British formulation, the sovereign reigns but does not rule, for the sovereign is under the law and not above it, ruling only by approval of Parliament and acting only on the advice of her ministers. The heir apparent is Prince Charles, Prince of Wales (b. 1948), followed by his son, Prince William. William married Catherine Middleton, a commoner, on 29 April 2011. She is now known as the Duchess of Cambridge.

The United Kingdom is governed, in the name of the sovereign, by Her Majesty's Government—a body of ministers who are the leading members of whichever political party the electorate has voted into office and who are responsible to Parliament. Parliament itself, the supreme legislative authority in the realm, consists of the sovereign, the House of Lords, and the House of Commons. Northern Ireland had its own parliament (Stormont) subordinate to Westminster; however, because of civil strife in Ulster, the Stormont was prorogued on 30 March 1972, and direct rule was imposed from Westminster. After several abortive attempts over the next decade to devise a system of home-rule government acceptable to both Protestant and Catholic leaders, the 78-member Northern Ireland Assembly was established in 1982, but it was dissolved in 1986. As a result of the 1998 "Good Friday Agreement," a Catholic-Protestant power-sharing government came into being in 1999. It was suspended in October 2002, and direct rule from London returned. However, after long negotiations, elections for the Northern Ireland Assembly were held in March 2007. Leaders of the Assembly were sworn in on 8 May 2007, ending five years of direct rule from London.

In 1979, proposals for the establishment of elected legislatures in Wales and Scotland failed in the former and, though winning a bare plurality, fell short of the required margin for approval (40% of all eligible voters) in the latter. Regional parliaments for Scotland and Wales were ratified by referendum in 1997, however, and they began their first sessions in 1998.

The sovereign formally summons and dissolves Parliament. The House of Lords, whose size has been greatly reduced, used to count about 1,200 peers, including hereditary peers, spiritual peers (archbishops and bishops of the Church of England), and life peers (eminent persons unwilling to accept a hereditary peerage). Over the centuries, its powers have gradually been lessened; today, its main function is to bring the wide experience of its members (741 in 2010) into the process of lawmaking. As of 2010, the House of Commons had 650 members. A general election must be held every five years but is often held sooner. All British subjects 18 years old and over may vote in national elections; women won equal franchise with men in 1922. Citizens of Ireland resident in Britain may also vote, as may British subjects abroad for a period of five years after leaving the United Kingdom.

Each Parliament may during its lifetime make or unmake any law. Parliamentary bills may be introduced by either house, unless they deal with finance or representation; these are always introduced in the Commons, which has ultimate authority for lawmaking. The House of Lords may not alter a financial measure or delay for longer than a year any bill passed by the Commons in two successive sessions. Bills passed by both houses receive the traditional royal assent and become law as acts of Parliament; no bill has received a royal veto for more than 200 years. The Speaker of the Parliament is the chief officer of the House of Commons. The Speaker is nonpartisan and functions impartially. The first female Speaker was elected in 1992.

Executive power is vested in the prime minister, who, though nominally appointed by the sovereign, is traditionally the leader of the majority party in Parliament. The prime minister is assisted by ministers, also nominally appointed by the sovereign, who are chosen from the majority party and mostly from the Commons, which must approve the government's general policy and the more important of its specific measures. The most senior ministers, about 20, compose the cabinet, which meets regularly to decide policy on major issues. Ministers are responsible collectively to Parliament for all cabinet decisions; individual ministers are responsible to Parliament for the work of their departments. There are around 30 major central government departments, each staffed by members of the permanent civil service.

The British constitution is made up of parliamentary statutes, common law, and traditional precepts and practices known as conventions, all evolved through the centuries. Largely unwritten, it has never been codified and is constantly evolving.

14 POLITICAL PARTIES

UK parliamentary government based on the party system has evolved only during the past 100 years. Although the 18th-century terms "Whig" and "Tory" indicated certain political leanings, there was no clear-cut division in Parliament and no comprehensive party organization. Not until the 19th-century Reform Acts enfranchised millions of new voters did the modern party system develop. The British party system is based on the assumption that there are at least two parties in the Commons, each with a sufficiently united following to be able to form an alternative government at any time. This assumption is recognized in the fact that the largest minority party is officially designated as Her Majesty's

Opposition; its leader, who designates a "shadow government," is paid a salary from public funds.

The main political parties represented in Parliament today are the Labour Party, the Conservative Party, and the Liberal Democrats (a coalition of the Liberal and Social Democratic parties, which voted in favor of a formal merger in 1988). From time to time during the past 50 years, other parties have arisen or have splintered off from the main groups, only to disappear or to become reabsorbed. The Fascists, who were of some significance before World War II, no longer put up candidates for elections. The British Communist Party has not elected a candidate to Parliament since 1950.

Since World War I, the Labour Party has replaced the Liberal Party, a major force during the late 19th century, as the official opposition to a Conservative government. Founded in 1900 as the political arm of the already powerful trade union movement, the Labour Party was until 1918 a federation of trade unions and socialist groups and had no individual members. Today, its constituent associations consist of affiliated organizations (such as trade unions, cooperative societies, branches of socialist societies, and trade councils), as well as individual members organized into wards. Its program calls for public ownership of the means of production, improvement of the social and economic conditions of the people, defense of human rights, cooperation with labor and socialist organizations of other countries, and peaceful adjustment of international disputes. Between the world wars, it established two short-lived Labour governments while still a minority party, and then joined Churchill's coalition government in World War II. Returned to power with a huge majority in 1945, Labour instituted a program of full employment through planned production; established social services to provide adequate medical care, senior care, nutrition, and educational opportunities for all; began the nationalization of basic industries; and started to disband the empire by granting independence to India, Pakistan, Ceylon (now Sri Lanka), and Burma (Myanmar).

If the rapid rise of the Labour Party has been an outstanding feature of 20th-century British politics, the continuing vitality and adaptability of the Conservative Party, successor of the 18th-century Tories, has been no less remarkable. In foreign affairs, there has been little difference between the parties since World War II. Both have generally been firm allies of the United States, and both are pledged to the maintenance of NATO. The two parties have also been in general agreement about the country's social and economic needs. They differ mainly on the degree of state control to be applied to industry and commerce and on practical methods of application. Conservative emphasis is on free enterprise, individual initiative, and restraining the power of the unions. Even on these matters, however, pragmatism is the norm. In office, the Conservatives have let stand much of Labour's social program, and Labour, during Britain's economic difficulties in the late 1970s, imposed its own policy of wage restraints.

After World War II, Labour was in power during 1945–51, 1964–70, 1974–79, and 1997–2010; the Conservatives have held office during 1951–64, 1970–74, 1979–97 and since 2010. Scottish National Party members were decisive in the fall of the Labour government in March 1979, after Labour was unable to enact its program for limited home rule (including elected legislatures) in Scotland and Wales. In elections on 3 May 1979, after a campaign fought mainly on economic grounds, Conservatives won 339 seats, with 43.9% of the vote, to Labour's 268 seats, with 36.9%, and Margaret Thatcher replaced James Callaghan as prime minister. Amid growing dissension, the Labour Party moved leftward in the early 1980s and broke with the Conservatives over defense policy, committing itself to the removal of all nuclear weapons from the United Kingdom and, in 1986, to the removal of US nuclear bases. The Social Democratic Party, founded in 1981 by moderate former Labour ministers, had by 30 September 1982 obtained 30 seats in Parliament, 27 of whose occupants were breakaway Labour members. In the elections of 9 June 1983, the Conservatives increased their parliamentary majority, winning 397 seats and about 42% of the vote. The Labour Party captured 209 seats and 28% of the vote, its poorest showing in more than five decades. The Alliance of Liberals and Social Democrats won 25% of the vote but only 23 seats (Liberals 17, Social Democrats 6). Minor parties took 5% of the vote and 21 seats.

In the elections of 11 June 1987, the Conservatives won 376 seats and about 42% of the vote. The Labour Party won 229 seats and 31% of the vote. The Liberal-Social Democratic Alliance won nearly 23% of the vote but only 22 seats (Liberals 17, Social Democrats 5). Minor parties took about 4% of the vote and 23 seats: Ulster Unionist (Northern Ireland), 9; Democratic Unionist (Northern Ireland), 3; Scottish National Party, 3; Plaid Cymru (Welsh Nationalist), 3; Social Democratic and Labour Party (Northern Ireland), 3; Sinn Féin (Northern Ireland), 1; and Popular Unionist (Northern Ireland), 1.

The general election of 9 April 1992 resulted in a continuation of Conservative government under John Major with 42% of the vote and 336 seats. Labour followed with 34% of the vote and 271 seats. The Liberal Democrats took almost 18% of the vote, which netted 20 seats. Minor parties received 3% of the vote and 17 seats.

The Labour Party, under the leadership of Tony Blair, won a landslide victory in the general election of 1 May 1997, restoring it to power for the first time in 18 years. Of 659 possible seats, the Labour Party won 418 (43.1%), gaining 146 seats; the Conservative Party won only 165 seats (30.6%), losing 178 seats. The Liberal Democrats won 46 seats (16.7%), a gain of 26 seats since 1992 and the most seats held by the party since the 1920s. Other parties received 9.6% of vote, with the following representation after the 1997 elections: Ulster Unionist, 10; Scottish National, 6; Plaid Cymru, 4; Social Democrat and Labour, 3; Democratic Unionist, 2; Sinn Féin, 2; Independent, 2; and United Kingdom Unionist, 1.

The June 2001 election was called "the quiet landslide" following the major victory of the Labour Party in the 1997 election. Labour won 40.7% of the vote and secured 413 seats; the Conservative Party gained only one seat (166 total) and registered 31.7% of the vote. The Liberal Democrats gained six seats (52; 18.3% of the vote) from their historic high in 1997. Other parties received 9.3% of the vote, with the following representation after the 2001 election: Ulster Unionist, 6; Scottish National, 5; Democratic Unionist, 5; Plaid Cymru, 4; Sinn Féin, 4; Social Democrat and Labour, 3; and Independent, 1.

In the general election held on 5 May 2005, Labour lost 47 seats but retained its majority with 356 seats in Parliament (35.3% of the vote); the Conservatives gained 33 seats to end up with 198 (32.3% of the vote). The Liberal Democrats held 62 seats after gaining 11 (22.1% of the vote). Other parties garnered 10.3% of

the vote, with the following representation in Parliament after the election: Democratic Unionist Party, 9; Scottish National Party, 6; Sinn Féin, 5; Plaid Cymru, 3; Social Democrat and Labour Party, 3; Ulster Unionist Party, 1; Independent Kidderminster Hospital and Health Concern, 1; and others, 2.

In the May 2010 elections, the Conservative Party gained 299 seats in the House of Commons, followed by the Labour Party with 255 seats, and the Liberal Democrats with 54 seats. Since neither the Conservatives nor the Labour Party gained the required majority, the Conservatives aligned with the Liberal Democrats to form a coalition government, with David Cameron selected as the new prime minister.

15 LOCAL GOVERNMENT

The scope of local governing bodies is defined and limited by acts of Parliament, which also makes certain ministers responsible for the efficient functioning of local services. In England, local government is supervised by the Department of the Environment; the regional parliaments supervise local governments in Wales and Scotland; and Northern Ireland, which was supposed to also have devolved powers, was placed back under the supervision of the Department of the Environment for Northern Ireland.

From 1965 to 1985, Greater London, the nation's largest metropolitan area, was subdivided into 32 London boroughs; the Greater London Council was the chief administrative authority. Under the Local Government Act of 1985, however, the Greater London Council was abolished and its functions were transferred to London borough and metropolitan district councils, excepting certain services (such as police and fire services and public transport) now administered by joint borough and council authorities. The Labour Party government returned local government to London. However, the mayor's office has a limited budget and few policy powers. The mayor's office coordinates relationship among the different boroughs and controls local transport (Underground).

Under the Local Government Act of 1972, the county system that had prevailed throughout the rest of England and Wales was replaced by a two-tier structure of counties and districts. In the 1990s, local governmental structures were reorganized, and single-tier administrations with responsibility for all areas of local government were reestablished. The system is composed of unitary authorities, with shire counties split into nonmetropolitan districts. These in turn are subdivided into electoral wards and districts. In 2000, a two-tier structure was reestablished for London, which has 32 boroughs and the City of London. The unitary authority divisions were further revised in 2009 for all of England. Scotland is subject to the administration of both the UK government in Westminster and the Scottish executive in Edinburgh, and Wales is subject to the administration of Westminster and the National Assembly for Wales in Cardiff. Scotland is divided into 32 council areas, which in turn are divided into electoral wards and communities. Wales is subdivided into 22 unitary authorities, which in turn are divided into electoral divisions and communities. Northern Ireland is subject to the administration of both the UK government and the Northern Ireland Executive in Belfast. It is divided into 26 districts, which in turn are divided into electoral wards. The United Kingdom has more than 10,000 electoral wards/divisions. The minimum voting age in local elections is 18.

¹⁶JUDICIAL SYSTEM

The United Kingdom does not have a single body of law applicable throughout the realm. Scotland has its own distinctive system and courts; in Northern Ireland, certain spheres of law differ in substance from those operating in England and Wales. A feature common to all UK legal systems, however—and one that distinguishes them from many continental systems—is the absence of a complete code, since legislation and unwritten or common law are all part of the "constitution."

The main civil courts in England and Wales are county courts for small cases; senior courts include the Court of Appeal, the High Court of Justice, and the Crown Courts. In 2005 parliament passed the Constitutional Reform Act of 2005, which provided for a Supreme Court of the United Kingdom to abolish the appellate jurisdiction of the House of Lords and to reduce the role of the lord chancellor, among other changes. The Supreme Court began operations in 2009. In Scotland, civil cases are heard at the sheriff courts (corresponding roughly to the English county courts). Higher courts include the Court of Session and High Court of the Justiciary, the highest court of appeal.

In England, Wales, and Northern Ireland, 12-citizen juries must unanimously decide the verdict unless, with no more than two jurors dissenting, the judge directs them to return a majority verdict. Scottish juries of 15 persons are permitted to reach a majority decision and, if warranted, a verdict of "not proven."

The United Kingdom accepts the compulsory jurisdiction of the International Court of Justice with reservations.

¹⁷ARMED FORCES

After the general demobilization that followed World War II, compulsory national service for all eligible males over 19 years of age was introduced. Call-ups of national servicemen ceased in 1960, but those who had been trained formed part of the general reserve until June 1974, when the national service legislation expired. Reserves now form part of the long-term reserve established in 1964, composed of all men under 45 years of age who have served in the regular army since 28 February 1964, plus the highly trained units of the territorial army volunteer reserve. Home service forces are stationed in Northern Ireland, Gibraltar, and the Falkland Islands. Basing its defense policy on NATO, the British government in the 1970s reduced its overseas commitments. British troops participate in a number of peacekeeping missions. The United States has 9,800 military personnel stationed in the United Kingdom.

The International Institute for Strategic Studies reports that armed forces in the United Kingdom totaled 178,470 members in 2011. The force was comprised of 102,600 from the army, 35,480 from the navy, and 40,390 members of the air force. Armed forces represented 0.6% of the labor force in the United Kingdom. Defense spending totaled $52.3 billion and accounted for 2.4% of GDP.

¹⁸INTERNATIONAL COOPERATION

The United Kingdom became a charter member of the UN on 24 October 1945; it participates in the Economic Commission for Europe (ECE), the Economic Commission for Latin America and the Caribbean (ECLAC), and the Economic and Social Commission for Asia and the Pacific (ESCAP), as well as in all of the non-regional specialized agencies. The United Kingdom is a permanent member of the UN Security Council. The United Kingdom is also a member of the Council of Europe, the European Union (EU), NATO, the Organisation for Economic Co-operation and Development (OECD), the Organization for Security and Co-operation in Europe (OSCE), the African Development Bank, the Asian Development Bank, the Caribbean Development Bank, G-5. G-7, G-8, the Paris Club (G-10), and the World Trade Organization (WTO). The headquarters of the International Maritime Organization (IMO) is in London. The country holds observer status in the Organization of American States (OAS).

The Commonwealth of Nations, an organization of 49 states, provides a means for consultation and cooperation, especially on economic matters, between the United Kingdom and its former colonies. Its main coordinating organ is the Commonwealth Secretariat, which was established in London in 1965 and is headed by a secretary-general appointed by the heads of the member governments. The heads of governments hold biennial meetings; meetings also are held by diplomatic representatives known as high commissioners and among other ministers, officials, and experts.

Despite controversy within the nation itself, the United Kingdom has been a strong supporter of the US-led international war on terrorism. The country has support UN missions and operations in Kosovo (est. 1999), Liberia (est. 2003), Sierra Leone (est. 1999), Georgia (est. 1993), the DROC (est. 1999), and Cyprus (est. 1964), among others. The United Kingdom is part of the Australia Group, the Zangger Committee, the European Organization for Nuclear Research (CERN), the Nuclear Suppliers Group (London Group), the Nuclear Energy Agency, and the Organization for the Prohibition of Chemical Weapons. The nation holds guest status in the Nonaligned Movement.

In environmental cooperation, the United Kingdom is part of the Antarctic Treaty; the Basel Convention; Conventions on Biological Diversity, Whaling, and Air Pollution; Ramsar; CITES; the London Convention; International Tropical Timber Agreements; the Kyoto Protocol; the Montréal Protocol; MARPOL; the Nuclear Test Ban Treaty; and the UN Conventions on the Law of the Sea, Climate Change, and Desertification.

¹⁹ECONOMY

The United Kingdom—one of the most highly industrialized countries in the world and one of four countries in Western Europe with a trillion dollar economy (the others are Germany, France, and Italy)—lives by manufacture, trade, and financial and commercial services. Apart from coal and low-grade iron ore, some timber, building materials, and natural gas and North Sea oil, it has few natural resources. Agriculture provides 60% of the food needed with less than 2% of the labor force. The remainder of the United Kingdom's food supply and most raw materials for its industries has to be imported and paid for largely through exports of manufactures and services. The United Kingdom is one of the world's largest markets for food and agricultural products and one of the largest trading nations. Vast quantities of imported wheat, meat, butter, livestock feeds, tea, tobacco, wool, and timber have been balanced by exports of machinery, ships, locomotives, aircraft, and motor vehicles. The pattern of exports is gradually changing, however. Post–World War II reduction in output of textiles—once a leading British export—due to competition from Asia, and in coal output, because of competition from oil and mines in Europe, has been offset by industries such as electronics and chemicals. A major source of earnings is the variety of commercial services that stem from the United Kingdom's role as central banker of the sterling area. Shipping, income from overseas investment, insurance, and tourism also make up an important part of the economy. London ranks with New York as an international financial center. The United Kingdom was Europe's only significant energy exporter until 2005 when, as oil and gas reserves declined, it became a net importer.

Since the 1979–81 recession, the British economy had posted steady gains, until the global economic crisis in 2008. In the 1980s and 1990s, the government privatized many major companies, as well as a number of subsidiaries of nationalized industries and other businesses. Among the major companies privatized were British Telecom, British Gas, British Steel, British Airways, British Aerospace, Rolls-Royce, Austin Rover, Cable and Wireless, ICL, British water utilities, British Coal, and British Rail. Between 1983 and 1990, real GDP increased by nearly 25%. Inflation fell from 18% in 1980 to an annual rate of 1.9% by July 1987. However, it averaged 6.3% a year during 1988–92 before falling to 1.6% in 1993. From 1994 to 1997, annual growth was over 3%, but fell an average 2.5% from 1998 to 1999. The global economic slowdown of 2001–03, exacerbated by the high value of the pound and the bursting of the "new economy" bubble, slowed growth to 1.6%, which hurt manufacturing and exports. Real GDP growth stood at an average 2.3% from 2001–05. Inflation during that period averaged 1.5%. The GDP rate of change in the United Kingdom, as of 2010, was 1.3%. Inflation stood at 3.3%, and unemployment was reported at 7.9%.

The nation went into recession beginning in late 2008 as financial markets dropped in response to the global financial crisis. Two major UK banks were nationalized, while the British government took a significant share in two others. In April 2009, the government announced a new budget plan that included over $1 trillion in deficit spending over a five-year period and an increased income tax rate to 50% for citizens earning over £150,000 ($216,750). Under the new plan, total government expenditure was expected to expand from 59% of GDP in 2009 to 68% of GDP in 2010.

By contrast, in June 2010, the government enacted one of the toughest austerity plans in the industrialized world. Under the new plan, the vast majority of government departments would be subject to a 25% budget reduction. The departments for health and international aid spending were exempt from these cuts. Additionally, significant tax increases were announced, including an increase in the capital gains tax (to 28%) and a hike in the value added tax (VAT) from 17.5% to 20%.

20 INCOME

The CIA estimated that in 2010 the GDP of the United Kingdom was $2.2 trillion. The CIA defines GDP as the value of all final goods and services produced within a nation in a given year, computed on the basis of purchasing power parity (PPP) rather than value as measured on the basis of the rate of the exchange based on current dollars. The per capita GDP was estimated at $34,800. The annual growth rate of GDP was 1.3%. It was estimated that

agriculture accounted for 0.9% of GDP, industry 22.1%, and services 77.1%.

The World Bank reported in 2009 that household consumption in the United Kingdom totaled $1.42 trillion or about $22,574 per capita, measured in current US dollars rather than PPP. Household consumption includes expenditures of individuals, households, and nongovernmental organizations on goods and services, excluding the purchases of dwellings. It was estimated that household consumption was growing at an average annual rate of 3.1%. As of 2011, the most recent study by the World Bank reported that actual individual consumption in the United Kingdom accounted for 77.8% of GDP and 4.06% of world consumption. By comparison, the United States accounted for 25.44% of world individual consumption. The World Bank also estimated that 7.8% of the United Kingdom's GDP was spent on food and beverages, 15.4% on housing and household furnishings, 3.6% on clothes, 7.7% on health, 9.2% on transportation, 1.4% on communications, 8.3% on recreation, 7.2% on restaurants and hotels, and 12.7% on miscellaneous goods and services and purchases from abroad. According to the World Bank, remittances from citizens living abroad totaled $7.3 billion or about $116 per capita and accounted for approximately .3% of GDP.

The World Bank estimated that the United Kingdom, with 0.98% of the world's population, accounted for 3.46% of the world's GDP. By comparison, the United States, with 4.85% of the world's population, accounted for 22.51% of world GDP.

21 LABOR

As of 2010, the United Kingdom had a total labor force of 31.52 million people. Within that labor force, CIA estimates in 2006 noted that 1.4% were employed in agriculture, 18.2% in industry, and 80.4% in the service sector. The standard workweek is limited to 48 hours, which is averaged over a period of 17 to 26 weeks. Besides the statutory public holidays, most employees have at least four weeks' annual vacation with pay. Children under the age of 16 are not permitted to work unless it is part of an educational experience. Children under age 13 are prohibited from working in any capacity. As of 2011, the national minimum wage rate varied from £3.68 ($5.77) per hour to £6.08($9.52) per hour depending upon the employee's age. The minimum wage for apprentices was £2.60 ($4.08). Although these rates are insufficient to provide a decent living standard, the gap is presumed to be filled by a range of government benefits, which includes free medical care under the National Health Service.

The Employment Relations Act protects union organization, the statutory right to strike, and minimum employment standards. Nearly all trade unions of any size are affiliated with the Trades Union Congress (TUC), the national center of the trade union movement. There is also a separate Scottish Trades Union Congress. The legal status of the trade unions is defined by the Trade Union and Labor Relations Act of 1974. Restrictions on the power of the trade unions are embodied in the Employment Acts of 1980 and 1982 and in the Trade Union Act of 1984. According to the Department of Business, Innovation, and Skills in 2010, 26.6% of the British workforce was unionized. Hourly earnings for union members were 16.7% higher than non-union members in the workforce, and women were more likely than men to be union members.

22 AGRICULTURE

Agriculture in the United Kingdom is intensive and highly mechanized. Roughly 23% of the total land is used for agriculture, and the country's major crops include cereals, oilseed, potatoes, and vegetables. In Great Britain roughly 70% of the farms are primarily or entirely owner-occupied, but in Northern Ireland nearly all are.

Most British farms produce a variety of products. The type of farming varies with the soil and climate. The better farming land is generally in the lowlands. The eastern areas are predominantly arable, and the western predominantly for grazing. Mechanization and research have greatly increased agricultural productivity. The United Kingdom now produces about 60% of its total food needs, whereas prior to World War II (1939–45) it produced only about 33%, and in 1960, less than half. Cereal production in 2009 amounted to 22 million tons, fruit production to 409,678 tons, and vegetable production to 2.4 million tons.

23 ANIMAL HUSBANDRY

Livestock continues to be the largest sector of the farming industry. The United Kingdom raises some of the world's finest pedigreed livestock and is the leading exporter of pedigreed breeding animals. Most of the internationally famous breeds of cattle, sheep, hogs, and farm horses originated in the United Kingdom. In England and Wales, fattening of animals for food is the predominant activity in the southeast, the east, and the Midlands, while stock rearing is widespread in northern England and in Wales. In Scotland, dairying predominates in the southwest, cropping and fattening in the east, and sheep raising in the hilly regions. Northern Ireland's livestock industry provides 90% of its agricultural income.

The UN Food and Agriculture Organization (FAO) reported that the United Kingdom dedicated 11.6 million hectares (28.7 million acres) to permanent pasture or meadow in 2009. During that year, the country tended 159.3 million chickens, 9.9 million head of cattle, and 4.6 million pigs. The production from these animals amounted to 1.34 million tons of beef and veal, 1.7 million tons of pork, 1.78 million tons of poultry, 627,952 tons of eggs, and 14.8 million tons of milk. The United Kingdom also produced 74,500 tons of cattle hide and 65,393 tons of raw wool.

The most highly reputed beef breeds are Hereford and Aberdeen Angus; distinguished dairy breeds are Guernsey, Jersey, and Ayrshire. To ensure sound breeding, there is compulsory licensing of bulls. On 20 March 1996, the British government reported concern over a possible link between bovine spongiform encephalopathy (BSE, or the so-called "Mad Cow" disease) in cattle and a new variant of Creutzfeldt-Jakob disease in humans. BSE was first identified in the United Kingdom in 1986. Transmission of BSE to cattle occurs from contaminated meat and bone meal in concentrate feed, with sheep or cattle as the original source. The United Kingdom is the only country with a high incidence of the disease, and the epidemic was mainly due to recycling affected bovine material back to cattle before a ban on ruminant feed began in July 1988. As a result, consumption of beef dropped and many countries banned imports of British cattle and beef. In 2011, South Africa partially lifted its ban on British beef; South Africa was the United Kingdom's largest non-European market prior to the 1996 outbreak.

24 FISHING

Lying on the continental shelf, the British Isles are surrounded by waters mainly less than 90 m (300 ft) deep, which serve as excellent fishing grounds and breeding grounds for fish. Small fishing villages are found all along the coast, but the modern large-scale industry is concentrated at Hull, Grimsby, Fleetwood, Yarmouth, and Lowestoft in England. The major herring landings are made at numerous east coast ports of Scotland, notably Aberdeen. The fishing industry has been declining, but it remains important to Scotland, which accounts for a majority of the United Kingdom's fishing fleet. The United Kingdom had 8,430 decked commercial fishing boats in 2008. The annual capture totaled 596,004 tons according to the UN FAO. The export value of seafood totaled $1.87 billion.

The deep-sea fleet has declined primarily because the adoption by most nations, including the United Kingdom, of a 322-km (200-mi) fishery limit decreased the opportunity to fish in distant waters. Some of the larger vessels have, instead, turned to fishing for mackerel and herring off the west coast. Leading species caught in 2010 (by landing) were mackerel (161,000 tons), herring (67,000 tons), and haddock (34,000 tons).

Salmon farming takes place primarily in Scotland. The UK is in fact a net exporter of salmon, exporting 82,000 tons in 2010 while importing 57,000 tons. Domestic demand for seafood grew during the late 1990s due to public concerns over beef tainted by bovine spongiform encephalopathy (BSE, or Mad Cow disease).

25 FORESTRY

The Forestry Commission promotes development of afforestation and increased timber production. Clearance of forests for agriculture began in the Neolithic and Bronze Ages, so that by the time of the Domesday survey in 1086, only 15% of England was forested. There was a considerable degree of reforestation in the second half of the 20th century. The estimated total area of woodland in 2011 was 3.1 million hectares, or 12.7% of the total land area of the United Kingdom, up from 2.8 million in 2004. Roughly 42% of the area is in England, 45% in Scotland, 10% in Wales, and 3% in Northern Ireland. The Forestry Commission estimates that there are 3.8 million trees in the United Kingdom, 56% of which are in Scotland. The principal species in the forest area are spruces, pines, and oak, with smaller amounts of beech, ash, birch, and fir. Because of the high proportion of unproductive woodland, largely a legacy of over-felling during the two world wars, major efforts have been directed toward rehabilitation.

The UN FAO estimated the 2009 roundwood production at 7.51 million cu m (265.2 million cu ft). The value of all forest products, including roundwood, totaled $2.39 billion. Except for the two wartime periods, home woodlands have made only a limited contribution in this century to the national requirements in wood and wood products, almost 90% of which are met by imports. The United Kingdom imports softwood lumber from Canada, hardwood lumber and softwood plywood from the United States, hardwood veneer from Germany, hardwood plywood from Russia, and particleboard from Belgium.

26 MINING

Although the United Kingdom had comparatively few mineral resources (except for North Sea oil), it became a significant player in the world mining and mineral-processing industries due to the extensive range of UK companies that had interests in the international mineral industry. An organized coal-mining industry has been in existence for over 300 years, 200 years longer than in any other country, and has traditionally been by far the most important mineral industry. Mine production of ferrous and nonferrous metals has been declining for more than 30 years as reserves became depleted, necessitating imports for the large and important metal processing industry. Metals, chemicals, coal, and petroleum were among the country's leading industries in 2009, and fuels and chemicals ranked second and third, respectively, among export commodities. The industrial minerals sector has provided a significant base for expanding the extractive industries. The United Kingdom was a leading world producer and exporter of ball clay and kaolin; operations were mainly in Dorsetshire and Devonshire.

Other minerals extracted in 2009 included: common sand and gravel, 65.8 million tons (estimated); crushed limestone, 54.7 million tons (estimated); crushed dolomite, 5 million tons; crushed igneous rock, 40.1 million tons (estimated); china clay kaolin (dry weight sales), 1.06 million tons (reported); ball and pottery clay (dry weight sales), 727,000 tons (reported); potash, 600,000 tons (reported); dimension sandstone, 9,200,000 tons (estimated); gypsum and anhydrite, 1.7 million tons (estimated); fluorspar (all grades), 19,000 tons (estimated); and crushed chalk, 6 million tons (estimated). Lead and hematite iron ore were worked on a small scale. The output of iron ore (gross weight) dropped from an estimated 1,000 metric tons in 1999 to 100 metric tons in 2009. Alumina was produced from imported bauxite. Zinc and tungsten are no longer mined. In 2003, the United Kingdom also produced barite and witherite, bromine, hydraulic cement, clays (including fire clay, fuller's earth, and shale), feldspar (china stone), quicklime and hydrated lime, nitrogen, rock and brine salt, sodium compounds, slate, sulfur, pyrophyllite and soapstone talc, and titania. Most slate mining was in northern Wales, and the Penrhyn quarry, at Bethesda, was considered the world's largest slate mine; it has been in operation for more than 400 years.

Most nonfuel mineral rights in the United Kingdom were privately owned in 2009, except gold and silver, the rights to which were vested in the royal family and were known as Crown Rights. Onshore exploration activities were to be directed mainly toward precious metals, mainly gold. In Northern Ireland, the rights to license and to work minerals were vested in the state.

27 ENERGY AND POWER

The United Kingdom (UK) is the European Union's (EU) largest petroleum and natural gas producer, thanks to its offshore oil reserves in the North Sea. It is also one of Europe's largest consumers of energy. The World Bank reported in 2008 that the United Kingdom produced 385.3 billion kWh of electricity and consumed 372.2 billion kWh, or 5,936 kWh per capita. Roughly 90% of energy came from fossil fuels, while 7% came from alternative fuels.

The United Kingdom, as of 2011, had proven oil reserves estimated at 2.858 billion barrels, according to the *Oil and Gas Journal*. The bulk of these reserves are located in the North Sea, on the UK Continental Shelf. Sizable reserves also are located north of the Shetland Islands, with smaller amounts located in the North Atlantic. The United Kingdom also has Europe's largest onshore oil field, the Wytch Farm field. In 2011, oil production averaged an estimated 1.38 million barrels per day, with domestic consumption estimated at 1.63 million barrels per day (2010). The United Kingdom's crude oil refining capacity, as of 2009, totaled an estimated 1.86 million barrels per day. British Petroleum (BP) has the most refining capacity in the United Kingdom, operating a facility in Grangemouth, Scotland, and a facility in Coryton, England. The largest refinery in the United Kingdom is the Fawley facility, operated by ExxonMobil. The United Kingdom is simultaneously a major importer and exporter of oil. Since North Sea oil is a light, high-quality oil, the United Kingdom exports this oil and imports crude oils of various qualities. In 2009, imports of refined petroleum products averaged 493,528 barrels per day.

As of 2011, the United Kingdom's proven natural gas reserves were estimated at 9.04 trillion cu ft. In 2010, natural gas production totaled an estimated 1.99 trillion cu ft. Net exports of natural gas that year were estimated at 0.553 trillion cu ft.

The United Kingdom is a major producer of coal in the EU. In 2008, the country had recoverable coal reserves estimated at 251 million short tons. According to the UK Department for Business, Innovation, and Skills , formerly the Department of Trade and Industry, a total of 19.6 million short tons were produced in 2010. However, this figure is down by more than 80% from the early 1970s, and the demand for coal has also dwindled. In 1970 consumption fell from 175.9 million short tons to 55.4 million short tons in 2010. Falling domestic demand and a surge in cheap imported coal put coal imports at 29.4 million short tons in 2010.

28 INDUSTRY

The United Kingdom is one of the most highly industrialized countries in the world. The industrial sector of the economy declined in relative importance after 1973, because of the worldwide economic slowdown; however, output rose in 1983 and 1984 and in 1985 was growing at an annual rate of 3%. Manufacturing accounted for 25.1% of GDP in 1985, 22.3% in 1992, 26.3% in 2004, and 22.1% in 2010. Since World War II, some traditional industries have markedly declined—e.g., cotton textiles, steel, shipbuilding, locomotives—and their place has been taken by newer industries, such as electronics, offshore oil and gas products, and synthetic fibers. In the chemicals industry, plastics and pharmaceuticals have registered the most significant growth.

The pattern of ownership, organization, and control of industry is varied: public, private, and cooperative enterprises are all important. The public sector plays a significant role; however, since 1979 the government has sold off a number of companies and most manufacturing is conducted by private enterprise. Although the average firm is still fairly small, there has been a trend in recent years toward the creation of larger enterprises.

Metals, engineering, and allied industries—including steel, nonferrous metals, vehicles, and machinery—employ nearly half of all workers in manufacturing. The United Kingdom's automotive industry produced 1.27 million automobiles in 2010. Britain's aerospace industry is among the world's foremost. Rolls-Royce, which was privatized in 1987, is one of the principal aero-engine manufacturers in the world. British Aerospace, nationalized during 1978–80 but now privately owned again, manufactures civil aircraft, such military aircraft as the Harrier and the Hawk advanced trainer, and guided weapons, including the Rapier ground-to-air missile.

While the relative importance of the textile and clothing industries has declined considerably since World War II, the United Kingdom continues to produce high-quality woolen textiles. Nevertheless, foreign competition has significantly cut into the textile industry. Following the expiration of the World Trade Organization's longstanding system of textile quotas at the beginning of 2005, the EU signed an agreement with China in June 2005 that imposed new quotas on 10 categories of textile goods, limiting growth in those categories to between 8% and 12.5% a year. The agreement ran until 2007 and was designed to give European textile manufacturers time to adjust to a world of unfettered competition. However, barely a month after the EU-China agreement was signed, China reached its quotas for sweaters, followed soon after by blouses, bras, T-shirts, and flax yarn. Tens of millions of garments piled up in warehouses and customs checkpoints, which affected both retailers and consumers.

Certain smaller industries in the United Kingdom are noted for the quality of their craftsmanship—e.g. pottery, jewelry, goldware, and silverware. Other sectors are the cement industry (which focuses on the manufacture of Portland cement, a British invention); the rubber industry, the world's oldest; paper industries; and leather and footwear.

29 SCIENCE AND TECHNOLOGY

Great Britain, preeminent in the Industrial Revolution from the mid-18th to the mid-19th century, has a long tradition of technological ingenuity and scientific achievement. It was in the United Kingdom that the steam engine, spinning jenny, and power loom were developed, and where the first steam-powered passenger railway entered service. To British inventors also belongs credit for the miner's safety lamp, the friction match, the cathode ray tube, stainless steel, and the first calculating machine. One of the most famous scientific discoveries of the 20th century, the determination of the double-helix structure of the deoxyribonucleic acid (DNA) molecule, took place at the Laboratory of Molecular Biology at Cambridge University. In February 1997, the first successful cloning of an animal from an adult (resulting in "Dolly" the lamb) was performed at the Roslin Institute near Edinburgh, Scotland's leading animal research laboratory. The United Kingdom is also in the forefront of research in radio astronomy, laser holography, and superconductivity. Patent applications in science and technology as of 2009, according to the World Bank, totaled 15,985 in the United Kingdom. Public financing of science was 1.88% of GDP.

The leading government agency for supporting science and technology is the Ministry of Defense, which plays an important role in both the United Kingdom's national security and its role in NATO. In addition, government-industry cooperation in aerospace, biotechnology and electronics has opened new frontiers in science.

The most prestigious scientific institution in the United Kingdom is the Royal Society, founded in 1660 in London. The British Association for the Advancement of Science, headquar-

tered in London, promotes public understanding of science and technology.

30 DOMESTIC TRADE

London is the United Kingdom's leading wholesale and importing center, accounting for more than half the total wholesale turnover. Other important distribution centers are Liverpool, Manchester, Bristol, Glasgow, and Hull.

Normal banking hours are 9 a.m. to 5 p.m., Monday through Friday, but this may vary in country areas. Business hours in London are 9 a.m. to 5:30 p.m., Monday through Friday; shops in certain areas may be open to 7:30 one night a week, usually Wednesday or Thursday. Outside of London, the shops of each town or village may close for a half or full day at midweek. Saturday shopping hours are 9 a.m. to 5:30 p.m. Sunday shopping is becoming increasingly available, from 10 a.m. to 4 p.m. A value-added tax of 20% as of January 2011 applies to most goods and services.

31 FOREIGN TRADE

The United Kingdom is highly dependent on foreign trade. It must import almost all its copper, ferrous metals, lead, zinc, rubber, and raw cotton; most of its tin, raw wool, hides and skins, and many other raw materials; and about one-third of its food.

The United Kingdom's major export commodities are manufactured items, crude petroleum, chemicals, food, beverages, and tobacco. Top sectors for trade and investment in the United Kingdom in 2011 were aircraft and parts, apparel, automotive parts and service equipment, computers and peripherals, cosmetics and toiletries, drugs and pharmaceuticals, education and training, furniture, medical equipment, pollution control, renewable energy equipment, safety and security equipment, telecommunications equipment, and travel and tourism.

The United Kingdom imported $546.5 billion worth of goods and services in 2008, while exporting $405.6 billion worth of goods and services. Major import partners in 2009 were Germany, 12.9%; the United States, 9.7%; China, 8.9%; Netherlands, 7%; France, 6.7%; Belgium, 4.9%; and Norway, 4.8%. Its major export partners were the United States, 14.7%; Germany, 11.1%; France, 8%; Netherlands, 7.8%; Ireland, 6.9%; and Belgium, 4.7%.

Principal Trading Partners – United Kingdom (2010)

(In millions of US dollars)

Country	Total	Exports	Imports	Balance
World	971,997.0	410,297.0	561,700.0	-151,403.0
Germany	112,386.0	41,657.0	70,729.0	-29,072.0
United States	73,899.0	42,547.0	31,352.0	11,195.0
Netherlands	72,087.0	31,703.0	40,384.0	-8,681.0
France	61,523.0	28,686.0	32,837.0	-4,151.0
China	56,824.0	7,898.0	48,926.0	-41,028.0
Belgium	46,092.0	19,990.0	26,102.0	-6,112.0
Ireland	45,048.0	25,344.0	19,704.0	5,640.0
Italy	34,558.0	13,237.0	21,321.0	-8,084.0
Norway	33,546.0	4,043.0	29,503.0	-25,460.0
Spain	30,112.0	14,818.0	15,294.0	-476.0

(…) data not available or not significant.

(n.s.) not specified.

SOURCE: *2011 Direction of Trade Statistics Yearbook,* New York: United Nations, 2011.

32 BALANCE OF PAYMENTS

Throughout the 1960s, revaluations of other currencies adversely affected the pound sterling. Large deficits in the balance of payments appeared in 1964 and 1967, leading to devaluation in November 1967. Another run on sterling prompted a decision to let the pound float on 23 June 1972. The pound then declined steadily, dropping below a value of $2.00 for the first time on 9 March 1976. The oil crisis and the rise in commodity prices in 1974 were even harsher blows to the UK economy. Increasing unemployment, the worldwide recession, and a large budgetary deficit placed the government in an extremely difficult position, since replenishment of currency reserves cost more in terms of sterling, and the need to curb inflation prevented expansion in the economy. Borrowing from the oil-producing states and the EU helped finance the deficits, but a further approach to the IMF became necessary. During the late 1970s, the United Kingdom's visible trade balance was generally negative, although surpluses on invisibles sometimes were sufficient to produce a surplus in the current account.

Increased North Sea oil exports helped produce substantial trade surpluses in 1980–82. The United Kingdom has run a deficit in visible trade since 1983, reaching a peak of $47 billion in 1989, as consumer demand for imported goods ballooned. As recession took hold, imports fell, reducing the visible trade deficit dramatically in 1991. The devaluation of the pound, following the United Kingdom's late 1992 withdrawal from the EU's Exchange Rate Mechanism, increased the cost of imports at the end of 1992. However, the sterling's trade-weighted exchange rate index stabilized by 1995.

In recent years, the export-oriented manufacturing sector has been challenged by an overvalued exchange rate. The United Kingdom is a major overseas investor (especially in the United States) and has an extremely important service sector, dominated by banking and insurance, which consistently generates invisible trade credits. In 2010, the United Kingdom had a foreign trade deficit of $55 billion, amounting to 10.9% of GDP. That year, the current account balance was -$71.6 million.

33 BANKING AND SECURITIES

The United Kingdom is known for its expertise in the field of banking, ranking third in the world after New York and Tokyo. Most activity takes place in the City of London, which has the greatest concentration of banks and the largest insurance market in the world. Until the Labour government of Tony Blair disengaged it from the Treasury, the Bank of England, established in 1694 as a corporate body and nationalized in 1946, held the main government accounts, acted as government agent for the issue and registration of government loans and other financial operations, and was the central note-issuing authority, with the sole right to issue bank notes in England and Wales (some banks in Scotland and Northern Ireland have limited note-issuing rights). It administered exchange control for the Treasury and is responsible for the application of the government's monetary policy to other banks and financial institutions. After its separation from the Treasury, the Bank of England retained the power to establish interest rates, while the Treasury continued to reign in public spending.

In 1762, a club of securities dealers was formed in London to fix rules for market transactions, and in 1773 the first stock exchange was opened in London. In 1801, the London Stock Exchange was constructed on part of its present site. Since that time, it has provided a market for the purchase and sale of securities and has played an important part in providing new capital for industry. The Stock Exchange opened to international competition in October 1986, permitting wider ownership of member firms. Minimum rates of commission on stock sales were abolished. In April 1982, the London Gold Futures Market began operations; it is the only market in Europe making possible worldwide, round-the-clock futures dealings in the metal. In 2007, the London Stock Exchange merged with Borsa Italiana, creating the London Stock Exchange Group. As of 2010, the Exchange had a share trading value of $962 billion.

The banks handling most domestic business are mainly limited liability companies. The four major clearing commercial banking groups are Barclays, Lloyds, Midland, and National Westminster. These banks carry out most of the commercial banking in England and Wales. In Scotland, which has its own clearing system, there are three clearing banks: the Bank of Scotland, the Clydesdale Bank, and the Royal Bank of Scotland. Other institutions, notably the building societies, have begun to compete with the clearing banks by providing current and deposit account facilities.

The National Savings Movement, started in 1916, encourages widespread savings investment by small depositors in trustee savings banks and the National Savings and Investments Bank (formerly known as the Post Office Savings Bank), the largest organization of its kind in the world, with about 20,000 branches in post offices. Merchant banks are of great importance in the financing of trade, both domestic and overseas. In addition, about 275 overseas banks are directly represented in London.

After the "Big Bang"—the deregulation of the United Kingdom's financial markets—the Financial Services Act, which became law in November 1986, set out a system of self-regulating organizations (SROs) to oversee operations in different markets under the overall control of an umbrella body, the Securities and Investment

---

Balance of Payments – United Kingdom (2010)

(In billions of US dollars)

Current Account		**-71.6**
Balance on goods		-152.9
Imports	-563.2	
Exports	410.2	
Balance on services		69.6
Balance on income		42.5
Current transfers		-30.8
Capital Account		**5.0**
Financial Account		**63.6**
Direct investment abroad		-10.7
Direct investment in United Kingdom		47.0
Portfolio investment assets		-130.9
Portfolio investment liabilities		143.9
Financial derivatives		44.9
Other investment assets		-359.9
Other investment liabilities		329.2
Net Errors and Omissions		**13.0**
Reserves and Related Items		**-10.0**

(…) data not available or not significant.

SOURCE: *Balance of Payment Statistics Yearbook 2011*, Washington, DC: International Monetary Fund, 2011.

Board (SIB). In 1996 there were five SROs covering the main financial activities, and since April 1988 any firm conducting investment business must have authorization to do so from the appropriate SRO.

The United Kingdom was the first country to initiate bank rescue packages following the global economic crisis in 2008, with one bailout of £500 billion ($780 billion) in October 2008 and another of £50 billion ($78 billion) in January 2009. The discount rate, or the rate at which the central bank lends money in the short term, was 7.75% in 2010, up significantly from 0.5% in 2009. The commercial bank prime lending rate, the rate at which banks lend to customers, was 4% in 2011, a slight increase over the 2010 figure of 3.962%.

34 INSURANCE

London is the leading international insurance center. It is the largest insurance industry in Europe, and the third-largest in the world. In 2010, the industry managed investments totaling £1.7 trillion. Lloyd's, the world-famous society of private insurers, was originally established in the 17th century as a center for marine insurance but has since built up a worldwide market for other types of insurance.

In the mid-1990s, total life insurance in force came to £1.04 trillion. In the United Kingdom, third-party automobile liability, employers' liability, nuclear facility liability, oil pollution liability, aircraft operators' liability, and professional liability is compulsory, with the government having a monopoly on workers' compensation. As of 2010, according to the Association of British Insurers, the British insurance industry held approximately 13% of investments in the London stock market.

35 PUBLIC FINANCE

The onset of recession in 1990 led to an increased level of public borrowing—about £14 billion in 1991–92, or 2.25% of GDP. By 1993–94, the public sector borrowing requirement had risen to £50 billion, or 8.1% of GDP. In 1994, the government initiated a series of stringent fiscal measures designed to curb the spiraling public sector borrowing requirement (PSBR). Since 1998, the United Kingdom has taken aggressive steps to reform its public spending activities. Reforms included limits on expenditures, higher governmental accountability regarding spending, better resource budgeting, and improved spending flexibility.

The CIA estimated that in 2005 the United Kingdom's central government took in revenues of approximately $881.4 billion and had expenditures of $951 billion. Revenues minus expenditures totaled approximately -$69.6 billion. Public debt in 2005 amounted to 42.2% of GDP. Total external debt was $7.107 trillion. In 2010, the budget of the United Kingdom included $926.7 billion in public revenue and $1.154 trillion in public expenditures. The budget deficit amounted to 10.2% of GDP. Public debt was 76.5% of GDP, with $8.981 trillion of the debt held by foreign entities. The reduction of budget deficits was a priority for the British government in 2011. Austerity measures implemented in 2011 aimed to reduce annual deficits to about 1% of GDP by 2015.

36 TAXATION

Taxes on income include a graduated individual income tax and a corporation tax. Although personal income taxes are high rela-

Public Finance – United Kingdom (2008)		
(In millions of pounds, central government figures)		
Revenue and Grants	**560,902**	**100.0%**
Tax revenue	413,598	73.7%
Social contributions	117,955	21.0%
Grants	5,440	1.0%
Other revenue	23,909	4.3%
Expenditures	**627,814**	**100.0%**
General public services	97,199	15.5%
Defense	36,742	5.9%
Public order and safety	27,130	4.3%
Economic affairs	59,644	9.5%
Environmental protection	6,030	1.0%
Housing and community amenities	7,576	1.2%
Health	107,854	17.2%
Recreational, culture, and religion	8,122	1.3%
Education	75,970	12.1%
Social protection	201,377	32.1%

(…) data not available or not significant.

SOURCE: *Government Finance Statistics Yearbook 2010*, Washington, DC: International Monetary Fund, 2010.

tive to the United States, they have been reduced several times since 1980.

As of 2011, the United Kingdom imposed a corporate profits income tax rate between 21% and 29.75%. Capital gains are taxed at the standard corporate rate, but nonresident companies are generally not taxed on capital gains derived from the sale of shares in a resident subsidiary company. However, companies that derive capital gains from the sale of assets that are located in and are used to carry on business activity in the United Kingdom are subject to the capital gains tax. Dividends are not taxed. Income from interest and from royalties is subject to withholding taxes of 20% and 22%, respectively.

Income tax is charged on all income that has its origin in Britain and on all income arising abroad of persons resident in Britain. However, the United Kingdom has entered into agreements with many countries to provide relief from double taxation. Generally, the United Kingdom has a progressive personal income tax structure with a top rate of 50%. For the 2010/11 fiscal year, a 20% rate was applied to taxable income up to £35,000 ($54,565). A 40% rate was applied on income up to £150,000 ($233,850), with a 50% rate on income above that amount.

In January 1973, a value-added tax (VAT) was introduced with a standard rate of 10%, replacing the purchase tax and bringing the UK's tax policy into harmony with the EU. In 1991, the standard rate was increased to 17.5% and in 1997, the reduced rate, applied to some medicines, medical equipment, heating oil, gas, electricity, small service businesses and some transportation services, was lowered from 8% to 5%. The VAT increased to 20% in 2011. A zero rate applies to most foods, books, newspapers and periodicals, and certain other goods. Services such as insurance, health, education, and land and rents are also exempt. Other taxes are levied on petroleum products, tobacco, and alcoholic drinks. There are also various stamp duties.

³⁷CUSTOMS AND DUTIES

Import licensing and quotas were the general rule in the United Kingdom between 1939 and 1959. For select items from specified countries or groups of countries, an individual license was required for each import. In June 1959, however, the United Kingdom began to remove important controls on virtually all raw materials and basic foodstuffs and on some machinery imported from the United States. With UK entry into the free-trade area of the EU, a tariff-free area was created. In addition, the United Kingdom uses the EU's common external tariff for non-EU imports. Rates range from 2–14% on most goods. The four principal types of import charges are customs duties, agricultural levies, value-added taxes, and excise duties on goods such as alcohol, tobacco, and tobacco products. The United Kingdom also levies a VAT on imports with a standard rate of 20%, with reduced rates ranging from 0% to 5%.

³⁸FOREIGN INVESTMENT

London is considered Europe's top financial and business center. London is the headquarters for some 130 of the top 500 global companies. With few exceptions, the United Kingdom does not discriminate between nationals and foreign individuals, and imposes few impediments to foreign ownership. Public-sector procurement policies seek best value and best practice regardless of national origin. The privatization of state-owned utilities is ongoing and offers additional opportunities for foreign investment.

The United Kingdom's outward FDI has normally exceeded its inward flow. Before World War I, British overseas investments were valued at more than $30 billion (adjusted into 1960 dollars). Even in the period between the two world wars, British foreign investments remained remarkably high. After World War II, the United Kingdom, having given up many of its overseas dependencies and having incurred enormous foreign debts to wage the war, had to liquidate a large part of its overseas holdings. As its economy recovered, the United Kingdom again began to invest overseas. From 1955 to 1964, gross total private capital outflow was at an annual average of £300 million. The abolition of exchange controls in 1979 also encouraged overseas investment. By 1985, private British investment overseas (direct and portfolio) had risen to £76.7 billion. The United Kingdom was the fourth-largest source of outward FDI, after the United States, France, and Spain. 54% of this went to countries in Europe, and 25% to North America.

Over the 10-year period from 1992 to 2002, foreign direct investment (FDI) inflow totaled $484.5 billion, the second highest in the world (after the United States by some distance: the United States' 10-year total was $1.3 trillion). In 1997, FDI inflow rose 60% over 1996 to $33.3 billion, placing the United Kingdom third in the world, behind the United States and China. FDI inflow peaked in 2000 at $116.6 billion (a fourth-place finish, behind the United States, Belgium-Luxembourg, and Germany), and then fell to $62 billion in the economic slowdown of 2001. From 2001–05, FDI inflows averaged 2.9% of GDP. Foreign direct investment (FDI) in the United Kingdom was a net inflow of $72.9 billion according to World Bank figures published in 2009. FDI represented 3.35% of GDP.

³⁹ECONOMIC DEVELOPMENT

Like many other industrialized nations of the West, the United Kingdom has sought to combine steady economic growth with a high level of employment, increased productivity, and continuing improvement in living standards. Attainment of these basic objectives was hindered after World War II by recurrent deficits in the balance of payments and by severe inflationary pressures. As a result, economic policy has chiefly been directed toward correcting these two underlying weaknesses in the economy. When crises have arisen, emergency measures have often conflicted with long-term objectives. In 1967, for example, the government devalued the pound by 14% in order to improve the balance-of-payments position, but simultaneously increased taxes and reduced the growth rate of public expenditures in order to restrain home demand in both public and private sectors. Since the almost uninterrupted upward trend in prices resulted principally from the tendency for money income to rise faster than the volume of production, the government sought to institute a policy designed to align the rise in money income with increases in productivity.

Various bodies have been set up to foster economic development and improve industrial efficiency, notably the National Economic Development Council, which was established in 1962 to coordinate industry before it was abolished in 1992. Another important body, the National Enterprise Board was set up in 1974 to help plan industrial investment, particularly in manufacturing and export industries; the NEB was combined with the National Research and Development Corp. in 1981 to form the British Technology Group, which was privatized in 1991. The Labour government in the 1970s began to de-emphasize increased social services and government participation in the economy and to stress increased incentives for private investment. (A notable exception was in the exploitation of North Sea oil resources.) General investment incentives included tax allowances on new buildings, plants, and machinery. The Conservative government elected in 1979 sought to reduce the role of government in the economy by improving incentives, removing controls, reducing taxes, moderating the money supply, and privatizing several large state-owned companies. This policy was continued by succeeding Conservative governments into the 1990s. The election of a Labour government in 1997 did not reverse this trend. Indeed, privatization is now widely accepted by most of the Labour Party (with the exception of the dwindling numbers of the wing of the party with strong ties to trade unions).

The United Kingdom has long been a major source of both bilateral aid (direct loans and grants) and multilateral aid (contributions to international agencies) to developing countries. To coordinate the overall aid program and its proportions of bilateral and multilateral aid, capital aid, and technical assistance, the Ministry of Overseas Development was set up in 1962. Its functions were subsequently taken over by the Overseas Development Administration (ODA) and are now administered by the Department for International Development (DFID). Since 1958, the terms for development loans have progressively softened, and a policy of interest-free loans for the poorest developing countries was introduced in 1965. Unlike other donors, the United Kingdom provides funds to the recipient governments, rather than funding individual projects. International development funds accounted for 0.56% of gross national income in 2010.

The most important issue facing Britain in the early 2000s was membership in the Economic and Monetary Union (EMU). Labour Prime Minister Tony Blair decided to opt out of EMU at its inception in 1998 and promised a referendum on British membership. By 2005, however, there was little or no prospect of the United Kingdom holding a referendum on joining the EMU over the succeeding five years. The opposition Conservatives opposed abandoning the pound and had the support of a majority of the British population on the issue. The global economic crisis in 2008 and the debt crisis within the Eurozone adversely affected the UK and its position within the EU. Conservative Prime Minister David Cameron vetoed a treaty in December 2011 designed to prevent a Eurozone crisis.

Another long-term economic problem facing the United Kingdom is the aging of its population and the pressures this phenomenon will place on its pension system. By 2035, the number of pensioners in the United Kingdom will rise by 45% as the postwar baby boomer generation retires; by 2050, the increase will reach 55%. If these people are to maintain their standards of living in relation to the rest of society, either the state pension age must be raised or workers must pay more taxes to support the aging population. In an effort to contain rising costs throughout the government, the government announced austerity measures in 2011 that were expected to last through 2017, with the goal of reducing budget deficits from 10% of GDP (2010) to about 1% in 2015.

40 SOCIAL DEVELOPMENT

A gradually evolved system of social security, placed in full operation in 1948, provides national insurance, industrial injuries insurance, family allowances, and national assistance throughout the United Kingdom. The National Insurance scheme provides benefits for sickness, unemployment, maternity, and widowhood, as well as guardian's allowances, retirement pensions, and death grants. The program is financed by contributions from employees, employers, and the government. A percentage of these contributions are allocated to the National Health Service, which provides extensive benefits to workers and their families. Retirement pensions cover men at 65 and women at 60, and benefits increase annually to adjust for cost of living. The first work injury law was instituted in 1897 and currently covers all employees with the exception of the self-employed. There is a universal child benefit and tax credit to residents with one or more children, funded by the government.

Financial assistance for the poor is provided through a system of benefits in the form of a supplementary pension for those over statutory retirement age and a supplementary allowance for others. It also provides temporary accommodation for the homeless in specially designated reception centers. For poverty-stricken families in which the head of the household is in full-time employment, a family income supplement is paid. Maternity benefits cover women who have been employed for 26 weeks.

Equal opportunity between the sexes is provided for by law, although discrimination against women continues. Sexual harassment is a problem in the workplace and women on average earn 18% less than men. Violence against women persists; however, there are many laws and substantial penalties providing protection.

The government at all levels recognizes the legal right to freedom of religion. Human rights organizations have criticized legislation in Northern Ireland that denies suspects the right to immediate legal counsel and the right to silence. There are also some security-related restrictions on the freedoms of assembly and association in Northern Ireland.

Although racial discrimination is prohibited by law, people of Asian and African origin are subject to discrimination and harassment. Ethnic minorities are also more likely to be stopped and searched by police. Police shot and killed an unarmed black man, Mark Duggan, on 4 August 2011 in North London. A peaceful protest occurred on 6 August, during which protestors marched to the police station. Anti-police riots broke out that evening and continued in North London and other places in London and throughout England through 10 August. The riots sparked debate about larger social and economic problems in the United Kingdom.

41 HEALTH

A comprehensive National Health Service (NHS), established in 1948, provides full medical care to all residents of the United Kingdom. NHS delivers health care through 129 health authorities, each of which receives money from the government and then purchases a preset amount of treatment each year from hospitals. Included are general medical, dental, pharmaceutical, and optical services; hospital and specialist services (in patients' homes when necessary) for physical and mental illnesses; and local health authority services (maternity and child welfare, vaccination, prevention of illness, health visiting, home nursing, and other services). The patient is free to choose a family doctor from any in the service, subject to the physician's acceptance. General tax revenues meet most of the cost of the NHS; the remainder is paid through National Health Insurance contributions and charges for certain items, including eyeglasses and prescription drugs. Compared with other OECD countries, the United Kingdom's per capita expenditure on health care is low. In 2011, the country spent 8.7% of its GDP on health care, amounting to $3,285 per person.

Life expectancy has increased from 50 years at birth in 1900 to 80.05 years in 2011. Rising living standards, medical advances, the growth of medical facilities and their general availability, and the smaller size of the family are some factors in the improved health of the British people. In 2011, there were 27 physicians, 103 nurses and midwives, and 34 hospital beds per 10,000 inhabitants. Deaths from infectious diseases have been greatly reduced, although the proportion of deaths from circulatory diseases—including heart attacks and strokes—and cancer has risen. Infant mortality has decreased from 142 per 1,000 live births in 1900–02 to 4.62 in 2011. The total fertility rate in 2011 was estimated at 1.91 children born per woman. In 2008, the maternal mortality rate, according to the World Bank, was 12 per 100,000 births. A high portion of women used birth control.

All specialist and auxiliary health services in England are the direct responsibility of the secretary of state for social services. In Wales, Scotland, and Northern Ireland, the corresponding services and administrative bodies fall under the respective secretaries of state. All hospitals, except a few run mostly by religious orders, are also in the NHS. The United Kingdom implemented major reforms in its health care services, including improvements in virtually all facets of the program. Areas of concern included incidence of coronary/stroke, cancer, accidents, mental illness, and HIV/AIDS. Half the British population is currently overweight. These high rates have been attributed to a sedentary lifestyle during leisure time.

In 2011, it was estimated that 86% of children were vaccinated against measles. Since 1982, to help control the spread of AIDS, the government has funded and implemented measures for blood testing, research, public education, and other social services relating to the disease. The HIV/AIDS adult prevalence rate was 0.2% in 2009.

42 HOUSING

Over 50% of families now live in a post-1945 dwelling. Most homeowners finance their purchase through a home mortgage loan from a building society, bank, insurance company, or other financial institution. New houses are built by both the public and private sectors, but most are built by the private sector for sale to owner-occupiers. The main providers of new subsidized housing are housing associations, which own, manage, and maintain over 600,000 homes in England alone. Local housing authorities were in the past primarily concerned with slum clearance; however, large-scale clearance virtually ended in the mid-1980s, with emphasis shifting to modernization of substandard homes and community improvement.

According to the Department of Communities and Local Government, between 2001 and 2010, 1.5 million more dwellings appeared in the United Kingdom, for a total of 23.5 million. As of 2008, 37% of this stock was semi-detached housing. In 2007, 15.4 million of these dwellings were owner-occupied.

Projections from the Department of Communities and Local Government predict that there will be 27.5 million households in the UK by 2033. One-third of this growth will be in London and southeast England. Some 19% of the population is expected to live alone.

43 EDUCATION

Although responsibility for education in the United Kingdom rests with the central government, schools are mainly administered by local education authorities. Overall, the United Kingdom has a literacy rate of 99%. Public expenditure on education represented 5.5% of GDP in 2009. The majority of primary students attend state schools that are owned and maintained by local education authorities. A small minority attend voluntary schools mostly run by the churches and also financed by the local authorities.

Education is compulsory for all children between the ages of 5 and 16. Since 1989, the government has introduced a "National School Curriculum" in England and Wales comprised of four key stages: five to seven (infants); 7 to 11 (juniors); 11 to 14 (pre-GCSE); and 14 to 16 (GCSE). Similar reforms are being introduced in Scotland and Northern Ireland. The main school examination, the General Certificate of Secondary Education (GCSE), is taken in England, Wales, and Northern Ireland at around the age of 16. A separate exam system exists in Scotland. Of the 2,500 registered independent schools, the largest and most important (Winchester, Eton, Harrow, and others) are known in England as "public schools." Many have centuries of tradition behind them and are world famous. The academic year runs from September to July.

In 2008, the World Bank estimated that 100% of age-eligible children in the United Kingdom were enrolled in primary school. Secondary enrollment for age-eligible children stood at 93%. Tertiary enrollment was estimated at 57%. Of those enrolled in tertiary education, there were 100 male students for every 140 female students. Most students complete their primary education.

Including the Open University, a nonresidential institution whose courses are conducted by television and radio broadcasts and correspondence texts, Britain had about 100 universities in 2010 (compared with 17 in 1945). As a result of legislation, nearly all polytechnics have become universities and started awarding their own degrees in 1993. The well-known Universities of Oxford and Cambridge date from the 12th and 13th centuries, respectively; the Scottish universities of St. Andrews, Glasgow, Aberdeen, and Edinburgh from the 15th and 16th centuries. Besides the universities, there were more than 800 other institutions of higher education, including technical, art, and commercial colleges run by local authorities.

In November 2010, university students across the country began participating in a series of demonstrations, walkouts, marches, and other protest events over the government's plan to decrease university funding and raise the tuition cap from about $5,198 per year to more than $14,220 per year. Two major demonstrations took place outside of the headquarters for the Conservative party and the Liberal Democrat party. The proposed plan cuts public university funding by up to 40%, thus making the raised tuition cap necessary as schools will need to find other measures to meet costs. Under the plan, schools that expect to charge more than $9,480 per year (6,000 pounds) are required to develop special access agreements with the national Office for Fair Access, through which the university commits to developing special programs to recruit and assist low-income students. These schools will also be required to participate in the national scholarships program. The plan will raise the amount offered to low-income students as maintenance grants (funds that help the student cover basic expenses while studying full-time) from $4,590 per year to $5,135 per year for those from households with an annual income of less than $39,500. The government will continue to offer low-interest loans to students. These loans are typically paid back with payments based on a percentage of the students' income once they have graduated and found employment. Students have 30 years to pay off the loans, after which any remaining amount is forgiven. The plan was passed by Parliament and is expected to go into effect in September 2012. With these changes, the average student loan debt upon graduation is expected to rise from $47,390 to $60,000.

44 LIBRARIES AND MUSEUMS

London has more than 500 libraries, among them the British Library, which is the national library and the largest library in the United Kingdom, with over 150 million items in 2011 and an average acquisition rate of about 3 million items per year. Special collections and treasures include the Magna Carta, a notebook of Leonardo da Vinci, original manuscripts of Jane Austen and James Joyce (among others), and musical manuscripts of G.F. Handel and the Beatles (among others). There is a branch location of the British Library at Boston Spa, West Yorkshire. The National Library of Scotland, with about seven million volumes, is in Edinburgh, and the National Library of Wales, with some four million volumes, in Aberystwyth. Each of these is a copyright library, entitled to receive a copy of every new book published in the United Kingdom. The Bodleian Library at Oxford University is also a copyright library with about 6.7 million volumes; there are nine branch locations of the Bodleian in Oxford. Oxford University sponsors over 100 departmental libraries. The Cambridge University Library, also a copyright library, has 5.9 million volumes throughout five locations.

Other major libraries in London include the University of London Central Library (two million volumes), the London Library (the largest public subscription library), the Science Museum Library (600,000), the Victoria and Albert Museum Art Library, the Public Record Office (containing such national historical treasures as the Domesday Book), and the libraries of such institutions as the Royal Institute of International Affairs (140,000), the Royal Commonwealth Society (150,000), the Royal Geographical Society (150,000), the Royal Academy of Arts (22,000), and the National Library for the Blind. In 2002, a Women's Library opened in London, giving a home to publications documenting women's lives in Britain.

There are major libraries at the Universities of Edinburgh (2.4 million), Glasgow (1.4 million), Queen's University in Belfast (1.1 million), and St. Andrew's (920,000). Manchester Metropolitan University has one million volumes.

London has about 395 public libraries. The South Western Regional Library System links the public libraries of Bristol, Devon, Foursite (Somerset, South Gloucestershire, North Somerset, Bath and North East Somerset), Gloucestershire, Swindon, and Wiltshire. The Edinburgh City Libraries maintain a central library and 25 branch libraries, as well as a mobile unit and two lending locations, plus several hospitals. Over 50 public libraries in Scotland were established through the assistance of the industrialist Andrew Carnegie. Nearly all of the public libraries in Scotland are linked via the Internet. Public libraries in Northern Ireland are managed by five regional Education and Library Boards. The Belfast Education and Library Board maintains the Belfast Central Library and 20 community public libraries, as well as two mobile libraries.

The United Kingdom is a museum-lover's dream. Almost every city and large town has museums of art, archaeology, and natural history. There are more than 1,000 museums and art galleries, ranging from nearly two dozen great national institutions to small collections housed in a few rooms. London has the British Museum (founded 1759), with its vast collections of archaeological and ethnographic material from all over the world, and the Victoria and Albert Museum, including extensive collections of works of fine and applied arts. The National Gallery, the Tate Gallery, and the National Portrait Gallery are among other prestigious London art museums. Other museums located in London include the London Transport Museum (founded 1978), the National Maritime Museum (1934), the Natural History Museum (1963), and the Science Museum (1857). There is also a collection of royal ceremonial dress at Kensington Palace, and the Sherlock Holmes Museum, featuring Victorian memorabilia, opened in 1990. The Tate Gallery of Modern Art, featuring rotating exhibits arranged by theme, opened in May 2000. There are important museums and art galleries in Liverpool, Manchester, Leicester, Birmingham, Bristol, Norwich, Southampton, York, Glasgow, Leeds, and other

cities. Oxford and Cambridge each have many museums, and several other universities also have important collections. Private art collections in historic family mansions are open to the public at specified times.

The National Museum and Gallery of Wales and the Museum of Welsh Life are in Cardiff. There is also a Welsh State Museum in Llanberis. The national museums of Scotland include the Royal Museum, the Museum of Scotland, and the National War Museum of Scotland, all in Edinburgh. The Museum of Scottish Country Life is in East Kilbride. There are at least three museums in Scotland that celebrate the life and work of native poet Robert Burns. The Ulster Museums and the Northern Irish Folk Museum are in Belfast.

45 MEDIA

The United Kingdom operates a technologically advanced international and domestic telecommunications system. Domestic services are provided by a mix of fiber-optic systems, buried cables, and microwave radio relay stations. International service is provided by 40 coaxial submarine cables, 12 satellite ground stations, and no less than 8 large international switching centers. In 2009, the CIA reported that there were 32 million telephone landlines in the United Kingdom. In addition to landlines, mobile phone subscriptions averaged 130 per 100 people. There were 219 FM radio stations, 431 AM radio stations, and 3 shortwave radio stations. Internet users numbered 83 per 100 citizens. In 2010, the country had about 7.03 million Internet hosts. Prominent newspapers in 2010, with circulation numbers listed parenthetically, included the *Guardian* (345,884), the *Financial Times* (434,196), and the *Daily Mail* (2,214,117), as well as 129 other major newspapers. There are some 2,000 weekly papers, numerous specialized papers, and about 7,000 periodicals in circulation throughout the United Kingdom.

Radio and television broadcasting services are provided by the British Broadcasting Corp. (BBC), which was established as a public corporation in 1927, and by the Independent Television Commission (ITC) and the Radio Authority, commercial concerns whose powers are defined in the Independent Broadcasting Authority (IBA) Act of 1973. The BBC broadcasts on two television channels and the Independent Television Commission broadcasts on ITV and Channel Four, which began operating in 1982. BBC Radio offers five national radio networks in the medium- and long-wave bands, as well as FM programming and an overseas service in 37 languages. Both the BBC and IBA operate local radio services; the BBC has 39 local stations (including 2 for the Channel Islands). In September of 1992, the first national commercial radio station, Classic FM, was inaugurated. Since then, several commercial stations have entered the market.

During the 2000s, the newspaper with the highest circulation was the tabloid *News of the World*, which distributed nearly 4 million papers per week. The publication printed its final issue in July 2011, closing down abruptly in the wake of a phone-hacking scandal that shook even the highest ranks of Rupert Murdoch's News International. Investigations documented the hacking of phones of celebrities, royalty, and politicians, but the revelation that reporters had hacked the cell phone of Milly Dowler, a murdered 11-year-old girl, led to public outrage, evidence of police bribery, and the resignation of high-level employees and police and government officials. Further investigations were pending in the United Kingdom and the United States as of early 2012, where News Corporation, the media conglomerate that houses News International, is headquartered.

Wales has five daily newspapers: *South Wales Echo, South Wales Evening Post, Western Mail, South Wales Argus,* and *Evening Leader*. Scotland has six morning, five evening, and four Sunday papers, plus the Scottish editions of the *Daily Mail* and the *Sunday Express*. The *Glasgow Herald* and *The Scotsman*, an Edinburgh paper, are the most influential. Others include: *Sunday Mail, Daily Record, Evening Times, The Press and Journal, Courier and Advertiser,* and *Evening News*. About 120 weekly papers are published in Scottish towns. Northern Ireland has two morning papers, one evening paper, and one Sunday paper, all published in Belfast, plus a number of weeklies. The largest is the evening paper, *Belfast Telegraph* (circulation 94,602).

Britain's ethnic minorities publish over 60 newspapers and magazines, most of them weekly, fortnightly, or monthly. These include the Chinese *Sing Tao* and *Wen Wei Po*, the Urdu *Daily Jang,* and the Arabic *Al-Arab* (the foregoing are all dailies), as well as newspapers in Gujarati, Bengali, Hindi and Punjabi. The *Weekly Journal,* aimed at Britain's black community, was begun in 1992.

The periodicals published weekly, monthly, and quarterly in the United Kingdom cover a huge range of special interests. Leading opinion journals are *New Statesman, The Economist,* and *Spectator*. The *Times Literary Supplement* is highly influential in cultural affairs. The chief news agency is Reuters, a worldwide organization servicing British papers with foreign and Commonwealth news and the world press with British and foreign news.

Although there is no government censorship of news or opinion, the Official Secrets Act, stringent libel and slander laws, and restrictions governing the disclosure of court proceedings do impose limitations on press freedom. In addition, the press regulates itself through the Press Council, which adjudicates complaints about newspaper practices from local officials and the public. Views critical of the government are well established.

46 ORGANIZATIONS

The national body representing British industry is the Confederation of British Industry, incorporated in 1965 and directly or indirectly representing about 250,000 companies. The Association of British Chambers of Commerce (founded in 1860) has 240 affiliated UK chambers. Agricultural organizations include the National Farmers' Union, agricultural cooperative societies, and other specialized associations. There are numerous professional associations for nearly every occupation. While some of these include members from all of the United Kingdom, there are also several associations particularly for Scottish businesses and professionals.

A vast number of organizations exist within the United Kingdom. Voluntary social service organizations number in the thousands. Social work on a national scale is carried out largely under religious sponsorship. Cooperation between Protestant churches is fostered by the British Council of Churches. The Council of Christians and Jews works for cooperation between these faiths. The principal coordinating body in general social service is the National Council of Social Service. There are national chapters of the Red Cross Society, Amnesty International, Greenpeace, Habitat for Humanity, and other major international organizations.

The British Council promotes a wider knowledge of the United Kingdom and its people abroad and develops cultural relations with other countries. There are more than 300 learned societies. The Arts Council of Great Britain (founded in 1946) promotes the fine arts and higher artistic standards, and advises government bodies on artistic matters. The Royal Academy and the Royal Scottish Academy are other leading bodies in the arts. The National Book League, the Royal Society of Literature, the British Academy, the English Association, the Bibliographical Society, and other groups foster interest in literature, language, and scholarship. There are also numerous clubs for hobbyists, enthusiasts, and fans with a wide variety of interests.

The Arts Council of Wales was established in 1967. Arts and Cultural organizations in Scotland include the Royal Scottish Academy of Music and Drama; the Royal Celtic Society; the Royal Scottish Academy of Painting, Sculpture and Architecture; the Royal Scottish Country Dance Society; the Scottish Arts Council; and the Scottish Games Association. Clan associations are also popular in Scotland, with many providing genealogical research and social events and contact. The Ulster Historical Foundation in Belfast is a prominent genealogical research group.

The National Council for Voluntary Youth Services includes most of the large youth groups. The leading political parties, major religious denominations, and some adult voluntary organizations, such as the Red Cross, also maintain youth organizations, as do the Scouts Association and the Girl Guides Association. There are numerous sports associations for participants of all ages. The Scottish Games Association specifically promotes traditional Highland games.

47 TOURISM, TRAVEL, AND RECREATION

The United Kingdom is a popular tourist destination, rich in natural as well as cultural attractions. Landscapes range from farmlands and gardens to sandy beaches, moors, and rocky coasts. Architectural sights include stone and thatched cottages, stately country houses, mansions, and castles. Among the many historic dwellings open to the public are the Welsh castles Cilgerran (11th century), Dolbadarn (12th century), and Conway and Caernarvon (both 13th century); the 10-century-old Traquair House near Peebles, the oldest continuously inhabited house in Scotland, and the Palace of Holyroodhouse in Edinburgh; and Warwick Castle, near Stratford-upon-Avon, the birthplace of William Shakespeare. Distinguished cathedrals include St. Paul's in London and those in Canterbury, Exeter, Norwich, Winchester, and York. At Bushmills, in Northern Ireland, the oldest distillery in the world may be visited, and some of Scotland's 100 malt whiskey distilleries also offer tours.

Among London's extraordinary attractions are Buckingham Palace, the Tower of London, and Westminster Abbey. Of the wide range of entertainment available, London is particularly noted for its theater, including the Royal Shakespeare Company. Folk music may be heard throughout the United Kingdom; traditional community gatherings for music and dancing, called ceilidhs, are held in Scotland, often in pubs, and Edinburgh is the site of one of the world's largest folk festivals, as well as an annual festival of classical music and other performing arts.

Scotland, where golf developed in the 15th century, has many superb golf courses, as does the rest of the United Kingdom; some

70 Highland Games and Gatherings take place in Scotland from May to September. Other popular sports include fishing, riding, sailing, rugby, cricket, and football (soccer). Wimbledon is the site of perhaps the world's most prestigious tennis competition. London hosted the summer Olympics in 1908 and 1948, and was scheduled to host again in 2012. England hosted and won the World Cup soccer championship in 1966.

In principle, foreigners entering the United Kingdom must have a valid passport and a visa issued by British consular authorities abroad. However, citizens of Ireland do not need a passport, and citizens of OECD, Commonwealth, and Latin American countries, among others, need no visa.

The *Tourism Factbook*, published by the UN World Tourism Organization, reported 29.9 million incoming tourists to the United Kingdom in 2009, who spent a total of $38.5 billion. Of those incoming tourists, there were 22.2 million from Europe. There were 1.25 million hotel beds available in the United Kingdom, which had an occupancy rate of 43%. The estimated daily cost to visit London, the capital, was $518. The cost of visiting other cities averaged $265.

⁴⁸FAMOUS PERSONS

Rulers and Statesmen

English rulers of renown include Alfred the Great (849–99), king of the West Saxons, who defeated and held off the Danish invaders; William I (the Conqueror, 1027–87), duke of Normandy, who conquered England (1066–70) and instituted many changes in the structure of English government and society; Henry II (1133–89), who centralized the power of the royal government, and his sons Richard I (the Lion-Hearted, 1157–99), leader of the Third Crusade, and John (1167?–1216), from whom the barons wrested the Magna Carta; Edward I (1239–1307), who subdued Wales and established the parliamentary system; Edward III (1312–77), who for a time conquered part of France, and did much to promote English commerce; Henry VIII (1491–1547), who separated the Anglican Church from the Roman Catholic Church and centralized administrative power; Elizabeth I (1533–1603), during whose reign, begun in 1558, England achieved great commercial, industrial, and political power, and the arts flourished; and Victoria (1819–1901), under whom Britain attained unprecedented prosperity and empire.

Among the statesmen distinguished in English history are Thomas à Becket (1118?–70), archbishop of Canterbury, who defended the rights of the church against the crown; Simon de Montfort, earl of Leicester (1208?–65), who in 1265 summoned the first Parliament; and Thomas Wolsey (1475?–1530), cardinal, archbishop of York, and Henry VIII's brilliant lord chancellor. Oliver Cromwell (1599–1658) established a republican and Puritan Commonwealth. Sir Robert Walpole, first earl of Oxford (1676–1745), unified cabinet government in the person of the prime minister and laid the foundations for free trade and a modern colonial policy. As England moved increasingly toward democratic government, important progress was achieved under the liberal statesmen William Pitt, first earl of Chatham (1708–78); his son William Pitt (1759–1806); and Charles James Fox (1749–1806). Outstanding statesmen of the 19th century were William Wilberforce (1759–1833); Henry John Temple, third Viscount Palmerston (1784–1865); Sir Robert Peel (1788–1850); Benjamin Disraeli, earl of Beaconsfield (1804–81); and William Ewart Gladstone (1809–98). Twentieth-century leaders include David Lloyd George, first earl of Dwyfor (1863–1945), prime minister during World War I; and Sir Winston Leonard Spencer Churchill (1874–1965), prime minister during World War II, historian, and winner of the Nobel Prize for literature in 1953. In 1979, Margaret (Hilda Roberts) Thatcher (b. 1925) became the nation's first woman prime minister. The reigning monarch since 1952 has been Queen Elizabeth II (b. 1926). The heir to the throne is Charles, prince of Wales (b. 1948), whose marriage on 29 July 1981 to Lady Diana Frances Spencer (1961–1997; at marriage, Diana, princess of Wales) was seen by a worldwide television audience of 750 million people.

Explorers and Navigators

British explorers and navigators played an important part in charting the course of empire. Sir Martin Frobisher (1535?–94), who set sail from England in search of the Northwest Passage, reached Canada in 1576. Sir Francis Drake (1545?–96) was the first Englishman to sail around the world. John Davis (1550?–1605) explored the Arctic and Antarctic, sailed to the South Seas, and discovered the Falkland Islands. Henry Hudson (d. 1611) explored the Arctic regions and North America. Sir Walter Raleigh (1552?–1618) was a historian and poet, as well as a navigator and colonizer of the New World. James Cook (1728–79) charted the coasts of Australia and New Zealand. Scottish-born David Livingstone (1813–73) explored central Africa while doing missionary work. Welsh-born Henry Morton Stanley (John Rowlands, 1841–1904) was sent by a US newspaper to find Livingstone in 1871 and, having done so, returned for further exploration of Africa. Sir Richard Francis Burton (1821–90), an Orientalist known for his translation of the *Arabian Nights,* and John Hanning Speke (1827–64) explored central Africa while searching for the source of the Nile.

Great British military figures include John Churchill, first duke of Marlborough (1650–1722), who attained many victories in the War of the Spanish Succession and in later campaigns against the French; Horatio, Viscount Nelson (1758–1805), the foremost British naval hero, whose career was climaxed by victory and death at Trafalgar; the Irish-born soldier-statesman Arthur Wellesley, first Duke of Wellington (1769–1852), whose brilliant campaigns culminated in the defeat of Napoleon at Waterloo; General Charles George Gordon (1833–85), who gained victories in China, acquiring the nickname "Chinese," and died while fighting against the Mahdi in Khartoum; Field Marshal Viscount Montgomery (Bernard Law Montgomery, 1887–1976), British military leader during World War II; Welsh-born Thomas Edward Lawrence (1888–1935), known as "Lawrence of Arabia," who led the Arabs in uprisings against the Turks during World War I; and Lord Mountbatten of Burma (Louis Battenberg, 1900–1979), supreme Allied commander in Southeast Asia (1943–46) and last viceroy and first governor-general of India (1946–48).

Philosophers and Legal Scholars

Sir Thomas Littleton (1407?–81) wrote *Tenures,* a comprehensive work on English land law that was used as a textbook for over three centuries. Sir Edward Coke (1552–1634), a champion of the common law, wrote the *Institutes of the Laws of England,* popularly known as *Coke on Littleton.* Sir William Blackstone (1723–

80) wrote *Commentaries on the Laws of England,* which became a basic text in modern legal education and strongly influenced the evolution of jurisprudence in the United States as well as in Britain. The jurist-philosopher Jeremy Bentham (1748–1832) championed liberal law reform.

Roger Bacon (1214?–92), philosopher and scientist, wrote treatises ranging over the whole field of human knowledge. John Duns Scotus (1265?–1308) was a Scottish-born dialectician and theologian. William of Ockham (1300?–1349) laid the foundation of the modern theory of the separation of church and state. John Wesley (1703–91) was the founder of Methodism. Chief among modern philosophers are Thomas Hobbes (1588–1679), John Locke (1632–1704), the Irish-born bishop and idealist thinker George Berkeley (1685–1753), John Stuart Mill (1806–73), Alfred North Whitehead (1861–1947), George Edward Moore (1873–1958), Ludwig Joseph Johann Wittgenstein (b. Austria, 1889–1951), and Sir Alfred Jules Ayer (b. 1910–1989). A philosopher and mathematician who widely influenced contemporary social thought was Bertrand Arthur William Russell, third Earl Russell (1872–1970).

Historians and Economists

Noted historians include Raphael Holinshed (d. 1580?), Edward Gibbon (1737–94), John Emerich Edward Dalberg-Acton, first Baron Acton (1834–92), William Edward Hartpole Lecky (1836–1903), John Richard Green (1837–83), Frederic William Maitland (1850–1906), George Macaulay Trevelyan (1876–1962), Giles Lytton Strachey (1880–1932), Sir Lewis Bernstein Namier (1880–1960), Arnold Joseph Toynbee (1889–1975), Edward Hallett Carr (1892–1982), E.P. Thompson (1924–1993), Eric Hobsbawm (1917–), Catherine Hall (1946–), Linda Colley (1949–), and David Cannadine (1950–).

Thomas Robert Malthus (1766–1834) and David Ricardo (1772–1823) were among the first modern economists. Robert Owen (1771–1858) was an influential Welsh-born socialist, industrial reformer, and philanthropist. Walter Bagehot (1826–77) was a distinguished critic and social scientist. The theories of John Maynard Keynes (Baron Keynes, 1883–1946) have strongly influenced the economic practices of many governments in recent years. Sir James George Frazer (1854–1941), a Scottish-born anthropologist and author of *The Golden Bough,* was a pioneer in the fields of comparative religion and comparative mythology. Herbert Spencer (1820–1903) was an influential economic and social philosopher. Sir Arthur John Evans (1851–1941) was an archaeologist who explored the ruins of ancient Crete. Anna Freud (b. Austria, 1895–1982), daughter of Sigmund Freud, and Melanie Klein (b. Austria, 1882–1960) were psychoanalysts influential in the study of child development. Noted anthropologists include Sir Edward Burnett Tylor (1832–1917); Polish-born Bronislaw Kasper Malinowski (1884–1942); Louis Seymour Bazett Leakey (1903–72) and his wife, Mary Leakey (1913–96), who discovered important fossil remains of early hominids in Tanzania; and Ashley Montagu (1905–1999).

Scientists

Present-day concepts of the universe largely derive from the theories of the astronomer and physicist Sir James Hopwood Jeans (1877–1946), the astronomers Sir Arthur Stanley Eddington (1882–1946) and Sir Fred Hoyle (1915–2001), and the radio as-

tronomers Sir Martin Ryle (1918–84) and Anthony Hewish (b. 1924), who shared the Nobel Prize for physics in 1974. Other British scientists and inventors who won fame for major contributions to knowledge include William Harvey (1578–1657), physician and anatomist, who discovered the circulation of the blood; Irish-born Robert Boyle (1627–91), physicist and chemist, who investigated the properties of gases; Sir Isaac Newton (1642–1727), natural philosopher and mathematician, who discovered gravity and made important advances in calculus and optics; German-born physicist Gabriel Daniel Fahrenheit (1686–1736), who introduced the temperature scale named after him; James Watt (1736–1819), the Scottish-born engineer who invented the modern condensing steam engine; Edward Jenner (1749–1823), who discovered the principle of vaccination; the great chemists John Dalton (1766–1844), who advanced the atomic theory, and Sir Humphry Davy (1778–1829); George Stephenson (1781–1848), inventor of the locomotive steam engine; Michael Faraday (1791–1867), a chemist and physicist noted for his experiments in electricity; Scottish-born geologist Sir Charles Lyell (1797–1875), the father of modern geology; Charles Darwin (1809–82), the great naturalist who advanced the theory of evolution; James Prescott Joule (1818–89), a physicist who studied heat and electrical energy; Thomas Henry Huxley (1825–95), a biologist who championed Darwin's theory; James Clerk Maxwell (1831–79), the Scottish-born physicist who developed the hypothesis that light and electromagnetism are fundamentally of the same nature; Sir Alexander Fleming (1881–1955), bacteriologist, who received the 1945 Nobel Prize for medicine for the discovery of penicillin in 1928; and Francis Harry Compton Crick (1916–2004) and Maurice Hugh Frederick Wilkins (New Zealand, 1916–2004), two of the three winners of the 1962 Nobel Prize in physiology or medicine for their research into the structure of the DNA molecule. UK citizen Charles Kao (b. 1933, Shanghai, China) was named as a co-recipient of the 2009 Nobel Prize in Physics for his work in developing fiber-optic cables.

Konstantin Novoselov (b. 1974) and Andrei Geim (b. 1958), professors at Manchester University, were awarded the 2010 Nobel Prize in physics for research on graphene, a flat one-atom thick layer of carbon that is nearly transparent, extremely strong, and a good conductor of electricity. The material has potential for a wide variety of uses in electronics and computer systems. Novoselov and Geim were among the first to isolate the material from graphite, which is widely used in pencils. Novoselov holds British and Russian citizenship, whereas Geim is a Dutch national. Manchester native Robert G. Edwards (b. 1925) was awarded the 2010 Nobel Prize in Medicine for the development of human in vitro fertilization therapy. Edwards's research led to the birth of the first test tube baby, Louise Brown, in 1978.

Literature and the Arts

Geoffrey Chaucer (1340?–1400) wrote the *Canterbury Tales* and other works that marked the height of medieval English poetry. Other major medieval poets were John Gower (1325?–1408) and William Langland (1332?–1400?). William Caxton (1422–91) was the first English printer. Sir Thomas Malory (fl. 1470) derived from French and earlier English sources the English prose epic traditionally known as *Morte d'Arthur.* Two religious reformers who translated the Bible into English, making it accessible to the common people, were John Wycliffe (1320?–84), who made the first complete translation, and William Tyndale (1492?–1536), who made the first translation from the original languages instead of Latin.

During the reign of Elizabeth I, England's golden age, emerged the dramatist and poet William Shakespeare (1564–1616), a giant of English and world literature, and a galaxy of other fine poets and playwrights. Among them were Edmund Spenser (1552?–99), Irish-born author of the *Faerie Queene;* the poet and soldier Sir Philip Sidney (1554–86); and the dramatists Christopher Marlowe (1564–93) and Ben Jonson (1572–1637). Outstanding writers of the Stuart period include the philosopher, scientist, and essayist Francis Bacon (1561–1626), first Baron Verulam Viscount St. Albans; John Donne (1572–1631), the greatest of the metaphysical poets; the lyric poet Robert Herrick (1591–1674); John Milton (1608–74), author of *Paradise Lost* and other poems and political essays; John Bunyan (1628–88), who created the classic allegory *Pilgrim's Progress;* and the poet, playwright, and critic John Dryden (1631–1700). The greatest Restoration dramatists were William Wycherley (1640–1716) and William Congreve (1670–1729). Two authors of famous diaries mirroring the society of their time were John Evelyn (1620–1706) and Samuel Pepys (1633–1703).

Distinguished writers of the 18th century include the Irish-born satirist Jonathan Swift (1667–1745), author of *Gulliver's Travels;* the essayists Joseph Addison (1672–1719) and Sir Richard Steele (1672–1729), whose journals were the prototypes of modern magazines; the poets Alexander Pope (1688–1744) and Thomas Gray (1716–71); the critic, biographer, and lexicographer Samuel Johnson (1709–84); and the Irish-born playwrights Oliver Goldsmith (1730?–74), also a poet and novelist, and Richard Brinsley Sheridan (1751–1816). The poet and artist William Blake (1757–1827) worked in a unique mystical vein.

The English Romantic movement produced a group of major poets, including William Wordsworth (1770–1850); Samuel Taylor Coleridge (1772–1834); George Noel Gordon Byron, sixth Lord Byron (1788–1824); Percy Bysshe Shelley (1792–1822); and John Keats (1795–1821). Victorian poets of note included Alfred, Lord Tennyson (1809–92); Elizabeth Barrett Browning (1806–61); her husband, Robert Browning (1812–89); Dante Gabriel Rossetti (1822–82); his sister, Christina Georgina Rossetti (1830–94); Algernon Charles Swinburne (1837–1909); and Gerard Manley Hopkins (1844–89). Edward FitzGerald (1809–83) is famous for his free translations of Omar Khayyam's *Rubáiyát.* Matthew Arnold (1822–88) was a noted poet and critic. Other prominent critics and essayists include Charles Lamb (1775–1834), William Hazlitt (1778–1830), Thomas De Quincey (1785–1859), John Ruskin (1819–1900), Leslie Stephen (1832–1904), and William Morris (1834–96). Thomas Babington Macaulay (1800–1859) was a distinguished statesman, essayist, and historian. John Henry Cardinal Newman (1801–90) was an outstanding Roman Catholic theologian. Irish-born Oscar Fingal O'Flahertie Wills Wilde (1854–1900) was famous as a playwright, novelist, poet, and wit.

Major poets of the 20th century include Alfred Edward Housman (1859–1936); Walter John de la Mare (1873–1956); Dame Edith Sitwell (1887–1964); US-born Thomas Stearns Eliot (1888–1965), winner of the Nobel Prize in 1949; Wystan Hugh Auden (1907–73); Welsh-born Dylan Thomas (1914–53); Philip Larkin

(1922–85); and Ted Hughes (1930–98). Prominent critics include Frank Raymond Leavis (1895–1978) and Sir William Empson (1906–84).

The English novel's distinguished history began with Daniel Defoe (1660–1731), Samuel Richardson (1689–1761), Henry Fielding (1707–54), and Laurence Sterne (1713–68). It was carried forward in the 19th century by Jane Austen (1775–1817); William Makepeace Thackeray (1811–63); Charles Dickens (1812–70); Charles Reade (1814–84); Anthony Trollope (1815–82); the Brontë Sisters, Charlotte (1816–55) and Emily (1818–48); George Eliot (Mary Ann Evans, 1819–80); George Meredith (1828–1909); Samuel Butler (1835–1902); and Thomas Hardy (1840–1928), who was also a poet. The mathematician Lewis Carroll (Charles Lutwidge Dodgson, 1832–98) became world-famous for two children's books, *Alice in Wonderland* and *Through the Looking Glass.* Rudyard Kipling (1865–1936), author of novels, stories, and poems, received the Nobel Prize for literature in 1907. Sir Arthur Conan Doyle (1859–1930) is known throughout the world as the creator of Sherlock Holmes.

Twentieth-century fiction writers of note include the Polish-born Joseph Conrad (Teodor Józef Konrad Korzeniowski, 1857–1924); Herbert George Wells (1866–1946), who was also a popular historian and a social reformer; Arnold Bennett (1867–1931); John Galsworthy (1867–1933), also a playwright, who received the Nobel Prize in 1932; William Somerset Maugham (1874–1965), also a playwright; Edward Morgan Forster (1879–1970); Virginia Woolf (1882–1941); David Herbert Lawrence (1885–1930); Joyce Cary (1888–1957); Katherine Mansfield (b. New Zealand, 1888–1923); Dame Agatha Christie (1881–1976), also a playwright; Dame Ivy Compton-Burnett (1892–1969); Dame Rebecca West (b. Ireland, 1892–1983), also known for her political writings and as an active feminist; Aldous Huxley (1894–1963); John Boynton Priestley (1894–1984), also a playwright; Irish-born Robert Ranke Graves (1895–1985), also a poet, novelist, scholar, and critic; George Orwell (Eric Blair, 1903–50), also a journalist and essayist; Evelyn Waugh (1903–66); Graham Greene (1904–91); Anthony Dymoke Powell (1905–2000); Henry Green (Henry Vincent Yorke, 1905–74); Charles Percy Snow (Baron Snow, 1905–80), also an essayist and a physicist; William Golding (1911–93), Nobel Prize winner in 1983; Lawrence George Durrell (b. India, 1912–90); Anthony Burgess (1917–93); Doris Lessing (b. Iran, 1919); John Le Carré (David John Moore Cornwell, b. 1931), and Ian McEwan (b. 1948). The dominant literary figure of the 20th century was George Bernard Shaw (1856–1950), Dublin-born playwright, essayist, critic, and wit. Sir Kingsley William Amis (1922–1995) was a novelist, poet, critic, and teacher; his son Martin Amis (b. 1949) became a novelist as well. Dame Antonia Susan "A.S." Byatt (b. 1936) has been hailed by some as one of the great postmodern novelists in England. Byatt's younger sister Margaret Drabble (b. 1939) is a novelist as well. Fay Weldon (b. 1931) is a novelist, short story writer, playwright, and essayist whose work has been associated with feminism. Hanif Kureishi (b. 1954) is a Pakistani-British playwright, author, and director. Kazuo Ishiguro (b. 1954) is a British author of Japanese origin. Joanne "J.K." Rowling (b. 1965) is most famous as author of the Harry Potter fantasy series. Zadie Smith (b. 1975) has been celebrated as one of Britain's most talented young authors. The playwright-composer-lyricist Sir Noel Coward (1899–1973) directed and starred in many of his sophisticated comedies. Harold Pinter (1930–2008) was a highly influential playwright; he was awarded the Nobel Prize for literature in 2005.

Actors and Actresses

The British stage tradition dates back to Richard Burbage (d. 1619), the greatest actor of Shakespeare's time, and Edmund Kean (1787–1833), the greatest tragedian of the Romantic era. Luminaries of the modern theater are Dame Ellen Alicia Terry (1848–1928), Dame Sybil Thorndike (1882–1976), Dame Edith Evans (1888–1976), Sir Ralph Richardson (1902–83), Sir John Gielgud (1904–2000), Laurence Olivier (Baron Olivier of Brighton, 1907–1989), Sir Michael Redgrave (1908–85), and Derek George Jacobi (b. 1938). Prominent stage directors are Peter Stephen Paul Brook (b. 1925) and Sir Peter Reginald Frederick Hall (b. 1930). Major contributors to the cinema have included the comic actor and director Charlie (Sir Charles Spencer) Chaplin (1889–1977); the directors Sir Alexander Korda (Sandor Corda, b.Hungary, 1893–1956), Sir Alfred Hitchcock (1899–1980), Sir Carol Reed (1906–76), Sir David Lean (1908–91), Sir Richard Attenborough (b. 1923), and Stephen Frears (b. 1941); and actors Cary Grant (Archibald Alexander Leach, 1904–86), Sir Alec Guinness (1914–2000), Deborah Kerr (1921–2007), Welsh-born Richard Burton (1925–84), Belgian-born Audrey Hepburn (1929–1993), Sir Thomas Sean Connery (b. 1930), Irish-born Peter O'Toole (b. 1932), Dame Elizabeth Taylor (1932–2011), Sir Michael Caine (b. 1933), Dame Maggie Natalie Smith (b. 1934), Dame Judi Dench (b. 1934), Glenda Jackson (b. 1936), Albert Finney (b. 1936), Vanessa Redgrave (b. 1937), Jacqueline Bisset (b. 1944), Miranda Richardson (b. 1958), Ralph Fiennes (b. 1962), Tilda Swinton (b. 1960), Rachel Weisz (b. 1971), and Kate Winslet (b. 1975).

Architects

Great English architects were Inigo Jones (1573–1652) and Sir Christopher Wren (1632–1723). Famous artists include William Hogarth (1697–1764), Sir Joshua Reynolds (1723–92), Thomas Gainsborough (1727–88), Joseph Mallord William Turner (1775–1851), John Constable (1776–1837), the illustrator Aubrey Beardsley (1872–98), Graham Sutherland (1903–80), Francis Bacon (b. Ireland, 1910–92), and David Hockney (b. 1937). Roger Eliot Fry (1866–1934) and Kenneth Mackenzie Clark (Lord Clark, 1903–83) were influential art critics. Sir Jacob Epstein (b. US, 1880–1959), Henry Moore (1898–1986), and Dame Barbara Hepworth (1903–75) are world-famous British sculptors. The most famous British potter was Josiah Wedgwood (1730–95).

Composers

English composers of note include John Dunstable (1370?–1453), whose works exerted a profound influence on continental musicians; William Byrd (1543–1623) and Orlando Gibbons (1583–1625), who were proficient in both sacred and secular music; the great lutenist and songwriter John Dowland (1563–1626); the madrigalists John Wilbye (1574–1638) and Thomas Weelkes (1575?–1623); Henry Purcell (1659?–95), a brilliant creator of vocal and chamber works; German-born George Frederick Handel (Georg Friedrich Händel, 1685–1759), a master of baroque operas, oratorios, and concerti; and Sir Arthur Seymour Sullivan (1842–1900), whose musical settings of the librettos of Sir William

Schwenk Gilbert (1836–1911) are among the most popular comic operas of all time. Significant 20th-century figures include Sir Edward Elgar (1857–1934), Frederick Delius (1862–1934), Ralph Vaughan Williams (1872–1958), Sir William Walton (1902–83), Sir Michael Kemp Tippett (1905–98), Edward Benjamin Britten (Baron Britten, 1913–76), Peter Maxwell Davies (b. 1934), and, in popular music, John Winston Lennon (1940–80) and James Paul McCartney (b. 1942) of the Beatles. Notable performers include pianists Dame Myra Hess (1890–1965) and Sir Clifford Curzon (1907–82), violinist Sir Yehudi Menuhin (1916–1999), guitarist-lutenist Julian Bream (b. 1933), singers Sir Peter Pears (1910–86) and Dame Janet Baker (b. 1933), and conductors Sir Thomas Beecham (1879–1961), Sir Adrian Boult (1889–1983), Sir John Barbirolli (1899–1970), Sir Georg Solti (b. Hungary, 1912–1997), and Sir Colin Davis (b. 1927).

Athletes

Notable British athletes include Sir Roger Bannister (b. 1929), who on 6 May 1954 became the first person to run a mile in under four minutes; golfer Tony Jacklin (b. 1944), winner of the British Open in 1969 and the US Open in 1970; three-time world champion John Young "Jackie" Stewart (b. 1939), a Scottish race-car driver; and the yachtsman Sir Francis Chichester (1901–72), winner of the first single-handed transatlantic race (1970) and the first sailor to make a solo circumnavigation of the globe (1966–67). Tennis player Sarah Virginia Wade (b. 1945) won three Grand Slam singles titles and five Grand Slam doubles titles; she is particularly remembered for winning the women's singles title at Wimbledon in the championship's centenary year in 1977.

Natives of Scotland and Wales

Duncan I (r. 1034–40) was the first ruler of the historical kingdom of Scotland. Macbeth (r. 1040–57), who killed Duncan and seized the throne, furnished the subject of one of Shakespeare's greatest plays. Margaret (d. 1093), Duncan's daughter-in-law, reformed the Church, won fame for piety and charity, and was made a saint. William Wallace (1272?–1306) led a rebellion against the English occupation. Robert the Bruce (1274–1329), ruler of Scotland (1306–29), won its independence from England. Mary, Queen of Scots (Mary Stuart, 1542–87), a romantic historical figure, is the subject of many plays and novels. Her son James VI (1566–1625) became England's King James I.

Before the union with England, outstanding poets writing in Scottish include Robert Henryson (1425?–1500?), William Dunbar (1460?–1520?), Gavin Douglas (1474–1522), and Sir David Lindsay (1490?–1555). One of the finest Scottish poets was William Drummond (1585–1649). Sir Thomas Urquhart (1611–60) produced a noted translation of Rabelais. John Knox (1514?–72) was the founder of Presbyterianism. David Hume (1711–76) was an outstanding philosopher and historian. Economist and philosopher Adam Smith (1723–90) influenced the development of world economy and politics. James Boswell (1740–95) wrote the brilliant *Life of Samuel Johnson*. The 18th century produced several important poets, notably Allan Ramsay (1686–1758), James Thomson (1700–48), James Macpherson (1736–96), and the national poet of Scotland, Robert Burns (1759–96). A major 19th-century essayist and social critic was Thomas Carlyle (1795–1881). Scottish novelists of prominence include Tobias George Smollett (1721–71); Sir Walter Scott (1771–1832); Robert Louis Stevenson (1850–94), also a poet; John Buchan, first Lord Tweedsmuir (1875–1940); and Sir James Matthew Barrie (1860–1937), who also wrote popular plays.

Distinguished figures who were active primarily in Wales include the 6th-century monk Dewi (d. 588?), who became St. David, the patron saint of Wales; Rhodri the Great (844–77), who attained rule over most of Wales and founded two great ruling houses; Howel the Good (Hywel Dda, 910–50), whose reformed legal code became the standard of Welsh law for centuries; the Lord Rhys ap Gruffydd (1155–97), ruler of southern Wales, who founded the national Eisteddfod; Dafydd ap Gwilym (fl. 1340–70), a remarkable poet; and Owen Glendower (Owain ap Gruffydd, 1359?–1416), the national hero of Wales, who led a rebellion against English rule. Bishop William Morgan (1541?–1604) made a Welsh translation of the Bible which, with revisions, is still in use. Among literary figures are Ellis Wynne (1671–1734), Daniel Owen (1836–95), and Sir Owen Morgan Edwards (1858–1920).

Two natives of Northern Ireland—Betty Williams (b. 1943), a Protestant, and Mairead Corrigan (b. 1944), a Roman Catholic—received the Nobel Peace Prize (awarded in 1977) for their leadership of a peace movement in Ulster.

49 DEPENDENCIES

British overseas dependencies include the British Indian Ocean Territory and St. Helena (described in the *Africa* volume under UK African Dependencies), Bermuda, the British Antarctic Territory, the British Virgin Islands, the Cayman Islands, the Falkland Islands, The Turks and Caicos Islands, and Anguilla and Montserrat (described in the *Americas* volume under UK American Dependencies).

Gibraltar

The colony of Gibraltar (5.83 sq km/2.25 sq mi in area), the smallest UK dependency, is a narrow peninsula connected to the southwest coast of Spain. From a low, sandy plain in the north, it rises sharply in the 430 m (1,400 ft) Rock of Gibraltar, a shrub-covered mass of limestone, with huge caves. Gibraltar has a pleasantly temperate climate, except for occasional hot summers. Average annual rainfall is 89 cm (35 in). There is a rainy season from December to May. The resident civilian population, almost entirely of European origin, was estimated at 29,034 in mid-2012. Gibraltar is an important port of call for cargo and passenger ships. There is a naval base at the northeast gate of the Strait of Gibraltar and a military airfield that is used by private companies. Telegraph, radio, and television are privately operated. The telephone system is government owned.

Known as Calpe in ancient times, Gibraltar was successively occupied by Phoenicians, Carthaginians, Romans, and Visigoths. Its strategic value was recognized early. In AD 711, it was captured by Moors under Tariq, and since then it has been known as Jabal Tariq or Gibraltar. It remained in Moor hands, except for short periods, until Spain took it in 1462. In 1704, a combined English-Dutch fleet captured Gibraltar, and it was officially transferred to Britain by the Treaty of Utrecht in 1713. Since 1964, Spain has tried to negotiate the return of Gibraltar to Spanish control. However, in a referendum held in 1967, Gibraltarians voted overwhelmingly (12,138–44) to retain their link with Britain. Since then, Spain has continued to raise the issue at the UN and put

direct pressure on the Gibraltarians by closing the land frontier between the peninsula and the Spanish mainland and suspending the ferry service between Gibraltar and Algeciras; the border was reopened to limited pedestrian traffic in December 1982 and fully reopened in February 1985.

Under the 1969 constitution, Gibraltar is governed by a House of Assembly with 18 members, 15 of whom are elected by popular vote. The governor (who is also commander of the fortress) retains direct responsibility for defense and external affairs and can intervene in domestic affairs.

Gibraltar was once largely dependent on British subsidies, but in the late 1990s it made the transition to private sector industry. Tourism (with about six million visitors annually), reexports (largely fuel for shipping), shipping services, and duties on consumer goods contribute to the economy. Local industries are tobacco and coffee processing. The Gibraltar pound is at par with the British pound. The financial sector accounts for about 15% of GDP. There is an income tax and an estate duty.

Illiteracy is negligible. Education is compulsory between the ages of 5 and 15. There are 12 primary schools, two single-sex comprehensive secondary schools, and the College of Further Education. The armed forces have their own schools; attendance by civilian children is available. Languages spoken at home include Spanish, Italian, and Portuguese, but the language of business and schools is English. The colony has a serious housing shortage.

Pitcairn Island

Pitcairn is a mountainous island of volcanic origin about 4.5 sq km (1.75 sq mi) in area, located in the South Pacific at 25°4′ S and 130°6′ W. Three smaller islands (Henderson, Ducie, and Oeno) associated with Pitcairn are uninhabited. Pitcairn Island was discovered in 1767 by the British and settled in 1790 by H.M.S. *Bounty* mutineers and the Polynesian women who accompanied them from Tahiti. The population, mainly descendants of the *Bounty* mutineers, after reaching a peak of 233 in 1937, decreased to 120 in 1962, 52 in 1992, and 48 in 2011. Most of the younger members of the community have migrated to New Zealand. The climate is warm, with very little change throughout the year.

There is one village, Adamstown. Pitcairn is administered, together with the three other small islands, as a UK colony by the UK high commissioner in New Zealand. The local government consists of an island magistrate and a 10-member Island Council. Six of the Council's members are elected. New Zealand dollars are used locally. There is no port or harbor; goods from ships are conveyed ashore in longboats. Cargo ships plying the route between Panama and New Zealand call periodically.

The main occupation is subsistence agriculture. A small surplus of fresh fruit and vegetables is sold to passing ships. Fish are abundant. Imports, mainly food, come from New Zealand. Fruit, woven baskets, carved curios, and stamps are sold to ships' passengers.

50 BIBLIOGRAPHY

Alexander, Yonah, ed. *Combating Terrorism: Strategies of Ten Countries.* Ann Arbor: University of Michigan Press, 2002.

Childs, Peter, and Mike Storry, eds. *British Cultural Identities.* 3rd ed. New York: Routledge, 2010.

Cook, Chris. *The Longman Handbook of Modern British History, 1714–1995*. 3rd ed. New York: Longman, 1996.

Foster, R. F., ed. *The Oxford History of Ireland*. New York: Oxford University Press, 2001.

Gagnon, Alain G., and James Tully, eds. *Multinational Democracies*. New York: Cambridge University Press, 2001.

Livesey, James. *Civil Society and Empire: Ireland and Scotland in the Eighteenth-century Atlantic World*. New Haven, CT: Yale University Press, 2009.

McElrath, Karen, ed. *HIV and AIDS: A Global View*. Westport, CT: Greenwood Press, 2002.

Menéndez, Alarcón A. V. *The Cultural Realm of European Integration: Social Representations in France, Spain, and the United Kingdom*. Westport, CT: Praeger Publishers, 2004.

Norton, Philip. *The British Polity*. 5th ed. Boston, MA: Longman, 2011.

O'Neill, Michael, ed. *Devolution and British Politics*. New York: Pearson/Longman, 2004.

Sampanis, Maria. *Preserving Power through Coalitions: Comparing the Grand Strategy of Great Britain and the United States*. Westport, CT: Praeger, 2003.

Summers, Randal W., and Allan M. Hoffman, eds. *Domestic Violence: A Global View*. Westport, CT: Greenwood Press, 2002.

United Kingdom Investment and Business Guide: Strategic and Practical Information. Washington, DC: International Business Publications USA, 2012.

VATICAN CITY

The Holy See (State of the Vatican City)
Santa Sede (Stato della Città del Vaticano)

CAPITAL: Vatican City

FLAG: The flag consists of two vertical stripes, yellow at the hoist and white at the fly. On the white field, in yellow, are the crossed keys of St. Peter, the first pope, surmounted by the papal tiara (triple crown).

ANTHEM: *Inno e Marcia Pontificale (Hymn and Pontifical March).*

MONETARY UNIT: In 1930, after a lapse of 60 years, the Vatican resumed issuance of its own coinage—the lira (L)—but it agreed to issue no more than 300 million lire in any year. There are coins of 10, 20, 50, 100, and 500 lire. Both Italy and the Vatican adopted the euro as official currency in 2002. The euro is divided into 100 cents. There are coins in denominations of 1, 2, 5, 10, 20, and 50 cents and 1 euro and 2 euros. There are notes of 5, 10, 20, 50, 100, 200, and 500 euros. The Vatican lira is fixed at 1,936.17 lire per euro. €1 = $1.371 (or $1 = €0.72939) as of September 2011.

WEIGHTS AND MEASURES: The metric system is in use.

HOLIDAYS: Roman Catholic religious holidays; the coronation day of the reigning pope; days when public consistory is held.

TIME: 1 p.m. = noon GMT.

¹LOCATION, SIZE, AND EXTENT

Located within Rome, Vatican City is the smallest state in the world. It is a roughly triangular area of 0.44 sq km (0.17 sq mi) lying near the west bank of the Tiber River and to the west of the Castel Sant'Angelo. On the W and S it is bounded by the Leonine Wall. The Vatican area comprises the following: St. Peter's Square, enclosed by Giovanni Lorenzo Bernini's quadruple colonnade; St. Peter's Basilica, the largest Christian church in the world, to which the square serves as an entrance; a quadrangular area north of the square in which there are administrative buildings and Belvedere Park; the pontifical palaces, or the Vatican proper, lying west of Belvedere Park; and the Vatican Gardens, which occupy about half the acreage.

Outside Vatican City itself, extraterritoriality is exercised over a number of churches and palaces in Rome, notably the Lateran Basilica and Palace in the Piazza San Giovanni, the Palace of San Callisto at the foot of the Janiculum hill, and the basilicas of Santa Maria Maggiore and San Paolo fuori le Mura. Extraterritoriality outside the city of Rome extends to the papal villa and its environs (almost 40 hectares/100 acres) at Castel Gandolfo, 24 km (15 mi) SE of Rome, and to the area (about 420 hectares/1,040 acres) at Santa Maria di Galeria, some 19 km (12 mi) N of Rome, where a Vatican radio station was established in 1957.

²TOPOGRAPHY

Vatican City lies on a slight hill not far from the Tiber River.

³CLIMATE

Winters are mild, and although summer temperatures are high during the day, the evenings are cold. Temperatures in January av- erage 7°C (45°F); in July, 24°C (75°F). There is little rain from May to September; October and November are the wettest months.

⁴FLORA AND FAUNA

The gardens are famous for their fine collection of orchids and other exotic flora. Vatican City, being entirely urban, does not have a distinctive fauna.

⁵ENVIRONMENT

The environment of Vatican City is similar to that of Rome (see Italy). Though there are no specific endangered species, according to a 2006 report issued by the International Union for Conserva- tion of Nature and Natural Resources (IUCN) there are five spe- cies with minimal or least concern. These are the long-tailed field mouse, the European water vole, the Crucian carp, the bank vole, and the red fox.

⁶POPULATION

The US Central Intelligence Agency (CIA) estimates the popula- tion of the Vatican in 2011 to be 832, which placed it last among the 196 nations of the world. The median age in the Vatican was 37.6 years. The population's annual rate of change was 0.004%.

The UN estimated that 100% of the population lived in urban areas, and that urban populations had an annual rate of change of 0.1%.

⁷MIGRATION

Does not apply.

⁸ETHNIC GROUPS

Although the citizenry of the Vatican includes cardinals and other clergymen from all parts of the world, most of the inhabitants are

Italian. The members of the Swiss Guard are a notable exception. Pope Benedict XVI is German.

⁹LANGUAGES

Italian is the official language of Vatican City, but Latin is the official language of the Holy See (the seat of jurisdiction of the pope as spiritual leader) and is employed for most papal encyclicals and other formal pronouncements. As the ordinary working language, Italian is in greater use. French, German, and other languages are also used.

¹⁰RELIGIONS

Vatican City is the center of the worldwide organization of the Roman Catholic Church and the seat of the pope. Roman Catholicism is the official religion and the primary business of the state itself.

¹¹TRANSPORTATION

Vatican City is easily reached by the public transportation system of Rome. It has its own railroad station, with 862 m (2,828 ft) of track which connect to Italy's network at Rome's Saint Peter's station. Vatican City also has a helicopter landing pad.

¹²HISTORY

Since the time of St. Peter, regarded by the Church as the first pope, Rome has been the seat of the popes, except in periods of great turbulence, when the pontiffs were forced to take refuge elsewhere, most notably in Avignon, France, from 1309 to 1377. The Roman papal residence before modern times was usually in the Lateran or Quirinal rather than in the Vatican Palace.

The Vatican City State and the places over which the Vatican now exercises jurisdiction are the sole remnants of the States of the Church, or Papal States, which at various times, beginning in 755, included large areas in Italy and, until the French Revolution, even parts of southern France. Most of the papal domain fell into the hands of King Victor Emmanuel II in 1860 in the course of the unification of Italy. By 1870, Pope Pius IX, supported by a garrison of French troops, retained rule over only the besieged city of Rome and a small territory surrounding it. Upon the withdrawal of the French garrison to take part in the Franco-Prussian War, the walls of Rome were breached by the besieging forces on 20 September, and the city fell. On 2 October, following a plebiscite, the city was annexed to the kingdom of Italy and made the national capital.

In May 1871, the Italian government promulgated a Law of Guarantees, which purported to establish the relations between the Italian kingdom and the papacy. The enactment declared the person of the pope to be inviolate, guaranteed him full liberty in his religious functions and in the conduct of diplomatic relations, awarded an annual indemnity in lieu of the income lost when the Papal States were annexed, and provided the right of extraterritoriality over the Vatican and the papal palaces. Pius IX refused to accept the law or the money allowance; he and his successors chose to become "prisoners of the Vatican." Until 1919, Roman Catholics were prohibited by the papacy from participating in the Italian government.

The so-called "Roman Question" was brought to an end by the conclusion on 11 February 1929 of three Lateran treaties between the Vatican and Italy. One treaty recognized the full sovereignty of the Vatican and established its territorial extent. Another treaty was a concordat establishing the Roman Catholic Church as the state church of Italy. The remaining treaty awarded the Vatican 750 million old lire in cash and one billion old lire in interest-bearing state bonds in lieu of all financial claims against Italy for annexing the Papal States. The constitution of the Italian Republic, adopted in 1947, substantially embodies the terms of the Lateran treaties. In 1962–65, the Vatican was the site of the Second Vatican Council, the first worldwide council in almost a century. Convened by Pope John XXIII and continued under Paul VI, the Council resulted in modernization of the Church's role in spiritual and social matters.

Ecumenism was the hallmark of the reign (1963–78) of Pope Paul VI. In a move to further Christian unity, he met with Athenagoras, the ecumenical patriarch of the Eastern Orthodox Church, in Jerusalem in 1964. In 1973, Paul VI conferred with the Coptic Orthodox patriarch of Alexandria; later in that same year, he met the exiled Dalai Lama, the first such meeting between a pope and a Buddhist leader. Steps were also taken to improve Roman Catholic-Jewish relations, including a 1965 declaration that Jews are not to be held collectively guilty of the death of Jesus. On doctrinal questions Pope Paul VI was generally conservative, reaffirming papal infallibility, disciplining dissident priests, and reiterating traditional Church opposition to all "artificial" methods of contraception, including abortion and sterilization. In September 1972, the concept of an all-male celibate priesthood was upheld.

Pope Paul VI was succeeded by Pope John Paul I, who reigned for only 34 days. John Paul I's sudden death, on 28 September 1978, brought about the election of Polish Cardinal Karol Wojtyla as John Paul II, the first non-Italian pontiff elected in over 450 years. On 13 May 1981, John Paul II was wounded in Vatican Square by a Turkish gunman, who is serving a life sentence. The alleged accomplices, three Bulgarians and three Turks, were acquitted of conspiracy in the assassination attempt on 29 March 1986 because of lack of evidence.

During his reign (1978–2005), John Paul II traveled widely, a practice begun by Paul VI. He also established himself as a conservative in doctrinal matters, as indicated in 1982 by his elevation to the status of personal prelature of Opus Dei, an international organization of 72,000 laity and priests known for its doctrinal fidelity. He spent much of his papacy condemning materialism and moral laxity. During John Paul II's papacy, the Lateran treaties of 1929 were superseded in 1984 by a new concordat under which the pope retained temporal authority over Vatican City but Roman Catholicism was no longer Italy's state religion.

Throughout the 1990s, John Paul II tried to build bridges to the Islamic world. Iran's president visited the Vatican in 1999 and a controversial trip to Iraq to talk to Saddam Hussein was cancelled that same year. He also traveled to Israel in March 2000 where he visited different Holocaust memorials and went to Bethlehem to reaffirm the Holy See's support for an independent Palestinian homeland.

John Paul II came out against embryonic or stem-cell research in 2001, stating it would lead to other evils such as "euthanasia and infanticide"; Following the 11 September 2001 terrorist attacks on the United States, John Paul II urged harmony between Christians and Muslims. He initially stated that conflicts must

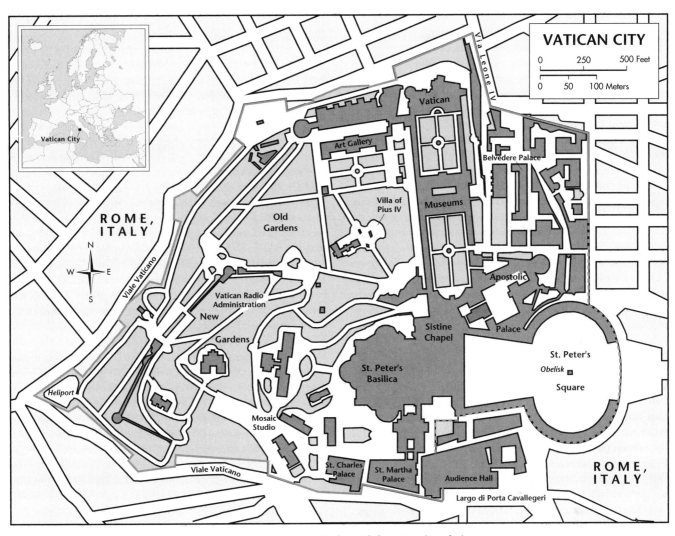

BOUNDARY LENGTHS: Italy, 3.2 kilometers (2 miles).

not be resolved by force, but by peaceful negotiation; however, he subsequently indicated the United States might need to use force against terrorists in the name of self-defense. When the Al Aqsa intifada—begun in September 2000 in Israel and the West Bank and Gaza Strip—intensified in the spring of 2002, John Paul II appealed for peace in the region, saying "nothing is resolved by war." He also reasserted his firm belief in peace over the use of force during the 2002–03 diplomatic and military crisis in Iraq. Nevertheless, his criticism of the conflict did not prevent war. Following the defeat of the Saddam Hussein regime in April 2003, John Paul II stated the Iraqi people should be responsible for the rebuilding of Iraq, while working closely with the international community, meaning the UN.

The Vatican announced in December 2002 it would open its archives relating to interactions with Nazi Germany from 1922–39 to scholars. The Catholic Church has been criticized for not doing enough to stop the persecution of Jews during the Holocaust.

Following the eruption of sex scandals in the United States regarding pedophile priests, John Paul II called for an emergency meeting with US cardinals in April 2002. US bishops had approved a "zero tolerance" policy on priests accused of sexual abuse, which would have priests suspended immediately following an accusation of abuse, but the Vatican demanded certain protections for the rights of priests.

In May 2003, the Vatican officially confirmed the pope suffered from Parkinson's disease. Despite his illness and his suffering from severe arthritis, John Paul II continued to travel extensively until his death on 2 April 2005.

Cardinal Joseph Ratzinger, a close confidant of John Paul II, was chosen on 19 April 2005 as the next pope, choosing the name Pope Benedict XVI. Ratzinger, originally from Cologne, Germany, was 78 years old at the time of his election; this made him the oldest pope to be elected in more than 100 years. He predicted that his tenure would be short and that his primary purpose would be to complete John Paul II's work. He was formally installed as pope on 24 April 2005. As a cardinal, Ratzinger was known as a hardline advocate of Vatican orthodoxy. He strongly opposed abortion, homosexuality, and religious pluralism. A long-time friend and ally of John Paul II, Ratzinger's selection as pope was greeted with dismay by more liberal factions within the Catholic Church.

Many feared that he would divide, rather than unite, Catholics worldwide. In the early months of his papacy, Pope Benedict XVI supported the conservative stance of his predecessor.

In October 2005, the Vatican completed a document that appeared to somewhat relax its stance against homosexuality. A change in policy on those entering the priesthood suggested that gay men who had lived a chaste life for at least three years prior to their admission to a seminary would be eligible. Previously, the Vatican banned homosexuals from priesthood, regardless of their status.

Pope Benedict XVI made his trip to the Middle East as pontiff and head of the Vatican state in May 2009. The trip was seen as an opportunity to strengthen ties between the Roman Catholic Church and Jewish and Muslim leaders. It was also a chance for the pope to express concern and offer support in securing peace for the region. The pope spoke on the need for religious freedom as a fundamental human right and reiterated the Vatican's stand for a two-state solution to the Israeli-Palestinian conflict. In efforts to reach out to a new generation of Catholics, the Vatican has launched a number of Internet-based social networking applications.

The Vatican and the Russian Federation furthered their relationship in 2009 by establishing full diplomatic ties. The announcement represented a significant movement in a relationship that has historically been strained. Under communism, the Soviet Union maintained a posture of hostility toward all religion. Then, with the fall of the Soviet Union, the Russian Orthodox Church began accusing the Vatican of spiritual encroachment, placing pressure on the Russian government to keep relations cool.

Accusations and revelations of priests' sexual abuse of children have continued to plague the Vatican. A serious conflict erupted between the Vatican and Ireland in 2011. The Irish government released a report detailing efforts of the Vatican to protect its priests by interfering with secular investigations of abuse. The Vatican responded by removing its ambassador and denying the obstructionist claims. The Irish prime minister and other government officials suggested that the actions of the Vatican may have violated Irish government laws protecting children. The debate asked broader questions about the legal relationship between the Catholic Church and historically Catholic states.

13 GOVERNMENT

The pope is simultaneously the absolute sovereign of the Vatican City State and the head of the Roman Catholic Church throughout the world. Since 1984, the pope has been represented by the cardinal secretary of state in the civil governance of Vatican City. In administering the government of the Vatican, the pope is assisted by the Pontifical Commission for the Vatican City State. Religious affairs are governed under the pope's direction by a number of ecclesiastical bodies known collectively as the Roman Curia.

The Pontifical Commission consists of seven cardinals and a lay special delegate, assisted since 1968 by a board of 21 lay advisers. Under the commission are the following: a central council (heading various administrative offices); the directorships of museums, technical services, economic services (including the postal and telegraph systems), and medical services; the guard; the Vatican radio system and television center; the Vatican observatory;

and the directorship of the villa at Castel Gandolfo, the traditional summer residence of popes.

Much of the work of the Roman Curia is conducted by offices called sacred congregations, each headed by a cardinal appointed for a five-year period. These are the Sacred Congregation for the Doctrine of the Faith (responsible for faith and morals, including the examination and, if necessary, prohibition of books and other writings), the Sacred Congregation for Bishops (diocesan affairs), the Sacred Congregation for the Eastern Churches (relations between Eastern and Latin Rites), the Sacred Congregation for the Sacraments, the Sacred Congregation for Divine Worship, the Sacred Congregation for the Clergy, the Sacred Congregation for Religious Orders and Secular Institutes (monastic and lay communities), the Sacred Congregation for the Evangelization of Peoples (missions), the Sacred Congregation for the Causes of Saints (beatification and canonization), and the Sacred Congregation for Catholic Education (seminaries and religious schools). There are also secretariats for Christian unity, non-Christians, and non-believers, and there are permanent and temporary councils and commissions for various other functions.

A pope serves from his election until death. On his decease, the College of Cardinals is called into conclave to choose a successor from their number. The usual method is to vote on the succession; in this case, the cardinal who receives two-thirds plus one of the votes of those present is declared elected. Pending the election, most Vatican business is held in abeyance.

Before the reign of Pope John XXIII, the size of the College of Cardinals was limited to 70. Pope John raised the membership to 88, and his successor, Pope Paul VI, increased the number to 136. Paul VI also decreed that as of 1 January 1971, cardinals would cease to be members of departments of the Curia upon reaching the age of 80 and would lose the right to participate in the election of a pope.

In 2010 Pope Benedict XVI appointed 24 new cardinals. Cardinals serve as the pope's closest advisors, with most representing large dioceses from around the world or serving as the heads of various Vatican departments. Twenty of the cardinals appointed in 2010 were young enough to be added to the conclave charged with electing the next pope. Cardinal electors, as conclave members are called, must be under the age of 80 years old. Ten of the appointed cardinals were Italian, a fact that to some suggested that the successor to Pope Benedict would be Italian.

14 POLITICAL PARTIES

Does not apply.

15 LOCAL GOVERNMENT

Does not apply.

16 JUDICIAL SYSTEM

For ordinary legal matters occurring within Vatican territory, there is a tribunal of first instance. Criminal cases are tried in Italian courts. There are three tribunals at the Vatican for religious cases. The Apostolic Penitentiary determines questions of penance and absolution from sin. The Roman Rota deals principally with marital issues but is also competent to handle appeals from any decisions of lower ecclesiastical courts. In exceptional cases, the Supreme Tribunal of the Apostolic Signature hears appeals from the Rota, which ordinarily is the court of last resort.

New codes of canon law for the government of the Latin Rite churches and the administration of the Curia were promulgated in 1918 and 1983. Eastern Rite churches have their own canon law.

17 ARMED FORCES

The papal patrol force now consists only of the Swiss Guard, who, sometimes armed with such ceremonial weapons as halberds, walk their posts in picturesque striped uniforms supposedly designed by Michelangelo (1475–1564). The force was founded in 1506 and is recruited from several Roman Catholic cantons of Switzerland. With about 110 men, the Papal Swiss Guard is considered to be the world's smallest army. The Guard is charged with the personal protection of the pope and serves as a security force during public audiences and masses with the pope. Requirements for membership in the guard are very strict. New recruits must be single, male, Catholic, Swiss, and under the age of 30. They must be in excellent health and with irreproachable reputations. Prerequisites include two to three years of college or professional training and completion of military training in the Swiss Army.

In May 2009, a commander of the Guard told reporters that the inclusion of women in the force might be possible in the future. There is also a civilian security force, responsible to the Central Office of Security, that protects Vatican personnel and property, and the art treasures owned by the Church. The Vatican maintains its own jail.

Italy is responsible for more substantive defense issues.

18 INTERNATIONAL COOPERATION

Vatican City's diplomatic relations are conducted by its secretariat of state and the Council for Public Affairs of the Church. The Vatican holds permanent observer status in the United Nations and several specialized agencies, such as UNESCO, IAEA, UNEP, WHO, WFP, United Nations Center for Human Settlements (UNCHS), and the FAO. The Vatican is also an observer with the African Union and the WTO. It is a member of the OSCE, holds a guest seat in the Nonaligned Movement, and participates in the Organization for the Prohibition of Chemical Weapons (OPCW).

19 ECONOMY

The Vatican, as essentially an administrative center, is dependent for its support on the receipt of charitable contributions (known as Peter's Pence), the fees charged to those able to pay for the services of the congregations and other ecclesiastical bodies, and interest on investments. Contributions to Peter's Pence are non-budgetary and used for charity, disaster relief, and church support in developing countries. Funds are also raised from the sale of stamps, religious literature, mementos, and museum admissions. Vatican City's economy is not commercial in the standard sense.

The labor force is small and is primarily employed in services and small industry. Most of the people working in the Vatican (dignitaries, priests, nuns, guards, and 3,000 lay workers) live outside the city.

In 2009 the Vatican had revenues totaling $314.4 million and expenditures reaching $319.6 million. Statistics from 2008 had stated revenues of $355.5 million and expenditures of $356.8 million.

20 INCOME

The incomes and living standards of lay workers employed in the Holy See are comparable to those of workers in the city of Rome, Italy.

21 LABOR

The labor force consists mainly of priests and other ecclesiastics, who serve as consultants or councilors; about 3,000 laborers, who live outside the Vatican; the guards; the nuns, who do the cooking, cleaning, laundering, and tapestry repair; and the cardinals, archbishops, bishops, and other higher dignitaries. Some ecclesiastical officials live outside Vatican City and commute from the secular city. The Association of Vatican Lay Workers, a trade union, has 1,800 members.

Lay employees of the Vatican have always had to be Roman Catholics and swear loyalty to the Pope. Under a new set of rules of conduct implemented in October 1995, new employees have to sign a statement binding them to observe the moral doctrines of the Roman Catholic Church.

22 AGRICULTURE

Does not apply.

23 ANIMAL HUSBANDRY

Does not apply.

24 FISHING

Does not apply.

25 FORESTRY

Does not apply.

26 MINING

Does not apply.

27 ENERGY AND POWER

As of 2011, virtually all electric power was supplied by Italy; the Vatican produced a small amount of power from solar panels.

28 INDUSTRY

A studio in the Vatican produces mosaic work, and a sewing establishment produces uniforms. There is a large printing plant, the Vatican Polyglot Press, which produces coins, medals, and postage stamps.

29 SCIENCE AND TECHNOLOGY

The Vatican promotes the study of science and mathematics through the Pontifical Academy of Sciences, which dates from 1603. The Vatican Observatory was begun by Pope Gregory XIII.

It has modern instruments, an astrophysics laboratory, and a more than 22,000-volume library.

³⁰DOMESTIC TRADE

The Vatican is basically a noncommercial economy, with no major imports or exports. Primary domestic industries include printing, mosaics, and staff uniforms. Products for retail sale are primarily postage stamps, tourist souvenirs, and publications.

³¹FOREIGN TRADE

The Vatican does not have a formal foreign trade sector. Its entire economy is based on tourism and donations (known as Peter's Pence) from Catholics around the world. However, the Vatican remains extremely wealthy despite its complete lack of natural resources because of the priceless artwork it possesses.

³²BALANCE OF PAYMENTS

Does not apply.

³³BANKING AND SECURITIES

The Vatican bank, known as the Institute for Religious Works (Istituto per le Opere di Religione—IOR), was founded in 1942. It carries out fiscal operations and invests and transfers the funds of the Vatican and of Roman Catholic religious communities throughout the world. The Administration of the Patrimony of the Holy See manages the Vatican's capital assets.

Spurred by a money laundering investigation in 2010, the Vatican revealed that it would be putting new rules in place to counter financial crimes and make financial activities within the country more transparent. Beginning in 2011, a pope-appointed Authority of Financial Information served as a financial watchdog for the Vatican. The Vatican also created laws to prevent money laundering and terror financing in all worldwide locations of the Holy See where financial transactions are made. The Vatican sought to earn a place on the European Union's "white list," a roster of countries with transparent banking and strong anti-money-laundering rules.

³⁴INSURANCE

Does not apply.

³⁵PUBLIC FINANCE

State income is derived from fees paid by the public for visiting the art galleries and from the sale of Vatican City postage stamps, tourist mementos, and publications. The Vatican also receives income in the form of voluntary contributions (Peter's Pence) from all over the world and from interest on investments. Contributions to Peter's Pence are non-budgetary and used for charity, disaster relief, and church support in developing countries. The Prefecture for Economic Affairs coordinates Vatican finances.

In both 2008 and 2009, the Vatican had budget deficits of $1.3 million and $5.2 million, respectively.

³⁶TAXATION

Residents of Vatican City pay no taxes.

³⁷CUSTOMS AND DUTIES

Vatican City imposes no customs tariffs.

³⁸FOREIGN INVESTMENT

Foreign direct investment (FDI) in the Vatican was unreported according to World Bank figures published in 2009.

³⁹ECONOMIC DEVELOPMENT

The Vatican administers industrial, real estate, and artistic holdings valued in the hundreds of millions of dollars. Investments have been in a wide range of enterprises, with makers of contraceptives and munitions specifically excepted.

⁴⁰SOCIAL DEVELOPMENT

Celibacy is required of all Roman Catholic clergy, except permanent deacons. The Church upholds the concept of family planning through such traditional methods as rhythm and abstinence but resolutely opposes such "artificial methods" as contraceptive pills and devices, as well as abortion and sterilization. Five important papal encyclicals—*Rerum Novarum* (1870), *Quadragesimo Anno* (1931), *Mater et Magistra* (1961), *Pacem in Terris* (1963), and *Laborem Exercens* (1981)—have enunciated the Church position on matters of workers' rights and social and international justice.

In 2011 the Vatican called on bishops around the world to make the fight against sexual abuse of minors by clerics a priority. The church planned to create organized procedures for combating such sexual abuse by 2012.

⁴¹HEALTH

The Department of Health and Welfare, under the Pontifical Commission for the Vatican City State, is responsible for health matters.

⁴²HOUSING

A small portion of the Vatican Palace (about 200 out of 1,000 rooms) serve as the residence for the pope, the secretary of state, high court officials, high officials in close attendance to the pope, and some administrative and scientific officials. Quarters for the Swiss Guard and the gendarmes are also located in the palace. Some officials and visitors find housing in Italy just outside of the Vatican borders.

⁴³EDUCATION

The Vatican is a major center for higher education for Roman Catholic clergy, particularly those being trained for upper level church positions. Adult literacy is 100%. About 65 papal educational institutions are scattered throughout Rome; some of the more important (all prefixed by the word "Pontifical") are the Gregorian University, the Biblical Institute, the Institute of Oriental Studies, the Lateran Athenaeum, the Institute of Christian Archaeology, and the Institute of Sacred Music.

Vatican archives are also a major source for outside academic researchers.

⁴⁴LIBRARIES AND MUSEUMS

The Apostolic Library of the Vatican is one of the most famous in the world. Founded in 1450 by Pope Nicholas V, the collection includes more than 1.1 million books, 72,000 manuscripts, 8,300 incunabula, 80,000 archival files, and 100,000 engravings. The Vatican Secret Archives, so called because originally they were strictly private records of the Vatican affairs, were opened to students in 1880. Literary scholars come from all over the world to study the collection of manuscripts. In 1994, librarians began entering the entire card catalogue of printed books into a computerized file accessible via the Internet.

In addition to more than a dozen museums, some of which figure among the greatest in the world, Vatican City includes as part of its decoration frescoes painted by Raphael (in the Stanze), Michelangelo (in the Sistine and Pauline Chapels), and other great Renaissance artists. In April 1994, after more than 14 years of careful cleaning, Michelangelo's frescoes became fully visible again. Among the museums in the Vatican are the Pius Clementine, the Chiaramonti, and New Wing (exhibiting antique sculpture); the Gregorian Etruscan and the Gregorian Egyptian museums; the Pinacoteca (paintings); the Collection of Modern Religious Art; the frescoed chapels, rooms, and galleries; and the Sacred and the Profane museums, which are administered by the Vatican Library.

⁴⁵MEDIA

The state maintains its own telegraph and postal facilities and a 5,120-line automatic telephone exchange tied into the Italian system. Radio Vatican, founded in 1931, comprises two facilities, one in Vatican City proper and the other outside Rome at Santa Maria di Galeria. Its broadcasts are transmitted worldwide via shortwave, AM, and FM radio stations, satellite, and the Internet. Programs in 34 languages are broadcast regularly.

There is also one television station. The Vatican Television Center (CTV), founded in 1983, produces and distributes religious programs. In addition to taped programs, CTV transmits live broadcasts of the Pope's Sunday and Wednesday audiences, as well as other papal events.

Vatican City is an important center for publishing. A semiofficial newspaper of wide fame, *L'Osservatore Romano*, founded in 1861, is published daily in Italian, with an estimated 2011 circulation of 70,000 copies. It is published weekly in English, Spanish, Portuguese, German, and French. Beginning in1934, the Vatican has also published *L'Osservatore della Domenica*, an illustrated weekly. The *Acta Apostolicae Sedis* (Record of the Apostolic See) appears regularly on a monthly basis and occasionally at other times; it publishes papal encyclicals and other official papers. An annual, the *Annuario Pontificio*, is issued as a record of the Vatican and the Roman Catholic hierarchy. The International Religious Press Service (Agenzia Internazionale Fides—AIF), founded in 1927, distributes news of missionary activity and publishes *Information* (weekly, in various languages, including English), *Documentation* (irregular), and *Photographic Service* (weekly).

The book publishers for the Vatican are the Vatican Editions (Libreria Editrice Vaticana), the Vatican Apostolic Library (Biblioteca Apostolica Vaticana), and the Vatican Polyglot Press (Tipografia Poliglotta Vaticana).

In May 2009, Pope Benedict XVI joined Facebook by posting the Pope2You application portal. The portal offered news and information on the pope's speeches and activities and also provided additional applications for iPhone users. The Facebook portal is available in English, French, German, Italian, and Spanish and is supervised by the Pontifical Council for Social Communications. Earlier in the year, a channel on YouTube was opened for the pope. The official Vatican website was launched in 1995; in 2010 the Vatican had 68 Internet hosts.

⁴⁶ORGANIZATIONS

The organizations at the Vatican are chiefly learned societies devoted to theology, science, archaeology, liturgy, and martyrdom. The Pontifical Academy of Sciences promotes study in mathematics and the physical and natural sciences. The Pontifical Council for Culture, founded in 1982, focuses on the study of unbelief and religious indifference, particularly concerning the cause and effect of nonreligious or antireligious attitudes in various cultures. The Apostleship of the Sea, based in the Vatican, is an organization of ship, port, and nautical school chaplains (and other sailors) that offers a wide variety of support to maritime workers and their families. Caritas International, representing social service organizations in 200 countries, is based in the Vatican. The World Federation of Catholic Medical Associations is also based in the Vatican.

⁴⁷TOURISM, TRAVEL, AND RECREATION

The Vatican is regularly visited by tourists in Rome, by pilgrims attracted by the jubilees proclaimed by the pope every 25 years, and by other special occasions. While there are no public accommodations in the Vatican, special inexpensive facilities are often arranged in Rome for pilgrims. No passport or identification is usually needed for admission to the public parts of the Vatican.

⁴⁸FAMOUS PERSONS

By virtue of their position of world importance, many popes are persons of fame. Among those who greatly increased the secular power of the papacy were St. Gregory I (the Great, 540?–604), pope from 590 to 604, who also was influential in matters of doctrine, liturgy, and missionary work; St. Gregory VII (Hildebrand, 1020?–1085), pope from 1073 to 1085, who engaged in conflict with Holy Roman Emperor Henry IV, forcing him to do public penance at the village of Canossa, and later was driven from Rome by him; and Alexander VI (Rodrigo Lanzol y Borja, b. Spain, 1431?–1503), pope from 1492 to 1503, who also divided colonial territories in the New World between Spain and Portugal.

The most significant 19th-century pope was Pius IX (Giovanni Maria Mastai-Ferretti, 1792–1878), pope from 1846 to 1878, who lost the Papal States to the kingdom of Italy and convened the First Vatican Council (1869–70), which established the doctrine of papal infallibility in matters of faith and morals. The first popes who reigned since the establishment of the Vatican City State in 1929 were Pius XI (Achille Damiano Ratti, 1857–1939), from 1922 to 1939, and Pius XII (Eugenio Pacelli, 1876–1958), from 1939 to 1958.

John XXIII (Angelo Giuseppe Roncalli, 1881–1963), pope from 1958 to 1963, made history by convening the Second Vatican

Council (1962–65), by altering the text of the canon of the mass for the first time since the 7th century, and by strongly defining the position of the Church on problems of labor and social progress (in his encyclical *Mater et Magistra* of June 1961). His greatest achievement was generally considered to be his eighth encyclical, *Pacem in Terris* (issued on 10 April 1963), a profound plea for peace, in which he hailed the UN as a defender of human rights.

Paul VI (Giovanni Battista Montini, 1897–1978), pope from 1963 to 1978, continued Pope John's effort to attain unity of the Christian world. On 4 October 1965, he addressed the UN General Assembly, appealing for world peace and international cooperation. He presided over the concluding sessions of the Second Vatican Council and traveled to many places, including the Holy Land.

Albino Luciani (1912–78), patriarch of Venice, was elected pope on 26 August 1978 and took the name John Paul I. He died on 28 September after a reign of only 34 days. His successor, John Paul II (Karol Wojtyla, 1920–2005), was elevated to the papacy on 16 October 1978. This former archbishop of Cracow was not only the first Polish pope but also the first non-Italian pope since the Renaissance. Despite suffering severe wounds in a 1981 assassination attempt, John Paul II continued to travel widely. To the dismay of Jewish and other leaders, John Paul II granted Austrian President Kurt Waldheim (b.1918) an audience in June 1987, despite accusations that Waldheim had taken part in war crimes during World War II when he was an officer in the German army. John Paul II opposed abortion, contraception, homosexuality, divorce, the ordination of women, capital punishment, embryonic stem cell research, euthanasia, and war. He died on 2 April 2005.

A German pope, Pope Benedict XVI (Joseph Alois Ratzinger, b.1927) succeeded John Paul II in 2005 and continued the traditional Catholic doctrines mapped out by his predecessor.

49 DEPENDENCIES

The Vatican has no territories or colonies.

50 BIBLIOGRAPHY

Duursma, Jorri. *Self-Determination, Statehood, and International Relations of Micro-States: The Cases of Liechtenstein, San Marino, Monaco, Andorra, and the Vatican City.* New York: Cambridge University Press, 1996.

Eccardt, Thomas M. *Secrets of the Seven Smallest States of Europe.* New York: Hippocrene Books, 2005.

Hartt, Frederick. *Michelangelo Buonarroti.* New York: H.N. Abrams, 2004.

Lucerne, Sam. *Theocracies.* Edina, MN: Abdo Publishing Company, 2011.

McDowell, Bart. *Inside the Vatican.* Washington, DC: National Geographic Society, 2005.

Norwich, John Julius. *Absolute Monarchs: History of the Papacy.* New York: Random House, 2011.

Political Chronology of Europe. London, Eng.: Europa, 2001.

Tronzo, William, ed. *St. Peter's in the Vatican.* New York: Cambridge University Press, 2005.

INDEX TO COUNTRIES AND TERRITORIES

This alphabetical list includes countries and dependencies (colonies, protectorates, and other territories) described in the encyclopedia. Countries and territories described in their own articles are followed by the continental volume (printed in *italics*) in which each appears. Country articles are arranged alphabetically in each volume. For example, Argentina, which appears in *Americas*, is listed this way: Argentina—*Americas*. Dependencies are listed here with the title of the volume in which they are treated, followed by the name of the article in which they are dealt with. In a few cases, an alternative name for the same place is given in parentheses at the end of the entry. The name of the volume *Asia and Oceania* is abbreviated in this list to *Asia*.

ISBN-13: 978-1-4144-3395-0
ISBN-10: 1-4144-3395-6

90000

9 781414 433950

Albania

Andorra

Armenia

Austria

Croatia

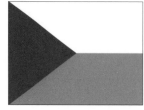
Czech Republic

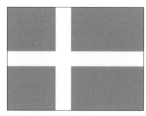
Denmark

Estonia

Greece

Hungary

Iceland

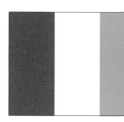
Ireland

Lithuania

Luxembourg

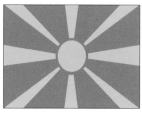
Macedonia

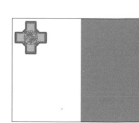
Malta

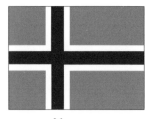
Norway

Poland

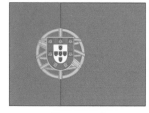
Portugal

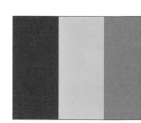
Romania

Slovenia

Spain

Sweden

Switzerland